S0-AXN-992

UNIVERSITY CASEBOOK SERIES®

PROSSER, WADE, AND SCHWARTZ'S

TORTS

CASES AND MATERIALS

THIRTEENTH EDITION

by

VICTOR E. SCHWARTZ
Adjunct Professor of Law, University of Cincinnati College of Law
Chairman, Public Policy Group, Shook, Hardy & Bacon L.L.P.
Washington, D.C.

KATHRYN KELLY
Professor of Law, The Catholic University of America

DAVID F. PARTLETT
Asa Griggs Candler Professor of Law, Emory University School of Law

444 Cedar Street, Suite 700
St. Paul, MN 55101
1-877-888-1330

Printed in the United States of America

ISBN: 978-1-60930-407-2

For Deborah Ann Underhill and the late Barbara Rosalie Wilner Schwartz Bromberg, two women who helped shape my life for the better

VES

Per le belle ragazze di musica

KK

For Nan, Anne, and Will

DFP

PREFACE

This is the 13th edition of a work first published in 1951, authored then by one of the most insightful minds in the law of torts during the 20th century, William Lloyd Prosser. He established a tradition of excellence in scholarship combined with ease of use. That tradition was continued and enhanced for almost three decades by our late colleague, Dean John W. Wade. Each of them contributed not just to the learning of countless students through their work on this casebook, but also to the development of the law through their scholarly writings and service as reporters to the American Law Institute Restatement of Torts (Second).

The casebook has benefitted from a half century of learning from many other sources and we, the current authors, Victor Schwartz, Kathryn Kelly, and David Partlett, feel a special sense of responsibility to be faithful to that tradition while keeping it current. As we worked on this edition, we did more than read cases (thousands of cases), statutes, and law review articles. We consulted with law professors who have adopted our book in the past, as well as with those who had not, about how it could be improved. Through emails, letters, and telephone calls, they sent us their thoughts. Some of their ideas were broad and conceptual, others were technical, and a few were chastising; the book benefitted from all of them. We sought comments from students who have studied from our book, including former students, now practicing lawyers, who took time from their busy law practices to send us cases, comment on the trends they observe from the frontlines of tort law, and share their reflections on the best ways to prepare for the practice of tort law.

With that goal and all of those suggestions in mind, we eliminated cases that were deemed unproductive; we pruned cases that were thought too lengthy; we added cases, not for the purpose of "change," but to make the subject more interesting and to assure that current and vital issues are discussed. The law has seen many changes in the last two decades. We would like to highlight three of them. First, a new Restatement of Torts (Third) is being published by the American Law Institute in segments. Victor Schwartz has served as an Adviser to all three sections. The first major step was the Restatement (Third) of Torts: Products Liability. The Products Liability chapter includes a focus on the new Restatement. The next step was the Restatement (Third) of Torts: Apportionment of Liability that was published in 2000. It is featured primarily in the chapter on Joint Tortfeasors. The third is the Restatement (Third) of Torts: Liability for Physical and Emotional Harm, published in 2010 and 2012. It is featured throughout. Second, while fully respecting the traditional common law development of torts, we have drawn attention to the role of modern legislatures in creating, and limiting the domain of, tort law and the response of the state judiciary to that phenomenon. The outcome of this struggle between the courts and the legislatures over the shaping of America's tort law is yet to be written. As much as tort law has moved dramatically to the center stage of social policy and political gamesmanship, it continues to be the subject of jurisprudential probing at a time of rapid technological change. Although we cannot cabin this rich debate, we have, throughout the book, provided references to it. Third, this edition appears at a time of rapid globalization of the law. In defamation, for example, old doctrines based upon publications confined to regions are strained to the breaking point when publications pulsate instantaneously to all corners of the globe via the Internet. Finally, in the book's last chapter, we invite exploration of compensation schemes beyond tort liability. The legal challenges presented by the catastrophic and tragic consequences of the terrorist attack of September 11, 2001, still resound over a decade later. More recently, the landmark Health Care legislation of 2010 has rekindled the debate about reform of medical malpractice litigation.

Throughout the text, we have held fast to a cardinal principle that has been a hallmark of this text for six decades: the casebook is not used to present any particular philosophy of tort law. We leave that to the law reviews, the Congressional testimony, and the amicus briefs. This casebook aspires to provide teachers with the raw material to inform and challenge students to learn the law and to think critically about it.

While the size and breadth of this casebook may give pause to some, we believe that all students should be given an opportunity if they wish to peruse topics excluded due to exigencies of class coverage. The casebook easily can be adapted for use in a first-year course of different credit hours and in optional advanced courses.

As in previous editions of this casebook, the deletion of a part of the text from a published opinion is indicated by the use of lacunae (* * *). When only citations are omitted, the letter "c" is used for "citation." To indicate that several citations have been deleted, "cc" is used. The letter is capitalized or not, depending on whether the citation was placed in the middle of a sentence or started a new sentence.

Those of you learning torts from this casebook will make the law in the 21st century. That is an important undertaking. We hope that you will find the first step of that undertaking, learning torts from this 13th Edition, challenging and enjoyable.

VICTOR SCHWARTZ
KATHRYN KELLY
DAVID PARTLETT

April 2015

WILLIAM L. PROSSER
Late Professor of Law, University of California,
Hastings College of Law

JOHN W. WADE
Late Dean and Distinguished Professor of Law,
Vanderbilt University School of Law

ACKNOWLEDGMENTS

Pictures. Grateful acknowledgment is made to the following for their kind assistance in locating or their courtesy in supplying or granting permission to publish pictures:

Picture of Dean John W. Wade. Mary Moody Wade.

Picture of Dean William L. Prosser. Hastings College of Law.

Palsgraf picture. William J. Pallas, Assistant General Counsel, Long Island Railroad.

Wagon Mound pictures. John Fairfax & Sons, Ltd., Sydney, N.S.W., Australia.

MacPherson Buick Model. Buick Motor Division of General Motors Corporation.

Picture of Justice Brennan. The National Portrait Gallery, Washington, D.C.

Pictures of New York Court of Appeals and of some individual Justices. Professor Robert J. Tyman, Albany Law School.

Pictures of California Supreme Court and of individual Justices. Professor T.A. Smedley, Hastings Law School.

Pictures of Supreme Court of Oregon. Retired Justice Ralph M. Holman.

Pictures of the parties and house in Katko v. Briney. Bruce A. Palmer, Esq., Oskaloosa, Iowa.

Picture of the New Jersey Supreme Court. Stephen W. Townsend, Clerk of the Court.

Especial appreciation is due to Ms. Bernice Loss, of the Art Collection at Harvard Law School, for her courtesy in making available the following pictures: Lords Abinger, Blackburn, Cairns, and Herschell, Lord Justice Bowen, Chief Justices Holt and Tindall, Justice Holmes, Judge Learned Hand, and Dean Bohlen.

Reprints. Appreciative acknowledgment is also made to the following for permission to include the indicated selections:

American Law Institute. Certain sections from the Restatement (Second) of Torts, from the Restatement (Third) of Torts: Products Liability, and from the Restatement (Third) of Torts: Liability for Physical and Emotional Harm.

National Conference of Commissioners on Uniform State Laws. Certain Uniform and Model Acts.

Matthew Bender & Co. Three paragraphs from A. Larson, The Law of Workmen's Compensation.

Mr. Schwartz gratefully acknowledges the assistance of Christopher E. Appel on Chapter 15, Products Liability.

SUMMARY OF CONTENTS

TABLE OF CONTENTS

TABLE OF CASES

The principal cases are in bold type.

UNIVERSITY CASEBOOK SERIES®

PROSSER, WADE, AND SCHWARTZ'S

TORTS

CASES AND MATERIALS

THIRTEENTH EDITION

CHAPTER 1

DEVELOPMENT OF LIABILITY BASED UPON FAULT

"Tort" comes from the Latin word "tortus," which means twisted, and the French word "tort," which means injury or wrong. A tort is a civil wrong, other than a breach of contract, for which the law provides a remedy. This area of law imposes duties on persons to act in a manner that will not injure other persons. A person who breaches a tort duty has committed a tort and may be liable to pay damages in a lawsuit brought by a person injured because of that tort.

Over the years, tort law has been principally a part of the common law, developed by the courts through the opinions of the judges in the cases before them. Within some areas of tort law, however, statutes have long been common—e.g., trespass to real property, limitation of actions, wrongful death actions; and in recent years the legislature has had an increasingly more significant role in modifying the common law.

Modern Tort Law—Beyond the Casebooks Into the Field of Public Debate. From the time this casebook began with its first edition in the early 1950's, tort law was of concern primarily to law students, law professors, and attorneys who practiced in the field. The public, in general, knew very little, if anything, about the subject. In the past few decades, however, this has changed quite dramatically. Prior to coming to law school, you probably read about healthcare providers who were unable to obtain affordable medical malpractice coverage, about people injured through someone else's fault who could not recover compensation because the cost of the lawsuit would have been more than they could recover, or about manufacturers going out of business or declining to put new and useful products on the market, all because of problems in the area of "tort law."

The Federal Government and all state governments have examined these issues and legislation affecting tort law has multiplied in recent years. As you study the law of torts, you may find that you will be reading news stories about the subject from a new perspective. You may decide that many stories oversimplify the tort system and perhaps miss critical points. It is important to pay attention to these stories because the subject you are studying is dynamic, complex, and at the center of major public policy debates.

In studying the subject, you should consider the major purposes of tort law: (1) to provide a peaceful means for adjusting the rights of parties who might otherwise "take the law into their own hands"; (2) to deter wrongful conduct; (3) to encourage socially responsible behavior; (4) to restore injured parties to their original condition, insofar as the law can do this, by compensating them for their injury; and (5) to vindicate individual rights of redress. Should people always be compensated when they have been injured by the action of another? If your answer to this question is in the affirmative, think about whether it is always necessary to have a trial, with a plaintiff, a defendant, and lawyers. On the other hand, if tort law should not compensate every person who is injured by another, what are appropriate rules and standards to determine whom to compensate and under what circumstances? This is the primary problem to which the law of torts addresses itself. Consider also how tort law evolves to meet changing circumstances—the great virtue of the common law. See Schwartz, Silverman & Goldberg, Neutral Principles of Stare Decisis in Tort Law, 58 S.C. L.Rev. 317 (2005) (suggesting principles for departure from traditional common law concepts).

The casebook will explore the system that has been accused of having caused these crises. Evaluate it carefully, and remember that you are not only learning a legal subject, but also becoming an educated citizen who can and should participate in the debate about the direction tort law should take through the 21st century.

Historical Origins. Historians have differed as to how the law of torts began. There is one theory that it originated with liability based upon "actual intent and actual personal culpability," with a strong moral tinge, and slowly formulated external standards that took less account of personal fault. O. Holmes, The Common Law, Lecture I (1881). It seems quite likely that the most flagrant wrongs were the first to receive redress.

Another, and more generally accepted theory, is that the law began by imposing liability on those who caused physical harm, and gradually developed toward the acceptance of moral standards as the basis of liability. Wigmore, Responsibility for Tortious Acts: Its History, 7 Harv.L.Rev. 315, 383 & 441 (1894). Ames, Law and Morals, 22 Harv.L.Rev. 97 (1908). An alternative theory is that there has been no steady progression from liability without fault to liability based on fault. The difference between no-fault periods and fault-based periods is, rather, one of degree. Isaacs, Fault and Liability, 31 Harv.L.Rev. 954, 965 (1918).

Certainly at one time the law was not very much concerned with the moral responsibility of the defendant. "The thought of man shall not be tried," said Chief Justice Brian, in Y.B. 7 Edw. IV, f. 2, pl. 2 (1468), "for the devil himself knoweth not the thought of man." The courts were interested primarily in keeping the peace between individuals by providing a substitute for private vengeance, as the party injured was just as likely to take the law into his own hands when the injury was an innocent one. The person who hurt another by unavoidable accident or in self-defense was required to make good the damage inflicted. "In all civil acts," it was said, in Lambert v. Bessey, T.Raym. 421, 83 Eng.Rep. 220 (K.B.1681), "the law doth not so much regard the intent of the actor, as the loss and damage of the party suffering."

Forms of action. In the early English law, after the Norman conquest, remedies for wrongs were dependent upon the issuance of writs to bring the defendant into court. In the course of the thirteenth century, the principle was established that no one could bring an action in the King's common law courts without the King's writ. As a result of the jealous insistence of the nobles and others upon the prerogatives of their local courts, the number of writs that the King could issue was limited, and their forms were strictly prescribed. There were, in other words, "forms of action," and unless the plaintiff's claim could be fitted into the form of some established and recognized writ, the plaintiff could not seek money damages in the King's courts. The result was a highly formalized system of procedure that governed and controlled the law as to the substance of the wrongs that might be remedied. You may learn more about how the forms of action affected the law of procedure in your civil procedure classes.

Two common law writs are the genesis of tort law—the writ of trespass and the writ of trespass on the case, often called action on the case. Here, "trespass" is used in the general sense of doing something to hurt or offend someone rather than the more specific sense of harming someone by intruding onto their land.

The form of action in trespass originally had a criminal character. It would lie only in cases of forcible breaches of the King's peace, and it was only on this basis that the royal courts assumed jurisdiction over the wrong. The purpose of the remedy was at first primarily that of punishment of the crime; but to this there was added later the satisfaction of the injured party's claim for redress. If the defendant was found guilty, damages were awarded to the successful plaintiff, and the defendant was imprisoned, and allowed to purchase his release by payment of a fine. What similarity remains between tort and crime is to be traced to this common beginning. See Woodbine, The Origin of the Action of Trespass, 33 Yale L.J. 799 (1923), 34 Yale L.J. 343 (1934); F. Maitland, The Forms of Action at Common Law, 65 (1941).

The writ of trespass on the case developed out of the practice of applying, in cases in which no writ could be found in the Register to cover the plaintiff's claim, for a special writ, in the nature of trespass, drawn to fit the particular case. Historians have differed as to the origin of this practice. Attempts to trace it are found in C. Fifoot, History and Sources of the Common Law: Tort and Contract, 66–74 (1949), and Kiralfy, The Action on the Case, Chapter I (1951).

Whatever may have been its origin, it was through this action on the case, rather than through trespass, that most of modern tort and contract law developed. Thus, in the field of tort law, actions for nuisance, conversion, deceit, defamation, malicious prosecution, interference with economic relations, and the modern action for negligence all developed out of the action on the case.

The distinction between trespass and case lay in the direct and immediate application of force to the person or property of the plaintiff. Trespass would lie only for direct and forcible injuries; case, for other tangible injuries to person or property. The classic illustration of this distinction is that of a log thrown into the highway. A person struck by the rolling log could maintain trespass against the thrower, since the injury was direct and immediate; but one who came along later and was hurt by stumbling over the stationary log could maintain only an action on the case. Leame v. Bray, 3 East 593, 102 Eng.Rep. 724 (1802).

Note that the distinction was not one between intentional and negligent conduct. The emphasis was upon the causal sequence, rather than the character of the defendant's wrong. Trespass would lie for all forcible, direct injuries, whether or not they were intended, while the action on the case might be maintained for injuries intended but not forcible or not direct. There were two additional significant points of difference between the two actions. Trespass, because of its quasi-criminal character, required no proof of any actual damage, since the invasion of the plaintiff's rights by the criminal conduct was regarded as a tort in itself; while in the action on the case, which developed purely as a civil remedy, there could ordinarily be no liability unless actual damage was proved. Also, in its earlier stages trespass was identified with the view that liability might be imposed without regard to the defendant's fault, while case always had required proof of culpability: either a wrongful intent or wrongful conduct (negligence).

The criminal aspect of trespass disappeared in 1697, when the statute of 5–6 William & Mary, c. 12, abolished the fine and left the action as an exclusively civil remedy. Out of adherence to precedent, however, the courts continued to allow the action even though no real injury was suffered. They were, however, disinclined to extend the scope of trespass beyond the existing precedents, perhaps because of the belief that punishment was primarily the function of the criminal law and the civil action should be used only to compensate for harm done. This explains why in modern law there is a requirement of proving actual damages except in cases of assault, offensive but harmless battery, false imprisonment, and trespass to land. If harm was done, the injured party could still sue in case and recover, even though the defendant's wrong did not amount to a trespass. If no harm was done, the recovery of punitive damages in a civil action was limited to the most flagrant cases, where the criminal law did not apply or was not effective as a deterrent.

Hulle v. Orynge
(The Case of Thorns)

King's Bench, 1466.
Y.B.M. 6 Edw. IV, folio 7, placitum 18.

BRIAN. In my opinion if a man does a thing he is bound to do it in such a manner that by his deed no injury or damage is inflicted upon others. As in the case where I erect a building, and when the timber is being lifted a piece of it falls upon the house of my neighbor and bruises his house, he will have a good action, and that, although the erection of my house was lawful and the timber fell without my intent.

Similarly, if a man commits an assault upon me and I cannot avoid him if he wants to beat me, and I lift my stick in self-defense in order to prevent him, and there is a man in back of me and I injure him in lifting my stick, in that case he would have an action against me, although my lifting the stick was lawful to defend myself and I injured him without intent.

NOTES AND QUESTIONS

1. This passage, translated from the Norman French, is one of the few bits and fragments of the early English law of torts that have come down to us. Although Brian, who became Chief Justice of the Court of

Common Pleas in 1471, was apparently only arguing as counsel in this case, he appears to have been summarizing accepted law.

Weaver v. Ward

King's Bench, 1616.
Hobart 134, 80 Eng.Rep. 284.

Weaver brought an action of trespass of assault and battery against Ward. The defendant pleaded, that he was amongst others by the commandment of the Lords of the Council a trained soldier in London, of the band of one Andrews captain; and so was the plaintiff, and that they were skirmishing with their muskets charged with powder for the exercise in re militari [in a military matter], against another captain and his band; and as they were so skirmishing the defendant casualiter & per infortunium & contra voluntatem suam [accidentally and by misfortune and against his will] in discharging his piece did hurt and wound the plaintiff, which is the same, & c. absque hoc [without this], that he was guilty aliter sive alio modo [otherwise or in another manner].

And upon demurrer by the plaintiff, judgment was given for him; for though it were agreed, that if men tilt or turney in the presence of the King, or if two masters of defence playing their prizes kill one another, that this shall be no felony; or if a lunatick kill a man, or the like, because felony must be done animo felonico [with a felonious mind]; yet in trespass, which tends only to give damages according to hurt or loss, it is not so; and therefore if a lunatick hurt a man, he shall be answerable in trespass; and therefore no man shall be excused of a trespass (for this is in the nature of an excuse, and not of a justification, prout ei bene licuit [as is properly permitted to him]), except it may be judged utterly without his fault.

As if a man by force take my hand and strike you, or if here the defendant had said, that the plaintiff ran cross his piece when it was discharging, or had set forth the case with the circumstances, so as it had appeared to the Court that it had been inevitable and that the defendant had committed no negligence to give occasion to the hurt.

NOTES AND QUESTIONS

1. This is the earliest known case in which it was clearly recognized that a defendant might not be liable, even in a trespass action, for a purely accidental injury occurring entirely without his fault. Note that the burden rests upon the defendant to plead and prove his freedom from all fault.

2. The next two centuries saw a gradual blurring of the distinction between trespass and case. The procedural distinction is now long antiquated, although some vestige of it still remains in jurisdictions retaining common law pleading in a modified form. Modern law has almost entirely abandoned the artificial classification of injuries as direct and indirect, and looks instead to the intent or negligence of the wrongdoer.

3. The first step was taken when the action on the case was held to cover injuries that were merely negligent but were directly inflicted, as in Williams v. Holland, 10 Bing. 112, 131 Eng.Rep. 848 (1833) (plaintiff's cart

was overturned by collision with wheel of defendant's gig, which was engaged in a race with another gig). Although this left the plaintiff an election between trespass and case, the action of case came to be used quite generally in all cases of negligence, whether direct or indirect, while trespass remained as the remedy for intentional injuries inflicted by acts of violence. Terms such as battery, assault, and false imprisonment, which were varieties of trespass, gradually came to be associated only with intent, and negligence emerged as a separate tort. The shift was a slow one, and the courts seem to have been quite unconscious of it at the time. When in the nineteenth century the old forms of action were replaced in most jurisdictions by code procedure, the new classification remained. Prichard, Trespass, Case and the Rule in Williams v. Holland, Cambridge L.J. 234 (1964). There was occasional confusion, and some talk, for example, of a negligent battery, as in Anderson v. Arnold's Ex'r, 79 Ky. 370 (1881), but, in general, these old trespass terms are now restricted to actions involving intentional conduct.

4. Although we no longer have "forms of action," it usually is helpful from the vantage point of advocacy to place one's claim under a tort label that will be familiar to the court—e.g., "battery," "assault," "negligence," "defamation," "nuisance"—and that is still the common practice in both state and federal courts.

5. With certain exceptions, actions for injuries to the person, or to tangible property, now require proof of an intent to inflict them or of failure to exercise proper care to avoid them. As to the necessity of proving actual damage, the courts have continued the distinctions found in the older actions of trespass and case. Thus, whether damage is essential to the existence of a cause of action for a particular tort depends largely upon its ancestry in terms of the old procedure.

6. Thoughtful perspectives on the problems presented in this chapter can be found in Malone, Ruminations on the Role of Fault in the History of the Common Law of Torts, 31 La.L.Rev. 1 (1970) and David Ibbetson, A Historical Introduction to the Law of Obligations (Oxford University Press 2000).

Brown v. Kendall

Supreme Judicial Court of Massachusetts, 1850.
60 Mass. (6 Cush.) 292.

This was an action of trespass for assault and battery. * * * [Two dogs, owned by plaintiff and defendant, were fighting. Defendant tried to separate them by hitting them with a stick. In doing so he backed up toward the plaintiff, and in raising his stick over his shoulder, struck plaintiff in the eye, injuring him.]

Whether it was necessary or proper for the defendant to interfere in the fight between the dogs; whether the interference, if called for, was in a proper manner, and what degree of care was exercised by each party on the occasion; were the subject of controversy between the parties, upon all the evidence in the case * * *

[The trial judge, refusing to give requested instructions to the contrary, instructed the jury that if hitting the dogs was a necessary act which defendant was under a duty to do, defendant was required to use only ordinary care in doing it; but if it were only a proper and permissible act, defendant was liable unless he exercised extraordinary care; and that the burden of proving the extraordinary care was on the defendant.]

The jury under these instructions returned a verdict for the plaintiff; whereupon the defendant alleged exceptions.

SHAW, C.J. This is an action of trespass, *vi et armis*, brought by George Brown against George K. Kendall, for an assault and battery. * * * The facts set forth in the bill of exceptions preclude the supposition, that the blow, inflicted by the hand of the defendant upon the person of the plaintiff, was intentional. The whole case proceeds on the assumption, that the damage sustained by the plaintiff, from the stick held by the defendant, was inadvertent and unintentional; and the case involves the question how far, and under what qualifications, the party by whose unconscious act the damage was done is responsible for it. We use the term "unintentional" rather than involuntary, because in some of the cases, it is stated, that the act of holding and using a weapon or instrument, the movement of which is the immediate cause of hurt to another, is a voluntary act, although its particular effect in hitting and hurting another is not within the purpose or intention of the party doing the act.

It appears to us, that some of the confusion in the cases on this subject has grown out of the long-vexed question, under the rule of the common law, whether a party's remedy, where he has one, should be sought in an action of the case, or of trespass. This is very distinguishable from the question, whether in a given case, any action will lie. The result of these cases is, that if the damage complained of is the immediate effect of the act of the defendant, trespass *vi et armis* lies; if consequential only, and not immediate, case is the proper remedy. [Cc]

In these discussions, it is frequently stated by judges, that when one receives injury from the direct act of another, trespass will lie. But we think this is said in reference to the question, whether trespass and not case will lie, assuming that the facts are such, that some action will lie. These *dicta* are no authority, we think, for holding, that damage received by a direct act of force from another will be sufficient to maintain an action of trespass, whether the act was lawful or unlawful, and neither wilful, intentional, or careless. * * * [Evidence showed that the striking of plaintiff was not intentional, but rather done as he was backing up and plaintiff, behind him, was moving forward.]

We think, as the result of all the authorities, the rule is correctly stated by Mr. Greenleaf, that the plaintiff must come prepared with evidence to show either that the *intention* was unlawful, or that the defendant was *in fault;* for if the injury was unavoidable, and the conduct of the defendant was free from blame, he will not be liable. 2 Greenl. Ev. §§ 85 to 92; [c]. If, in the prosecution of a lawful act, a casualty purely accidental arises, no action can be supported for an injury arising therefrom. [Cc] In applying these rules to the present case, we can perceive no reason why the instructions asked for by the defendant ought not to have been given; to this effect, that if both plaintiff and defendant at the time of the blow were using ordinary care, or if at that time the defendant was using ordinary care, and the plaintiff was not, or if at that time, both the plaintiff and defendant were not using ordinary care, then the plaintiff could not recover.

In using this term, ordinary care, it may be proper to state, that what constitutes ordinary care will vary with the circumstances of cases. In general, it means that kind and degree of care, which prudent and cautious men would use, such as is required by the exigency of the case, and such as is necessary to guard against probable danger. A man, who should have occasion to discharge a gun, on an open and extensive marsh, or in a forest, would be required to use less circumspection and care, than if he were to do the same thing in an inhabited town, village, or city. To make an accident, or casualty, or as the law sometimes states it, inevitable accident, it must be such an accident as the defendant could not have avoided by the use of the kind and degree of care necessary to the exigency, and in the circumstances in which he was placed.

We are not aware of any circumstances in this case, requiring a distinction between acts which it was lawful and proper to do, and acts of legal duty. There are cases, undoubtedly, in which officers are bound to act under process, for the legality of which they are not responsible, and perhaps some others in which this distinction would be important. We can have no doubt that the act of the defendant in attempting to part the fighting dogs, one of which was his own, and for the injurious acts of which he might be responsible, was a lawful and proper act, which he might do by proper and safe means. If, then, in doing this act, using due care and all proper precautions necessary to the exigency of the case, to avoid hurt to others, in raising his stick for that purpose, he accidentally hit the plaintiff in his eye, and wounded him, this was the result of pure accident, or was involuntary and unavoidable, and therefore the action would not lie. * * *

The court instructed the jury, that if it was not a necessary act, and the defendant was not in duty bound to part the dogs, but might with propriety interfere or not as he chose, the defendant was responsible for the consequences of the blow, unless it appeared that he was in the exercise of extraordinary care, so that the accident was inevitable, using the word not in a strict but a popular sense. This is to be taken in connection with the charge afterwards given, that if the jury believed, that the act of interference in the fight was unnecessary, (that is, as before explained, not a duty incumbent on the defendant,) then the burden of proving extraordinary care on the part of the defendant, or want of ordinary care on the part of the plaintiff, was on the defendant.

The court are of opinion that these directions were not conformable to law. If the act of hitting the plaintiff was unintentional, on the part of the defendant, and done in the doing of a lawful act, then the defendant was not liable, unless it was done in the want of exercise of due care, adapted to the exigency of the case, and therefore such want of due care became part of the plaintiff's case, and the burden of proof was on the plaintiff to establish it. [Cc]

Perhaps the learned judge, by the use of the term extraordinary care, in the above charge, explained as it is by the context, may have intended nothing more than that increased degree of care and diligence, which the exigency of particular circumstances might require, and which men of ordinary care and prudence would use under like circumstances, to guard against danger. If such was the meaning of this part of the charge, then it does not differ from our views, as above explained. But we are of opinion, that the other part of the charge, that the burden of proof was on the defendant, was incorrect. Those facts which are essential to enable the plaintiff to recover, he takes the burden of proving. The evidence may be offered by the plaintiff or by the defendant; the question of due care, or want of care, may be essentially connected with the main facts, and arise from the same proof; but the effect of the rule, as to the burden of proof, is this, that when the proof is all in, and before the jury, from whatever side it comes, and whether directly proved, or inferred from circumstances, if it appears that the defendant was doing a lawful act, and unintentionally hit and hurt the plaintiff, then unless it also appears to the satisfaction of the jury, that the defendant is chargeable with some fault, negligence, carelessness, or want of prudence, the plaintiff fails to sustain the burden of proof, and is not entitled to recover.

New trial ordered.

NOTES AND QUESTIONS

1. Why a new trial? Why not simply a judgment for the defendant?

2. What has gone on in the law since Hulle v. Orynge in 1466? How would Justice Shaw have decided Weaver v. Ward?

3. This decision is the earliest clear statement of the rule commonly applied: liability must be based on legal fault.

4. While Brown v. Kendall dealt with a defendant who was separating dogs, many tort defendants in Massachusetts at the time were industrial employers. Does this fact, plus the social policy of the time, have a bearing on the legal change reflected in the opinion? See Schwartz, The Character of Early American Tort Law, 36 U.C.L.A. L. Rev. 641, 667–670 (1989).

5. In some jurisdictions, the old distinction between trespass and case survived into the Twentieth Century, in the form of decisions holding that if the injury is one for which trespass would lie, the defendant must sustain the burden of proving that he was not at fault, while if only case would lie the burden of proving fault is on the plaintiff. The distinction was not finally abandoned in England until Fowler v. Lanning, [1959] 1 Q.B. 426.

Cohen v. Petty

Court of Appeals of the District of Columbia, 1933.
62 App.D.C. 187, 65 F.2d 820.

GRONER, ASSOCIATE JUSTICE. Plaintiff's declaration [complaint] alleged that on December 14, 1930, she was riding as a guest in defendant's automobile; that defendant failed to exercise reasonable care in its operation, and drove it at a reckless and excessive rate of speed so that he lost control of the car and propelled it off the road against an embankment on the side of the road, as the result of which plaintiff received permanent injuries. The trial judge gave binding instructions [directed a verdict], and the plaintiff appeals.

There were four eyewitnesses to the accident, namely, plaintiff and her sister on the one side, and defendant and his wife on the other. All four were occupants of the car. Defendant was driving the car, and his wife was sitting beside him. Plaintiff and her sister were in the rear seat. * * * After passing the Country Club, and when somewhere near Four Corners and five or six miles from Silver Spring, the automobile suddenly swerved out of the road, hit the abutment of a culvert, and ran into the bank, throwing plaintiff and her sister through the roof of the car onto the ground.

Plaintiff's sister estimated the speed of the car just before the accident somewhere between thirty-five and forty miles an hour, and plaintiff herself, who had never driven a car, testified she thought it was nearer forty-five. The place of the accident was just beyond a long and gradual curve in the road. Plaintiff testified that just before the accident, perhaps a minute, she heard the defendant, who, as we have said, was driving the car, exclaim to his wife, "I feel sick," and a moment later heard his wife exclaim in a frightened voice to her husband, "Oh, John, what is the matter?" Immediately thereafter the car left the road and the crash occurred. Her sister, who testified, could not remember anything that occurred on the ride except that, at the time they passed the Country Club, the car was being driven about thirty-five or forty miles an hour and that the occupants of the car were engaged in a general conversation. The road was of concrete and was wide. Plaintiff, when she heard defendant's wife exclaim, "What is the matter?" instead of looking at the driver of the car, says she continued to look down the road, and as a result she did not see and does not know what subsequently occurred, except that there was a collision with the embankment.

Defendant's evidence as to what occurred just before the car left the road is positive and wholly uncontradicted. His wife, who was sitting beside him, states that they were driving along the road at the moderate rate of speed when all of a sudden defendant said, "Oh, Tree, I feel sick"—defendant's wife's name is Theresa, and he calls her Tree. His wife looked over, and defendant had fainted. "His head had fallen back and his hand had left the wheel and I immediately took hold of the wheel with both hands, and then I do not remember anything else until I waked up on the road in a strange automobile." The witness further testified that her husband's eyes were closed when she looked, and that his fainting and the collision occurred in quick sequence to his previous statement, "Oh, Tree, I feel so sick." The defendant himself testified that he had fainted just before the crash, that he had never fainted before, and that so far as he knew he was in good health, that on the day in question he had had breakfast late, and had had no luncheon, but that he was not feeling badly until the moment before the illness and the fainting occurred. * * *

The sole question is whether, under the circumstances we have narrated, the trial court was justified in taking the case from the jury. We think its action was in all respects correct.

It is undoubtedly the law that one who is suddenly stricken by an illness, which he had no reason to anticipate, while driving an automobile, which renders it impossible for him to control the car, is not chargeable with negligence. [Cc]

In the present case the positive evidence is all to the effect that defendant did not know and had no reason to think he would be subject to an attack such as overcame him. Hence negligence cannot be predicated in this case upon defendant's recklessness in driving an automobile when he knew or should have known of the possibility of an accident from such an event as occurred.

As the plaintiff wholly failed to show any actionable negligence prior to the time the car left the road, or causing or contributing to that occurrence, and as the defendant's positive and uncontradicted evidence shows that the loss of control was due to defendant's sudden illness, it follows the action of the lower court was right. Even if plaintiff's own evidence tended more strongly than it does to imply some act of negligence, it would be insufficient to sustain a verdict and judgment upon proof such as the defendant offered here of undisputed facts, for in such a case the inference must yield to uncontradicted evidence of actual events.

Affirmed.

NOTES AND QUESTIONS

1. Defendant, asleep on the rear seat of an automobile, unconsciously pushed with his foot against the front seat in which plaintiff, the driver, was sitting. Plaintiff's arms were forced off the wheel, the car crashed into a culvert and overturned, and plaintiff was injured. Is defendant liable? Lobert v. Pack, 337 Pa. 103, 9 A.2d 365 (1939) (defendant not liable because he did not act with volition). The Restatement (Third) Reporters note that the cases are "impressively unanimous" in finding no liability for injuries that occur due to an actor's sudden and unforeseeable seizure or loss of consciousness. Restatement (Third) of Torts: Liability for Physical and Emotional Harm § 11(b), comment *d* (2010) and Reporters' Notes thereto.

2. Defendant, driving an automobile, fell asleep at the wheel. The car went into the ditch and injured the plaintiff. Is defendant liable for his conduct while he is asleep? What if he knew that he was getting sleepy and continued to drive? Is this not always the case? At least one court has found that falling asleep at the wheel of a car is always negligence unless the driver was suddenly overcome with illness. Bushnell v. Bushnell, 103 Conn. 583, 131 A. 432 (1925). Defendant became so frightened when she realized that her brakes were not working that she fainted and was thus unconscious when she collided with plaintiff's car. Liability? Kohler v. Sheffert, 250 Iowa 899, 96 N.W.2d 911 (1959) (fact that she was unconscious at time of collision did not excuse previous negligence in causing the situation that frightened her).

3. Knowing that he was subject to epileptic seizures, driver had a seizure while driving and lost control of the car, which ran into the plaintiff and injured him. Is driver liable? Eleason v. Western Casualty & Surety Co., 254 Wis. 134, 35 N.W.2d 301 (1948) (liability based on testimony that driver knew he was subject to "spells" that could render him unconscious even though he did not know he had epilepsy). What if he had never had a seizure before? Moore v. Capital Transit Co., 226 F.2d 57 (D.C.Cir.1955), cert. denied, 350 U.S. 966 (1956) (no liability because never had spell before and no reason to anticipate).

4. A patient was given prescription drugs and discharged from the hospital, without being warned that they would impair his mental and physical abilities. The patient drove his automobile, lost control and struck a tree, injuring his passenger. Is the driver liable to his passenger? Is his doctor? Is the manufacturer of the drugs? Cf. Kirk v. Michael Reese Hospital and Medical Center, 117 Ill.2d 507, 111 Ill.Dec. 944, 513 N.E.2d 387 (1987) and McKenzie v. Hawaii Permanente Medical Group, Inc., 98 Haw. 296, 47 P.3d 1209 (2002).

5. Do you agree with the result of the principal case? What about the argument that anyone who drives an automobile should bear the risk that others will be injured if he loses consciousness while driving, and should be liable for their loss? In a case where an epileptic had an unanticipated seizure, plaintiff's counsel argued most strongly that since defendant had liability insurance, he should bear the risk. Do you find this argument for strict liability persuasive? See Hammontree v. Jenner, 20 Cal.App.3d 528, 97 Cal.Rptr. 739 (1971). The court rejected this contention.

Spano v. Perini Corp.

Court of Appeals of New York, 1969.
25 N.Y.2d 11, 250 N.E.2d 31, 302 N.Y.S.2d 527, on remand,
33 A.D.2d 516, 304 N.Y.S.2d 15 (1969).

FULD, CHIEF JUDGE. The principal question posed on this appeal is whether a person who has sustained property damage caused by blasting on nearby property can maintain an action for damages without a showing that the blaster was negligent. Since 1893, when this court decided the case of Booth v. Rome, W. & O.T.R.R. Co., 140 N.Y. 267, 35 N.E. 592, 24 L.R.A. 105, it has been the law of this State that proof of negligence was required unless the blast was accompanied by an actual physical invasion of the damaged property—for example, by rocks or other material being cast upon the premises. We are now asked to reconsider that rule.

The plaintiff Spano is the owner of a garage in Brooklyn which was wrecked by a blast occurring on November 27, 1962. There was then in that garage, for repairs, an automobile owned by the plaintiff Davis which he also claims was damaged by the blasting. Each of the plaintiffs brought suit against the two defendants who, as joint venturers, were engaged in constructing a tunnel in the vicinity pursuant to a contract with the City of New York. * * *

It is undisputed that, on the day in question (November 27, 1962), the defendants had set off a total of 194 sticks of dynamite at a construction site which was only 125 feet away from the damaged premises. Although both plaintiffs [also] alleged negligence in their complaints, no attempt was made to show that the defendants had failed to exercise reasonable care or to take necessary precautions when they were blasting. Instead, they chose to rely, upon the trial, solely on the principle of absolute liability * * *

The concept of absolute liability in blasting cases is hardly a novel one. The overwhelming majority of American jurisdictions have adopted such a rule. [Cc] Indeed, this court itself, several years ago, noted that a change in our law would "conform to the more widely (indeed almost universally) approved doctrine that a blaster is absolutely liable for any damages he causes, with or without trespass". [C]

We need not rely solely however upon out-of-state decisions in order to attain our result. Not only has the rationale of the *Booth* case [c] been overwhelmingly rejected elsewhere but it appears to be fundamentally inconsistent with earlier cases in our own court which had held, long before *Booth* was decided, that a party was absolutely liable for damages to neighboring property caused by explosions. (See, e.g., Hay v. Cohoes Co., 2 N.Y. 159; Heeg v. Licht, 80 N.Y. 579.) In the *Hay* case (2 N.Y. 159, supra), for example, the defendant was engaged in blasting an excavation for a canal and the force of the blasts caused large quantities of earth and stones to be thrown against the plaintiff's house, knocking down his stoop and part of his chimney. The court held the defendant *absolutely* liable for the damage caused * * *

Although the court in *Booth* drew a distinction between a situation—such as was presented in the *Hay* case—where there was "a physical invasion" of, or trespass on, the plaintiff's property and one in which the damage was caused by "setting the air in motion, or in some other unexplained way," [c], it is clear that the court, in the earlier cases, was not concerned with the particular manner by which the damage was caused but by the simple fact that any explosion in a built-up area was likely to cause damage. Thus, in Heeg v. Licht, 80 N.Y. 579, the court held that there should be absolute liability where the damage was caused by the accidental explosion of stored gunpowder, even in the absence of a physical trespass (p. 581):

"The defendant had erected a building and stored materials therein, which from their character were liable to and actually did explode, causing injury to the plaintiff. The fact that the explosion took place tends to establish that the magazine was dangerous and liable to cause damage to the property of persons residing in the vicinity. * * * The fact that the magazine was liable to such a contingency, which could not be guarded against or averted by the greatest degree of care and vigilance, evinces its dangerous character, * * * In such a case, the rule which exonerates a party engaged in a lawful business, when free from negligence, has no application."

Such reasoning should, we venture, have led to the conclusion that the *intentional* setting off of explosives—that is, blasting—in an area in which it was likely to cause harm to neighboring property similarly results in absolute liability. However, the court in the *Booth* case rejected such an extension of the rule for the reason that "[t]o exclude the defendant from blasting to adapt its lot to the contemplated uses, at the instance of the plaintiff, would not be a compromise between conflicting rights, but an extinguishment of the right of the one for the benefit of the other" [c]. The court expanded on this by stating, "This sacrifice, we think, the law does not exact. Public policy is sustained by the building up of towns and cities and the improvement of property. Any unnecessary restraint on freedom of action of a property owner hinders this."

This rationale cannot withstand analysis. The plaintiff in *Booth* was not seeking, as the court implied, to "exclude the defendant from blasting" and thus prevent desirable improvements to the latter's property. Rather, he was merely seeking compensation for the damage which was inflicted upon his own property as a result of that blasting. The question, in other words, was not *whether* it was lawful or proper to engage in blasting but *who* should bear the cost of any resulting damage—the person who engaged in the dangerous activity or the innocent neighbor injured thereby. Viewed in such a light, it clearly appears that *Booth* was wrongly decided and should be forthrightly overruled * * *

[The court then remanded the case to the appellate division to determine the sufficiency of the evidence on causation because the appellate division had affirmed the trial court judge on the sole ground that no negligence had been proven and thus had no occasion to consider whether the blasting caused the plaintiffs' damage.]

NOTES AND QUESTIONS

1. The early common law absolute or strict liability of the Weaver v. Ward type has persisted stubbornly in connection with trespass to real property and has been exorcised only in mid-Twentieth Century. Thus, in Randall v. Shelton, 293 S.W.2d 559 (Ky.1956), defendant's truck ran over a large stone in the gravel highway and the tire cast it out so that it hit plaintiff, who was standing in her yard, and injured her. The appellate court found no negligence and held that the defendant's motion for judgment notwithstanding the verdict should have been granted. To do this, it had to overrule an earlier Kentucky case in which a runaway street car invaded plaintiff's property and did damage. The special rule for trespass explains some of the early New York cases discussed in the opinion of the principal case.

2. The procedural distinction long made in New York, between an action of trespass for blasting causing physical invasion by casting rocks on the plaintiff's land, for which there was strict liability, and the action of nuisance for vibration or concussion that shook plaintiff's house to pieces, which would require proof of negligence, was denounced as a marriage of procedural technicality with scientific ignorance. This distinction, abandoned by New York in the principal case, has lost its significance in states that apply strict liability to blasting operations because blasting is an abnormally dangerous activity. See, e.g., Stocks v. CFW Construction Co., Inc., 472 So.2d 1044 (Ala.1985). The question of strict liability for damage by blasting and other activities that have been deemed extrahazardous or abnormally dangerous is considered at greater length in Chapter 14.

3. For the present, it is sufficient to note that this case represents one type of situation in which strict liability may be applied, without any showing of intent or negligence, by the majority of the courts that have considered the question. This has sometimes been called absolute liability, or liability without fault. The first Restatement of Torts § 519 (1938) conferred the name of "ultrahazardous activities" upon these cases. The drafters of Restatement (Second) of Torts § 519 (1977) concluded that a better name is "abnormally dangerous activities," since the emphasis is more upon the abnormal character of what the defendant does in relation to the surroundings than upon the high degree of danger. That label was retained by the drafters of Restatement (Third) of Torts: Liability for Physical and Emotional Harm § 20 (2010).

4. Strict liability also has been imposed upon manufacturers of products when defects in their wares have caused injury. This position is now generally followed when the defect causing the injury is due to an error in the manufacturing process. There is less agreement as to the application of strict liability for failure to use a safer design or to warn of dangers. This application of strict liability to products liability is discussed in Chapter 15.

5. Strict liability involves a good many issues that are to be considered later in Chapters 14 and 15. For present purposes, note merely that there are three possible bases of tort liability:

A. Intentional conduct.

B. Negligent conduct that creates an unreasonable risk of causing harm.

C. Conduct that is neither intentional nor negligent but that subjects the actor to strict liability because of public policy.

6. These will be considered in turn, which will carry us through Chapter 15. The remainder of this book covers particular fields of case law in which special problems arise, and in most of which intent, negligence, and strict liability are all involved and intermingled as possible bases for recovery.

CHAPTER 2

INTENTIONAL INTERFERENCE WITH PERSON OR PROPERTY

1. INTENT

Garratt v. Dailey

Supreme Court of Washington, 1955.
46 Wash.2d 197, 279 P.2d 1091.

HILL, JUSTICE. The liability of an infant for an alleged battery is presented to this court for the first time. Brian Dailey (age five years, nine months) was visiting with Naomi Garratt, an adult and a sister of the plaintiff, Ruth Garratt, likewise an adult, in the back yard of the plaintiff's home, on July 16, 1951. It is plaintiff's contention that she came out into the back yard to talk with Naomi and that, as she started to sit down in a wood and canvas lawn chair, Brian deliberately pulled it out from under her. The only one of the three present so testifying was Naomi Garratt. (Ruth Garratt, the plaintiff did not testify as to how or why she fell.) The trial court, unwilling to accept this testimony, adopted instead Brian Dailey's version of what happened, and made the following findings:

"III. * * * that while Naomi Garratt and Brian Dailey were in the back yard the plaintiff, Ruth Garratt, came out of her house into the back yard. Some time subsequent thereto defendant, Brian Dailey, picked up a lightly built wood and canvas lawn chair which was then and there located in the back yard of the above described premises, moved it sideways a few feet and seated himself therein, at which time he discovered the plaintiff, Ruth Garratt, about to sit down at the place where the lawn chair had formerly been, at which time he hurriedly got up from the chair and attempted to move it toward Ruth Garratt to aid her in sitting down in the chair; that due to the defendant's small size and lack of dexterity he was unable to get the lawn chair under the plaintiff in time to prevent her from falling to the ground. That plaintiff fell to the ground and sustained a fracture of her hip, and other injuries and damages as hereinafter set forth.

"IV. That the preponderance of the evidence in this case establishes that when the defendant, Brian Dailey moved the chair in question *he did not have any wilful or unlawful purpose* in doing so; that *he did not have any intent to injure the plaintiff, or any intent to bring about any unauthorized or offensive contact with her person* or any objects appurtenant thereto; that the circumstances which immediately preceded the fall of the plaintiff established that the defendant, *Brian Dailey, did not have purpose, intent or design to perform a prank or to effect an assault and battery upon the person of the plaintiff.*" (Italics ours, for a purpose hereinafter indicated.)

It is conceded that Ruth Garratt's fall resulted in a fractured hip and other painful and serious injuries. To obviate the necessity of a retrial in the event this court determines that she was entitled to a judgment against Brian Dailey, the amount of her damage was found to be $11,000. Plaintiff appeals from a judgment dismissing the action and asks for the entry of a judgment in that amount or a new trial.

The authorities generally, but with certain notable exceptions, [c] state that when a minor has committed a tort with force he is liable to be proceeded against as any other person would be. * * *

In our analysis of the applicable law, we start with the basic premise that Brian, whether five or fifty-five, must have committed some wrongful act before he could be liable for appellant's injuries. * * *

It is urged that Brian's action in moving the chair constituted a battery. A definition (not all-inclusive but sufficient for our purpose) of a battery is the intentional infliction of a harmful bodily contact upon another. * * *

We have in this case no question of consent or privilege. We therefore proceed to an immediate consideration of intent and its place in the law of battery. In the comment on clause (a) of § 13, the Restatement says:

"*Character of Actor's Intention.* In order that an act may be done with the intention of bringing about a harmful or offensive contact or an apprehension thereof to a particular person, either the other or a third person, the act must be done for the purpose of causing the contact or apprehension or with knowledge on the part of the actor that such contact or apprehension is substantially certain to be produced." [C]

We have here the conceded volitional act of Brian, i.e., the moving of a chair. Had the plaintiff proved to the satisfaction of the trial court that Brian moved the chair while she was in the act of sitting down, Brian's action would patently have been for the purpose or with the intent of causing the plaintiff's bodily contact with the ground, and she would be entitled to a judgment against him for the resulting damages. [Cc]

The plaintiff based her case on that theory, and the trial court held that she failed in her proof and accepted Brian's version of the facts rather than that given by the eyewitness who testified for the plaintiff. After the trial court determined that the plaintiff had not established her theory of a battery (i.e., that Brian had pulled the chair out from under the plaintiff while she was in the act of sitting down), it then became concerned with whether a battery was established under the facts as it found them to be.

In this connection, we quote another portion of the comment on the "Character of actor's intention," relating to clause (a) of the rule from [Restatement, (First) Torts, 29, § 13]:

"It is not enough that the act itself is intentionally done and this, even though the actor realizes or should realize that it contains a very grave risk of bringing about the contact or apprehension. Such realization may make the actor's conduct negligent or even reckless but unless he realizes that to a substantial certainty, the contact or apprehension will result, the actor has not that intention which is necessary to make him liable under the rule stated in this section."

A battery would be established if, in addition to plaintiff's fall, it was proved that, when Brian moved the chair, he knew with substantial certainty that the plaintiff would attempt to sit down where the chair had been. If Brian had any of the intents which the trial court found, in the italicized portions of the findings of fact quoted above, that he did not have, he would of course have had the knowledge to which we have referred. The mere absence of any intent to injure the plaintiff or to play a prank on her or to embarrass her, or to commit an assault and battery on her would not absolve him from liability if in fact he had such knowledge. [C] Without such knowledge, there would be nothing wrongful about Brian's act in moving the chair and, there being no wrongful act, there would be no liability.

While a finding that Brian had no such knowledge can be inferred from the findings made, we believe that before the plaintiff's action in such a case should be dismissed there should be no question but that the trial court had passed upon that issue; hence, the case should be remanded for clarification of the findings to specifically cover the question of Brian's knowledge, because intent could be inferred therefrom. If the court finds that he had such knowledge the necessary intent will be established and the plaintiff will be entitled to recover, even though there was no purpose to injure or embarrass the plaintiff. [C] If Brian did not have such knowledge, there was no wrongful act by him and the basic premise of liability on the theory of a battery was not established.

It will be noted that the law of battery as we have discussed it is the law applicable to adults, and no significance has been attached to the fact that Brian was a child less than six years of age when the alleged battery occurred. The only circumstance where Brian's age is of any consequence is in determining what he knew, and there his experience, capacity, and understanding are of course material.

From what has been said, it is clear that we find no merit in plaintiff's contention that we can direct the entry of a judgment for $11,000 in her favor on the record now before us.

Nor do we find any error in the record that warrants a new trial. * * *

The cause is remanded for clarification, with instructions to make definite findings on the issue of whether Brian Dailey knew with substantial certainty that the plaintiff would attempt to sit down where the chair which he moved had been, and to change the judgment if the findings warrant it. * * *

Remanded for clarification.

[On remand, the trial judge concluded that it was necessary for him to consider carefully the time sequence, as he had not done before; and this resulted in his finding "that the arthritic woman had begun the slow process of being seated when the defendant quickly removed the chair and seated himself upon it, and that he knew, with substantial certainty, at that time that she would attempt to sit in the place where the chair had been." He entered judgment for the plaintiff in the amount of $11,000, which was affirmed on a second appeal in Garratt v. Dailey, 49 Wash.2d 499, 304 P.2d 681 (1956).]

NOTES AND QUESTIONS

1. The trial court judge found that plaintiff suffered damages in the amount of $11,000. For most intentional torts, the court will award *nominal* damages even if no actual damages were proved. Of course, if the plaintiff does prove actual damages, as she did in this case, defendant is liable for those actual damages. How would Ms. Garratt's lawyer prove actual damages? See Chapter 10, Damages.

2. Note that the trial judge was the finder of fact both times. Why do you think his findings of fact were different the second time? Might he have been influenced by the appellate court's view of the facts as well as its pronouncement of the law?

3. Can a child five years and nine months old have an intent to do harm to another? And if so, how can that intent be "fault"? Suppose that a boy of seven, playing with a bow and arrow, aims at the feet of a girl of five but the arrow hits her in the eye. Is he liable? Weisbart v. Flohr, 260 Cal.App.2d 281, 67 Cal.Rptr. 114 (1968) (yes).

4. Can a four-year-old child who strikes his babysitter in the throat, crushing her larynx, be held liable for an intentional tort? Bailey v. C.S., 12 S.W.3d 159 (Tex. App. 2000) (rejecting argument that four-year-old was incapable of intent). What about a two-year-old child who bites an infant? See Fromenthal v. Clark, 442 So.2d 608 (La.App.1983), cert. denied, 444 So.2d 1242 (1984) (affirming trial court ruling that two-year-old was too young to form intent).

5. At common law, parents are not liable for the torts of their children unless the plaintiff can show some fault on the part of the parents through, for example, negligence in supervising the child. (We will explore Negligence in Chapter 4.) Some states enacted statutes that make parents liable for their child's malicious torts. Can a young child commit a tort in a "malicious" state of mind? Ortega v. Montoya, 97 N.M. 159, 637 P.2d 841 (1981) (eight-year-old boy *could* be capable of willful and malicious conduct and it was for jury to determine whether he had acted in such a manner).

Wagner v. State

Supreme Court of Utah, 2005.
2005 UT 54, 122 P.3d 599.

[Mrs. Wagner was standing in line at a K-Mart store when she was suddenly attacked from behind by Mr. Giese who grabbed her by the head and hair and threw her to the ground. Mr. Giese was a mentally disabled patient accompanied by state employees who had brought him to K-Mart as part of his treatment program and remained there to supervise him. Mrs. Wagner and her husband filed claims against the State. The trial court granted a 12(b)(6) motion to dismiss based on the State's argument that the attack constituted a battery, a tort for which the State has retained immunity from suit. The appellate court affirmed that ruling and the Wagners then petitioned the Utah Supreme Court for review. It too affirmed.]

WILKINS, ASSOCIATE CHIEF JUSTICE: * * * The Wagners argue that Mr. Giese's attack could not legally constitute a battery because that intentional tort requires the actor to intend harm or offense through his deliberate contact, an intent Mr. Giese was mentally incompetent to form. The State, on the other hand, argues that the only intent required * * * is simply the intent to make a contact. The contact must be harmful or offensive by law, but the actor need not intend harm so long as he intended contact.

* * * While there is some variation among the definitions of the tort of battery, Prosser and Keeton on the Law of Torts § 8, at 33–34 (W. Page Keeton et al. eds., 5th ed.1984) (hereinafter Prosser), Utah has adopted the Second Restatement of Torts to define the elements of this intentional tort, including the element of intent. * * *

We conclude that the plain language of the Restatement, the comments to the Restatement, Prosser and Keeton's exhaustive explanation of the meaning of intent as described in the Restatement, and the majority of case law on the subject in all jurisdictions including Utah, compels us to agree with the State that only intent to make contact is necessary.

In order for a contact to constitute a battery at civil law, two elements must be satisfied. First, the contact must have been deliberate. Second, the contact must have been harmful or offensive at law. We hold that the actor need not intend that his contact be harmful or offensive in order to commit a battery so long as he deliberately made the contact and so long as that contact satisfies our legal test for what is harmful or offensive.

Section 2 of the Restatement (Second) of Torts defines the term "act" as "an external manifestation of the actor's will and does not include any of its results, even the most direct, immediate, and intended." Id. § 2. To illustrate this point, the comments clarify that when an actor points a pistol at another person and pulls the trigger, the act is the pulling of the trigger. Id. at cmt. c. The consequence of that act is the "impingement of the bullet upon the other's person." Id. It would be improper to describe the act as "the shooting," since the shooting is actually the conflation of the act with the consequence. For another example, the act that has taken place when one intentionally strikes another with his fist "is only the movement of the actor's hand and not the contact with the others body immediately established." Id. Thus, presuming that the movement was voluntary rather than spastic, whether an actor has committed an intentional or negligent contact with another, and thus a tort sounding in battery or negligence, depends not upon whether he intended to move his hand, but upon whether he intended to make contact thereby.

The example the Restatement sets forth to illustrate this point is that of an actor firing a gun into the Mojave Desert. Restatement (Second of Torts) § 8A cmt. a. In both accidental and intentional shootings, the actor intended to pull the trigger. Id. Battery liability, rather than liability sounding in negligence, will attach only when the actor pulled the trigger in order to shoot another person, or knowing that it was substantially likely that pulling the trigger would lead to that result. Id. § 8A cmts. a & b. An actor who intentionally fires a bullet, but who does not realize that the bullet would make contact with another person, as when "the bullet hits a person who is present in the desert without the actor's knowledge," is not liable for an intentional tort. Id.

* * * We agree with the Wagners that not all intentional contacts are actionable as batteries, and that the contact must be harmful or offensive in order to be actionable. We do not agree, however, that, under our civil law, the actor must appreciate that his act is harmful or offensive in order for his contact to constitute a battery. * * *

Prosser echoed the Restatement when he clarified that "[t]he intent with which tort liability is concerned is not necessarily a hostile intent, or a desire to do harm. Rather, it is an intent to bring about a result which will invade the interests of another in a way that the law forbids." Prosser, supra, § 8, at 36. * * * [Prosser] lists as one type of intentional tort the act of "intentionally invading the rights of another under a mistaken belief of committing no wrong." Id. § 8, at 37.

* * * For example, a man who decides to flatter a woman he spots in a crowd with an unpetitioned-for kiss, one of the examples of battery Prosser provides, Prosser, supra, § 9, at 41–42, would find no objection under the Wagners' proposed rule so long as his intentional contact was initiated with no intent to injure or offend. He would be held civilly liable for his conduct only if he intended to harm or offend her through his kiss. A woman in such circumstances would not enjoy the presumption of the law in favor of preserving her bodily integrity; instead, her right to be free from physical contact with strangers would depend upon whether she could prove that the stranger hoped to harm or offend her through his contact. So long as he could show that he meant only flattery and the communication of positive feelings towards her in stroking her, kissing her, or hugging her, she must be subjected to it and will find no protection for her bodily integrity in our civil law.

* * * We recognize that, in this instance, the retained immunity doctrine bars the caretakers of a handicapped person from taking responsibility for the conduct of their charge. It is unfortunate, and perhaps it is improvident of the State to retain immunity in this area. But it is not our role as a judiciary to override the legislature in this matter; it is for us only to interpret and apply the law as it is. We will not limit the recoveries of all other plaintiffs similarly injured by defining the tort of battery in such a way as to make it far more burdensome for plaintiffs to satisfy its elements and recover, nor will we distort the plain language of the Restatement so as to elevate an actor's "right" to deliberately touch others at will over an individual's right to the preservation of her bodily integrity.

* * * Applying the rule we have laid out today to the facts of this case, it is clear that Mr. Giese's attack constituted a battery upon Mrs. Wagner. There is no allegation that his action was the result of an involuntary muscular movement or spasm. Further, the Wagners concede that Mr. Giese affirmatively attacked her; they do not argue that he made muscular movements that inadvertently or accidentally brought him into contact with her.

* * * So long as he intended to make that contact, and so long as that contact was one to which Mrs. Wagner had not given her consent, either expressly or by implication, he committed a battery. Because battery is a tort for which the State has retained immunity, we affirm the court of appeals' decision to dismiss the case for failure to state a claim.

[Concurring opinion omitted.]

NOTES AND QUESTIONS

1. *Distinguish*:

A. The intent to do an act. The defendant throws a rock.

B. The intent to bring about the consequences of the act. The rock hits someone. Liability for intentional torts is premised on the intent to bring about the consequences. For battery, the consequence is a touching. The touching must be harmful or offensive.

C. The intent to bring about a specific harm (e.g., broken leg). This is sufficient to establish intent, but not necessary.

D. An actor's knowledge that particular consequences (e.g., touching that is harmful or offensive) are substantially certain to follow is sufficient to establish intent.

E. An actor's knowledge that she is merely risking particular consequences (e.g., touching that is harmful or offensive) is not sufficient to establish intent—although it may be negligence if the risk is an unreasonable one under the circumstances.

F. The motive for the act. Defendant's motive is irrelevant. Hudgens v. Prosper, Inc., 2011 WL 8181959 (Utah Dist. Ct. 2011) (allegations of intent sufficient even if motive was to provide incentive to team members and increase profits rather than to injure plaintiff).

2. *Distinguish*:

A. The defendant does not act. He is carried onto plaintiff's land against his will. Smith v. Stone, Style 65, 82 Eng.Rep. 533 (1647) (no liability).

B. He acts intentionally, but under fear or threats. Twelve armed men compel him to enter plaintiff's land and steal a horse. Gilbert v. Stone, Style 72, 82 Eng.Rep. 539 (1648) (intent, but may have excuse if acted under duress).

C. He acts intentionally, but without any desire to affect the plaintiff, or any certainty that he will do so. He rides a horse, which runs away with him and runs the plaintiff down. Gibbons v. Pepper, 1 Ld.Raym. 38, 91 Eng.Rep. 922 (1695) (no liability if someone else struck the horse; liability if defendant's spurring caused runaway).

D. He acts with the desire to affect the plaintiff, but for an entirely permissible or laudable purpose. He shoots the plaintiff in self-defense or while a soldier defending his country. See Chapter 3, Privileges (satisfies intent requirement but may result in no liability if conduct is privileged).

3. It may not seem important to distinguish between negligent and intentionally wrongful conduct: the defendant usually will be held liable to

the plaintiff in either situation. Nevertheless, the distinction may be legally significant. In addition to the principal case, consider the following:

A. Will defendant be liable for punitive damages? See Chapter 10, Section 3.

B. Will the defense of contributory negligence be available to defendant? See page 623, note 7.

C. Will defendant's employer be liable under the doctrine of *respondeat superior*? See page 711, note 3.

D. How far will the law trace the consequences of defendant's wrongful act? See Tate v. Canonica, 180 Cal.App.2d 898, 5 Cal.Rptr. 28 (1960) (more inclined to find defendant's conduct was legal cause of harm if tort was intentional) and R.D. v. W.H., 875 P.2d 26 (Wyo.1994) (court imposes higher degree of responsibility on those who commit intentional act).

E. Will the defendant be reimbursed through a liability insurance policy? See Allstate Ins. Co. v. Hiseley, 465 F.2d 1243 (10th Cir.1972) (applying Oklahoma law) (following an incident outside a bar, one car pursued another at speeds over 100 miles an hour and then bumped it, causing its driver to lose control and crash) and Automobile Ins. Co. of Hartford v. Cook, 7 N.Y.3d 131, 850 N.E.2d 1152, 818 N.Y.S.2d 176 (2006) (insured shot an acquaintance in self -defense inside insured's home). Pryor, The Stories We Tell: Intentional Harm and the Quest for Insurance Funding, 75 Tex.L.Rev. 1721 (1997).

F. Has the state statute of limitations run? Baska v. Scherzer, 283 Kan. 750, 156 P.3d 617 (2007) (statute of limitations for intentional tort applies to cause of action brought against two teenagers who hit the mother of one of their friends when the mother stepped between them to stop a fight).

G. Will an employer be subject to liability to an employee in spite of a general worker compensation immunity shield? Some state worker compensation statutes provide an exception to the immunity for intentional wrongdoing. Does an employer's intentional failure to train an employee to perform a dangerous task supply the requisite intent to injure under the worker compensation intentional injury exception? See Reed Tool Co. v. Copelin, 689 S.W.2d 404 (Tex.1985). What about an employer's deliberate exposure of employees to dangerous products? See Millison v. E.I. du Pont de Nemours & Co., 101 N.J. 161, 501 A.2d 505 (1985) and Bardere v. Zafir, 102 A.D.2d 422, 477 N.Y.S.2d 131, aff'd, 63 N.Y.2d 850, 472 N.E.2d 37, 482 N.Y.S.2d 261 (1984) (plaintiff must show "specific acts [by the employer] directed at causing harm to particular employees").

H. Will the plaintiff be able to bring a cause of action against the United States, which may be liable for the negligent acts of its employees, but not for their intentional acts? See note 5B, page 699.

4. Do you think that a court's characterization of a defendant's conduct as "negligent" or "intentional" sometimes might be influenced by the legal effect of its finding? Since the court is not bound by either party's characterization of the events, such influence could occur, but only in close cases. At the receiving dock of a meatpacking plant, plaintiff was unloading a truck when a government meat inspector leapt out at him, screamed

"boo," pulled his wool stocking cap over his eyes, and jumped on his back. Plaintiff fell forward and struck his face on some meat hooks, severely injuring his mouth and teeth. Plaintiff's complaint was for negligent conduct, apparently because the defendant's employer, the United States, would be liable for its employee's negligence, but not his battery. Cf. Lambertson v. United States, 528 F.2d 441 (2d Cir.1976), cert. denied, 426 U.S. 921 (1976) (court did not permit plaintiff to recover by "dressing up the substance" of battery in the "garments" of negligence). See also Wright v. University of Utah, 876 P.2d 380, 386 (Utah App. 1994) (describing plaintiff's attempt to circumvent the governmental immunity statute by recasting her claim as one sounding in negligence rather than battery as "fruitless, albeit creative").

5. For a discussion of the treatment of intent in English and American tort law, see Finnis, "Intention in Tort Law" in Owen, Philosophical Foundations of Tort Law 229 (Clarenden Press 1995). See also Restatement (Third) of Torts: Liability for Physical and Emotional Harm § 1 (2010).

Ranson v. Kitner

Appellate Court of Illinois, 1889.
31 Ill.App. 241.

CONGER, J. This was an action brought by appellee against appellants to recover the value of a dog killed by appellants, and a judgment rendered for $50.

The defense was that appellants were hunting for wolves, that appellee's dog had a striking resemblance to a wolf, that they in good faith believed it to be one, and killed it as such.

Many points are made, and a lengthy argument failed to show that error in the trial below was committed, but we are inclined to think that no material error occurred to the prejudice of appellants.

The jury held them liable for the value of the dog, and we do not see how they could have done otherwise under the evidence. Appellants are clearly liable for the damages caused by their mistake, notwithstanding they were acting in good faith.

We see no reason for interfering with the conclusion reached by the jury, and the judgment will be affirmed.

NOTES AND QUESTIONS

1. Did the defendant intend to kill the dog? The court calls it "mistake." Why not accident?

2. Defendant fuel oil distributor had a contract to deliver oil to a residence. One day, during the delivery, the oil overflowed and damaged surrounding lawn and shrubberies. The tank overflowed because it already had been filled by another company, hired by the new owner. The previous owner apparently had not canceled his contract when he moved. Is the fuel oil distributor liable for trespass? Serota v. M. & M. Utilities, Inc., 55 Misc.2d 286, 285 N.Y.S.2d 121 (1967) (reasonable mistake no defense to trespass).

3. Defendant, seeking to confront the driver who frightened his horses the previous day, pushed back the hat of the wrong man. Does he intend to touch him? Seigel v. Long, 169 Ala. 79, 53 So. 753 (1910). What if a surgeon operates on the wrong patient? Gill v. Selling, 125 Or. 587, 267 P. 812 (1928). Defendant cuts and removes timber from plaintiff's land under a reasonable belief that it was on his own land. Did he intend to take plaintiff's timber? Perry v. Jefferies, 61 S.C. 292, 39 S.E. 515 (1901). After purchasing some sheep, defendant butcher was driving them down the road into town when some of plaintiff's sheep became intermingled with them. Defendant stopped and sorted most of plaintiff's sheep out of the herd, but plaintiff proved that four of his were taken into town and butchered with those defendant's. Were defendant's actions intentional? Dexter v. Cole, 6 Wis. 319, 70 Am.Dec. 465 (1857). Generally, mistake as to the identity of the person or animal does not negate intent and thus defendant is liable.

4. On the other hand, some of the defendant's privileges depend, not upon the existence of a fact, but upon the reasonable belief that the fact exists. Defendant, seeing the plaintiff reach for a handkerchief in his pocket, reasonably believes that he is reaching for a gun, and strikes plaintiff to defend himself. See page 110. Mistakes as to the existence of a privilege, like self-defense, are dealt with in Chapter 3 in connection with the privilege itself.

McGuire v. Almy

Supreme Judicial Court of Massachusetts, 1937.
297 Mass. 323, 8 N.E.2d 760.

QUA, JUSTICE. This is an action of tort for assault and battery. The only question of law reported is whether the judge should have directed a verdict for the defendant.

The following facts are established by the plaintiff's own evidence: In August, 1930, the plaintiff was employed to take care of the defendant. The plaintiff was a registered nurse and was a graduate of a training school for nurses. The defendant was an insane person. Before the plaintiff was hired she learned that the defendant was a "mental case and was in good physical condition," and that for some time two nurses had been taking care of her. The plaintiff was on "24 hour duty." The plaintiff slept in the room next to the defendant's room. Except when the plaintiff was with the defendant, the plaintiff kept the defendant locked in the defendant's room. * * *

On April 19, 1932, the defendant, while locked in her room, had a violent attack. The plaintiff heard a crashing of furniture and then knew that the defendant was ugly, violent and dangerous. The defendant told the plaintiff and a Miss Maroney, "the maid," who was with the plaintiff in the adjoining room, that if they came into the defendant's room, she would kill them. The plaintiff and Miss Maroney looked into the defendant's room, "saw what the defendant had done," and "thought it best to take the broken stuff away before she did any harm to herself with it." They sent for a Mr. Emerton, the defendant's brother-in-law. When he arrived the defendant was in the middle of her room about ten feet from the door, holding upraised the leg of a low-boy as if she were going to strike. The plaintiff stepped into the room and walked toward the defendant, while Mr. Emerton and Miss Maroney remained in the doorway. As the plaintiff approached the defendant and tried to take hold of the defendant's hand which held the leg, the defendant struck the plaintiff's head with it, causing the injuries for which the action was brought.

The extent to which an insane person is liable for torts has not been fully defined in this Commonwealth. * * *

Turning to authorities elsewhere, we find that courts in this country almost invariably say in the broadest terms that an insane person is liable for his torts. As a rule no distinction is made between those torts which would ordinarily be classed as intentional and those which would ordinarily be classed as negligent, nor do the courts discuss the effect of different kinds of insanity or of varying degrees of capacity as bearing upon the ability of the defendant to understand the particular act in question or to make a reasoned decision with respect to it, although it is sometimes said that an insane person is not liable for torts requiring malice of which he is incapable. Defamation and malicious prosecution are the torts more commonly mentioned in this connection. * * * These decisions are rested more upon grounds of public policy and upon what might be called a popular view of the requirements of essential justice than upon any attempt to apply logically the underlying principles of civil liability to the special instance of the mentally deranged. Thus it is said that a rule imposing liability tends to make more watchful those persons who have charge of the defendant and who may be supposed to have some interest in preserving his property; that as an insane person must pay for his support, if he is financially able, so he ought also to pay for the damage which he does; that an insane person with abundant wealth ought not to continue in unimpaired enjoyment of the comfort which it brings while his victim bears the burden unaided; and there is also a suggestion that courts are loath to introduce into the great body of civil litigation the difficulties in determining mental capacity which it has been found impossible to avoid in the criminal field.

The rule established in these cases has been criticized severely by certain eminent text writers both in this country and in England, principally on the ground that it is an archaic survival of the rigid and formal mediaeval conception of liability for acts done, without regard to fault, as opposed to what is said to be the general modern theory that liability in tort should rest upon fault. Notwithstanding these criticisms, we think, that as a practical matter, there is strong force in the reasons underlying these decisions. They are consistent with the general statements found in the cases dealing with the liability of infants for torts, [cc] including a few cases in which the child was so young as to render his capacity for fault comparable to that of many insane persons, [cc]. Fault is by no means at the present day a universal prerequisite to liability, and the theory that it should be such has been obliged very recently to yield at several points to what have been thought to be paramount considerations of public good. Finally, it would be difficult not to recognize the persuasive weight of so much authority so widely extended.

But the present occasion does not require us either to accept or to reject the prevailing doctrine in its entirety. For this case it is enough to say that where an insane person by his act does intentional damage to the person or property of another he is liable for that damage in the same circumstances in which a normal person would be liable. This means that in so far as a particular intent would be necessary in order to render a normal person liable, the insane person, in order to be liable, must have been capable of entertaining that same intent and must have entertained it in fact. But the law will not inquire further into his peculiar mental condition with a view to excusing him if it should appear that delusion or other consequence of his affliction has caused him to entertain that intent or that a normal person would not have entertained it. * * *

Coming now to the application of the rule to the facts of this case, it is apparent that the jury could find that the defendant was capable of entertaining and that she did entertain an intent to strike and to injure the plaintiff and that she acted upon that intent. See American Law Institute Restatement, Torts, §§ 13, 14. We think this was enough. * * *

[The rest of the opinion holds that whether the plaintiff consented to the attack or assumed the risk of it is an issue to be left to the jury. There was no evidence that the defendant had previously attacked any one or made any serious threat to do so. The plaintiff had taken care of the defendant for fourteen months without being attacked. When the plaintiff entered the room the defendant was breaking up the furniture, and it could be found that the plaintiff reasonably feared that the defendant would do harm to herself. Under such circumstances it cannot be ruled as a matter of law that the plaintiff assumed the risk.]

Judgment for the plaintiff on the verdict.

NOTES AND QUESTIONS

1. Can someone who is mentally ill have an intent to do harm to another? And if so, how can such an intent be "fault"? How does the insane person differ from the automobile driver who loses consciousness due to a heart attack or stroke or other illness, as in Cohen v. Petty, page 9?

2. Note that the tort law standards differ from the criminal law standards for holding the mentally ill responsible for their actions. Polmatier v. Russ, 206 Conn. 229, 537 A.2d 468 (1988) (defendant liable for battery of plaintiff's decedent even though he was found not guilty by reason of insanity in criminal case arising out of same incident); Delahanty v. Hinckley, 799 F.Supp. 184 (D.D.C. 1992) (rejecting defendant's argument that he should not be liable to plaintiff police officer who was injured when defendant shot at President Reagan because he was in a "deluded and psychotic state of mind" and found not guilty by reason of insanity in criminal case).

3. Despite criticism, the American decisions are unanimous in their agreement with the principal case. Mentally disabled persons may be held responsible for their intentional torts as long as plaintiff can prove that they formed the requisite intent. Restatement (Second) § 895J (1979). See also White v. Muniz, 999 P.2d 814 (Colo. 2000) (in battery claim against

defendant with Alzheimer's, plaintiff must prove defendant desired to cause contact that was offensive or harmful).

4. Mental illness may prevent the specific kind of intent necessary for certain torts, such as deceit, that require the plaintiff to prove that the defendant knew that he was not speaking the truth. See Irvine v. Gibson, 117 Ky. 306, 77 S.W. 1106 (1904) (slander requires proof that defendant knew the statement was false) and Chaddock v. Chaddock, 130 Misc. 900, 226 N.Y.S. 152 (1927) (fraud requires proof that defendant knew the statement was false).

5. An action also may lie against persons responsible for caring for the mentally ill person, based on negligent supervision, but only if a caretaking responsibility has been assumed. Familial relationship only is not enough. Rausch v. McVeigh, 105 Misc.2d 163, 431 N.Y.S.2d 887 (1980) (cause of action for negligent supervision against parents of 22-year-old autistic son who attacked his therapist); Shirdon v. Houston, 2006 WL 2522394 (Ohio App.) (no duty to supervise adult son even though father knew his son could be aggressive and combative); and Kaminski v. Town of Fairfield, 216 Conn. 29, 578 A.2d 1048 (1990) (accord).

6. Several jurisdictions have carved out a narrow exception to this general rule, holding that an institutionalized mentally disabled patient who cannot control or appreciate the consequences of his conduct cannot be held liable for injuries caused to those employed to care for the patient. The jurisdictions that have addressed this issue have done so both in the context of intentional torts and negligence. Gould v. American Family Mutual Ins. Co., 198 Wis.2d 450, 543 N.W.2d 282 (1996) (negligence action brought against patient with Alzheimer's); Creasy v. Rusk, 730 N.E.2d 659 (Ind. 2000) (same); Anicet v. Gant, 580 So.2d 273 (Fla.App.1991) (assault and battery against twenty-three-year-old man suffering from "irremediable mental difficulties" who was unable to control himself from acts of violence). California recently extended this exception to in-home care givers. Gregory v. Cott, 59 Cal.4th 996, 331 P.3d 179, 176 Cal.Rptr.3d 1 (2014) (in-home care giver hired through agency injured while caring for Alzheimer's patient). There, the ruling was based on primary implied assumption of the risk, which will be discussed in Chapter 12.

7. *Intoxication.* What if the defendant is intoxicated? Does intoxication preclude a showing of intent? Bar patron passed out or fell asleep at bar and other patrons agreed to drive him home. Bar employee helped patron from bar and was putting him into the back seat of a car when he began shouting obscenities and kicked the employee in the face, seriously injuring him. Sufficient intent for battery? Janelsins v. Button, 102 Md.App. 30, 648 A.2d 1039 (1994) (voluntary intoxication does not vitiate intent).

Talmage v. Smith

Supreme Court of Michigan, 1894.
101 Mich. 370, 59 N.W. 656.

MONTGOMERY, J. The plaintiff recovered in an action of trespass. The case made by plaintiff's proofs was substantially as follows: * * * Defendant had on his premises certain sheds. He came up to the vicinity of the sheds, and saw six or eight boys on the roof of one of

FACTS

them. He claims that he ordered the boys to get down, and they at once did so. He then passed around to where he had a view of the roof of another shed, and saw two boys on the roof. The defendant claims that he did not see the plaintiff, and the proof is not very clear that he did, although there was some testimony from which it might have been found that he was within his view. Defendant ordered the boys in sight to get down, and there was testimony tending to show that the two boys in defendant's view started to get down at once. Before they succeeded in doing so, however, defendant took a stick, which is described as being two inches in width, and of about the same thickness, and about 16 inches long, and threw it in the direction of the boys; and there was testimony tending to show that it was thrown at one of the boys in view of the defendant. The stick missed him, and hit the plaintiff just above the eye with such force as to inflict an injury which resulted in the total loss of the sight of the eye. * * * George Talmage, the plaintiff's father, testifies that defendant said to him that he threw the stick, intending it for Byron Smith,—one of the boys on the roof,—and this is fully supported by the circumstances of the case. * * *

The circuit judge charged the jury as follows: "If you conclude that Smith did not know the Talmage boy was on the shed, and that he did not intend to hit Smith, or the young man that was with him, but simply, by throwing the stick, intended to frighten Smith, or the other young man that was there, and the club hit Talmage, and injured him, as claimed, then the plaintiff could not recover. If you conclude that Smith threw the stick or club at Smith, or the young man that was with Smith,—intended to hit one or the other of them,—and you also conclude that the throwing of the stick or club was, under the circumstances, reasonable, and not excessive, force to use towards Smith and the other young man, then there would be no recovery by this plaintiff. But if you conclude from the evidence in this case that he threw the stick, intending to hit Smith, or the young man with him,—to hit one of them,—and that that force was unreasonable force, under all the circumstances, then [the defendant] would be doing an unlawful act, if the force was unreasonable, because he had no right to use it. He would be liable then for the injury done to this boy with the stick. * * * "[The jury rendered a verdict for the plaintiff.]

We think the charge is a very fair statement of the law of the case. * * * The right of the plaintiff to recover was made to depend upon an intention on the part of the defendant to hit somebody, and to inflict an unwarranted injury upon some one. Under these circumstances, the fact that the injury resulted to another than was intended does not relieve the defendant from responsibility. * * *

The judgment will be affirmed, with costs.

NOTES AND QUESTIONS

1. This doctrine of "transferred intent" was derived originally from the criminal law and dates back to the time when tort damages were awarded as a side issue in criminal prosecutions. It is familiar enough in the criminal law, and has been applied in many tort cases where the defendant has shot at A, struck at him, or thrown a punch or rock at him, and unintentionally hit B instead. See, for example, Lopez v. Surchia, 112

Cal.App.2d 314, 246 P.2d 111 (1952) (shooting); Carnes v. Thompson, 48 S.W.2d 903 (Mo.1932) (striking with pliers); Baska v. Scherzer, 283 Kan. 750, 156 P.3d 617 (2007) (while throwing punches at each other, teenagers hit a woman who stepped between them to stop the fight); Singer v. Marx, 144 Cal.App.2d 637, 301 P.2d 440 (1956) (throwing a rock).

2. The doctrine is discussed in Prosser, Transferred Intent, 45 Tex.L.Rev. 650 (1967). The conclusion there is that it applies whenever both the tort intended and the resulting harm fall within the scope of the old action of trespass—that is, where both involve direct and immediate application of force to the person or to tangible property. There are five torts that fell within the trespass writ: battery, assault, false imprisonment, trespass to land, and trespass to chattels. When the defendant intends any one of the five, and accomplishes any one of the five, the doctrine applies and the defendant is liable, even if the plaintiff was not the intended target. Restatement (Third) of Torts § 33, comment *c*, (2010) suggests courts likely would apply transferred intent to Conversion actions as well.

3. Thus defendant is liable when he shoots to frighten A (assault) and the bullet unforeseeably hits a stranger (battery). Brown v. Martinez, 68 N.M. 271, 361 P.2d 152 (1961) (facts similar to principal case—defendant fired warning shot to scare intruders away from his watermelon patch and hit plaintiff whom he did not know was there) and Hall v. McBryde, 919 P.2d 910 (Colo.App.1996) (firing at passing car and hitting neighbor). Or when he shoots at a dog (trespass to chattels) and hits a boy scout (battery). Corn v. Sheppard, 179 Minn. 490, 229 N.W. 869 (1930). What if defendant, believing a house to be empty, intends arson (trespass to chattels) and accomplishes battery (sleeping man killed by smoke inhalation)? Cf. Lewis v. Allstate Ins. Co., 730 So.2d 65 (Miss. 1998).

4. On the other hand, when either the tort intended or the one accomplished does not fall within the trespass action, the doctrine does not apply. Clark v. Gay, 112 Ga. 777, 38 S.E. 81 (1901) (defendant committed murder in plaintiff's house and plaintiff sought value of house because his family refused to live there after the murder); McGee v. Vanover, 148 Ky. 737, 147 S.W. 742 (1912) (defendant inflicted beating on A, causing mental distress to plaintiff bystander).

2. BATTERY

Cole v. Turner

Nisi Prius, 1704.
6 Modern Rep. 149, 90 Eng.Rep. 958.

At Nisi Prius, upon evidence in trespass for assault and battery, Holt, C.J., declared:

1. That the least touching of another in anger is a battery.

2. If two or more meet in a narrow passage, and without any violence or design of harm, the one touches the other gently it will be no battery.

3. If any of them use violence against the other, to force his way in a rude inordinate manner, it is a battery; or any struggle about the passage, to that degree as may do hurt, is a battery.

NOTES AND QUESTIONS

1. Defendant approached the plaintiff in an offensive manner, took hold of the breast of his coat, and said that he demanded satisfaction. Is this a battery? United States v. Ortega, 4 Wash.C.C. 531, 27 Fed.Cas. 359 (E.D.Pa.1825). What about spitting in the plaintiff's face? Alcorn v. Mitchell, 63 Ill. 553 (1872). Or forcibly removing his hat? Seigel v. Long, 169 Ala. 79, 53 So. 753 (1910). Or an attempted search of his pockets? Piggly-Wiggly Alabama Co. v. Rickles, 212 Ala. 585, 103 So. 860 (1925). Or touching her private parts? Skousen v. Nidy, 90 Ariz. 215, 367 P.2d 248 (1961). Cf. Gates v. State, 110 Ga.App. 303, 138 S.E.2d 473 (1964) (stranger touching woman on the buttocks). All are examples of offensive touching.

2. What about tapping plaintiff on the shoulder to attract his attention? "Pardon me, sir, could you direct me, etc."? Coward v. Baddeley, 4 H. & N. 478, 157 Eng.Rep. 927 (1859). Tapping someone on the shoulder to get their attention is a common example of touching that is not offensive.

Wallace v. Rosen

Court of Appeals of Indiana, 2002.
765 N.E.2d 192.

KIRSCH, J. Mable Wallace appeals the jury verdict in favor of Indianapolis Public Schools (IPS) and Harriet Rosen, a teacher for IPS. On appeal, Wallace raises the following issues:

I. Whether the trial court erred in refusing to give her tendered jury instruction regarding battery. * * *

We affirm.

FACTS AND PROCEDURAL HISTORY

[Rosen was a teacher at Northwest High School in Indianapolis. On April 22, 1994, the high school had a fire drill while classes were in session. The drill was not previously announced to the teachers and occurred just one week after a fire was extinguished in a bathroom near Rosen's classroom. On the day the alarm sounded, Wallace, who was recovering from foot surgery, was at the high school delivering homework to her daughter Lalaya. Wallace saw Lalaya just as Wallace neared the top of a staircase and stopped to speak to her. Two of Lalaya's friends also stopped to talk. Just then, the alarm sounded and students began filing down the stairs while Wallace took a step or two up the stairs to the second floor landing. As Rosen escorted her class to the designated stairway she noticed three or four people talking together at the top of the stairway and blocking the students' exit. Rosen did not recognize any of the individuals but approached "telling everybody to move it." Wallace, with her back to Rosen, was unable to hear Rosen over the noise of the alarm and Rosen had to touch her on the back to get her attention. Rosen then told Wallace, "you've got to get moving because this is a fire drill." At trial, Wallace testified that Rosen pushed her and she slipped and fell down the stairs. Rosen denied pushing Wallace, but admitted touching her back. At the close of the trial, the trial court judge refused to give the jury an instruction concerning civil battery that was requested by plaintiff. The jury found in favor of IPS and Rosen on the negligence count, and Wallace appealed.]

DISCUSSION AND DECISION

* * *

I. Battery Instruction

Wallace first argues that it was error for the trial court to refuse to give the jury the following tendered instruction pertaining to battery:

> A battery is the knowing or intentional touching of one person by another in a rude, insolent, or angry manner.
>
> Any touching, however slight, may constitute an assault and battery.
>
> Also, a battery may be recklessly committed where one acts in reckless disregard of the consequences, and the fact the person does not intend that the act shall result in an injury is immaterial. * * *

The Indiana Pattern Jury Instruction for the intentional tort of civil battery is as follows: "A battery is the knowing or intentional touching of a person against [his] [her] will in a rude, insolent, or angry manner." 2 Indiana Pattern Jury Instructions (Civil) 31.03 (2d ed. Revised 2001).[2] Battery is an intentional tort. [C] In discussing intent, Professors Prosser and Keeton made the following comments:

> In a loose and general sense, the meaning of "intent" is easy to grasp. As Holmes observed, even a dog knows the difference between being tripped over and being kicked. This is also the key distinction between two major divisions of legal liability—negligence and intentional torts. . . .
>
> It is correct to tell the jury that, relying on circumstantial evidence, they may infer that the actor's state of mind was the same as a reasonable person's state of mind would have been. Thus, . . . the defendant on a bicycle who rides down a person in full view on a sidewalk where there is ample room to pass may learn that the factfinder (judge or jury) is unwilling to credit the statement, "I didn't mean to do it."
>
> On the other hand, the mere knowledge and appreciation of a risk—something short of substantial certainty—is not intent. The defendant who acts in the belief or consciousness that the act is causing an appreciable risk of harm to another may be negligent, and if the risk is great the conduct may be characterized as reckless or wanton, but it is not an intentional wrong. In such cases the distinction between

2 The Indiana Pattern Jury Instructions are prepared under the auspices of the Indiana Judges Association and the Indiana Judicial Conference Criminal and Civil Instruction Committees. Although not formally approved for use, they are tacitly recognized by Indiana Trial Rule 51(E). [C]

intent and negligence obviously is a matter of degree. The line has to be drawn by the courts at the point where the known danger ceases to be only a foreseeable risk which a reasonable person would avoid, and becomes in the mind of the actor a substantial certainty.

The intent with which tort liability is concerned is not necessarily a hostile intent, or a desire to do any harm. Rather it is an intent to bring about a result which will invade the interests of another in a way that the law forbids. The defendant may be liable although intending nothing more than a good-natured practical joke, or honestly believing that the act would not injure the plaintiff, or even though seeking the plaintiff's own good. W. PAGE KEETON et al., PROSSER AND KEETON ON THE LAW OF TORTS, § 8, at 33, 36–37 (5th ed.1984) (footnotes omitted).

[Witnesses] testified that Rosen touched Wallace on the back causing her to fall down the stairs and injure herself. For battery to be an appropriate instruction, the evidence had to support an inference not only that Rosen intentionally touched Wallace, but that she did so in a rude, insolent, or angry manner, i.e., that she intended to invade Wallace's interests in a way that the law forbids.

Professors Prosser and Keeton also made the following observations about the intentional tort of battery and the character of the defendant's action: "In a crowded world, a certain amount of personal contact is inevitable and must be accepted. *Absent expression to the contrary, consent is assumed to all those ordinary contacts which are customary and reasonably necessary to the common intercourse of life, such as a tap on the shoulder to attract attention*, a friendly grasp of the arm, or a casual jostling to make a passage. . . ."

The time and place, and the circumstances under which the act is done, will necessarily affect its unpermitted character, and so will the relations between the parties. A stranger is not to be expected to tolerate liberties which would be allowed by an intimate friend. But unless the defendant has special reason to believe that more or less will be permitted by the individual plaintiff, the test is what would be offensive to an ordinary person not unduly sensitive as to personal dignity. KEETON et al., § 9, at 42 (emphasis added). * * *

[The court quoted from the trial transcript concerning the nature of the touching.]

Viewed most favorably to the trial court's decision refusing the tendered instruction, the foregoing evidence indicates that Rosen placed her fingertips on Wallace's shoulder and turned her 90 degrees toward the exit in the midst of a fire drill. The conditions on the stairway of Northwest High School during the fire drill were an example of Professors Prosser and Keeton's "crowded world." Individuals standing in the middle of a stairway during the fire drill could expect that a certain amount of personal contact would be inevitable. Rosen had a responsibility to her students to keep them moving in an orderly fashion down the stairs and out the door. Under these circumstances, Rosen's touching of Wallace's shoulder or back with her fingertips to get her attention over the noise of the alarm cannot be said to be a rude, insolent, or angry touching. Wallace has failed to show that the trial court abused its discretion in refusing the battery instruction. * * *

[Other issues raised by the appeal were then discussed.]

Affirmed. [The concurring opinions are omitted.]

NOTES AND QUESTIONS

1. Has the law of battery undergone any substantial changes since Cole v. Turner in 1704?

2. Do you agree that there was not enough evidence to let the jury decide whether the touching was offensive? The concurring opinion notes that there was testimony that the teacher had grabbed plaintiff's arm or shoulder to turn her around and that when plaintiff told her she was a parent, the teacher responded, "I don't care who you are, move it."

3. Note that the court refers to Indiana's pattern jury instruction on battery. Many jurisdictions have pattern or sample instructions that are available to the parties to use in requesting the instructions for their particular cases.

4. In the principal case, in a section omitted from this excerpt, the court noted that the third paragraph of the proposed instruction—that battery may be recklessly committed—was not an accurate statement of Indiana law and could have misled or confused the jury under the facts of the case. The court's discussion of the intent requirement makes it clear that it is an essential element. With the modern shift of emphasis to intent and negligence, as distinguished from trespass and case, "battery" has become exclusively an intentional tort. Thus there is no battery when defendant negligently, or even recklessly, drives his car into plaintiff and injures him, without intending to hit him. Cook v. Kinzua Pine Mills Co., 207 Or. 34, 293 P.2d 717 (1956). The same shift of emphasis accounts for the modern cases allowing recovery when the contact inflicted is not direct and immediate, but indirect.

RESTATEMENT (SECOND) OF TORTS (1965)

"§ 13. Battery: Harmful Contact

"An actor is subject to liability to another for battery if

"(a) he acts intending to cause a harmful or offensive contact with the person of the other or a third person, or an imminent apprehension of such a contact, and

"(b) a harmful contact with the person of the other directly or indirectly results."

"§ 18. Battery: Offensive Contact

"(1) An actor is subject to liability to another for battery if

"(a) he acts intending to cause a harmful or offensive contact with the person of the other or a third person, or an imminent apprehension of such a contact, and "(b) an offensive contact with the person of the other directly or indirectly results.

"(2) An act which is not done with the intention stated in Subsection (1, a) does not make the actor liable to the other for a mere offensive contact with the other's person although the act involves an unreasonable risk of inflicting it and, therefore, would be negligent or reckless if the risk threatened bodily harm."

NOTES AND QUESTIONS

1. When defendant intentionally causes plaintiff to undergo an offensive contact and the resulting injuries are more extensive than a reasonable person might have anticipated, the defendant will still be liable for those injuries. See Baldinger v. Banks, 26 Misc.2d 1086, 201 N.Y.S.2d 629 (1960) (six-year-old boy shoves four-year-old girl) (broken elbow); Harrigan v. Rosich, 173 So.2d 880 (La.App.1965) (defendant, wishing to get rid of the plaintiff, pushed him with his finger, and said, "Go home, old man.") (detached retina).

2. In Vosburg v. Putney, 80 Wis. 523, 50 N.W. 403 (1891), one schoolboy, during a class hour, playfully kicked another on the shin. He intended no harm, and the touch was so slight that the plaintiff did not actually feel it. It had, however, the effect of "lighting up" an infection in the leg from a previous injury, and as a result the plaintiff suffered damages found by the jury to be $2,500. The court found liability for battery even though the injury could not have been foreseen. The case is entertainingly and exhaustively discussed in Zile, Vosburg v. Putney: A Centennial Story, [1992] Wis.L.Rev. 877 (1992).

3. Does it make any difference if the defendant is trying to help the plaintiff? In Clayton v. New Dreamland Roller Skating Rink, Inc., 14 N.J.Super. 390, 82 A.2d 458 (1951), cert. denied, 13 N.J. 527, 100 A.2d 567 (1953), plaintiff fell at a skating rink and broke her arm. Over the protests of plaintiff and her husband, defendant's employees, one of whom was a prize fight manager who had first aid experience, proceeded to manipulate the arm in an attempt to set it. Is this battery?

4. While her husband was helping her get dressed in her hospital room the day after her back surgery, patient found a washable tattoo of a rose on her lower abdomen. Surgeon says he had placed it there to improve her spirits and help her heal and that none of his other patients had complained. Patient is very upset. Does she have a cause of action for battery? If so, what would her damages be? See Todd McHale, "Doctor is Sued for Giving Woman Tattoo in Surgery," Burlington County Times, July 17, 2008, at 1, available at 2008 WLNR 13781779.

5. Can the plaintiff make the defendant liable for contact that would not be offensive to a reasonable person, such as a tap on the shoulder to attract attention, by specifically forbidding that conduct? The Restatement (Second) of Torts § 19, leaves the question open. See Richmond v. Fiske, 160 Mass. 34, 35 N.E. 103 (1893), where defendant, against orders, entered plaintiff's bedroom and woke him up to present a milk bill. This was held to be battery, but no doubt it would be offensive to a reasonable person.

6. Can there be liability for battery for a contact of which plaintiff is unaware at the time? Did Sleeping Beauty have a cause of action against

Prince Charming? What if an unauthorized surgical operation is performed while plaintiff is under an anaesthetic? Does it make any difference whether the operation is harmful or beneficial? See Mohr v. Williams, page 100.

7. Does the exposure to a virus, such as herpes, through sexual activity constitute a battery? Does consent to the sexual activity operate as a defense? See Doe v. Johnson, 817 F.Supp. 1382 (W.D.Mich.1993) (battery action alleged in transmission of HIV; consent to intercourse does not bar action). Liability in Tort for the Sexual Transmission of Disease: Genital Herpes and the Law, 70 Cornell L.Rev. 101 (1984).

8. Does a mortician who embalms a body unaware that it was infected with the AIDS virus have a cause of action for battery? Cf., Funeral Services by Gregory v. Bluefield Community Hospital, 186 W.Va. 424, 413 S.E.2d 79 (1991). What about the patients of a dentist who does not disclose he has AIDS? What if the dentist always wore gloves during treatment procedures? Would the reasonable person find such touching offensive? See Brzoska v. Olson, 668 A.2d 1355 (Dela. 1995).

Fisher v. Carrousel Motor Hotel, Inc.

Supreme Court of Texas, 1967.
424 S.W.2d 627.

[Action for assault and battery. Plaintiff, a mathematician employed by NASA, was attending a professional conference on telemetry equipment at defendant's hotel. The meeting included a buffet luncheon. As plaintiff was standing in line with others, he was approached by one of defendant's employees, who snatched the plate from his hand, and shouted that a "Negro could not be served in the club." Plaintiff was not actually touched, and was in no apprehension of physical injury; but he was highly embarrassed and hurt by the conduct in the presence of his associates. The jury returned a verdict for $400 actual damages for his humiliation and indignity, and $500 exemplary (punitive) damages in addition. The trial court set aside the verdict and gave judgment for the defendants notwithstanding the verdict. This was affirmed by the Court of Civil Appeals. Plaintiff appealed to the Supreme Court.]

GREENHILL, JUSTICE * * * Under the facts of this case, we have no difficulty in holding that the intentional grabbing of plaintiff's plate constituted a battery. The intentional snatching of an object from one's hand is as clearly an offensive invasion of his person as would be an actual contact with the body. "To constitute an assault and battery, it is not necessary to touch the plaintiff's body or even his clothing; knocking or snatching anything from plaintiff's hand or touching anything connected with his person, when done in an offensive manner, is sufficient." Morgan v. Loyacomo, 190 Miss. 656, 1 So.2d 510 (1941).

Such holding is not unique to the jurisprudence of this State. In S.H. Kress & Co. v. Brashier, 50 S.W.2d 922 (Tex.Civ.App.1932, no writ), the defendant was held to have committed "an assault or trespass upon the person" by snatching a book from the plaintiff's hand. The jury findings in that case were that the defendant "dispossessed plaintiff of the book" and caused her to suffer "humiliation and indignity."

The rationale for holding an offensive contact with such an object to be a battery is explained in 1 Restatement (Second) of Torts § 18 (Comment p. 31) as follows:

> "Since the essence of the plaintiff's grievance consists in the offense to the dignity involved in the unpermitted and intentional invasion of the inviolability of his person and not in any physical harm done to his body, it is not necessary that the plaintiff's actual body be disturbed. Unpermitted and intentional contacts with anything so connected with the body as to be customarily regarded as part of the other's person and therefore as partaking of its inviolability is actionable as an offensive contact with his person. There are some things such as clothing or a cane or, indeed, anything directly grasped by the hand which are so intimately connected with one's body as to be universally regarded as part of the person."

We hold, therefore, that the forceful dispossession of plaintiff Fisher's plate in an offensive manner was sufficient to constitute a battery, and the trial court erred in granting judgment notwithstanding the verdict on the issue of actual damages. * * *

Damages for mental suffering are recoverable without the necessity for showing actual physical injury in a case of willful battery because the basis of that action is the unpermitted and intentional invasion of the plaintiff's person and not the actual harm done to the plaintiff's body. Restatement (Second) of Torts § 18. Personal indignity is the essence of an action for battery; and consequently the defendant is liable not only for contacts which do actual physical harm, but also for those which are offensive and insulting. [Cc]. We hold, therefore, that plaintiff was entitled to actual damages for mental suffering due to the willful battery, even in the absence of any physical injury. [The court then held that the defendant corporation was liable for the tort of its employee.]

The judgments of the courts below are reversed, and judgment is here rendered for the plaintiff for $900 with interest from the date of the trial court's judgment, and for costs of this suit.

NOTES AND QUESTIONS

1. What if the plate had been snatched without a racial epithet? Or, suppose the waiter had not touched plaintiff's plate, but said in a loud voice, "Get out, we don't serve Negroes here!"? What if the doorman at the hotel shouted a racial epithet and kicked plaintiff's car when he was about to leave. Battery? Cf. Van Eaton v. Thon, 764 S.W.2d 674 (Mo.App.1988) (defendant struck horse plaintiff was riding).

2. Does the utilization of the tort of battery confuse things? Why not characterize what happened as "intentional infliction of emotional harm"? Might the case be regarded as one of imaginative lawyering, assuming the state was not ready to recognize intentional infliction of emotional harm as a tort? What other remedies might have been available to plaintiff? Compare this with the *State Rubbish Collectors* case, page 53.

3. Defendant, unreasonably suspecting the plaintiff of shoplifting, forcibly seized a package from under her arm and opened it. Morgan v.

Loyacomo, 190 Miss. 656, 1 So.2d 510 (1941) (battery). Defendant deliberately blew pipe smoke in plaintiff's face, knowing she was allergic to it. Richardson v. Hennly, 209 Ga.App. 868, 434 S.E.2d 772 (1993), rev'd on other grounds, 264 Ga. 355, 444 S.E.2d 317 (1994) (battery). Defendant, coming up behind coworker in break room, snatched a ten dollar bill from his hand. Reynolds v. MacFarlane, 322 P.3d 755, 759 (Utah App. 2014) (quoting Prosser and Keeton on the Law of Torts: "contact with the plaintiff's clothing, or with a cane, a paper, or any other object held in plaintiff's hand" is enough for bodily contact).

4. A is standing with his arm around B's shoulder and leaning on him. C, passing by, violently jerks B's arm, as a result of which A falls down. To whom is C liable for battery? Reynolds v. Pierson, 29 Ind.App. 273, 64 N.E. 484 (1902).

3. ASSAULT

I de S et ux. v. W de S

At the Assizes, 1348.
Y.B.Lib.Ass. folio 99, placitum 60.

I de S and M, his wife, complain of W de S concerning this, that the said W, in the year, etc., with force and arms did make an assault upon the said M de S and beat her. And W pleaded not guilty. And it was found by the verdict of the inquest that the said W came at night to the house of the said I and sought to buy of his wine, but the door of the tavern was shut and he beat upon the door with a hatchet which he had in his hand, and the wife of the plaintiff put her head out of the window and commanded him to stop, and he saw and he struck with the hatchet but did not hit the woman. Whereupon the inquest said that it seemed to them that there was no trespass since no harm was done.

THORPE, C.J. There is harm done and a trespass for which he shall recover damages since he made an assault upon the woman, as has been found, although he did no other harm. Wherefore tax the damages, etc. And they taxed the damages at half a mark. Thorpe awarded that they should recover their damages, etc., and that the other should be taken. And so note that for an assault a man shall recover damages, etc.

NOTES AND QUESTIONS

1. This is the great-grandparent of all assault cases. Why allow the action if "no harm was done"?

Western Union Telegraph Co. v. Hill

Court of Appeals of Alabama, 1933.
25 Ala.App. 540, 150 So. 709.

Action for damages for assault by J.B. Hill against the Western Union Telegraph Company. From a judgment for plaintiff, defendant appeals.

SAMFORD, JUDGE. The action in this case is based upon an alleged assault on the person of plaintiff's wife by one Sapp, an agent of defendant in charge of its office in Huntsville, Ala. The assault complained of consisted of an attempt on the part of Sapp to put his hand on the person of plaintiff's wife coupled with a request that she come behind the counter in defendant's office, and that, if she would come and allow Sapp to love and pet her, he "would fix her clock."

The first question that addresses itself to us is, Was there such an assault as will justify an action for damages? * * *

While every battery includes an assault, an assault does not necessarily require a battery to complete it. What it does take to constitute an assault is an unlawful attempt to commit a battery, incomplete by reason of some intervening cause; or, to state it differently, to constitute an actionable assault there must be an intentional, unlawful, offer to touch the person of another in a rude or angry manner under such circumstances as to create in the mind of the party alleging the assault a well-founded fear of an imminent battery, coupled with the apparent present ability to effectuate the attempt, if not prevented. * * *

What are the facts here? Sapp was the agent of defendant and the manager of its telegraph office in Huntsville. Defendant was under contract with plaintiff to keep in repair and regulated an electric clock in plaintiff's place of business. When the clock needed attention, that fact was to be reported to Sapp, and he in turn would report to a special man, whose duty it was to do the fixing. At 8:13 o'clock p.m. plaintiff's wife reported to Sapp over the phone that the clock needed attention, and, no one coming to attend the clock, plaintiff's wife went to the office of defendant about 8:30 p.m. There she found Sapp in charge and behind a desk or counter, separating the public from the part of the room in which defendant's operator worked. The counter is four feet and two inches high, and so wide that, Sapp standing on the floor, leaning against the counter and stretching his arm and hand to the full length, the end of his fingers reaches just to the outer edge of the counter. The photographs in evidence show that the counter was as high as Sapp's armpits. Sapp had had two or three drinks and was "still slightly feeling the effects of whisky; I felt all right; I felt good and amiable." When plaintiff's wife came into the office, Sapp came from towards the rear of the room and asked what he could do for her. She replied: "I asked him if he understood over the phone that my clock was out of order and when he was going to fix it. He stood there and looked at me a few minutes and said: 'If you will come back here and let me love and pet you, I will fix your clock.' This he repeated and reached for me with his hand, he extended his hand toward me, he did not put it on me; I jumped back. I was in his reach as I stood there. He reached for me right along here (indicating her left shoulder and arm)." The foregoing is the evidence offered by plaintiff tending to prove assault. Per contra, aside from the positive denial by Sapp of any effort to touch Mrs. Hill, the physical surroundings as evidenced by the photographs of the locus tend to rebut any evidence going to prove that Sapp could have touched plaintiff's wife across that counter even if he had reached his hand in her direction unless she was leaning against the counter or Sapp should have stood upon something so as to elevate him and allow him to reach beyond the counter. However, there is testimony tending to prove that, notwithstanding the width of the counter and the height of Sapp, Sapp could have reached from six to eighteen inches beyond the desk in an effort to place his hand on Mrs. Hill. The evidence as a whole presents a question for the jury. This was the view taken by the trial judge, and in the several rulings bearing on this question there is no error. * * *

[Reversed on the ground that Sapp had not acted within the scope of his employment.]

NOTES AND QUESTIONS

1. Defendant, standing three or four feet from plaintiff, made a "kissing sign" at her by puckering his lips and smacking them. He did not touch her and made no effort to kiss her or to use any force. Is this an assault? Fuller v. State, 44 Tex.Crim. 463, 72 S.W. 184 (1903) (leering alone is not enough). Defendant Ku Klux Klan members dressed in KKK robes and carrying guns rode around in a shrimp boat on Galveston Bay from dock to dock frightening Vietnamese fishermen and their families. What would the family members have to prove to recover for assault? See, Vietnamese Fishermen's Ass'n v. Knights of the K.K.K., 518 F.Supp. 993 (S.D.Tex.1981) (applying Texas law).

2. Defendant, a hundred yards from plaintiff, starts running toward him, throwing rocks as he runs. At what point does this become an assault? Cf. State v. Davis, 23 N.C. (1 Ired.) 125, 35 Am.Dec. 735 (1840) (at the point where defendant is close enough so that plaintiff's apprehension of imminent contact is reasonable).

3. What about mere preparation, such as bringing a gun along for an interview? Penny v. State, 114 Ga. 77, 39 S.E. 871 (1901).

4. What if the threat is not imminent? Brower v. Ackerley, 88 Wash.App. 87, 943 P.2d 1141, 1145 (1997) (threats of future action—"I'm going to find out where you live and kick your ass" and "you're finished; cut you in your sleep"—not imminent enough to state cause of action for assault.) Does a complaint state a cause of action for assault if one paragraph of the complaint asserts that the defendants threatened to strike the plaintiffs with blackjacks and that the threats placed the plaintiffs in fear that a battery will be committed against them and a subsequent paragraph asserts that the defendants showed the plaintiffs that the defendants were carrying blackjacks? Cucinotti v. Ortmann, 399 Pa. 26, 159 A.2d 216 (1960) ("words in themselves, no matter how threatening, do not constitute an assault").

5. Is there an assault if defendant threatens the plaintiff with an unloaded gun? See Allen v. Hannaford, 138 Wash. 423, 244 P. 700 (1926). Suppose the gun remains lying in defendant's lap? See Castiglione v. Galpin, 325 So.2d 725 (La.App.1976).

6. In State v. Barry, 45 Mont. 598, 124 P. 775 (1912), it was held that there was no assault where the plaintiff did not learn that a gun was aimed at him with intent to shoot him until it was all over. The Restatement (Second) of Torts § 22, has agreed. See also Reynolds v. MacFarlane, 322 P.3d 755, 758 (Utah App. 2014) (no assault where ten dollar bill was snatched from plaintiff's hand from behind because no

evidence that plaintiff was aware of defendant's impending action to grab the bill before defendant completed the act of taking the bill).

7. A major distinction between a criminal assault and an assault in tort is that for criminal assault, a victim need not have an apprehension of contact. A criminal assault occurs if the defendant intends to injure the victim and has the ability to do so. Commonwealth v. Slaney, 345 Mass. 135, 185 N.E.2d 919 (1962). For the tort of assault, the victim must have an apprehension of contact, and it is not necessary that the defendant have the actual ability to carry out the threatened contact. Depending upon the jurisdiction, a defendant could be subject to either criminal prosecution or civil damages, or both.

8. Although the court uses the term "fear" of an imminent battery, assault requires only apprehension or anticipation. Suppose Hill had a black belt in karate and was contemptuous of Sapp? Assault? Cf. Brady v. Schatzel, [1911] Q.St.R. 206, 208 (police officer testified he was not afraid when defendant pulled a gun on him because he did not believe he would fire it). Why might a lawyer plead and try to prove fear if it is not a necessary element of the tort?

9. What if these words are accompanied by a threatening gesture? Assault?

A. With his hand upon his sword, "If it were not assize-time, I would not take such language from you." Tuberville v. Savage, 1 Modern Rep. 3 (1699).

B. "Were you not an old man, I would knock you down." State v. Crow, 23 N.C. (1 Ired.) 375 (1841).

C. "If it were not for your gray hairs, I would tear your heart out." Commonwealth v. Eyre, 1 Serg. & Rawle 347 (Pa.1815).

D. "I have a great mind to hit you." State v. Hampton, 63 N.C. 13 (1868).

E. "If you do not pay me my money, I will have your life"? Keefe v. State, 19 Ark. 190 (1857).

10. Can words make an assault out of conduct that would otherwise not be sufficient for the tort? Suppose that while defendant and plaintiff are engaged in a violent quarrel, defendant reaches for his hip pocket. Does it make any difference whether he says, "I'll blow your brains out," or "Pardon me, I need a handkerchief"?

11. What about words that threaten harm from an independent source? "Look out! There is a rattlesnake behind you!"

4. FALSE IMPRISONMENT

Big Town Nursing Home, Inc. v. Newman

Court of Civil Appeals of Texas, 1970.
461 S.W.2d 195.

MCDONALD, CHIEF JUSTICE. This is an appeal by defendant Nursing Home from a judgment for plaintiff Newman for actual and exemplary damages in a false imprisonment case.

Plaintiff Newman sued defendant Nursing Home for actual and exemplary damages for falsely and wrongfully imprisoning him against his will from September 22, 1968 to November 11, 1968. * * *

Plaintiff is a retired printer 67 years of age, and lives on his social security and a retirement pension from his brother's printing company. He has not worked since 1959, is single, has Parkinson's disease, arthritis, heart trouble, a voice impediment, and a hiatal hernia. He has served in the army attaining the rank of Sergeant. He has never been in a mental hospital or treated by a psychiatrist. Plaintiff was taken to defendant nursing home on September 19, 1968, by his nephew who signed the admission papers and paid one month's care in advance. Plaintiff had been arrested for drunkenness and drunken driving in times past (the last time in 1966) and had been treated twice for alcoholism. Plaintiff testified he was not intoxicated and had nothing to drink during the week prior to admission to the nursing home. The admission papers provided that patient "will not be forced to remain in the nursing home against his will for any length of time." Plaintiff was not advised he would be kept at the nursing home against his will. On September 22, 1968, plaintiff decided he wanted to leave and tried to telephone for a taxi. Defendant's employees advised plaintiff he could not use the phone, or have any visitors unless the manager knew them, and locked plaintiff's grip and clothes up. Plaintiff walked out of the home, but was caught by employees of defendant and brought back forceably, and thereafter, placed in Wing 3 and locked up. Defendant's Administrator testified Wing 3 contained senile patients, drug addicts, alcoholics, mentally disturbed, incorrigibles and uncontrollables, and that "they were all in the same kettle of fish." Plaintiff tried to escape from the nursing home five or six times but was caught and brought back each time against his will. He was carried back to Wing 3 and locked and taped in a "restraint chair", for more than five hours. He was put back in the chair on subsequent occasions. He was not seen by the home doctor for some 10 days after he was admitted, and for 7 days after being placed in Wing 3. The doctor wrote the social security office to change payment of plaintiff's social security checks without plaintiff's authorization. Plaintiff made every effort to leave and repeatedly asked the manager and assistant manager to be permitted to leave. The home doctor is actually a resident studying pathology and has no patients other than those in two nursing homes. Finally, on November 11, 1968, plaintiff escaped and caught a ride into Dallas, where he called a taxi and was taken to the home of a friend. During plaintiff's ordeal he lost 30 pounds. There was never any court proceeding to confine plaintiff. * * *

False imprisonment is the direct restraint of one person of the physical liberty of another without adequate legal justification. There is ample evidence to sustain [the jury's finding that plaintiff was falsely imprisoned]. * * *

Defendant placed plaintiff in Wing 3 with insane persons, alcoholics and drug addicts knowing he was not in such category; punished plaintiff by locking and taping him in the restraint chair; prevented him from using the telephone for 51 days; locked up his clothes; told him he could not be released from Wing 3 until he began to obey the rules of the home; and detained him for 51 days during which period he was demanding to be released and attempting to escape. * * *

Defendant may be compelled to respond in exemplary damages if the act causing actual damages is a wrongful act done intentionally in violation of the rights of plaintiff. [Cc]

Defendant acted in the utter disregard of plaintiff's legal rights, knowing there was no court order for commitment, and that the admission agreement provided he was not to be kept against his will. * * *

Court of Appeals < Holding

[The court of appeals found that the amount of damages was excessive and offered plaintiff a remittitur. Plaintiff subsequently agreed to the remittitur and the judgment below, so reformed, was affirmed.]

NOTES AND QUESTIONS

1. Plaintiff has a ticket to enter defendant's race track, but defendant refuses to admit him because the stewards have banned him from the track. False imprisonment? Marrone v. Washington Jockey Club, 35 App.D.C. 82 (1910) (mere refusal to admit not false imprisonment). Plaintiff attempts to enter a dance hall during a public dance, but is prevented by defendant who is under the mistaken belief that she is under eighteen. False imprisonment? Cullen v. Dickenson, 33 S.D. 27, 144 N.W. 656 (1913) (no). Suppose the exclusion is based on race or religion? There may be a civil rights action, but not false imprisonment. See 42 U.S.C. § 2000a, page 79, note 4.

2. Can there be false imprisonment in a moving automobile? Cieplinski v. Severn, 269 Mass. 261, 168 N.E. 722 (1929) (yes). In a city? Allen v. Fromme, 141 App.Div. 362, 126 N.Y.S. 520 (1910) (yes). In the state of Rhode Island? Texas? Cf. Albright v. Oliver, 975 F.2d 343 (7th Cir.1992) (in dicta, court notes that actionable confinement could be "as large as an entire state"). When plaintiff is not permitted to leave the country? Cf. Shen v. Leo A. Daly Co., 222 F.3d 472 (8th Cir. 2000) (applying Nebraska law) (although difficult to define exactly how close the restraint must be, the country of Taiwan is clearly too great an area within which to be falsely imprisoned).

3. If one exit of a room or a building is locked with plaintiff inside, but another reasonable means of exit is left open, there is no imprisonment. Davis & Allcott Co. v. Boozer, 215 Ala. 116, 110 So. 28 (1926) (door through which plaintiff had entered was locked but other door was not); Furlong v. German-American Press Ass'n, 189 S.W. 385, 389 (Mo.1916) ("If a way of escape is left open which is available without peril of life or limb, no imprisonment"). See also the classic case of Bird v. Jones, 7 A. & E., N.S., 742, 115 Eng.Rep. 668 (1845) (the portion of Hammersmith Bridge across the Thames River ordinarily used as a footpath was obstructed by seats that defendant had erected for viewing a regatta on the river and defendant's agents refused to let plaintiff pass along the footpath; no false imprisonment because plaintiff could have returned the way he had come or crossed the bridge in the carriage way).

4. The Restatement (Second) of Torts § 36, comment *a*, treats the means of escape as unreasonable if it involves exposure of the person

(plaintiff in the water and defendant steals his clothes), material harm to the clothing, or danger of substantial harm to another. Plaintiff would not be required to make his escape by crawling through a sewer.

5. A means of escape is not a reasonable one if the plaintiff does not know of its existence, and it is not apparent. Talcott v. National Exhibition Co., 144 App.Div. 337, 128 N.Y.S. 1059 (1911).

6. What if it's just a joke? Employees of airline that prides itself on being a "fun-loving, spirited company" arranged for local police officers to perform a mock arrest of a new employee, complete with handcuffs and a suggestion that she find someone to post bail, as a prank to celebrate the end of her probation. Fuerschbach v. Southwest Airlines Co., 439 F.3d 1197 (10th Cir. 2006) (applying New Mexico law) (neither brevity of seizure nor its characterization as a prank enabled officers to avoid liability).

7. Along with battery and assault, false imprisonment has now become exclusively an intentional tort. The Restatement (Second) of Torts § 35, comment *h*, points out, however, that for negligence resulting in the confinement of another a negligence action will lie, but only if some actual damage results. Cf. Mouse v. Central Sav. & Trust Co., 120 Ohio St. 599, 7 Ohio L.Abs. 334, 167 N.E. 868 (1929). What would be the result if defendant double-parks his automobile and thus prevents plaintiff from driving to an important business meeting? False imprisonment is also like battery and assault in that no actual damages need be proved. Nominal damages may be awarded. Banks v. Fritsch, 39 S.W.3d 474 (Ky. App. 2001) (teacher who chained student to tree because of repeated absenteeism liable for nominal damages if student could not prove actual damages).

Parvi v. City of Kingston

Court of Appeals of New York, 1977.
41 N.Y.2d 553, 362 N.E.2d 960, 394 N.Y.S.2d 161.

[Police, responding to a complaint, found two brothers engaged in a noisy quarrel in an alley behind a commercial building. Plaintiff was with them, apparently trying to calm them. According to police testimony, all three were showing "the effects of alcohol." Plaintiff told the police he had no place to go, so rather than arrest him, they took him outside the city limits to an abandoned golf course to "dry out." There was conflicting testimony as to whether he went willingly. Within an hour, plaintiff had wandered 350 feet and onto the New York State Thruway, where he was struck by a car and severely injured. On cross-examination, he admitted he had no recollection of what happened that night.

Action for false imprisonment. The trial court dismissed the case and the Appellate Division affirmed.]

FUCHSBERG, JUSTICE. * * * [The element of] consciousness of confinement is a more subtle and more interesting subissue in this case. On that subject, we note that, while respected authorities have divided on whether awareness of confinement by one who has been falsely imprisoned should be a *sine qua non* for making out a case, [cc] *Broughton* [v. State of New York], 37 N.Y.2d p. 456, 373 N.Y.S.2d p. 92, 335 N.E.2d p. 313 has laid that question to rest in this State. Its holding gives recognition to the fact that false imprisonment, as a dignitary tort, is not suffered unless its victim knows of the dignitary invasion. Interestingly, the Restatement (Second) of Torts § 42 too has taken the position that there is no liability for intentionally confining another unless the person physically restrained knows of the confinement or is harmed by it.

However, though correctly proceeding on that premise, the Appellate Division, in affirming the dismissal of the cause of action for false imprisonment, erroneously relied on the fact that Parvi, after having provided additional testimony in his own behalf on direct examination, had agreed on cross that he no longer had any *recollection* of his confinement. In so doing, that court failed to distinguish between a later recollection of consciousness and the existence of that consciousness at the time when the imprisonment itself took place. The latter, of course, is capable of being proved though one who suffers the consciousness can no longer personally describe it, whether by reason of lapse of memory, incompetency, death or other cause. Specifically, in this case, while it may well be that the alcohol Parvi had imbibed or the injuries he sustained, or both, had had the effect of wiping out his recollection of being in the police car against his will, that is a far cry from saying that he was not conscious of his confinement at the time when it was actually taking place. And, even if plaintiff's sentient state at the time of his imprisonment was something less than total sobriety, that does not mean that he had no conscious sense of what was then happening to him. To the contrary, there is much in the record to support a finding that the plaintiff indeed was aware of his arrest at the time it took place. By way of illustration, the officers described Parvi's responsiveness to their command that he get into the car, his colloquy while being driven to Coleman Hill and his request to be let off elsewhere. At the very least, then, it was for the jury, in the first instance, to weigh credibility, evaluate inconsistencies and determine whether the burden of proof had been met. * * *

Reversed.

BREITEL, CHIEF JUDGE (dissenting). * * * [P]laintiff has failed even to make out a prima facie case that he was conscious of his purported confinement, and that he failed to consent to it. His memory of the entire incident had disappeared; at trial, Parvi admitted that he no longer had any independent recollection of what happened on the day of his accident, and that as to the circumstances surrounding his entrance into the police car, he only knew what had been suggested to him by subsequent conversations. In light of this testimony, Parvi's conclusory statement that he was ordered into the car against his will is insufficient, as a matter of law, to establish a prima facie case. * * *

NOTES AND QUESTIONS

1. In addition to the false imprisonment claim, could plaintiff have filed a negligence claim based on the police officers' conduct? For a more recent case with eerily similar facts, see Deuser v. Vecera, 139 F.3d 1190 (8th Cir.1998) (plaintiff's decedent who had been briefly detained by park rangers for public drunkenness, but not arrested, was released in a parking lot, and wandered onto interstate where he was killed by motorist).

2. The mother of a feverish and disoriented 16-year-old boy instructed a police officer to take her son to a particular hospital where her family physician was meeting them. Is there false imprisonment if the officer intentionally takes the boy to a different hospital? Cf. Haisenleder v. Reeder, 114 Mich.App. 258, 318 N.W.2d 634 (1982). Or what if the plaintiff, a sufferer from diabetes who is unconscious from insulin shock, is wrongfully arrested and confined in jail overnight in the belief that he is drunk, but is released before he regains consciousness. Is there a tort? See Prosser, False Imprisonment: Consciousness of Confinement, 55 Colum.L.Rev. 847 (1955); Restatement (Second) of Torts § 42.

3. Called upon to make an emergency evaluation, a doctor diagnoses a person as mentally ill and has her detained in a mental institution. Is this false imprisonment? See Williams v. Smith, 179 Ga.App. 712, 348 S.E.2d 50 (1986) (no false imprisonment if statutory commitment procedures were followed even if doctor was negligent in diagnosis); Foshee v. Health Mgt. Assocs., 675 So.2d 957 (Fla.App.1996) (false imprisonment if statutory commitment procedures were not followed by nurse who physically prevented patient from leaving a psychiatric facility and coerced her into signing voluntary admission papers). What if a hospital detains a woman for two hours while its staff initiates involuntary commitment proceedings because she is agitated and threatened suicide? Riffe v. Armstrong, 197 W.Va. 626, 477 S.E.2d 535 (1996) (hospital's action justified in light of plaintiff's condition upon arrival).

Hardy v. LaBelle's Distributing Co.

Supreme Court of Montana, 1983.
203 Mont. 263, 661 P.2d 35.

GULBRANDSON, JUSTICE. * * * Defendant, LaBelle's Distributing Company (LaBelle's) hired Hardy as a temporary employee on December 1, 1978. She was assigned duty as a sales clerk in the jewelry department.

On December 9, 1978, another employee for LaBelle's, Jackie Renner, thought she saw Hardy steal one of the watches that LaBelle's had in stock. Jackie Renner reported her belief to LaBelle's showroom manager that evening.

On the morning of December 10, Hardy was approached by the assistant manager of LaBelle's jewelry department and told that all new employees were given a tour of the store. He showed her into the showroom manager's office and then left, closing the door behind him.

There is conflicting testimony concerning who was present in the showroom manager's office when Hardy arrived. Hardy testified that David Kotke, the showroom manager, Steve Newsom, the store's loss prevention manager, and a uniformed policeman were present. Newsom and one of the policemen in the room testified that another policeman, instead of Kotke, was present.

Hardy was told that she had been accused of stealing a watch. Hardy denied taking the watch and agreed to take a lie detector test. According to conflicting testimony, the meeting lasted approximately from twenty to forty-five minutes.

Hardy took the lie detector test, which supported her statement that she had not taken the watch. The showroom manager apologized to Hardy the next morning and told her that she was still welcome to work at LaBelle's. The employee who reported seeing Hardy take the watch also apologized. The two employees then argued briefly, and Hardy left the store.

Hardy brought this action claiming that defendants had wrongfully detained her against her will when she was questioned about the watch.

On appeal Hardy raises basically two issues: (1) Whether the evidence is sufficient to support the verdict and judgment and (2) Whether the District Court erred in the issuance of its instructions.

The two key elements of false imprisonment are the restraint of an individual against his will and the unlawfulness of such restraint. [Cc] The individual may be restrained by acts or merely by words which he fears to disregard. [Cc]

Here, there is ample evidence to support the jury's finding that Hardy was not unlawfully restrained against her will. While Hardy stated that she felt compelled to remain in the showroom manager's office, she also admitted that she wanted to stay and clarify the situation. She did not ask to leave. She was not told she could not leave. No threat of force or otherwise was made to compel her to stay. Although she followed the assistant manager into the office under pretense of a tour, she testified at trial that she would have followed him voluntarily if she had known the true purpose of the meeting and that two policemen were in the room. Under these circumstances, the jury could easily find that Hardy was not detained against her will. [Cc] See also, Meinecke v. Skaggs (1949), 123 Mont. 308, 213 P.2d 237, and Roberts v. Coleman (1961), 228 Or. 286, 365 P.2d 79. * * *

[The court also found that the District Court did not err in issuance of jury instructions on the law of false imprisonment, and affirmed the District Court's judgment in favor of defendants.]

NOTES AND QUESTIONS

1. The Restatement suggests that, in addition to physical barriers, a false imprisonment can be accomplished by force, threat of force, duress, or asserted legal authority. Restatement (Second) of Torts §§ 37–41 (1965).

2. False imprisonment has not been extended beyond such direct duress to person or to property. As the principal case shows, persuading someone it is in her best interest to stay is not enough. If the plaintiff submits merely to persuasion, and accompanies the defendant to clear himself of suspicion, without any implied threat of force, the action does not lie. Hunter v. Laurent, 158 La. 874, 104 So. 747 (1925); James v. MacDougall & Southwick Co., 134 Wash. 314, 235 P. 812 (1925). Suppose the defendant says to the plaintiff, "You must remain in this room, or I will never speak to you again"? Compare Fitscher v. Rollman & Sons Co., 31 Ohio App. 340, 167 N.E. 469 (1929), where defendant threatened to make a scene on the street unless plaintiff remained.

3. Retention of plaintiff's property sometimes may provide the "restraint" necessary to constitute false imprisonment. See Fischer v.

Famous-Barr Co., 646 S.W.2d 819 (Mo.App.1982), where plaintiff set off the security alarm when exiting a store because the salesperson forgot to remove the sensor tag from an article of clothing she had purchased. Because an employee of the store took possession of the bag containing her purchases, plaintiff felt she had to follow the employee back to the fourth floor where she had made her purchase. Compare Marcano v. Northwestern Chrysler-Plymouth Sales, Inc., 550 F.Supp. 595 (N.D.Ill.1982), where plaintiff went to a car dealership to discuss a dispute over payments on her loan and voluntarily gave her keys to the dealer so he could inspect the car. The dealer locked the car and kept the keys. Plaintiff stayed at the dealership for five hours. The court held that there was no false imprisonment because she could have left and because the intention of defendant was not to confine her personally, but only to keep the car.

4. An employee is suspected of stealing property from her employer and is told a trip to her home is necessary to recover the property. If the employee feels mentally compelled for fear of losing her job to go in an automobile with her supervisor to her home, has she been confined involuntarily? See Faniel v. Chesapeake & Potomac Tel. Co., 404 A.2d 147 (D.C.App.1979) (fear of losing one's job is a powerful incentive, but it does not render behavior involuntary).

5. It is generally agreed that false imprisonment resembles assault, in that threats of future action are not enough. Thus the action does not lie where the defendant merely threatens to call the police and have the plaintiff arrested unless he remains. Sweeney v. F.W. Woolworth Co., 247 Mass. 277, 142 N.E. 50 (1924); Priddy v. Bunton, 177 S.W.2d 805 (Tex.Civ.App.1943).

6. On the shopkeeper's privilege to detain a suspected thief, see Bonkowski v. Arlan's Department Store, page 122.

Enright v. Groves

Colorado Court of Appeals, 1977.
39 Colo.App. 39, 560 P.2d 851.

SMITH, JUDGE. Defendants Groves and City of Ft. Collins appeal from judgments entered against them upon jury verdicts awarding plaintiff $500 actual damages and $1,000 exemplary damages on her claim of false imprisonment * * *.

The evidence at trial disclosed that on August 25, 1974, Officer Groves, while on duty as a uniformed police officer of the City of Fort Collins, observed a dog running loose in violation of the city's "dog leash" ordinance. He observed the animal approaching what was later identified as the residence of Mrs. Enright, the plaintiff. As Groves approached the house, he encountered Mrs. Enright's eleven-year-old son, and asked him if the dog belonged to him. The boy replied that it was his dog, and told Groves that his mother was sitting in the car parked at the curb by the house. Groves then ordered the boy to put the dog inside the house, and turned and started walking toward the Enright vehicle.

Groves testified that he was met by Mrs. Enright with whom he was not acquainted. She asked if she could help him. Groves responded by demanding her driver's license. She replied by giving him her name and address. He again demanded her driver's license, which she declined to produce. Groves thereupon advised her that she could either produce her driver's license or go to jail. Mrs. Enright responded by asking, "Isn't this ridiculous?" Groves thereupon grabbed one of her arms, stating, "Let's go!" * * *

She was taken to the police station where a complaint was signed charging her with violation of the "dog leash" ordinance and bail was set. Mrs. Enright was released only after a friend posted bail. She was later convicted of the ordinance violation. * * *

Appellants contend that Groves had probable cause to arrest Mrs. Enright, and that she was in fact arrested for and convicted of violation of the dog-at-large ordinance. They assert, therefore, that her claim for false imprisonment or false arrest cannot lie, and that Groves' use of force in arresting Mrs. Enright was permissible. We disagree.

False arrest arises when one is taken into custody by a person who claims but does not have proper legal authority. W. Prosser, Torts § 11 (4th ed.). Accordingly, a claim for false arrest will not lie if an officer has a valid warrant or probable cause to believe that an offense has been committed and that the person who was arrested committed it. Conviction of the crime for which one is specifically arrested is a complete defense to a subsequent claim of false arrest. [Cc]

Here, however, the evidence is clear that Groves arrested Mrs. Enright, not for violation of the dog leash ordinance, but rather for refusing to produce her driver's license. This basis for the arrest is exemplified by the fact that he specifically advised her that she would either produce the license or go to jail. We find no statute or case law in this jurisdiction which requires a citizen to show her driver's license upon demand, unless, for example, she is a driver of an automobile and such demand is made in that connection. * * *

Here, there was no testimony that Groves ever even attempted to explain why he was demanding plaintiff's driver's license, and it is clear that she had already volunteered her name and address. Groves admitted that he did not ask Mrs. Enright if she had any means of identification on her person, instead he simply demanded that she give him her driver's license.

We conclude that Groves' demand for Mrs. Enright's driver's license was not a lawful order and that refusal to comply therewith was not therefore an offense in and of itself. Groves was not therefore entitled to use force in arresting Mrs. Enright. Thus Groves' defense based upon an arrest for and conviction of a specific offense must, as a matter of law, fail. * * *

Judgment affirmed.

NOTES AND QUESTIONS

1. It is not necessary that the defendant be an officer to assert authority of law. Suppose a filling station attendant asserts legal authority to detain the plaintiff, believing he had stolen cash from the station? Daniel v. Phillips Petroleum Co., 229 Mo.App. 150, 73 S.W.2d 355 (1934).

(upholding jury verdict for plaintiff). Plaintiff, alighting from defendant's train, fell and broke his leg. Defendant's conductor told plaintiff that the law required him to remain and fill out a statement about the accident. Plaintiff did so, and his cab was held for fifteen or twenty minutes, during which plaintiff was in considerable pain, while the statement was filled out and signed. This was held to be false imprisonment. Whitman v. Atchison, T. & S.F.R. Co., 85 Kan. 150, 116 P. 234 (1911).

2. A private citizen who physically aids a police officer in making a false arrest can be held liable to plaintiff for false imprisonment. If, however, the police officer requests assistance, the private citizen will not be liable unless he knows the arrest is an unlawful one. See Restatement (Second) of Torts §§ 45A and 139.

3. Merely providing information to the police, even if it turns out to be incorrect information, is not enough to support a claim of false imprisonment. Holcomb v. Walter's Dimmick Petroleum, Inc., 858 N.E.2d 103, 107 (Ind. 2006) ("Liability will not be imposed when the defendant does nothing more than detail his version of the facts to a policeman and ask for his assistance, leaving it to the officer to determine what is the appropriate response, at least where his representation of the facts does not prevent the intelligent exercise of the officer's discretion.") See also Highfill v. Hale, 186 S.W.3d 277 (Mo. 2006) (because deputy's decision to arrest neighbors for stalking was based at least partly on deputy's own investigation, complainant was not liable).

Whittaker v. Sandford

Supreme Judicial Court of Maine, 1912.
110 Me. 77, 85 A. 399.

[Plaintiff was a member and her husband was a minister of a religious sect, of which defendant was the leader. The sect had a colony in Maine and at Jaffa (now part of Tel Aviv), the latter of which plaintiff had joined. Plaintiff decided to abandon the sect and to return to America. While she and her four children were in Jaffa awaiting passage on a steamer, defendant offered her passage back to America on his yacht. When plaintiff told defendant that she was afraid that he would not let her off the yacht until she was "won to the movement again," defendant assured her repeatedly that under no circumstances would she be detained on board. Plaintiff accepted this assurance and sailed for America on the yacht. On arrival in port, defendant refused to furnish her with a boat so that she could leave the yacht, saying it was up to her husband whether she could leave. When plaintiff raised the issue with her husband, he said it was up to defendant, the leader of the sect and the owner of the yacht. She remained on board for nearly a month, during which time defendant and plaintiff's husband attempted to persuade her to rejoin the sect. On several occasions, plaintiff, always in the company of her husband, was allowed to go ashore to the mainland and to various islands. She was not allowed to leave the yacht unaccompanied. She finally obtained her release and that of her four children with the assistance of the sheriff and a writ of habeas corpus. She then brought this action for false imprisonment. The jury returned a verdict in her favor for $1100. Defendant excepted to the court's instructions, and appealed from an order denying his motion for a new trial.]

SAVAGE, J. * * * The court instructed the jury that the plaintiff to recover must show that the restraint was physical, and not merely a moral influence; that it must have been actual physical restraint, in the sense that one intentionally locked into a room would be physically restrained but not necessarily involving physical force upon the person; that it was not necessary that the defendant, or any person by his direction, should lay his hand upon the plaintiff; that if the plaintiff was restrained so that she could not leave the yacht Kingdom by the intentional refusal to furnish transportation as agreed, she not having it in her power to escape otherwise, it would be a physical restraint and unlawful imprisonment. We think the instructions were apt and sufficient. If one should, without right, turn the key in a door, and thereby prevent a person in the room from leaving, it would be the simplest form of unlawful imprisonment. The restraint is physical. The four walls and the locked door are physical impediments to escape. Now is it different when one who is in control of a vessel at anchor, within practical rowing distance from the shore, who has agreed that a guest on board shall be free to leave, there being no means to leave except by rowboats, wrongfully refuses the guest the use of a boat? The boat is the key. By refusing the boat he turns the key. The guest is as effectually locked up as if there were walls along the sides of the vessel. The restraint is physical. The impassable sea is the physical barrier. * * *

A careful study of the evidence leads us to conclude that the jury were warranted in finding that the defendant was guilty of unlawful imprisonment. This, to be sure, is not an action based upon the defendant's failure to keep his agreement to permit the plaintiff to leave the yacht as soon as it should reach shore. But his duty under the circumstances is an important consideration. It cannot be believed that either party to the agreement understood that it was his duty merely to bring her to an American harbor. The agreement implied that she was to go ashore. There was no practical way for her to go ashore except in the yacht's boats. The agreement must be understood to mean that he would bring her to land, or to allow her to get to land, by the only available means. The evidence is that he refused her a boat. His refusal was wrongful. The case leaves not the slightest doubt that he had the power to control the boats, if he chose to exercise it. It was not enough for him to leave it to the husband to say whether she might go ashore or not. She had a personal right to go on shore. If the defendant personally denied her the privilege, as the jury might find he did, it was a wrongful denial.

NOTES AND QUESTIONS

1. A woman tells her boyfriend she does not want to see him anymore, but agrees to ride with him just to the store and back. When they return to her parents' house and she opens the car door, the boyfriend suddenly starts the car off, making it dangerous for her to exit the moving vehicle. False imprisonment? See Noguchi v. Nakamura, 2 Haw.App. 655, 638 P.2d 1383 (1982).

2. In Talcott v. National Exhibition Co., 144 App.Div. 337, 128 N.Y.S. 1059 (1911), plaintiff was one of a crowd seeking admission to the baseball game between the Chicago Cubs and the New York Giants that played off the tie for the 1908 National League pennant. This was necessary because of a one-to-one tie in an earlier game between the same teams, produced when Fred Merkle of the Giants pulled his famous "bonehead play" in failing to touch second base. For two fascinating accounts of that game told by other players in it, see L. Ritter, The Glory of Their Times 98–100 and 124–218 (1966); the book has a picture of the after-game crowd in the Polo Grounds at page 126. The Giants, who would have won the pennant except for the Merkle error, lost the playoff game. Plaintiff succeeded in entering an enclosure where tickets were sold, but found that he could not get in to the stands. Defendant closed the entrance gates behind him to prevent injuries from the crush. There was another exit, but because defendant failed to inform plaintiff of its existence, he remained within the enclosure for more than an hour. In his action for false imprisonment, a verdict and judgment in his favor were affirmed. It was held that while the defendant might have been justified in closing the gates, it was then under a duty to inform plaintiff of the other exit.

3. Members of a religious cult are abducted by their relatives and subjected to deprogramming. Is this false imprisonment? Eilers v. Coy, 582 F.Supp. 1093 (D.Minn.1984).

4. Plaintiff boarded a plane in Washington, D.C., for a flight to New York where he was to attend a reception at the United Nations. After sitting on the tarmac for over an hour waiting for his flight to take off, plaintiff realized he would miss the reception and demanded to be returned to the terminal. Is the airline liable for failing to allow him to leave the airplane after it had pulled away from the gate? After it had sat on the tarmac for an hour? Somewhere above New Jersey? See Abourezk v. New York Airlines, 895 F.2d 1456 (D.C.Cir.1990) (no duty to release passenger until plane reached New York absent exigent circumstances not present in the case).

5. INTENTIONAL INFLICTION OF EMOTIONAL DISTRESS

State Rubbish Collectors Ass'n v. Siliznoff

Supreme Court of California, 1952.
38 Cal.2d 330, 240 P.2d 282.

[The State Rubbish Collectors Association sued Siliznoff to collect on certain notes. Siliznoff sought cancellation of the notes because of duress and want of consideration. In addition, he sought general and punitive damages because of alleged "assaults" made on him. The evidence was that Siliznoff had collected the trash from the Acme Brewing Company, which the Association regarded as within the territory of another member of the Association named Abramoff. The defendant was called before the Association and ordered to pay over the collected money to Abramoff, as a result of which he signed the notes in question. Further facts appear in the opinion.

The jury returned a verdict for Siliznoff on the original complaint and on the counterclaim. Siliznoff obtained a judgment against the Association for $1,250 general and special damages and $4,000 punitive damages. The Association appealed the judgment.]

TRAYNOR, J. * * * Plaintiff's primary contention is that the evidence is insufficient to support the judgment. Defendant testified that: * * *

Andikian [an inspector of the Association] told defendant that " 'We will give you up till tonight to get down to the board meeting and make some kind of arrangements or agreements about the Acme Brewery, or otherwise we are going to beat you up.' * * * He says he either would hire somebody or do it himself. And I says, 'Well, what would they do to me?' He says, well, they would physically beat me up first, cut up the truck tires or burn the truck, or otherwise put me out of business completely. He said if I didn't appear at that meeting and make some kind of an agreement that they would do that, but he says up to then they would let me alone, but if I walked out of that meeting that night they would beat me up for sure." Defendant attended the meeting and protested that he owed nothing for the Acme account and in any event could not pay the amount demanded. He was again told by the president of the association that "that table right there [the board of directors] ran all the rubbish collecting in Los Angeles and if there was any routes to be gotten that they would get them and distribute them among their members * * *." After two hours of further discussion defendant agreed to join the association and pay for the Acme account. He promised to return the next day and sign the necessary papers. He testified that the only reason "they let me go home, is that I promised that I would sign the notes the very next morning." The president "made me promise on my honor and everything else, and I was scared, and I knew I had to come back, so I believe he knew I was scared and that I would come back. That's the only reason they let me go home." Defendant also testified that because of the fright he suffered during his dispute with the association he became ill and vomited several times and had to remain away from work for a period of several days.

Plaintiff contends that the evidence does not establish an assault against defendant because the threats made all related to action that might take place in the future; that neither Andikian nor members of the board of directors threatened immediate physical harm to defendant. [C] We have concluded, however, that a cause of action is established when it is shown that one, in the absence of any privilege, intentionally subjects another to the mental suffering incident to serious threats to his physical well-being, whether or not the threats are made under such circumstances as to constitute a technical assault.

In the past it has been frequently stated that the interest in emotional and mental tranquillity is not one that the law will protect from invasion in its own right. [Cc] As late as 1934 the Restatement of Torts took the position that "The interest in mental and emotional tranquillity and, therefore, in freedom from mental and emotional disturbance is not, as a thing in itself, regarded as of sufficient importance to require others to refrain from conduct intended or recognizably likely to cause such a disturbance." Restatement, Torts, § 46, comment *c*. The Restatement explained the rule allowing recovery for the mere apprehension of bodily harm in traditional assault cases as an historical anomaly (§ 24, comment *c*), and the rule allowing recovery for insulting conduct by an employee of a common carrier as justified by the necessity of securing for the public comfortable as well as safe service (§ 48, comment *c*).

The Restatement recognized, however, that in many cases mental distress could be so intense that it could reasonably be foreseen that illness or other bodily harm might result. If the defendant intentionally subjected the plaintiff to such distress and bodily harm resulted, the defendant would be liable for negligently causing the plaintiff bodily harm. Restatement, Torts, §§ 306, 312. Under this theory the cause of action was not founded on a right to be free from intentional interference with mental tranquillity, but on the right to be free from negligent interference with physical well-being. A defendant who intentionally subjected another to mental distress without intending to cause bodily harm would nevertheless be liable for resulting bodily harm if he should have foreseen that the mental distress might cause such harm.

The California cases have been in accord with the Restatement in allowing recovery where physical injury resulted from intentionally subjecting the plaintiff to serious mental distress. [Cc]

The view has been forcefully advocated that the law should protect emotional and mental tranquillity as such against serious and intentional invasions, [cc] and there is a growing body of case law supporting this position. [Cc] In recognition of this development the American Law Institute amended section 46 of the Restatement of Torts in 1947 to provide:

"One who, without a privilege to do so, intentionally causes severe emotional distress to another is liable (a) for such emotional distress, and (b) for bodily harm resulting from it."

In explanation it is stated that "The interest in freedom from severe emotional distress is regarded as of sufficient importance to require others to refrain from conduct intended to invade it. Such conduct is tortious. The injury suffered by the one whose interest is invaded is frequently far more serious to him than certain tortious invasions of the interest in bodily integrity and other legally protected interests. In the absence of a privilege, the actor's conduct has no social utility; indeed it is anti-social. No reason or policy requires such an actor to be protected from the liability which usually attaches to the wilful wrongdoer whose efforts are successful." (Restatement of the Law, 1948 Supplement, Torts, § 46, comment *d*.)

There are persuasive arguments and analogies that support the recognition of a right to be free from serious, intentional and unprivileged invasions of mental and emotional tranquillity. If a cause of action is otherwise established, it is settled that damages may be given for mental suffering naturally ensuing from the acts complained of [cc], and in the case of many torts, such as assault, battery, false imprisonment and defamation, mental suffering will frequently constitute the principal element of damages. [C] In cases where mental suffering constitutes a major element of damages it is anomalous to deny recovery because the defendant's intentional misconduct fell short of producing some physical injury.

It may be contended that to allow recovery in the absence of physical injury will open the door to unfounded claims and a flood of litigation, and that the requirement that there be physical injury is necessary to insure that serious mental suffering actually occurred. The jury is ordinarily in a better position, however, to determine whether outrageous conduct results in mental distress than whether that distress in turn results in physical injury. From their own experience jurors are aware of the extent and character of the disagreeable emotions that may result from the defendant's conduct, but a difficult medical question is presented when it must be determined if emotional distress resulted in physical injury. [C] Greater proof that mental suffering occurred is found in the defendant's conduct designed to bring it about than in physical injury that may or may not have resulted therefrom. * * *

In the present case plaintiff caused defendant to suffer extreme fright. By intentionally producing such fright it endeavored to compel him either to give up the Acme account or pay for it, and it had no right or privilege to adopt such coercive methods in competing for business. In these circumstances liability is clear. * * *

The judgment is affirmed.

NOTES AND QUESTIONS

1. Why not assault? Why not false imprisonment? Assuming neither tort occurred, how many attorneys in 1952 would have thought of bringing a cross-complaint, as counterclaims are known in California, in this case for "intentional infliction of emotional harm"? How many judges would have adopted it?

2. But what form of tort has been unleashed? Is it as definite in character as those that arose out of the writ of trespass? What would the result have been in the main case if the Association had only threatened to close down Siliznoff's business, but had not made threats to his physical well-being? Do you agree that the jury can more easily determine whether conduct is outrageous than whether physical injury resulted from emotional harm? If so, does this fact suggest that a claim should be allowed?

3. Kentucky has referred to the tort as a gap filler: "Clearly, the conduct in question must be extreme, or outrageous and intolerable. It must violate generally accepted standards of decency and morality. It must be more than bad manners, and must cause severe emotional distress, not just hurt feelings. Many instances of criminal conduct would likely qualify, but any conduct that shocks the conscience could be unlawful as well because others have the right to be free of such conduct, even if the conduct does not rise to the level of a crime. The purpose behind recognizing the tort of intentional infliction of emotional distress was to allow a cause of action for severe emotional distress, caused by truly outrageous behavior, where there was no remedy because the victim did not have an injury directly to his person or intangible personal attributes such as reputation. The tort is grounded in harassing or abusive behaviors that cause severe

emotional distress. To this extent, it is a 'gap-filler' tort. . . . And while the intentional infliction of emotional distress could be pleaded alternatively, a litigant cannot prevail on both a negligence claim and an intentional infliction of emotional distress claim on the same set of facts." Childers v. Geile, 367 S.W.3d 576, 581 (Ky. 2012) (internal citations omitted).

4. The seminal case to allow recovery for the intentional infliction of mental distress as a distinct tort was Wilkinson v. Downton, [1897] 2 Q.B. 57, in which a practical joker amused himself by telling the plaintiff that her husband had been smashed up in an accident, was lying at The Elms in Leytonstone with both legs broken, and that she was to go to him at once in a cab with two pillows to fetch him home. The shock to her nervous system caused serious physical illness with permanent consequences, and at one time threatened her reason. The cause of action through which defendant was held liable is unclear to the reader of the opinion and apparently to the court as well.

5. *Interference with Human Bodies.* Before the recognition of a separate tort for intentional infliction of emotional distress, a number of courts had allowed recovery for mental distress at the intentional mutilation or disinterment of a dead body or for interference with proper burial. See, for example, Alderman v. Ford, 146 Kan. 698, 72 P.2d 981 (1937); Gostkowski v. Roman Catholic Church, 262 N.Y. 320, 186 N.E. 798 (1933); Papieves v. Lawrence, 437 Pa. 373, 263 A.2d 118 (1970). In these and later cases, the courts have talked of a property right in the body, said to be in the next of kin or a group of close relatives, which serves as a foundation for the action for mental disturbance. See, for example, Whaley v. County of Tuscola, 58 F.3d 1111 (6th Cir.1995) (discussing Ohio and Michigan law) (unauthorized removal of corneas and eyeballs by coroner). In Gadbury v. Bleitz, 133 Wash. 134, 233 P. 299 (1925), where the body was held without burial with demand for payment of another debt, the court avoided difficulties surrounding right of ownership by recognizing that the tort was in reality the intentional infliction of mental distress upon the survivors by extreme outrage. In accord, Gray Brown-Service Mortuary, Inc. v. Lloyd, 729 So.2d 280, 285 (Ala. 1999) ("It has long been the law of Alabama that mistreatment of burial places and human remains will support the recovery of damages for mental suffering.")

6. *Common Carriers and Innkeepers* have been held to a higher standard of conduct and sometimes held liable for using insulting language to their passengers and patrons. See, e.g., Lipman v. Atlantic Coast Line R.R. Co., 108 S.C. 151, 93 S.E. 714 (1917) (carrier); Emmke v. De Silva, 293 F. 17 (8th Cir. 1923) (hotel). But cf. Wallace v. Shoreham Hotel Corp., 49 A.2d 81 (D.C. Mun. App. 1946) (restaurant patron did not state cause of action based on waiter's insult); Bethel v. N.Y.C. Transit Authority, 92 N.Y.2d 348, 681 N.Y.S.2d 201, 703 N.E.2d 1214 (1998) (abolishing higher standard of care for common carriers); and Nunez v. Professional Transit Mgt. of Tucson, Inc., 229 Ariz. 117, 271 P.3d 1104 (2012) (abandoning the "highest degree of care standard" for common carriers).

7. As the principal case indicates, § 46 of the Restatement of Torts was changed in the 1948 Supplement to recognize the cause of action for the intentional infliction of severe emotional distress, called "outrage" in some jurisdictions. As with any newly recognized cause of action, the courts in each jurisdiction must struggle with what its contours will be. What

sorts of conduct constitutes "extreme and outrageous" conduct? Are words alone enough? Should the plaintiff's individual vulnerabilities be taken into account? How does the jury determine whether the emotional distress is "severe"? Is it necessary that the defendant intended to cause the mental disturbance, or that it be substantially certain to follow, within the rule stated in Garratt v. Dailey, page 17?

Slocum v. Food Fair Stores of Florida

Supreme Court of Florida, 1958.
100 So.2d 396.

DREW, JUSTICE. This appeal is from an order dismissing a complaint for failure to state a cause of action. Simply stated, the plaintiff sought money damages for mental suffering or emotional distress, and an ensuing heart attack and aggravation of pre-existing heart disease, allegedly caused by insulting language of the defendant's employee directed toward her while she was a customer in its store. Specifically, in reply to her inquiry as to the price of an item he was marking, he replied: "If you want to know the price, you'll have to find out the best way you can * * * you stink to me." She asserts, in the alternative, that the language was used in a malicious or grossly reckless manner, "or with intent to inflict great mental and emotional disturbance to said plaintiff."

No great difficulty is involved in the preliminary point raised as to the sufficiency of damages alleged, the only direct injury being mental or emotional with physical symptoms merely derivative therefrom. [C] While that decision would apparently allow recovery for mental suffering, even absent physical consequences, inflicted in the course of other intentional or malicious torts, it does not resolve the central problem in this case, i.e. whether the conduct here claimed to have caused the injury, the use of insulting language under the circumstances described, constituted an actionable invasion of a legally protected right. Query: does such an assertion of a deliberate disturbance of emotional equanimity state an independent cause of action in tort?

Appellant's fundamental argument is addressed to that proposition. The case is one of first impression in this jurisdiction, and she contends that this Court should recognize the existence of a new tort, an independent cause of action for intentional infliction of emotional distress.

A study of the numerous references on the subject indicates a strong current of opinion in support of such recognition, in lieu of the strained reasoning so often apparent when liability for such injury is predicated upon one or another of several traditional tort theories. * * *

A most cogent statement of the doctrine covering tort liability for insult has been incorporated in the Restatement of the Law of Torts, 1948 supplement, sec. 46, entitled "Conduct intended to cause emotional distress only." It makes a blanket provision for liability on the part of "one, who, without a privilege to do so, intentionally causes severe emotional distress to another," indicating that the requisite intention exists "when the act is done for the purpose of causing the distress or with knowledge * * * that severe emotional distress is substantially certain to be produced by [such] conduct." Comment (a), Sec. 46, supra. Abusive language is, of course, only one of the many means by which the tort could be committed.

However, even if we assume, without deciding, the legal propriety of that doctrine, a study of its factual applications shows that a line of demarcation should be drawn between conduct likely to cause mere "emotional distress" and that causing "severe emotional distress," so as to exclude the situation at bar. [C] "So far as it is possible to generalize from the cases, the rule which seems to be emerging is that there is liability only for conduct exceeding all bounds which could be tolerated by society, of a nature especially calculated to cause mental damage of a very serious kind." [C] And the most practicable view is that the functions of court and jury are no different than in other tort actions where there is at the outset a question as to whether the conduct alleged is so legally innocuous as to present no issue for a jury. [C]

This tendency to hinge the cause of action upon the degree of the insult has led some courts to reject the doctrine in toto. [C] Whether or not this is desirable, it is uniformly agreed that the determination of whether words or conduct are actionable in character is to be made on an objective rather than subjective standard, from common acceptation. The unwarranted intrusion must be calculated to cause "severe emotional distress" to a person of ordinary sensibilities, in the absence of special knowledge or notice. There is no inclination to include all instances of mere vulgarities, obviously intended as meaningless abusive expressions. While the manner in which language is used may no doubt determine its actionable character, appellant's assertion that the statement involved in this case was made to her with gross recklessness, etc., cannot take the place of allegations showing that the words were intended to have real meaning or serious effect.

A broader rule has been developed in a particular class of cases, usually treated as a distinct and separate area of liability originally applied to common carriers. Rest.Torts, per. ed., sec. 48. The courts have from an early date granted relief for offense reasonably suffered by a patron from insult by a servant or employee of a carrier, hotel, theater, and most recently, a telegraph office. The existence of a special relationship, arising either from contract or from the inherent nature of a non-competitive public utility, supports a right and correlative duty of courtesy beyond that legally required in general mercantile or personal relationships. [Cc]

In view of the concurrent development of the cause of action first above described, there is no impelling reason to extend the rule of the latter cases. Their rationale does not of necessity cover the area of business invitees generally, where the theory of respondeat superior underlying most liabilities of the employer would dictate some degree of conformity to standards of individual liability. This factor, together with the stringent standards of care imposed in a number of the carrier cases [c], may have influenced the treatment of the subject by editors of the Restatement, where the statement of the carrier doctrine is quite limited in scope and classified separately from the section covering the more general area of liability under consideration. But whether or not these rules are ultimately adopted in this jurisdiction, the facts of the present case cannot be brought within their reasonable intendment.

Affirmed.

NOTES AND QUESTIONS

1. Why is the intentional infliction of mental disturbance by the insult not a tort in itself?

2. "Against a large part of the frictions and irritations and clashing of temperaments incident to participation in a community life, a certain toughening of the mental hide is a better protection than the law could ever be. * * * Of course there is danger of getting into the realm of the trivial in this matter of insulting language. No pressing social need requires that every abusive outburst be converted into a tort; upon the contrary, it would be unfortunate if the law closed all the safety valves through which irascible tempers might legally blow off steam." Magruder, Mental and Emotional Disturbance in the Law of Torts, 49 Harv.L.Rev. 1033, 1035, 1053 (1936). What if animal rights protesters came to plaintiff's place of business and to his house, making speeches through bullhorns and chanting slogans that included the phrase "we know where you sleep at night"? Ortberg v. Goldman Sachs Group, 64 A.3d 158, 164 (D.C. 2014) (conduct complained of is part and parcel "of the frictions and irritations and clashing of temperaments incident to participation in a community life," especially life in a society that recognizes a right to public political protest).

3. None of these was found actionable: Halliday v. Cienkowski, 333 Pa. 123, 3 A.2d 372 (1939) ("Scotch bitch," "bastard," and "bum"); Atkinson v. Bibb Mfg. Co., 50 Ga.App. 434, 178 S.E. 537 (1935) (foreman cursing discharged woman with open knife in his hand); Kramer v. Ricksmeier, 159 Iowa 48, 139 N.W. 1091 (1913) (profanity and abuse over the telephone, with threats of future violence); Barry v. Baugh, 111 Ga.App. 813, 143 S.E.2d 489 (1965) ("crazy"); and Booker v. Silverthorne, 111 S.C. 553, 99 S.E. 350, 351 (1919) ("You are a God damned liar. If I were there, I would break your God damned neck.") (language attributed to defendant "merits severest condemnation and subjects the user to the scorn and contempt of his fellow men. But it is not civilly actionable.").

4. What if the slurs or insults focus on racial, ethnic, or sexual characteristics? Most courts have found them not so outrageous as to be intolerable in a civilized society. See, for example, Harville v. Lowville Central School Dist., 245 A.D.2d 1106, 667 N.Y.S.2d 175 (App. Div. 1997) (student called "Polish Nazi" by teacher); Ugalde v. W.A. McKenzie Asphalt Co., 990 F.2d 239 (5th Cir. 1993) (applying Texas law) (worker called "wetback" by supervisor); Taggart v. Drake Univ., 549 N.W.2d 796 (Iowa 1996) (in fit of temper, dean addresses faculty member as "young woman" and refers to her in a "sexist and condescending manner"). Such words may be considered along with other conduct, however, in making a claim. Contreras v. Crown Zellerbach Corp., 88 Wash.2d 735, 736, 565 P.2d 1173, 1174 (1977) ("continuous humiliation and embarrassment by reason of racial jokes, slurs and comments made in his presence" by coworkers and supervisors held to state a claim).

5. In rare circumstances, the First Amendment's free speech clause may provide a defense to state tort actions, including claims for intentional infliction of emotional distress. Plaintiff Snyder's son Mathew was killed in action in Iraq and his funeral was held at his parish church in Westminster, Maryland. Defendant Phelps and members of his family and congregation picketed on public land adjacent to public streets near Mathew's funeral. The Westboro Baptist Church congregation believes that God hates and punishes the United States for its tolerance of homosexuality, particularly in America's military. The picket signs reflected that belief. A jury found that defendants were liable to Snyder for intentional infliction of emotional distress, but the Supreme Court found that the speech was protected by the First Amendment and vacated the judgment. Snyder v. Phelps, 131 S.Ct. 1207, 1219 (U.S. 2011). ("What Westboro said, in the whole context of how and where it chose to say it, is entitled to 'special protection' under the First Amendment, and that protection cannot be overcome by a jury finding that the picketing was outrageous.")

6. Note the last sentence of the opinion in the principal case. The Supreme Court of Florida did not adopt intentional infliction of emotional distress until almost thirty years later. Metropolitan Life Ins. Co. v. McCarson, 467 So.2d 277 (Fla. 1985).

Harris v. Jones

Court of Appeals of Maryland, 1977.
281 Md. 560, 380 A.2d 611.

MURPHY, CHIEF JUDGE. * * * The plaintiff, William R. Harris, a 26-year-old, 8-year employee of General Motors Corporation (GM), sued GM and one of its supervisory employees, H. Robert Jones, in the Superior Court of Baltimore City. The declaration alleged that Jones, aware that Harris suffered from a speech impediment which caused him to stutter, and also aware of Harris' sensitivity to his disability, and his insecurity because of it, nevertheless "maliciously and cruelly ridiculed * * * [him] thus causing tremendous nervousness, increasing the physical defect itself and further injuring the mental attitude fostered by the Plaintiff toward his problem and otherwise intentionally inflicting emotional distress." It was also alleged in the declaration that Jones' actions occurred within the course of his employment with GM and that GM ratified Jones' conduct.

The evidence at trial showed that Harris stuttered throughout his entire life. While he had little trouble with one syllable words, he had great difficulty with longer words or sentences, causing him at times to shake his head up and down when attempting to speak.

During part of 1975, Harris worked under Jones' supervision at a GM automobile assembly plant. Over a five-month period, between March and August of 1975, Jones approached Harris over 30 times at work and verbally and physically mimicked his stuttering disability. In addition, two or three times a week during this period, Jones approached Harris and told him, in a "smart manner," not to get nervous. As a result of Jones' conduct, Harris was "shaken up" and felt "like going into a hole and hide."

On June 2, 1975, Harris asked Jones for a transfer to another department; Jones refused, called Harris a "troublemaker" and chastised him for repeatedly seeking the assistance of his committeeman, a representative who handles employee grievances. On this occasion, Jones, "shaking his head up and down" to imitate Harris, mimicked his pronunciation of the word "committeeman," which Harris pronounced "mmitteeman." * * *

Harris had been under the care of a physician for a nervous condition for six years prior to the commencement of Jones' harassment. He admitted that many things made him nervous, including "bosses." Harris testified that Jones' conduct heightened his nervousness and his speech impediment worsened. He saw his physician on one occasion during the five-month period that Jones was mistreating him; the physician prescribed pills for his nerves.

Harris admitted that other employees at work mimicked his stuttering. Approximately 3,000 persons were employed on each of two shifts, and Harris acknowledged the presence at the plant of a lot of "tough guys," as well as profanity, name-calling and roughhousing among the employees. He said that a bad day at work caused him to become more nervous than usual. He admitted that he had problems with supervisors other than Jones, that he had been suspended or relieved from work 10 or 12 times, and that after one such dispute, he followed a supervisor home on his motorcycle, for which he was later disciplined.

On this evidence, * * * the jury awarded Harris $3,500 compensatory damages and $15,000 punitive damages against both Jones and GM. [This was reversed by the Court of Special Appeals.]

In concluding that the intentional infliction of emotional distress, standing alone, may constitute a valid tort action, the Court of Special Appeals relied upon Restatement (Second) of Torts, ch. 2, Emotional Distress, § 46 (1965), which provides, in pertinent part:

> "§ 46. Outrageous Conduct Causing Severe Emotional Distress
>
> "(1) One who by extreme and outrageous conduct intentionally or recklessly causes severe emotional distress to another is subject to liability for such emotional distress, and if bodily harm to the other results from it, for such bodily harm."

The court noted that the tort was recognized, and its boundaries defined, in W. Prosser, Law of Torts § 12, at 56 (4th ed. 1971), as follows:

> "So far as it is possible to generalize from the cases, the rule which seems to have emerged is that there is liability for conduct exceeding all bounds usually tolerated by decent society, of a nature which is especially calculated to cause, and does cause, mental distress of a very serious kind."

The trend in other jurisdictions toward recognition of a right to recover for severe emotional distress brought on by the intentional act of another is manifest. Indeed, 37 jurisdictions appear now to recognize the tort as a valid cause of action. * * *

[F]our elements * * * must coalesce to impose liability for intentional infliction of emotional distress:

(1) The conduct must be intentional or reckless;

(2) The conduct must be extreme and outrageous;

(3) There must be a causal connection between the wrongful conduct and the emotional distress;

(4) The emotional distress must be severe. * * *

[The intermediate Court of Special Appeals had found that the first two elements were established but reversed on the ground that the last two elements were not.]

Whether the conduct of a defendant has been "extreme and outrageous," so as to satisfy that element of the tort, has been a particularly troublesome question. Section 46 of the Restatement, comment *d*, states that "Liability has been found only where the conduct has been so outrageous in character, and so extreme in degree, as to go beyond all possible bounds of decency, and to be regarded as atrocious, and utterly intolerable in a civilized community." The comment goes on to state that liability does not extend, however: "to mere insults, indignities, threats, annoyances, petty oppressions, or other trivialities. The rough edges of our society are still in need of a good deal of filing down, and in the meantime plaintiffs must necessarily be expected and required to be hardened to a certain amount of rough language, and to occasional acts that are definitely inconsiderate and unkind. * * * "

In determining whether conduct is extreme and outrageous, it should not be considered in a sterile setting, detached from the surroundings in which it occurred. [C] The personality of the individual to whom the misconduct is directed is also a factor. "There is a difference between violent and vile profanity addressed to a lady, and the same language to a Butte miner and a United States marine." Prosser, Intentional Infliction of Mental Suffering: A New Tort, 37 Mich.L.Rev. 874, 887 (1939). * * *

It is for the court to determine, in the first instance, whether the defendant's conduct may reasonably be regarded as extreme and outrageous; where reasonable men may differ, it is for the jury to determine whether, in the particular case, the conduct has been sufficiently extreme and outrageous to result in liability. * * *

While it is crystal clear that Jones' conduct was intentional, we need not decide whether it was extreme or outrageous, or causally related to the emotional distress which Harris allegedly suffered.[2] The fourth element of the tort—that the emotional distress must be severe—was not established by legally sufficient evidence justifying submission of the case to the jury. That element of the tort requires the plaintiff to show that he suffered a *severely* disabling emotional response to the defendant's conduct. The severity of the emotional

[2] The fact that Harris may have had some pre-existing susceptibility to emotional distress does not necessarily preclude liability if it can be shown that the conduct intensified the pre-existing condition of psychological stress. [Cc]

distress is not only relevant to the amount of recovery, but is a necessary element to any recovery. * * *

Assuming that a causal relationship was shown between Jones' wrongful conduct and Harris' emotional distress, we find no evidence, legally sufficient for submission to the jury, that the distress was "severe" within the contemplation of the rule requiring establishment of that element of the tort. The evidence that Jones' reprehensible conduct humiliated Harris and caused him emotional distress, which was manifested by an aggravation of Harris' pre-existing nervous condition and a worsening of his speech impediment, was vague and weak at best. * * * While Harris' nervous condition may have been exacerbated somewhat by Jones' conduct, his family problems antedated his encounter with Jones and were not shown to be attributable to Jones' actions. Just how, or to what degree, Harris' speech impediment worsened is not revealed by the evidence. Granting the cruel and insensitive nature of Jones' conduct toward Harris, and considering the position of authority which Jones held over Harris, we conclude that the humiliation suffered was not, as a matter of law, so intense as to constitute the "severe" emotional distress required to recover for the tort of intentional infliction of emotional distress.

Judgment affirmed; costs to be paid by appellant.

NOTES AND QUESTIONS

1. *Conduct Exceeding All Bounds Usually Tolerated by Decent Society.* How culpable must defendant's conduct be before it reaches the level of being extreme enough to be deemed tortious? Some guidelines can be found in decided cases. For example, it is generally held that the mere solicitation of a woman to illicit intercourse is not only not an assault but does not give rise to any other cause of action. Reed v. Maley, 115 Ky. 816, 74 S.W. 1079 (1903). "The view being, apparently, that there is no harm in asking." Magruder, Mental and Emotional Disturbance in the Law of Torts, 49 Harv.L.Rev. 1033, 1055 (1936). Jones v. Clinton, 990 F.Supp. 657, 677 (E.D.Ark.1998) (applying Arkansas law) ("While the Court will certainly agree that plaintiff's allegations describe offensive conduct, the Court, as previously noted, has found that the Governor's alleged conduct does not constitute sexual assault. Rather, the conduct as alleged by plaintiff describes a mere sexual proposition or encounter, albeit an odious one. . . . The Court is not aware of any authority holding that such a sexual encounter or proposition of the type alleged in this case, without more, gives rise to a claim of outrage.")

In Samms v. Eccles, 11 Utah 2d 289, 358 P.2d 344 (1961), a married woman was hounded by continued telephone calls from May to December, some of them late at night; and on one occasion defendant came to her home and made an indecent exposure of his person. The court stated that under usual circumstances solicitation would not be actionable ("It seems to be a custom of long standing and one which in all likelihood will continue"), but found the "aggravated circumstances" in this case sufficient to make the defendant liable.

Plaintiff alleged that her rabbi had induced her to enter into a sexual relationship with him in the guise of therapy to assist her in finding a husband. Marmelstein v. Kehillat New Hempstead: The Rav Aron Jofen Community Synagogue, 11 N.Y.3d 15, 22, 892 N.E.2d 375, 862 N.Y.S.2d 311 (2008) (even if plaintiff could prove that her acquiescence was obtained through lies, manipulation, or other morally opprobrious conduct, the rabbi's conduct was not so outrageous in character and extreme in degree so as to go beyond all possible bounds of decency and be utterly intolerable in a civilized community).

2. Courts are reluctant to subject either internal family disputes or petty but strongly felt antagonisms to the sanctions of tort law. However, when conduct exceeds all reasonable bounds of behavior tolerated by society, courts are likely to find that a claim has been stated. Cf. Miller v. Currie, 50 F.3d 373 (6th Cir.1995) (applying Ohio law) (plaintiff's brother and sister-in-law and the employees of a nursing home prevented her from seeing her ninety-eight-year old mother); Halio v. Lurie, 15 A.D.2d 62, 222 N.Y.S.2d 759 (1961) (man who had jilted a woman wrote her jeering verses and taunting letters); Jackson v. Brown, 904 P.2d 685 (Utah 1995) (last minute cancellation of wedding not enough for outrage, but courting woman, proposing, and making arrangements for wedding including applying for license while married to someone else may be); Smith v. Malouf, 722 So.2d 490 (Miss. 1998) (teenager and her parents hid her location from the father of her baby so that baby could be secretly placed with strangers for adoption); Flamm v. Van Nierop, 56 Misc.2d 1059, 291 N.Y.S.2d 189 (1968) (defendant constantly drove behind plaintiff at a "dangerously close distance," phoned him unnecessarily at his home and business and either hung up or remained on the line in silence, and "dashed" at him in public places).

3. Is filing a frivolous lawsuit against someone conduct that is sufficiently outrageous to permit recovery for intentional infliction of emotional distress? After being injured in a fight in a parking lot that was poorly lit, crowded, and chaotic, plaintiff identified a man as her assailant even though she only had a vague impression of the physical characteristics of the person responsible for breaking her leg and someone else had apologized for causing her injury. After the man she identified was found not guilty on the criminal charges arising out of her identification, plaintiff filed a civil suit against the man. He counterclaimed for intentional infliction of emotional distress. Davis v. Currier, 704 A.2d 1207 (Maine 1997) (no cause of action for intentional infliction of emotional distress); Swerdlick v. Koch, 721 A.2d 849 (R.I. 1998) (no cause of action against neighbor who repeatedly photographed and maintained a log of activity in attempt to prove plaintiffs were illegally operating a mail-order business out of their home). What if a juror, found in contempt for failing to show up one day two weeks into the trial of someone accused of torturing and killing six people, was placed alone in a jail cell with the alleged murderer, was questioned and berated by the alleged murderer, and was laughed at by the jailors who placed her there? Johnson v. Wayne County, 213 Mich.App. 143, 540 N.W.2d 66 (1995) (states a cause of action).

4. What if a hospital had a policy of placing patients infected with the HIV virus in the same rooms as patients who were not, without disclosing that fact? Patient accidentally used his roommate's razor to shave and was then informed by the roommate that roommate was infected with HIV. Patient alleges that the hospital's conduct is outrageous and that

he suffered severe emotional distress as a result. Liability? What other information would you like to have before deciding this issue? Bain v. Wells, 936 S.W.2d 618 (Tenn.1997). Suppose a surgeon, angry at an operating-room nurse, throws a surgical drape into her face, covering her with the patient's blood and tissue. Both the nurse and the patient underwent a series of tests for HIV, hepatitis, and other communicable diseases. All were negative. Is her testimony that she feared for her life and suffered severe emotional distress at the thought of the risk sufficient? Grantham v. Vanderzyl, 802 So.2d 1077 (Ala. 2001) (court finds as a matter of law that the mere fear of contracting a disease, without actual exposure to it, cannot be sufficient to cause the level of distress necessary for tort of outrage).

5. Is there any common theme or set of similar factors running through the following cases?

A. State Rubbish Collectors Association v. Siliznoff, page 53.

B. Defendant, a private detective representing that he was a police officer, threatened to charge the plaintiff, a resident alien, with espionage unless she turned over to him certain private letters in her possession. She suffered severe mental disturbance and was made seriously ill. The defendant was held liable. Janvier v. Sweeney, [1919] 2 K.B. 316.

C. Defendants, school authorities, called a high school girl to the school office and bullied and badgered her for a considerable length of time, threatening her with prison and with public disgrace for herself and her family, unless she confessed to immoral conduct with various men. They succeeded in extorting from her a confession of misconduct, of which she was innocent. She suffered severe mental disturbance and resulting illness. Defendants were held liable. Johnson v. Sampson, 167 Minn. 203, 208 N.W. 814 (1926). See also Hunt v. State, 69 A.3d 360 (Del. 2013) (uniformed police officer threatened eight-year-old child while questioning him without parental permission about a bullying incident at school).

D. *Collecting Agencies.* While reasonable attempts to collect a debt lead to no liability, even though they may be expected to, and do, cause serious mental distress, more extreme conduct may produce a different result. Defendant, a creditor, had plaintiff called to the telephone of her neighbor, with the message that it was an emergency call. Defendant began the conversation by telling plaintiff that "this is going to be a shock; it is as much of a shock to me to have to tell you as it will be to you." When plaintiff said that she was prepared for the message, the defendant let her have it: "This is the Federal Outfitting Company—why don't you pay your bill?" Plaintiff suffered severe nervous shock and resulting serious illness. A complaint alleging these facts was held to state a cause of action. Bowden v. Spiegel, Inc., 96 Cal.App.2d 793, 216 P.2d 571 (1950). A veterinarian and an animal hospital threaten to "do away with" plaintiffs' dog unless plaintiffs paid in cash a bill for treating the dog for injuries suffered when struck by an automobile. See Lawrence v. Stanford and Ashland Terrace Animal Hospital, 655 S.W.2d 927 (Tenn.1983). See also Cadle Co. v. Hobbs, 673 So.2d 1363 (La. App. 1996) (implying that because plaintiff was African-American, no one would take her word against debt collector's).

E. There are similar cases involving the outrageous tactics of insurance adjusters seeking to force a settlement. Continental Cas. Co. v.

Garrett, 173 Miss. 676, 161 So. 753 (1935). See also, as to refusal of a liability insurer to settle a claim, Fletcher v. Western Nat. Life Ins. Co., 10 Cal.App.3d 376, 89 Cal.Rptr. 78 (1970). When the insurance company is reasonable in its refusal to settle a claim, it will not be held liable simply because its client happened to be an excessive worrier about fiscal problems. See Rossignol v. Noel, 289 A.2d 691 (Me.1972).

F. Other cases have involved evicting landlords, Kaufman v. Abramson, 363 F.2d 865 (4th Cir.1966), and even high pressure salesmen. See Turner v. ABC Jalousie Co., 251 S.C. 92, 160 S.E.2d 528 (1968).

Does this statement capture the common theme? "Whether an actor's conduct is extreme and outrageous depends on the facts of each case, including the relationship of the parties, whether the actor abused a position of authority over the other person, whether the other person was especially vulnerable and the actor knew of the vulnerability, the motivation of the actor, and whether the conduct was repeated or prolonged." Restatement (Third) of Torts: Liability for Physical and Emotional Harm § 46, comment *d* (2012).

6. Many cases, like the principal case, arise out of workplace behavior. Anderson v. Oklahoma Temp. Svcs., Inc., 925 P.2d 574 (Okla. App. 1996) (supervisor's use of profanity, smoking around employee after being asked to stop, and vulgar behavior not enough to state a cause of action for extreme and outrageous conduct) and Ford v. Revlon, Inc., 153 Ariz. 38, 734 P.2d 580 (1987) (employer liable for intentional infliction of emotional distress of plaintiff due to co-employee's actions in repeatedly subjecting plaintiff to physical assaults and vulgar remarks). In the employment context, some courts have held that a plaintiff's status as an employee should entitle him to a greater degree of protection from insult and outrage by a supervisor with authority over him than if he were a stranger while others do not. Compare Alcorn v. Anbro Eng'g, Inc., 2 Cal.3d 493, 468 P.2d 216, 86 Cal.Rptr. 88 (1970) with Texas Farm Bureau Mut. Ins. Cos. v. Sears, 84 S.W.3d 604, 611 (Tex. 2002) (while an employer's conduct might in some instances be unpleasant, the employer must have some discretion to "supervise, review, criticize, demote, transfer, and discipline" its workers; thus, only very unusual employment disputes will give rise to cause of action for intentional infliction of emotional distress).

7. *Vulnerability of Plaintiff.* The plaintiff's sensitivities may be a factor in deeming defendant's conduct extreme and outrageous. Cf. Korbin v. Berlin, 177 So.2d 551 (Fla.App.1965), where defendant approached a six-year-old girl and said to her: "Do you know that your mother took a man away from his wife? Do you know that God is going to punish them? Do you know that a man is sleeping in your mother's room? God will punish them." It was alleged that the child suffered serious mental distress and resulting physical injury. Should a demurrer to a complaint pleading these facts be overruled? Cf. Delta Fin. Co. v. Ganakas, 93 Ga.App. 297, 91 S.E.2d 383 (1956) (eleven-year-old child home alone frightened by threats she would be taken to jail if she did not open door for defendant seeking to repossess television set). Drejza v. Vaccaro, 650 A.2d 1308 (D.C.App.1994) (outrageousness of police officer's conduct while interviewing rape victim must be evaluated in light of the fact that it occurred only an hour after the rape, when she would be expected to be more susceptible to emotional distress). Brandon v. County of Richardson, 261 Neb. 636, 624 N.W.2d 604

(2001) (same). After fourteen years, Plaintiff's illness made her no longer able to care for her two beloved Appaloosa horses, so she made arrangements for them to be pastured on defendants' property. Although defendants assured her they would take good care of the horses and return them to her if they could no longer keep them, they in fact sold them to a buyer for slaughter within a week of when they arrived. When plaintiff came to visit them and discovered them gone, defendants lied about their whereabouts and covered up the sale until it was too late for plaintiff to save the horses from the slaughter house. Burgess v. Taylor, 44 S.W.3d 806 (Ky. App. 2001) (in upholding jury verdict for plaintiff, court notes it appropriate to take into account defendants' knowledge of plaintiff's vulnerability to emotional distress based on her attachment to the horses).

8. Should special protection be accorded to pregnant women? When a creditor came to the house of a woman seven months pregnant and screamed profanity, abuse, and accusations of dishonesty in the presence of others and she suffered severe emotional disturbance which resulted in a miscarriage, she was allowed to recover in Kirby v. Jules Chain Stores Corp., 210 N.C. 808, 188 S.E. 625 (1936). See Bartow v. Smith, 149 Ohio St. 301, 78 N.E.2d 735 (1948), a holding that otherwise was overruled by Yeager v. Local Union 20, 6 Ohio St.3d 369, 453 N.E.2d 666 (1983).

9. Should protection also be given to the hypersensitive or idiosyncratic plaintiff? In one early landmark case, protection was allowed. Plaintiff, an eccentric woman who had in the past been treated for mental illness, believed that her ancestors had concealed a pot of gold by burying it. After a fortune teller gave her a map that purportedly showed the land upon which the pot was buried, she spent months digging for it. Defendants filled a pot with rocks and dirt and buried it where plaintiff would find it, placing a note on it that directed the finder to gather all the heirs and wait three days before opening it. A large number of townspeople, including the practical jokers, the heirs, a judge, and other town officials, gathered at the local bank to observe plaintiff open the pot in circumstances of extreme public humiliation. She suffered acute mental distress, with resulting serious illness, which apparently further unsettled her reason and contributed to her early death. The "pot of gold" came in the form of a judgment to her heirs against the practical jokers. Nickerson v. Hodges, 146 La. 735, 84 So. 37 (1920).

10. *Severe Emotional Distress.* All jurisdictions require that the plaintiff prove *severe* not just *mere* emotional distress. This is frequently characterized as distress so severe that no reasonable person could be expected to endure it. Note that unlike most torts, the severity of the damage affects not just how much the plaintiff will recover, but whether the plaintiff recovers at all.

11. *Proof of Severe Emotional Distress.* Testimony that the plaintiff was upset and cried will not be enough. Hatch v. State Farm Fire and Cas. Co., 930 P.2d 382, 397 (Wyo. 1997) ("evidence of crying, being upset and uncomfortable is insufficient to demonstrate severe emotional distress that attains a level no reasonable person could be expected to endure"). Some jurisdictions require that the severe emotional distress be proved by expert witness testimony. Vallinoto v. DiSandro, 688 A.2d 830, 838 (R.I. 1997) (plaintiff must produce "competent medical evidence showing objective physical manifestation of her alleged psychic injuries"). Most, however, do

not generally require expert proof to establish severe emotional distress caused by defendant's conduct, preferring to rely on such factors as the flagrant and serious nature of the defendant's conduct, subjective testimony from plaintiff and others, and physical symptoms, if present. Miller v. Willbanks, 8 S.W.3d 607 (Tenn. 1999) (collecting cases from other jurisdictions); Kloepfel v. Bokor, 149 Wash.2d 192, 66 P.3d 630 (2003) (rejecting argument that objective symptomatology is required to prove severe emotional distress); Brandon v. County of Richardson, 261 Neb. 636, 624 N.W.2d 604 (2001) (noting connection between outrageousness of conduct and proof of severe emotional distress); Sacco v. High Country Independent Press, Inc., 271 Mont. 209, 896 P.2d 411 (1995) (evidence of physical injury not necessary to determine whether plaintiff suffered severe emotional distress).

Taylor v. Vallelunga

District Court of Appeal of California, 1959.
171 Cal.App.2d 107, 339 P.2d 910.

O'DONNELL, JUSTICE pro tem. * * * In the first count, plaintiff Clifford Gerlach alleges that on December 25, 1956, defendants struck and beat him causing him bodily injury for which he seeks damages. In the second count, plaintiff and appellant Gail E. Taylor incorporates by reference the charging allegations of the first count and proceeds to allege that she is the daughter of plaintiff Clifford Gerlach, that she was present at and witnessed the beating inflicted upon her father by defendants, and that as a result thereof, she suffered severe fright and emotional distress. She seeks damages for the distress so suffered. It is not alleged that any physical disability or injury resulted from the mental distress. A general demurrer to the second count of the complaint was interposed by defendants. The demurrer was sustained and appellant was granted ten days leave to amend. Appellant failed to amend and judgment of dismissal of the second count was entered. The appeal is from the judgment of dismissal.

The California cases have for some time past allowed recovery of damages where physical injury resulted from intentionally subjecting the plaintiff to serious mental distress. [C] In the Siliznoff case [page 53] the Supreme Court extended the right of recovery to situations where no physical injury follows the suffering of mental distress, saying that "a cause of action is established when it is shown that one, in the absence of any privilege, intentionally subjects another to the mental suffering incident to serious threats to his physical well-being, whether or not the threats are made under such circumstances as to constitute a technical assault." [C] In arriving at this result the court relied in substantial part upon the development of the law in this field of torts as traced by the American Law Institute, and it quotes with approval [c] section 46, as amended, of the Restatement of Torts, (Restatement of the Law, 1948 Supplement, Torts, § 46) which reads: "One who, without a privilege to do so, intentionally causes severe emotional distress to another is liable (a) for such emotional distress, and (b) for bodily harm resulting from it." In explanation of the meaning of the term "intentionally" as it is employed in said section 46, the Reporter says in subdivision (a) of that section: "An intention to cause severe emotional distress exists when the act is done for the purpose of causing the distress or with knowledge on the part of the actor that severe emotional distress is substantially certain to be produced by his conduct. See Illustration 3." Illustration 3 referred to reads as follows: "A is sitting on her front porch watching her husband B, who is standing on the sidewalk, C, who hates B and is friendly to A, *whose presence is known to him,* stabs B, killing him. C is liable to A for the mental anguish, grief and horror he causes." [Emphasis added.]

The failure of the second count of the complaint in the case at bar to meet the requirements of section 46 of the Restatement of Torts is at once apparent. There is no allegation that defendants knew that appellant was present and witnessed the beating that was administered to her father; nor is there any allegation that the beating was administered for the purpose of causing her to suffer emotional distress, or, in the alternative, that defendants knew that severe emotional distress was substantially certain to be produced by their conduct. * * *

Judgment affirmed.

NOTES AND QUESTIONS

1. Plaintiff's proof of intent is relatively straightforward if the conduct is aimed at the plaintiff or if plaintiff can show that defendant knew that extreme emotional distress was substantially certain to follow from the conduct. Blakeley v. Shortal's Estate, 236 Iowa 787, 20 N.W.2d 28 (1945) (Shortal committed suicide by slitting his own throat in Blakely's kitchen). Generally, committing a murder or a suicide is not a tort against an eyewitness; however, it may be if the act is directed at the plaintiff or if defendant knew that extreme emotional distress was substantially certain to follow. Lourcey v. Scarlett, 146 S.W.3d 48 (Tenn. 2004) (plaintiff, while delivering mail, encountered Scarlett and his wife, who was nude from the waist up, in the middle of the road. Scarlett asked for help and then, while plaintiff was calling 911, Scarlett shot his wife, turned toward the plaintiff, and shot himself); Mahnke v. Moore, 197 Md. 61, 77 A.2d 923, 927 (1951) (overturning demurrer where child's father killed her mother with a shotgun in her presence, kept child in cottage with her mother's body for a week, then killed himself with shotgun, spattering child with his blood). Why not use "transferred intent"? See note 2, page 31.

2. As California did in the principal case, many jurisdictions continue to require that the conduct not only be intentional and outrageous, but also directed at the plaintiff or take place in the presence of the plaintiff, with the defendant's awareness. Christensen v. Superior Court of Los Angeles Cty., 54 Cal.3d 868, 2 Cal.Rptr.2d 79, 820 P.2d 181 (1991) (claim of family members for intentional infliction of emotional distress arising out of mishandling of remains of family members did not state cause of action because it did not allege that conduct was directed at family members or done in their presence); Koontz v. Keller, 52 Ohio App. 265, 3 N.E.2d 694 (1936) (recovery denied where defendant murdered plaintiff's sister and plaintiff later discovered body); Ellsworth v. Massacar, 215 Mich. 511, 184 N.W. 408 (1921) (plaintiff later discovered attack on her husband). But see Doe v. Roman Catholic Diocese of Nashville, 154 S.W.3d 22 (Tenn. 2005) (conduct need not be directed at a specific person or occur in the presence of the plaintiff).

3. Consider how you would prove intent in a case arising out of these facts: After a fatal car accident, a state trooper forwarded horrific photographs taken at the accident site of a teenage girl's decapitated body to some of the trooper's family and friends, who in turn forwarded them to others, and the photos ended up posted on numerous websites. The teenage girl's parents and sisters sought damages for their severe emotional distress. The distress was extreme and it was caused by the trooper's outrageous conduct. But could you prove that the state trooper did it for the purpose of causing distress to the family or with knowledge that with substantial certainty his action would bring about such distress when he knew nothing about the teenager's family? See Catsouras v. Dept. of Cal. Hwy. Patrol, 181 Cal.App.4th 856, 104 Cal.Rptr.3d 352 (2010) (court found allegations of intent were sufficient to withstand demurrer and then case settled before trial).

4. The Restatement (Second) § 46(2) would allow recovery if defendant knows of bystander's presence *and* (1) the conduct was directed at a member of bystander's immediate family or (2) bystander suffers bodily harm as a result of her distress. Hill v. Kimball, 76 Tex. 210, 13 S.W. 59 (1890) (defendant inflicted a bloody battery upon two people in the presence of a pregnant woman who suffered a miscarriage as the result of her mental disturbance). What does it mean to be "present"? Bevan v. Fix, 42 P.3d 1013 (Wyo. 2002) (claim on behalf of young children who could hear their mother being attacked in adjacent hallway) ("sensory and contemporaneous observance of defendant's acts," does not necessarily require being able to see what is happening). Restatement (Third) of Torts: Liability for Physical and Emotional Harm § 46, comment *m* ("contemporaneous perception of the event") (2012).

5. Some courts, however, have permitted recovery even though plaintiff was not present. Knierim v. Izzo, 22 Ill.2d 73, 174 N.E.2d 157 (1961) (defendant threatened a woman that he would murder her husband and then carried out the threat outside of her presence); Schurk v. Christensen, 80 Wash.2d 652, 497 P.2d 937 (1972) (mother of five-year-old permitted to recover against teenage babysitter who molested child). In R.D. v. W.H., 875 P.2d 26 (Wyo. 1994), the husband and minor child of decedent sued her stepfather for events leading to her death by suicide. Plaintiffs alleged that the stepfather had sexually abused the decedent, provided her with a firearm with which she attempted suicide, and then provided her with prescription narcotics with which she killed herself. Although emphasizing that the generally better practice is to limit recovery to plaintiffs who were present during the outrageous conduct, the court recognized a narrow exception for this case.

6. How far should these narrow exceptions go? Should there be a cause of action on behalf of those who witness the assassination of the president? For those who saw it live on television? For those who saw it replayed a few minutes later? The next day? On the first anniversary? Restatement (Third) of Torts: Liability for Physical and Emotional Harm § 46, comment *i* (2012) (noting that courts generally do not allow recovery for bystanders' emotional distress even though it is substantially certain to follow).

7. The classic articles on the infliction of mental distress are Magruder, Mental and Emotional Distress in the Law of Torts, 49

Harv.L.Rev. 1033 (1936); Prosser, Insult and Outrage, 44 Cal.L.Rev. 40 (1956); Wade, Tort Liability for Abusive and Insulting Language, 4 Vand.L.Rev. 63 (1950); Partlett, Tort Liability and the American Way: Reflections on Liability for Emotional Distress, Am.J. Comp.L. 601 (1997); and Kircher, The Four Faces of Tort Law: Liability for Emotional Harm, 90 Marq. L. Rev. 789 (2007) (including an appendix with case law from all fifty-one jurisdictions).

6. TRESPASS TO LAND

Dougherty v. Stepp

Supreme Court of North Carolina, 1835.
18 N.C. 371.

This was an action of trespass quare clausum fregit, tried at Buncombe on the last Circuit, before his Honor Judge Martin. The only proof introduced by the plaintiff to establish an act of trespass, was, that the defendant had entered on the unenclosed land of the plaintiff, with a surveyor and chain carriers, and actually surveyed a part of it, claiming it as his own, but without marking trees or cutting bushes. This, his Honor held not to be a trespass, and the jury under his instructions, found a verdict for the defendant, and the plaintiff appealed. * * *

RUFFIN, CHIEF JUSTICE. In the opinion of the Court, there is error in the instructions given to the jury. The amount of damages may depend on the acts done on the land, and the extent of injury to it therefrom. But it is an elementary principle, that every unauthorized, and therefore unlawful entry, into the close of another, is a trespass. From every such entry against the will of the possessor, the law infers some damage; if nothing more, the treading down the grass or herbage, or as here, the shrubbery. * * *

Let the judgment be reversed, and a new trial granted.

NOTES AND QUESTIONS

1. We are here concerned only with intentional trespass to land. There may be negligent entry onto land, but it is governed by the ordinary rules applicable to negligence actions. One of these is that when the entry upon the land is merely negligent, proof of some actual damage is essential to the cause of action. Restatement (Second) of Torts § 165. Thus, the word "trespass" may be used to describe the kind of interest that defendant has invaded but usually is reserved for an intentional invasion of that interest—the right to exclusive possession of land.

2. Because the cause of action is for exclusive possession of land, it belongs to the party with the right of possession. If there is a tenant, it would be the tenant who could bring the trespass action. The owner also might have a claim, for trespass on the case, but that requires a showing of actual damage to the owner's reversionary interest. Owner would have to show some permanent injury to the property that would affect him after it reverted to him.

3. The trespass is intentional even when the defendant enters the land in the honest and reasonable belief that it is his own. See Glade v. Dietert, 156 Tex. 382, 387, 295 S.W.2d 642, 645 (1956) (dictum). Cf. Ranson v. Kitner, page 25 and Serota v. M. & M. Utilities, Inc., 55 Misc.2d 286, 285 N.Y.S.2d 121 (1967), page 25, note 2.

4. In a trespass action, plaintiff will be awarded nominal damages if there are no actual (compensatory) damages. Why nominal damages when the trespass does no harm? Why bother? The explanation sometimes given is that the action of trespass is frequently either a suit intended to try title or is directed at the vindication of the legal right, without which the defendant's conduct, if repeated, might ripen into a prescriptive right—the entitlement to use the land in a particular way granted to a longtime user even though the user did not have the owner's explicit permission. Hence there is no room for the application of the maxim, *de minimis non curat lex.* See 1 T. Street, Foundations of Legal Liability, 25 (1906). Suppose a car equipped with a panoramic digital camera drove down a private road and pulled into a driveway and photographed plaintiff's residence and swimming pool and those photographs were then posted as part of the Street View program of Google Maps. Trespass? Boring v. Google Inc., 362 Fed.Appx. 273 (3d Cir. 2010) (applying Pennsylvania law) (reinstating plaintiffs' trespass claim, court noted that "it may well be that, when it comes to proving damages from the alleged trespass, the Borings are left to collect one dollar and whatever sense of vindication that may bring, but that is for another day"). At common law, one reason underlying the rule was to keep the peace. Is the rule justified today? What about punitive damages? Should they be available if only nominal damages were awarded? See Jacque v. Steenberg Homes, Inc., 209 Wis.2d 605, 563 N.W.2d 154 (1997) (upholding punitive damages award even though no compensatory damages were proved where defendant had bulldozed a path in the snow across plaintiff's field to deliver a mobile home despite plaintiff's repeated refusals to permit the defendant to cross his land to make the delivery).

5. When a trespassory invasion is found, the fact that defendant's conduct was socially useful or even beneficial to plaintiff does not affect liability. See Longenecker v. Zimmerman, 175 Kan. 719, 267 P.2d 543 (1954) (even if jury finds that defendant's trimming of plaintiff's trees was beneficial to the trees, at least nominal damages would be available).

6. Of course, if the plaintiff does suffer compensatory damages, those too are recoverable in the trespass action. What about emotional distress damages? Defendant landlord, seeking to persuade tenants to vacate a townhouse, entered the premises without their consent, changed the locks on the garage, blocked the driveway, and repeatedly threatened and harassed the tenants. Johnson v. Marcel, 251 Va. 58, 465 S.E.2d 815 (1996) (where alleged trespass is deliberate and accompanied by aggravating circumstances, emotional distress damages may be recovered even in the absence of physical injury).

7. In addition to a cause of action for trespass, the plaintiff might have a cause of action for ejectment. Ejectment would lie if the defendant was in possession of the land, rather than just having been on it temporarily. A judgment in plaintiff's favor would entitle plaintiff to the sheriff's help in removing the defendant from her land. If the plaintiff is in

possession of the land, but the defendant is claiming to own it, a quiet title action would lie.

8. Since the tort protects plaintiff's right to exclusive possession of his land, traditionally there has been a requirement that the invasion be a physical one, which usually must be accomplished by a tangible mass, like a person, a fence, a building, or equipment. Intangible intrusions like smoke, odor, light, and noise are not typically actionable under a trespass theory. Thus, in Amphitheaters, Inc. v. Portland Meadows, 184 Or. 336, 198 P.2d 847 (1948), it was held to be no trespass where race track lights were reflected onto plaintiff's outdoor movie theater. See also Schuman v. Greenbelt Homes, Inc., 212 Md.App. 451, 69 A.3d 512 (2013) (cigarette smoke from neighbor's apartment not trespass) and Babb v. Lee Cty. Landfill, 405 S.C. 129, 747 S.E.2d 468 (2013) (odor from landfill not actionable trespass). Would any other action lie? Trespass has often been contrasted with the tort of nuisance, which protects plaintiff's use and enjoyment of the land. In an action for nuisance, courts usually require some actual damage, do not require a physical invasion of land, and take into account the social utility of defendant's activity. See Chapter 16, Nuisance. What about pesticide that drifts on to neighboring land? Johnson v. Paynesville Farmers Union Co-Op., 817 N.W.2d 693 (Minn. 2012) (not trespass because claim is that it interferes with the enjoyment and use of the land as an organic farm, not with possession of the land). What about microscopic particles of heavy metal from defendant's copper smelting plant that accumulate on neighbors' land? What about noise (sound waves) from a shooting gallery that invade the land on which an elementary school sits? With respect to invasions of the land by intangible items, courts consistently have required a showing of actual damage, as is required in a nuisance action, even when sometimes referring to it as "intangible trespass."

Herrin v. Sutherland

Supreme Court of Montana, 1925.
74 Mont. 587, 241 P. 328.

* * * [T]he defendant, while engaged in hunting ducks and other migratory game birds, and while standing on the lands of another, repeatedly discharged a Winchester shotgun at water fowl in flight over plaintiff's said premises * * * "to plaintiff's damage in the sum of $10." * * *

After defendant's general demurrer * * * was overruled, he declined to answer, and his default was entered. Upon the suggestion of counsel for plaintiff that only nominal damages would be demanded, the court rendered judgment in favor of the plaintiff for damages in the sum of $1. From this judgment the defendant has appealed.

CALLAWAY, C.J. * * * It must be held that when the defendant, although standing upon the land of another, fired a shotgun over plaintiff's premises, dwelling and cattle, he interfered with the "quiet, undisturbed, peaceful enjoyment of the plaintiff," and thus committed a technical trespass at least. The plaintiff was the owner of the land. "Land," says Blackstone, "in its legal significance has an indefinite extent, upwards as well as downwards; whoever owns the land possesses all the space upwards to an indefinite extent; such is the maxim of the law." * * *

Sir Frederick Pollock, in the tenth edition of his valuable work on Torts, page 363, observes that it has been doubted whether it is a trespass to pass over land without touching the soil, as one may in a balloon, or to cause a material object as a shot fired from a gun, to pass over it. * * * Continuing, he observes:

> "As regards shooting, it would be strange if we could object to shots being fired point blank across our land only in the event of actual injury being caused, and the passage of the foreign object in the air above our soil being thus a mere incident and a distinct trespass to person or property."

But he concludes that when taking into account the extreme flight of projectiles fired from modern artillery which may pass thousands of feet above the land, the subject is not without difficulty. That shortly it will become one of considerable importance is indicated by the rapid approach of the airplane as an instrumentality of commerce, as is suggested in a valuable note found in 32 Harvard Law Review, 569. However, it seems to be the consensus of the holdings of the courts in this country that the air space, at least near the ground, is almost as inviolable as the soil itself. * * * It is a matter of common knowledge that the shotgun is a firearm of short range. To be subjected to the danger incident to and reasonably to be anticipated from the firing of this weapon at water fowl in flight over one's dwelling house and cattle would seem to be far from inconsequential, and while plaintiff's allegations are very general in character, it cannot be said that a cause of action is not stated, for nominal damages at least. * * *

The judgment is affirmed.

NOTES AND QUESTIONS

1. A, disturbed at night by the howling of a cat atop B's shed, shoots the cat. The bullet remains in the cat, and neither bullet nor cat touches the ground. Is this a trespass to B's land? Davies v. Bennison, (1927) 22 Tasmanian L.Rep. 52 (Austl.).

2. During a dispute between neighbors over a backyard fence, one of them extends her arm over the fence, without touching it. Is this a trespass? Hannabalson v. Sessions, 116 Iowa 457, 90 N.W. 93 (1902) (mere fact that plaintiff did not step across the boundary line does not make her any less a trespasser if she reached her arm across the line). What about eaves that overhang plaintiff's property? Smith v. Smith, 110 Mass. 302 (1872) (eaves of barn overhanging neighbor's property constitute trespass).

3. *"Cujus est solum, ejus est usque ad coelum et ad inferos."* [Whose is the soil, his it is also unto the sky and the depths.] Coke, Littleton, 4a.

4. The Restatement of Torts, §§ 159, 194, had provided that air travel was a trespass but may be privileged. For historical treatment, see R. Wright, The Law of Air Space (1968). Restatement (Second) of Torts § 159, now provides that air travel is a trespass only if it "enters into immediate reaches of the air space next to the land, and * * * interferes substantially with the others' use and enjoyment of the land."

5. In effect, the Restatement approach changes a fundamental aspect of the tort of trespass (see Dougherty v. Stepp, page 72). Some courts have been more explicit in doing so and have held that flight by aircraft is never trespassory and plaintiff's remedy lies in negligence or nuisance. See Atkinson v. Bernard, Inc., 223 Or. 624, 355 P.2d 229 (1960); Nestle v. Santa Monica, 6 Cal.3d 920, 496 P.2d 480, 101 Cal.Rptr. 568 (1972). What is the disadvantage to plaintiff in these approaches?

6. When government overflights have substantially affected habitability of the land below, a court may find a "taking" within the meaning of the Fifth Amendment to the United States Constitution and the government will be required to compensate the owner. See, for example, Brown v. United States, 73 F.3d 1100 (Fed.Cir.1996) (owners of recreational ranch sought compensation for taking based on noise from low overflights by Air Force planes doing touch and go exercises at adjacent airstrip in remote West Texas, near Mexican border). See also, R. Epstein, Takings: Private Property and the Power of Eminent Domain, pp. 41–49 (1985). Local government is subject to the same constitutional responsibility. See Griggs v. Allegheny County, 369 U.S. 84 (1962) (county operated airport).

7. For treatment of noise and vibration as a nuisance and of the application of inverse condemnation, see Boomer v. Atlantic Cement Co., Inc., 26 N.Y.2d 219, 257 N.E.2d 870, 309 N.Y.S.2d 312 (1970), page 867. Remedies for ground damage as the result of airline crashes are considered in the chapters on Negligence, Chapter 4, and Strict Liability, Chapter 14.

8. The interest in the possession of land also extends below the surface, and may present similar problems and similar limitations. In Edwards v. Sims, 232 Ky. 791, 24 S.W.2d 619 (1929), plaintiff discovered that the cave that defendant had developed, advertised, and turned into a tourist attraction ran a considerable distance under plaintiff's land. Plaintiff sought to compel a survey of the cave, an injunction to stop the trespasses of the tourists, and an accounting for a portion of defendant's profits. The trial court ordered the survey and the appellate court refused to prohibit it, relying on the maxim "*cujus est solum*" [note 3 above], and noting that the owner of realty is "entitled to the free and unfettered control of his own land above, upon and beneath the surface. So whatever is in a direct line between the surface of the land and the center of the earth belongs to the owner of the surface." The dissent thought the principle should not extend so far above or so far below the land that the owner could not make use of it. Cf. Boehringer v. Montalto, 142 Misc. 560, 254 N.Y.S. 276 (1931) (sewer line at depth of 150 feet not trespass because beyond where owner could reasonably use land); Chance v. BP Chemicals, 77 Ohio St.3d 17, 670 N.E.2d 985 (1996) (in case involving industrial waste that had been injected far below the surface of defendant's land and then migrated to far below the surface of plaintiff's land, court noted that property rights are no longer as clear-cut as they were before airplanes and injection wells). In mining cases, most jurisdictions hold that it is a trespass to mine under the land of another, but some of the western states provide that the miner is permitted to follow the vein wherever it may lead, so long as it is unbroken.

Rogers v. Board of Road Com'rs for Kent County

Supreme Court of Michigan, 1947.
319 Mich. 661, 30 N.W.2d 358.

REID, JUSTICE. Plaintiff instituted this suit to recover damages because of the death of her husband, Theodore Rogers, which plaintiff claims was caused by the trespass and negligence of the defendant board of county road commissioners. Defendant filed a motion to dismiss, based on the pleadings and on the ground of governmental immunity. The lower court granted defendant's motion and dismissed the cause. Plaintiff appeals from the judgment of dismissal of her cause.

Plaintiff claims that for two winter seasons previous to the date of the fatal injury to her husband the defendant board of road commissioners had obtained a license to place a snow fence in decedent's field parallel to the roadway past decedent's farm. Plaintiff claims in her declaration that the placing of the snow fence there was with the distinct understanding and agreement between the defendant and decedent that all of the fence together with the anchor posts should be removed by defendant at the end of each winter season when the necessity for snow fences for that season no longer existed. . . . [T]he defendant's agents and employees removed the snow fence but did not remove a steel anchor post which protruded from 6 to 8 inches above the ground. Plaintiff further claims that the place where the post was located was a meadow where the grass grew to a considerable height, so that the anchor post was entirely hidden, and that on July 23, 1945, after decedent's [plaintiff's?] husband had mowed several swaths around the field where the snow fence had been, with his mowing machine attached to his neighbor's tractor, and without any negligence or want of proper method of operation on his part, the mowing bar struck the steel stake and as a result of the impact decedent was forcibly thrown from the seat of the mowing machine to and upon the wheels of the mowing machine and upon the ground. * * *

The court dismissed plaintiff's cause of action, ruling that the action was plainly an action based upon negligence, that there was no basis for any finding of trespass and that the defense of governmental immunity applied to the facts set forth in plaintiff's declaration.

Failure to remove the anchor stake upon expiration of the license to have it on defendant's [decedent's?] land was a continuing trespass and is alleged by plaintiff to have been a proximate cause of the damage for which she seeks to recover.

"§ 160. Failure to remove a thing placed on the land pursuant to a license or other privilege

"A trespass, actionable under the rule stated in § 158, may be committed by the continued presence on the land of a structure, chattel or other thing which the actor or his predecessor in legal interest therein has placed thereon

"(a) with the consent of the person then in possession of the land, if the actor fails to remove it after the consent has been effectively terminated, or "(b) pursuant to a privilege conferred on the actor irrespective of the possessor's consent, if the actor fails to remove it after the privilege has been terminated, by the accomplishment of its purpose or otherwise." Restatement of the Law, Torts, p. 368. * * *

[The court also concluded that sovereign immunity did not apply.]

The judgment of the court dismissing the cause of action is reversed and the cause remanded for such further proceedings as shall be found necessary.

NOTES AND QUESTIONS

1. At common law, trespass would not lie unless defendant entered the land illegally (breaking of the close). As the principal case reflects, the distinction between trespass and case is no longer controlling, and a trespass can arise today when a visitor who entered land with the consent of the possessor "overstays" his welcome. Of course, the visitor must be aware that he no longer has the possessor's consent to remain. Mitchell v. Mitchell, 54 Minn. 301, 55 N.W. 1134 (1893) (Widow admitted administrators of her husband's estate into her house to pick up his books but then asked them to leave when they tried to take all the books in the house, including some that were hers rather than her late husband's. They refused to leave and stayed for several hours, attempting to persuade her to turn over the books, thus committing a trespass from the time she asked them to leave.).

2. A privileged entry onto the land of another may be limited not only by time and space, but also by purpose. In Brown v. Dellinger, 355 S.W.2d 742 (Tex.Civ.App.1962), two children, who had been permitted to play in their neighbor's yard, on one occasion ignited a charcoal burner in the garage and caused $28,000 worth of damages. They were treated as trespassers. In Copeland v. Hubbard Broadcasting, Inc., 526 N.W.2d 402 (Minn.App.1995), the Copelands gave permission to their veterinarian to bring with him to their home a student who said she was considering a career in veterinary medicine. She did not disclose that she was an employee of a local television station doing a report on their veterinarian's practice. While in plaintiffs' home, she secretly videotaped the treatment of their cat. When the videotape of their home was broadcast as part of the report, the Copelands sued for trespass. The court found that there was a trespass because the entrant moved beyond the scope of the Copelands' invitation by using the visit for something other than educational or vocational purposes.

3. *Consequences of Trespass.* Note that in the principal case the defendant is held liable to the plaintiff for the death of her husband resulting from the trespass, without any question of negligence in failing to remove the anchor post. See Prosser, Transferred Intent, 45 Tex.L.Rev. 650, 658–671 (1967). Compare the following:

A. Defendant, a trespasser, entered plaintiff's blacksmith shop and built a fire in the forge. After he left, and without any showing of negligence on the part of defendant, the shop caught fire and was destroyed. Defendant was held liable for the loss of the shop on the basis of the trespass. Wyant v. Crouse, 127 Mich. 158, 86 N.W. 527 (1901).

B. Defendant's employee, delivering a package at plaintiff's residence, entered a side door into a sun porch, left the door open, and crossed the porch to knock at an inner door. Plaintiff's child, whom defendant did not see, fell through the open door and was injured. The jury was permitted to find that he was a trespasser, and to return a verdict against defendant. Keesecker v. G.M. McKelvey Co., 141 Ohio St. 162, 47 N.E.2d 211 (1943).

C. Plaintiffs, husband and wife, arrived home to find a parked car blocking their driveway. Defendants, neighbors of the plaintiffs, were loading the trunk with tools that they had just used to dig a trench across plaintiffs' driveway. Defendants and plaintiffs argued about the trench. Plaintiff went into the house to call the police. When she returned three minutes later, she found her husband lying face-down in a mud puddle and saw the defendants driving away. Husband was pronounced dead from a heart attack in the Emergency Room. Court held that damages (heart attack) caused by a trespasser need not be foreseeable to be compensable. Baker v. Shymkiv, 6 Ohio St.3d 151, 451 N.E.2d 811 (1983).

4. *Restrictions on Right to Exclude Persons from Premises*. Public utilities, innkeepers, and common carriers cannot exclude members of the public. Restatement (Second) of Tort § 191 (1965). Federal and state statutes require certain landowners and possessors of land to make their premises open to the public without discrimination. See, for example, 42 U.S.C. § 2000a (1965) (all places of public accommodation whose business affects interstate commerce must serve customers "without discrimination or segregation on the ground of race, color, religion, or national origin"). A private individual may control an area so extensive that it becomes "public" for the purposes of First Amendment freedom of speech provisions. See, for example, Marsh v. Alabama, 326 U.S. 501 (1946) (company town). A few states provide similar restrictions. See, for example, Robins v. Pruneyard Shopping Ctr., 23 Cal.3d 899, 153 Cal.Rptr. 854, 592 P.2d 341 (1979) (privately owned shopping mall).

7. TRESPASS TO CHATTELS

Glidden v. Szybiak

Supreme Court of New Hampshire, 1949.
95 N.H. 318, 63 A.2d 233.

Actions at law under the provisions of R.L. c. 180, §§ 23, 24, to recover for a dog bite sustained by the plaintiff Elaine Glidden upon September 29, 1946, and for medical expenses incurred by her father, Harold Glidden. Trial by the Court, with verdicts for the plaintiffs. The plaintiff Elaine Glidden, who was four years old at the time of the occurrence here involved, left her home about noon on the day of her injury, to go to a neighborhood store for candy. On the porch of the store Elaine encountered a dog named Toby and engaged in play with him. She eventually climbed on his back and pulled his ears. The dog snapped at her and bit her nose, inflicting wounds for which a recovery is sought. She was treated by two physicians and a successful result obtained. Such scars as were left are "in no way disfiguring but discernible on close view." The dog Toby was owned by the defendant

Jane Szybiak, an unmarried daughter of the other two defendants, 26 years of age at the time of the trial, living with her parents. * * * The defendants also excepted to the denial of their motions for judgment at the close of the evidence. The Court also made the following finding: "Elaine is found to have been of such tender years as to be incapable of being guilty of contributory negligence in her conduct toward the dog Toby. If she was too young to be guilty of negligence, she cannot be found to have been guilty of a trespass or a tort at the time she received her injury." To this finding the defendants duly excepted.

BRANCH, CHIEF JUSTICE. The statute under which these actions were brought reads as follows: "23. Liability of owner. Any person to whom or to whose property damage may be occasioned by a dog not owned or kept by him shall be entitled to recover such damage of the person who owns or keeps the dog, or has it in possession, unless the damage was occasioned to him while he was engaged in the commission of a trespass or other tort."

It is the contention of the defendants that the plaintiff Elaine was engaged in the commission of a trespass at the time of her injury and is, therefore, barred from recovery under the statute. The law in regard to a trespass to chattels is thus summarized in the Restatement of the Law of Torts, s. 218: "One who without consensual or other privilege to do so, uses or otherwise intentionally intermeddles with a chattel which is in possession of another is liable for a trespass to such person if, (a) the chattel is impaired as to its condition, quality or value, or (b) the possessor is deprived of the use of the chattel for a substantial time, or (c) bodily harm is thereby caused to the possessor or harm is caused to some person or thing in which the possessor has a legally protected interest." In comment (f) to clauses (a) and (b), it is pointed out that "the interest of a possessor of a chattel in its inviolability, unlike the similar interest of a possessor of land, is not given legal protection by an action for nominal damages for harmless intermeddlings with the chattel. * * * Sufficient legal protection of the possessor's interest in the mere inviolability of his chattel is afforded by his privilege to use reasonable force to protect his possession against even harmless interference."

No claim was advanced at the trial that the dog Toby was in any way injured by the conduct of the plaintiff Elaine. Consequently she could not be held liable for a trespass to the dog. Consequently her conduct did not constitute a trespass which will prevent her recovery under the statute here invoked. * * *

Judgment on the verdict against the defendant Jane. * * *

NOTES AND QUESTIONS

1. Why does the court need to address the question of the elements of trespass to chattels in a dog bite case?

2. The earliest cases in which trespass was applied to chattels involved asportation, or carrying off, and a special form of the writ, known as trespass de bonis asportatis ("d.b.a.") was developed for such situations. Later the action was extended to cases where the chattels were damaged but not taken, as where animals were killed or beaten. It at last became applicable to any physical interference with a chattel in the possession of

the plaintiff. Thus Parker v. Mise, 27 Ala. 480, 62 Am.Dec. 776 (1855) (shooting dog); Bruch v. Carter, 32 N.J.L. 554 (1867) (moving horse from one place to another); Cole v. Schweer, 159 Ill.App. 278 (1910) (releasing fish).

3. Trespass to chattels is now quite universally limited to intentional interferences with them. Thus in Mountain States Tel. & Tel. Co. v. Horn Tower Const. Co., 147 Colo. 166, 363 P.2d 175 (1961), it was held that there was no trespass when defendant unintentionally severed plaintiff's telephone conduit. An action would lie for negligent interference that causes damage, but that action has been absorbed into the general field of negligence actions, and no longer is called trespass.

4. As in the case of trespass to land, the conduct is treated as intentional even though the defendant acts under an innocent mistake, as where he drives off the plaintiff's sheep, believing that they are his own. Dexter v. Cole, 6 Wis. 319, 70 Am.Dec. 465 (1857).

5. Unlike trespass to land, trespass to chattels will not lie unless there is actual dispossession or actual damage to the chattel itself or to its owner or his property. Wintringham v. Lafoy, 7 Cow. 735 (N.Y.1827) (holding that where an officer mistakenly levied execution upon goods belonging to the plaintiff, the deprivation of possession was regarded as damage in itself, and no other is required). But where there is merely interference with the chattel, as by laying hands on a horse or an automobile, the few American decisions have held that the action cannot be maintained without proof of actual damages. Marentille v. Oliver, 2 N.J.L. 379 (1808); Paul v. Slason, 22 Vt. 231, 54 Am.Dec. 75 (1850); Graves v. Severens, 40 Vt. 636 (1868). In accord is the Restatement (Second) of Torts, § 218. What should be the result if defendant places a Yankees bumper sticker on a Red Sox fan's car?

6. English writers have contended that the analogy of trespass to land should apply to trespass to chattels and that there is a real necessity for an action for nominal damages to protect property from intermeddlers. See Salmond and Heuston, Torts 89–90 (20th ed. 1992), citing several British cases apparently holding this, including Thurston v. Charles, 21 T.L.R. 659 (K.B.1905), holding liability for showing a private letter to an unauthorized person (£400 damages).

7. The development of the action of trover, which evolved into the tort of conversion, provided a convenient substitute for trespass to chattels in most situations. Trespass to chattels survives as a possible remedy for interferences when the plaintiff wants to keep the chattel and sue for the harm rather than allow defendant to keep the chattel in exchange for its full market value. See, for example, Van Eaton v. Thon, 764 S.W.2d 674 (1988) (diminution in value of horse, which became "head-shy" after incident in which defendant struck it in jaw with his fist) and the next principal case.

CompuServe Inc. v. Cyber Promotions, Inc.

United States District Court, Southern District of Ohio, 1997.
962 F.Supp. 1015.

GRAHAM, DISTRICT JUDGE. This case presents novel issues regarding the commercial use of the Internet, specifically the right of an online computer service to prevent a commercial enterprise from sending unsolicited electronic mail advertising to its subscribers.

Plaintiff CompuServe Incorporated ("CompuServe") is one of the major national commercial online computer services. It operates a computer communication service through a proprietary nationwide computer network. In addition to allowing access to the extensive content available within its own proprietary network, CompuServe also provides its subscribers with a link to the much larger resources of the Internet. This allows its subscribers to send and receive electronic messages, known as "e-mail," by the Internet. Defendants Cyber Promotions, Inc. and its president Sanford Wallace are in the business of sending unsolicited e-mail advertisements on behalf of themselves and their clients to hundreds of thousands of Internet users, many of whom are CompuServe subscribers. CompuServe has notified defendants that they are prohibited from using its computer equipment to process and store the unsolicited e-mail and has requested that they terminate the practice. Instead, defendants have sent an increasing volume of e-mail solicitations to CompuServe subscribers. CompuServe has attempted to employ technological means to block the flow of defendants' e-mail transmission to its computer equipment, but to no avail.

This matter is before the Court on the application of CompuServe for a preliminary injunction which would extend the duration of the temporary restraining order issued by this Court on October 24, 1996 and which would in addition prevent defendants from sending unsolicited advertisements to CompuServe subscribers. * * *

Defendants refer to this as "bulk e-mail," while plaintiff refers to it as "junk e-mail." In the vernacular of the Internet, unsolicited e-mail advertising is sometimes referred to pejoratively as "spam."[1] * * *

Over the past several months, CompuServe has received many complaints from subscribers threatening to discontinue their subscription unless CompuServe prohibits electronic mass mailers from using its equipment to send unsolicited advertisements. CompuServe asserts that the volume of messages generated by such mass mailings places a significant burden on its equipment which has finite processing and storage capacity. CompuServe receives no payment from the mass mailers for processing their unsolicited advertising. * * *

In an effort to shield its equipment from defendants' bulk e-mail, CompuServe has implemented software programs designed to screen out the messages and block their receipt. In response, defendants have modified their equipment and the messages they send in such a fashion

---

[1] This term is derived from a skit performed on the British television show Monty Python's Flying Circus, in which the word "spam" is repeated to the point of absurdity in a restaurant menu.

as to circumvent CompuServe's screening software. Allegedly, defendants have been able to conceal the true origin of their messages by falsifying the point-of-origin information contained in the header of the electronic messages. Defendants have removed the "sender" information in the header of their messages and replaced it with another address. Also, defendants have developed the capability of configuring their computer servers to conceal their true domain name and appear on the Internet as another computer, further concealing the true origin of the messages. By manipulating this data, defendants have been able to continue sending messages to CompuServe's equipment in spite of CompuServe's protests and protective efforts. Defendants assert that they possess the right to continue to send these communications to CompuServe subscribers. CompuServe contends that, in doing so, the defendants are trespassing upon its personal property. * * *

CompuServe predicates this aspect of its motion for a preliminary injunction on the common law theory of trespass to personal property or to chattels, asserting that defendants' continued transmission of electronic messages to its computer equipment constitutes an actionable tort.

Trespass to chattels has evolved from its original common law application, concerning primarily the asportation of another's tangible property, to include the unauthorized use of personal property: Its chief importance now, is that there may be recovery . . . for interferences with the possession of chattels which are not sufficiently important to be classed as conversion, and so to compel the defendant to pay the full value of the thing with which he has interfered. Trespass to chattels survives today, in other words, largely as a little brother of conversion. Prosser & Keeton, Prosser and Keeton on Torts, § 14, 85–86 (1984). * * *

Both plaintiff and defendants cite the Restatement (Second) of Torts to support their respective positions. In determining a question unanswered by state law, it is appropriate for this Court to consider such sources as the restatement of the law and decisions of other jurisdictions. [Cc]

The Restatement § 217(b) states that a trespass to chattel may be committed by intentionally using or intermeddling with the chattel in possession of another. Restatement § 217, comment *e* defines physical "intermeddling" as follows: . . . intentionally bringing about a physical contact with the chattel. The actor may commit a trespass by an act which brings him into an intended physical contact with a chattel in the possession of another[.] Electronic signals generated and sent by computer have been held to be sufficiently physically tangible to support a trespass cause of action. [Cc] It is undisputed that plaintiff has a possessory interest in its computer systems. Further, defendants' contact with plaintiff's computers is clearly intentional. Although electronic messages may travel through the Internet over various routes, the messages are affirmatively directed to their destination.

Defendants, citing Restatement (Second) of Torts § 221, which defines "dispossession," assert that not every interference with the personal property of another is actionable and that physical dispossession or substantial interference with the chattel is required. Defendants then argue that they did not, in this case, physically dispossess plaintiff of its equipment or substantially interfere with it. However, the Restatement (Second) of Torts § 218 defines the circumstances under which a trespass to chattels may be actionable: One who commits a trespass to a chattel is subject to liability to the possessor of the chattel if, but only if, (a) he dispossesses the other of the chattel, or (b) the chattel is impaired as to its condition, quality, or value, or (c) the possessor is deprived of the use of the chattel for a substantial time, or (d) bodily harm is caused to the possessor, or harm is caused to some person or thing in which the possessor has a legally protected interest. Therefore, an interference resulting in physical dispossession is just one circumstance under which a defendant can be found liable. Defendants suggest that "unless an alleged trespasser actually takes physical custody of the property or physically damages it, courts will not find the 'substantial interference' required to maintain a trespass to chattel claim." * * * To support this rather broad proposition, defendants cite only two cases which make any reference to the Restatement. In Glidden v. Szybiak, 95 N.H. 318, 63 A.2d 233 (1949), the court simply indicated that an action for trespass to chattels could not be maintained in the absence of some form of damage. The court held that where plaintiff did not contend that defendant's pulling on her pet dog's ears caused any injury, an action in tort could not be maintained. 63 A.2d at 235. In contrast, plaintiff in the present action has alleged that it has suffered several types of injury as a result of defendants' conduct. In Koepnick v. Sears Roebuck & Co., 158 Ariz. 322, 762 P.2d 609 (1988) the court held that a two-minute search of an individual's truck did not amount to a "dispossession" of the truck as defined in Restatement § 221 or a deprivation of the use of the truck for a substantial time. It is clear from a reading of Restatement § 218 that an interference or intermeddling that does not fit the § 221 definition of "dispossession" can nonetheless result in defendants' liability for trespass.

* * * In the present case, any value CompuServe realizes from its computer equipment is wholly derived from the extent to which that equipment can serve its subscriber base. Michael Mangino, a software developer for CompuServe who monitors its mail processing computer equipment, states by affidavit that handling the enormous volume of mass mailings that CompuServe receives places a tremendous burden on its equipment. * * * Defendants' more recent practice of evading CompuServe's filters by disguising the origin of their messages commandeers even more computer resources because CompuServe's computers are forced to store undeliverable e-mail messages and labor in vain to return the messages to an address that does not exist. * * * To the extent that defendants' multitudinous electronic mailings demand the disk space and drain the processing power of plaintiff's computer equipment, those resources are not available to serve CompuServe subscribers. Therefore, the value of that equipment to CompuServe is diminished even though it is not physically damaged by defendants' conduct.

Next, plaintiff asserts that it has suffered injury aside from the physical impact of defendants' messages on its equipment. Restatement

§ 218(d) also indicates that recovery may be had for a trespass that causes harm to something in which the possessor has a legally protected interest. Plaintiff asserts that defendants' messages are largely unwanted by its subscribers, who pay incrementally to access their e-mail, read it, and discard it. Also, the receipt of a bundle of unsolicited messages at once can require the subscriber to sift through, at his expense, all of the messages in order to find the ones he wanted or expected to receive. These inconveniences decrease the utility of CompuServe's e-mail service and are the foremost subject in recent complaints from CompuServe subscribers. * * *

Many subscribers have terminated their accounts specifically because of the unwanted receipt of bulk e-mail messages. * * * Defendants' intrusions into CompuServe's computer systems, insofar as they harm plaintiff's business reputation and goodwill with its customers, are actionable under Restatement § 218(d). * * *

Defendants argue that plaintiff made the business decision to connect to the Internet and that therefore it cannot now successfully maintain an action for trespass to chattels. Their argument is analogous to the argument that because an establishment invites the public to enter its property for business purposes, it cannot later restrict or revoke access to that property, a proposition which is erroneous under Ohio law. * * *

Based on the foregoing, plaintiff's motion for a preliminary injunction is GRANTED. The temporary restraining order filed on October 24, 1996 by this Court is hereby extended in duration until final judgment is entered in this case. Further, defendants Cyber Promotions, Inc. and its president Sanford Wallace are enjoined from sending any unsolicited advertisements to any electronic mail address maintained by plaintiff CompuServe during the pendency of this action. It is so ORDERED.

NOTES AND QUESTIONS

1. You probably will run into cases in your other classes, as well as this one, where you will see the courts struggling with the application of traditional legal concepts to the new frontier of the Internet. Notice that both plaintiffs and defendants used the Restatement (Second) of Torts to support their arguments that defendant's conduct was trespass to chattels *vel non*. If you had been CompuServe's lawyer, would you have remembered the *Glidden* case and thought to apply its principles to your client's problem with spam?

2. Beyond spam, plaintiffs have sought recovery for trespass to chattels where their web sites were visited by data search and collection robots, sometimes known as spiders, that seek to collect information (like email addresses) to use to create searchable databases, Web catalogues, and comparison shopping services. See, for example, eBay, Inc. v. Bidder's Edge, Inc., 100 F. Supp.2d 1058 (N.D. Cal. 2000) and Register.com, Inc. v. Verio, Inc., 356 F.3d 393 (2d Cir. 2004) (applying New York law) (both finding that although the activity of the defendant alone would not incapacitate plaintiffs' systems, others would soon follow and the combined effect would).

3. What if a disgruntled former worker barrages a company's email system with messages that go to all 30,000 of its employees? Trespass to chattels? Intel Corp. v. Hamidi, 30 Cal.4th 1342, 71 P.3d 296, 1 Cal.Rptr.3d 32 (2003) (no trespass to chattels because no showing that the six messages sent over eighteen months either damaged or impaired computer system in a way that affected its functioning even though each message went to all 30,000 employees).

4. Could a CompuServe subscriber bring her own cause of action for trespass to chattels against Cyber Promotions for interference with her own computer?

8. CONVERSION

(A) NATURE OF THE TORT

Pearson v. Dodd

United States Court of Appeals, District of Columbia Circuit, 1969.
410 F.2d 701, cert. denied, 395 U.S. 947, 89 S.Ct. 2021, 23 L.Ed.2d 465 (1969).

J. SKELLY WRIGHT, CIRCUIT JUDGE: This case arises out of the exposure of the alleged misdeeds of Senator Thomas Dodd of Connecticut by newspaper columnists Drew Pearson and Jack Anderson. The District Court has granted partial summary judgment to Senator Dodd, appellee here, finding liability on a theory of conversion. At the same time, the court denied partial summary judgment on the theory of invasion of privacy. Both branches of the court's judgment are before us on interlocutory appeal. We affirm the District Court's denial of summary judgment for invasion of privacy and reverse its grant of summary judgment for conversion.

The undisputed facts in the case were stated by the District Court as follows: "* * * [O]n several occasions in June and July, 1965, two former employees of the plaintiff, at times with the assistance of two members of the plaintiff's staff, entered the plaintiff's office without authority and unbeknownst to him, removed numerous documents from his files, made copies of them, replaced the originals, and turned over the copies to the defendant Anderson, who was aware of the manner in which the copies had been obtained. The defendants Pearson and Anderson thereafter published articles containing information gleaned from these documents."

[The court also discussed the separate count of invasion of privacy].

The District Court ruled that appellants' receipt and subsequent use of photocopies of documents which appellants knew had been removed from appellee's files without authorization established appellants' liability for conversion. We conclude that appellants are not guilty of conversion on the facts shown.

Dean Prosser has remarked that "[c]onversion is the forgotten tort." That it is not entirely forgotten is attested by the case before us. History has largely defined its contours, contours which we should now follow except where they derive from clearly obsolete practices or abandoned theories.

Conversion is the substantive tort theory which underlay the ancient common law form of action for trover. A plaintiff in trover alleged that he had lost a chattel which he rightfully possessed, and that the defendant had found it and converted it to his own use. With time, the allegations of losing and finding became fictional, leaving the question of whether the defendant had "converted" the property the only operative one.

The most distinctive feature of conversion is its measure of damages, which is the value of the goods converted. The theory is that the "converting" defendant has in some way treated the goods as if they were his own, so that the plaintiff can properly ask the court to decree a forced sale of the property from the rightful possessor to the converter.

Because of this stringent measure of damages, it has long been recognized that not every wrongful interference with the personal property of another is a conversion. Where the intermeddling falls short of the complete or very substantial deprivation of possessory rights in the property, the tort committed is not conversion, but the lesser wrong of trespass to chattels.

The Restatement (Second) of Torts has marked the distinction by defining conversion as: "* * * [A]n intentional exercise of dominion or control over a chattel which so seriously interferes with the right of another to control it that the actor may justly be required to pay the other the full value of the chattel." Less serious interferences fall under the Restatement's definition of trespass [to chattels].

The difference is more than a semantic one. The measure of damages in trespass is not the whole value of the property interfered with, but rather the actual diminution in its value caused by the interference. More important for this case, a judgment for conversion can be obtained with only nominal damages, whereas liability for trespass to chattels exists only on a showing of actual damage to the property interfered with. Here the District Court granted partial summary judgment on the issue of liability alone, while conceding that possibly no more than nominal damages might be awarded on subsequent trial. Partial summary judgment for liability could not have been granted on a theory of trespass to chattels without an undisputed showing of actual damages to the property in question.

It is clear that on the agreed facts appellants committed no conversion of the physical documents taken from appellee's files. Those documents were removed from the files at night, photocopied, and returned to the files undamaged before office operations resumed in the morning. Insofar as the documents' value to appellee resided in their usefulness as records of the business of his office, appellee was clearly not substantially deprived of his use of them.

This of course is not an end of the matter. It has long been recognized that documents often have value above and beyond that springing from their physical possession. They may embody information or ideas whose economic value depends in part or in whole upon being kept secret. The question then arises whether the information taken by means of copying appellee's office files is of the type which the law of conversion protects. The general rule has been that ideas or information are not subject to legal protection, but the law has developed exceptions to this rule. Where information is gathered and arranged at some cost and sold as a commodity on the market, it is properly protected as property. Where ideas are formulated with labor and inventive genius, as in the case of literary works or scientific researches, they are protected. Where they constitute instruments of fair and effective commercial competition, those who develop them may gather their fruits under the protection of the law.

The question here is not whether appellee had a right to keep his files from prying eyes, but whether the information taken from those files falls under the protection of the law of property, enforceable by a suit for conversion. In our view, it does not. The information included the contents of letters to appellee from supplicants, and office records of other kinds, the nature of which is not fully revealed by the record. Insofar as we can tell, none of it amounts to literary property, to scientific invention, or to secret plans formulated by appellee for the conduct of commerce. Nor does it appear to be information held in any way for sale by appellee, analogous to the fresh news copy produced by a wire service. * * *

Because no conversion of the physical contents of appellee's files took place, and because the information copied from the documents in those files has not been shown to be property subject to protection by suit for conversion, the District Court's ruling that appellants are guilty of conversion must be reversed.

So ordered.

NOTES AND QUESTIONS

1. Conversion is a tort whose detailed complications exceed the time that can conveniently be allotted to it in any Torts course. There are thousands of conversion cases, but most of them have been concerned with settling the title to disputed goods, and there are relatively few in which the tort itself has been in issue. The topic of conversion has tended to be shunted back and forth between the courses in Torts and Property. Many of the practical problems relating to title and conversion are covered in Article 2 of the Uniform Commercial Code and law school courses in sales or commercial law.

2. The hand of history lies heavily on the tort. It is the lineal descendant of the old common law action of trover and for that reason is commonly listed under the heading "Trover and Conversion." (You may have seen a reference to it this way in your Civil Procedure course. Because it developed out of a common law writ, parties are entitled to a jury trial in such actions brought in federal courts.) Trespass and trover were both actions founded upon possession, and for some centuries they remained as alternative remedies for the wrongful taking or damaging of chattels. There was, however, one important difference between them, as to the measure of damages. The theory of trespass to chattels was that the plaintiff remained the owner of the chattel, with possession merely interrupted or interfered with, so that when the chattel was returned, the owner had to accept it and recovery was limited to damages to the chattel, or to reimbursement for the time it was missing. The theory of trover was that the defendant, by

"converting" the chattel to the defendant's own use had appropriated the plaintiff's property, for which he was required to make compensation—generally computed as market value at the time and place of conversion. The defendant did not have the option of simply returning the chattel and paying damages for repair of the chattel or for compensation for the time it was gone.

3. Plaintiff was holding a ten dollar bill loosely in his hand when defendant snatched it. Defendant immediately returned the bill, taunting "that was too easy." Conversion? Trespass to chattels? Cf. Reynolds v. MacFarlane, 322 P.3d 755, 759 (Utah App. 2014).

4. In each of the following cases, was the interference with the plaintiff's chattel serious enough to warrant an action for conversion?

A. Plaintiff and defendant owned a house as tenants in common. During a dispute over ownership, defendant notified plaintiff that if he did not remove his furniture she would have it removed. She did so, informing him of the location. Zaslow v. Kroenert, 29 Cal.2d 541, 176 P.2d 1 (1946) (no conversion, trespass to chattels for which plaintiff may recover only actual damages suffered by reason of the loss of use of the property).

B. Similar facts, except that defendant removes the furniture to a warehouse at a distance, so that plaintiff is subject to substantial inconvenience and expense in recovering it. This is a conversion. Forsdick v. Collins, 1 Starkie 173, 171 Eng.Rep. 437 (1816); and cf. Electric Power Co. v. Mayor of New York, 36 App.Div. 383, 55 N.Y.S. 460 (1899).

C. Similar facts, except that defendant does not notify plaintiff. This is a conversion. McGonigle v. Victor H.J. Belleisle Co., 186 Mass. 310, 71 N.E. 569 (1904); Borg & Powers Furniture Co. v. Reiling, 213 Minn. 539, 7 N.W.2d 310 (1942).

D. Similar facts, except that defendant stores the furniture in his own name, with the intent to keep it for himself. This is a conversion. Hicks Rubber Co., Distributors v. Stacy, 133 S.W.2d 249 (Tex.Civ.App.1939).

E. Similar facts, except that while the furniture is in the warehouse, and before plaintiff can remove it, it is destroyed by fire. This is a conversion. McCurdy v. Wallblom Furniture & Carpet Co., 94 Minn. 326, 102 N.W. 873 (1905).

5. What would plaintiff show as actual damages to support a cause of action for trespass to chattels if the dispossession was not serious enough for conversion?

6. A conversion may occur when one who is authorized to use a chattel uses it in a manner exceeding the authorization. See Swish Mfg. Southeast v. Manhattan Fire & Marine Ins., 675 F.2d 1218 (11th Cir.1982) (applying Georgia law) (lease permitted use of aircraft for transporting passengers but lessee used aircraft for transportation of contraband). A type of case that once was common is Doolittle v. Shaw, 92 Iowa 348, 60 N.W. 621 (1894). Defendant rented a horse from plaintiff, to be driven to Manchester and back. Defendant drove the horse six or seven miles into the country beyond Manchester, without damaging it. It was held that this was not a conversion. But if the horse had been seriously injured in an accident while it was beyond Manchester, with or without the defendant's fault,

there would have been a conversion. Palmer v. Mayo, 80 Conn. 353, 68 A. 369 (1907); Baxter v. Woodward, 191 Mich. 379, 158 N.W. 137 (1916).

7. Is a human body part "property" that can be converted? Plaintiff's spleen was removed as part of his treatment for cancer. Later, plaintiff discovered that his doctors had used cells from the removed spleen to develop a cell line for which they obtained a patent. The patent was then licensed for commercial development. Does plaintiff have a conversion action against the doctors and the commercial developer? See Moore v. Regents of the University of California, 51 Cal.3d 120, 793 P.2d 479, 271 Cal.Rptr. 146 (1990) (no conversion for excised body parts). Accord, Culpepper v. Pearl Street Bldg., Inc., 877 P.2d 877 (Colo. 1994) (in action by parents against those involved in mistaken cremation of son's body, court ruled there is no property right in a body that would support a conversion claim). Most courts do, however, recognize that the next of kin have some protected interests in the possession for burial or cremation and to prevent mutilation of the body, sometimes called a quasi-property right. See, for example, Whaley v. County of Tuscola, 58 F.3d 1111 (6th Cir.1995) (unauthorized removal of corneas and eyes during autopsies) (discussing Ohio and Michigan law re protected interests of next of kin to possess and prevent mutilation of body). Those rights do not extend to being informed that body parts had been withheld by the coroner for further testing or the right to later claim the withheld body parts for interment or disposal. Albrecht v. Treon, 118 Ohio St.3d 348, 889 N.E.2d 120 (2008) (answering in the negative certified question from federal district court that had before it a putative class action against all of Ohio's coroners) and In re Certified Question from U.S. District Court for the E.D. of Mich., 488 Mich. 1, 793 N.W.2d 560 (2010) (no Michigan case law gives next of kin a possessory right to decedent's brain following a lawful forensic examination).

8. What if defendant went through the trash in the common area of an office building and took plaintiff's papers? Conversion? Greenpeace, Inc. v. Dow Chemical Co., 97 A.3d 1053 (D.C. App. 2014) (no recognized property interest in anything that was purposefully thrown away or abandoned).

9. Is an Internet domain name a form of intangible property that can be converted? Kremen v. Cohen, 337 F.3d 1024 (9th Cir. 2003) (applying California law) (finding that plaintiff's complaint stated a cause of action for conversion of the domain name sex.com).

The Restatement (Second) of Torts has undertaken to identify the factors that influence courts in determining if a conversion has taken place when there has been interference with a chattel. It provides:

"§ 222A. What Constitutes Conversion

"(1) Conversion is an intentional exercise of dominion or control over a chattel which so seriously interferes with the right of another to control it that the actor may justly be required to pay the other the full value of the chattel.

"(2) In determining the seriousness of the interference and the justice of requiring the actor to pay the full value the following factors are important:

"(a) the extent and duration of the actor's exercise of dominion or control;

"(b) the actor's intent to assert a right in fact inconsistent with the other's right of control;

"(c) the actor's good faith;

"(d) the extent and duration of the resulting interference with the other's right of control;

"(e) the harm done to the chattel;

"(f) the inconvenience and expense caused to the other."

The ways in which an actor may convert a chattel—i.e., intentionally exercise dominion and control over it that so seriously interferes with the owner's right to control it that it is just to require the actor to pay its full value—include the following:

(1) acquiring possession of it—e.g., stealing the chattel;

(2) damaging or altering it—e.g., intentionally running over an animal and killing it;

(3) using it—e.g., a bailee seriously violates the terms of the bailment;

(4) receiving it—e.g., obtaining possession after a purchase from a thief;

(5) disposing of it—e.g., a bailee wrongfully sells the chattel;

(6) misdelivering it—e.g., delivery to wrong person by mistake so that the chattel is lost; and

(7) refusing to surrender it—e.g., bailee refuses to return the chattel.

See Restatement (Second) of Torts § 223 and following sections.

(B) EFFECT OF GOOD FAITH

An individual may be subject to liability for conversion although he was not subjectively at fault. This can occur in at least two ways:

1. When the defendant intends to affect the chattel in a manner inconsistent with the plaintiff's right of control, the fact that he acted in good faith and under a reasonable mistake does not prevent liability for conversion. Thus, if a bailee delivers goods to an imposter or on the basis of a forged document, he is liable to the bailor or owner. See Baer v. Slater, 261 Mass. 153, 158 N.E. 328 (1927) (defendant delivers goods to imposter); Potomac Ins. Co. v. Nickson, 64 Utah 395, 231 P. 445 (1924) (garage delivers car to person who presented a stolen duplicate parking ticket); Suzuki v. Small, 214 App.Div. 541, 212 N.Y.S. 589 (1925) (steel sent to wrong company). Compare Ranson v. Kitner, page 25.

Some special rules have developed at common law for the protection of bailees and servants who deal with the chattels of third persons under directions from their bailors or employers. These are rules of commercial convenience and the reason underlying them is clearly the practical necessity of permitting someone to receive goods for storage or safekeeping or transportation, without inquiry as to the title of the person from whom they are received. If, for example, a garage accepting an automobile for overnight parking were to be held liable for conversion when it turned out to be a stolen car, there would be few people willing to operate parking garages.

This privilege does not extend to a case in which the goods are in the hands of the bailee and they are claimed from him by both the bailor and the true owner. In this case, the bailee is required, at his peril, to see that he delivers to the right person, and he becomes liable for conversion if he delivers to the wrong one. To avoid this risk, the law provides interpleader or other modern statutes that permit the contested goods to be deposited in court.

2. The other major area in which an innocent conversion may take place concerns good faith purchasers, those who buy the goods not knowing they were converted. An innocent purchaser cannot obtain title from a thief because the thief does not have title. The purchaser acts at her peril and may be sued in conversion by the true owner. O'Keeffe v. Snyder, 83 N.J. 478, 416 A.2d 862 (1980) (title to three of Georgia O'Keeffe's paintings could not have passed to the putative owner because the artist testified that they had been stolen from her late husband's gallery some thirty years before they reappeared at defendant's gallery). The good faith purchaser is protected, however, if the goods were obtained by the converter through fraud rather than theft because title passes in a fraudulent transaction subject to the equitable right of rescission. That is, when the seller discovers the fraud, he can rescind the sale and take back the title. But, the right to rescind for fraud is terminated when a bona fide purchaser acquires both title and possession from the defrauding party. Phelps v. McQuade, 220 N.Y. 232, 115 N.E. 441 (1917) (jewels sold on credit to imposter who sold them to bona fide purchaser and then disappeared without paying for them could not be reclaimed by jewelers from bona fide purchaser because title had passed before the sale could be rescinded for fraud). There is thus a distinction between stolen goods, as to which the legal title does not pass and a bona fide purchaser is therefore not protected, and goods obtained by fraud, as to which the title does pass, subject to an equitable right of rescission, which is cut off by a bona fide purchase. Finally, the Uniform Commercial Code provides that a bona fide purchaser is protected in a sale by goods from a merchant "who deals in goods of that kind." U.C.C. § 2–403(2).

Consider whether a bona fide purchaser is protected under these circumstances: 1) Teenager leaves his bicycle in the front yard and it is stolen by a thief who cleans it up and sells it to college student through an ad on Craigslist. College student is a converter and would have to pay teenager the full value of the bicycle. 2) Teenager is tricked into trading his bicycle for a foreign stamp the trickster claims is worth at least a thousand dollars. By the time teenager learns the stamp is worthless, the bicycle has been sold to college student. College student is not a converter and teenager has lost the right to rescind the deal. 3) Teenager leaves his bicycle at a shop that sells and repairs bicycles. Merchant sells the bicycle to college student. College student is not a converter because the merchant "deals in goods of that kind." In all three scenarios, teenager would have a cause of action for conversion against the thief, trickster, or merchant. The college student may be easier to find, however.

Money and negotiable instruments (e.g., checks) may not be treated the same way as tangible chattels. Kelley Kar Co. v. Maryland Casualty Co., 142 Cal.App.2d 263, 298 P.2d 590 (1956). If thief steals teenager's twenty dollar bill and trades it to college student for two tens, college student is not a converter and teenager's only recourse is against thief.

(C) NECESSITY OF DEMAND; RETURN OF CHATTEL

Demand. Some states have followed the rule that possession by a bona fide purchaser or other innocent converter is not in itself a sufficiently serious defiance of the owner's rights and hold that the possessor is liable only if refusing to return the goods on demand. In most states, however, a conversion occurs as soon as the defendant takes dominion and control over the goods in a manner inconsistent with plaintiff's ownership. In these states, there may be a separate act of conversion for an initial taking of possession and for a later refusal to return on demand, and the owner can elect between them. Restatement (Second) of Torts § 229.

Return. When a converter offers to return the converted goods and the owner accepts, the return does not bar the action for conversion, but it must be taken into account to reduce the damages recovered. If the chattel is in the same condition as when it was taken, has not changed in value and the plaintiff has suffered no special damage through being deprived of possession, the effect may be to reduce his recovery to nominal damages.

When the plaintiff refuses to accept the offered return, the older rule was that the defendant could not force the goods back upon him in reduction of the damages. The plaintiff could insist upon the full value of the goods as the measure of damages, and the defendant had to keep them. The English courts and some American jurisdictions have held that when the conversion is an innocent one committed under an honest mistake, the court may require the plaintiff to take back the goods and credit the defendant with their value in any case in which the goods are undamaged and there has been no change in the plaintiff's position. The matter is within the sound discretion of the trial court, and even in these jurisdictions there is no absolute right to the return as a matter of law. See Rutland & W.R. Co. v. Bank of Middlebury, 32 Vt. 639 (1860). The Restatement (Second) of Torts has followed this approach in § 922.

Payment of the chattel's value by a converter to the original owner effectuates a common law forced sale of the chattel and precludes the original owner's further recovery of damages for subsequent conversions. Baram v. Farugia, 606 F.2d 42 (3d Cir.1979) (applying Pennsylvania law) (Trainer of race horse gave horse to defendants as payment of trainer's debt. Plaintiff, owner of race horse, filed a conversion action against defendants and was awarded value of horse and punitive damages. On appeal, court found that because plaintiff already had collected the full value of the horse from trainer, the acceptance of that payment was a "forced sale" to trainer and thus plaintiff did not have a conversion action against defendants.) Is a judgment for plaintiff sufficient for this purpose too?

(D) DAMAGES

The measure of damages for conversion is the value of the property converted. Usually, this is the market value—what the property could have been sold for in the open market by a willing seller to a willing buyer. For elaboration on this and indication of other recoverable damages, see Restatement (Second) of Torts § 927.

The market value is determined at the time and place of the conversion. The theory is that if the chattel is available on the market, the owner should mitigate damages by purchasing another chattel. This need not be done at the very moment of the conversion. While some courts would give him the highest intermediate value between the time of conversion and the time of the suit or the judgment, the rule approved by most commentators is the highest intermediate value between the time of conversion and a reasonable time for making a replacement. If there is no market value, other methods may be used, such as manufacturing cost, less depreciation. See Restatement (Second) of Torts § 911.

Sometimes the property destroyed or damaged has little market worth, but has a particular value to the owner. Damages cannot be recovered for sentiment alone, but if defendant's conduct is outrageous, plaintiff may be able to recover damages for emotional harm suffered from the loss. See La Porte v. Associated Independents, Inc., 163 So.2d 267 (Fla.1964) (trash collector killed pet dachshund by throwing garbage can at it); Womack v. Von Rardon, 133 Wash.App. 254, 135 P.3d 542 (2006) (teenagers took cat from porch, doused it with gasoline, and set it on fire). In cases where the converted chattels were of limited extrinsic or market value, the original or replacement cost or cost of repair of the chattel may be awarded. Lakewood Engineering and Mfg. Co. v. Quinn, 91 Md.App. 375, 604 A.2d 535 (1992) (allowing replacement value of household items lost in fire). Damages for a chattel that is the product of creative effort as to which no original or replacement cost can fairly be assigned may be based upon the value of the time that it took or would take to create the chattel. Wood v. Cunard, 192 F. 293 (2d Cir. 1911) (taking into account the value of two years of intermittent labor required to reproduce lost manuscript); Rajkovich v. Alfred Mossner Co., 199 Ill.App.3d 655, 557 N.E.2d 496, 145 Ill.Dec. 726 (1990) (compensating for 172 hours of architectural time at specified rate necessary to redo damaged architectural drawings); United States v. Arora, 860 F.Supp. 1091 (D. Md. 1994) (compensation based on hourly rate of lab technician to recreate cell line destroyed by rival scientist); U.D.C. v. Vossoughi, 963 A.2d 1162 (D.C. 2009) (colleagues testified as to value of college professor's class notes, teaching materials, research notes, laboratory equipment, and experiments in progress); Redwine v. Fitzhugh, 78 Wyo. 407, 329 P.2d 257 (1958) (allowing recovery for value of seed and for labor expended in sowing and cultivating seed).

Punitive damages may be allowed when the conversion was malicious but not when it was done innocently.

(E) WHAT MAY BE CONVERTED

Because of its origin as an action against the finder of lost goods, trover was limited to the conversion of things that were capable of being lost and found. It would lie for any chattel, but not for land, which in the eyes of the law could not be lost. Hence the dispossession or withholding of real property could not be a conversion. Nor could the severance of timber, minerals, crops or fixtures attached to the land. Once there was severance, however, the goods became chattels and the plaintiff could bring trover for their removal from the land. These rules are still applied.

Since intangible rights, such as those of a stockholder in a corporation, could not be lost and found, the original common law rule was that they could not be the subject of a conversion. This has been considerably modified. See Rubin, Conversion of Choses in Action, 10 Fordham L.Rev. 415 (1941). It was first held that damages could be recovered for the conversion of intangible rights when they were merged and identified with a special instrument, such as a promissory note, a check, a bill of lading or a stock certificate, and that instrument itself was converted. This has now been generally extended to permit recovery for the conversion of rights of a kind customarily merged with such an instrument, such as those of a stockholder, without any conversion of the stock certificate itself. Herrick v. Humphrey Hardware Co., 73 Neb. 809, 103 N.W. 685 (1905) (refusal to register a transfer on the books of the corporation, depriving the new owner of his rights as a stockholder). What about data stored electronically on a computer? Thyroff v. Nationwide Mut. Ins. Co., 8 N.Y.3d 283, 864 N.E.2d 1272, 832 N.Y.S.2d 873 (2007) (answering certified question in the affirmative, court found personal and client information of former insurance agent's stored on computer that belonged to insurance company to be property for purposes of agent's conversion claim).

What if an attorney who is leaving a law firm takes with her the files of seventy of the firm's clients? Is she liable for conversion of the files? Is the law firm who becomes her new employer? See Parker v. Kowalsky & Hirschhorn, 124 Md.App. 447, 722 A.2d 441, 447 (1999) ("While we agree with the lower court's conclusion that [first law firm] stated a viable cause of action in conversion against [attorney], we do not believe that this allegation demonstrates that [first law firm] had a possessory interest in the fees that were received by [second law firm, from work performed for clients whose files had been converted.]")

(F) WHO MAY MAINTAIN THE ACTION

Trover, like trespass, was founded upon the plaintiff's possession. From this has come the rule that anyone in possession of a chattel at the time of a conversion can maintain an action for it. Thus a finder can recover for conversion. See Aigler, Rights of Finders, 21 Mich.L.Rev. 664, 57 Am.L.Rev. 511 (1928); Moreland, Rights of Finders, 16 Ky.L.J. 1 (1927). The same is true of a bailee to whom the chattel is loaned, although he has no other interest in it, or a sheriff who has seized it on execution.

Recovery has been permitted even when the plaintiff's possession is wrongful and in defiance of the true owner. Thus one converter may recover from another. Jeffries v. Great Western R. Co., 5 El. & Bl. 802, 119 Eng.Rep. 680 (1856). In this case, however, the plaintiff usually has had some colorable claim of right to the chattel; and it has been held that in the absence of such a claim there is no recovery. Turley v. Tucker, 6 Mo. 583, 35 Am.Dec. 449 (1840); Rexroth v. Coon, 15 R.I. 35, 23 A. 37 (1885).

Trover was also extended to permit recovery by one who did not have possession, but had the immediate right to it, as in the case of a bailor at will who was entitled to possession on demand. Manders v. Williams, 4 Exch. 339, 154 Eng.Rep. 1242 (1849). Or a mortgagee after default. Nichols & Shepard Co. v. Minnesota Threshing Mfg. Co., 70 Minn. 528, 73 N.W. 415 (1897). This, too, has carried over into the modern law of conversion.

CHAPTER 3

PRIVILEGES

1. CONSENT

O'Brien v. Cunard S.S. Co.

Supreme Judicial Court of Massachusetts, 1891.
154 Mass. 272, 28 N.E. 266.

Tort, for an assault, and for negligently vaccinating the plaintiff, who was a steerage passenger on the defendant's steamship. The trial court directed a verdict for the defendant, and the plaintiff brings exceptions. [Plaintiff alleged that she suffered ulceration at the site and blistering all over her body due either to contamination of the vaccine or of the vaccination site. There was conflicting medical expert testimony as to the cause of her injuries.]

KNOWLTON, J. * * * To sustain the first count, which was for an alleged assault, the plaintiff relied on the fact that the surgeon who was employed by the defendant vaccinated her on ship-board, while she was on her passage from Queenstown to Boston. On this branch of the case the question is whether there was any evidence that the surgeon used force upon the plaintiff against her will. In determining whether the act was lawful or unlawful, the surgeon's conduct must be considered in connection with the surrounding circumstances. If the plaintiff's behavior was such as to indicate consent on her part, he was justified in his act, whatever her unexpressed feelings may have been. In determining whether she consented, he could be guided only by her overt acts and the manifestations of her feelings. [Cc] It is undisputed that at Boston there are strict quarantine regulations in regard to the examination of emigrants, to see that they are protected from small-pox by vaccination, and that only those persons who hold a certificate from the medical officer of the steam-ship, stating that they are so protected, are permitted to land without detention in quarantine, or vaccination by the port physician. It appears that the defendant is accustomed to have its surgeons vaccinate all emigrants who desire it, and who are not protected by previous vaccination, and give them a certificate which is accepted at quarantine as evidence of their protection. Notices of the regulations at quarantine, and of the willingness of the ship's medical officer to vaccinate such as needed vaccination, were posted about the ship in various languages, and on the day when the operation was performed the surgeon had a right to presume that she and the other women who were vaccinated understood the importance and purpose of vaccination for those who bore no marks to show that they were protected. By the plaintiff's testimony, which, in this particular, is undisputed, it appears that about 200 women passengers were assembled below, and she understood from conversation with them that they were to be vaccinated; that she stood about 15 feet from the surgeon, and saw them form in a line, and pass in turn before him; that he "examined their arms, and, passing some of them by, proceeded to vaccinate those that had no mark;" that she did not hear him say anything to any of them; that upon being passed by they each received a card, and went on deck; that when her turn came she showed him her arm; he looked at it, and said there was no mark, and that she should be vaccinated; that she told him she had been vaccinated before, and it left no mark; "that he then said nothing; that he should vaccinate her again;" that she held up her arm to be vaccinated; that no one touched her; that she did not tell him she did not want to be vaccinated; and that she took the ticket which he gave her, certifying that he had vaccinated her, and used it at quarantine. She was one of a large number of women who were vaccinated on that occasion, without, so far as appears, a word of objection from any of them. They all indicated by their conduct that they desired to avail themselves of the provisions made for their benefit. There was nothing in the conduct of the plaintiff to indicate to the surgeon that she did not wish to obtain a card which would save her from detention at quarantine, and to be vaccinated, if necessary, for that purpose. Viewing his conduct in the light of the surrounding circumstances, it was lawful; and there was no evidence tending to show that it was not. The ruling of the court on this part of the case was correct. * * *

Exceptions overruled.

NOTES AND QUESTIONS

1. With the principal case, contrast Mulloy v. Hop Sang, 1 W.W.R. 714 (Alberta C.A.) (1935). Patient arrived at the hospital with a hand that had been badly injured in an automobile accident wrapped in cloth, telling the surgeon to fix it but not cut it off as he wanted to have it looked after in his hometown. The surgeon replied that he would do whatever was necessary once the anesthesia was administered and he was able to get a look at the hand. Patient did not reply. Surgeon amputated his hand. Appellate court ruled that consent had not been given where patient with limited English did not reply or make objections to surgeon's statement that he would do what was necessary.

2. Suppose that in the course of an argument defendant announces that he is going to punch plaintiff in the nose. Plaintiff stands his ground but says and does nothing, and defendant punches him. Is there consent?

3. On a park bench in the moonlight, a young man informs his fiancée that he is going to kiss her. She says and does nothing, and he kisses her. Is he liable for battery? What if it's their first date? What if he is a stranger who has just sat down next to her when he makes his announcement?

Hackbart v. Cincinnati Bengals, Inc.

United States Court of Appeals, Tenth Circuit, 1979.

601 F.2d 516, cert. denied, 444 U.S. 931, 100 S.Ct. 275, 62 L.Ed.2d 188 (1979).

WILLIAM E. DOYLE, CIRCUIT JUDGE. The question in this case is whether in a regular season professional football game an injury which is inflicted by one professional football player on an opposing player can give rise to liability in tort where the injury was inflicted by the intentional striking of a blow during the game.

The injury occurred in the course of a game between the Denver Broncos and the Cincinnati Bengals, which game was being played in Denver in 1973. The Broncos' defensive back, Dale Hackbart, was the recipient of the injury and the Bengals' offensive back, Charles "Booby" Clark, inflicted the blow which produced it. * * *

The trial court's finding was that Charles Clark, "acting out of anger and frustration, but without a specific intent to injure * * * stepped forward and struck a blow with his right forearm to the back of the kneeling plaintiff's head and neck with sufficient force to cause both players to fall forward to the ground." Both players, without complaining to the officials or to one another, returned to their respective sidelines since the ball had changed hands and the offensive and defensive teams of each had been substituted. Clark testified at trial that his frustration was brought about by the fact that his team was losing the game. * * *

Despite the fact that the defendant Charles Clark admitted that the blow which had been struck was not accidental, that it was intentionally administered, the trial court ruled as a matter of law that the game of professional football is basically a business which is violent in nature, and that the available sanctions are imposition of penalties and expulsion from the game. Notice was taken of the fact that many fouls are overlooked; that the game is played in an emotional and noisy environment; and that incidents such as that here complained of are not unusual. * * *

Indeed, the evidence shows that there are rules of the game which prohibit the intentional striking of blows. Thus, Article 1, Item 1, Subsection C, provides that: "All players are prohibited from striking on the head, face or neck with the heel, back or side of the hand, wrist, forearm, elbow or clasped hands." Thus the very conduct which was present here is expressly prohibited by the rule which is quoted above.

The general customs of football do not approve the intentional punching or striking of others. That this is prohibited was supported by the testimony of all of the witnesses. They testified that the intentional striking of a player in the face or from the rear is prohibited by the playing rules as well as the general customs of the game. Punching or hitting with the arms is prohibited. Undoubtedly these restraints are intended to establish reasonable boundaries so that one football player cannot intentionally inflict a serious injury on another. Therefore, the notion is not correct that all reason has been abandoned, whereby the only possible remedy for the person who has been the victim of an unlawful blow is retaliation. * * *

In sum, having concluded that the trial court did not limit the case to a trial of the evidence bearing on defendant's liability but rather determined that as a matter of social policy the game was so violent and unlawful that valid lines could not be drawn, we take the view that this was not a proper issue for determination and that plaintiff was entitled to have the case tried on an assessment of his rights and whether they had been violated. * * *

Reversed and remanded for a new trial.

NOTES AND QUESTIONS

1. In order to recover, plaintiff must show that defendant acted intentionally, not just that he violated the game's safety rules. See Gauvin v. Clark, 404 Mass. 450, 537 N.E.2d 94 (1989) (jury found college hockey player did not act willfully when his stick struck other player in abdomen). Greer v. Davis, 921 S.W.2d 325 (Tex.App.1996) (question for jury whether base runner acted intentionally or merely negligently in colliding with catcher rather than sliding or stepping out of baseline to avoid the tag).

2. Plaintiff and defendant were opposing players in a family softball game. Defendant, sliding into second base, knocked the plaintiff down and broke two bones in his ankle. Is there liability? Tavernier v. Maes, 242 Cal.App.2d 532, 51 Cal.Rptr. 575 (1966). What other facts do you want to know about the game to decide if the plaintiff consented to the contact? Would it make a difference if the conduct occurred while players were warming up rather than during the game? Cf. Savino v. Robertson, 273 Ill.App.3d 811, 210 Ill.Dec. 264, 652 N.E.2d 1240 (1995) (no difference).

3. What about a course of rough-house practical joking between the parties in the past? Wartman v. Swindell, 54 N.J.L. 589, 25 A. 356 (1892). Wulf v. Kunnath, 285 Neb. 472, 827 N.W.2d 248 (2013) (doctors and nurses joking around in break room at lunch time when one thumped the other on the back of the neck).

4. Defendant taps plaintiff on the shoulder to attract his attention for a reasonable purpose. May consent be assumed? Wiffin v. Kincard, 2 Bos. & P.N.R. 471, 127 Eng.Rep. 713 (1807); Coward v. Baddeley, 4 Hurl. & N. 478, 157 Eng.Rep. 927 (1859); Wallace v. Rosen, 765 N.E.2d 192 (Ind. App. 2002), page 32. Is this a battery, to begin with?

5. Local custom permits the public to take fish from small lakes and ponds. Defendant passes over plaintiff's property to reach such a lake. Consent? See Marsh v. Colby, 39 Mich. 626 (1878).

Mohr v. Williams

Supreme Court of Minnesota, 1905.
95 Minn. 261, 104 N.W. 12.

[Plaintiff consulted defendant, an ear specialist, concerning trouble with her right ear. On examining her, he found a diseased condition of the right ear, and she consented to an operation upon it. When she was unconscious under the anaesthetic, defendant concluded that the condition of the right ear was not serious enough to require an operation; but he found a more serious condition of the left ear, which he decided required an operation. Without reviving the plaintiff to ask her permission, he operated on the left ear. The operation was skillfully performed, and was successful. Plaintiff nevertheless brought an action for battery. In the court below the jury returned a verdict in favor of the plaintiff for $14,322.50. The trial judge denied defendant's motion for judgment notwithstanding the verdict, but granted a new trial on the ground that the damages were excessive. Both parties appeal.]

BROWN, J. * * * The evidence tends to show that, upon the first examination of plaintiff, defendant pronounced the left ear in good condition, and that, at the time plaintiff repaired to the hospital to submit to the operation on her right ear, she was under the impression that no difficulty existed as to the left. In fact, she testified that she had not previously experienced any trouble with that organ. It cannot be doubted that ordinarily the patient must be consulted, and his consent given, before a physician may operate upon him. * * *

The physician impliedly contracts that he possesses, and will exercise in the treatment of patients, skill and learning, and that he will exercise reasonable care and exert his best judgment to bring about favorable results. The methods of treatment are committed almost exclusively to his judgment, but we are aware of no rule or principle of law which would extend to him free license respecting surgical operations. Reasonable latitude must, however, be allowed the physician in a particular case; and we would not lay down any rule which would unreasonably interfere with the exercise of his discretion, or prevent him from taking such measures as his judgment dictated for the welfare of the patient in a case of emergency. If a person should be injured to the extent of rendering him unconscious, and his injuries were of such a nature as to require prompt surgical attention, a physician called to attend him would be justified in applying such medical or surgical treatment as might reasonably be necessary for the preservation of his life or limb, and consent on the part of the injured person would be implied. And again, if, in the course of an operation to which the patient consented, the physician should discover conditions not anticipated before the operation was commenced, and which, if not removed, would endanger the life or health of the patient, he would, though no express consent was obtained or given, be justified in extending the operation to remove and overcome them. But such is not the case at bar. The diseased condition of plaintiff's left ear was not discovered in the course of an operation on the right, which was authorized, but upon an independent examination of that organ, made after the authorized operation was found unnecessary. Nor is the evidence such as to justify the court in holding, as a matter of law, that it was such an affection [affliction?] as would result immediately in the serious injury of plaintiff, or such an emergency as to justify proceeding without her consent. She had experienced no particular difficulty with that ear, and the questions as to when its diseased condition would become alarming or fatal, and whether there was an immediate necessity for an operation, were, under the evidence, question of fact for the jury.

The contention of defendant that the operation was consented to by plaintiff is not sustained by the evidence. At least, the evidence was such as to take the question to the jury. This contention is based upon the fact that she was represented on the occasion in question by her family physician; that the condition of her left ear was made known to him, and the propriety of an operation thereon suggested, to which he made no objection. It is urged that by his conduct he assented to it, and that plaintiff was bound thereby. It is not claimed that he gave his express consent. It is not disputed but that the family physician of plaintiff was present on the occasion of the operation, and at her request. But the purpose of his presence was not that he might participate in the operation, nor does it appear that he was authorized to consent to any change in the one originally proposed to be made. Plaintiff was naturally nervous and fearful of the consequences of being placed under the influence of anaesthetics, and the presence of her family physician was requested under the impression that it would allay and calm her fears. The evidence made the question one of fact for the jury to determine.

The last contention of defendant is that the act complained of did not amount to an assault and battery. This is based upon the theory that, as plaintiff's left ear was in fact diseased, in a condition dangerous and threatening to her health, the operation was necessary, and having been skillfully performed at a time when plaintiff had requested a like operation on the other ear, the charge of assault and battery cannot be sustained; that, in view of these conditions, and the claim that there was no negligence on the part of defendant, and an entire absence of any evidence tending to show an evil intent, the court should say, as a matter of law, that no assault and battery was committed, even though she did not consent to the operation. In other words, that the absence of a showing that defendant was actuated by a wrongful intent, or guilty of negligence, relieves the act of defendant from the charge of an unlawful assault and battery. We are unable to reach that conclusion, though the contention is not without merit. It would seem to follow from what has been said on the other features of the case that the act of defendant amounted at least to a technical assault and battery. If the operation was performed without plaintiff's consent, and the circumstances were not such as to justify its performance without, it was wrongful; and, if it was wrongful, it was unlawful. As remarked in 1 Jaggard on Torts, 437, every person has a right to complete immunity of his person from physical interference of others, except in so far as contact may be necessary under the general doctrine of privilege; and any unlawful or unauthorized touching of the person of another, except it be in the spirit of pleasantry, constitutes an assault and battery. In the case at bar, as we have already seen, the question whether defendant's act in performing the operation upon plaintiff was authorized was a question for the jury to determine. If it was unauthorized, then it was, within what we have said, unlawful. It was a violent assault, not a mere pleasantry; and, even though no negligence is shown, it was wrongful and unlawful. The case is unlike a criminal prosecution for assault and battery, for there an unlawful intent must be shown. But that rule does not apply to a civil action, to maintain which it is sufficient to show that the assault complained of was wrongful and unlawful or the result of negligence. [C]

The amount of plaintiff's recovery, if she is entitled to recover at all, must depend upon the character and extent of the injury inflicted upon her, in determining which the nature of the malady intended to be healed and the beneficial nature of the operation should be taken into consideration, as well as the good faith of the defendant.

Order affirmed.

[Reference to the records of the District Court of Ramsey County, Minnesota, discloses that on the second trial the plaintiff received a verdict and judgment for $39. There was no appeal.]

NOTES AND QUESTIONS

1. Why did plaintiff's attorney sue under a theory of battery instead of ordinary negligent medical malpractice? Should there be recovery if defendant used all reasonable care in the operation? Cf. Rogers v. Board of Road Commissioners, page 77.

2. Plaintiff, a boy 15 years of age, was run over by a train and his foot was crushed. When he arrived at the hospital he was unconscious and bleeding. Defendant, the house surgeon, concluded that immediate amputation of the foot was necessary to save the boy's life. Finding no relatives present, he performed the operation. Is he liable? Why? Luka v. Lowrie, 171 Mich. 122, 136 N.W. 1106 (1912).

3. What if the plaintiff had remained conscious, and had insisted on prohibiting the operation, saying that he would rather die than lose his foot? See Mulloy v. Hop Sang, 1 W.W.R. 714 (Alberta C.A.) (1935) (automobile accident victim arrived at hospital asking that his badly injured hand be treated but not amputated). Construction worker, believing that he saw "666, the sign of the devil" on his hand cut it off with a power saw. His co-workers rushed him and his severed hand, packed in ice, to the hospital. A hand surgeon was standing by ready to attempt to reattach it. Patient refused permission, saying it was against his religion. What should surgeon do? See "Man Who Lost Hand Loses Lawsuit," Virginia-Pilot & Ledger Star, Sept. 10, 1997 at B1 available at 1997 WLNR 2200014.

4. Medical care providers may act in the absence of express consent if (1) the patient is unable to give consent (unconscious, intoxicated, mentally ill, incompetent); (2) there is a risk of serious bodily harm if treatment is delayed; (3) a reasonable person would consent to treatment under the circumstances; and (4) the physician has no reason to believe this patient would refuse treatment under the circumstances. See, e.g., Kozup v. Georgetown U. Hosp., 851 F.2d 437 (D.C.Cir.1988) (parents' consent to baby's transfusion was not implied simply because it was necessary to save baby's life where there was no showing that there was no time to seek consent); Stewart-Graves v. Vaughn, 162 Wash.2d 115, 170 P.3d 1151 (2007) (father's consent implied as a matter of law even though he was in nearby waiting room because there was no meaningful opportunity for a deliberate, informed decision concerning treatment where failure to treat would have meant certain and immediate death of newborn).

5. The principal case has been regarded for years as the leading case on unauthorized operations. It is still sound law. Most surgery is performed in hospitals, which have their own rules and standardized practices, including consent forms. In many cases, it has been found that the consent is sufficiently general in its terms to justify the physician in doing whatever the physician believes necessary in the course of the operation. See for example Rothe v. Hull, 352 Mo. 926, 180 S.W.2d 7 (1944); Baxter v. Snow, 78 Utah 217, 2 P.2d 257 (1931). Does that mean the consent should be as broadly worded as possible? What if an obstetrician who has privileges at a hospital fails to obtain consent for a blood transfusion? The obstetrician

would be liable. Would the hospital? Ward v. Lutheran Hospitals & Homes Soc. of Am., Inc., 963 P.2d 1031 (Alaska 1998) (noting that overwhelming weight of authority holds that hospital does not owe duty to patient to obtain consent for treatment when patient is under care of independent physician).

6. Plaintiff consents to an operation under general anesthesia on the condition that her own physician be present during the procedure. He was not. Is consent vitiated? Pugsley v. Privette, 220 Va. 892, 263 S.E.2d 69 (1980) (jury verdict on battery claim upheld). What if the plaintiff specifically insists that the procedure shall go thus far, and no further? For example, she consents to an incision and an examination of her stomach under ether, but expressly forbids anything more. If the surgeon goes ahead and removes a tumor found there, is he liable? Schloendorff v. Society of New York Hospital, 211 N.Y. 125, 105 N.E. 92 (1914) (yes—every adult of sound mind has the right to determine what shall be done with her body). What if patient limits her consent to female health care providers, explaining that her religious beliefs prohibit her from being seen unclothed by a member of the opposite sex? During surgery, a male nurse sees and touches her as part of proper medical treatment. Liability for battery? Cohen v. Smith, 269 Ill.App.3d 1087, 207 Ill.Dec. 873, 648 N.E.2d 329 (1995) (violation of plaintiff's right to bodily integrity by unconsented to touching is the essence of battery). What if the consent form states anesthesia will be administered by "a physician privileged to practice anesthesia" and an EMT in training is permitted to do her first intubation on the patient? Mullins v. Parkview Hosp., Inc., 865 N.E.2d 608 (Ind. 2007) (battery claim stated against anesthesiologist but not student EMT who did not know that consent had not been obtained). What if patient, about to undergo an MRI, limits her consent to particular drugs—Demerol and morphine—because she is concerned about an allergic reaction. The nurse gives her fentanyl. Battery? Duncan v. Scottsdale Med. Imaging Ltd., 205 Ariz. 306, 70 P.3d 435 (2003) (rejecting argument that the patient consented to the administration of pain medication and therefore the nature of the procedure was the same no matter which drug was used). What if a patient withdraws her consent during the procedure? Schreiber v. Physicians Ins. Co. of Wisconsin, 223 Wis.2d 417, 588 N.W.2d 26 (1999) (withdrawal of consent means that physician must conduct new informed consent discussion, cannot continue to rely on previously given consent); Coulter v. Thomas, 33 S.W.3d 522 (Ky. 2000) (withdrawal of consent while medical procedure in progress must be unquestionable response from clear and rational mind and it must be medically feasible for doctor to stop).

7. May a competent, informed adult refuse medical treatment that is necessary to preserve life? Thor v. Superior Court, 5 Cal.4th 725, 855 P.2d 375, 21 Cal.Rptr.2d 357 (1993) (right to refuse treatment not limited to those who are suffering from terminal conditions).

8. Brother Joseph Fox, an 83-year-old member of the Marianists, a Roman Catholic order, had previously expressed a desire not to have his life artificially prolonged by extraordinary means of treatment if there was no reasonable hope for recovery. During surgery to repair a hernia, he suffered permanent brain damage due to cardiac arrest. Was his refusal of extraordinary means of treatment (a respirator) still effective after he became incompetent? Matter of Storar, 52 N.Y.2d 363, 438 N.Y.S.2d 266,

420 N.E.2d 64, cert. denied, 454 U.S. 858 (1981). This issue is resolved in many jurisdictions by statutory provisions for "living wills" or "advance directives" that state the patient's consent and limitations on treatment.

9. When plaintiff refused to consent to a transfusion on religious grounds, the court in Application of the President and Directors of Georgetown College, 331 F.2d 1000 (D.C.Cir.1964), granted a declaratory judgment to proceed, with the judge who issued the emergency order finding that the patient felt that it would not be her responsibility if the judge ordered the transfusion. A similar request was denied in In re Osborne, 294 A.2d 372 (D.C.App.1972), where a bedside hearing disclosed that the patient would regard a transfusion under any circumstances as violative of his religious beliefs. See also Stamford Hospital v. Vega, 236 Conn. 646, 674 A.2d 821 (1996) (patient competent to make decisions entitled to refuse blood transfusion even if that decision is fatal).

10. What happens if health care personnel ignore a "do not resuscitate order"? If the patient (or his family) has a cause of action for battery, what is the measure of damages? Campbell v. Delbridge, 670 N.W.2d 108 (Iowa 2003) (plaintiff entitled to emotional distress damages for unauthorized transfusion); Anderson v. St. Francis-St. George Hospital, Inc., 77 Ohio St.3d 82, 671 N.E.2d 225 (1996) (where the battery was physically harmless, plaintiff entitled only to nominal damages, not compensatory damages for wrongful living or wrongful prolongation of life.) See also Oddi, The Tort of Interference with the Right to Die: The Wrongful Living Cause of Action, 75 Geo. L. J. 625 (1986) and Milani, Better Off Dead Than Disabled?: Should Courts Recognize a "Wrongful Living" Cause of Action When Doctors Fail to Honor Patients' Advance Directives?, 54 Wash. & Lee L. Rev. 149 (1997).

11. All of the cases above assume an adult plaintiff. In the case of a minor child, consent of the parent is necessary for any medical procedure, except in an emergency. Zoski v. Gaines, 271 Mich. 1, 260 N.W. 99 (1935) (9½ years) (tonsillectomy); Bonner v. Moran, 126 F.2d 121 (D.C.Cir.1941) (15 years) (skin graft). A minor 17 or 18 years of age, however, has been held capable of legally consenting, at least to minor procedures, Gulf & S.I.R. Co. v. Sullivan, 155 Miss. 1, 119 So. 501 (1928) (smallpox vaccination), but not to major ones, Lacey v. Laird, 166 Ohio St. 12, 139 N.E.2d 25 (1956) (nose job). Is consent from a parent necessary to prescribe contraception? The right of mature teenage females to give or withhold consent to abortions is governed by statute in most jurisdictions and the statutes, in turn, must fall within constitutional parameters.

12. When a parent refuses on religious or other grounds to allow a hospital to provide medical treatment for a child, courts are likely to grant a hospital's application to overrule the parent if the treatment is for a life threatening condition, but not if it only will improve the child's comfort or appearance. Compare In re Sampson, 29 N.Y.2d 900, 328 N.Y.S.2d 686, 278 N.E.2d 918 (1972) (approving) with In re Green, 448 Pa. 338, 292 A.2d 387 (1972) (disallowing).

13. Can parents "consent" on behalf of their child to be a donor in a transplant operation for the benefit of a sibling? See Hart v. Brown, 29 Conn.Supp. 368, 289 A.2d 386 (1972) (approving parents' consent to have one twin donate a kidney to the other). Can a guardian consent to an incompetent's donation of an organ? See Strunk v. Strunk, 445 S.W.2d 145

(Ky.1969) (approving donation by mentally incompetent adult to his brother, noting that because of their close relationship the donor's well-being would be more jeopardized by the loss of his brother than the loss of his kidney). Can a parent consent to a child's participation in nontherapeutic research in which there is a risk of injury or damage to the health of the child? Grimes v. Kennedy Krieger Institute, Inc., 366 Md. 29, 782 A.2d 807 (2001) (parent cannot consent). Does the mother's consent to an abortion prevent the child who was injured by the failed abortion from bringing a personal injury action against the physician? Vandervelden v. Victoria, 177 Wis.2d 243, 502 N.W.2d 276 (App.1993) (no battery action on behalf of child because parent had consented to procedure).

De May v. Roberts

Supreme Court of Michigan, 1881.
46 Mich. 160, 9 N.W. 146.

MARTSON, C.J. The declaration in this case in the first count sets forth that the plaintiff was at a time and place named a poor married woman, and being confined in child-bed and a stranger, employed in a professional capacity defendant De May who was a physician; that defendant visited the plaintiff as such, and against her desire and intending to deceive her wrongfully, etc., introduced and caused to be present at the house and lying-in room of the plaintiff and while she was in the pains of parturition the defendant Scattergood, who intruded upon the privacy of the plaintiff, indecently, wrongfully and unlawfully laid hands upon her and assaulted her, the said Scattergood, which was well known to defendant De May, being a young unmarried man, a stranger to the plaintiff and utterly ignorant of the practice of medicine, while the plaintiff believed that he was an assistant physician, a competent and proper person to be present and to aid her in her extremity. * * *

The evidence on the part of the plaintiff tended to prove the allegations of the declaration. On the part of the defendants evidence was given tending to prove that Scattergood very reluctantly accompanied Dr. De May at the urgent request of the latter; that the night was a dark and stormy one, the roads over which they had to travel in getting to the house of the plaintiff were so bad that a horse could not be rode or driven over them; that the doctor was sick and very much fatigued from overwork, and therefore asked the defendant Scattergood to accompany and assist him in carrying a lantern, umbrella and certain articles deemed necessary upon such occasions; that upon arriving at the house of the plaintiff the doctor knocked, and when the door was opened by the husband of the plaintiff, De May said to him "that I had fetched a friend along to help carry my things;" he, plaintiff's husband, said all right, and seemed to be perfectly satisfied. They were bid to enter, treated kindly and no objection whatever made to the presence of defendant Scattergood. That while there Scattergood, at Dr. De May's request, took hold of plaintiff's hand and held her during a paroxysm of pain, and that both of the defendants in all respects throughout acted in a proper and becoming manner actuated by a sense of duty and kindness. * * *

Dr. De May therefore took an unprofessional young unmarried man with him, introduced and permitted him to remain in the house of the plaintiff, when it was apparent that he could hear at least, if not see all that was said and done, and as the jury must have found, under the instructions given, without either the plaintiff or her husband having any knowledge or reason to believe the true character of such third party. It would be shocking to our sense of right, justice and propriety to doubt even but that for such an act the law would afford an ample remedy. To the plaintiff the occasion was a most sacred one and no one had a right to intrude unless invited or because of some real and pressing necessity which it is not pretended existed in this case. The plaintiff had a legal right to the privacy of her apartment at such a time, and the law secures to her this right by requiring others to observe it, and to abstain from its violation. The fact that at the time, she consented to the presence of Scattergood supposing him to be a physician, does not preclude her from maintaining an action and recovering substantial damages upon afterwards ascertaining his true character. In obtaining admission at such a time and under such circumstances without fully disclosing his true character, both parties were guilty of deceit, and the wrong thus done entitles the injured party to recover the damages afterwards sustained, from shame and mortification upon discovering the true character of the defendants. * * *

Judgment for plaintiff affirmed.

NOTES AND QUESTIONS

1. The court says that the plaintiff consented to Scattergood's presence "supposing him to be a physician" and that the defendants introduced him without "fully disclosing his true character." In order for a consent to be valid, how much does defendant have to disclose? What if the plaintiff asks no questions? Under what circumstances can consent be assumed? Breast cancer patient, on a routine visit to her oncologist's office, is shown into a private examining room. Her doctor arrives, accompanied by another man, who is introduced as someone who is following his work. She says nothing. Following her doctor's instructions, she disrobes and he examines her breasts and lower abdomen in the other man's presence. As she leaves the office, she asks the receptionist who the other man is and is told he is a "drug salesman." Consent? Cf. Sanchez-Scott v. Alza Pharmaceuticals, 86 Cal.App.4th 365, 103 Cal.Rptr.2d 410 (2001) (because true status of drug company representative was not disclosed to patient, no consent was implied by failure to object).

2. Defendant calls on plaintiff, a woman with an artificial leg, in her house. Representing himself to be a doctor referred by the company that made her leg, he induces her to remove her dress, expose her person, and to permit him to touch her. He is in fact a doctor, but of theology. Battery? Cf. Commonwealth v. Gregory, 132 Pa.Super. 507, 1 A.2d 501 (1938) (consent not valid because defendant led plaintiff to belief he was a physician when he was not). Defendant gives plaintiff some chocolate candy, which contains an irritant poison. In ignorance of this fact, plaintiff eats the candy, and is made ill. Is there liability for a battery? Cf. Commonwealth v. Stratton, 114 Mass. 303, 19 Am.Rep. 350 (1873) (consent not valid because defendant did

not disclose the food had been laced with "love powder"). Defendant represents himself to be a licensed physician, but he is not. Cf. Taylor v. Johnston, 985 P.2d 460 (Alaska 1999) (battery claim may lie if person falsely claiming to be physician touches patient, even for purpose of providing medical treatment). O'Brien v. Synnott, 193 Vt. 546, 72 A.3d 331 (Vt. 2013) (consent not valid because nurse in hospital did not disclose that blood draw was for law enforcement analysis rather than medical treatment).

On the effect, in general, of fraud and mistake on consent, see Restatement (Second) of Torts § 892B.

3. Suppose that A consents to sexual intercourse with B, in ignorance of the fact that B has a sexually transmitted disease. A contracts the disease. Has she a battery action against B? Kathleen K. v. Robert B., 150 Cal.App.3d 992, 198 Cal.Rptr. 273 (1984). Crowell v. Crowell, 180 N.C. 516, 105 S.E. 206 (1920); cf. De Vall v. Strunk, 96 S.W.2d 245 (Tex.Civ.App.1936). A woman consents to sexual intercourse with a man only after he assured her that "I can't possibly get anyone pregnant," knowing that the statement was false. She then suffers an ectopic pregnancy and must undergo surgery, which saves her life but makes her sterile. Liability? Barbara A. v. John G., 145 Cal.App.3d 369, 193 Cal.Rptr. 422 (1983). Does it make a difference if he also does not know? See McPherson v. McPherson, 712 A.2d 1043 (Me.1998) (no liability because husband who infected wife with venereal disease neither knew nor had reason to know that he was infected). A wife consents to sexual intercourse with her husband, in ignorance of the fact that he is having an affair. After learning of the affair, she sues him for battery, claiming that her consent was obtained by fraud. Liability? Neal v. Neal, 125 Idaho 617, 873 P.2d 871 (1994) (plaintiff's battery claim should have gone to the jury on the issue of consent even though defendant husband proved that she also had consented to sexual intercourse *after* she learned of the affair).

4. Law Professor agrees to appear in the dunking booth at a law school fair. She was told that the proceeds would be donated to a fund to provide debt reduction for students who embark on public interest careers but later learned that the students spent the money on a fancy graduation reception for their parents. Consent valid? Consent induced by fraud or misrepresentation as to a collateral matter, rather than fraud as to the essential character of the act itself, will not invalidate consent. See Restatement (Second) of Torts §§ 55, 57 (1965).

5. *"Informed Consent."* The doctrine of "informed consent" requires a physician or surgeon to disclose to the patient the risks of proposed medical or surgical treatment. If she does not do so, she may be liable when injury results from the treatment. In early cases, this liability was placed on the ground of battery, by analogy to De May v. Roberts, and the cases in the preceding notes. Among the cases so holding have been Bang v. Charles T. Miller Hospital, 251 Minn. 427, 88 N.W.2d 186 (1958) and Gray v. Grunnagle, 423 Pa. 144, 223 A.2d 663 (1966). Around 1960, the failure to disclose the risk began to be treated as a breach of the doctor's professional duty, and hence as a matter of negligence. The cases now generally proceed on that basis. The matter is therefore treated in Chapter 4, Negligence. When the physician exceeds the boundaries of consent, the matter is still treated as battery as set forth in Mohr v. Williams.

6. Note that most of the "consent induced by fraud" cases involve battery. What if the underlying tort is trespass? Compare these two cases against ABC, which broadcasts PrimeTime Live. Plaintiff, an ophthalmic surgeon who owned several clinics, was approached by a producer of PrimeTime Live and told the show was doing a segment on cataract operations. The producer told plaintiff that the segment would not involve ambush interviews or undercover surveillance and would be fair and balanced. Plaintiff cooperated by permitting film crews and interviews of doctors, patients, and technicians at his clinic in Chicago. Unbeknownst to plaintiff, the producer also had dispatched seven undercover test "patients" equipped with concealed cameras to other clinic locations owned by plaintiff. The resulting show was very critical of the clinics. Plaintiff sued for trespass, claiming the consent given to the seven test patients with concealed cameras was induced by fraud. Liability? Desnick v. American Broadcasting Co., Inc., 44 F.3d 1345 (7th Cir.1995) (applying Illinois law) (no trespass because not an interference with the ownership or possession of land). Plaintiff, the Food Lion grocery store chain, was the target of a PrimeTime Live exposé on meat handling. Employees of ABC created false identities and applied for work at several Food Lion stores. While working for Food Lion, they filmed various activities with hidden cameras. Food Lion sued for trespass, claiming its consent to the ABC employees' presence in its deli and meatpacking departments was obtained by fraud. Food Lion, Inc. v. Capital Cities/ABC, Inc., 194 F.3d 505 (4th Cir. 1999) (applying North and South Carolina law) (jury verdict of trespass affirmed). See also Copeland v. Hubbard Broadcasting, Inc., 526 N.W.2d 402 (Minn.App.1995) (reporter posing as student interested in observing veterinarian liable in trespass to pet owners who allowed her in their home to observe). For a discussion of the invasion of privacy claims in these cases, see Chapter 18, Privacy.

7. Plaintiff is in a bar, so intoxicated that he does not know what he is doing when he agrees to "Indian wrestle" with defendant. Valid consent? Cf. Hollerud v. Malamis, 20 Mich.App. 748, 174 N.W.2d 626 (1969) (consent ineffective if plaintiff incapable of expressing rational will).

8. *Consent to Illegal Activity.* Plaintiff consented to participate in a prize fight, an illegal activity in that state. He died as a result of a blow received in the fight and his estate filed a battery claim against the other fighter who demurred on the basis of consent. Is consent to an illegal act a valid consent? Hart v. Geysel, 159 Wash. 632, 294 P. 570 (1930) (recognizing split of authority among jurisdictions as to whether consent to an illegal act is valid consent); Janelsins v. Button, 102 Md.App. 30, 648 A.2d 1039 (1994) (same). The question of when plaintiff's consent should be invalidated because defendant violated a criminal statute may depend on several considerations: (a) the policy of denying compensation to an intentional wrongdoer who himself may have committed a crime and been injured as a result of it; (b) the effect of deterring him, and others like him, by denying him recovery if he gets hurt; (c) the effect of potential liability in deterring defendant and others like him; (d) the fact that plaintiff has after all been intentionally battered by defendant; (e) the policy expressed by the maxim, *In pari delicto potior est conditio defendentis* [In equal guilt, the position of the defendant is the stronger]. Even states that generally recognize the validity of consent to an illegal act will not deny recovery to those whom the statute making the conduct illegal was designed to protect.

For example, plaintiff, a 15-year-old girl, consents to intercourse with a 50-year-old man in a state with criminal penalties for men who have sexual relations with children that age. Most courts have held plaintiff's consent to be ineffective. See Gaither v. Meacham, 214 Ala. 343, 108 So. 2 (1926). A competent adult woman, however, cannot maintain an action for her own seduction, even if intercourse between unmarried adults is illegal in the state. See Rouse v. Creech, 203 N.C. 378, 166 S.E. 174 (1932). Defendant provides plaintiff's decedent with sleeping pills, knowing he intends to use them to commit suicide. The state's criminal law prohibits both aiding and abetting suicide and attempted suicide. Schwartz, Civil Liability for Causing Suicide: A Synthesis of Law and Psychiatry, 24 Vand.L.Rev. 217, 220–222 (1971), evaluating the factors set forth above, suggests that a claim should be allowed. Would family members of those who commit suicide using the Kevorkian suicide machine have a cause of action against Dr. Kevorkian?

2. SELF-DEFENSE

The privilege of self-defense is covered in Criminal Law, and detailed discussion must be left to that course. Cases involving tort liability are infrequent. When they arise, the criminal law rules are carried over and applied without much variation. The following brief summary will indicate how self-defense fits into the tort picture:

1. *Existence of Privilege.* Anyone is privileged to use reasonable force to defend himself against a threatened battery on the part of another. The recognition of this privilege came about 1400, and it always has been an affirmative defense to be pleaded and proved by the defendant. In some jurisdictions, the burden of proof is reversed if the defendant is a police officer. Then, plaintiff would have to show as his prima facie battery case that the use of force was unreasonable (and thus not privileged). See, for example, Edson v. City of Anaheim, 63 Cal.App.4th 1269, 74 Cal.Rptr.2d 614 (1998) (collecting cases from other jurisdictions). The trial court judge will make the initial determination whether a self-defense instruction is warranted by the facts. See, for example, Goldfuss v. Davidson, 79 Ohio St.3d 116, 679 N.E.2d 1099 (1997) in which the Supreme Court of Ohio approved the trial court judge's refusal to give a jury instruction on self-defense where defendant fired a shot from his kitchen window at two men who had broken in to his pole barn. Defendant and his family were inside the house with all the doors locked, the police had been called, the pole barn was a hundred feet from the house, and the men were running away when defendant fired.

2. *Retaliation.* The privilege is one of defense against threatened battery, and not one of retaliation. When the battery is no longer threatened, the privilege terminates; and thereafter the original victim himself becomes liable for battery. Germolus v. Sausser, 83 Minn. 141, 85 N.W. 946 (1901) (defendant had grabbed a whip away from plaintiff and then knocked him unconscious); cf. Drabek v. Sabley, 31 Wis.2d 184, 142 N.W.2d 798 (1966) (battery and false imprisonment of boy who had thrown a snowball at defendant).

Even if a person initially was an aggressor, once he has retreated he has a right to self-defense against the person he initially threatened. Edgar v. Emily, 637 S.W.2d 412 (Mo.App.1982) (After coming to his sister's house armed with a stick, defendant walked back to his car intending to leave. At that point, the sister's husband came out of the house and grabbed defendant's shirt sleeve, which ripped as he tried to leave. The two men began fighting and the sister came at defendant with a hatchet or hammer and hit him in the face with her fist. He then hit his sister with the stick).

3. *Reasonable Belief.* The privilege exists when the defendant reasonably believes that the force is necessary to protect himself against battery, even though there is in fact no necessity. This is an instance in which a reasonable mistake on the part of the actor will protect him. The reason that the rule in Ranson v. Kitner, page 25, is not applied is apparently the importance attached by the courts to "self-preservation as the first law of nature." Smith v. Delery, 238 La. 180, 114 So.2d 857 (1959) (newspaper delivery boy shot while retrieving his dog from the back of defendant's house); Bunten v. Davis, 82 N.H. 304, 133 A. 16 (1926) (defendant fired at plaintiff and his companions who were out riding around on the Fourth of July setting off fireworks).

A. Plaintiff and defendant were on bad terms. They met in the highway, and defendant accosted plaintiff, asking why plaintiff had been slandering him. Plaintiff, who had a reputation for shooting people, suddenly put his hand into his pocket. Defendant, believing that he was about to draw a revolver, struck him on the head with a cane and knocked him down. It was held that the jury should have been instructed that defendant was liable only if he did not have reasonable grounds to fear an immediate attack by plaintiff. Keep v. Quallman, 68 Wis. 451, 32 N.W. 233 (1887).

B. Defendant ejected from a dance an intoxicated individual named Noble, who had not paid his admission fee. Defendant was then informed that Noble was outside, "getting some bricks." Defendant stepped into the doorway, looking out into the darkness for Noble. At this moment, plaintiff, arriving late for the dance, came running rapidly up the steps, which were dimly lighted. Defendant, believing that he was being attacked by Noble, struck plaintiff and knocked him down the steps. Defendant was held not liable. Crabtree v. Dawson, 119 Ky. 148, 83 S.W. 557 (1904).

4. *Provocation.* Should insults, verbal threats, or opprobrious language justify the exercise of self-defense? Almost every court that has passed upon the question has held that they do not. See Crotteau v. Karlgaard, 48 Wis.2d 245, 179 N.W.2d 797 (1970) ("Get out of the way, you dumb son of a bitch"); Prell Hotel Corp. v. Antonacci, 86 Nev. 390, 469 P.2d 399 (1970) ("hateful, degrading name"). In many states, the offending words can be introduced to oppose the imposition of punitive damages on the party claiming to have been provoked. Manning v. Michael, 188 Conn. 607, 452 A.2d 1157 (1982) (provocation does not justify battery but may limit liability to actual damages).

Although the general rule of law is relatively clear, its application in the context of a particular dispute may not be. If the abusive words are accompanied by an actual threat of physical violence reasonably warranting an apprehension of imminent bodily harm, one may be privileged to defend, (see Silas v. Bowen, 277 F.Supp. 314 (D.S.C.1967)); and one does not have to wait for the blow to fall before acting, (see Martin v. Estrella, 107 R.I. 247, 266 A.2d 41 (1970)). Further, when accompanied by an overt hostile act, oral abuse may amount to a challenge to fight and thus may constitute consent in some jurisdictions. Restatement (Second) of Torts § 69.

5. *Amount of Force.* The privilege is limited to the use of force that is or reasonably appears to be necessary for protection against a threatened battery. Differences in age, size and relative strength are proper considerations. Thus, a 5′6″, 135-pound middle-aged man was permitted to ward off a 6′6″, 230-pound young athlete with a shot aimed near his feet. Silas v. Bowen, 277 F.Supp. 314 (D.S.C.1967) (it missed and hit plaintiff). Similarly a small ten-year-old was permitted to throw a broom at a larger ten-year-old in McDonald v. Terrebonne Parish School Bd., 253 So.2d 558 (La.App.1971), cert. denied, 260 La. 128, 255 So.2d 353 (1971) (it missed and took out plaintiff's eye). But a teenage boy engaged in a fistfight with another was not justified in using a baseball bat to protect himself from threatened injury in Andrepont v. Naquin, 345 So.2d 1216 (La.App.1977). To justify resistance with a deadly weapon, defendant must have a reasonable apprehension of loss of life or great bodily injury. See Greenberg v. Mobil Oil Corp., 318 F.Supp. 1025 (N.D.Tex.1970). Generally, defendant has the burden of proving that the use of force was reasonable under the circumstances, although some jurisdictions shift the burden to the plaintiff if the defendant is a police officer. See, for example, Edson v. City of Anaheim, 63 Cal.App.4th 1269, 74 Cal.Rptr.2d 614 (1998) (collecting cases from other jurisdictions).

6. *Retreat Before Use of Deadly Force.* One basic disagreement in approach to the privilege of self-defense focuses on whether the defendant must retreat if he can do so without increasing his danger, rather than stand his ground and use deadly force. All agree that he may stand his ground and use any force short of that likely to cause serious injury. The common law rule was that, rather than kill his assailant or seriously wound him, defendant must first "retreat to the wall." A minority of the American courts still apply this rule, and it is adopted by the Restatement (Second) of Torts § 65 (1965). Even the Restatement, however, does not require retreat within one's own home. The Restatement provides that the victim may use deadly force if there is the slightest reasonable doubt that the retreat can be safely made, and "in determining whether his doubt is reasonable every allowance must be made for the predicament in which his assailant has placed him." Restatement (Second) of Torts § 65, comment *g*. The majority have insisted upon a higher importance of the dignity and honor of the individual and have held that the defendant may stand his ground and use deadly force, and even kill his assailant without having first to retreat. A recent wave of legislation goes even further, extending the area in which one can stand his ground and use deadly force to include any place where he has a right to be, no longer limiting it to his home or place of work. See, for example, Fla. Stat. Ann. § 776.013(3) and 18 Pa. C.S.A. § 505(b).

7. *Injury to Third Party.* A small number of cases have dealt with the situation in which the defendant, defending himself against A, unintentionally harms B instead. The privilege of self-defense is carried over, and the defendant is held not to be liable to B in the absence of some negligence toward him. And in determining whether there is negligence, the emergency, and the necessity of defense against A, are still to be considered. Morris v. Platt, 32 Conn. 75 (1864); Shaw v. Lord, 41 Okl. 347, 137 P. 885 (1914). Cf. Thompson v. Beliauskas, 341 Mass. 95, 167 N.E.2d 163 (1960) (defense of property).

3. DEFENSE OF OTHERS

1. *Nature of Privilege.* A privilege similar to that of self-defense is recognized for the defense of third persons. The early common law recognized a feudal privilege in the master of the household to defend members of his family and his servants against attack. Most of the cases have involved members of the same family defending one another, or the relation of master and servant, as in Frew v. Teagarden, 111 Kan. 107, 205 P. 1023 (1922), but the privilege is not so limited.

As in the case of self-defense, the closest questions concern whether defendant used reasonable force in the circumstances. For cases upholding the privilege, see e.g., Boyer v. Waples, 206 Cal.App.2d 725, 24 Cal.Rptr. 192 (1962) (plaintiff, who had previously made serious threats to members of defendant's family and was seen outside the defendant's home at night with an object in hand that looked like dynamite, but was, in fact, a flashlight, was shot and wounded); McCullough v. McAnelly, 248 So.2d 7 (La.App.1971), cert. denied, 259 La. 748, 252 So.2d 451 (1971) (three teenaged boys attacked defendant's son and would not desist when warned; father shot and wounded one). Compare Lopez v. Surchia, 112 Cal.App.2d 314, 246 P.2d 111 (1952) (defendant shot boy who was fighting with defendant's son on front lawn—force exceeded privilege).

2. *Reasonable Mistake.* One question over which the courts have differed is that of the effect of a reasonable mistake as to the necessity for taking action. Some courts hold that the intervenor steps into the shoes of the person he is defending, and is privileged only when that person would be privileged to defend himself. If it turns out that he has intervened to help the aggressor, he is liable. Robinson v. Decatur, 32 Ala.App. 654, 29 So.2d 429 (1947); cf. State v. Wenger, 58 Ohio St.2d 336, 390 N.E.2d 801 (Ohio 1979) (in criminal prosecution of bystander who struck plain clothes police officer making lawful arrest, court cited tort law that defendant had privilege only to extent that the one he was defending would have had). Other courts hold that the defendant is privileged to use reasonable force to defend another even when he is mistaken in his belief that intervention is necessary, so long as his mistake was reasonable. The Restatement (Second) of Torts § 76 has adopted this position.

4. DEFENSE OF PROPERTY

Katko v. Briney

Supreme Court of Iowa, 1971.
183 N.W.2d 657.

MOORE, CHIEF JUSTICE. The primary issue presented here is whether an owner may protect personal property in an unoccupied boarded-up farm house against trespassers and thieves by a spring gun capable of inflicting death or serious injury.

We are not here concerned with a man's right to protect his home and members of his family. Defendants' home was several miles from the scene of the incident to which we refer infra.

Plaintiff's action is for damages resulting from serious injury caused by a shot from a 20-gauge spring shotgun set by defendants in a bedroom of an old farm house which has been uninhabited for several years. Plaintiff and his companion * * * had broken and entered the house to find and steal old bottles and dated fruit jars which they considered antiques. * * *

The jury returned a verdict for plaintiff and against defendants for $20,000 actual and $10,000 punitive damages.

After careful consideration of defendants' motions for judgment notwithstanding the verdict and for new trial, the experienced and capable trial judge overruled them and entered judgment on the verdict. Thus we have this appeal by defendants. * * *

Mr. and Mrs. Edward Briney in front of their vacant farmhouse near Oskaloosa, Iowa.

[The house was inherited from Mrs. Briney's grandparents and had been unoccupied for some time. There had been a series of intrusions and thefts.] Defendants through the years boarded up the windows and doors in an attempt to stop the intrusions. They had posted "no trespass" signs on the land several years before 1967. The nearest one was 35 feet from the house. On June 11, 1967 defendants set "a shotgun trap" in the north bedroom. After Mr. Briney cleaned and oiled his 20-gauge shotgun, the power of which he was well aware, defendants took it to the old house where they secured it to an iron bed with the barrel pointed at the bedroom door. It was rigged with wire from the doorknob to the gun's trigger so it would fire when the door was opened. Briney first pointed the gun so an intruder would be hit in the stomach but at Mrs. Briney's suggestion it was lowered to hit the legs. He admitted he did so "because I was mad and tired of being tormented" but "he did not intend to injure anyone." He gave no explanation of why he used a loaded shell and set it to hit a person already in the house. Tin was nailed over the bedroom window. The spring gun could not be seen from the outside. No warning of its presence was posted. * * *

[Plaintiff] entered the old house by removing a board from a porch window which was without glass. * * * As he started to open the north bedroom door the shotgun went off striking him in the right leg above the ankle bone. Much of his leg, including part of the tibia, was blown away. Only by * * * assistance [from his accomplice] was plaintiff able to get out of the house and after crawling some distance was put in his vehicle and rushed to a doctor and then to a hospital. He remained in the hospital 40 days. * * *

Plaintiff Marvin E. Katko

There was undenied medical testimony plaintiff had a permanent deformity, a loss of tissue, and a shortening of the leg. * * *

The main thrust of defendants' defense in the trial court and on this appeal is that "the law permits use of a spring gun in a dwelling or warehouse for the purpose of preventing the unlawful entry of a burglar or thief." * * *

Instruction 6 stated: "An owner of premises is prohibited from willfully or intentionally injuring a trespasser by means of force that either takes life or inflicts great bodily injury; and therefore a person owning a premise is prohibited from setting out 'spring guns' and like dangerous devices which will likely take life or inflict great bodily injury, for the purpose of harming trespassers. The fact that the trespasser may be acting in violation of the law does not change the rule. The only time when such conduct of setting a 'spring gun' or a like dangerous device is justified would be when the trespasser was committing a felony of violence or a felony punishable by death, or where the trespasser was endangering human life by his act." * * *

The overwhelming weight of authority, both textbook and case law, supports the trial court's statement of the applicable principles of law. * * *

Restatement of Torts § 85, 180, states: "The value of human life and limb, not only to the individual concerned but also to society, so outweighs the interest of a possessor of land in excluding from it those whom he is not willing to admit thereto that a possessor of land has, as is stated in § 79, no privilege to use force intended or likely to cause death or serious harm against another whom the possessor sees about to enter his premises or meddle with his chattel, unless the intrusion threatens death or serious bodily harm to the occupiers or users of the premises. * * * A possessor of land cannot do indirectly and by a mechanical device that which, were he present, he could not do immediately and in person. Therefore, he cannot gain a privilege to install, for the purpose of protecting his land from intrusions harmless to the lives and limbs of the occupiers or users of it, a mechanical device whose only purpose is to inflict death or serious harm upon such as may intrude, by giving notice of his intention to inflict, by mechanical means and indirectly, harm which he could not, even after request, inflict directly were he present." * * *

The facts in Allison v. Fiscus, 156 Ohio St. 120, 100 N.E.2d 237, decided in 1951, are very similar to the case at bar. There plaintiff's right to damages was recognized for injuries received when he feloniously broke a door latch and started to enter defendant's warehouse with intent to steal. As he entered a trap of two sticks of dynamite buried under the doorway by defendant owner was set off and plaintiff seriously injured. The court held the question whether a particular trap was justified as a use of reasonable and necessary force against a trespasser engaged in the commission of a felony should have been submitted to the jury. The Ohio Supreme Court recognized plaintiff's right to recover punitive or exemplary damages in addition to compensatory damages. * * *

In addition to civil liability many jurisdictions hold a landowner criminally liable for serious injuries or homicide caused by spring guns or other set devices. [Cc] * * *

[The court declined to rule on whether punitive damages were allowable because defendant's attorney had not raised that issue in the trial court.]

Study and careful consideration of defendants' contentions on appeal reveal no reversible error.

Affirmed.

LARSON, JUSTICE [dissented, noting that the trial judge's instructions "failed to tell the jury it could find the installation was not made with the intent or purpose of striking or injuring the plaintiff," that the principle espoused by the court had never been applied to a burglar, but only "in the case of a mere trespasser in a vineyard," and that punitive damages should not be allowed where the injured party's conduct was criminal.]

NOTES AND QUESTIONS

1. Katko pled guilty to petty larceny and received a 30-day suspended sentence and a $50 fine. The Brineys had to sell 80 acres of their 120-acre farm in order to pay the judgment in this case. A strange development later arose between the parties. When the 80 acres were put up for judgment sale and there were no bids above the minimum price of $10,000, three neighbors borrowed money to purchase the land for a dollar more, expecting to hold it for the Brineys until they won their appeal. When they did not win, the neighbors leased the land back to them for enough to pay taxes and interest costs on the money the neighbors had borrowed. Several years later when land values rose, the neighbors offered to sell it back to Brineys at a price they could not afford. One of the neighbors then bought the property from the others for $16,000 and sold it to his son for $16,500. The Brineys and Katko, to whom the Brineys still owed money from the judgment, then sued the neighbors, arguing that the land was being held in trust for the Brineys and that they were therefore entitled to the profit from the increase in value. Just before the case came to trial, it was settled for a sum large enough to pay the remainder of Brineys' judgment to Katko. Further background about the case can be found in Palmer, Katko v. Briney: A Study in American Gothic, 56 Iowa L.Rev. 1219 (1971).

2. The United Press International (UPI) reported the results of the trial court decision in this case, stating in part that Katko was "shot and seriously injured in the *home* of Mr. and Mrs. Edward Briney." (Emphasis added.) A public outcry about the decision resulted in the introduction of "Briney Bills" in several state legislatures. The Nebraska Legislature enacted a self-defense act that provided in part that "no person * * * shall be placed in * * * jeopardy * * * for protecting, by any means necessary, himself, his family, or his real or personal property * * *." The statute was held to be unconstitutional by the Supreme Court of Nebraska on the ground of improper delegation of sentencing authority. See State v. Goodseal, 186 Neb. 359, 183 N.W.2d 258 (1971), cert. denied, 404 U.S. 845 (1971).

3. The privilege to defend one's land against an intruder is limited to unlawful intrusions. Thus, there is no privilege to use force to defend against those who are authorized to enter. Magnuson v. Billmayer, 189 Mont. 458, 616 P.2d 368 (1980) (land owner not justified in using force to stop workers removing telephone poles where telephone company had easement). Possessor who used force to defend property in a reasonably

mistaken belief that he was entitled to privilege is not protected unless the intruder in some way misled the possessor as to his identity or authorization.

4. As in the case of self-defense, the privilege to defend property is limited to the use of force reasonably necessary to the situation as it appears to the defendant. What constitutes reasonable force is normally a question for the jury, but there are several recognized limitations. When the invasion is peaceful and occurs in the presence of the possessor, the use of any force at all will be unreasonable unless a request has been made to depart. Chapell v. Schmidt, 104 Cal. 511, 38 P. 892 (1894) (defendant caned elderly person who was picking flowers); Emmons v. Quade, 176 Mo. 22, 75 S.W. 103 (1903) (mill worker used a club on a twelve-year-old boy who was trying to scoop up grain that had been left in a railroad car after it was unloaded). A request does not have to be made, however, when the conduct of the intruder would indicate to a reasonable person that it would be useless or that it could not safely be made in time. See Higgins v. Minaghan, 78 Wis. 602, 47 N.W. 941 (1891) (mob approaching house firing guns in air, shouting, and drumming on pans).

5. *Use of Force Calculated to Cause Death or Serious Injury.* The principal case caused a good deal of discussion about when, if ever, force calculated to cause death or serious injury may be utilized to defend property. Cases involving burglars or thieves attempting to recover from their intended victims are rare.

A. In Ilott v. Wilkes, 3 B. & Ald. 304, 106 Eng.Rep. 674 (1820), it was held that a landowner who placed spring guns on his land to keep off poachers was not liable to a trespasser who was shot. The result of this decision was a storm of public disapproval, which led to an act of Parliament making the setting of such devices a crime. In Bird v. Holbrook, 4 Bing. 628, 130 Eng.Rep. 911 (1828), a case which arose before the statute was passed, but was decided afterward, the court overruled the *Ilott* case and a defendant who set a spring gun was held liable to a trespasser.

B. Most American courts, including the Iowa Supreme Court, and the Restatement (Second) of Torts § 85 (1965) have followed Bird v. Holbrook. Many jurisdictions have placed the restrictions on the use of deadly force in their state statutory codes. See statutes collected in Posner, Killing or Wounding to Protect a Property Interest, 14 J.L. & Econ. 201, 228–232 (1971).

C. The general rule prohibiting deadly force is modified in some states if defendant gives the plaintiff clear notice of the danger. See Starkey v. Dameron, 92 Colo. 420, 21 P.2d 1112 (1933) (dictum); State v. Marfaudille, 48 Wash. 117, 92 P. 939 (1907). This is especially likely to occur when defendant's use of force involved a vicious dog. See Hood v. Waldrum, 58 Tenn.App. 512, 434 S.W.2d 94 (1968); Sappington v. Sutton, 501 P.2d 814 (Okl.1972). Compare Loomis v. Terry, 17 Wend. 496, 31 Am.Dec. 306 (N.Y.1837) (no warning, defendant liable). Barbed wire may give notice in and of itself. See Quigley v. Clough, 173 Mass. 429, 53 N.E. 884 (1899). What privilege is operating in these cases? In most jurisdictions, even posted warnings will not protect the landholder if he would not be privileged to use this amount of force were he there in person. See State v. Plumlee, 177 La. 687, 149 So. 425 (1933); State v. Childers, 133 Ohio St. 508, 14 N.E.2d 767 (1938).

D. When the invader threatens the personal safety of the defendant or his family, the defendant may use deadly force if it is necessary in the circumstances. This is likely to occur when the invader attempts to enter the homestead at night. See Tipsword v. Potter, 31 Idaho 509, 174 P. 133 (1918); Coleman v. New York & N.H.R. Co., 106 Mass. 160 (1870).

E. There also is a privilege to use reasonable force to prevent the commission of a crime. With a serious felony, the amount of permissible force is greater, and some states have permitted deadly force. See Tex. Civ. Prac. & Rem. Code Ann. § 83.001 (crime prevention statute provides immunity from civil suit for defendant who uses deadly force to prevent certain crimes, including kidnapping, murder, sexual assault, and robbery) and Ariz. Rev. Stat. §§ 13–411 and 13–413 (no civil liability for person using deadly force to prevent certain crimes, including arson of an occupied structure, burglary in the first or second degree, manslaughter, sexual conduct with a minor, child molestation, and armed robbery). In those jurisdictions that do not permit the use of deadly force to defend property, would it make a difference if the property was a government laboratory where deadly biological agents were stored for research?

F. What if the landholder claims that he intended only to frighten and not to injure the intruder? How does this correlate with the doctrine of transferred intent? See Allison v. Fiscus, 156 Ohio St. 120, 100 N.E.2d 237 (1951) (defendant argued that he did not think the two sticks of dynamite buried in the floor of tool shed would injure anyone). In Goldfuss v. Davidson, 79 Ohio St.3d 116, 679 N.E.2d 1099 (1997), defendant yelled at men he saw running away from his pole barn and fired from his kitchen window warning shots "over their heads" to try to get them to stop until the police arrived. One of the men was killed by the shots and his father filed a wrongful death action against defendant. The court found no prejudicial error in the trial court judge's instruction that the jury was to determine whether defendant's discharge of a firearm was reasonably necessary to prevent the theft of his property. The jury awarded $150,000 to the estate of the thief.

6. The limitations on the possessor's privilege may also restrict his power to eject the plaintiff from his property into a position of unreasonable physical danger. Thus a teenager stealing a ride on a railroad train cannot be thrown off at thirty miles an hour. Chesapeake & O. Ry. Co. v. Ryan's Adm'r, 183 Ky. 428, 209 S.W. 538 (1919). In Depue v. Flateau, 100 Minn. 299, 111 N.W. 1 (1907), plaintiff, a travelling cattle buyer, called at defendant's farmhouse on a cold winter evening, and was asked to stay for dinner. After dinner plaintiff was overcome by a "fainting spell," and became very weak and seriously ill. He asked permission to stay overnight, which was refused. Defendant led him out to his sleigh, put him into it, adjusted the robes around him, and threw the reins, which he was too weak to hold, over his shoulders. Defendant then started the horses on the road to town. Plaintiff was found the following morning by the side of the road about three-quarters of a mile away, badly frost-bitten, and nearly frozen to death. Case was permitted to go to the jury. Suppose the landowner places a drunken guest in his car to go home?

7. On the other hand, if the plaintiff's presence endangers the personal safety of those on the premises, the privilege of self-defense, or that of defense of third persons, may justify the ejection. In Tucker v. Burt,

152 Mich. 68, 115 N.W. 722 (1908), plaintiff, the mother-in-law of the janitor of an apartment house, fell ill with a highly contagious disease. Defendant, the owner of the building, ejected her. It was held that defendant was not liable. One of the interesting facts about Tucker v. Burt is that the plaintiff's description of her trip from her daughter's apartment (from which she was ejected by defendant landlord) to her own apartment includes walking a block to the street car stop, two street car rides (including a transfer), and then walking two blocks to her apartment. She obviously exposed many more people to her illness during the trip than she would have had she stayed put at her daughter's apartment. How could that point be used in the case to support a public policy argument in favor of plaintiff's recovery from her daughter's landlord?

5. RECOVERY OF PROPERTY

Hodgeden v. Hubbard

Supreme Court of Vermont, 1846.
18 Vt. 504, 46 Am.Dec. 167.

[Trespass for assault and battery, and for taking and carrying away a stove. Plaintiff buyer had purchased the stove on credit at the warehouse of defendants. Defendants discovered almost at once that plaintiff had misrepresented his assets and credit and that he was financially irresponsible. They immediately started out in pursuit, and overtook the plaintiff about two miles away, where they took the stove away from him by force. His resistance was such that the defendants applied force to his person with "great rudeness and outrage." Plaintiff drew a knife, and he was forcibly held by one of the defendants while the other took possession of the stove.

The court charged the jury that, although plaintiff was guilty of misrepresentation and fraud in obtaining the stove, the defendants were still not justified in forcibly taking it from him, or using force against his person, but must resort to redress by legal process; and that if they found that the force was used, the defendants would be liable. Verdict for plaintiff for $1.00 damages. Exceptions by defendants.]

WILLIAMS, CH. J. It is admitted, in this case, that the property in the stove did not pass to the plaintiff, that, though the plaintiff obtained possession of the stove, yet it was by such means of falsehood and fraud, criminal in the eye of the law, as made the possession unlawful, and that, although the consent of the owner was apparently obtained to the delivery of the possession to the plaintiff, yet, as it respects the plaintiff, and so far as the right of property was concerned, no such consent was given. * * *

In the present case the defendants had clearly a right to retake the property, thus fraudulently obtained from them, if it could be done without unnecessary violence to the person, or without breach of the peace. * * *

In this case before us it is stated, that it did not appear "how much force was used, or its character," before the defendants were assaulted by the plaintiff. To obtain possession of the property in question no violence to the person of the plaintiff was necessary, or required, unless from his resistance. * * * The plaintiff had no lawful possession, nor any right to resist the attempt of the defendants to regain the property, of which he had unlawfully and fraudulently obtained the possession. By drawing his knife he became the aggressor, inasmuch as he had no right thus to protect his fraudulent attempt to acquire the stove, and the possession of the same, and it was the right of the defendants to hold him by force, and, if they made use of no unnecessary violence, they were justified; if they were guilty of more, they were liable. * * *

The judgment of the county court is reversed.

NOTES AND QUESTIONS

1. The privilege of an owner dispossessed of a chattel to use force to recapture it appears to have been first recognized in cases in which there was only a momentary interruption of his possession, so that it was easy to regard him as in effect defending his original possession rather than interfering with that of another. This was extended later to situations in which the wrongdoer had obtained the chattel by *force or fraud*, and had made his escape with it, but the pursuit was "fresh." These limitations have continued to be applied to the privilege. As to the requirement of force or fraud, see Watson v. Rheinderknecht, 82 Minn. 235, 84 N.W. 798 (1901) (in breach of contract action—no force or fraud—defendant seller not entitled to take back his sheep from buyer).

2. *Fresh pursuit* is limited to prompt discovery of the dispossession, and prompt and persistent efforts to recover the chattel. Any undue lapse of time during which the pursuit has not been commenced, or has come to a halt, will mean that the owner is no longer privileged to fight himself back into possession, but must resort to the law. Restatement (Second) of Torts § 103. A resort to any force at all will not be justified until a *demand* has been made for the return of the property; but this is not required when it reasonably appears that demand would be useless or dangerous. Restatement (Second) of Torts § 104.

3. The privilege is limited to force reasonable under the circumstances. Hamilton v. Barker, 116 Mich. 684, 75 N.W. 133 (1898) (defendant could use only the force necessary to recover the plums gathered from his tree by plaintiff). As in the case of the defense of possession, it is not *reasonable* to use *force* calculated to inflict serious bodily harm to protect a property interest. Gortarez v. Smitty's Super Valu, Inc., 140 Ariz. 97, 680 P.2d 807 (1984) (shopowner's use of a choke hold on teenage boy after chasing him in parking lot because of suspected shoplifting was not reasonable). Restatement (Second) of Torts § 106. If the wrongdoer resists, the owner may use any force reasonably required to prevent the property from being taken and to defend his own person. Gyre v. Culver, 47 Barb. (N.Y.) 592 (1867) (persistent efforts of plaintiff to take the wood she had gathered from defendant's property even after defendant had taken it from her justified use of additional force by defendant).

4. How much force would be reasonable to defend a pet? During an argument, defendant's former girlfriend grabbed his small dog and took it to her car, refusing to release it even after defendant kicked her car. Defendant then pulled plaintiff's hair and hit her in the face with a closed

fist. Reasonable? Cf. Raynes v. Rogers, 183 Vt. 513, 955 A.2d 1135 (2008) (in considering whether protective order under abuse-prevention statute should issue, court discusses privilege to defend property (the dog) but does not decide whether this was reasonable force).

5. The courts are not agreed as to whether a clause in the contract giving the seller the privilege to use force is effective. A few of the older decisions have held that it is. Lambert v. Robinson, 162 Mass. 34, 37 N.E. 753 (1894); W.T. Walker Furniture Co. v. Dyson, 32 App.D.C. 90 (1908). The prevailing view of the later decisions is that the clause is void as inviting a breach of the peace. Girard v. Anderson, 219 Iowa 142, 257 N.W. 400 (1934), is one of the best decisions. Is the problem one of the scope of the privilege of recapture or whether consent should be invalidated?

6. The retaking of possession by a seller under a conditional sale, on default by the buyer, is now controlled by § 9–609 of the Uniform Commercial Code, which provides that a secured party has on default the right to take possession of the collateral without judicial process if this can be done without breach of the peace.

Bonkowski v. Arlan's Department Store

Court of Appeals of Michigan, 1968.
12 Mich.App. 88, 162 N.W.2d 347.

NEAL E. FITZGERALD, JUDGE. This appeal from a jury verdict for false arrest and slander, rendered against the defendant store whose agent stopped and questioned the plaintiff whom he suspected of larceny, surprisingly presents questions that are novel to the appellate courts of this jurisdiction.

The plaintiff, Mrs. Marion Bonkowski, accompanied by her husband, had left the defendant's Saginaw, Michigan store about 10:00 p.m. on the night of December 18, 1962 after making several purchases, when Earl Reinhardt, a private policeman on duty that night in the defendant's store, called to her to stop as she was walking to her car about 30 feet away in the adjacent parking lot. Reinhardt motioned to the plaintiff to return toward the store and when she had done so, Reinhardt said that someone in the store had told him the plaintiff had put three pieces of costume jewelry into her purse without having paid for them. Mrs. Bonkowski denied she had taken anything unlawfully, but Reinhardt told her he wanted to see the contents of her purse. On a cement step in front of the store, plaintiff emptied the contents of her purse into her husband's hands. The plaintiff produced sales slips for the items she had purchased, and Reinhardt, satisfied that she had not committed larceny, returned to the store.

Plaintiff brought this action against Earl Reinhardt and Arlan's Department Store, seeking damages on several counts. She complains that as a result of defendant's tortious acts she has suffered numerous psychosomatic symptoms, including headaches, nervousness, and depression. Arlan's Department Store filed a third-party complaint against Earl Reinhardt's employer, Gerald Kaweck, doing business as Michigan Security Police Service, who defaulted. On the counts of false arrest and slander the case went to the jury, who returned a verdict of

$43,750. The defendant's motions for judgment notwithstanding the verdict, remittitur, and new trial were denied by the trial court. * * *

We conclude the plaintiff established a case entitling her to go to the jury on a charge of false arrest. [The court first concluded that the private policeman Reinhardt was the agent of defendant department store, which was responsible for his acts.]

To the common-law tort of false arrest, privilege is a common-law defense, and we recognize as applicable here a privilege similar to that recognized by the American Law Institute in the Restatement (Second) of Torts. In section 120A, the Institute recognizes a privilege in favor of a merchant to detain for reasonable investigation a person whom he reasonably believes to have taken a chattel unlawfully. We adopt the concept embodied in section 120A, and we state the rule for this action as follows: if defendant Arlan's agent, Earl Reinhardt, reasonably believed the plaintiff had unlawfully taken goods held for sale in the defendant's store, then he enjoyed a privilege to detain her for a reasonable investigation of the facts.

The Commissioners' [sic; Institute's] comment states the strong reason behind recognizing such a privilege:

"The privilege stated in this section is necessary for the protection of a shopkeeper against the dilemma in which he would otherwise find himself when he reasonably believes that a shoplifter has taken goods from his counter. If there were no such privilege, he must either permit the suspected person to walk out of the premises and disappear, or must arrest him, at the risk of liability for false arrest if the theft could not be proved." 1 Restatement (Second) of Torts, page 202.

That the problem of shoplifting, faced by merchants, has reached serious dimensions is common knowledge, and we find compelling reason to recognize such a privilege, similar to that recognized in other jurisdictions. [Cc]

In Montgomery Ward & Co., Inc., v. Freeman, the United States Court of Appeals for the Fourth Circuit, in a case arising in Virginia and involving a detention considerably longer than the detention here of [Mrs.] Bonkowski, reversed a verdict for the plaintiff because of the trial court's too narrow instruction on the point of justifiable detention and sent the case back, stating that "the instruction should submit the reasonableness of the detention to the jury and should set out the facts which, if found, would constitute reasonable grounds for the defendant's conduct." 199 F.2d 720, 724.

The privilege we recognize here goes beyond that set forth in the Restatement, for the Commissioners [sic] there stated a caveat that "the Institute expresses no opinion as to whether there may be circumstances under which this privilege may extend to the detention of one who has left the premises but is in their immediate vicinity." 1 Restatement (Second) of Torts page 202.

In their comment, the Commissioners [sic] state that, by their caveat, in the absence of express authority, they intended to leave the question open. 1 Restatement (Second) of Torts page 204. We think the privilege should be so extended here because we think it entirely reasonable to apply it to the circumstances of the case at bar, for the reason that a merchant may not be able to form the reasonable belief justifying a detention for a reasonable investigation before a suspected person has left the premises. In *Montgomery Ward,* supra, the court recognized the privilege as applicable even though the plaintiff was stopped by a manager after she had left the store.

On remand, on the cause for false arrest, therefore, it will be the duty of the jury to determine in accordance with the rule we have set down, whether or not the defendant's agent, Earl Reinhardt, reasonably believed the plaintiff had unlawfully taken any goods held for sale at the defendant's store. If the jury finds the defendant's agent did so reasonably believe, then it must further determine whether the investigation that followed was reasonable under all the circumstances. If the jury finds the defendant does not come within this privilege, then from the facts as discussed above, it could find a false arrest. * * *

Reversed and remanded for new trial in accordance with this opinion. The award of costs to await final determination of the cause.

[In Bonkowski v. Arlan's Department Store, 383 Mich. 90, 174 N.W.2d 765 (1970), the Supreme Court of Michigan dismissed the false imprisonment claim on the ground that there was insufficient evidence that defendant intended to take plaintiff into custody. In dictum, the court affirmed the existence of the privilege.]

NOTES AND QUESTIONS

1. Shoplifting is a major problem for merchants. It costs them, in the aggregate, hundreds of millions of dollars every year, which the public of course pays. It puts the merchant in the dilemma that, if he has the suspected person arrested he may be liable for false imprisonment if there was no theft or if a jury fails to convict, while if he does nothing, and permits the suspect to walk out, the merchandise and all hope of proof will disappear forever.

2. Although some states have adopted this privilege by case law (see Collyer v. S.H. Kress Co., 5 Cal.2d 175, 54 P.2d 20 (1936)), it is statutory in many jurisdictions. The scope of the privilege differs in the various states and it is hazardous for an attorney to advise a client about the privilege without researching the current state law. The more important variables include the following:

A. Whether force can be utilized and, if so, how much? The Restatement would allow reasonable force short of bodily harm. A "request" to stay must be made if it is practicable to do so. See Restatement (Second) of Torts § 120A, comment *k*. If the merchant is not allowed to use force, is the privilege of any real benefit?

B. What constitutes "reasonable grounds" or "probable cause" to detain a shopper and whether that issue is to be decided by the court or a jury? See Moore v. Pay'N Save Corp., 20 Wash.App. 482, 581 P.2d 159 (1978) (court uses analogous probable cause reasoning from criminal cases); Turner v. Hudson Salvage, Inc., 709 So.2d 425 (Miss.1998) (unreasonable for second employee to detain plaintiff after first employee had questioned her and determined she had not stolen shoes).

C. What constitutes a reasonable time or manner of detention? The Virginia statute specifies that the detention cannot exceed an hour. Va. Code § 18.2–105.1. Most courts would agree that defendant is liable when he demands a signed confession, and says that he will detain the plaintiff until it is signed. Moffatt v. Buffums' Inc., 21 Cal.App.2d 371, 69 P.2d 424 (1937); W.T. Grant Co. v. Owens, 149 Va. 906, 141 S.E. 860 (1928). Defendant also is liable when he threatens to detain the plaintiff until he pays. Cox v. Rhodes Avenue Hospital, 198 Ill.App. 82 (1916).

D. Whether the privilege should extend beyond the premises? Should the answer to this problem vary with the type of business in which the defendant is engaged?

E. Who is entitled to the privilege? Some states have extended the privilege beyond merchants to suppliers of services when defendant has failed to pay. See Standish v. Narragansett S.S. Co., 111 Mass. 512, 15 Am.Rep. 66 (1873) (boat ride).

3. The merchant's privilege usually does not extend to protection against an action for defamation. See Chapter 17.

Re-entry upon Real Property

4. May one use force to retake possession of real property? A minority of states permit an individual who has the legal right to immediate possession of land to attempt to retake possession by use of reasonable force short of causing death or serious injury. See Shorter v. Shelton, 183 Va. 819, 33 S.E.2d 643 (1945) (hotel manager knocked on door, put his foot in door, and pushed his way into room to remove plaintiff's possessions).

5. Most states provide the lawful owner with a quick and inexpensive remedy usually called "Forcible Entry and Detainer." This fact has led a growing number of courts to hold that the rightful owner can retake possession of his land only if he does not use force. Further, the party in peaceful possession may have a claim for assault and battery or trespass to his goods occurring in the course of a forcible entry. See Lobdell v. Keene, 85 Minn. 90, 88 N.W. 426 (1901). A claim for intentional infliction of emotional harm has been allowed when the invading owner's conduct was extreme and outrageous. See Daluiso v. Boone, 71 Cal.2d 484, 455 P.2d 811, 78 Cal.Rptr. 707 (1969) (during dispute over boundary of plaintiff's almond ranch, neighbor tore down fence that had stood for decades despite 85-year-old plaintiff's pleas to stop and resolve the matter by discussion or in court).

6. The basic policy decision inherent in these cases can be traced to a 1381 statute, 5 Richard II, c. 2, which made it a criminal offense for one entitled to possession of land to enter and recover it by force. Aside from a temporary aberration in Newton v. Harland, 1 Man. & G. 644, 133 Eng.Rep. 490 (1840), however, the English courts did not utilize the statute to allow the party in peaceful possession a civil claim against the invader. See Turner v. Meymott, 1 Bing. 158, 130 Eng.Rep. 64 (1823), and Hemmings v. Stoke Poges Golf Club, [1920] 1 K.B. 720.

6. NECESSITY

Surocco v. Geary

Supreme Court of California, 1853.
3 Cal. 69, 58 Am.Dec. 385.

MURRAY, CHIEF JUSTICE. This was an action, commenced in the court below, to recover damages for blowing up and destroying the plaintiffs' house and property, during the fire of the 24th of December, 1849.

Geary, at that time Alcalde of San Francisco, justified, on the ground that he had authority, by virtue of his office, to destroy said building, and also that it had been blown up by him to stop the progress of the conflagration then raging.

It was in proof, that the fire passed over and burned beyond the building of the plaintiffs', and that at the time said building was destroyed, they were engaged in removing their property, and could, had they not been prevented, have succeeded in removing more, if not all of their goods.

The cause was tried by the court sitting as a jury, and a verdict rendered for the plaintiffs, from which the defendant prosecutes this appeal under the Practice Act of 1850.

The only question for our consideration is, whether the person who tears down or destroys the house of another, in good faith, and under apparent necessity, during the time of a conflagration, for the purpose of saving the buildings adjacent, and stopping its progress, can be held personally liable in an action by the owner of the property destroyed. * * *

The right to destroy property, to prevent the spread of a conflagration, has been traced to the highest law of necessity, and the natural rights of man, independent of society or civil government. "It is referred by moralists and jurists to the same great principle which justifies the exclusive appropriation of a plank in a shipwreck, though the life of another be sacrificed; with the throwing overboard goods in a tempest, for the safety of a vessel; with the trespassing upon the lands of another, to escape death by an enemy. It rests upon the maxim, *Necessitas inducit privilegium quod jura privata*" [Necessity provides a privilege for private rights].

The common law adopts the principles of the natural law, and places the justification of an act otherwise tortious precisely on the same ground of necessity. [C]

This principle has been familiarly recognized by the books from the time of the saltpetre case, and the instances of tearing down houses to prevent a conflagration, or to raise bulwarks for the defense of a city, are made use of as illustrations, rather than as abstract cases, in which its exercise is permitted. At such times, the individual rights of property give way to the higher laws of impending necessity.

A house on fire, or those in its immediate vicinity, which serve to communicate the flames, becomes a nuisance, which it is lawful to abate, and the private rights of the individual yield to the considerations of general convenience, and the interests of society. Were it otherwise, one stubborn person might involve a whole city in ruin, by refusing to allow the destruction of a building which would cut off the flames and check the progress of the fire, and that, too, when it was perfectly evident that his building must be consumed. * * *

The counsel for the respondent has asked, who is to judge of the necessity of the destruction of property?

This must, in some instances, be a difficult matter to determine. The necessity of blowing up a house may not exist, or be as apparent to the owner, whose judgment is clouded by interest, and the hope of saving his property, as to others. In all such cases the conduct of the individual must be regulated by his own judgment as to the exigencies of the case. If a building should be torn down without apparent or actual necessity, the parties concerned would undoubtedly be liable in an action of trespass. But in every case the necessity must be clearly shown. It is true, many cases of hardship may grow out of this rule, and property may often in such cases be destroyed, without necessity, by irresponsible persons, but this difficulty would not be obviated by making the parties responsible in every case, whether the necessity existed or not.

The legislature of the State possess the power to regulate this subject by providing the manner in which buildings may be destroyed, and the mode in which compensation shall be made; and it is to be hoped that something will be done to obviate the difficulty, and prevent the happening of such events as those supposed by the respondent's counsel.

In the absence of any legislation on the subject, we are compelled to fall back upon the rules of the common law.

The evidence in this case clearly establishes the fact, that the blowing up of the house was necessary, as it would have been consumed had it been left standing. The plaintiffs cannot recover for the value of the goods which they might have saved; they were as much subject to the necessities of the occasion as the house in which they were situate; and if in such cases a party was held liable, it would too frequently happen, that the delay caused by the removal of the goods would render the destruction of the house useless.

The court below clearly erred as to the law applicable to the facts of this case. The testimony will not warrant a verdict against the defendant.

Judgment reversed.

NOTES AND QUESTIONS

1. Defendant is fighting a forest fire that threatens an entire county. From an airplane he sprays fire-retardant chemicals onto plaintiff's land, which damage plaintiff's timber. Is defendant liable? Cf. Stocking v. Johnson Flying Service, 143 Mont. 61, 387 P.2d 312 (1963). During floods along the Mississippi River, the town of Prairie du Rocher, Illinois blew up a levee, deliberately flooding a plain north of town to relieve pressure on another levee protecting the historic town. According to newspaper reports,

the dynamiting of the levee saved the town but ruined farmland above the town because the floodwaters carried away the rich topsoil. Could the owner of the farm recover for the loss to that property? See Lev, " 'Trap' Appears to Hold Back Flood From Town," Chicago Tribune (Aug. 5, 1993).

2. Defendant, a public officer, burns the clothing worn by a person who has died of smallpox. Is he liable to the heir, the new owner of the clothing? Cf. Seavey v. Preble, 64 Me. 120 (1874); State v. Mayor of Knoxville, 80 Tenn. 146, 47 Am.Rep. 331 (1883). Putnam v. Payne, 13 Johns. (N.Y.) 312 (1816) (shooting mad dog in the street). South Dakota Dept. of Health v. Heim, 357 N.W.2d 522 (S.D.1984) (state destroyed plaintiff's herd of elk, which were suffering from a contagious disease).

3. In December, 1941, the United States Army destroyed stored petroleum, terminal facilities, and vital parts of the plant of an oil company in Manila, in order to prevent them from falling into the hands of the advancing Japanese army. It was held that this was privileged, and not a compensable taking for public use, the theory of the majority being that it was not the Army's conduct but an act of war that was the cause of the destruction. See United States v. Caltex, Inc., 344 U.S. 149 (1952). Contra, that the Crown has no such privilege, Burmah Oil Co., Ltd. v. Lord Advocate, [1964] 2 All E.R. 348.

4. To be privileged, must the defendant be a public officer? In Harrison v. Wisdom, 54 Tenn. 99 (1872), private citizens of the town of Clarksville, Tenn., destroyed all the liquor in the town just before the entry of the Union army. It was held that the court properly charged the jury that if they found that there was imminent danger, and a real public necessity, this was privileged. To the same effect is Restatement (Second) of Torts §§ 196 and 262. Suppose it only appeared to be necessary?

5. Even if the "champion of the public" is not liable, should not the city or other community, whose interests he protects, be required to make compensation to the plaintiff? See Hall and Wigmore, Compensation for Property Destroyed to Stop the Spread of a Conflagration, 1 Ill.L.Rev. 501 (1907), written just after the San Francisco earthquake of 1906 and Wegner v. Milwaukee Mutual Ins. Co., 479 N.W.2d 38 (Minn.1991) (holding municipality liable for damage done to plaintiff's house by SWAT team using tear gas and "flash-bang" grenades to force out suspected felon who had taken refuge there). Some jurisdictions have provided for compensation by statute.

6. Constitutional provisions against taking private property for public use without due compensation do not apply to action under the police power to protect the public against the spread of contagious diseases or devastating fires and floods or other exigencies. See, e.g., Kelley v. Story County Sheriff, 611 N.W.2d 475 (Iowa 2000) (claim by owner of rental property for damage done by sheriff's office while breaking in to make an arrest was not a taking of private property under Iowa Constitution but exercise of police power for which there could be no recovery) and Customer Co. v. City of Sacramento, 10 Cal.4th 368, 895 P.2d 900, 41 Cal.Rptr.2d 658 (1995) (rejecting claim under just compensation clause of California Constitution of owner of convenience store that was substantially damaged by SWAT team attempting to flush out fugitive). The Government must show that the danger to the public was imminent and the taking was a necessity, not just a convenience. See TrinCo Inv. Co. v. United States, 722

F.3d 1375 (Fed. Cir. 2013) (landowner seeking compensation for timber lost due to Forest Service's intentionally lighting of fires to manage a group of wildfires).

Vincent v. Lake Erie Transp. Co.

Supreme Court of Minnesota, 1910.
109 Minn. 456, 124 N.W. 221.

Action by R.C. Vincent and others against the Lake Erie Transportation Company. Verdict for plaintiffs. From an order denying a new trial, defendant appeals.

O'BRIEN, J. The steamship Reynolds, owned by the defendant, was for the purpose of discharging her cargo on November 27, 1905, moored to plaintiffs' dock in Duluth. While the unloading of the boat was taking place a storm from the northeast developed, which at about 10 o'clock p.m., when the unloading was completed, had so grown in violence that the wind was then moving at 50 miles per hour and continued to increase during the night. There is some evidence that one, and perhaps two, boats were able to enter the harbor that night, but it is plain that navigation was practically suspended from the hour mentioned until the morning of the 29th, when the storm abated, and during that time no master would have been justified in attempting to navigate his vessel, if he could avoid doing so. After the discharge of the cargo the Reynolds signaled for a tug to tow her from the dock, but none could be obtained because of the severity of the storm. If the lines holding the ship to the dock had been cast off, she would doubtless have drifted away; but, instead, the lines were kept fast, and as soon as one parted or chafed it was replaced, sometimes with a larger one. The vessel lay upon the outside of the dock, her bow to the east, the wind and waves striking her starboard quarter with such force that she was constantly being lifted and thrown against the dock, resulting in its damage, as found by the jury, to the amount of $500.

We are satisfied that the character of the storm was such that it would have been highly imprudent for the master of the Reynolds to have attempted to leave the dock or to have permitted his vessel to drift away from it. * * * Nothing more was demanded of them than ordinary prudence and care, and the record in this case fully sustains the contention of the appellant that, in holding the vessel fast to the dock, those in charge of her exercised good judgment and prudent seamanship. * * *

The appellant contends by ample assignments of error that, because its conduct during the storm was rendered necessary by prudence and good seamanship under conditions over which it had no control, it cannot be held liable for any injury resulting to the property of others, and claims that the jury should have been so instructed. An analysis of the charge given by the trial court is not necessary, as in our opinion the only question for the jury was the amount of damages which the plaintiffs were entitled to recover, and no complaint is made upon that score.

The situation was one in which the ordinary rules regulating property rights were suspended by forces beyond human control, and if, without the direct intervention of some act by the one sought to be held liable, the property of another was injured, such injury must be attributed to the act of God, and not to the wrongful act of the person sought to be charged. If during the storm the Reynolds had entered the harbor, and while there had become disabled and been thrown against the plaintiffs' dock, the plaintiffs could not have recovered. Again, if while attempting to hold fast to the dock the lines had parted, without any negligence, and the vessel carried against some other boat or dock in the harbor, there would be no liability upon her owner. But here those in charge of the vessel deliberately and by their direct efforts held her in such a position that the damage to the dock resulted, and, having thus preserved the ship at the expense of the dock, it seems to us that her owners are responsible to the dock owners to the extent of the injury inflicted. * * *

In Ploof v. Putnam, 81 Vt. 471, 71 A. 188 (1908), the Supreme Court of Vermont held that where, under stress of weather, a vessel was without permission moored to a private dock at an island in Lake Champlain owned by the defendant, the plaintiff was not guilty of trespass, and that the defendant was responsible in damages because his representative upon the island unmoored the vessel, permitting it to drift upon the shore, with resultant injuries to it. If, in that case, the vessel had been permitted to remain, and the dock had suffered an injury, we believe the shipowner would have been held liable for the injury done.

Theologians hold that a starving man may, without moral guilt, take what is necessary to sustain life; but it could hardly be said that the obligation would not be upon such person to pay the value of the property so taken when he became able to do so. And so public necessity, in times of war or peace, may require the taking of private property for public purposes; but under our system of jurisprudence compensation must be made.

Let us imagine in this case that for the better mooring of the vessel those in charge of her had appropriated a valuable cable lying upon the dock. No matter how justifiable such appropriation might have been, it would not be claimed that, because of the overwhelming necessity of the situation, the owner of the cable could not recover its value.

This is not a case where life or property was menaced by any object or thing belonging to the plaintiff, the destruction of which became necessary to prevent the threatened disaster. Nor is it a case where, because of the act of God, or unavoidable accident, the infliction of the injury was beyond the control of the defendant, but is one where the defendant prudently and advisedly availed itself of the plaintiff's property for the purpose of preserving its own more valuable property, and the plaintiffs are entitled to compensation for the injury done.

Order affirmed.

[The dissenting opinion of LEWIS, J. is omitted.]

NOTES AND QUESTIONS

1. The cases all appear to be in agreement with the principal case concerning defendant's obligation to compensate plaintiff even though the

intentional entry onto land was privileged and thus not tortious. See Newcomb v. Tisdale, 62 Cal. 575 (1881); Bohlen, Incomplete Privilege to Inflict Intentional Invasions of Interests of Property and Personality, 39 Harv.L.Rev. 307 (1926); and Ripstein, Tort Law in a Liberal State, 1 J. of Tort Law, Iss. 2, Article 3 (2007) (discussing jurisprudential basis of incomplete privilege for trespass). See also Restatement (Second) of Torts, §§ 197 and 263. If defendant has not been at fault, why should he pay? Note that the court's statement about compensation for public necessity is not generally the case. Perhaps the court is referring to takings pursuant to public domain rather than emergency taking or destroying property pursuant to police powers.

2. What result in the principal case if it was necessary to moor the vessel to allow crewmen to escape onto land? See Mouse's Case, 12 Co.Rep. 63, 77 Eng.Rep. 1341 (1609) (no compensation for loss of casket that was thrown overboard to keep the Gravesend to London ferry from capsizing during a great tempest).

3. A traveler upon the public highway is normally held to be privileged to turn out to avoid an obstruction (snowdrifts, ice, washouts, rock slides, downed tree), and to pass over the abutting land. Morey v. Fitzgerald, 56 Vt. 487, 48 Am.Rep. 811 (1884); Irwin v. Yeagar, 74 Iowa 174, 37 N.W. 136 (1888). See also Dodwell v. Missouri Pac. R. Co., 384 S.W.2d 643 (Mo.1964) (boy crawling through train that blocked crossing); Ploof v. Putnam, 81 Vt. 471, 71 A. 188 (1908) (discussed in principal case).

4. Can a homeless person who moves into a vacant house use private necessity to defend against a trespass action? See London Borough of Southwark v. Williams, [1971] 1 Ch. 734, [1971] 2 All. E.R. 175 (rejecting necessity defense) and Restatement (Second) of Torts § 263 (1965) (requiring threat of serious, imminent harm). Can a protester use private necessity to defend against a trespass action? Cases, most involving criminal rather than civil trespass, consistently hold that necessity is not available to trespassers making various protests against war, use of nuclear weapons, availability of abortions, and the draft.

5. An extortioner arrives at the office of business tycoon and threatens to drop a package of explosives if not paid $1 million. Business tycoon attempts to placate him, but when the negotiations fail, the extortioner drops the package. Is the tycoon liable if he leaps behind a bystander and is thereby protected from the blast? If he pulls the bystander in front of himself? Cf. Laidlaw v. Sage, 158 N.Y. 73, 52 N.E. 679 (1899).

6. Should the necessity privilege ever extend to the taking of life? In criminal law the answer has generally been "no." Thus, in Arp v. State, 97 Ala. 5, 12 So. 301 (1893), the court affirmed the trial court's refusal to allow the defendant to be excused on the basis that two other men armed with shotguns had been present and threatened to shoot him unless he killed the deceased. On the other hand, § 2.09 of the Model Penal Code permits duress as a defense if the force or threat of force was such that a person "of reasonable firmness in his situation would be unable to resist." Which is the better approach in tort law?

7. In Regina v. Dudley, 15 Cox C.C. 624, 14 Q.B.D. 273 (1884), four survivors of a shipwreck were adrift in an open boat, a thousand miles from land, and dying of hunger. Three of them killed the fourth, a boy, and ate

him. They were held criminally liable for his death. See Simpson, Cannibalism and the Common Law (1984) for an interesting exploration of the social mores of the time and how those mores influence the law and vice versa. In United States v. Holmes, 1 Wall.Jr. 1, 26 Fed.Cas. 360 (E.D.Pa.1842), after a passenger ship had hit an iceberg and sunk, nine members of her crew and thirty-two passengers were adrift in a badly overloaded lifeboat. The wind freshened, the sea began to rise, and the boat was in imminent danger of being swamped. The crew then threw overboard six of the passengers to lighten the boat. The following morning the survivors were rescued by a passing ship. Holmes, who had taken a leading part in throwing the passengers over, was tried for manslaughter, convicted and sentenced to hard labor for a long term, which the court subsequently reduced to six months. The president later remitted the sentence. The story is told in full in Hicks, Human Jettison (1927). What if the family members of those thrown overboard had sued Holmes for wrongful death? What should be the position of tort law in these situations?

8. For an exhaustive and most stimulating discussion about the theoretical jurisprudence of many of these problems, see Fuller, The Case of the Speluncean Explorers, 62 Harv.L. Rev. 616 (1949) and Robert Cover, Justice Accused: Antislavery and the Judicial Process (Yale University Press 1984 ed.).

7. AUTHORITY OF LAW

The defense of legal authority is a subject for a course in itself. It can only be touched on here. Police officers, military personnel, prison officials, regulatory inspectors, or officials at mental health facilities may act under authority of law, engaging in conduct that otherwise would be tortious. If the defendant is duly commanded or authorized by law to do what he does, he is of course not liable for doing it. The problem is to discover how far the legal sanction extends. For example, the police are privileged to enter a home to serve an arrest warrant, but reporters accompanying them on a media ride-along are not. Wilson v. Layne, 526 U.S. 603 (1999) (because law had not been clear before decision, qualified immunity protected police officer).

Arrest

One common form of action under authority of law is arrest of the person, which consists of taking him into the custody of the law. An arrest may be made under a warrant, which is a signed order issued by a court directing that the person in question be arrested; or it may be made without a warrant.

Arrest under a warrant, or the seizure of goods under civil process, to which the same rules apply, is an act generally considered to be "ministerial," so that the officer is liable only if he acts improperly as, for example, by using excessive force. If the court issuing the warrant is entirely without jurisdiction to do it, it is commonly held that the invalid order affords the officer no protection. Warren v. Kelley, 80 Me. 512, 15 A. 49 (1888) (state court had no jurisdiction to issue attachment to enforce lien on seagoing vessel because admiralty jurisdiction is exclusive to federal court); Smith v. Hilton, 147 Ala. 642, 41 So. 747 (1906) (conversion action for bale of cotton that was seized pursuant to attachment order issued by man whose term as a justice of peace had expired). But if the court has general jurisdiction to issue similar process, it is generally held that the officer is privileged if the warrant is "fair on its face," even though there may have been errors and irregularities in its issuance that affected the jurisdiction of the court in the particular case. Vittorio v. St. Regis Paper Co., 239 N.Y. 148, 145 N.E. 913 (1924); David v. Larochelle, 296 Mass. 302, 5 N.E.2d 571 (1936). The officer does not have to investigate the propriety of a warrant that appears valid.

Even if the warrant is entirely valid, however, it does not protect the officer unless he actually carries out the order given him, even though he makes a perfectly reasonable mistake in good faith. Thus an officer who has a warrant for the arrest of A, and who reasonably believes B to be A and arrests him, is liable to B for false arrest unless he can show that he acted with due diligence to identify the person arrested. After being stopped for speeding, Robert Pierson was told that there was an outstanding warrant for the arrest of "Ronald Pierson" who sometimes went by the name "Robert." The description and birth date on the warrant matched, but the speeding driver claimed the fugitive was actually his twin brother who sometimes used his name. The officer, who had "heard that song before," arrested him anyway. Fingerprinting at the police station revealed Robert was telling the truth and he sued for false arrest. Pierson v. Multnomah Cty., 301 Or. 48, 718 P.2d 738 (1986) (jury question whether police officer had met his burden of proving due diligence).

Arrest without a warrant may be made by a police officer, or by a private citizen. The common law imposed limitations upon the authority of each, with that of the private citizen, as might be expected, more narrowly restricted. The original common law rules concerning arrest without a warrant were as follows:

1. Either an officer or a citizen may arrest without a warrant to prevent a felony, or a breach of the peace (public offense done by violence or likely to cause an immediate disturbance of public order) that is being committed or reasonably appears about to be committed, in his presence.

2. An officer may make an arrest if he has information that affords reasonable grounds for thinking that a felony has been committed and that he has the right person. The citizen may arrest without a warrant if a felony has in fact been committed, and he has reasonable grounds to suspect the person arrested; but his authority depends upon the fact of the crime, and he must take the full risk if none has been committed.

3. For a past breach of the peace that is not a felony, an officer or a citizen may arrest without a warrant only if the offense was committed in his presence and he is in fresh pursuit.

4. For mere misdemeanors the old common law rule was that neither the officer nor the citizen could arrest without a warrant. This has now been modified in some jurisdictions to extend the power to arrest to an officer when the misdemeanor is committed in his presence.

5. Even if an arrest would be lawful, an officer may be subject to liability if he uses excessive force in the process of apprehending the suspect. Most of the cases focus on this issue.

The common law rules have been modified by statute in many jurisdictions.

8. DISCIPLINE

Parent and Child. There are a number of relationships in which the necessity of some orderly discipline gives persons who have the control of others the privilege of exercising reasonable force and restraint upon them. One of the most important examples of this privilege is that given to a parent or one who is deemed to stand in place of a parent. See Clasen v. Pruhs, 69 Neb. 278, 95 N.W. 640 (1903) (six-year-old child sent from Germany to Nebraska to live with maternal aunt; aunt claimed discipline privilege in suit brought by child claiming aunt had whipped her); Fortinberry v. Holmes, 89 Miss. 373, 42 So. 799 (1907) (one caring for a child "who was to be taken and treated as one of the children of the family"). The scope of the privilege was rarely tested for many years because parents were held to be immune from suits by their children. Interestingly enough, this very immunity was first recognized in a case where a court may have been unwilling to delineate the scope of the privilege. See Hewellette v. George, 68 Miss. 703, 9 So. 885 (1891) (claim of false imprisonment based on parent's confining daughter to mental institution). The Restatement suggests several factors to use to determine whether the conduct was within the privilege of discipline or falls outside of it: age, sex, and condition of child; nature of the child's offense and the apparent motive for it; influence of child's conduct as example on other children in same family; whether force or confinement is reasonably necessary and appropriate to compel obedience; whether it is disproportionate to the offense, unnecessarily degrading, or likely to cause serious or permanent harm. Restatement (Second) of Torts § 150 (1965).

Generally, the privilege of parents to discipline their children also covers those who are temporarily responsible for them. This may include other family members, teenage babysitters, adult daycare providers, housekeepers, piano teachers, school bus drivers, and others. The amount of force that is acceptable may be less than what would be acceptable for a parent to use. Restatement (Second) of Torts § 150(a).

While some early decisions stated that a parent delegates his authority to discipline his child to a teacher when the youngster is in school, the teacher's privilege to discipline is more properly predicated on the need to maintain reasonable order in the classroom and other school facilities. See LaFrentz v. Gallagher, 105 Ariz. 255, 462 P.2d 804 (1969) (swearing at umpire during P.E. class); Suits v. Glover, 260 Ala. 449, 71 So.2d 49 (1954) (scuffling in school hallway). Thus discipline may be exercised even though the parent objects. Most litigation has concerned the scope of the privilege.

First, there is some uncertainty as to whether it extends to activities conducted away from school that have only a slight connection with the educational program. Second, an instructor will be subject to liability for using "excessive" force. See Johnson v. Horace Mann Mut. Ins. Co., 241 So.2d 588 (La.App.1970). Significant variables gleaned from the cases include (1) the nature of the punishment, (2) the conduct of the student, (3) the age and physical condition of the student, and (4) the motive of the instructor, e.g., did he act in anger or out of dislike, rather than in an attempt to discipline. See Story v. Martin, 217 So.2d 758 (La.App.1969); Tinkham v. Kole, 252 Iowa 1303, 110 N.W.2d 258 (1961). Finally, most school systems today tightly regulate the use of corporal punishment, so most of the litigation in this area involves interpretation of specific state statutes or school board regulations rather than the common law. See, for example, Rinehart v. Board of Education, 87 Ohio App.3d 214, 621 N.E.2d 1365 (1993).

Corporal punishment has been held not to violate the due process clause or the Eighth Amendment privilege against cruel and unusual punishment. Ingraham v. Wright, 430 U.S. 651 (1977) (child's liberty interest is subject to historical limitations expressed in the common law privilege).

Others. Other examples of the privilege of discipline are those of military and naval officers over their subordinates, which are largely governed by military law and dealt with by courts martial; and the authority of the master of a ship over both the crew and the passengers. Again the privilege, in the latter case, is limited to force reasonable under the circumstances; and the captain will be liable if he puts a passenger in irons for calling him the landlord of a floating hotel. King v. Franklin, 1 F. & F. 360, 175 Eng.Rep. 764 (1858).

9. JUSTIFICATION

Sindle v. New York City Transit Authority

New York Court of Appeals, 1973.
33 N.Y.2d 293, 307 N.E.2d 245, 352 N.Y.S.2d 183.

JASEN, JUDGE. At about noon on June 20, 1967, the plaintiff, then 14 years of age, boarded a school bus owned by the defendant, New York City Transit Authority, and driven by its employee, the defendant Mooney. It was the last day of the term at the Elias Bernstein Junior High School in Staten Island and the 65 to 70 students on board the bus were in a boisterous and exuberant mood. Some of this spirit expressed itself in vandalism, a number of students breaking dome lights, windows, ceiling panels and advertising poster frames. There is no evidence that the plaintiff partook in this destruction.

The bus made several stops at appointed stations. On at least one occasion, the driver admonished the students about excessive noise and damage to the bus. When he reached the Annadale station, the driver discharged several more passengers, went to the rear of the bus, inspected the damage and advised the [remaining] students that he was taking them to the St. George police station.

The driver closed the doors of the bus and proceeded, bypassing several normal stops. * * *

The plaintiff, joined with his father, then commenced an action to recover damages for * * * false imprisonment. * * * At the close of the plaintiffs' case, the court denied defendants' motion to amend their answers to plead the defense of justification. The court also excluded all evidence bearing on the justification issue.

We believe that it was an abuse of discretion for the trial court to deny the motion to amend and to exclude the evidence of justification. It was the defendants' burden to prove justification—a defense that a plaintiff in an action for false imprisonment should be prepared to meet—and the plaintiffs could not have been prejudiced by the granting of the motion to amend. The trial court's rulings precluded the defendants from introducing any evidence in this regard and were manifestly unfair. Accordingly, the order of the Appellate Division must be reversed and a new trial granted.

In view of our determination, it would be well to outline some of the considerations relevant to the issue of justification. In this regard, we note that, generally, restraint or detention, reasonable under the circumstances and in time and manner, imposed for the purpose of preventing another from inflicting personal injuries or interfering with or damaging real or personal property in one's lawful possession or custody is not unlawful. (Cf. Penal Law, §§ 35.20, 35.25; see, also, General Business Law, § 218, which affords a retail merchant a defense to an action for false arrest and false imprisonment where a suspected shoplifter is reasonably detained for investigation or questioning.) Also, a parent, guardian or teacher entrusted with the care or supervision of a child may use physical force reasonably necessary to maintain discipline or promote the welfare of the child. (Penal Law, § 35.10.)

Similarly, a school bus driver, entrusted with the care of his student-passengers and the custody of public property, has the duty to take reasonable measures for the safety and protection of both—the passengers and the property. In this regard, the reasonableness of his actions—as bearing on the defense of justification—is to be determined from a consideration of all the circumstances. At a minimum, this would seem to import, a consideration of the need to protect the persons and property in his charge, the duty to aid the investigation and apprehension of those inflicting damage, the manner and place of the occurrence, and the feasibility and practicality of other alternative courses of action. * * *

For the reasons stated, the order of the Appellate Division should be reversed and the case remitted for a new trial.

NOTES AND QUESTIONS

1. What privileges did the court rely on "by analogy"? Are there others—not mentioned by the court—that might be relevant?

2. Can you think of other examples of conduct that might "justify" an apparent intentional tort although they do not fit within the traditional common law privileges discussed in this chapter? In Peterson v. Sorlien, 299 N.W.2d 123 (Minn.1980), cert. denied, 450 U.S. 1031 (1981), the Supreme Court of Minnesota held that the parent-child relationship justified limitations the defendant parents placed upon their adult child's

mobility during "deprogramming" that would otherwise support a judgment of false imprisonment. See LeMoult, Deprogramming Members of Religious Sects, 46 Fordham L.Rev. 599, 635 (1978).

CHAPTER 4

NEGLIGENCE

1. HISTORY

Negligence was scarcely recognized as a separate tort before the early part of the nineteenth century. Prior to that time, the word had been used in a very general sense to describe the breach of any legal obligation, or to designate a mental element, usually one of inadvertence or inattention or indifference, entering into the commission of other torts. As a result, some writers once maintained that negligence was merely one way of committing any tort, just as some courts, for example, spoke occasionally of a "negligent battery," meaning a negligent touching that was harmful or offensive.

One of the earliest appearances of what we now know as the tort of negligence was in the liability of those who professed to be competent in certain "public" callings. A common carrier, an innkeeper, a blacksmith, or a surgeon was regarded as holding himself out to the public as one in whom confidence might be reposed, and hence as assuming an obligation to give proper service, for the breach of which, by any negligent conduct, he might be liable. But in other fields such as trespass and nuisance the idea developed, thinly disguised, that there might be liability for negligence; and in later years the action on the case produced a large, undigested group of situations in which negligence was the essence of the tort.

Somewhere around the year 1825, negligence began to emerge out of the action on the case, and to be recognized as a separate basis of tort liability, independent of other causes of action. Its rise coincided to a marked degree with the Industrial Revolution in England. "It was probably stimulated a good deal by the enormous increase of industrial machinery in general and by the invention of railways in particular. At that time railway trains were notable neither for speed nor for safety. They killed any object from a Minister of State to a wandering cow, and this naturally reacted upon the law." P. Winfield, Law of Tort 404 (5th ed. 1950).

The separate recognition of negligence was undoubtedly greatly encouraged by the disintegration of the old forms of action, and the disappearance of the distinction between direct and indirect injuries, found in trespass and case. Intentional injuries, whether direct or indirect, began to be grouped as a distinct field of liability, and negligence took separate form as the basis for unintended torts. Today, it is widely recognized that distinct problems and principles, as well as distinct questions of policy, arise in negligence cases.

For more on the history of negligence in early law, and its development as an independent tort, see Winfield, The History of Negligence in the Law of Torts, 42 L.Q.Rev. 184 (1926); Wigmore, Responsibility for Tortious Acts: Its History, 7 Harv.L.Rev. 315, 441, 453 (1894); and Langbein, Lerner, and Smith, History of the Common

Law: The Development of Anglo-American Institutions (Walters Kluwer 2009).

For a view from the trenches, see Kelley & Wendt, What Judges Tell Juries about Negligence: A Review of Pattern Jury Instructions, 77 Chi-Kent L.Rev. 587 (2002) (collecting and discussing pattern jury instructions on various negligence issues from all states).

2. ELEMENTS OF CAUSE OF ACTION

"Negligent" is the word often used to describe the conduct of the person being evaluated. But a cause of action for negligence requires more than negligent conduct. The traditional formula for the elements necessary to the cause of action includes the following:

1. A **duty** to use reasonable care. This is an obligation recognized by the law, requiring the actor to conform to a certain standard of conduct, for the protection of others against unreasonable risks.

2. A failure to conform to the required standard. This is commonly called **breach** of the duty. These two elements make up what the courts refer to as negligent behavior; but the term frequently is applied to the second alone. Thus it may be said that the defendant was negligent (acted unreasonably), but is not liable because he was under no duty to the plaintiff to use reasonable care. Whether a duty is owed is a question of law for the court to decide. Whether the duty was breached is usually a question for the jury. See Cabral v. Ralphs Grocery Co., 51 Cal.4th 764, 122 Cal.Rptr.3d 313, 248 P.3d 1170, 1175 (2011) ("we preserve the crucial distinction between a determination that the defendant owed the plaintiff no duty of ordinary care, which is for the *court* to make, and a determination that the defendant did not breach the duty of ordinary care, which in a jury trial is for the *jury* to make"). The judge, of course, can always determine (as he did in the next principal case) that no reasonable jury could find that the duty was breached under those circumstances.

3. A reasonably close causal connection between the conduct and the resulting injury. This is commonly called **causation**. Causation involves a combination of two elements—causation in fact and legal or "proximate" causation. They receive separate treatment in Chapters 5 and 6.

4. Actual loss or **damage** resulting to the interests of another. The action for negligence developed chiefly out of the old form of action on the case; and it retained the rule of that action that pleading and proof of damage was an essential part of the plaintiff's case. Nominal damages to vindicate a technical right cannot be recovered in a negligence action if no actual damage has occurred. See, for example, Right v. Breen, 277 Conn. 364, 890 A.2d 1287 (2006) (reiterating common law rule allowing recovery only upon proof of causation and actual damages where plaintiff's right was negligently—rather than intentionally—invaded). If defendant's risk-creating negligent conduct threatens but does not harm plaintiff, however, he may be able to obtain an injunction and stop the activity as a "nuisance." While the modern law of torts has retained the requirement that proof of damage is an essential part of the law of negligence, the question of what

constitutes damage is less certain than it once was. Has the plaintiff suffered damage if the wrongful act causes her to fear that she will develop a disease in the future or reduces her chance of surviving a disease? See Chapter 10, Damages.

Although the negligence formula is useful in segregating and drawing attention to the elements of the cause of action the courts require, it is misleading to view the elements as discrete. None of the elements can really be defined except by reference to the others or as always containing within each element the same concepts. Professor David Owen has counted about 30 states that divide up the elements into the four above and about 20 that organize them into a three-element construct of duty, breach, and injury proximately caused by breach. Professor Owen argues that the more precise way to conceptualize the elements is to divide into five categories, with cause in fact and proximate cause listed separately. Owen, The Five Elements of Negligence, 35 Hofstra L. Rev. 1671 (2007).

Another commonly used rubric for negligence is conduct that falls below the standard of care established by law for the protection of others against the unreasonable risk of harm.

Most of the cases in this chapter involve the allegedly negligent conduct of the defendant from whom the plaintiff is seeking compensatory damages. Sometimes, however, it is the *plaintiff's* conduct that is being measured against the standard of the reasonable person because the defendant has pled the affirmative defense of contributory negligence: the defendant is claiming the plaintiff's conduct was negligent and that the plaintiff's negligent conduct also contributed to the cause of plaintiff's injuries. Chapter 12, Defenses, will explore this affirmative defense in detail. For now, keep in mind that the standard—reasonable care under the circumstances—applies to all parties, whether they are plaintiffs or defendants in a particular case.

3. A NEGLIGENCE FORMULA

Lubitz v. Wells

Superior Court of Connecticut, 1955.
19 Conn.Sup. 322, 113 A.2d 147.

TROLAND, JUDGE. The complaint alleges that James Wells was the owner of a golf club and that he left it for some time lying on the ground in the backyard of his home. That thereafter his son, the defendant James Wells, Jr., aged eleven years, while playing in the yard with the plaintiff, Judith Lubitz, aged nine years, picked up the golf club and proceeded to swing at a stone lying on the ground. In swinging the golf club, James Wells, Jr., caused the club to strike the plaintiff about the jaw and chin.

Negligence alleged against the young Wells boy is that he failed to warn his little playmate of his intention to swing the club and that he did swing the club when he knew she was in a position of danger.

In an attempt to hold the boy's father, James Wells, liable for his son's action, it is alleged that James Wells was negligent because although he knew the golf club was on the ground in his backyard and that his children would play with it, and that although he knew or "should have known" that the negligent use of the golf club by children would cause injury to a child, he neglected to remove the golf club from the backyard or to caution James Wells, Jr., against the use of the same.

The demurrer challenges the sufficiency of the allegations of the complaint to state a cause of action or to support a judgment against the father, James Wells.

It would hardly be good sense to hold that this golf club is so obviously and intrinsically dangerous that it is negligence to leave it lying on the ground in the yard. The father cannot be held liable on the allegations of this complaint. [Cc]

The demurrer is sustained.

NOTES AND QUESTIONS

1. Why might the boy be found negligent if the father was not?

2. Is a householder negligent for leaving in his backyard an object such as a baseball bat or a hose with a nozzle, which one child might pick up and swing at another? What if the object had been a hoe? A pitchfork? A loaded shotgun?

3. What result in the principal case if plaintiff had tripped over the golf club? Cf. Johnson v. Krueger, 36 Colo.App. 242, 539 P.2d 1296 (1975).

4. A twelve-year-old boy lost his eye from a pellet from a slingshot fired by his eleven-year-old playmate. Was it negligence to provide the slingshot to the boy by selling it to him? See Moning v. Alfono, 400 Mich. 425, 254 N.W.2d 759 (1977).

5. Defendant parks his car on the edge of a city street without a curb, in front of a house where a mother and a 13-month old toddler are sitting on a front porch, about 16 feet away. Defendant goes across the street to visit a friend there. He comes back in 5 minutes, gets in the car and drives off. There is a bump that he thought was a paving stone, but that turned out to be the toddler who had crawled under the car. Was he negligent? Should he have checked under his car before pulling away from the curb? Williams v. Jordan, 208 Tenn. 456, 346 S.W.2d 583 (1961).

Blyth v. Birmingham Waterworks Co.

Court of Exchequer, 1856.
11 Exch. 781, 156 Eng.Rep. 1047.

[Defendants had installed water mains in the street, with fire plugs at various points. The plug opposite the plaintiff's house sprung a leak during a severe frost, because the connection between the plug and the water main was forced out by the expansion of freezing water. As a result, a large quantity of water escaped through the earth and into plaintiff's house, causing damage. The apparatus had been laid down 25 years ago, and had worked well during that time. The trial court left the question of defendant's negligence to the jury, which returned a verdict for plaintiff. Judgment was entered on the verdict, and defendant appealed.]

ALDERSON, B. I am of opinion that there was no evidence to be left to the jury. The case turns upon the question, whether the facts proved show that the defendants were guilty of negligence. Negligence is the omission to do something which a reasonable man, guided upon those considerations which ordinarily regulate the conduct of human affairs, would do or doing something which a prudent and reasonable man would not do. The defendants might have been liable for negligence, if unintentionally, they omitted to do that which a reasonable person would have done, or did that which a person taking reasonable precautions would not have done. A reasonable man would act with reference to the average circumstances of the temperature in ordinary years. The defendants had provided against such frosts as experience would have led men, acting prudently, to provide against; and they are not guilty of negligence, because their precautions proved insufficient against the effects of the extreme severity of the frost of 1855, which penetrated to a greater depth than any which ordinarily occurs south of the polar regions. Such a state of circumstances constitutes a contingency against which no reasonable man can provide. The result was an accident for which the defendants cannot be held liable.

Verdict to be entered for the defendants.

[The concurring opinions of MARTIN, B., and BRAMWELL, B., are omitted.]

NOTES AND QUESTIONS

1. In 1951, plaintiff's goods, in freight cars in the yards of defendant railroad company at Topeka, were destroyed by a flood that swept over the yards. There never had been any prior flood that had come anywhere near the yards; and when defendant first learned that the water was likely to reach them, it was too late to move the cars. Is defendant negligent in not moving them sooner? Ismert-Hincke Milling Co. v. Union Pacific R. Co., 238 F.2d 14 (10th Cir.1956) (applying Kansas law) (flood was much more severe and came much sooner than was anticipated by anyone due to unheard of torrential rains that fell without advance notice in the watershed). During Hurricane Katrina, a casino barge floated free of its moorings and traveled roughly one mile, finally alliding with and coming to rest on top of the Biloxi Beachfront Hotel. Eli Investments, LLC v. Silver Slipper Casino Venture, LLC, 118 So.3d 151 (Miss. 2013) (expert testified that storm surge caused by Hurricane Katrina was foreseeable in light of prior storm history in the Gulf of Mexico).

2. Is a contractor building a skyscraper in Chicago required to take precautions against an earthquake? In San Francisco?

3. Could it be negligence to fail to take precautions against a stroke of lightning near an oil storage tank? Tex-Jersey Oil Corp. v. Beck, 292 S.W.2d 803 (Tex.Civ.App.1956). On a golf course? Compare Hames v. State of Tennessee, 808 S.W.2d 41 (Tenn.1991) with Maussner v. Atlantic City Country Club, Inc., 299 N.J.Super. 535, 691 A.2d 826 (1997). What else would you like to know before deciding this?

4. To refill the gasoline tank on a tractor, a farm worker was removing the bunghole cap from a drum used to distribute gasoline when a spark caused by the damaged threads (from repeated hammering on it during its nine-year life) caused flames to burst from it. In the negligence action against the company that owned the drum and distributed the gasoline, witnesses claimed that "no such happening had ever before been heard of by them" and thus the owner should not be liable for failing to anticipate the danger. Gulf Refining v. Williams, 183 Miss. 723, 185 So. 234 (1938) (affirming jury verdict for the plaintiff because the defendants knew (or should have known) of the condition of the bunghole cap and that such condition gave rise to a risk of harm even if they were not aware of incidents where the exact risk had manifested itself).

Pipher v. Parsell

Supreme Court of Delaware, 2007.
930 A.2d 890.

HOLLAND, JUSTICE. The plaintiff-appellant, Kristyn Pipher ("Pipher"), appeals from the Superior Court's judgment as a matter of law in favor of the defendant-appellee, Johnathan Parsell ("Parsell"). Pipher argues that the Superior Court erred when it ruled that, as a matter of law, Parsell was not negligent. We agree and hold that the issue of Parsell's negligence should have been submitted to the jury.

Facts

On March 20, 2002, around 6 p.m., Pipher, Parsell and Johnene Beisel ("Beisel"), also a defendant,[3] were traveling south on Delaware Route 1 near Lewes, Delaware, in Parsell's pickup truck. All three were sitting on the front seat. Parsell was driving, Pipher was sitting in the middle, and Beisel was in the passenger seat next to the door. They were all sixteen-years-old at the time.

As they were traveling at 55 mph, Beisel unexpectedly "grabbed the steering wheel causing the truck to veer off onto the shoulder of the road." Parsell testified that Beisel's conduct caused him both shock and surprise. Although Beisel's conduct prompted him to be on his guard, Parsell further testified that he did not expect Beisel to grab the wheel again. Nevertheless, his recognition of how serious Beisel's conduct was, shows he was aware that he now had someone in his car who had engaged in dangerous behavior.

Parsell testified that he did nothing in response to Beisel's initial action. Approximately thirty seconds later, Beisel again yanked the steering wheel, causing Parsell's truck to leave the roadway, slide down an embankment and strike a tree. Pipher was injured as a result of the collision.

Pipher's testimony at trial was for the most part consistent with Parsell's testimony. Pipher recalled that the three occupants in the vehicle were talking back and forth and that the mood was light as they drove south on Route 1. She also testified that after Beisel yanked the

[3] Pipher was awarded $70,150.00 in damages against Beisel. However, Beisel was not located before, during, or after trial.

steering wheel for the first time, Parsell was able to regain control of the truck. According to Pipher, despite the dangerous nature of the conduct, Parsell and Beisel just laughed about it like it was a joke. Pipher testified she felt that Beisel grabbed the steering wheel a second time because Parsell "laughed it off" the first time.

At trial, Parsell acknowledged that he could have taken different steps to try to prevent Beisel from grabbing the steering wheel a second time. First, Parsell acknowledged, he could have admonished Beisel not to touch the steering wheel again. Second, he acknowledged that he could have pulled over to the side of the road and required Beisel to get into the back seat. Third, Parsell acknowledged that he could have warned Beisel that he would put her out of the vehicle.

The trial judge concluded that, as a matter of law, Parsell had no duty to do anything after Beisel yanked the wheel the first time because it would be reasonable for the driver to assume that it would not happen again. The trial judge also ruled that (1) there was no negligence in failing to discharge the dangerous passenger and (2) that failing to admonish the dangerous passenger was not negligence. * * *

Duty of Driver

A "driver owes a duty of care to her [or his] passengers because it is foreseeable that they may be injured if, through inattention or otherwise, the driver involves the car she [or he] is operating in a collision." [C] Almost forty-five years ago, this Court held that a minor who operates a motor vehicle on the highways of Delaware will be held to the same standard of care and "must accord his [or her] own passengers the same diligence and protection which is required of an adult motorist under similar circumstances." * * *

Pipher argues that after Beisel grabbed the steering wheel initially, Parsell was on notice that a dangerous situation could reoccur in the truck. Pipher further argues that once Parsell had notice of a possibly dangerous situation, he had a duty to exercise reasonable care to protect his passengers from that harm. Finally, Pipher concludes that Parsell was negligent when he kept driving without attempting to remove, or at least address, that risk.

In a similar case, the Supreme Court of Vermont held a driver was liable for damages resulting from the passenger seizing the driver's arm. [C] In that case, a drunken passenger known for being a "playful fellow," and having previously attempted to shake hands with the driver of the vehicle over the course of fifteen minutes, then seized the arm of the driver, causing the vehicle to collide with a farm wagon. The Vermont Court held that the knowledge the passenger was "a playful fellow" and had in the course of the ride "persisted in trying to shake hands" with the driver "should have forecast the peril of an accident to an operator of reasonable prudence and vigilance." [Cc] In such cases, the driver is expected to make a reasonable attempt to prevent the passenger from taking such actions again.

In general, where the actions of a passenger that cause an accident are not foreseeable, there is no negligence attributable to the driver. [C] But, when actions of a passenger that interfere with the driver's safe operation of the motor vehicle are foreseeable, the failure to prevent such conduct may be a breach of the driver's duty to either other passengers or to the public. [Cc] Under the circumstances of this case, a reasonable jury could find that Parsell breached his duty to protect Pipher from Beisel by preventing Beisel from grabbing the steering wheel a second time.

Conclusion

The issue of Parsell's alleged breach of duty to Pipher, the foreseeability of Beisel's repeat conduct, and the proximate cause of Pipher's injuries were all factual determinations that should have been submitted to the jury. [C] Accordingly, the judgment of the Superior Court, that was entered as a matter of law, is reversed. This matter is remanded for further proceedings in accordance with this opinion.

NOTES AND QUESTIONS

1. Note that the passenger who grabbed the wheel also was a defendant in the case. What would the cause of action against her have been?

2. Why does the Delaware Supreme Court refer to a Vermont case?

3. Do you think the Delaware Supreme Court would have ruled that the case should have gone to the jury if the accident had occurred the first time the passenger grabbed the wheel?

4. The court's ruling suggests that the sixteen-year-old driver had 30 seconds (between the first and second grabs) to do something to prevent the passenger from grabbing the wheel the second time. Should the driver's age and inexperience be taken into account in evaluating his response? This issue will be explored in the next section, at page 172.

5. In Tullgren v. Amoskeag Mfg. Co., 82 N.H. 268, 133 A. 4 (1926), defendant escorted an employee with a "sick headache" home and left her to walk about 700 feet over a difficult road. On reaching her home she died. On motion for rehearing after reversing a directed verdict for defendant, the court said in part: "Danger consists in the risk of harm, as well as the likelihood of it, and a danger calling for anticipation need not be of more probable occurrence than less. If there is some probability of harm sufficiently serious that ordinary men would take precautions to avoid it, then failure to do so is negligence. That the danger will more probably than otherwise not be encountered on a particular occasion does not dispense with the exercise of care. One who crosses a railroad track may not reasonably anticipate that a train will in fact be met but, by reason of the risk that one may be, he is called upon to do what is reasonably required to find out. In going around a sharp turn on a highway, where the view is obstructed, a driver may be careless toward opposite travel in speed or other ways, though the probabilities may be against meeting any one. If the chance is so great that ordinary men would drive differently, then it is careless not to do so. * * * The test is not of the balance of probabilities, but of the existence of some probability of sufficient moment to induce action to avoid it on the part of a reasonable mind."

6. Could there be an unreasonable risk of harm in mislabeling a bottle of water as "kerosene"? In Pease v. Sinclair Refining Co., 104 F.2d 183 (2d Cir.1939), plaintiff, a high school science teacher, wrote to

defendant requesting an advertised free "science exhibit," consisting of bottles of petroleum products. Defendant sent him the exhibit and plaintiff, in preparation for an experiment, poured what was labeled "kerosene" onto metallic sodium to preserve it. Unfortunately, the bottle actually contained water, which caused an explosion seriously injuring the teacher. Do you see how the circumstances can make a difference?

7. The toilet in a railway coach car was heated by steam passing through an uninsulated iron pipe that went around the corner under the wash basin and a water cooler. Plaintiff, a passenger, fainted and fell with her face against the pipe, seriously burning it. Is the railroad negligent? Hauser v. Chicago, Rhode Island & Pacific Ry., 205 Iowa 940, 219 N.W. 60 (1928) (not unreasonable to fail to insulate pipe that ran underneath the wash basin and water cooler).

8. Bartender allowed an Akita (large dog that stood three feet high) to remain in the bar. Dog bit one of the customers in the face. Negligence? Rowland v. Log Cabin, Inc., 2003 S.D. 20, 658 N.W.2d 76 (2003) ("Whether a reasonable person would have realized that a large, unknown dog roaming free in a small bar with drunken patrons involved an unreasonable risk of harm is a question for a jury.")

9. Is it unreasonable conduct to send someone a text message if you know they are driving and will view the text while driving? Kubert v. Best, 432 N.J.Super. 495, 75 A.3d 1214 (App. 2013) ("We conclude that a person sending text messages has a duty not to text someone who is driving if the texter knows, or has special reason to know, the recipient will view the text while driving.")

Chicago, B. & Q.R. Co. v. Krayenbuhl

Supreme Court of Nebraska, 1902.
65 Neb. 889, 91 N.W. 880.

[Action to recover for personal injuries sustained by plaintiff, a child four years old, in playing on a railroad turntable maintained by defendant. The trial resulted in a verdict and judgment for plaintiff, and defendant brings error.

The turntable was located between two branches of defendant's line. A path or footway, in common use by the general public and by plaintiff's family, passed within about 70 feet of the turntable. The turntable had a movable bolt by which it could be held in position and was provided with a padlock. The defendant's rules required its employees to keep the turntable locked when not in use, but there was evidence that this rule was frequently disregarded and that one of the staples was so loose that the turntable could be unfastened without difficulty. Plaintiff, in company with other young children, found the turntable unlocked and unguarded. Plaintiff got on the turntable, and when the other children set it in motion, plaintiff's foot was caught between the rails and severed at the ankle joint.

The court first held that the fact that the children were trespassers on the defendant's property did not deprive them of the right to enforce defendant's duty to use reasonable care to make its premises safe. As to this, see Chapter 9, Owners and Occupiers of Land.]

ALBERT, C. * * * It is true, as said in Loomis v. Terry, 17 Wend. 496, 31 Am.Dec. 306, "the business of life must go forward"; the means by which it is carried forward cannot be rendered absolutely safe. * * * The business of life is better carried forward by the use of dangerous machinery; hence the public good demands its use, although occasionally such use results in the loss of life or limb. It does so because the danger is insignificant, when weighed against the benefits resulting from the use of such machinery and for the same reason demands its reasonable, most effective, and unrestricted use, up to the point where the benefits resulting from such use no longer outweigh the danger to be anticipated from it. At that point the public good demands restrictions. For example, a turntable is a dangerous contrivance, which facilitates railroading; the general benefits resulting from its use outweigh the occasional injuries inflicted by it; hence the public good demands its use. We may conceive of means by which it might be rendered absolutely safe, but such means would so interfere with its beneficial use that the danger to be anticipated would not justify their adoption; therefore the public good demands its use without them. But the danger incident to its use may be lessened by the use of a lock which would prevent children, attracted to it, from moving it; the interference with the proper use of the turntable occasioned by the use of such lock is so slight that it is outweighed by the danger to be anticipated from an omission to use it; therefore the public good, we think demands the use of the lock. The public good would not require the owner of a vacant lot on which there is a pond to fill up the pond or inclose the lot with an impassable wall to insure the safety of children resorting to it, because the burden of doing so is out of proportion to the danger to be anticipated from leaving it undone. [C] But where there is an open well on a vacant lot, which is frequented by children, of which the owner of the lot has knowledge, he is liable for injuries sustained by children falling into the well, because the danger to be anticipated from the open well, under the circumstances, outweighs the slight expense or inconvenience that would be entailed in making it safe. * * *

Hence, in all cases of this kind in the determination of the question of negligence, regard must be had to the character and location of the premises, the purpose for which they are used, the probability of injury therefrom, the precautions necessary to prevent such injury, and the relations such precautions bear to the beneficial use of the premises. The nature of the precautions would depend on the particular facts in each case. In some cases a warning to the children or the parents might be sufficient; in others, more active measures might be required. But in every case they should be such as a man of ordinary care and prudence would observe under like circumstances. If, under all the circumstances, the owner omits such precautions as a man of ordinary care and prudence, under like circumstances, would observe, he is guilty of negligence. * * *

[The judgment was reversed for error in instructions to the jury amounting to improper comment on the evidence.]

NOTES AND QUESTIONS

1. There are risks associated with the operation of trains, airplanes, automobiles, snowmobiles. How does the jury decide whether the risk is an unreasonable one (negligent) or not? In addition to the factors discussed by the court in the principal case, note that the court mentions that the defendant had an internal policy or rule that the turntable be kept locked when it was not in use. Such a policy can be used as evidence of what the standard of care should be, but it is not determinative of the issue. See, for example, Morgan v. Scott, 291 S.W.3d 622 (Ky. 2009) (adopting and then failing to follow its own in-house rule that a salesperson accompany a prospective buyer on a test drive does not impose a duty to do so on car dealership) and Jenkins v. Jordan Valley Water Conservancy Dist., 2013 UT 59, 321 P.3d 1049, 1051 (2013) (internal determination that a pipeline should be replaced does not establish a tort law duty to do so because internal decisions may be made for any number of reasons—convenience, caution, maximization of budget, mistake—having little to do with the standard of care).

2. Defendant, excavating in the highway, set out an open flare pot at night to give warning of the excavation. It left the flare pot until 10:00 a.m. in a street in which it knew that children were accustomed to play. A child meddled with the flare pot and was seriously burned. Should defendant be liable? Why? Would it make a difference if the child was injured at 10:00 a.m. or 10:00 p.m.? Ott v. Washington Gas Light Co., 205 F.Supp. 815 (D.D.C.1962), aff'd, 317 F.2d 138 (D.C.Cir.1963).

Davison v. Snohomish County

Supreme Court of Washington, 1928.
149 Wash. 109, 270 P. 422.

BEALS, J. Plaintiffs instituted this action against Snohomish county as defendant, seeking to recover damages alleged to have been suffered by them as the result of negligence of defendant in the construction and maintenance of the elevated approach to a bridge known as the Bascule bridge across Ebey slough. In the southwesterly approach to this bridge there is a right angle turn towards the south just easterly of the slough, and at this point the causeway or approach to the bridge is at quite an elevation above the ground level. The bridge itself is approximately 18 feet wide; the approach leading to the bridge proper at the curve just to the east of the bridge increases in width to a maximum of 30.9 feet, narrowing again to 18 feet at the end of the turn.

At about 8 o'clock in the evening of November 11, 1926, plaintiffs were driving their Ford automobile toward the city of Snohomish, and proceeded to cross the bridge from the west to east at a low rate of speed. Plaintiff Edwin F. Davison was driving, and, as the car rounded the curve to the east of the slough, he lost control, the car skidded, struck the railing on the east or outer edge of the approach just around the curve, broke through the railing, and, with plaintiffs, fell to the ground. Both plaintiffs suffered severe and painful injuries, and the automobile was wrecked; for all of which damage plaintiffs prayed for judgment in a large amount.

Defendant answered plaintiffs' complaint, denying all the allegations of negligence on its part and affirmatively pleading contributory negligence on the part of plaintiffs. The action came on regularly for trial, and resulted in a verdict in plaintiffs' favor in the sum of $2,500. Defendant seasonably moved for judgment in its favor notwithstanding the verdict, or, in the alternative, for a new trial. Both of these motions were denied by the trial court, which thereupon entered judgment upon the verdict, from which judgment defendant appeals. * * *

[Respondents contended that the bridge was unsafe because of] the insufficiency of the railing or guard to prevent respondents' automobile from skidding off the approach * * *.

The use of the automobile as a means of transportation of passengers and freight has, during recent years, caused certain changes in the law governing the liability of municipalities in respect to the protection of their roads by railings or guards. A few years ago, when people traveled either on foot or by horse-drawn vehicles, a guardrail could to a considerable extent, actually prevent pedestrians or animals drawing vehicles from accidentally leaving the roadbed; but as a practical proposition, municipalities cannot be required to protect long stretches of roadway with railings or guards capable of preventing an automobile, moving at a rapid rate, from leaving the road if the car be in any way deflected from the roadway proper and propelled against the railing. As was said by this court in the case of Leber v. King County, 69 Wash. 134, 124 P. 397:

"Roads must be built and traveled, and to hold that the public cannot open their highways until they are prepared to fence their roads with barriers strong enough to hold a team and wagon when coming in violent contact with them, the condition being the ordinary condition of the country, would be to put a burden upon the public that it could not bear. It would prohibit the building of new roads and tend to the financial ruin of the counties undertaking to maintain the old ones."

This principle applies with special force to elevated causeways constructed of wood, such as the approach from which respondents' automobile fell, as upon such a structure the railing can be anchored or secured only to the deck of the causeway. Upon the ground, in situations of special danger, strength can be given to a guard or railing by driving posts into the earth, and a guard of any desired strength can be constructed in that manner. A concrete viaduct can be constructed with side walls of considerable resisting power; but the same degree of protection cannot be expected from a guard or railing along the side of an elevated frame causeway or viaduct. Respondents introduced some testimony to the effect that the posts which supported the railing were, to some extent, rotted. We have carefully considered this testimony, and, for the purposes of this opinion, assume that it was true; but we still do not think that it was sufficient to take the case to the jury upon the question of appellant's negligence in connection with the condition of the railing at the time of the accident. * * *

The judgment is reversed, with directions to dismiss the action.

NOTES AND QUESTIONS

1. Compare a later decision of the same court in Bartlett v. Northern Pacific R. Co., 74 Wash.2d 881, 447 P.2d 735 (1968). With almost identical facts the trial court had granted summary judgment to the defendant on the basis of the *Davison* case. The Supreme Court reversed and remanded, saying: "The reasoning in *Davison* * * * was based on the impracticality as a matter of engineering and on prohibitive costs. We do not consider the ideas of the court, expressed 40 years ago, as necessarily authoritative on the engineering and financial phases of the same problem today. We are satisfied that the parties should have the opportunity of presenting their evidence as to the practicality (cost wise or otherwise) of guardrails or barriers on dangerous or misleading roadways to stop slow-moving vehicles."

2. Note that in the principal case experts testified to provide expertise and to assist the parties in establishing the standard of care. Where the behavior to be evaluated is so distinctly related to some science, profession, or occupation as to be beyond the ken of the average layperson, expert testimony to establish what the standard of care is required. See, e.g., Burke v. Air Intern., Inc., 685 F.3d 1102 (D.C. Cir. 2012) (applying D.C. law) (in case where former British soldier was injured while providing private security to an NGO in Afghanistan, court found that the precise precautions a security contractor should take in a war zone are plainly beyond the ken of the average layperson and thus needed to be established by expert testimony).

3. In determining whether a choice of alternatives is reasonable, must the risk of harm to third persons be taken into account? Defendant's engineer, operating a train, unexpectedly finds a truck load of furniture on a crossing ahead of him. He can stop the train abruptly and avoid the collision, but if he does he will almost certainly throw his passengers about and injure them. What is he to do? Lucchese v. San Francisco-Sacramento R. Co., 106 Cal.App. 242, 289 P. 188 (1930) (conduct to be evaluated in light of all the circumstances, including possible injury to others). Defendant, driving a truck heavily loaded with pipe, is suddenly confronted with a situation requiring him to stop suddenly or injure the plaintiff's intestate. If he stops the pipe may be expected to shift forward and crush him to death. What is he to do? Thurmond v. Pepper, 119 S.W.2d 900 (Tex.Civ.App.1938) (the reasonable care standard does not hold him to a higher duty to preserve deceased from injury than to preserve himself). Who decides? The tort law does not answer the question what the defendant should do but rather whether he will be liable to someone he injures for failing to do it.

United States v. Carroll Towing Co.

United States Circuit Court of Appeals, Second Circuit, 1947.
159 F.2d 169.

[Libel in admiralty for the sinking of libelant's barge, the *Anna C.* The *Anna C* was owned by the Conners Co. and had been chartered to the Pennsylvania Railroad Co., which had loaded it with a cargo of flour that belonged to the United States. The charter required that the Conners Co. provide a bargee between the hours of 8:00 a.m. and 4:00 p.m. Carroll Towing Co. was the owner of a tug whose servants negligently shifted the *Anna C*'s mooring lines, causing her to break free from her pier. After the *Anna C* broke away, she drifted up against a tanker at the next pier down the North River. Unbeknownst to those in the harbor responding to the problem, the tanker's propeller broke a hole in the *Anna C* at or near her bottom. She careened, dumped her cargo of flour belonging to the United States, and sank. The United States sought compensation for the flour and Conners Co. sought compensation for the barge. Carroll Towing Co. argued that the barge could have been kept afloat and her cargo saved if it had been known that she had been damaged by the propeller, but because her bargee had gone ashore, there was no one on board to observe that she was leaking. The trial court divided the damages, according to the admiralty rule, because it found Conners Co. partly responsible for the loss of the cargo and the barge in not having a custodian on board the barge at the time.]

Judge Learned Hand

LEARNED HAND, CIRCUIT JUDGE. * * * [The court reviewed a number of decisions in other cases involving absentee bargees.] It appears from the foregoing review that there is no general rule to determine when the absence of a bargee or other attendant will make the owner of the barge liable for injuries to other vessels if she breaks away from her moorings. However, in any cases where he would be so liable for injuries to others, obviously he must reduce his damages proportionately, if the injury is to his own barge. It becomes apparent why there can be no such general rule, when we consider the grounds for such a liability. Since there are occasions when every vessel will break from her moorings, and, since, if she does, she becomes a menace to those about her, the owner's duty, as in other similar situations, to provide against resulting injuries is a function of three variables: (1) The probability that she will break away; (2) the gravity of the resulting injury, if she does; (3) the burden of adequate precautions. Possibly it serves to bring this notion into relief to state it in algebraic terms: if the probability be called P; the injury L; and the burden B; liability depends upon whether B is less than L multiplied by P; i.e., whether B is less than PL.

Applied to the situation at bar, the likelihood that a barge will break from her fasts, and the damage she will do, vary with the place and time; for example, if a storm threatens, the danger is greater; so it is, if she is in a crowded harbor where moored barges are constantly being shifted about. On the other hand, the barge must not be the bargee's prison, even though he lives aboard; he must go ashore at times. * * * We hold that it is not in all cases a sufficient answer to a bargee's absence without excuse, during working hours, that he has properly made fast his barge to a pier, when he leaves her. In the case at bar the bargee left at five o'clock on the afternoon of January 3rd, and the flotilla broke away at about two o'clock in the afternoon of the following day, twenty-one hours afterwards. The bargee had been away all the time, and we hold that his fabricated story was affirmative evidence that he had no excuse for his absence. At the locus in quo—especially during the short January days and in the full tide of war activity—barges were being constantly drilled in and out. Certainly it was not beyond reasonable expectation that, with the inevitable haste and bustle, the work might not be done with adequate care. In such circumstances we hold—and that is all that we do hold—that it was a fair requirement that the Conners Co. should have a bargee aboard (unless he had some excuse for his absence), during the working hours of daylight.

[Conners Co. was found partly responsible for the losses.]

NOTES AND QUESTIONS

1. In Conway v. O'Brien, 111 F.2d 611, 612 (2d Cir.1940), Judge Learned Hand stated in part: "The degree of care demanded of a person by an occasion is the resultant of three factors: the likelihood that his conduct will injure others, taken with the seriousness of the injury if it happens, and balanced against the interest which he must sacrifice to avoid the risk. All these are practically not susceptible of any quantitative estimate, and the second two are generally not so, even theoretically. For this reason a solution always involves some preference, or choice between incommensurables, and it is consigned to a jury because their decision is thought most likely to accord with commonly accepted standards, real or fancied." Is this statement consistent with the approach taken in the principal case? Is a court well equipped to weigh these considerations? A jury?

2. In Florida, in a lawsuit against the United States, plaintiff alleged that the United States had acted negligently in failing to provide adequate security for the handling of anthrax samples, resulting in the death of plaintiff's husband who was exposed to anthrax when the newspaper for

whom he worked received an envelope from an unknown person containing anthrax that was traced to Fort Detrick. United States v. Stevens, 994 So.2d 1062, 1067 (Fla. 2008) (answering a certified question from the Eleventh Circuit) ("as a general proposition, the greater the risk of harm to others that is created by a person's chosen activity, the greater the burden or duty to avoid injury to others becomes. Thus, as the risk grows greater, so does the duty, because the risk to be perceived defines the duty that must be undertaken.")

3. An urban electric utility fails to insulate its high tension wires and the decedent is electrocuted when his ladder comes in contact with a wire. Negligence? Amici curiae "complain of the increased costs of more adequate insulation. When the likelihood of danger to human life is to be balanced against the costs of insulation, we do not think the latter is a good argument." Kingsport Util. v. Brown, 201 Tenn. 393, 299 S.W.2d 656 (1955).

4. Plaintiff fell and injured her wrist while removing her shoes to go through airport security. She alleged that the Transportation Security Administration ("TSA") was negligent in failing to provide a chair in the passenger screening area. Barnes v. United States, 485 F.3d 341, 343 (6th Cir. 2007) (applying Tennessee law in a Federal Tort Claims Act case). The trial court judge granted summary judgment for the government and the appellate court affirmed: "[A]cceptance of the plaintiff's argument would impose a burden that is not commensurate with the apparently small likelihood and gravity of the potential harm. * * * The TSA provided passengers the ability to stabilize themselves by placing a hand on the table near the x-ray machine. Although the TSA could have provided a chair and the Government does not dispute that such an option was feasible, requiring the TSA to do so would impose a general burden that potentially far exceeds the benefit of providing a chair in this particular case. In particular, there would be an affirmative duty on premises owners to provide chairs anytime footwear must be removed, including entrances to mosques and temples, and entrances to homes in stormy weather, or indeed whenever someone must simply bend down, as when retrieving an item at the grocery store that is located on the bottom shelf. The possibility of an occasional fall does not warrant the widespread precautionary provision of chairs."

5. Defendant left her car unlocked and its engine running in her own driveway when she went to retrieve the pocketbook that she had forgotten. In the three minutes she was gone, a thief high on meth stole her car, got into a highspeed chase with police, and caused a crash that seriously injured plaintiffs. Plaintiffs argued that the burden on defendant was low—she could easily have removed her keys from the ignition and locked her car before returning to her house. The court, in affirming the trial court's grant of summary judgment for the defendant noted that the "burden that this factor addresses is not, however, the effortlessness in removing the keys, but rather the burden that will result from imposing a duty not to leave the motor running temporarily in a vehicle parked in one's driveway. It must be remembered that the imposition of a duty not to leave the motor running in a vehicle in one's driveway would apply across the board, and would create potential liability for every person in Wyoming who, on a cold winter day, starts his or her car to warm it up and defrost the windshield before driving upon the public highways." Lucero v. Holbrook, 288 P.3d 1228, 1235 (Wyo. 2012).

RESTATEMENT (THIRD) OF TORTS:
LIABILITY FOR PHYSICAL AND EMOTIONAL HARM (2010)

§ 3. Negligence

A person acts negligently if the person does not exercise reasonable care under all the circumstances. Primary factors to consider in ascertaining whether the person's conduct lacks reasonable care are the foreseeable likelihood that the person's conduct will result in harm, the foreseeable severity of any harm that may ensue, and the burden of precautions to eliminate or reduce the risk of harm.

A note about the Restatement of Torts: The original Restatement of Torts, with Francis Bohlen as Reporter, was a four volume work that was published over several years and was completed 1939. William Prosser and then John Wade shepherded the Restatement Second, which was begun in the late 1950's and finally completed in 1979. When the American Law Institute concluded that tort law had evolved so much that a Restatement Third was appropriate, it divided the work into separate portions, each taking up an important subfield. The first one to be completed was Products Liability, published in 1998, and which will be discussed in Chapter 15. The second, Apportionment of Liability, was published in 2000, and will be discussed principally in Chapter 7. The third area is being published in two volumes and is called Liability for Physical and Emotional Harm. The first volume, published in 2010, includes liability for intentional physical harm and for negligence causing physical harm, duty, strict liability, factual cause, and scope of liability (traditionally called proximate cause). The second volume, dealing with affirmative duties, emotional harm, landowner liability, and liability of actors who retain independent contractors, was published in 2012. Some areas of the law (like the elements of the specific intentional torts) have not changed since the Second Restatement was published and thus remain in effect. Where applicable, references to both the Second and Third Restatements are included.

---

4. THE STANDARD OF CARE

(A) THE REASONABLE PRUDENT PERSON

Vaughan v. Menlove

Court of Common Pleas, 1837.
3 Bing. (N.C.) 468, 132 Eng.Rep. 490.

[Defendant built a hay rick near the boundary of his land not far from the plaintiff's cottages. It was alleged that the rick was likely to ignite, thereby endangering the plaintiff's cottages, of which the defendant had notice; that the defendant was negligent in maintaining the rick in this dangerous condition; and that the rick did ignite and the fire spread to plaintiff's land, burning his cottages. Defendant denied that he was negligent.]

At the trial it appeared that the rick in question had been made by the defendant near the boundary of his own premises; that the hay was in such a state when put together, as to give rise to discussions on the probability of fire; that though there [were] conflicting opinions on the subject, yet during a period of five weeks, the defendant was repeatedly warned of his peril; that his stock was insured; and that upon one occasion, being advised to take the rick down to avoid all danger, he said, "he would chance it." He made an aperture or chimney through the rick; but in spite, or perhaps in consequence of his precaution, the rick at length burst into flames from the spontaneous heating of its materials; the flames communicated to the defendant's barn and stables, and thence to the plaintiff's cottages, which were entirely destroyed.

Chief Justice Tindal

PATTERSON, J., before whom the cause was tried, told the jury that the question for them to consider, was, whether the fire had been occasioned by gross negligence on the part of the defendant; adding, that he was bound to proceed with such reasonable caution as a prudent man would have exercised under such circumstances.

A verdict having been found for the plaintiff, a rule nisi for a new trial was obtained, on the ground that the jury should have been directed to consider, not, whether the defendant had been guilty of gross negligence with reference to the standard of ordinary prudence, a standard too uncertain to afford any criterion; but whether he had acted bona fide to the best of his judgment; if he had, he ought not to be responsible for the misfortune of not possessing the highest order of intelligence. The action under such circumstances, was of the first impression.

TINDAL, C.J. I agree that this is a case primae impressionis; but I feel no difficulty in applying to it the principles of law as laid down in other cases of a similar kind. * * * [T]hough the defendant did not himself light the fire, yet mediately, he is as much the cause of it as if he had himself put a candle to the rick; for it is well known that hay will ferment and take fire if it be not carefully stacked. It has been decided that if an occupier burns weeds so near the boundary of his own land that damage ensues to the property of his neighbor, he is liable to an action for the amount of injury done, unless the accident were occasioned by a sudden blast which he could not foresee. * * *

It is contended, however, that the learned Judge was wrong in leaving this to the jury as a case of gross negligence, and that the question of negligence was so mixed up with reference to what would be the conduct of a man of ordinary prudence that the jury might have thought the latter the rule by which they were to decide; that such a rule would be too uncertain to act upon; and that the question ought to have been whether the defendant had acted honestly and bona fide to the best of his own judgment. * * * The care taken by a prudent man has always been the rule laid down; and as to the supposed difficulty of applying it, a jury has always been able to say whether, taking that rule as their guide, there has been negligence on the occasion in question.

Instead, therefore, of saying that the liability for negligence should be co-extensive with the judgment of each individual, which would be as variable as the length of the foot of each individual, we ought rather to adhere to the rule which requires in all cases a regard to caution such as a man of ordinary prudence would observe. That was in substance the criterion presented to the jury in this case, and therefore the present rule must be discharged.

[The concurring opinions of PARK and VAUGHAN, JJ., are omitted. GASLEE, J., concurred in discharging the rule.]

NOTES AND QUESTIONS

1. How can an honest mistake in judgment be "fault"? Based on the evidence as summarized by Chief Justice Tindal, what other argument could defendant's lawyer have made on behalf of his client?

2. "If, for instance, a man is born hasty and awkward, is always hurting himself or his neighbors, no doubt his congenital defects will be allowed for in the courts of Heaven, but his slips are no less troublesome to his neighbors than if they sprang from guilty neglect. His neighbors accordingly require him, at his peril, to come up to their standard, and the courts which they establish decline to take his personal equation into account." Holmes, The Common Law 108 (1881). See also Seavey, Negligence—Subjective or Objective? 41 Harv.L.Rev. 1 (1927).

3. The standard formula for instructing the jury has been that of "a reasonable man of ordinary prudence." Variations on this have, however, been upheld, if they obviously mean the same thing. Thus the "ordinarily prudent man," Osborne v. Montgomery, 203 Wis. 223, 234 N.W. 372 (1931); the "typical prudent man," Warrington v. New York Power & Light Corp., 252 App.Div. 364, 300 N.Y.S. 154 (1937); the "average person of ordinary prudence," Charbonneau v. MacRury, 84 N.H. 501, 153 A. 457 (1931).

"The 'reasonable man' has been described by Greer, L.J. as 'the man in the street' or 'the man in the Clapham omnibus', or, as I recently read in an American author, 'the man who takes the magazines at home, and in the evening pushes the lawn mower in his shirt sleeves.'" Hall v. Brooklands Club, [1933] 1 K.B. 205, 224. For whimsical treatments, see A. Herbert, Uncommon Law 1–6 (7th ed. 1952); R. Megarry, The Clapham Omnibus, in Miscellany-at-Law 260 (1955).

4. The courts have quite jealously guarded the integrity of the instruction to the jury, and in particular the entirely hypothetical character of the "reasonable man." Thus in Freeman v. Adams, 63 Cal.App. 225, 218 P. 600 (1923), it was held reversible error to charge the jury that:

> "In determining what a reasonable and prudent man would do under the circumstances, you will remember that presumably a jury is composed of such reasonable and prudent persons, and you may each ask yourself, Did the defendants do, or fail to do, anything which, under the circumstances, I would not have done or would have done?"

Historically, courts referred to this mythical person in the masculine gender. The form used here and in modern jury instructions is the reasonable, prudent person.

5. "[I]n applying the universally accepted standard of care: that of the ordinary, reasonable and prudent man under the circumstances, the term 'ordinary' should be given its true meaning by not requiring the conduct of an extraordinarily careful person. Such an 'ordinary' man is not necessarily a supercautious individual devoid of human frailties and constantly preoccupied with the idea that danger may be lurking in every direction about him at any time. We appreciate that to require such constant apprehension of danger from every possible source would indeed be beyond normal conduct and would be too exacting a standard." Whitman v. W.T. Grant Co., 16 Utah 2d 81, 395 P.2d 918, 920 (1964).

Delair v. McAdoo

Supreme Court of Pennsylvania, 1936.
324 Pa. 392, 188 A. 181.

KEPHART, CHIEF JUSTICE. Plaintiff brought an action in trespass to recover for damages to his person and property sustained as a result of a collision between his automobile and that owned by the defendant. The accident occurred when defendant, proceeding in the same direction as plaintiff, sought to pass him. As defendant drew alongside of plaintiff, the left rear tire of his car blew out, causing it to swerve and come into contact with the plaintiff's car. The latter's theory at trial was that defendant was negligent in driving with defective tires. The jury found for plaintiff in the sum of $7,500. The court below granted defendant a new trial on the ground that the verdict was excessive, but refused his motion for a judgment n.o.v. Its ruling on the latter motion is here for review. * * *

It has been held in other states that the question whether a particular person is negligent in failing to know that his tires are in too poor a condition for ordinary operation on the highways is a question of fact for the jury. [Cc] In the instant case the testimony relative to the defect was as follows: A witness for the plaintiff stated that the tire "was worn pretty well through. You could see the tread in the tire—the inside lining." The witness later described this inside lining as the "fabric." The fact that the tire was worn through to and into the fabric over its entire area was corroborated by another witness. The repairman who replaced the tire which had blown out stated that he could see "the breaker strip" which is just under the fabric of a tire. This testimony was contradicted by the defendant.

A jury is just as well qualified to pass judgment as to the risk of danger in the condition of an article in universal use under a given state of facts as experts. We have in this state more than a million automobiles and trucks, approximately two for every three families. Their daily use over the highways is common, and requires a certain amount of knowledge of the movable parts, particularly the tires; it is imperative that a duty or standard of care be set up that will be productive of safety for other users of the highways. Any ordinary individual, whether a car owner or not, knows that when a tire is worn through to the fabric, its further use is dangerous and it should be removed. When worn through several plies, it is very dangerous for further use. All drivers must be held to a knowledge of these facts. An owner or operator cannot escape simply because he says he does not know. He must know. The hazard is too great to permit cars in this condition to be on the highway. It does not require opinion evidence to demonstrate that a trigger pulled on a loaded gun makes the gun a dangerous instrument when pointed at an individual, nor could one escape liability by saying he did not know it was dangerous. The use of a tire worn through to the fabric presents a similar situation. The rule must be rigid if millions are to drive these instrumentalities which in a fraction of a second may become instruments of destruction to life and property. There is no series of accidents more destructive or more terrifying in the use of automobiles than those which come from "blow-outs." The law requires drivers and owners of motor vehicles to know the condition of those parts which are likely to become dangerous where the flaws or faults would be disclosed by a reasonable inspection. It will assume they do know of the dangers ascertainable by such examination.

Order affirmed.

NOTES AND QUESTIONS

1. This case is sent back for a new trial. In the light of the opinion, how should the trial judge instruct the jury?

2. Compare Michigan City v. Rudolph, 104 Ind.App. 643, 12 N.E.2d 970 (1938), holding that the driver is held to the knowledge that an

automobile will go out of control if it is driven fast through loose sand. What if the driver is a teenager who has just obtained her license?

3. What are the facts that every mentally competent adult should know? The law of gravity—something dropped will fall? Seaboard Air Line R. Co. v. Hackney, 217 Ala. 382, 115 So. 869 (1928). The principle of leverage—one end of a balanced board will fly up if the other is trod on? Cf. City of Huntingburg v. First, 15 Ind.App. 552, 43 N.E. 17 (1896). The fact that wood and paper will burn? Lillibridge v. McCann, 117 Mich. 84, 75 N.W. 288 (1898).

4. Suppose the individual has led a life that has not brought him into contact with information common in the particular community. A city dweller who never has seen a bull or a mule, or heard anything about their characteristics, visits a friend in the country, and makes a misguided attempt to fraternize with the animals. Tolin v. Terrell, 133 Ky. 210, 117 S.W. 290, 291 (1909) ("it is a matter of common knowledge and common experience that there is no telling when or under what circumstances a mule will or will not kick. The only way to escape danger from the feet of a mule is not to go within the radius of its heels.") A Notre Dame law student from Southern California, driving to the library in the midst of a lake effect snow storm, does not know that a driver is supposed to steer into a skid. Is it reasonable conduct not to?

5. Distinguish ignorance from the breach of a duty to find out. A stranger in a town is suddenly confronted with a purple traffic light. Can she continue to drive across town without stopping to find out what the light means? In Gobrecht v. Beckwith, 82 N.H. 415, 135 A. 20 (1926), defendant, a landlord, installed a gas heater in a closed and almost unventilated bathroom, in ignorance of the fact that it would fill the room with carbon monoxide. Plaintiff, a tenant, used the bathroom, lighted the heater, and was poisoned. It was held that it was unreasonable (negligent) for defendant not to make an inquiry or investigation as to the safety of the heater, but reasonable (not negligent) for plaintiff not to make an inquiry and to rely on the landlord.

6. Suppose persons who do not hold themselves out as having superior skills or knowledge do actually have them. Should they be required to exercise those superior skills or knowledge to avoid harm to others? For example, in the principal case, suppose the defect was a latent one, but defendant could easily have discovered it because his hobby was auto mechanics. Should he be held liable? The Restatement (Second) of Torts suggests an affirmative answer in § 289(b), comment *m*. Defendant in a medical malpractice case contended that patient, who also was a doctor, failed to tell him a crucial piece of information about his symptoms. Patient claimed he had told the doctor. The jury had to resolve the factual dispute at trial in deciding both negligence and contributory negligence. Should the jury consider the patient's superior knowledge (the significance of the symptom in making a diagnosis) in evaluating patient's conduct to determine contributory negligence? Jackson v. Axelrad, 221 S.W.3d 650 (Tex. 2007) (yes, citing Restatement (Second) of Torts § 289(b), comment *m*). See also Restatement (Third) of Torts: Liability for Physical and Emotional Harm § 12 (2010) (yes, to be taken into account). But see Fredericks v. Castora, 241 Pa.Super. 211, 360 A.2d 696 (1976) (court

refused to impose higher standard on truck driver despite twenty years' experience).

7. It is commonly held that the reasonable person will not forget what is actually known, and that forgetfulness does not excuse negligence. But when distracted attention, lapse of time or other similar factors make it reasonable to forget, it can be found that there is no negligence. See Ferrie v. D'Arc, 31 N.J. 92, 155 A.2d 257 (1959), rev'g, 55 N.J.Super. 65, 150 A.2d 83 (1959).

Trimarco v. Klein

Court of Appeals of New York, 1982.
56 N.Y.2d 98, 436 N.E.2d 502, 451 N.Y.S.2d 52.

FUCHSBERG, JUDGE. After trial by jury in a negligence suit for personal injuries, the plaintiff, Vincent N. Trimarco, recovered a judgment of $240,000. A sharply divided Appellate Division, 82 A.D.2d 20, 441 N.Y.S.2d 62, having reversed on the law and dismissed the complaint, our primary concern on this appeal is with the role of the proof plaintiff produced on custom and usage. The ultimate issue is whether he made out a case.

The controversy has its genesis in the shattering of a bathtub's glass enclosure door in a multiple dwelling in July, 1976. Taking the testimony most favorably to the plaintiff, as we must in passing on the presence of a prima facie case, we note that, according to the trial testimony, at the time of the incident plaintiff, the tenant of the apartment in which it happened, was in the process of sliding the door open so that he could exit the tub. It is undisputed that the occurrence was sudden and unexpected and the injuries he received from the lacerating glass most severe.

The door, which turned out to have been made of ordinary glass variously estimated as one sixteenth to one quarter of an inch in thickness, concededly would have presented no different appearance to the plaintiff and his wife than did tempered safety glass, which their uncontradicted testimony shows they assumed it to be. Nor was there any suggestion that defendants ever brought its true nature to their attention. * * *

As part of his case, plaintiff, with the aid of expert testimony, developed that, since at least the early 1950's, a practice of using shatterproof glazing materials for bathroom enclosures had come into common use, so that by 1976 the glass door here no longer conformed to accepted safety standards. This proof was reinforced by a showing that over this period bulletins of nationally recognized safety and consumer organizations along with official Federal publications had joined in warning of the dangers that lurked when plain glass was utilized in "hazardous locations", including "bathtub enclosures". * * * And, on examination of the defendants' managing agent, who long had enjoyed extensive familiarity with the management of multiple dwelling units in the New York City area, plaintiff's counsel elicited agreement that, since at least 1965, it was customary for landlords who had occasion to install glass for shower enclosures, whether to replace broken glass or to comply with the request of a tenant or otherwise, to do so with "some material such as plastic or safety glass".

In face of this record, in essence, the rationale of the majority at the Appellate Division was that, "assuming that there existed a custom and usage at the time to substitute shatterproof glass" and that this was a "better way or a safer method of enclosing showers" [c] unless prior notice of the danger came to the defendants either from the plaintiff or by reason of a similar accident in the building, no duty devolved on the defendants to replace the glass either under the common law or under section 78 of the Multiple Dwelling Law. * * *

Which brings us to the well-recognized and pragmatic proposition that when "certain dangers have been removed by a customary way of doing things safely, this custom may be proved to show that [the one charged with the dereliction] has fallen below the required standard" [c]. Such proof, of course, is not admitted in the abstract. It must bear on what is reasonable conduct under all the circumstances, the quintessential test of negligence.

It follows that, when proof of an accepted practice is accompanied by evidence that the defendant conformed to it, this may establish due care [c] and, contrariwise, when proof of a customary practice is coupled with a showing that it was ignored and that this departure was a proximate cause of the accident, it may serve to establish liability. [c]. Put more conceptually, proof of a common practice aids in "formulat[ing] the general expectation of society as to how individuals will act in the course of their undertakings, and thus to guide the common sense or expert intuition of a jury or commission when called on to judge of particular conduct under particular circumstances" (Pound, Administrative Application of Legal Standards, 44 ABA Rep, 445, 456–457).

The source of the probative power of proof of custom and usage is described differently by various authorities, but all agree on its potency. Chief among the rationales offered is, of course, the fact that it reflects the judgment and experience and conduct of many (2 Wigmore, Evidence [3d ed], § 461; Prosser, Torts [4th ed], § 33). Support for its relevancy and reliability comes too from the direct bearing it has on feasibility, for its focusing is on the practicality of a precaution in actual operation and the readiness with which it can be employed (Morris, Custom and Negligence, 42 Col.L.Rev. 1147, 1148). Following in the train of both of these boons is the custom's exemplification of the opportunities it provides to others to learn of the safe way, if that the customary one be. (See Restatement (Second) Torts § 295A, comments *a, b.*)

From all this it is not to be assumed customary practice and usage need be universal. It suffices that it be fairly well defined and in the same calling or business so that "the actor may be charged with knowledge of it or negligent ignorance" (Prosser, Torts [4th ed], § 33, p. 168; Restatement (Second) Torts § 295A, p. 62, comment *a*).

However, once its existence is credited, a common practice or usage is still not necessarily a conclusive or even a compelling test of negligence (1 Shearman & Redfield, Negligence [rev ed], § 10). Before it can be, the jury must be satisfied with its reasonableness, just as the jury must be satisfied with the reasonableness of the behavior which adhered to the custom or the unreasonableness of that which did not [c]. After all, customs and usages run the gamut of merit like everything else. That is why the question in each instance is whether it meets the test of reasonableness. As Holmes' now classic statement on this subject expresses it, "[w]hat usually is done may be evidence of what ought to be done, but what ought to be done is fixed by a standard of reasonable prudence, whether it usually is complied with or not" (Texas & Pacific Ry. Co. v. Behymer, 189 U.S. 468, 470, 23 S.Ct. 622, 622–23, 47 L.Ed. 905).

So measured, the case the plaintiff presented, even without the [evidence concerning a statute which applied only to construction after 1973 which the court held should not have been admitted], was enough to send it to the jury and to sustain the verdict reached. The expert testimony, the admissions of the defendant's manager, the data on which the professional and governmental bulletins were based, the evidence of how replacements were handled by at least the local building industry for the better part of two decades, these in the aggregate easily filled that bill. Moreover, it was also for the jury to decide whether, at the point in time when the accident occurred, the modest cost and ready availability of safety glass and the dynamics of the growing custom to use it for shower enclosures had transformed what once may have been considered a reasonably safe part of the apartment into one which, in the light of later developments, no longer could be so regarded.

Furthermore, the charge on this subject was correct. The Trial Judge placed the evidence of custom and usage "by others engaged in the same business" in proper perspective, when, among other things, he told the jury that the issue on which it was received was "the reasonableness of the defendant's conduct under all the circumstances". He also emphasized that the testimony on this score was not conclusive, not only by saying so but by explaining that "the mere fact that another person or landlord may have used a better or safer practice does not establish a standard" and that it was for the jurors "to determine whether or not the evidence in this case does establish a general custom or practice".

Nevertheless, we reverse and order a new trial because the General Business Law sections [concerning the statute which did not apply] should have been excluded. * * *

Order reversed, with costs, and case remitted to Supreme Court, Bronx County, for a new trial in accordance with the opinion herein.

NOTES AND QUESTIONS

1. Who is interested in introducing evidence of the custom, plaintiff or defendant? Why? Do you see that industry custom is one way to show the jury what a reasonable person would do under the circumstances?

2. Defendant, driving an automobile on a private road, where no statute is applicable, violates the custom in the United States by driving on the left side of the road. In the absence of special circumstances, can he be

found negligent in doing so? Cf. Eamiello v. Piscitelli, 133 Conn. 360, 51 A.2d 912 (1947) (walking on wrong side of road). What about special circumstances? Suppose the right side of the road is full of dangerous potholes? Texas & Pacific R. Co. v. Behymer, 189 U.S. 468 (1903), quoted in the principal case, where it was railway custom to make up a train by bumping cars together with brakemen standing on top of them; and this was done on one occasion when the cars were covered with a sheet of ice.

3. What if the custom of the industry is a careless one? Defendant's tug boats were towing plaintiff's barges loaded with coal up the coast from Norfolk, Virginia to New York when they were lost in a gale off the Jersey Coast. The tugs were not equipped with a radio that would have allowed them to receive a warning from the Weather Bureau in time to pull into safety in the Delaware Breakwater. Defendants proved that it was the custom of barge lines not to provide radio receiving sets to the crews. In upholding the verdict against the defendants, Learned Hand wrote an oft-quoted passage, which summarizes the law in this area: "[I]n most cases reasonable prudence is in fact common prudence; but strictly it is never its measure; a whole calling may have unduly lagged in the adoption of new and available devices. It never may set its own tests, however persuasive be its usages. Courts must in the end say what is required; there are precautions so imperative that even their universal disregard will not excuse their omission." The T.J. Hooper, 60 F.2d 737 (2d Cir.1932).

4. What if a custom violates a statute? Suppose everyone in town habitually jaywalks, crossing the street in the middle of the block? Cf. Fowler v. Key System Transit Lines, 37 Cal.2d 65, 230 P.2d 339 (1951) (even if conduct is against law, custom may be used to show expectations).

5. Are there customs that are so clearly unreasonable that they are not even to be admitted as evidence of due care? In Mayhew v. Sullivan Mining Co., 76 Me. 100 (1884), defendant mining company did not guard or even light ladder-holes in the platforms in its mine. A workman fell through such a hole and was injured. Barrow, J.: "If the defendants had proved that in every mining establishment that has existed since the days of Tubal Cain, it has been the practice to cut ladder-holes in their platforms, situated as this was while in daily use for mining operations, without guarding or lighting them, and without notice to contractors or workmen, it would have no tendency to show that the act was consistent with ordinary prudence or a due regard for the safety of those who were using their premises by their invitation."

Cordas v. Peerless Transportation Co.

City Court of New York, New York County, 1941.
27 N.Y.S.2d 198.

CARLIN, JUSTICE. This case presents the ordinary man—that problem child of the law—in a most bizarre setting. As a lonely chauffeur in defendant's employ he became in a trice the protagonist in a breath-bating drama with a denouement almost tragic. It appears that a man, whose identity it would be indelicate to divulge, was feloniously relieved of his portable goods by two nondescript highwaymen in an alley near 26th Street and Third Avenue, Manhattan; they induced him to relinquish his possessions by a strong argument ad hominem couched in the convincing cant of the criminal and pressed at the point of a most persuasive pistol. Laden with their loot, but not thereby impeded, they took an abrupt departure, and he, shuffling off the coil of that discretion which enmeshed him in the alley, quickly gave chase through 26th Street toward 2d Avenue, whither they were resorting "with expedition swift as thought" for most obvious reasons. Somewhere on that thoroughfare of escape they indulged the stratagem of separation ostensibly to disconcert their pursuer and allay the ardor of his pursuit. He then centered on for capture the man with the pistol, whom he saw board the defendant's taxicab which quickly veered south toward 25th Street on 2d Avenue, where he saw the chauffeur jump out while the cab still in motion, continued toward 24th Street; after the chauffeur relieved himself of the cumbersome burden of his fare the latter also is said to have similarly departed from the cab before it reached 24th Street.

The chauffeur's story is substantially the same except that he states that his uninvited guest boarded the cab at 25th Street while it was at a standstill waiting for a less colorful fare; that his "passenger" immediately advised him "to stand not upon the order of his going but go at once," and added finality to his command by an appropriate gesture with a pistol addressed to his sacroiliac. The chauffeur in reluctant acquiescence proceeded about fifteen feet, when his hair, like unto the quills of the fretful porcupine, was made to stand on end by the hue and cry of the man despoiled, accompanied by a clamorous concourse of the law-abiding who paced him as he ran; the concatenation of "stop thief," to which the patter of persistent feet did maddingly beat time, rang in his ears as the pursuing posse all the while gained on the receding cab with its quarry therein contained. The hold-up man sensing his insecurity suggested to the chauffeur that in the event there was the slightest lapse in obedience to his curt command that he, the chauffeur, would suffer the loss of his brains, a prospect as horrible to an humble chauffeur as it undoubtedly would be to one of the intelligentsia.

The chauffeur, apprehensive of certain dissolution from either Scylla, the pursuers, or Charybdis, the pursued, quickly threw his car out of first speed in which he was proceeding, pulled on the emergency, jammed on his brakes and, although he thinks the motor was still running, swung open the door to his left and jumped out of his car. He confesses that the only act that smacked of intelligence was that by which he jammed the brakes in order to throw off balance the hold-up man, who was half-standing and half-sitting with his pistol menacingly poised. Thus abandoning his car and passenger the chauffeur sped toward 26th Street and then turned to look; he saw the cab proceeding south toward 24th Street, where it mounted the sidewalk. The plaintiff-mother and her two infant children were there injured by the cab, which, at the time, appeared to be also minus its passenger, who, it appears, was apprehended in the cellar of a local hospital where he was pointed out to a police officer by a remnant of the posse, hereinbefore mentioned. He did not appear at the trial. The three aforesaid plaintiffs and the husband-father sue the defendant for damages, predicating their respective causes of action upon the contention that the chauffeur was negligent in abandoning the cab under the aforesaid circumstances. Fortunately the injuries sustained were comparatively slight. * * *

Negligence has been variously defined but the common legal acceptation is the failure to exercise that care and caution which a reasonable and prudent person ordinarily would exercise under like conditions or circumstances. * * * Negligence is "not absolute or intrinsic," but "is always relevant to some circumstances of time, place or person." In slight paraphrase of the world's first bard it may be truly observed that the expedition of the chauffeur's violent love of his own security outran the pauser, reason, when he was suddenly confronted with unusual emergency which "took his reason prisoner." The learned attorney for the plaintiffs concedes that the chauffeur acted in an emergency, but claims a right to recovery upon the following proposition taken verbatim from his brief: "It is respectfully submitted that the value of the interest of the public at large to be immune from being injured by a dangerous instrumentality such as a car unattended while in motion is very superior to the right of a driver to abandon same while it is in motion, even when acting under the belief that his life is in danger and by abandoning same he will save his life."

To hold thus under the facts adduced herein would be tantamount to a repeal by implication of the primal law of nature written in indelible characters upon the fleshy tablets of sentient creation by the Almighty Law-giver, "the supernal Judge who sits on high." There are those who stem the turbulent current for bubble fame, or who bridge the yawning chasm with a leap for the leap's sake, or who "outstare the sternest eyes that look, outbrave the heart most daring on the earth, pluck the young sucking cubs from the she-bear, yea, mock the lion when he roars for prey" to win a fair lady, and these are the admiration of the generality of men; but they are made of sterner stuff than the ordinary man upon whom the law places no duty of emulation. The law would indeed be fond if it imposed upon the ordinary man the obligation to so demean himself when suddenly confronted with a danger, not of his creation, disregarding the likelihood that such a contingency may darken the intellect and palsy the will of the common legion of the earth, the fraternity of the ordinary man—whose acts or omissions under certain conditions make the yardstick by which the law measures culpability or innocence, negligence or care. * * *

Returning to our chauffeur. If the philosophic Horatio and the martial companions of his watch were "distilled almost to jelly with the act of fear" when they beheld "in the dead vast and middle of the night" the disembodied spirit of Hamlet's father stalk majestically by "with a countenance more in sorrow than in anger," was not the chauffeur, though unacquainted with the example of these eminent men-at-arms more amply justified in his fearsome reactions when he was more palpably confronted by a thing of flesh and blood bearing in its hand an engine of destruction which depended for its lethal purpose upon the quiver of a hair? When Macbeth was cross-examined by Macduff as to any reason he could advance for his sudden dispatch of Duncan's grooms he said in plausible answer, "Who can be wise, amazed, temperate and furious, loyal and neutral in a moment? No man." * * *

Kolanko v. Erie Railroad Co., 215 App.Div. 82, 86, 212 N.Y.S. 714, 717, says: "The law in this state does not hold one in an emergency to the exercise of that mature judgment required of him under circumstances where he has an opportunity for deliberate action. He is not required to exercise unerring judgment, which would be expected of him, were he not confronted with an emergency requiring prompt action." The circumstances provide the foil by which the act is brought into relief to determine whether it is or is not negligent. If under normal circumstances an act is done which might be considered negligent, it does not follow as a corollary that a similar act is negligent if performed by a person acting under an emergency, not of his own making, in which he suddenly is faced with a patent danger with a moment left to adopt a means of extrication.

The chauffeur—the ordinary man in this case—acted in a split second in a most harrowing experience. To call him negligent would be to brand him coward; the court does not do so in spite of what those swaggering heroes, "whose valor plucks dead lions by the beard", may bluster to the contrary. The court is loathe to see the plaintiffs go without recovery even though their damages were slight, but cannot hold the defendant liable upon the facts adduced at the trial. Motions, upon which decision was reserved, to dismiss the complaint are granted, with exceptions to plaintiffs. Judgment for defendant against plaintiffs dismissing their complaint upon the merits.

NOTES AND QUESTIONS

1. Compare Vincent v. Lake Erie Transp. Co., page 129. Why a different result? Would it make any difference if plaintiff in the principal case had been killed or seriously injured? Should it? Some legal scholars have observed that society tends to prevent direct taking of life while permitting indirect, but statistically certain, deaths. See Calabresi, Reflections on Medical Experiments in Humans, 98 Daedalus 387 (1969).

2. Distinguish the sudden emergency doctrine from the situation where the defendant is unable to act due to sudden illness. The sudden emergency instruction is intended only for circumstances in which a defendant "has acted in response to a perceived peril and has made a choice which in hindsight may be regarded as unwise or ill-considered, but which was not unreasonable or imprudent under the stress of surrounding circumstances." Hagenow v. Schmidt, 842 N.W.2d 661 (Iowa 2014). It is not appropriate when it is physically impossible for the defendant to act volitionally. Hancock-Underwood v. Knight, 277 Va. 127, 670 S.E.2d 726 (2009) (sudden emergency instruction not applicable where driver suffered acute medical crisis and lost consciousness).

3. To qualify as a sudden emergency, the event must be unforeseen, sudden, and unexpected. Compare Lifson v. City of Syracuse, 17 N.Y.3d 492, 934 N.Y.S.2d 38, 958 N.E.2d 72 (2011) (blinding effect of setting sun's rays common and expected, no sudden emergency instruction) with Regenstreif v. Phelps, 142 S.W.3d 1 (Ky. 2004) (encounters with "black ice" on street, falling boulders, swooping airplanes, and darting children and animals all sudden emergencies). The judge makes the threshold determination whether the sudden emergency instruction is to be given and then the jury decides whether there was a sudden and unforeseen

emergency not of the defendant's own making and, if so, whether her response was reasonable under the circumstances. Four teenagers were driving home from the beach when a back seat passenger pulled the strings of the driver's bikini top, causing the top to fall and her breasts to be exposed. She reacted by letting go of the wheel to cover herself and lost control of the car. Is driver entitled to the sudden emergency instruction? Pelletier v. Lahm, 111 A.D.3d 807, 975 N.Y.S.2d 135 (N.Y. App. 2012), aff'd, 24 N.Y.3d 966, 19 N.E.3d 491 (2014) (majority of panel affirmed trial court judge's decision to give instruction but dissent pointed out that same passenger had engaged in other distracting conduct like opening an umbrella in the back seat and thus that it was not a sudden and unforeseen event).

4. The emergency does not excuse the actor from complying with the standard of the reasonable person. The actor's conduct still may be found to be unreasonable even in light of the emergency. Regenstreif v. Phelps, 142 S.W.3d 1, 5 (Ky. 2004) ("The sudden emergency doctrine is merely an expression of the reasonably prudent person standard of care. It expresses the notion that the law requires no more from an actor than is reasonable to expect in the event of an emergency."). Kreidt v. Burlington N. R.R., 615 N.W.2d 153, 156 (N.D. 2000) ("The sudden emergency doctrine is not so much doctrine as an illustration of how negligence law is applied in a specific situation.").

5. There is general agreement that if the emergency is created by the negligence of the actor, the emergency doctrine does not apply. See for example Lunzer v. Pittsburgh & L.E.R. Co., 296 Pa. 393, 145 A. 907 (1929) (driver put himself in position of peril by driving onto railroad tracks even though he saw train approaching) and Frisby v. Agerton Logging, Inc., 323 Ark. 508, 915 S.W.2d 718 (1996) (driver put himself in position of peril by driving in ruts down middle of road). It has been said, however, that it is not the conduct after the emergency has arisen that the law does not excuse, but the negligent conduct that brought it about. Windsor v. McKee, 22 S.W.2d 65 (Mo.App.1929).

6. Are there situations in which one may be required to anticipate an emergency and be prepared to meet it? What if defendant is driving past a school and a child suddenly comes darting out of a driveway on a bicycle? Lederer v. Connecticut Co., 95 Conn. 520, 111 A. 785 (1920); Conery v. Tackmaier, 34 Wis.2d 511, 149 N.W.2d 575 (1967). See also Restatement (Second) Torts § 290, comment *k* (motorist required to take into account the likelihood that child on sidewalk may suddenly dart into street). What if defendant's car hydroplaned, causing her to lose control, cross the median strip, and hit another car? She requested the emergency doctrine instruction, but the court found it was not warranted because the "occurrence of standing water on a roadway during a heavy rainstorm is simply another matter of common experience. The hazard this occurrence presents, including the possibility of hydroplaning, is one the driver of a vehicle along the roadway must anticipate and exercise reasonable care to avoid." Herr v. Wheeler, 272 Va. 310, 634 S.E.2d 317, 317 (2006).

7. In the principal case, unlike in most negligence cases, the judge acted as a trier of fact. In cases where the jury acts as the fact-finder, legal disputes surrounding the emergency doctrine arise in regard to whether a judge should have instructed a jury about "the reasonable person in an

emergency." See Miler v. Reilly, 21 Md.App. 465, 319 A.2d 553 (1974) (failure to apply emergency brake). Since the jury is usually instructed to view the reasonable person "in the circumstances," why insist upon a separate instruction? Lockhart v. List, 542 Pa. 141, 665 A.2d 1176 (1995) (reaffirming that separate sudden emergency instruction should be given to explain context for judging behavior in light of circumstances). Should the defendant have to alert the plaintiff that it plans to seek the instruction? In other words, is it an affirmative defense? Willis v. Westerfield, 839 N.E.2d 1179 (Ind. 2006) (although the proponent of the emergency doctrine bears the burden of establishing that the instruction should be given, it is not an affirmative defense that must be pled in the answer).

8. Not all jurisdictions permit a separate jury instruction, many finding that it puts undue emphasis on the one aspect of the circumstances and thus confuses juries. See, for example, Bedor v. Johnson, 292 P.3d 924 (Colo. 2013) (abolishing separate jury instruction on emergency doctrine and collecting cases with similar holdings from other jurisdictions).

Roberts v. State of Louisiana

Court of Appeal of Louisiana, 1981.
396 So.2d 566.

LABORDE, JUDGE. In this tort suit, William C. Roberts sued to recover damages for injuries he sustained in an accident in the lobby of the U.S. Post Office Building in Alexandria, Louisiana. Roberts fell after being bumped into by Mike Burson, the blind operator of the concession stand located in the building.

Plaintiff sued the State of Louisiana, through the Louisiana Health and Human Resources Administration, advancing two theories of liability: respondeat superior and negligent failure by the State to properly supervise and oversee the safe operation of the concession stand. The stand's blind operator, Mike Burson, is not a party to this suit although he is charged with negligence.

[The trial court ordered plaintiff's suit dismissed.]

We affirm the trial court's decision for the reasons which follow.

On September 1, 1977, at about 12:45 in the afternoon, operator Mike Burson left his concession stand to go to the men's bathroom located in the building. As he was walking down the hall, he bumped into plaintiff who fell to the floor and injured his hip. Plaintiff was 75 years old, stood 5′ 6″ and weighed approximately 100 pounds. Burson, on the other hand, was 25 to 26 years old, stood approximately 6′ and weighed 165 pounds. * * *

Even though Burson was not joined as a defendant, his negligence or lack thereof is crucial to a determination of the State's liability. Because of its importance, we begin with it.

Plaintiff contends that operator Mike Burson traversed the area from his concession stand to the men's bathroom in a negligent manner. To be more specific, he focuses on the operator's failure to use his cane even though he had it with him in his concession stand.

In determining an actor's negligence, various courts have imposed differing standards of care to which handicapped persons are expected to perform. Professor William L. Prosser expresses one generally recognized modern standard of care as follows:

"As to his physical characteristics, the reasonable man may be said to be identical with the actor. The man who is blind . . . is entitled to live in the world and to have allowance made by others for his disability, and he cannot be required to do the impossible by conforming to physical standards which he cannot meet. . . . At the same time, the conduct of the handicapped individual must be reasonable in the light of his knowledge of his infirmity, which is treated merely as one of the circumstances under which he acts . . . It is sometimes said that a blind man must use a greater degree of care than one who can see; but it is now generally agreed that as a fixed rule this is inaccurate, and that the correct statement is merely that he must take the precautions, be they more or less, which the ordinary reasonable man would take if he were blind." W. Prosser, *The Law of Torts,* Section 32, at Page 151–52 (4th ed. 1971).

A careful review of the record in this instance reveals that Burson was acting as a reasonably prudent blind person would under these particular circumstances.

Mike Burson is totally blind. Since 1974, he has operated the concession stand located in the lobby of the post office building. It is one of twenty-three vending stands operated by blind persons under a program funded by the federal government and implemented by the State through the Blind Services Division of the Department of Health and Human Resources. Burson hired no employees, choosing instead to operate his stand on his own. * * *

On the date of the incident in question, Mike Burson testified that he left his concession stand and was on his way to the men's bathroom when he bumped into plaintiff. He, without hesitancy, admitted that at the time he was not using his cane, explaining that he relies on his facial sense which he feels is an adequate technique for short trips inside the familiar building. Burson testified that he does use a cane to get to and from work.

Plaintiff makes much of Burson's failure to use a cane when traversing the halls of the post office building. Yet, our review of the testimony received at trial indicates that it is not uncommon for blind people to rely on other techniques when moving around in a familiar setting. For example George Marzloff, the director of the Division of Blind Services, testified that he can recommend to the blind operators that they should use a cane but he knows that when they are in a setting in which they are comfortable, he would say that nine out of ten will not use a cane and in his personal opinion, if the operator is in a relatively busy area, the cane can be more of a hazard than an asset. * * *

The only testimony in the record that suggests that Burson traversed the halls in a negligent manner was that elicited from plaintiff's expert witness, William Henry Jacobson. Jacobson is an instructor in peripathology, which he explained as the science of movement within the surroundings by visually impaired individuals. Jacobson, admitting that he conducted no study or examination of Mike Burson's mobility skills and that he was unfamiliar with the State's vending program, nonetheless testified that he would require a blind person to use a cane in traversing the areas outside the concession stand. * * *

Upon our review of the record, we feel that plaintiff has failed to show that Burson was negligent. Burson testified that he was very familiar with his surroundings, having worked there for three and a half years. He had special mobility training and his reports introduced into evidence indicate good mobility skills. He explained his decision to rely on his facial sense instead of his cane for these short trips in a manner which convinces us that it was a reasoned decision. Not only was Burson's explanation adequate, there was additional testimony from other persons indicating that such a decision is not an unreasonable one. Also important is the total lack of any evidence in the record showing that at the time of the incident, Burson engaged in any acts which may be characterized as negligence on his part. For example, there is nothing showing that Burson was walking too fast, not paying attention, et cetera. Under all of these circumstances, we conclude that Mike Burson was not negligent.

Our determination that Mike Burson was not negligent disposes of our need to discuss liability on the part of the State.

For the above and foregoing reasons, the judgment of the trial court dismissing plaintiff's claims against defendant is affirmed and all costs of this appeal are assessed against the plaintiff-appellant.

Affirmed.

NOTES AND QUESTIONS

1. Accord, as to the other physical characteristics: Otterbeck v. Lamb, 85 Nev. 456, 456 P.2d 855 (1969) (deafness); Stephens v. Dulaney, 78 N.M. 53, 428 P.2d 27 (1967) (no sense of smell); Mahan v. State, to Use of Carr, 172 Md. 373, 191 A. 575 (1937) (short stature, unable to see over hood of automobile); Storjohn v. Fay, 246 Neb. 454, 519 N.W.2d 521 (1994) (epilepsy); Hodges v. Jewel Cos., 72 Ill.App.3d 263, 28 Ill.Dec. 571, 390 N.E.2d 930 (1979) (paralysis).

2. Is a blind person negligent in going out on the street unaccompanied? See Hill v. Glenwood, 124 Iowa 479, 100 N.W. 522 (1904), where a blind man was the injured party. Suppose he had gone out without a cane. Smith v. Sneller, 147 Pa.Super. 231, 24 A.2d 61, 63 aff'd, 345 Pa. 68, 26 A.2d 452 (1942). ("A blind man may not rely wholly upon his other senses to warn him of danger but must use the devices usually employed, to compensate for his blindness.")

3. Should it make any difference if the party with a physical disability is a plaintiff or a defendant?

4. Suppose that instead of being physically disabled, the actor has superior endowments—he is stronger, can see farther, or distinguishes scents better than a bloodhound. Is it sufficient for him to exercise ordinary abilities or must he exercise his superior ones? Cf Restatement (Second) of

Torts § 289(b), comment *m* and Restatement (Third) of Torts: Liability for Physical and Emotional Harm § 12 (2010) (suggesting that actor should be held to higher standard but not citing any cases relating to superior physical characteristics as distinguished from superior knowledge).

5. What about the obligation of the defendant to take the possibility of such a disability as blindness into account? See Fletcher v. Aberdeen, 54 Wash.2d 174, 338 P.2d 743 (1959). ("While a city . . . owes no more than due, ordinary, or reasonable care toward a blind or other physically afflicted or handicapped pedestrian, in respect of the condition of walkways, the effect of the affliction or handicap may be considered in determining whether the required degree of care has been exercised").

6. The Americans with Disabilities Act ("ADA"), 42 U.S.C. §§ 12101–12213 (1990), is designed to require accommodations in all areas (employment, public service, public accommodation, telecommunication) where a disabled person might encounter unnecessary difficulties. In what ways might the ADA affect tort law?

7. *Intoxication.* Although intoxication arguably could be classified as a physical disability, the courts have consistently refused to make any allowance for it where it is "voluntary," or even negligent. Why? Is voluntary intoxication negligence in itself? What if the defendant indulged in a drug that impairs physical abilities? Cf. Janelsins v. Button, 102 Md.App. 30, 648 A.2d 1039 (1994) (in battery action by bartender against patron, court noted that voluntary intoxication does not vitiate intent).

8. What is defendant's obligation toward one who is intoxicated? One of the most famous judicial utterances is in Robinson v. Pioche, Bayerque & Co., 5 Cal. 460 (1885): "A drunken man is as much entitled to a safe street as a sober one, and much more in need of it."

Robinson v. Lindsay

Supreme Court of Washington, 1979.
92 Wash.2d 410, 598 P.2d 392.

UTTER, CHIEF JUSTICE. [Billy Anderson, age 13 years, was driving a snowmobile belonging to defendant Lindsay, pulling plaintiff Kelly Robinson on an innertube attached to the snowmobile. Plaintiff's thumb was severed when it was caught in the tow rope. The thumb was reattached, but still not fully functional at the time of trial. Plaintiff filed suit against Billy Anderson and Lindsay, the owner of the snowmobile.] An action seeking damages for personal injuries was brought on behalf of Kelly Robinson who lost full use of a thumb in a snowmobile accident when she was 11 years of age. The petitioner, Billy Anderson, 13 years of age at the time of the accident, was the driver of the snowmobile. After a jury verdict in favor of Anderson, the trial court ordered a new trial.

The single issue on appeal is whether a minor operating a snowmobile is to be held to an adult standard of care. The trial court failed to instruct the jury as to that standard and ordered a new trial because it believed the jury should have been so instructed. We agree and affirm the order granting a new trial.

The trial court instructed the jury under WPI 10.05 that: "In considering the claimed negligence of a child, you are instructed that it is the duty of a child to exercise the same care that a reasonably careful child of the same age, intelligence, maturity, training and experience would exercise under the same or similar circumstances." Respondent properly excepted to the giving of this instruction and to the court's failure to give an adult standard of care.

The question of what standard of care should apply to acts of children has a long historical background. Traditionally, a flexible standard of care has been used to determine if children's actions were negligent. Under some circumstances, however, courts have developed a rationale for applying an adult standard.

In the courts' search for a uniform standard of behavior to use in determining whether or not a person's conduct has fallen below minimal acceptable standards, the law has developed a fictitious person, the "reasonable man of ordinary prudence." That term was first used in Vaughan v. Menlove, 132 Eng.Rep. 490 (1837).

Exceptions to the reasonable person standard developed when the individual whose conduct was alleged to have been negligent suffered from some physical impairment, such as blindness, deafness, or lameness. Courts also found it necessary, as a practical matter, to depart considerably from the objective standard when dealing with children's behavior. Children are traditionally encouraged to pursue childhood activities without the same burdens and responsibilities with which adults must contend. [C] As a result, courts evolved a special standard of care to measure a child's negligence in a particular situation.

In Roth v. Union Depot Co., 13 Wash. 525, 43 P. 641 (1896), Washington joined "the overwhelming weight of authority" in distinguishing between the capacity of a child and that of an adult. As the court then stated, at page 544, 43 P. at page 647: "[I]t would be a monstrous doctrine to hold that a child of inexperience—and experience can come only with years—should be held to the same degree of care in avoiding danger as a person of mature years and accumulated experience."

The court went on to hold, at page 545, 43 P. at page 647: "The care or caution required is according to the capacity of the child, and this is to be determined, ordinarily, by the age of the child. * * * [A] child is held * * * only to the exercise of such degree of care and discretion as is reasonably to be expected from children of his age."

* * * In the past we have always compared a child's conduct to that expected of a reasonably careful child of the same age, intelligence, maturity, training and experience. This case is the first to consider the question of a child's liability for injuries sustained as a result of his or her operation of a motorized vehicle or participation in an inherently dangerous activity.

Courts in other jurisdictions have created an exception to the special child standard because of the apparent injustice that would occur if a child who caused injury while engaged in certain dangerous activities were permitted to defend himself by saying that other children similarly situated would not have exercised a degree of care higher than his, and he is, therefore, not liable for his tort. Some courts have couched the exception in terms of children engaging in an activity which is normally one for adults only. See, e.g., Dellwo v. Pearson, 259 Minn. 452, 107 N.W.2d 859 (1961) (operation of a motorboat). We believe a better rationale is that when the activity a child engages in is inherently dangerous, as is the operation of powerful mechanized vehicles, the child should be held to an adult standard of care.

Such a rule protects the need of children to be children but at the same time discourages immature individuals from engaging in inherently dangerous activities. Children will still be free to enjoy traditional childhood activities without being held to an adult standard of care. Although accidents sometimes occur as the result of such activities, they are not activities generally considered capable of resulting in "grave danger to others and to the minor himself if the care used in the course of the activity drops below that care which the reasonable and prudent adult would use * * *." Daniels v. Evans, 107 N.H. 407, 408, 224 A.2d 63, 64 (1966).

Other courts adopting the adult standard of care for children engaged in adult activities have emphasized the hazards to the public if the rule is otherwise. We agree with the Minnesota Supreme Court's language in its decision in Dellwo v. Pearson, supra, 259 Minn. at 457–58, 107 N.W.2d at 863:

"Certainly in the circumstances of modern life, where vehicles moved by powerful motors are readily available and frequently operated by immature individuals, we should be skeptical of a rule that would allow motor vehicles to be operated to the hazard of the public with less than the normal minimum degree of care and competence."

Dellwo applied the adult standard to a twelve-year-old defendant operating a motor boat. Other jurisdictions have applied the adult standard to minors engaged in analogous activities. Goodfellow v. Coggburn, 98 Idaho 202, 203–04, 560 P.2d 873 (1977) (minor operating tractor); Williams v. Esaw, 214 Kan. 658, 668, 522 P.2d 950 (1974) (minor operating motorcycle); Perricone v. DiBartolo, 14 Ill.App.3d 514, 520, 302 N.E.2d 637 (1973) (minor operating gasoline-powered minibike); Krahn v. LaMeres, 483 P.2d 522, 525–26 (Wyo.1971) (minor operating automobile). The holding of minors to an adult standard of care when they operate motorized vehicles is gaining approval from an increasing number of courts and commentators. [C]

The operation of a snowmobile likewise requires adult care and competence. Currently 2.2 million snowmobiles are in operation in the United States. 9 Envir.Rptr. (BNA) 876 [1978 Current Developments]. Studies show that collisions and other snowmobile accidents claim hundreds of casualties each year and that the incidence of accidents is particularly high among inexperienced operators. [C]

At the time of the accident, the 13-year-old petitioner had operated snowmobiles for about 2 years. When the injury occurred, petitioner was operating a 30-horsepower snowmobile at speeds of 10–20 miles per hour. The record indicates that the machine itself was capable of 65 miles per hour. Because petitioner was operating a powerful motorized vehicle, he should be held to the standard of care and conduct expected of an adult.

The order granting a new trial is affirmed.

NOTES AND QUESTIONS

1. The standard used by a majority of jurisdictions usually is stated to be "what it is reasonable to expect of children of like age, intelligence and experience." See Restatement (Second) of Torts § 283A and Restatement (Third) of Torts: Liability for Physical and Emotional Harm § 10 (2010); Cleveland Rolling-Mill Co. v. Corrigan, 46 Ohio St. 283, 20 N.E. 466 (1889). This means that more may be required of a child of superior intelligence.

2. After the judge has determined which standard, the jury applies it to the particular set of facts before it. Ordinarily, the question whether the child complied with the standard is one left to the jury; but if the only conclusion to be drawn from the evidence is that the child has behaved unreasonably in view of the child's estimated capacity, the judge may direct a verdict against the child.

3. A few courts use arbitrary age limits. See Price v. Kitsap Transit, 125 Wash.2d 456, 886 P.2d 556 (1994) (declining to abandon conclusive presumption that children under six are incapable of negligence). For example, a child under the age of seven may be, as a matter of law, incapable of any negligence; one between seven and 14 may be presumed incapable, but may be proved capable; one over 14 may be presumed capable, but may be proved incapable. Patterson v. Central Mills, Inc., 112 F.Supp.2d 681 (N.D. Ohio 2000) (noting that Ohio law presumes that children ages seven to 14 are incapable of negligence). These arbitrary rules have been taken over from the common law rules as to the capacity of children to commit crime, originally derived from civil law. Even the courts that usually make a case-by-case determination rather than using arbitrary age limits will hold that extremely young children are without the capacity. See, for example, Mastland, Inc. v. Evans Furniture, Inc., 498 N.W.2d 682 (Iowa 1993) (child under three who started fire playing with cigarette lighter in his crib was not capable of negligence as a matter of law even though Iowa had rejected the per se rules on the capacity of children for negligence) and Verni v. Johnson, 295 N.Y. 436, 68 N.E.2d 431 (1946) (children under four incapable of negligence over dissent's view that no fixed rule should be established). Restatement (Third) of Torts: Liability for Physical and Emotional Harm § 10(b) (2010) provides that children less than five years of age are incapable of negligence.

4. The maximum age to which the special rule as to children has been applied appears to be 17, in Charbonneau v. MacRury, 84 N.H. 501, 153 A. 457 (1931). In Atlanta Gas Light Co. v. Brown, 94 Ga.App. 351, 94 S.E.2d 612 (1956), it was "presumed" that a 20-year-old was as capable as an adult. Indiana applies the adult standard to everyone over the age of 14. Penn Harris Madison School Corp. v. Howard, 861 N.E.2d 1190 (Ind. 2007).

5. As reflected in the decision in the principal case, the Restatement (Second) of Torts has taken the position that the special rule for children should not be applied when the actor engages "in an activity which is normally undertaken only by adults, and for which adult qualifications are required." What activities fit that category? Thus far the adult standard

has been found applicable when a child was driving an automobile, Nielsen v. Brown, 232 Or. 426, 374 P.2d 896 (1962); a motorboat, Dellwo v. Pearson, 259 Minn. 452, 107 N.W.2d 859 (1961); a motorcycle, Harrelson v. Whitehead, 236 Ark. 325, 365 S.W.2d 868 (1963) and Daniels v. Evans, 107 N.H. 407, 224 A.2d 63 (1966); a motor scooter, Adams v. Lopez, 75 N.M. 503, 407 P.2d 50 (1965); and when a teen-ager was playing golf, Neumann v. Shlansky, 58 Misc.2d 128, 294 N.Y.S.2d 628 (1968), aff'd, 63 Misc.2d 587, 312 N.Y.S.2d 951 (1970) (Gullota, J., dissenting), aff'd, 36 A.D.2d 540, 318 N.Y.S.2d 925 (1971). In contrast, the special standard for children was applied to those who were bicycle riding, Williams v. Gilbert, 239 Ark. 935, 395 S.W.2d 333 (1965) and Bixenman v. Hall, 251 Ind. 527, 242 N.E.2d 837 (1968); deer hunting, Purtle v. Shelton, 251 Ark. 519, 474 S.W.2d 123 (1971); building a fire outdoors, Farm Bureau Ins. Group v. Phillips, 116 Mich.App. 544, 323 N.W.2d 477 (1982); and downhill skiing, Goss v. Allen, 70 N.J. 442, 360 A.2d 388 (1976). Restatement (Third) of Torts: Liability for Physical and Emotional Harm § 10(c) (2010) would apply the adult standard to children engaged in "dangerous activity that is characteristically undertaken by adults" and would include the use of firearms in that category. Comment *f*.

6. There are some decisions in which a similar allowance has been made for the physical and mental deficiencies of old age, but all have involved plaintiffs and have tended to focus on particular infirmities rather than age itself. Tobia v. Cooper Hospital University Med. Ctr., 136 N.J. 335, 643 A.2d 1 (1994) (holding that infirmities, including those caused by age, should be taken into account in determining whether comparative negligence instruction is appropriate in case where eighty-five year-old patient fell while getting off a gurney in emergency room). LaCava v. New Orleans, 159 So.2d 362 (La.App.1964); Johnson v. St. Paul City R. Co., 67 Minn. 260, 69 N.W. 900 (1897); Kitsap County Transp. Co. v. Harvey, 15 F.2d 166 (9th Cir.1926). See also Restatement (Third) of Torts: Liability for Physical and Emotional Harm § 11, comment *c* (2010).

Breunig v. American Family Ins. Co.

Supreme Court of Wisconsin, 1970.
45 Wis.2d 536, 173 N.W.2d 619.

[Action for personal injuries received by plaintiff when his truck was struck by an automobile driven on the wrong side of the highway by Mrs. Erma Veith. The action was brought against Mrs. Veith's automobile insurance company under Wisconsin procedure that permits direct action against a liability insurer. The jury returned a verdict for plaintiff, and defendant appealed.]

HALLOWS, CHIEF JUSTICE. There is no question that Erma Veith was subject at the time of the accident to an insane delusion which directly affected her ability to operate her car in an ordinarily prudent manner and caused the accident. * * *

The evidence established that Mrs. Veith, while returning home after taking her husband to work, saw a white light on the back of the car ahead of her. She followed this light for three or four blocks. Mrs. Veith could not remember anything else except landing in a field, lying on the side of the road, and people talking. She recalled awaking in the hospital.

The psychiatrist testified Mrs. Veith told him she was driving on a road when she believed that God was taking ahold of the steering wheel and was directing her car. She saw the truck coming and stepped on the gas in order to become air-borne because she knew she could fly because Batman does it. To her surprise she was not air-borne before striking the truck, but after the impact she was flying. * * * The psychiatrist testified Erma Veith was suffering from "schizophrenic reaction, paranoid type, acute." He stated that from the time Mrs. Veith commenced following the car with the white light and ending with the stopping of her vehicle in the cornfield, she was not able to operate the vehicle with her conscious mind, and that she had no knowledge or forewarning that such illness or disability would likely occur. * * *

The case was tried on the theory that some forms of insanity are a defense to and preclude liability for negligence. [C] Not all types of insanity vitiate responsibility for a negligent tort. The question of liability in every case must depend upon the kind and nature of the insanity. The effect of the mental illness or mental hallucination must be such as to affect the person's ability to understand and appreciate the duty which rests upon him to drive his car with ordinary care, or if the insanity does not affect such understanding and appreciation, it must affect his ability to control his car in an ordinarily prudent manner. And in addition, there must be an absence of notice or forewarning to the person that he may be suddenly subject to such a type of insanity or mental illness. * * *

The policy basis of holding a permanently insane person liable for his tort is: (1) Where one of two innocent persons must suffer a loss it should be borne by the one who occasioned it; (2) to induce those interested in the estate of the insane person (if he has one) to restrain and control him; and (3) the fear an insanity defense would lead to false claims of insanity to avoid liability. * * *

The cases holding an insane person liable for his torts have generally dealt with pre-existing insanity of a permanent nature and the question here presented was neither discussed nor decided. The plaintiff cites Sforza v. Green Bus Lines (1934) 150 Misc. 180, 268 N.Y.S. 446; Shapiro v. Tchernowitz (1956) 3 Misc.2d 617, 155 N.Y.S.2d 1011; Johnson v. Lambotte (1961) 147 Colo. 203, 363 P.2d 165, for holding insanity is not a defense in negligence cases. *Sforza* and *Shapiro* are New York trial court decisions which do not discuss the question here presented and are unconvincing. In *Johnson,* the defendant was under observation by order of the county court and was being treated in a hospital for "chronic schizophrenic state of paranoid type." On the day in question, she wanted to leave the hospital and escaped therefrom and found an automobile standing on a street with its motor running a few blocks from the hospital. She got into the car and drove off, having little or no control of the car. She soon collided with the plaintiff. Later she was adjudged mentally incompetent and committed to a state hospital. *Johnson* is not a case of sudden mental seizure with no forewarning. The defendant knew she was being treated for mental disorder and hence would not come under the nonliability rule herein stated.

We think the statement that insanity is no defense is too broad when it is applied to a negligence case where the driver is suddenly overcome without forewarning by a mental disability or disorder which incapacitates him from conforming his conduct to the standards of a reasonable man under like circumstances. These are rare cases indeed, but their rarity is no reason for overlooking their existence and the justification which is the basis of the whole doctrine of liability for negligence, i.e., that it is unjust to hold a man responsible for his conduct which he is incapable of avoiding and which incapability was unknown to him prior to the accident.

We need not reach the question of contributory negligence of an insane person or the question of comparative negligence as those problems are not now presented. All we hold is that a sudden mental incapacity equivalent in its effect to such physical causes as a sudden heart attack, epileptic seizure, stroke, or fainting should be treated alike and not under the general rule of insanity.

An interesting case holding this view in Canada is Buckley & Toronto Transp. Comm'n v. Smith Transport, Ltd. [1946] Ont.Rep. 798, 4 Dom.L.Rep. 721, which is almost identical on the facts with the case at bar. There, the court found no negligence when a truck driver was overcome by a sudden insane delusion that his truck was being operated by remote control of his employer and as a result he was in fact helpless to avert a collision.

[The court then considered whether Mrs. Veith had any warning or knowledge that would reasonably lead her to believe that hallucinations would occur and be such as to affect her driving an automobile. It concluded that, notwithstanding the testimony of the psychiatrist that in his opinion she did not, there was sufficient evidence of her past conduct to permit the jury to conclude that she believed she had a special relationship to God and was the chosen one to survive at the end of the world, and that she could believe that God would take over the direction of her life to the extent of driving her car. The question was held therefore to be properly left to the jury. Various other questions were also considered.]

Judgment affirmed.

NOTES AND QUESTIONS

1. Most courts do not make any allowance for the mental illness of the defendant—the defendant is judged by the standard of the reasonable person. See, for example, Johnson v. Lambotte, 147 Colo. 203, 363 P.2d 165 (1961); Cross v. Kent, 32 Md. 581 (1870); Williams v. Hays, 143 N.Y. 442, 38 N.E. 449 (1894); Ellis v. Fixico, 174 Okl. 116, 50 P.2d 162 (1935). This is true even in the case of "sudden insanity." See Kuhn v. Zabotsky, 9 Ohio St.2d 129, 224 N.E.2d 137 (1967).

2. Is this policy in accord with current understanding of mental illness? Does an "insane" defendant actually "know" about his condition and have the ability to make a rational decision not to drive? Cf. C.T.W. v. B.C.G., 809 S.W.2d 788 (Tex.App.1991) (pedophile negligent for failing to

seek professional help and to avoid situations where he would be alone with children). Should an exception be made for someone who is in treatment? See Shuman, Therapeutic Jurisprudence and Tort Law: A Limited Subjective Standard of Care, 46 SMU L.Rev. 409 (1992) (suggesting adoption of limited subjective standard of care for the mentally ill defendant who initiated treatment prior to allegedly negligent conduct). Should an exception be made for someone who is institutionalized and has injured a paid caretaker? See note 6, page 29, re jurisdictions that have carved out a narrow exception for institutionalized mentally disabled patients unable to control or appreciate the consequences of their conduct, which results in injury to a paid caretaker.

3. Who was the actual "defendant" in the principal case? What bearing does that have on the issue?

4. Why treat the diminished capacity of mentally disabled adults differently from the diminished capacity of children? What if the defendant is suffering from Alzheimer's Disease? Should that be treated as a mental illness (no exception made, defendant held to the reasonable person standard) or a physical condition (defendant held to standard of reasonable person with Alzheimer's)? See Gould v. American Family Mutual Ins. Co., 198 Wis.2d 450, 543 N.W.2d 282 (1996). What if someone's mental capacity is so limited that he is more like a child than an adult? Compare Restatement (Second) § 283(B) (no allowance is made for "lack of intelligence") and Restatement (Third) of Torts: Liability for Physical and Emotional Harm § 11(c) (2010) (no allowance for mental or emotional disability) with Lynch v. Rosenthal, 396 S.W.2d 272 (Mo.App.1965) (expert testimony that farm hand's IQ of 65 meant that his mental ability was less than that of a 10-year-old child considered in evaluating his contributory negligence).

5. In most of the cases we have read on the standard for negligence, the courts are considering the conduct of the defendant; some are considering the conduct of the plaintiff in order to determine whether the plaintiff's own negligence contributed to the cause of the accident. The effect of such a finding will be explored in more detail in Chapter 12, Defenses. With very few exceptions, the courts have consistently stated that the determination whether the reasonable person standard was met is the same, whether the actor is a defendant or a plaintiff, despite some argument that it should be different. A couple of jurisdictions have exhibited some flexibility in cases involving mental health patients against their health care providers in medical malpractice actions involving the failure to prevent the patient's suicide. Maunz v. Perales, 276 Kan. 313, 76 P.3d 1027 (2003) (jury should use capacity based standard in determining comparative fault of patient who committed suicide in action against psychiatrist who had treated him). Dodson v. South Dakota Dept. of Human Services, 703 N.W.2d 353 (S.D. 2005) (same).

(B) THE PROFESSIONAL

Heath v. Swift Wings, Inc.

Court of Appeals of North Carolina, 1979.
40 N.C.App. 158, 252 S.E.2d 526.

On 3 August 1975 a Piper 180 Arrow airplane crashed immediately after takeoff from the Boone-Blowing Rock Airport. * * * [On board the plane were the pilot, Fred Heath, his wife, their son, and a family friend, Vance Smathers. All were killed in the crash. This action alleges that the negligence of the pilot Fred Heath caused the crash. It was brought by the estates of the wife and son against the estate of the pilot (their husband and father) and Swift Wings, the owner of the airplane. Valerie Heath, the daughter of the pilot and his wife, was the sole survivor of the Heath family and the heir to the estates.]

Plaintiff's evidence, except to the extent it is quoted from the record, is briefly summarized as follows: Mary Payne Smathers Curry, widow of Vance Smathers, observed the takeoff of the Piper aircraft shortly after 5:00 o'clock on 3 August 1975. She observed Fred Heath load and reload the passengers and luggage, apparently in an effort to improve the balance of the aircraft. He also "walked around [the airplane] and looked at everything * * *." The airplane engine started promptly and the plane was taxied to the end of the runway where it paused for approximately five minutes before takeoff. The airplane came very close to the end of the runway before takeoff. However "[t]he engine sounded good the entire time, and she did not recall hearing the engine miss or pop or backfire." After takeoff, the airplane "gained altitude but it didn't go up very high" and then "leveled off pretty low". * * *

William B. Gough, Jr., a free-lance mechanical engineering consultant and pilot, testified concerning the operation and flight performance of the Piper 180 Arrow. He testified concerning the many factors affecting the takeoff capabilities of the Piper and the calculations to be made by the pilot before takeoff, utilizing flight performance charts. He testified that in his opinion, according to his calculations, the pilot should have used flaps to aid in the takeoff. Furthermore, he stated that in his opinion the reasonably prudent pilot should have made a controlled landing in the cornfield shortly after takeoff if he were experiencing difficulty attaining flight speed, and that if he had done so [all] would have survived. * * *

After the customary motions at the conclusion of all the evidence, the case was submitted to the jury upon voluminous instructions by the trial court. The jury returned a verdict answering the following issue as indicated: "1. Was Fred Heath, Jr., negligent in the operation of PA–28R 'Arrow' airplane on August 3, 1975 as alleged in the complaint?" Answer: "No". Plaintiff appeals assigning error to the exclusion of certain evidence and to the charge to the jury. * * *

MORRIS, CHIEF JUDGE. * * * Assignment of error No. 4 is directed to the trial court's charge concerning the definition of negligence and the applicable standard of care:

"Negligence, ladies and gentlemen of the jury, is the failure of someone to act as a reasonably and careful and prudent person would under the same or similar circumstances. Obviously, this could be the doing of something or the failure to do something, depending on the circumstances. With respect to aviation negligence could be more specifically defined as the failure to exercise that degree of ordinary care and caution, which an ordinary prudent pilot having the same training and experience as Fred Heath, would have used in the same or similar circumstances."

It is a familiar rule of law that the standard of care required of an individual, unless altered by statute, is the conduct of the reasonably prudent man under the same or similar circumstances. [Cc] While the standard of care of the reasonably prudent man remains constant, the quantity or degree of care required varies significantly with the attendant circumstances. [Cc]

The trial court improperly introduced a subjective standard of care into the definition of negligence by referring to the "ordinary care and caution, which an ordinary prudent pilot *having the same training and experience as Fred Heath,* would have used in the same or similar circumstances." (Emphasis added.) We are aware of the authorities which support the application of a greater standard of care than that of the ordinary prudent man for persons shown to possess special skill in a particular endeavor. See generally Prosser, Law of Torts (4th ed.) § 32. Indeed, our courts have long recognized that one who engages in a business, occupation, or profession must exercise the requisite degree of learning, skill, and ability of that calling with reasonable and ordinary care. See e.g., Insurance Co. v. Sprinkler Co., 266 N.C. 134, 146 S.E.2d 53 (1966) (fire sprinkler contractor); Service Co. v. Sales Co., 261 N.C. 660, 136 S.E.2d 56 (1964) (industrial designer); Hunt v. Bradshaw, 242 N.C. 517, 88 S.E.2d 762 (1955) (physician); Hodges v. Carter, 239 N.C. 517, 80 S.E.2d 144 (1954) (attorney). Furthermore, the specialist within a profession may be held to a standard of care greater than that required of the general practitioner. [C] Nevertheless, the professional standard remains an objective standard. For example, the recognized standard for a physician is established as "the standard of professional competence and care customary in similar communities among physicians engaged in his field of practice." Dickens v. Everhart, 284 N.C. at 101, 199 S.E.2d at 443.

Such objective standards avoid the evil of imposing a different standard of care upon each individual. The instructions in this case concerning the pilot's standard of care are misleading at best, and a misapplication of the law. They permit the jury to consider Fred Heath's own particular experience and training, whether outstanding or inferior, in determining the requisite standard of conduct, rather than applying a minimum standard generally applicable to all pilots. The plaintiff is entitled to an instruction holding Fred Heath to the objective minimum standard of care applicable to all pilots. * * *

This matter was well tried by both counsel for plaintiff and counsel for defendants, and several days were consumed in its trial. Nevertheless, for prejudicial errors in the charge, there must be a

New trial.

HARRY C. MARTIN and CARLTON, JJ., concur.

NOTES AND QUESTIONS

1. In evaluating professional services cases, the basic principles involved are relatively uncomplicated: the reasonable prudent person takes on the profession of the actor and an objective standard is applied. See The Germanic, 196 U.S. 589 (1905) (shipmaster—"external standard" applied by Justice Holmes).

2. The standard is expressed in objective form—the knowledge, training and skill (or ability and competence) of an ordinary member of the profession. See, e.g., Centman v. Cobb, 581 N.E.2d 1286 (Ind.App.1991) (holding defendant who had just graduated from medical school and was doing an internship at hospital to same standard of care as a physician) and Arpin v. U.S., 521 F.3d 769 (7th Cir. 2008) (applying Illinois law) (noting that the majority rule holds residents to the same standard of care as physicians who have completed their residency in the same field of medicine). "Average" member is incorrect instruction because this would literally mean that half of the members could not meet the standard. See, e.g., Nowatske v. Osterloh, 198 Wis.2d 419, 543 N.W.2d 265 (1996) (finding that "average" should be eliminated from pattern jury instruction) and Corbitt v. Tatagari, 804 A.2d 1057 (Del. 2002) ("It is not the standard of care of the most highly skilled, nor is it necessarily that of average members of this profession, since those who have somewhat less than average skills may still possess the degree of skill and care to treat patients competently.") Cf. Gridley v. Johnson, 476 S.W.2d 475 (Mo.1972) (phrase "in good standing" held to be too vague).

3. The "professional" contracts to render services, but the suit is usually in tort for damage caused by negligence. There is no need to contract specifically to exercise the ordinary skill of the professional—the law imposes the duty. Ordinarily, the professional is liable only for negligence, because the service performed does not have a guaranteed result. The service provider may choose to provide a guarantee, which would be enforceable through contract law. Absent such an express contract for a particular result, the cause of action is in tort. See, e.g., Sciacca v. Polizzi, 403 So.2d 728 (La.1981) (cause of action for injuries caused by IUD sounded in tort rather than contract despite plaintiff's explicit wording in complaint because no specific guarantees were made by physician); Sullivan v. O'Connor, 363 Mass. 579, 296 N.E.2d 183 (1973) (plastic surgeon promised plaintiff Hedy Lamarr's nose); Haase v. Starnes, 323 Ark. 263, 915 S.W.2d 675 (1996) (ads promised a full, growing head of hair for life). What about an attorney's statement that if client's liquor license was not granted by the Liquor Control Commission, he would "kick ass" at the court of appeals? McComas v. Bocci, 166 Or.App. 150, 996 P.2d 506 (2000) (attorney had denied making statement and court found that statement, if made, constituted a gratuitous prediction that attorney had no contractual duty to produce). For a perspective on how jurors react to tort and contract claims in the same case, see the interviews with jurors from the Sullivan v. O'Connor case (plastic surgeon promised Hedy Lamarr's nose) in Danzig and Watson, The Capability Problem in Contract Law 22–28 (2d ed. 2004).

4. *Expert Testimony.* Because the professional is engaged in work that is technical in nature—not a matter of "common knowledge"—a lay jury is not in a position to understand without assistance the nature of the work or the application of the standard of care to this work. Thus, a plaintiff must offer expert testimony on the standard of care in order to establish her case. See, for example, Aetna Ins. Co. v. Hellmuth, Obata & Kassabaum, Inc., 392 F.2d 472 (8th Cir.1968) (applying Missouri law) (expert testimony required to establish reasonable standard of professional care of architect when issues presented are beyond the ordinary competency of lay jurors) and Wong v. Ekberg, 148 N.H. 369, 807 A.2d 1266 (2002) (expert testimony required to establish standard of care for attorney for pretrial preparation of criminal defense case).

5. Professional negligence is commonly called malpractice. On the subject in general, see D. Partlett, Professional Negligence (1985); Restatement (Second) of Torts § 299A.

6. Representative treatments of negligence for the major professions include the following:

Accountants. Causey, Duties and Liabilities of Public Accountants (7th ed. 2001).

Architects and Engineers: Sweet, Legal Aspects of Architecture, Engineering, and the Construction Process (9th ed. 2012).

Attorneys. Mallen & Smith, Legal Malpractice (2015 ed.) and Bertschi, The Law of Lawyer's Liability: A Fifty-state Survey (2012).

Clergy. Some parishioners have attempted to persuade their jurisdictions to recognize a separate tort for clergy malpractice, although none of them has yet succeeded. See, for example, Nally v. Grace Com. Church of the Valley, 47 Cal.3d 278, 763 P.2d 948, 253 Cal.Rptr. 97 (1988), cert. denied 490 U.S. 1007 (1989) (failure to refer son to psychiatrist when he threatened suicide during pastoral counseling); Destefano v. Grabrian, 763 P.2d 275 (Colo.1988) (priest engaged in intimate relationship with parishioner during marital counseling); Byrd v. Faber, 57 Ohio St.3d 56, 565 N.E.2d 584 (1991) (same); Schieffer v. Catholic Archdiocese, 244 Neb. 715, 508 N.W.2d 907 (1993) (same); Bladen v. First Presbyterian Church, 857 P.2d 789 (Okla.1993) (same); Cherepski v. Walker, 323 Ark. 43, 913 S.W.2d 761 (1996) (same); F.G. v. MacDonell, 150 N.J. 550, 696 A.2d 697 (1997) (same). Most of the cases involve allegations that the cleric engaged in consensual sexual relations with an adult parishioner, with some of the complaints also alleging that the parishioner was receiving marital counseling from the cleric. Others allege that the consent was obtained through intimidation or fraud. Marmelstein v. Kehillat New Hempstead: The Rav Aron Jofen Community Synagogue, 11 N.Y.3d 15, 22, 892 N.E.2d 375, 862 N.Y.S.2d 311 (2008) (plaintiff alleged that her rabbi had induced her to enter into a sexual relationship with him in the guise of therapy to assist her in finding a husband). The courts appear reluctant to recognize a new cause of action where the alleged acts already give rise to an existing cause of action (counseling malpractice or battery) or where such a recognition would entangle the court in defining reasonable conduct within the context of religious tenets. See also Lightman v. Flaum, 736 N.Y.S.2d 300, 97 N.Y.2d 128, 761 N.E.2d 1027 (2001) (declining to recognize cause of action for breach of fiduciary duty where rabbi disclosed—in affidavit in support of husband's bid for child custody—information about wife that she had confided in him during spiritual counseling, expressing fear of entanglement in sorting out whether the disclosure was in accord with religious tenets). But see Doe v. Evans, 814 So.2d 370 (Fla. 2002) (permitting breach of fiduciary duty case to go forward against a Catholic priest based on alleged abuse of marital counseling relationship).

Designer of Group Health Insurance Plan. Coyne & Delany Co. v. Selman, 98 F.3d 1457 (4th Cir. 1996) (applying Virginia law).

Doctors, Dentists, and Veterinarians. Pegalis & Wachsman, American Law of Medical Malpractice (3rd ed. 2005); Schafler, "Dental Malpractice: Legal and Medical Handbook" (3rd ed. 1996); see also Price v. Brown, 545 Pa. 216, 680 A.2d 1149 (1996) (distinguishing veterinary malpractice from bailment in case involving death of pet).

Pharmacists. Brushwood, Pharmacy Malpractice: Law and Regulations (2nd ed. 1998). See also Kowalski v. Rose Drugs, 2011 Ark. 44, 378 S.W.3d 109 (2011) (joining majority of jurisdictions that impose no general duty to warn on pharmacists); Cottam v. CVS Pharmacy, 436 Mass. 316, 764 N.E.2d 814 (2002) (noting that pharmacists have no general duty to warn customers of potential side effects of prescription drugs but, by providing list of some side effects to customer, assume a duty to warn of all side effects) (collecting cases from other jurisdictions); and Happel v. Wal-Mart Stores, Inc., 199 Ill.2d 179, 262 Ill.Dec. 815, 766 N.E.2d 1118 (2002) (pharmacy owes duty to warn either customer or her prescribing physician that drug was contraindicated for patient with allergies that pharmacist knew patient had).

Teachers. Courts generally have refused to recognize educational malpractice, partly because of difficulties in determining why the student failed to learn, partly because it would be difficult to choose among various educational theories to set the standard, and partly because of problems in financing an award. See, for example, Brantley v. District of Columbia, 640 A.2d 181, 183 (D.C.App.1994) ("There is thus overwhelming judicial authority for the proposition that public school authorities' failure to educate students, or to assign them to the correct school or program, does not give rise to a suit for money damages") and Page v. Klein Tools, Inc., 461 Mich. 703, 610 N.W.2d 900 (2000) (allowing a claim for negligent instruction would avoid the practical reality that, in the end, it is the student who is responsible for his knowledge, including the limits of that knowledge.) But see Ethan Huff and Aaron Tang, "The New Education Malpractice Litigation," 99 Va. L.Rev. 419 (2013) (arguing that the new data-driven, value-added models should cause a rethinking of the rejection of educational malpractice claims). Contrast the educational malpractice claims with Sain v. Cedar Rapids Community School Dist., 626 N.W.2d 115 (Iowa 2001) (cause of action against guidance counselor for negligent misrepresentation of NCAA regulations to student athlete not educational malpractice and thus should have survived summary judgment) and Christensen v. Southern Normal School, 790 So.2d 252 (Ala. 2001) (distinguishing breach of contract and fraud claims from educational malpractice).

7. The standard is appropriately modified for specialists in a particular profession holding themselves out to have higher skills. Aves v. Shah, 997 F.2d 762 (10th Cir.1993) (applying Kansas law) (physician who

held herself out as a specialist in obstetrics could not object to jury instruction that held her to the higher standard of care of a specialist); Duffey Law Office v. Tank Transport, Inc., 194 Wis.2d 674, 535 N.W.2d 91 (App. 1995) (attorney who held himself out as specialist in labor law held to higher standard).

8. Professionals providing their services *pro bono* owe the same duty of care as those whose services are compensated. See Becker v. Janinski, 15 N.Y.S. 675, 677 (1891) ("Whether the patient be a pauper or a millionaire, whether he be treated gratuitously or for reward, the physician owes him precisely the same measure of duty, and the same degree of skill and care.")

Hodges v. Carter

Supreme Court of North Carolina, 1954.
239 N.C. 517, 80 S.E.2d 144.

Civil action to recover compensation for losses resulting from the alleged negligence of defendant D.D. Topping and H.C. Carter, now deceased, in prosecuting, on behalf of plaintiff, certain actions on fire insurance policies.

On 4 June 1948 plaintiff's drug store building located in Bellhaven, N.C., together with his lunch counter, fixtures, stock of drugs and sundries therein contained, was destroyed by fire. At the time plaintiff was insured under four policies of fire insurance against loss of, or damage to, said mercantile building and its contents. He filed proof of loss with each of the four insurance companies which issued said policies. The insurance companies severally rejected the proofs of loss, denied liability, and declined to pay any part of the plaintiff's losses resulting from said fire.

H.C. Carter and D.D. Topping were at the time attorneys practicing in Beaufort and adjoining counties. As they were the ones from whom plaintiff seeks to recover, they will hereafter be referred to as the defendants. * * *

On 3 May 1949 defendants, in behalf of plaintiff, instituted in the Superior Court of Beaufort County four separate actions—one against each of the four insurers. Complaints were filed and summonses were issued, directed to the sheriff of Beaufort County. In each case the summons and complaint, together with copies thereof, were mailed to the Commissioner of Insurance of the State of North Carolina. The Commissioner accepted service of summons and complaint in each case and forwarded a copy thereof by registered mail to the insurance company named defendant therein.

Thereafter each defendant [insurance company] made a special appearance and moved to dismiss the action against it for want of proper service of process for that the Insurance Commissioner was without authority, statutory or otherwise, to accept service of process issued against a foreign insurance company doing business in this State. [The statute provided that the Insurance Commissioner could *be served*. At that time, service meant personal delivery; there was no statutory authorization for service by mail. The attorneys followed a local custom of mailing the summons instead of having it served personally on the Insurance Commissioner. The insurance companies argued that the Insurance Commissioner did not have the authority to accept what amounted to substituted service by mail.] When the special appearance and motion to dismiss came on for hearing at the February Term 1950, the judge presiding concluded that the acceptance of service of process by the Insurance Commissioner was valid and served to subject the movants to the jurisdiction of the court. Judgment was entered in each case denying the motion therein made. Each defendant excepted and appealed. This Court reversed. Hodges v. New Hampshire Fire Insurance Co., 232 N.C. 475, 61 S.E.2d 372. See also Hodges v. Home Insurance Co., 233 N.C. 289, 63 S.E.2d 819.

On 4 March 1952 plaintiff instituted this action in which he alleges that the defendants were negligent in prosecuting his said actions in that they failed to (1) have process properly served, and (2) sue out alias summonses at the time the insurers filed their motions to dismiss the actions for want of proper service of summons, although they then had approximately sixty days within which to procure the issuance thereof.

Defendants, answering, deny negligence and plead good faith and the exercise of their best judgment.

At the hearing in the court below the judge, at the conclusion of plaintiff's evidence in chief, entered judgment of involuntary nonsuit. Plaintiff excepted and appealed.

BARNHILL, CHIEF JUSTICE. * * * Ordinarily when an attorney engages in the practice of the law and contracts to prosecute an action in behalf of his client, he impliedly represents that (1) he possesses the requisite degree of learning, skill, and ability necessary to the practice of his profession and which others similarly situated ordinarily possess; (2) he will exert his best judgment in the prosecution of the litigation entrusted to him; and (3) he will exercise reasonable and ordinary care and diligence in the use of his skill and in the application of his knowledge to his client's cause. [Cc]

An attorney who acts in good faith and in an honest belief that his advice and acts are well founded and in the best interest of his client is not answerable for a mere error of judgment or for a mistake in a point of law which has not been settled by the court of last resort in his State and on which reasonable doubt may be entertained by well-informed lawyers. [Cc]

Conversely, he is answerable in damages for any loss to his client which proximately results from a want of that degree of knowledge and skill ordinarily possessed by others of his profession similarly situated, or from the omission to use reasonable care and diligence, or from the failure to exercise in good faith his best judgment in attending to the litigation committed to his care. [Cc]

When the facts appearing in this record are considered in the light of these controlling principles of law, it immediately becomes manifest that plaintiff has failed to produce a scintilla of evidence tending to show that defendants breached any duty the law imposed upon them when they accepted employment to prosecute plaintiff's actions against his insurers or that they did not possess the requisite learning and skill required of an attorney or that they acted otherwise than in the utmost good faith.

The Commissioner of Insurance is the statutory process agent of foreign insurance companies doing business in this State, G.S. § 58–153, Hodges v. New Hampshire Insurance Co., 232 N.C. 475, 61 S.E.2d 372, and when defendants mailed the process to the Commissioner of Insurance for his acceptance of service thereof, they were following a custom [mailing of Complaint and Summons to Commissioner of Insurance rather than personal service upon him] which had prevailed in this State for two decades or more. Foreign insurance companies had theretofore uniformly ratified such service, appeared in response thereto, filed their answers, and made their defense. The right of the Commissioner to accept service of process [by mail] in behalf of foreign insurance companies doing business in this State had not been tested in the courts. Attorneys generally, throughout the State, took it for granted that under the terms of G.S. § 58–153 such acceptance of service was adequate. And, in addition, the defendants had obtained the judicial declaration of a judge of our Superior Courts that the acceptance of service by the Commissioner subjected the defendants to the jurisdiction of the court. Why then stop in the midst of the stream and pursue some other course?

Doubtless this litigation was inspired by a comment which appears in our opinion on the second appeal, Hodges v. Home Insurance Co., 233 N.C. 289, 63 S.E.2d 819. However, what was there said was pure dictum, injected—perhaps ill advisedly—in explanation of the reason we could afford plaintiff no relief on that appeal. We did not hold, or intend to intimate, that defendants had been in any wise neglectful of their duties as counsel for plaintiff.

The judgment entered in the court below is

Affirmed.

NOTES AND QUESTIONS

1. The dictum in the Hodges v. Home Ins. Co. case, referred to in the last major paragraph of the principal case, reads as follows: "At the time defendant entered its motion to dismiss the original action, the plaintiff still had more than sixty days in which to sue out an alias summons and thus keep his action alive. He elected instead to rest his case upon the validity of the service had. The unfortunate result is unavoidable." The statute of limitations had run and no new suit could be brought. As a result the loss fell on the insured. Is this where it should fall?

2. It is not legal malpractice to fail to advocate for or anticipate a substantial change in law requiring an overruling of controlling precedent. Minkina v. Frankl, 16 N.E.3d 492 (Mass. App. 2014). Nor is it malpractice to fail to anticipate correctly the resolution of an unsettled legal principle. Smith v. McLaughlin, 769 S.E.2d 7 (Va. 2015). Note that the principal case lists three areas in which an attorney's conduct may be questioned. *Possession of knowledge or skill.* Defendant attorney, representing a wife in a divorce proceeding, failed to claim for his client her interests under the California community property law in her husband's retirement benefits. The attorney mistakenly believed that they were not subject to the claim.

The trouble was that he failed to research the topic and would have found the law relatively clear that the retirement benefits were community property. The court upheld a judgment for $100,000. Smith v. Lewis, 13 Cal.3d 349, 530 P.2d 589, 118 Cal.Rptr. 621 (1975). Professionals are not expected to know everything, just what the ordinary member of the profession does. See, Lucas v. Hamm, 56 Cal.2d 583, 364 P.2d 685, 15 Cal.Rptr. 821 (1961), where a will had trust provisions that violated the rules against perpetuities and against restraints on alienation. Of these topics, it was said that "few, if any, areas of the law have been more fraught with more confusion or concealed traps for the unwary draftsman," and the court held the attorney not liable.

3. *Exercise of Best Judgment.* While most treatments of the standard of care for professionals have been confined to the element of knowledge and skill, there are, as the opinion in this case indicates, two other significant elements. The first is the exercise of a discerning judgment. It is usually expressed by saying that the professional is not liable for a "mere error of judgment." Crosby v. Jones, 705 So.2d 1356 (Fla.1998) (tactical decisions or decisions made on debatable point of law are not actionable so long as attorney exercises best judgment); Thomas v. Bethea, 351 Md. 513, 718 A.2d 1187 (1998) (recommendation to settle); Wood v. McGrath, North, Mullin & Kratz, 256 Neb. 109, 589 N.W.2d 103 (1999) (recommendation to settle without disclosing that settlement agreement conceded issues that client might have won was not exercise of best judgment); Black v. Shultz, 530 F.3d 702 (8th Cir.2008) (applying Nebraska law) (during legal representation on sexual harassment claim against employer, advice whether to accept severance package from employer and whether to seek other job were possible grounds for legal malpractice claim). The same language is used for doctors, particularly in the use of discretion in making a diagnosis. See Blankenship v. Baptist Memorial Hosp., 26 Tenn.App. 131, 168 S.W.2d 491 (1942). Jury instructions must be worded carefully so that jury is not misled into thinking that professional is not liable so long as she exercised *her* "best judgment" even if that best judgment was in fact below the accepted standard of care. Pleasants v. Alliance Corp., 209 W.Va. 39, 543 S.E.2d 320 (2000) (while noting that "mistake of judgment" jury instruction is still used in many jurisdictions, court finds that it wrongfully injects an element of subjectivity into evaluation of standard of care).

4. *Use of Due Care.* The other element involves the professional's use of due care in the application of the professional's skill and knowledge. This element describes steps that are mechanical rather than discretionary and hence because such steps implicate no professional judgment, courts are more likely to find liability. A prime illustration of this type of negligence for lawyers is failure to file a suit before the running of the statute of limitations. For doctors it would be failure to obtain the requisite data on which to exercise trained discretion to develop a diagnosis, by, for example, failing to read the test results.

5. While engaged in litigation, an attorney may run into problems involving all three aspects of the standard care. See the treatment in Woodruff v. Tomlin, 616 F.2d 924 (6th Cir.1980) (applying Tennessee law), alleging negligence in the conduct of personal injury litigation arising out of an automobile accident. The Report of an ABA study, Profile of Legal Malpractice Claims: 2008–2011, found that the most frequent areas of

malpractice claims against lawyers are real estate (20%), personal injury (16%), family law (12%), and estate and probate (11%). The most common alleged errors are failure to know or properly apply the law (13%), procrastination or failure to follow up (9%), inadequate discovery or investigation (8%), planning error or error in procedure choice (7%), and lost file, document, or evidence (7%).

6. Just as the patient-plaintiff in a medical malpractice case must show that the patient would have recovered, in attorney negligence cases the plaintiff-client must show that but for the attorney's negligence the client would have been successful in prosecuting or defending the claim. See Togstad v. Vesely, Otto, Miller & Keefe, 291 N.W.2d 686 (Minn.1980). See also Chapter 5, notes 6–9, pages 289–290. On this causation issue, do you think it would be more difficult for a plaintiff-client to bring a successful attorney-negligence case where the claim is that the attorney inadequately prepared for trial or where the claim is that the attorney missed the statute of limitations?

Boyce v. Brown

Supreme Court of Arizona, 1938.
51 Ariz. 416, 77 P.2d 455.

LOCKWOOD, JUDGE. Berlie B. Boyce and Nannie E. Boyce, his wife, hereinafter called plaintiffs, brought suit against Edgar H. Brown, hereinafter called defendant, to recover damages for alleged malpractice by the defendant upon the person of Nannie E. Boyce. The case was tried to a jury and, at the close of the evidence for plaintiffs, the court granted a motion for an instructed verdict in favor of the defendant, on the ground that there was no competent testimony that he was guilty of any acts of commission or omission sufficient, as a matter of law to charge him with malpractice. Judgment was rendered on the verdict, and, after the usual motion for new trial was overruled, this appeal was taken. * * *

The sole question for our consideration, therefore, is whether, taking the evidence as strongly as is reasonably possible in support of plaintiffs' theory of the case, as we must do when the court instructs a verdict in favor of defendant, there was sufficient evidence to sustain a judgment in favor of plaintiffs. * * *

About September 1, 1927, plaintiffs engaged the services of defendant, who for many years had been a practicing physician and surgeon in Phoenix, to reduce a fracture of Mrs. Boyce's ankle. This was done by means of an operation which consisted, in substance, of making an incision at the point of fracture, bringing the broken fragments of bone into apposition, and permanently fixing them in place by means of a metal screw placed in the bone. Defendant continued to attend Mrs. Boyce for three or four weeks following such operation until a complete union of the bone had been established, when his services terminated. There is no serious contention in the record that defendant did not follow the approved medical standard in the treatment of the fractured bone up to this time. No further professional relations existed between the parties until seven years later, in November, 1934, when Mrs. Boyce again consulted him, complaining that her ankle was giving her considerable pain. He examined the ankle, wrapped it with adhesive tape, and then filed the edge of an arch support, which he had made for her seven years before, and which, from use, had grown so thin that the edge was sharp. About a week later he removed the bandage. Her ankle, however, did not improve after this treatment, but continued to grow more painful until January, 1936, some two years later. At this last-mentioned time she returned to defendant, who again examined the ankle. A few days later she went to visit Dr. Kent of Mesa, who, on hearing the history of the case, and noticing some discoloration and swelling, caused an X-ray of the ankle to be made. This X-ray showed that there had been some necrosis of the bone around the screw. Dr. Kent operated upon Mrs. Boyce, removing the screw, and she made an uneventful recovery, the ankle becoming practically normal.

There are certain general rules of law governing actions of malpractice, which are almost universally accepted by the courts, and which are applicable to the present situation. We state them as follows: (1) One licensed to practice medicine is presumed to possess the degree of skill and learning which is possessed by the average member of the medical profession in good standing in the community in which he practices, and to apply that skill and learning, with ordinary and reasonable care, to cases which come to him for treatment. If he does not possess the requisite skill and learning, or if he does not apply it, he is guilty of malpractice. [C] (2) Before a physician or surgeon can be held liable as for malpractice, he must have done something in his treatment of his patient which the recognized standard of good medical practice in the community in which he is practicing forbids in such cases, or he must have neglected to do something which such standard requires. [C] (3) In order to sustain a verdict for the plaintiffs in an action for malpractice, the standard of medical practice in the community must be shown by affirmative evidence, and, unless there is evidence of such a standard, a jury may not be permitted to speculate as to what the required standard is, or whether the defendant has departed therefrom. [Cc] (4) Negligence on the part of a physician or surgeon in the treatment of a case is never presumed, but must be affirmatively proven, and no presumption of negligence nor want of skill arises from the mere fact that a treatment was unsuccessful, failed to bring the best results, or that the patient died. [C] (5) The accepted rule is that negligence on the part of a physician or surgeon, by reason of his departure from the proper standard of practice, must be established by expert medical testimony, unless the negligence is so grossly apparent that a layman would have no difficulty in recognizing it. [Cc] (6) The testimony of other physicians that they would have followed a different course of treatment than that followed by the defendant is not sufficient to establish malpractice unless it also appears that the course of treatment followed deviated from one of the methods of treatment approved by the standard in that community. [C]

With these principles of the law governing the relation of physician and patient, and malpractice actions arising out of that relation as a guide, let us consider the record to see whether plaintiffs presented sufficient evidence to sustain a judgment in their favor. Two questions present themselves to us: (a) What was the treatment which defendant gave Mrs. Boyce in November, 1934? and (b) What was the medical standard which he was required to conform to, under all the circumstances, in giving her treatment at that time? The treatment given, according to her own testimony, consisted in an ordinary examination of the ankle, the smoothing of an arch support which she was then wearing, and the wrapping of the ankle with adhesive tape, with the suggestion that the tape be left on for a few days. About a week later Mrs. Boyce returned and the tape was taken off. The evidence does not show that she ever came back to defendant for further treatment in November, 1934, or, indeed, until January, 1936. The next question is whether the examination and treatment given by defendant departed from the established standard for cases like that of Mrs. Boyce. The only testimony we have which, in any manner, bears upon medical standards or the proper treatment of Mrs. Boyce in November, 1934, is that of Dr. Kent, who performed the operation on the ankle in January, 1936, and of defendant. The latter testified that he did what was required by Mrs. Boyce's condition as it existed then. Dr. Kent's testimony as to the condition he found in 1936, and what he did, is clear and distinct. He was asked as to how long prior to that time the screw should have been removed, and stated that he could not answer; that, if the ankle was in the same condition as it was when he operated, he would say that the screw should have been removed, but that it was impossible for him to testify as to when the condition justifying removal arose. He was questioned more fully and answered substantially that his first conclusion, if he had been in the position of defendant, when Mrs. Boyce called on the latter in November, 1934, would have been that arthritis in the ankle joint was causing the pain, but that he would not have been fully satisfied without having an X-ray made of the ankle. On cross-examination he testified that the method of uniting bone used by defendant was a standard one, and that the screw was not removed, as a rule, unless it made trouble. Nowhere, however, did Dr. Kent testify as to what was the proper standard of medical care required at the time defendant treated Mrs. Boyce in 1934, or as to whether, in his opinion, the treatment given deviated from that standard. The nearest he came to such testimony was the statement that he personally would have had an X-ray taken, but he did not say the failure to do so was a deviation from the proper standard of treatment.

Counsel for plaintiffs, in their oral argument, apparently realized the weakness of their evidence on the vital point of what the proper medical standard required in 1934, and based their claim of negligence almost entirely upon the failure of defendant to take an X-ray of Mrs. Boyce's ankle at that time. They urge that this comes within the exception to the general rule, in that a failure to do so is such obvious negligence that even a layman knows it to be a departure from the proper standard. We think this contention cannot be sustained. It is true that most laymen know that the X-ray usually offers the best method of diagnosing physical changes of the interior organs of the body, and particularly of the skeleton, short of an actual opening of the body for ocular examination, but laymen cannot say that in all cases where there is some trouble with the internal organs that it is a departure from standard medical practice to fail to take an X-ray. Such things are costly and do not always give a satisfactory diagnosis, or even as good a one as other types of examination may give. In many cases the taking of an X-ray might be of no value and put the patient to unnecessary expense, and, in view of the testimony in the present case as to the arthritis which Mrs. Boyce had, and which Dr. Kent testified would have been his first thought as to the cause of Mrs. Boyce's pain in 1934, we think it is going too far to say that the failure to take an X-ray of Mrs. Boyce's ankle at that time was so far a departure from ordinary medical standards that even laymen would know it to be gross negligence. Since, therefore, there was insufficient evidence in the record to show that defendant was guilty of malpractice, under the rules of law above set forth, the court properly instructed a verdict in favor of the defendant.

The judgment of the superior court is affirmed.

NOTES AND QUESTIONS

1. In the principal case, do you suppose that the defendant was not negligent or just not proved to be negligent? Did plaintiff lose because her attorney failed to ask the right questions of Dr. Kent or because Dr. Kent really did not believe that Dr. Brown violated the standard of care in failing to take the x-ray? Why didn't Mrs. Boyce's attorney choose a different expert witness?

2. *Customary Practice (Violation of).* It is not enough that an expert witness testify that he would not personally follow the defendant's practice; he must also testify that the practice did not conform with the standard of care of an ordinary member of the profession. See, e.g., Johnson v. Riverdale Anesthesia Assocs., 275 Ga. 240, 563 S.E.2d 431 (2002) (because the standard of care in medical malpractice cases is that which is employed by the medical profession generally, and not what one individual physician would do under the same or similar circumstances, how a testifying medical expert personally would have treated a patient is not relevant to the issue of whether a physician committed malpractice). It may, however, be admissible to challenge the credibility of the expert witness if the witness's own practice is different from what he asserts for the standard of care. Condra v. Atlanta Orthopaedic Group, P.C., 285 Ga. 667, 681 S.E.2d 152 (2009).

3. Proof that a professional violated the standard of care usually must be established by expert testimony, unless the negligence is so obvious that it is within the common knowledge and experience of lay jurors. See, e.g., Welte v. Bello, 482 N.W.2d 437 (Iowa 1992) (during surgery on her nose, patient suffered third-degree burns on her arm caused by anesthesia that escaped from vein into surrounding tissue); Dickerson v. Fatehi, 253 Va. 324, 484 S.E.2d 880 (1997) (following surgery on her neck, patient had severe pain in her right arm and hand and 20 months later it was discovered that surgeon had failed to remove a hypodermic needle with a plastic attachment from the surgical site). Failure to file the complaint within the statute of limitations may not require expert witness testimony in a legal malpractice case. Yager v. Clauson, 101 A.3d 6 (N.H. 2014) (remanding to trial court to determine whether the facts of this case require an expert or are within the realm of common knowledge). For a detailed discussion of the common knowledge exception and scores of examples of rulings whether conduct was within the common knowledge

exception, see King, The Common Knowledge Exception to the Expert Testimony Requirement for Establishing the Standard of Care in Medical Malpractice, 59 Ala. L. Rev. 51 (2007). See also McGathey v. Brookwood Health Svcs., 143 So.3d 95 (Ala. 2013) (during arthroscopic shoulder surgery, patient suffered burns on her arm from a metal bar used to hold it in place during surgery that had not cooled sufficiently after having been sterilized by heating it) and the res ipsa loquitur cases, note 4, page 258.

4. The requirement of expert testimony to establish the standard of care applies to malpractice cases across the professions. See, for example, Singh v. Krueger, 39 Kan.App.2d 637, 183 P.3d 1, 4 (2008) ("The intricacies of the interplay between state and federal jurisdiction, the customs of a particular court, and the federal law surrounding immigration and deportation are all specialized areas of the law about which a lay juror would not know.") and Davis v. Enget, 779 N.W.2d 126, 127 (N.D. 2010) (plaintiff may have a firm belief that defendants' representation was insufficient, but his lay opinion cannot supplant that of an expert because the nature of the alleged errors are not so egregious or obvious that a layperson could perceive them).

5. *Customary Practice (Compliance with).* For the professions in general, evidence as to customary practice is admissible and may prove very influential. For the medical profession, it is usually found to be controlling and the jury are usually told that the plaintiff cannot recover unless the plaintiff proves that the defendant's conduct was not in accord with recognized medical practice. There are very few cases where the plaintiff has been allowed to recover despite the fact that the defendant health care provider complied with the customary practice of the profession. See Helling v. Carey, 83 Wash.2d 514, 519 P.2d 981 (1974) (ophthalmologist held negligent as a matter of law for failing to routinely test patients under age 40 for glaucoma despite expert testimony from both sides that the standards of the profession did not require such testing of patients that age; decision based on balancing court's perception of seriousness of potential risk against cost of test). This decision has been criticized by the commentators and reversed by the Washington legislature. See e.g., King, In Search of a Standard of Care for the Medical Profession: The "Accepted Practice" Formula, 28 Vand.L.Rev. 1213 (1975) and Keeton, Medical Negligence—The Standard of Care, 10 Tex.Tech.L.Rev. 351 (1979). For an interesting pair of cases with opposite results on this issue in the context of the obligation of a blood bank to do surrogate testing to screen for the AIDS virus before the AIDS antibody test was available, see Osborn v. Irwin Memorial Blood Bank, 5 Cal.App.4th 234, 7 Cal.Rptr.2d 101 (1992) ("professional prudence is defined by actual or accepted practice within a profession, rather than theories about what 'should' have been done"; j.n.o.v. for blood bank upheld) and United Blood Services v. Quintana, 827 P.2d 509 (Colo.1992) (applicable standard of care adopted by a profession, as established by expert testimony, is presumed to constitute due care for those practicing in that profession, but that presumption may be rebutted; plaintiffs entitled to new trial and opportunity to prove universal practice of blood banks was negligent). See also Peters, The Quiet Demise of Deference to Custom: Malpractice Law at the Millennium, 57 Wash. & Lee L. Rev. 163 (2000) (arguing that traditional deference to custom is eroding in many states).

Morrison v. MacNamara

District of Columbia Court of Appeals, 1979.
407 A.2d 555.

[Appellant Morrison reported to appellee medical laboratory in Washington, D.C., for a urethral smear test, which was physically invasive, for trichomonas, a urinary tract infection. The test was administered while Morrison was standing. Morrison had an adverse reaction to the test—he fainted and struck his head on a metal blood pressure stand and on the floor, causing permanent loss of his senses of smell and taste, among other injuries.

At trial, Morrison presented an expert witness from Michigan who testified that the test often causes the patient to feel faint and that the "national standard of care" requires that the patient sit or lie down during the test. The trial court refused to instruct the jury that a national standard of care applied, instead instructing them that a local standard applied. Morrison appeals that ruling. The defendants presented expert witnesses from Washington area laboratories who testified that they always administered the test with the patient standing.]

NEWMAN, CHIEF JUDGE: * * * At the close of all the evidence, appellant submitted several jury instructions which were based on the national standard of care. Appellant maintained that in view of the national certification of the laboratory, the laboratory was under a duty to adhere to nationally accepted standards for administering the urethral smear test, and that the jury should be so instructed. Appellees argued that the laboratory owed only the duty to adhere to that standard of medical care recognized in the Washington, D.C. metropolitan area. The trial court agreed with appellees.

* * * In medical malpractice, a term referring to ordinary negligence concepts in the area of medical diagnosis, treatment, and the like, the duty of care is generally formulated as that degree of reasonable care and skill expected of members of the medical profession under the same or similar circumstances. * * *

The locality rule states that the conduct of members of the medical profession is to be measured solely by the standard of conduct expected of other members of the medical profession in the same locality or the same community. [Cc]

This doctrine is indigenous to American jurisprudence and appears to have developed in the late nineteenth century. [Cc] The rule was designed to protect doctors in rural areas who, because of inadequate training and experience, and the lack of effective means of transportation and communication, could not be expected to exhibit the skill and care of urban doctors. * * *

In addition, it was argued that in view of the ability of urban areas to attract the most talented doctors, a rule which would hold rural doctors to urban standards of care would precipitate the departure of doctors from rural areas and thereby leave rural communities without sufficient medical care. [Cc] In sum, the locality rule was premised on the notion that the disparity in education and access to advances in medical science between rural and urban doctors required that they be held to different standards of care.

The cases in this jurisdiction exhibit a lack of uniformity on the issue of the geographic area in which the conduct of members of the medical profession is to be measured. For example, a number of cases state that members of the medical profession are held to the skill and learning exercised by members of their profession in the District of Columbia. [Cc] In other cases, the standard is referred to as that degree of care exercised by other members of the medical profession in the District or a similar locality. [Cc] Finally, a number of cases have articulated the medical standard of care without referring to any geographic limitation whatsoever. [Cc] Since courts in this jurisdiction were never directly presented with this issue, the empirical validity of the assumptions behind the locality rule has not previously been examined.

Even a cursory analysis of the policy behind the locality doctrine reveals that whatever relevance it has to the practice of medicine in remote rural communities, it has no relevance to medical practice in the District of Columbia. Clearly the nation's capital is not a community isolated from recent advances in the quality of care and treatment of patients. Rather, it is one of the leading medical centers in quality health care. * * *

Moreover, any purported disparity between the skills of practitioners in various urban centers has for the most part been eliminated. Unlike the diversified and often limited training that was available a hundred years ago, medical education has been standardized throughout the nation through a system of national accreditation. [Cc] Moreover, the significant improvements in transportation and communication over the past hundred years cast further doubt on continued vitality of the doctrine. * * * In sum, the major underpinnings of the locality doctrine no longer obtain. The locality rule has been quite properly criticized as a relic of the nineteenth century which has no relevance to the realities of modern medical practice. [Cc]

Quite apart from the locality rule's irrelevance to contemporary medical practice, the doctrine is also objectionable because it tends to immunize doctors from communities where medical practice is generally below that which exists in other communities from malpractice liability. [Cc] Rather than encouraging medical practitioners to elevate the quality of care and treatment of patients to that existing in other communities, the doctrine may serve to foster substandard care, by testing the conduct of medical professionals by the conduct of other medical professionals in the same community.

The locality rule is peculiar to medical malpractice. Architects are not held to a standard of conduct exercised by other architects in the District or a similar locality. [C] Moreover, the conduct of lawyers is not measured solely by the conduct of other lawyers in the District or a similar community. [Cc]

Despite these criticisms, the locality rule is still followed in several jurisdictions. * * *

Courts which have abandoned the locality rule have taken different approaches in defining the geographical boundary within which the conduct of a medical practitioner is to be measured. For example, a number of courts have modified the locality rule by extending the geographical reference group of the standard of care to include that of "the same or similar localities." [Cc]

This approach has been criticized because of the difficulty in determining whether two communities are similar. [Cc] In addition, the similar locality formulation has been criticized for containing the same deficiencies as the traditional locality rule, *i.e.,* if the standard of conduct in a similar community is substandard, the similar locality rule would immunize those medical professionals whose conduct conforms to the substandard medical practice in a similar community. [Cc]

Other courts, noting that medical standards have been nationalized largely through a system of national board certification, have adopted a national standard of care, and accordingly have eliminated any reference to a geographically defined area in their formulation of the standard of care applicable to medical professionals. [Cc] The import of these decisions is that health care professionals who are trained according to national standards and who hold themselves out to the public as such, should be held to a national standard of care.

We are in general agreement with those courts which have adopted a national standard of care. Varying geographical standards of care are no longer valid in view of the uniform standards of proficiency established by national board certification. * * *

Although we have found no cases which address the issue of the standard of care applicable to a clinical laboratory, the same reasons which justify the application of a national standard of care to physicians and hospitals appear to apply with equal validity to medical laboratories. Medical laboratories are often staffed and operated by doctors who undergo the same rigorous training as other physicians. The opportunities for keeping abreast of medical advances that are available to doctors are equally available to clinical laboratories. Indeed medical laboratories are often an integral part of a hospital. [C] Moreover, clinical laboratories generally conduct many of the routine tests that would normally be performed by physicians and hospitals. Accordingly, they owe similar duties in their care and treatment of patients. [C]

Thus we hold that at least as to board certified physicians, hospitals, medical laboratories, and other health care providers, the standard of care is to be measured by the national standard. It follows that an instruction which compares a nationally certified medical professional's conduct exclusively with the standard of care in the District or a similar community is erroneous.

In the present case, appellees concede that they are a nationally certified medical laboratory and that they hold themselves out to the public as such. Appellant's expert witness testified at trial that the proper procedure to be employed in conducting a urethral smear test, according to national standards, is with the patient in a sitting or prone position. Appellees' expert witnesses who were all from the Washington metropolitan area testified that they were not aware of any national standards for conducting the test and that they always conducted the test with the patient in a standing position. However, the trial court instructed the jury that the appellees' conduct is to be compared solely with the standard of care prevailing in Washington, D.C. Thus, in effect the jury was instructed to ignore the testimony of appellant's expert witness on the standard of care. This instruction was error. The conflict in expert testimony was for the jury to resolve. Accordingly, we vacate the judgment in favor of appellees and order a new trial. * * * Reversed.

NOTES AND QUESTIONS

1. What happens on remand at the new trial if each side's experts give the same testimony but the jury is given the correct instruction on considering expert testimony?

2. It was traditional with the medical profession to state the standard of knowledge and skill in terms of a practitioner in good standing in the local community in which the defendant practices. This is sometimes known as the "strict locality" rule. As the principal case notes, it arose in the days in which medical education was not standardized and there was wide variance in the knowledge, skill, and practices of doctors in different parts of the country, particularly between rural and urban areas. The locality rule has not been generally followed in regard to the other professions. See, e.g., Russo v. Griffin, 147 Vt. 20, 510 A.2d 436 (1986) (adopting statewide standard of care in attorney malpractice case); Chapman v. Bearfield, 207 S.W.3d 736, 740 (Tenn. 2006) ("while there may be local *rules of practice* within the various judicial districts of our State, there are no local *standards of care*"); and Hamilton v. Sommers, 2014 S.D. 76, 855 N.W.2d 855 (2014) (while locality may be relevant to the expectations a client has of his lawyer, a statewide focus would usually be appropriate.) But the expert must actually be qualified to opine on the standard of care and the qualification is more than just familiarizing himself with the case law of that state. Phillips v. Wilks, Lukoff & Bracegirdle, LLC, ___ A.3d ___, 2014 WL 4930693 (Del. 2014) (although competency requirements are not designed to preclude all testimony from out-of-state experts, expert witnesses must be "well acquainted or thoroughly conversant" with the degree of skill ordinarily employed in the local community and locality where the alleged malpractice occurred).

3. Critics charged that the strict locality rule in medical malpractice cases reinforced the status quo of care in any given community, served as a disincentive for the elevation of the standard of care, and sometimes made it difficult for the plaintiff to locate an expert witness if physicians within the same community were reluctant to testify against each other. See, e.g., McGulpin v. Bessmer, 241 Ia. 1119, 43 N.W.2d 121 (1950) (criticizing requirement of expert testimony of physician from same community).

4. Most jurisdictions now have adopted a "similar community in similar circumstances" test, which is designed to balance the need to avoid evaluating a general practitioner in a rural area by the same standards as a specialist in an urban teaching hospital with the need of the plaintiff for access to expert testimony. See, e.g., Cox v. Board of Hosp. Mgrs. for City of Flint, 467 Mich. 1, 651 N.W.2d 356 (2002) (reaffirming same or similar community as standard of care to be applied to nurse). But see Vergara v.

Doan, 593 N.E.2d 185 (Ind.1992) (standard of care does not focus on locality but uses it as one of factors to be considered, along with advances in profession, availability of facilities, and whether health care provider was specialist or general practitioner); Idaho Code Ann. § 6–1012 (standard of health care practice of the community in which such care allegedly was or should have been provided); and Nestorowich v. Ricotta, 97 N.Y.2d 393, 740 N.Y.S.2d 668, 767 N.E.2d 125 (N.Y. 2002) (quoting New York common law locality rule).

5. Some jurisdictions have gone further and adopted a "national standard," especially for specialists who are certified by a national board within their specialty areas. See, e.g., Shilkret v. Annapolis Emergency Hosp. Ass'n., 276 Md. 187, 349 A.2d 245 (1975) (because "medical profession itself recognizes national standards for specialists that are not determined by geography, the law should follow suit"); Hall v. Hilbun, 466 So.2d 856 (Miss.1985) (adopting a nationwide standard for care and skill but not for resources); and Jordan v. Bogner, 844 P.2d 664 (Colo.1993) ("family practice" specialist who delivered baby in rural area held to national standard because specialist); Sheeley v. Memorial Hospital, 710 A.2d 161 (R.I.1998) (abandoning "same or similar" community test for national standard). But see Robinson v. LeCorps, 83 S.W.3d 718 (Tenn. 2002) (same or similar community even though surgeon was specialist, based on language of statute).

6. As the critics of the strict locality rule had pointed out, the locality rule can create serious injustice in some situations. Does the rule in the principal case create injustice for the medical profession? Suppose it spawns "professional experts" who travel from city to city, testifying in medical malpractice cases against doctors.

7. To reduce the costs of defending professional malpractice claims where the plaintiff is ultimately unable to produce an expert witness to testify that the standard of care was violated, many jurisdictions require that the plaintiff have obtained an expert opinion before filing suit or shortly thereafter. Some of those statutes apply to all professionals and others apply only to medical malpractice. See, e.g., Pa. Rule of Civ. P. 1042.1 (certificate of merit must be filed within 60 days of filing of complaint in all professional malpractice cases); N.J. Stats. Ann. 2A:53A–26 (affidavit of merit must be filed within 60 days of filing of complaint in all malpractice actions against a licensed professional); Florida Stat. 766.104 (complaint in medical negligence case must contain certificate of counsel that a reasonable investigation gave rise to a good faith belief that grounds for negligence exist); and Ohio Rule of Civ. P. 10(D)(2) (affidavit of merit must be filed with complaint in action containing medical, dental, optometric, or chiropractic claim). If the case is filed in federal court, must the plaintiff comply with the requirement? Liggon-Redding v. Sugarman, 659 F.3d 258 (3d Cir. 2011) (Pennsylvania's affidavit of merit statute is substantive state law under *Erie* analysis and thus had to be applied by federal court applying Pennsylvania malpractice law).

Scott v. Bradford

Supreme Court of Oklahoma, 1979.
606 P.2d 554.

DOOLIN, JUSTICE. This appeal is taken by plaintiffs in trial below, from a judgment in favor of defendant rendered on a jury verdict in a medical malpractice action.

Mrs. Scott's physician advised her she had several fibroid tumors on her uterus. He referred her to defendant surgeon. Defendant admitted her to the hospital where she signed a routine consent form prior to defendant's performing a hysterectomy. After surgery, Mrs. Scott experienced problems with incontinence. She visited another physician who discovered she had a vesico-vaginal fistula which permitted urine to leak from her bladder into the vagina. This physician referred her to an urologist who, after three surgeries, succeeded in correcting her problems.

Mrs. Scott, joined by her husband, filed the present action alleging medical malpractice, claiming defendant failed to advise her of the risks involved or of available alternatives to surgery. She further maintained had she been properly informed she would have refused the surgery.

The case was submitted to the jury with instructions to which plaintiffs objected. The jury found for defendant and plaintiffs appeal. * * *

The issue involved is whether Oklahoma adheres to the doctrine of informed consent as the basis of an action for medical malpractice, and if so did the present instructions adequately advise the jury of defendant's duty.

Anglo-American law starts with the premise of thoroughgoing self-determination, each man considered to be his own master. This law does not permit a physician to substitute his judgment for that of the patient by any form of artifice. The doctrine of informed consent arises out of this premise.

Consent to medical treatment, to be effective, should stem from an understanding decision based on adequate information about the treatment, the available alternatives, and the collateral risks. This requirement, labeled "informed consent," is, legally speaking, as essential as a physician's care and skill in the *performance* of the therapy. The doctrine imposes a duty on a physician or surgeon to inform a patient of his options and their attendant risks. If a physician breaches this duty, patient's consent is defective, and physician is responsible for the consequences.

If treatment is completely unauthorized and performed without any consent at all, there has been a battery. However, if the physician obtains a patient's consent but has breached his duty to inform, the patient has a cause of action sounding in negligence for failure to inform the patient of his options, regardless of the due care exercised at treatment, assuming there is injury. * * *

The first buds of court decisions heralding this new medical duty are found in Salgo v. Leland Stanford, Jr., University Board of Trustees, 154 Cal.App.2d 560, 317 P.2d 170 (1957). That court grounded the disclosure requirement in negligence law holding a physician violates a duty to his patient and subjects himself to liability if he withholds any facts which are necessary to form the basis of an intelligent consent by the patient to the proposed treatment. The court strongly suggested a physician is obligated not only to disclose *what* he intends to do, but to supply information which addresses the question of *whether* he should do it. This view was a marked divergence from the general rule of "professional standard of care" in determining what must be disclosed. Under that standard, earlier decisions seemed to perpetuate medical paternalism by giving the profession sweeping authority to decide unilaterally what is in the patient's best interests. Under the "professional standard of care" a physician needed only to inform a patient in conformance with the prevailing medical practice in the community.

More recently, in perhaps one of the most influential informed consent decisions, Canterbury v. Spence, 150 U.S.App.D.C. 263, 464 F.2d 772 (D.C.Cir.1972), cert. den. 409 U.S. 1064, the doctrine received perdurable impetus. Judge Robinson observed that suits charging failure by a physician adequately to disclose risks and alternatives of proposed treatment were not innovative in American law. He emphasized the fundamental concept in American jurisprudence that every human being of adult years and sound mind has a right to determine what shall be done with his own body. True consent to what happens to one's self is the informed exercise of a choice. This entails an opportunity to evaluate knowledgeably the options available and the risks attendant upon each. It is the prerogative of every patient to chart his own course and determine which direction he will take.

The decision in *Canterbury* recognized the tendency of some jurisdictions to turn this duty on whether it is the custom of physicians practicing in the community to make the particular disclosure to the patient. That court rejected this standard and held the standard measuring performance of the duty of disclosure is conduct which is reasonable under the circumstances: "[We cannot] ignore the fact that to bind disclosure obligations to medical usage is to arrogate the decision on revelation to the physician alone." We agree. A patient's right to make up his mind whether to undergo treatment should not be delegated to the local medical group. What is reasonable disclosure in one instance may not be reasonable in another. We decline to adopt a standard based on the professional standard. We, therefore, hold the scope of a physician's communications must be measured by his patient's need to know enough to enable him to make an intelligent choice. In other words, full disclosure of all *material risks* incident to treatment must be made. There is no bright line separating the material from the immaterial; it is a question of fact. A risk is material if it would be likely to affect patient's decision. When non-disclosure of a particular risk is open to debate, the issue is for the finder of facts.

This duty to disclose is the first element of the cause of action in negligence based on lack of informed consent. However, there are exceptions creating a privilege of a physician not to disclose. There is no need to disclose risks that either ought to be known by everyone or are already known to the patient. Further, the primary duty of a physician is to do what is best for his patient and where full disclosure would be detrimental to a patient's total care and best interests a physician may withhold such disclosure, for example, where disclosure would alarm an emotionally upset or apprehensive patient. Certainly too, where there is an emergency and the patient is in no condition to determine for himself whether treatment should be administered, the privilege may be invoked.

The patient has the burden of going forward with evidence tending to establish prima facie the essential elements of the cause of action. The burden of proving an exception to his duty and thus a privilege not to disclose, rests upon the physician as an affirmative defense.

[The court then discussed the requirements of causation and damages in informed consent cases.]

In summary, in a medical malpractice action a patient suing under the theory of informed consent must allege and prove:

(1) defendant physician failed to inform him adequately of a material risk before securing his consent to the proposed treatment;

(2) if he had been informed of the risks he would not have consented to the treatment;

(3) the adverse consequences that were not made known did in fact occur and he was injured as a result of submitting to the treatment.

As a defense, a physician may plead and prove plaintiff knew of the risks, full disclosure would be detrimental to patient's best interests or that an emergency existed requiring prompt treatment and patient was in no condition to decide for himself.

Because we are imposing a new duty on physicians, we hereby make this opinion prospective only, affecting those causes of action arising after the date this opinion is promulgated.

The trial court in the case at bar gave rather broad instructions upon the duty of a physician to disclose. The instructions objected to did instruct that defendant should have disclosed material risks of the hysterectomy and feasibility of alternatives. Instructions are sufficient when considered as a whole they present the law applicable to the issues. Jury found for defendant. We find no basis for reversal.

Affirmed. * * *

NOTES AND QUESTIONS

1. The doctrine of informed consent developed first as a basis for vitiating the consent and holding that an action of battery would lie, but it proved to be too strong a remedy for the evil it purported to cure. The battery theory is now generally abandoned, except, of course, where the physician did not obtain any consent at all or exceeded the scope of consent. See, e.g., Mohr v. Williams, page 100. Pennsylvania is one of a few jurisdictions that continue to categorize informed consent as a battery action. Thus, it applies only to surgery or other invasive procedures, and not to the prescribing of drugs. Morgan v. Rose, 550 Pa. 202, 704 A.2d 617 (1997) (reaffirming battery basis for action but noting statute extends

informed consent requirement to radiation, chemotherapy, blood transfusions, and experimental drug therapy).

2. With the widespread abandonment of the battery rationale, the courts held that the question was whether the doctor was negligent in failing to disclose the nature, consequences, risks, and alternatives of any proposed treatment. This brought into play the doctrine of customary practice and the need of having expert medical testimony concerning the practice of a physician using customary care. Thus, if the cause of action is for informed consent, the plaintiff, like the plaintiff in the principal case, usually needs an expert witness, while she does not need an expert witness if the cause of action is for battery. Because of gum disease, plaintiff was advised to have her teeth extracted. Her dentist anesthetized her entire oral cavity and began a full extraction of all thirty-two of her teeth. Plaintiff says dentist never told her he was planning to extract all her teeth at one visit and did not obtain her consent to do so. Dentist, arguing that the case was based on lack of informed consent, moved for summary judgment because plaintiff did not have an expert witness to establish the standard—the usual and customary information given to patients to procure consent in similar situations. The Tennessee Supreme Court found the case was for medical battery, not lack of informed consent, and did not require an expert witness: "Lack of informed consent in a medical malpractice action under Tenn. Code Ann. § 29–16–118 operates to negate a patient's authorization for a procedure thereby giving rise to a cause of action for battery. [C] There is, however, no prior authorization or consent in a medical battery case to be negated by expert testimony. The primary consideration in a medical battery case is simply whether the patient knew and authorized a procedure. This determination does not require the testimony of an expert witness." Blanchard v. Kellum, 975 S.W.2d 522, 524 (Tenn.1998). See also Walls v. Shreck, 265 Neb. 683, 658 N.W.2d 686 (2003) (no expert testimony needed to establish standard for informed consent if surgeon operated on right eye after obtaining consent to operate on left eye).

3. This traditional, professional standard, which focuses on what physicians usually tell patients about a particular procedure, continues to be the rule in many jurisdictions. Some jurisdictions, however, have changed the test from what the *reasonable physician* would disclose to what the *reasonable patient* would want to know. See Culbertson v. Mernitz, 602 N.E.2d 98 (Ind.1992) for a discussion of the competing policy concerns present in the alternative standards. If a state adopts the "reasonable patient" standard, does the patient still need expert testimony to establish a prima facie case? Carr v. Strode, 79 Haw. 475, 904 P.2d 489 (1995) (plaintiff retains the burden of providing expert medical testimony as to the nature of risks inherent in a particular treatment, the probabilities of therapeutic success, the frequency of the occurrence of particular risks, and the nature of available alternatives to treatment). If a state adopts the "reasonable patient" standard, is the doctor permitted to introduce expert witness testimony concerning the informed consent? Marsingill v. O'Malley, 128 P.3d 151 (Alaska 2006) (In response to late night call from patient in abdominal pain, physician recommended she go to emergency room but did not speculate as to what might be wrong or the gravity of her condition. She decided to "tough it out for awhile," her husband later found her unconscious, and she suffered serious consequences from delaying her trip

to the emergency room. Doctor was permitted to offer expert testimony about what the reasonable patient would want to know in those circumstances.)

4. Note that the physician is required to inform about "material" risks. What does that mean? Is a 1–3 percent possibility material? Martin v. Richards, 192 Wis.2d 156, 531 N.W.2d 70 (1995) (in light of serious consequences, including death, a 1–3 percent possibility is not remote). Canterbury v. Spence, 464 F.2d 772 (D.C.Cir.1972) (although the risk of a complication may be small, such risk may be significant to a patient's decision in light of the potentially severe consequences).

5. Most informed consent cases involve whether to disclose particular risks of treatment or particular alternatives to treatment. What if the physician fails to tell the patient that she could do nothing at all and the condition might disappear on its own? Wecker v. Amend, 22 Kan.App.2d 498, 918 P.2d 658 (1996) (if doing nothing is medically acceptable alternative, which was contested in case, then patient must be so informed). What if the physician fails to tell the patient of the risks of refusing a diagnostic test? Truman v. Thomas, 27 Cal.3d 285, 611 P.2d 902, 165 Cal.Rptr. 308 (1980) (physician liable for failing to warn patient of risk of refusing pap smear screening test for cervical cancer). What if the physician fails to inform the patient of the availability of an alternative diagnostic test? Compare Martin v. Richards, 192 Wis.2d 156, 531 N.W.2d 70 (1995) (physician liable for failing to inform parents of child who suffered head injury in bicycle accident of availability of CAT scan) with Hall v. Frankel, 190 P.3d 852 (Colo. App. 2008) (physician does not have a duty to disclose the availability of diagnostic and treatment procedures he or she has concluded are not medically indicated; errors of this sort are covered by claims of negligence). What if physician fails to inform patient of psychological (not physical) risks of a procedure? Curtis v. MRI Imaging Services II, 327 Or. 9, 956 P.2d 960 (1998) (physician may be liable for failing to inform patient of possible claustrophobic effects of MRI procedure). What if the physician fails to inform the patient that her condition has changed since the original informed consent was given? After suffering pregnancy complications, patient agreed to stay in hospital and be monitored for several weeks and to postpone the birth of her baby as long as possible to allow him time to develop. During the ensuing weeks, tests revealed that her condition was worsening, but she alleged that the physician failed to tell her that. If he had told her, she would have withdrawn her agreement to wait and sought earlier delivery of her son. Is this a failure of informed consent? McQuitty v. Spangler, 410 Md. 1, 976 A.2d 1020 (2009) (finding that it could be).

6. Most informed consent cases are against physicians. If the treating physician with privileges at a hospital fails to obtain consent to a blood transfusion, does the hospital have a duty to obtain consent? Does the blood bank that provided the blood? Ward v. Lutheran Hospitals & Homes Soc. of Am., Inc., 963 P.2d 1031 (Alaska 1998) (noting that overwhelming weight of authority holds that hospital does not owe duty to patient to obtain consent for treatment when patient is under care of independent physician—not an employee of the hospital—and finding that neither hospital nor blood bank owed patient a duty). But see Bryant v. HCA Health Svces., 15 S.W.3d 804 (Tenn. 2000) (such a duty might exist if

federal regulations required hospital to obtain consent as requirement for its participation in FDA study of medical device).

Moore v. The Regents of the University of California

Supreme Court of California, 1990.
51 Cal.3d 120, 793 P.2d 479, 271 Cal.Rptr. 146.

Opinion by PANELLI, J.:

[Plaintiff, John Moore, first visited UCLA Medical Center in October 1976, shortly after being diagnosed with hairy-cell leukemia. Defendant Golde, his treating physician at UCLA, withdrew blood, bone marrow, and other bodily substances to test them. Dr. Golde then recommended that Moore's spleen be removed. Based upon Dr. Golde's representation that the removal of the spleen was necessary to slow down the progress of the disease, Moore consented to the recommended surgery. Moore alleged that Dr. Golde "formed the intent and made the arrangements to obtain portions of his spleen following the removal" to use them in research which was unrelated to Moore's medical care. Moore returned to UCLA Medical Center several times between November 1976 and September 1983 at Dr. Golde's direction and based on Dr. Golde's representations that the follow up was necessary for his treatment. After relocating to the Seattle area, Moore continued to return to UCLA because he had been told the procedures could only be performed there. In fact, Dr. Golde and some colleagues had discovered that Moore's cells were unusually useful in the genetic research they were performing. Dr. Golde and others developed and patented a cell line from Mr. Moore's cells and then licensed it for commercial development to Genetics Institute and Sandoz Pharmaceuticals, also named as defendants in the action.

Plaintiffs filed a complaint containing thirteen causes of action, including inter alia, conversion and lack of informed consent and breach of fiduciary duty for failing to disclose the financial interest of the defendants. The trial court sustained a demurrer to the conversion count and then dismissed the entire complaint without ruling on the other counts because of its view that the other counts simply repeated the inadequate allegations of the conversion count. The Court of Appeal reversed on the conversion count, holding that it did state a cause of action for conversion, agreed that the informed consent count against the commercial defendants was not adequate but directed the trial court to give Moore leave to amend, and directed the trial court to consider the remaining causes of action that had not been ruled upon. This appeal followed.]

* * *

A. Breach of Fiduciary Duty and Lack of Informed Consent

Moore repeatedly alleges that Golde failed to disclose the extent of his research and economic interests in Moore's cells before obtaining consent to the medical procedures by which the cells were extracted. These allegations, in our view, state a cause of action against Golde for invading a legally protected interest of his patient. This cause of action can properly be characterized either as the breach of a fiduciary duty to disclose facts material to the patient's consent or, alternatively, as the performance of medical procedures without first having obtained the patient's informed consent.

Our analysis begins with three well-established principles. First, "a person of adult years and in sound mind has the right, in the exercise of control over his own body, to determine whether or not to submit to lawful medical treatment." [Cc] Second, "the patient's consent to treatment, to be effective, must be an informed consent." [C] Third, in soliciting the patient's consent, a physician has a fiduciary duty to disclose all information material to the patient's decision. [Cc]

These principles lead to the following conclusions: (1) a physician must disclose personal interests unrelated to the patient's health, whether research or economic, that may affect the physician's professional judgment; and (2) a physician's failure to disclose such interests may give rise to a cause of action for performing medical procedures without informed consent or breach of fiduciary duty.

To be sure, questions about the validity of a patient's consent to a procedure typically arise when the patient alleges that the physician failed to disclose medical risks, as in malpractice cases, and not when the patient alleges that the physician had a personal interest, as in this case. The concept of informed consent, however, is broad enough to encompass the latter. "The scope of the physician's communication to the patient * * * must be measured by the patient's need, and that need is whatever information is material to the decision." [C]

Indeed, the law already recognizes that a reasonable patient would want to know whether a physician has an economic interest that might affect the physician's professional judgment. As the Court of Appeal has said, "[c]ertainly a sick patient deserves to be free of any reasonable suspicion that his doctor's judgment is influenced by a profit motive." * * *

It is important to note that no law prohibits a physician from conducting research in the same area in which he practices. Progress in medicine often depends upon physicians, such as those practicing at the university hospital where Moore received treatment, who conduct research while caring for their patients.

Yet a physician who treats a patient in whom he also has a research interest has potentially conflicting loyalties. This is because medical treatment decisions are made on the basis of proportionality—weighing the benefits to the patient against the risks to the patient. As another court has said, "the determination as to whether the burdens of treatment are worth enduring for any individual patient depends upon the facts unique in each case," and "the patient's interests and desires are the key ingredients of the decision-making process." [C] A physician who adds his own research interests to this balance may be tempted to order a scientifically useful procedure or test that offers marginal, or no, benefits to the patient. The possibility that an interest extraneous to the patient's health has affected the physician's judgment is something that a reasonable patient would want to know in deciding whether to consent to a proposed course of treatment. It is material to the patient's decision and, thus, a prerequisite to informed consent. [C]

Golde argues that the scientific use of cells that have already been removed cannot possibly affect the patient's medical interests. The argument is correct in one instance but not in another. If a physician has no plans to conduct research on a patient's cells at the time he recommends the medical procedure by which they are taken, then the patient's medical interests have not been impaired. In that instance the argument is correct. On the other hand, a physician who does have a preexisting research interest might, consciously or unconsciously, take that into consideration in recommending the procedure. In that instance the argument is incorrect: the physician's extraneous motivation may affect his judgment and is, thus, material to the patient's consent.

We acknowledge that there is a competing consideration. To require disclosure of research and economic interests may corrupt the patient's own judgment by distracting him from the requirements of his health. But California law does not grant physicians unlimited discretion to decide what to disclose. Instead, "it is the prerogative of the patient, not the physician, to determine for himself the direction in which he believes his interests lie." [C] "Unlimited discretion in the physician is irreconcilable with the basic right of the patient to make the ultimate informed decision * * *." [C]

However, we made that statement in the context of a physician-patient relationship unaffected by possible conflicts of interest. Cobbs v. Grant, supra, permits a physician acting solely in the patient's best interests to consider whether excessive disclosure will harm the patient. Disclosure of possible conflicts of interest raises different considerations. To illustrate, a physician who orders a procedure partly to further a research interest unrelated to the patient's health should not be able to avoid disclosure with the argument that the patient might object to participation in research. In some cases, however, a physician's research interest might play such an insignificant role in the decision to recommend a medically indicated procedure that disclosure should not be required because the interest is not material. By analogy, we have not required disclosure of "remote" risks [c] that "are not central to the decision to administer or reject [a] procedure." [C]

Accordingly, we hold that a physician who is seeking a patient's consent for a medical procedure must, in order to satisfy his fiduciary duty and to obtain the patient's informed consent, disclose personal interests unrelated to the patient's health, whether research or economic, that may affect his medical judgment.

* * *

[The court then discussed the specific allegations of the complaint relating to each of the medical procedures. First, Moore did not state a cause of action with respect to the original drawing of blood and tissue samples because Dr. Golde did not yet know of the rare nature of Moore's cells. Second, Moore stated a cause of action with respect to the surgical removal of the spleen even though the surgery had therapeutic value for Moore because Moore alleged that Dr. Golde planned to keep the removed spleen for scientific research but did not disclose that to Moore. Third, the postoperative takings of bodily tissues were done at a time when Dr. Golde had an undisclosed financial interest in them and even though they had no therapeutic purpose. Thus the complaint stated a cause of action against Dr. Golde for those procedures.

The court found that the remaining defendants could be liable to Moore for a failure of informed consent if they were vicariously liable for Dr. Golde's actions and ruled that Moore could amend his complaint to attempt to state a lack of informed consent cause of action against them.

On the conversion issue, see note 7, page 90, the Court decided that the traditional common law doctrine of conversion did not cover Moore's cells and that the common law doctrine should not be expanded to cover this kind of case. Case remanded.

The concurring and dissenting opinions are omitted.]

NOTES AND QUESTIONS

1. Note that California uses the *reasonable patient* rather than the *reasonable physician* test for informed consent. Do you think the court would have made the same ruling on the informed consent issue if California followed the *reasonable physician* test?

2. What will happen next in the case? If the jury finds for the plaintiff on the informed consent cause of action, what would the damages be? Will Moore share in the profits of the cell line started by his spleen?

3. Most risks that must be disclosed relate directly to the therapy or procedure. What about risks relating to the physician or the physician's capacity to perform? See, e.g., Curran v. Buser, 271 Neb. 332, 711 N.W.2d 562 (2006) (alleged failure to disclose that surgeon's surgical privileges had been restricted for one year, ending just nine days before patient's surgery) and Faya v. Almaraz, 329 Md. 435, 620 A.2d 327 (1993) (HIV status of surgeon). Compare Hidding v. Williams, 578 So.2d 1192 (La.App.1991) (alcoholism) (must disclose) with Albany Urology Clinic v. Cleveland, 272 Ga. 296, 528 S.E.2d 777 (2000) (cocaine use) (no duty to disclose). Suppose the doctor exaggerates his experience with the procedure. Is that enough by itself to vitiate consent? Compare Johnson v. Kokemoor, 199 Wis.2d 615, 545 N.W.2d 495 (1996) (comparative morbidity/mortality rates for the procedure between surgeons experienced in procedure and those inexperienced like himself must be disclosed); Howard v. University of Medicine and Dentistry of N.J., 172 N.J. 537, 800 A.2d 73 (2002) (misrepresented or exaggerated physician experience would have to significantly increase a risk of procedure in order to affect the decision of reasonably prudent patient and thus incur liability for informed consent); and Duttry v. Patterson, 565 Pa. 130, 771 A.2d 1255 (2001) (surgeon's personal characteristics and experience were irrelevant to informed consent claim).

4. *Causation.* Informed consent raises one problem that can be only mentioned at this early point in the course. Liability is being imposed even though there was no negligence in performing the operation or administering the treatment. If so, it must be on the basis that if the risk

had been disclosed the patient would not have agreed to be subjected to the risk by undergoing the operation or the treatment. How do we know? Can we rely on the patient's testimony after the risk has manifested itself? Can we resort to the reasonable prudent person again? Is that true causation?

5. Other causation problems can arise with professional services. If an attorney negligently lets the statute of limitations run without filing suit, what is he liable for? Compensatory damages client would have won minus contingent fee and expenses? See notes 6–9, pages 289–290. Punitive damages? See note 8, page 578.

6. Some of the professional-services cases involve another problem to be taken up later. Is the defendant liable to people who were not clients of the defendant? A lawyer draws up a will or trust that is invalid. Can the intended beneficiary of a legacy recover after the testator dies? Fabian v. Lindsay, 410 S.C. 475, 765 S.E.2d 132 (2014) (aligning itself with majority of courts that permit beneficiaries of will to recover as third-party beneficiaries against attorney whose drafting error defeats or diminishes client's intent). Should a divorce client's fiancée be able to recover from the lawyer whose lack of diligence in obtaining the divorce meant that client died before he was able to marry fiancée? Scott v. Burgin, 97 A.3d 564 (D.C. App. 2014) (duty of care does not extend to fiancée). Cf. Prudential Ins. Co. v. Dewey, Ballantine, Bushby, Palmer & Wood, 80 N.Y.2d 377, 590 N.Y.S.2d 831, 605 N.E.2d 318 (1992) (law firm may be liable to non-client who relied on opinion letter).

Does an architect owe a duty of care to future homeowners in the design of a residential building when the architect's client was the condo building's developer? Beacon Residential Community Assn. v. Skidmore, Owings & Merrill LLP, 59 Cal.4th 568, 173 Cal.Rptr.3d 752, 327 P.3d 850 (2014) (yes, where architect is a principal architect on the project, not subordinate to other design professionals). But see Bily v. Arthur Young & Co., 3 Cal.4th 370, 11 Cal.Rptr.2d 51, 834 P.2d 745 (1992) (no liability to non-client of accounting firm).

A physician negligently advises a patient exposed to hepatitis that if she remains symptom free for six weeks she has not contracted the disease and is not contagious. The advice should have been six months rather than six weeks. Patient refrains from sexual intercourse for eight weeks after the exposure and then resumes sexual intercourse with plaintiff. Both patient and plaintiff are diagnosed with hepatitis. Does plaintiff have a medical malpractice cause of action against the physician? See DiMarco v. Lynch Homes, 525 Pa. 558, 583 A.2d 422 (1990) (yes). Physician administers oral polio vaccine to infant and fails to inform parents that they might contract polio from infant. Does father have negligence case against physician? Tenuto v. Lederle Labs., 90 N.Y.2d 606, 687 N.E.2d 1300, 665 N.Y.S.2d 17 (1997) (yes). Physician treats patient for disease that is genetically transferable. Physician does not tell patient to warn her children that they too may develop the disease. Does patient's adult daughter have a medical malpractice cause of action against physician? Pate v. Threlkel, 661 So.2d 278 (Fla.1995) (maybe, if standard of care can be shown to include warning patient). In attempting to determine the cause of child's developmental delays, pediatrician orders genetic testing. Through a mistake either by the lab or the pediatrician, one crucial test was omitted. The child's father and stepmother were told that the genetic tests were all normal. The father reported that to the mother. Years later, the mother remarried and bore another child who suffered from the same genetic abnormality. Does mother have a medical malpractice action against the pediatrician of child of whom father and stepmother have custody? Molloy v. Meier, 679 N.W.2d 711 (Minn. 2004) (yes, pediatrician had met at least once with biological mother and thus owed duty to her as well as to patient).

Physician treats patient for epilepsy, which is controlled by medication for years. Patient then has a seizure while on medication. Physician fails to warn him not to drive. Patient has seizure while driving and kills the plaintiff's intestate. Does the family of the woman who was killed in the car accident caused by the seizure have a cause of action against physician? Compare Praesel v. Johnson, 967 S.W.2d 391 (Tex.1998) (no) and Jarmie v. Troncale, 306 Conn. 578, 50 A.3d 802 (2012) (no duty to non-patient motorist) with McKenzie v. Hawai'i Permanente Medical Group, Inc., 98 Haw. 296, 47 P.3d 1209 (2002) and Burroughs v. Magee, 118 S.W.3d 323 (Tenn. 2003) (physician owes duty to non-patient injured in automobile accident caused by adverse reaction to medication if physician negligently failed to warn patient that medication could impair driving ability).

Does a therapist owe a duty to the parents of a patient? Compare Ryder v. Mitchell, 54 P.3d 885 (Colo. 2002) (no duty to mother who claimed therapist was negligent in diagnosing children's symptoms and reporting to new therapist her opinion that mother was alienating children from father) and Hungerford v. Jones, 143 N.H. 208, 722 A.2d 478 (1998) (answering certified question) (in case involving repressed memory recovery techniques, therapist owes duty to accused parent of patient undergoing treatment for suspected sexual abuse when public accusations are made). Health care providers allegedly provided negligent treatment to mentally ill patient who killed his wife. Can her estate bring suit against health care providers? Tedrick v. Community Resource Center, Inc., 235 Ill.2d 155, 336 Ill.Dec. 210, 920 N.E.2d 220 (2009) (no cause of action absent physician-patient relationship).

7. What if the patient is injured during an examination conducted at the request of an employer, insurer, or other third person or pursuant to court order during litigation? Most courts have found that the physician owes a limited duty, sounding in medical malpractice, to examine the patient without harming her but not to provide diagnosis or treatment. See, for example, Harris v. Kreutzer, 271 Va. 188, 624 S.E.2d 24 (2006) (automobile accident victim alleged that she was injured by clinical psychologist who examined her pursuant to court order to determine the nature and extent of the brain injury she was alleging in her automobile accident case) (collecting cases from other jurisdictions). What if the treating physician consults with another physician about the case before making his treatment decision but the physician who provided the informal consultation did not agree to treat the patient, did not review the patient's records, and never met the patient? See, for example, Jennings v. Badgett, 2010 OK 7, 230 P.3d 861 (2010) (no physician-patient relationship established under those circumstances) (collecting cases from other jurisdictions).

8. Not all actions taken by professionals are malpractice. Some would be ordinary negligence. Why does it matter whether the allegedly

unreasonable conduct is classified as professional malpractice or ordinary negligence? In many states, there are prerequisites to filing medical malpractice claims, including presenting the claim first to an expert panel. Patient's family alleged that a hospital was negligent in failing to provide adequate backup power for life support systems and patient died in the aftermath of Hurricane Katrina when the power failed. Medical malpractice or ordinary negligence? Lacoste v. Pendleton Methodist Hospital, 966 So.2d 519 (La. 2007) (finding the claim sounded in ordinary negligence and thus did not have to be submitted to the medical review panel before suit was filed). The statute of limitations may be different for ordinary negligence and medical malpractice. J.B. v. Sacred Heart Hosp., 635 So.2d 945 (Fla.1994) (plaintiff contracted AIDS because hospital failed to tell him his brother had AIDS and how to care for him while transporting him to another medical facility; court found failure was ordinary negligence rather than medical malpractice).

The "Medical Malpractice Crisis" and Statutory Change in the Common Law

Three times during the last 25 years (the latter part of the 1970's, the mid-1980's, and the early 21st century) an increase in the number of medical malpractice suits produced sharp increases in the premiums for, and, in some instances, unavailability of malpractice liability insurance. This in turn produced alarm within the profession and demands that the state legislatures find ways of alleviating the "crisis" caused by the burden of the malpractice insurance premiums and the unavailability of insurance. Although some have pointed to the economics of the insurance industry as the source of most of the increase, much of the blame was placed by the lobbyists on the law of negligence, and various modifications of the substantive law of torts were passed by concerned state legislatures. See Logue, Toward a Tax Based Explanation of the Liability Insurance Crisis, 82 Va.L.Rev. 895 (1996). Almost every state passed legislation of some sort. The state statutes have varied considerably and there is no particular pattern to them. See Sanders & Joyce, "Off to the Races": The 1980s Tort Crisis and the Law Reform Process, 27 Hous.L.Rev. 207 (1990). Changes were made in the standard of care, the doctrine of informed consent (see page 199), the doctrine of res ipsa loquitur (see page 251), the collateral source rule (see page 566), the statute of limitations (see page 652), imposing limits on the amount that could be received for pain and suffering or on the total amount recovered in a malpractice action, and prohibiting the setting forth in a complaint of the amount of the relief requested. Many states required a certificate of merit upon filing or very early in the case, others capped damages, and some required submission to an expert board for screening or to arbitration before filing suit. The impact of the reform initiatives are difficult to discern. Viscusi and Born, Medical Malpractice in the Wake of Liability Reform, 24 J.Legal Stud. 463 (1995); Thorpe, The Medical Malpractice "Crisis": Recent Trends and the Impact of State Tort Reforms, Health Affairs 20 (2004); Sharkey, Unintended Consequences of Medical Malpractice Damages Caps, 80 NYU L.Rev. 391 (2005) (empirical analysis of impact of damages caps); and Wenner, "State's Malpractice Data Offer Ammo for Both Sides," The Patriot-News (March 9, 2010) (reporting on ten-year study of Pennsylvania medical malpractice lawsuits, including years before and after changes by legislature to medical malpractice claims) available at 2010 WLNR 5027772.

State supreme courts have held a number of the statutory provisions listed above to be unconstitutional for various reasons; but most of the states still have some of the statutory modifications in effect. See, for example, Smith v. Schulte, 671 So.2d 1334 (Ala.1995) (cap on damages in medical malpractice cases violates state constitutional guarantees of equal protection and right to jury trial). An attorney must therefore carefully research state statutes as well as common law in this area.

A recent study published in the New England Journal of Medicine of malpractice data from 1991–2005 showed 7.4% of all physicians had a malpractice claim, with 1.6% having a claim leading to a payment. The proportion of physicians facing a claim each year ranged from 19.1% in neurosurgery, 18.9% in thoracic-cardiovascular surgery, and 15.3% in general surgery to 5.2% in family medicine, 3.1% in pediatrics, and 2.6% in psychiatry. The study authors estimated that by the age of 65, 75% of physicians in low-risk specialties face a malpractice claim, as compared with 99% of physicians in high-risk specialties. Jena, Seabury, Lakdawalla, and Chandra, "Malpractice Risk According to Physician Specialty," 365 New Eng. J. Med. 629 (Aug. 18, 2011).

(C) AGGRAVATED NEGLIGENCE

1. *"Degrees" of Care.* It is obvious, and elementary, that the care required by the standard of the reasonable person will vary according to the risk. As the danger increases, the actor is required to exercise caution commensurate with it, and so to be more careful. Those who deal with things that are *known to be dangerous*, such as explosives or electricity, must exercise more care than one who is merely walking down the street. Likewise, those who have accepted a special responsibility toward others, as in the case of *a common carrier* responsible for the safety of passengers, must exercise more care in accordance with the duty undertaken. On many occasions, this has been expressed in instructions to the jury, approved on appeal, that the carrier, or the person dealing with special danger, must exercise "the highest degree of care," or "the utmost caution characteristic of very careful prudent persons." See, for example, Bayer v. Crested Butte Mountain Resort, Inc., 960 P.2d 70 (Colo.1998) (ski lift operator must exercise highest degree of care commensurate with the lift's practical operation); Peck v. Fanion, 124 Conn. 549, 1 A.2d 143, 144 (1938) (jury instruction on negligence against common carrier—taxicab—should have been "highest degree of care and skill which reasonably may be expected of intelligent and prudent persons engaged in such a business"); Pennsylvania Co. v. Roy, 102 U.S. 451, 455 (1880) (railroad owes greatest possible care and diligence when conveying persons by the "powerful and dangerous agency of steam"). On "reasonable care" vs. "extraordinary care" regarding the use of firearms, see the opinions in Everette v. New Kensington, 262 Pa.Super. 28, 396 A.2d 467 (1978).

There are many other decisions in which this type of instruction has been held to be error, on the ground that there are no "degrees" of care recognized by the law, but merely amounts of care, greater or less; that the care required of the actor is always the same under the traditional formula, that of a reasonable person under like circumstances; and that the greater danger, or the greater responsibility, are merely circumstances that require a greater amount of care. See Flowers v. Torrance Memorial Hospital Med. Ctr., 8 Cal.4th 992, 884 P.2d 142, 35 Cal.Rptr.2d 685 (1994) ("There are no 'degrees' of care as a matter of law; there are only different amounts of care, as a matter of fact"); Bethel v. N.Y.C. Transit Authority, 92 N.Y.2d 348, 355, 681 N.Y.S.2d 201, 703 N.E.2d 1214, Union Traction 1218 (1998) ("we conclude that the rule of a common carrier's duty of extraordinary care is no longer viable. Rather, a common carrier is subject to the same duty of care as any other potential tortfeasor—reasonable care under all of the circumstances of the particular case.") and Nunez v. Prof. Transit Mgt. of Tucson, 229 Ariz. 117, 271 P.3d 1104 (2012) (moving from heightened duty to exercise the highest degree of care practicable to ordinary negligence standard and applying decision retroactively).

2. *"Degrees" of Negligence.* A different attempt, carried to considerable lengths in the last century, has been to distinguish "degrees" of negligence, breaking it down into different kinds of conduct, with different legal consequences. This idea was lifted from the Roman law by Chief Justice Holt in a bailment case, Coggs v. Bernard, 2 Ld.Raym. 909, 92 Eng.Rep. 107 (1704) (defendant volunteered—without compensation—to move barrels of brandy from one cellar to another and one of the barrels broke). As it developed, the distinction was made between "slight" negligence, defined as a failure to use great care; ordinary negligence, or failure to use reasonable care; and "gross" negligence, which is failure to exercise even slight care. See Green, High Care and Gross Negligence, 23 Ill.L.Rev. 4 (1928); Elliott, Degrees of Negligence, 6 So.Cal.L.Rev. 91 (1932).

These distinctions were subjected to a good deal of criticism almost from the start. In Wilson v. Brett, 11 M. & W. 113, 152 Eng.Rep. 737 (1843), Baron Rolfe made a much quoted statement that gross negligence is merely the same thing as ordinary negligence, "with the addition of a vituperative epithet." In some of the very early cases, this was true. "Gross negligence" was an expression used to mean nothing more than negligence. See, for example, Vaughan v. Menlove, page 155. But when it is intended to mean more, "gross" negligence is readily understood by the ordinary person as involving an extreme departure from ordinary standards of conduct, and it is very probable that Judge Magruder's students at the Harvard Law School knew what he meant when he explained "Chief Justice Rugg's famous distinctions among negligence, gross negligence and recklessness as being the distinctions among a fool, a damned fool, and a God-damned fool." Harvard Law Record, April 16, 1959.

In practice, however, it proved extraordinarily difficult to set any lines of demarcation; and these distinctions filled the courts with vexatious appeals in which they were asked to rule upon particular conduct as a matter of law. During the latter half of the nineteenth century, the courts of Illinois and Kansas were deluged with appeals, as a result of their adoption of a rule that contributory negligence was not a defense when the negligence of the defendant was found to be "gross," and that of the plaintiff "slight" in comparison. Both courts finally threw up their hands and threw out the distinctions, declaring that henceforth only one kind of negligence, measured by the standard of the reasonable person, was to be recognized. The story is told in Malone, The Formative Era of Contributory Negligence, 41 Ill.L.Rev. 151 (1946).

Since then, "gross" and "slight" negligence have been under a cloud, and discredited with the courts. They have largely lost their significance in the common law, both in England and in most states. Some vestiges still remain in the law of bailments, where some courts still hold that a gratuitous bailee owes his bailor only the duty of slight care, and so is liable only for gross negligence in looking after the goods. See, for example, Altman v. Aronson, 231 Mass. 588, 121 N.E. 505 (1919) (prospective purchaser of silk found that sample was not of the quality he sought so he sent it back to seller but it was lost in transit). The words "gross negligence" occasionally appear as words of art in automobile guest statutes. In that context, they have been construed to mean "the absence of slight care." See, for example, Hennon v. Hardin, 78 Ga.App. 81, 50 S.E.2d 236 (1948) (allegation that defendant drove car 70 m.p.h. around a 45 degree curve, and then attempted to pass another car on the curve). On occasion they have been treated as synonyms for "recklessness." See Jackson v. Edwards, 144 Fla. 187, 197 So. 833 (1940) (allegation that defendant drove a truck at night at 60 m.p.h. down the center of the highway, colliding with truck traveling in opposite direction). The term is, perhaps, more popular with legislatures than with the courts. See, for example, the Clean Air Act, 33 U.S.C. § 1321(b)(7)(D) and In re Oil Spill by Oil Rig Deepwater Horizon in Gulf of Mexico, on April 20, 2010, 21 F.Supp.3d 657, 732 (E.D. La. 2014) (finding that defendant acted with "gross negligence" under the Clean Water Act).

3. *Willful, Wanton, and Reckless Conduct.* Another distinction is made by some courts based on defendant's state of mind. The effect is to establish an intermediate class of conduct, between negligence (including gross negligence) and intentional torts, which in some respects takes on the character of each. This type of conduct usually is defined as consisting of a deliberate and conscious disregard for a known high degree of probability of harm to another. See Restatement (Second) of Torts § 500 (1965) and Restatement (Third) of Torts: Liability for Physical and Emotional Harm § 2 (2010). This level of conduct is the threshold for punitive damages in many jurisdictions (see Chapter 10, Damages) and for particular causes of action in others. See, for example, Hickingbotham v. Burke, 140 N.H. 28, 662 A.2d 297 (1995) (recognizing cause of action for social host liability if service of alcohol was reckless) and Crawn v. Campo, 136 N.J. 494, 643 A.2d 600 (1994) (noting that majority of jurisdictions require plaintiff injured in recreational sports activity to prove that defendant's conduct was reckless, not merely negligent, in order to recover).

Automobile Guest Statutes

The use of the expressions "recklessness," "gross negligence" and "willful and wanton conduct" evolved for the most part in connection with statutes providing that the driver of an automobile is liable only for some form of aggravated misconduct to one who is riding as a guest in a car.

The principle of limiting the duty that a driver owes to an automobile guest originated in the Massachusetts case of Massaletti v.

Fitzroy, 228 Mass. 487, 118 N.E. 168 (1917). The court derived the principle from what it regarded as an analogous situation—the relationship between a gratuitous bailee and his bailor. While the *Massaletti* decision had only a minor impact on the case law of other states, it had an enormous impact on state legislatures. Over half the states adopted guest statutes, with quite a bit of variation in their categories and exceptions.

The many legislatures that followed *Massaletti* were persuaded by a persistent lobby on the part of some automobile liability insurance companies. Rationales included the possibility of collusion between host and injured guest in manufacturing a claim against the host's insurer, a fair allocation of a limited insurance fund to pedestrians and persons in other cars in preference to "guests," and savings in fuel by encouraging car pools.

The statutes filled the courts with cases, in which a good many knotty little problems of interpretation arose; and the efforts of many courts to get around the statute in cases of manifest hardship led to some rather peculiar law. First of all, who was a "guest"? What was the effect of sharing expenses, of the host's business interest in offering the ride, of an employer's order prohibiting the driver from taking free riders, of stowaways, of a passenger's demand to be let out of the car? Once each state had settled those questions, there was the further problem of whether the driver's conduct in the particular case fit into the state's definition of "gross negligence," "recklessness," or "willful and wanton." A major component was whether or not plaintiff needed to prove that the defendant had actual knowledge of the risk involved. See, for example, Bailey v. Brown, 34 Ohio St.2d 62, 63 Ohio Op.2d 92, 295 N.E.2d 672 (1973) (turning left at intersection in front of oncoming vehicle without first coming to complete stop and without being aware of oncoming vehicle could not be characterized as willful or wanton misconduct) and Williamson v. McKenna, 223 Or. 366, 354 P.2d 56 (1960) (turning left at intersection in front of oncoming vehicle without signaling is negligence but, without more, could not be regarded as facing a manifest danger with indifference as to the plaintiff's safety).

In Brown v. Merlo, 8 Cal.3d 855, 506 P.2d 212, 106 Cal.Rptr. 388 (1973), the Supreme Court of California held that the California guest statute denied "equal protection of the laws" to nonpaying automobile guests. See also Ramey v. Ramey, 273 S.C. 680, 258 S.E.2d 883 (1979) (South Carolina guest statute unconstitutional). Other state supreme courts found their guest statutes unconstitutional under state or federal constitutional provisions, and most state legislatures have repealed their guest statutes, recognizing their incompatibility with modern notions of risk distribution. See Woods, Goodbye and Good Riddance, 16 Cumb.L.Rev. 263 (1986) for a history of automobile guest statutes. The statutes remain in effect only in Alabama. Coffey v. Moore, 948 So.2d 544 (Ala. 2006) (deciding that the bailee of a rental car who was injured when a companion was driving is not a guest under the Alabama guest statute § 32–1–2). In 2010, Nebraska repealed its guest statute.

The legacy of the guest statutes is each state's definition of aggravated negligence, which today most often arises when juries decide whether to award punitive damages. See Chapter 10, Damages.

5. RULES OF LAW

Pokora v. Wabash Ry. Co.

Supreme Court of the United States, 1934.
292 U.S. 98, 54 S.Ct. 580, 78 L.Ed. 1149.

[Plaintiff, driving a truck, approached a level railroad crossing at which defendant had four tracks. Because of boxcars standing on the first track, five or ten feet to the north of the crossing, he could not see the tracks to the north. He stopped, looked as well as he could, and listened, but heard no bell or whistle. He then drove slowly ahead, and when he reached the main track was struck by a passenger train from the north, coming at a speed of about thirty miles an hour. The trial court in the Southern District of Illinois directed a verdict for defendant, on the ground that plaintiff's conduct was contributory negligence as a matter of law, and this was affirmed by the Seventh Circuit Court of Appeals. Certiorari was granted by the Supreme Court.]

MR. JUSTICE CARDOZO delivered the opinion of the Court. * * * The Circuit Court of Appeals (one judge dissenting) affirmed, resting its judgment on the opinion of this court in B. & O.R. Co. v. Goodman, 275 U.S. 66, 48 S.Ct. 24, 72 L.Ed. 167. * * *

The argument is made, however, that our decision in B. & O.R. Co. v. Goodman, supra, is a barrier in the plaintiff's path, irrespective of the conclusion that might commend itself if the question were at large. There is no doubt that the opinion in that case is correct in its result. Goodman, the driver, traveling only five or six miles an hour, had, before reaching the track, a clear space of eighteen feet within which the train was plainly visible. With that opportunity, he fell short of the legal standard of duty established for a traveler when he failed to look and see. This was decisive of the case. But the court did not stop there. It added a remark, unnecessary upon the facts before it, which has been a fertile source of controversy. "In such circumstances it seems to us that if a driver cannot be sure otherwise whether a train is dangerously near he must stop and get out of his vehicle, although obviously he will not often be required to do more than to stop and look."

There is need at this stage to clear the ground of brushwood that may obscure the point at issue. We do not now inquire into the existence of a duty to stop, disconnected from a duty to get out and reconnoitre. The inquiry, if pursued, would lead us into the thickets of conflicting judgments. Some courts apply what is often spoken of as the Pennsylvania rule, and impose an unyielding duty to stop, as well as to look and listen, no matter how clear the crossing or the tracks on either side. * * *

Other courts, the majority, adopt the rule that the traveler must look and listen, but that the existence of a duty to stop depends upon the circumstances, and hence generally, even if not invariably, upon the judgment of the jury. * * * The subject has been less considered in this court, but in none of its opinions is there a suggestion that at any and every crossing the duty to stop is absolute, irrespective of the danger.

Not even in B. & O.R. Co. v. Goodman, supra, which goes farther than the earlier cases, is there support for such a rule. To the contrary, the opinion makes it clear that the duty [to stop] is conditioned upon the presence of impediments whereby sight and hearing become inadequate for the traveler's protection.

Choice between these diversities of doctrine is unnecessary for the decision of the case at hand. Here the fact is not disputed that the plaintiff did stop before he started to cross the tracks. If we assume that by reason of the box cars, there was a duty to stop again when the obstructions had been cleared, that duty did not arise unless a stop could be made safely after the point of clearance had been reached. * * * For reasons already stated, the testimony permits the inference that the truck was in the zone of danger by the time the field of vision was enlarged. No stop would then have helped the plaintiff if he remained seated on his truck, or so the triers of fact might find. His case was for the jury, unless as a matter of law he was subject to a duty to get out of the vehicle before it crossed the switch, walk forward to the front, and then, afoot, survey the scene. We must say whether his failure to do this was negligence so obvious and certain that one conclusion and one only is permissible for rational and candid minds.

Standards of prudent conduct are declared at times by courts, but they are taken over from the facts of life. To get out of a vehicle and reconnoitre is an uncommon precaution, as everyday experience informs us. Besides being uncommon, it is very likely to be futile, and sometimes even dangerous. If the driver leaves his vehicle when he nears a cut or curve, he will learn nothing by getting out about the perils that lurk beyond. By the time he regains his seat and sets his car in motion, the hidden train may be upon him. * * * Often the added safeguard will be dubious though the track happens to be straight, as it seems that this one was, at all events as far as the station, about five blocks to the north. A train traveling at a speed of thirty miles an hour will cover a quarter of a mile in the space of thirty seconds. It may thus emerge out of obscurity as the driver turns his back to regain the waiting car, and may then descend upon him suddenly when his car is on the track. Instead of helping himself by getting out, he might do better to press forward with all his faculties alert. So a train at a neighboring station, apparently at rest and harmless, may be transformed in a few seconds into an instrument of destruction. At times the course of safety may be different. One can figure to oneself a roadbed so level and unbroken that getting out will be a gain. Even then the balance of advantage depends on many circumstances and can be easily disturbed.

Where was Pokora to leave his truck after getting out to reconnoitre? If he was to leave it on the switch, there was the possibility that the box cars would be shunted down upon him before he could regain his seat. The defendant did not show whether there was a locomotive at the forward end, or whether the cars were so few that a locomotive could be seen. If he was to leave his vehicle near the curb, there was even stronger reason to believe that the space to be covered in going back and forth would make his observations worthless. One must remember that while the traveler turns his eyes in one direction, a train or a loose engine may be approaching from the other.

Illustrations such as these bear witness to the need for caution in framing standards of behavior that amount to rules of law. The need is the more urgent when there is no background of experience out of which the standards have emerged. They are then, not the natural flowerings of behavior in its customary forms, but rules artificially developed, and imposed from without. Extraordinary situations may not wisely or fairly be subjected to tests or regulations that are fitting for the commonplace or normal. In default of the guide of customary conduct, what is suitable for the traveler caught in a mesh where the ordinary safeguards fail him is for the judgment of a jury. * * * The opinion in Goodman's Case has been a source of confusion in the federal courts to the extent that it imposes a standard for application by the judge, and has had only wavering support in the courts of the states. We limit it accordingly.

The judgment should be reversed, and the cause remanded for further proceedings in accordance with this opinion.

It is so ordered.

NOTES AND QUESTIONS

1. In Baltimore & Ohio R. Co. v. Goodman, 275 U.S. 66 (1927), Justice Holmes concluded his opinion with: "It is true * * * that the question of due care very generally is left to the jury. But we are dealing with a standard of conduct, and when the standard is clear it should be laid down once and for all by the courts." Do you think that Justice Holmes really intended to declare a rule to which there could be no possible exceptions? How would he handle exceptional circumstances?

2. The *Goodman* decision created something of a furor. See Note, Aftermath of the Supreme Court's Stop, Look and Listen Rule, 43 Harv.L.Rev. 926 (1930). Notwithstanding all the criticism, the general rule has held up. In nearly all jurisdictions, it is usually still negligence as a matter of law not to look and listen when approaching a known railroad crossing, and not to slow down or even stop when obstructed vision or something else in the situation calls for it. See, for example, Chicago, R.I. & P.R. Co. v. McFarlin, 336 F.2d 1 (10th Cir.1964) (applying New Mexico law).

3. But over the years many cases arose in which special circumstances made it unreasonable to apply the rule. Thus crossing gates were left open, as in Wabash R. Co. v. Glass, 32 F.2d 697 (6th Cir.1929). Or the driver relied on the absence of a customary flagman or flasher signal, as in Wabash R. Co. v. Walczak, 49 F.2d 763 (6th Cir.1931). Or it was clear that the conduct specified would have added nothing to the driver's safety, as in Torgeson v. Missouri-Kansas-Texas R. Co., 124 Kan. 798, 262 P. 564 (1928). Railroad crossing accidents are still quite common. National Transportation Safety Board, Safety Study at Passive Grade Crossings, vii (1998) (more than 4,000 accidents per year at passive and active railroad crossings).

4. A similar fate—the development of exceptions—has overtaken many "rules of law." For example, in nearly all jurisdictions, the "range of

vision" rule of law applies. That is, it is negligent to drive an automobile at such a speed that it is impossible to stop within the range of vision. See, for example, Tapp v. Blackmore Ranch, Inc., 254 Neb. 40, 575 N.W.2d 341 (1998) (driver rear-ended disabled vehicle on highway) and Nickell v. Russell, 247 Neb. 112, 525 N.W.2d 203 (1995) (driver's pickup truck struck body lying on gravel road in the middle of the night). Usually this is true. But the "rule" has given way to exceptions in unusual circumstances, such as when the driver is suddenly blinded by the lights of an approaching car, as in Emerson v. Bailey, 102 N.H. 360, 156 A.2d 762 (1959). Or a car ahead with a visible tail-light turns out to be backing up. Cerny v. Domer, 13 Ohio St.2d 117, 235 N.E.2d 132 (1968). Or there is a dense fog, and a sudden obstacle of an entirely unusual and unexpected kind turns up, such as the house being moved in the middle of the street in Morehouse v. Everett, 141 Wash. 399, 252 P. 157 (1926).

5. Compare the "rule" that a pedestrian crossing the street must continue to look all the way across. McKinney v. Yelavich, 352 Mich. 687, 90 N.W.2d 883 (1958) contains an excellent discussion of reducing negligence to fixed rules in this situation. See also Scott v. City of Lynchburg, 241 Va. 64, 399 S.E.2d 809 (1991) (when plaintiff knows of existence of condition but forgets about it and falls in, off, or over it, he is contributorily negligent as a matter of law).

6. VIOLATION OF STATUTE

Osborne v. McMasters

Supreme Court of Minnesota, 1889.
40 Minn. 103, 41 N.W. 543.

Action for damages by M. Osborne, administrator, against S.R. McMasters, for the death of plaintiff's intestate, resulting from the use of poison sold without a label by defendant's clerk in the course of his employment. Judgment for plaintiff, and defendant appeals.

MITCHELL, J. Upon the record in this case it must be taken as the facts that defendant's clerk in his drug-store, in the course of his employment as such, sold to plaintiff's intestate a deadly poison without labeling it "Poison," as required by statute; that she, in ignorance of its deadly qualities, partook of the poison which caused her death. * * * It is now well settled, certainly in this state, that where a statute or municipal ordinance imposes upon any person a specific duty for the protection or benefit of others, if he neglects to perform that duty he is liable to those for whose protection or benefit it was imposed for any injuries of the character which the statute or ordinance was designed to prevent, and which were proximately produced by such neglect. * * * It is immaterial whether the duty is one imposed by the rule of common law requiring the exercise of ordinary care not to injure another, or is imposed by a statute designed for the protection of others. In either case the failure to perform the duty constitutes negligence, and renders the party liable for injuries resulting from it. The only difference is that in the one case the measure of legal duty is to be determined upon common-law principles, while in the other the statute fixes it, so that the violation of the statute constitutes conclusive evidence of negligence, or, in other words, negligence *per se*. The action in the latter case is not a statutory one, nor does the statute give the right of action in any other sense, except that it makes an act negligent which otherwise might not be such, or at least only evidence of negligence. All that the statute does is to establish a fixed standard by which the fact of negligence may be determined. The gist of the action is still negligence, or the non-performance of a legal duty to the person injured. * * *

Judgment affirmed.

NOTES AND QUESTIONS

1. Consider the remarks of Traynor, J. in Clinkscales v. Carver, 22 Cal.2d 72, 136 P.2d 777 (1943): "A statute that provides for a criminal proceeding only does not create a civil liability; if there is no provision for a remedy by civil action to persons injured by a breach of the statute it is because the Legislature did not contemplate one. A suit for damages is based on the theory that the conduct inflicting the injuries is a common-law tort, in this case the failure to exercise the care of a reasonable man at a boulevard stop. The significance of the statute in a civil suit for negligence lies in its formulation of a standard of conduct that the court adopts in the determination of such liability. (See Holmes, The Common Law, 120–129 (1881); Morris, The Relation of Criminal Statutes to Tort Liability, 46 Harv.L.Rev. 453 (1932).) The decision as to what the civil standard should be still rests with the court, and the standard formulated by a legislative body in a police regulation or criminal statute becomes the standard to determine civil liability only because the court accepts it. In the absence of such a standard the case goes to the jury, which must determine whether the defendant has acted as a reasonably prudent man would act in similar circumstances. The jury then has the burden of deciding not only what the facts are but what the unformulated standard is of reasonable conduct. When a legislative body has generalized a standard from the experience of the community and prohibits conduct that is likely to cause harm, the court accepts the formulated standards and applies them."

2. Why give any effect at all in a civil action for negligence to a statute that merely specifies a crime and provides for a criminal penalty? What about the following arguments?

A. The reasonable person will always obey the criminal law. Is this true? Should it be a question for the jury? What about a statute such as the legendary one providing that when two railroad trains approach a crossing each shall stop and neither shall move forward until the other has passed by?

B. The legislature intended, or is "presumed" to have intended, a civil remedy for the violation. What is the probability as to the state of mind of the legislature: (1) it did intend to provide a civil remedy, but did not say so; (2) it intended not to provide one and therefore omitted it; (3) it never thought about the matter at all?

C. The statute gives rise to a right. A right without a remedy is useless and the court supplies an appropriate remedy. *Ubi ius ibi remedium.*

D. The court adopts the standard of conduct from the criminal statute and lays it down as a rule of law in the civil action. See the preceding section. See Chapter 23, Torts in the Age of Statutes, on the effect of statutes on torts other than negligence.

E. Allowing a jury to find that behavior is reasonable when the legislature has condemned the behavior as unlawful creates a dissonance and denies "institutional comity" between judiciary and legislature. Restatement (Third) of Torts: Liability for Physical and Emotional Harm § 14 comment *c* (2010) (discussing rationale for negligence per se).

3. What if a criminal statute is invalid for criminal prosecutions? For example, an ordinance establishing a stop sign at a particular intersection was never properly published, as required for the adoption of such ordinances. Does this prevent the court, in a negligence action, from adopting the stop as a required standard of conduct? A number of cases say no. See Lewis v. Miami, 127 Fla. 426, 173 So. 150 (1937); Ponca City v. Reed, 115 Okl. 166, 242 P. 164 (1925); Clinkscales v. Carver, 22 Cal.2d 72, 136 P.2d 777 (1943). What if the statute is that of a neighboring jurisdiction where the violation took place? Cf. Gaines-Tabb v. ICI Explosives, USA, Inc., 160 F.3d 613 (10th Cir.1998) (applying Oklahoma law) (victims of bombing of Oklahoma City federal building filed negligence per se claim based on violation of Kansas fertilizer labeling statute against manufacturer of ammonium nitrate, which was used to construct the bomb).

4. Is the court required to accept a statute's definition of reasonable conduct as controlling? See the next three cases.

(A) APPLICABILITY OF STATUTE

Stachniewicz v. Mar-Cam Corp.

Supreme Court of Oregon, 1971.
259 Or. 583, 488 P.2d 436.

HOLMAN, JUSTICE. The patron of a drinking establishment seeks to recover against the operator for personal injuries allegedly inflicted by other customers during a barroom brawl. The jury returned a verdict for defendant. Plaintiff appealed.

From the evidence introduced, the jury could find as follows:

A fight erupted in a bar between a group of persons of American Indian ancestry, who were sitting in a booth, and other customers who were at an adjacent table with plaintiff. One of plaintiff's friends had refused to allow a patron from the booth to dance with the friend's wife because the stranger was intoxicated. Thereafter, such threats as, "Hey, Whitey, how big are you?" were shouted from the booth at plaintiff and his companions. One of the persons at the table, after complaining to the bartender, was warned by him, "Don't start trouble with those guys." Soon thereafter, those individuals who had been sitting in the booth approached the table and one of them knocked down a person who was talking to a member of plaintiff's party. With that, the brawl commenced.

After a short melee, someone shouted "Fuzz!" and those persons who had been sitting in the booth ran out a door and into the parking lot, with one of plaintiff's friends in hot pursuit. Upon reaching the door, the friend discovered plaintiff lying just outside with his feet wedging the door open.

Plaintiff suffered retrograde amnesia and could remember nothing of the events of the evening. No one could testify to plaintiff's whereabouts at the time the band in the booth went on the warpath or to the cause of the vicious head injuries which plaintiff displayed when the brawl was ended.

The customers in the booth had been drinking in defendant's place of business for approximately two and one-half hours before the affray commenced.

The principal issue is whether, as plaintiff contends, violations of ORS 471.410(3) and of Oregon Liquor Control Regulation No. 10–065(2) constitute negligence as a matter of law. The portion of the statute relied on by plaintiff reads as follows:

"(3) No person shall give or otherwise make available any alcoholic liquor to a person visibly intoxicated * * *."

The portion of the regulation to which plaintiff points provides:

"(2) No licensee shall permit or suffer any loud, noisy, disorderly or boisterous conduct, or any profane or abusive language, in or upon his licensed premises, or permit any visibly intoxicated person to enter or remain upon his licensed premises."

The trial court held that a violation of either the statute or the regulation did not constitute negligence per se. It refused requested instructions and withdrew allegations of negligence which were based on their violation.

A violation of a statute or regulation constitutes negligence as a matter of law when the violation results in injury to a member of the class of persons intended to be protected by the legislation and when the harm is of the kind which the statute or regulation was enacted to prevent. [Cc] The reason behind the rule is that when a legislative body has generalized a standard from the experience of the community and prohibits conduct that is likely to cause harm the court accepts the formulation. Justice Traynor in Clinkscales v. Carver, 22 Cal.2d 72, 136 P.2d 777 (1943).

However, in addition, it is proper for the court to examine preliminarily the appropriateness of the standard as a measure of care for civil litigation under the circumstances presented. F. James, Jr., "Statutory Standards and Negligence in Accident Cases," 11 La.L.Rev. 95, 111–12 (1950–51); Restatement (Second) of Torts § 286, comment *d* (1965). The statute in question prevents making available alcohol to a person who is *already visibly intoxicated.* This makes the standard particularly inappropriate for the awarding of civil damages because of the extreme difficulty, if not impossibility, of determining whether a third party's injuries would have been caused, in any event, by the already inebriated person. Unless we are prepared to say that an alcoholic drink given after visible intoxication is the cause of a third party's injuries as a matter of law, a concept not advanced by anyone, the standard would be one almost impossible of application by a factfinder in most circumstances. * * *

The regulation promulgated by the commission is an altogether different matter. * * *

ORS 471.030, entitled "Purpose of Liquor Control Act," provides, in part, as follows:

"(1) The Liquor Control Act shall be liberally construed so as:

"(a) To prevent the recurrence of abuses associated with saloons or resorts for the consumption of alcoholic beverages." * * *

An examination of the regulation discloses that it concerns matters having a direct relation to the creation of physical disturbances in bars which would, in turn, create a likelihood of injury to customers. A common feature of our western past, now preserved in story and reproduced on the screen hundreds of times, was the carnage of the barroom brawl. No citation of authority is needed to establish that the "abuses associated with saloons," which the Liquor Control Act seeks to prevent, included permitting on the premises profane, abusive conduct and drunken clientele (now prohibited by the regulation) which results in serious personal injuries to customers in breach of the bar owner's duty to protect his patrons from harm. We find it reasonable to assume that the commission, in promulgating the regulation, intended to prevent these abuses, and that they had in mind the safety of patrons of bars as well as the general peace and quietude of the community. In view of the quoted purpose of the Act and of the history of injury to innocent patrons of saloons, we cannot assume otherwise.

In addition, we see no reason why the standard is not an appropriate one for use in the awarding of civil damages. Because plaintiff was within the class of persons intended to be protected by the regulation and the harm caused to him was the kind the statute was intended to prevent, we hold that the trial court erred in not treating the alleged violations of the regulation as negligence as a matter of law. * * *

We believe it would be fair for the jury to infer, in the circumstances set forth in the statement of the facts, that plaintiff was injured by one of the persons in the booth who had created the disturbance and that the injuries would not have occurred except for defendant's violation of the commission's regulation, as alleged.

The judgment of the trial court is reversed and the case is remanded for a new trial.

NOTES AND QUESTIONS

1. Why does the opinion identify the "ancestry" of the bar patrons sitting in the booth?

2. What is the basis upon which a court seeks to select or reject a criminal statute as a standard of care in a particular tort suit? The court must determine each of the following.

A. The party seeking to charge the other with violation of the statute is a *member of the class* the legislature intended to protect. See Thomas v. Baltimore & O.R. Co., 19 Md.App. 217, 310 A.2d 186 (1973) (plaintiff who knew of location of railway crossing not in class to be protected by regulation requiring warning); Erickson v. Kongsli, 40 Wash.2d 79, 240

P.2d 1209 (1952) (landowner's property damaged by collision that resulted when defendant made a left turn in front of an oncoming vehicle—not in class to be protected); Distad v. Cubin, 633 P.2d 167 (Wyo.1981) (violation of regulations on emergency treatment not negligence per se when plaintiff did not appear to need emergency care—not in class to be protected); Long v. Daly, 156 P.3d 994 (Wyo. 2007) (driver injured by collision with cattle that had escaped railroad's fence not within class of persons to be protected by statute requiring railroad to maintain fence along railroad right of way because statute was aimed at protecting livestock owners from loss of cattle); Lockhart v. Loosen, 943 P.2d 1074 (Okla.1997) (plaintiff, who had contracted herpes from her husband after his extramarital affair with defendant, could not use negligence per se to prove her case because she was not in the class of persons the legislature intended to protect in passing legislation that prohibited those with venereal disease from marrying or engaging in sexual intercourse while infectious). Horvath v. Ish, 134 Ohio St.3d 48, 979 N.E.2d 1246 (2012) (statutory responsibilities of ski-area operators and ski-area visitors designed by the legislature to be reciprocal and thus statute does not establish a duty of care that applies between skiers).

What result in the principal case if a waiter had been injured in the mêlée?

B. The *hazard* that caused injury was one the legislature intended to protect against. The leading case on the "different hazard" is Gorris v. Scott, L.R. 9 Ex. 125 (1874), where a contagious diseases act required that animals shipped by boat be kept in pens, to avoid the spread of disease. Plaintiff's sheep were washed overboard from defendant's boat during a storm, because they were not in pens. It was held that the violation of the statute did not make the defendant liable for the loss of the sheep.

What result in the principal case if plaintiff had been injured when another patron had stumbled and fallen upon him?

C. Whether it is *appropriate* to impose tort liability for violations of the statute. See Stevens v. Luther, 105 Neb. 184, 180 N.W. 87 (1920) (six mile an hour speed limit); Stafford v. Chippewa Valley Electric R. Co., 110 Wis. 331, 85 N.W. 1036 (1901) (requirement that a street car bell be rung continuously); Ridge v. Cessna Aircraft Co., 117 F.3d 126 (4th Cir. 1997) (applying Virginia law) (FAA regulations for guidelines and standards of conduct for pilots too general to warrant application as negligence standard).

3. The Restatement (Second) of Torts spells out in greater detail these requirements in § 286, and it states in § 288:

"The court will not adopt as the standard of conduct of a reasonable man the requirements of a legislative enactment or an administrative regulation whose purpose is found to be exclusively

(a) to protect the interests of the state or any subdivision of it as such, or

(b) to secure to individuals the enjoyment of rights or privileges to which they are entitled only as members of the public, or

(c) to impose upon the actor the performance of a service which the state or any subdivision of it undertakes to give the public, or

(d) to protect a class of persons other than the one whose interests are invaded, or

(e) to protect another interest than the one invaded, or

(f) to protect against other harm than that which has resulted, or

(g) to protect against any other hazards than that from which the harm has resulted."

4. Because state legislative history may be scanty and also difficult to obtain, there may be wide latitude for a court to decide who is in the "class" or what the "hazard" was that the legislature had in mind. On occasion the court may rely on the title or the preamble of the statute. Compare Kelly v. Henry Muhs Co., 71 N.J.L. 358, 59 A. 23 (1904) (firefighter not permitted to use statute requiring elevator shafts to be guarded because title and body of statute referred to safety of employees) with Drake v. Fenton, 237 Pa. 8, 85 A. 14 (1912) (firefighter permitted to use similar statute because its title was regulation of building safety and was not limited to employee safety).

5. *Federal Statutes and Regulations.* There is no "doctrine" of negligence per se in federal law. Because there is no general federal common law of negligence as a result of Erie R. Co. v. Tompkins, 304 U.S. 64 (1938), the federal courts are in no position to adopt a criminal statutory rule of conduct as a civil rule of conduct replacing the general standard of care. The result is that they find it necessary to "imply" a civil action from the criminal statute, thus placing the responsibility for the action on the Congress. See Chapter 23, Torts in the Age of Statutes. Should violation of a federal statute be a basis for finding negligence per se under state common law? Surprisingly, there is very little explicit consideration of this issue, with most courts appearing to assume that federal statutes can be used to set the standard of care. See Steagall v. Dot Mfg. Corp., 223 Tenn. 428, 446 S.W.2d 515 (1969), where the court assumed that violation of the Federal Hazardous Substances Act might be negligence per se but found no proximate cause. In a case of first impression in Idaho, a state court found that violation of Occupational Safety and Health Administration regulations constituted negligence per se as a matter of state law. Sanchez v. Galey, 112 Idaho 609, 733 P.2d 1234 (1986). In diversity cases where they are applying state law, most federal courts have assumed that the state court would apply negligence per se to a federal statute or regulation. See Orthopedic Equip. Co. v. Eutsler, 276 F.2d 455 (4th Cir.1960) (Federal Food, Drug & Cosmetic Act—Virginia law); Gober v. Revlon, Inc., 317 F.2d 47 (4th Cir.1963) (same—California law); Ridge v. Cessna Aircraft Co., 117 F.3d 126 (4th Cir.1997) (FAA regulations—Virginia law; inapplicable for other reasons). See also Howard v. Zimmer, 299 P.3d 463 (Okla. 2014) (answering certified question from federal court and specifically finding that an Oklahoma negligence per se action can be based on violation of the federal Medical Device Amendments Act) and Restatement (Third) of Torts: Liability for Physical and Emotional Harm § 14 comment *a* (2010) (recognizing that most states will use federal statutes for negligence per se). But see St. Luke Hospital, Inc. v. Straub, 354 S.W.3d 529 (Ky. 2011) (negligence per se is codified in Kentucky and it does not extend to federal statutes and regulations).

6. *Ordinances.* Generally, ordinances have been treated in the same manner as statutes, although a few states give a lesser effect to ordinances than they do to statutes.

7. *Administrative Regulations.* Unlike Oregon in the principal case, some states give regulations promulgated under the authority of administrative agencies lesser effect than statutes. See, e.g., Chambers v. St. Mary's School, 82 Ohio St.3d 563, 697 N.E.2d 198 (1998) (violation of administrative rule does not constitute negligence per se, but may be admissible as evidence of negligence); Elliott v. S.D. Warren Co., 134 F.3d 1 (1st Cir.1998) (applying Maine law) (OSHA regulation, at best, is on par with statute and thus evidence of negligence under Maine law); Morris, The Role of Administrative Safety Measures in Negligence Actions, 28 Tex.L.Rev. 143 (1949). Is an OSHA regulation that applies to employers admissible against the manufacturer of an allegedly defective machine used in the workplace? Hansen v. Abrasive Engineering and Mfg., Inc., 317 Or. 378, 856 P.2d 625 (1993) (admitted and given same weight as industry custom). Against the employee to prove contributory negligence per se? Leaf v. Goodyear Tire & Rubber Co., 590 N.W.2d 525 (Iowa 1999) (not admitted because purpose is protection of employee).

8. *Advisory Codes, Voluntary Industry Standards.* Advisory safety codes promulgated by governmental authority, industry, or voluntary associations may be admissible, though not binding, on the issue of negligence if properly identified and shown through expert testimony to have general acceptance in the industrial community. See Lemery v. O'Shea Dennis, Inc., 112 N.H. 199, 291 A.2d 616 (1972); Philo, Use of Safety Standards, Codes and Practices in Tort Litigation, 41 N.D.Law. 1 (1965).

Ney v. Yellow Cab Co.

Illinois Supreme Court, 1954.
2 Ill.2d 74, 117 N.E.2d 74.

MAXWELL, JUSTICE. * * * The Appellate Court here affirmed the trial court's judgment fixing liability on the defendant for violation of a section of the Uniform Traffic Act. The plaintiff charged that defendant, by its servant, negligently permitted its taxicab to remain unattended on a Chicago street without first stopping the engine or locking the ignition or removing the key, contrary to a section of said act. The undisputed facts reveal that a thief stole the taxicab and while in flight ran into plaintiff's vehicle causing property damage. Defendant's motion to dismiss the complaint was based on the theory that the acts or omissions of the defendant did not constitute actionable negligence, nor the proximate cause of the damage. Briefly stated, plaintiff contended that the defendant's violation of the statute was negligence and the proximate cause of the damage.

The statute in question, section 92 of article XIV of the Uniform Traffic Act, provides: "(a) No person driving or in charge of a motor vehicle shall permit it to stand unattended without first stopping the engine, locking the ignition and removing the key, or when standing upon any perceptible grade without effectively setting the brake thereon and turning the front wheels to the curb or side of the highway.

(b) No person shall operate or drive a motor vehicle who is under fifteen years of age." Ill.Rev.Stat.1953, chap. 95½, par. 189; Jones Ann.Stat. 85.221.

The defendant takes the position that this particular statute is not an antitheft measure but is a traffic regulation, the violation of which could impose no liability on the owner or operator of the vehicle for the misconduct of a thief, for the reason that, under such circumstances, the violation of the statute is not actionable negligence in that the misconduct is neither negligence with relation to the resulting injury, nor its proximate cause. The plaintiff, on the other hand, contends that the statute is a safety measure for the benefit of the public; that its violation is prima facie evidence of negligence; and that reasonable persons might reasonably foresee that its violation could result in the consequences which occurred here. The plaintiff further contends that irrespective of the statute there would be a common-law liability under the same circumstances, and that in either event the questions of negligence and proximate cause are, under the facts alleged and admitted here, questions of fact and not questions of law. * * *

We have carefully studied the reasoning of our Appellate Courts and the courts of the other jurisdictions, in the light of these distinctions, and conclude that the issue presented requires our determination of the following [question: What was the legislative intention?] * * *

Labeling of the statute does not solve the problem. Defendant urges that the statute is a traffic regulation and not an antitheft measure, and from this premise reasons to a conclusion of nonliability. It seems to argue that if it were an antitheft measure liability would attach in this case. * * * We think the key to the construction of the statute with regard to the legislative intention appears in the statute itself. The requirement that the brakes be set and the wheels turned to the curb on a grade is no material theft deterrent. The second subparagraph of the section prohibiting persons under fifteen years of age from operating a motor vehicle indicates to us that the legislature was thinking about the danger to the public in permitting persons lacking in experience, judgment, knowledge and maturity to operate such vehicles. We cannot but conclude that this entire section is a public safety measure. This being so, what harm did the legislature foresee and attempt to prevent by prohibiting the leaving of an unattended motor vehicle with the key in the ignition? The motor vehicle with the key in its ignition in itself could obviously do no harm.

Consequently, there enters into our consideration the question of foreseeability as to intervention of outside agencies not under the control of the person in charge of the motor vehicle. The drawing of lines of demarcation in problems of cause and effect is often difficult in the study of formal logic and these difficulties are not minimized in the field of jurisprudence. We cannot say that the legislature intended to distinguish between certain types of outside agencies without expressing such distinction. Such a distinction would be too tenuous a ground to serve as a basis for decision in view of the broad general sweep of the statutory language employed. The legislature has here used clear and express terms making it the duty of persons in charge of motor vehicles to do certain acts upon leaving their vehicles unattended. The motivation of such legislation is not the State's desire to punish but rather its interest in public welfare for protection of life, limb and property by prevention of recognized hazards.

The violation of the statute is prima facie evidence of negligence under the prevailing rule of this State. * * *

The speed and power of automobiles have increased to the extent that safety experts are now showing keen awareness of their potentials even in the hands of rightful owners and careful operators. Incidents of serious havoc caused by runaway thieves or irresponsible juveniles in stolen or "borrowed" motor vehicles frequently shock the readers of the daily press. With this background must come a recognition of the probable danger of resulting injury consequent to permitting a motor vehicle to become easily available to an unauthorized person through violation of the statute in question. * * *

[The court here discussed the proximate cause (covered in Chapter 6) issue raised by the parties, including the foreseeability that a thief would steal the car and injure someone.]

For the foregoing reasons, it is our opinion that the Appellate Court was correct in affirming the judgment of the municipal court of Chicago.

Judgment affirmed.

HERSHEY, J., dissenting. The majority opinion is contradictory within itself. It first concludes that section 92 of article XIV of the Uniform Traffic Act [C] is not an antitheft statute, but is, in fact, a public safety measure. Although the opinion fails to answer in specific fashion its question as to what harm the legislature foresaw and attempted to prevent by the passage of this act, it does ultimately determine that the statute was to prevent accidents caused by a thief in stealing the vehicle. This determination is manifest by the majority's adoption of the Appellate Court determination. The majority thus finds the statute, or at least that part of the statute rendering it unlawful to fail to remove the keys from a parked vehicle, to be an antitheft measure. * * *

The majority concludes that all parts of this statute, except that portion referring to the keys, indicate an intention on the part of the legislature to prevent harm to the public by an inadvertent or negligent movement of a parked vehicle, or through its being driven by a young person devoid of experience, judgment, knowledge, or maturity. It finds that the legislature's purpose in relation to those portions of the statute was not to deter theft. However, the majority then concludes that the portion directing the removal of the keys from the vehicle was to prevent the operation of the vehicle and possible public harm by a thief in flight. The slightest experience renders everyone cognizant of the fact that the removal of automobile ignition keys is only a minor deterrent, if any, to the theft of an automobile and a subsequent flight from detection and pursuit. Consequently, it is only reasonable and logical to construe the legislature's intention in the passage of this portion of the statute in the same light as is attributed to the remainder of the section. One can only conclude, therefore, that the legislature required the removal of the key to prevent a mere negligent or inadvertent starting of the automobile and an ensuing uncontrolled movement thereof. Obviously the legislature could not presume by such legislation to prevent a wilful movement of the vehicle by an unauthorized person. * * *

NOTES AND QUESTIONS

1. The principal case illustrates how much discretion a court may have in determining the purpose of a statute. Was the purpose of this key-in-the-car statute to prevent theft of the car, with resulting loss to the owner and his insurance company and an increased burden on the police? Cf. Anderson v. Theisen, 231 Minn. 369, 43 N.W.2d 272 (1950). To prevent the car from being started up by children or other irresponsible people? Cf. Bouldin v. Sategna, 71 N.M. 329, 378 P.2d 370 (1963). To prevent joy-riding teenagers from "taking it out for a spree"? Cf. Kozicki v. Dragon, 255 Neb. 248, 583 N.W.2d 336 (1998) (statute is for protection of users of public streets; teenage thief testified that four or five of the cars she had previously stolen had ended up wrecked). To prevent it from being stolen by a tense thief, endangering people in the vicinity while trying to make his getaway?

2. Observe that the two opinions in this case argue for a single purpose. May there not be more than one purpose? Cf. Hines v. Foreman, 243 S.W. 479 (Tex.Com.App.1922). The statute prohibited use of a "cut-out" in the exhaust pipe leading to the muffler, in order to make a zooming or roaring noise. Plaintiff had his cut-out open driving down the streets of a Texas city. He approached a railroad track, where, unknown to him because of the noise of the cut-out, there was a train coming and he was engaged in a race that ended in a tie. The issue was whether he was contributorily negligent, and he claimed that the statute was irrelevant because its purpose was to prevent harassing noises. Held, it had a double purpose, and one of them was to eliminate noises preventing him from hearing traffic hazards.

3. Who makes the decision as to the purpose of the statute—judge or jury?

4. Who decides whether that statute applies to the conduct? Roberts v. Randall, 51 P.3d 204 (Wyo.2002) (trial court judge correctly determined that statutes governing "rules of the road" for "motor vehicles" applied to drivers of snowmobiles in case where plaintiff alleged that defendant was on wrong side of road that had been closed during winter to regular traffic and approved as a snowmobile trail).

5. Both opinions in the principal case became heavily involved in the problem of proximate cause. In theory, there should be no problem of proximate cause if the event is within the hazard that the statute is intended to avert. By deciding the purpose of the statute, the court implicitly finds proximate cause. Is there an element of begging the question by following this procedure? But it may simplify some of the difficulties of proximate cause. Look for it later when the subject of proximate cause is taken up.

6. A statute requires that a seller of a "deadly weapon receive positive identification" of the purchaser from two residents of the state, and keep a record of name, age, address and other details. Defendant sells a gun without complying, and the purchaser uses it on the plaintiff in the

course of an armed robbery. Defendant is liable for fines under the statute. Should the defendant also be liable in negligence to the plaintiff? Cf. Hetherton v. Sears, Roebuck & Co., 593 F.2d 526 (3d Cir.1979), second appeal, 652 F.2d 1152 (3d Cir.1981) (applying Delaware law). Fertilizer manufacturer sells ammonium nitrate, allegedly in violation of various federal and state labeling statutes. Terrorist uses it to construct bomb. Should the manufacturer be liable? Gaines-Tabb v. ICI Explosives, USA, Inc., 160 F.3d 613 (10th Cir.1998) (applying Oklahoma law) (case brought by victims of bombing of Oklahoma City federal building dismissed due to lack of causal link between alleged statutory violations and injury).

7. A county ordinance provides that a "Pit Bull Terrier" must be "secured by an unbreakable or unseverable leash and maintained under the control of an adult" whenever it is out of its kennel. Owner's 15-year-old son had a pit bull terrier on front steps in unfenced yard without a leash when 12-year-old plaintiff and two of her friends walked by on the sidewalk. One of the girls got into an argument with the boys who threatened to "sic" the dog on the girls. Owner's son said something to dog and dog ran toward the girls. Plaintiff turned to flee the dog and ran into the path of a car. Is plaintiff within the protected class? Is her injury, suffered when fleeing the approaching pit bull, the kind of injury the statute was designed to prevent? Is the standard of conduct of the statute otherwise appropriate for use? Moore v. Myers, 161 Md.App. 349, 868 A.2d 954 (2005) (yes).

Perry v. S.N. and S.N.

Texas Supreme Court, 1998.
973 S.W.2d 301.

PHILLIPS, CHIEF JUSTICE. * * * This is a suit for injuries arising out of the abuse of children at a day care center. Plaintiffs filed suit individually and as next friends of their two children, alleging that defendants witnessed the abuse and failed to report it to the police or child welfare officials. The sole issue before us is whether plaintiffs may maintain a cause of action for negligence per se based on the Family Code, which requires any person having cause to believe a child is being abused to report the abuse to state authorities and makes the knowing failure to do so a misdemeanor. See TEX FAM. CODE §§ 261.101(a), 261.109 (formerly TEX. FAM. CODE §§ 34.01, 34.07). The trial court granted summary judgment for defendants, but the court of appeals reversed and remanded plaintiffs' negligence per se and gross negligence claims for trial. [C] We reverse the judgment of the court of appeals and render judgment that plaintiffs take nothing. Because plaintiffs did not preserve their common law negligence claims, we do not decide whether there should be a common law duty to report child abuse in some circumstances.

B.N. and K.N. attended a day care center operated by Francis Keller and her husband Daniel Keller from March 25, 1991, to August 28, 1991. Their parents, S.N. and S.N., allege that during that period, Daniel Keller regularly abused B.N. and K.N. and other children at the center both physically and sexually. Mr. and Mrs. N. brought suit against the Kellers and three of the Kellers' friends, Douglas Perry,

Janise White, and Raul Quintero. Plaintiffs claim that Francis Keller confided in White at an unspecified time that Daniel Keller had "abusive habits toward children." They further allege that on one occasion in August 1991, while visiting the Kellers, defendants Perry, White, and Quintero all saw Daniel Keller bring a number of children out of the day care center into the Kellers' adjoining home and sexually abuse them. The record does not indicate whether B.N. and K.N. were among these children. According to plaintiffs, Perry, White, and Quintero did not attempt to stop Daniel Keller from abusing the children or report his crimes to the police or child welfare authorities. * * *

Mr. and Mrs. N. alleged only that Perry, White, and Quintero were negligent per se because they violated a statute requiring any person who "has cause to believe that a child's physical or mental health or welfare has been or may be adversely affected by abuse" to file a report with the police or the Department of Protective and Regulatory Services. [C] Plaintiffs also asserted gross negligence and common law negligence claims. They claimed that Perry, White, and Quintero's failure to report the abuse proximately caused them harm by permitting the day care center to remain open, thus enabling Daniel Keller to continue abusing the children at the center. They sought damages for pain, mental anguish, and medical expenses, as well as loss of income when they could not work outside the home because of B.N. and K.N.'s injuries.

Perry, White, and Quintero moved for summary judgment on the sole ground that plaintiffs failed to state a cause of action. * * *

The trial court granted Perry, White, and Quintero's motions for summary judgment and severed plaintiffs' claims against those three defendants from their suit against the Kellers, which is not before us. * * * When the ground for the trial court's decision is that plaintiffs failed to state a cause of action, we must take the allegations in the pleadings as true in determining whether a cause of action exists. [C]

The court of appeals affirmed the summary judgment on plaintiffs' common law negligence claims but reversed and remanded for trial on the issues of negligence per se and gross negligence, holding that a violation of the Family Code's child abuse reporting requirement is negligence per se. [C] Mr. and Mrs. N. have not appealed the court of appeals' judgment affirming the summary judgment against them on common law negligence. Therefore, the question of whether Texas should impose a new common law duty to report child abuse on the facts of this case is not before us. * * *

"It is fundamental that the existence of a legally cognizable duty is a prerequisite to all tort liability." Graff v. Beard, 858 S.W.2d 918, 919 (Tex.1993). The court of appeals found a duty in the [mandatory child abuse reporting statute.] * * *

All persons have a duty to obey the criminal law in the sense that they may be prosecuted for not doing so, but this is not equivalent to a duty in tort. See, e.g., Smith v. Merritt, 940 S.W.2d 602, 607–08 (Tex.1997) (statute making it a crime to furnish alcohol to persons under age 21 did not impose a tort duty on social hosts). "It is well-established that the mere fact that the Legislature adopts a criminal statute does not mean that this court must accept it as a standard for civil liability." [C] "The considerations which warrant imposing tort liability are not identical with those which warrant criminal conviction," Morris, The Role of Criminal Statutes in Negligence Actions, 49 COLUM. L. REV. 21, 22–23 (1949), and we will not apply the doctrine of negligence per se if the criminal statute does not provide an appropriate basis for civil liability. * * *

Before we begin our analysis of whether section 261.109 of the Family Code is an appropriate basis for tort liability, we emphasize that we must look beyond the facts of this particular case to consider the full reach of the statute. We do not decide today whether a statute criminalizing only the type of egregious behavior with which these defendants are charged—the failure of eyewitnesses to report the sexual molestation of preschool children—would be an appropriate basis for a tort action. That is not the statute the Legislature passed. Rather, the issue before us is whether it is appropriate to impose tort liability on any and every person who "has cause to believe that a child's physical or mental health or welfare has been or may be adversely affected by abuse or neglect and knowingly fails to report." [C] Cf. Leonard, The Application of Criminal Legislation to Negligence Cases: A Reexamination, 23 SANTA CLARA L. REV. 427, 457–66 (1983) (contrasting the rigidity of statutory standards with the flexibility of case-by-case common law determinations of duty and breach).

The threshold questions in every negligence per se case are whether the plaintiff belongs to the class that the statute was intended to protect and whether the plaintiff's injury is of a type that the statute was designed to prevent. [Cc] Texas's first mandatory child abuse reporting statute, from which Family Code section 261.101(a) is derived, stated that "the purpose of this Act is to protect children who . . . are adversely affected by abuse or neglect." [C] Similarly, the current Family Code provision governing the investigation of reports of child abuse states that "the primary purpose of the investigation shall be the protection of the child." [C]

B.N. and K.N. are within the class of persons whom the child abuse reporting statute was meant to protect, and they suffered the kind of injury that the Legislature intended the statute to prevent. [Footnote omitted.] But this does not end our inquiry. [C] The Court must still determine whether it is appropriate to impose tort liability for violations of the statute. [C] This determination is informed by a number of factors, some discussed by the court of appeals in this case and others derived from past negligence per se decisions of Texas courts and from scholarly analysis. These factors are not necessarily exclusive, nor is the issue properly resolved by merely counting how many factors lean each way. Rather, we set out these considerations as guides to assist a court in answering the ultimate question of whether imposing tort liability for violations of a criminal statute is fair, workable, and wise.

We first consider the fact that, absent a change in the common law, a negligence per se cause of action against these defendants would derive the element of duty solely from the Family Code. At common law there is generally no duty to protect another from the criminal acts of a third party or to come to the aid of another in distress. [Cc] Although there are exceptions to this no-duty rule, see, e.g., Lefmark Management Co. v. Old, 946 S.W.2d 52, 53 (Tex.1997) (noting that under some circumstances, person in control of premises has duty to protect invitees from crime), this case does not fall within any of the established exceptions, and Mr. and Mrs. N. have not asked this Court to impose on persons who are aware of child abuse a new common law duty to report it or take other protective action.

In contrast, the defendant in most negligence per se cases already owes the plaintiff a pre-existing common law duty to act as a reasonably prudent person, so that the statute's role is merely to define more precisely what conduct breaches that duty. [Cc] For example, the overwhelming majority of this Court's negligence per se cases have involved violations of traffic statutes by drivers and train operators—actors who already owed a common law duty to exercise reasonable care toward others on the road or track. [Cc]

When a statute criminalizes conduct that is also governed by a common law duty, as in the case of a traffic regulation, applying negligence per se causes no great change in the law because violating the statutory standard of conduct would usually also be negligence under a common law reasonableness standard. [Cc] But recognizing a new, purely statutory duty "can have an extreme effect upon the common law of negligence" when it allows a cause of action where the common law would not. In such a situation, applying negligence per se "brings into existence a new type of tort liability." Burnette v. Wahl, 284 Ore. 705, 588 P.2d 1105, 1109 (Or.1978). The change tends to be especially great when, as here, the statute criminalizes inaction rather than action.

Some commentators contend that the term "negligence per se" does not even apply when the statute on which civil liability is based corresponds to no common law duty. See Keeton et al., Prosser & Keeton on the Law of Torts § 36, at 221 n.9; Forell, The Statutory Duty Action in Tort: A Statutory/Common Law Hybrid, 23 IND. L. REV. 781, 782 (1990). While our definition has never been so restrictive, this Court in fact has created a new duty by applying negligence per se on only one occasion. * * * Thus, based on both this Court's past practice and the observations of noted scholars, we conclude that the absence of a relevant common law duty should be considered in deciding whether to apply negligence per se to the Family Code's reporting provision.

The court of appeals in this case listed several factors to consider in deciding whether to apply negligence per se. [Cc] According to the court of appeals, the principal factors favoring negligence per se are that the Legislature has determined that compliance with criminal statutes is practicable and desirable and that criminal statutes give citizens notice of what conduct is required of them. [C] As considerations against negligence per se, the court of appeals cautioned that some penal statutes may be too obscure to put the public on notice, may impose liability without fault, or may lead to ruinous monetary liability for relatively minor offenses. [C] The first of these factors is not helpful because it points the same way in every case: the very existence of a criminal statute implies a legislative judgment that its requirements are practicable and desirable. The court of appeals' remaining factors, however, are pertinent to our analysis.

On the question of notice, this Court has held that one consideration bearing on whether to apply negligence per se is whether the statute clearly defines the prohibited or required conduct. [Cc] The Family Code's reporting requirement is triggered when a person "has cause to believe that a child's physical or mental health or welfare has been or may be adversely affected by abuse or neglect." [C] In this case, defendants allegedly were eyewitnesses to sexual abuse. Under these facts, there is no question that they had cause to believe abuse was occurring, and thus that the statute required them to make a report. In many other cases, however, a person may become aware of a possible case of child abuse only through second-hand reports or ambiguous physical symptoms, and it is unclear whether these circumstances are "cause to believe" that such conduct "may be" taking place.[6] [C] A statute that conditions the requirement to report on these difficult judgment calls does not clearly define what conduct is required in many conceivable situations. (Footnote omitted.)

The next factor the court of appeals considered was whether applying negligence per se to the reporting statute would create liability without fault. [C] We agree with the court of appeals that it would not, because the statute criminalizes only the "knowing" failure to report. * * * This characteristic of the statute weighs in favor of imposing civil liability.

Our next consideration is whether negligence per se would impose ruinous liability disproportionate to the seriousness of the defendant's conduct. In analyzing this factor, the court of appeals treated child abuse as the relevant conduct. [C] ("The abuse of children has become notorious."). The conduct criminalized by section 261.109, however, is not child abuse but the failure to report child abuse. Through its penal laws, the Legislature has expressed a judgment that abuse and non-reporting deserve very different legal consequences. * * * [The Court contrasted the severe penalty for the offense committed by the abuser, five to ninety-nine years in prison and a fine of up to $10,000, with the penalty provided for failure to report, no more than six months in jail and a $2,000 fine.] This evidence of legislative intent to penalize non-reporters far less severely than abusers weighs against holding a person who fails to report suspected abuse civilly liable for the enormous damages that the abuser subsequently inflicts. The specter of disproportionate liability is particularly troubling when, as in the case of the reporting statute, it is combined with the likelihood of "broad and wide-ranging liability" by collateral wrongdoers * * *

---

[6] Determining whether abuse is or may be occurring in a particular case is likely to be especially difficult for untrained laypersons. Texas is one of a minority of states that require any person who suspects child abuse to report it. See O'Brien & Flannery, The Pending Gauntlet to Free Exercise: Mandating that Clergy Report Child Abuse, 25 LOY. L.A. L. REV. 1, 24–25 & n.127 (1991) (collecting statutes). Most states place such a requirement only on professionals who may be expected to know more than the average person about recognizing child abuse and who have a professional relationship with and responsibility for children. * * *

Finally, in addition to the factors discussed by the court of appeals, we have also looked to whether the injury resulted directly or indirectly from the violation of the statute. * * * [T]he indirect relationship between violation of such a statute and the plaintiff's ultimate injury is a factor against imposing tort liability. * * *

We conclude by noting that for a variety of reasons, including many of those we have discussed, most other states with mandatory reporting statutes similar to Texas's have concluded that the failure to report child abuse is not negligence per se. [Cc]

* * * Because a decision to impose negligence per se could not be limited to cases charging serious misconduct like the one at bar, but rather would impose immense potential liability under an ill-defined standard on a broad class of individuals whose relationship to the abuse was extremely indirect, we hold that it is not appropriate to adopt Family Code section 261.109(a) as establishing a duty and standard of conduct in tort. Therefore, Mr. and Mrs. N. and their children may not maintain a claim for negligence per se or gross negligence based on defendants' violation of the child abuse reporting statute. Because plaintiffs did not appeal the court of appeals' adverse decision on their common law negligence claims, we do not consider whether Texas should impose a common law duty to report or prevent child abuse.

For the foregoing reasons, we reverse the judgment of the court of appeals and render judgment that plaintiffs take nothing.

NOTES AND QUESTIONS

1. The principal case (at footnote 6) indicates that the Texas statute imposes a reporting obligation on everyone while most such statutes impose it only on professionals like doctors, nurses, teachers, and social workers who may be expected to know more about identifying child abuse than a layperson. Would that distinction make a difference in the use of the statute to establish negligence per se? Compare Landeros v. Flood, 17 Cal.3d 399, 551 P.2d 389, 131 Cal.Rptr. 69 (1976) (doctor's failure to recognize and report proper basis for negligence per se) with Arbaugh v. Board of Education, 214 W.Va. 677, 591 S.E.2d 235 (2003) (teacher's failure to report not proper basis for negligence per se).

2. Generally, if the plaintiff is not permitted to use the statute to prove the standard of conduct, the plaintiff's case defaults to the reasonable person standard and may still succeed if the plaintiff can prove that the defendant failed to act as the reasonable person would act. Why did the plaintiffs in this case not have the chance to argue to the jury that the defendants failed to act as a reasonable person would act under the circumstances?

3. Who makes the decision whether the provision of the Family Code can be used as the basis for negligence per se—judge or jury?

4. *Licensing Statutes.* What if the day care center in the principal case had been operating without a license required by statute? Could that serve as the basis for a negligence per se jury instruction? Most courts have refused to use licensing statutes to establish the standard of care. Brown v. Shyne, 242 N.Y. 176, 151 N.E. 197 (N.Y. 1926) (chiropractor not licensed to practice medicine); Hertz Driv-Ur-Self System v. Hendrickson, 109 Colo. 1,

121 P.2d 483 (1942) (violation of statute prohibiting renting of car to someone who did not have operator's permit); Fuller v. Sirois, 97 N.H. 100, 82 A.2d 82 (1951) (driving motor vehicle after operator's license was suspended for reckless driving); Cullip v. Domann, 266 Kan. 550, 972 P.2d 776 (1999) (hunting without license not basis for negligence per se in case where fellow hunter was injured by accidental discharge of firearm); and Michaels v. Avitech, Inc., 202 F.3d 746 (5th Cir. 2000) (applying Texas law) (pilot did not have current license). See generally Gregory, Breach of Criminal Licensing Statutes in Civil Litigation, 36 Cornell L.Q. 622 (1951) and Restatement (Third) of Torts: Liability for Physical and Emotional Harm § 14 comment *h* (2010). Plaintiff is injured by fireworks that had been brought into the state in violation of a state statute. May defendant use the violation of the statute to show the plaintiff's contributory negligence? Horstmeyer v. Golden Eagle Fireworks, 534 N.W.2d 835 (N.D.1995) (violation of statute does not establish negligent conduct because, by analogy to licensing cases, the violation did not cause the harm).

5. Could a crime victim be liable for failing to report a crime as required by state and federal statutes? An accountant discovered that his bookkeeper had embezzled money from one of his client's accounts. He fired her and then negotiated the return of the money in exchange for not reporting her to the police. In the meantime, bookkeeper got a job at a law firm and embezzled money from it. Law firm then sued accountant and client alleging, *inter alia*, negligence per se based on federal and state statutes that require crimes to be reported. The Texas Appeals Court found that the statutes were for the protection of the state's interest in apprehending felons and that even if they could be construed as for the protection of the general public, like the law firm, use of the statutes to impose liability on those who failed to report criminal behavior would not be an appropriate use of the statutes. San Benito Bank & Trust v. Landair Travels, 31 S.W.3d 312 (Tex. App. 2000).

6. The fact that a statute is inapplicable, because it is not intended for the protection of the class of persons in which the plaintiff is included, or because it was not intended for protection against the hazards, or because it is otherwise inappropriate for such use, does not necessarily rule it out entirely as evidence bearing on the issue of negligence. Thus in Hansen v. Kemmish, 201 Iowa 1008, 208 N.W. 277 (1926), a statute, intended only to prevent the misbreeding of animals, provided that hogs should be confined by fences of specified strength. Defendant fenced his hogs with a fence of less strength. One of them broke through the fence, escaped into the highway, and wrecked plaintiff's car. It was held that, while the statute did not define a standard of conduct to be adopted as a matter of law, the jury could consider it as bearing on the kind of fence necessary for the effective confinement of hogs.

7. The effect of the violation of criminal (and other) statutes and regulations on the law of torts is not confined by any means to the tort of negligence and the doctrine of negligence per se. It has been generally recognized that in furtherance of the purpose of particular legislation and to insure its effectiveness, a court may, despite the absence of a provision to this effect, supply a civil action for damages according relief to a person for whose benefit conduct of another was either proscribed or required by the

legislation. Restatement (Second) of Torts § 874A. The usual explanation is that the right is "implied" from the legislation. See Chapter 23, Torts in the Age of Statutes.

(B) EFFECT OF STATUTE

Martin v. Herzog

Court of Appeals of New York, 1920.
228 N.Y. 164, 126 N.E. 814.

CARDOZO, J. The action is one to recover damages for injuries resulting in death.

Plaintiff and her husband, while driving toward Tarrytown in a buggy on the night of August 21, 1915, were struck by the defendant's automobile coming in the opposite direction. They were thrown to the ground, and the man was killed. At the point of the collision the highway makes a curve. The car was rounding the curve when suddenly it came upon the buggy, emerging, the defendant tells us, from the gloom. Negligence is charged against the defendant, the driver of the car, in that he did not keep to the right of the center of the highway [c]. Negligence is charged against the plaintiff's intestate, the driver of the wagon, in that he was traveling without lights [c]. There is no evidence that the defendant was moving at an excessive speed. There is none of any defect in the equipment of his car. The beam of light from his lamps pointed to the right as the wheels of his car turned along the curve toward the left; and looking in the direction of the plaintiff's approach, he was peering into the shadow. The case against him must stand, therefore, if at all, upon the divergence of his course from the center of the highway. The jury found him delinquent and his victim blameless. The Appellate Division reversed, and ordered a new trial. [Plaintiff now appeals to the Court of Appeals.]

* * * We think the unexcused omission of the statutory signals is more than some evidence of negligence. It is negligence in itself. Lights are intended for the guidance and protection of other travelers on the highway. Highway Law, § 329a. By the very terms of the hypothesis, to omit, willfully or heedlessly, the safeguards prescribed by law for the benefit of another that he may be preserved in life or limb, is to fall short of the standard of diligence to which those who live in organized society are under a duty to conform. That, we think, is now the established rule in this state. [Cc]

In the case at hand, we have an instance of the admitted violation of a statute intended for the protection of travelers on the highway, of whom the defendant at the time was one. Yet the jurors were instructed in effect that they were at liberty in their discretion to treat the omission of lights either as innocent or as culpable. They were allowed to "consider the default as lightly or gravely" as they would (Thomas, J., in the court below). They might as well have been told that they could use a like discretion in holding a master at fault for the omission of a safety appliance prescribed by positive law for the protection of a workman. [Cc] Jurors have no dispensing power, by which they may relax the duty that one traveler on the highways owes under the statute to another. It is error to tell them that they have. The omission of these lights was a wrong, and, being wholly unexcused, was also a negligent wrong. No license should have been conceded to the triers of the facts to find it anything else.

We must be on our guard, however, against confusing the question of negligence with that of the causal connection between the negligence and the injury. A defendant who travels without lights is not to pay damages for his fault, unless the absence of lights is the cause of the disaster. A plaintiff who travels without them is not to forfeit the right to damages, unless the absence of lights is at least a contributing cause of the disaster. To say that conduct is negligence is not to say that it is always contributory negligence. "Proof of negligence in the air, so to speak, will not do." Pollock Torts (10th Ed.) p. 472.

We think, however, that evidence of a collision occurring more than an hour after sundown between a car and an unseen buggy, proceeding without lights, is evidence from which a causal connection may be inferred between the collision and the lack of signals. [Cc] If nothing else is shown to break the connection, we have a case, prima facie sufficient, of negligence contributing to the result.

We are persuaded that the tendency of the charge, and of all the rulings, following it, was to minimize unduly, in the minds of the triers of the facts, the gravity of the decedent's fault. Errors may not be ignored as unsubstantial, when they tend to such an outcome. A statute designed for the protection of human life is not to be brushed aside as a form of words, its commands reduced to the level of cautions, and the duty to obey attenuated into an option to conform.

The order of the Appellate Division should be affirmed, and judgment absolute directed on the stipulation in favor of the defendant, with costs in all courts.

[The dissenting opinion of HOGAN, J., is omitted.]

NOTES AND QUESTIONS

1. Who used violation of a statute to establish the standard of care in this case?

2. The majority of the courts take the position stated by Cardozo in this case, that when a statute applies to the facts, an *unexcused* violation is "negligence per se," which must be declared by the court and not left to the jury. See, for example, Schlimmer v. Poverty Hunt Club, 597 S.E.2d 43 (Va. 2004).

3. A few states treat violation of a statute as giving rise to a "presumption" of negligence, which becomes negligence as a matter of law unless the presumption is rebutted. Since usually it can be rebutted only by showing an excuse for the violation, this appears to come out at much the same place as the "negligence per se" rule. See, for example, Bacon v. Lascelles, 165 Vt. 214, 678 A.2d 902 (1996) and the next principal case.

4. A minority of states hold that the violation is only evidence of negligence, which the jury may accept or reject as it sees fit. See, for example, Paramount Development Corp., 249 Md. 188, 238 A.2d 869 (1968).

Zeni v. Anderson

Supreme Court of Michigan, 1976.
397 Mich. 117, 243 N.W.2d 270.

WILLIAMS, JUSTICE. * * * The accident which precipitated this action occurred one snowy morning, March 7, 1969, when the temperature was 11° F, the sky was clear and the average snow depth was 21 inches. Plaintiff Eleanor Zeni, then a 56-year-old registered nurse, was walking to her work at the Northern Michigan University Health Center in Marquette. Instead of using the snow-covered sidewalk, which in any event would have required her to walk across the street twice to get to her job, she traveled along a well-used pedestrian snowpath, with her back to oncoming traffic.

Defendant Karen Anderson, a college student, was driving within the speed limit in a steady stream of traffic on the same street. Ms. Anderson testified that she had turned on the defroster in the car and her passenger said she had scraped the windshield. An eyewitness whose deposition was read at trial, however, testified that defendant's windshield was clouded and he doubted that the occupants could see out. He also testified that the car was traveling too close to the curb and that he could tell plaintiff was going to be hit.

Defendant's car struck the plaintiff on the driver's right side. Ms. Anderson testified she first saw the plaintiff between a car parked on the right-hand side of the road and defendant's car, and that she did not hear nor feel her car strike Ms. Zeni. The eyewitness reported seeing plaintiff flip over the fender and hood. He said when he went over to help her his knees were on or inside the white line delineating a parking space. A security officer observed blood stains on the pavement approximately 13 feet from the curb.

Ms. Zeni's injuries were serious and included an intra-cerebral subdural hematoma which required neurosurgery. She has retrograde amnesia and therefore, because she does not remember anything from the time she began walking that morning until sometime after the impact, there is no way to determine whether she knew defendant was behind her. Following an extended period of convalescence, plaintiff, still suffering permanent disability, could return to work on only a part-time basis.

Testimony at trial indicated that it was common for nurses to use the roadway to reach the Health Center, and a security officer testified that in the wintertime it was safer to walk there than on the one sidewalk. Apparently, several days before the accident, Ms. Zeni had indeed fallen on the sidewalk. Although she was not hurt when she fell, the Director of University Security was hospitalized when he fell on the walk.

Defendant, however, maintained that plaintiff's failure to use that sidewalk constituted contributory negligence because, she said, it violated M.C.L.A. § 257.655; M.S.A. § 9.2355, which requires:

"Where sidewalks are provided, it shall be unlawful for pedestrians to walk upon the main traveled portion of the highway. Where sidewalks are not provided, pedestrians shall, when practicable, walk on the left side of the highway facing traffic which passes nearest." * * *

[There was a jury verdict for plaintiff in the trial court. The court of appeals reversed because of instructions on the subject of last clear chance. Discussion of last clear chance is omitted.]

A. Violation of Statute as Rebuttable Presumption. In a growing number of states, the rule concerning the proper role of a penal statute in a civil action for damages is that violation of the statute which has been found to apply to a particular set of facts establishes only a prima facie case of negligence, a presumption which may be rebutted by a showing on the part of the party violating the statute of an adequate excuse under the facts and circumstances of the case. The excuses may not necessarily be applicable in a criminal action, since, in the absence of legislatively-mandated civil penalties, acceptance of the criminal statute itself as a standard of care in a civil action is purely discretionary. See Comment and Illustrations, 2 Restatement (Second) of Torts § 288A, pp. 33–37. * * *

This is the approach we follow today. * * *

[An] attraction of this approach is that it is fair. "If there is sufficient excuse or justification, there is ordinarily no violation of a statute and the statutory standard is inapplicable." Satterlee v. Orange Glenn School Dist. of San Diego County, 29 Cal.2d 581, 594, 177 P.2d 279, 286 (1947) (dissenting in part). It would be unreasonable to adhere to an automatic rule of negligence "where observance would subject a person to danger which might be avoided by disregard of the general rule." Tedla v. Ellman, 280 N.Y. 124, 131–132, 19 N.E.2d 987, 991 (1939).

The approach is logical. Liability without fault is not truly negligence, and in the absence of a clear legislative mandate to so extend liability, the courts should be hesitant to do so on their own. Because these are, after all, criminal statutes, a court is limited in how far it may go in plucking a statute from its criminal milieu and inserting it into the civil arena. The rule of rebuttable presumption has arisen in part in response to this concern, and in part because of the reluctance to go to the other extreme and in effect, discard or disregard the legislative standard. * * *

B. Violation of Statute as Negligence Per Se. While some Michigan cases seem to speak of negligence per se as a kind of strict liability, Holbert v. Staniak, 359 Mich. 283, 290, 102 N.W.2d 186 (1960), an examination indicates that there are a number of conditions that attempt to create a more reasonable approach than would result from an automatic application of a per se rule.

[Reference is made here to the court's construing the statute, determining its purpose, and applying principles of proximate cause.]

Despite such limitations, the judge-made rule of negligence per se has still proved to be too inflexible and mechanical to satisfy thoughtful commentators and judges. It is forcefully argued that no matter how a court may attempt to confine the negligence per se doctrine, if defendant is liable despite the exercise of due care and the availability of a reasonable excuse, this is really strict liability, and not negligence.

Prosser, The Law of Torts (4th ed.), § 36, p. 197. Since it is always possible that the Legislature's failure to deal specifically with the question of private rights was not accidental, and that there might have been no legislative intent to change the law of torts, such treatment of the statute may well be a gross perversion of the legislative will. It is troublesome, too, that "potentially ruinous civil liability" may follow from a "minor infraction of petty criminal regulations", [c] or may, in a jurisdiction burdened by contributory negligence, serve to deprive an otherwise deserving plaintiff of a much-needed recovery. * * *

C. Violation of Statute as Evidence of Negligence. Just as the rebuttable presumption approach to statutory violations in a negligence context apparently arose, at least in part, from dissatisfaction with the result of a mechanical application of the per se rule, a parallel development in our state with respect to infractions of ordinances and of administrative regulations, has been that violations of these amount to only evidence of negligence. [Cc]

We have not, however, chosen to join that small minority which has decreed that violation of a statute is only evidence of negligence. In view of the fairness and ease with which the rebuttable presumption standard has been and can be administered, we believe the litigants are thereby well served and the Legislature is given appropriate respect.

D. Application of Statutory Standard to This Case. We have seen, therefore, that while some of our Michigan cases seem to present negligence per se as an unqualified rule, the fact of the matter is that there are a number of qualifications which make application of this rule not really a per se approach at all. Not only must the statutory purpose doctrine and the requirement of proximate cause be satisfied, but the alleged wrongdoer has an opportunity to come forward with evidence rebutting the presumption of negligence.

An accurate statement of our law is that when a court adopts a penal statute as the standard of care in an action for negligence, violation of that statute establishes a prima facie case of negligence, with the determination to be made by the finder of fact whether the party accused of violating the statute has established a legally sufficient excuse. If the finder of fact determines such an excuse exists, the appropriate standard of care then becomes that established by the common law. Such excuses shall include, but shall not be limited to, those suggested by the Restatement (Second) of Torts § 288A, and shall be determined by the circumstances of each case.

In the case at bar, moreover, the statute itself provides a guideline for the jury, for a violation will not occur when it is impracticable to use the sidewalk or to walk on the left side of a highway. This is ordinarily a question for the finder of fact, [c] and thus the statute itself provides not only a legislative standard of care which may be accepted by the court, but a legislatively mandated excuse as well. * * *

* * * [W]e find the jury was adequately instructed as to the effect of the violation of this particular statute on plaintiff's case. * * *

The Court of Appeals is reversed and the trial court is affirmed. Costs to plaintiff.

NOTES AND QUESTIONS

1. Section 288A of the Second Restatement, referred to in the principal case, reads as follows:

> (1) An excused violation of a legislative enactment or an administrative regulation is not negligence.
>
> (2) Unless the enactment or regulation is construed not to permit such excuse, its violation is excused when
>
> (a) the violation is reasonable because of the actor's incapacity;
>
> (b) he neither knows nor should know of the occasion for compliance;
>
> (c) he is unable after reasonable diligence or care to comply;
>
> (d) he is confronted by an emergency not due to his own misconduct;
>
> (e) compliance would involve a greater risk of harm to the actor or to others.

This list is "not intended to be exclusive." See also Restatement (Third) of Torts: Liability for Physical and Emotional Harm § 15 (2010) (comparable list of excused violations).

2. The principal case classifies the approaches to the question of what effect to give to the violation of a statute into three groups: (1) negligence per se, (2) prima facie (rebuttable presumption) negligence, and (3) some evidence of negligence. Most commentators would agree with this classification, but there may be disagreement on which states fall into which of the first two groups. The Restatement (Second) espouses the negligence per se approach, but permits excuses as indicated in § 288A. The excuses are ones commonly permitted by the courts. Thus, an unexcused violation is negligence per se. The second classification (prima facie negligence or rebuttable presumption) applies to jurisdictions in which the issue goes to the jury even when there is no credible evidence of a recognized excuse, but merely testimony that the defendant acted with due care. See, for example, Gillingham v. Stephenson, 209 W.Va. 741, 551 S.E.2d 663 (2001) (in case where driver of van that rear-ended pickup violated statutes that prohibited following too closely, driving in excess of speed reasonable for conditions, and failing to maintain control of vehicle, issue of negligence is one for jury because driver testified he hit black ice and jury could have concluded that he acted reasonably under the circumstances). The third category is for jurisdictions that provide the violation is some evidence of negligence, but not conclusive.

3. How might the following situations be decided?

A. A statute provides that no vehicle shall be driven on the highway at night without a tail light. Without any fault or knowledge of defendant, his tail light goes out while he is driving at night, and as a result plaintiff is injured in a collision with him. Brotherton v. Day & Night Fuel Co., 192 Wash. 362, 73 P.2d 788 (1937). What if defendant discovered that the light was out, but continued to drive carefully to a near-by filling station? Taber v. Smith, 26 S.W.2d 722 (Tex.Civ.App.1930).

B. A statute prohibits automobile drivers from passing at an intersection. Defendant approaches an intersection concealed from view and not marked by any warning sign, of whose existence he is ignorant, and as he reaches it attempts to pass. Hullander v. McIntyre, 78 S.D. 453, 104 N.W.2d 40 (1960).

C. A child, too young to know or appreciate the statute, crosses a street in the middle of the block. Morby v. Rogers, 122 Utah 540, 252 P.2d 231 (1953); Maker v. Wellin, 214 Or. 332, 327 P.2d 793 (1958). Suppose an adult does not know of the jaywalking statute?

D. Defendant truck driver drives on the left side of the road in order to pass under a bridge that is not high enough for his truck on the right side and runs head on into motorcycle. Brown v. Roadway Express, Inc., 169 Vt. 633, 740 A.2d 352 (1999) (no excuse; finding of negligence as a matter of law upheld). Defendant drives on the left side of the road to avoid hitting a child who has darted out from the right. Burlie v. Stephens, 113 Wash. 182, 193 P. 684 (1920) (excuse). Would it be negligence *not* to violate the statute? Perhaps. But see Monreal v. Tobin, 61 Cal.App.4th 1337, 72 Cal.Rptr.2d 168 (1998) (driver who was traveling at posted speed limit did not owe a duty to speed up or move to a slower lane when approached from rear by vehicle traveling 25 m.p.h. in excess of posted speed limit even though there was testimony that "normal" speed on that stretch of interstate was at least 10 m.p.h. in excess of speed limit).

4. Certain types of statutes are commonly interpreted to make the defendant liable without regard to any excuse for the violation. They include

A. Child labor acts, providing under criminal penalty that no minor under a minimum age shall be employed in certain occupations, as in Krutlies v. Bulls Head Coal Co., 249 Pa. 162, 94 A. 459 (1915); Blanton v. Kellioka Coal Co., 192 Ky. 220, 232 S.W. 614 (1921).

B. Pure Food Acts that prohibit the commercial sale of adulterated food. Doherty v. S.S. Kresge Co., 227 Wis. 661, 278 N.W. 437 (1938); Bolitho v. Safeway Stores, 109 Mont. 213, 95 P.2d 443 (1939).

C. The Federal Safety Appliance Act, requiring that railway cars used in interstate commerce be equipped with automatic couplers and other safety devices, in good operating condition. O'Donnell v. Elgin, J. & E. R. Co., 338 U.S. 384 (1949). Accord, St. Louis S.W. R. Co. v. Williams, 397 F.2d 147 (5th Cir.1968) (Boiler Inspection Act).

D. "Safe place" statutes, requiring lights and other protection in tenement houses, or premises open to the public. Monsour v. Excelsior Tobacco Co., 115 S.W.2d 219 (Mo.App.1938); Smulczeski v. City Center of Music and Drama, 3 N.Y.2d 498, 169 N.Y.S.2d 1, 146 N.E.2d 769 (1957).

E. Statutes prohibiting the sale of firearms and other dangerous objects to minors.

5. When liability without fault is imposed because no excuse is permitted, it often is held that the legislative purpose cannot be given full effect unless the defenses of contributory negligence and assumption of risk are made unavailable against the plaintiff.

6. *Reasonable Care Per Se?* Suppose defendant shows that he complied with all applicable statutes and administrative regulations.

Should his conduct be deemed "reasonable care per se"? See Soproni v. Polygon Apartment Partners, 137 Wash.2d 319, 971 P.2d 500 (1999) (compliance with legislative or administrative regulatory standards is merely relevant evidence that may be considered by the trier of fact—building code) and Wilson v. Piper Aircraft Corp., 282 Or. 61, 577 P.2d 1322 (1978) (accord—FAA safety standards). Thus, at common law, compliance with a statute is not determinative of negligence, it is only evidence of due care.

7. Some states have modified the common law in particular types of cases by statute. Indiana, for example, in products liability cases provides that compliance with "applicable codes, standards, regulations, or specifications established, adopted, promulgated, or approved by the United States or by Indiana, or by an agency of the United States or Indiana" establishes a rebuttable presumption that the manufacturer or seller was not negligent. Indiana Code § 34–20–5–1, discussed in Schultz v. Ford Motor Co., 857 N.E.2d 977 (Ind. 2006) (finding it proper to inform jury of statutory presumption). Wisconsin provides a rebuttable presumption that the product is not defective. Wisc. Stat. Ann. § 895.047(3)(b). Michigan has limited the liability of drug manufacturers and sellers if the drug was approved for safety and efficacy by the FDA and labeled in compliance with FDA standards. Mich. Comp. Laws § 600.2946(5). Note that most of these are products liability statutes and some apply only to products regulated by the FDA. Should the answer depend on how completely the product or activity is regulated by government? See preemption discussion, Chapter 15, Products Liability, and Chapter 23, Torts in the Age of Statutes.

7. PROOF OF NEGLIGENCE

(A) COURT AND JURY: CIRCUMSTANTIAL EVIDENCE

Goddard v. Boston & Maine R.R. Co.

Supreme Judicial Court of Massachusetts, 1901.
179 Mass. 52, 60 N.E. 486.

Action by Wilfred H. Goddard against the Boston & Maine Railroad Company for personal injuries received by falling upon a banana skin lying upon the platform at defendant's station at Boston. The evidence showed that [plaintiff] was a passenger who had just arrived, and was about the length of the car from where he alighted when he slipped and fell. There was evidence that there were many passengers on the platform. Verdict directed for defendant, and plaintiff excepts.

HOLMES, C.J. The banana skin upon which the plaintiff stepped and which caused him to slip may have been dropped within a minute by one of the persons who was leaving the train. It is unnecessary to go further to decide the case.

Exceptions overruled.

Anjou v. Boston Elevated Railway Co.

Supreme Judicial Court of Massachusetts, 1911.
208 Mass. 273, 94 N.E. 386.

Action by Helen G. Anjou against the Boston Elevated Railway Company. Verdict was directed for defendant, and the case reported.

RUGG, J. The plaintiff arrived on one of defendant's cars on the upper level of the Dudley Street terminal; other passengers arrived on the same car, but it does not appear how many. She waited until the crowd had left the platform, when she inquired of one of defendant's uniformed employés the direction to another car. He walked along a narrow platform, and she, following a few feet behind him toward the stairway he had indicated, was injured by slipping upon a banana peel. It was described by several who examined it in these terms: It "felt dry, gritty, as if there were dirt upon it," as if "trampled over a good deal," as "flattened down, and black in color," "every bit of it was black, there wasn't a particle of yellow," and as "black, flattened out and gritty." It was one of the duties of employés of the defendant, of whom there was one at this station all the time, to observe and remove whatever was upon the platform to interfere with the safety of travelers. These might have been found to be the facts.

The inference might have been drawn from the appearance and condition of the banana peel that it had been upon the platform a considerable period of time, in such position that it would have been seen and removed by the employés of the defendant if they had been reasonably careful in performing their duty. Therefore there is something on which to base a conclusion that it was not dropped a moment before by a passenger, and Goddard v. Boston & Maine R.R., 179 Mass. 52, 60 N.E. 486 is plainly distinguishable. The obligation rested upon the defendant to keep its station reasonably safe for its passengers. It might have been found that the platform was suffered to remain in such condition as to be a menace to those rightfully walking upon it. Hence there was evidence of negligence on the part of the defendant, which should have been submitted to the jury. [Cc]

In accordance with the terms of the report, let the entry be:

Judgment for the plaintiff for $1,250 with costs.

[Normally, this case would have been reversed for a new trial. For some reason (perhaps to avoid expense of a new trial), defense counsel apparently agreed to an entry of judgment against his client if he lost on appeal.]

Joye v. Great Atlantic and Pacific Tea Co.

United States Court of Appeals, Fourth Circuit, 1968.
405 F.2d 464.

CRAVEN, CIRCUIT JUDGE: Willard Joye slipped and fell on a banana in defendant's A & P supermarket. In his diversity suit in the district court the jury returned a verdict for him in the amount of $10,000 and defendant appeals. We reverse because we are unable to find in the record sufficient evidence to present a jury issue as to constructive notice to defendant of a dangerous condition. Without such notice, in the context of the case, and under South Carolina law which we must apply, the district court should have granted defendant's Rule 50(b) motion for judgment n.o.v. * * *

There was no evidence that the A & P (1) put the banana on the floor or (2) had actual notice of its presence. Thus plaintiff's case turns on the sufficiency of the evidence to establish constructive notice. [C]

Plaintiff offered no direct evidence below as to how long the banana had been on the floor before the accident. The circumstantial evidence taken most favorably to the plaintiff shows that the floor may not have been swept for as long as 35 minutes. No one saw the banana until *after* Joye fell on it. It was then described as dark brown in color, having dirt and sand on it. There was dirt on the floor near the banana, and the banana was sticky around the edges. From this evidence we think the jury could not tell whether the banana had been on defendant's floor for 30 seconds or 3 days. * * *

Because it cannot be determined from the evidence how long (even the broadest range of approximation) the banana may have been on the floor, we reverse the judgment of the district court and remand to that court with instructions to enter judgment in favor of the defendant, The Great Atlantic & Pacific Tea Company.

Reversed.

Ortega v. Kmart Corp.

Supreme Court of California, 2001.
114 Cal.Rptr.2d 470, 26 Cal.4th 1200, 36 P.3d 11.

CHIN, J. * * *

Richard M. Ortega (plaintiff) was shopping at the Torrance Kmart store (Kmart) when he slipped on a puddle of milk on the floor adjacent to the refrigerator and suffered significant injuries to his knee, including ligament tears. Less than a year later, plaintiff sued Kmart for personal injuries. At trial, plaintiff testified he did not notice whether the puddled milk was fresh or odorous, warm or cold. He could not present evidence showing how long the milk had been on the floor. Nonetheless, plaintiff claimed that because the evidence showed Kmart had not inspected the premises in a reasonable period of time prior to the accident, a jury could infer the puddle was on the floor long enough for Kmart employees to have discovered and remedied it. * * *

Kmart's former store manager testified that although the store keeps no written inspection records, all Kmart employees are trained to look for and clean up any spills or other hazards. He also stated that several employees work in the pantry aisles next to the milk refrigerator, and that every 15 to 30 minutes an employee usually walked the aisle where plaintiff slipped. When asked whether the milk could have been on the floor for five minutes or two hours, the manager testified that in light of the staffing, it would be "hard for something [to] be on the floor for more than 15 or 30 minutes." He did admit, however, that the milk could have been on the floor for as long as two hours. On the day of the accident, the manager testified that management would not have had any idea if the aisle where the accident occurred was inspected at any time during that day. Kmart claimed that plaintiff failed to carry his burden of showing the milk puddle existed for a sufficient time to establish constructive notice to the store. [C]

The jury returned a verdict in plaintiff's favor, and awarded him $47,200 in damages. [The trial court judge denied Kmart's motion for a new trial or a j.n.o.v. and entered judgment on the verdict.] Kmart appealed [and the Court of Appeals affirmed the judgment against Kmart. The California Supreme Court granted review.] * * *

It is well established in California that although a store owner is not an insurer of the safety of its patrons, the owner does owe them a duty to exercise reasonable care in keeping the premises reasonably safe. * * *

A store owner exercises ordinary care by making reasonable inspections of the portions of the premises open to customers, and the care required is commensurate with the risks involved. [C] If the owner operates a self-service grocery store, where customers are invited to inspect, remove, and replace goods on shelves, "the exercise of ordinary care may require the owner to take greater precautions and make more frequent inspections than would otherwise be needed to safeguard against the possibility that such a customer may create a dangerous condition by disarranging the merchandise" and creating potentially hazardous conditions. * * *

Courts have also held that where the plaintiff relies on the failure to correct a dangerous condition to prove the owner's negligence, the plaintiff has the burden of showing that the owner had notice of the defect in sufficient time to correct it. [C] The courts' reasoning is that if the burden of proving lack of notice were placed on the owner in a slip-and-fall case, where the source of the dangerous condition or the length of time it existed cannot be shown, failure to meet the burden would require a finding of liability, effectively rendering the owner an insurer of the safety of those who enter the premises. [C] Several courts believe that shifting the burden to the defendant would, contrary to existing negligence law, permit an inference of negligence to be drawn against the owner based solely on the fact that the fall or accident occurred. [Cc]

The plaintiff need not show actual knowledge where evidence suggests that the dangerous condition was present for a sufficient period of time to charge the owner with constructive knowledge of its existence. Knowledge may be shown by circumstantial evidence "which is nothing more than one or more inferences which may be said to arise reasonably from a series of proven facts." [C] Whether a dangerous condition has existed long enough for a reasonably prudent person to have discovered it is a question of fact for the jury, and the cases do not impose exact time limitations. Each accident must be viewed in light of its own unique circumstances. [C] The owner must inspect the premises or take other proper action to ascertain their condition, and if, by the exercise of reasonable care, the owner would have discovered the condition, he is liable for failing to correct it. [C] In this case, we consider how a plaintiff may establish a defendant's constructive knowledge. * * *

We conclude that plaintiffs still have the burden of producing evidence that the dangerous condition existed for at least a sufficient time to support a finding that the defendant had constructive notice of the hazardous condition. [C] We also conclude, however, that plaintiffs may demonstrate the storekeeper had constructive notice of the dangerous condition if they can show that the site had not been inspected within a reasonable period of time so that a person exercising due care would have discovered and corrected the hazard. [C] In other words, if the plaintiffs can show an inspection was not made within a particular period of time prior to an accident, they may raise an inference the condition did exist long enough for the owner to have discovered it. [C] It remains a question of fact for the jury whether, under all the circumstances, the defective condition existed long enough so that it would have been discovered and remedied by an owner in the exercise of reasonable care.

For the above reasons, we affirm the Court of Appeal's judgment. [Justice Kennard's concurring opinion is omitted.]

Jasko v. F.W. Woolworth Co.

Supreme Court of Colorado, 1972.
177 Colo. 418, 494 P.2d 839.

[Plaintiff was injured when she slipped on a piece of pizza that was on the terrazzo floor near the "pizza-hoagie counter" in defendant's store. Trial court judge directed a verdict for defendant and intermediate appeals court affirmed.]

GROVES, JUSTICE. * * * We address ourselves solely to the necessity of notice of the specific condition, which under the facts of this case is of first impression in this court. * * *

In her attempt to meet the requirement of notice, plaintiff did not claim or show that the alleged pizza was placed or dropped on the floor directly by the defendant or its employees, or that defendant knew of its presence. [C] Rather, it was her contention that defendant's method of selling pizza was one which leads inescapably to such mishaps as her own, and that in such a situation conventional notice requirements need not be met. We agree.

The dangerous condition was created by the store's method of sale. The steps taken to constantly clean the floor show that the store owner recognized the danger.

The practice of extensive selling of slices of pizza on waxed paper to customers who consume it while standing creates the reasonable probability that food will drop to the floor. Food on a terrazzo floor will create a dangerous condition. In such a situation, notice to the proprietor of the specific item on the floor need not be shown.

The basic notice requirement springs from the thought that a dangerous condition, when it occurs, is somewhat out of the ordinary. * * * In such a situation the storekeeper is allowed a reasonable time, under the circumstances, to discover and correct the condition, unless it is the direct result of his (or his employees') acts. However, when the operating methods of a proprietor are such that dangerous conditions are continuous or easily foreseeable, the logical basis for the notice requirement dissolves. Then, actual or constructive notice of the specific condition need not be proved. * * *

The ruling of the Court of Appeals is reversed and the cause remanded to it for further remand to the trial court and new trial.

H.E. Butt Groc. Co. v. Resendez

Supreme Court of Texas, 1999.
988 S.W.2d 218.

PER CURIAM

Can mere display of produce for customer sampling constitute an unreasonable risk of harm to customers? The court of appeals said yes. [Footnotes omitted throughout.] We say no. We reverse the court of appeals' judgment and render judgment that plaintiff take nothing.

While shopping at an H.E. Butt Grocery Company store, Maria Resendez slipped and fell near two grape displays. She sued HEB for negligence, alleging that the customer sampling display posed an unreasonable risk of harm that caused her injuries. The trial court rendered judgment on a jury verdict for Resendez. The court of appeals affirmed.

From the undisputed evidence, we know that HEB had two grape displays in its produce section. One display table contained grapes bagged in cellophane and sitting in boxes. The other display table contained a bowl of loose grapes for customer sampling. The customer sampling bowl was level, sitting on ice and recessed about five inches below the table's surface. Each display table had a three-inch railing around its edges. The floor of the entire produce section was a non-skid surface and floor mats were in place around the display tables. There were also warning cones near the grape displays.

The court of appeals concluded that HEB's grape display, allowing for customer sampling, was some evidence of an unreasonable risk of harm to store customers. As a matter of law, though, the mere fact that a store has a customer sampling display cannot, without more, be evidence of a condition on the premises that poses an unreasonable risk of harm.

For Resendez to recover from HEB, she had the burden to prove that (1) HEB had actual or constructive knowledge of a condition on the premises, (2) the condition posed an unreasonable risk of harm, (3) HEB did not exercise reasonable care to reduce or to eliminate the risk, and (4) HEB's failure to use such care proximately caused her injuries.

Resendez, like the plaintiff in *Corbin* [v. Safeway Stores, Inc., 648 S.W.2d 292 (Tex. 1983)], claims that HEB's customer sampling display resulted in an unreasonable risk of harm. However, Resendez presented no evidence that the display created an unreasonable risk of customers falling on grapes. In *Corbin*, there was more evidence than the mere existence of a display. It was the manner in which Safeway displayed the grapes—in a slanted bin over a linoleum tile floor with no protective floor mat—that created an unreasonable risk of customer falls from grapes falling on the floor. Here, there is no evidence that the manner of display created an unreasonable risk.

Accordingly, we grant HEB's petition for review, and without hearing oral argument, reverse the court of appeals' judgment and render judgment that Resendez take nothing.

NOTES AND QUESTIONS

1. Can these cases be reconciled?

2. Why not require the defendant to prove that it was not negligent—that is, that it was not responsible for the substance plaintiff slipped on? Plaintiff has no information as to what defendant's employees have or have not done; defendant knows, or can perhaps find out. Some courts have done so. Compare Lanier v. Wal-Mart Stores, Inc., 99 S.W.3d 431 (Ky. 2003) (if plaintiff shows that there was foreign substance on floor and that substance caused fall, burden shifts to defendant to show that employees neither caused substance to be on floor nor had sufficient time to have discovered and removed it) with Wintersteen v. Food Lion, Inc., 344 S.C. 32, 542 S.E.2d 728 (2001) and Rallis v. Demoulas Super Markets, Inc., 159 N.H. 95, 977 A.2d 527 (N.H. 2009) (both declining to depart from the traditional burden of proof allocation). Who should make the decision about the burden of proof allocation—the court or the legislature? See Owens v. Publix Supermarkets, Inc., 802 So.2d 315 (Fla. 2001) (more black bananas) (shifting burden of proof to defendant) and Fla. Stat. 768.0710 (modifying *Owens*).

3. To what extent is plaintiff's disadvantage remedied by modern discovery procedure that provides both parties access to relevant information, including that within the possession of the other party?

4. Plaintiff has three separate burdens of proof on the issue of negligence—the burden of pleading, the burden of coming forward with enough evidence to avoid summary judgment or a directed verdict against him and, if he hurdles that, the burden of persuading the trier of fact to find in his favor. In most situations, plaintiff discharges the first burden by alleging sufficient facts in his complaint and the second by convincing the judge that reasonable jurors could find on a more-probable-than-not basis that plaintiff's contention is correct. Plaintiff must then persuade the jury that the preponderance of the evidence is in his favor. Generally speaking, determination of reasonable care, either the defendant's or the plaintiff's, is not susceptible to summary adjudication and must be resolved by the jury. Only rarely is it appropriate for the judge to grant summary judgment or direct a verdict in favor of one party or the other on the issue of negligence. See, e.g., Bell v. Leatherwood, 206 Ga.App. 550, 425 S.E.2d 679 (1992) (reasonable care should be question for jury except in plain, palpable, and indisputable cases where reasonable minds could not disagree).

5. Think about how you would prove negligence in some of the other cases you have read. Suppose an employee leaves a company-sponsored banquet at which alcohol was served and then rear ends another car at a stoplight. Plaintiff files suit against the employee and the employer, alleging that the employer served the employee when she was obviously intoxicated. Against the employee you could probably use eyewitness testimony to establish the fact that she had rear ended the plaintiff's car

and a rule of law or negligence per se or the reasonable person standard to establish that such conduct was negligent. What about the case against the employer? Perhaps you could find an eyewitness to say employee was obviously intoxicated at the banquet. What if the police officer called to the scene of the accident would testify that she was obviously intoxicated there? Is that enough? Cf. Fairbanks v. J.B. McLoughlin Co., Inc., 131 Wash.2d 96, 929 P.2d 433 (1997) ("[Employer] relies on the [testimony] from those attending the banquet which uniformly state that [employee] did not appear intoxicated. Nonetheless, [employee] appeared obviously intoxicated to both [plaintiff] Fairbanks and to Officer Asheim. Officer Asheim in particular noted that she smelled of alcohol, slurred her speech, stumbled as she got out of the car, and staggered when she walked. A police officer's subjective observation that the employee was obviously intoxicated shortly after leaving the banquet may raise an inference that she was obviously intoxicated when the employer served her, provided that the employee did not consume any alcohol after leaving the banquet and provided that no time remains unaccounted for between the banquet and the subsequent observation. [C] Because a reasonable jury could find based on [employee]'s own testimony that she left the banquet at 10:30 p.m. and was involved in the accident just 20 minutes later, Fairbanks' and Officer Asheim's observations were sufficient to raise a factual issue as to whether she was obviously intoxicated at the banquet.")

6. What if the product that plaintiff claims was negligently designed or manufactured disappears after the accident? How does plaintiff prove that it was made by defendant? Plaintiff was injured by a multipiece truck rim that was reassembled and then either used on another truck or placed against the wall. No one could identify it by the time the suit was filed and at least six different companies manufacture three-piece rims. Healey v. Firestone Tire & Rubber Co., 640 N.Y.S.2d 860, 87 N.Y.2d 596, 663 N.E.2d 901 (1996) (identity of manufacturer may be established by circumstantial evidence if product itself is destroyed after use, but there was insufficient circumstantial evidence available in this case to do so).

7. What if there is enough circumstantial evidence to identify the part and its manufacturer, but the part itself has disappeared and the manufacturer argues that it cannot defend itself without being able to examine the part to ascertain whether it failed, why it failed, or if its failure caused the accident? Bachmeier v. Wallwork Truck Ctrs., 544 N.W.2d 122 (N.D.1996) (summary judgment for manufacturer upheld where plaintiff had failed to preserve truck hub that allegedly failed due to a faulty design where manufacturer argued that failure might have been due to negligent maintenance). What if one of the parties actually destroys the evidence? Vodusek v. Bayliner Marine Corp., 71 F.3d 148 (4th Cir.1995) (expert retained by plaintiff destroyed boat while conducting his accident investigation; trial court judge acted within his discretion to instruct jury that it could draw negative inference from loss of evidence for which party—through its agent—was responsible). See also note 2, page 1091, Spoliation of Evidence.

8. Problems involved in proving facts in tort cases, as any trial lawyer will affirm, are often more challenging than developing the relevant rules of law. Courses in evidence, trial practice, and clinics will further develop these skills.

(B) RES IPSA LOQUITUR

Byrne v. Boadle

Court of Exchequer, 1863.
2 H. & C. 722, 159 Eng.Rep. 299.

[Action for negligence. The plaintiff's evidence was that he was walking in a public street past the defendant's shop, and that a barrel of flour fell upon him from a window above the shop, knocked him down, and seriously injured him. There was no other evidence. The Assessor was of the opinion that there was no evidence of negligence for the jury, and nonsuited the plaintiff, reserving leave to him to move the Court of Exchequer to enter the verdict for him for £50 damages. Plaintiff obtained a rule nisi.]

Charles Russell [attorney for defendant] now shewed cause. First, there was no evidence to connect the defendant or his servants with the occurrence. * * * It is consistent with the evidence that the purchaser of the flour was superintending the lowering of it by his servant, or it may be that a stranger was engaged to do it without the knowledge or authority of the defendant. [Pollock, C.B. The presumption is that the defendant's servants were engaged in removing the defendant's flour; if they were not it was competent to the defendant to prove it.]

Secondly, assuming the facts to be brought home to the defendant or his servants, these facts do not disclose any evidence for the jury of negligence. The plaintiff was bound to give affirmative proof of negligence. But there was not a scintilla of evidence, unless the occurrence is of itself evidence of negligence. There was not even evidence that the barrel was being lowered by a jigger-hoist as alleged in the declaration. [Pollock, C.B. There are certain cases of which it may be said res ipsa loquitur, and this seems one of them. In some cases the Courts have held that the mere fact of the accident having occurred is evidence of negligence, as, for instance, in the case of railway collisions.]

POLLOCK, C.B. We are all of opinion that the rule must be absolute to enter the verdict for the plaintiff. The learned counsel was quite right in saying that there are many accidents from which no presumption of negligence can arise, but I think it would be wrong to lay down as a rule that in no case can a presumption of negligence arise from the fact of an accident. Suppose in this case the barrel had rolled out of the warehouse and fallen on the plaintiff, how could he possibly ascertain from what cause it occurred? It is the duty of persons who keep barrels in a warehouse to take care that they do not roll out, and I think that such a case would, beyond all doubt, afford prima facie evidence of negligence. A barrel could not roll out of a warehouse without some negligence, and to say that a plaintiff who is injured by it must call witnesses from the warehouse to prove negligence seems to me preposterous. * * * The present case upon the evidence comes to this, a man is passing in front of the premises of a dealer in flour, and there falls down upon him a barrel of flour. I think it apparent that the barrel was in the custody of the defendant who occupied the premises, and who is responsible for the acts of his servants who had the control of it; and in my opinion the fact of its falling is prima facie evidence of negligence, and the plaintiff who was injured by it is not bound to show that it could not fall without negligence, but if there are any facts inconsistent with negligence it is for the defendant to prove them.

[The concurring opinions of BRAMWELL, B., CHANNELL, B., and PIGOTT, B., are omitted.]

NOTES AND QUESTIONS

1. What kind of evidence of defendant's negligence has plaintiff offered? How persuasive is it? What about the possibility that some trespasser entered the premises and rolled the barrel out of the window? Suppose the defendant in the principal case was merely a deliverer of flour and not the owner of the shop? Cf. Hake v. George Wiedemann Brewing Co., 23 Ohio St.2d 65, 52 Ohio Op.2d 366, 262 N.E.2d 703 (1970).

2. *Res Ipsa Loquitur.* "The thing speaks for itself." This is an old phrase, found in Cicero and other ancient writers; and it has been used from time to time in other connections in the law. Chief Baron Pollock was an English gentleman, with a classical education, as was counsel to whom he spoke. Just what did he mean by it? This question has been put in Latin: Res ipsa loquitur, sed quid in infernos dicet?

3. There has been considerable denunciation of the use of the phrase in negligence cases. See, for example, Bond, C.J., dissenting in Potomac Edison Co. v. Johnson, 160 Md. 33, 152 A. 633 (1930): "It adds nothing to the law, has no meaning which is not more clearly expressed for us in English, and brings confusion to our legal discussions. It does not represent a doctrine, is not a legal maxim, and is not a rule." Also Lord Shaw, in Ballard v. North British R. Co., [1923] Sess.Cas.H.L. 43, 56: "If that phrase had not been in Latin, nobody would have called it a principle." South Carolina does not follow the doctrine. Watson v. Ford Motor Co., 389 S.C. 434, 699 S.E.2d 169 (2010).

4. Shortly after 1870, this principle became entangled and confused with an older and quite different rule. In Christie v. Griggs, 2 Camp. 79, 170 Eng.Rep. 1088 (1809), the axle of a stagecoach broke and a passenger was injured. Sir James Mansfield declared that the burden lay upon the common carrier to prove that the injury was not caused by its negligence. Later decisions explained this on the basis of the special responsibility that the carrier had undertaken under its contract to transport the passenger safely. The two principles became intermingled and ultimately merged in cases of injuries to passengers under the name of "res ipsa loquitur"; and much of the confusion that has surrounded the doctrine is due to this merger.

5. The first attempt to state the rule of Byrne v. Boadle was that of Chief Justice Erle in Scott v. London & St. Katherine Docks Co., 3 H. & C. 596, 159 Eng.Rep. 665 (1865): "There must be reasonable evidence of negligence; but where the thing is shown to be under the management of the defendant or his servants, and the accident is such as in the ordinary course of things does not happen if those who have the management use proper care, it affords reasonable evidence, in the absence of explanation by the defendants, that the accident arose from want of care." These remain the two core requirements of the doctrine, although you will sometimes see a third requirement listed in opinions. Some jurisdictions added a

requirement that the event not have been brought about by the actions of the plaintiff. Usually, however, the conduct of the plaintiff is considered when evaluating causation and comparative negligence, which will be discussed later in Chapter 5, Causation, and Chapter 12, Defenses. See, for example, Giles v. New Haven, 228 Conn. 441, 455, 636 A.2d 1335, 1341 (1994) (res ipsa loquitur applies even if plaintiff's conduct contributed to injuries; jury to apply comparative negligence principles to account for plaintiff's conduct) and McGuire v. Davidson Manufacturing Corp., 398 F.3d 1005 (8th Cir. 2005) (applying Iowa law) (finding that Iowa would join the majority of states that eliminated the requirement that plaintiff show his own conduct did not contribute to accident and instead consider plaintiff's conduct as part of comparative negligence).

6. *Defendant's Superior Knowledge.* It has sometimes been said that the basis of res ipsa loquitur is the defendant's superior knowledge, or ability to obtain evidence, as to just what has occurred; or in other words, that the purpose of the rule is to "smoke out" evidence that the defendant has or can get, and the plaintiff cannot. This policy underpinning is stated as a third requirement in some jurisdictions. See Reese v. Memorial Hospital, 955 P.2d 425, 427 (Wyo.1998) ("If the circumstances do not show or suggest that defendant should have superior knowledge, or if the plaintiff himself possesses equal or superior means of explaining the occurrence, the rule may not properly be invoked."); Sides v. St. Anthony's Medical Ctr., 258 S.W.3d 811 (Mo. 2008) (reiterating that the third requirement of res ipsa loquitur is "the defendant possesses superior knowledge or means of information as to the cause of the occurrence"); and DeBusscher v. Sam's East, Inc., 505 F.3d 475, 481 (6th Cir. 2007) (applying Michigan law) (reciting requirement under Michigan law that "evidence of true explanation of event must be more readily accessible to the defendant than to the plaintiff" and applying to facts of case where portable basketball goal fell on shopper). Most jurisdictions hold that res ipsa loquitur applies even though the defendant's knowledge is not superior to that of the plaintiff. See, for example, Johnson v. Foster, 202 So.2d 520 (Miss.1967) (car unaccountably leaves highway and overturns; both parties dead); Nicol v. Geitler, 188 Minn. 69, 247 N.W. 8 (1933) (similar; guest passenger dead, driver disappeared); Burkett v. Johnston, 39 Tenn.App. 276, 282 S.W.2d 647 (1955) (similar; both dead); Haasman v. Pacific Alaska Air Express, 100 F.Supp. 1 (D.Alaska 1951), aff'd, 198 F.2d 550 (9th Cir.1952) (lost plane); Judson v. Giant Powder Co., 107 Cal. 549, 40 P. 1020 (1895) (nitroglycerin factory blew up; the "witnesses who saw and knew, like all things else around, save the earth itself, were scattered to the four winds").

McDougald v. Perry

Supreme Court of Florida, 1998.
716 So.2d 783.

WELLS, J. * * * Lawrence McDougald sued Henry Perry and Perry's employer, C & S Chemical, Inc., (collectively referred to as respondents), for personal injuries sustained in an accident which occurred on July 26, 1990, on U.S. Highway 60 West, in Bartow, Florida. On July 26, McDougald was driving behind a tractor-trailer which was driven by Perry. The trailer was leased by C & S from Ryder

Truck Rentals, Inc. As Perry drove over some railroad tracks, the 130-pound spare tire came out of its cradle underneath the trailer and fell to the ground. The trailer's rear tires then ran over the spare, causing the spare to bounce into the air and collide [with] the windshield of McDougald's Jeep Wagoneer.

The spare tire was housed in an angled cradle underneath the trailer and was held in place by its own weight. Additionally, the tire was secured by a four to six-foot long chain with one-inch links, which was wrapped around the tire. Perry testified that he believed the chain to be the original chain that came with the trailer in 1969. Perry also stated that, as originally designed, the chain was secured to the body of the trailer by a latch device. At the time of the accident, however, the chain was attached to the body of the trailer with a nut and bolt.

Perry testified that he performed a pretrip inspection of the trailer on the day of the accident. This included an inspection of the chain, although Perry admitted that he did not check every link in the chain. After the accident, Perry noticed that the chain was dragging under the trailer. Perry opined that one of the links had stretched and slipped from the nut which secured it to the trailer. [Footnote omitted.] The judge instructed the jury on the doctrine of res ipsa loquitur. The jury subsequently returned a verdict in McDougald's favor.

On appeal, the district court reversed with instructions that the trial court direct a verdict in respondents' favor. The district court concluded that the trial court erred by * * * [instructing the jury on res ipsa loquitur.] For the reasons expressed herein, we quash the decision below and approve the ... application of res ipsa loquitur to the circumstances of a wayward automobile wheel accident.

* * * In Marrero [v. Goldsmith, 486 So. 2d 530 (Fla.1986)], we stated:

> Res ipsa loquitur is a Latin phrase that translates "the thing speaks for itself." Prosser and Keaton, Law of Torts § 39 (5th ed. 1984). It is a rule of evidence that permits, but does not compel, an inference of negligence under certain circumstances. "The doctrine of res ipsa loquitur is merely a rule of evidence. Under it an inference may arise in aid of the proof." [C] In Goodyear [Tire & Rubber Co. v. Hughes Supply, Inc., 358 So.2d 530 (Fla. 1982)], a products liability case, we explained the doctrine as follows:
>
> It provides an injured plaintiff with a common-sense inference of negligence where direct proof of negligence is wanting, provided certain elements consistent with negligent behavior are present. Essentially the injured plaintiff must establish that the instrumentality causing his or her injury was under the exclusive control of the defendant, and that the accident is one that would not, in the ordinary course of events, have occurred without negligence on the part of the one in control. [Cc]

In concluding that it was reversible error for the trial court to give the res ipsa loquitur instruction, the Second District determined that "McDougald failed to prove that this accident would not, in the ordinary course of events, have occurred without negligence by the defendants." [C] The court explained that, "the mere fact that an accident occurs does not support the application of the doctrine." Id. In support of the Second District's conclusion, respondents cite to Burns v. Otis Elevator Co., 550 So.2d 21 (Fla.App.1989), in which the Third District stated:

To prevail at trial, plaintiff must still present sufficient evidence, beyond that of the accident itself, from which the jury may infer that the accident would not have occurred but for the defendants' breach of due care. [C] Respondents assert that this language means that res ipsa loquitur did not apply in this case because "there was no expert or other testimony or evidence that the failure of the safety chain and the spare tire's exit onto the roadway would not ordinarily occur in the absence of [respondents'] negligence." [C]

The Second and Third Districts misread and interpret too narrowly what we stated in Goodyear. We did not say, as those courts conclude, that "the mere fact that an accident occurs does not support the application of the doctrine." Rather, we stated:

> *An injury standing alone, of course, ordinarily does not indicate negligence. The doctrine of res ipsa loquitur simply recognizes that in rare instances an injury may permit an inference of negligence if coupled with a sufficient showing of its immediate, precipitating cause.* [C] (emphasis added).

Goodyear and our other cases permit latitude in the application of this common-sense inference when the facts of an accident in and of themselves establish that but for the failure of reasonable care by the person or entity in control of the injury producing object or instrumentality the accident would not have occurred. On the other hand, our present statement is not to be considered an expansion of the doctrine's applicability. We continue our prior recognition that res ipsa loquitur applies only in "rare instances."

The following comments in section 328D of Restatement (Second) of Torts (1965) capture the essence of a proper analysis of this issue:

> c. Type of event. The first requirement for the application of the rule stated in this Section is a basis of past experience which reasonably permits the conclusion that such events do not ordinarily occur unless someone has been negligent. There are many types of accidents which commonly occur without the fault of anyone. The fact that a tire blows out, or that a man falls down stairs is not, in the absence of anything more, enough to permit the conclusion that there was negligence in inspecting the tire, or in the construction of the stairs, because it is common human experience that such events all too frequently occur without such negligence. On the other hand there are many events, such as those of objects falling from the defendant's premises, the fall of an elevator, the escape of gas or water from mains or of electricity from wires or appliances, the derailment of trains or the explosion of boilers, where the conclusion is at least permissible that such things do not usually happen unless someone has been negligent. To such events res ipsa loquitur may apply.

> d. Basis of conclusion. In the usual case the basis of past experience from which this conclusion may be drawn is common to the community, and is a matter of general knowledge, which the court recognizes on much the same basis as when it takes judicial notice of facts which everyone knows. It may, however, be supplied by the evidence of the parties; and expert testimony that such an event usually does not occur without negligence may afford a sufficient basis for the inference. Such testimony may be essential to the plaintiff's case where, as for example in some actions for medical malpractice, there is no fund of common knowledge which may permit laymen reasonably to draw the conclusion. On the other hand there are other kinds of medical malpractice, as where a sponge is left in the plaintiff's abdomen after an operation, where no expert is needed to tell the jury that such events do not usually occur in the absence of negligence.

Restatement (Second) of Torts § 328D cmts. c–d (1965).

We conclude that the spare tire escaping from the cradle underneath the truck, resulting in the tire ultimately becoming airborne and crashing into McDougald's vehicle, is the type of accident which, on the basis of common experience and as a matter of general knowledge, would not occur but for the failure to exercise reasonable care by the person who had control of the spare tire. As the Fifth District noted [in another case], the doctrine of res ipsa loquitur is particularly applicable in wayward wheel cases. * * * [C]ommon sense dictates an inference that both a spare tire carried on a truck and a wheel on a truck's axle will stay with the truck unless there is a failure of reasonable care by the person or entity in control of the truck. Thus an inference of negligence comes from proof of the circumstances of the accident.

Furthermore, we do not agree with the Second District [in this case] that McDougald failed to establish this element because "other possible explanations exist to explain the failure of the chain." [C] Such speculation does not defeat the applicability of the doctrine in this case. As one commentator has noted:

> The plaintiff is not required to eliminate with certainty all other possible causes or inferences. . . . All that is required is evidence from which reasonable persons can say that on the whole it is more likely that there was negligence associated with the cause of the event than that there was not.

W. Page Keeton, et al., Prosser and Keaton on the Law of Torts, § 39, at 248 (5th ed. 1984). * * *

Accordingly, we quash the decision below, and remand this case with directions that the district court reinstate the trial court's judgment as to respondents' liability based upon the jury's verdict and for further proceedings consistent with the district court's decision on issues related to damages.

It is so ordered.

HARDING, C.J., and OVERTON, SHAW, KOGAN and PARIENTE, JJ., concur.

ANSTEAD, J., concurring.

I fully concur in the majority opinion, and write separately to note that this case presents a classic scenario whereby an aged appellate opinion giving rise to a legal doctrine in the distant past still illuminates and informs today's society. The thread of common sense in human experience ties today's decision to an opinion voiced by Baron Pollock in the 1863 decision in Byrne v. Boadle, 2 Hurlet & C. 722, 159 Eng. Rep. 299 (Ex. 1863). In Byrne a pedestrian was struck by a barrel which fell from a window of the defendant's flour business. * * * [The opinion then quotes Pollack's opinion in full (see page 1091).]

We can hardly improve upon this explanation for our decision today. The common law tradition is alive and well.

NOTES AND QUESTIONS

1. How does the court know that this accident would be unlikely to occur in absence of negligence on the part of defendant? How could an attorney persuade the court that this was true? What other possible explanations for the failure of the chain could defendant have argued? What about the possibility that the chain had been tampered with at a truck stop?

2. What would you expect the rule to be when a plane, flying through smooth air, suddenly and without any warning strikes a "bump," and a passenger is thrown from his seat? Cudney v. Midcontinent Airlines, 363 Mo. 922, 254 S.W.2d 662 (1953); Ness v. West Coast Airlines, Inc., 90 Idaho 111, 410 P.2d 965 (1965). Or hot tea is spilled into his lap from a tray? Lazarus v. Eastern Air Lines, 292 F.2d 748 (D.C.Cir.1961). (None permit application of res ipsa loquitur.)

3. How persuasive is the inference of negligence in the following cases? Should res ipsa loquitur be allowed?

A. When automatic doors close on a person, the owner is at fault. Compare the majority and dissenting opinions in Kmart Corp. v. Bassett, 769 So.2d 282 (Ala. 2000) (no res ipsa loquitur instruction because no evidence that such a malfunction does not ordinarily happen in the absence of negligence; claiming that majority of jurisdictions would allow a res ipsa instruction when automatic door malfunctions).

B. When a human body falls upon a work of art, the person who fell was negligent. See Krebs v. Corrigan, 321 A.2d 558 (D.C.App.1974) (yes).

C. When a heavy tool falls off a shelf at a store and injures a shopper's foot, a store employee was negligent. Hagler v. Coastal Farm Holdings, Inc., 354 Or. 132, 309 P.3d 1073 (2013) (no).

D. When an automobile leaves the travelled portion of a highway and overturns or crashes into a stationary object, the driver was at fault. Badela v. Karpowich, 152 Conn. 360, 206 A.2d 838 (1965) (yes).

E. When a fertilizer plant explodes, the person in control of the plant was negligent. Collins v. N-Ren Corp., 604 F.2d 659 (10th Cir.1979) (applying Oklahoma law) (yes).

F. When an escalator comes to a sudden stop, the company responsible for its manufacture and maintenance is at fault. Compare the majority and dissenting opinions in Barretta v. Otis Elevator Co., 242 Conn. 169, 698 A.2d 810 (1997) (no res ipsa loquitur instruction because no evidence such a malfunction ordinarily does not happen in the absence of negligence; such evidence not necessary because ordinary, common experience is enough to suggest it).

G. When cattle escape onto the highway, the rancher is at fault. Roberts v. Weber & Sons, 248 Neb. 243, 533 N.W.2d 664 (1995) (agreeing with courts that have found res ipsa loquitur instruction appropriate, but noting an even split among jurisdictions that have faced the issue).

H. When an experienced skier falls on his first run down the mountain, the equipment was negligently maintained. Mrotek v. Coal River Canoe Livery, Ltd., 214 W.Va. 490, 590 S.E.2d 683 (2003) (res ipsa loquitur has no application to "falling while skiing—which is an extremely frequent incident that can occur without any negligence.")

4. Note that in the principal case the defendant had argued that the plaintiff needed expert witness testimony to support his argument that the accident would not normally have occurred in the absence of negligence. Although the court rejected the argument in that case, there may be times when it is not within common knowledge that the event would not ordinarily occur in the absence of negligence, for example, when professional malpractice is at issue. In which of the following cases could the trial court judge find without the help of an expert that what happened does not ordinarily happen in the absence of negligence?

A. Patient continues to experience complications three months after surgery, so a second operation is performed and a laparotomy sponge, left in her during the first surgery, is removed. Coleman v. Rice, 706 So.2d 696 (Miss.1997).

B. Plaintiff is returned to her hospital room after surgery, and left in an unconscious condition for an hour. When she regains consciousness, she has a second-degree burn on her stomach in the exact shape of a hot water bottle. Cf. Timbrell v. Suburban Hosp., 4 Cal.2d 68, 47 P.2d 737 (1935).

C. Dentist operates on wrong side of patient's mouth during surgery to remove impacted wisdom teeth, apparently because x-ray was mislabeled. Pacheco v. Ames, 149 Wash.2d 431, 69 P.3d 324 (2003).

D. After surgery for a tumor of the spinal cord, plaintiff begins to hemorrhage. Defendant surgeon, having failed in other efforts to stop the bleeding, reopens the incision and packs the wound with a cellulosic material and sews it up. Plaintiff wakes up paralyzed below the incision. Brannon v. Wood, 251 Or. 349, 444 P.2d 558 (1968).

E. A few days after abdominal surgery to enhance her chances to become pregnant, plaintiff loses function in her left leg. Connors v. University Assocs., 4 F.3d 123 (2d Cir.1993) (applying Vermont law).

F. Shortly after undergoing a bilateral mastectomy, plaintiff experiences numbness in her right arm, which was subsequently diagnosed as ulnar neuropathy, degenerative nerve damage affecting her right hand. Mireles v. Broderick, 117 N.M. 445, 872 P.2d 863 (1994).

G. Plaintiff has permanent paralysis of her vocal cord after surgery to remove her thyroid. Hightower-Warren v. Silk, 548 Pa. 459, 698 A.2d 52 (1997).

5. The courts found only the first three of the above to be within common experience. Suppose that in all the other cases, the plaintiff has an expert that will testify that the injury is one that does not ordinarily occur in the absence of negligence. Should that expert be permitted to testify? Wouldn't the use of expert witness testimony in a res ipsa loquitur case be contradictory? After all, the "thing" is hardly speaking for itself if an expert is involved. Most, but not all, courts permit the plaintiff to use expert witness testimony to establish that the event does not ordinarily happen in the absence of negligence. See, for example, Mireles v. Broderick, 117 N.M. 445, 448, 872 P.2d 863, 866 (1994) ("the central issue is not whether common knowledge alone is sufficient to establish an inference of negligence. Rather, the issue is whether there is a factual predicate sufficient to support an inference that the injury was caused by the failure of the party in control to exercise due care. The requisite probability of negligence may exist independently of the common knowledge of the jurors. The common-knowledge exception to the expert testimony rule may inform but does not delimit the application of res ipsa loquitur."); States v. Lourdes Hospital, 100 N.Y.2d 208, 792 N.E.2d 151, 762 N.Y.S.2d 1 (2003) (aligning New York with majority of jurisdictions that permit expert witness testimony to supplement jury's understanding of whether an injury ordinarily would occur in absence of negligence, but noting that some jurisdictions permit res ipsa loquitur to be used only when the matter lies within the ken of a layperson); Sides v. St. Anthony's Medical Ctr., 258 S.W.3d 811 (Mo. 2008) (collecting cases from other jurisdictions and noting that "a vast majority" permit expert testimony to establish requirements for res ipsa loquitur in medical malpractice cases). The requirement of expert witness testimony on the subject whether the accident would have happened in the absence of negligence is not limited to malpractice cases. See Fricke, The Use of Expert Evidence in Res Ipsa Loquitur Cases, 5 Vill.L.Rev. 59 (1959). Cf. Newell v. Westinghouse Electric Corp., 36 F.3d 576 (7th Cir.1994) (applying Indiana law) (plaintiff permitted to present expert witness testimony that particular elevator failure would not ordinarily happen in the absence of negligent maintenance).

6. As part of medical malpractice reform legislation (see page 210), a number of states have codified the res ipsa loquitur doctrine, limiting its application to specific types of medical mishaps. See, for example, 18 Del. Code Ann. § 6853(e) (providing for a rebuttable presumption of negligence without expert medical testimony if injury is caused by foreign bodies unintentionally left in the body following surgery, an explosion or fire originating in a substance used for treatment, or a surgical procedure on the wrong patient or the wrong part of the body) and Nev. Rev. Stat. 41A.100 (providing for a rebuttable presumption without expert medical testimony if injury was caused by a foreign substance other than medication or prosthetic device unintentionally left in body after surgery, an explosion or fire originating in a substance used for treatment, an unintended burn caused by heat, radiation or chemicals, injury to a part of the body not directly involved in treatment, or a procedure performed on wrong patient or wrong body part).

Larson v. St. Francis Hotel

District Court of Appeal of California, 1948.
83 Cal.App.2d 210, 188 P.2d 513.

BRAY, JUSTICE. The accident out of which this action arose was apparently the result of the effervescence and ebullition of San Franciscans in their exuberance of joy on V-J day, August 14, 1945. Plaintiff (who is not included in the above description), while walking on the sidewalk on Post Street adjoining the St. Francis Hotel, just after stepping out from under the marquee, was struck on the head by a heavy, over-stuffed arm chair, knocked unconscious, and received injuries for which she is asking damages from the owners of the hotel. Although there were a number of persons in the immediate vicinity, no one appears to have seen from whence the chair came nor to have seen it before it was within a few feet of plaintiff's head, nor was there any identification of the chair as belonging to the hotel. However, it is a reasonable inference that the chair came from some portion of the hotel. For the purposes of this opinion, we will so assume, in view of the rule on nonsuit cases that every favorable inference fairly deducible from the evidence must be drawn in favor of plaintiff, and that all the evidence must be construed most strongly against the defendants. [C]

At the trial, plaintiff, after proving the foregoing facts and the extent of her injuries, rested, relying upon the doctrine of res ipsa loquitur. On motion of defendant the court granted a nonsuit. The main question to be determined is whether under the circumstances shown, the doctrine applies. The trial court correctly held that it did not.

In Gerhart v. Southern California Gas Co., 56 Cal.App.2d 425, 132 P.2d 874, 877, cited by plaintiff, the court sets forth the test for the applicability of the doctrine. "* * * for a plaintiff to make out a case entitling him to the benefit of the doctrine, *he must prove* (1) that there was an accident; (2) that the thing or instrumentality which caused the accident was at the time of and prior thereto under the *exclusive* control and management of the defendant; (3) *that the accident was such that in the ordinary course of events, the defendant using ordinary care, the accident would not have happened.* * * * The doctrine of res ipsa loquitur applies only where the cause of the injury is shown to be under the exclusive control and management of the defendant and can have no application * * * to a case having a divided responsibility where an unexplained accident may have been attributable to one of several causes, for some of which the defendant is not responsible, and when it appears that the injury was caused by one of two causes for one of which defendant is responsible but not for the other, plaintiff must fail, if the evidence does not show that the injury was the result of the former cause, or leaves it as probable that it was caused by one or the other." [Emphasis added.]

Applying the rule to the facts of this case, it is obvious that the doctrine does not apply. While, as pointed out by plaintiff, the rule of exclusive control "is not limited to the actual physical control but applies to the right of control of the instrumentality which causes the injury" it is not clear to us how this helps plaintiff's case. A hotel does not have exclusive control, either actual or potential, of its furniture.

Guests have, at least, partial control. Moreover, it cannot be said that with the hotel using ordinary care "the accident was such that in the ordinary course of events * * * it would not have happened." On the contrary, the mishap would quite as likely be due to the fault of a guest or other person as to that of defendants. The most logical inference from the circumstances shown is that the chair was thrown by some such person from a window. It thus appears that this occurrence is not such as ordinarily does not happen without the negligence of the party charged, but, rather, one in which the accident ordinarily might happen despite the fact that the defendants used reasonable care and were totally free from negligence. To keep guests and visitors from throwing furniture out windows would require a guard to be placed in every room in the hotel, and no one would contend that there is any rule of law requiring a hotel to do that. * * *

The judgment appealed from is affirmed.

NOTES AND QUESTIONS

1. Plaintiff hotel guest is seriously injured by extremely hot water from the bathtub faucet. Court agreed that did not ordinarily happen in the absence of negligence, but found hotel was not in exclusive control because guest controlled the mix of hot and cold water. Carroll v. Faust, 311 Ill.App.3d 679, 244 Ill.Dec. 291, 725 N.E.2d 764 (2000).

2. A one-pound tape measure attached to the belt of a construction worker on a 50-story tower slipped off the belt and struck a delivery man who had just stepped out of his van on the street below. Would res ipsa loquitur apply to a suit brought by the delivery man against the construction company? See Mark Santora, "Falling Tape Measure Kills Man at Jersey City Construction Site," N.Y. Times, Nov. 4, 2014, available at 2014 WLNR 30801473.

3. Hot water escapes through a ruptured fitting on a radiator in a tenant's apartment, causing personal injury and damaging property. Should defendant landlord's "right to control" the instrumentality be sufficient to invoke res ipsa loquitur? See Niman v. Plaza House, Inc., 471 S.W.2d 207 (Mo.1971), noted 38 U.Mo.L.Rev. 371 (1973); Errico v. LaMountain, 713 A.2d 791 (R.I.1998) (landlord had statutory right to enter premises; tenant entitled to res ipsa loquitur jury instruction after balcony railing gave way when she leaned against it).

4. Some of the older cases required that defendant have "exclusive control." Thus, in Kilgore v. Shepard Co., 52 R.I. 151, 158 A. 720 (1932), plaintiff sat down on a chair in defendant's store, and it collapsed and injured him. Recovery was denied because plaintiff, and not defendant, was in "control" of the chair at the time. Modern cases tend to focus more on the Restatement (Second) § 328(D)(1)(b) language "other responsible causes, including the conduct of the plaintiff and third persons, are sufficiently eliminated by the evidence" rather than strictly on the traditional "exclusive control" language. See the next principal case.

Cruz v. DaimlerChrysler Motors Corp.

Supreme Court of Rhode Island, 2013.
66 A.3d 446.

[Minivan owner was cleaning the inside of his minivan when both front airbags suddenly deployed and injured him. He and his wife filed suit against the minivan's manufacturer and the dealer who had sold the used minivan to him three years before the accident. After manufacturer sought bankruptcy protection, plaintiffs voluntarily dismissed the claims against it and proceeded against the dealer based on negligence and negligent misrepresentation. Plaintiffs then received permission to file an amended complaint adding a count seeking recovery based on the doctrine of res ipsa loquitur, which the court noted is not an independent cause of action, but rather a doctrine under which a plaintiff may establish a prima facie case of negligence.]

INDEGLIA, J. for the Court.

Airbags are a relatively modern safety feature in passenger vehicles; they are designed to deploy in the event of a collision. When the airbags in a stationary vehicle unexpectedly deploy, as they did in this case, something has gone wrong. The question presented in this appeal is whether the hearing justice correctly concluded that the seller of that vehicle could not be held legally responsible for the resulting harm. * * *

Ricky Smith [the car dealership] moved for summary judgment on all counts on October 28, 2010. Regarding plaintiffs' claim for negligence, it argued that plaintiffs "ha[d] produced no evidence to show that the [airbag] incident took place as a result of a defect which [it] knew or should have known of or that even existed in the vehicle when it was sold." It highlighted the lack of expert testimony about why the airbags had deployed—a matter beyond the common knowledge of a layperson. The plaintiffs could not make out a claim for negligence using the doctrine of res ipsa loquitur, it argued, because [defendant] Ricky Smith had no control over the vehicle and plaintiffs had not eliminated other potential causes for the incident. * * *

[P]laintiffs argued that the facts presented "a classic case for the application of the doctrine of res ipsa loquitur, which was intended to eliminate the very evidentiary strictures applicable to proving proximate cause cited by Ricky Smith." * * *

The matter came before a justice of the Superior Court on February 1, 2011. On the negligence claim, she found that plaintiffs "ha[d] failed to produce evidence that [Ricky Smith] caused harm to [them]." She noted that plaintiffs had produced no evidence, such as an inspection report or expert testimony, to demonstrate that Ricky Smith was negligent. She also found that plaintiffs could not make out a claim for negligence using the doctrine of res ipsa loquitur [nor had they produced sufficient evidence on the negligent misrepresentation claim]. * * * Accordingly, the trial justice granted Ricky Smith's motion for summary judgment on all counts. * * *

The four elements of negligence are "a legally cognizable duty owed by a defendant to a plaintiff, a breach of that duty, proximate causation between the conduct and the resulting injury, and the actual loss or damage." [C] Because plaintiffs lack direct proof of Ricky Smith's negligence, they have attempted to make out a prima facie negligence claim through the doctrine of res ipsa loquitur. This doctrine "establishes inferential evidence of a defendant's negligence * * * and casts upon a defendant the burden of rebutting the same to the satisfaction of the jury." [C] Before addressing whether the hearing justice erred in finding that plaintiffs could not maintain a negligence claim against Ricky Smith based on res ipsa loquitur, we first provide an overview of this doctrine.

In Parrillo v. Giroux Co., 426 A.2d 1313, 1320 (R.I.1981), this Court adopted § 328D of the Restatement (Second) Torts. This approach permits an inference of negligence on a defendant's part when:

"(a) the event is of a kind which ordinarily does not occur in the absence of negligence; (b) other responsible causes, including the conduct of the plaintiff and third persons, are sufficiently eliminated by the evidence; and (c) the indicated negligence is within the scope of the defendant's duty to the plaintiff." Restatement (Second) Torts § 328D(1) at 156 (1965). In adopting this approach, Parrillo expressly disavowed a previous requirement that res ipsa loquitur applied only where the defendant had exclusive control of the instrumentality which harmed the plaintiff. * * *

We take this opportunity to reaffirm Parrillo's adoption of § 328D of the Restatement (Second) Torts. * * * To the extent that our prior decisions are inconsistent with Parrillo, they are no longer to be followed.

After reviewing our precedent on the doctrine of res ipsa loquitur and carefully examining the facts of this case, we conclude that plaintiffs cannot avail themselves of this doctrine to make out a claim for negligence against Ricky Smith. Roughly three years passed between the purchase of the vehicle in December 1998 and the airbag malfunction in December 2001. The plaintiffs assert that Ricky Smith had a duty to discover whatever defect made the vehicle's airbags spontaneously deploy. This assertion assumes that the vehicle was defective when it was sold. Had the airbags deployed shortly after plaintiffs purchased the vehicle, res ipsa loquitur might have permitted that inference, but it is not supported by these facts.

We agree with plaintiffs' assertion that "[t]he spontaneous deployment of air bags [sic] while a passenger is cleaning out a vehicle is an event which ordinarily does not occur in the absence of negligence." However, "[i]t is * * * insufficient to show that the accident is of the kind that does not ordinarily occur without negligence; the negligence must point to the defendant." [C] In this case, "other responsible causes" have not been "sufficiently eliminated by the evidence." [C] Accordingly, we hold that the hearing justice properly granted summary judgment in Ricky Smith's favor on plaintiffs' negligence claim. * * *

[The court also affirmed the trial court's granting of summary judgment on the negligent misrepresentation count.]

NOTES AND QUESTIONS

1. A television catches fire in plaintiff's home. How does he persuade a court to invoke res ipsa loquitur against the manufacturer when the television left the factory several months before the incident in question? See Gast v. Sears Roebuck & Co., 39 Ohio St.2d 29, 68 Ohio Op.2d 17, 313 N.E.2d 831 (1974). Generally, what should the plaintiff do to eliminate his own conduct as a cause of the accident? Is it enough that he testifies that he did nothing unusual, and only made use of the thing furnished him by defendant for the purpose for which it was furnished? See also Metropolitan Property and Cas. Ins. Co. v. Deere and Co., 302 Conn. 123, 25 A.3d 571 (2011) (discussing product "malfunction theory" and noting its origins in res ipsa loquitur principles) and note 3, page 820.

2. Must the possibility that the event has been caused by the conduct of a third person, for which defendant is not responsible, be entirely eliminated? Defendant parks on the side of a hill. Shortly afterward, without explanation, the automobile runs away down the hill and injures plaintiff. What are the possibilities? Can plaintiff get to the jury? Glaser v. Schroeder, 269 Mass. 337, 168 N.E. 809 (1929); Borg & Powers Furniture Co. v. Clark, 194 Minn. 305, 260 N.W. 316 (1935). A court allowed plaintiff's case to be heard by the jury although there was a four-hour lapse of time after defendant parked her car. See Hill v. Thompson, 484 P.2d 513 (Okl.1971). An escalator comes to a sudden halt, injuring plaintiff who sues the department store owner. Holzhauer v. Saks & Co., 346 Md. 328, 697 A.2d 89 (1997) (res ipsa loquitur not applicable because evidence showed emergency stop buttons were accessible to patrons and thus escalator was not in exclusive control of defendant).

3. *Car Leaving Highway.* There is general agreement that the fact that an automobile leaves the traveled portion of the highway and overturns, or crashes into a stationary object, is enough, in the absence of explanation, to make out a res ipsa loquitur case against the driver. Badela v. Karpowich, 152 Conn. 360, 206 A.2d 838 (1965); Bavis v. Fonte, 241 Md. 123, 215 A.2d 739 (1966); Tanski v. Jackson, 269 Minn. 304, 130 N.W.2d 492 (1964); and Bagby v. Commonwealth, 424 S.W.2d 119 (Ky.1968).

4. *Collisions Between Vehicles.* There is general agreement that when plaintiff's car collides with defendant's, neither driver has a res ipsa loquitur case against the other. Why? When the collision injures a third person, such as a passenger or a bystander on the sidewalk, most of the decisions have held that the passenger or bystander does not have a res ipsa loquitur case against either driver.

5. *Common Carriers.* When one of the vehicles is operated by a common carrier, and the injury is to its passenger, some courts apply res ipsa loquitur against the carrier alone. See Capital Transit Co. v. Jackson, 80 U.S.App.D.C. 162, 149 F.2d 839 (1945). But see Reardon v. Boston Elevated R. Co., 247 Mass. 124, 141 N.E. 857 (1923) and Bethel v. N.Y.C. Transit Authority, 92 N.Y.2d 348, 355, 681 N.Y.S.2d 201, 703 N.E.2d 1214, 1218 (1998) (abandoning higher duty for common carriers in part because it results in different standards applying to different parties involved in the same accident). Why res ipsa loquitur against the carrier, but not against the other driver, when the evidence against each is the same? The reason sometimes given is that, since the carrier is held to the highest degree of

care, it is more probable that the collision was due to some negligence on the part of the carrier than of the other driver. See James, Proof of the Breach in Negligence Cases, 37 Va.L.Rev. 179 (1951); cf. Simpson v. Gray Line Co., 226 Or. 71, 358 P.2d 516 (1961), holding that a tire blowout on a bus creates a res ipsa loquitur case against the carrier. A better explanation may be simply that this is a survival of the older rule that once placed the burden of proof upon the carrier; and that its basis is the special responsibility undertaken toward the passenger.

6. *Medical Malpractice and Res Ipsa Loquitur.* The interaction between the general requirement that the standard of care in a medical malpractice case be proved by expert testimony and the use of res ipsa loquitur is illustrated by the next principal case.

James v. Wormuth

Court of Appeals of New York, 2013.
21 N.Y.3d 540, 997 N.E.2d 133, 974 N.Y.S.2d 308.

RIVERA, J. * * * [When Dr. Wormuth discovered that the guide wire placed to assist him in locating the area of patient's lung to be biopsied had dislodged, he conducted a 20-minute manual search for the wire, but was unable to find it. At that point, Dr. Wormuth determined that it was better for the patient to end the surgical procedure and leave the wire. Defendant informed plaintiff after the surgery that he had done so and why. Several weeks later, patient returned, complaining of pain that she attributed to the wire and Dr. Wormuth performed a second operation to remove it. Patient then filed this malpractice action.]

Plaintiff's evidence at trial consisted of her testimony about, among other things, her discussion with Dr. Wormuth after the procedure, the postoperative pain and its impact on her ability to work, as well as the testimony of two of her clients as to the apparent disruption to her work caused by the pain, and Dr. Wormuth's testimony describing the procedure and his decision to leave the wire inside the plaintiff. Plaintiff also introduced several medical records relating to both procedures, including Dr. Wormuth's file, operation reports, a surgical pathology report, and an X-ray report produced during the period between the two procedures.

At the close of plaintiff's case, defendants moved to dismiss for failure to establish a prima facie case of medical malpractice. Defendants argued that plaintiff failed to show a deviation from accepted standards of medical practice, and also that such deviation was the proximate cause of the plaintiff's injury. Defendants pointed specifically to plaintiff's failure to present any expert proof on the standard of practice. Anticipating plaintiff's response, defendants argued that res ipsa loquitur was inapplicable because there was no evidence of any error by Dr. Wormuth that caused the wire to become dislodged.

Plaintiff objected to the motion and argued that expert testimony was unnecessary because Dr. Wormuth admitted that he intentionally left the wire inside the plaintiff. Therefore, a jury could infer negligence given that there was no medical reason to leave the wire lodged in plaintiff, and defendant could have obtained a C-arm [special X-ray machine that was used in the second surgery] to locate and remove it. Plaintiff asserted that res ipsa loquitur necessarily applied because the wire was a foreign object that could only have been left in the plaintiff as a result of the doctor's negligence. * * *

[The trial court judge granted a directed verdict to defendant at the close of plaintiff's case and that ruling was affirmed by the appellate division. This appeal followed.]

Ordinarily, a plaintiff asserting a medical malpractice claim must demonstrate that the doctor deviated from acceptable medical practice, and that such deviation was a proximate cause of the plaintiff's injury [cc]. The theory of res ipsa loquitur is applied to occurrences "[w]here the actual or specific cause of an accident is unknown" [c]. Under such circumstances, "a jury may . . . infer negligence merely from the happening of an event and the defendant's relation to it" [cc]. To establish a prima facie case of negligence in support of a res ipsa loquitur charge, plaintiff must establish three elements:

[1.] the event must be of a kind that ordinarily does not occur in the absence of someone's negligence;

[2.] it must be caused by an agency or instrumentality within the exclusive control of the defendant; and

[3.] it must not have been due to any voluntary action or contribution on the part of the plaintiff [cc].

Further, in the context of a medical malpractice case based upon a foreign object, "[r]es ipsa loquitur is applicable where . . . [the object] is unintentionally left in a patient following an operative procedure." [Cc]

* * * Plaintiff, having chosen to pursue a theory of the case which focused on defendant's intentional choice to leave the wire in the plaintiff, rather than the initial dislodgement of the wire, was required to establish that the doctor's judgment deviated from accepted community standards of practice, and that such deviation was a proximate cause of the plaintiff's injury. * * *

It is clear from the record that the doctor explained his decision to leave the wire in terms of his medical assessment of what was best for the patient under the circumstances. Defendant's testimony that it was his professional judgment to leave the wire [because it would be riskier to extend the period under which the plaintiff was anaesthetized and to make a larger incision in order to find and remove the wire] could not be assessed by the jury based on the "common knowledge of lay persons." [Cc] Therefore, evidence clearly was needed, in the form of expert opinion to assist a jury's understanding of whether this occurrence would have "take[n] place in the absence of negligence." [C] Plaintiff, however, wholly failed to present any such evidence of the standards of practice, and therefore her complaint was properly dismissed.

To the extent counsel argued that res ipsa loquitur applies because the wire could only have dislodged due to the doctor's negligence, plaintiff failed to establish the elements of res ipsa, specifically that Dr. Wormuth had exclusive control [cc]. Dr. Wormuth testified that there were other medical personnel involved in the process of inserting the wire and transporting the plaintiff prior to the doctor's discovery that the wire had dislodged. Plaintiff did not produce any evidence to the contrary. Instead, plaintiff's counsel appears to have believed that the control element was satisfied because the doctor had control over the operation. Whether the doctor was in control of the operation does not address the question of whether he was in exclusive control of the instrumentality, because several other individuals participated to an extent in the medical procedure. Given that plaintiff failed to produce any evidence that the doctor had exclusive control of the wire, or sufficient proof that "eliminate[s] within reason all explanations for the injury other than the defendant's negligence," the control element clearly has not been satisfied [c]. Although the control requirement does not mean that "the possibility of other causes must be altogether eliminated, . . . [the] likelihood must be so reduced that the greater probability lies at defendant's door" [c].

Plaintiff's argument that the wire should be treated as a foreign object in support of her res ipsa claim is unpersuasive because her theory of the case was the doctor negligently chose to leave the wire. Thus, this case is distinguishable from those involving objects left unintentionally, where, as plaintiff argues, no decision to leave the object has been made which must be measured against a standard of care. * * * "As advantageous as the res ipsa loquitur inference is for a plaintiff unable to adduce direct evidence of negligence, application of the [evidentiary] doctrine does not relieve a plaintiff of the burden of proof." [C]

Accordingly, the Appellate Division order should be affirmed, with costs.

NOTES AND QUESTIONS

1. In the health care setting, a few courts have shifted the burden of proof to the defendants to prove they were not negligent in the case of an unconscious patient unable to identify who among the various health care providers had caused an injury while he was unconscious during a medical procedure that ordinarily would not have happened in the absence of *someone's* negligence. See, for example, Ybarra v. Spangard, 25 Cal.2d 486, 154 P.2d 587 (1944) (patient suffered paralysis of right shoulder during appendectomy; burden shifted to doctors, nurses, and anesthesiologist to prove he or she did not cause the injury). The *Ybarra* decision was approved and followed, upon similar facts, in Frost v. Des Moines Still College of Osteopathy, 248 Iowa 294, 79 N.W.2d 306 (1956) and Beaudoin v. Watertown Memorial Hosp., 32 Wis.2d 132, 145 N.W.2d 166 (1966), but rejected in Rhodes v. De Haan, 184 Kan. 473, 337 P.2d 1043 (1959) and Talbot v. Dr. W.H. Groves' Latter-Day Saints Hosp., Inc., 21 Utah 2d 73, 440 P.2d 872 (1968).

2. What if the patient sues the hospital that is responsible for the conduct of the nurses, but does not include the surgeon and the anesthesiologist as defendants? Darrah v. Bryan Memorial Hospital, 253 Neb. 710, 571 N.W.2d 783 (1998) (summary judgment for hospital because plaintiff did not eliminate surgeon and anesthesiologist as possible sources of injury).

3. Assuming that the judge finds the prerequisites for the use of res ipsa loquitur have been shown, what is the effect on the lawsuit? See the next principal case.

Sullivan v. Crabtree

Court of Appeals of Tennessee, 1953.
36 Tenn.App. 469, 258 S.W.2d 782.

FELTS, JUDGE. Plaintiffs sued for damages for the death of their adult son, Robert Sullivan, who was killed while a guest in a motor truck which swerved off the highway and overturned down a steep embankment. Suit was brought against both the owner and the driver of the truck, but a nonsuit was taken as to the owner, and the case went to trial against the driver alone. There was a verdict and judgment in his favor, and plaintiffs appealed in error.

The truck was a large trailer-tractor truck * * *. Its driver Crabtree * * * permitted Sullivan to ride with him as a guest in the cab of the truck.

The road on which he was driving was a paved first-class Federal-state highway (U.S. 41, Tenn. 2), but coming down the mountain from Monteagle to Pelham it had a number of moderate grades and pretty sharp curves. It was midafternoon, and the weather was dry and clear. As Crabtree was approaching a curve another truck overtook and passed him, and just after it did so, Crabtree's truck suddenly swerved from his right side over to his left, ran off the left shoulder, overturned down a steep embankment, and crushed Sullivan to death.

Defendant testified that there was some loose gravel on the road, which had perhaps been spilled there by trucks hauling gravel, and the pavement was broken a little on the right-hand side; and that when he "hit the edge of the curve on the right-hand side" he "lost control of the truck," and it turned from his right side across to the left, and ran off the shoulder of the highway. On cross-examination he further said:

"Q. Can you tell the Jury now what caused you to lose control of the truck and permit it to run off the road down the embankment? A. No. The brakes could have gave way, or the brakes could have grabbed or it could have been a particular wheel grabbed, because on a tractor, if the brakes happen to grab on it, the load is so much heavier than the tractor, it whips either way and takes control of the tractor and you have nothing to do with it.

"Q. Did that happen in this case? A. It is possible. * * *

"Q. You can't tell us just what did cause the accident or cause you to lose control of the truck? A. Probably hitting the edge of the pavement or it could have been several different things. Like one going off the mountain, if it is pulled out with the wrecker, you don't know whether a hose got connected up in there and when you turned the curve break a hose, cut it or break it loose. The brakes are cut on and off with a catch there like that, and it is easy for a hose to get loose."

Such being the undisputed facts, plaintiffs contend that defendant was guilty, as a matter of law, of negligence causing the death sued for, and that there was no evidence to support a verdict for defendant. They show a duty of care owing by defendant to the deceased under our rule that a driver must use ordinary care for the safety of his guest [c] and to make out a breach of that duty, or proximate negligence, they invoke the rule of res ipsa loquitur.

They insist that the facts of this case brought it within the rule of res ipsa loquitur requiring a finding of negligence, in the absence of an explanation disproving negligence; that since there was no such explanation, since defendant did not know why he lost control of the truck or what caused the accident, the jury were bound to find that it was caused by his negligence and could not reasonably render a verdict in his favor. * * *

The maxim res ipsa loquitur means that the facts of the occurrence evidence negligence; the circumstances unexplained justify an inference of negligence. In the principle of proof employed, a case of res ipsa loquitur does not differ from an ordinary case of circumstantial evidence. Res ipsa loquitur is not an arbitrary rule but rather "a common sense appraisal of the probative value of circumstantial evidence." Boykin v. Chase Bottling Works, 32 Tenn.App. 508, 520–523, 222 S.W.2d 889, 896.

This maxim does not generally apply to motor vehicle accidents but it may apply to such an accident where the circumstances causing it were within the driver's control and the accident was such as does not usually occur without negligence. So where a motor vehicle, without apparent cause, runs off the road and causes harm, the normal inference is that the driver was negligent, and res ipsa loquitur is usually held to apply. * * *

So we agree with learned counsel for plaintiffs that the facts of this case brought it within the maxim res ipsa loquitur. The accident was such as does not usually occur without negligence, and the cause of it was in control of the driver, or rather it resulted from his loss of control of the truck, which he could not explain.

While we agree that these facts made a case of res ipsa loquitur, we do not agree that they, though unexplained, required an inference or finding of negligence, or that the jury could not reasonably refuse to find negligence and return a verdict for defendant, or that there was no evidence to support their verdict for him.

It is true there has been confusion in the cases as to the procedural effect of res ipsa loquitur, some cases giving it one and some another of these three different effects:

(1) It warrants an *inference* of negligence which the jury may draw or not, as their judgment dictates. [Cc]

(2) It raises a *presumption* of negligence which requires the jury to find negligence if defendant does not produce evidence sufficient to rebut the presumption. [Cc]

(3) It not only raises such a presumption but also *shifts the ultimate burden of proof* to defendant and requires him to prove by a preponderance of all the evidence that the injury was not caused by his negligence. [Cc]

The effect of a case of res ipsa loquitur, like that of any other case of circumstantial evidence varies from case to case, depending on the particular facts of each case; and therefore such effect can no more be fitted into a fixed formula or reduced to a rigid rule than can the effect of other cases of circumstantial evidence. The only generalization that can be safely made is that, in the words of the definition of res ipsa loquitur, it affords "reasonable evidence," in the absence of an explanation by defendant, that the accident arose from this negligence.

The weight or strength of such "reasonable evidence" will necessarily depend on the particular facts of each case, and the cogency of the inference of negligence from such facts may of course vary in degree all the way from practical certainty in one case to reasonable probability in another.

In exceptional cases the inference may be so strong as to require a directed verdict for plaintiff, as in cases of objects falling from defendant's premises on persons in the highway, such as Byrne v. Boadle (1863), 2 H. & C. 722, 159 Eng.Reprint 299 (a barrel of flour fell from a window of defendant's warehouse); McHarge v. M.M. Newcomer & Co., 117 Tenn. 595, 100 S.W. 700, 9 L.R.A.N.S. 298, N.S., 298 (an awning roller fell from defendant's building); and Turnpike Co. v. Yates, supra (a toll gate or pole fell on a traveler); cf. Annotation, 153 A.L.R. 1134.

In the ordinary case, however, res ipsa loquitur merely makes a case for the jury—merely permits the jury to choose the inference of defendant's negligence in preference to other permissible or reasonable inferences. [Cc]

We think this is true in the case before us. The cause of the death sued for was defendant's loss of control of the truck. This may have been due to his own negligence, or it may have been due to no fault of his—an unavoidable accident resulting from the brakes giving way or the breaking of some part of the control mechanism of the truck. Since such conflicting inferences might be reasonably drawn from the evidence, it was for the jury to choose the inference they thought most probable; and we cannot say that there was no evidence to support their verdict for defendant. * * *

All the assignments of error are overruled and the judgment of the Circuit Court is affirmed.

NOTES AND QUESTIONS

1. Most cases are in accord with the principal case as to the procedural effect of res ipsa loquitur: it warrants the *inference* of negligence that the jury may draw or not, as its judgment dictates. See George Foltis, Inc. v. New York, 287 N.Y. 108, 38 N.E.2d 455 (1941) and Hubbard v. Mellion, 48 Kan.App.2d 1005, 302 P.3d 1084 (2013) (whether the inference of negligence arising from res ipsa loquitur will be convincing to a jury is a question to be answered by that jury). Others hold that res ipsa loquitur creates a rebuttable presumption and some that it shifts the burden of proof to the defendant.

2. Suppose plaintiff, the guardian of her sister who was confined to a nursing home, proved at trial that her sister had gone into a coma because

she received an overdose of a drug used to treat diabetes. The patient did not have diabetes and her chart did not indicate the administration of any medication other than sterile water as a placebo when she complained of pain. Is this enough evidence to warrant a res ipsa loquitur jury instruction? Now suppose that defendant nursing home proves that it did not have that drug in its pharmacy because no patient in its care used it, that patient frequently was visited by her family and had visited her sister's home two weeks before the overdose, that her sister was diabetic and had the drug in her home for her own treatment, and that patient had become addicted to prescription drugs and was a "known drug seeker." Think about this case in the context of each possible effect of res ipsa loquitur. Could the jury draw an inference of negligence on the part of the nursing home? Did defendant nursing home rebut a presumption of negligence on the part of the nursing home? Did defendant nursing home prove that its negligence did not cause patient's overdose? See Harder v. F.C. Clinton, Inc., 948 P.2d 298 (Okla.1997).

3. As the principal case notes, there may be exceptional cases where the inference of negligence will be so compelling that the jury cannot be permitted to reject it, and a verdict must be directed for the plaintiff in the absence of evidence to explain it away. One such case is the head-on collision of two trains on the same track in Moore v. Atchison, T. & S.F.R. Co., 28 Ill.App.2d 340, 171 N.E.2d 393 (1960). "The time will probably never come when a collision resulting from an attempt to have two trains going at full speed, in opposite directions, pass each other, on the same track, will not be held to be negligence in law." Rouse v. Hornsby, 67 Fed. 219, 221 (8th Cir.1895).

4. Some courts have given res ipsa loquitur a greater procedural effect when the action is brought by an injured passenger against his carrier. See, for example, Greyhound Corp. v. Brown, 269 Ala. 520, 113 So.2d 916 (1959) and Transcontinental Bus System v. Simons, 367 P.2d 160 (Okla.1961), shifting the burden of proof to the defendant. This is apparently a carry-over from the original rule that, because of the special responsibility undertaken by the carrier, it had the burden of proof. See note 5, page 264.

5. *Effect of Pleading Specific Acts of Negligence.* At least four positions have been taken by the courts, as to whether the plaintiff, by his specific pleading of negligence, is precluded from relying upon res ipsa loquitur: (a) that he cannot rely on it at all; (b) that he may take advantage of res ipsa loquitur to the extent that the inference of negligence to be drawn supports the specific allegations; (c) that he may rely on res ipsa loquitur only if the specific pleading is accompanied by a general allegation of negligence; and (d) that it is available without regard to the form of the pleading. Which is the best rule? Do you see how each of the positions might impact on the plaintiff in a particular case? See discussion in Vogreg v. Shepard Ambulance Co., 47 Wash.2d 659, 289 P.2d 350 (1955).

6. Similar positions have been taken as to the effect of the introduction at trial of specific evidence of negligent conduct. What if the plaintiff's specific evidence tells the complete story of how the accident happened and just what the defendant did? Is there any room for the application of res ipsa loquitur? Stahlecker v. Ford Motor Co., 266 Neb. 601, 667 N.W.2d 244 (2003) ("Because the [plaintiffs] have alleged specific

acts of negligence on the part of both Ford and Firestone, the doctrine of res ipsa loquitur is inapplicable to this case.") Augspurger v. Western Auto Supply Co., 257 Iowa 777, 134 N.W.2d 913 (1965) (res ipsa loquitur not applicable because plaintiff, injured by a metallic particle that flew off while auto mechanic was using hammer and chisel to remove a ball bearing, testified in detail about the accident and its cause—there were no unknown factors); Dover Elevator Co. v. Swann, 334 Md. 231, 638 A.2d 762 (1994) (expert's opinion as to the specific cause of the elevator misleveling precluded reliance on res ipsa loquitur). Consider the following: "When the plaintiff shows that the railway car in which he was a passenger was derailed, there is an inference that the defendant railroad has somehow been negligent. When the plaintiff goes further and shows that the derailment was caused by an open switch, the plaintiff destroys any inference of other causes; but the inference that the defendant has not used proper care in looking after its switches is not destroyed, but considerably strengthened. If the plaintiff goes further still and shows that the switch was left open by a drunken switchman on duty, there is nothing left to infer; and if the plaintiff shows that the switch was thrown by an escaped convict with a grudge against the railroad, the plaintiff has proven himself out of court." W. Prosser and W. Keeton, Torts, 260 (5th ed. 1984).

CHAPTER 5

CAUSATION IN FACT

1. SINE QUA NON

Perkins v. Texas and New Orleans R. Co.

Supreme Court of Louisiana, 1962.
243 La. 829, 147 So.2d 646.

SANDERS, JUSTICE. This is a tort action. Plaintiff, the 67-year-old widow of Tanner Perkins, seeks damages for the death of her husband in the collision of an automobile, in which he was riding, with a train of the defendant railroad. [After a bench trial, t]he district court awarded damages. The Court of Appeal affirmed. We granted certiorari to review the judgment of the Court of Appeal.

The tragic accident which gave rise to this litigation occurred at the intersection of Eddy Street and The Texas and New Orleans Railroad Company track in the town of Vinton, Louisiana, at approximately 6:02 a.m., after daylight, on September 28, 1959. At this crossing Eddy Street runs north and south, and the railroad track, east and west. Involved was a 113-car freight train pulled by four diesel engines traveling east and a Dodge automobile driven by Joe Foreman in a southerly direction on Eddy Street. Tanner Perkins, a guest passenger, was riding in the front seat of the automobile with the driver.

Located in the northwest quadrant of the intersection of the railroad track and Eddy Street was a warehouse five hundred feet long. A "house track" paralleled the main track on the north to serve the warehouse. This warehouse obstructed the view to the west of an automobile driver approaching the railroad crossing from the north on Eddy Street. It likewise obstructed the view to the north of trainmen approaching the crossing from the west. Having previously served on this route, the engineer and brakeman were aware of this obstruction.

To warn the public of the approach of trains, the defendant railroad had installed at the crossing an automatic signal device consisting of a swinging red light and a bell. At the time of the accident, this signal was operating. A standard Louisiana railroad stop sign and an intersection stop sign were also located at the crossing.

Proceeding east, the train approached the intersection with its headlight burning, its bell ringing, and its whistle blowing.

The engineer, brakeman, and fireman were stationed in the forward engine of the train. The engineer was seated on the right or south side, where he was unable to observe an automobile approaching from the left of the engine. The brakeman and fireman, who were seated on the left or north side of the engine, were looking forward as the train approached the intersection. These two crewmen saw the automobile emerge from behind the warehouse. At that time the front wheels of the automobile were on or across the north rail of the house track. The fireman estimated that the train was approximately 60 feet from the crossing when the automobile emerged from behind the warehouse. The brakeman, however, estimated that the train was 30 to 40 feet from the crossing at the time the automobile came into view. Both crewmen immediately shouted a warning to the engineer, who applied the emergency brakes. The train struck the right side of the automobile and carried it approximately 1250 feet. The two occupants were inside the automobile when it came to rest. Both were killed.

The speed of the automobile in which Tanner Perkins was riding was variously estimated from 3–4 miles per hour to 20–25 miles per hour.

The plaintiff and defendant railroad concede in their pleadings that Joe Foreman, the driver of the automobile, was negligent in driving upon the track in front of the train and that his negligence was a proximate cause of the death of Tanner Perkins.

It is conceded that the railroad's safety regulations imposed a speed limit of 25 miles per hour on trains in the town of Vinton. The plaintiff has conceded in this Court that this self-imposed speed limit was a safe speed at the crossing. The train was in fact traveling at a speed of 37 miles per hour.

Applicable here is the rule that the violation by trainmen of the railroad's own speed regulations adopted in the interest of safety is evidence of negligence. * * *

We find, as did the Court of Appeal, that the trainmen were negligent in operating the train 12 miles per hour in excess of the speed limit.

* * * [T]he prime issue in this case is whether the excessive speed of the train was a cause in fact of the fatal collision.

It is fundamental that negligence is not actionable unless it is a cause in fact of the harm for which recovery is sought. It need not, of course, be the sole cause. Negligence is a cause in fact of the harm to another if it was a substantial factor in bringing about that harm. Under the circumstances of the instant case, the excessive speed was undoubtedly a substantial factor in bringing about the collision if the collision would not have occurred without it. On the other hand, if the collision would have occurred irrespective of such negligence, then it was not a substantial factor. [Cc]

In the instant case the train engineer testified that at a speed of 25 miles per hour he would have been unable to stop the train in time to avoid the accident. Other facts of record support his testimony in this regard. With efficient brakes, the mile-long train required 1250 feet to stop at a speed of 37 miles per hour. It is clear, then, that even at the concededly safe speed of 25 miles per hour, the momentum of the train would have, under the circumstances, carried it well beyond the crossing. This finding, of course, does not fully determine whether the collision would have been averted at the slower speed. The automobile was also in motion during the crucial period. This necessitates the further inquiry of whether the automobile would have cleared the track and evaded the impact had the train been moving at a proper speed at the time the trainmen observed the automobile emerge from behind the warehouse. Basic to this inquiry are the speed of the automobile and the driving distance between it and a position of safety. [C]

The testimony of the witnesses is in hopeless conflict as to the speed of the automobile at the time of the collision.

* * * Despite these deficiencies in the evidence, the plaintiff argues that had the train been traveling at a proper speed the driver of the automobile would "conceivably" have had some additional time to take measures to avert disaster and the deceased would have had some additional time to extricate himself from danger. Hence, the plaintiff reasons, the collision and loss of life "might not" have occurred.

On the facts of this case, we must reject the escape theory advanced in this argument. Because of the deficiencies in the evidence which we have already noted, it is devoid of evidentiary support. The record contains no probative facts from which the Court can draw a reasonable inference of causation under this theory. In essence, the argument is pure conjecture.

Based upon the evidence of record, it appears almost certain that the fatal accident would have occurred irrespective of the excessive speed of the train. It follows that this speed was not a substantial factor in bringing about the accident.

We conclude that the plaintiff has failed to discharge the burden of proving that the negligence of the defendant was a cause in fact of the tragic death. The judgment in favor of plaintiff is manifestly erroneous.

For the reasons assigned, the judgment of the Court of Appeal is reversed, and the plaintiff's suit is dismissed at her cost.

NOTES AND QUESTIONS

1. In the principal case, if the collision was a cause of the plaintiffs' deaths, why did the defendant avoid liability?

2. Driver is driving 30 m.p.h. in a 25 m.p.h. zone in a thunderstorm. Her speed causes her car to be passing under a tree just as it is struck by lightning and falls onto the car, injuring passenger. Does passenger have a negligence cause of action against driver? Note that if she had been driving even faster they would have been past that point before the tree fell. The Third Restatement treats this as a scope of liability question. Restatement (Third) of Torts § 30, illustration 1 (2010).

3. Defendant truck driver negligently failed to signal for a left turn. Plaintiff crashed into the truck. Can defendant win the case by establishing that plaintiff was not looking and would not have seen the signal if it had been given? Rouleau v. Blotner, 84 N.H. 539, 152 A. 916 (1931) ("if he were a deaf man, the failure to sound whistle, bell or horn would be immaterial").

4. Defendant excavates a hole in the sidewalk, and leaves it unguarded and unlighted. Plaintiff, a traveler on the sidewalk, accidentally falls into it in the dark. Is defendant's negligence a cause of his injury? Probably. What if a third person negligently bumps into plaintiff, and knocks him into the hole? Village of Carterville v. Cook, 129 Ill. 152, 22 N.E. 14 (1889) (yes). Suppose the third person intentionally shoves him into it? Milostan v. Chicago, 148 Ill.App. 540 (1909) (no).

5. The mate of defendant's steam trawler falls overboard, and disappears immediately. Defendant's lifeboat is lashed to the deck instead of being suspended from davits, and is equipped with only one oar. Is this negligence a cause of his death? Ford v. Trident Fisheries Co., 232 Mass. 400, 122 N.E. 389 (1919) (no).

6. Defendant, cutting ice on a lake, was negligent in failing to fence the opening as required by statute, in failing to give warning of its location, and in not having ropes or other appliances at hand to rescue anyone who fell in. Plaintiff's horses ran away, plunged into the opening, and were drowned. The evidence was that the horses were uncontrollable and could not have been stopped or directed, and that they went under the ice and could not have been rescued. Is defendant's negligence a cause of their loss? Stacy v. Knickerbocker Ice Co., 84 Wis. 614, 54 N.W. 1091 (1893) (no).

7. When the North Tower of the World Trade Center collapsed on 9/11, flaming debris landed on a building known as 7 World Trade Center ("7WTC"), which had been built over an underground ConEd electrical substation. Firefighters assessing the scene found there were multiple fires in the building and evidence of structural damage from the flying debris. Because the building already had been evacuated and searched for survivors, there was no water to use due to the breaking of the Vesey Street water main when the Towers collapsed, and 400 firefighters already had been lost in the collapse of the Towers, the firefighters drew a perimeter around the building and let it burn. It collapsed several hours later, destroying the ConEd substation underneath it. ConEd's insurance company sought to recover from the owners of the building, arguing that an unfought fire would not have caused the building to collapse if it had been properly designed and constructed. The court upheld the trial court judge's grant of summary judgment to the owners, finding that plaintiff failed to prove that the design alternatives argued by its experts to the design and construction of 7WTC more than a decade earlier would have prevented its collapse under the conditions present on 9/11. Aegis Ins. Services, Inc. v. 7 World Trade Co., LLP, 737 F.3d 166 (2d Cir. 2013) (applying New York law).

8. Defendant failed to include a warning on a can of refrigerant. Plaintiff started using it without reading the instructions. Was defendant's failure to warn a cause of plaintiff's injury? Technical Chemical Co. v. Jacobs, 480 S.W.2d 602 (Tex.1972) (no). See also Motus v. Pfizer Inc., 358 F.3d 659 (9th Cir. 2004) (applying California law) (since doctor failed to read manufacturer's published warnings before prescribing drug, plaintiff could not show that a stronger warning would have averted injury to her husband); Harvey v. Washington, 95 S.W.3d 93 (Mo. 2003) (since kidney specialist had independent information re patient's condition, failure of neurologist to advocate dialysis was not cause of patient's death); Kovach v. Caligor Midwest, 913 N.E.2d 193 (Ind. 2009) (since patient was given a full cup of red liquid in a clear cup instead of the prescribed half cup, there was no causal link between the medicine cup manufacturer's failure to warn that the cup was not suited as a precision measuring device and the overdose that caused the injury); and Peart v. Dorel Juvenile Group, Inc., 456 Fed.Appx. 446 (5th Cir. 2012) (applying Louisiana law) (even if warning on step stool that collapsed was inadequate, plaintiff failed to

prove causation because she admitted that she had not read the warning stickers attached to the step stool before she used it).

9. Defendant railroad violated a statute in failing to display a warning sign at a railroad crossing. Plaintiff, who was injured at the crossing, knew from prior experience of the danger. Was defendant's negligence a cause in fact of plaintiff's injuries? Thomas v. Baltimore & Ohio R. Co., 19 Md.App. 217, 310 A.2d 186 (1973) (no—plaintiff had crossed over tracks only 15 minutes earlier on his way to quarry).

10. Texas uses the term "producing cause" for causation and had been defining it for the jury as "an efficient, exciting, or contributing cause that, in a natural sequence, produces the incident in question. There may be more than one producing cause." Texas Pattern Jury Charge 71.3. Recently, the Texas Supreme Court moved away from its traditional jury instruction and to defining "producing cause" as being a "substantial factor in bringing about an injury, and without which the injury would not have occurred." Ford Motor Co. v. Ledesma, 242 S.W.3d 32, 46 (Tex. 2007). See also Restatement (Third) of Torts: Liability for Physical and Emotional Harm § 26 (2010) on "but for" causation; Abraham, Self-Proving Causation, 99 Va. L. Rev. 1811 (2013); and Hart and Honoré, Causation in the Law (2d ed. 1985).

2. PROOF OF CAUSATION

Reynolds v. Texas & Pac. Ry. Co.

Court of Appeals of Louisiana, 1885.
37 La.Ann. 694.

[Plaintiff and his wife sought damages against defendant company for injuries she suffered when she fell down a stairway.]

FENNER, J. * * * The train was behind time. Several witnesses testify that passengers were warned to "hurry up." Mrs. Reynolds, a corpulent woman, weighing two hundred and fifty pounds, emerging from the bright light of the sitting-room, which naturally exaggerated the outside darkness, and hastening down these unlighted steps, made a misstep in some way and was precipitated beyond the narrow platform in front and down the slope beyond, incurring the serious injuries complained of. [The trial court, without a jury, gave judgment to the plaintiffs for $2,000 in damages. Defendant appealed.]

[Defendant] contends that, even conceding the negligence of the company in [failing to light the stairway or provide a handrail], it does not follow that the accident to plaintiff was necessarily caused thereby, but that she might well have made the misstep and fallen even had it been broad daylight. We concede that this is possible, and recognize the distinction between post hoc and propter hoc. But where the negligence of the defendant greatly multiplies the chances of accident to the plaintiff, and is of a character naturally leading to its occurrence, the mere possibility that it might have happened without the negligence is not sufficient to break the chain of cause and effect between the negligence and the injury. Courts, in such matters, consider the natural and ordinary course of events, and do not indulge in fanciful suppositions. The whole tendency of the evidence connects the accident with the negligence. * * *

Judgment affirmed.

NOTES AND QUESTIONS

1. If a life preserver had been thrown to a drowning man, would he have caught it and been saved? Kirincich v. Standard Dredging Co., 112 F.2d 163 (3d Cir.1940). Would an adequate number of campus police have prevented trespassing boys from shooting a student in the eye with an air rifle? Stockwell v. Board of Trustees of Leland Stanford Junior University, 64 Cal.App.2d 197, 148 P.2d 405 (1944). How are these questions to be decided? Who should decide them?

2. The owners of Tower Two of the World Trade Center sued American Airlines for the destruction of the tower on September 11th, arguing that a twenty-one minute delay between when a flight attendant reported the hijacking to American and when American reported it to the FAA was a cause of their loss. The FAA, learning of the hijacking from the Control Tower at Boston Center six minutes after American learned of it from its flight attendant, caused two military jets to scramble, and sent them to air space near Long Island where they were waiting for military personnel to establish the precise location of the plane. Time ran out and the American flight crashed into Tower One. Seventeen minutes later, the United flight crashed into Tower Two. Was the alleged delay in reporting the hijacking of the American plane a cause of the damage to Tower Two? In re September 11 Litigation, 594 F.Supp.2d 374 (S.D.N.Y. 2009) (granting summary judgment to American, finding that plaintiffs had not proved that the six-minute gap between when American was told of the hijacking and when the FAA learned of it from the Boston Control Tower was enough time to have stopped the destruction of Tower Two).

Gentry v. Douglas Hereford Ranch, Inc.

Supreme Court of Montana, 1998.
290 Mont. 126, 962 P.2d 1205.

[Defendant Bacon was planning to hunt deer on his wife's grandmother's ranch while his wife and a friend of theirs, Barbara Gentry, painted the interior of the grandmother's new house. After starting a fire in the fireplace, Bacon left to go get his rifle from where he had parked his car. He then returned to the new house to get the ranch pickup, holding his rifle on his shoulder with his right hand. As he was approaching a wooden deck adjacent to the house and accessed by two wooden steps, Barbara Gentry came out of the house to get a radio from the pickup. Bacon stumbled and his rifle discharged, the bullet struck Barbara Gentry in the head, and she died several weeks later from the head injury. Her husband brought wrongful death and survival actions against Bacon, the ranch company owned by the grandmother, and a cattle company that leased part of the ranch. The complaint alleged that Bacon had been negligent in his handling of the rifle, that the other defendants were liable for Bacon's negligence because he was their agent, that the other defendants had been negligent in maintaining the deck stairs in a dangerous condition, and that the combined negligence of Bacon and the other defendants had caused the injury. After Bacon sought bankruptcy protection, he was voluntarily dismissed from the case. The trial court judge entered summary judgment in favor of the ranch company defendants and plaintiff appealed on several grounds.]

TRIEWEILER, J. * * *

ISSUE 1

Did the District Court err when it concluded as a matter of law that the [ranch company] defendants were not negligent? * * *

A negligence action requires proof of four elements: (1) existence of a duty; (2) breach of the duty; (3) causation; and (4) damages. If the plaintiff fails to offer proof of one of these elements, the action in negligence fails and summary judgment in favor of the defendant is proper. [C] The causation element requires proof of both cause in fact and proximate cause. * * *

In Busta v. Columbus Hospital Corp. (1996), 276 Mont. 342, 916 P.2d 122, 139, we held that:

> In those cases which do not involve issues of intervening cause, proof of causation is satisfied by proof that a party's conduct was a cause-in-fact of the damage alleged. As stated in Prosser and Keeton on Torts § 41, at 266 (5th ed. 1984), a party's conduct is a cause-in-fact of an event if "the event would not have occurred but for that conduct; conversely, the defendant's conduct is not a cause of the event, if the event would have occurred without it."

* * * We limit our discussion, however, to our conclusion that Gentry failed to prove cause in fact.

Gentry alleged that the ranch company [defendants] . . . were negligent by failing to maintain the stairs to the deck adjoining the "new house" in a reasonably safe condition. He contended that the bottom stair was unstable and that the area leading to it was cluttered by debris, including a drain pipe, electric wires, and rocks. However, the defendants' motions for summary judgment were based on Bacon's testimony that he was unable to attribute his fall to any of those conditions. When he was deposed on May 2, 1997, he gave the following testimony in response to the following questions:

Q: Do you remember stumbling as you started up the steps?

A: I don't remember hardly anything.

. . .

Q: And you don't remember exactly where you were when you began to stumble; is that right?

A: That's correct.

Q: And you don't know whether it was—whether there was even some object that caused you to slip or stumble; is that right?

A: I don't remember anything.

. . .

Q: You don't remember where you were?

A: No.

Q: And from the time after the rifle discharged, you don't know exactly where you were when you fell or what caused you to fall; is that right?

A: Correct.

. . .

Q: And you don't recall if you had even reached the steps at the time that you fell; is that right?

A. That's correct.

. . .

Q: Did you want to add something?

A: Yes. I've stated umpteen numerous times that I don't remember if I tripped or if I was just clumsy or if I missed the step or hit it or whatever. I've stated that and stated that, and I don't recall.

Bacon also testified that while he had stumbled climbing those same steps prior to the incident in question, he had done so as the result of his own clumsiness, and not because of the condition of the steps.

In response to Bacon's deposition testimony, which was cited to the District Court in support of the defendants' motions for summary judgment, Gentry cited the District Court, and now cites this Court, to the following statement made by Bacon during an interview with investigators on November 16, 1995.

TW: Okay. So, you remember stumbling, and you don't remember on what?

BB: No, I don't remember if I went to step up on the step or if . . . there's a rock there also underneath the step to keep it level. I don't think it was that, I think it was the step.

Gentry contends that based on this isolated statement a reasonable finder of fact could infer that it was the step which caused Bacon's fall. However, earlier in the same interview, he was asked the following question and gave the following answer:

TW: Do you remember what you stumbled on?

BB: No I don't.

Furthermore, when asked in his deposition whether, at the time of his November 16 statement, he had remembered what caused him to fall, he testified that he had not. That testimony was consistent with his statement on the date of the incident in which he stated that he did not know how he fell.

Finally, even the isolated statement relied on by Gentry does not support the contention that it was the condition of the step or the area surrounding the step which caused Bacon to stumble and fall. The most that could be inferred was that he was about to ascend the stairs when he did stumble and fall. Why he stumbled and fell would still require speculation. In the context of summary judgment proceedings, we have previously held that neither a suspicion nor speculation is sufficient to defeat a motion for summary judgment. In Benson v. Diehl (1987), 228 Mont. 199, 203, 745 P.2d 315, 317, we held that:

> A suspicion, regardless of how particularized it may be, is not sufficient to sustain an action or to defeat a motion for summary judgment. Unsupported conclusory or speculative statements do not raise a genuine issue of material fact. The trial court has no duty to anticipate possible proof. [C]

The facts presented in this case are similar to those presented in [an earlier Montana case]. In that case, the plaintiff sought damages for injuries she sustained while walking on property owned by the defendant. She was injured when she stumbled over some object on the property. However, she was unable to identify what it was that caused her to stumble. We affirmed summary judgment for the defendant for the following reasons:

> More importantly, the fact is undisputed that the appellant cannot describe what caused her injury. She does not know if it was merely a mound of dirt or an old corral pole.
>
> In an action for negligence, a plaintiff must produce evidence from which it can be reasonably inferred that negligent conduct on the part of the defendant or its agents was the proximate cause of the plaintiff's injuries. [C] Here, the appellant simply does not know exactly what caused her injury. As noted above, the respondents cannot be the insurers of the appellant and held liable for her injury merely because an accident happened on their land. [C]

Likewise, Gentry has offered no substantial evidence that any condition on the property [of defendants] caused Bacon to stumble and fall immediately before his rifle discharged and struck the decedent, Barbara Gentry. Therefore, we conclude that cause in fact cannot be proven as a matter of law, and the District Court did not err when it held that the [ranch company] defendants . . . were not negligent in a manner that contributed to the injuries and death of Barbara Gentry. * * *

[The court then ruled that the ranch company defendants were not vicariously responsible for Bacon's negligent handling of the rifle since he was not an employee or agent of the companies.]

We affirm the judgment of the District Court.

NOTES AND QUESTIONS

1. In the principal case, if the steps were negligently maintained, why did the court affirm the trial court's entry of judgment in favor of the ranch company defendants? In light of Reynolds v. Texas & Pac. Ry. Co., what change in the facts would have been enough to get the principal case to the jury?

2. What happened to Bacon? Why doesn't he have to compensate plaintiff? Wasn't his negligent handling of the rifle a cause in fact of the injury to plaintiff's wife?

3. Notice the court's allusion to cause in fact and proximate cause as two separate analyses. Proximate cause will be discussed in Chapter 6.

4. A woman on board a cruise ship stepped into the bathtub in her cabin to take a shower. She slipped and injured herself. The bathtub had four anti-skid strips running parallel to each other from the middle to the back of the tub. After the accident, she noticed that there was sufficient space between the strips so that her foot could just fit between them. She does not know where her feet were when she slipped. Assuming that she could prove that the placement of the anti-skid strips was negligent, is the cruise ship liable for her injures? Fedorczyk v. Caribbean Cruise Lines, Ltd., 82 F.3d 69, 75 (3d Cir.1996) ("Even though we must draw all legitimate inferences in Fedorczyk's favor, the inference that she was standing between the strips at the time of the accident, because her feet could fit between the strips, is not an appropriate inference to be drawn. The possibility of the existence of an event does not tend to prove its probability.")

Kramer Service, Inc. v. Wilkins

Supreme Court of Mississippi, 1939.
184 Miss. 483, 186 So. 625.

[The plaintiff, a guest in the defendant's hotel, received a cut on his forehead from a piece of glass that fell from a broken transom when the plaintiff opened the door. There was evidence that the condition of disrepair had existed long enough to charge defendant with notice of it. The wound did not heal, and two years after the injury plaintiff went to a specialist in skin diseases, who found that at the point of the injury a skin cancer had developed, which was not fully cured at the time of the trial, some three years after the original injury. The defendant appeals a jury verdict for the plaintiff.]

GRIFFITH, JUSTICE. * * * Appellant requested an instruction to the effect that the cancer or any prolongation of the trouble on account thereof should not be taken into consideration by the jury, but this instruction was refused.

Two physicians or medical experts, and only two, were introduced as witnesses, and both were specialists in skin diseases and dermal traumatisms. One testified that it was possible that a trauma such as appellee suffered upon his temple, could or would cause a skin cancer at the point of injury, but that the chances that such a result would ensue from such a cause would be only one out of one hundred cases. The other testified that there is no causal connection whatever between trauma and cancer, and went on to illustrate that if there were such a connection nearly every person of mature age would be suffering from cancer. * * *

There is one heresy in the judicial forum which appears to be Hydraheaded, and although cut off again and again, has the characteristic of an endless renewal. That heresy is that proof that a past event possibly happened, or that a certain result was possibly caused by a past event, is sufficient, in probative force to take the question to a jury. Such was never the law in this state, and we are in accord with almost all of the other common-law states. * * * It is not enough that negligence of one person and injury to another coexisted, but the injury must have been caused by the negligence. Post hoc ergo propter hoc is not sound as evidence or argument. Nor is it sufficient for a plaintiff, seeking recovery for alleged negligence by another toward the plaintiff, to show a possibility that the injury complained of was caused by negligence. Possibilities will not sustain a verdict. It must have a better foundation. * * *

Taking the medical testimony in this case in the strongest light in which it could be reasonably interpreted in behalf of the plaintiff, this testimony is that as a possibility a skin cancer could be caused by an injury such as here happened, but as a probability the physicians were in agreement that there was or is no such a probability.

And the medical testimony is conclusive on both judge and jury in this case. That testimony is undisputed that after long and anxious years of research the exact cause of cancer remains unknown—there is no dependably known origin to which it can be definitely traced or ascribed. If, then, the cause be unknown to all those who have devoted their lives to a study of the subject, it is wholly beyond the range of the common experience and observation of judges and jurors, and in such a case medical testimony when undisputed, as here, must be accepted and acted upon in the same manner as is other undisputed evidence; otherwise the jury would be allowed to resort to and act upon nothing else than the proposition post hoc ergo propter hoc, which, as already mentioned, this Court has long ago rejected as unsound, whether as evidence or as argument.

In all other than the exceptional cases now to be mentioned, the testimony of medical experts, or other experts, is advisory only; but we repeat that where the issue is one which lies wholly beyond the range of the experience or observation of laymen and of which they can have no appreciable knowledge, courts and juries must of necessity depend upon and accept the undisputed testimony of reputable specialists, else there would be no substantial foundation upon which to rest a conclusion. * * *

Affirmed as to liability; reversed and remanded on the issue of the amount of the damages [in allowing recovery for the skin cancer in addition to the original cut on the forehead].

NOTES AND QUESTIONS

1. Why not decide this case on the basis of Reynolds v. Texas & Pacific Ry. Co.? How much is proved by the fact that, out of a good many square inches of skin on the human body, the cancer developed at the exact point of the unhealed cut? Compare Emery v. Tilo Roofing Co., 89 N.H. 165, 195 A. 409 (1937), where a fire started at a place on a roof where workmen had been smoking cigarettes, shortly after they had left it. The court upheld the jury's verdict, finding that the most probable possibility was that the fire was caused by a cigarette stub. A woman develops a rare and fatal lung disease after taking an overdose of a drug that had been negligently prescribed by her doctor. The lung disease had not been linked to exposure to the drug in any other patient; very few women had ever received such a high dose. Her expert testified that the onset and

progression of her symptoms matched those of others who had developed the lung disease when exposed to other drugs (mainly chemotherapy) known to induce pulmonary disease. She had been exposed to no other known causes of the lung disease. Is this enough to prove causation? Zuchowicz v. United States, 140 F.3d 381, 390 (2d Cir.1998) (applying Connecticut law in a Federal Tort Claims Act case) (upholding trial court judge's finding of causation based on expert's testimony).

2. In a medical malpractice case, the plaintiff's expert is prepared to testify that the cause of plaintiff's injury was the mobilization of her esophagus during surgery. Defendant's experts would testify that there are several possible causes for the injury, the least likely of which is the mobilization. Should the judge permit the defendants' experts to testify since they are expressing their opinions in terms of "possibility" rather than "probability"? Wilder v. Eberhart, 977 F.2d 673 (1st Cir. 1992) (applying New Hampshire law) (defendants' experts should have been permitted to testify because defendant need not prove another cause, only persuade the trier of fact that the plaintiff's putative cause was not the probable cause). See also Stinson v. England, 69 Ohio St.3d 451, 633 N.E.2d 532 (1994) (even though cause espoused by defendant's expert had a likelihood of less than fifty percent, it had a greater likelihood than the theory proposed by plaintiff's expert); Williams v. 8th Judicial Dist. Crt. of Nevada, 262 P.3d 360 (Nev. 2011) (because defense expert is seeking to controvert a key element of the plaintiff's prima facie case, as long as his or her alternative causation theory or theories are competent and supported by relevant evidence or research, they need not be stated as being more likely than not); and Martinez v. Johns Hopkins Hosp., 212 Md. App. 634, 70 A.3d 397 (2013) (defendant hospital entitled to offer proof of negligence and causation against nonparty midwife as part of its denial of liability).

3. What if plaintiff's proof shows three possible causes of a fireball shooting out of her oven, all of which can be traced to the manufacturer, but none of which is more likely than not? Under Kentucky law, a plaintiff must isolate the cause of the injury only where an alternative cause relieves the defendant of liability. Here, all three possible scenarios traced back to a defect in the stove's design or to a component part. Thus, plaintiff's proof of causation against the manufacturer was adequate. Siegel v. Dynamic Cooking Systems Inc., 501 Fed.Appx. 397 (6th Cir. 2012) (applying Kentucky law).

4. Cases dealing with *informed consent*, pages 199–210, can present a special problem in the area of cause in fact. Assume that patient proves that doctor failed to inform him of a material risk, that the applicable standard of care (whether physician or patient based) was violated, and that the risk manifested itself. How does patient prove causation? Should plaintiff patient be able to hurdle the issue if he testifies that he would not have undergone the medical procedure if defendant physician had informed him of the risk? Sard v. Hardy, 281 Md. 432, 379 A.2d 1014, 1025 (1977), quoting Canterbury v. Spence, 150 U.S.App.D.C. 263, 464 F.2d 772, 791 (1972), ("Such a test puts the physician in 'jeopardy of the patient's hindsight and bitterness.' ") Some courts have said that an objective test is preferable, i.e., what would a prudent person in the patient's position have decided if adequately informed of the peril? Aronson v. Harriman, 321 Ark. 359, 901 S.W.2d 832 (1995) (plaintiff's failure to testify that he would not

have undergone the surgery if he had been informed of the risk of paralysis did not defeat his claim; test is what a reasonable person would have decided if adequately informed). Others have insisted that the test must be subjective in order to fully protect the underlying concept of bodily integrity. Flanagan v. Wesselhoeft, 712 A.2d 365, 370 (R.I.1998) ("The essential inquiry then is not which course of treatment the trial justice, expert medical professionals, or even a reasonable person might elect. Rather, 'the patient's right to make his decision in the light of his [or her] own individual value judgment is the very essence of his freedom of choice' "). See also Hartke v. McKelway, 707 F.2d 1544 (D.C.Cir.1983) (discussing proof problems that could arise under either objective or subjective tests).

5. Should a broadcasting company be held liable for airing scenes of violent acts on television, when those scenes may incite others to perform similar acts? See Olivia N. v. National Broadcasting Co., Inc., 74 Cal.App.3d 383, 141 Cal.Rptr. 511 (1977), cert. denied, 435 U.S. 1000 (1978) (nine-year-old girl "artificially raped" with a bottle by her attackers, also minors, who had watched a similar incident depicted in a television drama); and McCollum v. CBS, Inc., 202 Cal.App.3d 989, 249 Cal.Rptr. 187 (1988) (no liability for suicide of teenager listening to rock music that parents claimed incited suicide) (collecting cases attempting to impose liability on media defendants for inciting various illegal and violent acts). Putting aside for the moment the First Amendment issues surrounding the imposition of tort liability on media defendants, what problems in proving causation would a plaintiff encounter?

Herskovits v. Group Health Cooperative of Puget Sound

Supreme Court of Washington, 1983.
99 Wash.2d 609, 664 P.2d 474.

DORE, JUSTICE. This appeal [from the trial court's action in granting defendant's motion for summary judgment] raises the issue of whether an estate can maintain an action for professional negligence as a result of failure to timely diagnose lung cancer, where the estate can show probable reduction in statistical chance for survival but cannot show and/or prove that with timely diagnosis and treatment, decedent probably would have lived to normal life expectancy.

Both counsel advised that for the purpose of this appeal we are to *assume* that the respondent Group Health Cooperative of Puget Sound and Dr. William Spencer negligently failed to diagnose Herskovits' cancer on his first visit to the hospital and *proximately* caused a 14 percent reduction in his chances of survival. It is undisputed that Herskovits had less than a 50 percent chance of survival at all times herein.

The main issue we will address in this opinion is whether a patient, with less than a 50 percent chance of survival, has a cause of action against the hospital and its employees if they are negligent in diagnosing a lung cancer which reduces his chances of survival by 14 percent. * * *

We are persuaded by the reasoning of the Pennsylvania Supreme Court in Hamil v. Bashline, 481 Pa. 256, 392 A.2d 1280 (1978). While *Hamil* involved an original survival chance of greater than 50 percent, we find the rationale used by the *Hamil* court to apply equally to cases such as the present one, where the original survival chance is less than 50 percent. The plaintiff's decedent was suffering from severe chest pains. His wife transported him to the hospital where he was negligently treated in the emergency unit. The wife, because of the lack of help, took her husband to a private physician's office, where he died. In an action brought under the wrongful death and survivorship statutes, the main medical witness testified that if the hospital had employed proper treatment, the decedent would have had a substantial chance of surviving the attack. The medical expert expressed his opinion in terms of a 75 percent chance of survival. It was also the doctor's opinion that the substantial loss of a chance of recovery was the result of the defendant hospital's failure to provide prompt treatment. The defendant's expert witness testified that the patient would have died regardless of any treatment provided by the defendant hospital.

The *Hamil* court distinguished the facts of that case from the general tort case in which a plaintiff alleges that a defendant's act or omission set in motion a force which resulted in harm. In the typical tort case, the "but for" test, requiring proof that damages or death probably would not have occurred "but for" the negligent conduct of the defendant, is appropriate. In *Hamil* and the instant case, however, the defendant's act or omission failed in a *duty* to protect against harm from *another source*. Thus, as the *Hamil* court noted, the fact finder is put in the position of having to consider not only what *did* occur, but also what *might have* occurred. *Hamil* states at p. 271: "Such cases by their very nature elude the degree of certainty one would prefer and upon which the law normally insists before a person may be held liable. Nevertheless, in order that an actor is not completely insulated because of uncertainties as to the consequences of his negligent conduct, Section 323(a) [of the Restatement of Torts (Second)] tacitly acknowledges this difficulty and permits the issue to go to the jury upon a less than normal threshold of proof." (Footnote omitted.) The *Hamil* court held that once a plaintiff has demonstrated that the defendant's acts or omissions have increased the risk of harm to another, such evidence furnishes a basis for the jury to make a determination as to whether such increased risk was in turn a substantial factor in bringing about the resultant harm. * * *

Both counsel have agreed for the purpose of arguing this summary judgment, that the defendants were negligent in failing to make a diagnosis of cancer on Herskovits' initial visit in December 1974, and that such negligence was the proximate cause of reducing his chances of survival by 14 percent. It is undisputed that Herskovits had less than a 50 percent chance of survival at that time. Based on this agreement and Dr. Ostrow's deposition and affidavit, a prima facie case is shown. We reject Group Health's argument that plaintiffs *must show* that Herskovits "probably" would have had a 51 percent chance of survival if the hospital had not been negligent. We hold that medical testimony of a reduction of chance of survival from 39 percent to 25 percent is sufficient evidence to allow the proximate cause issue to go to the jury.

Causing reduction of the opportunity to recover (loss of chance) by one's negligence, however, does not necessitate a total recovery against the negligent party for all damages caused by the victim's death. Damages should be awarded to the injured party or his family based only on damages caused directly by premature death, such as lost earnings and additional medical expenses, etc.

We reverse the trial court and reinstate the cause of action.

[This lead opinion was concurred in by only one other judge, ROSELLINI, J. Three judges dissented, urging that the traditional proximate cause standard should be maintained. The concurring opinion of PEARSON, J., joined by three judges, differed from Justice Dore's opinion in urging that the issues should be framed by looking at the injury as the reduced chance of survival, *not* as the death as conceptualized by Justice Dore. Damages would then be calculated based on that loss.]

NOTES AND QUESTIONS

1. Washington, through the principal case, was one of the first jurisdictions to find a way to allow the plaintiff to recover in a medical malpractice case even though the plaintiff could not prove that it was more likely than not that the malpractice had caused the death of the patient. Notice that it does so by allowing the case to go to the jury as long as the plaintiff shows some reduction in the chance of survival. Some jurisdictions permit recovery in such cases only if the lost chance was a substantial factor in producing the harm. See, e.g., McKellips v. St. Francis Hosp., Inc., 741 P.2d 467, 471 (Okla.1987) ("An evolving trend has developed to relax the standard for sufficiency of proof of causation ordinarily required of a plaintiff to provide a basis upon which the jury may consider causation in the 'lost chance of survival' cases") and Pipe v. Hamilton, 274 Kan. 905, 56 P.3d 823 (2002) (holding that a 10% chance of survival satisfies the "substantial probability of survival" requirement). In such a case, how should the jury assess damages? If the jury finds that the malpractice was a substantial factor in bringing about the patient's death, does the physician pay the full amount of the wrongful death damages? That is the approach taken by some jurisdictions. See DeBurkarte v. Louvar, 393 N.W.2d 131 (Iowa 1986) (criticizing those jurisdictions that permit the plaintiff to collect the full amount of the damages).

2. Other jurisdictions have analyzed the issue by viewing the patient's injury as the loss of the opportunity for a better outcome, rather than as the death or worse outcome. In those jurisdictions, the patient is permitted to recover damages, but only a proportion of the full amount. See, e.g., McMackin v. Johnson Cty. Healthcare Ctr., 88 P.3d 491 (Wyo. 2004) (loss of chance to avoid fatal stroke attributed to defendants' negligence); Lord v. Lovett, 146 N.H. 232, 770 A.2d 1103 (2001) (loss of opportunity for substantially better outcome because defendants misdiagnosed spinal cord injury); Dillon v. Evanston Hospital, 199 Ill.2d 483, 264 Ill.Dec. 653, 771 N.E.2d 357 (2002) (recognizing and joining trend toward allowing compensation for increased risk of future injury as long as it can be shown to a reasonable degree of certainty that the defendant's wrongdoing created the increased risk); Matsuyama v. Birnbaum, 452 Mass. 1, 890 N.E.2d 819 (2008) (recognizing loss of chance as injury and

setting out steps by which jury should calculate portion of damages to be awarded as compensation); and Dickhoff v. Green, 836 N.W.2d 321 (Minn. 2013) (adopting "proportional recovery approach" in which jury is asked to determine the total amount of damages and the percentage by which the chance of a favorable outcome was reduced, with the damage award being a multiple of those numbers). In a recent opinion, almost thirty years after *Herskovits*, Washington has adopted the proportional approach and extended the doctrine to include loss of a chance of a better outcome, if the ultimate harm is some serious injury short of death. Mohr v. Grantham, 172 Wash.2d 844, 262 P.3d 490 (2011) (formally adopting the view of the *Herskovits* plurality that the injury is the lost chance).

3. Some jurisdictions have refused either to relax the traditional causation requirement or recognize a cause of action for a reduced chance of recovery. See, e.g., Kemper v. Gordon, 272 S.W.3d 146, 152 (Ky. 2009) (recognizing public policy arguments in favor of traditional causation rules and holding "there remains great wisdom in ensuring that our laws offer redress for those wronged by medical malpractice based on reasonable probabilities and substantial cause, not on chance and mere possibility"); Smith v. Parrott, 175 Vt. 375, 833 A.2d 843 (2003) (less than 50% chance of recovering from paralysis); Joshi v. Providence Health System of Oregon Corp., 342 Or. 152, 149 P.3d 1164 (2006) (loss of 30% chance of surviving stroke due to alleged delay in proper diagnosis and treatment not compensable under wrongful death act); Jones v. Owings, 318 S.C. 72, 456 S.E.2d 371 (1995) (less than 50% chance of surviving lung cancer reduced to 20% chance of survival); Fennell v. Southern Maryland Hosp. Center, 320 Md. 776, 580 A.2d 206 (1990) (40% chance of surviving acute bacterial meningitis lost due to failure to do lumbar puncture after CT Scan suggested inflammatory process); Marcantonio v. Moen, 406 Md. 395, 959 A.2d 764 (2008) (declining to revisit decision that loss of chance doctrine is not recognized in Maryland); Mich. Comp. Laws Ann. § 600.2912a(2) ("In an action alleging medical malpractice, the plaintiff has the burden of proving that he or she suffered an injury that more probably than not was proximately caused by the negligence of the defendant or defendants. In an action alleging medical malpractice, the plaintiff cannot recover for loss of an opportunity to survive or an opportunity to achieve a better result unless the opportunity was greater than 50%."); and S.D. Cod. L. § 20–9–1.1 (reversing judicial adoption of loss of chance doctrine and returning to traditional rule of causation).

4. Almost all of the loss of a chance cases involve medical malpractice. Should the doctrine extend beyond medical malpractice? Hardy v. Southwestern Bell Telephone Co., 910 P.2d 1024 (Okla.1996) (declining to extend loss of chance doctrine to negligence action against telephone company for design flaw in 911 system that made it impossible for woman to reach 911 during her husband's heart attack due to volume of calls seeking purchase of Garth Brooks concert tickets); Lowmack v. Century Products Co., 139 F.3d 890 (4th Cir.1998) (upholding trial court judge's prediction that Virginia would not extend loss of chance doctrine to negligent design claim against child car seat manufacturer); Grant v. American National Red Cross, 745 A.2d 316 (D.C. App. 2000) (upholding summary judgment for defendant who had failed to use a screening test that plaintiff alleged had a 40% chance of identifying virus in blood

transfusion because traditional "more likely than not" causation test rather than loss of a chance doctrine was applicable).

5. For a general discussion of development of this area of law, see Restatement (Third) of Torts: Physical and Emotional Harm § 26, comment *n* (2010); King, Causation, Valuation, and Chance in Personal Injury Torts Involving Preexisting Conditions and Future Consequences, 90 Yale L.J. 1353 (1981) (cited in concurring opinion of principal case); King, "Reduction of Likelihood" Reformulation and Other Retrofitting of the Loss-of-a-Chance Doctrine, 28 U. Mem. L. Rev. 492 (1998) (author's proposed reformulation of doctrine after fifteen years of its development in the courts); and Noah, An Inventory of Mathematical Blunders in Applying the Loss-of-a-Chance Doctrine, 24 Review of Litigation 369 (2005).

6. *Attorney Malpractice Cases.* Establishing causation in fact can be a substantial burden in a suit against an attorney for professional negligence. An attorney fails to file a suit for his client before the statute of limitations runs. What must the client prove besides negligence? That the client would have won the original lawsuit? The amount of the damages the jury would have awarded in the original lawsuit? That the award in the original lawsuit was collectible? See Schmidt v. Coogan, 181 Wash.2d 661, 335 P.3d 424 (2014) (noting that a majority of jurisdictions require plaintiff to prove that he would have won the case, how much the award would have been, and that the award was collectible, but agreeing with minority that defendant must plead and prove uncollectibility of judgment as affirmative defense); Paterek v. Petersen & Ibold, 118 Ohio St.3d 503, 890 N.E.2d 316 (2008) (accord, except that burden of proving award collectible is placed on plaintiffs); Akin, Gump, Strauss, Hauer & Feld, L.L.P. v. National Development and Research Corp., 299 S.W.3d 106 (Tex. 2009) (accord, and ruling that plaintiff must prove that judgment would have been collectible at time that it would have been entered). But see Vahila v. Hall, 77 Ohio St.3d 421, 674 N.E.2d 1164 (1997) (recognizing that proof of causation usually dictates that plaintiff prove merits of underlying litigation, but declining to adopt rule that plaintiff must show that she would have won and recognizing that some plaintiffs may show that they suffered the damages of a less favorable result).

7. Suppose the attorney was negligent in failing to cite to the court relevant cases that might have avoided jail for his client. What must the client prove in an action against the attorney? Compare Humphries v. Detch, 227 W.Va. 627, 712 S.E.2d 795 (W.Va. 2011) (joining the majority of jurisdictions that require plaintiff show that he is actually innocent of the underlying criminal offense); Coscia v. McKenna & Cuneo, 25 Cal.4th 1194, 25 P.3d 670, 108 Cal.Rptr.2d 471 (2001) (client convicted of criminal offense must obtain reversal of conviction or other exoneration by postconviction relief to establish proof of actual innocence in subsequent malpractice action); and Rantz v. Kaufman, 109 P.3d 132 (Colo. 2005) (client may pursue legal malpractice action against attorneys while pursuing postconviction relief, but noting that a final determination on the ineffective assistance of counsel issue might have preclusive effect in malpractice action).

8. Client company co-signed a ten-year lease on a building for one of its wholly owned subsidiaries and then later sold that subsidiary to another company. Client claims that it instructed the lawyers who represented it in

the sale to negotiate to eliminate its contingent liability for rent on the building the subsidiary was using. Lawyers failed to do so, former subsidiary went bankrupt, and client was forced to pay $2.6 million under the lease. How does the client prove that the lawyer's failure to try to negotiate the elimination of the contingent liability caused its loss? "Proof of causation is often difficult in legal malpractice cases involving representation in litigation—the vast majority of such cases—because it is so difficult, yet vital, to estimate what difference a lawyer's negligence made in the actual outcome of a trial or other adversary proceeding. [Cc] How many criminal defendants, required as they are to prove that their lawyer's ineffective assistance prejudiced them, succeed in overturning their convictions on this ground? Proof of causation is even more difficult in a negotiating situation, because while there is (at least we judges like to think there is) a correct outcome to most lawsuits, there is no 'correct' outcome to a negotiation. Not only does much depend on the relative bargaining skills of the negotiators, on the likely consequences to each party if the negotiations fall through, and on luck, so that the element of the intangible and the unpredictable looms large; but there is no single 'right' outcome in a bargaining situation even in principle. Every point within the range bounded by the lowest offer that one party will accept and the highest offer that the other party will make is a possible transaction or settlement point, and none of these points is 'correct' or 'incorrect.' " Nicolet Instrument Corp. v. Lindquist & Vennum, 34 F.3d 453, 455 (7th Cir.1994) (applying Wisconsin law). See also Viner v. Sweet, 30 Cal.4th 1232, 70 P.3d 1046, 135 Cal.Rptr.2d 629 (2003) (discussing proof issues in transaction legal malpractice cases and noting that plaintiffs may use circumstantial evidence and are not limited to the testimony of their business adversaries to prove what other or additional terms the adversaries would have agreed to).

9. Do you see parallels between the medical loss of a chance cases and the attorney malpractice cases? See Kramer v. Lewisville Memorial Hospital, 858 S.W.2d 397 (Tex.1993) (if court were to adopt the loss of chance doctrine in the context of medical malpractice action before it, "it is doubtful that there is any principled way we could prevent its application to similar actions involving other professions. If, for example, a disgruntled or unsuccessful litigant loses a case that he or she had a less than 50 percent chance of winning, but is able to adduce expert testimony that his or her lawyer negligently reduced this chance by some degree, the litigant would be able to pursue a cause of action for malpractice under the loss of chance doctrine.") (Citations and footnote omitted.)

Daubert v. Merrell Dow Pharmaceuticals, Inc.

United States Court of Appeals, Ninth Circuit, 1995.
43 F.3d 1311.

KOZINSKI, J. On remand from the United States Supreme Court, we undertake "the task of ensuring that an expert's testimony both rests on a reliable foundation and is relevant to the task at hand." Daubert v. Merrell Dow Pharmaceuticals, Inc., 125 L. Ed. 2d 469, 113 S. Ct. 2786, 2799 (1993).

I

A. Background

Two minors brought suit against Merrell Dow Pharmaceuticals, claiming they suffered limb reduction birth defects because their mothers had taken Bendectin, a drug prescribed for morning sickness to about 17.5 million pregnant women in the United States between 1957 and 1982. [Cc] This appeal deals with an evidentiary question: whether certain expert scientific testimony is admissible to prove that Bendectin caused the plaintiffs' birth defects.

For the most part, we don't know how birth defects come about. We do know they occur in 2–3% of births, whether or not the expectant mother has taken Bendectin. [C] Limb defects are even rarer, occurring in fewer than one birth out of every 1000. [C] But scientists simply do not know how teratogens (chemicals known to cause limb reduction defects) do their damage: They cannot reconstruct the biological chain of events that leads from an expectant mother's ingestion of a teratogenic substance to the stunted development of a baby's limbs. * * *

Not knowing the mechanism whereby a particular agent causes a particular effect is not always fatal to a plaintiff's claim. Causation can be proved even when we don't know precisely *how* the damage occurred, if there is sufficiently compelling proof that the agent must have caused the damage *somehow*. One method of proving causation in these circumstances is to use statistical evidence. If 50 people who eat at a restaurant one evening come down with food poisoning during the night, we can infer that the restaurant's food probably contained something unwholesome, even if none of the dishes is available for analysis. This inference is based on the fact that, in our health-conscious society, it is highly unlikely that 50 people who have nothing in common except that they ate at the same restaurant will get food poisoning from independent sources.

It is by such means that plaintiffs here seek to establish that Bendectin is responsible for their injuries. * * *

The opinions proffered by plaintiffs' experts do not, to understate the point, reflect the consensus within the scientific community. The FDA—an agency not known for its promiscuity in approving drugs—continues to approve Bendectin for use by pregnant women because "available data do not demonstrate an association between birth defects and Bendectin." U.S. Department of Health and Human Services News, No. P80–45 (Oct. 7, 1980). Every published study here and abroad—and there have been many—concludes that Bendectin is not a teratogen. In fact, apart from the small but determined group of scientists testifying on behalf of the Bendectin plaintiffs in this and many other cases, there doesn't appear to be a single scientist who has concluded that Bendectin causes limb reduction defects.

It is largely because the opinions proffered by plaintiffs' experts run counter to the substantial consensus in the scientific community that we affirmed the district court's grant of summary judgment the last time the case appeared before us. The standard for admissibility of expert testimony in this circuit at the time was the so-called *Frye* test:

Scientific evidence was admissible if it was based on a scientific technique generally accepted as reliable within the scientific community. * * * We found that the district court properly applied this standard, and affirmed. The Supreme Court reversed, holding that *Frye* was superseded by [the adoption of] Federal Rule of Evidence 702, 113 S. Ct. at 2794, and remanded for us to consider the admissibility of plaintiffs' expert testimony under this new standard.

B. Procedural Issues

* * *

[The Ninth Circuit decided the case did not need to be remanded to the trial court judge to make an initial determination of admissibility under the standard newly articulated by the Supreme Court and that the admissibility of one of the defendant's expert's affidavits, challenged by plaintiffs, was irrelevant.]

II

A. Brave New World

Federal judges ruling on the admissibility of expert scientific testimony face a far more complex and daunting task in a post-*Daubert* world than before. The judge's task under *Frye* is relatively simple: to determine whether the method employed by the experts is generally accepted in the scientific community. [C] Under *Daubert*, we must engage in a difficult, two-part analysis. First, we must determine nothing less than whether the experts' testimony reflects "scientific knowledge," whether their findings are "derived by the scientific method," and whether their work product amounts to "good science." [C] Second, we must ensure that the proposed expert testimony is "relevant to the task at hand," [c], i.e., that it logically advances a material aspect of the proposing party's case. The Supreme Court referred to this second prong of the analysis as the "fit" requirement. [C]

The first prong of *Daubert* puts federal judges in an uncomfortable position. The question of admissibility only arises if it is first established that the individuals whose testimony is being proffered are experts in a particular scientific field; here, for example, the Supreme Court waxed eloquent on the impressive qualifications of plaintiffs' experts. [C] Yet something doesn't become "scientific knowledge" just because it's uttered by a scientist; nor can an expert's self-serving assertion that his conclusions were "derived by the scientific method" be deemed conclusive[.] * * *

The task before us is more daunting still when the dispute concerns matters at the very cutting edge of scientific research, where fact meets theory and certainty dissolves into probability. As the record in this case illustrates, scientists often have vigorous and sincere disagreements as to what research methodology is proper, what should be accepted as sufficient proof for the existence of a "fact," and whether information derived by a particular method can tell us anything useful about the subject under study.

Our responsibility, then, unless we badly misread the Supreme Court's opinion, is to resolve disputes among respected, well-credentialed scientists about matters squarely within their expertise, in areas where there is no scientific consensus as to what is and what is not "good science," and occasionally to reject such expert testimony because it was not "derived by the scientific method." Mindful of our position in the hierarchy of the federal judiciary, we take a deep breath and proceed with this heady task.

B. Deus ex Machina

* * *

How do we figure out whether scientists have derived their findings through the scientific method or whether their testimony is based on scientifically valid principles? Each expert proffered by the plaintiffs assures us that he has "utilized the type of data that is generally and reasonably relied upon by scientists" in the relevant field, [c], and that he has "utilized the methods and methodology that would generally and reasonably be accepted" by people who deal in these matters, [c]. The [Supreme] Court held, however, that federal judges perform a "gatekeeping role," *Daubert*, 113 S. Ct. at 2798; to do so they must satisfy themselves that scientific evidence meets a certain standard of reliability before it is admitted. This means that the expert's bald assurance of validity is not enough. Rather, the party presenting the expert must show that the expert's findings are based on sound science, and this will require some objective, independent validation of the expert's methodology.

While declining to set forth a "definitive checklist or test," [c], the [Supreme] Court did list several factors federal judges can consider in determining whether to admit expert scientific testimony under Fed. R. Evid. 702: whether the theory or technique employed by the expert is generally accepted in the scientific community; whether it's been subjected to peer review and publication; whether it can be and has been tested; and whether the known or potential rate of error is acceptable. [c] We read these factors as illustrative rather than exhaustive; similarly, we do not deem each of them to be equally applicable (or applicable at all) in every case. Rather, we read the Supreme Court as instructing us to determine whether the analysis undergirding the experts' testimony falls within the range of accepted standards governing how scientists conduct their research and reach their conclusions.

One very significant fact to be considered is whether the experts are proposing to testify about matters growing naturally and directly out of research they have conducted independent of the litigation, or whether they have developed their opinions expressly for purposes of testifying. That an expert testifies for money does not necessarily cast doubt on the reliability of his testimony, as few experts appear in court merely as an eleemosynary gesture. But in determining whether proposed expert testimony amounts to good science, we may not ignore the fact that a scientist's normal workplace is the lab or the field, not the courtroom or the lawyer's office. * * *

We have examined carefully the affidavits proffered by plaintiffs' experts, as well as the testimony from prior trials that plaintiffs have introduced in support of that testimony, and find that none of the experts based his testimony on preexisting or independent research. While plaintiffs' scientists are all experts in their respective fields, none claims to have studied the effect of Bendectin on limb reduction defects before being hired to testify in this or related cases.

If the proffered expert testimony is not based on independent research, the party proffering it must come forward with other objective, verifiable evidence that the testimony is based on "scientifically valid principles." One means of showing this is by proof that the research and analysis supporting the proffered conclusions have been subjected to normal scientific scrutiny through peer review and publication. * * *

Peer review and publication do not, of course, guarantee that the conclusions reached are correct; much published scientific research is greeted with intense skepticism and is not borne out by further research. But the test under *Daubert* is not the correctness of the expert's conclusions but the soundness of his methodology. * * * That the research is accepted for publication in a reputable scientific journal after being subjected to the usual rigors of peer review is a significant indication that it is taken seriously by other scientists, i.e., that it meets at least the minimal criteria of good science. *Daubert*, 113 S. Ct. at 2797 ("scrutiny of the scientific community is a component of 'good science' "). If nothing else, peer review and publication "increase the likelihood that substantive flaws in methodology will be detected."[7]

Bendectin litigation has been pending in the courts for over a decade, yet the only review the plaintiffs' experts' work has received has been by judges and juries, and the only place their theories and studies have been published is in the pages of federal and state reporters. (Footnote omitted.) None of plaintiffs' experts has published his work on Bendectin in a scientific journal or solicited formal review by his colleagues. Despite the many years the controversy has been brewing, no one in the scientific community—except defendant's experts—has deemed these studies worthy of verification, refutation or even comment. It's as if there were a tacit understanding within the scientific community that what's going on here is not science at all, but litigation.[9]

Establishing that an expert's proffered testimony grows out of pre-litigation research or that the expert's research has been subjected to

[7] For instance, peer review might well have brought to light the more glaring arithmetical errors in the testimony presented by plaintiffs' experts in other Bendectin cases. See DeLuca v. Merrell Dow Pharmaceuticals, Inc., 791 F. Supp. 1042, 1048 (D.N.J.1992), aff'd, 6 F.3d 778 (3d Cir.1993).

[9] There may well be good reasons why a scientific study has not been published. For example, it may be too recent or of insufficiently broad interest. [C] These reasons do not apply here. Except with respect to the views expressed in this litigation, plaintiffs' experts have been well-published, see, e.g., Crescitelli Aff. at 3 (authored 125 formal papers, 80–100 short notes or abstracts, a half-dozen reviews, and articles concerning antihistamines and related compounds), and the opinions they proffer, if supported by sound methodology, would doubtless be greedily devoured by the machinery of peer review. A conclusion that Bendectin causes birth defects would be of significant public interest both in this country (where millions of women have taken Bendectin and the FDA continues to approve its use) and abroad (where Bendectin is still widely used). That plaintiffs' experts have been unable or unwilling to publish their work undermines plaintiffs' claim that the findings these experts proffer are "grounded in the methods and procedures of science" and "derived by the scientific method." [C]

peer review are the two principal ways the proponent of expert testimony can show that the evidence satisfies the first prong of Rule 702. Where such evidence is unavailable, the proponent of expert scientific testimony may attempt to satisfy its burden through the testimony of its own experts. For such a showing to be sufficient, the experts must explain precisely how they went about reaching their conclusions and point to some objective source—a learned treatise, the policy statement of a professional association, a published article in a reputable scientific journal or the like—to show that they have followed the scientific method, as it is practiced by (at least) a recognized minority of scientists in their field. [C]

Plaintiffs have made no such showing. * * * We've been presented with only the experts' qualifications, their conclusions and their assurances of reliability. Under *Daubert*, that's not enough. * * *

Were this the only question before us, we would be inclined to remand to give plaintiffs an opportunity to submit additional proof that the scientific testimony they proffer was "derived by the scientific method." *Daubert*, however, establishes two prongs to the Rule 702 admissibility inquiry. [C] We therefore consider whether the testimony satisfies the second prong of Rule 702: Would plaintiffs' proffered scientific evidence "assist the trier of fact to . . . determine a fact in issue"? Fed. R. Evid. 702.

C. No Visible Means of Support

In elucidating the second requirement of Rule 702, *Daubert* stressed the importance of the "fit" between the testimony and an issue in the case: "Rule 702's 'helpfulness' standard requires a valid scientific connection to the pertinent inquiry as a precondition to admissibility." 113 S. Ct. at 2796. Here, the pertinent inquiry is causation. In assessing whether the proffered expert testimony "will assist the trier of fact" in resolving this issue, we must look to the governing substantive standard, which in this case is supplied by California tort law.

Plaintiffs do not attempt to show causation directly; instead, they rely on experts who present circumstantial proof of causation. Plaintiffs' experts testify that Bendectin is a teratogen because it causes birth defects when it is tested on animals, because it is similar in chemical structure to other suspected teratogens, and because statistical studies show that Bendectin use increases the risk of birth defects. Modern tort law permits such proof, but plaintiffs must nevertheless carry their traditional burden; they must prove that their injuries were the result of the accused cause and not some independent factor. In the case of birth defects, carrying this burden is made more difficult because we know that some defects—including limb reduction defects—occur even when expectant mothers do not take Bendectin, and that most birth defects occur for no known reason.

California tort law requires plaintiffs to show not merely that Bendectin increased the likelihood of injury, but that it more likely than not caused their injuries. [C] In terms of statistical proof, this means that plaintiffs must establish not just that their mothers' ingestion of Bendectin increased somewhat the likelihood of birth defects, but that it more than doubled it—only then can it be said that Bendectin is more likely than not the source of their injury. Because the background rate of limb reduction defects is one per thousand births, plaintiffs must show that among children of mothers who took Bendectin the incidence of such defects was more than two per thousand.[13]

None of plaintiffs' epidemiological experts claims that ingestion of Bendectin during pregnancy more than doubles the risk of birth defects. * * * While plaintiffs' epidemiologists make vague assertions that there is a statistically significant relationship between Bendectin and birth defects, none states that the relative risk is greater than two. These studies thus would not be helpful, and indeed would only serve to confuse the jury, if offered to prove rather than refute causation. A relative risk of less than two may suggest teratogenicity, but it actually tends to disprove legal causation as it shows that Bendectin does not double the likelihood of birth defects. * * *

[W]hat plaintiffs must prove is not that Bendectin causes some birth defects, but that it caused their birth defects. To show this, plaintiffs' experts would have had to testify either that Bendectin actually caused plaintiffs' injuries (which they could not say) or that Bendectin more than doubled the likelihood of limb reduction birth defects (which they did not say).

As the district court properly found below, "the strongest inference to be drawn for plaintiffs based on the epidemiological evidence is that Bendectin could possibly have caused plaintiffs' injuries." * * * Plaintiffs do not quantify this possibility, or otherwise indicate how their conclusions about causation should be weighted, even though the substantive legal standard has always required proof of causation by a preponderance of the evidence. Unlike these experts' explanation of their methodology, this is not a shortcoming that could be corrected on remand; plaintiffs' experts could augment their affidavits with independent proof that their methods were sound, but to augment the substantive testimony as to causation would require the experts to change their conclusions altogether. Any such tailoring of the experts' conclusions would, at this stage of the proceedings, fatally undermine any attempt to show that these findings were "derived by the scientific method." Plaintiffs' experts must, therefore, stand by the conclusions they originally proffered, rendering their testimony inadmissible under the second prong of Fed. R. Evid. 702.

Conclusion

The district court's grant of summary judgment is AFFIRMED.

---

[13] No doubt, there will be unjust results under this substantive standard. If a drug increases the likelihood of birth defects, but doesn't more than double it, some plaintiffs whose injuries are attributable to the drug will be unable to recover. There is a converse unfairness under a regime that allows recovery to everyone that may have been affected by the drug. Under this regime, all potential plaintiffs are entitled to recover, even though most will not have suffered an injury that can be attributed to the drug. One can conclude from this that unfairness is inevitable when our tools for detecting causation are imperfect and we must rely on probabilities rather than more direct proof. In any event, this is a matter to be sorted out by the states, whose substantive legal standards we are bound to apply. [C]

NOTES AND QUESTIONS

1. Before you tackle the substantive issues in this case, make sure you understand its procedural posture. What is the question before the Ninth Circuit? What route did the case take to get to this point? What happens next in the case?

2. *Daubert* was one of the most closely watched cases on the issue of the admissibility of scientific causation evidence that has arisen in the last three decades. What courts (besides federal courts in the Ninth Circuit) are bound by the Supreme Court's decision in the case?

3. Judge Kozinski notes that judges, not trained in science, must evaluate scientific evidence. In a case that turned on the question whether the claimant's Parkinson's disease was caused by exposure to manganese, Judge Sutton explained why judges are charged with this responsibility:

> "The sort of hypothesis Dr. Carlini presented can play a valuable role both in medicine, where, if the costs of action are low, doctors may want to act on hypotheses without further support, and in science generally, where all discoveries start as untested hypotheses. From this perspective, criticizing Dr. Carlini's hypothesis for being speculative would be like criticizing a sapling for being short. Some hypotheses become scientific theories and others do not.
>
> But that is not the issue. The issue is the reliability of his opinion from a legal perspective. And what science treats as a useful but untested hypothesis the law should generally treat as inadmissible speculation. As the Supreme Court has explained, "[t]he scientific project is advanced by broad and wide-ranging considerations of a multitude of hypotheses, for those that are incorrect will eventually be shown to be so. . . . Conjectures . . . are of little use, however, in the project of reaching a quick, final, and binding legal judgment—often of great consequence—about a particular set of events in the past." Daubert, 509 U.S at 597, 113 S.Ct. 2786. . . .
>
> This is an imperfect system, to be sure. Both sides agree that Mr. Tamraz is a good man who suffers from a terrible disease; we now force him to take the chance of prevailing at trial a second time, with less evidence than before [because Dr. Carlini's testimony is excluded]. If he does not, yet it turns out ten years from now that manganese causes his disease, that result will seem unfair. But the alternative route—allowing the law to get ahead of science—would be just as unfair. Such an approach would destroy jobs and stifle innovation unnecessarily. . . . [S]ee also, e.g., Gina Kolata, Panel Confirms No Major Illness Tied to Implants, N.Y. Times, June 21, 1999, at A1 (describing how scientists concluded, after years of litigation, billions in settlements and the bankruptcy of a major manufacturer, that no evidence tied breast implants to health problems). Rule 702 at all events has drawn the line for us, and we must enforce it."

Tamraz v. Lincoln Elec. Co., 620 F.3d 665, 677–678 (6th Cir. 2010).

4. Does the court's gatekeeper function apply only to novel scientific theories? In Kumho Tire Co. v. Carmichael, 526 U.S. 137 (1999), the Supreme Court resolved a split among the circuits and ruled that the gatekeeper function applied to all expert testimony, not just scientific testimony. Thus, in that case, the trial court judge had to decide whether the opinion of a tire failure analyst was based on reliable methodology. See also Barabin v. AstenJohnson, Inc., 740 F.3d 457, 464 (9th Cir. 2014) ("Just as the district court cannot abdicate its role as gatekeeper, so too must it avoid delegating that role to the jury.")

5. Why does the opinion talk about California tort law?

6. Notice the parallel between the proposed testimony of some of plaintiffs' experts in this case and the plaintiff's expert in Kramer Service, Inc. v. Wilkins, page 282: Bendectin or a cut *could* cause the harm, not it *did* cause the harm.

7. Some courts refer to the causation analysis in toxic substance exposure cases as having two steps, proof of general causation (toxin is capable of causing the medical condition or ailment) and proof of specific causation (exposure to toxin caused this plaintiff's condition). See, for example, Terry v. Caputo, 115 Ohio St.3d 351, 875 N.E.2d 72 (2007) (adopting analysis for Ohio and collecting cases from other jurisdictions in case involving exposure to mold). Thus, in the absence of direct proof of causation, establishing causation in fact against a defendant requires scientifically reliable proof that the plaintiff's exposure to the defendant's product more than doubled his risk of contracting the disease through epidemiological studies or similarly reliable scientific testimony. Plaintiff then must show that his own exposure was comparable to that of the subjects of the studies. See, for example, Bostic v. Georgia-Pacific Corp., 439 S.W.3d 332 (Tex. 2014) (asbestos exposure case).

8. In the principal case, footnote 13 of the opinion alludes to an issue with which the courts have been struggling. In cases involving exposure to other drugs or chemicals, unlike in the principal case, there may be clear evidence that a particular substance increases the risk of harm. That is, the experts generally agree that exposure to the substance increases the incidence of a particular disease. Application of the traditional preponderance rule to such cases may result in unfairness to both plaintiffs and defendants. Do you see why? Suppose expert testimony established that the incidence of a particular birth defect in the general population was 4 births per 1000 and that it was 6 births per 1000 in the population of those exposed to a toxic substance. Assume that the testimony would show that this is a statistically significant difference. A plaintiff with a birth defect would have difficulty proving to the court that his particular birth defect was caused by the toxic substance and was not one of the four naturally occurring. (As Judge Kozinski noted, plaintiff would be unable to do that in California.) On the other hand, if the tort system requires the defendant to compensate each person born with a birth defect, the defendant is paying for three times the risk created by producing the toxic substance. See Rubanick v. Witco Chemical Corp., 125 N.J. 421, 593 A.2d 733 (1991) (adopting a broadened standard for determining the reliability and admissibility of scientific theories of causation in toxic tort cases). See also, Restatement (Third) of Torts: Liability for Physical and Emotional Harm § 28, comment *c* and Reporters' Note thereto discussing various

approaches to proving causation in toxic exposure cases. Finally, although California and other jurisdictions require plaintiff to show that the risk was doubled by the defendant's conduct, this use of the statistic to establish a threshold might not meet the approval of the epidemiologists. See, for example, McIvor, The "Doubles the Risk" Test for Causation and Other Related Judicial Misconceptions about Epidemiology," in Tort Law: Challenging Orthodoxy (Hart 2013) and Restatement (Third) of Torts § 28(a), comment *c* (4) (2010).

9. Generally, a plaintiff in a tort case must establish causation by a preponderance of the evidence. In claims made in no-fault systems like worker compensation or in proceedings setting governmental safety standards, however, the burden of establishing causation may be lower than preponderance of the evidence. See, e.g., McAllister v. Workmen's Compensation Appeals Bd., 69 Cal.2d 408, 445 P.2d 313, 71 Cal.Rptr. 697 (1968) ("reasonable probability" enough to show that firefighter's lung cancer was caused by repeated inhalation of smoke during career); CSX Transp., Inc. v. McBride, 131 S.Ct. 2360 (U.S. 2011) (to establish liability under FELA, a railroad worker need not satisfy the common-law proximate cause standard but, instead, need only demonstrate that the railroad's negligence played a part, no matter how small, in bringing about the injury); and Industrial Union Dept., AFL-CIO v. American Petroleum Inst., 448 U.S. 607, 655–656 (1980) (OSHA "has no duty to calculate the exact probability of harm" or "to support its finding that a significant risk exists with anything approaching scientific certainty" in setting standards for workplace exposure to toxic substances).

3. CONCURRENT CAUSES

Hill v. Edmonds

Supreme Court of New York, Appellate Division, 1966.
26 A.D.2d 554, 270 N.Y.S.2d 1020.

MEMORANDUM BY THE COURT. In a negligence action to recover damages for personal injury, plaintiff appeals from a judgment of the Supreme Court, Queens County, entered June 21, 1965, which dismissed the complaint as against defendant Bragoli upon the court's decision at the close of plaintiff's case upon a jury trial. * * *

At the close of plaintiff's case the court dismissed the complaint against the owner of a tractor truck who on a stormy night left it parked without lights in the middle of a road where the car in which plaintiff was a passenger collided with it from the rear. From the testimony of the driver of the car the court concluded that she was guilty of negligence and was solely responsible for the collision. That testimony was that she saw the truck when it was four car lengths ahead of her and that she saw it in enough time to turn. At other points, however, she indicated that she did not know just what happened, that she swerved to avoid the truck, "and the next thing I knew I woke up. I was unconscious." Assuming, *arguendo,* that she was negligent, the accident could not have happened had not the truck owner allowed his unlighted vehicle to stand in the middle of the highway. Where separate acts of negligence combine to produce directly a single injury each tortfeasor is responsible for the entire result, even though his act alone might not have caused it. [Cc] Accordingly, the complaint against the truck owner must be reinstated and a new trial had.

NOTES AND QUESTIONS

1. As a horse-drawn street car stopped for a railroad crossing, the railroad's employee negligently raised the crossing gates, even though a train was approaching. The street car driver negligently proceeded onto the crossing without looking, whereupon the railroad employee lowered the gates, shutting in the street car on the railroad track. Passengers on the street car, seeing the train coming, stampeded in panic, and plaintiff, one of the passengers, was pushed off of the car and injured. Who is liable? Washington & Georgetown R. Co. v. Hickey, 166 U.S. 521 (1897) (upholding jury verdict against both defendants).

2. Plaintiff's horse fell into an excavation made by a traction company building a street car line and left unguarded at night. It scrambled out, and promptly fell into a second and nearby excavation, left in the street by the town authorities. After it climbed out again, and in consequence of both falls, the horse took fright and ran away. The horse was injured and the wagon was broken. The traction company and the town were acting independently. Carstesen v. Stratford, 67 Conn. 428, 35 A. 276 (1896) (each could be liable for the entire damage).

Anderson v. Minneapolis, St. P. & S. St. M. Ry. Co.

Supreme Court of Minnesota, 1920.
146 Minn. 430, 179 N.W. 45.

LEES, C. This is a fire case brought against the defendant railway company. * * * Plaintiff had a verdict. The appeal is from an order denying a motion in the alternative for judgment notwithstanding the verdict or for a new trial. * * *

[A forest fire, which originated in a bog and was found by the jury to have been caused by the negligence of the defendant, swept over a large area. It merged with another fire of independent and uncertain origin, and the combined fires burned over plaintiff's property. The defendant contends that the following instruction to the jury was in error:]

"If the plaintiff was burned out by some fire other than the bog fire, which other fire was not set by one of the defendant's engines, then, of course, defendant is not liable. * * * If plaintiff was burned out by fire set by one of the defendant's engines in combination with some other fire not set by any of its engines, then it is liable.

"If you find that other fire or fires not set by one of defendant's engines mingled with one that was set by one of the defendant's engines, there may be difficulty in determining whether you should find that the fire set by the engine was a material or substantial element in causing plaintiff's damage. If it was, the defendant is liable, otherwise it is not. * * *

"If you find that the bog fire was set by the defendant's engine and that some greater fire swept over it before it reached the plaintiff's land, then it will be for you to determine whether that bog fire * * * was a material or substantial factor in causing plaintiff's damage. If it was * * * the defendant is liable. If it was not, the defendant is not liable."

The following proposition is stated in defendant's brief and relied on for reversal:

> "If plaintiff's property was damaged by a number of fires combining, one * * * being the fire pleaded * * * the others being of no responsible origin, but of such sufficient or superior force that they would have produced the damage to plaintiff's property regardless of the fire pleaded, then defendant was not liable."

This proposition is based on Cook v. Minneapolis, St. P. & S.S.M. Ry. Co., 98 Wis. 624, 74 N.W. 561. * * * If the Cook case merely declares that one who negligently sets a fire is not liable if another's property is damaged, unless it is made to appear that the fire was a material element in the destruction of the property, there can be no question about the soundness of the decision. But if it decides that if such fire combines with another of no responsible origin, and after the union of the two fires they destroy the property, and either fire independently of the other would have destroyed it, then irrespective of whether the first fire was or was not a material factor in the destruction of the property, there is no liability, we are not prepared to adopt the doctrine as the law of this state. If a fire set by the engine of one railroad company unites with a fire set by the engine of another company, there is joint and several liability, even though either fire would have destroyed plaintiff's property. But if the doctrine of the Cook case is applied and one of the fires is of unknown origin, there is no liability. * * * [T]here [should] be liability in such a case. We, therefore hold that the trial court did not err in refusing to instruct the jury in accordance with the rule laid down in the Cook case. * * *

We find no error requiring a reversal, and hence the order appealed from is affirmed.

NOTES AND QUESTIONS

1. As plaintiff was driving his horse and wagon down a narrow road, two motorcycles, independently operated by two defendants, roared past him, one on each side. The horse took fright and ran away, and plaintiff was injured. Either motorcycle alone would have been sufficient to frighten the horse. Who is liable? Corey v. Havener, 182 Mass. 250, 65 N.E. 69 (1902).

2. A stabs B with a knife. C then fractures B's skull with a rock. Either injury would be fatal. B dies from the effect of both. Who is liable for his death? See these criminal law cases on the issue of concurrent causation. Wilson v. State, 24 S.W. 409 (Tex.Cr.App.1893); People v. Lewis, 124 Cal. 551, 57 P. 470 (1899). Should the answer be the same in criminal and tort law?

3. While plaintiff is suffering from terminal cancer, he is negligently hit by defendant's automobile and killed. How does this case differ from the

principal case and those cited in note 2? See Follett v. Jones, 252 Ark. 950, 481 S.W.2d 713 (1972). Plaintiff is standing in the path of an avalanche when defendant negligently shoots and kills him. Or plaintiff is about to embark for Europe on a ship, when defendant negligently shoots and kills him; a week later the ship runs into an iceberg and sinks with everyone on board. Is the result the same? Teenager is sitting on the top of a bridge when he leans over, loses his balance, and falls. As he fell, he reached out instinctively and grabbed a wire that brought electricity for the lights on the bridge at night. Due to defendant's negligence, he was electrocuted when he touched the wire. Evidence showed that he would have been killed or seriously injured in the fall if he had not been electrocuted. What damages did the defendant cause? Dillon v. Twin State Gas & Elec. Co., 85 N.H. 449, 163 A. 111 (1932) (jury must decide his probable future but for the touching of the live wire). See Peaslee, Multiple Causation and Damage, 47 Harv.L.Rev. 1127 (1934); King, Causation, Valuation and Chance in Personal Injury Torts Involving Preexisting Conditions and Future Consequences, 90 Yale L.J. 1353 (1981); Stapleton, Choosing What We Mean by "Causation" in the Law, 73 Mo. L.Rev. 433 (2008).

4. The "substantial factor" test would retain "but for" causation as an essential precondition except in situations, such as the principal case, in which two or more actively operating forces, for only one of which the defendant was responsible, combine to bring about the harm, while each alone would have been sufficient to bring about the harm. See Restatement (Second) of Torts §§ 431–433 (1965) and Restatement (Third) of Torts: Liability for Physical and Emotional Harm §§ 27 and 36 (2010). "Substantial factor" was taken by the trial judge in the *Anderson* case from an article by Jeremiah Smith, Legal Cause in Actions of Tort, 25 Harv.L.Rev. 103, 223, 229 (1911). It obviously has the advantage of eliminating cases in which the defendant has made a proved, but insignificant, contribution to the result—as where he throws a lighted match into a forest fire. See generally Fischer, Causation in Fact in Omission Cases, 1992 Utah L.Rev. 1335 (discussing difficult proof problems in cases involving a party's failure to act to prevent harm).

5. California has clarified the use of the "but for" test and "substantial factor" test in its jury instructions, noting that the "but for" test remains operable for all negligence cases except those involving concurrent independent causes, where the "substantial factor" test should be used. Viner v. Sweet, 30 Cal.4th 1232, 70 P.3d 1046, 135 Cal.Rptr.2d 629 (2003). Virginia has disapproved, in a mesothelioma case, the use of the term "substantial contributing factor," noting that jurors might hear it either to require something just more than *de minimus* or to require a higher than the ordinary standard of proof. Ford Motor Co. v. Boomer, 285 Va. 141, 736 S.E.2d 724, 732 (2013) ("The exposure must have been 'a' sufficient cause: if more than one party caused a sufficient exposure, each is responsible. Other sufficient causes, whether innocent or arising from negligence, do not provide a defense.")

6. A number of defendants spew pollution into the air and damage plaintiffs' property, but plaintiffs cannot show which defendant caused what damage. How do plaintiffs establish the causal link between each defendant's conduct and their injuries? Cf. Michie v. Great Lakes, 495 F.2d 213 (6th Cir. 1974) (applying Michigan tort law in a nuisance case). Over

his forty-year career as a pipe fitter at a shipyard in Baltimore, worker was exposed to many different types of products containing asbestos manufactured by many different defendants. What evidence does he have to produce against each defendant so that a reasonable jury could conclude exposure to that defendant's product was a substantial factor in bringing about his asbestosis? See Lohrmann v. Pittsburgh Corning Corp., 782 F.2d 1156, 1162 (4th Cir. 1986) (applying Maryland law) ("To support a reasonable inference of substantial causation from circumstantial evidence, there must be evidence of exposure to a specific product on a regular basis over some extended period of time in proximity to where the plaintiff actually worked.") Many jurisdictions use this frequency, regularity, proximity test in toxic exposure cases involving multiple possible defendants and substances for evaluating whether the plaintiff can survive a motion for summary judgment or for a directed verdict and get his case before the jury. See, for example, Holcomb v. Georgia Pacific, LLC, 289 P.3d 188 (Nev. 2012) and Smith v. Union Carbide Corp., 130 So.3d 66 (Miss. 2013). Worker's job is to clean and recondition fifty-five gallon drums that had been used to transport petroleum products and other chemicals. Neither his employer nor the owners of the drums warned him of the risks associated with inhaling fumes from the drums. He developed stomach and liver cancer. His expert witness will testify that several of the chemicals to which he was exposed are carcinogens, each of which could have caused his cancer. Should the frequency, regularity, proximity test be extended to this situation? James v. Bessemer Processing Co., Inc., 155 N.J. 279, 714 A.2d 898 (1998) (yes). What if there is only one of the defendants before the court? Should that defendant be able to introduce evidence that plaintiff was exposed to the asbestos products of others who are not present? Nolan v. Weil-McLain, 233 Ill.2d 416, 331 Ill.Dec. 140, 910 N.E.2d 549 (2009) (sending back for a new trial because trial court had excluded evidence of exposure caused by non-parties that defendant sought to introduce to show that it was not a substantial factor in causing plaintiff's mesothelioma).

4. PROBLEMS IN DETERMINING WHICH PARTY CAUSED THE HARM

Summers v. Tice

Supreme Court of California, 1948.
33 Cal.2d 80, 199 P.2d 1.

Actions by Charles A. Summers against Harold W. Tice and against Ernest Simonson for negligently shooting plaintiff while hunting. From judgments for plaintiff, defendants appeal, and the appeals were consolidated pursuant to stipulation.

[Plaintiff and the two defendants were members of a hunting party. Both defendants negligently fired, at the same time, at a quail and in the plaintiff's direction. Plaintiff was struck in the eye by a shot from one gun. There was no other satisfactory evidence.]

CARTER, J. * * * The problem presented in this case is whether the judgment against both defendants may stand. It is argued by defendants that they are not joint tort feasors, and thus jointly and severally liable, as they were not acting in concert, and that there is not sufficient evidence to show which defendant was guilty of the negligence which caused the injuries—the shooting by Tice or that by Simonson. * * * The one shot that entered plaintiff's eye was the major factor in assessing damages and that shot could not have come from the gun of both defendants. It was from one or the other only.

It has been held that where a group of persons are on a hunting party, or otherwise engaged in the use of firearms, and two of them are negligent in firing in the direction of a third person who is injured thereby, both of those so firing are liable for the injury suffered by the third person, although the negligence of only one of them could have caused the injury. * * *

These cases speak of the action of defendants as being in concert as the ground of decision, yet it would seem they are straining that concept and the more reasonable basis appears in Oliver v. Miles, 144 Miss. 852, 110 So. 666. There two persons were hunting together. Both shot at some partridges and in so doing shot across the highway injuring plaintiff who was traveling on it. The court stated they were acting in concert and thus both were liable. The court then stated: "We think that * * * each is liable for the resulting injury to the boy, although no one can say definitely who actually shot him. *To hold otherwise would be to exonerate both from liability, although each was negligent, and the injury resulted from such negligence.*" [Emphasis added.] * * *

When we consider the relative position of the parties and the results that would flow if plaintiff was required to pin the injury on one of the defendants only, a requirement that the burden of proof on that subject be shifted to defendants becomes manifest. They are both wrongdoers—both negligent toward plaintiff. They brought about a situation where the negligence of one of them injured the plaintiff, hence it should rest with them each to absolve himself if he can. The injured party has been placed by defendants in the unfair position of pointing to which defendant caused the harm. If one can escape the other may also and plaintiff is remediless. Ordinarily defendants are in a far better position to offer evidence to determine which one caused the injury. This reasoning has recently found favor in this Court. * * *

[T]he same reasons of policy and justice shift the burden to each of defendants to absolve himself if he can—relieving the wronged person of the duty of apportioning the injury to a particular defendant, apply here where we are concerned with whether plaintiff is required to supply evidence for the apportionment of damages. If defendants are independent tort feasors and thus each liable for the damage caused by him alone, and, at least, where the matter of apportionment is incapable of proof, the innocent wronged party should not be deprived of his right to redress. The wrongdoers should be left to work out between themselves any apportionment. * * *

The judgment is affirmed.

NOTES AND QUESTIONS

1. In accord, on similar facts, Cook v. Lewis, [1952] 1 Dom.L.Rep. 1, [1951] S.C.Rep. 830. The Restatement (Second) of Torts § 433B and

Restatement (Third) of Torts: Liability for Physical and Emotional Harm § 28(b) have approved the rule. But see Leuer v. Johnson, 450 N.W.2d 363 (Minn. 1990) (on similar facts, granting summary judgment to defendants because plaintiff could not prove that it was more likely than not that either had been the one whose shot hit him).

2. As plaintiff got out of her car to purchase some tomatoes, she was approached by two dogs, both of which barked and snapped at her. Trying to get away and return to her car, she turned her back and was bitten by one of them. The incident took place on the common driveway between the homes of next door neighbors who allowed their two dogs, which were of similar size and appearance, to run freely between their two properties. Plaintiff filed suit against both dog owners, but is unable to identify which dog bit her. Should the trial court judge enter summary judgment for the owners? Hood v. Hagler, 606 P.2d 548 (Okla.1979) (court relied upon principal case to shift burden of proof to defendant owners to prove that his dog was not the one.) Suppose the defendants produce evidence that the neighbor across the street has two dogs of a similar breed that they have had to chase away from their property on numerous occasions? Which parties should have to prove what?

3. Two automobiles, negligently driven by A and B, collide. Immediately, a car negligently driven by C piles into the wreck. Somewhere in the process plaintiff, a passenger in A's car, is killed. There is no other evidence. What result? Cummings v. Kendall, 41 Cal.App.2d 549, 107 P.2d 282 (1940); Murphy v. Taxicabs of Louisville, Inc., 330 S.W.2d 395 (Ky.1959). See also Restatement (Third) of Torts: Liability for Physical and Emotional Harm § 28 comment *k*, illustration 10. (Jury should be instructed that *if* it finds the injury was the result of both collisions, all defendants would be liable for the entirety of the harm. If it finds that injury was the result of one collision, burden shifts to each defendant to prove his negligence was not the cause. If no defendant can meet his burden of proof, the defendants are all liable.)

4. Should it make any difference in the principal case if plaintiff sues only one defendant, without joining the other? What if there had been ten hunters in the principal case and plaintiff only joined two?

Sindell v. Abbott Laboratories

Supreme Court of California, 1980.
26 Cal.3d 588, 607 P.2d 924, 163 Cal.Rptr. 132, cert. denied, 449 U.S. 912, 101 S.Ct. 285, 66 L.Ed.2d 140 (1980).

MOSK, JUSTICE. This case involves a complex problem both timely and significant: may a plaintiff, injured as the result of a drug administered to her mother during pregnancy, who knows the type of drug involved but cannot identify the manufacturer of the precise product, hold liable for her injuries a maker of a drug produced from an identical formula?

[Plaintiff alleged that her mother ingested a drug, diethylstilbestrol (DES), which was marketed by the defendants, five drug companies. The drug also was marketed by approximately 195 other companies, not joined as defendants. The drug, a synthetic estrogen, was given to plaintiff's mother while she was pregnant with plaintiff to prevent miscarriage. Plaintiff, now an adult, alleged that she developed cancer as a result of her exposure to the drug. She also indicated that she could not identify the manufacturer of the drug. The trial court dismissed the action.

This court held that (1) Summers v. Tice did not apply because not all the defendants were before the court, and (2) there was no "concert of action" among the defendants. See page 303].

A third theory upon which plaintiff relies is the concept of industry-wide liability, or according to the terminology of the parties, "enterprise liability." This theory was suggested in Hall v. E.I. Du Pont De Nemours & Co., Inc. (E.D.N.Y.1972) 345 F.Supp. 353. In that case, plaintiffs were 13 children injured by the explosion of blasting caps in 12 separate incidents which occurred in 10 different states between 1955 and 1959. The defendants were six blasting cap manufacturers, comprising virtually the entire blasting cap industry in the United States, and their trade association. There were, however, a number of Canadian blasting cap manufacturers which could have supplied the caps. The gravamen of the complaint was that the practice of the industry of omitting a warning on individual blasting caps and of failing to take other safety measures created an unreasonable risk of harm, resulting in the plaintiffs' injuries. The complaint did not identify a particular manufacturer of a cap which caused a particular injury.

The court reasoned as follows: there was evidence that defendants, acting independently, had adhered to an industry-wide standard with regard to the safety features of blasting caps, that they had in effect delegated some functions of safety investigation and design, such as labelling, to their trade association, and that there was industry-wide cooperation in the manufacture and design of blasting caps. In these circumstances, the evidence supported a conclusion that all the defendants jointly controlled the risk. Thus, if plaintiffs could establish by a preponderance of the evidence that the caps were manufactured by one of the defendants, the burden of proof as to causation would shift to all the defendants. The court noted that this theory of liability applied to industries composed of a small number of units, and that what would be fair and reasonable with regard to an industry of five or ten producers might be manifestly unreasonable if applied to a decentralized industry composed of countless small producers. * * *

We decline to apply this theory in the present case. At least 200 manufacturers produced DES; *Hall*, which involved 6 manufacturers representing the entire blasting cap industry in the United States, cautioned against application of the doctrine espoused therein to a large number of producers. (345 F.Supp. at p. 378.)

Moreover in *Hall,* the conclusion that the defendants jointly controlled the risk was based upon allegations that they had delegated some functions relating to safety to a trade association. There are no such allegations here, and we have concluded above that plaintiff has failed to allege liability on a concert of action theory. * * *

If we were confined to the theories of *Summers* and *Hall,* we would be constrained to hold that the judgment must be sustained. Should we require that plaintiff identify the manufacturer which supplied the DES used by her mother or that all DES manufacturers be joined in the action, she would effectively be precluded from any recovery. As defendants candidly admit, there is little likelihood that all the manufacturers who made DES at the time in question are still in business or that they are subject to the jurisdiction of the California courts. There are, however, forceful arguments in favor of holding that plaintiff has a cause of action.

In our contemporary complex industrialized society, advances in science and technology create fungible goods which may harm consumers and which cannot be traced to any specific producer. The response of the courts can be either to adhere rigidly to prior doctrine, denying recovery to those injured by such products, or to fashion remedies to meet these changing needs. * * *

The most persuasive reason for finding plaintiff states a cause of action is that advanced in *Summers*: as between an innocent plaintiff and negligent defendants, the latter should bear the cost of the injury. Here, as in *Summers,* plaintiff is not at fault in failing to provide evidence of causation, and although the absence of such evidence is not attributable to the defendants either, their conduct in marketing a drug the effects of which are delayed for many years played a significant role in creating the unavailability of proof.

From a broader policy standpoint, defendants are better able to bear the cost of injury resulting from the manufacture of a defective product. As was said by Justice Traynor in *Escola* [v. Coca Cola Bottling Co.], "[t]he cost of an injury and the loss of time or health may be an overwhelming misfortune to the person injured, and a needless one, for the risk of injury can be insured by the manufacturer and distributed among the public as a cost of doing business." (24 Cal.2d 462, 150 P.2d 441; see also Rest.2d Torts, § 402A, comment *c*, 349–350.) The manufacturer is in the best position to discover and guard against defects in its products and to warn of harmful effects; thus, holding it liable for defects and failure to warn of harmful effects will provide an incentive to product safety. [Cc] These considerations are particularly significant where medication is involved, for the consumer is virtually helpless to protect himself from serious, sometimes permanent, sometimes fatal, injuries caused by deleterious drugs.

Where, as here, all defendants produced a drug from an identical formula and the manufacturer of the DES which caused plaintiff's injuries cannot be identified through no fault of plaintiff, a modification of the rule of *Summers* is warranted. As we have seen, an undiluted *Summers* rationale is inappropriate to shift the burden of proof of causation to defendants because if we measure the chance that any particular manufacturer supplied the injury-causing product by the number of producers of DES, there is a possibility that none of the five defendants in this case produced the offending substance and that the responsible manufacturer, not named in the action, will escape liability.

But we approach the issue of causation from a different perspective: we hold it to be reasonable in the present context to measure the likelihood that any of the defendants supplied the product which allegedly injured plaintiff by the percentage which the DES sold by each of them for the purpose of preventing miscarriage bears to the entire production of the drug sold by all for that purpose. Plaintiff asserts in her briefs that Eli Lilly and Company and 5 or 6 other companies produced 90 percent of the DES marketed. If at trial this is established to be the fact, then there is a corresponding likelihood that this comparative handful of producers manufactured the DES which caused plaintiff's injuries, and only a 10 percent likelihood that the offending producer would escape liability.

If plaintiff joins in the action the manufacturers of a substantial share of the DES which her mother might have taken, the injustice of shifting the burden of proof to defendants to demonstrate that they could not have made the substance which injured plaintiff is significantly diminished. * * *

RULE

The presence in the action of a substantial share of the appropriate market also provides a ready means to apportion damages among the defendants. Each defendant will be held liable for the proportion of the judgment represented by its share of that market unless it demonstrates that it could not have made the product which caused plaintiff's injuries. * * *

Under this approach, each manufacturer's liability would approximate its responsibility for the injuries caused by its own products. Some minor discrepancy in the correlation between market share and liability is inevitable; therefore, a defendant may be held liable for a somewhat different percentage of the damage than its share of the appropriate market would justify. It is probably impossible, with the passage of time, to determine market share with mathematical exactitude. * * * As we said in *Summers* with regard to the liability of independent tortfeasors, where a correct division of liability cannot be made "the trier of fact may make it the best it can." (33 Cal.2d at 88, 199 P.2d at 5.)

We are not unmindful of the practical problems involved in defining the market and determining market share, but these are largely matters of proof which properly cannot be determined at the pleading stage of these proceedings. Defendants urge that it would be both unfair and contrary to public policy to hold them liable for plaintiff's injuries in the absence of proof that one of them supplied the drug responsible for the damage. Most of their arguments, however, are based upon the assumption that one manufacturer would be held responsible for the products of another or for those of all other manufacturers if plaintiff ultimately prevails. But under the rule we adopt, each manufacturer's liability for an injury would be approximately equivalent to the damages caused by the DES it manufactured.

The judgments are reversed.

BIRD, C.J., and NEWMAN and WHITE, JJ., concur.

RICHARDSON, CLARK and MANUAL, JJ., dissent.

NOTES AND QUESTIONS

1. Five state supreme courts have chosen to retain in DES cases the traditional common law requirement that the plaintiff prove the identity of the tortfeasor in order to recover. Zafft v. Eli Lilly and Co., 676 S.W.2d 241,

247 (Mo.1984); Mulcahy v. Eli Lilly and Co., 386 N.W.2d 67 (Iowa 1986); Smith v. Eli Lilly and Co., 137 Ill.2d 222, 560 N.E.2d 324, 148 Ill.Dec. 22 (1990); Gorman v. Abbott Lab., 599 A.2d 1364 (R.I.1991); and Sutowski v. Eli Lilly & Co., 82 Ohio St.3d 347, 696 N.E.2d 187 (1998). See also Reiter v. Pneumo Abex, LLC, 417 Md. 57, 8 A.3d 725 (2010) (in asbestos case, noting that Maryland does not recognize market share liability) and Gianvito v. Premo Pharma. Labs., Inc., 93 A.D.3d 546, 940 N.Y.S.2d 272 (N.Y. App. 2012) (applying New Jersey law) (in DES case, finding that New Jersey does not apply market share theory of liability).

2. California and the five state supreme courts that have followed its lead and fashioned some theory to allow a DES plaintiff to recover even if she cannot identify the manufacturer of the drug that injured her have done so in a variety of ways.

A. California requires the plaintiff to bring before the court defendants representing a "substantial share" of the market. A defendant is dismissed from the case if it can prove that it did not manufacture the drug taken by the plaintiff's mother. Assuming that the plaintiff can prove her case, each of the remaining defendants is severally liable for only that portion of the plaintiff's damages that corresponds to the percentage of its share of the market. Brown v. Superior Crt., 44 Cal.3d 1049, 751 P.2d 470, 245 Cal.Rptr. 412 (1988).

B. New York has not specified how many of the defendants need to be joined in order to use a market share theory of recovery. It does not allow a defendant to exculpate itself by proving that it did not manufacture the drug taken by the plaintiff's mother. As in California, each of the defendants is severally liable for only that portion of the plaintiff's damages that corresponds to the percentage of its share of the market. There is no joint and several liability. Market is defined as the national market. Hymowitz v. Eli Lilly and Co., 73 N.Y.2d 487, 539 N.E.2d 1069, 541 N.Y.S.2d 941 (1989).

C. Washington and Florida require the plaintiff to file suit against only one defendant, with that defendant then impleading others, if it so chooses. A defendant is dismissed from the case if it can prove that it did not manufacture the drug taken by the plaintiff's mother. The remaining defendants are then presumed to have an equal share of the entire DES market and the burden of proof shifts to each defendant to prove its actual share of the market. If a defendant succeeds in proving that its actual share is less than its presumptive share, it is only liable for that portion of plaintiff's damages that corresponds to its actual market share. The remaining defendants (those unable to prove their actual market shares) have their presumptive shares adjusted upward to again reflect 100% of the market. If there are no defendants unable to prove their actual market share, and plaintiff has not joined all defendants, the plaintiff may be unable to collect the full amount of her damages. Martin v. Abbott Labs., 102 Wash.2d 581, 689 P.2d 368 (1984); Conley v. Boyle Drug Co., 570 So.2d 275 (Fla.1990).

D. Wisconsin adopted a "risk contribution theory," requiring the plaintiff to file suit against only one defendant, with that defendant impleading others. A defendant is dismissed from the case if it can prove that it did not manufacture the drug taken by the plaintiff's mother. The jury, using comparative negligence principles, assigns to the remaining defendants shares of liability based on the amount of "risk" they contributed rather than their market share. Market share is only one of several factors considered by the jury in its assessment of risk. Collins v. Eli Lilly Co., 116 Wis.2d 166, 342 N.W.2d 37 (1984).

E. Michigan recognized alternative liability (like Summers v. Tice). If plaintiff joined all possible manufacturers as defendants, the burden of proof shifted to each defendant to prove that it did not make the DES that injured the plaintiff. Any defendants unable to exculpate themselves were then jointly and severally liable, apparently on a per capita rather than a market share basis. Abel v. Eli Lilly and Co., 418 Mich. 311, 343 N.W.2d 164 (1984). Does this ruling survive the Michigan legislature's action restricting joint and several liability? See Napier v. Osmose, Inc., 399 F.Supp.2d 811 (W.D. Mich. 2005) (finding that legislature's action precludes the use of alternative liability in a case against pesticide manufacturers).

3. Suppose the plaintiff has contact with more than one state. Her mother took DES in Louisiana where she was living at the time. When plaintiff was a toddler, the family moved to Washington where plaintiff grew up and as a teenager learned that she had been exposed to DES *in utero*. Plaintiff moved to California to attend college and met her husband there and has resided there since then. In California, she learned that she suffered DES-related injuries that preclude her from bearing children. She filed suit against DES manufacturers in federal court in the District of Columbia, urging the court to apply market share liability because her mother cannot identify which DES manufacturer's drug she took. Which state's law applies? Netherland v. Eli Lilly and Co., 2006 WL 626922 (D.D.C.).

4. Most courts have declined to apply market share theories of liability outside the DES context. See, e.g., Sheffield v. Eli Lilly and Co., 144 Cal.App.3d 583, 192 Cal.Rptr. 870 (1983) (vaccine); Goldman v. Johns-Manville Sales Corp., 33 Ohio St.3d 40, 514 N.E.2d 691 (1987) (asbestos); Lee v. Baxter Healthcare Corp., 721 F.Supp. 89 (D.Md.1989), aff'd, 898 F.2d 146 (4th Cir.1990) (breast implants); Rogers v. AAA Wire Products, Inc., 182 Wis.2d 263, 513 N.W.2d 643 (1994) (wire bread cart in grocery store); Bly v. Tri-Continental Indust, Inc., 663 A.2d 1232 (D.C.App.1995) (benzene in gasoline); Skipworth v. Lead Indust. Assn, Inc., 547 Pa. 224, 690 A.2d 169 (1997) (lead paint); and St. Louis v. Benjamin Moore & Co., 226 S.W.3d 110 (Mo. 2007) (lead paint). But see Smith v. Cutter Biological, Inc., 72 Haw. 416, 823 P.2d 717 (1991) (blood clotting protein); King v. Cutter Labs., 714 So.2d 351 (Fla.1998) (sending blood clotting protein case back for full evidentiary hearing to determine whether products manufactured by various defendants were sufficiently uniform in risk of infection to justify application of market share theory); and Thomas v. Mallett, 285 Wis.2d 236, 701 N.W.2d 523 (2005) (extending risk contribution apportionment to lead poisoning case against paint pigment manufacturers). After *Thomas*, the Wisconsin state legislature limited the application of risk contribution apportionment for claims arising from exposure to products other than DES "to return tort law to its historical, common law roots." Wisc. Stat. Ann. § 895.046.

5. Those of you writing for a law review and wondering if anyone reads your efforts should know that the *Sindell* decision was based on a

student law review contribution. See Comment, DES and a Proposed Theory of Enterprise Liability, 46 Fordham L.Rev. 963 (1978).

6. Courts that have adopted one of the alternative liability theories have had to decide how many of the defendants must be before the court (all? a substantial share? one?), what the plaintiff must prove about her efforts to identify the manufacturer of the DES that injured her (nothing? some effort? due diligence?), whether a defendant can avoid liability by proving that it did not manufacture the DES taken by the plaintiff's mother (plaintiff's mother remembers round blue tablets, defendant marketed red capsules), who will absorb the shares of defendants who are not present or who are judgment proof (plaintiff? all defendants who were sued by plaintiff? defendants impleaded by other defendants? defendants who are unable to prove they were not the manufacturer?), how the defendants will share the liability (per capita? risk contribution? market share?), what the relevant market is (plaintiff's state? region where plaintiff's mother took DES? suppliers of the pharmacy at which her mother filled her prescription? all DES manufacturers? only those that made round blue tablets?).

7. The complaint in *Sindell* contained allegations of strict liability, breach of warranty, and fraud, as well as negligence. Should the underlying theory of recovery make a difference as to whether the court relaxes the traditional burden of proof for causation? See Brown v. Superior Court, 44 Cal.3d 1049, 751 P.2d 470, 245 Cal.Rptr. 412 (1988) (strict liability, breach of warranty, and fraud not available in DES market share case) and King v. Cutter Labs., 714 So.2d 351 (Fla.1998) (reiterating that market share applies only in negligence actions).

8. Compare the plaintiffs in the Bendectin litigation (*Daubert*) and in the DES litigation (*Sindell*). Both faced difficulty in proving causation under traditional negligence principles. In what ways were their proof difficulties different?

9. What if plaintiff *admits* that he did not use defendant's drug, instead taking a generic version, but claims the defendant's misrepresentations about the drug caused his injury because his prescribing physician relied upon them? In re Darvocet, Darvon, and Propoxyphene Prod. Liab. Litig., 756 F.3d 917 (6th Cir. 2014) (affirming the dismissal of misrepresentation claims because a claim for injury caused by a product must be supported by an allegation that the plaintiff was exposed to the product). See also Victor E. Schwartz et al., Warning: Shifting Liability to Manufacturers of Brand-Name Medicines When the Harm Was Allegedly Caused by Generic Drugs Has Severe Side Effects, 81 Fordham L.Rev. 1835, 1857–58 (2013) (noting that almost all courts have dismissed such claims) and pages 835 to 839.

CHAPTER 6

PROXIMATE OR LEGAL CAUSE

Atlantic Coast Line R. Co. v. Daniels

Court of Appeals of Georgia, 1911.
8 Ga.App. 775, 70 S.E. 203.

POWELL, J. * * * Cause and effect find their beginning and end in the limitless and unknowable. Therefore courts, in their finitude, do not attempt to deal with cause and effect in any absolute degree, but only in such a limited way as is practical and as is within the scope of ordinary human understanding. Hence arbitrary limits have been set, and such qualifying words as "proximate" and "natural" have come into use as setting the limits beyond which the courts will not look in the attempt to trace the connection between a given cause and a given effect. A plaintiff comes into court alleging, as an effect, some injury that has been done to his person or to his property. He shows that antecedent to the injury a wrongful act of another person occurred, and that, if this wrongful act had not occurred, the injury complained of would not (as human probabilities go) have occurred. We then say, in common speech, that the wrong was a cause of the injury. But to make such a standard (that, if the cause had not existed, the effect would not have occurred) the basis of legal responsibility would soon prove very unsatisfactory; for a *reductio ad absurdum* may be promptly established by calling to mind that, if the injured person had never been born, the injury would not have happened. So the courts ask another question: Was the wrongful act the proximate cause? * * *

NOTES AND QUESTIONS

1. "Proximate cause is deep and muddy water into which many men, wise and otherwise, have ventured." White v. Southern Ry. Co., 151 Va. 302, 319, 144 S.E. 424, 429 (1928). For the not very illuminating term "proximate," we are indebted to Francis Bacon, Lord Chancellor, who in his time committed other sins. His maxim was *In jure non remota causa, sed proxima, spectatur.* [In law, not the remote cause but the nearest one is looked to.] According to the Random House Dictionary of the English Language (unabridged edition), proximate means "1. next; nearest; immediately before or after in order * * * 2. close, very near * * * " How important is the matter of physical distance between defendant's conduct and plaintiff's injury?

2. What about nearness or remoteness as to time? In City of Brady, Texas v. Finklea, 400 F.2d 352, 357 (5th Cir.1968) (applying Texas law), an electrician was electrocuted by wires suspended from a transformer cross arm that had been negligently installed by the city over 28 years before. The court stated that "lapse of time is but one element to be considered along with all relevant facts in the case."

3. The Restatement (Second) of Torts § 431 advocated the term "legal cause" as a more descriptive term than proximate cause. Is its meaning clearer? Is it more helpful in understanding the nature of

proximate cause? Thus far, most courts have been inclined to retain the terminology of "proximate cause." The Restatement (Third) of Torts (2010) has abandoned the term "legal" cause—in part because it is not being used by the courts—and has entitled Chapter 6 "Scope of Liability (Proximate Cause)." Both terms are often used to include cause in fact, a necessary predicate to an inquiry about proximate cause. If cause in fact is not present, then there is no need to inquire whether there is proximate cause.

4. Articles, notes, and comments on "proximate cause" are legion. The topic has had a peculiar fascination for legal writers, and most of them have used it as a springboard to launch their own theories as to the proper basis of legal liability. At one extreme, there have been attempts to reduce it all to definite mechanical rules, as in Beale, The Proximate Consequences of an Act, 33 Harv.L.Rev. 633 (1920). At the other extreme, there has been a rejection of all rules, and the position that the court must decide each case according to its ideas of "justice," as in Edgerton, Legal Cause, 72 U.Pa.L.Rev. 211, 343 (1924). See also, Stapleton, Choosing What We Mean By "Causation" in the Law, 73 Mo. L.Rev. 433 (2008). Important landmarks of discussion have been books by Leon Green, The Rationale of Proximate Cause (1927); Robert Keeton, Legal Cause in the Law of Torts (1963); and Hart and Honoré, Causation in the Law of Torts (2d ed. 1985).

5. Here is an articulation of the difference between cause in fact and proximate cause from the Tennessee Supreme Court: "The distinction between cause in fact and proximate, or legal, cause is not merely an exercise in semantics. The terms are not interchangeable. Although both cause in fact and proximate, or legal, cause are elements of negligence that the plaintiff must prove, they are very different concepts. Cause in fact refers to the cause and effect relationship between the defendant's tortious conduct and the plaintiff's injury or loss. Thus, cause in fact deals with the 'but for' consequences of an act. The defendant's conduct is a cause of the event if the event would not have occurred but for that conduct. In contrast, proximate cause, or legal cause, concerns a determination of whether legal liability should be imposed where cause in fact has been established. Proximate or legal cause is a policy decision made by the legislature or the courts to deny liability for otherwise actionable conduct based on considerations of logic, common sense, policy, precedent and 'our more or less inadequately expressed ideas of what justice demands or of what is administratively possible and convenient.' " Snyder v. LTG Lufttechnische GmbH, 955 S.W.2d 252 (Tenn.1997) (citations omitted).

6. As you read the cases in this chapter, remember that proximate cause is a concept that cuts off liability even though there is cause in fact. "An actor's liability is limited to those harms that result from the risks that made the actor's conduct tortious." Restatement (Third) of Torts § 29 Limitations on Liability for Tortious Conduct (2010).

1. UNFORESEEABLE CONSEQUENCES

Ryan v. New York Central R.R. Co.

Court of Appeals of New York, 1866.
35 N.Y. 210, 91 Am.Dec. 49.

HUNT, J. On the 15th day of July, 1854, in the city of Syracuse, the defendant, by the careless management, or through the insufficient condition of one of its engines, set fire to its woodshed, and a large quantity of wood therein. The plaintiff's house, situated at a distance of one hundred and thirty feet from the shed, soon took fire from the heat and sparks, and was entirely consumed, notwithstanding diligent efforts were made to save it. A number of other houses were also burned by the spreading of the fire. The plaintiff brings this action to recover from the railroad company the value of his building thus destroyed. The judge at the Circuit nonsuited the plaintiff, and the General Term of the fifth district affirmed the judgment.

The question may be thus stated: A house in a populous city takes fire, through the negligence of the owner or his servant; the flames extend to and destroy an adjacent building: Is the owner of the first building liable to the second owner for the damage sustained by such burning?

It is a general principle that every person is liable for the consequences of his own acts. He is thus liable in damages for the proximate results of his own acts, but not for remote damages. It is not easy at all times to determine what are proximate and what are remote damages. * * *

If an engineer upon a steamboat or locomotive in passing the house of A., so carelessly manages its machinery that the coals and sparks from its fires fall upon and consume the house of A., the railroad company or the steamboat proprietors are liable to pay the value of the property thus destroyed. [C] Thus far the law is settled and the principle is apparent. If, however, the fire communicates from the house of A. to that of B., and that is destroyed, is the negligent party liable for his loss? And if it spreads thence to the house of C., and thence to the house of D., and thence consecutively through the other houses until it reaches and consumes the house of Z., is the party liable to pay the damages sustained by these twenty-four sufferers? The counsel for the plaintiff does not distinctly claim this, and I think it would not be seriously insisted that the sufferers could recover in such case. Where then is the principle upon which A. recovers and Z. fails? * * *

I prefer to place my opinion upon the ground that in the one case, to-wit, the destruction of the building upon which the sparks were thrown by the negligent act of the party sought to be charged, the result was to have been anticipated the moment the fire was communicated to the building; that its destruction was the ordinary and natural result of its being fired. In the second, third or twenty-fourth case, as supposed, the destruction of the building was not a natural and expected result of the first firing. That a building upon which sparks and cinders fall should be destroyed or seriously injured must be expected, but that the fire should spread and other buildings be consumed is not a necessary or an usual result. That it is possible, and that it is not infrequent, cannot be denied. The result however depends, not upon any necessity of a further communication of the fire, but upon a concurrence of accidental circumstances, such as the degree of the heat, the state of the atmosphere, the condition and materials of the adjoining structures and the direction of the wind. These are accidental and varying circumstances. The party has no control over them, and is not responsible for their effects.

My opinion therefore is, that this action cannot be sustained, for the reason that the damages incurred are not the immediate but the remote result of the negligence of the defendants. The immediate result was the destruction of their own wood and sheds; beyond that, it was remote. * * *

To sustain such a claim as the present, and to follow the same to its legitimate consequences, would subject to a liability against which no prudence could guard, and to meet which no private fortune would be adequate. * * * A man may insure his own house or his own furniture, but he cannot insure his neighbor's building or furniture, for the reason that he has no interest in them. To hold that the owner must not only meet his own loss by fire, but that he must guarantee the security of his neighbors on both sides, and to an unlimited extent, would be to create a liability which would be the destruction of all civilized society. No community could long exist under the operation of such a principle. In a commercial country each man, to some extent, runs the hazard of his neighbor's conduct, and each, by insurance against such hazards, is enabled to obtain a reasonable security against loss. To neglect such precaution, and to call upon his neighbor on whose premises a fire originated, to indemnify him instead, would be to award a punishment quite beyond the offense committed. It is to be considered also that if the negligent party is liable to the owner of a remote building thus consumed, he would also be liable to the insurance companies who should pay losses to such remote owners. The principle of subrogation would entitle the companies to the benefit of every claim held by the party to whom a loss should be paid. * * *

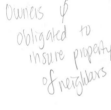

The remoteness of the damage, in my judgment, forms the true rule on which the question should be decided, and which prohibits a recovery by the plaintiff in this case.

Judgment should be affirmed.

NOTES AND QUESTIONS

1. Shortly after the principal case was decided, New York modified the rule to allow recovery of the first adjoining landowner, as distinct from the first building. Webb v. Rome, W. & O.R. Co., 49 N.Y. 420, 10 Am.Rep. 389 (1872). And then to the first property to which the fire jumps, although it is not adjoining. Homac Corp. v. Sun Oil Co., 258 N.Y. 462, 180 N.E. 172 (1932). The New York Court of Appeals has said that the *Ryan* case "should not be extended beyond the precise facts that appear therein," (Frace v. N.Y.L.E. & W.R. Co., 143 N.Y. 182, 189, 38 N.E. 102 (1894)), but on occasion the shadow of the old rule has barred a nonadjacent landowner's

claim. See Rose v. Pennsylvania R. Co., 236 N.Y. 568, 142 N.E. 287 (1923). Other courts have rejected the "first building" test. Decisions in other jurisdictions on fires spreading for a substantial distance have held the defendant liable. See, for example, Smith v. London & S.W.R. Co., [1870] L.R. 6 C.P. 14; Hoyt v. Jeffers, 30 Mich. 181 (1874); E.T. & H.K. Ide v. Boston & Maine R. Co., 83 Vt. 66, 74 A. 401 (1909).

2. At the opposite extreme from the principal case is Atchison, T. & S.F.R. Co. v. Stanford, 12 Kan. 354, 15 Am.Rep. 362 (1874), where a railroad that negligently set a fire next to its tracks was held liable to the owner of a farm nearly four miles away, to whose property the fire spread. Kansas had, at the time of the decision, many miles of uninsured grain, and its community attitude toward railroads was not necessarily the same as that of New York. Do these factors account for the difference in opinions? Is there any reason why the two states should have the same rule? What if the same railroad operates in both states?

3. Policy considerations weighed heavily in the principal case. How important was insurance? Could the defendant railroad have purchased liability insurance to cover this situation? Probably not. See Fischer & Jerry, Teaching Torts Without Insurance: A Second-Best Solution, 45 St. Louis L.J. 857, 860 (2001) (identifying 1886 as the date of the first liability insurance policy in the United States and noting that it only covered claims by employees, not claims by the general public). Should the fact that the plaintiff could have purchased accident or fire insurance be utilized to restrict the liability of a negligent defendant to consequences that are less than reasonably foreseeable? Why? The mention of "insurance" as a decisional factor in the opinion of the principal case sustained academic interest for over 100 years. For examples, see Green & Smith, No-Fault and Jury Trial II, 50 Tex.L.Rev. 1297, 1303 (1972); Smith, The Miscegenetic Union of Liability Insurance and the Tort Process in the Personal Injury Claims System, 54 Cornell L.Rev. 645, 666 (1969); and Weinrib, Causation & Wrongdoing, 63 Chi.-Kent L.Rev. 407 (1987).

Bartolone v. Jeckovich

Supreme Court of New York, Appellate Division, 1984.
103 A.D.2d 632, 481 N.Y.S.2d 545.

DENMAN, JUSTICE. On October 4, 1976 plaintiff was involved in a four-car chain reaction collision in Niagara Falls for which defendants were found liable. Plaintiff sustained relatively minor injuries consisting of whiplash and cervical and lower back strain for which he was treated with muscle relaxants and physical therapy but was not hospitalized. Subsequently, however, he suffered an acute psychotic breakdown from which he has not recovered. The theory on which plaintiff's case was tried was that the accident aggravated a pre-existing paranoid schizophrenic condition which has totally and permanently disabled him. * * *

At the time of the accident, plaintiff was a 48 year old man who lived alone in one room and worked out of a union hall as a carpenter. He was very proud of his physique and his strength, spending on the average of four hours daily at the local YMCA engaged in body building. On weekends, in order to conserve his strength, he pursued nonphysical interests such as painting and sculpture, singing and playing the guitar and trombone. Since the accident, plaintiff has been in a degenerative psychotic condition in which he is withdrawn, hostile, delusional, hears voices and sees shadows, refuses to cut his hair, shave or bathe and no longer participates in any of his former interests. In the words of his treating psychiatrist, he is "a life lost."

Three psychiatrists and one neurosurgeon testified on behalf of plaintiff. From their testimony a strange and sad profile emerged: Plaintiff's mother had died of cancer when he was a very young boy. His sister had also died of cancer. Probably as a consequence, plaintiff had developed a fear and dislike of doctors and engaged in body building in order to avoid doctors and ward off illness. His bodily fitness was extremely important to him because it provided him with a sense of control over his life so that he was able to function in a relatively normal way. * * * Because he had such an intense emotional investment in his body, his perception of this impairment made him incapable of his former physical feats and he was thus deprived of the mechanism by which he coped with his emotional problems. As a consequence, he deteriorated psychologically and socially as well. * * *

Defendants' expert, who had never seen the plaintiff, even at trial, agreed that plaintiff suffered from schizophrenia but stated that, in his opinion, it had not been exacerbated by the accident and that [he] was merely attempting to make money. The jury, who had an opportunity to see the plaintiff and hear his testimony, returned a verdict of $500,000. The court set that verdict aside stating that there was no basis on which the jury could conclude that plaintiff's total mental breakdown could be attributed to a minor accident.

We find, to the contrary, that there was ample proof in the record to support the jury's verdict. There is precedent for such determination. In *Bonner v. United States,* 339 F.Supp. 640, plaintiff was a passenger in a car which was rear-ended. She received a whiplash injury resulting in cervical spasms and lumbar-sacral strain for which she was treated with muscle relaxants and physiotherapy. She later developed numbness, headaches, hearing difficulties, inability to keep her eyes open, deteriorated personal hygiene, degeneration in appearance, facial tics and jerking and twitching of her head, all of which were determined to be of a psychological rather than neurological origin. The psychiatric testimony established that she had a pre-existing underlying psychotic illness with which she was able to cope until the accident but that the accident had precipitated a chronic psychosis which was totally disabling.

In *Steinhauser v. Hertz Corp.,* 421 F.2d 1169 (2d Cir.), plaintiff, a 14-year-old girl, was riding as a passenger in a car with her parents when it was struck by another vehicle. The occupants did not suffer any bodily injuries. Within minutes after the accident, plaintiff began to behave in a bizarre manner. After a series of hospitalizations, she was diagnosed as suffering from a "schizophrenic reaction—acute—undifferentiated." The other evidence at trial was similar to the evidence in the case before us. Prior to the accident she had a " 'prepsychotic' personality" and displayed a predisposition to abnormal behavior. * * * Nevertheless, there was testimony that, had it not been for the accident, she might have been able to lead a normal life and that the accident was the precipitating cause of her psychosis. The trial court did not allow plaintiff's counsel to elicit testimony as to whether the accident could have been an aggravating cause of her condition. In reversing a verdict of no cause for action, the United States Court of Appeals for the Second Circuit stated that the evidence made clear that plaintiff had some degree of pathology which was activated into schizophrenia by the emotional trauma connected with the accident and that she was entitled to have that issue fairly weighed by a jury.

The circumstances of those cases as well as those of the case before us illustrate the truth of the old axiom that a defendant must take a plaintiff as he finds him and hence may be held liable in damages for aggravation of a pre-existing illness (see *McCahill v. New York Transp. Co.*, 201 N.Y. 221, 94 N.E. 616). Nor may defendants avail themselves of the argument that plaintiff should be denied recovery because his condition might have occurred even without the accident. [Cc]

The record presents ample evidence that plaintiff, although apparently suffering from a quiescent psychotic illness, was able to function in a relatively normal manner but that this minor accident aggravated his schizophrenic condition leaving him totally and permanently disabled.

Accordingly, the order should be reversed and the jury's verdict reinstated.

Order unanimously reversed with costs, motion denied and verdict reinstated.

NOTES AND QUESTIONS

1. One of the illustrations running through the English cases, originating in Dulieu v. White, [1901] 2 K.B. 669, 679, is that of the man with the thin skull, who suffers death when an ordinary man would have had only a bump on the head. It is thus often referred to as the "eggshell skull" doctrine.

2. The courts are agreed upon the rule stated in this case when unforeseeable consequences follow from a *physical* injury to the person of the plaintiff. Keegan v. Minneapolis & St. L.R. Co., 76 Minn. 90, 78 N.W. 965 (1899) (death from inflammation of the heart resulting from a sprained ankle); Ominsky v. Charles Weinhagen & Co., 113 Minn. 422, 129 N.W. 845 (1911) (loss of hair from fright); Thompson v. Lupone, 135 Conn. 236, 62 A.2d 861 (1948) (obesity delayed recovery from normal period of two weeks to eight months: "The defendants took her as they found her"); Fuller v. Merten, 173 Or.App. 592, 22 P.3d 1221 (2001) (plaintiff's neck fractured in collision because osteoporosis had rendered her bones brittle and more susceptible to injury). See also Restatement (Third) of Torts: Liability for Physical and Emotional Harm § 31 (2010): When an actor's tortious conduct causes harm to a person that, because of a preexisting physical or mental condition or other characteristics of the person, is of a greater magnitude or different type than might reasonably be expected, the actor is nevertheless subject to liability for all such harm to the person.

3. A few courts have limited the doctrine to pre-existing *physical* conditions. Munn v. Algee, 924 F.2d 568, 576 (5th Cir.1991) (stating that

Mississippi has applied the "eggshell skull" rule only to pre-existing physical conditions and declining to extend its scope to cover the plaintiff's religious beliefs, which had prevented her from undergoing a blood transfusion); Ragin v. Harry Macklowe Real Estate Co., 6 F.3d 898 (2d Cir.1993) (in housing discrimination case, upholding the trial court judge's decision not to consider as part of emotional damages the effect of the discrimination in light of plaintiffs' past traumatic experiences with race discrimination). Most courts, however, include the fragile psyche as well as the fragile skull. In addition to the principal case, see Steinhauser v. Hertz Corp., 421 F.2d 1169 (2d Cir.1970) (applying New York law) (schizophrenia triggered by car accident) and Malcolm v. Broadhurst, [1970] 3 All E.R. 508, 511 (Q.B.D.) ("there is no difference in principle between an eggshell skull and an eggshell personality").

4. Note that the doctrine applies only to the proximate cause issue, not to the determination of reasonable care (negligence) or defect (strict liability). Those determinations are made in light of the ordinary person. See Vaughn v. Nissan Motor Corp., 77 F.3d 736, 738 (4th Cir.1996) (applying South Carolina law) ("The tortfeasor's duty of care is measured by the ordinary person, but the plaintiff's injuries may not be. In short, if Nissan breached its objective duty of care, it must take its victim as it finds her.")

In re Arbitration Between Polemis and Furness, Withy & Co., Ltd.

Court of Appeal, 1921.
[1921] 3 K.B. 560.

BANKES, L.J. By a time charter party dated February 21, 1917, the respondents chartered their vessel to the appellants. * * * The vessel was employed by the charterers to carry a cargo to Casablanca in Morocco. The cargo included a quantity of benzine or petrol in cases. While discharging at Casablanca a heavy plank fell into the hold in which the petrol was stowed, and caused an explosion, which set fire to the vessel and completely destroyed her. The owners claimed the value of the vessel from the charterers, alleging that the loss of the vessel was due to the negligence of the charterers' servants. The charterers contended * * * that the damages claimed were too remote. The claim was referred to arbitration and the arbitrators stated a special case for the opinion of the Court. Their findings of fact are as follows: The arbitrators found that the ship was lost by fire; that the fire arose from a spark igniting the petrol vapor in the hold; that the spark was caused by the falling board coming into contact with some substance in the hold; and that the causing of the spark could not reasonably have been anticipated from the falling of the board, though some damage to the ship might reasonably have been anticipated, and stated the damages at £196,165 1s. 11d. * * *

In the present case the arbitrators have found as a fact that the falling of the plank was due to the negligence of the defendants' servants. The fire appears to me to have been directly caused by the falling of the plank. Under these circumstances I consider that it is immaterial that the causing of the spark by the falling of the plank could not have been reasonably anticipated. The appellants' junior counsel sought to draw a distinction between the anticipation of the extent of damage resulting from a negligent act and the anticipation of the type of damage resulting from such an act. He admitted that it could not lie in the mouth of a person whose negligent act had caused damage to say that he could not reasonably have foreseen the extent of the damage, but he contended that the negligent person was entitled to rely upon the fact that he could not reasonably have anticipated the type of damage which resulted from his negligent act. I do not think that the distinction can be admitted. Given the breach of duty which constitutes the negligence, and given the damage as a direct result of that negligence, the anticipations of the person whose negligent act has produced the damage appear to me to be irrelevant. I consider that the damages claimed are not too remote. * * *

SCRUTTON, L.J. * * * The second defense is that the damage is too remote from the negligence, as it could not be reasonably foreseen as a consequence. * * * [I]f the act would or might probably cause damage, the fact that the damage it in fact causes is not the exact kind of damage one would expect is immaterial, so long as the damage is in fact directly traceable to the negligent act, and not due to the operation of independent causes having no connection with the negligent act, except that they could not avoid its results. Once the act is negligent, the fact that its exact operation was not foreseen is immaterial. * * * In the present case it was negligent in discharging cargo to knock down the planks of the temporary staging, for they might easily cause some damage either to workmen, or cargo, or the ship. The fact that they did directly produce an unexpected result, a spark in an atmosphere of petrol vapor which caused a fire, does not relieve the person who was negligent from the damage which his negligent act directly caused.

For these reasons the experienced arbitrators and the judge appealed from came, in my opinion, to a correct decision, and the appeal must be dismissed with costs.

Appeal dismissed.

[The concurring opinion of WARRINGTON, L.J., is omitted.]

NOTES AND QUESTIONS

1. The "rule" of this case has had considerable support in the United States. See, e.g., Christianson v. Chicago, St. P., M. & O.R. Co., 67 Minn. 94, 69 N.W. 640 (1896) ("consequences which follow in unbroken sequence, without an intervening efficient cause, from the original negligent act are natural and proximate"); Ramsey v. Carolina-Tennessee Power Co., 195 N.C. 788, 143 S.E. 861 (1928) (power company's negligently installed power line was damaged by railroad's negligent shunting of its cars on spur that caused them to derail and strike some transformers; plaintiff's intestate was a worker at a laundry who was killed by shock when he touched the laundry machine powered by that line). What is the reason underlying the rule? Is the rule similar in nature to the early common law distinction between trespass and case? See page 3. What supported that rule?

2. Was the petrol vapor in the hold an independent cause? Was the entire chain of events foreseeable? Was it negligence to start to unload with petrol vapor permeating the hold?

3. Distinguish between unforeseeability of the result that has occurred and unforeseeability of the manner in which it is brought about. It is quite generally agreed that the latter will not relieve the defendant of responsibility. A remarkable illustration is Bunting v. Hogsett, 139 Pa. 363, 21 A. 31 (1891), where negligent operation of defendant's "dinky" engine caused a collision with a train on a crossing. Just before the collision the engineer of the dinky reversed the engine, shut off the steam, and jumped. The collision jarred loose the throttle, and the engine backed up, gathering momentum, and traveled around a loop in the track the dinky was on to a second crossing, where there was a second collision with the train. Plaintiff, a passenger on the train, was injured in the second collision. Defendant was held liable. See also Colonial Inn Motor Lodge, Inc. v. Gay, 288 Ill.App.3d 32, 223 Ill.Dec. 674, 680 N.E.2d 407 (1997) (driver who negligently backed into building, severing natural gas line of air conditioning unit was responsible for explosion that destroyed building even though he might not have foreseen the exact manner in which damage from his negligent driving would occur).

4. Families of some of the victims of September 11th terrorist attacks have filed tort claims against airlines, airport security companies, and airport operators for negligently failing to prevent the attacks. The defendants argued that the terrorist acts were not reasonably foreseeable. The trial court judge denied the defendants' motion to dismiss, finding that "the crash of the airplanes was within the class of foreseeable hazards resulting from negligently performed security screening. While it may be true that terrorists had not before deliberately flown airplanes into buildings, the airlines reasonably could foresee that crashes causing death and destruction on the ground was a hazard that would arise should hijackers take control of a plane." In re September 11 Litigation, 280 F.Supp.2d 279, 296 (S.D.N.Y. 2003).

5. *Intentional Torts.* In Derosier v. New England Tel. & Tel. Co., 81 N.H. 451, 130 A. 145 (1925), the court made the following statement of policy, which has been much quoted: "In determining how far the law will trace causation and afford a remedy, the facts as to the defendant's intent, his imputable knowledge, or his justifiable ignorance are often taken into account. The moral element is here the factor that has turned close cases one way or the other. For an intended injury the law is astute to discover even very remote causation. For one which the defendant merely ought to have anticipated it has often stopped at an earlier stage of the investigation of causal connection. And as to those where there was neither knowledge nor duty to foresee, it has usually limited accountability to direct and immediate results."

This is undoubtedly true, although it has represented a general and often unexpressed tendency rather than any clear and definite lines of demarcation. There have, however, been decisions in which liability for intended injury has been carried farther than for the same injury negligently inflicted. Compare, for example, as to suicide resulting from intentional misconduct, the cases cited on page 24 in note 4D with those on pages 355–359 for suicide resulting from negligent conduct. See also Restatement (Third) of Torts § 33 (2010) (actor who intentionally or recklessly causes harm is subject to liability for a broader range of harms than the harms for which that actor would be liable if only acting negligently).

Overseas Tankship (U.K.) Ltd. v. Morts Dock & Engineering Co., Ltd. "Wagon Mound No. 1"

Privy Council, 1961.
[1961] A.C. 388.

[Plaintiff Morts Dock operated a wharf for shipbuilding and ship repairing in the Port of Sydney, Australia. The freighter Wagon Mound, owned by the defendants, was moored about 600 feet away. While she was taking on a load of furnace oil from a barge, Wagon Mound's crew left a valve open on one of the tanks and furnace oil flowed from it into the harbor. As the oil spread across the surface of the water, it came in contact with the slipways of plaintiff's wharf, and interfered with their use, thus causing minor damage, which was so slight that plaintiff made no claim for it. A few days later, the oil was ignited when cotton waste floating on its surface was set fire by molten metal dropped from the wharf by plaintiff's workmen. The fire seriously damaged the wharf and two ships docked alongside of it. The trial court specifically found that defendants "did not know and could not reasonably be expected to have known" that the oil (which was stated by counsel to have a flash point of about 170° F.) was capable of being set afire when spread on water. Judgment was given for the plaintiff, which was affirmed by the Supreme Court of New South Wales. Defendants appealed to the Privy Council, where the decision was reversed. After reviewing In re Polemis, page 320, and a number of subsequent English decisions, the Privy Council continued:]

Morts Dock after the fire

VISCOUNT SIMONDS: * * * [I]t does not seem consonant with current ideas of justice or morality that for an act of negligence, however slight or venial, which results in some trivial foreseeable damage the actor should be liable for all consequences however unforeseeable and however grave, so long as they can be said to be "direct." It is a principle of civil liability, subject only to qualifications which have no present relevance, that a man must be considered to be responsible for the probable consequences of his act. To demand more of him is too harsh a rule, to demand less is to ignore that civilized order requires the observance of a minimum standard of behaviour. * * *

[I]f it is asked why a man should be responsible for the natural or necessary or probable consequences of his act (or any other similar description of them) the answer is that it is not because they are natural or necessary or probable, but because, since they have this quality, it is judged by the standard of the reasonable man, that he ought to have foreseen them. Thus it is that over and over again it has happened that in different judgments in the same case and sometimes in a single judgment liability for a consequence has been imposed on the ground that it was reasonably foreseeable or alternatively on the ground that it was natural or necessary or probable. The two grounds have been treated as coterminous, and so they largely are. * * *

It is not the act but the consequences on which tortious liability is founded. Just as (as it has been said) there is no such thing as negligence in the air, so there is no such thing as liability in the air. Suppose an action brought by A for damage caused by the carelessness (a neutral word) of B, for example a fire caused by the careless spillage of oil. It may of course become relevant to know what duty B owed to A, but the only liability that is in question is the liability for damage by fire. It is vain to isolate the liability from its content and to say that B is or is not liable and then to ask for what damage he is liable. For his liability is in respect of that damage and no other. If, as admittedly it is, B's liability (culpability) depends on the reasonable foreseeability of the consequent damage, how is that to be determined except by the foreseeability of the damage which in fact happened—the damage in suit? And, if that damage is unforeseeable so as to displace liability at large, how can the liability be restored so as to make compensation payable?

Morts Dock was never rebuilt

But, it is said, a different position arises if B's careless act has been shown to be negligent and has caused some foreseeable damage to A. Their Lordships have already observed that to hold B liable for consequences however unforeseeable of a careless act, if, but only if, he is at the same time liable for some other damage however trivial, appears to be neither logical nor just. This becomes more clear if it is supposed that similar unforeseeable damage is suffered by A and C but other foreseeable damage, for which B is liable, by A only. A system of law which would hold B liable to A but not to C for the similar damage suffered by each of them could not easily be defended. Fortunately, the attempt is not necessary. For the same fallacy is at the root of the proposition. It is irrelevant to the question whether B is liable for unforeseeable damage that he is liable for foreseeable damage, as irrelevant as would the fact that he had trespassed on Whiteacre be to the question whether he had trespassed on Blackacre. Again suppose a claim by A for damage by fire by the careless act of B. Of what relevance is it to that claim that he has another claim arising out of the same careless act? It would surely not prejudice his claim if that other claim failed; it cannot assist it if it succeeds. Each of them rests on its own bottom and will fail if it can be established that the damage could not reasonably be foreseen. * * * As Lord Denning said in King v. Phillips, [1953] 1 Q.B. 429 at p. 441, there can be no doubt since Bourhill v. Young that the test of *liability for shock* is foreseeability of *injury by shock*. Their Lordships substitute the word "fire" for "shock" and endorse this statement of the law. * * *

[The action for damages caused by negligence was dismissed. The case was remanded to the Full Court of New South Wales for disposition of an alternative claim for liability on the basis of nuisance, since their Lordships thought that it would not be proper for them to come to any conclusion upon the material before them. The plaintiff decided not to proceed further with its claim based on nuisance, and the litigation ended with this decision of the Privy Council.]

NOTES AND QUESTIONS

1. Note that the owners of Morts Dock would have been able to recover for the damage to the property done by the oil itself if a claim had been made for that. The rule of this case has been the underlying premise of many decisions in the United States. See, e.g., Mauney v. Gulf Refining Co., 193 Miss. 421, 9 So.2d 780 (1942) ("The area within which liability is imposed is that which is within the circle of reasonable foreseeability").

2. The Restatement (Third) of Torts § 29 (2010) articulates scope of liability in these terms: "An actor's liability is limited to those harms that result from the risks that made the actor's conduct tortious." Consider each of these cases and think about whether plaintiff's harm was within risk of defendant's conduct.

A. When defendant served "foul smelling" shrimp, he risked causing patron to become ill, but not causing someone else to slip on her vomit. Crankshaw v. Piedmont Driving Club, 115 Ga.App. 820, 156 S.E.2d 208 (1967).

B. When defendant bus driver drove at an unreasonable speed in a snowstorm, he risked a collision with another vehicle, but not creating a snow-swirl that would blind another driver who followed in his wake. Metts v. Griglak, 438 Pa. 392, 264 A.2d 684 (1970).

C. When defendant manufacturer supplied a defective metal ring on a dog collar, it risked causing the owner to lose his dog, but not causing the plaintiff to be bitten by the dog. Oehler v. Davis, 223 Pa.Super. 333, 298 A.2d 895 (1972) (products liability case applying proximate cause principles of negligence law).

D. When defendant gas station employee permitted customer to pump gas while engine was still running, he risked fire or explosion but not that car would roll backward and injure plaintiff who was pumping gas at adjacent pump. Di Ponzio v. Riordan, 89 N.Y.2d 578, 657 N.Y.S.2d 377, 679 N.E.2d 616 (1997) (car left with its engine running unattended at pump while customer went inside to pay).

E. When defendant contractor improperly welded angle iron in place when installing ceiling in new wrestling room in high school, it risked injury to foreseeable occupants of room when angle iron dropped from ceiling, but not injury to high school maintenance worker who fell from ladder while trying to reinstall the angle iron. Virden v. Betts and Beer Construction Co., 656 N.W.2d 805 (Iowa 2003) (maintenance worker's fall was not a reasonably foreseeable or probable consequence of contractor's negligence).

F. When the manager of Hardwick Hall, a historic property, failed to post a warning against swimming in a pond that could be a source of Weil's disease, it risked a swimmer contracting that disease but not that the swimmer would drown. Darby v. The National Trust, [2001] EWCA Civ 189, [2001] PIQR 27.

G. When defendant day care center's negligence allowed a child to consume rat poison, it risked the child becoming ill, but not that the relatives with whom the child was residing would lose custody of the child because the child's subsequent minor bruises would become accentuated by the effects of the poison and be mistaken for the results of child abuse. Lewis v. Kehoe Academy, 346 So.2d 289 (La.App.1977).

3. Professor (later Judge) Robert E. Keeton suggested a general rule that helps to explain Wagon Mound No. 1 and other cases that espouse its approach to proximate cause. One of his three formulations of the rule is "A negligent actor is legally responsible for that harm, and only that harm, of which the negligent aspect of his conduct is a cause in fact." R. Keeton, Legal Cause in the Law of Torts, 9 (1963). How helpful is this formulation? Compare it to the rule as to violation of statutes intended to protect plaintiffs against a particular risk. See note 2B, page 223. Should the same rule apply when there is no statute, and the defendant's conduct creates only a particular risk? Or do the written law and the policy of strict statutory construction afford a reason to make a distinction?

4. The Privy Council was the highest appellate court for the Commonwealth but its decisions were only binding in the country where the case arose, so there was initially some doubt whether the case would be accepted by the English courts. This was finally set to rest in Doughty v. Turner Mfg. Co., [1964] 1 Q.B. 518, where an asbestos cement cover was

knocked into a vat filled with an extremely hot solution of sodium cyanide, which might have been expected to splash some of the molten substance upon anyone standing nearby. Although no such injuries were sustained when the cover was initially knocked into the vat, a short time later the molten liquid erupted and caused injury to the plaintiff. His recovery in the trial court was reversed, because there was no reason for anyone to expect the eruption, which was determined to have been caused by a chemical reaction between the liquid and the lid.

5. Other English decisions have made it clear that there are some limits on the requirement of foreseeability laid down in Wagon Mound No. 1. Thus the way in which the event occurs need not be foreseeable, so long as the event itself is to be anticipated. Hughes v. Lord Advocate, [1963] A.C. 837. And the rule as to the thin skull, where the particular consequences of an actual personal injury are unforeseeable, continues to be applied. Smith v. Leech Brain & Co., [1962] 2 Q.B. 405.

Overseas Tankship (U.K.) Ltd. v. Miller Steamship Co. "Wagon Mound No. 2"

Privy Council, 1966.
[1967] 1 A.C. 617.

[The accident facts are the same as in the preceding case, but this action was brought, on the grounds of nuisance and negligence, by the owners of the two ships docked at the wharf. The trial court, Walsh, J., made more elaborate findings on the issue of foreseeability, as follows:

"(1) Reasonable people in the position of the officers of the *Wagon Mound* would regard the furnace oil as very difficult to ignite upon water. (2) Their personal experience would probably have been that this had very rarely happened. (3) If they had given attention to the risk of fire from the spillage, they would have regarded it as a possibility, but one which could become an actuality only in very exceptional circumstances. (4) They would have considered the chances of the required exceptional circumstances happening whilst the oil remained spread on the harbour waters as being remote. (5) I find that the occurrence of damage to the plaintiff's property as a result of the spillage not reasonably foreseeable by those for whose acts the defendant would be responsible. * * * (8) Having regard to those findings, and because of finding (5), I hold that the claim of each of the plaintiffs, framed in negligence, fails."

Judgment for the defendants was affirmed by the Supreme Court of New South Wales, and plaintiffs appealed to the Privy Council.]

LORD REID [After holding that the count in nuisance added nothing, since it too requires proof of foreseeability, the Court turned to the negligence count.] It is now necessary to turn to the respondents' submission that the trial judge was wrong in holding that damage from fire was not reasonably foreseeable. * * *

In *The Wagon Mound (No. 1)* the Board were not concerned with degrees of foreseeability because the finding was that the fire was not foreseeable at all. So Lord Simonds had no cause to amplify the statement that the "essential factor in determining liability is whether the damage is of such a kind as the reasonable man should have foreseen." But here the findings show that some risk of fire would have been present to the mind of a reasonable man in the shoes of the ship's chief engineer. So the first question must be what is the precise meaning to be attached in this context to the words "foreseeable" and "reasonably foreseeable."

[The court here referred to Bolton v. Stone, [1951] A.C. 850, where the risk that a cricket ball would be driven out of the grounds and strike a plaintiff on an unfrequented public road was held to be "so small that in the circumstances a reasonable man would have been justified in disregarding it and taking no steps to eliminate it."]

But it does not follow that, no matter what the circumstances may be, it is justifiable to neglect a risk of such a small magnitude. A reasonable man would only neglect such a risk if he had some valid reason for doing so, e.g., that it would involve considerable expense to eliminate the risk. He would weigh the risk against the difficulty of eliminating it. * * *

In the present case there was no justification whatever for discharging the oil into Sydney Harbour. Not only was it an offence to do so, but it involved considerable loss financially. If the ship's engineer had thought about the matter, there could have been no question of balancing the advantages and disadvantages. From every point of view it was both his duty and his interest to stop the discharge immediately.

It follows that in their Lordships' view the only question is whether a reasonable man having the knowledge and experience to be expected of the chief engineer of the *Wagon Mound* would have known that there was a real risk of the oil on the water catching fire in some way; if it did, serious damage to ships or other property was not only foreseeable but very likely. * * *

The findings show that he ought to have known that it is possible to ignite this kind of oil on water, and that the ship's engineer probably ought to have known that this had in fact happened before. The most that can be said to justify inaction is that he would have known that this could only happen in very exceptional circumstances. But this does not mean that a reasonable man would dismiss such a risk from his mind and do nothing when it was so easy to prevent it. If it is clear that the reasonable man would have realized or foreseen and prevented the risk, then it must follow that the appellant is liable in damages. * * *

Appeal (of the ship owners) allowed.

NOTES AND QUESTIONS

1. What is the difference between Wagon Mound No. 1 and No. 2? Is the law that was applied different or is there a difference in the facts before the court? Do you suppose the attorneys representing the ship plaintiffs benefitted from the experience of the attorneys representing Morts Dock? How might the presentation of the case be affected by the fact that the plaintiffs are different?

2. Has *Polemis* come in again by the back door, in the guise of foreseeability of the remotely possible? Are there many events that the

reasonable person would not recognize as possible, with at least a slight degree of risk?

3. Compare the formula of Learned Hand in United States v. Carroll Towing Co., page 151. How does it relate to this case?

4. Suppose homeowners disassemble a trampoline and leave its parts in their yard about 38 feet from a gravel road at the edge of their property. A few weeks later, during the night, a thunderstorm blows the top of the trampoline onto the road. Several hours later, plaintiff, driving by, swerves to avoid the obstruction in the road. He lost control of his car and was severely injured. Should the courts consider foreseeability as part of a duty analysis or part of a proximate cause analysis? In Thompson v. Kaczinski, 774 N.W.2d 829, 839 (Iowa 2009), the Iowa Supreme Court relied upon the (then) draft of Restatement (Third) § 29 to decide that foreseeability should be part of the scope of liability analysis. That is, "when scope of liability arises in a negligence case, the risks that make an actor negligent are limited to foreseeable ones, and the factfinder must determine whether the type of harm that occurred is among those reasonably foreseeable potential harms that made the actor's conduct negligent." The court then applied that reasoning and found that whether serious injury to a motorist was within the range of harms risked by property owners' actions in leaving disassembled trampoline in yard was for the jury to determine.

Palsgraf v. Long Island R.R. Co.

Court of Appeals of New York, 1928.
248 N.Y. 339, 162 N.E. 99.

CARDOZO, C.J. Plaintiff was standing on a platform of defendant's railroad after buying a ticket to go to Rockaway Beach. A train stopped at the station, bound for another place. Two men ran forward to catch it. One of the men reached the platform of the car without mishap, though the train was already moving. The other man, carrying a package, jumped aboard the car, but seemed unsteady as if about to fall. A guard on the car, who had held the door open, reached forward to help him in, and another guard on the platform pushed him from behind. In this act, the package was dislodged, and fell upon the rails. It was a package of small size, about fifteen inches long, and was covered by a newspaper. In fact it contained fireworks, but there was nothing in its appearance to give notice of its contents. The fireworks when they fell exploded. The shock of the explosion threw down some scales at the other end of the platform many feet away. The scales struck the plaintiff, causing injuries for which she sues.

The conduct of the defendant's guard, if a wrong in its relation to the holder of the package, was not a wrong in its relation to the plaintiff, standing far away. Relatively to her it was not negligence at all. Nothing in the situation gave notice that the falling package had in it the potency of peril to persons thus removed. Negligence is not actionable unless it involves the invasion of a legally protected interest, the violation of a right. "Proof of negligence in the air, so to speak, will not do." Pollock, Tort (11th Ed.) p. 455 * * *.

The plaintiff, as she stood upon the platform of the station, might claim to be protected against intentional invasion of her bodily security. Such invasion is not charged. She might claim to be protected against unintentional invasion by conduct involving in the thought of reasonable men an unreasonable hazard that such invasion would ensue. These, from the point of view of the law, were the bounds of her immunity, with perhaps some rare exceptions, survival for the most part of ancient forms of liability, where conduct is held to be at the peril of the actor. [C] If no hazard was apparent to the eye of ordinary vigilance, an act innocent and harmless, at least to outward seeming, with reference to her, did not take to itself the quality of a tort because it happened to be a wrong, though apparently not one involving the risk of bodily insecurity, with reference to some one else. "In every instance, before negligence can be predicated of a given act, back of the act must be sought and found a duty to the individual complaining, the observance of which would have averted or avoided the injury." McSherry, C.J., in West Virginia Central & P.R. Co. v. State, 96 Md. 652, 666, 54 A. 669, 671. [Cc]

"The ideas of negligence and duty are strictly correlative." Bowen, L.J., in Thomas v. Quartermaine, 18 Q.B.D. 685, 694. The plaintiff sues in her own right for a wrong personal to her, and not as the vicarious beneficiary of a breach of duty to another.

A different conclusion will involve us, and swiftly too, in a maze of contradictions. A guard stumbles over a package which has been left upon a platform. It seems to be a bundle of newspapers. It turns out to be a can of dynamite. To the eye of ordinary vigilance, the bundle is abandoned waste, which may be kicked or trod on with impunity. Is a passenger at the other end of the platform protected by the law against the unsuspected hazard concealed beneath the waste? If not, is the result to be any different, so far as the distant passenger is concerned, when the guard stumbles over a valise which a truckman or a porter has left upon the walk? The passenger far away, if the victim of a wrong at all, has a cause of action, not derivative, but original and primary. His claim to be protected against invasion of his bodily security is neither greater nor less because the act resulting in the invasion is a wrong to another far removed. In this case, the rights that are said to have been violated, the interests said to have been invaded, are not even of the same order. The man was not injured in his person or even put in danger. The purpose of the act, as well as its effect, was to make his person safe. If there was a wrong to him at all, which may very well be doubted, it was a wrong to a property interest only, the safety of his package. Out of this wrong to property, which threatened injury to nothing else, there has passed, we are told, to the plaintiff by derivation or succession a right of action for the invasion of an interest of another order, the right to bodily security. The diversity of interests emphasizes the futility of the effort to build the plaintiff's right upon the basis of a wrong to some one else. Even then, the orbit of the danger as disclosed to the eye of reasonable vigilance would be the orbit of the duty. * * *

Scene of *Palsgraf* accident, taken a few years later but with no change in features

The argument for the plaintiff is built upon the shifting meanings of such words as "wrong" and "wrongful," and shares their instability. What the plaintiff must show is "a wrong" to herself; i.e., a violation of her own right, and not merely a wrong to some one else, nor conduct, "wrongful" because unsocial, but not "a wrong" to any one. * * * The risk reasonably to be perceived defines the duty to be obeyed and risk imports relation; it is risk to another or to others within the range of apprehension. [C] This does not mean, of course, that one who launches a destructive force is always relieved of liability, if the force, though known to be destructive, pursues an unexpected path. "It was not necessary that the defendant should have had notice of the particular method in which an accident would occur, if the possibility of an accident was clear to the ordinarily prudent eye." Munsey v. Webb, 231 U.S. 150, 156. [Cc] Some acts, such as shooting, are so imminently dangerous to any one who may come within reach of the missile however unexpectedly, as to impose a duty of prevision not far from that of an insurer. Even today, and much oftener in earlier stages of the law, one acts some times at one's peril. [Cc] Under this head, it may be, fall certain cases of what is known as transferred intent, an act willfully dangerous to A resulting by misadventure in injury to B. [Cc] These cases aside, wrong is defined in terms of the natural or probable, at least when unintentional. [Cc] The range of reasonable apprehension is at times a question for the court, and at times, if varying inferences are possible, a question for the jury. Here, by concession, there was nothing in the situation to suggest to the most cautious mind that the parcel wrapped in newspaper would spread wreckage through the station. If the guard had thrown it down knowingly and willfully, he would not have threatened the plaintiff's safety, so far as appearances could warn him. His conduct would not have involved, even then, an unreasonable probability of invasion of her bodily security. Liability can be no greater where the act is inadvertent.

Negligence, like risk, is thus a term of relation. Negligence in the abstract, apart from things related, is surely not a tort, if indeed it is understandable at all. * * *

The law of causation, remote or proximate, is thus foreign to the case before us. The question of liability is always anterior to the question of the measure of the consequences that go with liability. If there is no tort to be redressed, there is no occasion to consider what damage might be recovered if there were a finding of a tort. We may assume, without deciding, that negligence, not at large or in the abstract, but in relation to the plaintiff, would entail liability for any and all consequences, however novel or extraordinary. [Cc]

There is room for argument that a distinction is to be drawn according to the diversity of interests invaded by the act, as where conduct negligent in that it threatens an insignificant invasion of an interest in property results in an unforeseeable invasion of an interest of another order, as, e.g., one of bodily security. Perhaps other distinctions may be necessary. We do not go into the question now. The consequences to be followed must first be rooted in a wrong.

The judgment of the Appellate Division and that of the Trial Term should be reversed, and the complaint dismissed, with costs in all courts.

ANDREWS, J. (dissenting). Assisting a passenger to board a train, the defendant's servant negligently knocked a package from his arms. It fell between the platform and the cars. Of its contents the servant knew and could know nothing. A violent explosion followed. The concussion broke some scales standing a considerable distance away. In falling, they injured the plaintiff, an intending passenger.

Upon these facts, may she recover the damages she has suffered in an action brought against the master? The result we shall reach depends upon our theory as to the nature of negligence. Is it a relative concept—the breach of some duty owing to a particular person or to particular persons? Or, where there is an act which unreasonably threatens the safety of others, is the doer liable for all its proximate consequences, even where they result in injury to one who would generally be thought to be outside the radius of danger? This is not a mere dispute as to words. We might not believe that to the average mind the dropping of the bundle would seem to involve the probability of harm to the plaintiff standing many feet away whatever might be the case as to the owner or to one so near as to be likely to be struck by its fall. If, however, we adopt the second hypothesis, we have to inquire only as to the relation between cause and effect. We deal in terms of proximate cause, not of negligence. * * *

But we are told that "there is no negligence unless there is in the particular case a legal duty to take care, and this duty must be one which is owed to the plaintiff himself and not merely to others." Salmond Torts (6th Ed.) 24. This I think too narrow a conception. Where there is the unreasonable act, and some right that may be affected there is negligence whether damage does or does not result.

That is immaterial. Should we drive down Broadway at a reckless speed, we are negligent whether we strike an approaching car or miss it by an inch. The act itself is wrongful. It is a wrong not only to those who happen to be within the radius of danger, but to all who might have been there—a wrong to the public at large. Such is the language of the street. Such the language of the courts when speaking of contributory negligence. * * *

Due care is a duty imposed on each one of us to protect society from unnecessary danger, not to protect A, B, or C alone.

It may well be that there is no such thing as negligence in the abstract. "Proof of negligence in the air, so to speak, will not do." In an empty world negligence would not exist. It does involve a relationship between man and his fellows, but not merely a relationship between man and those whom he might reasonably expect his act would injure; rather, a relationship between him and those whom he does in fact injure. If his act has a tendency to harm some one, it harms him a mile away as surely as it does those on the scene. * * *

The proposition is this: Every one owes to the world at large the duty of refraining from those acts that may unreasonably threaten the safety of others. Such an act occurs. Not only is he wronged to whom harm might reasonably be expected to result, but he also who is in fact injured, even if he be outside what would generally be thought the danger zone. There needs be duty due the one complaining, but this is not a duty to a particular individual because as to him harm might be expected. Harm to some one being the natural result of the act, not only that one alone, but all those in fact injured may complain. We have never, I think, held otherwise. * * * Unreasonable risk being taken, its consequences are not confined to those who might probably be hurt. * * * An overturned lantern may burn all Chicago. We may follow the fire from the shed to the last building. We rightly say the fire started by the lantern caused its destruction.

A cause, but not the proximate cause. What we do mean by the word "proximate" is that, because of convenience, of public policy, of a rough sense of justice, the law arbitrarily declines to trace a series of events beyond a certain point. This is not logic. It is practical politics. Take our rule as to fires. Sparks from my burning haystack set on fire my house and my neighbor's. I may recover from a negligent railroad. He may not. Yet the wrongful act as directly harmed the one as the other. We may regret that the line was drawn just where it was, but drawn somewhere it had to be. We said the act of the railroad was not the proximate cause of our neighbor's fire. Cause it surely was. The words we used were simply indicative of our notions of public policy. Other courts think differently. * * *

Take the illustration given in an unpublished manuscript by a distinguished and helpful writer on the law of torts. A chauffeur negligently collides with another car which is filled with dynamite, although he could not know it. An explosion follows. A, walking on the sidewalk nearby, is killed. B, sitting in a window of a building opposite, is cut by flying glass. C, likewise sitting in a window a block away, is similarly injured. And a further illustration: A nursemaid, ten blocks away, startled by the noise, involuntarily drops a baby from her arms to the walk. We are told that C may not recover while A may. As to B it is a question for court or jury. We will agree that the baby might not. Because, we are again told, the chauffeur had no reason to believe his conduct involved any risk of injuring either C or the baby. As to them he was not negligent.

But the chauffeur being negligent in risking the collision, his belief that the scope of the harm he might do would be limited is immaterial. His act unreasonably jeopardized the safety of any one who might be affected by it. C's injury and that of the baby were directly traceable to the collision. Without that, the injury would not have happened. C had the right to sit in his office, secure from such dangers. The baby was entitled to use the sidewalk with reasonable safety.

The true theory is, it seems to me, that the injury to C, if in truth he is to be denied recovery, and the injury to the baby, is that their several injuries were not the proximate result of the negligence. And here not what the chauffeur had reason to believe would be the result of his conduct, but what the prudent would foresee, may have a bearing—may have some bearing, for the problem of proximate cause is not to be solved by any one consideration. It is all a question of expediency. There are no fixed rules to govern our judgment. There are simply matters of which we may take account. * * * There is in truth little to guide us other than common sense.

There are some hints that may help us. The proximate cause, involved as it may be with many other causes, must be, at the least, something without which the event would not happen. The court must ask itself whether there was a natural and continuous sequence between cause and effect. Was the one a substantial factor in producing the other? Was there a direct connection between them, without too many intervening causes? Is the effect of cause on result not too attenuated? Is the cause likely, in the usual judgment of mankind, to produce the result? Or, by the exercise of prudent foresight, could the result be foreseen? Is the result too remote from the cause, and here we consider remoteness in time and space. [C] Clearly we must so consider, for the greater the distance either in time or space, the more surely do other causes intervene to affect the result. When a lantern is overturned, the firing of a shed is a fairly direct consequence. Many things contribute to the spread of the conflagration—the force of the wind, the direction and width of streets, the character of intervening structures, other factors. We draw an uncertain and wavering line, but draw it we must as best we can.

* * * Once again, it is all a question of fair judgment, always keeping in mind the fact that we endeavor to make a rule in each case that will be practical and in keeping with the general understanding of mankind.

Here another question must be answered. In the case supposed, it is said, and said correctly, that the chauffeur is liable for the direct effect of the explosion, although he had no reason to suppose it would follow a collision. "The fact that the injury occurred in a different manner than that which might have been expected does not prevent the chauffeur's negligence from being in law the cause of the injury." But the natural results of a negligent act—the results which a prudent man would or should foresee—do have a bearing upon the decision as to proximate cause. We have said so repeatedly. What should be foreseen? No human foresight would suggest that a collision itself might injure one a block away. On the contrary, given an explosion, such a possibility might be reasonably expected. I think the direct connection, the foresight of which the courts speak, assumes prevision of the explosion, for the immediate results of which, at least, the chauffeur is responsible.

It may be said this is unjust. Why? In fairness he should make good every injury flowing from his negligence. Not because of tenderness toward him we say he need not answer for all that follows his wrong. We look back to the catastrophe, the fire kindled by the spark, or the explosion. We trace the consequences, not indefinitely, but to a certain point. And to aid us in fixing that point we ask what might ordinarily be expected to follow the fire or the explosion.

This last suggestion is the factor which must determine the case before us. The act upon which defendant's liability rests is knocking an apparently harmless package onto the platform. The act was negligent. For its proximate consequences the defendant is liable. If its contents were broken, to the owner; if it fell upon and crushed a passenger's foot, then to him; if it exploded and injured one in the immediate vicinity, to him also as to A in the illustration. Mrs. Palsgraf was standing some distance away. How far cannot be told from the record—apparently 25 or 30 feet, perhaps less. Except for the explosion, she would not have been injured. We are told by the appellant in his brief, "It cannot be denied that the explosion was the direct cause of the plaintiff's injuries." So it was a substantial factor in producing the result—there was here a natural and continuous sequence—direct connection. The only intervening cause was that, instead of blowing her to the ground, the concussion smashed the weighing machine which in turn fell upon her. There was no remoteness in time, little in space. And surely, given such an explosion as here, it needed no great foresight to predict that the natural result would be to injure one on the platform at no greater distance from its scene than was the plaintiff. Just how no one might be able to predict. Whether by flying fragments, by broken glass, by wreckage of machines or structures no one could say. But injury in some form was most probable.

Under these circumstances I cannot say as a matter of law that the plaintiff's injuries were not the proximate result of the negligence. That is all we have before us. The court refused to so charge. No request was made to submit the matter to the jury as a question of fact, even would that have been proper upon the record before us.

The judgment appealed from should be affirmed, with costs.

POUND, LEHMAN and KELLOGG, JJ., concur with CARDOZO, C.J.

ANDREWS, J., dissents in opinion in which CRANE and O'BRIEN, JJ., concur.

Judgment reversed, etc.

NOTES AND QUESTIONS

1. Plaintiff on a motion for reargument pointed out that Mrs. Palsgraf stood much closer to the scene of the explosion than the majority opinion would suggest. Would this fact be likely to alter Judge Cardozo's decision in the case? See Palsgraf v. Long Island R. Co., 249 N.Y. 511, 164 N.E. 564 (1928).

2. A study of the record in this case indicates that the testimony at trial was different from the "ball of fire" facts in the opinion. No one testified to seeing the scale fall over. An appreciable interval elapsed after the first noise and smoke, during which Mrs. Palsgraf said to her daughter, "Elizabeth, turn your back." Then, "the scale blew and hit me in the side." Plaintiff's original complaint, before amendment, alleged that the scale was knocked over by a stampede of frightened passengers. If that is what happened, would Judge Cardozo allow Mrs. Palsgraf to recover for her injuries? Would Judge Andrews?

The news story in the New York Times for August 25, 1924, p. 1, col. 4, differs in numerous details. It lists 13 persons injured, including Helen Polsgraf [sic], whose injury was "shock." It describes the events as happening at 11:25 a.m. at the East New York station, under the Atlantic Avenue stations, and a transfer point. There was a large crowd of excursionists, "jostling and pushing" to board a Jamaica express train. Three men, each carrying a large package, sought to board the train and a package fell to the tracks below. [The witnesses had testified that the package fell between the car and the tracks and was dragged along as the car moved.] A large explosion rocked the car and tore away part of the platform and "overthrew a penny weighing machine more than ten feet away," smashing the glass and wrecking its mechanism. The police surmised that the three men, who disappeared, were Italians "bound for an Italian celebration somewhere on Long Island, where fireworks and bombs were to play an important role." The police decided that the event was an accident, with the man dropping the exploding package being jostled by the crowd. One of the other men dropped his parcel in the station as he fled, and it was found to contain fireworks of various kinds.

Further discussion of the facts is to be found in Prosser, Palsgraf Revisited, 52 Mich.L.Rev. 1 (1953); J. Noonan, Persons and Masks of the Law, c. 4 (1976); Palsgraf Kin Tell Human Side of Famed Case, 66 Harv.L.Record [No. 8] 1 (Apr. 14, 1978); and Wm. H. Manz, Palsgraf: Cardozo's Urban Legend?, 107 Dickinson L. Rev. 785 (2003). On the relationship of the case to the Restatement of Torts, see Prosser and Noonan, supra, and R. Keeton, A Palsgraf Anecdote, 56 Tex.L.Rev. 513 (1978).

3. Accepting the facts as stated, Mrs. Palsgraf was a passenger. She had bought her ticket, and started her trip by going upon the platform. Did the defendant owe her no duty? Was there no relation between them? This is ignored by both opinions. See Goldberg and Zipursky, The Moral of *MacPherson*, 146 U. Pa. L. Rev. 1733 (1998) (critiquing Prosser's influence on tort law through his treatment of the duty concept in proximate cause cases like *Palsgraf*).

4. How does the decision square with *In re Polemis*, page 320? The Restatement of Torts approved both cases, in § 281, and in § 433, comment *e*. Are they consistent?

5. Both opinions in *Palsgraf* have been cited hundreds of times; almost every practicing lawyer knows the case by name and it has served as a stimulus for legal writers to work out their own ideas, and endeavor to line up "duty" and "proximate cause."

6. How important is all this as a practical matter? How often will a case involve direct causation and an unforeseeable plaintiff? In one recurring situation, a vehicle negligently strikes someone whose body then strikes plaintiff who had been in a position of apparent safety. Is plaintiff "unforeseeable"? A number of courts have allowed recovery. See Kommerstad v. Great N.R. Co., 120 Minn. 376, 139 N.W. 713 (1913); Alabama Great S.R. Co. v. Chapman, 80 Ala. 615, 2 So. 738 (1887); Wolfe v. Checker Taxi Co., 299 Mass. 225, 12 N.E.2d 849 (1938). On the other hand, the Supreme Court of Pennsylvania has twice declared that this fact pattern presents an "unforeseeable" plaintiff. See Wood v. Pennsylvania R. Co., 177 Pa. 306, 35 A. 699 (1896) (train); Dahlstrom v. Shrum, 368 Pa. 423, 84 A.2d 289 (1951) (bus). What if a train strikes a commuter who had dashed across the tracks in front of it due to the commuter's negligence—not the railroad's—and the commuter's body strikes plaintiff who is standing a hundred feet away awaiting her own train? Foreseeable plaintiff? Cf. Zokhrabov v. Jeung-Hee Park, 357 Ill. Dec. 637, 963 N.E.2d 1035 (Ill. App. 2011) (reversing trial court's grant of summary judgment for defendant commuter's estate based on defendant's "no duty" argument and remanding for jury to consider breach and proximate cause).

7. Families of some of the victims of September 11th terrorist attacks have filed claims against airlines, airport security companies, and airport operators for negligently failing to prevent the attacks. The defendants admitted that they owed a duty to their passengers, but argued that they did not owe a duty to protect those on the ground. Were those present in the Twin Towers foreseeable plaintiffs? Note that New York, the home of the *Palsgraf* decision, is also the source of controlling law for this diversity case. In re September 11 Litigation, 280 F.Supp.2d 279, 293 (S.D.N.Y. 2003) ("We live in the vicinity of busy airports, and we work in tall office towers, depending on others to protect us from the willful desire of terrorists to do us harm. . . . [Defendants] perform their screening duties, not only for those boarding airplanes, but also for society generally. It is both their expectation, and ours, that the duty of screening was performed for the benefit of passengers and those on the ground, including those present in the Twin Towers on the morning of September 11, 2001.")

8. What about a bank that issued letters of credit that helped finance terrorist activities by paying for supplies that were converted into chemical weapons? In Stutts v. De Dietrich Group, 2006 WL 1867060 (E.D.N.Y.), plaintiffs who had been injured by exposure to sarin nerve gas, mustard gas, and other chemical weapons stored in facilities in Iraq sought relief from the banks that had supplied the letters of credit and the suppliers of the raw materials for the chemical weapons. In dismissing their complaint, the court relied upon *Palsgraf*:

> In *Palsgraf v. Long Island R.R.*, 248 N.Y. 339, 344 (1928), Judge Cardozo, although in a decidedly different context and yet with

peculiar relevance to what we decide here, penned the following familiar phrase: "The risk reasonably to be perceived defines the duty to be obeyed." What the plaintiffs essentially ask the Court to accept is that by providing letters of credit to the manufacturers of chemicals, the Bank Defendants should have perceived the risk that those chemicals would be sold to Iraq; that Saddam Hussein would use those chemicals to manufacture lethal weapons; that those weapons would be stockpiled in a location that would one day be bombed by coalition forces; that the bombs would hit and detonate those weapons; that the detonation would cause the toxic emissions to be released; that those emissions would permeate the atmosphere; that the plaintiffs would be present in that atmosphere, inhale those emissions and sustain the injuries alleged. Given that procession of events, this Court is driven to conclude that there was nothing to suggest to the most cautious mind that a letter of credit would cause the harm the plaintiffs allege. To attribute such foresight to the Banks is to attribute a prescience that is beyond human ken.

9. For some cases following the majority opinion in *Palsgraf,* see Busta v. Columbus Hospital Corp., 276 Mont. 342, 916 P.2d 122, 133 (1996) ("Any discussion of foreseeability as it relates to liability law begins with the oft-cited decision of the Court of Appeals of New York in Palsgraf v. Long Island Railroad Co."); Edwards v. Honeywell, Inc., 50 F.3d 484 (7th Cir.1995) (Indiana, which follows *Palsgraf*'s exclusion of the unforeseeable victim, would not permit firefighter's widow to recover in case against alarm company whose negligence caused a delay in the notification of the fire department); Tucker v. Collar, 79 Ariz. 141, 285 P.2d 178 (1955) (defective machinery supplied by defendant to a tenant started a fire that burned the landlord's building); Radigan v. W.J. Halloran Co., 97 R.I. 122, 196 A.2d 160 (1963) (defendant negligently brought a crane into contact with an uninsulated high tension power line, and electricity passed through the crane, through an electrical conduit in the ground, and burned a hole in a gas main, which ultimately resulted in explosion of gas on the third floor of a fire station).

The *Palsgraf* dissenting opinion has been followed in other jurisdictions. See Stephenson v. Universal Metrics, Inc., 251 Wis.2d 171, 641 N.W.2d 158 (2002) (noting that Wisconsin follows the approach of the dissent in the "well-known *Palsgraf* decision"); Jackson v. B. Lowenstein & Bros., 175 Tenn. 535, 136 S.W.2d 495 (1940) (customer in department store fell on a defective mat at the top of the stairway, and then her potential rescuer jostled another customer who fell and injured plaintiff who was around the corner of the stairs).

Yun v. Ford Motor Co.

Superior Court of New Jersey, Appellate Division, 1994.
276 N.J.Super. 142, 647 A.2d 841.

VILLANUEVA, J. * * *

I.

On November 27, 1988, between 11:10 p.m. and 11:40 p.m., Chang was a passenger in a 1987 Ford van owned and driven by his daughter, Yun Cho Shim (Yun), northbound in the local lanes of the Garden State Parkway (Parkway). While driving on the Parkway returning from Atlantic City, Yun heard a "rattling type" noise coming from the rear of the van. * * * [T]he plastic cover and spare tire and part of the support bracket which was screwed to the rear of the van landed directly behind Yun's van and then rolled across both lanes of traffic or were pushed there by another vehicle, ultimately coming to a rest against the wooden guard rail separating the Parkway lanes.

Yun safely drove the van onto the right berm of the highway and stopped. Chang, a rear seat passenger who was sixty-five years old at the time, exited the vehicle, then ran across two lanes of the dark, rain-slicked Parkway and retrieved the spare tire and some of the other parts. During the course of returning back to the Ford van across the Parkway, Chang was struck by the vehicle operated by defendant Precious Linderman. * * *

[Yun, as representative of her father's estate, sued the Lindermans, the driver and owner of the car; Ford, the manufacturer of the van; Miller, the manufacturer of the spare tire assembly; Universal, which converted the chassis and installed the spare tire assembly; Castle, the dealer; and Kim's Mobile Service Center, which had changed the oil about a month before the accident and pointed out to Ms. Yun that the spare tire assembly was bent. She instructed Kim not to fix it because it had been damaged in an accident and she was waiting for the other driver's insurance company to handle having it repaired.]

II.

With a broad brush, plaintiffs seek to reverse the summary judgment granted to all defendants except Lindermans [who had settled]. Plaintiffs in their appellate argument do not even mention any of the defendants by name or capacity, rather they assert that the issue of proximate cause is a question for the jury.

Plaintiffs abandoned their claim against Ford apparently because the evidence showed that the spare tire assembly was not part of the vehicle when it left Ford's factory. At the motion for summary judgment the plaintiffs' attorney specifically told the court that he did "not oppose the motion made by Ford Motor Company." Having so stated, plaintiffs have no standing to appeal against Ford. [Cc]

III.

Kim, in its motion for summary judgment, relied upon the lack of proximate cause argument made by the other defendants but also asserted that there was no legal basis for plaintiffs' claim against Kim. Furthermore, plaintiffs' expert did not impute any negligence against

Kim. Rather, he opined that the defect was weld failure with which Kim had nothing to do.

Kim alerted Chang and Yun to the problem but Chang and Yun told Kim that they did not want Kim to repair it. Kim had no duty to repair and therefore did not breach any duty. [C] An order or judgment will be affirmed on appeal if it is correct, even though the judge gave the wrong reasons for it. [Cc] This is true even if the judge erroneously declined to reach the merits of the issue. [C]

IV.

Because the initial complaint was filed on May 17, 1990, it falls within the scope of the Products Liability Act * * * The Act does not affect the requirement of causation, which is an essential element of an action based in either strict liability or negligence. [Cc]

Accordingly, plaintiffs must prove that the alleged defect in the spare tire bracket assembly proximately caused the injuries sustained by Chang. [C] Proximate cause is "any cause which in the natural and continuous sequence, unbroken by an efficient intervening cause, produces the result complained of and without which the result would not have occurred." [Cc]

Proximate cause has been described as a standard for limiting liability for the consequences of an act based "upon mixed considerations of logic, common sense, justice, policy and precedent." [Cc] Proximate cause "must be limited to those causes which are so closely connected with the result and of such significance that the law is justified in imposing liability." [C] Under the most liberal interpretation, conduct constituting proximate cause "need only be a cause which sets off a foreseeable sequence of consequences, unbroken by any superseding cause, and which is a substantial factor in producing the particular injury." [C] Thus, our focus must be on whether Chang's conduct was reasonably foreseeable versus "highly extraordinary," thereby breaking the chain of causation. [C]

The present case presents extraordinary circumstances. After Ford manufactured a van, spare tire assembly was attached to the van by Universal. Assuming plaintiffs' allegations are true, an alleged defect in the spare tire assembly caused the spare tire and other parts to fall off the van and roll across the Parkway. Because the van in which Chang was traveling came safely to rest at the side of the Parkway, his actions were "highly extraordinary." Chang's attempt to retrieve the parts involved crossing the Parkway in both directions—an activity which cannot be described as anything short of extraordinarily dangerous, if not suicidal, as the action proved. In the process of returning from the middle of the Parkway, Chang was struck by Mrs. Linderman and fatally injured. Although cited in the context of the foreseeability of a person's emotional reaction to a given event, the New Jersey Supreme Court aptly noted in Caputzal [v. The Lindsay Co., 48 N.J. 69, 222 A.2d 513 (1966)], supra: "Generally a defendant's standard of conduct is measured by the reaction to be expected of normal persons. . . ." [C]

Logic and fairness dictate that liability should not extend to injuries received as a result of Chang's senseless decision to cross the Parkway under such dangerous conditions. Common sense should have persuaded Chang, who was only a passenger, to wait for assistance or abandon the bald tire and damaged assembly. The van could have been driven safely home. * * *

[T]he alleged defect in the spare tire assembly did not injure Chang. The driver of the van was able to pull the vehicle to the side of the road safely and without incident. Chang's injury occurred after he decided to leave the vehicle and cross the Parkway and return where he was struck. At most, the presence of the spare tire created a "condition upon which the subsequent intervening force acted" and in such case there is no proximate cause relationship between the defective product and the injury. [Cc]

A tortfeasor will be held responsible for his negligent conduct if it is a "substantial factor" in bringing about plaintiff's injuries. [C] Where, however, concurrent forces are involved, the manufacturer of a defective product may negate strict liability upon a showing of an intervening, superseding cause or the existence of another "sole proximate cause" of the resulting injury. [Cc] Assuming, arguendo, that the spare tire assembly was a substantial factor in causing Chang's injuries, Chang's highly extraordinary and dangerous actions in crossing the Parkway twice with complete disregard for his own personal safety clearly constitute a superseding and intervening cause of his own injuries. * * * The danger involved in crossing a busy highway at night should be apparent to an adolescent, let alone an adult sixty-five years of age.

The allegedly defective product (the spare tire carrier) did not cause Chang's injuries. Chang's and Yun's joint decision, thirty days before this accident, not to repair the allegedly defective assembly and Chang's flagrant disregard for his personal safety by crossing the Parkway late at night and the injuries he received when struck by Linderman's vehicle constitute intervening superseding causes. Logic, common sense, justice and fairness dictate that the alleged product defect was not a proximate cause of Chang's injury.

Usually, the issue of proximate cause is reserved for the jury's determination. [Cc] In certain cases, however, the issue of proximate cause has been held so intertwined with issues of policy as to be treated as a matter of law for the court to determine. [C] This is especially true where the manner or type of harm caused to the plaintiff is unexpected. As the Supreme Court stated in Caputzal: "the idea of non-liability for the highly extraordinary consequence as a question of law for the court has already been recognized in this state." [C] This position is consistent with that of the Restatement (Second) Torts § 435(2) (1965): The actor's conduct may be held not to be a legal cause of harm to another where after the event and looking back from the harm to the actor's negligent conduct, it appears to the court highly extraordinary that it should have brought about the harm. * * *

In Jensen v. Schooley's Mountain Inn, 216 N.J. Super. 79, 522 A.2d 1043 (App.Div.), certif. denied, 108 N.J. 181 (1987), the defendant bar served alcoholic beverages to Jensen while he allegedly was visibly intoxicated. After leaving the bar, Jensen drove eight miles, where he "parked his car and, for some unknown reason, began climbing a tree." Id. at 80. The branches of the tree apparently could not support Jensen's weight and one broke, causing Jensen to fall twenty feet to the river bank. Jensen either fell or rolled into the river and drowned. Accepting as true plaintiffs' allegations that the defendant negligently and wrongfully served Jensen, we nonetheless affirmed the trial court's granting of summary judgment in favor of the defendant. We stressed: [L]egal responsibility for the consequences of an act cannot be imposed without limit. The events here transgress the judicial line beyond which liability should not be extended as a matter of fairness or policy. [Id. at 82, 522 A.2d 1043 (citations omitted).]

That principle is equally applicable herein. It was not reasonably foreseeable to defendants that if the spare wheel assembly was defective, and the driver-owner of the car and Chang refused to have it repaired and later while they were driving on the Parkway at night, it fell off but they safely brought the car to a stop on a berm, that Chang would then violate the law by twice crossing the Parkway to go to the median to retrieve the parts and be killed by a passing car. Furthermore, reasonable people could not differ that the continued driving for thirty days with knowledge of the defect and the senseless, and illegal crossing of the Parkway were intervening superseding causes of the accident which broke the chain of causation.

Affirmed.

BAIME, J., concurring and dissenting: I agree that the judgment in favor of Ford Motor Company should be affirmed because plaintiffs offered no opposition to that defendant's motion for a dismissal of the complaint. [Cc] So too, my careful review of the record fails to disclose facts sufficient to support a negligence claim against Kim's Mobile Service Center. Consequently, the judgment in favor of that defendant should also be affirmed. [C] However, I part company with my colleagues in their affirmance of the Law Division's judgment as to the remaining defendants. I believe that plaintiff's submissions relating to proximate cause were sufficient to defeat the defendants' motion for summary judgment. * * *

Ordinarily, questions of proximate cause are left to the jury for its factual determination. [Cc] Likewise, questions of intervening cause are generally within the jury's domain. [Cc] Prosser and Keeton have instructed that: if reasonable persons could differ, either because relevant facts are in dispute or because application of the legal concept of "proximate cause" to the case at hand is an evaluative determination as to which reasonable persons might differ, the issue of "proximate cause" is submitted to the jury with appropriate instructions on the law.

Thus, in any case where there might be reasonable difference of opinion as to the foreseeability of a particular risk, the reasonableness of the defendant's conduct with respect to it, or the normal character of an intervening cause, the question is for the jury, subject of course to suitable instructions from the court as to the legal conclusion to be drawn as the issue is determined either way. By far the greater number of the cases which have arisen have been of this description; and to this extent it may properly be said that "proximate cause is ordinarily a question of fact for the jury, to be solved by the exercise of good common sense in the consideration of the evidence of each particular case." [Prosser and Keeton on Torts § 45 at 321 (5th ed. 1984).]

Applying these principles, I am convinced that reasonable persons might differ regarding whether the plaintiff's death was proximately caused by the defective spare tire assembly. A jury could find that it was reasonably foreseeable the tire would dislodge and fall onto the roadway while the van was in operation and that the operator or passenger might sustain injuries in his or her attempt to retrieve it. Indeed, some might think it odd if the operator or passenger were to abandon the tire and drive off, especially where, as shown by the record here, traffic is "very light," and "visibility [is] good." And if the operator or passenger were negligent in his or her attempt to retrieve the tire, this would be reflected within the calculus of comparative fault. In other words, the entire incident could reasonably be viewed within an "objective 'realm of foreseeability.'" [C] A jury could also reasonably find that the harm that resulted was not proximately caused by the defective assembly and that fairness and logic demand that defendants be absolved from responsibility. I am of the view that the issue is reasonably debatable and one that should be submitted to the jury for its determination.

I note one final point before leaving the subject. While I recognize the power and duty of a trial judge to bar the jury from considering the question of proximate cause where the consequences of a negligent act are so extraordinary that as a matter of law they cannot be considered "natural," that authority should be exercised sparingly. We judges are strange creatures. It is not that we are less brave than others, but rather by reason of our training, if not our nature, we tend to the conservative. For most of us, prudence and caution are the watchwords. We are rarely rewarded for taking risks. But the rest of the population does not always act the way we do. What may appear strange to judges might seem rather ordinary to others. It thus generally makes sense to have lay people, not judges, make decisions on the question of proximate cause, grounded as that concept is in considerations of foreseeability and fairness. And in that context, a jury might well find it rather ordinary for a person to venture on to the highway on a clear night when there is little traffic in order to retrieve a spare tire that has become dislodged from his vehicle. I would thus reverse as to all defendants except Ford Motor Company and Kim's Mobile Service Center.

[The New Jersey Supreme Court issued a per curiam opinion, reversing the appellate division for the reasons expressed in Judge Baime's dissent. That decision too drew a dissenting opinion. Yun v. Ford Motor Co., 143 N.J. 162, 669 A.2d 1378 (1996).]

NOTES AND QUESTIONS

1. What happens to the case after the New Jersey Supreme Court opinion?

2. The trial court judge, a majority of the panel at the appellate division, and one of seven New Jersey Supreme Court judges found no proximate cause as a matter of law. One dissenting judge at the appellate division and six supreme court judges thought a reasonable jury could find in plaintiff's favor against some of the defendants. What do you think? Note Judge Baime's point about the difficulty inherent in a judge (as opposed to

the jury) making decisions about what the reasonable person would do. Do you find that argument persuasive?

3. As in *Palsgraf*, there are differences in emphasis in the recitation of the facts in the two opinions. For example, the majority calls the Garden State Parkway "dark, rain-slicked," while the dissent notes that traffic was "very light," and "visibility good." Do you see other examples?

4. If you were representing one of the parties in this case, what would you say to your client about proximate cause and how it was likely to be viewed by the judge or jury? How would you advise your client on whether to settle the case or take it to trial? To appeal?

5. Dealer negligently failed to tighten lug bolts on the wheels of Hairston's newly purchased automobile. A wheel fell off and Hairston brought the car safely to a stop on a bridge. A van stopped behind Hairston's auto, and the driver offered to assist Hairston. Hairston got out and was standing behind his car when Alexander's flatbed truck rammed into the van stopped behind Hairston, propelling the van into Hairston, who was killed. The court held the dealer liable even though the conduct of the driver of the flatbed truck was "inexcusable," because his conduct was not "so highly improbable and extraordinary an occurrence in this series of events as to bear no reasonable connection to the harm threatened" by the dealer's original negligence. Alexander's negligent driving was therefore in the "area of risk created by the negligence" of dealer not tightening the lug bolts. Hairston v. Alexander Tank and Equipment Co., 310 N.C. 227, 311 S.E.2d 559, 567 (1984).

6. Doctor negligently performed a sterilization procedure and patient became pregnant and gave birth to child with a serious birth defect. Doctor is liable for medical and other costs associated with patient's pregnancy. Is he also liable for the medical costs associated with baby's birth defect and parents' emotional distress due to baby's ill health? Simmerer v. Dabbas, 89 Ohio St.3d 586, 733 N.E.2d 1169 (2000) (even though a negligently performed sterilization may lead to conception and birth of unhealthy child, proximate cause is not established because it contemplates liability for a probable or likely result, not merely a possible one).

7. In addition to unforeseeable consequences, the doctrine of proximate cause may be used to cut off liability even though there is cause in fact in cases involving other acts that intervene in the causal link between the defendant's act and the plaintiff's injury.

2. INTERVENING CAUSES

Derdiarian v. Felix Contracting Corp.

New York Court of Appeals, 1980.
51 N.Y.2d 308, 414 N.E.2d 666, 434 N.Y.S.2d 166.

[Defendant Felix Contracting Corporation, in performing a contract to install an underground gas main in Mount Vernon, N.Y., had excavated a worksite in the street. Plaintiff Derdiarian, employee of a subcontractor, was engaged in sealing the gas main.]

COOKE, CHIEF JUDGE. * * * On the afternoon of November 21, 1973, defendant James Dickens suffered an epileptic seizure and lost consciousness, allowing his vehicle to careen into the work site and strike plaintiff with such force as to throw him into the air. When plaintiff landed, he was splattered over his face, head and body with 400 degree boiling hot liquid enamel from a kettle struck by the automobile. The enamel was used in connection with sealing the gas main. Although plaintiff's body ignited into a fire ball, he miraculously survived the incident.

At trial, plaintiff's theory was that defendant Felix had negligently failed to take adequate measures to insure the safety of workers on the excavation site. * * *

To support his claim of an unsafe work site, plaintiff called as a witness Lawrence Lawton, an expert in traffic safety. According to Lawton, the usual and accepted method of safeguarding the workers is to erect a barrier around the excavation. Such a barrier, consisting of a truck, a piece of heavy equipment or a pile of dirt, would keep a car out of the excavation and protect workers from oncoming traffic. The expert testified that the barrier should cover the entire width of the excavation. He also stated that there should have been two flagmen present, rather than one, and that warning signs should have been posted advising motorists that there was only one lane of traffic and that there was a flagman ahead.

[The trial court judge entered a judgment on the jury verdict in favor of plaintiff. Defendant Felix appealed, arguing there was insufficient evidence for the jury to have found proximate cause between its conduct and plaintiff's injuries. The Appellate Division affirmed.]

* * * Defendant Felix now argues that plaintiff was injured in a freakish accident, brought about solely by defendant Dickens' negligence, and therefore there was no causal link, as a matter of law, between Felix' breach of duty and plaintiff's injuries.

The concept of proximate cause, or more appropriately legal cause, has proven to be an elusive one, incapable of being precisely defined to cover all situations * * *.

Where the acts of a third person intervene between the defendant's conduct and the plaintiff's injury, the causal connection is not automatically severed. In such a case, liability turns upon whether the intervening act is a normal or foreseeable consequence of the situation created by the defendant's negligence. [Cc] If the intervening act is extraordinary under the circumstances, not foreseeable in the normal course of events, or independent of or far removed from the defendant's conduct, it may well be a superseding act which breaks the causal nexus. [Cc] Because questions concerning what is foreseeable and what is normal may be the subject of varying inferences, as is the question of negligence itself, these issues generally are for the fact finder to resolve.

There are certain instances, to be sure, where only one conclusion may be drawn from the established facts and where the question of legal cause may be decided as a matter of law. Those cases generally involve independent intervening acts which operate upon but do not flow from the original negligence. Thus, for instance, we have held that where an automobile lessor negligently supplies a car with a defective trunk lid, it is not liable to the lessee who, while stopped to repair the trunk, was injured by the negligent driving of a third party. [Lessee had pulled into a parking space at the curb and was shutting the trunk when another automobile, parked several car lengths behind, jumped ahead and severely injured him.] [C] Although the renter's negligence undoubtedly served to place the injured party at the site of the accident, the intervening act was divorced from and not the foreseeable risk associated with the original negligence. And the injuries were different in kind than those which would have normally been expected from a defective trunk. In short, the negligence of the renter merely furnished the occasion for an unrelated act to cause injuries not ordinarily anticipated. [C]

By contrast, in the present case, we cannot say as a matter of law that defendant Dickens' negligence was a superseding cause which interrupted the link between Felix' negligence and plaintiff's injuries. From the evidence in the record, the jury could have found that Felix negligently failed to safeguard the excavation site. A prime hazard associated with such dereliction is the possibility that a driver will negligently enter the work site and cause injury to a worker. That the driver was negligent, or even reckless, does not insulate Felix from liability. [Cc] Nor is it decisive that the driver lost control of the vehicle through a negligent failure to take medication, rather than a driving mistake. [C] The precise manner of the event need not be anticipated. The finder of fact could have concluded that the foreseeable, normal and natural result of the risk created by Felix was the injury of a worker by a car entering the improperly protected work area. An intervening act may not serve as a superseding cause, and relieve an actor of responsibility, where the risk of the intervening act occurring is the very same risk which renders the actor negligent.

In a similar vein, plaintiff's act of placing the kettle on the west side of the excavation does not, as a matter of law, absolve defendant Felix of responsibility. Serious injury, or even death, was a foreseeable consequence of a vehicle crashing through the work area. The injury could have occurred in numerous ways, ranging from a worker being directly struck by the car to the car hitting an object that injures the worker. Placement of the kettle, or any object in the work area, could affect how the accident occurs and the extent of injuries. That defendant could not anticipate the precise manner of the accident or the exact extent of injuries, however, does not preclude liability as a matter of law where the general risk and character of injuries are foreseeable. * * *

For the foregoing reasons, the order of the Appellate Division should be affirmed, with costs.

NOTES AND QUESTIONS

1. Why does the opinion focus on the contractor? What about the driver? Shouldn't he be liable?

2. Note that when courts have decided that the intervening act should cut off liability, it is labelled a "superseding" cause. This is the language used by most courts. But see Control Techniques, Inc. v. Johnson, 762 N.E.2d 104 (Ind. 2002) (Indiana uses the terms "superseding" and "intervening" interchangeably to refer to an act of another that cuts off the liability of the original actor if the ultimate injury was not reasonably foreseeable as the natural and probable consequence of the negligent act).

3. *Foreseeability of Intervening Force.* The test for determining whether an intervening force constitutes a superseding cause is often couched in terms of foreseeability. See Restatement (Second) of Torts § 447 (1965). A person is deemed to have foreseen the normal consequences of his conduct, but is not responsible for extraordinarily negligent intervening acts of third persons. On considerations important in determining whether an intervening force is a superseding cause, see Restatement (Second) of Torts § 442 (1965) and Restatement (Third) of Torts: Liability for Physical and Emotional Harm § 34 (2010). Consider whether the defendant should be liable in the cases that follow.

4. A wrecking company failed to secure a condemned house during salvage, prior to demolition. Trespassers using the house for shelter accidentally started a fire that spread to the building next door. Testimony established that the neighborhood was one frequented by "vagrants" and that it was the custom of the industry to lock and board up buildings during salvage to keep trespassers out. Aetna Ins. Co. v. 3 Oaks Wrecking and Lumber Co., 65 Ill.App.3d 618, 382 N.E.2d 283, 21 Ill.Dec. 919 (1978) (jury verdict for plaintiff affirmed).

5. Defendant sets off an auto alarm at 4:00 a.m. while attempting to repossess a car. In the resulting confusion, a neighbor is shot. Is the negligent handling of a gun foreseeable under those circumstances or one that interrupts the causal link? Griffith v. Valley of Sun Recovery & Adjustment Bureau, Inc., 126 Ariz. 227, 613 P.2d 1283 (1980) (question of fact for jury).

6. Around 9:30 p.m., a man, distraught because he recently had been fired from his job at the power company, climbed up a 34,000-volt power pole and threatened to electrocute himself. A crowd formed. About midnight, the police chief of the city ordered the power shut off, the power company complied, and portions of the city went dark. An hour later, two teenagers on their way home from a concert were driving through the city. Driver noticed about 100 yards before an intersection that streetlights and traffic lights were out. He drove through the intersection without stopping because he "wasn't quite up on the rules of the road." His car collided with another car in the intersection and his passenger sued both drivers, the city, the power company, and the man who had threatened suicide. Who should be liable? Quirke v. City of Harvey, 266 Ill.App.3d 664, 203 Ill.Dec. 536, 639 N.E.2d 1355 (1994).

7. Defendant, under an obligation to furnish a safe place to work, set plaintiff, its employee, at cleaning a coin-operated vending machine with gasoline in a small room in which there was a lighted gas heater with an open flame. While he was working, a rat escaped from the vending machine and ran to take refuge under the heater, where its fur, impregnated with gasoline fumes, caught fire from the flame. The rat "returned in haste and flames to its original hideout," and exploded the gasoline vapor inside the

vending machine, injuring the plaintiff. Is defendant liable? United Novelty Co. v. Daniels, 42 So.2d 395 (Miss.1949).

8. A radio station with an extensive teenage audience conducted a contest that rewarded the first contestant to locate a peripatetic disc jockey. Two minors driving in separate automobiles attempted to follow the disc jockey's automobile to its next stop. In the course of their pursuit, at speeds up to 80 m.p.h., one of the minors negligently forced a car off the highway, killing the driver. Wrongful death action was filed against the radio station. What result? Weirum v. RKO Gen., Inc., 15 Cal.3d 40, 539 P.2d 36, 123 Cal.Rptr. 468 (1975). On April Fool's Day, defendant encouraged his daughter to call a friend of his and pretend that she was home alone and frightened. The friend, concerned about the child, jumped into his pick-up truck to go to the child. In his haste, he ran a stop sign and collided with plaintiff's motorcycle. Plaintiff was seriously injured and sued both the driver and the instigator of the practical joke. Who should be liable? Kolar v. Bergo, 280 Mont. 262, 929 P.2d 867 (1996).

9. Note that a plaintiff's own conduct can constitute an intervening cause that breaks the causal connection between defendant's negligence and the injury. However, in order to be a superseding cause, plaintiff's conduct must be more than contributory negligence that would be relevant in apportioning negligent conduct. For example, in Mesick v. State of New York, 118 A.D.2d 214, 504 N.Y.S.2d 279 (1986), plaintiff's conduct was not a superseding cause of his injuries when he swung himself from a rope tied to a tree branch out over a water hole and fell onto jagged rocks. There was evidence that the defendant, State of New York, was aware that the rope had been tied to the tree and was used by people who swam at the water hole.

10. Some jurisdictions have backed away from giving a separate jury instruction on superseding cause, finding that the substance of the doctrine is covered by the proximate cause instruction. Barry v. Quality Steel Products, Inc., 263 Conn. 424, 440, 820 A.2d 258, 268 (2003) ("the term superseding cause merely describes more fully the concept of proximate cause when there is more than one alleged act of negligence, and is not functionally distinct from the determination of whether an act is a proximate cause of the injury suffered by the plaintiff").

11. *Act of God.* One standard type of "intervening force" is called an "act of God," "vis major" or "force of nature." In Kimble v. Mackintosh Hemphill Co., 359 Pa. 461, 59 A.2d 68, 71–72 (1948), defendant was not relieved of liability when a section of a negligently maintained roof crashed, falling onto and killing plaintiff's decedent. The defendant claimed that the roof collapsed as a result of extremely high winds. The court stated, "We cannot say that the intervening cause [of the high winds] was vis major. One who fails in his duty to remedy a defective or dangerous condition is liable for injuries resulting therefrom, although the immediate cause of the injury is the wind. [Cc] The causal connection is not broken, and the original wrongdoer is liable for the injury sustained." Note how the issue in *Kimble* differs from Blyth v. Birmingham Waterworks Co., page 142. Is it consistent in principle with the *Anderson* "twin fires" case, page 300? The Restatement (Second) § 450 defines force of nature, and § 451 outlines the consideration that will make the force of nature a superseding cause. Restatement (Third) of Torts: Liability for Physical and Emotional Harm

§ 34, comment *d* (2010) provides that the actor is liable, even for the result of an extraordinary force of nature, if the risks of that force of nature were risks against which the actor should have taken adequate precautions. In which of the following situations does the intervening force of nature interrupt the causal link between defendant's act and plaintiff's injury?

A. Defendant did not inspect a telephone pole for 14 years and it is then felled during a 12-inch snowfall and injures plaintiff. Bowman v. Columbia Tel. Co., 406 Pa. 455, 179 A.2d 197 (1962) (jury verdict for plaintiff upheld).

B. In the dead of winter, defendant ships plaintiff's apples in an unheated car through the state of Maine. A cold spell sets in, and the apples are frozen. Fox v. Boston & Maine R. Co., 148 Mass. 220, 19 N.E. 222 (1889) (liability).

C. Defendant's negligence damages canvas coverings designed to protect plaintiff's pineapple plants from frost. Before they can be replaced, the plants are killed by a frost. Benedict Pineapple Co. v. Atlantic Coast Line R. Co., 55 Fla. 514, 46 So. 732 (1908) (liability).

D. Defendant charter plane company negligently fails to supply one of its planes with sufficient fuel. The pilot is forced to make an emergency landing on a small island in the Pacific. A volcano erupts and kills a passenger. Cf. Doss v. Big Stone Gap, 145 Va. 520, 134 S.E. 563 (1926) (car struck by crash landing airplane while car was on road detour that took it near airstrip because defendant had negligently failed to maintain the road from which the car detoured; no liability).

With respect to the use of the term "act of God" as shorthand for this concept, see the criticism in Goldberg v. R. Grier Miller & Sons, Inc., 408 Pa. 1, 182 A.2d 759, 763 (1962). Note that the court is criticizing the term, not the concept.

> Judges should have no difficulty in describing these incidents of cosmic convulsion or fierce agitation of the elements, without referring to them as 'acts of God.'
>
> The English language is rich, not poor. In its vast wardrobe there are words with which to clothe every thought, concept and phenomenal thing so as to make that thing readily identifiable by the jury no matter how lacking in formal or higher education it might be. Thus, we have storms, tempests, tornadoes, cyclones, hurricanes, blizzards, monsoons, typhoons, twisters, siroccos, gales, southwesters, duststorms, snowstorms, sandstorms, whirlwinds, wind eddies, not to mention tidal waves, earthquakes, volcanic eruptions and all the other pyrotechnical spectacles of nature which at times turn the world into a stage of colossal drama, were it not that the resulting human suffering robs the blazing scenes of theatrical perspective.
>
> Not only is there no need, but it is actually confusing, to tell the jury that they must determine whether a given mundane turbulence is an 'act of God.' The jury is not chosen to determine what should be rendered unto Caesar and what is to be rendered unto God. The Trial Judge should instruct the jury that they are to decide whether the alleged blizzard (if a blizzard is blamed for the proved damage), or the cloudburst (if a cloudburst is accused

of upsetting the normal state of affairs), or whatever phenomenon in the meteorological armory is accused of doing the damage,-the judge is to direct the jury to decide whether that phenomenon of weather was so unpredictable, so extensive, and so unprecedented in vehemence and destructive fury, that the defendant could not have made preparations to prevent or mitigate the catastrophic effects.

12. Remember that there may be more than one proximate cause of an injury and, therefore, more than one defendant may be held liable. Do you see why it would be prejudicial to the plaintiff to instruct the jury that the defendant's negligence must be "the" proximate cause of the injury?

Watson v. Kentucky & Indiana Bridge & R.R. Co.

Court of Appeals of Kentucky, 1910.
137 Ky. 619, 126 S.W. 146.

[Through the negligence of the defendant railroad, a tank car full of gasoline was derailed and its valve broken, so that the gasoline ran into the street. One Duerr struck a match, igniting the gasoline vapor, and an explosion followed, injuring plaintiff, a bystander. Duerr testified that he struck the match to light a cigar, and that when he dropped the match the explosion occurred before it reached the ground. Other witnesses testified that Duerr had said to a companion, "Let's go set the damn thing on fire," that he struck the match against a fence and deliberately threw it into the gasoline vapor. The trial court directed a verdict for the defendant, and plaintiff appealed.]

SETTLE, J. * * * The lighting of the match by Duerr having resulted in the explosion, the question is, was that act merely a contributing cause, or the efficient and, therefore, proximate cause of appellant's injuries? The question of proximate cause is a question for the jury. In holding that Duerr in lighting or throwing the match acted maliciously or with intent to cause the explosion, the trial court invaded the province of the jury. There was, it is true, evidence tending to prove that the act was wanton or malicious, but also evidence conducing to prove that it was inadvertently or negligently done by Duerr. It was therefore for the jury and not the court to determine from all the evidence whether the lighting of the match was done by Duerr inadvertently or negligently, or whether it was a wanton and malicious act. * * *

If the presence on Madison street in the city of Louisville of the great volume of loose gas that arose from the escaping gasoline was caused by the negligence of the appellee Bridge & Railroad Company it seems to us that the probable consequence of its coming in contact with fire and causing an explosion was too plain a proposition to admit of doubt. Indeed, it was most probable that some one would strike a match to light a cigar or for other purposes in the midst of the gas. In our opinion, therefore, the act of one lighting and throwing a match under such circumstances cannot be said to be the efficient cause of the explosion. It did not of itself produce the explosion, nor could it have done so without the assistance and contribution resulting from the primary negligence, if there was such negligence, on the part of the appellee Bridge & Railroad Company in furnishing the presence of the gas in the street. This conclusion, however, rests upon the theory that Duerr inadvertently or negligently lighted and threw the match in the gas.

If, however, the act of Duerr in lighting the match and throwing it into the vapor or gas arising from the gasoline was malicious, and done for the purpose of causing the explosion, we do not think appellees would be responsible, for while the appellee Bridge & Railroad Company's negligence may have been the efficient cause of the presence of the gas in the street, and it should have understood enough of the consequences thereof to have foreseen that an explosion was likely to result from the inadvertent or negligent lighting of a match by some person who was ignorant of the presence of the gas or of the effect of lighting or throwing a match in it, it could not have foreseen or deemed it probable that one would maliciously or wantonly do such an act for the evil purpose of producing the explosion. Therefore, if the act of Duerr was malicious, we quite agree with the trial court that it was one which the appellees could not reasonably have anticipated or guarded against, and in such case the act of Duerr, and not the primary negligence of the appellee Bridge & Railroad Company, in any of the particulars charged, was the efficient or proximate cause of appellant's injuries. The mere fact that the concurrent cause or intervening act was unforeseen will not relieve the defendant guilty of the primary negligence from liability, but if the intervening agency is something so unexpected or extraordinary as that he could not or ought not to have anticipated it, he will not be liable, and certainly he is not bound to anticipate the criminal acts of others by which damage is inflicted and hence is not liable therefor.

For the reasons indicated, the judgment is * * * reversed as to the Bridge & Railroad Company, and the cause remanded for a new trial consistent with the opinion.

NOTES AND QUESTIONS

1. *Intervening Criminal Acts.* The principal case continues to be cited frequently, although the Kentucky Supreme Court has noted that criminal conduct no longer automatically interrupts the causal link in Kentucky. Britton v. Wooten, 817 S.W.2d 443, 451 (1991) (whether the spark that ignited trash negligently allowed to accumulate next to building was ignited accidentally, negligently, intentionally, or even criminally, it may still have been foreseeable and thus would not cut off liability).

2. It is probably impossible to state any comprehensive rule as to when a defendant will be liable for the intervening criminal act of a third person. See Restatement (Second) of Torts §§ 448–449 (1965) and Restatement (Third) of Torts: Liability for Physical and Emotional Harm § 34, comment *e* (2010) (intervening acts that are unforeseeable, unusual, or highly culpable may be outside the scope of the risk). Some of the more common situations in which liability has been found are the following:

A. Defendant, by contract or otherwise, is under a duty to protect plaintiff against criminal misconduct, and fails to do so. See, e.g., Silva v. Showcase Cinemas Concessions of Dedham, Inc., 736 F.2d 810, 813 (1st Cir.1984), cert. denied, 469 U.S. 883 (1984) (applying Massachusetts law), where the court held that a jury could reasonably find that a proximate cause of plaintiff's being stabbed to death was the theatre's failure to patrol adequately its premises.

Sixth grade class was taken from school to a nearby park for a drug awareness program. Student did not appear at the meeting place to return to school and teacher left without her. Walking home alone, she was accosted by students from a nearby junior high school and raped. Bell v. Board of Educ. of the City of New York, 90 N.Y.2d 944, 687 N.E.2d 1325, 665 N.Y.S.2d 42 (1997) (question of fact for jury whether intervening act of another is itself the foreseeable harm that shaped the duty imposed and thus defendant who failed to guard against such conduct would not be relieved of liability).

B. Defendant's affirmative act destroys or defeats a protection that plaintiff has placed around his person or property to guard them against crime. Defendant, who has leased floor space in plaintiff's jewelry store, goes to the store on a holiday, and leaves the key in the front door. Garceau v. Engel, 169 Minn. 62, 210 N.W. 608 (1926). Cf. Southwestern Bell Tel. Co. v. Adams, 199 Ark. 254, 133 S.W.2d 867 (1939) (defendant left windows of plaintiff's warehouse open).

C. Defendant brings into association with plaintiff a person whom he knows or should know to be peculiarly likely to commit crime, under circumstances creating a recognizable unreasonable risk that he will do so. The security agency for an apartment building hired a security guard with a violent record. The guard used his passkey to gain access to plaintiff's apartment, where he assaulted her. Easley v. Apollo Detective Agency, 69 Ill.App.3d 920, 26 Ill.Dec. 313, 387 N.E.2d 1241 (1979). Compare Hines v. Garrett, 131 Va. 125, 108 S.E. 690 (1921), where a railroad negligently carried an 18-year-old past her station, and then put her off the train near a place known locally as "Hoboes' Hollow," which the court described as known to be frequented by hoboes, tramps, and questionable characters. On her walk back to town, she was raped by two different unidentified persons. Is the railroad company liable? (Carrier would be liable if it had reason to know of risk to passenger's safety.)

D. Defendant has taken custody of a person of dangerous criminal tendencies, and fails to restrain him. Matron held liable for policeman's death when he was stabbed by juveniles who escaped from a youth center. Christensen v. Epley, 36 Or.App. 535, 585 P.2d 416 (1978). Contra, and much criticized, was Henderson v. Dade Coal Co., 100 Ga. 568, 28 S.E. 251 (1897), where a company using convict labor negligently guarded a brutal and vicious convict with a record of sexual offenses, and he escaped and raped the plaintiff. What if the convict were only a forger, with no record of violence, and he held up plaintiff with a gun in the course of his escape? Cf. Williams v. State, 308 N.Y. 548, 127 N.E.2d 545 (1955) (no liability because no reason to anticipate violence).

3. The following cases will help to test one's understanding of the rules and policy implications involved with regard to intervening criminal acts:

A. The State of New York was negligent in having only one attendant in a maximum-security closed ward. This led to the escape of a known dangerous psychotic. Some four hours after this occurred the escapee chanced upon an automobile with the keys in it, drove away, and collided with plaintiff's automobile. Should the State be liable for this consequence? Dunn v. State, 29 N.Y.2d 313, 277 N.E.2d 647, 327 N.Y.S.2d 622 (1971) (no proximate cause).

B. Defendant insurance company issued a policy on the life of a child, payable to her aunt as beneficiary. Under state law sale of such a policy was prohibited because the aunt did not have an insurable interest in the life of the child. The aunt murdered the child in the hope of collecting the life insurance. Should the insurance company be liable to the child's parents in a wrongful death action? See Liberty Nat'l Life Ins. Co. v. Weldon, 267 Ala. 171, 100 So.2d 696 (1957) (yes, because type of harm statute designed to protect against).

C. While driving a Ford Explorer in a remote area in the early morning hours, driver's Firestone Wilderness AT radial tire failed, rendering her vehicle inoperable. While she was stranded, a stranger raped and murdered her. Her parents sued Ford and Firestone, alleging that defendants should have foreseen that a defective tire could expose drivers to criminal behavior, such as might be encountered in dark parking lots or during breakdowns in remote areas. Should the manufacturers be held liable for driver's wrongful death? Stahlecker v. Ford Motor Co., 266 Neb. 601, 667 N.W.2d 244 (2003) (upholding trial court judge's ruling that general awareness that there are "bad people in society who do bad things" was insufficient to establish foreseeability).

D. Promoters of a gun show were negligent in providing security and several minors were able to gain admission and steal handguns and ammunition. Later that night, while deliberately skidding their car on snow-covered roads to slide into trash cans, they were confronted by plaintiffs. One of the teenagers shot both of the plaintiffs with a gun stolen from the gun show. Should the promoters be liable? Pavlides v. Niles Gun Show, Inc., 93 Ohio App.3d 46, 637 N.E.2d 404 (1994) (reasonable minds could differ whether such criminal conduct was foreseeable).

E. Driver was on her way home when a fifteen-year-old dropped a twenty-pound chunk of concrete from an overpass onto her car, killing her. Her family filed suit against the highway department, alleging that the negligence of its employees in inadequately fencing the overpass, allowing loose pieces of concrete to be left there, and failing to light it properly caused the death. Should the highway department be liable? State ex rel. Missouri Hwy. and Transp. Com. v. Dierker, 961 S.W.2d 58 (Mo.1998) (no proximate cause).

F. Teenager purchased a one-pint container of a drain cleaner called Liquid Fire from Ace Hardware and took it with her to the home of a classmate, confronting classmate on her front porch about an incident involving teenager's boyfriend. They argued and teenager threw the Liquid Fire at her classmate. It missed the target and hit classmate's brother who was seriously burned. The brother sued Ace Hardware and Liquid Fire's manufacturer, claiming they should be held strictly liable for selling an inherently dangerous product. Briscoe v. Amazing Products, Inc., 23 S.W.3d 228 (Ky. App. 2000) (intentional criminal conduct of teenager is a factor of such extraordinary, unforeseeable nature as to relieve the original wrongdoers of liability). Plaintiff also had argued that defendants failed to provide adequate warnings of the severity of the injury the product would cause when brought into contact with skin. As a review of cause in fact, think about why that allegation would fail.

G. Defendant manufactured ammonium nitrate, a chemical used in both fertilizer and explosives, and sold it through several intermediaries to a terrorist who mixed it with fuel oil and used it to blow up the Murrah Federal Building in Oklahoma City. Plaintiffs, who were injured or whose family members were killed in the blast, allege that the chemical sold to the farm co-op was explosive grade rather than fertilizer grade. Should the manufacturer or the farm co-op that sold the chemical be liable? Gaines-Tabb v. ICI Explosives, USA, Inc., 160 F.3d 613, 620 (10th Cir.1998) (applying Oklahoma law) ("When the intervening act is intentionally tortious or criminal, it is more likely to be considered independent.") See also Port Authority of N.Y. and N.J. v. Arcadian Corp., 189 F.3d 305 (3d Cir.1999) (applying New York and New Jersey law) (accord, World Trade Center bombing).

4. *Keys Left in Car.* One fairly common proximate-cause puzzle involves an intervening criminal act and subsequent negligence by the intervenor. This occurs when defendant leaves keys in the ignition of his unlocked automobile. A thief drives off with the vehicle and negligently injures plaintiff in a subsequent collision. See, for example, Kozicki v. Dragon, 255 Neb. 248, 583 N.W.2d 336 (1998) (teenage thief testified that four or five of the cars she had stolen had ended up wrecked and police officer submitted affidavit that stolen vehicles are more likely to be involved in accidents). For treatment when a statute or ordinance is involved, see Ney v. Yellow Cab Co., page 225 and notes thereafter. When there is no statute or ordinance involved, some courts have declined to impose liability on the owner unless the vehicle has been left in an area where the crime is especially likely to happen. See Hergenrether v. East, 61 Cal.2d 440, 393 P.2d 164, 39 Cal.Rptr. 4 (1964). Other courts leave the decision of proximate cause to the jury. See Herrera v. Quality Pontiac, 134 N.M. 43, 73 P.3d 181 (2003) (case brought by victims of head-on collision with stolen vehicle against owner who had left unlocked car with keys in ignition at service station should have gone to jury for determination of proximate cause). Should the owner of the lot where an unlocked vehicle is left be liable? Cf. Kim v. Budget Rent A Car, 143 Wash.2d 190, 15 P.3d 1283 (2001) (no liability for damage done by van stolen from parking lot of administrative office of rental car company). The fact that the vehicle is an extraordinarily dangerous one may also be a circumstance that suggests liability. See Richardson v. Ham, 44 Cal.2d 772, 285 P.2d 269 (1955) (26-ton bulldozer left unlocked and unguarded at construction site).

5. *Intervening Intentional Misconduct.* What if the conduct is not necessarily criminal, but at least intentional? Defendant service station attendant sold a small amount of gasoline to six-year-old Penny Jones. Penny falsely told the attendant that her mother had requested it. Later that day, Penny's four-year-old half-sister Candy threw a lighted match into the gasoline and the ensuing flames ignited her legs and dress. Is defendant liable? Can the principal case be distinguished? See Jones v. Robbins, 289 So.2d 104 (La.1974). See also, Kush v. City of Buffalo, 59 N.Y.2d 26, 449 N.E.2d 725, 462 N.Y.S.2d 831 (1983) (plaintiff was injured by chemicals negligently stored by defendant and then stolen by two teenagers).

6. In Village of Carterville v. Cook, 129 Ill. 152, 22 N.E. 14 (1889), defendant excavated a hole in the sidewalk and a third person negligently jostled the plaintiff into it. Defendant was held liable. What if the third person had deliberately pushed plaintiff into the hole? Alexander v. New Castle, 115 Ind. 51, 17 N.E. 200 (1888); Milostan v. Chicago, 148 Ill.App. 540 (1909).

7. Defendant left the door of its elevator shaft unlocked and unguarded. A stranger, impersonating an elevator boy, politely ushered plaintiff through the door. She fell down the shaft and was injured. Is defendant liable? Cole v. German Savings & Loan Society, 124 Fed. 113 (8th Cir.1903).

8. In Parness v. Tempe, 123 Ariz. 460, 600 P.2d 764 (App.1979), a young boy was pushed to the ground by two others at a neighborhood recreation center. The center did not provide adequate supervision. Should it be liable for the intentional conduct of others? In Stevens v. Des Moines Independent Community School Dist., 528 N.W.2d 117 (Iowa 1995), the school failed to adequately supervise the corridors at a middle school and plaintiff was beaten by another student. Is the student's intentional act a superseding cause?

9. Defendant engaged in an extramarital affair with plaintiff's husband. Plaintiff alleges that defendant knew or should have known that she had a sexually transmitted disease and failed to warn plaintiff's husband that she was infectious. Plaintiff contracted the disease from her husband and filed suit against defendant for damages. Is the conduct of plaintiff's husband an intentional act that is a superseding cause that cuts off liability? Lockhart v. Loosen, 943 P.2d 1074 (Okla.1997) (would be superseding cause *if* husband knew of disease because defendant's silence—which could have been a proximate cause of plaintiff's injury—would then be a mere condition).

Fuller v. Preis

New York Court of Appeals, 1974.
35 N.Y.2d 425, 322 N.E.2d 263, 363 N.Y.S.2d 568.

BREITEL, CHIEF JUDGE. Plaintiff executor, in a wrongful death action, recovered a jury verdict for $200,000. The Appellate Division set aside the verdict and judgment in favor of plaintiff executor and dismissed the complaint. In doing so, that court noted that even if it were not to dismiss the complaint, it would set the verdict aside as contrary to the weight of the credible evidence. Plaintiff executor appeals.

Decedent, Dr. Lewis, committed suicide some seven months after an automobile accident from which he had walked away believing he was uninjured. In fact he had suffered head injuries with consequences to be detailed later. The theory of the case was that defendants, owner and operator of the vehicle which struck decedent's automobile, were responsible in tort for the suicide as a matter of proximate cause and effect. The issue is whether plaintiff's evidence of cause of the suicide was sufficient to withstand dismissal of the complaint.

There should be a reversal of the order of the Appellate Division and a new trial ordered. * * *

[An] act of suicide, as a matter of law, is not a superseding cause in negligence law precluding liability. An initial tort-feasor may be liable for the wrongful acts of a third party if foreseeable (see Restatement (Second) of Torts § 442A). * * *

Thus, there is neither public policy nor precedent barring recovery for suicide of a tortiously injured person driven "insane" by the consequence of the tortious act. [Cc] * * *

[T]his case was tried for all purposes in accordance with the prevailing law. Indeed, the jury was instructed, primarily, upon the theory of liability for a suicide by an accident victim suffering from ensuing mental disease, who was unable to control the "irresistible impulse" to destroy himself. The theory of the trial, therefore, determines the rule to be applied on the appeal.

Dr. Lewis was physically and mentally healthy immediately prior to the automobile accident in which he struck his head against the interior of his own vehicle. After the accident he suffered several epileptic seizures, often with unconsciousness. Before the accident he had never suffered a seizure. For seven months between the accident and his death, Dr. Lewis experienced no fewer than 38 separate seizures. * * *

The only authentic issue is whether the suicide was an "irresistible impulse" caused by traumatic organic brain damage. * * *

On the day of the suicide, only seven months after the accident, when Dr. Lewis had had three seizures, his daughter tried to speak with him but he did not respond. After the third seizure he seemed unable to recognize his wife, had a strange look, and locked himself in the bathroom. Twenty minutes later, his wife heard him mutter, "I must do it, I must do it", and then a gunshot rang out. Dr. Lewis had shot himself in the head and died the following day. * * *

In tort law, as contrasted with criminal law, there is recognition that one may retain the power to intend, to know, and yet to have an irresistible impulse to act and therefore be incapable of voluntary conduct. * * *

The issue in this case was, precisely, whether Dr. Lewis, who obviously knew what he was doing and intended to do what he did, nevertheless, was, because of mental derangement, incapable of resisting the impulse to destroy himself. Precedents and modern knowledge say that that could have been. The jury found that it was so. * * *

Of course, there may be and undoubtedly have been cases where the causal nexus becomes too tenuous to permit a jury to "speculate" as to the proximate cause of the suicide. * * *

A suicide is a strange act and no rationalistic approach can fit the act into neat categories of rationality or irrationality. When the suicide is preceded by a history of trauma, brain damage, epileptic seizures, aberrational conduct, depression and despair, it is at the very least a fair issue of fact whether the suicide was the rational act of a sound mind or the irrational act or irresistible impulse of a deranged mind evidenced by a physically damaged brain. It would be illogical to conclude otherwise. Consequently, although the Appellate Division in exercise of its supervisory power to review the facts could set the jury verdict aside, it was impermissible for it to dismiss the complaint.

Since the Appellate Division, in reversing, stated that in any event it would have set the verdict aside as contrary to the weight of the evidence, the verdict in favor of plaintiff may not be reinstated and a new trial is required.

Accordingly, the order of the Appellate Division should be reversed, with costs, and a new trial directed.

NOTES AND QUESTIONS

1. Courts generally view suicide as a deliberate, intentional act. See Cleveland v. Rotman, 297 F.3d 569 (7th Cir. 2002) (applying Illinois law) (upholding summary judgment for defendant where estate had not alleged that decedent was mentally unstable and court assumed that decedent was a "competent adult who clearly understood what he was doing and intentionally took his own life") and Rollins v. Wachenhut Services, Inc., 703 F.3d 122 (D.C. Cir. 2012) (applying D.C. law) (recognizing that most jurisdictions, including D.C., view suicide as an intervening, intentional act that breaks the chain of causation and dismissing estate's complaint against decedent's employer for negligently providing him with a gun with which he committed suicide while on guard duty).

2. Early decisions steadfastly denied claims based on causing suicide if the decedent had even the slightest awareness of what he was doing. See Scheffer v. Railroad Co., 105 U.S. 249 (1881) (death by suicide eight months after injury in train accident); Daniels v. New York, N.H. & H.R. Co., 183 Mass. 393, 67 N.E. 424 (1903) ("An act of suicide resulting from a moderately intelligent power of choice, even though the choice is determined by a disordered mind, should be deemed a new and independent, efficient cause of the death that immediately ensues."). Even when defendant had engaged in conduct likely to cause severe emotional distress, courts found decedent's cognitive understanding of her act made it a superseding cause. Lancaster v. Montesi, 216 Tenn. 50, 390 S.W.2d 217 (1965) (after suffering physical and emotional abuse, "paramour" of defendant wrote a suicide note, left apartment, traveled to bridge, and then jumped off).

Liability for suicide following a negligent act was broadened somewhat when some courts permitted recovery if the decedent's injury caused an irresistible impulse to commit suicide. In addition to the principal case, see Tate v. Canonica, 180 Cal.App.2d 898, 5 Cal.Rptr. 28, 40 (1960) ("where the negligent wrong only causes a mental condition in which the injured person is able to realize the nature of the act of suicide and has the power to control it if he so desires, the act then becomes an independent intervening force and the wrongdoer cannot be held liable for the death. On the other hand, if the negligent wrong causes mental illness which results in an uncontrollable impulse to commit suicide, then the wrongdoer may be held liable for the death."). Kivland v. Columbia Orthopaedic Group., LLP, 331 S.W.3d 299 (Mo. 2011) (jury question whether pain due to medical malpractice had robbed patient of his ability to act rationally and, therefore, his suicide was not voluntary). Most courts found an irresistible impulse only when decedent acted in a sudden frenzy; if decedent left a note or purchased poison or otherwise evidenced planning, the courts found decedent was in control and therefore denied recovery. In one decision, the court relied on the efficient manner in which the decedent had prepared for and cut his throat to deny recovery. Brown v. American Steel and Wire Co., 43 Ind.App. 560, 88 N.E. 80 (1909). See also Long v. Omaha & C.B. St. R. Co., 108 Neb. 342, 187 N.W. 930 (1922) (decedent purchased a shell for his shotgun, took it home, loaded gun, and shot himself).

For modern cases applying the irresistible impulse exception and discussing the development of the doctrine, see Clift v. Narragansett Television, 688 A.2d 805 (R.I. 1996) and Corales v. Bennett, 567 F.3d 554 (9th Cir. 2009) (applying California law) (after being "sternly lectured" for leaving campus the day before without permission, eighth grader attended classes, spoke with friends about what had happened, went home, talked to his mother by telephone, wrote a detailed suicide note, and then shot himself—uncontrollable impulse not shown).

Contrast these with the approach taken by the House of Lords in Corr v. IBC Vehicles Ltd., [2008] 1 A.C. 884, [2008] 2 All E.R. 943, unanimously permitting recovery for the death of plaintiff by suicide about six years after the accident that caused him severe head injuries and three months after he had been admitted to the hospital after taking a drug overdose. The personal injury case had been filed three years after the accident and was still pending at the time plaintiff took his life by jumping from the top of a car park. His widow was substituted as the party representing his estate on the personal injury claim and also sought recovery under the wrongful death act. Both sides agreed that he had the capacity to manage his own affairs, that his intellectual ability and appreciation of danger were not affected, and that he acted deliberately with the intention of killing himself. The court found that a severe depressive episode caused by the accident had impaired his capacity to make reasoned and informed judgments about his future and thus his suicide did not cut off liability between the defendant's negligence and the damages for his death sought by his widow.

3. Courts are more likely to permit a claim where the tort was intentional. See R.D. v. W.H., 875 P.2d 26 (Wyo.1994) (stepfather had sexually abused the decedent, provided her with a firearm with which she attempted suicide, and then later provided her with prescription narcotics with which she killed herself) and Cauverien v. De Metz, 20 Misc.2d 144, 188 N.Y.S.2d 627 (Sup.Ct.1959) (defendants converted a diamond that decedent had on consignment, refusing to return it or pay for it, deliberately blackening decedent's reputation and ruining his livelihood, and causing him an irresistible impulse to end his life).

4. Some worker compensation cases have allowed a claim when a work-related accident was a substantial factor in the decedent's becoming incapable of normal judgment and then committing suicide. Would that be an appropriate rule for tort law? See Clift v. Narragansett Television, 688 A.2d 805 (R.I. 1996) (noting that the analysis of the worker compensation cases has not been adopted in the tort cases).

5. Suppose a criminal defense attorney was negligent in defending her client and he committed suicide in jail after being wrongfully convicted? Is the attorney liable for the client's death? McLaughlin v. Sullivan, 123

N.H. 335, 461 A.2d 123 (1983) (denying liability because connection between negligence in the practice of law and decedent's suicide twelve hours after arriving in jail is too attenuated) and McPeake v. William T. Cannon, 381 Pa.Super. 227, 553 A.2d 439 (1989) (accord in case where client leapt from fifth floor window of courthouse upon being found guilty).

6. An affirmative duty to use care to prevent suicide is sometimes imposed by tort law upon certain classes of defendants. There, plaintiff's suicide would not be an intentional act that supersedes defendant's negligence. Jacoves v. United Merchandising Corp., 9 Cal.App.4th 88, 11 Cal.Rptr.2d 468 (1992) (suicide itself was the foreseeable risk and cannot, therefore, be a superseding cause).

7. What if defendant negligently sells a gun, ammunition, or drugs to plaintiff who uses it to commit suicide? Scoggins v. Wal-Mart Stores, Inc., 560 N.W.2d 564 (Iowa 1997) (ammunition sold to minor; plaintiff's act is superseding cause) (collecting cases); Runyon v. Reid, 510 P.2d 943 (Okla.1973) (barbiturates sold without refill authorization; plaintiff's act is superseding cause). The cases suggest that the result might have been otherwise if defendants had had reason to suspect the intent of the purchaser. Compare the cases on liability of a seller of liquor, note 6, page 371.

McCoy v. American Suzuki Motor Corp.

Supreme Court of Washington, 1998.
136 Wash.2d 350, 961 P.2d 952.

SANDERS, J. * * * At 5:00 p.m. on a cold November evening James McCoy drove eastbound on Interstate 90 outside Spokane as the car which preceded him, a Suzuki Samurai, swerved off the roadway and rolled. McCoy stopped to render assistance, finding the driver seriously injured. Shortly thereafter a Washington State Patrol trooper arrived on the scene and asked McCoy to place flares on the roadway to warn approaching vehicles. McCoy did so, but concerned the flares were insufficient, continued further and positioned himself a quarter-mile from the accident scene with a lit flare in each hand, manually directing traffic to the inside lane.

By 6:50 p.m., almost two hours after the accident, the injured driver and passenger of the Suzuki were removed and the scene was cleared, leaving only the trooper and McCoy on the roadway. McCoy walked back on the shoulder of the roadway to his car with a lit flare in his roadside hand. When McCoy was within three or four car-lengths of the trooper, the trooper pulled away without comment. Moments later McCoy was struck from behind while still walking on the roadway's shoulder by a hit-and-run vehicle.

McCoy and his wife filed a multicount complaint against the driver of the Suzuki for negligent driving; the passenger of the Suzuki for negligently grabbing the steering wheel when the car was fishtailing, further causing it to lose control; the State for the negligence of the trooper; and American Suzuki Motor Corporation and its parent corporation, Suzuki Motor Company, Ltd., for its allegedly defective Samurai which allegedly caused the wreck in the first place. We presently consider only McCoy's claim against Suzuki. * * *

Suzuki moved for summary judgment asserting: (1) the rescue doctrine does not apply to product liability actions; and (2) even if it does, McCoy must still, but cannot, prove Suzuki proximately caused his injuries. The trial court found the rescue doctrine applies to product liability actions but concluded any alleged defect in the Suzuki was not the proximate cause of McCoy's injuries and, accordingly, granted summary judgment of dismissal. * * *

[McCoy appealed the dismissal and the Court of Appeals reversed, finding the rescue doctrine applies in product liability actions just as it does in negligence actions, but that an injured rescuer need not prove the defendant proximately caused his injuries. Instead the court concluded the rescuer need only prove the defendant proximately caused the danger and that the rescuer was injured while rescuing.]

The Rescue Doctrine

The rescue doctrine is invoked in tort cases for a variety of purposes in a variety of scenarios. The doctrine, as here asserted, allows an injured rescuer to sue the party which caused the danger requiring the rescue in the first place. [C] As Justice Cardozo succinctly summarized, the heart of this doctrine is the notion that "danger invites rescue." Wagner v. International Ry. Co., 232 N.Y. 176, 133 N.E. 437, 437, 19 A.L.R.1 (1921). This doctrine serves two functions. First, it informs a tort-feasor it is foreseeable a rescuer will come to the aid of the person imperiled by the tort-feasor's actions, and, therefore, the tort-feasor owes the rescuer a duty similar to the duty he owes the person he imperils. [Cc] Second, the rescue doctrine negates the presumption that the rescuer assumed the risk of injury when he knowingly undertook the dangerous rescue, so long as he does not act rashly or recklessly. [C]

To achieve rescuer status one must demonstrate: (1) the defendant was negligent to the person rescued and such negligence caused the peril or appearance of peril to the person rescued; (2) the peril or appearance of peril was imminent; (3) a reasonably prudent person would have concluded such peril or appearance of peril existed; and (4) the rescuer acted with reasonable care in effectuating the rescue. [C] The Court of Appeals found McCoy demonstrated sufficient facts of rescuer status to put the issue of whether he met the four requirements * * * to the jury. [C] Suzuki does not question this finding. Nor will we.

Does the Rescue Doctrine Apply in Product Liability Actions?

Suzuki argues the rescue doctrine may not be invoked in product liability actions. Suzuki contends the [Washington product liability statute] supplants all common law remedies and contends the rescue doctrine is nothing more than a common law remedy. We disagree. The rescue doctrine is not a common law remedy. Rather, it is shorthand for the idea that rescuers are to be anticipated and is a reflection of a societal value judgment that rescuers should not be barred from bringing suit for knowingly placing themselves in danger to undertake a rescue. We can conceive of no reason why this doctrine should not apply with equal force when a product manufacturer causes the danger. * * * We adopt the Court of Appeals analysis on this point and conclude the rescue doctrine may be invoked in product liability actions just as it may in ordinary negligence actions.

Must Plaintiff Show Proximate Causation Under the Rescue Doctrine?

McCoy argues the rescue doctrine relieves the rescuer-plaintiff of proving the defendant's wrongdoing proximately caused his injuries. McCoy asserts a rescuer may prevail in a suit by showing the defendant proximately caused the danger and that, while serving as rescuer, the plaintiff was injured. The Court of Appeals agreed stating the rescue doctrine "varies the ordinary rules of negligence." McCoy, 86 Wash. App. at 110 (citing Solgaard v. Guy F. Atkinson Co., 6 Cal. 3d 361, 491 P.2d 821, 99 Cal. Rptr. 29 (1971)).

The Court of Appeals erred on this point. * * * [The rescuer, like any other plaintiff, must still show the defendant proximately caused his injuries.]

In Maltman [v. Sauer, 84 Wash.2d 975, 530 P.2d 254 (1975)] a rescue helicopter was called to the scene of an auto accident to transport one of the injured to the hospital. However, the rescue helicopter crashed on the way to the scene killing the entire crew. A wrongful death suit was brought on behalf of the deceased crew members under the rescue doctrine against the party which allegedly caused the car accident in the first place. We * * * concluded, as a matter of law, the car accident was not the proximate cause of the helicopter crash and, accordingly, dismissed. [C]

We adhere to *Maltman* noting its requirement that a rescuer show the defendant proximately caused his injuries is in keeping with general principles of liability.

Did Suzuki Proximately Cause McCoy's Injuries?

Concluding that the rescue doctrine may apply to a product liability action and that the rescuer must show the defendant proximately caused his injuries, we question whether McCoy has demonstrated Suzuki proximately caused his injuries. * * *

Here, Suzuki argues, it was totally unforeseeable that a rescuer such as McCoy would be injured by a third vehicle under these particular facts and, accordingly, Suzuki asks us to rule in its favor on this issue as a matter of law. We find the issue of foreseeability of the intervening cause is sufficiently close that it should be decided by a jury, not the court. A jury might consider the position of the rescuer, the negligence of the oncoming motorist, if any, and many other factors.

McCoy cites In re Estate of Keck v. Blair, 71 Wash. App. 105, 108–09, 856 P.2d 740 (1993). In Keck a rescuer aided a driver who had been drinking and who caused an accident. As the rescuer escorted the driver across the highway to safety, a car approached and the rescuer had barely enough time to push the person he was rescuing to safety but was himself hit and instantly killed. The Court of Appeals allowed the decedent's estate to bring suit against the person he was rescuing under the rescue doctrine. The court held it could not say as a matter of law whether the original accident was the proximate cause of decedent's injuries and accordingly remanded the case for jury determination. The facts of the present case are not sufficiently different from those of Keck to take the issue from the jury.

In the present case, if the Suzuki Samurai is found to be defective the jury could find it foreseeable that the Suzuki Samurai would roll and that an approaching car would cause injury to either those in the Suzuki Samurai or to a rescuer, depending on the specific facts to be proved. We note sister jurisdictions have reached the same conclusion under similar facts. * * *

As numerous cases illustrate, the court often exercises its gatekeeper function by dismissing an action without trial for lack of legal cause if the defendant's actions are too remote a cause of plaintiff's injuries. In *Maltman* we dismissed the action, reasoning the party causing the principal accident should not be liable for the subsequent crash of a rescue helicopter hundreds of miles away because the helicopter crash was simply too remote a result of the principal accident. In *Hartley* [v. State, 103 Wash.2d 768, 698 P.2d 77 (1985)] the estate of a decedent killed by a drunk driver sued the State for failing to revoke the drunk driver's license. There we similarly dismissed reasoning the State should not be held liable for injuries caused by a driver simply because the State failed to revoke that driver's license. [C] Such fault on the State's behalf was again too remote a cause of the ensuing injury to impose liability.

Here, we do not find the alleged fault of Suzuki, if proved, to be so remote from these injuries that its liability should be cut off as a matter of law. Certainly the alleged fault of Suzuki is not as remote as the fault of the defendants in *Maltman* and *Hartley* and, thus, we must distinguish their results. Accordingly, we will not dismiss this case for lack of legal causation. Instead we remand the case for trial consistent with this opinion. * * *

NOTES AND QUESTIONS

1. What happens to the case after the Washington Supreme Court opinion? What must McCoy prove at trial in order to recover from Suzuki?

2. The opinion quotes Judge Cardozo's famous pronouncement in Wagner v. International Ry. Co., 232 N.Y. 176, 180, 133 N.E. 437, 437–38 (1921): "Danger invites rescue." In that opinion, he went on to say "[t]he cry of distress is the summons to relief. The law does not ignore these reactions of the mind in tracing conduct to its consequences. It recognizes them as normal. It places their effects within the range of the natural and probable. The wrong that perils life is a wrong to the imperiled victim; it is a wrong also to his rescuer. . . . The risk of rescue, if only it be not wanton is born of the occasion. The emergency begets the man. The wrongdoer may not have foreseen the coming of a deliverer. He is accountable as if he had."

3. A few of the numerous legal problems raised by the "rescue doctrine" are noted here. By his efforts the rescuer may injure himself, as in *McCoy* and *Wagner*, or the rescuee, or a third person. Are the proximate cause issues the same? Should the defendant be liable for all of these injuries? See Restatement (Third) of Torts: Liability for Physical and Emotional Harm § 32 (2010) (the scope of the actor's liability includes any harm to a person resulting from that person's efforts to aid or to protect the

imperiled person or property, so long as the harm arises from a risk that inheres in the effort to provide aid).

4. *Rescuer Sues Rescuee.* House caught fire because water heater was negligently installed too close to insulation. Passerby saw smoke and stopped to assist family in escaping. Husband broke bedroom window and lowered child to passerby. Husband was then trying to clear away more glass to make a wider opening when wife pushed him aside and dove head first out window. Passerby was injured trying to break her fall. Passerby sued installer of water heater and wife. Rescue doctrine applies to installer. Does it also apply to rescuee wife? See Williams v. Foster, 281 Ill.App.3d 203, 217 Ill.Dec. 9, 666 N.E.2d 678 (1996) (court raised but did not reach issue because it found wife was not negligent in jumping from burning building). See also In re Estate of Keck v. Blair, 71 Wash.App. 105, 856 P.2d 740 (1993) (cited in the principal case) (permitting case against rescuee); Sears v. Morrison, 90 Cal.Rptr.2d 528, 76 Cal.App.4th 577 (1999) (permitting case against rescuee); Lowrey v. Horvath, 689 S.W.2d 625 (Mo.1985) (rescue doctrine extends to plaintiff's decedent killed while trying to rescue defendant from well). Suppose the rescuee was in the act of taking his own life and clearly did not want to be rescued? See Talbert v. Talbert, 22 Misc.2d 782, 199 N.Y.S.2d 212 (1960) (son's case against father allowed to proceed for recovery of injuries sustained while breaking garage door window to rescue father from attempted suicide).

5. What if the attempt at rescue is *utterly foolish*? A passenger about to alight from defendant's train hands her baby to a man on the platform. The train unexpectedly starts up and carries her away. A bystander heroically snatches up the child and runs after the train. He runs the length of the platform, losing ground steadily, and stumbles over a baggage truck at the far end. The child is injured. Liability? Atchison, T. & S.F.R. Co. v. Calhoun, 213 U.S. 1 (1909) (no liability). Cf. Robinson v. Butler, 226 Minn. 491, 33 N.W.2d 821 (1948) (no liability where excited passenger seized steering wheel of automobile to help avoid collision). Suppose the rescuer was mistaken and the rescuee was not actually in danger? Cf. Ellmaker v. Goodyear Tire & Rubber Co., 372 S.W.2d 650 (Mo.App.1963) (doctrine applies as long as mistake was a reasonable one).

6. An active-duty marine in town as a recruiter was having a drink at a bar with a blonde woman known only as "Dimples" when a grease fire flared up at the grill where hamburgers were being cooked just outside the bar. The fire was extinguished but the grill attendant could not turn off the gas because the valve was too hot. At that point, the marine took off his shirt, wrapped it around his hand, walked up to the grill, and turned the gas off just as the fire flared up and burned him. He sued the bar in negligence and the bar argued everything was under control, the fire department was on its way, and that no one was in danger until the marine placed himself there. Judge Cardozo's "normal" reaction of a rescuer or an utterly foolish one? Clinkscales v. Nelson Securities, Inc., 697 N.W.2d 836 (Iowa 2005) (should have been question for the jury).

7. Suppose the lawsuit is based on *product liability* rather than negligence? In addition to the principal case, see Dillard v. Pittway Corp., 719 So.2d 188 (Ala.1998) (smoke detector manufacturer liable to neighbor who was injured trying to rescue elderly residents from boarding house fire) and Govich v. North American Systems, Inc., 112 N.M. 226, 814 P.2d

94 (1991) (manufacturer of coffee maker that started house fire may be liable to resident who entered home to rescue his guide dog).

8. What about the *rescuer of a rescuer*? Richards v. Kansas Electric Power Co., 126 Kan. 521, 268 P. 847 (1928) (father rushed to rescue of son who had been knocked down by live wire that son was trying to keep away from house during thunderstorm); Brown v. Ross, 345 Mich. 54, 75 N.W.2d 68 (1956) (dropping his teenage son off at work at gas station, father saw car accident that damaged pump and started fire; after pulling his car away, he went back and took fire extinguisher from son and sent him to call fire department, just as explosion occurred); Richardson v. United States, 248 F.Supp. 99 (E.D.Okl.1965) (mother injured while rescuing son who was in a position of peril because he was attempting to rescue father who drowned due to negligence of defendant); Govich v. North American Systems, Inc., 112 N.M. 226, 814 P.2d 94 (1991) (mother injured rescuing adult son from his burning home, which he had entered to rescue his guide dog).

9. Suppose the injured *rescuer is a professional*—a police officer, a firefighter, a lifeguard, a paramedic. Most states do not permit recovery by professionals, at least against the property owner or driver whose negligence occasioned the response, under the so-called "firefighter's rule" or the "professional rescuer's rule." The rationale for the rule is sometimes grounded in premises liability distinctions between licensees and invitees (see Chapter 9, Owners and Occupiers of Land), sometimes grounded in assumption of risk principles, and sometimes in public policy considerations including that those professionals already have been compensated for their potentially hazardous duty. See, e.g., Fordham v. Oldroyd, 2007 UT 74, 171 P.3d 411 (2007) (state trooper injured while getting flares from his trunk sued driver whose car had crashed due to icy and snowy road conditions) and Nowicki v. Pigue, 430 S.W.3d 765 (Ark. 2013) (state roadside assistance worker injured after stopping to assist the driver of a tractor trailer who had run out of gas sued driver for running out of gas and not putting warning markers or reflectors behind the stalled truck). The rule operates to preclude recovery only if the risk created was the type of risk reasonably anticipated by the job. Compare Smith v. Tully, 665 A.2d 1333 (R.I.1995) (police officer injured in altercation with an intoxicated person armed with a knife in a bar after responding to call from bar employee barred by firefighter's rule) with Solgaard v. Guy F. Atkinson Co., 6 Cal.3d 361, 491 P.2d 821, 99 Cal.Rptr. 29 (1971) (doctor who had agreed to provide medical services at construction site not barred when he was injured in seeking to reach injured person trapped in landslide). The firefighter's rule has been limited or abolished in some jurisdictions. See, e.g., Cole v. Hubanks, 272 Wis.2d 539, 681 N.W.2d 147 (2004) (does not apply to police officer attacked by stray dog while she was trying to capture it); Espinoza v. Schulenburg, 212 Ariz. 215, 129 P.3d 937 (2006) (does not apply to off-duty EMT who stopped to assist car accident victims); Tucker v. Shoemake, 354 Md. 413, 731 A.2d 884 (1999) (does not apply if alleged negligence was independent and not related to situation requiring police response); and Ruiz v. Mero, 189 N.J. 525, 917 A.2d 239 (2007) (recognizing that New Jersey legislature has abolished the "firefighter's rule," thus allowing police officer who responded to call for assistance at bar and was attacked by bar patrons to sue bar owner for inadequate security).

California has used assumption of the risk principles and public policy arguments to bar the lawsuit of an in-home caregiver who was attacked by the Alzheimer's patient she was being paid to care for. Gregory v. Cott, 59 Cal.4th 996, 331 P.3d 179, 176 Cal.Rptr.3d 1 (2014) (claims arising from inherent occupational hazards first developed as the "firefighter's rule," which precludes firefighters and police officers from suing members of the public for the conduct that makes their employment necessary). See also Chapter 12's discussion of primary implied assumption of the risk at pages 644–648.

10. *Attempt to Escape from Danger Created by Defendant.* The cases generally agree that the defendant who caused the danger will be liable to someone who is injured trying to escape from it. The classic decision is Tuttle v. Atlantic City R. Co., 66 N.J.L. 327, 49 A. 450 (1901), where a freight car jumped a track and lunged across the street. Plaintiff, on the sidewalk, ran from the car, fell and injured her knee. She was allowed to recover. See also Kroeger v. Safranek, 161 Neb. 182, 72 N.W.2d 831 (1955) (after collision that drove a truck into a cornfield on the side of the road, driver was electrocuted by wires from a utility pole knocked down by his truck as it left the road); Thornton v. Weaber, 380 Pa. 590, 112 A.2d 344 (1955) (teen driver lost control on curve and hit utility pole, downing wires that electrified the metal guardrails and cable on shoulder of road so that driver and passenger were electrocuted when they tried to climb back onto road from meadow where truck had come to rest after accident).

11. *Attempt to Alleviate Harm Caused by Defendant.* The primary example of this is the case in which a physician treats the plaintiff's injuries and negligently aggravates them. Is the original defendant liable for the aggravation? The usual answer is in the affirmative. Fairchild v. S.C. Dept. of Transp., 398 S.C. 90, 727 S.E.2d 407 (2011) (defendant driver suggested that plaintiff's headaches were caused by overmedication; plaintiff entitled to jury instruction that driver also would be liable for damages from physician's negligence). In Banks v. Elks Club, 301 S.W.3d 214 (Tenn. 2010), the plaintiff's injuries from collapse of chair at Elks Club were made worse by medical malpractice of orthopedic surgeon and then of nursing home where she contracted infection. The nursing home would be liable for the infection, the surgeon for the medical malpractice and the infection, the Elks Club for all of the injuries. In this context, the court notes that the surgeon is both a successive tortfeasor and an original tortfeasor. Suppose the injured party is being taken by an ambulance to the hospital for treatment. An accident en route causes additional injuries. Should it make any difference whether the second collision was caused by (1) the speed of the ambulance because of the emergency, (2) the negligence of the ambulance driver though no emergency was involved, or (3) the negligence of a third party in running into the ambulance? Atherton v. Devine, 602 P.2d 634 (Okla.1979); Anaya v. Superior Court, 78 Cal.App.4th 971, 93 Cal.Rptr.2d 228 (2000) (driver liable for plaintiff's death in helicopter crash en route to hospital after automobile accident). The intervening negligence may be so unusual that the court holds it to be superseding, as in Purchase v. Seelye, 231 Mass. 434, 121 N.E. 413 (1918), where the hospital made a mistake and operated on the wrong patient. See Restatement (Third) of Torts: Liability for Physical and Emotional Harm § 35 (2010) (original tortfeasor liable for enhanced harm unless it arises from harm different from harm incident to normal efforts to render aid).

12. *Second Injury Caused by Weakened Condition Resulting from First Injury.* There are some recurrent patterns falling into this classification, in which the cases have indicated a more or less crystallized response, holding the first defendant liable for the second injury. The first involves the onset of a disease likely to attack one in a weakened condition—for example, pneumonia in Beauchamp v. Saginaw Mining Co., 50 Mich. 163, 15 N.W. 65 (1883), or streptococcus infection in Wallace v. Ludwig, 292 Mass. 251, 198 N.E. 159 (1935). An earlier distinction depending on the time when the germs invaded the body has been abandoned, but it will still make a difference whether the disease was of a type that would attack a healthy person and produce the same result. See, e.g., Case of Upham, 245 Mass. 31, 139 N.E. 433 (1923) (appendicitis).

Another type of case involves a second breaking of a limb that had not fully recovered its original strength. The plaintiff usually recovers for the second injury. Squires v. Reynolds, 125 Conn. 366, 5 A.2d 877 (1939); Mitchell v. Legarsky, 95 N.H. 214, 60 A.2d 136 (1948). Factors that may affect the holding, however, include the length of time between the accidents, the location and nature of the second injury, the reasonableness of the plaintiff's conduct, and the character of the second accident. See Linder v. Payette, 64 Idaho 656, 135 P.2d 440 (1943) (no recovery where plaintiff drowned while fishing when boat capsized; defendant was responsible for plaintiff's arm being in a plaster cast weighing eight pounds).

3. PUBLIC POLICY

Kelly v. Gwinnell

Supreme Court of New Jersey, 1984.
96 N.J. 538, 476 A.2d 1219.

[Defendant Gwinnell, after having driven coworker Zak home, spent an hour or two at Zak's home before leaving to return to his own home. During that time, Gwinnell consumed two or three drinks of scotch on the rocks with Zak and his wife. Zak accompanied Gwinnell outside to his car, chatted with him, and watched as Gwinnell drove off to go home. On the way home, Gwinnell was involved in a head-on collision with an automobile operated by plaintiff Marie Kelly, who was seriously injured. Kelly sued Gwinnell and Gwinnell's employer, and those defendants in turn sued the Zaks in a third party action. Thereafter, plaintiff amended her complaint to include the Zaks as direct defendants. The trial court granted the Zaks' motion for summary judgment holding that as a matter of law a host is not liable for the negligence of an adult social guest who has become intoxicated at the host's home. The appellate court affirmed, noting that New Jersey has no Dram Shop Act imposing liability on the provider of alcoholic beverages and that New Jersey common law liability had been extended to a social host only when the guest was a minor.]

WILENTZ, C.J. This case raises the issue of whether a social host who enables an adult guest at his home to become drunk is liable to the victim of an automobile accident caused by the drunken driving of the guest. Here the host served liquor to the guest beyond the point at which the guest was visibly intoxicated. We hold the host may be liable under [certain] circumstances. * * *

"Negligence is tested by whether the reasonably prudent person at the time and place should recognize and foresee an unreasonable risk or likelihood of harm or danger to others." [Cc] When negligent conduct creates such a risk, setting off foreseeable consequences that lead to plaintiff's injury, the conduct is deemed the proximate cause of the injury. "[A] tortfeasor is generally held answerable for the injuries which result in the ordinary course of events from his negligence and it is generally sufficient if his negligent conduct was a substantial factor in bringing about the injuries." [Cc]

Under the facts here defendant provided his guest with liquor, knowing that thereafter the guest would have to drive in order to get home. Viewing the facts most favorably to plaintiff (as we must, since the complaint was dismissed on a motion for summary judgment), one could reasonably conclude that the Zaks must have known that their provision of liquor was causing Gwinnell to become drunk, yet they continued to serve him even after he was visibly intoxicated. By the time he left, Gwinnell was in fact severely intoxicated. A reasonable person in Zak's position could foresee quite clearly that this continued provision of alcohol to Gwinnell was making it more and more likely that Gwinnell would not be able to operate his car carefully. Zak could foresee that unless he stopped providing drinks to Gwinnell, Gwinnell was likely to injure someone as a result of the negligent operation of his car. * * *

[T]he only question remaining is whether a duty exists to prevent such risk or, realistically, whether this Court should impose such a duty. * * *

When [a] court determines that a duty exists and liability will be extended, it draws judicial lines based on fairness and policy. In a society where thousands of deaths are caused each year by drunken drivers, where the damage caused by such deaths is regarded increasingly as intolerable, where liquor licensees are prohibited from serving intoxicated adults, and where long-standing criminal sanctions against drunken driving have recently been significantly strengthened to the point where the Governor notes that they are regarded as the toughest in the nation, see Governor's Annual Message to the N.J. State Legislature, Jan. 10, 1984, the imposition of such a duty by the judiciary seems both fair and fully in accord with the State's policy. * * *

We therefore [expand our prior decisions that limited liability to licensees who served liquor for profit or social hosts who served liquor to a minor and] hold that a host who serves liquor to an adult social guest, knowing both that the guest is intoxicated and [that he] will thereafter be operating a motor vehicle, is liable for injuries inflicted on a third party as a result of the negligent operation of a motor vehicle by the adult guest when such negligence is caused by the intoxication. We impose this duty on the host to the third party because we believe that the policy considerations served by its imposition far outweigh those asserted in opposition. While we recognize the concern that our ruling will interfere with accepted standards of social behavior; will intrude on and somewhat diminish the enjoyment, relaxation, and camaraderie that accompany social gatherings at which alcohol is served; and that such gatherings and social relationships are not simply tangential benefits of a civilized society but are regarded by many as important, we believe that the added assurance of just compensation to the victims of drunken driving as well as the added deterrent effect of the rule on such driving outweigh the importance of those other values. * * * We therefore reverse the [summary] judgment in favor of the defendants Zak and remand the case. * * *

GARIBALDI (dissenting). * * * The majority need not parade the horrors that have been caused by drunk drivers to convince me that there is always room for stricter measures against intoxicated drivers. I too am concerned for the injured victim of a drunken driver. However, the almost limitless implications of the majority's decision lead me to conclude that the Legislature is better equipped to effectuate the goals of reducing injuries from drunken driving and protecting the interests of the injured party, without placing such a grave burden on the average citizen of this state. * * *

My reluctance to join the majority is not based on any exaggerated notion of judicial deference to the Legislature. Rather, it is based on my belief that before this Court plunges into this broad area of liability and imposes high duties of care on social hosts, it should carefully consider the ramifications of its actions. * * *

[T]his Court has, in the past, imposed civil liability on commercial licensees who serve alcoholic beverages to intoxicated patrons. Commercial licensees are subject to regulation by both the Alcoholic Beverage Commission (ABC) and the Legislature. It is reasonable to impose tort liability on licensees based on their violation of explicit statutes and regulations.

I have no quarrel with the imposition of such liability because of the peculiar position occupied by the licensee. A social host, however, is in a different position. * * *

A significant difference between an average citizen and a commercial licensee is the average citizen's lack of knowledge and expertise in determining levels and degrees of intoxication. Licensed commercial providers, unlike the average citizen, deal with the alcohol-consuming public every day. This experience gives them some expertise with respect to intoxication that social hosts lack. A social host will find it more difficult to determine levels and degrees of intoxication. * * *

The nature of home entertaining compounds the social host's difficulty in determining whether a guest is obviously intoxicated before serving the next drink. In a commercial establishment, there is greater control over the liquor; a bartender or waitress must serve the patron a drink. Not so in a home when entertaining a guest. At a social gathering, for example, guests frequently serve themselves or guests may serve other guests. Normally, the host is so busy entertaining he does not have time to analyze the state of intoxication of the guests. * * * Furthermore, the commercial bartender usually does not drink on the job. The social host often drinks with the guest, as the Zaks did here. * * *

Further, it is not clear from the Court's opinion to what lengths a social host must go to avoid liability. Is the host obligated to use physical force to restrain an intoxicated guest from drinking and then from driving? Or is the host limited to delay and subterfuge tactics short of physical force? What is the result when the host tries to restrain the guest but fails? Is the host still liable? The majority opinion is silent on the extent to which we must police our guests.

The most significant difference between a social host and a commercial licensee, however, is the social host's inability to spread the cost of liability. The commercial establishment spreads the cost of insurance against liability among its customers. The social host must bear the entire cost alone. * * *

[The social host] may not have sufficient insurance to cover the limitless liability that the Court seeks to impose. These people may lose everything they own if they are found liable as negligent social hosts under the Court's scheme. The individual economic cost to every New Jersey citizen should be weighed before today's result is reached. * * *

NOTES AND QUESTIONS

1. The New Jersey legislature later modified the decision by statute to limit liability in several ways. Under the statute, liability of the social host extends only to third parties (i.e., not the intoxicated person); there is an irrebuttable presumption that anyone whose blood alcohol level tested at less than 0.10% was not visibly intoxicated and a rebuttable presumption that anyone whose blood alcohol level is between 0.10% and 0.15% was not visibly intoxicated; and the social host is not jointly and severally liable, which means the social host would pay only a portion of the judgment, even if the driver is insolvent.

2. The traditional common law view was that the drinker's voluntary consumption and subsequent negligence was the sole "proximate" cause of the third party's injury and that a person who sold or gave liquor to an intoxicated adult drinker was not liable for subsequent injuries caused by his intoxication. A seminal decision is Cruse v. Aden, 127 Ill. 231, 20 N.E. 73 (1889) where a wife filed suit against her husband's friend for giving her husband two drinks while he was a guest at the friend's house. While returning home on horseback, the husband was thrown from the horse and died. The Illinois Supreme Court refused to impose liability, finding no cause of action for giving "a glass of intoxicating liquor to a friend as a mere act of courtesy and politeness." Illinois has reaffirmed this decision, holding that for "over one century, this court has spoken with a single voice to the effect that no social host liability exists in Illinois." Charles v. Seigfried, 165 Ill.2d 482, 209 Ill.Dec. 226, 651 N.E.2d 154 (1995). See also Ferreira v. Strack, 652 A.2d 965 (R.I.1995). Almost all state supreme courts ruling on this issue have declined to impose liability on a social host when the recipient of the alcohol is an adult. See, e.g., Klein v. Raysinger, 504 Pa. 141, 470 A.2d 507, 510 (1983) ("Thus, the great weight of authority supports the view that in the case of an ordinary able-bodied man it is the consumption of the alcohol, rather than the furnishing of the alcohol, which is the proximate cause of any subsequent occurrence").

3. Why no liability? Could the social hosts argue that the consequences of their serving alcohol were not foreseeable? "The paucity of cases in this country imposing social host liability cannot be explained solely on the ground that a social host does not, as a matter of law, create a reasonably foreseeable risk of harm to highway travelers in serving an alcoholic drink to a drunken guest. The risk created by serving liquor to an intoxicated person who is about to operate a motor vehicle is far too apparent to permit the conclusion that the social host's act could not have been the 'proximate' cause of a third person's injury. The reluctance of courts to impose liability in these circumstances has been founded, rightly or wrongly, on policy considerations, particularly consideration of the effect that a rule of social host liability would have on a multitude of personal relationships in a variety of social settings." McGuiggan v. New England Telephone & Telegraph Co., 398 Mass. 152, 496 N.E.2d 141, 145 (1986). What about the argument that the legislature is a better forum for such a dramatic departure from the common law? "We conclude that the General Assembly, not this Court, should decide whether to create a cause of action for dram shop liability or social host liability. The General Assembly heavily regulates the sale and use of alcohol and by so doing has clearly announced its intent to occupy exclusively the field of policy making in that subject area. Furthermore, the parties raise controversial and competing public policy questions which the General Assembly can more effectively debate, consider and resolve through the legislative process." Shea v. Matassa, 918 A.2d 1090 (Del. 2007) (declining to recognize social host liability). Willis v. Omar, 954 A.2d 126 (R.I. 2008) (accord).

4. New Hampshire imposes liability if the social host's service of alcohol was reckless. Hickingbotham v. Burke, 140 N.H. 28, 662 A.2d 297 (1995) (expressed as highly unreasonable conduct, involving an extreme departure from ordinary care, in a situation where a high degree of danger is apparent). In dicta, Massachusetts has hinted it would impose liability under the appropriate circumstances. McGuiggan v. New England Telephone & Telegraph Co., 398 Mass. 152, 496 N.E.2d 141 (1986) (no liability in this case because no evidence that guest was obviously intoxicated when served). New Mexico's Liquor Liability statute imposes liability on social hosts who provide alcoholic beverages "recklessly in disregard of the rights of others." N.M. Stat. Ann. § 41–11–1. Delfino v. Griffo, 150 N.M. 97, 257 P.3d 917 (2011) (drug company representatives purchased drinks for a doctor office's staff member at three different bars over an eight hour period beginning with lunch).

5. In contrast to almost universal rejection of social host liability for serving adult guests, many jurisdictions have imposed liability on those who serve alcohol to minors. See Wiener v. Gamma Phi Chapter of Alpha Tau Omega Fraternity, 258 Or. 632, 485 P.2d 18 (1971) (fraternity found negligent for serving beer to minor who subsequently injured third party in automobile accident); cf. Sutter v. Hutchings, 254 Ga. 194, 327 S.E.2d 716 (1985) (defendant mother who purchased keg of beer for consumption at party for high school friends of defendant daughter may be liable to estate of driver who was killed when minor party guest ran a red light leaving party); Hansen v. Friend, 118 Wash.2d 476, 824 P.2d 483 (1992) (two adult companions held liable to estate of minor who drowned while intoxicated after defendants had provided minor with alcohol on overnight fishing trip). What if the driver is not a minor (is 18 or older) but is under the legal

drinking age? Marcum v. Bowden, 372 S.C. 452, 643 S.E.2d 85 (2007) (holding social host liable for underage drinker's negligence but doing so only prospectively). But see Smith v. Merritt, 940 S.W.2d 602 (Tex.1997) and Charles v. Seigfried, 165 Ill.2d 482, 209 Ill.Dec. 226, 651 N.E.2d 154 (1995) (both declining to impose liability even where guest is minor). Why are courts more willing to impose liability when a minor is involved? What if the social host is also a minor? Kapres v. Heller, 536 Pa. 551, 640 A.2d 888 (1994) (declining to impose liability on social host who is a minor).

6. *Commercial Dispensers of Liquor.* The common law imposed liability on neither social hosts nor commercially licensed vendors. Warr v. JMGM Group, LLC, 433 Md. 170, 70 A.3d 347 (2013) (deferring to legislature and declining to change law to recognize duty). Many state legislatures have changed this for commercial vendors through Dram Shop Acts. These acts generally provided a civil cause of action (as well as criminal sanctions) against commercial furnishers of alcohol for damages resulting from a consumer's intoxicated state. In addition, many states that are without a Dram Shop Act have enacted alcohol-beverage control laws, the violation of which may constitute negligence per se, as it did in the case of Stachniewicz v. Mar-Cam Corp., 259 Or. 583, 488 P.2d 436 (1971), page 220. Licensed vendors' supplying of liquor to patrons has become widely recognized as a proximate cause of injuries attributable to intoxicated persons. But see Ling v. Jan's Liquors, 237 Kan. 629, 703 P.2d 731 (1985) (listing jurisdictions that do not recognize such liability) and Shea v. Matassa, 918 A.2d 1090 (Del. 2007) (declining to recognize common law dram shop liability). Most courts have been unwilling to extend liability on these grounds to a social host. What are the policy considerations and tort law principles differentiating a licensee and a social host? See Page, The Law of Premises Liability §§ 12.1–24 (3rd ed. 2001).

7. *Employers.* Some courts also have imposed liability on employers where employees became intoxicated at work or at a work-related social event and then injured someone while driving intoxicated. See, e.g., Dickinson v. Edwards, 105 Wash.2d 457, 716 P.2d 814 (1986) (alcohol served at employer-sponsored "banquet"); Otis Engineering Corp. v. Clark, 668 S.W.2d 307 (Tex.1983) (employee sent home because discovered by supervisor to be intoxicated at work); Slade v. Smith's Management Corp., 119 Idaho 482, 808 P.2d 401 (1991) (employee struck and killed pedestrian on way home from company party). But see, Overbaugh v. McCutcheon, 183 W.Va. 386, 396 S.E.2d 153 (1990) (no liability for employer of driver who struck another car on way home from office Christmas party) and Johnston v. KFC National Management Co., 71 Haw. 229, 788 P.2d 159, 162 (1990) (employee injured someone after office Christmas party, "we find no clear judicial trend toward modifying the traditional common law, nor any statutory enactment or policy which leads this court to conclude that a change in the common law is appropriate at this time.")

8. *Designated Driver.* At a company awards dinner at a country club, the bartender refused further service to one of the guests because she thought he had had too much to drink. Based on an assurance from a colleague that he would drive him home, the bartender resumed serving him. The colleague later changed his mind and left the country club without him. Driving himself home, he crossed the center line and struck another vehicle head on, killing its driver. Should the colleague be liable to

the estate of the driver who was killed? Stephenson v. Universal Metrics, Inc., 251 Wis.2d 171, 641 N.W.2d 158 (2002) (finding that public policy considerations precluded the imposition of liability on the designated driver).

9. *Entrustment.* A car owner lends his vehicle to a person who is obviously intoxicated. The driver negligently runs into plaintiff. Should the owner be liable? See Deck v. Sherlock, 162 Neb. 86, 75 N.W.2d 99 (1956) (owner denied that driver was intoxicated, but court found jury question based on circumstances that included owner drinking with driver earlier on day of accident and owner knowing that driver's license had been revoked for driving while intoxicated). K-Mart sells a gun to a visibly intoxicated person who shoots the plaintiff. Should K-Mart be liable? Kitchen v. K-Mart, 697 So.2d 1200 (Fla.1997) (recognizing negligent entrustment in case involving sale of firearm). Suppose the owner does not know bailee is intoxicated at the time but does know he is an alcoholic. See Powell v. Langford, 58 Ariz. 281, 119 P.2d 230 (1941) (wife's knowledge that husband was alcoholic who had previously been involved in accidents while driving intoxicated was enough even though she had no knowledge of intoxication on the day of the accident). Should it make any difference that the automobile is given outright rather than loaned? Compare Estes v. Gibson, 257 S.W.2d 604 (Ky.1953) (no liability where title was in son's name and mother was merely a donor) with Kahlenberg v. Goldstein, 290 Md. 477, 431 A.2d 76 (1981) (liability where father purchased car for son whom he knew to be an incompetent driver). What if the defendant loaned money to her grandson to buy a car knowing that he had a drinking problem? What if the car dealer from whom the grandson purchased the car was also aware of the problem? Cf. Vince v. Wilson, 151 Vt. 425, 561 A.2d 103 (1989) (both the relative who financed purchase and the dealer could be liable where both knew that driver had no license because he had repeatedly failed test). Many courts have recognized the analogy between negligent sale of alcohol and the tort of negligent entrustment. See Buchanan v. Merger Enterprises, Inc., 463 So.2d 121, 126 (Ala.1984).

Enright v. Eli Lilly & Co.

Court of Appeals of New York, 1991.
77 N.Y.2d 377, 570 N.E.2d 198, 568 N.Y.S.2d 550.

[Plaintiff Karen Enright's grandmother ingested DES as a miscarriage preventive during a pregnancy that resulted in the birth of plaintiff Patricia Enright in 1960. Plaintiff Patricia Enright alleges that she developed abnormalities of her reproductive system due to her in utero exposure to DES and that these abnormalities resulted in several miscarriages and the premature birth of plaintiff Karen Enright. Karen suffers from cerebral palsy and other disabilities that plaintiffs attribute to her premature birth and thus to her grandmother's ingestion of DES. Karen Enright's claims were dismissed by the trial court and she appealed. The appellate division affirmed the dismissal of the causes of action based on negligence, breach of warranty and fraud, but reinstated the strict liability count, holding that the strong public policy in favor of providing a remedy for DES victims justified recognizing a strict products liability cause of action. Patricia Enright's claim for her own injuries and her husband's derivative claim for loss of consortium were not affected by the trial court's ruling and were still pending.]

WACHTLER, CHIEF JUDGE. * * *

The tragic DES tale is well documented in this Court's decisions and need not be recounted here (see, e.g., Hymowitz v. Lilly & Co., supra; Bichler v. Lilly & Co., 55 N.Y.2d 571, 450 N.Y.S.2d 776, 436 N.E.2d 182). It is sufficient to note that between 1947 and 1971, the drug, a synthetic estrogen-like substance produced by approximately 300 manufacturers, was prescribed for use and ingested by millions of pregnant women to prevent miscarriages. In 1971, the Food and Drug Administration banned the drug's use for the treatment of problems of pregnancy after studies established a link between in utero exposure to DES and the occurrence in teen-age women of a rare form of vaginal and cervical cancer. Plaintiffs allege that in utero exposure to DES has since been linked to other genital tract aberrations in DES daughters, including malformations or immaturity of the uterus, cervical abnormalities, misshapen Fallopian tubes and abnormal cell and tissue growth, all of which has caused in this population a marked increase in the incidence of infertility, miscarriages, premature births and ectopic pregnancies.

The Legislature and this Court have both expressed concern for the victims of this tragedy by removing legal barriers to their tort recovery—barriers which may have had their place in other contexts, but which in DES litigation worked a peculiar injustice because of the ways in which DES was developed, marketed and sold and because of the insidious nature of its harm. * * *

More recently, this Court responded to the fact that—for a variety of reasons unique to the DES litigation context—a DES plaintiff generally finds it impossible to identify the manufacturer of the drug that caused her injuries. We held that liability could be imposed upon DES manufacturers in accordance with their share of the national DES market, notwithstanding the plaintiff's inability to identify the manufacturer particularly at fault for her injuries [c].

In the present case, we are asked to do something significantly different. We are asked, not to remove some barrier to recovery that presents unique problems in DES cases, but to recognize a cause of action not available in other contexts simply (or at least largely) because this is a DES case.

In Albala v. City of New York, 54 N.Y.2d 269, 271, 445 N.Y.S.2d 108, 429 N.E.2d 786, supra, we were presented with the question "whether a cause of action lies in favor of a child for injuries suffered as a result of a preconception tort committed against the mother." There, the mother suffered a perforated uterus during the course of an abortion. Four years later, she gave birth to a brain-damaged child, whose injuries were allegedly attributable to the defendants' negligence in perforating the mother's uterus. We declined, as a matter of policy, to recognize a cause of action on behalf of the child, believing that to do so would "require the extension of traditional tort concepts beyond manageable bounds" [c]. Among other things, we were concerned with "the staggering implications of any proposition which would honor claims assuming the breach of an identifiable duty for less than a perfect birth" and the difficulty, if such a cause of action were recognized, of confining liability by other than artificial and arbitrary boundaries [c].

The case now before us differs from *Albala* only in that the mother's injuries in this case were caused by exposure to DES instead of by medical malpractice. A different rule is justified, therefore, only if that distinction alters the policy balance we struck in *Albala*.

The primary thrust of plaintiffs' argument and the Appellate Division's decision is that DES itself alters that balance. From the Legislature's actions in modifying the applicable Statute of Limitations and reviving time-barred DES cases and from our adoption of a market-share liability theory in *Hymowitz,* plaintiffs perceive a public policy favoring a remedy for DES-caused injuries sufficient to overcome the countervailing policy considerations we identified in *Albala.* The implication, of course, is that the public interest in providing a remedy for those injured by DES is stronger than the public interest in providing a remedy for those injured by other means—medical malpractice, for example. We do not believe that such a preference has been established. * * *

In the present case, however, neither plaintiffs, the Appellate Division, nor the dissent has identified any unique feature of DES litigation that justifies the novel proposition they advance—recognition of a multigenerational cause of action that we have refused to recognize in any other context. The fact that this is a DES case does not by itself justify a departure from the *Albala* rule.

Closer to the mark, though still falling short, is plaintiffs' second argument. They note that *Albala* was a negligence case and that we left open the question whether a different result might obtain under a strict products liability theory, because of the potentially different policy considerations in such a case [c]. Having now examined the question in the context of this particular strict products liability claim, we find no basis for reaching a different conclusion than we did in *Albala.* * * *

Despite these considerations, the countervailing ones remain strong enough to preclude us from recognizing a cause of action here. To begin, the concerns we identified in *Albala* are present in equal measure here. The nature of the plaintiffs' injuries in both cases—birth defects—and their cause—harm to the mothers' reproductive systems before the children were conceived—are indistinguishable for these purposes. They raise the same vexing questions with the same "staggering implications" [c]. As in *Albala,* the cause of action plaintiffs ask us to recognize here could not be confined without the drawing of artificial and arbitrary boundaries. For all we know, the rippling effects of DES exposure may extend for generations. It is our duty to confine liability within manageable limits (see, [c]; Prosser, Palsgraf Revisited, 52 Mich.L.Rev. 1, 27). Limiting liability to those who ingested the drug or were exposed to it in utero serves this purpose.

At the same time, limiting liability in this fashion does not unduly impair the deterrent purposes of tort liability. The manufacturers remain amenable to suit by all those injured by exposure to their product, a class whose size is commensurate with the risk created. In addition, we note that the tort system is not the only means of encouraging prescription drug safety; the Federal Food and Drug Administration has primary responsibility for that task [c]. We do not suggest, as some have (see, id.), that for this reason the judicial system should abandon its traditional role. But in light of the FDA's responsibility in this area, the need for the tort system to promote prescription drug safety is at least diminished.

That the product involved here is a prescription drug raises other considerations as well. First, as in most prescription drug cases [c], liability here is predicated on a failure to warn of dangers of which the manufacturers knew or with adequate testing should have known. Such a claim, though it may be couched in terms of strict liability, is indistinguishable from a negligence claim [c]. Concepts of reasonable care and foreseeability are not divorced from this theory of liability, as they may be under other strict products liability predicates. Thus, the effort to distinguish this case from *Albala* is strained.

More important, however, is recognition that public policy favors the availability of prescription drugs even though most carry some risks (see, Brown v. Superior Ct., 44 Cal.3d 1049, 245 Cal.Rptr. 412, 751 P.2d 470, 478–479; Restatement [Second] of Torts § 402A, comment *k;*) [c]. That is not to say that drug manufacturers should enjoy immunity from liability stemming from their failure to conduct adequate research and testing prior to the marketing of their products. They do not enjoy such immunity, as evidenced by our recognition of liability in favor of those who have been injured by ingestion or in utero exposure to DES. But we are aware of the dangers of overdeterrence—the possibility that research will be discouraged or beneficial drugs withheld from the market. These dangers are magnified in this context, where we are asked to recognize a legal duty toward generations not yet conceived.

The dissent would have us believe that this case involves nothing but application of straightforward strict products liability doctrine. But this case is fundamentally different in the same way that *Albala* was fundamentally different from other negligence cases. In neither this case nor *Albala* was the infant plaintiff exposed to the defendants' dangerous product or negligent conduct; rather, both were injured as a consequence of injuries to the reproductive systems of their mothers. * * *

In sum, the distinctions between this case and *Albala* provide no basis for a departure from the rule that an injury to a mother which results in injuries to a later-conceived child does not establish a cause of action in favor of the child against the original tort-feasor. For this reason, we decline to recognize a cause of action on behalf of plaintiff Karen Enright.

* * *

[Dissenting opinion of JUSTICE HANCOCK omitted.]

NOTES AND QUESTIONS

1. In a comparable case, Ohio also found no liability because of the remoteness in time and causation. Grover v. Eli Lilly & Co., 63 Ohio St.3d 756, 591 N.E.2d 696 (1992).

2. Is an emergency room doctor liable to the friend who brought the patient for treatment for not telling the friend to be tested for meningitis? "The Court is once again at a familiar place: defining legal duty in a negligence case, in particular determining where to fix the limit of a doctor's malpractice liability for professional advice allegedly given to someone not his patient. This sort of line-drawing—a policy-laden determination reflecting a balance of competing concerns—is invariably difficult not only because it looks in part to an unknowable future but also because it is in a sense arbitrary, hard to explain to the person just on the other side of the line, especially when grievous injury is alleged. Human compassion and rigorous logic resist the exercise. If this person can recover, why not the next? Yet line-drawing is necessary because, in determining responsibility for negligent acts, common law courts also must look beyond the immediate facts and take into account the larger principles at stake, including the need 'to limit the legal consequences of wrongs to a controllable degree.'" McNulty v. City of New York, 100 N.Y.2d 227, 234, 792 N.E.2d 162, 167, 762 N.Y.S.2d 12, 17 (2003) (Kaye, C.J., concurring). Would the doctor be liable if the friend fainted while observing emergency room treatment of patient? Murillo v. Seymour Ambulance Assn., Inc., 264 Conn. 474, 823 A.2d 1202 (2003) (repeated attempts to insert IV in preparation for emergency surgery) (no duty to bystander).

3. Employer or land owner acts negligently in exposing worker to a toxin. Should employer or land owner be liable to family members of the worker who themselves become ill through exposure to the toxin at home? Compare Holdampf v. A.C. & S., Inc., 5 N.Y.3d 486, 840 N.E.2d 115, 806 N.Y.S.2d 146 (2005) (second-hand exposure to asbestos fibers while laundering husband's clothes—no liability): In re Certified Question from the Fourteenth Dist. Ct. App. of Tex., 479 Mich. 498, 740 N.W.2d 206 (2007) (second-hand exposure to asbestos fibers while laundering clothes of step-father who had worked on defendant's premises—no liability); and Doe v. Pharmacia & Upjohn Co., 388 Md. 407, 879 A.2d 1088 (2005) (exposure to HIV-2 through unprotected intercourse with husband who became infected while working as lab technician at defendant's viral production facility—no liability) with Olivo v. Owens-Illinois, Inc., 186 N.J. 394, 895 A.2d 1143 (2006) (second-hand exposure to asbestos fibers while laundering clothes of husband who had worked on defendant's premises—liability) and Satterfield v. Breeding Insulation Co., 266 S.W.3d 347 (Tenn. 2008) (daughter's second-hand exposure to asbestos fibers through living in same household as worker—liability). In jurisdictions like New Jersey and Tennessee that permit claims by family members, what about someone who commuted each day with worker in a car pool? Sat next to him on the bus? Would they too have claims?

4. What are the public policy considerations in each of the following situations? Where should the line be drawn?

A. The day after he performed surgery on a twelve-year-old girl, doctor learned that the blood with which she was transfused included HIV antibodies and thus that she probably had been exposed to HIV. He did not tell her or her parents until she was seventeen and was diagnosed with AIDS. In the meantime, she had infected her boyfriend. He sued physician for failing to inform the patient or her parents of the exposure, the risk that she might develop AIDS, and the risk to her sexual partners. Should the boyfriend be able to recover? See Reisner v. UCLA, 31 Cal.App.4th 1195, 37 Cal.Rptr.2d 518 (1995) (appellate court reversed judgment on the pleadings, allowing boyfriend's case to proceed). What if boyfriend infected someone else before he found out? Could she recover? What if the woman he infected had a baby who developed AIDS from exposure to her mother? Could the baby recover from the doctor?

B. After a procedure to enhance his fertility, the patient's sperm count actually was lower, allegedly as a result of the urologist's malpractice. Patient and his wife both filed suit for malpractice. She sought recovery for her pain, suffering, and mental anguish due to the failed IVF procedures that she later underwent in attempting to conceive a child and for her inability to bear her husband's genetic children. Does her complaint state a cause of action against her husband's doctor? Cohen v. Cabrini Medical Ctr., 94 N.Y.2d 639, 730 N.E.2d 949, 709 N.Y.S.2d 151 (2000) (dismissing claim because imposition of duty does not turn merely on foreseeability of the harm but also public policy considerations). After a vasectomy, patient claimed that doctor provided negligent post-operative advice and care that resulted in patient's wife becoming pregnant. Does patient's wife have a cause of action against doctor? Dehn v. Edgecombe, 384 Md. 606, 865 A.2d 603 (2005) (court declined to permit wife's claim to proceed because it would expand traditional tort concepts beyond manageable bounds since the rationale would cover all potential sexual partners of the patient).

C. A drug company failed to warn physicians of possible risks associated with prescribing a drug for children under particular circumstances. Child suffered permanent damage after taking drug. Parents sued pediatrician and drug company. Can pediatrician recover for his pain and suffering caused by knowing the child was injured through the drug he prescribed and by the litigation itself? Cf. Washington State Physicians Ins. Exch. & Assn., 122 Wash.2d 299, 858 P.2d 1054 (1993) (drug company argued that physician's damages were too remote; case decided on narrower grounds).

D. Should an attorney be liable to the intended beneficiaries of a will? Or the fiancée of a divorce client? Scott v. Burgin, 97 A.3d 564 (D.C. App. 2014) (client died before divorce and thus pension went to wife instead of fiancée). Some jurisdictions permit such an action, but others limit legal malpractice actions to clients. See Chapter 8, Duty of Care, pages 434–437.

E. Should a pharmacy that filled a prescription for hydrocodone be liable for the injuries caused by its customer while she was driving under the influence of the drug? Sanchez v. Wal-Mart Stores, Inc., 221 P.3d 1276 (Nev. 2009) (finding no duty to protect general public from customer driving under the influence of controlled substance).

5. The following cases all involve causes of action against various media defendants. What public policy issues are implicated in the courts' decisions regarding proximate cause?

A. Plaintiff is wounded by gunmen who also killed his father. He learned the gunmen had been hired by a business associate of his father's through a "Gun for Hire" ad in a magazine for mercenaries. Plaintiff seeks compensation for his gunshot wounds and, along with his brother, for the wrongful death of his father from the publisher of the magazine, claiming that the publisher should have foreseen that the ad would result in violent criminal activity. How might plaintiffs prove that the result was foreseeable to the publisher? What other factors should the court consider? Compare Eimann v. Soldier of Fortune Magazine, 880 F.2d 830 (5th Cir.1989), cert. denied, 493 U.S. 1024 (1990) (applying Texas law) (denying liability) with Braun v. Soldier of Fortune Magazine, Inc., 968 F.2d 1110 (11th Cir.1992), cert. denied, 506 U.S. 1071 (1993) (applying Georgia law) (upholding liability). Soldier of Fortune magazine stopped accepting personal ads and narrowly avoided bankruptcy in the wake of the *Braun* case. How far should the courts go to protect the First Amendment rights of the publisher? What about new media? Should a website be liable for facilitating the illegal sale of a firearm that was used to murder plaintiff's decedent? Cf. Vesely v. Armslist LLC, 762 F.3d 661 (7th Cir. 2014) (applying Illinois law) (dismissing complaint because no duty on part of website to protect plaintiff's decedent from criminal conduct of defendant).

B. James Perry murdered an eight-year-old quadriplegic boy, the boy's mother, and the boy's private duty nurse. Perry had been hired by the boy's father who was after the $2 million that his son had received in settlement for the injuries that had left him paralyzed. In negotiating with the father, planning the murders, and executing them, Perry had followed the detailed instructions and advice of the book *Hit Man: A Technical Manual for Independent Contractors*, published by Paladin Enterprises. Is Paladin a proximate cause of the deaths? Should the First Amendment preclude liability? Rice v. Paladin Enterprises, Inc., 128 F.3d 233 (4th Cir.1997) (applying Maryland law).

C. Defendants went on a shooting spree, during which they killed someone and seriously injured plaintiff, a clerk in a convenience store. Plaintiff's complaint alleged that the killers were trying to emulate characters in the movie *Natural Born Killers*, which they watched repeatedly, sometimes under the influence of mind-altering drugs. Warner Brothers and Producer Oliver Stone are among the defendants named. Plaintiff claims they used violent imagery that was intended to cause its viewers to imitate it. If plaintiff can prove her allegations, should Warner Brothers and Oliver Stone be liable? Byers v. Edmondson, 712 So.2d 681 (La.App.1998).

D. Student walked into the lobby of his high school in Paducah, Kentucky, and shot several of his fellow students. Their parents sued companies that had produced movies, video games, and Internet sites that they alleged had "desensitized the shooter to violence" and "caused" him to kill the other students. Do the defendants owe a duty to protect third parties from how watchers or players of their products process the ideas and images presented? Was it foreseeable that someone would react in this way? Was the violent, criminal action a superseding cause? James v. Meow Media, Inc., 300 F.3d 683, 701 (6th Cir. 2002) (applying Kentucky law) (no liability because no duty).

E. Man who was "ambushed" at a taping of the Jenny Jones Show by revelation that fellow guest had crush on him shot fellow guest several days later back in their hometown. Do the producers of the show have a duty to protect one guest from the criminal acts of another? Graves v. Warner Bros., 253 Mich.App. 486, 656 N.W.2d 195 (2002) (majority holds no duty, but dissent would hold that "as a matter of public policy, if defendants, for their own benefit, wish to produce 'ambush' shows that can conceivably create a volatile situation, they should bear the risk, if a guest is psychologically unstable or criminally dangerous by being charged with that knowledge in the context of any foreseeability analysis.")

6. For an interesting analysis of the tort issues arising out of the cases against media defendants, see Anderson, "Incitement and Tort Law," 37 Wake Forest L. Rev. 957 (2002).

BY WAY OF SYNTHESIS

The problem involved in the cases in this chapter is whether defendant's liability to plaintiff should be cut off even though the defendant's conduct was both negligent and a factual cause of the plaintiff's injury. Is there a system by which this problem can be handled and a test by which to make the determination?

1. It may first be suggested that the problem can be raised and treated by the court in connection with any one of the four elements of a negligence case—duty, breach of duty, causation or damage. The duty approach, for example, is espoused in the majority opinion in *Palsgraf* and is rather frequently used in cases of the unforeseeable plaintiff. Certain types of damage may be held not to be the basis of recovery. Negligence may be held not to be directed to the plaintiff. But most courts have treated the question in the causation element.

The problem is a difficult one, but the length of the treatment in this casebook and the amount of time allotted it in most courses may perhaps give an exaggerated impression of its importance. In the great majority of cases, the problem does not arise at all; it comes up only in the fraction of actions that involve unusual fact situations. How is it to be handled when it does arise?

There are many legal tests that have been devised by the courts and legal scholars—some rather precise and almost mechanical and some very broad and general. The more precise ones give an illusion of certainty. As a matter of fact, almost every jurisdiction has two distinct and apparently unrelated lines of authority—one with a broad scope of liability and the other with a narrow scope. They do not help the court especially to reach a decision on a case before it, but they do help substantially in explaining the decision after it has been reached.

This is not a situation, however, in which precision and certainty are essential. Neither party to the action engaged in his conduct in reliance upon a "rule" of proximate cause. The principal task of the court is to do justice as between these parties in their present situation. For this purpose, a weighing, evaluative process is required, rather than a clear-cut rule of law. This suggests the use of a standard similar to the one for determining whether a person was negligent (what a reasonable, prudent person would do under the same or similar circumstances). A standard allows the taking into consideration of competing factors or policy elements. Often these policy elements are not articulated or brought out into the open. For an analysis of some of them, see L. Green, Judge and Jury, Ch. 4, 5 (1930).

2. There are two general approaches to the problem of proximate cause—the hindsight, or direct-causation, approach and the foreseeability approach. Practically every jurisdiction has used both, at one time or another. In many instances they would be likely to produce the same result, but not always. In theory the foresight approach would produce a smaller ambit of liability.

But foreseeability is an accordion concept, depending upon the detail and precision with which foresight is required. Many torts teachers have found it helpful to express foreseeability in terms of the risk idea. "This position has been justified as more rational, since the factors which define negligence should also limit liability for negligence; as easier to administer, since it fixes the nearest thing to a definite boundary of liability which is possible; and more just, since negligence may consist of only a slight deviation from the community standard of conduct, and even be free from all moral blame, while its consequences may be catastrophic, and out of all proportion to the fault." Prosser and Keeton, Torts 282 (5th ed. 1984), citing Pollock, Liability for Consequences, 38 Law Q.Rev. 165 (1922).

There is much force in these arguments, but they suggest far more in the way of certainty and precision than the test warrants. Consider a single illustration, adapted from Judge Magruder's opinion in Marshall v. Nugent, 222 F.2d 604 (1st Cir.1955) (applying New Hampshire law).

Suppose that a truck is driven at excessive speed. It is relatively easy to say that the total risk, made up of the aggregate of all of the possibilities of harm, whether they are very probable or fantastic, is so great that the reasonable man of ordinary prudence would not do this, and therefore the driver is negligent. How easy is it, by a process of fragmentation of the risk, to separate out particular consequences and intervening factors, and to say that they are, or are not, significant parts of the original total foreseeable risk? Is it "foreseeable," in any sense that the reasonable driver could have the possibility in mind, and so take precautions against it, that

(a) The driver will hit another car and kill someone?

(b) The car with which he collides will be thrown out of control, and hit a third car, or even a fourth? Springer v. Pacific Fruit Exchange, 92 Cal.App. 732, 268 P. 951 (1928).

(c) He will endanger a child in the street, and a person who tries to rescue her will sustain a broken arm? Wagner v. International R. Co., note 2, page 362.

(d) The truck will narrowly miss a pregnant woman, who will be frightened into a miscarriage? Cf. Mitnick v. Whalen Bros., 115 Conn. 650, 163 A. 414 (1932).

(e) He will hit a pedestrian, who will be left helpless in the street, and be run over by another car? Bunda v. Hardwick, 376 Mich. 640, 138 N.W.2d 305 (1965).

(f) He will cause a collision, which will leave wrecked cars blocking the highway, and another driver will run into the wreckage? Holmberg v. Villaume, 158 Minn. 442, 197 N.W. 849 (1924).

(g) He will hit a pedestrian, and while the pedestrian is unconscious, his watch will be stolen? Cf. Brauer v. New York Central R. Co., 91 N.J.L. 190, 103 A. 166 (1918).

(h) The person he injures will contract pneumonia or another infection because of his weakened condition, and die of it? See page 366, note 12.

(i) The injured person may suffer a second accident six months later while he is walking on crutches? Squires v. Reynolds, page 366, note 12.

(j) The person he injures will receive negligent medical treatment, and die or be further injured because of it? Jess Edwards, Inc. v. Goergen, page 365, note 11.

(k) The truck will knock a car up against a stone wall. The wall is weakened and, as a result, a stone falls off the top a day later and injures a pedestrian. Cf. In re Guardian Casualty Co., 253 App.Div. 360, 2 N.Y.S.2d 232 (1938).

All of these things have happened and there have been holdings that each was "proximate." Is it perhaps overloading the risk concept to make it the basis for determining each of these situations?

Like the purpose-of-the-statute test (see note 2B, page 223), from which it is derived, the risk test often approaches a begging of the question. One decides how broadly or narrowly to express the purpose of the statute or the scope of the risk of an act of common law negligence with an awareness of what the result of that decision will be and with the decision perhaps influenced by it.

And yet, despite all of these difficulties, the risk approach, viewed entirely as an approach rather than as a definitive test, can be very helpful. It poses the problem in a way that can help to direct the line of thought of the decision-maker. If the idea is expressed in terms of a reasonably close relation between the harm threatened (or the risk created) and the injury incurred, then it is put in the form of a standard instead of a rule, and the need to exercise discretion in its application is made apparent. See Prosser, Selected Topics on the Law of Torts, 191, 233, 242 (1954); Wade, Book Review, 8 Vand.L.Rev. 657, 660–663 (1955).

3. From the consideration of the cases in this chapter, you should have obtained a "feel" for the problem, so that it is possible to tell promptly whether the answer is clear or so difficult that litigation may be warranted. You are not expected to be sure of the answer for all cases, but you should identify fact patterns in which application of the principles of proximate cause have become fairly well crystallized—for example, the thin-skull and rescue situations, social host liability, and third-generation DES plaintiffs.

You should have become acquainted with the various legal tests and their ramifications and be able (1) to use or respond to them in argument, (2) to present a lucid and logical legal argument for a particular result, and (3) to utilize or respond to such modifying adjectives for the word "cause" as active, efficient, natural and probable, foreseeable or unforeseeable, proximate, nearest and superseding and such terms as risk, unbroken sequence, just or expedient result, or dependent or independent intervening cause.

You ought to know how to argue the facts as well as the law. An illustration may be helpful in this regard. In Hines v. Morrow, 236 S.W. 183 (Tex.Civ.App.1921), defendant negligently left a mudhole in a highway. A's car drove into it and got stuck. B, a man with a wooden leg, attempted to pull A's car out of the mud with a tow rope. His wooden leg got stuck in the mud, and in order to extricate himself B took hold of the tail gate of the tow truck. As the truck moved, a loop in the tow rope lassoed his good leg and broke it. Clarence Morris in Proximate Cause in Minnesota, 34 Minn.L.Rev. 185 (1950), attributes the "peg leg" decision in the *Hines* case to the summary of the facts in plaintiff's brief, as follows: "The case stated in briefest form, is simply this: Appellee was on the highway, using it in a lawful manner, and slipped into this hole, created by appellant's negligence, and was injured in attempting to extricate himself."

If the plaintiff had used the same approach in stating the issue in Koehler v. Waukesha Milk Co., 190 Wis. 52, 208 N.W. 901 (1926), he would have said that the defendant left a glass milk bottle on the plaintiff's doorstep with a slight chip near the top, and the decedent perished as a result—with the consequence that he would probably have lost the case. Instead, he explained that the decedent had picked the bottle up and scratched a finger. The scratch had become infected, the infection had gone into blood poisoning (before the advent of penicillin), and the decedent died.

4. If a trial court decides "as a matter of law" that the defendant's conduct was not a proximate cause of the plaintiff's injury, it dismisses the complaint, grants summary judgment, or directs a verdict for the defendant. This has happened in many of the cases in this chapter. If there is an issue of proximate cause in the case and the trial court decides to let it go to the jury, it must instruct the jury as to the nature of the problem that it is to decide. What does the court say? There is no consensus. Model instructions from three different states illustrate the variety.

Arkansas. Model Jury Instructions AMI 501. "The law frequently uses the expression 'proximate cause,' with which you may not be familiar. When I use the expression 'proximate cause,' I mean a cause which, in a natural and continuous sequence, produces damage and without which the damage would not have occurred. [This does not mean that the law recognizes only one proximate cause of damage. To the contrary, if two or more causes work together to produce damage, then you may find that each of them was a proximate cause.]"

AMI 503. "[Defendant] contends and has the burden of proving that following any act or omission on his part an event intervened that in itself caused any damage completely independent of his conduct. If you so find, then his act or omission was not a proximate cause of any damage resulting from the intervening event. [The fact that other cause(s) intervened between any act or omission on the part of [defendant,] and the damage for which claim is made, would not relieve [defendant] of liability if the damage is reasonably foreseeable as a natural and probable result of any act or omission on the part of [defendant].]"

Illinois. Ill. Pattern Jury Instr.-Civ. 15.01. "When I use the expression 'proximate cause,' I mean a cause that, in the natural or ordinary course of events, produced the plaintiff's injury. [It need not be the only cause, nor the last or nearest cause. It is sufficient if it combines with another cause resulting in the injury.]"

Florida. 401.12 a. Legal cause generally. "Negligence is a legal cause of [loss] [injury] [or] [damage] if it directly and in natural and continuous sequence produces or contributes substantially to producing such [loss] [injury] [or] [damage], so that it can reasonably be said that, but for the negligence, the [loss] [injury] [or] [damage] would not have occurred."

Are these instructions meaningful to the average jury? Is that necessary? Would they do as the test for the court to apply? Would they produce the same result in such cases as *Palsgraf, Derdiarian v. Felix Contracting Co.* and *Fuller v. Preis*? Is it better for them to be complex and accurate, or simple and understandable? Do they suggest that the court should be more ready to decide the case itself or turn it over to the jury? See Mikell, Jury Instructions and Proximate Cause: An Uncertain Trumpet in Georgia, 27 Ga. St.B.J. 60 (1990) for a discussion of several empirical studies concerning the jury's understanding of the instruction on proximate cause.

4. SHIFTING RESPONSIBILITY

Usually, when the defendant has negligently created a risk of harm to the plaintiff, the failure of a third person to intervene and take some action to prevent the risk from being realized, that is, to prevent the harm, will not affect the liability of the defendant when the harm in fact occurs. If, for example, the defendant negligently sets a grass fire that is burning toward the plaintiff's building, the failure of someone else to put out the fire does not relieve the defendant. Wiley v. West Jersey R. Co., 44 N.J.L. 247 (1882). The fact that the third person was under a duty to the plaintiff to extinguish the fire, and would be liable to the plaintiff for his failure to do so, makes no difference to the defendant's liability.

Thus in Diehl v. Fidelity Philadelphia Trust Co., 159 Pa.Super. 513, 49 A.2d 190 (1946), the defendant Metropolitan negligently discharged steam onto the sidewalk in front of a building owned by Fidelity. The steam condensed and froze, forming a coating of invisible ice on the pavement. With notice of the situation, Fidelity failed to clean off the ice although it was under a duty to do so. Plaintiff, a pedestrian, slipped on the ice, fell, and was injured. It was held that the failure of Fidelity to perform its duty did not relieve Metropolitan of liability, and that the two were both liable.

This is the usual conclusion in situations of this nature. There are, however, a few cases in which the conduct of the third person, whether action or inaction, has been held to relieve the defendant because the responsibility has been shifted from his shoulders. For example, suppose defendant construction company left dynamite caps lying about and they were found by children whose parent confiscated them. If the parent then left them where child found them and was injured, the responsibility is held to have shifted to the parent, relieving the originally negligent defendant. See Peterson v. Martin, 138 Minn. 195, 164 N.W. 813 (1917); Pittsburg Reduction Co. v. Horton, 87 Ark. 576, 113 S.W. 647 (1908); Calkins v. Albi, 163 Colo. 370, 431 P.2d 17 (1967).

Although it may be said in these cases that the risk created by the defendant has terminated, the risk is still there, and very much alive. What has happened is that another person has taken control of it. When should that fact shield the original wrongdoer? Consider this situation. Plaintiff alleged that her daughter's physician negligently misdiagnosed her as having chronic tonsillitis and referred her to an ENT specialist. Specialist, after performing tonsillectomy, prescribed too high a dose of a pain killer and child suffered brain damage. Is the physician who referred the patient to the specialist liable for the specialist's negligence? In Spicer v. Osunkoya, 32 A.3d 347 (Del. 2011), the court noted that other jurisdictions consistently have held that the original physician is not liable for the negligence of the specialist unless the referring physician had reason to know the specialist was incompetent. Plaintiff attempted to avoid this result by arguing that the referring physician was himself negligent in diagnosing the patient's condition and that his medical malpractice was a proximate cause of the injury. The court rejected the argument, applying the principles of Restatement (Second) of Torts § 452, comment *f*, and finding that the full responsibility for "control of the situation and prevention of the threatened harm" had passed to the specialist and specialist's alleged malpractice was a superseding cause as a matter of law.

CHAPTER 7

JOINT TORTFEASORS

1. LIABILITY AND JOINDER OF DEFENDANTS

Bierczynski v. Rogers

Supreme Court of Delaware, 1968.
239 A.2d 218.

HERRMANN, JUSTICE. This appeal involves an automobile accident in which the plaintiffs claim that the defendant motorists were racing on the public highway, as the result of which the accident occurred.

The plaintiffs Cecil B. Rogers and Susan D. Rogers brought this action against Robert C. Race and Ronald Bierczynski, ages 18 and 17 respectively, alleging concurrent negligences in that they violated various speed statutes and various other statutory rules of the road, and in that they failed to keep a proper lookout and failed to keep their vehicles under proper control. The jury, by answer to interrogatories in its special verdict, expressly found that Race and Bierczynski were each negligent and that the negligence of each was a proximate cause of the accident. Substantial verdicts were entered in favor of the plaintiffs against both defendants jointly. The defendant Bierczynski appeals therefrom. The defendant Race does not appeal; rather, he joins with the plaintiffs in upholding the judgment below.

[The evidence justified a finding that Bierczynski and Race were engaged in a speed contest, as they came down a hill side-by-side at twice the legal speed. Ahead of them was the car of the plaintiffs, in the westbound lane. As they approached it, Race tried to get his car back into the eastbound lane. He lost control of it, and careened sideways, at about 70 miles per hour, into the front of plaintiffs' car. Bierczynski remained in the proper lane at all times, and brought his car to a stop in it, about 35 feet from the area of collision. It did not come in contact with the plaintiffs' vehicle.]

In many States, automobile racing on a public highway is prohibited by statute, the violation of which is negligence per se. [Cc] Delaware has no such statute. Nevertheless, speed competition in automobiles on the public highway is negligence in this State, for the reason that a reasonably prudent person would not engage in such conduct. This conclusion is in accord with the general rule, prevailing in other jurisdictions which lack statutes on the subject, that racing motor vehicles on a public highway is negligence. [Cc]

It is also generally held that all who engage in a race on the highway do so at their peril, and are liable for injury or damage sustained by a third person as a result thereof, regardless of which of the racing cars directly inflicted the injury or damage. The authorities reflect generally accepted rules of causation that all parties engaged in a motor vehicle race on the highway are wrongdoers acting in concert, and that each participant is liable for harm to a third person arising from the tortious conduct of the other, because he has induced and encouraged the tort. [Cc]

We subscribe to those rules; and hold that, as a general rule, participation in a motor vehicle race on a public highway is an act of concurrent negligence imposing liability on each participant for any injury to a non-participant resulting from the race. If, therefore, Race and Bierczynski were engaged in a speed competition, each was liable for the damages and injuries to the plaintiffs herein, even though Bierczynski was not directly involved in the collision itself. Bierczynski apparently concedes liability if a race had, in fact, [still] been in progress [at the time of the accident]. Clearly there was ample evidence to carry to the jury the issue of a race—and with it, implicit therein, the issue of proximate cause as to Bierczynski. * * *

We find no error as asserted by the appellant. The judgments below are affirmed.

NOTES AND QUESTIONS

1. Defendant Bierczynski is held liable to the plaintiffs even though his car did not come into contact with them because he acted in concert with defendant Race to cause injury to plaintiffs. Observe that there is also a civil procedure issue lurking beneath the holding of this case. The civil procedure rules of joinder govern whether the causes of action that the plaintiffs have against each of the two defendants can be joined together in a single lawsuit.

2. *Joinder.* Originally, English law permitted joinder in the same lawsuit of multiple defendants only if those defendants had acted in concert, as in the principal case. Thus, under the old common law rules of joinder, Race and Bierczynski could have been joined as defendants, but defendants who had not acted in concert could not have been joined in the same action. See Sadler v. Great Western Ry. Co., [1896] A.C. 450 (delivery carts and vans belonging to two different companies, acting independently, blocked either end of a street, preventing access to plaintiff's land—separate actions required). Modern procedural codes or rules of civil procedure are based on principles of convenience and provide that joinder is permitted when the plaintiff's claims arise from "the same transaction, occurrence, or series of transactions or occurrences;" and "any question of law or fact common to all defendants will arise in the action." See Fed.R.Civ.P. 20(a)(2) and its state law counterparts. Joinder, therefore, is now permitted when the defendants acted in concert, when the defendants acted independently to cause the same harm, and even when the defendants acted independently to cause different harms.

3. Most jurisdictions, while *permitting* the plaintiff to join multiple defendants in the same action, do not *require* that the plaintiff do so. The plaintiff has the right to sue one tortfeasor alone, without joining others who also may be liable. The defendant cannot, over the plaintiff's objection, compel the joinder of the others. See Sox v. Hertz Corp., 262 F.Supp. 531 (D.S.C.1967) and Magnuson v. Kelsey-Hayes Co., 844 S.W.2d 448 (Mo.App.1992) (defendant cannot prevent the voluntary dismissal of co-defendant by plaintiff if defendant had not filed a cross-claim against co-defendant). Although the defendant cannot affect the cause of action

between the plaintiff and other potential defendants, the defendant can enforce whatever right to contribution or indemnity the defendant may have against another potential defendant by impleading, bringing a third-party complaint against, that other party or by later bringing a separate lawsuit for contribution or indemnity against the other party. See Knell v. Feltman, page 409.

4. *Liability.* "Joint and several liability" means that each of several tortfeasors can be sued jointly with the others for the amount of the plaintiff's loss, and that each is also individually liable for the full amount of plaintiff's damages. The plaintiff can collect from any one of them or any group of them.

5. There are three types of factual situations in which joint and several liability usually is imposed. The principal case illustrates the first—that in which the tortfeasors acted in concert. The classic discussion is Prosser, Joint Torts and Several Liability, 25 Calif.L.Rev. 413 (1937).

A. Three defendants, acting in concert, set upon the plaintiff. One held him, which was false imprisonment; another battered him; the third stole his silver buttons. All three were held liable for the entire damages. Smithson v. Garth, 3 Lev. 324, 83 Eng.Rep. 711 (1691). Cf. Garrett v. Garrett, 228 N.C. 530, 46 S.E.2d 302 (1948) and the echoes of Romeo and Juliet in Tricoli v. Centalanza, 100 N.J.L. 231, 126 A. 214 (1924).

B. Suppose that assailant attacks and beats the plaintiff. Assailant's brother takes no part in the attack, but encourages him to do it and prevents plaintiff's wife from interfering. Is brother liable? Hilmes v. Stroebel, 59 Wis. 74, 17 N.W. 539 (1883) (all liable who encouraged or incited assailant); Thompson v. Johnson, 180 F.2d 431 (5th Cir. 1950) (applying Mississippi law) (brothers liable because engaged in common enterprise and prevented plaintiff's wife from helping him). What if he merely stands by and approves, but does nothing active? The mere presence at the commission of a tort does not render an observer liable as if he were a participant.

C. Did the principal case involve an express or implied agreement to injure plaintiff? If not, why are defendants deemed joint tortfeasors? Did they participate in the joint creation of a negligent risk? See Lemons v. Kelly, 239 Or. 354, 360–61, 397 P.2d 784, 787 (1964).

D. Suppose, in the principal case, that Race and Bierczynski had not been drag racing, but had entered a contest to see which one could get first from one point in the city to another, with each selecting his own route. Race was speeding and hit the plaintiffs. Should Bierczynski, who went by a different route, be liable? Would it make any difference whether Bierczynski was also speeding? Whether the point of the contest was to see who could drive the fastest or who picked the shortest route?

6. Four friends (Cole, Woods, Hill, and Carrera) decided to travel to a farm belonging to Cole's grandfather to go shooting. On the way, Woods fell asleep. Cole hatched a plan to frighten Woods. He persuaded Hill and Carrera to load their guns to fire only one shell or bullet. Upon arrival at the farm, the pickup truck was driven into a barn, Woods was left asleep in the truck, and the guns were prepared. Following the plan, all three of them fired their guns into the ground near the truck, awakening plaintiff. They then pointed their guns at Woods, saying "it's time to die," and pulled

the triggers. Cole's and Carrera's guns produced a click as Cole had planned, but Hill's gun discharged, killing Woods. The representative of Woods' estate filed suit against Cole, alleging that he had acted in concert with Hill to negligently injure Woods. Would Cole be liable under traditional common law rules of joint and several liability? What if the jurisdiction has amended its common law rule to provide for apportionment of liability and otherwise limiting joint and several liability? Woods v. Cole, 181 Ill.2d 512, 230 Ill.Dec. 204, 693 N.E.2d 333 (1998) (no indication that legislature intended to abolish well-established principle of common law that those who act in concert are jointly and severally liable when it limited joint and several liability for indivisible harm). See also Restatement (Third) of Torts: Apportionment of Liability § 15 (2000) (Reporters' Note listing statutes that retain joint and several liability for concerted action even though abolishing it for indivisible injury cases).

7. The second situation in which joint and several liability may be imposed is that in which defendants fail to perform a common duty to the plaintiff. Included in this category are cases involving the liability of two parties based on their relationship to each other, e.g., the liability of a master for acts of the servant, the liability of an employer for the acts of the employee, the liability of the seller for a defect in a product manufactured by someone else. Marcon v. Kmart Corp., 573 N.W.2d 728 (Minn.App.1998) (under Minnesota statute governing joint and several liability, seller Kmart liable for entire $8 million award based on jury's finding that sled was defective because bankrupt manufacturer had failed to warn of risks of kneeling on sled). See Chapters 13 and 15 for discussions of vicarious liability and liability of seller of product for defects in product.

8. The third category of cases imposing joint and several liability, and the last in time of the three to be recognized by the common law, is that involving defendants who acted independently to cause an indivisible harm. As you read the cases that follow, keep in mind that the defendants might have acted either simultaneously or successively. Does this make a difference? Should it?

Coney v. J.L.G. Industries, Inc.

Supreme Court of Illinois, 1983.
97 Ill.2d 104, 454 N.E.2d 197, 73 Ill.Dec. 337.

[Wrongful death and survival claims were brought by Coney as administrator of the estate of Clifford M. Jasper. Jasper died while operating a hydraulic aerial work platform, manufactured by defendant, and the claims are based on strict products liability. Defendant argued that Jasper had committed contributory negligence and that his employer, V. Jobst & Sons, also had contributed to the plaintiff's injuries by failing to provide a "groundman," and by failing to "instruct and train Jasper on the operation of the platform." Three questions were certified to the Supreme Court on interlocutory appeal:

> "Whether the doctrine of comparative negligence or fault is applicable to actions or claims seeking recovery under products liability or strict liability in tort theories?
>
> Whether the doctrine of comparative negligence or fault eliminates joint and several liability?

> Whether the retention of joint and several liability in a system of comparative negligence or fault denies defendants equal protection of the laws in violation of the Federal and state constitutions?"

The Illinois Supreme Court's answer to the first question was in the affirmative. This issue will be considered in more detail in the chapters on Defenses and Product Liability.]

THOMAS J. MORAN, JUSTICE: * * * The common law doctrine of joint and several liability holds joint tortfeasors responsible for the plaintiff's entire injury, allowing plaintiff to pursue all, some, or one of the tortfeasors responsible for his injury for the full amount of the damages. [Cc]

Defendant asserts joint and several liability is a corollary of the contributory negligence doctrine. Prior to *Alvis* [v. Ribar, 85 Ill.2d 1, 421 N.E.2d 886, 52 Ill.Dec. 23 (1981), judicially adopting pure comparative negligence in Illinois], a plaintiff who was guilty of even slight contributory negligence was barred from recovery. Defendant maintains that joint and several liability balanced this inequity by permitting a faultless plaintiff to collect his entire judgment from any defendant who was guilty of even slight negligence. With the adoption of comparative negligence where damages are apportioned according to each party's fault, defendant argues it is no longer rational to hold a defendant liable beyond his share of the total damages. * * *

Generally, four reasons have been advanced [by plaintiff] for retaining joint and several liability:

> (1) The feasibility of apportioning fault on a comparative basis does not render an indivisible injury "divisible" for purposes of the joint and several liability rule. A concurrent tortfeasor is liable for the whole of an indivisible injury when his negligence is a proximate cause of that damage. In many instances, the negligence of a concurrent tortfeasor may be sufficient by itself to cause the entire loss. The mere fact that it may be possible to assign some percentage figure to the relative culpability of one negligent defendant as compared to another does not in any way suggest that each defendant's negligence is not a proximate cause of the entire indivisible injury.
>
> (2) In those instances where the plaintiff is not guilty of negligence, he would be forced to bear a portion of the loss should one of the tortfeasors prove financially unable to satisfy his share of the damages.
>
> (3) Even in cases where a plaintiff is partially at fault, his culpability is not equivalent to that of a defendant. The plaintiff's negligence relates only to a lack of due care for his own safety while the defendant's negligence relates to a lack of due care for the safety of others; the latter is tortious, but the former is not.
>
> (4) Elimination of joint and several liability would work a serious and unwarranted deleterious effect on the ability of an

injured plaintiff to obtain adequate compensation for his injuries. [Cc]

In adopting comparative negligence, this court eliminated the total bar to recovery which a plaintiff had faced under contributory negligence. In return for allowing a negligent plaintiff to recover, this court said fairness requires that a plaintiff's damages be "reduced by the percentage of fault *attributable to him*." (Emphasis added.) (Alvis v. Ribar (1981), 85 Ill.2d 1, 25, 52 Ill.Dec. 23, 421 N.E.2d 886.) Were we to eliminate joint and several liability as the defendant advocates, the burden of the insolvent or immune defendant would fall on the plaintiff; in that circumstance, plaintiff's damages would be reduced beyond the percentage of fault *attributable to him*. We do not believe the doctrine of comparative negligence requires this further reduction. Nor do we believe this burden is the price plaintiffs must pay for being relieved of the contributory negligence bar. The *quid pro quo* is the reduction of plaintiff's damages. What was said in American Motorcycle Association v. Superior Court (1978), 20 Cal.3d 578, 590, 578 P.2d 899, 906, 146 Cal.Rptr. 182, 189, is applicable here: "[F]airness dictates that the 'wronged party should not be deprived of his right to redress,' * * * '[t]he wrongdoers should be left to work out between themselves any apportionment.' " * * *

Now, under *Alvis,* damages are allocated according to fault. As such, defendant argues, *Alvis* mandates that a tortfeasor should be liable only to the extent that his negligent acts or omissions produced the damages.

We find nothing in *Alvis* which mandates either a shift in who shall bear the risk of the insolvent defendant or the elimination of joint and several liability. Defendant has not cited nor have we found persuasive judicial authority for the proposition that comparative negligence compels the abolition of joint and several liability. On the contrary, most jurisdictions which have adopted comparative negligence have retained the doctrine. Therefore, we hold that our adoption of comparative negligence in *Alvis* does not change the longstanding doctrine of joint and several liability. * * *

Therefore, in response to the questions posed, we conclude that (1) comparative fault is applicable to strict products liability actions; (2) comparative fault does not eliminate joint and several liability; and (3) retention of joint and several liability does not deny defendants equal protection of the laws. * * *

Affirmed and remanded, with directions.

Bartlett v. New Mexico Welding Supply, Inc.

Court of Appeals of New Mexico, 1982.
98 N.M. 152, 646 P.2d 579, cert. denied, 98 N.M. 336, 648 P.2d 794.

WOOD, JUDGE * * * The automobile accident involved three vehicles. The car in front of plaintiffs' car signaled a right hand turn. This lead car turned into and then pulled out of a service station in a very fast motion. Plaintiff Jane Bartlett slammed on her brakes to avoid hitting the lead car. Defendant's truck was behind plaintiffs' car. Defendant's driver applied his brakes; however, the truck skidded into the rear of plaintiffs' car.

The driver of the lead car is unknown. Plaintiffs sued defendant on a theory of negligence. Defendant contended that the negligence of the unknown driver "caused or contributed to cause" the accident and resulting damages. * * *

The jury answered "special questions." It determined that plaintiffs' damages were $100,000.00, that plaintiffs were not negligent, that defendant was negligent, that defendant's negligence contributed to the accident and plaintiffs' damages to the extent of 30%, that the unknown driver was negligent and this negligence contributed to the accident and plaintiffs' damages to the extent of 70%.

Plaintiffs moved that judgment be entered in their favor in the amount of $100,000.00. This motion was not granted. Instead, the trial court ordered a new trial [based on the jury instructions concerning comparative negligence]. * * *

We granted defendant's application for an interlocutory appeal.

In this case, in using the term "joint and several liability," we mean that either of two persons whose concurrent negligence contributed to cause plaintiffs' injury and damage may be held liable for the entire amount of the damage caused by them.

It is not disputed that this is a common law rule which existed in New Mexico prior to Scott v. Rizzo, 96 N.M. 682, 634 P.2d 1234 (1981), which adopted the opinion of the Court of Appeals in Claymore v. City of Albuquerque. In *Claymore,* this Court adopted pure comparative negligence. * * *

The question is whether, in a comparative negligence case, a concurrent tortfeasor is liable for the entire damage caused by concurrent tortfeasors. * * * The premise for the question to be answered is that, under the common law rule, either the defendant or the unknown driver could be held liable for the damage caused by their combined negligence.

The question has been answered in several states; most of these decisions are not helpful because the answer depended upon the contents of a comparative negligence statute. [The court discusses rulings in a number of states.]

The foregoing discussion shows that joint and several liability, for concurrent tortfeasors, has been retained by judicial decision in pure comparative negligence states. We recognize that this retention accords with 2 Restatement (Second) of Torts § 433A (1965). See, comment *h* to § 433A. Retention also accords with the Uniform Comparative Fault Act, § 2.

The retention of joint and several liability ultimately rests on two grounds; neither ground is defensible.

The first ground is the concept that a plaintiff's injury is "indivisible." The California Supreme Court, in American Motorcycle Ass'n [v. Superior Court, 20 Cal.3d 578, 146 Cal.Rptr. 182, 578 P.2d 899 (1978)] supra, followed this ground when it stated: "[T]he simple feasibility of apportioning fault on a comparative negligence basis does not render an indivisible injury 'divisible' for purposes of the joint and several liability. * * * In other words, the mere fact that it may be possible to assign some percentage figure to the relative culpability of one negligent defendant as compared to another does not in any way suggest that each defendant's negligence is not a proximate cause of the entire indivisible injury."

Thus, under the California Supreme Court decision, a concurrent tortfeasor, 1% at fault, is liable for 100% of the damage caused by concurrent tortfeasors, on the basis that the tortfeasor, 1% at fault, caused the entire damage. A practical answer, in this case, is that the jury found that defendant was 30% at fault and caused 30% of the damage.

Prosser, Law of Torts, 4th Edition, § 41, p. 241, states: "The law of joint tortfeasors rests very largely upon recognition of the fact that each of two or more causes may be charged with a single result."

Prosser, "Joint Torts and Several Liability," 25 Cal.L.Rev. 413 (1936–37), states that the rule holding a concurrent tortfeasor for the entire loss "grew out of the common law concept of the unity of the cause of action; the jury could not be permitted to apportion the damages, since there was but one wrong." The "unity" concept, in turn was based on common law rules of pleading and joinder. * * *

Joint and several liability is not to be retained in our pure comparative negligence system on a theory of one indivisible wrong. The concept of one indivisible wrong, based on common law technicalities, is obsolete, and is not to be applied in comparative negligence cases in New Mexico. [C]

The second ground is that joint and several liability must be retained in order to favor plaintiffs; a plaintiff should not bear the risk of being unable to collect his judgment. We fail to understand the argument. Between one plaintiff and one defendant, the plaintiff bears the risk of the defendant being insolvent; on what basis does the risk shift if there are two defendants, and one is insolvent? In our case, the risk factor arises because the concurrent tortfeasor, 70% at fault, is unknown. * * *

Joint and several liability is not to be retained in our pure comparative negligence system on the basis that a plaintiff must be favored.

We hold that defendant is not liable for the entire damage caused by defendant and the unknown driver. Defendant, as a concurrent tortfeasor, is not liable on a theory of joint and several liability. * * *

The trial court properly instructed the jury to consider the negligence and damage resulting from the negligence of the unknown driver.

The order granting a new trial is reversed. The cause is remanded with instructions to enter judgment in favor of plaintiffs, against defendant, for the 30% of plaintiffs' damages caused by defendant.

NOTES AND QUESTIONS

1. In these two cases, the negligent conduct of more than one actor combined to produce a particular injury to the plaintiff. The negligence of each of them is found to be a proximate cause of that injury. The injury has therefore been treated as indivisible and this has commonly been regarded as the third situation in which the principle of joint and several liability should be applied. But this doctrine of joint and several liability, as the opinions in the principal cases note, originally was based upon two other major tort principles that have been changing. One principle involves contributory negligence, which at common law barred plaintiff's recovery but has been changed in all but a few states so that it now has the effect of diminishing the amount of plaintiff's recovery (details in Chapter 12, Section 1). A second principle involves contribution among joint tortfeasors, which was not allowed at early common law but is now generally permitted, usually by statute. A joint tortfeasor paying more than his share of the plaintiff's damages may recover from the other joint tortfeasors on either a per capita basis or a comparative-fault basis (this chapter, Section 3). The question being asked by many courts is whether the doctrine of joint and several liability, which was premised on these two principles, also should change. See, e.g., McIntyre v. Balentine, 833 S.W.2d 52, 58 (Tenn.1992) (adopting comparative negligence and abolishing joint and several liability), page 626. See also Restatement (Third) of Torts: Apportionment of Liability § 20 (2000) for an extensive discussion of the various ways in which the states have resolved these questions.

2. Defendants in states that adopted comparative negligence urged that the concept of comparative negligence should be applied to compare the negligence of the defendants to each other as well as to compare the negligence of the defendants to the plaintiff and that each defendant be responsible for only that part of the injury that the percentage of fault apportioned to him bears to the total negligence of all tortfeasors. Otherwise, it is claimed, he will not be treated fairly. If each tortfeasor is identifiable (unlike the driver of the "lead" car in the *Bartlett* case), not protected by immunity (unlike the employer in the *Coney* case), subject to the jurisdiction of the court, and solvent, this form of liability will produce exactly the same result as the traditional system of joint and several liability, aided by contribution among joint tortfeasors based on percentage fault, would produce. Contribution is unnecessary if there is no joint and several liability.

3. The principal difference between the two systems arises when the shares of one or more tortfeasors cannot be collected from them. Under joint and several liability, the plaintiff can collect from one (or more) of the tortfeasors (sometimes called the "Deep Pocket") and leave it up to that defendant either to obtain contribution from the others or to bear the loss alone. Under several liability, each tortfeasor pays no more than his apportioned share, and the injured party bears the loss of any uncollectible share. Which is the fairer method? Some courts have found that the public policy reasons for requiring tortfeasors rather than injured persons to bear the burden of uncollectible portions of the damages continue to control even with the adoption of comparative negligence. See, e.g., American Motorcycle Assn. v. Superior Crt., 20 Cal.3d 578, 578 P.2d 899, 146

Cal.Rptr. 182 (1978) (quoted in both principal cases); Kaeo v. Davis, 68 Haw. 447, 719 P.2d 387 (1986).

4. Some states, adopting a provision of the 1977 Uniform Comparative Fault Act also included in the 2002 Uniform Apportionment of Tort Responsibility Act, have attempted to ameliorate the effect of an insolvent defendant by providing for a reallocation of the share of the insolvent defendant among the other parties (including the plaintiff, if he is at fault) according to their respective percentages of fault. V. Schwartz, Comparative Negligence § 19.04 (5th ed. 2010) (listing states).

5. How should a nonparty actor be treated? Note that in the *Bartlett* case, the 70% tortfeasor was a "hit and run" driver, and therefore not a party to the action. Is it appropriate to determine the percentage attributable to a nonparty? Chronister v. Bryco Arms, 125 F.3d 624 (8th Cir.1997) (applying Missouri law) (noting that neither legislature nor courts had addressed issue whether fault can be apportioned to a nonparty). See also V. Schwartz, Comparative Negligence § 15.05 (5th ed. 2010) (discussing ways states have treated absent tortfeasors). Do you see why it might affect the nonparty as well as the parties? One court has found that assigning a share of comparative responsibility to a nonparty violates the due process rights of the nonparty. Plumb v. Fourth Judicial District Court, 279 Mont. 363, 927 P.2d 1011 (1996) (in slip and fall case against shopping center, shopping center sought to reduce its liability by proving nonparty physician's malpractice in treating plaintiff—damage to physician's reputation) and another has found it unconstitutional because the State constitution grants to the judiciary rather than the legislature the power over the court's rules of pleadings, practice, and procedure. Johnson v. Rockwell Automation, Inc., 2009 Ark. 241, 308 S.W.3d 135 (2009) (answering certified question from federal court).

6. If the unidentified tortfeasor should later be found and sued, would the determination of fault in the prior case be binding? Would the plaintiff or any of the tortfeasors be able to use collateral estoppel to prevent relitigation of the allocation of fault?

7. What if the nonparty is identified but immune from suit by the plaintiff? Should that be treated differently from nonparties who were not joined for other reasons? Worker is injured when he reaches into a cotton baler to clear some loose cotton away from a protective switch. The opening through which he reached should have been covered by a plate that had been bolted on by the manufacturer of the baler. Worker sues manufacturer. The manufacturer argues that the employer, who permitted the protective plate to be removed in violation of manufacturer's instructions, is at least partially at fault for the injury. Should the jury be permitted to allocate a percentage of fault to the employer, immune from a suit by the worker through the exclusive remedy provision of the state worker compensation law? Compare Snyder v. LTG Lufttechnische GmbH, 955 S.W.2d 252 (Tenn.1997) (jury may consider actions of employer in deciding whether manufacturer is liable, but may not assess fault against the employer) with Mack Trucks, Inc. v. Tackett, 841 So.2d 1107 (Miss. 2003) (under comparative negligence statute, jury should allocate fault to employer even though employer immune from suit by plaintiff). Whether the immune tortfeasor is allocated a percentage of fault may depend on the type of immunity. Carroll v. Whitney, 29 S.W.3d 14 (Tenn. 2000) (resident

physicians in medical malpractice case who were immune because they were employees of the state could have fault allocated to them even though an employer immune through worker compensation statute could not).

8. What if the nonparty is an intentional tortfeasor and the party was negligent in failing to protect the plaintiff? Should the intentional conduct be compared to the negligent conduct? Brandon v. County of Richardson, 261 Neb. 636, 624 N.W.2d 604 (2001) (in case where county sheriff's department negligently failed to protect rape victim, after rape was reported to them, from being killed by rapists, intentional conduct of killers could not be compared to negligent conduct of county); Hutcherson v. City of Phoenix, 192 Ariz. 51, 961 P.2d 449 (1998) (in case where 911 operator's negligence in categorizing call caused shooting death of two people being attacked by former boyfriend of one of them, jury found that City was 75% at fault and killer was 25% at fault); Welch v. Southland Corp., 134 Wash.2d 629, 952 P.2d 162 (1998) (in case brought by patron who was shot by thief at 7–11 convenience store, statute did not permit jury to compare negligent conduct of owner to intentional conduct of thief); Ozaki v. Association of Apartment Owners of Discovery Bay, 87 Haw. 273, 954 P.2d 652 (App.), rev'd on other grounds, 87 Haw. 265, 954 P.2d 644 (1998) (in case where woman was murdered in her apartment by her paramour, negligent conduct of condominium complex security could be compared to intentional conduct of murderer, but condominium association would be subject to joint and several liability for murderer's share). See also Restatement (Third) of Torts: Apportionment of Liability § 24 (2000) for an extensive discussion of the cluster of issues arising in cases involving negligent failure to protect against intentional conduct.

9. During the last two decades, the traditional common law doctrine of joint and several liability for all joint tortfeasors has been changed in some way in most jurisdictions (including the jurisdictions of the principal cases) by either legislative enactments as part of "tort reform" movements or by judicial decisions. About ten jurisdictions have abolished joint and several liability. See, e.g., Alaska, Florida, and Wyoming. About ten have retained traditional joint and several liability. See, e.g., Maryland, Massachusetts, and Rhode Island. Others have modified it in various ways so, for example, that it does not apply 1) to noneconomic damages like pain and suffering or emotional distress (see, e.g., California); or 2) to defendants whose percentage of fault is below a certain threshold (see e.g., Iowa and Texas); or 3) to certain types of defendants (see e.g., New Mexico for product sellers); or 4) to certain types of actions (see, e.g., Idaho, which still applies joint and several liability only to cases involving intentional torts, hazardous wastes, medical and pharmaceutical products and Connecticut, which applies it to product liability claims). There are many other variations and some of the jurisdictions combine more than one element of change. Which is preferable? Do they all address the same "problem"?

Restatement (Third) of Torts: Apportionment of Liability § 27 (2000) takes no position as to whether joint and several liability, several liability, or some combination thereof should govern the liability of tortfeasors whose independent acts cause an indivisible injury. Instead, it leaves that to be determined by local law and then proposes several alternative tracks for addressing related issues, depending on the resolution of the basic question.

Most jurisdictions that have in some way modified joint and several liability for those acting independently to cause an indivisible harm will still apply it to those acting in concert. See, for example, Minn. Stat. Ann. § 604.02(2) (persons who act in a common scheme or plan that results in injury) and Reilly v. Anderson, 727 N.W.2d 102 (Iowa 2006) (finding that Iowa legislature did not intend to eliminate joint and several liability for those who acted in concert in action against driver and passenger where passenger was steering while driver took hit from a bong—concerted action does not have to be in context of an intentional tort to give rise to joint and several liability).

10. Would it be desirable to have the judge explain to the jury the consequences of their decision in setting the percentage of fault? See Kaeo v. Davis, 68 Haw. 447, 719 P.2d 387 (1986). (city wanted jury told that it would have to pay the whole verdict even if only 1% of fault was allocated to it by jury because co-defendant driver who had run into utility pole, injuring plaintiff passenger, was insolvent).

11. See generally Restatement (Third) of Torts: Apportionment of Liability (2000).

2. SATISFACTION AND RELEASE

Bundt v. Embro

Supreme Court of New York, Queens County, 1965.
48 Misc.2d 802, 265 N.Y.S.2d 872.

[Action by five plaintiffs, who were passengers in one or the other of two automobiles that collided. The actions were against the owners and drivers, as well as a contractor who was repairing the highway and who had negligently obstructed the view of a stop sign. Defendants moved to amend their answers to interpose the defense of discharge and satisfaction when plaintiffs recovered a judgment for the same injuries against the State of New York in the Court of Claims and this judgment had been satisfied.]

WILLIAM B. GROAT, JUSTICE. * * * "[I]t is elementary law that one who has been injured by the joint wrong of several parties may recover his damages against either or all; but, although there may be several suits and recoveries, there can be but one satisfaction. [Cc] The reason of the rule is that while there may be many perpetrators of a wrongful act, each of whom is separately liable, yet the act and its consequences are indivisible, and the injured person is, therefore, limited to a single satisfaction." [C] * * *

Nor does this court agree with plaintiffs' argument that the rule that the satisfaction of the judgment against one joint tort feasor discharges the others has no application to a Court of Claims judgment. Section 8 of the Court of Claims Act states:

"The state hereby waives its immunity from liability and action and hereby assumes liability and consents to have the same determined in accordance with the same rules of law as applied to actions in the supreme court against individuals or corporations, provided the claimant complies with the limitations of this article."

"By the adoption of such section the State places itself as to those making claims against the State, in the same position as a private individual or a corporation would be for his or its negligence." [C]

The Court of Claims determined that the state was negligent and the plaintiffs were awarded judgments for the injuries sustained. If defendants are joint tort feasors with the state, the fact that the judgment satisfied is a Court of Claims judgment should not prevent application of a rule which prevents double recovery for a single injury.

The state may also be a joint tortfeasor [c]. While the sovereign has always been immune from suit at common law, " '[w]hen, however, the state confers upon a court jurisdiction to hear and determine all claims against it, or all claims of a particular class, the situation in that court is the same as if the claim were against a private individual or corporation.' " [Cc]

Therefore, if the trial court shall determine that the defendants were in fact joint tort feasors with the state, the satisfaction of a judgment against the state would operate as a discharge of the defendants.

Accordingly, leave to amend is granted to the defendants.

NOTES AND QUESTIONS

1. The original English joinder rule, now altered by statute, was that the plaintiff could obtain but one judgment against one or more "joint tortfeasors." Only those who acted in concert or were vicariously liable for each other's actions were called "joint tortfeasors" at that time. Since the act of each was the act of all, it was considered that there was only one cause of action against all of them, which was "merged" in the judgment, so that the judgment against one alone, even if unsatisfied, barred any later action against another. This rule is now repudiated everywhere in the United States. The plaintiff may bring a series of separate actions against multiple tortfeasors liable for the same damage, and take each to judgment, as long as he only collects on one. Why would the plaintiff do that? Can you think of examples, other than the one in the principal case involving suit against a governmental entity in a designated court?

2. Suppose the plaintiff is unhappy with the amount of damages set by the first court and does not collect on that judgment? Cf. Nielson v. Spanaway General Med. Clinic, Inc., 135 Wash.2d 255, 956 P.2d 312 (1998) (plaintiff's dissatisfaction with the amount of damages may be the basis for an appeal, but it does not prevent the application of collateral estoppel in the second action, requested by the second set of defendants to estop the plaintiffs from relitigating the amount of the damages).

3. A quite distinct principle developed in England, and carried over to the United States, that the plaintiff was entitled to only one compensation, and that *full satisfaction* of his claim, by full payment, would prevent its further enforcement. This rule is equitable in its nature,

and its purpose is to prevent unjust enrichment. It is this principle that is being applied in the principal case.

4. A necessary corollary to the rule that there be only one full satisfaction of a claim through satisfaction of the judgment was that any *partial satisfaction* of the claim must be credited to the other parties who are also liable. All states provide for some type of credit against the judgment for partial satisfaction of the judgment by a joint tortfeasor. The judgment is either reduced dollar for dollar by the amount of any partial satisfaction, often referred to as a *pro tanto reduction*, or reduced on a percentage basis. See, e.g., Va. Code Ann. § 8.01–35.1 ("reduced by any amount stipulated by the covenant or the release, or in the amount of the consideration paid for it, whichever is the greater"); Jones v. Ahlberg, 489 N.W.2d 576 (N.D.1992) (non-settling defendant receives credit for percentage of fault that the settling defendant represents). Restatement (Third) of Torts: Apportionment of Liability § 26 (2000), recognizing that each possibility has its advantages and disadvantages, recommends a percentage credit based on comparative responsibility. Think about how each scheme would influence the parties' settlement negotiations under different factual scenarios.

5. What if the settling defendant has not paid the settlement amount by the time of the entry of judgment against the nonsettling defendant? Garcia v. Duro Dyne Corp., 156 Cal.App.4th 92, 67 Cal.Rptr.3d 100 (2007) (no credit given for amount specified in release since it had not been paid due to settling defendant's pending bankruptcy; court noted that nonsettling defendant would be entitled to reimbursement if settling defendant ever paid).

6. What if the claim is reduced to a judgment against one tortfeasor (like the principal case), but the amount of the damages is agreed by the parties rather than adjudicated by the court (unlike the principal case)? Plaintiff, a teenage minor, was riding in the front seat of a truck when the door flew open while the driver was turning a corner. Plaintiff fell out and was injured. His mother filed suit against the driver of the truck and obtained a consent judgment against him in the amount of the driver's (relatively low) automobile liability policy coverage limit and that judgment was paid. Later, plaintiff sued Chrysler, the manufacturer of the truck, alleging that the truck door flew open due to defective design or manufacture. Chrysler sought summary judgment, arguing that the previous (consent) judgment, which had been satisfied, operated to discharge Chrysler. Plaintiff argued that the prior judgment was not a full compensation for his injuries even if it was a full satisfaction of the consent judgment. Abandoning previous decisions that had treated all judgments the same, whether they were the result of consent or adjudication, Oklahoma concluded that satisfaction of a consent judgment should be treated like a settlement and release (partial satisfaction) and not like a judgment (full satisfaction). Kirkpatrick v. Chrysler Corp., 920 P.2d 122 (Okla.1996). If New York had made such a ruling, would it change the result in the principal case?

7. What if the jury's allocation of fault does not match the amount of the settlement? Kiss v. Jacob, 138 N.J. 278, 650 A.2d 336 (1994) (if plaintiff makes a particularly good bargain in settlement and the ultimate percentage of negligence attributed to the settling defendant is less than

the amount of the settlement, plaintiff will benefit by the excess amount, just as plaintiff runs the risk of a low settlement).

8. Suppose the trial occurs in a jurisdiction that reduces the amount of the plaintiff's recovery by the percentage of the plaintiff's comparative negligence. (See Chapter 12, Defenses.) Does the trial court judge first subtract the amount of the settlement and then reduce it by the percentage of plaintiff's fault or vice versa? Whalen v. Kawasaki Motors Corp., 680 N.Y.S.2d 435, 92 N.Y.2d 288, 703 N.E.2d 246 (1998) (subtracting amount of settlement from judgment and then reducing it by percentage of fault attributed by jury to plaintiff, noting that New York's adoption of the settlement-first method is in accord with prevailing trend). Suppose the trial occurs in a jurisdiction that places a cap on the amount of the damages. (See Chapter 10, Damages.) Does the trial court judge first reduce the jury verdict to the cap and then credit the amount of a settlement or vice versa? Compare Fairfax Hosp. Sys., Inc. v. Nevitt, 249 Va. 591, 457 S.E.2d 10 (1995) (reducing to amount of cap and then subtracting amount of settlement) with Teeter v. Missouri Hwy. and Transp. Com'n, 891 S.W.2d 817 (Mo. 1995) (subtracting amount of settlement first and then reducing to amount of cap applicable to actions against state highway department).

9. Suppose the trial occurs in a jurisdiction that has eliminated joint and several liability. Would the nonsettling defendant still be entitled to a setoff? McReynolds v. Krebs, 290 Ga. 850, 725 S.E.2d 584 (2012) (setoff not applicable because settling and nonsettling defendants are no longer jointly and severally liable under 2005 statute eliminating joint and several liability) and Duncan v. Cessna Aircraft Co., 665 S.W.2d 414 (Tex. 1984) (settlement does not reflect the amount of harm caused by the remaining defendants and likewise should not affect their liability). Suppose the trial occurs in a jurisdiction that has limited joint and several liability to economic damages only. Would the nonsettling defendant be entitled to a setoff for the economic damages? How would the settlement be allocated between economic and non-economic losses? Wells v. Tallahassee Memorial Regional Medical Ctr., Inc., 659 So.2d 249 (Fla.1995) (nonsettling defendant entitled to setoff for economic damages only, with settlement proceeds to be divided between economic and noneconomic damages in the same proportion as the jury's award.) What if the settling defendant is found by the jury not to be liable? Gouty v. Schnepel, 795 So.2d 959 (Fla. 2001) (no setoff because setoff statute presumes joint liability).

10. Payments made by the tortfeasor's liability insurance company are of course made on the tortfeasor's behalf and therefore credited against the judgment. At common law, payments that were not made by, or on behalf of, the tortfeasor are not credited to the benefit of the tortfeasors, even though this means plaintiff may receive more in compensation than he suffered in losses. If, for example, a plaintiff's medical treatment is provided for free by plaintiff's spouse or paid for by some source collateral to the defendant, such as a relative, employer, or health insurance company, the defendant should not "be permitted to profit by any gratuity extended to his victim, and consequently, the reasonable value of said services should be recoverable." Burke v. Byrd, 188 F.Supp. 384 (N.D.Fla.1960) (plaintiff entitled to reasonable value of medical treatment provided free to him as member of military). This—the so-called collateral-

source rule—applies to insurance policies maintained by the injured party, to gratuities to him, to employment benefits, and to benefits from social legislation. Approximately half of the states have modified the common law collateral source rule by statute, usually as part of "tort reform" statutes. See Chapter 10, Damages.

Cox v. Pearl Investment Co.

Supreme Court of Colorado, 1969.
168 Colo. 67, 450 P.2d 60.

HODGES, JUSTICE. This is a negligence case which terminated in the trial court with a summary judgment in favor of the defendant on a showing that a purported release had been executed by the plaintiffs in favor of a joint tort-feasor. The common law rule of law that the release of one tort-feasor releases all others who may have liability was applied by the trial court.

As plaintiffs in the trial court, Mr. and Mrs. Cox sought recovery of damages for injuries which Mrs. Cox sustained when she fell on property owned by the defendant Pearl Investment Company. * * * When the summary judgment motion was considered by the trial court, it was shown that the tenant, Goodwill Industries, had previously paid the plaintiffs $2500 in consideration of the plaintiffs' execution of a document entitled "Covenant Not to Proceed with Suit." * * *

[The plaintiffs' assignment of error brings into focus an important issue concerning the legal effect to be given to the "Covenant Not to Proceed with Suit" involved here.] The trial court denominated it a release and, without ascribing any dignity to the expressed words that the plaintiffs reserved "the right to sue any other person or persons against whom they may have or assert any claim on account of damages arising out of the above described accident," ruled that it therefore barred any action against the defendant as a joint tort-feasor.

Although Price v. Baker, 143 Colo. 264, 352 P.2d 90 supports the trial court, we no longer deem it advisable to further impose on our body of law the harshness and rigidity of the rule and rationale of *Price*. * * * In our present analysis of this issue, we are drawn toward only one conclusion. We can no longer countenance the continuation of a rule of law which is not only harsh and illogical, but which gives refuge and absolution to wrongdoers by depriving a litigant under these circumstances of probable just and full compensation for his injuries caused by wrongdoers. It is not possible to visualize any reasonable or compelling justification for persisting in the application of this harsh and unrealistic rule except on the basis of ancient formalisms, the reasons for which no longer prevail. * * *

In *Price,* we declared "this state has long followed the universal rule that the release of one joint tort-feasor is a release of all." We hereby confirm this to be still the rule in Colorado. Also, we agree with the proposition that a joint tort-feasor is not ipso facto released by a covenant not to sue. We do, however, now state that the instrument involved in Price v. Baker, which is substantially identical to the writing involved in the case at bar, was improvidently interpreted to be an absolute and full release of all joint tort-feasors.

The manifest intent of the parties to a contract should always be given effect unless it be in violation of law or public policy. This is fundamental in contract law. Where a contract has the effect of releasing one joint tort-feasor but expressly reserves the right to sue others who may be liable, it should not in law be treated otherwise. The expressed reservation in this instrument of the right to sue other joint tort-feasors evinces a clear-cut manifestation that the plaintiffs were not receiving full compensation; and if this is borne out, their right to bring an action against others who were the cause of their damages should not be foreclosed. The danger of over compensation or double compensation is no excuse for barring a claim against joint tort-feasors. Obviously, no court would permit the accomplishment of this possible contingency. And certainly, the non-settling joint tort-feasor is not prejudiced, but rather, he is benefited for he would be entitled to have the amount of the judgment reduced by the amount paid by his co-tortfeasor. * * *

To be particularly noted is the early case of Matheson v. O'Kane, 211 Mass. 91, 97 N.E. 638. The facts therein are quite similar to the facts of the instant case in that the released parties were authorized to plead the instrument in bar to any action filed by the plaintiffs. It was held that this did not constitute a release of other defendants and further stated:

"* * * But where it is evident that the consideration paid to the plaintiff was not intended to be full compensation for his injuries, and the agreement signed by him although in form a release was clearly intended to preserve the liability of those who were not parties to it, many of the courts have sought to give effect to that intention by construing the agreement as in legal effect a covenant not to sue and not a technical release." 4 Restatement of Torts § 885 which is modeled after numerous cases like *Matheson,* supra, provides that a release will be construed as a covenant not to sue where the right to proceed against the remaining tort-feasors is expressly reserved. This section emphasizes the importance of the expressed intent of the contracting parties.

In the supplemental brief of the defendant, it is urged that *Price,* supra, establishes the rule in Colorado that the document involved there which is essentially identical to the instrument here is an absolute release of all joint tort-feasors and therefore, should not now be repudiated under the doctrine of stare decisis. This doctrine is assiduously followed by this court. However, when, as here, a prior decision is adverse to the rules of fundamental law and initiates a harsh and unrealistic rule, we believe it becomes incumbent upon us at the first opportunity presented to make a necessary change.

Accordingly, the judgment is reversed and the cause remanded to the trial court for further proceedings not inconsistent with the views expressed herein.

NOTES AND QUESTIONS

1. Distinguish between judgment and satisfaction of the judgment. Plaintiffs may proceed to judgment against as many tortfeasors as they

wish, although some issues may be affected by collateral estoppel. Satisfaction is receiving full compensation for the injury, based either on the plaintiff's valuation of the case (settlement) or the jury's (verdict). A plaintiff's claim is satisfied when the judgment is actually paid after the trial or when a settlement reflecting the full amount of plaintiff's claim is actually paid. A plaintiff may receive only one satisfaction for an injury.

2. Distinguish between satisfaction and release. Satisfaction is acceptance of full compensation for the injury. A release is a surrender of the plaintiff's claim, which may be for only partial compensation or for no compensation at all. Releases in the early common law were under seal, which disposed of the question of consideration, and thus could be given for no compensation.

3. Distinguish between a release and a covenant not to sue. The theory of the covenant is that plaintiff does not surrender the cause of action, but contracts not to sue on it. The right is retained, but there is agreement not to enforce it. The protection to the defendant is that if the plaintiff sues, defendant will have a counterclaim for breach of the covenant, in which the damages will equal any recovery by the plaintiff plus the expenses of defending the suit. It is generally recognized by the courts that the covenant is a mere procedural device, invented by the ingenuity of counsel to get around the traditional effect of a release at common law.

4. In early common law the only "joint tortfeasors" were those who acted in concert. Because the act of one was the act of all, a release to one of them was held to release the others, since there was but one cause of action, which was surrendered. Confusion as to the meaning of "joint tortfeasors" carried this rule over in the early American decisions to those who acted independently but could be joined in the same lawsuit because they were liable for the same damages. In addition, perhaps because of abolition of the seal, release sometimes was confused with satisfaction. See Abb v. Northern Pacific R. Co., 28 Wash. 428, 68 P. 954 (1902) (a release, even with express reservation of rights against other tortfeasors, is "conclusive evidence of satisfaction"). The result was, almost everywhere, an original American rule that a release of one tortfeasor releases all who are liable for the same damages, regardless of compensation paid or reservation of rights.

5. That original rule to the effect that the release of one joint tortfeasor releases all has been extensively changed, by decision or by statute.

A. Some states distinguish between a release and a covenant not to sue, and hold that the release necessarily releases other tortfeasors, but the covenant does not unless full compensation has been paid.

B. Some states hold that a release with express reservation of rights against other tortfeasors is to be treated as a covenant not to sue, regardless of words of release.

C. Some states hold that even a release without such a reservation does not release other tortfeasors unless it shows an intention to do so or full compensation has been paid. Leung v. Verdugo Hills Hosp., 55 Cal.4th 291, 145 Cal.Rptr.3d 553, 282 P.3d 1250 (2012).

D. Statutes in some states have provided that a release with an express reservation of rights against other tortfeasors does not release them. For example, the Uniform Joint Obligations Act, § 4. Or that they are released only when the terms so provide. Uniform Contribution Among Tortfeasors Act, § 4(a). A release usually is a separate document, but does not need to be. Bank drafts (checks) from insurance companies frequently have a general release printed on them. See Cupidon v. Alexis, 335 Md. 230, 643 A.2d 385 (1994) (language on face of check constitutes release).

6. In some jurisdictions, a release of the negligent agent (like the driver in an automobile accident or the doctor in a medical malpractice action) also releases the principal who is vicariously liable for the agent's conduct (like the employer of the driver or the doctor). Compare Booth v. Gades, 788 N.W.2d 701 (Minn. 2010) (release of firefighter also discharges City, his employer) and J & J Timber Co. v. Broome, 932 So.2d 1 (Miss. 2006) (release of driver also releases his employer, even though express reservation of rights against employer) with JFK Medical Ctr. v. Price, 647 So.2d 833 (Fla.1994) (release of doctor does not release hospital employer) and Woodrum v. Johnson, 210 W.Va. 762, 559 S.E.2d 908 (2001) (collecting cases and noting broad and diverse disagreement, finding no release).

7. Driver negligently runs into the plaintiff and breaks his leg. Physician negligently treats the break, with the result that the leg is permanently shorter. Suppose that plaintiff accepts a payment from driver for the original injury and releases him, expecting to hold physician liable for the aggravation. When he sues physician, physician relies on the common law rule as to the effect of the release of a joint tortfeasor. Assuming that driver's liability extends to the total injury (see page 388), some cases have held that physician was released by the release of driver. Thompson v. Fox, 326 Pa. 209, 192 A. 107 (1937). Others, however, have declined to apply the rule to release successive tortfeasors. Lujan v. Healthsouth Rehabilitation Corp., 120 N.M. 422, 902 P.2d 1025 (1995); Fieser v. St. Francis Hosp. & School of Nursing, 212 Kan. 35, 510 P.2d 145 (1973).

8. Suppose there is only one tortfeasor. A release is signed on the basis of assumed injuries. It turns out that the injuries are actually much more extensive than assumed. What can the injured party do? Ordinarily he must seek to set the release aside on the ground of fraud, mistake, duress, or undue influence. Most courts will not permit plaintiff to avoid the terms of the release if the mistake is about the extent of the injury or its consequences. Mack v. Albee Press, 263 A.D. 275, 32 N.Y.S.2d 231 (1942), aff'd without opinion, 288 N.Y. 623, 42 N.E.2d 617 (1942) (plaintiff settled claim for bruised toe, only later to develop gangrene and suffer the amputation of his leg). Some courts have set aside releases where the plaintiff believed she had no personal injury (having settled her property damage claim), when in fact her injuries were serious. Williams v. Glash, 789 S.W.2d 261 (Tex.1990). This issue is discussed in more detail in other courses, such as Restitution or Remedies. See also Dobbs, Remedies, § 11.9 (2d ed. 1993).

9. Some courts will still enforce a *general release* ("any and all other persons who are or may be liable for injuries arising out of said accident") even in favor of joint tortfeasors who did not participate in the settlement that generated the release. Enos v. Key Pharmaceuticals, Inc., 106 F.3d 838

(8th Cir.1997) (applying South Dakota law) (general release executed as part of settlement with physicians in medical malpractice case by parents of minor who suffered brain damage while taking asthma medication operated to release drug manufacturers in later suit based on product liability and fraud). But see Russ v. General Motors Corp., 111 Nev. 1431, 906 P.2d 718 (1995) (general release executed as part of settlement with driver in negligence case operates to release car manufacturer in later suit based on product liability against automobile manufacturer only if parties to release intended such a result) and Hess v. Ford Motor Co., 117 Cal.Rptr.2d 220, 27 Cal.4th 516, 41 P.3d 46 (2002) (similar facts, language of release ignored because based on "mutual mistake" supported by testimony of plaintiff, his attorney, and the claims adjustor who had negotiated the settlement for the other driver).

10. Should an attorney be liable (in professional malpractice) for failing to advise a client that a general release forecloses lawsuits against other tortfeasors? See Collas v. Garnick, 425 Pa.Super. 8, 624 A.2d 117 (1993) (alleging client lost opportunity to sue tortfeasor because attorney failed to advise her of the effect of signing a general release as part of a settlement; malpractice action allowed).

Elbaor v. Smith

Supreme Court of Texas, 1992.
845 S.W.2d 240.

[As a result of an automobile accident, plaintiff Smith suffered serious injuries, including a compound fracture of her left ankle. Dr. Syrquin treated her in the emergency room of Dallas/Fort Worth Medical Center ("D/FW Medical Center") on the night of the accident and then eight days later she was transferred to Arlington Community Hospital ("ACH") where she was treated by Drs. Elbaor (an orthopedic surgeon), Stephens (a plastic surgeon), and Gatmaitan (an infectious disease specialist). Ms. Smith received treatment at other facilities from other specialists over the next few years and ultimately, her ankle joint was fused. She filed a medical malpractice action against Dr. Syrquin and D/FW Medical Center and against Drs. Elbaor, Stephens, and Gatmaitan and ACH. Prior to trial, Ms. Smith settled and dismissed her claims against D/FW Medical Center and non-suited her claim against Dr. Gatmaitan. She also entered into "Mary Carter" settlement agreements with Dr. Syrquin, Dr. Stephens, and ACH. Those agreements provided that those defendants would pay her a total of $425,010, remain as defendants, participate in the trial of the case, and be paid back all or part of the settlement money paid to Ms. Smith out of the recovery against the remaining defendant, Dr. Elbaor. Dr. Elbaor requested that the Mary Carter agreements be voided as against public policy or, alternatively, that the settling defendants be dismissed from the trial. The trial court denied this request, the case proceeded to trial, and the jury awarded Ms. Smith damages in the amount of $2,253,237, allocating responsibility between Dr. Elbaor (88%) and Dr. Syrquin (12%). After deducting the credits for the settlements, the trial court entered a judgment against Dr. Elbaor for $1,872,848. The court of appeals affirmed.]

GONZALEZ, JUDGE * * *

Although the Mary Carter agreements were not entered into evidence, the trial judge was troubled by them and he took remedial measures to mitigate their harmful effects by reapportioning the peremptory challenges, changing the order of proceedings to favor Dr. Elbaor, allowing counsel to explain the agreements to the jury, and instructing the jury regarding the agreements.

During the trial, the settling defendants' attorneys, who sat at the table with Dr. Elbaor's attorneys, vigorously assisted Ms. Smith in pointing the finger of culpability at Dr. Elbaor. This created some odd conflicts of interest and some questionable representations of fact. For example, although Ms. Smith's own experts testified that [ER physician] Dr. Syrquin committed malpractice [by closing the wound too soon], her attorney stated during voir dire and in her opening statement that Dr. Syrquin's conduct was "heroic" and that [orthopedic surgeon] Dr. Elbaor's negligence caused Ms. Smith's damages. And during her closing argument, Ms. Smith's attorney urged the jury to find that Dr. Syrquin had not caused Ms. Smith's damages. This is hardly the kind of statement expected from a plaintiff's lawyer regarding a named defendant. ACH and Drs. Syrquin and Stephens had remained defendants of record, but their attorneys asserted during voir dire that Ms. Smith's damages were "devastating," "astoundingly high," and "astronomical." Furthermore, on cross examination they elicited testimony from Ms. Smith favorable to her and requested recovery for pain and mental anguish. The settling defendants' attorneys also abandoned their pleadings on Ms. Smith's contributory negligence, argued that Ms. Smith should be awarded all of her alleged damages, and urged that Dr. Elbaor was 100 percent liable.

The term "Mary Carter agreement" has been defined in different ways by various courts and commentators.[13]

* * *

A Mary Carter agreement exists, under our definition, when the plaintiff enters into a settlement agreement with one defendant and goes to trial against the remaining defendant(s). The settling defendant, who remains a party, guarantees the plaintiff a minimum payment, which may be offset in whole or in part by an excess judgment recovered at trial. [Cc] This creates a tremendous incentive for the settling defendant to ensure that the plaintiff succeeds in obtaining a sizable recovery, and thus motivates the defendant to assist greatly in the plaintiff's presentation of the case (as occurred here). Indeed, Mary Carter agreements generally, but not always, contain a clause requiring the settling defendant to participate in the trial on the plaintiff's behalf.

Given this Mary Carter scenario, it is difficult to surmise how these agreements promote settlement. Although the agreements do secure the

---

[13] The majority of cases and commentators define "Mary Carter agreement" as one in which the settling defendant possesses a financial stake in the outcome of the case and the settling defendant remains a party to the litigation. [Cc] Many cases also describe other requisite elements of a Mary Carter agreement, such as secrecy. [C] Other cases and commentators argue that a Mary Carter agreement exists any time the settling defendant possesses a financial interest in the plaintiff's recovery. [Cc]

partial settlement of a lawsuit, they nevertheless nearly always ensure a trial against the non-settling defendant. [Cc] Mary Carter agreements frequently make litigation inevitable, because they grant the settling defendant veto power over any proposed settlement between the plaintiff and any remaining defendant. [C] Thus, "only a mechanical jurisprudence could characterize Mary Carter arrangements as promoting compromise and discouraging litigation—they plainly do just the opposite." * * *

Many jurisdictions have decided to tolerate the ill effects of Mary Carter agreements, presumably because they believe that the agreements promote settlement. Some have sought to mitigate the agreements' harmful skewing of the trial process by imposing prophylactic protections. Indeed, Texas previously has taken such an approach [c] Smithwick, 724 S.W.2d at 8–12 (Spears, J., concurring).[19] These protective measures generally seek to remove the secrecy within which Mary Carter agreements traditionally have been shrouded. See Slusher v. Ospital, 777 P.2d 437, 440 (Utah 1989) (secrecy is the essence of a Mary Carter agreement).

Justice Spears rightly noted in Smithwick the falsity of the premise upon which the prophylactic protection approach is founded, namely, the promotion of equitable settlements. [C] Mary Carter agreements instead: present to the jury a sham of adversity between the plaintiff and one co-defendant, while these parties are actually allied for the purpose of securing a substantial judgment for the plaintiff and, in some cases, exoneration for the settling defendant. [Cc] The agreements pressure the "settling" defendant to alter the character of the suit by contributing discovery material, peremptory challenges, trial tactics, supportive witness examination, and jury influence to the plaintiff's cause. [C] These procedural advantages distort the case presented before a jury that came "to court expecting to see a contest between the plaintiff and the defendants [and] instead sees one of the defendants cooperating with the plaintiff." Smithwick, 724 S.W.2d at 9 (Spears, J., concurring). Mary Carter agreements not only allow plaintiffs to buy support for their case, they also motivate more culpable defendants to "make a 'good deal' [and thus] end up paying little or nothing in damages." [Cc] Remedial measures cannot overcome nor sufficiently alleviate the malignant effects that Mary Carter agreements inflict upon our adversarial system. No persuasive public policy justifies them, and they are not legitimized simply because this practice may continue in the absence of these agreements. The Mary Carter agreement is simply an unwise and champertous device that has failed to achieve its intended purpose.

* * *

As a matter of public policy, this Court favors settlements, but we do not favor partial settlements that promote rather than discourage

---

19 The guidelines provided in the Smithwick concurrence require that Mary Carter agreements: (1) are discoverable; (2) should be fully disclosed "to the trial court before trial or immediately after the agreement is formed;" (3) should be considered by the trial court in allowing jury strikes and ruling on witness examination; and (4) should be fully disclosed to the jury at the start of the trial. Smithwick, 724 S.W.2d at 8–11.

further litigation. And we do not favor settlement arrangements that skew the trial process, mislead the jury, promote unethical collusion among nominal adversaries, and create the likelihood that a less culpable defendant will be hit with the full judgment. The bottom line is that our public policy favoring fair trials outweighs our public policy favoring partial settlements.

This case typifies the kind of procedural and substantive damage Mary Carter agreements can inflict upon our adversarial system. Thus, we declare them void as violative of sound public policy.

* * *

[Reversed and remanded for new trial.]

Dissenting opinion by Justice Doggett, joined by Justices Mauzy and Gammage.

* * *

In the instant case the trial court took great care to safeguard procedurally the adversarial nature and fairness of its proceedings. Nothing about the agreements now under attack was hidden from anyone. The court appropriately solicited and welcomed suggestions from Elbaor and the other parties as to what and when to tell the jury about the Mary Carter agreements. At voir dire, the court informed prospective jury members that ACH and Syrquin, by participating in the trial, could recover all or a portion of the amounts paid in settlement to Smith, depending on the size of the verdict. An additional warning was extended regarding the possibility of witness bias arising from the agreements. The implications of the agreements were also explored by various counsel during voir dire.

To offset any disadvantage to Elbaor resulting from the agreements, the trial court gave him the same number of peremptory challenges as those of Smith and the three settling defendants together. Recognizing that these settling parties effectively were no longer aligned against one another, the trial court denied them the customary right of an opponent to lead each other's witnesses. Finally, the order of presentation was changed to guarantee that Elbaor always had the final opportunity to present evidence and examine witnesses. While Elbaor specifically complains of a lack of forcefulness in Smith's assertion of her claim against Syrquin, her counsel criticized Syrquin beginning in voir dire, though crediting his efforts to save Smith's life. Since in some multi-party suits co-defendants become aligned against one another, Elbaor might have found Syrquin and Stephens blaming him for Smith's injury even in the absence of the Mary Carter agreements. Despite Elbaor's concession that "the trial court [correctly] followed Texas law when it disclosed the Mary Carter agreements and implemented the other procedures to protect [him]," the majority rejects these procedures as "missing the point," thereby renewing its commitment to limit the role of the jury in the truth-seeking process. [C] Simply because jurors may initially expect the plaintiff to have interests adverse to all defendants does not mean that they are incapable of understanding that certain defendants have an incentive for the plaintiff to succeed. Indeed the same may occur in some multiparty litigation where no Mary Carter agreement is involved. The trial cannot be a "sham of adversity," when the jury, as here, is fully aware of this shift in alliances. Nor does the trial become less adversarial merely because some of the parties have switched sides—the names may have changed but the struggle is left intact. So long as at least two parties with antagonistic interests remain, the likelihood that the truth will emerge is not diminished.

Accordingly, most jurisdictions allow Mary Carter agreements when trial courts implement similar procedural safeguards to those adopted here. [Cc] In rejecting the full disclosure approach, today's opinion embraces a decidedly minority view accepted in only "a couple of states" that have previously chosen to prohibit such agreements. [C]

* * *

The elitist view that ordinary people acting as jurors are incapable of determining the facts after full disclosure has once again prevailed. While protecting the litigation process from deleterious agreements, this court should avoid precipitous action with uncertain consequences for so many litigants, particularly when, as here, the parties have exercised considerable care and the trial court has conscientiously monitored the proceedings.

NOTES AND QUESTIONS

1. As the opinion in the principal case suggests, Mary Carter agreements were named after an agreement discussed in the case of Booth v. Mary Carter Paint Co., 202 So.2d 8 (Fla.App.1967), and sometimes are called Gallagher covenants, Loan Receipt Agreements, or High/Low agreements. As the dissent pointed out, most jurisdictions permit the agreements as long as they are disclosed to the court and the other parties. See, for example, Reynolds v. Amchem Products Inc., 8 N.Y.3d 717, 872 N.E.2d 232, 840 N.Y.S.2d 546 (2007) (new trial ordered because high-low agreement between plaintiff and one defendant disclosed to trial court but not to other defendant) and Carter v. Tom's Truck Repair, Inc., 857 S.W.2d 172, 176 (Mo.1993) ("There is a strong public policy against allowing secret agreements to work a fraud on either the nonsettling defendant(s), the jury, or the trial court. However, there are also strong public policy considerations in favor of allowing plaintiffs to control their own cases and settle with defendants as they choose. This court finds no reason that these policies cannot coexist, even in the presence of a Mary Carter Agreement, so long as the other defendant is not deceived. [C] Like the court of appeals, we are convinced that the appropriate solution is to examine these troublesome agreements on a case-by-case basis rather than brand them all as outcasts.") A few, like Texas in the principal case, have found them void as against public policy even when disclosed. Interestingly, Florida, the home of the case that gave the agreement its name, has followed the lead of the principal case and no longer permits such agreements, even if they are disclosed. Dosdourian v. Carsten, 624 So.2d 241 (Fla.1993). See also Bernstein and Klerman, "An Economic Analysis of Mary Carter Settlement Agreements," 83 Geo.L.J. 2215 (1995).

2. The case is a good illustration of the ways in which strategy in a multiparty case can cause shifting alliances whether or not there is a Mary

Carter agreement. See also Newman v. Ford Motor Co., 975 S.W.2d 147 (Mo.1998).

3. Note that Justice Doggett's dissenting opinion chides the majority for "once again" allowing an "elitist view" of the jury system to prevail. What does that tell you about the process of decision making at the Texas Supreme Court?

3. CONTRIBUTION AND INDEMNITY

Knell v. Feltman

United States Court of Appeals, District of Columbia, 1949.
85 U.S.App.D.C. 22, 174 F.2d 662.

WILBUR K. MILLER, CIRCUIT JUDGE. On May 19, 1945 Evelyn Langland and her husband were guest passengers in an automobile owned and operated by Kenneth E. Knell. At 12th Street and Pennsylvania Avenue, in the District of Columbia, the car in which they were riding collided with a taxicab owned by Ralph L. Feltman and operated by his employee, as a result of which Mrs. Langland was seriously injured. She and her husband sued Feltman to recover damages. After answering, Feltman filed a third-party complaint against Knell, asserting the collision was caused by the contributing or sole negligence of Knell.

[The jury found, in answer to special interrogatories, that both Feltman's employee and Knell were negligent, that the negligence of each contributed to the collision, and that plaintiffs' damages were $11,500. The court then awarded judgment in favor of plaintiffs against Feltman for $11,500, and upon payment of this by Feltman, judgment in favor of Feltman against Knell for $5,750. Knell argued that contribution should not be available because plaintiff passengers had not alleged that Knell was a joint tortfeasor with Feltman.]

Is Feltman to be denied contribution because the Langlands neither asked nor obtained judgment against Knell? The gist of Knell's argument on this question is that the right to contribution exists only between tortfeasors liable in common to the plaintiff; that his liability to the plaintiff was not established by a judgment against him in favor of the plaintiffs; that, therefore, his and Feltman's common liability to the Langlands was not established, and that consequently Feltman cannot have contribution from him. * * *

In addition to being balked by Rule 14(a) [of the Federal Rules of Civil Procedure, which provides that a defendant may bring into the action another person who may be liable to him for all or any part of the damages, even though the plaintiff does not seek a judgment against him], the appellant's theory that there can be no contribution unless the plaintiff has first obtained a judgment against both wrongdoers is untenable for still another reason. The right to seek contribution belongs to the tortfeasor who has been forced to pay, and the existence of the right cannot logically depend upon a selection of defendants made by the plaintiff. If it did so depend, the caprice or whim of the plaintiff, or his deliberate intention to fasten liability on one defendant alone, could preclude that defendant from having contribution to which he might otherwise be entitled. Moreover, such an application of the contribution doctrine would open the way to collusion between a plaintiff, and one against whom he has a cause of action to impose liability solely upon another against whom he has a cause of action for the same wrong.

For these reasons, we see no substance in the suggestion that contribution between concurrent tortfeasors can be enforced only if both are judgment debtors of the plaintiff.

We come now to consider whether the fact that Knell personally participated in the commission of the tort takes this case out of the ruling in George's Radio, [Inc. v. Capital Transit Co., 75 U.S.App.D.C. 187, 126 F.2d 219 (1942),] where both wrongdoers were "vicariously" negligent.

This consideration logically leads to an examination of the interesting history of the no-contribution doctrine, which is conventionally said to begin with Merryweather v. Nixan, 8 Term Rep. 186, 101 Eng.Rep. 1337 (K.B.1799). The plaintiff and defendant in that case had injured a mill by taking or damaging its machinery and the plaintiff, having satisfied the judgment of the mill owner, sued for contribution. The trial judge non-suited on the ground that "no contribution could by law be claimed as between joint wrongdoers." On appeal, affirming the trial court, Kenyon, C.J., stated "that he had never before heard of such an action having been brought, where the former recovery was for a tort." In 1799, the word "tort" was used only to describe wrongs of a wilful or intentional character.

Due to the brevity of the report and a misleading headnote, the Merryweather case has often been cited in support of the sweeping proposition that no contribution can be had between joint tortfeasors. It is plain, however, that the ruling of the case was limited to the denial of contribution between wilful or intentional wrongdoers.

Nevertheless, after a period of adherence to the true Merryweather holding, the majority of American courts have long flatly said there can be no contribution between joint or concurrent tortfeasors, without distinguishing between those who are intentional wrongdoers and those whose unpurposed negligence results in a tort.

Widespread revulsion against that rule, which Chief Justice Groner said "is not sustainable upon any fair basis of reasoning, is wrong, and should be overruled", was demonstrated when [many legislatures reversed and courts repudiated the rule.] * * *

We conclude that when a tort is committed by the concurrent negligence of two or more persons who are not intentional wrongdoers, contribution should be enforced; that a joint judgment against such tort-feasors is not a prerequisite to contribution between them, and it is immaterial whether they were, or any of them was, personally negligent. In other words, we adopt for the District of Columbia, without exception or reservation, the rule stated by Chief Justice Groner in the George's Radio case "that when the parties are not intentional and wilful wrongdoers, but are made so by legal inference or intendment, contribution may be enforced." * * *

Affirmed.

NOTES AND QUESTIONS

1. As the opinion in the principal case notes, the common law rule that there could be no contribution among joint tortfeasors had its origin in 1799 in the case of Merryweather v. Nixan, 8 T.R. 186, 101 Eng.Rep. 1337 [K.B.1799]. There is a very meager report of the case, but it seems clear that there had been a joint judgment against two defendants in an action for conversion and that they had acted in concert, since they were joined at a time when joinder was possible only on this basis. One defendant was denied contribution from the other, apparently on the ground that he had acted intentionally and his claim rested upon what was, in the eyes of the law, entirely his own wrong.

2. The early American cases denied contribution in cases of willful misconduct, although some allowed it when the tort committed by the claimant was a matter of negligence or mistake. Once the door was thrown open to joinder in one action of those tortfeasors who had acted independently to cause the same harm, the origin of the "no contribution" rule and the reason for it were lost to sight, and contribution was denied among all "joint tortfeasors." This was the majority common law rule in the United States early in the twentieth century. Most of the early twentieth century commentators advocated a right to contribution, at least when the claimant was not an intentional wrongdoer, on the ground that it is unfair to saddle the entire burden of a loss, for which two are responsible, upon one alone, while the other goes scot free. See Bohlen, Contribution and Indemnity Between Tortfeasors, 21 Cornell L.Q. 522 (1936) and Leflar, Contribution and Indemnity Between Tortfeasors, 81 U.Pa.L.Rev. 130 (1932).

3. By the middle of the twentieth century, a substantial majority of the states permitted contribution, either by statute or judicial decision. See, e.g., Safeway Stores, Inc. v. Raytown, 633 S.W.2d 727 (Mo.1982). Three successive uniform acts have provided for it. See Uniform Contribution Among Tortfeasors Act (1939), Uniform Contribution Among Tortfeasors Act (1955), and Uniform Comparative Fault Act (1979). The Restatement (Third) of Torts: Apportionment of Liability § 23 (2000) has adopted this position. But see Muncie Power Prods., Inc. v. United Technologies Automotive, Inc., 328 F.3d 870 (6th Cir. 2003) (applying Indiana law) (Indiana adheres to the traditional common law rule prohibiting contribution among joint tortfeasors).

4. As jurisdictions recognized contribution among joint tortfeasors, they applied a rule of allocation, by analogy to contribution among sureties, on an equal-division basis—half and half if there are two tortfeasors, by thirds if there are three, and so on. With the advent of comparative negligence, most jurisdictions have changed and make the division according to the relative fault of the parties. In accord, the Uniform Comparative Fault Act and Restatement (Third) of Torts: Apportionment of Liability § 23(b), comment *e* (2000).

5. The traditional common law rule that contribution is not permitted among *intentional* wrongdoers has persisted, and there seems little inclination to change it. It has been codified in many jurisdictions.

6. Keep in mind that contribution is neither necessary nor permitted in jurisdictions that have eliminated joint and several liability. After a single car accident, passenger sued driver and driver's employer. Before trial, passenger settled with both defendants. Settling defendants then filed a contribution claim against the State, arguing that its negligence in maintaining the road contributed to the accident. Washington had limited joint and several liability by statute and its scope did not include this situation. Thus, settling defendants were not entitled to contribution. Kottler v. State of Washington, 136 Wash.2d 437, 449, 963 P.2d 834, 841 (1998) (settling defendants "settled in the eyes of the law only for their proportionate shares of total liability. Absent joint and several liability[,] they simply have no claim for contribution under the statute.")

Yellow Cab Co. of D.C., Inc. v. Dreslin

United States Court of Appeals, District of Columbia Circuit, 1950.
86 U.S.App.D.C. 327, 181 F.2d 626.

PROCTOR, CIRCUIT JUDGE. The question here concerns contribution between tortfeasors where the judgment creditor is the wife of the tortfeasor against whom contribution is sought.

A taxicab of appellant (hereafter called "Cab Co."), driven by its agent, and an automobile, driven by appellee (hereafter called "Dreslin"), collided. Dreslin's wife and others in his car were injured. They sued the Cab Co. for damages. Dreslin joined with them, claiming for loss of consortium, medical expenses for Mrs. Dreslin and damages to his automobile. Among its defenses, the Cab Co. pleaded contributory negligence of Dreslin. It also cross-claimed against him for damages to the taxicab and for contribution for any sums recovered by the other plaintiffs against it. The jury's verdict established the collision to have been caused by concurrent negligent operation of the two cars. Accordingly judgments for varying amounts were entered in favor of all plaintiffs except Dreslin. In addition a declaratory judgment was entered allowing the Cab Co. contribution against Dreslin upon the several judgments except that of Mrs. Dreslin. This was disallowed because, as the Court held, "the right to contribution arises from a joint liability," and as Dreslin was not liable in tort to his wife, there was no joint liability between him and the Cab Co. as to her. This appeal is confined to that single question.

We agree with the conclusion of the trial court. Neither husband nor wife is liable for tortious acts by one against the other. That is the common law rule. It prevails today in the District of Columbia. * * *

The rights of contribution arise out of a common liability. The rule "hinges on the doctrine that general principles of justice require that in the case of a common obligation, the discharge of it by one of the obligors without proportionate payment from the other, gives the latter an advantage to which he is not equitably entitled." [C] Contribution, then, depends upon joint liability. An injured party plaintiff in the suit from which a right of contribution develops must have had a cause of action against the party from whom contribution is sought. Here there was no liability by Dreslin to his wife,—no right to action against him and the Cab Co., hence nothing to which a right of contribution could attach.

The argument that it would be inequitable to allow Mrs. Dreslin to be "enriched" at the sole expense of the Cab Co., permitting her husband, equally at fault, to escape any of the burden, overlooks the fact that preservation of domestic peace and felicity is the policy upon which the rule of immunity between husband and wife is based. * * *

The judgment is affirmed.

NOTES AND QUESTIONS

1. Most states agree that non-immune tortfeasors may not seek contribution or indemnity from those who are immune. See Landis v. Hearthmark, LLC, 232 W.Va. 64, 750 S.E.2d 280 (W.Va. 2013) (product seller of fire starter gel could not seek contribution from parents of child injured while using it); Sears, Roebuck & Co. v. Huang, 652 A.2d 568 (Del. 1995) (owner and manufacturer of escalator could not seek contribution from parent whose failure to supervise child contributed to injury); Crotta v. Home Depot, Inc., 249 Conn. 634, 732 A.2d 767 (1999) (accord, collecting cases from other jurisdictions); Bond v. Pittsburgh, 368 Pa. 404, 84 A.2d 328 (1951) (charitable immunity). See Chapter 12, Section 3, Immunities.

2. A similar problem arises in connection with worker compensation statutes, which prevent the employee from suing the employer in tort. Almost all courts have construed their state's statute as cutting off all possible liability, but a few courts have disagreed. For a stimulating discussion of this controversial issue, see 7 Larson's, Workers' Compensation Law § 121 (2012). Restatement (Third) of Torts: Apportionment of Liability § 23, comment *j* (2000) takes no position on this.

3. What if the plaintiff does not file against one of the tortfeasors before the statute of limitations has run? Can the tortfeasor against whom the plaintiff did file in time and who has paid a judgment collect contribution even though the other tortfeasor is protected by the statute of limitations against any action by the injured person? See Keleket X-Ray Corp. v. United States, 275 F.2d 167 (D.C.Cir.1960) and Cooper v. Philadelphia Dairy Products Co., 34 N.J.Super. 301, 112 A.2d 308 (1955) (both allowing claim). Restatement (Third) of Torts: Apportionment of Liability § 23, comment *k* (2000) permits contribution under these circumstances. What if the party from whom contribution is sought is protected by a statute of repose? Estate of Ryan v. Heritage Trails Assocs., Inc., 745 N.W.2d 724 (Iowa 2008) (no contribution claim permitted because plaintiffs never had a claim against the manufacturer due to operation of statute of repose).

4. In most jurisdictions, a party who is sued for negligence may file a cross-claim for contribution if plaintiff joined both tortfeasors, may join (implead) another person as a third-party defendant from whom he is seeking contribution, or may bring a separate action for contribution. Some states permit the claim for contribution to be made as a motion for contribution even though no cross-claim had been filed. See, for example, Lerman v. Heeman, 347 Md. 439, 701 A.2d 426 (1997). West Virginia requires that the contribution claim be brought as a crossclaim or third-party claim in the action by the plaintiff. It cannot be brought as a separate

claim. Charleston Area Medical Center, Inc. v. Parke-Davis, 217 W.Va. 15, 614 S.E.2d 15 (2005) (answering certified question from Fourth Circuit).

5. *Contribution Sought by Settling Defendant.* Most states permitting contribution do not require that a judgment be obtained against a tortfeasor before he pays and seeks contribution. He may settle out of court with the injured party and then obtain contribution. Of course, in addition to proving that the other party is a joint tortfeasor, he has the burden of proving that the amount of the settlement was reasonable. This position is endorsed by Restatement (Third) of Torts: Apportionment of Liability § 23, comment *h* (2000).

6. *Contribution Sought by Nonsettling Defendant.* A is injured by the combined negligence of B and C. A accepts $100,000 from B and gives him a covenant not to sue (or release retaining rights). A proceeds to trial against C and obtains a judgment for $500,000. In a jurisdiction that gives C a percentage setoff against the judgment, C would pay only his share and no contribution would be necessary. In a jurisdiction that provides for a *pro tanto* (dollar for dollar) setoff against the judgment, C pays $400,000 ($500,000 minus the credit for the partial satisfaction of the claim, see note 4, page 398.) Can C obtain contribution from B? See the next case and the notes that follow it.

Slocum v. Donahue

Court of Appeals of Massachusetts, 1998.
44 Mass.App.Ct. 937, 693 N.E.2d 179.

After Robert Donahue pleaded guilty to motor vehicle homicide in the death of [the Slocums'] eighteen month old son, the Slocums filed a civil action against the Donahues alleging negligence and gross negligence. The Donahues then filed a third-party complaint against Ford Motor Company (Ford), denying negligence and [in the alternative seeking contribution and indemnity,] alleging that Ford was negligent and was in breach of warranties of merchantability and fitness for a particular use. The Donahues claim that, when Robert Donahue was in the car prior to the accident, he inadvertently pushed the floor mat on the driver's side, under the throttle. When he later started to back the car down his driveway, the engine began to race and, although he repeatedly stepped on the brakes, his car continued to accelerate. The car's rear wheels hit the curb across the street from his house, became airborne, turned, and then hit a fence. When he got out of the car, he saw Todd Slocum lying on the lawn. The Donahues' expert would testify at trial that the floor mat was defective, permitting it to interfere with the operation of the vacuum booster which caused the power brakes to fail to function.[4]

Prior to trial, the Slocums and Ford signed a settlement agreement providing that Ford would pay $150,000 to the Slocums in exchange for a release of any claim. Ford then moved for summary judgment as to the Donahues' [contribution and indemnity] claims and on the grounds that the settlement was made in good faith and, pursuant to G.L. c.

[4] Robert Donahue claims that he pleaded guilty in the criminal case because he feared receiving the maximum sentence if he proceeded to trial.

231B, § 4, that all claims for contribution were thereby extinguished, and that there was no basis for the Donahues' claims for indemnity. * * * The Donahues appeal from the final judgment dismissing their third-party complaint against Ford.[5] We affirm.

1. Right to contribution. Under G.L. c. 231B, § 4, as inserted by St.1962, c. 730, § 1, "When a release . . . is given in good faith to one of two or more persons liable in tort for the same injury: . . . (b) It shall discharge the tortfeasor to whom it is given from all liability for contribution to any other tortfeasor." The Donahues argue on appeal that the settlement between Ford and the Slocums was not made in good faith and was collusive both because the amount of the settlement was for less than the value of the case and because Ford allegedly told the Slocums that Ford would allow them to use its experts so that the Donahues' attempt to attribute liability to Ford at trial would be unsuccessful.

The seminal Massachusetts case construing this statute in this context, Noyes v. Raymond, 28 Mass.App.Ct. 186, 548 N.E.2d 196 (1990), controls the instant case in material respects. * * *

As in *Noyes*, there were facts before the judge showing that the settlement between Ford and the Slocums was fair and reasonable. It was reasonably predictable that damages would be high and that a jury would find liability on the part of Robert Donahue, in view of the fact that he pleaded guilty in the criminal case and on the basis of his admission in his deposition that, prior to the accident, he was drinking from a bottle of vodka that he kept under the driver's seat in a brown bag. Given these facts, it was not unreasonable to think that a jury might not find any liability on the part of Ford.

According to the Donahues' attorney, in February of 1995, counsel for Ford notified the Donahues' attorney that Ford was proposing a settlement offer totaling $300,000 with $150,000 to be contributed by Ford, $125,000 by Liberty Mutual Insurance Company (the policy limits of the Donahues' insurance carrier), and $25,000 by the Donahues personally.[6] The Donahues' attorney responded that she would discuss the matter with her clients, but that $25,000 was not an amount that her clients would be financially able to contribute to the settlement. Apparently the subsequent negotiations between the Slocums and Ford occurred without the Donahues' participation. In May, 1995, the Slocums settled with Ford for $150,000. *Noyes* instructs that the purpose of the contribution statute is to promote settlement, that a low settlement figure alone is not evidence of "bad faith," and that settlements should be routinely approved without extended hearings if the purpose of the statute is to be served. Further, the court in *Noyes* observed that lack of good faith was evidenced by "collusion, fraud, dishonesty, and other wrongful conduct." [C] In these circumstances Ford's settlement with the Slocums for an amount contemplated as its

---

[5] After the entry of judgment in the third-party action in the lower court, the case of the Slocums against Robert Donahue proceeded to trial. The jury returned a verdict against Donahue.

[6] Counsel for the Slocums had earlier indicated to Ford's counsel that they would consider settling this matter with all parties for a total settlement package of $400,000.

contribution to a total settlement package does not indicate bad faith or collusion.

As to the Donahues' contention that the Slocums' use of experts originally retained by Ford is evidence of collusion, we disagree. [Footnote omitted.] In Commercial Union Ins. Co. v. Ford Motor Co., 640 F.2d 210 (9th Cir.), cert. denied, 454 U.S. 858 (1981), cited by the Donahues, the court found that the settlement was collusive because, to some extent, it was "dictated by the tactical advantage of removing a deep-pocket defendant because of the experts it could produce" and, therefore, "[was] not made in 'good faith' consideration of the relevant liability of all parties." Id. at 214. [Footnote omitted.] The Donahues' argument suggests that there was bad faith here because the Slocums were not interested in the deep pocket of Ford, but settled with Ford because they believed that Ford was not responsible for the death of their son. Such a speculation does not trigger the necessity for a more extensive hearing on the issue of good faith. See McDermott, Inc. v. AmClyde, 511 U.S. 202, 213 n. 16, 216–217 (1994) (while recognizing "the cursory nature of most good-faith hearings," also noted "the large potential for unfairness" in "the pro tanto rule untamed by good-faith hearings"). The motion for summary judgment was properly allowed.

2. Right to indemnity. "Under G.L. c. 231B, contribution is allowed between joint tortfeasors who cause another, by reason of their wrongdoing, to incur injury or damage. In addition, . . . the statute permits a plaintiff to settle with one joint tortfeasor and still have recourse against remaining tortfeasors (subject to the limitations stated in the statute). The right to contribution, unlike the right to indemnity, is based on the shared fault of the joint tortfeasors. Indemnity, on the other hand, allows someone who is without fault, compelled by operation of law to defend himself against the wrongful act of another, to recover from the wrongdoer the entire amount of his loss, including reasonable attorney's fees." [C] "[I]ndemnity is permitted only when the would-be indemnitee does not join in the negligent act." [Cc] "This right to indemnity is limited to those cases in which the would-be indemnitee is held derivatively or vicariously liable for the wrongful act of another." [C]

If the claim against Ford had gone to trial and Ford had been found liable to the Donahues,[9] it would have been as a result of its negligence or breach of warranty. [Footnote omitted.] "Such liability will not be derivative or vicarious in nature, nor will it be constructive rather than actual. Accordingly, the third-party plaintiffs are not entitled to indemnification. . . ." [C]

Once Ford settled with the Slocums, the sole question for the fact finder was whether Todd Slocum's death was caused by defendant Robert Donahue's negligence. [Footnote omitted.] Robert Donahue was free to claim that he was not negligent and that Todd Slocum's death was caused by Ford's negligence in selling a defective product. Under no set of circumstances could the jury properly have held the Donahues liable to the Slocums for the conduct of Ford. Further, in holding Robert Donahue negligent (as they did; see note 5, supra) the jury concluded

[9] The Slocums never made a direct claim against Ford.

that he was solely negligent (or was a joint tortfeasor with Ford). His liability is not vicarious and he is not entitled to indemnification from Ford. If Ford had remained in the case, any liability on its part would have been as a joint tortfeasor, and contribution would have been required. Indemnity would not have been appropriate.[12] "Contribution and indemnity are mutually exclusive remedies." [C] Summary judgment on the issue of indemnification was appropriate. * * *

Judgment affirmed.

NOTES AND QUESTIONS

1. *Contribution.* The Massachusetts statute providing for no contribution from settling defendants is based on the 1955 Uniform Act, § 4. It is also endorsed by Restatement (Third) of Torts: Apportionment of Liability § 23, comment *i* (2000).

2. Not all jurisdictions protect a settling defendant from contribution; some permit the nonsettling defendant to seek contribution from the settling defendant. This is the position of the 1939 Uniform Act, § 4. Do you see why this approach might discourage settlement? Lavoie v. Celotex Corp., 505 A.2d 481, 483 (Me.1986) (Although encouraging settlement to help reduce the burden upon the judicial system is an important principle, it should not be followed to the detriment of nonsettling defendants.)

3. Note that in Massachusetts, and other jurisdictions following the position of the 1955 Uniform Act, a settlement with the plaintiff protects the settling defendant from a contribution claim brought by a nonsettling defendant, as long as the settlement is in good faith. How is good faith to be determined? See Kornhauser and Revesz, "Settlements Under Joint and Several Liability," 68 N.Y.U.L.Rev. 427 (1993) (collecting cases and noting that courts are divided on whether a "good faith" determination should involve only an inquiry concerning the absence of collusion or also should include a determination of the adequacy of the settlement).

4. *Indemnity.* The opinion in the principal case also explains the difference between contribution and indemnity. Although the terms are frequently linked in a phrase and both may be pleaded in a complaint, as in the principal case, they are actually distinct concepts. Traditionally, while contribution allowed a tortfeasor to be partially reimbursed for money paid in judgment or settlement, indemnity was available to shift the entire cost of the judgment or settlement from a tortfeasor whose liability to the plaintiff was not based on its own wrongful conduct, but imposed on it by law because of its relationship with the tortfeasor whose wrongful conduct caused the injury. For example, the employer's liability for its employee's conduct, the automobile owner's liability for a driver's conduct, the retailer's liability for the manufacturer's product would give rise to a cause of action for indemnity, or full reimbursement for the liability to the injured party. (See Chapters 13 and 15). In addition, the right to indemnity can arise through agreement, sometimes referred to as a "hold harmless" clause

[12] If, as the Donahues claimed, any damages sustained by the Slocums were caused not by the negligence or gross negligence of the Donahues (but, rather, solely as a result of Ford's breach of warranty) this would have constituted an absolute defense to the Slocum's action but would not provide the basis for an indemnity claim. [C]

in a contract. See also Restatement (Third) of Torts: Apportionment of Liability § 22 (2000).

5. In some states, a doctrine of "equitable indemnity" developed, usually to avoid restrictive contribution statutes that provided for pro rata contribution even though one of the tortfeasors was substantially more culpable than the other. In those jurisdictions, indemnity was sometimes permitted if the indemnitor was "actively" negligent while the indemnitee was "passively" negligent or if the indemnitor was "primarily" liable while the indemnitee was "secondarily" liable. With the development of comparative responsibility principles, this form of indemnity has been curtailed. Tolbert v. Gerber Indus., Inc., 255 N.W.2d 362 (Minn.1977) (in light of Minnesota's adoption of comparative negligence, contribution rather than equitable indemnity is appropriate vehicle for allocating loss between negligent manufacturer and negligent installer); Owens v. Truckstops of America, 915 S.W.2d 420 (Tenn.1996) (claim for indemnity can no longer be based on active-passive negligence because that distinction subsumed into newly adopted doctrine of comparative fault).

4. APPORTIONMENT OF DAMAGES

Bruckman v. Pena

Colorado Court of Appeals, 1971.
29 Colo.App. 357, 487 P.2d 566.

DWYER, JUDGE. * * * Plaintiff was injured on July 21, 1964, when the car in which he was riding collided with a truck driven by the defendant Bruckman and owned by the defendant Armored Motors Service. On June 11, 1965, plaintiff was injured in a second collision and certain injuries he had sustained in the first collision were aggravated. This action was commenced on June 25, 1965, and the only defendants named in the action are the owner and driver of the truck involved in the first collision.

[The jury returned a verdict in favor of plaintiff William Pena in the sum of $50,000.]

In seeking reversal, defendants assert that the court was in error in one of its instructions to the jury. * * *

The instruction complained of concerns the amount of damages recoverable from the defendants. The first part of the instruction, which is a proper statement of the law applicable to the case, is as follows:

> "If you find that after the collision complained of Plaintiff, William Pena, had an injury which aggravated the ailment or disability received in the collision complained of, the Plaintiff is entitled to recover for the injury or pain received in the collision complained of; but he is not entitled to recover for any physical ailment or disability which he may have incurred subsequent to the collision.
>
> "Where a subsequent injury occurs which aggravated the condition caused by the collision, it is your duty, if possible, to apportion the amount of disability and pain between that

caused by the subsequent injury and that caused by the collision."

In addition to this correct statement of the law, the court further instructed the jury: "But if you find that the evidence does not permit such an apportionment, then the Defendants are liable for the entire disability." Defendants argue that this last statement in the instruction is in error. * * *

It is the general rule that one injured by the negligence of another is entitled to recover the damages proximately caused by the act of the tort-feasor, and the burden of proof is upon the plaintiff to establish that the damages he seeks were proximately caused by the negligence of the defendant. In accordance with this general rule, we hold that the instruction is in error because it permits the plaintiffs to recover damages against the defendants for injuries which the plaintiff received subsequent to any act of negligence on the part of the defendants and from causes for which the defendants were in no way responsible. The instruction erroneously places upon the defendants the burden of proving that plaintiff's disability can be apportioned between that caused by the collision here involved and that caused by the subsequent injury in order to limit their liability to the damages proximately caused by their negligence. Counsel for plaintiffs argues that the rules concerning apportionment of disability announced by our Supreme Court in Newbury v. Vogel, 151 Colo. 520, 379 P.2d 811, should also apply here. In *Newbury,* the Court stated:

> "We find the law to be that where a pre-existing diseased condition exists, and where after trauma aggravating the condition disability and pain result, and no apportionment of the disability between that caused by the pre-existing condition and that caused by the trauma can be made, in such case, even though a portion of the present and future disability is directly attributable to the pre-existing condition, the defendant, whose act of negligence was the cause of the trauma, is responsible for the entire damage."

The pre-existing condition in the *Newbury* case was of non-traumatic origin, but the rules there announced also apply where the pre-existing condition was caused by trauma. [C] The reasons for the adoption of the *Newbury* rules are not present here. It is one thing to hold a tort-feasor who injures one suffering from a pre-existing condition liable for the entire damage when no apportionment between the pre-existing condition and the damage caused by the defendant can be made, but it is quite another thing to say that a tort-feasor is liable, not only for the damage which he caused, but also for injuries subsequently suffered by the injured person. We hold that the defendants here cannot be held liable for the plaintiff's subsequent injury and this is so whether or not such damage can be apportioned between the two injuries.

The plaintiffs also rely on the case of Maddux v. Donaldson, 362 Mich. 425, 108 N.W.2d 33, 100 A.L.R.2d 1. This case involved a chain-type collision, and plaintiff's injuries resulted from successive impacts which to all intents and purposes were concurrent. The court there held that where independent concurring negligent acts have proximately caused injury and damage which cannot be apportioned between the tort-feasors, each tort-feasor is jointly and severally liable for all of the injury and damage. This rule is not applicable where, as here, the second injury or aggravation of the first injury is attributable to a distinct intervening cause without which the second injury or aggravation would not have occurred. * * *

Judgments reversed and cause remanded for a new trial on the issues of damages alone.

NOTES AND QUESTIONS

1. *Concurrent Tortfeasors.* A and B, driving separate cars, negligently collide. One car bounces over on the sidewalk, hits C and injures him. C's injury is indivisible and therefore not apportionable. A and B are each liable for the full injury. Seattle-First Nat'l Bank v. Shoreline Concrete Co., 91 Wash.2d 230, 588 P.2d 1308 (1978). If A and B separately hit the plaintiff and the combined effect of the two accidents is that C dies, the death is treated as an indivisible result for which each is liable. Glick v. Ballentine Produce Inc., 396 S.W.2d 609 (Mo.1965). See also Maddux v. Donaldson, 362 Mich. 425, 108 N.W.2d 33 (1961) (chain reaction collision in which successive impacts were practically speaking concurrent) (discussed in principal case).

2. *Successive Tortfeasors (Unrelated Incidents).* What if, unlike in the principal case, it had been the second tortfeasor who was the defendant? Plaintiff suffered injury to his right elbow in March and was under a physician's care because of continued pain and swelling when, about a month later, he was in an automobile accident in which his elbow again was injured. In an action based on the automobile accident, the trial court judge found no basis for apportioning damages to the elbow between the March and April accidents. Lovely v. Allstate Ins. Co., 658 A.2d 1091 (Me.1995) (second tortfeasor liable for whole injury where damages could not be apportioned). See also Montalvo v. Lapez, 77 Haw. 282, 884 P.2d 345 (1994) (noting that whether plaintiff recovered could depend upon which unrelated tortfeasor is before the court).

3. *Successive Tortfeasors (Related Incidents).* In the principal case, the court found that plaintiff had the burden of proving what damages plaintiff had suffered in the first accident, for which defendants were responsible, and that defendants could not be held responsible for the second, independent accident. What if the second incident was not independent? Driver negligently strikes pedestrian, breaking his leg. While pedestrian is lying helpless in street, bicyclist negligently runs over his arm. At the hospital, pedestrian is treated negligently by physician, aggravating his leg injury. Driver would be responsible for all injuries. Bicyclist would be responsible for only the arm injury. Physician would be responsible for aggravation of leg injury. See note 11, page 365. See also Harsh v. Petroll, 584 Pa. 606, 887 A.2d 209 (2005) (employer of trucker who rear-ended car would be liable for injuries caused in initial collision and for death of occupants who died when car burst into flame due to defect in car's fuel system for which manufacturer was liable based on crashworthiness) and Payne v. Hall, 139 N.M. 659, 137 P.3d 599 (N.M. 2006) (clinic where late term abortion was begun would be liable for injuries caused by malpractice at hospital to which patient was sent for completion of abortion

if jury found that clinic had committed malpractice). This is often referred to as the "original tortfeasor doctrine" because the original tortfeasor is liable, along with the later acting tortfeasor, for the plaintiff's enhanced injuries. Banks v. Elks Club Pride of Tenn., 301 S.W.3d 214 (Tenn. 2010) (club where plaintiff was injured when chair collapsed liable for injuries along with doctors who committed malpractice when treating her for back injury caused by chair collapse).

Consider this scenario. Would you characterize it as a "related" incident? After suffering personal injury in a car accident, plaintiff scheduled a consultation with a lawyer to discuss representation. At the lawyer's office, he was sitting in the firm's conference room when his chair collapsed, causing him to hit his head and land on the floor. Would the driver of the car by liable for the injury in the lawyer's office? Cf. Friedrich v. Fetterman and Assocs., P.A., 137 So.3d 362 (Fla. 2013).

4. *Proof Issues.* A comment on the principal case in 49 Den.L.J. 115 (1972), indicates that there was testimony in the trial below that plaintiff had suffered permanent brain damage in each of the accidents and that it was impossible to apportion the damage between them. How can the jury apportion? Compare McAllister v. Pennsylvania R. Co., 324 Pa. 65, 187 A. 415 (1936), where plaintiff suffered, six months apart, an injury to each leg, with some combined effect on the back. The doctor treating the first injury had died. The court held that there is a "reasonable basis of apportionment" when there is "some evidence to sustain the apportionment made, even though, due to circumstances of the particular case, the proofs do not attain the degree of precision which would make possible an exact dividing line between the injuries." In Loui v. Oakley, 50 Haw. 260, 438 P.2d 393 (1968), involving four accidents, the court held that the jury should be told to make a "rough estimate" and if that were impossible, "to apportion the damages equally among the various accidents." For a particularly challenging factual scenario, see Montalvo v. Lapez, 77 Haw. 282, 884 P.2d 345 (1994) (apportionment of damages in case involving injury to plaintiff's back during rear-end chain reaction automobile accident in which plaintiff had a congenital condition that made him more susceptible to back injuries, previously had been injured in another automobile accident, had been the victim of assaults that included blows to his spine and face, and had himself engaged in activities—boogey boarding and pushing a car with a flat tire—that exacerbated his back injuries). See also Restatement (Third) of Torts: Apportionment of Liability § 26 (2000).

5. *Successive Tortfeasors (Related Incidents) (Allocation Between Actors).* What if plaintiff only sues the second actor? Plaintiff was passenger in the car of an intoxicated driver that left the road and struck a tree, bursting into flames a few minutes later. Plaintiff sued only the manufacturer of the car for the injuries suffered in the fire, alleging that a defect in the car had led to the fire. Should manufacturer be able to put on evidence of the driver's intoxication and excessive speed that caused the initial crash and seek an apportionment of the damages between it and the driver? See D'Amario v. Ford Motor Co., 806 So.2d 434 (Fla. 2001) (adopting minority view—evidence not permitted because important to maintain distinction between fault in causing the accident and fault in causing additional or enhanced injuries) and Fla. Stat. Ann. § 768.81(3)(b) (legislature changed result—Florida now with majority in permitting jury

to compare fault of original tortfeasor and product manufacturer responsible for enhanced injuries in allocating fault). Under the original tortfeasor doctrine, the driver would be responsible for all the injuries suffered in the collision, including the burn injuries. Why would a passenger choose only to sue the manufacturer and not include the driver in the suit? See Egbert v. Nissan Motor Co., Ltd., 228 P.3d 737 (Utah 2010) (noting that the elimination of joint and several liability complicates the question whether majority or minority approach is chosen).

CHAPTER 8

DUTY OF CARE

In Heaven v. Pender, 11 Q.B.D. 503 (C.A.1883), Brett, M.R., declared, "[t]he proposition * * * is that whenever one person is by circumstances placed in such a position with regard to another that every one of ordinary sense * * * would at once recognize that if he did not use ordinary care and skill in his own conduct with regard to those circumstances, he would cause danger of injury to the person or property of the other, a duty arises to use ordinary care and skill to avoid such danger."

This passage was much quoted by courts and writers, notwithstanding the fact that ten years later, Brett, who had become Lord Esher, was forced to retreat from his own words. See Le Lievre v. Gould, [1893] 1 Q.B. 491 (C.A.) (holding that a surveyor did not owe a duty to the mortgagees to exercise care in issuing certificates, and therefore, mortgagees could not maintain an action against surveyor for negligence).

The Restatement Third, Torts: Liability for Physical and Emotional Harm, § 7 (2012) states a principle for the proper role of the duty concept in negligence:

Duty

(a) An actor ordinarily has a duty to exercise reasonable care when the actor's conduct creates a risk of physical harm.

(b) In exceptional cases, when an articulated countervailing principle or policy warrants denying or limiting liability in a particular class of cases, a court may decide that the defendant has no duty or that the ordinary duty of reasonable care requires modification.

Where a person creates through his or her negligence a risk of physical harm a duty is imposed. A driver of an automobile owes a general duty of care to others whom he reasonably foresees will be injured through his or her driving.

This chapter explores the limits of liability and where courts have denied or curtailed liability. Recall the limits to liability articulated in *Palsgraf*, supra page 329. If the defendant's conduct creates a risk of physical injury to the plaintiff, a duty of care will ordinarily be owed by the defendant to the plaintiff. However, the scope of the duty may be contested. The courts often provide reasons of social policy in delimiting liability as identified in paragraph (b) above.

The areas of the law in which duty is of vital concern lie beyond the core of wrongful acts causing physical harm. There are three areas, the subject matter of this chapter, in which a duty of care is central in establishing liability.

(1) The, often wrongful, act of a third party or a natural event has caused physical harm to plaintiff that defendant has failed to take affirmative steps to prevent or ameliorate;

(2) The negligent act causes non-physical harm, i.e., emotional distress or pure economic loss; and

(3) The negligent act causes losses in birth or conception where the traditional categorizations of personhood are incapable of bestowing a cause of action. This third area demonstrates that technological advances and social change may give rise to new interests that may be protected by negligence.

It is within the concept of duty that the frontier arenas of negligence are recognized and the courts are put to the test of how far to expand the domain of negligence.

1. PRIVITY OF CONTRACT

Historically, the contract action developed considerably later than tort liability. Along with it, it remained possible to maintain the old tort action on the case in any situation where it had already been recognized. The result was a distinction, generally recognized, between "nonfeasance," where the defendant had done no more than make a promise and break it, and "misfeasance," where he had attempted performance but done the wrong thing. The tort/contract boundary was the prime analytical division in the law of obligations. That division became demarcated by the description that the duty in contract arose out of the agreement of the parties, while in tort it arose by operation of law. The language of duty became entrenched in the law of negligence because the contract/tort distinction rested on the source of the obligation. See D. J. Ibbetson, A Historical Introduction to the Law of Obligations (1999) at 170–173.

Nonfeasance. In general, when there is only the promise and the breach, only the contract action will lie, and no tort action can be maintained. A good illustration is Louisville & Nashville R. Co. v. Spinks, 104 Ga. 692, 30 S.E. 968 (1898), where the defendant invited plaintiff to come to Cincinnati for employment and promised that if it did not employ him, it would furnish him with transportation back to Atlanta. He came, fell ill, and was not employed. Defendant refused to give him a ticket to Atlanta, and he was forced to walk the whole way, suffering "much from pain, weariness and blistered feet." It was held that his only remedy was an action on the contract and no tort action would lie. See also Newton v. Brook, 134 Ala. 269, 32 So. 722 (1902), where defendants contracted to prepare a body for shipment by a certain train and then did nothing. Again it was held that there was no tort remedy.

To this general rule there are a few recognized exceptions. One is that a public utility or common carrier that has undertaken the duty of serving the public becomes liable in tort when it fails to do so, whether or not it has made a contract. See, for example, Nevin v. Pullman Palace-Car Co., 106 Ill. 222, 46 Am.Rep. 688 (1883); Zabron v. Cunard S.S. Co., 151 Iowa 345, 131 N.W. 18 (1911). Another is that a defendant who makes a contract without the intention to perform is regarded as committing a form of misrepresentation or fraud for which a tort action of deceit will lie. See Burgdorfer v. Thielemann, infra page 1146. Promises or undertakings may form the foundation of a special relationship sufficient to impose a duty of care in negligence to take affirmative action to protect a person from harm. See Section 2.

Misfeasance. When the defendant misperforms the contract, the possibility of recovery in tort is greatly augmented. In some instances this is merely the survival of the older tort action, as when a carrier remains liable in tort, as well as for breach of contract, for negligent injury to a passenger, or for loss of his baggage. In the United States this has gradually been extended to virtually any type of contract. One of the leading cases is Flint & Walling Mfg. Co. v. Beckett, 167 Ind. 491, 79 N.E. 503 (1906), where the defendant negligently installed a windmill on the plaintiff's barn, and it collapsed and wrecked the barn. In all these cases the question may arise whether the defendant has gone so far in his performance, as distinguished from mere preparation for it, as to have undertaken a tort duty. Two cases that further delve into this concept are Hart v. Ludwig, 347 Mich. 559, 79 N.W.2d 895 (1956), and Kozen v. Comstock, 270 F.2d 839 (5th Cir. 1959).

Election and Gravamen. In many cases it is thus possible to maintain an action in either contract or tort. When this is true, a number of questions may arise as to different rules of law applicable to the two actions. For example, a particular court may have jurisdiction over one type of action but not the other, or certain remedies, such as summary judgment, attachment, or arrest of the defendant may be available in one action but not the other. Different statutes of limitations may apply. Different rules as to the damages may prevail, especially in regard to punitive damages or for emotional harm. Some defenses, such as infancy or the statute of frauds, may be set up against one action and not the other.

In these situations the courts have proceeded along two different lines. One is to permit the plaintiff to choose the theory of his action and dispose of the particular question accordingly. Thus in Doughty v. Maine Cent. Transp. Co., 141 Me. 124, 39 A.2d 758 (1944), an action for personal injuries received by a passenger through the negligence of the carrier would be barred by the statute of limitations if the action were in tort, but not if it were in contract. It was held that the plaintiff, having elected to treat his action as one for breach of contract, was not barred by the tort statute.

On the other hand, some courts will not give plaintiff such latitude. Rather, the court will determine the "gravamen" or "gist" of the action, which is to say the essential facts on which the plaintiff's claim rests. Thus in Webber v. Herkimer & Mohawk St. R. Co., 109 N.Y. 311, 16 N.E. 358 (1888), another case of a passenger injured by a carrier's negligence, it was held that the action was essentially founded on the negligence and that it was governed by the tort rather than the contract statute of limitations. See also the ample discussion of the tort versus contract cause of action problem in Victorson v. Bock Laundry Mach. Co., 37 N.Y.2d 395, 335 N.E.2d 275, 373 N.Y.S.2d 39 (1975), overruling

Mendel v. Pittsburgh Plate Glass Co., 25 N.Y.2d 340, 253 N.E.2d 207, 305 N.Y.S.2d 490 (1969) (personal injury—breach of implied warranty).

The liability of professionals directly raises the issue because plaintiff and defendant are usually in a contractual relationship. Can a client sue his attorney for negligently caused losses in both tort and contract? In most instances the courts have not restricted the cause of action to breach of contract, Collins v. Reynard, 154 Ill.2d 48, 607 N.E.2d 1185, 180 Ill.Dec. 672 (1992) (reversing appellate court that found lawyer malpractice cognizable in contract but not in tort).

As these cases suggest, there is little consistency in the decisions, even in a single state, although many courts have tended to look to the policy underlying the particular rule of law or statute to be applied in order to assist themselves in making the characterization.

The famous discussion of this topic is Prosser, The Borderland of Tort and Contract, in W. Prosser, Selected Topics on the Law of Torts, 380, at 429–450 (1954).

Winterbottom v. Wright

Exchequer of Pleas, 1842.
10 M. & W. 109, 152 Eng.Rep. 402.

[Defendant Wright, a manufacturer and repairer of mail coaches, contracted with the Postmaster General, Mr. Atkinson, to keep the coaches in a safe and secure condition. Defendant failed to comply with his promise and plaintiff Winterbottom, a mail coach driver, was seriously injured when a vehicle broke down due to lack of repair.]

LORD ABINGER, C.B. I am clearly of opinion that the defendant is entitled to our judgment. We ought not to permit a doubt to rest upon this subject, for our doing so might be the means of letting in upon us an infinity of actions. * * * There is no privity of contract between these parties; and if the plaintiff can sue, every passenger, or even any person passing along the road, who was injured by the upsetting of the coach, might bring a similar action. Unless we confine the operation of such contracts as this to the parties who entered into them, the most absurd and outrageous consequences, to which I can see no limit, would ensue. Where a party becomes responsible to the public, by undertaking a public duty, he is liable, though the injury may have arisen from the negligence of his servant or agent. So, in cases of public nuisances, whether the act was done by the party as a servant, or in any other capacity, you are liable to an action at the suit of any person who suffers. Those, however, are cases where the real ground of the liability is the public duty, or the commission of the public nuisance. There is also a class of cases in which the law permits a contract to be turned into a tort; but unless there has been some public duty undertaken, or public nuisance committed, they are all cases in which an action might have been maintained upon the contract. Thus, a carrier may be sued either in assumpsit or case; but there is no instance in which a party, who was not privy to the contract entered into with him, can maintain any such action. The plaintiff in this case could not have brought an action on the contract; if he could have done so, what would have been his situation, supposing the Postmaster-General had released the defendant? That would, at all events, have defeated his claim altogether. By permitting this action, we should be working this injustice, that after the defendant had done everything to the satisfaction of his employer, and after all matters between them had been adjusted, and all accounts settled on the footing of their contract, we should subject them to be ripped open by this action of tort being brought against him.

ALDERSON, B. I am of the same opinion. The contract in this case was made with the Postmaster-General alone; and the case is just the same as if he had come to the defendant and ordered a carriage, and handed it at once over to Atkinson. If we were to hold that the plaintiff could sue in such a case, there is no point at which such actions would stop. The only safe rule is to confine the right to recover to those who enter into the contract: if we go one step beyond that, there is no reason why we should not go fifty. The only real argument in favour of the action is, that this is a case of hardship; but that might have been obviated, if the plaintiff had made himself a party to the contract. * * *

Lord Abinger

ROLFE, B. The breach of the defendant's duty stated in this declaration, is his omission to keep the carriage in a safe condition, and when we examine the mode in which that duty is alleged to have arisen, we find a statement that the defendant took upon himself, to wit, under and by virtue of the said contract, the sole and exclusive duty, charge, care, and burden of the repairs, state and condition of the said mail-coach, and, during all the time aforesaid, it had become and was the sole and exclusive duty of the defendant, to wit, under and by virtue of his said contract, to keep and maintain the said mail-coach in a fit, proper, safe, and secure state and condition. The duty, therefore, is shewn to have arisen solely from the contract; and the fallacy consists in the use of that word "duty." If a duty to the Postmaster-General be meant, that is true; but if a duty to the plaintiff be intended (and in that sense the word is evidently used), there was none. This is one of those unfortunate cases in which there certainly has been damnum, but it is damnum absque injuriâ; it is, no doubt, a hardship upon the plaintiff to be without a remedy, but by that consideration we ought not to be influenced. Hard cases, it has been frequently observed, are apt to introduce bad law.

Judgment for the defendant.

NOTES AND QUESTIONS

1. Although the principal case involved nonfeasance, it was universally interpreted as applying to any negligence of the defendant, including misfeasance; and this resulted in many decisions holding that the seller of a chattel was under no liability, in contract or in tort, to anyone other than his immediate buyer. The first major service rendered by Professor Bohlen to the law was to point out this error in his article, The Basis of Affirmative Obligations in the Law of Tort, 44 Am.L.Reg., N.S., 209, 280–285, 289–310 (1905), also in F. Bohlen, Studies in the Law of Torts, 33 (1926). This same point is made by Stapleton, Duty of Care and Economic Loss: A Wider Agenda, 107 L.Q.Rev. 249, 250 (1991).

MacPherson v. Buick Motor Co.

Court of Appeals of New York, 1916.
217 N.Y. 382, 111 N.E. 1050.

Action by Donald C. MacPherson against the Buick Motor Company. From a judgment of the Appellate Division (160 App. Div. 55, 145 N.Y. Supp. 462), affirming a judgment of the Supreme Court for plaintiff, defendant appeals.

FACTS

alleged neg.

CARDOZO, J. The defendant is a manufacturer of automobiles. It sold an automobile to a retail dealer. The retail dealer resold to the plaintiff. While the plaintiff was in the car it suddenly collapsed. He was thrown out and injured. One of the wheels was made of defective wood, and its spokes crumbled into fragments. The wheel was not made by the defendant; it was bought from another manufacturer. There is evidence, however, that its defects could have been discovered by reasonable inspection, and that inspection was omitted. There is no claim that the defendant knew of the defect and willfully concealed it. * * * The charge is one, not of fraud, but of negligence. The question to be determined is whether the defendant owed a duty of care and vigilance to any one but the immediate purchaser.

[The court discusses competing lines of precedents. One group of cases suggested that the manufacturer owed a duty of care to ultimate purchasers only when the product was "inherently dangerous." Some courts confined this classification to guns, poisons or other products whose normal function it was to injure or destroy. Other decisions suggested that a manufacturer would breach a duty of care to a foreseeable user of the product if the product was likely to cause injury if negligently made.]

Judge Cardozo

We hold * * * that * * * [i]f the nature of a thing is such that it is reasonably certain to place life and limb in peril when negligently made, it is then a thing of danger. Its nature gives warning of the consequences to be expected. If to the element of danger there is added knowledge that the thing will be used by persons other than the purchaser, and used without new tests, then, irrespective of contract, the manufacturer of this thing of danger is under a duty to make it carefully. That is as far as we are required to go for the decision of this case. There must be knowledge of a danger, not merely possible, but probable. It is possible to use almost anything in a way that will make it dangerous if defective. That is not enough to charge the manufacturer with a duty independent of his contract. Whether a given thing is dangerous may be sometimes a question for the court and sometimes a question for the jury. There must also be knowledge that in the usual course of events the danger will be shared by others than the buyer. Such knowledge may often be inferred from the nature of the transaction. But it is possible that even knowledge of the danger and of the use will not always be enough. The proximity or remoteness of the relation is a factor to be considered. We are dealing now with the liability of the manufacturer of the finished product, who puts it on the market to be used without inspection by his customers. If he is negligent, where danger is to be foreseen, a liability will follow. * * * We have put aside the notion that the duty to safeguard life and limb, when the consequences of negligence may be foreseen, grows out of contract and nothing else. We have put the source of the obligation where it ought to be. We have put its source in the law.

There is nothing anomalous in a rule which imposes upon A., who has contracted with B., a duty to C. and D. and others according as he knows or does not know that the subject-matter of the contract is intended for their use. We may find an analogy in the law which measures the liability of landlords. If A. leases to B. a tumbledown house, he is not liable, in the absence of fraud, to B.'s guests who enter it and are injured. This is because B. is then under the duty to repair it, the lessor has the right to suppose that he will fulfill that duty, and, if he omits to do so, his guests must look to him. Bohlen, Affirmative Obligations in the Law of Torts, 44 Am. Law Reg., N.S., 341. But if A. leases a building to be used by the lessee at once as a place of public entertainment, the rule is different. There injury to persons other than the lessee is to be foreseen, and foresight of the consequences involves the creation of a duty. [C]

In this view of the defendant's liability there is nothing inconsistent with the theory of liability on which the case was tried. It is true that the court told the jury that "an automobile is not an inherently dangerous vehicle." The meaning, however, is that danger is not to be expected when the vehicle is well constructed. The court left it to the jury to say whether the defendant ought to have foreseen that the car, if negligently constructed, would become "imminently dangerous." Subtle distinctions are drawn by the defendant between things inherently dangerous and things imminently dangerous, but the case does not turn upon these verbal niceties. If danger was to be expected as reasonably certain, there was a duty of vigilance, and this whether you call the danger inherent or imminent. In varying forms that thought was put before the jury. We do not say that the court would not have been justified in ruling as a matter of law that the car was a dangerous thing. If there was any error, it was none of which the defendant can complain.

We think the defendant was not absolved from a duty of inspection because it bought the wheels from a reputable manufacturer. It was not merely a dealer in automobiles. It was responsible for the finished product. It was not at liberty to put the finished product on the market without subjecting the component parts to ordinary and simple tests. [C] Under the charge of the trial judge nothing more was required of it. The obligation to inspect must vary with the nature of the thing to be inspected. The more probable the danger the greater the need of caution. * * *

The judgment should be affirmed with costs.

[The dissenting opinion of WILLARD BARTLETT, C.J., is omitted.]

NOTES AND QUESTIONS

1. The privity limitation lasted longer with regard to those who perform services. It is clear today, however, that an individual who undertakes to make a repair owes a duty to use care to those who may be foreseeably injured in case the repair is negligently made. See Kalinowski v. Truck Equipment Company, 237 App. Div. 472, 261 N.Y.S. 657 (1933) (failure properly to repair broken axle on a truck, defendant repair company liable to those he should expect to be in the vicinity of the vehicle); Nagy v. McEachern, 28 Mich.App. 439, 184 N.W.2d 556 (1970) (failure adequately to repair safety catch on rifle).

2. Liability for physical injury arising out of a failure to repair turns on whether the contractor gave an undertaking. In Wroblewski v. Otis Elevator Co., 9 A.D.2d 294, 193 N.Y.S.2d 855 (3d Dept.1959), a repairer inspected an elevator and assured plaintiff that it was in working order. If the repairer had done nothing at all, the case might have been deemed one of nonfeasance and the privity limitation might have applied. In Levine v. Sears Roebuck & Co., 200 F.Supp. 2d 180 (E.D.N.Y. 2002), plaintiff was injured when she tripped over a dishwasher door hanging open below its normal position. A maintenance agreement between plaintiff and defendant was insufficient to support liability in the absence of an assurance or misrepresentation by defendant.

When there is an assurance to an owner that a repair has been made even though nothing has in fact been done, many modern courts have found misfeasance and thus a breach of duty even to third parties. See, for example, Moody v. Martin Motor Co., 76 Ga.App. 456, 46 S.E.2d 197 (1948) (finding that the defendant owed a duty of care to plaintiff employee, where defendant falsely assured plaintiff's employer that it had repaired the vehicle whose unsafe condition allegedly caused plaintiff's injury).

3. If defendant commences performance and then omits to complete performance, he has committed misfeasance just as if he had performed negligently, and will likely be liable. For example: Smith v. State, 921 P.2d 632 (Alaska 1996) (finding that defendant assumed a duty by attempting to repair fluoride problem in water supply and would be liable for plaintiff's injuries from fluoride poisoning if defendant either failed to address fluoride problem or was negligent in addressing fluoride problem). For other recent cases illustrating this principle, see Restatement (Third) of Torts § 42 cmt. c, reporter's note (Proposed Final Draft No. 1, 2005).

4. A physician prescribes a drug to a patient without warning her of its soporific effect. The patient takes the drug, falls asleep at the wheel of her automobile, and thereby injures a third party. Is the physician liable to the third party? Joy v. Eastern Maine Medical Center, 529 A.2d 1364 (Me.1987) (duty of care); Kirk v. Michael Reese Hospital & Medical Center, 117 Ill.2d 507, 513 N.E.2d 387, 111 Ill.Dec. 944 (1987) (no duty of care); McKenzie v. Hawaii Permanente Med. Group, Inc., 98 Hawaii 296, 47 P.3d 1209 (2002) (physician owes a duty to non-patient third parties to warn patient about treatment's effect on driving ability, where the circumstances are such that the reasonable patient could not have been expected to be aware of the risk without the physician's warning); Wilschinsky v. Medina, 108 N.M. 511, 775 P.2d 713 (1989) (physicians owe a duty to persons injured by patients driving automobiles from a doctor's office when the patient has just been injected with drugs known to affect judgment and driving ability).

H.R. Moch Co. v. Rensselaer Water Co.

Court of Appeals of New York, 1928.
247 N.Y. 160, 159 N.E. 896.

CARDOZO, C.J. The defendant, a waterworks company under the laws of this state, made a contract with the city of Rensselaer for the supply of water during a term of years. Water was to be furnished to the city for sewer flushing and street sprinkling; for service to schools and public buildings; and for service at fire hydrants, the latter service at the rate of $42.50 a year for each hydrant. Water was to be furnished to private takers within the city at their homes and factories and other industries at reasonable rates, not exceeding a stated schedule. While this contract was in force a building caught fire. The flames, spreading to the plaintiff's warehouse near by, destroyed it and its contents. The defendant, according to the complaint, was promptly notified of the fire, "but omitted and neglected after such notice, to supply or furnish sufficient or adequate quantity of water, with adequate pressure to stay, suppress, or extinguish the fire before it reached the warehouse of the plaintiff, although the pressure and supply which the defendant was equipped to supply and furnish, and had agreed by said contract to supply and furnish, was adequate and sufficient to prevent the spread of the fire to and the destruction of the plaintiff's warehouse and its contents." By reason of the failure of the defendant "to fulfill the provisions of the contract between it and the city of Rensselaer," the plaintiff is said to have suffered damage, for which judgment is demanded. A motion, in the nature of a demurrer, to dismiss the complaint, was denied at Special Term. The Appellate Division reversed by a divided court. * * *

We think the action is not maintainable as one for a common-law tort. * * *

If conduct has gone forward to such a stage that inaction would commonly result, not negatively merely in withholding a benefit, but positively or actively in working an injury, there exists a relation out of which arises a duty to go forward. [C] So the surgeon who operates without pay is liable, though his negligence is the omission to sterilize his instruments * * *; the engineer though his fault is in the failure to shut off steam * * *; the maker of automobiles, at the suit of some one other than the buyer, though his negligence is merely in inadequate inspection [c]. The query always is whether the putative wrongdoer has advanced to such a point as to have launched a force or instrument of harm, or has stopped where inaction is at most a refusal to become an instrument for good. * * *

The plaintiff would have us hold that the defendant, when once it entered upon the performance of its contract with the city, was brought into such a relation with every one who might potentially be benefited through the supply of water at the hydrants as to give to negligent performance, without reasonable notice of a refusal to continue, the quality of a tort. * * * We are satisfied that liability would be unduly and indeed indefinitely extended by this enlargement of the zone of duty. The dealer in coal who is to supply fuel for a shop must then answer to the customers if fuel is lacking. The manufacturer of goods, who enters upon the performance of his contract must answer, in that view, not only to the buyer, but to those who to his knowledge are looking to the buyer for their own sources of supply. Every one making a promise having the quality of a contract will be under a duty to the promisee by virtue of that promise, but under another duty, apart from contract, to an indefinite number of potential beneficiaries when performance has begun. The assumption of one relation would mean the involuntary assumption of a series of new relations, inescapably hooked together. Again we may say in the words of the Supreme Court of the United States, "The law does not spread its protection so far." Robins Dry Dock & Repair Co. v. Flint, 275 U.S. 303. * * *

We think the action is not maintainable as one for the breach of a statutory duty. * * *

The judgment should be affirmed, with costs.

NOTES AND QUESTIONS

1. What if the city's own property were destroyed by fire because of lack of sufficient water pressure? Town of Ukiah v. Ukiah Water & Improvement Co., 142 Cal. 173, 75 P. 773 (1904); Inhabitants of Milford v. Bangor Ry. & Elec. Co., 106 Me. 316, 76 A. 696 (1909).

2. The rule from the principal case was applied in a case involving an accident caused by the New York City blackout of 1977 in which the court held that the power company owed no duty of care to the plaintiff, a tenant in a building who fell down a dark stairway during the power outage. Strauss v. Belle Realty Co., 65 N.Y.2d 399, 482 N.E.2d 34, 492 N.Y.S.2d 555 (1985); see also Goldstein v. Consolidated Edison Co. of New York, 115 A.D.2d 34, 499 N.Y.S.2d 47 (1st Dep't 1986) (same); but see Hall v. Consolidated Edison Corp., 104 Misc.2d 565, 428 N.Y.S.2d 837 (N.Y. Sup. Ct. 1980) (liability where plaintiff fell in the darkened hallway after defendant cut off power without notice).

3. The principal case represents the majority rule. However, some courts have allowed recovery. See Harlan Water Co. v. Carter, 220 Ky. 493, 295 S.W. 426 (1927) (reasoning that plaintiff was a third-party beneficiary of the contract with the city); Fisher v. Greensboro Water-Supply Co., 128

N.C. 375, 38, S.E. 912 (1901) (reasoning that the defendant breached a duty undertaken); Mugge v. Tampa Waterworks Co., 52 Fla. 371, 42 So. 81 (1906) (same); Doyle v. South Pittsburgh Water Co., 414 Pa. 199, 199 A.2d 875 (1964) (reasoning that defendant had entered on performance).

4. If defective water is in fact supplied under a contract with the city, the defendant may be liable to an individual for resulting injury, such as typhoid fever. Hayes v. Torrington Water Co., 88 Conn. 609, 92 A. 406 (1914) ("The duty which a water company owes to the public and to its customers is that of exercising reasonable care and diligence in providing an adequate supply of wholesome water at all times"). See also Horton v. North Attleboro, 302 Mass. 137, 19 N.E.2d 15 (1939) (lead poisoning of water supply).

5. There is much the same difference of opinion on the failure of a telephone company to render service under a contract with a private individual, as a result of which a third party is injured. See, for example, Mentzer v. New England Tel. & Tel. Co., 276 Mass. 478, 177 N.E. 549 (1931) (no liability); Adams v. Carolina Tel. & Tel. Co., 59 N.C.App. 687, 297 S.E.2d 785 (1982) (liability). The same reasoning has been applied to fire alarm companies in denying liability to third parties injured by negligent operation of the system, Edwards v. Honeywell, 50 F.3d 484 (7th Cir. 1995) (applying Indiana law), fireman killed when dispatcher negligently delayed in sending fire department to the call.

Clagett v. Dacy

Court of Special Appeals of Maryland, 1980.
47 Md.App. 23, 420 A.2d 1285.

WILNER, JUDGE. Appellants were the high bidders at a foreclosure sale, but because the attorneys conducting the sale failed to follow the proper procedures, the sale was set aside. This occurred twice. Ultimately, the debtor discharged the loan, thus "redeeming" his land, and appellants lost the opportunity to acquire the property and make a profit on its resale. They sued the attorneys in the Circuit Court for Prince George's County to recover their loss, alleging that the attorneys in question owed them, as bidders, a duty to use care and diligence and to conduct the sale "properly and carefully." By sustaining the attorneys' demurrer without leave to amend, the court concluded that no such duty existed—at least not one from which an action for damages will arise; and, by affirming that order, we shall indicate our concurrence with the court's conclusion. * * *

Although [Prescott v. Coppage, 266 Md. 562, 296 A.2d 150 (1972)] has a most unusual factual setting, it does seem to suggest a modest relaxation of the strict privity requirement to the extent of allowing a true third party beneficiary to sue an attorney as he could sue any other defaulting or tortious party to a contract made for his benefit. This extension is not unique to Maryland. [C]

It is, however, a limited one with a special utility. It is most often seen and applied in actions based on drafting errors in wills and other such documents or on erroneous title reports—errors that, by their very nature, will likely have a long or delayed effect and will most probably impact upon persons other than the attorney's immediate employer, [cc] although it has been applied in other contexts as well. See Donald v. Garry, 19 Cal.App.3d 769, 97 Cal.Rptr. 191 (1971) (creditor who assigned claim to collection agency for collection allowed to sue agency's attorney for negligence in prosecuting his claim).

The *Coppage* Court made clear that only those persons who qualify under the normal rules for determining third party beneficiaries will be afforded the privileged status *vis à vis* attorney defendants; i.e., creditor beneficiaries. [Cc] This would seem to limit the extension to actions based upon contract, to which the third party beneficiary theory is peculiarly applicable, and would not supply a basis for permitting third parties to sue attorneys on a pure negligence theory—violation of some general duty arising in the absence of an underlying contractual attorney-client relationship.

In Donald v. Garry, supra, the California court utilized the concept expressed in Restatement (Second) of Torts § 324A [1979], to support a third party action, concluding that "[a]n attorney may be liable for damage caused by his negligence *to a person intended to be benefited by his performance* irrespective of any lack of privity of contract between the attorney and the party to be benefited." (Emphasis supplied.) The context of this, as noted above, was an action by the true creditor against the collection agency attorney, and the court was careful to mention that "the transaction in which the respondent's negligence occurred was intended primarily for the benefit of [the creditor]. Respondent was retained to collect an account due him."

It will, moreover, take more than general conclusory allegations to satisfy that requirement. Attorneys are not quite the free agents as some others are in the world of commerce. There are well-recognized limitations, judicially imposed and enforced, upon how they may conduct themselves, and who they may, and may not, represent in certain situations. Except in very limited circumstances, they may not represent or act for conflicting interests in a transaction; their manifest duty of loyalty to their employer/client forbids it. See, for example, Code of Professional Responsibility, Canon 5, EC5–14, 5–15, 5–16, 5–19, 5–22; DR5–105.

These limitations, predominant but not necessarily exclusive with attorneys, must, of necessity, be taken into account when dealing with actions founded upon an implied duty owed by an attorney to a person who is not his direct employer/client, or upon an employment relationship alleged to arise by implication rather than by express agreement. Thus, the duties or obligations inherent in an attorney-client relationship will not be presumed to flow to a third party and will not be presumed to arise by implication when the effect of such a presumption would be tantamount to a prohibited or improbable employment, absent the clearest exposition of facts from which such an employment may be fairly and rationally inferred.

When judged against these principles, it becomes clear that the Declaration at issue here has failed to state a cause of action. It does not sufficiently allege a proper standing on the part of appellants to sue the appellee attorneys; nor, from what *is* alleged, could it do so. Appellees were engaged to represent the mortgagee (deed of trust beneficiary), not the bidders, whose interest would likely be in conflict with that of the mortgagee. The mortgagee's economic interest, and legal obligation, is to secure the highest possible price for the property, whereas the bidders' goal is to pay as little as possible. It is evident, in that circumstance, that an attorney could not lawfully represent both the mortgagee and the bidder in the transaction; and it will not be lightly presumed or inferred that appellees did so.

Nor may the prohibited employment be inferred from an allegation that appellees' fees would ultimately be paid from the proceeds of sale. The mere fact that those fees, along with the other costs of the proceeding, may be taken from the purchase price paid by the successful bidder does not mean that the purchaser is actually paying the fees. Quite the contrary. The debtor/mortgagor ultimately pays the fees and all other costs, for he gets only the net surplus (if any) available after all such fees and costs are discharged. The bidder pays only for the property, not the cost of selling it; and he is not, therefore, the client (express or implied) of the attorney engaged to sell the property.

Judgment affirmed; appellants to pay the costs.

NOTES AND QUESTIONS

1. One place in which the privity limitation is still significant is the area of professional relationships.

2. *Attorneys.* As the principal case reflects, the privity limitation on the scope of duty has also been utilized by attorneys when they have committed an act of professional negligence. In many jurisdictions the privity limitation is still strictly applied.

3. The first major inroad on the privity rule as applied to attorneys occurred in California in Biakanja v. Irving, 49 Cal.2d 647, 320 P.2d 16 (1958) (finding exception to the privity requirement along the lines of the principal case); cf. Brammer v. Taylor, 175 W.Va. 728, 338 S.E.2d 207 (1985). In Lucas v. Hamm, 56 Cal.2d 583, 364 P.2d 685, 15 Cal.Rptr. 821 (1961), cert. denied, 368 U.S. 987 (1962), the court indicated that the new rule would be applied to an actual attorney; however, the court found that the defendant was not negligent in drafting a will provision that ran afoul of the rule against perpetuities.

Connecticut followed this lead in Licata v. Spector, 26 Conn.Supp. 378, 225 A.2d 28 (1966). New York disagreed; see Victor v. Goldman, 74 Misc.2d 685, 344 N.Y.S.2d 672 (1973), aff'd, 43 A.D.2d 1021, 351 N.Y.S.2d 956 (1974).

4. Cases in which attorneys have been held liable to third parties generally have involved beneficiaries of wills. See Heyer v. Flaig, 70 Cal.2d 223, 449 P.2d 161, 74 Cal.Rptr. 225 (1969), where an attorney neglected to advise his client that her pending marriage would affect her intent to have all of her property flow to her daughters. But, whenever an attorney's work product is primarily for the benefit of a third party, potential liability can arise. See Donald v. Garry, 19 Cal.App.3d 769, 97 Cal.Rptr. 191 (1971) (attorney hired by collection agency liable to individual creditor). Vereins-Und Westbank v. Carter, 691 F.Supp. 704 (S.D.N.Y.1988) (attorney's opinion letter, written at client's request but with plaintiff's reliance in mind). Should it matter that a testator's attorney intentionally drafted a

will in such a way that a testamentary beneficiary failed to receive what the testator intended to leave her? See Kirgan v. Parks, 60 Md.App. 1, 478 A.2d 713 (1984).

5. Although the "rule" is long established in California, the courts struggle with its application in specific cases. For example, should an attorney be liable to an apparently intended beneficiary charitable organization when his client gave him an incorrect name of the group and this voided that provision of the will? See Ventura County Humane Society v. Holloway, 40 Cal.App.3d 897, 115 Cal.Rptr. 464 (1974). See also Roberts v. Ball, Hunt, Hart, Brown and Baerwitz, 57 Cal.App.3d 104, 128 Cal.Rptr. 901 (1976); and Goodman v. Kennedy, 18 Cal.3d 335, 556 P.2d 737, 134 Cal.Rptr. 375 (1976), both holding for the defendant. For discussion see Partlett, Professional Negligence (1985) pages 78–85. Liability in these cases generally does not depend upon the plaintiff's reasonable reliance. The issue is hotly debated elsewhere. See White v. Jones, [1995] 2 A.C. 207 (H.L.) and Cooper v. Hobart, [2001] 3 S.C.R. 537 (both finding a duty of care).

2. FAILURE TO ACT

Compare the following two cases. Both ask whether universities have a duty to protect their students, but in distinctly different contexts. How do the decisions comport with one another? Do you agree with the outcomes?

Commonwealth v. Peterson

Supreme Court of Virginia, 2013.
286 Va. 349, 749 S.E.2d 307.

OPINION BY JUSTICE CLEO E. POWELL

This appeal arises out of wrongful death suits filed against the Commonwealth by the administrators (hereinafter "Administrators") of the estates of Erin Nicole Peterson and Julia Kathleen Pryde, two murder victims of the tragic 2007 mass shooting at Virginia Polytechnic Institute and State University (hereinafter "Virginia Tech"). [C] In this case, we hold that even if there was a special relationship between the Commonwealth and students of Virginia Tech, under the facts of this case, there was no duty for the Commonwealth to warn students about the potential for criminal acts by third parties. Therefore, we will reverse the judgment of the circuit court.

I. FACTS AND PROCEEDINGS

On the morning of April 16, 2007, at approximately 7:30 a.m., the Virginia Tech Police Department received a call that an incident had occurred in the West Ambler Johnston Hall dormitory but the specifics of what had happened were unknown. When officers arrived they found two gunshot victims: a female and a male clad in only his boxer shorts. Although officers from the Virginia Tech Police Department were the first on the scene, the Blacksburg Police Department led the investigation. At least one member of the Virginia State Police also joined the investigation. During the investigation, police came to believe that they were investigating a domestic homicide because there were no signs of forced entry or a robbery. They believed that a "targeted shooting" had occurred because the shooting was in a "less conspicuous area . . . kind of hidden in the back"[2] making it "easier for the suspect to get in and get out without being noticed." Police believed that this was an isolated incident that posed no danger to others and that the shooter had fled the area. They did not believe that a campus lockdown was necessary.

At the crime scene, police observed a bloody footprint and were determined to locate the source of the print. Police also learned that the female's boyfriend was a gun enthusiast.

Once the female's boyfriend was identified as a person of interest, a "Be On The Lookout" ("BOLO") went out for him. The police located the boyfriend at approximately 9:45 a.m. Officers described him as appearing "[s]hocked" and "[s]cared." The boyfriend told the police that he was en route to Virginia Tech from Radford University where he attended school because, while he was in his 9 a.m. class, he heard from a friend who attended Virginia Tech who told him what had happened. He explained that he had dropped his girlfriend off that morning around 7 a.m. and then headed to Radford University for his 8 a.m. class. The boyfriend consented to a search of his vehicle and shoes. He also allowed the police to conduct a gunshot residue test. As police spoke with the boyfriend, they received word that there were "active shots" in Norris Hall. Officers quickly took the boyfriend's contact information, told him that they would be in touch, and left for the Virginia Tech campus.

Police subsequently executed a search warrant of the home of the boyfriend of the female victim found in West Ambler Johnston Hall. They found nothing.

Charles W. Steger, the President of Virginia Tech, testified that he learned of "a shooting" at approximately 8 a.m. and he called a meeting of a group of administrators tasked with campus safety, called the University Policy Group (hereinafter "Policy Group"), to assess the situation and handle the release of information pertaining thereto. Shortly after 8 a.m., President Steger spoke with Wendell Flinchum, the Chief of the Virginia Tech Police Department, and learned that a female and a male student had been shot, at least one of whom was dead, that the shootings appeared targeted, likely domestic in nature, and that the shooter had likely left the campus. The Policy Group convened around 8:30 a.m. During this meeting, Steger learned that the police were on the lookout for the female victim's boyfriend as a person of interest. * * * [A notice to the Governor's office stated a "gunman was on the loose"]. Steger instructed a Policy Group member to compose a campus notice, and following revisions and a technical difficulty with the computer system, it was sent out by campus-wide "blast e-mail" at 9:26 a.m. The notice stated that "[a] shooting incident occurred at West Ambler Johnston [Hall] earlier this morning. Police are on the scene

---

2 The officers described the area as being one that you would not even know was there if you did not live there.

and investigating" and advised students to be alert for anything suspicious. * * *

At approximately 9:45 a.m. the mass shooting at Norris Hall began. At 9:50 a.m. a second campus-wide "blast e-mail" was sent stating that "[a] gunman is loose on campus. Stay in buildings until further notice. Stay away from all windows." Erin Peterson, 18, and Julia Pryde, 23, were among the victims murdered in Norris Hall. Police later identified Seung-Hui Cho as the shooter.

* * * The day after the shootings, police learned that the gun used to murder the two people in West Ambler Johnston Hall matched the one Cho used in Norris Hall. Police later found bloody clothing belonging to Cho that had the DNA from one of the victims of the West Ambler Johnston Hall shooting on it.

The Administrators filed wrongful death claims in Montgomery County Circuit Court against Cho's estate, the Commonwealth and eighteen other individuals, including Steger. * * * [The cases were consolidated and several motions resulted in the Commonwealth being named as the only defendant]. The Administrators claimed that the Commonwealth was liable for the actions of the Commonwealth's employees at the university pursuant to the Virginia Tort Claims Act ("VTCA") [C]. They alleged that a special relationship existed between the Commonwealth's employees at Virginia Tech and Peterson and Pryde that gave rise to the Commonwealth's duty to warn Peterson and Pryde of third party criminal acts and that the Commonwealth's failure to warn them was the proximate cause of their deaths and the Administrators' losses. The Commonwealth argued that there was no foreseeable harm to the students and that the evidence failed to establish that any alleged breach of a duty of care was the proximate cause of the deaths. * * * The jury returned a verdict in favor of the Administrators awarding $4 million to each family. Upon the Commonwealth's motion, the court reduced each verdict to $100,000 in accordance with the VTCA, [C] * * * This appeal follows.

II. ANALYSIS

On appeal, the Commonwealth argues that

1. The circuit court erred in finding that the Commonwealth, Virginia Tech, and/or their employees had a special relationship with Peterson and Pryde that imposed a duty, and therefore, erred in instructing the jury that there was such a duty, in submitting the case to the jury and in entering judgment on the jury's verdict.

2. Even assuming that the Commonwealth, Virginia Tech or their employees had a relevant special relationship under Virginia law, the evidence adduced did not give rise to a duty to warn of third party criminal acts, and therefore, the circuit court erred in submitting the case to the jury and in entering judgment on the jury's verdict.

* * *

We hold that the facts in this case do not give rise to a duty for the Commonwealth to warn students of the potential for third party criminal acts. * * *

As a general rule, a person does not have a duty to warn or protect another from the criminal acts of a third person. [C] "This is particularly so when the third person commits acts of assaultive criminal behavior because such acts cannot reasonably be foreseen." [C] However, the general rule does not apply in all situations. " 'There are narrow exceptions to this rule,' but the application of those exceptions 'is always fact specific and, thus, not amenable to a bright-line rule for resolution.' " Taboada v. Daly Seven, Inc., 271 Va. 313, 322–23, 626 S.E.2d 428, 432 (2006) [C]. Before an exception comes into play, the facts must establish the existence of a special relationship.

" '[W]hether a legal duty in tort exists is a pure question of law' " to be reviewed de novo. [Cc]. To prevail, the plaintiff must establish that there is a special relationship, either between the plaintiff and the defendant or between the third party criminal actor and the defendant. The necessary special relationship may be one that has been recognized as a matter of law . . . or it may arise from the factual circumstances of a particular case. [C] For the purposes of this opinion, we will assume without deciding that the threshold requirement that such a special relationship exists is satisfied on these facts.

Having assumed without deciding that a special relationship exists, the question becomes whether, as a matter of law, under the facts and circumstances of this case, the Commonwealth had a duty to warn students about the potential for third party criminal acts. "The law determines the duty, and the jury, upon the evidence, determines whether the duty has been performed." [C]

A review of our prior cases indicates that in order for a duty to be imposed upon a defendant, the degree of the foreseeability of harm that the plaintiff must establish depends on the nature of the special relationship. We have recognized two levels of foreseeable harm: known or reasonably foreseeable harm, Taboada, 271 Va. at 325–26, and "imminent probability of harm," the heightened degree of foreseeability that arises where the defendant "knows that criminal assaults against persons are occurring, or are about to occur, on the premises," based upon "notice of a specific danger just prior to the assault." [C]. Certain special relationships such as that of a common carrier/passenger, innkeeper/guest, and employer/employee impose a duty to warn when the danger of third party criminal acts is known or reasonably foreseeable. [Cc]

In instances, however, where the special relationship was that of business owner/invitee or landlord/tenant, we have imposed a duty to warn of third party criminal acts only where there was "an imminent probability of injury" from a third party criminal act. [C]. Thus, the duty to warn of danger from third party criminal acts has remained an exception to the general rule. [C]

Where the standard was that the duty to warn or protect was present when there was "an imminent probability of injury" from a third party criminal act, this Court has held that the duty to warn existed, as a matter of law, in the unusual situation where an on-duty police officer failed to intervene when he responded to the scene of a motor vehicle accident and observed one driver attack a bystander who had stopped to render assistance. [C]

More frequently, however, this Court has concluded that facts relied upon in particular cases fail to establish a duty, as a matter of law, to protect against third party criminal acts. [Cc].

In cases where it was alleged that a special relationship gave rise to the duty to warn because the danger of harm from third party criminal acts was known or reasonably foreseeable, this Court has similarly, frequently concluded that the duty to warn was not present as a matter of law. See A.H., 255 Va. at 221–22, 495 S.E.2d at 486 (stating that an employer has no duty to protect an employee from third party criminal acts unless the danger is "known or reasonably foreseeable" as a matter of law and concluding that knowledge of similar assaults in the preceding five years was not sufficient); Connell, 93 Va. at 58, 24 S.E. at 469 (common carrier "cannot be deemed to have anticipated nor be expected to guard and protect [a passenger] against a crime so horrid, and happily so rare, as that of murder.").

In only rare circumstances has this Court determined that the duty to protect against harm from third party criminal acts exists. See Taboada, 271 Va. at 325–26 (concluding that, like a common carrier, an innkeeper has a "duty of utmost care and diligence" to protect guests from third party criminal acts where the danger is known or reasonably foreseeable, and holding that where—over a three year period immediately prior to the attack—hotel employees had called police 96 times to report criminal conduct including robberies, malicious woundings, shootings, and other criminally assaultive acts, the hotel knew of the danger and had received a warning from police that "guests were at a specific imminent risk of harm," these were sufficient averments to survive a demurrer and, if proven, to establish the duty as a matter of law).

Here, even if this Court were to apply the less stringent standard of "know or have reasonably foreseen," there simply are not sufficient facts from which this Court could conclude that the duty to protect students against third party criminal acts arose as a matter of law. In this case, the Commonwealth knew that there had been a shooting in a dormitory in which one student was critically wounded and one was murdered. The Commonwealth also knew that the shooter had not been apprehended. At that time, the Commonwealth did not know who the shooter was, as law enforcement was in the early stages of its investigation of the crime. However, based on representations from three different police departments, Virginia Tech officials believed that the shooting was a domestic incident and that the shooter may have been the boyfriend of one of the victims. Most importantly, based on the information available at that time, the defendants believed that the shooter had fled the area and posed no danger to others. This is markedly different from the situation presented in Taboada, 271 Va. at 325–26, where police had specifically warned the innkeepers that guests were at risk prior to the time that the plaintiff in that case was shot by a trespasser. Based on the limited information available to the Commonwealth prior to the shootings in Norris Hall, it cannot be said that it was known or reasonably foreseeable that students in Norris Hall would fall victim to criminal harm. Thus, as a matter of law, the Commonwealth did not have a duty to protect students against third party criminal acts.

III. CONCLUSION

Assuming without deciding that a special relationship existed between the Commonwealth and Virginia Tech students, based on the specific facts of this case, as a matter of law, no duty to warn students of harm by a third party criminal arose. Thus, we will reverse the trial court's judgment holding that a duty arose and enter final judgment in favor of the Commonwealth.

Reversed and final judgment.

Hegel v. Langsam

Court of Common Pleas of Ohio, 1971.
29 Ohio Misc. 147, 55 Ohio Ops.2d 476, 273 N.E.2d 351.

BETTMAN, JUDGE. This matter is before the Court on defendant's motion for judgment on the pleadings. The gravamen of plaintiff's position is that the defendants permitted the minor plaintiff, a seventeen year old female student from Chicago, Illinois, enrolled at the University, to become associated with criminals, to be seduced, to become a drug user and further allowed her to be absent from her dormitory and failed to return her to her parents' custody on demand.

In our opinion plaintiffs completely misconstrue the duties and functions of a university. A university is an institution for the advancement of knowledge and learning. It is neither a nursery school, a boarding school nor a prison. No one is required to attend. Persons who meet the required qualifications and who abide by the university's rules and regulations are permitted to attend and must be presumed to have sufficient maturity to conduct their own personal affairs.

We know of no requirement of the law and none has been cited to us placing on a university or its employees any duty to regulate the private lives of their students, to control their comings and goings and to supervise their associations.

We do not believe that O.R.C. 3345.21 requiring a university to maintain "law and order" on campus, nor O.R.C. 2151.41, making it a crime to contribute to the delinquency of a child, have any bearing on the fact situation before us.

For these reasons we hold that plaintiffs have failed to state a cause of action and defendants' motion for judgment on the pleadings should be granted. * * *

NOTES AND QUESTIONS

1. Other cases have cited *Hegel* in discussing a University's duty with regard to the private activities of its students. *See*: Bradshaw v. Rawlings, 612 F.2d 135 (1979) (Holding that duty of protection could not be imposed simply based on college regulation prohibiting alcohol consumption at off-campus college-sponsored events. Not sufficient to place college in custodial relationship with its students); *see also* Univ. of Denver v. Whitlock, 744 P.2d 54 (1987) (Holding that student-university

relationship does not create a "special relationship" or a duty for the university to take reasonable measures to protect student from accidental trampoline-related injuries at fraternity houses, notwithstanding affiliations or housing agreements between the fraternity and the university).

2. Compare with Duarte v. State, 84 Cal.App.3d 729, 148 Cal.Rptr. 804 (1978), holding a university liable for rape and murder in a student dormitory. Reconcilable? Is a university liable for injuries sustained by a student athlete engaged in the sport? In Davidson v. Univ. of N. Carolina at Chapel Hill, 142 N.C.App. 544 (2001), the court held that the defendant university owed a duty of care to a cheerleader who sustained injuries during practice. It highlighted the mutually beneficial nature of the parties' relationship, as both derived benefits from each other. It also discussed the high level of control the university had over its cheerleaders with regard to grades and alcohol consumption, which made reasonable the belief that the university would provide a higher level of protection from injury. How does this fit with the preceding cases?

3. The duty to rescue is much debated. Opinions divide on the common law's presumption against a duty of affirmative opinions on the basis of its unethical message, its morality, and its behavioral effects. It is unsurprising that with these shifting foundations exceptions to the no-duty rule make up the bulk of the law. These exceptions had grown into an unruly amalgam but have been helpfully tamed by the Restatement (Third) of Torts: Physical & Emotional Harm, Chapter 7 (2012). The base rule is articulated in § 37: An actor whose conduct has not created a risk of physical harm to another has no duty of care to the other unless a court determines that one of the affirmative duties provided in §§ 38–44 is applicable. Thus § 38 stipulates the role of a statutory obligation to protect another as one foundation for a duty of affirmative action. Under § 39 an actor's conduct may have created the risk conditions whereby an actor has a duty to exercise reasonable care to prevent or minimize harm. The actor's conduct must have increased the chances of the harm. A duty under § 40 is owed where the actor has a special relationship with the injured person. The last two principal cases address aspects of such duties. The duty may be founded on the special relationship between the victim and the defendant. § 41. The next three cases are examples of this principle. Under §§ 42 and 43 the duty can be generated by undertakings and reliance. Under § 44 an actor who acts to take charge of a vulnerable person may owe him a duty.

L.S. Ayres & Co. v. Hicks

Supreme Court of Indiana, 1942.
220 Ind. 86, 40 N.E.2d 334.

[Plaintiff, a boy six years old, accompanied his mother to defendant's department store while she was shopping. Plaintiff fell, and got his fingers caught in defendant's escalator. Defendant unreasonably delayed stopping the escalator, as a result of which plaintiff's injuries were aggravated. Judgment for plaintiff, and a new trial denied. Defendant appeals.]

SHAKE, C.J. [after holding that there was no negligence in the construction of the escalator]. It may be observed, on the outset, that there is no general duty to go to the rescue of a person who is in peril. So, in Hurley, Adm'r, v. Eddingfield, 1901, 156 Ind. 416, 59 N.E. 1058, it was held that a physician was not liable for failing without any reason to go to the aid of one who was violently ill and who died from want of medical attention which was otherwise unavailable. The effect of this rule was aptly illustrated by Carpenter, C.J., in Buch v. Amory Mfg. Co., 1897, 69 N.H. 257, 260, 44 A. 809, 810, as follows:

"With purely moral obligations the law does not deal. For example, the priest and Levite who passed by on the other side were not, it is supposed, liable at law for the continued suffering of the man who fell among thieves, which they might, and morally ought to have prevented or relieved."

There may be principles of social conduct so universally recognized as to be demanded that they be observed as a legal duty, and the relationship of the parties may impose obligations that would not otherwise exist. Thus, it has been said that, under some circumstances, moral and humanitarian considerations may require one to render assistance to another who has been injured, even though the injury was not due to negligence on his part and may have been caused by the negligence of the injured person. Failure to render assistance in such a situation may constitute actionable negligence if the injury is aggravated through lack of due care. [C] The case of Depue v. Flatau, 1907, 100 Minn. 299, 111 N.W. 1, lends support to this rule. It was there held that one who invited into his house a cattle buyer who called to inspect cattle which were for sale owed him the duty, upon discovering that he had been taken severely ill, not to expose him to danger on a cold winter night by sending him away unattended while he was in a fainting and helpless condition.

After holding that a railroad company was liable for failing to provide medical and surgical assistance to an employee who was injured without its fault but who was rendered helpless, by reason of which the employee's injuries were aggravated, it was said with the subsequent approval of this court, in Tippecanoe Loan, etc., Co. v. Cleveland, etc., R. Co., 1915, 57 Ind.App. 644, 649, 650, 104 N.E. 866, 868.

"In some jurisdictions the doctrine has been extended much further than we are required to do in deciding this case. It has been held to apply to cases where one party has been so injured as to render him helpless by an instrumentality under the control of another, even though no relation of master and servant, or carrier and passenger, existed at the time. It has been said that the mere happening of an accident of this kind creates a relation which gives rise to a legal duty to render such aid to the injured party as may be reasonably necessary to save his life, or to prevent a serious aggravation of his injuries, and that this subsequent duty does not depend on the negligence of the one party, or the freedom of the other party from contributory negligence, but that it exists irrespective of any legal responsibility for the original injury."

From the above cases it may be deduced that there may be a legal obligation to take positive or affirmative steps to effect the rescue of a person who is helpless or in a situation of peril, when the one proceeded against is a master or invitor, or when the injury resulted from use of an instrumentality under the control of the defendant. Such an obligation may exist although the accident or original injury was caused by the negligence of the plaintiff or through that of a third person and without any fault on the part of the defendant. Other relationships may impose a like obligation, but it is not necessary to pursue that inquiry further at this time.

In the case at bar the appellee was an invitee and he received his initial injury in using an instrumentality provided by the appellant and under its control. Under the rule stated above and on the authority of the cases cited this was a sufficient relationship to impose a duty upon the appellant. Since the duty with which we are presently concerned arose after the appellee's initial injury occurred, the appellant cannot be charged with its anticipation or prevention but only with failure to exercise reasonable care to avoid aggravation. * * *

Since the appellee was only entitled to recover for an aggravation of his injuries, the jury should have been limited and restricted in assessing the damages to the injuries that were the proximate result of the appellant's actionable negligence. * * *

The judgment is reversed with directions to sustain the appellant's motion for a new trial.

NOTES AND QUESTIONS

1. The reasoning in these torts claims may be usefully compared to cases stemming from deprivation of constitutional rights. In DeShaney v. Winnebago County Department of Social Services, 489 U.S. 189 (1989), the mother of an abused child sued the state of Wisconsin. She alleged that the failure of state welfare officers to protect her child from repeated beatings (at the hands of his father) breached her child's constitutionally protected due process rights under the 14th Amendment. The court found, however, that due process conferred "no affirmative right to government aid * * * [thus] the State cannot be held liable * * * for injuries that could have been averted had it chosen to provide them." If, however, the state officers had acted to protect the child and had failed to do so, his due process rights would have been implicated. The distinction was put by Judge Posner as whether the state is the "doer of harm rather than merely an inept rescuer, just as the Roman state was a doer of harm when it threw Christians to lions." K.H. Through Murphy v. Morgan, 914 F.2d 846, 849 (7th Cir.1990). Thus, "once the state assumes custody of a person, it owes him a rudimentary duty of safekeeping no matter how perilous his circumstances when he was free." The distinction tracks tort law—there is no duty to rescue but, having effected it, the "rescuer" is "not entitled to harm the person whom he has rescued." Restatement (Third), § 40(b)(7) (2012) includes in the special relationships generating a duty to protect a charge of a custodian where (a) the custodian is required by law to take custody or voluntarily takes custody of the other; and (b) the custodian has a superior ability to protect the other.

J.S. and M.S. v. R.T.H.

Supreme Court of New Jersey, 1998.
155 N.J. 330, 714 A.2d 924.

HANDLER, J., delivered the unanimous opinion of the Court.

In this case, two young girls, ages 12 and 15, spent substantial periods of recreational time with their neighbor at his horse barn, riding and caring for his horses. Betraying the trust this relationship established, the neighbor, an older man, sexually abused both girls for a period of more than a year. Following the man's conviction and imprisonment for these sexual offenses, the girls, along with their parents, brought this action against the man and his wife for damages, contending that the wife's negligence rendered her, as well as her husband, liable for their injuries. The man conceded liability for both the intentional and negligent injuries that he inflicted on the girls by his sexual abuse. His wife, however, denied that, under the circumstances, she could be found negligent for the girls' injuries.

This case presents the issue of whether a wife who suspects or should suspect her husband of actual or prospective sexual abuse of their neighbors' children has any duty of care to prevent such abuse. And, if there is such a duty, does a breach of that duty constitute a proximate cause of the harm that results from sexual abuse.

Defendants R.T.H. and R.G.H., husband and wife (called "John" and "Mary" for purposes of this litigation), moved into a house in Vineland, New Jersey, and became next-door neighbors of plaintiffs, J.S. and M.S. and their two daughters, C.S. and M.S.

John, 64 years old, was charged with sexually assaulting the two sisters over a period of more than a year. He pled guilty to endangering the welfare of minors and was sentenced to eighteen months in state prison. Plaintiffs, as the natural parents and guardians ad litem of their two daughters, filed a complaint against John alleging intentional, reckless, and/or negligent acts of sexual assault against each of the two girls. In an amended complaint, plaintiffs added Mary as a defendant, alleging that she "was negligent in that she knew and/or should have known of her husband's proclivities/propensities" and that as a result of her negligence the two girls suffered physical and emotional injury.

Defendants filed a joint answer in which they denied plaintiffs' allegations. In an amended answer, Mary offered the defenses that she owed no duty to plaintiffs, that any alleged negligence on her part was not the proximate cause of any injuries or damages sustained by plaintiffs, and that any damages sustained by plaintiffs were the result of actions by a third party over whom she exercised no control. Mary also filed a crossclaim for contribution and indemnification against John, alleging that even if plaintiffs' allegations were proven, John was the primary, active, and sole culpable cause of any injuries to the plaintiffs.

* * *

The trial court entered summary judgment on behalf of Mary. On appeal, the Appellate Division reversed the order and remanded for entry of an order granting plaintiffs extended discovery. [C]

This Court granted defendant's petition for certification. [C]

* * *

In determining whether a duty is to be imposed, courts must engage in a rather complex analysis that weighs and balances several, related factors, including the nature of the underlying risk of harm, that is, its foreseeability and severity, the opportunity and ability to exercise care to prevent the harm, the comparative interests of, and the relationships between or among, the parties, and, ultimately, based on considerations of public policy and fairness, the societal interest in the proposed solution.

Foreseeability of the risk of harm is the foundational element in the determination of whether a duty exists. [C] The "ability to foresee injury to a potential plaintiff" is "crucial" in determining whether a duty should be imposed. [C]

Foreseeability as a component of a duty to exercise due care is based on the defendant's knowledge of the risk of injury and is susceptible to objective analysis. [C] That knowledge may be an actual awareness of risk. [C] Such knowledge may also be constructive; the defendant may be charged with knowledge if she is "in a position" to "discover the risk of harm." [C] In some cases where the nature of the risk or the extent of harm is difficult to ascertain, foreseeability may require that the defendant have a "special reason to know" that a "particular plaintiff" or "identifiable class of plaintiffs" would likely suffer a "particular type" of injury. Further, when the risk of harm is that posed by third persons, a plaintiff may be required to prove that defendant was in a position to "know or have reason to know, from past experience, that there [was] a likelihood of conduct on the part of [a] third person[ ]" that was "likely to endanger the safety" of another.

"The question whether there is a 'duty' merely begs the more fundamental question whether the plaintiff's interests are entitled to legal protection against the defendant's conduct." [C] The imposition of a duty thus requires an evaluation and a balancing of the conflicting interests of the respective parties. [C] That assessment necessarily includes an examination of the relationships between and among the parties. Also implicated in this analysis is an assessment of the defendant's "responsibility for conditions creating the risk of harm" and an analysis of whether the defendant had sufficient control, opportunity, and ability to have avoided the risk of harm. [C]

Ultimately, the determination of the existence of a duty is a question of fairness and public policy. [C] In fixing the limits of liability as a matter of public policy, courts must draw on "notions of fairness, common sense, and morality." [C] Public policy must be determined in the context of contemporary circumstances and considerations. See, e.g., Kelly v. Gwinnell, 96 N.J. 538, 544–45, 476 A.2d 1219 (1984) (noting that in a society growing increasingly intolerant of drunken driving, the imposition of a duty on social hosts "seems both fair and fully in accord with the State's policy"). Thus, "'duty' is not a rigid formalism" that remains static through time, but rather is a malleable concept that "must of necessity adjust to the changing social relations and exigencies and man's relation to his fellows." [C]

The Court, in its determination whether to impose a duty, must also consider the scope or boundaries of that duty. [C] The scope of a duty is determined under "the totality of the circumstances," and must be "reasonable" under those circumstances. [C] Factors to be taken into consideration include the risk of harm involved and the practicality of preventing it. [C] When the defendant's actions are "relatively easily corrected" and the harm sought to be prevented is "serious," it is fair to impose a duty. [C] In the final analysis, the "reasonableness of action" that constitutes such a duty is "an essentially objective determination to be made on the basis of the material facts" of each case. [C]

Here, a man criminally sexually assaulted unrelated, adolescent children whom he had befriended. The defendant is the spouse of the wrongdoer. The abuse occurred on her own property over an extended period of time. The tortious, assaultive conduct is of a type that is extremely difficult to identify, anticipate, and predict. While these considerations bear on all of the factors that are relevant in determining whether a duty of care should be recognized and imposed on the spouse, they bear materially on the primary element of foreseeability.

Although conduct involving sexual abuse is often secretive, clandestine, and furtive, a number of factors are relevant when determining whether or not it is foreseeable to a wife that her husband would sexually abuse a child. These include whether the husband had previously committed sexual offenses against children; the number, date, and nature of those prior offenses; the gender of prior victims; the age of prior victims; where the prior offenses occurred; whether the prior offense was against a stranger or a victim known to the husband; the husband's therapeutic history and regimen; the extent to which the wife encouraged or facilitated her husband's unsupervised contact with the current victim; the presence of physical evidence such as pornographic materials depicting children and the unexplained appearance of children's apparel in the marital home; and the extent to which the victims made inappropriate sexual comments or engaged in age-inappropriate behavior in the husband and wife's presence. [C]

Moreover, there is some empirical support for the conclusion that sexual abuse of a child, while extremely difficult to detect or anticipate, is a risk that can be foreseen by a spouse. This evidence indicates that an extremely high percentage of child sexual molesters are men, many of whom are married. U.S. Dept. of Justice, Bureau of Justice Statistics, Child Victimizers: Violent Offenders and Their Victims 5 (March 1996). The vast majority of child victims are female and many child victims fall prey to an immediate relative or a family acquaintance; most of these sexual assaults are committed either in the offender's home or the victim's home. [C] Given those factors, the wife of a sexual abuser of children is in a unique position to observe firsthand telltale signs of sexual abuse. A wife may well be the only person with the kind of knowledge or opportunity to know that a particular person or particular class of persons is being sexually abused or is likely to be abused by her husband. [C]

These considerations warrant a standard of foreseeability in this case that is based on "particular knowledge" or "special reason to know" that a "particular plaintiff" or "identifiable class of plaintiffs" would suffer a "particular type" of injury. [Cc] "Particularized foreseeability" in this kind of case will conform the standard of foreseeability to the empirical evidence and common experience that indicate a wife may often have actual knowledge or special reason to know that her husband is abusing or is likely to abuse an identifiable victim and will accommodate the concerns over the inherent difficulties in predicting such furtive behavior. That test of foreseeability will also ensure that the wife is not subject to a broad duty that may expose her to liability to every child whom her husband may threaten and harm. Foreseeability under that definitional standard is neither unrealistic nor unfair.

The nature of the parties' interests bears on the need to recognize a duty of care. "There can be no doubt about the strong policy of this State to protect children from sexual abuse and to require reporting of suspected child abuse." That policy is so obvious and so powerful that it can draw little argument. It is an interest that is massively documented.

The Legislature has dealt comprehensively with the subject of child abuse and has enacted a plethora of statutes designed to prevent the sexual abuse of children. For example, N.J.S.A. 9:6–8.10 requires any person having reasonable cause to believe that a child has been subject to abuse to report the abuse immediately to the Division of Youth and Family Services. The duty to report is not limited to professionals, such as doctors, psychologists, and teachers, but is required of every citizen. [C] Indeed, friends or neighbors are often in the best position to fulfill this statutory duty because they are the people "who frequently hear or observe acts of child abuse." [C]

* * *

"Megan's Law," N.J.S.A. 2C:7–1 to –11, provides yet more evidence of the State's intolerance of sexual abuse of children. In affirming the constitutionality of the community notification and registration requirements of Megan's Law for convicted sex offenders, this Court recognized the enormous public interest in protecting society from the threat of potential molestation, rape, or murder of women and children. [C]

While the interest in protecting children from sexual abuse is great, this Court must also take into consideration defendants' interests in a stable marital relationship and in marital privacy. [C] That interest traditionally found expression in the common-law doctrine of interspousal immunity wherein one spouse could not sue or be sued by another, [c] and the testimonial disqualification wherein one spouse was not permitted to testify for or against the other [c]. Both courts and scholars, however, increasingly questioned whether the doctrine of marital immunity actually succeeded in promoting the marital tranquility and privacy it was designed to serve. [C]

Public Interest considerations

Moreover, the societal interest in enhancing marital relationships cannot outweigh the societal interest in protecting children from sexual abuse. The child-abuse reporting statute itself has mandated that balance—it applies to every citizen, including a spouse. [Cc]

Considerations of fairness and public policy also govern whether the imposition of a duty is warranted. [C] Public policy considerations based in large measure on the comparative interests of the parties support overwhelmingly the recognition of a duty of care in these circumstances. This Court has recognized that the sexual abuse of children not only traumatizes the victims, but also exacts a heavy toll on society: [The court details research demonstrating the adverse consequences of sexual abuse on victims and on society.]

Considerations of fairness implicate the scope as well as the existence of a duty. In defining the duty to be imposed, the court must weigh the ability and opportunity of the defendant to exercise reasonable care. Defendant contends that the imposition of a duty to prevent her husband from engaging in sexual abuse of another person would be unfair. She argues that sexual offenses are extremely difficult to combat and that she did not necessarily have the power, the ability, or the opportunity to control her husband and should not be expected or required to police his conduct continuously. However, fairness concerns in these circumstances can be accommodated by a flexible duty of care that requires a spouse, when there is particularized foreseeability of harm of sexual abuse to a child, to take reasonable steps to prevent or warn of the harm. [C]

Holding on I1

Considerations of foreseeability, the comparative interests and relationships of the parties, and public policy and fairness support the recognition of a duty of care. Based in large measure on the strong public policy of protecting children from sexual abuse, we conclude that there is a sound, indeed, compelling basis for the imposition of a duty on a wife whose husband poses the threat of sexually victimizing young children.

Closely-related to the recognition of a duty, however, is the issue of proximate causation, which must also be considered in determining whether any liability may be allowed for the breach of such a duty. Proximate causation is "that combination of 'logic, common sense, justice, policy and precedent' that fixes a point in the chain of events, some foreseeable and some unforeseeable, beyond which the law will bar recovery." [C]

It does not seem highly extraordinary that a wife's failure to prevent or warn of her husband's sexual abuse or his propensity for sexual abuse would result in the occurrence or the continuation of such abuse. The harm from the wife's breach of duty is both direct and predictable. There is little question, here, that the physical and emotional injuries allegedly suffered by the girls are hardly an extraordinary result of John's acts of molestation and that their victimization is not an extraordinary consequence of Mary's own negligence. Mary's negligence could be found to be a proximate cause of plaintiffs' injuries. [C]

Accordingly, we hold that when a spouse has actual knowledge or special reason to know of the likelihood of his or her spouse engaging in sexually abusive behavior against a particular person or persons, a spouse has a duty of care to take reasonable steps to prevent or warn of the harm. Further, we hold that a breach of such a duty constitutes a proximate cause of the resultant injury, the sexual abuse of the victim.

It may be found that the relationship between the next-door neighbors' in this case had been close. Mary knew that the neighbors' adolescent girls were visiting at her home nearly every day and that they spent considerable amounts of time there alone with her husband. Moreover, she never "confronted" her husband about the unsupervised time he was spending with the girls. At both the trial level and on appeal, Mary conceded for the purposes of argument that "at all relevant times" she "knew or should have known of her husband's proclivities/propensities." Thus, it may be determined that it was particularly foreseeable that John was abusing the young girls. Further, the evidence at trial could support a finding of negligence on Mary's part. It is inferable, as explained by the Appellate Division, that Mary could have discharged her duty by confronting her husband and warning him, by insisting or seeing that the girls were not invited to ride or care for the horses, by keeping a watchful eye when she knew the girls to be visiting with her husband, by asking the girls' parents to ensure that the children not visit when she was not present, or by warning the girls or their parents of the risk she perceived. [C] Finally, the evidence may be found sufficient to support the determination that the harm suffered by the girls was not a highly extraordinary result of the breach of that duty.

We affirm the judgment of the Appellate Division.

NOTES AND QUESTIONS

1. In the principal case Mary, the wife, could be said to be in position of knowledge and control where she could take reasonable steps to protect the vulnerable plaintiffs. In other contexts the defendant is in a relationship where he or she is expected to take measures against the risks posed by another to a third party. A parent may have a duty to protect others against dangers posed by his or her dependent child. Nieuwendorp v. Am. Family Ins. C., 529 N.W.2d 594 (Wis. 1995). Other relationships include employer and employee, automobile owner and driver, and persons who have taken charge of dangerous lunatics, criminals and persons with contagious diseases. In Otis Engineering Corp. v. Clark, 668 S.W.2d 307 (Tex.1983), a drunken employee, after being told to go home, killed the plaintiff's husband in an automobile accident. The court grounded the duty on the defendant employer's ability to control the intoxicated employee.

An interesting case is Connolly v. Nicollet Hotel, 254 Minn. 373, 95 N.W.2d 657 (1959), where a convention in the defendant's hotel got out of hand and started menacing everybody and everything in the vicinity, and the management was held to be under a duty to make reasonable efforts to control it. Does a passenger in an automobile who is aware that the driver has been drinking heavily have an affirmative duty to warn other passengers who do not realize the driver's potentially impaired condition? See VanHaverbeke v. Bernhard, 654 F.Supp. 255 (S.D.Ohio 1986). Cf.

Pulka v. Edelman, 40 N.Y.2d 781, 358 N.E.2d 1019, 390 N.Y.S.2d 393 (1976) (automobile garage and customers driving out over a sidewalk outside the exit).

2. In a case similar to the principal case, the plaintiff, a minor between the ages of 14 to 18, had been invited to stay at defendant's house for the period of time. During this period, plaintiff entered a sexual relationship with defendant's "live-in male friend." The latter was convicted of criminal sexual contact and plaintiff brought a suit asserting that defendant had failed to protect her from sexual abuse. The Supreme Court of Minnesota found that the defendant owed plaintiff a duty of care, stressing the vulnerability of minors in sexual abuse cases and the social need to protect them. Bjerke v. Johnson, 742 N.W.2d 660 (2007). But cf. Berry v. Watchtower Bible and Tract Society, 152 N.H. 407, 879 A.2d 1124 (2005) (finding that church congregations and elders owed no duty to protect child victims of sexual abuse after mother had frequently told the defendants that father was abusing the daughter; court affirmed the narrow duty).

3. In Schurk v. Christensen, 80 Wash.2d 652, 497 P.2d 937 (1972), defendants' son, while acting as a baby-sitter, sexually molested a neighbor's five-year-old daughter. The neighbors suffered severe emotional harm when they learned this fact from their daughter and they sued defendants. What should be the major legal and factual issues in the case? Distinguish this case from Haselhorst v. State, 240 Neb. 891, 485 N.W.2d 180 (1992), where the plaintiff parents suffered emotional distress when they discovered that their children had been sexually assaulted by a foster child placed with them by the Nebraska Department of Social Services. In Randi W. v. Muroc Joint Unified School District, 14 Cal.4th 1066, 60 Cal.Rptr.2d 263, 929 P.2d 582 (1997), the California Supreme Court held that a former employer of a teacher had owed a duty to a molested student not to misrepresent the fitness of that teacher to a school district proposing to hire him. The defendant former employer knew of charges and complaints of sexual misconduct by the employee-teacher. After being hired, the teacher molested plaintiff.

Tarasoff v. Regents of University of California

Supreme Court of California, 1976.
17 Cal.3d 425, 551 P.2d 334, 131 Cal.Rptr. 14.

[Posenjit Poddar was an out-patient under the care of a psychologist, Dr. Lawrence Moore, at Cowell Memorial Hospital of the University of California. During the course of treatment, Dr. Moore learned from Poddar that he intended to kill Tatiana Tarasoff because she had spurned Poddar's romantic advances.

On the basis of this information, Dr. Moore had the campus police detain Poddar, apparently at the hospital. Poddar was released shortly afterward. Despite disagreement among the psychiatrists the final decision was that no further action should be taken to confine Poddar. This judgment proved to be mistaken; two months later Poddar shot and then repeatedly stabbed Tatiana. Plaintiffs, Tatiana's parents, brought a wrongful death claim against the four psychiatrists. Plaintiffs claimed that they should be liable because they failed to confine Poddar.

The court rejected this claim because California Government Code Section 856 cloaked the doctors with tort immunity with regard to this type of decision. Plaintiffs also claimed that defendants should be liable for Tatiana's death because they failed to warn her or them about Poddar's threat.]

TOBRINER, JUSTICE. * * * The second cause of action can be amended to allege that Tatiana's death proximately resulted from defendants' negligent failure to warn Tatiana or others likely to apprise her of her danger. Plaintiffs contend that as amended, such allegations of negligence and proximate causation, with resulting damages, establish a cause of action. Defendants, however, contend that in the circumstances of the present case they owed no duty of care to Tatiana or her parents and that, in the absence of such duty, they were free to act in careless disregard of Tatiana's life and safety. * * *

Although * * * under the common law, as a general rule, one person owed no duty to control the conduct of another [cc], nor to warn those endangered by such conduct [cc], the courts have carved out an exception to this rule in cases in which the defendant stands in some special relationship to either the person whose conduct needs to be controlled or in a relationship to the foreseeable victim of that conduct (see Rest.2d Torts, supra, §§ 315–320). * * *

Although plaintiffs' pleadings assert no special relation between Tatiana and defendant therapists, they establish as between Poddar and defendant therapists the special relation that arises between a patient and his doctor or psychotherapist. Such a relationship may support affirmative duties for the benefit of third persons. Thus, for example, a hospital must exercise reasonable care to control the behavior of a patient which may endanger other persons. A doctor must also warn a patient if the patient's condition or medication renders certain conduct, such as driving a car, dangerous to others.

Although the California decisions that recognize this duty have involved cases in which the defendant stood in a special relationship *both* to the victim and to the person whose conduct created the danger, we do not think that the duty should logically be constricted to such situations. Decisions of other jurisdictions hold that the single relationship of a doctor to his patient is sufficient to support the duty to exercise reasonable care to protect others against dangers emanating from the patient's illness. The courts hold that a doctor is liable to persons infected by his patient if he negligently fails to diagnose a contagious disease [c] or, having diagnosed the illness, fails to warn members of the patient's family. * * *

Defendants contend, however, that imposition of a duty to exercise reasonable care to protect third persons is unworkable because therapists cannot accurately predict whether or not a patient will resort to violence. In support of this argument amicus representing the American Psychiatric Association and other professional societies cites numerous articles which indicate that therapists, in the present state of the art, are unable reliably to predict violent acts; their forecasts, amicus claims, tend consistently to overpredict violence, and indeed are more often wrong than right. Since predictions of violence are often erroneous, amicus concludes, the courts should not render rulings that predicate the liability of therapists upon the validity of such predictions. * * *

We recognize the difficulty that a therapist encounters in attempting to forecast whether a patient presents a serious danger of violence. Obviously we do not require that the therapist, in making that determination, render a perfect performance; the therapist need only exercise "that reasonable degree of skill, knowledge, and care ordinarily possessed and exercised by members of [that professional specialty] under similar circumstances." * * *

In the instant case, however, the pleadings do not raise any question as to failure of defendant therapists to predict that Poddar presented a serious danger of violence. On the contrary, the present complaints allege that defendant therapists did in fact predict that Poddar would kill, but were negligent in failing to warn.

Amicus contends, however, that even when a therapist does in fact predict that a patient poses a serious danger of violence to others, the therapist should be absolved of any responsibility for failing to act to protect the potential victim. In our view, however, once a therapist does in fact determine, or under applicable professional standards reasonably should have determined, that a patient poses a serious danger of violence to others, he bears a duty to exercise reasonable care to protect the foreseeable victim of that danger. * * *

The risk that unnecessary warnings may be given is a reasonable price to pay for the lives of possible victims that may be saved. We would hesitate to hold that the therapist who is aware that his patient expects to attempt to assassinate the President of the United States would not be obligated to warn the authorities because the therapist cannot predict with accuracy that his patient will commit the crime.

Defendants further argue that free and open communication is essential to psychotherapy [c]; that "unless a patient * * * is assured that * * * information [revealed by him] can and will be held in utmost confidence, he will be reluctant to make the full disclosure upon which diagnosis and treatment * * * depends." (Sen.Com. on Judiciary, comment on Evid.Code, § 1014.) The giving of a warning, defendants contend, constitutes a breach of trust which entails the revelation of confidential communications.

We recognize the public interest in supporting effective treatment of mental illness and in protecting the rights of patients to privacy [c] and the consequent public importance of safeguarding the confidential character of psychotherapeutic communication. Against this interest, however, we must weigh the public interest in safety from violent assault. The Legislature has undertaken the difficult task of balancing the countervailing concerns. In Evidence Code section 1014, it established a broad rule of privilege to protect confidential communications between patient and psychotherapist. In Evidence Code section 1024, the Legislature created a specific and limited exception to the psychotherapist-patient privilege: "There is no privilege * * * if the psychotherapist has reasonable cause to believe that the patient is in such mental or emotional condition as to be dangerous to himself or to the person or property of another and that disclosure of the communication is necessary to prevent the threatened danger." * * *

Our current crowded and computerized society compels the interdependence of its members. In this risk-infested society we can hardly tolerate the further exposure to danger that would result from a concealed knowledge of the therapist that his patient was lethal. If the exercise of reasonable care to protect the threatened victim requires the therapist to warn the endangered party or those who can reasonably be expected to notify him, we see no sufficient societal interest that would protect and justify concealment. The containment of such risks lies in the public interest. For the foregoing reasons, we find that plaintiffs' complaints can be amended to state a cause of action against defendants Moore, Powelson, Gold, and Yandell and against the Regents as their employer, for breach of a duty to exercise reasonable care to protect Tatiana. * * *

[WRIGHT, C.J., and SULLIVAN and RICHARDSON, JJ., concurred and dissented in part; and CLARK and MCCOMB, JJ., dissented.]

NOTES AND QUESTIONS

1. In his dissent Justice Clark agreed with the majority that when a psychiatrist, in terminating a patient, increases the risk of his violence toward a particular individual, a duty to warn should arise. However, he could find neither precedent nor reason to support a duty to warn solely based on the psychiatrist-patient relationship. Other courts have agreed that the relationship does not ground a duty to warn. The Virginia Supreme Court in Nasser v. Parker, 249 Va. 172, 455 S.E.2d 502 (1995), found that the principal case "is at odds with [its] interpretation of the Restatement's provisions relating to one's duty to control the conduct of a third person." Id. at 177, 504. Plaintiff must show defendant had "taken charge" of third person within the meaning of Restatement (Second) § 319 (1979), id. at 178, 504. This was not the case in *Tarasoff*, nor in this case where defendants had released the victim's former boyfriend from the hospital without warning victim of the release.

The degree of control necessary to generate a duty of care was raised in Estates of Morgan v. Fairfield Family Counseling Ctr., 77 Ohio St.3d 284, 673 N.E.2d 1311 (1997). In this case, the victim's son had been in outpatient care of the defendants. Their negligent misdiagnosis and treatment of the patient's schizophrenia led to the patient shooting and killing his parents and wounding his sister. Defendant's control over the patient was attenuated. The court found that a want of close control, in itself, does not determine that a duty should not be imposed. Rather, the court insisted on a balancing of factors: "(1) the psychotherapist's ability to control the outpatient; (2) the public's interest in safety from violent assault; (3) the difficulty inherent in attempting to forecast whether a patient represents a substantial risk of physical harm to others; (4) the goal of placing the mental patient in the least restrictive environment and safeguarding importance of maintaining the confidential nature of psychotherapeutic communications." Id. at 297, 1322.

2. Describe the duty that should be imposed on a physician who finds that her patient is HIV positive. Should she warn the patient's sexual

partners? See, In Estate of Behringer (M.D.) v. Medical Center at Princeton, 249 N.J.Super. 597, 592 A.2d 1251 (1991) (dicta). It has been held that physicians owe a duty to unidentified third persons, but may fulfill duty by informing patient of risks of transmission of AIDS. See Reisner v. Regents of Univ. of Cal., 31 Cal.App.4th 1195, 37 Cal.Rptr.2d 518 (1995); A diagnosis of Rocky Mountain spotted fever in a patient may give rise to a duty in the physician to warn the patient's family that they have been exposed to ticks carrying the disease, Bradshaw v. Daniel, 854 S.W.2d 865 (Tenn. 1993).

3. The duty to protect subsumes a duty to warn. Does it include a duty to commit or retain custody? Currie v. United States, 644 F.Supp. 1074 (M.D.N.C.1986); Estates of Morgan v. Fairfield Family Counseling Ctr., 77 Ohio St.3d 284, 673 N.E.2d 1311 (1997) (stating that a fear of undue confinement caused by the imposition of a duty has no reliable statistical support). Other actions may be called for, e.g. in Lundgren v. Fultz, 354 N.W.2d 25 (Minn.1984), blocking return of guns to paranoid schizophrenic patient obsessed with weapons.

4. Is there a "dangerous patient" exception to Psychotherapist-Patient privilege? Authorities are split. The 8th Circuit said no in United States v. Ghane, 673 F.3d 771 (8th Cir. 2012): " '[T]he scope [or contours] of a privilege and the decision whether to establish a new privilege [or to adopt an exception thereto] are mixed questions of fact . . . which we review de novo.' * * * In Jaffee, the Court observed in a footnote: '[W]e do not doubt that there are situations in which the privilege must give way, for example, if a serious threat of harm to the patient or to others can be averted only by means of a disclosure by the therapist.' [C] Arising from this dictum is a 'dangerous patient' exception to the psychotherapist-patient privilege discussed, but often rejected, by circuit courts. United States v. Auster [C] (recognizing that an exception to the privilege exists and can be useful in a criminal trial, but refusing to apply it on the facts of the case because the patient knew his communication to his therapist was not confidential); United States v. Chase, [C] (holding that even if a patient knows that a threat is not made in confidence, any statements made to the therapist are privileged in a federal trial); Hayes, [C] (analyzing and ultimately rejecting the dangerous patient exception to the federal psychotherapist-patient testimonial privilege); United States v. Glass [C] (restricting the application of the exception to situations where the threat was serious when it was uttered and its disclosure was the only means of averting harm).' "

What of this exception with regard to *Peterson*, infra 437? Much has been made of the gunman's mental health and Virginia Tech's knowledge of his condition. What if the plaintiffs focused their case differently in light of these facts? Would the outcome differ? Should it? See Commonwealth of Va., Va. Tech Review Panel, Rep. on Mass Shootings at Virginia Tech 31–62 (2007).

5. In the principal case the duty was owed to an identified victim. When the threat is not pointed, but general, the authorities are split. In Thompson v. County of Alameda, 27 Cal.3d 741, 614 P.2d 728, 167 Cal.Rptr. 70 (1980), a juvenile offender was released into his mother's custody despite his history of violence and known desire to kill a young child if he were set free. He accomplished this within twenty-four hours of

his release when he killed the plaintiff's son. The court reasoned that no duty of care obtained because the generalized threat here, in juxtaposition to the direct threat in the principal case, would have been an ineffective guard against violence and might have adversely impacted the patient's rehabilitation. Accord: Brady v. Hopper, 570 F.Supp. 1333 (D.Colo.1983), aff'd, 751 F.2d 329 (10th Cir.1984) (suit against John Hinckley's psychiatrist by victims of the attempted assassination of President Reagan); Rousey v. United States, 115 F.3d 394 (6th Cir.1997) (applying Maine law, holding that duty to warn requires identification of victims).

6. In the principal case it was assumed, for the purposes of the appeal, that the defendant clinicians had predicted Poddar's dangerousness. This issue, however, is often live. Although it is rare for mental health clinicians to be liable, by reason of failure to reasonably predict violence, those professionals have remained anxious lest courts too readily conclude that violence can be accurately predicted. See Menendez v. Superior Court, 11 Cal. Rptr. 2d 92, 834 P.2d 786 (1992) (with regard to the "dangerous patient exception," the "reasonableness" of the requisite "reasonable cause to believe" is determined in light of the standards of the psychotherapeutic community. The test is objective and must consider all relevant circumstances. It is based on prevailing norms among psychotherapists but allows broad discretion to the individual psychotherapist.). See also White v. United States, 780 F.2d 97 (D.C.Cir.1986), and Tamsen v. Weber, 166 Ariz. 364, 802 P.2d 1063 (App.1990).

7. In Bellah v. Greenson, 81 Cal.App.3d 614, 146 Cal.Rptr. 535 (1978), the court found no duty to warn when a psychiatrist had failed to alert a patient's parents that the patient had suicidal propensities and was running risks by consorting with heroin addicts. Likewise, in Nally v. Grace Community Church of the Valley, 47 Cal.3d 278, 763 P.2d 948, 253 Cal.Rptr. 97 (1988), a religious counsellor was found to owe no duty to refer a suicidal young man to a mental health professional. In contrast, school counsellors owed a duty to warn the parents of a thirteen-year-old girl of a suicidal statement made at school. The dangers were acute and the burdens of warning the parents light. Eisel v. Board of Education of Montgomery County, Md., 324 Md. 376, 597 A.2d 447 (1991).

8. You overhear a conversation while in line at the supermarket. In it a person reveals that he intends to rob a nearby jewelry store. Do you have a duty? If so, what is expected of you in discharging the duty?

3. PURE ECONOMIC LOSS

The citadel of privity has now been vanquished. In most cases the fact that *A* was in a contractual relationship with *B* alone cannot defeat a claim that a duty was owed by *A* to *C* to prevent causing *C* foreseeable physical injury. A last bastion survives, however. If the harm is pure economic loss, the courts take more seriously the claim that liability should be restricted. Pure economic loss arises when a person suffers pecuniary loss not consequent upon injury to his person or property. The cases fall into two categories:

(1) Negligent misrepresentation or misstatement causing economic loss; and

(2) Negligent acts causing economic loss.

The former category is treated in detail in Chapter 21. The paradigmatic cases relate to auditor or accountant liability. An auditor retained by a corporation completes a negligent audit which is then relied upon by a third person to his detriment. Does that third person have a cause of action against the negligent auditors? Does privity describe the limits of liability or does the auditor owe a duty to a class of persons outside privity of contract? Benjamin Cardozo, the champion of the assault on the privity citadel, held back from imposing a duty of care in negligence. Ultramares Corporation v. Touche, infra page 1130. The courts, nevertheless, have found duties of care to parties outside privity of contract, sometimes narrowly, sometimes broadly, in a way reminiscent of the hesitation that has surrounded the scope of the duty in negligence for emotional distress. See Daley v. La Croix infra page 469.

The latter category—negligent acts causing economic loss—held firmly against the proponents of wider tort liability.

State of Louisiana ex rel. Guste v. M/V Testbank

United States Court of Appeals, Fifth Circuit (en banc), 1985.
752 F.2d 1019, cert. denied, 477 U.S. 903, 106 S.Ct. 3271, 91 L.Ed.2d 562 (1986).

HIGGINBOTHAM, CIRCUIT JUDGE: We are asked to abandon physical damage to a proprietary interest as a prerequisite to recovery for economic loss in cases of unintentional maritime tort. We decline the invitation.

I. In the early evening of July 22, 1980, the M/V Sea Daniel, an inbound bulk carrier, and the M/V Testbank, an outbound container ship, collided at approximately mile forty-one of the Mississippi River Gulf outlet. At impact, a white haze enveloped the ships until carried away by prevailing winds, and containers aboard Testbank were damaged and lost overboard. The white haze proved to be hydrobromic acid and the contents of the containers which went overboard proved to be approximately twelve tons of pentachlorophenol, PCP, assertedly the largest such spill in United States history. The United States Coast Guard closed the outlet to navigation until August 10, 1980 and all fishing, shrimping, and related activity was temporarily suspended in the outlet and four hundred square miles of surrounding marsh and waterways. * * * [Numerous lawsuits, representing various interests,] were filed and consolidated before the same judge in the Eastern District of Louisiana. * * *

Defendants moved for summary judgment as to all claims for economic loss unaccompanied by physical damage to property. The district court granted the requested summary judgment as to all such claims except those asserted by commercial oystermen, shrimpers, crabbers and fishermen who had been making a commercial use of the embargoed waters. * * *

On appeal a panel of this court affirmed, concluding that claims for economic loss unaccompanied by physical damage to a proprietary interest were not recoverable in maritime tort. 728 F.2d 748 (5th

Cir.1984). The panel, as did the district court, pointed to the doctrine of Robins Dry Dock & Repair Co. v. Flint, 275 U.S. 303 (1927), and its development in this circuit. Judge Wisdom specially concurred, agreeing that the denial of these claims was required by precedent, but urging reexamination en banc. We then took the case en banc for that purpose. After extensive additional briefs and oral argument, we are unpersuaded that we ought to drop physical damage to a proprietary interest as a prerequisite to recovery for economic loss. To the contrary, our reexamination of the history and central purpose of this pragmatic restriction on the doctrine of foreseeability heightens our commitment to it. Ultimately we conclude that without this limitation foreseeability loses much of its ability to function as a rule of law. * * *

III. The meaning of Robins Dry Dock v. Flint, 275 U.S. 303 (1927) (Holmes, J.) is the flag all litigants here seek to capture. We turn first to that case and to its historical setting.

Robins broke no new ground but instead applied a principle, then settled both in the United States and England, which refused recovery for negligent interference with "contractual rights." Stated more broadly, the prevailing rule denied a plaintiff recovery for economic loss if that loss resulted from physical damage to property in which he had no proprietary interest. See, e.g., Byrd v. English, 117 Ga. 191, 43 S.E. 419 (1903); Cattle v. Stockton Waterworks Co., 10 Q.B. 453, 457 (C.A.1875). See also James, Limitations on Liability for Economic Loss Caused by Negligence: A Pragmatic Appraisal, 25 Vand.L.Rev. 43, 44–46 (1972) (discussing history of the rule); Carpenter, Interference with Contract Relations, 41 Harv.L.Rev. 728 (1928). Professor James explains this limitation on recovery of pure economic loss: "The explanation * * * is a pragmatic one: the physical consequences of negligence usually have been limited, but the indirect economic repercussions of negligence may be far wider, indeed virtually open-ended." James, supra, at 45.

Decisions such as *Stockton* illustrate the application of this pragmatic limitation on the doctrine of foreseeability. The defendant negligently caused its pipes to leak, thereby increasing the plaintiff's cost in performing its contract to dig a tunnel. The British court, writing fifty-two years before *Robins,* denied the plaintiff's claim. The court explained that if recovery were not contained, then in cases such as Rylands v. Fletcher, L.R. 1 Ex. 265 (1866), the defendant would be liable not only to the owner of the mine and its workers "but also to * * * every workman and person employed in the mine, who in consequence of its stoppage made less wages than he would otherwise have done." Id. at 457. [C]

1. In *Robins,* the time charterer of a steamship sued for profits lost when the defendant dry dock negligently damaged the vessel's propeller. The propeller had to be replaced, thus extending by two weeks the time the vessel was laid up in dry dock, and it was for the loss of use of the vessel for that period that the charterer sued. The Supreme Court denied recovery to the charterer, noting: " * * * no authority need be cited to show that, as a general rule, at least, a tort to the person or property of one man does not make the tort-feasor liable to another merely because the injured person was under a contract with

that other unknown to the doer of the wrong. The law does not spread its protection so far * * * " 275 U.S. at 309. * * *

2. The principle that there could be no recovery for economic loss absent physical injury to a proprietary interest was not only well established when *Robins Dry Dock* was decided, but was remarkably resilient as well. * * * Indeed this limit on liability stood against a sea of change in the tort law. Retention of this conspicuous bright-line rule in the face of the reforms brought by the increased influence of the school of legal realism is strong testament both to the rule's utility and to the absence of a more "conceptually pure" substitute. The push to delete the restrictions on recovery for economic loss lost its support and by the early 1940's had failed. See W. Prosser, *Law of Torts* § 129, at 938–940 (4th ed. 1971). In sum, it is an old sword that plaintiffs have here picked up.

3. Plaintiffs would confine *Robins* to losses suffered for inability to perform contracts between a plaintiff and others, categorizing the tort as a species of interference with contract. When seen in the historical context described above, however, it is apparent that *Robins Dry Dock* represents more than a limit on recovery for interference with contractual rights. Apart from what it represented and certainly apart from what it became, its literal holding was not so restricted. If a time charterer's relationship to its negligently injured vessel is too remote, other claimants without even the connection of a contract are even more remote. * * *

The language and the cases the *Robins* Court pointed to as "good statement[s]" of the principle make plain that the charterer failed to recover its delay claims from the dry dock because the Court believed them to be too remote. Notably, although the dry dock company did not know of the charter party when it damaged the propeller, delay losses by users of the vessel were certainly foreseeable. Thus, *Robins* was a pragmatic limitation imposed by the Court upon the tort doctrine of foreseeability.

In a sense, every claim of economic injury rests in some measure on an interference with contract or prospective advantage. It was only in this sense that profits were lost in *Byrd v. English* when the electrical power to plaintiffs printing plant was cut off. The printing company's contractual right to receive power was interfered with, and in turn, its ability to print for its customers was impinged. That the printing company had a contract with the power company did not make more remote the relationship between its loss of profits and the tortious acts. To the contrary, the contract reduced this remoteness by defining an orbit of predictable injury smaller than if there were no contract between the power company and the printer. When the loss is economic rather than physical, that the loss caused a breach of contract or denied an expectancy is of no moment. If a plaintiff connected to the damaged chattels by contract cannot recover, others more remotely situated are foreclosed *a fortiori*. Indisputably, the *Robins Dry Dock* principle is not as easily contained as plaintiff would have it. * * *

4. This circuit has consistently refused to allow recovery for economic loss absent physical damage to a proprietary interest. [The court discusses in detail its own decisions and those of other circuits. It

gives particular attention to Petitions of Kinsman Transit Co., 388 F.2d 821 (2d Cir.1968) (Kinsman II, described in this casebook, infra page 469); and Union Oil Co. v. Oppen, 501 F.2d 558 (9th Cir.1974), described infra page 468].

IV. Plaintiffs urge that the requirement of physical injury to a proprietary interest is arbitrary, unfair, and illogical, as it denies recovery for foreseeable injury caused by negligent acts. At its bottom the argument is that questions of remoteness ought to be left to the trier of fact. Ultimately the question becomes who ought to decide—judge or jury—and whether there will be a rule beyond the jacket of a given case. * * *

Those who would delete the requirement of physical damage have no rule or principle to substitute. Their approach fails to recognize limits upon the adjudicating ability of courts. We do not mean just the ability to supply a judgment; prerequisite to this adjudicatory function are preexisting rules, whether the creature of courts or legislatures. Courts can decide cases without preexisting normative guidance but the result becomes less judicial and more the product of a managerial, legislative or negotiated function.

Review of the foreseeable consequences of the collision of the [two ships in this case] demonstrates the wave upon wave of successive economic consequences and the managerial role plaintiffs would have us assume. The vessel delayed in St. Louis may be unable to fulfill its obligation to haul from Memphis, to the injury of the shipper, to the injury of the buyers, to the injury of their customers. Plaintiffs concede, as do all who attack the requirement of physical damage, that a line would need to be drawn—somewhere on the other side, each plaintiff would say in turn, of its recovery. Plaintiffs advocate not only that the lines be drawn elsewhere but also that they be drawn on an ad hoc and discrete basis. The result would be that no determinable measure of the limit of foreseeability would precede the decision on liability. We are told that when the claim is too remote, or too tenuous, recovery will be denied. Presumably then, as among all plaintiffs suffering foreseeable economic loss, recovery will turn on a judge or jury's decision. There will be no rationale for the differing results save the "judgment" of the trier of fact. Concededly, it can "decide" all the claims presented, and with comparative if not absolute ease. The point is not that such a process cannot be administered but rather that its judgments would be much less the products of a determinable rule of law. In this important sense, the resulting decisions would be judicial products only in their draw upon judicial resources.

The bright line rule of damage to a proprietary interest, as most, has the virtue of predictability with the vice of creating results in cases at its edge that are said to be "unjust" or "unfair." Plaintiffs point to seemingly perverse results, where claims the rule allows and those it disallows are juxtaposed—such as vessels striking a dock, causing minor but recoverable damage, then lurching athwart a channel causing great but unrecoverable economic loss. The answer is that when lines are drawn sufficiently sharp in their definitional edges to be reasonable and predictable, such differing results are the inevitable result—indeed, decisions are the desired product. But there is more.

The line drawing sought by plaintiffs is no less arbitrary because the line drawing appears only in the outcome—as one claimant is found too remote and another is allowed to recover. The true difference is that plaintiffs' approach would mask the results. The present rule would be more candid, and in addition, by making results more predictable, serves a normative function. It operates as a rule of law and allows a court to adjudicate rather than manage.[12]

V. That the rule is identifiable and will predict outcomes in advance of the ultimate decision about recovery enables it to play additional roles. Here we agree with plaintiffs that economic analysis, even at the rudimentary level of jurists, is helpful both in the identification of such roles and the essaying of how the roles play. Thus it is suggested that placing all the consequence of its error on the maritime industry will enhance its incentive for safety. While correct, as far as such analysis goes, such *in terrorem* benefits have an optimal level. Presumably, when the cost of an unsafe condition exceeds its utility there is an incentive to change. As the costs of an accident become increasing multiples of its utility, however, there is a point at which greater accident costs lose meaning, and the incentive curve flattens. When the accident costs are added in large but unknowable amounts the value of the exercise is diminished.

With a disaster inflicting large and reverberating injuries through the economy, as here, we believe the more important economic inquiry is that of relative cost of administration, and in maritime matters administration quickly involves insurance. Those economic losses not recoverable under the present rule for lack of physical damage to a proprietary interest are the subject of first party or loss insurance. The rule change would work a shift to the more costly liability system of third party insurance. For the same reasons that courts have imposed limits on the concept of foreseeability, liability insurance might not be readily obtainable for the types of losses asserted here. As Professor James has noted, "[s]erious practical problems face insurers in handling insurance against potentially wide, open-ended liability. From an insurer's point of view it is not practical to cover, without limit, a liability that may reach catastrophic proportions, or to fix a reasonable premium on a risk that does not lend itself to actuarial measurement." James, supra, at 53. By contrast, first party insurance is feasible for many of the economic losses claimed here. Each businessman who might be affected by a disruption of river traffic or by a halt in fishing activities can protect against that eventuality at a relatively low cost since his own potential losses are finite and readily discernible. Thus, to the extent that economic analysis informs our decision here, we think that it favors retention of the present rule. * * *

VI. Plaintiffs seek to avoid the *Robins* rule by characterizing their claims as damages caused by a public nuisance. They suggest that when

[12] Fuller, The Forms and Limits of Adjudication, 92 Harv.L.Rev. 353, 396 (1978). This case illustrates how our technocratic tradition masks a deep difference in attitudes toward the roles of a judiciary. The difference between the majority and dissenting opinions is far more than a choice between competing maritime rules. The majority is driven by the principle of self ordering and modesty for the judicial role; the dissent accepts a role of management which can strain the limits of adjudication.

a defendant unreasonably interferes with public rights by obstructing navigation or negligently polluting a waterway he creates a public nuisance for which recovery is available to all who have sustained "particular damages." * * *

* * * With economic losses such as the ones claimed here the problem is to determine who among an entire community that has been commercially affected by an accident has sustained a pecuniary loss so great as to justify distinguishing his losses from similar losses suffered by others. Given the difficulty of this task, we see no jurisprudential advantage in permitting the use of nuisance theory to skirt the *Robins* rule. * * *

VII. In conclusion, having reexamined the history and central purpose of the doctrine of *Robins Dry Dock* as developed in this circuit, we remain committed to its teaching. Denying recovery for pure economic losses is a pragmatic limitation on the doctrine of foreseeability, a limitation we find to be both workable and useful. Nor do we find persuasive plaintiffs' arguments that their economic losses are recoverable under a public nuisance theory, as damages for violation of federal statutes, or under state law.

Accordingly, the decision of the district court granting summary judgment to defendants on all claims for economic losses unaccompanied by physical damage to property is affirmed.

GEE, CIRCUIT JUDGE, with whom CLARK, CHIEF JUDGE, joins, concurring: * * * It is my thesis that the dispute-resolution systems of courts are poorly equipped to manage disasters of such magnitude and that we should be wary of adopting rules of decision which, as would that contended for by the dissent, encourage the drawing of their broader aspects before us. * * * Such a system as ours works tolerably well in the traditional case for which it was developed, where the stakes are limited to who owns the farm or to some other finite benefit. Its deficiencies become immediately and painfully apparent, however, when the consideration of factors inherently extraneous to the dispute becomes necessary or desirable to resolving it. Of these factors, perhaps the most often encountered is that of financial reality. * * *

Extending theories of liability may not always be the more moral course, especially in such a case as this, where the extension, in the course of awarding damages to unnumbered claimants for injuries that are unavoidably speculative, may well visit destruction on enterprise after enterprise, with the consequent loss of employment and productive capacity which that entails.

[GARWOOD and WILLIAMS, JJ., concurred specially in separate opinions.]

WISDOM, CIRCUIT JUDGE, with whom ALVIN B. RUBIN, POLITZ, TATE, and JOHNSON, CIRCUIT JUDGES, join, dissenting.

Robins is the Tar Baby of tort law in this circuit. And the brierpatch is far away. This Court's application of *Robins* is out of step with contemporary tort doctrine, works substantial injustice on innocent victims, and is unsupported by the considerations that justified the Supreme Court's 1927 decision. * * *

The * * * bar for claims of economic loss unaccompanied by any physical damage conflicts with conventional tort principles of foreseeability and proximate cause. I would analyze the plaintiffs' claims under these principles, using the "particular damage" requirement of public nuisance law as an additional means of limiting claims. Although this approach requires a case-by-case analysis, it comports with the fundamental idea of fairness that innocent plaintiffs should receive compensation and negligent defendants should bear the cost of their tortious acts. Such a result is worth the additional costs of adjudicating these claims, and this rule of liability appears to be more economically efficient. Finally, this result would relieve courts of the necessity of manufacturing exceptions totally inconsistent with the expanded *Robins* rule of requiring physical injury as a prerequisite to recovery. * * *

II. THE INAPPLICABILITY OF *Robins Dry Dock* TO THIS CASE. Whatever the pragmatic justification for the original holding in *Robins,* the majority has extended the case beyond the warrant of clear necessity in requiring *a physical injury* for a recovery of economic loss in cases such as the one before the court. *Robins* prevented plaintiffs who were neither proximately nor foreseeably injured by a tortious act or product from recovering solely by claiming a contract with the injured party. The wisdom of this rule is apparent. This rule, however, has been expanded now to bar recovery by plaintiffs who would be allowed to recover if judged under conventional principles of foreseeability and proximate cause. * * *

Robins held only that if a defendant's negligence injures party *A,* and the plaintiff suffers loss of expected income or profits because it had a contract with *A,* then the plaintiff has no cause of action based on the defendant's negligence. * * *

It is a long step from *Robins* to a rule that requires *physical damage* as a prerequisite to recovery in maritime tort. The majority believes that the plaintiff's lack of any contractual connection with an injured party, taken with the *Robins* rule, forecloses liability: "If a plaintiff connected to the damaged chattels by contract cannot recover, others more remotely situated are foreclosed *a fortiori.*"

This conclusion follows readily from the reasoning that if uninjured contracting parties are barred from recovery, and if contracting parties have a closer legal relationship than non-contracting parties, then a party who is not physically injured and who does not have a contractual relation to the damage is surely barred.

This argument would be sound in instances where the plaintiff suffered no loss *but for a contract* with the injured party. We would measure a plaintiff's connection to the tortfeasor by the only line connecting them, the contract, and disallow the claim under *Robins.* In the instant case, however, some of the plaintiffs suffered damages whether or not they had a contractual connection with a party physically injured by the tortfeasor. These plaintiffs do not need to rely on a contract to link them to the tort. The collision proximately caused their losses, and those losses were foreseeable. These plaintiffs are therefore freed from the *Robins* rule concerning the recovery of those who suffer economic loss because of an injury to a party with whom they have contracted.

Because *Robins* provides an overly restrictive bar on recovery, courts have over the years developed a number of exceptions. The traditional exceptions allow recovery for certain husband-wife claims, recovery for negligent interference with contract when the interference results from a tangible injury to the contractor's person or property, and recovery for persons employed on fishing boats to recover for lost income when the employment contract is disrupted by a third party's negligent injury to the ship or equipment. * * * [The opinion discusses other cases.]

One cannot deny that *Robins*'s policy of limiting the set of plaintiffs who can recover for a person's negligence and damage to physical property provides a "bright line" for demarcating the boundary between recovery and nonrecovery. Physical harm suggests a proximate relation between the act and the interference. At bottom, however, the requirement of a tangible injury is artificial because it does not comport with accepted principles of tort law. Mrs. Palsgraf, although physically injured, could not recover. Many other plaintiffs, although physically uninjured, can recover. * * *

With deference to the majority, I suggest, notwithstanding their well reasoned opinion, that the utility derived from having a "bright line" boundary does not outweigh the disutility caused by the limitation on recovery imposed by the physical-damage requirement. *Robins* and its progeny represent a wide departure from the usual tort doctrines of foreseeability and proximate cause. Those doctrines, as refined in the law of public nuisance, provide a rule of recovery that compensates innocent plaintiffs and holds the defendants liable for much of the harm proximately caused by their negligence.

III. AN ALTERNATE RULE OF RECOVERY. Rather than limiting recovery under an automatic application of a physical damage requirement, I would analyze the plaintiffs' claims under the conventional tort principles of negligence, foreseeability, and proximate causation. I would confine *Robins* to the "factual contours" of that case: A plaintiff's claim may be barred only if the claim is derived solely through contract with an injured party. The majority's primary criticism of this approach to a determination of liability is that it is potentially open ended. Yet, there are well-established tort principles to limit liability for a widely-suffered harm. Under the contemporary law of public nuisance, courts compensate "particularly" damaged plaintiffs for harms suffered from a wide-ranging tort, but deny recovery to more generally damaged parties. Those parties who are foreseeably and proximately injured by an oil spill or closure of a navigable river, for example, and who can also prove damages that are beyond the general economic dislocation that attends such disasters, should recover whether or not they had contractual dealings with others who were also damaged by the tortious act. The limitation imposed by "particular" damages, together with refined notions of proximate cause and foreseeability, provides a workable scheme of liability that is in step with the rest of tort law, compensates innocent plaintiffs, and imposes the costs of harm on those who caused it.

* * *

IV. ADVANTAGES OF THE ALTERNATE RULE OF RECOVERY. The advantages of this alternate rule of recovery are that it compensates damaged plaintiffs, imposes the cost of damages upon those who have caused the harm, is consistent with economic principles of modern tort law, and frees courts from the necessity of creating a piecemeal quilt of exceptions to avoid the harsh effects of the *Robins* rule. * * *

If tort law fails to compensate plaintiffs or to impose the cost of damages on those who caused the harm, it should be under a warrant clear of necessity. When a rule of law, once extended, leads to inequitable results and creates principles of recovery that are at odds with the great weight of tort jurisprudence, then that rule of law merits scrutiny. A strict application of the extension denies recovery to many plaintiffs who should be awarded damages. Conventional tort principles of foreseeability, proximate causation, and "particular" damages would avoid such unfairness.

It is true that application of foreseeability and proximate causation would necessitate case-by-case adjudication. But I have a more optimistic assessment of courts' ability to undertake such adjudication than the majority.[38] Certainly such an inquiry would be no different from our daily task of weighing such claims in other tort cases.

The majority opinion also states that the *Robins* rule, being free from the vagaries of factual findings in a case-by-case determination, serves an important normative function because it is more predictable and more "candid." Normative values would also be served, however, by eliminating a broad categorical rule that is insensitive to equitable and social policy concerns that would support allowing the plaintiffs' claims in many individual cases. In assessing "normative concerns", the courts' compass should be a sense of fairness and equity, both of which are better served by allowing plaintiffs to present their claims under usual tort standards. It is not clear, moreover, that a jury's finding of negligence in a case-by-case determination is "less the product of a determinable rule of law" when the finder of fact is guided in its determination by rules of law. The jury's finding of liability in this case

---

[38] The majority criticizes foreseeability because it necessitates a case-by-case determination of liability. But this criticism of "foreseeability" as the criterion for judgment applies with equal force to well-established tort law for physical injury. The unquestioned concepts of foreseeability and proximate cause as established in *Palsgraf* and its progeny are open to the same condemnation that the majority makes of a rule of liability that would abandon *Robins:* "The result would be that no determinable measure of the limit of foreseeability would precede the decision on liability. We are told that where a claim is too remote, or too tenuous, recovery will be denied. Presumably then, as among all plaintiffs suffering foreseeable economic loss, recovery will turn on a judge['s] or jury's decision. * * * The point is not that such a process cannot be administered but rather that its judgments would be much less the product of a determinable rule of law." [C]

The majority opinion favors a bright line rule, as opposed to a case-by-case determination of liability, because it enables courts to "adjudicate" rather than to "manage." A bright line rule such as the one the majority proposes, however, requires no adjudication whatsoever. Judges need merely to preside over a self-executing system of limited liability where recovery is predicated upon an easily determined physical injury. The application of such a rule, rather than a case-by-case determination, seems more "management" than adjudication.

would be no more "lawless" than a finding of proximate cause, foreseeability, and particular damages in a physical damage case. * * *

The economic arguments regarding allocation of loss that purportedly favor the *Robins* rule of nonliability are not as clear to me as they appear to be to the majority. It is true that denial of recovery may effectively spread the loss over the victims. It is not certain, however, that victims are generally better insurers against the risk of loss caused by tortious acts having widespread consequences. Although the victims do possess greater knowledge of their circumstances and their potential damages, we do not know whether insurance against these types of losses is readily available to the businesses that may be affected. We do know that insurance against this kind of loss is already available for shippers. Imposition of liability upon the shippers helps ensure that the potential tortfeasor faces incentives to take the proper care. The majority's point is well taken that the incentives to avoid accidents do not increase once potential losses pass a certain measure of enormity. But in truth we have no idea what this measure is: Absent hard data, I would rather err on the side of receiving little additional benefit from imposing additional quanta of liability than err by adhering to *Robins'* inequitable rule and bar victims' recovery on the mistaken belief that a "marginal incentive curve" was flat, or nearly so. If a loss must be borne, it is no worse if a "merely" negligent defendant bears the loss than an innocent plaintiff absorb the damages.

V. CONCLUSION. The *Robins* approach restricts liability more severely than the policies behind limitations on liability require and imposes the cost of the accident on the victim, who is usually not in a superior position to obtain insurance to cover this loss. I would apply a rule of recovery based on conventional tort principles of proximate cause and foreseeability and limit eligibility only by the requirement that a claimant prove "particular" damages.

ALVIN B. RUBIN, CIRCUIT JUDGE, with whom WISDOM, POLITZ and TATE, CIRCUIT JUDGES, join, dissenting. * * * *Robins* should not be extended beyond its actual holding and should not be applied in cases like this, for the result is a denial of recompense to innocent persons who have suffered a real injury as a result of someone else's fault. We should not flinch from redressing injury because Congress has been indifferent to the problem.

NOTES AND QUESTIONS

1. The principal case follows the clear majority rule, but disagreement in the opinions in the case indicates the current ferment. The case is discussed by Atiyah, Economic Loss in the United States, 5 Oxford J. of Legal Stud. 485 (1985). For a strong, but isolated, case holding liability, see People Express Airlines, Inc. v. Consolidated Rail Corp., 100 N.J. 246, 495 A.2d 107 (1985) (tank car accident producing toxic fumes requiring evacuation of plaintiff's offices at Newark Airport, resulting in economic loss).

2. The foundational authority in the Common Law world establishing no duty is Justice Holmes's opinion in Robins Dry Dock & Repair Co. v. Flint, supra. But see Goldberg, Recovery of Pure Economic

Loss in Tort: Another Look at Robins Dry Dock v. Flint, 20 J. of Legal Stud. 249 (1991), noting that "[t]ort law is under constant pressure to extend the boundaries of what constitutes a compensable injury" and that *Robins* is inapposite in many contexts in which it has been employed to deny liability. He finds a requirement for "some intellectual apparatus for evaluating the myriad of claims for recovery of mere economic loss."

3. The rule in *Robins* was a backwater in American law until recently: Jane Stapleton, Comparative Economic Loss: Lessons from Case-Law-Focused "Middle Theory," 50 UCLA L.Rev 531–536 (2002). The American Law Institute has focused and refined discussion of recovery of economic loss through injury to person or property not belonging to the claimant in § 7 and under public nuisance in § 8 of Chapter 1 of its Restatement of the Law (Third): Torts: Liability for Economic Harm (Preliminary Draft No. 2). The courts and Congress have created some inroads to permit recovery for pure economic loss. Fishermen suffering disruption to their livelihood by defendant's negligent conduct have been permitted to recover for consequent economic losses: Union Oil Co. v. Oppen, 501 F.2d 588 (9th Cir. 1974). Where state and federal law on the issue conflict, state law may prevail in allowing a foreseeability analysis to permit recovery for pure economic loss contrary to the *Robins* rule. See In re Complaint of Nautilus Motor Tanker Co., 900 F. Supp. 697 (D.N.J. 1995). Private rights of action for recovery for pure economic loss is also available under federal statute in the case of oil spills by the Oil Pollution Act (OPA), 33 U.S.C. § 2702; the proximity of the connection between the economic loss and spill event is still being worked out in the courts. See, e.g., Ballard Shipping Co. v. Beach Shellfish, 32 F.3d 623, 631 (1st Cir. 1994). For a recent and controversial discussion of how far liability should extend under OPA, see John C. Goldberg, Liability for Economic Loss in Connection with the Deepwater Horizon Spill. (November 22, 2010), available at: http://nrs.harvard.edu/urn-3:HUL.InstRepos:4595438.

4. Although the rule in *Robins* has been adopted throughout Anglo American law, the roots are independent. Often applied in the admiralty context in the United States, in England the rule is traceable to traditional common law. See Cattle v. Stockton Waterworks Co. 10 Q.B. 453 (1875). Limited exceptions to the *Robins* rule have been crafted, although they are remarkably inconsistent. For example, the rule relating to defects in structures is viewed as falling within the *Robins* rule in England, Murphy v. Brentwood District Council [1991] 1 A.C. 398 (H. L.), but not so in Canada, Winnipeg Condominium Corporation no. 36. v. Bird Construction Co. Ltd. (1995) 121 D.L.R. (4th) 193. In Australia, the High Court took the position in Bryan v. Maloney (1995) 182 C.L.R. 609 that a subsequent buyer of property could sue a builder for the loss of value when the latent defect was manifested, but qualified that holding in Woolcock Street Investments v. CDG (2004) 216 C.L.R. 515, refusing to extend liability for structural defects to commercial premises.

5. The High Court of Australia extended liability for pure economic loss to a potato grower whose statutorily prohibited importation of non-certified seed caused harm to his neighboring potato growers under considerations of foreseeability, proximity, and policy. See Perre v. Apand Pty Ltd, 198 CLR 180; HCA 36 (1999) (Austl.). Lost profits due to actual or perceived contamination by genetically modified (GM) crops has been

another contested area for economic loss litigation internationally. See Karinne Ludlow & Stuart J. Smith, The Quandary of Agricultural Biotechnology, Pure Economic Loss, and Non-adopters: Comparing Australia, Canada, and the United States, 53 Jurimetrics J. 7 (2011).

6. When the loss arises from the defectiveness of a good or structure, the proper action may be a products liability claim. See East. River Steamship Corp. v. Transamerica Delaval, Inc. 476 U.S. 858 (U.S. 1986) (holding no duty for the manufacturer to compensate for economic loss when economic loss from repairs resulted from faulty construction of ship turbines and noting this "was most naturally understood as a warranty claim"). See discussion infra of the tort aspects of warranty, pages 770–781. How is the damage to be characterized in these cases:

A. the defective engine explodes causing the ship to sink; liability to the injured crew, and to the ship's owner for the loss of his ship?

B. design defect in a fishing vessel's hydraulic system causes her to catch fire and sink; the accident destroys, in addition to the vessel, equipment added after the initial sale, namely a skiff, a fishing net, and spare parts: Saratoga Fishing Co. v. J. M. Martinac & Co., 520 U.S. 875 (1997)?

C. the defective engine threatens to explode, necessitating drydocking and repairs and resulting in wasted hire charges and a loss of profits? Colleton Preparatory Academy v. Hoover Universal, 379 S.C. 181, 666 S.E.2d 247 (2008) (duty extends to economic loss where the breach threatens physical or bodily harm).

D. the defective engine does not work at all when the manufacturer knew the purpose to which the engine would be put?

7. The courts do not always restrict liability via the duty issue. In Petitions of Kinsman Transit Co., 388 F.2d 821 (2d Cir.1968), supra Chapter 6, Kaufman J. employed a proximate cause analysis to deny recovery for economic losses suffered by wheat owners when Buffalo harbor was blocked due to the defendant's negligence.

4. EMOTIONAL DISTRESS

Daley v. LaCroix

Supreme Court of Michigan, 1970.
384 Mich. 4, 179 N.W.2d 390.

T.M. KAVANAGH, JUDGE. * * * On July 16, 1963, about 10:00 p.m., defendant was traveling west on 15 Mile Road near plaintiffs' farm in Macomb county. Defendant's vehicle left the highway, traveled 63 feet in the air and 209 feet beyond the edge of the road and, in the process, sheared off a utility pole. A number of high voltage lines snapped, striking the electrical lines leading into plaintiffs' house and caused a great electrical explosion resulting in considerable property damage.

Plaintiffs claimed, in addition to property damage, that Estelle Daley suffered traumatic neurosis, emotional disturbance and nervous upset, and that Timothy Daley suffered emotional disturbance and nervousness as a result of the explosion and the attendant circumstances. * * *

The Court of Appeals (13 Mich.App. 26, 163 N.W.2d 666) affirmed the trial court's grant of a directed verdict upon the ground that Michigan law denies recovery for negligently caused emotional disturbance absent a showing of physical impact. * * *

Recovery for mental disturbance caused by defendant's negligence, but without accompanying physical injury or physical consequences or any independent basis for tort liability, has been generally denied with the notable exception of the *sui generis* cases involving telegraphic companies and negligent mishandling of corpses. * * *

[However], compensation for a purely mental component of damages where defendant negligently inflicts an *immediate physical injury* has always been awarded as "parasitic damages." * * *

The final bastion against allowing recovery [for negligent infliction of emotional harm] is the requirement of some impact upon the person of the plaintiff. It is this doctrine and its continued vitality in our State which we must now consider. * * *

In the landmark decision of Victorian Railways Commissioners v. Coultas, 13 A.C. 222 (1888), recovery for a much disputed damage to plaintiff's nervous system caused by defendant's oncoming train was denied upon the ground that:

"Damages arising from mere sudden terror unaccompanied by any actual physical injury, but occasioning a nervous or mental shock, cannot under such circumstances, their Lordships think, be considered a consequence which, in the ordinary course of things, would flow from the negligence of the gate-keeper. If it were held that they can, it appears to their Lordships that it would be extending the liability for negligence much beyond what that liability has hitherto been held to be. Not only in such a case as the present, but in every case where an accident caused by negligence had given a person a serious nervous shock, there might be a claim for damages on account of mental injury. The difficulty which now often exists in case of alleged physical injuries of determining whether they were caused by the negligent act would be greatly increased, and a wide field opened for imaginary claims."

As a further hedge against fraudulent or fancied claims and the feared flood of litigation, a large number of American courts in adopting the Victorian Railways Commissioners rule superimposed the additional requirement of a contemporaneous physical impact. * * *

The leading American authority of Mitchell v. Rochester Ry. Co. (1896), 151 N.Y. 107, 45 N.E. 354, with "remorseless logic" stated the position as follows (pp. 109, 110, 45 N.E. p. 354):

"Assuming that fright cannot form the basis of an action, it is obvious that no recovery can be had for injuries resulting therefrom. That the result may be nervous disease, blindness, insanity, or even a miscarriage, in no way changes the principle. These results merely show the degree of fright, or the extent of the damages. * * * Therefore the logical result of the respondent's concession would seem to be, not only that no recovery can be had for mere fright, but also that none can be had for injuries which are the direct consequences of it. * * * These considerations lead to the conclusion that no recovery can be had for injuries sustained by fright occasioned by the negligence of another, where there is no immediate personal injury." * * *

The life of the law, however, has not been logic but experience. Bowing to the onslaught of exceptions[9] and the growing irreconcilability between legal fact and decretal fiction, a rapidly increasing majority of courts have repudiated the "requirement of impact" and have regarded the physical consequences themselves or the circumstances of the accident as sufficient guarantee.

Pertinently, the New York Court of Appeals in Battalla v. State (1961), 10 N.Y.2d 237, 219 N.Y.S.2d 34, 176 N.E.2d 729, expressly overruled its Mitchell v. Rochester Ry. Co., decision, supra, observing at page 239, 219 N.Y.S.2d at page 36, 176 N.E.2d at page 730:

"Before passing to a resume of the evolution of the doctrine in this State, it is well to note that it has been thoroughly repudiated by the English courts which initiated it, rejected by a majority of American jurisdictions, abandoned by many which originally adopted it, and diluted, through numerous exceptions, in the minority which retained it. Moreover, it is the opinion of the scholars that *the right* to bring an action should be enforced."

Based upon close scrutiny of our precedential cases and the authority upon which they rested and cognizant of the changed circumstances relating to the factual and scientific information available, we conclude that the "impact" requirement of the common law should not have a continuing effect in Michigan and we therefore overrule the principle to the contrary contained in our previous cases.

We hold that where a definite and objective physical injury is produced as a result of emotional distress proximately caused by defendant's negligent conduct, the plaintiff in a properly pleaded and proved action may recover in damages for such physical consequences to himself notwithstanding the absence of any physical impact upon plaintiff at the time of the mental shock.

The rule we adopt today is, of course, subject to familiar limitations.

Generally, defendant's standard of conduct is measured by reactions to be expected of normal persons. Absent specific knowledge of plaintiff's unusual sensitivity, there should be no recovery for

[9] The divergent approaches of the courts to find an exception to the Rochester Ry. Co. rule is excellently summarized by Prosser, Torts (3d Ed.), pages 350, 351:

"Apart from some quite untenable notions of causal connection, the theory seems to be that the 'impact' affords the desired guarantee that the mental disturbance is genuine. But the same courts have found 'impact' in minor contacts with the person which play no part in causing the real harm, and in themselves can have no importance whatever. 'Impact' has meant a slight blow, a trifling burn or electric shock, a trivial jolt or jar, a forcible seating on the floor, dust in the eye, or the inhalation of smoke. The requirement has even been satisfied by a fall brought about by a faint after a collision, or the plaintiff's own wrenching of her shoulder in reaction to the fright. 'The magic formula 'impact' is pronounced; the door opens to a full joy of a complete recovery.' A Georgia circus case has reduced the whole matter to a complete absurdity by finding 'impact' where the defendant's horse 'evacuated his bowels' into the plaintiff's lap."

hypersensitive mental disturbance where a normal individual would not be affected under the circumstances. * * *

Further, plaintiff has the burden of proof that the physical harm or illness is the *natural result* of the fright proximately caused by defendant's conduct. In other words, men of ordinary experience and judgment must be able to conclude, after sufficient testimony has been given to enable them to form an intelligent opinion, that the physical harm complained of is a natural consequence of the alleged emotional disturbance which in turn is proximately caused by defendant's conduct. * * *

In view of the above holding it becomes necessary to discuss another issue raised by plaintiffs—whether, considering the evidence in the light most favorable to plaintiffs, sufficient evidence was presented to create a jury question. Denying plaintiffs' motion for a new trial which sought to set aside the directed verdict against plaintiffs Timothy and Estelle Daley, the trial court reasoned:

"There was no expert or medical testimony offered on behalf of the minor, Timothy. Extremely vague lay testimony was offered to the effect he was nervous. It was so vague and uncertain it did not, in the court's opinion, reach the dignity of possessing any evidentiary value whatever. It afforded the jury nothing into which the jury could put its 'damage-assessment teeth'." Vachon v. Todorovich, 356 Mich. 182[, 97 N.W.2d 122].

"On behalf of Estelle Daley, Dr. Goldin, a psychiatrist, testified. Direct and cross examination were extensive. He testified clearly that she had been neurotic since childhood and the incident complained of did not cause her neurosis. Dr. Goldin indicated the incident could have broken down her 'balances' somewhat although she did not consult him until a year after the accident.

"The lay testimony was of the same type as was given in Timothy's claim. It was vague and uncertain and indefinite."

From an examination of the evidence presented on behalf of Timothy Daley, we believe that, even though the question is a close one, on favorable view, he presented facts from which under our new rule as announced in this case, a jury could reasonably find or infer a causal relation between defendant's alleged negligence and the injuries alleged. We conclude that Timothy Daley should be given an opportunity to prove his alleged cause of action, if he can do so, at a new trial.

Plaintiff Estelle Daley's claim that she suffered physical consequences naturally arising from the fright proximately caused by defendant's conduct is amply supported by the record. Her sudden loss of weight, her inability to perform ordinary household duties, her extreme nervousness and irritability, repeatedly testified to by plaintiffs, are facts from which a jury could find or infer a compensable physical injury.

The plaintiffs' testimony is also supported by the medical expert witness, who diagnosed plaintiff Estelle Daley as "a chronic psychoneurotic * * * in partial remission," and who attributed this state or condition to the explosion directly caused by defendant's acts:

"Q. I want to ask one more question, from everything that you know about this case, Doctor, do you feel there is a causal relationship between the explosion of July, 1963 and the symptoms that she has shown that you have reported?

"A. Yes, the trauma is the triggering point for her breaking the balance in her.

"Q. By trauma?

"A. Any trauma, may be emotional trauma or physical trauma, in this case having this explosive sound that she heard and the fears that were attendant with the explosive sounds."

We hold * * * that this record presents sufficient facts from which a jury could reasonably find, or infer therefrom, a causal relationship between the fright occasioned by defendant's negligence and the injuries alleged in plaintiffs' complaint. The trial court erred in taking plaintiff Estelle Daley's case from the jury. [Cc] It follows that the trial court also erred in striking plaintiff Leonard H. Daley's claim for medical expenses.

The order of the trial court granting directed verdicts against plaintiffs Estelle Daley and Timothy Daley and the Court of Appeals' affirmance thereof are reversed and the causes remanded for new trials. * * *

Costs shall abide the final result.

DETHMERS, T.G. KAVANAGH, ADAMS and BLACK, JJ., concurred with T.M. KAVANAGH.

BRENNAN, CHIEF JUSTICE (dissenting). If this were a case where a definite and objective physical injury was produced without impact by the negligent act of the defendant, it might be appropriate to adopt the rule set forth in the Restatement (Second) of Torts § 436(2) (1979).

This is not such a case. Plaintiffs did not suffer definite and objective physical injury. Plaintiffs suffered, if anything, indefinite and subjective injury. Traumatic neurosis, emotional disturbance and nervous upset are the very type of complaints which ought to be eliminated by restricting "no impact" cases to those in which a definite and objective physical injury occurs.

I would affirm the trial court's grant of directed verdict.

KELLY, J., concurred with BRENNAN, C.J.

NOTES AND QUESTIONS

1. Most jurisdictions do not apply the "impact" rule, although some continue to champion it, e.g., R.J. v. Humana of Florida, 652 So.2d 360 (Fla. 1995); and Lee v. State Farm Mut. Ins. Co., 272 Ga. 583, 533 S.E.2d 82 (2000).

2. The policy reasons for and against allowing recovery despite the absence of an impact are vigorously and colorfully expounded in the dissenting opinions in two Pennsylvania cases. In Bosley v. Andrews, 393 Pa. 161, 169, 142 A.2d 263, 267 (1958), Musmanno, J., dissented against the continued application of the impact rule. In Niederman v. Brodsky, 436

Pa. 401, 413, 261 A.2d 84, 90 (1970), Bell, C.J., dissented against the overruling of the impact rule.

3. Where the plaintiff has narrowly escaped imminent and serious harm to his own physical well being, the courts have readily allowed recovery upon a demonstration of ensuing mental disturbance. See Falzone v. Busch, 45 N.J. 559, 214 A.2d 12 (1965) (pedestrian almost struck by automobile).

4. When plaintiff's alleged emotional suffering stems from other causes, the cases are more difficult to decide. Thus:

A. Defendant sold plaintiff a water softener that caused a rusty discoloration of the water in plaintiff's home. Plaintiff noticed the discoloration after she drank a cup of coffee made from this water and claimed she suffered a heart attack as a result of her shock. The court denied her claim. See Caputzal v. Lindsay Co., 48 N.J. 69, 222 A.2d 513 (1966). Is the denial of a claim best placed on the ground of proximate cause or duty? In the most famous and foundational case of English and Commonwealth tort law, Donoghue v. Stevenson, [1932] A.C. 562, the House of Lords decided that the relationship of the manufacturer of ginger beer and eventual consumer gave rise to a duty of care. Mrs. Stevenson claimed she had suffered severe shock as a result of witnessing the decomposed remains of a snail emerge from a bottle of ginger beer made by Donoghue, some of which she had already drunk.

B. Mrs. Donoghue's American "cousin," Ms. Ellington, was more imaginative. She thought that the Coca-Cola she was drinking contained a worm. It was in fact a piece of Good-N-Plenty candy that did not touch her lips. Should she be able to recover for her emotional distress? See Ellington v. Coca-Cola Bottling Co., 717 P.2d 109 (Okl.1986) (finding that plaintiff could recover for proven physical injury induced by mental anguish or mental anguish induced by physical injury). In another Coca-Cola case, plaintiffs, after drinking the contents, believed they saw a condom lurking in the bottle. They undertook HIV tests and suffered emotional distress. The "condom" was actually mold. Coca-Cola Bottling Co. v. Hagan, 813 So.2d 167 (Fla.App. 2002) (recognizing that the impact rule did not bar recovery for mental anguish unaccompanied by physical injury against a defendant responsible for providing a plaintiff with food or beverage containing a foreign substance, the plaintiffs failed to establish a reasonable fear of contracting AIDS to permit recovery). Is it appropriate to insist on a standard of normality? How would this comport with the thin skull cases?

5. Should fear of becoming ill or dying at a later date be compensable? The question often arises in litigation over toxic torts and latent diseases. What criteria should be applied? Is the impact rule really at issue here? For example:

A. *Asbestos.* A person incurs asbestosis (scarring of the lung) resulting from asbestos exposure. In addition to recovering for this injury, should he also be able to recover damages for fear of contracting lung cancer? See Jackson v. John-Manville Sales Corp. 781 F.2d 394 (5th Cir. 1986), cert. denied. 478 U.S. 1022 (1986). Suppose there has been asbestos exposure, but no illness has yet occurred? The Supreme Court, in Norfolk v.

Ayers, 538 U.S. 135 (2003), required that the fear of contracting cancer must be genuine and severe.

B. *HIV/AIDS*. Courts have split regarding whether actual exposure is necessary to permit recovery for fear of contracting HIV/AIDS. See Majca v. Beekil, 183 Ill.2d 407, 233 Ill.Dec 810, 701 N.E.2d 1084 (1998) (denying damages for fear of contracting HIV from cut from scalpel left in waste basket and requiring actual exposure to HIV). But cf. Williamson v. Waldman, 150 N.J. 232, 696 A.2d 14 (1997), rejecting the actual exposure test for a reasonableness standard of the emotional distress measured by "a level of knowledge of the disease that is then-current, accurate, and generally available to the public." But compare, Hedgepeth v. Whitman Walker Clinic, 22 A.3d 789 (DC 2011), where District of Columbia Court of Appeals, sitting *en banc,* held that a plaintiff who was told he was HIV positive when he in fact was not, and suffered depression during the five years he dealt with the misdiagnosis, had a cause of action for the negligent infliction of emotional distress against the doctor and clinic. The court expanded the "zone of physical danger" concept generally applied to tort actions: . . . the zone of physical danger requirement imposes an unnecessary limitation upon, and is not to be applied indiscriminately in all cases to, claims of emotional distress brought against a defendant who has a relationship with the plaintiff, or has undertaken an obligation to the plaintiff, and whose negligence causes serious emotional distress to the plaintiff. A duty to avoid negligent infliction of serious emotional distress will be recognized where the defendant has an obligation to care for the plaintiff's emotional well-being or the plaintiff's emotional well-being is necessarily implicated by the nature of the defendant's undertaking to or relationship with the plaintiff, and serious emotional distress is especially likely to be caused by the defendant's negligence.

C. *Cancer from Other Toxic Exposure*. A seaman was soaked in toxic chemicals, causing physical injury. Should he be compensated for emotional distress for fear of developing cancer? See Hagerty v. L&L Marine Services, Inc. 788 F.2d 315 (5th Cir. 1986) (finding that fear of contracting cancer later in life was a present state of mental anguish and recoverable). Toxic tort cases introduce a plethora of problems—numerosity, wide distribution of claims, long latency periods, indeterminate proof of harm and multiple sources of responsibility. The majority of courts have denied recovery. But see discussion § 47, comment k Restatement Third (2012) (collecting cases)

6. How should a court determine what is or is not a "physical injury"? Should it be left to the jury to decide the question on the basis of conflicting expert testimony? Is there any viable alternative to the "physical injury threshold"? Consider the statement of Judge McEntee in Petition of the United States, 418 F.2d 264 (1st Cir.1969): "The term 'physical' is not used in its ordinary sense for purposes of applying the 'physical consequences' rule. Rather, the word is used to indicate that the condition or illness for which recovery is sought must be one susceptible of objective determination. Hence, a definite nervous disorder is a 'physical injury' sufficient to support an action for damages for negligence." In Johnson v. Ruark Obstetrics & Gynecology Assoc., 327 N.C. 283, 303–4, 395 S.E.2d 85, 97 (1990), the court held that recovery depended upon proof of "severe emotional distress" which meant "any emotional or mental disorder, such as, for example, neurosis, psychosis, chronic depression,

phobia, or any other type of severe and disabling emotional or mental condition which may be generally recognized and diagnosed by professionals trained to do so."

7. Uncertainties of tracing causation from defendant's conduct to plaintiff's injuries have formed a basic rationale for adhering to the impact rule. The Supreme Court of Virginia has sponsored a procedural safeguard on this issue: plaintiff must prove causation in fact by "clear and convincing" evidence. Womack v. Eldridge, 215 Va. 338, 210 S.E.2d 145 (1974). Yet the courts have often pointed to medical scientific knowledge as a reason for extending liability, e.g.:

> There is * * * nothing unusual or peculiar in the recognition by the law that compensable injury may be caused just as much by a direct assault upon the mind or the nervous system as by direct physical contact with the body. This is no more than the natural and inevitable result of the growing appreciation by modern medical science of recognizable causal connections between shock to the nervous system and physical or psychiatric illness.

Alcock v. Chief Constable of the South Yorkshire Police, [1992] 1 A.C. 310, at 406–407 (House of Lords) per Lord Oliver. In Flax v. DaimlerChrysler Corp., 272 S.W.3d 521 (Tenn. 2008), the court insisted that to establish his claim, plaintiff was required to "present expert medical or scientific evidence that he had suffered a severe emotional injury," id., 528.

8. Most states retain the physical manifestation requirement, but two exceptions are well recognized. The death-telegram rule (recovery for emotional harm resulting from negligent transmission by a telegraph company of a message announcing death) is a minority rule but followed by a number of the states. See Johnson v. State, 37 N.Y.2d 378, 334 N.E.2d 590, 372 N.Y.S.2d 638 (1975); Mentzer v. Western Union Tel. Co., 93 Iowa 752, 62 N.W. 1 (1895); Western Union Tel. Co. v. Redding, 100 Fla. 495, 129 So. 743 (1930); Camper v. Minor, 915 S.W.2d 437, 443 (Tenn.1996) (recognizing the exception); Oswald v. LeGrand, 453 N.W.2d 634, 639 (Iowa 1990) (recognizing the exception). The Federal rule allows recovery if physical harm results. Kaufman v. Western Union Tel. Co., 224 F.2d 723 (5th Cir.1955), cert. denied, 350 U.S. 947 (1956).

The second exception involves negligent interference with dead bodies. See Lott v. State, 32 Misc.2d 296, 225 N.Y.S.2d 434 (1962); Christensen v. Superior Court, 230 Cal.App.3d 798, 271 Cal.Rptr. 360 (1990), superseded, 54 Cal.3d 868, 820 P.2d 181, 2 Cal.Rptr.2d 79 (1991) (defendant mortuaries and crematoriums mishandling of about 16,000 decedents); Dufour v. Westlawn Cemeteries, Inc., 639 So.2d 843 (La.Ct.App. 1994); Contreraz v. Michelotti-Sawyers, 271 Mont. 300, 896 P.2d 1118 (1995); but see Gonzalez v. Metropolitan Dade County Public Health Trust, 651 So.2d 673, 675 (Fla.1995) (recognizing the difficulty of distinguishing between normal grief and emotional distress from mishandling of a dead body, court affirmed Florida law requiring plaintiff prove physical injury or wanton and willful conduct by the defendant to maintain an action for mental anguish based upon mishandling of a dead body). Corso v. Crawford Dog and Cat Hosp., 97 Misc.2d 530, 415 N.Y.S.2d 182 (1979) (substitution in casket of cat for beloved pet dog).

Thing v. La Chusa

Supreme Court of California, In Bank 1989.
48 Cal.3d 644, 771 P.2d 814, 257 Cal.Rptr. 865.

EAGLESON, JUSTICE.

The narrow issue presented by the parties in this case is whether the Court of Appeal correctly held that a mother who did not witness an accident in which an automobile struck and injured her child may recover damages from the negligent driver for the emotional distress she suffered when she arrived at the accident scene. The more important question this issue poses for the court, however, is whether the "guidelines" enunciated by this court in Dillon v. Legg (1968) 68 Cal.2d 728, 69 Cal.Rptr. 72, 441 P.2d 912, are adequate, or if they should be refined to create greater certainty in this area of the law.

[In *Dillon*, the court had enunciated a test based upon whether defendant should have reasonably foreseen the injury to plaintiff, the victim's mother, who had suffered emotional distress. This foreseeability test of duty demanded courts "take in account such factors as the following: (1) Whether plaintiff was located near the scene of the accident as contrasted with one who was a distance away from it. (2) Whether the shock resulted from a direct emotional impact upon plaintiff from the sensory and contemporaneous observance of the accident, as contrasted with learning of the accident from others after its occurrence. (3) Whether plaintiff and the victim were closely related, as contrasted with an absence of any relationship or the presence of only a distant relationship."]

* * *

On December 8, 1980, John Thing, a minor, was injured when struck by an automobile operated by defendant James V. La Chusa. His mother, plaintiff Maria Thing, was nearby, but neither saw nor heard the accident. She became aware of the injury to her son when told by a daughter that John had been struck by a car. She rushed to the scene where she saw her bloody and unconscious child, whom she believed was dead, lying in the roadway. Maria sued defendants, alleging that she suffered great emotional disturbance, shock, and injury to her nervous system as a result of these events, and that the injury to John and emotional distress she suffered were proximately caused by defendants' negligence.

The trial court granted defendants' motion for summary judgment, ruling that, as a matter of law, Maria could not establish a claim for negligent infliction of emotional distress because she did not contemporaneously and sensorily perceive the accident.

* * *

[N]egligence cases permitting recovery of damages for emotional distress had developed in California at the time *Siliznoff* [supra Chapter II], [C], was decided. Initially, however, in negligence cases the right to recover for emotional distress had been limited to circumstances in which the victim was himself injured and emotional distress was a "parasitic" item of damages, or if a plaintiff who had been in the "zone of danger" did not suffer injury from impact, but did suffer physical injury as a result of the emotional trauma. [C]

* * *

* * * [I]n Amaya v. Home Ice, Fuel & Supply Co., supra, * * * the court had declined the opportunity to broaden the right to recover for emotional distress.

* * * [A]fter confirming that the "impact rule" making a contemporaneous physical impact a prerequisite to recovery for negligently induced fright or shock was not applicable in California, [the court] held damages could not be recovered by persons outside the zone of danger created by the defendant's negligence even when that shock was reflected in physiological symptoms.

* * *

The *Amaya* view was short lived, however. Only five years later, the decision was overruled in *Dillon v. Legg,* supra.

In *Dillon* * * *, the issue was limited. The mother and sister of a deceased infant each sought damages for "great emotional disturbance and shock and injury to her nervous system" which had caused them great mental pain and suffering. Allegedly these injuries were caused by witnessing the defendant's negligently operated vehicle collide with and roll over the infant as she lawfully crossed a street. The mother was not herself endangered by the defendant's conduct. The sister may have been. The trial court had therefore granted the defendant's motion for judgment on the pleadings as to the mother, but had denied it with respect to the sister of the decedent. Faced with the incongruous result demanded by the "zone of danger" rule which denied recovery for emotional distress and consequent physical injury unless the plaintiff himself had been threatened with injury, the court overruled *Amaya.*

* * *

The difficulty in defining the limits on recovery * * * was rejected as a basis for denying recovery, but the court did recognize that "to limit the otherwise potentially infinite liability which would follow every negligent act, the law of torts holds defendant amenable only for injuries to others which to defendant at the time were reasonably foreseeable." [C] * * * Thus, while the court indicated that foreseeability of the injury was to be the primary consideration in finding duty, it simultaneously recognized that policy considerations mandated that infinite liability be avoided by restrictions that would somehow narrow the class of potential plaintiffs. But the test limiting liability was itself amorphous.

In adopting foreseeability of the injury as the basis of a negligent actor's duty, the *Dillon* court identified the risks that could give rise to that duty as both physical impact and emotional disturbance brought on by the conduct. Having done so, the *Dillon* court conceded: "We cannot now predetermine defendant's obligation in every situation by a fixed category; no immutable rule can establish the extent of that obligation for every circumstance of the future." [C] * * *

* * *

The expectation of the *Dillon* majority that the parameters of the tort would be further defined in future cases has not been fulfilled. Instead, subsequent decisions of the Courts of Appeal and this court, have created more uncertainty. And, just as the "zone of danger" limitation was abandoned in *Dillon* as an arbitrary restriction on recovery, the *Dillon* guidelines have been relaxed on grounds that they, too, created arbitrary limitations on recovery. Little consideration has been given in post-*Dillon* decisions to the importance of avoiding the limitless exposure to liability that the pure foreseeability test of "duty" would create and towards which these decisions have moved.

Both the physical harm and accident or sudden occurrence elements were eliminated, however, in Molien v. Kaiser Foundation Hospitals, 27 Cal.3d 916, 167 Cal.Rptr. 831, 616 P.2d 813, at least as to those plaintiffs who could claim to be "direct victims" of the defendant's negligence. The court held in *Molien* that a defendant hospital and doctor owed a duty directly to the husband of a patient who had been diagnosed erroneously as having syphilis, and had been told to so advise the husband in order that he could receive testing and, if necessary, treatment.

In finding the existence of a duty to the husband of the patient, the court reasoned that the risk of harm to the husband was reasonably foreseeable, and that the tortious conduct was directed to him as well as the patient. [C] The status of the plaintiff mother in *Dillon* was distinguished as she suffered her injury solely as a "percipient witness" to the infliction of injury on another. She was therefore a "bystander" rather than a "direct victim." * * * The limitations on recovery for emotional distress that had been suggested in the *Dillon* "guidelines" were not applicable to "direct" victims of a defendant's negligence.

The subtleties in the distinction between the right to recover as a "bystander" and as a "direct victim" created what one Court of Appeal has described as an "amorphous nether realm" [Cc] * * *

"The problem * * * is: how are we to distinguish between 'direct victim' cases and 'bystander' cases? * * * The inference suggested is that a 'direct victim' is a person whose emotional distress is a reasonably foreseeable consequence of the conduct of the defendant. This does not provide criteria which delimit what counts as reasonable foreseeability. It leads into the quagmire of novel claims which the Supreme Court foresaw as an unacceptable consequence of a 'pure' foreseeability analysis * * *." * * * [C]

"[F]oreseeability," the court noted later in Newton v. Kaiser Foundation Hospitals, 184 Cal.App.3d 386, 391, 228 Cal.Rptr. 890, "is endless because foreseeability, like light, travels indefinitely in a vacuum." *Molien,* supra, thus, left to future cases the "unenviable tasks of distinguishing bystander from direct victim cases and establishing limits for the latter * * * with a 'foreseeable' diversity of results."

* * * In order to avoid limitless liability out of all proportion to the degree of a defendant's negligence, and against which it is impossible to insure without imposing unacceptable costs on those among whom the

risk is spread, the right to recover for negligently caused emotional distress must be limited.

We acknowledged and addressed one aspect of this problem in Elden v. Sheldon (1988) 46 Cal.3d 267, 250 Cal.Rptr. 254, 758 P.2d 582, holding that cohabitation, without formal marriage, did not constitute the close relationship contemplated by the *Dillon* guidelines and that foreseeability of injury alone does not justify imposition of liability for negligently caused emotional distress. In so doing, we again recognized that policy considerations justify restrictions on recovery for emotional distress notwithstanding the sometimes arbitrary result, and that the court has an obligation to establish those restrictions. *Elden* confirmed that those policy considerations include both the burden on the courts in applying vaguely defined criteria and the importance of limiting the scope of liability for negligence. If the consequences of a negligent act are not limited an intolerable burden is placed on society. A "bright line in this area of the law is essential." [C] * * *

The issue resolved in *Elden* was too narrow to create that "bright line" * * * This case, however, presents a broader question and thus affords the court a better opportunity to meet its obligation to create a clear rule under which liability may be determined. In so doing we balance the impact of arbitrary lines which deny recovery to some victims whose injury is very real against that of imposing liability out of proportion to culpability for negligent acts. We also weigh in the balance the importance to the administration of justice of clear guidelines under which litigants and trial courts may resolve disputes.

* * *

The impact of personally observing the injury-producing event in most, although concededly not all, cases distinguishes the plaintiff's resultant emotional distress from the emotion felt when one learns of the injury or death of a loved one from another, or observes pain and suffering but not the traumatic cause of the injury. Greater certainty and a more reasonable limit on the exposure to liability for negligent conduct is possible by limiting the right to recover for negligently caused emotional distress to plaintiffs who personally and contemporaneously perceive the injury-producing event and its traumatic consequences.

Similar reasoning justifies limiting recovery to persons closely related by blood or marriage since, in common experience, it is more likely that they will suffer a greater degree of emotional distress than a disinterested witness to negligently caused pain and suffering or death. Such limitations are indisputably arbitrary since it is foreseeable that in some cases unrelated persons have a relationship to the victim or are so affected by the traumatic event that they suffer equivalent emotional distress. As we have observed, however, drawing arbitrary lines is unavoidable if we are to limit liability and establish meaningful rules for application by litigants and lower courts.

No policy supports extension of the right to recover * * * to a larger class of plaintiffs. Emotional distress is an intangible condition experienced by most persons, even absent negligence, at some time during their lives. Close relatives suffer serious, even debilitating, emotional reactions to the injury, death, serious illness, and evident suffering of loved ones. These reactions occur regardless of the cause of the loved one's illness, injury, or death. That relatives will have severe emotional distress is an unavoidable aspect of the "human condition." The emotional distress for which monetary damages may be recovered, however, ought not to be that form of acute emotional distress or the transient emotional reaction to the occasional gruesome or horrible incident to which every person may potentially be exposed in an industrial and sometimes violent society. Regardless of the depth of feeling or the resultant physical or mental illness that results from witnessing violent events, persons unrelated to those injured or killed may not now recover for such emotional upheaval even if negligently caused. Close relatives who witness the accidental injury or death of a loved one and suffer emotional trauma may not recover when the loved one's conduct was the cause of that emotional trauma. The overwhelming majority of "emotional distress" which we endure, therefore, is not compensable.

Unlike an award of damages for intentionally caused emotional distress which is punitive, the award * * * simply reflects society's belief that a negligent actor bears some responsibility for the effect of his conduct on persons other than those who suffer physical injury. In identifying those persons and the circumstances in which the defendant will be held to redress the injury, it is appropriate to restrict recovery to those persons who will suffer an emotional impact beyond the impact that can be anticipated whenever one learns that a relative is injured, or dies, or the emotion felt by a "disinterested" witness. The class of potential plaintiffs should be limited to those who because of their relationship suffer the greatest emotional distress. When the right to recover is limited in this manner, the liability bears a reasonable relationship to the culpability of the negligent defendant.

The elements which justify and simultaneously limit an award of damages for emotional distress caused by awareness of the negligent infliction of injury to a close relative are * * * the traumatic emotional effect on the plaintiff who contemporaneously observes both the event or conduct that causes serious injury to a close relative and the injury itself. Even if it is "foreseeable" that persons other than closely related percipient witnesses may suffer emotional distress, this fact does not justify the imposition of what threatens to become unlimited liability for emotional distress on a defendant whose conduct is simply negligent. Nor does such abstract "foreseeability" warrant continued reliance on the assumption that the limits of liability will become any clearer if lower courts are permitted to continue approaching the issue on a "case-to-case" basis some 20 years after *Dillon*.

We conclude, therefore, that a plaintiff may recover damages for emotional distress caused by observing the negligently inflicted injury of a third person if, but only if, said plaintiff: (1) is closely related to the injury victim; (2) is present at the scene of the injury-producing event at the time it occurs and is then aware that it is causing injury to the victim; and (3) as a result suffers serious emotional distress—a reaction beyond that which would be anticipated in a disinterested witness and which is not an abnormal response to the circumstances. * * *

Experience has shown that, contrary to the expectation of the *Dillon* majority, * * * there are clear judicial days on which a court can foresee forever and thus determine liability but none on which that foresight alone provides a socially and judicially acceptable limit on recovery of damages for that injury.

The undisputed facts establish that plaintiff was not present at the scene of the accident in which her son was injured. She did not observe defendant's conduct and was not aware that her son was being injured. She could not, therefore, establish a right to recover for the emotional distress she suffered when she subsequently learned of the accident and observed its consequences. The order granting summary judgment was proper.

The judgment of the Court of Appeal is reversed.

Each party shall bear its own costs on appeal.

LUCAS, C.J., and PANELLI and ARGUELLES, JJ., concur. JUSTICE KAUFMAN concurred but disagreed with the reasoning of the majority and dissent, finding that *Dillon* ought to be overruled and liability be confined to those in the zone of danger put in fear of their *own* safety. JUSTICE BROUSSARD dissented.

NOTES AND QUESTIONS

1. The principal case traces a distinction between direct and bystander victims. The distinction is treated more satisfactorily by Justice Mosk in his dissent. The "direct victim" cases are denoted by a "special relationship" between the plaintiff and defendant. In *Molien*, supra, defendant physician had plaintiff directly in mind when giving advice to his patient, plaintiff's wife. In Marlene F. v. Affiliated Psychiatric Medical Clinic, Inc., 48 Cal.3d 583, 588–592, 257 Cal.Rptr. 98, 770 P.2d 278, 281–293 (1989), the court held that minor patients' mother had a good cause of action against defendant therapist who had allegedly molested the patients. The mother and children were in family therapy. In Carey v. Lovett, 132 N.J. 44, 622 A.2d 1279 (1993), the court found that the unique connection between mother and her baby allows mother a *direct* claim for emotional distress caused by false information that her baby was stillborn when it was born alive. The father's claim, however, was limited by the *indirect* bystander requirements. Similarly, in Burgess v. Superior Court, 2 Cal.4th 1064, 831 P.2d 1197, 9 Cal.Rptr.2d 615 (1992), mother suffered emotional distress because of defendant physician's negligent delivery of child. She was a patient of the defendant and thus regarded as a direct victim. See also Schwarz v. Regents of University of California, 226 Cal.App.3d 149, 276 Cal.Rptr. 470 (1990), rejecting a father's claim for emotional distress as a result of negligent psychiatric treatment of his child; the father was not involved in the treatment. The English House of Lords in W v. Essex County Council, [2002] 2 A.C. 592, allowed to stand a claim against the local social services department when officials placed a boy "G" in plaintiffs' house knowing that the boy had committed acts of sexual abuse in the past. G committed similar acts of sexual abuse against plaintiffs' four young children in consequence of which plaintiffs alleged they had suffered emotional distress. Such direct relationship cases are within § 47 (b) of the Restatement (Third) (2012) that imposes liability

where the negligent conduct "causes serious emotional harm to another occurring in the course of specified categories of activities, undertakings, or relationships in which negligent conduct is especially likely to cause serious emotional harm."

2. A woman in therapy recovers memories of sexual abuse perpetrated upon her by her father when she was a child. The woman accuses her father who, protesting his innocence, suffers emotional distress. Father believes that the memories were induced by the therapy. Does the therapist owe a duty of care to the father? The growing body of case law is contradictory. See Flanders v. Cooper, 706 A.2d 589 (Me.1998) (finding no duty of care because the duty might restrict treatment choices of health care professionals and hence intrude on professional patient relationship); Doe v. McKay, 183 Ill.2d 272, 233 Ill.Dec. 310, 700 N.E.2d 1018 (1998). But see Sawyer v. Midelfort, 227 Wis.2d 124, 595 N.W.2d 423 (1999) (finding a duty of care to those accused of abuse for emotional injuries caused).

3. As the principal case shows, the twists and turns in bystander liability have been manifold. Some courts have adopted the foreseeability test: Ramsey v. Beavers, 931 S.W.2d 527 (Tenn.1996) (foreseeability requiring consideration of relevant factors, position of plaintiff, degree of injury, relationship to injured party, and proof of severe emotional injury); Clohessy v. Bachelor, 237 Conn. 31, 675 A.2d 852 (1996) (adopting a rule of "reasonable foreseeability if bystander satisfies the following conditions: (1) he or she is closely related to the injury victim, such as the parent or the sibling of the victim; (2) emotional injury of the bystander is caused by the contemporaneous sensory perception of the event or conduct that causes the injury or by arriving on the scene soon thereafter and before substantial change has occurred in the victim's condition or location; (3) injury of the victim must be substantial, resulting in his or her death or serious physical injury; and (4) bystander's emotional injury must be serious, beyond that which would be anticipated in a disinterested witness and which is not the result of an abnormal response."); Gabaldon v. Jay-Bi Property Management, Inc., 122 N.M. 393, 925 P.2d 510 (1996) (adopting contemporaneous sensory perception as a requirement; mother called to scene of son's near drowning in wave pool arrived too late to fall within class of persons owed a duty of care); Bowen v. Lumbermens Mutual Casualty Co., 183 Wis.2d 627, 517 N.W.2d 432 (1994) (rejecting the zone of impact rule and adopting a framework that "should be free of artificial, vague and inconsistent rules," and hence articulating a rule that guards against false claims and overdue burdens on actors: factors employed are (1) victim's serious injury or death, (2) close familial relationship, (3) direct perception of accident or coming immediately upon its aftermath).

Others have criticized the *Dillon* foreseeability test as too broad in imposing sweeping liability. Tobin v. Grossman, 24 N.Y.2d 609, 249 N.E.2d 419, 301 N.Y.S.2d 554 (1969). In New York the zone of damages test was adopted in and Bovsun v. Sanperi, 61 N.Y.2d 219, 461 N.E.2d 843, 473 N.Y.S.2d 357 (1984). Eschewing the foreseeability test, Minnesota has opted for a zone of danger test, Stadler v. Cross, 295 N.W.2d 552 (Minn. 1980). Responding to Professor Jane Stapleton's severe critique of the state of the law in the area of emotional distress, *In Restraint of Tort*, in THE FRONTIERS OF LIABILITY, Vol. 2 83 (Peter Birks, ed., Oxford: Oxford

University Press, 1994), the Australian High Court in *Tame v. New South Wales; Annetts v. Australian Stations Pty Ltd*, (2002) 191 ALR 449; [2002] HCA 35 (Austl.) attempted a principled restatement of the law grounded in a balancing relational and foreseeability considerations.

4. The limits of *Thing* were tested in In re Air Crash Disaster Near Cerritos, 967 F.2d 1421 (9th Cir.1992), where the plaintiff, having left her house shortly before, returned to find her house ablaze with her husband and two children inside; part of an Aeromexico jetliner had crashed into it. See also Wilks v. Hom, 2 Cal.App.4th 1264, 3 Cal.Rptr.2d 803 (1992) in which the "sensory and contemporaneous observance of the accident" requirement was satisfied when an explosion severely injured the plaintiff's daughter and blew the plaintiff out of the house. She did not see her daughter being injured but was contemporaneously aware of that fact.

5. What of rescuers who tend to the wounded at the scene of an air crash disaster? In White v. Chief Constable of the South Yorkshire Police, [1999] 2 A.C. 455, the House of Lords disallowed claims by the police who were involved in the aftermath of the tragedy in attempting to resuscitate victims and carrying the dead and injured. Some courts draw within the fold of liability those relatives who come in the "aftermath" of the accident. Stressing contemporaneity, the observation must be "shortly thereafter," with the scene intact from the accident: Colbert v. Moomba Sports, Inc., 163 Wash.2d 43, 176 P.3d 497 (2008) (watching rescue attempts and body discovered were too remote in law).

5. UNBORN CHILDREN

Endresz v. Friedberg

New York Court of Appeals, 1969.
24 N.Y.2d 478, 248 N.E.2d 901, 301 N.Y.S.2d 65.

FULD, CHIEF JUDGE. * * * The plaintiff, Janice Endresz, seven months pregnant, was injured in an automobile accident in the winter of 1965 and two days later was delivered of stillborn twins, a male and a female. Four actions in negligence were brought against the persons assertedly responsible for the accident. In the first two actions—one for the wrongful death of each child—the plaintiff Steve Endresz, Janice's husband, suing as administrator, seeks damages of $100,000 by reason of the distributees' "loss of anticipated * * * care, comfort and support during the minority and majority" of each infant and for "medical, hospital and funeral expenses incurred by reason of the death" of the children. * * *

On motion of the defendants, the court at Special Term * * * dismissed the first two suits for wrongful death. * * *

This court has already decided that a wrongful death action may not be maintained for the death of an unborn child. [Cc] This view is held by a number of other jurisdictions and, although there is authority to the contrary, further study and thought confirm the justice and wisdom of our earlier decisions.

Chief Justice Fuld

Section 5–4.1 of the EPTL (L.1966, ch. 952, eff. Sept. 1, 1967), * * * declares, insofar as pertinent, that "The personal representative * * * of a decedent who is survived by distributees may maintain an action to recover damages for a wrongful act, neglect or default which caused the decedent's death against a person who would have been liable to the decedent by reason of such wrongful conduct if death had not ensued." Before there may be a "decedent", there must, perforce, be birth, a person born alive, and, although the statute, enacted in 1847 (L.1847, ch. 450), is silent on the subject, it is fairly certain that the Legislature did not intend to include an "unborn" foetus within the term "decedent". Indeed, it was not until 1951, more than 100 years later, that this court—overruling a long-standing decision (Drobner v. Peters, 232 N.Y. 220, 133 N.E. 567, 20 A.L.R. 1503 [1921])—decided that "a child viable but *in utero,* if injured by tort, should, when born, be allowed to sue." (Woods v. Lancet, 303 N.Y. 349, 353, 102 N.E.2d 691, 693, 27 A.L.R.2d 1250.) If, before *Woods,* a child so injured had no right of action, still less was such an action intended to lie on behalf of one who, never seeing the light of day, was deprived of life while still in its mother's womb.

Our decision in the *Woods* case (303 N.Y. 349, 102 N.E.2d 691, supra) does not require us, as suggested, to reinterpret the wrongful death statute to provide compensation to the distributees of a stillborn foetus for "pecuniary injuries" resulting from its death apart from those sustained by the mother and father in their own right. The *Woods* decision, as the court recognized in Matter of Logan, 3 N.Y.2d 800, 166 N.Y.S.2d 3, 144 N.E.2d 644, supra, simply brought the common law of this State into accord with the demand of natural justice which requires recognition of the legal right of every human being to begin life unimpaired by physical or mental defects resulting from the negligence of another. The considerations of justice which mandate the recovery of damages by an infant, injured in his mother's womb and born deformed through the wrong of a third party, are absent where the foetus, deprived of life while yet unborn, is never faced with the prospect of impaired mental or physical health.

In the latter case, moreover, proof of pecuniary injury and causation is immeasurably more vague than in suits for prenatal injuries. * * *

Beyond that, since the mother may sue for any injury which she sustained in her own person, including her suffering as a result of the stillbirth, and the father for loss of her services and consortium, an additional award to the "distributees" of the foetus would give its parents an unmerited bounty and would constitute not compensation to the injured but punishment to the wrongdoer. [Cc]

A leading law review article on the subject has clearly pointed up the differences in the two situations (Gordon, The Unborn Plaintiff, 63 Mich.L.Rev. 579, 594–595):

"The hardship of many of the decisions denying relief [in prenatal injury cases] lay in the fact that they required an infant to go through life * * * bearing the seal of another's fault. There is no such justification in the wrongful death situation. * * *

"A fundamental basis of tort law is the provision for compensation of an innocent plaintiff for the loss he has suffered. Tort law is not, as a general rule, premised upon punishing the wrongdoer. It is not submitted that the tortious destroyer of a child in utero should be able to escape completely by killing instead of merely maiming. But it is submitted that to compensate the parents any further than they are entitled by well-settled principles of law and to give them a windfall through the estate of the fetus is blatant punishment."

* * * Even if, as science and theology teach, the child begins a separate "life" from the moment of conception, it is clear that, "except in so far as is necessary to protect the child's own rights" (Matter of Roberts, 158 Misc. 698, 699, 286 N.Y.S. 476, 477), the law has never considered the unborn foetus as having a separate "juridical existence" (Drabbels v. Skelly Oil Co., 155 Neb. 17, 22, 50 N.W.2d 229) or a legal personality or identity "until it sees the light of day." (Matter of Peabody, 5 N.Y.2d 541, 547, 186 N.Y.S.2d 265, 270, 158 N.E.2d 841, 844, 845.) * * *

It is argued that it is arbitrary and illogical to draw the line at birth, with the result that the distributees of an injured foetus which survives birth by a few minutes may have a recovery while those of a stillborn foetus may not. However, such difficulties are always present where a line must be drawn. To make viability rather than birth the test would not remove the difficulty but merely relocate it and increase a hundredfold the problems of causation and damages. Thus, one commentator aptly observed that (Wenger, Developments in the Law of Prenatal Wrongful Death, 69 Dickinson L.Rev. 258, 268), "since any limitation will be arbitrary in nature, a tangible and concrete event would be the most acceptable and workable boundary. Birth, being a definite, observable and significant event, meets this requirement."

In light of all these considerations, then, we do not feel that, on balance and as a matter of public policy, a cause of action for pecuniary loss should accrue to the distributees of a foetus stillborn by reason of the negligence of another; the damages recoverable by the parents in their own right afford ample redress for the wrong done. Decidedly applicable here is the rule that "[l]iability for damages caused by wrong ceases at a point dictated by public policy or common sense." [C] * * *

The order appealed from should be affirmed, without costs.

BURKE, JUDGE (dissenting in part). * * * The illogicalness of the majority's position was aptly demonstrated by the Supreme Court of Wisconsin, in the analogous case of Kwaterski v. State Farm Mut. Auto. Ins. Co., 34 Wis.2d 14, 20, 148 N.W.2d 107, 110, in these terms: "If no right of action is allowed, there is a wrong inflicted for which there is no remedy. Denying a right of action for negligent acts which produce a stillbirth leads to very incongruous results. For example, a doctor or midwife whose negligent acts in delivering a baby produced the baby's death would be legally immune from a lawsuit. However, if they badly injured the child they would be exposed to liability. Such a rule would produce the absurd result that an unborn child who was badly injured by the tortious acts of another, but who was born alive, could recover while an unborn child, who was more severely injured and died as the result of the tortious acts of another, could recover nothing." * * *

In summary, I am of the opinion that it is both illogical and unreasonable to distinguish between injuries wrongfully inflicted upon a viable foetus which result in death just prior to the infant's separation from the mother and those which cause either permanent injuries or death itself, but at some short interval after birth has occurred. I, therefore, dissent from that portion of the majority opinion which affirms the dismissal of the wrongful death actions by the personal representatives of these stillborn foetus.

KEATING, J., concurred.

NOTES AND QUESTIONS

1. The question of whether any duty is owed to unborn children has undergone substantial change in the law and still is not free from controversy. At one time, the answer was a simple one: no claim was allowed. See, e.g., Dietrich v. Inhabitants of Northampton, 138 Mass. 14, 52 Am.Rep. 242 (1884).

2. The reasons for denial of recovery were threefold: First, it was assumed that the fetus had no separate existence from its mother. This hypothesis was later found to be inaccurate as a matter of medical science.

Second, it was thought that the problems of proving causation in fact would be overwhelming. Medical science was of assistance here also, although highly speculative questions about causation still arise. For example, can physical trauma to a mother cause a child to be born with Down's Syndrome? Compare Sinkler v. Kneale, 401 Pa. 267, 164 A.2d 93 (1960) (allowing plaintiff to attempt to prove a case), with Puhl v. Milwaukee Auto. Ins. Co., 8 Wis.2d 343, 99 N.W.2d 163 (1959) (finding that plaintiff had not met her burden of proof after trial).

Third, damages were thought to be too speculative. How could the jury accurately estimate a new born baby's loss of earning power? In spite of the difficulties involved, is it clear that the child has suffered a loss and would often need medical treatment in the future? Is this a sufficient reason to allow a claim?

3. Beginning in 1946 with the case of Bonbrest v. Kotz, 65 F.Supp. 138 (D.D.C.1946), an overwhelming majority of jurisdictions has held that the reasons supporting the denial of a claim were no longer persuasive and has allowed a cause of action for prenatal injuries when they were inflicted on a viable fetus who was subsequently born alive.

4. Suppose plaintiff alleges that defendant's wrongful conduct adversely affected the mother's ability to produce normal children prior to conception? Recovery has been allowed in several cases. See Bergstreser v. Mitchell, 577 F.2d 22 (8th Cir.1978) (negligent performance of caesarean—subsequent child had birth difficulties producing brain damage); Renslow v. Mennonite Hosp., 67 Ill.2d 348, 10 Ill.Dec. 484, 367 N.E.2d 1250 (1977) (wrong Rh-type blood transfusion to a 13-year-old produced injury to her child years later); Lazevnick v. General Hosp., 499 F.Supp. 146 (M.D.Pa.1980) (similar); Walker v. Rinck, 604 N.E.2d 591 (Ind.1992) (similar). The New York Court of Appeals was scathing in its condemnation of *Renslow,* Albala v. City of New York, 54 N.Y.2d 269, 429 N.E.2d 786, 445 N.Y.S.2d 108 (1981).

5. A majority of states uphold a civil claim for the wrongful death of an unborn child. See, e.g., Sprangler v. Bechtel, 958 N.E.2d 458 (Ind. 2011), where parents of a stillborn baby were able to bring a wrongful death action against the hospital and nurses; Volk v. Baldazo, 103 Idaho 570, 651 P.2d 11 (1982); Vaillancourt v. Medical Center Hosp., Inc., 139 Vt. 138, 425 A.2d 92 (1980); but the authorities are not consistently in favor of liability, e.g., Milton v. Cary Medical Center, 538 A.2d 252 (Me.1988); Witty v. American General Capital Dist., Inc., 727 S.W.2d 503 (Tex.1987). In some jurisdictions courts have interpreted "death of a person" in the state wrongful death statute to include only individuals who were born alive. See Bayer v. Suttle, 23 Cal.App.3d 361, 100 Cal. Rptr. 212 (1st Dist. 1972); Stern v. Miller, 348 So.2d 303 (Fla. 1997); and Wartelle v. Women's and Children's Hospital, Inc., 704 So.2d 778 (La. 1997). As the principal case reflects, other courts have gone beyond the matter of legislative intent (was there any?) and weighed policy considerations that support the grant or denial of a claim. Suppose the child dies during the delivery process? Duncan v. Flynn, 342 So.2d 123 (Fla.App.1977) and Shaw v. Jendzejec, 717 A.2d 367 (Me. 1998). Some states have explicitly clarified the issue. See e.g. Tex. Civ. Prac. & Rem. Code § 71.001(4) (providing that "individual," for the purposes of the wrongful death act, includes "an unborn child at every stage of gestation from fertilization until birth") and Tex. Civ. Prac. & Rem. Code § 71.003(c)(4) (providing that the wrongful death statute does not apply to claims "for the death of an individual who is an unborn child that

is brought against . . . a physician or other health care provider licensed in this state, if the death directly or indirectly is caused by, associated with, arises out of, or relates to a lawful medical or health care practice or procedure of the physician or health care provider").

6. As the principal case predicts, if a wrongful death action is available for the death of an unborn fetus, the issue then is posed of whether the action should extend beyond independent viability of the fetus. Thibert v. Milka, 419 Mass. 693, 646 N.E.2d 1025 (1995) (holding that a fetus with a gestational age of sixteen weeks was not viable and thus could not recover under a wrongful death action).

7. In upholding the principal case, the Court of Appeals of New York recently overruled prior authority in holding a physician owed a duty to an expectant mother where the physician's negligence caused a miscarriage or stillbirth; the mother was entitled to damages for emotional distress: Broadnax v. Gonzalez, 2 N.Y.3d 148, 777 N.Y.S.2d 416, 809 N.E.2d 645 (2004). But see Sheppard-Mobley v. King, 4 N.Y.3d 627, 797 N.Y.S.2d 403, 830 N.E.2d 301 (2005) (refusing to extend *Brodnax's* holding to the case of a mother whose infant was born alive albeit with birth defects, court held that the array of actions available were sufficient, not requiring a cause of action to fill a remedial gap).

8. Should a pregnant woman owe a duty of care to take reasonable precautions to protect her fetus from harm? Grodin v. Grodin, 102 Mich.App. 396, 301 N.W.2d 869 (1980) (liability of mother taking an antibiotic while pregnant that discolored the infant's teeth); but cf. Stallman v. Youngquist, 125 Ill.2d 267, 531 N.E.2d 355, 126 Ill.Dec. 60 (1988) (fetus subsequently born alive has no cause of action against mother for unintentional infliction of prenatal injuries (injuries sustained in auto accident)). The split in authority is reflected in Chenault v. Huie, 989 S.W.2d 474 (Tex.App.1999) (holding in an action arising from injuries to child allegedly caused by mother's drug and alcohol use during pregnancy; Texas law recognizes no general legal duty owed by a mother to her fetus). But cf. Bonte v. Bonte, 136 N.H. 286, 616 A.2d 464 (1992) ("recognizing a child born alive has a cause of action against his or her mother for negligent conduct that results in prenatal injury"). See Finley, A Breach in the Silence: Including Women's Issues in a Torts Course, 1 Yale J.L. & Feminism 41 (1989).

9. *A,* a broker for surrogate mother contracts, engages *B* to have a baby for *C*. *B* is artificially inseminated with *C*'s semen. *C*'s semen carries a disease that causes birth defects to (a) the offspring or (b) *B*'s child by her husband. Does *A* owe a duty to reasonably protect *C*? *B*? And the offspring? See Stiver v. Parker, 975 F.2d 261 (6th Cir.1992), finding an affirmative duty to *C* and *B* by dint of the "special relationship" between the brokers and the parties to the arrangement (supra); the court emphasized the commercial aspects of the arrangement in finding the duty. The duty to the "offspring" was not discussed; should a duty to the surrogate offspring be imposed?

Procanik by Procanik v. Cillo

Supreme Court of New Jersey, 1984.
97 N.J. 339, 478 A.2d 755.

POLLOCK, J. The primary issue on this appeal is the propriety of a grant of a partial summary judgment dismissing a "wrongful life" claim brought by an infant plaintiff through his mother and guardian *ad litem.* That judgment, which was granted on the pleadings, dismissed the claim because it failed to state a cause of action upon which relief may be granted. [C]

The infant plaintiff, Peter Procanik, alleges that the defendant doctors * * * negligently failed to diagnose that his mother, Rosemary Procanik, had contracted German measles in the first trimester of her pregnancy. As a result, Peter was born with congenital rubella syndrome. Alleging that the doctors negligently deprived his parents of the choice of terminating the pregnancy, he seeks general damages for his pain and suffering and for "his parents' impaired capacity to cope with his problems." He also seeks special damages attributable to the extraordinary expenses he will incur for medical, nursing, and other health care. The Law Division granted defendants' motion to dismiss, and the Appellate Division affirmed. * * *

Justices Daniel J. O'Hern, Alan B. Handler, Robert L. Clifford, Robert Wilentz, Sidney M. Schreiber, Stewart G. Pollock and Marie L. Garibaldi.

We granted certification, 95 N.J. 176, 470 A.2d 403 (1983). We now conclude that an infant plaintiff may recover as special damages the extraordinary medical expenses attributable to his affliction, but that he may not recover general damages for emotional distress or for an impaired childhood. * * * Accepting as true the plaintiff's allegations, [c] the complaint discloses the following facts. * * *

On June 9, 1977, during the first trimester of her pregnancy with Peter, Mrs. Procanik consulted the defendant doctors and informed Dr. Cillo "that she had recently been diagnosed as having measles but did not know if it was German measles." Dr. Cillo examined Mrs. Procanik and ordered "tests for German Measles, known as Rubella Titer Test." The results "were 'indicative of past infection of Rubella.'" Instead of ordering further tests, Dr. Cillo negligently interpreted the results and told Mrs. Procanik that she "had nothing to worry about because she had become immune to German Measles as a child." In fact, the "past infection" disclosed by the tests was the German measles that had prompted Mrs. Procanik to consult the defendant doctors.

Ignorant of what an accurate diagnosis would have disclosed, Mrs. Procanik allowed her pregnancy to continue, and Peter was born on December 26, 1977. Shortly thereafter, on January 16, 1978, he was diagnosed as suffering from congenital rubella syndrome. As a result of the doctors' negligence, Mr. and Mrs. Procanik were deprived of the choice of terminating the pregnancy, and Peter was "born with multiple birth defects," including eye lesions, heart disease, and auditory defects. The infant plaintiff states further that "he has suffered because of his parents' impaired capacity to cope with his problems," and seeks damages for his pain and suffering and for his "impaired childhood."

In April 1983, while this matter was pending in the Appellate Division, Peter moved to amend the first count to assert a claim to recover, as special damages, the expenses he will incur as an adult for medical, nursing, and related health care services. In its opinion, the Appellate Division denied without prejudice leave to amend. * * *

In this case we survey again the changing landscape of family torts. See Schroeder v. Perkel, 87 N.J. 53, 71, 432 A.2d 834 (1981). Originally that landscape presented a bleak prospect both to children born with birth defects and to their parents. If a doctor negligently diagnosed or treated a pregnant woman who was suffering from a condition that might cause her to give birth to a defective child, neither the parents nor the child could maintain a cause of action against the negligent doctor. *Gleitman v. Cosgrove,* 49 N.J. 22, 227 A.2d 689 (1967).

Like the present case, *Gleitman* involved a doctor who negligently treated a pregnant woman who had contracted German measles in the first trimester of her pregnancy. Reasoning from the premise that the doctor did not cause the infant plaintiff's birth defects, the *Gleitman* Court found it impossible to compare the infant's condition if the defendant doctor had not been negligent with the infant's impaired condition as a result of the negligence. Measurement of "the value of life with impairments against the nonexistence of life itself" was, the Court declared, a logical impossibility. [C] Consequently, the Court rejected the infant's claim.

The Court denied the parents' claim for emotional distress and the costs of caring for the infant, because of the impossibility of weighing the intangible benefits of parenthood against the emotional and monetary injuries sustained by them. Prevailing policy considerations, which included a reluctance to acknowledge the availability of abortions and the mother's right to choose to terminate her pregnancy, prevented the Court from awarding damages to a woman for not having an abortion. Another consideration was the Court's belief that "[i]t is basic to the human condition to seek life and hold on to it however heavily burdened." [C]

In the seventeen years that have elapsed since the *Gleitman* decision, both this Court and the United States Supreme Court have reappraised, albeit in different contexts, the rights of pregnant women and their children. The United States Supreme Court has recognized that women have a constitutional right to choose to terminate a pregnancy. Roe v. Wade, 410 U.S. 113 (1973). Recognition of that right by the high court subsequently influenced this Court in Berman v. Allan, 80 N.J. 421, 404 A.2d 8 [1979].

In *Berman,* the parents sought to recover for their emotional distress and for the expenses of raising a child born with Down's Syndrome. Relying on *Roe v. Wade,* the Court found that public policy now supports the right of a woman to choose to terminate a pregnancy. [C] That finding eliminated one of the supports for the *Gleitman* decision—i.e., that public policy prohibited an award for depriving a woman of the right to choose whether to have an abortion. Finding that a trier of fact could place a dollar value on the parents' emotional suffering, the *Berman* Court concluded "that the monetary equivalent of this distress is an appropriate measure of the harm suffered by the parents." [C]

Nonetheless, the Court rejected the parents' claim for "medical and other expenses that will be incurred in order to properly raise, educate and supervise the child." [C] The Court reasoned that the parents wanted to retain "all the benefits inhering in the birth of the child—i.e., the love and joy they will experience as parents—while saddling defendants with enormous expenses attendant upon her rearing." Id. Such an award would be disproportionate to the negligence of the defendants and constitute a windfall to the parents. Id.

The *Berman* Court also declined to recognize a cause of action in an infant born with birth defects. Writing for the Court, Justice Pashman reasoned that even a life with serious defects is more valuable than non-existence, the alternative for the infant plaintiff if his mother chose to have an abortion. [C]

More recently we advanced the parents' right to compensation by permitting recovery of the extraordinary expenses of raising a child born with cystic fibrosis, including medical, hospital, and pharmaceutical expenses. Schroeder v. Perkel, 87 N.J. at 68–69, 432 A.2d 834. No claim on behalf of the infant was raised in that case, [c] and we elected to defer consideration of such a claim until another day. [C] That day is now upon us, and we must reconsider the right of an infant in a "wrongful life" claim to recover general damages for diminished childhood and pain and suffering, as well as special damages for medical care and the like.

The terms "wrongful birth" and "wrongful life" are but shorthand phrases that describe the causes of action of parents and children when negligent medical treatment deprives parents of the option to terminate a pregnancy to avoid the birth of a defective child. See Schroeder v. Perkel, supra, 87 N.J. at 75–76, 432 A.2d 834 (Handler, J., concurring and dissenting). In the present context, "wrongful life" refers to a cause of action brought by or on behalf of a defective child who claims that but for the defendant doctor's negligent advice to or treatment of its parents, the child would not have been born. "Wrongful birth" applies to the cause of action of parents who claim that the negligent advice or treatment deprived them of the choice of avoiding conception or, as here, of terminating the pregnancy. [Cc]

Both causes of action are distinguishable from the situation where negligent injury to a fetus causes an otherwise normal child to be born in an impaired condition. [Cc] In the present case, the plaintiffs do not allege that the negligence of the defendant doctors caused the congenital rubella syndrome from which the infant plaintiff suffers. Neither do plaintiffs claim that the infant ever had a chance to be a normal child. The essence of the infant's claim is that the defendant doctors wrongfully deprived his mother of information that would have prevented his birth.

Analysis of the infant's cause of action begins with the determination whether the defendant doctors owed a duty to him. The defendant doctors do not deny they owed a duty to the infant plaintiff, and we find such a duty exists. [Cc] In evaluating the infant's cause of action, we assume, furthermore, that the defendant doctors were negligent in treating the mother. Moreover, we assume that their negligence deprived the parents of the choice of terminating the pregnancy and of preventing the birth of the infant plaintiff.

Notwithstanding recognition of the existence of a duty and its breach, policy considerations have led this Court in the past to decline to recognize any cause of action in an infant for his wrongful life. The threshold problem has been the assertion by infant plaintiffs not that they should not have been born without defects, but that they should not have been born at all. [*Gleitman*] The essence of the infant's cause of action is that its very life is wrongful. [*Berman*] Resting on the belief that life, no matter how burdened, is preferable to non-existence, the *Berman* Court stated that the infant "has not suffered any damage cognizable at law by being brought into existence." [C] Although the premise for this part of the *Berman* decision was the absence of cognizable damages, the Court continued to be troubled, as it was in *Gleitman,* by the problem of ascertaining the measure of damages. [C]

The courts of other jurisdictions have also struggled with the issues of injury and damages when faced with suits for wrongful life. Although two intermediate appellate courts in New York and California recognized an infant's claim for general damages, those decisions were rejected by the courts of last resort in both jurisdictions. * * *

Other courts have uniformly found that the problems posed by the damage issues in wrongful life claims are insurmountable and have refused to allow the action on behalf of the infant. [Cc]

Even when this Court declined to recognize a cause of action for wrongful life in *Gleitman* and *Berman,* dissenting members urged recognition of that claim. * * *

Recently we recognized that extraordinary medical expenses incurred by parents on behalf of a birth-defective child were predictable, certain, and recoverable. [*Schroeder*] * * *

When a child requires extraordinary medical care, the financial impact is felt not just by the parents, but also by the injured child. As a practical matter, the impact may extend beyond the injured child to his brothers or sisters. Money that is spent for the health care of one child is not available for the clothes, food, or college education of another child.

Recovery of the cost of extraordinary medical expenses by either the parents or the infant, but not both, is consistent with the principle that the doctor's negligence vitally affects the entire family. * * *

Law is more than an exercise in logic, and logical analysis, although essential to a system of ordered justice, should not become a instrument of injustice. Whatever logic inheres in permitting parents to recover for the cost of extraordinary medical care incurred by a birth-defective child, but in denying the child's own right to recover those expenses, must yield to the injustice of that result. The right to recover the often crushing burden of extraordinary expenses visited by an act of medical malpractice should not depend on the "wholly fortuitous circumstance of whether the parents are available to sue." [Cc]

The present case proves the point. Here, the parents' claim is barred by the statute of limitations. Does this mean that Peter must forego medical treatment for his blindness, deafness, and retardation? We think not. His claim for the medical expenses attributable to his birth defects is reasonably certain, readily calculable, and of a kind daily determined by judges and juries. We hold that a child or his parents may recover special damages for extraordinary medical expenses incurred during infancy, and that the infant may recover those expenses during his majority. * * *

In restricting the infant's claim to one for special damages, we recognize that our colleagues, Justice Schreiber and Justice Handler, disagree with us and with each other. From the premise that "man does not know whether non-life would have been preferable to an impaired life," [c] Justice Schreiber concludes that a child does not have a cause of action for wrongful life and, therefore, that "it is unfair and unjust to charge the doctors with the infant's medical expenses." [C] Justice Handler reaches a diametrically opposite conclusion. He would allow the infant to recover not only his medical expenses, but also general damages for his pain and suffering and for his impaired childhood.

We find, however, that the infant's claim for pain and suffering and for a diminished childhood presents insurmountable problems. The philosophical problem of finding that such a defective life is worth less than no life at all has perplexed not only Justice Schreiber, but such other distinguished members of this Court as Chief Justice Weintraub, [c] Justice Proctor, [c] and Justice Pashman, [c]. We need not become preoccupied, however, with these metaphysical considerations. Our decision to allow the recovery of extraordinary medical expenses is not premised on the concept that non-life is preferable to an impaired life, but is predicated on the needs of the living. We seek only to respond to the call of the living for help in bearing the burden of their affliction.

Sound reasons exist not to recognize a claim for general damages. Our analysis begins with the unfortunate fact that the infant plaintiff never had a chance of being born as a normal, healthy child. Tragically, his only choice was a life burdened with his handicaps or no life at all. The congenital rubella syndrome that plagues him was not caused by the negligence of the defendant doctors; the only proximate result of their negligence was the child's birth.

The crux of the problem is that there is no rational way to measure non-existence or to compare non-existence with the pain and suffering of his impaired existence. Whatever theoretical appeal one might find in recognizing a claim for pain and suffering is outweighed by the essentially irrational and unpredictable nature of that claim. Although damages in a personal injury action need not be calculated with mathematical precision, they require at their base some modicum of rationality.

Underlying our conclusion is an evaluation of the capability of the judicial system, often proceeding in these cases through trial by jury, to appraise such a claim. Also at work is an appraisal of the role of tort law in compensating injured parties, involving as that role does, not only reason, but also fairness, predictability, and even deterrence of future wrongful acts. In brief, the ultimate decision is a policy choice summoning the most sensitive and careful judgment.

From that perspective it is simply too speculative to permit an infant plaintiff to recover for emotional distress attendant on birth defects when that plaintiff claims he would be better off if he had not been born. Such a claim would stir the passions of jurors about the nature and value of life, the fear of non-existence, and about abortion. That mix is more than the judicial system can digest. We believe that the interests of fairness and justice are better served through more predictably measured damages—the cost of the extraordinary medical expenses necessitated by the infant plaintiff's handicaps. Damages so measured are not subject to the same wild swings as a claim for pain and suffering and will carry a sufficient sting to deter future acts of medical malpractice.

As speculative and uncertain as is a comparison of the value of an impaired life with non-existence, even more problematic is the evaluation of a claim for diminished childhood. The essential proof in such a claim is that the doctor's negligence deprives the parents of the knowledge of the condition of the fetus. The deprivation of that information precludes the choice of terminating the pregnancy by abortion and leaves the parents unprepared for the birth of a defective child, a birth that causes them emotional harm. The argument proceeds that the parents are less able to love and care for the child, who thereby suffers an impaired childhood. [Cc]

Several considerations lead us to decline to recognize a cause of action for impaired childhood. At the outset, we note the flaw in such a claim in those instances in which the parents assert not that the information would have prepared them for the birth of the defective child, but that they would have used the information to prevent that birth. Furthermore, even its advocates recognize that a claim for "the kind of injury suffered by the child in this context may not be readily divisible from that suffered by her wronged parents." Berman v. Allan, supra, 80 N.J. at 445, 404 A.2d 8 (Handler, J., concurring and dissenting). We believe the award of the cost of the extraordinary medical care to the child or the parents, when combined with the right of the parents to assert a claim for their own emotional distress, comes closer to filling the dual objectives of a tort system: the compensation of injured parties and the deterrence of future wrongful conduct. * * *

The judgment of the Appellate Division is affirmed in part, reversed in part, and the matter is remanded to the Law Division. The infant plaintiff shall have leave to file an amended complaint asserting a claim for extraordinary medical, hospital, and other health care expenses.

[The gist of the separate partially dissenting opinions of HANDLER and SCHREIBER, JJ., is described in the majority opinion.]

NOTES AND QUESTIONS

1. In Smith v. Cote, 128 N.H. 231, 513 A.2d 341 (1986), the court dealt with a factually similar case: the defendants, obstetricians and gynecologists, had not tested their patient for rubella early in the pregnancy when she had an untrammelled right to an abortion. The child was born with congenital rubella syndrome. In a thorough analysis, Justice Batchelder found that suits of this kind, by parents and children, had been spawned by scientific advances in detection of abnormalities in fetus and in the pregnancy risk factors and the Supreme Court's decision in Roe v. Wade, 410 U.S. 113 (1973). (The Supreme Court in Planned Parenthood of Southeastern Pennsylvania v. Casey, 505 U.S. 833 (1992), refused to overrule Roe v. Wade, supra, but substituted that decision's trimester division with the more flexible criterion that the state may regulate provided a woman's right to choose an abortion is not unduly burdened.) Taking the actions separately, he supported the wrongful birth action—the parents' action—as comporting with accepted tort doctrine. The difficulty of measuring damages could not undermine the action. As to damages, the court found, they should be limited to extraordinary costs even beyond the age of majority. This figure could include extraordinary maternal care, susceptible to valuation, made necessary by the child's condition. Also recoverable were the parent's pecuniary losses resulting from the emotional distress, in seeking medical help or counselling. However, general emotional distress was not compensable.

After an examination of the law supporting the wrongful life action, including the principal case, the court, in *Smith*, nevertheless, was not moved to allow the child a wrongful life action for the following reasons.

A. Distinguishing the right to die cases (see Cruzan by Cruzan v. Director, Missouri Dept. of Health, 497 U.S. 261 (1990)) the issue is "not protection of the impaired child's right to choose nonexistence over life but whether legal injury has occurred as a result of the defendant's conduct

* * * [The court] has no business in declaring that among the living are people who should never have been born." Id., 249.

B. Recognition of the claim would stigmatize the child's life as wrongful, cutting against policies of removing social disabilities.

C. The contingent nature of the loss valuation is beyond the capacity of the courts proceeding by way of predictable rules.

On the last point, the principal case fashioned a pragmatic compromise—special damages for extraordinary expenses. The New Hampshire Court referred to Justice Schreiber's opinion, dissenting in part from the majority's opinion in the principal case:

> The position that a child may recover special damages despite the failure of his underlying theory of wrongful life violates the moral code underlying our system of justice from which the fundamental principles of tort law are derived.

Procanik v. Cillo, 97 N.J. 339, 370, 478 A.2d 755, 772 (1984).

2. An older but related line of cases concerns situations where a woman has conceived or become pregnant due to the tortious action of the defendant. In these cases the child is not necessarily handicapped but the pregnancy was not wanted. Generally, the cause of action is in negligence for: (1) lack of informed consent or (2) negligent performance of a sterilization operation. Burke v. Rivo, 406 Mass. 764, 551 N.E.2d 1 (1990), is an example of the former (failure to advise plaintiff of the risks of recanalization in sterilization operation) and Marciniak v. Lundborg, 153 Wis.2d 59, 450 N.W.2d 243 (1990), an example of the latter (negligence in performance of "laparoscopy with bilateral fallopian tube cautery"). Both cases accepted the legitimacy of the cause of action and addressed the issue of the measure of damages. Damages flowing directly from the operation and pregnancy were readily recoverable: these include cost of the operation and corrective surgery, loss of earnings during pregnancy, medical expenses surrounding pregnancy and hospitalization, and husband's loss of consortium. Pain and suffering and emotional distress are usually recoverable. The difficult issue was whether the costs of rearing the child should be recoverable. Against a strong dissent supported by weighty authority, the majority in *Burke* decided that "the cost of rearing a normal healthy but (at least initially) unwanted child [were recoverable if the parents'] reason for seeking sterilization was founded on economic and financial considerations." The same arguments rejected by the majority in *Burke* were also dismissed in *Marciniak:* the awarding of damages for the costs of child rearing would not psychologically harm the child nor "debase the sanctity of human life." The argument that the plaintiffs had not mitigated their damages by putting the child out to adoption or by aborting met the same fate: it was not reasonable to force this choice on the plaintiffs. On the issue of offsetting the benefits of the child against the detriments the court turned to § 920 Restatement of Torts (Second) (1979), embodying the principle that damages resulting from an invasion of one interest are not diminished by showing another interest has been benefited. Thus emotional benefit could not be set off against financial detriments.

Are you concerned in drawing a distinction on the grounds of motivation for the operation?

3. Few jurisdictions allow actions for wrongful life. The most poignant cases result from a negligent failure to detect the genetic disease Tay-Sachs Syndrome, a devastating disease characterized by severe mental retardation and physical disability limiting life to a few painful years. In Schloss v. Miriam Hospital, No. C.A. 98–2076, 1999 WL 41875 (R.I.Super.1999), the Rhode Island court allowed a wrongful birth action but rejected the wrongful life claim where the child was born with Tay-Sachs after negligent genetic testing. The court found the moral issues beggared their judicial ability, and unlike the few cases in California, Washington, and New Jersey that had recognized the claim, here the wrongful birth action accorded compensation for the injury. In the few that recognize wrongful life, the damages have been curtailed as to include only extraordinary expenses arising from the condition with which the child is afflicted. Harbeson v. Parke-Davis, Inc., 98 Wn. 2d 460, 656 P.2d 483 (1983). No general damages for pain and suffering are awarded. Turpin v. Sortini, 31 Cal.3d 220, 643 P.2d 954, 182 Cal.Rptr. 337 (1982). The California Court of Appeal in Curlender v. Bio-Science Laboratories, 106 Cal.App.3d 811, 165 Cal.Rptr. 477 (1980), allowed pain and suffering damages, where the plaintiff's parents had obtained blood tests from the defendant lab in order to ascertain whether their offspring was likely to suffer from Tay-Sachs disease. The lab was negligent in performing the blood tests. In *Sortini* the court found that general damages were not awardable since no principles were available to discern whether an injury was suffered in being born rather than not, and that the balancing of incommensurable elements in general damages, the joy of life versus the pain of it, made the calculus too speculative. Extraordinary expenses, on the other hand, could have been estimated with some certainty and no setoff of highly subjective elements would be allowable under the § 920 Restatement of Torts (Second) (1979) principle. The majority's reasoning was savaged by Justice Mosk's dissent. Do you consider that the plaintiff ought to be precluded from recovery of pain and suffering in cases of this kind?

4. The grounding of wrongful life and birth actions on the missed opportunity to abort the fetus has proved controversial. North Carolina and Missouri courts have refused to recognize actions thus premised, see Peters, Rethinking Wrongful Life: Bridging the Boundary Between Tort and Family Law, 67 Tul.L.Rev. 397, 415 (1992) (also listing various state legislation proscribing such claims). The Court of Appeals of Michigan in Taylor v. Kurapati, 236 Mich.App. 315, 600 N.W.2d 670 (1999), took the extraordinary step of repudiating its past recognition of the wrongful birth action. It found that it had developed a "misshapen jurisprudence" in its recognition of the action but total rejection of the wrongful life action and its partial rejection of the wrongful conception action. Such a tort, it found, must be expressed through legislative action.

5. What actions may be available if the abortion is performed but was unnecessary or negligently advised? Parent's action, Martinez v. Long Island Jewish Hillside Medical Center, 70 N.Y.2d 697, 512 N.E.2d 538, 518 N.Y.S.2d 955 (1987) (recognition of action for mental anguish and depression resulting from the unnecessary abortion, derived not from what happened to fetus but from breach of duty owed to mother) and Acuna v. Turkish, 192 N.J. 399, 930 A.2d 416 (2007). Fetus's action?

6. Should parents be liable in a wrongful life action? In Zepeda v. Zepeda, 41 Ill.App.2d 240, 190 N.E.2d 849 (1963), a child sued his father for wrongfully begetting him as an illegitimate child by deceiving his mother that he would marry her when in fact he was already married. Recovery denied. What of an institution that fails to protect a vulnerable patient from being raped? Does the child have an action? The answer was "no" in Williams v. State of New York, 18 N.Y.2d 481, 223 N.E.2d 343, 276 N.Y.S.2d 885 (1966) and again "no," after a lower court "yes," in Cowe v. Forum Group, Inc., 541 N.E.2d 962, 964 (Ind.App.1989), aff'd in part and vacated in part, 575 N.E.2d 630 (Ind.1991). In *Curlender,* supra note 3, the court suggested that parents may be liable for a conscious decision to conceive and allow to be born a seriously impaired infant. The California legislature quickly responded by relieving the parents of liability. § 43.6 Civil Code, 1981.

7. In Canesi ex rel. Canesi v. Wilson, 158 N.J. 490, 730 A.2d 805 (1999), the parents of a child born with bilateral limb reduction brought an action against two obstetricians involved with the mother's pregnancy. Plaintiffs alleged that the defendants were negligent in failing to warn them of the risks posed by the drug Provera and to take diagnostic measures to ascertain the presence of the defect. Two possible causes arose, the first in informed consent and the second in wrongful birth. The court held that for the former, plaintiffs must prove that the negligence caused the bilateral limb reduction. For the latter—the wrongful birth action—such proof was unnecessary. The appropriate inquiry was "whether the defendant's negligence was the proximate cause of the parents' loss of the option to make an informed and meaningful decision either to terminate the pregnancy or to give birth to a potentially defective child." Id. at 818. In other words, medical causation is not essential in a wrongful birth action. The majority reasoning is criticized by Pollock, J. dissenting, who finds the "majority's result is unprecedented in any jurisdiction." Id. at 825.

CHAPTER 9

OWNERS AND OCCUPIERS OF LAND

1. OUTSIDE THE PREMISES

Taylor v. Olsen

Supreme Court of Oregon, 1978.
282 Or. 343, 578 P.2d 779.

LINDE, JUSTICE. Plaintiff sued for damages for injuries she sustained when her car, on a dark and windy January evening, struck a tree which shortly before had splintered and fallen across a * * * road. The trial court directed verdicts for * * * Marion Olsen, the adjoining landowner who was alleged to be in possession of the location. Plaintiff appeals from the judgment entered on the directed verdict for Olsen. * * *

We think * * * that, except for extreme situations, the question of the landowner's or possessor's attention to the condition of his roadside trees under a general standard of "reasonable care to prevent an unreasonable risk of harm" is to be decided as a question of fact upon the circumstances of the individual case. The extent of his responsibility either to inspect his trees or only to act on actual knowledge of potential danger cannot be defined simply by categorizing his land as "urban" or "rural." Surely it is not a matter of zoning or of city boundaries but of actual conditions. No doubt a factfinder will expect more attentiveness of the owner of an ornamental tree on a busy sidewalk [cc] than of the United States Forest Service * * *, but the great variety of intermediate patterns of land use, road use, traffic density, and preservation of natural stands of trees in urban and suburban settings prevents a simple "urban-rural" classification.

* * * [T]he onus on a homeowner of inspecting a few trees in his yard is modest, but the "practical difficulty of continuously examining each tree in the untold number of acres of forests" or in "sprawling tracts of woodland adjacent to or through which a road has been built [can be] so potentially onerous as to make property ownership an untenable burden. This would be particularly true for an absentee landowner." [C] It is less obviously true, however, for one who is engaged in logging or in actively developing the land. * * *

In this case, the road in question was a two-lane blacktop highway serving a number of communities * * *. There was testimony that it was used by an average 790 vehicles a day; in other words, a fallen tree might encounter a vehicle within an average of about two minutes, depending on the time of day. Defendant had purchased the land adjoining the road in 1973 for logging purposes, and during the five or six weeks before the accident he had logged about half the timber on his land. This included the trees adjacent to the tree on the county's right-of-way that eventually fell onto the road. Under these circumstances we conclude * * * that it would be a jury question whether defendant had taken reasonable care to inform himself of the condition of this tree, provided there was evidence that an inspection would have disclosed its hazardous condition.

The evidence is that after the tree broke and fell onto the road, the center of the tree at the point of the break proved to be decayed. However, the decay did not extend through the bark, or even to the surface below the bark except perhaps in a few places. Only by chopping or boring into the trunk of the tree would there have been a substantial chance of discovering the decay. Thus the question is not so much whether defendant had some responsibility to give his attention to the safety of this tree left behind by his logging operations as, rather, how far that responsibility extends.

There was no evidence to suggest that chopping or drilling into the trunk would have been a normal or expected way to examine a standing tree in the absence of external indications that it might not be structurally sound. * * *

It requires some evidence either that the defendant should have been on notice of possible decay in this tree, or that cutting through the bark to the trunk is a common and ordinary method of examining trees generally. In the absence of such evidence, it was not error to direct a verdict for the defendant.

Affirmed.

NOTES AND QUESTIONS

1. With regard to most conditions on land that arise in the state of nature, most courts have held that there is no duty upon the landholder to protect persons outside the premises. See Roberts v. Harrison, 101 Ga. 773, 28 S.E. 995 (1897) (foul swamp); Brady v. Warren, [1900] 2 Ir.Rep. 632 (rabbits).

2. An exception has evolved with regard to trees, and there is agreement that the landowner is liable for negligence if he knows, or should have known, that the tree is defective and fails to take reasonable precautions. Turner v. Ridley, 144 A.2d 269 (Mun.App.D.C.1958); Plesko v. Allied Inv. Co., 12 Wis.2d 168, 107 N.W.2d 201 (1961). Foreseeability alone is insufficient to show actual or constructive knowledge when the tree is healthy: Lewis v. Krussel, 101 Wash.App. 178, 2 P.3d 486 (2000).

3. The rule was clear at one time that the owner of land abutting on a rural highway is under no duty to inspect it to discover defects in trees. Chambers v. Whelen, 44 F.2d 340 (4th Cir.1930); O'Brien v. United States, 275 F.2d 696 (9th Cir.1960). The trend, however, is toward factor balancing. Miles v. Estate of Christensen, 724 N.E.2d 643, 646 (Ind. Ct. App. 2000) (calling for "a more sophisticated analysis of the duty question, requiring a consideration of factors such as traffic patterns and land use in the relevant area" and concluding, in accord with the principal case, that "one who owns land, whether it be classified as 'urban' or 'rural,' may owe a duty of reasonable care as to natural land conditions that threaten outsiders.").

4. In Sprecher v. Adamson Cos., 30 Cal.3d 358, 636 P.2d 1121, 178 Cal.Rptr. 783 (1981), the landowner's general immunity for harm outside the premises caused by natural conditions was abolished, and an uphill landowner was found to owe a duty of care to a downhill landowner to control a landslide condition. This decision was followed in Moeller v. Fleming, 136 Cal.App.3d 241, 186 Cal.Rptr. 24 (1982), where a landowner could be sued by a pedestrian who slipped on an irregular break in the sidewalk that was caused by tree roots from the landowner's adjacent property. See also Leakey v. National Trust for Places of Historic Interest or Natural Beauty, [1980] 1 Q.B. 485 (CA) (repudiating the rule distinguishing natural and artificial hazards in finding the National Trust liable for the collapse of the Burrow Mump, a famous conical hill). Compare Restatement (First) of Torts, § 363 (no liability for injuries resulting from natural conditions of the land other than trees growing near a highway), with Restatement (Second) of Torts, § 840(2) (urban landowner liable for failure to exercise reasonable care to prevent an unreasonable risk of harm to persons using the highway; liability of rural landowner left open), and Restatement (Third) of Torts: Physical & Emotional Harm § 54(b) (2012) (rejecting the distinction between rural and urban land; duty only if the land is commercial, the landowner knows of the risk or the risk is obvious).

5. Some states recognize a "self-help" rule, under which a landowner can resort to self-help and cut off tree branches and roots intruding onto his property from adjoining property. See, e.g., Melnick v. C.S.X. Corp., 68 Md.App. 107, 510 A.2d 592 (1986), limiting remedy to "self-help" for incidents of healthy trees, as the most efficient and equitable way to resolve the problem.

Salevan v. Wilmington Park, Inc.

Superior Court of Delaware, 1950.
45 Del. (6 Terry) 290, 72 A.2d 239.

WOLCOTT, JUDGE. The plaintiff brings suit for personal injuries received when struck in the back by a baseball while walking on East Thirtieth Street in the City of Wilmington, past the ball park of the defendant.

The defendant is the owner of land * * * on which is located the ball park in question. The business of the defendant is the maintenance and renting of the ball park and its facilities and has been carried on by the defendant for over eight years. * * *

[I]t appears that in the course of an average ball game, 16 to 18 foul balls come from inside the park into Thirtieth Street and, of them, an average of 2 or 3 foul balls come from within the park over the 10-foot fence and into the area along Thirtieth Street through which the plaintiff was passing at the time of the injury. The manager of the defendant testified that, on an average, 68 baseball games were played at Wilmington Park during the baseball season.

The plaintiff does not contend that the defendant is an insurer of persons lawfully using the highways and sidewalks adjacent to its ball park, but does contend that the defendant, as a landowner, has the duty to exercise reasonable care in the use of its land so as to prevent injury to travelers lawfully using the highways adjacent thereto. The plaintiff contends that the defendant had notice of the passage of baseballs outside of its park into East Thirtieth Street to the danger of persons using that public street, and that the failure of the defendant to take reasonable precautions to safeguard the public was negligence. * * *

It is clear that the public has a right to the free and unmolested use of the public highways, and that abutting landowners may not so use their land as to interfere with the rights of persons lawfully using the highways. * * *

The inherent nature of the game of baseball * * * is such as to require the landowner to take reasonable precautions for the protection of the traveling public. What precautions are reasonable must depend upon the facts and circumstances of the particular case. Only those precautions are required which the inherent nature of the game and its past history in the particular location make necessary for the protection of a person lawfully using the highways. * * *

While the defendant has shown that consideration was given by it to the protection of the public at the time the park was first built, the fact remains that despite the precautions taken, baseballs went out of its park into the public highway and that the defendant either knew that baseballs went out of its park or, under the circumstances, should have known. The evidence is not seriously contradicted that baseballs went out of the park into Thirtieth Street within the area through which the plaintiff was passing at the time of her injury two or three times in each game played in the defendant's park.

Under the circumstances, it seems clear to me that while the defendant took precautions to protect people passing along Thirtieth Street, those precautions were insufficient. It further seems clear that the defendant knew, or should have known, that the precautions taken initially were insufficient to protect the public engaged in its lawful right, that is, using the highways. This circumstance puts the case at bar squarely within the rule I have drawn from the reported decisions, and if this were a jury trial, would be sufficient to submit the case to the jury and would compel, in my opinion, the jury to return a verdict for the plaintiff. Accordingly, my conclusion is that judgment should be entered for the plaintiff.

Judgment being entered for the plaintiff, it remains to determine in what amount that judgment should be. Under the circumstances, I believe the sum of $2500.00 will adequately compensate the plaintiff for the injuries received as a result of the negligence of the defendant.

NOTES AND QUESTIONS

1. Once a landowner alters a condition of his land, it becomes an "artificial" one for the purposes of tort law and the owner must exercise reasonable care for the protection of those outside of the premises. Thus Towaliga Falls Power Co. v. Sims, 6 Ga.App. 749, 65 S.E. 844 (1909) (damming a stream to form a malarial pond); Ettl v. Land & Loan Co., 122 N.J.L. 401, 5 A.2d 689 (1939) (piling sand where the wind may blow it). This obligation will also arise with regard to a condition that may appear, on the surface, to be a natural one. See, e.g., Coates v. Chinn, 51 Cal.2d 304, 332 P.2d 289 (1958) (cultivated trees). But see, Langer v. Goode, 21

N.D. 462, 131 N.W. 258 (1911) (no liability for growth and spread of weeds when cultivation was a contributing cause).

2. The landowner is not liable for the normal flow of surface water, which is regarded as a "natural" condition. Livezey v. Schmidt, 96 Ky. 441, 29 S.W. 25 (1895); Middlesex County v. McCue, 149 Mass. 103, 21 N.E. 230 (1889). On the same principle, it is generally held that an abutting owner is under no duty to remove snow and ice that falls naturally upon the highway. See Albertie v. Louis & Alexander Corp., 646 A.2d 1001 (D.C. 1994). However, if the owner has altered the condition of the premises so that surface water or snow is discharged upon the highway, he may be directly held liable for negligence or nuisance. Compare Tremblay v. Harmony Mills, 171 N.Y. 597, 64 N.E. 501 (1902) (liability when downspout resulted in flow of water and ice to sidewalk), with Holschbach v. Wash. Park Manor, 280 Wis. 2d 264, 694 N.W.2d 492 (Ct. App. 2005) (no liability for artificial downspout pouring water on sidewalk because it operated as intended). The fine-spun distinction between hazards naturally arising and those caused by human agency is "not only inconvenient, but also lacks * * * any logical foundation." Goldman v. Hargrave, [1967] 1 A.C. 645 (Privy Council) (liability for bush fire in the hot Australian summer).

3. Some courts, though, have extended an owner's responsibility for abutting sidewalks. Stewart v. 104 Wallace St., Inc., 87 N.J. 146, 432 A.2d 881 (1981) (commercial owner liable for failing to maintain abutting sidewalks in reasonably good condition), and Cogliati v. Ecco High Frequency Corp., 92 N.J. 402, 456 A.2d 524 (1983) (current owner and predecessor in title liable for poorly maintained public sidewalks).

4. Suppose the plaintiff is injured outside the premises by something subject to the control of the owner of the premises? Compare Blake v. Dunn Farms Inc., 274 Ind. 560, 413 N.E.2d 560 (1980) (horse running out on highway when landowner was not animal's keeper), with Klobnak v. Wildwood Hills, Inc., 688 N.W.2d 799 (Iowa 2004) (horses running out on highway when landowner owned and kept the horses). Compare Leary v. Lawrence Sales Corp., 442 Pa. 389 (1971) (no duty when food dropped on shopping-center mall two feet from defendant's premises), with Tolu v. Ayodeji, 945 A.2d 596 (D.C. 2008) (duty when construction employees deposited debris in neighbor's yard).

5. Courts have held that landowners have a duty to maintain natural and artificial conditions on private land such that they do not dangerously obscure highway visibility. Physicians Plus Ins. Corp. v. Midwest Mut. Ins. Co., 254 Wis. 2d 77, 646 N.W.2d 777 (2002) (tree on private land obscuring stop sign); Justice v. CSX Transp., Inc., 908 F.2d 119 (7th Cir. 1990) (driver's view obstructed by placement of railway cars on private land).

6. A large body of case law has developed concerning the obligation of landowners to users of the highway who stray onto private land. Compare Hayes v. Malkan, 26 N.Y.2d 295, 258 N.E.2d 695, 310 N.Y.S.2d 281 (1970) (no duty when plaintiff crashed into a utility pole because the pole was on private property rather than public land), with Coates v. S. Md. Elec. Coop., Inc., 354 Md. 499, 731 A.2d 931 (1999) (declining to adopt the distinction between public or private land and noting that the trend is toward a "flexible approach" grounded in foreseeability).

7. Most courts agree that a landholder owes a duty to a traveler who accidentally falls into excavations on land immediately adjoining the highway. See Downes v. Silva, 57 R.I. 343, 190 A. 42 (1937), where the excavation was created or maintained by the landowner; Zens v. Chicago, Milwaukee, St. Paul & Pac.R.R. Co., 386 N.W.2d 475 (S.D.1986). Durst v. Wareham, 132 Kan. 785, 297 P. 675 (1931) (rickety shed collapsed on motorist who slid off the road); Ind. Limestone Co. v. Staggs, 672 N.E.2d 1377 (Ind. Ct. App. 1996) (plaintiff's car skidded into quarry 25 feet from sharp curve in the road).

8. The rule has even been extended, in several cases, to those who deviate intentionally from the highway for some casual purpose connected with travel. Gibson v. Johnson, 69 Ohio App. 19, 42 N.E.2d 689 (1941) (stepping out to allow others to pass); Lacanfora v. Goldapel, 37 A.D.2d 721, 323 N.Y.S.2d 990 (1971) (knobless door close to sidewalk opened when child leaned on it, precipitating him to 12-foot drop).

9. In Murray v. McShane, 52 Md. 217 (1879), plaintiff, walking along the public sidewalk, sat down on defendant's doorstep to tie his shoe, and was injured when a brick fell on him out of the doorway. He was allowed to recover. In Foley v. H.F. Farnham Co., 135 Me. 29, 188 A. 708 (1936), where two pedestrians stopped to rest on the doorsill of a factory and were injured when a sign fell on them, recovery was denied. What is the difference?

10. There is no liability as to dangers a considerable distance from the highway. Hardcastle v. South Yorkshire R. & R.D.R. Co., 4 H. & N. 67, 157 Eng.Rep. 761 (1859); Gaboury v. Ireland Rd. Grace Brethren, Inc., 446 N.E.2d 1310 (Ind. 1983) (cable in church parking lot). In Flint v. Bowman, 42 Tex.Civ.App. 354, 93 S.W. 479 (1906), plaintiff was driving along a highway obliterated by fifteen inches of snow. He missed a right turn, and continued on across the defendant's land for nearly half a mile until he drove into an abandoned and unguarded well. Is the defendant liable to him?

11. When the land has a deceptive appearance of being a continuation of the public way, a duty may be imposed on the landholder to guard a trap or excavation even though the hazard is actually a considerable distance within private property. See Louisville & Nashville R. Co. v. Anderson, 39 F.2d 403 (5th Cir. 1930); Holmes v. Drew, 151 Mass. 578, 25 N.E. 22 (1890). In such a case the entrant on the land may be deemed to be invited and not a trespasser. Is this inconsistent with the rule of Ranson v. Kitner, supra page 25?

2. ON THE PREMISES

(A) TRESPASSERS

Sheehan v. St. Paul & Duluth Ry. Co.

United States Circuit Court of Appeals, Seventh Circuit, 1896.
76 Fed. 201.

[Action for damages for personal injury. While plaintiff was walking on defendant's railroad track, his foot slipped and became caught between the rail and a cattle guard. He was unable to extricate his shoe, or to get at it to untie it. Defendant's train approached, and ran over his foot. Defendant's train crew did not see him until the train was almost upon him, and it was too late to stop it. The trial court directed a verdict for defendant, on the ground that "upon the undisputed facts of the case, this injury did not occur through any wrongful action upon the part of the defendant." Plaintiff appeals.]

SEAMAN, DISTRICT JUDGE. * * * The plaintiff, at the time of his injury, was neither in the relation of passenger nor of one in a public crossing or place in which the public were licensed to travel, but, upon the undisputed facts, was a mere intruder on the tracks of the defendant,—technically, a trespasser; and this record excludes any of the elements of implied license or invitation to such use which have given rise to much discussion and diversity of views in the courts. Therefore the inquiry is here squarely presented: What is the duty which a railway company owes to a trespasser on its tracks, and how and when does the duty arise? The decisions upon this subject uniformly recognize that the trespasser cannot be treated as an outlaw; and, at the least, that, if wantonly injured in the operation of the railroad, the company is answerable in damages. Clearly, then, an obligation is placed upon the company to exercise some degree of care when the danger becomes apparent. Is it, however, bound to foresee or assume that rational beings will thus enter as trespassers in a place of danger, and to exercise in the running of its trains the constant vigilance in view of that probability which is imposed for public crossings? There are cases which would seem to hold this strict requirement [cc]; but by the great preponderance of authority, in this country, and in England, the more reasonable doctrine is pronounced, in effect, as follows: That the railroad company has the right to a free track in such places; that it is not bound to any act or service in anticipation of trespassers thereon; and that the trespasser who ventures to enter upon a track for any purpose of his own assumes all risks of the conditions which may be found there, including the operation of engines and cars. * * *

The well-established and just rule which holds the railroad company to the exercise of constant and strict care against injury through its means is applicable only to the relation on which it is founded, of an existing duty or obligation. This active or positive duty arises in favor of the public at a street crossing or other place at which it is presumable that persons or teams may be met. It is not material, so far as concerns this inquiry, whether the place is one for which a lawful right of passage exists, as it is the fact of notice to the company, arising out of its existence and the probability of its use, which imposes the positive duty to exercise care; the requirement of an extreme degree of care being superadded because of the hazards which attend the operations of the company. The case of a trespasser on the track, in a place not open to travel, is clearly distinguishable in the absence of this notice to the company. There is no constructive notice upon which to base the obligation of constant lookout for his presence there, and no actual notice up to the moment the trainmen have discovered the fact of his peril. As that peril comes wholly from his unauthorized act and temerity, the risk, and all positive duty of care for his safety, rests with the trespasser. The obligation of the company and its operatives is not, then, pre-existing, but arises at the moment of discovery, and is negative in its nature,—a duty, which is common to human conduct, to make all reasonable effort to avert injury to others from means which can be controlled. This is the issue presented here. It excludes all inquiry respecting the character of the roadbed, cattle guard, locomotive, brake appliances, or other means of operation, or of the speed or manner of running the train up to the moment of notice, because no breach of positive duty is involved. It is confined to the evidence relating to the discovery by the engineer and fireman of the plaintiff's peril, and to the efforts then made to avert the injury, and, out of that, to ascertain whether, in any view which may justly be taken, it is shown that these men, or the engineer, in disregard of the duty which then confronted them, neglected to employ with reasonable promptness the means at hand for stopping the train. * * *

The court was clearly justified in directing a verdict for the defendant, and the judgment is affirmed.

NOTES AND QUESTIONS

1. How valid are the following explanations, commonly given for the nonliability to the trespasser:

A. His presence is not reasonably to be anticipated. Suppose a railroad company, as well as everyone else, knows that people do habitually trespass on its right of way?

B. The trespasser assumes the risk. What if he does not know there is any risk or is a child too young to assume it? See Santora v. New York, N.H. & H.R. Co., 211 Mass. 464, 98 N.E. 90 (1912), where a child 27 months old got onto a railroad track and was run over.

C. He is contributorily negligent or is himself a wrongdoer not entitled to legal protection.

2. Although not clear from the principal case, the foundational rule was that a landowner could not be liable to a trespasser. From this rule, courts began to carve out exceptions.

3. The rule stated in the principal case is commonly applied to a wide variety of dangerous conditions on the land, including dangerous machinery and defective construction.

4. The landowner's immunity toward trespassers extends to the members of his household. Sohn v. Katz, 112 N.J.L. 106, 169 A. 838 (1934). It does not extend to adjoining landowners. Fitzpatrick v. Penfield, 267 Pa. 564, 109 A. 653 (1920).

5. The courts have not favored the immunity to trespassers, and have tended to erode it with exceptions. The first exception is that of a trespasser whose presence has been discovered. Frederick v. Philadelphia Rapid Transit Co., 337 Pa. 136, 10 A.2d 576 (1940) (plaintiff fell from subway platform onto track, train automatically stopped by "tripper," crew drove on without making adequate inspection).

A. The earliest cases finding liability to a trespasser were those of spring guns or traps deliberately set for him. From these cases the rule developed that the defendant was not allowed to injure the trespasser negligently by an act specifically directed at him, as in Palmer v. Gordon,

173 Mass. 410, 53 N.E. 909 (1899); Magar v. Hammond, 183 N.Y. 387, 76 N.E. 474 (1906); or recklessly by conduct in conscious disregard of his danger; Trico Coffee Co. v. Clemens, 168 Miss. 748, 151 So. 175 (1933).

B. From such decisions the rule developed that the defendant is liable for injury to a trespasser for conduct that is "wilful or wanton." Thus in Bremer v. Lake Erie & W.R. Co., 318 Ill. 11, 148 N.E. 862 (1925), the defendant was held liable when its engineer recklessly ran past a signal and injured a trespasser on the train who had not been discovered.

C. In a number of states it is still held that there is no liability even to a discovered trespasser unless the defendant's conduct is wilful or wanton. Some of these jurisdictions have defined "wilful and wanton," as in the principal case, to include a failure to use ordinary care after discovery of the trespasser's presence. See Sloniker v. Great N.R. Co., 76 Minn. 306, 79 N.W. 168 (1899); Cain v. Johnson, 755 A.2d 156 (R.I. 2000).

D. The great majority of the courts have now discarded "wilful and wanton" as a limitation, and have held that when the presence of the trespasser is discovered there is a duty to use ordinary care to avoid injuring him by active operations. This duty includes the control of operating forces, such as machinery already in motion, or a warning against it. Maldonado v. Jack M. Berry Grove Corp., 351 So.2d 967 (Fla.1977); Alexander v. Medical Associates Clinic, 646 N.W.2d 74 (Iowa 2002).

E. Cases involving passive conditions on the land, as distinguished from active operations, have been infrequent. It was once held that the defendant had no duty to warn a trespasser whom he saw walking into a concealed danger. This apparently has now given way to the rule that he must at least warn the trespasser. Martin v. Jones, 122 Utah 597, 609, 253 P.2d 359 (1953); Restatement (Second) of Torts § 337.

6. The second exception is that of frequent trespassers on a very limited area of the land. The defendant is required to anticipate the trespassers and to exercise reasonable care in his activities for their protection. In Imre v. Riegel Paper Corp., 24 N.J. 438, 132 A.2d 505 (1957), the existence of a well-defined path across the land was held to be sufficient evidence of frequent trespass.

7. The third exception is that of *tolerated intruders.* This is sometimes explained or justified on the theory that the defendant's continued toleration of the trespasses amounts to permission to use the land, so that the plaintiff becomes a licensee. In most cases, however, the mere fact that a railway company or other defendant has failed to take steps to prevent trespassing, which would be burdensome, expensive, and perhaps futile, is not in itself any indication that it consents to the entry. See Restatement (Second) of Torts § 330 (1965), comment *c;* Bohlen, The Duty of a Landowner Toward Those Entering His Premises of Their Own Right, 69 U.Pa.L.Rev. 142, 237 (1921).

8. Other exceptions include dangerous conditions obvious to an owner, Restatement (Second) of Torts §§ 342–343 (1965); and trapped trespassers in peril. Pridgen v. Boston Hous. Auth., 364 Mass. 696, 308 N.E.2d 467 (1974).

9. Restatement (Third) of Torts addresses the dilemma of the duty owed to trespassers by distinguishing between ordinary trespassers and

"flagrant" trespassers. While land owners would owe an ordinary trespasser a duty of reasonable care, they would only owe a flagrant trespasser the duty not to act in an intentional, willful, or wanton manner to cause physical harm. The reasonable duty of care would still attach in the case of imperiled and helpless trespassers. See RESTATEMENT (THIRD) OF TORTS: PHYSICAL AND EMOTIONAL HARM § 52 (2012) cmts. a, g. It should be noted that the bifurcation has been controversial and some states have retained and passed specific legislation preserving the no duty rule.

10. There is a division of authority over whether a defendant using the land by permission of the owner shares the immunity of the owner toward trespassers. See, e.g., Humphrey v. Twin State Gas & Electric Co., 100 Vt. 414, 139 A. 440 (1927). Thus gratuitous licensees, invitees and holders of easements have been held liable in some cases and not in others. The Restatement (Second) of Torts §§ 383–386, has endeavored to resolve the conflict with the statement that persons on the premises who are doing work or creating artificial conditions *on behalf* of the possessor are subject to the same liability, and entitled to the same immunity, as the possessor; but that other persons on the land with his permission have no such immunity. This logical approach serves to explain the greater number of cases, though by no means all. See, Dzenutis v. Dzenutis, 200 Conn. 290, 304, 512 A.2d 130, 137 (1986); Muckey v. Dittoe, 235 Neb. 250, 454 N.W.2d 682 (1990).

11. Elsewhere in the Common Law world the law relating to trespassers has gone through similar contortions. The English House of Lords attempted, in conflicting voices, to state a rule in British Railways Board v. Herrington [1972] A.C. 877. Holding, the duty owed to trespassers, is less than that of reasonable care, and one of "common humanity." The rule was not a panacea and legislation was enacted, see infra note 3, page 527.

(B) LICENSEES

Barmore v. Elmore

Appellate Court of Illinois, Second District, 1980.
83 Ill.App.3d 1056, 403 N.E.2d 1355, 38 Ill.Dec. 751.

LINDBERG, JUSTICE. Plaintiff, Leon Barmore ("plaintiff"), appeals from an order of the Circuit Court of Winnebago County directing a verdict in favor of defendants, Thomas Elmore, Sr., and Esther Elmore ("defendants").

On August 8, 1977, at approximately 5:30 or 6:00 p.m., plaintiff came to the defendants' home. Both plaintiff and Thomas Elmore, Sr. ("Thomas, Sr.") were officers of a Masonic Lodge and plaintiff's purpose in making the visit was to discuss lodge business. During the course of plaintiff's visit, codefendant, Thomas Elmore, Jr., ("Thomas, Jr."), the defendants' 47-year old son, entered the living room with a steak knife. Thomas, Jr. said "You've been talking about me," and advanced toward plaintiff. Thomas, Sr. tried to restrain his son while plaintiff left the house. However, Thomas, Jr. was able to get away from his father, and he followed plaintiff out of the house where he stabbed the plaintiff several times in the chest area. Thomas, Sr. followed his son out of the house and, when he saw that plaintiff had been injured, he summoned help.

* * * [P]laintiff's basic contention is that defendants, as landowners, were negligent in failing to protect him from a dangerous condition upon their premises—namely their son who had a history of mental illness. The extent of defendants' duty in this regard is based in part on whether the plaintiff had the status of an invitee or of a licensee at the time he visited the premises of the defendants.

* * * In order for a person to be classified as an invitee it is sufficient that he go on the land in furtherance of the owner's business. It is not necessary that the invited person gain an advantage by his entry on the land. [C] A social guest is considered a licensee and has been defined as one who enters the premises of the owner by permission, but for the licensee's own purposes. Therefore, a social guest is a person who goes on another's property for companionship, diversion, or entertainment. [C]

The duty owed by the owner of premises towards an invitee is greater than that owed towards a licensee. [C] A social guest as a licensee, generally must take the premises of his host as he finds them. However, the owner of the premises has a duty to warn the licensee of any hidden dangers which are unknown to his guest, of which he, the owner, has knowledge, and to refrain from injuring his guest willfully or wantonly. [Cc] Towards an invitee, the owner of the premises has a duty to exercise reasonable care in keeping the premises reasonably safe for use by the invitee. [C] There may be circumstances by which this duty is extended to include the responsibility to protect the invitee from criminal attacks by third parties. [C]

Plaintiff asserts that sufficient evidence was presented at trial to establish his status as an invitee at the time of the incident. Specifically, plaintiff argues that Illinois courts have recognized that the transaction of business of a fraternal organization carries with it such a status. * * *

Here, although there is evidence that Thomas, Sr. permitted lodge members to come to his home to pay their dues, the primary benefit of this service ran not to the defendant himself, but rather to the fraternal organization of which both parties were members. In sum, we conclude that plaintiff is best categorized as a licensee—social guest and thus the only duty owed to the plaintiff by the defendants was to warn him of hidden dangers unknown to the plaintiff of which the defendants had knowledge.

There is no question that defendants failed to warn plaintiff of the danger that their son might attack a house guest before the attack was underway. Thus the issue becomes whether under the facts of this case defendants had a duty to do so. Plaintiff contends that he presented sufficient evidence by which a jury could have concluded that the defendants had knowledge of previous incidents which would charge them with a duty to anticipate the criminal acts of their son toward the plaintiff. We disagree. [The Court summarizes the evidence.]

Verdicts should be directed and judgments n.o.v. entered "only in those cases in which all of the evidence, when viewed in its aspect most favorable to the opponent, so overwhelmingly favors movant that no contrary verdict based on that evidence could ever stand." [C] In our view, the evidence so overwhelmingly established that the defendants did not know or have reason to know of the possibility that Thomas, Jr. would commit a criminal act toward plaintiff that no contrary verdict could ever stand. Although they did know that their son had a history of mental problems and had been hospitalized several times, and also that approximately ten years before the present incident their son had been involved in what could be characterized as two or three violent incidents, the length of time which had passed would not give them reason to know that their son would engage in violent behavior in August, 1977. This conclusion is buttressed by the fact that plaintiff had previous contact with Thomas, Jr. without incident.

Accordingly, the judgment * * * is affirmed.

NOTES AND QUESTIONS

1. As in the case of trespassers, it was at first held that there was no duty to a licensee except to refrain from inflicting wilful or wanton injury; and there are still courts which hold this. Carter v. Baltimore Gas & Electric Co., 25 Md.App. 717, 336 A.2d 790 (1975); Hill v. Baltimore & Ohio R. Co., 153 F.2d 91 (7th Cir.1946) (Illinois law). See also, Illinois C. R. Co. v. White, 610 So.2d 308 (Miss. 1992) (affirming the rule that the duty owed to licensees, like trespassers, is to refrain from inflicting willful and wanton injury, but modifying the rule so that "the railroad's duty does not always depend upon the rigid common-law classifications of the injured."). Courts often define "wilful or wanton" to include a failure to exercise ordinary care after the presence of the licensee has been discovered, or should reasonably have been expected. Atlantic Coast Line R. Co. v. Heath, 57 Ga.App. 763, 196 S.E. 125 (1938); Jackson v. Pennsylvania R. Co., 176 Md. 1, 3 A.2d 719 (1939).

2. Most courts have now overruled older decisions and hold that the defendant, in conducting active operations, is under a duty of reasonable care toward licensees. This duty extends not only to licensees who are discovered, but to those whose presence might reasonably be anticipated. Babcock & Wilcox Co. v. Nolton, 58 Nev. 133, 71 P.2d 1051 (1937); Le Poidevin v. Wilson, 111 Wis.2d 116, 330 N.W.2d 555 (Wis. 1983).

3. If defendant landholder knows about a dangerous, latent condition on his premises that a visitor is likely to encounter, he is under a duty to warn the licensee about it. Laube v. Stevenson, 137 Conn. 469, 78 A.2d 693 (1951), involving a dangerous condition on a stairwell, is an excellent case illustrating difference in result between a defendant who knew and one who did not know about the hazard. In 2012, however, the majority opinion in *Laube* was superseded by a statute requiring the standard of care owed to a social invitee to be the same as that owed to a business invitee. CONN. GEN. STAT. ANN. § 52–577a (West). See also Barry v. Cantrell, 150 Ga.App. 439, 258 S.E.2d 61 (1979) (hammock tied to dead tree); Rushton v. Winters, 331 Pa. 78, 200 A. 60 (1938) (defective porch railing).

The Restatement (Second) of Torts § 342 subjects the landholder to liability if he had "reason to know" about the unsafe condition. Even in this modern age when householder's liability insurance is common, this extension has not always been met with approval.

4. In some jurisdictions the licensee category is broken down into two subgroups, the ordinary licensee and the "bare" licensee. The latter group includes salespersons, canvassers and social visitors who "drop in" without an express invitation. As might be expected, the duty owed to "bare" licensees is less than that owed to ordinary licensees. See Kight v. Bowman, 25 Md.App. 225, 333 A.2d 346, 350 (1975); Wilson v. Goodrich, 218 Iowa 462, 252 N.W. 142 (1934); cf. Scheibel v. Lipton, 156 Ohio St. 308, 102 N.E.2d 453 (1951). In other states, the word "bare" is simply an uncomplimentary epithet applied to all licensees.

5. *Social Guests.* Ever since Southcote v. Stanley, 1 H. & N. 247, 156 Eng.Rep. 1195 (1856), the decisions have been essentially uniform in holding that a social guest, although he is invited, and even urged to come, is not in law an invitee but is to be treated as merely a licensee. See, for example, Stevens v. Dovre, 248 Md. 15, 234 A.2d 596 (1967); cf. CONN. GEN. STAT. ANN. § 52–577a (West) ("The standard of care owed to a social invitee shall be the same as the standard of care owed to a business invitee."), *supra* note 3 at page 512.

6. An incidental service rendered to an occupier by a social guest does not clothe that social guest an invitee. Thompson v. Katzer, 86 Wash.App. 280, 936 P.2d 421 (Div. 2 1997).

7. Should the rule be changed? Does a social guest anticipate that the premises will be made reasonably safe for his benefit? What about the uninvited social guest, salesperson or canvasser? Does the host receive a "benefit" from a purely social guest? Is it enough to impose a duty of reasonable care? For an incisive analysis of the rule relating to social guests, see Burrell v. Meads, 569 N.E.2d 637 (Ind.1991) (holding that social guests are entitled to a standard of reasonable care from host landowners because social guests are invitees).

8. Should the host be liable for protecting third parties from acts of intoxicated guests? See Kelly v. Gwinnell, 96 N.J. 538, 476 A.2d 1219 (1984), supra page 366. Should parents be liable if they leave teenagers "home alone" and a drunken guest injures plaintiff in a motor vehicle accident after leaving a party at their house? See Morella v. Machu, 235 N.J.Super. 604, 563 A.2d 881 (App.Div.1989).

(C) INVITEES

Campbell v. Weathers

Supreme Court of Kansas, 1941.
153 Kan. 316, 111 P.2d 72.

[Defendant, as tenant of a part of a building in the city of Wichita, operated a lunch counter and cigar stand. Plaintiff entered defendant's place of business, loitered in the front part of the premises for fifteen or twenty minutes without making any purchase, and then went to the back part of the building to use the toilet. He stepped into an open trap door in a dark hallway, and was injured. In his action for negligence, the trial court sustained defendant's demurrer to the evidence and plaintiff appeals.]

WEDELL, J. * * * The first issue to be determined is the relationship between plaintiff and the lessee. Was plaintiff a trespasser, a licensee or an invitee? The answer must be found in the evidence. A part of the answer is contained in the nature of the business the lessee conducted. It is conceded lessee operated a business which was open to the public. Lessee's business was that of selling cigars and lunches to the public. It was conceded in oral argument, although the abstract does not reflect it, that the lessee also operated a bar for the sale of beer, but that beer was not being sold on Sunday, the day of the accident. Plaintiff had been a customer of the lessee for a number of years. He resided in the city of Wichita. He was a switchman for one of the railroads. He stopped at the lessee's place of business whenever he was in town. He had used the hallway and toilet on numerous occasions, whenever he was in town, and had never been advised that the toilet was not intended for public use. * * *

That the public had a general invitation to be or to become lessee's customers cannot be doubted. * * * Can we say, as a matter of law, in view of the record in this particular case, appellant had no implied invitation to use the toilet simply because he had not made an actual purchase before he was injured? * * *

The evidence of lessee's own employees was that the toilet was not regarded as a private toilet. * * * In a densely populated business district such a privilege may have constituted a distinct inducement to bring, not only old customers like appellant, but prospective customers into lessee's place of business. * * * But we need not rest our conclusion that appellant was an invitee upon the fact that according to the unqualified evidence, not only customers but everybody was permitted to use the toilet.

The writer cannot subscribe to the theory that a regular customer of long standing is not an invitee to use toilet facilities required by law to be provided by the owner of a restaurant, simply because the customer had not actually made a purchase on the particular occasion of his injury, prior to his injury. * * * Women do a great deal of shopping. They sometimes shop all day in their favorite stores and fail to make a single purchase. Shall courts say, as a matter of law, they were not invitees of the business simply because on a particular occasion they had not yet made a purchase? No business concern would contend that they were not invitees unless perchance an injury had occurred. Men frequently, during spare moments, step into a place of business, which they patronize regularly, where drinks, cigars and lunches are sold. They may not have intended definitely to presently make a purchase. They may, nevertheless, become interested, for example, in a new brand of cigars on display which they may purchase then or on some future occasion. Would the owner or operator of the business contend that they were not invitees? We do not think so. Then why should courts arbitrarily say so, as a matter of law? * * *

Manifestly this does not imply that a trespasser or a mere licensee who enters the premises on a personal errand for the advancement of his own interest or benefit is entitled to the protection due to an invitee.

In the case of Kinsman v. Barton & Co., 141 Wash. 311, 251 P. 563, that court had occasion to determine what constituted an invitee, and said:

"An invitee is one who is either expressly or impliedly invited onto the premises of another in connection with the business carried on by that other. * * * If one goes into a store with a view of then, or at some other time, doing some business with the store, he is an invitee." * * *

Of course, if it appears that a person had no intention of presently or in the future becoming a customer he could not be held to be an invitee, as there would be no basis for any thought of mutual benefit. * * *

The order sustaining the demurrer of the lessee is reversed.

NOTES AND QUESTIONS

1. In Indermaur v. Dames, L.R. 1 C.P. 274 (1866), a journeyman gasfitter came to defendant's sugar refinery to test a patent gas regulator installed there by his employer. He fell down an open and unguarded shaft in the floor, and was injured. It was held that the defendant owed him a duty of reasonable care to make the premises safe for him, because he came "on business which concerns the occupier, and upon his invitation, express or implied."

From this case, those who enter premises "upon business which concerns the occupier" acquired the name of invitees. The early cases left it unclear whether "business" was used in a commercial sense, referring to profit motive, or whether it referred only to the defendant's affairs, as when we say the thing is my own business, and none of yours. Most of the early decisions did not mention any commercial motive behind the invitation, and were decided solely upon the ground that the defendant had thrown his premises open and "invited" the plaintiff to use them. See Corby v. Hill, 4 C.B. N.S. 556 (1858); Sweeny v. Old Colony & Newport R. Co., 10 Allen (92 Mass.) 368, 87 Am.Dec. 644 (1865); Gillis v. Pennsylvania R. Co., 59 Pa. 129, 98 Am.Dec. 317 (1868).

The Restatement (Second) of Torts, in § 332, discarded the term "invitees," and referred instead to "business visitors." The theory adopted was that the duty of affirmative care to make the premises safe is the price that the occupier must pay for the present or prospective economic benefit to be derived from the visitor's presence. See Restatement (Third) of Torts: Liability for Physical and Emotional Harm §§ 40, 51 (2012). It appears to have originated in Campbell, Law of Negligence 63–64 (2d ed. 1878) and was espoused by the Reporter of the First Restatement in Bohlen, The Basis of Affirmative Obligations in the Law of Tort, 44 Am.L.Reg., N.S., 209, 227 (1905); Bohlen, The Duty of a Landowner Towards Those Entering His Premises of Their Own Right, 69 U.Pa.L.Rev. 142, 340, 342 (1920).

2. Actual or potential pecuniary benefit is easily made out in the case of customers who intend to buy, or who are merely "shopping." How valid is the attempt to find it in the following situations:

A. Children accompany parents to stores or other places of business, where nothing is to be bought for the child. Anderson v. Cooper, 214 Ga. 164, 104 S.E.2d 90 (1958). Or adult friends accompany the customer. Goldsmith v. Cody, 351 Mich. 380, 88 N.W.2d 268 (1958).

B. Friends meet passengers at a railway station, or see them off. McCann v. Anchor Line, 79 F.2d 338 (2d Cir.1935). Or a potential passenger has not yet obtained a ticket on an airline. Suarez v. Trans World Airlines, Inc., 498 F.2d 612 (7th Cir.1974).

C. Tourists are invited to go through factories. Gilliland v. Bondurant, 51 S.W.2d 559 (Mo.App.1932), aff'd, 332 Mo. 881, 59 S.W.2d 679 (1933).

3. In all of the following instances the plaintiff has been held to be an invitee:

A. Those attending free public meetings. Bunnell v. Waterbury Hosp., 103 Conn. 520, 131 A. 501 (1925) (Salvation Army); Howe v. Ohmart, 7 Ind.App. 32, 33 N.E. 466 (1893) (literary society); Geiger v. Simpson M.E. Church, 174 Minn. 389, 219 N.W. 463 (1928) (social meeting at church).

B. Spectators at public amusements, entering on a free pass. Recreation Centre Corp. v. Zimmerman, 172 Md. 309, 191 A. 233 (1937); Mesa v. Spokane World Exposition, 18 Wash.App. 609, 570 P.2d 157 (1977).

C. Entering a bank to get change for a $20 bill. First Nat'l Bank of Birmingham v. Lowery, 263 Ala. 36, 81 So.2d 284 (1955).

D. Coming to get things advertised to be given away. Roper v. Commercial Fibre Co., 105 N.J.L. 10, 143 A. 741 (1928) (ashes and boxes); Edwards v. Gulf Oil Corp., 69 Ga.App. 140, 24 S.E.2d 843 (1943) (comic books at filling station).

E. Use of state or municipal land open to the public. Caldwell v. Village of Island Park, 304 N.Y. 268, 107 N.E.2d 441 (1952) (park); Lowe v. Gastonia, 211 N.C. 564, 191 S.E. 7 (1937) (golf course); Ashworth v. City of Clarksburg, 118 W.Va. 476, 190 S.E. 763 (1937) (swimming pool).

F. Visitors in national parks. Adams v. United States, 239 F.Supp. 503 (E.D.Okl.1965); Smith v. United States, 117 F.Supp. 525 (N.D.Cal.1953) (camper).

4. Most courts have rejected the old rule that plaintiff's status on public land depends on whether he was entering the premises for the purpose for which they were open to the public (invitee) or whether he entered the premises for an unintended purpose (licensee). See Home Ins. Co. v. Spears, 267 Ark. 704, 590 S.W.2d 71 (1979). In other words, on public land, the state, city or county owes to all persons coming on the premises a duty to use reasonable care to keep the premises safe.

5. In Guilford v. Yale Univ., 128 Conn. 449, 23 A.2d 917 (1942), plaintiff attended a class reunion on the Yale campus. Late at night, seeking to urinate, he proceeded into a dark area, fell over a low retaining wall to a level ten feet below, and was injured. It was held that he was an invitee, without regard to any question of "mutual benefit." Is this one of the purposes for which Old Eli invites its alumni to return to the hallowed elms?

6. What if a customer, in an attempt to find the restroom, is injured on another part of the premises? Knapp v. Conn. Theatrical Corp., 122 Conn. 413, 190 A. 291 (1937).

Whelan v. Van Natta

Court of Appeals of Kentucky, 1964.
382 S.W.2d 205.

[Plaintiff came into defendant's grocery store, and purchased some cigarettes. He then asked about a box for his son. Defendant, who was busy behind the counter, replied, "Go back in the backroom. You will find some back there." Plaintiff went to the rear of the store, and opened the door of the storage room. The room was dark, and the light was not turned on. In hunting around for a box, plaintiff fell into an unseen stair well, and was injured. The defendant testified that he did not warn plaintiff of the existence of the stair well, that the light in the room had been on that morning, and that he did not know whether it was still on when the plaintiff fell.

On these facts, the court gave judgment for the defendant, and plaintiff appealed.]

MONTGOMERY, JUDGE. * * * The trial court held that appellant was a licensee at the time of his fall, to whom appellee owed no duty to provide a safe place, save and except to have abstained from doing any intentional or willful act endangering his safety or knowingly letting appellant run upon a hidden peril. [C] Appellant contends that he entered the store on business with appellee and thus had the status of an invitee and that he still occupied this status when he fell and was injured. The question is: "Did the status of appellant change from invitee to licensee after he made his purchase and went into the storage room to obtain the box?" The status of appellant determines the degree of responsibility of appellee.

Pertinent discussion of the scope of the invitation is contained in Torts, Restatement of the Law, Second, Chapter 13, Section 332, page 67 as follows:

"The possessor of land is subject to liability to another as an invitee only for harm sustained while he is on the land within the scope of his invitation. Thus an invitee ceases to be an invitee after the expiration of a reasonable time within which to accomplish the purpose for which he is invited to enter, or to remain. Whether at the expiration of that time he becomes a trespasser or a licensee will depend upon whether the possessor does or does not consent to his remaining on the land.

"Likewise, the visitor has the status of an invitee only while he is on the part of the land to which his invitation extends—or in other words, the part of the land upon which the possessor gives him reason to believe that his presence is desired for the purpose for which he has come. In determining the area included within the invitation, the purpose for which the land is held open, or the particular business purpose for which the invitation is extended is of great importance. * * *

"If the invitee goes outside of the area of his invitation, he becomes a trespasser or a licensee, depending upon whether he goes there without the consent of the possessor, or with such consent. Thus one who goes into a shop which occupies part of the building, the rest of which is used as the possessor's residence, is a trespasser if he goes into the residential part of the premises without the shopkeeper's consent;

but he is a licensee if the shopkeeper permits him to go to the bathroom, or invites him to pay a social call."

Judgment affirmed.

NOTES AND QUESTIONS

1. What if the visitor is invited to go to an unusual part of the premises, such as a stock room, to make his own selection of goods? Bullock v. Safeway Stores, 236 F.2d 29 (8th Cir.1956). See also Lavitch v. Smith, 224 Or. 498, 356 P.2d 531 (1960) (salesman invited into private office); Crown Cork & Seal Co. v. Kane, 213 Md. 152, 131 A.2d 470 (1957) (truck driver's helper forced to wait, going to smoking room).

2. What if the visitor is injured taking a shortcut to the parking lot? Nicoletti v. Westcor, Inc., 131 Ariz. 140, 639 P.2d 330 (1982).

3. The scope of the duty owed by an occupant to an invitee is one of reasonable care in all the circumstances. Even though the danger is known to the plaintiff, the defendant may be found to be negligent if it is not too difficult to eliminate the danger and he should reasonably anticipate that the plaintiff might still be injured by it; Wilk v. Georges, 267 Or. 19, 514 P.2d 877 (duty not necessarily discharged by posting warning signs). On the issue of "reasonable care," see Preuss v. Sambo's of Arizona, Inc., 130 Ariz. 288, 635 P.2d 1210, 1211 (1981); see also Restatement (Second) of Torts, §§ 343, 343A.

4. When an obvious hazard is also a natural one such as snow, ice or rainwater, a number of jurisdictions hold that the invitor owes no duty to any invitee who slips or falls because of the hazard. See Sidle v. Humphrey, 13 Ohio St.2d 45, 233 N.E.2d 589 (1968). But cf. Richardson v. Corvallis Pub. Sch. Dist. No. 1, 286 Mont. 309, 950 P.2d 748 (Mont. 1997). In *Richardson*, the court did not focus on whether or not the condition was "natural," but rather whether it was open and obvious. The court adopted the following standard of care: "The possessor of the premises is not liable to persons foreseeably upon the premises for physical harm caused to them by any activity or condition on the premises whose danger is known or obvious to them, unless the possessor should anticipate the harm despite such knowledge or obviousness." *Richardson* retained the no duty rule but provided an exception based on foreseeable harm notwithstanding an obvious risk, in accord with Restatement (Second) of Torts, § 343A(1).

5. As elsewhere, the duty is not confined to injuries caused solely because of the condition of the premises. The Illinois Supreme Court in Marshall v. Burger King Corporation, 222 Ill.2d 422, 305 Ill.Dec. 897, 856 N.E.2d 1048 (2006) examined the degree of foreseeability necessary to impose a duty of care where the deceased customer of the fast food restaurant was fatally injured by a car that crashed through the wall of the restaurant and struck the customer. The majority found that the duty extended to protect customers from the negligent acts of third persons even though defendant restaurant had no notice of prior similar incidents. Precedents requiring a particularized notice of the type of damages were overruled in favor of a broad forseeability test for the duty of care. Restatement (Second) of Torts § 344, comment *f* was interpreted to require an inquiry of all surrounding circumstances of the accident as establishing

foreseeability. The dissent strongly objected to finding a duty because of the burdens it would impose on businesses in defendant's position.

6. There are two lines of cases concerning an invitor's duty to an invitee injured at the hands of third party criminal conduct. Injured parties assert either that (1) the invitor has failed to take reasonable measures to reduce the likelihood of dangerous criminal activity posing a danger to invitees or that (2) the invitor's actions (or those of her servant) in the face of the crime negligently endangered the invitee. Two other lines of cases concern an invitor's duty to an invitee injured at the hands of third-party criminal elements. Injured parties assert either that (1) the invitor has failed to take reasonable measures to reduce the likelihood of dangerous criminal activity posing a danger to invitees or that (2) the invitor's actions (or those of her servant) in face of the crime negligently endangered the invitee.

In the former category, the courts have sometimes found a duty to protect entrants as in Erickson v. Curtis Investment Co., 447 N.W.2d 165 (Minn.1989), wherein a duty of care was imposed on the operator or owner of a parking ramp facility toward a customer who was raped in her parked car. The court stressed the particular focus and opportunity for criminals and their criminal activities in structures of this kind. The duty was expressed in terms of reasonable care to deter, requiring the jury to weigh "the likelihood of the risk with the financial and practical feasibility of the means to meet that risk * * *." In contrast, the Michigan Supreme Court in Williams v. Cunningham Drug Stores, Inc., 429 Mich. 495, 418 N.W.2d 381 (1988), found that the proprietor of a drug store owed no duty to hire armed guards to deter robberies and associated violence in a high crime area. The defendant was found not to have sufficient control and any duty would be difficult to apply. The duty to use care may apply to discovery of the dangerous criminal, cf. Townsley v. Cincinnati Gardens, Inc., 39 Ohio App.2d 5, 68 Ohio Op.2d 72, 314 N.E.2d 409 (1974) (dictum); to becoming aware of his dangerous character, cf. Repka v. Rentalent Inc., 477 P.2d 470 (Colo.App.1970); or to giving a warning of the danger, see Sinn v. Farmers' Deposit Sav. Bank, 300 Pa. 85, 150 A. 163 (1930).

In respect of the latter category—the invitor's actions in the face of a crime—the courts have shown a disinclination to second guess actions taken in the exigencies of an ongoing crime. In Boyd v. Racine Currency Exchange, Inc., 56 Ill.2d 95, 306 N.E.2d 39 (1973), the plaintiff's decedent was shot by a robber when a teller, behind a bullet-proof shield, refused to comply with the robber's demand for money or access to a restricted area. The court found that to impose a duty of compliance would benefit criminals and endanger "future business invitees."

7. In another line of cases, a landowner may be liable to injuries sustained by an invitee for the intentional acts of others falling short of criminal behavior. Reasonable precautions must be taken to prevent an intoxicated patron from harming another, McFarlin v. Hall, 127 Ariz. 220, 619 P.2d 729 (1980). Similarly, a duty extends to taking reasonable precautions to maintain order in a movie theater—such as preventing reasonably foreseeable violence to a patron in the parking lot following a movie. In Colorado a cinema owner was sued for injuries to patrons injured when another movie-goer discharged a gun in a Batman movie. Silva v. Showcase Cinemas Concessions of Dedham, Inc., 736 F.2d 810 (1st

Cir.1984), cert. denied, 469 U.S. 883 (1984). The duty may also extend to adjacent property, particularly entrances to the business premises if the business is aware of a dangerous condition and fails to warn invitees or take precautions. Banks v. Hyatt Corp., 722 F.2d 214 (5th Cir.1984).

(D) PERSONS OUTSIDE THE ESTABLISHED CATEGORIES

(1) CHILDREN

Courts have been reluctant to apply to child trespassers or licensees the same limited-duty rules that would be applicable to adults. By various legal devices, most of them have imposed on landowners the duty to exercise a higher standard of care toward children. A principal reason for this is society's interest in protecting children from serious injury. See Green, Landowners' Responsibility to Children, 27 Tex.L.Rev. 1 (1948).

The Attractive Nuisance Doctrine. The first major inroad serving to raise the duty owed to child trespassers and licensees developed over a hundred years ago—it was known as the "attractive nuisance" or "turntable" doctrine. See Sioux City & Pac. R. Co. v. Stout, 84 U.S. (17 Wall.) 657 (1873); Keffe v. Milwaukee & St. Paul R. Co., 21 Minn. 207, 18 Am.Rep. 393 (1875). These cases arose when a young child entered railroad property and was seriously injured while playing on an unlocked turntable. The courts decided that when a landholder sets before young children a temptation that he has reason to believe will lead them into danger, he must use ordinary care to protect them from harm. The courts relied on English precedents where defendants who set traps baited with strong smelling meat on their land were held liable when dogs were lured upon the land and killed in the traps.

On the basis of the turntable decisions, the doctrine acquired the misleading name "attractive nuisance." The word "nuisance" was used because of a supposed analogy to conditions dangerous to children outside the premises. The word "attractive" was applied because courts regarded it as essential that the child be lured or enticed onto the premises.

Justice Holmes, in United Zinc & Chemical Co. v. Britt, 258 U.S. 268 (1922), forestalled the doctrine's growth. In this case, two children trespassed on defendant's land and then discovered a pool of water, apparently clear but actually poisoned with sulfuric acid. The children went into the water and were harmed. Justice Holmes held that the attractive-nuisance doctrine did not apply because the children were not attracted onto the land and induced to trespass in the first instance by the thing that injured them. While at first receiving a favorable response, the *Britt* case was later rejected by a substantial majority of states.

Restatement of Torts § 339. The question of what duty should be owed to child trespassers or licensees occupied considerable time and thought in the preparation of the First Restatement of Torts. The result of these efforts was § 339, which became one of the most influential provisions of the entire Restatement. The authors abandoned the fictitious language of "attractive nuisance" and substituted the title "Artificial Conditions

Highly Dangerous to Trespassing Children." As readopted, with only a few modifications, in the Restatement (Second) of Torts, it reads:

> "A possessor of land is subject to liability for physical harm to children trespassing thereon caused by an artificial condition upon the land if
>
> (a) the place where the condition exists is one upon which the possessor knows or has reason to know that children are likely to trespass, and
>
> (b) the condition is one of which the possessor knows or has reason to know and which he realizes or should realize will involve an unreasonable risk of death or serious bodily harm to such children, and
>
> (c) the children because of their youth do not discover the condition or realize the risk involved in intermeddling with it or in coming within the area made dangerous by it, and
>
> (d) the utility to the possessor of maintaining the condition and the burden of eliminating the danger are slight as compared with the risk to children involved, and
>
> (e) the possessor fails to exercise reasonable care to eliminate the danger or otherwise to protect the children."

It is clear that the Restatement (Second) of Torts rejected the *Britt* case. It was not essential that the child be attracted or lured onto the premises by the thing that injured him. The Restatement (Second), § 339, however, has been superseded by § 51 of the Restatement (Third) (2012), which provides that a possessor of land owes a duty of reasonable care to entrants on the land with regard to natural and artificial conditions, among other things. Comment l addresses child trespassers and indicates that the principles behind § 339 of the Restatement (Second) remain relevant to determining whether a possessor of land exercised reasonable care under § 51 of the Restatement (Third).

The Reporter's Note reveals that courts that have adopted a unitary duty of reasonable care to all entrants have decided cases regarding child trespassers without reference to § 339 of the Restatement (Second). See Silva v. Union Pac. R.R. Co., 85 Cal. App. 4th 1024, 102 Cal. Rptr. 2d 668 (2000). Yet, § 339 of the Restatement (Second) remains popular with courts that retain the status-based duties for landowners.

The Restatement (Second), § 343B, which extended the duty in § 339 to child licensees and invitees, has also been superseded by § 51 of the Restatement (Third).

(2) PERSONS PRIVILEGED TO ENTER IRRESPECTIVE OF LANDOWNER'S CONSENT

Public employees or officials do not fit very well into any of the categories that the law has established for the classification of visitors. They are not trespassers, since they are privileged to enter. This privilege is independent of any permission, consent or license of the occupier; they would be privileged to enter and could insist upon doing so even if the landholder made an active objection. They normally do not come for any of the purposes for which the premises are held open to the public, and frequently they do not enter for any benefit of the occupier, or under circumstances which would justify any expectation that the place has been prepared to receive them.

Many courts have still struggled to place public officers and employees within the category of invitees. Some public officers enter for a purpose connected with defendant's business, and are essential to it, since without them it could not legally be carried on. This is true, for example, of sanitary and safety inspectors, who are commonly held to be invitees. Swift & Co. v. Schuster, 192 F.2d 615 (10th Cir.1951); Atchley v. Berlen, 87 Ill.App.3d 61, 408 N.E.2d 1177, 42 Ill.Dec. 468 (1980). Economic advantage may also be made out in the case of a garbage collector, a city water-meter reader or a postman. Finnegan v. Fall River Gas-Works Co., 159 Mass. 311, 34 N.E. 523 (1893); Paubel v. Hitz, 339 Mo. 274, 96 S.W.2d 369 (1936).

On the other hand, both firemen and policemen have generally been held to enter under a bare license conferred by the law, and so to be no more than licensees. This means, however, that if defendant knows they are present, he must warn them of known dangers which they are unlikely to discover. James v. Cities Serv. Oil Co., 66 Ohio App. 87, 31 N.E.2d 872 (1939), aff'd, 140 Ohio St. 314, 23 Ohio Ops. 571, 43 N.E.2d 276 (1942); Rogers v. Cato Oil & Grease Co., 396 P.2d 1000 (Okl.1964).

The general frustration with categorizing policemen and firemen into common law categories has prompted some courts to abandon the category system as applied to public officers and simply apply a general negligence, reasonable care standard. See Mounsey v. Ellard, 363 Mass. 693, 297 N.E.2d 43 (1973); Armstrong v. Mailand, 284 N.W.2d 343 (Minn.1979). Oregon abolished the fireman's rule in Christensen v. Murphy, 296 Or. 610, 678 P.2d 1210 (1984).

The Restatement (Third) in § 51 deals with firefighters and other professional rescuers. Since § 51 provides for a unified duty owed to entrants it eliminates the need to classify separately the status of firefighters, police officers, and other professional rescuers. Most jurisdictions that limit the possessor's liability to rescuers do so on grounds other than the rescuer's status on the land. One approach is that, since professional rescuers, and their workers compensation payments are paid by the tax payers, it would be unfair to hold tax payers liable for injuries suffered by the rescuers, thereby charging the tax payer twice. See Roberts v. Vaughn, 459 Mich. 282, 587 N.W.2d 249 (1998). Other courts have grounded the limitation of liability on assumption of risk and public policy concerns. See Zanghi v. Niagara Frontier Transp. Comm'n, 85 N.Y.2d 423, 649 N.E.2d 1167 (1995); Syracuse Rural Fire Dist. v. Pletan, 254 Neb. 393, 577 N.W.2d 527 (1998); Aetna Cas. & Sur. Co. v. Vierra, 619 A.2d 436 (R.I. 1993). Yet, some jurisdictions continue to base liability to rescuers on land-possessor duties. See Levandoski v. Cone, 267 Conn. 651, 841 A.2d 208 (2004).

At least five different answers have been given to the question of how public officials are to be treated. They have been: (1) classified as licensees, (2) classified as invitees, (3) held as entitled to the duty owed to licensees or invitees depending upon the highest duty which the landowner already owed to some other person at that place and time, (4) given a separate classification, with a special duty owed to it, and (5) held entitled to reasonable care under all the circumstances.

Private Persons. The same kinds of problems, with some additional complications, exist in regard to private individuals who come on the premises for self-protection or to rescue or aid someone. They may be privileged as a matter of law to enter, regardless of the landowner's consent. Should the duty owed to them be derivative, depending upon the classification of the person being rescued? What would be the effect of that person's contributory negligence? If the duty owed is an independent one owed to the rescuer in his own right, do all of the possible answers listed in the previous paragraph apply? Perhaps all of this is an appropriate introduction to the next Section.

(E) REJECTION OR MERGING OF CATEGORIES

Rowland v. Christian

Supreme Court of California, 1968.
69 Cal.2d 108, 443 P.2d 561, 70 Cal.Rptr. 97.

PETERS, JUSTICE. Plaintiff appeals from a summary judgment for defendant Nancy Christian in this personal injury action.

[The evidence was that plaintiff was a social guest in defendant's apartment; that he asked to use the bathroom; and that while there he was injured when a cracked handle of the cold water faucet on the basin broke and severed tendons and nerves on his right hand. Also that defendant had known for two weeks that the handle was cracked and had complained to the manager of the building, but that she did not say anything to the plaintiff as to its condition.]

One of the areas where this court and other courts have departed from the fundamental concept that a man is liable for injuries caused by his carelessness is with regard to the liability of a possessor of land for injuries to persons who have entered upon that land. It has been suggested that the special rules regarding liability of the possessor of land are due to historical considerations stemming from the high place which land has traditionally held in English and American thought, the dominance and prestige of the landowning class in England during the formative period of the rules governing the possessor's liability, and the heritage of feudalism. [C]

[The court reviewed the various confusing rules and exceptions that had been applied in California to licensees.]

The cases dealing with the active negligence and the trap exceptions are indicative of the subtleties and confusion which have resulted from application of the common law principles governing the liability of the possessor of land. Similar confusion and complexity exist as to the definitions of trespasser, licensee, and invitee. [C]

California Supreme Court
Front row: McComb, Traynor, C.J., Peters
Back row: Burke, Tobriner, Mosk, Sullivan

In refusing to adopt the rules relating to the liability of a possessor of land for the law of admiralty, the United States Supreme Court stated: "The distinctions which the common law draws between licensee and invitee were inherited from a culture deeply rooted to the land, a culture which traced many of its standards to a heritage of feudalism. In an effort to do justice in an industrialized urban society, with its complex economic and individual relationships, modern commonlaw courts have found it necessary to formulate increasingly subtle verbal refinements, to create subclassifications among traditional commonlaw categories, and to delineate fine gradations in the standards of care which the landowner owes to each. Yet even within a single jurisdiction, the classifications and subclassifications bred by the common law have produced confusion and conflict. As new distinctions have been spawned, older ones have become obscured. Through this semantic morass the common law has moved, unevenly and with hesitation, towards 'imposing on owners and occupiers a single duty of reasonable care in all circumstances.' " (Footnotes omitted.) (Kermarec v. Compagnie Generale, 358 U.S. 625, 630–631.) * * *

There is another fundamental objection to the approach to the question of the possessor's liability on the basis of the common law distinctions based upon the status of the injured party as a trespasser, licensee, or invitee. Complexity can be borne and confusion remedied where the underlying principles governing liability are based upon proper considerations. Whatever may have been the historical justifications for the common law distinctions, it is clear that those distinctions are not justified in the light of our modern society and that the complexity and confusion which has arisen is not due to difficulty in applying the original common law rules—they are all too easy to apply in their original formulation—but is due to the attempts to apply just rules in our modern society within time-worn terminology.

> Without attempting to labor all of the rules relating to the possessor's liability, it is apparent that the classifications of trespasser, licensee, and invitee, the immunities from liability predicated upon those classifications, and the exceptions to those immunities, often do not reflect the major factors which should determine whether immunity should be conferred upon the possessor of land. Some of those factors, including the closeness of the connection between the injury and the defendant's conduct, the moral blame attached to the defendant's conduct, the policy of preventing future harm, and the prevalence and availability of insurance, bear little, if any, relationship to the classifications of trespasser, licensee and invitee and the existing rules conferring immunity.

Although in general there may be a relationship between the remaining factors and the classifications of trespasser, licensee, and invitee, there are many cases in which no such relationship may exist. Thus, although the foreseeability of harm to an invitee would ordinarily seem greater than the foreseeability of harm to a trespasser, in a particular case the opposite may be true. The same may be said of the issue of certainty of injury. The burden to the defendant and consequences to the community of imposing a duty to exercise care with resulting liability for breach may often be greater with respect to trespassers than with respect to invitees, but it by no means follows that this is true in every case. In many situations, the burden will be the same, i.e., the conduct necessary upon the defendant's part to meet the burden of exercising due care as to invitees will also meet his burden with respect to licensees and trespassers. The last of the major factors, the cost of insurance, will, of course, vary depending upon the rules of liability adopted, but there is no persuasive evidence that applying ordinary principles of negligence law to the land occupier's liability will materially reduce the prevalence of insurance due to increased cost or even substantially increase the cost.

Considerations such as these have led some courts in particular situations to reject the rigid common law classifications and to approach the issue of the duty of the occupier on the basis of ordinary principles of negligence. [Cc] And the common law distinctions after thorough study have been repudiated by the jurisdiction of their birth. (Occupiers' Liability Act, 1957, 5 and 6 Eliz. 2, ch. 31.)

A man's life or limb does not become less worthy of protection by the law nor a loss less worthy of compensation under the law because he has come upon the land of another without permission or with permission but without a business purpose. Reasonable people do not ordinarily vary their conduct depending upon such matters, and to focus upon the status of the injured party as a trespasser, licensee, or invitee in order to determine the question whether the landowner has a duty of care, is contrary to our modern social mores and humanitarian values. The common law rules obscure rather than illuminate the proper considerations which should govern determination of the question of duty. * * *

Once the ancient concepts as to the liability of the occupier of land are stripped away, the status of the plaintiff relegated to its proper place in determining such liability, and ordinary principles of negligence applied, the result in the instant case presents no substantial difficulties. As we have seen, when we view the matters presented on the motion for summary judgment as we must, we must assume defendant Miss Christian was aware that the faucet handle was defective and dangerous, that the defect was not obvious, and that plaintiff was about to come in contact with the defective condition, and under the undisputed facts she neither remedied the condition nor warned plaintiff of it. Where the occupier of land is aware of a concealed condition involving in the absence of precautions an unreasonable risk of harm to those coming in contact with it and is aware that a person on the premises is about to come in contact with it, the trier of fact can reasonably conclude that a failure to warn or to repair the condition constitutes negligence. Whether or not a guest has a right to expect that his host will remedy dangerous conditions on his account, he should reasonably be entitled to rely upon a warning of the dangerous condition so that he, like the host, will be in a position to take special precautions when he comes in contact with it. * * *

The judgment is reversed.

BURKE, J. I dissent. In determining the liability of the occupier or owner of land for injuries, the distinctions between trespassers, licensees and invitees have been developed and applied by the courts over a period of many years. They supply a reasonable and workable approach to the problems involved, and one which provides the degree of stability and predictability so highly prized in the law. The unfortunate alternative, it appears to me, is the route taken by the majority in their opinion in this case; that such issues are to be decided on a case by case basis under the application of the basic law of negligence, bereft of the guiding principles and precedent which the law has heretofore attached by virtue of the relationship of the parties to one another.

Liability for negligence turns upon whether a duty of care is owed, and if so, the extent thereof. Who can doubt that the corner grocery, the large department store, or the financial institution owes a greater duty of care to one whom it has invited to enter its premises as a prospective customer of its wares or services than it owes to a trespasser seeking to enter after the close of business hours and for a nonbusiness or even an antagonistic purpose? I do not think it unreasonable or unfair that a social guest (classified by the law as a licensee, as was plaintiff here) should be obliged to take the premises in the same condition as his host finds them or permits them to be. Surely a homeowner should not be obliged to hover over his guests with warnings of possible dangers to be found in the condition of the home (e.g., waxed floors, slipping rugs, toys in unexpected places, etc., etc.). Yet today's decision appears to open the door to potentially unlimited liability despite the purpose and circumstances motivating the plaintiff in entering the premises of another, and despite the caveat of the majority that the status of the parties may "have some bearing on the question of liability * * *," whatever the future may show that language to mean.

In my view, it is not a proper function of this court to overturn the learning, wisdom and experience of the past in this field. Sweeping modifications of tort liability law fall more suitably within the domain of the Legislature, before which all affected interests can be heard and which can enact statutes providing uniform standards and guidelines for the future.

I would affirm the judgment for defendant.

MCCOMB, J., concurred.

NOTES AND QUESTIONS

1. Criticism of the categories as a vehicle for determining the duty a possessor of land owes to a visitor or intruder is not new. See Bohlen, The Duty of a Landholder Towards Those Entering His Premises of Their Own Right, 69 U.Pa.L.Rev. 142 (1921), also in F. Bohlen, Studies in the Law of Torts, 136, 163 (1926); Lord Denning in Dunster v. Abbott, [1953] 2 All E.R. 1572, 1574 (C.A.).

The principal case has "shown sustained persuasive influence." Robert L. Rabin, *Rowland v. Christian*: Hallmark of an Expansionary Era, Torts Stories, Rabin and Sugarman (eds.) (2003) 73, at 91. The Restatement (Third) of Torts, § 51 (2012) proposes a general duty of reasonable care to entrants on land for natural, artificial, and land possessor created risks. The Supreme Court of Nevada in Foster v. Costco Wholesale Corporation, 291 P.3d 150 (2012) adopts the provision in discussing liability for open and obvious dangers on the premises.

2. California has declined to apply the rule from the principal case when the injured plaintiff is a trespassing criminal. Cal. Civ. Code § 847 (West).

3. In 1957, a Report of the Law Reform Committee, the Occupiers' Liability Act, 5 & 6 Eliz. II, c. 31, was adopted in England. The Act declared the occupier's common duty of care to all lawful visitors (thus excluding trespassers) upon his land, and enumerated various factors to be considered in determining whether that duty had been discharged. The English law was subsequently supplemented by a duty to treat all trespassers with "common humanity." See British Railways Board v. Herrington, [1972] A.C. 877 (House of Lords). Eventually statutory reform came in Occupiers' Liability Act, 1984, to provide a duty owed to unlawful entrants where: (1) the occupier is aware of the danger or has reasonable grounds to believe that it exists; (2) he knows or has reasonable grounds to believe that the other is in, or may come into, the vicinity of the danger; and (3) the risk is one against which, in all the circumstances of the case, he may reasonably be expected to offer the other some protection.

4. In Hopkins v. Fox & Lazo Realtors, 132 N.J. 426, 625 A.2d 1110 (1993), the court held that a real estate broker owed a duty to a person inspecting the house during an open-house. The duty was one to take reasonable care in preventing foreseeable harm to its open-house customers. The duty was owed in addition to that of the owner to the entrant. The court applied the principal case, finding that approximately fourteen jurisdictions had completely abrogated the various categories of entrants, while "many others" had eliminated the distinction between licensees and business invitees. Other jurisdictions, however, have reaffirmed the retention of the categories. Whaley v. Lawing, 352 So.2d 1090 (Ala.1977); Bailey v. Pennington, 406 A.2d 44 (Del.1979); Huyck v. Hecla Mining Co., 101 Idaho 299, 612 P.2d 142 (1980); Murphy v.

Baltimore Gas & Elec. Co., 290 Md. 186, 428 A.2d 459 (1981) (trespassers only); Buchanan v. Prickett & Son, Inc., 203 Neb. 684, 279 N.W.2d 855 (1979); Moore v. Denune & Pipic, Inc., 26 Ohio St.2d 125, 269 N.E.2d 599 (1971); Younce v. Ferguson, 106 Wash.2d 658, 724 P.2d 991 (1986); Pinnell v. Bates, 838 So.2d 198 (Miss. 2002) (cogent argument for maintaining the distinction); Woodty v. Weston's Lamplighter Motels, 171 Ariz. 265, 830 P.2d 477, 480 (1992); Sims v. Giles, 343 S.C. 708, 541 S.E.2d 857, 861 (2001); Musch v. H-D Elec. Co-op., Inc., 460 N.W.2d 149, 151 (S.D. 1990); Franconia Assocs. v. Clark, 250 Va. 444, 463 S.E.2d 670, 672–73 (1995); Buzzell v. Jones, 151 Vt. 4, 556 A.2d 106, 108 (1989); Carter v. Kinney 896 S.W.2d 926, 930 (Mo. 1995); Lohrenz v. Lane 787 P.2d 1274 (Okla. 1990).

5. While there is considerable agreement that the general negligence standard should be applied to all persons invited or permitted on the premises, there is less accord as to how the trespasser should be handled. Some cases deliberately apply it to a trespasser. In Mark v. Pacific Gas & Elec. Co., 7 Cal.3d 170, 496 P.2d 1276, 101 Cal.Rptr. 908 (1972), a college student was electrocuted when he attempted to unscrew a street lamp located outside his apartment bedroom window. The Supreme Court of California reaffirmed that the negligence standard would be applied to trespassers. Many of the cases adopting *Rowland* have not involved trespass, and in some that have raised the issue the courts have not extended the duty to the benefit of trespassers: Wood v. Camp, 284 So.2d 691 (Fla.1973); Nelson v. Freeland, 349 N.C. 615, 507 S.E.2d 882 (1998); Peterson v. Balach, 294 Minn. 161, 199 N.W.2d 639 (1972), Mounsey v. Ellard, 363 Mass. 693, 297 N.E.2d 43 (1973); O'Leary v. Coenen, 251 N.W.2d 746 (N.D. 1977); Poulin v. Colby College, 402 A.2d 846 (Me. 1979); Baltimore Gas & Elec. Co. v. Flippo, 348 Md. 680, 705 A.2d 1144 (1998); Heins v. Webster County, 250 Neb. 750, 552 N.W.2d 51; Ford v. Board of County Comm'rs, 118 N.M. 134, 879 P.2d 766 (1994); Ragnone v. Portland Sch. Dist. No. 1J, 291 Ore. 617, 633 P.2d 1287 (1981); Tantimonico v. Allendale Mut. Ins. Co., 637 A.2d 1056 (R.I. 1994); Hudson v. Gaitan, 675 S.W.2d 699 (Tenn. 1984); Clarke v. Beckwith, 858 P.2d 293 (Wyo. 1993).

3. LESSOR AND LESSEE

Borders v. Roseberry

Supreme Court of Kansas, 1975.
216 Kan. 486, 532 P.2d 1366.

PRAGER, JUSTICE. * * * The sole point raised on this appeal by the plaintiff, Gary D. Borders, is that the trial court committed reversible error in concluding as a matter of law that a landlord of a single-family house is under no obligation or duty to a social guest of his tenant to repair or remedy a known condition whereby water dripped from the roof onto the front steps of a house fronting north, froze and caused the social guest to slip and fall.

Traditionally the law in this country has placed upon the lessee as the person in possession of the land the burden of maintaining the premises in a reasonably safe condition to protect persons who come upon the land. It is the tenant as possessor who, at least initially, has the burden of maintaining the premises in good repair. [Cc]

The relationship of landlord and tenant is not in itself sufficient to make the landlord liable for the tortious acts of the tenant. [Cc]

When land is leased to a tenant, the law of property regards the lease as equivalent to a sale of the premises for the term. The lessee acquires an estate in the land, and becomes for the time being the owner and occupier, subject to all of the responsibilities of one in possession, both to those who enter onto the land and to those outside of its boundaries. Professor William L. Prosser in his Law of Torts, 4th Ed. § 63, points out that in the absence of agreement to the contrary, the lessor surrenders both possession and control of the land to the lessee, retaining only a reversionary interest; and he has no right even to enter without the permission of the lessee. There is therefore, as a general rule, no liability upon the landlord, either to the tenant or to others entering the land, for defective conditions existing at the time of the lease.

The general rule of non-liability has been modified, however, by a number of exceptions which have been created as a matter of social policy. Modern case law on the subject today usually limits the liability of a landlord for injuries arising from a defective condition existing at the time of the lease to six recognized exceptions. These exceptions are as follows:

1. Undisclosed dangerous conditions known to lessor and unknown to the lessee.

This exception is stated in Restatement (Second) of Torts § 358 as follows:

"§ 358. Undisclosed Dangerous Conditions Known to Lessor

"(1) A lessor of land who conceals or fails to disclose to his lessee any condition, whether natural or artificial, which involves unreasonable risk of physical harm to persons on the land, is subject to liability to the lessee and others upon the land with the consent of the lessee or his sublessee for physical harm caused by the condition after the lessee has taken possession, if

"(a) the lessee does not know or have reason to know of the condition or the risk involved, and

"(b) the lessor knows or has reason to know of the condition, and realizes or should realize the risk involved, and has reason to expect that the lessee will not discover the condition or realize the risk.

"(2) If the lessee [sic] actively conceals the condition, the liability stated Subsection (1) continues until the lessee discovers it and has reasonable opportunity to take effective precautions against it. Otherwise the liability continues only until the vendee has had reasonable opportunity to discover the condition and to take such precautions." * * *

It should be pointed out that this exception applies [in Kansas] only to latent conditions and not to conditions which are patent or reasonably discernible to the tenant. [C]

2. Conditions dangerous to persons outside of the premises.

This exception is stated in Restatement (Second) of Torts § 379 as follows:

"§ 379. Dangerous Conditions Existing When Lessor Transfers Possession

"A lessor of land who transfers its possession in a condition which he realizes or should realize will involve unreasonable risk of physical harm to others outside of the land, is subject to the same liability for physical harm subsequently caused to them by the condition as though he had remained in possession."

The theory of liability under such circumstances is that where a nuisance dangerous to persons outside the leased premises (such as the traveling public or persons on adjoining property) exists on the premises at the time of the lease, the lessor should not be permitted to escape liability by leasing the premises to another. * * *

3. Premises leased for admission of the public. [§ 359]

The third exception arises where land is leased for a purpose involving the admission of the public. The cases usually agree that in that situation the lessor is under an affirmative duty to exercise reasonable care to inspect and repair the premises before possession is transferred, to prevent any unreasonable risk or harm to the public who may enter. * * *

4. Parts of land retained in lessor's control which lessee is entitled to use. [§§ 360, 361]

When different parts of a building, such as an office building or an apartment house, are leased to several tenants, the approaches and common passageways normally do not pass to the tenant, but remain in the possession and control of the landlord. Hence the lessor is under an affirmative obligation to exercise reasonable care to inspect and repair those parts of the premises for the protection of the lessee, members of his family, his employees, invitees, guests, and others on the land in the right of the tenant. * * *

5. Where lessor contracts to repair. [§ 357]

At one time the law in most jurisdictions and in Kansas was that if a landlord breached his contract to keep the premises in good repair, the only remedy of the tenant was an action in contract in which damages were limited to the cost of repair or loss of rental value of the property. Neither the tenant nor members of his family nor his guests were permitted to recover for personal injuries suffered as a result of the breach of the agreement. [C] In most jurisdictions this rule has been modified and a cause of action given in tort to the injured person to enable him recovery for his personal injuries. * * *

In Steele v. Latimer, 214 Kan. 329, 521 P.2d 304, we held that the provisions of a municipal housing code prescribing minimum housing standards are deemed by implication to become a part of a lease of urban residential property, giving rise to an implied warranty on the part of the lessor that the premises are habitable and safe for human occupancy in compliance with the pertinent code provisions and will remain so for the duration of the tenancy. Such an implied warranty creates a contractual obligation on the lessor to repair the premises to keep them in compliance with the municipal housing standards as set forth in a municipal housing code.

6. Negligence by lessor in making repairs. [§ 362]

When the lessor does in fact attempt to make repairs, whether he is bound by a covenant to do so or not, and fails to exercise reasonable care, he is held liable for injuries to the tenant or others on the premises in his right, if the tenant neither knows nor should know that the repairs have been negligently made. * * * [The court found the first five exceptions not applicable in this case.]

[Exception six] comes into play only when the lessee lacks knowledge that the purported repairs have not been made or have been negligently made. Here it is undisputed that the tenant had full knowledge of the icy condition on the steps created by the absence of guttering. It seems to us that the landlord could reasonably assume that the tenant would inform his guest about the icy condition on the front steps. We have concluded that the factual circumstances do not establish liability on the landlord on the basis of negligent repairs made by him.

In his brief counsel for the plaintiff vigorously argues that the law should be changed to make the landlord liable for injuries resulting from a defective condition on the leased premises where the landlord has knowledge of that condition. He has not cited any authority in support of his position, nor does he state with particularity how the existing law pertaining to a landlord's liability should be modified. We do not believe that the facts and circumstances of this case justify a departure from the established rules of law discussed above.

The judgment of the district court is affirmed.

NOTES AND QUESTIONS

1. Courts universally agree that the lessor must disclose all known concealed dangerous conditions existing at the time of the transfer of possession. The liability extends not only to the tenant, and the members of his family, but to his employees, his social guests and others on the premises in his right, and to a subtenant to whom he leases the premises. Most courts find it sufficient that the lessor has information that would lead a reasonable person to conclude that the danger may exist, and that if he does he must disclose such information to the tenant. See Cesar v. Karutz, 60 N.Y. 229, 19 Am.Rep. 164 (1875) ("reasonable notice"); Cutter v. Hamlen, 147 Mass. 471, 18 N.E. 397 (1888) ("should have known"); Rhoades v. Seidel, 139 Mich. 608, 102 N.W. 1025 (1905) (same).

2. Until about 1965, courts held that when a landlord's covenant or contract to repair is broken, the only remedy is a contract action for the breach. However, the modern majority approach derives a lessor's liability from failure to perform a contract to repair. Lessors are thus liable for resulting injuries to the tenant, the members of his family and their guests. The Restatement (First) of Torts, § 357, adopted the minority position, and this has been continued in the Restatement (Second) and Restatement (Third), § 53 (2012).

Pagelsdorf v. Safeco Ins. Co. of America

Supreme Court of Wisconsin, 1979.
91 Wis.2d 734, 284 N.W.2d 55.

CALLOW, JUSTICE. We dispose of this appeal by addressing the single issue of the scope of a landlord's duty toward his tenant's invitee who is injured as a result of defective premises. Abrogating the landlord's general cloak of immunity at common law, we hold that a landlord must exercise ordinary care toward his tenant and others on the premises with permission.

The defendant Richard J. Mahnke owned a two-story, two-family duplex. There were four balcony porches: one in front and one in back of each flat. Mahnke rented the upper unit to John and Mary Katherine Blattner. * * *

[Plaintiff Pagelsdorf was assisting Mrs. Blattner move some furniture. He leaned against the railing for the second-floor front balcony, and it collapsed with him. The railing had a dryrot condition and should have been replaced. The trial court put the case to the jury in terms of plaintiff's being a licensee of Mahnke, the landlord, and the jury found by special verdict that he had no knowledge of the defective condition of the railing. Judgment was entered on the verdict, dismissing the complaint.]

The question on which the appeal turns is whether the trial court erred in failing to instruct the jury that Mahnke owed Pagelsdorf a duty to exercise ordinary care in maintaining the premises.

Prior to December 10, 1975, the duty of an occupier of land toward visitors on the premises was determined in Wisconsin law on a sliding scale according to the status of the visitor. * * * In Antoniewicz v. Reszcynski, 70 Wis.2d 836, 854–55, 236 N.W.2d 1, 10 (1975), we abolished, prospectively, the distinction between the different duties owed by an occupier to licensees and to invitees. * * *

The classification of visitors identified the degree of duty of the possessor or occupier of the premises. [C] When the property is leased, the duty of the landlord was controlled by a different rule: That, with certain exceptions, a landlord is not liable for injuries to his tenants and their visitors resulting from defects in the premises. [C] The general rule of nonliability was based on the concept of a lease as a conveyance of property and the consequent transfer of possession and control of the premises to the tenant. [Cc]

There are exceptions to this general rule of nonliability. * * * The rule of nonliability persists despite a decided trend away from application of the general rule and toward expansion of its exceptions. [Cc]

None of the exceptions to the general rule are applicable to the facts of this case. * * *

Therefore, if we were to follow the traditional rule, Pagelsdorf was not entitled to an instruction that Mahnke owed him a duty of ordinary care. We believe, however, that the better public policy lies in the abandonment of the general rule of nonliability and the adoption of a rule that a landlord is under a duty to exercise ordinary care in the maintenance of the premises.

Such a rule was adopted by the New Hampshire court in Sargent v. Ross, 113 N.H. 388, 308 A.2d 528 (1973). The plaintiff's four-year-old child fell to her death from an outdoor stairway of a residential building owned by the defendant. In a wrongful death action against the landlord, the plaintiff claimed the stairs were too steep and the railing inadequate. The jury awarded the plaintiff damages, and the landlord appealed from a judgment entered on the verdict. After eliminating the established exceptions to the rule of nonliability, the court concluded that the rule had nothing to recommend itself in a contemporary, urban society and ought to be abandoned. Instead, general principles of negligence should apply. The court stated that the " 'quasi-sovereignty of the landowner' " had its genesis in "agrarian England of the dark ages." [C] Whatever justification the rule might once have had, there no longer seemed to be any reason to except landlords from a general duty of exercising ordinary care to prevent foreseeable harm. The court reasoned that the modern trend away from special immunities in tort law and the recognition of an implied warranty of habitability in an apartment lease transaction argued in favor of abolishing the common law rule of nonliability. Accordingly, a landlord's conduct should be appraised according to negligence principles. Questions of control, hidden defects, and common use would be relevant only as bearing on the general determination of negligence, including foreseeability and unreasonableness of the risk of harm.

In *Antoniewicz,* [c] we cited *Sargent* as one of many cases whose reasoning supported the abolition of the common law distinctions between licensees and invitees. The policies supporting our decision to abandon these distinctions concerning a land occupier's duty toward his visitors compel us, in the instant case, to abrogate the landlord's general cloak of immunity toward his tenants and their visitors. Having recognized that modern social conditions no longer support special exceptions for land occupiers, it is but a short step to hold that there is no remaining basis for a general rule of nonliability for landlords. Arguably, the landlord's relinquishment of possession, and consequently control of the premises, removes this case from the sweep of the policies embodied in *Antoniewicz.* We are not so persuaded. One of the basic principles of our tort law is that one is liable for injuries resulting from conduct foreseeably creating an unreasonable risk to others. [C] Public policy limitations on the application of this principle are shrinking. [Cc]

The modern-day apartment lease is regarded as a contract, not a conveyance. Pines v. Perssion, 14 Wis.2d 590, 111 N.W.2d 409 (1961). In *Pines* we determined that modern social conditions called for judicial recognition of a warranty of habitability implied in an apartment lease. * * *

It would be anomalous indeed to require a landlord to keep his premises in good repair as an implied condition of the lease, yet immunize him from liability for injuries resulting from his failure to do so. We conclude that there is no remaining justification for the landlord's general cloak of common law immunity and hereby abolish the general common law principle of nonliability of landlords toward persons injured as a result of their defective premises. * * *

At trial plaintiffs' counsel requested the jury be instructed that Mahnke owed Pagelsdorf, as his invitee, a duty of ordinary care. Pagelsdorf's proposed special verdict inquired whether Mahnke was "negligent in failing to keep the guardrail in question in a reasonably good state of repair." Thus Pagelsdorf preserved the assigned error for appeal. We simply reach the result he seeks by a different means. [C] * * *

Generally, a decision overruling or repudiating other cases is given retrospective operation. [C] The rule of landlords' nonliability was riddled with many exceptions; thus reliance on the rule could not have been great. [C] We find no reason to depart from the general rule of retrospective operation of the mandate herein.

In conclusion, a landlord owes his tenant or anyone on the premises with the tenant's consent a duty to exercise ordinary care. If a person lawfully on the premises is injured as a result of the landlord's negligence in maintaining the premises, he is entitled to recover from the landlord under general negligence principles. Issues of notice of the defect, its obviousness, control of the premises, and so forth are all relevant only insofar as they bear on the ultimate question: Did the landlord exercise ordinary care in the maintenance of the premises under all the circumstances?

Judgment reversed and cause remanded for proceedings consistent with this opinion.

NOTES AND QUESTIONS

1. The "implied warranty of habitability" creates a duty on the part of the lessor to deliver the premises in a habitable condition. As seen in the principal case, it has been utilized by a number of courts in recent years to hold lessors legally accountable. See Knight v. Hallsthammer, 29 Cal.3d 46, 623 P.2d 268, 171 Cal.Rptr. 707 (1981); Lemle v. Breeden, 51 Haw. 426, 462 P.2d 470 (1969); Marini v. Ireland, 56 N.J. 130, 265 A.2d 526 (1970). These decisions did not abolish the general limitation on a landlord's duty in tort, but rather provided tenants only with a defense to an eviction action or a right to withhold rent until repairs were made.

Efforts by lessors to immunize themselves against liability through exculpatory clauses in leases have been held to be void as against public policy, at least insofar as they seek to immunize lessors against damages cause by negligence in maintaining common areas. Cappaert v. Junker, 413 So.2d 378 (Miss 1982).

2. What damages should be available to lessees for lessor's negligence? In Simon v. Solomon, 385 Mass. 91, 431 N.E.2d 556 (1982), the court upheld damages to the tenant for emotional distress caused by the landlord's substandard maintenance of her apartment, after evidence showed that water and sewage from an adjoining area flooded her basement apartment approximately 30 times. In a similar vein, see 49 Prospect Street Tenants Ass'n v. Sheva Gardens, 227 N.J.Super. 449, 547 A.2d 1134 (App.Div.1988), affirming jury award for emotional distress where the landlord of rent controlled premises failed to maintain utility

services, rid the building of vermin, repair broken windows and evict squatters. Do you see an appropriate role for tort law in these circumstances?

3. In Becker v. IRM Corp., 38 Cal.3d 454, 213 Cal.Rptr. 213, 698 P.2d 116 (1985), the California Supreme Court imposed strict liability to landlords for injuries caused by latent structural defects in the premises. The decision attracted a fire-storm of criticism and was repudiated in Peterson v. Superior Court of Riverside County, 10 Cal.4th 1185, 43 Cal.Rptr.2d 836, 899 P.2d 905 (1995) (holding that a tenant could not reasonably expect a landlord to have eliminated defects of which the landlord was unaware and which would have not been disclosed by a reasonable inspection).

Kline v. 1500 Massachusetts Ave. Apartment Corp.

United States Court of Appeals, District of Columbia Circuit, 1970.
141 U.S.App.D.C. 370, 439 F.2d 477.

[Plaintiff Sarah B. Kline, a lessee of defendant, sustained serious injuries when she was criminally assaulted and robbed at approximately 10:15 P.M. while she was in the common hallway of a large (585-unit) combination office-apartment building. Although a doorman had been employed in the past, the entrances to the building were left unguarded at the time plaintiff was assaulted. This procedure was followed in spite of the fact that defendant lessor had notice of an increasing number of assaults, larcenies and robberies being perpetrated against the tenants in and from the common hallways of the building.]

WILKEY, CIRCUIT JUDGE. The appellee apartment corporation states that there is "only one issue presented for review * * * whether a duty should be placed on a landlord to take steps to protect tenants from foreseeable criminal acts committed by third parties". The District Court as a matter of law held that there is no such duty. We find that there is, and that in the circumstances here the applicable standard of care was breached. We therefore reverse and remand to the District Court for the determination of damages for the appellant. * * *

In this jurisdiction, certain duties have been assigned to the landlord because of his *control* of common hallways, lobbies, stairwells, etc., used by all tenants in multiple dwelling units. * * *

While [prior cases have] dealt with a physical defect in the building leading to plaintiff's injury, the rationale as applied to predictable criminal acts by third parties is the same. The duty is the landlord's because by his control of the areas of common use and common danger he is the only party who has the *power* to make the necessary repairs or to provide the necessary protection.

As a general rule, a private person does not have a duty to protect another from a criminal attack by a third person. We recognize that this rule has sometimes in the past been applied in landlord-tenant law, even by this court. Among the reasons for the application of this rule to landlords are: judicial reluctance to tamper with the traditional common law concept of the landlord-tenant relationship; the notion that the act of a third person in committing an intentional tort or crime is a superseding cause of the harm to another resulting therefrom; the oftentimes difficult problem of determining foreseeability of criminal acts; the vagueness of the standard which the landlord must meet; the economic consequences of the imposition of the duty; and conflict with the public policy allocating the duty of protecting citizens from criminal acts to the government rather than the private sector.

But the rationale of this very broad general rule falters when it is applied to the conditions of modern day urban apartment living, particularly in the circumstances of this case. The rationale of the general rule exonerating a third party from any duty to protect another from a criminal attack has no applicability to the landlord-tenant relationship in multiple dwelling houses. The landlord is no insurer of his tenants' safety, but he certainly is no bystander. And where, as here, the landlord has notice of repeated criminal assaults and robberies, has notice that these crimes occurred in the portion of the premises exclusively within his control, has every reason to expect like crimes to happen again, and has the exclusive power to take preventive action, it does not seem unfair to place upon the landlord a duty to take those steps which are within his power to minimize the predictable risk to his tenants. * * *

[I]nnkeepers have been held liable for assaults which have been committed upon their guests by third parties, if they have breached a duty which is imposed by reason of the innkeeper-guest relationship. By this duty, the innkeeper is generally bound to exercise reasonable care to protect the guest from abuse or molestation from third parties, be they innkeeper's employees, fellow guests, or intruders, if the attack could, or in the exercise of reasonable care, should have been anticipated.

Liability in the innkeeper-guest relationship is based as a matter of law either upon the innkeeper's supervision, care, or control of the premises, or by reason of a contract which some courts have implied from the entrustment by the guest of his personal comfort and safety to the innkeeper. In the latter analysis, the contract is held to give the guest the right to expect a standard of treatment at the hands of the innkeeper which includes an obligation on the part of the latter to exercise reasonable care in protecting the guest.

Other relationships in which similar duties have been imposed include landowner-invitee, businessman-patron, employer-employee, school district-pupil, hospital-patient, and carrier-passenger. In all, the theory of liability is essentially the same: that since the ability of one of the parties to provide for his own protection has been limited in some way by his submission to the control of the other, a duty should be imposed upon the one possessing control (and thus the power to act) to take reasonable precautions to protect the other one from assaults by third parties which, at least, could reasonably have been anticipated. * * *

As between tenant and landlord, the landlord is the only one in the position to take the necessary acts of protection required. He is not an insurer, but he is obligated to minimize the risk to his tenants. Not only as between landlord and tenant is the landlord best equipped to guard against the predictable risk of intruders, but even as between landlord and the police power of government, the landlord is in the best position to take the necessary protective measures. * * *

We * * * hold in this case that the applicable standard of care in providing protection for the tenant is that standard which this landlord himself was employing in October 1959 when the appellant became a resident on the premises at 1500 Massachusetts Avenue. * * * [W]e hold that the same relative degree of security should have been maintained. * * *

Having said this, it would be well to state what is not said by this decision. We do not hold that the landlord is by any means an insurer of the safety of his tenants. His duty is to take those measures of protection which are within his power and capacity to take, and which can reasonably be expected to mitigate the risk of intruders assaulting and robbing tenants. The landlord is not expected to provide protection commonly owed by a municipal police department; but as illustrated in this case, he is obligated to protect those parts of his premises which are not usually subject to periodic patrol and inspection by the municipal police. We do not say that every multiple unit apartment house in the District of Columbia should have those same measures of protection which 1500 Massachusetts Avenue enjoyed in 1959, nor do we say that 1500 Massachusetts Avenue should have precisely those same measures in effect at the present time. Alternative and more up-to-date methods may be equally or even more effective. * * *

The landlord is entirely justified in passing on the cost of increased protective measures to his tenants, but the rationale of compelling the landlord to do it in the first place is that he is the only one who is in a position to take the necessary protective measures for overall protection of the premises, which he owns in whole and rents in part to individual tenants.

Reversed and remanded to the District Court for the determination of damages.

[MACKINNON, J., dissented.]

NOTES AND QUESTIONS

1. How important is the fact that the assault occurred in a common passageway? Suppose the attacker had waited outside Mrs. Kline's apartment, forced his way in and attacked her in the living room. Liability? Cf. Wassell v. Adams, 865 F.2d 849 (7th Cir.1989) (plaintiff assaulted when she opened her motel door late at night). How does *Kline* differ from those holding a landlord liable when a tenant trips on a defective condition in a common hallway?

2. Prior to the 1970s, courts found no duty obligation in the instant case. See Goldberg v. Housing Auth. of Newark, 38 N.J. 578, 186 A.2d 291 (1962); Bass v. New York, 38 A.D.2d 407, 330 N.Y.S.2d 569 (1972), aff'd, 32 N.Y.2d 894, 300 N.E.2d 154, 346 N.Y.S.2d 814 (1973) (municipally-owned dwelling treated as privately owned); Daniels v. Shell Oil Co., 485 S.W.2d 948 (Tex.Civ.App.1972). Some courts adhere to the no duty rule, unless the landlord actively "assumes a duty": Feld v. Merriam, 506 Pa. 383, 485 A.2d

742 (1984). The main arguments against imposing that duty are stated in the principal case.

Also, it is said that a tenant makes a choice as to where to live and in effect "assumes the risk" of injury from criminal elements in a low security building. What about the contention that the *Kline* decision places the costs of crime on those who can least afford it—the rent-paying tenants? Who is in the better position to take measures against these criminal activities? Even though the victim's conduct may not immunize the landlord from liability, defenses and apportionment of blame to her, under principles of contribution, may shift to her prime responsibility and the burden of the loss. See Ellen M. Bublick, Citizen No-Duty Rules: Rape Victims and Comparative Fault, 99 Colum. L. Rev. 1413 (1999) for an effective critique of rules that allow this result.

3. Today there are several decisions finding the landlord liable to tenant or its employee or agent for an attack by a third person when the attack was foreseeable and reasonable steps to increase security would have prevented it. See Graham v. M & J Corp., 424 A.2d 103 (D.C.App.1980); Holley v. Mt. Zion Terrace Apts., 382 So.2d 98 (Fla.App.1980); Jardel Co. v. Hughes, 523 A.2d 518 (Del.1987); and Lay v. Dworman, 732 P.2d 455 (Okl.1986). A few courts have extended the warranty of habitability to include security. See Trentacost v. Brussel, 82 N.J. 214, 412 A.2d 436 (1980); Secretary of HUD v. Layfield, 88 Cal.App.3d Supp. 28, 152 Cal.Rptr. 342 (1978); Brownstein v. Edison, 103 Misc.2d 316, 425 N.Y.S.2d 773 (1980).

4. Courts struggle to determine whether third-party criminal acts were sufficiently foreseeable to impose liability. Some courts have focused exclusively on previous similar incidents, see, e.g., Madden v. C & K Barbecue Carryout, Inc., 758 S.W.2d 59 (Mo. 1988). Other courts have looked to the "totality of the circumstances" to determine foreseeability, see Isaacs v. Huntington Memorial Hospital, 38 Cal.3d 112, 695 P.2d 653, 211 Cal.Rptr. 356 (1985) (evidence of similar incidents in establishing foreseeability relevant but not essential); Seibert v. Vic Regnier Builders, 253 Kan. 540, 856 P.2d 1332 (1993) (same). In the wake of decisions such as the principal case and *Isaacs*, District of Columbia and California courts have limited the potential for liability by requiring a "heightened showing of foreseeability" in cases involving third-party criminal acts. See Potts v. District of Columbia, 697 A.2d 1249 (D.C. 1997); Wiener v. Southcoast Childcare Centers, Inc., 32 Cal.4th 1138, 12 Cal.Rptr.3d 615, 88 P.3d 517 (2004).

Judge Posner had harsh words for the "heightened foreseeability" approach adopted by District of Columbia and California courts: "These cases . . . invoke the rather old-fashioned formula that a criminal act, being deliberate, is an 'intervening' or 'supervening' cause that severs the 'causal chain' that would otherwise connect the negligence of the party who failed to prevent the criminal act to the injury to the victim. This is legal mumbo-jumbo. The practical question (and law should try to be practical) is whether the defendant knows or should know that the risk is great enough, in relation to the cost of averting it, to warrant the defendant's incurring the cost." Shadday v. Omni Hotels Mgmt. Corp., 477 F.3d 511 (7th Cir. 2007) (applying Indiana law). Should courts require a heightened showing of foreseeability to recover for injuries resulting from third party criminal acts? Should this requirement be imposed on hotel guests to the same degree that it is imposed on tenants who live in the area? Is there any basis for a principled distinction between these two types of plaintiffs?

5. Defining the extent of a landlord's duty to protect tenants is problematic. In Sherman v. Concourse Realty Corp., 47 A.D.2d 134, 365 N.Y.S.2d 239 (1975), the landlord of a 200-tenant multiple dwelling removed a lock cylinder from the building's security buzzer system which had been installed as a condition for a rent increase. Plaintiff-tenant was assaulted by an intruder. See also Tan v. Arnel Management Co., 170 Cal.App.4th 1087, 88 Cal.Rptr.3d 754 (2009), where a carjacker shot the plaintiff in an ungated common area in his apartment complex. The court found a duty to protect the plaintiff from the third party criminal act because the landlord failed to implement security measures that were neither "socially [nor] financially onerous." It took a sliding scale approach: "The higher [the] burden to be imposed on the landowner, the higher the degree of foreseeability is required." Id. at 1095.

6. Should the liability imposed on landlords be extended to condominium boards and their members? See Frances T. v. Village Green Owners Ass'n, 42 Cal.3d 490, 723 P.2d 573, 229 Cal.Rptr. 456 (1986) and Martinez v. Woodmar IV Condos. Homeowners Ass'n, 189 Ariz. 206, 941 P.2d 218 (1997).

CHAPTER 10

DAMAGES

Many law students take a separate course in Remedies that will cover the issues in this chapter in more detail and will cover other damages issues not relevant to tort law. For additional discussion of damages topics see Dobbs, Law of Remedies (2d ed. 1993). Because the valuation of the plaintiff's injuries is integral to the operation of the tort system, it is important to at least get an overview of some of the specific damages issues in tort litigation.

Proof of damages is an essential part of plaintiff's causes of action in negligence and strict liability, stemming historically from the actions on the case. In these actions, damage is the gist of the action. Recall that elsewhere, in actions based on trespass—most of the intentional torts—the cause of action is complete upon showing an invasion of the protected interest. Whether the plaintiff's skull was fractured by a deliberate blow, an act of negligence, or a product that was defectively designed, the amount of damages the defendant will have to pay to compensate the plaintiff for the skull fracture is the same.

The question of how much damage plaintiff suffered is often at the heart of the dispute between plaintiff and defendant. In the course of settlement negotiations, defendant may be willing to concede the issue of liability, but vigorously dispute the amount plaintiff is claiming for damages. Also, a good deal of trial time and effort is devoted to the topic of how much plaintiff should recover.

Some matters already considered in the chapter on duty (such as the question whether plaintiff can recover for negligent infliction of emotional harm where there has been no physical damage) and the chapters on causation (whether the injury for which plaintiff seeks compensation was caused by the defendant) also can be viewed as damages questions. In this chapter, it is assumed that plaintiff has been injured, that defendant is liable for plaintiff's injury, and that the law would allow some monetary recovery. The question here is deceptively simple: how much?

As part of the "tort reform" movement during the last three decades, over half the states passed legislation affecting the common law of damages in some way. In order to understand and appreciate the effect of this legislation, you must first consider the traditional scheme of tort damages. Let us begin with some basic vocabulary and some underlying themes.

NOTES AND QUESTIONS

Although injunctive relief is sometimes available as a remedy through tort lawsuits, money damages are the most commonly sought form of relief. There are three basic kinds of money damages in tort law:

1. *Nominal Damages.* These consist of a small sum of money (usually six cents or a dollar) awarded to the plaintiff in order to vindicate rights, make the judgment available as a matter of record in order to

prevent the defendant from acquiring prescriptive rights, and carry a part of the costs of the action. The amount of the award, so long as it is trivial, is unimportant.

2. *Compensatory Damages.* These are intended to represent the closest possible financial equivalent of the loss or harm suffered by the plaintiff, to make the plaintiff whole again, to restore the plaintiff to the position the plaintiff was in before the tort occurred. Most of this chapter is concerned with these damages.

3. *Punitive Damages.* These are an additional sum, over and above the compensation of the plaintiff, awarded in order to punish the defendant, to make an example of defendant, and to deter defendant and others from engaging in similar tortious conduct.

4. *Some Underlying Themes.* First, the purpose of *compensatory* damages is to restore the plaintiff to pre-injury status as far as possible. Second, the only tool at the jury's disposal for "making the plaintiff whole again" is money. All losses, even non-economic ones, must somehow be translated into money damages. Third, all damages, whether past, present, or future, must be included in one lump sum award, on the particular day the verdict is returned, in that single lawsuit that the plaintiff is permitted to bring. Fourth, judicial review of jury verdict amounts is relatively limited. Most jurisdictions allow new trials only if the award is so high or low that it "shocks the conscience." Finally, because the purpose of *punitive* damages is to punish and deter, they are focused on behavior and characteristics of the defendant rather than the plaintiff.

5. As you read the next two principal cases, think about how the lawyers used the discovery process to develop the information on damages and how it was presented, through the testimony of lay and expert witnesses.

1. PERSONAL INJURIES

Anderson v. Sears, Roebuck & Co.

United States District Court, Eastern District of Louisiana, 1974.
377 F.Supp. 136.

CASSIBRY, DISTRICT JUDGE. On April 23, 1970 the Britains' home was completely consumed by a fire which was ignited by a defective Sears' heater. Both Mildred [Anderson] Britain and her infant daughter, Helen Britain, were severely burned and Helen Britain suffered multiple permanent injuries. * * * [The jury awarded $2,000,000 in compensatory damages for Helen's injuries and the defendants moved for a new trial or, in the alternative, remittitur.]

The legal standard on which to gauge a jury verdict for remittitur purposes is the "maximum recovery rule". [Cc] This rule directs the trial judge to determine whether the verdict of the jury exceeds the maximum amount which the jury could reasonably find and if it does, the trial judge may then reduce the verdict to the highest amount that the jury could properly have awarded. Functionally, the maximum recovery rule both preserves the constitutionally protected role of the jury as finder of facts and prevents the predilections of the judge from infecting the jury's determination. Thus, the court's task is to ascertain, by scrutinizing all of the evidence as to each element of damages, what amount would be the maximum the jury could have reasonably awarded. In this case there are five cardinal elements of damages; past physical and mental pain; future physical and mental pain; future medical expenses; loss of earning capacity and permanent disability and disfigurement.

Past Physical and Mental Pain. The infant child Helen Britain, was almost burned to death in the tragic fire that swept her home. She was burned over forty per cent of her entire body; third degree burns cover eighty per cent of her scalp and second and third degree burns of the trunk and of her extremities account for the remainder. Helen Britain's immediate post-trauma treatment required hospitalization for twenty-eight days, during which time the child developed pneumonia, required numerous transfusions, suffered fever, vomiting, diarrhea, and infection, and underwent skin graft surgery, under general anesthesia, to her scalp, which was only partially successful. Keloid scarring caused webbing and ankylosis of the child's extremities and severely limited their motion. The child's fingers became adhered together; scarring bent the arm at the elbow in a burdensome, fixed position; and thick scarring on the thighs and on the side of and behind the knees impaired walking.

This child had to undergo subsequent hospitalizations for further major operations and treatment. The second major operation under general anesthesia was undertaken to graft new skin from the back and stomach to the remaining bare areas of the scalp. The third operation under general anesthesia was an attempt to relieve the deformity of her left hand caused by the webbing scars which bound down the fingers of that hand. A fourth operation under general anesthesia was performed to reduce scars which had grown back on the left hand again webbing the fingers. I cannot envisage the breadth and intensity of the pain experienced by Helen Britain throughout this ordeal.

The undisputed testimony reveals that one of the most tragic aspects of this case is that the horrible mental and emotional trauma caused to this child occurred at an age which medical experts maintain is crucial to a child's entire psyche and personality formation. Helen Britain's persistent emotional and mental disturbance is evidenced by bed wetting, nightmares, refusing to sleep alone, withdrawal, and speech impediments. Dr. Cyril Phillips, a psychiatrist, and Dr. Diamond both indicated that the child manifested to them, even at this early age, emotional illness and retarded mental growth.

The evidence reflects that an award of six hundred thousand dollars for this element of damages alone would not be unreasonable.

Future Physical and Mental Pain. There is clear evidence that the stretching, pulling, and breaking down of scars inherent in growth will continue to cause severe pain and a crippling limitation of motion in varying degrees to all of Helen Britain's upper and lower extremities. Very little can be done to improve the condition of the scalp which will never be able to breathe, sweat or grow hair. There will be risks, trauma and pain, both physical and mental, with each of the recommended twenty-seven future operations which will extend over most of the child's adult life, if she is in fact fortunate enough to be able to risk undergoing these recommended surgeries. Furthermore, Helen Britain must vigilantly guard against irritation, infection and further injury to the damaged and abnormal skin, scars and grafts because any injury, however slight, can generate cancer in these adynamic areas.

The inherent stresses and tensions of each new phase of life will severely tax this little girl's debilitated and delicate mental and emotional capacity. Throughout her future life expectancy of seventy-five years, it is reasonable to expect, that she will be deprived of a normal social life and that she will never find a husband and raise a family. On top of this, Helen Britain will always be subjected to rejection, stares and tactless inquiries from children and adults.

The court concludes that an award of seven hundred fifty thousand dollars for this element of damages alone would not be excessive.

Future Medical Expenses. A large award for future medical expenses is justified. The uncontradicted testimony was that Helen Britain would need the guidance, treatment and counseling of a team of doctors, including plastic surgeons, psychiatrists and sociologists, throughout her lifetime. Add to this the cost of the twenty-seven recommended operations and the cost of private tutoring necessitated by the child's mental and emotional needs and the jury could justifiably award a figure of two hundred and fifty thousand dollars to cover these future expenses.

Loss of Earning Capacity. The evidence of Helen Britain's disabilities both physical, mental and emotional was such that this court holds that the jury could properly find that these disabilities would prevent her from earning a living for the rest of her life. Not only do the physical impairments to her extremities disable her but her emotional limitations require avoiding stress and the combined effect is the permanent incapacity to maintain serious employment.

The jury was provided with actuarial figures which accurately calculated both the deduction of interest to be earned and the addition of an inflationary buffer, on any award made for future loss of earning capacity. In view of these incontrovertible projections at trial, it was within the province of the jury to award as much as $330,000.00 for the loss of earning capacity.

Permanent Disability and Disfigurement. The award for this element of damage must evaluate in monetary terms the compensation due this plaintiff for the permanent physical, mental and emotional disabilities and disfigurements proved by the evidence adduced at trial. A narration treating Miss Britain's permanent disabilities and disfigurements would be lengthy and redundant; therefore, I resort to listing.

1. The complete permanent loss of 80% of the scalp caused by the destruction of sweat glands, hair follicles and tissue—all of which effects a grotesque disfigurement and freakish appearance.

2. The permanent loss of the normal use of the legs.

3. The permanent impairment of the left fingers and hand caused by recurring webbing and resulting in limited motion.

4. The permanent impairment of the right hand caused by scars and webbing of the fingers.

5. The permanent injury to the left elbow and left arm with ankylosis and resulting in a crippling deformity.

6. The permanent destruction of 40% of the normal skin. As a result of this a large portion of the body is covered by "pigskin." Pigskin resembles the dry, cracked skin of an aged person and is highly susceptible to irritation from such ordinary things as temperature changes and washing.

7. Permanent scars over the majority of the body where skin donor sites were removed.

8. The permanent impairment of speech.

9. The loss of three years of formative and impressionable childhood.

10. Permanently reduced and impaired emotional capacity.

11. The permanent impairment of normal social, recreational and educational life.

12. The permanent imprint of her mother's hand on her stomach.

Considering each of the foregoing items, the court concludes that the jury had the prerogative of awarding up to $1,100,000 for this element of damages.

By totaling the estimated maximum recovery for each element of damages, the jury's actual award is placed in proper perspective. According to my calculations the maximum jury award supported by the evidence in this case could have been $2,980,000. Obviously, the jury's $2,000,000 verdict is well within the periphery established by the maximum award test.

The defendants assert three other grounds for a remittitur. They contend that there was error in the verdict since the verdict exceeded the amount prayed for in the plaintiff's pleadings. This contention fails because the plaintiffs' pleadings were amended subsequent to the jury verdict to conform to the evidence and the verdict of the jury. This amendment was permitted by the court in accordance with law. [Cc]

[Defendants] argue that the introduction of photographs of the plaintiff was inflammatory. Since a part of plaintiff's claim for damages is for disfigurement and the humiliation and embarrassment resulting therefrom, I hold that these photographs were properly admitted to show the condition of the plaintiff as she appeared to others, at the time they were taken. [Cc]

The defendants suggest that the presence of the child in the courtroom and in the corridors of the courthouse in some way inflamed or prejudiced the jury. This allegation is unfounded; the defendants have not pointed out any wrongful conduct on the part of Helen Britain, her parents, or counsel for plaintiffs. Helen Britain was well behaved and quiet the entire time she was in the courtroom.

Accordingly I hold that there was not any bias, prejudice, or any other improper influence which motivated the jury in making its award.

The defendants' motions for a remittitur are denied.

Richardson v. Chapman

Supreme Court of Illinois, 1997.
175 Ill.2d 98, 221 Ill.Dec. 818, 676 N.E.2d 621.

MILLER, J. * * * [Plaintiff Keva Richardson was the driver of a car with plaintiff Ann McGregor as a passenger. While they were stopped at a traffic light, their car was struck from behind by a semi-trailer driven by defendant Chapman who was employed by defendant Tandem/Carrier. At the trial, the judge directed a verdict in favor of the plaintiffs on the question of liability. Determining only the plaintiffs' damages, the jury returned verdicts against them in favor of Richardson and McGregor in the amounts of $22,358,814 and $102,215, respectively. The intermediate appellate court rejected the defendants' challenges to the amounts of damages awarded by the jury and defendants appealed.]

In their initial challenge to the damages verdicts, the defendants complain of certain testimony introduced by plaintiff Richardson concerning the calculation of the present value of her future economic losses. The defendants maintain that Professor Charles Linke, who testified as Richardson's economist, improperly used non-neutral, actual figures in describing to the jury the calculation of present cash value. Richardson's life expectancy at the time of trial, in May 1990, was 54.5 years. Relying on information and figures supplied by Richardson's primary physician, Professor Linke testified that the present cash value of her future medical expenses had a lower bound of $7,371,914 and an upper bound of $9,570,034. The lower bound figure assumed a discount rate one percentage point higher than the growth rate; the upper bound figure assumed that the two rates would be equal. The difference between the two numbers was based on different assumptions concerning future growth rates and interest rates. Professor Linke also provided testimony regarding the present cash value of Richardson's lost future earnings. Assuming a work history of 27.5 years, Professor Linke found that the present cash value of Richardson's lost income was between $854,107 and $971,944; using a longer work history of 35.8 years, Professor Linke arrived at a range of $1,068,343 to $1,265,363. Again, the differences between the two ranges were based on the witness' different assumptions regarding future growth and interest rates. * * *

We conclude that Professor Linke's approach was a reasonable one; by using a differential between the two rates, he did not have to make a prediction of future growth and inflation rates. Professor Linke was consistent in his treatment of inflation, and he did not adopt a method that would undercompensate or overcompensate the plaintiff. [Cc]

The defendants next contend that the damages awarded to the plaintiffs are excessive. Before resolving this question, we will briefly summarize the evidence presented at trial regarding the two women's injuries.

Keva Richardson was 23 years old at the time of the accident. She grew up in Pampa, Texas, and received a bachelor's degree in elementary education in May 1987 from Texas Tech University. While in college, she participated in a number of athletic activities and was, by all accounts, a popular, happy person. After graduating from college, Keva obtained a position as a flight attendant with American Airlines. She planned to work in that capacity for several years before returning to school to gain a post-graduate degree in education; her ultimate goal was to teach. Keva met Ann McGregor in the flight attendant training program, and the two decided to room together upon completion of their training. At the conclusion of the program, they were assigned to the Chicago area, and they had moved there just several days before the accident occurred.

Following the accident, Keva was initially taken to Highland Park Hospital for treatment. Because of the seriousness of her injuries, however, Keva was transferred that morning to Northwestern Memorial Hospital. Dr. Giri Gereesan, an orthopedic surgeon specializing in spinal surgery, determined that Keva had incurred a fracture of the fifth cervical vertebra, which severely damaged her spinal cord and resulted in incomplete quadriplegia. Dr. Gereesan performed surgery on Keva on December 1, 1987, to stabilize her spine so that she would be able to support her head; the surgery did not repair the damage to her spinal cord, and no treatment exists that could do so.

Keva was transferred to the Rehabilitation Institute of Chicago in December 1987, where she came under the care of Dr. Gary Yarkony. Keva was initially dependent on others in all aspects of her daily life. At the Rehabilitation Institute she learned how to perform a number of basic tasks, such as sitting in a wheelchair, transferring from a bed to a wheelchair, brushing her teeth, washing her face, and putting on loose-fitting tops. Keva's initial stay at the Rehabilitation Institute lasted until April 1988, when she moved to her parents' home in Texas. Keva returned to the Rehabilitation Institute in 1988 and in 1989 for follow-up visits. Keva also required hospitalization in Texas on three subsequent occasions for treatment of conditions arising from the accident.

Testifying in Keva's behalf at trial, Dr. Gary Yarkony, who had served as her primary physician at the Rehabilitation Institute, described Keva's current condition. He explained that she cannot use her legs and that she has only limited functioning in her arms, with loss of control of her fingers and fine muscles in her hands. She suffers pain in her legs and shoulders. Her chest and abdomen are paralyzed, and she has restrictive pulmonary disease. In addition, she has no control over her bladder or bowel functions and requires assistance in emptying them. As a consequence of her physical condition, she is at risk for bladder infections, pneumonia, and pressure ulcers. Keva also suffered a number of facial injuries in the accident. Some of these scars were later repaired through plastic surgery, but others remain.

At trial, Keva's mother, Dixie Richardson, described her daughter's current activities and the level of care necessary to assist her in her daily routine. Keva requires help in taking a shower and getting dressed. She cannot put on underwear, socks, or pants by herself but is able to put on pullover shirts and sweaters. With assistance, she can brush her teeth, apply makeup, and put in her contact lenses. She is unable to cut food or button a sweater. She can push her wheelchair on a smooth, level surface but otherwise needs assistance. In her own testimony, Keva said that she is self-conscious about her appearance now and the impression she makes on others. She said that the thing she misses most is just being able to get up in the morning and begin her day; now she requires the assistance of others, throughout the day.

The jury awarded Richardson a total of $22,358,814 in damages, divided among the following six elements: $258,814 for past medical care; $11,000,000 for future medical care; $900,000 for past and future lost earnings; $3,500,000 for disability; $2,100,000 for disfigurement; and $4,600,000 for pain and suffering. In challenging Richardson's award of damages, the defendants first argue that the sum of the future medical costs found by the jury—$11,000,000—is not supported by the evidence, for it exceeds even the larger of the two figures supplied by Professor Linke, $9,570,034. The defendants contend that the decision to award Richardson nearly $1.5 million more illustrates the jury's failure to properly determine damages in this case.

In response, Richardson argues that the larger award may simply be attributable to the jury's decision to make an award of expenses that she is likely to incur in the future but that were not specifically included in the calculations performed by Professor Linke. Richardson notes that Dr. Yarkony, in compiling for Linke's use the list of likely future medical costs, did not assign specific values to certain items, such as the expenses of future hospitalizations and the costs of wheelchairs and a specially equipped van. Richardson thus argues that the jury's decision to award an amount for future medical costs greater than Professor Linke's higher estimate might simply reflect the jury's desire to compensate her for those unspecified but likely expenses. We agree with Richardson that the trier of fact enjoys a certain degree of leeway in awarding compensation for medical costs that, as shown by the evidence, are likely to arise in the future but are not specifically itemized in the testimony. [Cc] In the present case, however, the amount awarded by the jury for future medical costs is nearly $1.5 million more than the higher of the two figures claimed at trial by Richardson. Notably, Professor Linke did not rely on the projections by the General Accounting Office (GAO) of the growth of future medical care costs, mentioned in the partial concurrence. Professor Linke explained that the GAO's study included a large number of technology-based items, while the main expense to be incurred by Richardson will be wages for attendant care. Given the disparity between the trial testimony and the jury's eventual award, we will not attribute the entire difference between those sums simply to miscellaneous costs Richardson is likely to incur in the future. For these reasons, we conclude that it is appropriate, by way of remittitur, to reduce by $1 million the nearly $1.5 million differential between the award for Richardson's future medical expenses and the higher figure presented in the testimony. This adjustment allows Richardson recovery for expected future medical costs for which no specific estimates were introduced, yet is not so large that it represents a departure from the trial testimony.

We do not agree with the defendants, however, that the remainder of the award of damages to Richardson, including the sums for pain and suffering, disability, and disfigurement, is duplicative or excessive or lacks support in the record. The determination of damages is a question reserved to the trier of fact, and a reviewing court will not lightly substitute its opinion for the judgment rendered in the trial court. [Cc] An award of damages will be deemed excessive if it falls outside the range of fair and reasonable compensation or results from passion or prejudice, or if it is so large that it shocks the judicial conscience. [C] When reviewing an award of compensatory damages for a nonfatal injury, a court may consider, among other things, the permanency of the plaintiff's condition, the possibility of future deterioration, the extent of the plaintiff's medical expenses, and the restrictions imposed on the plaintiff by the injuries. [C]

Here, it was the jury's function to consider the credibility of the witnesses and to determine an appropriate award of damages. We cannot say that the present award to Richardson is the result of passion or prejudice, "shocks the conscience," or lacks support in the evidence. * * *

The defendants also contend that the jury's award of damages to Ann McGregor is excessive. McGregor was 22 years old at the time of the accident. She grew up in Houston, Texas, and graduated from Southern Methodist University in May 1987 with a degree in psychology. Like Keva Richardson, McGregor was accepted after graduation for a position as a flight attendant with American Airlines. As mentioned earlier, the two women met while enrolled in the flight attendant training program and were sharing an apartment in the Chicago area at the time of the accident. Following the accident, McGregor was taken to Highland Park Hospital, where she was treated and released that day; she was then off work for about two weeks. A laceration she suffered on her forehead eventually healed, with only minimal scarring. At trial McGregor testified that she continues to suffer from nightmares about the accident. The jury awarded McGregor a total of $102,215 in damages, divided among the following components: $1,615 for past medical expenses, $600 for lost earnings, and $100,000 for pain and suffering.

* * * [W]e believe that the award of $100,000 for pain and suffering is, in these circumstances, excessive. McGregor was not seriously injured in the accident, incurring a laceration on her forehead, which left only a slight scar. The jury declined to award McGregor any compensation for disfigurement; rather, the bulk of her recovery consisted of compensation for pain and suffering. We conclude that a more appropriate figure for pain and suffering would be $50,000, which would reduce her total damages to $52,215. By way of remittitur, we accordingly reduce the judgment entered in favor of McGregor and against Tandem/Carrier and Chapman to that amount.

[The court then ruled on various matters relating to contribution and indemnity issues among the defendants.]

For the reasons stated, the judgment of the appellate court is affirmed in part, reversed in part, and vacated in part, and the judgment of the circuit court of Cook County is affirmed in part, reversed in part, and vacated in part. * * * In the absence of consent to the entry of a remittitur by each plaintiff within 21 days of the filing of this opinion or any further period in which the mandate is stayed, her individual action will be remanded to the circuit court of Cook County for a new trial on the question of damages. * * *

MCMORROW, J., concurring in part and dissenting in part: I concur in the opinion of my colleagues in all but one respect: I do not agree with the majority that it is proper to order a remittitur of the jury's award of damages to Keva Richardson for present cash value of future medical expenses or the jury's award to Ann MacGregor for pain and suffering.

In determining the total verdict awarded to Richardson, the jury considered extensive evidence relating to six separate components of damages. As noted by the majority, Richardson "suffered devastating, disabling injuries." The appellate court majority's unpublished opinion describes her condition: "After the collision, doctors determined that the communication connection between Richardson's brain and the rest of her body had become severed and she was rendered a quadriplegic. Richardson was soon placed in traction with tongs affixed to her skull by driving screws into the side of her head. She was also placed in a roto-rest bed with 25 pound weights attached to her body for traction. Eventually, Richardson underwent surgery to stabilize her spine so it could support the weight of her head which hung like a rag doll's head. In that operation, bone from her hips was grafted to her cervical spine with the use of metal plates and screws. The surgery did not repair the injury to Richardson's spinal cord, nor does medical technology yet exist to rectify the injury."

Other evidence related Richardson's need for assistance every six hours to empty her bladder by catheterization and daily assistance to empty her bowel, over which she permanently lacks control. She has lost the use of her legs, fingers, and the fine muscles of her hand. Her chest and abdomen are paralyzed. She is subject to risk of serious infections and other conditions and, according to the evidence, having a child would be life-threatening. The appellate court opinion further stated that Richardson "may expect to be hospitalized on a regular basis for the balance of her life."

The jury awarded $11 million to compensate Richardson for her future medical needs. To this sum the majority applies a remittitur of $1 million, based on the majority's observation that the jury's award for this element of damages exceeded by $1.5 million the testimony of economist Charles Linke regarding the "upper bound" of the present cash value of Richardson's future medical needs. Linke explained that he calculated a "lower bound" present value ($7.4 million) and an "upper bound" present value ($9.5 million). His figures were derived from different assumptions regarding the relationship of the rate of interest to the rate of growth. In explaining his economic assumptions and methods, Linke also noted that there were different accounting methods that could be used to calculate Richardson's future medical needs. The one he employed yielded a more conservative figure for medical care than that used by the General Accounting Office, which, according to Linke, would yield the conclusion that "the present value of

Keva Richardson's care needs would be approximately 12.1 million dollars." * * *

Dr. Yarkony testified, "This is the basic minimum care not covering any hospital admissions for emergencies, complications, and the like." He further testified that in his opinion Richardson would continue to require hospitalizations in the future caused by complications related to her spinal cord injury, including infections, pressure sores, pneumonia, and blood clots. * * *

Nothing in the record or the itemized jury verdict indicates that the jury departed from its customary duty to weigh the evidence and assess damages that would fairly compensate Richardson for her permanent and disabling injuries. The jury's award for future medical expenses, which arguably exceeded certain testimony, does not warrant the conclusion that the jury's determination was a departure from the flexible range of damages that was reasonably supported by the facts. There is no indication that the jury's award was the product of passion or prejudice. In fact, with respect to a different component of damages, i.e, Richardson's past and future lost earnings, the jury awarded a sum that was $1.265 million less than the higher of the testimonial estimates presented for that item of damages. If experts' estimates of a person's future income losses or medical expenses were an exact science capable of mathematical precision, there would be no need to have a jury make the final determination of proven damages. * * *

Similarly, I depart from the majority's holding that Ann MacGregor's damages award of $100,000 for pain and suffering was excessive. The majority orders a remittitur of $50,000 as a "more appropriate figure for pain and suffering." [C] The majority appears to base its conclusion on the relatively minor injury MacGregor sustained, noting that she suffered a laceration on her forehead that healed with only minimal scarring. Although the majority views the award of $100,000 as overly generous for a facial laceration that did not result in permanent disfigurement, the majority substitutes its own subjective judgment for the jury's evaluation of the evidence. The record indicates that MacGregor's lacerated forehead took six months to heal. The record further indicates that she suffered ongoing trauma, including recurrent nightmares resulting from the rear-end collision that left the other occupant of the car a quadriplegic. The jury, as finder of fact, had the superior ability to assess the evidence, including MacGregor's testimony relating to her traumatic and painful experience. I am aware of no sound reason to nullify the function of the jury and arbitrarily reduce MacGregor's award for pain and suffering to $50,000. Therefore, I cannot concur in the reasoning or result of the majority with respect to the reduction by remittitur of both plaintiffs' verdicts.

For the reasons stated, I concur in part and dissent in part from the judgment of the majority.

JUSTICE FREEMAN joins in this partial concurrence and partial dissent.

NOTES AND QUESTIONS

1. The principal cases present a catalogue of many of the major elements of damages in a personal injury case. Think about the time and

thought plaintiffs' attorneys devoted to developing proof of these items. Although both cases were based on negligence, similar items of damage can occur in actions based on intentional torts or strict liability.

2. The court in the *Anderson* case rejected defendants' argument that the child's presence inflamed or prejudiced the jury. Generally, a party is entitled to attend the trial and will be excluded only if there is disruptive conduct. Cary v. Oneok, Inc., 940 P.2d 201 (Okla.1997) (new trial ordered in case involving six-year-old burn victim who had been excluded from the courtroom during the liability phase of the case). This entitlement may be based on the federal Constitution's due process clause or a state constitution's right to jury trial or access to courts clause. Jordan v. Deery, 778 N.E.2d 1264 (Ind. 2002) (finding an ancillary right to be present in courtroom in Indiana Constitution's right to trial by jury and discussing cases in other jurisdictions).

3. In the *Richardson* case, note the difference in detail between the majority's and the dissent's description of plaintiffs' injuries and treatment. The dissent added detail from the intermediate appellate court opinion which, in turn, was gleaned from the trial transcript. Keep in mind when you are reading appellate opinions that their summary of testimony below is often cooler and more detached than the way it actually was given at the trial court level. In terms of strategy, do you think plaintiff McGregor benefitted from joining her claim with plaintiff Richardson or would she have been better off bringing it separately?

4. Note the courts' recitation of the standard in each of the jurisdictions for granting a new trial based on the amount of the damages. See notes 21–23.

5. *Evidence of Damages.* Proof of damages is an important part of plaintiff's cause of action, whether based on intentional conduct, negligence, or strict liability. There have been extensive developments over the past several decades in techniques for presenting this proof. For example, attorneys have made growing use of "demonstrative evidence." This form of evidence consists of tangible items such as charts, photographs, videos, models, and computer simulations. The purpose of this evidence is to bring home to the jury the total extent of plaintiff's injury. Much of this was pioneered by San Francisco attorney Melvin M. Belli, who showed empirically how demonstrative evidence can greatly enlarge the amount of a plaintiff's verdict. See Belli, Demonstrative Evidence and the Adequate Award, 22 Miss.L.J. 284 (1951). Experts may be used to project earnings, to detail plaintiff's medical difficulties, both physical and psychological, and in a variety of other ways. This is treated in more detail in courses in Evidence and Trial Practice.

6. It has become customary to divide damages in a personal injury case into separate categories. One classification is between "special" and "general" damages; another is between "economic" and "non-economic" damages. The two classifications are not always coterminous, but in personal injury cases lost earnings and medical and other expenses are treated as special damages subject to objective measurement of the economic loss, while pain and suffering and emotional distress are treated as general damages whose loss—although real—is fundamentally non-economic. You will sometimes hear attorneys discussing a case ask, as a

preliminary question, how much the "specials" are. The specials are all of the plaintiff's out of pocket expenses or economic losses.

Economic Losses

7. *Medical Expenses.* As the principal cases indicate, the plaintiff is compensated for reasonable medical expenses. Medical expenses may include bills for hospitals, doctors (including psychiatrists), physical therapists, nurses, medication, x-rays, crutches, wheel chairs, braces, travel to a different climate, etc. Past medical expenses are proved at trial by submitting the bills into evidence or through testimony. Future medical expenses (e.g., surgery that the plaintiff will need or medication plaintiff takes) must be proved by expert testimony establishing the anticipated need and predicted cost. Note that in the *Richardson* case the future medical expenses were proved by the testimony of two experts. Plaintiff's treating physician testified as to the medical care she was likely to need and an economist testified as to the likely cost of those procedures, based on assumptions about the rise in medical care costs over the time period in issue. Plaintiff will be able to recover unless the costs incurred were not related to the tortious injury, were unnecessary (trips to three medical specialists where one would have been reasonable), or excessively high (hourly fees higher than reasonable).

8. What if plaintiff suffers a relatively minor injury but fears developing a more serious condition because the defendant's act put the plaintiff at risk for it? Can plaintiff recover for that increased risk? Petriello v. Kalman, 215 Conn. 377, 576 A.2d 474 (1990) (allowing jury to consider plaintiff's risk of future bowel obstruction due to surgeon's negligence). Could she recover for her fear of developing the disease? Majca v. Beekil, 183 Ill.2d 407, 233 Ill.Dec. 810, 701 N.E.2d 1084 (1998) (allowing recovery if plaintiff can prove actual exposure to HIV and collecting AIDS cases from other jurisdictions).

If the plaintiff has no current physical illness or disease but alleges that the defendant negligently exposed the plaintiff to a toxic substance that increased the plaintiff's risk of contracting a disease in the future, may the plaintiff recover for the increased risk itself or for the costs of *medical monitoring* in order to detect the disease early if it does develop? Compare Caronia v. Philip Morris USA, Inc., 22 N.Y.3d 439, 982 N.Y.S.2d 40, 5 N.E.3d 11 (2013) (answering certified question from Second Circuit) (no medical monitoring for smokers for increased risk of lung cancer but no physical injury); Lowe v. Philip Morris USA Inc., 344 Or. 403, 183 P.3d 181 (2008) (same); In re Hanford Nuclear Reservation Litigation, 534 F.3d 986 (9th Cir. 2008) (under Price-Anderson Act, no medical monitoring for exposure to nuclear radiation); and Metro-North Commuter Railroad Co. v. Buckley, 521 U.S. 424 (1997) (not permitted in FELA case) with Bower v. Westinghouse Elec. Corp., 206 W.Va. 133, 522 S.E.2d 424 (1999) (recovery permitted for medical monitoring for exposure to toxic substances); Meyer v. Fluor Corp., 220 S.W.3d 712 (Mo. 2007) (medical monitoring claim permitted for children exposed to lead from lead smelter); Sinclair v. Merck & Co., 195 N.J. 51, 948 A.2d 587 (2008) (medical monitoring permitted for negligent exposure to toxic chemicals but not for product liability actions); Donovan v. Philip Morris USA, Inc., 455 Mass. 215, 914 N.E.2d 891 (2009) (medical monitoring recognized in negligence cases if claimant can show at least subcellular changes and that early detection and prompt treatment would significantly decrease risk of death or severity of disease) and Exxon Mobil Corp. v. Albright, 433 Md. 303, 71 A.3d 30 (2013) (recognizing medical monitoring as a form of relief—as distinguished from a cause of action—and determining that it should be accomplished through an equity fund administered by a trustee).

9. *Lost Wages.* If the plaintiff was employed at a fixed wage at the time of injury, the wages lost during the time of injury are relatively easy to calculate. For example, if an attorney who works for the Department of Justice loses two months from work because of an injury suffered in an automobile accident, she will be able to recover from the defendant responsible for her injury for two months' pay. The damages calculation is more complicated if the plaintiff was not employed at the time of the injury. For example, if the attorney was at home caring for two small children at the time of the injury, damages probably would be calculated on the basis of the cost of replacement care for her two children.

10. *Loss or Impairment of Future Earning Capacity.* If the injury is one from which the plaintiff does not recover and reenter the workforce, the measure of damages will include loss of earning capacity (sometimes called loss of future earnings) or impairment of earning capacity. First, the jury must be persuaded that the injury is permanent. See, e.g., Byrum v. Maryott, 26 Md.App. 130, 337 A.2d 142 (1975) (discussion of adequacy of expert witness testimony re permanency of injury). Then, expert testimony is needed to assist the jury in estimating what the plaintiff would have earned during the plaintiff's lifetime. As indicated in the *Anderson* case, even a very young plaintiff who would not be expected to engage in employment until the distant future may recover for the loss of future earnings. So may a plaintiff who was, at the time of injury, temporarily unemployed or voluntarily out of the workforce (e.g., while caring for family members or going to school in preparation to starting a new career). The jury is assisted in its estimate of lifetime earnings by the presentation of expert testimony on issues like life expectancy and the earnings of the average high school graduate, violinist, mechanic, fourth grade teacher, used car salesman, minister, nurse, etc., as appropriate. The jury is instructed that it is to rely on tables of life expectancy and average earnings only as a general guideline in determining how long plaintiff might be expected to live and how much he might be expected to earn. The jury may consider how individual factors such as plaintiff's "sex, prior state of health, nature of daily employment and its perils, manner of living, personal habits, and individual characteristics" will affect the life expectancy figure provided by a mortality table and the likelihood that plaintiff actually would achieve the positions, jobs, or promotions being predicted for him. See Volz v. Dresser, 150 Pa.Super. 371, 28 A.2d 493 (1942) (instructing jury to take into account characteristics of plaintiff in applying mortality tables) and South Carolina Finance Corp. v. West Side Finance Co., 236 S.C. 109, 113 S.E.2d 329, 336 (1960) ("The law does not require absolute certainty of data upon which lost profits are to be estimated, but all that is required is such reasonable certainty that damages may not be based wholly upon speculation and conjecture, and it is sufficient if there is a certain standard or fixed method by which profits sought to be recovered may be estimated and determined with a fair degree of accuracy.")

What if the plaintiff is claiming he would have earned millions as a professional athlete? Compare Sheppard v. Crow-Barker-Paul No. 1 Ltd. P'ship, 192 Ariz. 539, 968 P.2d 612 (1998) (affirming trial court judge's refusal to let the jury speculate on star high school basketball player's possible earnings during a professional career) with Felder v. Physiotherapy Assocs., 215 Ariz. 154, 158 P.3d 877 (2007) (expert permitted to testify re plaintiff's potential earnings in major league baseball where plaintiff already was playing on minor league team at time of injury).

What if an undocumented worker suffers a permanent injury? Can he seek future lost wages? See Grocers Supply, Inc. v. Cabello, 390 S.W.3d 707 (Tex. App. 2012) (finding that Texas tort law, which does not require U.S. citizenship or possession of work authorization in order to recover damages for lost earning capacity, is not preempted by federal immigration law) and Balbuena v. IDR Realty LLC, 6 N.Y.3d 338, 845 N.E.2d 1246, 812 N.Y.S.2d 416 (2006) (finding that federal immigration law does not preempt worker's common law right to damages for future lost wages but that jury should consider absence of work authorization in determining amount just as it would any other relevant fact or consideration in determining the likely amount of lost future wages).

It is loss of earning capacity that is being calculated and most people do not continue to earn money for their entire lives. Thus, the jury may consider the prospects for change in plaintiff's earning capacity, taking into account not only the nature of the person's employment, but also the fact that in growing older the person may be expected to earn more, and that a point is ultimately reached at which an older person will earn less or nothing at all. Note that in the *Richardson* case the economist calculated lost earnings based on two different work life expectancies (27.5 years and 35.8 years). Why did he do that?

11. *Damage Calculation: Present Value.* In personal injury actions, a plaintiff is awarded a lump sum to compensate for all future pecuniary losses, such as loss of future wages or future medical expenses. Most jurisdictions require that the lump sum award for future losses be reduced to its "present value." That is, the jury is instructed to award the amount of money in a lump that will produce for the plaintiff the amount the plaintiff would have earned or will need for a future operation. For example, plaintiff is a child whose back was injured. The back injury requires surgery, but not until the child has stopped growing. Thus, the medical testimony is that the child will need an operation ten years from the time of trial and that the cost of that operation is estimated to be $5,000. The jury must award the child enough money (principal) at the time of trial so that the principal plus the interest it will earn will equal $5,000 at the end of 10 years. Similarly, if the plaintiff is an adult who had been earning $50,000 a year and had a worklife expectancy of 10 years at the time of trial, the jury must award the adult enough money (principal) at the time of trial so that the adult will have an earnings stream of $50,000 a year for the next 10 years with no principal remaining at the end of the 10 years. The present value is computed by formula or by reference to tables once it has been determined at what interest rate to assume the plaintiff will be able to invest the lump sum (principal). Expert witnesses frequently differ as to the predicted interest rate, usually called the "discount rate" in this

context, that should be used. In addition to the *Richardson* opinion, see generally, Restatement (Second) of Torts § 913A.

12. *Future Inflation.* Plaintiffs' attorneys have argued that the jury should not merely reduce lump sum awards to present value based on estimated interest payments, but also should consider the countervailing effect of future inflation. They contend that an upward price movement is probable and that valuing future damages in terms of present prices does not fully compensate the victim. To continue the examples used earlier, it may be argued at trial that although the back operation costs $5,000 today, inflation will make its cost $6,000 in ten years and that today's $50,000 a year salary will be $52,000 next year. Most jurisdictions have recognized the need to adjust for expected future inflation in some way. Differences have arisen, however, with respect to the proper means to account for inflation, and how to mesh calculations for inflation with those for discount for present value. Three general methods have dominated the discussion: (a) the "inflation-discount method," which seeks to avoid undercompensation by increasing expected future earnings to account for inflation, and then discounting to present value by the market interest rate. Turcotte v. Ford Motor Co., 494 F.2d 173 (1st Cir.1974); (b) the "real interest method," whereby the "real" interest rate is perceived to be stable (between one percent and three percent) regardless of the level of inflation. Doca v. Marina Mercante Nicaraguense, S.A., 634 F.2d 30 (2d Cir.1980); and (c) the "total offset method," which assumes as a matter of law that the market interest rate that would be used to discount damage awards is completely offset by inflation in computing lost future income. Beaulieu v. Elliott, 434 P.2d 665 (Alaska 1967); State v. Guinn, 555 P.2d 530 (Alaska 1976); Kaczkowski v. Bolubasz, 491 Pa. 561, 421 A.2d 1027 (1980).

In Jones & Laughlin Steel Corp. v. Pfeifer, 462 U.S. 523 (1983), the Supreme Court reviewed various approaches and concluded that it should not establish one method as the exclusive federal rule for use in federal causes of action in federal courts. The Court observed that there are two stages in calculating damages (estimation of the lost stream of income or the cost of the surgery in the future and selection of an appropriate discount rate) and found that inflation should be included in both stages. Although the Court declined to establish any one method as the federal rule, it did note the attractiveness of the total offset method. This would amount to no discounting at all. Such a system would be easy to administer, but would it be fair? Is this a problem arising out of the highly inflationary decade of the 1970's with less impact now? To return to the example, would the court allow a party to demonstrate that there are different inflation rates for medical services than for the general inflation index? Note that the economist in the *Richardson* case testified that he had modified the GAO's projections for the cost of future medical services because he thought they were too focused on technology-based items and that Ms. Richardson's needs would primarily be for attendant care.

13. *Federal Income Tax.* Plaintiff's award for personal injuries is not subject to the federal income tax. Under Section 104(a)(2) of the Internal Revenue Code, a tort victim can exclude from gross income the amount of compensatory damages received on account of personal injuries. Punitive damages, however, are considered income. O'Gilvie v. United States, 519 U.S. 79 (1996). A problem arises when the award, or a part of it, is to

compensate for a loss that would have been subject to income tax. The primary instance is compensation for lost wages. If no reduction is made in the award, the injured plaintiff receives more for wages than if he had not been injured. For this reason, some courts have held that the "tax-free" nature of the award must be taken into account in setting the amount of the award. Caldwell v. Haynes, 136 N.J. 422, 643 A.2d 564 (N.J. 1994) (plaintiff has burden of producing evidence of net income for lost future wages). Other authorities have taken the position that to deduct the anticipated tax saving from the recovery would nullify the tax benefit conferred by Congress. Spencer v. A-1 Crane Svc., Inc., 880 S.W.2d 938 (Tenn.1994).

Most courts have refused to take into account the "tax-free" nature of the award because of concern about the speculative character of the amount of a potential deduction, at least insofar as it applies to future earnings. There is no way of telling what the tax rates will be in the future, nor what exemptions, deductions and other income the plaintiff would have, so as to determine what tax bracket he would be in. For these reasons, most courts have been inclined toward the position that in the case of the average taxpayer no adjustment should be made, and the plaintiff should receive the benefit of the windfall. In fact, most jurisdictions do not tell the jury that the award is tax free. But see Norfolk & Western Ry. Co. v. Liepelt, 444 U.S. 490 (1980) (Supreme Court in Federal Employers' Liability Act case allows jury to be told that award is tax exempt). There is a good debate on the pertinent policy issues between Judges Friendly and Lumbard in McWeeney v. New York, N.H. & H.R. R. Co., 282 F.2d 34 (2d Cir.1960), cert. denied, 364 U.S. 870 (1960).

14. *Interest.* Tort damages for personal injuries are generally unliquidated. No precise sum of damages is sought by the complaint. The jury must set a value on the loss suffered by plaintiff. Consequently, courts traditionally have not permitted the plaintiff to collect interest on the award until judgment is entered or until a verdict is reached. This rule has been criticized as discouraging settlements because it is to defendant's advantage to keep the money as long as possible without having to pay interest on it. Legislatures in some states have enacted statutes that provide for interest on the amount of the award from the date of the injury, the date of a demand of payment from the plaintiff, the date the cause of action was filed, or the date the expense actually was incurred by the plaintiff. See, e.g., Nev.Rev.Stats.Ann. § 17.130 and N.H.Rev.Stat.Ann. § 524:1–b. The plaintiff must pay federal income tax on any pre-judgment interest. Brabson v. United States, 73 F.3d 1040 (10th Cir.1996).

What is your view? Should plaintiff be paid interest on his claim? If so, when should interest obligations begin? Should interest cover both special and general damages? Even in the absence of statute, the jury may consider the time that has elapsed between the harm and the time of determining the amount of damages. See In re Air Crash Disaster Near Chicago, 644 F.2d 633 (7th Cir.1981) (applying Illinois law) (although the relevant statute did not specify that prejudgment interest could be awarded, it could be allowed as one element of "fair and just compensation"). On interest in general, see Restatement (Second) of Torts § 913.

Non-Economic Losses

15. *Physical Pain and Suffering, Mental Anguish.* In an action for a personal injury the plaintiff may recover damages for general or non-economic damages. They include not only suffering prior to the trial, but also any suffering reasonably certain to result from the injury in the future. Since pain, suffering and mental anguish are not capable of being reduced to any precise equivalent in money, there can be no fixed standard by which damages for them can be measured. The best that can be done is to leave the question to the jury, subject to control by the court, to fix a reasonable amount as compensation. It may be reversible error if the jury does not make an award for pain and suffering. Bowers v. Sprouse, 254 Va. 428, 492 S.E.2d 637 (1997) (jury award for exact amount of specials is inadequate as a matter of law, even if those damages were controverted; plaintiff experienced pain, suffering, and inconvenience and is entitled to be compensated for that). See also, Red Lake Band of Chippewa Indians v. United States, 1990 WL 515095 (D.D.C. 1990), rev'd on other grounds, 936 F.2d 1320 (D.C.Cir.1991) (In assessing damages in a bench trial in a suit against the United States under the Federal Tort Claims Act, the court noted that plaintiff "spoke little of his emotional distress and inconvenience or annoyance. Indeed, he gave sparse testimony on this. The court takes note of [plaintiff's] stoic nature. It also is aware of [plaintiff's] age, schooling, and health, and recognizes that he had to speak English in court, when this may not be his tongue of choice. Stoics unwilling or unable to orate on their anger, fear, worry, or pain feel these no less keenly than the voluble. When the law entitles a man to damages he should not be penalized for his reserve. The court has kept all this in mind when finding facts about damages. . . .") What about plaintiff's anxiety about payment of medical bills for treatment of injuries suffered in automobile accident? Warren v. Ballard, 266 Ga. 408, 467 S.E.2d 891 (1996) (finding no recovery for anxiety about paying medical bills).

What if plaintiff suffered emotional distress damages without any physical injury? A police officer went through a Burger King drive-thru staffed by two employees, both of whom had criminal records. Due to an uneasy feeling, the police officer lifted the top of the bun and observed a "slimy, clear and white phlegm glob" on the meat patty. DNA testing revealed that it was the saliva of one of the Burger King employees. Police officer alleged that he suffered ongoing emotional trauma from the incident, including vomiting, nausea, food anxiety, and sleeplessness, and has sought treatment by a mental health professional. Liability under Washington's product liability statute? Bylsma v. Burger King Corp., 176 Wash.2d 555, 293 P.3d 1168 (2013) (answering certified question from Ninth Circuit in the affirmative, if plaintiff can show emotional distress was a reasonable reaction and was manifested by objective symptomatology).

The general damages portion of the award may consist of several different elements. The most common is the physical pain caused by the injury. This may be of relatively short duration and be over by the time of trial (past pain and suffering) or it may be a chronic symptom that the medical experts predict plaintiff will always have (future pain and suffering). Plaintiff must be conscious to recover for this element of damages. Thus, whether the plaintiff was conscious after the accident but before death may be a hotly contested issue in some cases. How might the plaintiff's attorney prove conscious pain and suffering if the plaintiff cannot testify? Ghotra v. Bandila Shipping, Inc., 113 F.3d 1050 (9th Cir.1997) (applying maritime law) (affidavit from doctor opining that it was "highly likely" that decedent was conscious for ten seconds following accident not enough to overcome defendant's motion for summary judgment on the issue of pain and suffering where eyewitness testimony and autopsy report indicated that decedent was not conscious after injury and prior to death).

Loss of Function or Appearance. Plaintiff also may be able to recover for other types of loss. For example, there are holdings that allow a jury to award a recovery for the loss of sense of taste and smell, Purdy v. Swift & Co., Indus. Indem. Exch., 34 Cal.App.2d 656, 94 P.2d 389 (1939); incontinence, Thoren v. Myers, 151 Neb. 453, 37 N.W.2d 725 (1949); impotency and loss of desire for sexual intercourse, Sullivan v. City and County of San Francisco, 95 Cal.App.2d 745, 214 P.2d 82 (1950); change of personality and change of attitude towards others, Fjellman v. Weller, 213 Minn. 457, 7 N.W.2d 521 (1942); insomnia and inability to drive a car, Napier v. DuBose, 45 Ga.App. 661, 165 S.E. 773 (1932); fear of injury to an unborn child, Domenico v. Kaherl, 160 Me. 182, 200 A.2d 844 (1964); scars and other disfigurements, Gray v. Washington Water Power Co., 30 Wash. 665, 71 P. 206 (1903).

Emotional Distress from Legal Malpractice. Should plaintiff be entitled to pain and suffering damages in a legal malpractice action? Lickteig v. Alderson, Ondov, Leonard & Sween, 556 N.W.2d 557 (Minn.1996) (emotional distress may be an element of damages only if plaintiff suffers physical injury; if plaintiff was exposed to physical injury due to the negligence of another and develops physical symptoms after emotional distress; or if emotional distress results from a direct invasion of rights such as in slander, libel, malicious prosecution, seduction or other willful, wanton, or malicious conduct) and Schmidt v. Coogan, 181 Wash.2d 661, 335 P.3d 424 (2014) (emotional distress damages are available for attorney negligence only if emotional distress is foreseeable due to the particularly egregious (or intentional) conduct of an attorney or the sensitive or personal nature of the representation—not for loss of compensation in a slip and fall case).

Can you see the policy implications of allowing such damages in a legal malpractice case? Compare Miranda v. Said, 836 N.W.2d 8 (Iowa 2013) (although emotional distress damages generally require showing of either intentional conduct of defendant or physical injury to plaintiff, such damages were allowed in legal malpractice action in immigration matter that resulted in parents being separated from their young child) with Dombrowski v. Bulson, 19 N.Y.3d 347, 948 N.Y.S.2d 208, 971 N.E.2d 338, 341 (2012) ("We see no compelling reason to depart from the established rule limiting recovery in legal malpractice actions to pecuniary damages. Allowing this type of recovery [for emotional distress] would have, at best, negative and, at worst, devastating consequences for the criminal justice system. Most significantly, such a ruling could have a chilling effect on the willingness of the already strapped defense bar to represent indigent accused. Further, it would put attorneys in the position of having an incentive not to participate in post-conviction efforts to overturn wrongful convictions. We therefore hold that plaintiff does not have a viable claim for [emotional distress] damages and the complaint should be dismissed in its entirety.").

Litigation-Induced Stress. Should plaintiff be able to recover for the anxiety and stress that accompanies litigation? Most courts have not recognized it as a separate component of damages. School Dist. v. Nilsen, 271 Or. 461, 534 P.2d 1135 (1975) (this type of stress inherent in most litigation); Buoy v. ERA Helicopters, Inc., 771 P.2d 439 (Alaska 1989) (litigation-induced depression); Stoleson v. United States, 708 F.2d 1217, 1223 (7th Cir.1983) (alleged tortfeasor should have the right to defend himself without thereby multiplying his damages); Picogna v. Board of Education, 143 N.J. 391, 671 A.2d 1035 (1996) (not appropriate element of pain and suffering damages).

16. *Loss of Enjoyment of Life.* As the cases in note 15 illustrate, most jurisdictions allow plaintiffs to recover for the loss of specific aspects of their lives as part of the recovery for pain and suffering, while some categorize it as a separate element of damages. Golden Eagle Archery, Inc. v. Jackson, 116 S.W.3d 757, 768 (Tex. 2003) ("Courts across the country have struggled with whether loss of enjoyment of life is compensable at all, and if so, whether it is part of pain and suffering, mental anguish, or physical impairment or is a separate, independent category of damages.") (collecting cases). These are sometimes called "hedonic damages." McGee v. AC and S, Inc., 933 So.2d 770 (2006) (holding that loss of enjoyment of life is a separate element of hedonic damages; dissent traces history of use of term "hedonic" damages and argues that it should not be separated from general damages). See also McClurg, Dead Sorrow: A Story About Loss and a New Theory of Wrongful Death Damages, 85 B.U. L. Rev. 1 (2005) (discussing the confusion surrounding the term and its use by various courts to describe different types of damages).

17. *Per-diem Argument.* A controversial technique of counsel for the plaintiff in arguing to the jury has been to break physical and mental suffering down into days, hours, or even minutes, set a value on each unit, and multiply it by the total number of the units that pain and suffering has lasted and may be expected to last. It is not permitted in some jurisdictions because it tends to give the appearance of mathematical precision, through the use of a formula, to something that is by its nature neither mathematical nor precise and because it ignores the fact that once the "threshold" of pain is crossed, the body tends to adjust to it and the suffering to diminish. See, e.g., Affett v. Milwaukee & Suburban Transport Corp., 11 Wis.2d 604, 106 N.W.2d 274 (1960); Reid v. Baumgardner, 217 Va. 769, 232 S.E.2d 778 (1977). A majority of jurisdictions, however, permit the argument, assuming that defendant's counsel can point out any flaws in the argument and that the jury will not be misled. See, e.g., Weeks v. Holsclaw, 306 N.C. 655, 295 S.E.2d 596 (1982); Debus v. Grand Union Stores of Vermont, 159 Vt. 537, 621 A.2d 1288 (1993). See also Joseph H. King, Jr., "Counting Angels and Weighing Anchors: Per Diem Arguments for Noneconomic Personal Injury Tort Damages," 71 Tenn. L. Rev. 1 (2003) (arguing that courts should not permit the per diem argument to be used).

18. Assuming that plaintiff is awarded damages for future pain and suffering, should that amount be reduced to its present value? Most courts have held that since damages for pain and suffering do not have a precise market value, they need not be reduced to present value. See Texas & Pac.

R. Co. v. Buckles, 232 F.2d 257 (5th Cir.), cert. denied, 351 U.S. 984 (1956). A few courts have indicated that a rough attempt at reduction is better than no effort at all. See In re Millard's Estate, 251 Iowa 1282, 105 N.W.2d 95 (1960); Abbott v. Northwestern Bell Tel. Co., 197 Neb. 11, 246 N.W.2d 647 (1976). A California court has left the decision to the discretion of the jury. Garfoot v. Avila, 213 Cal.App.3d 1205, 261 Cal.Rptr. 924 (1989).

19. The idea of awarding money damages for pain and suffering is not without its critics. Do these damages do any good? Do they help plaintiff bear the pain? A legal-medical study concluded that damages should be allowed only for pain that has a physiological basis. See Peck, Compensation for Pain: A Reappraisal in Light of New Medical Evidence, 72 Mich.L.Rev. 1355 (1974). What of the argument that an award for pain and suffering is an indirect way of taking care of the plaintiff's attorney's fees, thus allowing the plaintiff the full amount of the pecuniary loss? See page 563 re legislative alterations to common law recovery for pain and suffering.

20. *Reduced Life Expectancy.* Traditionally, American authority has denied any damages for the shortening of the plaintiff's life expectancy itself, as distinguished from loss of prospective earnings. There have been three major factors responsible for this: the belief that the common law rule against compensating for loss of life except as provided by statute must preclude compensation for shortening life; the fear that duplication of damages may result; and unwillingness to enter a field filled with incalculable variables. See Farrington v. Stoddard, 115 F.2d 96 (1st Cir.1940); O'Leary v. United States Lines Co., 111 F.Supp. 745 (D.Mass.1953); Rhone v. Fisher, 224 Md. 223, 167 A.2d 773 (1961); and Paladino v. Campos, 145 N.J.Super. 555, 368 A.2d 429 (1976).

Judicial Control of Amounts Recovered

21. A trial judge (through a motion for a new trial) or an appellate panel (on appeal) can disturb the jury's finding on the amount of the damages only if the verdict is so excessive or so inadequate as to demonstrate that the jury acted contrary to the law—in passion or prejudice rather than according to their instructions. The test for disturbing a jury award on the amount of damages is expressed in various ways. The principal cases referred to the "maximum amount which the jury could reasonably find" and whether the amount "shocks the conscience." Other courts have used terms like "grossly" excessive or inadequate, "inordinate," or "outrageous." Meals v. Ford Motor Co., 417 S.W.3d 414, 425 (Tenn. 2013) ("A jury has wide latitude in assessing non-economic damages. We trust jurors to use their personal experiences and sensibilities to value the intangible harms such as pain, suffering, and the inability to engage in normal activities. This task is made more difficult in a catastrophic injury case. It is not our role to second-guess the jury and to substitute our judgment; but it is our role to protect against a verdict that is excessive.")

22. If the judicial review of the verdict concludes that the award was grossly excessive or grossly inadequate, the judge(s) must then decide whether to set aside the verdict and grant a new trial on both liability and damages, or to allow the liability portion of the verdict to stand and to grant a new trial on damages alone. Maier v. Santucci, 697 A.2d 747 (Del. 1997) (new trial on damages ordered where jury, in rear-end collision, back injury case, awarded $0 damages to plaintiff after trial court judge had

directed a verdict for plaintiff on liability). Usually, a whole new trial is granted. A partial new trial, on damages only, is the appropriate remedy only if the judge is persuaded that whatever influenced the jury to act inappropriately in setting the amount of damages did not also taint the liability verdict. Tedder v. American Railcar Indus., Inc. v. 739 F.3d 1104 (8th Cir. 2014) (FELA action) ("We favor new trials over remittiturs when a court finds that passion or prejudice has influenced a jury's damage award on the theory that such passion or prejudice may also have influenced the jury's determinations in other phases of the trial.")

23. *Remittitur and Additur.* If the judge decides to grant a new trial on damages alone, the judge may make the grant conditional. To avoid the expense, inconvenience and delay of new trials in these cases, trial courts frequently, in cases of excessive verdicts, grant a motion for a new trial that is conditioned upon the refusal of the plaintiff to accept a lesser amount. This order is called a remittitur and was at issue in both principal cases. When the verdict is inadequate, the trial judge may grant the motion for a new trial conditioned on the defendant's refusal to pay a larger sum set by the court. This order is called an additur or an increscitur. The trial court must explain its reasoning so that the appellate court can ensure that the trial court judge did not merely substitute its opinion for that of the jury's. He v. Miller, 207 N.J. 230, 24 A.3d 251 (2012) (jury's award is entitled to presumption of correctness, which should only be overcome if award "shocks the conscience of the court or is wide of the mark and pervaded by a sense of wrongness"). It has generally been held that remittitur does not violate the guaranty of jury trial contained in the federal and state constitutions. On the other hand the power of additur has been denied to the federal courts by a 5–4 decision of the Supreme Court, Dimick v. Schiedt, 293 U.S. 474 (1935). The decisions as to the constitutionality of additur under state constitutions are split, with some courts interpreting their state constitutions to permit additur in the state court and others finding that additur in a state court action violates their state constitutions as the Supreme Court had found that it would violate the Seventh Amendment in an action in federal court.

In the *Richardson* case, what happens after the Illinois Supreme Court decision? Will there be a new trial?

Legislative Control of Amounts Recovered

24. In response to tort reform efforts, about half of the state legislatures have passed laws that in some way affect the amount of damages recoverable. Many of these statutes apply only to particular types of claims (e.g., medical malpractice claims, claims against the government), while others cover all tort actions seeking recovery for personal injury, but apply only to non-economic injuries. Compare R.R.S. Neb. § 44–2825 (medical malpractice only, $1,750,000 total recovery) with Md.Cts. & Jud.Proc.Code Ann. § 11–108 (all personal injury actions, $815,000 for non-economic damages in 2015, increasing $15,000 a year thereafter).

25. Some of the legislative caps on damages have been found unconstitutional, particularly those limited to certain causes of action, but most have survived constitutional scrutiny. Compare Lebron v. Gottlieb Memorial Hosp., 237 Ill.2d 217, 930 N.E.2d 895 (2010) (cap of $500,000 on noneconomic injuries in medical malpractice actions is unconstitutional violation of separation of powers clause); Watts v. Lester E. Cox Medical

Ctr., 376 S.W.3d 633 (Mo. 2012) (cap of $350,000 on non-economic damages for medical malpractice actions violates right to jury trial of state constitution); and Estate of McCall v. U.S., 134 So.3d 894 (Fla. 2014) (answering certified question from federal court in FTCA case) (cap of $500,000 for noneconomic damages for wrongful death actions violates equal protection clause of state constitution) with Fein v. Permanente Medical Group, 38 Cal.3d 137, 695 P.2d 665, 211 Cal.Rptr. 368 (1985) (legislature may expand or limit recoverable damages so long as its action is rationally related to a legitimate state interest); Miller v. Johnson, 295 Kan. 636, 289 P.3d 1098 (2012) (statutory cap of $250,000 on noneconomic damages in medical malpractice actions had rational basis and thus did not violate state equal protection clause); MacDonald v. City Hosp., Inc., 227 W.Va. 707, 715 S.E.2d 405 (2011) (statutory damages cap of $500,000 did not violate the state constitutional right to a jury trial, separation of powers, equal protection, special legislation, or the "certain remedy" provisions); and Arbino v. Johnson & Johnson, 116 Ohio St.3d 468, 880 N.E.2d 420 (2007) (upholding cap on noneconomic damages on most tort actions and noting that similar statutes previously had been held unconstitutional).

26. In addition to the question whether the caps will survive constitutional challenges, the legislative alterations of the common law raise other issues. Is the jury to be told of the cap? How does the cap apply to multiple causes of action arising out of the same incident? Where comparative negligence reduces the verdict by a percentage, which is to be applied first, the percentage reduction or the cap?

Montgomery Ward & Co., Inc. v. Anderson

Supreme Court of Arkansas, 1998.
334 Ark. 561, 976 S.W.2d 382.

NEWBERN, J. * * * On November 14, 1994, appellee Shirley Anderson was badly injured in a fall while shopping in appellant's Montgomery Ward store in Little Rock. Montgomery Ward personnel sent her to the hospital at the University of Arkansas for Medical Sciences ("UAMS") to be treated. Ms. Anderson had surgical and other medical-services expenses at UAMS totaling $24,512.45. Montgomery Ward moved in limine to prohibit Ms. Anderson from presenting the total amount billed by UAMS as proof of her medical expenses and asked that her evidence be limited to the actual amount for which she would be responsible to pay. In response, Ms. Anderson stated that, through her attorney, she had reached an agreement with UAMS that UAMS would discount the bill by fifty per cent. Ms. Anderson asserted that the collateral-source rule would prohibit Montgomery Ward from introducing evidence of the discount.

The Trial Court denied the motion in limine, ruling that the negotiated discount with UAMS was a collateral source, and allowed evidence of the entire amount billed by UAMS. Montgomery Ward urges that the ruling and the denial of the motion for new trial made on the same basis were erroneous. * * *

We have held that the collateral-source rule applies unless the evidence of the benefits from the collateral source is relevant for a purpose other than the mitigation of damages. [C] The issue, then, is whether the forgiveness of a debt for medical services is a collateral source to be sheltered by the rule. There is no Arkansas authority dealing directly with that precise issue, but our cases explaining the policy behind the rule support the Trial Court's ruling. * * *

Although those cases [relied on by the trial court judge] do not directly answer the question in this case, they deal with analogous situations and explain the policy behind the collateral-source rule. A trial court must "exclude evidence of payments received by an injured party from sources 'collateral' to . . . the wrongdoer, such as private insurance or government benefits. . . ." Bell v. Estate of Bell, 318 Ark. 483, 490, 885 S.W.2d 877, 880 (1994). [Cc] Recoveries from collateral sources "do not redound to the benefit of a tortfeasor, even though double recovery for the same damage by the injured party may result." Bell v. Estate of Bell, 318 Ark. at 490, 885 S.W.2d at 880; [c].

In the Bell case, we recognized that commentators had criticized the rule as being "incongruous with the compensatory goal of the tort system" and that some jurisdictions had modified or abrogated the rule. * * *

We also noted that the rule had been extended to cases in other areas of the law, such as unemployment compensation received during a period later held to have resulted from a wrongful discharge under the Teacher Fair Dismissal Act. [C] In a later case, [c], a defendant argued that the collateral-source rule was inequitable because it resulted in a windfall to the plaintiff. We disposed of the argument by explaining the policy behind the rule as follows: "Whether she received the money from her employer or from an insurance policy, she, rather than the alleged tortfeasor, is entitled to the benefit of the collateral source, even though in one sense a double recovery occurs. [C] The law rationalizes that the claimant should benefit from the collateral source recovery rather than the tortfeasor, since the claimant has usually paid an insurance premium or lost sick leave, whereas to the tortfeasor it would be a total windfall." [C] That statement of policy and the cases cited favor including discounted and gratuitous medical services within the shelter of the collateral-source rule. There is no evidence of record showing that Montgomery Ward had anything to do with procuring the discount of Ms. Anderson's bill by UAMS. The rationale of the rule favors her, just as it would had she been compensated by insurance for which she had arranged. * * *

We recognize four situations in which the rule does not apply. . . . They are cases in which a collateral source of recovery may be introduced (1) to rebut the plaintiff's testimony that he or she was compelled by financial necessity to return to work prematurely or to forego additional medical care; (2) to show that the plaintiff had attributed his condition to some other cause, such as sickness; (3) to impeach the plaintiff's testimony that he or she had paid his medical expenses himself; (4) to show that the plaintiff had actually continued to work instead of being out of work, as claimed. [Cc] This Court has also allowed evidence of collateral sources when the plaintiff opens the door to his or her financial condition. [Cc] The Trial Court ruled that none of the exceptions applied to the facts at hand, and an examination of the abstract indicates that ruling was correct. There is no testimony by the plaintiff that arguably invokes any of the exceptions.

The Restatement (Second) of Torts § 920A(2) provides guidance on this issue and explains that the general rule is that "[p]ayments made to or benefits conferred on the injured party from other sources are not credited against the tortfeasor's liability, although they cover all or a part of the harm for which the tortfeasor is liable." Comment *b* to that Restatement section explains that, if the plaintiff is responsible for the benefit received, the law allows the plaintiff to keep it. Further, if the benefit was a gift to the plaintiff from a third party or established for the plaintiff by law, the plaintiff should not be deprived of the advantage that it confers. Another way to state the rule is to say that "it is the tortfeasor's responsibility to compensate for all harm that he [or she] causes, not confined to the net loss that the injured party receives." Restatement (Second) of Torts § 920A comment *b*. Comment *c* (3) indicates that gratuities of cash or services are collateral sources that are not subtracted from a plaintiff's recovery. The comment gives the example of a doctor who does not charge for medical services.

Other authority indicates that a substantial number of jurisdictions addressing the issue have held that the plaintiff may recover the reasonable value of nursing care or services rendered gratuitously for the plaintiff's benefit. [C] The primary issue remaining today is how to value the services, [c], but that issue is determined in this case by the total medical bill submitted to Ms. Anderson by UAMS.

Montgomery Ward cites cases from Massachusetts, New York, and Illinois for the proposition that gratuitous medical services may not be an item of recovery because the policy behind the collateral-source rule does not apply where the plaintiff has incurred no expense or obligation for the services needed. [Cc] We are, however, persuaded by cases holding that gratuitous medical services do fall under the collateral-source rule. * * *

We choose to adopt the rule that gratuitous or discounted medical services are a collateral source not to be considered in assessing the damages due a personal-injury plaintiff. It is the rule recommended by the Restatement (Second) of Torts, and it is consistent with our oft-stated policy of allowing the innocent plaintiff, instead of the tortfeasor defendant, to receive any windfall associated with the cause of action. Accordingly, we hold that the Trial Court did not err by excluding evidence of the UAMS discount as a collateral source.

Affirmed.

NOTES AND QUESTIONS

1. What is a motion in limine?

2. What if the health care provider's write-off was negotiated in advance by the plaintiff's health insurance company? Would the evidence of the write-off still be excluded by the collateral source rule? Compare Howell v. Hamilton Meats & Provisions, Inc., 52 Cal.4th 541, 129 Cal.Rptr.3d 325, 257 P.3d 1130 (2011) (the negotiated rate differential is not a collateral payment or benefit subject to the collateral source rule and thus is admissible) with White v. Jubitz Corp., 347 Or. 212, 219 P.3d 566 (2009)

(evidence of what Medicare paid to patient's medical providers—reflecting Medicare write-offs—was inadmissible).

3. *Collateral Source Rule.* As the principal case suggests, the collateral source or collateral benefits rule is applied when the plaintiff receives compensation from any source collateral to the tortfeasor. Those sources may include health or medical insurance, life insurance, disability insurance, employee benefits (sick leave, vacation pay), or governmental benefits (free care at Veteran's Hospital or through Medicare). Helfend v. Southern Cal. Rapid Transit Dist., 2 Cal.3d 1, 465 P.2d 61, 84 Cal.Rptr. 173 (1970). But see Washington v. Barnes Hospital, 897 S.W.2d 611 (Mo.1995) (availability of free public school special education and therapy services admissible in case where plaintiff's expert had testified about the cost of private school education because plaintiff did not pay for or bargain for free services and services were not contingent on plaintiff's financial need or special status as some government programs are). The rule does not apply, however, to payments made by the defendant or by a joint tortfeasor or one who mistakenly thinks he is a tortfeasor, or by an insurance company or other person who makes payment on behalf of a tortfeasor. See, in general, Restatement (Second) of Torts § 920A and note 4, page 398.

4. When benefits are conferred upon the plaintiff gratuitously, as when a plaintiff is nursed without charge by the spouse, the prevailing rule is that plaintiff is entitled to recover the reasonable value of the services from the defendant, since they are a gift to the plaintiff, and not to the defendant, and should not reduce the liability of the latter. Strand v. Grinnell Auto. Garage Co., 136 Iowa 68, 113 N.W. 488 (1907); Wells v. Minneapolis Baseball & Athletic Ass'n, 122 Minn. 327, 142 N.W. 706 (1913). A minority rule, however, does not permit the plaintiff to recover for the value of services provided without charge to plaintiff. See Coyne v. Campbell, 11 N.Y.2d 372, 183 N.E.2d 891, 230 N.Y.S.2d 1 (1962).

5. As the principal case states, plaintiff may recover double when the collateral source rule is applied. This is not usually the case, however. Paid sick leave will reduce the amount of sick leave the plaintiff has to use for illness or other injuries. Health insurance contracts and government programs providing benefits typically provide that the insured must pay back the benefits that were provided from the proceeds of a judgment or settlement with a tortfeasor. See, for example, Administrative Comm. of Wal-Mart Stores, Inc. Assoc. Health and Welfare Plan v. Shank, 500 F.3d 834 (8th Cir. 2007) (upholding judgment reimbursing health insurance plan for amounts paid on behalf of insured after recovery from third party tortfeasor) and US Airways, Inc. v. McCutchen, 133 S.Ct. 1537 (U.S. 2013) (upholding reimbursement of health insurance plan for amounts paid on behalf of insured from settlement between insured and tortfeasor but requiring plan to pay its share of insured's attorneys' fees).

6. Over half of the states have modified the common law collateral source rule by statute, usually as part of "tort reform" movements. Some of the modifications apply only to particular causes of action (e.g., medical malpractice). About half of those provide that the information concerning the collateral source is admissible in evidence (see e.g., Ariz.Rev.Stat. § 12–565) without indicating what the jury is to do with that information, while others specify that the award is to be reduced by the amount of the collateral source (see, e.g., N.Y. C.P.L.R. § 4545(c)). Some of these statutes

have been found unconstitutional, while others have survived constitutional challenge. Compare Carson v. Maurer, 120 N.H. 925, 424 A.2d 825 (1980) (unconstitutional) with Barme v. Wood, 37 Cal.3d 174, 689 P.2d 446, 207 Cal.Rptr. 816 (1984) and Reid v. Williams, 964 P.2d 453 (Alaska 1998) (constitutional). The Kansas legislature tried three times (1976, 1986, and 1992) to limit the common law collateral source rule and each time the Kansas Supreme Court found the statute unconstitutional. See Thompson v. KFB Insurance Co., 252 Kan. 1010, 850 P.2d 773 (1993).

7. *Loss of Consortium.* Most states recognize a claim by the spouse of an injured person for loss of conjugal relations, society, companionship, household services, etc. during the time period that the injured person is recovering or for a permanent loss. The claim is derivative of the injured person's and in most states must be joined in the same cause of action as the injured person's. Should loss of consortium be available for relationships not formalized by marriage? Should loss of consortium be available for damage to the parent child relationship? See a more detailed discussion of these issues in Chapter 22, Section 2, Family Relations.

8. *Expenses of Litigation.* Under the English practice, the winning party, whether plaintiff or defendant, recovers his expenses of litigation, including attorney's fees. This is not the practice in the United States in regard to litigation in general, or tort litigation in particular. The practice of having each side bear its own expenses often is referred to as the "American Rule." See Restatement (Second) of Torts § 914. Alaska is an exception. Alaska Civil Rule 82. It is sometimes suggested that in a personal injury case, as a practical matter, the award for pain and suffering may have the effect of allowing the plaintiff to pay the attorney and still retain compensation for economic losses.

Chapter 21, Misuse of Legal Procedure, covers the tort action for bringing a suit held to be frivolous or for using legal procedure for an improper purpose—"abuse of process." It also treats statutes and Rules of Court providing for the trial judge to impose a sanction—usually payment of attorney's fees—for conduct of this nature.

9. *The Contingent Fee.* Lawyers who represent plaintiffs in personal injury litigation usually are paid on the basis of a contingent fee contract. Under this arrangement, the lawyer agrees to render professional services for a fee that is based on a percentage of the amount the client recovers in the case. If there is no recovery, the lawyer receives no fee. The percentage of the contingent fee varies, sometimes depending upon whether the case is settled or tried, or on the size of recovery. A common contingent fee is 30%–40%. If for some reason no figure is set by attorney and client, or there is later a dispute about the amount of the figure, an attorney may bring an action against the former client for a *quantum meruit* recovery. See e.g., Nugent v. Downs, 230 So.2d 597 (La.App.1970) (setting a fee of 30%). In certain situations the amount of the contingent fee may be fixed by statute. For example, the Federal Tort Claims Act makes it a crime for an attorney to obtain a contingent fee greater than 25% of the judgment or settlement of the suit against the United States Government or 20% of a settlement through the administrative procedure before suit. 28 U.S.C. § 2678. Jurors are not informed about the contingent fee and they are not to add that fee to their verdict. Thus, it is a basic part of the tort damage system that plaintiff absorbs the costs of bringing a law suit. The contingent fee may

result in an attorney being compensated far beyond or far below what would be a "reasonable fee" for the effort expended. Also, it may create a conflict of interest between attorney and client as to whether to accept a settlement. The lawyer, of course, is obligated by the Rules of Professional Responsibility to place the interests of the client first. On the other hand, the contingent fee system has allowed injured persons of limited means to obtain good legal services when they are injured. Also, individual "fees" look less exorbitant when one considers that plaintiff attorneys also lose cases, thus receiving no compensation for the work on those cases. See Symposium: Contingency Fee Financing of Litigation in America, Third Annual Clifford Seminar on Tort Law and Social Policy, 47 DePaul L.Rev. 227 (1998).

10. *The Hourly Fee.* In contrast to lawyers who represent plaintiffs, most lawyers who represent defendants are paid for their services based on an hourly fee for the work done. In many of the cases you have read, the payments to the lawyer for the defendant actually were made by the defendant's liability insurance carrier, which had agreed by contract to indemnify the insured for any expenses associated with defending itself in lawsuits arising from its alleged negligence, including attorney fees. In others, the defendant had no insurance or was self-insured and made the payments. Attorneys working under this system are sometimes accused of doing more work than is necessary to prepare the case for trial or of delaying settlement talks to keep the case, and their payments for services rendered in the meantime, alive. Such conduct would be a violation of the Rules of Professional Responsibility.

11. *Champerty and Maintenance.* Champerty is an agreement whereby a person with no interest in a lawsuit agrees to aid in or carry on its litigation in consideration of a share of the proceeds. Maintenance is meddling in a lawsuit by assisting either party with means to carry it on. Both were illegal at common law as an "offense against public justice, as it keeps alive strife and contentions, and perverts the remedial process of the law into an engine of oppression." Key v. Vattier, 1 Ohio 132, 143 (1823). For a modern version, see Rancman v. Interim Settlement Funding Corp., 99 Ohio St.3d 121, 789 N.E.2d 217 (2003) (finding void an agreement between an automobile accident victim and company who advanced her funds, with repayment secured by the proceeds of the claim based on the accident). Contingent fee arrangements do not run afoul of these common law principles because the client, not the attorney, retains control of the litigation and because the client must pay for the out-of-pocket expenses associated with the litigation like court filing fees, costs of obtaining transcripts, and fees of expert witnesses.

12. *Structured Settlements and Periodic Payment of Judgments.* When an injury is very serious, large damages are likely to be involved. The traditional common law treatment is to provide for lump-sum damages, with the money to go to the injured party to spend or invest as he sees fit. The lump sum is paid after a jury verdict to satisfy the judgment or before a trial as part of a settlement agreement. During the last few decades attorneys have begun using structured settlements to settle some cases. A structured settlement is any settlement that provides that payments are to be made periodically instead of in a lump sum. The periodic payments can be tailored to meet the individual plaintiff's needs (e.g., monthly income for

someone unable to work, four annual payments to begin when a minor reaches college age). The primary advantage of the structured settlement is its favorable tax treatment. As long as the agreement meets certain requirements, the income earned on the principal is tax free. 26 U.S.C. § 130. If the money had been paid in a lump sum, the principal would not have been taxable income to the plaintiff but the interest earned on the principal would have been. For example, under a properly structured settlement agreement, the defendant may pay $50,000 to purchase an annuity that would pay the plaintiff $380 per month for life with fifteen years guaranteed. Thus, the plaintiff would receive $68,400 guaranteed and would receive $192,000 if the plaintiff lived out his life expectancy.

There has been some interest in arranging for periodic payments after a judgment has been awarded and many states have enacted some form of periodic payment legislation to permit, or in some instances require, periodic payment of damages. See, e.g., Fla.Stat. § 768.78; Md.Cts. & Judic.Proc. § 11–109; and N.Y. CPLR §§ 5031 and 5041.

2. PHYSICAL HARM TO PROPERTY

Damages for physical harm to land or chattels is closely tied in with the concept of value, or in other words, what the property is worth. If a chattel is completely destroyed, or is converted by the defendant for his own use, the measure of damages is its entire value at the time and place of the tort. If it is damaged, but not destroyed or converted, the damages are measured by the difference in value before and after the injury. If there is merely deprivation of use, as in the case of dispossession for a limited time, the damages consist of the value of the use of which the plaintiff has been deprived.

Value necessarily involves the idea of some standard by which it can be determined—the financial equivalent of the property, or the harm to it. In the vast majority of the cases, whether the harm is to chattels or to land, the standard set for value is the market value of the property. The theory underlying this is that the plaintiff, given this financial equivalent, can go out on the open market and replace the property by buying other property freely offered for sale. See, generally, Restatement (Second) of Torts § 911.

Market value usually is defined as what the property in question could probably have been sold for on the open market, in the ordinary course of voluntary sale by a leisurely seller to a willing buyer. Thus, it is not the cost to the seller, or the asking price, nor is it what could be obtained on a forced sale. Since value must be looked at from the point of view of one who is complaining of being deprived of the thing valued, it is the highest price that could have been realized, and not the lowest price at which there could reasonably have been a sale.

Market value ordinarily is determined on the basis of the market at the place where the wrong occurred. When there is no available market at that place, there is resort to the nearest market, with allowance made for the costs of transportation to and from it. If the goods were intended by the plaintiff for use, these transportation costs will be added to the market price when determining damages; but if they were intended for sale, they will be deducted.

Market value also is ordinarily determined as of the time of the wrong. There is, however, one group of cases in which subsequent increases in value have been taken into account. These arise where there is conversion of goods of the kind commonly traded on exchanges, such as stocks and bonds, and commodities such as grain. The same exception is made as to cases of breach of contract to sell such goods to the plaintiff. Even here, some courts refuse to consider subsequent increase in value, and adhere strictly to the value at the time of the wrong. Most of the American courts have made some kind of allowance for an increase. See Restatement (Second) of Torts § 927.

Occasionally, chattels have no market value because they are not salable. Or, plaintiff may argue that the market value would not be adequate compensation. In some of these cases, there may be recovery of the value to the owner, as distinguished from value to others. This is true of family heirlooms and other articles that have a purely personal value to the plaintiff and no one else. It is also true, in general, of clothing, books, pictures, furniture and household goods, which will be worth more to the owner than their value to a second-hand store. The "personal value" so awarded is determined by consideration of whatever factors may be relevant, such as original cost of the property, the use made of it, and its condition at the time of the wrong. See, for example, Campins v. Capels, 461 N.E.2d 712 (Ind.App.1984) ("those items generally capable of generating sentimental feelings, not just emotions peculiar to the owner"); Shaffer v. Honeywell, Inc., 249 N.W.2d 251 (S.D.1976) (trophies won at horse shows); Brown v. Frontier Theatres, Inc., 369 S.W.2d 299 (Tex.1963) (grandmother's wedding veil); Brousseau v. Rosenthal, 110 Misc.2d 1054, 443 N.Y.S.2d 285 (1980) (dog); Southern Express Co. v. Owens, 146 Ala. 412, 41 So. 752 (1906) (unpublished manuscript); Mieske v. Bartell Drug Co., 92 Wash.2d 40, 593 P.2d 1308 (1979) (family's home movies). But see C & O Ry. Co. v. May, 120 Va. 790, 92 S.E. 801 (1917) (no damages other than fair market value allowed for family portraits).

For pets, these other factors might include the animal's training and characteristics as well as veterinary expenses for the animal. Brousseau v. Rosenthal, 110 Misc.2d 1054, 443 N.Y.S.2d 285 (1980) (trained guard dog belonging to elderly woman); Burgess v. Shampooch Pet Industries, Inc., 35 Kan.App.2d 458, 131 P.3d 1248 (2006) (measure of damages may include reasonable and customary cost of necessary veterinary care and treatment even though that exceeds pet's fair market value); and Leith v. Frost, 387 Ill.App.3d 430, 326 Ill.Dec. 418, 899 N.E.2d 635 (2008) (same). Most courts have not been persuaded by the argument that the owners of pets should be able to recover emotional distress or loss of consortium damages. McDougall v. Lamm, 211 N.J. 203, 48 A.3d 312 (2012) (pet owners can be awarded costs in excess of the animal's value that represent pecuniary losses associated with medical treatment, damages based on the intrinsic value of the pet, or specific performance of an agreement as between the pet's co-owners but not emotional distress damages); Scheele v. Dustin, 188 Vt. 369, 98 A.2d 697 (2010) (noneconomic damages—as distinct from alternate means of valuing a pet's monetary worth—are not available in trespass to chattels action); Carbasho v. Musulin, 217 W.Va. 359, 618 S.E.2d 368 (2005) (no damages for sentimental value, mental suffering, or emotional distress for death of dog); Kondaurov v. Kerdasha, 271 Va. 646, 629 S.E.2d 181 (2006) (no recovery for emotional distress or mental anguish suffered due to injury to dog); Anzalone v. Kragness, 356 Ill.App.3d 365, 292 Ill.Dec. 331, 826 N.E.2d 472 (2005) (loss to owner may include an element of the owner's feelings for cat but the amount is severely restricted because pet is item of personal property); Goodby v. Vetpharm, Inc., 974 A.2d 1269, 1272 (Vt. 2009) (no recovery for loss of consortium due to death of cats). See also Restatement (Third) of Torts § 47, comment *m* (2012) (recognizing that pets are often quite different from other chattels in terms of emotional attachment, but declining to extend damages for emotional distress for chattels, including pets).

The Texas Supreme Court refused to expand its common law and referred the plaintiff to the legislature for any change in the law: "Under Texas common law, the human-animal bond, while undeniable, is uncompensable, no matter how it is conceived in litigation—as a measure of property damages (including 'intrinsic value' or 'special value . . . derived from the attachment that an owner feels for his pet'), as a personal-injury claim for loss of companionship or emotional distress, or any other theory. The packaging or labeling matters not: Recovery rooted in a pet owner's feelings is prohibited. We understand that limiting recovery to market (or actual) value seems incommensurate with the emotional harm suffered, but pet-death actions compensating for such harm, while they can certainly be legislated, are not something Texas common law should enshrine." Strickland v. Medlen, 397 S.W.3d 184, 198 (Tex. 2013).

A few state legislatures have provided for recovery in addition to market value for loss of pets. See, for example, Tenn. Code Ann. § 44–17–403 (providing for up to $5,000 in noneconomic damages for loss of pet dog or cat that is killed through intentional or negligent act while pet is on property of owner or caretaker or under control and supervision of owner or caretaker but not including certain situations like professional negligence against veterinarian, dog that was worrying livestock, or those acting on behalf of public health or animal welfare).

When the property is not destroyed or converted, but only damaged, the measure becomes one of the difference in value before and after the wrong. The cost of repairing the land or chattel is admissible in evidence, on the assumption that it amounts to a restoration of the original value; but it is not conclusive, and may be challenged by either side as excessive or inadequate for the purpose. Restatement (Second) of Torts § 928. The cost of repairs may not exceed the value of the chattel prior to the injury. See Smith v. Brooks, 337 A.2d 493 (D.C.App.1975).

When there is only temporary deprivation of use, as by dispossession for a limited period, the measure becomes one of the rental value of the property for that period—or in other words, the amount which the owner could have obtained in the market by renting out the property, or the cost to him of renting similar property for the specified time.

Consequential damages may be recovered for the conversion of property, or for harm to it, when they are "proximately" caused. These might include, for example, the reasonable expense of trying to recover possession of the property, or loss of a profitable bargain resulting from deprivation of the goods, and the like. Parroski v. Goldberg, 80 Wis. 339, 50 N.W. 191 (1891) (cost of recovering horses) and Preble v. Hanna, 117 Or. 306, 244 P. 75 (1926) (lost profits while locked out of business). An interesting case in which market value, damages for deprivation of use, and punitive damages all were recovered is Glass v. Brunt, 157 Kan. 27, 138 P.2d 453 (1943) (conversion of equipment resulted in lost sales).

3. PUNITIVE DAMAGES

Punitive damages, sometimes called exemplary or vindictive damages, or "smart money," consist of an additional sum, over and above the compensation of the plaintiff for the harm suffered, awarded for the purpose of punishing the defendant, of admonishing the defendant not to do it again, and of deterring others from following defendant's example. They originated in England in the days of George III, in situations of outrageous abuses of authority by government officers, in cases such as Huckle v. Money, 2 Wils.K.B. 206, 95 Eng.Rep. 768 (1763). Plaintiff, a journeyman printer, was seized by the King's messenger on a general warrant, issued without probable cause, and held in custody for six hours on suspicion of having printed a pamphlet very critical of the King. Although he was treated "very civilly" and given "beef-steaks and beer" and thus suffered little in actual damages, a large jury verdict was upheld because the evidence showed that the "Magna Charta" had been violated and thus exemplary damages were warranted. These principles were then adopted in the United States.

The policy of awarding punitive damages in tort cases has been a subject of much dispute. It has been condemned as undue compensation to the plaintiff beyond his just deserts, in the form of a criminal fine that should be paid to the state if to anyone and fixed by the caprice of the jury, without any standards, and without any of the usual safeguards of criminal procedure, such as proof of guilt beyond a reasonable doubt, the privilege against self-incrimination, and even the rule against double jeopardy—since, in most places, the defendant may still be punished for the crime after he has been mulcted in the tort action.

Punitive damages have been defended as a salutary method of discouraging evil motives, as a partial remedy for the refusal of American civil procedure to allow compensation for the expenses of litigation including counsel fees, as a way of diverting plaintiff's desire for revenge into peaceful channels, and as an incentive to bring into court and redress a long array of petty cases of outrage and oppression, that in practice escape the notice of busy prosecuting attorneys occupied with serious crime and that a private individual would otherwise find not worth the trouble and expense of a lawsuit. See, for example, Mathias v. Accor Econ. Lodging, Inc., 347 F.3d 672, 677 (7th Cir. 2003) (applying Illinois law). Plaintiffs, guests at a national hotel chain where they paid about $100 a night for their room, were bitten by bedbugs. Evidence at trial revealed that the hotel had been aware of the infestation for months, had declined the recommendation of its exterminator that the hotel be closed for a thorough treatment, had been moving guests who complained or refunding their money, and had designated some rooms not to be rented until treated. It was one of those rooms that plaintiffs spent the night in. On that particular night, 190 of the hotel's 191 rooms were occupied, even though many of them had been designated as not to be rented until treated. Bedbug bites are not dangerous, but are painful and unsightly. Jury verdict was for $5,000 in compensatory damages and $186,000 in punitive damages. On appeal, hotel argued that the maximum allowable punitive damages award was $20,000 (a four-to-one ratio of punitive damages to compensatory damages). The Seventh Circuit upheld the jury's verdict, noting that the "defendant's behavior was outrageous but the compensable harm done was slight and at the same time difficult to quantify because a large element of it was emotional. And the defendant may well have profited from its misconduct because by concealing the infestation it was able to keep renting rooms. Refunds were frequent but may have cost less than the cost of closing the hotel for a thorough fumigation. The hotel's attempt to pass off the bedbugs as ticks, which some guests might ignorantly have thought less unhealthful, may have postponed the instituting of litigation to rectify the hotel's misconduct. The award of punitive damages in this case thus serves the additional purpose of limiting the defendant's ability to profit from its fraud by escaping detection and (private) prosecution."

Cheatham v. Pohle

Supreme Court of Indiana, 2003.
789 N.E.2d 467.

BOEHM, J. * * *

After Doris Cheatham and Michael Pohle divorced in 1994, Pohle retained photographs he had taken of Cheatham in the nude as well as photos of the two engaged in a consensual sexual act. In early 1998, Pohle made photocopies of the photographs, added Cheatham's name, her work location and phone number, her new husband's name, and her attorney's name, and proceeded to distribute at least sixty copies around the small community where both he and Cheatham still lived and worked. Cheatham sued, alleging invasion of privacy and intentional infliction of emotional distress, and the jury awarded her $100,000 in compensatory damages and $100,000 in punitive damages.

Indiana Code section 34–51–3–6, enacted in 1995, provides:

> (a) Except as provided in IC 13–25–4–10, when a judgment that includes a punitive damage award is entered in a civil action, the party against whom the judgment was entered shall pay the punitive damage award to the clerk of the court where the action is pending.
>
> (b) Upon receiving the payment described in subsection (a), the clerk of the court shall:
>
> (1) pay the person to whom punitive damages were awarded twenty-five percent (25%) of the punitive damage award; and

(2) pay the remaining seventy-five percent (75%) of the punitive damage award to the treasurer of state, who shall deposit the funds into the violent crime victims compensation fund established by IC 5–2–6.1–40. * * *

[Cheatham argued that the new statute providing that 75% of the punitive damages be paid to the state violated the Takings Clauses found in both the Indiana Constitution and the Fifth Amendment of the United States Constitution and that it violated other provisions of the Indiana Constitution.]

I. Punitive Damages in Indiana

In assessing the claim that the allocation statute takes property without just compensation, it is essential to understand the nature of a claim for punitive damages. The purpose of punitive damages is not to make the plaintiff whole or to attempt to value the injuries of the plaintiff. Rather, punitive damages, sometimes designated "private fines" or "exemplary damages," have historically been viewed as designed to deter and punish wrongful activity. As such, they are quasi-criminal in nature. [Cc]

As a matter of federal [Constitutional] law, state legislatures have broad discretion in authorizing and limiting the award of punitive damages, just as they do in fashioning criminal sanctions. BMW of N. Am. Inc. v. Gore, 517 U.S. 559 (1996). Victims in a criminal case have no claim to benefit from criminal sanctions. [Cc] For the same reason, it has been consistently held that civil plaintiffs have no right to receive punitive damages. [Cc]

To the extent punitive damages are recoverable, they are a creature of the common law. [Cc] As we have repeatedly held in other contexts, the legislature is free to create, modify, or abolish common law causes of action. [C] And, as a matter of federal constitutional law, no person has a vested interest or property right in any rule of common law. [C] As a result, the General Assembly is free to eliminate punitive damages completely, as other states have done, and also has wide discretion in modifying this "quasi-criminal" sanction. Indeed, several jurisdictions have chosen not to recognize punitive damages as an acceptable award in any form.[1]

Indiana, like several other states, has chosen an intermediate ground—permitting juries to award punitive damages and thereby inflict punishment on the defendant, but placing restrictions on the amount the plaintiff may benefit from the award. The facts warranting punitive damages must be established by clear and convincing evidence. [C] Whether punitive damages may be awarded is usually a question of fact. [C]

In sum, Indiana law recognizes a right to assert a claim to be compensated for a cognizable wrong and to recover on that claim to the extent the law allows. But a number of consequences flow from the fundamentally different nature of a claim to punitive damages. The

---

[1] In Nebraska punitive damages are constitutionally prohibited. [C] In Louisiana, Massachusetts, New Hampshire, and Washington, punitive damages are permitted only if expressly authorized by statute. [Cc]

financial condition of the defendant is relevant, [c], which it would not be if the goal were to compensate the plaintiff, as opposed to deterring or punishing the defendant. (Footnote omitted.) Proof is required by a clear and convincing standard rather than a preponderance of the evidence standard. [C] For our purposes, the essential point is that because punitive damages do not compensate the plaintiff, the plaintiff has no right or entitlement to an award of punitive damages in any amount. Unlike a claim for compensatory damages, the trier of fact is not required to award punitive damages even if the facts that might justify an award are found. [C].

II. Claims Under State and Federal Taking Clauses

* * * [A]ny interest the plaintiff has in a punitive damages award is a creation of state law. The plaintiff has no property to be taken except to the extent state law creates a property right. [C] The Indiana legislature has chosen to define the plaintiff's interest in a punitive damages award as only twenty-five percent of any award, and the remainder is to go to the Violent Crime Victims' Compensation Fund. The award to the Fund is not the property of the plaintiff. Nor is her prejudgment claim a property interest. Rather, the claim she had before satisfaction was, pursuant to statute, a claim to only one fourth of any award of punitive damages. As a result, there is no taking of any property by the statutory directive that the clerk transfer a percentage of the punitive damages award to the Fund.

A claim for punitive damages can be sustained only if it is accompanied by a viable claim for compensatory damages. [Cc] Cheatham thus claims that an award for punitive damages is "connected to" a claim for actual damages. From this, Cheatham reasons that because she has a right to compensatory damages, she must have a right to punitive damages as well. This confuses necessary preconditions with sufficient ones. To be sure, a claim for compensatory damages is a prerequisite to a claim for punitive damages, but it does not follow that it is adequate to confer a right to that claim.

Several states have statutes that allocate punitive damages to the state in some form similar to the Indiana version. BMW of N. Am., Inc., 517 U.S. at 616, App. to Opinion of Ginsburg, J. (Ginsburg, J., dissenting); [Cc]. Of the state courts that have addressed the issue, only the Colorado Supreme Court has found an unconstitutional taking of property, while statutes in Alaska, Oregon, Georgia, Florida and Iowa have been upheld. * * *

[The Court concluded that neither the Takings Clauses of the Federal and Indiana Constitutions nor the other provisions of the Indiana Constitution were violated by the statute.] The judgment of the trial court is affirmed.

[The dissenting opinion of DICKSON, J. is omitted.]

NOTES AND QUESTIONS

1. *Intentional Torts.* Punitive damages are generally permitted when defendant has committed an intentional tort such as assault, battery, false imprisonment, conversion, trespass, malicious prosecution, or intentional

infliction of emotional harm, as the defendant did in the principal case. Defendant's conduct need not be motivated by personal hatred; it is enough if it has the character of "outrage." Jones v. Fisher, 42 Wis.2d 209, 166 N.W.2d 175 (1969) (couple forcibly removed denture from former employee's mouth to hold as collateral because they had loaned her the money to have the dental work done and were upset when she quit her job before she had paid the money back). Some states permit malice to be inferred from a conscious indifference to the consequences of conduct. Yeakley v. Doss, 370 Ark. 122, 257 S.W.3d 895 (2007) (defendant had admitted that he was intoxicated and at fault for automobile accident; plaintiff entitled to introduce evidence of two prior DWI convictions in support of claim for punitive damages). Others limit them to situations where the plaintiff proves "evil motive, intent to injure, ill will, or fraud, i.e., 'actual malice.'" Exxon Mobil Corp. v. Albright, 433 Md. 303, 71 A.3d 30, 57 (2013). There are times when a technically intentional tort may be committed without malice. For example, a defendant unknowingly buys a stolen article or falsely imprisons a person whom he unreasonably believes to have stolen his property or unwittingly operates on the wrong patient.

In one case, couple seeking to adopt specifically asked for a healthy infant from a healthy family. Adoption agency, pursuant to a policy of not disclosing family information if it was not hereditary and might interfere with the bonding between adoptive parent and child, told them baby was healthy and did not tell them that baby's biological father was a paranoid schizophrenic and that baby's biological mother's father had been hospitalized for treatment of schizophrenia. Adopted baby had numerous behavioral problems as a child and, as a young adult, was diagnosed with paranoid schizophrenia. Couple filed suit against agency for fraud/wrongful adoption. Court found that trial court's granting of summary judgment on behalf of agency on punitive damages claim was appropriate. Although the actions were intentional, they were not malicious or vindictive and thus did not warrant punitive damages. Ross v. Louise Wise Svs., Inc., 8 N.Y.3d 478, 868 N.E.2d 189, 836 N.Y.S.2d 509 (2007).

2. *Negligent Torts.* Conduct short of intentional wrongdoing also may be sufficient to justify punitive damages in most jurisdictions. Courts use a variety of formulas to spell this out, including "reckless disregard for the rights of others," Allman v. Bird, 186 Kan. 802, 353 P.2d 216 (1960); or "willful misconduct, wantonness, recklessness, or want of care indicative of indifference to consequences," In re Air Crash Disaster Near Chicago, 644 F.2d 594 (7th Cir.1981), cert. denied, 454 U.S. 878 (1981). Conduct that is merely negligent, even if it causes severe damage, is insufficient to justify punitive damages. This is usually held to be true of "grossly negligent" conduct when that term is used as a synonym for "extreme carelessness" as opposed to "recklessness." Doe v. Isaacs, 265 Va. 531, 579 S.E.2d 174 (2003) (conduct of hit-and-run drunk driver was gross negligence, but not the willful recklessness that would support punitive damages). But see Williams v. Wilson, 972 S.W.2d 260 (Ky.1998) (new statutory punitive damages standard, which required "subjective awareness" that conduct would result in human death or bodily harm, violated state constitutional jural rights doctrine because recovery for conduct that was grossly negligent was well-established common law right in Kentucky).

3. *Strict Liability in Tort.* Should punitive damages be available in a cause of action based on strict liability? Fischer v. Johns-Manville Corp., 103 N.J. 643, 512 A.2d 466 (1986) (defendant unsuccessfully argued that the concept of strict liability for products that theoretically focuses on the condition of the product rather than the conduct of the manufacturer, is incompatible with the concept of punitive damages, which is based on the defendant's malicious conduct); Owens-Illinois, Inc. v. Zenobia, 325 Md. 420, 601 A.2d 633 (1992) (evidence necessary to sustain punitive damages award goes far beyond that necessary to sustain a compensatory damages award in a strict liability claim, but such an approach is open to plaintiff; "actual malice" requirement is satisfied in product liability case by showing of actual knowledge of the defect and conscious or deliberate disregard of the foreseeable harm resulting from the defect).

4. *Estate as Defendant.* Should punitive damages be available against the estate of a deceased tortfeasor? How are the goals of punishment and deterrence served in that situation? In a case with facts very similar to those of the principal case, plaintiff's former boyfriend distributed photocopies of sexually explicit photographs of her that he had taken during their relationship, including her address, telephone number, and captions that implied that she was a prostitute. The photocopies were distributed throughout the community, including places that would ensure that they would be seen by plaintiff's minor children, her mother, her brother, and her employer. The distribution finally stopped when plaintiff filed a complaint including counts of defamation, intentional infliction of emotional distress, and false light invasion of privacy. The tortfeasor committed suicide before the trial and his sister, the executrix of his estate, was substituted as a defendant. Should a jury award of punitive damages be upheld? G.J.D. v. Johnson, 552 Pa. 169, 713 A.2d 1127 (1998) (permitting award of punitive damages against estate, but noting that the majority of jurisdictions do not). See also In re Vajgrt, 801 N.W.2d 570 (Iowa 2011) (noting that Iowa is among the approximately thirty states that do not permit awards of punitive damages against estates for the conduct of the decedent). See Chapter 11, Wrongful Death and Survival, note 10, page 613.

5. Arizona voters amended their state constitution to prohibit aliens who were present in the state in violation of federal immigration law from recovering punitive damages. Ariz. Rev. Stat. Constitution, Art. II, § 35.

6. Can the plaintiff recover punitive damages if she has suffered no compensable harm? Note that the principal case says that Indiana has such a requirement. Others have deemed it sufficient that the plaintiff prove the elements of her underlying cause of action, even if the jury does not actually award compensatory damages. Clark v. McClurg, 215 Cal. 279, 9 P.2d 505 (1932). Can an award of nominal damages support an award of punitive damages? Jacque v. Steenberg Homes, Inc., 209 Wis.2d 605, 563 N.W.2d 154 (1997) (general rule that compensatory damages are required for award of punitive damages does not apply in case of intentional tort of trespass; defendant had bulldozed a path in the snow across plaintiff's field to deliver a mobile home despite plaintiff's repeated refusals to give permission to defendant to cross his land to make delivery of the mobile home).

7. In a medical malpractice action, jury found that patient's medical records had been altered in a way that made it more difficult for her to prove her case. The alteration in the records did not, however, affect her treatment so it did not cause any of her damages. Does a showing of actual malice permit the imposition of punitive damages if the malicious conduct did not cause compensable harm? Moskovitz v. Mt. Sinai Medical Ctr., 69 Ohio St.3d 638, 635 N.E.2d 331 (1994) (not necessary that malicious intent necessary to sustain an award of punitive damages must itself have proximately caused compensable harm as long as plaintiff also proves compensable harm in suit). See also note 2, page 1091, re spoliation of evidence.

8. *Legal Malpractice Claims.* Suppose an attorney negligently fails to pursue a personal injury claim on behalf of client who was injured in an automobile accident and the client therefore loses the chance to recover compensatory and punitive damages against the driver. Client's damages in the malpractice case against the attorney would include the amount client proves she would have recovered but for the attorney's malpractice. Does the claim against the attorney include the punitive damages client might have obtained from the driver? Compare Ferguson v. Lieff, Cabraser, Heimann & Bernstein, 135 Cal.Rptr.2d 46, 30 Cal.4th 1037, 69 P.3d 965 (2003) (after analysis of public policy issues, court concludes lost punitive damages are not part of claim against legal malpractice defendant); Tri-G, Inc. v. Burke, Bosselman & Weaver, 222 Ill.2d 218, 305 Ill.Dec. 584, 856 N.E.2d 389 (2006) (accord); and Osborne v. Keeney, 399 S.W.3d 1 (Ky. 2012) (accord, surveying cases) with Jacobsen v. Oliver, 201 F.Supp.2d 93 (D.D.C. 2002) (interpreting District of Columbia law to include lost punitive damages as part of legal malpractice damages) and Haberer v. Rice, 511 N.W.2d 279 (S.D. 1994) (accord).

9. The decisions usually hold that punitive damages are a windfall to the plaintiff, not a right and that the jury has complete discretion to refrain from awarding them in any case. In addition to the principal case, see Harrison v. Ely, 120 Ill. 83, 11 N.E. 334 (1887) (emphasizing that plaintiff's showing of malice authorizes the jury to award punitive damages but does not require it to).

State Farm Mutual Automobile Ins. Co. v. Campbell

Supreme Court of the United States, 2003.
538 U.S. 408, 123 S.Ct. 1513, 155 L.Ed.2d 585.

JUSTICE KENNEDY delivered the opinion of the Court.

We address once again the measure of punishment, by means of punitive damages, a State may impose upon a defendant in a civil case. The question is whether, in the circumstances we shall recount, an award of $145 million in punitive damages, where full compensatory damages are $1 million, is excessive and in violation of the Due Process Clause of the Fourteenth Amendment to the Constitution of the United States.

I

In 1981, Curtis Campbell (Campbell) was driving with his wife, Inez Preece Campbell, in Cache County, Utah. He decided to pass six vans traveling ahead of them on a two-lane highway. Todd Ospital was driving a small car approaching from the opposite direction. To avoid a head-on collision with Campbell, who then was driving on the wrong side of the highway and toward oncoming traffic, Ospital swerved onto the shoulder, lost control of his automobile, and collided with a vehicle driven by Robert G. Slusher. Ospital was killed, and Slusher was rendered permanently disabled. The Campbells escaped unscathed.

In the ensuing wrongful death and tort action, Campbell insisted he was not at fault. Early investigations did support differing conclusions as to who caused the accident, but "a consensus was reached early on by the investigators and witnesses that Mr. Campbell's unsafe pass had indeed caused the crash." 65 P.3d 1134, 1141 (Utah 2001). Campbell's insurance company, petitioner State Farm Mutual Automobile Insurance Company (State Farm), nonetheless decided to contest liability and declined offers by Slusher and Ospital's estate (Ospital) to settle the claims for the policy limit of $50,000 ($25,000 per claimant). State Farm also ignored the advice of one of its own investigators and took the case to trial, assuring the Campbells that "their assets were safe, that they had no liability for the accident, that [State Farm] would represent their interests, and that they did not need to procure separate counsel." [C] To the contrary, a jury determined that Campbell was 100 percent at fault, and a judgment was returned for $185,849, far more than the amount offered in settlement.

At first State Farm refused to cover the $135,849 in excess liability. Its counsel made this clear to the Campbells: " 'You may want to put for sale signs on your property to get things moving.' " [C] Nor was State Farm willing to post a supersedeas bond to allow Campbell to appeal the judgment against him. Campbell obtained his own counsel to appeal the verdict. * * *

In 1989, the Utah Supreme Court denied Campbell's appeal in the wrongful death and tort actions. Slusher v. Ospital, 777 P.2d 437. State Farm then paid the entire judgment, including the amounts in excess of the policy limits. The Campbells nonetheless filed a complaint against State Farm alleging bad faith, fraud, and intentional infliction of emotional distress. * * *

[After a jury found that State Farm's decision not to settle was unreasonable, a second jury addressed] State Farm's liability for fraud and intentional infliction of emotional distress, as well as compensatory and punitive damages. The Utah Supreme Court aptly characterized this phase of the trial:

"State Farm argued during phase II that its decision to take the case to trial was an 'honest mistake' that did not warrant punitive damages. In contrast, the Campbells introduced evidence that State Farm's decision to take the case to trial was a result of a national scheme to meet corporate fiscal goals by capping payouts on claims company wide. This scheme was referred to as State Farm's 'Performance, Planning and Review,' or PP & R, policy. To prove the existence of this scheme, the trial court allowed the Campbells to introduce extensive expert testimony regarding fraudulent practices by State Farm in its nation-wide operations. Although State Farm moved prior to phase II of the trial for the exclusion of such evidence and continued to object to it at trial, the trial court ruled that such evidence was admissible to determine whether State Farm's conduct in the Campbell case was indeed intentional and sufficiently egregious to warrant punitive damages." [C]

Evidence pertaining to the PP & R policy concerned State Farm's business practices for over 20 years in numerous States. Most of these practices bore no relation to third-party automobile insurance claims, the type of claim underlying the Campbells' complaint against the company. The jury awarded the Campbells $2.6 million in compensatory damages and $145 million in punitive damages, which the trial court reduced to $1 million and $25 million respectively. Both parties appealed.

The Utah Supreme Court sought to apply the three guideposts we identified in [*BMW of North America, Inc. v.*] *Gore* [c], and it reinstated the $145 million punitive damages award. Relying in large part on the extensive evidence concerning the PP & R policy, the court concluded State Farm's conduct was reprehensible. The court also relied upon State Farm's "massive wealth" and on testimony indicating that "State Farm's actions, because of their clandestine nature, will be punished at most in one out of every 50,000 cases as a matter of statistical probability," [c], and concluded that the ratio between punitive and compensatory damages was not unwarranted. Finally, the court noted that the punitive damages award was not excessive when compared to various civil and criminal penalties State Farm could have faced, including $10,000 for each act of fraud, the suspension of its license to conduct business in Utah, the disgorgement of profits, and imprisonment. [C] We granted certiorari. [C]

II

We recognized in *Cooper Industries, Inc. v. Leatherman Tool Group, Inc.*, 532 U.S. 424 (2001) that in our judicial system compensatory and punitive damages, although usually awarded at the same time by the same decisionmaker, serve different purposes. [C] Compensatory damages "are intended to redress the concrete loss that the plaintiff has suffered by reason of the defendant's wrongful conduct." [C] (citing Restatement (Second) of Torts § 903, pp. 453–454 (1979)). By contrast, punitive damages serve a broader function; they are aimed at deterrence and retribution. [C]; see also *Gore*, supra, at 568 ("Punitive damages may properly be imposed to further a State's legitimate interests in punishing unlawful conduct and deterring its repetition"); *Pacific Mut. Life Ins. Co. v. Haslip*, 499 U.S. 1 (1991) ("Punitive damages are imposed for purposes of retribution and deterrence").

While States possess discretion over the imposition of punitive damages, it is well established that there are procedural and substantive constitutional limitations on these awards. [Cc] The Due Process Clause of the Fourteenth Amendment prohibits the imposition of grossly excessive or arbitrary punishments on a tortfeasor [Cc]; see also [*Gore*] at 587 (BREYER, J., concurring) ("This constitutional concern, itself harkening back to the Magna Carta, arises out of the basic unfairness of depriving citizens of life, liberty, or property, through the application, not of law and legal processes, but of arbitrary coercion"). The reason is that "elementary notions of fairness enshrined in our constitutional jurisprudence dictate that a person receive fair notice not only of the conduct that will subject him to punishment, but also of the severity of the penalty that a State may impose." [Cc] To the extent an award is grossly excessive, it furthers no legitimate purpose and constitutes an arbitrary deprivation of property. * * *

Our concerns are heightened when the decisionmaker is presented, as we shall discuss, with evidence that has little bearing as to the amount of punitive damages that should be awarded. Vague instructions, or those that merely inform the jury to avoid "passion or prejudice," [C] do little to aid the decisionmaker in its task of assigning appropriate weight to evidence that is relevant and evidence that is tangential or only inflammatory.

In light of these concerns, in *Gore* [c], we instructed courts reviewing punitive damages to consider three guideposts: (1) the degree of reprehensibility of the defendant's misconduct; (2) the disparity between the actual or potential harm suffered by the plaintiff and the punitive damages award; and (3) the difference between the punitive damages awarded by the jury and the civil penalties authorized or imposed in comparable cases. [C] We reiterated the importance of these three guideposts in *Cooper Industries* and mandated appellate courts to conduct *de novo* review of a trial court's application of them to the jury's award. [C] Exacting appellate review ensures that an award of punitive damages is based upon an " 'application of law, rather than a decisionmaker's caprice.' " [C]

III

Under the principles outlined in *BMW of North America, Inc. v. Gore*, this case is neither close nor difficult. It was error to reinstate the jury's $145 million punitive damages award. We address each guidepost of *Gore* in some detail.

A

"The most important indicium of the reasonableness of a punitive damages award is the degree of reprehensibility of the defendant's conduct." [C] We have instructed courts to determine the reprehensibility of a defendant by considering whether: the harm caused was physical as opposed to economic; the tortious conduct evinced an indifference to or a reckless disregard of the health or safety of others; the target of the conduct had financial vulnerability; the conduct involved repeated actions or was an isolated incident; and the harm was the result of intentional malice, trickery, or deceit, or mere accident. [C] The existence of any one of these factors weighing in favor of a plaintiff may not be sufficient to sustain a punitive damages award; and the absence of all of them renders any award suspect. It should be presumed a plaintiff has been made whole for his injuries by compensatory damages, so punitive damages should only be awarded if the defendant's culpability, after having paid compensatory damages, is so reprehensible as to warrant the imposition of further sanctions to achieve punishment or deterrence. [C].

Applying these factors in the instant case, we must acknowledge that State Farm's handling of the claims against the Campbells merits no praise. * * * While we do not suggest there was error in awarding punitive damages based upon State Farm's conduct toward the Campbells, a more modest punishment for this reprehensible conduct could have satisfied the State's legitimate objectives, and the Utah courts should have gone no further.

This case, instead, was used as a platform to expose, and punish, the perceived deficiencies of State Farm's operations throughout the country. The Utah Supreme Court's opinion makes explicit that State Farm was being condemned for its nationwide policies rather than for the conduct directed toward the Campbells. * * * ("This is a very important case. . . . It transcends the Campbell file. It involves a nationwide practice. And you, here, are going to be evaluating and assessing, and hopefully requiring State Farm to stand accountable for what it's doing across the country, which is the purpose of punitive damages")[quoting argument to jury]. * * *

A State cannot punish a defendant for conduct that may have been lawful where it occurred. [Cc] Nor, as a general rule, does a State have a legitimate concern in imposing punitive damages to punish a defendant for unlawful acts committed outside of the State's jurisdiction. * * *

For a more fundamental reason, however, the Utah courts erred in relying upon this and other evidence: The courts awarded punitive damages to punish and deter conduct that bore no relation to the Campbells' harm. A defendant's dissimilar acts, independent from the acts upon which liability was premised, may not serve as the basis for punitive damages. A defendant should be punished for the conduct that harmed the plaintiff, not for being an unsavory individual or business. * * *

B

Turning to the second *Gore* guidepost, we have been reluctant to identify concrete constitutional limits on the ratio between harm, or potential harm, to the plaintiff and the punitive damages award. [Cc] We decline again to impose a bright-line ratio which a punitive damages award cannot exceed. Our jurisprudence and the principles it has now established demonstrate, however, that, in practice, few awards exceeding a single-digit ratio between punitive and compensatory damages, to a significant degree, will satisfy due process. In *Haslip*, in upholding a punitive damages award, we concluded that an award of more than four times the amount of compensatory damages might be close to the line of constitutional impropriety. [C]. We cited that 4-to-1 ratio again in *Gore*. [C] The Court further referenced a long legislative history, dating back over 700 years and going forward to today, providing for sanctions of double, treble, or quadruple damages to deter and punish. [C] While these ratios are not binding, they are instructive. They demonstrate what should be obvious: Single-digit multipliers are more likely to comport with due process, while still achieving the State's goals of deterrence and retribution, than awards with ratios in range of 500 to 1, [c], or, in this case, of 145 to 1.

Nonetheless, because there are no rigid benchmarks that a punitive damages award may not surpass, ratios greater than those we have previously upheld may comport with due process where "a particularly egregious act has resulted in only a small amount of economic damages." * * * The converse is also true, however. When compensatory damages are substantial, then a lesser ratio, perhaps only equal to compensatory damages, can reach the outermost limit of the due process guarantee. The precise award in any case, of course, must be based upon the facts and circumstances of the defendant's conduct and the harm to the plaintiff.

In sum, courts must ensure that the measure of punishment is both reasonable and proportionate to the amount of harm to the plaintiff and to the general damages recovered. In the context of this case, we have no doubt that there is a presumption against an award that has a 145-to-1 ratio. The compensatory award in this case was substantial; the Campbells were awarded $1 million for a year and a half of emotional distress. This was complete compensation. The harm arose from a transaction in the economic realm, not from some physical assault or trauma; there were no physical injuries; and State Farm paid the excess verdict before the complaint was filed, so the Campbells suffered only minor economic injuries for the 18-month period in which State Farm refused to resolve the claim against them. The compensatory damages for the injury suffered here, moreover, likely were based on a component which was duplicated in the punitive award. Much of the distress was caused by the outrage and humiliation the Campbells suffered at the actions of their insurer; and it is a major role of punitive damages to condemn such conduct. Compensatory damages, however, already contain this punitive element. See Restatement (Second) of Torts § 908, comment *c*, p. 466 (1977) ("In many cases in which compensatory damages include an amount for emotional distress, such as humiliation or indignation aroused by the defendant's act, there is no clear line of demarcation between punishment and compensation and a verdict for a specified amount frequently includes elements of both"). * * *

C

The third guidepost in *Gore* is the disparity between the punitive damages award and the "civil penalties authorized or imposed in comparable cases." [C] We note that, in the past, we have also looked to criminal penalties that could be imposed. [Cc] The existence of a criminal penalty does have bearing on the seriousness with which a State views the wrongful action. When used to determine the dollar amount of the award, however, the criminal penalty has less utility. Great care must be taken to avoid use of the civil process to assess criminal penalties that can be imposed only after the heightened protections of a criminal trial have been observed, including, of course, its higher standards of proof. Punitive damages are not a substitute for the criminal process, and the remote possibility of a criminal sanction does not automatically sustain a punitive damages award.

Here, we need not dwell long on this guidepost. The most relevant civil sanction under Utah state law for the wrong done to the Campbells appears to be a $10,000 fine for an act of fraud, [c], an amount dwarfed by the $145 million punitive damages award. The Supreme Court of Utah speculated about the loss of State Farm's business license, the disgorgement of profits, and possible imprisonment, but here again its references were to the broad fraudulent scheme drawn from evidence of out-of-state and dissimilar conduct. This analysis was insufficient to justify the award.

IV

An application of the *Gore* guideposts to the facts of this case, especially in light of the substantial compensatory damages awarded (a portion of which contained a punitive element), likely would justify a punitive damages award at or near the amount of compensatory damages. The punitive award of $145 million, therefore, was neither reasonable nor proportionate to the wrong committed, and it was an irrational and arbitrary deprivation of the property of the defendant. The proper calculation of punitive damages under the principles we have discussed should be resolved, in the first instance, by the Utah courts.

The judgment of the Utah Supreme Court is reversed, and the case is remanded for proceedings not inconsistent with this opinion.

It is so ordered.

[The dissenting opinions of JUSTICES SCALIA, THOMAS, and GINSBURG are omitted.]

Exxon Shipping Co. v. Baker

Supreme Court of the United States, 2008.
554 U.S. 471, 128 S.Ct. 2605, 171 L.Ed.2d 570.

JUSTICE SOUTER delivered the opinion of the Court. * * *

[One of the questions of maritime law before the Court is whether the award of $2.5 billion in this case is greater than maritime law should allow in the circumstances. We hold that the award here should be limited to an amount equal to the compensatory damages.

On March 24, 1989, the supertanker *Exxon Valdez* grounded on Bligh Reef off the Alaskan coast, fracturing its hull and spilling millions of gallons of crude oil into Prince William Sound. Its owner settled state and federal claims for environmental damage, with payments exceeding $1 billion, and this action by respondent Baker and others, including commercial fishermen and native Alaskans, was brought for economic losses to individuals dependent on Prince William Sound for their livelihoods. Evidence showed that just before the accident the captain had inexplicably left the bridge even though he was the only officer licensed to navigate that difficult part of the passage, that blood alcohol testing done by the Coast Guard when it responded to the accident indicated that the captain had been drinking, and that Exxon had some knowledge of the captain's alcoholism. There was conflicting testimony as to whether Exxon officials knew of the captain's backsliding.]

[I]n most American jurisdictions the amount of the punitive award is generally determined by a jury in the first instance, and that "determination is then reviewed by trial and appellate courts to ensure that it is reasonable." [Cc] Many States have gone further by imposing statutory limits on punitive awards, in the form of absolute monetary caps, see, *e.g.*, Va.Code Ann. § 8.01–38.1 (Lexis 2007) ($350,000 cap), a maximum ratio of punitive to compensatory damages, see, *e.g.*, Ohio Rev.Code Ann. § 2315.21(D)(2)(a) (Lexis 2001) (2:1 ratio in most tort cases), or, frequently, some combination of the two, see, *e.g.*, Alaska Stat. § 09.17.020(f) (2006) (greater of 3:1 ratio or $500,000 in most actions). The States that rely on a multiplier have adopted a variety of ratios, ranging from 5:1 to 1:1.

Despite these limitations, punitive damages overall are higher and more frequent in the United States than they are anywhere else. * * * [The Court references various statistical studies of punitive damages awards, noting that their authors draw conflicting conclusions as to their extent and their impact.]

The real problem, it seems, is the stark unpredictability of punitive awards. Courts of law are concerned with fairness as consistency, and evidence that the median ratio of punitive to compensatory awards falls within a reasonable zone, or that punitive awards are infrequent, fails to tell us whether the spread between high and low individual awards is acceptable. The available data suggest it is not. * * *

Starting with the premise of a punitive-damages regime, these ranges of variation might be acceptable or even desirable if they resulted from judges' and juries' refining their judgments to reach a generally accepted optimal level of penalty and deterrence in cases involving a wide range of circumstances, while producing fairly consistent results in cases with similar facts. [C] But anecdotal evidence suggests that nothing of that sort is going on. One of our own leading cases on punitive damages, with a $4 million verdict by an Alabama jury, noted that a second Alabama case with strikingly similar facts produced "a comparable amount of compensatory damages" but "no punitive damages at all." [*BMW of No. America, Inc. v.*] *Gore,* 517 U.S. 559, 565 [1996]. * * *

The Court's response to outlier punitive damages awards has thus far been confined by claims at the constitutional level, and our cases have announced due process standards that every award must pass. See, *e.g., State Farm Mut. Automobile Ins. Co. v. Campbell,* 538 U.S. 408, 425 * * * (2003); *Gore,* 517 U.S., at 574–575. Although "we have consistently rejected the notion that the constitutional line is marked by a simple mathematical formula," [c], we have determined that "few awards exceeding a single-digit ratio between punitive and compensatory damages, to a significant degree, will satisfy due process," [c]; "[w]hen compensatory damages are substantial, then a lesser ratio, perhaps only equal to compensatory damages, can reach the outermost limit of the due process guarantee," [c].

* * *

[Our review of punitive damages today], considers not their intersection with the Constitution, but the desirability of regulating them as a common law remedy for which responsibility lies with this Court as a source of judge-made law in the absence of statute. Whatever may be the constitutional significance of the unpredictability of high punitive awards, this feature of happenstance is in tension with the function of the awards as punitive, just because of the implication of unfairness that an eccentrically high punitive verdict carries in a system whose commonly held notion of law rests on a sense of fairness in dealing with one another. Thus, a penalty should be reasonably predictable in its severity, so that even Justice Holmes's "bad man" can look ahead with some ability to know what the stakes are in choosing one course of action or another. See The Path of the Law, 10 Harv. L.Rev. 457, 459 (1897). And when the bad man's counterparts turn up from time to time, the penalty scheme they face ought to threaten them with a fair probability of suffering in like degree when they wreak like damage. * * *

With that aim ourselves, we have three basic approaches to consider, one verbal and two quantitative. As mentioned before, a number of state courts have settled on criteria for judicial review of punitive-damages awards that go well beyond traditional "shock the conscience" or "passion and prejudice" tests. * * *

These examples [from state law] leave us skeptical that verbal formulations, superimposed on general jury instructions, are the best insurance against unpredictable outliers. Instructions can go just so far in promoting systemic consistency when awards are not tied to specifically proven items of damage (the cost of medical treatment, say), and although judges in the States that take this approach may well produce just results by dint of valiant effort, our experience with attempts to produce consistency in the analogous business of criminal sentencing leaves us doubtful that anything but a quantified approach will work. A glance at the experience there will explain our skepticism.

* * *

It is instructive, then, that in the last quarter century federal sentencing rejected an "indeterminate" system, with relatively unguided discretion to sentence within a wide range, under which "similarly situated offenders were sentenced [to], and did actually serve, widely disparate sentences." [C] Instead it became a system of detailed guidelines tied to exactly quantified sentencing results, under the authority of the Sentencing Reform Act of 1984, [c].

* * *

This is why our better judgment is that eliminating unpredictable outlying punitive awards by more rigorous standards than the constitutional limit will probably have to take the form adopted in those States that have looked to the criminal-law pattern of quantified limits. One option would be to follow the States that set a hard dollar cap on punitive damages, [c], a course that arguably would come closest to the criminal law, rather like setting a maximum term of years. The trouble is, though, that there is no "standard" tort or contract injury, making it difficult to settle upon a particular dollar figure as appropriate across the board. And of course a judicial selection of a dollar cap would carry a serious drawback; a legislature can pick a figure, index it for inflation, and revisit its provision whenever there seems to be a need for further tinkering, but a court cannot say when an issue will show up on the docket again. [C]

The more promising alternative is to leave the effects of inflation to the jury or judge who assesses the value of actual loss, by pegging punitive to compensatory damages using a ratio or maximum multiple. * * *

Still, some will murmur that this smacks too much of policy and too little of principle. [C] But the answer rests on the fact that we are acting here in the position of a common law court of last review, faced with a perceived defect in a common law remedy. Traditionally, courts have accepted primary responsibility for reviewing punitive damages and thus for their evolution, and if, in the absence of legislation, judicially derived standards leave the door open to outlier punitive-damages awards, it is hard to see how the judiciary can wash its hands of a problem it created, simply by calling quantified standards legislative. [Cc]

History certainly is no support for the notion that judges cannot use numbers. The 21-year period in the rule against perpetuities was a judicial innovation, [c], and so were exact limitations periods for civil actions[.] * * * [The Court then noted many examples of ratios to set amounts in state punitive damages legislation and in federal treble damages statutes.]

There is better evidence of an accepted limit of reasonable civil penalty, however, in several studies mentioned before, showing the median ratio of punitive to compensatory verdicts, reflecting what juries and judges have considered reasonable across many hundreds of punitive awards. [C] We think it is fair to assume that the greater share of the verdicts studied in these comprehensive collections reflect reasonable judgments about the economic penalties appropriate in their particular cases.

These studies cover cases of the most as well as the least blameworthy conduct triggering punitive liability, from malice and avarice, down to recklessness, and even gross negligence in some jurisdictions. The data put the median ratio for the entire gamut of circumstances at less than 1:1, [c], meaning that the compensatory award exceeds the punitive award in most cases. In a well-functioning system, we would expect that awards at the median or lower would roughly express jurors' sense of reasonable penalties in cases with no earmarks of exceptional blameworthiness within the punishable spectrum (cases like this one, without intentional or malicious conduct, and without behavior driven primarily by desire for gain, for example) and cases (again like this one) without the modest economic harm or odds of detection that have opened the door to higher awards. It also seems fair to suppose that most of the unpredictable outlier cases that call the fairness of the system into question are above the median; in theory a factfinder's deliberation could go awry to produce a very low ratio, but we have no basis to assume that such a case would be more than a sport, and the cases with serious constitutional issues coming to us have naturally been on the high side, [cc]. On these assumptions, a median ratio of punitive to compensatory damages of about 0.65:1 probably marks the line near which cases like this one largely should be grouped. Accordingly, given the need to protect against the possibility (and the disruptive cost to the legal system) of awards that are unpredictable and unnecessary, either for deterrence or for measured retribution, we consider that a 1:1 ratio, which is above the median award, is a fair upper limit in such maritime cases.

Applying this standard to the present case, we take for granted the District Court's calculation of the total relevant compensatory damages at $507.5 million. [C] A punitive-to-compensatory ratio of 1:1 thus yields maximum punitive damages in that amount.

We therefore vacate the judgment and remand the case for the Court of Appeals to remit the punitive damages award accordingly.

It is so ordered.

JUSTICE ALITO took no part in the consideration or decision of this case. [The concurring and dissenting opinions are omitted.]

NOTES AND QUESTIONS

1. The first principal case is one in a series of Supreme Court decisions, beginning in 1991, setting Due Process limits on the authority of a state to impose punitive damages in a civil case. If you were seated on the Utah Supreme Court, how would you rule on remand? What is the Constitutionally permitted amount of punitive damages for this case? "When considered in light of all of the *Gore* reprehensibility factors, we conclude that a 9-to-1 ratio between compensatory and punitive damages, yielding a $9,018,780.75 punitive damages award, serves Utah's legitimate goals of deterrence and retribution within the limits of due process." Campbell v. State Farm Mutual Automobile Ins. Co., 2004 UT. 34, 98 P.3d 409, 418, *cert. denied*, 543 U.S. 874, 125 S.Ct. 114 (2004).

2. Note that the opinion in the first principal case, as part of the discussion of the *Gore* reprehensibility guideposts, holds that the jury may not punish the defendant for conduct that occurred outside of the state. In its next consideration of the Due Process limits on punitive damages, the Supreme Court ruled that the jury may not punish the defendant for injury that it inflicted on nonparties. Philip Morris USA v. Williams, 549 U.S. 346 (2007). As a trial court judge, how would you permit the plaintiff to introduce evidence that the conduct was reprehensible because it could have injured many people while protecting the defendant from being punished for injuries to others? Here is the Ninth Circuit's Model Jury Instruction on this issue. Does it accomplish those goals? "In considering the amount of any punitive damages, consider the degree of reprehensibility of the defendant's conduct, including whether the conduct that harmed the plaintiff was particularly reprehensible because it also caused actual harm or posed a substantial risk of harm to people who are not parties to this case. You may not, however, set the amount of any punitive damages in order to punish the defendant for harm to anyone other than the plaintiff in this case." The plaintiff's lawyer during the closing argument is not permitted to ask the jury to consider all those, like his client, who had been exposed to the drug in the United States. Ray v. Allergan, Inc., 863 F.Supp.2d 552 (E.D.Va. 2012).

3. Is defendant subject to punitive damages if its product complied with government standards? Compare Wyeth v. Rowatt, 244 P.3d 765 (Nev. 2012) (manufacturer's alleged compliance with regulations promulgated by Food and Drug Administration governing labeling and drug testing, by

itself, did not absolve it of punitive damages) and Ariz. Rev. Stat. § 12–689 (no punitive damages if "product, activity or service complied with all statutes of this state or the United States or standards, rules, regulations, orders or other actions of a government agency pursuant to statutory authority that are relevant and material to the event or risk allegedly causing the harm.").

4. *Calculation of Amount.* There is a strong tradition in many jurisdictions of requiring that the punitive damages award bear some reasonable relation to the compensatory award. This usually is expressed in terms of a factor to be considered by the jury, although some jurisdictions have set firmer guidelines by statute. Fla. Stat. § 768.73 (greater of three times compensatory or $500,000 except under certain specified circumstances when it is greater of four times or $2,000,000); Colo. Rev. Stat. §§ 13–21–102(1)(a) and (3) (one times compensatory or three times compensatory under specified circumstances); and N.J. Stat. § 2A:15–5.14 (greater of five times compensatory or $350,000). Some jurisdictions have imposed a cap on the amount of punitive damages. Va. Code Ann. § 8.01–38.1 ($350,000).

The United States Supreme Court, in the second principal case, was sitting as a common law court in its admiralty jurisdiction, trying to determine what standards should be applied to determine the maximum amount of a punitive damages award. It arrived at a 1:1 ratio as "the fair upper limit" for maritime cases. Exxon Shipping Co. v. Baker, 554 U.S. 471, 512 (2008). Because it is not a constitutional ruling, this determination does not bind the states. Do you think it might influence their decisions about their own punitive damages regimes?

5. Within the limits set by a cap or ratio, what factors should the jury consider in setting the amount of punitive damages? In California, the jury may consider "the character of defendant's act, the nature and extent of the harm to the plaintiff and the wealth of the defendant." See Coats v. Construction & Gen. Laborers Local No. 185, 15 Cal.App.3d 908, 93 Cal.Rptr. 639 (1971). Oregon advises the jury to consider the likelihood that serious harm would arise from the misconduct, the degree of defendant's awareness of the misconduct, the profitability of the misconduct, the duration of the misconduct and any concealment of it, the attitude and conduct of defendant upon discovery of the misconduct, the financial condition of the defendant, and the total deterrent effect of other punishment imposed for the same conduct. Ore. Rev. Stat. § 30.925. South Carolina directs the jury to consider the degree of culpability, the duration of the conduct, the awareness or concealment of conduct, the existence of similar past conduct, the likelihood that the award will deter defendant or other, whether the award is reasonably related to the harm likely to result, the defendant's ability to pay, and any other factors deemed appropriate. Atlas Food Sys. and Svcs., Inc. v. Crane Nat. Vendors, Inc., 99 F.3d 587 (4th Cir.1996). The fact that the defendant's wealth is considered may justify different awards against two defendants who engaged in equally culpable conduct. See Joab, Inc. v. Thrall, 245 So.2d 291 (Fla.App.1971).

6. Where defendant's wealth is relevant to the determination of the amount of punitive damages, who has the burden of producing that evidence? Compare Anderson v. Latham Trucking Co., 728 S.W.2d 752 (Tenn.1987) (either plaintiff or the defendant may offer proof of the

financial condition of defendant but it is not essential or mandatory that the record contain any such evidence to sustain an award of punitive damages) with Adams v. Murakami, 54 Cal.3d 105, 813 P.2d 1348, 284 Cal.Rptr. 318 (1991) (plaintiff has burden). Where defendant's wealth is not relevant, financial records are neither admissible nor discoverable. Corbetta v. Albertson's, Inc., 975 P.2d 718 (Colo.1999) (because punitive damages tied to amount of compensatory damages, no discovery of financial records permitted). How is the defendant's financial status to be measured? By net worth or annual sales or profits?

7. Some courts permit the defendant to show that he has been criminally punished for the same wrong or punished in an earlier civil suit in an effort to lower the amount of punitive damages imposed. Compare Hanover Ins. Co. v. Hayward, 464 A.2d 156 (Me.1983) (fact-finder may consider whether criminal liability has been imposed as one factor in determining whether an award of damages would serve as a meaningful deterrent) with Owens-Illinois, Inc. v. Zenobia, 325 Md. 420, 601 A.2d 633 (1992) (after discussing proof problems associated with such a proffer, court declined to "impose this onerous burden on the trial court"). See also Ore. Rev. Stat. § 30.925(2)(g) and Owens-Corning Fiberglas Corp. v. Malone, 972 S.W.2d 35 (Tex.1998) (evidence of paid punitive damages awards and past settlements that specified amounts for punitive damages relevant when offered in mitigation of punitive damages). Are there tactical reasons why defense counsel may decline this opportunity?

8. *Procedural Issues.* Most jurisdictions permit the jury to consider evidence, like the wealth of the defendant, in awarding punitive damages that would be irrelevant and unduly prejudicial on the liability and compensatory damages aspects of the case. Therefore, many jurisdictions have developed various safeguards to protect against the misuse of that evidence. Some require that the plaintiff make a prime facie showing of entitlement to punitive damages before permitting discovery of financial information. Others require that the trial be bifurcated so that the jury does not hear evidence of defendant's financial status until after it has ruled on liability, compensatory damages, and liability for punitive damages. Campen v. Stone, 635 P.2d 1121 (Wyo.1981) (adopting bifurcation procedure through case law); Cal. Civ. Code Ann. § 3295(d) (requiring bifurcation on request of defendant in case seeking punitive damages); Kan. Stat. Ann. § 60–3701(a)–(b) (trier of fact determines liability for punitive damages, then court determines amount).

9. The applicable burden of proof for establishing entitlement to punitive damages is clear and convincing evidence in most jurisdictions. This standard is between "preponderance of the evidence" and the criminal standard "beyond a reasonable doubt." See Rodgriguez v. Suzuki Motor Corp., 936 S.W.2d 104 (Mo.1996) (adopting the higher standard because punitive damages are extraordinary and harsh and listing twenty-four jurisdictions that adopted the higher standard by statute and seven other jurisdictions that adopted it by judicial decision).

10. Like Indiana in the *Cheatham* case, some jurisdictions have directed that a portion of the punitive damages award be paid to a state fund. Ga. Code Ann. § 51–12–5.1(e)(2) (three-quarters of punitive damages award, less proportionate share of costs and attorneys' fees, must be paid to state treasury); Iowa Code § 668A.1(2)(b) (in certain circumstances, 75% of

punitive damages, after payment of costs and counsel fees, goes to civil reparations trust fund); Ore.Rev.Stat. § 31.735 (60% to compensation fund for crime victims). The Ohio Supreme Court has done so without benefit of legislature. Dardinger v. Anthem Blue Cross & Blue Shield, 98 Ohio St.3d 77, 781 N.E.2d 121 (2002) (ordering portion of $30 million award to go to cancer research fund at state university). Do you see why no state provides that all of the award go to a state fund? What would be the incentive for the claimant and the claimant's attorney to pursue the punitive damages case? Should the jury be told that a portion of the punitive damages goes to the state? Honeywell v. Sterling Furniture Co., 310 Or. 206, 797 P.2d 1019 (1990) (no, because jury might be encouraged to award damages for improper reason—to enhance state account) and Ford v. Uniroyal Goodrich Tire Co., 267 Ga. 226, 476 S.E.2d 565 (1996) (no, because it is irrelevant to jury's consideration of the amount who will benefit from the award or how much plaintiff will ultimately receive).

11. *Vicarious Liability for Punitive Damages.* Some courts take the position that a party can be liable for punitive damages only for the party's own conduct and not vicariously liable for the acts of others, like agents or employees. Others take the position that when the agent or employee commits an act that makes the agent liable for punitive damages, the principal or employer should be liable as well. An especially vigorous opinion to this effect is found in Goddard v. Grand Trunk Ry., 57 Me. 202, 2 Am.Rep. 39 (1869). Most courts take the middle position of the Restatement (Second) of Torts § 909 (1977) and hold that the principal (whether an individual or corporation) is liable only if the principal authorized or ratified the act, was reckless in employing or retaining the agent, or the agent was employed in a managerial capacity and was acting in the scope of employment. See, e.g., Chuy v. Philadelphia Eagles Football Club, Inc., 595 F.2d 1265 (3d Cir.1979) (applying Pennsylvania law) and Purvis v. Prattco, Inc., 595 S.W.2d 103 (Tex.1980).

12. Defendants sometimes carry liability insurance that provides for reimbursement of "all sums" incurred in defending tort lawsuits against them. Should the insurance company be able to avoid paying the punitive damages portion of an award by arguing that it is against public policy to permit the insured to shift the burden of punishment to an insurance company? Jurisdictions have split on this issue. Compare Allen v. Simmons, 533 A.2d 541 (R.I.1987) (burden of satisfying punitive damage award should remain with wrongdoer and not be spread upon the blameless through higher insurance premiums) with Whalen v. On-Deck, Inc., 514 A.2d 1072 (Del.1986) (wrongdoer who is insured would still be punished through higher insurance premiums or loss of insurance); Hensley v. Erie Ins. Co., 168 W.Va. 172, 283 S.E.2d 227 (1981) (increased cost of insurance has some deterrent effect and punishment is not the only use of punitive damages; additional compensation to plaintiff is part of reason for award); and Westchester Fire Ins. Co. v. Admiral Ins. Co., 152 S.W.3d 172 (Tex. App. 2004) (declining to hold insurability of punitive damages is against public policy in absence of clear indication from either legislature or supreme court).

CHAPTER 11

WRONGFUL DEATH AND SURVIVAL

At common law, the cause of action for personal injury was extinguished by the death of either the plaintiff or the defendant: it was said the cause of action was "interred with the bones." Moreover, there was no separate cause of action that arose to compensate the family of the person who was injured for the losses suffered by the family. Thus, as Dean Prosser has said, "it was more profitable for the plaintiff to kill a man than to scratch him." By mid-19th century this was beginning to change. First, in England with the passage of Lord Campbell's Act (1846), sometimes called the Compensation to Relatives Act, and later with the Survival of Actions Legislation (1934), Parliament abrogated the common law rules. In the United States, state by state, changes were made by statute to the common law rules. Now, in every state, there is some form of recovery for the death of another due to tortious conduct. In most states, there are two statutes that change the common law in this area: the *survival statute* and the *wrongful death statute*.

Although the statutes vary by jurisdiction, basically the *survival statute* reverses the common law rule by providing that a cause of action for personal injury survives the death of the plaintiff or the defendant or both. The cause of action decedent would have had survives the death of either party. If it is a defendant who has died, the claim may be brought against the defendant's estate. If it is a plaintiff who has died, usually the claim can be brought by the executor or administrator of the estate on behalf of the estate. Note that the cause of the death of the plaintiff may be independent of the defendant's wrongdoing.

Under the *wrongful death statute*, on the other hand, a new cause of action is created by the death of an individual due to the tortious conduct of another. It is a new, independent cause of action created on behalf of certain beneficiaries designated by the statute. It is to be brought by one of the beneficiaries on behalf of all of them or by the personal representative of the decedent. Sometimes the statute provides for categories or classes of beneficiaries, giving priority to one class of beneficiaries (spouse and minor children) over others (adult children).

1. WRONGFUL DEATH

Moragne v. States Marine Lines, Inc.

Supreme Court of the United States, 1970.
398 U.S. 375, 90 S.Ct. 1772, 26 L.Ed.2d 339.

MR. JUSTICE HARLAN delivered the opinion of the Court. We brought this case here to consider whether The Harrisburg, 119 U.S. 199, in which this Court held in 1886 that maritime law does not afford a cause of action for wrongful death, should any longer be regarded as acceptable law.

The complaint sets forth that Edward Moragne, a longshoreman, was killed while working aboard the vessel Palmetto State in navigable waters within the State of Florida. Petitioner, as his widow and representative of his estate, brought this suit in a state court against respondent States Marine Lines, Inc., the owner of the vessel, to recover damages for wrongful death and for the pain and suffering experienced by the decedent prior to his death. The claims were predicated upon both negligence and the unseaworthiness of the vessel. * * *

The Court's opinion in *The Harrisburg* acknowledged that the result reached had little justification except in primitive English legal history—a history far removed from the American law of remedies for maritime deaths. * * *

One would expect, upon an inquiry into the sources of the common-law rule, to find a clear and compelling justification for what seems a striking departure from the result dictated by elementary principles in the law of remedies. Where existing law imposes a primary duty, violations of which are compensable if they cause injury, nothing in ordinary notions of justice suggests that a violation should be nonactionable simply because it was serious enough to cause death. On the contrary, that rule has been criticized ever since its inception, and described in such terms as "barbarous." [Cc] Because the primary duty already exists, the decision whether to allow recovery for violations causing death is entirely a remedial matter. It is true that the harms to be assuaged are not identical in the two cases: in the case of mere injury, the person physically harmed is made whole for his harm, while in the case of death, those closest to him—usually spouse and children—seek to recover for their total loss of one on whom they depended. This difference, however, even when coupled with the practical difficulties of defining the class of beneficiaries who may recover for death, does not seem to account for the law's refusal to recognize a wrongful killing as an actionable tort. One expects, therefore, to find a persuasive, independent justification for this apparent legal anomaly.

Legal historians have concluded that the sole substantial basis for the rule at common law is a feature of the early English law that did not survive into this century—the felony-merger doctrine. [Cc] According to this doctrine, the common law did not allow civil recovery for an act that constituted both a tort and a felony. The tort was treated as less important than the offense against the Crown, and was merged into, or pre-empted by, the felony. [Cc] The doctrine found practical justification in the fact that the punishment for the felony was the death of the felon and the forfeiture of his property to the Crown; thus, after the crime had been punished, nothing remained of the felon or his property on which to base a civil action. Since all intentional or negligent homicide was felonious, there could be no civil suit for wrongful death.

The first explicit statement of the common-law rule against recovery for wrongful death came in the opinion of Lord Ellenborough, sitting at *nisi prius,* in Baker v. Bolton, 1 Camp. 493, 170 Eng.Rep. 1033 (1808). That opinion did not cite authority, or give supporting reasoning, or refer to the felony-merger doctrine in announcing that "[i]n a Civil court, the death of a human being could not be complained of as an injury." Ibid. Nor had the felony-merger doctrine seemingly been cited as the basis for the denial of recovery in any of the other reported wrongful-death cases since the earliest ones, in the 17th century. [Cc] However, it seems clear from those first cases that the rule of Baker v. Bolton did derive from the felony-merger doctrine, and that there was no other ground on which it might be supported even at the time of its inception. * * *

The historical justification marshaled for the rule in England never existed in this country. In limited instances American law did adopt a vestige of the felony-merger doctrine, to the effect that a civil action was delayed until after the criminal trial. However, in this country the felony punishment did not include forfeiture of property; therefore, there was nothing, even in those limited instances, to bar a subsequent civil suit. [Cc]

Nevertheless, despite some early cases in which the rule was rejected as "incapable of vindication," [cc] American courts generally adopted the English rule as the common law of this country as well. * * *

It was suggested by some courts and commentators that the prohibition of nonstatutory wrongful-death actions derived support from the ancient common-law rule that a personal cause of action in tort did not survive the death of its possessor [c], and the decision in Baker v. Bolton itself may have been influenced by this principle. [C] However, it is now universally recognized that because this principle pertains only to the victim's own personal claims, such as for pain and suffering, it has no bearing on the question whether a dependent should be permitted to recover for the injury he suffers from the victim's death. [Cc]

We need not, however, pronounce a verdict on whether *The Harrisburg,* when decided, was a correct extrapolation of the principles of decisional law then in existence. A development of major significance has intervened, making clear that the rule against recovery for wrongful death is sharply out of keeping with the policies of modern American maritime law. * * *

[L]egislatures both here and in England began to evidence unanimous disapproval of the rule against recovery for wrongful death. The first statute partially abrogating the rule was Lord Campbell's Act, 9 & 10 Vict., c. 93 (1846), which granted recovery to the families of persons killed by tortious conduct, "although the Death shall have been caused under such Circumstances as amount in Law to Felony."

In the United States, every State today has enacted a wrongful-death statute. [C] The Congress has created actions for wrongful deaths of railroad employees, Federal Employers' Liability Act; of merchant seamen, Jones Act, [c]; and of persons on the high seas, Death on the High Seas Act, [c]. Congress has also, in the Federal Tort Claims Act,[c], made the United States subject to liability in certain circumstances for negligently caused wrongful death to the same extent as a private person. [C]

These numerous and broadly applicable statutes, taken as a whole, make it clear that there is no present public policy against allowing recovery for wrongful death. The statutes evidence a wide rejection by the legislatures of whatever justifications may once have existed for a general refusal to allow such recovery. This legislative establishment of policy carries significance beyond the particular scope of each of the statutes involved. The policy thus established has become itself a part of our law, to be given its appropriate weight not only in matters of statutory construction but also in those of decisional law. See Landis, Statutes and the Sources of Law, in Harvard Legal Essays 213, 226–227 (1934).

Professor Landis has said, "much of what is ordinarily regarded as 'common law' finds its source in legislative enactment." Landis, supra, at 214. It has always been the duty of the common-law court to perceive the impact of major legislative innovations and to interweave the new legislative policies with the inherited body of common-law principles—many of them deriving from earlier legislative exertions.

[The court then concluded that it was sometimes the duty of the common law court to bend to the weight of legislative authority and noted that Congress by its failure to enact a specific remedy did not intend to forestall recovery for wrongful death in admiralty and that the doctrine of *stare decisis* does not preclude a change in law.]

Respondents argue that overruling *The Harrisburg* will necessitate a long course of decisions to spell out the elements of the new "cause of action." We believe these fears are exaggerated, because our decision does not require the fashioning of a whole new body of federal law, but merely removes a bar to access to the existing general maritime law. In most respects the law applied in personal-injury cases will answer all questions that arise in death cases. * * *

The one aspect of a claim for wrongful death that has no precise counterpart in the established law governing nonfatal injuries is the determination of the beneficiaries who are entitled to recover. General maritime law, which denied any recovery for wrongful death, found no need to specify which dependents should receive such recovery. On this question, petitioner and the United States argue that we may look for guidance to the expressions of Congress, which has spoken on this subject in the Death on the High Seas Act, the Jones Act, and the Longshoremen's and Harbor Workers' Compensation Act. Though very similar, each of these provisions differs slightly in the naming of dependent relatives who may recover and in the priority given to their claims. * * *

We do not determine this issue now, for we think its final resolution should await further sifting through the lower courts in future litigation. For present purposes we conclude only that its existence affords no sufficient reason for not coming to grips with *The Harrisburg*. If still other subsidiary issues should require resolution, such as particular questions of the measure of damages, the courts will not be without persuasive analogy for guidance. Both the Death on the High Seas Act and the numerous state wrongful-death acts have been implemented with success for decades. The experience thus built up counsels that a suit for wrongful death raises no problems unlike those that have long been grist for the judicial mill.

In sum, in contrast to the torrent of difficult litigation that has swirled about *The Harrisburg* * * * and the problems of federal-state accommodation [it] occasioned, the recognition of a remedy for wrongful death under general maritime law can be expected to bring more placid waters. That prospect indeed makes for, and not against, the discarding of *The Harrisburg.*

We accordingly overrule *The Harrisburg,* and hold that an action does lie under general maritime law for death caused by violation of maritime duties. The judgment of the Court of Appeals is reversed, and the case is remanded to that court for further proceedings consistent with this opinion. It is so ordered.

Reversed and remanded.

NOTES AND QUESTIONS

1. American maritime law was the last island for the common law rule that "the death of a human being could not be complained of as an injury." Baker v. Bolton, 1 Camp. 493, 170 Eng.Rep. 1033 (N.P.1808). Lord Ellenborough did not supply reasons for his rule, but later sympathizers with his result have given at least two. First, allowing a claim would lead jurors to award runaway damages and, second, it is "immoral" to place a monetary value on a human life.

2. The principal case is unusual in making a major change away from the common law rule by the process of judicial decision, rather than by action of the legislature. In its subsequent decision of Sea-Land Services, Inc. v. Gaudet, 414 U.S. 573 (1974), the Supreme Court elaborated on its holding that there is a maritime common law cause of action for wrongful death. It held that the fact that the decedent had previously recovered damages for loss of wages, pain and suffering, and medical expenses did not interfere with the independent common law cause of action for wrongful death resulting from the original injury, so that the later action was not precluded by res judicata. Recovery for wrongful death was held to cover damages for (1) "loss of support, * * * [including] all the financial support that the decedent would have made to his dependents had he lived," (2) "the monetary value of services the decedent provided and would have continued to provide but for his wrongful death * * * [including] the nurture, training, education, and guidance that a child would have received had not the parent been wrongfully killed * * * [plus] services the decedent performed at home or for his spouse," (3) "compensation for loss of society * * *, [including] a broad range of mutual benefits each family member receives from the others' continued existence, including love, affection, care, attention, companionship, comfort and protection," and (4) "damages for funeral expenses * * * in circumstances where the decedent's dependents have either paid for the funeral or are liable for its payment." The potential for double liability coming from the awards to the decedent for loss of future wages and to the dependents for loss of support was held to be controlled by the law of collateral estoppel, but it has continued to be a cause of concern to some courts. See Alfone v. Sarno, 87 N.J. 99, 432 A.2d 857 (1981) for a discussion of duplication of damages in such cases. Note

also that most states permit a wrongful death action on behalf of beneficiaries only if the decedent had not recovered damages arising out of the accident before his death. See note 14, page 615.

3. All fifty states have some form of statutory action for the recovery of the wrongful death of another. Most of the statutes were modeled after Lord Campbell's Act, mentioned by Justice Harlan. These statutes vary in many important respects and the material considered in this Chapter is necessarily only introductory in nature. Lawyers have the benefit of an excellent treatise on the subject that treats the statutes individually and provides a wealth of information on state-specific issues. See S. Speiser, Recovery for Wrongful Death and Injury (4th ed. 2005). The topic of wrongful death differs from many others in the law of torts because it is statutory. Courts must engage in the process of statutory construction and fathoming legislative intent. This is not an easy process with regard to wrongful death statutes because there is rarely much legislative history and most statutes are over one hundred years old. It also means that the court has less flexibility in meeting new circumstances than it might have with common law causes of action.

4. Representative wrongful death statutes from two states provide as follows:

South Carolina

"*Civil Action for Wrongful Act Causing Death.* Whenever the death of a person shall be caused by the wrongful act, neglect or default of another and the act, neglect or default is such as would, if death had not ensued, have entitled the party injured to maintain an action and recover damages in respect thereof, the person who would have been liable, if death had not ensued, shall be liable to an action for damages, notwithstanding the death of the person injured, although the death shall have been caused under such circumstances as make the killing in law a felony. In the event of the death of the wrongdoer, such cause of action shall survive against his personal representative." S.C.Code § 15–51–10.

"*Beneficiaries of Action for Wrongful Death; By Whom Brought.* Every such action shall be for the benefit of the wife or husband and child or children of the person whose death shall have been so caused, and, if there be no such wife, husband, child or children, then for the benefit of the parent or parents, and if there be none such, then for the benefit of the heirs of the person whose death shall have been so caused. Every such action shall be brought by or in the name of the executor or administrator of such person." Id. § 15–51–20.

Kentucky

"*Action for Wrongful Death—Personal Representative to Prosecute—Distribution of Amount Recovered.* (1) Whenever the death of a person results from an injury inflicted by the negligence or wrongful act of another, damages may be recovered for the death from the person who caused it, or whose agent or servant caused it. If the act was willful or the negligence gross, punitive damages may be recovered. The action shall be prosecuted by the personal representative of the deceased. (2) The amount recovered, less funeral expenses and the cost of administration and costs of recovery including the attorney fees, not included in the recovery from the defendant, shall be for the benefit of and go to the kindred of the deceased in the following order: (a) If the deceased leaves a widow or husband, and no children or their descendants, then the whole to the widow or husband. (b) If the deceased leaves a widow and children or a husband and children, then one-half (1/2) to the widow or husband and the other one-half (1/2) to the children of the deceased. (c) If the deceased leaves a child or children, but no widow or husband, then the whole to the child or children. (d) If the deceased leaves no widow, husband or child, then the recovery shall pass to the mother and father of the deceased, one (1) moiety each, if both are living; if the mother is dead and the father is living, the whole thereof shall pass to the father; and if the father is dead and the mother living, the whole thereof shall go to the mother. In the event the deceased was an adopted person, 'mother' and 'father' shall mean the adoptive parents of the deceased. (e) If the deceased leaves no widow, husband or child, and if both father and mother are dead, then the whole of the recovery shall become a part of the personal estate of the deceased, and after the payment of his debts the remainder, if any, shall pass to his kindred more remote than those above named, according to the law of descent and distribution." Ky. Rev. Stat. § 411.130.

5. *Proper Party*. Note that both of these statutes provide that the action is to be brought by the personal representative of the deceased for the benefit of the named beneficiaries. Some statutes provide that the action can be brought by the beneficiaries themselves. In a jurisdiction that provides that the wrongful death action for a minor child must be brought by his "surviving mother or father," can his grandmother bring the action? The child had lived with the grandmother and she alleged that she was his "psychological" or "de facto" mother and that the parents had agreed to her bringing the action. Goodleft v. Gullickson, 556 N.W.2d 303 (N.D.1996) (grandmother not entitled to bring claim even though she had been in *loco parentis*; trial court should permit parents to substitute themselves as parties). In a jurisdiction that provides the action can be brought by the parent only if there is no surviving spouse or child, what happens if an (adult) child was killed by his spouse? Can decedent's mother bring the action despite the fact that there is a surviving spouse in prison? Carringer v. Rodgers, 276 Ga. 359, 578 S.E.2d 841 (2003) (holding that the equity powers of the court can be used to permit mother to bring action even though literal reading of statute would not allow).

Beneficiaries

6. The original Lord Campbell's Act specified that the action was for the benefit of the husband, wife, parent or child of the deceased, and many American acts have limited recovery to a similar group of beneficiaries. Interpretation problems often arise.

7. *Spouse*. All of the states provide that the lawful spouse is a designated beneficiary. Lewis v. Allis-Chalmers Corp., 615 F.2d 1129 (5th Cir.1980) (applying Louisiana law) (but former wife may not recover). The cases have been consistent in refusing to extend the definition of spouse to unmarried cohabitants. See, e.g., Nieto v. City of Los Angeles, 138 Cal.App.3d 464, 188 Cal.Rptr. 31 (1982) (fiancé may not recover); Raum v. Restaurant Assocs., Inc., 252 A.D.2d 369, 675 N.Y.S.2d 343 (1998) (unmarried couples living together, whether heterosexual or homosexual, are not "spouses" within the wrongful death statute and thus have no cause of action); Holguin v. Flores, 122 Cal.App.4th 428, 18 Cal.Rptr.3d 749

(2004) (unmarried cohabitants have no right to sue under wrongful death act).

8. *Domestic Partner, Civil Union Party, Reciprocal Beneficiary.* Several jurisdictions have made wrongful death benefits available to domestic partners (e.g., Cal. Code Civ. Proc. § 377.60); civil union parties (Colo. Rev. Stat. Ann. 14–15–101); or reciprocal beneficiaries (Haw. Rev. Stat. 663–3(b)(3)). Note that each of these is a legal status requiring compliance with particular formalities to acquire the status. Wrongful death benefits would not be available if the parties had not complied with the formalities before the death occurred, even if they were eligible to do so. To what extent are those benefits available outside the state that bestowed them? Should a party to a Vermont civil union be permitted to sue under the New York wrongful death statute? Langan v. St. Vincent's Hosp., 25 A.D.3d 90, 802 N.Y.S.2d 476 (2005) (not permitted to bring action under New York wrongful death statute).

9. *Child.* Most jurisdictions provide that children of the decedent are beneficiaries, although some put them in a different category from spouses and allow them to recover only if there is no surviving spouse.

10. *Stepchild.* Did the legislature intend to cover stepchildren? Most cases have held no. See, e.g., in Steed v. Imperial Airlines, 12 Cal.3d 115, 524 P.2d 801, 115 Cal.Rptr. 329 (1974) (statute later amended to cover stepchildren if they had been financially dependent on decedent) and Balas v. Smithkline Beecham Corp., 2009 WL 1708831 (Tex. App. 2009) (unadopted stepchildren not beneficiaries under wrongful death statute).

11. *Child Born out of Wedlock.* Until the late 1960's a majority of American courts held that children born out of wedlock were not intended beneficiaries under the statute, unless the statute said so. Contra, Armijo v. Wesselius, 73 Wash.2d 716, 440 P.2d 471 (1968) (child permitted to bring a claim for the death of his natural father when the latter had both acknowledged and contributed to the support of the child). The Supreme Court then held that the Louisiana Wrongful Death Statute constituted a denial of equal protection of the laws when it precluded a child born out of wedlock from bringing a wrongful death claim upon the death of her mother. Levy v. Louisiana, 391 U.S. 68 (1968). The court also struck down a Louisiana provision that barred the claim of a mother for the wrongful death of her child born out of wedlock. Glona v. American Guarantee & Liability Ins. Co., 391 U.S. 73 (1968). Although some jurisdictions require that a father have acknowledged paternity or that paternity have been adjudicated before the death in order for a wrongful death action to be brought by him, most permit the showing of paternity to be made after the death of the child. Brookbank v. Gray, 74 Ohio St.3d 279, 658 N.E.2d 724 (1996) (status of beneficiary may not be created after death, but it may be proved) (citing cases from other jurisdictions). Washington's requirement that the father have contributed regularly to financial support of the child in order to recover for the child's wrongful death was found to violate Washington's Equal Rights Amendment since the same requirement was not imposed on the mother. Guard v. Jackson, 132 Wash.2d 660, 940 P.2d 642 (1997).

12. *Unborn Child.* Should parents be able to obtain recovery for the death of an unborn child? Every jurisdiction has a cause of action for prenatal injuries to a viable unborn child who is born alive. Some, however,

will not allow recovery if the child is stillborn. See e.g., Kandel v. White, 339 Md. 432, 663 A.2d 1264 (1995) (no cause of action under either wrongful death or survival statute for fetus who was not born alive); Tanner v. Hartog, 696 So.2d 705 (Fla.1997) (same, but parents have cause of action for their own pain and suffering and for medical expenses); Smith v. Borello, 370 Md. 227, 804 A.2d 1151 (2002) (same, mother can recover medical expenses and pain and suffering related to miscarriage, but not for solatium or loss of consortium damages). But see Aka v. Jefferson Hospital Assn., 344 Ark. 627, 42 S.W.3d 508 (2001) (reversing earlier ruling that a viable fetus who was stillborn is not a person for the purposes of the wrongful death act and noting that eight jurisdictions still follow that interpretation of their statutes). Others will not allow recovery if the child was not viable at the time of injury, even if born alive. Miller v. Kirk, 120 N.M. 654, 905 P.2d 194 (1995). But see Connor v. Monkem Co., Inc., 898 S.W.2d 89 (Mo.1995) and Farley v. Sartin, 195 W.Va. 671, 466 S.E.2d 522 (1995) (both permitting wrongful death action for unborn child even when injured prior to viability). See also Chapter 8, page 484. Illinois is one of the states that permit a wrongful death action to be brought on behalf of an unborn child injured before viability. Plaintiffs filed a wrongful death claim against a fertility clinic, claiming that it had failed to cryopreserve their blastocyst for future implantation. Miller v. American Infertility Group of Ill., 386 Ill.App.3d 141, 325 Ill.Dec. 298, 897 N.E.2d 837 (2008) (finding Wrongful Death Act applied only to the loss of an embryo that has been implanted in the mother and thus did not apply to loss of blastocyst).

13. *Parent.* In most jurisdictions, a parent is a beneficiary only if a child dies without a spouse or children. Some of those statutes require the parents of adult children to show financial dependence in order to qualify as a beneficiary. See, for example, Philippides v. Bernard, 151 Wash.2d 376, 88 P.3d 939 (2004) (no cause of action under wrongful death statute unless parents can show they were financially dependent on decedent). Other jurisdictions provide that the parent is a beneficiary even if there are minor children. Florida is such a jurisdiction while Louisiana is not. Decedent lived in Florida with his parents and worked on an oil rig off the Louisiana coast in international waters. He was killed in a helicopter crash in Louisiana on his way to the oil rig. When he died, he left behind three survivors, his parents and young son. His parents filed a wrongful death action in Florida on behalf of themselves and his son. His son's mother filed a wrongful death action in Louisiana on behalf of his son. Which wrongful death statute controls? See Yelton v. PHI, Inc., 669 F.3d 577 (5th Cir. 2012) (affirming trial court's dismissal of parents' action after determination that Louisiana law applied in action arising out of helicopter crash that occurred in Louisiana). For a discussion of the measure of damages when the decedent is a minor child, see the next principal case.

14. *Next of Kin.* Some statutes provide that the next of kin is a beneficiary, as long as that person can show financial loss. A Roman Catholic nun who belonged to the order the Sisters of St. Ursula was killed when the car she was driving was struck by a drunk driver who ran a stop sign. She had been a member of her religious community for almost forty years and had taken a vow of poverty that meant that all her income went to the community for the common good. Her death caused her community to lose about $250,000 that she would have earned over the rest of her lifetime. Is the religious community her next of kin and therefore a

beneficiary under the wrongful death statute? Buchert v. Newman, 90 Ohio App.3d 382, 629 N.E.2d 489 (1993) (not next of kin under statute even though community showed financial dependence on decedent).

The Vermont Supreme Court has rejected the argument of the owners of two cats who allegedly died as the result of a mistake in the dosage of their hypertension medication that it should extend the wrongful death act to cover them. Goodby v. Vetpharm, Inc., 974 A.2d 1269, 1272 (Vt. 2009). "We note that under the Wrongful Death Act people may recover only for the loss of their next of kin, which can exclude recovery in many cases for the loss of many close relatives, such as grandparents or grandchildren, nieces, nephews, aunts, and uncles, as well as for the loss of nonrelatives like stepchildren, fiancés, or other closely held companions. [C] Viewed from this perspective, plaintiffs request a judicial expansion of law to recover for loss of a pet what the law does not allow for loss of a broad variety of critically loved human beings. Whether the familial quality of companionship between humans and their pets is relatively new or ancient, plaintiffs seek a dramatic alteration to the law."

15. If no designated beneficiaries are living at the time of the wrongful death, the action fails. See, for example, Tait v. Wahl, 97 Wash.App. 765, 987 P.2d 127 (1999) (no cause of action in wrongful death because decedent died without spouse or children (Tier 1) and without parents or siblings who were financially dependent on her (Tier 2) even though her niece and niece's children were financially dependent on her). A problem of statutory interpretation occurs if the beneficiary dies after the person has been wrongfully killed, but before an action has begun or even after commencement of the action, but before judgment. How are courts to decide these things? Compare Murrell v. Springdale Memorial Hospital, 330 Ark. 121, 952 S.W.2d 153 (1997) (summary judgment for medical malpractice defendants is appropriate upon death of widower of patient) and Thomas v. Eads, 400 N.E.2d 778 (Ind.App.1980) (no award for wrongful death unless at the commencement of the action, and also at the time of awarding damages, there be living some person or persons in the class of beneficiaries set by statute) with Gray v. Goodson, 61 Wash.2d 319, 378 P.2d 413 (1963) (once a right of action for wrongful death has accrued, the subsequent death of a beneficiary does not abate the action, but the benefit of the action survives to the beneficiary's estate, with the measure of damages recoverable to the estate limited to the amount of loss sustained by the beneficiary prior to his death) and McDaniel v. Bullard, 34 Ill.2d 487, 216 N.E.2d 140 (1966) (cause of action for wrongful death accrues at time of death and survives death of sole beneficiary, whose estate may maintain the cause of action).

16. *Allocation of Proceeds Among Beneficiaries.* Most jurisdictions provide for some formal mechanism by which the court can allocate the proceeds among the beneficiaries. California, for example, provides that there is only one cause of action for wrongful death and that if one of the beneficiaries chooses not to join in the action as a plaintiff, he can be made a nominal defendant. The court has jurisdiction to adjudicate the claim even if not all beneficiaries are present. Patient died, allegedly as a result of medical malpractice, and his widow and minor children brought a wrongful death action, naming his adult daughter from a previous marriage as a nominal defendant. She was never served, however, and did

not learn about the settlement with the malpractice defendants until the proceeds had been distributed to the widow and minor children. Does she have a cause of action against the malpractice defendants? Against the widow for a share of the proceeds? Ruttenberg v. Ruttenberg, 53 Cal.App.4th 801, 62 Cal.Rptr.2d 78 (1997) (no cause of action against medical malpractice defendants because court had power to adjudicate that action and thus to bind her; no cause of action for share of proceeds because that amount represented only the loss to the widow and minor children; cause of action against the widow for omitting daughter from wrongful death action, thereby causing her to lose her opportunity to prove damages in that action); Wilmot v. Wilmot, 203 Ariz. 565, 58 P.3d 507 (2002) (where statute provided that widow could bring wrongful death action on behalf of herself and surviving children, she could not settle claim without obtaining consent from adult children from previous marriage); Parr v. Parr, 16 S.W.3d 332 (Mo. 2000) (discussing allocation of proceeds among widow, adult children, and elderly parents of fifty-five year old decedent); Corder v. Corder, 41 Cal.4th 644, 161 P.3d 172, 61 Cal.Rptr.3d 660 (2007) (discussing allocation of proceeds between widow and adult daughter from previous marriage where daughter presented evidence that decedent at time of his death was planning to leave wife because she had not kept the promise made at their wedding eight months before to stop working as a prostitute).

Selders v. Armentrout

Supreme Court of Nebraska, 1973.
190 Neb. 275, 207 N.W.2d 686.

MCCOWN, JUSTICE. * * * Three minor children (aged 15, 13, and 9) were killed in an automobile accident due to the negligent conduct of defendants. Their parents brought these wrongful death actions. The sole issue on this appeal involves the proper elements and measure of damages in a tort action in Nebraska for the wrongful death of a minor child. The [trial] court essentially instructed the jury that except for medical and funeral expenses, the damages should be the monetary value of the contributions and services which the parents could reasonably have expected to receive from the children less the reasonable cost to the parents of supporting the children.

The defendants contend that the measure of damages is limited to pecuniary loss and that the instructions to the jury correctly reflect the measure and elements of damage. The plaintiffs assert that the loss of the society, comfort, and companionship of the children are proper and compensable elements of damage, and that evidence of amounts invested or expended for the nurture, education, and maintenance of the children before death is proper. * * *

[A] broadening concept of the measure and elements of damages for the wrongful death of a minor child has been in the development stage for many years. [Cc] Following a discussion of the rigid common law rules limiting recovery for wrongful death to the loss of pecuniary benefits, Prosser states: "Recent years, however, have brought considerable modification of the rigid common law rules. It has been recognized that even pecuniary loss may extend beyond mere contributions of food, shelter, money or property; and there is now a decided tendency to find that the society, care and attention of the deceased are 'services' to the survivor with a financial value, which may be compensated. This has been true, for example, not only where a child has been deprived of a parent, * * * but also where the parent has lost a child * * *." Prosser, Law of Torts (4th Ed.), § 127, p. 908.

The original pecuniary loss concept and its restrictive application arose in a day when children during minority were generally regarded as an economic asset to parents. Children went to work on farms and in factories at age 10 and even earlier. This was before the day of child labor laws and long before the day of extended higher education for the general population. A child's earnings and services could be generally established and the financial or pecuniary loss which could be proved became the measure of damages for the wrongful death of a child. Virtually all other damages were disallowed as speculative or as sentimental.

The damages involved in a wrongful death case even today must of necessity deal primarily with a fictitious or speculative future life, as it might have been had the wrongful death not occurred. For that reason, virtually all evidence of future damage is necessarily speculative to a degree. The measure and elements of damage involved in a wrongful death case, however, have been excessively restrictive as applied to a minor child in contrast to an adult. Modern economic reality emphasizes the gulf between the old concepts of a child's economic value and the new facts of modern family life. To limit damages for the death of a child to the monetary value of the services which the next of kin could reasonably have expected to receive during his minority less the reasonable expense of maintaining and educating him stamps almost all modern children as worthless in the eyes of the law. In fact, if the rule was literally followed, the average child would have a negative worth. This court has already held that contributions reasonably to be expected from a minor, not only during his minority but afterwards, may be allowed on evidence justifying a reasonable expectation of pecuniary benefit. [Cc] Even with that modification, the wrongful death of a child results in no monetary loss, except in the rare case, and the assumption that the traditional measure of damages is compensatory is a pure legal fiction.

Particularly in the last decade, a growing number of courts have extended the measure of damages to include the loss of society and companionship of the minor child, even under statutes limiting recovery to pecuniary loss or pecuniary value of services less the cost of support and maintenance, or similar limitations. [Cc]

In this state, the statute has not limited damages for wrongful death to pecuniary loss but this court has imposed that restriction. For an injury to the marital relationship, the law allows recovery for the loss of the society, comfort, and companionship of a spouse. This court has allowed such a recovery for the wrongful death of a wife. [C] There is no logical reason for treating an injury to the family relationship resulting from the wrongful death of a child more restrictively. It is no more difficult for juries and courts to measure damages for the loss of the life of a child than many other abstract concepts with which they are required to deal. We hold that the measure of damages for the wrongful death of a minor child should be extended to include the loss of the society, comfort, and companionship of the child. To the extent this holding is in conflict with prior decisions of this court, they are overruled. * * *

The judgment of the trial court as to liability is affirmed, the judgment as to damages is reversed and the cause remanded for trial on the issue of damages only, consistent with our holding in this opinion.

WHITE, CHIEF JUSTICE (dissenting). * * * I submit that the majority opinion, which arbitrarily and in one stroke, after 50 years of settled law and without public hearing or consideration of the different interests and policies involved, and in violation of the 1945 legislative policy clearly announced in the statute, and unrepealed, simply throws open a death claim for a minor child to a sympathy and sentiment contest in the award of money, and is a serious mistake for us to make.

NOTES AND QUESTIONS

1. The original Lord Campbell's Act, as interpreted by the Court of Queen's Bench, and wrongful death statutes in the United States patterned after that law were intended to limit damages to "pecuniary" losses caused by the death of a loved one. This was to meet concerns of common law judges, like Justice White in the principal case, that awards made for emotional losses arising from another's death would know no bounds. In most states, pecuniary loss is measured by having the trier of fact attempt to determine the monetary contribution that decedent would have made during his lifetime to the plaintiff beneficiary. This is frequently referred to as a loss-to-beneficiaries statute. As in the case of permanent injuries discussed in Chapter 10, the trier of fact is aided by mortality tables, income projections, and expert testimony. Pecuniary loss also may include the market value of any services that the decedent performed for the beneficiary. Most states measure the economic loss by calculating the "joint life expectancy" of the decedent and each beneficiary, i.e., the period of loss is the life expectancy of the decedent or the life expectancy of the beneficiary, whichever is shorter. See, e.g., Runyon v. District of Columbia, 463 F.2d 1319 (D.C.Cir.1972) (interpreting District of Columbia's statute). Beginning with the 19th century cases and continuing today, most jurisdictions recognized that the economic loss suffered by a child due to the death of a parent includes loss of training, education, guidance, and nurture as well as direct financial support. See, e.g., McKay v. New England Dredging Co., 92 Me. 454, 43 A. 29 (1899) (education and training that children receive from parent "are of actual and commercial value to them").

2. Although most states measure the damages based on the loss to the beneficiaries, some use the loss to the decedent's estate. This is frequently referred to as a loss-to-estate statute. In those jurisdictions, how should lost earnings be calculated? Should the jury award the probable worth of the decedent's gross earnings through his worklife expectancy? Should an estimate of the decedent's own living expenses be deducted and the net amount awarded to the beneficiaries? See Wehner v. Weinstein, 191 W.Va. 149, 444 S.E.2d 27 (1994) (choosing to permit jury to award gross amount, but recognizing that most jurisdictions require the deduction of decedent's projected living expenses).

3. In Alabama, damages are based on the extent of the defendant's culpability. The plaintiff's pecuniary loss is immaterial. A separate action survives for the decedent's actual damages, but that is limited to damages that occurred before death. King v. National Spa and Pool Institute, Inc., 607 So.2d 1241 (Ala. 1994).

4. As the principal case reflects, the pecuniary-loss limitation is problematic when a minor child has been killed and his parents bring a wrongful death claim; however, even in those states that adhere to the pecuniary-loss standard, substantial damages have been upheld on the theory that the child eventually would have made a monetary contribution to the parents.

5. A growing number of courts have taken the route of the principal case and allowed recovery for "loss of companionship" or consortium of a deceased family member. Some do so by finding that loss of society and companionship is an element of pecuniary damages. Hancock v. Chattanooga-Hamilton Cty. Hosp. Auth., 54 S.W.3d 234 (Tenn. 2001) (noting that thirty-two states allow recovery for filial consortium damages and joining those that do so by interpreting "pecuniary loss" to include consortium damages). Also, some states have amended their wrongful death statutes to provide specifically for recovery for loss of companionship in all cases, not just those involving the death of a minor child. See, e.g., Haw.Rev.Stat. § 663–3 ("pecuniary injury and loss of love and affection").

Some jurisdictions have built in a protection against runaway damages by placing a ceiling on damages for nonpecuniary losses. See Kan.Stat.Ann. § 60–1903 ($250,000); Me.Rev.Stat.Ann. tit. 18–A, § 2–804 ($500,000); Or. Rev. Stat. Ann. § 31.710 ($500,000); and Hughes v. PeaceHealth, 344 Or. 142, 178 P.3d 225 (2008) (upholding constitutionality of damages cap as applied in wrongful death action). In a case upholding its cap on noneconomic losses in wrongful death actions, Maryland noted that the cap applied per wrongful death claim, not per claimant or beneficiary. The jury allocates the damages among the beneficiaries. Dixon v. Ford Motor Co., 433 Md. 137, 70 A.3d 328 (2013). Florida had a cap of $1 million dollars for noneconomic damages for wrongful death actions based on medical malpractice, but its Supreme Court found that limitation violated the Equal Protection Clause of the Florida state constitution. Estate of McCall v. U.S., 134 So.3d 894 (Fla. 2014) (answering certified question in FTCA case).

6. What elements of proof would be required in a jurisdiction permitting recovery for loss of companionship damages? Where it is the spouse who is seeking recovery, evidence of happiness or discord in the marriage is admissible on the issue of damages. Should the trier of fact be informed that a plaintiff has remarried since the death of decedent spouse? Most courts have held that this information should be withheld from the jury because the jury is not permitted to consider it when assessing the amount of the damages. Groesbeck v. Napier, 275 N.W.2d 388 (Iowa 1979) (noting that overwhelming majority of jurisdictions do not permit remarriage to reduce damages). What if decedent's child was later adopted by her stepfather? Should she still be allowed to recover under the wrongful death statute for the death of her natural father? Rich v. Taser Intern., Inc., 2012 WL 4490845 (D. Nev. 2012) (applying Nevada law) (predicting that Nevada would permit recovery).

Consider the court's summary of parents' proof on this issue after the death of their child in Anderson v. Lale, 88 S.D. 111, 216 N.W.2d 152, 159 (1974): "The record in this case shows that the decedent was seven years of age and a bright, affectionate, kindly child who did well in school and church activities. She was an energetic, active, obedient, helpful child and an integral part of a close-knit family." The award of damages for the loss of consortium must be tied to the economic value of the services lost. In Fontenot v. Taser Intern., Inc., 736 F.3d 318 (4th Cir. 2013) (applying North Carolina law), the trial court judge granted a new trial on damages because plaintiff parents of decedent teenager, who died after being shocked with a Taser, failed to present any evidence showing that his services, care, and companionship had a value approaching the $1000–$2000 per week, per parent that their lawyer had argued in closing argument. Additionally, there was no testimony concerning whether, and for what duration, the parents reasonably expected their teenage son to continue providing services such as babysitting his younger siblings and assisting with household chores.

Suppose the mother of two very young children gave custody to her ex-husband and then left their hometown in Iowa for an unknown destination. Over the next few months, she made one telephone call to her ex-husband and one to her sister's house and then she was never heard from again. Fourteen years later, her family learned that she had been killed by a drunk driver while walking along the side of the road in Casper, Wyoming, shortly after the telephone call made to her sister's house. Because she had no identification with her, it took the police that long to identify her. In a wrongful death action brought on behalf of her two children—now teenagers—what damages would they be able to recover? Knowles v. Corkill, 51 P.3d 859 (Wyo. 2002) (jury awarded zero damages, apparently concluding that children had failed to prove they suffered a loss of probable future companionship, society, and comfort). Suppose the wrongful death beneficiary is the decedent's brother. How does brother prove the nature of the relationship between himself and decedent? Dubaniewicz v. Houman, 180 Vt. 367, 910 A.2d 897 (2006) (closeness of physical, emotional, and psychological relationship can be proved by living arrangements of parties, harmony of family relations, and commonality of interests and activities).

7. Some states go beyond damages for "loss of companionship" and also provide for damages based on "grief." See, e.g., Ark. Stat. Ann. § 16–62–102(f)(2) ("When mental anguish is claimed as a measure of damages under this section, mental anguish will include grief normally associated with the loss of a loved one.") and Kan.Stat.Ann. § 60–1904 ("mental anguish, suffering or bereavement"). But see N.J.S. 2A:31–5 (bill that would have added recovery for mental anguish and emotional pain and suffering vetoed by Governor). See also Knowles v. Corkill, 51 P.3d 859, 863 (Wyo. 2002), distinguishing between damages for loss of companionship and damages for grief: "Put simply, loss of probable future companionship, society and comfort entails the loss of positive benefits, while mental anguish represents an emotional reaction to the wrongful death."

8. Almost half of the wrongful death statutes as originally enacted included a cap on recovery. The caps represented a response to the concern that the new cause of action would create unlimited liability and the possibility of runaway jury verdicts. The limitations ranged from $5,000 to

$20,000. Over time the limitations were raised and then eliminated. No modern American jurisdiction caps recovery for pecuniary losses, although some do limit recovery for non-pecuniary losses. See note 25 and Chapter 10, page 562. Do the general tort reform statutory caps on non-economic damages apply to wrongful death actions? United States v. Streidel, 329 Md. 533, 620 A.2d 905 (1993) (Maryland cap applicable to "personal injury actions" does not apply to wrongful death action); Cole v. Sullivan, 110 Md.App. 79, 676 A.2d 85 (1996) (Maryland legislature then amended statute to extend cap to wrongful death actions).

9. Can a wrongful death recovery include compensation for lost estate tax benefits? Plaintiff, ninety-seven years of age, died in 2008 following a car accident and a wrongful death action was filed on behalf of his beneficiaries against the driver and owner of the other car. The suit alleged that because he had died in 2008, his federal estate tax bill was over a million dollars, significantly more that if he had lived until 2009 due to a change in the tax laws. Beim v. Hulfish, 216 N.J. 484, 83 A.3d 31 (2014) (alleged damages do not give rise to a "pecuniary" loss within the meaning of the wrongful death statute).

10. Should punitive damages be awarded to the beneficiary in cases involving reckless or intentional conduct? About half of the states permit punitive damages to be awarded in a wrongful death action. Some of those jurisdictions have statutes that specifically authorize punitive damages; others have interpreted their statutes, although silent on the subject, to permit an award of punitive damages. See S. Speiser, Recovery for Wrongful Death and Injury § 8.7 (4th ed. 2005); Simeone v. Charron, 762 A.2d 442 (R.I. 2000) (declining to allow for award of punitive damages in absence of express language authorizing or broad language that could be interpreted to include such damages); Durham v. U-Haul International, 745 N.E.2d 755 (Ind. 2001) (court rules that longstanding interpretation of wrongful death act is that its purpose is compensatory and does not include punitive damages; if legislature does not agree, it can amend statute). Oklahoma has a separate statute that covers the wrongful death of a minor child. 12 Okl. St. § 1055. It does not list punitive damages as a permissible element of recovery even though the general wrongful death statute does. 12 Okl. St. § 1053. The mother of three minor children killed in a head on collision with a drunk driver on the wrong side of the road filed suit against the driver and the bars where he had been drinking. She sought both compensatory damages and punitive damages. Should punitive damages be permitted? Roach v. Jimmy D. Enters., 912 P.2d 852 (Okla.1996) (yes because general wrongful death statute and statute for death of minor child should be read in conjunction with each other).

2. SURVIVAL

Murphy v. Martin Oil Co.

Supreme Court of Illinois, 1974.
56 Ill.2d 423, 308 N.E.2d 583.

[Suit for negligently causing the death of plaintiff's husband. The husband was injured in a fire on defendant's premises, survived for nine days, and then died from the injuries. The claim was in two counts:

(1) under the Wrongful Death Statute and (2) under the Survival Statute. The trial court dismissed the second count. The intermediate appellate court allowed the claim in part. Both parties appealed to the State Supreme Court.]

WARD, JUSTICE. Count I of the complaint claimed damages for wrongful death under the Illinois Wrongful Death Act. * * * The language of section 1 of the statute is:

> "Whenever the death of a person shall be caused by wrongful act, neglect or default, and the act, neglect or default is such as would, if death had not ensued, have entitled the party injured to maintain an action and recover damages in respect thereof, then and in every such case the person who or company or corporation which would have been liable if death had not ensued, shall be liable to an action for damages, notwithstanding the death of the person injured, and although the death shall have been caused under such circumstances as amount in law to felony." * * *

The second count of the complaint asked for damages for the decedent's physical and mental suffering, for loss of wages for the nine-day period following his injury and for the loss of his clothing worn at the time of injury. These damages were claimed under the common law and under our survival statute, which provides that certain rights of action survive the death of the person with the right of action. (Ill.Rev.Stat.1971, ch. 3, par. 339.) The statute states:

> "In addition to the actions which survive by the common law, the following also survive: actions of replevin, actions to recover damages for an injury to the person (except slander and libel), actions to recover damages for an injury to real or personal property or for the detention or conversion of personal property, actions against officers for misfeasance, malfeasance, or nonfeasance of themselves or their deputies, actions for fraud or deceit, and actions provided in Section 14 of Article VI of 'An Act relating to alcoholic liquors', approved January 31, 1934, as amended."

On this appeal we shall consider: (1) whether the plaintiff can recover for the loss of wages which her decedent would have earned during the interval between his injury and death; (2) whether the plaintiff can recover for the destruction of the decedent's personal property (clothing) at the time of the injury; (3) whether the plaintiff can recover damages for conscious pain and suffering of the decedent from the time of his injuries to the time of death.

This State in 1853 enacted the Wrongful Death Act and in 1872 enacted the so-called Survival Act (now section 339 of the Probate Act). This court first had occasion to consider the statutes in combination in 1882 in Holton v. Daly, 106 Ill. 131. The court * * * held that the Wrongful Death Act provided the exclusive remedy available when death came as a result of given tortious conduct. In considering the Survival Act the court stated that it was intended to allow for the survival of a cause of action only when the injured party died from a cause other than that which caused the injuries which created the cause of action. Thus, the court said, an action for personal injury would not survive death if death resulted from the tortious conduct which caused the injury.

This construction of the two statutes persisted for over 70 years. [Cc] Damages, therefore, under the Wrongful Death Act were limited to pecuniary losses, as from loss of support, to the surviving spouse and next of kin as a result of the death. [C] Under the survival statute damages recoverable in a personal injury action, as for conscious pain and suffering, loss of earnings, medical expenses and physical disability, could be had only if death resulted from a cause other than the one which gave rise to the personal injury action. * * *

In Prosser, Handbook of the Law of Torts (4th ed. 1971), at page 901, it is said: "[T]he modern trend is definitely toward the view that tort causes of action and liabilities are as fairly a part of the estate of either plaintiff or defendant as contract debts, and that the question is rather one of why a fortuitous event such as death should extinguish a valid action. Accordingly, survival statutes gradually are being extended; and it may be expected that ultimately all tort actions will survive to the same extent as those founded on contract." And at page 906 Prosser observes that where there have been wrongful death and survival statutes the usual holding has been that actions may be concurrently maintained under those statutes. The usual method of dealing with the two causes of action, he notes, is to allocate conscious pain and suffering, expenses and loss of earnings of the decedent up to the date of death to the survival statute, and to allocate the loss of benefits of the survivors to the action for wrongful death.

As the cited comments of Prosser indicate, the majority of jurisdictions which have considered the question allow an action for personal injuries in addition to an action under the wrongful death statute, though death is attributable to the injuries. Recovery for conscious pain and suffering is permitted in most of these jurisdictions. [Citing cases from 21 different jurisdictions.]

Too, recovery is allowed under the Federal Employers' Liability Act for a decedent's conscious pain and suffering provided it was not substantially contemporaneous with his death. [Cc]

We consider that those decisions which allow an action for fatal injuries as well as for wrongful death are to be preferred to this court's holding in Holton v. Daly that the Wrongful Death Act was the only remedy available when injury resulted in death.

The holding in *Holton* was not compelled, we judge, by the language or the nature of the statutes examined. The statutes were conceptually separable and different. The one related to an action arising upon wrongful death; the other related to a right of action for personal injury arising during the life of the injured person.

The remedy available under *Holton* will often be grievously incomplete. There may be a substantial loss of earnings, medical expenses, prolonged pain and suffering, as well as property damage sustained, before an injured person may succumb to his injuries. To say that there can be recovery only for his wrongful death is to provide an obviously inadequate justice. Too, the result in such a case is that the wrongdoer will have to answer for only a portion of the damages he caused. Incongruously, if the injury caused is so severe that death results, the wrongdoer's liability for the damages before death will be extinguished. It is obvious that in order to have a full liability and a full recovery there must be an action allowed for damages up to the time of death, as well as thereafter. Considering "It is more important that the court should be right upon later and more elaborate consideration of the cases than consistent with previous declarations" [c], we declare *Holton* and the cases which have followed it overruled. * * *

[T]he judgment of the appellate court is affirmed insofar as it held that an action may be maintained by the plaintiff for loss of property and loss of wages during the interval between injury and death, and that judgment is reversed insofar as it held that the plaintiff cannot maintain an action for her decedent's pain and suffering.

NOTES AND QUESTIONS

1. Under English common law as it was received by American courts, personal injury tort actions died with the person of the plaintiff or the defendant. For the historical background of this rule see W. Prosser & W. Keeton, Torts 940 (5th ed. 1984) and materials cited.

2. In almost every jurisdiction today survival statutes have modified these rules. At the very least, these statutes provide that causes of action for injury to all tangible property survive the death of either party. The majority of statutes also allow personal injury actions to survive. Only a few states permit claims for intangible interests of personalty (such as intentional infliction of emotional harm or defamation) to survive.

3. Two survival statutes are presented below. What are the important differences between them?

South Carolina

"*Survival of Right of Action.* Causes of action for and in respect to any and all injuries and trespasses to and upon real estate and any and all injuries to the person or to personal property shall survive both to and against the personal or real representative, as the case may be, of a deceased person and the legal representative of an insolvent person or a defunct or insolvent corporation, any law or rule to the contrary notwithstanding." S.C.Code § 15–5–90.

Kentucky

"*What Action Shall Survive.* No right of action for personal injury or for injury to real or personal property shall cease or die with the person injuring or injured, except actions for slander, libel, criminal conversation, and so much of the action for malicious prosecution as is intended to recover for the personal injury. For any other injury an action may be brought or revived by the personal representative, or against the personal representative, heir or devisee, in the same manner as causes of action founded on contract." Ky. Rev. Stat. 411.140.

4. *Proper Party.* Generally, survival actions are brought by the executor or administrator of the estate and a recovery becomes an asset of that estate, with the recovery subject to the claims of creditors of the estate and the net proceeds (after debts and taxes are paid) distributed with the rest of the estate to the heirs under the will or intestacy statute. Damages

are based on loss to the estate rather than on loss to the dependents or other survivors. See S. Speiser, Recovery for Wrongful Death and Injury § 1.13 (4th ed. 2005).

5. The major argument against survival statutes is that they may result in a windfall to distant relatives who cared very little about the decedent and were not in any way dependent on the decedent. Do you find the argument persuasive? The survival action may be the only recourse for someone who is not named as a beneficiary in the wrongful death statute. See, e.g., Warner v. McCaughan, 77 Wash.2d 178, 460 P.2d 272 (1969) (parents of college student who could not recover under wrongful death act because they were not financially dependent on decedent college student could bring survival action because they were heirs to her estate).

6. As the principal case notes, most states have both survival and wrongful death statutes. There are then two causes of action that may be maintained separately or concurrently to successful judgment. But see ACandS, Inc. v. Redd, 703 So.2d 492 (Fla.App.1997) (in Florida, personal injury cause of action abates with death of claimant and recovery is only through wrongful death action) (holding that spouse's loss of consortium claim also abates with death of primary claimant) and Capone v. Philip Morris USA, Inc., 116 So.3d 363 (Fla. 2013) (provision of Wrongful Death Act stating that personal injury action pending at time of decedent's death from the underlying injury shall "abate" causes case to be suspended until personal representative of decedent's estate is added as party to pending action and receives reasonable opportunity to amend complaint to state damages sought under a wrongful death claim). Where both actions are allowed, the courts must control the damages in each action so as to avoid holding the defendant liable twice for the same elements of recovery. A good case struggling with the problem is Pezzulli v. D'Ambrosia, 344 Pa. 643, 26 A.2d 659 (1942).

7. Funeral and burial expenses, if paid by the beneficiaries, ordinarily are allocated to the wrongful death action. The pain and suffering of the decedent are allocated to the survival action, as are medical expenses. Decedent's loss of potential earnings during normal life expectancy is also assigned to the survival action. But since it is out of these future earnings that decedent would have been expected to provide support for family, or to have made contributions to them, it is obvious that there would be a double recovery to the extent that they were allowed to recover for the loss when both actions are maintained. A frequent solution has been to allow in the survival action the potential earnings of the decedent during life expectancy, reduced to their present value, and to deduct the probable cost of maintenance of family, which would then be allocated to the death action. See, for example, First Nat'l Bank in Greensburg v. M. & G. Convoy, Inc., 106 F.Supp. 261 (W.D.Pa.1952); and Wetzel v. McDonnell Douglas Corp., 491 F.Supp. 1288 (E.D.Pa.1980).

8. Recovery for decedent's pain and suffering is allowed only if the decedent was conscious prior to death. See, e.g., Dubaniewicz v. Houman, 180 Vt. 367, 910 A.2d 897 (2006) (no expert medical testimony that murder victim was conscious after being shot; state trooper's testimony suggesting that decedent moved from one room to another before dying was too speculative to support an award for pain and suffering). Thus, courtroom battles between medical experts have developed over this factual issue

when the decedent lived only a short time after injury. Compare Fialkow v. DeVoe Motors, Inc., 359 Mass. 569, 270 N.E.2d 798 (1971) (evidence of gasping, gurgling and heavy breathing insufficient to show consciousness) with Campbell v. Leach, 352 Mass. 367, 225 N.E.2d 594 (1967) (evidence that decedent cried out sufficient to support an award).

9. Should the claim include pain and suffering that occurred before the physical injury, sometimes called "pre-impact fright"? Several courts have permitted recovery in the context of airplane crashes. See, e.g., Shu-Tao Lin v. McDonnell Douglas Corp., 742 F.2d 45 (2d Cir.1984) (applying New York law). A few have applied it in other contexts. Beynon v. Montgomery Cablevision Ltd. Partnership, 351 Md. 460, 718 A.2d 1161 (1998) (jury verdict of $1,000,000 for pre-impact fright of 2 seconds based on evidence of 71′ skidmarks left by plaintiff's vehicle before it rear ended tractor trailer, killing plaintiff instantly) (collecting cases from other jurisdictions).

10. Should a claim for punitive damages survive the death of the claimant? Most jurisdictions permit the estate to recover for all damages, including punitive damages, that the decedent would have had. But see Froud v. Celotex Corporation, 98 Ill.2d 324, 74 Ill.Dec. 629, 456 N.E.2d 131 (1983) (in Illinois, punitive damages ablate with the death of the claimant). Should a claim for punitive damages survive the death of the tortfeasor? Who would be punished? Tortfeasor distributed photocopies of sexually explicit photographs of his former girlfriend throughout the community, particularly where her mother, minor children, and employer would see them. She filed suit against him to stop the distribution and seeking compensatory and punitive damages. The tortfeasor committed suicide before the trial and his sister, the executrix of his estate, was substituted as a defendant. Should the estate be liable for punitive damages? G.J.D. v. Johnson, 552 Pa. 169, 713 A.2d 1127 (1998) (permitting award of punitive damages against estate, but noting that the majority of jurisdictions do not). See also Crabtree v. Estate of Crabtree, 837 N.E.2d 135 (Ind. 2005) (joining majority of jurisdictions that do not permit award of punitive damages against estate); In re Vajgrt, 801 N.W.2d 570 (Iowa 2011) (noting that Iowa is among the approximately thirty states that do not permit awards of punitive damages against estates for the conduct of the decedent); and Chapter 10, Section 3, Punitive Damages.

A Note on Defenses

The interrelationship of wrongful death and survival statutes and defenses, although presented at this point, will be better appreciated by the reader after completion of Chapter 12 on Defenses. The discussion is based on W. Prosser & W. Keeton, Torts 954–60 (5th ed. 1984).

11. *Defenses Based on Conduct or Status of the Decedent.* Since the survival statute merely continues the decedent's own cause of action beyond his death, any defenses that might have been set up against decedent if decedent had lived are still available to the defendant. The contrary might perhaps have been expected of the wrongful death acts, which create a separate and independent cause of action, founded upon the death itself, for the benefit of the designated beneficiaries. The original Lord Campbell's Act, however, contained an express provision limiting the death action to those cases in which the deceased might have recovered damages if he had lived; and this provision has been carried over into most

of the American acts, or has been read into them by implication when it does not expressly appear. It obviously is intended at least to prevent recovery for death when the decedent could never at any time have maintained an action, as where the act that caused the death was not tortious.

On the same theoretical basis, but with less apparent justification, there has been general agreement denying recovery when the defendant's conduct has been tortious toward the decedent and has caused his death, thus causing loss to the innocent beneficiaries, but the defendant would have had a defense available against the decedent. This has been true of contributory and comparative negligence, assumption of risk or consent to the defendant's conduct, as well as privileges such as self-defense or defense of property. See also Restatement (Third) of Torts: Apportionment of Liability § 6 (2000). Many of the courts that have considered the question have given the same effect to the immunity of one member of a family for torts against another, although there is a strong minority view to the contrary, based upon the theory that death destroys the reason for the immunity.

12. *Defenses Based on Conduct of the Beneficiaries Under the Statute or Heirs of the Estate.* Defenses available against the beneficiaries or heirs based on their own conduct offer a still more troublesome problem, on which the courts have not agreed. When the action is brought under a survival act, it is in theory still on behalf of the decedent, and the negligence of even a sole heir has been held not to prevent recovery through contributory negligence doctrine since the heir is not the plaintiff. Under the usual wrongful death act, the recovery is for the beneficiaries, and the contributory or comparative negligence or the consent or assumption of risk of a sole beneficiary or of all beneficiaries generally is held to preclude the action, on the same principle that would bar any other plaintiff in interest. A few statutes have been construed to the contrary.

When only one of several beneficiaries is contributorily negligent, the prevailing view is that the action is not barred for those who were not negligent, but that recovery is diminished to the extent of the share of damages of the negligent beneficiary, who is denied all share in the proceeds. The same conclusion has been reached for assumption of risk. Generally, the negligence of one parent is not imputed to the other in a claim arising out of the death of their child. See, for example, Teeter v. Missouri Hwy. and Transp. Com., 891 S.W.2d 817 (Mo.1995) (mother's contributory fault in driving vehicle in which her passenger daughter was killed cannot be attributed to father where both mother and father are wrongful death beneficiaries).

13. *Comparative Negligence.* Under comparative negligence systems, there is the possibility of having the jury consider both the negligence of a beneficiary and the decedent since the negligence of either one—standing alone—may not automatically bar a claim. The process is not as complicated as it may appear: the jury simply allocates a percentage of negligence to the beneficiary and the decedent and then reduces the award to the beneficiary by that total amount. In modified comparative negligence systems, recovery by that beneficiary is precluded if the threshold is reached. Where both parent beneficiaries may have been contributorily negligent, their negligence would be added in assessing the threshold for

recovery in a modified comparative negligence jurisdiction. Curtis v. States Family Practice, LLC, 20 Neb.App. 234, 823 N.W.2d 224 (2012) (in medical malpractice action, jury found each parent 25% responsible, so parents' combined responsibility was not less than that of defendants and thus judgment was entered for defendants).

14. *Effect of Personal Injury Action Brought Before Death.* Most courts have held that a judgment for or against the decedent in an action for his injuries commenced during his lifetime, or the compromise and release of such an action, will operate as a bar to any subsequent suit founded upon his death. See Thompson v. R.J. Reynolds Tobacco Co., 760 F.3d 913, 917 (8th Cir. 2014) (applying Missouri law) ("As a result of the 2003 judgment in his personal injury suit, Michael Thompson no longer had a viable claim against the cigarette manufacturers at the time of his death, and his family is barred from bringing such a claim now."); Boeken v. Philip Morris USA Inc., 48 Cal.4th 788, 108 Cal.Rptr.3d 806, 230 P.3d 342 (Cal. 2010) (widow's prior loss of consortium claim precluded her wrongful death claim); and Union Bank of California v. Copeland Lumber Yards, Inc., 213 Or.App. 308, 160 P.3d 1032 (2007) (surveying other jurisdictions and noting that clear weight of authority finds wrongful death actions precluded if decedent had litigated to judgment or settled a personal injury action before his death). This has the effect of placing in the decedent's hands the power to sell out the claim of the beneficiaries before it has come into existence because their action is regarded as "derivative," arising out of and dependent upon the wrong done to him. The courts undoubtedly have been influenced by a fear of a double recovery. This is possible because the decedent would be allowed to recover for the prospective earnings lost through his diminished work life expectancy, out of which any financial benefits receivable by the beneficiaries would be expected to come.

Opposed to this risk is the counter-danger of an improvident settlement by an optimistic individual, confident that he is not going to die, that takes no account of shortened life expectancy or of the interests of the beneficiaries. Because of this, there is a minority view that neither a judgment in his action nor his release of his claim will bar the action for wrongful death. See, for example, Thompson v. Wing, 70 Ohio St.3d 176, 637 N.E.2d 917 (1994) (medical malpractice judgment during patient's lifetime did not bar subsequent wrongful death claim by her beneficiaries because it is an independent claim; court notes that this is minority view). See also Brown v. Drillers, Inc., 630 So.2d 741 (La.1994) (release signed by personal injury claimant and his wife releases subsequent claim by wife as wrongful death beneficiary only if release unequivocally reflects that parties contemplated a release of future wrongful death claim). The possibility of double compensation either has been ignored, on the ground that legally it could not arise, or has been met by a credit against the award to the death beneficiaries, of the amount found to have been paid to the decedent covering the permanent destruction of his earning capacity. Riggs v. Georgia-Pacific LLC, 345 P.3d 1219 (Utah 2015) (noting that double recovery is impermissible and therefore that it would be improper for the court in the wrongful death action to award lost wages since compensation for those already had been recovered in the previous personal injury action).

If the statute of limitations on the personal injury action had run before the decedent's death, some jurisdictions have held that the statute runs against the death action only from the date of death, even though at that time the decedent's own action would have been barred while he was living. See, e.g., Evans v. Southern Ohio Medical Ctr., 103 Ohio App.3d 250, 659 N.E.2d 326 (1995) (wrongful death claim not barred even though underlying medical malpractice action was). Others hold that it runs from the time of the original injury and consequently that the death action may be lost before it ever has accrued. See, e.g., Russell v. Ingersoll-Rand Co., 841 S.W.2d 343 (Tex.1992) (wrongful death action, because it is dependent on underlying personal injury action, may not be brought if statute of limitations expired on personal injury action before decedent's death); Edwards v. Fogarty, 962 P.2d 879 (Wyo.1998) (accord, noting that this is the majority rule); and Okeke v. Craig, 782 So.2d 281 (Ala. 2000) (accord).

15. *Statutes of Limitation.* The wrongful death statutes of many states contain their own time period within which to bring the action for wrongful death. In those states, that time limit rather than the general statute of limitations controls the wrongful death action. Because the action is a creature of statute rather than of the common law, filing within the limitation period is an essential element of the cause of action. Limitations of the remedy are to be treated as limitations of the right. Deckert v. Burns, 75 S.D. 229, 62 N.W.2d 879 (1954) (dictum recognizing rule as "the general holding"). It is not subject to the tolling provisions of the general statute of limitations. See, e.g., Moreno v. Sterling Drug, Inc., 787 S.W.2d 348 (Tex. 1990) (noting that "overwhelming majority of states" that require cause of action to be filed within two years of death have refused to apply the discovery rule or other equitable tolling measures); Ortiz v. Gavenda, 590 N.W.2d 119, 590 N.W.2d 119 (Minn. 1999) (civil procedure relation back rule could not be used to avoid effect of statute of limitations); Taylor v. Black & Decker Mfg. Co., 21 Ohio App.3d 186, 486 N.E.2d 1173 (1984) (not tolled by beneficiary's minority); and Trentadue v. Buckler Lawn Sprinkler, 479 Mich. 378, 738 N.W.2d 664 (2007) (discovery rule not applicable to wrongful death statute of limitations even though beneficiary did not discover the identity of the person who raped and murdered decedent until DNA evidence identified him more than 15 years later—negligence case against defendant who was murderer's employer and decedent's landlord dismissed). But see LaFage v. Jani, 166 N.J. 412, 766 A.2d 1066 (2001) (recognizing tolling for beneficiaries who are minors).

Although statutes of limitations usually are considered procedural and thus governed by the law of the forum, where the time limitation is within the statute creating the right, that jurisdiction's law controls even if the foreign forum's law would have considered the action timely. Ramsay v. Boeing Co., 432 F.2d 592 (5th Cir. 1970) (because Belgian five year limit was a condition to bringing suit and thus a matter of substantive law where the airplane crash occurred, federal court sitting in diversity did not apply the longer six year statute of limitations of Mississippi). In states whose wrongful death statutes do not contain a separate time limit and in those that provide a wrongful death remedy through an expanded survival action, the statute of limitations for personal injury is applied. In those jurisdictions, the tolling provisions of the general statute of limitations (e.g., for minors, discovery rule) usually are applied.

The accrual of the cause of action (when does the statute begin to run?) is dependent on the wording of the wrongful death statute. Some specify that the cause of action accrues at death. Of those statutes that do not specify the accrual of the cause of action, some have interpreted their statutes as providing that the cause of action accrues at death while others have held that the action accrues at the time of injury.

16. *Two Separate Actions.* Most jurisdictions provide for both wrongful death and survival actions and most of the time those two actions are joined in one lawsuit. That is not always the case, however, and it is important to keep in mind that they are two distinct causes of action, each with its own requirements. Some jurisdictions, for example, use the survival statute only for situations where the decedent died from an unrelated cause and use the wrongful death statute for claims arising from situations where the decedent died due to the actions of the defendant. See Capone v. Philip Morris USA, Inc., 116 So.3d 363 (Fla. 2013) and Sears v. Griffin, 771 N.E.2d 1136 (Ind. 2002). Some jurisdictions require that a lawsuit for the personal injury claim have been filed in order for the claim to survive. Motorist was injured in a collision with another vehicle. Doctors who treated him at the hospital failed to diagnose fractures in his vertebrae. He and his wife filed suit against the driver of the other vehicle for his personal injuries. He died while that lawsuit was pending. His representative then filed a wrongful death action against both the driver and the doctors and tried to amend the personal injury complaint against the driver to include a survival claim against the doctors. Because the Alabama survival statute provides that unfiled tort claims do not survive the death of the claimant, the doctors sought to dismiss the estate's claim against them. The estate's representative argued that the amended complaint should relate back to the filing of the original complaint, before patient's death. Should it? Malcolm v. King, 686 So.2d 231 (Ala.1996) (medical malpractice claim against doctors is distinct claim from negligence claim against driver and does not relate back; no survival cause of action against medical malpractice defendants; wrongful death action against both driver and doctors could proceed). In wrongful death action against tobacco company, wrongful death beneficiaries sought to prove that cigarettes caused decedent's lung cancer and that the cancer caused his death. Tobacco company argued that his death was caused by a blood clot that lodged in his heart and was a complication of surgery that he had undergone to treat urinary tract problems unrelated to the lung cancer. Jury returned a verdict that found that the death was unrelated to lung cancer. Beneficiaries, who were also the heirs to his estate's survival action, argued that they should at least be able to recover for damages suffered by decedent during his lifetime. Neither smoker during his lifetime nor his heirs after his death had filed a personal injury or survival action, however. Judgment for the tobacco company on the wrongful death action was affirmed. Wilks v. American Tobacco Co., 680 So.2d 839 (Miss.1996).

CHAPTER 12

DEFENSES

1. PLAINTIFF'S CONDUCT

(A) CONTRIBUTORY NEGLIGENCE

Butterfield v. Forrester

King's Bench, 1809.
11 East 59, 103 Eng.Rep. 926.

This was an action on the case for obstructing a highway, by means of which obstruction the plaintiff, who was riding along the road, was thrown down with his horse, and injured, & c. At the trial before Bayley J. at Derby, it appeared that the defendant, for the purpose of making some repairs to his house, which was close by the road side at one end of the town, had put up a pole across this part of the road, a free passage being left by another branch or street in the same direction. That the plaintiff left a public house not far distant from the place in question at 8 o'clock in the evening in August, when they were just beginning to light candles, but while there was light enough left to discern the obstruction at 100 yards distance: and the witness, who proved this, said that if the plaintiff had not been riding very hard he might have observed and avoided it: the plaintiff however, who was riding violently, did not observe it, but rode against it, and fell with his horse and was much hurt in consequence of the accident; and there was no evidence of his being intoxicated at the time. On this evidence Bayley J. directed the jury, that if a person riding with reasonable and ordinary care could have seen and avoided the obstruction; and if they were satisfied that the plaintiff was riding along the street extremely hard, and without ordinary care, they should find a verdict for the defendant: which they accordingly did.

Vaughan Serjt. now objected to this direction, on moving for a new trial; and referred to Buller's Ni.Pri. 26(a), where the rule is laid down, that "if a man lay logs of wood across a highway; though a person may with care ride safely by, yet if by means thereof my horse stumble and fling me, I may bring an action."

BAYLEY, J. The plaintiff was proved to be riding as fast as his horse could go, and this was through the streets of Derby. If he had used ordinary care he must have seen the obstruction; so that the accident appeared to happen entirely from his own fault.

LORD ELLENBOROUGH, C.J. A party is not to cast himself upon an obstruction which has been made by the fault of another, and avail himself of it, if he do not himself use common and ordinary caution to be in the right. In cases of persons riding upon what is considered to be the wrong side of the road, that would not authorize another purposely to ride up against them. One person being in fault will not dispense with another's using ordinary care for himself. Two things must concur to support this action, an obstruction in the road by the fault of the defendant, and no want of ordinary care to avoid it on the part of the plaintiff.

PER CURIAM. Rule refused.

NOTES AND QUESTIONS

1. Consider the basic options available to the law in connection with how to treat the fact that plaintiff's negligence contributed to the happening of the accident. First, the law could completely bar plaintiff's claim. This approach, called contributory negligence, was taken by the court in *Butterfield*. What does it have to recommend it?

Second, the law could completely ignore plaintiff's culpable conduct. This is the approach taken under most Worker Compensation Acts and No-Fault Automobile Accident Reparation Systems. The advantage to the plaintiff is obvious. Do you also see its philosophical underpinnings?

Third, the law could adopt one of the first two options as a general rule and then set up other rules making exceptions for designated situations. This is what the common law later did—generally adopting option 1, but allowing exceptions to it. Note that this is still an all-or-nothing approach in the individual case; the fact that the cases may average out as a whole provides cold comfort to the parties to the particular case. Is it desirable to leave to the jury the question of whether to allow the plaintiff to recover all or nothing? This may have been the practice prior to the principal case. See Cruden v. Fentham, 2 Esp. 685, 170 Eng.Rep. 496 (N.P.1799); Clay v. Wood, 5 Esp. 44, 170 Eng.Rep. 732 (N.P.1803).

Fourth, the law could compare plaintiff's fault with that of defendant and reduce plaintiff's damages according to the measure of fault. This approach, usually called comparative negligence or comparative fault, has been expressly adopted in one form or another in 46 states, by statute or judicial decision. Contributory negligence continues to be a complete bar to recovery in only four states (Alabama, Maryland, Virginia, North Carolina) and the District of Columbia.

What are the advantages and disadvantages of each approach?

2. In 1854 a Pennsylvania judge reflected the feelings of many of his brethren when he called the defense of contributory negligence a "rule from time immemorial" and ventured to guess that it was "not likely to be changed for all time to come." Pennsylvania R. Co. v. Aspell, 23 Pa. 147, 149 (1854). While the judge was a poor historian (a form of comparative negligence was applied by English Admiralty Courts long before the *Butterfield* decision), he did rather well as a prognosticator of the law late into the 20th century. The defense had great appeal and sticking power in the United States. It was even adopted in Louisiana—a state that could easily have utilized its code and civil law tradition to adopt a comparative negligence approach. See Malone, Comparative Negligence—Louisiana's Forgotten Heritage, 6 La.L.Rev. 125 (1945).

3. The following theories all have been advanced from time to time in explanation or justification of the defense. Which of them are valid?

A. The defense has a penal basis, and plaintiff is denied recovery as punishment for misconduct. See Barker v. Kallash, 63 N.Y.2d 19, 468

N.E.2d 39, 479 N.Y.S.2d 201 (1984) (teenager, who was injured while building a pipe bomb, filed suit against nine-year-old who had sold him the firecrackers from which he extracted the gun powder for the pipe bomb). See also Cole v. Taylor, 301 N.W.2d 766 (Iowa 1981) (convicted murderer cannot bring action against her therapist for negligently failing to prevent her from shooting her ex-husband) and Price v. Purdue Pharma Co., 920 S.2d 479 (Miss. 2006) (patient who illegally obtained prescription narcotic by simultaneously seeking treatment from several doctors and filling duplicative prescriptions at different pharmacies may not bring action against doctors, pharmacies, or drug manufacturer). This rationale sometimes is applied even in comparative negligence jurisdictions to prevent plaintiff's recovery.

B. Plaintiff is required to come into court with "clean hands," and the court will not aid one whose own fault has participated in causing his injury.

C. A rule of negligence is designed to encourage optimal care by both interacting parties. Usually, primary liability will suffice in promoting that level of care, but it may be inadequate where one party acts negligently and the other has an opportunity to avoid the accident. Without the defense of contributory negligence, the injured party may face a diluted incentive to take due care and the system may incur more administrative costs as well. See Landes & Posner, The Economic Structure of Tort Law 73–77 (1987).

D. Plaintiff's negligence is an intervening, superseding cause, which makes the defendant's negligence no longer "proximate." What if two negligently driven automobiles collide and injure both drivers and a pedestrian who was in no way negligent. The pedestrian could recover from either driver, but neither driver could recover from the other. Does the "proximate cause" analysis vary as applied to each of the potential plaintiffs? The plaintiff's negligence can be viewed as an act that stops the defendant's responsibility for the wrongful conduct. Without the intervention of the plaintiff's action, corrective justice notions would demand that the defendant rectify the wrong toward the plaintiff. For an examination of corrective justice issues, see Symposium, Corrective Justice and Formalism: The Care One Owes One's Neighbors, 77 Iowa L.Rev. 403 (1992).

4. The defense of contributory negligence should be distinguished from the rule on avoidable consequences or mitigation of damages, discussed at pages 635 to 637. The doctrine of avoidable consequences is invoked *after* plaintiff has been injured. Also, remember that plaintiff's conduct may be such that it is the sole proximate cause of the injury, even if defendant too was negligent. Cf. Soto v. NYC Transit Authority, 6 N.Y.3d 487, 846 N.E.2d 1211, 813 N.Y.S.2d 701 (2006). Plaintiff was among four teenagers who had been drinking, got tired waiting for a subway train to take them home, and started walking between stations on a catwalk that ran parallel to the tracks. When they heard a train coming from behind them, they began running to try to catch the train at the next station. Plaintiff, in the midst of the line of running teens, suffered serious injury when the train struck him as he moved around a signal box that jutted out onto the catwalk. Defendant argued that the plaintiff's conduct was the sole cause of his injuries but plaintiff argued that the conduct of both plaintiff and defendant (in failing to stop the train before it struck him) contributed

to the cause of his injuries and should be compared. The judge denied the defendant's motion for a directed verdict and the jury returned a verdict against the defendant, attributing 75% of the responsibility to the plaintiff. The Court of Appeals upheld the denial of the directed verdict by a split vote of 4 to 3.

5. The common law rule of contributory negligence often produced results that a court or jury regarded as unjust. Whenever a rule of law regularly produces unjust results or lags behind social and economic developments, courts develop ameliorating practices and a group of exceptions for avoiding its application. This tenet of judicial behavior, which might be called the Erosion Principle, has occurred in a number of important areas in the law of torts. Can you think of some other illustrations? Over the years, the courts created a number of judicial devices to ameliorate the harsh effects of the rule of contributory negligence as a complete bar to recovery.

A. *Burden of Proof.* The burden of pleading and proving contributory negligence is on the defendant. See e.g., Brown v. Piggly-Wiggly Stores, 454 So.2d 1370 (Ala.1984) (contributory negligence is an affirmative defense). This is also true of comparative negligence. See Restatement (Third) of Torts: Apportionment of Liability § 4 (2000).

B. *Leaving the Question of Contributory Negligence to the Jury.* Courts have been very reluctant to take the issue of contributory negligence away from the jury through summary judgment, directed verdict, or judgment as a matter of law. See e.g., Lazar v. Cleveland Electric Illuminating Co., 43 Ohio St.2d 131, 331 N.E.2d 424 (1975) (plaintiff grabbed an uninsulated high tension wire) and Urban v. Wait's Supermarket, Inc., 294 N.W.2d 793 (S.D.1980) (plaintiff tripped over a watermelon in a store aisle). But courts will do so if no reasonable jury could find in favor of the plaintiff. Burleson v. RSR Group Fla., Inc., 981 So.2d 1109 (Ala. 2007) (contributory negligence as a matter of law where gun accidentally discharged when it fell from holster to desk when plaintiff was placing holster on rack with live round in chamber in line with hammer and manual safety not engaged).

C. *Causation in Fact.* Plaintiff's negligence will bar recovery only if it is a substantial factor in bringing about the result. See, for example, Bahm v. Pittsburgh & Lake Erie R. Co., 6 Ohio St.2d 192, 217 N.E.2d 217 (1966) (jury instruction that plaintiff's recovery was barred if his conduct directly and proximately contributed "in any degree" to bring about the accident was error; quoted phrase must be eliminated so it is clear that plaintiff's conduct must be a substantial factor in bringing about the accident); Hofstrom v. Share, 295 N.J.Super. 186, 684 A.2d 981 (1996) (negligence of plaintiff in failing to follow emergency room physician instructions to return immediately if condition worsened not relevant because defendant's experts did not establish that her conduct was a substantial factor in her injuries).

D. *Proximate Cause.* Courts have subtly confined the defense by narrowly limiting the scope of proximate cause as applied to risks that plaintiff exposed himself to by his act of negligence. Prime examples are Furukawa v. Uoshio Ogawa, 236 F.2d 272 (9th Cir.1956) (applying California law) (negligence as to danger of falling, but not of falling upon a hook) and Smithwick v. Hall & Upson Co., 59 Conn. 261, 21 A. 924 (1890) (negligence as to danger of slipping off an unguarded icy ledge, but not of wall collapsing on plaintiff).

What should happen to these holdings when a jurisdiction adopts comparative negligence?

6. *Dual Standards of Care.* Professor Fleming James argued that the different treatment of plaintiff's contributory negligence as compared with defendant's negligence should be recognized as a formal rule, but the courts steadfastly have refused to do so. See Restatement (Third) of Torts: Apportionment of Liability § 3, comment *a* (2000). See also James, Contributory Negligence, 62 Yale L.J. 691 (1953); James and Dickinson, Accident Proneness and Accident Law, 63 Harv.L.Rev. 769 (1950).

Applicability of Contributory Negligence in Particular Circumstances

7. *Defendant Engaged in Intentional, Wanton or Willful or Reckless Conduct.* It is standard hornbook law that contributory negligence is not a defense to an intentional tort. See W. Prosser & W. Keeton, Torts 462 (5th ed. 1984). Thus, one cannot defend against a battery by arguing that the plaintiff was negligent in failing to duck. The same general rule has been extended in almost every jurisdiction to situations in which defendant engaged in "wanton and willful" or reckless conduct. It is said that this conduct differs from negligence not only in degree, but also in kind and, therefore, the defense of contributory negligence is inapplicable. See, e.g., Kasanovich v. George, 348 Pa. 199, 34 A.2d 523, 525 (1943) ("Negligence consists of inattention or inadvertence, whereas wantonness exists where the danger to the plaintiff, though realized, is so recklessly disregarded that, even though there be no actual intent, there is at least a willingness to inflict injury, a conscious indifference to the perpetration of the wrong.") and Adkisson v. City of Seattle, 42 Wash.2d 676, 258 P.2d 461, 467 (1953) ("Wanton misconduct is not negligence, since it involves intent rather than inadvertence, and is positive rather than negative.")

8. *Strict Liability.* See Chapter 14, pages 761–765 and Chapter 15, pages 822–829.

9. *Defendant Violates a Statute.* Generally, contributory negligence is still held to be a defense although defendant was negligent *per se* because of violation of a statute. See Brown v. Derry, 10 Wash.App. 459, 518 P.2d 251 (1974) (motorist transported individual on outside of vehicle). Certain statutes, however, are deemed to abrogate the defense. See generally Prosser, Contributory Negligence as Defense to Violation of Statute, 32 Minn.L.Rev. 105 (1948).

A. *Statutes Explicitly Abolishing the Defense in Limited Situations.* Sometimes the legislature explicitly abolishes the contributory negligence defense in a limited situation. An example is under the Federal Employers Liability Act ("F.E.L.A") when defendant has violated a federal safety standard and that caused the injury. See 45 U.S.C. § 53.

B. *Statutes Intended to Protect a Plaintiff Unable to Protect Himself.* Statutes prohibiting child labor, the sale of firearms to minors, the sale of liquor to intoxicated persons, and those that require safety devices to protect factory workers, have been held to be in this category. The court must determine that the "statute [was] enacted to protect a class of persons from their inability to exercise self-protective care." Restatement (Second) of Torts § 483.

Davies v. Mann

Exchequer, 1842.
10 M. & W. 546, 152 Eng.Rep. 588.

At the trial, before Erskine, J., at the last Summer Assizes for the county of Worcester, it appeared that the plaintiff, having fettered the fore feet of an ass belonging to him, turned it into a public highway, and at the time in question the ass was grazing on the off side of the road about eight yards wide, when the defendant's waggon, with a team of three horses, coming down a slight descent, at what the witness termed a smartish pace, ran against the ass, knocked it down, and the wheels passing over it, it died soon after. The ass was fettered at the time, and it was proved that the driver of the waggon was some little distance behind the horses. The learned Judge told the jury, that though the act of the plaintiff, in leaving the donkey on the highway so fettered as to prevent his getting out of the way of carriages travelling along it, might be illegal, still, if the proximate cause of the injury was attributable to the want of proper conduct on the part of the driver of the waggon, the action was maintainable against the defendant; and his Lordship directed them, if they thought that the accident might have been avoided by the exercise of ordinary care on the part of the driver, to find for the plaintiff. The jury found their verdict for the plaintiff, damages 40s.

Godson now moved for a new trial, on the ground of misdirection.

LORD ABINGER, C.B. I am of opinion that there ought to be no rule in this case. The defendant has not denied that the ass was lawfully in the highway, and therefore we must assume it to have been lawfully there; but even were it otherwise, it would have made no difference, for as the defendant might, by proper care, have avoided injuring the animal, and did not, he is liable for the consequences of his negligence, though the animal may have been improperly there.

PARKE, B. * * * [A]lthough the ass may have been wrongfully there, still the defendant was bound to go along the road at such a pace as would be likely to prevent mischief. Were this not so, a man might justify the driving over goods left on a public highway, or even over a man lying asleep there, or the purposely running against a carriage going on the wrong side of the road.

NOTES AND QUESTIONS

1. "The groans, ineffably and mournfully sad, of Davies' dying donkey, have resounded around the earth. The last lingering gaze from the soft, mild eyes of this docile animal, like the last parting sunbeams of the softest day in spring, has appealed to and touched the hearts of men. There has girdled the globe a band of sympathy for Davies' immortal 'critter.' Its ghost, like Banquo's ghost, will not down at the behests of the people who are charged with inflicting injuries, nor can its groanings be silenced by the ranting and excoriations of carping critics. The law as enunciated in that

case has come to stay." McLain, J., in Fuller v. Illinois Cent. R. Co., 100 Miss. 705, 717, 56 So. 783 (1911).

2. Later commentators rationalized the holding in the principal case into what has come to be known as the doctrine of *last clear chance.* As the title indicates, the notion is that if the defendant had the opportunity to avoid the accident after the opportunity was no longer available to the plaintiff, the defendant is the one who should bear the loss. Note that under this doctrine the whole loss is still placed on one party or the other. Does this accomplish justice between the parties?

3. The doctrine of last clear chance is one of fearful and wonderful complexity. Some jurisdictions restricted its use to cases where the plaintiff was helpless and unable to avoid the danger created by the defendant's negligence, while others permitted its use if the plaintiff was merely inattentive to the danger. Some required the defendant to have discovered that the plaintiff was helpless, while others allowed its use if the defendant should have discovered that the plaintiff was helpless. See Restatement (Second) of Torts §§ 479 and 480, grouping the patterns around the nature of the plaintiff's conduct. The jurisdictions that still follow the common law rule of contributory negligence apply the exception of last clear chance in at least one of its many forms. For several modern cases in which the courts struggle to untangle its many threads to find the one applicable to the facts of the cases, see Belton v. WMATA, 20 F.3d 1197 (D.C.Cir.1994) (Plaintiff, dressed in a Batman cape and roaming the streets of Georgetown taunting motorists, banged on a bus door as the driver turned the corner. He slid under the bus and was injured. Whether bus driver's negligence was antecedent to plaintiff's and also operating after plaintiff's negligence was question for jury.); Williams v. Harrison, 255 Va. 272, 497 S.E.2d 467 (1998) (Plaintiff and defendant and two of their friends were driving their four cars through a suburban neighborhood at a speed of 60 m.p.h. when the second and third cars in the line collided with each other. Jury instruction on last clear chance not available because plaintiff did not show that he was unconscious of his peril.); WMATA v. Johnson, 726 A.2d 172 (D.C.App.1999) (on certified question, court rules that the last clear chance doctrine does not apply to intentional act of woman who committed suicide by jumping into path of oncoming subway train in suit by her estate seeking recovery from transit authority for subway train operator's negligent failure to stop in time); Penn Harris Madison School Corp. v. Howard, 861 N.E.2d 1190 (Ind. 2007) (Indiana retains contributory negligence in cases against governmental entities) (last clear chance does not apply where student who had designed a rig for Peter Pan to fly in a school play was injured while testing it during rehearsal—no evidence that school could have done anything to avert or prevent the injuries after plaintiff put himself in position of danger by jumping from ladder).

4. The last clear chance doctrine has been called a "transitional doctrine," a way station on the road to comparative negligence. James, Last Clear Chance: A Transitional Doctrine, 47 Yale L.J. 704 (1938). Its effect, for many years, however, was to freeze the transition rather than to hasten it. The opinion in the next principal case recounts the transition from contributory negligence as a complete bar to recovery to comparative negligence in the various jurisdictions in the United States.

(B) COMPARATIVE NEGLIGENCE

McIntyre v. Balentine

Supreme Court of Tennessee, 1992.
833 S.W.2d 52.

DROWOTA, J.

In this personal injury action, we granted Plaintiff's application for permission to appeal in order to decide whether to adopt a system of comparative fault in Tennessee. * * *

In the early morning darkness of November 2, 1986, Plaintiff-Harry Douglas McIntyre and Defendant-Clifford Balentine were involved in a motor vehicle accident resulting in severe injuries to Plaintiff. The accident occurred in the vicinity of Smith's Truck Stop in Savannah, Tennessee. As Defendant-Balentine was traveling south on Highway 69, Plaintiff entered the highway (also traveling south) from the truck stop parking lot. Shortly after Plaintiff entered the highway, his pickup truck was struck by Defendant's Peterbilt tractor. At trial, the parties disputed the exact chronology of events immediately preceding the accident.

Both men had consumed alcohol the evening of the accident. After the accident, Plaintiff's blood alcohol level was measured at .17 percent by weight. Testimony suggested that Defendant was traveling in excess of the posted speed limit.

Plaintiff brought a negligence action against Defendant-Balentine and [the lessee of the truck]. Defendants answered that Plaintiff was contributorially negligent, in part due to operating his vehicle while intoxicated. After trial, the jury returned a verdict stating: "We, the jury, find the plaintiff and the defendant equally at fault in this accident; therefore, we rule in favor of the defendant."

* * *

[After judgment was entered for Defendants on the verdict, Plaintiff brought an appeal alleging the trial court erred (1) by refusing to instruct the jury regarding the doctrine of comparative negligence and (2) in admitting evidence of intoxication. The Court of Appeals affirmed, holding that comparative negligence is not the law in Tennessee and that the evidence of intoxication was properly admitted. This appeal followed.]

I.

The common law contributory negligence doctrine has traditionally been traced to Lord Ellenborough's opinion in Butterfield v. Forrester, 11 East 60, 103 Eng.Rep. 926 (1809). There, plaintiff, "riding as fast as his horse would go," was injured after running into an obstruction defendant had placed in the road. Stating as the rule that "one person being in fault will not dispense with another's using ordinary care," plaintiff was denied recovery on the basis that he did not use ordinary care to avoid the obstruction. [C]

The contributory negligence bar was soon brought to America as part of the common law, see Smith v. Smith, 19 Mass. 621, 624 (1825), and proceeded to spread throughout the states. See H.W. Woods, The Negligence Case: Comparative Fault § 1:4 (1978). This strict bar may have been a direct outgrowth of the common law system of issue pleading; issue pleading posed questions to be answered "yes" or "no," leaving common law courts, the theory goes, no choice but to award all or nothing. See J.W. Wade, W.K. Crawford, Jr., and J.L. Ryder, Comparative Fault In Tennessee Tort Actions: Past, Present and Future, 41 Tenn.L.Rev. 423, 424–25 (1974). A number of other rationalizations have been advanced in the attempt to justify the harshness of the "all-or-nothing" bar. Among these: the plaintiff should be penalized for his misconduct; the plaintiff should be deterred from injuring himself; and the plaintiff's negligence supersedes the defendant's so as to render defendant's negligence no longer proximate. [Cc]

In Tennessee, the rule as initially stated was that "if a party, by his own gross negligence, brings an injury upon himself, or contributes to such injury, he cannot recover;" for, in such cases, the party "must be regarded as the author of his own misfortune." [C] In subsequent decisions, we have continued to follow the general rule that a plaintiff's contributory negligence completely bars recovery. [Cc]

Equally entrenched in Tennessee jurisprudence are exceptions to the general all-or-nothing rule: contributory negligence does not absolutely bar recovery where defendant's conduct was intentional, [cc]; where defendant's conduct was "grossly" negligent, [cc]; where the defendant had the "last clear chance" with which, through the exercise of ordinary care, to avoid plaintiff's injury, [cc]; or where plaintiff's negligence may be classified as "remote." [Cc]

In contrast, comparative fault has long been the federal rule in cases involving injured employees of interstate railroad carriers, [c], and injured seamen. [Cc] See generally V. Schwartz, Comparative Negligence § 1.4(A) (2d ed. 1986).

Similarly, by the early 1900s, many states, including Tennessee, had statutes providing for the apportionment of damages in railroad injury cases. See V. Schwartz, supra, at § 1.4. * * *

Between 1920 and 1969, a few states began utilizing the principles of comparative fault in all tort litigation. [C] Then, between 1969 and 1984, comparative fault replaced contributory negligence in 37 additional states. [C] In 1991, South Carolina became the 45th state to adopt comparative fault, see Nelson v. Concrete Supply Co., 303 S.C. 243, 399 S.E.2d 783 (1991), leaving Alabama, Maryland, North Carolina, Virginia, and Tennessee as the only remaining common law contributory negligence jurisdictions.

Eleven states have judicially adopted comparative fault. Thirty-four states have legislatively adopted comparative fault.

* * *

II.

Over 15 years ago, we stated, when asked to adopt a system of comparative fault:

> We do not deem it appropriate to consider making such a change unless and until a case reaches us wherein the pleadings and proof present an issue of contributory negligence accompanied by advocacy that the ends of justice will be served by adopting the rule of comparative negligence.

Street v. Calvert, 541 S.W.2d [576] at 586 [Tenn.1976]. Such a case is now before us. After exhaustive deliberation that was facilitated by extensive briefing and argument by the parties, amicus curiae, and Tennessee's scholastic community, we conclude that it is time to abandon the outmoded and unjust common law doctrine of contributory negligence and adopt in its place a system of comparative fault. Justice simply will not permit our continued adherence to a rule that, in the face of a judicial determination that others bear primary responsibility, nevertheless completely denies injured litigants recompense for their damages.

We recognize that this action could be taken by our General Assembly. However, legislative inaction has never prevented judicial abolition of obsolete common law doctrines, especially those, such as contributory negligence, conceived in the judicial womb. [C] Indeed, our abstinence would sanction "a mutual state of inaction in which the court awaits action by the legislature and the legislature awaits guidance from the court," Alvis v. Ribar, 85 Ill.2d 1, 421 N.E.2d 886, 896, 52 Ill.Dec. 23 (1981), thereby prejudicing the equitable resolution of legal conflicts.

Nor do we today abandon our commitment to stare decisis. While "confidence in our courts is to a great extent dependent on the uniformity and consistency engendered by allegiance to stare decisis, * * * mindless obedience to this precept can confound the truth and foster an attitude of contempt." Hanover [v. Ruch], 809 S.W.2d at 898 [(Tenn. 1991)].

III.

Two basic forms of comparative fault are utilized by 45 of our sister jurisdictions, these variants being commonly referred to as either "pure" or "modified." In the "pure" form[5] a plaintiff's damages are reduced in proportion to the percentage negligence attributed to him; for example, a plaintiff responsible for 90 percent of the negligence that caused his injuries nevertheless may recover 10 percent of his damages. In the "modified" form[6] plaintiffs recover as in pure jurisdictions, but only if

---

5 The 13 states utilizing pure comparative fault are Alaska, Arizona, California, Florida, Kentucky, Louisiana, Mississippi, Missouri, Michigan, New Mexico, New York, Rhode Island, and Washington. See V. Schwartz, supra, at § 2.1. [Michigan has since moved to the "50 percent" modified form. Ed.]

6 The 21 states using the "50 percent" modified form: Connecticut, Delaware, Hawaii, Illinois, Indiana, Iowa, Massachusetts, Minnesota, Montana, Nevada, New Hampshire, New Jersey, Ohio, Oklahoma, Oregon, Pennsylvania, South Carolina, Texas, Vermont, Wisconsin, and Wyoming. The 9 states using the "49 percent" form: Arkansas, Colorado, Georgia, Idaho, Kansas, Maine, North Dakota, Utah, and West Virginia. Two states, Nebraska and South

the plaintiff's negligence either (1) does not exceed ("50 percent" jurisdictions) or (2) is less than ("49 percent" jurisdictions) the defendant's negligence. See generally V. Schwartz, supra, at §§ 3.2, 3.5.

Although we conclude that the all-or-nothing rule of contributory negligence must be replaced, we nevertheless decline to abandon totally our fault-based tort system. We do not agree that a party should necessarily be able to recover in tort even though he may be 80, 90, or 95 percent at fault. We therefore reject the pure form of comparative fault.

We recognize that modified comparative fault systems have been criticized as merely shifting the arbitrary contributory negligence bar to a new ground. See, e.g. Li v. Yellow Cab Co., 13 Cal.3d 804, 532 P.2d 1226, 119 Cal.Rptr. 858 (1975). However, we feel the "49 percent rule" ameliorates the harshness of the common law rule while remaining compatible with a fault-based tort system. [C] We therefore hold that so long as a plaintiff's negligence remains less than the defendant's negligence the plaintiff may recover; in such a case, plaintiff's damages are to be reduced in proportion to the percentage of the total negligence attributable to the plaintiff.

In all trials where the issue of comparative fault is before a jury, the trial court shall instruct the jury on the effect of the jury's finding as to the percentage of negligence as between the plaintiff or plaintiffs and the defendant or defendants. Accord Colo.Rev.Stat. § 13–21–111.5(5) (1987). The attorneys for each party shall be allowed to argue how this instruction affects a plaintiff's ability to recover.

IV.

Turning to the case at bar, the jury found that "the plaintiff and defendant [were] equally at fault." Because the jury, without the benefit of proper instructions by the trial court, made a gratuitous apportionment of fault, we find that their "equal" apportionment is not sufficiently trustworthy to form the basis of a final determination between these parties. Therefore, the case is remanded for a new trial in accordance with the dictates of this opinion.

V.

We recognize that today's decision affects numerous legal principles surrounding tort litigation. For the most part, harmonizing these principles with comparative fault must await another day. However, we feel compelled to provide some guidance to the trial courts charged with implementing this new system.

First, and most obviously, the new rule makes the doctrines of remote contributory negligence and last clear chance obsolete. The circumstances formerly taken into account by those two doctrines will henceforth be addressed when assessing relative degrees of fault.

Second, in cases of multiple tortfeasors, plaintiff will be entitled to recover so long as plaintiff's fault is less than the combined fault of all tortfeasors.

Dakota, use a slight-gross system of comparative fault. See V. Schwartz, supra, at § 2.1. [Nebraska has since moved to the "50 percent" modified form. Ed.]

Third, today's holding renders the doctrine of joint and several liability obsolete. Our adoption of comparative fault is due largely to considerations of fairness: the contributory negligence doctrine unjustly allowed the entire loss to be borne by a negligent plaintiff, notwithstanding that the plaintiff's fault was minor in comparison to defendant's. Having thus adopted a rule more closely linking liability and fault, it would be inconsistent to simultaneously retain a rule, joint and several liability, which may fortuitously impose a degree of liability that is out of all proportion to fault.[7]

Further, because a particular defendant will henceforth be liable only for the percentage of a plaintiff's damages occasioned by that defendant's negligence, situations where a defendant has paid more than his "share" of a judgment will no longer arise, and therefore the Uniform Contribution Among Tort-feasors Act, T.C.A. §§ 29–11–101 to 106 (1980), will no longer determine the apportionment of liability between codefendants.

Fourth, fairness and efficiency require that defendants called upon to answer allegations in negligence be permitted to allege, as an affirmative defense, that a non-party caused or contributed to the injury or damage for which recovery is sought. In cases where such a defense is raised, the trial court shall instruct the jury to assign this nonparty the percentage of the total negligence for which he is responsible. However, in order for a plaintiff to recover a judgment against such additional person, the plaintiff must have made a timely amendment to his complaint and caused process to be served on such additional person. Thereafter, the additional party will be required to answer the amended complaint. The procedures shall be in accordance with the Tennessee Rules of Civil Procedure.

Fifth, until such time as the Tennessee Judicial Conference Committee on Civil Pattern Jury Instructions promulgates new standard jury instructions, we direct trial courts' attention to the suggested instructions and special verdict form set forth in the appendix to this opinion.

VI.

The principles set forth today apply to (1) all cases tried or retried after the date of this opinion, and (2) all cases on appeal in which the comparative fault issue has been raised at an appropriate stage in the litigation.

* * *

For the foregoing reasons, the judgment of the Court of Appeals is reversed in part and affirmed in part [on other issue on appeal relating to admissibility of evidence of intoxication], and the case is remanded to the trial court for a new trial in accordance with the dictates of this opinion. The costs of this appeal are taxed equally to the parties.

---

[7] Numerous other comparative fault jurisdictions have eliminated joint and several liability. See, e.g., Alaska Stat. § 09.17.080(d) (Supp.1991); Colo.Rev.Stat. § 13–21–111.5(1) (1987); Kan.Stat.Ann. § 60–258a(d) (Supp.1991); N.M.Stat.Ann. § 41–3A–1 (1989); N.D.Cent.Code § 32–03.2–02 (Supp.1991); Utah Code Ann. § 78–27–38, –40 (1992); Wyo.Stat.Ann. § 1–1–109(d) (1988).

NOTES AND QUESTIONS

1. Note the court's discussion of the history of the shift from contributory negligence to comparative negligence and of the policy issues underlying each of the doctrines.

2. Only four states (Alabama, Maryland, North Carolina, and Virginia) and the District of Columbia continue to apply the common law doctrine that contributory negligence is a complete bar to recovery. See Williams v. Delta International Mach. Corp., 619 So.2d 1330, 1333 (Ala.1993) ("We have heard hours of oral argument; we have read numerous briefs; we have studied cases from other jurisdictions and law review articles; and in numerous conferences we have discussed in depth this issue and all of the ramifications surrounding such a change. After this exhaustive study and these lengthy deliberations, the majority of the Court, for various reasons, has decided that we should not abandon the doctrine of contributory negligence, which has been the law in Alabama for approximately 162 years.") and Coleman v. Soccer Ass'n of Columbia, 432 Md. 679, 69 A.3d 1149 (2013) (declining to abandon common law doctrine of contributory negligence because such a change involves fundamental and basic public policy considerations properly left to legislature).

3. As the principal case tells you, most of the 46 jurisdictions that have adopted comparative negligence have done so by legislation with only a dozen doing so by judicial decision. Even in some jurisdictions that first adopted comparative negligence by decision, the legislature has since acted to establish a comprehensive statutory scheme. See, e.g., Goetzman v. Wichern, 327 N.W.2d 742 (Iowa 1982) and Iowa Code Ann. § 668.3; Alvis v. Ribar, 85 Ill.2d 1, 421 N.E.2d 886, 52 Ill.Dec. 23 (1981) and 735 Ill. Comp. Stat. 5/2–1116.

4. Do you think that behavior will differ according to whether contributory negligence or some form of comparative negligence is the rule? The law and economics literature has explored this issue. The comparative negligence rule also has been advocated by reference to game theory. Orr, The Superiority of Comparative Negligence, 20 J. Legal Stud. 119 (1991). What about litigation costs? Do you think that more litigation, more hotly contested, and less susceptible to settlement, would be generated under comparative fault? Is "fairness" enough to justify comparative negligence if it is less efficient? See also, Cane, Atiyah's Accidents, Compensation and the Law 124–125 (4th ed. 1987).

5. Note that the Tennessee Supreme Court in adopting comparative negligence had to make a number of other decisions. What type of comparative negligence? What about the continuing effect of ameliorating doctrines like last clear chance? In multiple defendant cases, does the jury compare the fault of the plaintiff to each defendant or to all of the defendants combined? Should joint and several liability survive the adoption of comparative negligence? Should the fault of a non-party be considered by the jury in its apportionment of fault? What should the jury be told about the impact of its allocation of fault? When should the new rules take effect? The notes that follow discuss how these and other issues have been resolved in other jurisdictions adopting comparative negligence.

6. *Types of Comparative Negligence.* After deciding against the "all or nothing" approach of contributory negligence, the court or legislature

must decide the effect of the plaintiff's contributory negligence on plaintiff's recovery.

A. *Pure.* About a dozen jurisdictions (e.g., Arizona, California, New York, and Washington) and several federal statutes (e.g., F.E.L.A., Jones Act) have adopted the pure comparative negligence approach. In those jurisdictions, the plaintiff's recovery is reduced by the percentage fault attributable to the plaintiff. See also Restatement (Third) of Torts: Apportionment of Liability § 7 (2000).

B. *Modified (Plaintiff "Not as Great as").* About a dozen jurisdictions (e.g., Arkansas, Colorado, Nebraska, and Tennessee) have adopted a modified form of comparative negligence in which the plaintiff's recovery is reduced by the percentage of fault attributable to the plaintiff as long as the plaintiff's fault is "not as great as" the defendant's. If the plaintiff's fault is equal to or greater than the defendant's, the plaintiff is completely barred from recovery. Maine's statute authorizes the jury to reduce the damages to "such extent as the jury thinks just and equitable having regard to the claimant's share in the responsibility for the damage," without actually requiring that it be proportional. Thus, the jury may reduce the amount of damages by more than the percentage of fault attributable to the plaintiff. Pelletier v. Fort Kent Golf Club., 662 A.2d 220 (Maine 1995) (interpreting 14 Maine Rev.Stat. § 156).

C. *Modified (Plaintiff "Not Greater than").* About twenty jurisdictions (e.g., Connecticut, New Jersey, Texas, and Wisconsin) have adopted a modified form of comparative negligence in which the plaintiff's recovery is reduced by the percentage of fault attributable to the plaintiff as long as the plaintiff's fault is "not greater than" the fault of the defendant's. If the plaintiff's fault is greater than the defendant's, the plaintiff is completely barred from recovery.

The two modified forms of comparative negligence produce a different result only in the 50/50 case. Although this distinction may not seem very important in theory, it is important as a practical matter because a 50/50 apportionment is an appealing one to juries and therefore common. See also Best & Donahue, Jury Nullification in Modified Comparative Negligence Regimes, 79 U. Chi. L. Rev. 945 (2012) (finding that juries in modified comparative negligence jurisdictions are 67% less likely to assign fault in excess of 50% to the plaintiff than juries in pure comparative negligence jurisdictions).

D. *Slight.* South Dakota is the only remaining jurisdiction that apportions damages so long as plaintiff's negligence "was slight in comparison with the negligence of the defendant"; otherwise, plaintiff is barred from recovery. What constitutes "slight" contributory negligence is a "relative and variable term [that defies] precise definition and prohibits an arbitrary mathematical ratio limitation." Crabb v. Wade, 84 S.D. 93, 167 N.W.2d 546 (1969). But see Wood v. City of Crooks, 559 N.W.2d 558 (S.D. 1997) (apparently setting a thirty percent ceiling as to what constitutes more than slight as a matter of law) and S.D. Codified Laws 20–9–2 (amending the statute to prohibit juries from revealing their determination of the relative negligence of each party, apparently to prevent the parties from knowing their relative fault).

7. *What Is Being Compared?* In comparative negligence jurisdictions, what is the jury being asked to compare? Should fault be apportioned according to the nature of the parties' conduct (whose conduct was worse) or the proximity of the causal relationship between the conduct and the injuries (whose conduct contributed more to the cause of the injury) or some combination of the two? Eaton v. McLain, 891 S.W.2d 587 (Tenn.1994) (cataloguing the approaches of various jurisdictions).

8. *Mechanics of Apportionment.* Some statutes use a special verdict or special interrogatory procedure by which the jurors inform the court as to (1) what percentage of fault was attributable to each party and (2) how much damage each claimant suffered. The court then computes the damages. Is this procedure better or is it better to let the jury return a general verdict? See, for example, In re Asbestos Litigation Pusey Trial Group, 669 A.2d 108 (Del. 1995) (establishing order of questions for jury to consider re effect of plaintiffs' smoking in lung cancer cases brought against asbestos defendants).

9. *Burden of Proof.* The burden of proof is on the defendant to show both that the plaintiff was negligent and that the plaintiff's negligent conduct was a proximate cause of the plaintiff's injuries. See Restatement (Third) of Torts: Apportionment of Liability § 4 (2000).

10. *Should the Jury Be Instructed as to the Legal Consequences of Their Verdict?* For example, in a modified comparative negligence jurisdiction, a percentage change of a single point can mean the plaintiff recovers almost half of her damages or none of them. See Kaeo v. Davis, 68 Haw. 447, 719 P.2d 387 (1986) (jury should be told). See also Reporters' Notes to Restatement (Third) of Torts: Apportionment of Liability § 7, comment *n* (2000).

11. *Multiple Parties.* In a modified comparative negligence system, if there are several defendants, should plaintiff's negligence be compared with that of each defendant individually or with all of them together? Compare Wis. Stat. 895.045(1) (against each) with N.J. Stat. § 2A:15–5.1 (against all) and Restatement (Third) of Torts: Apportionment of Liability § 7, comment *n* (2000) (noting that almost all jurisdictions use "against all").

12. *Application to Persons Not Made Party to the Action.* Should their proportion of the fault be assessed and taken into consideration?

13. *Immunity.* Should the fault of an immune actor be considered? That decision may depend on the type of immunity at issue: Snyder v. LTG Lufttechnische GmbH, 955 S.W.2d 252 (Tenn.1997) (jury may consider actions of immune employer in deciding whether manufacturer of product used by worker is liable, but may not assess fault against the employer); Carroll v. Whitney, 29 S.W.3d 14 (Tenn. 2000) (jury may allocate fault to resident physicians who were immune because they were employees of state); Sears, Roebuck & Co. v. Huang, 652 A.2d 568 (Dela. 1995) (parental negligence in supervising child who was injured by escalator may be considered by jury in deciding whether escalator manufacturer is liable, but jury may not assess fault against mother); Y.H. Investments, Inc. v. Godales, 690 So.2d 1273 (Fla.1997) (jury, in assessing fault against owner of apartment building responsible for guardrail that was in violation of statute, could consider fault of mother of injured two-year-old plaintiff); and

Mack Trucks, Inc. v. Tackett, 841 So.2d 1107 (Miss. 2003) (permitting fault to be allocated to immune employer).

14. *Relationship to Contribution.* What should be done if a separate statute provides for pro rata per capita contribution?

15. *Should Joint and Several Liability Be Abolished?* As the principal case indicates, some states have eliminated joint and several liability after adopting comparative negligence, while others have retained it. See Fernanders v. Marks Construction of S.C., Inc., 330 S.C. 470, 499 S.E.2d 509 (1998) (declining to abolish joint and several liability in wake of adoption of comparative negligence and collecting cases and statutes from other jurisdictions). See also the cases and notes at pages 388–396.

16. *Effect of Comparative Negligence on Certain Common Law Doctrines.* (a) *Last clear chance.* Like Tennessee in the principal case, most courts have found that the doctrine is no longer necessary under comparative negligence, while others have retained it even after switching to comparative negligence. See Restatement (Third) of Torts: Apportionment of Liability § 3, comment *b* (2000). (b) *Res ipsa loquitur.* Should it still be necessary for the plaintiff to present evidence that no negligent conduct on his part contributed to the injury? (c) *Negligence per se.* The conduct of either plaintiff or defendant may violate a statute. Should either of these affect the percentage of negligence? (d) *Imputed negligence.* (e) *Punitive damages.* (f) *Avoidable consequences.* (g) *Trial Judge's Control of Jury* (remittitur or additur).

17. *Types of Defendant's Conduct Subject to Application of Comparative Fault.* Comparative fault is, of course, applicable to negligence. What about an intentional tort? If defendant swings at plaintiff, should the damages be reduced because of plaintiff's negligent failure to duck? The answer would be no in a contributory negligence jurisdiction and in most comparative negligence jurisdictions as well. Ezzell v. Miranne, 84 S.3d 641 (La. App. 2011). What about recklessness? Willful and wanton misconduct? Compare Berberich v. Jack, 392 S.C. 278, 709 S.E.2d 607 (2011) (homeowner's ordinary negligence could be compared with contractor's recklessness for comparative negligence purposes) with Burke v. 12 Rothschild's Liquor Mart, Inc., 148 Ill.2d 429, 170 Ill.Dec. 633, 593 N.E.2d 522 (1992) (qualitative difference between negligence and willful/wanton conduct means that they cannot be compared and comparative negligence is thus not a defense to intentional or willful/wanton conduct). Violation of a "higher degree of care" imposed on a common carrier? Strict liability for abnormally dangerous activities (Chapter 14), or for products liability based on strict liability or breach of warranty (Chapter 15)? Fuchsgruber v. Custom Accessories, Inc., 244 Wis.2d 758, 628 N.W.2d 833 (2001) (in strict product liability cases, jury asked to determine extent to which plaintiff's injuries were attributable to his own negligence as compared to the product's defectiveness). Defendant maintains a nuisance (Chapter 16); should all nuisances be treated alike? He makes a misrepresentation that plaintiff relies upon to his detriment (Chapter 21); should intentional and negligent misrepresentations be treated alike?

18. *Extent to Which Plaintiff's Condition or the Nature of His Conduct Affects the Application of Comparative Fault.* Assume plaintiff is a minor or aged, or is mentally or physically impaired; or is an automobile guest in a

state that has a different standard of care for them; he is a trespasser or licensee on defendant's land; or acted recklessly (all problems treated in earlier chapters). See, for example, Christensen v. Royal School District No. 160, 156 Wash.2d 62, 124 P.3d 283 (2005) (answering certified question from federal district court) (although contributory negligence of minor generally is available to compare in negligence suits brought by minors, in suit against school district for negligence in hiring and supervising teacher accused of sexual abuse of middle school student, court rules that minor under the age of 16 has no duty to protect herself from sexual abuse by teacher) and Gregoire v. City of Oak Harbor, 170 Wash.2d 628, 244 P.3d 924 (2010) (jailor's special duty to inmates includes protecting against suicide, to which assumption of the risk and contributory negligence cannot be defenses) (collecting cases from other jurisdictions).

19. See V. Schwartz, Comparative Negligence (5th ed. 2010) (supplemented annually); H. Woods and B. Deere, Comparative Fault (3d ed. 1996) (supplemented annually); and Comparative Negligence Symposium, 23 Mem. St. U.L.Rev. (1992).

FAILURE TO TAKE ADVANCE PRECAUTIONS AGAINST INJURY AND MITIGATION OF DAMAGES AFTER INJURY

1. *Before Injury*: Plaintiff negligently fails to wear his seatbelt and is more seriously injured than he would have been if he had worn it. Should plaintiff's failure to wear a seatbelt be considered in his case against the other driver? Against the vehicle manufacturer? See Restatement (Third) of Torts: Apportionment of Liability § 3, comment *b*, illus. 3 (2000) (unless there is a statute precluding consideration, such conduct should be taken into account). Compare Estep v. Mike Ferrell Ford Lincoln-Mercury, 223 W.Va. 209, 672 S.E.2d 345 (2008) (West Virginia statute prohibits introduction of evidence that plaintiff was not wearing seatbelt even in crashworthiness cases against car manufacturer as long as plaintiff stipulates to a 5% reduction in damages) with Stokes v. Montana Thirteenth Judicial Dist. Court, 361 Mont. 279, 259 P.3d 754 (2011) (joining majority of jurisdictions that interpret their statutes to permit evidence of seatbelt use or nonuse in cases against the manufacturer raising crashworthiness issues but not the driver of the other car). See also Restatement (Third) of Torts: Products Liability § 16, comment *f* (1998) (Reporters' Note lists jurisdictions that have statutes that do not permit plaintiff's damages to be reduced by failure to wear a seatbelt and those that do). Texas is one of the jurisdictions where admissibility of seatbelt nonuse is *not* governed by statute. It recently decided to permit that evidence to be admitted as part of the consideration of comparative negligence where the defendant was the driver of the other vehicle. Nabors Well Services, Ltd. v. Romero, 456 S.W.3d 553 (Tex. 2015) (noting that holding is not merely correct interpretation of the comparative negligence statute but also promotes sound public policy).

In a case where the jury found that the plaintiff was 90% at fault for her injuries due to her failure to use the shoulder harness of her seatbelt, should her damages award be reduced by 5% as provided by the seatbelt statute or 90% as provided by the comparative fault statute? Klinke v. Mitsubishi Motors Corp., 458 Mich. 582, 581 N.W.2d 272 (1998) (5% cap on reduction applicable only against another driver, not against manufacturer of car).

2. Suppose plaintiff motorcyclist fails to wear a helmet in violation of state criminal law. Defendant negligently crashes into him. Should the court allow defendant to show that plaintiff's injuries would have been less severe if he had worn the helmet? Rogers v. Frush, 257 Md. 233, 262 A.2d 549 (1970) (failure to wear helmet not admissible to show contributory negligence or failure to mitigate damages) and McKinley v. Casson, 80 A.3d 618 (Del. 2013) (because neither statutory nor common law duty to wear motorcycle helmet, nonuse not relevant to comparative negligence). What if a parent does not secure a child in a child safety seat in violation of state law? Cf. Thurel v. Varghese, 207 A.D.2d 220, 621 N.Y.S.2d 633 (N.Y. App. 1995) (court did not reach question because statute was applicable only to operator of vehicle and mother who was holding unrestrained baby in backseat was not operator).

3. In what other situations might there be a duty imposed on plaintiff to take self-precaution against the negligence of others? Should neighbors have to wear masks in an area polluted by a factory? Should they have to wear hard hats when walking near a negligently maintained construction site? Where should the line be drawn? The conceptual problem underlying these cases is not new. Many tort law students of the 1930's and 1940's spent hours studying the case of Mahoney v. Beatman, 110 Conn. 184, 147 A. 762 (1929). Plaintiff drove an automobile at excessive speed and defendant negligently crossed over the median and collided with it. The proof was clear that plaintiff's speed was not responsible for the collision, but it did increase his damages. How should the court have decided the case? See Green, Mahoney v. Beatman: A Study in Proximate Cause, 39 Yale L.J. 532 (1930) and Gregory, Judge Maltbie's Dissent in Mahoney v. Beatman, 24 Conn.B.J. 78 (1950).

4. *After Injury.* The so-called duty to mitigate damages in tort law, sometimes called the doctrine of avoidable consequences, actually is merely a rule that does not allow recovery of those damages that plaintiff could have avoided by reasonable conduct on the part of the plaintiff after a legal wrong has been committed by defendant. It is distinguished from the defense of contributory or comparative negligence, which is unreasonable conduct on the part of plaintiff that contributes to the happening of the accident or injury in the first place. See, for example, Searles v. Fleetwood Homes of Pa., Inc., 878 A.2d 509 (Me. 2005) (distinguishing between comparative negligence and mitigation of damages).

5. The failure to submit to surgery that a reasonable person would undergo to mitigate injury can limit plaintiff's damages for both loss of wages and pain and suffering. See Young v. American Export Isbrandtsen Lines, Inc., 291 F.Supp. 447 (S.D.N.Y.1968) (plaintiff refused surgery that doctor testified would have repaired cartilage and allowed him to return to work). The mere fact that there is some risk involved, even with a chance of fatality, may not bar the application of the avoidable consequences rule. See Bowers v. Lumbermens Mut. Casualty Co., 131 So.2d 70 (La.App.1961). See also Hayes v. United States, 367 F.2d 340 (2d Cir.1966) (claim under FTCA for fall in post office). Cf. Ramkumar v. Grand Style Transp. Enters., Inc., 998 N.E.2d 801 (N.Y. 2013) (plaintiff making no-fault claim was asked why he was no longer going to physical therapy). Is this consistent with the

principle inherent in the law of battery that individuals should have the right to decide whether another person can violate their physical being? Why impose an obligation to mitigate damages?

6. In some cases, the plaintiff's failure to undergo reasonable medical treatment is motivated by the plaintiff's religious beliefs. How should this affect the doctrine? Some courts would not admit evidence of the plaintiff's religious beliefs while others permit the jury to consider it as part of their determination of reasonableness. How might the First Amendment affect the application of the tort doctrine? See Munn v. Algee, 924 F.2d 568 (5th Cir. 1991) (finding neither the Establishment Clause nor the Free Exercise Clause violated); Williams v. Bright, 230 A.D.2d 548, 658 N.Y.S.2d 910 (1997) ("[W]e hold that the pattern jury instruction must be supplemented here with the following direction: 'In considering whether the plaintiff acted as a reasonably prudent person, you may consider the plaintiff's testimony that she is a believer in the Jehovah's Witness faith, and that as an adherent of that faith, she cannot accept any medical treatment which requires a blood transfusion. I charge you that such belief is a factor for you to consider, together with all the other evidence you have heard, in determining whether the plaintiff acted reasonably in caring for her injuries, keeping in mind, however, that the overriding test is whether the plaintiff acted as a reasonably prudent person, under all the circumstances confronting her.' ").

7. Should the reduction in damages be considered a "defense"? See J. Goudkamp, Tort Law Defences (Hart Publishing 2014) (arguing that doctrines affecting the amount of damages—remedy restricting rules—should not be categorized as defenses.)

(C) ASSUMPTION OF RISK

(1) EXPRESS

Seigneur v. National Fitness Institute, Inc.

Court of Special Appeals of Maryland, 2000.
132 Md.App. 271, 752 A.2d 631.

SALMON, J. In this case, we are asked to examine the enforceability of an exculpatory clause found in a fitness club's contract. * * *

[Gerilynne Seigneur was injured while undergoing an initial evaluation at a fitness club owned and operated by National Fitness Institute, Inc. ("NFI"), a Maryland corporation operating an exercise and fitness facility in Montgomery County, Maryland. Ms. Seigneur, after deciding to begin a weight loss and fitness program, joined NFI on a one-month trial basis, having selected NFI over its competitors because her chiropractor had recommended it, it advertised as a fitness club that employed certified fitness and health specialists, and promised to provide programs that are "appropriate for your health status and fitness level." When she signed her membership contract, Ms. Seigneur disclosed that she had a history of serious lower back problems, including a herniated disc, and that her general physical condition was poor. As part of the application process, Ms. Seigneur was required to complete and sign a Participation Agreement that, besides informing the customer of NFI's payment and fee collection policies, contained the following clause:

> "Important Information: I, the undersigned applicant, agree and understand that I must report any and all injuries immediately to NFI, Inc. staff. It is further agreed that all exercises shall be undertaken by me at my sole risk and that NFI, Inc. shall not be liable to me for any claims, demands, injuries, damages, actions, or courses of action whatsoever, to my person or property arising out of or connecting with the use of the services and facilities of NFI, Inc., by me, or to the premises of NFI, Inc. Further, I do expressly hereby forever release and discharge NFI, Inc. from all claims, demands, injuries, damages, actions, or courses of action, and from all acts of active or passive negligence on the part of NFI, Inc., its servants, agents or employees."

During her initial evaluation on the weight machines, Ms. Seigneur felt a tearing or ripping sensation in her right shoulder. Since the incident, she has had pain and difficulty using her shoulder and has undergone shoulder surgery for a condition that her doctor attributed to the use of NFI's upper torso machine. She and her husband filed a negligence action against NFI, based on vicarious liability for the actions of the employee who conducted the evaluation and for its own negligence in hiring and failing to properly train the employee. NFI filed a motion to dismiss, treated by the court as a motion for summary judgment, arguing that the exculpatory clause contained in the Participation Agreement was valid and enforceable and that NFI was entitled to judgment as a matter of law. The Seigneurs responded by arguing that the Participation Agreement was a contract of adhesion and that the exculpatory clause was void as against public policy and that even if the clause did not violate public policy, the agreement was unclear and ambiguous, thus precluding summary judgment.]

Analysis

A. Validity of the Exculpatory Clause

To decide this case, we must first determine whether the exculpatory clause quoted at the beginning of this opinion unambiguously excused NFI's negligence. In construing the Participation Agreement, we are required to give legal effect to all of its unambiguous provisions. * * *

In Maryland, for an exculpatory clause to be valid, it need not contain or use the word "negligence" or any other "magic words." [Cc] An exculpatory clause "is sufficient to insulate the party from his or her own negligence as long as [its] language . . . clearly and specifically indicates the intent to release the defendant from liability for personal injury caused by the defendant's negligence. . . ." (internal quotations omitted) [Cc]

In the instant case, there is no suggestion that the agreement between NFI and Ms. Seigneur was the product of fraud, mistake, undue influence, overreaching, or the like. The exculpatory clause unambiguously provides that Ms. Seigneur "expressly hereby forever releases and discharges NFI, Inc. from all claims, demands, injuries, damages, actions, or courses of action, and from all acts of *active or passive negligence on the part of NFI, Inc., its servants, agents or employees*." (emphasis added). Under these circumstances, we hold that this contract provision expresses a clear intention by the parties to release NFI from liability for all acts of negligence. * * *

B. Public Policy Exception

More than one hundred years ago, it was noted that "the right of parties to contract as they please is restricted only by a few well defined and well settled rules, and it must be a very plain case to justify a court in holding a contract to be against public policy." [Cc] This legal principle continues to hold true today.

In Maryland, unambiguous exculpatory clauses are generally held to be valid in the absence of legislation to the contrary. * * * The Court of Appeals, in Wolf v. Ford, 335 Md. 525, 644 A.2d 522 (1994), said: It is quite possible for the parties expressly to agree in advance that the defendant is under no obligation of care for the benefit of the plaintiff, and shall not be liable for the consequences of conduct which would otherwise be negligent. There is in the ordinary case no public policy which prevents the parties from contracting as they see fit. (quoting W. Page Keeton, et al., Prosser and Keeton on the Law of Torts, § 68 (5th ed. 1984)).

Three exceptions have been identified where the public interest will render an exculpatory clause unenforceable. They are: (1) when the party protected by the clause intentionally causes harm or engages in acts of reckless, wanton, or gross negligence; (2) when the bargaining power of one party to the contract is so grossly unequal so as to put that party at the mercy of the other's negligence; and (3) when the transaction involves the public interest. [Cc]

Ms. Seigneur has not alleged that NFI's agents intentionally caused her harm, or engaged in reckless, wanton, or gross acts of negligence. She does assert, however, that the second and third exceptions are applicable.

Appellants argue that NFI "possesses a decisive advantage in bargaining strength against members of the public who seek to use its services." She also claims that she was presented with a contract of adhesion and that this is additional evidence of NFI's grossly disproportionate "bargaining power."

It is true that the contract presented to Ms. Seigneur was a contract of adhesion.[4] But that fact alone does not demonstrate that NFI had grossly disparate bargaining power. * * * [T]here were numerous other competitors providing the same non-essential services as NFI. The exculpatory clause was prominently displayed in the Participation Agreement and Ms. Seigneur makes no claim that she was unaware of this provision prior to her injury.

---

[4] "A contract of adhesion has been defined as one 'that is drafted unilaterally by the dominant party and then presented on a "take-it-or-leave-it" basis to the weaker party who has no real opportunity to bargain about its terms.' " Meyer v. State Farm Fire and Cas. Co., 85 Md. App. 83, 89, 582 A.2d 275 (1990) (quoting Restatement (Second) of Conflict of Laws § 187, comment *b*).

To possess a decisive bargaining advantage over a customer, the service offered must usually be deemed essential in nature. * * * [The court discussed two earlier Maryland cases that had found that parachute jumping and drag racing were not of an essential nature.] In Schlobohm [v. Spa Petite, Inc., 326 N.W.2d 920 (Minn. 1982)], the Court said:

In the determination of whether the enforcement of an exculpatory clause would be against public policy, the courts consider whether the party seeking exoneration offered services of great importance to the public, which were a practical necessity for some members of the public. As indicated above, courts have found generally that the furnishing of gymnasium or health spa services is not an activity of great public importance nor of a practical necessity. For example, in a negligence action brought against a health club and gym, the Court of Appeals of New York in Ciofalo v. Vic Tanney Gyms, Inc., 10 N.Y.2d 294, 297–98, 220 N.Y.S.2d 962, 964, 177 N.E.2d 925, 927 (1961), noted:

Here there is no special legal relationship and no overriding public interest which demand that this contract provision, voluntarily entered into by competent parties, should be rendered ineffectual. Defendant, a private corporation, was under no obligation or legal duty to accept plaintiff as a "member" or patron. Having consented to do so, it has the right to insist upon such terms as it deemed appropriate. Plaintiff, on the other hand, was not required to assent to unacceptable terms, or to give up a valuable legal right, as a condition precedent to obtaining employment or being able to make use of the services rendered by a public carrier or utility. She voluntarily applied for membership in a private organization, and agreed to the terms upon which the membership was bestowed. She may not repudiate them now.

Similarly, in Shields v. Sta-Fit, Inc., 79 Wn. App. 584, 903 P.2d 525, 528 (Wash.App. 1995), the Court pointed out that:

Health clubs are a good idea and no doubt contribute to the health of the individual participants and the community at large. But ultimately, they are not essential to the state or its citizens. And any analogy to schools, hospitals, housing (public or private) and public utilities therefore fails. Health clubs do not provide essential services.

We agree with the views expressed in *Schlobohm* and *Shields, supra.* The services offered by the appellee simply cannot be accurately characterized as "essential." * * *

The Washington metropolitan area, of which Montgomery County is a part, is home to many exercise and fitness clubs. Ms. Seigneur, like Ms. Wolf, was free to choose among scores of facilities providing essentially the same services. [C] She also had the option of purchasing her own fitness equipment and exercising at home or of exercising without any equipment by doing aerobic or isometric exercises. Ms. Seigneur's bargaining position was not grossly disproportionate to that of NFI.

[In a previous case], when defining what transactions affect public interests, this Court relied in part on a test enunciated in Tunkl v. Regents of the Univ. of California, 60 Cal. 2d 92, 383 P.2d 441, 32 Cal. Rptr. 33 (Ca. 1963). Quoting *Tunkl*, the Court stated that public interests are affected when the transaction exhibits some or all of the following characteristics. It concerns a business of a type generally thought suitable for public regulation. The party seeking exculpation is engaged in performing a service of great importance to the public, which is often a matter of practical necessity for some members of the public. The party holds himself out as willing to perform this service for any member of the public who seeks it, or at least for any member coming within certain established standards. As a result of the essential nature of the service, in the economic setting of the transaction, the party invoking exculpation possesses a decisive advantage of bargaining strength against any member of the public who seeks his services. In exercising a superior bargaining power the party confronts the public with a standardized adhesion contract of exculpation, and makes no provision whereby a purchaser may pay additional reasonable fees and obtain protection against negligence. Finally, as a result of the transaction, the person or property of the purchaser is placed under the control of the seller, subject to the risk of carelessness by the seller or his agents.

* * * Because of the fluid nature of the "public interest," strict reliance on the presence or absence of six fixed factors may be arbitrary. The *Tunkl* Court itself recognized that the public interest does not—and cannot—lend itself easily to definition, because "the social forces that have led to such characterization [of the public interest] are volatile and dynamic. No definition of the concept of public interest can be contained within the four corners of a formula." *Tunkl,* 60 Cal. 2d at 98, 383 P.2d at 444, 32 Cal. Rptr. at 36.

* * * The ultimate determination of what constitutes the public interest must be made considering the totality of the circumstances of any given case against the backdrop of current societal expectations. * * * [T]ransactions that affect the public interest [include not only] those involving the performance of a public service obligation, e.g., public utilities, common carriers, innkeepers, and public warehousemen [but] also includes those transactions, not readily susceptible to definition or broad categorization, that are so important to the public good that an exculpatory clause would be "patently offensive," such that "the common sense of the entire community would . . . pronounce it" invalid. [C]

NFI does not provide an essential public service such that an exculpatory clause would be "patently offensive" to the citizens of Maryland. The services offered by a health club are not of great importance or of practical necessity to the public as a whole. [C] Nor is a health club anywhere near as socially important as institutions or businesses such as innkeepers, public utilities, common carriers, or schools. * * *

JUDGMENT AFFIRMED

NOTES AND QUESTIONS

1. There are two basic issues involved when defendant asserts that plaintiff expressly assumed a risk. The first concerns whether the risk that injured plaintiff fell within the unambiguous terms of the agreement.

Suppose that plaintiff signed a release concerning inherent risks involved in horseback riding. Her own horse behaved well, but the guide's horse kicked her. Is that within the scope of the release? Wright v. Loon Mtn. Rec. Corp., 140 N.H. 166, 663 A.2d 1340 (1995) (question of fact for jury). Suppose that plaintiff signed a release concerning the inherent risks of motorcycle riding and was injured when she lost control of defendant's motorcycle during a test drive. She alleged that dealer was negligent in urging her to ride a motorcycle that was too big for her. Was dealer's negligence within the scope of the release? Thompson v. Hi Tech Motor Sports, Inc., 183 Vt. 218, 945 A.2d 368 (2008) (dealer's negligence not within scope of release relating to inherent dangers of motorcycle riding). After signing releases to enter the pit area of a county racetrack, several participants were injured when rockets from a fireworks display went astray and entered the pit area. They claimed injury by fireworks was not within the scope of the release. Grabill v. Adams County Fair and Racing Assn., 666 N.W.2d 592 (Iowa 2003) (fireworks are within the broad range of events that might transpire and cause injury on a racetrack). Must the release actually mention the word "negligence"? Compare Hyson v. White Water Mntn. Resorts, 265 Conn. 636, 829 A.2d 827 (2003) (release of liability only applies to negligence if express language said so) with the principal case (need not use the word "negligence" or any other magic words) and Sanislo v. Give Kids the World, Inc., 157 So.3d 256 (Fla. 2015) ("hold harmless and release . . . all claims" language is adequate). See also Restatement (Third) of Torts: Apportionment of Liability § 2, comment *c* (2000) (word "negligence" not necessary if language is otherwise clear and unequivocal).

2. The second issue is whether the contract itself violates public policy and therefore should not be enforced. The principal case sets forth considerations that underlie that determination. In light of those principles, how should a court rule on the enforceability of a document in which

A. An express assumption of risk clause is written into a contract of sale between two large corporations. See Delta Air Lines, Inc. v. McDonnell Douglas Corp., 503 F.2d 239 (5th Cir.1974) (applying California law) (enforceable because parties with equal bargaining power can allocate the risk of loss as they choose).

B. Ordinarily, a common carrier like a railroad may not require a pre-injury release of passengers. New York Cent. R. Co. v. Lockwood, 84 U.S. (17 Wall.) 357 (1873). What if passenger is given the opportunity to ride free on a common carrier, but he must relieve it of all liability to him for negligent acts committed in the course of transportation? See Gonzales v. Baltimore & Ohio R. Co., 318 F.2d 294 (4th Cir.1963) (applying West Virginia law) (enforceable).

C. A patient agreed to assume all risks that had been explained to her in connection with medical diagnosis and treatment in a hospital. Cudnik v. William Beaumont Hosp., 207 Mich.App. 378, 525 N.W.2d 891 (1994) (joining the "overwhelming majority" of jurisdictions that have found exculpatory agreements for providing of medical treatment invalid and unenforceable) and Covenant Health Rehab of Picayune v. Brown, 949 So.2d 732 (Miss. 2007) (limitation of damages clause in form admitting plaintiff to nursing home is unconscionable). As is a mandatory arbitration clause. Covenant Health & Rehabilitation of Picayune, LP v. Estate of Moulds ex rel. Braddock, 14 So.3d 695 (Miss. 2009). Suppose the patient did not have to pay for medical services. Should that make a difference? Tunkl v. Regents of Univ. of California, 60 Cal.2d 92, 383 P.2d 441, 32 Cal.Rptr. 33 (1963) (no) (discussed in principal case).

D. A day care center required a release as a condition of admission to the program. Gavin W. v. YMCA of Metropolitan Los Angeles, 131 Cal.Rptr.2d 168, 106 Cal.App.4th 662 (2003) (exculpatory agreement that purported to relieve child care provider of liability for its own negligence is void as against public policy).

E. What if the release covers gross negligence as well as negligence? City of Santa Barbara v. Superior Court, 41 Cal.4th 747, 161 P.3d 1095, 62 Cal.Rptr.3d 527 (2007) (joining "vast majority" of jurisdictions that find agreements unenforceable as to gross negligence).

3. A parent signs an assumption of the risk form on behalf of a minor child so that the child may attend ski-racing lessons, play recreational soccer, or enter a skateboard facility. Is the agreement enforceable against the parent who signed the agreement? against the other parent? against the child? Compare Scott v. Pacific West Mountain Resort, 119 Wash.2d 484, 834 P.2d 6 (1992) (parents can waive their own rights but not their minor child's) and Hojnowski v. Vans Skate Park, 187 N.J. 323, 901 A.2d 381 (2006) (accord) with Zivich v. Mentor Soccer Club, Inc., 82 Ohio St.3d 367, 696 N.E.2d 201 (1998) (mother waived her rights, and child's rights, and father's rights) and Sharon v. City of Newton, 437 Mass. 99, 769 N.E.2d 738 (2002) (father's waiver of rights effective as to injury incurred by teenage cheerleader). Should it make a difference whether the defendant is a commercial entity or non-commercial entity like a school or community-sponsored program? Compare Kirton v. Fields, 997 So.2d 349 (Fla. 2008) (finding pre-injury release signed by parent on behalf of minor is unenforceable against the minor or minor's estate in tort action arising from participation in commercial activity and noting that cases from other jurisdictions that enforced releases usually involved non-commercial entities like school or community-sponsored programs) with BJ's Wholesale Club, Inc. v. Rosen, 435 Md. 714, 80 A.3d 345 (2013) (upholding pre-injury release signed by father on behalf of child playing at store's children's play area, rejecting commercial v. non-commercial distinction). After *Kirton*, the Florida legislature acted to limit its holding to permit parents to release commercial activity providers for injuries that occurred as a result of the inherent risk of the activity. Fla. Stat. § 744.301(3).

4. In the principal case, would Mr. Seigneur's loss of consortium claim be barred by his wife's express assumption of the risk? With the principal case (barred), compare Huber v. Hovey, 501 N.W.2d 53 (Iowa 1993) (not barred because independent right under Iowa law) and Hardy v. St. Claire, 739 A.2d 368 (Maine 1999) (recognizing split in jurisdictions).

5. Must the agreement be in writing in order to constitute express assumption of the risk? See Boyle v. Revici, 961 F.2d 1060 (2d Cir.1992) (applying New York law) (assumption of the risk of unconventional treatment for cancer need not be in writing). Of course, it will be harder to prove if not in writing.

6. In any case involving express assumption of risk, an attorney must research not only tort law but also appropriate regulatory laws that may affect the validity of the documents. See, e.g., N.Y.Gen.Oblig.Law § 5–321 (declaring void exculpatory clauses in rental of real property).

7. As indicated in the next section, comparative negligence statutes may affect implied assumption of risk, but they do not affect an express assumption of risk. See Gilson v. Drees Bros., 19 Wis.2d 252, 120 N.W.2d 63, 67 (1963).

(2) IMPLIED

Rush v. Commercial Realty Co.

Supreme Court of New Jersey, 1929.
7 N.J.Misc. 337, 145 A. 476.

PER CURIAM. The case for the plaintiffs was that they were tenants of the defendant, which controlled the house wherein they lived and also the adjoining house, and provided a detached privy for the use of both houses; that Mrs. Rush having occasion to use this privy, went into it and fell through the floor, or through some sort of trap door therein, descended about nine feet into the accumulation at the bottom, and had to be extricated by use of a ladder. * * *

Taking the facts as the jury were entitled to find them, most favorably for the plaintiffs, the situation was that of a building under the control of the landlord for the use of tenants generally, and maintained by the landlord; a consequent duty of care in maintenance; a defective condition in the floor which the jury might say was due to negligent maintenance by the defendant; and an accident resulting therefrom. In such a situation it would seem that the argument for a nonsuit or for a direction [directed verdict] must be restricted to the questions of contributory negligence and assumption of risk. In dealing with these, it should be observed that Mrs. Rush had no choice, when impelled by the calls of nature, but to use the facilities placed at her disposal by the landlord, to wit, a privy with a trap door in the floor, poorly maintained. We hardly think this was the assumption of a risk; she was not required to leave the premises and go elsewhere. Whether it was contributory negligence to step on a floor, which she testified was in bad order, was a question for the jury to solve according to its finding of the conditions and her knowledge of them, or what she should have known of them; it does not seem to be a court question.

We conclude that there was no error in denying motions to take the case from the jury, and the judgment will accordingly be affirmed.

NOTES AND QUESTIONS

1. Is implied assumption of risk virtually the same as the consent defense to intentional torts? Assumption of risk, in the sense of consent, is sometimes called *volenti*, after the Latin maxim, *Volenti non fit injuria* [To the willing, there is no injury]. It requires actual knowledge of the particular risk, appreciation of its magnitude, and voluntary encountering of the risk. It is an affirmative defense for which the defendant bears the

burden of pleading, production, and proof. See In re Tobacco Litigation, 2014 WL 5545853 (W.Va. 2014) (distinguishing between the affirmative defense of assumption of the risk and other defenses such as lack of proximate cause, federal preemption, compliance with government regulations, etc., all of which are factors the jury could consider or limitations on what it could consider in determining whether plaintiffs had met their burden of proof).

2. In a number of states the defense of assumption of risk has been carried beyond the concept of consent and applied to any factual situation where the plaintiff consciously and voluntarily places himself in a position where he is subject to a known risk. The relationship of this type of assumption of risk to contributory negligence has given much trouble. Sometimes the distinction is drawn by saying that the "essence of contributory negligence is carelessness; of assumption of risk, venturousness. Thus an injured person may not have acted carelessly, may have exercised the utmost care, yet may have assumed, voluntarily, a known hazard." Hunn v. Windsor Hotel Co., 119 W.Va. 215, 193 S.E. 57 (1937) (plaintiff deliberately walked down defective steps when others, not greatly more inconvenient, were also available). Assumption of the risk involves the encountering of a subjectively known risk; contributory negligence may involve a plaintiff exposing himself to a danger of which he was subjectively unaware but which would have been apparent had he used due care. See Robinson v. BF Goodrich Tire Co., 444 Pa.Super. 640, 664 A.2d 616 (1995) and Wallace v. Rosen, 765 N.E.2d 192 (Ind. App. 2002) (distinguishing assumption of the risk and contributory negligence). This approach gives the defendant two separate defenses for the same conduct, as New Jersey did in the principal case. See also Thomas v. Panco Mgt. of Md., LLC, 423 Md. 387, 31 A.3d 583 (2011) (in case involving slip on black ice on sidewalk, court noted that jury should consider both whether plaintiff had assumed the risk and whether she was contributorily negligent).

3. Distinguish the following. Which defense or defenses would be available to defendant in each?

A. Plaintiff voluntarily enters into a relation with defendant, which he knows to involve some risk. He teaches a beginner to drive an automobile. Le Fleur v. Vergilia, 280 App.Div. 1035, 117 N.Y.S.2d 244 (1952) (assumed risk of driver's inexperience). She agrees to provide home health care to a patient with Alzheimer's. Gregory v. Cott, 59 Cal.4th 996, 331 P.3d 179, 176 Cal.Rptr.3d 1 (2014) (in-home care giver hired through agency injured while caring for Alzheimer's patient assumed the risk of injury because agitation and physical aggression are common symptoms).

B. Plaintiff knows that defendant's activity, or a condition created by him, involves some danger, but quite reasonably concludes that he can safely encounter it and proceeds. In an amusement park, he buys a ride on a moving belt that upsets the riders. See Judge Cardozo's terse opinion in Murphy v. Steeplechase Amusement Co., 250 N.Y. 479, 166 N.E. 173 (1929).

C. Plaintiff, fully aware of an unreasonable risk, voluntarily proceeds to encounter it. He consents to ride with a drunken driver on a dark night. Cf. Sutherland v. Davis, 286 Ky. 743, 151 S.W.2d 1021 (1941). She goes for a walk at night near a lagoon in a community in which she knows wild alligators are present. Landings Ass'n, Inc. v. Williams, 291 Ga. 397, 728 S.E.2d 577 (2012) (assumption of risk).

D. Plaintiff, having spent half an hour in an above ground swimming pool, knows that the water is only three feet deep, dives into it, and is injured when her head strikes the bottom. She testifies that she thought she could safely make a shallow dive and that the worst possible outcome was the risk that she would scrape the bottom of the pool on a poorly executed dive. Did she understand the magnitude of the risk? Sheehan v. The No. Am. Marketing Corp., 610 F.3d 144 (1st Cir. 2010) (applying Rhode Island law) (the risk of a poorly executed or botched dive is subsumed within the risk of diving generally and there are certain risks that are so self-evident that a person will be deemed to have understood them as a matter of law).

4. As the principal case indicates, it is essential to show that *plaintiff had actual knowledge* of the risk. The best way to show this, of course, is to secure a direct admission from plaintiff or someone who overheard him. See Vanderlei v. Heideman, 83 Ill.App.3d 158, 403 N.E.2d 756, 38 Ill.Dec. 525 (1980) (horseshoer testified he knew of risk of being kicked because he had been kicked several times before). But circumstantial evidence may be adequate for the jury to draw a reasonable inference. Cf. Wyly v. Burlington Indus., 452 F.2d 807 (5th Cir.1971) (applying Texas law) (plaintiff contestant in "National Lap Sitting Contest" promoting wrinkle-free slacks must have been aware of risk of chair collapsing when 14 college students sat on his lap). Thurmond v. Prince Wm. Prof. Baseball Club, Inc., 265 Va. 59, 574 S.E.2d 246 (2003) (adult spectator of ordinary intelligence familiar with the rules of baseball assumed the normal risks of watching game, including danger of being hit by a foul ball). C&M Builders, LLC v. Strub, 420 Md. 268, 22 A.3d 867, 883 (2011) ("In prior opinions, we have noted, with approval, the proposition formulated by Prosser and Keeton that 'there are certain risks which anyone of adult age must be taken to appreciate: the danger of slipping on ice, of falling through unguarded openings, of lifting heavy objects . . . and doubtless many others.' ") (finding assumption of risk as matter of law where HVAC contractor fell through unguarded stairwell opening in rowhouse). Suppose plaintiff is rendered incompetent by the accident. How can it be determined if he assumed the risk? See Farley v. M.M. Cattle Co., 549 S.W.2d 453 (Tex.Civ.App.1977) (court acknowledged that knowledge may be inferred from circumstances, but circumstances to justify inference not present in particular case).

5. The *scope of the risk assumed* must be addressed. Courts, unfavorably disposed to assumption of risk, place a narrow or specific gloss on "risk." See Hawthorne v. Gunn, 123 Cal.App. 452, 11 P.2d 411 (1932) (woman sitting on man's lap in a moving car assumes certain risks, but a collision is not among them). Does a hockey fan assume the risk of being struck in the face by an errant puck? Even if she deliberately buys a ticket for a seat low in the stands behind the plexiglass shield? Cf. Moulas v. PBC Prods., Inc., 213 Wis.2d 406, 570 N.W.2d 739 (App.1997), aff'd 217 Wis.2d 449, 576 N.W.2d 929 (1998) (no recovery for plaintiff). Does a football fan who holds season tickets for seats in the end zone assume the risk that a ball might soar over the net and hit him? That unruly fans might trample him while attempting to relieve him of a ball he caught? Cf. Telega v.

Security Bureau, Inc., 719 A.2d 372 (Pa.Super.1998) (being trampled by unruly fans not a risk inherent in or an ordinary part of watching football).

6. In addition to knowledge of the risk, plaintiff must proceed to encounter it "*voluntarily*." How much latitude does this concept give a court to define the scope of the defense? Defendant negligently maintains a highway, leaving a large mudhole in it. Plaintiff, knowing the condition of the highway, attempts to drive past the mudhole and, while keeping to the extreme edge of the road, slides off into the ditch and is injured. The assumption is not voluntary if plaintiff is away from home and has to get back, but is if there is a reasonably short and convenient detour at hand, in good condition. Pomeroy v. Westfield, 154 Mass. 462, 28 N.E. 899 (1891) (no defense because no alternative) and Campion v. Rochester, 202 Minn. 136, 277 N.W. 422 (1938) (defendant has burden of showing that safe alternative existed). On his own property, plaintiff was bitten by a vicious boar owned by a neighbor. The plaintiff had knowledge of the vicious propensities of the boar and yet left his house and exposed himself to the risk. See Marshall v. Ranne, 511 S.W.2d 255 (Tex.1974) (not voluntary because his only choices were to remain prisoner in his own house or to try to make it past the boar to his pickup truck). College failed to clear snow from dormitory parking lot so it was "crunchy with ice and snow." Plaintiff fell and broke her leg while crossing the parking lot to get to her car. If plaintiff is a student who lives in the dorm and has no other way out, it would not be voluntary. If plaintiff is student's mother who has come to visit her and bring her some money, it is voluntary. Morgan State University v. Walker, 397 Md. 509, 919 A.2d 21 (2007) (upholding trial court judge's granting of summary judgment to defendant based on plaintiff mother's assumption of the risk but noting that jury question would be created as to voluntariness if it had been student tenant who fell).

7. *Plaintiff's Protests.* The fact that plaintiff has protested against the defendant's conduct is of course important evidence that he does not consent to assume the risk. But having protested, he may thereafter, even though reluctantly, accept the situation, and as the courts have sometimes put it, "waive" the protest. Whether he does so is a question of fact, and usually a question for the jury. Often it will turn upon the existence of some reasonable alternative to the plaintiff's course. Compare Young v. Wheby, 126 W.Va. 741, 30 S.E.2d 6 (1944) (accepting ride with intoxicated driver is voluntary) with Ridgway v. Yenny, 223 Ind. 16, 57 N.E.2d 581 (1944) (accepting ride with reckless driver not voluntary because weather was bad and plaintiff was in unfamiliar neighborhood).

8. Assumption of the risk is not available as a matter of law in cases involving sexual abuse of a child. Bjerke v. Johnson, 742 N.W.2d 660 (Minn. 2007) (teenage plaintiff sued defendant owner of horse farm for negligently failing to protect her from the criminal sexual conduct of defendant's live-in boyfriend).

9. Historically, many jurisdictions divided implied assumption of the risk into categories of primary and secondary assumption of the risk. The category of *primary assumption of the risk* collects cases that might more accurately be described as cases where the defendant owed no duty to the plaintiff or where the defendant did not breach the limited duty owed to the plaintiff rather than that plaintiff assumed the risks inherent in the activity. For example, those who attend baseball games seated outside the

area behind home plate that is screened assume the risk of balls being batted into the stands during the game. This might also be expressed by saying the owner of the stadium had no duty to screen all the seats from balls or by saying that the owner did not breach its duty to plaintiff as long as it provided some seats that were screened from balls. See, for example, Cincinnati Baseball Club Co. v. Eno, 112 Ohio St. 175, 147 N.E. 86 (1925) (surveying cases in a number of jurisdictions and concluding that it is common knowledge that in baseball games hard balls are thrown and batted with great swiftness, that they are liable to be thrown or batted outside the lines of the diamond, and that spectators in positions that may be reached by such balls assume the risk thereof); South Shore Baseball, LLC v. DeJesus, 11 N.E.3d 903 (Ind. 2014) (spectator admitted she knew of risk of foul balls entering seating area not protected by netting); Cole v. Boy Scouts of America, 397 S.C. 247, 725 S.E.2d 476 (2011) (primary assumption of the risk includes risk that base runner in pickup softball game including Boy Scouts and their fathers will collide with catcher at home plate); Nigro v. NY Racing Ass'n, Inc., 3 A.D.3d 647, 939 N.Y.S.2d 565 (2012) (primary assumption of the risk applicable where experienced professional horse exercise rider appreciated risks posed by loose gravel on asphalt road intersecting dirt path she was on); Nalwa v. Cedar Fair, L.P., 55 Cal.4th 1148, 150 Cal.Rptr.3d 551, 290 P.3d 1158 (2012) (primary assumption of the risk applies to bumper car head-on collisions); and Werne v. Executive Women's Golf Ass., 158 N.H. 373, 969 A.2d 346 (2009) (plaintiff would only be able to recover if she could show that defendants created or allowed unreasonable risks beyond those risks inherent in the sport of glow golf—played at night with glow-in-the-dark balls). But see Coomer v. Kansas City Royals Baseball Corp., 437 S.W.3d 184 (Mo. 2014) (risk of injury from hotdog toss by mascot was not one of the risks inherent in being spectator at baseball game and thus was not covered by implied primary assumption of the risk).

10. The category of *secondary assumption of the risk* collects cases where the plaintiff acts voluntarily but unreasonably to encounter a known risk. Should those situations continue to bar the plaintiff from recovery after the adoption of comparative negligence? Consider Florida's answer in the next case.

Blackburn v. Dorta

Supreme Court of Florida, 1977.
348 So.2d 287.

[Several cases in the Florida District Court of Appeal had reached differing decisions on the issue of whether "the doctrine of assumption of risk is still viable as an absolute bar to recovery subsequent to adoption of the rule of comparative negligence in Hoffman v. Jones, 280 So.2d 431 (Fla.1973)." Three of them were consolidated by the state supreme court under its "conflict certiorari jurisdiction."]

SUNDBERG, JUSTICE. * * * Since our decision in Hoffman v. Jones, supra, contributory negligence no longer serves as a complete bar to plaintiff's recovery but is to be considered in apportioning damages according to the principles of comparative negligence. We are now asked to determine the effect of the *Hoffman* decision on the common law doctrine of assumption of risk. If assumption of risk is equivalent to contributory negligence, then *Hoffman* mandates that it can no longer operate as a complete bar to recovery. However, if it has a distinct purpose apart from contributory negligence, its continued existence remains unaffected by *Hoffman*. This question was expressly reserved in *Hoffman* as being not ripe for decision. 280 So.2d 431, 439.

At the outset, we note that assumption of risk is not a favored defense. There is a puissant drift toward abrogating the defense. The argument is that assumption of risk serves no purpose which is not subsumed by either the doctrine of contributory negligence or the common law concept of duty. It is said that this redundancy results in confusion and, in some cases, denies recovery unjustly. * * * The issue is most salient in states which have enacted comparative negligence legislation. Those statutes provide that the common law defense of contributory negligence no longer necessarily acts as a complete bar to recovery. The effect of these statutes upon the doctrine of assumption of risk has proved to be controversial. Joining the intensifying assault upon the doctrine, a number of comparative negligence jurisdictions have abrogated assumption of risk. Those jurisdictions hold that assumption of risk is interchangeable with contributory negligence and should be treated equivalently. Today we are invited to join this trend of dissatisfaction with the doctrine. For the reasons herein expressed, we accept the invitation.

At the commencement of any analysis of the doctrine of assumption of risk, we must recognize that we deal with a potpourri of labels, concepts, definitions, thoughts, and doctrines. The confusion of labels does not end with the indiscriminate and interchangeable use of the terms "contributory negligence" and "assumption of risk." In the case law and among text writers, there have developed categories of assumption of risk. Distinctions exist between *express* and *implied;* between *primary* and *secondary;* and between *reasonable* and *unreasonable* or, as sometimes expressed, *strict* and *qualified.* It will be our task to analyze these various labels and to trace the historical basis of the doctrine to unravel what has been in the law an "enigma wrapped in a mystery."

It should be pointed out that we are not here concerned with express assumption of risk which is a contractual concept outside the purview of this inquiry and upon which we express no opinion herein. * * *

The breed of assumption of risk with which we deal here is that which arises by implication or *implied* assumption of risk. Initially it may be divided into the categories of *primary* and *secondary*. The term primary assumption of risk is simply another means of stating that the defendant was not negligent, either because he owed no duty to the plaintiff in the first instance, or because he did not breach the duty owed. Secondary assumption of risk is an affirmative defense to an established breach of a duty owed by the defendant to the plaintiff.

* * *

It is apparent that no useful purpose is served by retaining terminology which expresses the thought embodied in primary assumption of risk. This branch (or trunk) of the tree of assumption of risk is subsumed in the principle of negligence itself. * * * An example of this concept is presented in the operation of a passenger train. It can be said that a passenger assumes the risk of lurches and jerks which are ordinary and usual to the proper operation of the train, but that he does not assume the risk of extraordinary or unusual lurches and jerks resulting from substandard operation of the train. The same issue can be characterized in terms of the standard of care of the railroad. Thus, it can be said that the railroad owes a duty to operate its train with the degree of care of an ordinary prudent person under similar circumstances which includes some lurching and jerking while a train is in motion or commencing to move under ideal circumstances. So long as the lurching or jerking is not extraordinary due to substandard conduct of the railroad, there is no breach of duty and, hence, no negligence on the part of the railroad. The latter characterization of the issue clearly seems preferable and is consistent with the manner in which the jury is instructed under our standard jury instructions.

Having dispensed with *express* and *primary-implied* assumption of risk, we recur to *secondary-implied* assumption of risk which is the affirmative defense variety that has been such a thorn in the judicial side. The affirmative defense brand of assumption of risk can be subdivided into the type of conduct which is reasonable but nonetheless bars recovery (sometimes called *pure* or *strict* assumption of risk), and the type of conduct which is unreasonable and bars recovery (sometimes referred to as *qualified* assumption of risk). [C] Application of pure or strict assumption of risk is exemplified by the hypothetical situation in which a landlord has negligently permitted his tenant's premises to become highly flammable and a fire ensues. The tenant returns from work to find the premises a blazing inferno with his infant child trapped within. He rushes in to retrieve the child and is injured in so doing. Under the pure doctrine of assumption of risk, the tenant is barred from recovery because it can be said he voluntarily exposed himself to a known risk. Under this view of assumption of risk, the tenant is precluded from recovery notwithstanding the fact that his conduct could be said to be entirely reasonable under the circumstances. [C] There is little to commend this doctrine of implied-pure or strict assumption of risk, and our research discloses no Florida case in which it has been applied. Certainly, in light of Hoffman v. Jones, supra, there is no reason supported by law or justice in this state to give credence to such a principle of law.

There remains, then, for analysis only the principle of implied-qualified assumption of risk, and it can be demonstrated in the hypothetical recited above with the minor alteration that the tenant rushes into the blazing premises to retrieve his favorite fedora. Such conduct on the tenant's part clearly would be unreasonable. Consequently, his conduct can just as readily be characterized as contributory negligence. It is the failure to exercise the care of a reasonably prudent man under similar circumstances. It is this last category of assumption of risk which has caused persistent confusion in the law of torts because of the lack of analytic difference between it and contributory negligence. If the only significant form of assumption of risk (implied-qualified) is so readily characterized, conceptualized, and verbalized as contributory negligence, can there be any sound rationale for retaining it as a separate affirmative defense to negligent conduct which bars recovery altogether? In the absence of any historical imperative, the answer must be no. We are persuaded that there is no historical significance to the doctrine of implied-secondary assumption of risk. * * *

Therefore, we hold that the affirmative defense of implied assumption of risk is merged into the defense of contributory negligence and the principles of comparative negligence enunciated in Hoffman v. Jones, supra, shall apply in all cases where such defense is asserted. * * *

It is so ordered.

NOTES AND QUESTIONS

1. Assumption of risk is not favored by the courts; and it has been cordially disliked by the friends of the plaintiff, because of its long history of defeating recovery in cases of genuine hardship—particularly in those of injuries to employees before the worker compensation acts. The first cases to refuse to recognize the defense involved the violation of statutes that were found to be enacted to protect a particular class of persons against their own consent and it was declared that the purpose of the statute would be defeated if the defense were allowed. Child labor acts afford the obvious example. Lenahan v. Pittston Coal Mining Co., 218 Pa. 311, 67 A. 642 (1907); Terry Dairy Co. v. Nalley, 146 Ark. 448, 225 S.W. 887 (1920). Some states had even abolished implied assumption of the risk as a separate defense before the adoption of comparative negligence. V. Schwartz, Comparative Negligence, § 9.04[b] (5th edition 2010).

2. *Comparative Negligence.* A growing number of courts are in accord with the holding of the principal case that implied secondary assumption of risk does not remain an affirmative defense separate and apart from contributory negligence. As the principal case reflects, the advent of comparative negligence is prompting courts to implement a merger of the defenses of contributory negligence and implied secondary assumption of risk. What are the reasons for this? Some comparative negligence statutes have treated assumption of risk the same as contributory negligence, but the merger may occur even if the comparative negligence statute is completely silent about assumption of risk. See Kopischke v. First Continental Corp., 187 Mont. 471, 610 P.2d 668 (1980); Monk v. Virgin Islands Water & Power Authority, 53 F.3d 1381 (3d Cir.1995) (applying Virgin Islands law) (distinguishing primary assumption of risk and collecting cases and statutes from other jurisdictions); Rountree v. Boise Baseball, LLC, 154 Idaho 167, 296 P.3d 373 (2013) (merging both primary and secondary implied assumption of the risk into comparative negligence); and Simmons v. Porter, 298 Kan. 299, 312 P.3d 345 (2013) (eliminating separate assumption of risk defense and remanding for consideration as comparative negligence). See also Restatement (Third) of Torts: Apportionment of Liability § 3, comment *c* (2000) (conduct of plaintiff who is actually aware of risk and voluntarily encounters it is evaluated under comparative negligence standard). But see Neb. Rev. Stat. § 25–21,185.12 (codifying assumption of the risk as a separate affirmative defense). Which approach do you prefer?

3. *Open and Obvious Danger*. While vacationing in Hawaii, plaintiff and her family got caught in a rainstorm and returned to their hotel room to dry off. Plaintiff went on the lanai to get a chair, slipped, slid across the balcony, and sustained injury to her foot when it got trapped under the lanai railing. Plaintiff knew the floor was wet. Did she assume the risk of injury when she stepped on to the lanai floor? Steigman v. Outrigger Ent., Inc., 126 Haw. 133, 267 P.3d 1238 (2011) (joining majority of states that have eliminated open and obvious danger as a bar to recovery and holding that the jury should consider any known or obvious characteristics of the danger as factors in the larger comparative negligence analysis). Broussard v. State Office of State Buildings, 113 So.3d 175 (La. 2013) (accord, UPS delivery man injured back pulling dolly into misaligned elevator). But see Armstrong v. Best Buy Co., Inc., 99 Ohio St.3d 79, 788 N.E.2d 1088, 1089 (2003) and O'Sullivan v. Shaw, 431 Mass. 201, 726 N.E.2d 951, 956–57 (2000) (analyzing open and obvious danger situation as a question of whether defendant owes any duty to plaintiff at all rather than as comparing the conduct of defendant and plaintiff).

2. STATUTES OF LIMITATIONS AND REPOSE

Teeters v. Currey

Supreme Court of Tennessee, 1974.
518 S.W.2d 512.

HENRY, JUSTICE. This malpractice action essentially involves a determination of whether the statute of limitation begins to run from the date of the injury or from the date of the discovery of the injury.

The admitted facts are that on June 5, 1970, plaintiff gave birth to a normal child. Defendant was the attending physician. Following delivery, because of edema, anemia, and other medical complications, he recommended that plaintiff have a bilateral tubal ligation, the purpose of which was to avoid future pregnancies. Defendant performed this surgery on June 6, 1970, and her recovery was uneventful.

On December 6, 1972 she was hospitalized at Newell Clinic and was attended by Dr. Edgar Atkin. Dr. Atkin discovered that she was pregnant. He so advised her and referred her to other physicians for obstetrical care.

On March 9, 1973 plaintiff was delivered of a premature child and there were severe complications. Pursuant to medical advice, another bilateral tubal ligation was performed on March 11, 1973.

Plaintiff instituted suit on November 15, 1973, three years, five months and nine days after the operation, but approximately eleven months after discovering her pregnancy.

Plaintiff alleges that during the course of this latter surgery it was discovered that the earlier surgery performed by the defendant was negligently and inadequately done and was not performed in accordance with proper standards of care and good medical practice. * * *

The defendant's answer pleads the statute of limitations and denies that he was guilty of any act of negligence. * * *

Section 28–304, T.C.A. applies to malpractice suits and provides that the action be "commenced within one (1) year after cause of action accrued."

When does the cause of action accrue?

In Bodne v. Austin, 156 Tenn. 366, 2 S.W.2d 104 (1928) the Court said: " * * * we have been referred to no authority holding that mere ignorance and failure to discover the existence of the cause of action, or the consequential damages resulting from the breach of duty or wrongful act, can prevent the running of the statute of limitations."

But this was in 1927 almost half a century ago.

In Albert v. Sherman, 167 Tenn. 133, 67 S.W.2d 140 (1934), the Court followed *Bodne.*

This was forty years ago. * * *

The time has come for us to re-examine the past holdings of our Appellate Courts in the light of contemporary standards of justice and of the holdings of the courts of last resort in other American jurisdictions. * * *

We recognize that statutes of limitations are * * * designed to promote stability in the affairs of men and to avoid the uncertainties and burdens inherent in defending stale claims.

In recognition of this, traditionally our courts have held that a right of action accrues immediately upon the infliction or occurrence of injury and that mere ignorance or failure of plaintiff to discover his cause of action or the subsequent resulting damage does not toll the statute. [C]

That this is a harsh and an oppressive rule there can be little doubt. To counter the casualties it has produced the courts have fashioned the so-called "discovery doctrine," under which the statute does not begin to run until the negligent injury is, or should have been discovered.

This concept has been adopted by judicial interpretation in at least a majority of the American states. [C] Some of these jurisdictions limit the application of the doctrine to "foreign objects"; the majority apply it to all medical malpractice cases. * * *

As evidence of the rapidity with which the various jurisdictions have embraced this equitable doctrine, the main volume of 80 A.L.R.2d, published in 1961, at page 388, lists *seven (7) states* as having adopted the discovery rule, viz., California, Colorado, Louisiana, Missouri, North Carolina, Pennsylvania and Texas.

The main volume of the appropriate Later Case Service, published in 1968, lists *twelve (12) additional states*, Arizona, Delaware, Hawaii, Idaho, Iowa, Maryland, Michigan, Montana, Nebraska, New Jersey, Utah and West Virginia.

The 1974 supplement lists *nine (9) more states,* Georgia, Illinois, Kansas, Kentucky, North Dakota, Oklahoma, Oregon, Rhode Island and Washington.

This brings the total to twenty-eight (28) states.

Add Tennessee to the list.

We adopt as the rule of this jurisdiction the principle that in those classes of cases where medical malpractice is asserted to have occurred through the negligent performance of surgical procedures, the cause of action accrues and the statute of limitations commences to run when the patient discovers, or in the exercise of reasonable care and diligence for his own health and welfare, should have discovered the resulting injury. All cases contra are overruled.

In the instant case the cause of action accrued when plaintiff discovered that she was pregnant, or in the exercise of reasonable care and diligence, she should have so discovered.

We add, in meticulous fairness to the trial judge, that in ruling as he did, he properly relied upon our precedents.

We here merely recede from prior cases in order to establish a rule which we are convinced will be productive of results more nearly consonant with the demands of justice and the dictates of ethics and morality.

Reversed and remanded. Appellee will pay all costs incident to this appeal.

HARBISON, JUSTICE, concurred in a separate opinion.

NOTES AND QUESTIONS

1. The statute of limitations is a complete bar to actions that do not meet its time limits. It is in no way dependent on the merits of the case. All states have some statute of limitation, although the time period within which the action must be brought varies in length. For actions sounding in tort, most states impose a two or three-year limitation. Even within each state, there is variation depending on the type of action that is brought. Statutes of limitations in tort law may vary in length, depending upon the basis of liability, the general subject matter of the claim, and the type of interest invaded. In most jurisdictions, the statute of limitations is satisfied by the filing of the complaint, but in a few it is not satisfied until the complaint and summons are served on defendant. See, for example, Sommervold v. Wal-Mart Inc., 709 F.3d 1234 (8th Cir. 2013) (applying South Dakota law) (in South Dakota an action is commenced as to each defendant when the summons is served on him). One of the first points a lawyer ascertains on undertaking a claim is what is the appropriate statute of limitations. Failure to meet its requirements is likely to be malpractice.

2. *Classification of Action for the Purpose of the Statutes of Limitations.* A good deal of judicial prose has been spent in classifying actions for the purpose of the statute of limitations. Is the action based on "intent" or "negligence?" See Spivey v. Battaglia, 258 So.2d 815 (Fla. 1972). Is an action for breach of warranty a matter of tort or contract? See, e.g., Heavner v. Uniroyal, Inc., 118 N.J.Super. 116, 286 A.2d 718 (1972). Does the two-year limitation of the product liability statute or the three-year limitation of the wrongful death statute apply to the action to recover damages for death caused by a defective airbag? Kambury v. DaimlerChrysler Corp., 334 Or. 367, 50 P.3d 1163 (2002) (applying more

specific product liability statute rather than general wrongful death statute). Is negligent conduct ordinary negligence or professional malpractice? J.B. v. Sacred Heart Hosp., 635 So.2d 945 (Fla.1994) (plaintiff contracted AIDS because hospital failed to tell him his brother had AIDS and how to care for him while transporting him to another medical facility; court found failure was ordinary negligence rather than medical malpractice). Cases that have defined the terms "contract," "tort," "intent" or "malpractice" in other legal contexts are not always helpful in solving classification problems involving the statute of limitations. Why?

3. *Accrual.* Most statutes of limitation provide that the time within which to file begins to run when the cause of action "accrues," leaving to the courts to fix that point. Since damage is an essential element of a cause of action based on negligence, most courts have held that the statute begins to run when there has been an actual injury to plaintiff's person or property. In most cases, that is easy to determine and not a subject of dispute between the parties. Some categories of cases have arisen, however, where the date of injury is not easily ascertainable or where the strict application of the time-of-injury rule works an apparent injustice. For example, in the principal case, when did the cause of action accrue? That is, when did "injury" occur? At the time the sterilization surgery was performed negligently or at the time of conception of the baby? See Nunnally v. Artis, 254 Va. 247, 492 S.E.2d 126 (1997) (on facts similar to principal case, court finds injury occurs at conception of baby) and Conner v. Hodges, 157 Idaho 19, 333 P.3d 130 (2014) (accord). Note that logically the court should reach this question first and then decide whether to recognize a discovery rule to toll the running of the statute of limitations.

4. *Continuing Tort.* In some professional malpractice cases, courts have found that the statute of limitations did not begin to run until the course of treatment was complete. See, e.g., Justice v. Natvig, 238 Va. 178, 381 S.E.2d 8 (1989) (surgeon) and Shumsky v. Eisenstein, 96 N.Y.2d 164, 750 N.E.2d 67 (attorney). This is sometimes referred to as a continuing tort. Should this concept be extended to other areas of the law? Plaintiff lived with defendant in an abusive relationship for ten years. The statute of limitations for assault and battery is one year. Plaintiff argues that "battered women's syndrome" prevented her from leaving the relationship. How should the courts treat the statute of limitations issue? Cusseaux v. Pickett, 279 N.J.Super. 335, 652 A.2d 789 (1994) (treating it as a continuing tort for statute of limitations purposes). Feltmeier v. Feltmeier, 207 Ill.2d 263, 278 Ill.Dec. 228, 798 N.E.2d 75 (2003) (alleged acts of domestic violence over eleven years were held to constitute a "continuous series of acts" for statute of limitations purposes).

5. The fact that a latent defect in a building may not manifest itself for years or even decades affects the application of the statute of limitations to builders, architects, and engineers. How long should these professionals be subject to liability? Is it reasonable to begin the running of the statute when the construction of the building is completed and the parties' professional relationship terminated? The client then can inspect the building and determine if the structure is sound. Compare Sosnow v. Paul, 43 A.D.2d 978, 352 N.Y.S.2d 502 (1974) (time of construction), with Malesev v. Board of County Rd. Comm'rs, 51 Mich.App. 511, 215 N.W.2d 598 (1974) (time of discovery). A number of state legislatures have enacted

special statutes of limitations dealing with malpractice by builders, architects, and engineers. See Knapp & Lee, Application of Special Statutes of Limitations Concerning Design and Construction, 23 St. Louis U.L.J. 351 (1979). If these classes of defendants are given special protection without any rational basis, the special statute of limitation may be found to be unconstitutional because it denies equal protection. Kallas Millwork Corp. v. Square D Co., 66 Wis.2d 382, 225 N.W.2d 454 (1975).

6. Problems with the time-of-injury rule also have arisen with regard to negligent acts of other professionals. When should the statute of limitations begin to run with regard to an attorney who has committed an act of malpractice? See Grunwald v. Bronkesh, 131 N.J. 483, 621 A.2d 459 (1993) (limitations period begins to run when the client suffers actual damage and discovers the damage was attributable to the attorney's negligent advice) and Draper v. Brennan, 142 N.H. 780, 713 A.2d 373 (1998) (where attorney commits malpractice in prosecution or defense of claim that results in litigation, statute of limitations on malpractice action is not affected by appeal of adverse ruling). See generally Chapter 22 of Mallen and Smith, Legal Malpractice (2015 ed.).

7. *Tolling.* Statutes of limitation contain within them provisions that toll (stop) the running of the time within which to file for various reasons. The most common of these are provisions that toll the statute for minors, for those legally insane or incompetent, and for those defendants who have concealed their identity through fraud or obstructed the filing of the action. Ordinarily, the tolling stops (clock begins running) when the minor reaches her majority or when the incompetent becomes competent again, for example, upon resuming consciousness after a coma. But what if the incompetence is permanent? In a few jurisdictions, the appointment of a guardian starts the clock of the statute of limitations and others have an outside time limit for filing actions on behalf of incompetent plaintiffs, whether or not they have been restored to competency by that time. In others, the appointment of a guardian does not affect the tolling provision of the statute of limitations because it does not remove the disability. Abels v. Genie Industries, Inc., 202 S.W.3d 99 (Tenn. 2006) (certified question from federal district court) (resolving issue for Tennessee and discussing other jurisdictions). What if, at the scene of an automobile accident, one of the drivers gave the police officer identification stolen from someone else and plaintiff did not discover driver's true identity until after the statute of limitations had run? Newman v. Walker, 270 Va. 291, 618 S.E.2d 336 (Va. 2005) (defendant's misrepresentation of his identity tolled the statute). Georgia's statute of limitations permits tolling for fraud only if the cause of action is itself based on fraud or the plaintiff has been prevented from discovering the defendant's identity by a separate independent actual fraud involving moral turpitude. In the cause of action brought by the estate of a murder victim against man who hired someone to murder her, the court found that murderer's motive was to conceal his identity to avoid apprehension by police, not to commit a fraud on the murder victim. Rai v. Reid, 294 Ga. 270, 751 S.E.2d 821 (2013) (no tolling).

In addition to tolling specified in the statute itself, many jurisdictions recognize equitable (not provided in statute) tolling where, for example, the defendant fraudulently concealed the injury from the plaintiff or concealed his own identity. See, e.g., Lakeman v. La France, 102 N.H. 300, 156 A.2d

123 (1959) (doctor allegedly concealed surgical malpractice from patient) and Bernson v. Browning-Ferris Indus. of Cal., Inc., 30 Cal.Rptr.2d 440, 873 P.2d 613, 7 Cal.4th 926 (1994) (defendants allegedly concealed their identity by anonymously publishing defamatory "dossier" on member of City Council). Such equitable tolling is not available, however, if it is someone other than defendant that concealed the identity of the defendant. Renaud v. Sigma-Aldrich Corp., 662 A.2d 711 (R.I.1995) (worker injured on job by chemical spill claimed that both her employer and the supplier of the chemical misled her as to identity of manufacturer of chemical's container, causing her to miss the statute of limitations in claim against that manufacturer).

Could equitable tolling be used to extend the statute of limitations where the attorney had failed to discover the correct period? "If the lawyer fails in this duty, the remedy is not to punish the defendant by depriving him of the protection of the statute of limitations; it is for the plaintiff to sue the lawyer who misadvised him for legal malpractice." Arteaga v. U.S., 711 F.3d 828 (7th Cir. 2013) (FTCA medical malpractice case).

8. *Discovery Rule.* As the principal case reflects, the time-of-damage rule can lead to difficulty in certain types of actions for medical malpractice. Some legislatures have specifically dealt with the problem and adopted a time-of-discovery rule for medical malpractice cases. See Conn.Gen.Stat., § 52–584 and R.S.Mo., § 516.105. In other jurisdictions, the discovery rule is a creature of the courts. Chase v. Sabin, 445 Mich. 190, 516 N.W.2d 60 (1994) (discovery rule applied to plaintiff who discovered that the loss of his eye, which had occurred 26 years previously after cataract surgery, was caused by negligence of nurse anesthetist) (later modified by statute). Some have limited the application of the time-of-discovery rule to situations where surgeons have left sponges, scalpels, or other objects in the patient's body. (This is referred to in the opinion in principal case as limiting the doctrine to "foreign objects.") They apply the time-of-damage rule to cases of negligent diagnosis or ingestion of a drug or toxic substance. A few states, in adopting a discovery rule, have placed an outside limit on claims. See, e.g., Tenn. Code Ann. § 29–26–116 (one year from discovery or three years from occurrence).

9. The discovery rule, first developed in medical malpractice cases like the principal case, has been extended in many jurisdictions to apply to any action based on a latent injury. See, e.g., Perlov v. G.D. Searle & Co., 621 F.Supp. 1146 (D.Md.1985) ("Although ordinarily that statute begins to run at the time of injury, in this case the Maryland 'discovery rule' should be utilized to determine when the cause of action accrued which is when the statute begins to run. Under this rule, the delayed filing of an action is tolerated for causes of action that are inherently unknowable, so the cause of action accrues only when 'the claimant in fact knew or reasonably should have known of the alleged wrongs.' ") The courts sometimes refer to "should have known" as being placed on inquiry notice. That is, the statute of limitations begins to run when a person gains sufficient knowledge of facts that would put a reasonable person on notice of the existence of a problem or potential problem such that he would inquire further about it. Buechel v. Five Star Quality Care, 745 N.W.2d 732 (Iowa 2008) (family of nursing home resident who was asphyxiated when her head was trapped between mattress and bed frame was on notice that there was a problem with the

bed even though they may not have known the nature of the defect). But see Lo v. Burke, 249 Va. 311, 455 S.E.2d 9 (1995) (Virginia does not recognize discovery rule).

10. The discovery rule itself can be narrow or broad depending on *what* the plaintiff has to discover to trigger the statute. Injury? Griffin v. Unocal Corp., 990 So.2d 291 (Ala. 2008) (abandoning "last exposure" rule and adopting rule that cause of action begins to run when injury is manifest). That the injury was caused by defendant's conduct or product? Brown v. E.I. DuPont de Nemours and Co., Inc., 820 A.2d 362 (Del. 2003) (statute of limitations for children born with birth defects did not begin to run at birth but when scientists first linked their birth defects to prenatal exposure to defendant's chemical) and Arroyo v. U.S., 656 F.3d 663 (7th Cir. 2011) (claim under FTCA based on alleged medical malpractice of clinic employees) (parents told that infant was injured due to bacterial infection contracted during delivery but were not told that clinic employees negligently failed to discover and treat the infection). That the defendant's conduct was negligent or its product defective? What about a child abuse case where the plaintiff only became aware through psychotherapy after becoming an adult that the actions of the defendant were tortious and that those actions caused the plaintiff's emotional problems? Pritzlaff v. Archdiocese of Milwaukee, 194 Wis.2d 302, 533 N.W.2d 780 (1995) (noting that many states recognize a special discovery rule for cases involving incest and other forms of child sexual abuse). Because fixing the time that plaintiff "should have discovered" something usually is dependent on fact finding by the jury, the discovery rule makes it unlikely that the defendant can obtain summary judgment based on the statute of limitations. Tucker v. Baxter Healthcare Corp., 158 F.3d 1046 (9th Cir.1998) (applying California law) (summary judgment precluded because question of fact as to when plaintiff suspected or should have suspected that her breast implants were likely cause of her autoimmune disease) and Clarke v. Abate, 194 Vt. 294, 80 A.3d 578 (2013) (in sex abuse case, jury should have been allowed to weigh inferences from the factual record regarding whether teenage plaintiff understood that defendant surgeon's conduct under guise of medical treatment was wrongful).

11. *Wrongful Death Actions*. See note 15, page 616.

12. *Complications of Injury or Second Disease*. Sometimes, plaintiff will develop a second, more serious injury after initial, less serious symptoms were noted. A patient is told by her doctor that she has pelvic inflammatory disease ("PID") in 1977 and that it probably was caused by an intrauterine device ("IUD"). In 1980, after months of difficulty trying to become pregnant, she is diagnosed as infertile due to the PID. In her case against the manufacturer of the IUD, when did the statute of limitations begin to run? See, e.g., Gnazzo v. G.D. Searle & Co., 973 F.2d 136 (2d Cir.1992) (applying Connecticut law) (statute begins to run when plaintiff discovers some form of actionable harm, not the fullest manifestation thereof); Klempka v. G.D. Searle & Co., 963 F.2d 168 (8th Cir.1992) (applying Minnesota law) (plaintiff who is aware of both her injury and the likely cause of her injury is not permitted to circumvent the statute of limitations by waiting for a more serious injury to develop from the same cause); Kemp v. G.D. Searle & Co., 103 F.3d 405 (5th Cir. 1997) (applying Mississippi law) (infertility is merely a sequela of PID and not a separate

disease). See also Shadle v. Pearce, 287 Pa.Super. 436, 430 A.2d 683 (1981) (dental malpractice cause of action accrued when patient first injured, not two years later when patient developed incapacitating complication); Golla v. General Motors Corp., 167 Ill.2d 353, 212 Ill.Dec. 549, 657 N.E.2d 894 (1995) (cause of action against car manufacturer based on alleged design defect of car seat accrued on day of accident, not a year later when plaintiff was diagnosed with reflex sympathetic dystrophy).

But what if the claimant, pressured by the statute of limitations, files suit, her case is adjudicated and *then* she develops a more serious disease? Traditional claim preclusion principles would bar a second action because a plaintiff is not permitted to split her claim. See, e.g., Gideon v. Johns-Manville Sales Corp., 761 F.2d 1129 (5th Cir.1985) (under Texas law, only one suit may be brought from all injuries caused by asbestos exposure) and Kiser v. A.W. Chesterton Co., 285 Va. 12, 736 S.E.2d 910 (2013) (answering certified question) (same). What if the plaintiff claims that the second injury is a new, separate injury rather than a complication of the first injury? In asbestos cases, a majority of jurisdictions have permitted a second action for cancer where the first disease was a non-malignant disease like asbestosis. See, e.g., Daley v. A.W. Chesterton, Inc., 614 Pa. 335, 37 A.3d 1175 (2012) (plaintiff can recover a second time from same asbestos exposure as long as plaintiff can show that he was later diagnosed with a separate and distinct malignant disease) and Sopha v. Owens-Corning Fiberglas Corp., 230 Wis.2d 212, 601 N.W.2d 627 (1999) (joining majority, but emphasizing this is narrow exception).

Plaintiff, who smoked from 1953 until 1991, was diagnosed with chronic obstructive pulmonary disease in 1989 and with periodontal disease in 1990. Plaintiff knew these conditions were caused by her smoking but did not bring suit for either of these ailments. In 2003, she was diagnosed with lung cancer and filed suit. Was her lawsuit barred by the one-year statute of limitations or is cancer a separate disease under California law? See Pooshs v. Phillip Morris USA, Inc., 51 Cal.4th 788, 123 Cal.Rptr.3d 578, 250 P.3d 181 (2011) (answering certified question) (if plaintiff can establish that lung cancer is separate and distinct disease from other two smoking-related diseases, action for lung cancer is not time barred).

13. *Which State's Law Applies?* Suppose the injury happened in one state but the lawsuit was filed in another. Which state's statute of limitations applies? Choice of law rules in most states provide that the law of the forum (state where the lawsuit is filed) determines the statute of limitations. Most states have "borrowing" rules as part of their statutes of limitations that provide that the forum's law applies unless the other jurisdiction's statute is shorter, in which case that jurisdiction's limitation is borrowed. This prevents states with longer statutes of limitations from having to hear lawsuits for claims that arose in other jurisdictions. See also Standard Fire Ins. Co. v. Ford Motor Co., 723 F.3d 690 (6th Cir. 2013) (applying Michigan choice of law rules) (Tennessee statute of repose applies to bar action filed in Michigan forum by plaintiff who lived in Tennessee based on vehicle fire that occurred in Tennessee against defendant headquartered in Michigan because Tennessee had a substantial interest in having its law applied and Michigan had little or no interest in a Tennessee incident involving a Tennessee resident).

14. *Notice-of-Claim Statutes.* Statutes that provide a limited waiver of sovereign immunity to allow tort claims against governmental entities frequently provide that a notice-of-claim must be made to the appropriate government agency within a particular time frame, in addition to a statute of limitation. The time period for the filing of the notice-of-claim may be very short. See, e.g., D.C. Code § 12–309 (6 months); N.M. Stat. Ann. § 41–4–16(A) (90 days); Va. Code Ann. § 8.01–195.6 (one year). See also Keller v. Tavarone, 262 Neb. 2, 628 N.W.2d 222 (2001) (dismissing medical malpractice claim against physician because he was employed by county hospital and notice-of-claim had not been filed within one year as required by the statute waiving sovereign immunity).

15. *Statutes of Repose.* A statute of limitation limits the time during which a cause of action can be brought. A statute of repose limits potential liability by limiting the time during which a cause of action can arise. Statutes of repose, which are substantive rather than procedural in nature, stem from the equitable concept that a time should arrive when a person is no longer responsible for a past act. Statutes of repose have been enacted primarily in the area of liability for architects and engineers and, more recently, for products liability. For example, Congress has provided an 18-year statute of repose for claims against manufacturers of small airplanes. See discussion of issues in Lyon v. Agusta, 252 F.3d 1078 (9th Cir. 2001) (court upheld summary judgment in cases arising out of 1993 crash of small airplane manufactured in Italy in 1970). Because the statute provides an outside time limit within which the action must commence (for example, 15 years from date of product's sale to consumer), the time period may run even before a person is injured. A few states with statutes of repose have made special exceptions for particular products such as asbestos or diethylstilbestrol (DES) that involve a long latency period between exposure and manifestation of injury.

Some state courts have declared statutes of repose unconstitutional based on equal protection or "open courts" provisions in state constitutions. See, e.g., DeYoung v. Providence Medical Ctr., 136 Wash.2d 136, 960 P.2d 919 (1998) (medical malpractice) and Dickie v. Farmers Union Oil Co., 611 N.W.2d 168 (N.D. 2000) (products liability). Other courts have upheld the statutes. See, e.g., McIntosh v. Melroe Co., 729 N.E.2d 972 (Ind. 2000) (products liability); Groch v. General Motors Corp., 117 Ohio St.3d 192, 883 N.E.2d 377 (2008) (products liability); and Damiano v. McDaniel, 689 So.2d 1059 (Fla.1997) (medical malpractice). Generally, the tolling provisions of the statutes of limitation do not apply to statutes of repose. See, for example, Albrecht v. General Motors Corp., 648 N.W.2d 87 (Iowa 2002) (Iowa's 15-year statute of repose for products liability actions not affected by fact that teenage motorist was a minor); Budler v. General Motors Corp., 268 Neb. 998, 689 N.W.2d 847 (2004) (Nebraska's 10-year statute of repose not affected by fact that claimant was a teenager when he was injured); Penley v. Honda Motor Co., 31 S.W.3d 181 (Tenn. 2000) (Tennessee's 10-year statute of repose for products liability actions not extended by plaintiff's mental incompetency due to pain killers taken during hospitalization after accident); and Simonsen v. Ford Motor Co., 196 Or.App. 460, 102 P.3d 710 (2004) (Oregon's 8-year statute of repose not tolled by plaintiff's disabling mental condition).

3. IMMUNITIES

An immunity differs from a privilege, or justification or excuse, although the difference is largely one of degree. A privilege avoids liability for tortious conduct only under particular circumstances, and because those circumstances make it just and reasonable that the liability should not be imposed. An immunity, on the other hand, avoids liability in tort under all circumstances, within the limits of the immunity itself. It is conferred not because of the particular facts, but because of the status or position or relationship of the favored defendant. It does not deny the tort, but rather the resulting liability. The immunity does not mean that conduct that would amount to a tort on the part of other defendants is not still equally tortious in character, but merely that for the protection of the particular defendant, or of interests that the defendant represents, absolution from liability is granted.

Congress and some state legislatures have created new immunities, often as part of tort reform movements, that were not present at common law. These vary by state and some are very specific, applying in only quite limited circumstances. For example, the federal *Biomaterials Access Assurance Act* created immunity for companies that provide biomaterials that are used to manufacture implantable medical devices. The manufacturer and seller of the device itself may be liable in negligence or strict liability, but the company that provided the raw materials is immune. 21 U.S.C. §§ 1601–1606. See also Mattern v. Biomet, Inc., 2013 WL 1314695 (D.N.J. 2013) (dismissing casting manufacturer whose sole role in the manufacturing process was to shape a raw piece of metal that eventually was incorporated into a hip implant). Congress, through the *Protection of Lawful Commerce in Arms Act*, also provided immunity to gun manufacturers in suits brought by those injured by gun-related criminal actions of others. 15 U.S.C. §§ 7901–7903.

About 24 states have statutes that allow a nonmanufacturer seller to be dismissed from a products liability lawsuit if the seller identifies the product manufacturer, the manufacturer is subject to the court's jurisdiction, and the manufacturer is able to satisfy any judgment. See, for example, N.J.S.A. 2A:58C–9; Rev. Stat. Mo. § 537.762; and Tex. Civ. Prac. & Rem. Code § 82.002. These statutes are sometimes described as "*innocent seller immunity*" provisions. Delaware's sealed container defense accomplishes a similar result although the seller remains subject to discovery as if it were still a party. 18 Del. C. § 7001.

Congress, through the *Coverdell Teacher Protection Act* for states that accept federal funds for particular programs, and some states, provide immunity to teachers. 20 U.S.C. § 6736 and Va. Code Ann. § 8.01–220.1:2.

The Maryland *Reduction of Lead Risk in Housing Act* granted to the owners of certain rental properties, under specified conditions, immunity from personal injury suits based on the plaintiffs' ingestion of lead in paint chips. The immunity provisions of that statute were found to violate the Maryland state constitution and severed from the law. Jackson v. Dackman Co., 422 Md. 357, 30 A.3d 854 (2011).

(A) JUDICIAL PROCEEDINGS

The "absolute privilege" to publish defamation in the course of judicial, legislative, or executive proceedings (pages 974–978) is really an immunity of those engaged in the proceedings, conferred because of the public interest in protecting them from suit. In the judicial context, the immunity is sometimes referred to as a litigation immunity. See, for example, Rabinowitz v. Wahrenberger, 406 N.J.Super. 126, 966 A.2d 1091 (2009) (litigation immunity protects attorney from tort liability for questions asked during deposition that plaintiffs alleged constituted intentional infliction of emotional distress). It may protect judges, attorneys, witnesses, court-appointed guardians ad litem, and court-appointed psychiatrists. See, for example, Muzingo v. St. Luke's Hospital, 518 N.W.2d 776 (Iowa 1994) (court-appointed psychiatrist immune from suit brought by woman injured by bomb planted in her car by her husband who had been examined by psychiatrist pursuant to involuntary commitment proceeding) and Simms v. Seaman, 308 Conn. 523, 69 A.3d 880 (2013) (attorney immune from claims of fraud and intentional infliction of emotional distress brought by former husband of client based on representations made during divorce proceedings). It also protects those who maintain evidence for criminal proceedings. Hoyer v. Utah (Div. of Wildlife Resources), 2009 UT 38, 212 P.3d 547 (2009) (in suit by amateur herpetologist seeking to recover damages for the death of over fifty boa snakes that were seized from his home and died while being held for use as evidence in criminal trial against him, judicial proceedings immunity protected state from tort suit).

(B) EMPLOYER IMMUNITY

Worker Compensation statutes in effect in all jurisdictions provide that employees may recover from their employers for work-related injuries without having to show any fault on the part of the employer. This alternative compensation system is described in more detail in Chapter 24, Compensation Systems as Substitutes for Tort Law. It is a complex area. The one aspect that is critical at this juncture is that because the statutes provide an alternative to the tort system, they confer immunity from tort liability on the employer and co-employees. Thus, under most circumstances, an employee who is injured on the job cannot file a tort claim against his employer or co-employees even if they were negligent.

(C) FAMILIES

Freehe v. Freehe

Supreme Court of Washington, 1972.
81 Wash.2d 183, 500 P.2d 771.

NEILL, ASSOCIATE JUSTICE. Plaintiff, Clifford Freehe, seeks compensation for personal injuries allegedly sustained due to defendant's negligent maintenance of a tractor and failure to warn plaintiff of the tractor's unsafe condition. The claim for relief would be just the normal action in tort for personal injury but for the fact that the defendant is the wife of the plaintiff, thus bringing into issue the doctrine of interspousal tort immunity.

The farm on which the accident took place is the separate property of defendant, doing business under the name of Hazel Knoblauch. The tractor involved in this accident, together with all other assets and income of the farm, were and remain the separate property of defendant. The business of the farm is carried on separately from any community business of the parties. Plaintiff has no interest in the farming operation. Neither was he employed by defendant.

The trial court granted defendant's motion for summary judgment solely on the basis of interspousal tort immunity. Plaintiff appeals. * * *

The rule of interspousal immunity or disability is of common law origin, court made and court preserved. * * * Our cases have referred to the historical arguments supporting the common law disability. One is the "supposed unity of husband and wife." [Cc]

The "supposed unity" of husband and wife * * * is not a reference to the common nature or loving oneness achieved in a marriage of two free individuals. Rather, this traditional premise had reference to a situation, coming on from antiquity, in which a woman's marriage for most purposes rendered her a chattel of her husband. * * *

The husband acquired the right to possession and use of his wife's real and personal property, and he was entitled to all of her choses in action, provided that he 'reduced them to possession' during marriage by some act by which he appropriated them to himself, such as collecting the money or obtaining judgment in a suit in his own name. In turn he became liable for the torts of his wife, committed either before or during the marriage." (footnotes omitted) W.L. Prosser, Torts ch. 23, § 122 (4th ed. 1971) at 859–60. At old common law, with the husband entitled to the chose in action for his own torts and liable to himself for his wife's torts against him, the rule of interspousal disability made sense.

Things have changed. * * * Neither spouse is liable for the separate debts of the other. RCW 26.16.200. * * * [E]ither spouse may sue the other for invasion of separate property rights. RCW 26.16.180. [Cc] Spouses are no longer individually liable for each other's torts unless they would be jointly liable if unmarried.

Modern realities do not comport with the traditional "supposed unity" of husband and wife. In our view, this concept of legal identity is no longer a valid premise for a rule of this interspousal disability.

A second major reason given for the disability is the notion that to allow a married person to sue his or her spouse for tort damages would be to destroy the peace and tranquility of the home. On reflection, we are convinced that this is a conclusion without basis. If a state of peace and tranquility exists between the spouses, then the situation is such that either no action will be commenced or that the spouses—who are, after all, the best guardians of their own peace and tranquility—will allow the action to continue only so long as their personal harmony is not jeopardized. If peace and tranquility is nonexistent or tenuous to begin with, then the law's imposition of a technical disability seems more likely to be a bone of contention than a harmonizing factor. * * *

A third reason advanced in support of maintaining the common law rule of disability is the suggestion that the injured spouse has an adequate remedy through the criminal and divorce laws. It has been observed that neither of these alternatives actually compensates for the damage done, or provides any remedy for nonintentional (negligent) torts. Prosser, supra, at pages 862–63. * * * To these reflections we add the observation that limiting the injured party to a divorce or criminal action against his or her tort-feasor spouse is quite inconsistent with any policy of preserving domestic tranquility. Thus, the argument based on suggested legal alternatives simply does not withstand analysis.

It has also been argued that to permit litigation between spouses over personal torts would flood the courts with a burdensome amount of trivial matrimonial disputes. * * * [T]his theoretical problem has not materialized elsewhere. Furthermore, should the courts find this possibility to be materializing, there is nothing to prevent application of established notions of "consent" or "assumption of risk" to minor annoyances associated with the ordinary frictions of wedlock. [C]

Respondent also suggests that another argument in favor of the disability rule is that to permit suits between spouses would encourage collusion and fraud where one or both of the spouses carries liability insurance. * * * In * * * Borst v. Borst, 41 Wash.2d at page 653, 251 P.2d at page 155, we stated:

"The courts may and should take cognizance of fraud and collusion when found to exist in a particular case. However, the fact that there may be greater opportunity for fraud or collusion in one class of cases than another does not warrant courts of law in closing the door to all cases of that class. Courts must depend upon the efficacy of the judicial processes to ferret out the meritorious from the fraudulent in particular cases. [C] If those processes prove inadequate, the problem becomes one for the legislature. [C] Courts will not immunize tort feasors from liability in a whole class of cases because of the possibility of fraud, but will depend upon the legislature to deal with the problem as a question of public policy."

We there cited, as an example of the ability of the legislature to cope with such a problem should it arise, the enactment of host-guest statutes (RCW 46.08.080, –.085, –.086) in automobile personal injury cases. We conclude that this possibility is not a valid premise for the common law disability rule.

Respondent also suggests that any change in the marital disability rule is a matter for the legislature * * * This argument ignores the fact that the rule is not one made or sanctioned by the legislature, but rather is one that depends for its origins and continued viability upon the common law. * * *

[The court then decided that the state's community property laws imposed no barrier to abandoning interspousal immunity.]

We are cognizant of the long standing nature of the common law rule of interspousal tort immunity. But we find more impelling the fundamental precept that, absent express statutory provision, or compelling public policy, the law should not immunize tort-feasors or deny remedy to their victims. With this in mind, we have reviewed the stated reasons for the common law rule, and have found all of them to be insufficient. Therefore, the rule of interspousal disability in personal injury cases is hereby abandoned. * * *

Reversed and remanded.

NOTES AND QUESTIONS

1. *General Abrogation.* The movement toward complete abrogation of interspousal immunity began with a dissenting opinion of the first Justice Harlan in Thompson v. Thompson, 218 U.S. 611 (1910). It is now the majority rule. Bozman v. Bozman, 376 Md. 461, 830 A.2d 450 (2003) (abrogating doctrine and noting that only a handful of states retain it) and Ellis v. Ellis, 169 P.3d 441 (Utah 2007) (abolishing doctrine for negligence claims in case where newlywed husband's negligent driving on honeymoon seriously injured wife). See generally Restatement (Second) of Torts § 895F.

2. Some decisions that have taken this step have placed heavy reliance on the state's married women's property act. See, e.g., Gilman v. Gilman, 78 N.H. 4, 95 A. 657 (1915); Fitzmaurice v. Fitzmaurice, 62 N.D. 191, 242 N.W. 526 (1932). These statutes, enacted in the mid-1800's, abrogated the common law disabilities of wives to sue or be sued in their own name and to buy, own, or sell property. Other decisions have construed the statutes as having no intent to affect interspousal immunity. See, e.g., Oken v. Oken, 44 R.I. 291, 117 A. 357 (1922). These latter decisions may be correct in measuring legislative intent. As the principal case reflects, arguments made in support of interspousal tort immunity are not necessarily related to legal restrictions on the rights of women.

3. *Partial Abrogation.* Most of the courts that still recognize the immunity have limited it. They refuse to apply it in one or more specific situations where they are certain that no good reason supports it.

A. After divorce or marital dissolution, spouses are permitted a claim for torts that occurred prior to and, in some jurisdictions, during the marriage. See, e.g., Gaston v. Pittman, 224 So.2d 326 (Fla.1969) (prior); Sanchez v. Olivarez, 94 N.J.Super. 61, 226 A.2d 752 (1967) (during). Claims also are permitted if either spouse is dead at the time the action is brought. Asplin v. Amica Mut. Ins. Co., 121 R.I. 51, 394 A.2d 1353 (1978).

B. When the tort occurred prior to the marriage, some states allow the claim. See, e.g., Childress v. Childress, 569 S.W.2d 816 (Tenn.1978); Berry v. Harmon, 329 S.W.2d 784 (Mo.1959). The reason given for allowing the claim is that the spouse should not lose a property right because of entering into a marriage.

C. When the tort is an intentional one such as battery, assault, or false imprisonment, most states allow the claim. See Lusby v. Lusby, 283 Md. 334, 390 A.2d 77 (1978) (husband and two accomplices forced wife's car off road by threatening her with rifle, kidnapped her, raped her, and threatened to kill her if she told anyone); McCulloh v. Drake, 24 P.3d 1162 (Wyo. 2001) (recognizing cause of action for intentional infliction of emotional distress during marriage).

4. The facts of the principal case are somewhat unusual as compared with most tort suits between spouses. The overwhelming majority of these cases have involved automobile accidents, and a number of courts have

expressly limited their elimination of the immunity in negligence actions to those situations. See Digby v. Digby, 120 R.I. 299, 388 A.2d 1 (1978); Richard v. Richard, 131 Vt. 98, 300 A.2d 637 (1973).

5. Suppose a wife sues her husband in tort for the injury she suffered because he prepared her food in a careless and unsanitary manner. Does she have a claim? Suppose the husband alleges that he suffered serious injury because his wife was negligent in leaving her shoes where he tripped on them? Would he then have a claim? In Beaudette v. Frana, 285 Minn. 366, 173 N.W.2d 416 (1969), the Supreme Court of Minnesota abolished interspousal immunity, but it also observed in dictum that: "There is an intimate sharing of contact within the marriage relationship, both intentional and unintentional, that is uniquely unlike the exposure among strangers. The risks of intentional contact in marriage are such that one spouse should not recover damages from the other without substantial evidence that the injurious contact was plainly excessive or a gross abuse of normal privilege. The risks of negligent conduct are likewise so usual that it would be an unusual case in which the trial court would not instruct the jury as to the injured spouse's peculiar assumption of risk." What if the husband alleges that the wife infected him with a sexually transmitted disease? Does the outcome depend on whether the conduct was intentional or negligent?

Zellmer v. Zellmer

Supreme Court of Washington, 2008.
164 Wash.2d 147, 188 P.3d 497.

MADSEN, J. * * * [Three-year-old Ashley McLellan drowned in a backyard swimming pool while under the supervision of her stepfather, Joel Zellmer. Ashley and her mother had moved into Zellmer's house three months before when Zellmer and her mother married. Ordinarily, Ashley went to day care while her mother worked, but on the day of the accident Ashley stayed home sick and Zellmer agreed to take care of her. According to Zellmer, he started a video for Ashley in her bedroom and then went downstairs to build a fire. About an hour later, he realized she was no longer in her room and saw that the sliding glass door leading to the backyard was open. He found Ashley floating in the swimming pool, pulled her out, and called 911. The paramedics resuscitated Ashley, but she died in the hospital two days later. Ashley's mother and father sued Zellmer for wrongful death, alleging several causes of action, including negligent supervision.

Zellmer moved for summary judgment, claiming that the parental immunity doctrine shielded him from liability for negligence in connection with Ashley's death because he stood *in loco parentis* to Ashley, having provided her with financial and emotional support, including housing, meals, and day care. In opposition to the summary judgment motion, Ashley's mother disputed Zellmer's characterization of his relationship with Ashley, denied that Zellmer supported Ashley financially (he was unemployed throughout their marriage), and asserted that she did not allow him to discipline Ashley because she did not think he knew Ashley well enough to do so.

The trial court granted summary judgment, concluding Zellmer necessarily stood *in loco parentis* to Ashley by virtue of assuming the status of stepparent: "when there is a marriage ceremony and there is a blended family and someone becomes a stepparent that the doctrine of parental immunity applies, and there does not have to be a finding of *in loco parentis*." Affirming the summary judgment, the Court of Appeals held that a stepparent is shielded by parental immunity from liability for negligent supervision of the child only if obligated to financially support a stepchild under the family support statute, an obligation that generally arises when a stepparent is married to the child's primary residential parent and lives in the same household with the child. Ashley's parents appealed to the Supreme Court of Washington.]

* * * In its original form, the parental immunity doctrine operated as a nearly absolute bar to suit by a child for personal injuries caused by a parent, no matter how wrongful the parent's conduct. [Cc] The parental immunity doctrine originated in three decisions near the turn of the last century and was quickly adopted by most states. [C] From its inception, however, the doctrine has been subject to extensive critical commentary. Like other courts, this court has disavowed several of the original rationales underlying the doctrine, while sharply limiting its scope. Today, no jurisdiction recognizes the original formulation of the common law parental immunity doctrine, and we need not repeat our reasons for retreating from it. [Cc]

The evolution of the parental immunity doctrine in Washington is consistent with the national trend. Washington was one of the first states to recognize the parental immunity doctrine. [C] However, this court has exercised its continuing duty to determine whether the doctrine remains supported by reason and common sense in view of changing social realities, and to modify it as necessary. [C] Like other jurisdictions, this court has substantially limited the scope of parental immunity in accordance with changing views of public policy on the family relation. A parent is not immune when acting outside his or her parental capacity. [Cc] For example, when operating a business or driving a car, a parent owes a child the same duty of reasonable care applicable to the world at large, and may be held liable notwithstanding the parent/child relationship. Even when acting in a parental capacity, a parent who abdicates his or her parental responsibilities by engaging in willful or wanton misconduct is not immune from suit.[2] [Cc]

But this court has consistently held a parent is not liable for ordinary negligence in the performance of parental responsibilities. * * * [The court here lists cases where parents allowed child to wander free in neighborhood and child was electrocuted at utility power station; where parent started backyard fire then left three-year-old son unattended, resulting in severe burns; where parents allowed sight-impaired child to ride motorbike, resulting in fatal crash; where divorced parent negligently injured children while transporting them home from a scheduled visitation; where parent instructed son to siphon gas, resulting in burn injuries; where parent failed to prevent

[2] "Willful" requires a showing of actual intent to harm, while "wanton" infers such intent from reckless conduct. [Cc]

child from wandering into neighbor's yard where she was burned by trash fire.]

There are two principal routes by which courts have concluded that children may not sue their parents for negligent supervision. Under the approach first articulated by the Wisconsin Supreme Court, courts recognize a limited form of parental immunity for personal injuries resulting from the negligent exercise of parental authority and ordinary parental discretion. *Goller v. White*, 20 Wis.2d 402, 122 N.W.2d 193 (1963). The American Law Institute subsequently approved *Goller,* although the approach codified in the *Restatement* is grounded in a concept of parental privilege rather than immunity. See Restatement (Second) of Torts § 895g (1979). Under the *Restatement,* "the proper inquiry concerns the tortious or privileged nature of a parent's act that causes injury to the child, not a special parental immunity from a child's action for personal torts as distinct from other kinds of claims." [C] Parents are not immune from suit by virtue of the parent/child relationship. The *Restatement* recognizes that in the course of exercising parental discipline and parental discretion, parents may be privileged to act in a manner that would be deemed tortious if directed at a stranger. [C]

States that either abolished the parental immunity doctrine or declined to adopt it in the first instance nonetheless have followed the *Restatement,* disallowing negligent supervision claims based on the concept of a parental privilege. [Cc]

There now appears to be nearly universal consensus that children may sue their parents for personal injuries caused by intentionally wrongful conduct. [Cc] However, the overwhelming majority of jurisdictions hold parents are not liable for negligent supervision of their child, whether stated in terms of a limited parental immunity (among jurisdictions that have partially abrogated the parental immunity doctrine), parental privilege (among those that either abolished the immunity doctrine outright or declined to adopt it in the first instance), or lack of an actionable parental duty to supervise. [Cc]

A minority of states have followed the lead of the California Supreme Court, allowing children to sue parents for negligent supervision under a "reasonable parent" standard. * * *

In a trio of cases decided in 1986, we "reaffirmed the vitality of the doctrine of parental immunity with respect to assertions of negligent supervision." [Cc] We expressly rejected the "reasonable parent" standard and concluded the better approach was to continue to recognize a limited form of parental immunity in cases of ordinary negligence when a parent is acting in a parental capacity. In explaining our decision, we stated: "Parents should be free to determine how the physical, moral, emotional, and intellectual growth of their children can best be promoted." [C] Parents should not routinely have to defend their child-rearing practices where their behavior does not rise to the level of wanton misconduct. There is no correct formula for how much supervision a child should receive at a given age.

The petitioners offer no persuasive arguments for overruling [the 1986 cases] [Cc]. Instead, they direct much of their criticism at long-discarded rationales underlying the original form of the parental immunity doctrine. . . . [T]he primary objective of the modern parental immunity doctrine is to avoid undue judicial interference with the exercise of parental discipline and parental discretion. This rationale remains as vital today as it was in 1986. Parents have a right to raise their children without undue state interference. [Cc]

The petitioners argue the parental immunity doctrine is inconsistent with our abolition of interspousal tort immunity. *See Freehe v. Freehe,* 81 Wash.2d 183, 500 P.2d 771 (1972), [c]. The concurrence/dissent similarly points to the erosion of judicial support for tort immunity as a basis for declining to extend the parental immunity doctrine to stepparents. [C] Unlike in the case of interspousal tort immunity, however, an important public policy interest continues to justify a limited form of parental immunity. * * * Even those states [like California and Minnesota] that have adopted the "reasonable parent" standard recognize that holding parents liable for ordinary negligence in connection with the discharge of parental duties threatens to unduly interfere with the parent/child relationship. [Cc]

The reasonable parent standard does not adequately protect against undue judicial interference in the parent/child relationship. First, it should be noted that substituting "parent" for "person" is of little consequence, as a judge or jury always is required to consider the status of the actor in applying the reasonable person standard in a negligence case. Thus, the "reasonable parent" standard is, in fact, the ordinary negligence standard. Subjecting parents to liability for negligent supervision inevitably allows judges and juries to supplant their own views for the parent's individual child-rearing philosophy.

Thus, we continue to agree with those jurisdictions that have declined to permit an action for negligent parental supervision, as it accords too little respect for family autonomy and parental discretion. [Cc] We adhere to the parental immunity doctrine as it relates to claims of negligent parental supervision. We reaffirm our holding in [the 1986 case] that parents are immune from suit for negligent parental supervision, but not for willful or wanton misconduct in supervising a child. * * *

[The court declined to make an exception for cases where the alleged negligence results in a child's death because, even though the relationship is no longer there to protect, the potential tort liability would have a chilling effect on a parent's exercise of parental discipline and parental discretion.]

Next, petitioners argue it would be inappropriate to extend the parental immunity doctrine to stepparents in view of the modern trend to limit or abolish it.

Notwithstanding the limitations courts have placed on the scope of conduct shielded by the parental immunity doctrine, a majority of states addressing the issue hold it applies to stepparents who stand *in loco parentis* to the same extent as to legal parents. [Cc]

Authority to the contrary exists only in jurisdictions where stepparents either have no legal obligation to support a child, [c] or where parental immunity otherwise bars suit in the case of motor vehicle torts[4] * * *.

No court has allowed a stepparent to claim parental immunity solely by virtue of his or her marriage to the injured child's biological parent. [C] This is consistent with the common law rule that a stepparent gains no parental rights and assumes no obligations merely by reason of the relationship. [C] On the other hand, a stepparent standing *in loco parentis* has a common law duty to support and educate a child to the same extent as does a natural parent. [C]

* * *

[The court then found that taking into account the short duration of the relationship, and viewing the facts in the light most favorable to the nonmoving party, a genuine issue of material fact exists as to whether Zellmer stood *in loco parentis* to Ashley, making summary judgment improper.] Thus, we reverse the summary judgment order and remand for further proceedings consistent with this opinion.

[The dissenting and concurring opinion is omitted. The three justices who signed that opinion would have limited parental immunity to birth or adoptive parents and not extended it to stepparents.]

NOTES AND QUESTIONS

1. Unlike the interspousal immunity doctrine, which was part of the common law of England, the immunity between parent and child is a homegrown product. In Hewllette v. George, 68 Miss. 703, 9 So. 885 (1891), the court applied the doctrine to bar a minor daughter's claim for false imprisonment against her mother, whom she alleged had wrongfully committed her to an insane asylum. Other states soon adopted the rule, applying it to actions for negligence as well as intentional torts. See, e.g., Mesite v. Kirchstein, 109 Conn. 77, 145 A. 753 (1929) (action against father for negligent driving); Roller v. Roller, 37 Wash. 242, 79 P. 788 (1905) (15-year-old girl attempting to bring a tort claim against her father for rape). The fact that the doctrine was not announced by any of the writers of common law did not seem to trouble courts because "it was unmistakably and indelibly carved upon the tablets of Mount Sinai." Small v. Morrison, 185 N.C. 577, 585–86, 118 S.E. 12, 16 (1923). Seven jurisdictions never recognized the immunity: District of Columbia, Hawaii, Nevada, North Dakota, South Dakota, Utah, and Vermont. See Herzfeld v. Herzfeld, 781 So.2d 1070 (Fla. 2001) (collecting cases).

2. *General Abrogation.* Abolition of the parent-child immunity has lagged behind the abolition of interspousal immunity. Only about a dozen jurisdictions have abandoned it completely. See, for example, Gibson v. Gibson, 3 Cal.3d 914, 479 P.2d 648, 92 Cal.Rptr. 288 (1971); Anderson v. Stream, 295 N.W.2d 595 (Minn.1980); and Broadbent v. Broadbent, 184

[4] Most jurisdictions abrogated parental immunity in the case of motor vehicle torts, reasoning that mandatory automobile liability insurance renders it unnecessary to bar suit in order to preserve family finances or family harmony. *See Warren* [*v. Warren*], 336 Md. at 622 n. 1, 650 A.2d 252 [(1994)] (noting only eight states continue to apply the parental immunity doctrine in cases of motor vehicle torts).

Ariz. 74, 907 P.2d 43 (1995) (discussed in the principal case) (all abolishing parental immunity and adopting reasonable and prudent parent standard).

3. *Partial Abrogation.* As in the case of interspousal immunity and as in the principal case, most states developed one or more exceptions to the general rule when they believed that the policies supporting it were inapplicable or were outweighed by the benefit of allowing a tort claim. Some of the more common exceptions include

A. When the action is for personal injury inflicted intentionally, or is "willful" or "wanton." The usual explanation has been that that conduct is so foreign to the relation as to take the case out of it. Henderson v. Woolley, 230 Conn. 472, 644 A.2d 1303 (1994) (answering certified question from federal court) (immunity doctrine does not bar action for sexual abuse, sexual assault, or sexual exploitation); Herzfeld v. Herzfeld, 781 So.2d 1070 (Fla. 2001) (accord); Eagan v. Calhoun, 347 Md. 72, 698 A.2d 1097 (1997) (parent-child immunity does not apply in case where children filed wrongful death action against father who had committed voluntary manslaughter of mother); and Newman v. Cole, 872 So.2d 138 (Ala. 2003) (wrongful death action permitted to proceed against father whose sixteen-year-old son died as a result of father's disciplining him for failure to perform household chores; intentional conduct must be proved by clear and convincing evidence).

B. When the relationship has been terminated before suit by the death of the parent or child or both. MFA Mut. Ins. Co. v. Howard Constr. Co., 608 S.W.2d 535 (Mo.App.1980). This includes action for the wrongful death of the child through the negligence of the parent. Mosier v. Carney, 376 Mich. 532, 138 N.W.2d 343 (1965). But see the principal case, declining to do so.

C. When the child has been legally emancipated. Fitzgerald v. Valdez, 77 N.M. 769, 427 P.2d 655 (1967) and Carricato v. Carricato, 384 S.W.2d 85 (Ky.1964). There is a good discussion of what constitutes emancipation in Gillikin v. Burbage, 263 N.C. 317, 139 S.E.2d 753 (1965) and Small v. Rockfeld, 66 N.J. 231, 330 A.2d 335 (1974).

D. When the defendant is a stepparent who has not adopted the child. Compare Rayburn v. Moore, 241 So.2d 675 (Miss. 1970) and Warren v. Warren, 336 Md. 618, 650 A.2d 252 (Md. 1994) (both refusing to extend immunity to stepparent even though he had provided financial support and treated child in same manner as his own children) with Lyles v. Jackson, 216 Va. 797, 223 S.E.2d 873 (1976) (stepparent protected by immunity if he stands *in loco parentis* to children) and the principal case (same; determination of whether stepfather was *in loco parentis* was a question of fact to be determined by the jury).

E. Many jurisdictions have abolished the immunity in the context of automobile accident cases, where the relationship is coincidental to the conduct. See, e.g., Broadwell v. Holmes, 871 S.W.2d 471 (Tenn.1994) (in context of automobile accident case, court limited parental immunity to conduct that constitutes the exercise of parental authority, the performance of parental supervision, and the provision of parental care and custody.).

4. *Liability Insurance.* The existence or availability of liability insurance has served as an important justification for the abolishment of the parent-child immunity. Nevertheless, some courts have been steadfast

in holding that the existence of insurance cannot "create liability or reduce the need for the immunity." See Maxey v. Sauls, 242 S.C. 247, 130 S.E.2d 570 (1963) and Squeglia v. Squeglia, 234 Conn. 259, 661 A.2d 1007 (1995) (plaintiff's reliance on the existence of liability insurance as a basis for discarding the doctrine is misplaced both as a matter of law and public policy). A few courts have even turned the insurance argument against the plaintiff and have said that its existence is a reason to uphold the immunity because it creates an opportunity for fraud and collusion against the insurance company. The insurance company does receive some protection against this possibility from the "failure to cooperate" clause that appears in the standard liability insurance policy. At least one court has abolished the immunity in negligence cases to the extent that the parent is protected by liability insurance. See Williams v. Williams, 369 A.2d 669 (Del.1976).

5. *Beyond Immunity: What Standard?* Once an immunity is abolished courts face novel questions regarding the extent of the duty owed by a brand new class of defendants. If the parent is alleged to have negligently injured the child while operating an automobile, the standard is what the reasonable driver would have done under the circumstances. But what if the allegation, like the ones in the principal case, is for negligent supervision of the child? See, for example, Poole v. Poole, 299 Mont. 435, 1 P.3d 936 (2000) (failure to act as reasonable parent supervising 11-year-old by allowing him to go to friend's house without ascertaining whether adult was present at other home). What is the standard? The reasonable person? The reasonable parent? Is there a difference? See e.g., Hartman v. Hartman, 821 S.W.2d 852 (Mo.1991) (parents not required to meet an idealized standard). For a good discussion of the issues and other factual examples, see Holodook v. Spencer, 36 N.Y.2d 35, 324 N.E.2d 338, 364 N.Y.S.2d 859 (1974) ("parents have always had the right to determine how much independence, supervision and control a child should have, and to best judge the character and extent of development of their child"); Shoemake v. Fogel, Ltd., 826 S.W.2d 933 (Tex.1992) ("The discharge of parental responsibilities, such as the provision of a home, food and schooling, entails countless matters of personal, private choice. In the absence of culpability beyond ordinary negligence, those choices are not subject to review in court."); Crotta v. Home Depot, Inc., 249 Conn. 634, 732 A.2d 767 (1999) ("Also, different cultural, educational and financial conditions affect the manner in which different parents supervise their children. Allowing a cause of action for negligent supervision would enable others, ignorant of a case's peculiar familial distinctions and bereft of any standards, to second-guess a parent's management of family affairs. . . ."); and Squeglia v. Squeglia, 234 Conn. 259, 661 A.2d 1007 (1995) ("The decision to maintain a dog in the home is an example of parental discretion, and permitting a minor child to be exposed to the dog is within the parental supervisory function. This maintenance of the home environment typifies the day-to-day exercise of parental discretion that the state would rather not disrupt."). What result if the child alleges that he suffered emotional harm because the parent failed to perform general parental duties? See Burnette v. Wahl, 284 Or. 705, 588 P.2d 1105 (1978) and at page 1215. Is this a matter that should be addressed by tort law?

6. *Parent Sues Minor Child.* What if it is the parent who sues the child? Should the parent child immunity protect the child? Most courts that

have considered the issue have found that because the underlying policy reasons would apply equally to such a case, immunity, to the extent recognized and including whatever exceptions have been recognized, should be reciprocal. See Ales v. Ales, 650 So.2d 482 (Miss.1995) (collecting cases) and Bentley v. Bentley, 172 S.W.3d 375 (Ky. 2005) (noting that parent v. child cases are far rarer but finding that the policy considerations would impact them in the same way).

7. *brothers & sisters*: Generally, courts have not recognized immunity between siblings. Lickteig v. Kolar, 782 N.W.2d 810 (Minn. 2010) (answering certified question from federal court) (noting no other jurisdiction has done so, court declines to apply doctrine of intrafamilial immunity to siblings).

8. *Contribution or Indemnity or Fault Allocation Against Parent.* Remember that the immunity also would protect the parent from actions by other tortfeasors sued by the child. See note 1, page 413. Many of the opinions addressing challenges to parental immunity come from claims of joint tortfeasors seeking contribution from parents rather than from children seeking compensation from parents. See, for example, Landis v. Hearthmark, LLC, 232 W.Va. 64, 750 S.E.2d 280 (W.Va. 2013) (answering certified questions). Seven-year-old plaintiff was seriously burned while trying to light a fire in fireplace using fire starter gel. He filed suit against the sellers of the product who in turn sought to have the conduct of his parents considered by the jury. Parents were upstairs and mother had given child permission to roast a marshmallow in the fireplace. The fire starter gel, which was for use in starting fires in wood pellet stoves, contained the directions to store it away from heat and flame and to "keep out of reach of children." The gel bottle was on a stand next to the fireplace and within plaintiff's reach. The Court held that the parental immunity doctrine precluded the product sellers from seeking contribution from the parents, but allowed them to present evidence of parents' conduct to argue comparative negligence, product misuse, and intervening cause.

(D) CHARITIES

Abernathy v. Sisters of St. Mary's

Supreme Court of Missouri, 1969.
446 S.W.2d 599.

HENLEY, CHIEF JUSTICE. This is an action by a patient against a hospital for $35,000 damages for personal injuries allegedly suffered as a result of negligence of defendant. Defendant moved for summary judgment, alleging that it is, and operates the hospital as, a benevolent, religious, nonprofit corporation and charitable institution and, therefore, is immune from liability for its torts. The motion was sustained, judgment was entered for defendant, and plaintiff appealed.

[Plaintiff alleged that defendant's employee negligently failed to assist him as he moved from his bed to the bathroom. Plaintiff fell and suffered multiple injuries.]

The doctrine of immunity of charitable institutions from liability for tort was adopted in this state in 1907 by a decision of the Kansas

City Court of Appeals in Adams v. University Hospital, 122 Mo.App. 675, 99 S.W. 453. * * *

[T]he court said, in effect, that it is better that the individual suffer injury without compensation from the negligent charitable institution than to risk the judicially assumed probability that the public and state would be deprived of the benefits of the charity; that the interest of the latter is so supreme that the former must be sacrificed to it. * * *

There can be no doubt that at the time of its adoption the exception was a rule of expediency justifiable then, and for some time thereafter, to encourage and protect charity as vital to the growth and development of the state, but the reasons for the exception to the rule do not exist today. * * * "Today charity is big business. It often is corporate both in the identity of the donor and in the identity of the donee who administers the charity. Tax deductions sometimes make it actually profitable for donors to give to charity. Organized corporate charity takes over large areas of social activity which otherwise would have to be handled by government, or even by private business. Charity today is a large-scale operation with salaries, costs and other expenses similar to business generally. It makes sense to say that this kind of charity should pay its own way, not only as to its office expenses but as to the expense of insurance to pay for torts as well." [C] Today public liability insurance is available to charitable institutions to indemnify them against losses by way of damages for their negligence, and it is common knowledge that most charitable institutions carry such insurance and pay the premiums thereon as a part of their normal cost of operation.[12] In the states where immunity has not been accorded charity, experience has shown that the apprehension expressed here and elsewhere that the purses of donors would be closed and the funds of charity depleted if these institutions were not granted immunity was not well founded. In the quarter century since the doctrine began its decline, there has been no indication in the states which have abolished immunity that its withdrawal has discouraged donations or that the funds of these institutions have been depleted resulting in their demise. * * *

The public is doubtless still interested in the maintenance of charitable institutions and we acknowledge society's debt to them and recognize their right to every benefit and assistance which the law can justly allow. But the day has arrived when these institutions must acknowledge the injustice of denying compensation to a person injured as a result of their negligence or the negligence of their agents or employees; when they must acknowledge that all persons, organizations and corporations stand equal before the law and must be bound or excused alike. They must recognize that " * * * immunity fosters neglect and breeds irresponsibility, while liability promotes care and caution * * *."

---

12 We do not make the existence of liability insurance the criterion of liability, as some states have done; we merely emphasize its availability and widespread use as a fact and circumstance that did not exist when the doctrine was adopted. We have held that the existence of liability insurance is immaterial on the issue of liability and adhere to that decision. * * *

[The court then discussed two of the principal arguments utilized to support charitable immunity—the "implied waiver" and "trust fund" theories.]

The theory of "implied waiver," namely, that he who accepts the benefit of charity impliedly agrees he will not assert against the institution any right of recourse for wrong done him is a mere fiction. The fiction is based upon impossibility in many instances. It is impossible to say that a conscious or unconscious grievously injured accident victim carried to the emergency room of a charitable hospital, or an ill person received at such hospital unconscious, or a conscious ill person who enters such hospital by arrangement of others waives his rights by accepting its benefits. To say that an insane person, a minor or babe in arms waives his rights when he receives or there is administered to him the benefits of *any* charitable institution does violence to the facts; such persons have no legal capacity to will away their rights. The waiver theory obviously cannot be applied alike to all persons and this fact points up the fallacy in relying upon it to support immunity as a rule of public policy.

The "trust fund" theory as support for the doctrine of immunity rests on an illogical, and therefore weak, foundation. The essence of the theory is that the institutions' funds, given and held for charitable purposes, cannot be used to *pay* judgments resulting from tort claims. Thus, the rationale of the theory is identified solely with the right to *satisfaction* of a judgment, rather than to the fundamental question of whether an injured person has a right to maintain an action and secure a judgment. If it is reasonable to say, and it is, that the existence of liability insurance does not create liability where none exists, then it is also reasonable to say that the inability to have satisfaction of a judgment does not create or support exemption from liability where exemption does not otherwise exist. * * *

Defendant and amici curiae recognize that the court has the authority to abolish or modify the doctrine of charitable immunity, but insist the doctrine as public policy is so deeply and firmly embedded in our law that if it is to be modified or abolished the change should be made by the legislature rather than the court.

It is neither realistic nor consistent with the common law tradition to wait upon the legislature to correct an outmoded rule of case law. Nor is legislative silence as instructive or persuasive. * * *

For the reasons stated, we hold that a nongovernmental charitable institution is liable for its own negligence and for the negligence of its agents and employees acting within the scope of their employment.

Having abolished the doctrine of charitable immunity, it remains for us to determine the point of departure from precedent. We are cognizant of the fact that retrospective application of our decision could result in great hardship to those institutions which have relied on our prior decisions upholding the doctrine of charitable immunity. Therefore, feeling that justice will best be served by prospective application of the decision announced today, we hold that the new rule shall apply to this case and to all future causes of action arising after November 10, 1969, the date of the filing of this opinion.

The judgment is reversed and the cause remanded for further proceedings.

DONNELLY, J., concurs in result in separate concurring opinion filed.

NOTES AND QUESTIONS

1. Charitable immunity originated in England in 1846 in Feoffees of Heriot's Hospital v. Ross, 12 C. & F. 507, 8 Eng.Rep. 1508 (1846). Although it was later repudiated in Mersey Docks Trustees v. Gibbs, 11 H.L.Cas. 686 (1866), it was taken up by Massachusetts in McDonald v. Massachusetts Gen. Hosp., 120 Mass. 432, 21 Am.Rep. 529 (1876), which was then followed in the United States. Prior to 1942, the immunity was accepted, sometimes with various minor limitations, by all but two or three of the American courts. In that year, Judge Rutledge, in what has become a landmark opinion, abolished the immunity for the District of Columbia. See President and Directors of Georgetown College v. Hughes, 130 F.2d 810 (D.C.Cir.1942). A substantial majority of the states now follow that decision, see Rabon v. Rowan Memorial Hosp. Inc., 269 N.C. 1, 152 S.E.2d 485 (1967) (collecting cases). Despite this trend, the immunity, at least on a qualified basis, is not without its defenders. See Moore v. Warren, 250 Va. 421, 463 S.E.2d 459 (1995) (public policy considerations underlie doctrine of charitable immunity that precludes action by beneficiary against charity so long as charity exercised due care in hiring and retention of agents); Abramson v. Reiss, 334 Md. 193, 638 A.2d 743 (1994) (charitable immunity doctrine based on trust fund theory precludes action against Jewish Community Center); George v. Jefferson Hosp. Assn., Inc., 337 Ark. 206, 987 S.W.2d 710 (1999) (entity created and maintained exclusively for charity may not have its assets diminished in favor of one injured by its agents) (dissent notes that state is in distinct minority in continuing to recognize immunity).

2. Some jurisdictions have made one or more inroads on the immunity, but have not abolished it completely. The more common incursions include (1) abolishing the immunity for charitable hospitals but retaining it for religious institutions and other charities, (2) limiting the immunity to recipients of the benefits of the charity, and (3) abolishing the immunity to the extent that the defendant is covered by liability insurance or to the extent that the judgment can be satisfied out of other nontrust fund assets. Picher v. Roman Catholic Bishop of Portland, 974 A.2d 286 (Maine 2009) (charitable immunity for negligence because insurance policy did not cover it, but no immunity for intentional torts).

3. Which organizations qualify for the immunity? Compare Ola v. YMCA of South Hampton Roads, 270 Va. 550, 621 S.E.2d 70 (2005) (YMCA qualifies as charity protected by immunity) with University of Va. Health Services Foundation v. Morris, 275 Va. 319, 657 S.E.2d 512 (2008) (foundation that employs physicians that staff U.Va. hospitals does not qualify as charity for immunity purposes).

4. New Jersey, by statute, provides immunity for negligent acts injuring any "beneficiary" of the works of the charity. N.J.S.A. 2A:53A–7. Does "beneficiary" include a paying patient at a hospital? A pedestrian walking past a church who is struck by a falling stone from a negligently maintained steeple while listening to its bells toll? An expectant mother

who belonged to a nonprofit group that used a church basement for its meetings who was injured while attending a meeting of her group at the church but who was not a parishioner? Some states provide limited charitable immunity tied to liability insurance coverage. See, e.g., Md. Cts. & Jud. Proc. § 5–632 (liability of charitable hospital limited to $100,000 if hospital obtains liability insurance in that amount).

5. During the last few decades, the general expansion of tort liability combined with the tight insurance market of the 1980's raised concerns about the ability of some charitable organizations to continue to provide services. Thus, some state legislatures acted to extend partial immunity to some charitable organizations. See, e.g., N.H.Rev.Stat.Ann. § 508:17 (limiting liability of charitable organization to $250,000 in action based on alleged negligence of volunteer). What if an individual volunteer is sued rather than or in addition to the organization? N.H. Rev. Stat. Ann. § 508:17 (immunity for volunteer so long as certain conditions met); Moore v. Warren, 250 Va. 421, 463 S.E.2d 459 (1995) (volunteer driver who was providing transportation to plaintiff was protected by the immunity of the charitable organization, the American Red Cross).

6. See generally Tremper, Compensation for Harm from Charitable Activity, 76 Cornell L.Rev. 401 (1991); Restatement (Second) of Torts § 895E, and Appendix.

(E) STATE AND LOCAL GOVERNMENTS

Clarke v. Oregon Health Sciences University

Supreme Court of Oregon, 2007.
343 Or. 581, 175 P.3d 418.

DE MUNIZ, C. J. * * * [Jordaan Clarke, a three-month old infant, was admitted to Oregon Health Sciences University Hospital (OHSU) for surgical repair of a congenital heart defect. After surgery, due to the negligence of OHSU's employees, he suffered prolonged oxygen deprivation causing him permanent brain damage. He is totally disabled and his guardian seeks over $17,000,000 in economic and noneconomic damages from OHSU and its employees. The individual employees sought dismissal of the suit against them pursuant to the provision of the Oregon Tort Claims Statute that makes the remedy against the state exclusive. The plaintiff challenged the constitutionality of that statute in light of the $200,000 damages cap applicable to tort actions against the state. The trial court judge granted judgment on the pleadings to the individual defendants based on the exclusive remedy provision and to the plaintiff against the state for $200,000. The Court of Appeals affirmed the judgment against the state but reversed the judgment for the individual defendants, finding the exclusive remedy provision in conjunction with the damages cap violated the Oregon Constitution. This appeal to the Supreme Court of Oregon followed.]

A. *Overview of the OTCA*

Before 1967, public bodies were immune from tort liability. [C] A person injured by the negligence of a public employee acting within the scope of his or her employment could pursue an action against the employee, but not against the public employer. [Cc] In 1967, the legislature enacted the [Oregon Tort Claims Act] OTCA, which partially waived immunity for public bodies. [C] The 1967 version of the OTCA included a monetary limitation on the state's liability, [c], but did not alter the liability of [individual] public officers, employees, or agents. [C] Those individuals, therefore, remained personally liable for torts committed within the course and scope of their employment. [C]

In 1975, the legislature amended the OTCA. The 1975 version required that public bodies indemnify officers, employees, and agents against tort claims "arising out of an alleged act or omission occurring in the performance of duty." [Cc] Additionally, the legislature extended the limitation on damages to claims against officers, employees, and agents of all public bodies. [Cc]

In 1991, the legislature again revised the OTCA. [C] That revision added language [c] that eliminated entirely any claim against any officer, employee, or agent for their work-related torts. [C] Pursuant to the 1991 amendments, the sole cause of action available for torts committed by public officers, employees, or agents is an action against the public body. [C] After that amendment, [the statute] now requires that, if an action is filed against a public officer, employee, or agent, the public body "shall be substituted as the only defendant." That substituted claim against the public body is subject to the OTCA's damages limitations. [Cc] The 1991 amendments were added at the request of the state, which asserted three reasons for the requested change. [C] First, because the law provided indemnification for state officers, naming the officers as parties "serve[d] no purpose." Second, some claimants had argued that the limitation on the liability of the state did not apply to the liability of individuals; therefore, the state sought to "plug that loophole." Finally, the state noted that "a lot of resources were spent" litigating which state officials are properly named in any given lawsuit. * * *

B. *Overview of Article 1, section 10*

[The Court discussed the interpretation of Article 1, section 10, the so-called Remedy Clause of the Oregon Constitution, noting that it can be traced to Edward Coke's commentary on the second sentence of the Magna Carta and that it made its way to the American colonies and then into many state Constitutions as those states joined the United States. Case law interpreting the Remedy Clauses found that their purpose is to "save from legislative abolishment those jural rights which had become well established prior to the enactment of our Constitution" and to "preserve the common-law right of action for injury to person or property." Thus, "while the legislature may change the remedy or the form of procedure, attach conditions precedent to is exercise, and perhaps abolish old and substitute new remedies, it cannot deny a remedy entirely." Oregon follows this analysis for Remedy Clause claims: Did the common law of Oregon recognize a cause of action for the alleged injury in 1857 when the Oregon Constitution was drafted? If it did and the legislature then abolished that common-law cause of action, has a constitutionally adequate substitute remedy been provided?]

C. *Plaintiff's claim against OHSU*

[The first issue we must address] is whether the common law would have recognized plaintiff's negligence claim against OHSU. OHSU contends that plaintiff would not have had a claim against it, because OHSU would have been entitled to sovereign immunity under the common law of Oregon. * * * We conclude that OHSU would have been entitled to sovereign immunity at common law because, among other reasons, OHSU is a state-created entity that performs functions traditionally performed by the state.

* * *

[The Court noted that the Oregon Constitution is framed on the premise that the state is immune from suit. Therefore, the court may not abolish the doctrine; only the legislature can waive or alter the immunity. The Court previously had ruled that, in addition to the state itself and its agencies, entities that are "instrumentalities" of the state, which are charged with carrying out one of the functions of government, are protected by the immunity. In earlier cases, the Court had determined that the Port of Portland, the State Board of Education, and the State Accident Insurance Fund were all instrumentalities of the State whose actions are covered by state immunity. Other public bodies, such as municipal corporations, also may be protected, but only when they are engaged in "governmental" as opposed to "proprietary" functions. Thus, liability for the actions of public bodies like municipal corporations depends on the nature of the function being performed as well as the status of the defendant.

Based on the stated purposes specified by the legislature in creating OHSU (promoting the public welfare of the people of the State of Oregon through providing education and health care), the entrusting of powers and duties of the state to the OHSU board and university officials, and OHSU's governance structure (board of directors appointed by Governor and confirmed by Senate), the Court finds that OHSU is an instrumentality of the state performing state functions. Thus, it would have been entitled to immunity at common law for all of its activities and the legislature's choice to limit its liability for tort claims does not violate the Remedy Clause.]

D. *Plaintiff's claim against the individual defendants*

Having concluded that the common law in Oregon in 1857 would not have recognized a cause of action for negligence against OHSU, we now address whether the OTCA's elimination of a cause of action against the individual defendants, combined with its damages limitation, survives scrutiny under Article I, section 10. * * *

On review, defendants offer several arguments supporting their assertion that the Court of Appeals erred in holding that the application of the OTCA in this case violated the Remedy Clause. First, defendants contend that Article I, section 10, guarantees only that a remedy of some kind be available, not that the remedy be of any certain type or amount. Therefore, in defendants' view, because plaintiff here has a remedy available to him in the form of an action against OHSU, there is no Article I, section 10, infirmity. Second, defendants assert that the Court of Appeals erred in comparing the amount of damages available under the OTCA to the amount of damages claimed by plaintiff. Defendants argue that "substantial," as that term had been used in this court's Remedy Clause jurisprudence, does not call for such a comparison; instead, defendants contend that "substantial" refers to the remedial *process* or, at the very most, that a substitute remedy need only be one that is not illusory or the practical equivalent of no remedy at all.

From the foregoing, the state contends that the court should review a legislatively substituted remedy on a categorical basis only. Put another way, the state suggests that the determination of whether a substitute remedy is adequate should not focus on the facts of an individual case, but instead should focus on the balance struck by the legislature in creating a substitute remedy. The state asserts that, unless a category of potential plaintiffs is left without a remedy, the legislative policy choice is conclusive.

On the other hand, plaintiff contends that the Remedy Clause protects both the procedure for seeking redress as well as the substance of that redress. Plaintiff argues further that, when the legislature abolishes a common-law remedy, it must provide a remedy that is "substantially equivalent" to the common-law remedy.

* * *

[T]his court consistently has held that Article I, section 10, is not merely an aspirational statement, but was intended by the framers of the Oregon Constitution to preserve for future generations, against legislative or other encroachment, the right to obtain a remedy for injury to interests in person, property, and reputation under circumstances in which Oregon law provided a remedy for those injuries when Oregon ratified its constitution. [C] However, as our review of the cases demonstrates, Article I, section 10, does not eliminate the power of the legislature to vary and modify both the form and the measure of recovery for an injury, as long as it does not leave the injured party with an "emasculated" version of the remedy that was available at common law.

* * *

We view plaintiff's economic damages of over $12 million as representative of the enormous cost of lifetime medical care currently associated with permanent and severe personal injuries caused by the medical negligence of a state officer, agent, or employee. Defendants do not argue that those damages do not constitute an "injury" within the meaning of the constitution. Nor does anything in the legislation suggest such a conclusion by the legislature. Yet, the legislature has completely eliminated an injured person's preexisting right to obtain a full recovery for those damages from the individual tortfeasors who negligently caused the injuries.

As we have explained, the legislature is authorized under Article I, section 10, to vary or modify the nature, the form, or the amount of recovery for a common-law remedy. However, that authority is not unlimited. To be clear, we respect the legislature's goal in amending the OTCA in 1991—the legislature was entitled to conclude that the goal of encouraging public employment of qualified health care professionals by protecting them from the demands of litigation and the threat of personal liability is an important one. However, there is simply nothing that we can discern from our state's history, or from the nature, the form, or the amount of recovery available for the preexisting common-law claim, that would permit this court to conclude that the limited remedy for permanent and severe injury caused by medical negligence that is now available under the OTCA meets the Article I, section 10, remedy requirement.

* * *

The decision of the Court of Appeals is affirmed. The judgment of the circuit court is reversed and the case is remanded to the circuit court for further proceedings.

[The concurring opinion is omitted. The concurring judges emphasized that the remedy limitation in OTCA cried out for a legislative solution. The Oregon State Legislature amended the damages limits effective July 1, 2009. The new limits provide for damages of $2 million for causes of action arising between July 1, 2014 and July 1, 2015. O.R.S. § 30.271]

NOTES AND QUESTIONS

1. The origin of the idea of governmental immunity at English common law often is attributed to the phrase "the King can do no wrong," but perhaps is more accurately described as necessarily a contradiction of the King's sovereignty to allow him to be sued as of right in his own courts. The doctrine evolved to mean that the government could not be sued without its consent and was firmly established in the common law when the United States was formed. Since the federal government and the state governments were all sovereigns, all were protected by the immunity. Although municipal corporations and other local entities are not sovereigns, the protection usually extended to them as well, although numerous judicial exceptions to their immunity were recognized. New York waived its sovereign immunity in 1929, the United States did so in 1946, and most states acted during the decades of the 1960s and 70s to limit sovereign immunity in various ways—including Oregon in 1967.

2. *State Governments.* Although the immunity of state governments from tort liability had its origins in English common law, it was given firmer underpinning in some state statutes and in some state constitutions that required legislative consent for the state to be liable in tort. Even when consent to suit was given, some state courts held that this was not "consent to liability" and they continued to apply the immunity.

3. *State Agencies and Instrumentalities.* In most states, sovereign immunity extends to state agencies and to instrumentalities of the state. The immunity has been held to extend to state agencies such as prisons, hospitals, educational institutions, state fairs, conservation districts, and commissions for public works. As in the principal case, the legislation creating the agency or instrumentality is examined to determine whether the agency or instrumentality is included in the immunity. Entities created after the state has adopted tort claim legislation may specify whether or

not they are protected and under what circumstances they can subject the state to liability.

4. *Municipal Corporations.* Municipal corporations, such as cities, school districts, and the like have a rather curious dual character. On the one hand, they are subdivisions of the state, acting as local governments. On the other, they are corporate bodies, capable of much the same acts and having much the same special interests and relations as private corporations. The absence of any constitutional or statutory provisions requiring consent to suit made it much easier than in the case of state government entities to develop exceptions to the rule of immunity. The principal exception was for activities that were deemed "proprietary" or "private" as contrasted with "governmental" functions. Courts imposed liability when the city or town engaged in activity that normally was carried out by the private sector of the economy and reserved the immunity for traditional governmental functions like administering elections, providing a judicial system, exercising police powers, etc. The distinction has produced a morass of confusion and inconsistency—nevertheless, many jurisdictions still use it. See, e.g., Steelman v. New Bern, 279 N.C. 589, 184 S.E.2d 239 (1971) (public street lighting governmental rather than proprietary); Casey v. Wake County, 45 N.C.App. 522, 263 S.E.2d 360 (1980) (county health department dispensing of IUD contraceptive medical device is governmental function); and Matter of World Trade Ctr. Bombing Litigation, 17 N.Y.3d 428, 957 N.E.2d 733, 933 N.Y.S.2d 164 (2011) (Port Authority performed both proprietary and governmental functions—allegations of failure to provide adequate security was governmental allocation of police resources, not commercial landlord's proprietary action).

5. As with charitable immunity, when the state has authorized a municipal corporation to purchase liability insurance, a number of courts have held that action to be an implied waiver of the immunity to the extent of the insurance. See, e.g., Ballew v. Chattanooga, 205 Tenn. 289, 326 S.W.2d 466 (1959); Bollinger v. Schneider, 64 Ill.App.3d 758, 381 N.E.2d 849, 21 Ill.Dec. 522 (1978).

6. *Abrogation.* Beginning in 1957 with Hargrove v. Cocoa Beach, 96 So.2d 130 (Fla.1957), there have been a number of decisions abrogating the immunity of municipal corporations even for governmental functions. Merrill v. Manchester, 114 N.H. 722, 332 A.2d 378 (1974) and Oroz v. Board of County Comm'rs of Carbon County, 575 P.2d 1155 (Wyo.1978) (except for judicial and legislative functions). Judicial respect for governmental immunity has been greater in regard to state government than for municipal corporations. When there has been no state constitutional barrier, some courts have abrogated the immunity. See, e.g., Jones v. State Highway Comm'n, 557 S.W.2d 225 (Mo.1977) (except in legislative, judicial, and executive functions) and Bulman v. Hulstrand Construction Co., 521 N.W.2d 632 (N.D.1994) (abrogation of immunity is prospective only, to allow Legislature to implement and plan in advance by securing liability insurance or by creating funds for self-insurance).

7. More commonly, state and municipal immunities have been abrogated by legislation and legislation regulating the matter may be enacted after judicial abrogation. Some statutes are modeled on the Federal Torts Claims Act, discussed at page 690. Others broadly provide that the state shall be liable to the same extent as any private individual. Rather

complex "codes" have been worked out in several states. See, e.g., Cal.Gov't Code §§ 810 et seq. and N.J.Stat.Ann. §§ 59:1–1 et seq. Today, every state provides for some tort claims against the government under some circumstances. Navigating the patchwork of waivers of immunity can be tricky. In some states, even the standard of conduct to which the governmental entity is held may vary, depending on how the claim is characterized. For example, in New Jersey, public entities can be held liable for dangerous conditions on public property only if the public entity acted in a "palpably unreasonable manner" in failing to protect against the condition but can be liable for injuries caused by the conduct of an employee under ordinary negligence principles. Which standard applies when someone is injured while climbing over a brick wall to escape a park in which she found herself trapped after taking a walk during her lunch hour? The gates were locked by a city employee hours before the scheduled closing time. Ogborne v. Mercer Cemetery Corp., 197 N.J. 448, 963 A.2d 828 (2009) (higher standard of "palpably unreasonable" applies because court interprets immunity broadly and waiver creating liability narrowly).

8. Most state schemes preserve some special privileges to the state as well as placing various procedural limits on the enforcement of the claims. For example, the state may cap the total amount of damages for which it is liable (as Oregon did in the principal case), create special courts of claims, or impose additional "notice of claim" requirements (see note 14, page 660). See generally Civil Actions Against State and Local Government, Its Divisions, Agencies, and Officers (Thomson 2d ed. 2002 with semi-annual updates) and Restatement (Second) of Torts §§ 895B (states), 895C (local governments). Damages caps usually are upheld, even when they represent a small portion of the plaintiff's damages. See, for example, Zauflik v. Pennsbury School Dist., 104 A.3d 1096 (Pa. 2014) (upholding $500,000 limit in face of $14 million jury verdict for student who lost her leg when school bus ran over her). How does that decision compare to the principal case?

9. Generally, even those states that have waived or limited governmental immunity have retained immunity for the judicial and legislative functions of the government. This immunity also extends to the agents of the government. Thus, a legislator may not be sued for how he voted or a judge for how she ruled.

10. As in the states where other immunities, like parental immunity, were abolished or limited, a state that abolished or limited governmental immunity and permitted recovery for some torts then had to grapple with how to define the duty owed to its citizens. New York's legislature had provided by statute that tort claims could be made against the state. In the next two principal cases, the court is faced with determining the duty owed by the government in its provision of emergency and protective services. The first case is against the City of New York for activities of its police department. The second is against a county for actions of its agency providing emergency response services. Each struggles with defining whether a duty is owed to the individual plaintiff, separate from the duty owed to the public, and what the scope of that duty is.

Riss v. New York

New York Court of Appeals, 1968.
22 N.Y.2d 579, 240 N.E.2d 860, 293 N.Y.S.2d 897.

[The description of the facts in this case is taken from the dissenting opinion of Judge Keating:

"Linda Riss, an attractive young woman, was for more than six months terrorized by a rejected suitor well known to the courts of this State, one Burton Pugach. This miscreant, masquerading as a respectable attorney, repeatedly threatened to have Linda killed or maimed if she did not yield to him: 'If I can't have you, no one else will have you, and when I get through with you, no one else will want you.' In fear for her life, she went to those charged by law with the duty of preserving and safeguarding the lives of the citizens and residents of this State. Linda's repeated and almost pathetic pleas for aid were received with little more than indifference. Whatever help she was given was not commensurate with the identifiable danger. On June 14, 1959 Linda became engaged to another man. At a party held to celebrate the event, she received a phone call warning her that it was her 'last chance.' Completely distraught, she called the police, begging for help, but was refused. The next day Pugach carried out his dire threats in the very manner he had foretold by having a hired thug throw lye in Linda's face. Linda was blinded in one eye, lost a good portion of her vision in the other, and her face was permanently scarred. After the assault the authorities concluded that there was some basis for Linda's fears, and for the next three and one-half years, she was given around-the-clock protection."]

BREITEL, J. This appeal presents, in a very sympathetic framework, the issue of the liability of a municipality for failure to provide special protection to a member of the public who was repeatedly threatened with personal harm and eventually suffered dire personal injuries for lack of such protection. * * * The issue arises upon the affirmance by a divided Appellate Division of a dismissal of the complaint, after both sides had rested but before submission to the jury. * * *

[T]his case involves the provision of a governmental service to protect the public generally from external hazards and particularly to control the activities of criminal wrongdoers. [Cc] The amount of protection that may be provided is limited by the resources of the community and by a considered legislative-executive decision as to how those resources may be deployed. For the courts to proclaim a new and general duty of protection in the law of tort, even to those who may be the particular seekers of protection based on specific hazards, could and would inevitably determine how the limited police resources of the community should be allocated and without predictable limits. This is quite different from the predictable allocation of resources and liabilities when public hospitals, rapid transit systems, or even highways are provided.

Before such extension of responsibilities should be dictated by the indirect imposition of tort liabilities, there should be a legislative determination that that should be the scope of public responsibility. * * *

When one considers the greatly increased amount of crime committed throughout the cities, but especially in certain portions of them, with a repetitive and predictable pattern, it is easy to see the consequences of fixing municipal liability upon a showing of probable need for and request for protection. To be sure these are grave problems at the present time, exciting high priority activity on the part of the national, State and local governments, to which the answers are neither simple, known, or presently within reasonable controls. To foist a presumed cure for these problems by judicial innovation of a new kind of liability in tort would be foolhardy indeed and an assumption of judicial wisdom and power not possessed by the courts.

* * *

For all of these reasons, there is no warrant in judicial tradition or in the proper allocation of the powers of government for the courts, in the absence of legislation, to carve out an area of tort liability for police protection to members of the public. Quite distinguishable, of course, is the situation where the police authorities undertake responsibilities to particular members of the public and expose them, without adequate protection, to the risks which then materialize into actual losses (Schuster v. City of New York, 5 N.Y.2d 75).

Accordingly, the order of the Appellate Division affirming the judgment of dismissal should be affirmed.

KEATING, JUDGE (dissenting). It is not a distortion to summarize the essence of the city's case here in the following language: "Because we owe a duty to everybody, we owe it to nobody." * * * To say that there is no duty is, of course, to start with the conclusion. The question is whether or not there should be liability for the negligent failure to provide adequate police protection.

The foremost justification repeatedly urged for the existing rule is the claim that the State and the municipalities will be exposed to limitless liability. The city invokes the specter of a "crushing burden" * * *.

The fear of financial disaster is a myth. The same argument was made a generation ago in opposition to proposals that the State waive its defense of "sovereign immunity". The prophecy proved false then, and it would now. * * *

Another variation of the "crushing burden" argument is the contention that, every time a crime is committed, the city will be sued and the claim will be made that it resulted from inadequate police protection. Here, again, is an attempt to arouse the "anxiety of the courts about new theories of liability which may have a far-reaching effect" * * *.

The instant case provides an excellent illustration of the limits which the courts can draw. No one would claim that, under the facts here, the police were negligent when they did not give Linda protection after her first calls or visits to the police station in February of 1959. The preliminary investigation was sufficient. If Linda had been attacked at this point, clearly there would be no liability here. When, however, as time went on and it was established that Linda was a reputable person, that other verifiable attempts to injure her or intimidate her had taken place, that other witnesses were available to support her claim that her life was being threatened, something more was required—either by way of further investigation or protection—than the statement that was made by one detective to Linda that she would have to be hurt before the police could do anything for her. * * *

More significant, however, is the fundamental flaw in the reasoning behind the argument alleging judicial interference. It is a complete oversimplification of the problem of municipal tort liability. What it ignores is the fact that indirectly courts are reviewing administrative practices in almost every tort case against the State or a municipality, including even decisions of the Police Commissioner * * *.

DeLong v. Erie County

New York Supreme Court, Appellate Division, 1982.
89 A.D.2d 376, 455 N.Y.S.2d 887.

HANCOCK, JUSTICE: * * * Before her death, Amalia DeLong, her husband, and their three young children resided at 319 Victoria Boulevard in the Village of Kenmore, a suburb of Buffalo located in Erie County. In October, 1976, the Village of Kenmore was one of the four communities outside of Buffalo fully served by the 911 emergency telephone system operated by the Central Police Services, an agency of Erie County[.] * * * At 9:29:29 in the morning of October 25, 1976 Amalia DeLong dialed 911 on her telephone and was immediately connected to the 911 room. The transcript of her call is as follows:

9:29:29	—Caller:	"Police?"
	—Complaint Writer:	"911."
	—Caller:	"Police, please come, 319 Victoria right away."
	—Complaint Writer:	"What's wrong?"
	—Caller:	"There's a burglar."
9:29:34	—Complaint Writer:	"In there now?"
	—Caller:	"I heard a burglar; I saw his face in the back; he was trying to break in the house; please come right away."
	—Complaint Writer:	"Okay, right away."
9:29:43	—Caller:	"Okay."

The complaint writer recorded the address on the complaint card as "219 Victoria"—not "319 Victoria". The call had lasted 14 seconds. [The evidence regarding police response time indicated that the decedent's life might have been saved if the police had not been misdirected to a nonexistent address.] As a result of the failure of proper police response, Amalia DeLong had received seven knife wounds: to the left side of the neck, the left side of the head, the second finger of the right hand, the nail of the third finger on the left hand, the thumb of the left hand, and a wound to the left shoulder. The laceration on the neck was fatal. It was deep and had severed the jugular vein and carotid artery on the left. The cuts on the fingers were described as being of a "defensive type".

* * *

The purpose of the 911 emergency or "hot line" system is to assist in the delivery of police services to the people in the communities served[.]* * *

On the morning of October 25, the complaint writer, in addition to mistakenly recording the address on the complaint card as 219 instead of 319 Victoria, failed to follow the instructions in four respects: (1) he did not ask the name of the caller; (2) he did not determine the exact location of the call; (3) he did not address the caller by name; (4) he did not repeat the address.

The operating procedures in effect on October 25, 1976 also called for follow-up action if, as with the DeLong call, the report came back to the dispatcher: "No such address." In such event, the dispatcher was required to notify the complaint writer or the 911 lieutenant (the Buffalo police lieutenant on duty in the 911 room) so that the tape recording of the call could be replayed, the Haines Directory and the street guides consulted, and other communities having street names identical or similar to the street name given by the caller immediately notified. On Amalia DeLong's call, no follow-up of any kind took place. The call was treated as a fake.

Our discussion of the questions raised concerning liability must start with Riss v. City of New York, 22 N.Y.2d 579, 293 N.Y.S.2d 897, 240 N.E.2d 860, in which the court found no legal responsibility for the tragic consequences of the city's failure to furnish police protection despite proof of Linda Riss' repeated and agonized pleas for assistance. In an opinion by then Associate Judge Breitel, the court, with one dissent, concluded: "[T]here is no warrant in judicial tradition or in the proper allocation of the powers of government for the courts, in the absence of legislation, to carve out an area of tort liability for police protection to members of the public." Quite distinguishable, of course, is the situation where the police authorities undertake responsibilities to particular members of the public and expose them, without adequate protection, to the risks which then materialize into actual losses [cc]. This fundamental rule remains the law [cc] when a relationship is created between the police and an individual which gives rise to a special duty, the municipality loses its governmental immunity and liability may result. Courts have found such a special duty to be owing to informers [c], undercover agents [c], persons under court orders of protection [c], and school children for whom the municipality has assumed the responsibility of providing crossing guards [cc]. * * *

It is not the establishment of the emergency call system to serve the Village of Kenmore, standing alone, which creates the duty. It is the holding out of the 911 number as one to be called by someone in need of assistance, Amalia DeLong's placing of the call in reliance on that holding out, and her further reliance on the response to her plea for immediate help: "Okay, right away." This is not a mere failure to furnish police protection owed to the public generally but a case where the municipality has assumed a duty to a particular person which it must perform "in a nonnegligent manner, [although without the] voluntary assumption of that duty, none would have otherwise existed" [c]. The complaint writer's acceptance of the call, his transmittal of the complaint card to the dispatcher and the dispatcher's radio calls to the police cars were affirmative actions setting the emergency machinery in motion. This voluntary assumption of a duty to act carried with it the obligation to act with reasonable care [c].

But, defendants remind us, failing to fulfill an undertaking to provide police protection does not result in municipal liability unless it be shown that the police conduct in some way increased the risk [c]. * * * In other words, defendants argue, although the hand may have been set to the task and withdrawn [c], it has resulted in no harm. We disagree.

While there could in this case be no direct evidence that Amalia DeLong relied to her ultimate detriment on the assurance of police assistance, the circumstantial evidence strongly suggests that she did so. Instead of summoning help from the Village police or from her neighbors (one of whom was a captain in the Kenmore Police Department), she waited for the response to her 911 call. Instead of taking her baby and going out the front door where she would have been safe, she remained defenseless in the house. * * *

[The court found that the jury's award of $200,000 for pain and suffering was "within reasonable bounds." The period of time of decedent's fatal encounter with her assailant was between 9:30 and 9:42 a.m.]

Accordingly, the judgment insofar as it awards damages for conscious pain and suffering, should be affirmed.

Judgment affirmed with costs.

[Concurring and dissenting opinions omitted.]

NOTES AND QUESTIONS

1. Do you agree with Judge Keating's dissent in the *Riss* case? Has New York decided that because the state government owes a duty to protect everyone it owes no duty to a particular crime victim? At what point does Ms. Riss move from being a member of the general public to being a particular person, like Ms. DeLong, to whom the government has assumed a duty? Suppose plaintiff's decedent had reported to police that she had been raped and that the assailants had threatened to kill her if she reported them. Less than a week later, assailants made good on their threat. Brandon v. County of Richardson, 252 Neb. 839, 566 N.W.2d 776 (1997) (holding special relationship was created when the victim went to law enforcement officials and offered to testify and aid in the prosecution of the assailants and that fact that she was the victim of the crime did not change this relationship). Suppose plaintiff's decedent placed a call to 911, stated an address and "heart attack," and then hung up before the dispatcher could obtain any additional information or respond. Is the caller a member of the general public (no duty) or someone with whom the county is in a special relationship (duty)? Cummins v. Lewis County, 156 Wash.2d 844, 133 P.3d 458 (2006) (no special relationship giving rise to duty because caller did not identify himself, did not receive any assurance of assistance from operator, and did not engage in dialogue with operator from which assurance could have been inferred). Suppose hospital staff called the police to report that a patient who had voluntarily committed himself for

treatment for mental illness had left the hospital grounds without telling anyone and wandered into the countryside. The police kept a lookout for him during routine patrols but did not search for him. He died of exposure. Is the patient a member of the general public (no duty) or someone with whom the county has a special relationship? Eves v. Anaconda-Deer Lodge County, 327 Mont. 437, 114 P.3d 1037 (2005) (no special relationship created by call from hospital to police).

2. The same issues also can arise outside of police protection cases. Suppose the state never inspects a chicken processing plant during its eleven years of operation and thus fails to find numerous fire safety violations. A fire there killed 25 workers and injured 55 others whose escape from the burning building was prevented or hindered by the fire safety violations. Does the state owe a duty to the workers? Stone v. North Carolina Dept. of Labor, 347 N.C. 473, 495 S.E.2d 711 (1998) (obligation to inspect runs to public at large, not individuals, and thus there is no liability). Suppose two children report that they are being sexually abused by their stepfather but state social workers, after promising to take action, do nothing to protect them. Sabia v. State of Vermont, 164 Vt. 293, 669 A.2d 1187 (1995) (obligation to protect children where report of abuse has been made runs to those children and state may be liable if it was negligent in not providing protection after promising to do so).

3. Many states and the federal government have eliminated the immunity for ministerial acts but retained it for *discretionary functions*. Discretionary functions are those where the government is acting to establish policy. Ministerial acts are those that implement or effectuate the policies. Do you see why the government is more appropriately held accountable for discretionary decisions through elections and the political process? Court review of discretionary decisions would interfere with democratic choices: how much money to spend on the police force, how many snow plows to buy, whether to build a new middle school or provide Internet access in public libraries. See, for example, Lane v. State of Vermont, 174 Vt. 219, 811 A.2d 190 (2002) (decisions of how to allocate snow plow operators, how many workers to call in for any given winter storm event, how many trucks to put on the road, and how much salt to use are discretionary functions) and Kohl v. City of Phoenix, 215 Ariz. 291, 160 P.3d 170 (2007) (decision which intersections have traffic signals and which do not is determination of "fundamental governmental policy" and therefore protected discretionary function).

Ministerial decisions, on the other hand, are not manifestations of public policy decisions and therefore can subject the government to liability if they are performed negligently. For example, the government may be liable if one of its agents negligently drives a car, negligently fails to maintain government premises, or negligently fails to maintain public roads. See, for example, Hensley v. Jackson County, 227 S.W.3d 491 (Mo. 2007) (negligent failure to maintain or repair stop sign) and Gregor v. Argenot Great Central Ins. Co., 851 So.2d 959 (La. 2003) (finding that enforcement of health code was mandatory, not discretionary, and therefore state could be jointly liable with restaurant for patron's death). Although some actions are easily categorized as discretionary or ministerial (city traffic engineer deciding where to put a traffic signal v. city traffic engineer running a red light while on city business), many actions are not so easily characterized. The next principal case raises that issue in the context of the Federal Tort Claims Act, the federal government's statutory waiver of immunity. Note also that even if the decision is a ministerial one (and thus no immunity), claimant still must show that there was some special relationship that gave rise to a duty, something more than the general duty owed to the public at large. Valdez v. City of New York, 18 N.Y.3d 69, 936 N.Y.S.2d 587, 960 N.E.2d 356 (2011) (must be an affirmative undertaking that creates justifiable reliance—not justifiable to rely on police officer's alleged statement that former boyfriend who had threatened plaintiff would be arrested immediately when plaintiff knew that police did not know location of former boyfriend).

4. For those who may be interested, here is a side note on the subsequent history of the personalities in the *Riss* case. Burton Pugach, the attorney who hired the "thug" who partially blinded Ms. Riss, served 14 years in prison for his crime. Six months after his release he again proposed to Ms. Riss. She accepted and the couple were married in 1974. See N.Y. Times Nov. 28, 1974, at 1, col. 4. In 1990, they were still married and Pugach was working as a paralegal while attempting to have his disbarment lifted so that he could again practice law. See Agus, City Legend: What They Did for Love, Newsday April 26, 1990, at 4. The disbarment was never lifted. In 1996, a nurse with whom Pugach had been having a five-year long extramarital affair reported to the police that he had threatened her when she attempted to end their affair. She claimed he said "It's 1959 all over again" and "I have tremendous contacts. All I have to do is tell them to do a job." Pugach admitted the affair, but denied that he had made any threats. He acted as his own lawyer at the criminal trial and his wife (the former Ms. Riss) testified as a character witness on his behalf. See Donohue and Kennedy, "Lover Lawyer Grills His Ex," Daily News April 22, 1997, at 8. Pugach was acquitted of several charges, but convicted of one count of harassment. He and his wife then filed a lawsuit against the nurse, alleging malicious prosecution based on the criminal charges and breach of confidentiality based on the nurse's disclosure of medical data about Linda (Riss) Pugach. Pugach v. Borja, 175 Misc.2d 683, 670 N.Y.S.2d 718 (1998). Does all this sound familiar? The Pugachs are the subject of an award-winning documentary, CRAZY LOVE (2007), directed by Dan Klores and Fisher Stevens.

(F) THE UNITED STATES

Deuser v. Vecera

United States Court of Appeals, Eighth Circuit, 1998.
139 F.3d 1190.

BOWMAN, CIRCUIT JUDGE. * * * On July 3–6, 1986, the event known as the Veiled Prophet (or VP) Fair was held on the grounds of the Jefferson National Expansion Memorial in St. Louis, Missouri (the site of the Gateway Arch). Because the Expansion Memorial is a national park (a special use permit was issued to the city of St. Louis for the Fair), the Secretary of the Interior is responsible for maintaining the park and its facilities and for providing services to visitors, functions generally carried out by the National Park Service. [C] The park is within the jurisdiction of the National Park Rangers. On the evening of July 4, 1986, many thousands of people were in attendance at the Fair, including Larry Deuser. Rangers David Vecera and Edward Bridges observed Deuser grabbing women on the buttocks, to the obvious outrage of the victims and others. The rangers warned Deuser, and continued to keep an eye on him. When he urinated in public, the rangers arrested him. As the rangers made their way to their tent with Deuser, he was argumentative with them and continued making rude comments to female visitors.

After conferring with chief ranger Dennis Burnett, the rangers elected to turn Deuser over to St. Louis police. But the police department was overwhelmed with the additional workload created by the Fair, and officers were unable or unwilling to process Deuser's arrest. At this point, the rangers, together with St. Louis police officer Lawrence King, decided to release Deuser, but away from the park so that he would not return to the Fair that evening.

There is some dispute between the parties about where Deuser was released, and also some question of the timing of the events that occurred that night. It is sufficient for our purposes to know the undisputed facts: Deuser was freed in a parking lot [behind the police station] somewhere in St. Louis [about 10 blocks from the Fair], alone and with no money and no transportation. At some time after that, he wandered onto an interstate highway [about a mile and a half away] and was struck and killed by a motorist. Deuser's blood alcohol level was 0.214 at the time of his death, well above the legal limit for intoxication. [Deuser's survivors brought several state and federal claims against both municipal and federal actors. This wrongful death action against the United States under the Federal Tort Claims Act ("FTCA") based on the allegedly negligent acts of the park rangers in deciding not to arrest him and to release him in the parking lot was dismissed by the trial court judge. The survivors appealed.] * * *

By enacting the FTCA, Congress opted to waive the sovereign immunity to civil suit enjoyed by the United States, and to give consent to be sued "for money damages . . . for injury or loss of property, or personal injury or death caused by the negligent or wrongful act or omission of any employee" of the United States acting within the scope of his employment. 28 U.S.C.A. § 1346(b)(1) (Supp.1997). The federal courts have subject matter jurisdiction over such claims "under circumstances where the United States, if a private person, would be liable to the claimant in accordance with the law of the place where the act or omission occurred." Id. But, as is true in other cases where Congress on behalf of the United States has waived sovereign immunity, amenability to suit is not without exception.

The exception relevant here is commonly known as the discretionary function exception. It is statutory and shields the government from civil liability for claims "based upon the exercise or performance . . . [of] a discretionary function or duty on the part of a federal agency or an employee of the Government, whether or not the discretion involved be abused." 28 U.S.C. § 2680(a) (1994). The exception "marks the boundary between Congress' willingness to impose tort liability upon the United States and its desire to protect certain governmental activities from exposure to suit by private individuals." [C]

To determine whether the discretionary function exception applies here to protect the rangers and the United States from suit, we engage in a two-step inquiry.

A.

First, we must consider whether the actions taken by the rangers as regards Deuser were discretionary, that is, "a matter of choice." Berkovitz [v. United States], 486 U.S. [531] at 536, [1988]. "[C]onduct cannot be discretionary unless it involves an element of judgment or choice." Id. It is axiomatic that a government employee has no such discretion "when a federal statute, regulation, or policy specifically prescribes a course of action for an employee to follow." Id. If the rangers had a policy they were to follow in releasing Deuser, as the appellants contend, "then there is no discretion in the conduct for the discretionary function exception to protect." Id. * * *

[The court then described the written Standard Operating Procedure ("SOP") for an arrest and the VP Fair Operations Handbook.] The opening paragraph of the Handbook's General Enforcement Guidelines makes it clear that the guidelines are in fact quite general and are for use by the rangers "in enforcement contacts[,] but in no way should [they] be construed as a substitute for sound judgement and discretionary action on the part of the Ranger." The guidelines then cover the areas of concern for enforcement by rangers during the Fair: traffic control; liquor law violations; city ordinances in effect for the duration of the Fair concerning alcoholic beverages, glass containers, and pets; access to the Arch; and a variety of crimes against persons from simple assault to murder. The Enforcement section of the Handbook then wraps up with a paragraph that makes it clear the rangers have wide latitude in making enforcement decisions:

> This will be a busy weekend and our holdover facilities at the 4th District may or may not be available per our existing agreement. Transport of federal prisoners to either St. Clair in Illinois or Cape Giraudeau [sic] in Missouri will tie up rangers that we can ill afford and create an extreme workload on the 7th of July [the first business day after the Fair] when we can least afford it. That does not mean we will not take appropriate action, only that our actions will be tempered with reality and arrests will only be on a "last resort" basis.

* * * The Handbook was intended to provide guidance to the rangers on the extent to which certain laws should be enforced during the Fair. Read as a whole, the Handbook suggests that enforcement in many circumstances might be relaxed during the event, so that arrests would be kept to a minimum. The rangers' "sound judgement and discretionary action" was to be exercised in the context of making decisions on whether to make an arrest at all; the Handbook never touches on the procedure to be followed in the event an arrest is made (except to note that holding facilities and rangers will be busy during the Fair). The Handbook did not override the standard operating procedures. [Footnote omitted.] Based on the record before us, it

appears the SOP for processing arrestees remained unchanged during the Fair. Still, that conclusion does not mean that the rangers were required to complete an arrest, that is, to charge and incarcerate a suspect, once he was in custody.

We know that Deuser was arrested by the rangers. The SOP to be followed when a person is arrested by a ranger at the Expansion Memorial is precise and, as to the salient points, mandatory. Appellants are correct that there was very little discretion to be exercised, at least for as long as Deuser was under arrest. And it seems that the rangers initially followed the prescribed procedure: they searched Deuser and handcuffed him before transporting him. After that, it is true that the SOP was not followed—but when Deuser was released in the parking lot, the arrest was terminated. He was free to go, and further arrest procedures—booking the prisoner and so forth—were irrelevant. Deuser was not charged with a crime, so there was no reason to follow the procedures for incarceration.

The question remains whether a ranger's decision to terminate an arrest made at the park during the Fair would require the same sort of judgment and choice as would the initial decision to make the arrest. We think that it would. There is nothing in either the SOP or the Handbook that sets forth a policy—whether discretionary or otherwise—for terminating an arrest. But we conclude that this is because the decision to terminate an arrest is closely akin to the decision to make the arrest in the first place. Law enforcement decisions of the kind involved in making or terminating an arrest must be within the discretion and judgment of enforcing officers. See, e.g., Redmond v. United States, 518 F.2d 811, 816–17 (7th Cir.1975) ("It cannot be denied that the Government has a duty to maintain law and order, but how best to fulfill this duty is wholly within the discretion of its officers . . ."). It would be impossible to put into a manual every possible scenario a ranger might encounter, and then to decide in advance for the ranger whether an arrest should be made and, once made, under what circumstances an arrest could be terminated. Just as the rangers had discretion to decide (within constitutional limits, of course) when and whether to make an arrest, so they had—and here exercised—discretion to terminate an arrest without charging the suspect. Under the terms of the Handbook, that discretion became even broader during the Fair.

We hold that terminating Deuser's arrest, that is, releasing him without charging him with a crime, was a discretionary function reserved to the judgment of the rangers.

B.

We move now to the second part of our inquiry. Notwithstanding the judgment involved in terminating Deuser's arrest, we must ask "whether that judgment is of the kind that the discretionary function exception was designed to shield." Berkovitz, 486 U.S. at 536, 108 S.Ct. at 1959. To be protected, the rangers' conduct must be "grounded in the social, economic, or political goals" of the Handbook's discretionary enforcement guidelines. United States v. Gaubert, 499 U.S. 315, 323, 111 S.Ct. 1267, 1274, 113 L.Ed.2d 335 (1991). * * *

We think the conduct of the rangers here is the classic example of a "permissible exercise of policy judgment." Berkovitz, 486 U.S. at 539, 108 S.Ct. at 1960. Social, economic, and political goals—all three—were the basis for the actions taken by the rangers.

An important function of the rangers during the Fair, according to the Handbook, was to serve and protect visitors to the park. Clearly, the decision to remove Deuser from the park served the social goals of protecting innumerable other fairgoers and ensuring that their enjoyment of the festivities was not diminished by the obnoxious and offensive behavior of a fellow attendee. Further, the decision to release Deuser, rather than to charge him for the offenses he committed, may have prevented a night of revelry that obviously was out of control from becoming a criminal conviction. And the rangers who otherwise would have spent considerable time booking Deuser were free to return to the Fair, possibly to prevent more serious or more dangerous crimes from being committed, or to apprehend the perpetrators of graver offenses, thereby continuing to further the goal of visitor protection.

The economic goals of the guidelines are clear, and are spelled out in some detail in the Handbook. Law enforcement manpower was expected to be stretched thin, both during the Fair and on the first business day following the Fair, when arrestees would have to be transported for court appearances. (In fact, the SOP tells rangers to expect the process to take all day, even under ordinary circumstances.) There were simply not enough officers to arrest and to charge all persons who might commit a crime at the park during the four-day Fair. The rangers' colleagues, St. Louis police department officers, were expected to be equally taxed with their own enforcement duties. Moreover, it was anticipated that the nearest holdover facility would be overcrowded with arrestees, meaning more miles and more manpower to transport suspects to alternative holdover facilities and to see to their arraignments. Releasing Deuser without charging him preserved already scarce law enforcement resources.

The political goals to be served by the guidelines concern law enforcement "territories." The Fair was not a National Park Service event. The Handbook acknowledges that "[t]he St. Louis Police Department is the lead agency for law enforcement." VP Fair 1986 Operations Handbook—Overview and Hindsight para. 6. As the chief ranger stated in the Handbook, the federal park rangers' "primary role is defined as resource protection followed by the things we do best, visitor services and visitor care." Id. When the police opted not to process Deuser's arrest, the rangers appropriately decided not to override the decision of "the lead agency for law enforcement." The Fair's success depended in part on all enforcement agencies involved working together toward a common goal, and the rangers acted properly to preserve that cooperation by releasing Deuser in this situation. Further, the Fair was designed to be an enjoyable event for the city, and it would have been unfortunate if overzealous federal law enforcement had dampened the festivities. * * *

[We hold that the conduct of the officers here was grounded in the social, economic, and political policies of the Handbook and thus within the discretionary function exception to the FTCA's waiver of sovereign immunity.]

The judgment of the District Court is affirmed.

NOTES AND QUESTIONS

1. *From Congress to the Courts*: Governmental immunity has barred tort suits against the United States for most of its history. The United States cannot be sued without its consent. Consent to be sued began to appear in the form of private bills by Congress authorizing particular plaintiffs to sue on particular claims. Apart from the obvious possibility of political influence, this of necessity involved considerable delay and inconvenience, as well as inflicting a considerable burden upon the time of Congress. In 1855 a Court of Claims was established to hear contract cases. This was initially merely an advisory court making recommendations to Congress, but in 1863 the Court of Claims was given the power to render effective judgments. There were also a number of minor statutes permitting suit upon particular types of claims, and in a few instances some of these even authorized some relief in tort. The great majority of the tort claims against the United States however, remained without any redress. The inconvenience caused by having to deal with private bills eventually pressured Congress to provide for a general tort remedy. Between 1919 and 1946, some 18 proposals were considered. Finally, on August 2, 1946, the Federal Tort Claims Act was enacted. It applies to all claims accruing on or after January 1, 1945. In effect, it represented the first judicial remedy of general application available to persons who suffered tortious injury to their person or property caused by employees of the United States Government.

2. Tort claims against the Federal Government are a major source of tort litigation today. As an author of a three-volume treatise on the subject has observed: "During recent years, it has not been uncommon to find that there were some 3,000 lawsuits against the United States under the Federal Tort Claims Act pending before the federal courts at one time involving claims of approximately $5 billion. New suits are filed at the rate of more than 1,500 each year. Administrative claims, presented by claimants each year to federal agencies [a prerequisite to filing suit], number some 10 to 20 times that amount. This large volume of tort claims . . . is understandable when you consider that the United States employs almost 5 million people, military and civilian, for whose tortious conduct it is answerable in damages under the Tort Claims Act. It operates more than half a million autos, trucks, and other vehicles. It flies huge fleets of aircraft and sails great numbers of ships. It maintains hundreds of hospitals and employs more than 85,000 doctors, dentists, nurses, and other medical personnel. It operates tens of thousands of post offices and buildings and other places for the transaction of government business. It maintains immense parks, builds highways, constructs dams, and engages in a vast variety of activities." Jayson, Handling Federal Tort Claims § 1.01.

3. The Federal Tort Claims Act is a subject for separate study. Only a few major issues under the Act will be noted here. It is of paramount importance to remember that a lawyer cannot assume that matters will be handled in "the ordinary way" under the Act. Here are a few examples:

A. A person seeking recovery must present his claim to the "appropriate Federal agency" before instituting suit. 28 U.S.C. § 2675. See note 14, page 660 re notice-of-claim requirements. Failure to exhaust the administrative remedy before filing the lawsuit results in a dismissal of the suit due to lack of subject matter jurisdiction. McNeil v. United States, 508 U.S. 106 (1993) (such is the case even where the plaintiff is a prisoner proceeding *pro se*).

B. Two different time deadlines must be met by the claimant. The claim with the administrative agency must be filed within two years of when the cause of action accrues and the lawsuit must then be filed within six months of when the agency mails the notice of final denial of the claim. 28 U.S.C. 2401(b). The cause of action accrues when claimant learns of his injury and its cause, not when he learns that the conduct that injured him was tortious. United States v. Kubrick, 444 U.S. 111 (1979) (medical malpractice). Federal law governs the interpretation of the statute of limitations and the Supreme Court has concluded that those deadlines are not jurisdictional and that the courts may apply equitable principles to toll the both limitations periods. U.S. v. Wong, 135 S.Ct. 1625 (U.S. 2015).

C. The lawsuit cannot be filed in state court because the federal district courts have exclusive jurisdiction. 28 U.S.C. § 1346(b). It must be filed in the district where the plaintiff resides or wherein the act or omission complained of occurred. 28 U.S.C. § 1402(b).

D. The suit will be tried by a judge and not a jury. 28 U.S.C. § 2402.

E. The plaintiff's attorney's contingent fee is subject to express regulation and collection of a higher fee constitutes a federal crime. 28 U.S.C. § 2678 (the maximum amount permitted is 25% of any judgment or settlement made after commencement of the action and 20% of any settlement obtained through the administrative procedure before filing suit).

4. The two principal sections of the Act are the jurisdiction and general liability sections. They were quoted in the principal case and are set out below:

The federal district courts "shall have exclusive jurisdiction of civil actions on claims against the United States, for money damages, accruing on or after January 1, 1945, for injury or loss of property, or personal injury or death caused by the negligent or wrongful act or omission of any employee of the Government while acting within the scope of his office or employment, under circumstances where the United States, if a private person, would be liable to the claimant in accordance with the law of the place where the act or omission occurred." 28 U.S.C. § 1346(b).

"The United States shall be liable, respecting the provisions of this title relating to tort claims, in the same manner and to the same extent as a private individual under like circumstances, but shall not be liable for interest prior to judgment or for punitive damages." 28 U.S.C. § 2674.

A. *Use of State Tort Law.* What problems of statutory interpretation can you glean from each section? Why do you think Congress did not enact a complete code of federal tort law rather than rely on the "law of the place where the tort occurred"? Should the liability of the federal government vary from state to state? Suppose local law would make a state governmental entity liable for failing to perform a governmental function like a safety inspection of a mine. Does that make the United States liable under the FTCA standard? United States v. Olson, 546 U.S. 43 (2005) (FTCA waives federal government's sovereign immunity only where local law would make a *private person* liable in tort, not where local law would make a state or municipal entity liable).

B. Would the United States be subject to *strict liability* under the Act? Suppose it engaged in an "abnormally dangerous" activity or manufactured a "defective" product? This matter would appear to have been finally put to rest in Laird v. Nelms, 406 U.S. 797 (1972) (no FTCA liability based on strict liability for ultrahazardous activity in case involving damage from military jets on training exercises breaking the sound barrier), where the Supreme Court held that the Act did not authorize suit against the government based on strict or absolute liability. Nevertheless, could you make an argument the other way based on language of the Act itself?

C. Recovery in many cases turns on the issue of whether a government officer or employee was "*acting within his office or employment*" for the purpose of the Act. Should this be decided as a matter of state or federal law? Williams v. United States, 350 U.S. 857 (1955) (state law of respondeat superior controls). Under a provision of the statute sometimes called the Westfall Act, a claim against the United States is the exclusive remedy and the individual employee is shielded from liability. 28 U.S.C. § 2679. Osborn v. Haley, 549 U.S. 225 (2007) (The Westfall Act's core purpose is to relieve covered employees from the cost and effort of defending the lawsuit and to place those burdens on the government.) This exclusive remedy provision shields the government employee even if another provision of the FTCA means that the United States also is immune. United States v. Smith, 499 U.S. 160 (1991) (claimant allegedly injured by medical malpractice of military doctor stationed in Italy has no cause of action against the doctor because of the exclusive remedy provision even though the FTCA provides no remedy because the cause of action arose outside of the United States).

5. The Act contains *13 specific exceptions* to the waiver of immunity in 28 U.S.C. § 2680. Most of them deal with specific activities of the government, such as the transmission of mail, the assessment or collection of customs duties, the imposition of quarantines, the fiscal operations of the Treasury, and the like, and in particular the combatant activities of military and naval forces in time of war. The Supreme Court of the United States has adhered to the proposition that it will not "extend the waiver of sovereign immunity more broadly than has been directed by Congress." United States v. Shaw, 309 U.S. 495, 502 (1940).

Suppose a postal customer trips over mail negligently left on her porch by the mail carrier. Does that fall within the exception for the "loss, miscarriage, or negligent transmission of letters or postal matter"? Dolan v. U.S. Postal Svs., 546 U.S. 481 (2006) (not within exception to waiver of immunity—claim could go forward). Suppose the mother of a soldier serving in Iraq had a letter she had sent to her son returned to her marked "DECEASED" even though her son was alive? Najbar v. United States, 649 F.3d 868 (8th Cir. 2011) (within exception to waiver—claim for emotional distress dismissed).

Three of the most important exceptions are for

A. "Any claim based upon an act or omission of an employee of the Government, exercising due care, in the execution of a statute or regulation, whether or not such statute or regulation be valid, or based upon the exercise or performance or the failure to *exercise or perform a discretionary function or duty* on the part of a federal agency or an employee of the Government, whether or not the discretion involved be abused." 28 U.S.C. § 2680(a). This was the issue in the principal case.

Problems regarding the interpretation of this section are not dissimilar from those that have arisen in suits against state and local governments after their abrogation of governmental immunity. In Berkovitz v. United States, 486 U.S. 531 (1988), cited in the principal case, plaintiff was a child who was left paralyzed and unable to breathe without a respirator when he contracted polio from a dose of oral polio vaccine. His parents filed suit against the manufacturer of the vaccine and against the United States alleging that the United States (through the Office of Biologics of the Food and Drug Administration) had wrongfully licensed the manufacturer to produce the vaccine and had wrongfully approved the release of the particular lot that had injured the plaintiff. The United States moved to dismiss, invoking the discretionary function exception and arguing that it applied to all regulatory activities. Justice Marshall delivered the unanimous opinion of the Court, holding that the discretionary function exception applied only to those activities that involve an element of judgment or choice and that are based on public policy considerations to further social, economic, or political goals. Because plaintiff had alleged that the FDA had knowingly released that lot to the public without testing it for compliance with safety standards, there was no discretion involved and the United States would be liable if plaintiff could prove his allegations. Justice Marshall noted that the FDA could have adopted a policy of testing only some batches and that such a decision would not be reviewable. Having made the decision to test all batches, however, the FDA had no discretion not to test each batch.

See also United States v. S.A. Empresa (Varig Airlines), 467 U.S. 797 (1984) (FAA decision to certify airplanes as airworthy without inspecting each one and only "spot-checking" them for compliance with safety standards is a discretionary function decision that cannot subject the United States to liability); Holbrook v. U.S., 673 F.3d 341 (4th Cir. 2012) (immunity for decision to issue FAA airworthiness certificate even if discretion was abused); Irving v. United States, 162 F.3d 154 (1st Cir.1998) (OSHA's failure to inspect machine that then injured plaintiff is within discretionary function exception to liability); In re Orthopedic Bone Screw Product Liability Litigation, 264 F.3d 344 (3d Cir. 2001) (FDA's decision to approve marketing of medical device is within discretionary function exception to sovereign immunity); Merando v. United States, 517 F.3d 160 (3d Cir. 2008) (National Park Service's determination of how to distribute its finite resources to locate and remove hazardous trees falls within discretionary function exception); Freeman v. United States, 556 F.3d 326 (5th Cir. 2009) (FEMA's decisions about when, where, and how to allocate limited resources during aftermath of Hurricane Katrina's landfall in the New Orleans area are the type of decisions that the discretionary function exception is designed to shelter from suit); In re Katrina Canal Breaches

Consolidated Litigation (Robinson v. United States), 696 F.3d 436 (5th Cir. 2012) (Army Corps of Engineers' decisions concerning design and maintenance of the Mississippi River Gulf Outlet channel are protected by discretionary function exception because those decisions were susceptible to policy considerations even though the actual reasons for the decisions were varied and sometimes unknown); and A.O. Smith Corp. v. U.S., 774 F.3d 359 (6th Cir. 2014) (Army Corps immune from suit brought by Grand Ole Opry and other property owners after thousand-year flood event because it used its discretion to balance Old Hickory dam's primary objectives: commercial navigation, hydropower, and replacement of natural valley water storage along with flood control).

B. "Any claim arising out of *assault, battery, false imprisonment, false arrest,* malicious prosecution, abuse of process, libel, slander, misrepresentation, deceit, or interference with contract rights: Provided, That, with regard to acts or omissions of investigative or law enforcement officers of the United States Government, the provisions of this chapter and section 1346(b) of this title shall apply to any claim arising, on or after the date of the enactment of this proviso, out of assault, battery, false imprisonment, false arrest, abuse of process, or malicious prosecution. For the purpose of this subsection, 'investigative or law enforcement officer' means any officer of the United States who is empowered by law to execute searches, to seize evidence, or to make arrests for violations of Federal law." 28 U.S.C. § 2680(h).

Do you see why the plaintiff in United States v. Lambertson, note 4, page 25, characterized his cause of action as one for negligence rather than battery when he was injured by a government meat inspector who leapt out at him, screamed "boo," pulled his wool stocking cap over his eyes, and jumped on his back?

What does "arising out of" mean? An off-duty U.S. Navy Corpsman fired rifle shots into a car passing by the hospital where he worked. Plaintiff alleged that other U.S. Naval employees knew he was intoxicated and brandishing a rifle and negligently failed to take steps to prevent the battery. Liability? See Sheridan v. United States, 487 U.S. 392 (1988) (negligence claim relating to conduct of employees other than shooter did not "arise out of" battery and thus is not barred by statutory exception to waiver).

The FTCA's intentional tort exception does not apply to medical battery by military or veterans' benefits health care providers. Levin v. United States, 133 S.Ct. 1224 (U.S. 2013). Thus, claimant would be able to bring a medical battery claim against the United States based on a Navy doctor allegedly operating without consent. The doctor himself would be immune under the exclusive remedy provision of the Westfall Act.

C. 28 U.S.C. § 2680(j) provides that the Federal Tort Claims Act does not apply to any "claim arising out of the *combatant activities of the military or naval forces, or the Coast Guard, during time of war.*"

The Feres Doctrine: the Supreme Court has held that the FTCA does not permit recovery for claims arising out of or in the course of *activity incident to any active duty service*. Feres v. United States, 340 U.S. 135 (1950). This exception is not stated in the FTCA and was implied by the Supreme Court. Rationales for the doctrine include the need for uniformity of law, the health and welfare benefits provided to servicemen and their dependents, the absence of private liability in like circumstances, and the potential for disrupting military discipline. The definition of "incident to service" has been exhaustively litigated over the past fifty years. Although most of the cases involve soldiers struck by government vehicles while on varying degrees of leave, others raise interesting policy issues. See, e.g., United States v. Stanley, 483 U.S. 669 (1987) (plaintiff injured by LSD experiment conducted by government without informing him of the risks was precluded from suit because experiments were "incident to service"); Kitowski v. United States, 931 F.2d 1526 (11th Cir.1991) (during training exercise for Rescue Swimmer School, recruit died after being repeatedly held underwater until he became unconscious and turned blue—no recovery because still incident to service even though egregious behavior); Minns v. United States, 155 F.3d 445 (4th Cir.1998) (claims brought by wives and children of Gulf War veterans for birth defects allegedly caused by inoculations and exposure to various toxins dismissed because injuries had their genesis in injuries to soldiers incident to service); Schnitzer v. Harvey, 389 F.3d 200 (D.C. Cir. 2004) (soldier injured when portion of ceiling collapsed on him while he was watching television in prison at Fort Leavenworth where he was serving a 29-year sentence for kidnapping, rape, and murder—injury suffered incident to service); and Witt v. U.S., 379 Fed.Appx. 559 (9th Cir. 2010) (medical malpractice during treatment of appendicitis in military hospital while service member on leave).

The *Feres* doctrine was extended to shield the government against contribution or indemnity claims brought by manufacturers of products sued by service personnel (Stencel Aero Eng'g Corp. v. United States, 431 U.S. 666 (1977), reh'g denied, 434 U.S. 882 (1977)) and to include injuries caused by non-military employees of the government (United States v. Johnson, 481 U.S. 681 (1987) (civilian employees of the FAA who guided a military helicopter into the side of a mountain)).

Shield extended to government contractors? This exception may extend its reach to shield from liability government contractors through preemption only if, during wartime, the contractor is integrated into combatant activities over which the military retains command authority. See, for example, Harris v. Kellogg Brown & Root Services, Inc., 724 F.3d 458 (3d Cir. 2013) (claim by soldier electrocuted while showering due to faulty pump not preempted because military did not have command authority over how maintenance was performed in barracks) and In re KBR, Inc. Burn Pit Litigation, 744 F.3d 326 (4th Cir. 2014) (for MDL cases, adopting Third Circuit test and remanding to trial court to determine if contractor performing waste management and water treatment functions in combat zone was integrated into military command authority).

6. If a claimant is unsuccessful under the Federal Tort Claims Act, all is not necessarily lost. It is still possible to obtain relief by private bill. This is a difficult procedure requiring full cooperation of a Representative, plus tremendous persistence by an attorney.

(G) PUBLIC OFFICERS

Public officers may be subject to personal liability for tortious conduct committed in the course of their official duties. Claims against them may be predicated on the common law of torts, special statutes (a prime example being the Civil Rights Act of 1871, 42 U.S.C. § 1983), or a provision of the United States Constitution. See Bivens v. Six Unknown Named Agents, 403 U.S. 388 (1971), page 1233.

In each of these situations the public official may be shielded from liability if the official's conduct comes within *common law official immunity*—a doctrine that is separate and apart from governmental immunity. Thus, even after governmental immunity has been abolished or limited, official immunity still may protect an individual public official. Conversely, when the state has not consented to be sued on a matter, a public official may be personally liable if the conduct does not come within the immunity discussed in this section.

In addition to common law immunity, as part of legislation waiving sovereign immunity, Congress and many state legislators have granted immunity to public employees through *exclusive remedy provisions*. The Federal Tort Claims Act, through the Westfall Act, provides that the remedy against the United States for negligent acts of its employees is exclusive of any remedy against the employee. 28 U.S.C. § 2679(b). See also Agnew v. Porter, 23 Ohio St.2d 18, 260 N.E.2d 830 (1970) (construing state statute that protected policemen from tort claims based on their operation of motor vehicles while responding to emergency calls) and the Oregon state statute discussed in the *Clarke* case in this section. Those statutes usually provide that the individual must be dismissed from the case if the Attorney General (under the FTCA) or the state equivalent certifies that the federal or state employee was operating within the scope of his employment when the injury-causing conduct occurred.

The common law immunity for public officers would appear to be based "not so much [on a] desire to protect an erring officer as * * * [on] a recognition of the need of preserving independence of action, without deterrence or intimidation by the fear of personal liability and vexatious suits." Restatement (Second) of Torts § 895D, comment *b*. See also the classic statement of Learned Hand, J., in Gregoire v. Biddle, 177 F.2d 579, 581 (2d Cir.1949) ("in the end [it is] better to leave unredressed the wrongs done by dishonest officers than to subject those who try to do their duty to the constant dread of retaliation.").

Legislators and judges have been granted *absolute immunity* for acts committed within the scope of their office even if they acted in bad faith. See, e.g., Tenney v. Brandhove, 341 U.S. 367 (1951) (legislators); Pierson v. Ray, 386 U.S. 547 (1967) (judges); Voelbel v. Town of Bridgewater, 144 N.H. 599, 747 A.2d 252 (1999) (town selectman's statements about termination of police chief made at town meeting were absolutely privileged because he was acting in legislative capacity). Some states have statutes that provide immunity to attorneys appointed to represent indigent criminal defendants. See Mooney v. Frazier, 225 W.Va. 358, 693 S.E.2d 333 (2010) (listing several). The Minnesota Supreme Court has created immunity for attorneys appointed to represent indigents, finding that conserving the limited resources of the State to provide indigent defense should be husbanded and not spent on defending legal malpractice claims. Dziubak v. Mott, 503 N.W.2d 771 (Minn.1993).

The President of the United States is absolutely immune for acts within the scope of his office. Nixon v. Fitzgerald, 457 U.S. 731 (1982). But presidential aides, like other federal government officials, are entitled only to a qualified immunity. Harlow v. Fitzgerald, 457 U.S. 800 (1982).

State executive officers in some states also have the benefit of absolute immunity with regard to common law torts committed in the course of their official duties. In other states, the immunity is qualified; in some, it depends upon whether the harmful action was taken in good faith, and in others it depends on whether the official had a reasonable basis for taking the action.

When the immunity is *qualified*, it becomes similar in an operative sense to a "privilege," see page 661, and perhaps the major reason to preserve the label of "immunity" is to signify that it applies to negligent as well as intentional conduct.

The Civil Rights Act of 1871 (42 U.S.C. § 1983) created a civil remedy against anyone operating under color of state law who deprived someone of their federal constitutional rights. It is also sometimes known as the "Ku Klux Klan Act" because it was designed to provide a civil remedy against abuses committed by the Klan and others in the Southern states following the Civil War. At the time, state officials were not providing enforcement of federal civil rights and the courts interpreted the newly enacted statute to create tort liability. (See Chapter 19, Civil Rights.) State employees sued under § 1983 have a qualified immunity if they act in good faith, based on an objective test. See Harlow v. Fitzgerald, 457 U.S. 800 (1982) (adopting objective test to determine "good faith") and Brosseau v. Haugen, 543 U.S. 194 (2004) ("Qualified immunity shields an officer from suit when she makes a decision that, even if constitutionally deficient, reasonably misapprehends the law governing the circumstances she confronted.") A state official may be deemed to have violated the act if he knew or reasonably should have known that his conduct would violate plaintiff's constitutional rights or if he took the action in bad faith. Kovacic v. Villarreal, 628 F.3d 209 (5th Cir. 2010) (official must have "fair warning" that his conduct is unconstitutional). The qualified immunity extends to private individuals temporarily retained by the government to carry out its work. Filarsky v. Delia, 132 S.Ct. 1657 (U.S. 2012) (lawyer hired to do internal investigation of firefighter's alleged fraud). Prosecutors have absolute immunity under § 1983. See Imbler v. Pachtman, 424 U.S. 409 (1976). Why should a prosecutor be distinguished from officials in the executive branch of the government?

Federal officials, unless they happen to be acting under color of state law, are not covered by § 1983 but may be sued for constitutional violations directly under the federal Constitution. (See discussion of Bivens v. Six Unknown Named Agents of Federal Bureau of Narcotics, 403 U.S. 388 (1971), at page 1233.) They too enjoy qualified immunity and also some federal employees enjoy special statutory immunity. Hui v. Castaneda, 559 U.S. 799 (U.S. 2010) (Public Health Service Act precludes *Bivens* actions against PHS personnel for constitutional violations arising out of their official duties.)

Official immunity is available only with respect to acts that are "discretionary" as opposed to "ministerial" in nature. This distinction, discussed in the area of governmental immunity, has not been an easy one to apply. Obviously, if the official was engaged in formulating policy at a high level in government, the conduct will be deemed "discretionary." Comment *f* to Section 895D of Restatement (Second) of Torts sets forth most of the factors courts have looked to when they have attempted to classify an official's conduct as "discretionary" or "ministerial."

The doctrine of vicarious liability is not applicable in § 1983 and *Bivens* actions to hold public officials liable for torts committed by lower echelon employees, at least when the official in no way personally participated in the wrongdoing. Ashcroft v. Iqbal, 556 U.S. 662, 676 (2009) ("Because vicarious liability is inapplicable to *Bivens* and § 1983 suits, a plaintiff must plead that each Government-official defendant, through the official's own individual actions, has violated the Constitution."). See also Carter v. Allan, 94 Idaho 190, 484 P.2d 739 (1971) (suit against mayor and city council for injuries caused by negligently constructed sidewalk dismissed—at the very least, personal participation in the alleged negligence would have to be shown).

The Westfall Act does not apply to *Bivens* and § 1983 actions. 28 U.S.C. § 2679(b)(2).

See Restatement (Second) of Torts § 895D and Civil Actions Against State and Local Government, Its Divisions, Agencies, and Officers (Thomson 2d ed. 2002 with semi-annual updates).

CHAPTER 13

VICARIOUS LIABILITY

A is negligent; B is not; C is injured by A's negligence. By reason of some relationship between A and B, B is responsible for A's actions, although B has played no part in it, has done nothing to aid or encourage it, and in fact may have done all that he possibly could to prevent it. The result may be that B, in C's action against him, becomes liable as a defendant for C's injuries, to the same extent as if he had been negligent himself. This is sometimes called "imputed negligence." More often it is called vicarious liability or *respondeat superior*, which may be freely translated, "look to the person higher up." The topic is covered in depth in the course in Agency. Only highlights closely related to torts are presented in this Chapter. Finally, in some circumstances the negligence of another may be imputed to the plaintiff to deny or limit plaintiff's recovery through contributory or comparative negligence.

1. RESPONDEAT SUPERIOR

The various rules that have imputed the negligence of one person to another in order to impose vicarious liability upon him as a defendant all have one thing in common. Each has involved an effort, sometimes openly declared by the court, more often unexpressed or tacitly assumed, to find a financially responsible defendant. The plaintiff is injured; his life may be utterly ruined if he is left without compensation. The person who has injured him is, or is likely to be, unable to pay that compensation. There is another who stands in such a relation to the wrongdoer that it is not unreasonable to make the responsibility his; and that other is more likely to be able to pay. So, without exonerating the actual wrongdoer, who remains liable to the plaintiff and will be required to indemnify the other to the extent that he is able to do so, the liability is imposed upon both. See Tony Honoré, The Morality of Tort Law, in Philosophical Foundations of Tort Law 73, 85 (David G. Owen ed., 1995) ("The conventional reasons given for holding that the employer ought to bear the risk of loss within certain limits for the employee's harmful conduct in the course of his work are that the employer (i) has control over the business, including the work of employees, and (ii) stands to profit from the employee's services. A combination of these reasons, it is generally thought, justifies us in imposing vicarious liability on the employer. As in outcome-responsibility, the person who, in a situation of uncertainty, has a degree of control over how it will turn out, and who stands to gain if it goes in his favor, must bear the risk that it will turn out to harm another.")

In one sense this is strict liability, since the new person who is held liable is without any fault of his own and becomes liable only by reason of his relation to the actual wrongdoer. In another it is not. The foundation of vicarious liability is still negligence or other fault on the part of someone. What the law does is to broaden the liability for that fault by imposing it upon an additional defendant who is himself without fault.

Bussard v. Minimed, Inc.

California Court of Appeal, 2003.
129 Cal.Rptr.2d 675, 105 Cal.App.4th 798.

RUBIN, J. * * *

[Minimed hired a pest control company to spray pesticide overnight to eliminate fleas at its facility. Around 7:00 a.m. the next day, Minimed clerical employee Irma Hernandez arrived for work and noticed a funny smell similar to "Raid." By 10 o'clock, she felt ill, with headache, nausea, and tightness in her chest. At noon, she told two supervisors she did not feel well enough to continue working and wanted to go home. One of them asked if she wanted to see the company doctor, but she declined. The other asked whether she felt well enough to drive home, and she said yes. Hernandez was one of nine workers who went home early feeling ill. While on her way home, Hernandez rear-ended Barbara Bussard, who was stopped at a red light. Hernandez told the police officer who responded to the accident scene that she had felt dizzy and lightheaded before the accident. Plaintiff Bussard filed this action against Hernandez for negligent driving and against her employer, Minimed, in vicarious liability under the doctrine of respondeat superior, alleging that Hernandez was acting within the scope of her employment when she was driving home ill from pesticide exposure. Minimed moved for summary judgment. It argued the "going-and-coming" rule meant Hernandez was not within the course and scope of her employment during her commute home. Accordingly, it should not be held vicariously liable under respondeat superior. The trial court agreed and entered summary judgment for Minimed. This appeal followed.]

Under the doctrine of respondeat superior, an employer is ordinarily liable for the injuries its employees cause others in the course of their work. Respondeat superior imposes liability whether or not the employer was itself negligent, and whether or not the employer had control of the employee. The doctrine's animating principle is that a business should absorb the costs its undertakings impose on others. * * *

The doctrine's application requires that the employee be acting within the course of her employment, which case law defines expansively. * * * Thus, acts necessary to the comfort, convenience, health, and welfare of the employee while at work, though strictly personal and not acts of service, do not take the employee outside the scope of employment. [C] Moreover, "where the employee is combining his own business with that of his employer, or attending to both at substantially the same time, no nice inquiry will be made as to which business he was actually engaged in at the time of injury, unless it clearly appears that neither directly nor indirectly could he have been serving his employer." [Cc] It is also settled that an employer's vicarious liability may extend to willful and malicious torts of an employee as well as negligence [under certain circumstances]. [C] Finally, an employee's tortious act may be within the scope of employment even if it contravenes an express company rule and confers no benefit to the employer. [Cc]

Despite the doctrine's wide reach, courts have not defined it so broadly as to include an employee's daily commute. "Case law has established the general rule that an employee is outside the scope of his employment while engaged in his ordinary commute to and from his place of work. [C] This principle is known as the 'going-and-coming rule' and is based on several theories. One is that the employment relationship is suspended from the time the employee leaves his job until he returns. Another is that during the commute, the employee is not rendering services to his employer." [Cc]

The going-and-coming rule is not ironclad, however, and allows for several exceptions. One exception applies when an employee endangers others with a risk arising from or related to work. In determining whether such danger arises from or is related to work, case law applies a foreseeability test. Our Supreme Court describes this type of foreseeability, which is different from the foreseeability of negligence, as employees' conduct that is neither startling nor unusual. "One way to determine whether a risk is inherent in, or created by, an enterprise is to ask whether the actual occurrence was a generally foreseeable consequence of the activity. . . . '[F]oreseeability' as a test for respondeat superior merely means that in the context of the particular enterprise an employee's conduct is not so unusual or startling that it would seem unfair to include the loss resulting from it among other costs of the employer's business. [Cc] . . . [Such a test is] useful because it reflects the central justification for respondeat superior: that losses fairly attributable to an enterprise—those which foreseeably result from the conduct of the enterprise—should be allocated to the enterprise as a cost of doing business." (internal quotations omitted) [C]

This test has been applied to employees who got into car accidents on the way home after drinking alcohol at work. Courts have found a sufficient link between the drinking and the accidents to make the collisions neither startling nor unusual, and thus foreseeable under respondeat superior. * * *

Hernandez suffered pesticide exposure at work to which she attributed illness and impaired driving. [Footnote omitted.] That an employee might not be fit to drive after breathing lingering pesticide fumes for several hours is not such a startling or unusual event that we find a car accident on Hernandez's commute home was unforeseeable. Hence, the trial court erred in finding the going-and-coming rule barred appellant's claim of respondeat superior. Indeed, the going-and-coming rule was an analytical distraction. The thrust of appellant's claim for vicarious liability was that Hernandez was an "instrumentality of danger" because of what had happened to her at work. [C] Although Hernandez's decision to drive home gave respondent an opening to raise the going-and-coming rule, the rule did not apply because her decision was a fortuity that must not obscure appellant's central claim that Hernandez's job had contributed to the accident. Thus, summary judgment for respondent was improper.

Respondent argues the foreseeability exception to the going-and-coming rule does not apply because it was not negligent. In support, respondent points to the absence of evidence that it contributed in any negligent manner to the underlying pesticide exposure. It also cites the uncontested fact that its supervisors diligently inquired into Hernandez's ability to drive before she went home. Respondent contrasts its seeming blamelessness with decisions [in other cases] imposing vicarious liability for drunken employees, suggesting liability attached to the employer in those decisions in part because the employer bore some responsibility for the employee's intoxication. Whatever merit respondent's argument might have in defeating appellant's theory that respondent was directly liable to her for ordinary negligence—a theory . . . [not here addressed]—it does not apply to vicarious liability. * * *

The judgment is reversed and the court is directed to enter a new and different order denying respondent Minimed, Inc.'s motion for summary judgment. Appellant to recover her costs on appeal.

COOPER, P. J., and BOLAND, J., concurred.

O'Shea v. Welch

United States Court of Appeals, Tenth Circuit, 2003.
350 F.3d 1101.

MCKAY, CIRCUIT JUDGE. * * *

[Mr. Welch, an Osco store manager, was driving from his store to the Osco District Office to deliver Kansas City Chiefs football tickets that had been obtained from a vendor to pass out among Osco managers. During his drive, Mr. Welch made a spur of the moment decision to pull into a service station for an estimate on some work he needed done on his car, striking O'Shea's car as he turned left in front of it. O'Shea filed suit against Welch for negligence in failing to yield and against Osco in vicarious liability. On cross-motions for summary judgment, the district court held that no reasonable jury could conclude that Mr. Welch was acting within the scope of his employment. The district court did not specifically decide whether the trip to the District Office was within Mr. Welch's scope of employment because it found that even if the trip had been within the scope of Mr. Welch's employment, the stop at the service station was not.]

Pursuant to Kansas law, an employer is only liable for injuries caused by an employee acting within the scope of his employment. [C] The following Kansas jury instruction is an accurate illustration of Kansas scope of employment law: "An employee is acting within the scope of [his employment] when [he] is performing services for which [he] has been [employed], or when [he] is doing anything which is reasonably incidental to [his employment]. The test is not necessarily whether this specific conduct was expressly authorized or forbidden by the employer[ ], but whether such conduct should have been fairly foreseen from the nature of the [employment] and the duties relating to it." [C] Unfortunately, there are no Kansas cases directly on point to help define the parameters of Kansas law. Therefore, in its grant of summary judgment for Osco, the district court relied substantially on two cases from other jurisdictions. * * * [The court described those two cases and concluded that their facts were not close enough to provide much guidance.]

Due to the absence of binding authority, Appellant urges us to decide that Kansas would adopt the "slight deviation" rule which it already follows in worker's compensation cases. Approximately half of the states . . . have applied some form of the slight deviation analysis in third-party liability cases. [C] Pursuant to this analysis, "it must be determined whether the employee was on a frolic or a detour; the latter is a deviation that is sufficiently related to the employment to fall within its scope, while the former is the pursuit of the employee's personal business as a substantial deviation from or an abandonment of the employment. If an employee wholly abandons, even temporarily, the employer's business for personal reasons, the act is not within the scope of employment, and the employer is not liable under respondeat superior for the employee's conduct during that lapse. A diversion from the strict performance of a task is not an abandonment of responsibility and service to an employer, unless the very character of the diversion severs the employment relationship. Acts that are necessary to the comfort, convenience, health, and welfare of the employee while at work are not outside the scope of employment, if the conduct is not a substantial deviation from the duties of employment." [C] Personal acts that are not far removed in time, distance, or purpose are deemed to be incidental to the employment. See, e.g., Restatement (Second) of Agency § 237 (1958). Our research has not revealed a single jurisdiction that has considered and rejected slight deviation analysis in third-party liability cases. Kansas has not had the occasion to consider the slight deviation analysis in such cases. However, it has adopted the analysis in worker's compensation cases. * * * [The Court concludes that Kansas would use the slight deviation analysis in third-party liability cases like this one.]

Mindful of the volume of authority which indicates that scope of employment is generally a jury question, we turn to the parameters of slight deviation analysis. * * * Dual purpose ventures may be considered within the scope of an employee's employment. [C]

Appellant argues that Mr. Welch was acting within the scope of his employment and made only a slight deviation from his business-related trip at the time the accident occurred. Several factors have been identified as helpful in determining whether an employee has embarked on a slight or substantial deviation. They include: (1) the employee's intent; (2) the nature, time, and place of the deviation; (3) the time consumed in the deviation; (4) the work for which the employee was hired; (5) the incidental acts reasonably expected by the employer; and (6) the freedom allowed the employee in performing his job responsibilities. [C]

Applying these factors to our case, and viewing the facts in a light most favorable to Appellant, Mr. Welch intended to get an estimate for non-emergency maintenance on a car used for business. In terms of purpose, it was maintenance to a vehicle used regularly in performing his job duties for Osco. While his stop was not for emergency maintenance for his car, his stop for routine maintenance on a car used for business purposes could be considered enough of a mixed purpose by a jury to keep him within the scope of his employment with Osco.

In terms of time and place, the accident occurred minutes and feet from the direct route to Osco's District Office. Mr. Welch was simply attempting to turn from the most direct route into a service station right off the main road. At the time of the accident, he had not entered the service station. He was technically still on the road en route to the District Office. Because the accident occurred on this road, not at the service station, a jury could decide that Mr. Welch had not yet abandoned his employment for a personal errand at the time of the accident. It is unclear how long the estimate would have taken. However, we do know that if he had deviated at the time of the accident, the length of the deviation was only a few minutes or less. Mr. Welch was an Osco store manager. A jury could find that an employee in a managerial position was given some freedom to attend to certain personal needs throughout the day. It is possible that Osco reasonably expected certain incidental acts to take place, especially when a store manager was en route from one store to another or from a store to the District Office. * * *

Assuming without deciding that Mr. Welch was acting within the scope of his employment in delivering the [football] tickets to the District Office, we hold that a reasonable jury could conclude that he was acting within the scope of his employment when he attempted to turn into the service station. * * *

The district court did not specifically decide whether Mr. Welch was in the scope of his employment in making the trip from his store to the District Office. It stated: "[W]hile the court would conclude from the record that genuine issues of material fact exist with respect to whether defendant Welch's delivery of the Chiefs tickets was within the scope of his employment, the court need not address this issue because it concludes that, as a matter of law, defendant Welch's attempted stop at the service station for routine vehicle maintenance was outside the scope of his employment." [C] We agree with the district court that summary judgment is inappropriate on this issue. Therefore, this issue must be remanded for trial as well. * * *

NOTES AND QUESTIONS

1. A prime example of vicarious liability is the doctrine of *respondeat superior* as discussed in the principal cases. It is triggered by the employee acting "within the scope of his employment." There have been literally thousands of cases exploring this issue.

As the first principal case notes, an employee's commuting to and from work is generally not considered within the scope of his employment. See also O'Toole v. Carr, 175 N.J. 421, 815 A.2d 471 (2003) (law firm partner who was driving from office to part-time job as municipal judge did not subject law firm to liability).

As the second principal case notes, the court often must determine whether the employee was on a *frolic* (abandonment of employer's business while in pursuit of employee's own personal business) or a *detour* (slight deviation from employer's own business for employee's own reasons). The phrase was first uttered by Baron Parke in Joel v. Morrison, [1834] 6 C. & P. 501, 172 Eng.Rep. 1338 and provides a colorful label for the sorting between liability and no liability. This sorting is almost always done by the jury. Mauk v. Wright, 367 F.Supp. 961 (M.D.Pa.1973) (football player on his own "free time" during training camp could still be deemed within the scope of employment when he caused car accident); Edgewater Motels, Inc. v. Gatzke, 277 N.W.2d 11 (Minn.1979) (employee's negligent handling of cigarette while filling out his expense report in his hotel room found by jury to be within scope); Valdiviez v. United States, 884 F.2d 196 (5th Cir.1989) (serviceman who donated blood contaminated with the AIDS virus while on duty was not acting in the scope of his employment and thus his employer, the United States, was not vicariously liable to the patient who contracted AIDS from a transfusion of contaminated blood).

Note that both principal cases consider similar cases from the related field of worker compensation coverage, where the court is also tasked with deciding whether a worker was acting within the scope of his employment in order to determine whether the worker can obtain worker compensation benefits if it is the worker who was injured. Although those cases are analogous, they are not always helpful to the court because the doctrines have different goals. See, for example, Teurlings v. Larson, 320 P.3d 1224, 1233 (Idaho 2014) ("Our decision not to borrow this concept [the coming and going rule and its exceptions from worker compensation cases] is based upon the different goals of workers' compensation and the doctrine of respondeat superior. A liberal interpretation of the scope of employment in workers' compensation cases is warranted in order to ensure certain recovery for injured workers, regardless of fault. [C] There is no such tradition of a liberal approach to course and scope questions when considering application of respondeat superior in order to impose tort liability onto an employer.").

2. Courts have long agreed that the employer cannot insulate himself from liability by imposing safety rules or by instructing his employees to proceed carefully—no matter how specific and detailed his orders may be. See Limpus v. London Gen. Omnibus Co., 1 H. & C. 526, 158 Eng.Rep. 993 (1862) (omnibus owner who had instructed driver to "drive his horses at a steady pace" and "not on any account to race with or obstruct another omnibus" was nonetheless liable when driver ignored those instructions, thereby injuring driver of another omnibus); Cosgrove v. Ogden, 49 N.Y. 255 (1872) (owner of lumber yard who had told employee not to pile lumber in street was nonetheless liable when employee did and pile fell on six-year-old boy, severely injuring him).

3. *Vicarious Liability for Intentional Torts (Compensatory Damages).* Respondeat superior is not limited to negligent torts. An employer may be held liable for the intentional torts of his employee when they are reasonably connected with the employment and so within its "scope." Thus the employer may be liable for assault and battery on the part of an employee trying to collect a debt, because the employee is acting in furtherance of the employer's business; and the same may be true of false imprisonment, malicious prosecution, defamation, deceit or intentional infliction of emotional distress. See Chuy v. Philadelphia Eagles Football Club, 595 F.2d 1265 (3d Cir.1979) (applying Pennsylvania law). But when the employee acts from purely personal motives, as for example out of a

desire to revenge the seduction of his wife, or in a quarrel in no way connected with the employer's interests, he is considered to have departed from his employment and the employer is not liable.

What should be the result: When a professional baseball pitcher intentionally "beans" a heckling spectator? Manning v. Grimsley, 643 F.2d 20 (1st Cir.1981) (applying Massachusetts law) (whether Orioles could be vicariously liable depended on whether jury found that pitcher acted against hecklers out of personal offense or because hecklers were interfering with his ability to do his job). When the head cook in the kitchen of a restaurant throws hot oil at the under cook, hitting both the under cook and a policeman who had been called to the scene to break up the fight? Yamaguchi v. Harnsmut, 130 Cal.Rptr.2d 706, 106 Cal.App.4th 472 (2003) (jury question). When a gas station attendant shoots a customer who refused to pay cash? Jefferson v. Rose Oil Co. of Dixie, 232 So.2d 895 (La.App.1970) (jury question even though attendant had not been authorized to collect payment by force). When a minister sexually assaults a parishioner? Compare Byrd v. Faber, 57 Ohio St.3d 56, 565 N.E.2d 584 (1991) (not in furtherance as a matter of law) and Gibson v. Brewer, 952 S.W.2d 239 (Mo.1997) ("intentional sexual misconduct and intentional infliction of emotional distress are not within the scope of employment of a priest") with Mullen v. Horton, 46 Conn.App. 759, 700 A.2d 1377 (1997) (reversing trial court's grant of summary judgment in favor of religious order in case involving consensual sexual relations between priest/psychologist and parishioner/patient: trier of fact could reasonably determine that sexual relationship with the plaintiff was an unauthorized, unethical, tortious method of pastoral counseling, but not an abandonment of church business). When a health care provider sexually assaults a patient during treatment? Lisa M. v. Henry Mayo Newhall Mem. Hosp., 12 Cal.4th 291, 907 P.2d 358, 48 Cal.Rptr.2d 510 (1995) (hospital may have set the stage, but the script was entirely his own) and Porter v. Harshfield, 329 Ark. 130, 948 S.W.2d 83 (1997) (outside scope). When the college debate coach kills one of his students with multiple stab wounds? Copeland v. Samford University, 686 So.2d 190 (Ala.1996) (even if debate coach was on university's business at beginning of confrontation over student's performance at practice, murder is a major deviation for which university is not responsible). When a nurse, who learned through her employment at a doctor's office that an acquaintance of her teenage daughter's had genital herpes reveals this to her teenage daughter and the daughter tells all their friends? Jones v. Baisch, 40 F.3d 252 (8th Cir. 1994) (applying Nebraska law) (outside scope) and Doe v. Guthrie Clinic, Ltd., 22 N.Y.3d 480, 5 N.E.3d 578 (2014) (no vicarious liability for unauthorized disclosure of confidential patient records by nurse because she was acting for purely personal reasons—warning her sister-in-law that her boyfriend was being treated for an STD). When a daycare worker strikes a baby's head against a cubby to stop her from crying? Baker v. St. Francis Hosp., 126 P.3d 602 (Okla. 2005) (jury question whether daycare worker was serving her own personal needs or trying to quiet baby as part of her job, even though in a wrongful manner).

4. *Vicarious Liability for Intentional Torts (Punitive Damages).* Most courts follow the position of the Restatement (Second) of Torts § 909 (1979) that the principal (whether an individual or corporation) is liable for punitive damages only if the principal authorized or ratified the act, was

reckless in employing or retaining the agent, or the agent was employed in a managerial capacity and was acting in the scope of employment. See also College Hospital, Inc. v. Superior Court, 8 Cal.4th 704, 882 P.2d 894, 34 Cal.Rptr.2d 898 (1994) (punitive damages against employer only available if employer was guilty of malice) and Chapter 10, note 11, page 591.

5. Distinguish *Negligence in Hiring or Retention of Employee.* To be distinguished from the vicarious liability cases are cases in which the employer is liable for its own negligence in hiring or retaining an employee without adequately checking the employee's background or failing to properly train the employee. Suppose discotheque retains an employee who had previously shot a patron. Later the employee shoots another patron. Should the discotheque be liable? See Freeman v. Bell, 366 So.2d 197 (La.App.1978). See also F & T Co. v. Woods, 92 N.M. 697, 594 P.2d 745 (1979) (employer retained an alleged rapist to deliver and repair home appliances and was sued by a rape victim) and Glomb v. Ginosky, 366 Pa.Super. 206, 530 A.2d 1362 (1987) (parents liable for retaining babysitter despite child's bruises and fears). What if the employer knew the employee had been convicted of a felony and hired him as a part of a rehabilitation program?

6. The search for the deep pocket can be crucial to plaintiff's recovery. Would it be legal malpractice *not* to join the employer and only file against the employee? Hand v. Howell, Sarto & Howell, 131 So.3d 599 (Ala. 2013) (failure to name alleged tortfeasor's corporate employer not legal malpractice where, as here, tortfeasor's insurance was adequate to cover settlement; rejecting plaintiff's argument that he might have obtained a higher settlement or a higher award from jury if the corporate employer had been named).

7. The master, principal, or employer can seek indemnity from the servant, agent, or employee. An indemnity award, of course, will only be collectable if the servant, agent, or employee has assets or liability insurance of his own. See pages 409–418.

2. INDEPENDENT CONTRACTORS

Murrell v. Goertz

Court of Appeals of Oklahoma, 1979.
597 P.2d 1223.

REYNOLDS, JUDGE. Mrs. C.L. Murrell, plaintiff in the trial court, appeals the order sustaining the motion for summary judgment in favor of co-defendant Oklahoma Publishing Company (appellee), in a suit for damages resulting from an alleged assault and battery by co-defendant Bruce Goertz.

On August 27, 1976, Bruce Goertz was making monthly collections for the delivery of appellant's morning newspaper, the Daily Oklahoman, which is published by appellee. Appellant questioned Goertz concerning damage to appellant's screen door caused by the newspaper carrier throwing the newspaper into it. An argument ensued culminating in appellant slapping Goertz who in turn struck appellant. As a result thereof, appellant was allegedly injured, requiring medical

treatment and subsequent hospitalization. Appellant filed suit in the District Court of Oklahoma County seeking a total of $52,500 for past and future medical expenses, pain and suffering, and exemplary damages.

Appellant's petition contends that Goertz was a servant of appellee either by agreement between the co-defendants, or by appellee creating the apparent belief in appellant that Goertz was a servant by allowing Goertz to deliver the paper, advertise that product, and to collect for accounts due. Both appellee and Goertz answered denying that Goertz was appellee's servant. * * * [Those who enter into a contract to have work performed are not vicariously responsible for the tortious acts of independent contractors.]

The line of demarcation between an independent contractor and a servant is not clearly drawn. An independent contractor is one who engaged to perform a certain service for another according to his own methods and manner, free from control and direction of his employer in all matters connected with the performance of the service except as to the result thereof. [C] The parties agree that the decisive test for determining whether a person is an employee or an independent contractor is the right to control the physical details of the work. [C] * * *

Appellant contends that the distribution of papers and the collection of money therefor is an integral part of appellee's business. Appellant cites the following factors as indicative of the high degree of control appellee possesses over the physical details of the work: ultimate control over the territorial boundaries of Goertz's route; appellee set a standard policy that paper deliveries be completed by 6 a.m.; appellee set policy that all papers were to be held by rubber bands; customers who were missed by the carrier called appellee to report it; complaints concerning the service were lodged with appellee; and new subscribers called appellee to initiate newspaper service.

Appellee submits that the affidavit of Russell Westbrook and Goertz's deposition reveal that Goertz had no contact with appellee. Westbrook stated that he was an independent newspaper distributor for appellee and that he employed Bruce Goertz as an independent carrier salesman. Westbrook further stated that Goertz was responsible only to him for the delivery of the newspapers and was in no way under the supervision, dominion, and control of appellee. By the terms of Westbrook's contract, he was an independent contractor and likewise not subject to the supervision, dominion, and control of appellee as to the manner and method of performing his job. Appellee further cites the statements of Westbrook and Goertz that Goertz was collecting money for Westbrook at the time of the incident with appellant, and that appellee received money only from Westbrook.

From a review of the record we conclude that the evidence is reasonably susceptible of but one inference. Bruce Goertz was hired as an independent carrier salesman by his friend Russell Westbrook, who was himself an independent contractor. Appellee had no input into the decision to hire Goertz and had no knowledge of his employment. Goertz had no direct contract with appellee in his business operations. While appellee established certain policies and standards to which all distributors and carriers were to adhere, such policies and standards do not rise to that level of supervision, dominion, and control over Goertz's day to day activities as to make him appellee's servant.

Affirmed.

NOTES AND QUESTIONS

1. According to a "general rule" that developed both in English and American law, one who arranges for work to be done by an independent contractor is not vicariously liable for the contractor's torts. The distinction between a servant or employee and an independent contractor has been said to lie in the fact that the latter does the work on his own time, in his own way, and under no one's directions but his own, so that the one who selected the contractor has no control or right of control over the manner in which it is done. It is therefore to be regarded as the contractor's own enterprise, and he, rather than the one who retained his services, is the proper party to be charged with the risk. Also, no doubt, there is in the picture, although not often expressed, the fact that, taken as a class, independent contractors are in the main financially responsible parties, at least to a far greater extent than employees, and thus there is less need to look for a deeper pocket.

2. Should the state be vicariously liable for the actions of foster parents when a foster child is injured due to the negligence of the foster parents? Mitzner v. State, 257 Kan. 258, 891 P.2d 435 (1995) (foster parents are independent contractors and state is not liable). Should the state be vicariously liable for the medical malpractice of those with whom it arranged to provide medical care to prisoners? Herbert v. District of Columbia, 716 A.2d 196 (D.C.App.1998) (state not liable for actions of independent contractors). Should a hospital be vicariously liable for the negligent acts of a radiologist, an independent contractor permitted to practice at the hospital? Estates of Milliron v. Francke, 243 Mont. 200, 793 P.2d 824 (1990) (no liability for independent contractor). Should a cruise ship be liable for the medical malpractice of the ship's doctor? Carnival Corp. v. Carlisle, 953 So.2d 461 (Fla. 2007) (applying maritime law) (no liability because no control over independent doctor's actions).

3. The "general rule" remains. But many exceptional situations have been recognized in which vicarious liability is imposed. The next principal case discusses one of those exceptions.

Maloney v. Rath

Supreme Court of California, 1968.
69 Cal.2d 442, 445 P.2d 513, 71 Cal.Rptr. 897.

[Defendant's automobile collided with a car driven by plaintiff because defendant's brakes failed. The trial court found that defendant had no reason to know the brakes were defective. Three months prior to the accident, defendant had her brakes overhauled by a mechanic, Peter Evanchik. The trial court determined that Evanchik's negligent repair was the cause of the accident and rendered a judgment in favor of defendant. Plaintiff appealed.

The Supreme Court of California first stated that it would not hold a motorist strictly liable for damage caused by brake failure. Although the state vehicle code required that brakes be maintained "in good working order," a failure to comply could be excused by the owner's exercise of "ordinary prudence," and the court found that defendant had met that standard of care. It then discussed the question of whether defendant vehicle owner could delegate the responsibility of making a brake repair to an independent contractor.]

TRAYNOR, JUSTICE. * * * Unlike strict liability, a nondelegable duty operates, not as a substitute for liability based on negligence, but to assure that when a negligently caused harm occurs, the injured party will be compensated by the person whose activity caused the harm and who may therefore properly be held liable for the negligence of his agent, whether his agent was an employee or an independent contractor. To the extent that recognition of nondelegable duties tends to insure that there will be [a] financially responsible defendant available to compensate for the negligent harms caused by that defendant's activity, it ameliorates the need for strict liability to secure compensation. * * *

[W]e have found nondelegable duties in a wide variety of situations and have recognized that the rules set forth in the Restatement of Torts with respect to such duties are generally in accord with California law. Such duties include those imposed by a public authority as a condition of granting a franchise [cc], the duty of a condemning agent to protect a severed parcel from damage [c], the duty of a general contractor to construct a building safely [c], the duty to exercise due care when an "* * * independent contractor is employed to do work which the employer should recognize as necessarily creating a condition involving an unreasonable risk of bodily harm to others unless special precautions are taken" [cc], the duty of landowners to maintain their property in a reasonably safe condition [cc], and to comply with applicable safety ordinances [cc], and the duty of employers and suppliers to comply with the safety provisions of the Labor Code [cc].

Restatement (Second) of Torts § 423 provides that "One who carries on an activity which threatens a grave risk of serious bodily harm or death unless the instrumentalities used are carefully * * * maintained, and who employs an independent contractor to * * * maintain such instrumentalities, is subject to the same liability for physical harm caused by the negligence of the contractor in * * * maintaining such instrumentalities as though the employer had himself done the work of * * * maintenance." Section 424 provides that "One who by statute or by administrative regulation is under a duty to provide specified safeguards or precautions for the safety of others is subject to liability to the others for whose protection the duty is imposed for harm caused by the failure of a contractor employed by him to provide such safeguards or precautions." Both of these sections point to a nondelegable duty in this case. The statutory provisions regulating the maintenance and equipment of automobiles constitute express legislative recognition of the fact that improperly maintained motor vehicles threaten "a grave risk of serious bodily harm or death." The responsibility for minimizing that risk or compensating for the failure to do so properly rests with the person who owns and operates the vehicle. He is the party primarily to be benefitted by its use; he selects the contractor and is free to insist upon one who is financially responsible and to demand indemnity from him; the cost of his liability insurance that distributes the risk is properly attributable to his activities; and the discharge of the duty to exercise reasonable care in the maintenance of his vehicle is of the utmost importance to the public.

In the present case it is undisputed that the accident was caused by a failure of defendant's brakes that resulted from her independent contractor's negligence in overhauling or in thereafter inspecting the brakes. Since her duty to maintain her brakes in compliance with the provisions of the Vehicle Code is nondelegable, the fact that the brake failure was the result of her independent contractor's negligence is no defense.

The judgment and the order denying the [plaintiff's] motion for judgment notwithstanding the verdict on the issue of liability are reversed and the case is remanded to the trial court for a new trial on the issue of damages only.

NOTES AND QUESTIONS

1. How does the imposition of liability on the theory of a nondelegable duty differ from strict liability?

2. There are several common situations where retaining an independent contractor will not insulate the party from vicarious liability:

A. *Nondelegable Duties.* There are certain responsibilities that courts will not permit to be delegated to an independent contractor. Or rather, the duty can be delegated to another (the car mechanic) but the responsibility for a negligent failure remains with the owner. *Maloney* contains a broad, but not totally complete, list of examples. There is no obvious criterion by which it can be determined whether a duty is "delegable" or not. In the last analysis, the cases represent *ad hoc* decisions that, as a matter of public policy, one cannot avoid particular responsibilities by retaining someone else to discharge them, because of the importance of the duty. Compare Westby v. Itasca County, 290 N.W.2d 437 (Minn. 1980) (county vicariously liable for an independent contractor's failure to clear the road of mud from an exploded beaver dam); Miller v. Martin, 838 So.2d 761 (La. 2003) (state vicariously liable for abuse inflicted upon children by foster parents because Department of Social Services' custodial duty is non-delegable); Jackson v. Power, 743 P.2d 1376 (Alaska 1987) (general acute care hospital's duty to provide emergency room care nondelegable and therefore facility liable for actions of independent physician in emergency room) with I.H. v. County of Lehigh, 610 F.3d 797 (3d. Cir. 2010) (applying Pennsylvania law) (foster care agency not vicariously liable for negligent driving of foster father because he was an independent contractor and the agency's duty did not fall into the nondelegable duty exception); Baptist Memorial Hospital System v. Sampson, 969 S.W.2d 945 (Tex.1998) (declining invitation of court of appeals to find a nondelegable duty for hospital emergency room); Broussard v. United States, 989 F.2d 171 (5th Cir.1993) (in FTCA case, hospital not liable for actions of emergency room physicians who were independent contractors); Estates of Milliron v.

Francke, 243 Mont. 200, 793 P.2d 824 (1990) (no nondelegable duty to provide radiology services); Fletcher v. South Peninsula Hosp., 71 P.3d 833 (Alaska 2003) (declining to extend non-delegable duty for emergency room to operating room); and Arizona v. Hicks, 219 Ariz. 328, 198 P.3d 1200 (2009) (state's duty to provide indigent criminal defendant with competent counsel was met when competent counsel was appointed; no vicarious liability under non-delegable duty doctrine for alleged malpractice of court-appointed attorney).

B. *Apparent Authority.* One who expressly or impliedly represents that another party is his servant or agent may be held vicariously liable for the latter's negligent acts to the extent of that representation. This result may occur even though the negligent party is an independent contractor or even when there is no employment or contractual relationship whatsoever between the negligent actor and the party making the representation.

This theory, called apparent authority, apparent agency, or agency by estoppel, allows an injured party who reasonably relies on the representation to hold the party who made the misrepresentation liable. The theory has sometimes been utilized to hold franchisors vicariously liable for the negligent conduct of their independent contractor franchisees. See Singleton v. International Dairy Queen, Inc., 332 A.2d 160 (Del.1975); Wood v. Holiday Inns, Inc., 508 F.2d 167 (5th Cir.1975) and Gizzi v. Texaco, Inc., 437 F.2d 308 (3d Cir.), cert. denied, 404 U.S. 829 (1971) (Texaco's advertising and other representations sufficient for a jury to determine that the company had vested "apparent authority" in a dealer who sold a van on his own behalf). But see O'Banner v. McDonald's Corp., 173 Ill.2d 208, 218 Ill.Dec. 910, 670 N.E.2d 632 (1996) (customer who was injured in slip and fall accident in bathroom did not show the justifiable reliance necessary to hold franchisor liable through apparent agency) and Patterson v. Domino's Pizza, LLC, 60 Cal.4th 474, 177 Cal.Rptr.3d 539, 333 P.3d 723 (2014) (no showing franchisor controlled day-to-day decisions). The theory also has been applied in cases holding hospitals vicariously liable for the medical malpractice of independent physicians practicing medicine on their premises. See, e.g., Seneris v. Haas, 45 Cal.2d 811, 291 P.2d 915 (1955) ("record reveals defendant did nothing to put [patient] on notice that the X-ray laboratory was not an integral part of the institution, and it cannot seriously be contended that [patient] should have inquired whether the individual actors who examined him were [hospital's] employees"); Clark v. Southview Hosp. & Family Health Ctr., 68 Ohio St.3d 435, 444, 628 N.E.2d 46, 53 (1994) ("A hospital may be held liable under the doctrine of agency by estoppel for the negligence of independent medical practitioners practicing in the hospital if it holds itself out to the public as a provider of medical services and in the absence of notice or knowledge to the contrary, the patient looks to the hospital, as opposed to the individual practitioner, to provide competent medical care."); and York v. Rush-Presbyterian-St. Luke's Medical Ctr., 222 Ill.2d 147, 305 Ill.Dec. 43, 854 N.E.2d 635 (2006) (hospital liable for independent anesthesiologist's malpractice because consent form did not disclose he was not employee of hospital, hospital employee assigned him to operating room, he wore scrubs and lab coat with hospital insignia on them, and he did not inform patient that he was independent). But see Simmons v. Tuomey Regional Med. Ctr., 341 S.C. 32, 533 S.E.2d 312 (2000) (cannot use doctrine if patient is treated in emergency room by patient's own physician or where patient is admitted to hospital by private, independent physician with staff privileges at hospital) and Baptist Memorial Hospital System v. Sampson, 969 S.W.2d 945 (Tex.1998) (emergency room patient failed to establish the reasonable reliance required for apparent authority because written consent form signed by patient before treatment explained that ER physicians were independent contractors and not employees of hospital). It also has been applied to hold a cruise line liable for the medical malpractice of an onboard nurse and doctor. Franza v. Royal Caribbean Cruises, Ltd., 772 F.3d 1225 (11th Cir. 2014) (applying maritime law) (ship doctor and nurse wore same uniform as rest of crew, doctor was introduced as a ship Officer, marketing materials described infirmary as staffed by cruise line crew, and patient was billed by cruise line for services of infirmary personnel).

C. *Inherently Dangerous Activities* or *Peculiar Risk of Harm.* Originally this came from Bower v. Peate, [1876] 1 Q.B.D. 321, where the foundation of plaintiff's building was undermined by an excavation. It is not limited to activities (such as blasting) that involve an extraordinarily high degree of danger and are thus classified as "abnormally dangerous" for the purposes of imposing strict liability on the actor. See Chapter 14. Rather, the exception is applicable when the activity involves a *peculiar risk of harm* that calls for more than ordinary precaution. This would be the case, for example, if a contractor were engaged to transport giant logs, six feet in diameter, over the highway, where an obvious special danger arises unless the logs are properly anchored and secured. Risley v. Lenwell, 129 Cal.App.2d 608, 277 P.2d 897 (1954). Or to fly a small private plane to a meeting in western Colorado. Huddleston v. Union Rural Electric Assn., 841 P.2d 282 (Colo. 1992). Or spray a potent herbicide capable of killing oak, birch, poplar, and maple trees. Brandenburg v. Briarwood Forestry Servs., LLC, 354 Wis.2d 413, 847 N.W.2d 395 (2014). Or to provide security to a manufacturing plant with armed guards. Pusey v. Bator, 94 Ohio St.3d 275, 762 N.E.2d 968 (2002). Or to transport prisoners from Florida to Montana in a van. Paull v. Park County, 352 Mont. 465, 218 P.3d 1198 (2009). Or the apprehension of fugitives by independent contractors hired by a defendant bail bondsman. Stout v. Warren, 176 Wash.2d 263, 290 P.3d 972 (2012). Or to sell ice cream to small children from an ice cream vending truck on a busy street. Wilson v. Good Humor Corp., 757 F.2d 1293 (D.C.Cir.1985). Under those circumstances, those injured by the contractor's negligence would be able to recover through vicarious liability from the person who hired the contractor. Suppose homeowner hired a roofing contractor to replace the roof on his home and a passerby was injured when the contractor's employee negligently dropped hot tar from the roof. The bystander would be able to sue the homeowner through this exception to the rule that homeowner is not liable for the actions of independent contractors. But what if the person injured is the roofer's own employee rather than a bystander? Privette v. Superior Court, 5 Cal.4th 689, 854 P.2d 721, 21 Cal.Rptr.2d 72 (1993) (exception not available for contractor's employee—no vicarious liability).

Negligence Collateral to Risk. The exception for inherently dangerous activities does not apply when the independent contractor's negligence is deemed "collateral" to the inherent risk of the activity: in other words, not recognizable in advance as particularly likely to occur or as calling for special precaution. For example, how should a court classify negligence on the part of a contractor in operating a wrecking crane? See Garczynski v.

Darin & Armstrong Co., 420 F.2d 941 (6th Cir.1970) (applying Michigan law) (affirming trial court's ruling that conduct of independent contractor crane operator in knocking a worker off a steel girder was collateral to the usual risk of operating a crane).

D. *"Illegal Activities."* One who contracts for performance of an illegal act is vicariously liable for any damage even if the agent is an independent contractor. See King v. Loessin, 572 S.W.2d 87 (Tex.Civ.App.1978) (company who hired private investigator to obtain copies of sales invoices from its competitors was liable for damage done during private investigator's break-in to competitor's offices) and Hester v. Bandy, 627 So.2d 833 (Miss. 1993) (dealer hired repossesor who trespassed to repossess van).

3. Distinguish *Negligence in the Selection of the Contractor.* If a company is negligent in selecting the contractor or in giving improper directions or equipment or in failing to stop any unreasonably dangerous practices that come to its attention, the company will be held liable for *its own* negligence, which has combined with that of the contractor. See Larson v. Wasemiller, 738 N.W.2d 300 (Minn. 2007) (noting that a majority of jurisdictions permit a claim of negligent credentialing against hospitals based on their negligence in granting of hospital privileges to independent physicians). This, of course, is not vicarious liability at all, but ordinary concurrent negligence.

3. JOINT ENTERPRISE

Popejoy v. Steinle

Supreme Court of Wyoming, 1991.
820 P.2d 545.

GOLDEN, JUSTICE. * * * On the morning of May 8, 1986, Connie Steinle, accompanied by her seven-year-old daughter and a niece, left the family ranch for Douglas, Wyoming. The purpose of the trip was to purchase a calf for the daughter to raise on the ranch. While en route to Douglas, the truck Connie was driving collided with a vehicle driven by Ronald Popejoy. Connie died as a result of the accident and Ronald sustained injuries initially diagnosed as a muscle strain. As a result of his injuries, Ronald received outpatient medical treatment at a local hospital. * * *

Approximately fifteen months after the accident Ronald Popejoy began experiencing severe pain in his neck and back. Because other treatments failed to correct the problem, he underwent two separate neurosurgeries to fuse cervical vertebrae. Following the second surgical procedure, Ronald attempted unsuccessfully to reopen Connie Steinle's estate which had been probated and closed more than a year earlier. The Popejoys then filed a creditor's claim against the estate [of Connie's husband, William,] as he had died in the interim following Connie's death [from an illness unrelated to Connie's accident]. After the Popejoys' creditor's claim was rejected, they filed a complaint against the personal representatives of William's estate. The complaint was premised on the theory that William and Connie Steinle were engaged in a joint venture when Connie embarked on her May 8, 1986 "business trip" to pick up the daughter's calf [and thus that William was liable for Connie's negligent driving].

* * *

[The trial court granted the Estate's motion for summary judgment, finding that a careful reading of the depositions and affidavits submitted to support the motion showed that William had no financial or other interest in the purpose of the trip to town, such that vicarious liability could be imposed upon him based on the alleged negligence of his wife. This appeal followed.]

The Popejoys seek to impute Connie Steinle's alleged negligence to her husband William's estate by claiming that the Steinles were engaged in a joint venture relationship at the time of the accident. "The burden of establishing the existence of a joint venture is upon the party asserting that the relationship exists." [Cc] Consequently, the Popejoys are required to demonstrate each of the elements of a joint venture relationship in order to prevail. They must also show that the joint venture relationship existed at the time of Connie's alleged negligent conduct. [C]

This court has never set forth a specific "test" of elements necessary to prove existence of a joint venture. The parties in this case and many courts from other jurisdictions frequently use the terms "joint venture" and "joint enterprise" interchangeably and the two terms are conceptually closely related. It has been stated that "[t]he term joint enterprise is often used interchangeably with joint venture, and it has been stated that when the term joint enterprise is used to describe a business or commercial undertaking, no significant differences between the terms may be drawn."

* * *

Although the Restatement [(Second) of Torts § 491 comment *c* at 548 (1965)] does not define elements of a joint venture, it does define the four elements of a joint enterprise as:

> (1) an agreement, express or implied, among the members of the group; (2) a common purpose to be carried out by the group; (3) community of pecuniary interest in that purpose, among the members; and (4) an equal right to a voice in the direction of the enterprise, which gives an equal right of control.

In *Holliday* [v. Bannister, 741 P.2d 89 (Wyo.1987)], we considered among several issues a claim that a father and son were engaged in a joint enterprise while together on a hunting trip. The plaintiff in *Holliday,* as personal representative for the estate of a hunter accidently shot and killed by the son, asserted that the father was vicariously liable for his son's negligence.

In Part II of the *Holliday* opinion and the cases and authorities cited therein, we emphasized the commercial and profit motive aspects of the "community of pecuniary interest" element of a joint enterprise or joint venture relationship. * * *

The Popejoys' claim in this case is premised on a theory of joint venture and the contention that William and Connie Steinle were engaged in securing an appreciable business asset for their family business at the time of the accident. In the type of business activity being alleged by the Popejoys, there are no significant differences between a joint venture and a joint enterprise. Thus, in determining the existence or nonexistence of a joint venture relationship in this case, we apply the same four-pronged joint enterprise test in *Holliday,* 741 P.2d at 93.

In support of its * * * motion for summary judgment, the Estate submitted several affidavits, depositions and other materials. The Steinle daughter who was accompanying her mother at the time of the accident and who was the intended recipient of the calf they were on their way to buy submitted an affidavit stating that her father did not ordinarily have any ownership interest in the cattle that she, her sisters and mother raised and owned. She also stated that she, her mother and sisters were primarily responsible for caring for the "pets" and other domestic animals raised on the ranch.

Carl Steinle, William's brother and one of two personal representatives of the Estate, submitted an affidavit indicating that Connie and the Steinle daughters regularly kept numerous farm animals as their own and that William would not have had any interest in the calf that was to be purchased. Further, he stated that the purpose of the trip was to purchase a calf for the daughter to raise as her own. A second Steinle daughter also submitted an affidavit confirming the purpose of the trip.

Other materials submitted with the motion supplemented the affidavits described above and included the affidavit and deposition of Roger Wesnitzer, a certified public accountant. After reviewing Steinle tax records, ranch journal books, bank records, livestock sales receipts and the other affidavits and depositions, Wesnitzer stated that other livestock raised by the Steinle daughters in the past had been given directly to the children by the parents. Further, he stated that while William Steinle bore the costs of raising such livestock on his ranch, sale proceeds went directly to the children. Similar "nonranch" cattle owned by the Steinle daughters in the past had been separately identified by brands owned by the daughters and sale proceeds had gone directly to the children. He stated that William and Connie did not share in any portion of livestock sale proceeds of their daughters' cattle. He concluded that it was his professional opinion that the trip in which Connie was killed and Ronald was injured did not involve a joint venture between William and Connie Steinle.

* * *

In attempting to demonstrate existence of a joint venture relationship, the Popejoys relied extensively on the affidavits provided by Ted Grooms, a certified public accountant. Grooms stated in his first affidavit that William and Connie Steinle did not separate their income and expenses with respect to their ranching activities and that Connie did much of the work around the ranch because of William's poor health. In his second affidavit, Grooms maintained that after reviewing all the depositions, affidavits, business and tax records submitted by the Steinles for the years 1982–1986 he was convinced that William and Connie were involved in a joint venture at the time of Connie's trip on May 8, 1986. Grooms stated that William's eventual purchase of the calf for his daughter a week after the accident, his efforts in raising and selling the calf, and the fact that the calf bore the brand of the daughter's older sister led him to the conclusion that a joint venture relationship existed between Connie and William. Finally, and significantly, he stated that it was his understanding that only a pecuniary interest and not an interest in profit was needed to show existence of a joint venture.

Noticeably missing from Grooms' testimony is any evidence that proceeds from the sale of the calf that Connie and the daughter were on their way to purchase on May 8, 1986, would not have gone solely to the daughter. Along the same lines, he found no evidence that proceeds from the actual sale of the calf that was eventually purchased for the daughter following the accident went to anyone other than the daughter. Thus, it appears that only the daughter had an actual pecuniary or financial interest in the profits of the sale of the calf that was to be purchased at the time of the accident.

The record in this case shows that Connie's trip to Douglas to purchase a calf for the couple's seven-year-old daughter was [not a joint venture of the ranch but] a family undertaking. * * *

In *Holliday,* this court adopted and applied a narrow definition of joint enterprise. See, e.g., W. Keeton, *Prosser and Keaton on the Law of Torts* § 72 (5th ed. 1984). By limiting the application of the doctrine to a venture having a distinct business or pecuniary purpose, we avoid the imposition of a basically commercial concept upon relationships not having this characteristic. [C] With our decision in this case, we reaffirm our holding in *Holliday* and continue to restrict application of the joint venture/joint enterprise doctrine in Wyoming.

After a careful review of the record, we hold that the Popejoys failed to demonstrate the existence of a genuine issue of material fact which would preclude summary judgment as a matter of law. William and Connie Steinle were not engaged in a joint venture when Connie attempted to drive to Douglas to purchase the calf for their daughter.

The decision of the trial court is affirmed.

NOTES AND QUESTIONS

1. The joint enterprise theory was developed by American courts to impose liability vicariously upon one person who is engaged in the same activity with another person committing the tortious act. The Restatement (Second) of Torts § 491, comment *c*, quoted in the principal case, sets out four elements required for liability to be imposed. Because of these elements, each member of the joint enterprise is held to be the agent of the other; each may therefore be held liable for the acts of the other.

2. Note the fact specific nature of the inquiry on joint enterprise in the principal case, including testimony from witnesses, documents reflecting the ranch's and the family's financial dealings, and expert testimony. The decision to allow the seven-year-old daughter to keep the

profit from the calf she raised turned out to have significant consequences years later.

3. This theory as a means of imposing vicarious liability is most commonly applied in automobile accident cases. It has been applied occasionally in other contexts. See, e.g., Cullinan v. Tetrault, 123 Me. 302, 122 A. 770 (1923) (one party purchases liquor for a party); see Shell Oil Co. v. Prestidge, 249 F.2d 413 (9th Cir.1957) (parties prospecting for oil). It generally does not apply to parties who take pleasure trips or other nonbusiness journeys together. Fugate v. Galvin, 84 Ill.App.3d 573, 406 N.E.2d 19, 22, 40 Ill.Dec. 318 (1980) (travel arrangements to meet a mutual friend not a joint venture); Lovell v. Brock, 330 Ark. 206, 952 S.W.2d 161 (1997) (hunting party). As in the principal case, joint ownership without more usually is not enough to impose vicarious liability; there must be some business purpose involved.

4. BAILMENTS

Malchose v. Kalfell

Supreme Court of North Dakota, 2003.
664 N.W.2d 508.

NEUMANN, JUSTICE. The Kalfells appeal from the trial court's judgment finding them liable in a negligence action arising out of an automobile accident. We affirm.

[Eric Kalfell and Kelly Malchose were involved in a motor vehicle accident. At the time of the accident, Eric Kalfell was driving a 1992 Pontiac Bonneville titled in the names of his parents, Lance and Lisa Kalfell. Malchose sued all three Kalfells seeking to recover damages against Eric Kalfell for negligence, and against his parents as owners of the car under the family car doctrine and negligent entrustment. After a bench trial, the trial court found Eric Kalfell at fault for negligence and his parents liable under the family car doctrine. The Kalfells appeal.]

The Kalfells argue the trial court erred * * * [on three grounds, one of which was] in determining Lance and Lisa Kalfell were liable under the family car doctrine because Eric Kalfell was an adult child living away from home, Eric was the [true] owner of the vehicle involved in the accident, and the car was not being used for family business. * * *

The family car doctrine places liability on the owner of a vehicle for negligent operation by a person using the vehicle with the express or implied consent of the owner for purposes of the business or pleasure of the owner's family. [C] The owner is not liable for his own negligence; he is vicariously liable for the tortious acts of the driver. * * * To be liable, the head of household need not own the vehicle, but must furnish it for the use, pleasure, and business of himself or a member of the family. Whether the family car doctrine applies is a question of fact. We will not set aside a trial court's findings of fact unless they are clearly erroneous. A trial court's findings of fact are clearly erroneous only if they are induced by an erroneous view of the law or, although there is some evidence to support the findings of fact, on the record as a whole we are left with a definite and firm conviction a mistake has been made.

Here, Lance and Lisa Kalfell were named on the vehicle's certificate of title as owners at the time of the accident. While the Kalfells presented evidence Eric Kalfell had used the vehicle as collateral for a loan, we agree with the trial court that this does not prove a transfer of ownership. Even if title had transferred to Eric Kalfell, the record shows he could not financially maintain the vehicle and attend college without Lance and Lisa Kalfell's support. Record evidence shows Lance and Lisa Kalfell purchased the vehicle and furnished it to Eric Kalfell. The Kalfells argue Eric Kalfell had moved away from the family ranch in Montana to attend college and he was, therefore, no longer a member of the family. Evidence presented at trial, however, showed Eric Kalfell was a member of the Kalfell family for the purposes of the family car doctrine. Eric Kalfell listed the family's ranch address on his driver's license, Lance and Lisa Kalfell claimed Eric Kalfell as a dependent on their tax return, and Lance and Lisa Kalfell financially supported Eric Kalfell while he was at college. Based on the record evidence, we conclude the trial court's findings of fact were not clearly erroneous and, in the totality of the circumstances, the trial court did not err in determining the family car doctrine applied. * * *

The trial court's judgment is affirmed.

[The concurring opinion of Justice Kapsner is omitted.]

NOTES AND QUESTIONS

1. Under the common law in most states, a bailment does not make a bailor vicariously liable for the acts of the bailee in the use of the chattel. Recall, for example, Lubitz v. Wells, the first negligence case of Chapter 4. There was no suggestion the father was vicariously liable for his son's negligent use of the golf club simply because the father was the owner of the golf club. Instead, the plaintiff attempted to prove that the father had acted negligently in leaving the golf club in the yard where he knew a child might find it and play with it.

2. The common law rule on bailments has been altered in many states by decision, as in the principal case, or by statute, especially with respect to automobiles.

A. *The Family Purpose Doctrine.* The "family purpose" or "family car" doctrine is a court-created legal fiction by which the owner of an automobile is held vicariously liable when the car is negligently driven by a member of the immediate household. The fiction is predicated on the assumption that the driver is implementing a "family purpose," even if the driver is only using the automobile for his own pleasure or convenience. The car must be driven with the permission of the owner, but this may be inferred from very general circumstances. Courts have consistently held the parents of teenager drivers liable even when the teenager was exceeding the scope of the permission. See, for example, Young v. Beck, 227 Ariz. 1, 251 P.3d 380 (2011) (teen not permitted to give rides to others was given permission to drive to friend's home to spend the night and then to drive home the next morning injured plaintiff during the night while driving around with several friends as they threw eggs at houses and parked cars). In general, it is limited to automobiles, but the court in Stewart v. Stephens, 225 Ga. 185, 166 S.E.2d 890 (1969), extended it to a "family motorboat." Who should be primarily liable as between a father or mother? What if the mother has custody of the child? See Starr v. Hill, 353 S.W.3d 478 (Tenn. 2011) (question of fact for jury whether noncustodial father, who was owner of vehicle that had been purchased for teenager's use pursuant to terms of divorce decree, had sufficient day-to-day control over teenager's use of vehicle to subject him to liability under family purpose doctrine).

B. *Presumption that Owner Controls the Vehicle.* Some older cases held that the mere presence of the owner in the car establishes his right of control over the driving, so that the owner becomes responsible for the acts of the driver as if the driver were the agent of the owner. See, for example, Boker v. Luebbe, 198 Neb. 282, 252 N.W.2d 297 (1977). A number of states have retreated from this position even when the parties are close relatives because it is unrealistic and may encourage dangerous back-seat driving, Bauer v. Johnson, 79 Ill.2d 324, 38 Ill.Dec. 149, 403 N.E.2d 237 (1980); Reed v. Hinderland, 135 Ariz. 213, 660 P.2d 464 (1983) (the mere presence of the owner in an automobile driven by another does not create any presumption of a master-servant relationship or joint enterprise; existence of such a relationship must be proved by the party asserting it in the same manner as any other issue in the case). This does not relieve the owner of a duty to object to or otherwise interfere with negligent driving as soon as becoming aware of it. The breach of that duty would trigger liability based on primary negligence on the part of the owner, not vicarious liability. See Sherman v. Korff, 353 Mich. 387, 91 N.W.2d 485 (1958). See also next principal case discussing imputing of the negligence of the driver to the contributory negligence of the passenger-owner.

C. *Automobile Consent Statutes.* Many states have statutes that make the owner of an automobile vicariously liable for injury caused by the negligent operation of the vehicle as long as it is being used with the owner's consent. Problems of statutory construction arising under those statutes include what constitutes "consent"; what happens when the scope of the consent is exceeded; and whether "owner" includes conditional sellers who have legal title but no power to control the vehicle. What if a parent co-signed on a car loan but was not listed as a co-owner on the title?

3. The "omnibus clause" in standard automobile liability insurance policies may lessen the need for the use of consent statutes. This clause provides that liability insurance for the designated automobile applies to the named insured, any member of the insured's household, and to any person using the automobile with the insured's permission, provided the use was within the scope of permission. Under what circumstances might the plaintiff still need the benefit of the consent statutes even if the automobile liability insurance policy covered the actions of the driver?

4. What if the owner is a rental car company? Should it be vicariously liable through automobile consent statutes or other theories of vicarious liability for the negligent driving of those to whom it rents cars? Many jurisdictions would hold the rental car company liable as the owner of the car. See, for example, Shuck v. Means, 302 Minn. 93, 226 N.W.2d 285 (1974) (Hertz held liable even though the driver of the vehicle was not the person who had rented it because driver had permission of person who had

rented it from Hertz) and Murdza v. Zimmerman, 99 N.Y.2d 375, 786 N.E.2d 440, 756 N.Y.S.2d 505 (2003) (company that had leased van to an employer could be held vicariously liable for accident caused by employee's boyfriend because lease had no restrictions on use of vehicle).

In 2005, Congress passed the Graves Amendment as part of the Safe, Accountable, Flexible, Efficient Transportation Equity Act, codified at 49 U.S.C. § 30106(a). It preempts state law and provides that there is no vicarious liability for injury or damage arising out of the use of a vehicle rented or leased by someone in the business of renting or leasing motor vehicles. It has been upheld as a constitutional exercise of federal preemption of state law. See, for example, Graham v. Dunkley, 50 A.D.3d 55, 852 N.Y.S.2d 169 (2008) (applying Graves Amendment to preempt New York tort law); Garcia v. Vanguard Car Rental USA, Inc., 540 F.3d 1242 (11th Cir. 2008) (applying Graves Amendment to preempt Florida tort law); Rogriguez v. Testa, 296 Conn. 1, 993 A.2d 955 (2010) (applying Graves Amendment to preempt Connecticut law and finding it a constitutionally valid exercise of Commerce Clause power); and Vargas v. Enterprise Leasing Co., 60 So.3d 1037 (Fla. 2011) (applying Graves Amendment to preempt Florida tort law and finding that it does not violate the Commerce Clause).

5. Do the policies that support an application of vicarious liability to owners of automobiles apply to any other bailors? Some attorneys have made enterprising, but unsuccessful, attempts to apply the same rule to private aircraft. See McCord v. Dixie Aviation Corp., 450 F.2d 1129 (10th Cir.1971) and McDaniel v. Ritter, 556 So.2d 303 (Miss.1989) (in granting summary judgment to owner, court notes nothing in Tennessee law that would change the common law rule of no vicarious liability for bailor).

6. *Vicarious Liability by Statute—Other.* There are other, occasional, instances of statutes creating vicarious liability. Some states have imposed the liability on owners of private aircraft, on municipalities for certain acts committed by a mob through so-called "anti-lynching" statutes, or on parents for certain intentional torts committed by their teenage children.

7. *Distinguish Negligent Entrustment.* All of the vicarious liability circumstances should be carefully distinguished from cases in which the plaintiff is arguing that the employer/owner/bailor was itself negligent in some way. Just as the employer may be negligent in hiring an employee (see note 5, page 713) and the hirer may be negligent in selecting the independent contractor (see note 3, page 720), the owner/bailor may be liable in entrusting the chattel to the bailee. This is frequently referred to as "negligent entrustment." See Wery v. Seff, 136 Ohio St. 307, 16 Ohio Ops. 445, 25 N.E.2d 692 (1940) (unlicensed minor driver); Snowhite v. State, 243 Md. 291, 221 A.2d 342 (1966) (owner knew driver was frequently intoxicated); Kahlenberg v. Goldstein, 290 Md. 477, 431 A.2d 76 (1981) (father funded purchase of automobile for son whom he knew to be an irresponsible driver); and Vince v. Wilson, 151 Vt. 425, 561 A.2d 103 (1989) (evidence that defendant who provided funding to grandnephew to purchase car knew he did not have driver's license, had failed driver's test several times, and abused alcohol and other drugs was sufficient to get negligent entrustment case to jury). This may occur not only with automobiles, but also with other chattels. See McBerry v. Ivie, 116 Ga.App. 808, 159 S.E.2d 108 (1967) (shotgun given to a young child); Miles v.

Harrison, 223 Ga. 352, 155 S.E.2d 6 (1967) (power mower); and LaFaso v. LaFaso, 126 Vt. 90, 223 A.2d 814 (1966) (cigarette lighter). But not computers. Finkel v. Dauber, 29 Misc.3d 325, 906 N.Y.S.2d 697 (2010) (computer not a dangerous instrument that could give rise to a negligent entrustment claim in a case against the parents of teenagers who had allegedly defamed plaintiff on their secret Facebook group). The plaintiff in the principal case had included negligent entrustment as part of her case against the parents of the college student driver, but the court did not have to reach that issue because it found the parents vicariously liable.

Some states recognize so-called "first party" negligent entrustment actions that permit the driver entrustee who should not have been entrusted with the car to make a claim against the owner entruster. See, for example, Martell v. Driscoll, 302 P.3d 375 (Kan. 2013) (driver injured by his own negligence in driving car alleged that owner should not have let him use it because owner knew that driver's license had been suspended after multiple DUIs and owner entruster therefore should be liable to driver entrustee for driver's injuries).

5. IMPUTED CONTRIBUTORY NEGLIGENCE

Smalich v. Westfall

Supreme Court of Pennsylvania, 1970.
440 Pa. 409, 269 A.2d 476.

EAGEN, JUSTICE. Two automobiles collided in Westmoreland County. One of the vehicles, owned by Julia Smalich, was operated by Felix Rush Westfall. Julia Smalich [was a] passenger in this automobile at the time. The other vehicle involved was operated by Stephanna Louise Blank. Julia Smalich suffered injuries in the collision which caused her death. * * *

The estate of Julia Smalich sought damages [against both Westfall and Blank] in both a wrongful death action and a survival action. * * *

The trial jury found that Westfall's negligent operation of the Smalich automobile was a proximate cause of the collision. That the trial record amply supports this finding is not and cannot be questioned. After trial, the court en banc ruled that, under the facts, the contributory negligence of Westfall must be imputed to the owner of the automobile [Smalich] as a matter of law and this precluded recovery by the Smalich Estate against defendant Blank [because at this time contributory negligence was a complete bar to recovery]. * * *

[A] plaintiff ought not to be barred from recovery against a negligent defendant by the contributory negligence of a third person unless the relationship between the plaintiff and the third person is such that the plaintiff would be vicariously liable as a defendant for the negligent acts of the third person: Prosser, The Law of Torts § 73 (3d ed. 1964). See also, Restatement (Second) Torts §§ 485, 486 and 491 (1965). Placed in the context of this case, a driver's negligence will not be imputed to a passenger, unless the relationship between them is such that the passenger would be vicariously liable as a defendant for the driver's negligent acts * * *. The relationship between the passenger and the driver is therefore a very critical one, worthy of careful analysis and consideration. * * * We therefore now state unequivocally that only a master-servant relationship or a finding of joint enterprise will justify the imputation of contributory negligence.

We have serious doubt that, in the ordinary situation, the mutual understanding of the owner-passenger and the driver is that the owner-passenger reserves a right to control over the physical details of driving or that the driver consents to submit himself to the control of a "back-seat driver." It seems more reasonable that the mutual understanding is that the driver will use care and skill to accomplish a result, retaining control over the manner of operation yet subject to the duty of obedience to the wishes of the owner-passenger as to such things as destination. Such would only constitute an agency relationship and not one of master-servant, although there are undoubtedly situations where the understanding might well be such as to constitute a master-servant relationship. * * *

The jury rendered a verdict for the plaintiffs against defendant Blank, and therefore, must have determined that Julia Smalich had relinquished her right to control her automobile to defendant Westfall. On the facts, such a conclusion is justified under the law as we have now stated it. Judgments n.o.v. should not, therefore, have been entered in favor of defendant Blank and against the Smalich Estate. These judgments are vacated, and the record remanded with directions to enter judgments in favor of the Smalich Estate and against defendant Blank in accordance with the jury's verdict. * * *

ROBERTS, JUSTICE, concurring. I am pleased that the Court today partially repudiates the imputed contributory negligence doctrine. I am unable to join the majority's opinion, however, because I believe that in adopting a limited "both ways" test, it falls short of accomplishing the degree of reform necessary in this area. I am particularly disturbed that the majority, in continuing to apply the doctrine to the master-servant relationship, places so much weight on the physical control a master has over a servant. I therefore can only concur in the result.

The imputed contributory negligence doctrine has been criticized on two grounds. For one, it is quite obvious that the doctrine is based on the absurd fiction that the owner-passenger has the "right" to control the vehicle. In the real world, however, a passenger can in no safe way exercise operational control over the vehicle in which he rides, even if he is the owner. * * *

A second weakness in the doctrine of imputed contributory negligence arises from the fact that courts have often failed to discern the difference between using the fiction of control to impute negligence when the owner-passenger is the defendant, and using it to impute contributory negligence when the owner-passenger is the plaintiff. The assumption has been that if the driver's negligence is imputed, it is only logical to likewise impute his contributory negligence. But there is no justification for imputing contributory negligence, other than "the strong psychological appeal of all rules case in the form of balanced and logical symmetry." * * *

[T]he [so-called] "both-ways test" has been strongly criticized. * * *

The Supreme Court of Minnesota re-examined the whole problem of imputed contributory negligence recently in a well-reasoned opinion that deserves close study. See Weber v. Stokley-Van Camp, Inc., 274 Minn. 482, 144 N.W.2d 540 (1966). There the court repudiated the application of the doctrine to the master-servant relation in automobile negligence cases, stressing the absurdity of the control argument, and the absence of need for a solvent defendant, unlike vicarious liability cases where the master properly is held accountable for the negligence of his servant.

I look forward to the day when this Court completes its reform in this area.

NOTES AND QUESTIONS

1. "Imputed contributory negligence" has acquired a bad reputation in the law, because of a set of rules that developed in the latter part of the 19th century, under which entirely innocent persons, seriously injured without any fault of their own, were barred from recovery against one person who negligently injured them, because they were charged with the negligence of another who had contributed to the injury. The result was that, of the three persons involved, the entire loss fell upon the only one who was free from all negligence. Most of this is now thoroughly discredited and obsolete. For a court decision that "completed the reform," at least in New York, in a well-reasoned decision, see Bibergal v. McCormick, 101 Misc.2d 794, 421 N.Y.S.2d 978 (1979) (declining to impute contributory negligence of driver of cab to owner of cab, his father). Imputed contributory negligence has been largely rejected in the following areas:

A. *Driver and Passenger*. An early English decision, Thorogood v. Bryan, 8 C.B. 115, 137 Eng.Rep. 452 (1849), "imputed" negligence of the driver of an omnibus to a passenger who was injured in a collision, so as to prevent recovery by the passenger against the other driver. The decision has long since been overruled in England. Although some decisions in United States jurisdictions followed it for a time, those cases also have been overruled. The principal case was based not on the passenger-driver relationship but on the owner-driver relationship. See also Pittman v. Frazer, 129 F.3d 983 (8th Cir. 1997) (applying Arkansas law) (where driver and passenger-owner of car that collided with train at railroad crossing were engaged in adulterous affair, jury could conclude that they were engaged in a joint enterprise so that negligence of driver could be imputed to passenger-owner thus preventing her estate from recovering against railroad). A passenger in an automobile can be charged with contributory negligence of his own if he, for example, grabbed the wheel, distracted the driver by untying the strings of her bikini top, or gave directions to turn the wrong way down a one-way street.

B. *Husband and Wife*. At common law a married woman's separate legal identity was merged with that of her husband. One result of this legal fiction was that if her spouse contributed to the happening of an accident, his negligence was imputed to her and would bar any claim against a negligent third party. All this is ancient history. Today, the contributory negligence of one spouse is no longer imputed to bar a recovery by the other, on the basis of the marital relation alone.

C. *Parent and Child.* The common law had no similar rule of legal identity as between parent and child. The child always has been held to be entitled to the separate ownership of his own property, to the enforcement of his causes of action, and to be liable as an individual for his own torts. On occasion a parent's negligence will be so substantial in regard to the accident that a court will treat the parent's negligent conduct as a superseding cause and bar the child's claim against the third party. Some courts may be reluctant to accept this argument and will regard it as an end run attempt to restore the old rules imputing contributory negligence. See, e.g., Caroline v. Reicher, 269 Md. 125, 304 A.2d 831 (1973), noted in 34 Md.L.Rev. 155 (1975) (parent's failure to supervise child will not relieve landlord of liability for child's consumption of paint containing lead). But see Lash v. Cutts, 943 F.2d 147 (1st Cir.1991) (applying Maine law), where a child was injured when he rode his tricycle down a neighbor's driveway into the path of a speeding car. The combined negligence of the child and the mother (in failing to properly supervise the child), which was imputed to the child, was greater than the negligence of the defendant driver, so the child collected nothing under Maine's modified comparative negligence scheme.

2. A general rule developed in many jurisdictions that contributory negligence will not be imputed unless negligence could be imputed. Many courts then accepted the converse of this proposition: if negligence can be imputed, contributory negligence will be also. This is the so-called "both-ways test" mentioned in the principal case. The both-ways test has been under a slow but steady attack. Many automobile consent statutes have been construed only to impose vicarious liability and not vicarious contributory negligence. See page 726, note 2C. See also White v. Yup, 85 Nev. 527, 458 P.2d 617 (1969) (construing family purpose doctrine to impose only vicarious liability and not vicarious contributory negligence).

3. *Employer and Employee.* Although largely abandoned, imputed negligence remains viable in a few areas. See generally Restatement (Third) of Torts: Apportionment of Liability § 5 (2000). The contributory negligence of the employee will be imputed to the plaintiff employer. After an accident involving a delivery truck and a motorcycle, the company that owned the delivery truck and employed the truck driver filed suit against the motorcyclist to recover for the damage to the truck and the worker compensation benefits paid to its driver. The jury found both the truck driver and the motorcyclist negligent and assessed percentages of fault to each of them. The percentage of fault of the truck driver was imputed to his employer, the plaintiff. Thomas Oil, Inc. v. Onsgaard, 298 Minn. 465, 215 N.W.2d 793 (1974). Suppose the motorcyclist had filed a counterclaim for his personal injury and was permitted to recover a portion of his damages from the company that owned the delivery truck and it sought indemnity or contribution from its employee, the driver?

4. *Derivative Claims.* When a claim is held to be derivative in nature, e.g., loss of consortium or wrongful death, the contributory negligence of an injured party usually will be imputed to the plaintiff because plaintiff's claim derived from that of the injured party. Thus, if the spouse of the motorcyclist in the previous note brought a loss of consortium claim, motorcyclist's contributory negligence would be imputed to spouse and would either defeat the claim or reduce the damages, depending on the

operation of the jurisdiction's comparative negligence regime. Similarly, the contributory negligence of a decedent not only affects his estate's ability to recover in a survival action, it is imputed to the beneficiaries in a wrongful death action and will affect their recovery as well. The imputation of contributory negligence in those circumstances is not based on principles of vicarious liability, but on the judgment of the court or legislature that plaintiff's claim is not independent in nature but is derived from and dependent on another party's claim.

5. How much does the so-called "deep-pocket" theory explain the doctrines discussed in this chapter? Put another way, is the doctrinal basis of imputed negligence actually based on courts trying to find a solvent defendant? The next two chapters explore a more direct route for this result—strict and products liability.

CHAPTER 14

STRICT LIABILITY

When a court imposes "strict liability" on a defendant, the defendant must pay damages although the defendant neither acted intentionally nor failed to live up to the objective standard of reasonable care that traditionally has been at the root of negligence law. Some courts and commentators call this "absolute liability." This description overstates the case because there are numerous defenses to an action for strict liability and sometimes, especially in some of the types of so-called "strict products liability" (Chapter 15), the requirement of fault creeps back into the system. Some group the cases in this chapter under the rubric "liability without fault." This description suggests that negligence and intentional tort causes of action are always based on fault, but there are many examples of imposition of liability without fault under the negligence and intentional tort bases of liability. Can you recall some?

As Dean Prosser observed: "Once the legal concept of 'fault' is divorced, as it has been, from the personal standard of moral wrongdoing, there is a sense in which liability with or without 'fault' must beg its own conclusion. The term requires such extensive definition, that it seems better not to make use of it at all, and to refer instead to strict liability, apart from either wrongful intent or negligence." W. Prosser & W. Keeton, Torts 538 (5th ed. 1984).

Thus far we have seen that most activities are judged on the basis of intent or negligence. This chapter focuses on activities that have been selected over the past two centuries by judges or, occasionally, legislatures to bear the burden of strict liability. Observe the rationales that underlie their judgments. Are they consistent? Are they sound? Should they be extended?

1. ANIMALS

One of the first areas selected by courts for the imposition of strict liability focused on the care and maintenance of particular animals in certain situations. Keep in mind that the basis of liability, whether it is strict liability or negligence, is imposed on those who *keep, possess, or harbor* the animal, not just the owner. Compare Snow v. Birt, 968 P.2d 177 (Colo. App.1998) (owners of house where child was bitten responsible even though dog belonged to their adult son who resided with them); Pawlowski v. American Fam. Mutual Ins. Co., 777 N.W.2d 67 (Wis. 2009) (owner of house responsible even though dog belonged to acquaintance of owner's daughter who was staying in owner's home while he was unemployed in informal arrangement whereby he did some home repairs and housekeeping in exchange for lodging); and Terral v. Louisiana Farm Bureau Casualty Ins. Co., 892 So.2d 732 (La. App. 2005) (testimony that dog spent most of its time on porch of defendant and ate food put out on porch for defendant's other dogs enough to sustain jury finding that defendant harbored dog even though he denied that it was his and testified that he did not allow it inside with his other dogs, had not taken it to vet, or bought it anything) with Auster v. Norwalk United Methodist Church (Auster II), 286 Conn. 152, 943 A.2d 391 (2008) (church not liable as "keeper" of dog that belonged to its employee who lived on church grounds with his family and dog); Blaha v. Stuard, 640 N.W.2d 85 (S.D. 2002) (seller of dog was no longer a possessor ten days after sale and transfer of dog to buyers); Miles v. Rich, 347 S.W.3d 477 (Mo. App. 2011) (Humane Society did not own, possess, harbor, or control the dog at the time it bit plaintiff—it had been adopted over a year before); and Hayes v. Adams, 987 N.E.2d 402 (Ill. App. 2013) (owner not liable where veterinarian's assistant had allowed dog to escape and it bit a child trying to assist in its recapture). See also Restatement (Second) of Torts § 514 (1977) and Restatement (Third) of Torts: Liability for Physical and Emotional Harm § 23, comment *f* (2010).

Worldwide Primates is a breeder of monkeys and other primates operating in southern Florida. During Hurricane Andrew, the primate cages were damaged and many escaped. A macaque monkey was captured by Gomez who sold it to Martinez who sold it to Scorza (a photographer whose specialty was photographing people with exotic animals) whom the monkey bit. Photographer sued Worldwide Primates for negligence in letting the monkey escape and strict liability for possessing a wild animal. Should Worldwide Primates be strictly liable? Scorza v. Martinez, 683 So.2d 1115 (Fla. App.1996) (strict liability not available against owner of escaped wild animal once someone else has taken possession of it).

Landowners are not responsible for harm done by wild animals on their property unless they reduce the wild animal to possession or control or introduce a non-indigenous animal into an area. Belhumeur v. Zilm, 157 N.H. 233, 949 A.2d 162 (2008) (landowner not strictly liable to neighbor attacked by wild bees living in tree on landowner's property). Cf. Landings Ass'n, Inc. v. Williams, 291 Ga. 397, 728 S.E.2d 577 (2012) (wild alligators in residential area).

Trespassing Animals. Somewhere around the middle of the fourteenth century, the courts began to recognize a rule making the owner of cattle liable when his animals caused damage while trespassing upon the plaintiff's land. The origin of the rule is somewhat obscure. It has been attributed to a fiction that the trespass of the animals was to be attributed to the owner, because he was in some way identified with them, and responsible for what they did. According to Glanville Williams, Liability for Animals 127–34 (1939), there was no such fiction, and the early cases were those in which the owner intentionally put his cattle upon the land of the plaintiff. Liability for mere escape originated as a deliberate extension designed to remedy a gap in the law; and because it came before the full development of the action on the case, it was identified with trespass, although the invasion was an indirect one. Out of this there developed the rule that the owner of animals of a kind likely to roam and do damage is strictly liable for their trespasses. The Restatement (Third) of Torts: Liability for Physical and Emotional Harm § 21, comment *b* (2010), while acknowledging the prevalence of the phrase "trespass," notes that animals cannot trespass (because they are incapable of intent) and suggests instead "intrusion." It remains to be seen whether this terminology catches on with the courts.

The kinds of animals for whose trespasses or intrusions their owner would be liable were limited, and they had a definite barnyard pattern. They included cattle, horses, sheep, hogs, and goats, as well as such common errant fowl as turkeys, in McPherson v. James, 69 Ill.App. 337 (1896), and chickens, in Adams Bros. v. Clark, 189 Ky. 279, 224 S.W. 1046 (1920), or even pigeons, in Taylor v. Granger, 37 A. 13 (R.I.1896).

On the other hand, such household favorites as dogs and cats were not included. Olson v. Pederson, 206 Minn. 415, 288 N.W. 856 (1939); McDonald v. Castle, 116 Okl. 46, 243 P. 215 (1925); Buckle v. Holmes, [1926] 2 K.B. 125; Bischoff v. Cheney, 89 Conn. 1, 92 A. 660 (1914). The reason sometimes given was that dogs and cats were of no value, which is of course clearly wrong; and that their trespasses were likely to be trivial and do no serious harm, which is unlikely to impress the owners of flowerbeds and poultry. A better explanation may be that of Glanville Williams, Liability for Animals 145–146 (1939), that dogs and cats are very difficult to confine or restrain, and the general custom of the community has permitted them to roam at large. In other words, the keeping of these household pets is so far sanctioned by general usage that an exception is made in their favor. McElroy v. Carter, 2006 WL 2805141 (Tenn. App. 2006) (noting that the strict liability that applies to trespassing livestock does not apply to trespassing cats). But see Baker v. Howard County Hunt, 171 Md. 159, 188 A. 223 (1936) (trespass rule applied to pack of dogs engaged in fox hunting).

An early and well established exception to the rule of strict liability for trespassing cattle and the like was the case of animals straying from a highway on which they were lawfully being driven. Tillett v. Ward, L.R. 10 Q.B.D. 17 (1882). This obviously arose out of the necessity of getting the animals to market. It was explained as in the nature of a servitude to which owners of lands adjoining the highway were subject; and it did not apply to other lands. Thus when cattle strayed from the highway across the lands of A, and thence onto the land of B, B could use strict liability even though A could not. Wood v. Snider, 187 N.Y. 28, 79 N.E. 858 (1907).

In the United States, the rule as to strict liability for animal trespass has had something of a checkered history. In the early days, many of the courts, particularly in the western part of the country where cattle were customarily permitted to graze at large on open range, rejected the common law rule as not suitable to the conditions of the country and established local custom. See for example Delaney v. Errickson, 10 Neb. 492, 6 N.W. 600 (1880) and Beinhorn v. Griswold, 27 Mont. 79, 69 P. 557 (1902). These cases are among the leading authorities for the proposition that, under state reception statutes, the common law of England is to be followed only when it is suitable and appropriate in the local context.

As the country became more settled, some states began to enact "fencing out" statutes, which provided that if the plaintiff fenced his land properly there was strict liability when animals broke through the fence. Otherwise, there was liability only if the owner of the animals was negligent. See for example Buford v. Houtz, 133 U.S. 320 (1890); Garcia v. Sumrall, 58 Ariz. 526, 121 P.2d 640 (1942); Hart v. Meredith, 196 Ill.App.3d 367, 553 N.E.2d 782, 143 Ill.Dec. 75 (1990) (application of fencing out statute to impose strict liability on farmer whose bull broke through fence and bred two of plaintiff's purebred Angus cows, causing plaintiff to lose the services of the cows in plaintiff's embryo transplant breeding operation).

As the country became still more settled, the conflict between the grazing interests and developing agricultural interests—or, in other words, as the motion pictures would have it, between the range men and the "nesters" along the creek bed or the cowboys and the farmers—resulted in many states in "fencing in" statutes, which required the owner of the animals to fence them in or otherwise restrain them, and made the owner strictly liable if he did not do so. Plaintiff's pickup truck hit a black cow standing in a dark road at midnight. Florida's fencing in statute requires the plaintiff to show defendant's intent or negligence in order to recover (i.e., no strict liability as long as animal was fenced in) if animals escape onto the highway. The only evidence is that defendant's gate could only be opened by human hands, that defendant himself had secured the gate the day before, that defendant had had no visitors after that, and that he did not know how the gate had been opened. Liability? Fisel v. Wynns, 667 So.2d 761 (Fla.1996) (summary judgment in favor of owner approved). Compare Larson-Murphy v. Steiner, 303 Mont. 96, 15 P.3d 1205 (2000) (motorist struck black bull on a dark night; no explanation for how bull escaped double enclosure; no evidence gate had been opened or tampered with; extended discussion of open range common law and statutes and the rules regarding responsibility for damage done by trespassing animals that developed from them; summary judgment for owners reversed and sent back for jury decision).

Finally, some states, particularly in the eastern part of the country, apply the common law rule (King v. Blue Mountain Forest Ass'n, 100 N.H. 212, 123 A.2d 151 (1956)) while others require proof of negligence. Hastings v. Sauve, 21 N.Y.3d 122, 967 N.Y.S.2d 658, 989 N.E.2d 940 (2014) (motorist injured when her vehicle collided with cow on public road could recover from owner if fence restraining animal had been negligently maintained).

Many states permit each county to choose the rule it wishes to apply. Thus in some states animals are permitted to run at large unless a county adopts a "fencing in" or a "fencing out" ordinance. There are states in which all four variants of the rule—common law strict liability, fencing out, fencing in, and no liability without fault—can be found in different counties.

Wild Animals. Under the common law of England, the owner or possessor of a nondomesticated animal (collectively referred to by courts as "wild animals" or animals "*ferae naturae*") was subject to strict liability if the animal injured anyone. See May v. Burdett, 9 Q.B. 101 (1846) (monkey bite); Filburn v. Peoples Palace and Aquarium Co., Ltd., 25 Q.B.Div. 258 (C.A.1890) (elephant attack); Johnson v. Swain, 787 S.W.2d 36 (Tex.1989) (bull elephant gore). On the other hand, the owner of a domestic animal such as a cat, dog, sheep, or horse was subject to strict liability only if the owner knew or had reason to know that the animal had dangerous propensities.

This led to interesting problems of classification. Obviously lions and tigers and bears ("oh my!") were deemed "wild animals." What about deer? Congress & Empire Spring Co. v. Edgar, 99 U.S. 645 (1878); Briley v. Mitchell, 238 La. 551, 115 So.2d 851 (1959) (wild). A hive of bees? Wilhelm v. Flores, 133 S.W.3d 726 (Tex. App. 2003) (hived bees usually considered domesticated and thus strict liability not applicable). A boar? Marshall v. Ranne, 511 S.W.2d 255 (Tex.1974) (domesticated).

The customs of the community influence the determination. In Burma an elephant is regarded as a domesticated animal, for which there is no strict liability. Maung Kayn Dun v. Ma Kyian, 2 Upper Burma Rulings, Civ. 570 (1900). Suppose an elephant is brought from Burma to England to perform in a circus. Behrens v. Bertram Mills Circus Ltd., [1957] 2 Q.B. 1 (wild—strict liability). How about a camel, which is now domesticated virtually everywhere it is found? McQuaker v. Goddard, [1940] 1 K.B. 687 (domestic—no strict liability). A ferret? Gallick v. Barto, 828 F.Supp. 1168 (M.D.Pa.1993) (finding that ferret is a wild animal even though evidence showed that approximately one million are kept as pets in United States).

The majority American position has followed the rule of strict liability in regard to wild animals. See Isaacs v. Powell, 267 So.2d 864 (Fla.App.1972) (chimpanzee); Franken v. Sioux Center, 272 N.W.2d 422 (Iowa 1978) (tiger); Whitefield v. Stewart, 577 P.2d 1295 (Okl.1978) (monkey). But see Wisconsin, which has not adopted strict liability for harboring of wild animals but instead applies a negligence standard that is modified by the fact that the owner is charged with the knowledge of the animal's "natural traits and habits." Ollhoff v. Peck, 177 Wis.2d 719, 503 N.W.2d 323 (1993) (negligence standard applied to musky).

Some courts have applied a negligence standard rather than strict liability with regard to the liability of persons who display wild animals to the public. See Hansen v. Brogan, 145 Mont. 224, 400 P.2d 265 (1965) (buffalo); Vaughan v. Miller Bros. "101" Ranch Wild West Show, 109 W.Va. 170, 153 S.E. 289 (1930) ("ape"). The trend is more pronounced with regard to public zoos, although some of those decisions are based on the fact that the legislature authorized the activity. See, e.g., City and County of Denver v. Kennedy, 29 Colo.App. 15, 476 P.2d 762 (1970). Contra: City of Mangum v. Brownlee, 181 Okl. 515, 75 P.2d 174 (1938). What about wild animals that roam freely in animal parks where visitors drive their cars?

Domestic Animals. As for domestic animals, the canard is often repeated that the common law rule is that a domestic animal such as a dog (or cat) is entitled to one bite. The cases do not bear this out. If the owner knows or has reason to know (scienter) that a domestic animal has vicious propensities, this is sufficient to classify that animal with wild ones and thus to impose strict liability. See Andrews v. Smith, 324 Pa. 455, 188 A. 146 (1936); Barger v. Jimerson, 130 Colo. 459, 276 P.2d 744 (1954); Harris v. Williams, 160 Okl. 103, 15 P.2d 580 (1932). Many of the cases show interesting and imaginative efforts to prove that the animal had such a temperament and that the owner was aware of it.

See, e.g., Walters v. Grand Teton Crest Outfitters, Inc., 804 F.Supp. 1442 (D.Wyo.1992) (whether plaintiff had proved mule had vicious propensities by showing it had thrown two previous riders and had rolled on its back before plaintiff had mounted it was question of fact for the jury); Zarek v. Fredericks, 138 F.2d 689 (3d Cir.1943) (applying Pennsylvania law) (dog snarled at guests and was almost always accompanied by his owners); Frederickson v. Kepner, 82 Cal.App.2d 905, 187 P.2d 800 (1947) (75-pound German police dog, served as watch dog at junkyard, and kept tied during day); Perkins v. Drury, 57 N.M. 269, 258 P.2d 379 (1953) (children warned to stay away from dog); Hill v. Moseley, 220 N.C. 485, 17 S.E.2d 676 (1941) (dog had bad reputation in the neighborhood); and Allen v. Cox, 285 Conn. 603, 942 A.2d 296 (2008) (where plaintiff was injured while trying to save her own cat from attack by neighbor's cat, owner's knowledge that its cat had a tendency to attack other animals did not necessarily imply knowledge of propensity to harm persons, but is enough to create jury question).

Can plaintiff show that the owner knew the animal had a vicious nature merely by showing that it belonged to a particular breed? Compare Montiero v. Silver Lake, 813 A.2d 978 (R.I. 2003) (pit bull—declining to create "species-specific" standard of care because that is better left to legislature); Carter v. Metro North Associates, 255 A.D.2d 251, 680 N.Y.S.2d 239 (1998) (reversing trial court judge's taking judicial notice of vicious nature of pit bulls); Bard v. Jahnke, 6 N.Y.3d 592, 848 N.E.2d 463, 815 N.Y.S.2d 16 (2006) (plaintiff's expert's statement that breeding bulls are generally dangerous and vicious animals not enough to establish particular animal's propensity); and Morgan v. Marquis, 50 A.3d 1 (Maine 2012) (Maine does not recognize pit bulls are per se abnormally dangerous, requiring plaintiff to prove that specific dog was known by owners to have dangerous propensity in order to recover in strict liability) with Poznanski v. Horvath, 788 N.E.2d 1255 (Ind. 2003) (recognizing that plaintiff could use evidence that dog belonged to breed known to exhibit vicious or dangerous tendencies as proof that owner knew particular animal had such tendencies, but declining to apply in case involving mixed-breed sheepdog) and City of Toledo v. Tellings, 114 Ohio St.3d 278, 871 N.E.2d 1152 (2007) (upholding as constitutional breed-specific regulations imposed on owners of pit bulls by City of Toledo).

Maryland has been on both sides of this issue recently. The Court of Appeals issued an opinion holding that strict liability applied to pit bulls or mixed-breed pit bulls without a showing of dangerous propensity. It then reconsidered that decision and limited its application to pure bred pit bulls. Tracey v. Solesky, 427 Md. 627, 50 A.3d 1075 (2012) (as amended on reconsideration). Then the Legislature acted. Md. Code Ann., Cts. & Jud. Proce. § 3–1901 (effective April 8, 2014) (eliminating "breed or heritage of the dog" as factor affecting liability).

Can plaintiff show that the owner knew an animal had a vicious propensity merely by showing that it belonged to a group (gaggle) of animals that did? Plaintiff was visiting defendant whom she had met through a message board for gardening enthusiasts to view some of defendant's plants. As plaintiff attempted to leave, she was frightened by a domestic goose that squawked at her and reached out as if it meant to bite her chest. She retreated to defendant's porch where defendant gave her a bamboo pole to fend off the birds. During her second attempt to leave, she was again attacked and broke her arm fleeing the birds. Plaintiff put on evidence that a police officer previously had been attacked by one of the geese, but that one had been confined elsewhere when plaintiff was attacked. Does plaintiff's claim fail because she cannot show that owner knew the particular goose that attacked that day had a dangerous propensity? Olier v. Bailey, 2015 WL 1611772 (Miss. 2015) (holding that when a person keeps a large group of essentially indistinguishable animals, some of which have exhibited dangerous propensities in the past, she can be liable for injuries attributable to characteristics that the animals have exhibited collectively).

Note that although many of the cases use the term "vicious," the test is really whether the animal has a "dangerous propensity abnormal to its class." Restatement (Second) of Torts § 509, comment *c* (1977) (large dog that owner knows has a tendency to "fawn violently" would be strictly liable for harm done by dog's playfulness or demonstrative show of affection). See also Bard v. Jahnke, 6 N.Y.3d 592, 848 N.E.2d 463, 815 N.Y.S.2d 16 (2006) (vicious propensity includes animal's propensity to do any act that might endanger the safety of the person or property of others in a given situation); Bauman v. Auch, 539 N.W.2d 320 (S.D.1995) (testimony that horse was flighty, high-strung, and spirited, not mean or vicious, enough to create jury question on issue whether strict liability should apply); and the Restatement (Third) of Torts: Liability for Physical and Emotional Harm § 23 (2010) ("dangerous tendencies abnormal for the animal's category").

If the plaintiff is unable to prove that the owner knew or should have known of a domestic animal's dangerous propensities, then strict liability does not apply and the plaintiff must prove negligence in order to recover. See, e.g., Duren v. Kunkel, 814 S.W.2d 935 (Mo.1991) (plaintiff not entitled to strict liability because failed to show that Limousin bull had any dangerous propensity different from any other bull of its breed or class, but was entitled to go to jury on question of owner's negligence in failing to protect plaintiff from animal); Bushnell v. Mott, 254 S.W.3d 451 (Tex. 2008) (although plaintiff's failure to show dogs had vicious propensity meant that strict liability did not apply, plaintiff presented evidence that owner was negligent in failing to stop dogs after attack had begun); and Vendrella v. Astriab Family Ltd. Partnership, 311 Conn. 301, 87 A.3d 546 (2014) (horse with no known tendency to nip or bite bit toddler's cheek) (collecting cases from other jurisdictions). But New York provides that the sole claim against owners of domestic animals is in strict liability based on a showing of dangerous propensity and does not allow an alternative negligence claim. Bard v. Jahnke, 6 N.Y.3d 592, 848 N.E.2d 463 (2006) (no companion common-law cause of action for negligence available if plaintiff cannot show requirement of scienter for strict liability where animal injured plaintiff in its own barn).

In many states, the common law regarding liability for dog bites has been changed by statute. These statutes usually do away with the necessity of plaintiff's proving scienter in order to recover. See, for example, Minn. Stat. Ann. § 347.22. The statutes also may list defenses—e.g., plaintiff committing a trespass or presence of warning signs. See, for example, the New Hampshire statute quoted in Glidden v. Szybiak, page 79. Colorado's statute provides an exception for "working" dogs. Robinson v. Legro, 325 P.3d 1053 (Colo. 2014) (interpreting exemption in case involving predator control dogs guarding sheep who attacked a bicyclist on federal land within a national forest where both had a permit to be). Almost all states also have a statute limiting common law liability for equine activities. See, for example, Ohio Rev. Code § 2305.321 and Loftin v. Lee, 341 S.W.3d 352 (Tex. 2011) (interpreting Tex. § 87.001–.005 and noting that all but five states have in some way limited the common law liability.)

Liability also is affected by statutory provisions requiring dogs to be muzzled or leashed. If a person is injured due to the failure of the owner to comply with such ordinance, negligence per se may apply. Wistafka v. Grotowski, 205 Ill.App. 529 (1917). As in all negligence per se cases, causation still must be proved. If the muzzling of the dog would not have prevented the injury, as where the dog does not bite the plaintiff but knocks him down, there is no causal connection between the injury and the violation of the statute, so plaintiff must prove negligence based on conduct other than the statutory violation. Kennet v. Sossnitz, 260 App.Div. 759, 23 N.Y.S.2d 961 (1940), aff'd, 286 N.Y. 623, 36 N.E.2d 459 (1941).

In Florida, a dog owner who displays an easily readable sign that says "BAD DOG" in a prominent place in his premises is not liable in strict liability to anyone who is at least 6 years old. Suppose an owner who displays such a sign says to an invitee, "Rex can be bad, but he can also be good." Rex is bad that day. See Noble v. Yorke, 490 So.2d 29 (Fla.1986) (cannot take advantage of statute if told plaintiff to ignore sign and enter side yard).

Should a landlord have a duty to tell a potential tenant that a neighbor owns a pit bull dog? See Wylie v. Gresch, 191 Cal.App.3d 412, 236 Cal.Rptr. 552 (1987) (no duty—"a vicious dog is a danger one might expect to encounter anywhere in our society").

2. ABNORMALLY DANGEROUS ACTIVITIES

Rylands v. Fletcher

In the Exchequer, 3 H. & C. 774, 159 Eng.Rep. 737, 1865.
In the Exchequer Chamber, L.R. 1 Ex. 265, 1866.

In the House of Lords, L.R. 3 H.L. 330, 1868.

[Action brought in 1861 and tried at the Liverpool Summer Assizes (1862). The material facts in the special case stated by the arbitrator were as follows:

The defendants were the owners of a mill. In order to supply it with water they constructed upon the nearby land of Lord Wilton, with his permission, a reservoir. The plaintiff under lease from Lord Wilton was working certain coal mines under lands close to but not adjoining the premises on which the reservoir was constructed. They worked their mine in the direction of the reservoir until they came upon certain old workings, part of which at least had been made and abandoned at a time beyond living memory. These workings consisted of horizontal passages and vertical shafts, the latter apparently filled with rubbish and marl similar to that of the solid earth surrounding them. The defendant employed a competent engineer and competent contractors to plan and construct the reservoir, and it was so planned and constructed solely by them upon a site, in the choice of which the defendants were guilty of no personal fault. In fact, the old mine workings lay beneath it and, continuing under the intermediate lands, communicated, at the point to which the plaintiff had pushed its workings in that direction, with the workings of the plaintiff. The contractors in excavating for the bed of the reservoir came upon five of the above mentioned vertical shafts; the sides or walls of these were of timber, but, because they were filled with soil of the same kind as that composing the surrounding ground, neither the contractors nor the defendants suspected that they were abandoned mine shafts. The arbitrator found that the defendants were guilty of no personal negligence or fault, but that the engineer and contractors had not in fact exercised proper care, with reference to the shafts discovered, to provide for the sufficiency of the reservoir to bear the pressure that it was designed to bear when in use.

The reservoir was completed in December, 1860, and the defendants had it partly filled. Within a few days, one of the shafts that had been met while excavating gave way and burst downward, letting the water into the abandoned workings beneath, through which it flowed, through the communications that the plaintiffs in working their mine had made between the two, into the plaintiffs' workings, flooding their mine.

The question for the opinion of the Court was whether the plaintiff was entitled to recover damages from the defendant by reason of the matters thus stated by the arbitrator.

In the Exchequer, judgment was given for the defendants by a 2-to-1 vote. Martin, B., said there was no trespass, because the damage was not "immediate," but "mediate or consequential." There was no nuisance, because the defendants were doing a lawful and reasonable act. The same rule must be applied to real property as to personal property, that there must be negligence on the part of the defendant to make him responsible. The plaintiff brought error to the Exchequer Chamber.]

BLACKBURN, J. * * * It appears from the statement in the case, that the plaintiff was damaged by his property being flooded by water which, without any fault on his part, broke out of a reservoir constructed on the defendants' land by the defendants' orders, and maintained by the defendants. * * *

The plaintiff, though free from all blame on his part, must bear the loss, unless he can establish that it was the consequence of some default for which the defendants are responsible. The question of law therefore arises, what is the obligation which the law casts on a person who, like the defendants, lawfully brings on his land something which though harmless whilst it remains there, will naturally do mischief if it escape out of his land. It is agreed on all hands that he must take care to keep in that which he has brought on the land and keeps there, in order that it may not escape and damage his neighbors; but the question arises whether the duty which the law casts upon him, under such circumstances, is an absolute duty to keep it in at his peril, or is, as the majority of the Court of Exchequer have thought, merely a duty to take all reasonable and prudent precautions, in order to keep it in, but no more. If the first be the law, the person who has brought on his land and kept there something dangerous, and failed to keep it in, is responsible for all the natural consequences of its escape. If the second be the limit of his duty, he would not be answerable except on proof of negligence, and consequently would not be answerable for escape arising from any latent defect which ordinary prudence and skill could not detect. * * *

Lord Blackburn

We think that the true rule of law is that the person who for his own purposes brings on his lands and collects and keeps there any thing likely to do mischief if it escapes, must keep it in at his peril, and if he does not do so, is prima facie answerable for all the damage which is the natural consequence of its escape. He can excuse himself by showing that the escape was owing to the plaintiff's default; or perhaps that the escape was the consequence of vis major, or the act of God; but as nothing of this sort exists here, it is unnecessary to inquire what excuse would be sufficient. The general rule, as above stated, seems on principle just. The person whose grass or corn is eaten down by the escaping cattle of his neighbor, or whose mine is flooded by the water from his neighbor's reservoir, or whose cellar is invaded by the filth of his neighbor's privy, or whose habitation is made unhealthy by the fumes and noisome vapors of his neighbor's alkali works, is damnified without any fault of his own; and it seems but reasonable and just that the neighbor, who has brought something on his own property which was not naturally there, harmless to others so long as it is confined to his own property, but which he knows to be mischievous if it gets on his neighbor's, should be obliged to make good the damage which ensues if he does not succeed in confining it to his own property. But for his act in bringing it there no mischief could have accrued, and it seems but just that he should at his peril keep it there, so that no mischief may accrue, or answer for the natural and anticipated consequences. And upon authority, this we think is established to be the law, whether the things so brought be beasts, or water, or filth, or stenches.

The case that has most commonly occurred and which is most frequently to be found in the books, is as to the obligation of the owner of cattle which he has brought on his land to prevent their escaping and doing mischief. The law as to them seems to be perfectly settled from early times; the owner must keep them in at his peril, or he will be answerable for the natural consequences of their escape; that is, with regard to tame beasts, for the grass they eat and trample upon, though not for an injury to the person of others, for our ancestors have settled that it is not the general nature of horses to kick, or bulls to gore; but if the owner knows that the beast has a vicious propensity to attack man, he will be answerable for that too. * * *

Judgment for the plaintiff.

Rylands and Horrocks [mill owners and reservoir builders] brought error to the House of Lords against the judgment of the Exchequer Chamber, which had reversed the judgment of the Court of Exchequer.

THE LORD CHANCELLOR (LORD CAIRNS). * * * My Lords, the principles in which this case must be determined appear to me to be extremely simple. The defendants, treating them as the owner or occupiers of the close on which the reservoir was constructed, might lawfully have used that close for any purpose for which it might in the ordinary course of the enjoyment of land be used; and if, in what I may term the natural user of that land, there had been any accumulation of water, either on the surface or underground, and if, by the operation of the laws of nature, that accumulation of water had passed off into the close occupied by the plaintiff, the plaintiff could not have complained that that result had taken place. If he had desired to guard himself against it, it would have been lain upon him to have done so, by leaving, or by interposing, some barrier between his close and the close of the defendants in order to have prevented that operation of the laws of nature.

Lord Cairns

As an illustration of that principle, I may refer to a case which was cited in the argument before your Lordships, the case of Smith v. Kendrick, in the Court of Common Pleas, 7 C.B. 515.

On the other hand, if the defendants, not stopping at the natural use of their close, had desired to use it for any purpose which I may term a non-natural use, for the purpose of introducing into the close that which in its natural condition was not in or upon it, for the purpose of introducing water either above or below ground in quantities and in a manner not the result of any work or operation on or under the land; and if in consequence of their doing so, or in consequence of any imperfection in the mode of their doing so, the water came to escape and to pass off into the close of the plaintiff, then it appears to me that that which the defendants were doing they were doing at their own peril; and, if in the course of their doing it the evil arose to which I have referred, the evil, namely, of the escape of the water and its passing away to the close of the plaintiff and injuring the plaintiff, then for the consequence of that, in my opinion, the defendants would be liable. As the case of Smith v. Kendrick is an illustration of the first principle to which I have referred, so also the second principle to which I have referred is well illustrated by another case in the same Court, the case of Baird v. Williamson, 15 C.B.N.S. 317, which was also cited in the argument at the bar. * * *

Judgment of the Court of Exchequer Chamber affirmed.

[The concurring opinion of LORD CRANWORTH is omitted.]

NOTES AND QUESTIONS

1. Why not liability simply for trespass to land? Or nuisance? The contractor who did the work was negligent in not discovering the abandoned mine shafts and blocking them up. Why was defendant not liable for the negligence of the person with whom he contracted to do the work? Would he be liable today?

2. Professor Simpson, in Legal Liability for Bursting Reservoirs: The Historical Context of Rylands v. Fletcher, 13 J.Leg.Stud. 209 (1984), states that bursting dams were a particular problem at the time and that events had prompted public inquiries and legislation concerning the liability of dam owners. The reservoir in this case was located in a part of Lancashire devoted to coal mining. Has this any significance?

3. How far does the opinion of Lord Cairns limit that of Blackburn in *Rylands?* What does he mean by a "natural use" of land? Something like trees, in a state of nature? Note that he relies on Smith v. Kendrick, 7 C.B. 515, 137 Eng.Rep. 205 (1849), where defendant's normal and usual mining operations resulted in the flow of percolating water from springs into plaintiff's adjoining mine, and defendant was held not liable. A parallel case is Zampos v. United States Smelting R. & M. Co., 206 F.2d 171 (10th Cir.1953) (applying Utah law) (summary judgment for defendant upheld because no showing that defendant did anything to affect natural flow of water). He relies also upon Baird v. Williamson, 15 C.B. (N.S.) 376, 143 Eng.Rep. 831 (1863), where defendant pumped the water from his mine to a higher level, from which it flowed into plaintiff's mine, and was held liable.

4. Subsequent decisions in England followed the distinction between "natural" and "nonnatural" uses of land made by Lord Cairns. In determining what is a nonnatural use, the English courts have looked not only to the character of the thing or activity in question, but also to the place and manner in which it is maintained, and its relation to its surroundings. The distinction between natural and non-natural use has enabled the courts to infuse notions of social and economic needs prevailing at a given time and place. The scope of natural use is to be confined so as to give proper scope to the basic rationale of the rule to compensate even though the operations may have been for the community's benefit. Transco v. Stockport MBC [2004] 2 A.C. 1 (House of Lords). Frustration about the proper bounds of liability led the High Court of Australia to collapse it into the general rule of negligence liability: Burnie Port Authority v. General Jones, (1994) 179 Comm. L. Rep. 520.

5. In the United States, Rylands v. Fletcher started out with approval in Ball v. Nye, 99 Mass. 582, 97 Am.Dec. 56 (1868) (percolation of filthy water) and Cahill v. Eastman, 18 Minn. 324, 10 Am.Rep. 184 (1872)

(water escaping from a tunnel). The case then was rejected in its entirety by three leading American courts in three years. Losee v. Buchanan, 51 N.Y. 476, 10 Am.Rep. 623 (1873); Marshall v. Welwood, 38 N.J.L. 339 (1876); Brown v. Collins, 53 N.H. 442, 16 Am.Rep. 372 (1873). The first two of these involved the explosion of ordinary steam boilers, and the third a runaway horse. They were clearly cases of customary, natural uses, to which the English courts would not have applied the rule. In each case the attack was directed at Blackburn's broad statement in the intermediate court, and the decision in the House of Lords was given little or no attention. Rylands v. Fletcher was treated as holding that the defendant is absolutely liable whenever anything whatever escapes from his control and causes damage. In other words, the rule of the case was misstated, and as misstated was rejected, in cases in which it had no proper application in the first place.

6. These decisions gave Rylands v. Fletcher a bad name, and it was rejected in several jurisdictions. For a time a majority of the courts that considered the case by name rejected it. In recent years the American trend has been very much in favor of approval of the case, and a majority now favor the case, including New Jersey, home of the *Marshall v. Welwood* opinion in the previous note. State, Dept. of Environmental Protection v. Ventron Corp., 94 N.J. 473, 468 A.2d 150, 157 (N.J. 1983) ("We believe it is time to recognize expressly that the law of liability has evolved so that a landowner is strictly liable to others for harm caused by toxic wastes that are stored on his property and flow onto the property of others. Therefore, we overrule Marshall v. Welwood and adopt the principle of liability originally declared in Rylands v. Fletcher. The net result is that those who use, or permit others to use, land for the conduct of abnormally dangerous activities are strictly liable for resultant damages."). What factors may have influenced recent courts to accept the *Rylands* principle? Have there been changes in society that made courts more willing to impose strict liability for hazardous activities? See Cities Service Co. v. State, 312 So.2d 799, 801 (Fla.App. 1975) ("In early days it was important to encourage persons to use their land by whatever means were available for the purpose of commercial and industrial development. In a frontier society there was little likelihood that a dangerous use of land could cause damage to one's neighbor. Today our life has become more complex. Many areas are overcrowded, and even the non-negligent use of one's land can cause extensive damages to a neighbor's property. Though there are still many hazardous activities which are socially desirable, it now seems reasonable that they pay their own way. It is too much to ask an innocent neighbor to bear the burden thrust upon him as a consequence of an abnormal use of the land next door. The doctrine of Rylands v. Fletcher should be applied in Florida.")

Miller v. Civil Constructors, Inc.

Illinois Court of Appeal, 1995.
272 Ill.App.3d 263, 209 Ill.Dec. 311, 651 N.E.2d 239.

BOWMAN, J. * * *

[Plaintiff, Gary Miller, was injured when a stray bullet ricocheted during the course of firearm practice in a nearby gravel pit and caused him to fall from a truck. Count I (against the owner of the gravel pit) and Count V (against the employer of the police officers engaged in firearm practice) alleged that those defendants were strictly liable for injuries to plaintiff arising from "ultrahazardous" activity for which defendants were legally responsible because of the owner's control of the premises or the police department's employees' discharge of firearms. The circuit court of Stephenson County dismissed the strict liability counts of the complaint and plaintiff appeals.]

The doctrine of strict liability, sometimes called absolute liability, has its genesis in the English rule of Rylands v. Fletcher (1868), L.R. 3 H.L. 330, wherein strict liability was imposed on the defendant owners of land for harm resulting from the abnormal or nonnatural use of the defendants' land which arose when water from defendants' reservoir flooded the adjoining mine of the plaintiff. Subsequent decisions interpreted the rule to be confined to things or activities which were "extraordinary," or "exceptional," or "abnormal" so that there was some special use bringing with it increased danger to others. (W. Keeton, D. Dobbs, R. Keeton, & D. Owen, Prosser & Keeton on the Law of Torts § 78, at 545–46 (5th ed. 1984).) From the decisions of the English courts the "rule" of Rylands which has emerged is that "the defendant will be liable when he damages another by a thing or activity unduly dangerous and inappropriate to the place where it is maintained, in the light of the character of that place and its surroundings." Prosser, § 78, at 547–48.

Most jurisdictions in this country have adopted the rule of Rylands to impose strict liability on owners and users of land for harm resulting from abnormally dangerous conditions and activities. [C] The best-known applications of the Rylands rule imposing strict liability on a defendant involve the storing and use of explosives and flammable materials. [Cc] * * *

[After discussing the alternative to strict liability, negligence, the court noted that the standard of care in negligence is a] flexible one which varies according to the particular circumstances. Imposing a duty of ordinary care, even where it may become a high degree of care under the particular circumstances, is quite different from imposing strict or absolute liability by classifying the activity ultrahazardous. Our review of the authorities thus discloses that the discharge of firearms resulting in injury ordinarily presents a question of negligence and that the standard of care is ordinary care—one which may be equated to a high degree of care because of the particular circumstances presented.

We return to the threshold question whether the use of firearms ought to be classified as an ultrahazardous activity. This type of inquiry is a question of law that we believe will be subjected to more rigorous, disciplined, and consistent analysis if we adopt the use of the Restatement principles and factors discussed, or at least implicitly considered, in prior decisions. [Cc] We expressly adopt the use of the Restatement principles and factors as an aid in deciding this type of question.

Section 519 of the Restatement states the general principle that "one who carries on an abnormally dangerous activity is subject to liability for harm to the person, land or chattels of another resulting from the activity, although he has exercised the utmost care to prevent the harm." [C] Section 520 of the Restatement sets forth several factors which we will consider in determining whether an activity is abnormally dangerous (ultrahazardous):

"(a) existence of a high degree of risk of some harm to the person, land or chattels of others;

(b) likelihood that the harm that results from it will be great;

(c) inability to eliminate the risk by the exercise of reasonable care;

(d) extent to which the activity is not a matter of common usage;

(e) inappropriateness of the activity to the place where it is carried on; and

(f) extent to which its value to the community is outweighed by its dangerous attributes."

While all of these factors are important and should be considered, ordinarily the presence of more than one factor, but not all of them, will be necessary to declare the activity ultrahazardous as a matter of law so as to hold the actor strictly liable. The essential question is whether the risk created is so unusual, either because of its magnitude or because of the circumstances surrounding it, as to justify the imposition of strict liability even though the activity is carried on with all reasonable care. (Restatement § 520, comment *f*, at 37–38.) Considerations of public policy also enter prominently into the decisions by our courts to impose strict liability (at least in product liability cases). [Cc] Particular consideration is also given to the appropriateness of the activity to the place where it is maintained, in light of the character of the place and its surroundings under the Rylands rule. [C]

The use of guns or firearms, even though frequently classified as dangerous or even highly dangerous, is not the type of activity that must be deemed ultrahazardous when the above-stated criteria are taken into consideration. First, the risk of harm to persons or property, even though great, can be virtually eliminated by the exercise of reasonable or even "utmost" care under the circumstances [C]. The doctrine of strict or absolute liability is ordinarily reserved for abnormally dangerous activities for which no degree of care can truly provide safety. There is a clear distinction between requiring a defendant to exercise a high degree of care when involved in a potentially dangerous activity and requiring a defendant to insure absolutely the safety of others when engaging in ultrahazardous activity. [C]

Second, the use of firearms is a matter of common usage and the harm posed comes from their misuse rather than from their inherent nature alone [c]. Third, the activity in this case was carried on at a firing range in a quarry located somewhere near the City of Freeport. We assume that the location was appropriate for such activity in the absence of further factual allegations in the complaint particularly describing the area as inappropriate for the target practice. Finally, the target practice is of some social utility to the community; this weighs against declaring it ultrahazardous where the activity was alleged to have been performed by law enforcement officers apparently to improve their skills in the handling of weapons.

In light of the above considerations, we conclude that plaintiff's allegations are legally insufficient to show that the activity should be declared ultrahazardous so as to subject defendants to claims premised on a theory of strict liability. [C]

The judgment of the circuit court of Stephenson County is affirmed.

Affirmed.

RATHJE and HUTCHINSON, JJ., concur.

NOTES AND QUESTIONS

1. Note that the principal case uses the terms "ultrahazardous" and "abnormally dangerous" activity. The first Restatement of Torts had used the term "ultrahazardous" and applied it to an activity that "necessarily involves a risk of serious harm to the persons, land or chattels of others which cannot be eliminated by the exercise of the utmost care and * * * is not a matter of common usage." § 520. The definition is categoric. If an activity is ultrahazardous, it would be so regarded no matter where it took place. This was the approach taken by the Alaska Supreme Court regarding storage of explosives in Yukon Equipment, Inc. v. Fireman's Fund Ins. Co., 585 P.2d 1206 (Alaska 1978). That case carried the approach so far that it found liability on the part of the company storing the explosives, even though they were stolen by the other defendant and deliberately set off to produce the explosion. (This situation is the subject of a caveat in the Restatement.)

2. The Second Restatement, on the other hand, uses the term "abnormally dangerous" and makes the decision depend on the nature of the location where the activity takes place. Consider, for example, whether a hardware store in a small town, keeping a small amount of dynamite for the benefit of farmers clearing fields of stumps, would be subject to strict liability. Cf. Barnes v. Zettlemoyer, 25 Tex.Civ.App. 468, 62 S.W. 111 (1901) (no strict liability). The Third Restatement retains the "abnormally dangerous" language and defines it as one that "creates a foreseeable and highly significant risk of physical harm even when reasonable care is exercised by all actors; and the activity is not one of common usage." Note that the "value to the community" factor is not included. Do you expect that the courts will follow the Restatement (Third)'s lead on this? Restatement (Third) of Torts: Liability for Physical and Emotional Harm § 20 (2010).

3. Opinions frequently recite that blasting is the paradigm for an abnormally dangerous activity. Most jurisdictions impose strict liability for blasting if it is done in an urban or residential area. Dyer v. Maine Drilling & Blasting, Inc., 984 A.2d 210, 216 (Maine 2009) ("[a]t least forty-one states have adopted some form of strict liability for blasting"). Some state that the nature of the location is important in determining whether the blasting activity is subject to strict liability, while others impose strict liability for use of explosives but not their storage. See Otero v. Burgess, 84 N.M. 575, 505 P.2d 1251 (1973); cf. Chavez v. Southern Pac. Transp. Co., 413 F.Supp. 1203 (E.D.Cal.1976) (keeping 18 bomb-loaded box cars in railroad yard

near town). Sometimes strict liability is accomplished by calling the blasting activity a nuisance, as in Gossett v. Southern R. Co., 115 Tenn. 376, 89 S.W. 737 (1905). (See Chapter 16.) A few courts, stressing the comparative safety with which blasting can be carried on by the exercise of due care, hold that strict liability is not applicable and there is liability only for negligence. Wadleigh v. Manchester, 100 N.H. 277, 123 A.2d 831 (1956).

Indiana Harbor Belt R.R. Co. v. American Cyanamid Co.

United States Court of Appeals, Seventh Circuit, 1990.
916 F.2d 1174.

POSNER, J.

American Cyanamid Company, the defendant in this diversity tort suit governed by Illinois law, is a major manufacturer of chemicals, including acrylonitrile, a chemical used in large quantities in making acrylic fibers, plastics, dyes, pharmaceutical chemicals, and other intermediate and final goods. On January 2, 1979, at its manufacturing plant in Louisiana, Cyanamid loaded 20,000 gallons of liquid acrylonitrile into a railroad tank car that it had leased from the North American Car Corporation. The next day, a train of the Missouri Pacific Railroad picked up the car at Cyanamid's siding. The car's ultimate destination was a Cyanamid plant in New Jersey served by Conrail rather than by Missouri Pacific. The Missouri Pacific train carried the car north to the Blue Island railroad yard of Indiana Harbor Belt Railroad, the plaintiff in this case, a small switching line that has a contract with Conrail to switch cars from other lines to Conrail, in this case for travel east. The Blue Island yard is in the Village of Riverdale, which is just south of Chicago and part of the Chicago metropolitan area.

The car arrived in the Blue Island yard on the morning of January 9, 1979. Several hours after it arrived, employees of the switching line noticed fluid gushing from the bottom outlet of the car. The lid on the outlet was broken. After two hours, the line's supervisor of equipment was able to stop the leak by closing a shut-off valve controlled from the top of the car. No one was sure at the time just how much of the contents of the car had leaked, but it was feared that all 20,000 gallons had, and since acrylonitrile is flammable at a temperature of 30 degrees Fahrenheit or above, highly toxic, and possibly carcinogenic [c], the local authorities ordered the homes near the yard evacuated. The evacuation lasted only a few hours, until the car was moved to a remote part of the yard and it was discovered that only about a quarter of the acrylonitrile had leaked. Concerned nevertheless that there had been some contamination of soil and water, the Illinois Department of Environmental Protection ordered the switching line to take decontamination measures that cost the line $981,022.75, which it sought to recover by this suit.

One count of the two-count complaint charges Cyanamid with having maintained the leased tank car negligently. The other count asserts that the transportation of acrylonitrile in bulk through the Chicago metropolitan area is an abnormally dangerous activity, for the consequences of which the shipper (Cyanamid) is strictly liable to the switching line, which bore the financial brunt of those consequences because of the decontamination measures that it was forced to take. * * *

[The trial court judge found that strict liability applied and granted summary judgment in favor of the plaintiff on that count. Defendant appealed.]

The question whether the shipper of a hazardous chemical by rail should be strictly liable for the consequences of a spill or other accident to the shipment en route is a novel one in Illinois[.] * * *

The parties agree that the question whether placing acrylonitrile in a rail shipment that will pass through a metropolitan area subjects the shipper to strict liability is, as recommended in Restatement (Second) of Torts § 520, comment *l* (1977), a question of law, so that we owe no particular deference to the conclusion of the district court. They also agree * * * that the Supreme Court of Illinois would treat as authoritative the provisions of the Restatement governing abnormally dangerous activities. The key provision is section 520, which sets forth six factors to be considered in deciding whether an activity is abnormally dangerous and the actor therefore strictly liable.

The roots of section 520 are in nineteenth-century cases. The most famous one is Rylands v. Fletcher, 1 Ex. 265, aff'd, L.R. 3 H.L. 300 (1868), but a more illuminating one in the present context is Guille v. Swan, 19 Johns. (N.Y.) 381 (1822). A man took off in a hot-air balloon and landed, without intending to, in a vegetable garden in New York City. A crowd that had been anxiously watching his involuntary descent trampled the vegetables in their endeavor to rescue him when he landed. The owner of the garden sued the balloonist for the resulting damage, and won. Yet the balloonist had not been careless. In the then state of ballooning it was impossible to make a pinpoint landing.

Guille is a paradigmatic case for strict liability. (a) The risk (probability) of harm was great, and (b) the harm that would ensue if the risk materialized could be, although luckily was not, great (the balloonist could have crashed into the crowd rather than into the vegetables). The confluence of these two factors established the urgency of seeking to prevent such accidents. (c) Yet such accidents could not be prevented by the exercise of due care; the technology of care in ballooning was insufficiently developed. (d) The activity was not a matter of common usage, so there was no presumption that it was a highly valuable activity despite its unavoidable riskiness. (e) The activity was inappropriate to the place in which it took place—densely populated New York City. The risk of serious harm to others (other than the balloonist himself, that is) could have been reduced by shifting the activity to the sparsely inhabited areas that surrounded the city in those days. (f) Reinforcing (d), the value to the community of the activity of recreational ballooning did not appear to be great enough to offset its unavoidable risks.

These are, of course, the six factors in section 520. They are related to each other in that each is a different facet of a common quest for a proper legal regime to govern accidents that negligence liability cannot adequately control. The interrelations might be more perspicuous if the six factors were reordered. One might for example start with (c), inability to eliminate the risk of accident by the exercise of due care. [C] The baseline common law regime of tort liability is negligence. When it is a workable regime, because the hazards of an activity can be avoided by being careful (which is to say, nonnegligent), there is no need to switch to strict liability. Sometimes, however, a particular type of accident cannot be prevented by taking care but can be avoided, or its consequences minimized, by shifting the activity in which the accident occurs to another locale, where the risk or harm of an accident will be less ((e)), or by reducing the scale of the activity in order to minimize the number of accidents caused by it ((f)). [Cc] By making the actor strictly liable—by denying him in other words an excuse based on his inability to avoid accidents by being more careful—we give him an incentive, missing in a negligence regime, to experiment with methods of preventing accidents that involve not greater exertions of care, assumed to be futile, but instead relocating, changing, or reducing (perhaps to the vanishing point) the activity giving rise to the accident. [C] The greater the risk of an accident ((a)) and the costs of an accident if one occurs ((b)), the more we want the actor to consider the possibility of making accident-reducing activity changes; the stronger, therefore, is the case for strict liability. Finally, if an activity is extremely common ((d)), like driving an automobile, it is unlikely either that its hazards are perceived as great or that there is no technology of care available to minimize them; so the case for strict liability is weakened.

The largest class of cases in which strict liability has been imposed under the standard codified in the Second Restatement of Torts involves the use of dynamite and other explosives for demolition in residential or urban areas. Restatement, supra, § 519, comment *d*; [c]. Explosives are dangerous even when handled carefully, and we therefore want blasters to choose the location of the activity with care and also to explore the feasibility of using safer substitutes (such as a wrecking ball), as well as to be careful in the blasting itself. Blasting is not a commonplace activity like driving a car, or so superior to substitute methods of demolition that the imposition of liability is unlikely to have any effect except to raise the activity's costs.

Against this background we turn to the particulars of acrylonitrile. Acrylonitrile is one of a large number of chemicals that are hazardous in the sense of being flammable, toxic, or both; acrylonitrile is both, as are many others. A table in the record . . . contains a list of the 125 hazardous materials that are shipped in highest volume on the nation's railroads. Acrylonitrile is the fifty-third most hazardous on the list. Number 1 is phosphorus (white or yellow), and among the other materials that rank higher than acrylonitrile on the hazard scale are anhydrous ammonia, liquified petroleum gas, vinyl chloride, gasoline, crude petroleum, motor fuel antiknock compound, methyl and ethyl chloride, sulphuric acid, sodium metal, and chloroform. The plaintiff's lawyer acknowledged at argument that the logic of the district court's opinion dictated strict liability for all 52 materials that rank higher than acrylonitrile on the list, and quite possibly for the 72 that rank lower as well, since all are hazardous if spilled in quantity while being shipped by rail. Every shipper of any of these materials would therefore be strictly liable for the consequences of a spill or other accident that occurred while the material was being shipped through a metropolitan area. The plaintiff's lawyer further acknowledged the irrelevance, on her view of the case, of the fact that Cyanamid had leased and filled the car that spilled the acrylonitrile; all she thought important is that Cyanamid introduced the product into the stream of commerce that happened to pass through the Chicago metropolitan area. Her concession may have been incautious. One might want to distinguish between the shipper who merely places his goods on his loading dock to be picked up by the carrier and the shipper who, as in this case, participates actively in the transportation. But the concession is illustrative of the potential scope of the district court's decision.

* * *

Cases . . . that impose strict liability for the storage of a dangerous chemical provide a potentially helpful analogy to our case. But they can be distinguished on the ground that the storer . . . has more control than the shipper.

So we can get little help from precedent, and might as well apply section 520 to the acrylonitrile problem from the ground up. To begin with, we have been given no reason * * * for believing that a negligence regime is not perfectly adequate to remedy and deter, at reasonable cost, the accidental spillage of acrylonitrile from rail cars. * * * [A]lthough acrylonitrile is flammable even at relatively low temperatures, and toxic, it is not so corrosive or otherwise destructive that it will eat through or otherwise damage or weaken a tank car's valves although they are maintained with due (which essentially means, with average) care. No one suggests, therefore, that the leak in this case was caused by the inherent properties of acrylonitrile. It was caused by carelessness—whether that of the North American Car Corporation in failing to maintain or inspect the car properly, or that of Cyanamid in failing to maintain or inspect it, or that of the Missouri Pacific when it had custody of the car, or that of the switching line itself in failing to notice the ruptured lid, or some combination of these possible failures of care. Accidents that are due to a lack of care can be prevented by taking care; and when a lack of care can * * * be shown in court, such accidents are adequately deterred by the threat of liability for negligence.

* * *

The district judge and the plaintiff's lawyer make much of the fact that the spill occurred in a densely inhabited metropolitan area. Only 4,000 gallons spilled; what if all 20,000 had done so? Isn't the risk that this might happen even if everybody were careful sufficient to warrant giving the shipper an incentive to explore alternative routes? Strict liability would supply that incentive. But this argument overlooks the fact that, like other transportation networks, the railroad network is a hub-and-spoke system. And the hubs are in metropolitan areas. Chicago is one of the nation's largest railroad hubs. In 1983, the latest date for which we have figures, Chicago's railroad yards handled the third highest volume of hazardous-material shipments in the nation. East St. Louis, which is also in Illinois, handled the second highest volume.

Office of Technology Assessment, Transportation of Hazardous Materials 53 (1986). With most hazardous chemicals (by volume of shipments) being at least as hazardous as acrylonitrile, it is unlikely—and certainly not demonstrated by the plaintiff—that they can be rerouted around all the metropolitan areas in the country, except at prohibitive cost. Even if it were feasible to reroute them one would hardly expect shippers, as distinct from carriers, to be the firms best situated to do the rerouting. * * *

The difference between shipper and carrier points to a deep flaw in the plaintiff's case. Unlike Guille * * * and unlike the storage cases, beginning with Rylands itself, here it is not the actors—that is, the transporters of acrylonitrile and other chemicals—but the manufacturers, who are sought to be held strictly liable. [C] A shipper can in the bill of lading designate the route of his shipment if he likes, [c] but is it realistic to suppose that shippers will become students of railroading in order to lay out the safest route by which to ship their goods? Anyway, rerouting is no panacea. Often it will increase the length of the journey, or compel the use of poorer track, or both. When this happens, the probability of an accident is increased, even if the consequences of an accident if one occurs are reduced; so the expected accident cost, being the product of the probability of an accident and the harm if the accident occurs, may rise. [C] It is easy to see how the accident in this case might have been prevented at reasonable cost by greater care on the part of those who handled the tank car of acrylonitrile. It is difficult to see how it might have been prevented at reasonable cost by a change in the activity of transporting the chemical. This is therefore not an apt case for strict liability.

* * *

In emphasizing the flammability and toxicity of acrylonitrile rather than the hazards of transporting it, as in failing to distinguish between the active and the passive shipper, the plaintiff overlooks the fact that ultrahazardousness or abnormal dangerousness is, in the contemplation of the law at least, a property not of substances, but of activities: not of acrylonitrile, but of the transportation of acrylonitrile by rail through populated areas. [C] Natural gas is both flammable and poisonous, but the operation of a natural gas well is not an ultrahazardous activity. [C] Whatever the situation under products liability law (section 402A of the Restatement), the manufacturer of a product is not considered to be engaged in an abnormally dangerous activity merely because the product becomes dangerous when it is handled or used in some way after it leaves his premises, even if the danger is foreseeable. [Cc] The plaintiff does not suggest that Cyanamid should switch to making some less hazardous chemical that would substitute for acrylonitrile in the textiles and other goods in which acrylonitrile is used. Were this a feasible method of accident avoidance, there would be an argument for making manufacturers strictly liable for accidents that occur during the shipment of their products (how strong an argument we need not decide). Apparently it is not a feasible method.

The relevant activity is transportation, not manufacturing and shipping. This essential distinction the plaintiff ignores. But even if the defendant is treated as a transporter and not merely a shipper, the plaintiff has not shown that the transportation of acrylonitrile in bulk by rail through populated areas is so hazardous an activity, even when due care is exercised, that the law should seek to create—perhaps quixotically—incentives to relocate the activity to nonpopulated areas, or to reduce the scale of the activity, or to switch to transporting acrylonitrile by road rather than by rail, perhaps to set the stage for a replay of Siegler v. Kuhlman[, 81 Wash. 2d 448, 502 P.2d 1181 (1972) (fire on highway caused by gasoline that leaked from overturned tanker truck)]. It is no more realistic to propose to reroute the shipment of all hazardous materials around Chicago than it is to propose the relocation of homes adjacent to the Blue Island switching yard to more distant suburbs. It may be less realistic. Brutal though it may seem to say it, the inappropriate use to which land is being put in the Blue Island yard and neighborhood may be, not the transportation of hazardous chemicals, but residential living. The analogy is to building your home between the runways at O'Hare.

The briefs hew closely to the Restatement, whose approach to the issue of strict liability is mainly allocative rather than distributive. By this we mean that the emphasis is on picking a liability regime (negligence or strict liability) that will control the particular class of accidents in question most effectively, rather than on finding the deepest pocket and placing liability there. At argument, however, the plaintiff's lawyer invoked distributive considerations by pointing out that Cyanamid is a huge firm and the Indiana Harbor Belt Railroad a fifty-mile-long switching line that almost went broke in the winter of 1979, when the accident occurred. Well, so what? A corporation is not a living person but a set of contracts the terms of which determine who will bear the brunt of liability. Tracing the incidence of a cost is a complex undertaking which the plaintiff sensibly has made no effort to assume, since its legal relevance would be dubious. We add only that however small the plaintiff may be, it has mighty parents: it is a jointly owned subsidiary of Conrail and the Soo line.

* * *

The judgment is reversed (with no award of costs in this court) and the case remanded for further proceedings, consistent with this opinion, on the plaintiff's claim for negligence.

Reversed and remanded, with directions.

NOTES AND QUESTIONS

1. In the Siegler v. Kulman case to which the opinion refers, the Supreme Court of Washington found that strict liability applied to the transportation of gasoline as freight in a tanker truck. The case arose out of an accident in which a high school student on her way home from her after school job came upon a gasoline spill that had just occurred on the highway when the tank trailer separated from the truck and overturned. The gasoline spill burst into flames as she reached it.

2. Activities (in addition to blasting) that have been held to be abnormally dangerous include transportation and storage of toxic

chemicals and inflammable liquids, pile driving, crop dusting, fumigation with toxic gases, testing of rockets, fireworks displays, operation of a plutonium production facility, operation of hazardous waste disposal sites, operation of oil wells, and storage of large quantities of water and other liquids. Note, however, that some of these activities also have been found *not* to be subject to strict liability. Compare Northglenn v. Chevron USA, Inc., 519 F.Supp. 515 (D. Colo. 1981) (strict liability applied to storage of large amounts of gasoline in underground tanks at service station near residential area) with Hudson v. Peavey Oil Co., 279 Or. 3, 566 P.2d 175 (1977) (no strict liability because filling stations are common in residential areas); Langan v. Valicopters, Inc., 88 Wash.2d 855, 567 P.2d 218 (1977) (strict liability for crop dusting) and Lawler v. Skelton, 241 Miss. 274, 130 So.2d 565 (1961) (negligence for crop dusting); Klein v. Pyrodyne Corp., 117 Wash.2d 1, 810 P.2d 917 (1991) (strict liability for fireworks display at 4th of July celebration) and Cadena v. Chicago Fireworks Mfg. Co., 297 Ill.App.3d 945, 232 Ill.Dec. 60, 697 N.E.2d 802 (1998) (using same §§ 519–520 analysis, court reaches opposite result).

3. These activities all involve the use of property. Can the abnormally dangerous or ultrahazardous activity theory be used to establish strict liability for other activities not involving the use of land? See Merrill v. Navegar, Inc., 75 Cal.App.4th 500, 89 Cal.Rptr.2d 146, 190 (1999) ("overwhelming majority of American courts have taken the position that the distribution or sale" of firearms is not subject to strict liability), rev'd on other grounds, 26 Cal.4th 465, 28 P.3d 116, 110 Cal.Rptr.2d 370 (2001); Tompson v. Mindis Metals, Inc., 692 So.2d 805 (Ala.1997) (sale of batteries to recycling facility—theory not applied). What about committing suicide by running automobile in closed garage of duplex? Laterra v. Treaster, 17 Kan.App.2d 714, 844 P.2d 724 (1992) (strict liability applied where plaintiff's decedent was asphyxiated by carbon monoxide that leaked from defendant's decedent's garage).

4. *"Common Usage."* Automobile accidents kill and injure more people and damage more property than any of the other activities listed, yet driving is not subject to strict liability in part because it is not abnormal. Similarly, the transmission of electricity and natural gas are considered matters of common usage and thus not subject to strict liability. See, e.g., Voelker v. Delmarva Power & Light Co., 727 F.Supp. 991 (D.Md.1989). What about driving an automobile under the influence of alcohol? See Goodwin v. Reilley, 176 Cal.App.3d 86, 221 Cal.Rptr. 374 (1985) (rejecting the application of strict liability). What about engaging in sexual intercourse while infected with a sexually transmitted disease? See Doe v. Johnson, 817 F.Supp. 1382 (W.D.Mich.1993) (in action seeking damages for transmission of HIV, the virus that causes AIDS, plaintiff's strict liability count was dismissed). What about the storage of firearms? Police officer's widow filed suit against homeowner who had allowed the man who lived with her to store a firearms collection in the basement of her home in a locked cabinet. His adult son whom she knew to have a history of mental illness and violence and to have been dishonorably discharged from the military had a key to the house and took a .357 magnum with which he shot police officer. Jupin v. Kask, 447 Mass. 141, 849 N.E.2d 829 (2006) (strict liability claim dismissed because storage of firearms in the home is not an unusual or extraordinary use of property).

5. *"Inappropriate for the Location."* Many of the differences in the holdings of the cases cited in note 2 can be explained on the basis of the location of the activity. See also the Reporter's Note to § 520 of the Restatement, classifying the cases according to the location of the activity.

6. What is the appropriate location for the producing of plutonium for an atomic bomb? In cases brought by its neighbors against the operators of the Hanford Nuclear Weapons Reservation, the Ninth Circuit determined that Washington state law would find the activity was abnormally dangerous and therefore one to which strict liability would apply under the § 520 factors even though there is no appropriate place to carry on such an activity. It also rejected defendants' argument that the "public duty" exception to strict liability (Restatement (Second) § 521) should apply since defendants were not public officers or employees carrying out their duties but private contractors doing their patriotic duty by producing plutonium for the war effort, charging the Government only $1 a year to run the facility. In re Hanford Nuclear Reservation Litigation, 534 F.3d 986 (9th Cir. 2008) (applying Washington law).

7. *Aviation—Ground Damage.* In early stages of commercial aviation, airlines were held strictly liable for ground damage resulting from a crash. This view is no longer justified in light of the safety record of air travel if the basis is an ultrahazardous or abnormally dangerous activity and most courts have retreated to a negligence standard. See Crosby v. Cox Aircraft Co., 109 Wash.2d 581, 746 P.2d 1198 (1987) (noting "modern trend" away from strict liability to negligence standard for ground damage from aviation accidents). See also Restatement (Third) of Torts: Liability for Physical and Emotional Harm § 20, comment *k* (2010) (Reporters' Note "A special note on aviation ground damage.")

8. *Policy Behind the Imposition of Strict Liability.* Strict liability is "founded upon a policy of the law that imposes upon anyone who for his own purposes creates an abnormal risk of harm to his neighbors, the responsibility of relieving against that harm when it does in fact occur. The defendant's enterprise, in other words, is required to pay its way by compensating for the harm it causes because of its special, abnormal and dangerous character." Restatement (Second) of Torts § 519, comment *d*. The liability "is applicable to an activity that is carried on with all reasonable care, and that is of such utility that the risk involved in it cannot be regarded as so great or so unreasonable as to make it negligence merely to carry it on." Id., § 520, comment *b*. Observe also, that the decision whether an activity is subject to strict liability is for the court, not the jury, to make. Id.

In other words, this liability is analogous to negligence per se, but it is not called negligence because a court makes a judgment that value to the community is sufficiently great that the mere participation in the activity is not to be stigmatized as wrongdoing in the negligence sense. The activity is simply required to pay its own way, without that stigma, but it does pay with full tort damages, including pain and suffering damages when personal injury is involved. Does it make for sound social policy to make a "non-negligent" defendant pay the same as a "negligent" one? Should courts, as contrasted with legislatures, make judgments as to which activities should be subject to "strict liability"? What practical difference do such judgments entail?

Of course, one who carries on an abnormally dangerous activity may also be negligent in the way in which he conducts it and therefore subject to liability on both bases.

3. LIMITATIONS ON STRICT LIABILITY

Foster v. Preston Mill Co.

Supreme Court of Washington, 1954.
44 Wash.2d 440, 268 P.2d 645.

HAMLEY, JUSTICE. Blasting operations conducted by Preston Mill Company frightened mother mink owned by B.W. Foster, and caused the mink to kill their kittens. Foster brought this action against the company to recover damages. His second amended complaint, upon which the case was tried, sets forth a cause of action on the theory of absolute liability * * *.

After a trial to the court without a jury, judgment was rendered for plaintiff in the sum of $1,953.68. The theory adopted by the court was that, after defendant received notice of the effect which its blasting operations were having upon the mink, it was absolutely liable for all damages of that nature thereafter sustained. * * *

The primary question presented by appellant's assignments of error is whether, on these facts, the judgment against appellant is sustainable on the theory of absolute liability.

[The court noted that in Washington there is strict liability in blasting cases whether the damage is caused by trespassory or non-trespassory invasions.]

However the authorities may be divided on the point just discussed, they appear to be agreed that strict liability should be confined to consequences which lie within the extraordinary risk whose existence calls for such responsibility. [Cc] This limitation on the doctrine is indicated in the italicized portions of the rule as set forth in Restatement of Torts, § 519:

> "Except as stated in §§ 521–4, one who carries on an ultrahazardous activity is liable to another whose person, land or chattels the actor should recognize as likely to be harmed by the unpreventable miscarriage of the activity for harm resulting thereto *from that which makes the activity ultrahazardous,* although the utmost care is exercised to prevent the harm." (Italics supplied.)

This restriction which has been placed upon the application of the doctrine of absolute liability is based upon considerations of policy. * * * "* * * It is one thing to say that a dangerous enterprise must pay its way within reasonable limits, and quite another to say that it must bear responsibility for every extreme of harm that it may cause. The same practical necessity for the restriction of liability within some reasonable bounds, which arises in connection with problems of 'proximate cause' in negligence cases, demands here that some limit be set. * * * This limitation has been expressed by saying that the defendant's duty to insure safety extends only to certain consequences. More commonly, it is said that the defendant's conduct is not the 'proximate cause' of the damage. But ordinarily in such cases no question of causation is involved, and the limitation is one of the policy underlying liability." Prosser on Torts, 457, § 60.

Applying this principle to the case before us, the question comes down to this: Is the risk that any unusual vibration or noise may cause wild animals, which are being raised for commercial purposes, to kill their young, one of the things which make the activity of blasting ultrahazardous?

We have found nothing in the decisional law which would support an affirmative answer to this question. The decided cases, as well as common experience, indicate that the thing which makes blasting ultrahazardous is the risk that property or persons may be damaged or injured by coming into direct contact with flying debris, or by being directly affected by vibrations of the earth or concussions of the air. * * *

The relatively moderate vibration and noise which appellant's blasting produced at a distance of two and a quarter miles was no more than a usual incident of the ordinary life of the community. See 3 Restatement of Torts 48, § 522, comment *a*. The trial court specifically found that the blasting did not unreasonably interfere with the enjoyment of their property by nearby landowners, except in the case of respondent's mink ranch.

It is the exceedingly nervous disposition of mink, rather than the normal risks inherent in blasting operations, which therefore must, as a matter of sound policy, bear the responsibility for the loss here sustained. We subscribe to the view expressed by Professor Harper . . . that the policy of the law does not impose the rule of strict liability to protect against harms incident to the plaintiff's extraordinary and unusual use of land. This is perhaps but an application of the principle that the extent to which one man in the lawful conduct of his business is liable for injuries to another involves an adjustment of conflicting interests. * * *

It is our conclusion that the risk of causing harm of the kind here experienced, as a result of the relatively minor vibration, concussion, and noise from distance blasting, is not the kind of risk which makes the activity of blasting ultrahazardous. The doctrine of absolute liability is therefore inapplicable under the facts of this case, and respondent is not entitled to recover damages.

The judgment is reversed.

NOTES AND QUESTIONS

1. In accord with the principal case, upon similar facts, are Madsen v. East Jordan Irrigation Co., 101 Utah 552, 125 P.2d 794 (1942) and Gronn v. Rogers Construction, Inc., 221 Or. 226, 350 P.2d 1086 (1960) (both declining to award damages in strict liability for loss of minks due to blasting activity).

2. Suppose defendant had known that plaintiff's mink might be frightened and kill their kittens. Should defendant be held liable? See Summit View, Inc. v. W.W. Clyde & Co., 17 Utah 2d 26, 403 P.2d 919 (1965) (liability in negligence—not strict liability—for unnecessarily parking heavy equipment near mink sheds during whelping season).

3. Without any negligence on the part of the defendant, his cow trespasses in plaintiff's garden. Plaintiff tries to drive the cow out, and the cow attacks and injures her. Strict liability? Troth v. Wills, 8 Pa.Super. 1, 6 (1897) ("the act of the animal was one to which a creature of that kind is naturally disposed on being disturbed while feeding; and it was so directly associated with the primary trespass that, unless the plaintiff's right to prevent a continuance of this be denied, there can be no ground for questioning the liability of the owner"); Nixon v. Harris, 15 Ohio St.2d 105, 238 N.E.2d 785 (1968) (accord). What if the cow wanders into plaintiff's barn and breaks through a rotten place in the floor; and plaintiff, entering the barn in the dark falls into the hole and is injured? Hollenbeck v. Johnson, 79 Hun 499, 29 N.Y.S. 945 (1894) (no proximate cause).

4. Defendant parades his circus elephants through the streets of a city. Plaintiff's skittish horse, seeing a large object pass at a distance of a city block, takes fright and runs away, and plaintiff is injured. Is there strict liability? Scribner v. Kelley, 38 Barb. 14 (N.Y.1862) (no liability because injury did not proceed from savage and ferocious nature of wild animal but from reaction of horse to large moving object); Bostock-Ferari Amusement Co. v. Brocksmith, 34 Ind.App. 566, 73 N.E. 281 (1905) (bear on leash on way to train station frightens horse; no liability because the injury did not result from any dangerous quality of the bear—he did nothing but walk docilely in the charge of his keeper).

5. Defendant keeps a vicious dog that he knows has attacked human beings. This dog, trotting peacefully down the street, accidentally runs into plaintiff and knocks him down. Strict liability? Cf. Koetting v. Conroy, 223 Wis. 550, 270 N.W. 625 (1936) (no strict liability because no evidence that act was either vicious or mischievous). See also Martinez v. Modenbach, 396 So.2d 471 (La.App.1981) (chasing dog back in to owner's yard, plaintiff slips on wet grass and falls).

Golden v. Amory

Supreme Judicial Court of Massachusetts, 1952.
329 Mass. 484, 109 N.E.2d 131.

LUMMUS, JUSTICE. The defendants owned a hydroelectric plant in Ludlow in the Red Bridge area. As a result of the hurricane of September 21, 1938, the Chicopee River overflowed and damaged the real estate of the several plaintiffs. In these actions of tort the first count of the several declarations alleged that no permit or decree or approval of the county commissioners was secured by the defendants for the construction, maintenance, and operation of the Alden Street dike. The second count alleged negligence in the maintenance of that dike. The judge directed verdicts for the defendants on the first count, and on the second count, after verdicts for the plaintiffs, entered verdicts for the defendants under leave reserved. To that action, as well as to the exclusion of certain evidence offered by the plaintiffs, the plaintiffs excepted.

* * *

The plaintiffs rely upon the rule stated in Fletcher v. Rylands, L.R., 1 Ex. 265, 279, and affirmed in Rylands v. Fletcher, L.R., 3 H.L. 330, 339–340, that "the person who for his own purposes brings on his lands and collects and keeps there anything likely to do mischief if it escapes, must keep it in at his peril, and, if he does not do so, is prima facie answerable for all the damage which is the natural consequence of its escape." That rule is the law of this Commonwealth. [Cc] But that rule does not apply where the injury results from "vis major, the act of God * * *, which the owner had no reason to anticipate." [Cc] In the present case the flood, as disclosed by the evidence, was plainly beyond the capacity of any one to anticipate, and was clearly an act of God. [C] For this reason the rule under discussion does not apply, and the defendants cannot be held liable for injury caused by the flood waters.

Upon the whole case, we find no error, either in the rulings of the judge or in his exclusion of evidence offered by the plaintiffs.

Exceptions overruled.

NOTES AND QUESTIONS

1. In accord are Nichols v. Marsland, L.R. 2 Ex.Div. 1 (1876) (dam washed out by extraordinary rainfall); Bratton v. Rudnick, 283 Mass. 556, 186 N.E. 669 (1933) (same); and Murphy v. Gillum, 73 Mo.App. 487 (1898) (seepage from dam embankment caused by unprecedented frost).

2. What if defendant's reservoir overflows because the owner of another reservoir upstream suddenly releases a large quantity of water? Box v. Jubb, 4 Ex.Div. 76 (1879) (no liability). The act of a third party over whom the defendant has no control does not give rise to liability even where defendant's activity is subject to strict liability. See, for example, Rickards v. Lothian, [1913] A.C. 263 (malicious third person plugged up defendant's lavatory basin and turned the water on full causing flood in flat below).

Sandy v. Bushey

Supreme Judicial Court of Maine, 1925.
124 Me. 320, 128 A. 513.

STURGIS, J. In the summer of 1923, the plaintiff turned his mare and colt out in the pasture of a neighbor. Other horses occupied the pasture during the season, including the defendant's three-year old colt. On July 14, 1923, the plaintiff went to the pasture to grain his mare, and, while so doing, was kicked by the defendant's horse and seriously injured. This action on the case is brought to recover damages for such injuries and, after verdict for the plaintiff, is before this court on a general motion.

By the common law the owners or keepers of domestic animals are not answerable for an injury done by them in a place where they have a

right to be, unless the animals in fact, and to the owners' knowledge, are vicious. If, however, a person keeps a vicious or dangerous animal which he knows is accustomed to attack and injure mankind, he assumes the obligation of an insurer against injury by such animal, and no measure of care in its keeping will excuse him. His liability is founded upon the keeping of such an animal when he has knowledge of its vicious propensities, and his care or negligence is immaterial. In an action for an injury caused by such an animal, the plaintiff has only to allege and prove the keeping, the vicious propensities, and the scienter. Negligence is not the ground of liability, and need not be alleged or proved. This rule of liability of keepers of domestic animals finds its origin in the ancient common law and, except as modified by statute in case of injuries by dogs, is retained as the rule of law in this class of cases in this state. [Cc]

A careful consideration of the evidence discloses facts which fairly tend to establish that the defendant's horse had exhibited a vicious and ugly disposition at various times prior to the day on which the plaintiff was injured, and notice of the animal's vicious propensities had been brought home to the defendant. Upon these issues the jury's verdict in favor of the plaintiff was fully warranted.

The defendant, however, says that the plaintiff was guilty of contributory negligence and cannot, therefore, recover in this action. We are unable to sustain this contention under the rule of liability adopted by this court. In those jurisdictions which have departed from the ancient common-law rule and declared negligence to be the ground of liability in actions for injuries by animals, the defense of contributory negligence has been recognized, and the injured party's failure to exercise due care will defeat his action. [Cc] In this state, however, the negligence doctrine has not been accepted, and contributory negligence in the strict sense of that term cannot be held to constitute a defense to the action. Exclusion of negligence as the basis of liability forbids the inclusion of contributory negligence as a defense. Something more than slight negligence or want of due care on the part of the injured party must be shown in order to relieve the keeper of a vicious domestic animal known to be such from his liability as an insurer.

In Muller v. McKesson, 73 N.Y. 195, 29 Am.Rep. 123, which may be fairly accepted as the leading case in this country upon the question of contributory negligence as a defense to an action of this character, Church, C.J., in stating the opinion of the court, says:

> "If a person with full knowledge of the evil propensities of an animal wantonly excites him, or voluntarily and unnecessarily puts himself in the way of such an animal, he would be adjudged to have brought the injury upon himself, and ought not to be entitled to recover. In such a case it cannot be said, in a legal sense, that the keeping of the animal, which is the gravamen of the offense, produced the injury. * * * But as the owner is held to a rigorous rule of liability on account of the danger to human life and limb, by harboring and keeping such animals, it follows that he ought not to be relieved from it by slight negligence or want of ordinary care. To enable an owner of such an animal to interpose this defense, acts should

be proved with notice of the character of the animal, which would establish that the person injured voluntarily brought the calamity upon himself." * * *

We are convinced that the principle announced by Chief Justice Church correctly defines the degree of responsibility which must be fixed upon the injured party in order to relieve the keeper of a known vicious animal from his liability as an insurer with which he is charged in this state. The fact must be established that the injury is attributable, not to the keeping of the animal, but to the injured party's unnecessarily and voluntarily putting himself in a way to be hurt knowing the probable consequences of his act, so that he may fairly be deemed to have brought the injury upon himself.

Applying this rule to the facts in the case before us, we are of the opinion that the prima facie case against the defendant, established by the evidence, is not rebutted by the plaintiff's acts or omissions. The plaintiff led his mare away from the other horses in the pasture and started to grain her, when the defendant's horse approached in a threatening manner. The plaintiff drove him away and turned to continue feeding the mare. The colt's return was silent and swift and his attack unexpected. It cannot be said that the plaintiff voluntarily put himself in a way to be injured by the defendant's horse, knowing the probable consequences of his act. The defendant is liable, as found by the jury.

Motion overruled.

NOTES AND QUESTIONS

1. The Restatement (Second) of Torts also has adopted the rule for both wild animals and abnormally dangerous activities. See §§ 515, 523, 524. Is this a logical rule? If ordinary contributory negligence is a defense when defendant is negligent, why is it not a defense when he is not even negligent?

2. Most states have adopted comparative negligence rules, reducing a plaintiff's damages by the plaintiff's percentage of negligence. If a plaintiff's negligence is no longer a complete bar to recovery, should it be a defense in strict liability cases as well as negligence cases? Is it true that conduct constituting negligence and conduct forming the basis for strict liability cannot be rationally compared? Plaintiff, who had been around cattle all his life, attempted to move a newborn calf away from the danger of a muddy river bank, with its mother unsecured and only a few feet away. She attacked as he put the calf down and injured him. Should plaintiff's actions completely bar his recovery? See Andrade v. Shiers, 564 So.2d 787 (La.App.1990) (plaintiff's fault compared to owners' strict liability; 80% of fault allocated to plaintiff). Restatement (Third) of Torts: Liability for Physical and Emotional Harm § 25 (2010) would apply comparative negligence principles to compare the negligence of the plaintiff to the strict liability of the defendant in cases involving abnormally dangerous activities and animals. Would you expect a jurisdiction to adopt Restatement (Third)'s position if it still applied the traditional rule that contributory negligence was a complete bar to recovery? Assuming a jurisdiction had adopted comparative negligence, would you expect it to be more likely to

adopt Restatement (Third)'s position if it had chosen pure or modified comparative negligence?

3. Defendant keeps a bear in a cage at a circus. Plaintiff crawls under the rope in front of the cage and goes within six inches of the bars. The bear slaps at him through the bars hitting him in the face and putting out his eye. Is defendant liable? Cf. Ervin v. Woodruff, 119 App.Div. 603, 103 N.Y.S. 1051 (1907) (no; plaintiff brought the calamity upon himself) and Heidemann v. Wheaton, 72 S.D. 375, 34 N.W.2d 492 (1948) (no; plaintiff voluntarily approached obvious danger). A customer at a service station put his hand in an unlocked box of snakes kept for public display. He was bitten by a rattlesnake. Is his claim barred? See Keyser v. Phillips Petroleum Co., 287 So.2d 364 (Fla.App.1973) (demurrer reversed; plaintiff entitled to opportunity to prove that he did not know dangers). Defendant raises exotic animals on her farm, including Siberian tigers. A man who is visiting the tenant who lives above the garage goes into defendant's backyard to pet a tiger through the fence. The tiger grabs his arm and pulls it through the fence. Is the owner strictly liable? Can she argue assumption of the risk as a defense? Plaintiff had visited the tenant on the farm about thirty times before the incident. Irvine v. Rare Feline Breeding Ctr., 685 N.E.2d 120 (Ind.App.1997) (strict liability applies to wild animals; question of fact for jury whether defendant proved assumption of risk).

4. Defendant is conducting blasting operations in proximity to a highway. He stations a flagman to stop traffic when a blast is about to be set off. Plaintiff drives past the flagman, and is injured by the blast. Should it make any difference whether plaintiff does not see the flagman because he is not looking, or sees him and deliberately drives past? See Worth v. Dunn, 98 Conn. 51, 62, 118 A. 467, 471 (1922) (plaintiff part of crowd that had gathered to watch demolition of wall and had been warned to move back) and Wells v. Knight, 32 R.I. 432, 80 A. 16 (1911) (occupants of buggy drove past defendant's employee who had tried to stop them from entering area where blasting charges had been set and were about to be set off).

5. *Legal Sanction.* Statutory sanction for defendant's conduct frequently has been held to preclude the application of strict liability, on the ground that the defendant cannot be held strictly liable for doing properly what the law has authorized him to do, although he will still of course be liable for any negligence. Thus the custodian of a public zoo may be held not subject to strict liability for harm done by the animals kept in it. Jackson v. Baker, 24 App.D.C. 100 (1904); Guzzi v. New York Zoological Society, 192 App.Div. 263, 182 N.Y.S. 257 (1920), aff'd, 233 N.Y. 511, 135 N.E. 897 (1922). This has been held to be true for gas or electric conduits laid in the street under legislative authority. Gould v. Winona Gas Co., 100 Minn. 258, 111 N.W. 254 (1907). Also for common carriers required by law to ship wild animals or explosives. Actiesselskabet Ingrid v. Central R. Co. of N.J., 216 Fed. 72 (2d Cir.1914); Pope v. Edward M. Rude Carrier Corp., 138 W.Va. 218, 75 S.E.2d 584 (1953).

The protection from strict liability also has been extended to a contractor doing such work as blasting for the state. Pumphrey v. J.A. Jones Const. Co., 250 Iowa 559, 94 N.W.2d 737 (1959). But see Smith v. Lockheed Propulsion Co., 247 Cal.App.2d 774, 56 Cal.Rptr. 128, 139–142 (1967) (strict liability applied to company testing rockets under contract with federal government) and In re Hanford Nuclear Reservation

Litigation, 534 F.3d 986 (9th Cir. 2008) (applying Washington law) (strict liability applied to companies managing nuclear weapons development for federal government).

6. The next chapter addresses the development of strict liability for "unreasonably dangerous" products. Is this analogous to the principle of strict liability for abnormally dangerous activities? See Arlington Forest Assoc. v. Exxon Corp., 774 F.Supp. 387 (E.D.Va.1991) (under § 519, strict liability attaches only to abnormally dangerous activities, not substances) and Indiana Harbor Belt R.R. Co. v. American Cyanamid Co., 916 F.2d 1174 (7th Cir.1990) ("ultrahazardousness or abnormal dangerousness is, in the contemplation of the law at least, a property not of substances, but of activities").

CHAPTER 15

PRODUCTS LIABILITY

"Products liability" is the umbrella term for the liability of a manufacturer, seller, or other supplier of chattels, to one who suffers physical harm caused by the chattel. Products liability may rest upon the manufacturer or supplier's negligence, upon a warranty theory, or upon strict liability in tort. Strict liability theories burst onto the scene only during the past fifty years, but have become the paramount basis of liability for manufacturers of products. This "revolution" in the common law of torts through the widespread adoption of strict products liability, however, is not as radical as it initially may seem. Developments in negligence and warranty law foreshadowed the adoption of strict liability in many jurisdictions. Moreover, elements of the law of negligence, especially the "reasonableness" standard, have crept back into the strict liability basis in cases alleging product design and warning defects.

The development of strict products liability law occurred initially through the courts, largely around the organizing principle of the American Law Institute's (ALI) Restatement (Second) of Torts (1965). This publication, in turn, had its intellectual roots in the views of some of the great scholars of tort law—Fleming James, William Prosser, Roger Traynor, and John Wade. The development of strict products liability represented a significant intellectual achievement whose influence runs far beyond the borders of the United States as Europe and other common law countries have utilized it as a model for their own efforts. See, e.g., the Product Liability Directive for the European Economic Community (85/374/EEC). As the courts worked out the kinks in the application of the Restatement (Second) formulation of strict products liability, significant changes and legal doctrines developed, many of which were recognized in Restatement (Third) of Torts: Products Liability (1998).

The development of strict products liability has been a controversial one. Manufacturers have claimed that the application of strict liability for design and warnings defect cases has kept good products off the market, inhibited product development, and created an unreasonable "tort tax" on products. Consumer groups and plaintiffs' lawyers deny these claims and argue that strict liability has acted as a surrogate policeman to make products safer. The assessment is complicated by the fact that the critics and supporters are not always defining "strict liability" in the same way. As you will discern from this chapter, courts have had a great deal of difficulty in defining strict liability in the context of design and warning cases. See Henderson & Eisenberg, The Quiet Revolution in Products Liability: An Empirical Study of Legal Change, 37 UCLA L. Rev. 479 (1990); G. Schwartz, The Beginning and the Possible End of the Rise of Modern American Tort Law, 26 Ga.L.Rev. 601 (1992); Cupp & Polage, The Rhetoric of Strict Products Liability Versus Negligence: An Empirical Analysis, 77 N.Y.U. L. Rev. 874 (2002); V. Schwartz & Tedesco, The Re-emergence of "Super Strict" Liability: Slaying the Dragon Again,

71 U. Cin. L. Rev. 917 (2003); Twerski, Chasing the Illusory Pot of Gold at the End of the Rainbow: Negligence and Strict Liability in Design Defect Litigation, 90 Marq. L. Rev. 7 (2006); Owen, The Evolution of Products Liability, 26 Rev. Litig. 955 (2007); and Stewart, Strict Liability for Defective Product Design: The Quest for a Well-Ordered Regime, 74 Brook. L. Rev. 1039 (2009). Legislative bodies at the state level also have become involved in shaping the law, sometimes intervening to alter common law doctrines. Congress has heard and "reheard" about the need for federal legislation, but it declined to act, leaving the development of products liability law to the states.

The ALI's Restatement (Third) (1998) is now a focal point for many judicial decisions. As will be explained in this chapter, the Restatement (Third) adopts a functional approach to products liability, with separate tests for defects in a product's manufacture, design, and warnings.

As you work your way through this chapter, think about the rationale for the system. Why is a liability rule necessary to assure product safety? Is the market a viable mechanism for weeding out unsafe products? Why or why not? If the market fails, should product safety be assured by government regulation given the institutional advantage of government in broad information gathering, cost-benefit evaluation, predictability, and uniformity? Should the questions asked be confined to ones of efficiency or should justice also be considered? See Wright, The Principles of Products Liability Law, 26 Rev. Litig. 1067 (2007) and Owen, The Moral Foundations of Products Liability Law: Toward First Principles, 68 Notre Dame L.Rev. 427 (1993).

The topic of products liability has sufficient material to support a separate law school course. Students and lawyers who practice in the area have the benefit of an excellent treatise: Owen, Products Liability Law (Thomson 3d ed. 2015) and a major multivolume work, regularly updated: Frumer and Friedman, Products Liability (LexisNexis). What follows is a taste of some of the common issues and basic theories of this burgeoning area of the law.

1. DEVELOPMENT OF THEORIES OF RECOVERY

(A) NEGLIGENCE

MacPherson v. Buick Motor Co.

Court of Appeals of New York, 1916.
217 N.Y. 382, 111 N.E. 1050.

[See page 428 in Chapter 8 for text of *MacPherson v. Buick Motor Co.* opinion.]

Buick Model 10 Runabout (1909)
(The model Mr. MacPherson purchased)

NOTES AND QUESTIONS

1. The early development of liability of a manufacturer or seller of chattels to third parties was strongly influenced by Winterbottom v. Wright, 10 M. & W. 109, 152 Eng.Rep. 402 (1842), page 426. The case was misinterpreted to state a general rule of nonliability of any contractor, including any supplier of a product, to third parties, whether in contract or in tort, and whether for nonfeasance or misfeasance. This misinterpretation was first pointed out by Professor Bohlen, the Reporter of the First Restatement, in a noted article in 1905. Bohlen, The Basis of Affirmative Obligations in the Law of Torts, 44 Am.L.Reg. (N.S.) 209, 280–85, 289–310 (1905). Nevertheless, most courts clung to the general rule while carving out a few exceptions for "inherently dangerous" products.

2. The principal case became a leading case, and a new point of departure. It is now accepted in all of the American jurisdictions, although one or two of them, such as Mississippi in State Stove Mfg. Co. v. Hodges, 189 So.2d 113 (Miss.1966), jumped over negligence to the strict liability basis of liability for cases against product sellers.

3. For a time some of the courts continued to use the language "inherently dangerous," although it was clear from the opinions that this meant no more than that substantial harm is to be anticipated if the chattel is defective. This seems to have faded out almost entirely. What finally emerged is a general rule imposing negligence liability upon all sellers of chattels—whether damage is to person or property, whether the manufacturer produced the whole product or a component part, and whether or not the injured person was the immediate purchaser.

4. Even with the advent of alternative means of recovery such as breach of warranty and strict liability, negligence continues to be an important cause of action for plaintiffs injured by products. Almost every product liability lawsuit includes a negligence count. Most plaintiffs' lawyers still try to prove negligence. Why? An experienced practitioner has observed: "More plaintiffs would prefer to present their respective cases to a jury on a negligence, rather than on a strict liability, basis. In McLuhanesque terms negligence is 'hot' and strict liability is 'cold.' It is easier to prevail by showing that the defendant did something wrong than that there is something technically defective about the product." Rheingold, The Expanding Liability of the Product Supplier: A Primer, 2 Hofstra L.Rev. 521, 531 (1974). Does the theoretical basis for a finding of liability affect a jury's willingness to award damages? Professors Cupp and Polage have concluded, based on their analysis of mock jurors' responses to negligence and strict liability jury instructions, that jurors may be more likely to find liability and to award higher damage amounts in negligence actions. Cupp & Polage, The Rhetoric of Strict Products Liability Versus Negligence: An Empirical Analysis, 77 N.Y.U. L. Rev. 874 (2002). Also, note that a finding by a jury that the defendant was negligent but there was no defect in the product may be an inconsistent verdict that requires a new trial. Kosmynka v. Polaris Indus., Inc., 462 F.3d 74 (2d Cir. 2006) (applying New York law) (granting new trial in ATV case due to an inconsistent jury verdict).

(B) WARRANTY

The action by the buyer of goods against the seller for breach of warranty is a hybrid, "born of the illicit intercourse of tort and contract," and partaking the characteristics of both. Originally a breach of warranty action arose from the tort action of trespass on the case for breach of an assumed duty. The wrong was conceived to be a form of misrepresentation, in the nature of deceit, and not at all clearly distinguished from it. In the latter part of the seventeenth century, decisions such as Cross v. Gardiner, 1 Show.K.B. 68, 89 Eng.Rep. 453 (1689), and Medina v. Stoughton, 1 Ld.Raym. 593, 91 Eng.Rep. 1297 (1700), established the fact that the tort action would lie for an affirmation of fact ("express warranty"), even one made without knowledge of its falsity and without negligence. As a result warranty became a form of strict liability in tort.

In Stuart v. Wilkins, 1 Doug. 18, 99 Eng.Rep. 15 (1778), it was first held that assumpsit would lie for breach of an express warranty as a part of the contract of sale. After that decision, and over a period of more than a century, warranties gradually came to be regarded as express or implied terms of the contract of sale, and the action on the contract became the usual remedy for any breach.

Warranty has, however, never entirely lost its original tort character. Even when the action is in the form of breach of contract, its basic tort character has sometimes been recognized by the application of statutes applicable to torts, such as survival of tort actions. Gosling v. Nichols, 59 Cal.App.2d 442, 139 P.2d 86 (1943). Or the statute of limitations for torts. Rubino v. Utah Canning Co., 123 Cal.App.2d 18, 266 P.2d 163 (1954). Or the application of the comparative negligence statute. JCW Electronics, Inc. v. Garza, 257 S.W.3d 701 (Tex. 2008) (finding that breach of implied warranty of merchantability is a "cause of action based on tort" and thus included within the comparative responsibility scheme enacted by the legislature using that language). Several jurisdictions allow recovery for wrongful death arising out of breach of warranty, when the action would not lie for an ordinary breach of contract. See for example Greco v. S.S. Kresge Co., 277 N.Y. 26, 12 N.E.2d 557 (1938); Kelley v. Volkswagenwerk Aktiengesellschaft, 110 N.H. 369, 268 A.2d 837 (1970).

The question began to be asked: if warranty is a matter of tort as well as contract and it can arise without any intent to make it a matter of contract, why should it require a contract between the parties? Why should it not arise, in tort, between parties who have not dealt at all with one another—or in other words, without privity of contract?

(1) EXPRESS WARRANTIES

Baxter v. Ford Motor Co.

Supreme Court of Washington, 1932.
168 Wash. 456, 12 P.2d 409.

HERMAN, J. During the month of May, 1930, plaintiff purchased a model A Ford town sedan from defendant St. John Motors, a Ford dealer, who had acquired the automobile in question by purchase from defendant Ford Motor Company. Plaintiff claims that representations were made to him by both defendants that the windshield of the automobile was made of nonshatterable glass which would not break, fly, or shatter. October 12, 1930, while plaintiff was driving the automobile through Snoqualmie pass, a pebble from a passing car struck the windshield of the car in question, causing small pieces of glass to fly into plaintiff's left eye, resulting in the loss thereof. Plaintiff brought this action for damages for the loss of his left eye and for injuries to the sight of his right eye. The case came on for trial, and, at the conclusion of plaintiff's testimony, the court took the case from the jury and entered judgment for both defendants. From that judgment, plaintiff appeals. * * *

The principal question in this case is whether the trial court erred in refusing to admit in evidence, as against respondent Ford Motor

Company, the catalogues and printed matter furnished by that respondent to respondent St. John Motors to be distributed for sales assistance. Contained in such printed matter were statements which appellant maintains constituted representations or warranties with reference to the nature of the glass used in the windshield of the car purchased by appellant. A typical statement, as it appears in appellant's exhibit for identification No. 1, is here set forth:

> "Triplex Shatter-Proof Glass Windshield. All of the new Ford cars have a Triplex shatter-proof glass windshield—so made that it will not fly or shatter under the hardest impact. This is an important safety factor because it eliminates the dangers of flying glass—the cause of most of the injuries in automobile accidents. In these days of crowded, heavy traffic, the use of this Triplex glass is an absolute necessity. Its extra margin of safety is something that every motorist should look for in the purchase of a car—especially where there are women and children."

Respondent Ford Motor Company contends that there can be no implied or express warranty without privity of contract, and warranties as to personal property do not attach themselves to, and run with, the article sold.

[The court here referred at length to Mazetti v. Armour & Co., 75 Wash. 622, 135 P. 633 (1913), in which a restaurant keeper was permitted to recover for damage to his business resulting when a customer was served defective canned food manufactured by the defendant.]

In the case at bar the automobile was represented by the manufacturer as having a windshield of nonshatterable glass "so made that it will not fly or shatter under the hardest impact." An ordinary person would be unable to discover by the usual and customary examination of the automobile whether glass which would not fly or shatter was used in the windshield. In that respect the purchaser was in a position similar to that of the consumer of a wrongly labeled drug, who has bought the same from a retailer, and who has relied upon the manufacturer's representation that the label correctly set forth the contents of the container. For many years it has been held that, under such circumstances, the manufacturer is liable to the consumer, even though the consumer purchased from a third person the commodity causing the damage. Thomas v. Winchester, 6 N.Y. 397, 57 Am.Dec. 455. The rule in such cases does not rest upon contractual obligations, but rather on the principle that the original act of delivering an article is wrong, when, because of the lack of those qualities which the manufacturer represented it as having, the absence of which could not be readily detected by the consumer, the article is not safe for the purposes for which the consumer would ordinarily use it.

The vital principle present in the case of Mazetti v. Armour & Co., supra, confronts us in the case at bar. In the case cited the court recognized the right of a purchaser to a remedy against the manufacturer because of damages suffered by reason of a failure of goods to comply with the manufacturer's representations as to the existence of qualities which they did not in fact possess, when the absence of such qualities was not readily discoverable, even though there was no privity of contract between the purchaser and the manufacturer.

Since the rule of caveat emptor was first formulated, vast changes have taken place in the economic structures of the English speaking peoples. Methods of doing business have undergone a great transition. Radio, billboards, and the products of the printing press have become the means of creating a large part of the demand that causes goods to depart from factories to the ultimate consumer. It would be unjust to recognize a rule that would permit manufacturers of goods to create a demand for their products by representing that they possess qualities which they, in fact, do not possess, and then, because there is no privity of contract existing between the consumer and the manufacturer, deny the consumer the right to recover if damages result from the absence of those qualities, when such absence is not readily noticeable.

"An exception to a rule will be declared by courts when the case is not an isolated instance, but general in its character, and the existing rule does not square with justice. Under such circumstances a court will, if free from the restraint of some statute, declare a rule that will meet the full intendment of the law." Mazetti v. Armour & Co., supra.

We hold that the catalogues and printed matter furnished by respondent * * * Ford Motor Company for distribution and assistance in sales were improperly excluded from evidence, because they set forth representations by the manufacturer that the windshield of the car which appellant bought contained Triplex nonshatterable glass which would not fly or shatter. The nature of nonshatterable glass is such that the falsity of the representations with reference to the glass would not be readily detected by a person of ordinary experience and reasonable prudence. Appellant, under the circumstances shown in this case, had the right to rely upon the representations made by respondent Ford Motor Company relative to qualities possessed by its products, even though there was no privity of contract between appellant and respondent Ford Motor Company. * * *

The trial court erred in taking the case from the jury and entering judgment for respondent Ford Motor Company. It was for the jury to determine under proper instructions, whether the failure of respondent Ford Motor Company to equip the windshield with glass which did not fly or shatter was the proximate cause of appellant's injury. * * *

Reversed, with directions to grant a new trial with reference to respondent Ford Motor Company; affirmed as to respondent St. John Motors.

[The second trial resulted in a verdict for plaintiff, and defendant Ford Motor Company appealed. In Baxter v. Ford Motor Co., 179 Wash. 123, 35 P.2d 1090 (1934), judgment entered on the verdict was affirmed. HOLCOMB, J., said in part:

"A new point arising out of the last trial, claimed as error, was in excluding testimony of an expert witness on behalf of appellant to the effect that there was no better windshield made than that used in respondent's car and in sustaining the objection to appellant's offer of proof on that point.

"No authorities are cited by appellant to sustain this claim, and we know of none. Indeed, it would seem that whether there was any better make of shatter-proof glass manufactured by any one at that time would be wholly immaterial, under the law as decided by us on the former appeal. Since it was the duty of appellant to know that the representations made to purchasers were true. Otherwise it should not have made them. If a person states as true material facts, susceptible of knowledge, to one who relies and acts thereon to his injury, if the representations are false, it is immaterial that he did not know they were false, or that he believed them to be true. * * *

"The court charged the jury that 'there is no proof of fraud in this case.' It has become almost axiomatic that false representations inducing a sale or contract constitute fraud in law. * * * However, the instruction, if it was error against respondent, was cured by the verdict of the jury favorable to respondent."]

NOTES AND QUESTIONS

1. Is this case an extension of a contract warranty to one who has made no contract with the defendant, or is it strict liability in tort for an innocent misrepresentation made to the plaintiff? Most of the cases have talked of "express warranty." In comparison, the Tennessee Supreme Court, in Ford Motor Co. v. Lonon, 217 Tenn. 400, 398 S.W.2d 240 (1966), reverted to the theory of misrepresentation. It relied on the Restatement (Second) of Torts § 402B, which addresses strict liability without using the word "warranty." The section reads:

> "One engaged in the business of selling chattels who, by advertising, labels, or otherwise, makes to the public a misrepresentation of a material fact concerning the character or quality of a chattel sold by him is subject to liability for physical harm to a consumer of the chattel caused by justifiable reliance upon the misrepresentation, even though (a) it is not made fraudulently or negligently, and (b) the consumer has not bought the chattel from or entered into any contract relation with the seller."

Tennessee later limited the *Lonon* innocent misrepresentation cause of action to cases involving personal injury or property damage, leaving plaintiffs who had suffered only economic losses to seek redress on breach of contract theories. First Nat'l. Bank of Louisville v. Brooks Farms, 821 S.W.2d 925 (Tenn.1991). See also Restatement (Third) of Torts: Products Liability § 9 (1998), allowing potential claims for "innocent misrepresentation of material fact concerning the product." Why should an innocent manufacturer be liable?

2. The principal case generally has been followed for express statements as to quality and safety made in advertising, on labels, in brochures, or other literature accompanying the product. It applies to property damage as well as personal injury. Should warranty liability flow from any express statement? Consider a drug treatment for Lyme disease that was accompanied by a drug store brochure from defendant that

advised "take with food or milk if upset stomach occurs." If taking the drug with dairy products decreased its absorption, allegedly causing plaintiff's complications, should the language provided by the drug store constitute an express warranty? Rite Aid Pharmacy v. Levy-Gray, 391 Md. 608, 894 A.2d 563 (2006) (finding language was warranty that drug's efficacy would not be adversely impacted by milk). What about the "safe and effective" language on drug labels? In re Avandia Marketing Sales Practices & Products Liab. Litig., 588 Fed.Appx. 171 (3d Cir. 2014) (applying New Jersey law) (because contraindications, risk factors, and possible side effects also were included on same label, "safe and effective" could not be read as an unqualified guarantee for all consumers).

3. Should a plaintiff be required to demonstrate reliance upon the representation, either in making the purchase or in using the product? Most courts require this, but some have not. Plaintiff, a minor, was seriously injured while driving intoxicated. He filed a breach of warranty claim against defendant beer manufacturer arguing that its advertising campaign induced him to purchase and consume beer and to drive while intoxicated. Liability? See Smith v. Anheuser-Busch, Inc., 599 A.2d 320 (R.I.1991) (upholding trial court's dismissal of complaint on ground that plaintiff could not demonstrate reasonable reliance on alleged representation in media advertising that driving while intoxicated is safe or acceptable). What about a plaintiff who bought a mace gun that had been advertised to "instantly stop and subdue entire groups," but it failed to stop an intruder who shot plaintiff after plaintiff had sprayed him. See Klages v. General Ordnance Equip. Co., 240 Pa.Super. 356, 367 A.2d 304 (1976) (rejecting manufacturer's argument that representations were mere puffery and that the plaintiff did not justifiably rely upon them). See also Restatement (Third) of Torts: Products Liability § 9 (1998) (liability for harm to person or property caused by misrepresentation of material fact).

4. Consumer Protection Acts have been enacted in a number of jurisdictions. Their violation usually is pled along with violations of express warranty claims. The statutes were first drafted to redress a grievance to the public at large and therefore avoid some of the basic requirements of tort law, including reliance and proof of damage. The remedy for these claims includes refund of the purchase price, punitive damages, and awards of attorney fees. If the plaintiff also seeks personal injury damages, is it enough for plaintiff to allege that the defendant made a misrepresentation pertaining to a fact about safety? See Aspinall v. Philip Morris Cos., Inc., 442 Mass. 381, 813 N.E.2d 476 (2004) (affirming certification of class of smokers with no requirement of showing health problems or reliance on manufacturer's representations) and Pelman v. McDonald's Corp., 396 F.3d 508 (2d Cir. 2005) (applying New York statute) (plaintiffs not required to show they relied on defendant's representations of nutritional value of food). But see Schwartz & Silverman, Common-Sense Construction of Consumer Protection Acts, 54 U. Kan. L. Rev. 1 (2006) (arguing that reliance and actual damages should be required for recovery).

5. What result if a tire manufacturer advertises, "If it saves your life once, it's a bargain," and plaintiff's decedent is killed when the product "blows out"? See Collins v. Uniroyal, Inc., 64 N.J. 260, 315 A.2d 16 (1974). Suppose the manufacturer of a grinding disc states that the product is

"stronger, sharper, and longer-lived than ever before available anywhere." The wheel breaks and injures plaintiff. See Jakubowski v. Minnesota Mining & Mfg., 80 N.J.Super. 184, 193 A.2d 275 (1963), rev'd on other grounds, 42 N.J. 177, 199 A.2d 826 (1964). Courts have stated that the promise of safety must be a specific one in order to constitute a warranty. What about old cigarette advertising such as "not a cough in a carload" or "more doctors smoke our brand"? Do they constitute express warranties? Cf. Cipollone v. Liggett Group, Inc., 893 F.2d 541 (3d Cir.1990), affirmed in part and reversed in part, 505 U.S. 504 (1992) (applying New Jersey law) (alleging breach of express warranty based on cigarette advertising). What if the plaintiff buys a cream to remove age spots on her skin that is labeled "safe," but that causes a severe irritation? Spiegel v. Saks 34th Street, 43 Misc.2d 1065, 252 N.Y.S.2d 852 (1964), aff'd mem., 26 A.D.2d 660, 272 N.Y.S.2d 972 (1966) (finding breach of express warranty). Do the words "minced pimento stuffed" on a jar of olives constitute an express warranty that the olives are entirely free of pits? Kolarik v. Cory Int'l. Corp., 721 N.W.2d 159 (Iowa 2006) (finding that to impart such a meaning would be unrealistic).

(2) IMPLIED WARRANTIES

Henningsen v. Bloomfield Motors, Inc.

Supreme Court of New Jersey, 1960.
32 N.J. 358, 161 A.2d 69.

[Plaintiff Mrs. Henningsen was badly injured while driving a 1955 Plymouth automobile, when "something went wrong" with the steering gear, and the car turned sharply to the right into a wall. The automobile had been manufactured by defendant Chrysler Corporation, and sold by it to defendant Bloomfield Motors, a retail dealer. Mr. Henningsen purchased it from Bloomfield, and gave it to his wife for Christmas.

When he purchased the car, Mr. Henningsen signed a contract, without reading 8½ inches of fine print on the back of it. Included in this fine print was a "warranty" clause, which provided that the manufacturer and the dealer gave no warranties, express or implied, except that they would make good at the factory any parts which became defective within 90 days after delivery of the car to the original purchaser, or before the car had been driven 4,000 miles, whichever event should first occur. In plaintiff's action against both defendants, negligence counts were dismissed by the trial court, and the cause was submitted to the jury solely on the issues of implied warranty of merchantability. Verdicts were returned for plaintiff against both defendants. Defendants appealed, and the appeal was certified directly to the Supreme Court.]

FRANCIS, J. * * * In the ordinary case of sale of goods by description an implied warranty of merchantability is an integral part of the transaction. R.S. 46:30–20, N.J.S.A. If the buyer, expressly or by implication, makes known to the seller the particular purpose for which the article is required and it appears that he has relied on the seller's skill or judgment, an implied warranty arises of reasonable fitness for that purpose. R.S. 46:30–21(1), N.J.S.A. The former type of warranty simply means that the thing sold is reasonably fit for the general purpose for which it is manufactured and sold. [Cc] As Judge Cardozo remarked in Ryan v. Progressive Grocery Stores (1931) 255 N.Y. 388, 175 N.E. 105, the distinction between a warranty of fitness for a particular purpose and of merchantability in many instances is practically meaningless. * * *

The uniform [sales] act codified, extended and liberalized the common law of sales. The motivation in part was to ameliorate the harsh doctrine of caveat emptor, and in some measure to impose a reciprocal obligation on the seller to beware. The transcendent value of the legislation, particularly with respect to implied warranties, rests in the fact that obligations on the part of the seller were imposed by operation of law, and did not depend for their existence upon express agreement of the parties. And of tremendous significance in a rapidly expanding commercial society was the recognition of the right to recover damages on account of personal injuries arising from a breach of warranty. [Cc] The particular importance of this advance resides in the fact that under such circumstances strict liability is imposed upon the maker or seller of the product. Recovery of damages does not depend upon proof of negligence or knowledge of the defect. [Cc]

As the Sales Act and its liberal interpretation by the courts threw this protective cloak about the buyer, * * * many manufacturers took steps to avoid these ever increasing warranty obligations. Realizing that the act governed the relationship of buyer and seller, they undertook to withdraw from actual and direct contractual contact with the buyer. They ceased selling products to the consuming public through their own employees and making contracts of sale in their own names. Instead, a system of independent dealers was established; their products were sold to dealers who in turn dealt with the buying public, ostensibly solely in their own personal capacity as sellers. In the past in many instances, manufacturers were able to transfer to the dealers burdens imposed by the act and thus achieved a large measure of immunity for themselves. * * *

There is no doubt that under early common-law concepts of contractual liability only those persons who were parties to the bargain could sue for a breach of it. In more recent times a noticeable disposition has appeared in a number of jurisdictions to break through the narrow barrier of privity when dealing with sales of goods in order to give realistic recognition to a universally accepted fact. The fact is that the dealer and the ordinary buyer do not, and are not expected to, buy goods, whether they be foodstuffs or automobiles, exclusively for their own consumption or use. Makers and manufacturers know this and advertise and market their products on that assumption; witness, the "family" car, the baby foods, etc. The limitations of privity in contracts for the sale of goods developed their place in the law when marketing conditions were simple, when maker and buyer frequently met face to face on an equal bargaining plane and when many of the products were relatively uncomplicated and conducive to inspection by a buyer competent to evaluate their quality. [C] With the advent of mass marketing, the manufacturer became remote from the purchaser, sales were accomplished through intermediaries, and the demand for the product was created by advertising media. In such an economy it became obvious that the consumer was the person being cultivated. Manifestly, the connotation of "consumer" was broader than that of "buyer." He signified such a person who, in the reasonable contemplation of the parties to the sale, might be expected to use the product. Thus, where the commodities sold are such that if defectively manufactured they will be dangerous to life or limb, then society's interests can only be protected by eliminating the requirement of privity between the maker and his dealers and the reasonably expected ultimate consumer. In that way the burden of losses consequent upon use of defective articles is borne by those who are in a position to either control the danger or make an equitable distribution of the losses when they do occur. As Harper & James put it, "The interest in consumer protection calls for warranties by the maker that *do* run with the goods, to reach all who are likely to be hurt by the use of the unfit commodity for a purpose ordinarily to be expected." 2 Harper & James, Torts, 1571, 1572. * * *

Accordingly, we hold that under modern marketing conditions, when a manufacturer puts a new automobile in the stream of trade and promotes its purchase by the public, an implied warranty that it is reasonably suitable for use as such accompanies it into the hands of the ultimate purchaser. * * *

In the light of these matters, what effect should be given to the express warranty in question which seeks to limit the manufacturer's liability to replacement of defective parts, and which disclaims all other warranties, express or implied? In assessing its significance we must keep in mind the general principle that, in the absence of fraud, one who does not choose to read a contract before signing it, cannot later relieve himself of its burdens. [C] And in applying that principle, the basic tenet of freedom of competent parties to contract is a factor of importance. But in the framework of modern commercial life and business practices, such rules cannot be applied on a strict, doctrinal basis. The conflicting interests of the buyer and seller must be evaluated realistically and justly, giving due weight to the social policy evinced by the Uniform Sales Act, the progressive decisions of the courts engaged in administering it, the mass production methods of manufacture and distribution to the public, and the bargaining position, occupied by the ordinary consumer in such an economy. * * *

[W]arranties originated in the law to safeguard the buyer and not to limit the liability of the seller or manufacturer. It seems obvious in this instance that the motive was to avoid the warranty obligations which are normally incidental to such sales. The language gave little and withdrew much. In return for the delusive remedy of replacement of defective parts at the factory, the buyer is said to have accepted the exclusion of the maker's liability for personal injuries, arising from the breach of the warranty, and to have agreed to the elimination of any other express or implied warranty. An instinctively felt sense of justice cries out against such a sharp bargain. But does the doctrine that a person is bound by his signed agreement, in the absence of fraud, stand in the way of any relief? * * *

The warranty before us is a standardized form designed for mass use. It is imposed upon the automobile consumer. He takes it or leaves it, and he must take it to buy an automobile. No bargaining is engaged in with respect to it. In fact, the dealer through whom it comes to the buyer is without authority to alter it; his function is ministerial—simply to deliver it. The form warranty is not only standard with Chrysler but, as mentioned above, it is the uniform warranty of the Automobile Manufacturers Association. * * *

The gross inequality of bargaining position occupied by the consumer in the automobile industry is thus apparent. There is no competition among the car makers in the area of the express warranty. Where can the buyer go to negotiate for better protection? Such control and limitation of his remedies are inimical to the public welfare and, at the very least, call for great care by the courts to avoid injustice through application of strict common-law principles of freedom of contract. Because there is no competition among the motor vehicle manufacturers with respect to the scope of protection guaranteed to the buyer, there is no incentive on their part to stimulate good will in that field of public relations. Thus, there is lacking a factor existing in more competitive fields, one which tends to guarantee the safe construction of the article sold. Since all competitors operate in the same way, the urge to be careful is not so pressing. See "Warranties of Kind and Quality," 57 Yale L.J. 1389, 1400 (1948). * * *

The task of the judiciary is to administer the spirit as well as the letter of the law. On issues such as the present one, part of that burden is to protect the ordinary man against the loss of important rights through what, in effect, is the unilateral act of the manufacturer. * * * In the framework of this case, illuminated as it is by the facts and the many decisions noted, we are of the opinion that Chrysler's attempted disclaimer of an implied warranty of merchantability and of the obligations arising therefrom is so inimical to the public good as to compel an adjudication of its invalidity. * * *

[The court then held that the dealer, Bloomfield Motors, would not be permitted to disclaim an implied warranty of fitness with respect to personal injuries caused by the automobile in question. The problem of whether retailers should be subject to strict liability is discussed at note 4, page 834.]

NOTES AND QUESTIONS

1. The first case to extend an implied warranty of the seller beyond privity of contract was Mazetti v. Armour & Co., 75 Wash. 622, 135 P. 633 (1913), which was a bad food case. It came upon the heels of a prolonged nation-wide agitation about dangerous food and was promptly followed in Mississippi and Kansas, and then in other states. For a period of time, courts struggled to evolve various ingenious theories, most of them with an obvious element of fiction—such as that the dealer was an agent of the consumer in purchasing from the manufacturer or third party beneficiary contracts and the like. Finally, in Coca-Cola Bottling Works v. Lyons, 145 Miss. 876, 111 So. 305 (1927), the Mississippi Supreme Court came up with the idea of an implied warranty running with the goods, by analogy to a covenant running with the land. By 1960 nearly half of the states had

accepted the special rule as to food, and five more reached the same result under pure food statutes. The development is traced in Prosser, The Assault Upon the Citadel, 69 Yale L.J. 1099 (1960).

2. A gradual extension beyond food began not long after 1950, first with other products for what might be called intimate bodily use, such as hair dye and clothing, and then to all products as in the principal case. The implied warranty theory is still used as a basis for product liability claims in Massachusetts. Haglund v. Philip Morris, Inc., 446 Mass. 741, 847 N.E.2d 315 (2006) (unreasonable use of the product may be a defense). Some states, however, require privity for product liability cases based on the implied warranty of merchantability. Compex Inter. Co., Ltd. v. Taylor, 209 S.W.3d 462 (Ky. 2006) (dismissing case against chair manufacturer because privity existed only between buyer and retailer).

3. The Uniform Sales Act, discussed in the principal case, was promulgated in 1906. Its warranty provisions were intended to apply only to buyer and seller. It was superseded by the Uniform Commercial Code (UCC). Article 2, which contains the warranty provisions, has been adopted in every state except Louisiana. While the UCC's implied-warranty provisions are similar to those in the Uniform Sales Act (UCC §§ 2–314 and 315), the Code extended warranties to certain third parties in Section 2–318.

4. *Disclaimers and Limitations on Damages.* The UCC, unlike the Uniform Sales Act, deals directly with the issue of disclaimers. The most important sections include 2–302 and 2–316, allowing sellers to disclaim warranties implied by the code in some circumstances. Some states have modified their version of the UCC to prohibit the exclusion or modification of implied warranties for consumer goods and services. See, e.g., Me.Rev.Stat.Ann., Tit. 11, § 2–316(5) and Mass.Gen. Laws Ann., Ch. 106, § 2–316A. The UCC also allows the seller to limit the damages available in the event of a breach—but restricts the seller's ability to do that in ways that impact on personal injury breach of warranty claims. Section 2–719(3) "Consequential damages may be limited or excluded unless the limitation or exclusion is unconscionable. Limitation of consequential damages for injury to the person in the case of consumer goods is prima facie unconscionable but limitation of damages where the loss is commercial is not."

5. *Notice.* Could the principal case have been decided the same way within the framework of the UCC? How? Like its predecessor, the UCC has a number of stumbling blocks in the way of a strict liability recovery in tort law. One of them is UCC § 2–607, which requires that a buyer must "within a reasonable time after he discovers or should have discovered the breach [of warranty] notify the seller or be barred from any remedy." The analogue Uniform Sales Act provision and the whole problem of the utility of warranty as a tort law remedy confronted Justice Traynor in the next case.

6. *Federal Acts.* Warranty and other safety issues are the subject of federal regulation.

A. *The "Magnuson-Moss Warranty Act,"* 15 U.S.C. §§ 2301–12, created a comprehensive regulatory system governing the form and to some degree the content of written warranties and warranties implied by state law. The Act applies to warranties offered to "consumers" by "suppliers" of "consumer products." The Act does not require that a warranty be given; rather, it regulates the scope of warranties that are provided. While it does not affect state personal injury actions, it will affect the nature and scope of disclaimers in the sale of most consumer products that are sold with a "warranty" in the United States.

B. *The Consumer Product Safety Act.* The Consumer Product Safety Act, 15 U.S.C. §§ 2051 et seq., created a federal agency, the Consumer Product Safety Commission ("CPSC"), that has regulatory power over consumer products that are not already subject to safety regulation by other federal agencies (such as the FDA). The CPSC is empowered to establish and enforce uniform safety standards for consumer products and to ban products from the market if they create an "unreasonable risk" of injury to the consumer. Section 2072 of the Act provides a federal tort remedy to persons who are injured as a result of a knowing violation of a safety standard or a rule of the CPSC. The powers of the CPSC were broadly enhanced in 2008 with the passage of the Consumer Product Safety Improvement Act.

C. *Other Federal Statutes.* The National Traffic and Motor Vehicle Safety Act of 1966 requires the Secretary of Transportation to establish motor vehicle safety standards. See 15 U.S.C. §§ 1381 et seq. Some of the other important federal regulatory acts relating to products include the Occupational Safety and Health Act (OSHA), 29 U.S.C. §§ 651 et seq., the Federal Hazardous Substances Act, 15 U.S.C.A. §§ 1261 et seq., the Poison Prevention Packaging Act, 15 U.S.C. §§ 1471 et seq., the Flammable Fabrics Act, 15 U.S.C. §§ 1191 et seq., and the Refrigerator Safety Act, 15 U.S.C. §§ 1211 et seq. While none of these acts creates specific civil tort remedies, violation of a specific standard issued under them may subject a defendant to liability on a negligence per se or implied tort theory. See note 5, page 224; note 7, page 235; and pages 1215–1246.

(C) STRICT LIABILITY IN TORT

Greenman v. Yuba Power Products, Inc.

Supreme Court of California, 1963.
59 Cal.2d 57, 377 P.2d 897, 27 Cal.Rptr. 697.

TRAYNOR, JUSTICE. Plaintiff brought this action for damages against the retailer and the manufacturer of a Shopsmith, a combination power tool that could be used as a saw, drill, and wood lathe. He saw a Shopsmith demonstrated by the retailer and studied a brochure prepared by the manufacturer. He decided he wanted a Shopsmith for his home workshop, and his wife bought and gave him one for Christmas in 1955. In 1957 he bought the necessary attachments to use the Shopsmith as a lathe for turning a large piece of wood he wished to make into a chalice. After he had worked on the piece of wood several times without difficulty, it suddenly flew out of the machine and struck him on the forehead, inflicting serious injuries. About ten and a half months later, he gave the retailer and the manufacturer written notice of claimed breaches of warranties and filed a complaint against them alleging such breaches and negligence.

After a trial before a jury, the court ruled that there was no evidence that the retailer was negligent or had breached any express warranty and that the manufacturer was not liable for the breach of any implied warranty. Accordingly, it submitted to the jury only the cause of action alleging breach of implied warranties against the retailer and the causes of action alleging negligence and breach of express warranties against the manufacturer. The jury returned a verdict for the retailer against plaintiff and for plaintiff against the manufacturer in the amount of $65,000. The trial court denied the manufacturer's motion for a new trial and entered judgment on the verdict. * * *

Plaintiff introduced substantial evidence that his injuries were caused by defective design and construction of the Shopsmith. His expert witnesses testified that inadequate set screws were used to hold parts of the machine together so that normal vibration caused the tailstock of the lathe to move away from the piece of wood being turned permitting it to fly out of the lathe. They also testified that there were other more positive ways of fastening the parts of the machine together, the use of which would have prevented the accident. The jury could therefore reasonably have concluded that the manufacturer negligently constructed the Shopsmith. The jury could also reasonably have concluded that statements in the manufacturer's brochure were untrue, that they constituted express warranties, and that plaintiff's injuries were caused by their breach.

The manufacturer contends, however, that plaintiff did not give it notice of breach of warranty within a reasonable time and that therefore his cause of action for breach of warranty is barred by section 1769 of the Civil Code. Since it cannot be determined whether the verdict against it was based on the negligence or warranty cause of action or both, the manufacturer concludes that the error in presenting the warranty cause of action to the jury was prejudicial.

Section 1769 of the Civil Code provides: "In the absence of express or implied agreement of the parties, acceptance of the goods by the buyer shall not discharge the seller from liability in damages or other legal remedy for breach of any promise or warranty in the contract to sell or the sale. But, if after acceptance of the goods, the buyer fails to give notice to the seller of the breach of any promise or warranty within a reasonable time after the buyer knows, or ought to know of such breach, the seller shall not be liable therefor." * * *

The notice requirement of section 1769, however, is not an appropriate one for the court to adopt in actions by injured consumers against manufacturers with whom they have not dealt. [Cc] "As between the immediate parties to the sale, [the notice requirement] is a sound commercial rule, designed to protect the seller against unduly delayed claims for damages. As applied to personal injuries, and notice to a remote seller, it becomes a booby-trap for the unwary. The injured consumer is seldom 'steeped in the business practice which justifies the rule,' [cc] and at least until he has had legal advice it will not occur to him to give notice to one with whom he has had no dealings." [Cc] It is true that in [four prior California cases cited] the court assumed that notice of breach of warranty must be given in an action by a consumer against a manufacturer. Since in those cases, however, the court did not consider the question whether a distinction exists between a warranty based on a contract between the parties and one imposed on a manufacturer not in privity with the consumer, the decisions are not authority for rejecting the rule. [Cc] We conclude, therefore, that even if plaintiff did not give timely notice of breach of warranty to the manufacturer, his cause of action based on the representations contained in the brochure was not barred.

Moreover, to impose strict liability on the manufacturer under the circumstances of this case, it was not necessary for plaintiff to establish an express warranty as defined in section 1732 of the Civil Code. A manufacturer is strictly liable in tort when an article he places on the market, knowing that it is to be used without inspection for defects, proves to have a defect that causes injury to a human being. Recognized first in the case of unwholesome food products, such liability has now been extended to a variety of other products that create as great or greater hazards if defective. [Cc]

Although in these cases strict liability has usually been based on the theory of an express or implied warranty running from the manufacturer to the plaintiff, the abandonment of the requirement of a contract between them, the recognition that the liability is not assumed by agreement but imposed by law [cc], and the refusal to permit the manufacturer to define the scope of its own responsibility for defective products [cc], make clear that the liability is not one governed by the law of contract warranties but by the law of strict liability in tort. Accordingly, rules defining and governing warranties that were developed to meet the needs of commercial transactions cannot properly be invoked to govern the manufacturer's liability to those injured by their defective products unless those rules also serve the purposes for which such liability is imposed.

We need not recanvass the reasons for imposing strict liability on the manufacturer. * * * The purpose of such liability is to insure that the costs of injuries resulting from defective products are borne by the manufacturers that put such products on the market rather than by the injured persons who are powerless to protect themselves. Sales warranties serve this purpose fitfully at best. [C] In the present case, for example, plaintiff was able to plead and prove an express warranty only because he read and relied on the representations of the Shopsmith's ruggedness contained in the manufacturer's brochure. Implicit in the machine's presence on the market, however, was a representation that it would safely do the jobs for which it was built. Under these circumstances, it should not be controlling whether plaintiff selected the machine because of the statements in the brochure, or because of the machine's own appearance of excellence that belied the defect lurking beneath the surface, or because he merely assumed that it would safely do the jobs it was built to do. It should not be controlling whether the details of the sales from manufacturer to retailer and from retailer to plaintiff's wife were such that one or more of the implied warranties of the sales act arose. [C] "The remedies of injured consumers ought not to be made to depend upon the intricacies of the law of sales." [Cc] To establish the manufacturer's liability it was sufficient that plaintiff proved that he was injured while using the Shopsmith in a way it was intended to be used as a result of a defect in design and manufacture of which plaintiff was not aware that made the Shopsmith unsafe for its intended use. * * *

The judgment is affirmed.

NOTES AND QUESTIONS

1. The *Greenman* decision, which might be characterized as the *MacPherson* of a later day, appeared two years before the final published draft of the Restatement (Second) of Torts § 402A:

§ 402A. Special Liability of Seller of Product for Physical Harm to User or Consumer

(1) One who sells any product in a defective condition unreasonably dangerous to the user or consumer or to his property is subject to liability for physical harm thereby caused to the ultimate user or consumer, or to his property, if

(a) the seller is engaged in the business of selling such a product, and

(b) it is expected to and does reach the user or consumer without substantial change in the condition in which it is sold.

(2) The rule stated in Subsection (1) applies although

(a) the seller has exercised all possible care in the preparation and sale of his product, and

(b) the user or consumer has not bought the product from or entered into any contractual relation with the seller.

It should be noted in passing that the law was moving so fast that this Section was actually drafted three times—first as applicable only to food and drink, next, as extended also to include products for "intimate bodily use," and finally, as applicable to all products.

2. Section 402A literally has swept the country. Only a few jurisdictions do not recognize a cause of action for strict liability for personal injury caused by a product and those jurisdictions use breach of implied warranty of liability in a comparable fashion. See Sensenbrenner v. Rust, Orling & Neale, 236 Va. 419, 374 S.E.2d 55 (1988); Smith v. Fiber Controls Corp., 300 N.C. 669, 268 S.E.2d 504 (1980) and N.C. Gen. Stat. Ann. § 99B–1.1 (declaring that "[t]here shall be no strict liability in tort in product liability actions"); Cline v. Prowler, Inc., 418 A.2d 968 (Del. 1980); and Cigna Ins. Co. v. Oy Saunatec, Ltd., 241 F.3d 1, 15 (1st Cir. 2001) ("Actions under Massachusetts law for breach of the implied warranty of merchantability are the functional equivalent of strict liability in other jurisdictions").

3. Now that almost all jurisdictions have followed the lead of the principal case and the Restatement (Second) and recognized some form of strict liability, should breach of implied warranty still survive as a separate cause of action? Compare Denny v. Ford Motor Co., 87 N.Y.2d 248, 639 N.Y.S.2d 250, 662 N.E.2d 730, 736 (1995) (as long as the legislature, through enactment of UCC, is the source of authority for a breach of implied warranty claim, "we are not free to merge the warranty cause of action with its tort-based sibling regardless of whether, as a matter of

policy, the contract-based warranty claim may fairly be regarded as a historical relic that no longer has any independent substantive value") with Restatement (Third) of Torts: Products Liability § 2 comment *n* (1998) (Restatement "contemplates that a well-coordinated body of law governing liability for harm to persons or property arising out of the sale of defective products requires a consistent definition of defect, and that the definition properly should come from tort law, whether the claim carries a tort label or one of implied warranty of merchantability").

4. Whether the liability rests upon negligence, warranty, or strict liability in tort, it applies to all types of products. Whatever limitations there may once have been as to food and drink, intimate bodily use, "inherent danger," or a high degree of danger, all have gone by the boards. The product is not even limited to those used by human beings; such things as animal feed and veterinary medication that may foreseeably cause harm only to property are within the liability.

5. Also gone by the boards is a rather foolish distinction that used to plague the food cases, between the product itself and the container in which it is sold. The two are now treated as one, so if a bottled beverage explodes, it no longer makes any difference whether it is due to a defect in the beverage or in the bottle. Would strict liability apply to the manufacturer of Tylenol for failure to make its packaging tamper proof? Cf. Elsroth v. Johnson & Johnson, 700 F.Supp. 151 (S.D.N.Y.1988) (cyanide poisoning due to breach of packaging by unknown third party).

6. With warranty language out of the way, a number of problems (including the notice requirement confronting the court in *Greenman*) disappear. For example, courts have held that a tort and not a contract statute of limitations applies to plaintiff's claim. The court in Greeno v. Clark Equip. Co., 237 F.Supp. 427, 429 (N.D.Ind.1965), stated that strict liability in tort is "hardly more than what exists under implied warranty when stripped of the contract doctrines of privity, disclaimer, requirements of notice of defect, and limitation through inconsistencies with express warranties."

7. A number of rationales have been advanced by legal writers in support of strict liability in tort. Which do you regard as sound?

A. The consumer finds it too difficult to prove negligence against the manufacturer of a product.

B. Strict liability provides an effective and necessary incentive to manufacturers to make their products as safe as possible.

C. Reputable manufacturers do in fact stand behind their products, replacing or repairing those that prove to be defective; and many of them issue express agreements to do so. Therefore all manufacturers should be responsible when an injury results from a normal use of a product.

D. The manufacturer is in a better position to protect against harm, by insuring against liability for it, and, by adding the cost of the insurance to the price of the product, to pass the loss on to the general public.

E. Strict liability already can be accomplished by a series of actions, in which the consumer first recovers from the retailer on a warranty theory, and liability based on warranties is then carried back through the intermediate dealers to the manufacturer. This process is time-consuming, expensive, and wasteful, so there should be a short-cut.

F. By placing the product on the market, the seller represents to the public that it is fit; and the seller intends and expects that it will be purchased and consumed in reliance upon that representation. The distributors and retailers are no more than a conduit, a mechanical device through which the product reaches the consumer.

G. The costs of accidents should be placed on the party best able to determine whether there are means to prevent that accident. When those means are less expensive than the costs of such accidents, responsibility for implementing them should be placed on the party best able to do so.

8. What about the danger of deterring manufacturers from introducing new products, or improving old ones? And what about the danger of frivolous claims? "The rats of Hamlin were as nought in comparison with that horde of mice which has sought refreshment within Coca-Cola bottles and died of a happy surfeit." Spruill, Privity of Contract as a Requisite for Recovery on Warranty, 19 N.C.L.Rev. 551, 566 (1941). Assuming that there will be groundless claims, are there ways the manufacturer can be protected from those claims without eliminating strict liability?

9. *Beyond Restatement (Second).* When the American Law Institute's (ALI) Restatement (Second) § 402A was drafted, a decision was made to use a singular definition of defect to cover all cases of product liability: "any product in a defective condition unreasonably dangerous to the user or consumer." Following this model, a single definition of defect was utilized when the European EC Product Liability Directive was drafted. As Restatement (Second) § 402A was applied by the courts, it became apparent that a single definition standard was being used to address very different types of defects.

The first type of defect, and the focus of the drafters of § 402A, is a manufacturing defect. Such a defect occurs when a product that injures a person does so because there is a flaw that is not in the general product line. It is a failure in quality control. As the cases suggest, strict product liability for this type of defect had been evolving for a substantial period of time. The second type, which is very different, is a defect attributable to failure of design. Here, an entire product line is challenged. The singular definition provided little or no guidelines to courts as to how liability should be imposed: Should fault be a basis? Should it be strict liability or absolute liability? The third type is a defect due to failure to warn. Restatement (Second) did not separate this type of defect in its "Black Letter" rule, but did address it separately in comment *j*, suggesting a fault predicate for failure to warn.

In the three decades that followed the publication of § 402A, literally thousands of cases wrestled with the problem of a singular definition of defect. As each jurisdiction struggled with its standard for liability in the context of each of the types of defect, it became apparent that the monolithic approach was such in name (strict liability) or number (§ 402A) only. In reality, the standards for each type of defect were somewhat different. In 1993, the American Law Institute began work on a new Restatement of Torts, with a specific focus on products liability. The process through which it was developed is told below and the critical section shifting the paradigm of Restatement (Second) § 402A is then reprinted.

2. PRODUCT DEFECTS

In the 1990's, the ALI began a five year process to develop the Restatement (Third) of Torts: Products Liability with a draft prepared by its Reporters, Professors Aaron Twerski of Brooklyn Law School and James Henderson of Cornell Law School. They were assisted by a 20-person Advisory Committee composed of judges, law professors, and practicing attorneys. The decision to once again "restate" the law of products liability was the result of case law interpretations of § 402A that had produced many new and challenging issues not anticipated in the early 1960's when § 402A was drafted.

After the Reporters produced an initial draft, it went through an intensive review process by the Advisory Committee, a Members Consultative Group, interest groups that were not members of the ALI, the ALI's Governing Council, and finally the ALI membership itself. A multiplicity of drafts went through the same process until May 1998 when the Final Draft was approved overwhelmingly by the ALI membership. The process is described in Schwartz, The Restatement (Third) of Torts: Products Liability: The American Law Institute's Process of Democracy and Deliberation, 26 Hofstra L.Rev. 743 (1998). Both the process by which the new Restatement was developed and the final product that was approved have been subject to criticism. See Shapo, In Search of the Law of Products Liability: The ALI Restatement Project, 48 Vand. L. Rev. 631 (1995) and Popper, Tort Reform Policy More Than State Law Dominates Section 2 of the Third Restatement, 8 Kan. J.L. & Pub. Pol'y 38 (1998). The Restatement, similar to UPLA, abandoned the single definition approach to defect and replaced it with separate functional rules for manufacturing defects, design defects, and defects due to failure to warn. There were some members of the ALI who believed that Restatement (Second) had it right, that judges needed latitude to shape the law, and that any further definition of defect would restrict them. Other ALI members supported the functional model, but differed as to whether the Reporters had arrived at the correct approach in defining each of the three separate categories. Only time will tell whether the new Restatement will receive the general acceptance that ultimately met the Restatement (Second) § 402A. In the nearly two decades since its publication, Restatement (Third) has been a major influence on the development of products liability law. Some courts have embraced its approach, others have not, but almost all have considered it. See, e.g., Tincher v. Omega Flex, Inc., 104 A.3d 328 (Pa. 2014) (declining to adopt Restatement (Third) but acknowledging appreciation of certain of its principles in the formation of Pennsylvania strict liability law). For a scholarly evaluation of its effect, see Symposium: The Products Liability Restatement: Was it a Success? 74 Brook. L. Rev. (2009). Here is the basic text defining product defectiveness from Restatement (Third) of Torts: Products Liability (1998):

TOPIC 1. PRODUCT DEFECTIVENESS

§ 1. Liability of Commercial Seller or Distributor for Harm Caused by Defective Products

> (a) One engaged in the business of selling or otherwise distributing products who sells or distributes a defective product is subject to liability for harm to persons or property caused by the defect.

§ 2. Categories of Product Defect

> A product is defective when, at the time of sale or distribution, it contains a manufacturing defect, is defective in design, or is defective because of inadequate instructions or warnings. A product:
>
> (a) contains a manufacturing defect when the product departs from its intended design even though all possible care was exercised in the preparation and marketing of the product;
>
> (b) is defective in design when the foreseeable risks of harm posed by the product could have been reduced or avoided by the adoption of a reasonable alternative design by the seller or other distributor, or a predecessor in the commercial chain of distribution, and the omission of the alternative design renders the product not reasonably safe;
>
> (c) is defective because of inadequate instructions or warnings when the foreseeable risks of harm posed by the product could have been reduced or avoided by the provision of reasonable instructions or warnings by the seller or other distributor, or a predecessor in the commercial chain of distribution, and the omission of the instructions or warnings renders the product not reasonably safe.

As you review the cases in the rest of this chapter, consider whether the monolithic approach of Restatement (Second) § 402A (1965) or the functional approach of Restatement (Third) of Torts: Products Liability (1998) better serves the goals of tort law.

(A) MANUFACTURING DEFECT

Rix v. General Motors Corp.

Supreme Court of Montana, 1986.
222 Mont. 318, 723 P.2d 195.

WEBER, J.

In 1978, Michael Rix was injured when the pickup he was driving was hit from behind by a 1978 General Motors Corporation (GMC) two ton chassis-cab, which had been equipped with a water tank after sale by the GMC dealer. Plaintiff sued GMC on a theory of strict liability in the Yellowstone County District Court. Following a jury verdict for GMC, plaintiff appeals. * * *

1. Did the trial court properly instruct the jury on strict liability?

* * *

Plaintiff contends he was injured by an unreasonably dangerous 1978 two ton chassis-cab, which had been placed in the stream of commerce by GMC. Premised on a theory of strict liability, he maintains the product was unreasonably dangerous because of both manufacturing and design defects.

The parties stipulated that the accident occurred because of brake failure. Expert testimony from both parties established that the fluids necessary to the braking system had escaped when a brake tube came out of a nut where it fastened to the top of the Hydrovac, a booster unit. Witnesses also testified that the brake tube came out of the nut either because the tube broke or was improperly flared.

Plaintiff contends that the tube broke because there was a manufacturing defect in the tube, basically a bad flare, when the truck came off the assembly line. Plaintiff also contends that the brake system on the truck, a single system, was defectively designed, and argues that GMC's knowledge of available technology coupled with the foreseeable use of the vehicle should have mandated a dual braking system, which provides extra braking power. Plaintiff maintains the accident would have been less severe or would not have happened had the truck been equipped with a dual system.

GMC agreed that the brake tube was defective, but contended that the tube had been altered after it left the GMC assembly line, so that the defective tube was not GMC's responsibility. GMC also contended that the single system was neither a design defect nor unreasonably dangerous, and that the accident would have occurred even if the truck had been equipped with a dual brake system.

Did the trial court properly instruct the jury on strict liability?

* * *

INSTRUCTION NO. 10

I will now define the doctrine of strict liability to you. Keep in mind that this is only a general definition, and must be considered along with the specific instructions on the same topic which follow. The general principle of strict liability as it applies in the State of Montana is:

(1) One who sells any product in a defective condition unreasonably dangerous to the user or consumer or to his property is subject to liability for physical harm thereby caused to the ultimate user or consumer, or to his property, if:

(a) the seller is engaged in the business of selling such a product, and

(b) it is expected and does reach the user or consumer without substantial change in the condition in which it is sold.

(2) The rule stated in Subsection (1) applies although

(a) the seller has exercised all possible care in the preparation and sale of his product, and

(b) the user or consumer has not bought the product from or entered into any contractual relation with the seller.

INSTRUCTION NO. 11

The plaintiff must establish three essential elements in order to recover under his theory of strict liability. They are as follows:

First, that the defendant General Motors Corporation manufactured and sold a product which at the time General Motors sold it was in a defective condition unreasonably dangerous to the consumer or user;

Second, that the product was expected to and did reach the ultimate consumer without substantial change in the condition it was in at the time it was sold; and

Third, that the defective condition in the product proximately caused injury to the plaintiff.

Jury instruction #10 is the same as Section 402A Restatement (Second) of Torts (1965). Plaintiff did not make an objection at the time the instruction was offered. Plaintiff objected to jury instruction #11 "on the grounds that the second standard improperly states Montana law regarding tracing requirement back to the manufacturer."

* * *

We will now discuss strict liability under a manufacturing defect theory. Under a manufacturing defect theory, the essential question is whether the product was flawed or defective because it was not constructed correctly by the manufacturer:

"[M]anufacturing defects, by definition, are 'imperfections that inevitably occur in a typically small percentage of products of a given design as a result of the fallibility of the manufacturing process. A [defectively manufactured] product does not conform in some significant aspect to the intended design, nor does it conform to the great majority of products manufactured in accordance with that design.' (Henderson, Judicial Review of Manufacturers' Conscious Design Choices: The Limits of Adjudication, 73 Col.L.Rev. 1531, 1543). Stated differently, a defectively manufactured product is flawed because it is misconstructed without regard to whether the intended design of the manufacturer was safe or not. Such defects result from some mishap in the manufacturing process itself, improper workmanship, or because defective materials were used in construction." [C]

Restatement (Second) of Torts, Section 402A (1965) has been adopted by this Court as the applicable law with regard to strict liability under a manufacturing defect theory. The Restatement view is continued in Instruction #10, previously quoted in this opinion. In the context of strict liability under a manufacturing defect theory, we conclude that instructions #10 and #11, as given by the District Court, are adequate. * * *

* * *

We reverse and remand [on other grounds] for a new trial in conformity with this opinion.

NOTES AND QUESTIONS

1. The distinction between defect in design and defect in manufacture (or construction) was not well developed in early strict liability cases. See, e.g., Greenman v. Yuba Power Prods., Inc., page 781, nor did the Restatement (Second) of Torts § 402A resolve the ambiguity. Today, the distinction is clearer and may be quite important in terms of strict liability theory. If a product has a material defect in construction that causes a personal injury to the user, strict liability usually will be imposed. The plaintiff's main problems will be in the area of factual proof—a topic developed at page 816. On the other hand, when plaintiff contends that the product is defectively designed or was accompanied by inadequate warnings, the test for defect varies by jurisdiction. See, e.g., Ford Motor Co. v. Ledesma, 242 S.W.3d 32 (Tex. 2007) (jury instruction for manufacturing defect that omitted requirement of "deviation from specifications or planned output" required new trial and noting that design defect claim requires showing of safer alternative design).

2. Note that the plaintiff has to prove that the product deviated from the seller's design or from the seller's other products of the same design, not what specific conduct of the manufacturer led to that defect. In the context of the principal case, the plaintiff only needs to show that the brakes failed because of a manufacturing defect in the tube (strict liability), not what assembly line actions led to that defect (negligent conduct of the manufacturer). What if the manufacturer could show that it had the best quality control procedures in the entire industry, that only one out of every one million tubes came off the assembly line with a defect, and that there was no way to detect those defects? That would constitute reasonable care and thus no liability under a negligence standard. Under a strict liability standard, however, the manufacturer would be liable. See Restatement (Third) of Torts: Products Liability § 2(a) (1998) (liability for manufacturing defect even though all possible care was exercised). If you represented a manufacturer whose product contained a manufacturing defect that caused injury to someone, would you advise your client to settle or litigate?

3. The manufacturer in this case was claiming that the defect was not present when it left the assembly line, but was introduced by someone else who later altered the product. If that is so, the manufacturer would not be liable. No doubt anticipating this possibility, the plaintiff also has alleged a design defect—that the manufacturer should have provided for a dual braking system, which would have prevented the accident. Very few cases contain only a manufacturing defect claim. Based on the principal case, do you see why it would be to the plaintiff's advantage to bring a design defect claim in addition to the manufacturing defect claim? Do you see why there is almost always a design defect claim lurking within a manufacturing defect case?

(B) DESIGN DEFECT

Prentis v. Yale Mfg. Co.

Supreme Court of Michigan, 1984.
421 Mich. 670, 365 N.W.2d 176.

BOYLE, JUSTICE. This products liability action arose out of injuries sustained in an accident involving the operation of a hand-operated forklift manufactured by defendant. * * *

The facts of this case are not seriously in dispute. In April of 1970, plaintiff John Prentis, who was employed as foreman of the parts department at an automobile dealership, sustained a hip injury in an accident involving the use of a forklift manufactured by defendant Yale Manufacturing Company and sold to plaintiff's employer in 1952. The forklift was a stand-up or walking type, termed by defendant a "walkie hi-lo" model, rather than a riding or sit down variety. It was operated by lifting its handle up, much like the handle of a wagon. The forklift was estimated by plaintiff to weigh about two thousand pounds and was powered by a large battery, which had to be recharged every night. The machine was equipped with a hand controlled "dead-man" switch which normally prevented it from moving if the operator let go of the handle or controls. * * *

The accident in which Mr. Prentis was injured occurred late in the day, and he testified that he was aware at the time that the battery charge on the forklift was running low. After using the machine to assist him in placing an engine inside the cargo area of a delivery van, while the forklift was in tow behind him on a slightly inclined ramp leading from the delivery bay, Mr. Prentis attempted to start the machine by working the handle up and down. When the machine experienced a power surge, he lost his footing and fell to the ground. It appears that plaintiff's injuries were a result of the fall only, as the machine did not hit or run over him, but continued past him and stopped when it ran into a parked car. Mr. Prentis received extensive treatment for multiple fractures of his left hip. * * *

The focus of plaintiffs' proofs at both trials was an alleged defect in the design of the forklift, and the substance of the expert witness's testimony was that the design of the forklift failed to properly incorporate the operator as a "human factor" into the machine's function, specifically because it did not provide a seat or platform for the operator. * * *

The development of the law of tort liability for physical injury caused by products is perhaps the most striking and dramatic of all the numerous stories in the portfolio of modern tort scenarios. When the societal goal of holding manufacturers accountable for the safety of their products has been threatened by the interposition of technical rules of law, it has been the rules that have gradually given way.

However, this has never meant that courts have been willing to impose absolute liability in this context and from their earliest application, theories of products liability have been viewed as tort doctrines which should not be confused with the imposition of absolute liability. * * *

Thus while courts have accepted the social policy rationale that those injured by defective products should be compensated for their injuries without being subject to the contractual intricacies of the law of sales, and have agreed that manufacturers can most effectively distribute the costs of injuries, they have never gone so far as to make sellers insurers of their products and thus absolutely liable for any and all injuries sustained from the use of those products.

Like the courts in every other state, whether a suit is based upon negligence or implied warranty, we require the plaintiff to prove that the product itself is actionable—that something is wrong with it that makes it dangerous. This idea of "something wrong" is usually expressed by the adjective "defective" and the plaintiff must, *in every case, in every jurisdiction,* show that the product was defective. [C]

As a term of art, "defective" gives little difficulty when something goes wrong in the manufacturing process and the product is not in its intended condition. In the case of a "manufacturing defect," the product may be evaluated against the manufacturer's own production standards, as manifested by that manufacturer's other like products.

However, injuries caused by the condition of a product may also be actionable if the product's design, which is the result of intentional design decisions of the manufacturer, is not sufficiently safe. Conscious design defect cases provide no such simple test. The very question whether a defect in fact exists is central to a court's inquiry. It is only in design defect cases that a court is called upon to supply the standard for defectiveness. Thus, the term "defect" in design cases is "an epithet—an expression for the legal conclusion rather than a test for reaching that conclusion." See Wade, On product "design defects" and their actionability, 33 Van. L.R. 551, 552 (1980).

At present, questions related to "design defects" and the determination of when a product is defective, because of the nature of its design, appear to be the most agitated and controversial issues before the courts in the field of products liability. A number of appellate courts, aware that they are engaged in the conscious task of molding the law of products liability, have become concerned that they are not differentiating with sufficient clarity between various theories of recovery in design defect cases. In response, they have sought to devise significant and well-articulated distinctions. At the same time, other courts have become concerned that the differentiation is too great, and have attempted to devise means of keeping the broad scope of liability in check. The result has been several cases in which the standard for liability in the design area has been very carefully examined by courts and often vigorously debated by the judges themselves. A survey of the important recent cases in neighboring jurisdictions suggests something of the creative ferment underlying what has been described as the "rich tapestry" of the developing common law of products liability.

The approaches for determination of the meaning of "defect" in design cases fall into four general categories. The first, usually associated with Dean Wade, employs a negligence risk-utility analysis, but focuses upon whether the manufacturer would be judged negligent if it had known of the product's dangerous condition at the time it was marketed. The second, associated with Dean Keeton, compares the risk and utility of the product at the time of trial. The third focuses on consumer expectations about the product. The fourth combines the risk-utility and consumer-expectation tests. While courts have included many other individual variations in their formulations, the overwhelming consensus among courts deciding defective design cases is in the use of some form of risk-utility analysis, either as an exclusive or alternative ground of liability. Risk-utility analysis in this context always involves assessment of the decisions made by manufacturers with respect to the design of their products. * * *

The risk-utility balancing test is merely a detailed version of Judge Learned Hand's negligence calculus. See United States v. Carroll Towing Co., 159 F.2d 169, 173 (2d Cir.1947). As Dean Prosser has pointed out, the liability of the manufacturer rests "upon a departure from proper standards of care, so that the tort is essentially a matter of negligence."

Although many courts have insisted that the risk-utility tests they are applying are not negligence tests because their focus is on the *product* rather than the manufacturer's *conduct,* [c] the distinction on closer examination appears to be nothing more than semantic. As a common-sense matter, the jury weighs competing factors presented in evidence and reaches a conclusion about the judgment or decision (*i.e., conduct*) of the manufacturer. The underlying negligence calculus is inescapable. As noted by Professor Birnbaum:

"When a jury decides that the risk of harm outweighs the utility of a particular design (that the product is not as safe as it *should* be) it is saying that in choosing the particular design and cost tradeoffs, the manufacturer exposed the consumer to greater risk of danger than he should have. Conceptually and analytically, this approach bespeaks negligence." Birnbaum, Unmasking the test for design defect: From negligence [to warranty] to strict liability to negligence, 33 Van.L.R. 593, 610 (1980) * * *

The competing factors to be weighed under a risk-utility balancing test invite the trier of fact to consider the alternatives and risks faced by the manufacturer and to determine whether in light of these the manufacturer exercised reasonable care in making the design choices it made. Instructing a jury that weighing factors concerning conduct and judgment must yield a conclusion that does not describe conduct is confusing at best.

The Model Uniform Product Liability Act (UPLA) was published in 1979 by the Department of Commerce for voluntary use by the states. The act adopts a negligence or fault system with respect to design defects. It is important to examine the rationale underlying the UPLA's adoption of negligence as the criteria for liability in design defect cases. The drafters rejected, as a reason for application of strict liability to design defect cases, the theory of risk distribution wherein the product seller distributes the costs of all product-related risks through liability insurance. They believe that a "firmer liability foundation" than strict liability is needed in a design defect case because the whole product line is at risk. Furthermore, the drafters believed that a fault system would provide greater incentives for loss prevention.

The approach of the UPLA has been approved by several commentators, whose analysis is also instructive. First, unlike manufacturing defects, design defects result from deliberate and documentable decisions on the part of manufacturers, and plaintiffs should be able to learn the facts surrounding these decisions through liberalized modern discovery rules. Access to expert witnesses and technical data are available to aid plaintiffs in proving the manufacturer's design decision was ill considered.

Second, to the extent that a primary purpose of products liability law is to encourage the design of safer products and thereby reduce the incidence of injuries, a negligence standard that would reward the careful manufacturer and penalize the careless is more likely to achieve that purpose. A greater incentive to design safer products will result from a fault system where resources devoted to careful and safe design will pay dividends in the form of fewer claims and lower insurance premiums for the manufacturer with a good design safety record. The incentive will result from the knowledge that a distinction is made between those who are careful and those who are not.

Third, a verdict for the plaintiff in a design defect case is the equivalent of a determination that an entire product line is defective. It usually will involve a significant portion of the manufacturer's assets and the public may be deprived of a product. Thus, the plaintiff should be required to pass the higher threshold of a fault test in order to threaten an entire product line. The traditional tort law of negligence better serves this purpose.

Fourth, a fault system incorporates greater intrinsic fairness in that the careful safety-oriented manufacturer will not bear the burden of paying for losses caused by the negligent product seller. It will also follow that the customers of the careful manufacturer will not through its prices pay for the negligence of the careless. As a final bonus, the careful manufacturer with fewer claims and lower insurance premiums may, through lower prices as well as safer products, attract the customers of less careful competitors.

We find the formula adopted by the UPLA on the question of defective design to have the merit of being clear and understandable. We recognize that in products liability cases against manufacturers based upon alleged defects in the design of a product, the courts of this state have attempted to avoid both the notion of fault implicit in negligence and the harshness of no-fault implicit in absolute liability. Thus, on the basis of the heritage of contract and sales law underlying concepts of implied warranty, we have in the past approved instructions that attempted to focus a jury's attention on the condition of a product rather than on the reasonableness of the manufacturer's conduct or decision. We are persuaded that in so doing in the context of cases against the manufacturers of products *based upon allegations of defective design,* we have engaged in a process that may have served to confuse, rather than enlighten, jurors, who must ultimately apply understandable guidelines if they are to justly adjudicate the rights and duties of all parties. Imposing a negligence standard for design defect litigation is only to define in a coherent fashion what our litigants in this case are in fact arguing and what our jurors are in essence analyzing. Thus we adopt, forthrightly, a pure negligence, risk-utility test in products liability actions against manufacturers of products, where liability is predicated upon defective design.

We hold that in this products liability action against a manufacturer for an alleged defect in the design of its product, where the jury was properly instructed on the theory of negligent design, the trial judge's refusal to instruct on breach of warranty was not reversible error. Such instructions could have created juror confusion and prejudicial error. Indeed, such an instruction would have been repetitive and unnecessary and could have misled the jury into believing that plaintiff could recover on the warranty count even if it found there was no "defect" in the design of the product.

* * *

This holding is based upon the recognition that under the common law of products liability, in an action against the manufacturer of a product based upon an alleged defect in its design, "breach of implied warranty and negligence involve identical evidence and require proof of exactly the same elements." * * *

Applying these principles to the facts of this case, although plaintiffs alleged that their injuries were proximately caused by defendant's negligence and breach of an implied warranty, their evidence and proofs at trial focused on the single claim that the defendant *defectively designed* the "walkie hi-lo" forklift, because it failed to provide a seat or platform for the operator. Thus, recovery under either theory required the jury to determine that the forklift was defectively designed by defendant. [C] The factual inquiry was: whether the design of defendant's forklift was "unreasonably dangerous" because it did not contain a seat or platform for the operator. [C]

The trial court properly recognized that the standards of liability under the theories of implied warranty and negligence were indistinguishable and that instructions on both would only confuse the jury. Accordingly, the trial judge's instructions regarding the standard of care and theories of liability properly informed the jury of defendant's legal duties as the manufacturer of the forklift. The court set forth the necessary elements for determining whether defendant defectively designed the forklift when it stated:

> "A manufacturer of a product made under a plan or design which makes it dangerous for uses for which it is manufactured is, [however,] subject to liability to others whom he should expect to use the product or to be endangered by its probable use from physical harm caused by his failure to exercise reasonable care in the adoption of a safe plan or design.
>
> "A manufacturer has a duty to use reasonable care in designing his product and guard it against a foreseeable and unreasonable risk of injury and this may even include misuse which might reasonably be anticipated."

In essence, the jury was instructed to consider whether the manufacturer took reasonable care in light of any reasonably foreseeable use of the product which might cause harm or injury. [C]

Therefore we hold that in a products liability action against a manufacturer, based upon defective design, the jury need only be instructed on a single unified theory of negligent design.

The judgment of the Court of Appeals is reversed, and the judgment of the trial court is reinstated.

WILLIAMS, C.J., and BRICKLEY and RYAN, JJ., concur.

CAVANAGH, J., concurring in result.

LEVIN, JUSTICE (dissenting) [with opinion].

NOTES AND QUESTIONS

1. When is a product to be regarded as "defective" in design for the purposes of imposing strict liability? Many courts and commentators have struggled with this broad issue and the principal case presents a thorough judicial discussion of the topic. See also Caterpillar Tractor Co. v. Beck, 593 P.2d 871, 880 (Alaska 1979) ("Design defects present the most perplexing problems in the field of strict products liability because there is no readily ascertainable external measure of defectiveness. While manufacturing flaws can be evaluated against the intended design of the product, no such objective standard exists in the design defect context.")

2. As indicated in the notes following Greenman v. Yuba Power Prods., Inc., page 781, the great majority of the states adopted the rule of § 402A of the Restatement. Most utilized the language of § 402A and spoke of the requirement that the product be unreasonably dangerous, but some espoused strict liability while refusing to accept the Restatement terminology. As the states developed their tests for design defect, many of them appeared to be requiring negligence or at least some showing of fault, despite their explicit adoption of strict liability. See Restatement (Third) of Torts: Products Liability § 2 comment *a* (1998) (recognizing this phenomenon.

3. "*Crashworthiness.*" A difference existed at one time on the issue whether an automobile was "defective" if it had not been designed to minimize injury to occupants during a collision. In Evans v. General Motors Corp., 359 F.2d 822 (7th Cir.1966) (applying Indiana law), a new X-frame design for a car body turned out to be less safe than a conventional rectangular frame when the car was hit from the side. The court held, however, that the manufacturer was under no duty to design an accident-proof or crash-proof car, since the intended purpose of automobiles did not include its participation in a collision. Two years later another federal court in Larsen v. General Motors Corp., 391 F.2d 495 (8th Cir.1968) (applying Michigan law), disagreed, holding that because the risk of collision was foreseeable, the design must reflect that. The *Larsen* view swept the field. See Blankenship v. General Motors Corp., 185 W.Va. 350, 406 S.E.2d 781 (1991) (noting unanimous support for *Larsen* rule) and Restatement (Third) of Torts: Products Liability § 16 comment *a* (1998). How far does the manufacturer's duty to protect the occupant in an accident extend? Consider a four-door hardtop convertible that leaves the road, rolls over,

and lands on its top. A corner of the roof collapses on the driver and paralyzes him. Plaintiff's expert testifies that a roll bar or roll cage would have prevented the disabling injury, that roll cages were technically feasible at the time the car was manufactured, and in use on race cars. But no mass-produced automobile had ever been built this way. Liability? Although most of the crashworthiness or enhanced injuries cases involve automobiles, not all of them do. See, e.g., Smith v. Ariens Co., 375 Mass. 620, 377 N.E.2d 954 (1978) (snowmobile); Camacho v. Honda Motor Co., Ltd., 741 P.2d 1240 (Colo.1987) (motorcycle); Tafoya v. Sears Roebuck & Co., 884 F.2d 1330 (10th Cir.1989) (riding lawnmower); Hillrichs v. Avco Corp., 478 N.W.2d 70 (Iowa 1991) (corn picker). Does the manufacturer owe a duty to the occupants of the *other* vehicle? See Rennert v. Great Dane Ltd., 543 F.3d 914 (7th Cir. 2008) (applying Illinois law) (manufacturer does not owe duty to protect those who collide with its vehicle; court notes some conflicting authority in other jurisdictions).

The crashworthiness claim against the manufacturer requires proof that the defect enhanced plaintiff's injuries, but what if it is difficult to apportion the injuries between the original tortfeasor who caused the crash and the manufacturer? See Green v. Ford Motor Co., 942 N.E.2d 791 (Ind. 2011) (answering certified question) (jury may allocate fault between plaintiff for causing crash and manufacturer for enhanced injury if jury finds that plaintiff's conduct was a proximate cause of the harm for which he is seeking damages) and Egbert v. Nissan Motor Co., 228 P.3d 737 (Utah 2010) (discussing cases from other jurisdictions deciding whether to place burden of apportioning injury on plaintiff or manufacturer).

4. *Category Liability and Products Such as Whiskey, Tobacco, and Butter.* The Restatement (Second) § 402A (1965) cautioned that products whose inherent characteristics made them dangerous were not to be considered "unreasonably dangerous." In language frequently quoted by the courts that adopted § 402A strict liability, comment *i* provides that "Good whiskey is not unreasonably dangerous merely because it will make some people drunk, and is especially dangerous to alcoholics. . . . Good tobacco is not unreasonably dangerous merely because the effects of smoking may be harmful; . . . . Good butter is not unreasonably dangerous merely because, if such be the case, it deposits cholesterol in the arteries and leads to heart attacks; . . . ." See also Buckingham v. R.J. Reynolds Tobacco Co., 142 N.H. 822, 713 A.2d 381 (1998) (in context of second-hand smoke case, dismissing strict liability claim against cigarette manufacturers, citing comment *i*) and Godoy v. E.I. Du Pont de Nemours and Co., 319 Wis.2d 91, 768 N.W.2d 674 (2009) (white lead carbonate pigment cannot be defective in design based on presence of lead, a characteristic ingredient of the product). These principles can be found in the Restatement (Third) of Torts, but only with respect to design liability. In Restatement (Third) of Torts: Products Liability § 2, comment *d*, tobacco was not specifically mentioned but alcoholic beverages, firearms, and above-ground swimming pools were used as examples. The principle stated was that "widely distributed products" could only be subject to liability for defective design if a plaintiff proved that a "reasonable alternative design" was available. Is there one for a cigarette? Adamo v. Brown & Williamson Tobacco Corp., 11 N.Y.3d 545, 872 N.Y.S.2d 415, 900 N.E.2d 966 (2008) (claimant did not show that proposed alternative design—cigarette with lower levels of tar and nicotine—has the same function or utility).

5. Unlike Michigan in the principal case, many jurisdictions instruct the jury on all available causes of action, negligence, breach of warranty, and strict liability. See, for example, Castro v. QVC Network, Inc., 139 F.3d 114 (2d Cir.1998) (under New York law, jury should be instructed separately on strict liability and breach of warranty in case involving roasting pan). See also Restatement (Third) of Torts: Products Liability § 2 comment *n* (1998) (rules are stated functionally rather than in terms of traditional doctrinal categories so that as long as the requirements are met all theories of liability may be used to bring claim).

O'Brien v. Muskin Corp.

Supreme Court of New Jersey, 1983.
94 N.J. 169, 463 A.2d 298.

POLLOCK, J. Plaintiff, Gary O'Brien, seeks to recover in strict liability for personal injuries sustained because defendant, Muskin Corporation, allegedly marketed a product, an above-ground swimming pool, that was defectively designed and bore an inadequate warning. In an unreported decision, the Appellate Division reversed the judgment for defendants and remanded the matter for trial. We granted certification, [c] and now modify and affirm the judgment of the Appellate Division. * * *

O'Brien sued to recover damages for serious personal injuries sustained when he dove into a swimming pool at the home of Jean Henry, widow of Arthur Henry, now Jean Glass. Ultimately, plaintiff sued as defendants not only Muskin Corporation, the manufacturer, but also Kiddie City Inc., the distributor of the pool, charging them with placing a defectively designed pool in the stream of commerce. * * *

Muskin, a swimming pool manufacturer, made and distributed a line of above-ground pools. Typically, the pools consisted of a corrugated metal wall, which the purchaser placed into an oval frame assembled over a shallow bed of sand. This outer structure was then fitted with an embossed vinyl liner and filled with water.

In 1971, Arthur Henry bought a Muskin pool and assembled it in his backyard. The pool was a twenty-foot by twenty-four-foot model, with four-foot walls. An embossed vinyl liner fit within the outer structure and was filled with water to a depth of approximately three and one-half feet. At one point, the outer wall of the pool bore the logo of the manufacturer, and below it a decal that warned "DO NOT DIVE" in letters roughly one-half inch high.

On May 17, 1974, O'Brien, then twenty-three years old, arrived uninvited at the Henry home and dove into the pool. A fact issue exists whether O'Brien dove from the platform by the pool or from the roof of the adjacent eight-foot high garage. As his outstretched hands hit the vinyl-lined pool bottom, they slid apart, and O'Brien struck his head on the bottom of the pool, thereby sustaining his injuries.

In his complaint, O'Brien alleged that Muskin was strictly liable for his injuries because it had manufactured and marketed a defectively designed pool. In support of this contention, O'Brien cited the slippery quality of the pool liner and the lack of adequate warnings.

At trial, both parties produced experts who testified about the use of vinyl as a pool liner. One of the plaintiff's witnesses, an expert in the characteristics of vinyl, testified that wet vinyl was more than twice as slippery as rubber latex, which is used to line in-ground pools. The trial court, however, sustained an objection to the expert's opinion about alternative kinds of pool bottoms, specifically whether rubber latex was a feasible liner for above-ground pools. The expert admitted that he knew of no above-ground pool lined with a material other than vinyl, but plaintiff contended that vinyl should not be used in above-ground pools, even though no alternative material was available. A second expert testified that the slippery vinyl bottom and lack of adequate warnings rendered the pool unfit and unsafe for its foreseeable uses.

Muskin's expert testified that vinyl was not only an appropriate material to line an above-ground pool, but was the best material because it permitted the outstretched arms of the diver to glide when they hit the liner, thereby preventing the diver's head from striking the bottom of the pool. Thus, he concluded that in some situations, specifically those in which a diver executes a shallow dive, slipperiness operates as a safety feature. Another witness, Muskin's customer service manager, who was indirectly in charge of quality control, testified that the vinyl bottom could have been thicker and the embossing deeper. A fair inference could be drawn that deeper embossing would have rendered the pool bottom less slippery.

At the close of the entire case, the trial court instructed the jury on the elements of strict liability, both with respect to design defects and the failure to warn adequately. The court, however, then limited the jury's consideration to the adequacy of the warning. That is, the court took from the jury the issue whether manufacturing a pool with a vinyl liner constituted either a design or manufacturing defect.

Strict liability law, a relatively recent but rapidly growing legal phenomenon, has received uneven treatment from scholars, legislatures and courts. Underlying the various responses is a shared concern about the allocation of the risk of loss upon manufacturers, distributors and others in the stream of commerce for injuries sustained by the public from unsafe products.

One of the policy considerations supporting the imposition of strict liability is easing the burden of proof for a plaintiff injured by a defective product, a policy that is achieved by eliminating the requirement that the plaintiff prove the manufacturer's negligence. [C] Generally speaking, a plaintiff has the burden of proving that (1) the product was defective; (2) the defect existed when the product left the hands of the defendant; and (3) the defect caused injury to a reasonably foreseeable user. [C] Proof that the product was defective requires more than a mere showing that the product caused the injury. The necessity of proving a defect in the product as part of the plaintiff's *prima facie* case distinguishes strict from absolute liability, and thus prevents the manufacturer from also becoming the insurer of a product. [Cc]

Fundamental to the determination of a products liability case, including one predicated on a defective design or inadequate warning, is the duty of the manufacturer to foreseeable users. The duty includes warning foreseeable users of the risks inherent in the use of that product, [c] and not placing defective products on the market. [Cc] A manufacturer who breaches these duties is strictly liable to an injured party. That liability reflects the policy judgment that by marketing its product, a manufacturer assumes responsibility to members of the public who are injured because of defects in that product. Restatement (Second) of Torts § 402A comment *c* (1965). * * *

Critical, then, to the disposition of products liability claims is the meaning of "defect". The term is not self-defining and has no accepted meaning suitable for all strict liability cases. Implicit in the term "defect" is a comparison of the product with a standard of evaluation; something can be defective only if it fails to measure up to that standard. [C] Speaking generally, defects may be classified as design defects or manufacturing defects. In cases alleging manufacturing defects, as distinguished from design defects, defining the standard, and thus the meaning of "defect," is relatively easy. For example, the injury-causing product may be measured against the same product as manufactured according to the manufacturer's standards. If the particular product used by the plaintiff fails to conform to those standards or other units of the same kind, it is defective. An apt illustration is a mass-produced product that comes off the assembly line missing a part. The question in those cases becomes whether the product as produced by the manufacturer conformed to the product as intended. [C]

The considerations are more subtle when a plaintiff alleges that a product is defective due to any feature of its design, including the absence or inadequacy of accompanying warnings. In design defect or failure-to-warn cases, the product has been manufactured as intended and cannot be "defective" by comparison to a standard set by the manufacturer. [C] Rather, the standard to measure the product reflects a policy judgment that some products are so dangerous that they create a risk of harm outweighing their usefulness. From that perspective, the term "defect" is a conclusion rather than a test for reaching that conclusion. [C]

Although the appropriate standard might be variously defined, one definition, based on a comparison of the utility of the product with the risk of injury that it poses to the public, has gained prominence. To the extent that "risk-utility analysis," as it is known, implicates the reasonableness of the manufacturer's conduct, strict liability law continues to manifest that part of its heritage attributable to the law of negligence. [Cc] Risk-utility analysis is appropriate when the product may function satisfactorily under one set of circumstances, yet because of its design present undue risk of injury to the user in another situation.

Another standard is the consumer expectations test, which recognizes that the failure of the product to perform safely may be viewed as a violation of the reasonable expectations of the consumer. [C] In this case, however, the pool fulfilled its function as a place to swim. The alleged defect manifested itself when the pool was used for diving.

> * * * [S]ome factors relevant in risk-utility analysis are:
>
> (1) The usefulness and desirability of the product—its utility to the user and to the public as a whole.
>
> (2) The safety aspects of the product—the likelihood that it will cause injury, and the probable seriousness of the injury.
>
> (3) The availability of a substitute product which would meet the same need and not be as unsafe.
>
> (4) The manufacturer's ability to eliminate the unsafe character of the product without impairing its usefulness or making it too expensive to maintain its utility.
>
> (5) The user's ability to avoid danger by the exercise of care in the use of the product.
>
> (6) The user's anticipated awareness of the dangers inherent in the product and their avoidability, because of general public knowledge of the obvious condition of the product, or of the existence of suitable warnings or instructions.
>
> (7) The feasibility, on the part of the manufacturer, of spreading the loss by setting the price of the product or carrying liability insurance. [C] * * *

By implication, risk-utility analysis includes other factors such as the "state-of-the-art" at the time of the manufacture of the product. [C] The "state-of-the-art" refers to the existing level of technological expertise and scientific knowledge relevant to a particular industry at the time a product is designed. [C] Although customs of an industry may be relevant, [c] because those customs may lag behind technological development, they are not identical with the state-of-the-art. [Cc] A manufacturer may have a duty to make products pursuant to a safer design even if the custom of the industry is not to use that alternative. [C] * * *

Although state-of-the-art evidence may be dispositive on the facts of a particular case, it does not constitute an absolute defense apart from risk-utility analysis. [C] The ultimate burden of proving a defect is on the plaintiff, but the burden is on the defendant to prove that compliance with state-of-the-art, in conjunction with other relevant evidence, justifies placing a product on the market. Compliance with proof of state-of-the-art need not, as a matter of law, compel a judgment for a defendant. State-of-the-art evidence, together with other evidence relevant to risk-utility analysis, however, may support a judgment for a defendant. In brief, state-of-the-art evidence is relevant to, but not necessarily dispositive of, risk-utility analysis. That is, a product may embody the state-of-the-art and still fail to satisfy the risk-utility equation.

The assessment of the utility of a design involves the consideration of available alternatives. If no alternatives are available, recourse to a unique design is more defensible. The existence of a safer and equally efficacious design, however, diminishes the justification for using a challenged design.

The evaluation of the utility of a product also involves the relative need for that product; some products are essentials, while others are luxuries. A product that fills a critical need and can be designed in only one way should be viewed differently from a luxury item. Still other products, including some for which no alternative exists, are so dangerous and of such little use that under the risk-utility analysis, a manufacturer would bear the cost of liability of harm to others. That cost might dissuade a manufacturer from placing the product on the market, even if the product has been made as safely as possible. Indeed, plaintiff contends that above-ground pools with vinyl liners are such products and that manufacturers who market those pools should bear the cost of injuries they cause to foreseeable users.

A critical issue at trial was whether the design of the pool, calling for a vinyl bottom in a pool four feet deep, was defective. The trial court should have permitted the jury to consider whether, because of the dimensions of the pool and slipperiness of the bottom, the risks of injury so outweighed the utility of the product as to constitute a defect. In removing that issue from consideration by the jury, the trial court erred. To establish sufficient proof to compel submission of the issue to the jury for appropriate fact-finding under risk-utility analysis, it was not necessary for plaintiff to prove the existence of alternative, safer designs. Viewing the evidence in the light most favorable to plaintiff, even if there are no alternative methods of making bottoms for above-ground pools, the jury might have found that the risk posed by the pool outweighed its utility.

In a design-defect case, the plaintiff bears the burden of both going forward with the evidence and of persuasion that the product contained a defect. To establish a *prima facie* case, the plaintiff should adduce sufficient evidence on the risk-utility factors to establish a defect. With respect to above-ground swimming pools, for example, the plaintiff might seek to establish that pools are marketed primarily for recreational, not therapeutic purposes; that because of their design, including their configuration, inadequate warnings, and the use of vinyl liners, injury is likely; that, without impairing the usefulness of the pool or pricing it out of the market, warnings against diving could be made more prominent and a liner less dangerous. It may not be necessary for the plaintiff to introduce evidence on all those alternatives. Conversely, the plaintiff may wish to offer proof on other matters relevant to the risk-utility analysis. It is not a foregone conclusion that plaintiff ultimately will prevail on a risk-utility analysis, but he should have an opportunity to prove his case. * * *

We modify and affirm the judgment of the Appellate Division reversing and remanding the matter for a new trial.

CLIFFORD, J., concurring in result. SCHREIBER, J., concurring and dissenting [with opinion].

For affirmance as modified—CHIEF JUSTICE WILENTZ, and JUSTICES CLIFFORD, HANDLER, POLLOCK and O'HERN.

NOTES AND QUESTIONS

1. *Risk Utility Balancing Test for Design Defect.* Many jurisdictions use some form of risk utility analysis for design defect cases. See, e.g., Branham v. Ford Motor Co., 390 S.C. 203, 701 S.E.2d 5 (2010) (adopting risk utility balancing as the exclusive test for design defects). See also Restatement (Third) of Torts: Products Liability § 2 comment *a* (1998). Should the test be the utility to the individual who was injured or to society as a whole? See, e.g., In re Fosamax Prod. Liab. Litig., 509 Fed.Appx. 69 (2d Cir. 2013) (applying Florida law) (as part of risk utility balancing test, jury should be instructed to consider the risks and benefits to the public as a whole, as opposed to directing the jury to consider the drug from the perspective of either a particular user or a sub-category of users).

2. *Consumer Expectations Test for Design Defect.* A few jurisdictions use the consumer expectations test for design defect cases. See Godoy v. E.I. Du Pont de Nemours and Co., 319 Wis.2d 91, 768 N.W.2d 674 (2009) (Prosser, J., concurring) (noting that only six states use the consumer expectations test as the exclusive test for analyzing defective design claims). The Third Restatement treats "consumer expectations" as a factor to consider. But whose expectations are to be considered? Those of the ordinary consumer? Those of a bystander injured by the product? See Horst v. Deere & Co., 319 Wis.2d 147, 769 N.W.2d 536 (2009) (whether product is defective depends on expectations of ordinary consumer, not expectations of bystander). See Restatement (Third) of Torts: Products Liability § 2 comments *f* and *g* (1998) (consumer expectations one factor, among many, in risk-utility balancing).

3. Some jurisdictions permit both the consumer expectations test and the risk utility balancing test to be used to prove that a product was defectively designed. See, e.g., Tincher v. Omega Flex, Inc., 104 A.3d 328 (Pa. 2014) (plaintiff is master of the claim and may allege facts to make a prima facie case upon either theory or both). How should the trial court choose which jury instruction to give in each case? Could both be given? Illinois has noted that the two tests are not *theories of liability* but *methods of proof* by which a plaintiff may show that the element of unreasonable dangerousness is met. Mikolajczyk v. Ford Motor Co., 231 Ill.2d 516, 327 Ill.Dec. 1, 901 N.E.2d 329 (2008) (finding that both tests may be utilized in a strict liability design defect case to prove that the product is "unreasonably dangerous"; that which jury instruction would be appropriate depends on the issues raised by the pleadings and evidence; and that if both are appropriate, consumer expectations should be treated as one factor in the risk utility analysis).

4. *Reasonable Alternative Design.* Unlike the principal case, most jurisdictions require that the plaintiff prove an alternative feasible design in order to prove design defect. See, e.g., Beech v. Outboard Marine Corp., 584 So.2d 447 (Ala.1991) (defect must be shown by safer, practical, alternative design) and Tex. Civ. Prac. & Rem. Code Ann. § 82.005 ("In a products liability action in which a claimant alleges a design defect, the burden is on the claimant to prove . . . there was a safer alternative design"). See also Restatement (Third) of Torts: Products Liability § 2(b) (1998) ("is defective in design when the foreseeable risks of harm posed by the product could have been reduced or avoided by the adoption of a reasonable alternative design") and Reporters' Note to § 2 comment *d*

(survey of cases dealing with requirement of reasonable alternative design). But see Potter v. Chicago Pneumatic Tool Co., 241 Conn. 199, 694 A.2d 1319 (1997) (alternative feasible design is only one factor to be considered, citing principal case). One of the greatest battles among members of the ALI developing the Third Restatement was whether the plaintiff should be required to prove a reasonable alternate design in design defect cases. Is this simply a battle over theory? What is the requirement's practical effect? At this point, it appears that most, but not all, state courts require such proof. See Twerski and Henderson, Manufacturers' Liability for Defective Product Designs: The Triumph of Risk-Utility, 74 Brooklyn L. Rev. 1061 (2009).

5. Are there products that are so dangerous and of such low social utility that liability should be imposed even if there is no reasonable alternative design? What about ammunition that is designed in a way that dramatically increases the wounding power of the bullet? Victims of a shooting spree on the Long Island Railroad brought claims against the manufacturer of the "Black Talon" bullets that were used. McCarthy v. Olin Corp., 119 F.3d 148, 155 (2d Cir.1997) (applying New York law) ("the risk of injury to be balanced with the utility is a risk not intended as the primary function of the product. There is no reason to search for an alternative safer design where the product's sole utility is to kill and maim"). New Jersey, the home of the principal case, also has a statute imposing such liability. N.J. Stat. Ann. § 2A:58C–3(b) (practical and technically feasible alternative design not necessary if product is egregiously unsafe or ultra-hazardous and product has little or no usefulness). Acknowledging that there is only scant authority for such a position, Restatement (Third) of Torts: Products Liability § 2 comment *e* (1998) recognizes the possibility of such liability through a comment. Judge Calabresi, dissenting in *McCarthy*, suggested that the Black Talon bullets would qualify as "manifestly unreasonable" products under the Restatement formulation.

6. *State of the Art.* A key issue in design liability cases is whether a defendant can avoid liability by showing compliance with the "state of the art" at the time the product was made. The concept of "state of the art" for products has become muddled because different courts ascribe different meanings to the term. Sometimes the term is confused with evidence of compliance with "industry customs," which is introduced to show the defendant's reasonableness or to rebut allegations of product defect. The better use of the term is as a label for the requirement for the best scientific and medical technology that is practically and economically feasible at the time the product was made or marketed. The product thus is evaluated in light of knowledge and technology available at the time of manufacture rather than at the time of trial. See Restatement (Third) of Torts: Products Liability § 2 comment *d* (1998).

7. *Open and Obvious Danger.* A few courts have held that an "open and obvious" or "patent" danger is an absolute defense to a design defect case. Most jurisdictions, however, have rejected the obviousness of the danger as a bar to recovery and instead consider it as one factor in the risk utility balancing test. See e.g., Perkins v. Wilkinson Sword, Inc., 83 Ohio St.3d 507, 700 N.E.2d 1247 (1998) (in case where children were killed in fire they started while playing with cigarette lighter, court ruled that

obvious danger of cigarette lighter was factor to be considered in risk-utility analysis, but was not determinative); Calles v. Scripto-Tokai Corp., 224 Ill.2d 247, 309 Ill.Dec. 383, 864 N.E.2d 249 (2007) (utility lighter; accord); and Timpte Indus., Inc. v. Gish, 286 S.W.3d 306 (Tex. 2009) (top rail on side of trailer; obviousness of danger is not itself a bar to liability but is an important consideration and may even be decisive in a particular case).

8. *Applicability to Prescription Drugs and Medical Devices.* Most jurisdictions have declined to apply true strict liability to the design of prescription drugs, following comment *k* to Restatement (Second) of Torts § 402A, which provided for no strict liability in the case of unavoidably unsafe products. Comment *k* used prescription drugs as an example of such products, noting that "The seller of such products, again with the qualification that they are properly prepared and marketed, and proper warning is given, . . . is not to be held to strict liability for unfortunate consequences attending their use, merely because he has undertaken to supply the public with an apparently useful and desirable product, attended with a known but apparently reasonable risk." Should *all* products requiring a prescription fall into the "unavoidably unsafe" category or should that determination be made on a case by case basis? Compare Brown v. Superior Court, 44 Cal.3d 1049, 751 P.2d 470, 245 Cal.Rptr. 412 (1988) (DES; applies to all) with White v. Wyeth Lab., 40 Ohio St.3d 390, 533 N.E.2d 748 (1988) (vaccine; case-by-case determination whether unavoidably unsafe). Restatement (Third) of Torts: Products Liability has a separate section governing liability for sellers and distributors of prescription drugs and medical devices. It would impose liability for harm caused by defective design, whether grounded in negligence or strict liability, only if "the foreseeable risks of harm posed by the drug or medical device are sufficiently great in relation to its therapeutic benefits that reasonable health-care providers, knowing of such foreseeable risks and therapeutic benefits, would not prescribe the drug or medical device for any class of patients." Restatement (Third) of Torts: Products Liability § 6(c) (1998). See also Lance v. Wyeth, 85 A.3d 434 (Pa. 2014) (recognizing claim for negligent drug design). Note that strict liability would be available if the drug or medical device was alleged to have a *manufacturing* defect. See Transue v. Aesthetech Corp., 341 F.3d 911 (9th Cir. 2003) (applying Washington law) (strict liability instruction should have been given to jury where plaintiff alleged that her silicone breast implants had a manufacturing defect) and Restatement (Third) of Torts § 6 comment *c* (1998).

9. *Applicability to Food.* Courts have struggled with whether to impose strict liability on vendors of food when suit is based on an injury-producing substance in food. One group of cases has applied a "foreign-natural" test. Under this theory, strict liability is only applicable if the injury-causing substance is a piece of glass, wire, or other substance "foreign" to the food. If the substance is natural, like bone fragments in meat, pits in cherries, or shells in nuts, strict liability is not available and the plaintiff must prove negligence in the preparation of the food in order to recover. See, e.g., Mexicali Rose v. Superior Court, 1 Cal.4th 617, 4 Cal.Rptr.2d 145, 822 P.2d 1292 (1992) (no strict liability for throat injury from chicken bone in chicken enchilada). Another line of cases provides that regardless whether the injury-producing substance is natural or foreign, strict liability will lie if the consumer of the product would not

reasonably have expected to find the substance in the product. See, e.g., Jackson v. Nestle-Beich, Inc., 147 Ill.2d 408, 589 N.E.2d 547, 168 Ill.Dec. 147 (1992) (broken tooth from biting pecan shell from can of chocolate-covered pecan-caramel candy); Schafer v. JLC Food Systems, Inc., 695 N.W.2d 570 (Minn. 2005) (plaintiff could not identify object in pumpkin muffin that caused her throat injury); and Pinkham v. Cargill, Inc., 55 A.3d 1 (Maine 2012) (adopting "reasonable expectations" test in case of alleged bone fragments in turkey). Restatement (Third) of Torts: Products Liability § 2 comment *h* and § 7 (1998) (endorsing the latter position).

10. *Allergic Reaction.* An allergic reaction to a drug or product may occur because of an individual's unusual susceptibility to an ingredient. Since the product is reasonably fit for the ordinary user, it might be said that there is no defect and thus no recovery for any allergic reaction. Most jurisdictions have handled this as a failure to warn issue and imposed a duty on the manufacturer to warn of possible adverse reactions only if it knew or should have known of the risk. What if the allergy is common to a number of potential users? See, e.g., Braun v. Roux Distributing Co., 312 S.W.2d 758 (Mo.1958) (3–4%); Simeon v. Doe (Sweet Pepper Grill), 618 So.2d 848 (La.1993) (no strict liability against bar owner for serving oysters containing a bacteria common to Gulf region, which was not harmful to most people; plaintiff entitled to try to prove failure to warn if plaintiff could show that owner knew or had reason to know that individuals like plaintiff with a pre-existing liver or kidney disease could become ill from consuming oysters in which the bacteria was present). See note 7, page 812.

(C) WARNINGS DEFECT

Anderson v. Owens-Corning Fiberglas Corp.

Supreme Court of California, 1991.
53 Cal.3d 987, 810 P.2d 549, 281 Cal.Rptr. 528.

PANELLI, J.

In this case we consider the issue "whether a defendant in a products liability action based upon an alleged failure to warn of a risk of harm may present evidence of the state of the art, i.e., evidence that the particular risk was neither known nor knowable by the application of scientific knowledge available at the time of manufacture and/or distribution." (Order on grant of review, May 3, 1990.) As will appear, resolution of this evidentiary issue requires an examination of the failure-to-warn theory as an alternate and independent basis for imposing strict liability and a determination of whether knowledge, actual or constructive, is a component of strict liability on the failure-to-warn theory. It is manifest that, if knowledge or knowability is a component, state-of-the-art evidence is relevant and, subject to the normal rules of evidence, admissible.

We conclude that * * * the California courts, either expressly or by implication, have to date required knowledge, actual or constructive, of potential risk or danger before imposing strict liability for a failure to warn. The state of the art may be relevant to the question of knowability and, for that reason, should be admissible in that context. Exclusion of state-of-the-art evidence, when the basis of liability is a failure to warn, would make a manufacturer the virtual insurer of its product's safe use, a result that is not consonant with established principles underlying strict liability.

Defendants are or were manufacturers of products containing asbestos. Plaintiff Carl Anderson filed suit in 1984, alleging that he contracted asbestosis and other lung ailments through exposure to asbestos and asbestos products (i.e., preformed blocks, cloth and cloth tape, cement, and floor tiles) while working as an electrician at the Long Beach Naval Shipyard from 1941 to 1976. Plaintiff allegedly encountered asbestos while working in the vicinity of others who were removing and installing insulation products aboard ships. * * * [After a verdict for defendants, the trial court granted a new trial and the parties argued on appeal the admissibility of state of the art evidence in a failure to warn case.]

Defendants contend that, if knowledge or knowability is irrelevant in a failure-to-warn case, then a manufacturer's potential liability is absolute, rendering it the virtual insurer of the product's safe use. Plaintiff, on the other hand, argues that to impose the requirement of knowledge or knowability improperly infuses a negligence standard into strict liability in contravention of the principles set out in our decisions from Greenman v. Yuba Power Products, Inc. (1963) 59 Cal.2d 57 [27 Cal.Rptr. 697, 377 P.2d 897, 13 A.L.R.3d 1049] to Brown v. Superior Court (1988) 44 Cal.3d 1049 [245 Cal.Rptr. 412, 751 P.2d 470]. Plaintiff also urges that, although some courts have assumed that knowledge or knowability is a condition of strict liability for failure to warn, the issue has not been definitively resolved in this court.

Greenman v. Yuba Power Products, Inc., supra, 59 Cal.2d 57, established the doctrine of strict liability in California: "[a] manufacturer is strictly liable in tort when an article he places on the market, knowing that it is to be used without inspection for defects, proves to have a defect that causes injury to a human being." [C] "The purpose of such liability is to insure that the costs of injuries resulting from defective products are borne by the manufacturers that put such products on the market rather than by the injured persons who are powerless to protect themselves." [Cc] The strict liability doctrine achieves its goals by "reliev[ing] an injured plaintiff of many of the onerous evidentiary burdens inherent in a negligence cause of action." [Cc]

Strict liability, however, was never intended to make the manufacturer or distributor of a product its insurer. "From its inception, * * * strict liability has never been, and is not now, absolute liability. * * * [U]nder strict liability the manufacturer does not thereby become the insurer of the safety of the product's user." * * *

Whatever the ambiguity of *Brown*, we hereby adopt the requirement, as propounded by the Restatement Second of Torts and acknowledged by the lower courts of this state and the majority of jurisdictions, that knowledge or knowability is a component of strict liability for failure to warn.

One of the guiding principles of the strict liability doctrine was to relieve a plaintiff of the evidentiary burdens inherent in a negligence cause of action. [C] Indeed, it was the limitations of negligence theories that prompted the development and expansion of the doctrine. The proponents of the minority rule, including the Court of Appeal in this case, argue that the knowability requirement, and admission of state-of-the-art evidence, improperly infuse negligence concepts into strict liability cases by directing the trier of fact's attention to the conduct of the manufacturer or distributor rather than to the condition of the product. Similar claims have been made as to other aspects of strict liability, sometimes resulting in limitations on the doctrine and sometimes not. * * *

However, the claim that a particular component "rings of" or "sounds in" negligence has not precluded its acceptance in the context of strict liability. * * * [T]he doctrine of strict liability was a judicial creation and, in reaching our conclusion, we blended or accommodated the "theoretical and semantic distinctions between the twin principles of strict products liability and traditional negligence." [C] * * *

[T]he strict liability doctrine has incorporated some well-settled rules from the law of negligence and has survived judicial challenges asserting that such incorporation violates the fundamental principles of the doctrine. It may also be true that the "warning defect" theory is "rooted in negligence" to a greater extent than are the manufacturing—or design-defect theories. The "warning defect" relates to a failure extraneous to the product itself. Thus, while a manufacturing or design defect can be evaluated without reference to the conduct of the manufacturer [c], the giving of a warning cannot. The latter necessarily requires the communicating of something to someone. How can one warn of something that is unknowable? If every product that has no warning were defective per se and for that reason subject to strict liability, the mere fact of injury by an unlabelled product would automatically permit recovery. That is not, and has never been, the purpose and goal of the failure-to-warn theory of strict liability. Further, if a warning automatically precluded liability in every case, a manufacturer or distributor could easily escape liability with overly broad, and thus practically useless, warnings. [C]

We * * * reject the contention that every reference to a feature shared with theories of negligence can serve to defeat limitations on the doctrine of strict liability. Furthermore, despite its roots in negligence, failure to warn in strict liability differs markedly from failure to warn in the negligence context. Negligence law in a failure-to-warn case requires a plaintiff to prove that a manufacturer or distributor did not warn of a particular risk for reasons which fell below the acceptable standard of care, i.e., what a reasonably prudent manufacturer would have known and warned about. Strict liability is not concerned with the standard of due care or the reasonableness of a manufacturer's conduct. The rules of strict liability require a plaintiff to prove only that the defendant did not adequately warn of a particular risk that was known or knowable in light of the generally recognized and prevailing best scientific and medical knowledge available at the time of manufacture and distribution. Thus, in strict liability, as opposed to negligence, the reasonableness of the defendant's failure to warn is immaterial.

Stated another way, a reasonably prudent manufacturer might reasonably decide that the risk of harm was such as not to require a warning as, for example, if the manufacturer's own testing showed a result contrary to that of others in the scientific community. Such a manufacturer might escape liability under negligence principles. In contrast, under strict liability principles the manufacturer has no such leeway; the manufacturer is liable if it failed to give warning of dangers that were known to the scientific community at the time it manufactured or distributed the product. Whatever may be reasonable from the point of view of the manufacturer, the user of the product must be given the option either to refrain from using the product at all or to use it in such a way as to minimize the degree of danger. [C] "When, in a particular case, the risk qualitatively (e.g., of death or major disability) as well as quantitatively, on balance with the end sought to be achieved, is such as to call for a true choice judgment, medical or personal, the warning must be given. [Fn. omitted.]" [C] Thus, the fact that a manufacturer acted as a reasonably prudent manufacturer in deciding not to warn, while perhaps absolving the manufacturer of liability under the negligence theory, will not preclude liability under strict liability principles if the trier of fact concludes that, based on the information scientifically available to the manufacturer, the manufacturer's failure to warn rendered the product unsafe to its users.

The foregoing examination of the failure-to-warn theory of strict liability in California compels the conclusion that knowability is relevant to imposition of liability under that theory. Our conclusion not only accords with precedent but also with the considerations of policy that underlie the doctrine of strict liability.

We recognize that an important goal of strict liability is to spread the risks and costs of injury to those most able to bear them.[14] However, it was never the intention of the drafters of the doctrine to make the manufacturer or distributor the insurer of the safety of their products. It was never their intention to impose absolute liability.

Conclusion

Therefore, in answer to the question raised in our order granting review, a defendant in a strict products liability action based upon an alleged failure to warn of a risk of harm may present evidence of the state of the art, i.e., evidence that the particular risk was neither known nor knowable by the application of scientific knowledge available at the time of manufacture and/or distribution. The judgment of the

---

14 The suggestion that losses arising from unknowable risks and hazards should be spread among all users to the product, as are losses from predictable injuries or negligent conduct, is generally regarded as not feasible. Not the least of the problems is insurability. (See Henderson, Coping with Time Dimension in Products Liability (1981) 69 Cal.L.Rev. 919, 948–949; Wade, On the Effect in Product Liability of Knowledge Unavailable Prior to Marketing (1983) 58 N.Y.U.L.Rev. 734.) Dean Wade stated the dilemma, but provided no solution:

"How does one spread the potential loss of an unknowable hazard? How can insurance premiums be figured for this purpose? Indeed, will insurance be available at all? Spreading the loss is essentially a compensation device rather than a tort concept. Providing compensation should not be the sole basis for imposing tort liability, and this seems more emphatically so in the situation where the defendant is no more able to insure against unknown risks than is the plaintiff." (58 N.Y.U.L.Rev. at p. 755.)

Court of Appeal is affirmed with directions that the matter be remanded to the trial court for proceedings in accord with our decision herein.

[The concurring and dissenting opinions are omitted.]

NOTES AND QUESTIONS

1. Would you have predicted this decision from the jurisdiction that was the first to adopt strict liability less than thirty years before in *Greenman v. Yuba Power Products, Inc.*, page 781, 27 Cal.Rptr. 697, 377 P.2d 897?

2. Justice Mosk in a concurring and dissenting opinion to the principal case noted the convergence of strict liability and negligence theories of liability in failure-to-warn cases and urged the court to consider "the possibility of holding that failure-to-warn actions lie solely on a negligence theory." Is the distinction between the two worth preserving? Note that the approach of Restatement (Third) of Torts: Products Liability § 2 (1998) eliminates this potential confusion by organizing liability by type of alleged defect (manufacturing, design, warning) rather than by theory of recovery (negligence, breach of warranty, strict liability).

3. In warnings cases, most courts still apply a fault-based standard by requiring the plaintiff to show that the manufacturer knew or should have known of risks that injured plaintiff. See, e.g., Vassallo v. Baxter Healthcare Corp., 428 Mass. 1, 696 N.E.2d 909, 923 (1998) ("In recognition of the clear judicial trend regarding the duty to warn in products liability cases, and the principles stated in Restatement (Third) of Torts: Products Liability § 2(c) and comment *m*, we hereby revise our law to state that a defendant will not be held liable under an implied warranty of merchantability for failure to warn or provide instructions about risks that were not reasonably foreseeable at the time of sale or could not have been discovered by way of reasonable testing prior to marketing the product.").

4. Often a case involves claims based on both defective design and inadequate warnings. Should the fact that a product contains a good warning overcome the effect of a design problem—i.e., should a warning about a design hazard preclude liability, or should the manufacturer be required to eliminate the defective design condition? See, e.g., Uniroyal Goodrich Tire Co. v. Martinez, 977 S.W.2d 328 (Tex.1998) (warning on tire did not relieve manufacturer of liability for defective design); Rogers v. Ingersoll-Rand Co., 144 F.3d 841 (D.C.Cir.1998) (applying District of Columbia law) (warning is one factor to consider in risk-utility analysis, but warnings alone will not save a product from being unreasonably dangerous, citing Restatement (Third)); and Chow v. Reckitt & Colman, Inc., 17 N.Y.3d 29, 926 N.Y.S.2d 377, 950 N.E.2d 113 (2011) (even with adequate warning on container that was ignored by plaintiff, jury still may find utility of lye did not outweigh the risk inherent in marketing it as a drain cleaner). See Restatement (Third) of Torts: Products Liability § 2 comment *l* (1998) (warnings are not a substitute for a reasonably safe design).

5. *Obvious Dangers and Generally Known Risks.* Most jurisdictions have found no duty to warn of obvious dangers or of risks that are generally known. See e.g., Glittenberg v. Doughboy Recreational Indus., 441 Mich.

379, 491 N.W.2d 208 (1992) (diving into shallow water of above ground swimming pool) (collecting cases); American Tobacco Co. v. Grinnell, 951 S.W.2d 420 (Tex.1997) (defendant established that health risks of smoking cigarettes were commonly known when plaintiff began smoking, but did not establish that addictive quality of cigarettes was commonly known); Joseph E. Seagram & Sons, Inc. v. McGuire, 814 S.W.2d 385 (Tex.1991) (danger of developing alcoholism from prolonged and excessive consumption of alcoholic beverages is within ordinary knowledge common to the community); Mills v. Giant, 508 F.3d 11 (D.C. Cir. 2007) (applying District of Columbia law) (risk that milk will cause lactose intolerant consumers to experience temporary gas and related stomach discomfort is widely known). See also Restatement (Third) of Torts: Products Liability § 2(c) and comment *j* (1998) (no duty because warning will not reduce risk and may diminish significance of warnings about non-obvious risks).

6. In which of these situations is there a duty to warn or does the failure to warn make the product defective? Should a manufacturer of a perfume have to warn that the product is highly inflammable and should not be poured on a lit candle? See Moran v. Faberge, Inc., 273 Md. 538, 332 A.2d 11 (1975). Should a manufacturer of pointed darts have to warn that they might injure someone's eye? See Atkins v. Arlans Dept. Store of Norman, Inc., 522 P.2d 1020 (Okl.1974). Should the manufacturer of a Jeep CJ have to warn the driver not to ride with his bare foot outside of the vehicle while travelling on a highway? See Smith v. American Motors Sales Corp., 215 Ill.App.3d 951, 576 N.E.2d 146, 159 Ill.Dec. 477 (1991). Should the manufacturer of a pickup truck have to warn of the dangers involved in riding unrestrained in the cargo bed of the pickup truck? See Josue v. Isuzu Motors, 87 Haw. 413, 958 P.2d 535 (1998). Should the manufacturer of a machine that dispenses coffee and hot chocolate have to warn that the hot chocolate can cause second degree burns if spilled on skin? See McCroy v. Coastal Mart, Inc., 207 F.Supp.2d 1265 (D. Kan. 2002). Who decides? See Restatement (Third) of Torts: Products Liability § 2 comment *j* (1998) (stating that jury should decide if reasonable minds may differ as to whether risk is obvious or generally known).

7. *Allergic Reactions and Hypersensitivity.* If a product is dangerous only to hypersensitive persons, do manufacturers have a duty to provide warnings if they know or should know of such dangers? Most jurisdictions impose a duty to warn if the ingredient is one to which a substantial number of persons are allergic. Proving that a substantial number are affected is the plaintiff's burden. Just as in other determinations of duty, courts will consider the severity of the harm as a factor. See Restatement (Third) of Torts: Products Liability § 2 comment *k* (1998).

8. Why not always require a warning? They cost the manufacturer very little to provide in most circumstances. Might the proliferation of warnings in obvious danger situations dilute the impact of necessary warnings? See Restatement (Third) of Torts: Products Liability § 2 comment *j* (1998) (recognizing that requiring warnings of obvious or generally known risks could reduce efficacy of warnings generally). If the manufacturer chooses to supply a warning that the law would not have required, has the manufacturer exposed itself to additional liability by assuming a duty?

9. *Adequacy of Warning.* The determination whether the warning was adequate is usually left to the jury who in turn rely on expert testimony. Consider a manufacturer's warning that its adhesive was highly flammable, that it should be used only in a well-ventilated area, and that all open flames should be extinguished before use. Plaintiff was injured when the pilot light of a gas stove ignited fumes from the adhesive. Was the warning defective if it did not specifically mention "pilot lights" as examples of open flames? Cf. Burch v. Amsterdam Corp., 366 A.2d 1079 (D.C.1976).

10. *Sophisticated Users.* Should the extent of expertise of the known user be taken into account? See Garrett v. Nissen Corp., 84 N.M. 16, 498 P.2d 1359 (1972) (experienced trampoline user landed on his head and suffered a paralyzing spinal injury); Lawley v. Chevron Chem. Co., 720 So.2d 922 (Ala.1998) (plastic pipe manufacturer did not have duty to warn gas company or its employees because it was common knowledge among workers that failure to take certain precautions would greatly increase danger from static electricity build up); Johnson v. American Standard, Inc., 43 Cal.4th 56, 74 Cal.Rptr.3d 108, 179 P.3d 905 (2008) (manufacturer of HVAC system that contained refrigerant had no duty to warn trained and certified HVAC technician of risks associated with using heat on pipes to repair system because technician was sophisticated user); and Carrel v. National Cord & Braid Corp., 447 Mass. 431, 852 N.E.2d 100 (2006) (sophisticated user jury instruction was appropriate in case against bungee cord manufacturer whose cords had been sold through intermediary to Boy Scout organization that ran camp).

11. *Learned Intermediary Rule.* In cases involving pharmaceuticals, most courts hold that warnings and instructions should be provided to the physician, who is a "learned intermediary" between the drug company and the patient and the best person to understand the patient's needs and assess the risks and benefits of a particular course of treatment. Centocor, Inc. v. Hamilton, 372 S.W.3d 140 (Tex. 2012) (noting at least thirty-five states have adopted some form of the learned intermediary doctrine). The physician will then decide which warnings to pass on to the patient in light of the patient's particular condition and needs and using the physician's professional judgment. See Restatement (Third) of Torts: Products Liability § 6(d)(1) and comment *b* (1998). The doctrine has been extended from prescription drugs to prescription medical devices. See, for example, Rohde v. Smiths Medical, 165 P.3d 433 (Wyo. 2007) (implantable venous access device for administration of chemotherapy). Many jurisdictions do not apply the learned intermediary rule in situations where the manufacturer is aware that there will be no medical provider to provide learned advice or where the patient is expected to take an active role in the selection of the product. Cf. Mazur v. Merck & Co., 964 F.2d 1348 (3d Cir.1992) (applying Pennsylvania law) (in case involving MMR vaccination at public school, court noted "mass immunization exception" to learned intermediary rule where prescription drugs are dispensed without an individualized medical balancing of the risks and benefits to the user) and MacDonald v. Ortho Pharmaceutical Corp., 394 Mass. 131, 475 N.E.2d 65 (1985) (manufacturer of oral contraceptive must warn consumers directly because they often are actively involved in the decision to use the birth control pill and the physician usually has a relatively passive role). In those situations, the duty to warn is satisfied by a warning to the consumer rather than to the

learned intermediary. See also Restatement (Third) of Torts: Products Liability § 6(d)(2) and comments *b* and *e* (1998) (warning must be given directly to patient in situation where health-care provider's role is diminished by circumstances).

12. What if the manufacturer of a prescription drug that treats baldness, allergies, or erectile dysfunction, markets the product directly to the general public rather than to physicians? Should that affect the use of the learned intermediary doctrine? Perez v. Wyeth Labs. Inc., 161 N.J. 1, 734 A.2d 1245 (1999) (holding that learned intermediary doctrine does not apply when product is marketed directly to consumers because direct marketing belies the premises upon which the doctrine is based). Restatement (Third) of Torts: Products Liability § 6 comment *e* (1998) (leaving to developing law whether warnings must be given directly to patients in circumstances where governmental regulation mandates direct information or where manufacturer is advertising to public). What if the manufacturer of a generic drug had failed to update its warning but learned intermediary testified that he had read and relied on the warning provided by the brand manufacturer? Brinkley v. Pfizer Inc., 772 F.3d 1133 (8th Cir. 2014) (applying Arkansas law) (no causal link between failure to update label and patient's injury).

13. Should the "learned intermediary" doctrine be available for products used in the workplace? In other words, should the employer be responsible for warning and instructing its employees about use of the product because of the employer's control of the worksite, its knowledge of the hazards associated with products it has purchased, and its ability to instruct its employees on how to protect against those hazards? See, e.g., Adams v. Union Carbide Corp., 737 F.2d 1453 (6th Cir.1984), cert. denied, 469 U.S. 1062 (1984) (applying Ohio law) (chemical manufacturer satisfied duty by warning its buyer, plaintiff's employer). Sometimes the product is unpackaged or in a liquid or dust form, sold to the employer in bulk containers, so it would be difficult for the manufacturer to attach its warnings directly onto the product. See Hoffman v. Houghton Chemical Corp., 434 Mass. 624, 751 N.E.2d 848 (2001) (discussing the difference between the bulk supplier doctrine and sophisticated user defense in product liability failure to warn action brought by estates of workers killed in explosion at ink manufacturing plant allegedly caused by defendant's chemicals). What if the manufacturer relies upon a purchaser to warn its employees or others of the risks associated with the use of its product and the purchaser fails to so warn? Mississippi Valley Silica Co., Inc. v. Eastman, 92 So.2d 666 (Miss. 2012) (manufacturer's reliance must be a reasonable one). See Restatement (Third) of Torts: Products Liability § 2 comment *i* (1998) (no general rule whether manufacturer must warn users directly or can rely on intermediary to relay warning; standard is one of reasonableness under the circumstances).

14. *Presumption that Warning Will Be Read and Heeded.* In many jurisdictions plaintiff is entitled to a presumption that the user would have read and heeded an adequate warning. Compare Coffman v. Keene Corp., 133 N.J. 581, 628 A.2d 710 (1993) (collecting cases) (adopting presumption) with Rivera v. Philip Morris, Inc., 125 Nev. 18, 209 P.3d 271 (2009) (rejecting presumption and leaving burden of proof on plaintiff). This presumption, based on language in comment *j* to Restatement (Second) of

Torts § 402A (1965), assists the plaintiff in proving causation after the plaintiff has proved an inadequate warning. How might that presumption be rebutted? Suppose defendant introduces evidence in an asbestos case that plaintiff smoked despite warning labels on cigarettes? That plaintiff never wore a seatbelt? That plaintiff was indifferent to matters of personal health? Is this enough to rebut the presumption? Nelson v. Ford Motor Co., 150 F.3d 905 (8th Cir.1998) (applying Missouri law) (plaintiff admitted that he had not read instructions before using jack to change tire because he thought he already knew how to use it); Sharpe v. Bestop, Inc., 158 N.J. 329, 730 A.2d 285 (1999) (plaintiff, who had argued that he would have worn a seatbelt if the manufacturer of the soft top installed on his Jeep CJ had warned him to do so, admitted that he had not followed the warning by the Jeep manufacturer on the sun visor to wear seatbelts at all times). Defendant's evidence may be so strong that the court finds as a matter of law that an adequate warning would not have been heeded. Bachtel v. TASER Intern., Inc., 747 F.3d 965 (8th Cir. 2014) (applying Missouri law) (officer ignored warnings and training he was given in use of TASER). What if defendant demonstrates through empirical evidence that there is no common experience on which the courts can premise the presumption that the general public reads and heeds warnings? See Coffman v. Keene Corp., 133 N.J. 581, 628 A.2d 710 (1993) (recognizing validity of defendant's argument, bolstered by "a plethora of data and studies," but adopting the presumption anyway, based on public policy considerations).

15. *Post-Sale Duty to Warn.* In addition to the duty to provide warnings at the time a product is marketed, some courts impose a duty on the manufacturer to provide post-sale warnings about risks that are discovered or that develop after the sale. See Restatement (Third) of Torts: Products Liability § 10 and comments *a–i* (1998) (post-sale duty to warn determined by balancing factors, including obviousness of danger, its seriousness, the burden on the manufacturer to locate those who should be warned, and the likelihood of harm). Compare Jones v. Bowie Indus., Inc., 282 P.2d 316 (Alaska 2013) (adopting Restatement standard) and Brown v. Crown Equip. Corp., 960 A.2d 1188 (Me. 2008) (answering certified question) (declining to adopt Restatement (Third) formulation but finding a post-sale duty to warn in negligence law where, several years after sale of forklift, manufacturer became aware of new types of shelving that posed a risk of injury to forklift operators but did not warn plaintiff's employer of those risks) with Jablonski v. Ford Motor Co., 353 Ill.Dec. 327, 955 N.E.2d 1138 (2011) (finding no post-sale duty to warn if product was not defective at time of sale).

16. *Post-Sale Duty to Recall.* Very few courts have extended a manufacturer's post-sale obligations beyond a duty to take reasonable steps to provide warnings. Traditionally, product recall has been a function of federal administrative agencies rather than of the tort system. See Consumer Product Safety Act, 15 U.S.C. § 2064; National Traffic and Motor Vehicle Safety Act, 15 U.S.C. § 1414. Most courts that have considered the issue have declined to impose such a duty. See Ford Motor Co. v. Reese, 300 Ga.App. 82, 684 S.E.2d 279 (2009) and Ostendorf v. Clark Equipment Co., 122 S.W.3d 530 (Ky. 2003) (both collecting cases). See also Adams v. Genie Indus., Inc., 14 N.Y.3d 535, 903 N.Y.S.2d 318, 929 N.E.2d 380 (2010) (" We have never imposed a post-sale duty to recall or retrofit a product.") and Restatement (Third) of Torts: Products Liability § 11 (1998) (liability for

failure to act as reasonable person would in recalling product only if governmental directive requires or manufacturer voluntarily undertakes recall).

3. PROOF

Friedman v. General Motors Corp.

Supreme Court of Ohio, 1975.
43 Ohio St.2d 209, 72 Ohio Ops.2d 119, 331 N.E.2d 702.

[While waiting in line to purchase gas, Plaintiff Morton Friedman turned his engine off. When it was his turn, he turned the ignition key on his 17-month-old 1966 Oldsmobile, allegedly while the gearshift selector was in the "drive" position. The car "leaped forward, and so startled [him] that he could not regain control before the automobile ran wild * * *." Morton and three members of his family were injured in the crash.

Morton brought a claim against General Motors, the manufacturer of the vehicle. At the close of his case, the trial court granted General Motor's motion for a directed verdict on the ground that plaintiff had not proved that the vehicle was defective. The intermediate appellate court reversed the trial judge's decision and General Motors appealed to the Supreme Court of Ohio.]

PAUL W. BROWN, JUSTICE. The single issue presented by this appeal is whether the evidence introduced by the plaintiffs was of sufficient quality to overcome the defendant's motion for a directed verdict. The Court of Appeals, having thoroughly examined the entire record, concluded that reasonable minds could differ upon the evidence presented and reversed the judgment directing a verdict for the defendant. We affirm.

To sustain their allegation against General Motors, the plaintiffs were required to prove that the Oldsmobile Toronado, manufactured and sold by the defendant, was defective; that the defect existed at the time the product left the factory; and that the defect was the direct and proximate cause of the accident and injuries. [Cc]

A defect may be proven by circumstantial evidence, where a preponderance of that evidence establishes that the accident was caused by a defect and not other possibilities, although not all other possibilities need be eliminated. [Cc]

In our judgment, the evidence presented by the plaintiffs established a prima facie case of defect for which defendant General Motors would be liable.

From the testimony of [the retailer-dealer] and Morton Friedman, the jury could have found that the linkages and adjustments existing at the time of the accident were the original, factory set, adjustments, and that the defective condition, if the evidence established defect, was a defect created by the manufacturer and not by some third person after delivery.

Based upon the testimony of Morton Friedman, his wife, and his son, the jury might have concluded that the Toronado had always been started in Park, thus affording no opportunity for discovery of the alleged defect. Further, because the gear shift indicator and transmission had always operated properly, the jury might have inferred that when the gear shift indicator registered in Drive after the accident, it accurately reflected the position of the transmission.

From the testimony of eye witnesses to, and participants in, the accident, the jury might have concluded that, when Friedman started the Toronado at the Sohio station, it accelerated immediately upon ignition; that the automobile's transmission was therefore in a forward position; and that the transmission jammed, upon impact, in that same forward position.

From the testimony of [expert witnesses produced by plaintiff,] the jury could have found that, subsequent to the accident, the Toronado started with the gear shift indicator in Drive position. Based upon English's testimony, the jury might have concluded further that, upon ignition, the front wheels accelerated to a speed of 30 miles per hour in five seconds.

Finally, the record clearly established that the Toronado could not have started unless the contacts in the neutral start switch were in Neutral or Park position. Even though the transmission gears and gear shift indicator were in Drive, if the contacts in the neutral start switch were in Neutral or Park, the ignition key would start the automobile, and the front wheels would immediately rotate. In light of other facts presented, this possibility approaches probability.

Because the trial court granted the defendant's motion for a directed verdict, we must construe the evidence most strongly in favor of the plaintiffs, so as to determine if reasonable minds could differ. From the evidence heretofore summarized, we believe the jury might reasonably have concluded that the defendant was guilty of manufacturing a defective automobile, which directly and proximately caused the accident. For that reason, the judgment of the Court of Appeals is affirmed.

Judgment affirmed.

STERN, JUSTICE (dissenting). * * * In products liability cases, proof that a defect existed is often difficult and complex. Frequently the product in dispute will have been destroyed, beyond any possibility of analysis, or be so complex that a plaintiff would have a greater difficulty in determining the presence of a defect than would the manufacturer. In most cases, proof of the defect must necessarily be by circumstantial evidence and inference. No general rule can adequately apply to the wide range of such cases, each involving a different mixture of fact and inference, but fundamental to any such case is that some defect must be proved. As Prosser states, in Strict Liability to the Consumer in California, 18 Hastings L.J. 9, 52–54:

"The mere fact of an accident, as where an automobile goes into the ditch, does not make out a case that the product was defective; nor does the fact that it is found in a defective condition after the event, when it appears equally likely that it was caused by the accident itself. The addition of other facts, tending to show that the defect existed before the accident, may make out a case, and so may expert testimony. So likewise may proof that other similar products made by the defendant met with similar misfortunes, or the elimination of other causes by satisfactory evidence. In addition, there are some accidents, as where a beverage bottle explodes or even breaks while it is being handled normally, as to which there is human experience that they do not ordinarily occur without a defect. As in cases of res ipsa loquitur, the experience will give rise to the inference, and it may be sufficient to sustain the plaintiff's burden of proof."

Although plaintiff's evidence may be sufficient to permit an inference that something was wrong with the car, that alone is not sufficient to establish a defect, except perhaps in cases, analogous to res ipsa loquitur, in which ordinary human experience tells us that the event could not happen without a defect. The instant case is not such a case, for driver error, failure of some part, accidental or unwitting damage to the car, and other possibilities do provide other explanations. * * *

The particular defect that plaintiff alleges is that the indicator and the transmission gear linkages were both malaligned in a similar fashion, relative to the neutral starter switch, so that the car as manufactured could start in Drive rather than, as intended, only in Park and Neutral. There are various ways in which that particular fact could be proved, by means of several types of evidence. Keeton, Manufacturer's Liability: The Meaning of Defect in the Manufacture and Design of Products, 20 Syracuse L.Rev. 559, for example, suggests five ways by which the particular fact could be proved. [C]

(1) Plaintiff might introduce evidence by an expert based upon an examination of the product in question following the happening of the damaging event. Expert evidence would be direct evidence of an identifiable defect. In the instant case, two expert witnesses testified, and neither was able to point out an identifiable defect. Both testified that the car could be started in an indicated Drive position, but neither identified a cause for that based upon their examination. The only explanation, offered by one of the experts, was that the pointer was probably damaged.

(2) There may simply be evidence of a damaging event occurring in the course of or following use of a product, whether by the testimony of the user or otherwise. This may be sufficient in the case where, as a matter of common knowledge, a defect is the probable cause. As already indicated, the instant case is not one involving such common knowledge.

(3) A plaintiff may produce both evidence of a damaging event occurring in the course of or following the use of a product and expert evidence that the most likely probable cause was attributable to a defect in the product being used at the time. In the instant case, the only expert who was qualified to state such an opinion, the company expert called as a witness by the plaintiff, was not asked to state whether a defect was the probable cause, and in fact made clear in his testimony that he believed it probable that there was no defect and that the apparent starting of the car in Drive was probably caused by

damage from the accident to the indicator. He stated only that it was possible for various components to be malaligned as plaintiffs' theory required.

(4) In addition to evidence of an accident and the probable cause of such accident, evidence could be introduced to negate the existence of 'probable causes' not attributable to the maker. This type of evidence was not introduced in the instant case, except with respect to the issue of maintenance on the car in the 17 months after delivery.

(5) In some cases, the physical evidence of the actual condition of the product after the accident would be such that a layman could infer that it was defective. No such physical evidence was introduced in the instant case.

The sum of the evidence [in this case] is * * * only that something unusual happened in the car, and that a possible explanation of that happening is a defect. * * *

The same difficulty arises with regard to the issue of whether the claimed defect existed at the time the car left the hands of the defendant. * * * Here, the car was 17 months old, there was no expert testimony that the claimed defect was one which would probably have existed at the time the car was manufactured, and common experience does not permit any such inference. * * *

I agree with the trial judge that plaintiffs failed to submit sufficient evidence from which it could be inferred that a defect existed in the Friedman car at the time it left the hands of the defendant.

NOTES AND QUESTIONS

1. As the principal case reflects, problems relating to proof may be equally as important as legal theory in products liability actions. Plaintiff must be prepared to show:

A. That the product that injured plaintiff was, in fact, manufactured by defendant. Suppose an alleged manufacturer's name or trademark appeared on the product. Should that be sufficient? See Restatement (Third) of Torts: Products Liability § 14 (1998) (one who sells or distributes a product as its own that was manufactured by another is subject to same liability as if it were the product's manufacturer). Suppose plaintiff is injured by a common product that has no trademark. How does he prove it was manufactured by defendant? Suppose an entire industry produces allegedly defective products, but plaintiff cannot identify who made the one that injured him? See Sindell v. Abbott Laboratories, page 305 (DES). In those cases, the plaintiff was able to prove that a product caused his or her injury, but was unable to prove which manufacturer made the particular product involved. In other words, the plaintiff was unable to prove that any particular manufacturer was the cause in fact of the injury. Some courts have developed a variety of theories to get the plaintiff past the requirement of proving actual causation. Other courts have refused to take this step and have applied the traditional rule that the plaintiff must prove the particular manufacturer's product caused his or her injury. See note 1, page 308.

B. That the product was defective and plaintiff was injured as a result. The principal case and the cases in the prior section are illustrative of this problem. After a plane crash, should plaintiff have to eliminate the possibility of negligent flying? See Restatement (Third) of Torts: Products Liability § 3 (1998) (permitting inference of defect based on circumstantial evidence if incident of kind that ordinarily occurs as a result of product defect and other possible causes are negated).

C. That the defect was present in the product at the time of sale, not introduced by a distributor or installer or repairer. This was an issue in the Rix v. General Motors Corp. case at page 788.

2. *Effect of Government Safety Statute or Regulation*. Paralleling the doctrine of *negligence per se*, most jurisdictions provide that a *violation of* a product safety statute or regulation makes the product defective as a matter of law. Restatement (Third) of Torts: Products Liability § 4(a) (1998) (taking the position that such a violation will deem the product defective with respect to the risks sought to be reduced by the statute or regulation).

The mirror image of that situation is where the product *complied with* government safety standards. Most jurisdictions permit the defendant to introduce evidence of compliance with government standards on the question whether the manufacturer was negligent, or, in a strict liability case, whether the product was defective. Should the jury be permitted to "second guess" the governmental agency that set the standard? Most jurisdictions allow the jury to do just that. The manufacturer's compliance with government standards is evidence that the jury may consider, but is not bound by. A regulatory standard issued by the federal government may preempt (completely preclude the bringing of) state claims only in the limited circumstance that the court determines that Congress intended such preemption. See also Restatement (Third) of Torts: Products Liability § 4(b) (1998) (providing that compliance with an applicable product safety statute or administrative regulation can be considered in determining defect, but is not determinative). A few jurisdictions provide that compliance with government standards precludes imposition of punitive damages and some jurisdictions create a rebuttable presumption that the product was not defective. See, for example, Ariz. Rev. Stat. § 12–869 (no punitive damages if manufactured in accordance with government agency approval); Schultz v. Ford Motor Co., 857 N.E.2d 977 (Ind. 2006) (discussing jury instruction for Indiana statute that provides a rebuttable presumption that manufacturer was not negligent or product was not defective if manufacturer proves that it complied with applicable government safety regulations); and N.J. 2A–58C–4 (rebuttable presumption for FDA approved warnings). Michigan provides that the manufacturer or seller of a drug approved by FDA has an absolute defense to products liability actions if the drug and its labeling were in compliance with FDA's approval, unless plaintiff alleges fraud or bribery in obtaining the approval. Taylor v. Smithkline Beecham Corp., 468 Mich. 1, 658 N.W.2d 127 (2003).

3. Strictly speaking, since negligence is not in question, *res ipsa loquitur* has no application to a strict liability case, but the inferences that are the core of the doctrine also are applicable to strict liability. In other words, the fact that the product failed in a way that caused injury may, in a proper case, give rise to a permissible inference that it was defective and

that the defect existed when it left the hands of the defendant. See Myrlak v. Port Authority of New York and New Jersey, 157 N.J. 84, 723 A.2d 45 (1999) (discussing the doctrines of *res ipsa loquitur* for proof of negligence and indeterminate defect for strict liability in case involving the sudden collapse of chair in which worker was seated that had been placed in service only five weeks before); Allstate Ins. Co. v. Hamilton Beach/Proctor Silex, Inc., 473 F.3d 450 (2d Cir. 2007) (applying Vermont law) (plaintiff's expert traced origin of house fire to coffee maker that had just been removed from box and used for the first time on the day of the fire); and Hickerson v. Pride Mobility Prods. Corp., 470 F.3d 1252 (8th Cir. 2006) (applying Missouri law) (house fire and motorized wheelchair with rechargeable battery; product liability claim can be proved by inference from circumstantial evidence without proof of specific defect). As with *res ipsa loquitur* in negligence cases, plaintiff must provide sufficient evidence to exclude other causes of accident not attributable to product malfunction. Ramos v. Howard Industries, Inc., 10 N.Y.3d 218, 885 N.E.2d 176, 855 N.Y.S.2d 412 (2008) (although plaintiff not required to identify a specific defect in transformer that exploded, he did have to provide evidence that excluded other possible causes like improper installation). Generally, under those circumstances, plaintiff is not required to prove a specific defect. This is referred to in some jurisdictions as the "general defect" theory and in others as malfunction theory. White v. Mazda Motor of Am., Inc., 313 Conn. 610, 99 A.3d 1079 (2014) (malfunction theory must be pled in complaint to give manufacturer fair notice). See Restatement (Third) of Torts: Products Liability § 3 comment *c* (1998).

4. The most convincing evidence is a direct showing of what went wrong. Good advice to a client is to "save the pieces," but often the client disposes of them before he consults an attorney. If the product is destroyed in the accident, plaintiff will be left in the uncertain sphere of circumstantial proof.

5. *Rule on Excluding Evidence of Product Improvements to Prove Defect.* Should plaintiff be able to show that defendant redesigned or repaired his product after the accident occurred? What are the policy considerations? Most states do not permit the evidence of subsequent improvements to prove negligence or other culpable conduct. Should that exclusion also apply to actions based on strict liability? While a few courts will admit this evidence if the underlying theory of liability is strict liability rather than negligence, most preclude its introduction. See, for example, Federal Rule of Evidence 407 (evidence of subsequent remedial measures not admissible to prove negligence, defect, or need for warning but may be admitted to prove ownership, control or feasibility of precautionary measures) and Scott v. Dutton-Lainson Co., 774 N.W.2d 501 (Iowa 2009) (not admissible under Iowa evidence law in design defect case because negligence principles are used to determine design defect liability).

6. When a defect arises long after purchase, plaintiff is confronted with another facet of the problem of establishing that the product was defective or unreasonably unsafe. It has often been said that the seller does not warrant that a product will not eventually wear out. McNally v. Chrysler Motors Corp., 55 Misc.2d 128, 284 N.Y.S.2d 761 (Sup.Ct.1967) (proof that hydraulic brakes leaked in 1963 was no proof brakes were defective when sold in 1961).

4. DEFENSES

(A) PLAINTIFF'S CONDUCT

Daly v. General Motors Corp.

Supreme Court of California, 1978.
20 Cal.3d 725, 575 P.2d 1162, 144 Cal.Rptr. 380.

[Suit for death of the driver of an Opel automobile, thrown from his car in an accident, because of an alleged defect of the door latch. There was evidence that the driver did not use the shoulder harness system or lock the door, and that he was intoxicated. The case was submitted to the jury, which found for the defendant.]

RICHARDSON, JUSTICE. The most important of several problems which we consider is whether the principles of comparative negligence expressed by us in Li v. Yellow Cab Co. (1975) 13 Cal.3d 804, 119 Cal.Rptr. 858, 532 P.2d 1226, apply to actions founded on strict products liability. We will conclude that they do. * * *

From its inception * * * strict liability has never been, and is not now, absolute liability. As has been repeatedly expressed, under strict liability the manufacturer does not thereby become the insurer of the safety of the product's user. [Cc] On the contrary, the plaintiff's injury must have been caused by a "defect" in the product. Thus the manufacturer is not deemed responsible when injury results from an unforeseeable use of its product. [Cc] Furthermore, we have recognized that though most forms of contributory negligence do not constitute a defense to a strict products liability action, plaintiff's negligence is a complete defense when it comprises assumption of risk. [Cc] As will thus be seen, the concept of strict products liability was created and shaped judicially. In its evolution, the doctrinal encumbrances of contract and warranty, and the traditional elements of negligence, were stripped from the remedy, and a new tort emerged which extended liability for defective product design and manufacture beyond negligence but short of absolute liability.

In Li v. Yellow Cab Co., supra, 13 Cal.3d 804, 119 Cal.Rptr. 858, 532 P.2d 1226, we introduced the other doctrine with which we are concerned, comparative negligence. We examined the history of contributory negligence, the massive criticism directed at it because its presence in the slightest degree completely barred plaintiff's recovery, and the increasing defection from the doctrine. * * *

We stand now at the point of confluence of these two conceptual streams, having been greatly assisted by the thoughtful analysis of the parties and the valuable assistance of numerous amici curiae. We are by no means the first to consider the interaction of these two developing principles. As with the litigants before us, responsible and respected authorities have reached opposing conclusions stressing in various degrees the different considerations which we now examine.

Those counseling against the recognition of comparative fault principles in strict products liability cases vigorously stress, perhaps equally, not only the conceptual, but also the semantic difficulties incident to such a course. The task of merging the two concepts is said to be impossible, that "apples and oranges" cannot be compared, that "oil and water" do not mix, and that strict liability, which is not founded on negligence or fault, is inhospitable to comparative principles. The syllogism runs, contributory negligence was only a defense to negligence, comparative negligence only affects contributory negligence, therefore comparative negligence cannot be a defense to strict liability. [Cc] While fully recognizing the theoretical and semantic distinctions between the twin principles of strict products liability and traditional negligence, we think they can be blended or accommodated.

The inherent difficulty in the "apples and oranges" argument is its insistence on fixed and precise definitional treatment of legal concepts. In the evolving areas of both products liability and tort defenses, however, there has developed much conceptual overlapping and interweaving in order to attain substantial justice. The concept of strict liability itself, as we have noted, arose from dissatisfaction with the wooden formalisms of traditional tort and contract principles in order to protect the consumer of manufactured goods. Similarly, increasing social awareness of its harsh "all or nothing" consequences led us in *Li* to moderate the impact of traditional contributory negligence in order to accomplish a fairer and more balanced result. We acknowledged an intermixing of defenses of contributory negligence and assumption of risk and formally effected a type of merger. "As for assumption of risk, we have recognized in this state that this defense overlaps that of contributory negligence to some extent * * *." (*Li*, supra). * * *

We think, accordingly, the conclusion may fairly be drawn that the terms "comparative negligence," "contributory negligence" and "assumption of risk" do not, standing alone, lend themselves to the exact measurements of a micrometer-caliper, or to such precise definition as to divert us from otherwise strong and consistent countervailing policy considerations. Fixed semantic consistency at this point is less important than the attainment of a just and equitable result. The interweaving of concept and terminology in this area suggests a judicial posture that is flexible rather than doctrinaire. * * *

Given all of the foregoing, we are, in the wake of *Li,* disinclined to resolve the important issue before us by the simple expedient of matching linguistic labels which have evolved either for convenience or by custom. Rather, we consider it more useful to examine the foundational reasons underlying the creation of strict products liability in California to ascertain whether the purposes of the doctrine would be defeated or diluted by adoption of comparative principles. We imposed strict liability against the manufacturer and in favor of the user or consumer in order to relieve injured consumers "from *problems of proof* inherent in pursuing negligence * * * and warranty * * * remedies * * *." * * * As we have noted, we sought to place the burden of loss on manufacturers rather than "injured persons *who are powerless to protect themselves.*" [quoting Greenman v. Yuba Power Products, Inc., supra, page 781.] * * *

The foregoing goals, we think, will not be frustrated by the adoption of comparative principles. Plaintiffs will continue to be relieved of proving that the manufacturer or distributor was negligent in the production, design, or dissemination of the article in question. Defendant's liability for injuries caused by a defective product remains strict. The principle of protecting the defenseless is likewise preserved, for plaintiff's recovery will be reduced *only* to the extent that his own lack of reasonable care contributed to his injury. The cost of compensating the victim of a defective product, albeit proportionately reduced, remains on defendant manufacturer, and will, through him, be "spread among society." However, we do not permit plaintiff's own conduct relative to the product to escape unexamined, and as to that share of plaintiff's damages which flows from his own fault we discern no reason of policy why it should, following *Li,* be borne by others. Such a result would directly contravene the principle announced in *Li,* that loss should be assessed equitably in proportion to fault. * * *

A second objection to the application of comparative principles in strict products liability cases is that a manufacturer's incentive to produce safe products will thereby be reduced or removed. While we fully recognize this concern we think, for several reasons, that the problem is more shadow than substance. First, of course, the manufacturer cannot avoid its continuing liability for a defective product even when the plaintiff's own conduct has contributed to his injury. The manufacturer's liability, and therefore its incentive to avoid and correct product defects remains; its exposure will be lessened only to the extent that the trier finds that the victim's conduct contributed to his injury. Second, as a practical matter a manufacturer, in a particular case, cannot assume that the user of a defective product upon whom an injury is visited will be blameworthy. * * *

In passing, we note one important and felicitous result if we apply comparative principles to strict products liability. This arises from the fact that under present law when plaintiff sues in negligence his own contributory negligence, however denominated, may diminish but cannot wholly defeat his recovery. When he sues in strict products liability, however, his "assumption of risk" *completely bars* his recovery. Under *Li,* as we have noted, "assumption of risk" is merged into comparative principles. [Cc] The consequence is that after *Li* in a negligence action, plaintiff's conduct which amounts to "negligent" assumption of risk no longer defeats plaintiff's recovery. Identical conduct, however, in a strict liability case acts as a complete bar under rules heretofore applicable. Thus, strict products liability, which was developed to free injured consumers from the constraints imposed by traditional negligence and warranty theories, places a consumer plaintiff in a worse position than would be the case were his claim founded on simple negligence. This, in turn, rewards adroit pleading and selection of theories. The application of comparative principles to strict liability obviates this bizarre anomaly by treating alike the defenses to both negligence and strict products liability actions. In each instance the defense, if established, will reduce but not bar plaintiff's claim.

A third objection to the merger of strict liability and comparative fault focuses on the claim that, as a practical matter, triers of fact, particularly jurors, cannot assess, measure, or compare plaintiff's negligence with defendant's strict liability. We are unpersuaded by the argument and are convinced that jurors are able to undertake a fair apportionment of liability. * * *

We note that the majority of our sister states which have addressed the problem, either by statute or judicial decree, have extended comparative principles to strict products liability. * * *

Of the three decisions which have declined to apply comparative negligence to strict liability, two have noted their reliance on state comparative negligence statutes which are expressly confined to "negligence" actions. [Cc] At least three jurisdictions have applied comparative negligence statutes to strict liability actions, despite language arguably limiting the statute application to negligence. [Cc] Finally, one court has judicially extended a "pure" form of comparative fault to the traditional strict liability defense of "product misuse," despite the existence of a statutory scheme of "modified" comparative negligence. (General Motors Corp. v. Hopkins (Tex.1977) 548 S.W.2d 344, 351–352.)

Moreover, we are further encouraged in our decision herein by noting that the apparent majority of scholarly commentators has urged adoption of the rule which we announce herein. * * *

We find additional significance in the provisions of the proposed Uniform Comparative Fault Act (Act). * * * Our attention has been called to the action of the Conference [of Commissioners on Uniform State Laws] in August 1977, wherein it approved adoption of the Act by a vote of 40 states to 8 (California voting favorably). The Act is the distillation of approximately five years of discussion, analysis, and contribution by a special committee and a review committee of the Conference. We quote portions of [it] * * *.

Having examined the principal objections and finding them not insurmountable, and persuaded by logic, justice, and fundamental fairness, we conclude that a system of comparative fault should be and it is hereby extended to actions founded on strict products liability. In such cases the separate defense of "assumption of risk," to the extent that it is a form of contributory negligence, is abolished. While, as we have suggested, on the particular facts before us, the term "equitable apportionment of loss" is more accurately descriptive of the process, nonetheless, the term "comparative fault" has gained such wide acceptance by courts and in the literature that we adopt its use herein. * * *

It is readily apparent that the foregoing broad expressions of principle do not establish the duties of the jury with that fixed precision which appeals to minds trained in law and logic. Nonetheless, rather than attempt to anticipate every variant and nuance of circumstance and party that may invoke comparative principles in a strict products liability context, we deem it wiser to await a case-by-case evolution in the application of the broad principles herein expressed.

By extending and tailoring the comparative principles announced in *Li,* supra, to the doctrine of strict products liability, we believe that we move closer to the goal of the equitable allocation of legal responsibility for personal injuries. We do so by relying on what Professor Schwartz aptly terms a "predicate of fairness." In making liability more commensurate with fault we undermine neither the theories nor the policies of the strict liability rule. In *Li* we took "a first step in what we deem to be a proper and just direction, * * *." [C] We are convinced that the principles herein announced constitute the next appropriate and logical step in the same direction.

The judgment is reversed.

[TOBRINER, CLARK and MANUEL, JJ., concurred; CLARK, J. filed a concurring opinion; JEFFERSON, J. (assigned), concurred in part and dissented in part and filed an opinion in which BIRD, C.J., concurred; MOSK, J., filed a dissenting opinion.]

NOTES AND QUESTIONS

1. Most jurisdictions have followed the lead of the principal case and extended comparative negligence principles to strict liability products liability actions. A few jurisdictions, however, either have refused to recognize the doctrine of comparative fault in product liability cases or have limited it to situations in which plaintiff has assumed the risk. Shipler v. General Motors Corp., 271 Neb. 194, 710 N.W.2d 807 (2006) (interpreting comparative negligence statute to preclude use of comparative negligence defense in product liability actions based on strict liability).

2. A number of decisions are in accord with the Restatement (Second) of Torts, holding that a product user's negligence in failing to discover a defect in the product, or to guard against a possible defect, is not a defense. See, e.g., General Motors Corp. v. Sanchez, 997 S.W.2d 584 (Tex.1999) (consumer has no duty to discover or guard against a product defect, but other consumer conduct is subject to comparative responsibility); Star Furniture Co. v. Pulaski Furniture Co., 171 W.Va. 79, 297 S.E.2d 854 (1982) (accord). What is the reason for this rule? Is fault irrelevant under strict liability? Or is the rule based on the theory that a purchaser may assume the product is safe? The Restatement (Second) appeared simply to carry over the rule from the approach taken in the area of Abnormally Dangerous Activities. See pages 761–763. Restatement (Third) of Torts: Products Liability § 17 comment *d* (1998) does not limit the forms or categories of plaintiff's conduct that may be taken into account to apportion damages under comparative negligence principles.

3. *Assumption of Risk.* When plaintiff voluntarily confronts a known hazard, the Restatement (Second) and some courts would bar the claim. Ferraro v. Ford Motor Co., 423 Pa. 324, 223 A.2d 746 (1966) (driving truck with knowledge that wheels would lock on left turns and accelerator pedal tended to dislodge). See also Reott v. Asia Trend, Inc., 618 Pa. 228, 55 A.3d 1088 (2012) (explaining that in voluntary assumption of the risk, manufacturer must show that user knew of a defect and yet voluntarily and unreasonably proceeded to use the product whereas misuse of the product is use that was "unforeseeable or outrageous" but does not require user's knowledge of the defect).

Other courts would subject the plaintiff to the same fault apportionment as in comparative negligence. Bonds v. Snapper Power Equip. Co., 935 F.2d 985 (8th Cir.1991) (applying Arkansas law) (jury instructed to compare negligence of plaintiff in reaching under lawn mower that had tipped over); King v. Kayak Mfg. Corp., 182 W.Va. 276, 387 S.E.2d

511 (1989) (jury instructed to compare negligence of plaintiff in diving into above ground swimming pool). See pages 644–652 and Restatement (Third) of Torts: Products Liability § 17 comment *d* (1998). Which approach has the better basis in logic and policy?

Ford Motor Co. v. Matthews

Supreme Court of Mississippi, 1974.
291 So.2d 169.

RODGERS, PRESIDING JUSTICE. Earnest Matthews was killed as a result of being run over by his tractor and dragged underneath a disc attachment. It was alleged that Matthews was standing beside his tractor when he started it, and the tractor was in gear at the time. The Ford tractor in question was equipped with a starter safety switch which was designed to prevent the tractor from being started in gear. It is the position of the plaintiff-administratrix that the plunger connected with the safety switch was defective and allowed the tractor to be started in gear.

[The trial court, sitting without a jury, found for the plaintiff-administratrix and entered a judgment against Ford in the amount of $74,272.65. Ford appealed.]

The appellant Ford contends that Matthews' act of standing on the ground and starting the tractor while in gear was a misuse of the product. It is argued that such misuse is an absolute limitation on Ford's liability. The basic authority for this position is Comment (h), Restatement (Second) of Torts § 402A, which reads in part: "A product is not in a defective condition when it is safe for normal handling and consumption. If the injury results from abnormal handling * * * the seller is not liable." [Restatement (Second) of Torts § 402A, at 351.] Several cases are cited by appellant to illustrate this proposition. However, in the cases cited, the court either found that there was no defect and the accident was caused by a misuse, or even if there were a defect, it played no part in the causation of the accident. Here the situation is clearly distinguishable. It is apparent that the failure of the safety switch to prevent the tractor from cranking in gear was a cause of the accident. The failure of the decedent to make sure the tractor was in neutral before starting [, if that were true] may be characterized as the omission of a customary precaution, although there is no evidence that he was warned of this danger, or that he knew of the danger. Nevertheless, this was not such a misuse of the tractor as to relieve Ford from its strict liability for the defective condition of the tractor.

Although misuse of a product that causes an injury is normally a bar to strict liability, it is said that: " * * * [T]he manufacturer is not liable for injuries resulting from abnormal or unintended use of his product, *if such use was not reasonably foreseeable. The issue is one of foreseeability and misuse may be foreseeable."* (Emphasis added). 1 Frumer and Friedman, Products Liability § 15.01, at 351 (1973).

A recent law review writer expressed it in this manner: "In strict liability cases the same duty to foresee certain unintended uses has been recognized, and ordinarily the factual issue of the foreseeability of a particular use has been left to the jury." Noel, Defective Products:

Abnormal Use, Contributory Negligence, and Assumption of Risk, 25 Vand.L.Rev. 93, 97 (1972).

It is admitted that the tractor in question was designed to prevent its starting in gear. It is apparent that it could be foreseen by Ford that one day a tractor operator might carelessly crank the engine without first making certain that it was not in gear (as recommended in the owner's manual), especially if he were aware of the purpose of the safety switch system. In short, even if Matthews were guilty of negligence, such negligence was reasonably foreseeable by Ford and is not a bar to an action based on strict liability resulting from a defective tractor. * * *

[W]e are of the opinion that the total sum determined by the trial judge to be due was not excessive and the case should be affirmed.

Affirmed.

NOTES AND QUESTIONS

1. When plaintiff uses a product in a manner unintended by the manufacturer, courts often treat this conduct as a defense. On the other hand, could the matter be viewed more logically as an issue of duty or defect? What is the obligation of a manufacturer to produce a product that will withstand misuse? Evidence concerning a misuse or alteration of the product could be used to argue that there was no defect in the product (failure of prime facie case), that any defect in the product did not cause the plaintiff's injury (no causation), or that the plaintiff's unreasonable conduct in contributing to the cause of the accident should reduce the plaintiff's recovery (affirmative defense of comparative fault). See also Restatement (Third) of Torts: Products Liability § 2 comment *p* and § 15 comment *b* (1998) (product misuse, alteration, and modification, whether by third party or plaintiff, are relevant to issues of defect, causation, and comparative responsibility).

2. Whether regarded as a matter of defect or causation, the manufacturer is not subject to liability for an unforeseeable abnormal use of its product. Thus, a manufacturer was not liable in a case involving an above-ground swimming pool that was installed in the ground with a deck built around it, disguising the fact that the pool was shallow from the plaintiff who was injured while diving. Amatulli v. Delhi Construction Corp., 77 N.Y.2d 525, 571 N.E.2d 645, 569 N.Y.S.2d 337 (1991).

3. Before the advent of strict liability, there were many negligence cases holding that the seller is not liable when the injury is brought about by an abnormal use of the chattel. See, for example, McCready v. United Iron & Steel Co., 272 F.2d 700 (10th Cir.1959) (applying Oklahoma law) (casements for window frames used by worker as ladder) and Dubbs v. Zak Bros. Co., 38 Ohio App. 299, 175 N.E. 626 (1931) (shoes far too small for plaintiff's feet caused blisters). Even in cases based on negligence, there are some unusual uses of a product that the seller had to anticipate, and against which the seller was required to guard, at least to the extent of a warning. Phillips v. Ogle Aluminum Furniture, Inc., 106 Cal.App.2d 650, 235 P.2d 857 (1951) (standing on a chair).

4. As the principal case reflects, courts have shown a willingness to let juries determine whether an alleged product misuse was foreseeable.

Are the following misuses foreseeable and thus ones for which the product manufacturer could be liable? An 11-year-old boy rides a vacuum cleaner as if it were a toy car and his penis slips through an opening in the casing and is seriously injured by the fan blades. See Larue v. National Union Elec. Corp., 571 F.2d 51 (1st Cir.1978) (applying Maine law) (in upholding jury verdict, court noted that jury could have found that the intrusion of the boy's penis into the fan was within the class of dangers foreseeable to the manufacturer even though the precise circumstances of the accident might not have been). A two-year-old was being given a ride by her great-grandmother on a riding mower in a small wooden box attached to the mower's fender that the owner had made for her dog to ride in. When the mower hit a tree stump, the child was thrown off, the operator jumped off to pick up the child, and the riderless mower ran over the child's leg. See Erkson v. Sears, Roebuck & Co., 841 S.W.2d 207 (Mo.App.1992) (finding use of mower was not intended or foreseeable). A child is injured while playing with a disposable cigarette lighter. Compare Griggs v. BIC Corp., 981 F.2d 1429 (3d Cir.1992) (applying Pennsylvania law) (finding use by children of cigarette lighter was not intended or reasonably foreseeable) with Bean v. BIC Corp., 597 So.2d 1350 (Ala.1992) (finding jury question whether foreseeability of product misuse required manufacturer to design a child-proof cigarette lighter). While inhaling fumes from butane fuel cans to "get high," a man suffered cardiac arrest. Cf. Pavlik v. Lane Ltd., 135 F.3d 876 (3d Cir.1998) (applying Pennsylvania law) (discussing adequacy of warning and proximate cause in decision reversing summary judgment in favor of fuel distributor). A teenager is injured while attempting to ride the moving pendulum of an oil well pump. Payne v. Gardner, 56 So.3d 229 (La. 2011) (upholding summary judgment based on finding that riding the pumping unit was not a reasonably anticipated use). See Restatement (Third) of Torts: Products Liability § 2 comment *p* (1998) (noting that foreseeable product misuse must be considered in determining whether an alternative design should have been adopted).

5. Does it make any difference whether the "misuse" or "abnormal use" is that of the plaintiff or of a third party? In Jacobsen v. Ford Motor Co., 365 N.C. 468, 723 S.E.2d 753 (2012), the court found that manufacturer could raise affirmative defense of modification based on evidence that father had placed shoulder restraint behind his daughter's chest when he placed her in car). Can the conduct, whether plaintiff's or a third party's, be used by defendant to argue no defect, no causation, or an affirmative defense such as comparative negligence?

(B) PREEMPTION AND OTHER GOVERNMENT ACTIONS

In the past decade, the question whether a state product liability claim is preempted by a federal law has been litigated in the context of several different federal statutes. Supreme Court guidance on the issue has developed gradually. For example, in Medtronic, Inc. v. Lohr, 518 U.S. 470 (1996), Justice Breyer posed this hypothetical to illustrate why state common law claims, as well as state regulatory agency rules, might be preempted by Congress: "Imagine that, in respect to a particular hearing aid component, a federal MDA regulation requires a 2-inch wire, but a state agency regulation requires a 1-inch wire. If the federal law, embodied in the '2-inch' MDA regulation, pre-empts the state '1-inch' agency regulation, why would it not similarly pre-empt a state-law tort action that premises liability upon the defendant manufacturer's failure to use a 1-inch wire (say, an award by a jury persuaded by expert testimony that use of a more than 1-inch wire is negligent)? The effects of the state agency regulation and the state tort suit are identical. To distinguish between them for pre-emption purposes would grant greater power (to set state standards 'different from, or in addition to,' federal standards) to a single state jury than to state officials acting through state administrative or legislative lawmaking processes. Where Congress likely did not focus specifically upon the matter, . . . , I would not take it to have intended this anomalous result." Justice Breyer's concurring opinion, 518 U.S. 470, 504.

Express Preemption. In statutory schemes where Congress has made its intent to preempt state law clear, the courts have no choice. The state law is preempted by the federal law and, as a practical matter, the manufacturer need comply only with the federal statute and the regulations issued under it. What language creates the preemption? Even in cases of express preemption, the Court must decide which claims are preempted. See, for example, Cipollone v. Liggett Group, Inc., 505 U.S. 504 (1992) (in tobacco case, state tort law claims for failure to warn preempted, but claims for breach of express warranty would not be). What if the plaintiff can prove that the manufacturer misrepresented or withheld critical information from the agency charged with issuing the standard? Buckman Co. v. Plaintiffs' Legal Committee, 531 U.S. 341 (2001) (in products liability litigation involving medical device, state-law fraud-on-the-FDA claims are preempted because they inevitably would conflict with the FDA's responsibility to police fraud consistently with the FDA's other objectives).

Implied Preemption. Where Congress has not made its intent clear, the courts must determine whether preemption is warranted and which claims are to be preempted. This requires a case by case analysis of whether a claim is preempted, both because the statutes themselves vary and because some claims under a given statute may be preempted while others are not under what are sometimes called "frustration of purpose preemption" and "impossibility preemption." The National Highway Traffic Safety Administration promulgated standards that permitted automobile manufacturers to include either an airbag or an alternative form of passive restraints. Should a plaintiff be able to bring a crashworthiness claim based on the manufacturer's failure to include an airbag? Geier v. American Honda Motor Co., 529 U.S. 861 (2000) (finding claim preempted because otherwise NHTSA's purpose in encouraging development of various forms of passive restraints to ascertain which was more effective would be frustrated). NHTSA's vehicle safety standard for windows permits a manufacturer to use either tempered glass or laminated glass in side windows. Plaintiff's expert testified that laminated glass is more likely to keep a passenger's body from being ejected during an accident. Should plaintiff be able to bring a crashworthiness claim based on the manufacturer's use of tempered glass on the side windows? Compare Morgan v. Ford Motor Co., 224 W.Va. 62, 680 S.E.2d 77 (2009) (finding claim preempted because otherwise NHTSA's purpose in allowing both, motivated in part by safety concerns relating to increase in neck injuries with laminated glass, would be frustrated) with Lake v. Memphis Landsmen, LLC, 405 S.W.3d 47 (Tenn. 2013) (concluding that NHTSA merely narrowed the range of manufacturer's acceptable choices for glazing materials but did not intend to preclude states from imposing liability for the choice of tempered glass). Implied preemption also can occur when a tort claim would create a situation where it would be impossible for a defendant to comply both with what the plaintiff in the tort claim is arguing should have been done and with what the federal law requires.

See also the discussion of preemption in the area of prescription drugs and medical devices at note 3, page 838.

Government Contractor Defense. Suppose the government acts not to set standards or specifications but as a purchaser mandating a particular design? Should a manufacturer be liable for a design defect in a product manufactured to government specifications pursuant to a contract with the government? In Boyle v. United Technologies Corp., 487 U.S. 500 (1988), the family of a Navy pilot killed in a helicopter crash during a training exercise sued the helicopter manufacturer alleging a defect in the design of the escape hatch. The manufacturer urged the court to recognize a defense based on the fact that the government itself had made the design decision. The Supreme Court ruled that a contractor could be immune from liability for an allegedly defective product if the manufacturer could show that (1) the United States approved reasonably precise specifications, (2) the equipment conformed to those specifications, and (3) the contractor warned the United States about the dangers in the use of the equipment that were known to the contractor but not to the United States. The contractor has the burden of proving each of the elements of the defense. The defense is available even if the product was based on a design originally developed for another buyer as long as the United States approved the aspect of the design that the plaintiff claims is defective. Getz v. Boeing Co., 654 F.3d 852 (9th Cir. 2011) (finding preemption of state products liability claim brought by survivors of helicopter crash in Afghanistan involving Chinook helicopter initially developed for the RAF).

5. DEFENDANTS OTHER THAN PRINCIPAL MANUFACTURERS/HARM OTHER THAN PERSONAL INJURY

(A) OTHER SUPPLIERS OF CHATTELS

Peterson v. Lou Bachrodt Chevrolet Co.

Supreme Court of Illinois, 1975.
61 Ill.2d 17, 329 N.E.2d 785.

SCHAEFER, JUSTICE. On September 3, 1971, Maradean Peterson, age 11, and her brother, Mark Peterson, age 8, were struck by an automobile while they were walking home from school. Maradean Peterson died on the day of the accident, and Mark Peterson suffered severe injuries, including the amputation of one of his legs. The automobile involved in the accident was a used 1965 Chevrolet. James A. Peterson, administrator of the estate of Maradean Peterson, and Mark Peterson, by James A. Peterson, his father and next friend, brought this action against the driver of the used car, its owners, and the defendant involved in the appeal, Lou Bachrodt Chevrolet Company.

[The trial court dismissed two counts of the complaint and this ruling is before the supreme court on appeal.]

One of the challenged counts sought recovery for the wrongful death of the daughter, the other for the injuries to the son. Each count alleged that the defendant, Lou Bachrodt Chevrolet Company, had sold the 1965 Chevrolet on June 11, 1971, in the ordinary course of business, and that at the time the automobile left the defendant's control it was defective and not reasonably safe for driving and operation in that:

> "(a) A spring or springs in the left front wheel braking system was missing at the time of its sale;
>
> "(b) One of the left rear brake shoes was completely worn out at the time of the sale;
>
> "(c) A part of the cylinder braking system in the left rear wheel was missing at the time of the sale."

It was alleged that the injuries and death were a direct and proximate result of the defective conditions.

* * *

In Suvada v. White Motor Co. (1965), 32 Ill.2d 612, 210 N.E.2d 182, we held that a manufacturer is liable under a theory of strict liability if the plaintiffs "prove that their injury or damage resulted from a condition of the product, that the condition was an unreasonably dangerous one and that the condition existed at the time it left the manufacturer's control." [C] In Dunham v. Vaughan & Bushnell Mfg. Co. (1969), 42 Ill.2d 339, 247 N.E.2d 401, strict liability was imposed upon a wholesaler through whose warehouse the packaged product passed unopened. In that case we pointed out: "The strict liability of a retailer arises from his integral role in the overall producing and marketing enterprise and affords an additional incentive to safety." [C] The plaintiffs now ask that the same liability be imposed upon a defendant who is outside of the original producing and marketing chain. We decline to do so.

One of the basic grounds supporting the imposition of strict liability upon manufacturers is that losses should be borne by those "who have created the risk and reaped the profit by placing the product in the stream of commerce." [C] Imposition of liability upon wholesalers and retailers is justified on the ground that their position in the marketing process enables them to exert pressure on the manufacturer to enhance the safety of the product. [Cc] A wholesaler or retailer who neither creates nor assumes the risk is entitled to indemnity. [Cc] Therefore, although liability is imposed upon anyone who is engaged in the business of selling the product (Restatement (Second) of Torts § 402A (1965)), the loss will ordinarily be ultimately borne by the party that created the risk.

There is no allegation that the defects existed when the product left the control of the manufacturer. Nor is there any allegation that the defects were created by the used car dealer. [C] If strict liability is imposed upon the facts alleged here, the used car dealer would in effect become an insurer against defects which had come into existence after the chain of distribution was completed, and while the product was under the control of one or more consumers. See Restatement (Second) of Torts § 402A, comment *f*. * * *

The judgment of the Appellate Court, Second District, is reversed.

Appellate court reversed; circuit court affirmed.

GOLDENHERSH, JUSTICE (dissenting). I dissent. The rationale underlying the application of strict liability to a manufacturer is that losses should be borne by those "who have created the risk and reaped the profit by placing the product in the stream of commerce." (Suvada v. White Motor Co., [c]) In Dunham v. Vaughan & Bushnell Mfg. Co., [c], strict liability was made applicable to a wholesaler and retailer for the reason that "these considerations apply with equal compulsion to all elements in the distribution system." * * *

In Galluccio v. Hertz Corp., 1 Ill.App.3d 272, 274 N.E.2d 178, appeal denied, 49 Ill.2d 575, the appellate court held strict liability applicable to the lessor of a motor vehicle. No reason presents itself for not applying the principle to a used car dealer who places in the stream of commerce a vehicle rendered unreasonably dangerous by reason of a defect discoverable upon reasonable inspection.

I am aware of the argument made by defendant and *amici curiae* that many vehicles are sold "as is" and that the cost of repairs in some instances might exceed the value of the vehicle. These pleadings present no such issues, and assuming, *arguendo*, that in some future case they will arise, there is precedent for weighing the cost of remedying the dangerous condition against the nature and extent of the risk which it creates. [C]

I would affirm the judgment of the appellate court.

NOTES AND QUESTIONS

1. The Restatement (Second) of Torts § 402A and most courts in their initial decision implementing strict products liability on tort or warranty theories limited its reach to defendants "in the business of selling products." Part of the development of strict liability law in the next two decades focused on (1) which defendants fit within this definition and (2) whether other defendants also should be included.

2. *Used Products*. As the principal case reflects, many courts decline to impose strict liability on sellers of used products, but not all do. Compare Peterson v. Idaho First Nat'l Bank, 117 Idaho 724, 791 P.2d 1303 (1990) (declining to apply strict liability to sale of mobile home by bank that sold it after repossessing it) with Gaumer v. Rossville Truck and Tractor Co., Inc., 292 Kan. 749, 257 P.3d 292 (2011) (applying strict liability to sale of used farm equipment by dealer) (collecting cases). See also Restatement (Third) of Torts: Products Liability § 8 (1998) (focusing on consumer expectations to limit liability in cases involving used goods). If strict liability is applied, can

a seller of a used product avoid it by selling the product "as is" or "with all faults"? The jurisdictions are split on this issue. See Restatement (Third) of Torts: Products Liability § 8 comment *k* and Reporters' Notes thereto (1998) (collecting cases).

3. *Lessors and Bailors of Chattels.* See Restatement (Third) of Torts: Products Liability § 20 comment *c* (1998) (including lessors in defining an entity that "sells or otherwise distributes" a product).

4. *Retailers, Wholesalers, and Distributors.* Most jurisdictions extended strict liability to these sellers in the chain of distribution. As Justice Traynor indicated in Vandermark v. Ford Motor Co., 61 Cal.2d 256, 391 P.2d 168, 37 Cal.Rptr. 896 (1964): "In some cases the retailer may be the only member of the enterprise reasonably available to the injured plaintiff. In other cases, the retailer himself may play a substantial part in insuring that the product is safe or may be in a position to exert pressure on the manufacturer to that end." The Restatement (Third) of Torts: Products Liability § 20 (1998) includes all sellers in the chain of distribution, including retailers and wholesalers, in the same category as product manufacturers. The Uniform Product Liability Act would hold retailers and wholesalers liable only for their own acts of negligence unless the manufacturer was out of business or unreachable through judicial process. Approximately twenty-four state legislatures have enacted these types of provisions limiting the liability of non-manufacturer product sellers. See, e.g., Ga.Code Ann. § 51–1–11.1; Minn.Stat. § 544.41; and Wash.Rev.Code § 7.72.040. See Chapter 12, page 661.

5. *Occasional Sellers.* A seller who does not hold himself out as having any knowledge or skill in the commercial sense will not be subject to strict liability. See Restatement (Third) of Torts: Products Liability § 1 comment *c* (1998) (applies only to those engaged in the business of selling or otherwise distributing the type of product that injured the plaintiff); New Texas Auto Auction Service v. Gomez de Hernandez, 249 S.W.3d 400 (Tex. 2008) (auctioneer not subject to strict liability); and Jaramillo v. Weyerhaeuser Co., 12 N.Y.3d 181, 906 N.E.2d 387, 878 N.Y.S.2d 659 (2009) (answering certified question) (company that periodically disposed of equipment it no longer needed by sale to other companies was not strictly liable as a product seller to employee of buyer who was injured by equipment).

6. *Owners.* The owner of a product may be subject to liability for negligence, but not for strict liability since the owner receives products from the stream of commerce; the owner does not place the product in the stream of commerce merely by offering it to a guest. Burnett v. Covell, 191 P.3d 985 (Ala. 2008) (plaintiff was visitor to law office who was injured when the chair that he was offered by attorney who owned it collapsed).

7. *Manufacturer of Component Parts or Raw Materials.* The maker of a component part not subject to further processing or substantial change in the manufacturing process is likely to be subject to strict liability if there is a defect in that part or material. The component maker or raw material supplier also may be liable if he substantially participates in integrating the component or raw material into a defective product. See Buonanno v. Colmar Belting Co., Inc., 733 A.2d 712 (R.I.1999) and Restatement (Third) of Torts: Products Liability § 5(b)(1) (1998).

8. *Corporate Acquisitions/Successor Liability.* When one company acquires another, how should this affect liability for defective products? Should the acquiring corporation be subject to claims based on products manufactured and sold before the takeover? Generally, the successor corporation is liable only if it agreed to assume liability, the transfer was a fraudulent one, the two corporations merged, or the successor is essentially a continuation of the original company. See Restatement (Third) of Torts: Products Liability § 12 (1998). Some courts have gone further, holding a corporation that acquired substantially all of the assets of another corporation liable if it continues the product line. See, for example, Mettinger v. Glove Slicing Mach. Co., Inc., 153 N.J. 371, 709 A.2d 779 (1998).

Wyeth, Inc. v. Weeks

Supreme Court of Alabama, 2014.
159 So.3d 649.

[Danny Weeks alleges that he suffered injury as a result of his long-term use of the prescription drug metoclopramide to treat his gastric acid reflux and that the drug's warning label was inadequate to inform his doctor of the risks of long-term use. He and his wife sued the drug companies that made the brand-name version of the drug, Reglan®, even though the medication that Danny took was not made by defendants but by generic manufacturers. Defendants moved to dismiss or, in the alternative, for summary judgment, arguing that because plaintiff admitted that defendants did not make the drugs he took that defendants owed him no duty and are entitled to judgment as a matter of law. The federal trial court for the Middle District of Alabama certified to the Alabama Supreme Court the following question:

"Under Alabama law, may a drug company be held liable for fraud or misrepresentation (by misstatement or omission), based on statements it made in connection with the manufacture or distribution of a brand-name drug, by a plaintiff claiming physical injury from a generic drug manufactured and distributed by a different company?"]

BOLIN, J.

* * * At the outset, we limit the question posed to manufacturers of prescription drugs and not to any distributors thereof. The Weekses' complaint alleges that three brand-name manufacturers, Wyeth, Pfizer, Inc., and Schwarz Pharma, Inc. (hereinafter collectively referred to as "Wyeth"), falsely and deceptively misrepresented or knowingly suppressed facts about Reglan or metoclopramide such that Danny Weeks's physician, when he prescribed the drug to Danny, was materially misinformed and misled about the likelihood that the drug would cause the movement disorder tardive dyskinesia and related movement disorders. The Weekses contend that Wyeth had a duty to warn Danny's physician about the risks associated with the long-term use of metoclopramide and that the Weekses, as third parties, have a right to hold Wyeth liable for the alleged breach of that duty. * * *

Wyeth * * * argues that this Court has never extended third-party-fraud liability to a defendant who did not manufacture the product about which the plaintiff is complaining. We again note that prescription medication is unlike other consumer products. Unlike "construction machinery," "lawnmowers," or "perfume," which are "used to make work easier or to provide pleasure," a prescription drug "may be necessary to alleviate pain and suffering or to sustain life." [C] Prescription medication is heavily regulated by the FDA. It can be obtained only through a health-care provider who can make a determination as to the benefits and risks of a drug for a particular patient. Also, the Weekses' claims are not based on the manufacturing of the product but instead allege that the label—drafted by the brand-name manufacturer and required by federal law to be replicated verbatim on the generic version of the medication—failed to warn. Moreover, the brand-name manufacturer is under a continuing duty to supply the FDA with postmarketing reports of serious injury and can strengthen its warnings on its own accord. [C] In contrast, a generic manufacturer's label must be the same as the brand-name manufacturer's label, and the generic manufacturer cannot unilaterally change its warning label. * * *

A prescription-drug manufacturer fulfills its duty to warn the ultimate users of the risks of its product by providing adequate warnings to the learned intermediaries who prescribe the drug. Once that duty is fulfilled, the manufacturer has no further duty to warn the patient directly. However, if the warning to the learned intermediary is inadequate or misrepresents the risk, the manufacturer remains liable for the injuries sustained by the patient. The patient must show that the manufacturer failed to warn the physician of a risk not otherwise known to the physician and that the failure to warn was the actual and proximate cause of the patient's injury. In short, the patient must show that, but for the false representation made in the warning, the prescribing physician would not have prescribed the medication to his patient.

Wyeth argues that there is no relationship between Wyeth and the Weekses so as to create a duty on Wyeth's part to adequately warn the Weekses and that the simple fact that it may be foreseeable that a physician would rely on Wyeth's representations in its warning label in determining whether a prescription drug originally manufactured by Wyeth was appropriate for a particular patient did not create a relationship between Wyeth and the patient. * * *

Wyeth's argument completely ignores the nature of prescription medication. The Weekses cannot obtain Reglan or any other prescription medication directly from a prescription-drug manufacturer. The only way for a consumer to obtain a prescription medication is for a physician or other medical professional authorized to write prescriptions (i.e., a learned intermediary) to prescribe the medication to his or her patient. This Court has adopted the learned-intermediary doctrine, which provides that a prescription-drug manufacturer fulfills its duty to warn users of the risk associated with its product by providing adequate warnings to the learned intermediaries who prescribe the drug and that, once that duty is fulfilled, the manufacturer owes no further duty to the ultimate consumer. When the warning to the prescribing health-care professional is inadequate, however, the manufacturer is directly liable to the patient for damage resulting from that failure. The substitution of a generic drug for its brand-name equivalent is not fatal to the Weekses' claim because the Weekses are not claiming that the drug Danny ingested was defective; instead, the Weekses' claim is that Wyeth fraudulently misrepresented or suppressed information concerning the way the drug was to be taken and, as discussed, the FDA mandates that the warning on a generic-drug label be the same as the warning on the brand-name-drug label and only the brand-name manufacturer may make unilateral changes to the label. * * *

We answer the certified question as follows: Under Alabama law, a brand-name-drug company may be held liable for fraud or misrepresentation (by misstatement or omission), based on statements it made in connection with the manufacture of a brand-name prescription drug, by a plaintiff claiming physical injury caused by a generic drug manufactured by a different company. Prescription drugs, unlike other consumer products, are highly regulated by the FDA. Before a prescription drug may be sold to a consumer, a physician or other qualified health-care provider must write a prescription. The United States Supreme Court in *Wyeth v. Levine*, [555 U.S. 555, 578 (2009)] recognized that Congress did not preempt common-law tort suits, and it appears that the FDA traditionally regarded state law as a complementary form of drug regulation: The FDA has limited resources to monitor the approximately 11,000 drugs on the market, and manufacturers have superior access to information about their drugs, especially in the postmarketing phase as new risks emerge; state-law tort suits uncover unknown drug hazards and provide incentives for drug manufacturers to disclose safety risks promptly and serve a distinct compensatory function that may motivate injured persons to come forward with information. * * *

In the context of inadequate warnings by the brand-name manufacturer placed on a prescription drug manufactured by a generic manufacturer, it is not fundamentally unfair to hold the brand-name manufacturer liable for warnings on a product it did not produce because the manufacturing process is irrelevant to misrepresentation theories based, not on manufacturing defects in the product itself, but on information and warning deficiencies, when those alleged misrepresentations were drafted by the brand-name manufacturer and merely repeated, as allowed by the FDA, by the generic manufacturer.

In answering the question of law presented to us by the federal court, we emphasize the following: We are not turning products-liability law (or tort law for that matter) on its head, nor are we creating a new tort of "innovator liability" as has been suggested. Instead, we are answering a question of law involving a product that, unlike any other product on the market, has unprecedented federal regulation. Nothing in this opinion suggests that a plaintiff can sue Black & Decker for injuries caused by a power tool manufactured by Skil based on labeling or otherwise. The unique relationship between brand-name and generic drugs as a result of federal law and FDA regulations, combined with the learned-intermediary doctrine and the fact that representations regarding prescription drugs are made not to the plaintiff but to a third party, create the sui generis context in which we find prescription medication. * * *

Question Answered.

NOTES AND QUESTIONS

1. The principal case, which permitted liability against one product manufacturer for harms allegedly caused by another manufacturer's product, is a minority approach. See also Conte v. Wyeth, Inc., 168 Cal.App.4th 89 (Cal. App. 2008). Other courts examining this issue in the pharmaceutical context have rejected as unsound so-called "innovator liability." Huck v. Wyeth, Inc., 850 N.W.2d 353 (Iowa 2014). See also Schwartz et al., Warning: Shifting Liability to Manufacturers of Brand-Name Medicines When the Harm was Allegedly Caused by Generic Drugs Has Severe Side Effects, 80 Fordham L. Rev. 1835 (2013). Less than a year after the *Weeks* decision, the Alabama legislature passed a law the purpose of which was to overrule *Weeks*. Ala. Code 1975 § 6–5–530. Should state legislatures overrule state Supreme Court cases? When and why?

2. Product liability involving pharmaceuticals introduces a number of important public policy considerations. Does subjecting a brand-name drug manufacturer to liability for harm caused to someone taking a generic version of the drug result in safer drugs for the public or does this liability rule deter companies from investing in the development of new, more effective drugs? Is it fair to subject any manufacturer to liability for harms caused by another manufacturer's product?

3. Pharmaceutical cases present an interesting dynamic in product liability for another reason: preemption. (See pages 829 to 831.) Because the Food and Drug Administration (FDA) comprehensively regulates both the approval and warnings of prescription drugs and medical devices, the issue has arisen whether a plaintiff may assert an inadequate warning claim related to an FDA-approved drug. In 2009, the U.S. Supreme Court answered this question in Wyeth v. Levine, 555 U.S. 555 (2009), cited in the principal case, finding that Congress's delegation to FDA of drug labeling oversight did not preempt state product liability claims for failure to warn about a drug's risks. In 2011, however, the Court reached the opposite conclusion with respect to FDA-approved generic drugs such as the one plaintiff took in the principal case. See PLIVA, Inc. v. Mensing, 131 S. Ct. 2567 (2011) (holding that federal labeling law for generic drugs generally preempts a plaintiff's failure to warn claim because generic drug manufacturers must use the same warning label that was approved by the FDA for the branded drug). The Supreme Court later made clear that the preemption defense for generic drugs extended to claims based on defective design. Mutual Pharm. Co. v. Bartlett, 133 S. Ct. 2466 (2013). These decisions followed a 2008 ruling by the Court that failure to warn claims related to FDA-approved medical devices were similarly preempted. See Riegel v. Medtronic, Inc., 552 U.S. 312 (2008). Thus, the current law governing pharmaceutical product liability is that failure to warn claims against a brand-name drug manufacturer are allowed, but claims against a generic drug manufacturer or the manufacturer of an FDA-approved medical device generally are barred. Do you see why Mr. Weeks sued Wyeth instead of the manufacturer of the generic drugs he took? Do you believe this to be a sensible approach or do the distinctions in Congress's

liability regime, as interpreted by the Supreme Court, appear somewhat arbitrary?

(B) SERVICES

Hector v. Cedars-Sinai Medical Ctr.

Court of Appeals of California, 1986.
180 Cal.App.3d 493, 225 Cal.Rptr. 595.

SPENCER, J.

Plaintiff Frances J. Hector appeals from an order dismissing her second and third causes of action against defendant following the granting of defendant's motion for partial summary judgment.

Plaintiff filed a complaint against Cedars-Sinai Medical Center (Cedars-Sinai) and American Technology, Inc., alleging personal injury resulting from the implantation of a defective pacemaker. The pacemaker was manufactured by American Technology, Inc., and implanted at Cedars-Sinai by plaintiff's physician, Dr. Eugene Kompaniez.

The complaint contained three causes of action: negligence, strict liability and breach of warranty. Cedars-Sinai moved for partial summary judgment on plaintiff's second and third causes of action, strict liability and breach of warranty, alleging as a matter of law there were no triable issues of fact. The trial court granted the motion. Plaintiff subsequently requested and received dismissal of the first cause of action, negligence, against Cedars-Sinai. The trial court then issued its order dismissing the second and third causes of action.

Plaintiff contends the trial court erred in finding Cedars-Sinai was exempt from the application of the strict products liability doctrine. For the reasons set forth below, we disagree. * * *

On appeal, the court first recalls the origin of the application of strict liability in California: Greenman v. Yuba Power Products, Inc. (1963) 59 Cal.2d 57 [27 Cal.Rptr. 697, 377 P.2d 897] held that " '[a] manufacturer is strictly liable in tort when an article he places on the market, knowing that it is to be used without inspection for defects, proves to have a defect that causes injury to a human being.' " [C] The court then notes the expansion of the doctrine to impose strict liability on others in the chain of distribution, not merely manufacturers. [C] For example, Vandermark v. Ford Motor Co. (1964) 61 Cal.2d 256 [37 Cal.Rptr. 896, 391 P.2d 168] extends strict liability to retailers since they are "engaged in the business of distributing goods to the public" and "are an integral part of the overall producing and marketing enterprise that should bear the cost of injuries resulting from defective products." * * *

After surveying the cases which expand the scope of strict liability, the Silverhart [v. Mount Zion Hosp., 20 Cal.App.3d 1022, 98 Cal.Rptr. 187 (1971)] court observes: "A significant common element running through the cases is that each of the defendants against whom the standard of strict liability has been applied played an integral and vital part in the overall production or marketing enterprise. At the very least the defendant in each case was a link in the chain of getting goods from the manufacturer to the ultimate user or consumer. * * * [para.] Plaintiff seeks to extend the doctrine of strict liability to a hospital that furnishes, in connection with the care and treatment of a patient, a product that proves to have a defect that causes injury to the patient. The theory upon which she seeks to predicate such liability is that the hospital is a 'supplier' of such product and, therefore, should be subject to the same standard of liability as any other supplier of articles or products." [C]

The court then examines two key cases in which strict liability has not been applied to the medical profession: "In Magrine v. Krasnica [(1967)] 94 N.J.Super. 228 [227 A.2d 539], affirmed 100 N.J.Super. 223 [241 A.2d 637], and 53 N.J. 259 [250 A.2d 129], the court declined to apply the doctrine of strict liability to a dentist whose drill, with a latent defect, broke while he was working on his patient, causing injury to the patient. The court stated, 'Of * * * meaningful significance is a recognition that the essence of the transaction between the retail seller and the consumer relates to the article sold. The seller is in the business of supplying the product to the consumer. It is that, and that alone, for which he is paid. A dentist or a physician offers, and is paid for, his professional services and skill. That is the essence of the relationship between him and his patient.' [C]

The foregoing statement in Magrine was cited with approval in Carmichael v. Reitz [(1971)] 17 Cal.App.3d 958, 979. * * * In Carmichael it was held that the doctrine of strict liability did not apply to a doctor who prescribed a drug which produced untoward results in a patient. In that case we find the following rationale: '[There] is a difference in status or classification between those upon whom the courts have heretofore imposed the doctrine of strict liability and a physician who prescribes an ethical drug to achieve a cure of the disorders for which the patient has sought his professional services. The former act basically as mere conduits to the distribution of the product to the consumer; the latter sells or furnishes his services as a healer of illnesses. The physician's services depend upon his skill and judgment derived from his specialized training, knowledge, experience, and skill. The physician prescribes the medicine in the course of chemotherapy only as a chemical aid or instrument to achieve a cure. A doctor diagnosing and treating a patient normally is not selling either a product or insurance. One of the requisites which the Restatement prescribes for the imposition of strict liability is that 'the seller is engaged in the business of selling such product.' " [Cc]

The Silverhart court was "persuaded that the rationale of Magrine and Carmichael applies with equal force to a hospital in the exercise of its primary function which is to provide medical services. A hospital is not ordinarily engaged in the business of selling any of the products or equipment it uses in providing such services. The essence of the relationship between a hospital and its patients does not relate essentially to any product or piece of equipment it uses but to the professional services it provides." [C] The court notes, however, that "this principle does not apply where the hospital is engaged in activities not integrally related to its primary function of providing medical services, such as the situation where the hospital operates a gift shop which sells a defective product." [C] The court concludes the rule of strict liability cannot be applied to defendant hospital. * * *

Cases dealing with blood transfusions and products reflect the same considerations when declining to apply strict liability to hospitals, although there is additional statutory justification for treating these items as services rather than sales. Shepard v. Alexian Brothers Hosp. (1973) 33 Cal.App.3d 606 [109 Cal.Rptr. 132] states: "It needs no extended discussion to perceive that a hospital is primarily devoted to the care and healing of the sick. The supplying of blood by the hospital is entirely subordinate to its paramount function of furnishing trained personnel and specialized facilities in an endeavor to restore the patient's health. Providing medicine or supplying blood is simply a chemical aid or instrument utilized to accomplish the objective of cure or treatment. The patient who enters a hospital goes there not to buy medicine or pills, not to purchase bandages, iodine, serum or blood, but to obtain a course of treatment. [Cc] It is also obvious that in the normal commercial transaction contemplated in the strict liability cases the essence of the transaction relates solely to the article sold, the seller is in the business of supplying the product to the consumer, and it is that, and that alone, for which he is paid. [C] The foregoing marked distinctions compel the conclusion that a hospital is not engaged in the business of distributing blood to the public and does not put the blood as a product on the market in order to profit therefrom." [C]

Turning to the facts in the instant case, Howard Allen, M.D., Director of the Cedars-Sinai Cardiac Noninvasive Laboratory states in his declaration that the specific model and type of pacemaker to be implanted in a patient is specified by the surgeon. The surgeon ordinarily contacts the manufacturer's representative to provide for delivery of the pacemaker to the operating room when it is to be implanted. The pacemaker may be sterilized and ready for implantation when it is delivered to the hospital; the manufacturer's representative or the surgeon may pretest the pacemaker, but the hospital employees do not.

Dr. Allen indicated Cedars-Sinai does not routinely stock pacemakers, nor is it in the business of recommending, selling, distributing or testing pacemakers. The treatment provided by Cedars-Sinai in relation to implantation of pacemakers includes pre-and post-operative care, nursing care, a surgical operating room and technicians. * * *

The essence of the relationship between hospital and patient is the provision of professional medical services necessary to effect the implantation of the pacemaker—the patient does not enter the hospital merely to purchase a pacemaker but to obtain a course of treatment which includes implantation of a pacemaker. [Cc] As a provider of services rather than a seller of a product, the hospital is not subject to strict liability for a defective product provided to the patient during the course of his or her treatment. * * *

Unlike the products sold in a hospital gift shop, for which the hospital is strictly liable * * *, the pacemaker provided to the patient is necessary to the patient's medical treatment. While the hospital itself does not use its own medical skill or knowledge in providing its services in connection with the provision of the pacemaker for the patient, the hospital still is engaged in the process of providing everything necessary to furnish the patient with a course of treatment. In this regard, the hospital's actions concerning the provision of the pacemaker are "integrally related to its primary function of providing medical services." * * *

Of equal importance, the policy considerations behind the imposition of strict product liability would not be served by its application here. Strict liability is imposed "to insure that the cost of injuries resulting from defective products are borne by the manufacturers who put such products on the market rather than by the injured persons who are powerless to protect themselves." [Cc] Further, since the defendant profits from the sale of the products, it is in a good strategic position to protect itself by inquiring about or testing the products, promoting safety through pressure on the manufacturer, selling another product which is not defective, or insuring itself and distributing the risk of injury among the public as a cost of doing business. [Cc]

Plaintiff asserts the imposition of strict liability will result in lower costs for health care, since the hospital no longer will be able to charge high fees for processing the paperwork for pacemakers ordered by physicians for their patients. But because the overall charges to the patients must equal the overall expenditures by the hospital, any decrease in the charge on pacemakers necessarily would mean an increase in another charge, and there would be no overall decrease in the cost to the consumer of health care. Moreover, if a hospital is to be considered a seller who places a product on the market and who must bear the cost of injuries resulting from defective products, it will have to insure itself and distribute the risk of injury among the public as a cost of doing business. This necessarily will result in higher costs for health care.

In the instant case, the hospital does not select the pacemaker for the patient, but the selection is made by the treating physician. Thus, the hospital is in a poor position to protect itself by inquiring about or testing the devices, pressuring the manufacturer to promote product safety or selling a different pacemaker which is not defective. The imposition of strict liability would force the hospital to become involved in the selection process. This might provide added protection to the patient; it might also increase the cost of hospital services. But once the hospital began using its medical knowledge to aid in the selection of a pacemaker, it would be in the position of providing professional medical services, for which it could not be held strictly liable. Thus, there would be no ultimate advantage to putting the hospital in the position of having to take part in the selection process.

For the foregoing reasons, we conclude Cedars-Sinai is not "engaged in the business of selling" pacemakers, but is a provider of medical services which included the provision of the pacemaker implanted in plaintiff. Inasmuch as the hospital is not a seller, it cannot be held strictly liable for injuries to plaintiff caused by defects in the pacemaker. Accordingly, the trial court did not err in granting the motion for partial summary judgment.

The order is affirmed.

NOTES AND QUESTIONS

1. The sales-service distinction grew out of the fact that breach of implied warranty was a basis for early strict liability cases. The distinction is perpetuated by the language of the Uniform Commercial Code, of Restatement (Second) § 402A, and of Restatement (Third) of Torts: Products Liability § 19(b) (1998). Judicial reluctance to extend strict liability to services has two underlying policy rationales. In a service transaction, there is no mass production and distribution, and hence no real ability to spread the risk of loss to consumers. Moreover, service transactions do not involve a group of consumers needing protection from a remote and unknown manufacturer. See La Rossa v. Scientific Design Co., 402 F.2d 937 (3d Cir.1968) (applying New Jersey law) (refusing to apply strict liability to engineering company involved in construction of chemical plant).

2. Attempts to extend strict liability to services generally have failed. See, for example, Madison v. American Home Products Corp., 358 S.C. 449, 595 S.E.2d 493 (2004) (pharmacist is not a seller of drug but provider of service and thus no strict liability). There have been several attempts in recent years to impose strict liability on health care providers whose patients were injured during the course of their treatment by various products, including breast implant, hip prosthesis, electro-surgical grounding pad, hypodermic needle, spinal rod, and temporomandibular joint implant. Almost all of these have been unsuccessful. See In re Breast Implant Product Liability Litigation, 331 S.C. 540, 503 S.E.2d 445 (1998) (surgeons not subject to strict liability) (collecting cases).

3. In many situations, as in the principal case, the transaction will have characteristics of both a sale and a service. In those cases, the courts will not apply strict liability if the transaction is predominately a service, with only an incidental transfer of goods. Compare Stafford v. International Harvester Co., 668 F.2d 142 (2d Cir.1981) (applying New York and Pennsylvania law) (no strict liability because repair of truck steering mechanism was predominately a service transaction) and Hennigan v. White, 199 Cal.App.4th 395, 130 Cal.Rptr.3d 856 (2011) (same for cosmetologist's application of permanent makeup pigment) with O'Laughlin v. Minnesota Natural Gas Co., 253 N.W.2d 826 (Minn.1977) (strict liability applied because installation of furnace was service incidental to sale of furnace).

4. *Blood, Blood Products, and Human Tissue.* Most jurisdictions exempt the providers of blood and blood products and, in most cases, human tissue from strict liability, usually by statute. This protection extends not only to the physician or other healthcare provider, but also to a commercial supplier. See, e.g., Palermo v. LifeLink Foundation, Inc., 152 So.3d 1099 (Miss. 2014) (human tissue supplier provides a service and is not a manufacturer or seller subject to strict products liability law). Such suppliers are liable only if the plaintiff can prove negligence. The Restatement (Third) of Torts: Products Liability § 19(c) and comment *c*

(1998) exempts human blood and human tissue from its coverage. Is a sperm bank providing a service or selling a product? Cf. Donovan v. Idant Labs., 625 F.Supp.2d 256 (E.D. Pa. 2009) (applying New York law) (plaintiff's action fails because if the sperm was defective or did not live up to its warranty, to place plaintiff in the position which she would have occupied had the product not been distributed would be to alter plaintiff's genetic identity so that she would be someone else), aff'd, D.D. v. Idant Labs., 374 Fed.Appx. 319, 323 (3d Cir. 2010) ("she, like any other child, does not have a protected right to be born free of genetic defects").

5. Consider whether the following should be held to be products, thus subjecting the defendants to strict liability.

Animals. A store that does not usually carry parrots orders one as a favor to one of its employees. The employee's spouse contracts a disease from the parrot. Strict liability? Compare Latham v. Wal-Mart Stores, Inc., 818 S.W.2d 673 (Mo.App.1991) (animal not a product) with Beyer v. Aquarium Supply Co., 94 Misc.2d 336, 404 N.Y.S.2d 778 (1977) (hamster is a product). See also Blaha v. Stuard, 2002 S.D. 19, 640 N.W.2d 85, 89 (2002) (yellow Labrador dog) (collecting cases) ("living creatures . . . are by their nature in a constant process of internal development and growth and they are also participants in a constant interaction with the environment around them as part of their development. Thus, living creatures have no fixed nature and cannot be products as a matter of law") and Restatement (Third) of Torts: Products Liability § 19 comment *b* (1998) (a living animal sold commercially in a diseased condition is a product).

Charts and Maps. An airplane crashes into the side of Johnson Hill (elevation 2257 feet) on a snowy night, allegedly because the pilot was using an aeronautical chart sold by defendant that did not show Johnson Hill, but did show a nearby hill with an elevation of only 1991 feet. Strict liability? See Fluor Corp. v. Jeppesen & Co., 170 Cal.App.3d 468, 216 Cal.Rptr. 68 (1985) and Brocklesby v. United States, 767 F.2d 1288 (9th Cir.1985) (applying Colorado law) (holding that mass production and marketing of aeronautical charts requires defendant to bear the costs of accidents caused by defects in them).

Books and Games. Plaintiff is injured while body surfing in Hawai'i on his honeymoon. Does he have a strict liability action against the publisher of a guide book for failing to warn him that wave and water conditions on a particular beach were dangerous to swimmers? See Birmingham v. Fodor's Travel Publications, Inc., 73 Haw. 359, 833 P.2d 70 (1992) (declining to extend strict liability to the ideas and expressions in a book). Accord, Winter v. G.P. Putnam's Sons, 938 F.2d 1033 (9th Cir.1991) (applying California law) (plaintiff was poisoned by wild mushrooms collected by referring to the Encyclopedia of Mushrooms); Smith v. Linn, 386 Pa.Super. 392, 563 A.2d 123 (1989) (plaintiff died after following Last Chance Diet book); Watters v. TSR, Inc., 904 F.2d 378 (6th Cir.1990) (applying Kentucky law) (in case where boy allegedly committed suicide because of influence of game Dungeons and Dragons, court declined to apply strict liability, noting that the doctrine of strict liability has never been extended to words or pictures). See page 377 for a discussion of proximate cause and First Amendment issues arising out of *Watters* and similar cases and page 1110 for a discussion of possible misrepresentation claims. See also Restatement (Third) of Torts: Products Liability § 19 comment *d* (1998)

("Although a tangible medium such as a book, itself clearly a product, delivers the information, the plaintiff's grievance in such cases is with the information, not with the tangible medium.") What if the plaintiff developed a rash while reading the book because the ink used was contaminated with a toxic substance? Cf. James v. Meow Media, Inc., 300 F.3d 683, 701 (6th Cir. 2002) (applying Kentucky law) ("Certainly if a video cassette exploded and injured its user, we would hold it a 'product' and its producer strictly liable for the user's physical damages.") (dicta).

Computer Software. The Ninth Circuit suggested in dicta that it thought California would apply strict liability to computer software that "fails to yield the result for which it was designed." Winter v. G.P. Putnam's Sons, 938 F.2d 1033, 1036 (9th Cir.1991). Should the law of defect be the same for computer software as it is for other products?

Electricity. Plaintiff is injured by electricity supplied by defendant. Strict liability? See Schriner v. Pennsylvania Power & Light Co., 348 Pa.Super. 177, 501 A.2d 1128 (1985) (electricity is a service while passing through transmission lines but becomes a product after it passes through the meter to the user's abode) and Stein v. Southern California Edison, 7 Cal.App.4th 565, 8 Cal.Rptr.2d 907 (1992) (strict liability applied to defendant whose employees' actions while repairing a transformer caused a high-voltage arc to enter plaintiff's home, exploding their meter, and setting their house on fire). See also Restatement (Third) of Torts: Products Liability § 19 comment *d* (1998).

Who makes the determination whether something is a product for strict liability purposes? In some jurisdictions, the statute imposing strict liability provides the definition. In others, it is left to the common law. In either case, it is the judge, rather than the jury, who decides whether the situation fits within the statutory definition or is one to which strict liability should apply.

6. *Endorsers, Licensors, and Franchisors.* Courts may extend strict liability to a trademark licensor or franchiser, particularly if the licensor retains the right to control the quality of the product on which the trademark is used. The few courts that have considered the liability of endorsers of products have not imposed strict liability. See, e.g., Hanberry v. Hearst Corp., 276 Cal.App.2d 680, 81 Cal.Rptr. 519 (1969) (consumer's reliance on Good Housekeeping's "seal of approval" may give rise to liability for negligence or negligent misrepresentation, but not strict liability).

7. *Organizations that Set Standards.* What about an organization that sets voluntary standards that have significant influence on its members? Should the organization be liable if the standards are set too low? Should strict liability apply to the organization? Cf. Snyder v. American Ass'n. of Blood Banks, 144 N.J. 269, 676 A.2d 1036 (1996) (holding association of blood banks and blood-banking professionals liable for negligence in the formulation of standards for screening blood donations for HIV).

8. Even if strict liability does not apply, one who renders a service to another is under a duty to exercise reasonable care in doing so and is liable for any negligence to anyone who may foreseeably be expected to be injured. If cases alleging design defects and failure to warn are based on a risk-utility analysis, how important is the classification of something as a

product for the purpose of imposing strict liability? See Restatement (Third) of Torts: Products Liability § 19 comment *a* (1998) (suggesting that the distinction is less important in design and warnings cases).

9. Recall that some services may be considered "abnormally dangerous activities." See Chapter 14, pages 740–758. In this area, the two roads of strict liability come together.

(C) HARM OTHER THAN PERSONAL INJURY

1. *Economic Loss Resulting from Personal Injury.* Lost wages and medical expenses are common forms of economic loss that result from personal injury to plaintiff and are recoverable, along with plaintiff's other losses, in a strict liability action. Most jurisdictions also permit loss of consortium claims based on personal injury in products liability cases. See Restatement (Third) of Torts: Products Liability § 21 comments *b* and *c* (1998).

2. *Economic Loss Without Personal Injury or Property Damage.* Because product liability law was developed largely to provide compensation to plaintiffs who suffered personal injury or property damage, its applicability to other types of harm is limited. An action in strict liability does not lie when the product itself simply did not perform as expected. See, e.g., Seely v. White Motor Co., 63 Cal.2d 9, 403 P.2d 145, 45 Cal.Rptr. 17 (1965) (Traynor, C.J.) (truck "galloped" and did not perform properly). Chief Justice Traynor explained, however, that if there was an express warranty (including a relevant misrepresentation regarding the quality of the product), a tort action might be maintained on that basis. The *Seely* case has been followed by a majority of courts, including New Jersey, which originally had rejected it. Alloway v. General Marine Industries, 149 N.J. 620, 695 A.2d 264 (1997). The courts of many jurisdictions have been strongly influenced by the United States Supreme Court opinion in an admiralty case, East River S.S. Corp. v. Transamerica Delaval, Inc., 476 U.S. 858 (1986). See Chapter 8, Section 3, Pure Economic Loss.

The issue of what constitutes a personal injury also may be implicated by a case alleging a defective product. Consider a product liability claim by a condom user against the condom manufacturer seeking recovery of the costs of an unwanted pregnancy. Did the product simply fail to perform as expected or was there physical harm for which the manufacturer should be strictly liable? Cf. Miceli v. Ansell, Inc., 23 F.Supp.2d 929 (N.D.Ind.1998) (finding that Indiana would consider pregnancy to be a "harm" for the purposes of its product liability statute).

3. A few courts have recognized an exception to the rule that excludes recovery for pure economic loss when the alleged defect creates an "unreasonable risk" of injury to persons, even though no one actually was injured. Under those circumstances, economic losses resulting from damage to the product itself may be compensable. See, e.g., Vulcan Materials Co. v. Driltech, Inc., 251 Ga. 383, 306 S.E.2d 253 (1983) (permitting compensation for defective product itself if it fails in a sudden and calamitous manner). But see Lincoln General Ins. Co. v. Detroit Diesel Corp., 293 S.W.3d 487 (Tenn. 2009) (fire in engine of bus

caused damage to bus only; joining majority of jurisdictions in declining to recognize exception for product failure that is part of sudden, calamitous event) and Dobrovolny v. Ford Motor Co., 281 Neb. 86, 793 N.W.2d 445 (2011) (whether the damage to vehicle occurs gradually over time or through an abrupt, accident-like event, purchaser is confined to recovery in contract if the loss is purely economic). Do you think this distinction should make a difference in whether a tort claim is available?

4. *Damage to Property.* Section 402A covers damage to property as well as persons and most courts have agreed with this extension of strict liability beyond personal injury. See, e.g., Morrow v. Caloric Appliance Corp., 372 S.W.2d 41 (Mo.1963) (defective stove set fire to a house). When the product itself is destroyed by a defect in it most courts treat this as an economic loss not recoverable in tort. Sapp v. Ford Motor Co., 386 S.C. 143, 687 S.E.2d 47 (2009) (alleged defect in cruise control switch caused fire that damaged only truck itself; no tort liability under economic loss rule).

5. When the defective product is used in the process of manufacturing another product and that other product is ruined as a result, this may be treated as damage to property and recovery allowed under strict liability. Suppose the owner of a building seeks to recover from asbestos sellers for the costs of abating asbestos insulation from its building. Is this merely the failure of the product to provide safe heat-retention or has other property (the building) been damaged by the asbestos product? See Restatement (Third) of Torts: Products Liability § 21 comment *e* (1998) (property damage). See also Dean v. Barrett Homes, Inc., 204 N.J. 286, 8 A.3d 766 (2010) (holding that home owners did not have products liability action for cost of replacing defective synthetic stucco because of the economic loss rule, but could recover for damage caused to their home by the allegedly defective stucco because that was damage to property).

6. When a retailer suffers economic loss through a tort suit brought against him by a party injured by the product, it usually can shift that loss to the manufacturer by way of an indemnity action. What if the driver of an allegedly defective car seeks reimbursement from the manufacturer for the damages he paid to an injured passenger? Should strict liability apply to that indemnity claim? Cf. Dixon v. Chicago and North Western Transportation Co., 151 Ill.2d 108, 176 Ill.Dec. 6, 601 N.E.2d 704 (1992) (indemnity not allowed under Illinois law because plaintiff driver was not free of fault in accident). When the manufacturer has sold a retailer bad food and this in turn has driven his customers away, there is a well-aged precedent that would allow recovery. See Mazetti v. Armour & Co., 75 Wash. 622, 135 P. 633 (1913).

6. LEGISLATION AND PRODUCTS LIABILITY

1. *Uniform Commercial Code.* Article 2 of the Uniform Commercial Code, which governs breach of warranty for the sale of goods, has been enacted in all states except Louisiana. Common law

and statutory breach of warranty have had an important influence on the development of the law of product liability.

2. *Restatement (Second) of Torts § 402A*. Beginning in the 1960's, statutes directly applicable to the tort law were enacted in some jurisdictions. For example, some states enacted Restatement (Second) of Torts § 402A through legislation while it was being adopted judicially in most jurisdictions.

3. *Tort Reform: The Legislature Enters the Tort Law Arena*. As indicated earlier in this chapter, product liability insurance rates increased dramatically in the 1970's. As a result, a number of states enacted comprehensive statutory schemes to decrease the size and number of recoveries against manufacturers and sellers. Those changes were principally in the areas of statutes of limitation and repose, the significance of state of the art evidence, the effect of alteration or misuse of the product, and the limitation of strict liability against non-manufacturing sellers. Do these changes to the common law seem fair to you?

4. *Uniform Product Liability Act*. The same pressures that led state legislators to change product liability law at the state level also affected the Federal government. In 1976, the Ford Administration established a Federal Interagency Task Force on product liability to study the problem. Chaired by Professor Victor Schwartz, the Task Force continued into the Carter Administration and issued a Final Report in November 1977. One of the conclusions of that Final Report was that product liability law would be more stable if, as under the Uniform Commercial Code, there was less variation in the laws of the states. Thus, the Uniform Product Liability Act ("UPLA") was offered as a model for state enactment. Some legislatures have enacted portions of UPLA, sometimes modifying its contents. Thus, even in these few states, product liability law has retained its variety. Some courts have used UPLA as a basis for changes in common law. See Prentis v. Yale Mfg. Co., page 792. UPLA also was a predicate for the basic structure of Restatement (Third) of Torts: Products Liability (1998) in taking a functional, as compared to theoretical, approach to the subject.

5. *Tort Reform in the State Legislatures and Congress*. The next two decades saw a shift in approach away from product liability-specific statutes to more broadly applicable tort reform legislation. Those changes were principally in the areas of caps on damages, modification or elimination of joint and several liability, changes in the standards for awarding punitive damages, changes in the collateral source rule, and regulation of attorney contingency fees. In some states, the reform legislation was limited to particular categories of tort liability such as product liability or medical malpractice.

Because many businesses and insurers concluded that the product liability problem could not be solved on a state by state basis, federal legislation was introduced that would preempt state tort law in a number of areas. A predicate for federal action is that product liability insurance rates are set on a nationwide, not a state-by-state, basis. The factual basis for this rate setting is that, on average, the vast majority of goods manufactured in a particular state are shipped beyond its borders. Therefore, legislative product liability action in one state can only provide predictability for a limited number of cases for businesses in that state. Proponents of federal legislation argued that product manufacturers need uniform rules to do business in interstate commerce so that rights and obligations with respect to the same product would not vary simply because a person was injured in one state or another. While many in Congress agreed that there was a clear basis for federal product liability law, there was considerable controversy about the substance of the proposed legislation. Moreover, with each session of Congress, the focus of the legislation, like the reform movement in the states, drifted away from the core of product liability law—establishing the standard for design defects, manufacturing defects, and defects based on failure to warn—into areas of general tort law such as whether there should be limits or caps on punitive damages and whether the doctrine of joint and several liability should be limited.

When the Republicans took over Congress in 1994, an effort was made to expand draft legislation dealing with punitive damages and joint and several liability beyond product liability to all tort claims that arose in interstate commerce. Democratic Members found it ironic that Republicans and business groups, usually proponents of states' rights, were calling for broad-based federal tort reform, and the effort was doomed. Those who supported product liability reform returned to the concept of a bill that would address only product liability claims. After vetoing a version of a product liability bill, the Clinton Administration indicated that it could support federal product liability legislation that did not contain limits on punitive damages or joint and several liability. At that point, proponents of the legislation differed as to whether this limited legislation was "worth the effort." With the proponents divided, and the opponents united, the movement for general federal product liability reform met its end. No general federal product liability legislation has been considered since 1998 and it is unlikely to arise as an issue in the foreseeable future, even with Republican control of both houses of Congress.

Limited liability reforms have had more success. For example, the General Aviation Revitalization Act, which applies an 18-year statute of repose for general aviation products, was enacted into law in 1994. See Schwartz and Lorber, "The General Aviation Revitalization Act: How Rational Civil Justice Reform Revitalized an Industry," 67 J. Air L. & Com. 1269 (2002). In 1998, Congress enacted the Biomaterials Assurance Access Act, which limits the liability of suppliers of biomaterials used in medical implants. While state and local legislative efforts have brought some harmony to product liability law among states, a wide variance still exists. This is particularly the case with respect to rules related to design liability.

6. *Tort Reform in the 21st Century.* State legislatures have remained active in considering and enacting tort reform during the 21st century. This effort has included very specific product liability reforms as well as more broad laws that apply to any tort action. Some legislative efforts to limit liability have been struck down by state supreme courts pursuant to provisions of their state constitutions. Such rulings implicate a broader debate about who will make America's tort

law, courts or legislatures. Those arguing for more legislative intervention contend that legislators can take a more comprehensive view of a subject—holding hearings to obtain more information and broader prospective views—than a court that is focused on the limited factual situation and the arguments of two adversarial parties in a particular case. Those who contend that courts should develop product liability law point to decisions such as those set forth in this case book. They argue that judges are best suited to handle nuances of law that legislators may miss and that incremental change can reduce unintended consequences. This debate about who should make product liability law and general tort law—courts or legislatures—will continue throughout your practice. See Chapter 23, Torts in the Age of Statutes.

In the 21st century, you will be the consumers and manufacturers of products, the attorneys who represent them in litigation and counsel them in risk prevention, and the judges, regulators, and legislators who make the law relating to product liability. How will you change the law?

CHAPTER 16

NUISANCE

The term "nuisance" is surrounded by a great deal of legal confusion. The word itself, which is taken over from the French, means nothing more than harm, annoyance or inconvenience. The courts customarily speak of "a" nuisance as if it were a type of conduct on the part of the defendant or a condition created by him. Actually it is neither. The word refers to a kind of interest invaded, a type of damage or harm. Nuisance is a field of liability, rather than a particular tort.

Nuisance covers two fields of liability—public nuisance and private nuisance. The two fields represent distinct kinds of damage or harm. The two have little in common and are unrelated except as each involves the basic idea of causing harm or inconvenience to someone, which is common to all torts. It is only by the accident of historical development that the same word is used to cover the two; but the use of the common term has led to the application of much the same rules to both.

Public Nuisance. The earliest cases involved purprestures, encroachments upon the royal domain or the public highway. An obstruction of the public highway is still a typical public nuisance. The remedy was gradually extended to cover other miscellaneous invasions of the public right. The remedy was exclusively criminal until the fifteenth century, when it was first recognized that a private individual who had suffered special injury could maintain a tort action.

In the United States, public nuisances are now very largely covered by statute. There are many types of specific criminal provisions covering such things as black currant plants, buildings where narcotics are sold, or waters where mosquitoes breed. In addition, many states have broad criminal statutes covering "public nuisances" without attempting to define them, which are construed to include anything that would have been a public nuisance at common law.

The Restatement (Second) of Torts § 821B defines a public nuisance as "an unreasonable interference with a right common to the general public," and then provides that "circumstances that may sustain a holding that an interference with a public right is unreasonable include the following: (a) whether the conduct involves a substantial interference with the public health, the public safety, the public peace, the public comfort or the public convenience, or (b) whether the conduct is proscribed by a statute, ordinance or administrative regulation, or (c) whether the conduct is of a continuing nature or has produced a permanent or long-lasting effect and, to the actor's knowledge, has a substantial detrimental effect upon the public right."

Private Nuisance. This form of the tort action developed as an unreasonable interference with the use or enjoyment of a property interest in land. It is essentially a tort to an owner or possessor of land. It is distinguished from trespass, in that it did not require a physical entry upon the plaintiff's premises, although it might accompany a trespass. The Minnesota Supreme Court recently provided a detailed discussion relating the differences between the torts of nuisance and trespass. See Johnson v. Paynesville Farmers Union Coop. Oil Co., 817 N.W.2d 693 (Minn. 2012)(holding farmer's claim that pesticide drift caused interference with the use and enjoyment of land for organic production stated a claim for private nuisance, but did not interfere with his right of exclusive possession to support an action in trespass).

The interference might be with the physical condition of the premises, as by blasting or vibration that damages a house; with the health of the occupant, as by unsanitary conditions on adjoining property; with his comfort or convenience, as by smoke, odors, noise or heat; or merely with his peace of mind, as in the case of a nearby bawdy house or funeral parlor. A threat of future injury may be treated as a present menace and interference with enjoyment, as in the case of stored explosives or a vicious dog.

Particular conduct may result in both a public and a private nuisance. The plaintiff may then proceed on either ground, or both, to the extent that she can make out her cause of action.

1. WHAT CONSTITUTES AN ACTION IN NUISANCE?

Philadelphia Electric Company v. Hercules, Inc.

United States Court of Appeals, Third Circuit, 1985.
762 F.2d 303.

A. LEON HIGGINBOTHAM, JR., CIRCUIT JUDGE. This is an appeal from a final judgment of the district court in favor of Philadelphia Electric Company ("PECO") and against Hercules, Inc. ("Hercules") in the amount of $394,910.14, and further ordering Hercules to take all appropriate action to eliminate pollution on a property owned by PECO in Chester, Pennsylvania. The case was tried to a jury on theories of public and private nuisance. For the reasons set forth in the opinion that follows, we will reverse the judgment against Hercules on PECO's claims, and vacate the injunction. * * *

[The property in question, "the Chester site," had been owned, prior to October 1971, by the Pennsylvania Industrial Chemical Corporation ("PICCO"), where it operated a hydrocarbon resin manufacturing plant. PICCO sold the facility to "Gould" in 1971. Gould sold the site to PECO in 1974. PECO had owned an adjoining site and had full opportunity to inspect and investigate the condition of the property. Subsequently Hercules, Inc. became the successor to PICCO, expressly assuming all debts, obligations and liabilities. This action is therefore held properly brought against Hercules. The court treats the relationship between defendant Hercules and plaintiff PECO as "that of a vendor and remote vendee of land." It holds that the sale of the site was subject to the rule of caveat emptor, being between two commercial corporations with no misrepresentation or concealment and full opportunity to inspect.

In 1980 the Pennsylvania Department of Environmental Resources ("DER") discovered that resinous materials similar to those once produced by PICCO were seeping into the Delaware River and directed

PECO to develop and act on a plan to eliminate the situation. In all PECO spent or lost almost $400,000.

PECO brought suit against Hercules for the damages and an injunction requiring defendant to abate any further pollution. The district court granted both. The suit is based on private nuisance, public nuisance and indemnity.]

Restatement (Second) of Torts § 821D defines a "private nuisance" as "a nontrespassory invasion of another's interest in the private use and enjoyment of land." The briefs and arguments, as well as the district court's opinion, 587 F.Supp. at 152–54, give much attention to the questions of whether the condition created by Hercules on the Chester site amounted to a nuisance, and whether Hercules remains liable for the nuisance even after vacating the land. For the purposes of our decision, we may assume that Hercules created a nuisance, and that it remains liable for this condition. See *Restatement (Second) of Torts* § 840A. The crucial and difficult question for us is *to whom* Hercules may be liable.

The parties have cited no case from Pennsylvania or any other jurisdiction, and we have found none, that permits a purchaser of real property to recover from the seller on a private nuisance theory for conditions existing on the very land transferred, and thereby to circumvent limitations on vendor liability inherent in the rule of *caveat emptor*. In a somewhat analogous circumstance, courts have not permitted *tenants* to circumvent traditional limitations on the liability of *lessors* by the expedient of casting their cause of action for defective conditions existing on premises (over which they have assumed control) as one for private nuisance. [Cc] In *Harris v. Lewistown Trust Co.*, 326 Pa. 145, 191 A. 34 (1937), [c] the Supreme Court of Pennsylvania held that the doctrine that a landlord not in possession may be liable for injuries resulting from a "condition amounting to a nuisance" is confined to "the owners or occupants of near-by property, persons temporarily on such property, or persons on a neighboring highway or other places."[6] [C] Recovery on this theory was not available to tenants or their invitees: "A breach of duty owed to one class of persons cannot create a cause of action in favor of a person not within the class. A plaintiff must show that as to him there was a breach of duty." [C] 326 Pa. at 152, 191 A. at 38. Similarly, under the doctrine of *caveat emptor* Hercules owed only a limited duty to Gould and, in turn, to PECO. PECO concedes that this duty was not violated. PECO cannot recover in private nuisance for the violation of a duty Hercules may have owed to others—namely, its neighbors.

We believe that this result is consonant with the historical role of private nuisance law as a means of efficiently resolving conflicts between *neighboring*, contemporaneous land uses. * * * Neighbors, unlike the purchasers of the land upon which a nuisance exists, have no opportunity to protect themselves through inspection and negotiation. The record shows that PECO acted as a sophisticated and responsible

[6] Cf. Restatement (Second) of Torts § 840A and comment *c* thereto ("If the vendor or lessor has himself created on the land a condition that results in a nuisance, * * * *his responsibility toward those outside of his land* is such that he is not free to terminate his liability to them * * * by passing the land itself on to a third person.") (emphasis added).

purchaser—inquiring into the past use of the Chester site, and inspecting it carefully. We find it inconceivable that the price it offered Gould did not reflect the possibility of environmental risks, even if the exact condition giving rise to this suit was not discovered. * * *

Where, as here, the rule of *caveat emptor* applies, allowing a vendee a cause of action for private nuisance for conditions existing on the land transferred—where there has been no fraudulent concealment—would in effect negate the market's allocations of resources and risks, and subject vendors who may have originally sold their land at appropriately discounted prices to unbargained-for liability to remote vendees. * * * Such an extension of common law doctrine is particularly hazardous in an area, such as environmental pollution, where Congress and the state legislatures are actively seeking to achieve a socially acceptable definition of rights and liabilities. We conclude that PECO did not have a cause of action against Hercules sounding in private nuisance.

The doctrine of public nuisance protects interests quite different from those implicated in actions for private nuisance, and PECO's claim for public nuisance requires separate consideration. Whereas private nuisance requires an invasion of another's interest in the private use and enjoyment of land, a public nuisance is "an unreasonable interference with a right common to the general public." Restatement (Second) of Torts § 821B(1). An action for public nuisance may lie even though neither the plaintiff nor the defendant acts in the exercise of private property rights.[11] As William Prosser once wrote: "There are, then, two and only two kinds of nuisance, which are quite unrelated except in the vague general way that each of them causes inconvenience to someone, and in the common name, which naturally has led the courts to apply to the two some of the same substantive rules of law. A private nuisance is narrowly restricted to the invasion of interests in the use and enjoyment of land. It is only a tort, and the remedy for it lies exclusively with the individual whose rights have been disturbed. A public nuisance is a species of catch-all low-grade criminal offense, consisting of an interference with the rights of the community at large, which may include anything from the blocking of a highway to a gaming-house or indecent exposure. Although as in the case of other crimes, the normal remedy is in the hands of the state, a public nuisance may also be a private one, when it interferes with private land. The seeds of confusion were sown when courts began to hold that a tort action would lie even for a purely public nuisance if the plaintiff had suffered 'particular damage.'" Prosser, Private Action for Public Nuisance, 52 Va.L.Rev. 997, 999 (1966).

In analyzing the public nuisance claim, we are not concerned with the happenstance that PECO now occupies the very land PICCO occupied when it allegedly created the condition that has polluted the Delaware River waters, or that the continuing source of that pollution is located on that land. The question before us is whether PECO has

[11] Thus, commercial fishermen and clam diggers operating in public waters can recover on a public nuisance theory for harm to the waters and marine life caused by oil discharged from a tanker in transit. See Burgess v. M/V Tamano, 370 F.Supp. 247 (D.Me.1973).

standing to bring an individual action for damages or injunctive relief for interference with a public right.

Restatement (Second) of Torts § 821C(1) provides: "In order to recover damages in an individual action for a public nuisance, one must have suffered harm of a kind different from that suffered by other members of the public exercising the right common to the general public that was the subject of interference."

The same requirements apply to individual plaintiffs seeking injunctive relief. Restatement (Second) of Torts § 821C(2); Prosser, supra, 52 Va.L.Rev. at 1006. PECO argues that the expense it incurred in cleaning up the offending condition constituted the harm requisite for standing to sue for public nuisance. We disagree. Though pecuniary harm certainly may be harm of a different kind from that suffered by the general public, see Restatement (Second) of Torts § 821C comment *h*,[14] we find in this case no allegation or evidence that PECO suffered this harm "exercising the right common to the general public that was the subject of interference." The public right that was interfered with was the right to "pure water". [C] PECO does not allege that it used the waters of the Delaware River itself, or that it was directly harmed in any way by the pollution of those waters. Thus, this is not a case "where an established business made commercial use of the public right with which the defendant interfered." [C] If PECO—as a riparian landowner—had suffered damage to its land or its operations as a result of the pollution of the Delaware, it would possibly have a claim for public nuisance. But the condition of the Chester site was not the *result* of the pollution, it was the *cause* of it. DER required PECO, as owner of the Chester site, to remove the sources of the pollution. PECO has been specially harmed only in the exercise of its private property rights over the Chester site. PECO has suffered no "particular damage" in the exercise of a right common to the general public, and it lacks standing to sue for public nuisance.

* * *

We emphasize that our decision today should not be interpreted as standing for the general proposition that a party that contaminates land, or the successors to its assets, can escape liability by the expedient of selling the land. To the contrary, it would seem that there are many avenues by which such a party may be held accountable.[20] We hold only that in this case the purchaser of that land, PECO—though

---

[14] It may be that under Pennsylvania law harm of a *magnitude* greater than that suffered by the general public is sufficient to confer standing. See Pennsylvania Society for the Prevention of Cruelty to Animals v. Bravo Enterprises, 428 Pa. 350, 360, 237 A.2d 342, 348 (1968). This distinction is not, however, important in the instant case. As the discussion that follows points out, even if PECO has suffered a harm both different in kind and greater in degree than that suffered by the general public, it has not suffered that harm in the exercise of a right common to the general public. Cf. Burgess v. M/V Tamano, 370 F.Supp. 247 (D.Me.1973) (businesses operating on beach did not have standing to sue for pollution of swimming waters, even though they lost customers as a result).

[20] For example, Hercules could be liable to neighboring landowners in private nuisance, or to users of Delaware River waters in public nuisance. DER or the federal Environmental Protection Agency may be able to proceed directly against Hercules on statutory or public nuisance theories.

we recognize that it acted as a responsible corporate citizen—had no cause of action against the vendor's successor, Hercules, for private nuisance, public nuisance, or common law indemnity.

For the foregoing reasons, the injunction requiring Hercules to clean up the Chester site will be vacated, and the judgment of the district court on PECO's claims against Hercules will be reversed.

NOTES AND QUESTIONS

1. The plaintiff must suffer an injury that is different in kind from that suffered by the general public to sustain an action for public nuisance. Courts have struggled to distinguish between differences in kind and differences in degree. Consider, however, the following:

A. Defendant obstructs a public highway, forcing travelers to detour. Plaintiff, on his way to work, has to travel over the highway twice a day. Cf. Borton v. Mangus, 93 Kan. 719, 145 P. 835 (1915).

B. The same facts, except that plaintiff drives into the unguarded and unlighted obstruction and sustains personal injury. Cf. Leahan v. Cochran, 178 Mass. 566, 60 N.E. 382 (1901).

C. The same facts, except that the obstructed highway cuts off ingress and egress to plaintiff's land. Pilgrim Plywood Co. v. Melendy, 110 Vt. 12, 1 A.2d 700 (1938). Is it enough that there is serious interference? Gates v. Bloomfield, 243 Iowa 671, 53 N.W.2d 279 (1952).

D. Noise and smoke from defendant's factory amounting to a public nuisance also interfere seriously with plaintiff's use and enjoyment of his land. Soap Corp. of America v. Reynolds, 178 F.2d 503 (5th Cir. 1949); Morris v. Haledon, 24 N.J.Super. 171, 93 A.2d 781 (1952).

2. Why should it be necessary to have an injury different in kind from that of the general public? Is it because the harm suffered by the public is so trivial? Or because there would be such a flood of suits? Why not allow a class action? Or permit one member of the public to sue for an injunction that would eliminate the nuisance? In most states the district attorney or other official may sue for abatement. See, e.g., State ex rel. Swann v. Pack, 527 S.W.2d 99 (Tenn. 1975), cert. denied, 424 U.S. 954 (1976) (snake-handling); Boyles v. City of Topeka, 271 Kan. 69, 21 P.3d 974 (2001) (unsightly trash heap).

3. *Public Nuisance and Environmental Protection.* Public nuisance has had a close connection with environmental concerns, although the "difference in kind" rule has limited its use by private citizens in seeking to control environmental hazards. Given the hurdle in the ability of private citizens to enforce environmental laws through nuisance actions, many federal environmental laws contain citizen suit provisions that enable citizens who do not suffer particularized harm to proceed with claims for an injunction and damages paid to the federal treasury. See, e.g., the Federal Water Pollution Control Act, 33 U.S.C. § 1365, and the Clean Air Act, 42 U.S.C § 7604. An individual seeking to secure a remedy of private damages must proceed under public or private nuisance. Not surprisingly, environmental hazards regulated by statute may also be the subject of public nuisance actions. For a successful example of a pairing of a public nuisance action with state and federal environmental enforcement, see City

of Portland v. Boeing Co., 179 F. Supp. 2d 1190 (D. Or. 2001) (finding liability for chemical contamination of groundwater under public nuisance, state Superfund law, and federal environmental law under the Comprehensive Environmental Response, Compensation and Liability Act (CERCLA)). Others have been less successful, see Connecticut v. American Elec. Power Co., 406 F. Supp. 2d 265 (S.D.N.Y. 2005) (dismissing action against electric utilities to obtain injunctive emissions cap); California v. General Motors Corp., 2007 WL 2726871 (N.D. Cal. Sept. 17, 2007) (dismissing action against automakers to obtain relief from, inter alia, sea-water intrusion into freshwater areas and prolonged heat waves, both allegedly caused by automobile emissions); Comer v. Murphy Oil, USA, 2007 WL 6942285 (S.D. Miss. Aug. 30, 2007), (dismissing an action based in part on public nuisance theories against oil, coal, and chemical companies alleging their emissions of greenhouse gases increase the frequency and intensity of hurricanes in the Gulf of Mexico). A recently popular area of nuisance litigation regarding environmental harm is hydraulic fracturing or "fracking" for the production of oil and natural gas. Parr v. Aruba Petroleum, Inc., No. CC–11–01650–E (Dallas County Ct., Tex., Mar. 8, 2011), in which a jury awarded Wise County Texas residents $2.95 million in damages on the basis of private nuisance, is considered the first anti-fracking verdict in the United States. Cities have failed in establishing viable public nuisance suits for lead paint. See In re Lead Paint Litigation, 191 N.J. 405, 924 A.2d 484 (2007); (rejecting public nuisance claim by 26 municipalities against lead paint manufacturers); State v. Lead Industries Assoc., 951 A.2d 428 (R.I. 2008); St. Louis v. Benjamin Moore & Co., 226 S.W.3d 110 (Mo. 2007). Remedies sought under public nuisance may also be preempted by federal environmental law. See Am. Elec. Power Co. v. Connecticut, 131 S. Ct. 2527 (2011) (holding that the Clean Air Act required the Environmental Protection Agency to set the limitations on emissions requested in the remedy, thus preempting the common law public nuisance claim for the contribution of factory emissions to global warming). The Supreme Court of Iowa recently provided a detailed discussion of the relationship between nuisance law and environmental statutes after the Supreme Court's holding in *American Electric Power Company*. See Freeman v. Grain Processing Corp., 848 N.W.2d 58 (Iowa 2014).

4. *The Expanding Realm of Public Nuisance.* Recent actions have expanded into areas well beyond those contemplated as within the bailiwick of public nuisance. For example, actions have been brought in all of the following areas:

A. *Street Gang Violence:* The California Supreme Court, in People ex rel. Gallo v. Acuna, 14 Cal. 4th 1090, 60 Cal.Reptr. 2d 277, 929 P.2d 596 (1997), enjoined, at the suit of the city of San Jose, street gang members from conducting their violent and intimidating gang-like activities in a San Jose neighborhood. The court found that citizens had suffered particular damage through activities that constituted a public nuisance.

B. *Handgun Liability:* Cities have brought public nuisance actions against the handgun industry seeking reimbursement for police, emergency, and medical costs stemming from accidental shootings and homicides. Victims who suffered either physical trauma resulting from an assault with a gun or emotional distress upon experiencing or witnessing the events could bring a public nuisance claim against the gun manufacturers for the manufacture, marketing, and distribution of firearms. Ileto v. Glock, Inc., 349 F.3d 1191 (9th Cir. 2003). But see City of Philadelphia v. Berretta U.S.A. Corp., 277 F.3d 415 (3d Cir. 2002)(holding that even though illegal use of firearms may constitute a public nuisance, the defendant was not liable because the handguns were no longer under its control). Suits such as *Glock* motivated Congress to pass the Protection of Lawful Commerce in Arms Act (PCLAA), 15 U.S.C. §§ 7901 et seq., which required the dismissal of any pending or future claims against federally licensed gun manufacturers and distributors based upon a general tort theory of liability. See City of New York v. Beretta U.S.A. Corp., 524 F. 3d 384, 388–89 (2d Cir. 2008), dismissing nuisance claims brought under New York's criminal nuisance statute), Ileto v. Glock, Inc., 565 F.3d 1126 (9th Cir. 2009) (same for claims under California statute).

C. *Methamphetamine Production:* In Ashley Cty. v. Pfizer, 552 F.3d 659 (8th Cir. 2009), the court rejected the county's public nuisance claim against pharmaceutical manufacturers premised on the use of their products in methamphetamine production.

5. *Public or Private Nuisance?* It is commonplace for plaintiffs to file an action in both public and private nuisance, though instances where the elements of both causes of action are satisfied are somewhat rare. This issue was raised recently in a controversy regarding the contamination of non-genetically modified rice with genetically modified rice in Missouri and Arkansas. See In re Genetically Modified Rice Litig., 666 F. Supp. 2d 1004, 1018 (E.D. Mo. 2009). On motion for summary judgment, the court dismissed the action for public nuisance, finding that the plaintiff had presented no evidence for public harm from the contamination. The court sustained the action for private nuisance on grounds that controversy remained over issues of fact regarding whether the contamination and resulting damage to the market for non-GM producers had interfered with the use of their land. Recalling the discussion of Chapter 8, can you hypothesize why these claims were not barred under the pure economic loss doctrine?

2. LIABILITY FOR PRIVATE NUISANCE

Private nuisance actions typically arise either through the intentional or negligent conduct of the defendant. Intentional nuisances occur when the defendant knows that his conduct interferes with the plaintiff's use and enjoyment of her property, or is substantially certain to do so. Negligence is the basis of liability when the defendant has not intentionally interfered with the protected property interest but has failed to exercise reasonable care to avoid the interference. Strict liability may be imposed when the defendant's activity poses extreme danger to the plaintiff's enjoyment and use of his property. See Heeg v. Licht, 80 N.Y. 579 (1880)(holding the defendant liable for the explosion of a powder magazine that had existed for some time). More recently, strict liability theories of nuisance have been proposed to hold hydraulic fracturing operations responsible for groundwater contamination, though individuals have yet to succeed in the application of this theory. See Neal J. Manor, Note, "What the Frack?" Why Hydraulic Fracturing Is Abnormally Dangerous and Whether Courts Should Allow Strict

Liability Causes of Action, 4 Ky. J. Eq. Ag. & Nat'l Res. L. 459 (2011–2012).

The following cases represent instances of intentional private nuisance. Do you see why? The cases have different determinations regarding liability. How would you reconcile them?

Morgan v. High Penn Oil Co.

Supreme Court of North Carolina, 1953.
238 N.C. 185, 77 S.E.2d 682.

Civil action to recover temporary damages for a private nuisance, and to abate such nuisance by injunction.

[Plaintiff owned a tract of nine acres of land, on which he had his dwelling, a restaurant, and accommodations for thirty-two trailers. Defendant owned an adjoining tract on which it operated an oil refinery, at a distance of 1,000 feet from plaintiff's dwelling. Plaintiff's evidence was that for some hours on two or three different days each week the refinery emitted nauseating gases and odors in great quantities, which invaded plaintiff's land and other tracts of land within a distance of two miles, in such density as to render persons of ordinary sensitiveness uncomfortable and sick. This substantially impaired the use and enjoyment of plaintiff's land. Defendant failed to put an end to this atmospheric pollution after notice and demand from plaintiff to abate it.

Defendant's evidence was that the oil refinery was a modern plant of the type approved, known and in general use for renovating used lubricating oils; that it was not so constructed or operated as to give out noxious gases or odors in annoying quantities, and that it had not annoyed the plaintiff or other persons save on a single occasion when it suffered a brief mechanical breakdown.

The trial judge submitted to the jury the question whether the refinery was so maintained and operated as to create a nuisance. The jury returned a special verdict saying that there was a nuisance, and assessed plaintiff's damages at $2,500. The trial court entered judgment on this verdict, and enjoined defendant from continuing the nuisance. Defendant appealed.]

ERVIN, JUSTICE. * * * [The] defendant assigns as error the disallowance of its motion for a compulsory nonsuit. * * *

The High Penn Oil Company contends that the evidence is not sufficient to establish either an actionable or an abatable private nuisance. This contention rests on a twofold argument somewhat alternative in character. The High Penn Oil Company asserts primarily that private nuisances are classified as nuisances *per se* or at law, and nuisances *per accidens* or in fact; that when one carries on an oil refinery upon premises in his rightful occupation, he conducts a lawful enterprise, and for that reason does not maintain a nuisance *per se* or at law; that in such case the oil refinery can constitute a nuisance *per accidens* or in fact to the owner of neighboring land if, but only if, it is constructed or operated in a negligent manner; that there was no testimony at the trial tending to show that the oil refinery was constructed or operated in a negligent manner; and that consequently the evidence does not suffice to establish the existence of either an actionable or an abatable private nuisance. * * *

A nuisance *per se* or at law is an act, occupation or structure which is a nuisance at all times and under any circumstances, regardless of location or surroundings. [Cc] Nuisances *per accidens* or in fact are those which become nuisances by reason of their location, or by reason of the manner in which they are constructed, maintained, or operated. [Cc] The High Penn Oil Company also asserts with complete correctness that an oil refinery is a lawful enterprise and for that reason cannot be a nuisance *per se* or at law. [Cc] The High Penn Oil Company falls into error, however, when it takes the position that an oil refinery cannot become a nuisance *per accidens* or in fact unless it is constructed or operated in a negligent manner.

Negligence and nuisance are distinct fields of liability. [Cc] While the same act or omission may constitute negligence and also give rise to a private nuisance *per accidens* or in fact, and thus the two torts may coexist and be practically inseparable, a private nuisance *per accidens* or in fact may be created or maintained without negligence. [Cc] Most private nuisances *per accidens* or in fact are intentionally created or maintained, and are redressed by the courts without allegation or proof of negligence. [Cc] * * *

Much confusion exists in respect to the legal basis of liability in the law of private nuisance because of the deplorable tendency of the courts to call everything a nuisance, and let it go at that. [Cc] The confusion on this score vanishes in large part, however, when proper heed is paid to the sound proposition that private nuisance is a field of tort liability rather than a single type of tortious conduct; that the feature which gives unity to this field of tort liability is the interest invaded, namely, the interest in the use and enjoyment of land; that any substantial nontrespassory invasion of another's interest in the private use and enjoyment of land by any type of liability forming conduct is a private nuisance; that the invasion which subjects a person to liability for private nuisance may be either intentional or unintentional; that a person is subject to liability for an intentional invasion when his conduct is unreasonable under the circumstances of the particular case; and that a person is subject to liability for an unintentional invasion when his conduct is negligent, reckless or ultrahazardous. [Cc].

An invasion of another's interest in the use and enjoyment of land is intentional in the law of private nuisance when the person whose conduct is a question as a basis for liability acts for the purpose of causing it, or knows that it is resulting from his conduct, or knows that it is substantially certain to result from his conduct. Restatement (Second) of the Law of Torts, § 825; [Cc]. A person who intentionally creates or maintains a private nuisance is liable for the resulting injury to others regardless of the degree of care or skill exercised by him to avoid such injury. [Cc] One of America's greatest jurists, the late Benjamin N. Cardozo, made this illuminating observation on this aspect of the law:

"Nuisance as a concept of the law has more meanings than one. The primary meaning does not involve the element of negligence as one of its essential factors. One acts sometimes at one's peril. In such circumstances, the duty to desist is absolute whenever conduct, if persisted in, brings damage to another. Illustrations are abundant. One who emits noxious fumes or gases day by day in the running of his factory may be liable to his neighbor though he has taken all available precautions. He is not to do such things at all, whether he is negligent or careful." McFarlane v. City of Niagara Falls, 247 N.Y. 340, 160 N.E. 391.

When the evidence is interpreted in the light most favorable to the plaintiff, it suffices to support a finding that in operating the oil refinery the High Penn Oil Company intentionally and unreasonably caused noxious gases and odors to escape onto the nine acres of the plaintiff to such a degree as to impair in a substantial manner the plaintiff's use and enjoyment of his land. This being so, the evidence is ample to establish the existence of an actionable private nuisance, entitling the plaintiff to recover temporary damages from the High Penn Oil Company. [Cc] When the evidence is taken in the light most favorable to the plaintiff, it also suffices to warrant the additional inference that the High Penn Oil Company intends to operate the oil refinery in the future in the same manner as in the past; * * * and that the issuance of an appropriate injunction is necessary to protect the plaintiff against the threatened irreparable injury. * * *

For the reasons given, the evidence is sufficient to withstand the motion of the High Penn Oil Company for a compulsory nonsuit.

[A new trial was ordered, however, because of an error in instructions to the jury.]

Carpenter v. The Double R Cattle Company, Inc.

Supreme Court of Idaho, 1985.
108 Idaho 602, 701 P.2d 222.

BAKES, JUSTICE. * * * Plaintiff appellants are homeowners who live near a cattle feedlot owned and operated by respondents. Appellants filed a complaint in March, 1978, alleging that the feedlot had been expanded in 1977 to accommodate the feeding of approximately 9,000 cattle. Appellants further alleged that "the spread and accumulation of manure, pollution of river and ground water, odor, insect infestation, increased concentration of birds, . . . dust and noise" allegedly caused by the feedlot constituted a nuisance. After a trial on the merits a jury found that the feedlot did not constitute a nuisance. The trial court then also made findings and conclusions that the feedlot did not constitute a nuisance. * * *

The case was assigned to the Court of Appeals which reversed and remanded for a new trial. The basis for this reversal was that the trial court did not give a jury instruction based upon subsection (b) of Section 826 of the Restatement (Second) of Torts. That subsection allows for a finding of a nuisance even though the gravity of harm is outweighed by the utility of the conduct if the harm is "serious" and the payment of damages is "feasible" without forcing the business to discontinue.

This Court granted defendant's petition for review. We hold that the instructions which the trial court gave were not erroneous, being consistent with our prior case law and other persuasive authority. We further hold that the trial court did not err in not giving an instruction based on subsection (b) of Section 826 of the Second Restatement, which does not represent the law in the State of Idaho. * * *

The Court of Appeals * * * adopted the new subsection (b) of Section 826 of the Second Restatement partially because of language in Koseris [v. J.R. Simplot Co., 82 Idaho 263, 352 P.2d 235 (1960)], which reads: "We are constrained to hold that the trial court erred in sustaining objections to those offers of proof [evidence of utility of conduct], since they were relevant as bearing upon the issue whether respondents, in seeking injunctive relief, were pursuing the proper remedy; nevertheless, on the theory of damages which respondents had waived, the ruling was correct." 82 Idaho at 270, 352 P.2d at 239.

The last phrase of the quote, relied on by the Court of Appeals, is clearly *dictum,* since the question of utility of conduct in a nuisance action for damages was not at issue in *Koseris*. It is very doubtful that this Court's *dictum* in *Koseris* was intended to make such a substantial change in the nuisance law. * * * The case of McNichols v. J.R. Simplot Co., 74 Idaho 321, 262 P.2d 1012 (1953) should be viewed as the law in Idaho that in a nuisance action seeking damages the interests of the community, which would include the utility of the conduct, should be considered in the determination of the existence of a nuisance. The trial court's instructions in the present case were entirely consistent with *McNichols*. A plethora of other modern cases are in accord. * * *

The State of Idaho is sparsely populated and its economy depends largely upon the benefits of agriculture, lumber, mining and industrial development. To eliminate the utility of conduct and other factors listed by the trial court from the criteria to be considered in determining whether a nuisance exists, as the appellant has argued throughout this appeal, would place an unreasonable burden upon these industries. We see no policy reasons which should compel this Court to accept appellant's argument and depart from our present law. Accordingly, the judgment of the district court is affirmed and the Court of Appeals decision is set aside. * * *

BISTLINE, JUSTICE, dissenting. * * * I applaud the efforts of the Court of Appeals to modernize the law of nuisance in this state. I am not in the least persuaded to join the majority with its narrow view of nuisance law as expressed in the majority opinion.

The majority today continues to adhere to ideas on the law of nuisance that should have gone out with the use of buffalo chips as fuel. We have before us today homeowners complaining of a nearby feedlot—not a small operation, but rather a feedlot which accommodates 9,000 cattle. The homeowners advanced the theory that after the expansion of the feedlot in 1977, the odor, manure, dust, insect infestation and increased concentration of birds which accompanied all of the foregoing, constituted a nuisance. If the odoriferous quagmire created by 9,000 head of cattle is *not* a nuisance, it is difficult for me to imagine what is. * * *

I agree wholeheartedly that the interests of the community should be considered in determining the existence of a nuisance. However, where this primitive rule of law fails is in recognizing that in our society, while it may be desirable to have a serious nuisance continue because the utility of the operation causing the nuisance is great, at the same time, those directly impacted by the serious nuisance deserve some compensation for the invasion they suffer as a result of the continuation of the nuisance. This is exactly what the more progressive provisions of § 826(b) of the Restatement (Second) of Torts addresses. Clearly, § 826(b) recognizes that the continuation of the serious harm must remain feasible. See especially comment on clause (b), subpart f of § 826 of the Restatement. What § 826(b) adds is a method of compensating those who must suffer the invasion without putting out of business the source or cause of the invasion. This does not strike me as a particularly adventuresome or far-reaching rule of law. In fact, the fairness of it is overwhelming. * * *

We should not be adopting a rule of preference which suggests that if the community interest is preferred any other interest must be disregarded. Instead, § 826(b) accommodates adverse interests by contemplating continuation of the facility which creates the nuisance while compensating those who suffer the direct impact of the nuisance—in the instant case the homeowners who live in the vicinity of the feedlot.

The majority's rule today suggests that part of the cost of industry, agriculture or development must be borne by those unfortunate few who have the fortuitous luck to live in the immediate vicinity of a nuisance producing facility. Frankly, I think this naive economic view is ridiculous in both its simplicity and its outdated view of modern economic society. The "cost" of a product includes not only the amount it takes to produce such a product but also includes the external costs: the damage done to the environment through pollution of air or water is an example of an external cost. In the instant case, the nuisance suffered by the homeowners should be considered an external cost of operating a feedlot and producing beef for public consumption. I do not believe that a few should be required to pay this extra cost of doing business by going uncompensated for a nuisance of this sort. * * *

The majority today blithely suggests that because the State of Idaho is sparsely populated and because our economy is largely dependent on agriculture, lumber, mining and industrial development, we should forego compensating those who suffer a serious invasion. If humans are such a rare item in this state, maybe there is all the more reason to protect them from the discharge of industry. At a minimum, we should compensate those who suffer a nuisance at the hands of industry and agriculture. What the majority overlooks is that the cost of development should not be absorbed by few, but rather should be spread out and paid by all. I am not convinced that agriculture or industry will be put out of business by requiring compensation for the nuisance they generate. * * *

The decision of the Court of Appeals is an outstanding example of a judicial opinion which comes from a truly exhaustive and analytical review. See 105 Idaho 320, 669 P.2d 643 (1983). * * *

[The decision was 3 to 2.]

NOTES AND QUESTIONS

1. Judicial balancing of factors in the determination of liability is redolent of the central test in negligence articulated by Learned Hand. See Pendergrast v. Aiken, 293 N.C. 201, 236 S.E.2d 787 (1977) ("Reasonableness is a question of fact to be determined in each case by weighing the gravity of the harm to the plaintiff against the utility of the conduct of the defendant. Determination of the gravity of the harm involves consideration of the extent and character of the harm to the plaintiff, the social value which the law attaches to the type of use which is invaded, the suitability of the locality for that use, the burden on plaintiff to minimize the harm, and other relevant considerations arising upon the evidence. Determination of the utility of the conduct of the defendant involves consideration of the purpose of the defendant's conduct, the social value which the law attaches to that purpose, the suitability of the locality for the use defendant makes of the property, and other relevant considerations arising upon the evidence."); and Freeman v. Blue Ridge Paper Prods., 229 S.W.3d 694, 705 (Tenn. Ct. App. 2007) (same as *Pendergrast*). But in Jost v. Dairyland Power Cooperative, 45 Wis.2d 164, 172 N.W.2d 647 (1969), the court was hostile to a balancing test when the nuisance was intentional and the damage "substantial."

2. Liability rules in nuisance thus govern the use of property. The framework of the rules reveal this underlying objective: Michelman, Property, Utility and Fairness, 80 Harv.L.Rev. 1165 (1967); Epstein, Nuisance Law: Corrective Justice and Its Utilitarian Constraints, 8 J.Leg.Stud. 49 (1979). Note that it was the application of liability rules to competing uses of property that led Ronald Coase to his Nobel prize scholarship in The Problem of Social Cost, 3 J.L. & Econ. 1 (1960). Legal rules, however, may be of limited influence in guiding the behavior of neighbors whose use of land conflicts, see Ellickson, Order Without Law: How Neighbors Settle Disputes (1991) (informal social norms are chosen outside the shadow of the law whose content maximizes the objective welfare of group members).

3. Recurring circumstances establish doctrines in nuisance law:

A. *Hypersensitivity.* It is generally held that the harm must be of a kind that would be suffered by a normal person in the community. Rogers v. Elliott, 146 Mass. 349, 15 N.E. 768 (1888) (plaintiff, in highly nervous condition from sunstroke, affected by ringing of church bell); Beckman v. Marshall, 85 So.2d 552 (Fla.1956) (noise of children playing in nursery); Venuto v. Owens-Corning Fiberglas Corp., 22 Cal.App.3d 116, 99 Cal.Rptr. 350 (1971) (allergic reactions); Jenkins v. CSX Transportation, Inc., 906 S.W.2d 460 (Tenn.Ct.App.1995) (allergic reaction to creosote).

Suppose that most people in the vicinity are hardened to the discomfort of noise, smoke, dust, vibration or odors from the defendant's factory, and do not object. Does this prevent the plaintiff from maintaining an action for a nuisance, if a normal person would be affected?

B. *Sensitive Uses of Land.* What if the defendant engages in an activity that is normally harmless to his neighbors, but the plaintiff is making an abnormally sensitive use of his land, which is adversely affected? Defendant operates a race track at night, and his flood lights, directed downward, are reflected with a light approximately equal to that of the full moon. This would be inoffensive to the ordinary landowner in the vicinity; but the plaintiff has an outdoor motion picture screen, on which his pictures are made less visible, and he loses customers. Is defendant liable on the basis of nuisance? Amphitheaters, Inc. v. Portland Meadows, 184 Or. 336, 198 P.2d 847 (1948).

Plaintiff has installed an effective solar heating system on the roof of his house. Defendant proposes to construct a house on adjoining land that will shade the heating system and impair its operation and refuses to change the location of the house sufficiently to avoid the shading. Plaintiff sues for an injunction. What problems are raised? See Prah v. Maretti, 108 Wis.2d 223, 321 N.W.2d 182 (1982) (nuisance liability), but cf. Tenn v. 889 Associates, Ltd., 127 N.H. 321, 500 A.2d 366 (1985) (nuisance liability applicable but not established).

C. *Locality*. In Euclid v. Ambler Realty Co., 272 U.S. 365, 388 (1926), the case in which the Supreme Court first upheld the constitutionality of zoning legislation, Justice Sutherland said: "A nuisance may be merely a right thing in the wrong place, like a pig in the parlor instead of the barnyard." It also is important where the barnyard is located. Thus, in William Aldred's Case, 9 Co.Rep. 576, 77 Eng.Rep. 816 (1610), one of the very first reported cases on private nuisance, the action was brought for maintaining a hogstye next to the plaintiff's house. Defendant "moved in arrest of judgment, that the building of the house for hogs was necessary for the sustenance of man; and one ought not to have so delicate a nose, that he cannot bear the smell of hogs * * * but it was resolved that the action for it is * * * well maintainable."

4. *Right to Farm Statutes*. Right to Farm Statutes have been enacted in all fifty states. They follow a pattern of preventing new residents from restricting established agricultural practices. See Leaf River Forest Prod., Inc. v. Ferguson, 662 So.2d 648, 661 (Miss. 1995). The intent of the legislature is to prevent the encroaching urban population from destroying farmland by placing the blame on plaintiffs who "come to the nuisance," and therefore, should not be given a remedy at law. If the statute bestows an immunity for nuisance suit on those carrying on certain "agricultural" activities, the issue of unconstitutional taking arises. The statutory immunity may be construed as the creation of an easement over the complainant's land in favor of the party enjoying the immunity. See Gacke v. Pork Xtra, 684 N.W.2d 168 (Iowa 2004); Bormann v. Bd. of Supervisors, 584 N.W.2d 309 (Iowa 1998). But compare Craig v. County of Chatham, 356 N.C. 40, 565 S.E.2d 172 (2002) (holding that state hog farm laws form a "complete and integrated regulatory scheme" preempting local regulation). The rise of agritourism has pushed the limit of right-to-farm laws in preempting actions for private nuisance. Several courts have addressed the question of whether noise from concerts or farm attractions may properly be considered agriculture to preempt a cause of action. For a well-developed discussion of the issue, see Shore v. Maple Lane Farms, LLC, 411 S.W.3d 405 (Tenn. 2013)(holding that plaintiff successfully presented a prima facie claim for private nuisance regarding noise from concerts associated with a neighboring farm's harvest festivals). See also In re Appeal of Stagebrush Promotions, Inc., 512 A.2d 776 (Pa. Commw. Ct. 1986)(affirming denial of a

township's conditional use permit application for a farm to host "spring flings" for college students).

5. The judicial function of zoning via liability rules calls for an examination of its relationship with public zoning regulations and environmental agency controls. On these questions, see Ellickson, Alternatives to Zoning, Covenants, Nuisance Rules, and Fines as Land Use Controls, 40 U.Chi.L.Rev. 681 (1973).

3. DEFENSES

Relationship with Contributory Negligence

1. When there is an intentional private nuisance, contributory negligence is not a defense, as in the case of other intentional torts. Higginbotham v. Kearse, 111 W.Va. 264, 161 S.E. 37 (1931); Phillips Ranch, Inc. v. Banta, 273 Or. 784, 543 P.2d 1035 (1975).

2. When the nuisance arises out of negligence, most courts recognize that contributory negligence eliminates or reduces recovery. See Timmons v. Reed, 569 P.2d 112 (Wyo. 1977); McFarlane v. Niagara Falls, 247 N.Y. 340, 160 N.E. 391 (1928) (leading case); Denny v. Garavaglia, 333 Mich. 317, 52 N.W. 521 (1952); RESTATEMENT (SECOND) OF TORTS § 840B.

3. When the nuisance is based on strict liability, contributory negligence of the plaintiff failing to discover the danger is not a defense, but if he discovers the danger and deliberately proceeds to encounter it, his contributory negligence or assumption of risk may affect his recovery. For example, if a defendant is blasting in dangerous proximity to a highway and plaintiff negligently fails to observe a warning sign, drives past it, and is hurt by the blast, he may recover. However, if the plaintiff sees the sign or flagman who warns him not to proceed and insists on doing so, he cannot recover. See Worth and Dunn, 98 Conn. 51, 118 A. 467 (1922). For a case that addresses the issue of comparative negligence, see Tint v. Sanborn, 211 Cal. App. 3d 1225, 259 Cal. Reptr. 902 (Cal. Ct. App. 1989)(view of San Francisco obstructed by trees on adjoining property).

Self-Help to Abate a Nuisance

1. The privilege of self-help to abate a nuisance is analogous to the privilege of using reasonable force to protect the possession of land against trespass. Self-help is only available to those to whom the condition is a nuisance. There are several additional guiding principles toward the application of self-help.

A. A public nuisance may only be abated by a private individual in the instance that the nuisance causes or threatens special damage to the individual, apart from the general public. Corthell v. Holmes, 87 Me. 24, 32 A. 715 (1894); Nation v. District of Columbia, 34 App. D.C. 453 (1910).

B. The privilege of abating conditions outside the actor's premises is predicated upon the existence of an actual nuisance, and that an honest mistaken belief will not justify the action. Humphery's Oil Co. v. Liles, 262 S.W. 1058 (Tex. Civ. App. 1924), aff'd, 277 S.W. 100 (Com. App. 1925).

C. The application of reasonable force according to the necessities of the situation may extend to the destruction of valuable property.

Amoskeag Mfg. Co. v. Goodale, 46 N.H. 53 (dam); Maryland Tel. and Tel. Co. v. Ruth, 106 Md. 644, 68 A. 358 (1907) (telephone pole).

D. Abating a nuisance will not excuse unnecessary or unreasonable damage. For example, a neighbor may not burn down an adjoining house because it is used for prostitution. See Moody v. Bd. of Supervisors of Niagara Cty., 46 Barb. 659 (N.Y. 1886).

E. Abating a nuisance does not justify inflicting personal injury or a breach of the peace. Walker v. Davis, 139 Tenn. 475, 202 S.W. 78 (1918).

F. The individual exercising self-help must notify the wrongdoer of the existence of the condition and demand the condition's removal prior to exercising the privilege. An exception to this principle is if the wrongdoer is already aware of the problem and making the demand would be futile. Hickey v. Michigan Central R. Co., 96 Mich. 498, 55 N.W. 989 (1893).

2. *Tree and Plant Related Actions:* A common scenario in which self-help arises is in the situation of tree or plant related nuisances. In some instances, such as overhanging branches, an action for nuisance will not lie unless and until a landowner has attempted self-help, where self-help would cure the nuisance. For an instructive discussion of four common approaches to self-help requirements in such cases, see Iny v. Collom, 13 Misc. 3d 75, 827 N.Y.S.2d. 416 (2006). See also RESTATEMENT (SECOND) OF TORTS §§ 839–40. The courts have considered factors such as increased population density and diminishing agricultural activity in determining whether trees and plants constitute a nuisance. For example, the Virginia Supreme Court overruled its precedent that a plant or tree must be considered noxious to assess liability, finding that a tree or plant could constitute a nuisance where self-help was ineffective and the trees or branches posed imminent danger or actual harm. Fancher v. Fagella, 274 Va. 549, 650 S.E.2d 519 (2007), following Lane v. W.J. Curry & Sons, 92 S.W.3d 355 (Tenn. 2002)(this is known as the Hawaii rule). How does this rule compare with RESTATEMENT (SECOND) OF TORTS §§ 839–40? What do you think is the better approach?

4. NUISANCE REMEDIES

Compare and contrast the remedies adopted by the courts in addressing nuisance problems in the following cases. What are the consequences of the different approaches taken by the courts?

Boomer v. Atlantic Cement Co., Inc.

Court of Appeals of New York, 1970.
26 N.Y.2d 219, 257 N.E.2d 870, 309 N.Y.S.2d 312.

BERGAN, J. Defendant operates a large cement plant near Albany. These are actions for injunction and damages by neighboring land owners alleging injury to property from dirt, smoke and vibration emanating from the plant. A nuisance has been found after trial, temporary damages have been allowed; but an injunction has been denied.

The public concern with air pollution arising from many sources in industry and in transportation is currently accorded ever wider recognition accompanied by a growing sense of responsibility in State and Federal Governments to control it. Cement plants are obvious sources of air pollution in the neighborhoods where they operate.

But there is now before the court private litigation in which individual property owners have sought specific relief from a single plant operation. The threshold question raised by the division of view on this appeal is whether the court should resolve the litigation between the parties now before it as equitably as seems possible; or whether, seeking promotion of the general public welfare, it should channel private litigation into broad public objectives.

A court performs its essential function when it decides the rights of parties before it. Its decision of private controversies may sometimes greatly affect public issues. Large questions of law are often resolved by the manner in which private litigation is decided. But this is normally an incident to the court's main function to settle controversy. It is a rare exercise of judicial power to use a decision in private litigation as a purposeful mechanism to achieve direct public objectives greatly beyond the rights and interests before the court.

Effective control of air pollution is a problem presently far from solution even with the full public and financial powers of government. In large measure adequate technical procedures are yet to be developed and some that appear possible may be economically impracticable.

It seems apparent that the amelioration of air pollution will depend on technical research in great depth; on a carefully balanced consideration of the economic impact of close regulation; and of the actual effect on public health. It is likely to require massive public expenditure and to demand more than any local community can accomplish and to depend on regional and interstate controls.

A court should not try to do this on its own as a by-product of private litigation and it seems manifest that the judicial establishment is neither equipped in the limited nature of any judgment it can pronounce nor prepared to lay down and implement an effective policy for the elimination of air pollution. This is an area beyond the circumference of one private lawsuit. It is a direct responsibility for government and should not thus be undertaken as an incident to solving a dispute between property owners and a single cement plant—one of many—in the Hudson River valley.

The cement making operations of defendant have been found by the court at Special Term to have damaged the nearby properties of plaintiffs in these two actions. The total damage to plaintiffs' properties is, however, relatively small in comparison with the value of defendant's operation and with the consequences of the injunction which plaintiffs seek.

The ground for the denial of injunction, notwithstanding the finding both that there is a nuisance and that plaintiffs have been damaged substantially, is the large disparity in economic consequences of the nuisance and of the injunction. This theory cannot, however, be sustained without overruling a doctrine which has been consistently reaffirmed in several leading cases in this court and which has never been disavowed here, namely that where a nuisance has been found and where there has been any substantial damage shown by the party complaining an injunction will be granted.

The rule in New York has been that such a nuisance will be enjoined although marked disparity be shown in economic consequence between the effect of the injunction and the effect of the nuisance.

The problem of disparity in economic consequence was sharply in focus in Whalen v. Union Bag & Paper Co., 208 N.Y. 1, 101 N.E. 805. A pulp mill entailing an investment of more than a million dollars polluted a stream in which plaintiff, who owned a farm, was "a lower riparian owner." The economic loss to plaintiff from this pollution was small. This court, reversing the Appellate Division reinstated the injunction granted by the Special Term against the argument of the mill owner that in view of "the slight advantage to plaintiff and the great loss that will be inflicted on defendant" an injunction should not be granted [c]. "Such a balancing of injuries cannot be justified by the circumstances of this case," Judge Werner noted [c]. He continued: "Although the damage to the plaintiff may be slight as compared with the defendant's expense of abating the condition, that is not a good reason for refusing an injunction" [c].

Thus the unconditional injunction granted at Special Term was reinstated. The rule laid down in that case, then, is that whenever the damage resulting from a nuisance is found not "unsubstantial," viz., $100 a year, injunction would follow. This states a rule that had been followed in this court with marked consistency. * * *

Although the court at Special Term and the Appellate Division held that injunction should be denied, it was found that plaintiffs had been damaged in various specific amounts up to the time of the trial and damages to the respective plaintiffs were awarded for those amounts. The effect of this was, injunction having been denied, plaintiffs could maintain successive actions at law for damages thereafter as further damage was incurred.

The court at Special Term also found the amount of permanent damage attributable to each plaintiff, for the guidance of the parties in the event both sides stipulated to the payment and acceptance of such permanent damage as a settlement of all the controversies among the parties. The total of permanent damages to all plaintiffs thus found was $185,000. This basis of adjustment has not resulted in any stipulation by the parties.

This result at Special Term and at the Appellate Division is a departure from a rule that has become settled; but to follow the rule literally in these cases would be to close down the plant at once. This court is fully agreed to avoid that immediately drastic remedy; the difference in view is how best to avoid it. [Footnote by Court: Respondent's investment in the plant is in excess of $45,000,000. There are over 300 people employed there.]

One alternative is to grant the injunction but postpone its effect to a specified future date to give opportunity for technical advances to permit defendant to eliminate the nuisance; another is to grant the injunction conditioned on the payment of permanent damages to plaintiffs which would compensate them for the total economic loss to their property present and future caused by defendant's operations. * * * [T]he court chooses the latter alternative.

If the injunction were to be granted unless within a short period—e.g., 18 months—the nuisance be abated by improved methods, there would be no assurance that any significant technical improvement would occur.

The parties could settle this private litigation at any time if defendant paid enough money and the imminent threat of closing the plant would build up the pressure on defendant. If there were no improved techniques found, there would inevitably be applications to the court at Special Term for extensions of time to perform on showing of good faith efforts to find such techniques.

Moreover, techniques to eliminate dust and other annoying by-products of cement making are unlikely to be developed by any research the defendant can undertake within any short period, but will depend on the total resources of the cement industry nationwide and throughout the world. The problem is universal wherever cement is made.

For obvious reasons the rate of the research is beyond control of defendant. If at the end of 18 months the whole industry has not found a technical solution a court would be hard put to close down this one cement plant if due regard be given to equitable principles.

On the other hand, to grant the injunction unless defendant pays plaintiffs such permanent damages as may be fixed by the court seems to do justice between the contending parties. All of the attributions of economic loss to the properties on which plaintiffs' complaints are based will have been redressed.

The nuisance complained of by these plaintiffs may have other public or private consequences, but these particular parties are the only ones who have sought remedies and the judgment proposed will fully redress them. The limitation of relief granted is a limitation only within the four corners of these actions and does not foreclose public health or other public agencies from seeking proper relief in a proper court.

It seems reasonable to think that the risk of being required to pay permanent damages to injured property owners by cement plant owners would itself be a reasonable effective spur to research for improved techniques to minimize nuisance.

The power of the court to condition on equitable grounds the continuance of an injunction on the payment of permanent damages seems undoubted. [Cc]

The damage base here suggested is consistent with the general rule in those nuisance cases where damages are allowed. "Where a nuisance is of such a permanent and unabatable character that a single recovery can be had, including the whole damage past and future resulting therefrom, there can be but one recovery" [c].

Thus it seems fair to both sides to grant permanent damages to plaintiffs which will terminate this private litigation. The theory of damage is the "servitude on land" of plaintiffs imposed by defendant's nuisance. * * *

The judgment, by allowance of permanent damages imposing a servitude on land, which is the basis of the actions, would preclude future recovery by plaintiffs or their grantees [c].

This should be placed beyond debate by a provision of the judgment that the payment by defendant and the acceptance by plaintiffs of permanent damages found by the court shall be in compensation for a servitude on the land.

Although the Trial Term has found permanent damages as a possible basis of settlement of the litigation, on remission the court should be entirely free to re-examine this subject. It may again find the permanent damage already found; or make new findings.

The orders should be reversed, without costs, and the cases remitted to Supreme Court, Albany County to grant an injunction which shall be vacated upon payment by defendant of such amounts of permanent damage to the respective plaintiffs as shall for this purpose be determined by the court.

JASEN, J. dissenting. I agree with the majority that a reversal is required here, but I do not subscribe to the newly enunciated doctrine of assessment of permanent damages, in lieu of an injunction, where substantial property rights have been impaired by the creation of a nuisance. * * *

I see grave dangers in overruling our long-established rule of granting an injunction where a nuisance results in substantial continuing damage. In permitting the injunction to become inoperative upon the payment of permanent damages, the majority is, in effect, licensing a continuing wrong. It is the same as saying to the cement company, you may continue to do harm to your neighbors so long as you pay a fee for it. Furthermore, once such permanent damages are assessed and paid, the incentive to alleviate the wrong would be eliminated, thereby continuing air pollution of an area without abatement.

It is true that some courts have sanctioned the remedy here proposed by the majority in a number of cases, but none of the authorities relied upon by the majority are analogous to the situation before us. In those cases, the courts, in denying an injunction and awarding money damages, grounded their decision on a showing that the use to which the property was intended to be put was primarily for the public benefit. Here, on the other hand, it is clearly established that the cement company is creating a continuing air pollution nuisance primarily for its own private interest with no public benefit.

This kind of inverse condemnation [c] may not be invoked by a private person or corporation for private gain or advantage. Inverse condemnation should only be permitted when the public is primarily served in the taking or impairment of property. [Cc] The promotion of the interests of the polluting cement company has, in my opinion, no public use or benefit.

Nor is it constitutionally permissible to impose servitude on land, without consent of the owner, by payment of permanent damages where the continuing impairment of the land is for a private use. [Cc] This is made clear by the State Constitution (art. I, § 7, subd. [a]) which provides that "[p]rivate property shall not be taken for *public use* without just compensation" (emphasis added). It is, of course, significant that the section makes no mention of taking for a *private* use.

In sum, then, by constitutional mandate as well as by judicial pronouncement, the permanent impairment of private property for private purposes is not authorized in the absence of clearly demonstrated public benefit and use.

I would enjoin the defendant cement company from continuing the discharge of dust particles upon its neighbors' properties unless, within 18 months, the cement company abated this nuisance. * * *

NOTES AND QUESTIONS

1. The principal case is highly controversial, but addresses some of the challenges faced by the courts in deliberating whether to award an injunction. Why should the court eschew the award of an injunction? How would parties negotiate once an injunction was granted? If injunctions were routinely awarded, predict how operators, like Atlantic, would respond prior to establishing the plant causing pollution.

2. Consider an alternative argument. The right of eminent domain is given to public authorities exercising powers to take private property with the award of just compensation for the public benefit. By setting damages in the principal case, is the court providing a means for the (private) defendant to buy the plaintiff's property rights? If the court is setting the price for the defendant to purchase such rights, how should the quantum be assessed? Should it be confined to the diminution in value of the property? Extended to the personal annoyance suffered by the property holder? Farber, Reassessing Boomer: Justice, Efficiency, and Nuisance Law, Property Law and Legal Education: Essays in Honor of John E. Cribbett 7, 17 (P. Hay & M. Hoeflich eds., 1988) suggests that the formula should not be confined to the diminution in value but rather by the market value to purchase buffer rights. What if the bargaining costs were too great? See Kaplow and Shavell, Property Rules versus Liability Rules: An Economic Analysis, 109 Harv. L. Rev. 713 (1996).

3. Most courts do not adopt a categorical position regarding whether an injunction should be granted. Instead, once it has been determined that there is a nuisance the court engages in a process called "balancing of the equities" to see whether the issuance of an injunction is the most appropriate remedy. Courts consider a number of factors in this equitable determination, including: the character or extent of the harm suffered by or threatened to the plaintiff, the good faith or intentional misconduct of the defendant or his efforts to avoid injury to defendant, the financial investments of the parties and the relative economic harm each will suffer from the grant or denial of an injunction, and the interest of the general public in the continuance of the defendant's enterprise. See Estancias Dallas Corp. v. Schultz, 500 S.W.2d 217 (Tex. Civ. App. Beaumont 1973) (affirming the issuance of an injunction because little to no evidence was presented in favor of the public benefit of the operation of the apartment complex); Southwestern Constr. Co. v. Liberto, 385 So. 2d 633 (Ala. 1980)(highlighting that the determination of the balancing of the equities is

to be made after the determination of a nuisance and holding that the trial court's issuance of an injunction was adequately supported by the evidence presented in the case). See also Laycock, The Neglected Defense of Undue Hardship (and the Doctrinal Train Wreck in *Boomer v. Atlantic Cement*), criticizing the economic analysis for its failure to weigh adequately the defense of undue hardship that would leave the plaintiff to a damages remedy if the costs of compliance with the injunction disproportionately outweighed the benefits; and arguing that *Boomer* was not an innovation but that the defense of undue hardship had been well-established in New York as elsewhere.

4. In Little Joseph Realty, Inc. v. Babylon, 41 N.Y.2d 738, 363 N.E.2d 1163, 395 N.Y.S.2d 428 (1977), the court refused to apply the *Boomer* principle when an asphalt plant was located in violation of a zoning ordinance and the lower court conditioned an injunction on payment of permanent damages and abatement of the most offensive aspects. "[W]hen a continuing use flies in the face of a valid zoning restriction it must, subject to the existence of any appropriate equitable defenses, be enjoined unconditionally."

5. The principal case influenced the 1970 amendments to the Clean Air Act. In testimony before the Senate Committee, the majority opinion was criticized for not inducing industry to improve the state of technology. Judge Jasen's proposal of a conditional injunction was praised; S. 3229, S. 3466, and S. 3546, Subcomm. on Air and Water of the Senate Comm. on Public Works, 91st Cong., 2d Sess., part 2, at 849 (1970). Thus the Clean Air Act Amendment added strict deadlines called "technology-forcing" for industry compliance.

Spur Industries, Inc. v. Del E. Webb Development Co.

Supreme Court of Arizona, 1972.
108 Ariz. 178, 494 P.2d 700.

CAMERON, VICE CHIEF JUSTICE. From a judgment permanently enjoining the defendant, Spur Industries, Inc., from operating a cattle feedlot near the plaintiff Del E. Webb Development Company's Sun City, Spur appeals. Webb cross-appeals. Although numerous issues are raised, we feel that it is necessary to answer only two questions. They are:

1. Where the operation of a business, such as a cattle feedlot is lawful in the first instance, but becomes a nuisance by reason of a nearby residential area, may the feedlot operation be enjoined in an action brought by the developer of the residential area?

2. Assuming that the nuisance may be enjoined, may the developer of a completely new town or urban area in a previously agricultural area be required to indemnify the operator of the feedlot who must move or cease operation because of the presence of the residential area created by the developer?

[Farming had existed in the general area involved (about 14 to 15 miles west of urban Phoenix) prior to 1950. The property owned by Spur was well suited for cattle feeding, and Spur's predecessors began this activity. In 1959 Del Webb began to develop Sun City, some distance from Spur. The development progressed rapidly and expanded, coming into closer proximity to Spur.]

By December 1967, Del Webb's property had extended south to Olive Avenue and Spur was within 500 feet of Olive Avenue to the north. * * * Del Webb filed its original complaint alleging that in excess of 1,300 lots in the southwest portion were unfit for development for sale as residential lots because of the operation of the Spur feedlot.

Del Webb's suit complained that the Spur feeding operation was a public nuisance because of the flies and the odor which were drifting or being blown by the prevailing south to north wind over the southern portion of Sun City. At the time of the suit, Spur was feeding between 20,000 and 30,000 head of cattle, and the facts amply support the finding of the trial court that the feed pens had become a nuisance to the people who resided in the southern part of Del Webb's development. The testimony indicated that cattle in a commercial feedlot will produce 35 to 40 pounds of wet manure per day, per head, or over a million pounds of wet manure per day for 30,000 head of cattle, and that despite the admittedly good feedlot management and good housekeeping practices by Spur, the resulting odor and flies produced an annoying if not unhealthy situation as far as the senior citizens of southern Sun City were concerned. There is no doubt that some of the citizens of Sun City were unable to enjoy the outdoor living which Del Webb had advertised and that Del Webb was faced with sales resistance from prospective purchasers as well as strong and persistent complaints from the people who had purchased homes in that area. * * *

Where the injury is slight, the remedy for minor inconveniences lies in an action for damages rather than in one for an injunction. [c]. Moreover, some courts have held, in the "balancing of conveniences" cases, that damages may be the sole remedy. * * *

We have no difficulty, however, in agreeing with the conclusion of the trial court that Spur's operation was an enjoinable public nuisance as far as the people in the southern portion of Del Webb's Sun City were concerned. * * *

It is clear that as to the citizens of Sun City, the operation of Spur's feedlot was both a public and a private nuisance. They could have successfully maintained an action to abate the nuisance. Del Webb, having shown a special injury in the loss of sales, had a standing to bring suit to enjoin the nuisance. [Cc] The judgment of the trial court permanently enjoining the operation of the feedlot is affirmed. * * *

In the so-called "coming to the nuisance" cases, the courts have held that the residential landowner may not have relief if he knowingly came into a neighborhood reserved for industrial or agricultural endeavors and has been damaged thereby:

"Plaintiffs chose to live in an area uncontrolled by zoning laws or restrictive covenants and remote from urban development. In such an area plaintiffs cannot complain that legitimate agricultural pursuits are being carried on in the vicinity, nor can plaintiffs, having chosen to build in an agricultural area, complain that the agricultural pursuits carried on in the area depreciate the value of their homes. The area being *primarily agricultural,* any opinion reflecting the value of such property must take this factor into account. The standards affecting the value of residence property in an urban setting, subject to zoning controls and controlled planning techniques, cannot be the standards by which agricultural properties are judged.

"People employed in a city who build their homes in suburban areas of the county beyond the limits of a city and zoning regulations do so for a reason. Some do so to avoid the high taxation rate imposed by cities, or to avoid special assessments for street, sewer and water projects. They usually build on improved or hard surface highways, which have been built either at state or county expense and thereby avoid special assessments for these improvements. It may be that they desire to get away from the congestion of traffic, smoke, noise, foul air and the many other annoyances of city life. But with all these advantages in going beyond the area which is zoned and restricted to protect them in their homes, they must be prepared to take the disadvantages." Dill v. Excel Packing Company, 183 Kan. 513, 525, 526, 331 P.2d 539, 548, 549 (1958). * * *

Were Webb the only party injured, we would feel justified in holding that the doctrine of "coming to the nuisance" would have been a bar to the relief asked by Webb, and, on the other hand, had Spur located the feedlot near the outskirts of a city and had the city grown toward the feedlot, Spur would have to suffer the cost of abating the nuisance as to those people locating within the growth pattern of the expanding city. * * *

There was no indication in the instant case at the time Spur and its predecessors located in western Maricopa County that a new city would spring up, full-blown, alongside the feeding operation and that the developer of that city would ask the court to order Spur to move because of the new city. Spur is required to move not because of any wrongdoing on the part of Spur, but because of a proper and legitimate regard of the courts for the rights and interests of the public.

Del Webb, on the other hand, is entitled to the relief prayed for (a permanent injunction), not because Webb is blameless, but because of the damage to the people who have been encouraged to purchase homes in Sun City. It does not equitably or legally follow, however, that Webb, being entitled to the injunction, is then free of any liability to Spur if Webb has in fact been the cause of the damage Spur has sustained. It does not seem harsh to require a developer, who has taken advantage of the lesser land values in a rural area as well as the availability of large tracts of land on which to build and develop a new town or city in the area, to indemnify those who are forced to leave as a result.

Having brought people to the nuisance to the foreseeable detriment of Spur, Webb must indemnify Spur for a reasonable amount of the cost of moving or shutting down. It should be noted that this relief to Spur is limited to a case wherein a developer has, with foreseeability, brought into a previously agricultural or industrial area the population which makes necessary the granting of an injunction against a lawful business and for which the business has no adequate relief.

It is therefore the decision of this court that the matter be remanded to the trial court for a hearing upon the damages sustained by the defendant Spur as a reasonable and direct result of the granting of the permanent injunction. Since the result of the appeal may appear novel and both sides have obtained a measure of relief, it is ordered that each side will bear its own costs.

Affirmed in part, reversed in part, and remanded for further proceedings consistent with this opinion.

NOTES AND QUESTIONS

1. The majority rule is that the plaintiff is not barred from recovery for either a public or a private nuisance by the sole fact that he "comes to the nuisance" by buying property adjoining it. See Restatement (Second) of Torts § 840D; see also Chase v. Eldred Borough, 902 A.2d 992 (Pa. Cmwlth. Ct. 2006) (nuisance constituted by a hail of baseballs from outfield 20 feet away; injunction to prevent play until the town built a protective fence; plaintiff had bought house with knowledge of the baseball field in operation for 50 years).

2. The rule is not, however, an absolute one; and particularly in cases where other factors are more or less balanced, the fact that the plaintiff has come to the nuisance may be important and even decisive. An interesting case is East St. Johns Shingle Co. v. Portland, 195 Or. 505, 246 P.2d 554 (1952), where the plaintiff's shingle mill relied for its supply of logs upon rafting through a slough from the Columbia River. Defendant city discharged sewage into the river, which polluted the slough and fouled the logs, thus interfering seriously with plaintiff's business. When the plaintiff had bought its property twenty years before, the city was already polluting the slough; but with the growth of the community, the condition gradually became worse. The health of the city of Portland depended in large measure upon the sewage disposal, and there was no other way to dispose of it. It was held that plaintiff was not entitled either to an injunction or to damages.

3. Defendant does not acquire a prescriptive right to continue the nuisance through adverse use, unless during the necessary period an action might have been maintained for it. Ireland v. Bowman & Cockrell, 130 Ky. 153, 113 S.W. 56 (1908); Holsman v. Boiling Spring Bleaching Co., 14 N.J.Eq. 335 (1862). By the majority rule, one cannot acquire a prescriptive right to maintain a *public* nuisance, no matter how long it has continued, even though plaintiff brings suit for damages personal to himself. Gundy v. Merrill, 250 Mich. 416, 230 N.W. 163 (1930); Smejkal v. Empire Lite-Rock, Inc., 274 Or. 571, 547 P.2d 1363 (1976); and Foster Auto Parts, Inc. v. City of Portland, 171 Ore. App. 278, 15 P.3d 573 (2000).

4. The adjustment of the equities in the principal case by requiring indemnity is a new approach and the reverse of *Boomer*. It adds to the court's repertoire of remedies. How can these remedies be adjusted or combined to produce the fairest and most effective result? Suppose that newly arrived neighbors had obtained the injunction. How would the moving costs be apportioned? This topic has been the subject of some stimulating studies of the law of nuisance. See Calabresi & Melamed, Property Rules, Liability Rules and Inalienability: One View of the

Cathedral, 85 Harv.L.Rev. 1089 (1972); Lewin, Compensated Injunction on the Evolution of Nuisance Law, 71 Iowa L.Rev. 775 (1986); Kaplow and Shavell, Property Rules Versus Liability Rules: An Economic Analysis, 109 Harv. L. Rev. 713 (1996) (asserting that many variables, besides externalities, need to be taken into account in choosing between a liability and property rule). For discussion of various rules, their implications and desirability see also Symposium: Property Rules, Liability Rules, and Inalienability: A Twenty-Five Year Retrospective, 106 Yale L.J. 2083 (1997).

Other Torts Involving Invasion of Interests in Real Property

Besides Trespass and Nuisance, there are two additional commonly recognized torts arising on behalf of a landowner or possessor of real property because of damage to his interests in the land. They are

1. *Interference with the Support of Land.* This applies to both lateral support and subjacent support. If the withdrawal of the support is sufficient to cause a subsidence of the land in its natural condition—i.e., "naturally necessary support" is withdrawn—the liability is strict and no showing of fault on the part of the defendant is required. Damage to artificial additions to the land is also included. If the withdrawal of support would not have caused a subsidence of the land in its natural condition but does cause subsidence because of artificial additions to the land, then liability may still exist but it depends upon a finding that the actor's conduct was negligent. See Bonomi v. Backhouse, El.Bl. & El. 622, 120 Eng.Rep. 643 (1859), aff'd, 9 H.L. 503, 11 Eng.Rep. 825 (1861); Blake Constr. Co. v. United States, 218 Ct.Cl. 163, 585 F.2d 998 (1978); St. Louis-S.F.R.R. v. Wade, 607 F.2d 126 (5th Cir.1979); St. Joseph Light & Power Co. v. Kaw Valley Tunneling, 589 S.W.2d 260 (Mo.1979). On subsidence caused by withdrawal of ground water, see Friendswood Dev. Co. v. Smith-Southwest Industries, Inc., 576 S.W.2d 21 (Tex.1978), Sipriano v. Great Spring Waters of Am., Inc., 1 S.W.3d 75 (Tex. 1999), and Maddocks v. Giles, 728 A.2d 150 (Me. 1999). See also Restatement (Second) of Torts §§ 817–821 (1979).

2. *Interference with the Use of Water.* This tort covers three types of water: water in a watercourse or lake in or adjoining the land ("riparian rights"), ground water (sometime called subterranean water or underground water) and surface waters (from precipitation). On the subject of riparian rights, there are three distinct legal theories for determination of the rights involved. The first, adopted in England and used by a few American states, is the natural-flow theory—the right to have the water flow as it was wont to flow in nature, qualified only by the right of each riparian owner to make a limited use of it. The second, adopted in a majority of American states, is the reasonable-use theory—the right to be free from unreasonable uses that cause harm to the proprietor's own reasonable use. The third, adopted largely in the states of the west, is the prior-appropriation rule, that beneficial use of the water is the basis of the right to it and that priority of use is the basis of the division of it between appropriators when there is not enough for all. The reasonable-use theory is the most flexible and adaptable one, and it has succeeded in adapting to both of the other two in terms of the factors affecting the determination of when a use is reasonable. It is now distinctly the majority rule. In a

number of states, there are statutory provisions modifying the common law rules.

On the use of "ground water" (subsurface water), there are also several theories: (1) the English rule of absolute ownership, (2) the American rule of reasonable use, a rule of correlative rights, and (3) the rule that an "underground stream" is treated like a surface stream. Here too, the adaptable reasonable-use rule is growing in number of adherents, and there are statutory modifications in some states. As for surface waters, there is general agreement that a landowner can use as much of them as he needs.

The subject is canvassed in Chapter 41 of the Restatement (Second) of Torts §§ 841–864.

CHAPTER 17

DEFAMATION

The term "tort" deriving from the Latin *tortus,* meaning twisted, is apt for the tort of defamation in two senses. The conduct involved is twisted, or crooked; and the law governing it is twisted, or wrenched sadly out of shape by its historical development. As one commentator put it, the law of defamation was "[m]arred in the making." 1 THOMAS ATKINS STREET, THE FOUNDATIONS OF LEGAL LIABILITY: A PRESENTATION OF THE THEORY AND DEVELOPMENT OF THE COMMON LAW 273 (1906). Rules and distinctions originating from ancient controversies over jurisdiction, long since obsolete, nevertheless became frozen and crystallized.

Originally the common law courts took no jurisdiction over any defamation, leaving it to be dealt with by the local seigniorial courts. When these fell into decay, the ecclesiastical courts began to take jurisdiction over slander, regarding it as a sin and punishing it with penance. Since the cases all involved oral defamation, slander became identified with word of mouth. When the ecclesiastical courts in turn began to lose their power, there was in the sixteenth century a slow infiltration of tort actions for slander into the common law courts. The excuse for this invasion of church jurisdiction was that some "temporal" damage had been done, distinct from the mere "spiritual" offense, and that it was properly a matter for the king's courts to redress. A long conflict of jurisdiction, part of the broader contest between church and state, finally fixed this as a requirement for any slander action at common law. See Ogden v. Turner, (1703) 87 Eng. Rep. 862 (K.B.); 6 Mod. Rep. 104 (Eng); Davies v. Gardiner, (1593) 79 Eng. Rep. 1155 (K.B.); Popham 37 (Eng.); Matthew v. Crass, (1614) 79 Eng. Rep. 276 (K.B.); Cro. Jac. 323 (Eng.). The result was that slander became actionable only in those cases where special damage of a "temporal" or pecuniary character was proved or could reasonably be assumed.

About the beginning of the seventeenth century, the Court of Star Chamber began independently to punish the crime of libel, in order to suppress the seditious publications that had multiplied with the spread of printing. In the earliest cases the libels were political, and the crime was a form of sedition. It was gradually extended to non-political libels, and still later tort damages were awarded to the person defamed, probably in order to provide a legal substitute for the duel when it was forbidden. When the Star Chamber was abolished, jurisdiction over libel in turn passed to the common law courts. Through this process, libel became identified with printed or written defamation, while slander remained oral. Instead of merging the two torts, the courts maintained their separate identity, as well as the rules that had grown up around slander.

In the sixteenth and seventeenth centuries the judges were annoyed by the flood of rather frivolous actions let loose upon them once their jurisdiction over slander was established, and were reluctant to extend the possibilities of recovery. In addition, further development of the law of defamation was arrested when it encountered the rising tide of sentiment in favor of freedom of speech and the press, which, together with the odium attached to the memory of the Star Chamber and its political prosecutions, made any action for defamation an unpopular one, and the court somewhat reluctant in dealing with it.

Few commentators have had a kind word to say about the general condition of the common law of defamation as it finally developed. Many calls have been made for its complete overhaul and reform. Some studies have been undertaken with this end in view. But they have failed to accomplish any really worthwhile results. The outstanding historical treatment is Richard H. Helmholz, *Introduction* to SELECT CASES ON DEFAMATION TO 1600, *IN* 101 THE PUBLICATIONS OF THE SELDON SOCIETY (Richard H. Helmholz ed., 1985).

In 1964, a new reformer entered the field. The United States Supreme Court decided the case of *N.Y. Times Co. v. Sullivan*, 376 U.S. 254 (1964), see infra page 922, holding that the free-speech and free-press provisions of the First Amendment, as applied through the Fourteenth Amendment, affected the common law of defamation.

Since that time, the decisions under the First Amendment have produced numerous changes in the law of defamation, some of them very far ranging in effect. The Supreme Court itself is still slowly feeling its way on the course to take. The Court has wavered and changed its position on several matters, so that a good deal of uncertainty remains as to the extent of present law and future change in it. For this reason, the first part of this chapter will be primarily concerned with the common law of defamation, with only incidental references to constitutional holdings. Beginning with *N.Y. Times Co. v. Sullivan*, see infra page 922, the emphasis will be placed on the constitutional developments.

The law of torts involves a careful balancing of conflicting individual and social interests, with the establishment of principles, rules and standards for the purpose of enabling the court to reach the appropriate result in the particular case. In this chapter, you will observe that the same kind of balancing of interests is followed. Social concepts about the function of reputation have shifted from protection of honor to protection of property. This individual interest has had to be reconciled with the public interest in freedom of expression, not only as developed by the common law, but more recently by dint of the First Amendment. See Robert C. Post, The Social Foundations of Defamation Law: Reputation and the Constitution, 74 Cal. L. Rev. 691 (1986). This maelstrom of interests sometimes creates serious difficulties in maintaining orderly organization in the tort law of defamation. It is a stimulating and sometimes frustrating process to contemplate and study.

1. NATURE OF A DEFAMATORY COMMUNICATION

Belli v. Orlando Daily Newspapers, Inc.

United States Court of Appeals, Fifth Circuit, 1967.
389 F.2d 579, cert. denied 393 U.S. 825, 89 S.Ct. 88, 21 L.Ed.2d 96 (1968).

WISDOM, CIRCUIT JUDGE. This action for damages for libel and slander is based on a false statement relating to Mr. Melvin Belli. Belli, an attorney of national prominence, is well known in the legal profession for his pioneering in the development of demonstrative evidence as a trial tactic and his success in obtaining large judgments for plaintiffs in personal injury suits. He is well known to the general public because of his representation of Jack Ruby and others in the public eye.

In March 1964 Mr. Leon Handley, an attorney in Orlando, Florida, in a conversation with Miss Jean Yothers, a columnist for the Orlando Evening Star, repeated a story he had heard concerning Belli. Handley told Yothers that the Florida Bar Association had invited Belli to serve as a member of one of the panels on the program of the Association at its 1955 Convention in Miami Beach. Belli agreed, with the understanding that "since there were no funds provided in the budget for payment per se for his contribution as a lawyer to the program the Florida Bar instead would pick up the hotel tab for himself and his wife during their stay." According to Handley, after Mr. and Mrs. Belli left Florida, the Association discovered that the Bellis "ran up a bunch of [clothing] bills" which they charged to their hotel room. The derogatory portion of the story was admittedly false: The Bellis had not charged any purchases to their hotel account. Unfortunately for all, Jean Yothers reported, with embellishments, this nine-year old story in her gossip column in the Orlando Evening Star for March 19, 1964.[2] * * *

---

[2] The article appeared in the Orlando Evening Star under the title "On the Town" by Jean Yothers and headed "Florida Bar Got the Bill". The full text is as follows:

Jack Ruby's flamboyant attorney Melvin Belli of San Francisco makes an indelible impression whither he goeth.

Consider the time he and Mrs. Belli were in Miami six or so years ago and Belli was a member of a panel at a program-meeting of the Florida Bar.

Here's what happened:

In making arrangements for Belli's participation it had been pointed out to him that since there were no funds provided in the budget for payment per se for his contribution as a lawyer to the program, the Florida Bar instead would pick up the hotel tab for himself and his wife during their stay.

Belli agreed.

Oops!

A local attorney remembers, with embarrassed chagrin, how the plan backfired on the Florida Bar.

After the well-dressed Mr. Belli and his well-dressed wife left town, the hotel where they had been staying received clothing bills amounting to hundreds of $s. The Bellis had shopped in Miami stores and charged clothing bills to their hotel rooms.

The Florida Bar had been taken.

It was hard to stomach but the Board of Governors of the Florida Bar picked up the Bellis' bill.

After all, that was the plan!

The district court dismissed Belli's complaint for failure to state a claim upon which relief could be granted. The court relied on the erroneous assumption that the determination whether a statement is a libel (or slander) per se is solely for the court. We consider it a close question whether the publication is so clearly defamatory that as a matter of law the case should not be submitted to the jury. We hold, however, that the publication itself, without reference to extrinsic facts, is capable of carrying a defamatory meaning. It is for a jury to determine whether it was so understood by the "common mind". We reverse and remand. * * *

In Florida and in many states * * * a libel per se is "any publication which exposes a person to distrust, hatred, contempt, ridicule, obloquy". For example, in Briggs v. Brown, 55 Fla. 417, 46 So. 325, 330 (1908) the court states the formula for libels per se as follows:

"A civil action for libel will lie when there has been a false and unprivileged publication by letter or otherwise which exposes a person to distrust, hatred, contempt, ridicule, or obloquy * * * or which has a tendency to injure such person in his office, occupation, business, or employment. If the publication is false and not privileged, and is such that its natural and proximate consequence necessarily causes injury to a person in his personal, social, official, or business relations or life, wrong and injury are presumed and implied, and such publication is actionable per se." * * *

We find that the general law and Florida law are in agreement with Dean Prosser's conclusion: "It is for the court *in the first instance* to determine whether the words are reasonably capable of a particular interpretation, or whether they are necessarily so; it is then for the jury to say whether they were in fact understood as defamatory. If the language used is open to two meanings * * * it is for the jury to determine whether the defamatory sense was the one conveyed." (Emphasis added.) Prosser, Law of Torts § 106, at 765 (1963). * * *

Both judge and jury play a part in determining whether language constitutes libel. The Supreme Court has delineated these roles in Washington Post Co. v. Chaloner, 1919, 250 U.S. 290:

"A publication claimed to be defamatory must be read and construed in the sense in which the readers to whom it is addressed would ordinarily understand it. * * * When thus read, if its meaning is so unambiguous as to reasonably bear but one interpretation, it is for the judge to say whether that signification is defamatory or not. If, upon the other hand, it is capable of two meanings, one of which would be libelous and actionable and the other not, it is for the jury to say, under all the circumstances surrounding its publication, including extraneous facts admissible in evidence, which of the two meanings would be attributed to it by those to whom it is addressed or by whom it may be read." * * *

The district court in this case completely excised the jury's role, a position it could take only on the assumption that the publication unambiguously carried no defamatory meaning. Since the court did not spell out its reasons, the defendants in their briefs have attempted to articulate the rationale for the holding below.

The defendants argue that the article did not "hurt" Belli as an attorney, did not imply that he was "losing his touch with demonstrative evidence", did not affect his ability to "obtain those 'more adequate awards' for seamen and railroad workers for which he is so justly famous". In effect, so the argument runs, the article was nothing more than caustic comment on the acuteness of the Florida Bar Association. Belli simply "showed the Florida lawyers that their agreement was somewhat more favorable to him tha[n] they—in their naiveté—contemplated". In its harshest sense, they say, "the article implies no more than that Mr. Belli 'put one over' on the Florida Bar", which is "not quite the same as conning a destitute widow out of her homestead". In short, Mr. Belli just got "a little more out of the agreement than the Bar Association contemplated".

The defendants make a case—just barely—for the view that the article is capable of being reasonably interpreted as non-defamatory. But since the article on its face is also capable of carrying a defamatory meaning, it is for the jury to decide whether the words were in fact so understood.

The plaintiff contends, in his brief, "No person reading the headline and the article *sub judice* * * * could conclude other than that Melvin Belli, both as a lawyer and as a private citizen is grasping, conniving, contemptible, dishonest; a cheat, swindler, trickster, deceiver, defrauder; a person to be avoided, shunned and distrusted." Without benefit of the defendants' cavalier reading of the article or the plaintiff's retort hyperbolic, we consider that the bare bones of the article are capable of carrying the meaning that Belli tricked and deceived the Florida Bar Association out of hundreds of dollars worth of clothes. * * *

The author's comment seems intended to insure the common reader's understanding of what purportedly happened. The common reader is likely to understand "take", just as Miss Yothers must have understood it. A recent dictionary defines it: "To cheat, deceive"; other dictionaries agree with this definition. The man in the street is likely to understand that hotel expenses do not include "hundreds of dollars worth of clothing". But any doubts the reader might have as to what purportedly happened are likely to be resolved by the reference to Belli's "plan" to "take" the Florida Bar. We hold that a jury might reasonably conclude that the conduct imputed to Belli was incompatible with the standards of an ethical lawyer and as such violated one of the four traditional categories of libel per se. A jury might also conclude that such conduct subjected Belli to contempt, and ridicule, humiliating him socially and injuring him professionally.

The Court has some doubt whether the publication in question carries a non-defamatory meaning. The Court has very little doubt that it carries a defamatory meaning. The Court has concluded however that the final determination of the issue of defamation should be made by a jury.

The story is nine years old. It was not made within the context of a discussion of an important public issue. Nevertheless, the delimiting effect of the law of libel on First Amendment rights and a free press impels the Court not to excise the role of the jury. "Since one's reputation is the view which others take of him * * * [w]hether an idea injures a person's reputation depends upon the opinions of those to whom it is published." Developments in the Law: Defamation, 69 Harv.L.Rev. 875, 881–82 (1956). Thus, because it is impractical, even unreliable, to depend upon in-court testimony of recipients of the particular publication for determining whether that publication is defamatory, a logical function of the jury is to decide whether the plaintiff has been lowered in the esteem of those to whom the idea was published. * * *

We reverse the dismissal of the district court and remand the case for further proceedings consistent with this opinion.

NOTES AND QUESTIONS

1. The older definition of defamation was that of a communication to a third person, "which is calculated to injure the reputation of another, by exposing him to hatred, contempt, or ridicule, is a libel." This appears to have originated with Baron Parke, in Parmiter v. Coupland, (1840) 151 Eng. Rep. 340 (Exch.) 342; 6 M. & W. 104, 109 (Eng.): It is still often repeated by the courts. For a modern articulation of the definition, see Gorman v. Wolpoff & Abramson, LLP, 584 F.3d 1147 (9th Cir. 2009) (citing definition of libel under California law as set forth in Cal. Civ. Code § 45); McLeod v. State, 206 P.3d 956 (Mont. 2009) (citing definition of libel under Montana law as set forth in Mont. Code Ann. § 27–1–802).

2. When the question has arisen, the later cases have recognized that this definition is too narrow. Defamation is rather a communication that tends to damage the plaintiff's "reputation," more or less in the popular sense—that is, to diminish the respect, good will, confidence or esteem in which he is held, or to excite adverse or unpleasant feelings about him. And this is the case even though decent citizens would regard him only with pity.

3. Which of the following are in themselves defamatory?

"He is under treatment for mental illness." Cowper v. Vannier, 156 N.E.2d 761 (Ill. App. Ct. 1959). "He refuses to pay his just debts." Thompson v. Adelberg & Berman, 205 S.W. 558 (Ky. 1918). "His parents were never married." Cf. Harris v. Nashville Trust Co., 162 S.W. 584 (Tenn. 1914). "He is a liar." Murphy v. Harty, 393 P.2d 206 (Or. 1964). A motion picture portrays an identifiable woman as having been raped by Rasputin. Youssoupoff v. Metro-Goldwyn-Mayer Pictures, Ltd., (1934) 50 T.L.R. 581 (A.C) (Eng.). His face "resembles a hard-boiled egg," "roly-poly, like a rubber beach toy," "relentlessly small town in fashion and horizon." Raymer v. Doubleday & Co., 615 F.2d 241 (5th Cir. 1980). "Sinatra's Mouthpiece." Rudin v. Dow Jones & Co., 510 F. Supp. 210 (S.D.N.Y. 1981). "He is a son of a bitch." Cf. White v. Valenta, Cal. Rptr. 241 (Cal. Dist. Ct. App. 1965); Bryson v. News Am. Publ'ns, Inc., 672 N.E.2d 1207 (Ill. 1996) ("I remembered what a slut she was and forgot about the sorriness I'd been holding onto for her.").

Grant v. Reader's Digest Ass'n

United States Circuit Court of Appeals, Second Circuit, 1945.
151 F.2d 733.

L. HAND, CIRCUIT JUDGE. This is an appeal from a judgment dismissing a complaint in libel for insufficiency in law upon its face. The complaint alleged that the plaintiff was a Massachusetts lawyer, living in that state; that the defendant, a New York corporation, published a periodical of general circulation, read by lawyers, judges and the general public; and that one issue of the periodical contained an article entitled "I Object To My Union in Politics," in which the following passage appeared:

"And another thing. In my state the Political Action Committee has hired as its legislative agent one, Sidney S. Grant, who but recently was a legislative representative for the Massachusetts Communist Party."

The innuendo then alleged that this passage charged the plaintiff with having represented the Communist Party in Massachusetts as its legislative agent, which was untrue and malicious. Two questions arise: (1) What meaning the jury might attribute to the words; (2) whether the meaning so attributed was libellous. * * * The case therefore turns upon whether it is libellous in New York to write of a lawyer that he has acted as agent of the Communist Party, and is a believer in its aims and methods.

The interest at stake in all defamation is concededly the reputation of the person assailed; and any moral obliquity of the opinions of those in whose minds the words might lessen that reputation, would normally be relevant only in mitigation of damages. A man may value his reputation even among those who do not embrace the prevailing moral standards; and it would seem that the jury should be allowed to appraise how far he should be indemnified for the disesteem of such persons. That is the usual rule. [Cc] The New York decisions define libel, in accordance with the usual rubric, as consisting of utterances which arouse "hatred, contempt, scorn, obloquy or shame," and the like. [Cc] However, the opinions at times seem to make it a condition that to be actionable the words must be such as would so affect "right-thinking" people. * * * The same limitation has apparently been recognized in England [c]; and it is fairly plain that there must come a point where that is true. As was said in Mawe v. Piggott, Irish Rep. 4 Comm.Law, 54, 62, among those "who were themselves criminal or sympathized with crime," it would expose one "to great odium to represent him as an informer or prosecutor or otherwise aiding in the detection of crime"; yet certainly the words would not be actionable. Be that as it may, in New York, if the exception covers more than such a case, it does not go far enough to excuse the utterance at bar. Katapodis v. Brooklyn Spectator, Inc., 287 N.Y. 17, 38 N.E.2d 112 * * * held that the imputation of extreme poverty might be actionable; although certainly "right-thinking people" ought not to shun, or despise, or otherwise condemn one because he is poor. Indeed, the only declaration of the Court of Appeals [c] leaves it still open whether it is not libellous to say that a man is insane. [Cc]

We do not believe, therefore, that we need say whether "right-thinking" people would harbor similar feelings toward a lawyer, because he had been an agent for the Communist Party, or was a sympathizer with its aims and means. It is enough if there be some, as there certainly are, who would feel so, even though they would be "wrong-thinking" people if they did. * * *

Judgment reversed; cause remanded.

NOTES AND QUESTIONS

1. In accord with this decision are two excellent, and lengthy, opinions arising out of a similar charge, in Herrmann v. Newark Morning Ledger Co., 138 A.2d 61 (N.J. Super. Ct. App. Div. 1958), *aff'd on reh'g*, 140 A.2d 529 (N.J. Super. Ct. App. Div. 1958).

2. The leading case is Peck v. Tribune Co., 214 U.S. 185 (1909), where defendant, by mistake, published plaintiff's picture accompanying a testimonial signed by another woman, who was a nurse, in praise of the merits of Duffy's Pure Malt Whiskey. Holmes, J.: "If the advertisement obviously would hurt the plaintiff in the estimation of an important and respectable part of the community, liability is not a question of a majority vote." 214 U.S. at 190. Massachusetts courts have kept the Holmesian faith: King v. Globe Newspaper Co., 512 N.E.2d 241 (Mass. 1987) (finding that because statement about plaintiff governor had both a libelous and a non-libelous meaning, trial judge could not enter summary judgment for defendant).

3. What about the statement that plaintiff is obtaining a divorce? Gersten v. Newark Morning Ledger Co., 145 A.2d 56 (N.J. Super. Ct. Law Div. 1958). Or that a business man is a "price cutter"? Meyerson v. Hurlbut, 98 F.2d 232 (D.C. Cir. 1938). Or that a kosher meat dealer sells bacon? Braun v. Armour & Co., 173 N.E. 845 (N.Y. 1930). The issue is embedded in time, place, and culture. Jones v. R.L. Polk & Co., 67 So. 577 (Ala. 1915) (to be described as "colored" defamatory); Natchez Times Publ'g Co. v. Dunigan, 72 So.2d 681 (Miss. 1954) (to be listed as a "negro" in the telephone book is defamatory); but not so in England, Forbes v. King, (1833) 1 Dowl. 672 (K.B.) 673 (Eng.) (writing that plaintiff is a "Man Friday" is not defamatory). An imputation of homosexuality? Nowark v. Maguire, 22 A.D.2d 901 (N.Y. App. Div. 1964); Buck v. Savage, 323 S.W.2d 363 (Tex. Civ. App. 1959); Hayes v. Smith, 832 P.2d. 1022 (Colo. App. 1991); Starks v. McCabe, 49 Va. Cir. 554 (Va. Cir. Ct. 1998).

4. There must, however, be an element of discredit or disgrace, even in the eyes of the particular segment of the community. Thus if a Democrat is called a Republican, it is quite probable that unpleasant feelings would be aroused against him in the minds of some other Democrats; but it can scarcely be regarded as defamatory. Cf. Steinman v. Roberts, 23 A.D.2d 693 (N.Y. App. Div. 1965) ("liberal"); Haas v. Evening Democrat Co., 107 N.W.2d 444 (Iowa 1961) ("conservative").What of a publication saying a woman is a "feminist"?

5. A statement that plaintiff has informed the police about crime has been held not to be defamatory. Why? Mawe v. Piggott, (1869) 4 Ir. R.-C.L. 54; Rose v. Borenstein, 119 N.Y.S.2d 288 (1953); Byrne v. Deane, (1937) 1 K.B. 818 (Eng.). In the last case the allegation was that the plaintiff had

"ratted" to the police about fellow club members' illegal gambling on club premises. Yet the goodwill of fellow club members may be vital to a person's functioning in society. Why have a test that fails to undergird the individual's interest in being free of imputations that tend to estrange her from those with whom social intercourse is most important?

Pleading Defamation

6. When the meaning that defames the plaintiff is clear upon the face of the words uttered, the cause of action is made out by pleading, and proving, the words themselves and their communication to a third person. However, defamers can be highly creative, imaginative, and devious in conveying a defamatory imputation in words or conduct. As the RESTATEMENT (SECOND) OF TORTS § 563 cmt. c (1977) states, defamatory matter may be communicated "by innuendo, by figure of speech, by expressions of belief, by allusion or by irony or satire . . . or by words spoken in jest if not so understood." DAVID ELDER, DEFAMATION: A LAWYER'S GUIDE § 1:7 (2002 & Supp. 2004), provides a list of authorities exemplifying the importance of context in arriving at defamatory meaning.

Where the meaning is not clear, the plaintiff must plead the context that renders the words or conduct defamatory. The defamatory imputation may arise from the juxtaposition of material, as where an actress participates in a commercial ad with sexually explicit pornography. She was libeled because of the implication that she willingly participated in pornography. Geary v. Goldstein, 831 F. Supp. 269, 277–78 (S.D.N.Y. 1993). The matter may be defamatory by making material omissions. For example, omitting to report the presence of two other persons at shooting gave rise to the implication that plaintiff was having an affair with suspect's husband. Memphis Publ'g Co. v. Nichols, 569 S.W.2d 412 (Tenn. 1978).

The law of pleading the defamation is arcane and technical. For example, take the words: "He burned down his own barn." This the plaintiff would have a perfect right to do if he chose, and on its face the statement does not defame him. Here the courts very early set up quite technical rules as to the way in which the action must be pleaded; and although these have been relaxed slightly here and there, they are in the main still rather rigidly followed. In such a case the plaintiff must plead:

A. The defamatory words, "He burned down his own barn."

B. The publication: communication of the words to a third person. "Defendant spoke these words to X."

C. Extrinsic facts, because of which the words were reasonably understood to convey a meaning defaming the plaintiff. This is called the "inducement." For example, X knew that plaintiff had insurance on the barn.

D. A formal allegation that the words were spoken of and concerning plaintiff. This is called the "colloquium." "He (meaning the plaintiff) burned down his own barn."

E. An allegation of the particular defamatory meaning conveyed by the words. This is called the "innuendo." In this case, that the words were understood by X to mean that plaintiff had burned the barn in order to defraud the insurance company, which would be the crime of arson.

F. Special damages, when they are necessary to the cause of action.

7. Both the colloquium and the innuendo must be reasonable in the light of the words spoken and the facts pleaded in the inducement. If the words, together with such facts, do not fairly support the defamatory meaning pleaded, no cause of action is made out. See also Davis v. R.K.O. Radio Pictures, Inc., 191 F.2d 901 (8th Cir. 1951) (colloquium); Grice v. Holk, 108 So. 2d 359 (Ala. 1949) (innuendo).

Kilian v. Doubleday & Co., Inc.

Supreme Court of Pennsylvania, 1951.
367 Pa. 117, 79 A.2d 657.

HORACE STERN, JUSTICE. In this action for libel the jury rendered a verdict in favor of defendant. Plaintiff appeals from the refusal of the court below to grant him a new trial.

This is the way in which the allegedly libelous article came to be written:—At the American University in Washington a course in English was conducted by Don M. Wolfe, the students being disabled veterans of World War II. The course consisted, in part, of the writing by the students of essays or stories about their personal experiences in the war; their compositions would be submitted to Dr. Wolfe, who suggested corrections and revisions. Dr. Wolfe conceived the idea of having these stories published in book form, and, after an original publication by another concern, he entered into a contract with defendant, Doubleday & Company, for that purpose. Each student in the class, 53 in all, contributed at least one article. The book was published under the title "The Purple Testament", and it was advertised in the jacket as consisting of "the native eloquence of *absolute honesty,*" and as constituting "the fragments of their [the authors'] *own intimate experiences.*" Some 9000 copies were sold and distributed throughout the United States. Among the articles was one by Joseph M. O'Connell which gave rise to the present suit.

O'Connell was a soldier who had been seriously injured during the course of the Normandy invasion and was hospitalized from August to October, 1944, at a station hospital about 12 miles from Lichfield, England, where there was a large replacement depot. In the original draft of the article which he wrote he narrated incidents said to have occurred at the Lichfield camp and which, he testified at the trial, were described to him by individuals who had allegedly witnessed them. Dr. Wolfe, to whom he submitted the draft several times, stated that he "thought it was interesting, and that it was the first time he had heard about it", but twice returned it with the suggestion that O'Connell should use "more descriptive detail", that he should "make it more vivid", that it "did not have in it the sights, sounds and bits of conversation necessary to make the story readable". The result was that whereas O'Connell had originally written the article in the third person he now wrote it, in order to "make it more vivid", in the first person, purporting that the incidents he narrated occurred under his own personal observation and in his own experience.

The story, as it finally appeared in "The Purple Testament", may be condensed as follows:—I [O'Connell] and my buddy, while being transferred in an ambulance from one hospital to another in England, reached a big army camp near Lichfield. The camp was dreary and ugly; it reminded me of the rotten, filthy German prison camps I had seen in France. As we lay in the ambulance we heard a loud voice outside shouting: "Just let me catch one of you sons o'bitches loaf on this detail and you'll get twenty lashes when you get back tonight." A group of four men came to carry us into the hospital; they were all dressed in blue pants and shirts with a large letter "P" sewed on their clothes. The same loud voice I had heard a few minutes before said: "You're not supposed to talk to these ______ prisoners." A big heavy-set sergeant stepped closer to me and said, "All they are is a bunch of cowards. They are too yellow to go back to combat. They'll be glad to go back when they finish with this prison." The sergeant ordered them to carry us into the hospital; as they were placing me there in my bed I noticed that one of them had all the fingers of his right hand missing and three fingers of his left. Could such things be allowed in our army? If so, it was being covered up by the brass, and the brass were making suckers of the American people. A ward attendant limping around outside the room came in and said: "I was blown out of a tank; all the muscle of my right leg was blown away. * * * I came through this way on my way [back] to combat. One day the old man (Colonel ______) ordered us out on a ten-mile hike. After about two miles I fell flat on my face. They ordered me on, but I couldn't go. So the next day they took me before the old dictator. He ordered me before a quick court martial. I got six months of hard labor. The doctor said I was unfit for hard labor, so they assigned me to this hospital. I'm still a prisoner. The other night a guard caught me stealing a piece of bread from the kitchen, and I got fifty lashes for it." * * * In the morning the old colonel himself came along to inspect the hospital. He wasn't a big guy, but he was stockily built. Behind his glasses his eyes were mean. He looked like a man who enjoys seeing another man suffer. He was surrounded by a lot of other officers. None of them looked good to me. After one scowling glance at Red [my buddy] and me, he left. As we were being carried down the hall of the ward the big sergeant was clubbing a G.I. in a corner, while some officers looked on. I only hoped that some day I would meet up with that big sergeant and the rest of the people that ran that prison. The death chair would be too good for them. But as always, Colonel ______ and the rest of the responsible officers will be protected by the big brass. Mark my word, Colonel ______ and his bullies will get off light. That is Lichfield justice.

It is not questioned that by "Colonel ______", the "old dictator", and "the old colonel", was meant Colonel Kilian, the present plaintiff, who was the commanding officer of the Lichfield camp. At the end of the article as published there was appended a footnote which Dr. Wolfe himself had added and which stated:—"On August 29, 1946, the Associated Press reported that Colonel James A. Kilian was convicted 'of permitting cruel and unusual punishment of American soldiers.' He was reprimanded by the military court and fined $500.—Editor." This insertion was obviously intended to give the impression that what was said or implied in the article in regard to Colonel Kilian was corroborated by his conviction, and further that, as the author of the article had predicted, he "got off light".

The fact in regard to plaintiff's trial before a military court in 1946 is this:—He was charged with *authorizing, aiding and abetting* the imposition of cruel, unusual and unauthorized punishments upon prisoners in confinement at the depot of which he was the Commanding Officer. The punishments referred to were itemized in the charge. A second specification was that he *knowingly permitted* the imposition of such punishments. As to the first specification—authorizing, aiding and abetting—he was acquitted; as to the second specification—knowingly permitting—he was acquitted of *knowingly* permitting and found guilty merely of *permitting;* in other words, he was convicted of neglect, but not of actual wrongdoing or of acquiescing in what occurred. Moreover, many of the alleged punishments specified in the charge as having been "permitted" were deleted by the court because they were not supported by the evidence. * * *

As affirmative defense to the action defendant pleaded justification on the ground that the publication was "a *true and accurate account of events which were observed by the author of the article in question.*" How is that defense supported by the testimony presented at the trial? As far as O'Connell being an eye-witness of any of the alleged happenings at the camp is concerned, he admitted on the witness stand that he never was at Lichfield; therefore, his article, in that respect, was wholly false. Defendant produced as witnesses three soldiers who *were* at Lichfield, who testified to punishments inflicted on them or observed by them as imposed on others, but none of the incidents they described tended to prove that a single one of the events narrated in the O'Connell article actually occurred; therefore such testimony was not properly admissible to prove the truth of the publication. While, in order to support a defense of truth, it is necessary merely to prove that it was *substantially* true, and while, therefore, if the testimony of those witnesses had shown a variance merely in the details of the events described in the article it would nevertheless have been admissible as giving support to the plea of truth, it furnished no such support by proving that other and wholly different incidents occurred although these also may have been equally blameworthy. * * * "Specific charges cannot be justified by showing the plaintiff's general bad character; and if the accusation is one of particular misconduct, such as stealing a watch from A, it is not enough to show a different offense, even though it be a more serious one, such as stealing a clock from A, or six watches from B." Prosser on Torts, p. 855, § 95. * * * None of defendant's testimony showed any instances at the camp, as alleged in O'Connell's article, of lashing, of cursing prisoners, of having a soldier whose fingers were missing act as a stretcher bearer, of ordering a badly wounded veteran on a ten-mile hike. * * * It is obvious that there was not a shred of testimony presented at the trial to prove either that the author of the article saw any of the events he narrated, or that those events or even substantially similar ones occurred, or that plaintiff was aware of any such happenings, or that he sanctioned them, or that he was a "dictator", or that in his very appearance he looked like a man who would enjoy seeing another man suffer. The court, therefore, was in error in submitting to the jury, as it did, the question whether the publication was substantially true. * * *

Judgment reversed and new trial awarded.

NOTES AND QUESTIONS

1. Under the common law the defense that the defamatory statement was true was not open to the defendant in a prosecution for criminal libel. That crime was originated to suppress sedition, and later extended to prevent breaches of the peace, and neither was likely to be minimized if the defamation were true. Hence the criminal courts took no account of any freedom to publish the truth. The Case de Libellis Famosis, (1605) 77 Eng. Rep. 250 (K.B.); 5 Co. Rep. 125 a (Eng.); The King v. Franklin, (1731) 25 Eng. Rep. 499 (Ch.); W. Kel. 76 (Eng.). This explains the statement, usually attributed to Lord Mansfield, that "the greater the truth the greater the libel." In the Unites States, the Supreme Court has held that a criminal libel statute is unconstitutional if it imposes a penalty for making a true statement about a public official. Garrison v. Louisiana, 379 U.S. 64 (1964). However, a criminal libel prosecution of public persons (and private persons) is sustainable if "calculated falsehood" is proved.

2. The criminal law rule never was applied to civil actions. Johns v. Gittings, (1589) 78 Eng. Rep. 495 (Q.B.); Cro. Eliz. 239 (Eng.); Hilsden v. Mercer, (1623) 79 Eng. Rep. 586 (K.B.); Cro. Jac. 677 (Eng.).At common law there has been general agreement that an action of defamation will lie only if the statement is both defamatory and false. Statutes in a few states and judicial decisions in some others have indicated that an action may lie even for a true statement if it was not made for good motives and justifiable ends. E.g., Hutchins v. Page, 72 A. 689 (N.H. 1909). But a statute of this nature was held unconstitutional as a violation of the First Amendment in Farnsworth v. Tribune Co., 253 N.E.2d 408 (Ill. 1969). This is probably the result that the United States Supreme Court would reach if the issue were presented to it, except where the requirement of "good motives and justifiable ends" was directed to private defendants subsequent to a defamation implicating no public concern.

Even where true and thus not actionable as defamation, a statement may support a cause of action for invasion of privacy. See Hall v. Post, 372 S.E.2d 711 (N.C. 1988), see infra page 1022.

3. *Burden of Proof.* It has long been customary for the plaintiff to allege in his complaint that the statement is false. The common law raised a presumption of the falsity of all statements that were defamatory. As a result truth has been consistently treated as an affirmative defense, which the defendant must raise and on which he has the burden of proof. Supreme Court decisions engendered doubt about the soundness of this common law position. In the 1986 decision of Phila. Newspapers, Inc. v. Hepps, 475 U.S. 767 (1986), see infra page 958, the Supreme Court in a 5-to-4 decision held that in an action against a "media defendant for speech of public concern," the plaintiff had the burden of proving falsity.

4. As the principal case indicates, the determination is whether the statement is substantially true. See, e.g., Sun Printing & Publ'g Ass'n v. Schenck, 98 F. 925 (2d Cir. 1900) (finding that specific charge of crime not justified by proof of another and more serious crime); Crellin v. Thomas, 247 P.2d 264 (Utah 1952) (charge that plaintiff was a "whore" not shown by evidence that she worked for a short time as a "dance hall girl" or "percentage girl"); see Restatement (Second) of Torts §§ 581A, 613 (1977); St. Surin v. V.I. Daily News, 21 F.3d 1309 (3d Cir. 1994) (finding that a

statement indicating that plaintiff was under criminal investigation, implied by references to a "prosecutor" in the headline and the U.S. Attorney's office in the article's body, was not coextensive with the truth that he was being investigated by the Environmental Protection Agency). In *St. Surin*, the sting of the article was found to be factually untrue. Whereas in Smith v. Maldonado, 85 Cal. Rptr.2d 397 (Cal. Ct. App. 1999), a factually true newspaper report could not be rendered defamatory by the defendant highlighting a passage in the report and distributing it to third parties.

In the principal case, O'Connell, the writer of the story, states that some of the "events" were told to him by other persons. Suppose that the story had been told to him, but it was untrue. Liability on his part?

Neiman-Marcus v. Lait

United States District Court, Southern District of New York, 1952.
13 F.R.D. 311.

IRVING R. KAUFMAN, DISTRICT JUDGE. * * * The defendants are authors of a book entitled "U.S.A. Confidential". The plaintiffs are the Neiman-Marcus Company, a Texas corporation operating a department store at Dallas, Texas, and three groups of its employees. They allege that the following matter libelled and defamed them: * * *

"He [Stanley Marcus, president of plaintiff Neiman-Marcus Company] may not know that some Neiman models are call girls—the top babes in town. The guy who escorts one feels in the same league with the playboys who took out Ziegfeld's glorified. Price, a hundred bucks a night.

"The salesgirls are good, too—pretty, and often much cheaper—twenty bucks on the average. They're more fun, too, not as snooty as the models. We got this confidential, from a Dallas wolf.

"Neiman-Marcus also contributes to the improvement of the local breed when it imports New York models to make a flash at style shows. These girls are the cream of the crop. Oil millionaires toss around thousand-dollar bills for a chance to take them out.

"Neiman's was a women's specialty shop until the old biddies who patronized it decided their husbands should get class, too. So Neiman's put in a men's store. Well, you should see what happened. You wonder how all the faggots got to the wild and woolly. You thought those with talent ended up in New York and Hollywood and the plodders got government jobs in Washington. Then you learn the nucleus of the Dallas fairy colony is composed of many Neiman dress and millinery designers, imported from New York and Paris, who sent for their boy friends when the men's store expanded. Now most of the sales staff are fairies, too." * * *

[Plaintiffs sued in the following groups:]

(1) Nine individual models who constitute the entire group of models at the time of the publication * * *;

(2) Fifteen salesmen of a total of twenty-five suing on their own behalf and on behalf of the others * * *;

(3) Thirty saleswomen of a total of 382 suing on their own behalf and on behalf of the others. * * *

[T]he following propositions are rather widely accepted:

(1) Where the group or class libelled is large, none can sue even though the language used is inclusive. [Cc]

(2) Where the group or class libelled is small, and each and every member of the group or class is referred to, then any individual member can sue. [Cc]

Conflict arises when the publication complained of libels *some* or *less than all* of a designated small group. Some courts say no cause of action exists in any individual of the group. [Cc] Other courts in other states would apparently allow such an action. [Cc] * * *

[I]t is the opinion of this Court that the plaintiff salesmen, of whom it is alleged that "most * * * are fairies" have a cause of action in New York and most likely other states * * * Defendants' motion to dismiss as to the salesmen for failure to state a claim upon which relief can be granted is denied.

The plaintiff saleswomen are in a different category. The alleged defamatory statement in defendants' book speaks of the saleswomen generally. While it does not use the word "all" or similar terminology, yet it stands unqualified. However, the group of saleswomen is extremely large, consisting of 382 members at the time of publication. No specific individual is named in the alleged libelous statement. I am not cited to a single case which would support a cause of action by an individual member of any group of such magnitude. * * *

Giving the plaintiff saleswomen the benefit of all legitimate favorable inferences, the defendants' alleged libel cannot reasonably be said to concern more than the saleswomen as a class. There is no language referring to some ascertained or ascertainable person. Nor is the class so small that it follows that defamation of the class infects the individual of the class. This Court so holds as a matter of law since it is of the opinion that no reasonable man would take the writer seriously and conclude from the publication a reference to any individual saleswoman. [Cc]

While it is generally recognized that even where the group is large, a member of the group may have a cause of action if some particular circumstances point to the plaintiff as the person defamed, no such circumstances are alleged in the amended complaint. * * *

Accordingly, it is the opinion of this Court that as a matter of law the individual saleswomen do not state a claim for libel upon which relief can be granted and the motion to dismiss their cause of action is granted. * * *

The amended complaint is dismissed with leave to file separate complaints as to the two groups of individuals and the corporation, all in conformity with this opinion.

NOTES AND QUESTIONS

1. For which of the following statements may an individual member of the group or class maintain an action for defamation?

Watson v. Detroit Journal Co., 107 N.W. 81 (Mich. 1906). "That jury was bribed." Byers v. Martin, 2 Colo. 605 (Colo. 1875). "The election board is crooked." Story v. Jones, 52 Ill. App. 112 (Ill. App. Ct. 1893). "All men are liars." *Psalms* 116:11.

2. RESTATEMENT (SECOND) OF TORTS § 564A (1977) states: "One who publishes defamatory matter concerning a group or class of persons is subject to liability to an individual member of it if, but only if, (a) the group or class is so small that the matter can reasonably be understood to refer to the member, or (b) the circumstances of publication reasonably give rise to the conclusion that there is particular reference to the member." For an article defending the Restatement rule, see Nat Stern, The Certainty Principle as Justification for the Group Defamation Rule, 40 Ariz. St. L.J. 951 (2008). No recovery was allowed when defendant, addressing three men, said: "One of you is a crook." Cohn v. Brecher, 192 N.Y.S.2d 877 (N.Y. Spec. Term 1959). Other cases include: Friends of Gong v. Pac. Culture, 109 Fed. App'x 442 (2d Cir. 2004) (concerning defamatory statements about non-plaintiff practitioners of Falun Gong, the practice of Falun Gong itself, or entire group of New York-based Falun Gong Devotees); Alvord-Polk, Inc. v. F. Schumacher & Co., 37 F.3d 996, 1015 (3d Cir. 1994) (concerning defamatory statement by defendants referring to over 800 dealers as pirates); Mich. United Conservation Clubs v. CBS News, 485 F. Supp. 893 (W.D. Mich. 1980) (involving case where plaintiffs were several of more than a million hunters allegedly defamed by television networks' portrayal of hunters). However, recovery was allowed in Ball v. White, 143 N.W.2d 188 (Mich. Ct. App. 1966) (one out of five); Forbes v. Johnson, 50 Ky. (11 B. Mon.) 48 (1850) (statement that a note had been altered by A or by B); Hardy v. Williamson, 12 S.E. 874 (Ga. 1891) (eleven engineers employed by one company, "or some of them").

3. The "numerical" approach to group libel has found approval in a number of jurisdictions. See Restatement (Second) of Torts § 564A, cmt. b (1977) (noting that the groups that are generally successful in pursuing group libel actions number 25 or less). See also Church of Scientology Int'l v. Time Warner, Inc., 806 F. Supp. 1157 (S.D.N.Y. 1992) (Church of Scientology International claimed it was defamed by a Time article; nearly two hundred entities constituted the Church; thus general references were not "of and concerning" the plaintiff; four specific references could be so construed); Tex. Beef Group v. Winfrey, 11 F. Supp. 2d 858 (N.D. Tex. 1998) (finding that the segment of program describing the dangers of Mad Cow Disease in the United States did not identify the Texas Panhandle ranchers who brought the action for the decline in their business following the program).

A minority of jurisdictions, though, have begun to question this "numerical" approach. In McCullough v. Cities Serv. Co., 676 P.2d 833 (Okla. 1984), the plaintiff sought to bring an action as an osteopath based upon a publication that attacked generally that branch of the medical profession. The court held that the plaintiff's action was not maintainable noting that there were 19,686 doctors of osteopathy in the United States.

Although size alone was not determinative, it was an important factor in determining whether the "intensity of suspicion" cast upon the plaintiff was sufficient to give him a right to maintain a personal action. In Brady v. Ottaway Newspapers, Inc., 84 A.D.2d 226 (N.Y. App. Div. 1981), and individual police officer sued newspaper over an article claiming that unidentified members of the police department of the City of Newburgh, numbering fifty-three people, had in essence aided and abetted police corruption. Here, the court rejected the "numerical" rule and instead adopted "intensity of suspicion" test, holding that the specificity of the charge, the high degree of organization in the police department, and the prominence of the department in the community outweighed the problems associated with a group defamation of this size. What of allegation that Nat'l Football League players take steroids? See Fawcett Publ'ns, Inc. v. Morris, 377 P.2d 42 (Okla. 1962), *cert. denied*, 376 U.S. 513 (1964) (holding that statement concerning unidentifiable members of University of Oklahoma football team used illegal amphetamines was actionable).

4. *N.Y. Times Co. v. Sullivan*, see infra page 922, touches the issue of identification where the plaintiff if a public official. The Supreme Court pointed to the implications for free speech should public officials assert that a criticism of governmental action identify them as individuals. "Public authorities must not be permitted to stifle commentary concerning their conduct by simply substituting individuals as plaintiffs in a defamation action." Edgartown Police Patromen's Ass'n v. Johnson, 522 F. Supp. 1149 (D. Mass. 1981) the matter was clarified by the court in Rosenblatt v. Baer, 383 U.S. 75 (1966), requiring that if the individual were to be identified to ground an action in defamation, he or she must establish that the defamatory matter specifically identify him or her. The reasonable reader must associate the plaintiff with the defamatory imputation for a reason beyond his public capacity and responsibility. Plaintiff, a member of a group, will base a good cause of action by pleading and proving that the publication implicates his or her individual shortcomings.

In the small Virginia town of Elkton (population about 2,000), M. Lee Dearing, the mayor of Elkton, published a series of articles accusing the Elkton police of a litany of wrongdoing. The force had five to eight officers. That fact that the publications were "of and concerning" the officers, including the plaintiff, was plain. However, the Virginia Supreme Court in Dean v. Dearing, 561 S.E.2d 686 (Va. 2002), held that the First amendment was a bar to plaintiff grounding a defamation action. It found no extrinsic facts were pleaded that pointed to individual officers. For a trenchant critique of *Dean* in its failure to apply precedent and in its policy implications, see David A. Elder, Small Town Police Forces, Other Governmental Entities and the Misapplication of the First Amendment to the Small Group Defamation Theory—A Plea for Fundamental Fairness for Mayberry, 6 U. Pa. J. Const. L. 881 (2004). For a recommendation for a simplification of the law, see Joseph H. King, Jr., Reference to the Plaintiff Requirement in Defamatory Statements Directed at Groups, 35 WAKE FOREST L. REV. 343 (2000).

5. Immediately after the Second World War, social concern, resulting in some legislation, focused on group defamation directed at, among others, Jews, Catholics, and African-Americans. An Illinois Act, conferring protection on racial minorities from defamation, survived a

constitutional challenge in Beauharnais v. Illinois, 343 U.S. 250 (1952). First Amendment jurisprudence has since undermined the validity of such legislation, see *N.Y. Times Co. v. Sullivan*, infra page 922 & *Hustler Magazine v. Falwell*, infra page 1040. Racial hate speech has returned as a social issue. At the same time, pornography and sexual harassment have been perceived as social evils. See Catharine MacKinnon, Pornography, Civil Rights, and Speech, 20 HARV. C.R.-C.L. L. REV. 1 (1985). For a powerful argument that hate speech should be regulated as part of our commitment to human dignity and to inclusion and respect for members of vulnerable minorities, see Jeremy Waldron, The Harm in Hate Speech (2012). Again, the debate has turned to appropriate legal response within the confines of the First Amendment. In R.A.V. v. City of St. Paul, 505 U.S. 377 (1992), the U.S. Supreme Court reviewed the constitutionality of St. Paul's Bias-Motivated Crime Ordinance, which proscribed actions arousing "anger, alarm, or resentment in others on the basis of race, color, creed, religion or gender." The petitioner and others were charged with the criminal offense. They had burned a cross in the backyard of an African-American family. The legislation was found unconstitutional because it regulated only some violence-inducing speech and because it controlled content and threatened censorship of ideas. First Amendment Jurisprudence, and the law of defamation, is imbued with the idea of individual rights. Is it legitimate to shift to a recognition of group rights? Why should the "victims" of this speech bear the burden of the benefit of the public's free-speech interest? See Frederick Schauer, Uncoupling Free Speech, 92 COLUM. L. REV. 1321 (1992) (suggesting a public scheme for compensating victims).

6. *Who Can Be Defamed?* Any living person can be defamed. Even a child ten minutes old may have a cause of action if called a bastard. On the other hand, it is generally agreed that there can be no actionable defamation of the dead, since there is no living person whose reputation is affected. Bello v. Random House, Inc., 422 S.W.2d 339 (Mo. 1967); Flynn v. Higham, 197 Cal. Rptr. 145 (Cal. Ct. App. 1983) (dismissed action by the late actor Errol Flynn's children alleging that defendant's defamed their father by saying he was a homosexual Nazi spy).The defamation of the dead may, however, also defame the living, as where it is said that the plaintiff's deceased mother was not married to his father. Marrill v. Post Publ'g Co., 83 N.E. 419 (Mass. 1908); see also Meeropol v. Nizer, 381 F. Supp. 29 (S.D.N.Y. 1974).

7. A corporation can have no reputation in the personal sense, and cannot be defamed, for example, by being accused of unchastity. Neither can a partnership, as such. "The venereal disease was not a partnership malady. That was individual property." Gilbert v. Crystal Fountain Lodge, 4 S.E. 905, 906 (Ga. 1887) (Bleckley, C.J.). However, a corporation may maintain an action for defamation that casts an aspersion upon its honesty, credit, efficiency, or other business or moral character. Brown & Williamson Tobacco Corp. v. Jacobson, 827 F.2d 1119, 1122 (7th Cir. 1987) (finding that company was defamed by report alleging practice of inducing youth to smoke by presenting cigarettes as an "illicit pleasure" and associating tobacco with "pot, wine, beer, and sex"). A charitable or benevolent corporation not operated for profit, may establish a good cause of action since defamation affecting its character or operations may deprive it of gifts or other sources of revenue. Bos. Nutrition Soc'y v. Stare, 173

N.E.2d 812 (Mass. 1961); R.H. Bouligny, Inc. v. United Steelworkers of America, 154 S.E.2d 344 (N.C. 1967). The same is true of a partnership, or an unincorporated association, such as a labor union, to the extent that the latter is recognized as a legal entity capable of bringing suit. Stone v. Textile Examiners & Shrinkers Emp'rs' Ass'n, 137 A.D. 655 (N.Y. App. Div. 1910). Should a governmental entity be entitled to maintain an action in libel for words that reflect on it in its government and administrative functions? See Derbyshire CC v. Times Newspapers Ltd., [1993] A.C. 534 (H.L.) 547 (appeal taken from Eng.) (distinguishing governmental entities as bodies that should be open to "uninhibited public criticism" and thus holding that, in contrast to corporations, they should not enjoy a right to sue in libel). See also City of Chicago v. Tribune Co., 139 N.E. 86 (Ill. 1923).

Bindrim v. Mitchell

Court of Appeal of California, Second District, 1979.
92 Cal.App.3d 61, 155 Cal.Rptr. 29, hearing denied by California Supreme Court, 1979; cert. denied 444 U.S. 984, 100 S.Ct. 490, 62 L.Ed.2d 412 (1979), reh. denied 444 U.S. 1040, 100 S.Ct. 713, 62 L.Ed.2d 675 (1980).

[Plaintiff, Paul Bindrim, a Ph.D. and licensed psychologist, used what he designated as a "nude marathon in group therapy as a means of helping people to shed their psychological inhibitions with the removal of their clothes." Defendant Gwen Davis Mitchell, a successful novelist, registered in Bindrim's nude-therapy program, telling him that she was participating for therapeutic reasons only, and signing a contract "not to take photographs, write articles or in any manner disclose who has attended the workshop or what has transpired." Shortly thereafter, she contracted with defendant Doubleday for a novel based on the nude-therapy technique. The novel was written and published under the title of *Touching,* with a principal character, Dr. Simon Herford, using the technique.

Claiming that he was defamed by the depiction, plaintiff brought an action of libel against the two defendants. There was a jury verdict for the plaintiff in the trial court for substantial damages, and the court granted a motion for new trial conditioned on plaintiff's accepting a remittitur. Both plaintiff and the two defendants appealed.]

KINGSLEY, ASSOCIATE JUSTICE. * * * [Defendants] claim that, even if there are untrue statements, there is no showing that plaintiff was identified as the character Simon Herford, in the novel "Touching."

[They] allege that plaintiff failed to show he was identifiable as Simon Herford, relying on the fact that the character in "Touching" was described in the book as a "fat Santa Claus type with long white hair, white sideburns, a cherubic rosy face and rosy forearms" and that Bindrim was clean shaven and had short hair. Defendants rely in part on Wheeler v. Dell Publishing Co., 300 F.2d 372 (7th Cir. 1962), which involved an alleged libel caused by a fictional account of an actual murder trial. The *Wheeler* court said (at p. 376):

"In our opinion, any reasonable person who read the book and was in a position to identify Hazel Wheeler with Janice Quill would more likely conclude that the author created the latter in an ugly way so that none would identify her with Hazel Wheeler. It is important to note that while the trial and locale might suggest Hazel Wheeler to those who knew the Chenoweth family, suggestion is not identification. In [Levey v. Warner Bros. Pictures, 57 F.Supp. 40 (S.D.N.Y.1944),] the court said those who had seen her act may have been reminded of her by songs and scenes, but would not reasonably identify her."

However, in *Wheeler* the court found that no one who knew the real widow could possibly identify her with the character in the novel. In the case at bar, the only differences between plaintiff and the Herford character in "Touching" were physical appearance and that Herford was a psychiatrist rather than psychologist. Otherwise, the character Simon Herford was very similar to the actual plaintiff. We cannot say, as did the court in *Wheeler,* that no one who knew plaintiff Bindrim could reasonably identify him with the fictional character. Plaintiff was identified as Herford by several witnesses and plaintiff's own tape recordings of the marathon sessions show that the novel was based substantially on plaintiff's conduct in the nude marathon.

Defendant also relies on Middlebrooks v. Curtis Publishing Co., 413 F.2d 141 (4th Cir. 1969), where the marked dissimilarities between the fictional character and the plaintiff supported the court's finding against the reasonableness of identification. In *Middlebrooks,* there was a difference in age, an absence from the locale at the time of the episode, and a difference in employment of the fictional character and plaintiff; nor did the story parallel the plaintiff's life in any significant manner. In the case at bar, apart from some of those episodes allegedly constituting the libelous matter itself, and apart from the physical difference and the fact that plaintiff had a Ph.D., and not an M.D., the similarities between Herford and Bindrim are clear, and the transcripts of the actual encounter weekend show a close parallel between the narrative of plaintiff's novel and the actual real life events. Here, there were many similarities between the character, Herford, and the plaintiff Bindrim and those few differences do not bring the case under the rule of *Middlebrooks.* [C] There is overwhelming evidence that plaintiff and "Herford" were one. * * *

Defendants contend that the fact that the book was labeled as being a "novel" bars any claim that the writer or publisher could be found to have implied that the characters in the book were factual representations not of the fictional characters but of an actual nonfictional person. That contention, thus broadly stated, is unsupported by the cases. The test is whether a reasonable person, reading the book, would understand that the fictional character therein pictured was, in actual fact, the plaintiff acting as described. [C] Each case must stand on its own facts. In some cases, such as Greenbelt Pub. Assn. v. Bresler, 398 U.S. 6 (1970), an appellate court can, on examination of the entire work, find that no reasonable person would have regarded the episodes in the book as being other than the fictional imaginings of the author about how the character he had created would have acted. * * * Whether a reader, identifying plaintiff with the "Dr. Herford" of the book, would regard the passages herein complained of as mere fictional embroidering or as reporting actual language and conduct, was for the jury. Its verdict adverse to the defendants cannot be overturned by this court. * * *

Defendants raise the question of whether there is "publication" for libel where the communication is to only one person or a small group of persons rather than to the public at large. Publication for purposes of defamation is sufficient when the publication is to only one person other than the person defamed. [C] Therefore [it is] irrelevant whether all readers realized plaintiff and Herford were identical.

[The opinion also discusses whether the depiction was defamatory, the application of the "actual malice" test of New York Times v. Sullivan, infra page 922, the fact-opinion dichotomy, and damage issues.]

The judgment, as modified on the motion for a new trial, is further modified as [to damages.] * * *

Otherwise the judgment is affirmed. Neither party shall recover costs on appeal.

JEFFERSON, ASSOCIATE JUSTICE, concurring. * * * The dissent finds error in the instruction given the jury on the issue of identification. The use of the word "reasonably" in the instruction dissipates the dissent's view that only one person was required to understand the defamatory meaning. If one person "reasonably" understood the defamatory character of the language used, it describes what readers generally would "reasonably" understand. I see no basis for the dissent's view that the instruction had the result of mulcting defendants for the exercise of their first amendment right to comment on the nude marathon. The first amendment right to comment does *not* include the right to commit libel. * * *

"Of course the fictional setting does not insure immunity when a reasonable man would understand that the fictional character was a portrayal of the plaintiff. 'Reputations may not be traduced with impunity, whether under the literary forms of a work of fiction or in jest.' " [C]

FILES, PRESIDING JUSTICE (dissenting). * * * Defendants' novel describes a fictitious therapist who is conspicuously different from plaintiff in name, physical appearance, age, personality and profession.

Indeed the fictitious Dr. Herford has none of the characteristics of plaintiff except that Dr. Herford practices nude encounter therapy. Only three witnesses, other than plaintiff himself, testified that they "recognized" plaintiff as the fictitious Dr. Herford. All three of those witnesses had participated in or observed one of plaintiff's nude marathons. The only characteristic mentioned by any of the three witnesses as identifying plaintiff was the therapy practiced. * * *

Plaintiff's brief discusses the therapeutic practices of the fictitious Dr. Herford in two categories: Those practices which are similar to plaintiff's technique are classified as identifying. Those which are unlike plaintiff's are called libelous because they are false. Plaintiff has thus resurrected the spurious logic which Professor Kalven found in the position of the plaintiff in New York Times v. Sullivan, infra page 922. Kalven wrote: "There is revealed here a new technique by which defamation might be endlessly manufactured. First, it is argued that, contrary to all appearances, a statement referred to the plaintiff; then, that it falsely ascribed to the plaintiff something that he did not do, which should be rather easy to prove about a statement that did not refer to plaintiff in the first place. * * * " Kalven, The New York Times Case: A Note on "The Central Meaning of the First Amendment," 1964 The Supreme Court Review 191, 199.

Even if we accept the plaintiff's thesis that criticism of nude encounter therapy may be interpreted as libel of one practitioner, the evidence does not support a finding in favor of plaintiff.

Whether or not a publication to the general public is defamatory is "whether in the mind of the average reader the publication, considered as a whole, could reasonably be considered as defamatory." [C]

The majority opinion contains this juxtaposition of ideas: "Secondly, defendants' [proposed] instructions that the jury must find that a substantial segment of the public did, in fact, believe that Dr. Simon Herford was, in fact, Paul Bindrim * * * was properly refused. For the tort of defamation, publication to one other person is sufficient."

The first sentence refers to the question whether the publication was defamatory of plaintiff. The second refers to whether the defamatory matter was published. The former is an issue in this case. The latter is not. Of course, a publication to one person may constitute actionable libel. But this has no bearing on the principle that the allegedly libelous effect of a publication to the public generally is to be tested by the impression made on the average reader. * * *

From an analytical standpoint, the chief vice of the majority opinion is that it brands a novel as libelous because it is "false," i.e., fiction; and infers "actual malice" from the fact that the author and publisher knew it was not a true representation of plaintiff. From a constitutional standpoint the vice is the chilling effect upon the publisher of any novel critical of any occupational practice, inviting litigation on the theory "when you criticize my occupation, you libel me."

I would reverse the judgment.

NOTES AND QUESTIONS

1. The colloquium, or reference to the plaintiff, need not be to him by name if it is reasonably understood as referring to him. Peagler v. Phoenix Newspapers, Inc., 560 P.2d 1216 (Ariz. 1977); cf. Youssoupoff v. Metro-Goldwyn Mayer Pictures, (1934) 50 T.L.R. 581 (A.C) (Eng.) (motion picture purportedly based on historical events; plaintiff identifiable as person raped by Rasputin). But if the words are not reasonably understood to refer to the plaintiff, there is no defamatory imputation identifying plaintiff. Boyce & Isley v. Cooper, 568 S.E.2d 893 (N.C. Ct. App. 2002); Chapman v. Byrd, 475 S.E.2d 734 (N.C. Ct. App. 1996). When the plaintiff is not expressly identified, the issue is whether a reader with knowledge of the surrounding circumstances could have reasonably understood that the words referred to the plaintiff. The standard against which the material is read or understood changes with the medium. A daily newspaper is read loosely so that factual variations in the story may not prevent the plaintiff from being reasonably identified by the story. See Morgan v. Odhams Press Ltd., (1971) 1 W.L.R. 1239 (H.L.) 1248 (Lord Morris of Borth-y-Gest) (appeal taken from Court of Appeal), for a discussion of these issues. The

fewer the number of persons who are possessed with knowledge of the surrounding circumstances that identify the plaintiff, the less the damages that may be awarded.

2. Look at the latter part of the opinion in *N.Y. Times Co. v. Sullivan*, see infra p. 922, referring to the purported reference to Police Commissioner in the advertisement. Has it any relevance here?

3. If the novel *Touching* had contained a statement after the title page that this was a work of fiction and any similarity to existing persons was unintended, would that have made a difference? Stanton v. Metro Corp., 438 F.3d 119 (1st Cir. 2006) (holding that article about teen sexuality accompanied by photograph of various young people, including plaintiff, was susceptible of defamatory meaning despite statement that "the individuals pictured are unrelated to the people or events described in this story").

4. For other recent cases offering variations to the problem of defamation in fiction, see Pring v. Penthouse Int'l, Ltd., 695 F.2d 438 (10th Cir. 1982), *cert. denied*, 462 U.S. 1132 (1983) (2–1 decision) (reversing decision by the trial court for the real Miss Wyoming concerning a salacious story about a Miss Wyoming who performed on television at a Miss America Pageant sexual feats too fantastic to be believed); Geisler v. Petrocelli, 616 F.2d 636 (2d Cir. 1980) (holding that plaintiff known to defendant, with identical name to that of the major character in a novel about a transsexual tennis player, allowed to recover); Springer v. Viking Press, 90 A.D.2d 315 (N.Y. App. Div. 1982), *aff'd*, 458 N.E.2d 1256 (1983) (holding that plaintiff, former girl friend of author of a novel, given the same name as minor character in the book and similar physical characteristics, not allowed to recover because of insufficient basis for identifying the two); Haynes v. Alfred A. Knopf, Inc., 8 F.3d 1222 (7th Cir. 1993) (plaintiffs featured in book on social history of black migration from the South to the North; no recovery in defamation or breach of privacy); Flip Side, Inc. v. Chicago Tribune Co., 564 N.E.2d 1244 (1990) (plaintiff, an Illinois business, claimed defamation for use of name "Flipside" for character in "Dick Tracy" comic strip; held similarity is not sufficient where depiction was so clearly fictional.). Persons making libelous statements can be held liable for damages resulting from repetition or republication of the libelous statement. *See* Restatement (Second) of Torts § 576 (1977). In Brown v. First Nat'l Bank, 193 N.W.2d 547 (Iowa 1972), the court held defendant bank liable for libel for republication of information given to newspaper reporter about an investigation at the bank into missing funds. Here, the plaintiff had been terminated after failing a polygraph test, and the bank manager had relayed information to the newspaper for two articles concerning the situation, although neither article mentioned the plaintiff herself; plaintiff claimed that the articles accused her of embezzlement. The court ruled that the bank was liable for any and all republications of the information through gossip and rumor, since it was a natural and probable result of giving the information to the newspaper. Similarly, in Moore v. Allied Chem. Corp., 480 F. Supp. 364 (E.D. Va. 1979), defendant was held liable for rebroadcast of a "60 Minutes" story on the plight of employees at defendant's corporation from a supposedly toxic chemical produced by the plaintiff. The court ruled that the libel concerning the toxic chemical could be expected to be repeated any time "60 Minutes"

discussed the situation concerning defendant's employees. Do you see problems with the modern genre of television docudramas? See Erwin Chemerinsky, Tucker Lecture, Law and Media Symposium, 66 WASH. & LEE L. REV. 1449 (2009), for interesting comments also incorporating the "invasion of privacy" tort.

5. One of the most fascinating areas of defamation law today is that of defamation involving works of fiction. See, e.g., Symposium, Defamation in Fiction, 51 Brook. L. Rev. 223 (1985) (including eleven articles and covering over 200 pages). On the principal case, see Stephen Louis, Libel in Fiction: A Chilling Decision for Authors, 6 Art & L. 3 (1980). See Rodney A. Smolla, Let the Author Beware: The Rejuvenation of the American Law of Libel, 132 U. Pa. L. Rev. 1, 42–47 (1983), for an excellent article placing the issue of defamation in fictional works in context.

2. LIBEL AND SLANDER

The erratic and anomalous development of the law of defamation has led to the survival until the present day of two forms of action for defamatory publication. One is libel, which originally concerned written or printed words; the other is slander, which was originally oral.

The prime significance of the distinction lies in the requirement of proof of damages. It has long been the rule as to slander that it is necessary to prove "special damages" (i.e. pecuniary loss), Terwilliger v. Wands, see infra page 905, unless the words spoken come within one of the four classes of what is called slander per se. Libel, on the other hand, did not require special damages to be actionable, though there was some disagreement on whether this applied to libel which was not defamatory on its face. The distinction has been an important one. Defamatory communications often do not produce pecuniary loss, and it is often impossible to prove when it does exist. The result is that for many types of slander no relief may be available. A natural question is, why should there be a difference? Is it solely a matter of history? Since the remarks of Sir James Mansfield, in *Thorley v. Lord Kerry*, (1812) 128 Eng. Rep. 367 (C.P.) 371; 4 Taunt. 355 (Mansfield, C.J.) (Eng.), there has been no real effort to defend the distinction: "But the distinction has been made between written and spoken slander as far back as Charles the Second's time, and the difference has been recognized by the Courts for at least a century back."

So long as the difference as to the requirement of special damages continues to be applied, however, it becomes necessary to draw the distinction between what is slander and what is libel. This is itself a question not at all free from difficulty. As it took form in the seventeenth century, the distinction was one between words that were written or printed and those that were oral. But not long afterward, libel was extended to include defamatory pictures, signs, statues, motion pictures and the like, and even conduct carrying a defamatory implication, such as hanging the plaintiff in effigy, or erecting a gallows before his door. From this it was concluded that libel is communicated by the sense of sight, while slander is conveyed by the sense of hearing. On the other hand, slander was soon extended to include transitory gestures, such as the signals of a deaf-mute or, as in Bennett v. Norban,

151 A.2d 476 (Pa. 1959), the act of a storekeeper in publicly stopping a woman and searching her shopping bag. Furthermore, it was held to be a publication of a libel to: read a defamatory writing aloud, as in Bander v. Metro. Life Ins. Co., 47 N.E.2d 595 (Mass. 1943); read words aloud (by person other than the one defamed), expected to be and in fact written down, as in the case of dictation to a stenographer in Ostrowe v. Lee, 175 N.E. 505 (N.Y. 1931); or make a statement to a newspaper reporter in *Valentine v. Gonzalez*, 190 A.D. 490 (N.Y. App. Div. 1920). This has led some authorities to conclude that the distinction turns on embodiment of the defamation in some more or less permanent physical form.

The advent of new methods of communication such as radio and television left the courts floundering to formulate the distinction, and led the RESTATEMENT (SECOND) OF TORTS § 568 (1977), to state that:

> "(1) Libel consists of the publication of defamatory matter by written or printed words, by its embodiment in physical form or by any other form of communication that has the potentially harmful qualities characteristic of written or printed words.
>
> (2) Slander consists of the publication of defamatory matter by spoken words, transitory gestures or by any form of communication other than those stated in Subsection (1).
>
> (3) The area of dissemination, the deliberate and premeditated character of its publication and the persistence of the defamation are factors to be considered in determining whether a publication is a libel rather than a slander."

Shor v. Billingsley

Supreme Court, New York County, Special Term, 1956.
4 Misc.2d 857, 158 N.Y.S.2d 476.

[Action of defamation for a nationwide telecast. One person on the program "ad-libbed" the remark: "Want to know something? I wish I had as much money as he [plaintiff] owes * * * [to] everybody—oh, a lot of people." One count in the complaint was based on this remark.]

HECHT, JUSTICE. * * * That leaves for consideration the real problem in the case—whether the first cause of * * * action based upon a telecast not read from a prepared script sounds in libel or in slander.

This precise question has not been passed upon by our appellate courts, nor apparently in any other jurisdiction. Hartmann v. Winchell held that the "utterance of defamatory remarks, *read from a script* into a radio microphone and broadcast, constitute[s] publication of libel", 296 N.Y. [296,] at page 298, 73 N.E.2d [30,] at page 31, italics supplied. It expressly did not reach the question "whether broadcasting defamatory matter which has not been reduced to writing should be held to be libellous because of the potentially harmful and widespread effects of such defamation." [C] Fuld, J., concurring, held that it should "because of the likelihood of aggravated injury inherent in such broadcasting" [c].

Sorensen v. Wood, 123 Neb. 348, 353, 243 N.W. 82 (1932), likewise held libelous radio broadcasts read from a written script; Meldrum v. Australian Broadcasting Co. Ltd., [1932] Vict.L.R. 425, to the contrary, was specifically rejected in Hartmann v. Winchell, supra. * * *.

When account is taken of the vast and far-flung audience reached by radio today—often far greater in number than the readers of the largest metropolitan newspaper [c] it is evident that the broadcast of scandalous utterances is in general as potentially harmful to the defamed person's reputation as a publication by writing. That defamation by radio, in the absence of a script or transcription, lacks the measure of durability possessed by written libel, in nowise lessens its capacity for harm. Since the element of damage is, historically, the basis of the common-law action for defamation [c], and since it is as reasonable to presume damage from the nature of the medium employed when a slander is broadcast by radio as when published by writing, both logic and policy point the conclusion that defamation by radio should be actionable per se. * * *

It is true that "the delivery of the same speech over an amplifier to a vast audience in a stadium" would still be treated as a slander despite the fact that it may cause infinitely more damage than a writing seen by few, [c]. But such a speech falls so inescapably within the conventional definition of slander that in the foregoing situation "abolition of the line between libel and slander would * * * be too extreme a break with the past to be achieved without legislation." [C] But it does not follow that a court is equally powerless when dealing with the new media of radio and television. * * *

Our own courts experience no difficulty in applying the law of libel to the new instrumentality of the motion picture because "in the hands of a wrongdoer these devices have untold possibilities toward producing an effective libel". * * *

Accordingly, the motion to dismiss is denied as to the first three causes of action. * * *

NOTES AND QUESTIONS

1. This decision was affirmed without opinion by the Appellate Division, First Department. *Shor v. Billingsley*, 158 N.Y.S.2d 476 (N.Y. Spec. Term 1956), *aff'd*, 169 N.Y.S.2d 416 (N.Y. App. Div. 1957).

2. The matter is now primarily regulated by statute. Most of the statutes, enacted under lobbying from broadcasting companies, provide that any broadcast defamation is to be treated as slander, whether there is a script or not. See Donald H. Remmers, Recent Legislative Trends in Defamation by Radio, 64 HARV. L. REV. 727 (1951). In Great Britain, the Defamation Act, (1952) 15 & 16 Geo. 6 & 1 Eliz. 2, c. 66 (Gr. Brit.), provides that any broadcast is libel.

Terwilliger v. Wands

Court of Appeals of New York, 1858.
17 N.Y. 54, 72 Am.Dec. 420.

Action for slander. The plaintiff proved by La Fayette Wands that the defendant asked him, Wands, what the plaintiff was running to Mrs. Fuller's so much for; he knew he went there for no good purpose; Mrs. Fuller was a bad woman, and plaintiff had a regular beaten path across his land to Fuller's; defendant said plaintiff went there to have intercourse with Mrs. Fuller, and that plaintiff would do all he could to keep Mrs. Fuller's husband in the penitentiary so that he could have free access there. * * *

The only damages proved were that the plaintiff was prostrated in health and unable to attend to business after hearing of the reports circulated by the defendant. A motion for a nonsuit was sustained * * *.

STRONG, J. The words spoken by the defendant not being actionable of themselves, it was necessary, in order to maintain the action, to prove that they occasioned special damages to the plaintiff. The special damages must have been the natural, immediate and legal consequence of the words. * * *

The special damages relied upon are not of such a nature as will support the action. * * * It is injuries affecting the reputation only which are the subject of the action. In the case of slanderous words actionable per se, the law, from their natural and immediate tendency to produce injury, adjudges them to be injurious, though no special loss or damage can be proved. "But with regard to words that do not apparently and upon the face of them import such defamation as will of course be injurious, it is necessary that the plaintiff should aver some particular damage to have happened." (3 Bl.Com. 124.) As to what constitutes special damages, Starkie mentions the loss of a marriage, loss of hospitable gratuitous entertainment, preventing a servant or bailiff from getting a place, the loss of customers by a tradesman; and says that in general whenever a person is prevented by the slander from receiving that which would otherwise be conferred upon him, though gratuitously, it is sufficient. * * *

It necessarily follows from the rule that the words must be disparaging to character, that the special damage to give an action must flow from disparaging it. * * * In the present case the words were defamatory, and the illness and physical prostration of the plaintiff may be assumed, so far as this part of the case is concerned, to have been actually produced by the slander, but this consequence was not, in a legal view, a natural, ordinary one, as it does not prove that the plaintiff's character was injured. The slander may not have been credited by or had the slightest influence upon any one unfavorable to the plaintiff; and it does not appear that anybody believed it or treated the plaintiff any different from what they would otherwise have done on account of it. The cause was not adapted to produce the result which is claimed to be special damages. Such an effect may and sometimes does follow from such a cause but not ordinarily; and the rule of law was framed in reference to common and usual effects and not those which are accidental and occasional. * * *

Where there is no proof that the character has suffered from the words, if sickness results it must be attributed to the apprehension of loss of character, and such fear of harm to character, with resulting sickness and bodily prostration, cannot be such special damage as the law requires for the action. The loss of character must be a substantive loss, one which has actually taken place. * * *

Judgment affirmed.

NOTES AND QUESTIONS

1. When special damages must be pleaded and proved to make out a cause of action for slander, the common law rule developed that the damages must be of a pecuniary character. This was a carry-over from the old conflict of jurisdiction with the ecclesiastical courts, and the rule that the king's court could take jurisdiction only where there was "temporal," as distinguished from "spiritual," harm. Hence, if no pecuniary loss is shown, it is not enough that the plaintiff has suffered acute mental distress and serious physical illness as a result of the defamation. Allsop v. Allsop, (1860) 157 Eng. Rep. 1292 (Exch.); 5 H. & N. 534 (Eng.); *Scott v. Harrison*, 2 S.E.2d 1 (N.C. 1939); Baugh v. Baugh, 512 So.2d 1283, 1286 (Miss. 1987) (dismissing case in which plaintiff failed to "suggest any damages of a pecuniary character said to have been caused him by what [defendant] said"); Galarneau v. Merrill Lynch, Pierce, Fenner & Smith Inc., 504 F.3d 189, 204 (1st Cir. 2007); Beverly Enters. v. Trump, 182 F.3d 183, 188 (3d Cir. 1999) ("[P]laintiff must go beyond a claim of injury to reputation and allege . . . 'actual and concrete damages capable of being estimated in money . . . .' " (quoting Altoona Clay Prods., Inc. v. Dun & Bradstreet, Inc., 246 F. Supp. 419, 422 (W.D. Penn. 1965)).

2. When the cause of action is once made out, either as libel or slander per se, or by proof of special damages of a pecuniary character, plaintiff may recover additional damages for his mental distress, wounded feelings and humiliation. Pion v. Caron, 129 N.E. 369 (Mass. 1921); Baker v. Winslow, 113 S.E. 570 (N.C. 1922).

3. The original rule was that the defendant was liable only for damages due to his own publication, and was not responsible for repetition by others. Vicars v. Wilcocks, (1806) 103 Eng. Rep. 244 (K.B.); 8 East 1 (Eng.); Hastings v. Stetson, 126 Mass. 329 (1879). Later decisions tend to hold that the original publisher is liable for damages due to a repetition that might reasonably have been anticipated. Elms v. Crane, 107 A. 852 (Me. 1919); Sawyer v. Gilmers, Inc., 126 S.E. 183 (N.C. 1925); Weaver v. Beneficial Finance Co., 98 S.E.2d 687 (Va. 1957) (illustrating a significant disagreement between the majority and dissenting justices on this issue); *see* Restatement (Second) of Torts § 576 (1977). See infra, pages 994–997.

4. The party repeating the defamation is himself liable for its publication, even though he states the source. Haines v. Campbell, 21 A. 702 (Md. 1891); Times Pub. Co. v. Carlisle, 94 Fed. 762 (8th Cir. 1899). He is held liable even though he states that he does not believe the imputation. Morse v. Times-Republican Printing Co., 100 N.W. 867 (Iowa 1904); Cobbs v. Chicago Defender, 31 N.E.2d 323 (Ill. App. Ct. 1941).

Slander Per Se

Four special kinds of slander are exceptions to the general common law rule, and actionable without proof of special damages. These are the following:

1. *Imputations of Major Crime.* The original basis for this exception seems to have been that the plaintiff was thus exposed to criminal prosecution. Later the emphasis shifted to the social ostracism involved and the probability that the plaintiff must have suffered some pecuniary loss, even though he could not prove it. Thus, the action lay without any proof of damage, even though the words made it clear that the plaintiff had been punished or pardoned, or that prosecution was barred by the statute of limitations. It is insufficient to accuse a person of being capable of a crime or to have criminal intent unless a criminal act is charged. Biondi v. Nassimos, 692 A.2d 103, 108 (N.J. Super. Ct. App. Div. 1997) (quoting Restatement (Second) of Torts § 571 cmt. c (1977)).

The courts struggled to define a distinction between major and minor crimes. The formula that most courts now follow is that the crime must be one involving "moral turpitude," defined as "an inherent baseness or vileness of principle in the human heart." It is not the categorization of the crime, but rather the character of the act charged, that is controlling. Not every trivial assault or battery involves "moral turpitude." However, an accusation that the plaintiff beat his mother was held in Sipp v. Coleman, 179 Fed. 997 (C.C.D. N.J. 1910), necessarily to do so.

2. *Loathsome Disease.* The basis of the exception for the imputation of certain diseases appears originally to have been simply the exclusion from society that would result. It began with venereal disease and leprosy, at a time when both were regarded as permanent, lingering and incurable. It was not applied to more contagious and equally repugnant disorders such as smallpox, from which one either recovered or died in a short time. James v. Rutlech, (1599) 76 Eng. Rep. 900 (K.B.); 4 Co. Rep. 17 a. (Eng.)

The advance of medical science and a better understanding of disease tended to freeze the exception within its original limits, and today accusations of insanity, tuberculosis or other communicable diseases are not included. Furthermore, since there would not be the same social avoidance of one who had recovered, it is well settled that the imputation that the plaintiff has had even a venereal disease in the past is not sufficient to be actionable without proof of special damage. *Bruce v. Soule,* 69 Me. 562 (1879). The importance of this exception has been slight, and there have been almost no cases applying it in this century. Has the situation changed with the advent of AIDS?

3. *Business, Trade, Profession or Office.* If the spoken words are likely to affect the plaintiff in his business, trade, profession or office, the probability of some "temporal" damage is sufficiently obvious. Any legitimate calling is included, "be it ever so base." Terry v. Hooper, (1763) 83 Eng. Rep. 325 (K.B.); 1 Lev. 115 (Eng.); cf. Fitzgerald v. Redfield, 51 Barb. 484 (N.Y. Gen. Term 1868) (lime-burner); Burtch v. Nickerson, 17 Johns. 217 (N.Y. 1819) (blacksmith). Even uncompensated offices of confidence or trust have been included. In Dietrich v. Hauser, 257 N.Y.S.2d 716 (N.Y. Spec. Term 1965), it was held slander per se to say of a club president that he was a cheat and a fraud.

The exception was limited to defamation of a kind incompatible with the proper conduct of the business, trade, profession or office itself. Thus, it is actionable without proof of special damage to say of an attorney that he is a shyster. Nolan v. Standard Publ'g Co., 216 P. 571 (Mont. 1923). Or of a school teacher that he has been guilty of improper conduct with his pupils. Thompson v. Bridges, 273 S.W. 529 (Ky. 1925). Or a chauffeur that he is habitually drinking. Louisville Taxicab & Transfer Co. v. Ingle, 17 S.W.2d 709 (Ky. 1929). Or of a bank, that it is insolvent, or of a merchant that his credit is bad. Ridgeway State Bank v. Bird, 202 N.W. 170 (Wis. 1925). Or of the governor of a state that he is indifferent to lynching and has approved the work of a mob. Caldwell v. Crowell-Collier Publn'g Co., 161 F.2d 333 (5th Cir. 194 7). The person must be employed in the profession at the time that the statement is made. *See* Restatement (Second) of Torts § 573, cmt. c (1977); Bassim v. Howlett, 594 N.Y.S.2d 381 (N.Y. App. Div. 1993) (holding that a doctor who had his license removed just after the defamatory statement could not maintain a cause of action because he was no longer a member of the medical profession).

4. *Serious Sexual Misconduct.* The principal application of this to date has been a charge imputing unchastity to a woman. In England this was not actionable per se, until the common law rule was changed by the Slander of Women Act, 1891, 54 & 55 Vict., c.51 (Eng.). Some of the American courts got around the rule, as in Kelly v. Flaherty, 14 A. 876 (R.I. 1888), by finding that the imputation was equivalent to a charge of the crime of adultery or fornication, which involved moral turpitude. Gradually this gave way to a recognition of the essentially damaging nature of the charge, and a fourth exception is now generally recognized. Hollman v. Brady, 233 F.2d 877 (9th Cir. 1956); Gnapinsky v. Goldyn, 128 A.2d 697 (N.J. 1957).

The assumption has always been that the imputation of unchastity is not so damaging to a man, and it is still held that this is not slander per se, unless it falls into one of the other slander exceptions. Hickerson v. Masters, 226 S.W. 1072 (Ky. 1921); Marion v. Davis, 114 So. 357 (Ala. 1927).

Is this consistent with constitutional law requirements and ideals of equality? *See* RESTATEMENT (SECOND) OF TORTS § 574 (1977); King v. Tanner, 539 N.Y.S.2d 617, 620 (N.Y. Sup. Ct. 1989) (suggesting that Terwilliger v. Wands, see supra page 905, would not survive equal protection scrutiny); Wardlaw v. Peck, 318 S.E.2d 270 (S.C. Ct. App. 1984) (refusing, on an interpretation of the old case law, to distinguish between men and women).

What about the imputation of homosexual conduct or characteristics? In Buck v. Savage, 323 S.W.2d 363 (Tex. Civ. App. 1959), the statement that plaintiff was "queer on" another man was held to amount to a charge of the crime of sodomy and so to be actionable per se. Plumley v. Landmark Chevrolet, 122 F.3d 308 (5th Cir. 1997).

However, changing social attitudes have prompted many jurisdictions to reconsider the law on this issue. Until 2012, appellate courts in New York had uniformly held that statements imputing homosexuality fell under the four categories of statements that rise to the level of defamation per se. In Yonaty v. Mincolla, 945 N.Y.S.2d 774 (App. Div. 2012), the New York Appellate Division held that the imputation of homosexuality is no longer defamation per se: "statements falsely describing a person as lesbian, gay or bisexual . . . are not defamatory per se." *Id.* at 776. *Yonaty* reflects the trend in courts "across the country that have repudiated similar precedents of their own." Note, Tort Law—Defamation—New York Appellate Division Holds That the Imputation of Homosexuality Is No Longer Defamation Per Se.—Yonaty v. Mincolla, 945 N.Y.S.2d 774 (App. Div. 2012), 126 Harv. L. Rev. 852 (2013). See Albright v. Morton, 321 F. Supp. 2d 130, 136 (D. Mass. 2004), *aff'd on other grounds*, 410 F.3d 69 (1st Cir. 2005) (applying Massachusetts law), *Hayes v. Smith*, 832 P.2d 1022, 1025–26 (Colo. App. 1991) (""false statements concerning homosexuality are not slander per se even though they arise in an employment context and are directed at plaintiff's business reputation"), Boehm v. Am. Bankers Ins. Grp., Inc., 557 So. 2d 91, 94 (Fla. Dist. Ct. App. 1990), Donovan v. Fiumara, 442 S.E.2d 572, 576–77 (N.C. Ct. App. 1994) ("[R]equiring allegation and proof of special damages as a condition of recovery."), *and* Lehman v. Wellens, No. 86–1665, 1987 WL 267191, at *1 (Wis. Ct. App. Apr. 8, 1987) (per curiam), for cases in other jurisdictions holding that false allegations of homosexuality are not defamatory per se. But see Nazeri v. Missouri Valley College, 860 S.W.2d 303, 312 (Mo. 1993) ("Despite the efforts of many homosexual groups to foster greater tolerance and acceptance, homosexuality is still viewed with disfavor, if not outright contempt, by a sizeable proportion of our population. . . . We hold that a false allegation of homosexuality is defamatory in Missouri.").

Libel Per Se and Libel Per Quod

The established rule at common law was to the effect that it is not necessary to prove special damages in order to maintain an action for libel. Some American decisions deviated from this rule, apparently through an initial mistake as to the meaning of the expression "libel per se." As applied to the requirement of proof of special damages, all libel was libel per se. But if the statement was not defamatory on its face and it was necessary to be aware of certain extrinsic (or unstated) facts in order to appreciate its defamatory implications, it was sometimes called libel per quod, meaning that the plaintiff must allege and prove those extrinsic facts in order to have a cause of action. Some American decisions, breaking away from the established rule, apparently assumed that if the communication was not defamatory on its face and was called libel per quod, it was not libel per se and required proof of special damages. But other cases deliberately adopted the rule. Case authority was divided and a vigorous debate developed between Dean Prosser and Professor Laurence Eldredge on the status of the authorities and the arguments for the two rules.

The RESTATEMENT (SECOND) OF TORTS § 569 (1977), provides that special damages are not required in any libel action. See Hinsdale v. Orange Cnty. Publ'ns, Inc., 217 N.E.2d 650 (N.Y. 1966); Muzikowski v. Paramount Pictures Corp., 477 F.3d 899 (7th Cir. 2007) (applying Illinois law).

3. PUBLICATION

Economopoulos v. A.G. Pollard Co.

Supreme Judicial Court of Massachusetts, 1914.
218 Mass. 294, 105 N.E. 896.

Action by George Economopoulos against A.G. Pollard Company. There was a verdict for defendant, and plaintiff brings exceptions.

This was an action of tort in three counts * * *; the third count charging defendant with falsely and maliciously charging plaintiff with larceny by words spoken of plaintiff, as follows: "You have stolen a handkerchief from us and have it in your pocket." There was evidence that a clerk of defendant stated in English to plaintiff, a Greek, that he had stolen a handkerchief, and that a Greek clerk stated to plaintiff in Greek that plaintiff had stolen a handkerchief. There was nothing to show that third persons heard the charge, excepting the floor walker.

LORING, J. * * * There was no evidence that anybody but the plaintiff was present when Carrier spoke to the plaintiff in English. There was no publication of this statement made in English, because on the evidence the words could not have been heard by any one but the plaintiff. [C]

Nor was there any evidence of publication of the Greek words spoken by Miralos, for although there was evidence that they were spoken in the presence of others, there was no evidence that any one understood them but the plaintiff. * * *

Exceptions overruled.

NOTES AND QUESTIONS

1. "Publication" is a word of art in defamation cases. It does not mean printing, writing or even publicity, but merely communication of the defamatory words to someone other than the person defamed. It is not enough that the words are spoken to the plaintiff himself, even in the presence of others, if no one else overhears them. Sheffill v. Van Deusen, 79 Mass. (13 Gray) 304 (1859) (concerning words spoken in a bakery). See also Food Lion v. Melton, 458 S.E.2d 580 (Va. 1995) (holding that circumstantial evidence alone was sufficient to show reasonable inference of overhearing when defendant used a "very loud tone of voice" and witnesses were "close by").

2. Defendant, in the presence of others who overhear him, calls plaintiff a "cocotte," which, according to the court, is a French word meaning either a prostitute or a poached egg. What else must plaintiff plead and prove in order to establish her cause of action? Rovira v. Boget, 148 N.E. 534 (N.Y. 1925). What if those hearing or reading the reference are too young to know the meaning of a word? Sullivan v. Sullivan, 48 Ill. App. 435 (Ill. App. Ct. 1892).

3. Sometimes the court presumes that some one has read and understood the defamatory words. The presumption has been employed regarding a publication in German, in a German-language newspaper that was circulated among German-speaking subscribers. Kimm v. Steketee, 12

N.W. 177 (Mich. 1882). This presumption has also be applied to a defamatory postcard sent through the mail. Ostro v. Safir, 1 N.Y.S.2d 377 (N.Y. Spec. Term 1937); Abofreka v. Alston Tobacco Co., 341 S.E.2d 622 (S.C. 1986) (regarding a statement on a bulletin board). Other cases hold that proof of actual reading is required in such a case. McKeel v. Latham, 162 S.E. 747, 748 (N.C. 1932).

4. Authority is conflicted on the issue of publications where the communications is from one officer, agent, or office of an organization to another. See Jerolamon v. Fairleigh Dickinson Univ., 488 A.2d 1064 (N.J. Super. Ct. App. Div. 1985) (holding that a report by university security guards to Director of Campus Safety and Provost was a publication). But cf. Perez v. Boatmen's Nat'l Bank, 788 S.W.2d 296 (Mo. App. Ct. 1990) ("[C]ommunications between officers of the same corporation in the due and regular course of the corporate business, or between different offices of the same corporation, are not publications to third persons." (quoting Hellesen v. Knaus Truck Lines, 370 S.W.2d 341, 344 (Mo. 1963)); Starr v. Pearle Vision, Inc., 54 F.3d 1548 (10th Cir. 1995). Under common law, employers generally enjoy a "qualified privilege," when discussing matters related to employment with individuals having a corresponding interest or duty. Restatement (Second) of Torts § 595 (1977). However, this privilege can be pierced if the employer acted recklessly or with malice. See, e.g., Lyons v. Nat'l Car Rental Sys., Inc., 30 F.3d 240, 244 (1st Cir. 1994). The law on internal communications and applicable defenses of qualified privilege is discussed in an illuminating way in Hagebak v. Stone, 61 P.3d 201 (2002) (holding that intra-corporate communications are only subject to a qualified privilege that can be rebutted by the plaintiff).

5. For a communication to a third party to be a publication, it must have been done intentionally or by a negligent act. *See* RESTATEMENT (SECOND) OF TORTS § 577 (1977). Thus, there is no publication when words are spoken by defendant directly to plaintiff, with no reason to suppose that any one can overhear, but they are in fact overheard by a concealed listener. *Hill v. Balkind* (1918) NZLR 740 (SC). However, when the words are spoken so loudly that defendant can expect that that someone may overhear, the defendant has published the defamatory imputation. McNichol v. Grandy, [1931] S.C.R. 696 (Can.).Where defendant mistakenly believed he had deleted a file from his hard drive, which was later accessed by third parties, held no publication. Morrow v. II Morrow, Inc., 911 P.2d 964 (Or. Ct. App. 1996); see also Smith v. Jones, 335 So.2d 896 (Miss. 1976) (holding that there was no publication where defendant was unaware that plaintiff's children were listening to conversation on another telephone line). In Tuman v. Genesis Assoc., 894 F. Supp. 183 (E.D. Pa. 1995), the court denied defendant's motion to dismiss a defamation claim for falsely implanting memories into plaintiffs' daughter during therapy sessions—including allegations of incest, rape, murder, and satanic ritualistic behavior—holding that where the defendants, although they did not personally make the statements, implanted the statements in plaintiffs' daughter's head and induced and encouraged her to make the defamatory claims and could be liable for such.

6. If the defamatory matter is sent by defendant to plaintiff himself in a sealed letter, which is unexpectedly opened and read by a third person, there is no publication. Barnes v. Clayton House Motel, 435 S.W.2d 616

(Tex. Civ. App. 1968). But there is liability if defendant knows, or should know, that plaintiff's spouse or secretary is in the habit of reading plaintiff's mail, or in the circumstances would likely read it, and the words are in fact read by such person. Rumney v. Worthley, 71 N.E. 316 (Mass. 1904); Roberts v. English Mfg. Co., 46 So. 752 (Ala. 1908). In the English case, Theaker v. Richardson, [1962] 1 W.L.R. 151 (Eng.), the defendant wrote a letter to the plaintiff (both members of their local district council and candidates in an imminent council election), accusing her of a list of misdeeds, and ended the letter saying: "[Y]ou are nothing but a lying low down brothel-keeping whore and thief. . . ." The letter was typed by the defendant and the envelope was addressed to the plaintiff. The plaintiff's husband entered the house, saw the letter on the mat and opened it, thinking it was an election address.

7. There is a publication when a telegraph company transmits a message or a third party orally repeats a message. The postal service does not make a publication when it delivers a letter. Nor is there a publication by the telephone company when its system is used for communication purposes. See Anderson v. New York Tel. Co., 320 N.E.2d 647 (N.Y. 1974). The same rule applied to an internet service provider (ISP) for emails sent through its servers. Lunney v. Prodigy Serv. Co., 723 N.E.2d 539 (N.Y. 1999), *cert. denied*, 529 U.S. 1098 (2000).

8. *Publication by Plaintiff.* Ordinarily the defendant is not liable for any publication made by the plaintiff alone, since it is considered that it is plaintiff's responsibility and not the defendant's. Lyle v. Waddle, 188 S.W.2d 770 (Tex. 1945). But suppose it is reasonable for the plaintiff to consult someone else about a defamatory communication made only to plaintiff and the defendant might expect this. The obvious case is that of the plaintiff who is blind or illiterate. Lane v. Schilling, 279 P. 267 (Or. 1929); cf. Hedgpeth v. Coleman, 111 S.E. 517 (N.C. 1922) (involving a child plaintiff).

9. A discharged employee of the defendant, seeking other employment, is asked by all prospective employers why he left his last job. In response, he repeats, and denies, the defamatory charge. Is defendant liable? The courts have come to inconsistent conclusions.

10. *Failure to Remove Defamation.* In several cases defendant has been held liable for failure to remove defamation posted on his premises. See Tidmore v. Mills, 32 So.2d 769 (Ala. Ct. App. 1947) (affirming judgment where defendant refused to remove sign comparing plaintiff to Hitler); Hellar v. Bianco, 244 P.2d 757 (Cal. Dist. Ct. App. 1952) (concerning statements about plaintiff's chastity written on bar toilet stall).The courts have not agreed upon a theory, and have struggled with "republication," "ratification," and negligent breach of a duty to remove. *See Scott v. Hull*, 22 Ohio App.2d 141, 259 N.E.2d 160 (Ohio Ct. App.1970) (holding that nonfeasance in the removal of defamatory graffiti from the exterior of defendant's building after notification was not actionable defamation).

Carafano v. Metrosplash.com, Inc.

United States Court of Appeals, Ninth Circuit, 2003.
339 F.3d 1119.

THOMAS, CIRCUIT JUDGE. This is a case involving a cruel and sadistic identity theft. In this appeal, we consider to what extent a computer match making service may be legally responsible for false content in a dating profile provided by someone posing as another person. Under the circumstances presented by this case, we conclude that the service is statutorily immune pursuant to 47 U.S.C. 230(c)(1).

I

Matchmaker.com is a commercial Internet dating service. For a fee, members of Matchmaker post anonymous profiles and may then view profiles of other members in their area, contacting them via electronic mail sent through the Matchmaker server. A typical profile contains one or more pictures of the subject, descriptive information such as age, appearance and interests, and answers to a variety of questions designed to evoke the subject's personality and reason for joining the service.

Members are required to complete a detailed questionnaire containing both multiple-choice and essay questions. In the initial portion of the questionnaire, members select answers to more than fifty questions from menus providing between four and nineteen options. Some of the potential multiple choice answers are innocuous; some are sexually suggestive. In the subsequent essay section, participants answer up to eighteen additional questions, including "anything that the questionnaire didn't cover." Matchmaker policies prohibit members from posting last names, addresses, phone numbers or e-mail addresses within a profile. Matchmaker reviews photos for impropriety before posting them but does not review the profiles themselves, relying instead upon participants to adhere to the service guidelines.

On October 23, 1999, an unknown person using a computer in Berlin posted a "trial" personal profile of Christianne Carafano in the Los Angeles section of Matchmaker. (New members were permitted to post "trial" profiles for a few weeks without paying.) The posting was without the knowledge, consent or permission of Carafano. The profile was listed under the identifier "Chase529."

Carafano is a popular actress. Under the stage name of Chase Masterson, Carafano has appeared in numerous films and television shows, such as "Star Trek: Deep Space Nine," and "General Hospital." Pictures of the actress are widely available on the Internet, and the false Matchmaker profile "Chase529" contained several of these pictures. Along with fairly innocuous responses to questions about interests and appearance, the person posting the profile selected "Playboy/Playgirl" for "main source of current events" and "looking for a one-night stand" for "why did you call." In addition, the open-ended essay responses indicated that "Chase529" was looking for a "hard and dominant" man with "a strong sexual appetite" and that she "liked sort of be [ ]ing controlled by a man, in and out of bed." The profile text did not include a last name for "Chase" or indicate Carafano's real name, but it listed two of her movies (and, as mentioned, included pictures of the actress).

In response to a question about the "part of the LA area" in which she lived, the profile provided Carafano's home address. The profile included a contact e-mail address, cmla2000@yahoo.com, which, when contacted, produced an automatic e-mail reply stating, "You think you are the right one? Proof it !!" [sic], and providing Carafano's home address and telephone number.

Unaware of the improper posting, Carafano soon began to receive messages responding to the profile. Although she was traveling at the time, she checked her voicemail on October 31 and heard two sexually explicit messages. When she returned to her home on November 4, she found a highly threatening and sexually explicit fax that also threatened her son. Alarmed, she contacted the police the following day. As a result of the profile, she also received numerous phone calls, voicemail messages, written correspondence, and e-mail from fans through her professional e-mail account. Several men expressed concern that she had given out her address and phone number (but simultaneously expressed an interest in meeting her). Carafano felt unsafe in her home, and she and her son stayed in hotels or away from Los Angeles for several months.

Sometime around Saturday, November 6, Siouxzan Perry, who handled Carafano's professional website and much of her e-mail correspondence, first learned of the false profile through a message from "Jeff." Perry exchanged e-mails with Jeff, visited the Matchmaker site, and relayed information about the profile to Carafano. Acting on Carafano's instructions, Perry contacted Matchmaker and demanded that the profile be removed immediately. The Matchmaker employee indicated that she could not remove the profile immediately because Perry herself had not posted it, but the company blocked the profile from public view on Monday morning, November 8. At 4:00 AM the following morning, Matchmaker deleted the profile.

Carafano filed a complaint in California state court against Matchmaker and its corporate successors, alleging invasion of privacy, misappropriation of the right of publicity, defamation, and negligence. The defendants removed the case to federal district court. The district court granted the defendants' motion for summary judgment in a published opinion. Carafano v. Metrosplash.com, Inc., 207 F. Supp. 2d 1055 (C.D. Cal.2002). The court rejected Matchmaker's argument for immunity under 47 U.S.C. § 230(c)(1) after finding that the company provided part of the profile content. [c] However, the court rejected Carafano's invasion of privacy claim on the grounds that her home address was "newsworthy" and that, in any case, Matchmaker had not disclosed her address with reckless disregard for her privacy. [c] Similarly, the court rejected Carafano's claims for defamation, negligence, and misappropriation because she failed to show that Matchmaker had acted with actual malice. [C]

II

The dispositive question in this appeal is whether Carafano's claims are barred by 47 U.S.C. § 230(c)(1), which states that "[n]o provider or user of an interactive computer service shall be treated as the publisher or speaker of any information provided by another information content provider." Through this provision, Congress granted most Internet services immunity from liability for publishing false or defamatory material so long as the information was provided by another party. As a result, Internet publishers are treated differently from corresponding publishers in print, television and radio. See Batzel v. Smith, 333 F.3d 1018, 1026–27 (9th Cir. 2003).

Congress enacted this provision as part of the Communications Decency Act of 1996 for two basic policy reasons: to promote the free exchange of information and ideas over the Internet and to encourage voluntary monitoring for offensive or obscene material. [C] Congress incorporated these ideas into the text of § 230 itself, expressly noting that "interactive computer services have flourished, to the benefit of all Americans, with a minimum of government regulation," and that "[i]ncreasingly Americans are relying on interactive media for a variety of political, educational, cultural, and entertainment services." 47 U.S.C. § 230(a)(4), (5). Congress declared it the "policy of the United States" to "promote the continued development of the Internet and other interactive computer services," "to preserve the vibrant and competitive free market that presently exists for the Internet and other interactive computer services," and to "remove disincentives for the development and utilization of blocking and filtering technologies." 47 U.S.C. § 230(b)(1), (2), (4).

In light of these concerns, reviewing courts have treated § 230(c) immunity as quite robust, adopting a relatively expansive definition of "interactive computer service" [footnote omitted] and a relatively restrictive definition of "information content provider." [footnote omitted] Under the statutory scheme, an "interactive computer service" qualifies for immunity so long as it does not also function as an "information content provider" for the portion of the statement or publication at issue.

We recently considered whether § 230(c) provided immunity to the operator of an electronic newsletter who selected and published an allegedly defamatory e-mail over the Internet. *Batzel*, 333 F.3d at 1030–32. We held that the online newsletter qualified as an "interactive computer service" under the statutory definition and that the selection for publication and editing of an e-mail did not constitute partial "creation or development" of that information within the definition of "information content provider." Although the case was ultimately remanded for determination of whether the original author intended to "provide" his e-mail for publication, [C] the *Batzel* decision joined the consensus developing across other courts of appeals that § 230(c) provides broad immunity for publishing content provided primarily by third parties. [Cc]

The fact that some of the content was formulated in response to Matchmaker's questionnaire does not alter this conclusion. Doubtless, the questionnaire facilitated the expression of information by individual users. However, the selection of the content was left exclusively to the user. The actual profile "information" consisted of the particular options chosen and the additional essay answers provided. Matchmaker was not responsible, even in part, for associating certain multiple choice responses with a set of physical characteristics, a group of essay answers, and a photograph. Matchmaker cannot be considered an "information content provider" under the statute because no profile has any content until a user actively creates it.

As such, Matchmaker's role is similar to that of the customer rating system at issue in Gentry v. eBay, Inc., 99 Cal. App. 4th 816, 121 Cal. Rptr. 2d 703 (2002). In that case, the plaintiffs alleged that eBay "was an information content provider in that it was responsible for the creation of information, or development of information, for the online auction it provided through the Internet." [C] Specifically, the plaintiffs noted that eBay created a highly structured Feedback Forum, which categorized each response as a "Positive Feedback," a "Negative Feedback," or a "Neutral Feedback." [C] In addition, eBay provided a color coded star symbol next to the user name of a seller who had achieved certain levels of "Positive Feedback" and offered a separate "Power Sellers" endorsement based on sales volume and Positive Feedback ratings. [C] The court concluded that § 230 barred the claims:

> Appellants' negligence claim is based on the assertion that the information is false or misleading because it has been manipulated by the individual defendants or other co-conspiring parties. Based on these allegations, enforcing appellants' negligence claim would place liability on eBay for simply compiling false and/or misleading content created by the individual defendants and other coconspirators. We do not see such activities transforming eBay into an information content provider with respect to the representations targeted by appellants as it did not create or develop the underlying misinformation. [C]

Similarly, the fact that Matchmaker classifies user characteristics into discrete categories and collects responses to specific essay questions does not transform Matchmaker into a "developer" of the "underlying misinformation."

We also note that, as with eBay, Matchmaker's decision to structure the information provided by users allows the company to offer additional features, such as "matching" profiles with similar characteristics or highly structured searches based on combinations of multiple choice questions. Without standardized, easily encoded answers, Matchmaker might not be able to offer these services and certainly not to the same degree. Arguably, this promotes the expressed Congressional policy "to promote the continued development of the Internet and other interactive computer services." 47 U.S.C. § 230(b)(1).

Carafano responds that Matchmaker contributes much more structure and content than eBay by asking 62 detailed questions and providing a menu of "pre-prepared responses." However, this is a distinction of degree rather than of kind, and Matchmaker still lacks responsibility for the "underlying misinformation."

Further, even assuming Matchmaker could be considered an information content provider, the statute precludes treatment as a publisher or speaker for "*any* information provided by *another* information content provider." 47 U.S.C. § 230(c)(1) (emphasis added). The statute would still bar Carafano's claims unless Matchmaker created or developed the particular information at issue. As the *Gentry* court noted,

> [T]he fact appellants allege eBay is an information content provider is irrelevant if eBay did not itself create or develop the content for which appellants seek to hold it liable. It is not inconsistent for eBay to be an interactive service provider and also an information content provider; the categories are not mutually exclusive. The critical issue is whether eBay acted as an information content provider with respect to the information that appellants claim is false or misleading. [C]

In this case, critical information about Carafano's home address, movie credits, and the e-mail address that revealed her phone number were transmitted unaltered to profile viewers. Similarly, the profile directly reproduced the most sexually suggestive comments in the essay section, none of which bore more than a tenuous relationship to the actual questions asked. Thus Matchmaker did not play a significant role in creating, developing or "transforming" the relevant information.

Thus, despite the serious and utterly deplorable consequences that occurred in this case, we conclude that Congress intended that service providers such as Matchmaker be afforded immunity from suit. Thus, we affirm the judgment of the district court, albeit on other grounds.

Affirmed.

NOTES AND QUESTIONS

1. Responding to demands and encourage ISPs to take measures to monitor material coming before children, Congress enacted the Communications Decency Act of 1996. The CDA grants broad immunity to ISPs. The protection extends to ISPs that fall within the definition of secondary publishers and, even more, to those that come within the terms of primary publishers. Blumenthal v. Drudge, 992 F. Supp. 44 (D.D.C. 1998). Does this immunity go too far? What incentives do ISPs have to self-regulate in light of such broad protections?

2. Courts have resoundingly interpreted immunity under § 230(c) broadly. See Zeran v. Am. Online, Inc., 129 F.3d 327 (4th Cir. 1997) (immunity for refusal to post a retraction for defamatory content that resulted in death threats to plaintiff); Universal Commc'ns Sys. v. Lycos, Inc., 478 F.3d 413 (1st Cir. 2007) (immunity for message board posts about plaintiff company's management and finances); Doe v. MySpace, Inc., 528 F.3d 413 (5th Cir. 2008) (immunity when minor used site to connect with older male who sexually assaulted her).

However, several courts have questioned the limits of the Act's coverage of "providers." In Doe v. GTE Corp., 347 F.3d 655 (7th Cir. 2003), Judge Easterbrook, writing for a unanimous panel, stated that § 230(c)(1) may be a definitional clause in which an entity "would become a 'publisher or speaker' and lose the benefit of 230(c)(2) if it created the objectionable information." In Jones v. Dirty World Entm't Recordings LLC, 755 F.3d 398 (6th Cir. 2014), the plaintiff, a high school teacher and professional cheerleader, sued defendant for featuring a user submission consisting of photos of the plaintiff with male companions captioned with statements that the plaintiff had tested positive for several sexually transmitted diseases. The Court of Appeals for the Sixth Circuit held that the website operator could be liable if it made a "material contribution to the alleged illegality" of the defamatory content, but that defendant's actions of selecting the photos to be featured on the website and adding a brief comment to the post did not constitute a material contribution. Consider also Fair Housing Council of San Fernando Valley v. Roommates.com, LLC, 521 F.3d 1157 (9th Cir. 2008) (holding that the website operator may "contribute to the content's illegality" if the "design" requires "users to input illegal information"). For an empirical analysis of cases interpreting § 230(c)(1), see David Ardia, Free Speech Savior or Shield for Scoundrels: An Empirical Study of Intermediary Immunity under Section 230 of the Communications Decency Act, 43 LOY. L.A. L. REV. 373 (2010). See also Marjorie Heins, The Brave New World of Social Media Censorship: How "Terms of Service" Abridge Free Speech, 127 HARV. L. REV. F. 325 (2014).

3. Courts have occasionally found creative ways of limiting immunity. In Barnes v. Yahoo!, Inc., 570 F.3d 1096 (9th Cir. 2009), the facts fitted the usual pattern, in that a third party posted nude pictures of plaintiff and offensive remarks on defendant's website. The case is notable because it shows how a plaintiff can avoid the immunity provisions by alleging a claim sounding in contract law; the court held that § 230(c)(1) did not bar plaintiff's promissory estoppel cause of action. To prevail in a promissory estoppel claim, the plaintiff must show that the defendant undertook to remove harmful content and failed to do so. A divided panel in Batzel v. Smith, 333 F.3d 1018 (9th Cir. 2003), discussed in the principal case, announced that immunity is maintained provided the ISP reasonably understood that the original source intended the content to be published online. The court held that the website operator could reasonably have concluded that an email containing statements that plaintiff possessed looted art work was intended for dissemination, even when the author of the email did not so intend.

Ogden v. Association of the United States Army

United States District Court, District of Columbia, 1959.
177 F.Supp. 498.

HOLTZOFF, DISTRICT JUDGE. The question presented for decision in this case is whether from the standpoint of the statute of limitations in an action for libel every sale or delivery of a copy of a book, periodical, or newspaper containing an alleged defamatory statement, creates a separate cause of action; or whether only one cause of action arises which accrues at the time of the first publication of one or more copies of the offending material. To formulate this question in another form, should the so-called modern "single publication rule" be the law of the District of Columbia? [The book containing the alleged libel was published in November, 1955. This suit was filed on June 25, 1959. The District of Columbia has a 1-year statute of limitations for defamation.]

The common law was originally to the effect that every sale or delivery of libelous matter was a new publication and that, therefore, a new cause of action accrued on each occasion. * * *

A leading English case on the subject is The Duke of Brunswick v. Harmer, 14 Q.B. 185, 117 Eng.Rep. 75, decided in 1849. It involved an issue of a newspaper published in 1830. A single copy was sold by the defendant seventeen years later and a suit for libel was predicated on this sale as a publication. The plea of the statute of limitations was overruled on the theory that each sale or delivery of a copy of the offending material gave rise to a new and separate cause of action. * * *

Under modern conditions the original common-law rule would give rise to an unnecessary multiplicity of suits and would practically destroy the statute of limitations as a statute of repose in actions for libel. There is no doubt, to be sure, that the number of copies of the offending publication that have been supplied to the public is a factor to be considered in determining the amount of damages to be awarded. In order to protect the plaintiff in this respect, however, it is not necessary to hold that every sale and delivery of an additional copy is a new publication and gives rise to a new cause of action.

[The court reviews decisions from many states adopting the single-publication rule and quotes the Uniform Single Publications Act, promulgated in 1952 and adopted in a number of other states.]

There are indeed a few States that expressly adhere to the original English rule in cases that were decided a great many years ago, [cc]. They are a small minority. * * *

* * * [T]he conclusion is inescapable that the modern American law of libel has adopted the so-called "single publication" rule; and, therefore, this principle must be deemed a part of the common law of the District of Columbia. In other words, it is the prevailing American doctrine that the publication of a book, periodical, or newspaper containing defamatory matter gives rise to but one cause of action for libel, which accrues at the time of the original publication, and that the statute of limitations runs from that date. It is no longer the law that every sale or delivery of a copy of the publication creates a new cause of action. * * *

The defendant's motion for summary judgment is granted.

NOTES AND QUESTIONS

1. American jurisdictions now generally agree with the principal case. Each edition of a newspaper, magazine, or book is held to be one separate publication. Christoff v. Nestle USA, Inc., 213 P.3d 132 (Ca. 2009) (thoroughly discussing the history of the single publication rule, including the common law rule and reasons for its rejection). This is true of each broadcast or rebroadcast over radio or television, and each exhibition of a motion picture. However, when a hundred different newspapers each publish in their own editions a news report supplied by the Associated Press, there a hundred publications. *See* RESTATEMENT (SECOND) OF TORTS § 577A (1977).

2. In Firth v. State, 775 N.E.2d 463 (N.Y. 2002), the New York Court of Appeals wrestled with the question of how to deal with the Internet in the context of the single publication rule. Plaintiff claimed that defendant had modified its website, after being made aware of a defamatory statement on it, without removing that statement. Plaintiff argued that, for

the purposes of the statute of limitations, the modification and reposting should be a second publication of the information on the Internet. The court disagreed, noting that the Internet is a unique media format that allows constant access to information by all persons. This also gives an individual the opportunity to modify a website without restriction at any time. Unlike a book or magazine that has specific publication runs, this constant modification, if counted as a publication, could create a morass of litigation and defeat the statute of limitations for Internet defamation. The court also held the mere addition of information to a website cannot serve as republication of any supposedly defamatory material already on the website. The court in Nationwide Bi-Weekly Admin., Inc. v. Belo Corp., 512 F.3d 137 (5th Cir. 2007), held that, under Texas law, the single publication rule applied to a website or internet publication.

3. The Internet has had, and will continue to have, an impact on how the law crafts defamation rules. The deep and ancient roots of the law are being challenged, as they were when the printing press was invented. In reading the cases to follow in Section 4, tracing the Supreme Court's inroads into defamation law, ask yourselves what values under the First Amendment are being promoted. Do the assumptions of free speech found in *New York Times* apply in the era of the Internet with the potential of citizens' unprecedented access to information and debate? Christopher S. Yoo, Free Speech and the Myth of the Internet as an Unintermediated Experience, 78 Geo. Wash. L. Rev. 697 (2010) (discussing the inevitable and arguably beneficial role of internet intermediaries, including last-minute network providers, search engines, social networking sites and smartphones, in promoting free speech); Bruce Johnson, Is the *New York Times* Rule Relevant in a Breitbarted World?, 19 Comm. L. & Pol'y 211 (2014) (arguing that the New York Times rule "is sufficiently hardy and relevant for America's dynamic and sometimes acrid marketplace of ideas").

4. BASIS OF LIABILITY

The early law imposed strict liability for defamation, as in the case of most other torts. See Holdsworth, Defamation in the Sixteenth and Seventeenth Centuries, 41 L.Q. Rev. 13 (1925).

During the Seventeenth Century, the courts were not at all anxious to encourage actions for defamation. The rule developed that the plaintiff must prove not only that the defendant intended to defame him, but that he was inspired by "malice," in the sense of spite, ill will, or a desire to do harm. Whitlock v. Horton, (1791) 79 Eng. Rep. 78 (Exch.); 1 Cro. Jac. 91 (Eng.); Crawford v. Middleton, (1793) 83 Eng. Rep. 308 (K.B.); 1 Lev. 82 (Eng.). Apparently this was carried over from the ecclesiastical law of slander, which was concerned with the moral sin of speaking ill of one's neighbor, and from criminal libel, which required at least a criminal intent. Van Vechten Veeder, History and Theory of the Law of Defamation, 4 Colum. L. Rev. 33 (1904); Note, Slander and Libel, 6 AM. L. REV. 593 (1872).

The historic case of Bromage v. Prosser, (1825) 107 Eng. Rep. 1051 (K.B.); 4 B. & C. 247 (Eng.), drew a distinction between "malice in fact and malice in law." Malice is necessary, it held, but in the ordinary defamation case, if the statement is false and defamatory and it was made intentionally, "the law implies such malice as is necessary to maintain the action." Factual malice, on the other hand, is not a necessary part of the plaintiff's case in an ordinary defamation action; but it may be important to refute a qualified privilege or to justify punitive damages. "Malice" has also come to be used, with a still different meaning, in the constitutional law cases set out in this Section.

Thus, malice implied in law consequently became a pure fiction, and therefore malice in fact was no longer requisite to prima facie defamation cases. Nevertheless, the courts continued to reference malice, and thus the term's role in defamation actions is one of profound confusion.

After *Bromage v. Prosser*, decisions imposing liability for unintended and innocent defamation. The classic case was the Scottish decision of Morrison v. Ritchie & Co., (1904) 4 F. 645 (Scot.). Here, the defendant newspaper company published a notice in good faith that plaintiff's wife had given birth to twins. It was held liable when the report proved false and was considered "defamatory in respect that the date stated was within two months of [the plaintiff's] marriage."

Then came Hulton v. Jones, [1910] A.C. 20 (appeal taken from Wales). In this case, the defendant newspaper published a report from a French correspondent from the resort of Dieppe, which contained a passage reading: " 'Whist! there is Artemus Jones with a woman who is not his wife, who must be, you know—the other thing!' whispers a fair neighbour of mine excitedly into her bosom friend's ear. Really, is it not surprising how certain of our fellow-countrymen behave when they come abroad?" Jones v. Hulton, [1909], 2 K.B. 444 at 445. The name Artemus Jones was fictitious, coined for the occasion after an American humorist named Artemus Ward. However, a real Artemus Jones, a North Wales barrister, sued. Although nothing connected him with the person parodied in the article apart from his name, he recovered on the ground that some of his friends understood the piece to refer to him. See Jeremiah Smith, *Jones v. Hulton*: Three Conflicting Views as to Defamation, 60 U. PA. L. REV. 365, 461 (1912); W.S. Holdsworth, A Chapter of Accidents in the Law of Libel, 57 L.Q. REV. 74 (1941).

In the United States, the leading case of Corrigan v. Bobbs-Merrill Co., 126 N.E. 260, 262 (N.Y. 1920), was similar. An author sent in a book manuscript purporting to be fictitious, and the publisher produced it without realizing that it referred in an identifiable way to a magistrate in the city of New York. "The fact that the publisher has no actual intention to defame a particular man or indeed to injure any one does not prevent recovery of compensatory damages by one who connects himself with the publication. . . . The question is not so much who was aimed at as who was hit." There were numerous cases in accord.

Secondary Publishers. There is one important exception. A vendor or distributor of a newspaper, magazine or book is called a "secondary publisher". A secondary publisher is not liable if it did not know about, and had no reason to suspect, libelous matter in the publication. See Vizetelly v. Mudie's Select Library Ltd., [1900] 2 Q.B. 170 (Eng.)

(concerning a lending library); Balabanoff v. Fossani, 81 N.Y.S.2d 732 (N.Y. Spec. Term 1948) (concerning a newspaper vendor); Grisham v. W. Union Tel. Co., 142 S.W. 271 (Mo. 1911) (finding that the telegram was innocent on its face).

A newspaper or book publishing company does not qualify as a secondary publisher and is subject to strict liability even though it innocently took the defamatory material from someone else without reason to be put on guard. However, republication of items received from wire services will not be subject to liability if (1) the service was reputable; (2) defendant did not know of the falsity; (3) the story itself does not reveal its falsity; and (4) no substantial change was made to the story.

There has been sharp disagreement as to how local radio and television networks are to be classified when they broadcast material directly from national networks or allow someone else to supply a program without opportunity for screening it. Holding that they are primary publishers: Sorensen v. Wood, 123 Neb. 348, 243 N.W. 82 (1932); Miles v. Louis Wasmer, Inc., 172 Wash. 466, 20 P.2d 847 (1933). See Sorensen v. Wood, 243 N.W. 82 (Neb. 1932); Miles v. Louis Wasmer, Inc., 20 P.2d 847 (Wash. 1933), for cases holding that they are primary publishers. See Kelly v. Hoffman, 61 A.2d 143 (N.J. 1948); Summit Hotel Co. v. Nat'l Broad. Co., 8 A.2d 302 (Pa. 1939); Auvil v. CBS "60 Minutes," 800 F. Supp. 928 (E.D. Wash. 1992), for cases holding that they are secondary publishers. A number of states have statutes, the enactment of which was supported by broadcasters, providing protection unless due care was not taken. The Restatement takes the position that a broadcasting station should be treated as an original publisher. RESTATEMENT (SECOND) OF TORTS § 581(2) (1977). *See* Marvin Ammori, The "New" *New York Times*: Free Speech Lawyering in the Age of Google and Twitter, 127 Harv. L. Rev. 2259 (2014); Jacob H. Rowbottom, In the Shadow of the Big Media: Freedom of Expression, 2014 Pub. L. 491. Before the promulgation of the Communications Decency Act of 1996 (CDA), 47 U.S.C. § 230, Internet service providers ("ISPs") were classified as secondary publishers. For further discussion, see supra page 917.

New York Times Co. v. Sullivan

Supreme Court of the United States, 1964.
376 U.S. 254, 84 S.Ct. 710, 11 L.Ed.2d 686.

JUSTICE BRENNAN delivered the opinion of the Court.

We are required in this case to determine for the first time the extent to which the constitutional protections for speech and press limit a State's power to award damages in a libel action brought by a public official against critics of his official conduct.

Respondent L.B. Sullivan is one of the three elected Commissioners of the City of Montgomery, Alabama. He testified that he was "Commissioner of Public Affairs and the duties are supervision of the Police Department, Fire Department, Department of Cemetery and Department of Scales." He brought this civil libel action against the four individual petitioners, who are Negroes and Alabama clergymen, and against petitioner the New York Times Company, a New York corporation which publishes the New York Times, a daily newspaper. A jury in the Circuit Court of Montgomery County awarded him damages of $500,000, the full amount claimed, against all the petitioners, and the Supreme Court of Alabama affirmed.

Justice Brennan

Respondent's complaint alleged that he had been libeled by statements in a full-page advertisement that was carried in the New York Times on March 29, 1960. Entitled "Heed Their Rising Voices," the advertisement began by stating that "As the whole world knows by now, thousands of Southern Negro students are engaged in wide-spread non-violent demonstrations in positive affirmation of the right to live in human dignity as guaranteed by the U.S. Constitution and the Bill of Rights." It went on to charge that "in their efforts to uphold these guarantees, they are being met by an unprecedented wave of terror by those who would deny and negate that document which the whole world looks upon as setting the pattern for modern freedom. * * * " Succeeding paragraphs purported to illustrate the "wave of terror" by describing certain alleged events. The text concluded with an appeal for funds for three purposes: support of the student movement, "the struggle for the right-to-vote," and the legal defense of Dr. Martin Luther King, Jr., leader of the movement, against a perjury indictment then pending in Montgomery.

The text appeared over the names of 64 persons, widely known for their activities in public affairs, religion, trade unions, and the performing arts. * * *

Of the 10 paragraphs of text in the advertisement, the third and a portion of the sixth were the basis of respondent's claim of libel. They read as follows:

Third paragraph: "In Montgomery, Alabama, after students sang 'My Country, 'Tis of Thee' on the State Capitol steps, their leaders were expelled from school, and truckloads of police armed with shotguns and tear-gas ringed the Alabama State College Campus. When the entire student body protested to state authorities by refusing to re-register, their dining hall was padlocked in an attempt to starve them into submission."

Sixth paragraph: "Again and again the Southern violators have answered Dr. King's peaceful protests with intimidation and violence. They have bombed his home almost killing his wife and child. They have assaulted his person. They have arrested him seven times—for 'speeding,' 'loitering' and similar 'offenses.' And now they have charged him with 'perjury'—a *felony* under which they could imprison him for *ten years.* * * * "

[Although plaintiff was not mentioned by name, he contended that these statements attributed misconduct to him as the Montgomery Commissioner who supervised the Police Department.]

It is uncontroverted that some of the statements contained in the two paragraphs were not accurate descriptions of events which occurred in Montgomery. Although Negro students staged a demonstration on the State Capitol steps, they sang the National Anthem and not "My Country, 'Tis of Thee." Although nine students were expelled by the State Board of Education, this was not for leading the demonstration at the Capitol, but for demanding service at a lunch counter in the Montgomery County Courthouse on another day. Not the entire student body, but most of it, had protested the expulsion, not by refusing to register, but by boycotting classes on a single day; virtually all the students did register for the ensuing semester. The campus dining hall was not padlocked on any occasion, and the only students who may have been barred from eating there were the few who had neither signed a preregistration application nor requested temporary meal tickets. Although the police were deployed near the campus in large numbers on three occasions, they did not at any time "ring" the campus, and they were not called to the campus in connection with the demonstration on the State Capitol steps, as the third paragraph implied. Dr. King had not been arrested seven times, but only four; and although he claimed to have been assaulted some years earlier in connection with his arrest for loitering outside a courtroom, one of the officers who made the arrest denied that there was such an assault.

On the premise that the charges in the sixth paragraph could be read as referring to him, respondent was allowed to prove that he had not participated in the events described. Although Dr. King's home had in fact been bombed twice when his wife and child were there, both of these occasions antedated respondent's tenure as Commissioner, and the police were not only not implicated in the bombings, but had made every effort to apprehend those who were. Three of Dr. King's four arrests took place before respondent became Commissioner. Although Dr. King had in fact been indicted (he was subsequently acquitted) on two counts of perjury, each of which carried a possible five-year sentence, respondent had nothing to do with procuring the indictment. * * *

The trial judge submitted the case to the jury under instructions that the statements in the advertisement were "libelous per se" and were not privileged, so that petitioners might be held liable if the jury found that they had published the advertisement and that the statements were made "of and concerning" respondent. * * *

Under Alabama law as applied in this case * * * once "libel per se" has been established, the defendant has no defense as to stated facts unless he can persuade the jury that they were true in all their particulars. [Cc] His privilege of "fair comment" for expressions of opinion depends on the truth of the facts upon which the comment is based. * * *

The First Amendment, said Judge Learned Hand, "presupposes that right conclusions are more likely to be gathered out of a multitude of tongues, than through any kind of authoritative selection. To many this is, and always will be, folly; but we have staked upon it our all." United States v. Associated Press, 52 F.Supp. 362, 372 (S.D.N.Y.1943). * * * Thus we consider this case against the background of a profound national commitment to the principle that debate on public issues should be uninhibited, robust and wide-open, and that it may well include vehement, caustic, and sometimes unpleasantly sharp attacks on government and public officials. [Cc] The present advertisement, as an expression of grievance and protest, on one of the major public issues of our time, would seem clearly to qualify for the constitutional protection. The question is whether it forfeits that protection by the falsity of some of its factual statements and by its alleged defamation of respondent.

Authoritative interpretations of the First Amendment guarantees have consistently refused to recognize an exception for any test of truth—whether administered by judges, juries, or administrative officials—and especially one that puts the burden of proving truth on the speaker. [C] The constitutional protection does not turn upon "the truth, popularity, or social utility of the ideas and beliefs which are offered." [C] As Madison said, "Some degree of abuse is inseparable from the proper use of everything; and in no instance is this more true than in that of the press." [C] * * *

If neither factual error nor defamatory content suffices to remove the constitutional shield from criticism of official conduct, the combination of the two elements is no less inadequate. [The Court here reviewed the history of the Sedition Act of 1798, which made it a crime to publish defamation against high officers of the United States, and reached the conclusion at this late date that the Act was unconstitutional.]

What a State may not constitutionally bring about by means of a criminal statute is likewise beyond the reach of its civil law of libel. The fear of damage awards under a rule such as that invoked by the Alabama courts here may be markedly more inhibiting than the fear of prosecution under a criminal statute. * * * Presumably a person charged with violation of [a criminal-libel] statute enjoys ordinary criminal-law safeguards such as the requirements of an indictment and of proof beyond a reasonable doubt. These safeguards are not available to the defendant in a civil action. * * *

The state rule of law is not saved by its allowance of the defense of truth. * * * A rule compelling the critic of official conduct to guarantee the truth of all his factual assertions—and to do so on pain of libel judgments virtually unlimited in amount—leads to a comparable "self-censorship." * * *

The constitutional guarantees require, we think, a federal rule that prohibits a public official from recovering damages for a defamatory falsehood relating to his official conduct unless he proves that the statement was made with "actual malice"—that is, with knowledge that it was false or with reckless disregard of whether it was false or not. An oft-cited statement of a like rule, which has been adopted by a number of state courts, is found in the Kansas case of Coleman v. MacLennan, 78 Kan. 711, 98 P. 281 (1908). The State Attorney General, a candidate for re-election and a member of the commission charged with the management and control of the state school fund sued a newspaper publisher for alleged libel in an article purporting to state facts relating to his official conduct in connection with a school-fund transaction. * * * In answer to a special question, the jury found that the plaintiff had not proved actual malice, and a general verdict was returned for the defendant. On appeal the Supreme Court of Kansas, in an opinion by Justice Burch, reasoned as follows:

"[I]t is of the utmost consequence that the people should discuss the character and qualifications of candidates for their suffrage. The importance to the state and to society of such discussions is so vast, and the advantages derived are so great that they more than counterbalance the inconvenience of private persons whose conduct may be involved, and occasional injury to the reputations of individuals must yield to the public welfare, although at times such injury may be great. The public benefit from publicity is so great and the chance of injury to private character so small that such discussion must be privileged." The court thus sustained the trial court's instruction as a correct statement of the law, saying:

"In such a case the occasion gives rise to a privilege qualified to this extent. Any one claiming to be defamed by the communication must show actual malice, or go remediless. This privilege extends to a great variety of subjects and includes matters of public concern, public men, and candidates for office." [C]

We hold today that the Constitution delimits a State's power to award damages for libel in actions brought by public officials against critics of their official conduct. Since this is such an action, the rule requiring proof of actual malice is applicable. * * *

[W]e consider that the proof presented to show actual malice lacks the convincing clarity which the constitutional standard demands, and hence that it would not constitutionally sustain the judgment for respondent under the proper rule of law. The case of the individual petitioners requires little discussion. Even assuming that they could constitutionally be found to have authorized the use of their names on the advertisement, there was no evidence whatever that they were aware of any erroneous statements or were in any way reckless in that regard. The judgment against them is thus without constitutional support.

As to the Times, we similarly conclude that the facts do not support a finding of actual malice. The statement by the Times' Secretary that, apart from the padlocking allegation, he thought the advertisement was "substantially correct," affords no constitutional warrant for the Alabama Supreme Court's conclusion that it was a "cavalier ignoring of the falsity of the advertisement, [from which] the jury could not have but been impressed with the bad faith of The Times, and its maliciousness inferable therefrom." The statement does not indicate malice at the time of the publication; even if the advertisement was not "substantially correct"—although respondent's own proofs tend to show that it was—that opinion was at least a reasonable one, and there was no evidence to impeach the witness' good faith in holding it. The Times' failure to retract upon respondent's demand, although it later retracted upon the demand of Governor Patterson, is likewise not adequate evidence of malice for constitutional purposes. Whether or not a failure to retract may ever constitute such evidence, there are two reasons why it does not here. *First,* the letter written by the Times reflected a reasonable doubt on its part as to whether the advertisement could reasonably be taken to refer to respondent at all. *Second,* it was not a final refusal, since it asked for an explanation on this point—a request that respondent chose to ignore. Nor does the retraction upon the demand of the Governor supply the necessary proof. It may be doubted that a failure to retract which is not itself evidence of malice can retroactively become such by virtue of a retraction subsequently made to another party. But in any event that did not happen here, since the explanation given by the Times' Secretary for the distinction drawn between respondent and the Governor was a reasonable one, the good faith of which was not impeached.

Finally, there is evidence that the Times published the advertisement without checking its accuracy against the news stories in the Times' own files.... We think the evidence against the Times supports at most a finding of negligence in failing to discover the misstatements, and is constitutionally insufficient to show the recklessness that is required for a finding of actual malice. * * *

We also think the evidence was constitutionally defective in another respect: it was incapable of supporting the jury's finding that the allegedly libelous statements were made "of and concerning" respondent.

There was no reference to respondent in the advertisement, either by name or official position. A number of the allegedly libelous statements * * * did not even concern the police. * * *

Although the statements may be taken as referring to the police, they do not on their face make even an oblique reference to respondent as an individual. * * *

This * * * has disquieting implications for criticism of governmental conduct. For good reason, "no court of last resort in this country has ever held, or even suggested, that prosecutions for libel on government have any place in the American system of jurisprudence." City of Chicago v. Tribune Co. (1923) 307 Ill. 595, 601, 139 N.E. 86, 88.

The present proposition would sidestep this obstacle by transmuting criticism of government, however impersonal it may seem on its face, into personal criticism, and hence potential libel of the officials of whom the government is composed. * * * We hold that such a proposition may not constitutionally be utilized to establish that an otherwise impersonal attack on governmental operations was a libel of an official responsible for those operations. * * *

The judgment of the Supreme Court of Alabama is reversed, and the case is remanded to that court for further proceedings not inconsistent with this opinion.

[The concurring opinions of JUSTICES BLACK and GOLDBERG are omitted. Both would categorically deny any action of defamation by a public official insofar as his public conduct is concerned. This was variously characterized as "an absolute, unconditional constitutional right to * * * say what one pleases about public affairs," "an absolute immunity for criticism of the way public officials do their public duty," and "an absolute privilege for criticism of official conduct." JUSTICE DOUGLAS joined in both opinions.]

NOTES AND QUESTIONS

1. For fuller accounts of this case and its background, see Harry Kalven, Jr., The *New York Times* Case: A Note on "The Central Meaning of the First Amendment," 1964 Sup. Ct. Rev. 191; Anthony Lewis, *New York Times v. Sullivan* Reconsidered: A Return to "The Central Meaning of the First Amendment," 83 Colum. L. Rev. 603 (1983); Samuel R. Pierce, Jr., The Anatomy of an Historic Decision: *New York Times Co. v. Sullivan*, 43 N.C. L. Rev. 315 (1964). See also Kermit L. Hall & Melvin I. Urofsky, *New York Times v. Sullivan*: Civil Rights, Libel Law, and the Free Press (2011); Paul Finkelman & Melvin L. Urofsky, Landmark Decisions of the United States Supreme Court (2d ed. 2008); Richard A. Epstein, Was *New York Times v. Sullivan* Wrong?, 53 U. Chi. L. Rev. 782 (1986).

2. *Fair Comment.* For many years before the principal case, the courts had developed, at common law and virtually without reference to the Constitution, a privilege of criticism of public officers and their official conduct. It usually was called the privilege of "fair comment," see *Milkovich v. Lorain Journal*, infra page 966.

The existence of this qualified privilege was not disputed. There was, however, a sharp division of authority on whether it was limited to "comment" or criticism, that is, the expression of opinion, or whether it extended to false statements of fact. About three-quarters of the courts that had considered the question held that the privilege was limited to the expression of opinion, and did not include misstatements of fact. This was the position taken by the Supreme Court of Alabama before it was reversed two years later. N.Y. Times Co. v. Sullivan, 144 So.2d 25 (Ala. 1962), *rev'd*, 376 U.S. 254 (1964)

The leading case to this effect was Post Pub. Co. v. Hallam, 59 Fed. 530 (6th Cir. 1893), an opinion of Judge (later President and Chief Justice) Taft. The reason he advanced was that if public men were to be subjected to false statements of fact, good men could not be found to take the positions. A vigorous minority, headed by Coleman v. MacLennan, 98 P. 281 (Kan.1908), and supported by most of the commentators, contended that the privilege extended to false statements of fact, so long as they were made in good faith. For an interpretive history of political libel in the United States, see NORMAN L. ROSENBERG, PROTECTING THE BEST MEN: AN INTERPRETIVE HISTORY OF THE LAW OF LIBEL (1986).

3. *Public Officials.* Rosenblatt v. Baer, 383 U.S. 75 (1966), involved comments about the supervisor of a county recreation area. The Court held that whether he was a public official was a question of federal law, not state law. The test was held to be whether "[t]he position in government has such apparent importance that the public has an independent interest in the qualifications and performance of the person who holds it, beyond the general public interest in the qualifications and performance of all governmental employees." Cf. Tucker v. Kilgore, 388 S.W.2d 112 (Ky.1964) (patrolman).

The *N.Y Times* rule applies to candidates for public office. Monitor Patriot Co. v. Roy, 401 U.S. 265 (1971); Ocala Star-Banner Co. v. Damron, 401 U.S. 295 (1971).

4. *Public Figures.* The *N.Y Times* rule was extended to apply to "public figures" in Curtis Pub. Co. v. Butts, 388 U.S. 130 (1967), and Associated Press v. Walker, 388 U.S. 130 (1967). Two cases were involved: a suit by (1) Coach Wally Butts of the University of Georgia (employed by a private corporation rather than the state) for story in the Saturday Evening Post charging him with conspiring with Coach Bear Bryant of the University of Alabama to "fix" a football game; and (2) Edwin A. Walker a well-known retired army general, against the Associated Press for a story regarding his alleged part in a student disturbance at the University of Mississippi involving enrollment of its first black student. Both were held to be public figures. Recovery below was reversed in *Walker,* but affirmed in *Butts.* For an interesting look on the factual background of the *Butts* case, see JAMES KIRBY, FUMBLE: BEAR BRYANT, WALLY BUTTS AND THE GREAT COLLEGE SCANDAL (1986).

The *Walker* and *Butts* opinions precipitated some confusion about the correct standard of proof for actual malice. Any doubt was resolved by the Court in Harte-Hanks Commns, Inc. v. Connaughton, 491 U.S. 657 (1989), infra page 934, when the Court "emphatically" adopted the standard of "knowledge or reckless disregard" enunciated in *New York Times*. In Dongguk Univ. v. Yale Univ., 734 F.3d 113 (2d Cir. 2013), a Korean university sued Yale for defamation. Yale publicly denied that it had ever confirmed a Korean art professor's bogus Ph.D. Yale did not check anything before its initial denial, but then later discovered it had, in fact, confirmed the bogus degree. Nonetheless, the court said the university was a public figure and that there was no actual malice.

5. *Matter of Public or General Interest.* Rosenbloom v. Metromedia, Inc., 403 U.S. 29 (1971), expanded the *N.Y.Times* knowing-or-reckless-disregard standard beyond public officials and public figures to apply to any matter of public or general interest. Rosenbloom had been arrested in a police drive against obscene books. Defendant, operating a radio news station, reported the arrest and used the terms "smut literature racket" and "girlie-book peddlers." Following acquittal of the criminal charges, plaintiff sued for libel. He recovered $25,000 in general damages and $725,000 in punitive damages, reduced by remittitur to $250,000. The Court of Appeals reversed, holding the *N.Y. Times* standard applied, though the plaintiff was not a public figure. The Supreme Court agreed.

Once again the Justices divided sharply. The plurality opinion was written by Justice Brennan, joined by Chief Justice Burger, and Justices Blackmun and Black concurred in the judgment but adhered to his absolute-privilege view. Justice White, J., concurred in the result on the ground that the report covered the official action of public officials. Justices Harlan and Marshall, JJ. (Joined by Justice Stewart), dissented in separate opinions deprecating the ad-hoc nature of a test depending upon whether an event was a matter of public or general interest and urged that the way for the Court to take care of the recurring cases was to limit the measure of recovery to "proven, actual damages" and to eliminate strict liability. Justice Douglas, J., did not participate in the case.

The plurality opinion of Justice Brennan remained the binding rule of constitutional law until it was repudiated in 1974 by Gertz v. Robert Welch, Inc., infra page 944. Does its spirit still live in Dun & Bradstreet, Inc. v. Greenmoss Builders, Inc., infra page 953?

The concept of "matters of public concern" is frequently used to identify the realm of information that attracts heightened First Amendment protection. In Bartnicki v. Vopper, 532 U.S. 514 (2001) Justice Stevens, writing for the Court, held a wiretapping statute unconstitutional when applied to defendants who had received and disseminated recordings of unlawfully obtained cell phone conversations. The content of the tapes was "truthful information of public concern," the distribution of which could not be punished under the law. Justice Breyer, joined by Justice O'Connor, emphasized that the holding was narrow because the expectation of privacy, a legitimate state interest, was low, considering the threat of violence made in the conversations. Chief Justice Rehnquist, joined by Justices Scalia and Thomas, criticized the "amorphous concept" of "public concern," finding that the Court's decision chilled, rather than enhanced, the free speech purposes of the First Amendment.

6. As with all revolutions, so with *New York Times:* many problems were left in its wake. The common law had to be reconciled with First Amendment principles. We now review the "wreckage" and subsequent "salvage" work of the courts. What is the meaning of actual malice? How does it affect the press? What of imputations concerning private persons? What of information that is purely private? What of the falsity presumption of defamatory imputations? What are public figures and officials? Do defamatory imputations in the form of opinion call forth a special analysis? The case law and academic commentary on the impact of *New York Times* and its progeny is multitudinous. David A. Anderson, Is Libel Law Worth Reforming, 140 U. Pa. L. Rev. 487, 488 nn.2–3 (1991), gives a sampling of the debate. The flow shows no signs of diminishing.

(A) ACTUAL MALICE, BURDENS OF PROOF, AND THE PRESS

St. Amant v. Thompson

Supreme Court of the United States, 1968.
390 U.S. 727, 88 S.Ct. 1323, 20 L.Ed.2d 262.

[Defendant St. Amant made a televised political speech, in the course of which he read questions that he had put to a union member, Albin, and Albin's answers. The answers falsely charged the plaintiff, a deputy sheriff, with criminal conduct. Plaintiff sued defendant for defamation, and was awarded damages by the trial judge. The judge then considered New York Times Co. v. Sullivan, supra page 922, decided after the trial, and denied a motion for a new trial. An intermediate appellate court reversed the judgment, finding that defendant had not acted with "actual malice" within the meaning of the New York Times rule. The Louisiana Supreme Court reversed, finding that there had been sufficient evidence that defendant had acted in "reckless disregard" of the truth. The Supreme Court granted certiorari.]

JUSTICE WHITE delivered the opinion of the Court. * * *

For purposes of this case we accept the determinations of the Louisiana courts that the material published by St. Amant charged Thompson with criminal conduct, that the charge was false, and that Thompson was a public official, and so had the burden of proving that the false statements about Thompson were made with actual malice as defined in New York Times Co. v. Sullivan and later cases. We cannot, however, agree with either the Supreme Court of Louisiana or the trial court that Thompson sustained this burden.

Purporting to apply the *New York Times* malice standard, the Louisiana Supreme Court ruled that St. Amant had broadcast false information about Thompson recklessly though not knowingly. Several reasons were given for this conclusion. St. Amant had no personal knowledge of Thompson's activities; he relied solely on Albin's affidavit although the record was silent as to Albin's reputation for veracity; he failed to verify the information with those in the union office who might have known the facts; he gave no consideration as to whether or not the statements defamed Thompson and went ahead heedless of the consequences; and he mistakenly believed he had no responsibility for the broadcast because he was merely quoting Albin's words.

These considerations fall short of proving St. Amant's reckless disregard for the accuracy of his statements about Thompson. "Reckless disregard," it is true, cannot be fully encompassed in one infallible definition. Inevitably its outer limits will be marked out through case-by-case adjudication, as is true with so many legal standards for judging concrete cases, whether the standard is provided by the Constitution, statutes, or case law. Our cases, however, have furnished meaningful guidance for the further definition of a reckless publication.

In *New York Times,* the plaintiff did not satisfy his burden because the record failed to show that the publisher was aware of the likelihood that he was circulating false information. In Garrison v. State of Louisiana, 379 U.S. 64 (1964), also decided before the decision of the Louisiana Supreme Court in this case, the opinion emphasized the necessity for showing that a false publication was made with a "high degree of awareness of * * * probable falsity." Mr. Justice Harlan's opinion in Curtis Publishing Co. v. Butts, 388 U.S. 130, 153 (1967), stated that evidence of either deliberate falsification or reckless publication "despite the publisher's awareness of probable falsity" was essential to recovery by public officials in defamation actions. These cases are clear that reckless conduct is not measured by whether a reasonably prudent man would have published, or would have investigated before publishing. There must be sufficient evidence to permit the conclusion that the defendant in fact entertained serious doubts as to the truth of his publication. Publishing with such doubts shows reckless disregard for truth or falsity and demonstrates actual malice.

It may be said that such a test puts a premium on ignorance, encourages the irresponsible publisher not to inquire, and permits the issue to be determined by the defendant's testimony that he published the statement in good faith and unaware of its probable falsity. Concededly the reckless disregard standard may permit recovery in fewer situations than would a rule that publishers must satisfy the standard of the reasonable man or the prudent publisher. But *New York Times* and succeeding cases have emphasized that the stake of the people in public business and the conduct of public officials is so great that neither the defense of truth nor the standard of ordinary care would protect against self-censorship and thus adequately implement First Amendment policies. Neither lies nor false communications serve the ends of the First Amendment, and no one suggests their desirability or further proliferation. But to insure the ascertainment and publication of the truth about public affairs, it is essential that the First Amendment protect some erroneous publications as well as true ones. We adhere to this view and to the line which our cases have drawn between false communications which are protected and those which are not.

The defendant in a defamation action brought by a public official cannot, however, automatically insure a favorable verdict by testifying that he published with a belief that the statements were true. The finder of fact must determine whether the publication was indeed made in good faith. Professions of good faith will be unlikely to prove persuasive, for example, where a story is fabricated by the defendant, is the product of his imagination, or is based wholly on an unverified anonymous telephone call. Nor will they be likely to prevail when the publisher's allegations are so inherently improbable that only a reckless man would have put them in circulation. Likewise, recklessness may be found where there are obvious reasons to doubt the veracity of the informant or the accuracy of his reports. * * *

Because the state court misunderstood and misapplied the actual malice standard which must be observed in a public official's defamation action, the judgment is reversed and the case remanded for further proceedings not inconsistent with this opinion.

[JUSTICES BLACK and DOUGLAS concurred in the judgment, on the ground that there should be an absolute privilege. JUSTICE FORTAS dissented, on the ground that the defendant had a duty to check the reliability of the statement, and hence that he published it in reckless disregard of the truth.]

NOTES AND QUESTIONS

1. Almost immediately after the New York Times decision, the Court discarded completely the old-fashioned meaning of "malice," so far as the constitutional restriction on defamation is concerned. Relying on *New York Times v. Sullivan,* supra page 922, and Garrison v. Louisiana, 379 U.S. 64 (1964), the Court held jury instructions impermissible because they failed to convey that a public official could only recover in libel if the defendants intended not merely to inflict harm, but to inflict harm through falsehood. Henry v. Collins, 380 U.S. 356 (1965).

2. The test of serious doubt in *St. Amant* is admittedly subjective in nature. In Herbert v. Lando, 441 U.S. 153 (1979), a public officer was obligated to prove knowledge or reckless disregard as to falsity in his libel action based on a "60 Minutes" report. The officer sought to depose the defendant with inquiries into his state of mind and communications with other participants in the editorial process. The defendant resisted on First Amendment grounds and the Second Circuit held for him (568 F.2d 974 (2d Cir. 1977)), declaring that the First Amendment grants him an absolute privilege regarding "his thoughts, opinions and conclusions with respect to the material gathered by him and about his conversations with his editorial colleagues." 441 U.S. at 158. The Supreme Court reversed, holding that previous decisions did not authorize or presage an editorial privilege of this nature and that it did not construe the First Amendment to authorize it as a matter of constitutional law. The holding was unanimous regarding questions on state of mind, but three justices had somewhat varying views regarding forced disclosure of communications between participants in the editorial process. On remand, the Court of Appeals held, on the basis of evidence in the new trial, that summary judgment should be granted to the defendant. Herbert v. Lando, 781 F.2d 298 (2d Cir. 1986).

On state of mind, would it be better to substitute an objective test for the subjective one? This does not require a negligence test, but could be based on the language of Justice White in *St. Amant:* "publisher's allegations . . . so inherently improbable that only a reckless man would have put them in circulation." A pointed example is Khawar v. Globe Int'l, Inc., 965 P.2d 696 (Cal. 1998), where the imputation that plaintiff was the real assassin of Robert Kennedy was in such hopeless collision with notorious and established facts, known to defendants, that it showed purposeful avoidance of the truth.

Harte-Hanks Communications, Inc. v. Connaughton

Supreme Court of the United States, 1989.
491 U.S. 657, 109 S.Ct. 2678, 105 L.Ed.2d 562.

JUSTICE STEVENS delivered the opinion of the Court.

A public figure may not recover damages for a defamatory falsehood without clear and convincing proof that the false "statement was made with 'actual malice'—that is, with knowledge that it was false or with reckless disregard of whether it was false or not." New York Times Co. v. Sullivan, 376 U.S. 254, 279–280 (1964). In Bose Corp. v. Consumers Union of United States, Inc., 466 U.S. 485 (1984) we held that judges in such cases have a constitutional duty to "exercise independent judgment and determine whether the record establishes actual malice with convincing clarity." [c] In this case the Court of Appeals affirmed a libel judgment against a newspaper without attempting to make an independent evaluation of the credibility of conflicting oral testimony concerning the subsidiary facts underlying the jury's finding of actual malice. We granted certiorari to consider whether the Court of Appeals' analysis was consistent with our holding in *Bose*.

Respondent, Daniel Connaughton, was the unsuccessful candidate for the office of Municipal Judge of Hamilton, Ohio, in an election conducted on November 8, 1983. Petitioner is the publisher of the Journal News, a local newspaper that supported the reelection of the incumbent, James Dolan. A little over a month before the election, the incumbent's Director of Court Services resigned and was arrested on bribery charges. A grand jury investigation of those charges was in progress on November 1, 1983. On that date, the Journal News ran a front-page story quoting Alice Thompson, a grand jury witness, as stating that Connaughton had used "dirty tricks" and offered her and her sister jobs and a trip to Florida "in appreciation" for their help in the investigation.

* * *

After listening to six days of testimony and three taped interviews—one conducted by Connaughton and two by Journal News reporters—and reviewing the contents of 56 exhibits, the jury was given succinct instructions accurately defining the elements of public figure libel and directed to answer three special verdicts. [footnote omitted] It unanimously found by a preponderance of the evidence that the November 1 story was defamatory and that it was false. It also found by clear and convincing proof that the story was published with actual malice. After a separate hearing on damages, the jury awarded Connaughton $5,000 in compensatory damages and $195,000 in punitive damages. Thereafter, the District Court denied a motion for judgment notwithstanding the verdict, and petitioner appealed.

The Court of Appeals affirmed. [c] It separately considered the evidence supporting each of the jury's special verdicts, concluding that neither the finding that the article was defamatory[3] nor the finding that it was false[4] was clearly erroneous.

II

Petitioner contends that the Court of Appeals made two basic errors. First, while correctly stating the actual malice standard announced in New York Times Co. v. Sullivan, supra, the court actually applied a less severe standard that merely required a showing of " 'highly unreasonable conduct constituting an extreme departure from the standards of investigation and reporting ordinarily adhered to by responsible publishers.' " (quoting Curtis Publishing Co. v. Butts, 388 U.S., at 155, 87 S.Ct. at 1991 (opinion of Harlan, J.)). Second, the court failed to make an independent *de novo* review of the entire record and therefore incorrectly relied on subsidiary facts implicitly established by the jury's verdict instead of drawing its own inferences from the evidence.

There is language in the Court of Appeals' opinion that supports petitioner's first contention. For example, the Court of Appeals did expressly state that the Journal News' decision to publish Alice Thompson's allegations constituted an extreme departure from professional standards. Moreover, the opinion attributes considerable weight to the evidence that the Journal News was motivated by its interest in the reelection of the candidate it supported and its economic interest in gaining a competitive advantage over the Cincinnati Enquirer, its bitter rival in the local market. Petitioner is plainly correct in recognizing that a public figure plaintiff must prove more than an extreme departure from professional standards and that a newspaper's motive in publishing a story—whether to promote an opponent's candidacy or to increase its circulation—cannot provide a sufficient basis for finding actual malice.

* * *

---

[3] The Court of Appeals observed that "the article was defamatory in its implication that Connaughton was an unethical lawyer and an undesirable candidate for the Hamilton Municipal judgeship who was capable of extortion, who was a liar and an opportunist not fit to hold public office, particularly a judgeship." [c]

[4] As to the finding of falsity, the Court of Appeals wrote: "Equally apparent from the jury's answer to the second special interrogatory is that it considered the published Thompson charges to be false. Its finding is understandable in light of the plaintiff's proof which disclosed that the *Journal*'s effort to verify her credibility ended in an avalanche of denials by knowledgeable individuals; [and] its inability to produce a single person who supported Thompson's accusations . . .

"Moreover, the jury obviously refused to credit the *Journal*'s construction of Connaughton's interview of October 31. It accepted Connaughton's express denials of each Thompson charge and considered the significant language interpreted by the *Journal* to constitute his admissions of those charges, when read in context, as nothing more than conjecture elicited by structured questions calculated to evoke speculation. Thus, upon reviewing the record in its entirety, this court concludes that the jury's determinations of the operational facts bearing upon the falsity of the article in issue were not clearly erroneous." [c]

It also is worth emphasizing that the actual malice standard is not satisfied merely through a showing of ill will or "malice" in the ordinary sense of the term. [c] Indeed, just last Term we unanimously held that a public figure "may not recover for the tort of intentional infliction of emotional distress . . . without showing . . . that the publication contains a false statement of fact which was made . . . with knowledge that the statement was false or with reckless disregard as to whether or not it was true." Hustler Magazine, Inc. v. Falwell, 485 U.S. 46. (1988). Nor can the fact that the defendant published the defamatory material in order to increase its profits suffice to prove actual malice. The allegedly defamatory statements at issue in the *New York Times* case were themselves published as part of a paid advertisement. If a profit motive could somehow strip communications of the otherwise available constitutional protection, our cases from *New York Times* to *Hustler Magazine* would be little more than empty vessels. Actual malice, instead, requires at a minimum that the statements were made with a reckless disregard for the truth. And although the concept of "reckless disregard" "cannot be fully encompassed in one infallible definition," St. Amant v. Thompson, supra, we have made clear that the defendant must have made the false publication with a "high degree of awareness of . . . probable falsity," [c] or must have "entertained serious doubts as to the truth of his publication," [c]

When the Court of Appeals opinion is read as a whole, it is clear that the conclusion concerning the newspaper's departure from accepted standards and the evidence of motive were merely supportive of the court's ultimate conclusion that the record "demonstrated a reckless disregard as to the truth or falsity of Thompson's allegations and thus provided clear and convincing proof of 'actual malice' as found by the jury." [c] Although courts must be careful not to place too much reliance on such factors, a plaintiff is entitled to prove the defendant's state of mind through circumstantial evidence, see Herbert v. Lando, 441 U.S. 153, 160, [c] and it cannot be said that evidence concerning motive or care never bears any relation to the actual malice inquiry. Thus, we are satisfied that the Court of Appeals judged the case by the correct substantive standard.

The question whether the Court of Appeals gave undue weight to the jury's findings—whether it failed to conduct the kind of independent review mandated by our opinion in *Bose*—requires more careful consideration. A proper answer to that question must be prefaced by additional comment on some of the important conflicts in the evidence. [The opinion canvasses the evidence.] * * *

V

The question whether the evidence in the record in a defamation case is sufficient to support a finding of actual malice is a question of law. Bose Corp. v. Consumers Union of United States, Inc., supra. This rule is not simply premised on common-law tradition, but on the unique character of the interest protected by the actual malice standard. Our profound national commitment to the free exchange of ideas, as enshrined in the First Amendment, demands that the law of libel carve out an area of " 'breathing space' " so that protected speech is not discouraged. *Gertz, supra.* The meaning of terms such as "actual malice"—and, more particularly, "reckless disregard"—however, is not readily captured in "one infallible definition." St. Amant v. Thompson, supra. Rather, only through the course of case-by-case adjudication can we give content to these otherwise elusive constitutional standards. *Bose, supra*. Moreover, such elucidation is particularly important in the area of free speech for precisely the same reason that the actual malice standard is itself necessary. Uncertainty as to the scope of the constitutional protection can only dissuade protected speech—the more elusive the standard, the less protection it affords. Most fundamentally, the rule is premised on the recognition that "[j]udges, as expositors of the Constitution," have a duty to "independently decide whether the evidence in the record is sufficient to cross the constitutional threshold that bars the entry of any judgment that is not supported by clear and convincing proof of 'actual malice.'" *Bose, supra*, at 511.

There is little doubt that "public discussion of the qualifications of a candidate for elective office presents what is probably the strongest possible case for application of the *New York Times* rule," Ocala Star-Banner Co. v. Damron, 401 U.S. 295 (1971), and the strongest possible case for independent review. As Madison observed in 1800, just nine years after ratification of the First Amendment:

> "Let it be recollected, lastly, that the right of electing the members of the government constitutes more particularly the essence of a free and responsible government. The value and efficacy of this right depends on the knowledge of the comparative merits and demerits of the candidates for public trust, and on the equal freedom, consequently, of examining and discussing these merits and demerits of the candidates respectively." 4 J. Elliot, Debates on the Federal Constitution 575 (1861).

This value must be protected with special vigilance. When a candidate enters the political arena, he or she "must expect that the debate will sometimes be rough and personal," Ollman v. Evans, 242 U.S.App.D.C. 301, 333, 750 F.2d 970, 1002 (1984) (en banc) (Bork, J., concurring), cert. denied, 471 U.S. 1127 (1985), and cannot "'cry Foul!' when an opponent or an industrious reporter attempts to demonstrate" that he or she lacks the "sterling integrity" trumpeted in campaign literature and speeches, Monitor Patriot Co. v. Roy, 401 U.S. 265. Vigorous reportage of political campaigns is necessary for the optimal functioning of democratic institutions and central to our history of individual liberty.

We have not gone so far, however, as to accord the press absolute immunity in its coverage of public figures or elections. If a false and defamatory statement is published with knowledge of falsity or a reckless disregard for the truth, the public figure may prevail. See Curtis Publishing Co. v. Butts, 388 U.S., at 162, (opinion of Warren, C.J.). A "reckless disregard" for the truth, however, requires more than a departure from reasonably prudent conduct. "There must be sufficient evidence to permit the conclusion that the defendant in fact entertained serious doubts as to the truth of his publication." *St. Amant, supra* at 731. The standard is a subjective one—there must be sufficient evidence to permit the conclusion that the defendant actually had a "high degree of awareness of . . . probable falsity." Garrison v. Louisiana, 379 U.S., at 74. As a result, failure to investigate before publishing, even when a reasonably prudent person would have done so, is not sufficient to establish reckless disregard. See *St. Amant, supra.* In a case such as this involving the reporting of a third party's allegations, "recklessness may be found where there are obvious reasons to doubt the veracity of the informant or the accuracy of his reports." *St. Amant, supra.*

In determining whether the constitutional standard has been satisfied, the reviewing court must consider the factual record in full. Although credibility determinations are reviewed under the clearly-erroneous standard because the trier of fact has had the "opportunity to observe the demeanor of the witnesses," *Bose, supra,* the reviewing court must " 'examine for [itself] the statements in issue and the circumstances under which they were made to see . . . whether they are of a character which the principles of the First Amendment . . . protect,' " *New York Times Co., supra.* Based on our review of the entire record, we agree with the Court of Appeals that the evidence did in fact support a finding of actual malice. Our approach, however, differs somewhat from that taken by the Court of Appeals. In considering the actual malice issue, the Court of Appeals identified 11 subsidiary facts that the jury "could have" found. * * * We agree that the jury *may* have found each of those facts, but conclude that the case should be decided in a less speculative ground

* * *

Given the trial court's instructions, the jury's answers to the three special interrogatories, and an understanding of those facts not in dispute, it is evident that the jury *must* have rejected (1) the testimony of petitioner's witnesses that Stephens was not contacted simply because Connaughton failed to place her in touch with the newspaper; (2) the testimony of Blount that he did not listen to the tapes simply because he thought they would provide him with no new information; and (3) the testimony of those Journal News employees who asserted that they believed Thompson's allegations were substantially true. When these findings are considered alongside the undisputed evidence, the conclusion that the newspaper acted with actual malice inexorably follows.

There is no dispute that Thompson's charges had been denied not only by Connaughton, but also by five other witnesses before the story was published. Thompson's most serious charge—that Connaughton intended to confront the incumbent judge with the tapes to scare him into resigning and otherwise not to disclose the existence of the tapes—was not only highly improbable, but inconsistent with the fact that Connaughton had actually arranged a lie detector test for Stephens and then delivered the tapes to the police. These facts were well known to the Journal News before the story was published. Moreover, because the newspaper's interviews of Thompson and Connaughton were captured on tape, there can be no dispute as to what was communicated, nor how it was said. The hesitant, inaudible, and sometimes unresponsive and improbable tone of Thompson's answers to various leading questions raise obvious doubts about her veracity.

Moreover, contrary to petitioner's contention that the prepublication interview with Connaughton confirmed the factual basis of Thompson's statements, review of the tapes makes clear that Connaughton unambiguously denied each allegation of wrongful conduct. * * * It is extraordinarily unlikely that the reporters missed Connaughton's denials simply because he confirmed certain aspects of Thompson's story.

It is also undisputed that Connaughton made the tapes of the Stephens interview available to the Journal News and that no one at the newspaper took the time to listen to them. Similarly, there is no question that the Journal News was aware that Patsy Stephens was a key witness and that they failed to make any effort to interview her. Accepting the jury's determination that petitioner's explanations for these omissions were not credible, it is likely that the newspaper's inaction was a product of a deliberate decision not to acquire knowledge of facts that might confirm the probable falsity of Thompson's charges. Although failure to investigate will not alone support a finding of actual malice, [c] the purposeful avoidance of the truth is in a different category.

There is a remarkable similarity between this case—and in particular, the newspaper's failure to interview Stephens and failure to listen to the tape recording of the September 17 interview at Connaughton's home—and the facts that supported the Court's judgement in Curtis Publishing Co. v. Butts, supra. In *Butts* the evidence showed that the Saturday Evening Post had published an accurate account of an unreliable informant's false description of the Georgia athletic director's purported agreement to "fix" a college football game. Although there was reason to doubt Thompson's story, the editors did not interview a witness who had the same access to the facts as the informant and did not look at films that revealed what actually happened at the game in question . . . This evidence of an intent to avoid the truth was not only sufficient to convince the plurality that there had been an extreme departure from professional publishing standards, but it was also sufficient to satisfy the more demanding *New York Times* standard . . . As in *Butts*, the evidence in the record in this case, when reviewed in its entirety, is "unmistakably" sufficient to support a finding of actual malice.

Affirmed.

NOTES AND QUESTIONS

1. *Actual Malice and Journalistic Enterprise.* As the principal case demonstrates, the inquiry is richly factual. Much will turn on defendant's knowledge and actions or omissions in respect of that knowledge. In Tavoulareas v. Piro, 817 F.2d 762 (D.C. Cir.) (en banc), *cert. denied*, 484 U.S. 870 (1987), cert. denied, 484 U.S. 870 (1987), the Court stressed that insufficient investigation alone, in the absence of serious doubts about the truth of statements, will not support a finding of actual malice. Reporter's ill will and a newspaper policy to find sensational stories are relevant but not sufficient in sustaining the burden of showing actual malice. The court warned that mere accumulation of factors will not meet the burden. But cf. Ball v. E.W. Scripps, 801 S.W.2d 684 (Ky.1990). In the absence of direct

proof establishing that the defendant "entertained serious doubts as to the truth of [its] publication," a jury may infer awareness of falsity if it finds "obvious reasons to doubt" the accuracy of the story, and that the defendant did not act reasonably in dispelling those doubts. Masson v. New Yorker Magazine, Inc., 960 F.2d 896 (9th Cir. 1992). Similarly, in St. Surin v. Virgin Islands Daily News, 21 F.3d 1309 (3d Cir. 1994), the court held that defendant could not obtain summary judgment where its editor was aware of changes in the article that made it false.

In Suzuki Motor Corp. v. Consumers Union of U.S. Inc., 330 F.3d 1110 (9th Cir. 2003) a divided *en banc* panel of the Ninth Circuit on re-hearing held that Suzuki had made a case sufficient to resist Consumer Union's motion for a summary judgment. Defendant had published a report stating that plaintiff's vehicle was subject to rollovers. Defendant had argued that the evidence did not establish the requisite actual malice according to the principle in Liberty Lobby, Inc. v. Anderson, 746 F.2d 1563 (D.C. Cir. 1984), vacated, 477 U.S. 242 (1986). The majority, applying the principal case, analyzed the argument on two bases, i.e., whether a reasonable jury could find by clear and convincing evidence that (1) defendant had a high degree of awareness of the probable falsity of the statement, and (2) defendant, in the face of obvious reasons to doubt the statement's accuracy, did not act to dispel doubts, thereby raising an inference that defendant knew of falsity. On both grounds, it was held that plaintiff had raised a genuine issue of material fact to resist a summary judgment. In a vehement dissent, Judge Kozinski was dismayed that after a truthful disclosure of the circumstances of the rollover test, the "information could be deemed malicious under *New York Times v. Sullivan* [c]." The willingness to produce reports to the public good would be dampened. Are you persuaded by Judge Kozinski?

A critical concern for the press is maintenance of confidentiality of its sources. Can plaintiff insist on disclosure of a source in discovery in fashioning her prima facie case of actual malice? Without the opportunity to depose the source, the chances of plaintiff resisting a motion for summary judgment will be slim. Southwell v. Southern Poverty Law Center, 949 F. Supp. 1303 (W.D. Mich.1996) (holding that confidential source need not be disclosed where plaintiff showed source was reliable and defendant failed to show that disclosure of source would yield evidence of malice confidential source need not be disclosed). For the interaction of emerging legal rules and journalism norms, see Brian C. Murchison et al., *Sullivan*'s Paradox: The Emergence of Judicial Standards of Journalism, 73 N.C. L. Rev. 7 (1994)(arguing that in applying actual malice and negligence standards state and federal judges consider and evaluate a wide range of journalistic behavior and *per force*, in a baleful manner, create norms of journalistic research, writing, and editing). For a transnational appraisal, see RUSSELL L. WEAVER ET AL., THE RIGHT TO SPEAK ILL: DEFAMATION, REPUTATION AND FREE SPEECH (2005)(examining and comparing defamation law in the United States, England, New Zealand, and Australia, noting the changing law and the willingness of media to publish in the shadow of various legal rules).

2. *Standards for Summary Judgment.* The standard on summary judgment is often critical. Anderson v. Liberty Lobby, 477 U.S. 242 (1986), examines the standard of proof in a motion for summary judgment, finding that it varies according to whether the plaintiff is a public figure under

New York Times or a private person under *Gertz*. Justice White stated: "In sum, we conclude that the determination of whether a given factual dispute requires submission to a jury must be guided by the substantive evidentiary standards that apply to the case. This is true at both the directed verdict and summary judgment stages. Consequently, where the *New York Times*, 'clear and convincing' evidence requirement applies, the trial judge's summary judgment inquiry as to whether a genuine issue exists will be whether the evidence presented is such that a jury applying that evidentiary standard could reasonably find for either the plaintiff or the defendant. Justices Brennan and Rehnquist, dissented in separate opinions, and the Chief Justice concurred with Justice Rehnquist.

3. *Fair Reporting—First Amendment Standards.* In Time, Inc. v. Pape, 401 U.S. 279 (1971), Time Magazine cited a report of the U.S. Commission of Civil Rights entitled *Justice,* listing instances of police brutality which were alleged in complaints to have occurred. The allegations of one complaint, involving plaintiff, were stated as facts. Held: "In light of the totality of what was said in *Justice,* we cannot agree that, when Time failed to state that the Commission in reporting the Monroe incident had technically confined itself to the allegations of a complaint, Time engaged in a 'falsification' sufficient in itself to sustain a jury finding of 'actual malice.' . . . Time's omission of the word 'alleged' amounted to the adoption of one of a number of possible rational interpretations of a document that bristled with ambiguities. The deliberate choice of such an interpretation, though arguably reflecting a misconception, was not enough to create a jury issue of 'malice' under *New York Times.* To permit the malice issue to go to the jury because of the omission of a word like 'alleged' . . . would be to impose a much stricter standard of liability on errors of interpretation or judgment than on errors of historic fact. . . . Nothing in this opinion is to be understood as making the word 'alleged' a superfluity in published reports of information damaging to reputation."

In Time, Inc. v. Firestone, 424 U.S. 448 (1976), Time Magazine published in its "Milestones" Section this item: "Divorced, by Russell A. Firestone, Jr., 41, heir to the tire fortune, Mary Alice Sullivan Firestone, 32, his third wife; a one time Palm Beach schoolteacher; on ground of extreme cruelty and adultery; after six years marriage, one son; in West Palm Beach Florida. The 17-month intermittent trial produced enough testimony of extramarital adventures on both sides, said the judge, 'to make Dr. Freud's hair curl.'" Although the publication's language was quite ambiguous, plaintiff demanded that Time retract its statement of adultery because, under Florida statute, she would not be entitled to the alimony she had been awarded if found guilty of such conduct. Time's refusal produced the libel action in which she was awarded $100,000 for mental distress. The Florida Supreme Court affirmed; but the Supreme Court reversed on the ground that there was never any intentional finding of fault by court or jury in the case. The Court distinguished *Pape* on the ground that it involved the *New York Times* standard (public figure) while *Firestone* involved the *Gertz* standard (private figure).

4. *Repetition of Defamation.* Observe that in neither *Pape* nor *Firestone* was the court concerned with the truth or falsity of the defamatory charge or the measure of defendant's fault in ascertaining it. The defendant would apparently not have been liable even if it had actually

known that the plaintiff was innocent of the charge, so long as the report of the official record was fair and accurate.

One is not ordinarily relieved of liability for repeating a defamatory charge, even if he indicates the source and accurately repeats it—even if he also says that he does not believe it. RESTATEMENT (SECOND) OF TORTS § 578 (1977).

5. *Fair Reporting.* At common law, there developed a special privilege, known as the "reporter's privilege" or as "record libel." It was a privilege because it did not exempt the defendant from liability unless his report was verbatim or a fair and accurate summary. *Pape* and *Firestone* now impose a constitutional requirement of fault in failing to make the report fair and accurate. It remains a privilege nonetheless. There is no liability for repetition of a defamatory statement, even if a defendant is at fault with regard to the relative truth of the charge itself, provided that the material carrying the defamatory imputation was an accurate report. An actual malice standard applies for reports on official actions providing a fair and accurate rendition. Milligan v. United States, 670 F.3d 686 (6th Cir. 2012) (holding that report of arrests is privileged even though police errors lead to plaintiff's wrongful arrest). See Restatement (Second) of Torts § 611 (1977). There is a good discussion in Gobin v. Globe Publ'g Co., 531 P.2d 76 (Kan. 1975), decided prior to *Firestone.*

The remaining problem involves the scope of the privilege, both at common law and under the more recent constitutional doctrine, and whether they will differ or coincide.

6. *The Privilege at Common Law.* This began as a privilege to report all official proceedings in the public interest. Wason v. Walter, (1868) 4 L.R.Q.B. 73 (Parliament); Terry v. Fellows, 21 La. Ann. 375 (1869) (concerning evidence or testimony given before session of legislative committee); Hahn v. Holum, 162 N.W. 432 (Wis. 1917) (proceeding before justice of the peace).

A privilege to report often attaches to information of public concern uttered at public meetings. The meetings need not be official but should be open to a wide segment of the public. Jackson v. Record Pub. Co., 178 S.E. 833 (S.C.1935) (words of a candidate at a political rally); Phoenix Newspapers v. Choisser, 312 P.2d 150 (Ariz.1957) (same, at Chamber of Commerce "forum"); Pulvermann v. A.S. Abell Co., 228 F.2d 797 (4th Cir. 1956) (speech made by candidate for President); Borg v. Boas, 231 F.2d 788 (9th Cir. 1956) (mass meeting held to urge calling a grand jury to investigate local law enforcement). In all of these cases, the matter reported has been one of public concern.

On the other hand, private meetings, not open to the public, have not been included. Kimball v. Post Pub. Co., 85 N.E. 103 (Mass.1908) (stockholders' meeting); Lewis v. Hayes, 132 P. 1022 (Cal.1913).

7. *Reports of Pleadings.* Authorities divide on whether an exception to the reporter's privilege in the case of pleadings filed with a court but not yet acted upon judicially. Comment e to section 611 of the RESTATEMENT (SECOND) OF TORTS recognizes the exception. For cases in favor: see Quigley v. Rosenthal, 327 F.3d 1044, 1062 (10th Cir. Colo. 2003); Flues v. New Nonpareil Co., 135 N.W. 1083 (Iowa 1912); Sanford v. Boston Herald-Traveler Corp., 61 N.E.2d 5 (Mass. 1945); Moreno v. Crookston Times

Printing Co., 610 N.W.2d 321 (Minn. 2000); Byers v. Meridian Printing Co., 408, 95 N.E. 917 (Ohio 1911). For those against, see Solaia Tech., LLC v. Specialty Publ. Co., 852 N.E.2d 825 (Ill.2006) (including dissent on this issue); Misao Yoshimura Kurata v. L.A. News Pub. Co., 40 P.2d 520 (Cal. Dist. Ct. App.1935); Johnson v. Johnson Pub. Co., 271 A.2d 696 (D.C. App. 1970); Paducah Newspapers, Inc. v. Bratcher, 118 S.W.2d 178 (Ky.1937).

8. *The Privilege Under the Constitution. Pape* and *Firestone* are the only Supreme Court cases on the subject. A significant issue is raised by Edwards v. National Audubon Soc'y, Inc., 556 F.2d 113 (2d Cir. 1977), *cert. denied,* 434 U.S. 1002 (1977), espousing a much broader privilege of "neutral reportage." The court announced as a "fundamental principle" that "when a responsible, prominent organization like the National Audubon Society makes serious charges against a public figure, the First Amendment protects the accurate and disinterested reporting of those charges, regardless of the reporter's private views regarding their validity. . . . What is newsworthy about such accusations is that they were made. We do not believe that the press may be required under the First Amendment to suppress newsworthy statements merely because it has serious doubts regarding their truth. . . . The public interest in being fully informed about controversies that often rage around sensitive issues demands that the press be afforded the freedom to report such charges without assuming responsibility for them." . . .

The court went on the explain that: "[L]iteral accuracy is not a prerequisite: if we are to enjoy the blessings of a robust and unintimidated press, we must provide immunity from defamation suits where the journalist believes, reasonably and in good faith, that his report accurately conveys the charges made."

The authorities are divided with the doctrine of neutral reportage constituting a minority rule. See BRUCE W. SANFORD, LIBEL AND PRIVACY (2d ed. 2008) The doctrine attracts four requirements:

a. The charges in the article must either relate to a current public controversy or create one in their own right (Barry v. Time, Inc., 584 F. Supp. 1110 (N.D. Cal. 1984); McManus v. Doubleday & Co., 513 F. Supp. 1383 (S.D.N.Y. 1981)).

b. The charge must be made by a public official or public figure, or by a prominent organization (Cianci v. New Times Publ. Co., 639 F.2d 54 (2d Cir. 1980); *McManus*, 513 F. Supp. 1383).

c. The charges must be about a public figure or a public official (Dixson v. Newsweek, Inc., 562 F.2d 626 (10th Cir. 1977)).

d. The reportage of the charges must be "neutral," that is, accurately and disinterestedly republished (*Cianci,* 639 F.2d 54; *Dixson* 562 F.2d 626; *Barry*, 584 F. Supp. 1110).

9. A newspaper, opposing a candidate for office, carries accurate stories about his business transactions affecting the government, but deliberately prepares slanted headlines, intended to give a misleading impression to a person who did not carefully read through the story as to the candidate's ethics. Can this be found to constitute reckless disregard as to falsity? Cf. McNair v. Hearst Corp., 494 F.2d 1309 (9th Cir. 1974); Sprouse v. Clay Commn, Inc., 211 S.E.2d 674 (W.Va.1975); Journal-Gazette Company v. Bandido's, Inc., 712 N.E.2d 446 (Ind.), *cert. denied,* 528 U.S.

1005 (1999) (adopting the minority "fair index" rule, i.e., if the headline is not a "fair index" of the substance, headline must be examined independently to determine its actionability in libel).

(B) PRIVATE PLAINTIFFS

Gertz v. Robert Welch, Inc.

Supreme Court of the United States, 1974.
418 U.S. 323, 94 S.Ct. 2997, 41 L.Ed.2d 789.

JUSTICE POWELL delivered the opinion of the Court. * * *

I. In 1968 a Chicago policeman named Nuccio shot and killed a youth named Nelson. The state authorities prosecuted Nuccio for the homicide and ultimately obtained a conviction for murder in the second degree. The Nelson family retained petitioner Elmer Gertz, a reputable attorney, to represent them in civil litigation against Nuccio.

Respondent publishes American Opinion, a monthly outlet for the views of the John Birch Society. Early in the 1960's the magazine began to warn of a nationwide conspiracy to discredit local law enforcement agencies and create in their stead a national police force capable of supporting a Communist dictatorship. As part of the continuing effort to alert the public to this assumed danger, the managing editor of American Opinion commissioned an article on the murder trial of Officer Nuccio. For this purpose he engaged a regular contributor to the magazine. In March 1969 respondent published the resulting article under the title "FRAME-UP: Richard Nuccio And The War On Police." The article purports to demonstrate that the testimony against Nuccio at his criminal trial was false and that his prosecution was part of the Communist campaign against the police.

In his capacity as counsel for the Nelson family in the civil litigation, petitioner attended the coroner's inquest into the boy's death and initiated actions for damages, but he neither discussed Officer Nuccio with the press nor played any part in the criminal proceeding. Notwithstanding petitioner's remote connection with the prosecution of Nuccio, respondent's magazine portrayed him as an architect of the "frame-up." According to the article, the police file on petitioner took "a big, Irish cop to lift." The article stated that petitioner had been an official of the "Marxist League for Industrial Democracy, originally known as the Intercollegiate Socialist Society, which has advocated the violent seizure of our government." It labeled Gertz a "Leninist" and a "Communist-fronter." It also stated that Gertz had been an officer of the National Lawyers Guild, described as a Communist organization that "probably did more than any other outfit to plan the Communist attack on the Chicago police during the 1968 Democratic Convention."

These statements contained serious inaccuracies. The implication that petitioner had a criminal record was false. Petitioner had been a member and officer of the National Lawyers Guild some 15 years earlier, but there was no evidence that he or that organization had taken any part in planning the 1968 demonstrations in Chicago. There was also no basis for the charge that petitioner was a "Leninist" or a

"Communist-fronter." And he had never been a member of the "Marxist League for Industrial Democracy" or the "Intercollegiate Socialist Society."

The managing editor of American Opinion made no effort to verify or substantiate the charges against petitioner. Instead, he appended an editorial introduction stating that the author had "conducted extensive research into the Richard Nuccio Case." And he included in the article a photograph of petitioner and wrote the caption that appeared under it: "Elmer Gertz of Red Guild harasses Nuccio." Respondent placed the issue of American Opinion containing the article on sale at newsstands throughout the country and distributed reprints of the article on the streets of Chicago.

Petitioner filed a diversity action for libel in the United States District Court for the Northern District of Illinois.

[The District Court denied defendant's motion to dismiss. After the evidence was in, it "ruled in effect that petitioner was neither a public official nor a public figure," and it submitted the issue of damages to the jury, which awarded $50,000. On further reflection the District Court concluded that the *New York Times* standard applied and entered judgment for defendant notwithstanding the jury verdict. This action was affirmed by the Court of Appeals for the Seventh Circuit, on the basis of Rosenbloom v. Metromedia, Inc., 403 U.S. 29 (1971), supra page 930, which had been decided in the meantime.]

II. The principal issue in this case is whether a newspaper or broadcaster that publishes defamatory falsehoods about an individual who is neither a public official nor a public figure may claim a constitutional privilege against liability for the injury inflicted by those statements. The Court considered this question on the rather different set of facts presented in Rosenbloom v. Metromedia, Inc. [c]. [The opinion describes in detail the facts and opinions in *Rosenbloom*.]

III. We begin with the common ground. Under the First Amendment there is no such thing as a false idea. However pernicious an opinion may seem, we depend for its correction not on the conscience of judges and juries but on the competition of other ideas. But there is no constitutional value in false statements of fact. Neither the intentional lie nor the careless error materially advances society's interest in "uninhibited, robust, and wide-open" debate on public issues. [C] They belong to that category of utterances which "are no essential part of any exposition of ideas, and are of such slight social value as a step to truth that any benefit that may be derived from them is clearly outweighed by the social interest in order and morality." Chaplinsky v. New Hampshire, 315 U.S. 568, 572 (1942).

Although the erroneous statement of fact is not worthy of constitutional protection, it is nevertheless inevitable in free debate. As James Madison pointed out in the Report on the Virginia Resolutions of 1798, "Some degree of abuse is inseparable from the proper use of every thing; and in no instance is this more true than in that of the press." 4 J. Elliot, Debates on the Federal Constitution of 1787, p. 571 (1876). And punishment of error runs the risk of inducing a cautious and restrictive exercise of the constitutionally guaranteed freedoms of speech and press. Our decisions recognize that a rule of strict liability that compels a publisher or broadcaster to guarantee the accuracy of his factual assertions may lead to intolerable self-censorship. Allowing the media to avoid liability only by proving the truth of all injurious statements does not accord adequate protection to First Amendment liberties. As the Court stated in New York Times Co. v. Sullivan, supra, at 279, "Allowance of the defense of truth, with the burden of proving it on the defendant, does not mean that only false speech will be deterred." The First Amendment requires that we protect some falsehood in order to protect speech that matters.

The need to avoid self-censorship by the news media is, however, not the only societal value at issue. If it were, this Court would have embraced long ago the view that publishers and broadcasters enjoy an unconditional and indefeasible immunity from liability for defamation. [Cc] Such a rule would, indeed, obviate the fear that the prospect of civil liability for injurious falsehood might dissuade a timorous press from the effective exercise of First Amendment freedoms. Yet absolute protection for the communications media requires a total sacrifice of the competing value served by the law of defamation.

The legitimate state interest underlying the law of libel is the compensation of individuals for the harm inflicted on them by defamatory falsehood. * * * The protection of private personality, like the protection of life itself, is left primarily to the individual States under the Ninth and Tenth Amendments. But this does not mean that the right is entitled to any less recognition by this Court as a basic of our constitutional system. [C]

Some tension necessarily exists between the need for a vigorous and uninhibited press and the legitimate interest in redressing wrongful injury. * * * In our continuing effort to define the proper accommodation between these competing concerns, we have been especially anxious to assure to the freedoms of speech and press that "breathing space" essential to their fruitful exercise. [C] To that end this Court has extended a measure of strategic protection to defamatory falsehood.

The New York Times standard defines the level of constitutional protection appropriate to the context of defamation of a public person. Those who, by reason of the notoriety of their achievements or the vigor and success with which they seek the public's attention, are properly classed as public figures and those who hold governmental office may recover for injury to reputation only on clear and convincing proof that the defamatory falsehood was made with knowledge of its falsity or with reckless disregard for the truth. This standard administers an extremely powerful antidote to the inducement to media self-censorship of the common-law rule of strict liability for libel and slander. And it exacts a correspondingly high price from the victims of defamatory falsehood. Plainly many deserving plaintiffs, including some intentionally subjected to injury, will be unable to surmount the barrier of the New York Times test. Despite this substantial abridgment of the state law right to compensation for wrongful hurt to one's reputation, the Court has concluded that the protection of the New York Times privilege should be available to publishers and broadcasters of defamatory falsehood concerning public officials and public figures. [C] We think that these decisions are correct, but we do not find their holdings justified solely by reference to the interest of the press and broadcast media in immunity from liability. Rather, we believe that the New York Times rule states an accommodation between this concern and the limited state interest present in the context of libel actions brought by public persons. For the reasons stated below, we conclude that the state interest in compensating injury to the reputation of private individuals requires that a different rule should obtain with respect to them.

Theoretically, of course, the balance between the needs of the press and the individual's claim to compensation for wrongful injury might be struck on a case-by-case basis. * * * But this approach would lead to unpredictable results and uncertain expectations, and it could render our duty to supervise the lower courts unmanageable. Because an ad hoc resolution of the competing interests at stake in each particular case is not feasible, we must lay down broad rules of general application. * * *

The first remedy of any victim of defamation is self-help—using available opportunities to contradict the lie or correct the error and thereby to minimize its adverse impact on reputation. Public officials and public figures usually enjoy significantly greater access to the channels of effective communication and hence have a more realistic opportunity to counteract false statements than private individuals normally enjoy. Private individuals are therefore more vulnerable to injury, and the state interest in protecting them is correspondingly greater.

More important than the likelihood that private individuals will lack effective opportunities for rebuttal, there is a compelling normative consideration underlying the distinction between public and private defamation plaintiffs. An individual who decides to seek governmental office must accept certain necessary consequences of that involvement in public affairs. He runs the risk of closer public scrutiny than might otherwise be the case. * * *

Those classed as public figures stand in a similar position. Hypothetically, it may be possible for someone to become a public figure through no purposeful action of his own, but the instances of truly involuntary public figures must be exceedingly rare. * * * Commonly, those classed as public figures have thrust themselves to the forefront of particular public controversies in order to influence the resolution of the issues involved. * * *

The communications media are entitled to act on the assumption that public officials and public figures have voluntarily exposed themselves to increased risk of injury from defamatory falsehood concerning them. No such assumption is justified with respect to a private individual. * * * He has relinquished no part of his interest in the protection of his own good name, and consequently he has a more compelling call on the courts for redress of injury inflicted by defamatory falsehood. Thus, private individuals are not only more vulnerable to injury than public officials and public figures; they are also more deserving of recovery.

For these reasons we conclude that the States should retain substantial latitude in their efforts to enforce a legal remedy for defamatory falsehood injurious to the reputation of a private individual. The extension of the New York Times test proposed by the Rosenbloom plurality would abridge this legitimate state interest to a degree that we find unacceptable. And it would occasion the additional difficulty of forcing state and federal judges to decide on an ad hoc basis which publications address issues of "general or public interest" and which do not—to determine, in the words of Mr. Justice Marshall, "what information is relevant to self-government." Rosenbloom v. Metromedia, Inc., 403 U.S., at 79. We doubt the wisdom of committing this task to the conscience of judges. Nor does the Constitution require us to draw so thin a line between the drastic alternatives of the New York Times privilege and the common law of strict liability for defamatory error. * * *

We hold that, so long as they do not impose liability without fault, the States may define for themselves the appropriate standard of liability for a publisher or broadcaster of defamatory falsehood injurious to a private individual. This approach provides a more equitable boundary between the competing concerns involved here. It recognizes the strength of the legitimate state interest in compensating private individuals for wrongful injury to reputation, yet shields the press and broadcast media from the rigors of strict liability for defamation. At least this conclusion obtains where, as here, the substance of the defamatory statement "makes substantial danger to reputation apparent." * * *

IV. Our accommodation of the competing values at stake in defamation suits by private individuals allows the States to impose liability on the publisher or broadcaster of defamatory falsehood on a less demanding showing than that required by New York Times. This conclusion is not based on a belief that the considerations which prompted the adoption of the New York Times privilege for defamation of public officials and its extension to public figures are wholly inapplicable to the context of private individuals. Rather, we endorse this approach in recognition of the strong and legitimate state interest in compensating private individuals for injury to reputation.

But this countervailing state interest extends no further than compensation for actual injury. For the reasons stated below, we hold that the States may not permit recovery of presumed or punitive damages, at least when liability is not based on a showing of knowledge of falsity or reckless disregard for the truth.

The common law of defamation is an oddity of tort law, for it allows recovery of purportedly compensatory damages without evidence of actual loss. Under the traditional rules pertaining to actions for libel, the existence of injury is presumed from the fact of publication. Juries may award substantial sums as compensation for supposed damage to reputation without any proof that such harm actually occurred. The largely uncontrolled discretion of juries to award damages where there is no loss unnecessarily compounds the potential of any system of liability for defamatory falsehood to inhibit the vigorous exercise of First Amendment freedoms. Additionally, the doctrine of presumed damages invites juries to punish unpopular opinion rather than to compensate individuals for injury sustained by the publication of a false fact. More to the point, the States have no substantial interest in securing for plaintiffs such as this petitioner gratuitous awards of money damages far in excess of any actual injury.

We would not, of course, invalidate state law simply because we doubt its wisdom, but here we are attempting to reconcile state law with a competing interest grounded in the constitutional command of the First Amendment. It is therefore appropriate to require that state remedies for defamatory falsehood reach no farther than is necessary to protect the legitimate interest involved. It is necessary to restrict defamation plaintiffs who do not prove knowledge of falsity or reckless disregard for the truth to compensation for actual injury. We need not define "actual injury," as trial courts have wide experience in framing appropriate jury instructions in tort actions. Suffice it to say that actual injury is not limited to out-of-pocket loss. Indeed, the more customary types of actual harm inflicted by defamatory falsehood include impairment of reputation and standing in the community, personal humiliation, and mental anguish and suffering. Of course, juries must be limited by appropriate instructions, and all awards must be supported by competent evidence concerning the injury, although there need be no evidence which assigns an actual dollar value to the injury.

We also find no justification for allowing awards of punitive damages against publishers and broadcasters held liable under state-defined standards of liability for defamation. In most jurisdictions jury discretion over the amounts awarded is limited only by the gentle rule that they not be excessive. Consequently, juries assess punitive damages in wholly unpredictable amounts bearing no necessary relation to the actual harm caused. And they remain free to use their discretion selectively to punish expressions of unpopular views. Like the doctrine of presumed damages, jury discretion to award punitive damages unnecessarily exacerbates the danger of media self-censorship, but, unlike the former rule, punitive damages are wholly irrelevant to the state interest that justifies a negligence standard for private defamation actions. They are not compensation for injury. Instead, they are private fines levied by civil juries to punish reprehensible conduct and to deter its future occurrence. In short, the private defamation plaintiff who establishes liability under a less demanding standard than that stated by New York Times may recover only such damages as are sufficient to compensate him for actual injury.

V. Notwithstanding our refusal to extend the New York Times privilege to defamation of private individuals, respondent contends that we should affirm the judgment below on the ground that petitioner is either a public official or a public figure. * * *

Respondent admits this but argues that petitioner's appearance at the coroner's inquest rendered him a "de facto public official." Our cases recognize no such concept. Respondent's suggestion would sweep all lawyers under the New York Times rule as officers of the court and distort the plain meaning of the "public official" category beyond all recognition. We decline to follow it.

Respondent's characterization of petitioner as a public figure raises a different question. That designation may rest on either of two alternative bases. In some instances an individual may achieve such pervasive fame or notoriety that he becomes a public figure for all purposes and in all contexts. More commonly, an individual voluntarily injects himself or is drawn into a particular public controversy and thereby becomes a public figure for a limited range of issues. In either case such persons assume special prominence in the resolution of public questions.

Petitioner has long been active in community and professional affairs. He has served as an officer of local civic groups and of various professional organizations, and he has published several books and articles on legal subjects. Although petitioner was consequently well known in some circles, he had achieved no general fame or notoriety in the community. * * * Absent clear evidence of general fame or notoriety in the community, and pervasive involvement in the affairs of society, an individual should not be deemed a public personality for all aspects of his life. It is preferable to reduce the public-figure question to a more meaningful context by looking to the nature and extent of an individual's participation in the particular controversy giving rise to the defamation.

In this context it is plain that petitioner was not a public figure. He played a minimal role at the coroner's inquest, and his participation related solely to his representation of a private client. He took no part in the criminal prosecution of Officer Nuccio. Moreover, he never discussed either the criminal or civil litigation with the press and was never quoted as having done so. He plainly did not thrust himself into the vortex of this public issue, nor did he engage the public's attention in an attempt to influence its outcome. We are persuaded that the trial court did not err in refusing to characterize petitioner as a public figure for the purpose of this litigation.

We therefore conclude that the New York Times standard is inapplicable to this case and that the trial court erred in entering judgment for respondent. Because the jury was allowed to impose liability without fault and was permitted to presume damages without proof of injury, a new trial is necessary. We reverse and remand for further proceedings in accord with this opinion.

It is so ordered.

[This opinion was joined by STEWART, MARSHALL, BLACKMUN and REHNQUIST, JJ.; BLACKMUN, J., stating in a concurring opinion that he found some difficulties with the majority opinion, but that he joined in it to attain a "definitive ruling."

BURGER, C.J., dissented, disapproving the requirement of negligence for private defamation and urging remand for a reinstatement of the jury verdict below. DOUGLAS, J., dissented on the basis of his absolute-privilege theory and would at least retain the *Rosenbloom* rule. BRENNAN, J., dissented and would retain the *Rosenbloom* rule. WHITE, J., dissented and would retain strict liability for private defamation.]

NOTES AND QUESTIONS

1. A requisite finding of fault for private defamation, adopted first in the principal case, had been urged in the dissenting opinion of Harlan, J., in Time, Inc. v. Hill, 385 U.S. 374 (1967) ("States should be free to hold the press to a duty of making a reasonable investigation of the underlying facts"), and the dissenting opinion of Justice Marshall, in Rosenbloom v. Metromedia, Inc., 403 U.S. 29 (1971) ("[o]nly constitutional caveat should be that absolute or strict liability * * * cannot be used"). Eliminating presumed and punitive damages had been urged in *Rosenbloom* in the dissenting opinion of Justice Marshall, (restrict "the award of damages to prove, actual injuries" and cut down on the "jury's wide ranging discretion * * * since the award will be based on essentially objective discernable factors"), and, to a large extent, in the dissenting opinion of Justice Harlan, ("[l]egitimate function of libel law must be understood as that of compensating individuals for actual, measurable harm caused by the conduct of others").

2. *Contracting the Coverage of the New York Times Standard.* In receding from the position taken in Rosenbloom v. Metromedia, Inc., 403 U.S. 29 (1971), where the *New York Times* standard of knowledge or reckless disregard applied to any matter of public or general interest, and holding that the standard applies only to public officials and public figures, the Court was speaking only of what the Constitution requires the states to do. That is, while the *NYTimes* standard must apply in a suit by a public person, states are not required to do this in a suit by a private person. States are nonetheless entirely free to do so if they wish.

A few courts have indicated that they will continue to require knowledge or reckless disregard where the publication touches matters of public or general interest. For example, see Sisler v. Gannett Co., 516 A.2d 1083 (N.J. 1986). However, in Turf Lawnmower Repair, Inc. v. Bergen Record Corp., 655 A.2d 417, 435 (N.J. 1995), the protection against the threat of defamation actions extended beyond that imposed by the Supreme Court by applying the actual malice standard "where the press's statement concerns businesses affecting the public's health and safety and businesses that are subject to substantial government regulation." The court recognized the "public benefits from having the press act as a consumer affairs watchdog." Thus, the court articulated "an actual-malice standard rather than a negligence standard, even for ordinary businesses, if the consumer fraud allegations in the article, if true, would constitute a violation of the Consumer Fraud Act." Id. at 435. For other contexts, the most appropriate standard was negligence in conformity with forty-two jurisdictions. Only Colorado, New Jersey, and Indiana apply non-negligence standard: Journal-Gazette Company v. Bandido's, Inc., 712 N.E.2d 446 (Ind.), *cert. denied*, 528 U.S. 1005 (1999) (confirming the actual malice standard for "matters of general or public concern," but against strong dissent). A majority of the courts decline to impose a requirement of knowledge or reckless disregard in an action by a private person. Mead Corporation v. Hicks, 448 So.2d 308 (Ala.1983); Stone v. Essex County Newspapers, Inc., 330 N.E.2d 161 (Mass.1975); Jacron Sales Co., Inc. v. Sindorf, 350 A.2d 688 (Md.1976); Cottrell v. NCAA, 975 So.2d 306 (Ala. 2007) ("If it is determined that the plaintiff is a private figure, then the plaintiff has the burden of establishing by a preponderance of the evidence that the defendant negligently published the defamatory statement."). Rouch v. Enquirer & News, 398 N.W.2d 245 (Mich.1986); Re v. Gannett Co., 480 A.2d 662 (Del. Super. Ct. 1984).

3. *Scope of Fault Requirement in Action by Private Person. Gertz* seemed to indicate that strict liability for defamation is unconstitutional. This would require fault in regard, at least, to the falsity of the statement. There still remain some unanswered questions on the scope of the requirement, however. For a general discussion of scope with regard to falsity and defamatory character, the mode of communication, and the nature of content, see Restatement (Second) of Torts § 580B cmts. *d–f* (1977). On the nature of the negligence standard, see id. cmts. *g–h*. The constitutional fault standard is probably applicable to the identification issue. What result in Hulton v. Jones, supra, under the *Gertz* test? Note that in *New York Times v. Sullivan*, supra, the Court found that the common law standard, turning on a reasonable reader's assumptions to identify the plaintiff, was constitutionally insufficient. Reference would have to be made to the plaintiff as an individual lest criticism of government be crimped. On the effect of the fault requirement on the whole system of conditional privileges, see id., comment *l*, and the Special Note preceding § 593. And see the discussion in Jacron Sales Co. v. Sindorf, 350 A.2d 688 (Md.1976), infra, p. 978.

Concerning the standard of care, Anderson has stated that, "suits under the negligence formula of *Gertz* have turned out the be rare." David A. Anderson, Is Libel Law Worth Reforming?, 140 U. Pa. L. Rev. 487, 503 (1991). Why?

4. *Nonmedia Defendants. New York Times* and *Gertz* both involved suits against members of the news media. Were their constitutional requirements confined to suits against media defendants? Although the Supreme Court has never expressly said so, the answer for the *Times* standard seems to be clearly, "no." In *Times* itself, the suit was also against private individuals who signed the political advertisement. See also Garrison v. Louisiana, 379 U.S. 64 (1964) (press conference); Henry v. Collins, 380 U.S. 356 (1965) (letter and telephone conversation); St. Amant v. Thompson, 390 U.S. 727 (1968), supra page 931 (televised political speech); Old Dominion Branch No. 496, Nat'l Ass'n of Letter Carriers v. Austin, 418 U.S. 264, 285 (1974) (newsletter). But cf. Hutchinson v. Proxmire, 443 U.S. 111, 133, n.16 (1979) (Supreme Court "has never decided . . . whether the *New York Times* standard can apply to an individual defendant rather than a media defendant"). In Milkovich v. Lorain Journal Co., infra page 966, the court was at pains to distinguish media from nonmedia defendants, but did not decide the force of the dichotomy.

There has been less agreement about the *Gertz* standard, the cases dividing almost evenly. But the opinions in *Greenmoss,* the next principal case, indicate that some of the current members of the Court would draw no distinction between media defendants and other defendants. Although in *Hepps*, infra page 958, the Supreme Court couched its decision to apply the burden of proof on the issue of the falsity of the publication only to media defendants. In Air Wisconsin v. Hoeper, 134 S. Ct 852 (2014), the Court found the burden of proof of falsity fell on the defendant regardless of its media or non-media status.

5. *When Is the Statement Defamatory?* Is this issue subject to constitutional constraint? The Supreme Court entertained the question in 1942 when it granted certiorari on the (2–1) holding in Sweeney v. Schenectady Union Pub. Co., 122 F.2d 288 (2d Cir. 1941). However, the Court handed down a per-curiam memorandum affirming the judgment "by an equally divided court." Schenectady Union Pub. Co. v. Sweeney, 316 U.S. 642 (1942). The Court has not accepted any other cases raising the issue.

6. *Damages.* Actual damages, as required by the Constitution under the holding in *Gertz,* are broader in scope than special damages, as required at common law for oral statements that are not slanderous per se. Special damages require pecuniary loss. Actual damages may include injury to reputation or emotional distress, without showing pecuniary loss, but the injury must be proved. It initially appeared that the purpose of this requirement was to give the trial and appellate courts greater control over the amount of damages that the jury can properly award. But the opportunity has not been utilized. Interestingly, the Texas Supreme Court awarded non-economic damages for injury to reputation in a defamation suit. See Texas Disposal Sys. Landfill, Inc. v. Waste Mgmt. Holdings, Inc., 219 S.W.3d 563 (Tex. Ct. App. 2014).

7. *Public and Private Plaintiffs.* The principal case turns its analysis on the characterization of the plaintiff. Under *Gertz,* all plaintiffs, public or private, in cases of public interest speech, may claim punitive and presumed damages where actual malice is proved. State law may dictate otherwise.

In Obsidian Finance Group, LLC v. Cox, 740 F.3d 1284 (9th Cir. 2014), the court addressed a "question of first impression": "What First Amendment protections are afforded a blogger sues for defamation?" Liability for a defamatory blog that involves a matter of public concern cannot be imposed without proof of fault and actual damages. The intersection between *Sullivan* and *Gertz* had not been explored in respect of this kind of Internet publication. Following the trend in other decisions, the court held that no distinction could be made between media and non-media defendants. Particularly in the age of the Internet the distinction is too unstable. The public figure status of the plaintiff and the public importance of the statement at issue are the First Amendment "touchstones."

(C) SPEECH OF PRIVATE CONCERN

Dun & Bradstreet, Inc. v. Greenmoss Builders, Inc.

Supreme Court of the United States, 1985.
472 U.S. 749, 105 S.Ct. 2939, 86 L.Ed.2d 593.

[Petitioner-defendant Dun & Bradstreet supplied confidential credit rating reports to subscribers. It sent a report to five subscribers, indicating that respondent-plaintiff Greenmoss Builders had filed a voluntary petition for bankruptcy. The report was totally false, the error resulting from petitioner's use of a 17-year-old high school student to review Vermont bankruptcy proceedings. He mistakenly attributed to respondent a bankruptcy petition filed by one of respondent's former employees, and from petitioner's failure to make routine checks of accuracy. Learning of the report, respondent called petitioner's regional office, explained the error and asked for a correction. Petitioner sent out a notice which respondent regarded as inadequate, and refused to disclose the identity of the five subscribers.

Respondent sued for libel and obtained a verdict for $50,000 in compensatory or presumed damages and $300,000 in punitive damages. The trial court granted a motion for a new trial, but respondent appealed to the Vermont Supreme Court, which reversed and reinstated the verdict on the ground that the constitutional requirements of the U.S. Supreme Court did not apply when the suit was against a non-media defendant. 143 Vt. 66, 461 A.2d 414 (1983). This court granted certiorari, and affirmed the holding, "although for reasons different from those relied on by the Vermont Supreme Court."]

JUSTICE POWELL announced the judgment of the Court and delivered an opinion, in which JUSTICE REHNQUIST and JUSTICE O'CONNOR joined.

In Gertz v. Robert Welch, Inc., 418 U.S. 323, we held that the First Amendment restricted the damages that a private individual could obtain from a publisher for a libel that involved a matter of public concern. More specifically, we held that in these circumstances the First Amendment prohibited awards of presumed and punitive damages for false and defamatory statements unless the plaintiff shows "actual malice," that is, knowledge of falsity or reckless disregard for the truth. The question presented in this case is whether this rule of *Gertz* applies when the false and defamatory statements do not involve matters of public concern. * * *

In *Gertz,* we held that the fact that [an] expression concerned a public issue did not by itself entitle the libel defendant to the constitutional protections of *New York Times.* These protections, we found, were not "justified solely by reference to the interest of the press and broadcast media in immunity from liability." [C] Rather, they represented "an accommodation between [First Amendment] concern[s] and the limited state interest present in the context of libel actions brought by public persons." [C] In libel actions brought by private persons we found the competing interests different. Largely because private persons have not voluntarily exposed themselves to increased risk of injury from defamatory statements and because they generally lack effective opportunities for rebutting such statements, [c] we found that the State possessed a "strong and legitimate * * * interest in compensating private individuals for injury to reputation." [C] Balancing this stronger state interest against the same First Amendment interest at stake in *New York Times,* we held that a State could not allow recovery of presumed and punitive damages absent a showing of "actual malice." Nothing in our opinion, however, indicated that this same balance would be struck regardless of the type of speech involved. * * *

We have never considered whether the *Gertz* balance obtains when the defamatory statements involve no issue of public concern. To make this determination, we must employ the approach approved in *Gertz* and balance the State's interest in compensating private individuals for injury to their reputation against the First Amendment interest in protecting this type of expression. This state interest is identical to the one weighed in *Gertz.* There we found that it was "strong and legitimate." [C] A State should not lightly be required to abandon it. * * *

The First Amendment interest, on the other hand, is less important than the one weighed in *Gertz.* We have long recognized that not all speech is of equal First Amendment importance. It is speech on " 'matters of public concern' " that is "at the heart of the First Amendment's protection." First National Bank of Boston v. Bellotti, 435 U.S. 765, 776. * * *

In contrast, speech on matters of purely private concern is of less First Amendment concern. [C] As a number of state courts, including the court below, have recognized, the role of the Constitution in regulating state libel law is far more limited when the concerns that activated *New York Times* and *Gertz* are absent. * * *

While * * * speech on matters not of public concern is not totally unprotected by the First Amendment [cc], its protections are less stringent. In *Gertz,* we found that the state interest in awarding presumed and punitive damages was not "substantial" in view of their effect on speech at the core of First Amendment concern. [C] This interest, however, is "substantial" relative to the incidental effect these remedies may have on speech of significantly less constitutional interest. The rationale of the common law rules has been the experience and judgment of history that "proof of actual damage will be impossible in a great many cases where, from the character of the defamatory words and the circumstances of publication, it is all but certain that serious harm has resulted in fact." [Cc] As a result, courts for centuries have allowed juries to presume that some damage occurred from many defamatory utterances and publications. * * * [Cc] This rule furthers the state interest in providing remedies for defamation by ensuring that those remedies are effective. In light of the reduced constitutional value of speech involving no matters of public concern, we hold that the state interest adequately supports awards of presumed and punitive damages—even absent a showing of "actual malice." * * *

The only remaining issue is whether petitioner's credit report involved a matter of public concern. In a related context, we have held that "[w]hether * * * speech addresses a matter of public concern must be determined by [the expression's] content, form, and context * * * as revealed by the whole record." Connick v. Myers, 461 U.S., at 147–148. These factors indicate that petitioner's credit report concerns no public issue. It was speech solely in the individual interest of the speaker and its specific business audience. [C] This particular interest warrants no special protection when—as in this case—the speech is wholly false and clearly damaging to the victim's business reputation. [Cc] Moreover, since the credit report was made available to only five subscribers, who, under the terms of the subscription agreement, could not disseminate it further, it cannot be said that the report involves any "strong interest in the free flow of commercial information." [C] There is simply no credible argument that this type of credit reporting requires special protection to ensure that "debate on public issues [will] be uninhibited, robust, and wide-open." New York Times Co. v. Sullivan, 376 U.S., at 270.

In addition, the speech here, like advertising, is hardy and unlikely to be deterred by incidental state regulation. [Cc] It is solely motivated by the desire for profit, which, we have noted, is a force less likely to be deterred than others. [C] Arguably, the reporting here was also more objectively verifiable than speech deserving of greater protection. [C] In any case, the market provides a powerful incentive to a credit reporting agency to be accurate, since false credit reporting is of no use to creditors. Thus, any incremental "chilling" effect of libel suits would be of decreased significance. * * *

We conclude that permitting recovery of presumed and punitive damages in defamation cases absent a showing of "actual malice" does not violate the First Amendment when the defamatory statements do not involve matters of public concern. Accordingly, we affirm the judgment of the Vermont Supreme Court.

[CHIEF JUSTICE BURGER and JUSTICE WHITE concurred in the judgment with separate opinions. They had dissented in *Gertz* and urged it to be overruled. They also wished to reevaluate the extent of application of New York Times v. Sullivan.]

JUSTICE BRENNAN, with whom JUSTICE MARSHALL, JUSTICE BLACKMUN and JUSTICE STEVENS join, dissenting. * * *

The four who join this opinion would reverse the judgment of the Vermont Supreme Court. We believe that, although protection of the type of expression at issue is admittedly not the "central meaning of the First Amendment," [c] *Gertz* makes clear that the First Amendment nonetheless requires restraints on presumed and punitive damage awards for this expression. The lack of consensus in approach to these idiosyncratic facts should not, however, obscure the solid allegiance the principles of *New York Times v. Sullivan* continue to command in the jurisprudence of this Court. * * *

When an alleged libel involves criticism of a public official or a public figure, the need to nurture robust debate of public issues and the requirement that all state regulation of speech be narrowly tailored coalesce to require actual malice as a prerequisite to any recovery. When the alleged libel involves speech that falls outside these especially important categories, we have held that the Constitution permits states significant leeway to compensate for actual damage to reputation. The requirement of narrowly tailored regulatory measures, however, always mandates at least a showing of fault and proscribes the award of presumed and punitive damages on less than a showing of actual malice. It has remained the judgment of the Court since *Gertz* that this comprehensive two-tiered structure best accommodates the values of the constitutional free speech guarantee and the states' interest in protecting reputation. * * *

In professing allegiance to *Gertz,* the plurality opinion protests too much. As Justice White correctly observes, Justice Powell departs completely from the analytic framework and result of that case: "*Gertz* was intended to reach any false statements * * * whether or not [they] implicate a matter of public importance." [C][11]

---

[11] One searches *Gertz* in vain for a single word to support the proposition that limits on presumed and punitive damages obtained only when speech involved matters of public

Even accepting the notion that a distinction can and should be drawn between matters of public concern and matters of purely private concern, however, the analyses presented by both JUSTICE POWELL and JUSTICE WHITE fail on their own terms. Both, by virtue of what they hold in this case, propose an impoverished definition of "matters of public concern" that is irreconcilable with First Amendment principles. The credit reporting at issue here surely involves a subject matter of sufficient public concern to require the comprehensive protections of *Gertz*. Were this speech appropriately characterized as a matter of only private concern, moreover, the elimination of the *Gertz* restrictions on presumed and punitive damages would still violate basic First Amendment requirements. * * *

The five Members of the Court voting to affirm the damage award in this case have provided almost no guidance as to what constitutes a protected "matter of public concern." JUSTICE WHITE offers nothing at all, but his opinion does indicate that the distinction turns on solely the subject matter of the expression and not on the extent or conditions of dissemination of that expression. [C] JUSTICE POWELL adumbrates a rationale that would appear to focus primarily on subject matter.[12]

The opinion relies on the fact that the speech at issue was "solely in the individual interest of the speaker and its *business* audience," [c] Analogizing explicitly to advertising, the opinion also states that credit reporting is "hardy" and "solely motivated by the desire for profit." [C] These two strains of analysis suggest that JUSTICE POWELL is excluding the subject matter of credit reports from "matters of public concern" because the speech is predominantly in the realm of matters of economic concern. * * *

Greenmoss Builders should be permitted to recover for any actual damage it can show resulted from Dun & Bradstreet's negligently false credit report, but should be required to show actual malice to receive

---

concern. *Gertz* could not have been grounded in such a premise. Distrust of placing in the courts the power to decide what speech was of public concern was precisely the rationale *Gertz* offered for rejecting the *Rosenbloom* plurality approach. [C] It would have been incongruous for the Court to go on to circumscribe the protection against presumed and punitive damages by reference to a judicial judgment as to whether the speech at issue involved matters of public concern. At several points the Court in *Gertz* makes perfectly clear the restrictions of presumed and punitive damages were to apply in all cases. [C]

Indeed, JUSTICE POWELL's opinion today is fairly read as embracing the approach of the *Rosenbloom* plurality to deciding when the Constitution should limit state defamation law. The limits imposed, however, are less stringent than those suggested by the *Rosenbloom* plurality. Under the approach of today's plurality, speech about matters of public or general interest receives only the *Gertz* protections against unrestrained presumed and punitive damages, not the full *New York Times v. Sullivan* protections against any recovery absent a showing of actual malice.

[12] Justice Powell also appears to rely in part on the fact that communication was limited and confidential. Given that his analysis also relies on the subject matter of the credit report, it is difficult to decipher exactly what role the nature and extent of dissemination plays in JUSTICE POWELL's analysis. But because the subject matter of the expression at issue is properly understood as a matter of public concern, it may well be that this element of confidentiality is crucial to the outcome as far as JUSTICE POWELL's opinion is concerned. In other words, it may be that JUSTICE POWELL thinks this particular expression could not contribute to public welfare because the public generally does not receive it. This factor does not suffice to save the analysis. * * *

presumed or punitive damages. Because the jury was not instructed in accordance with these principles, we would reverse and remand for further proceedings not inconsistent with this opinion.

NOTES AND QUESTIONS

1. On studying the *Gertz* case, would it have occurred to you that this case would have been decided this way? After reading *this* case, what do you think the Court will do when it reviews a case involving a private plaintiff in a matter not of public concern, when the question arises whether the *Gertz* requirement of defendant's fault is raised? What would be the effect of its decision either way?

2. Do you agree with the reasoning that the nature of this information militates against its production and dissemination being "chilled" by defamation liability? Can the hazards of liability be captured by the price charged for access to this information? How does this differ from political speech? May the susceptibility of the information to chilling describe a principled distinction between the categories of public and private concern? See Daniel A. Farber, Free Speech Without Romance: Public Choice and the First Amendment, 105 HARV. L. REV 554 (1991), for further discussion.

3. The principal case does appear to settle, at least for the time being, one issue that had never been specifically decided. This is the issue of whether different standards might constitutionally be applied to media defendants and nonmedia defendants. The Vermont Supreme Court had based its decision in *Greenmoss* on the ground that the defendant was not acting as a member of the news media. Although the Supreme Court affirmed, it pointedly stated that the affirmance was not based on the reasons given by the state supreme court. Justice Brennan stated in his dissenting opinion that he counted "at least six" Justices who "agree today that, in the context of defamation law, the rights of the institutional media are no greater and no less than those enjoyed by" others.

(D) FALSITY

Philadelphia Newspapers, Inc. v. Hepps

Supreme Court of the United States, 1986.
475 U.S. 767, 106 S.Ct. 1558, 89 L.Ed.2d 783.

[Plaintiffs were Maurice S. Hepps, principal stockholder of General Programming, Inc. (GPI), a corporation engaged in franchising a chain of "Thrifty Stores" (selling beer, soft drinks and snacks), plus GPI itself and some of the franchisees. The charges were that plaintiffs "had links to organized crime and used some of those links to influence the State's governmental processes, both legislative and administrative." They were published in a series of articles by defendant, Philadelphia Newspapers, Inc., in the Philadelphia Inquirer.

Suit was in the state court, where the court followed two statutes requiring (1) a private plaintiff to prove negligence or malice by the defendant and (2) the defendant to meet the burden of proving the truth of a defamatory statement. There was also a third statute ("a shield law") providing that no person employed by a public medium should be required to disclose the source of information obtained. Plaintiffs requested an instruction that the jury could draw a negative inference from the exercise of the shield law's privilege, and defendants requested an instruction that no reference could be drawn. The judge declined to give either instruction and the jury found for the defendants.

On appeal directly to the Pennsylvania Supreme Court, that court "held that to place the burden of showing truth on the defendant did not unconstitutionally inhibit free debate, and remanded the case for a new trial." This court granted certiorari.]

JUSTICE O'CONNOR delivered the opinion of the Court.

This case requires us once more to "struggl[e] * * * to define the proper accommodation between the law of defamation and the freedoms of speech and press protected by the First Amendment." Gertz v. Robert Welch, Inc., 418 U.S. 323, 325. In *Gertz,* the Court held that a private figure who brings a suit for defamation cannot recover without some showing that the media defendant was at fault in publishing the statements at issue. [C] Here, we hold that, at least where a newspaper publishes speech of public concern, a private-figure plaintiff cannot recover damages without also showing that the statements at issue are false. * * * [The opinion describes the holdings of *New York Times, Gertz* and *Greenmoss.*]

One can discern in these decisions two forces that may reshape the common-law landscape to conform to the First Amendment. The first is whether the plaintiff is a public official or figure, or is instead a private figure. The second is whether the speech at issue is of public concern. When the speech is of public concern and the plaintiff is a public official or public figure, the Constitution clearly requires the plaintiff to surmount a much higher barrier before recovering damages from a media defendant than is raised by the common law. When the speech is of public concern but the plaintiff is a private figure, as in *Gertz,* the Constitution still supplants the standards of the common law, but the constitutional requirements are, in at least some of their range, less forbidding than when the plaintiff is a public figure and the speech is of public concern. When the speech is of exclusively private concern and the plaintiff is a private figure, as in *Dun & Bradstreet,* the constitutional requirements do not necessarily force any change in at least some of the features of the common-law landscape.

Our opinions to date have chiefly treated the necessary showings of fault rather than of falsity. Nonetheless, as one might expect given the language of the Court in *New York Times,* a public-figure plaintiff must show the falsity of the statements at issue in order to prevail on a suit for defamation. * * *

Here, as in *Gertz,* the plaintiff is a private figure and the newspaper articles are of public concern. In *Gertz,* as in *New York Times,* the common-law rule was superseded by a constitutional rule. We believe that the common law's rule on falsity—that the defendant must bear the burden of proving truth—must similarly fall here to a constitutional requirement that the plaintiff bear the burden of showing falsity, as well as fault, before recovering damages.

There will always be instances when the factfinding process will be unable to resolve conclusively whether the speech is true or false; it is in those cases that the burden of proof is dispositive. Under a rule forcing the plaintiff to bear the burden of showing falsity, there will be some cases in which plaintiffs cannot meet their burden despite the fact that the speech is in fact false. The plaintiff's suit will fail despite the fact that, in some abstract sense, the suit is meritorious. Similarly, under an alternative rule placing the burden of showing truth on defendants, there would be some cases in which defendants could not bear their burden despite the fact that the speech is in fact true. Those suits would succeed despite the fact that, in some abstract sense, those suits are unmeritorious. Under either rule, then, the outcome of the suit will sometimes be at variance with the outcome that we would desire if all speech were either demonstrably true or demonstrably false. * * *

In a case presenting a configuration of speech and plaintiff like the one we face here, and where the scales are in such an uncertain balance, we believe that the Constitution requires us to tip them in favor of protecting true speech. To ensure that true speech on matters of public concern is not deterred, we hold that the common-law presumption that defamatory speech is false cannot stand when a plaintiff seeks damages against a media defendant for speech of public concern.

In the context of governmental restriction of speech, it has long been established that the government cannot limit speech protected by the First Amendment without bearing the burden of showing that its restriction is justified. * * * It is not immediately apparent from the text of the First Amendment, which by its terms applies only to governmental action, that a similar result should obtain here: a suit by a private party is obviously quite different from the government's direct enforcement of its own laws. Nonetheless, the need to encourage debate on public issues that concerned the Court in the governmental-restriction cases is of concern in a similar manner in this case involving a private suit for damages: placement by state law of the burden of proving truth upon media defendants who publish speech of public concern deters such speech because of the fear that liability will unjustifiably result. [Cc] Because such a "chilling" effect would be antithetical to the First Amendment's protection of true speech on matters of public concern, we believe that a private-figure plaintiff must bear the burden of showing that the speech at issue is false before recovering damages for defamation from a media defendant. To do otherwise could "only result in a deterrence of speech which the Constitution makes free." [C]

We recognize that requiring the plaintiff to show falsity will insulate from liability some speech that is false, but unprovably so. Nonetheless, the Court's previous decisions on the restrictions that the First Amendment places upon the common law of defamation firmly support our conclusion here with respect to the allocation of the burden of proof. In attempting to resolve related issues in the defamation context, the Court has affirmed that "[t]he First Amendment requires that we protect some falsehood in order to protect speech that matters." *Gertz,* 418 U.S., at 341. Here the speech concerns the legitimacy of the political process, and therefore clearly "matters." [C] To provide " 'breathing space' " [c] for true speech on matters of public concern, the Court has been willing to insulate even *demonstrably* false speech from liability, and has imposed additional requirements of fault upon the plaintiff in a suit for defamation. [Cc] We therefore do not break new ground here in insulating speech that is not even demonstrably false.

We note that our decision adds only marginally to the burdens that the plaintiff must already bear as a result of our earlier decisions in the law of defamation. The plaintiff must show fault. A jury is obviously more likely to accept a plaintiff's contention that the defendant was at fault in publishing the statements at issue if convinced that the relevant statements were false. As a practical matter, then, evidence offered by plaintiffs on the publisher's fault in adequately investigating the truth of the published statements will generally encompass evidence of the falsity of the matters asserted. * * * [T]he judgment of the Pennsylvania Supreme Court is reversed, and the case is remanded for further proceedings not inconsistent with this opinion.

JUSTICE BRENNAN, with whom JUSTICE BLACKMUN joins, concurring. * * *

JUSTICE STEVENS, with whom THE CHIEF JUSTICE, JUSTICE WHITE, and JUSTICE REHNQUIST join, dissenting. * * *

The Court, after acknowledging the need to " 'accommodat[e] * * * the law of defamation and the freedoms of speech and press protected by the First Amendment,' " [c] decides to override "the common-law presumption" retained by several states that "defamatory speech is false" because of the need "[t]o ensure that true speech on matters of public concern is not deterred." [C] I do not agree that our precedents require a private individual to bear the risk that a defamatory statement—uttered either with a mind toward assassinating his good name or with careless indifference to that possibility—cannot be proven false. By attaching no weight to the state's interest in protecting the private individual's good name, the Court has reached a pernicious result. * * *

While deliberate or inadvertent libels vilify private personages, they contribute little to the marketplace of ideas. In assaying the First Amendment side of the balance, it helps to remember that the perpetrator of the libel suffers from its failure to demonstrate the truth of its accusation only if the "private-figure" plaintiff first establishes that the publisher is at "fault," either that it published its libel with "actual malice" in the *New York Times* sense * * * or that it published with that degree of careless indifference characteristic of negligence. Far from being totally in the dark about "how much of the speech affected by the allocation of the burden of proof is true and how much is false," [c] the antecedent fault determination makes irresistible the inference that a significant portion of this speech is beyond the constitutional pale. This observation is almost tautologically true with regard to libels published with "actual malice." For that standard to be met, the publisher must come close to wilfully blinding itself to the falsity of its utterance. The observation is also valid, albeit to a lesser extent, with respect to defamations uttered with "fault." Thus, while the public's interest in an uninhibited press is at its nadir when the publisher is at fault or worse, society's "equally compelling" need for judicial redress of libelous utterances is at its zenith. * * * [C]

In my opinion deliberate, malicious character assassination is not protected by the First Amendment to the United States Constitution. That Amendment does require the target of a defamatory statement to prove that his assailant was at fault, and I agree that it provides a constitutional shield for truthful statements. I simply do not understand, however, why a character assassin should be given an absolute license to defame by means of statements that can be neither verified nor disproven. The danger of deliberate defamation by reference to unprovable facts is not a merely speculative or hypothetical concern. * * *

Even assuming that attacks on the reputation of a public figure should be presumed to be true, however, a different calculus is appropriate when a defamatory statement disparages the reputation of a private individual. In that case, the overriding concern for reliable protection of truthful statements must make room for "[t]he legitimate state interest underlying the law of libel"—"the compensation of individuals for the harm inflicted on them by defamatory falsehood." *Gertz,* 418 U.S. at 341. * * *

In my view, as long as publishers are protected by the requirement that the plaintiff has the burden of proving fault, there can be little, if any, basis for a concern that a significant amount of true speech will be deterred unless the private person victimized by a malicious libel can also carry the burden of proving falsity. The Court's decision trades on the good names of private individuals with little First Amendment coin to show for it. * * *

NOTES AND QUESTIONS

1. Who has the better of the argument? Remember, this is a decision of constitutional law, binding on both federal and state courts.

2. In Air Wisconsin Airlines v. Hoeper, 134 S. Ct 852 (2014) the Court reemphasized the place of falsity requiring, that if the immunity there claimed for the defendants depended upon the statute's intention to incorporate the free speech requirements under *N.Y. Times v. Sullivan*, the plaintiff would bear the burden of showing that the statements were materially false. Airline representatives had passed on information to the Transport Safety Administration ("TSA") that the plaintiff a pilot for the airline was mentally unstable, was potentially armed, and had been fired. TSA officials took the plaintiff off his flight. The Colorado Supreme Court had affirmed on the basis that the statement had been made recklessly as its truth or falsity. The Court cited the principal case to affirm the central place of proof of falsity in contrast to the common law's strict liability doctrine. It also took the view that it should have the power to decide the issue of the material falsity of the statement. This drew a partial dissent from Justice Scalia, with whom Justices Thomas and Kagan concurred, that the issue of material falsity was whether a jury could find it false in the estimation of the TSA official to whom it was published. The facts as established did not compel a finding of material falsity and so the matter must be put to a jury properly instructed. It was plausible for example that

the false statement of mental instability would have a material effect on the judgment of the TSA official. Should this judgment reside in the judge or jury?

3. The term "of public concern" has often been employed in garnering protection for speech carrying "First Amendment" importance. Does an article in defendant's tourist guidebook, "*Let's Go: Egypt and Israel,*" advising that proprietor of hostel had been sued for sexual harassment and warning readers to stay away, fall within *Hepps*, as a matter of "public concern" published by the "media"? Shaari v. Harvard Student Agencies, Inc., 691 N.E.2d 925 (Mass.1998). A newspaper article stating that plaintiff, a married woman, had contracted chlamydia, a sexually transmitted disease, is a matter of "public concern." Cox Enters., Inc. v. Thrasher, 442 S.E.2d 740 (Ga.1994).

4. The risk of falsity is shifted to the plaintiff under the principal case. The risk is thus moved from the enterprise to the individual. Since the enterprise is likely insured, does this make sense? See David A. Anderson, Is Libel Law Worth Reforming?, 140 U. Pa. L. Rev. 487, 547–49 (1991); Frederick Schauer, Uncoupling Free Speech, 92 Colum. L. Rev. 1321, 1339–43 (1992), for discussion on the above issue.

(E) PUBLIC FIGURES AND PUBLIC OFFICIALS

In *New York Times* the status of the plaintiff as a public official was critical to the publication receiving additional First Amendment protections. This was extended to public figures in Curtis Pub. Co. v. Butts, 388 U.S. 130 (1967). The question remained open of the protection that a "private" plaintiff could garner under the First Amendment. Putting aside the wrong turning in *Metromedia,* supra, *Gertz* provided the answer that the status of the plaintiff as "private" attracted a lesser, but still substantial, protection if the publication related to a matter of public concern. Beginning in *Gertz,* through many a long decision, the courts have searched for a definition of the term "public figure." A completion of the journey will likely cause students to agree that an articulation of the distinction is much like trying to nail a jellyfish to a wall, Rosanova v. Playboy Enters. 411 F. Supp. 440 (S.D.Ga.1976), *aff'd,* 580 F.2d 859 (5th Cir. 1978). The beginning point is found in *Gertz* where two rationales were deployed for imposing a greater burden on public figures: (1) their "access to the media," and (2) their assumption of risk—you must accept the heat in the kitchen if you enter. Public figures can be (1) limited (vortex) figures or (2) universal (unlimited). Very few are universal; most have thrust themselves into a public controversy.

In deciding whether a person may be a limited public figure, it is necessary first to inquire whether a "public controversy" exists. Mere public interest is not enough: many people are interested in the divorces of the wealthy, but curiosity does not a "public controversy" make. Time, Inc. v. Firestone, 424 U.S. 448 (1976). The issue must be one publicly debated with foreseeable and substantial ramifications for nonparticipants, Waldbaum v. Fairchild Publs, Inc., 627 F.2d 1287 (D.C. Cir.), *cert. denied,* 449 U.S. 898 (1980). A public controversy exists over the accreditation of a law school. Avins v. White, 627 F.2d 637 (3d Cir. 1980). It does not exist in respect of a bank's expenditures despite a great public interest in its wealth. Blue Ridge Bank v. Veribanc, 866 F.2d 681 (4th Cir. 1989). Dicta in one leading case, Wolston v. Reader's Digest Assn, 443 U.S. 157 (1979), suggests that a public controversy requires a division of opinion; the plaintiff could not have thrust himself into a "controversy" about communist espionage because "all responsible United States citizens understandably were and are opposed to it." Id. at 166 n. 8. Really?

Once a public controversy is identified, the issue then becomes whether the plaintiff's role was such that he is a limited public figure in the context of that controversy. In *Wolston,* Justice Rehnquist, citing the two *Gertz* rationales, announced that the second—the assumption of risk—was the more important. Plaintiff, the nephew of a couple who had pleaded guilty to espionage charges, had failed to answer a subpoena. Sixteen years later he was listed by the defendant as a Soviet agent who had been convicted. He never "voluntarily thrust" or "injected" himself into the controversy concerning investigations of Soviet espionage in the United States. A similar basis was relied upon in Hutchinson v. Proxmire, 443 U.S. 111 (1979), where plaintiff, director of a state mental hospital and adjunct professor at a state university, had applied for and obtained federal grants to study aggression in animals. Senator Proxmire, to illustrate his claim that federal funds were wasted on frivolous research, invented the "Golden Fleece of the Month Award," and gave it to the Navy and NASA for their grant to Hutchinson. Hutchinson was not a public figure because he had not thrust himself or his views into public controversies to influence others. Any controversy was of the Senator's making: he could not manufacture his own defense. The twin *Gertz* rationales were referred to in Khawar v. Globe Intl, Inc., 965 P.2d 696 (Cal.1998), where plaintiff was featured in a Globe article as a person implicated in the assassination of Senator Robert Kennedy. The Globe, with embellished headlines and an enhanced photograph, had lifted the story from a book written by Robert Morrow alleging that the Iranian Secret Police, at the time of the Shah had colluded with the Mafia in the assassination. Plaintiff at the time was a photographer and had placed himself on the stage to be photographed with the Senator. The California Supreme Court reasoned he was not a vortex public figure, particularly as he had not acquired such public prominence in relation to the controversy as to permit him media access to counter the defamatory statements.

Although an important factor, voluntary assumption of risk is not essential. Some persons may be deemed to be public figures even if they were drawn involuntarily into a public controversy: Johnny Carson's wife, Carson v. Allied News Co., 529 F.2d 206 (7th Cir. 1976); the leading prosecution witness in the Scottsboro case (1931), in which black youths were accused of raping the plaintiff and another white woman, Street v. Nat'l Broad. Co., 645 F.2d 1227 (6th Cir. 1981); and the only air traffic controller on duty in 1974 at Dulles Airport when a plane crashed, Dameron v. Washington Magazine, Inc., 779 F.2d 736 (D.C.Cir. 1985), *cert. denied*, 476 U.S. 1141 (1986). (opining that these involuntary cases would be "few and far between.") That prediction of judicial reticence may be questioned, however, in light of Atlanta Journal-Constitution v. Jewell, 555 S.E.2d 175 (Ga. Ct. App.2001) (deeming the hapless Richard Jewell, who was caught up in the Atlanta

Olympic bombing, a public figure), and Lohrenz v. Donnelly, 350 F.3d 1272 (D.C. Cir. 2003) (one of the first women combat pilots in the Navy was deemed a public figure). In Hatfill v. N.Y. Times Co., 532 F.3d 312 (4th Cir. 2008) the Court held that Steven Hatfill, a biodefense research scientist was a "limited purpose; public figure" in that he had "voluntarily thrust himself into the controversy surrounding the threat of bioterrorism and the nation's lack of preparedness." New York Times had named Hatfill in a series of articles as a suspect in the 2001 anthrax attacks. The court cited Hatfill's media appearances on the broad topic of bioterrorism as sufficient public engagement. The court characterized the controversy broadly and as not circumstantial to the events surrounding the anthrax attacks. Could this have an adverse impact on public debate?

General purpose or universal public figures are a select group. In *Hustler Magazine v. Falwell*, infra page 1040, the Reverend Jerry Falwell was found to be one. Robert C. Post, The Constitutional Concept of Public Discourse: Outrageous Opinion, Democratic Deliberation, and *Hustler Magazine v. Falwell*, 103 HARV. L. REV. 601 (1990), for thorough discussion on this issue in *Hustler*. Wells v. Liddy, 186 F.3d 505 (4th Cir. 1999), confirmed that "instances of truly involuntary public figures must be extremely rare." In this case Wells had been a secretary at the Democratic National Committee "DNC" for a short period in 1972 during the Watergate break-in. She had been mentioned by Liddy, commenting on Watergate many years afterwards, as a person connected with the organization of a prostitution ring and in possession of embarrassing information relating to John Dean, the White House Counsel. The court needed to determine whether [ ] qualified as an "involuntary" or "voluntary" public figure. "Before a plaintiff can be classified, as a matter of law, as a limited-purpose public figure, the defendant must prove" five necessary elements:

(1) the plaintiff has access to channels of effective communication;

(2) the plaintiff voluntarily assumed a role of special prominence in the public controversy;

(3) the plaintiff sought to influence the resolution or outcome of the controversy;

(4) the controversy existed prior to the publication of the defamatory statement; and

(5) the plaintiff retained public-figure status at the time of the alleged information.

Although Wells had made the contacts with the media, she had not tried to influence the merits of the controversy or thrust herself to the forefront of it. Time had changed the Watergate controversy and she was not a voluntary public figure in respect of its contemporary aspect.

Regarding the *involuntary* public figure examination, the District Court applied *Dameron*, whereas the Fourth Circuit Court of Appeals articulated a new test in an attempt to avoid resurrecting *Rosenbloom*. Accordingly, it defined an "involuntary public figure" as a person who has "pursued a course of conduct from which it was reasonably foreseeable, at the time of conduct, that public interest would arise."

The person must have been recognized as a "central figure" during the debate over the public controversy. On this criterion Wells was not a public figure: she was not a central figure, she was peripheral, a "footnote." Without a limiting criterion, the court was concerned that all persons connected with large public controversies would be swept up, treated as public figures, and "an individual's interest in privacy and protecting her reputation would be erased from the balance of defamation law."

Public officials are more easily identified. They are persons "who have, or appear to the public to have, substantial responsibility for or control over the conduct of governmental affairs," Rosenblatt v. Baer, 383 U.S. 75 (1966).

In *Wolston,* the Court emphasized the requirement of an objective approach in fashioning clear rules for those participating in public debate. Do you have a sense of clear rules prevailing? Given the absence of common law strict liability, how would you have fashioned the rules?

Although the classification is intensely factual—the person's position and responsibilities (public official) or the scope of the person's fame or connection with public affairs (public figures)—the courts regard it as a question of law, Kassel v. Gannett Co., 875 F.2d 935 (1st Cir. 1989) (staff psychologist for Veteran's Administration not a public official); White v. Mobile Press Register, Inc., 514 So.2d 902 (Ala.1987) (former E.P.A. official who was officer in corporation transporting hazardous waste is limited purpose public figure); Franklin v. Benevolent & Protective Order of Elks, 159 Cal. Rptr. 131 (Cal. Ct. App. 1979) (public school teacher is not a public figure); Johnston v. Corinthian Television Corp., 583 P.2d 1101 (Okla.1978) (high school wrestling coach is a public figure). Trustee in Bankruptcy is not a public figure, Obsidian Fin. Grp. v. Cox, 740 F.3d 1284 (9th Cir. 2014). But cf. O'Connor v. Burningham, 165 P.3d 1214 (Utah 2007) (denying public figure status to a high school basketball teacher/coach).

Note that a publication not attaching to a public official's public status does not attract constitutional protection. The higher public status of the official, the more extensive is the relevant public arena. *See, e.g.*, Hatfill v. N.Y. Times Co., 532 F.3d 312 (4th Cir. 2008). The inquiry is fact intensive, leading to a tendency of Federal District Courts to find a wide range of persons falling into the public classification. Marjorie Heins, The Brave New World of Social Media Censorship, 127 HARV. L. REV. F. 325 (2014).

(F) OPINION

Milkovich v. Lorain Journal Co.

Supreme Court of the United States, 1990.
497 U.S. 1, 110 S.Ct. 2695, 111 L.Ed.2d 1.

CHIEF JUSTICE REHNQUIST delivered the opinion of the Court.

Respondent J. Theodore Diadiun authored an article in an Ohio newspaper implying that petitioner Michael Milkovich, a local high school wrestling coach, lied under oath in a judicial proceeding about an incident involving petitioner and his team which occurred at a wrestling match. Petitioner sued Diadiun and the newspaper for libel, and the Ohio Court of Appeals affirmed a lower court entry of summary judgment against petitioner. This judgment was based in part on the grounds that the article constituted an "opinion" protected from the reach of state defamation law by the First Amendment to the United States Constitution. We hold that the First Amendment does not prohibit the application of Ohio's libel laws to the alleged defamations contained in the article.

This case is before us for the third time in an odyssey of litigation spanning nearly 15 years. [Cc]

Petitioner Milkovich, now retired, was the wrestling coach at Maple Heights High School in Maple Heights, Ohio. In 1974, his team was involved in an altercation at a home wrestling match with a team from Mentor High School. Several people were injured. In response to the incident, the Ohio High School Athletic Association (OHSAA) held a hearing at which Milkovich and H. Don Scott, the Superintendent of Maple Heights Public Schools, testified. Following the hearing, OHSAA placed the Maple Heights team on probation for a year and declared the team ineligible for the 1975 state tournament. OHSAA also censored Milkovich for his actions during the altercation. Thereafter, several parents and wrestlers sued OHSAA in the Court of Common Pleas of Franklin County, Ohio, seeking a restraining order against OHSAA's ruling on the grounds that they had been denied due process in the OHSAA proceeding. Both Milkovich and Scott testified in that proceeding. The court overturned OHSAA's probation and ineligibility orders on due process grounds.

The day after the court rendered its decision, respondent Diadiun's column appeared in the News-Herald, a newspaper which circulates in Lake County, Ohio, and is owned by respondent Lorain Journal Co. The column bore the heading "Maple beat the law with the 'big lie,'" beneath which appeared Diadiun's photograph and the words "TD Says." The carryover page headline announced "* * * Diadiun says Maple told a lie." The column contained the following passages:

> "'* * * a lesson was learned (or relearned) yesterday by the student body of Maple Heights High School, and by anyone who attended the Maple-Mentor wrestling meet of last Feb. 8.
>
> "'A lesson which, sadly, in view of the events of the past year, is well they learned early.
>
> "'It is simply this: If you get in a jam, lie your way out.
>
> "'If you're successful enough, and powerful enough, and can sound sincere enough, you stand an excellent chance of making the lie stand up, regardless of what really happened.
>
> "'The teachers responsible were mainly Maple wrestling coach, Mike Milkovich, and former superintendent of schools, H. Donald Scott.

* * *

" 'Anyone who attended the meet, whether he be from Maple Heights, Mentor, or impartial observer, knows in his heart that Milkovich and Scott lied at the hearing after each having given his solemn oath to tell the truth.

" 'But they got away with it.

" 'Is that the kind of lesson we want our young people learning from their high school administrators and coaches?

" 'I think not.' " [C]

* * *

Superintendent Scott had been pursuing a separate defamation action through the Ohio courts. Two years after its *Milkovich* decision, in considering Scott's appeal, the Ohio Supreme Court reversed its position on Diadiun's article, concluding that the column was "constitutionally protected opinion." Scott v. News-Herald, 25 Ohio St.3d 243, 254, 496 N.E.2d 699, 709 (1986). Consequently, the court upheld a lower court's grant of summary judgment against Scott.

The *Scott* court decided that the proper analysis for determining whether utterances are fact or opinion was set forth in the decision of the United States Court of Appeals for the D.C. Circuit in Ollman v. Evans, 242 U.S.App.D.C. 301, 750 F.2d 970 (1984), cert. denied, 471 U.S. 1127, 105 S.Ct. 2662, 86 L.Ed.2d 278 (1985). Under that analysis, four factors are considered to ascertain whether, under the "totality of circumstances," a statement is fact or opinion. These factors are: (1) "the specific language used"; (2) "whether the statement is verifiable"; (3) "the general context of the statement"; and (4) "the broader context in which the statement appeared." [C] The court found that application of the first two factors to the column militated in favor of deeming the challenged passages actionable assertions of fact. [C] That potential outcome was trumped, however, by the court's consideration of the third and fourth factors. With respect to the third factor, the general context, the court explained that "the large caption 'TD Says' * * * would indicate to even the most gullible reader that the article was, in fact, opinion." [C] As for the fourth factor, the "broader context," the court reasoned that because the article appeared on a sports page—"a traditional haven for cajoling, invective, and hyperbole"—the article would probably be construed as opinion. [C]

Subsequently, considering itself bound by the Ohio Supreme Court's decision in *Scott,* the Ohio Court of Appeals in the instant proceedings affirmed a trial court's grant of summary judgment in favor of respondents, concluding that "it has been decided, as a matter of law, that the article in question was constitutionally protected opinion." Milkovich v. News-Herald, 46 Ohio App.3d 20, at 23, 545 N.E.2d at 1324. The Supreme Court of Ohio dismissed petitioner's ensuing appeal for want of a substantial constitutional question. App. 119. We granted certiorari [c] to consider the important questions raised by the Ohio courts' recognition of a constitutionally-required "opinion" exception to the application of its defamation laws. We now reverse. [Cc]

* * * As the common law developed in this country, apart from the issue of damages, one usually needed only allege an unprivileged

publication of false and defamatory matter to state a cause of action for defamation. See, e.g., Restatement of Torts § 558 (1938); Gertz v. Robert Welch, Inc., supra. The common law generally did not place any additional restrictions on the type of statement that could be actionable. Indeed, defamatory communications were deemed actionable regardless of whether they were deemed to be statements of fact or opinion. See, e.g., Restatement of Torts, supra, §§ 565–567. As noted in the 1977 Restatement (Second) of Torts § 566, comment *a*:

> "Under the law of defamation, an expression of opinion could be defamatory if the expression was sufficiently derogatory of another as to cause harm to his reputation, so as to lower him in the estimation of the community or to deter third persons from associating or dealing with him. * * * The expression of opinion was also actionable in a suit for defamation, despite the normal requirement that the communication be false as well as defamatory.... This position was maintained even though the truth or falsity of an opinion—as distinguished from a statement of fact—is not a matter that can be objectively determined and truth is a complete defense to a suit for defamation."

However, due to concerns that unduly burdensome defamation laws could stifle valuable public debate, the privilege of "fair comment" was incorporated into the common law as an affirmative defense to an action for defamation. "The principle of 'fair comment' afford[ed] legal immunity for the honest expression of opinion on matters of legitimate public interest when based upon a true or privileged statement of fact." 1 F. Harper & F. James, Law of Torts § 5.28, p. 456 (1956) (footnote omitted). As this statement implies, comment was generally privileged when it concerned a matter of public concern, was upon true or privileged facts, represented the actual opinion of the speaker, and was not made solely for the purpose of causing harm. See Restatement of Torts, supra, § 606. "According to the majority rule, the privilege of fair comment applied only to an expression of opinion and not to a false statement of fact, whether it was expressly stated or implied from an expression of opinion." Restatement (Second) of Torts, supra, § 566 comment *a*. Thus under the common law, the privilege of "fair comment" was the device employed to strike the appropriate balance between the need for vigorous public discourse and the need to redress injury to citizens wrought by invidious or irresponsible speech.

[The court canvassed the authorities incorporating First Amendment safeguards.]

Respondents would have us recognize, in addition to the established safeguards discussed above, still another First Amendment-based protection for defamatory statements which are categorized as "opinion" as opposed to "fact." For this proposition they rely principally on the following dictum from our opinion in *Gertz:*

> "Under the First Amendment there is no such thing as a false idea. However pernicious an opinion may seem, we depend for its correction not on the conscience of judges and juries but on the competition of other ideas. But there is no constitutional value in false statements of fact." [C]

Judge Friendly appropriately observed that this passage "has become the opening salvo in all arguments for protection from defamation actions on the ground of opinion, even though the case did not remotely concern the question." *Cianci v. New Times Publishing Co.,* 639 F.2d 54, 61 (C.A.2 1980). Read in context, though, the fair meaning of the passage is to equate the word "opinion" in the second sentence with the word "idea" in the first sentence. Under this view, the language was merely a reiteration of Justice Holmes' classic "marketplace of ideas" concept. See Abrams v. United States, 250 U.S. 616, 630, 40 S.Ct. 17, 22, 63 L.Ed. 1173 (1919) (Holmes, J., dissenting) ("[T]he ultimate good desired is better reached by free trade in ideas * * * the best test of truth is the power of the thought to get itself accepted in the competition of the market").

Thus we do not think this passage from *Gertz* was intended to create a wholesale defamation exemption for anything that might be labeled "opinion." [C] Not only would such an interpretation be contrary to the tenor and context of the passage, but it would also ignore the fact that expressions of "opinion" may often imply an assertion of objective fact.

If a speaker says, "In my opinion John Jones is a liar," he implies a knowledge of facts which lead to the conclusion that Jones told an untruth. Even if the speaker states the facts upon which he bases his opinion, if those facts are either incorrect or incomplete, or if his assessment of them is erroneous, the statement may still imply a false assertion of fact. Simply couching such statements in terms of opinion does not dispel these implications; and the statement, "In my opinion Jones is a liar," can cause as much damage to reputation as the statement, "Jones is a liar." As Judge Friendly aptly stated: "[It] would be destructive of the law of libel if a writer could escape liability for accusations of [defamatory conduct] simply by using, explicitly or implicitly, the words 'I think.'" [C] It is worthy of note that at common law, even the privilege of fair comment did not extend to "a false statement of fact, whether it was expressly stated or implied from an expression of opinion." Restatement (Second) of Torts, supra, § 566 comment *a.*

Apart from their reliance on the *Gertz* dictum, respondents do not really contend that a statement such as, "In my opinion John Jones is a liar," should be protected by a separate privilege for "opinion" under the First Amendment. But they do contend that in every defamation case the First Amendment mandates an inquiry into whether a statement is "opinion" or "fact," and that only the latter statements may be actionable. They propose that a number of factors developed by the lower courts (in what we hold was a mistaken reliance on the *Gertz* dictum) be considered in deciding which is which. But we think the "'breathing space'" which "'freedoms of expression require in order to survive'" *Hepps,* supra (quoting *New York Times,* supra), is adequately secured by existing constitutional doctrine without the creation of an artificial dichotomy between "opinion" and fact.

Foremost, we think *Hepps* stands for the proposition that a statement on matters of public concern must be provable as false before there can be liability under state defamation law, at least in situations, like the present, where a media defendant is involved.[6] Thus, unlike the statement, "In my opinion Mayor Jones is a liar," the statement, "In my opinion Mayor Jones shows his abysmal ignorance by accepting the teachings of Marx and Lenin," would not be actionable. *Hepps* ensures that a statement of opinion relating to matters of public concern which does not contain a provably false factual connotation will receive full constitutional protection.[7]

Next, the *Bresler-Letter Carriers-Falwell* line of cases provide protection for statements that cannot "reasonably [be] interpreted as stating actual facts" about an individual. *Falwell,* 485 U.S., at 50, 108 S.Ct., at 879. This provides assurance that public debate will not suffer for lack of "imaginative expression" or the "rhetorical hyperbole" which has traditionally added much to the discourse of our Nation. [C]

The *New York Times-Butts* and *Gertz* culpability requirements further ensure that debate on public issues remains "uninhibited, robust, and wide-open," *New York Times,* supra. Thus, where a statement of "opinion" on a matter of public concern reasonably implies false and defamatory facts regarding public figures or officials, those individuals must show that such statements were made with knowledge of their false implications or with reckless disregard of their truth. Similarly, where such a statement involves a private figure on a matter of public concern, a plaintiff must show that the false connotations were made with some level of fault as required by *Gertz.* [Cc] Finally, the enhanced appellate review required by *Bose Corp.,* provides assurance that the foregoing determinations will be made in a manner so as not to "constitute a forbidden intrusion of the field of free expression." Bose, 466 U.S., at 499, 104 S.Ct., at 1959 (quotation omitted).

We are not persuaded that, in addition to these protections, an additional separate constitutional privilege for "opinion" is required to ensure the freedom of expression guaranteed by the First Amendment. The dispositive question in the present case then becomes whether or not a reasonable factfinder could conclude that the statements in the Diadiun column imply an assertion that petitioner Milkovich perjured himself in a judicial proceeding. We think this question must be answered in the affirmative. * * * This is not the sort of loose, figurative or hyperbolic language which would negate the impression that the writer was seriously maintaining petitioner committed the crime of perjury. Nor does the general tenor of the article negate this impression.

We also think the connotation that petitioner committed perjury is sufficiently factual to be susceptible of being proved true or false. A

---

[6] In *Hepps* the Court reserved judgment on cases involving nonmedia defendants, see 475 U.S., at 779, n. 4, 106 S.Ct., at 1565, n. 4, and accordingly we do the same. Prior to *Hepps,* of course, where public-official or public-figure plaintiffs were involved, the *New York Times* rule already required a showing of falsity before liability could result. Id., at 775, 106 S.Ct., at 1563.

[7] We note that the issue of falsity relates to the *defamatory* facts implied by a statement. For instance, the statement, "I think Jones lied," may be provable as false on two levels. First, that the speaker really did not think Jones had lied but said it anyway, and second that Jones really had not lied. It is, of course, the second level of falsity which would ordinarily serve as the basis for a defamation action, though falsity at the first level may serve to establish malice where that is required for recovery.

determination of whether petitioner lied in this instance can be made on a core of objective evidence by comparing, *inter alia,* petitioner's testimony before the OHSAA board with his subsequent testimony before the trial court. As the *Scott* court noted regarding the plaintiff in that case, "[w]hether or not H. Don Scott did indeed perjure himself is certainly verifiable by a perjury action with evidence adduced from the transcripts and witnesses present at the hearing. Unlike a subjective assertion, the averred defamatory language is an articulation of an objectively verifiable event." 25 Ohio St.3d, at 252, 496 N.E.2d, at 707. So too with petitioner Milkovich. [Cc]

The numerous decisions discussed above establishing First Amendment protection for defendants in defamation actions surely demonstrate the Court's recognition of the Amendment's vital guarantee of free and uninhibited discussion of public issues. But there is also another side to the equation; we have regularly acknowledged the "important social values which underlie the law of defamation," and recognize that "[s]ociety has a pervasive and strong interest in preventing and redressing attacks upon reputation." Rosenblatt v. Baer, 383 U.S. 75, 86 (1966). Justice Stewart in that case put it with his customary clarity:

> "The right of a man to the protection of his own reputation from unjustified invasion and wrongful hurt reflects no more than our basic concept of the essential dignity and worth of every human being—a concept at the root of any decent system of ordered liberty.
>
> * * *
>
> "The destruction that defamatory falsehood can bring is, to be sure, often beyond the capacity of the law to redeem. Yet, imperfect though it is, an action for damages is the only hope for vindication or redress the law gives to a man whose reputation has been falsely dishonored." [C]

We believe our decision in the present case holds the balance true. The judgment of the Ohio Court of Appeals is reversed and the case remanded for further proceedings not inconsistent with this opinion.

Reversed.

JUSTICE MARSHALL joined JUSTICE BRENNAN in dissenting.

NOTES AND QUESTIONS

1. Has the Supreme Court eroded protection of free speech?

A. Will the jury play a larger part under the rule in the principal case, than it did when opinion was constitutionally protected? The interpretation of whether the statement was a factual assertion is judged by the reasonable listener or reader. Yetman v. English, 811 P.2d 323 (Ariz.1991) (a politician calling another a "Communist"). It is for the court, and not the jury, to determine as a matter of law whether an alleged defamatory statement is one of fact or opinion. Williams v. Garraghty, 455 S.E.2d 209 (Va.1995). But cf. Greenbelt Cooperative Publg Assn v. Bresler, 398 U.S. 6 (1970) (use of word "blackmail," reviewing court deciding the word could be understood as "no more than rhetorical hyperbole . . ."). Knievel v. ESPN, 393 F.3d 1068 (9th Cir. 2005) (holding that a photograph of Knievel with his arms around his wife and another young woman, with a caption: "Evil Knievel proves that you're never too old to be a pimp" could not, as a matter of law, be interpreted as stating facts). Is expert evidence admissible on the question how the average person would understand the statement? Weller v. Am. Broad. Co., 283 Cal. Rptr. 644 (Cal. Ct. App. 1991) (evidence of linguistics expert to assist jury in determining how certain rhetorical devises or patterns of speech convey implied meanings). But cf. James v. San Jose Mercury News, Inc., 20 Cal. Rptr.2d 890 (Cal. Ct. App. 1993) (finding plaintiff's representation that he would present at trial testimony of an expert linguist to establish the impact of the defamatory statements on an average reader irrelevant at the summary judgment stage).

B. Will courts be encouraged to engage in close literal interpretation, de-emphasizing the context of the statement? Cf. Immuno AG. v. Moor-Jankowski, 567 N.E.2d 1270 (N.Y. 1991), *cert. denied*, 500 U.S. 954 (1991), vacated and remanded by the Supreme Court after its decision in the principal case. The New York court held that the letter to the scientific magazine was protected under the principal case but also found under the state constitution, that context played a larger part: "analysis . . . begins by looking at the content of the whole communication, its tone and apparent purpose." See Wachtel v. Storm, 796 F. Supp. 114 (S.D.N.Y. 1992) for decision focusing on the interpretation of the statement alone. Factual assertions were implied by the statement "outrageous overhead and unrelated business expenses." Context has re-emerged in the case law, at least in publications where a wide license is necessary to encourage vigorous public debate. In a letter to the editor assertions about the state of a farm were construed as opinion, Rudnick v. McMillan, 31 Cal. Rptr.2d 193 (Cal. Ct. App. 1994). Likewise in book reviews, assertions referable to the text of the book being evaluated are, although factually based, protected commentary. Moldea v. New York Times Co., 22 F.3d 310 (D.C. Cir.), *cert. denied*, 513 U.S. 875 (1994), wherein plaintiff was accused of "sloppy journalism." In remarkable fashion the court admitted a mistake in its earlier ruling in *Moldea I*, 15 F.3d 1137 (D.C. Cir. 1994). For a criticism of the turnabout, see David A. Logan, Of "Sloppy Journalism," "Corporate Tyranny," and Mea Culpas: The Curious Case of *Moldea v. New York Times*, 37 WM. & MARY L. REV. 161 (1995).

2. Is this a non-factual assertion, which cannot be proved false? What if the utterer of the statement did not in fact have this opinion of Jones but was motivated to destroy him socially? How is this to be distinguished from the *Falwell* case where Flynt, the publisher, intended to destroy Falwell's character? What of a statement that plaintiff is "a very poor lawyer"? In Sullivan v. Conway, 157 F.3d 1092 (7th Cir. 1998), Judge Posner held this to be an expression of opinion; no "reasonable listener" would take defendant to base the "opinion" on "knowledge of facts of the sort that can be evaluated in a defamation suit." Id. at 4. However, in Armstrong v. Simon & Schuster, Inc., 610 N.Y.S.2d 503 (N.Y. App. Div. 1994), *aff'd*, 649 N.E.2d 825 (N.Y. 1995), defendants published a book "Den of Thieves" about Michael Milken's financial dealings. Plaintiff, a well-known criminal defense attorney complained that a passage in the book described plaintiff as presenting a perjurious affidavit for execution.

Referring to the nature of the book, its tone and purpose, the court held that the assertions were of fact and not opinion. Similarly, in Flamm v. Am. Ass'n of Univ. Women, 201 F.3d 144 (2d Cir. 2000) (fact-laden attorney referral directory accusing plaintiff of being "an ambulance chaser" and taking only "slam dunk cases" was actionable; it amounted to a factual assertion that plaintiff engaged in "improper solicitation").

3. The principal case allows an assertion to be actionable where the *ex facie* opinion refers to underlying facts that are false and defamatory. In Flowers v. Carville, 310 F.3d 1118 (9th Cir. 2002), plaintiff claimed to have been defamed by defendants' characterizing the *Sun*, which published her story, as "trash" and by defendant's assertion that plaintiff had "doctored" tapes to support her version of an affair with the President. The former was dismissed as generally invective, but the latter implied facts that would impute to plaintiff a nefarious motive. See also LRX, Inc. v. Horizon Assoc. Joint Venture, 842 So. 2d 881 (Fla. Ct. App. 2003), *review denied,* 859 So. 2d 514 (Fla. 2003) (accusation of unauthorized legal practice, actionable).

4. Restaurant reviews have prompted litigation. Even if review statements could be reasonably regarded as asserting fact, the restaurant is a public figure and thus the plaintiff must show actual malice. Mr. Chow of New York v. Ste. Jour Azur S.A., 759 F.2d 219 (2d Cir. 1985), Terillo v. N.Y. Newsday, 519 N.Y.S.2d 914 (N.Y. Civ. Ct. 1987) (holding that a misstatement as to the ingredients in a dish, if it was done with actual malice, could be actionable defamation). TripAdvisor listed the plaintiff's resort in Pigeon Forge Tennessee as no.1 on its "2011 Dirtiest Hotels" list. Was this an assertion of fact or an opinion? Was this an opinion or an assertion of fact? The context and hyperbole militates against finding this an assertion of fact: Seaton v. TripAdvisor LLC., 728 F.3d 592 (6th Cir. 2013).

5. A humorous context will not prevent an interpretation that the statement constituted an assertion of fact. See Unelko v. Rooney, 912 F.2d 1049 (9th Cir. 1990). Andy Rooney on "60 Minutes," in discussing the "junk" he received in the mail, mentioned that the plaintiff's product "Rain-ex" which was designed to shed rain from windshields "didn't work." The court found this to be an implied assertion of objective fact; unlike the *Falwell* case it was not couched in base, figurative, or hyperbolic language. Are dry humorists in jeopardy?

6. The principal case in its terms does not apply where a private party publishes material of purely private concern about a non-public figure or official. The state law will apply. *Dun and Bradstreet*, supra page 953.

5. PRIVILEGES

The common law developed a number of defenses in order to protect the interest of free speech and political and public debate. The defense of fair comment has now been constitutionalized, in the manner just observed. The common law recognized that some speech was essential for the functioning of representative government and the administration of justice and hence gave precedence to this speech by according it an absolute privilege. In essence the nature of this speech could not be judicially reviewed. Other speech attracted a qualified or conditional privilege. This speech was not actionable, although defamatory, if it was communicated by the publisher to the recipient where both parties had a reciprocal duty and interest to communicate and receive it. A letter of reference is an example. If the purpose for the communication is outside the purpose of the privilege, the defense is lost. Similarly, if the communication is transmitted to persons who have no duty or interest to receive it, there is no privilege.

Despite the overwhelming bulk of constitutional law, these privileges remain important in defamation law.

(A) ABSOLUTE PRIVILEGE

NOTES AND QUESTIONS

1. *Judicial Privilege.* A judge has absolute immunity for defamatory words published in the course of judicial proceedings. An attorney says the plaintiff was not truthful and was "lower than a rattlesnake because a rattlesnake gives warning before it strikes." The trial is broadcast. Privilege attaches to the judge, the attorney and the radio station. The attorney's statement may be false and malicious but will be privileged if relevant and pertinent to the issues in the litigation. See Irwin v. Ashurst, 74 P.2d 1127 (Or. 1938). The privilege covers preliminary actions engaged in by a lawyer in good faith anticipation of litigation, e.g., demand letters, negotiations, and file investigations. Hawkins v. Harris, 661 A.2d 284 (N.J. 1995) (concerning statements of private investigator to potential witnesses during pretrial discussions).

2. The privilege extends also to witnesses, even though they testify voluntarily, and not under subpoena. It extends to a defamatory statement in a pleading filed in the action, as in Di Blasio v. Kolodner, 197 A.2d 245 (Md. 1964); and also to affidavits filed in a judicial proceeding, or filed for the purpose of reopening it after judgment, as in Fleming v. Adams, 153 N.Y.S.2d 964 (N.Y. Spec. Term 1956). What about pretrial interviews of potential witnesses? Compare Ascherman v. Natanson, 100 Cal. Rptr. 656 (Cal. Ct. App. 1972) (absolute immunity), *with* Delmonico v. Traynor, 116 So. 3d 1205 (Fla. 2013) (qualified immunity). For privilege attaching to report of pleadings, see supra note 7, page 942.

3. The privilege applies to the hearing of a sanity commission. Jarman v. Offutt, 80 S.E.2d 248 (N.C. 1954). Compare, for hearings before a grievance committee of the state bar association, Wiener v. Weintraub, 239 N.E.2d 540 (N.Y. 1968); Ramstead v. Morgan, 347 P.2d 594 (Or. 1959). When the proceedings of administrative agencies are found to be judicial in character, the same privilege applies to them. Robertson v. Industrial Insurance Co., 75 So. 2d 198 (Fla.1954) (revocation of insurance license). University grievance procedures were not to be regarded as quasi-judicial, Overall v. Univ. of Penn.,.412 F. 3d 492 (3d Cir. 2005), per Judge Alito at 498.

Once the privilege is found to exist, the only limitation on it is that what is said must be found to have some reasonable bearing upon or relation to the subject of inquiry. Even the judge cannot seize upon the occasion of a judicial proceeding to voice entirely unrelated defamation. La Porta v. Leonard, 97 A. 251 (N.J. 1916); Stahl v. Kincade, 192 N.E.2d 493

(Ind. App. 1963). Of course, the privilege does not extend to what is said outside of court. Bochetto v. Gibson, 860 A.2d 67 (Pa. 2004) (attorney faxed a copy of the complaint to a freelance reporter); Jacobs v. Adelson, 325 P.3d 1282 (Nev. 2014) (statements made to the media outside judicial proceedings).

But the required "relevance" or "pertinence" does not mean that what is said must come within the rules of evidence as to relevancy: and a great deal of latitude is allowed. Thus when a witness answers a question asked him and not objected to, he is privileged although both the question and the answer are entirely irrelevant to the proceeding. Harman v. Belk, 600 S.E.2d 43 (N.C. Ct. App. 2004) (during deposition for breach of contract litigation, witness discussed rumors that defendant "liked to hurt people, that he broke their knees" and that he "liked to blackmail people").And if he speaks under an honest, but mistaken belief as to what is called for, as when he misunderstands the question, he is privileged. Johnson v. Dover, 143 S.W.2d 1112 (Ark. 1940).

4. The result of the absolute privilege is that there is no civil remedy at all against the witness who gives perjured testimony in court, even though he does so in furtherance of a conspiracy to injure the plaintiff. Ginsburg v. Halpern, 118 A.2d 201 (Pa. 1955). On the other hand, it has been held that the privilege does not protect one not himself involved in the proceeding, who procures the false testimony. Bailey v. McGill, 100 S.E.2d 860 (N.C. 1957).

5. *Legislative Proceedings.* A similar absolute privilege is applied to members of Congress and of the state legislatures, in the performance of their legislative functions. See U.S. CONST. art. I, § 6, cl. 1 (speech and debate clause); Cochran v. Couzens, 42 F.2d 783 (D.C. Cir. 1930).

6. The common law rule was that the defamation, to be privileged, must have some relation to the business of the legislature. Coffin v. Coffin, 4 Mass. (1 Tyng) 1 (1808). Federal and state constitutional provisions have been construed, however, to extend the privilege to anything whatever said in the course of legislative proceedings themselves. Gravel v. United States, 408 U.S. 606 (1972) (holding that privilege extends beyond pure speech and debate when the matter is "an integral part of the deliberative and communicative processes by which members of Congress participate in" proceedings); Kilbourn v. Thompson, 103 U.S. 168 (1880).

7. The Supreme Court in Hutchinson v. Proxmire, 443 U.S. 111 (1979), focused on the scope of immunity under the speech and debate clause. Senator Proxmire gave "Golden Fleece of the Month Awards" to highlight what he considered wasteful federal spending. Hutchinson had been given federal grants for research on aggressive behavior in primates, for which the Senator gave a Golden Fleece Award. In a speech on the Senate Floor written by an aide, he demeaned Hutchinson's work. The speech was published in a press release and a summary distributed to Wisconsin constituents. The Supreme Court held that the Senator was "wholly immune" for his statements on the Senate Floor, but not immune for statements in the press releases and newsletters because they were not "essential to the deliberations of the Senate" and were not "part of the deliberative process." See also *Brooks v. Muldoon* [1973] 1 NZLR 1 (SC) (statement by Prime Minister to reporters outside Parliament).

8. The privilege extends to the hearings of the legislative body, and to witnesses testifying at such hearings. Kelly v. Daro, 118 P.2d 37 (Cal. Dist. Ct. App. 1941); Logan's Super Markets v. McCalla, 343 S.W.2d 892 (Tenn. 1961). In the last case, it was held that the testimony of the witness was subject to the same rules as to pertinence to the proceeding as in the case of the judicial proceeding immunity.

9. There is disagreement on whether the legislative privilege extends to local legislative bodies, such as city councils. The majority view grants an absolute privilege. See Butler v. Town of Argo, 871 So. 2d 1 (Ala. 2003). But cf. Vultaggio v. Yasko, 572 N.W.2d 450 (Wisc. 1998) (conditional privilege to those testifying at city council meetings).

10. In McDonald v. Smith, 472 U.S. 479 (1985), the Court dealt with the right to petition the government under the First Amendment. Those petitioning had no special constitutional status, but rather enjoyed a qualified privilege defeasible by proof of actual malice where, as in the case at hand, plaintiff was a public figure—a candidate for nomination as U.S. Attorney. Letters to the President and other executive and legislative leaders allegedly defamed plaintiff.

11. *Public Officials: Federal.* The Supreme Court in Barr v. Matteo, 360 U.S. 564 (1959), decided that the immunity the Court had previously given to executive officers of the Cabinet in Spalding v. Vilas, 161 U.S. 483 (1896) (Postmaster General), from defamation liability while acting as their duties required or inherently permitted, also extended to federal agents of lower standing. Rank is not the determinant, rather it is the scope of the official's duties.

12. If the publication took place within the scope of the federal official's office, or employment, no cause of action in defamation is available against the officer or the United States. A statutory immunity is granted to the official under amendments to the Federal Torts Claims Act (FTCA): Federal Employees Liability Reform and Tort Compensation Act of 1988, Pub.L. 100–694, 102 Stat. 4563. This immunity subsists even though the plaintiff is precluded from suing the United States: United States v. Smith, 499 U.S. 160 (1991) (Federal Employees Liability Reform Act immunized federal government physicians from malpractice liability even when the FTCA precludes recovery against the United States). It follows that no action in defamation is available since the United States has not waived sovereign immunity in respect of defamation (slander and libel). This has led to attempts to frame the action in negligence, thus permitting the action against the United States. Success has been mixed. Quinones v. United States, 492 F.2d 1269 (3d Cir. 1974) (claim of negligent record keeping accepted). Cf. Jimenez-Nieves v. United States, 682 F.2d 1 (1st Cir. 1982) (refusing to allow claims for injury to plaintiff's reputation when Social Security Administration stopped payment erroneously on plaintiff's benefit check).

13. *Public Officers: State.* High state officials have an absolute immunity in the discharge of their official duties. Jones v. State, 426 S.W.3d 50 (Tenn. 2013) (Department of Corrections Commissioner); Blair v. Walker, 349 N.E.2d 385 (Ill. 1976). This has been held to include press releases to inform the public of what they are doing. Hackworth v. Larson, 165 N.W.2d 705 (S.D. 1969) (state secretary of state but must not be extraneous to this informational purpose, Hutchinson v. Proxmire, supra).

14. Some state courts have adopted the federal position and extended the absolute privilege to officials of lower rank. See, e.g., Sheridan v. Crisona, 198 N.E.2d 359, 249 N.Y.S.2d 161 (N.Y. 1964) (President of the Borough of Queens accused city appraiser of "ignorance, distortion and incompetence"); Carradine v. State, 511 N.W.2d 733 (Minn. 1994) (absolute immunity for state trooper writing arrest report). Many state courts, however, hold that minor officials are entitled only to a qualified privilege. E.g., Ranous v. Hughes, 141 N.W.2d 251 (Wis. 1966); Gardner v. Hollifield, 533 P.2d 730 (Idaho 1975); Chamberlain v. Mathis, 729 P.2d 905 (Ariz. 1986) (doubting the efficacy of extending absolute immunity to minor officials and recommending an objective malice test for discharging the qualified immunity defense).

(B) CONDITIONAL OR QUALIFIED PRIVILEGE

Sindorf v. Jacron Sales Co., Inc.

Court of Special Appeals of Maryland, 1975.
27 Md.App. 53, 341 A.2d 856.

[Plaintiff Sindorf worked as salesman for Jacron Sales Co., Inc., (the parent company resident in Pennsylvania). He resigned after 18 months, as a result of a dispute over his sales practices. Jacron contended that he was selling to people without adequately checking their credit ratings and apparently held up payment of his commissions until they received payment for the sales. On resigning, Sindorf kept some of his inventory, "as partial payment of the commissions due me." He soon went to work as a salesman for Tool Box Corporation of Maryland.

At the suggestion of Langton, President of Pennsylvania Jacron, a call was made to William Brose, President of Tool Box, by Bob Fridkis, Vice President of Virginia Jacron, a subsidiary of Pennsylvania Jacron, to see whether Sindorf had started working for Tool Box before leaving Jacron. Fridkis and Brose, though competitors, were friends and had had similar conversations about employees before. In a long conversation, Fridkis learned that Sindorf had not gone to work for Tool Box until after his resignation from Jacron. Fridkis told Brose that "a few cash sales and quite a bit of merchandise was not accounted for" by Sindorf, and suggested that Brose had better "watch your stock real, real carefully on trucks and things." There were other derogatory insinuations.

The trial court held that Fridkis' conversation was conditionally privileged and that no malice was shown. It granted a motion by Jacron for a directed verdict.]

ORTH, CHIEF JUDGE. * * * The first * * * question to be resolved is whether Jacron enjoyed a conditional privilege to defame Sindorf. * * *

"In an action for defamation, the plaintiff's prima facie case is made out when he has established a publication to a third person for which the defendant is responsible, the recipient's understanding of the defamatory meaning, and its actionable character. It is then open to the defendant to set up various defenses, which to some extent have moderated the rigors of the law of libel and slander." W. Prosser, Law of Torts, 776 (4th ed., 1971). One of these defenses is privilege. "It rests upon the * * * idea, that conduct which otherwise would be actionable is to escape liability because the defendant is acting in furtherance of some interest of social importance, which is entitled to protection even at the expense of uncompensated harm to the plaintiff's reputation. The interest thus favored may be one of the defendant himself, of a third person, or of the general public. If it is one of paramount importance, considerations of policy may require that the defendant's immunity for false statements be absolute, without regard to his purpose or motive, or the reasonableness of his conduct." Id. This is absolute privilege. [C] "If it has relatively less weight from a social point of view, the immunity may be qualified, and conditional upon good motives and reasonable behavior. The defendant's belief in the truth of what he says, the purpose for which he says it, and the manner of publication, all of which are immaterial when no question of privilege is involved, may determine the issue when he enters the defense of such a conditional privilege." Prosser, at 776–777. In the words of Baron Parke in Toogood v. Spyring, 1 C.M. & R. 181, 149 Eng.Rep. 1044 (1834), a publication is conditionally privileged when it is "fairly made by a person in the discharge of some public or private duty, whether legal or moral, or in the conduct of his own affairs, in matters where his interest is concerned." * * * The types of interest which are protected by a qualified privilege are classified by Prosser, at 786, as interest of the publisher, interest of others, common interest of publisher and recipient, communications made to one who may act in the public interest, and fair comment on matters of public concern. [C] "The condition attached to all such qualified privileges is that they must be exercised in a reasonable manner and for a proper purpose. The immunity is forfeited if the defendant steps outside of the scope of the privilege, or abuses the occasion. * * * [It does not] include publication to any person other than those whose hearing of it is reasonably believed to be necessary or useful for the furtherance of that interest. * * * Any reasonable and appropriate method of publication may be adopted which fits the purpose of protecting the particular interest. The dictation of a business letter to a stenographer * * * may be privileged on proper occasion. * * * [T]he fact that the communication is incidentally read or overheard by a person to whom there is no privilege to publish it will not result in liability, if the method adopted is a reasonable and appropriate one under the circumstances." Prosser, at 792–794.

The burden is upon the defendant in the first instance to establish the existence of a privileged occasion for the publication, by proof of a proper interest or duty justifying the utterance of the words. "Whether the occasion was a privileged one, is a question to be determined by the court as an issue of law, unless of course the facts are in dispute, in which case the jury will be instructed as to the proper rules to apply." Id., at 796.

The rules of law as to conditional privilege followed in Maryland generally reflect the views of the authorities above discussed. [Cc]

Thus, the law of this State is that a defamatory publication is conditionally privileged when the occasion shows that the communicating party and the recipient have a mutual interest in the subject matter, or some duty with respect thereto. [Cc] Over seventy-five years ago the Court of Appeals established that where an employer gives a character of an employee the communication is conditionally privileged under the principle that the party communicating has a duty owed, even though such duty is not a legal one, but only a moral or social duty of imperfect obligation. This is so even though the defamatory information was given voluntarily rather than upon request. Fresh v. Cutter, 73 Md. 87, 92–94, 20 A. 774. * * * The authorities are in general agreement that where a former employer communicates with a new or prospective employer about a former employee, a conditional privilege arises from a discharge of duty owed to the new or prospective employer. * * *

The circumstances here * * * were that the defamer was the vice-president of the subsidiary of the corporation which was Sindorf's former employer, and that the communicator and recipient, even though competitors, had a close personal and business relationship. Whether based on a duty owed or a common interest, we think that a qualified privilege arose. In the absence of a dispute as to the facts, the existence *vel non* of a common interest or duty giving rise to a qualified privilege is a matter of law for the court. [Cc] There was no dispute here as to such facts. We conclude that the trial court did not err in holding as a matter of law that Fridkis, and therefore Jacron, had a conditional privilege to communicate the defamatory utterance to Brose.

The second * * * question is whether Jacron lost the privilege to defame. * * *

Because a conditional or qualified privilege is conditioned upon publication in a reasonable manner and for a proper purpose, it is defeasible. * * * The Court of Appeals said in Orrison v. Vance, 262 Md. at 295, 277 A.2d at 578: * * * "In determining an abuse of privilege all relevant circumstances are admissible, [c] including the defendant's reasonable belief in the truth of his statements, [c] the excessive nature of the language used, [c] whether the disclosures were unsolicited, id., and whether the communication was made in a proper manner and only to proper parties [c]."[7]

"Malice may be a jury question." [C] It is a jury question unless only one conclusion can be drawn from the evidence. Prosser, at 796. In other words, it is only when the evidence and all inferences fairly deducible therefrom lead to conclusions from which reasonable minds could not differ, that the issue of malice is one of law for the court and not one of fact for the jury. * * *

The motion for a directed verdict was primarily based on the theory that there was no sufficient showing by Sindorf of malice within the meaning of that word as defeating a conditional privilege. It appears

7 "Prosser said that the qualified privilege will be lost if the defendant publishes the defamation 'in the wrong state of mind.' At 794. He thought that the statement that the privilege is defeated if the publication is 'malicious' is misleading and discounted malice in this context as a 'meaningless and quite unsatisfactory term.' At 795. He concluded, at 796: 'Probably the best statement of the rule is that the defendant is required to act as a reasonable man under the circumstances, with due regard to the strength of his belief, the grounds that he has to support it, and the importance of conveying the information.' "

that the grant of the motion was substantially bottomed on that reason. We think that the grant of the motion was wrong. We believe that the evidence, when viewed as required by the rule pertaining to the grant *vel non* of a directed verdict, led to conclusions from which reasonable minds could differ. We start with the rule that the publisher's motive will be more carefully scrutinized if his statements are volunteered than if they are in response to an inquiry, in which latter instance, greater latitude is permitted. We observe that Fridkis clearly indicated that Sindorf had been fired, whereas, as far as the record shows, he resigned. It does not appear that Langton told Fridkis that Sindorf was fired, and if Fridkis did not in fact know that Sindorf was not fired, stating that he was fired could be found to be a reckless disregard of truth. * * *

We observe that the publisher will be liable if he publishes his statement to accomplish a distinct objective, which may be legitimate enough in itself but is not within the privilege. [C] We think that a reasonable person could conclude from the evidence that Fridkis's communication to Brose was an effort to pressure Sindorf into returning the material he was holding, or, perhaps, simply to ascertain, as Langton requested, the date of employment of Sindorf by Tool Box. Neither would be within the privilege. The short of it is that we cannot find, assuming the truth of all credible evidence on the issue of malice and of all inferences fairly deducible therefrom, and considering them in the light most favorable to Sindorf, that they lead to the conclusions, from which reasonable minds could not differ, that Fridkis, and through him, Jacron, did not abuse the privilege to defame by excessive publication or by use of the occasion for an improper purpose, or by lack of grounds for belief in the truth of what was said. Therefore, the question of malice was properly for the jury and the trial judge erred in granting the motion for a directed verdict. The issue of malice should have gone to the jury with appropriate instructions. We reverse the judgment and remand the case for a new trial. * * *

NOTES AND QUESTIONS

1. *Protection of Publisher's Own Interests.* A person has a qualified privilege to make defamatory statements in a reasonable effort to recover goods stolen from him; to collect money due him or prevent others from collecting it; to protest against the mismanagement of a concern in which he has a financial interest; to protect his own business against unfair competition; to protect his own personal safety; or to defend any other legitimate interest. See, e.g., Montgomery Ward & Co. v. Watson, 55 F.2d 184 (4th Cir. 1932) (employer accuses one employee, before others, of stealing from him); Gardner v. Standard Oil Co., 175 So. 203 (Miss. 1937) (employer warns employees that plaintiff is of bad character and they are not to deal with him). Park v. Hill, 380 F. Supp.2d 1002 (N.D. Iowa 2005) (in a letter to other bank shareholders, unsuccessful bidder for control of bank made statements about bank president; protecting his own financial interest and a common interest with other shareholders), Denardo v. Bax, 147 P.3d 672 (Alaska 2006) (defendant told coworkers that she believes plaintiff fellow coworker was stalking her).

2. Included in the privilege of protecting the defendant's own interest is the protection of his reputation against defamation on the part of others. The privilege is not limited merely to publication of the statement that the plaintiff is an unmitigated liar and the truth is not in him. The defendant may go further and attack the plaintiff's motives, to explain the defamation. Foretich v. Capital Cities/ABC, Inc., 37 F.3d 1541 (4th Cir. 1994) (when plaintiff accused defendant in-laws of molesting their grandchild, defendants' statements that plaintiff was "sick" and that her comments came "from the bottom of a cesspool" were a proportionate response). On the other hand, the privilege does not extend to an irrelevant matter, as, for example, a statement that the plaintiff beats his wife. Cf. Sternberg Mfg. Co. v. Miller, DuBrul & Peters Mfg. Co., 170 Fed. 298 (8th Cir. 1909).

3. *Protection of Interests of a Third Person.* The third person is usually the recipient of the communication but need not be. The privilege exists when the publisher reasonably believes that there is information that affects a sufficiently important interest of the third party and that he publishes the information under a legal duty or in accordance with "generally accepted standards of decent conduct." RESTATEMENT (SECOND) OF TORTS § 595 (1977). Thus, there is a privilege to answer the inquiry of a prospective employer of the plaintiff concerning his character or fitness for the position. Kevorkian v. Glass, 913 A.2d 1043 (R.I. 2007); Child v. Affleck, (1839) 109 Eng. Rep. 150 (K.B.); 9 B. & C. 403 (Eng.). And a bank is privileged to answer an inquiry about the plaintiff's credit from one who has been asked to sell him goods. Melcher v. Beeler, 110 P. 181 (Colo. 1910).

4. In determining whether the privilege should be granted, weight is given to the question of whether the information was requested by the recipient or was volunteered. Thus, volunteered statements were held not privileged in such cases as Watt v. Longsdon, (1930) 1 K.B. 130 (Eng.), and Burton v. Mattson, 166 P. 979 (Utah 1917), involving personal gossip. But there are occasions when it is appropriate to volunteer the information. De Van Rose v. Tholborn, 134 S.W. 1093 (Mo. 1911) (landlord informed that his tenant was undesirable).

5. *Common Interest.* The existence of a common interest between the publisher and the recipient gives rise to a privilege to speak regarding the common interest. Here there is more freedom to volunteer information. See RESTATEMENT (SECOND) OF TORTS § 596. Representative cases include Bereman v. Power Pub. Co., 27 P.2d 749 (Colo. 1933) (labor union); Slocinski v. Radwan, 144 A. 787 (N.H. 1929) (church members); Smith Bros. & Co. v. W.C. Agee & Co., 59 So. 647 (Ala. 1912) (common creditors). O'Connor v. Burningham, 165 P.3d 1214 (Utah 2007) (familial privilege when parents criticized the behavior of their daughters' basketball coach to the school board). A family relationship is given similar treatment. See RESTATEMENT (SECOND) OF TORTS § 597; Kroger Co. v. Young, 172 S.E.2d 720 (Va. 1970); Watt v. Longsdon, 1 K.B. 130 (Eng.); Gohari v. Darvish, 767 A.2d 321 (Md. 2001) (franchisor and franchisee discussing qualifications of potential new franchisee).

6. Recall that under *Gertz* liability could not attach to the defendant unless the plaintiff proved that the defendant was "at fault." If the plaintiff discharges her burden of proving that the defendant was negligent in the

publication, can defendant, nevertheless, raise the defense of qualified privilege? In other words, does negligence under *Gertz* subsume malice in discharging the defense of conditional or qualified privilege? The issue arose on appeal from the preceding, Jacron Sales Co., Inc. v. Sindorf, 350 A.2d 688 (Md. 1976), finding that the malice standard was stricter than negligence (under *Gertz*). It requires at least a "reckless disregard for the truth." The Virginia Supreme Court in Gazette, Inc. v. Harris, 325 S.E.2d 713 (Va. 1985), in adopting the *Gertz* negligence standard, maintained the defense of conditional or qualified immunity. (Id. at 727).

7. Courts all agree that the defendant cannot claim a qualified privilege if he knows that his defamatory statement is false or does not believe it to be true. Lawless v. Muller, 123 A. 104 (N.J.L. 1923); Russell v. Geis, 59 Cal. Rptr. 569 (Cal. Ct. App. 1967).

Prior to the *Gertz* revolution, a majority of American courts held that malice was evaluated by an objective criterion—did defendant have reasonable grounds for believing his statement to be true. A sizeable minority followed the English rules adopting the subjective criterion—defendant does not lose his privilege if he acted in good faith and not in reckless disregard as to the falsity of the statement. A.B.C. Needlecraft v. Dun & Bradstreet, 245 F.2d 775 (2d Cir. 1957). Because the requirements of *Gertz* would make the defense useless under the majority/objective criterion, the Restatement (Second) of Torts has adopted reckless-disregard as to the test for determining whether the privilege is lost. See § 600 and the Special Note preceding § 593. This position has been adopted in numerous cases. See Luster v. Retail Credit Co., 575 F.2d 609 (8th Cir. 1978); British Am. & E. Co. v. Wirth Ltd., 592 F.2d 75 (2d Cir. 1979); Moore v. Smith, 578 P.2d 26 (Wash. 1978). The attitude to malice as defeating privilege resulted from *Gertz*, but the Restatement does not adequately reflect the exception made by *Dun & Bradstreet v. Greenmoss*, supra page 953. Where matters of purely private concern are involved, the common law rules stand and no fault is necessary to be proved. This can be a matter of real practical moment.

8. The common law doctrine of "qualified privilege," in various forms, has been extended to protect free speech in other common law countries. Australia: *Lange v. Australian Broad. Corp.* (1997) 189 CLR 520; *Bashford v. Info. Austl. (Newsletter) Pty. Ltd.* (2004) 218 CLR 366 (articulating how the defense of qualified privilege is applied). New Zealand: *Lange v. Atkinson* [1997] 2 NZLR 22 (HC), *reconfirmed by* [1998] 3 NZLR 424 (CA). England: Reynolds v. Times Newspapers, Ltd., (2001) 2 A.C. 127 (H.L.); Jameel v. Wall Street Journal. Eur. SPRL (No. 3), [2007] 1 A.C. 359 (H.L.) (stressing the "liberalizing intention" of *Reynolds* and flexibility accorded to responsible journalism).

9. This necessarily means that "courts will find it desirable to reassess the circumstances under which it is appropriate to grant a conditional privilege. If a proper adjustment of the conflicting interests of the parties indicates that a publisher should be held liable for failure to use due care to determine the truth of the communication before publishing it, a conditional privilege is not needed and should not be held to apply." RESTATEMENT (SECOND) OF TORTS § 593, cmt. *c*. For application of this viewpoint to a privilege for credit-rating agencies, see § 595, comment *h*. If a plaintiff, as a public official, is already subject to the *New York Times*

standard, a conditional privilege can have no significance and is not held to exist. Wright v. Haas, 586 P.2d 1093 (Okl. 1978).

Can you envisage situations where a person unreasonably believing a statement to be true is justified in reporting it to others?

10. At common law there were two types of privileges that were unlike the others in that they did not depend upon the measure of fault on the part of the defendant regarding falsity of the defamatory communication. A defendant might successfully rely on the privilege even though he was aware of the fact that the statement was false. Instead the privilege was controlled by other restrictions. These are:

A. *Fair Reporting.* This privilege is to report public proceedings, public records and official acts. The restriction is that the report must be accurate and fair or disinterested. This has been treated supra, pages 942–944.

B. *Privilege to Provide Means of Publication.* When the author of the defamatory utterance is in fact privileged to publish it, those who provide him with the appropriate means of publication are likewise privileged to do so. Otherwise, of course, he would have great difficulty in making his communication. Thus if the author is privileged to publish his statement in a newspaper, the newspaper itself can be no less privileged; and the same is true of a stenographer taking dictation. See Israel v. Portland News Publg. Co., 53 P.2d 529 (Or. 1936); Western Union Tel. Co. v. Lesesne, 182 F.2d 135 (4th Cir. 1950); RESTATEMENT (SECOND) OF TORTS § 612 (1977).

C. *Fair Comment.* The media relied heavily upon this privilege prior to the imposition of constitutional limits on the tort. It allowed the publisher to offer criticism on matters of public concern including activities of public officials and figures and on subjects scientific, artistic, literary, and dramatic. The "freer the criticism is, the better it will be for the aesthetic welfare of the public." Lyon v. Daily Telegraph, [1943] K.B. 746 at 752 (Scott L.J.). The criticism must be comment or opinion, not a misstatement of fact. It must be *fair* in that it must be based upon true facts and express, within wide bounds, what an honest-minded person might conclude. Neely v. Wilson, 418 S.W.3d 52 (Tex. 2013) (asking whether "the gist of the broadcast was substantially true"). The opinion, however, need not be reasonable. The privilege might be abused and lost if the criticism did not represent the actual opinion of the critic, or if it were made solely for the purpose of causing harm to the person criticized. See generally the Restatement of Torts §§ 606–610 (1938). The holding in *Milkovich,* supra, may revivify the common law fair comment jurisprudence as constrained by the First Amendment. Thus, the defense of fair comment applies where a private person is defamed by broadcasts. Magnusson v. N.Y. Times, 98 P.3d 1070 (Okl. 2004) (applying Oklahoma law).

6. DEFAMATION GOES GLOBAL

In the well-known Australian High Court, *Dow Jones & Co. Inc. v. Gutnick* (2002) 210 CLR 575 (Austl.), an Australian businessman, Joseph Gutnick, sued an American magazine and publishing company in the Australian state of Victoria over an allegedly defamatory online article. Only five copies of the print edition were sent from New Jersey to be circulated in Australia, however, none had actually arrived in the jurisdiction. To establish an actionable tort in the jurisdiction, Gutnick resorted to the internet based publication (the internet version of the magazine had 550,000 international subscribers and 1,700 Australian-based credit cards). The law of Victoria applied as the place of publication; under Australian law, each download of the article in Victoria was a publication in that jurisdiction. Dow Jones' pleas of impracticality and free speech restriction were considered but rejected by the High Court. Justice Kirby lamented that the common law was bound by "judicial remarks in England in a case decided more than a hundred fifty years ago involving . . . a newspaper of miniscule circulation." (citing Duke of Brunswick v. Harmer, (1849) 117 E.R. 75; 14 Q.B. 185 (Eng.)).

The assumption of jurisdiction by English courts has been criticized as "libel tourism," where actions are brought in English courts by aggrieved persons against publishers who have been protected in the United States under the principles of protected in the United States under the principles of *N.Y. Times v. Sullivan*. Of particular note is litigation brought by Sheikh Khalid Salim A bin Mahfouz, who sued in England complaining he had been defamed in Rachel Ehrenfeld's book "Funding Evil: How Terrorism is Finance—and How to Stop It." The English High Court gave a default judgment in favor of the plaintiff. Concern rising to a political storm of political protest, about the implications of "libel tourism," prompted some legislatures, in particular, the U.S. Congress, to introduce legislation designed to protect Americans' First Amendment rights. David Anderson, Transnational Libel, 53 Va. J. Int'l L. 71 (2012). In 2010, Congress passed, unanimously (both in the House and the Senate), the Securing the Protection of our Enduring and Established Constitutional Heritage (SPEECH) Act, which makes foreign libel judgments unenforceable in U.S. courts, unless either the legislation applied offers at least as much protection as the U.S. First Amendment (concerning free speech), or the defendant would have been found liable even if the case had been heard under U.S. law. However, in practice, this act goes far beyond legitimate instances of "libel tourism," and makes recognition of any foreign defamation judgment virtually impossible. Still, this debate is nothing new and well exposes the differing balances of free speech, reputation, and individual dignity supporting different versions of defamation law. See Eric Barendt, Jurisdiction in Internet Libel Cases, 110 Penn. St. L. Rev. 727 (2006); David F. Partlett, The Libel Tourist and the Ugly American: Free Speech in an Era of Modern Global Communications, 47 U. Louisville L. Rev. 635 (2009); David F. Partlett & Barbara McDonald, International Publications and Protection of Reputation: A Margin of Appreciation but not Subservience?, 62 Ala. L. Rev. 477 (2011); Mark D. Rosen, Exporting the Constitution, 53 Emory L.J. 171 (2004). For a thorough comparison of the differing approaches to balancing free speech rights with other fundamental rights, see Casey Jo Cooper, Balancing the Scales: Adhuc Sub Judice Li Est or Trial by Media, 3 Int'l L.J. London * * * (2015).

In 2014, the Defamation Act of 2013, c. 26, took effect in the United Kingdom. The legislation, aimed at reforming the United Kingdom's status as a libel tourism destination, raised the threshold for complaints to defamation that caused serious harm to the plaintiff's reputation, including a requirement of actual or likely serious financial loss for corporate entities and a tighter *forum non conveniens* threshold. For a comparison of the provisions of the Defamation Act with the United States Supreme Court's approach to defamation, see Lord Lester, Two Cheers for the First Amendment, 8 Harv. L. & Pol'y Rev. 177 (2014).

Trout Point Lodge v. Handshoe

United States Court of Appeals, Fifth Circuit, 2014.
729 F.3d 481.

ELROD, CIRCUIT JUDGE. This case requires us to construe the newly-enacted Securing the Protection of our Enduring and Established Constitutional Heritage Act (the "SPEECH Act"), 28 U.S.C. § 4102. Appellants Trout Point Lodge, Ltd. ("Trout Point Lodge"), Vaughn Perret ("Perret"), and Charles Leary ("Leary") (collectively, "Trout Point") seek to enforce a defamation-based default judgment that they obtained against Appellee Doug K. Handshoe ("Handshoe") in Nova Scotia, Canada. We agree with the district court that Trout Point cannot satisfy its burden under the SPEECH Act to show that either (A) Nova Scotian law provided at least as much protection for freedom of speech and press in Handshoe's case as would be provided by the First Amendment and relevant state law, or (B) Handshoe would have been found liable for defamation by a Mississippi court. 28 U.S.C. § 4102. Accordingly, we AFFIRM.

I.

Handshoe, a Mississippi citizen, owns and operates Slabbed.org, a public-affairs blog with the tagline "Alternative New Media for the Gulf South." He describes Slabbed.org as a "forum for local residents and other interested parties to gather and share information regarding various political and legal issues that impact the Gulf Coast."

One of the blog's focal points over the last few years has been Aaron Broussard, the former Parish President of Jefferson Parish, Louisiana. Broussard was indicted in the United States District Court for the Eastern District of Louisiana and pleaded guilty to charges of bribery and theft in September 2012. Handshoe claims that Slabbed.org has been "instrumental" in reporting the "ongoing corruption scandal, indictment, and guilty plea" involving Broussard.

During his time in office, Broussard owned property in Nova Scotia. The property sat on Trout Point Road, very close to Trout Point Lodge, a hotel that Perret and Leary own and operate. In about January 2010, Handshoe began publishing entries on Slabbed.org alleging a link between Broussard and Trout Point Lodge, Perret, and Leary. At or near the same time, the Times-Picayune, a New Orleans newspaper, published an article indicating that Broussard had an ownership interest in Trout Point Lodge and that Jefferson Parish contractors had paid to rent the premises. The Times-Picayune retracted this assertion and issued a correction after Perret and Leary alerted the paper to purported "factual errors in [its] reporting." It appears that the corporate parent of the Times-Picayune also took the Slabbed.org blog offline after Perret and Leary demanded this retraction. The district court determined that Handshoe, "apparently in reaction to his blog being taken offline," found another web host for his site and "began an internet campaign to damage Perret and Leary." Specifically, Handshoe posted several updates regarding Trout Point Lodge, Perret, and Leary, which the district court noted "can be characterized as derogatory, mean spirited, sexist, and homophobic."

Trout Point filed suit in the Supreme Court of Nova Scotia (the "Nova Scotia Court") on September 1, 2011, alleging defamation and related claims. Trout Point's First Amended Statement of Claim referred to publications on Slabbed.org and related third-party web sites, which it asserted "were directly defamatory and were also defamatory by both true and false innuendo in that they would tend to lower the opinion or estimation of the plaintiffs in the eyes of others who read the defamatory publications as a series, or alternatively, in parts." At the outset, the First Amended Statement of Claim asserted four primary sources of reputational harm: (1) content linking Trout Point with the "Jefferson Parish Political Corruption Scandal," the "sting" of which was that "Trout Point Lodge and its owners were somehow involved in corruption, fraud, money laundering, and 'pay to play' schemes involving Jefferson Parish President Aaron Broussard and his administration"; (2) the "clear imputation" that Trout Point "misled investors and court officials in litigation" with the Atlantic Canada Opportunities Agency ("ACOA"), the "sting" of which was that "Leary perjured himself, investors were misled, businesses nefariously changed ownership, and that the ACOA litigation is ongoing, with the plaintiffs [losing] every step of the way"; (3) the "imputation" that the "Trout Point Lodge business is actively failing, near bankruptcy, having once relied on the good graces of Aaron Broussard," along with the "related imputation" that Perret and Leary "have had a series of failed businesses that used other people's money, creating a pattern," the "sting" of which was that Trout Points's "13-year-old business is on the verge of bankruptcy, that the plaintiffs will take the money and run, and that the plaintiffs are either con artists or have no business acumen whatsoever"; and (4) the "unabashed anti-gay, anti-homosexual rhetoric and rants of the defendant," used to "amplify and support the three other stings listed above" and "support[ ] and shore[ ] up all the other defamatory imputations."

The First Amended Statement of Claim continued to describe several specific blog posts on Slabbed.org, reciting much of the offensive language that Handshoe used to refer to Perret and Leary. Some of the alleged defamatory statements indicated Handshoe's poor opinion of Perret and Leary, for example, that they "had Champagne taste on a beer budget," "work as a unit to grift their way through life," and were either "first-class b-tches, common thugs, or plain ol' morons."

In stating its defamation claim, Trout Point generically alleged that Handshoe's publications were false and malicious. It did not, however, make any specific statements to refute the truth of the individual blog posts at issue. * * *

Trout Point purportedly served Handshoe with a notice of the First Amended Statement of Claim in Mississippi, but Handshoe did not appear in the Nova Scotia action. In December 2011, the Nova Scotia

Court entered a default judgment against Handshoe (the "Nova Scotia Judgment"). * * *

The Nova Scotia Court set the matter for a hearing to assess damages. At the hearing, Perret and Leary testified and offered additional evidence regarding Handshoe's allegedly defamatory statements and the damage that they inflicted on Trout Point Lodge, and Perret and Leary individually. * * * Ultimately, the court awarded Trout Point Lodge $75,000 in general damages, and Leary and Perret each $100,000 in general damages, $50,000 in aggravated damages, and $25,000 in punitive damages. It also awarded $2,000 in costs.

Trout Point enrolled the Nova Scotia Judgment in the Circuit Court of Hancock County, Mississippi, in March 2012 in an attempt to collect its damages award. Handshoe removed the action to the United States District Court for the Southern District of Mississippi pursuant to the SPEECH Act. * * *

The district court entered summary judgment in Handshoe's favor, finding that Trout Point failed to meet its burden under the SPEECH Act to show that "Handshoe was afforded at least as much protection for freedom of speech in [the Nova Scotia] action as he would have in a domestic proceeding or, alternatively, that Handshoe would have been found liable for defamation by a domestic court." Trout Point timely appealed.

II.

* * *

III.

This action depends on our interpretation of the SPEECH Act. The task of statutory interpretation begins and, if possible, ends with the language of the statute. * * *

Many commentators have explained that Congress enacted the SPEECH Act in 2010 in response to the perceived threat of "libel tourism," a form of international forum-shopping in which a plaintiff chooses to file a defamation claim in a foreign jurisdiction with more favorable substantive law. In enacting the statute, Congress found that "by seeking out foreign jurisdictions that do not provide the full extent of free-speech protections to authors and publishers that are available in the United States" and by suing United States authors or publishers in those foreign jurisdictions, some persons were "obstructing" the free expression rights of domestic authors and publishers and "chilling" domestic citizens' First Amendment interest in "receiving information on matters of importance." * * * It further found that "[g]overnments and courts of foreign countries scattered around the world have failed to curtail this practice . . . and foreign libel judgments inconsistent with United States [F]irst [A]mendment protections are increasingly common." Id.

With these findings in mind, the SPEECH Act provides that a domestic court "shall not recognize or enforce a foreign judgment for defamation" unless it satisfies both First Amendment and due process considerations. See 28 U.S.C. § 4102. We focus our inquiry on the statute's "First Amendment considerations" provision.

Under the "First Amendment considerations" provision of the SPEECH Act, a foreign defamation judgment is unrecognizable and unenforceable unless

(A) the defamation law applied in the foreign court's adjudication provided at least as much protection for freedom of speech and press in that case as would be provided by the [F]irst [A]mendment to the Constitution of the United States and by the constitution and law of the State in which the domestic court is located; or

(B) even if the defamation law applied in the foreign court's adjudication did not provide as much protection for freedom of speech and press as the [F]irst [A]mendment to the Constitution of the United States and the constitution and law of the State, the party opposing recognition or enforcement of that foreign judgment would have been found liable for defamation by a domestic court applying the [F]irst [A]mendment to the Constitution of the United States and the constitution and law of the State in which the domestic court is located.

§ 4102(a)(1).

Although there is no case law directly interpreting these two prongs, the plain language of the statute suggests two distinct options for a party seeking to enforce a foreign defamation judgment: one focused on the law applied by the foreign forum and one focused on the facts the parties presented in the foreign proceeding. Put differently, a party may enforce a foreign defamation judgment in a domestic court if either (A) the law of the foreign forum, as applied in the foreign proceeding, provides free-speech protection that is coextensive with relevant domestic law, or (B) the facts, as proven in the foreign proceeding, are sufficient to establish a defamation claim under domestic law. We address each prong in turn.

A.

There is no meaningful dispute that the law applied by the Nova Scotia Court provides less protection of speech and press than First Amendment and Mississippi law. Canadian defamation law is derivative of the defamation law of the United Kingdom, which has long been substantially less protective of free speech. As Justice Black noted in Bridges v. California:

No purpose in ratifying the Bill of Rights was clearer than that of securing for the people of the United States much greater freedom of religion, expression, assembly, and petition than the people of Great Britain had ever enjoyed. . . . Ratified as it was while the memory of many oppressive English restrictions on the enumerated liberties was still fresh, the First Amendment cannot reasonably be taken as approving prevalent English practices. On the contrary, the only conclusion supported by history is that the unqualified prohibitions laid down by the framers were intended to give to liberty of the press, as to the other liberties, the broadest scope that could be countenanced in an orderly society.

* * * Thus, while Canadian law generally comports with England's traditional common-law approach, the United States has parted ways with its northern neighbor in matters of free speech.

The most critical legal difference here is that a Canadian plaintiff—unlike a plaintiff subject to First Amendment and Mississippi state law—need not prove falsity as an element of its prima facie defamation claim. Rather, in Canada, truth is a defense that a defamation defendant may raise and, if so, must prove. Compare Grant v. Torstar, (2009) 3 S.C.R. 640, para. 28–32 (Can.) (holding that "falsity and damages are presumed" if a plaintiff proves the elements of a prima facie defamation case), with Blake v. Gannett Co., 529 So.2d 595, 602 (Miss.1988) (holding that a defamation plaintiff bears the burden of proving falsity). See Eugenie Brouillet, Free Speech, Reputation, and the Canadian Balance, 50 N.Y.L. Sch. L.Rev. 33, 52 (2006) ("In the Canadian common law, the courts have chosen a low threshold for the establishment by the plaintiff of a prima facie cause of action in defamation, offering considerable protection to his right to reputation. The balance in favor of free speech is restored by a number of defenses, but the burden of proof rests on the defendant. In comparison, . . . American laws both seem to show a certain bias towards freedom of expression and freedom of the press; the burden of proof of the wrongful nature of the injury to reputation lies in both cases with the person defamed." (footnote omitted)). Thus, Trout Point cannot satisfy the first prong of the First-Amendment considerations inquiry; that is, the law applied in the Nova Scotia proceeding did not provide at least as much protection for freedom of speech and press as Handshoe would have received under domestic law.

B.

The more challenging question in this case arises from the statute's second prong: whether a Mississippi court presented with the same facts and circumstances would have found Handshoe liable for defamation. The answer depends on whether the facts Trout Point proved in the Nova Scotia proceeding were sufficient to demonstrate falsity under the United States Constitution and Mississippi state law. In Mississippi, "[t]he threshold question in a defamation suit is whether the published statements are false. Truth is a complete defense to an action for libel. The plaintiff bears the burden to prove such falsity." Armistead v. Minor, 815 So.2d 1189, 1194 (Miss.2002) (quotations and citations omitted). Significantly, statements that are "substantially true" are not defamatory in Mississippi. Id. "As the United States Supreme Court has noted, minor inaccuracies do not amount to falsity so long as the substance, the gist, the sting, of the libelous charge be justified." Id. (internal quotation marks omitted) (quoting Masson v. New Yorker Magazine, Inc., 501 U.S. 496, 517, 111 S.Ct. 2419, 115 L.Ed.2d 447 (1991)).

Applying First Amendment and Mississippi law, the district court concluded that Trout Point failed to prove falsity in the Nova Scotia proceeding:

* * *

On appeal, Trout Point criticizes the district court's reasoning because it "hinges entirely upon the faulty premise that [Trout Point] failed to prove the falsity of the publications at issue." Trout Point relies on two key sources to establish the falsity of Handshoe's statements: (1) the allegations in Trout Point's First Amended Statement of Claim, deemed admitted by the Nova Scotia Judgment, and (2) the Nova Scotia Court's purported factual findings made in the course of awarding damages. In our view, neither is sufficient to establish that a Mississippi court confronted with the same facts and circumstances would have found Handshoe liable for defamation. We turn first to the allegations deemed admitted by Nova Scotia Judgment.

1.

In Mississippi, a plaintiff may obtain a default judgment when the defendant "has failed to plead or otherwise defend" the case. Miss. R. Civ. P. 55(a); see also Fed.R.Civ.P. 55(a). But a default judgment is not appropriate if the plaintiff's allegations are insufficient to state a claim. * * *

* * *

Applying these principles here, Trout Point failed to show that a state or federal court in Mississippi faced with the First Amended Statement of Claim would have awarded a default judgment in its favor. Although Handshoe's failure to answer or otherwise defend the case satisfies the basic prerequisite for default, the allegations in the First Amended Statement of Claim—particularly those regarding the falsity of Handshoe's statements—are not particularly well-pleaded for at least three reasons.

First, the First Amended Statement of Claim is unclear regarding whether all, or just some, of Handshoe's statements are false. At the outset, it indicates that Handshoe's statements were "defamatory by both true and false innuendo." (emphasis added). In explaining the particular statements at issue, the First Amended Statement of Claim repeatedly emphasizes that the statements were "defamatory," in that they would tend to lower one's opinion of Trout Point. But it specifically alleges falsity with respect to only a limited few of the statements, and offers no facts to rebut or undermine most of Handshoe's statements. Although Trout Point includes some generic allegations of falsity towards the end of its defamation claim—* * * this catch-all language offers little guidance regarding whether some or all of the statements are allegedly false, especially in light of the First Amended Statement of Claim's earlier reference to "true innuendo" as a source of harm.

For this reason, Trout Point cannot show that a state or federal court in Mississippi would grant a default judgment based on the First Amended Statement of Claim. Indeed, a Mississippi court has affirmed dismissal where a complaint failed to specify which of a series of statements constituted slander. * * * Similarly, here, a Mississippi court could deny a default judgment because the First Amended Statement of Claim does not clearly and specifically allege that each of the relevant statements is false.

Second, some of the publications at issue are statements of unverifiable opinion. For example, Trout Point based its defamation claim, in part, on the allegation that Handshoe used "unabashed anti-gay, anti-homosexual rhetoric and rants of the defendants" intended to "engender[ ] discrimination and hatred." The First Amended Statement of Claim complains that Handshoe referred to Perret and Leary as " 'girls,' 'blow buddies,' 'queer f-g scum,' and 'b-tches,' published more than one reference to a gay-themed movie, and posted video clips of movies and music videos commonly associated with gay stereotypes." While less grotesque, many of the other statements at issue also involve expressions of opinion; for example, that Trout Point had "Champagne taste on a beer budget," that Perret and Leary were a "litigious bunch," and that the Nova Scotia action was "foolish and frivolous."

Though offensive, these statements generally are not actionable in Mississippi. The Mississippi Supreme Court has recognized that "name calling and verbal abuse are to be taken as statements of opinion, not fact, and therefore will not give rise to an action for libel." * * * Here, although some of Handshoe's opinions certainly imply facts (e.g., that Trout Point was involved in the Aaron Broussard scandal), his bare "linguistic slings and arrows" do not. Indeed, counsel for Trout Point conceded at oral argument that Handshoe's offensive insults and opinion statements would not be actionable in Mississippi. Thus, Trout Point cannot show that a state or federal court in Mississippi would grant a default judgment on these opinion-based allegations.

Finally, a state or federal court in Mississippi could view some of the allegations in the First Amended Statement of Claim as legal conclusions, as opposed to well-pleaded facts. The Mississippi Supreme Court's decision in DynaSteel illustrates this point. 611 So.2d at 985. There, the court held that punitive damages were not recoverable on a default judgment because the allegations in the complaint, taken as true, were insufficient to support a finding of bad faith. Id. It stated:

* * * Given the legal significance attached to the word "falsity," Mississippi law requires Trout Point to do more than merely cry "false" to prove its claim. Therefore, even deemed admitted, the allegations likely would have been insufficient—without subsequent evidence, analysis, and fact-finding—to satisfy Trout Point's burden in a Mississippi court.

For these three reasons, Trout Point failed to show that the allegations in the First Amended Statement of Claim, standing alone and taken as true, would be sufficient to support a defamation claim in a Mississippi court. Trout Point asserts a second ground to establish falsity, however: the Nova Scotia Court's purported factual findings that Handshoe's statements were false and malicious. We turn next to that issue.

2.

As a threshold matter, the plain language of the SPEECH Act suggests that the purported "factual findings" of the Nova Scotia Court are irrelevant to the enforceability inquiry. The critical question is not whether the Nova Scotia Court found falsity, but rather whether a state or federal court in Mississippi faced with the allegations in the First Amended Statement of Claim would have done so. See § 4102(a)(1)(B) (requiring the party seeking to enforce the foreign defamation judgment to establish that the defendant "would have been found liable for defamation by a domestic court applying the [F]irst [A]mendment to the Constitution of the United States and the constitution and law of the State in which the domestic court is located"). Moreover, the Nova Scotia Court issued its factual findings at a damages hearing that occurred after it had already granted default judgment in favor of Trout Point.

But even assuming, arguendo, that the Nova Scotia Court's factual findings have some bearing on the enforceability inquiry, they are insufficient to demonstrate falsity. As the district court summarized, the Nova Scotia Court's oral decision "does not contain specific findings of fact with respect to the falsity of Handshoe's statements." Indeed, despite repeated entreaties at oral argument, Trout Point could not identify a single specific allegation in the Statement of Claim that the Nova Scotia Court found was actually false. Rather, the Nova Scotia Court noted generically that some statements were "erroneous," but remained silent as to the truth of others. The only statement with arguably global reach is that Handshoe's conduct was "outrageous" in the "face of true facts" about Trout Point. This simply is not direct enough to constitute a meaningful factual finding that all of Handshoe's statements were false.

In analyzing the Nova Scotia Court's oral opinion and purported factual findings, it is important to note that the court based its damages award on allegations and evidence that a Mississippi court would not have credited. * * * In sum, much of the conduct that underlies the Nova Scotia Court's oral opinion and damages award would not give rise to relief in Mississippi.

IV.

Before we conclude, we note that the SPEECH Act also contains a "jurisdictional considerations" provision, which requires "the party seeking recognition or enforcement of the foreign judgment" to show that "the exercise of personal jurisdiction by the foreign court comported with the due process requirements that are imposed on domestic courts by the Constitution of the United States." § 4102(b).

Handshoe asserts that Trout Point also failed to satisfy this provision because the Nova Scotia Court's exercise of personal jurisdiction over him did not comport with our nation's due process requirements. He makes a strong argument that Nova Scotia was not the "focal point" of the statements that preceded the First Amended Statement of Claim. * * *.

V.

For the above-stated reasons, Trout Point failed to satisfy its burden to show that either (1) Canadian law offers as much free speech protection as the United States Constitution and Mississippi state law, or (2) a Mississippi court presented with the same facts and circumstances would have found Handshoe liable for defamation. Accordingly, we hold that the Nova Scotia Judgment is unrecognizable and unenforceable. We AFFIRM.

NOTES AND QUESTIONS

1. *Trout Point Lodge* was the first appellate level ruling issued under the Act, affirming a lower court decision holding that a Nova Scotia Judgment was unrecognizable and unenforceable in the United States. As explained in the case and the prefatory note (see supra page 984), the SPEECH Act was a response to the perceived threat of "libel tourism"—"a

form of international forum-shopping in which a plaintiff chooses to file a defamation claim in a foreign jurisdiction with more favorable substantive law." However, many commentators have argued that the SPEECH Act goes too far and "systematic parochialism has the potential to cause harms that are greater than might be anticipated, because the Act's broad language makes it applicable to far more than just libel tourism." Mark D. Rosen, The SPEECH Act's Unfortunate Parochialism: Of Libel Tourism and Legitimate Pluralism, 53 Va. J. Int'l L. 99 (2012). For a thorough discussion on how American legislation, such as the SPEECH Act, is exporting American values and may negatively affect foreign recognition of American judgments, see Peter Hay, Favoring Local Interests—Some Justizkonflikt-Issues in American Perspective, *in* Grenzen überwinden-Prinzipien bewahren, Festschrift für Bernd von Hoffmann 634, 642–47 (Herbert Kronke & Karsten Thorn eds., 2011). Could any foreign libel judgments survive and receive recognition under this Act? Was *Trout Point Lodge* even an instance of libel tourism? See Partlett & McDonald, supra page 985.

7. REMEDIES

(1) *Damages.* As with most other torts the prime remedy for defamation is damages. For libel and for slander per se, it was presumed at common law that there were "general damages," the damages were "at large," and thus the jury were permitted to estimate the harm to plaintiff's reputation that they thought the defamation had caused, without the need of evidence to support the conclusion. This meant that there was little control by the court over the amount that the jury assessed. As a result of the holding in *Gertz v. Robert Welch*, Inc., supra page 944, damages were confined to "compensation for actual injury" unless plaintiff establishes actual malice. But see Dun & Bradstreet v. Greenmoss, supra page 953, where the common law position of presumed damages is restored for publications which are not of public concern.

To the extent that damages cover pecuniary, or out-of-pocket loss, an award of money damages is entirely appropriate, as it purports to make the plaintiff whole. These are the special damages that must be proved in the case of slander, if it is not actionable per se. The Supreme Court has explained, however, that "actual injury," may include "impairment of reputation and standing in the community, personal humiliation, and mental anguish and suffering," so long as there is adequate proof of these matters. This gives the court some control over the action of the jury and it remains to be seen whether the Supreme Court will take further steps to prevent the award of very large verdicts against news media in a manner that makes them a figurative sand bag. Significantly, most of the cases that the Court has entertained have involved large sums of money that can constitute a heavy burden on the news media.

There is something anomalous in attempting to convert general impairment of standing in the community, personal humiliation and mental anguish into a money award. What kind of conversion standard can there be? Would a better approach be to limit recovery to pecuniary loss but include within this concept the plaintiff's litigation expenses, including reasonable attorney's fees? This would utilize a much more objective standard and would pay the out-of-pocket costs to the plaintiff in vindicating his name. It might also have the effect of discouraging efforts to make the prosecution of the suit so expensive as to force the plaintiff to discontinue it. For a criticism of defamation law's preoccupation with money damages as a vindication of reputation, see John G. Fleming, Retraction and Reply: Alternative Remedies for Defamation, 12 Univ. Brit. Colum. L. Rev. 15 (1978).

Mitigation of Damages. Provocation by the plaintiff is generally regarded as admissible for the purpose of mitigating punitive damages. Palmer v. Mahin, 120 Fed. 737 (8th Cir. 1903). Under a minority holding, it may also be considered in mitigation of compensatory damages. Craney v. Donovan, 102 A. 640 (Conn. 1917); Conroy v. Fall River Herald News Co., 28 N.E.2d 729 (Mass. 1940). Where the defamatory statement would not be believed, the resultant damages are reduced: Bishop v. New York Times Co., 135 N.E. 845 (N.Y. 1922). Note that prior publication of the same defamatory matter is not considered in mitigating damages, cf., Sun Printing & Publishing Ass'n v. Schneck, 98 F. 925 (2d Cir. 1900).

The "Libel-Proof" Plaintiff. Plaintiffs may possess such an atrocious reputation that they are, in effect, immune from libel in a given suit. "The libel-proof plaintiff doctrine is to be applied with caution, since few plaintiffs will have so bad a reputation that they are not entitled to obtain redress for defamatory statements, even if their damages cannot be quantified and they receive only nominal damages." Guccione v. Hustler Magazine, Inc., 800 F.2d 298, 303 (2d Cir. 1986) (citations omitted). In Cerasani v. Sony Corp., 991 F.Supp. 343 (S.D.N.Y. 1998), the court found that plaintiff's reputation was so "badly tarnished" that he was "libel proof." Plaintiff was, the court found, a "convicted racketeer, Mafia associate, bank robber, and drug dealer." An unsuccessful prosecution did not rehabilitate him. See also Ray v. Time, Inc., 452 F.Supp. 618 (W.D. Tenn. 1976), *aff'd*, 582 F.2d 1280 (6th Cir. 1978) (holding that James Earl Ray, the purported assassin of Dr. Martin Luther King, Jr., was effectively libel proof). Lamb v. Rizzo, 391 F.3d 1133 (10th Cir.2004) (doctrine applied to convicted murderer and kidnapper). Defendant may plead true damaging facts relevant to the plaintiff's reputation but those must be "closely related to the false ones." The requirement of relevance guards against the introduction of evidence of a broad and boundless litany of plaintiff's discreditable acts of all kinds. Haynes v. Alfred A. Knopf, Inc., 8 F.3d 1222, 1229 (7th Cir. 1993).

Incremental Harm Doctrine. Suppose the plaintiff pleads as defamatory only part of a published work, while the rest of the publication contains other harmful but true statements. Under the incremental harm doctrine, if the defamatory portion does not go significantly beyond the harm done by the non-pleaded portions (if the defamatory portion adds no more than "incremental" additional harm), an action for defamation will not lie. The doctrine is a specific application of the doctrine that a plaintiff may be "libel proof." In Masson v. New Yorker Magazine, Inc., 895 F.2d 1535 (9th Cir. 1989), the Ninth Circuit relied on this "incremental harm" doctrine as an alternative basis for affirming the decision of the District Court. The Court ruled that "[g]iven the * * * many provocative, bombastic statements indisputably made by Masson and quoted by Malcolm, the additional damage caused [by the pleaded imputation] was nominal or non-existent, rendering the defamation claim as to this quote nonactionable." Id, at 1541. On appeal the Supreme Court stated that this "incremental harm" doctrine is not part of First Amendment jurisprudence although it may be accepted under state law. 501 U.S. 496 (1991). The Ninth Circuit noted that the doctrine was one of state law and quoted the words of then-Judge Scalia in Liberty Lobby, Inc. v. Anderson, 746 F.2d 1563, 1568 (D.C. Cir. 1984).

"The theory must be rejected because it rests upon the assumption that one's reputation is a monolith, which stands or falls in its entirety. The law, however, proceeds upon the optimistic premise that there is a little bit of good in all of us—or perhaps upon the pessimistic assumption that no matter how bad someone is, he can always be worse. . . . ('He was a liar and a thief, but for all that he was a good family man.')"

Judge Scalia concluded that the incremental harm doctrine is simply a "bad idea." *Liberty Lobby*, 746 F.2d at 1569. The Ninth Circuit agreed it was a "bad idea" and that therefore the incremental harm doctrine was not an "element of the California libel law." See also Maguire v. Journal Sentinel, Inc., 605 N.W.2d 881 (Wisc. Ct. App. 1999) (noting that Wisconsin has yet to adopt an incremental harm defense to defamation).

Other states have retained the incremental harm doctrine. See Tonnessen v. Denver Publ'g Co., 5 P.3d 959 (Colo. Ct. App. 2000); Jewell v. NYP Holdings, Inc., 23 F. Supp. 2d 348 (S.D.N.Y. 1998). (when defamatory and non-defamatory statements both referred to the same incident, harm was incremental); (applying the doctrine but finding that the defamatory portions added more than incremental harm when, compared to true statement that plaintiff was the "prime suspect," they stated that the noose was tightening" around him and that his arrest was only "a matter of time").

Bad Reputation. Evidence of a bad reputation may reduce the damages a plaintiff can recover. Generally, that evidence of bad reputation must relate to the content of the supposed defamation claimed. Towle v. St. Albans Publg Co., 165 A.2d 363 (Vt. 1960). "A defendant in an action for slander may introduce, for the purpose of reducing the damages, evidence to show that the plaintiff's general character or reputation is bad, but evidence of particular facts tending to establish the plaintiff's reputation is inadmissible." Small v. Chronical & Gazette Publishing Co., 267, 74 A.2d 544, 545 (N.H. 1950); see also Snively v. Record Publ'g Co., 198 P. 1, 7 (Cal. 1921). In Sclar v. Resnik, 192 Iowa 669, 185 N.W. 273 (1921), a defendant was charged with defamation in calling a plaintiff "a whore and an immoral woman." The defendant was allowed to enter evidence of the plaintiff's reputation, including that she was associated with a "house of ill fame" and was generally known to be an "inmate" of that establishment, to mitigate the harm of his statement to her reputation. Rumors are admissible if shown to be sufficiently widespread to affect the plaintiff's reputation. Blickenstaff v. Perrin, 27 Ind. 527 (1867); Stuart v. News Publ'g Co., 51 A. 709 (N.J.L. 1902). The law is a reflection of defamation's foundational concept that reputation is protected even if that reputation may not be deserved.

Punitive Damages. Punitive damages were freely awarded at common law, if "malice" in the literal sense of that term were shown. Gertz v. Robert Welch, Inc., supra page 944, has placed some limitations on this. It seems clear that in the absence of "malice" in the constitutional sense—i.e., knowledge or reckless disregard as to falsity—they cannot be awarded. The Court did not expressly hold whether they can be awarded then, but it seems later to have assumed that they can and *Dun and Bradstreet* permits such an award in the private figure/private speech context. Herbert v. Lando, 441 U.S. 153, 162 n.7 (1979). See, awarding punitive damages, Ayala v. Washington, 679 A.2d 1057 (D.C. 1996) (pilot plaintiff's defendant girlfriend told his employer and the FAA that he smoked marijuana during off-duty hours). Newspaper Publ'g Corp. v. Burke, 224 S.E.2d 132 (Va. 1976). See generally Note, Punitive Damages and Libel Law, 98 HARV. L. REV. 847 (1985). The Supreme Court in Pac. Mutual Life Ins. Co. v. Haslip, 499 US. 1 (1991), upheld as constitutional Alabama's scheme for awarding punitive damages in a case outside the defamation and First Amendment arena. The Court in its decision in State Farm Mutual Auto. Ins. Co. v. Campbell, 538 U.S. 408 (2003), page 578, provided the constitutional principles. Are these principles likely to differ in the defamation context?

Nominal Damages. Gertz v. Robert Welch held that a plaintiff cannot recover unless he proves "actual injury." If he proves that the statement is both defamatory and false, but does not prove actual injury, can he recover nominal damages? The Supreme Court has not ruled, nor does it indicate whether he can bring the initial action for the purpose of recovering only nominal damages and thus vindicating his name. It would seem, however, that the latter action ought to be allowed, and even favored. See discussion in Hearst Corp. v. Hughes, 466 A.2d 486 (Md. 1983).

(2) *Declaratory Relief.* The action brought solely for nominal damages, referred to immediately above, essentially seeks declaratory relief. Its purpose is to obtain a judicial determination that the statement about the plaintiff is false, and thus to vindicate his reputation—to make him whole, as far as the law can. Marc. A. Franklin, Good Names and Bad Law: A Critique of Libel Law and a Proposal, 18 U.S.F. L. Rev. 1 (1983), Anna L. Moore, Note, The Defamed Reputation: Will Declaratory Judgment Bill Provide Vindication?, 13 J. Legis. 72 (1986).

In a declaratory proceeding of this sort, should all of the requirements of an action for compensatory damage be imposed? If the plaintiff is not seeking to recover damages, but only a ruling that the statement was false, should he have to show that defendant was at fault regarding its falsity? Do privileges serve a useful purpose here? Would it be feasible to have the trial judge pose two separate questions to the jury—(1) was the statement false, and (2) was the defendant at fault regarding its falsity?

Judge Leval, who presided over Westmoreland v. CBS Inc., 596 F. Supp. 1170 (S.D.N.Y. 1984), has strongly supported a form of "no-money, no-fault suit," as "enhancing the primary object of the law of defamation: the restoration of a falsely damaged reputation." Pierre N. Leval, The No-Money, No-Fault. Libel Suit: Keeping Sullivan in Its Proper Place, 101 HARV. L. REV. 1287 (1988).

There were a number of trial innovations used in the famous *Westmoreland* and *Sharon* trials. One of special interest here was the use of "tripartite verdicts" in *Sharon.* Judge Sofaer instructed the jury to render separate special verdicts on whether the communication was defamatory, whether it was false, and whether the defendant was motivated by "actual malice." The verdicts were returned on separate days. Uses of this technique should be easily apparent.

(3) *Self-help.* "The first remedy of any victim of defamation is self-help—using available opportunities to contradict the lie or correct the error and thereby to minimize its adverse impact on reputation." Gertz v. Robert Welch, Inc., 418 U.S. 323, 344 (1974). Thus, the defamed party may make a response to the defamatory statement about him—provided he can find a suitable medium for making the response.

Right-of-Response Statutes. Several states have passed statutes requiring a public communications medium to give a right of response to a person who claims that he has been defamed by it. A Florida statute to this effect was held unconstitutional in Miami Herald Publ'g. Co. v. Tornillo, 418 U.S. 241 (1974). While the particular statute was overly broad and did not limit the requirement to cases in which there was a claim of actual defamation, the holding seems broad enough to cover a more limited statute. What about a statute requiring a newspaper to publish a news item of a defamation judgment obtained against it?

The person claiming to have been defamed may also go to the person publishing the defamation, explain that there has been a mistake and request a correction or a retraction. On the effect of refusal to retract after notice of falsity as evidence of "malice," see Morgan v. Dun & Bradstreet, Inc., 421 F.2d 1241 (5th Cir. 1970).

Retraction Statutes. There are retraction statutes in about thirty states. They vary considerably in their provisions, as to the types of defamation covered, the requirement of notice, the types of plaintiffs and defendants covered, and the effect of compliance. See, e.g., FLA. STAT. § 770. 02. Some may be outdated as a result of constitutional developments, as in applying only to "innocent misrepresentation," or in limiting recovery to "actual damages."

A retraction, to be effective, must be unequivocal and not partial or hesitant and hypothetical. Goolsby v. Forum Printing Co., 135 N.W. 661 (N.D. 1912). (retraction not full and fair when article entitled "Blind Pigger's Frightful Crime. Ran Amuck at Geneseo and Killed One Man" retracted with "It is now asserted that there was no murder. . . . The sensational story put Mr. Goolsby in the limelight in a manner that he does not desire."). Indeed, an "evasive" and "incomplete" retraction may be grounds for punitive damages. Burnett v. Nat'l Enquirer, Inc., 144

Cal.App.3d 991, 193 Cal. Rptr. 206 (1983), appeal dismissed, 465 U.S. 1014 (1984).

To the effect that the *Tornillo* case on right-of-reply statutes does not indicate the unconstitutionality of retraction statutes, see Brennan, J., concurring, in Miami Herald Pub. Co. v. Tornillo, 418 U.S. 241, 258 (1974). The Uniform Correction or Clarification of Defamation Act of 1993 (National Conference of Commissioners on Uniform State Laws) proposed mechanisms for correction and clarification to mend the "flaws in current law by providing strong incentives for parties in a defamation as an alternative to costly litigation."

(4) *Injunctive Relief.* Ever since the decision in Near v. Minnesota, 283 U.S. 697 (1931), it has been recognized that prior restraint of a publication runs afoul of the First Amendment. (On the *Near* case, see the thorough study in F. Friendly, Minnesota Rag (1981)). Nevertheless, it remains possible that injunctive relief might become a suitable supplement to other relief when it has been formally determined in court that a statement is both defamatory and false, and the defendant persists in continuing to publish it. An injunction, carefully worded so as not to be too broad, might be both appropriate and constitutional. In Tory v. Cochran, 544 U.S. 734 (2005) the United States Supreme Court granted certiorari to hear the issue of the constitutionality of the grant of a permanent injunction prohibiting continuing libels directed against the famous late trial lawyer, Johnnie Cochran. Cochran's death occurred before the appeal was heard, and the primary purpose of the injunction to prevent the coercion of Mr. Cochran lapsed. Thus the court in this light found the injunction an overly broad prior restraint upon speech. Common law courts weigh heavily the public interest in free speech when exercising discretions in granting injunctions:

The above remedial rubrics are brought together in the form of a Model Communicative Torts Act that seeks to limit and clarify the law, weigh First Amendment concerns, establish procedures, and remedies reflecting parties' realistic expectations, and promote as central features limited damages and encouragement of corrections and retractions. The Model Communicative Torts Act, 47 WASH. & LEE L. REV. 1 (1990).

The Report of the Libel Reform Project of the Annenberg Washington Program, Proposal for Reform of Libel Law (1988) sets forth a proposed Libel Reform Act that incorporates, among other reforms, retraction and reply, a declaratory judgment option and abolition of punitive damages. Anderson, Is Libel Law Worth Reforming?, 140 U. Pa. L. Rev. 487, 550–554 (1991), views the present law as a failure in that it denies defamation victims any remedy, but at the same time chills speech by encouraging high litigation costs and occasional large judgments. Anderson calls on the Supreme Court to instigate reform that would bring uniformity and reduce even more the role of the jury by a greater resort to summary judgment and judicial review, and perhaps take the assessment of damages out of the jury's hands.

CHAPTER 18

PRIVACY

The recognition and development of the "right of privacy" is perhaps the outstanding illustration of the influence of legal journals upon the courts. Prior to 1890, no English or American court had ever granted relief expressly based upon the invasion of this right, although there were cases that seem in retrospect to have been groping in that direction. For instance Judge Cooley had coined the phrase "the right to be let alone." See, e.g., DeMay v. Roberts, supra, page 106, Hardin v. Harshfield, 12 S.W. 779 (Ky.1890) (loss of marriage engagement caused by defendant's spreading a true tale of plaintiff's embarrassing combination of expelling *flatus* in a public place and her *lapsus linguae*—treated as slander).

"The Right to Privacy," written by Samuel D. Warren and Louis D. Brandeis, in 1890, was published in 4 Harvard Law Review 193. The article discussed several cases in which relief had been granted on the basis of defamation, breach of confidence, or of an implied contract for the publication of letters, portraits and the like. It concluded that these cases were, in reality, founded upon a broader principle entitled to separate recognition: the right of a private individual to be let alone and protected from unauthorized publicity in essentially private affairs.

One of the first states to consider the doctrine advanced by Warren and Brandeis was New York. After two lower courts apparently had accepted the article and recognized the right of privacy, it fell into the unfriendly hands of the Court of Appeals in Roberson v. Rochester Folding Box Co., 171 N.Y. 538, 64 N.E. 442 (1902), where the defendant used a picture of an attractive young woman in an advertisement without her permission. The court rejected the entire doctrine, as it denied the existence of any "right of privacy" at common law. It feared any recognition of such legal fiction would ignite a "vast amount of litigation," a slippery slope that would involve not only pictures, but "a comment upon one's looks, conduct, domestic relations or habits." It said that any such change in the law must be made by the legislature. The decision was met immediately with widespread public disapproval, which led to the enactment of a statute the following year, now New York Civil Rights Law §§ 50–51. It prohibits the use of the name, portrait or picture of any living person without prior written consent for "advertising purposes" or for "purposes of trade." Similar statutes were adopted in Virginia, Oklahoma, and Utah.

Three years later the same question was presented in Pavesich v. New England Life Ins. Co., 122 Ga. 190, 50 S.E. 68 (1905), when the defendant used the plaintiff's name and picture, together with a bogus testimonial, in an insurance advertisement. The court rejected the *Roberson* case, accepted the views of Warren and Brandeis, and recognized the existence of a distinct right of privacy. This became the leading case, but authority remained divided until the 1930's when the tide set in strongly in favor of recognition.

Today the right of privacy is clearly recognized by all but two or three states in one form or another, although not explicitly. Some states limit it to commercial uses of the plaintiff's name or likeness. Elsewhere in the common law world the courts generally refused, until recently, to recognize a tort for invasion of privacy. See Wainwright v. Home Office, [2004] 2 A.C. 406 (refusing to articulate a separate cause of action for invasion of privacy). Dean Prosser made a profound contribution to the law in synthesizing and categorizing the case law discerning that the law falls into four distinct rubrics that are exemplified by the following principal cases in this chapter. See Prosser, Privacy, 48 Calif.L.Rev. 383 (1960).

In the age of the internet the protection of data privacy has loomed large as an issue of social concern and legal regulation. Privacy is a protean term. No single definition is capable of capturing its scope. The term data privacy refers to the sharing, use, and collection of personal data. See Daniel Solove, Conceptualizing Privacy, 90 Cal. L. Rev. 1087 (2002). The American Law Institute has recently embarked on a new project, the Restatement of Data Privacy Principles. The process of drafts and comments has begun. The principles are drawn around Fair Information Practice Principles (FIPPs). These are designed to establish duties and responsibilities for entities that process personal data. They describe also the rights and duties that people should have regarding their data. There is thick jurisprudence around these principles, the sources of which are legislation, agency practices, the common law, and comparative international law and practice. This chapter addresses a subset of these sources, that is, the law of torts. It is a subset that has a long history and one that is most fraught in its capacity to clash with the constitutional protection of free speech. Whether or not a constitutional right of information privacy is recognized is debatable. The most recent treatment by the United States Supreme Court gives encouragement with a strong caveat. National Aeronautics and Space Administration v. Nelson, 131 S. Ct. 746 (2011). The Restatement process and the exigencies of international commerce and the drive of technology will give a great impetus to the field of data protection. If the past is prologue, the trumping power of the First Amendment will be a major influence in the shaping of the law in the next decade. Information that is of public interest attracts constitutional protection, the latest example of which is the case at the end of this chapter, Snyder v. Phelps, 562 U.S. 443 (2011).

Joe Dickerson & Associates, LLC v. Dittmar

Supreme Court of Colorado, En Banc., 2001.
34 P.3d 995.

JUSTICE BENDER delivered the Opinion of the Court.

I. INTRODUCTION

This appeal involves the tort of invasion of privacy by appropriation of another's name or likeness. The defendant published an article in a newsletter, identifying the plaintiff by name and including her picture, which detailed his investigation of the plaintiff's theft of bearer bonds and her subsequent criminal conviction. The plaintiff sued the defendant claiming that her privacy was invaded by appropriation of her name and likeness.

Ruling on the defendant's motion for summary judgment, the trial court held that even if the tort were cognizable in Colorado, the plaintiff's appropriation claim failed because she presented no evidence that her name or likeness had any value.

We hold that the tort of invasion of privacy by appropriation of another's name or likeness is cognizable under Colorado law. The elements of this tort are: (1) the defendant used the plaintiff's name or likeness; (2) the use of the plaintiff's name or likeness was for the defendant's own purposes or benefit, commercially or otherwise; (3) the plaintiff suffered damages; and (4) the defendant caused the damages incurred. A plaintiff's claim of invasion of privacy by appropriation of her name and likeness will not succeed, however, if the defendant's use of the plaintiff's name and likeness is privileged under the First Amendment. In this case, the defendant is entitled to summary judgment as a matter of law because we find that the defendant's use of the plaintiff's name and likeness in the context of an article about the plaintiff's crime and felony conviction is a matter of legitimate public concern and is, therefore, privileged. Hence, we reverse the court of appeals and return this case to that court with directions to reinstate the trial court's order granting summary judgment to the defendant.

II. FACTS AND PROCEEDINGS BELOW

Defendants Joe Dickerson & Associates, LLC and Joe Dickerson were hired during a child custody dispute to investigate plaintiff Rosanne Marie (Brock) Dittmar. During the course of this investigation, Dickerson noticed inconsistencies in the way Dittmar came to possess certain bearer bonds. He reported the results of his investigation to authorities. Thereafter, Dittmar was charged with and convicted of felony theft of these bonds.

Dickerson publishes a newsletter called "The Dickerson Report," which is sent free of charge to law enforcement agencies, financial institutions, law firms, and others. This report contains articles about financial fraud investigations, tips for avoiding fraud, activities of private investigator boards, information about upcoming conferences, and the like. Dickerson ran a series of articles in the report under the heading "Fraud DuJour." This column included such articles as "Fraud DuJour—Wireless Cable Investments," "Fraud DuJour—Prime Bank Instruments," and the article at issue here, "Fraud—DuJour Five Cases, 100%+ Recovery."

In this article, Dickerson related the role his firm played in five cases in recovering 100%—and in one case more than 100%—of the value of stolen assets. Dittmar's case was discussed first. Dickerson's article detailed how Dittmar, who worked as a secretary at a brokerage firm, stole a customer's bearer bonds from her place of employment and cashed them for personal use. In addition, the article described Dickerson's investigation of Dittmar, the fact that the jury convicted Dittmar of theft, and how the court ordered her to pay restitution to the theft victim. This article appears on the front page of The Dickerson Report, mentions Dittmar by name, and includes her photograph.

Dittmar sued Dickerson on a number of tort theories including defamation, outrageous conduct, and invasion of privacy by appropriation of another's name or likeness. The trial court granted summary judgment for Dickerson on all claims. With respect to Dittmar's claim for invasion of privacy by appropriation of another's name or likeness, the only claim relevant to this appeal, the trial court noted that Colorado has not explicitly recognized this tort. The trial court granted Dickerson's motion for summary judgment because, even assuming the tort was cognizable under Colorado law, Dittmar "present[ed] no evidence that her name or likeness had any value." The trial court noted that, under the definition of the tort in the Second Restatement of Torts, appropriation requires more than mere publication of the plaintiff's name or likeness:

> The value of a plaintiff's name is not appropriated by mere mention of it, or by reference to it in connection with legitimate mention of his public activities; nor is the value of his likeness appropriated when it is published for purposes other than taking advantage of his reputation, prestige, or other value associated with him, for purposes of publicity.

Restatement (Second) of Torts 652C, comment *d* (1976).

Dittmar appealed the trial court's dismissal of her appropriation claim. The court of appeals agreed with the trial court that this tort requires the defendant to appropriate certain values associated with the plaintiff's name or likeness: "In order for liability to exist, the defendant must have appropriated to his or her own use or benefit the reputation, prestige, social or commercial standing, public interest or other values of the plaintiff's name or likeness." [C] The court of appeals concluded, however, that the plaintiff raised issues of material fact regarding different aspects of the tort, namely the purpose of the publication and whether the use benefited Dickerson. [C] These issues of fact, the court of appeals reasoned, precluded summary judgment in favor of Dickerson. Hence, that court reversed the trial court's grant of summary judgment. [C]

Dickerson petitioned this court for certiorari on three issues: (1) whether the tort of invasion of privacy based on appropriation of another's name or likeness is cognizable under Colorado law; (2) if so, whether an appropriation claim requires evidence that the plaintiff's name has an exploitable value; and (3) whether the article constituted constitutionally protected speech.

We agree with the court of appeals' recognition of this tort but we disagree that a plaintiff must provide evidence of the value of her name and likeness when she seeks only personal damages. Because we find that the defendant's publication of the plaintiff's name and likeness in the context of an article about her crime and felony conviction is privileged under the First Amendment, we hold that the defendant is entitled to summary judgment as a matter of law.

III. ANALYSIS

A. Overview of the Appropriation Tort

In 1890, an influential law review article outlined the contours of the tort of invasion of privacy. Samuel D. Warren & Louis D. Brandeis,

The Right To Privacy, 4 Harv. L.Rev. 193 (1890). Warren and Brandeis suggested that increased abuses by the press required a remedy that would protect private individuals from mental distress and anguish. [C] They proposed that the right of privacy would protect a person's rights in their appearance, sayings, acts, and personal relations. [C] To Warren and Brandeis, the right of privacy did not involve property so much as the "more general immunity of the person—the right to one's personality." [C] In short, they desired to protect the individual's right "to be let alone." [C]

Over the years, almost every state has recognized, either statutorily or by case law, that one way that an individual's privacy can be invaded is when a defendant appropriates a plaintiff's name or likeness for that defendant's own benefit. While the exact parameters of this tort of invasion of privacy by appropriation of identity vary from state to state, it has always been clear that a plaintiff could recover for personal injuries such as mental anguish and injured feelings resulting from an appropriation. [C]

There has been a great deal of debate, however, over the ability of a plaintiff to recover for pecuniary loss resulting from an unauthorized commercial exploitation of her name or likeness. Courts initially had difficulty reconciling how a celebrity, well-known to the public, could recover under the misleading heading of "privacy." [C] Such plaintiffs often sought damages for commercial injury that resulted when defendants used plaintiffs' identities in advertising. [C]

Therefore, in the context of pecuniary damages, some courts and commentators have resorted by analogy to property law and have recognized a "right of publicity" which permits plaintiffs to recover for injury to the commercial value of their identities. [C]

In a seminal law review article, William Prosser described invasion of privacy as a complex of four related torts: (1) unreasonable intrusion upon the seclusion of another; (2) publicity that places another in a false light before the public; (3) public disclosure of embarrassing private facts about another; and (4) appropriation of another's name or likeness. [C] The first three of these four torts protect only personal interests. [C] But, perhaps in response to the simmering legal debate about the scope of the protection afforded by the appropriation tort, Prosser defined the appropriation tort as protective of both personal and economic interests. In doing so, Prosser emphasized the proprietary nature of the appropriation tort without removing it from the framework of privacy: "The interest protected is not so much a mental as a proprietary one, in the exclusive use of the plaintiff's name and likeness as an aspect of his identity." [C]

Thus, Prosser's formulation of the appropriation tort subsumed the two types of injuries—personal and commercial—into one cause of action that existed under the misleading label of "privacy." The privacy label is misleading both because the interest protected (name and/or likeness) is not "private" in the same way as the interests protected by other areas of privacy law and because the appropriation tort often applies to protect well-known "public" persons. Despite these problems, Prosser's view of the appropriation tort was ultimately incorporated into the Second Restatement of Torts. Restatement (Second) of Torts 652C.

Prosser's emphasis on the property-like aspects of the tort has led to a great deal of confusion in the law of privacy. [c] Some courts have partially rejected the Prosser formulation, choosing to distinguish claims for injury to personal feelings caused by an unauthorized use of a plaintiff's identity ("right of privacy") from claims seeking redress for pecuniary damages caused by an appropriation of the commercial value of the identity ("right of publicity"). [C] Thus, in those jurisdictions, the right of publicity is viewed as an independent doctrine distinct from the right of privacy. This view finds support in the Third Restatement of Unfair Competition, which recognizes that the right of publicity protects against commercial injury, while the right of privacy appropriation tort protects against personal injury. Restatement (Third) of Unfair Competition 346, cmts. *a* & *b* (1995).

Some jurisdictions attempt to follow Prosser's formulation of the tort and provide relief for both personal and commercial harm through a single common law or statutory cause of action. [C]

In other states, however, the parameters or even the existence of the appropriation tort remain undetermined. Such is the case in Colorado.

B. Colorado's Recognition of the Appropriation Tort

A brief review of the development of the tort of invasion of privacy in Colorado demonstrates that recognition of the appropriation tort is a natural outgrowth of our earlier precedent.

We have recognized that invasion of privacy is a cognizable tort under Colorado law. Rugg v. McCarty, 173 Colo. 170, 175, 476 P.2d 753, 755 (1970). In *Rugg,* we held that a plaintiff may assert a claim for invasion of privacy where a creditor unreasonably attempts collection of a debt in a manner that will foreseeably result in extreme mental anguish and embarrassment to the debtor.

Recently, we recognized the tort of invasion of privacy by unreasonable publicity given to another's private life. Ozer v. Borquez, 940 P.2d 371, 377 (Colo.1997). As in *Rugg,* we relied upon the fact that a majority of jurisdictions have recognized this tort. [C]

Similarly, the tort of invasion of privacy by appropriation of a plaintiff's name or likeness has been recognized throughout most of the United States, either statutorily or through the common law. Staruski v. Cont'l Tel. Co., 154 Vt. 568, 581 A.2d 266, 268 (1990) (stating that almost all states have recognized the tort). Further, neither the plaintiff nor the defendant in this case disputes that such a tort is cognizable in Colorado. We now hold that Colorado recognizes the tort of invasion of privacy by appropriation of an individual's name or likeness.

C. Elements of the Tort

Having recognized that the invasion of privacy by appropriation of name or likeness tort is recognized in Colorado, we now consider the elements of this tort.

The Second Restatement of Torts articulates the tort of appropriation of another's name or likeness, stating: "One who appropriates to his own use or benefit the name or likeness of another is subject to liability to the other for invasion of his privacy." Restatement (Second) of Torts 652C. The Colorado Civil Jury Instructions divide the tort into five distinct elements: (1) the defendant used the plaintiff's name or likeness; (2) the defendant sought to take advantage of the plaintiff's reputation, prestige, social or commercial standing, or any other value attached to the plaintiff's name, likeness, or identity; (3) the use of the plaintiff's name or likeness was for the defendant's own purposes or benefit, commercially or otherwise; (4) damages; and (5) causation. CJI-Civ. 4th 28:4 (2000).

The dispute in this case centers around the second element listed above, that defendant must appropriate "the reputation, prestige, social or commercial standing, or other value associated with the plaintiff's name or likeness." The defendant, Dickerson, argues that summary judgment in his favor is appropriate because the plaintiff, Dittmar, has presented no evidence that her name and likeness had any value.

The Colorado Civil Jury Instructions were developed from the comments to section 652C of the Second Restatement of Torts. Comment *c* implies that one element that a plaintiff must prove is that the plaintiff's identity has value, stating that "the defendant must have appropriated to his own use or benefit the reputation, prestige, social or commercial standing, public interest or other values of the plaintiff's name or likeness." Restatement (Second) of Torts 652C, comment *c*. Based on this and other comments to section 652C, some courts that follow the Restatement have explicitly required that one element of the tort is that the plaintiff's identity must have had pre-existing commercial value. [C]

However, as discussed above, the Restatement takes a property-oriented approach to the law of appropriation, an approach not wholly embraced in all jurisdictions. In the context of damages intended to remedy a proprietary injury to the plaintiff's commercial interests, it may make sense to require a plaintiff to prove the value of her identity, either as part of her proof of damages or as an element of the tort. This does not necessarily mean that the value of the plaintiff's identity is relevant when the plaintiff seeks damages only for her mental anguish.

It appears illogical to require the plaintiff to prove that her identity has value in order for her to recover for her personal damages. The market value of the plaintiff's identity is unrelated to the question of whether she suffered mental anguish as a result of the alleged wrongful appropriation. A plaintiff whose identity had no commercial value might still experience mental anguish based on an unauthorized use of her name and likeness. Of the numerous cases that have considered the tort of invasion of privacy by appropriation of the plaintiff's name or likeness, few have suggested that there is any requirement that the plaintiff prove the value of her identity as a prerequisite to recovery for mental suffering. Rather, a more typical summary of the law is found in Motschenbacher v. R.J. Reynolds Tobacco Co., where the 9th Circuit attempted to reconcile the relationship between commercial damages, mental anguish damages, and the requirement of value, stating:

> It is true that the injury suffered from an appropriation of the attributes of one's identity may be "mental and subjective"—in

> the nature of humiliation, embarrassment and outrage. However, where the identity appropriated has a commercial value, the injury may be largely, or even wholly, of an economic or material nature. [C]

Consistent with this approach, we decline to include the second element of value, as described by the Colorado Civil Jury Instructions, as a required element of the tort. Hence, we hold that the elements of an invasion of privacy by appropriation claim are: (1) the defendant used the plaintiff's name or likeness; (2) the use of the plaintiff's name or likeness was for the defendant's own purposes or benefit, commercially or otherwise; (3) the plaintiff suffered damages; and (4) the defendant caused the damages incurred.

Applying these elements in this case, we conclude that Dittmar, the plaintiff, alleged sufficient facts to satisfy each of the required elements. We do not require the plaintiff, who seeks only personal damages, to prove the value of her identity. Thus, her failure to do so is not fatal to her claim.

We note that the plaintiff does not seek commercial damages. Hence, we do not reach the question of whether Colorado permits recovery for commercial damages under either the rubric of privacy or under the right of publicity, or the question of whether the plaintiff must prove the value of her identity when she seeks commercial damages.

Thus, we hold that the trial court erred by granting summary judgment to the defendant on the grounds that the plaintiff failed to provide evidence of the value of her name or likeness.

D. Newsworthiness Privilege

Having defined the elements of the tort of invasion of privacy by appropriation of name or likeness, we now consider the defendant's argument that the trial court properly granted summary judgment in his favor because his publication of the plaintiff's name and picture was constitutionally protected speech as a matter of law. We note, as discussed below, that our review is de novo because this is a question of law.

Dickerson, the defendant, argues that his article relates to a matter of legitimate public concern and that, therefore, it is constitutionally protected speech. The plaintiff agrees that the circumstances surrounding her arrest and conviction are newsworthy and of legitimate public concern. She does not object to the fact that a local newspaper wrote articles regarding her crime, arrest, trial, and conviction, or that these articles identified her by name. Instead, she argues that the defendant's republication of these same facts in his newsletter, in conjunction with her name and picture, constitutes an invasion of her privacy. She characterizes Dickerson's newsletter as an "infomercial" that is "designed to promote Dickerson's private investigation firm and to attract business for the firm." Hence, she argues that the character of the defendant's article is primarily commercial and that it should not receive the protection of the First Amendment. Under the particular facts of this case, we disagree with the plaintiff's argument.

In the context of invasion of privacy by appropriation of name and likeness, there is a First Amendment privilege that permits the use of a plaintiff's name or likeness when that use is made in the context of, and reasonably relates to, a publication concerning a matter that is newsworthy or of legitimate public concern. [C]

In many situations, however, it is not altogether clear whether a particular use of a person's name or likeness is made for the purpose of communicating news or for the purpose of marketing a product or service. After all, many advertisements incorporate factual information as part of their sales message. [C] * * *

To resolve this question, courts must determine whether the character of the publication is primarily noncommercial, in which case the privilege will apply, or primarily commercial, in which case the privilege will not apply. [C] Under this test, an article that has commercial undertones may still be protected if it concerns a legitimate matter of public concern. [C] The question of whether a use of plaintiff's identity is primarily commercial or noncommercial is ordinarily decided as a question of law. [C] * * *

To determine whether the defendant's use of the plaintiff's name and likeness was for a primarily commercial or noncommercial purpose, we must first define "commercial speech." Commercial speech is speech that proposes a commercial transaction. [C] It is the content of the speech, not the motivation of the speaker, which determines whether particular speech is commercial. [C]

A profit motive does not transform a publication regarding a legitimate matter of public concern into commercial speech. [C] Many news publishers, including newspapers and magazines, are motivated by their desire to make a profit. Courts have repeatedly held that, in order to be actionable, the use of a plaintiff's identity must be more directly commercial than simply being printed in a periodical that operates for profit. [C] A contrary rule would preclude the publication of much news and other matters of legitimate public concern.

Applying the above principles to the instant case, we conclude that the defendant's publication was primarily noncommercial because it related to a matter of public concern, namely the facts of the plaintiff's crime and felony conviction. The defendant's article detailed how the plaintiff, who worked as a secretary at a brokerage firm, stole a customer's bearer bonds from her place of employment and cashed them for personal use. In addition, the article described the defendant's investigation of the plaintiff, the fact that the jury convicted the plaintiff of theft, and how the court ordered her to pay restitution to the theft victim. There can be no question that these details about the plaintiff's crime and conviction are matters of legitimate public concern. * * *

The fact that the defendant's article did not appear in a traditional newspaper does not change this result. We have previously stated that "[i]t is . . . well established that freedom of the press is not confined to newspapers or periodicals, but is a right of wide import and 'in its historic connotation comprehends every sort of publication which affords a vehicle of information and opinion.' " [C] This means that if the contents of an article are newsworthy when published by a local newspaper, then they do not cease to be newsworthy when subsequently communicated by a different sort of publisher.

Further, the fact that the defendant's reason for publishing the newspaper may have been his own commercial benefit does not necessarily render the speech "commercial." As noted above, a magazine or newspaper article is protected despite the fact that a publisher may publish a particular article in order to make a profit. Similarly, the defendant's speech is protected even if he intends it to result in profit to him, so long as the contents of the speech qualify for protection.

The defendant's profit motive does not affect the fact that the article relates to the arrest and circumstances of a felony conviction, which are matters of legitimate public concern. Therefore, we conclude that the defendant's publication was predominately a noncommercial publication. We hold that the publication of a plaintiff's name and likeness in connection with a truthful article regarding the plaintiff's felony conviction is privileged. As such, the plaintiff's claim of invasion of privacy by appropriation of name or likeness cannot prevail.

IV. CONCLUSION

Since the defendant's use of the plaintiff's name and picture is privileged under the First Amendment, we reverse the court of appeals and return this case to that court with directions to reinstate the trial court's order granting summary judgment to the defendant.

NOTES AND QUESTIONS

1. This was the first type of invasion of privacy to be recognized by the courts. Statutes in some states are limited to commercial appropriations of name or likeness. One example is New York, where the statute limits actions to appropriations for advertising purposes of trade. Griffin v. Law Firm of Harris, Beach, Wilcox, Rubin, and Levey, 126 Misc.2d 209, 481 N.Y.S.2d 963 (1984) aff'd, 112 A.D.2d 514, 490 N.Y.S.2d 919 (3d Dept.1985). Other courts, not restricted by statute, have allowed recovery for appropriations of the plaintiff's name for non-commercial purposes. State ex rel. Lafollette v. Hinkle, 131 Wash. 86, 229 P. 317 (1924) (use of name as candidate for office by political party); Hamilton v. Lumbermen's Mutual Cas. Co., 82 So.2d 61 (La.App.1955), (advertising in name of plaintiff for witness to an accident); Vanderbilt v. Mitchell, 72 N.J.Eq. 910, 67 A. 97 (1907) (providing father for child on birth certificate).

Should an action be available where Sears photographs a three and a half month old child in its studio and uses, without parental consent, the photograph for its own promotion? Slocum v. Sears Roebuck & Co., 542 So.2d 777 (La.App.1989) (invasion of infant's privacy occurred but the limited exhibition of the photograph, its flattering quality, and the age of the infant did not reach a threshold of seriousness to make the invasion actionable).

2. While most cases involve advertisements, other forms of commercial appropriation have resulted in liability. Edison v. Edison Polyform Mfg. Co., 73 N.J.Eq. 136, 67 A. 392 (1907) (use of name in title of corporation); Goodyear Tire & Rubber Co. v. Vandergriff, 52 Ga.App. 662, 184 S.E. 452 (1936) (impersonation to obtain secret information); Binns v.

Vitagraph Co. of America, 147 App.Div. 783, 132 N.Y.S. 237 (1911), aff'd, 210 N.Y. 51, 103 N.E. 1108 (1913) (motion picture based on incident in life of plaintiff, in which an actor represented him). Morse v. Studin, 283 A.D.2d 622, 725 N.Y.S.2d 93 (2001) (plastic surgeon's use of before and after photographs to promote business); Michaels v. Internet Entertainment Group, Inc., 5 F. Supp.2d 823 (C.D. Cal.1998) (publicizing plaintiffs' names and identities to advertise pornographic videos on the Internet).

3. There is no liability for the mere use of the same name as that of the plaintiff. Swacker v. Wright, 154 Misc. 822, 277 N.Y.S. 296 (1935) (novel); Nebb v. Bell Syndicate, Inc., 41 F.Supp. 929 (S.D.N.Y.1941) (comic strip).

4. *Right of Publicity.* The right of common law protects a person's "name and likeness from unwarranted intrusion or exploitation. . . ." Lugosi v. Universal Pictures, 25 Cal.3d 813, 160 Cal.Rptr. 323, 603 P.2d 425, 431 (1979). Whereas the privacy tort of misappropriation protects a plaintiff's personal dignity, the right of publicity action protects the commercial value of a plaintiff's personal image. Doe v. TCI Cablevision, 110 S.W.3d 363 (Mo. 2003). The former action requires that the defendant used the plaintiff's name or likeness to obtain some advantage, while the latter requires that the advantage be specifically commercial. Restatement (Second) of Torts § 652C.

In an era of media celebrity, the right has been widely litigated, especially in California before the Ninth Circuit Court of Appeals. California and eleven other states supplement, or displace in few instances, the common law right with statutory protections. Cal. Civ. Code § 3344(a) (1971). The right is not confined to "appropriation of name or likeness" but extends to identity. Thus, at common law and under California statute, causes of action have been stated for advertisements that used: a well-known race car driver's car to promote cigarettes (Motschenbacher v. R.J. Reynolds Tobacco Co., 498 F.2d 821 (9th Cir.1974)); a soundalike voice (Midler v. Ford Motor Co., 849 F.2d 460 (9th Cir.1988); a robot redolent of Vanna White (White v. Samsung Electronics America, Inc., 971 F.2d 1395 (9th Cir.1992)), rehearing en banc denied, 989 F.2d 1512 (9th Cir.1993)); and a birthname of a famous athlete (Abdul-Jabbar v. General Motors Corporation, 75 F.3d 1391 (9th Cir.1996)).

Courts elsewhere have taken the same approach, Carson v. Here's Johnny Portable Toilets, Inc., 698 F.2d 831 (6th Cir.1983) (holding actionable under Michigan common law distributor's use of "Here's Johnny" in conjunction with promotion of a portable lavatory); Ali v. Playgirl, Inc., 447 F.Supp. 723 (S.D.N.Y.1978) (holding publication of drawing of nude black man labeled "the greatest" entitled plaintiff to preliminary injunction under New York statutory and common law right of action); Onassis v. Christian Dior-New York, Inc., 122 Misc.2d 603, 472 N.Y.S.2d 254, aff'd, 110 A.D.2d 1095, 488 N.Y.S.2d 943 (1985) (holding plaintiff entitled to injunction under New York law for posing a look-alike of plaintiff in advertisement of defendant's product); Parks v. LaFace Records, 329 F.3d 437 (6th Cir. 2003) (entitling a song after civil rights movement icon actionable where there was no artistic nexus to the song's content). Note, however, that where the appropriation consists of copyrighted material, federal copyright statutes may preempt privacy actions. Laws v. Sony

Music Entertainment, Inc., 448 F.3d 1134 (9th Cir. 2006), cert. denied 549 U.S. 1252 (2007).

5. The inherently ambiguous nature of the right to publicity presents jurisprudential and practical issues. Is it an action to vindicate the privacy rights of the person, or is it a recognition of a separate property right—a form for intellectual property? If it is a property right, is it alienable and does it survive the death of the person? The majority favors such survivability, either by case law or by statute. Herman Miller, Inc. v. Palazzetti Imports and Exports, Inc., 270 F.3d 298 (6th Cir. 2001) (counting jurisdictions). Selling busts in the likeness of a deceased famous person, then, gives rise to right of publicity liability. Martin Luther King, Jr., Center for Social Change v. American Heritage Products, Inc., 250 Ga. 135, 296 S.E.2d 697 (1982).

Oftentimes the courts are not careful in distinguishing dignitary interests from the right to publicity. Contra, Doe v. TCI Cablevision, 110 S.W.3d 363 (Mo. 2003) for a discussion of damages that draws a careful bifurcation between the actions. Whereas the plaintiff in *Doe* brought a misappropriation action, the Missouri court concluded that the claim was more properly a publicity action. The recognition of a property right also allows for some cases to embrace unjust enrichment in justifying liability: Zacchini v. Scripps-Howard Broadcasting Co., 433 U.S. 562 (1977). What are the implications of allowing a remedy for unjust enrichment? Should damages be only economic or should they extend to non-economic losses, see Abdul-Jabbar v. General Motors Corp., 85 F.3d 407 (9th Cir. 1996) (damages for economic loss and for humiliation and mental distress in conclusions that he had abandoned his religion) and Petty v. Chrysler Corp., 343 Ill.App.3d 815, 278 Ill.Dec. 714, 799 N.E.2d 432 (2003) (court will presume damages for misappropriation of identity; actual and special damages available). Should an injunction be available?

6. *Constitutional Law.* The capacious protection of the right to privacy potentially invades the First Amendment. The principal case asserts a First Amendment interest in protecting "newsworthy" material. Take the leading Supreme Court decision in Zacchini v. Scripps-Howard Broadcasting Co., 433 U.S. 562 (1977). Plaintiff was an entertainer commercially performing a "human cannonball act" in which he was shot from a cannon into a net 200 feet away, the performance taking some 15 seconds. Defendant broadcasting station, though requested not to do so, took a film of the act and showed it on the evening news broadcast. Plaintiff's suit for damages was held not maintainable by the Supreme Court of Ohio because of the station's privilege to report in its newscasts matters of legitimate public interest, relying on New York Times Co. v. Sullivan, supra page 922 and Time, Inc. v. Hill, 385 U.S. 374 (1967), infra page 1035. The Supreme Court reversed.

Speaking for the majority, Justice White said: "The differences between [false-light privacy and appropriation privacy] are important. First, the State's interests in providing a cause of action in each instance are different. 'The interest protected' in permitting recovery for placing the plaintiff in a false light 'is clearly that of reputation, with the same overtones of mental distress as in defamation.' [C] By contrast, the State's interest in permitting a 'right of publicity' is in protecting the proprietary interest of the individual in his act in part to encourage such entertainment. As we later note, the State's interest is closely analogous to the goals of patent and copyright law, focusing on the right of the individual to reap the reward of his endeavors and having little to do with protecting feelings or reputation. Second, the two torts differ in the degree to which they intrude on dissemination of information to the public. In 'false light' cases the only way to protect the interests involved is to attempt to minimize publication of the damaging matter, while in 'right of publicity' cases the only question is who gets to do the publishing. An entertainer such as petitioner usually has no objection to the widespread publication of his act as long as he gets the commercial benefit of such publication. Indeed, in the present case petitioner did not seek to enjoin the broadcast of his act; he simply sought compensation for the broadcast in the form of damages. * * *

Wherever the line in particular situations is to be drawn between media reports that are protected and those that are not, we are quite sure that the First and Fourteenth Amendments do not immunize the media when they broadcast a performer's entire act without his consent. The Constitution no more prevents a State from requiring respondent to compensate petitioner for broadcasting his act on television than it would privilege respondent to film and broadcast a copyrighted dramatic work without liability to the copyright owner [cc], or to film and broadcast a prize fight [c], or a baseball game [c], where the promoters or the participants had other plans for publicizing the event. There are ample reasons for reaching this conclusion."

Speaking for the dissenters, Justice Powell said: "Rather than begin with a quantitative analysis of the performer's behavior—is this or is this not his entire act?—we should direct initial attention to the actions of the news media: what use did the station make of the film footage? When a film is used, as here, for a routine portion of a regular news program, I would hold that the First Amendment protects the station from a 'right of publicity' or 'appropriation' suit, absent a strong showing by the plaintiff that the news broadcast was a subterfuge or cover for private or commercial exploitation."

7. *Public Commentary Often Focuses upon Personalities.* Pursued by many but attained by few, fame is often accompanied by the price of others' exploitation of such status. In the course of public speech, celebrities are used to sell products, influence attitudes, and affect public discourse. The balance between free speech under the First Amendment on the privacy right is often at issue. In *White*, supra page 1011 the court held that Vanna White had made a supportable claim when a robot identifiable as a representation of her was featured in an ad for defendant's product. The Ninth Circuit rejected the application for rehearing en banc, 989 F.2d 1512 (9th Cir.1993). Judge Kozinski, joined by others, dissented, finding that the right to publicity had become too expansive and inconsistent with free speech notions, where actionability rests simply on the invocation of the "celebrity's image in the public's mind." Id. at 1514. The use of a bewigged robot may be a powerful way of expressing the durability of defendant's product: as the "Wheel of Fortune" has survived, so would defendant's product.

There is a large and accumulating number of authorities drawing the line between protection of the right of publicity and legitimate free expression. The Ninth Circuit has long experience. Downing v. Abercrombie & Fitch, 265 F.3d 994 (9th Cir. 2001) (use of well-known surfer's image actionable under the Lanham Act). The courts have found images protected if they contain "significant expressive content." Winter v. DC Comics, 30 Cal.4th 881, 134 Cal.Rptr.2d 634, 69 P.3d 473 (2003). But compare Doe v. TCT Cablevision, 110 S.W.3d 363 (Mo. 2003) (on facts similar to *Winter*, adopting a "predominant use" test). What of an art print of Tiger Woods winning the 1997 Masters? ETW Corp. v. Jireh Pub., Inc., 332 F.3d 915 (6th Cir. 2003) (finding Wood's publicity right was outweighed by society's interest in "artistic expression"). What of lithographs and T-shirts featuring the Three Stooges? Comedy III Productions v. Gary Saderup, 25 Cal.4th 387, 106 Cal.Rptr.2d 126, 21 P.3d 797 (2001) (adopting a test requiring the work have a transformative element as to make it a creative contribution).

Sanders v. American Broadcasting Companies, Inc., et al.

Supreme Court of California, 1999.
20 Cal.4th 907, 978 P.2d 67, 85 Cal.Rptr.2d 909.

WERDEGAR, J., Defendant Stacy Lescht, a reporter employed by defendant American Broadcasting Companies, Inc. (ABC), obtained employment as a "telepsychic" with the Psychic Marketing Group (PMG), which also employed plaintiff Mark Sanders in that same capacity. While she worked in PMG's Los Angeles office, Lescht, who wore a small video camera hidden in her hat, covertly videotaped her conversations with several coworkers, including Sanders.

Sanders sued Lescht and ABC for, among other causes of action, the tort of invasion of privacy by intrusion. Although a jury found for Sanders on the intrusion cause of action, the Court of Appeal reversed the resulting judgment in his favor on the ground that the jury finding for the defense on another cause of action, violation of Penal Code section 632, established Sanders could have had no reasonable expectation of privacy in his workplace conversations because such conversations could be overheard by others in the shared office space. We granted review to determine whether the fact that a workplace interaction might be witnessed by others on the premises necessarily defeats, for purposes of tort law, any reasonable expectation of privacy the participants have against covert videotaping by a journalist. We conclude it does not: In an office or other workplace to which the general public does not have unfettered access, employees may enjoy a limited, but legitimate, expectation that their conversations and other interactions will not be secretly videotaped by undercover television reporters, even though those conversations may not have been completely private from the participants' coworkers.

Although we reverse, for these reasons, the Court of Appeal's judgment for defendants, we do not hold or imply that investigative journalists necessarily commit a tort by secretly recording events and conversations in offices, stores or other workplaces. Whether a reasonable expectation of privacy is violated by such recording depends on the exact nature of the conduct and all the surrounding circumstances. In addition, liability under the intrusion tort requires that the invasion be highly offensive to a reasonable person, considering, among other factors, the motive of the alleged intruder. (Shulman v. Group W Productions, Inc. (1998) 18 Cal.4th 200, 231, 236). [c] The scope of our review in this case does not include any question regarding the offensiveness element of the tort, and we therefore express no view on the offensiveness or inoffensiveness of defendants' conduct. We hold only that, where the other elements of the intrusion tort are proven, the cause of action is not defeated as a matter of law simply because the events or conversations upon which the defendant allegedly intruded were not completely private from all other eyes and ears.

Factual and Procedural Background

In 1992, plaintiff Mark Sanders was working as a telepsychic in PMG's Los Angeles office, giving "readings" to customers who telephoned PMG's 900 number (for which they were charged a per-minute fee). The psychics' work area consisted of a large room with rows of cubicles, about 100 total, in which the psychics took their calls. Each cubicle was enclosed on three sides by five-foot-high partitions. The facility also included a separate lunchroom and enclosed offices for managers and supervisors. During the period of the claimed intrusion, the door to the PMG facility was unlocked during business hours, but PMG, by internal policy, prohibited access to the office by nonemployees without specific permission. An employee testified the front door was visible from the administration desk and a supervisor greeted any nonemployees who entered.

Defendant Stacy Lescht, employed by defendant ABC in an investigation of the telepsychic industry, obtained employment as a psychic in PMG's Los Angeles office. When she first entered the PMG office to apply for a position, she was not stopped at the front door or greeted by anyone until she found and approached the administration desk. Once hired, she sat at a cubicle desk, where she gave telephonic readings to customers. Lescht testified that while sitting at her desk she could easily overhear conversations conducted in surrounding cubicles or in the aisles near her cubicle. When not on the phone, she talked with some of the other psychics in the phone room. Lescht secretly videotaped these conversations with a "hat cam," i.e., a small camera hidden in her hat; a microphone attached to her brassiere captured sound as well. Among the conversations Lescht videotaped were two with Sanders, the first at Lescht's cubicle, the second at Sanders's. [The court described the relatively discrete nature of the conversation.]

[The court described the two causes of action, one statutory and the other the "common law tort of invasion of privacy by intrusion." The Court of Appeal reversed the judgment for plaintiffs entering a judgment for defendants.]

* * *

We granted plaintiff's petition for review and, by later order, limited the issues to be briefed and argued to the following: (1) whether a person who lacks a reasonable expectation of complete privacy in a conversation because it could be seen and overheard by coworkers (but not the general public) may nevertheless have a claim for invasion of privacy by intrusion based on a television reporter's covert videotaping of that conversation; (2) whether the jury's findings in the first phase of trial, on liability under section 632, legally precluded maintenance of a common law intrusion claim; and (3) whether the jury instructions in the second phase of trial, on liability for intrusion, were prejudicially erroneous.

Discussion

Question 1: May a person who lacks a reasonable expectation of complete privacy in a conversation because it could be seen and overheard by coworkers (but not the general public) nevertheless have a claim for invasion of privacy by intrusion based on a television reporter's covert videotaping of that conversation?

Answer: Yes.

Neither the trial court nor the Court of Appeal had the benefit of our recent decision in Shulman v. Group W Productions, Inc., supra. We therefore begin by recounting what we said in *Shulman* regarding the privacy element of an intrusion cause of action.

In *Shulman*, we adopted the definition of the intrusion tort articulated in Miller v. National Broadcasting Co., 187 Cal.app.3d at page 1482, and in the Restatement Second of Torts section 652B. The cause of action, we held, has two elements: (1) intrusion into a private place, conversation or matter, (2) in a manner highly offensive to a reasonable person. [c] The first element, we stated, is not met when the plaintiff has merely been observed, or even photographed or recorded, in a public place. [c] Rather, "the plaintiff must show the defendant penetrated some zone of physical or sensory privacy surrounding, or obtained unwanted access to data about, the plaintiff. The tort is proven only if the plaintiff had an objectively reasonable expectation of seclusion or solitude in the place, conversation or data source." [C]

While *Shulman* reiterated the requirement that an intrusion plaintiff have a reasonable expectation of privacy, neither in *Shulman* nor in any other case have we stated that an expectation of privacy, in order to be reasonable for purposes of the intrusion tort, must be of *absolute* or *complete* privacy. Indeed, our analysis of the issues in *Shulman* suggested, to the contrary, that mass media videotaping may constitute an intrusion even when the events and communications recorded were visible and audible to some limited set of observers at the time they occurred. In *Shulman*, a television producer had fitted a rescue nurse with a small microphone, by which the nurse's conversation with a severely injured accident victim was recorded. Although a number of other persons were participating in the rescue, the record on summary judgment, we noted, left unclear whether any nonparticipant members of the general public were present or could overhear any of the patient's communications to the nurse and other rescuers. [c] Partly on that basis, we found triable issues of fact as to the patient's reasonable expectation of privacy in her conversation with the nurse and other rescuers. [c] We thereby implied the plaintiff patient could have a reasonable expectation of privacy in her communications even if some of them may have been overheard by those involved in the rescue, but not by the general public.

Shulman's discussion of possible bases for a reasonable expectation of privacy on the patient's part also suggests that a person may reasonably expect privacy against the electronic recording of a communication, even though he or she had no reasonable expectation as to confidentiality of the communication's contents. [W]e stated: "" 'While one who imparts private information risks the betrayal of his confidence by the other party, a substantial distinction has been recognized between the secondhand repetition of the contents of a conversation and its simultaneous dissemination to an unannounced second auditor, whether that auditor be a person or a mechanical device . . . [S]uch secret monitoring denies the speaker an important aspect of privacy of communication-the right to control the nature and extent of the firsthand dissemination of his statements.' " [C]

This case squarely raises the question of an expectation of limited privacy. On further consideration, we adhere to the view suggested in *Shulman*: privacy, for purposes of the intrusion tort, is not a binary, all-or-nothing characteristic. There are degrees and nuances to societal recognition of our expectations of privacy: the fact that the privacy one expects in a given setting is not complete or absolute does not render the expectation unreasonable as a matter of law. Although the intrusion tort is often defined in terms of "seclusion" (see, e.g., Rest.2d Torts, 652B [Intrusion upon Seclusion]; *Shulman*, supra, 18 Cal.4th at p. 232 ["intrusion on seclusion"]), the seclusion referred to need not be absolute. "Like 'privacy,' the concept of 'seclusion' is relative. The mere fact that a person can be seen by someone does not automatically mean that he or she can legally be forced to be subject to being seen by everyone." (1 McCarthy, The Rights of Publicity and Privacy (1998) § 5.10[A][2], p. 5–120.1.)

Dietemann v. Time, Inc., supra, 449 F.2d 245 upon which the trial court relied, does, indeed, exemplify the idea of a legitimate expectation of limited privacy. Reporters for a news magazine deceitfully gained access to a quack doctor's home office, where they secretly photographed and recorded his examination of one of them. [C] The court held the plaintiff could, under California law, reasonably expect privacy from press photography and recording, even though he had invited the reporters-unaware of their true identity-into his home office: "Plaintiff's den was a sphere from which he could reasonably expect to exclude eavesdropping newsmen. He invited two of defendant's employees to the den. One who invites another to his home or office takes a risk that the visitor may not be what he seems, and that the visitor may repeat all he hears and observes when he leaves. But he does not and should not be required to take the risk that what is heard and seen will be transmitted by photograph or recording, or in our modern world, in full living color and hi-fi to the public at large. . . ." [C]

Equally illustrative of the general principle is Huskey v. National Broadcasting Co., Inc. (N.D. Ill. 1986) 632 F. Supp. 1282. The defendant's camera crew, visiting a federal prison, filmed plaintiff Huskey, an inmate, in the prison's "exercise cage," wearing only gym shorts and exposing his distinctive tattoos. The federal court rejected the defendant's contention no intrusion could have occurred because Huskey was "not secluded." [C] "Of course Huskey *could* be seen by guards, prison personnel and inmates, and obviously he was in fact seen by NBC's camera operator. But the mere fact a person can be seen by others does not mean that person cannot legally be 'secluded.' . . . Further, Huskey's visibility to some people does not strip him of the right to remain secluded from others. Persons are exposed to family members and invited guests in their own homes, but that does not mean they have opened the door to television cameras." [C] Whether the exercise cage could be considered an area of limited seclusion within the prison was a factual question for trial.

[The court cited numbers of cases illustrating the principle.] [I]n a famous early case, the presence of an unnecessary male observer at the home delivery of the plaintiff's child was held to be an intrusion, even though the delivery was also observed by the plaintiff's husband, the attending doctor and a woman assistant. (De May v. Roberts (1881) 46 Mich. 160 [9 N.W. 146, 148–149].) The existence of such limited privacy is not dependent on the plaintiff being in his or her home, as demonstrated by Huskey v. National Broadcasting Co., Inc., supra, 632 F.Supp. 1282, and many other cases. See also Pearson v. Dodd (D.C. Cir. 1969) 410 F.2d 701, 704 [133 App.D.C. 279] [intrusion tort protects against intrusion "whether by physical trespass or not, into spheres from which an ordinary man in a plaintiff's position could reasonably expect that the particular defendant should be excluded"].)

Defendants' claim, that a "complete expectation of privacy" is necessary to recover for intrusion, thus fails as inconsistent with case law as well as with the common understanding of privacy. Privacy for purposes of the intrusion tort must be evaluated with respect to the identity of the alleged intruder and the nature of the intrusion. As seen below, moreover, decisions on the common law and statutory protection of *workplace* privacy show that the same analysis applies in the workplace as in other settings; consequently, an employee may, under some circumstances, have a reasonable expectation of visual or aural privacy against electronic intrusion by a stranger to the workplace, despite the possibility that the conversations and interactions at issue could be witnessed by coworkers or the employer.

Doe by Doe v. B.P.S. Guard Services, Inc. (8th Cir. 1991) 945 F.2d 1422 illustrates the existence of limited, but reasonable, *visual* privacy in the workplace. A fashion show was being held at a convention center. The organizers had set up a curtained dressing area for the models, unaware that the area was visible on one of the convention center's security cameras. Guards in the security control room used the surveillance camera to watch and videotape the models changing clothes. [c] Nothing in the opinion suggests the curtained changing area, used by all the models and presumably accessible to the show's director and assistants, was a place of complete seclusion for any of the models. Nonetheless, the appellate court, in an action for common law invasion of privacy, had no difficulty discerning a reasonable expectation of privacy on the models' part, violated in this circumstance by a visual "invasion by strangers." [C]

Defendants' cited cases on workplace privacy do not establish a contrary rule. None of them hold or demonstrate that employee privacy in the workplace is nonexistent if not complete. More particularly, none hold or demonstrate that a worker necessarily loses all reasonable expectation of privacy against covert media videotaping merely because the worker's interactions and conversations may have been witnessed by some coworkers.

Finally, defendants rely on Com. v. Alexander (1998) 551 Pa. 1 [708 A.2d 1251] (*Alexander*) and Desnick v. American Broadcasting Companies, Inc. (7th Cir. 1995) 44 F.3d 1345 (*Desnick*). Both involved investigations into suspected misconduct by doctors; the investigation was by ABC in *Desnick* and by the Philadelphia police in *Alexander*. In both cases, patients or those posing as such, acting for the investigators, covertly recorded or videotaped the doctors' conversations with the patients in the doctors' offices. [C] Both courts rejected claims the taping illegally invaded the doctors' privacy.

In *Desnick*, the question was whether the covert videotaping by "testers" posing as patients was a tortious invasion of privacy. The appellate court held it was not, partly because "the only conversations that were recorded were conversations with the testers themselves." [C] "The test patients entered offices that were open to anyone expressing a desire for ophthalmic services and videotaped physicians engaged in professional, not personal, communications with strangers (the testers themselves)." [C]

The *Desnick* court characterized the doctor-patient relationship as one between a service provider and a customer and therefore viewed these parties' conversations in the medical office as essentially public conversations between strangers. We need not agree or disagree with this characterization in order to see that it renders the decision's reasoning inapplicable to the question before us. We are concerned here with interactions between coworkers rather than between a proprietor and customer. As the briefed question is framed, the interactions at issue here could not have been witnessed by the general public, although they could have been overheard or observed by other employees in the shared workplace.

To summarize, we conclude that in the workplace, as elsewhere, the reasonableness of a person's expectation of visual and aural privacy depends not only on who might have been able to observe the subject interaction, but on the identity of the claimed intruder and the means of intrusion. [c] For this reason, we answer the briefed question affirmatively: a person who lacks a reasonable expectation of complete privacy in a conversation, because it could be seen and overheard by coworkers (but not the general public), may nevertheless have a claim for invasion of privacy by intrusion based on a television reporter's covert videotaping of that conversation.

Defendants warn that "the adoption of a doctrine of *per se* workplace privacy would place a dangerous chill on the press' investigation of abusive activities in open work areas, implicating substantial First Amendment concerns." (Italics in original.) We adopt no such per se doctrine of privacy. We hold only that the possibility of being overheard by coworkers does not, as a matter of law, render unreasonable an employee's expectation that his or her interactions within a nonpublic workplace will not be videotaped in secret by a journalist. In other circumstances, where, for example, the workplace is regularly open to entry or observation by the public or press, or the interaction that was the subject of the alleged intrusion was between proprietor (or employee) and customer, any expectation of privacy against press recording is less likely to be deemed reasonable. Nothing we say here prevents a media defendant from attempting to show, in order to negate the offensiveness element of the intrusion tort, that the claimed intrusion, even if it infringed on a reasonable expectation of privacy, was "justified by the legitimate motive of gathering the news." (*Shulman*, supra, 18 Cal.4th at pp. 236–237.) As for possible First Amendment defenses, any discussion must await a later case, as no constitutional issue was decided by the lower courts or presented for our review here.

Disposition

The judgment of the Court of Appeal is reversed, and the cause is remanded to that court for further proceedings consistent with our opinion.

NOTES AND QUESTIONS

1. Physical intrusion upon seclusion or solitude has been recognized as a distinct form of invasion of privacy. Byfield v. Candler, 33 Ga.App. 275, 125 S.E. 905 (1924) (woman's stateroom on a steamboat); Welsh v. Pritchard, 125 Mont. 517, 241 P.2d 816 (1952) (landlord moving in on tenant); Sutherland v. Kroger Co., 144 W.Va. 673, 110 S.E.2d 716 (1959) (search of woman's shopping bag in store); K-Mart Corp. Store No. 7441 v. Trotti, 677 S.W.2d 632 (Tex.App.1984) (search of employee's locker). Are privacy rights violated by the mere presence of a video camera installed in a bathroom, even if it's inoperable? See Koeppel v. Speirs, 808 NW2d 177 (Iowa 2011) (holding that because the camera was capable of operation, a reasonable person would believe that his or her privacy had been invaded, thus establishing that an invasion occurred under the intrusion on solitude component of the tort.)

2. As to eavesdropping, see Rhodes v. Graham, 238 Ky. 225, 37 S.W.2d 46 (1931) (wire tapping); Roach v. Harper, 143 W.Va. 869, 105 S.E.2d 564 (1958) (microphone); Hamberger v. Eastman, 106 N.H. 107, 206 A.2d 239 (1964) (landlord "bugs" tenant's bedroom). Suppose a telephone user customarily records his telephone conversations without informing the other parties? Cf. Marks v. Bell Tel. Co., 460 Pa. 73, 331 A.2d 424 (1975). Suppose husband secretly videotapes in marital bedroom? Cf. In re Marriage of Tigges, 758 N.W.2d 824 (Iowa 2008).

On "telephone harassment," repeated telephone calls at unreasonable hours, see Donnel v. Lara, 703 S.W.2d 257 (Tex.App.1985); cf. Ruple v. Brooks, 352 N.W.2d 652 (S.D.1984) (obscene phone calls may create liability for intentional infliction of emotional distress). And see Nader v. General Motors Corp., 25 N.Y.2d 560, 255 N.E.2d 765, 307 N.Y.S.2d 647 (1970), involving a general campaign of harassment including lengthy surveillance, probing inquiries about Nader's political, social, racial and religious views and beliefs, his sexual behavior and attempts to entrap him in illicit relationships.

3. Some courts limit the tort of invasion of seclusion or solitude to actual physical invasion. Compare Davis v. Emmis Pub. Corp., 244 Ga.App. 795, 536 S.E.2d 809 (2000) (requiring physical invasion) with Lawlor v. N. Am. Corp. of Ill., 983 N.E.2d 414, 425 (2012), in which telephone records were gathered through misrepresentation to determine whether plaintiff violated a covenant not to compete. The Illinois Supreme Court adopted the Restatement (Second) of Torts definition of the tort of intrusion upon seclusion: " 'The intrusion itself makes the defendant subject to liability, even [where] there is no publication or other use of any kind of the * * * information * * * Today, we join the vast majority of other jurisdictions that recognize the tort of intrusion upon seclusion." See also Zimmermann v. Wilson, 81 F.2d 847 (3d Cir.1936) (unauthorized prying into private bank account); Frey v. Dixon, 141 N.J.Eq. 481, 58 A.2d 86 (1948) (invalid order requiring production of books and documents); Melvin v. Burling, 141 Ill.App.3d 786, 490 N.E.2d 1011, 95 Ill.Dec. 919 (1986) (harassed by intentional ordering of merchandise without consent). Cf. Galella v. Onassis, 487 F.2d 986 (2d Cir.1973) (continued surveillance and persistent harassment by taking photographs).

4. The invasion test has two interlinking elements. The intrusion must be into a private place, conversation, or matter, and must be highly offensive to a reasonable person. The essence of the first requirement is an objective expectation of privacy and it will vary with respect to the identity of the intruder or the nature of the intrusion. See Shulman v. Group W Productions, Inc., 18 Cal.4th 200, 74 Cal.Rptr.2d 843, 955 P.2d 469 (1998), discussed in the principal case. But compare Deteresa v. American Broadcasting Companies, Inc., 121 F.3d 460 (9th Cir.1997), discussed in the principal case, where plaintiff was an attendant on the flight taken by O.J. Simpson to Chicago after the murder of his former wife, Nicole Brown. Plaintiff refused an interview with ABC, but did speak on the street with an ABC reporter and was, without her knowledge, videotaped. The court as noted held that considering the circumstances she could not expect privacy, and defendant did not act offensively.

5. There is ordinarily no liability for taking the plaintiff's photograph in a public place. Gill v. Hearst Pub. Co., 40 Cal.2d 224, 253 P.2d 441 (1953) (Farmers' Market in Los Angeles); Berg v. Minneapolis Star & Tribune Co., 79 F.Supp. 957 (D.Minn.1948) (courtroom); Nelson v. Maine Times, 373 A.2d 1221 (Me.1977) (picture of small Indian child). But in Daily Times Democrat Co. v. Graham, 276 Ala. 380, 162 So.2d 474 (1964), where the plaintiff was photographed in a "Fun House" with her dress blown up over her head, it was held to be an invasion of privacy. The public nature of the place bears on the fundamental issue: the reasonable expectation of privacy. Where the interest protected is highly personal, for example of a sexual or intimate kind, psychological tranquility is at stake and the expectation of privacy is at its highest. However, knowingly exposing one's self in public excites no privacy right, even where the photograph is taken surreptitiously: Barnhart v. Paisano Publications, LLC, 457 F. Supp. 2d 590 (D. Md. 2006).

6. Intrusion upon seclusion is the aspect of the privacy tort that relates more closely to the concerns expressed by Warren and Brandeis in

the article cited by the "principal" case. Nonetheless, as the preceding notes demonstrate, the scope of the tort is continually tested as the press engages in modes of newsgathering that affect privacy interests. See J.H. Desnick v. American Broadcasting Companies, 44 F.3d 1345 (7th Cir.1995). Posner C.J. referred to First Amendment protection pertaining to defamation suits. He noted that "tabloid" style reporting was "often shrill, one-sided, and offensive, and sometimes defamatory." Yet it was entitled to protection. Id. at 1355. However, limits were drawn on capacity of the press to intrude in Food Lion v. Capital Cities/ABC, Inc., 194 F.3d 505 (4th Cir.1999) (holding that plaintiff supermarket chain had a cause of action in trespass where defendant had breached their duty of loyalty by secretly videotaping in plaintiff's non-public areas to which they had fraudulently obtained entry). Note that the tort in this form does not possess a publication element.

The media has no immunity from the general law in news-gathering. A breach of general law, as in Cohen v. Cowles Media Company, 501 U.S. 663 (1991) (discussed infra page 1033, does not raise First Amendment issues. The court in *Shulman*, discussed in the principal case, confirms this principle. Yet the First Amendment dimension does have a role because, as the *Shulman* court acknowledges, the issue of whether the intrusion was "highly offensive to a reasonable person" makes relevant offender's motivation in news-gathering. The court in *Food Lion*, for First Amendment reasons, disallowed damages flowing from the publication. Disallowing publication damages effectively detooths the tort. But cf. *Dietemann supra* allowing enhanced damages for subsequent publication. *Food Lion* has spawned considerable academic comment attempting to chart a rule that provides for ample and certain newsgathering prerogatives, but balances the privacy interests of individuals: Lidsky, Prying, Spying, and Lying: Intrusive Newsgathering and What the Law Should Do About It, 73 Tul.L.Rev. 173 (1998).

Hall v. Post

Supreme Court of North Carolina, 1988.
323 N.C. 259, 372 S.E.2d 711.

MITCHELL, JUSTICE. In the present case, this Court must decide whether claims for tortious invasion of privacy by truthful public disclosure of "private" facts concerning the plaintiffs are cognizable at law in North Carolina. We hold that they are not and reverse the decision of the Court of Appeals.

The plaintiffs, Susie Hall and her adoptive mother, Mary Hall, brought separate civil actions against the defendants for invasion of privacy. The actions were based upon two articles printed in The Salisbury Post and written by its special assignment reporter, Rose Post.

[O]n 18 July 1984, The Salisbury Post published an article by Rose Post which bore the headline "Ex-Carny Seeks Baby Abandoned 17 Years Ago." The article concerned the search by Lee and Aledith Gottschalk for Aledith's daughter by a previous marriage, whom she and her former husband had abandoned in Rowan County in September of 1967. The article told of Aledith's former marriage to a carnival barker named Clarence Maxson, the birth of their daughter in 1967, their abandonment of the child at the age of four months, events in Aledith's life thereafter, and her return to Rowan County after seventeen years to look for the child. The article indicated that Clarence Maxson had made arrangements in 1967 for a babysitter named Mary Hall to keep the child for a few weeks. Clarence and Aledith then moved on with the carnival, and Clarence later told Aledith that he had signed papers authorizing the baby's adoption.

Aledith was married to Lee Gottschalk in 1984, and they decided to travel to Rowan County to look for Aledith's child. The newspaper article of 18 July 1984 related the details of their unsuccessful search and then stated:

> If anyone, they say, knows anything about a little blonde baby left here when the county fair closed and the carnies moved on in September 1967, Lee and Aledith Gottschalk can be reached in Room 173 at the Econo Motel.

Shortly after the article was published, the Gottschalks were called at the motel and informed of the child's identity and whereabouts.

The defendants published a second article on 20 July 1984 reporting that the Gottschalks had located the child with the aid of responses to the earlier article. The second article identified the child as Susie Hall and identified her adoptive mother as Mary Hall. The article related the details of a telephone encounter between the Gottschalks and Mrs. Hall and described the emotions of both families.

The plaintiffs alleged that they fled their home in order to avoid public attention resulting from the articles. Each plaintiff alleged that she sought and received psychiatric care for the emotional and mental distress caused by the incident.

The defendants have contended at all times that the imposition of civil liability for their truthful public disclosure of facts about the plaintiffs would violate the First Amendment to the Constitution of the United States. The defendants have contended in the alternative that this Court should refuse to adopt any tort which imposes liability for such conduct as a part of the common law of this State.

Although the plaintiffs contended before the Court of Appeals that their claims constituted valid claims both for public disclosure of embarrassing private facts and for intrusion upon the plaintiffs' seclusion or solitude or into their private affairs, we agree with the Court of Appeals that the intrusion branch of the invasion of privacy tort is not involved here. [c] Therefore, we strictly limit our consideration in the present case to issues concerning the private facts branch of the invasion of privacy tort. We neither consider nor decide whether any other tort is constitutional or cognizable at law upon facts such as those presented here.

* * *

Since the publication of the nineteenth century Warren and Brandeis article in the Harvard Law Review, two different broad categories of privacy rights have evolved. [C] One is the *constitutional* right of privacy which protects personal privacy from certain types of *governmental* intrusion. [c] The other is the general right of privacy, violations of which have been viewed by some as giving rise to a tort composed of four branches, only one of which is of concern in the present case. This Court has recently acknowledged that, as to this general right to privacy:

> A review of the current tort law of all American jurisdictions reveals cases identifying at least four types of invasion of four different interests in privacy: (1) appropriation, for the defendant's advantage, of the plaintiff's name or likeness; (2) intrusion upon the plaintiff's seclusion or solitude or into his *private affairs;* (3) public disclosure of *private* facts about the plaintiff; and (4) publicity which places the plaintiff in a false light in the public eye. See W. Prosser, *Handbook of the Law of Torts* § 117 (4th ed. 1971) (emphasis added).

In the present case, we consider for the first time that branch of the invasion of privacy tort which is most commonly referred to as the "public disclosure of private facts." The plaintiffs have at all times acknowledged that the facts published about them by the defendants were true and accurate in every respect, but they contend, nevertheless, that they are entitled to recover.

Under the definition of the private facts tort set out in the Restatement (Second) of Torts, liability will be imposed for publication of "private facts" when "the matter publicized is of a kind that (a) would be highly offensive to a reasonable person, and (b) is not of legitimate concern to the public." Restatement (Second) of Torts § 652D (1977). That definition includes four elements: (1) publicity; (2) private facts; (3) offensiveness; and (4) absence of legitimate public concern. Id., commentary. With regard to what has become known as the "newsworthiness" or "public interest," i.e., "legitimate public concern" standard, the Restatement view is that:

> In determining what is a matter of legitimate public interest, account must be taken of the customs and conventions of the community; and in the last analysis what is proper becomes a matter of the *community mores.* The line is to be drawn when the publicity ceases to be the giving of information *to which the public is entitled,* and becomes a morbid and sensational prying into private lives for its own sake, with which a *reasonable member* of the public, with *decent* standards, would say that he has no concern. [C]

The private facts branch of the invasion of privacy tort was not recognized at common law in 1776 or at the times of adoption of either the Constitution or the Bill of Rights. It has never been recognized in England, Australia, New Zealand, Canada, or other jurisdictions sharing the heritage of the English common law. [C] After an extensive study, the British Committee on Privacy recommended that the invasion of privacy tort not be adopted in Great Britain, because its application would be too difficult and time consuming and would unnecessarily threaten free speech.

Although expressing constitutional and other reservations, this Court has recognized a general right of privacy as a part of the tort law of this State. (recognizing the "appropriation" branch of the tort). However, we have not recognized or applied either of the two branches of the tort which, because they arise from publicity, most directly affect First Amendment speech and press rights. Quite to the contrary, we have refused to recognize the branch of the invasion of privacy tort arising from publicity by which the defendant places the plaintiff in a *false* light in the public eye. Renwick v. News and Observer, 310 N.C. 312, 312 S.E.2d 405. We did so because "false light" claims often would duplicate or overlap existing claims for relief. [C] For the same reasons, we now hold that claims for invasions of privacy by publication of *true* but "private" facts are not cognizable at law in this State.

The Supreme Court of the United States has specifically declined to "address the broader question whether *truthful* publications *may ever* be subjected to civil or criminal liability consistently with the First and Fourteenth Amendments." Cox Broadcasting Corp. v. Cohn, 420 U.S. 469 (1975) (emphasis added). But see Smith v. Daily Mail Publishing Co., 443 U.S. 97, 99 S.Ct. 2667, 61 L.Ed.2d 399 (1979) (statute prohibiting publication of defendant-juvenile's name unconstitutional, because state's interest in protecting juveniles and ensuring their rehabilitation could not overcome defendants' rights of speech and press); Landmark Communications, Inc. v. Virginia, 435 U.S. 829, 98 S.Ct. 1535, 56 L.Ed.2d 1 (1978) (same result and reasoning where statute prohibited publishing information regarding confidential proceedings before state judicial review commission). We do not find it necessary to answer that "broader question" here. It is enough for us to decide here, as we did in *Renwick* that adoption of the tort sought by the plaintiffs would add to the existing tensions between the First Amendment and the law of torts and would be of little practical value to anyone.

This action between two non-governmental parties does not involve "a situation in which two constitutional interests must be balanced in apposition, but rather one in which state [tort] laws protecting privacy are constrained by the federal Constitution. As the constitutional right of privacy is not involved here, a reasonable argument certainly can be made that the First Amendment rights of speech and press control and prohibit recovery in these actions against the defendants for publishing the truth.

Further, the Supreme Court of the United States has consistently held that even *false* statements *which cause actual harm* must be given limited "breathing space." [C] To do otherwise would unduly limit the rights of free speech and press by causing writers and speakers to cautiously exercise those rights for fear of liability. Hustler Magazine v. Falwell, [C]. This in turn would reduce the vigor and limits of public debate. Surely, it would be reasonable to argue that the publication of *true* statements, such as those made by the defendants, are entitled to no less constitutional protection than that guaranteed *false* statements.

"[A] cause of action predicated on public disclosure of private facts depends for its success on the truthfulness of the published material." [C] The Supreme Court of the United States has specifically recognized that "it is here that claims of privacy *most directly confront* the constitutional freedoms of speech and press." Cox Broadcasting Corp. v.

Cohn, 420 U.S. at 489, 43 L.Ed.2d at 346 (emphasis added). Thus, it is obvious here, just as it was obvious in *Renwick* that the branch of the invasion of privacy tort which the plaintiffs seek to have us adopt is constitutionally suspect and, even if it ultimately manages to survive constitutional review, "would tend to add to the tension already existing between the First Amendment and the law of torts. . . ." Renwick v. News and Observer, 310 N.C. at 323, 312 S.E.2d at 412.

* * *

We conclude that any possible benefits which might accrue to plaintiffs are entirely insufficient to justify adoption of the constitutionally suspect private facts invasion of privacy tort which punishes defendants for the typically American act of broadly proclaiming the truth by speech or writing. Accordingly, we reject the notion of a claim for relief for invasion of privacy by public disclosure of true but "private" facts.

For the foregoing reasons, the decision of the Court of Appeals is reversed.

REVERSED.

FRYE, JUSTICE, concurring in result.

The majority holds that summary judgment was appropriately entered for the defendants in these cases in which the plaintiffs sought recovery for tortious invasion of privacy by public disclosure of private but true facts concerning the plaintiffs. I agree that plaintiffs have failed to forecast evidence sufficient to withstand defendants' motions for summary judgment and that summary judgment was appropriately entered against the plaintiffs. I therefore concur in the result reached by the majority.

I do not concur in the reasoning of the majority which leads it to "reject the notion of a claim for relief for invasion of privacy by public disclosure of true but 'private' facts." I do not accept the notion that the tension already existing between the First Amendment [sic] and the law of torts requires the non-recognition of a legitimate claim by a non-public figure against a media defendant for wrongfully publishing highly offensive private facts which are not of legitimate concern to the public. While public figures give up some of their rights to privacy in the public interest, I do not believe that the media should be given a license to pry into the private lives of ordinary citizens and spread before the public highly offensive but very private facts without any degree of accountability. Such is not required by either the federal or state constitutions.

The Supreme Court has specifically left unanswered the "question whether truthful publication of very private matters unrelated to public affairs could be constitutionally proscribed." Cox Broadcasting Corp. v. Cohn, supra. However, I agree with our Court of Appeals' conclusion that the resolution of the conflicting rights lies in the "application of a 'newsworthiness' or 'public interest' standard in determining what publications are constitutionally privileged and what publications are actionable." [C] Adopting this standard gives credence to the viewpoint that neither the right to privacy nor the right of freedom of the press is absolute.

[T]he chilling effect is minimized if the question of whether the published material is of legitimate concern to the public is initially a question of law for the trial court. This eliminates the fear voiced by the *amici* in their brief filed with this Court that if the question of public concern was one for the jury it would subject every print and broadcast journalist to an *ex post facto* jury of lay censors and would convert every news story about a private citizen into a potential jury issue. Therefore, if the court determines that every reasonable person applying the proper standard would have to conclude that the published matter was of legitimate concern to the public, then the publication would be privileged and the granting of summary judgment would be proper. [C]

In determining whether published information is of legitimate concern to the public, I would adopt the standard set out in the Restatement (Second) of Torts:

> [t]he line is to be drawn when the publicity ceases to be the giving of information to which the public is entitled, and becomes a morbid and sensational prying into private lives for its own sake, with which a reasonable member of the public, with decent standards, would say that he had no concern.

Restatement (Second) of Torts, § 652D comment *h*. [C]

In short, I would adopt the private facts tort consisting of the elements as stated in the Restatement (Second) of Torts. [The judge considered the elements of the tort.]

I now turn to the application of the legitimate public concern standard to the facts of the case *sub judice*. I do not agree with the Court of Appeals' conclusion that a reasonable juror could conclude that the articles at issue here constituted a "morbid and sensational prying into private lives for its own sake." On the contrary, the article was initiated when the biological mother, Aledith Gottschalk, returned to Salisbury in search of her daughter, whom she had abandoned seventeen years earlier. This was unquestionably a story of matters of public interest and concern. The central focus was on a mother's search for her abandoned daughter, and the events and emotions relating thereto. When defendants reported that Mrs. Gottschalk thought that her daughter might have been left with a Mary Hall, and subsequently that she had located her daughter, defendants were simply reporting the details of a news story that had arisen as a result of Mrs. Gottschalk's return. However much plaintiffs may have wished to keep their personal histories out of public view, they became a legitimate public concern upon Mrs. Gottschalk's return. "There are times when one, whether willingly or not, becomes an actor in an occurrence of public or general interest." Meetze v. Associated Press, 230 S.C. 330, 337, 95 S.E.2d 606, 609, (1956).

In summary, I would hold that the private facts tort is cognizable in this jurisdiction but that plaintiffs' forecast of evidence was insufficient to withstand defendants' summary judgment motion. Thus, I concur in the result reached by the majority in this case while disagreeing with the reasons given therefor.

NOTES AND QUESTIONS

1. This form of the tort of invasion of privacy acutely implicates interests of free speech. The authorities have been at pains to map the common law and to articulate restrictions imposed by the First Amendment.

2. *Common Law: The Right to Privacy.* The cases suggest that disclosure of an embarrassing private fact to only one or just a few persons does not amount to an invasion of privacy. Thus there is no invasion of privacy when defendant calls plaintiff's employer and asks his help in collecting a debt from plaintiff. Household Finance Corp. v. Bridge, 252 Md. 531, 250 A.2d 878 (1969); Timperley v. Chase Collection Service, 272 Cal.App.2d 697, 77 Cal.Rptr. 782 (1969); Contra Pack v. Wise, 155 So.2d 909 (La.Ct.App.1963), writ refused, 245 La. 84, 157 So.2d 231 (1963). These cases might well be explained, however, on the basis that defendant's disclosure was privileged as a legitimate means of collecting the debt. See also Restatement (Second) of Torts § 652G. For an example of how courts approach "public" disclosure, see Chisholm v. Foothill Capital Corp., 3 F. Supp. 2d 925 (N.D. Ill. 1998) ("If a plaintiff has a special relationship with the individuals to whom the matter was disclosed, the publicity requirement may be satisfied by disclosure to a small number of people."). See also Pachowitz v. LeDoux, 265 Wis.2d 631, 666 N.W.2d 88 (Wis. Ct. App. 2003) (medic's disclosure of plaintiff's drug overdose to plaintiff's friend-coworker constituted sufficient publicity). In determining whether the facts were communicated to a sufficient number of persons, the *Pachowtiz* court considered whether the person to whom defendant made the disclosure "was 'the biggest gossip in Muskego and West Allis Hospital' or whether 'she had the stiffest upper lip of anyone in the state.' " But see Restatement (Second) of Torts, § 652D cmt. a ("[I]t is not an invasion of the right of privacy . . . to communicate a fact concerning the plaintiff's private life to a single person or even to a small group of persons.") Accord C.L.D. v. Wal-Mart Stores, Inc., 79 F. Supp. 2d 1080 (D. Minn. 1999) (applying Minnesota law) (manager's disclosure to coworkers of embarrassing grounds for plaintiff's medical leave insufficient for the action).

3. One who intentionally seeks publicity, or puts himself in the public eye, as does an actor, professional baseball player, explorer or inventor, is often held to become a "public figure," and to have no right to complain of publicity that reasonably bears upon his public activity. Cohen v. Marx, 94 Cal.App.2d 704, 211 P.2d 320 (1949) (prize fighter); Koussevitzky v. Allen, Towne & Heath, Inc., 188 Misc. 479, 68 N.Y.S.2d 779 (1947), aff'd, 272 App.Div. 759, 69 N.Y.S.2d 432 (1947) (symphony conductor); Martin v. Dorton, 210 Miss. 668, 50 So.2d 391 (1951) (sheriff).

Others may incidentally become actors in an event of public interest—and become a public figure in relation to that event. Jones v. Herald Post Co., 230 Ky. 227, 18 S.W.2d 972 (1929) (plaintiff's husband murdered before her eyes); See also Berg v. Minneapolis Star & Tribune Co., 79 F.Supp. 957 (D.Minn.1948) (plaintiff engaged in divorce litigation); Stryker v. Republic Pictures Corp., 108 Cal.App.2d 191, 238 P.2d 670 (1951) (war hero); Elmhurst v. Pearson, 153 F.2d 467 (D.C.Cir.1946) (defendant in sedition trial), note 11 at page 1032.

Persons captured on film incidental to newsworthy reports have no cause of action. See Jacova v. Southern Radio and Television Co., 83 So.2d 34 (Fla.1955) (plaintiff present in store to make a purchase was filmed being interviewed by police subsequent to a raid of the store); Mark v. King Broadcasting, 27 Wash.App. 344, 618 P.2d 512 (1980) (plaintiff filmed for television broadcast from outside his store in relation to a story on Medicare fraud); Heath v. Playboy Enterprises, Inc., 732 F.Supp. 1145 (S.D.Fla.1990) (plaintiff, the daughter of Christopher Carson (son of Johnny), was photographed with her mother outside a courthouse after a paternity hearing; no action available).

4. *Common Law: Breach of Confidence.* The Reporters for the Restatement of Data Privacy Principles formulate the duty of confidentiality as follows: Whenever personal data is collected under an express or implied promise of confidentiality or a legal obligation of confidentiality, the entity collecting it shall maintain its confidentiality. A duty of confidentiality may also be based upon ethical standards, such as professional rules of conduct, or applicable law.

The English law has recognized a right to confidentiality as right in equity and has created an extensive right to privacy from it. (See note 6). It arises from the relationship of a giver of information to a recipient of it and confidence with which it is impressed. Neil Richards and Daniel Solove, Privacy's Other Path: Recovering the Law of Confidentiality, 96 Geo. L.J. 123 (2007). In Humphers v. First Interstate Bank of Oregon, 298 Or. 706, 696 P.2d 527 (1985), plaintiff birth mother agreed to place for adoption her child, born out of wedlock. An anonymous adoption was effected. Later, the child approached the doctor who had delivered her seeking her birth mother's identity. The doctor gave her a letter to the hospital which enabled her to obtain release of the sealed information by falsely stating that plaintiff had taken DES during her pregnancy and that her daughter needed the records for medical reasons. The plaintiff was distressed when located and sued the doctor's estate (he had died) for invasion of privacy and for unauthorized disclosure of the confidential information. The court held no recovery for invasion of privacy, but held for the plaintiff on her confidentiality claim. Similarly, in Doe v. Portland Health Centers, 99 Or.App. 423, 782 P.2d 446 (1989), a hospital employee disclosed information about a patient's suicide attempt to a person who subsequently publicized it widely. The patient's mother sued in breach of confidentiality and invasion of privacy, among other causes of action. The court agreed that plaintiff had no action under invasion of privacy because defendant's disclosure was not made to the public or a large number of persons. She also failed in her confidentiality action, since it was not her confidence which had been breached, although her claim in breach of contract, and the duty arising therefrom, was allowed to proceed.

Not all courts have maintained the distinction between the two actions: often the action, in substance for breach of confidence, is labelled an action for invasion of privacy: See Doe v. Roe, 93 Misc.2d 201, 400 N.Y.S.2d 668 (1977) (psychiatrist published a book recording the plaintiff patient's thoughts, feelings, and fantasies; actionable although patient not named). The confluence of the two actions may be observed in the following cases on disclosure of HIV status. Such disclosure of a private fact that may give rise to a breach of confidentiality claim (Estate of Behringer v. Medical

Center at Princeton, 249 N.J.Super. 597, 592 A.2d 1251 (1991) (hospital failed to preserve confidentiality of HIV antibody test results of patient)). Such disclosure may also give rise to an invasion of privacy claim. Urbaniak v. Newton, 226 Cal.App.3d 1128, 277 Cal.Rptr. 354 (1991) (disclosure of HIV status by defendant physician violated privacy rights of plaintiff when information was revealed by plaintiff to protect others who may come in contact with examining instrument). The later case was characterized as one of "public disclosure of true, embarrassing private facts * * *." But a better characterization would be as a breach of confidence claim where the information was disclosed within a relationship of confidence.

The action in breach of confidence, from a fiduciary relationship between the parties or from a confidential relationship: See Horne v. Patton, 291 Ala. 701, 287 So.2d 824 (1973) (physician's duty to patient); Street v. Hedgepath, 607 A.2d 1238 (D.C. App. 1992) (same). In the United States, the accumulating law has been conceptualized as providing a new action in tort: the relationship establishes a duty of confidentiality: Note, Breach of Confidence: An Emerging Tort, 82 Colum.L.Rev. 1426 (1982) is based on the relationship established between the person entrusting the information and the person receiving it.

5. Two important issues remain. First, the information must be confidential. If the information is in the public domain, there is nothing to protect. Messinger v. United States, 769 F.Supp. 935, 937 (D.Md.1991) ("It is axiomatic that in order to bring suit for breach of confidentiality, the information allegedly published without consent cannot have previously been made public in a legitimate manner").

See also Meetze v. Associated Press, 230 S.C. 330, 95 S.E.2d 606 (1956) (dates of birth and marriage); Stryker v. Republic Pictures Corp., 108 Cal.App.2d 191, 238 P.2d 670 (1951) (military service record); Bell v. Courier-Journal & Louisville Times Co., 402 S.W.2d 84 (Ky.1966) (tax delinquency); cf. Rome Sentinel Co. v. Boustedt, 43 Misc.2d 598, 252 N.Y.S.2d. 10 (1964) (death certificate). Second, even confidential information may be disclosed to appropriate parties on occasion. Thus, in Bryson v. Tillinghast, 749 P.2d 110 (Okla.1988), the plaintiff, while committing a rape, had been bitten on his penis. He sought medical treatment. No cause of action was maintainable against the physician who provided information to investigating police.

The recipient of the confidential information also may owe a duty to warn or protect persons who may be injured at the hands of the provider of the information: recall *Tarasoff,* supra (duty of mental health professionals to warn or protect third parties of dangers posed by patients). Presumably, if there is a tort duty to disclose information, there is no liability for doing so. See In re Viviano, 645 So.2d 1301 (La. Ct. App. 4th Cir. 1994), writ denied, 650 So.2d 254 (La. 1995) (holding that psychotherapist's disclosure of a patient's threats to a federal judge, who was an intended victim, and the FBI violated neither the patient's right of privacy nor the professional standard of care). Do the cases provide a dilemma for some classes of defendants?

6. In a number of cases, the English courts have developed the law on breach of confidence to protect privacy interests more broadly. Campbell v. Mirror Group Newspapers Ltd., [2004] 2 A.C. 457 (photograph published

of plaintiff celebrity supermodel on a public street leaving a "Narcotics Anonymous" group meeting was a breach of plaintiff's confidentiality that protects human autonomy and dignity, in the right to control dissemination of information about private life and the right to esteem and respect of people) and Douglas & Others v. Hello! Ltd. & Others, [2006] QB 125 (unauthorized photographs of the Douglas, Zeta-Jones wedding).

7. Defendant, an exasperated creditor, put up a placard in the show window of his garage, on the public street, stating that "Dr. W.R. Morgan owes an account here of $49.67. This account will be advertised as long as it remains unpaid." Brents v. Morgan, 221 Ky. 765, 299 S.W. 967 (1927). Cf. Hamilton v. Crown Life Ins. Co., 246 Or. 1, 423 P.2d 771 (1967).

8. On the requirement that the publicity be highly offensive to a person of ordinary sensitivities, see Bitsie v. Walston, 85 N.M. 655, 515 P.2d 659 (1973), cert. denied, 85 N.M. 639, 515 P.2d 643 (1973) (holding that traditional beliefs of the Navajo about taking a child's photograph were not sufficient to make the action highly offensive where defendant newspaper did not know of the beliefs).

9. *Constitutional Law.* The Supreme Court has stopped short of constitutionally condemning the tort. The Court in The Florida Star v. B.J.F., 491 U.S. 524 (1989), addressed the issue of civil liability of a newspaper which had published the name of the victim of a sexual offense in violation of a Florida statute. The newspaper reporter had lawfully copied the police report which mistakenly included the victim's name. Unlike the foundational case of Cox Broadcasting Corp. v. Cohn, 420 U.S. 469 (1975), the protected nature of accurate reports of *judicial* proceedings was not implicated. Nevertheless, the Court found the publication was not actionable under per se negligence theory because it was of "truthful information about a matter of public interest." Such publication could be proscribed only where it served to "further a state interest of the highest order."

The Court, however, did not completely eliminate the tort. Justice Marshall, delivering the Court's opinion, announced:

> Our holding today is limited. We do not hold that truthful publication is automatically constitutionally protected, or that there is no zone of personal privacy within which the State may protect the individual from intrusion by the press, or even that the State may never punish publication of the name of a victim of a sexual offence. We hold only that where a newspaper publishes truthful information which it has lawfully obtained, punishment may lawfully be imposed, if at all, only when narrowly tailored to a state interest of the highest order * * *.

Justice White, joined by the Chief Justice and Justice O'Connor, dissented. He was not sanguine about the future of the tort. Citing, Time, Inc. v. Hill, 385 U.S. 374 (1967), and the principal case, he concluded:

> [T]he trend in "modern" jurisprudence has been to eclipse an individual's right to maintain private any truthful information that the press wished to publish. * * * Today, we hit the bottom of the slippery slope.

In Bartnicki v. Vopper, 532 U.S. 514 (2001), defendants broadcast plaintiffs' taped cellphone conversations that had been intercepted and recorded by an unknown person in violation of federal and state law. The tape had been left with Vopper, a radio talk show host who, knowing of their illegal source, later broadcast the tapes, revealing plaintiffs' telephone numbers, together with private information about the teachers' union tactics in a labor dispute. Plaintiff Bartnicki received threatening phone calls. The Court held that illegally intercepted phone calls later broadcast by others were protected by the First Amendment. The holding, however, bristles with qualifications. The majority determined that the legal garnering of the tape was critical. In weighing the interests, privacy versus free speech, the Court's opinion puts much emphasis on the "newsworthiness" of the information weighing that against the privacy interests that were diminished. This was particularly the view of Justices Breyer and O'Connor, who pointed to the threat of violence in the conversation as eroding "legitimate interest in maintaining privacy," Id. at 539. The dissenting judges noted that want of enforcement reduced deterrence of illegal scanning. Protection of privacy by enforcement would increase speech. Professor Smolla regards *Bartnicki* as a "backhanded" victory for privacy. Smolla, Information as Contraband: The First Amendment and Liability for Trafficking in Speech, 96 Nw. U.L. Rev. 1099, 1149 (2002). He regards the justices as endorsing the tort with its "newsworthiness" defense. Id. at 1150.

10. The Colorado Supreme Court has identified at least one other area in which a State's interest may be of a sufficiently high order as to impinge on the First Amendment: protection of sexual assault victims' privacy, however newsworthy the facts. People v. Bryant, 94 P.3d 624 (Colo. 2004) (rape shield law prevented media from publishing transcript of *in camera* testimony concerning the sexual behavior of accuser prior and subsequent to her alleged rape by a basketball star).

11. Should individuals be given privacy protection to allow them to "make a new start in life?" Judicial attitudes have changed. Melvin v. Reid, 112 Cal.App. 285, 297 P. 91 (1931), is a widely cited privacy case. Gabrielle Darley, a prostitute, had been tried for murder and acquitted in a famous case. She subsequently married, left the state and "thereafter at all times lived an exemplary, virtuous, honorable and righteous life." Defendant produced and released a movie entitled "The Red Kimono" based on plaintiff's experiences, using her true maiden name and advertising the film as a true account.

These cases, however, are exceptional and the modern trend is to confine them. See Johnson v. Harcourt, Brace, Jovanovich, Inc., 43 Cal. App. 3d 880, 118 Cal. Rptr. 370 (Cal. Ct. App. 1974); Haynes v. Alfred A. Knopf, Inc., 8 F.3d 1222 (7th Cir. 1993); Gates v. Discovery Commc'ns, Inc., 34 Cal. 4th 679, 101 P.3d 552 (2004). Haynes v. Alfred A. Knopf, 8 F.3d 1222, 1231 (7th Cir.1993). In *Haynes*, Posner J. trenchantly discusses the case law. Plaintiff's early married life had been described at length in a book about African-American migration to the North. Plaintiff had reformed and was involved in community and church affairs when the book publicized his early and wayward ways. Posner J. found the publication was not actionable because although the disclosure may have deeply offended plaintiff, the facts were of a kind in which the public has a legitimate interest. Id. at 1232. The question turns on two criteria, "offensiveness and newsworthiness." Publications, particularly photographs that gratuitously ridicule, especially with a connotation, are actionable. In Gates v. Discovery Communications, Inc., 101 P.3d 552 (Calif. 2004) defendants' television producers and transmitters aired an account of a crime in which plaintiff was involved a dozen years prior. Citing the fact that the published information was on the public record, the court held the disclosure was not actionable. Any state interest on rehabilitation was found not to outweigh the interest in publication of truthful public information.

Beyond this, the state may have an interest to prevent the publication of true facts in vindication of a paramount social interest, Capra v. Thoroughbred Racing Ass'n of North America, Inc., 787 F.2d 463 (9th Cir.1986), cert. denied, 479 U.S. 1017 (1986) (disclosures of identity of persons in witness protection program).

12. In *The Florida Star,* as in other cases, the court emphasizes that the information could have been kept secret. Once it reached the "public domain" through lawful means, however, the media can publish it. What constitutional law restrictions apply to breach of confidence? In Cohen v. Cowles Media Company, 501 U.S. 663 (1991), the plaintiff gave information about a political candidate to reporters of the defendant newspapers, conditioned upon the promise that his identity remain confidential. The defendant newspapers published stories identifying the plaintiff as the source of the information. The plaintiff was fired by his employer. The majority found the plaintiff to have a good cause of action for the loss occasioned by the breach. The Court's opinion distinguished *The Florida Star* line of cases. Minnesota law "simply requires those making promises to keep them." In Ruzicka v. Conde Nast Publications, Inc., 999 F.2d 1319 (8th Cir.1993), Glamour magazine published a story about therapist-patient sexual abuse. Plaintiff gave information to the story's author on condition that she not be identified or identifiable. Story was published changing her name but supplying details allowing a reasonable recipient of the communication to identify her. (She was the only female law student or lawyer serving on the Minnesota Task Force Against Sexual Abuse.) Liability was based on a promissory estoppel theory. What measure of damages could be given? Would they include the harm done by the subsequent publications?

Is protection of confidentiality consistent with the tenets of the First Amendment? The government contracts with its employees to keep information secret. An employee subject to such a contract discloses the information. Is the employee (or former employee) liable for breach of confidence? Can a publisher of the information, knowing of its confidential nature, be held liable? May that publisher be enjoined from publication? These issues were aired in United States v. Marchetti, 466 F.2d 1309 (4th Cir.1972), cert. denied, 409 U.S. 1063 (1972) (former CIA agent revealed secrets in book in violation of agreement) and United States v. Snepp, 897 F.2d 138 (4th Cir.1990) (similar facts). The English and Commonwealth courts in the Spycatcher litigation wrestled with the same issues when a former M.I.5 agent in retirement in Tasmania wrote a book disclosing intelligence secrets. The British Government waged a global campaign to suppress the publication: Attorney-General v. Guardian Newspapers (No. 2), [1990] 1 A.C. 109.

Cantrell v. Forest City Publishing Co.

Supreme Court of the United States, 1974.
419 U.S. 245, 95 S.Ct. 465, 42 L.Ed.2d 419.

MR. JUSTICE STEWART delivered the opinion of the Court.

Margaret Cantrell and four of her minor children brought this diversity action in a federal district court for invasion of privacy against the Forest City Publishing Company, publisher of a Cleveland newspaper, The Plain Dealer, and against Joseph Eszterhas, a reporter formerly employed by The Plain Dealer, and Richard Conway, a Plain Dealer photographer. The Cantrells alleged that an article published in The Plain Dealer Sunday Magazine unreasonably placed their family in a false light before the public through its many inaccuracies and untruths. The District Judge struck the claims relating to punitive damages as to all the plaintiffs and dismissed the actions of three of the Cantrell children in their entirety, but allowed the case to go to the jury as to Mrs. Cantrell and her oldest son, William. The jury returned a verdict against all three of the respondents for compensatory money damages in favor of these two plaintiffs.

The Court of Appeals for the Sixth Circuit reversed, holding that, in the light of the First and Fourteenth Amendments, the District Judge should have granted the respondents' motion for a directed verdict as to all the Cantrells. Cantrell v. Forest City Publishing Co., 484 F.2d 150. We granted certiorari, 418 U.S. 909.

I. In December 1967, Margaret Cantrell's husband Melvin was killed along with 43 other people when the Silver Bridge across the Ohio River at Point Pleasant, West Virginia, collapsed. The respondent Eszterhas was assigned by The Plain Dealer to cover the story of the disaster. He wrote a "news feature" story focusing on the funeral of Melvin Cantrell and the impact of his death on the Cantrell family.

Five months later, after conferring with the Sunday Magazine editor of The Plain Dealer, Eszterhas and photographer Conway returned to the Point Pleasant area to write a follow-up feature. The two men went to the Cantrell residence, where Eszterhas talked with the children and Conway took 50 pictures. Mrs. Cantrell was not at home at any time during the 60 to 90 minutes that the men were at the Cantrell residence.

Eszterhas's story appeared as the lead feature in the August 4, 1968, edition of The Plain Dealer Sunday Magazine. The article stressed the family's abject poverty; the children's old, ill-fitting clothes and the deteriorating condition of their home were detailed in both the text and accompanying photographs. As he had done in his original, prize-winning article on the Silver Bridge disaster, Eszterhas used the Cantrell family to illustrate the impact of the bridge collapse on the lives of the people in the Point Pleasant area.

It is conceded that the story contained a number of inaccuracies and false statements. Most conspicuously, although Mrs. Cantrell was not present at any time during the reporter's visit to her home, Eszterhas wrote, "Margaret Cantrell will talk neither about what happened nor about how they are doing. She wears the same mask of non-expression she wore at the funeral. She is a proud woman. She says that after it happened, the people in town offered to help them out with money and they refused to take it." Other significant misrepresentations were contained in details of Eszterhas' descriptions of the poverty in which the Cantrells were living and the dirty and dilapidated conditions of the Cantrell home.

The case went to the jury on a so-called "false light" theory of invasion of privacy. In essence, the theory of the case was that by publishing the false feature story about the Cantrells and thereby making them the objects of pity and ridicule, the respondents damaged Mrs. Cantrell and her son William by causing them to suffer outrage, mental distress, shame, and humiliation.

II. In Time, Inc. v. Hill, 385 U.S. 374, the Court considered a similar false light, invasion of privacy action. The New York Court of Appeals had interpreted New York Civil Rights Law, McKinney's Consol.Laws, c. 6, §§ 50–51 to give a "newsworthy person" a right of action when his or her name, picture or portrait was the subject of a "fictitious" report or article. Material and substantial falsification was the test for recovery. [C] Under this doctrine the New York courts awarded the plaintiff James Hill compensatory damages based on his complaint that Life Magazine had falsely reported that a new Broadway play portrayed the Hill family's experience in being held hostage by three escaped convicts. This Court, guided by its decision in New York Times Co. v. Sullivan, 376 U.S. 254, which recognized constitutional limits on a State's power to award damages for libel in actions brought by public officials, held that the constitutional protections for speech and press precluded the application of the New York statute to allow recovery for "false reports of matters of public interest in the absence of proof that the defendant published the report with knowledge of its falsity or in reckless disregard of the truth." [C] Although the jury could have reasonably concluded from the evidence in the *Hill* case that Life had engaged in knowing falsehood or had recklessly disregarded the truth in stating in the article that "the story re-enacted" the Hill family's experience, the Court concluded that the trial judge's instructions had not confined the jury to such a finding as a predicate for liability as required by the Constitution. [C]

The District Judge in the case before us, in contrast with the trial judge in Time, Inc. v. Hill, did instruct the jury that liability could be imposed only if it concluded that the false statements in the Sunday Magazine feature article on the Cantrells had been made with knowledge of their falsity or in reckless disregard of the truth. No objection was made by any of the parties to this knowing-or-reckless-falsehood instruction. Consequently, this case presents no occasion to consider whether a State may constitutionally apply a more relaxed standard of liability for a publisher or broadcaster of false statements injurious to a private individual under a false-light theory of invasion of privacy, or whether the constitutional standard announced in Time, Inc. v. Hill applies to all false-light cases. Cf. Gertz v. Welch, Inc., 418 U.S. 323. Rather, the sole question that we need decide is whether the Court of Appeals erred in setting aside the jury's verdict.

III. At the close of the petitioners' case-in-chief, the District Judge struck the demand for punitive damages. He found that Mrs. Cantrell had failed to present any evidence to support the charges that the invasion of privacy "was done maliciously within the legal definition of that term." The Court of Appeals interpreted this finding to be a determination by the District Judge that there was no evidence of knowing falsity or reckless disregard of the truth introduced at the trial. Having made such a determination, the Court of Appeals held that the District Judge should have granted the motion for a directed verdict as to all respondents. 484 F.2d, at 155.

The Court of Appeals appears to have assumed that the District Judge's finding of no malice "within the legal definition of that term" was a finding based on the definition of "actual malice" established by this Court in New York Times Co. v. Sullivan, 376 U.S. 254, 280: "with knowledge that [a defamatory statement] was false or with reckless disregard of whether it was false or not." As so defined, of course, "actual malice" is a term of art, created to provide a convenient shorthand for the standard of liability that must be established before a State may constitutionally permit public officials to recover for libel in actions brought against publishers. As such, it is quite different from the common-law standard of "malice" generally required under state tort law to support an award of punitive damages. In a false-light case, common-law malice—frequently expressed in terms of either personal ill will toward the plaintiff or reckless or wanton disregard of the plaintiff's rights—would focus on the defendant's attitude toward the plaintiff's privacy, not towards the truth or falsity of the material published. See Time, Inc. v. Hill, 385 U.S., at 396 n. 12. See generally W. Prosser, Law of Torts 9–10 (4th ed.).

Although the verbal record of the District Court proceedings is not entirely unambiguous, the conclusion is inescapable that the District Judge was referring to the common-law standard of malice rather than to the *New York Times* "actual malice" standard when he dismissed the punitive damages claims. For at the same time that he dismissed the demands for punitive damages, the District Judge refused to grant the respondents' motion for directed verdicts as to Mrs. Cantrell's and William's claims for compensatory damages. And, as his instructions to the jury made clear, the District Judge was fully aware that the Time, Inc. v. Hill meaning of the *New York Times* "actual malice" standard had to be satisfied for the Cantrells to recover actual damages. Thus, the only way to harmonize these two virtually simultaneous rulings by the District Judge is to conclude, contrary to the decision of the Court of Appeals, that in dismissing the punitive damages claims he was not determining that Mrs. Cantrell had failed to introduce any evidence of knowing falsity or reckless disregard of the truth. This conclusion is further fortified by the District Judge's subsequent denial of the respondents' motion for judgment N.O.V. and alternative motion for a new trial.

Moreover, the District Judge was clearly correct in believing that the evidence introduced at trial was sufficient to support a jury finding that the respondents Joseph Eszterhas and Forest City Publishing Company had published knowing or reckless falsehoods about the

Cantrells. There was no dispute during the trial that Eszterhas, who did not testify, must have known that a number of the statements in the feature story were untrue. In particular, his article plainly implied that Mrs. Cantrell had been present during his visit to her home and that Eszterhas had observed her "wear[ing] the same mask of nonexpression she wore [at her husband's] funeral." These were "calculated falsehoods," and the jury was plainly justified in finding that Eszterhas had portrayed the Cantrells in a false light through knowing or reckless untruth.

The Court of Appeals concluded that there was no evidence that Forest City Publishing Company had knowledge of any of the inaccuracies contained in Eszterhas' article. However, there was sufficient evidence for the jury to find that Eszterhas' writing of the feature was within the scope of his employment at The Plain Dealer and that Forest City Publishing Company was therefore liable under traditional doctrines of *respondeat superior*. Although Eszterhas was not regularly assigned by The Plain Dealer to write for the Sunday Magazine, the editor of the magazine testified that as a staff writer for The Plain Dealer, Eszterhas frequently suggested stories he would like to write for the magazine. When Eszterhas suggested the follow-up article on the Silver Bridge disaster, the editor approved the idea and told Eszterhas the magazine would publish the feature if it was good. From this evidence, the jury could reasonably conclude that Forest City Publishing Company, publisher of The Plain Dealer should be held vicariously liable for the damage caused by the knowing falsehoods contained in Eszterhas' story.

For the foregoing reasons the judgment of the Court of Appeals is reversed and the case is remanded to that court with directions to enter a judgment affirming the judgment of the District Court as to the respondents Forest City Publishing Company and Joseph Eszterhas.

[JUSTICE DOUGLAS dissented, with opinion.]

NOTES AND QUESTIONS

1. This branch of the tort of invasion of privacy can be described as placing the plaintiff in an objectionable false light in the public eye. It goes back as far as Lord Byron v. Johnston, 2 Mer. 29, 35 Eng. Rep. 851 (1816), when Byron succeeded in enjoining the circulation of a bad poem that had been attributed to his pen. The Restatement (Second) of Torts § 652E explains that false-light actions protect the plaintiff's interest in "not being made to appear before the public . . . otherwise than as he is." Courts have likened this interest to the plaintiff's interest in possessing a good reputation.

Plaintiff, a war hero, was the subject of a motion picture produced by the defendant. In addition to portraying plaintiff's immense valor on the battlefield, defendant's film includes a detailed yet wholly fictitious narrative of plaintiff's private life, "including a non-existent romance with a girl." Is defendant liable to plaintiff for defamation? For invasion of privacy? See Restatement (Second) of Torts § 652 E, comment b, illustration 5. But see Crowley v. Fox Broadcasting Co., 851 F.Supp. 700 (D. Md. 1994) (requiring the elements of defamation be met in a false-light action). The tort focuses not on the truth or falsity of a statement, but on whether a statement leads the public to believe something false about the plaintiff. Phillips v. Lincoln County School Dist., 161 Or.App. 429, 984 P.2d 947 (1999). The false light must be shed on the individual plaintiff. Michigan United Conservation Clubs v. CBS News, 485 F.Supp. 893 (W.D. Mich 1980) (no action available to individual Michigan hunters for television documentary's offensive portrayal of hunters in Michigan generally).

Representative cases include Leverton v. Curtis Pub. Co., 192 F.2d 974 (3d Cir.1951) (picture of child, hurt in automobile accident, used to illustrate article, "They Ask to be Killed"); Peay v. Curtis Pub. Co., 78 F.Supp. 305 (D.D.C.1948) (picture of honest taxi driver illustrating article on the cheating propensities of taxi drivers); Douglass v. Hustler Magazine, Inc., 769 F.2d 1128 (7th Cir.1985), cert. denied, 475 U.S. 1094 (1986) (plaintiff allowed Playboy to run nude picture of her, but Hustler did it without permission; false light lies for implying that she would allow that magazine to carry the picture); Lerman v. Flynt Distributing Co., Inc., 745 F.2d 123 (2d Cir.1984), cert. denied, 471 U.S. 1054 (1985) (plaintiff identified as actress in photographs topless and in "orgy" scene in defendant's magazine); Peoples Bank and Trust Co. of Mountain Home v. Globe International Publishing, Inc., 978 F.2d 1065 (8th Cir.1992), aff'g 786 F.Supp. 791 (W.D.Ark.1992) (plaintiff, a ninety-five-year-old woman, had her photograph featured in defendant's tabloid reporting that an Australian woman of 101 had been forced to quit her job because an affair with a millionaire had left her pregnant; award of $850,000 in punitive damages); Kolegas v. Heftel Broadcasting Corp., 154 Ill.2d 1, 607 N.E.2d 201, 180 Ill.Dec. 307 (1992) (plaintiff placed in false light by defendant's disc jockey stating that plaintiff and his wife were in shotgun wedding and his wife and son had abnormally large heads; the imputations were highly offensive).

2. In Samuel v. Curtis Pub. Co., 122 F.Supp. 327 (N.D.Cal.1954), a woman stood on the edge of the Golden Gate bridge in San Francisco, about to jump. Plaintiff was photographed while trying to dissuade her. Two years later defendant published in its magazine an article on suicide, and used the picture as an illustration. This was held not to invade the plaintiff's privacy. In accord are Sarat Lahiri v. Daily Mirror, Inc., 162 Misc. 776, 295 N.Y.S. 382 (1937) (picture of Hindu illusionist illustrating article on the Indian rope trick); Oma v. Hillman Periodicals, 281 App.Div. 240, 118 N.Y.S.2d 720 (1953) (picture of boxer illustrating article on boxing); Kline v. Robert M. McBride & Co., 170 Misc. 974, 11 N.Y.S.2d 674 (1939) (picture of strike-breaker, book on strike-breaking). How are the two groups of cases to be distinguished?

3. In the privacy action, what becomes of the various safeguards thrown about the freedom of the press in defamation cases, such as the necessity of a defamatory innuendo, the requirement of proof of special damage when what is published is not actionable per se, the retraction statutes, and those requiring the filing of a bond for costs? See Prosser, Privacy, 48 Calif.L.Rev. 383, 422–23 (1960); Wade, Defamation and the Right of Privacy, 15 Vand.L.Rev. 1093 (1962). In Werner v. Times-Mirror Co., 193 Cal.App.2d 111, 14 Cal.Rptr. 208 (1961), the court recognized the

problem, and applied a retraction statute even to false statements about the plaintiff that were not defamatory.

4. At least 20 states and the District of Columbia expressly recognize false light invasion of privacy. Jurisdictions that reject the tort include: Colorado: Denver Publishing Co. v. Bueno, 54 P.3d 893 (2002); Minnesota: Markgraf v. Douglas Corporation., 468 N.W.2d 80 (Minn.App.1991); Lake v. Wal-Mart Stores, Inc., 582 N.W.2d 231, 235 (Minn.1998) (finding that false-light actions are similar to, but more expansive than, defamation actions, and as such create an unacceptable tension between tort law and the First Amendment); North Carolina: Renwick v. News and Observer Publishing Co., 310 N.C. 312, 312 S.E.2d 405 (1984); Hall v. Post and the Post Publishing Co., Inc., supra page 1022; Brown v. Pearson, 326 S.C. 409, 483 S.E.2d 477 (S.C. App. Ct. 1997); Texas: Cain v. Hearst Corporation, 878 S.W.2d 577 (Tex.1994) (plaintiff, a prison inmate with a shocking criminal record, claimed defendant's article actionable because it claimed he was a member of the "Dixie Mafia" and had killed as many as eight people; held tort should not be recognized, but against strong dissent). In Missouri, no action is available where a defamation action would be adequate to afford relief: Sullivan v. Pulitzer Broadcasting Co., 709 S.W.2d 475 (Mo.1986); Renner v. Donsbach, 749 F.Supp. 987 (W.D.Mo.1990); but in Meyerkord v. Zipatoni Co., 276 S.W.3d 319 (Mo. Ct. App. 2008) the court favored the cognizability of the tort. In Florida, the court rejected the tort as "failing to add anything distinctive to the law." Jews for Jesus, Inc. v. Rapp, 997 So.2d 1098 (Fla. 2008). Three other jurisdictions have found that state statutory rights to privacy exclude false-light actions: Howell v. New York Post Co., Inc., 81 N.Y.2d 115, 596 N.Y.S.2d 350, 612 N.E.2d 699 (1993); Zinda v. Louisiana Pacific Corp., 149 Wis.2d 913, 440 N.W.2d 548 (1989); and Falwell v. Penthouse Intern., Ltd., 521 F.Supp. 1204 (W.D. Va. 1981) (applying Virginia law).

5. *Constitutional Law*. As the principal case notes, Time, Inc. v. Hill, 385 U.S. 374 (1967) established that false-light cases involving matters of public concern require actual malice: that the defendant knew of the statement's falsity, or acted with reckless disregard of the statement's truth. Subsequently, the Court limited the malice requirement to statements concerning public figures, and held that mere negligence is sufficient for claims by private individuals. Gertz v. Robert Welch, Inc., supra page 944. *Gertz*, however, was a defamation case, and its effect on the *Time*'s false-light standard is not presumptive. The Court did not reconcile the two cases in the principal case here, and it remains unclear whether the *Gertz* relaxation applies to false-light cases, or whether the *Time* standard continues to require malice whenever the false-light case, regardless of the private character of the plaintiff, involves a matter of public concern. See, applying the negligence standard to a false-light case, Wood v. Hustler Mag., Inc., 736 F.2d 1084 (5th Cir.1984); Jones v. Palmer Communications, Inc., 440 N.W.2d 884, 894 (Iowa 1989) (the "false light" cases are subject to the same constitutional constraints as defamation cases); Crump v. Beckley Newspapers, Inc., 173 W.Va. 699, 320 S.E.2d 70 (1983) (holding that the inconsistency will be resolved in favor of *Gertz*; photograph of woman coal miner was used to illustrate an article about sexual harassment in mines). But cf. Lovgren v. Citizens First Nat'l Bank, 126 Ill.2d 411, 534 N.E.2d 987, 128 Ill.Dec. 542 (1989) (ruling that at common law a false light action requires a showing of at least reckless

falsification). Even though the resolution of the conflict between *Gertz* and *Time Inc.* is in doubt as to the libel of a private person where the material is of public interest, is there doubt where the material is of purely private interest?

Tennessee has attempted to reconcile the various policies evinced in the Supreme Court cases, favoring plaintiffs in wholly private matters and the First Amendment in matters of public discourse. West v. Media General Convergence, Inc., 53 S.W.3d 640 (Tenn. 2001) (requiring actual malice for claims by public figures and for claims involving matters of public concern brought by private individuals, but permitting a negligence standard for claims by private individuals involving matters of private concern).

Hustler Magazine v. Falwell

Supreme Court of the United States, 1988.
485 U.S. 46, 108 S.Ct. 876, 99 L.Ed.2d 41.

CHIEF JUSTICE REHNQUIST delivered the opinion of the Court.

Petitioner Hustler Magazine, Inc., is a magazine of nationwide circulation. Respondent Jerry Falwell, a nationally known minister who has been active as a commentator on politics and public affairs, sued petitioner and its publisher, petitioner Larry Flynt, to recover damages for invasion of privacy, libel, and intentional infliction of emotional distress. The District Court directed a verdict against respondent on the privacy claim, and submitted the other two claims to a jury. The jury found for petitioners on the defamation claim [on the ground that the "ad parody could not 'reasonably be understood as describing actual facts' about plaintiff or actual events in which he participated." It also] found for respondent on the claim for intentional infliction of emotional distress and awarded damages [of $200,000, including punitive damages]. We now consider whether this award is consistent with the First and Fourteenth Amendments of the United States Constitution.

The inside front cover of the November 1983 issue of Hustler Magazine featured a "parody" of an advertisement for Campari Liqueur that contained the name and picture of respondent and was entitled "Jerry Falwell talks about his first time." This parody was modeled after actual Campari ads that included interviews with various celebrities about their "first times." Although it was apparent by the end of each interview that this meant the first time they sampled Campari, the ads clearly played on the sexual double entendre of the general subject of "first times." Copying the form and layout of these Campari ads, Hustler's editors chose respondent as the featured celebrity and drafted an alleged "interview" with him in which he states that his "first time" was during a drunken incestuous rendezvous with his mother in an outhouse. The Hustler parody portrays respondent and his mother as drunk and immoral, and suggests that respondent is a hypocrite who preaches only when he is drunk. In small print at the bottom of the page, the ad contains the disclaimer, "ad parody—not to be taken seriously." The magazine's table of contents also lists the ad as "Fiction; Ad and Personality Parody." * * *

On appeal [from the District Court,] the United States Court of Appeals for the Fourth Circuit affirmed the judgment against petitioners. Falwell v. Flynt, 797 F.2d 1270 (C.A.4 1986). The court rejected petitioners' argument that the "actual malice" standard of New York Times Co. v. Sullivan, 376 U.S. 254 (1964), must be met before respondent can recover for emotional distress. The court agreed that because respondent is concededly a public figure, petitioners are "entitled to the same level of first amendment protection in the claim for intentional infliction of emotional distress that they received in [respondent's] claim for libel." 797 F.2d, at 1274. But this does not mean that a literal application of the actual malice rule is appropriate in the context of an emotional distress claim. In the court's view, the *New York Times* decision emphasized the constitutional importance not of the falsity of the statement or the defendant's disregard for the truth, but of the heightened level of culpability embodied in the requirement of "knowing * * * or reckless" conduct. Here, the *New York Times* standard is satisfied by the state-law requirement, and the jury's finding, that the defendants have acted intentionally or recklessly.[3] The Court of Appeals then went on to reject the contention that because the jury found that the ad parody did not describe actual facts about respondent, the ad was an opinion that is protected by the First Amendment. As the court put it, this was "irrelevant," as the issue is "whether [the ad's] publication was sufficiently outrageous to constitute intentional infliction of emotional distress." [C] Petitioners then filed a petition for rehearing en banc, but this was denied by a divided court. Given the importance of the constitutional issues involved, we granted certiorari.

This case presents us with a novel question involving First Amendment limitations upon a State's authority to protect its citizens from the intentional infliction of emotional distress. We must decide whether a public figure may recover damages for emotional harm caused by the publication of an ad parody offensive to him, and doubtless gross and repugnant in the eyes of most. Respondent would have us find that a State's interest in protecting public figures from emotional distress is sufficient to deny First Amendment protection to speech that is patently offensive and is intended to inflict emotional injury, even when that speech could not reasonably have been interpreted as stating actual facts about the public figure involved. This we decline to do.

At the heart of the First Amendment is the recognition of the fundamental importance of the free flow of ideas and opinions on matters of public interest and concern. "[T]he freedom to speak one's mind is not only an aspect of individual liberty—and thus a good unto itself—but also is essential to the common quest for truth and the vitality of society as a whole." Bose Corp. v. Consumers Union of United States, [c] Inc., 466 U.S. 485, 503–504 (1984). We have therefore been particularly vigilant to ensure that individual expressions of ideas remain free from governmentally imposed sanctions. The First Amendment recognizes no such thing as a "false" idea. *Gertz v. Robert Welch, Inc.*, 418 U.S. 323, 339 (1974). * * *

---

[3] Under Virginia law, in an action for intentional infliction of emotional distress a plaintiff must show that the defendant's conduct (1) is intentional or reckless; (2) offends generally accepted standards of decency or morality; (3) is causally connected with the plaintiff's emotional distress; and (4) caused emotional distress that was severe. 797 F.2d, at 1275, n. 4 (citing Womack v. Eldridge, 215 Va. 338, 210 S.E.2d 145 (1974)).

The sort of robust political debate encouraged by the First Amendment is bound to produce speech that is critical of those who hold public office or those public figures who are "intimately involved in the resolution of important public questions or, by reason of their fame, shape events in areas of concern to society at large." [C] Justice Frankfurter put it succinctly in Baumgartner v. United States, 322 U.S. 665, 673–674 (1944), when he said that "[o]ne of the prerogatives of American citizenship is the right to criticize public men and measures." Such criticism, inevitably, will not always be reasoned or moderate; public figures as well as public officials will be subject to "vehement, caustic, and sometimes unpleasantly sharp attacks," *New York Times,* supra, at 270. "[T]he candidate who vaunts his spotless record and sterling integrity cannot convincingly cry 'Foul!' when an opponent or an industrious reporter attempts to demonstrate the contrary." Monitor Patriot Co. v. Roy, 401 U.S. 265, 274 (1971).

Of course, this does not mean that *any* speech about a public figure is immune from sanction in the form of damages. Since *New York Times Co. v. Sullivan,* supra, we have consistently ruled that a public figure may hold a speaker liable for the damage to reputation caused by publication of a defamatory falsehood, but only if the statement was made "with knowledge that it was false or with reckless disregard of whether it was false or not." Id., at 279–280. False statements of fact are particularly valueless; they interfere with the truth-seeking function of the marketplace of ideas, and they cause damage to an individual's reputation that cannot easily be repaired by counterspeech, however persuasive or effective. See *Gertz,* 418 U.S., at 340, 344, n. 9. But even though falsehoods have little value in and of themselves, they are "nevertheless inevitable in free debate," id., at 340, and a rule that would impose strict liability on a publisher for false factual assertions would have an undoubted "chilling" effect on speech relating to public figures that does have constitutional value. "Freedoms of expression require 'breathing space.'" Philadelphia Newspapers, Inc. v. Hepps, 475 U.S. 767, 772 (1986) (quoting *New York Times,* 376 U.S., at 272). This breathing space is provided by a constitutional rule that allows public figures to recover for libel or defamation only when they can prove *both* that the statement was false and that the statement was made with the requisite level of culpability.

Respondent argues, however, that a different standard should apply in this case because here the State seeks to prevent not reputational damage, but the severe emotional distress suffered by the person who is the subject of an offensive publication. Cf. Zacchini v. Scripps-Howard Broadcasting Co., 433 U.S. 562 (1977) (ruling that the "actual malice" standard does not apply to the tort of appropriation of a right of publicity). In respondent's view, and in the view of the Court of Appeals, so long as the utterance was intended to inflict emotional distress, was outrageous, and did in fact inflict serious emotional distress, it is of no constitutional import whether the statement was a fact or an opinion, or whether it was true or false. It is the intent to cause injury that is the gravamen of the tort, and the State's interest in preventing emotional harm simply outweighs whatever interest a speaker may have in speech of this type.

Generally speaking the law does not regard the intent to inflict emotional distress as one which should receive much solicitude, and it is quite understandable that most if not all jurisdictions have chosen to make it civilly culpable where the conduct in question is sufficiently "outrageous." But in the world of debate about public affairs, many things done with motives that are less than admirable are protected by the First Amendment. In Garrison v. Louisiana, 379 U.S. 64 (1964), we held that even when a speaker or writer is motivated by hatred or ill-will his expression was protected by the First Amendment: "Debate on public issues will not be uninhibited if the speaker must run the risk that it will be proved in court that he spoke out of hatred; even if he did speak out of hatred, utterances honestly believed contribute to the free interchange of ideas and the ascertainment of truth." Id., at 73.

Thus, while such a bad motive may be deemed controlling for purposes of tort liability in other areas of the law, we think the First Amendment prohibits such a result in the area of public debate about public figures.

Were we to hold otherwise, there can be little doubt that political cartoonists and satirists would be subjected to damages awards without any showing that their work falsely defamed its subject. [The court discusses a number of well-known cartoon caricatures.]

Respondent contends, however, that the caricature in question here was so "outrageous" as to distinguish it from more traditional political cartoons. There is no doubt that the caricature of respondent and his mother published in Hustler is at best a distant cousin of the political cartoons described above, and a rather poor relation at that. If it were possible by laying down a principled standard to separate the one from the other, public discourse would probably suffer little or no harm. But we doubt that there is any such standard, and we are quite sure that the pejorative description "outrageous" does not supply one. "Outrageousness" in the area of political and social discourse has an inherent subjectiveness about it which would allow a jury to impose liability on the basis of the jurors' tastes or views, or perhaps on the basis of their dislike of a particular expression. An "outrageousness" standard thus runs afoul of our longstanding refusal to allow damages to be awarded because the speech in question may have an adverse emotional impact on the audience. * * * [A]s we stated in FCC v. Pacifica Foundation, 438 U.S. 726 (1978): "[T]he fact that society may find speech offensive is not a sufficient reason for suppressing it. Indeed, if it is the speaker's opinion that gives offense, that consequence is a reason for according it constitutional protection. For it is a central tenet of the First Amendment that the government must remain neutral in the marketplace of ideas." Id., at 745–746. See also Street v. New York, 394 U.S. 576, 592 (1969) ("It is firmly settled that . . . the public expression of ideas may not be prohibited merely because the ideas are themselves offensive to some of their hearers").

Admittedly, these oft-repeated First Amendment principles, like other principles, are subject to limitations. We recognized in Pacifica Foundation, that speech that is " 'vulgar,' 'offensive,' and 'shocking' " is "not entitled to absolute constitutional protection under all circumstances." 438 U.S., at 747. In Chaplinsky v. New Hampshire, 315

U.S. 568 (1942), we held that a state could lawfully punish an individual for the use of insulting " 'fighting' words—those which by their very utterance inflict injury or tend to incite an immediate breach of the peace." Id., at 571–572. These limitations are but recognition of the observation in Dun & Bradstreet, Inc. v. Greenmoss Builders, Inc., 472 U.S. 749, 758 (1985), that this Court has "long recognized that not all speech is of equal First Amendment importance." But the sort of expression involved in this case does not seem to us to be governed by any exception to the general First Amendment principles stated above.

We conclude that public figures and public officials may not recover for the tort of intentional infliction of emotional distress by reason of publications such as the one here at issue without showing in addition that the publication contains a false statement of fact which was made with "actual malice," *i.e.*, with knowledge that the statement was false or with reckless disregard as to whether or not it was true. This is not merely a "blind application" of the *New York Times* standard, [c] it reflects our considered judgment that such a standard is necessary to give adequate "breathing space" to the freedoms protected by the First Amendment.

Here it is clear that respondent Falwell is a "public figure" for purposes of First Amendment law. [He cannot recover in libel and] is thus relegated to his claim for damages awarded by the jury for the intentional infliction of emotional distress by "outrageous" conduct. But for reasons heretofore stated this claim cannot, consistently with the First Amendment, form a basis for the award of damages when the conduct in question is the publication of a caricature such as the ad parody involved here. The judgment of the Court of Appeals is accordingly

Reversed.

JUSTICE WHITE, concurring in the judgment. As I see it, the decision in New York Times v. Sullivan, 376 U.S. 254 (1964), has little to do with this case, for here the jury found that the ad contained no assertion of fact. But I agree with the Court that the judgment below, which penalized the publication of the parody, cannot be squared with the First Amendment.

NOTES AND QUESTIONS

1. Why is New York Times v. Sullivan, supra page 922, invoked?

2. Once the plaintiff is identified as a public figure and the speech is directed toward public debate in which the public figure is involved, the courts, consistent with the principal case, have permitted robust and vitriolic attack: Dworkin v. Hustler Magazine Inc., 867 F.2d 1188 (9th Cir.1989) (ad hominem attack on feminist who had advocated suppression of pornography). In *Milkovich* supra page 966, the principal case was treated as one of "imaginative expression" where the burden of falsity rests on the plaintiff. The reasoning implies that the principal case extends beyond public figures to private figures in matters of public interest. It follows that the principal case does not protect the publisher or utterer of statement from liability where the attack is directed to a private individual in a matter of no public interest: Esposito-Hilder v. SFX Broadcasting, 171

Misc.2d 286, 654 N.Y.S.2d 259 (1996) (plaintiff, who worked for a rival radio station, was identified by defendants in an "Ugliest Bride Contest"; held action for intentional infliction of emotional distress could lie, although no defamation action would lie since it asserted no facts about plaintiff).

3. Should limits be applied to speech in order to protect the viability of community norms that "inculcate the ideal of rational deliberation"? See Post, The Constitutional Concept of Public Discourse: Outrageous Opinion, Democratic Deliberation, and *Hustler Magazine v. Falwell,* 103 Harv.L.Rev. 601, 684 (1990).

4. The Reverend Falwell's mother proposes to bring an action for intentional infliction of emotional distress. Advise her.

Snyder v. Phelps

Supreme Court of the United States, 2011.
562 U.S. 443, 131 S.Ct. 1207, 179 L.Ed.2d 172.

CHIEF JUSTICE ROBERTS delivered the opinion of the Court.

A jury held members of the Westboro Baptist Church liable for millions of dollars in damages for picketing near a soldier's funeral service. The picket signs reflected the church's view that the United States is overly tolerant of sin and that God kills American soldiers as punishment. The question presented is whether the First Amendment shields the church members from tort liability for their speech in this case.

Fred Phelps founded the Westboro Baptist Church in Topeka, Kansas, in 1955. The church's congregation believes that God hates and punishes the United States for its tolerance of homosexuality, particularly in America's military. The church frequently communicates its views by picketing, often at military funerals. In the more than 20 years that the members of Westboro Baptist have publicized their message, they have picketed nearly 600 funerals.

Marine Lance Corporal Matthew Snyder was killed in Iraq in the line of duty. Lance Corporal Snyder's father selected the Catholic church in the Snyders' hometown of Westminster, Maryland, as the site for his son's funeral. Local newspapers provided notice of the time and location of the service.

Phelps became aware of Matthew Snyder's funeral and decided to travel to Maryland with six other Westboro Baptist parishioners (two of his daughters and four of his grandchildren) to picket. On the day of the memorial service, the Westboro congregation members picketed on public land adjacent to public streets near the Maryland State House, the United States Naval Academy, and Matthew Snyder's funeral. The Westboro picketers carried signs that were largely the same at all three locations. They stated, for instance: "God Hates the USA/Thank God for 9/11," "America is Doomed," "Don't Pray for the USA," "Thank God for IEDs," "Thank God for Dead Soldiers," "Pope in Hell," "Priests Rape Boys," "God Hates Fags," "You're Going to Hell," and "God Hates You."

The church had notified the authorities in advance of its intent to picket at the time of the funeral, and the picketers complied with police instructions in staging their demonstration. The picketing took place within a 10- by 25-foot plot of public land adjacent to a public street, behind a temporary fence. That plot was approximately 1,000 feet from the church where the funeral was held. Several buildings separated the picket site from the church. [c]. The Westboro picketers displayed their signs for about 30 minutes before the funeral began and sang hymns and recited Bible verses. None of the picketers entered church property or went to the cemetery. They did not yell or use profanity, and there was no violence associated with the picketing.

The funeral procession passed within 200 to 300 feet of the picket site. Although Snyder testified that he could see the tops of the picket signs as he drove to the funeral, he did not see what was written on the signs until later that night, while watching a news broadcast covering the event.

Snyder filed suit against Phelps, Phelps's daughters, and the Westboro Baptist Church (collectively Westboro or the church) in the United States District Court for the District of Maryland under that court's diversity jurisdiction. Snyder alleged five state tort law claims: defamation, publicity given to private life, intentional infliction of emotional distress, intrusion upon seclusion, and civil conspiracy. Westboro moved for summary judgment contending, in part, that the church's speech was insulated from liability by the First Amendment.

The District Court awarded Westboro summary judgment on Snyder's claims for defamation and publicity given to private life, concluding that Snyder could not prove the necessary elements of those torts.

A trial was held on the remaining claims. At trial, Snyder described the severity of his emotional injuries. He testified that he is unable to separate the thought of his dead son from his thoughts of Westboro's picketing, and that he often becomes tearful, angry, and physically ill when he thinks about it. Expert witnesses testified that Snyder's emotional anguish had resulted in severe depression and had exacerbated preexisting health conditions.

A jury found for Snyder on the intentional infliction of emotional distress, intrusion upon seclusion, and civil conspiracy claims, and held Westboro liable for $2.9 million in compensatory damages and $8 million in punitive damages. Westboro filed several post-trial motions, including a motion contending that the jury verdict was grossly excessive and a motion seeking judgment as a matter of law on all claims on First Amendment grounds. The District Court remitted the punitive damages award to $2.1 million, but left the jury verdict otherwise intact.

In the Court of Appeals, Westboro's primary argument was that the church was entitled to judgment as a matter of law because the First Amendment fully protected Westboro's speech. The Court of Appeals agreed. The court reviewed the picket signs and concluded that Westboro's statements were entitled to First Amendment protection because those statements were on matters of public concern, were not provably false, and were expressed solely through hyperbolic rhetoric.

We granted certiorari. [c].

To succeed on a claim for intentional infliction of emotional distress in Maryland, a plaintiff must demonstrate that the defendant intentionally or recklessly engaged in extreme and outrageous conduct that caused the plaintiff to suffer severe emotional distress. See *Harris* v. *Jones*, supra page 61. The Free Speech Clause of the First Amendment—"Congress shall make no law . . . abridging the freedom of speech"—can serve as a defense in state tort suits, including suits for intentional infliction of emotional distress. See, *e.g., Hustler Magazine, Inc.* v. *Falwell*, supra page 1040.

Whether the First Amendment prohibits holding Westboro liable for its speech in this case turns largely on whether that speech is of public or private concern, as determined by all the circumstances of the case. "[S]peech on 'matters of public concern' . . . is 'at the heart of the First Amendment's protection.' " *Dun & Bradstreet, Inc.* v. *Greenmoss Builders, Inc.*, supra page 953. The First Amendment reflects "a profound national commitment to the principle that debate on public issues should be uninhibited, robust, and wide-open." *New York Times Co.* v. *Sullivan*, supra page 922. That is because "speech concerning public affairs is more than self-expression; it is the essence of self-government." *Garrison* v. *Louisiana*, 379 U. S. 64, 74–75 (1964). Accordingly, "speech on public issues occupies the highest rung of the hierarchy of First Amendment values, and is entitled to special protection." *Connick* v. *Myers*, 461 U. S. 138, 145 (1983)

" '[N]ot all speech is of equal First Amendment importance,' " however, and where matters of purely private significance are at issue, First Amendment protections are often less rigorous. [c] That is because restricting speech on purely private matters does not implicate the same constitutional concerns as limiting speech on matters of public interest: "[T]here is no threat to the free and robust debate of public issues; there is no potential interference with a meaningful dialogue of ideas"; and the "threat of liability" does not pose the risk of "a reaction of self-censorship" on matters of public import.

We noted a short time ago, in considering whether public employee speech addressed a matter of public concern, that "the boundaries of the public concern test are not well defined." *San Diego* v. *Roe*, 543 U. S. 77, 83 (2004) (*per curiam*). Although that remains true today, we have articulated some guiding principles, principles that accord broad protection to speech to ensure that courts themselves do not become inadvertent censors.

Speech deals with matters of public concern when it can "be fairly considered as relating to any matter of political, social, or other concern to the community," *Connick, supra,* at 146, or when it "is a subject of legitimate news interest; that is, a subject of general interest and of value and concern to the public," *San Diego, supra,* at 83–84. [c] The arguably "inappropriate or controversial character of a statement is irrelevant to the question whether it deals with a matter of public concern." *Rankin* v. *McPherson*, 483 U. S. 378, 387 (1987).

Our opinion in *Dun & Bradstreet*, on the other hand, provides an example of speech of only private concern. In that case we held, as a general matter, that information about a particular individual's credit report "concerns no public issue." The content of the report, we explained, "was speech solely in the individual interest of the speaker and its specific business audience." That was confirmed by the fact that the particular report was sent to only five subscribers to the reporting service, who were bound not to disseminate it further. To cite another example, we concluded in *San Diego* v. *Roe* that, in the context of a government employer regulating the speech of its employees, videos of an employee engaging in sexually explicit acts did not address a public concern; the videos "did nothing to inform the public about any aspect of the [employing agency's] functioning or operation."

Deciding whether speech is of public or private concern requires us to examine the " 'content, form, and context' " of that speech, " 'as revealed by the whole record.' " As in other First Amendment cases, the court is obligated "to 'make an independent examination of the whole record' in order to make sure that 'the judgment does not constitute a forbidden intrusion on the field of free expression.' " *Bose Corp.* v. *Consumers Union of United States, Inc.*, 466 U. S. 485, 499 (1984). In considering content form, and context, no factor is dispositive, and it is necessary to evaluate all the circumstances of the speech, including what was said, where it was said, and how it was said.

The "content" of Westboro's signs plainly relates to broad issues of interest to society at large, rather than matters of "purely private concern." The placards read "God Hates the USA/Thank God for 9/11," "America is Doomed," "Don't Pray for the USA," "Thank God for IEDs," "Fag Troops," "Semper Fi Fags," "God Hates Fags," "Maryland Taliban," "Fags Doom Nations," "Not Blessed Just Cursed," "Thank God for Dead Soldiers," "Pope in Hell," "Priests Rape Boys," "You're Going to Hell," and "God Hates You." While these messages may fall short of refined social or political commentary, the issues they highlight—the political and moral conduct of the United States and its citizens, the fate of our Nation, homosexuality in the military, and scandals involving the Catholic clergy—are matters of public import. The signs certainly convey Westboro's position on those issues, in a manner designed, unlike the private speech in *Dun & Bradstreet*, to reach as broad a public audience as possible. And even if a few of the signs—such as "You're Going to Hell" and "God Hates You"—were viewed as containing messages related to Matthew Snyder or the Snyders specifically, that would not change the fact that the overall thrust and dominant theme of Westboro's demonstration spoke to broader public issues.

Apart from the content of Westboro's signs, Snyder contends that the "context" of the speech—its connection with his son's funeral—makes the speech a matter of private rather than public concern. The fact that Westboro spoke in connection with a funeral, however, cannot by itself transform the nature of Westboro's speech. Westboro's signs, displayed on public land next to a public street, reflect the fact that the church finds much to condemn in modern society. Its speech is "fairly characterized as constituting speech on a matter of public concern," *Connick*, 461 U. S., at 146, and the funeral setting does not alter that conclusion.

Snyder argues that the church members in fact mounted a personal attack on Snyder and his family, and then attempted to "immunize their conduct by claiming that they were actually protesting the United

States' tolerance of homosexuality or the supposed evils of the Catholic Church." We are not concerned in this case that Westboro's speech on public matters was in any way contrived to insulate speech on a private matter from liability. Westboro had been actively engaged in speaking on the subjects addressed in its picketing long before it became aware of Matthew Snyder, and there can be no serious claim that Westboro's picketing did not represent its "honestly believed" views on public issues. *Garrison*, 379 U. S., at 73. There was no preexisting relationship or conflict between Westboro and Snyder that might suggest Westboro's speech on public matters was intended to mask an attack on Snyder over a private matter.

Snyder goes on to argue that Westboro's speech should be afforded less than full First Amendment protection "not only because of the words" but also because the church members exploited the funeral "as a platform to bring their message to a broader audience." There is no doubt that Westboro chose to stage its picketing at the Naval Academy, the Maryland State House, and Matthew Snyder's funeral to increase publicity for its views and because of the relation between those sites and its views—in the case of the military funeral, because Westboro believes that God is killing American soldiers as punishment for the Nation's sinful policies.

Westboro's choice to convey its views in conjunction with Matthew Snyder's funeral made the expression of those views particularly hurtful to many, especially to Matthew's father. The record makes clear that the applicable legal term—"emotional distress"—fails to capture fully the anguish Westboro's choice added to Mr. Snyder's already incalculable grief. But Westboro conducted its picketing peacefully on matters of public concern at a public place adjacent to a public street. Such space occupies a "special position in terms of First Amendment protection." *United States* v. *Grace*, 461 U. S. 171, 180 (1983). "[W]e have repeatedly referred to public streets as the archetype of a traditional public forum," noting that " '[t]ime out of mind' public streets and sidewalks have been used for public assembly and debate." *Frisby* v. *Schultz*, 487 U. S. 474, 480 (1988).

That said, "[e]ven protected speech is not equally permissible in all places and at all times." *Id.,* at 479. Westboro's choice of where and when to conduct its picketing is not beyond the Government's regulatory reach—it is "subject to reasonable time, place, or manner restrictions" that are consistent with the standards announced in this Court's precedents. *Clark* v. *Community for Creative Non-Violence*, 468 U. S. 288, 293 (1984). Maryland now has a law imposing restrictions on funeral picketing, Md. Crim. Law Code Ann. § 10–205. To the extent these laws are content neutral, they raise very different questions from the tort verdict at issue in this case. Maryland's law, however, was not in effect at the time of the events at issue here, so we have no occasion to consider how it might apply to facts such as those before us, or whether it or other similar regulations are constitutional.

We have identified a few limited situations where the location of targeted picketing can be regulated under provisions that the Court has determined to be content neutral. In *Frisby*, for example, we upheld a ban on such picketing "before or about" a particular residence, 487 U.

S., at 477. In *Madsen* v. *Women's Health Center, Inc.*, we approved an injunction requiring a buffer zone between protesters and an abortion clinic entrance. 512 U. S. 753, 768 (1994). The facts here are obviously quite different, both with respect to the activity being regulated and the means of restricting those activities.

Simply put, the church members had the right to be where they were. Westboro alerted local authorities to its funeral protest and fully complied with police guidance on where the picketing could be staged. The picketing was conducted under police supervision some 1,000 feet from the church, out of the sight of those at the church. The protest was not unruly; there was no shouting, profanity, or violence.

The record confirms that any distress occasioned by Westboro's picketing turned on the content and view point of the message conveyed, rather than any interference with the funeral itself. A group of parishioners standing at the very spot where Westboro stood, holding signs that said "God Bless America" and "God Loves You," would not have been subjected to liability. It was what Westboro said that exposed it to tort damages.

Given that Westboro's speech was at a public place on a matter of public concern, that speech is entitled to "special protection" under the First Amendment.

The jury here was instructed that it could hold Westboro liable for intentional infliction of emotional distress based on a finding that Westboro's picketing was "outrageous." "Outrageousness," however, is a highly malleable standard with "an inherent subjectiveness about it which would allow a jury to impose liability on the basis of the jurors' tastes or views, or perhaps on the basis of their dislike of a particular expression." *Hustler*, 485 U. S., at 55. In a case such as this, a jury is "unlikely to be neutral with respect to the content of [the]speech," posing "a real danger of becoming an instrument for the suppression of . . . 'vehement, caustic, and sometimes unpleasan[t]' " expression. *Bose Corp.*, 466 U. S., at 510. Such a risk is unacceptable; "in public debate [we] must tolerate insulting, and even outrageous, speech in order to provide adequate 'breathing space' to the freedoms protected by the First Amendment." *Boos* v. *Barry*, 485 U. S. 312, 322 (1988). What Westboro said, in the whole context of how and where it chose to say it, is entitled to "special protection" under the First Amendment, and that protection cannot be overcome by a jury finding that the picketing was outrageous.

For all these reasons, the jury verdict imposing tort liability on Westboro for intentional infliction of emotional distress must be set aside.

The jury also found Westboro liable for the state law torts of intrusion upon seclusion and civil conspiracy. The Court of Appeals did not examine these torts independently of the intentional infliction of emotional distress tort. Instead, the Court of Appeals reversed the District Court wholesale, holding that the judgment wrongly "attache[d] tort liability to constitutionally protected speech." 580 F. 3d, at 226.

Snyder argues that even assuming Westboro's speech is entitled to First Amendment protection generally, the church is not immunized from liability for intrusion upon seclusion because Snyder was a member of a captive audience at his son's funeral. We do not agree. In most circumstances, "the Constitution does not permit the government to decide which types of otherwise protected speech are sufficiently offensive to require protection for the unwilling listener or viewer. Rather, . . . the burden normally falls upon the viewer to avoid further bombardment of [his] sensibilities simply by averting [his] eyes." *Erznoznik* v. *Jacksonville*, 422 U. S. 205, 210–211 (1975). As a result, "[t]he ability of government, consonant with the Constitution, to shut off discourse solely to protect others from hearing it is . . . dependent upon a showing that substantial privacy interests are being invaded in an essentially intolerable manner." *Cohen* v. *California*, 403 U. S. 15, 21 (1971).

As a general matter, we have applied the captive audience doctrine only sparingly to protect unwilling listeners from protected speech.

Here, Westboro stayed well away from the memorial service. Snyder could see no more than the tops of the signs when driving to the funeral. And there is no indication that the picketing in any way interfered with the funeral service itself. We decline to expand the captive audience doctrine to the circumstances presented here.

Because we find that the First Amendment bars Snyder from recovery for intentional infliction of emotional distress or intrusion upon seclusion—the alleged unlawful activity Westboro conspired to accomplish—we must likewise hold that Snyder cannot recover for civil conspiracy based on those torts.

Our holding today is narrow. We are required in First Amendment cases to carefully review the record, and the reach of our opinion here is limited by the particular facts before us. As we have noted, "the sensitivity and significance of the interests presented in clashes between First Amendment and [state law] rights counsel relying on limited principles that sweep no more broadly than the appropriate context of the instant case." *Florida Star* v. *B. J. F.*, supra page 1033.

Westboro believes that America is morally flawed; many Americans might feel the same about Westboro. Westboro's funeral picketing is certainly hurtful and its contribution to public discourse may be negligible. But Westboro addressed matters of public import on public property, in a peaceful manner, in full compliance with the guidance of local officials. The speech was indeed planned to coincide with Matthew Snyder's funeral, but did not itself disrupt that funeral, and Westboro's choice to conduct its picketing at that time and place did not alter the nature of its speech.

Speech is powerful. It can stir people to action, move them to tears of both joy and sorrow, and—as it did here—inflict great pain. On the facts before us, we cannot react to that pain by punishing the speaker. As a Nation we have chosen a different course—to protect even hurtful speech on public issues to ensure that we do not stifle public debate. That choice requires that we shield Westboro from tort liability for its picketing in this case.

The judgment of the United States Court of Appeals for the Fourth Circuit is affirmed.

It is so ordered

JUSTICE BREYER joined the Court's opinion in a separate concurrence. JUSTICE ALITO dissented stressing the "vicious verbal assault in this case" and that Snyder was a private figure. He stressed the limited scope of the tort of infliction of emotional distress.

NOTES AND QUESTIONS

1. The Chief Justice in the principal case admits and Justice Alito in dissent stresses the pain and hurt suffered by the plaintiffs. Why should a discrete and narrow sector of the public bear the costs of free speech for the benefit of the general public? Consider the reflections of the courts in Spano v. Perini Corp., supra page 12 and Surocco v. Geary supra page 126.

2. The Chief Justice describes the tort of intentional infliction of emotional distress as presenting too "malleable" a standard considering the need to allow for "vehement, caustic and sometimes unpleasant" expression. Thinking back to the tort, is its formulation inattentive to the need to provide scope for robust speech? Note in Gertz v. Robert Welch, Inc., supra page 944 the Court rejects the test in *Rosenbloom*, extending NYT v. Sullivan, based on the published matter being of public interest and concern. (See note 5. page 930). *Rosenbloom* was rejected in Gertz as abridging a legitimate state interest and residing too much "latitude to the conscience of judges." Does *Rosenbloom* ride again?

3. Even in respect of areas of consumer protection where the states have traditionally enjoyed considerable powers in protection of citizens, the Supreme Court has exercised First Amendment doctrine to limit regulations in favor of privacy and maintenance of doctor patient relationships. Sorrell v. IMS Health, Inc., 564 U.S. ___, 131 S. Ct. 2653 (2011).

CHAPTER 19

CIVIL RIGHTS

Ashby v. White

Court of King's Bench, 1702; House of Lords, 1703.
2 Ld.Raym. 938, 92 Eng.Rep. 126; 1 Brown P.C. 62, 1 Eng.Rep. 417.

HOLT, CHIEF JUSTICE. The single question in this case is, whether, if a free burgess of a corporation, who has an undoubted right to give his vote in the election of a burgess to serve in Parliament, be refused and hindered to give it by the officer, if an action on the case will lie against such officer.

I am of opinion that judgment ought to be given in this case for the plaintiff. My brothers differ from me in opinion, and they all differ from one another in the reasons of their opinion; but notwithstanding their opinion, I think the plaintiff ought to recover, and that this action is well maintainable, and ought to lie.

But to proceed, I will do these two things: first, I will maintain that the plaintiff has a right and privilege to give his vote: secondly, in consequence thereof, that if he be hindered in the enjoyment or exercise of that right, the law gives him an action against the disturber, and that this is the proper action given by the law. * * *

If the plaintiff has a right, he must of necessity have a means to vindicate and maintain it, and a remedy if he is injured in the exercise or enjoyment of it; and indeed it is a vain thing to imagine a right without a remedy; for want of right and want of remedy are reciprocal. * * * Where a new Act of Parliament is made for the benefit of the subject, if a man be hindered from the enjoyment of it, he shall have an action against such person who so obstructed him. * * * If then when a statute gives a right, the party shall have an action for the infringement of it, is it not as forcible when a man has his right by the common law? This right of voting is a right in the plaintiff by the common law, and consequently he shall maintain an action for the obstruction of it. * * *

And I am of opinion, that this action on the case is a proper action. My brother Powell indeed thinks, that an action upon the case is not maintainable, because here is no hurt or damage to the plaintiff; but surely every injury imports a damage, though it does not cost the party one farthing, and it is impossible to prove the contrary; for a damage is not merely pecuniary, but an injury imports a damage, when a man is thereby hindered of his right. * * *. So here in the principal case, the plaintiff is obstructed of his right, and shall therefore have his action. And it is no objection to say, that it will occasion multiplicity of actions; for if men will multiply injuries, actions must be multiplied too; for every man that is injured ought to have his recompence. Suppose the defendant had beat forty or fifty men, the damage done to each one is peculiar to himself, and he shall have his action. So if many persons receive a private injury by a publick nusance, every one shall have his action. * * *

But in the principal case my brother says, we cannot judge of this matter, because it is a Parliamentary thing. O! By all means be very tender of that. Besides it is intricate, and there may be contrariety of opinions. But this matter can never come in question in Parliament; for it is agreed that the persons for whom the plaintiff voted were elected; so that the action is brought for being deprived of his vote; and if it were carried for the other candidates against whom he voted, his damage would be less. To allow this action will make publick officers more careful to observe the constitution of cities and boroughs, and not to be so partial as they commonly are in all elections, which is indeed a great and growing mischief, and tends to the prejudice of the peace of the nation. But they say, that this is a matter out of our jurisdiction, and we ought not to inlarge it. I agree we ought not to incroach or inlarge our jurisdiction; by so doing we usurp both on the right of the Queen and the people: but sure we may determine on a charter granted by the King, or on a matter of custom or prescription, when it comes before us without incroaching on the Parliament. And if it be a matter within our jurisdiction, we are bound by our oaths to judge of it. This is a matter of property determinable before us. Was ever such a petition heard of in Parliament, as that a man was hindred of giving his vote, and praying them to give him remedy? The Parliament undoubtedly would say, take your remedy at law. It is not like the case of determining the right of election between the candidates. * * *

Therefore my opinion is, that the plaintiff ought to have judgment. * * *

[The opinions of GOULD, POWYS and POWELL, JJ., constituting the majority in the Court of King's Bench and reversing the jury verdict for the plaintiff, are omitted.

The report of the proceeding in the House of Lords concludes: "After hearing counsel on this writ of error, a debate ensued; and the question being put, Whether this judgment should be reversed? it was resolved in the affirmative. * * * It was therefore ordered and adjudged, that the said judgment should be reversed, and that the plaintiff should recover his damages assessed by the jury; and also, the further sum of 10£. for his costs, in this behalf sustained."]

NOTES AND QUESTIONS

1. Accord: Lane v. Mitchell, 153 Iowa 139, 133 N.W. 381 (1911); Valdez v. Gonzales, 50 N.M. 281, 176 P.2d 173 (1946).

"The objection that the subject matter of the suit is political is little more than a play upon words. Of course the petition concerns political action but it alleges and seeks to recover for private damage. That private damage may be caused by such political action and may be recovered for in a suit at law hardly has been doubted for over two hundred years. * * * If the defendants' conduct was a wrong to the plaintiff the same reasons that allow a recovery for denying the plaintiff a vote at a final election allow it for denying a vote at the primary election that may determine the final result." Holmes, J., in Nixon v. Herndon, 273 U.S. 536, 540 (1927).

2. A similar action lies for depriving a person of the right to hold political office. See, e.g., Hill v. Carr, 186 Ill.App. 515 (1914), and

Goetcheus v. Matthewson, 61 N.Y. 420 (1875), both indicating a right to emoluments. Cf. Sutton v. Adams, 180 Ga. 48, 178 S.E. 365 (1934); Judd v. Polk, 267 Ky. 408, 102 S.W.2d 325 (1937). On both of these torts, see Restatement (Second) of Torts § 865. The decision of Lord Holt was to influence the course of British constitutional history in its transformation to representative democracy. Cornish & Clark, Law and Society in England 1750–1950, 12 (1989).

3. In Morningstar v. Lafayette Hotel Co., 211 N.Y. 465, 105 N.E. 656 (1914), plaintiff was publicly refused service at the restaurant of the hotel where he resided. The reason was his refusal to pay a disputed bill of $1 for special service. Judgment had been given for the defendant. In reversing, Cardozo, J., said: "It is no concern of ours that the controversy at the root of this lawsuit may seem to be trivial. The fact supplies, indeed, the greater reason why the jury should not have been misled into the belief that justice might therefore be denied to the suitor. To enforce one's rights when they are violated is never a legal wrong, and may often be a moral duty. It happens in many instances that the violation passes with no effort to redress it—sometimes from praiseworthy forbearance, sometimes from weakness, sometimes from mere inertia. But the law, which creates a right, can certainly not concede that an insistence upon its enforcement is evidence of a wrong." On a common law action for refusal to serve, see Restatement (Second) of Torts § 866 (1979).

4. To discharge an employee for complying with her duty to serve on a jury will give rise to an action by the employee against the employer. Nees v. Hocks, 272 Or. 210, 536 P.2d 512 (1975); Hodges v. S.C. Toof & Co., 833 S.W.2d 896 (Tenn. 1992) (noting additionally that an action lies where the retaliatory discharge violates a clear public policy, as where an employee is fired for refusing to act illegally).

5. Should these torts be confined to an intentional interference with civil rights and duties, or should they extend to a negligent interference? Should they perhaps be restricted to a purposive interference? Consider the approach of English courts, which have adopted a "bad faith" requirement for the tort of misfeasance in public office. See, e.g., Three Rivers District Council v. Governor and Company of the Bank of England, [2003] 2 A.C. 1 (HL).

6. Despite the remarks of Judge Cardozo in note 3 supra, the tort action for damages sometimes proves not adequate and other remedies are needed. Thus, if a person is wrongfully prevented from voting and recovers in an action of tort, what is the measure of damages? Would it justify the plaintiff in bringing suit or the attorney in taking the case? How might this be handled?

For these reasons, in both the voting and refusal-of-service situations, statutory provisions for injunctive, criminal and administrative relief have largely replaced the common law action. As to voting rights, federal and state statutes control: Voting Rights Act of 1965, 42 U.S.C.A. § 1971. As to refusal of service, see particularly 42 U.S.C.A. § 2000a. Congress has enacted legislation relying, for its enforcement, on private rights of action. Two examples are the Sherman Act (Title 15, §§ 1–3, 104 Stat. 2880, Pub.L. 101–588) and RICO (Racketeer Influenced and Corrupt Organizations Act) (Title 18, §§ 1961–1968, 84 Stat. 941). Both statutes encourage litigation in furtherance of their aims by providing for the award of super-compensatory charges to private litigants. The Supreme Court in Sedima, S.P.R.L. v. Imrex Co., 473 U.S. 479 (1985), gave a broad interpretation to civil RICO. The parameters of the action are still in flux, see DeFalco v. Bernas, 244 F.3d 286 (2d Cir.2001) and notes, infra page 1247.

7. Tort law, either alone or arising out of statute, provides a way for the individual to assert rights against government. In this way it can be said to empower the individual in his relations with the state: thus the law functions as an ombudsman, see Wade, Tort Law as Ombudsman, 65 Or.L.Rev. 309 (1986).

8. The most pervasive cause of action arises from the Ku Klux Klan Act of 1871 wherein Congress, acting under the newly ratified Fourteenth Amendment, responded to the violence and lawlessness during Reconstruction. Section 1 of the Act is now codified as 42 U.S.C.A. § 1983 and provides:

> Every person who, under color of any statute, ordinance, regulation, custom, or usage of any State or Territory, subjects, or causes to be subjected, any citizen of the United States or other person within the jurisdiction thereof to the deprivation of any rights, privileges, or immunities secured by the Constitution and laws, shall be liable to the party injured in an action at law, suit in equity, or other proper proceeding for redress . . .

Very few actions were brought until the Supreme Court decision in Monroe v. Pape, 365 U.S. 167 (1961), which made it clear that the term "every person" included state officers such as state police. The late start has not diminished the power of the section; in fact, the courts have struggled to define its limits. Much of the debate turns on balancing the need to vindicate rights with the conviction that not every wrong needs to be remedied by a federal (as opposed to state) cause of action. Justice Scalia has excoriated the law flowing from Monroe v. Pape, supra. In his dissent in Crawford-El v. Britton, 523 U.S. 574 (1998), he describes *Monroe* as a case "that pours into the federal courts tens of thousands of suits each year, and engages this Court in a losing struggle to prevent the Constitution from degenerating into a general tort law," id. at 611. But compare, Eisenberg and Schwab, The Reality of Constitutional Tort Litigation, 72 Cornell L.Rev. 641 (1987) (empirical survey showed burden of § 1983 litigation was not excessive).

9. If the term "every person" included state officers such as state police, did it include local government? In Monell v. New York City Department of Social Services, 436 U.S. 658 (1978), the Supreme Court held, overruling *Monroe* in part, that a municipality may be held liable for a "policy" or "custom" that causes a constitutional violation. The Court thereby rejected *respondeat superior* liability under § 1983, holding that a municipality cannot be held liable for a civil rights violation merely because the tortfeasor was in that municipality's employ. *Monell*, 436 U.S. at 691. Given this liability requirement, could a municipality be liable for a single instance of a civil rights violation? Board of the County Commissioners of Bryan County, Oklahoma v. Brown, 520 U.S. 397 (1997) (holding that *Monell* does not create municipal liability for isolated failure to properly screen police applicant, but hypothesizing that the *Monell* test may permit single-instance liability in the case of a systemic failure to train

employees). The Court has been willing to find liability where municipal action has the force of law (in *Monroe*, supra), but has refused to create municipal liability solely for the action of municipal employees (in *Monell*). In Canton v. Harris, 489 U.S. 378 (1989), the Court established an approach to hard cases: a municipality may be liable for an individual employee's single instance of wrongful conduct when the plaintiff shows that a civil rights violation was a "highly predictable consequence" of the municipality's action, such that the conduct evinces policymakers' "deliberate indifference" to civil rights. Id. (finding liability for failure to properly train police officers); *Bryan County*, supra (distinguishing failure-to-train cases, which contain obvious potential for violations, from a failure-to-screen case where violation was not a "plainly obvious consequence" of hiring without scrutiny). Note the strong dissent of Justices Breyer, Stevens, and Ginsberg in *Bryan County* arguing for "reexamination" of the *Monell* holding as it relates to the "continued viability" of the "distinction between vicarious municipal liability and municipal liability based upon policy and custom."

State-created causes of action, in contrast to § 1983, may permit municipalities to be held vicariously liable. Washington v. Robertson Co., 29 S.W.3d 466 (Tenn. 2000) (finding the relevant action in the Tennessee Human Rights Act).

10. The Supreme Court has often reiterated that § 1983 is "not itself a source of substantive rights, but a method for vindicating federal rights elsewhere conferred by those parts of the United States Constitution and federal statutes that it describes." Baker v. McCollan, 443 U.S. 137 (1979). The remedial context in which the Court is asked to define constitutional rights influences the scope of the rights: Daryl Levinson, Rights Essentialism and Remedial Equilibration, 99 Colum. L. Rev. 857 (1999). Suits in some areas call for injunctions and declarative relief, others call for relief from criminal law sanctions (e.g. Fourth Amendment), yet others have clear damages common law antecedents. In the area of damages the courts are called upon to balance concerns about liability overreach affecting official decision-making. Limits are drawn by way of immunities, absolute and qualified. The underlying rights are sometimes circumscribed by reference to whether:

1. The interest is cognizable as a "life", "liberty', or "property" interest;
2. The interest was protected by the state;
3. There was a deprivation without due process of law. Paul v. Davis, 424 U.S. 693 (1976). The case has been controversial. The next principal case takes up the issue of identifying the rights that fall within the scope of § 1983.

A Section 1983 cause of action may be expressly excluded by Congress or impliedly precluded by an alternative remedial scheme. Wilder v. Virginia Hosp. Ass'n, 496 U.S. 498 (1990). The right under legislation must "unambiguously" confer "an enforceable right upon the Act's beneficiaries." Suter v. Artist M, 503 U.S. 347, 362 (1992) (holding that the Adoption Assistance and Child Welfare Act did not create such a right through the obligation imposed on states to provide "reasonable efforts" to maintain and reunify families). Similarly, no § 1983 action is available for disclosing a student's educational records in breach of the Family Educational Rights and Privacy Act (FERPA): Gonzaga University v. Doe, 536 U.S. 273 (2002). It is necessary to ascertain whether the claim arises under a specific constitutional provision, say the Fourth or Eighth Amendment or, more generally, under the rubric of substantive due process. If the violative activity falls into a specific constitutional provision, it must be analyzed within the purview of that constitutional provision and not under substantive due process. United States v. Lanier, 520 U.S. 259 (1997). This restrictive approach was reaffirmed in City of Ranchos Palos Verdes v. Abrams, 544 U.S. 113 (2005). Plaintiff had sued his municipality claiming that a denial of a zoning permit for a radio antenna on his property had violated obligations of the city imposed under Telecommunications Act of 1996. The Court found that Congressional intent guided the founding of the right to be enforced and that lack of intent is the "ordinary inference" in the presence of another statutory enforcement scheme. It follows that an abuse of governmental power that does not violate an individual's constitutional or federal legal rights is not actionable under § 1983: Collins v. City of Harker Heights, Tex., 503 U.S. 115 (1992) (failure of public employer to provide a safe working environment does not violate the 14th Amendment and is thus not actionable under § 1983).

11. Federal officers may be liable in tort for violations of the plaintiff's constitutional rights. See Bivens v. Six Unknown Named Agents of the Federal Bureau of Narcotics, 403 U.S. 388 (1971), infra page 1233. The Court, however, has hedged the scope of *Bivens* by considering any "special factors counseling hesitation" before fashioning such remedy. See Bush v. Lucas, 462 U.S. 367 (1983) (deferring to previously established "elaborate remedial system" in retaliatory demotion case); Chappell v. Wallace, 462 U.S. 296 (1983) (declining to provide *Bivens*-type remedy to enlisted military personnel against superior officers). Nor does *Bivens* liability extend to supervisory federal officials, except where such officials have pursued purposefully unconstitutional courses of action. See Ashcroft v. Iqbal, 556 U.S. 662, 129 S.Ct. 1937 (2009). Similarly, courts have refused to grant *Bivens* remedies against state officials. Vakas v. Rodriquez, 728 F.2d 1293 (10th Cir. 1984) (members of administrative board immune when acting in judicial capacities); Berrios v. Agosto, 716 F.2d 85 (1st Cir. 1983) (refusing to allow *Bivens* abrogation of legislative immunity).

12. Expanding liability has per force placed an emphasis on the defense of governmental immunity. See Chapter 12(3). See Imbler v. Pachtman, 424 U.S. 409 (1976) (absolute immunity for certain legislative and judicial officials); Butz v. Economou, 438 U.S. 478 (1978) (good-faith immunity for executive officials performing discretionary functions); Monell v. Department of Social Services, 436 U.S. 658 (1978) (governmental immunity); Pembaur v. City of Cincinnati, 475 U.S. 469 (1986) (municipal immunity, single act); Anderson v. Creighton, 483 U.S. 635, 638 (1987) (F.B.I. officials making a warrantless search of house have "a qualified immunity, shielding them from civil damages liability as long as their actions could reasonably have been thought consistent with the rights they are alleged to have violated"); Mireles v. Waco, 502 U.S. 9 (1991) (judge enjoyed absolute immunity when ordering that plaintiff be taken from another courtroom to appear before him). Harlow v. Fitzgerald, 457 U.S. 800 (1982) (officials shielded from liability if conduct does not "violate clearly established statutory or constitutional rights of which a reasonable

person would have known"). For an instructive application, see Hope v. Pelzer, 536 U.S. 730 (2002) (actions of prison guards sufficiently egregious to base an Eighth Amendment violation). The immunity enjoyed by public officials cannot be invoked by private defendants acting under "color of state law" threatened with a § 1983 suit: Wyatt v. Cole, 504 U.S. 158 (1992). Private prison guards were not entitled to qualified immunity from suit by prisoners charging a § 1983 violation. Richardson v. McKnight, 521 U.S. 399 (1997).

Camp v. Gregory

United States Court Of Appeals, Seventh Circuit, 1995.
67 F.3d 1286.

POSNER, CIRCUIT JUDGE. Anthony Young died on his sixteenth birthday. At the time of his death, Anthony was under the guardianship of the Illinois Department of Children and Family Services ("DCFS"). His aunt and former guardian, Elnora Camp, brought this suit contending that George Gregory, the DCFS caseworker assigned to Anthony, had denied Anthony substantive due process by failing to ensure that Anthony was placed in a safe living environment. The district court dismissed the suit, believing that the Supreme Court's decision in DeShaney v. Winnebago County Dep't of Social Services, 489 U.S. 189 (1989), shielded Gregory from liability for his decision where to place Anthony. Because the DCFS had assumed guardianship over Anthony, we do not think *DeShaney* necessarily bars Camp's due process claim. However, we do conclude that Gregory is entitled to qualified immunity, as prior caselaw did not make clear that a state official could be liable under facts analogous to those alleged here.

FACTS

* * *

The DCFS became Anthony's guardian on June 25, 1991, by order of the Circuit Court of Cook County, Illinois. Prior to that time, Camp had assumed guardianship of Anthony from his mother, whose medical condition rendered her unable to care for him. Camp ultimately sought appointment of another guardian, however, after concluding that she could not provide the highly structured and closely supervised environment necessary to assure Anthony's safety and well-being. The state court granted her request and by agreement appointed the DCFS Anthony's guardian. Gregory was subsequently assigned to be Anthony's caseworker.

A DCFS referral form completed by a probation officer assigned to the Cook County Juvenile Court recommended that Anthony be placed in a highly structured environment. Despite knowing that Camp could not provide the degree of supervision and care that Anthony required and that Anthony faced a greater than normal risk of physical harm while living in her home, Gregory returned him to Camp's care. Subsequently, he neglected to make any referral or application for any appropriate educational or guidance program and failed to follow up on Anthony's progress. Yet, on September 20, 1991, he represented under oath to the state court (which had retained jurisdiction over Anthony's case to monitor his progress) that Anthony had been returned to Camp at the request of the Camp family, that Anthony was attending school, and that he was "doing fine." [C] Each of these representations was false and Gregory knew as much.

Ten days later, on September 30, 1991, Camp wrote to Gregory noting that her previous telephone calls to him had gone unanswered. She requested information concerning appropriate referrals and advised Gregory that Anthony was not attending school and was "placing himself in situations jeopardizing his physical safety as well as his education." [C] She also reiterated that she could not ensure Anthony's safety.

Anthony remained in Camp's care until he died on December 30, 1991. Camp contends that his death resulted directly from Gregory's failure to arrange for Anthony to be placed in an appropriate environment and to be given the types of services he required in order to ensure his safety and well-being.

* * *

SUBSTANTIVE DUE PROCESS CLAIM

Relying on the Supreme Court's decision in DeShaney v. Winnebago County Dep't of Social Servs., 489 U.S. 189 (1989), Gregory argues that "Anthony had no constitutional right to have his DCFS caseworker protect him from being killed in a gang-related incident in his neighborhood." [C] * * * [T]he precise circumstances of Anthony's death are not at all clear at this juncture. Yet, it does seem reasonable, in light of what has been alleged, to assume that Anthony's death occurred outside of his home at the hands of someone other than a family member. The essence of Camp's claim, after all, is not that she or someone else in the Camp household posed a danger to Anthony, but that she was unable to protect him from dangers posed by others. And, indeed, Camp's counsel represented to us at oral argument that Anthony was shot and killed two blocks from Camp's home. Having this in mind, we take up two questions: first, whether, by virtue of it being appointed Anthony's guardian, the DCFS (and thus Gregory) acquired any duty to protect Anthony that it otherwise would not have under *DeShaney*; and second, whether that duty extends to dangers beyond the household in which the DCFS and Gregory placed Anthony. We understand Gregory to answer "no" to both inquiries. Our analysis begins with review of *DeShaney*.

A. DeShaney

In *DeShaney*, the Court held that due process did not require the state to protect a child from the abuse he suffered at the hands of his father. Joshua DeShaney had repeatedly been taken to the local emergency room with injuries that physicians suspected were due to physical abuse. At one point Joshua was temporarily placed in the custody of the hospital while a "Child Protection Team" evaluated his situation; however, the Team determined there was insufficient evidence that he was being abused to retain custody. Joshua was returned to his father's custody and, despite subsequent hospital admissions for injuries indicative of abuse, local officials failed to intervene. Ultimately, his father beat Joshua so severely that he was expected to spend the remainder of his life in an institution for the profoundly retarded.

Despite the fact that local officials had suspected ongoing abuse, the Court rejected the contention that they had deprived Joshua of his liberty in violation of due process by taking no action:

> Nothing in the language of the Due Process Clause itself requires the State to protect the life, liberty, and property of its citizens against invasion by private actors. The Clause is phrased as a limitation on the State's power to act, not as a guarantee of certain minimal levels of safety and security. It forbids the State itself to deprive individuals of life, liberty, or property without "due process of law," but its language cannot fairly be extended to impose an affirmative obligation on the State to ensure that those interests do not come to harm through other means. Nor does history support such an expansive reading of the constitutional text. . . . Its purpose was to protect the people from the State, not to ensure that the State protected them from each other. The Framers were content to leave the extent of governmental obligation in the latter area to the democratic political processes.

The Court acknowledged that "in certain limited circumstances the Constitution imposes upon the State affirmative duties of care and protection with respect to particular individuals." 489 U.S. at 198. Thus, when someone is incarcerated, the Eighth Amendment (via the Fourteenth) requires the State to provide him with adequate medical care. Estelle v. Gamble, 429 U.S. 97, 97 S. Ct. 285, 50 L. Ed. 2d 251 (1976). Similarly, substantive due process compels the State to take reasonable steps to ensure the safety of individuals involuntarily committed to its mental facilities. Youngberg v. Romeo, 457 U.S. 307, 102 S. Ct. 2452, 73 L. Ed. 2d 28 (1982).

> But these cases afford petitioners no help. Taken together, they stand only for the proposition that when the State takes a person into its custody and hold[s] him there against his will, the Constitution imposes upon it a corresponding duty to assume some responsibility for his safety and general well-being. The rationale for this principle is simple enough: when the State by the affirmative exercise of its power so restrains an individual's liberty that it renders him unable to care for himself, and at the same time fails to provide for his basic human needs—e.g., food, clothing, shelter, medical care, and reasonable safety—it transgresses the substantive limits on state action set by the Eighth Amendment and the Due Process Clause. The affirmative duty to protect arises not from the State's knowledge of the individual's predicament or from its expressions of intent to help him, but from the limitation which it has imposed on his freedom to act on his own behalf. In the substantive due process analysis, it is the State's affirmative act of restraining the individuals's freedom to act on his own behalf—through incarceration, institutionalization, or other similar restraint of personal liberty—which is the

> "deprivation of liberty" triggering the protections of the Due Process Clause, not its failure to act to protect his liberty interests against harms inflicted by other means.
>
> The *Estelle-Youngberg* analysis simply has no applicability in the present case. Petitioners concede that the harms Joshua suffered occurred not while he was in the State's custody, but while he was in the custody of his natural father, who was in no sense a state actor. While the State may have been aware of the dangers that Joshua faced in the free world, it played no part in their creation, nor did it do anything to render him any more vulnerable to them. That the State took temporary custody of Joshua does not alter the analysis, for when it returned him to his father's custody, it placed him in no worse position than that in which he would have been had it not acted at all; the State does not become the permanent guarantor of an individuals's safety by having once offered him shelter. Under these circumstances, the State had no constitutional duty to protect Joshua.

B. Gregory's Duty to Protect Anthony Generally

In essence, Gregory argues that this case is on all fours with *DeShaney*, and that he bore no duty to protect Anthony from a danger that neither he nor the State played any role in creating. Likewise, although it was Gregory who made the decision to return Anthony to the Camp household after a court had made the DCFS his guardian, Gregory reasons that in doing so he placed Anthony in no worse position than if he had taken no action whatsoever.

We believe the fact that the DCFS had been made Anthony's guardian represents a key point of distinction from *DeShaney*, however. Camp had sought to surrender her own guardianship responsibilities because she believed she could not provide him adequate care and supervision. With the agreement of both Camp and the state, the complaint tells us, the court made the DCFS Anthony's guardian. At that juncture, whether the DCFS had a duty to intervene on Anthony's behalf was moot; it had already assumed a role that made it constitutionally liable (at least to some extent) for Anthony's well-being.

That the DCFS had a cognizable duty to protect Anthony as his guardian is reflected in a series of cases holding government officials liable for placing minors in foster homes where they suffered abuse or neglect. Prominent among these is our opinion in K.H. through Murphy v. Morgan, 914 F.2d 846 (7th Cir.1990), which post-dates *DeShaney*. In that case, an abused child who had been removed from the custody of her parents was then shuffled among a series of foster homes in which she continued to suffer abuse and was deprived of the special care she required in view of her history. The child sued DCFS officials, contending that they had deprived her of due process by placing her in foster homes that they knew to be either abusive or unable to care for her properly. We agreed that the plaintiff might have a viable claim in this circumstance. We noted at the outset that the Due Process Clause quite clearly prohibits a public officer from intentionally harming an individual physically without justification, citing, inter alia, K. H. v. Morgan, 914 F.2d at 848. "The extension [of this principle] to the case in which the plaintiff's mental health is seriously impaired by deliberate and unjustified action is," we observed, "straightforward." Id. We proceeded to distinguish *DeShaney*:

> This is not a "positive liberties" case, like *DeShaney*, where the question was whether the Constitution entitles a child to governmental protection against physical abuse by his parents or other private persons not acting under the direction of the state. . . . Here, in contrast, the state removed a child from the custody of her parents; having done so, it could no more place her in a position of danger, deliberately and without justification, without thereby violating her rights under the due process clause of the Fourteenth Amendment than it could deliberately and without justification place a criminal defendant in a jail or prison in which his health or safety would be endangered, without violating his rights either under the cruel and unusual punishments clause of the Eighth Amendment (held applicable to the states through the Fourteenth Amendment) if he was a convicted prisoner, or the due process clause if he was awaiting trial. In either case the state would be a doer of harm rather than merely an inept rescuer, just as the Roman state was a doer of harm when it threw Christians to the lions.
>
> The Roman analogy is sound even if one concedes, as one must in the light of *DeShaney*, that the State of Illinois has no constitutional obligation to protect children from physical or sexual abuse by their parents. The state could have left K.H. to the tender mercies of her parents without thereby violating her rights under the Constitution. But having removed her from their custody the state assumed at least a limited responsibility for her safety. . . . The Illinois Department of Children and Family Services could not have subjected K.H. to sexual abuse and then defended on the ground that by doing this it did not make her any worse off than she would have been had she been left with her parents. . . . Once the state assumes custody of a person, it owes him a rudimentary duty of safekeeping no matter how perilous his circumstances were when he was free. The distinction follows the lines of tort law. There is no duty to rescue a bystander in distress, but having rescued him from certain death you are not privileged to kill him. This is not to say that you assume responsibility for his future welfare. You do not. Our point is only that the absence of a duty to rescue does not entitle the rescuer to harm the person whom he has rescued.

* * *

Thus, as our opinion in *K.H.* reflects, *DeShaney* does not preclude liability when the state, as guardian of a child, places that child in an environment where harm results. [Cc]

To be sure, there are differences between this case and *K.H.* First among them is that Gregory is not alleged to have placed Anthony in an abusive home, at least not one we would normally think of as abusive.

The complaint does not suggest that anyone in the Camp household was prone to strike Anthony, or to molest him, or to deprive him of food or clothing, or to denigrate him emotionally. The focus of *K.H.* was confined to this realm: "The only right in question in this case is the right of a child in state custody not to be handed over by state officers to a foster parent or other custodian, private or public, whom the state knows or suspects to be a child abuser." [C] Camp moves a step beyond this narrow right; her theory is that Gregory knowingly returned Anthony to a household that could not supervise and guide Anthony to the degree he required. This is a theory that *K.H.* neither addressed nor endorsed. * * * Thus, we believe a child placed in the guardianship of the state has a due process right not to be placed by the state with a custodian whom the state knows will fail to exercise the requisite degree of supervision over the child. This is precisely the right that Camp alleges Gregory denied to Anthony; and it is the denial of that right, she further alleges, which resulted in Anthony's death.

In this case, of course, Gregory did not place Anthony with a stranger, but returned him to his aunt. That fact is important for two reasons. First, our cases acknowledge a difference between the state placing a child with a relative and placing him with a foster home. Second, *DeShaney* emphasized that although the state may have been aware of the danger that Joshua faced in his family's home, it had done nothing to create those dangers nor had it done anything rendering Joshua more vulnerable to them. Neither of these points necessarily bars Camp's claim, however, in view of the facts alleged.

* * *

C. Duty to Protect Anthony from Violence Outside of the Home

Whether Gregory's duty extended to dangers outside of the household to which he had returned Anthony is a more novel and difficult question. Gregory argues that this aspect of Camp's claim makes the case even more compelling for him than DeShaney. In one sense he is no doubt correct. Government officials can and routinely do make assessments of the adults with whom children under the state's guardianship are placed. Thus, as we recognized in *K.H.*, if a DCFS caseworker places a child in a foster home where he knows the child will likely suffer abuse, he can be held liable. But to place on the caseworker a duty to evaluate and protect a child from dangers outside of the household is a great step beyond that. Given the widespread escalation of violence we have witnessed over the years, many a child may be in danger of injury at the hands of strangers when he is outside of his home, and public officials cannot be deemed constitutionally obligated to shield a child from all such dangers beyond the reasonable control of his parent or foster parent any more than the parents themselves can be.

Even so, a parent does not relinquish all responsibility once a child leaves the house. No one would think it reasonable, for example, for a parent to knowingly permit a toddler to wander the streets at will, confronting a gamut of risks from inattentive motorists to Mr. or Ms. Stranger Danger. We expect, instead, that the parent will have the child in hand, protecting him from danger that the child is otherwise unequipped to avoid. As the child matures, the degree to which his parent is expected to supervise his activities lessens, but it does not cease altogether. We still expect parents to see to it that their children attend school, obey statutory curfews, and stay out of trouble. Parents are not the insurers of their children's conduct, but when they fail to exercise a reasonable degree of supervision, they can be held liable for their omissions. See, e.g., Restatement (Second) of Torts § 316 (1965).

Commensurate with the parental obligation to supervise a child's activities outside the home is a duty on the part of the state not to place one of its charges with an adult that it knows will not or cannot exercise that responsibility. The DCFS regulations governing placement with relative caretakers recognize that responsibility, specifying as a pre-condition to approval that the DCFS staff must find that "supervision of the related child(ren) can be assured at all times including times when the related caregiver is employed or otherwise engaged in activity outside of the home." [C] Thus, we believe that when a DCFS caseworker places a child in a home knowing that his caretaker cannot provide reasonable supervision, and the failure to provide that degree of supervision and care results in injury to the child outside of the home, it might be appropriate, depending upon the facts culminating in the injury, for the caseworker to be held liable for a deprivation of liberty.

Liability must, nonetheless, be confined to what we believe will be a very narrow range of cases. Without attempting to identify all of the factors that might limit this category, we mention a few that come readily to mind. First, before a DCFS worker or other state official can be held liable for a placement decision, he must, as we indicated in *K.H.*, have failed to exercise bona fide professional judgment. [C] Second, a caretaker can be expected only to provide a reasonable degree of supervision to a minor in her care. * * *

Because the complaint does not detail the particular circumstances of Anthony's death, we cannot say one way or another whether this case would fit the criteria we have articulated. In light of our conclusion below that Gregory is entitled to qualified immunity, it does not matter; no factual development of the case is required.

* * *

[W]e cannot say that the amended complaint failed to state a claim upon which relief could be granted.

D. Qualified Immunity

A public official who has deprived someone of his constitutional right may nonetheless enjoy immunity from an award of damages if his actions were "objectively reasonable, meaning that [if] '[his] conduct does not violate clearly established statutory or constitutional rights of which a reasonable person would have known,' " he is immune from an action for civil damages. Supreme Video, Inc. v. Schauz, 15 F.3d 1435, 1438–39 (7th Cir.1994) (quoting Harlow v. Fitzgerald, 457 U.S. 800, 818 (1982)).

* * *

CONCLUSION

Although we believe that Camp's complaint alleged facts sufficient to state a claim for the deprivation of Anthony's liberty in violation of his Fourteenth Amendment right to substantive due process, we also conclude that Gregory is entitled to qualified immunity. Because Camp did not argue below that her complaint stated a separate procedural due process claim, we deem any such argument waived and need not consider its merits.

AFFIRMED

NOTES AND QUESTIONS

1. A "state-created danger" claim under § 1983 consists of four elements: direct and foreseeable harm; conduct by a state actor that shocks the conscience; a relationship between the state and the plaintiff whereby the plaintiff was a particularly foreseeable victim of the conduct; and a state actor's affirmative use of authority "in a way that created a danger to the citizen or that rendered the citizen more vulnerable to danger than had the state not acted at all." Bright v. Westmoreland County, 443 F.3d 276, 281 (3d Cir. 2006).

2. In dealing with the affirmative creation of risk, other courts have been less expansive than that in the principal case. In S.S. v. McMullen, 225 F.3d 960 (8th Cir. 2000), plaintiff brought a § 1983 claim against state family service officers where she had been released from state custody and returned to her father, although the officers knew that she would be exposed to a known pedophile. She was subsequently sodomized by the pedophile on at least two occasions. Applying *DeShaney*, and distinguishing the Seventh Circuit decision in *K.H.* through *Murphy v. Morgan*, supra, the court found that plaintiff's claim failed because the allegations did not show that by returning her to her father the officers had "created greater risks to her than the ones to which she was originally exposed." Id. at 968. It was as though the state had not acted. The dissent, relying on *K.H.*, found that S.S. was rescued from danger and that the child's fate thus fell into the hands of the state. The rescuer would be liable for "knowingly exposing a small girl to a convicted child molester." Id. A relative increase in some danger to which the plaintiff voluntarily exposed himself is not likely to trigger liability. See Johnson v. City of Seattle, 474 F.3d 634 (9th Cir. 2007) (plaintiffs voluntarily entered a crowd that subsequently became unruly; police department's decision to decrease active efforts to control the crowd's violence did not amount to creating a danger to plaintiffs).

3. Litigation began with prisons but has vigorously moved to state child services and to the schoolhouse. In Daniels v. Williams, 474 U.S. 327 (1986), the Court held that an official's negligent causation of loss or injury to life, liberty or property does not violate due process rights. The Due Process Clause does not extend a duty of due care to prisoners. Davidson v. Cannon, 474 U.S. 344 (1986). Much litigation has attended the protection of school pupils from sexual harassment and other abuse while in school. The questions in these cases are whether the student is in a special relationship denoted by control and whether the school has maintained a policy, practice or custom of deliberate indifference. Stoneking v. Bradford Area Sch. Dist., 882 F.2d 720 (3d Cir. 1989) (finding liability). Cf. Maldonado v. Josey, 975

F.2d 727 (10th Cir. 1992) (no liability); Johnson v. Dallas Indep. Sch. Dist., 38 F.3d 198 (5th Cir. 1994), cert. denied 514 U.S. 1017 (1995) (no liability). The courts are reluctant to extend liability beyond sexual abuse. Abeyta v. Chama Valley Indep. Sch. Dist., 77 F.3d 1253 (10th Cir. 1996) (no liability where teacher repeatedly called student a "prostitute" and allowed other students to taunt her).

4. In claims based on denial of substantive due process as in the principal case, the courts require that the behavior of the officer is so egregious, so outrageous, that it may be said to "shock the contemporary conscience." See County of Sacramento v. Lewis, 523 U.S. 833 (1998) (holding that a high-speed police chase, albeit unreasonable, did not "shock the conscience" in order to found an action). The need for this high threshold is dictated by the need to "preserve the constitutional proportions of constitutional claims, lest the Constitution be demoted to what [the Court has] called a font of tort law." Id. at 847 n.8. See also Schieber v. City of Philadelphia, 320 F.3d 409 (3d Cir. 2003) (holding that police failure to go further than cursory inquiries after 911 call reporting screams and choking noise did not "shock the conscience"; victim, daughter of plaintiffs, was raped and murdered); S.S. v. McMullen, supra note 1 (state officer's conduct in returning child to pedophile father's custody, despite knowing the danger of abuse, was not sufficiently outrageous as to "shock the conscience"). Cf. Rochin v. People of California, 342 U.S. 165 (1952) (repeatedly pumping suspect's stomach to retrieve illegal drugs "shocked the conscience"); Culberson v. Doan, 125 F. Supp. 2d 252 (S.D. Ohio 2000) (sheriff warned murderer of search for victim's body and delayed draining a pond so that murderer could successfully re-conceal the victim; conduct "shocked the conscience").

5. Many ills of modern society are catalogued in these claims. In Pinder v. Johnson, 54 F.3d 1169 (4th Cir.1995), plaintiff's children died in a fire. The perpetrator of the arson had been taken into custody earlier in the evening for an attempted arson. Plaintiff asked defendant, a police officer, whether it would be safe to leave her children and go to work in view of this attempted arson and others in the past. Defendant assured plaintiff that the perpetrator would be held in custody. He was not. He returned and carried out his plan. Judge Wilkinson, recounting the "genuinely tragic" circumstances and applying *DeShaney*, could not find the sufficient "custodial relationship" upon which to base an "affirmative constitutional duty." Promises alone do not create the required "special relationship." Moreover, it was held that an immunity covered defendant's acts because of the embryonic quality of the law. In Town of Castle Rock v. Gonzales, 545 U.S. 748 (2005), the Court held that the due process clause protects only against deprivation of benefits to which persons are legally entitled, from which entitlement stems a property right. The police had failed to heed plaintiff's repeated entreaties to enforce a restraining order, whereby the husband and father was afforded the opportunity to murder the couple's children. Justice Scalia, writing for the majority, did not interpret the Colorado restraining order statute as making mandatory the enforcement of such orders; indeed his opinion finds an implied reservation of discretion to peace officers in enforcement of the law "even in the presence of seemingly mandatory legislative commands." Id. at 761. Over Justice Souter's dissent, Justice Scalia finds that, even if the statute mandated the issuance of an arrest warrant, such was "an entitlement to nothing but

procedure" into which a property interest cannot be imputed. Id. at 764. Again declining to recognize the Fourteenth Amendment as a "font of tort law," the Court strained to interpret the legislation to bestow discretion to the police. Id. at 768.

6. Section 1983 is not the only source of private right of action. Title IX, 20 U.S.C. § 1681(a) provides: "No person in the United States shall, on the basis of sex, be excluded from participation in, be denied the benefits of, or be subjected to discrimination under any education program or activity receiving Federal financial assistance." 20 U.S.C. § 1681(a).

In Gebser v. Lago Vista Independent School Dist., 524 U.S. 274 (1998), the Court held that a school district may be liable for damages under Title IX where it is deliberately indifferent to known acts of teacher-student sexual harassment. Pointing out that the common law holds liable those put on notice of the tortious actions of third parties, the Court in Davis v. Monroe County Board of Education, 526 U.S. 629 (1999) held that Title IX liability could obtain where the abuse or harassment was "student-on-student." Such liability requires the plaintiff to establish the school was both aware of and deliberately indifferent to the harassment. Moreover, "such an action will lie only for harassment that is so severe, pervasive, and objectively offensive that it effectively bars the victim's access to an educational opportunity or benefit." Id. at 633.

7. The principal case utilizes causation rules and duty of care analysis canvassed in Chapter 8. The *Davis* case supra note 6 also draws on common-law duty of care. Do you agree that the common law would fix a school board with liability in the circumstances in *Davis*? Title IX extends to universities. Do you see a problem?

Memphis Community School Dist. v. Stachura

Supreme Court of the United States, 1986.
477 U.S. 299, 106 S.Ct. 2537, 91 L.Ed.2d 249.

[Respondent, a tenured teacher in the Memphis, Michigan, public schools, was suspended following parents' complaints about his teaching methods in a 7th-grade life science course that included the showing of allegedly sexually explicit pictures and films. While respondent was later reinstated, he, before being reinstated, brought suit in Federal District Court under 42 U.S.C. § 1983 against petitioner School District, Board of Education, Board Members, school administrators, and parents, alleging that his suspension deprived him of liberty and property without due process of law and violated his First Amendment right to academic freedom. He sought both compensatory and punitive damages. The District Court instructed the jury on the standard elements of compensatory and punitive damages and also charged the jury that additional compensatory damages could be awarded based on the value or importance of the constitutional rights that were violated. The jury found petitioners liable, awarding both compensatory and punitive damages. The Court of Appeals affirmed. (Facts from official syllabus.)]

JUSTICE POWELL delivered the opinion of the Court. * * *

We granted certiorari limited to the 474 U.S. 918, 106 S.Ct. 245, 88 L.Ed.2d 254 (1985) question whether the Court of Appeals erred in affirming the damages award in the light of the District Court's instructions that authorized not only compensatory and punitive damages, but also damages for the deprivation of "any constitutional right." 474 U.S. 918, 106 S.Ct. 245, 88 L.Ed.2d 254 (1985). We reverse, and remand for a new trial limited to the issue of compensatory damages. * * *

We have repeatedly noted that 42 U.S.C. § 1983 creates " 'a species of tort liability' in favor of persons who are deprived of 'rights, privileges, or immunities secured' to them by the Constitution." Carey v. Piphus, 435 U.S. 247, 253 (1978). [Cc] Accordingly, when § 1983 plaintiffs seek damages for violations of constitutional rights, the level of damages is ordinarily determined according to principles derived from the common law of torts. [Cc]

Punitive damages aside, damages in tort cases are designed to provide "*compensation* for the injury caused to plaintiff by defendant's breach of duty." 2 F. Harper, F. James & O. Gray, Law of Torts § 25.1, p. 490 (2d ed. 1986) (emphasis in original), quoted in Carey v. Piphus, supra. [Cc] To that end, compensatory damages may include not only out-of-pocket loss and other monetary harms, but also such injuries as "impairment of reputation * * *, personal humiliation, and mental anguish and suffering." Gertz v. Robert Welch, Inc., 418 U.S. 323, 350 (1974). See also Carey v. Piphus, supra, 435 U.S., at 264 (mental and emotional distress constitute compensable injury in § 1983 cases). Deterrence is also an important purpose of this system, but it operates through the mechanism of damages that are *compensatory*—damages grounded in determinations of plaintiffs' actual losses. * * * Congress adopted this common-law system of recovery when it established liability for "constitutional torts." Consequently, "the basic purpose" of § 1983 damages is "to *compensate persons for injuries* that are caused by the deprivation of constitutional rights." Carey v. Piphus, 435 U.S., at 254 (emphasis added). See also id., at 257 ("damages awards under § 1983 should be governed by the principle of compensation").

Carey v. Piphus represents a straightforward application of these principles. * * * Where no injury was present, no "compensatory" damages could be awarded.

The instructions at issue here cannot be squared with *Carey,* or with the principles of tort damages on which *Carey* and § 1983 are grounded. The jurors in this case were told that, in determining how much was necessary to "compensate [respondent] for the deprivation" of his constitutional rights, they should place a money value on the "rights" themselves by considering such factors as the particular right's "importance * * * in our system of government," its role in American history, and its "significance * * * in the context of the activities" in which respondent was engaged. These factors focus, not on compensation for provable injury, but on the jury's subjective perception of the importance of constitutional rights as an abstract matter. *Carey* establishes that such an approach is impermissible. The constitutional right transgressed in *Carey*—the right to due process of law—is central to our system of ordered liberty. We nevertheless held that *no* compensatory damages could be awarded for violation of that right absent proof of actual injury. *Carey,* 435 U.S., at 264. *Carey* thus makes clear that the abstract value of a constitutional right may not form the basis for § 1983 damages.[11]

Respondent nevertheless argues that *Carey* does not control here, because in this case a *substantive* constitutional right—respondent's First Amendment right to academic freedom—was infringed. The argument misperceives our analysis in *Carey.* That case does not establish a two-tiered system of constitutional rights, with substantive rights afforded greater protection than "mere" procedural safeguards. We did acknowledge in *Carey* that "the elements and prerequisites for recovery of damages" might vary depending on the interests protected by the constitutional right at issue. [C] But we emphasized that, whatever the constitutional basis for § 1983 liability, such damages must always be designed "to *compensate injuries* caused by the [constitutional] deprivation." [Cc] That conclusion simply leaves no room for noncompensatory damages measured by the jury's perception of the abstract "importance" of a constitutional right.

Nor do we find such damages necessary to vindicate the constitutional rights that § 1983 protects. See n. 11, supra. Section 1983 presupposes that damages that compensate for actual harm ordinarily suffice to deter constitutional violations. * * *

Moreover, damages based on the "value" of constitutional rights are an unwieldy tool for ensuring compliance with the Constitution. History and tradition do not afford any sound guidance concerning the precise value that juries should place on constitutional protections. Accordingly, were such damages available, juries would be free to award arbitrary amounts without any evidentiary basis, or to use their unbounded discretion to punish unpopular defendants. [C] Such damages would be too uncertain to be of any great value to plaintiffs, and would inject caprice into determinations of damages in § 1983 cases. We therefore hold that damages based on the abstract "value" or "importance" of constitutional rights are not a permissible element of compensatory damages in such cases. * * *

Respondent further argues that the challenged instructions authorized a form of "presumed" damages—a remedy that is both compensatory in nature and traditionally part of the range of tort law remedies. Alternatively, respondent argues that the erroneous instructions were at worst harmless error.

---

[11] We did approve an award of nominal damages for the deprivation of due process in *Carey.* 435 U.S., at 266. Our discussion of that issue makes clear that nominal damages, and not damages based on some undefinable "value" of infringed rights, are the appropriate means of "vindicating" rights whose deprivation has not caused actual, provable injury:

"Common-law courts traditionally have vindicated deprivations of certain 'absolute' rights that are not shown to have caused actual injury through the award of a nominal sum of money. By making the deprivation of such rights actionable for nominal damages without proof of actual injury, the law recognizes the importance to organized society that those rights be scrupulously observed; but at the same time, it remains true to the principle that substantial damages should be awarded only to compensate actual injury or, in the case of exemplary or punitive damages, to deter or punish malicious deprivations of rights." Ibid.

Neither argument has merit. Presumed damages are a *substitute* for ordinary compensatory damages, not a *supplement* for an award that fully compensates the alleged injury. When a plaintiff seeks compensation for an injury that is likely to have occurred but difficult to establish, some form of presumed damages may possibly be appropriate. [Cc]

In those circumstances, presumed damages may roughly approximate the harm that the plaintiff suffered and thereby compensate for harms that may be impossible to measure. As we earlier explained, the instructions at issue in this case did not serve this purpose, but instead called on the jury to measure damages based on a subjective evaluation of the importance of particular constitutional values. Since such damages are wholly divorced from any compensatory purpose, they cannot be justified as presumed damages.[14] Moreover, no rough substitute for compensatory damages was required in this case, since the jury was fully authorized to compensate respondent for both monetary and non-monetary harms caused by petitioners' conduct.

Nor can we find that the erroneous instructions were harmless. [Cc] When damages instructions are faulty and the verdict does not reveal the means by which the jury calculated damages, "[the] error in the charge is difficult, if not impossible, to correct without retrial, in light of the jury's general verdict." [C]

The jury was authorized to award three categories of damages: (i) compensatory damages for injury to respondent, (ii) punitive damages, and (iii) damages based on the jury's perception of the "importance" of two provisions of the Constitution. The submission of the third of these categories was error. * * *

The judgment of the Court of Appeals is reversed, and the case is remanded for further proceedings consistent with this opinion.

JUSTICE MARSHALL, with whom JUSTICE BRENNAN, JUSTICE BLACKMUN, and JUSTICE STEVENS join, concurring in the judgment.

---

[14] For the same reason, *Nixon v. Herndon,* 273 U.S. 536 (1927), and similar cases do not support the challenged instructions. * * *

Nixon followed a long line of cases, going back to Lord Holt's decision in *Ashby v. White,* 2 Ld.Raym. 938, 92 Eng.Rep. 126 (1703), authorizing substantial money damages as compensation for persons deprived of their right to vote in particular elections. [Cc] Although these decisions sometimes speak of damages for the value of the right to vote, their analysis shows that they involve nothing more than an award of presumed damages for a non-monetary harm that cannot easily be quantified:

> "In the eyes of the law th[e] right [to vote] is so valuable that damages are presumed from the wrongful deprivation of it without evidence of actual loss of money, property, or any other valuable thing, and the amount of the damages is a question peculiarly appropriate for the determination of the jury, because each member of the jury has personal knowledge of the value of the right." Ibid. * * *

See also *Ashby v. White, supra,* at 955, 92 Eng.Rep., at 137 (Holt, C.J.) ("As in an action for slanderous words, though a man does not lose a penny by reason of the speaking [of] them, yet he shall have an action"). The "value of the right" in the context of these decisions is the money value of the particular loss that the plaintiff suffered—a loss of which "each member of the jury has personal knowledge." It is *not* the value of the right to vote as a general, abstract matter, based on its role in our history or system of government. Thus, whatever the wisdom of these decisions in the context of the changing scope of compensatory damages over the course of this century, they do not support awards of non-compensatory damages such as those authorized in this case.

I agree with the Court that this case must be remanded for a new trial on damages. Certain portions of the Court's opinion, however, can be read to suggest that damages in § 1983 cases are necessarily limited to "out-of-pocket loss," "other monetary harms," and "such injuries as 'impairment of reputation * * *, personal humiliation, and mental anguish and suffering.' "

I do not understand the Court so to hold, and I write separately to emphasize that the violation of a constitutional right, in proper cases, may itself constitute a compensable injury. * * *

Following *Carey*, the courts of appeals have recognized that invasions of constitutional rights sometimes cause injuries that cannot be redressed by a wooden application of common-law damages rules. In Hobson v. Wilson, 237 U.S.App.D.C. 219, 275–281, 737 F.2d 1, 57–63 (1984), [c] plaintiffs claimed that defendant FBI agents had invaded their First Amendment rights to assemble for peaceable political protest, to associate with others to engage in political expression, and to speak on public issues free of unreasonable government interference. The District Court found that the defendants had succeeded in diverting plaintiffs from, and impeding them in, their protest activities. The Court of Appeals for the District of Columbia Circuit held that that injury to a First Amendment-protected interest could itself constitute compensable injury wholly apart from any "emotional distress, humiliation and personal indignity, emotional pain, embarrassment, fear, anxiety and anguish" suffered by plaintiffs. [C] The court warned, however, that that injury could be compensated with substantial damages only to the extent that it was "reasonably quantifiable"; damages should not be based on "the so-called inherent value of the rights violated."

I believe that the *Hobson* court correctly stated the law. * * * There is no reason why such an injury should not be compensable in damages. At the same time, however, the award must be proportional to the actual loss sustained.

The instructions given the jury in this case were improper because they did not require the jury to focus on the loss actually sustained by respondent. * * *

The Court therefore properly remands for a new trial on damages. I do not understand the Court, however, to hold that deprivations of constitutional rights can never themselves constitute compensable injuries. Such a rule would be inconsistent with the logic of *Carey,* and would defeat the purpose of § 1983 by denying compensation for genuine injuries caused by the deprivation of constitutional rights.

NOTES AND QUESTIONS

1. There is no damages award that can be made to vindicate the abstract value of deprivation of a constitutional right. This contrasts with damages awards for the intentional torts. The Justices refusal to swell damages for dignitary harm may be related to the Civil Rights Attorneys' Fees Act of 1976 wherein civil rights claimants may recover attorneys' fees. This encourages such suits and meets in an indirect way the objective of vindication. Municipalities are not ordinarily subject to punitive damages

in § 1983 cases. City of Newport v. Fact Concerts, Inc., 453 U.S. 247 (1981). The principal case has been applied broadly. In Heck v. Humphrey, 512 U.S. 477 (1994), the Court held that plaintiff's asserted § 1983 claim could not be established since the corresponding common law action in malicious prosecution would not lie in the circumstances. Thus a § 1983 cause of action for damages attributable to an unconstitutional conviction or sentence does not accrue until the conviction or sentence has been invalidated. Justice Souter, with whom Justices Blackmun, Stevens and O'Connor concurred, warned that while the malicious prosecution analogy was useful in starting analysis, congressional policy was the ultimate lodestar. While formal exhaustion of state remedies is not only unnecessary, but more is inconsistent with the scheme of § 1983, a court may be guided by federal principles, applying Patsy v. Board of Regents of Fla., 457 U.S. 496 (1982) (superceded in part by the Prison Litigation Reform Act of 1995, requiring the prisoners exhaust all state and federal administrative remedies before bringing suit under § 1983).

2. An iconoclastic view is presented by John Jeffries, Damages for Constitutional Violations: the Relation of Risk to Injury in Constitutional Torts, 75 Va. L. Rev. 1461 (1989). The article argues that the only damages encompassed relate to "constitutionally relevant injuries—that is, injuries within the risks that the constitutional prohibition seeks to avoid."

CHAPTER 20

MISUSE OF LEGAL PROCEDURE

Texas Skaggs, Inc. v. Graves

Court of Civil Appeals of Texas, 1979.
582 S.W.2d 863.

[Suit for malicious prosecution. Plaintiff-appellee, Mrs. Sharon Graves, had "worked as a checker in the Skaggs store but was fired for reasons not material to this case." She continued to purchase groceries at Skaggs and had given the store two checks totaling $34.70. The checking account was in her name, but she had left a few blank checks signed by her at home, for her husband to use. The couple had separated and, unknown to her, her husband had withdrawn all of her funds. She agreed to pay "as soon as she could get the money from the Skaggs' credit union." Over two weeks later, when she received her money from the credit union, she "purchased a money order and mailed it to Skaggs to cover the 'hot' checks."

The next day, Bill Pennington, a Skaggs manager, filed an "Incident Report" with the Texarkana, Arkansas, Police Department reporting Mrs. Graves for a violation of the Arkansas Hot Check Law. Four days later, he filed an affidavit for warrant of her arrest. Over a week later, when Mrs. Graves was shopping in the Skaggs store, a manager summoned the police, who came and arrested her. She tried to explain to police sergeant Larry Arnold that she had paid the checks, but he took her out of the store and to the police station where she was booked on a hot check charge. Arnold then telephoned Skaggs and learned that the checks had, in fact, been paid. Arnold then released Graves and returned the two checks to her (that had been attached to the Affidavit for Warrant of Arrest). Sgt. Arnold talked to an employee of Skaggs again that afternoon and when the person he was talking to learned that Graves had been released, that person (unidentified) told Arnold that he wanted Graves prosecuted and that he did not care if she had paid the checks. The next morning, March 4th, Arnold drove to Sharon Graves' home in Texas and told her that Skaggs intended to prosecute her that afternoon. Mrs. Graves immediately hired an attorney and appeared in Court. The municipal judge dismissed the case when the prosecution could not produce the "hot checks."]

RAY, JUSTICE. * * * In Arkansas, a cause of action for malicious prosecution consists of the following elements: (1) A criminal prosecution instituted or continued by the defendant against the plaintiff; (2) Termination of the proceedings in favor of the accused; (3) Absence of probable cause for the proceeding; (4) Malice; and, (5) Damages. * * *.

In response to special issues, the jury found that Graves did not know that her bank account had insufficient funds for the payment of the two checks; that Skaggs did not have probable cause to institute the prosecution of Sharon Graves; that Skaggs acted with malice; and, that the sum of $20,000.00 would reasonably compensate Graves for her actual damages.

Institution of Criminal Proceedings. The evidence is clear and undisputed that Skaggs initiated and continued the prosecution of Sharon Graves.

Termination of the Proceedings in Favor of the Accused. The record reflects that the case against Graves was dismissed in the Municipal Court of Texarkana, Arkansas, with the notation, "dismissed on basis checks not available for presentation of case." Skaggs argues that this type of termination is indecisive and is not sufficient to establish malicious prosecution. Prosser describes types of termination that are sufficient to sustain a malicious prosecution suit:

"On the other hand, it will be enough that the proceeding is terminated in such a manner that it cannot be revived, and the prosecutor, if he proceeds further, will be put to a new one. This is true, for example, of an acquittal in court, * * * the entry of a nolle prosequi or a dismissal, abandonment of the prosecution by the prosecuting attorney or the complaining witness, * * * where any of these things have the effect of ending the particular proceeding and requiring new process or other official action to commence a new prosecution. It may be said generally, that this is true whenever the charges or the proceeding are withdrawn on the initiative of the prosecution. * * *

"On the other hand, where charges are withdrawn or the prosecution is terminated at the instigation of the accused himself, or by reason of a compromise into which he has entered voluntarily, there is no sufficient termination in favor of the accused. * * * " W. Prosser, Torts Sec. 113, pp. 857, 858 (3rd ed.1964).

Prosser is in accord with the rule established by the Restatement (Second) of Torts, §§ 658, 659 (1977). The abandonment of the proceedings because a conviction has, in the natural course of events, become impossible or improbable, is a sufficient termination in favor of the accused. [C] We are of the opinion that this case was not dismissed on technical or procedural grounds, but was an abandonment of the prosecution by the prosecuting attorney and that the inferences to be drawn from the evidence support that conclusion. We are of the further opinion that because there was a dismissal for lack of incriminating evidence, Graves could have procured a finding of "not guilty" by the municipal court had the matter been pressed for a full trial by the prosecuting attorney. Closely connected with the element of successful termination is the defense that Graves was in fact guilty of the charge. This defense was available even if Graves had been acquitted of the criminal charge. The rational basis is that the law protects only the innocent and, if guilty, the plaintiff deserved the treatment complained of. Thus, Skaggs had the option to assert the defense that Graves was in fact guilty of the charge. There was apparently some attempt to prove this defense, but the jury rejected it.

Absence of Probable Cause. Graves had the burden of proving that the criminal proceeding was initiated or continued by Skaggs without probable cause; that is, Graves had to show that Skaggs had no honest or reasonable belief in the truth of the charge however suspicious the circumstances of Graves' acts. Probable cause has been defined by the Arkansas Supreme Court in *Hitson v. Sims,* 69 Ark. 439, 441, 64 S.W. 219, 220 (1901), as follows: " * * * such a state of facts known to the prosecutor, or such information received by him from sources entitled to credit, as would induce a man of ordinary caution and prudence to believe, and did induce the prosecutor to believe, that the accused is guilty of the crime alleged, and thereby caused the prosecution * * * "

However, it is stated in 22 Ark.L. Rev. 349: "Liability is imposed on the defendant where there are sufficient facts to indicate to a reasonable man that the plaintiff was guilty but the defendant himself knew better, i.e., a subjective test. Since the test requires more than mere unfounded suspicion the courts will hold a defendant liable in cases where a reasonable man would further investigate the facts."

The facts supporting the jury's finding of lack of probable cause are that Graves was well-known by the employees of Skaggs; that the two checks were relatively small; that the checks were used to pay for groceries alone and that no cash was obtained with the checks; that Graves could have obtained large amounts of cash because she knew all of the Skaggs' employees; that she could have cashed many checks obtaining cash, but did not; that the checks were written on her regular bank account and not some fictitious bank or bank account; that once she was notified that her two checks had been returned to Skaggs, she immediately agreed to make restitution; that Graves in fact mailed her money order to Skaggs prior to the time that prosecution was instituted; that Skaggs was aware of the restitution before her arrest; that Skaggs had agreed to await restitution and to accept payment for the checks when Graves received her money from the Skaggs credit union; that Skaggs, pursuant to its agreement with Graves, had accepted restitution but issued instructions that the prosecution continue; and, that Skaggs further insisted that the prosecution continue after having been apprised of the fact that Mrs. Graves had been arrested and released by the officer after the officer had called one of Skaggs' employees and learned that restitution had been made. From the foregoing facts, and the inferences to be drawn therefrom, the jury could have reasonably concluded that Graves did not intend to defraud Skaggs and that no probable cause existed to institute or continue the prosecution proceedings. As a defense, the burden of persuasion was on Skaggs to show that the complaining witness, Bill Pennington, believed in Graves' guilt at the time the original proceeding commenced and that this belief was supported with facts which would lead a reasonable, cautious or prudent man to the same conclusion, and which in fact did lead Pennington to this conclusion. Pennington was not called as a witness. The jury apparently believed that the testimony of Sharon Graves was more plausible than that of the employees at Skaggs and that Skaggs knew or should have known or found out from further investigation that Graves did not issue the checks knowing at the time of issuing them that she did not have sufficient funds in her bank account to cover the checks. The jury could have further believed that while a reasonable person might have concluded that Graves was guilty, Skaggs' employees knew better and should have further investigated the facts.

The "Arkansas Hot Check Law", Ark.Stat.Ann. Sec. 67–720 (Supp.1978) provides:

"It shall be unlawful for any person to procure any article or thing of value, * * * or for any other purpose to make or draw or utter or deliver, with intent to defraud, any check, * * * upon any bank, * * * knowing at the time of such making, * * * that the maker, * * * has not sufficient funds in, or on deposit with, such bank, * * * ".

Evidence of the requisite intent to defraud is supplied by Ark.Stat.Ann. Sec. 67–722 which provides that the making of a check, " * * * payment of which is refused by the drawee, shall be prima facie evidence of intent to defraud * * * ". While the statute raises the presumption of intent to defraud, such presumption may be rebutted by evidence explaining the transaction and where the evidence is sufficient to dispel any presumption of intent to defraud, the statute alone will not support a conviction under the Arkansas Hot Check Law. [Cc]. In the present case, there was no intent to defraud because there was ample evidence to support the jury finding that Graves did not know that she had insufficient funds in her bank account at the time of writing the checks with which to make payment of the two checks when they were processed for payment at her bank. And while restitution alone is not an absolute defense to the Arkansas Hot Check Law [c], the fact that Graves immediately agreed to make restitution and did in fact make restitution is some evidence that she did not intend to defraud Skaggs. Certainly, once Graves had made restitution and that fact was coupled with all the other facts known to Skaggs' employees, a conclusion that Skaggs had no probable cause to further insist upon the prosecution of Graves would be justified.

Malice. Regarding the element of malice, it is generally agreed that the lack of probable cause may give rise to an inference of malice, sufficient to carry the question to the jury. W. Prosser, Torts, Sec. 113, p. 868 (3rd ed. 1964). The courts require that malice in fact be shown in order to sustain a recovery for malicious prosecution. This is usually established by proving that the defendant had a wrongful or improper motive or was motivated by some purpose other than bringing a guilty person to justice, such as, using the prosecution as a means to recover property, to extort money, or to collect a debt. " * * * Hence, proof of malice need not be direct but may be inferred from circumstances surrounding the defendant's act. This does not mean the defendant must have acted out of hatred, ill will, spite or grudge." 22 Ark.L. Rev. 340, 353, supra. The jury could and probably did believe that Skaggs instituted the criminal proceedings without probable cause in an effort to collect the two checks. The jury finding that Skaggs acted with malice has ample support in the record. Certainly, Skaggs' insistence that the prosecution continue against Graves after she had been released by Sgt. Arnold following her arrest with the statement to the effect that Skaggs did not care if Graves had paid the checks, Skaggs wanted her prosecuted anyway, supports the inference that Skaggs continued to act maliciously.

Damages. Appellant argues that the jury verdict was so grossly excessive as to show that it was the result of passion, prejudice or other improper motives. No cases are cited to guide this Court in its determination of this issue. The general rule is as follows:

"Although the verdict is large and the trial court, in the exercise of a sound discretion, might properly have set it aside, the appellate court will not disturb the verdict, although it may seem too large, in the absence of circumstances tending to show that it was the result of passion, prejudice, or other improper motive, or that the amount fixed was not the result of a deliberate and conscientious conviction in the minds of the jury and the court, or so excessive as to shock a sense of justice in the minds of the appellate court." 17 Tex.Jur.2d Damages, Sec. 341, p. 415 (1960).

As stated in *Green v. Meadows,* 527 S.W.2d 496 (Tex.Civ.App. Houston-1st Dist. 1975, writ ref'd n.r.e.), there are no objective guidelines by which we can measure the money equivalent of mental pain.

"* * * Much discretion must be allowed the jury in fixing this amount. The trial judge refused to order a remittitur. We are unable to say that the jury's verdict is excessive to the extent that the judgment should be reversed for that reason only. * * * "

In *Green,* the jury had awarded the plaintiff $20,000.00 in a malicious prosecution suit.

The facts in the present case show that Sharon Graves has suffered substantial injury. She was arrested and paraded through the store by a uniformed policeman and the store manager in front of her friends and former fellow employees. She was taken to the police station where she was booked and suffered the humiliation of a criminal charge. She testified that because of this criminal record she was not hired by several prospective employers because of her arrest record which will follow her the rest of her life. The evidence supports the jury verdict. * * *

To recapitulate, the pleadings were adequate to support the judgment; there was sufficient evidence to establish that Skaggs had instituted and continued criminal prosecution against Sharon Graves; there was evidence that the proceeding was terminated in favor of Graves; that the evidence established an absence of probable cause for institution of the criminal proceedings against Graves; that the evidence supports the finding of malice; and, the evidence supports the jury finding of $20,000.00 in damages. * * *

NOTES AND QUESTIONS

1. *Institution of Criminal Proceedings.* This element may be met by (1) indictment or information or (2) the issuance of criminal process to bring the accused before a magistrate whose function is to determine whether he is guilty or is to be held for later determination or (3) arrest on a criminal charge. The commencement must have been either initiated or procured by the private prosecuting witness, or he must have played an active part in continuing the proceeding. See Wilson v. Yono, 65 Mich.App. 441, 237 N.W.2d 494 (1975). Giving evidence to authorities to initiate criminal prosecution is commonly referred to as "pressing charges" and is often the factual predicate in malicious criminal prosecution. The

defendant's malicious prosecution must be the proximate legal cause of the commencement of criminal charges. Where such defendant "simply gives a statement of fact to the authorities (assuming he does not know it to be false), and leaves the decision to prosecute solely in the hands of the authorities, who have the opportunity to conduct an independent evaluation, he is not regarded as having instigated the criminal action." Dorf v. Usher, 514 So.2d 68, 69 (Fla. Dist. Ct. App. 1987).

2. *Termination in Favor of the Accused.* This element is met by discharge by magistrate at a preliminary hearing, Tritchler v. West Virginia Newspaper Pub. Co., Inc., 156 W.Va. 335, 193 S.E.2d 146 (1972); grand jury refusal to indict, Davis v. Quille, 248 Md. 631, 237 A.2d 745 (1968); a nolle prosequi, Bickford v. Lantay, 394 A.2d 281 (Me.1978); dismissal, Green v. Warnock, 144 Kan. 170, 58 P.2d 1059 (1936); failure to prosecute for lack of evidence, Southern Farmers Ass'n v. Whitfield, 238 Ark. 607, 383 S.W.2d 506 (1964); quashing of indictment, Davis v. McCrory Corp., 262 So.2d 207 (Fla.App.1972); or acquittal, Singer Mfg. Co. v. Bryant, 105 Va. 403, 54 S.E. 320 (1906). It is not met by an indecisive termination, Weissman v. K-Mart Corp., 396 So.2d 1164 (Fla.App.1981); Hoog v. Strauss, 567 S.W.2d 353 (Mo.App.1978); or by the impossibility of bringing the accused to trial, Halberstadt v. New York Life Ins. Co., 194 N.Y. 1, 86 N.E. 801 (1909); however, the abandonment or termination must touch the merits and indicate "accused's innocence." MacFawn v. Kresler, 88 N.Y.2d 859, 644 N.Y.S.2d 486, 666 N.E.2d 1359 (1996); O'Brien v. Alexander, 101 F.3d 1479, 1486 (2d Cir. 1996) (applying New York law). New York has held that a termination is favorable when it is merely "not inconsistent with innocence." See Smith-Hunter v. Harvey, 95 N.Y.2d 191, 712 N.Y.S.2d 438, 734 N.E.2d 750 (2000) (holding that termination in a manner "such that the proceeding cannot be brought again, qualifies as a favorable termination for purposes of a malicious prosecution action"). The disposition of the underlying case need not reach the merits in all circumstances. The Restatement (Second) of Torts § 674, comment *j* (1977) enunciates a test that turns on the "circumstances under which the proceedings are withdrawn." In Cult Awareness Network v. Church of Scientology International, 177 Ill.2d 267, 278–79, 226 Ill.Dec. 604, 685 N.E.2d 1347, 1353 (1997), the court found that the Restatement's position "best balances the right of citizens to have free access to our courts and the right of the individual to be free from being haled into court without reason, thereby better serving the interests of justice."

3. *Lack of Probable Cause.*

A. *Mistake of Fact.* The private prosecutor must have reasonable grounds for believing that the accused is guilty of the criminal charge. But if the private prosecutor does not honestly believe that the accused was guilty, there is no probable cause. Hanson v. Couch, 360 So.2d 942 (Ala.1978).

A reasonable mistake will not destroy probable cause. The standard is akin to the reasonable person in a negligence case, but the difference is that probable cause is for the court, rather than the jury, to decide. The defendant's subjective knowledge is a question of fact for the jury under proper instructions; but whether, upon established facts, there was probable cause is not left to them. See generally Smith v. Tucker, 304 A.2d 303 (D.C.App.1973); Turner v. City of Chicago, 91 Ill.App.3d 931, 47 Ill.Dec.

476, 415 N.E.2d 481 (1980). If a reasonable person would investigate further to make more certain of the facts before instituting criminal proceedings and the private prosecutor fails to do so, he may be found to have acted without probable cause. Food Fair Stores, Inc. v. Kincaid, 335 So.2d 560 (Fla.App.1976); Lambert v. Sears, Roebuck & Co., 280 Or. 123, 570 P.2d 357 (1977).

In both Kroger Co. v. Standard, 283 Ark. 44, 670 S.W.2d 803 (1984), and Wal-Mart Stores, Inc. v. Yarbrough, 284 Ark. 345, 681 S.W.2d 359 (1984), a customer was accosted after leaving the store with an article not paid for. Disbelieving the customer's explanation, the store prosecuted for shoplifting and the jury acquitted. Suit for malicious prosecution by the customer, who obtained a jury award of compensatory damages and substantial punitive damages in each. The appellate court affirmed one case and reversed the other, by a divided vote each time.

B. *Mistake of Law.* A layman who institutes a criminal proceeding on facts that do not constitute a crime may be held to have acted without probable cause if he failed to consult an attorney before initiating the charges; there may be circumstances, however, under which such conduct is reasonable. See generally Restatement (Second) of Torts § 662, comment *i*. For a case law sampling, see Meadows v. Grant, 15 Ariz.App. 104, 486 P.2d 216 (1971); Ruff v. Eckerds Drugs, Inc., 265 S.C. 563, 220 S.E.2d 649 (1975). Some courts hold, however, that even a reasonable mistake of law will not support probable cause. See Thomas v. Kessler, 334 Pa. 7, 5 A.2d 187 (1939); Atkinson v. Birmingham, 44 R.I. 123, 116 A. 205 (1922).

4. *Effect of Various Occurrences on Determination of Probable Cause.*

A. *Action of Magistrate on Preliminary Hearing.* Discharge is conclusive of lack of probable cause unless it was not on the merits or was based on testimony of the accused at the hearing. Hawkins v. Hawkins, 32 N.C.App. 158, 231 S.E.2d 174 (1977); Huntley v. Harberts, 264 N.W.2d 497 (S.D.1978). Contra, Hoene v. Associated Dry Goods Corp., 487 S.W.2d 479 (Mo.1972). Commitment is evidence that there was probable cause. Davis v. Quille, 248 Md. 631, 237 A.2d 745 (1968). A similar distinction is made regarding action of a grand jury. Freides v. Sani-Mode Mfg. Co., 33 Ill.2d 291, 211 N.E.2d 286 (1965) (return of indictment by grand jury establishes rebuttable "prima facie probable cause").

B. *Outcome of Proceedings.* Abandonment by the private prosecutor is evidence of lack of probable cause. See Exxon Corp. v. Kelly, 281 Md. 689, 381 A.2d 1146 (1978). Conviction is usually held to be conclusive on existence of probable cause. Earley v. Harry's I.G.A., Inc., 223 Kan. 32, 573 P.2d 572 (1977); cf. J.C. Penney Co., Inc. v. Blush, 356 So.2d 590 (Miss.1978) (presumption). Acquittal does not have any effect, according to the majority rule. Meyer v. Nedry, 159 Or. 62, 78 P.2d 339 (1938); Kroger Texas Ltd. Partnership v. Suberu, 216 S.W.3d 788 (Tex. 2006) (alleged shoplifter's acquittal does not prove lack of probable cause).

C. Advice of counsel is conclusive on the issue of probable cause, if the advice is sought in good faith and is given after a full and fair disclosure of the facts within the accuser's knowledge and information. Varner v. Hoffer, 267 Or. 175, 515 P.2d 920 (1973); Bain v. Phillips, 217 Va. 387, 228 S.E.2d 576 (1976); Murray v. Wal-Mart, Inc., 874 F.2d 555 (8th Cir. 1989) (Arkansas law).

5. *"Malice."* This troublesome word turns up again in malicious prosecution, and has given its name to the action. Here, it does not necessarily mean hatred, spite or ill will, but rather a purpose in initiating the prosecution other than that of bringing a criminal to justice. "Malice" is constituted where defendant has used the prosecution to extort money from the accused, to recover property from him, to collect a debt, or to compel performance of a contract. Dislike and ill will, which are not uncommon toward any criminal, may not be enough for "malice," if the proper purpose is also found to exist. The courts have tended, however, to look to the primary objective of the defendant. This element is usually left to the jury, unless the facts in evidence permit only one decision. See Restatement (Second) of Torts § 668. It is generally agreed that the jury are to be instructed that lack of probable cause may be evidence of the existence of malice, but that malice is not evidence of lack of probable cause.

6. *Damages.* The plaintiff must have suffered damage from the prosecution; it is assumed by the law that some damage, such as harm to reputation, will necessarily follow. The same is true of humiliation and other mental suffering. There may, in addition, be recovery for any special damages that the plaintiff can prove, as for example those for arrest or imprisonment; discomfort or injury to health; and expenses, such as attorney's fees, incurred in defending the criminal case. Punitive damages are clearly appropriate for this tort and can be awarded at the discretion of the jury in most jurisdictions.

Malice is an ingredient in the determination of punitive damages. For a discussion of the differences in the meaning of "malice" for the substantive cause of action and for the purposes of determining entitlement to punitive damages, see Sanders v. Daniel International Corporation, 682 S.W.2d 803 (Mo. 1984). Malice inferred from want of probable cause is not sufficient to sustain punitive damage award where actual malice in punitive damages must be established on clear and convincing evidence. Montgomery Ward v. Wilson, 339 Md. 701, 664 A.2d 916 (1995).

Friedman v. Dozorc

Supreme Court of Michigan, 1981.
412 Mich. 1, 312 N.W.2d 585.

LEVIN, JUSTICE. * * * Leona Serafin entered Outer Drive Hospital in May, 1970, for treatment of gynecological problems. A dilation and curettage was performed by her physician, Dr. Harold Krevsky. While in the hospital, Mrs. Serafin was referred to the present plaintiff, Dr. Friedman, for urological consultation. Dr. Friedman recommended surgical removal of a kidney stone which was too large to pass, and the operation was performed on May 20, 1970. During the surgery, the patient began to ooze blood uncontrollably. Although other physicians were consulted, Mrs. Serafin's condition continued to worsen and she died five days after the surgery. An autopsy was performed the next day; the report identified the cause of death as thrombotic thrombocytopenic purpura, a rare and uniformly fatal blood disease, the cause and cure of which are unknown.

On January 11, 1972, attorneys Dozorc and Golden, the defendants in this action, filed a malpractice action on behalf of Anthony Serafin,

Jr., for himself and as administrator of the estate of Leona Serafin, against Peoples Community Hospital Authority, Outer Drive Hospital, Dr. Krevsky and Dr. Friedman, as well as another physician who was dismissed as a defendant before trial. * * * No expert testimony tending to show that any of the defendants had breached accepted professional standards in making the decision to perform the elective surgery or in the manner of its performance was presented as part of the plaintiff's case. The judge entered a directed verdict of no cause of action in favor of Dr. Friedman and the other defendants at the close of the plaintiff's proofs. The judge subsequently denied a motion for costs brought by codefendant Peoples Community Hospital Authority, pursuant to GCR 1963, 111.6. The Court of Appeals affirmed and this Court denied leave to appeal.

Dr. Friedman commenced the present action on March 17, 1976 in Oakland Circuit Court.

[The trial court granted summary judgment for the defendants. The Court of Appeals affirmed in part and reversed in part.]

This Court granted leave to appeal on both the plaintiff's application from that portion of the Court of Appeals decision affirming the dismissal of the causes of action sounding in negligence and abuse of process and on the defendants' application to cross-appeal from that portion of the decision reversing the dismissal of the cause of action for malicious prosecution. * * *

Plaintiff and amici in support urge this Court to hold that an attorney owes a present or prospective adverse party a duty of care, breach of which will give rise to a cause of action for negligence. We agree with the circuit judge and the Court of Appeals that an attorney owes no actionable duty to an adverse party.

Plaintiff and amici argue that an attorney who initiates a civil action owes a duty to his client's adversary and all other foreseeable third parties who may be affected by such an action to conduct a reasonable investigation and re-examination of the facts and law so that the attorney will have an adequate basis for a good-faith belief that the client has a tenable claim. Plaintiff contends that this duty is created by the Code of Professional Responsibility and by the Michigan General Court Rules. * * *

In a negligence action the question whether the defendant owes an actionable legal duty to the plaintiff is one of law which the court decides after assessing the competing policy considerations for and against recognizing the asserted duty. * * *

Assuming that an attorney has an obligation to his client to conduct a reasonable investigation prior to bringing an action, that obligation is not the functional equivalent of a duty of care owed to the client's adversary. We decline to so transform the attorney's obligation because we view such a duty as inconsistent with basic precepts of the adversary system. * * *

[C]reation of a duty in favor of an adversary of the attorney's client would create an unacceptable conflict of interest which would seriously hamper an attorney's effectiveness as counsel for his client. Not only would the adversary's interests interfere with the client's interests, the attorney's justifiable concern with being sued for negligence would detrimentally interfere with the attorney-client relationship. * * *

Because * * * a cause of action for negligence in favor of a client's adversary might unduly inhibit attorneys from bringing close cases or advancing innovative theories, or taking action against defendants who can be expected to retaliate, we decline to recognize a duty of due care to the adverse party. * * *

To recover upon a theory of abuse of process, a plaintiff must plead and prove (1) an ulterior purpose and (2) an act in the use of process which is improper in the regular prosecution of the proceeding. * * *

We need not decide whether plaintiff's pleadings sufficiently allege that the defendants had an ulterior purpose in causing process to issue, since it is clear that the plaintiff has failed to allege that defendants committed some irregular act in the use of process. * * * [A] summons and complaint are properly employed when used to institute a civil action, and thus plaintiff has failed to satisfy the second element required. * * *

We note that other courts that have addressed the question whether abuse of process is a possible theory of recovery in the context of a medical malpractice countersuit have found that mere commencement of an action for malpractice is not an improper use of process. [Cc]

Plaintiff relies upon the same allegations respecting defendants' conduct and their failure to meet professional standards which assertedly constitute negligence in contending that he has pled a cause of action for malicious prosecution. He argues that the question of probable cause in a malicious prosecution action against the attorney for an opposing party turns on whether the attorney fulfilled his duty to reasonably investigate the facts and law before initiating and continuing a lawsuit. If the attorney's investigation discloses that the claim is not tenable, then it is his obligation to discontinue the action. * * *

We agree with defendants that under Michigan law special injury remains an essential element of the tort cause of action for malicious prosecution of civil proceedings. * * *

The recognition of an action for malicious prosecution developed as an adjunct to the English practice of awarding costs to the prevailing party in certain aggravated cases where the costs remedy was thought to be inadequate and the defendant had suffered damages beyond the expense and travail normally incident to defending a lawsuit. In 1698 three categories of damage which would support an action for malicious prosecution were identified: injury to one's fame (as by a scandalous allegation), injury to one's person or liberty, and injury to one's property. To this day the English courts do not recognize actions for malicious prosecution of either criminal or civil proceedings unless one of these types of injury, as narrowly defined by the cases, is present.

A substantial number of American jurisdictions today follow some form of "English rule" to the effect that "in the absence of an arrest, seizure, or special damage, the successful civil defendant has no remedy, despite the fact that his antagonist proceeded against him maliciously and without probable cause." A larger number of jurisdictions, some say a majority, follow an "American rule" permitting actions for malicious prosecution of civil proceedings without requiring the plaintiff to show special injury. * * *

The plaintiff's complaint does not allege special injury. We are satisfied that Michigan has not significantly departed from the English rule and we decline to do so today. * * *

Since this Court has not heretofore declared that an action for malicious prosecution of civil proceedings may be maintained in the absence of special injury, it remains to be decided whether we should so hold today. * * *

Most commentators appear to favor abrogation of the special injury requirement to make the action more available and less difficult to maintain. Their counsel should, however, be evaluated skeptically. The lawyer's remedy for a grievance is a lawsuit, and a law student or tort professor may be particularly predisposed by experience and training to see the preferred remedy for a wrongful tort action as another tort action. In seeking a remedy for the excessive litigiousness of our society, we would do well to cast off the limitations of a perspective which ascribes curative power only to lawsuits.

We turn to a consideration of Dean Prosser's criticisms of the three reasons commonly advanced by courts for adhering to the English rule. First, to the assertion that the costs awarded to the prevailing party are intended as the exclusive remedy for the damages incurred by virtue of the wrongful litigation, Prosser responds that "in the United States, where the costs are set by statute at trivial amounts, and no attorney's fees are allowed, there can be no pretense at compensation even for the expenses of the litigation itself." This argument is compelling, but it does not necessarily justify an award of compensation absent the hardship of special injury or dictate that an award of compensation be assessed in a separate lawsuit. Second, to the arguments that an unrestricted tort of wrongful civil proceedings will deter honest litigants and that an innocent party must bear the costs of litigation as the price of a system which permits free access to the courts, Prosser answers that "there is no policy in favor of vexatious suits known to be groundless, which are a real and often a serious injury." But a tort action is not the only means of deterring groundless litigation, and other devices may be less intimidating to good-faith litigants. Finally, in response to the claim that recognition of the tort action will produce interminable litigation, Prosser argues that the heavy burden of proof which the plaintiff bears in such actions will safeguard bona fide litigants and prevent an endless chain of countersuits. But if few plaintiffs will recover in the subsequent action, one may wonder whether there is any point in recognizing the expanded cause of action. If the subsequent action does not succeed, both parties are left to bear the expenses of two futile lawsuits, and court time has been wasted as well.

* * *

[S]uccessful defense of the former action is no assurance of recovery in a subsequent tort action, but the unrestricted availability of such an action introduces a new strategic weapon into the arsenal of defense litigators, particularly those whose clients can afford to devote extensive resources to prophylactic intimidation.

* * * If the instant plaintiff's approach is adopted, all plaintiffs and their attorneys henceforth must also weigh the likelihood that if they persevere in the action and receive an unfavorable decision, they will not only take nothing but also be forced to defend an action for malicious prosecution of civil proceedings. * * * [T]his would push the pendulum too far in favor of the defense, more than is necessary to rectify the evil to which this effort is directed. * * *

The cure for an excess of litigation is not more litigation. Meritorious as well as frivolous claims are likely to be deterred. There are sure to be those who would use the courts and such an expanded tort remedy as a retaliatory or punitive device without regard to the likelihood of recovery or who would seek a means of recovering the actual costs of defending the first action without regard to whether it was truly vexatious. * * *

Apart from special injury, elements of a tort action for malicious prosecution of civil proceedings are (1) prior proceedings terminated in favor of the present plaintiff, (2) absence of probable cause for those proceedings, and (3) "malice," more informatively described by the Restatement as "a purpose other than that of securing the proper adjudication of the claim in which the proceedings are based."

The following discussion addresses the chief concern of this case: the conditions under which the attorney for an unsuccessful plaintiff may be held liable. * * *

The absence of probable cause in bringing a civil action may not be established merely by showing that the action was successfully defended. To require an attorney to advance only those claims that will ultimately be successful would place an intolerable burden on the right of access to the courts.

The Court of Appeals adopted, and plaintiff endorses, the standard for determining whether an attorney had probable cause to initiate and continue a lawsuit articulated in Tool Research & Engineering Corp. v. Henigson, 46 Cal.App.3d 675, 683–684, 120 Cal.Rptr. 291 (1975): "The attorney is not an insurer to his client's adversary that his client will win in litigation. Rather, he has a duty 'to represent his client zealously * * * [seeking] any lawful objective through legally permissible means * * * [and presenting] for adjudication any lawful claim, issue, or defense.' (ABA, Code of Professional Responsibility, EC 7–1, DR 7–101[A][1], * * *.) So long as the attorney does not abuse that duty by prosecuting a claim which a reasonable lawyer would not regard as tenable or by unreasonably neglecting to investigate the facts and law in making his determination to proceed, his client's adversary has no right to assert malicious prosecution against the attorney if the lawyer's efforts prove unsuccessful. * * *

"The attorney's obligation is to represent his client honorably and ethically, and he may, without being guilty of malicious prosecution, vigorously pursue litigation in which he is unsure of whether his client or the client's adversary is truthful, so long as that issue is genuinely in doubt."

The *Henigson* court also said: "An attorney has probable cause to represent a client in litigation when, after a reasonable investigation and industrious search of legal authority, he has an honest belief that his client's claim is tenable in the forum in which it is to be tried."

In our view, this standard, while well-intentioned, is inconsistent with the role of the attorney in an adversary system.

Our legal system favors the representation of litigants by counsel. Yet the foregoing standard appears skewed in favor of non-representation; the lawyer risks being penalized for undertaking to present the client's claim to a court unless satisfied, after a potentially substantial investment in investigation and research, that the claim is tenable.

* * *

Moreover, the *Henigson* standard suggests rather ominously that every time a lawyer representing, say, a medical malpractice plaintiff encounters a fact adverse to the client's position or an expert opinion that there was no malpractice, he must immediately question whether to persevere in the action. An attorney's evaluation of the client's case should not be inhibited by the knowledge that perseverance may place the attorney personally at risk; the next fact or the next medical opinion may be the one that makes the case, and such developments may occur even on the eve of trial.

Indeed, a jury-submissible claim of medical malpractice may sometimes be presented even without specific testimony that the defendant physician violated the applicable standard of care. Thus, a lawyer may proceed in the good-faith belief that his proofs will establish a prima facie case of medical malpractice without expert testimony, only to find that the court disagrees. Such conduct is not the equivalent of proceeding without probable cause. * * *

This Court has said, in opinions addressed to the tort of malicious prosecution, that malice may be inferred from the facts that establish want of probable cause, although the jury is not required to draw that inference. This rule, developed in cases where damages were sought from a lay person who initiated proceedings, fails to make sufficient allowance for the lawyer's role as advocate and should not be applied in determining whether a lawyer acted for an improper purpose.

A client's total lack of belief that the action he initiates or continues can succeed is persuasive evidence of intent to harass or injure the defendant by bringing the action. But a lawyer who is unaware of such a client's improper purpose may, despite a personal lack of belief in any possible success of the action, see the client and the claim through to an appropriate conclusion without risking liability. * * *

The Restatement defines the mental element of the tort of wrongful civil proceedings as "a purpose other than that of securing the proper adjudication of the claim in which the proceedings are based." A finding of an improper purpose on the part of the unsuccessful attorney must be supported by evidence independent of the evidence establishing that the action was brought without probable cause.

We affirm that portion of the Court of Appeals decision which upheld summary judgment in favor of defendants on plaintiff's claims sounding in negligence and abuse of process. With respect to plaintiff's claim for malicious prosecution, we reverse the decision of the Court of Appeals and affirm the trial court's grant of summary judgment; we do so on the ground that an action for malicious prosecution of a civil action may not be brought absent special injury and the plaintiff failed to plead special injury.

[LEVIN, JUSTICE concurred separately, suggesting that the Court devise a new rule authorizing the judge "to order payment of the prevailing party's actual expenses, including reasonable attorneys' fees and limited consequential damages, where the action was wrongfully initiated, defended or continued."]

NOTES AND QUESTIONS

1. The title of malicious prosecution is often expanded to cover not only criminal prosecutions but also frivolous or unwarranted civil actions. To avoid confusion, the latter action is sometimes called malicious civil prosecution. The Restatement gives it the title of wrongful civil proceedings.

2. In general, the elements of the cause of action are the same for both criminal and civil prosecutions. As the principal case indicates, the major variance involves the element of damages. In the case of a civil prosecution, damages are not presumed and must be proved. The American rule is that each party to a civil action bears his own expenses of litigation, including attorney's fees. In England, attorney's fees are normally awarded to the winning party, and as a result there is no occasion for awarding them in a subsequent tort action, as part of the damages. Around a third of the American states follow the so-called "English rule"—not in awarding attorney's fees to the winner but only in declining to allow recovery of attorney's fees as damages in the subsequent tort action. This result is distinctly anomalous: the damages that are an inevitable result of the tortious conduct and that always arise cannot be recovered, and the only recoverable damages are the abnormal special damages that are specifically proved. The Restatement (Second) of Torts meets this persistent anomaly by providing expressly for certain types of injuries, such as civil proceedings involving arrest of person or deprivation of property, or repetitive actions. See §§ 677–680. But see Johnson v. Calado, 159 Wis.2d 446, 464 N.W.2d 647 (1991), reaffirming adherence to the English rule. The courts have often resisted expansion of the tort of malicious prosecution or wrongful civil actions. The remedy for excessive litigation is best addressed by facilitating speedy resolution of litigation or authorizing sanctions for abuses. With the policy of reducing litigation in mind, the California Supreme Court in Brennan v. Tremco Inc., 25 Cal.4th 310, 105 Cal.Rptr.2d 790, 20 P.3d 1086 (2001), decided that an adverse finding in a contractual arbitration proceeding could not be a basis for a malicious prosecution action. But cf. where the arbitration is ordered by a court, see Stanley v. Superior Court, 130 Cal.App.3d 460, 181 Cal.Rptr. 878 (1982). See also *Brennan*, 20 P.3d at 1089.

3. Note the differences in the elements of probable cause and "malice." The courts pride themselves in being open to the public to settle civil disputes. What is required is not a better-than-even chance that the suit will be won, but a finding by the court that there was a reasonably good chance that it would. How does this concept apply when the original plaintiff was trying to persuade the court to change the law judicially?

If "malice" means bringing a civil action with an ulterior motive, how does this apply? Does it mean that the plaintiff brought the action with a subjective awareness that he had no actual chance of prevailing? Can the attorney be held liable? What is the effect of his failure to make an adequate investigation?

Is there real basis for requiring both lack of probable cause and "malice," or should either one be sufficient?

4. Is it feasible to arrange for award of appropriate litigation expenses in the original action, rather than requiring a second action in tort, with a different judge and jury? The cases have held that a countersuit, rather than a counterclaim in the same suit, is required, because there must have been a termination in favor of the plaintiff at the time the tort claim is filed; Lees v. Smith, 363 So.2d 974 (La. Ct. App. 1978). A few states have provided by statute for allowing counterclaims; see, e.g., Clark v. Baines, 150 Wash.2d 905, 84 P.3d 245 (2004) (discussing malicious prosecution counterclaim pursuant to Washington's relevant statutory cause of action, RCWA 4.24.350).

5. If the case is filed in federal court, another remedy may be available through Rule 11 of the Federal Rules of Civil Procedure. Rule 11 establishes the standards that attorneys and parties must meet when filing pleadings, motions, or other documents in court and the circumstances under which a court may impose sanctions for the violation of those standards. At its core, the rule requires that representations made to the court be based on the best of the person's knowledge, information, and belief, formed after an inquiry reasonable under the circumstances. Violations of the standard of conduct may subject the attorney or client to various sanctions designed to deter repetition of the conduct. If the principal case had been filed in federal court under the current version of Rule 11, defendants might have served motions for summary judgment (based on the absence of proof of violation of the standard of care) and for sanctions under Rule 11. The rule specifies that the plaintiffs would then have had twenty-one days to withdraw their complaint to avoid the imposition of sanctions. Rule 11 permits the trial court judge to sanction conduct without the filing of another action. Its primary purpose, however, is to streamline litigation. Rule 11 is not foremost intended to compensate the aggrieved party. Michigan enacted a statute responding to the principal case. For discussion see Wade, On Frivolous Litigation: A Study of Tort Liability and Procedural Sanctions, 14 Hofstra L. Rev. 433 (1986).

Grainger v. Hill

Court of Common Pleas, 1838.
4 Bing.N.C. 212, 132 Eng.Rep. 769.

TINDAL C.J. This is a special action on the case, in which the Plaintiff declares that he was the master and owner of a vessel which, in

September 1836, he mortgaged to the Defendants for the sum of 80£, with a covenant for repayment in September 1837, and under a stipulation that, in the mean time, the Plaintiff should retain the command of the vessel, and prosecute voyages therein for his own profit: that the Defendants, in order to compel the Plaintiff through duress to give up the register of the vessel, without which he could not go to sea, before the money lent on mortgage became due, threatened to arrest him for the same unless he immediately paid the amount: that, upon the Plaintiff refusing to pay it, the Defendants, knowing he could not provide bail, arrested him under a capias, indorsed to levy 95£ 17s. 6d., and kept him imprisoned, until, by duress, he was compelled to give up the register, which the Defendants then unlawfully detained; by means whereof the Plaintiff lost four voyages from London to Caen. * * * The Defendants pleaded the general issue; after a verdict for the Plaintiff, the case comes before us * * * under an application for a nonsuit. * * *

The * * * ground urged for a nonsuit is, that there was no proof of the suit commenced by the Defendants having been terminated. But the answer to this * * * namely, the omission to allege want of reasonable and probable cause for the Defendants' proceeding, is * * * that this is an action for abusing the process of the law, by applying it to extort property from the Plaintiff, and not an action for a malicious arrest or malicious prosecution, in order to support which action the termination of the previous proceeding must be proved, and the absence of reasonable and probable cause be alleged as well as proved. * * * If the course pursued by the Defendants is such that there is no precedent of a similar transaction, the Plaintiff's remedy is by an action on the case, applicable to such new and special circumstances; and his complaint being that the process of the law has been abused, to effect an object not within the scope of the process, it is immaterial whether the suit which that process commenced has been determined or not, or whether or not it was founded on reasonable and probable cause. * * *

Judgment for Plaintiff.

NOTES AND QUESTIONS

1. The principal case is the classic authority. A more contemporary case on abuse of process is Board of Education of Farmingdale Union Free School District v. Farmingdale Classroom Teachers Association, Inc., 38 N.Y.2d 397, 343 N.E.2d 278, 380 N.Y.S.2d 635 (1975), where, in litigation between the School District and the Teachers Association, the latter served subpoenas on all the teachers in the school system, requiring them to report to court at the same time. This harassment of the District was held to give rise to tort liability. See also Bell v. Icard, 986 S.W.2d 550 (Tenn.1999) (filing of conservatorship proceedings to "scuttle" an allied lawsuit); Ash v. Cohn, 119 N.J.L. 54, 194 A. 174 (1937) (body execution); Ginsberg v. Ginsberg, 84 A.D.2d 573, 443 N.Y.S.2d 439 (2d Dep't 1981) (in divorce action, defendant charged with using subpoena process "for the unjustified purpose of harassing [wife] and exhausting her financial resources in order to win a collateral advantage in the legal struggle over custody of the child"). Generally, liability is ascribed to the uses of process

that are "primarily" intended to achieve an ulterior or improper purpose. See, e.g., Greenberg v. Wolfberg, 890 P.2d 895 (Okla. 1994).

The tort of abuse of process is not available for merely filing a frivolous action, absent proof that the claim was filed for a collateral or ulterior purpose. Wells v. Orthwein, 670 S.W.2d 529 (Mo.App.1984); Martin v. Trevino, 578 S.W.2d 763 (Tex.Civ.App.1978) and In re Burzynski, 989 F.2d 733 (5th Cir. 1993) (Texas law setting forth elements of claim). The procurement or issuance of process with malicious intent, or without probable cause, is not actionable. To bring an action for medical malpractice to coerce a settlement by tying a physician up in litigation with its attendant time away from practice, while it may establish malice, does not constitute abuse of process. Detenbeck v. Koester, 886 S.W.2d 477 (Tex. App. 1994); accord, Commerce Bank, N.A. v. Plotkin, 255 Ill.App.3d 870, 194 Ill.Dec. 409, 627 N.E.2d 746 (1994) (action against developers by landowners). The tort of abuse of process is not delimited by the requirements of malicious prosecution: Brownsell v. Klawitter, 102 Wis.2d 108, 306 N.W.2d 41 (1981) (action for abuse of process may proceed without termination of action in favor of defendant, an essential element in malicious prosecution).

2. *The Tort of Spoliation of Evidence*. The integrity of the litigation process depends upon the availability of accurate and reliable information being made available in evidence. The California Supreme Court in Smith v. Superior Court, 151 Cal.App.3d 491, 198 Cal.Rptr. 829 (1984), implied a cause of action for failure to preserve evidence where a car dealership, accused of negligence in installing the wheels of a van, lost or destroyed parts of the vehicle. The van wheels had spun off the van injuring plaintiff as she drove past the van. The actions of the dealership relating to the van after the accident made investigation of the cause of the accident impossible. The Court of Appeals recognized a cause of action. It found that the expectation of preservation of evidence was akin to a "probable expectancy that the court must protect from the kind of interference alleged here." Id. at 502.

In Willard v. Caterpillar, Inc., 40 Cal.App.4th 892, 48 Cal.Rptr.2d 607 (1995), the court enunciated the elements of the tort of intentional spoliation of evidence

> (1) pending or probable civil litigation, (2) defendant's knowledge that litigation is pending or probable, (3) willful destruction of evidence, (4) intent to interfere with plaintiff's prospective civil suit, (5) a causal relationship between the evidence destruction and the inability to prove the lawsuit, and (6) damages. Id. at 911.

The development of the tort was, however, arrested in Cedars-Sinai Medical Center v. Superior Court, 18 Cal.4th 1, 74 Cal.Rptr.2d 248, 954 P.2d 511 (1998). The California Supreme Court held that:

> when the alleged intentional spoliation is committed by a party to the underlying cause of action to which the evidence is relevant and when the spoliation is or reasonably should have been discovered before the conclusion of the underlying litigation, it is preferable to rely on existing nontort remedies rather than creating a tort remedy. Id. at 4.

In a footnote, the court explicitly overruled *Smith* and *Willard* "to the extent they are inconsistent with [this holding]." Id. at 18 n.4.

In *Cedars-Sinai*, a hospital could not locate fetal monitoring strips that were allegedly critical to a plaintiff "prevailing in his malpractice action." Id. at 4–5. In response to the hospital's inability to produce these records, the guardian ad litem of the infant plaintiff attempted to amend his complaint to include an intentional spoliation of evidence claim. The trial court granted the motion to amend precipitating the California Supreme Court's review of the writ of mandate and subsequent holding that scaled back the tort remedy for the intentional spoliation of evidence.

The court ironically decried intentional spoliation of evidence as "a grave affront to the cause justice . . . deserv[ing] of [the court's] unqualified condemnation." Id. at 4. Despite the effect that the destruction of evidence has on "fairness and justice," the Court cited three concerns with the tort liability it originally created.

The first concern addressed by the Court involved "the conflict between a tort remedy for intentional first party spoliation and the policy against creating derivative tort remedies for litigation-related misconduct." Id. at 8. Deciding this conflict in favor of denying an independent tort remedy, the Court cited its traditional presumption against creating new derivative torts, the "spiral[ing]" burden of lawsuits, and other jurisdictions emphasis on the "finality of adjudication." Id. at 9–10. In addition, the court analogized the lack of an independent civil remedy for perjury as support for its conclusion.

The second concern for the Court was "the strength of existing nontort remedies for spoliation." Id. at 8. "Chief among these is the evidentiary inference that evidence which one party has destroyed or rendered unavailable was unfavorable to that party." Id. at 11. Other nontort remedies include the sometimes crippling sanctions imposed for violating discovery laws, id. at 12 (such as "dismissing part or all of the action, or granting a default judgment against the offending party"), and local bar associations' authority to firmly discipline lawyers that participate in the "suppression or destruction of evidence." Id. at 13 ("Lawyers are subject to discipline, including suspension and disbarment. . . ."). The deterrent effect of criminal penalties imposed on persons found guilty of intentionally destroying evidence provides more support for relying on the strength of existing nontort remedies.

The third and final concern for the *Cedars-Sinai* court was "the uncertainty of the fact of harm in spoliation cases." Id. at 8. In other words, "even if the jury infers from the act of spoliation that the spoliated evidence was somehow unfavorable to the spoliator, there will typically be no way of telling what precisely the evidence would have shown and how much it would have weighed in the victim's favor." Id. at 13–14. Furthermore, "if evidence would not have helped to establish plaintiff's case[,] an award of damages for its destruction would work a windfall for the plaintiff." Id. at 14. Jurisdictions remain divided. In Gribben v. Wal-Mart Stores, Inc., 824 N.E.2d 349 (Ind. 2005), the court rejected the test on the grounds that existing remedies within the original or intended litigation suffice. It follows that third-party spoliation might give rise to an independent tort where such parties are not subject to remedies available against parties to the original litigation. Compare Rizzuto v. Davidson Ladders, Inc., 280

Conn. 225, 905 A.2d 1165 (2006), wherein the Connecticut court adopted the action on the grounds that it most adequately serves the fundamental purpose of tort law: compensating injured parties, shifting such loss to the responsible parties, and deterring wrongful conduct.

Where the spoliation of evidence is at the hands of third parties or it is not intentional, the tort is even more problematic: Lueter v. State of California, 94 Cal.App.4th 1285, 115 Cal.Rptr.2d 68 (2002) (declining the recognize the tort of negligent spoliation of evidence).

The California courts' experience with the tort of spoliation of evidence has been volatile. In the space of fifteen years, California courts went from an expansive recognition of both intentional and negligent spoliation of evidence causes of action, to a narrow, uncertain toleration of the tort in only the rarest cases. It is reported that over twenty-seven jurisdictions have addressed the recognition of the tort. Six have adopted the tort of negligent spoliation, while seven have approved its intentional version. The Mississippi Supreme Court has succinctly stated an implicit truth of the action: the tort is available "only to dissatisfied plaintiffs and never to dissatisfied defendants." Dowdle Butane Gas Co., Inc. v. Moore, 831 So.2d 1124, 1134 (Miss. 2002) (action exists to compensate for the loss of prospective economic advantage in a separate lawsuit; only a plaintiff may have contemplated such advantage).

CHAPTER 21

MISREPRESENTATION

1. INTRODUCTION

"Misrepresentation runs all through the law of torts, as a method of accomplishing various types of tortious conduct which, for reasons of historical development or as a matter of convenience, usually are grouped under categories of their own. Thus a battery may be committed by feeding the plaintiff poisoned chocolates, or by inducing his consent to a physical contact by misrepresenting its character; false imprisonment may result from a pretense of authority to make an arrest, a trespass to land from fraudulent statements inducing another to enter, or a conversion from obtaining possession of goods by false representations; and a malicious lie may give rise to a cause of action for the intentional infliction of mental suffering. A great many of the common and familiar forms of negligent conduct, resulting in invasions of tangible interests of person or property, are in their essence nothing more than misrepresentation, from a misleading signal by a driver of an automobile about to make a turn, or an assurance that a danger does not exist, to false statements concerning a chattel sold, or non-disclosure of a latent defect by one who is under a duty to give warning. In addition, misrepresentation may play an important part in the invasion of intangible interests, in such torts as defamation, malicious prosecution, or interference with contractual relations. In all such cases the particular form which the defendant's conduct has taken has become relatively unimportant, and misrepresentation has been merged to such an extent with other kinds of misconduct that neither the courts nor legal writers have found any occasion to regard it as a separate basis of liability." WILLIAM L. PROSSER, LAW OF TORTS 683–84 (4th ed. 1971).

Misrepresentation as a distinct cause of action has usually been associated with the common law action of deceit. The law of negligent misrepresentation or misstatement has developed rapidly in the past few decades. The causes of action in misrepresentation normally protect economic interests and consequently the parameters of liability have been carefully controlled. A form of strict liability, although occasionally recognized, is mainly banished from the ambit of tort liability.

Misrepresentation is thus a very complex field. The complexity results primarily from the existence of numerous alternative remedies. They include:

1. The tort action of deceit.

2. An action for breach of contract, when the representation is found to be an express or implied term of the contract itself. In the case of the sale of chattels, this may take the form of an action for breach of warranty, which has definite tort characteristics of its own. The contract liability is of course a strict one, and requires no intent to deceive, negligence, or other fault than the breach of the contract itself.

3. A negligence action for negligent misrepresentation or misstatement. This is now recognized by nearly all courts where tangible injury to person or property results, and by most of the American jurisdictions where the only damage is financial loss.

4. A suit in equity to rescind the transaction or for other relief such as an equitable lien or a constructive trust.

5. An action at law for restitution to recover what the plaintiff has parted with, or the unjust enrichment which the defendant has received from it.

History. The action of deceit is of very ancient origin. There was an old writ of deceit known as early as 1201, which lay only in cases of what we would now call malicious prosecution. At a later period this writ was superseded by an action on the case in the nature of deceit, which became the general common law remedy for any misrepresentation, whether fraudulent or not, which resulted in actual damage. It was used to afford a remedy for many wrongs that we should now regard as breaches of contract, such as false warranties in the sale of goods. Its use was limited almost entirely to direct transactions between the plaintiff and the defendant, and it was treated as inseparable from some contract relation. In other words, tort and contract were not at all clearly distinguished.

"Caveat emptor"—let the buyer beware—was the rule. The buyer could garner protection by exacting a warranty from the seller. Thus in the picturesque old case of Chandelor v. Lopus, (1603) 79 Eng. Rep. 3 (Exch.); Cro. Jac. 4 (Eng.), a goldsmith sold a stone to the plaintiff, falsely stating that it was a bezar stone—a "calcareous concretion in the stomach of a goat," believed to have medicinal properties, particularly as a remedy against snake-bite. It was held that there was no liability, even though the seller knew his statement to be false, in the absence of an express undertaking to be bound. The only exception was in the sale of food and drink.

In 1789, in Pasley v. Freeman, (1789) 100 Eng. Rep. 450 (K.B.); 3 T.R. 51 (Eng.), the action of deceit was held to lie in a case where the plaintiff had had no dealings with the defendant, but had been induced by his misrepresentation to extend credit to a third person. After that date deceit was recognized as purely a tort action, and not necessarily founded upon a contract. At about the same time, in Stuart v. Wilkins, (1778) 99 Eng. Rep. 15 (K.B.); 1 Doug 18 (Eng.), the remedy for breach of warranty was taken over into the action of assumpsit, and it was thus established that it had a contract character. Thereafter the two lines of recovery slowly diverge, although some vestige of confusion between the two still remains, even today.

At the beginning of the Nineteenth Century the elements were in place to provide a wide liability for misrepresentations. These developments were put asunder by the momentous case of Derry v. Peek, infra at 1086. Deceit was established as the basis of tortious liability and deceit required an actual "intention to cheat." Nocton v. Ashburton, [1914] A.C. 932 (H.L.) 953 (Eng.), Dishonesty rather than negligence was the lodestar of liability. The tort requires a fraudulent misrepresentation relied upon by the plaintiff to his detriment. What is a "misrepresentation"?

2. CONCEALMENT AND NONDISCLOSURE

Swinton v. Whitinsville Savings Bank

Supreme Judicial Court of Massachusetts, 1942.
311 Mass. 677, 42 N.E.2d 808.

Action by Neil W. Swinton against Whitinsville Savings Bank to recover damages for alleged fraudulent concealment by defendant in sale of a house to plaintiff. From an order sustaining a demurrer to plaintiff's declaration, the plaintiff appeals.

QUA, JUSTICE. The declaration alleges that on or about September 12, 1938, the defendant sold the plaintiff a house in Newton to be occupied by the plaintiff and his family as a dwelling; that at the time of the sale the house "was infested with termites, an insect that is most dangerous and destructive to buildings"; that the defendant knew the house was so infested; that the plaintiff could not readily observe this condition upon inspection; that "knowing the internal destruction that these insects were creating in said house", the defendant falsely and fraudulently concealed from the plaintiff its true condition; that the plaintiff at the time of his purchase had no knowledge of the termites, exercised due care thereafter, and learned of them about August 30, 1940; and that, because of the destruction that was being done and the dangerous condition that was being created by the termites, the plaintiff was put to great expense for repairs and for the installation of termite control in order to prevent the loss and destruction of said house.

There is no allegation of any false statement or representation, or of the uttering of a half truth which may be tantamount to a falsehood. There is no intimation that the defendant by any means prevented the plaintiff from acquiring information as to the condition of the house. There is nothing to show any fiduciary relation between the parties, or that the plaintiff stood in a position of confidence toward or dependence upon the defendant. So far as appears the parties made a business deal at arm's length. The charge is concealment and nothing more; and it is concealment in the simple sense of mere failure to reveal, with nothing to show any peculiar duty to speak. The characterization of the concealment as false and fraudulent of course adds nothing in the absence of further allegations of fact. * * *

If this defendant is liable on this declaration every seller in liable who fails to disclose any nonapparent defect known to him in the subject of the sale which materially reduces its value and which the buyer fails to discover. Similarly it would seem that every buyer would be liable who fails to disclose any nonapparent virtue known to him in the subject of the purchase which materially enhances its value and of which the seller is ignorant. [C] The law has not yet, we believe, reached the point of imposing upon the frailties of human nature a standard so idealistic as this. That the particular case here stated by the plaintiff possesses a certain appeal to the moral sense is scarcely to be denied. Probably the reason is to be found in the facts that the infestation of buildings by termites has not been common in Massachusetts and constitutes a concealed risk against which buyers are off their guard. But the law cannot provide special rules for termites and can hardly attempt to determine liability according to the varying probabilities of the existence and discovery of different possible defects in the subjects of trade. The rule of nonliability for bare nondisclosure has been stated and followed by this court. * * * It is adopted in the American Law Institute's Restatement of Torts § 551. See Williston on Contracts, Rev.Ed., §§ 1497, 1498, 1499.

The order sustaining the demurrer is affirmed, and judgment is to be entered for the defendant. * * *

So ordered.

NOTES AND QUESTIONS

1. The classic statement of the effect of nondisclosure is that of Lord Cairns in Peek v. Gurney, (1873) 6 L.R.E. & I. App. 377 (H.L.) 403 (Lord Cairns) (Eng.) "Mere non-disclosure of material facts, however morally censurable, however that nondisclosure might be a ground in a proper proceeding at a proper time for setting aside an allotment or a purchase of shares, would in my opinion form no ground for an action in the nature of an action for misrepresentation. There must, in my opinion, be some active misstatement of fact, or, at all events, such a partial and fragmentary statement of fact, as that the withholding of that which is not stated makes that which is stated absolutely false." Perhaps the leading case espousing the view is Keates v. Earl of Cardogan, (1851) 138 Eng. Rep. 234 (C.P.); 10 C.B. 591 (Eng.)

2. What is the foundation of the "general rule" that an action of deceit will not lie for tacit nondisclosure, as distinguished from active misrepresentation?

3. Three different rules modifying the harshness of the common law position developed quite early:

A. The courts assumed a much more liberal attitude when the plaintiff sought rescission of the contract, or other equitable relief. Even mutual mistake as to a basic fact affecting the transaction is ordinarily held to be sufficient grounds for such relief; and the position of the defendant is not improved if he has knowledge of the plaintiff's mistake, failed to make disclosure, and took advantage of the situation. See, for example, Slade v. McIntyre, 11 Mass. L. Rep. 79, 1999 WL 1335106 (Mass. Super. 1999). See also Weintraub v. Krobatsch, 317 A.2d 68 (N.J. 1974) (discussing modern trend away from *Peek v. Gurney* in suits in equity).

B. Even in actions at law, the defendant was held liable for nondisclosure if the parties were in some confidential or fiduciary relation to one another, so that reliance upon good faith and full disclosure was justified. McDonough v. Williams, 92 S.W. 783 (Ark.1905); Brasher v. First Nat'l. Bank of Birmingham, 168 So. 42 (Ala. 1936). "For instance, the relations of trustee and cestui que trust, principal and agent, attorney and client, physician and patient, priest and parishioner, partners, tenants in common, husband and wife, parent and child, guardian and ward, and many others of like character." Farmers' State Bank of Newport v. Lamon,

231 P. 952 (Wash.1925). As to banker and customer, see Buxcel v. First Fidelity Bank, 601 N.W.2d 593 (S.D. 1999).

C. In addition, certain types of contracts, such as those of suretyship and guaranty, joint adventure, or insurance, were recognized as in themselves creating or involving something of a confidential relation, and hence as requiring the utmost good faith, and full and fair disclosure of all material facts.

4. An active concealment may constitute an act sufficient to base liability. The leading American case is Croyle v. Moses, 90 Pa. 250 (1879), where defendant, selling a horse to plaintiff, hitched him up short for the purpose of concealing the fact that the horse was a cribber and a windsucker.

5. Are words necessary to a misrepresentation? In Kuelling v. Roderick Lean Mfg. Co., 75 N.E. 1098 (N.Y. 1905), defendant sold a road roller with its defects concealed with putty and paint. To demonstrate that fraud remained remarkably stable during the course of the 20th century, see Reichelt v. Urban Inv. & Dev. Co., 577 F. Supp. 971 (N.D. Ill. 1984) (seller of home covered up cracks in home with fiberglass and paint).

6. Defendant, selling plaintiff sheets of aluminum, placed good undamaged sheets on top of bundles of sheets that were corroded or otherwise damaged. The bundles were bulky and heavy, and plaintiff did not take them apart. Is this deceit? Salzman v. Maldaver, 24 N.W.2d 161 (Mich. 1946).

7. Suppose the defendant, in possession of the facts, denies all knowledge in response to plaintiff's inquiry, and thereby discourages him from investigating further? Smith v. Beatty, 40 Am. Dec. 435 (N.C. 1843).

Griffith v. Byers Constr. Co. of Kansas, Inc.

Supreme Court of Kansas, 1973.
212 Kan. 65, 510 P.2d 198.

FROMME, JUSTICE. The purchasers of new homes in Woodlawn East Addition, City of Wichita, Kansas, brought separate actions for damages because of the saline condition of the soil of their homesites. These actions were filed on alternative theories, (1) breach of an implied warranty of fitness and (2) fraud in the concealment of a material matter. The actions were brought against the developer. This appeal is from an order granting summary judgments in favor of the developer, Byers Construction Co. of Kansas, Inc. (Byers).

The petitions allege that Byers developed and advertised the addition as a choice residential area. Prior to the time of development the addition was part of an abandoned oil field which contained salt water disposal areas which Byers knew or should have known would not sustain vegetation because of the saline content of the soil. It was alleged that Byers graded and developed the whole addition for homesites in such a manner that it became impossible for a purchaser to discover the presence of these salt areas. It further appears from allegations in the petitions and testimony in depositions that each of the plaintiffs selected a homesite which was located within a salt water disposal area. After houses were constructed attempts to landscape the homesites failed. Grass, shrubs and trees were planted and died because of the saline content of the soil. * * * No inquiry was made and no assurance was given by Byers on soil fertility.

The facts of this case appear to be unique for, although many cases can be found on a vendor-builder's liability for the sale of a defective home no cases are cited and we find none which discuss a developer's liability for defects arising from sterility of soil. The saline content of the soil of these homesites does not affect the structural qualities of the homes. The allegations of the petitions and deposition testimony indicate that landscaping is either impossible or highly expensive.

A real estate developer by subdividing and offering lots for sale as choice residential homesites does not by implication warrant the fertility of the soil of said lots. Liability on an implied warranty of soil fertility cannot reasonably be imposed upon the real estate developer in this case. * * *

Our next inquiry is directed to the claims based on fraud. The trial court held as a matter of law no claims for fraud could be maintained because of lack of privity between the developer and these appellants. The residential lots were sold to the builders who in turn constructed the houses and then deeded the improved lots to the appellants. * * *

The allegations of fraud appear to be viable issues for trial if nondisclosure of a known material defect in the lots constitutes actionable fraud as to the appellants.

This court has held that the purchaser may recover on the theory of fraud from a vendor-builder for nondisclosure of defects. In Jenkins v. McCormick, 184 Kan. 842, 339 P.2d 8, it is stated:

"Where a vendor has knowledge of a defect in property which is not within the fair and reasonable reach of the vendee and which he could not discover by the exercise of reasonable diligence, the silence and failure of the vendor to disclose the defect in the property constitutes actionable fraudulent concealment." * * *

This *Jenkins* rule approximates that stated in Restatement (Second) of Torts, § 551:

"(1) One who fails to disclose to another a thing that he knows may justifiably induce the other to act or refrain from acting in a business transaction is subject to the same liability to the other as though he had represented the nonexistence of the matter that he has failed to disclose, if, but only if, he is under a duty to the other to exercise reasonable care to disclose the matter in question.

"(2) One party to a business transaction is under a duty to disclose to the other before the transaction is consummated. * * *

"(e) Facts basic to the transaction, if he knows that the other is about to enter into it under a mistake as to them, and that the other, because of the relationship between them, the customs in the trade or other objective circumstances, would reasonably expect a disclosure of those facts."

* * * We see no reason why the rule in *Jenkins* should not be extended in the present case to a developer of residential lots.

The appellee Byers next contends, without agency, there can be no privity and without privity there can be no duty to disclose. Here, of course, appellants never dealt with the appellee, Byers. The duty to disclose the saline nature of the soil must extend to appellants if their fraud claims are to be upheld. However, the doctrine of privity provides no defense to appellee Byers if appellants were within a class of persons appellee intended to reach. * * *

Under the alleged facts of our present case, accepting the same in the light most favorable to the appellants, we must assume the appellee, Byers, had knowledge of the saline content of the soil of the lots it placed on the market. After the grading and development of the area this material defect in the lots was not within the fair and reasonable reach of the vendees, as they could not discover this latent defect by the exercise of reasonable care. The silence of the appellee, Byers, and its failure to disclose this defect in the soil condition to the purchasers could constitute actionable fraudulent concealment under the rule in Jenkins v. McCormick, supra. One who makes a fraudulent misrepresentation or concealment is subject to liability for pecuniary loss to the persons or class of persons whom he intends or has reason to expect to act or to refrain from action in reliance upon the misrepresentation or concealment.

Of course, the fraudulent concealment to be actionable has to be material to the transaction. A matter is material if it is one to which a reasonable man would attach importance in determining his choice of action in the transaction in question. (Restatement (Second) of Torts, § 538.) There is little doubt in this case a prospective purchaser of a residential building site would consider the soil condition a material factor in choosing a lot on which to build his home. It materially affected the value and acceptability of the homesite.

As to privity we do not believe it is important to categorize its existence under a particular legal theory. Suffice it to say the appellants were in that class of persons desiring building lots in a choice residential area whom appellee intended and had reason to expect would purchase and build their homes. The fact that title was first taken in the names of the builders did not change the identity of those who would be ultimately affected by any fraudulent misrepresentations or nondisclosure of material defects in the lots. The building contractors were acting on behalf of their respective purchasers as a conduit or temporary way station for the legal title which, it was understood, would pass on completion of the homes to the appellants. There is no lack of privity in this case which would prevent causes of action based on fraud, and, in this, the district court erred in entering summary judgments for the appellee, Byers. * * *

The order of the district court entering summary judgment in favor of the appellee is affirmed as to those claims based on implied warranty but reversed as to the alternative claims based on fraud, and these cases are remanded with instructions to proceed in accordance with the views expressed herein.

NOTES AND QUESTIONS

1. The principal case was applied in Ensminger v. Terminix Int'n. Co., 102 F.3d 1571 (10th Cir. 1996), where the buyers of a home, found to be infested with termites, brought an action in fraudulent misrepresentation against the termite company that, at the request of the seller, had inspected the house prior to its sale. The court stressed the unequal access to information in the hands of a specialist on whom reliance is rested.

2. The duty to disclose material information is much debated and replete with contradictory law. The information may be possessed exclusively by the buyer or by the seller. Sellers knowing of a termite infestation are often obligated to disclose; buyers knowing of particularly valuable gold deposits on the properties are generally found not to owe duty to disclose that information to the seller. When is it that parties assume the risk that information will not be disclosed?

3. A person in the contemplation of the provider of the information who will act upon the information as given, although not directly given to that person, may have an action against the information provider in both fraudulent and negligent misrepresentation. Thus, the issuer of a letter of credit intended to be acted upon for a third party in a transaction may be liable for a fraudulent and negligent misrepresentation. See Banca del Sempione v. Provident Bank of Md, 75 F.3d 951 (4th Cir. 1996) (applying Maryland law). The scope of liability is more narrowly circumscribed for fraudulent misrepresentation because of the intentional core of the tort. Thus, in the classic case of Peek v. Gurney, (1873) 6 L.R.E. & I. App. 377 (H.L.) 403 (Lord Cairns) (Eng.), corporate directors prepared a prospectus to induce the public to buy stock in the company. It was held that no liability would attach to persons who bought the stock from a stockholder. Under the RESTATEMENT (SECOND) OF TORTS § 531 (1977), a person who makes a misrepresentation is liable to the person or class of persons the maker intends, or "has reason to expect" will act in reliance upon the misrepresentation. Foreseeability alone is not sufficient; the tortfeasor must have information that would at least lead a reasonable person to conclude that there is an "especial" likelihood that it would influence persons in plaintiff's position. See Ernst & Young, L.L.P. v. Pac. Mutual Life Ins. Co., 51 S.W.3d 573 (Tex. 2001). With the more expansive definition of intent in the modern law, the courts, as in *Banca del Sempione*, have extended the range of persons able to recover in fraudulent misrepresentation. Note Cardozo's recognition of the limits of liability in *Ultramares*, infra page 1130.

3. BASIS OF LIABILITY

(A) TO THE RECIPIENT

Derry v. Peek

House of Lords, 1889.
14 App. Cas. 337.

[This action on the case was brought by Sir Henry William Peek against William Derry, chairman, and four directors of the Plymouth, Devonport and District Tramways Company, for the fraudulent misrepresentations of the defendant; whereby the plaintiff was induced to take shares in the company.

By Section 34 of the Tramways Act, 1870, which section was incorporated in the special Act, "all carriages used on any tramway shall be moved by the power prescribed by the special Act, and where no such power is prescribed, by animal power only."

Under Section 35 of the same Act, the vehicles used on the tramways might be moved by steam or mechanical power, with the consent of the Board of Trade, for fixed periods and subject to the regulations of the Board. In February, 1883, the defendants as directors of the company issued a prospectus.

The heading, which was in large type, was as follows: "Incorporated by special Act of Parliament authorizing the use of steam or mechanical motive power." It also contained the following paragraph: "One great feature of this undertaking to which considerable importance should be attached, is, that by the special Act of Parliament obtained the company has the right to use steam or mechanical motive power, instead of horses, and it is fully expected that by means of this a considerable saving will result in the working expenses of the line as compared with other tramways worked by horses," and there were other paragraphs further setting forth the advantages to be derived from steam as compared with horse power.

Soon after the issuing of the prospectus, a copy of which the plaintiff received, he applied for and was allotted shares in the company relying, as he alleged, upon the representations of this paragraph, believing the company had an absolute right to use steam and other mechanical power.

The company proceeded to construct its tramways, but the Board of Trade refused to consent to the use of steam or mechanical power except on certain portions of the tramway, and the corporations of Devonport refused their consent to the company opening the completed part of their lines until the remainder was ready for use. In consequence the company was wound up, and immediately thereafter the plaintiff brought this action against the defendants.

At the trial the defendants all testified that they knew that consent of the Board of Trade was required for the use of steam, but that they either thought that it had been obtained, or assumed that it was assured as a matter of course once the company had been incorporated by Act of Parliament with power to use steam.

STIRLING, JUSTICE, dismissed the action, having come to the conclusion that the directors all believed that the company had the rights stated in the prospectus and that their belief was not unreasonable, nor was their conduct so reckless or careless that they ought to be held liable in an action of deceit.

On appeal the judgment of Stirling, J., was reversed on the ground that while the defendants honestly believed that the statements in the prospectus were true, the statements were made without any reasonable grounds for believing them. The defendants appealed to the House of Lords. The House of Lords unanimously reversed the decisions of the Court below and unanimously restored the opinion of Stirling, J.]

LORD HERSCHELL. * * * "This action is one which is commonly called an action of deceit, a mere common-law action." This is the description of it given by Cotton, L.J., in delivering judgment. I think it important that it should be borne in mind that such an action differs essentially from one brought to obtain rescission of a contract on the ground of misrepresentation of a material fact. The principles which govern the two actions differ widely. Where rescission is claimed it is only necessary to prove that there was misrepresentation; then, however honestly it may have been made, however free from blame the person who made it, the contract, having been obtained by misrepresentation, cannot stand. In an action of deceit, on the contrary, it is not enough to establish misrepresentation alone; it is conceded on all hands that something more must be proved to cast liability upon the defendant, though it has been a matter of controversy what additional elements are requisite. I lay stress upon this because observations made by learned judges in actions for rescission have been cited and much relied upon at the bar by counsel for the respondent. Care must obviously be observed in applying the language used in relation to such actions to an action of deceit. * * *

I think the authorities establish the following propositions: First, in order to sustain an action of deceit there must be proof of fraud, and nothing short of that will suffice. Secondly, fraud is proved when it is shown that a false representation has been made (1) knowingly, or (2) without belief in its truth, or (3) recklessly, careless whether it be true or false. Although I have treated the second and third as distinct cases, I think the third is but an instance of the second, for one who makes a statement under such circumstances can have no real belief in the truth of what he states. To prevent a false statement being fraudulent there must, I think, always be an honest belief in its truth. And this probably covers the whole ground, for one who knowingly alleges that which is false has obviously no such honest belief. Thirdly, if fraud be proved, the motive of the person guilty of it is immaterial. It matters not that there was no intention to cheat or injure the person to whom the statement was made. * * *

In my opinion making a false statement through want of care falls far short of, and is a very different thing from, fraud, and the same may be said of a false representation honestly believed though on insufficient grounds. * * *

At the same time I desire to say distinctly that when a false statement has been made the questions whether there were reasonable grounds for believing it, and what were the means of knowledge in the possession of the person making it, are most weighty matters for consideration. The ground upon which an alleged belief was founded is a most important test of its reality. I can conceive of many cases where the fact that an alleged belief was destitute of all reasonable foundation would suffice of itself to convince the Court that it was not really entertained, and that the representation was a fraudulent one. So, too, although means of knowledge are * * * a very different thing from knowledge, if I thought that a person making a false statement had shut his eyes to the facts, or purposely abstained from inquiring into them I should hold that honest belief was absent, and that he was just as fraudulent as if he had knowingly stated that which was false. * * *

I quite admit that the statements of witnesses as to their belief are by no means to be accepted blindfolded. The probabilities must be considered. Whenever it is necessary to arrive at a conclusion as to the state of mind of another person, and to determine whether his belief under given circumstances was such as he alleges, we can only do so by applying the standard of conduct which our own experience of the ways of men has enabled us to form; by asking ourselves whether a reasonable man situated as the defendants were, with their knowledge and means of knowledge, might well believe what they state they did believe, and consider that the representations made were substantially true. * * *

I think the judgment of the Court of Appeals should be reversed. * * *

Order of the Court of Appeal reversed; order of STIRLING, J., restored.

NOTES AND QUESTIONS

1. Lord Bramwell in his speech approved the remark of Stirling J. in the lower court: "[M]ercantile men dealing with matters of business would be the first to cry out if I extended the notion of deceit into what is honestly done * * *." Liability was confined to deceit (fraud), breach of contract, and breach of fiduciary obligation. It was not until 1964 that the House of Lords in Hedley Byrne & Co. v. Heller & Partners Ltd., [1964] A.C. 465 (H.L.) (Eng.) extended liability to the situation where a person relied upon information negligently supplied by another in a "special relationship."

2. The principal case has influenced American courts. See Lambert v. Smith, 201 A.2d 491 (Md. 1964). In many of these states, however, a negligence action will lie for the pecuniary loss. See Int'l Prod. Co. v. Erie R.R. Co., infra page 1107.

3. The unreasonableness of the defendant's belief may be strong evidence that it does not in fact exist, and that conclusion may be reached as an inference of fact. For example, Kimber v. Young, 137 Fed. 744 (8th Cir. 1905); Palmacci v. Umpierrez, 121 F.3d 781 (1st Cir. 1997).

4. It is generally agreed that a bad motive, as distinguished from an intent to mislead, is not essential to the tort of deceit. The defendant is liable if he intended to deceive, notwithstanding the fact that he meant no

harm, was disinterested or intended to do the plaintiff a kindness. Polhill v. Walter, (1832) 110 Eng. Rep. 43 (K.B.); 3 B & Ad. 114 (Eng.) Nielsen v. Adams, 388 N.W.2d 840 (Ned. 1986). The presence or absence of bad motive may, however, affect the issue of punitive damages for deceit. Thompson v. Modern Sch. of Bus. & Correspondence, 190 P. 451 (Cal. 1920); Laughlin v. Hopkinson, 126 N.E. 591 (Ill. 1920).

5. Section 526 of the RESTATEMENT (SECOND) OF TORTS (1977) reads as follows:

> A misrepresentation is fraudulent if the maker
>
> (a) knows or believes that the matter is not as he represents it to be,
>
> (b) does not have the confidence in the accuracy of his representation that he states or implies, or
>
> (c) knows that he does not have the basis for his representation that he states or implies.

How does this fit with the definition of Lord Herschell in *Derry v. Peek*?

6. Suppose the plaintiff knows that the matter represented is one upon which the defendant could not have any definite knowledge? Thus a representation that there is water under land, and it will be found when a well is drilled. Harris v. Delco Prod., Inc., 25 N.E.2d 740 (Mass. 1940).

7. Suppose the defendant makes a statement that can reasonably be understood in two ways, one true and the other false. Plaintiff understands it in the false sense, and is misled, but defendant believes that plaintiff has understood in the true one. Will an action for deceit lie? Nash v. Minn. Title Ins. & Trust Co., 40 N.E. 1039 (Mass. 1895).

8. *Intersection of Free Speech and Misrepresentation.* In United States v. Alvarez, 132 S. Ct. 2537 (2012), the Supreme Court struck down the Stolen Valor Act of 2005, 18 U.S.C.A. § 704 (2006), which criminalized making false statements about having been awarded a military medal. The law was passed to stem instances where people falsely claimed to have received a medal in an attempt to protect the "valor" of those who really earned such medals. While a 6–3 majority of the Supreme Court agreed that the law was unconstitutional under the First Amendment's free speech protections, it could not agree on a single rationale. Four justices concluded that a statement's falsity is not enough, by itself, to exclude speech from First Amendment protection. Another two justices concluded that while false statements were entitled to some protection, the Stolen Valor Act was invalid because it could have achieved its objectives in less restrictive ways. Due to the negative reactions to the decision from the political community and veterans' organizations, Congress enacted a new version, the Stolen Valor Act of 2013, Pub. L. 113–12, 127 Stat. 448, which amended Title 18 of the U.S. Code to make it a crime for a person to fraudulently claim having received any of a series of particular military decorations with the intention of obtaining money, property, or other tangible benefit from convincing someone that he or she rightfully did receive that award.

International Products Co. v. Erie R.R. Co.

Court of Appeals of New York, 1927.
244 N.Y. 331, 155 N.E. 662.

[Plaintiff, an importer, was expecting a valuable consignment of goods to arrive on the steamer Plutarch, and had made arrangements with defendants to receive and store the goods until they could be reshipped. The shipment was covered by insurance until it reached the warehouse, and plaintiff desired to insure it after that time. Giving this reason for its question, it inquired of defendant where the goods would be stored. Defendant, taking time to obtain the information, replied that the goods were docked at Dock F, Weehawken. From this reply, plaintiff reasonably inferred that the goods were already received and stored, and obtained its insurance on this basis. The goods arrived later and were stored at Dock D. They were destroyed by fire, and plaintiff was unable to collect any insurance payments because of the misdescription. Plaintiff seeks to recover from defendant the sum it would have received if defendant's statement had been correct. The trial court directed a verdict for plaintiff, which was affirmed by the Appellate Division. Defendant appeals.]

ANDREWS, J. * * * Confining ourselves to the issues before us, we eliminate any theory of fraud or deceit. * * * [C] We come to the vexed question of liability for negligent language. In England the rule is fixed. "Generally speaking there is no such thing as liability for negligence in words as distinguished from act." Pollock on Torts (12th Ed.) p. 565; [c]. Dicta to the contrary may be found in earlier cases. * * * But since Derry v. Peek, L.R. 14 App.Cas. 337, although what was said was not necessary to the decision, the law is clearly to the effect "that no cause of action is maintainable for a mere statement, although untrue, and although acted upon to the damage of the person to whom the statement is made unless the statement be false to the knowledge of the person making it," [c] or, as said elsewhere, "we have to take it as settled that there is no general duty to use any care whatever in making statements in the way of business or otherwise, on which other persons are likely to act" [c]. * * *

These cases have not been without criticism. The denial, under all circumstances, of relief because of the negligently spoken or written word, is, it is said, a refusal to enforce what conscience, fair dealing, and the usages of business require. The tendency of the American courts has been towards a more liberal conclusion. The searcher of a title employed by one who delivers his abstract to another to induce action on the faith of it must exercise care. [C] So must a physician who assures a wife that she may safely treat the infected wound of her husband [c], or hired by another, examines a patient, and states the result of his diagnosis [c]. So of a telegraph company stating that a telegram was delivered when in fact it was not. [C] And the liability of such a company to the receiver for the erroneous transcription of a telegram has also sometimes been placed on this ground. [C]

In New York we are already committed to the American as distinguished from the English rule. In some cases a negligent statement may be the basis for a recovery of damages. * * * [In] Glanzer

v. Shepard, 233 N.Y. 236, 135 N.E. 275, [a] public weigher, hired by the seller to weigh goods, realizing that the buyer would rely on his certificate in paying therefor, was held liable for erroneous statements contained therein. * * *

The negligence was inferred from the issuance of a false certificate. That was the wrong for which a recovery was allowed. "Diligence was owing, not only to him who ordered, but to him also who relied."

Obviously, however, the rule we have adopted has its limits. Not every casual response, not every idle word, however damaging the result, gives rise to a cause of action. * * * Liability in such cases arises only where there is a duty, if one speaks at all, to give the correct information. And that involves many considerations. There must be knowledge, or its equivalent, that the information is desired for a serious purpose; that he to whom it is given intends to rely and act upon it; that, if false or erroneous, he will because of it be injured in person or property. Finally, the relationship of the parties, arising out of contract or otherwise, must be such that in morals and good conscience the one has the right to rely upon the other for information, and the other giving the information owes a duty to give it with care. [C] An inquiry made of a stranger is one thing; of a person with whom the inquirer has entered, or is about to enter into a contract concerning the goods which are, or are to be, its subject, is another. Even here the inquiry must be made as the basis of independent action. We do not touch the doctrine of caveat emptor. But in a proper case we hold that words negligently spoken may justify the recovery of the proximate damages caused by faith in their accuracy.

When such a relationship as we have referred to exists may not be precisely defined. All that may be stated is the general rule. In view of the complexity of modern business, each case must be decided on the peculiar facts presented. The same thing is true, however, in the usual action for personal injuries. There whether negligence exists depends upon the relations of the parties, the thing done or neglected, its natural consequences, and many other considerations. No hard and fast line may be drawn.

Here, as we view the facts, the duty to speak with care, if it spoke at all, rested on the defendant. We have [defendant] about to become the bailee of the plaintiff's goods; the inquiry made by [plaintiff] with whom [defendant] was dealing for the purpose as it knew of obtaining insurance; the realization that the information it gave was to be relied upon, and that, if false, the insurance obtained would be worthless. We have an inquiry such as might be expected in the usual course of business made of one who alone knew the truth. We have a negligent answer, untrue in fact, actual reliance upon it, and resulting proximate loss. True, the answer was not given to serve the purposes of the defendant itself. This we regard as immaterial.

If there was negligence justifying a recovery, we cannot hold the plaintiff guilty of contributory negligence as a matter of law. Whether or not it should have discovered the error by an inspection of the bill of lading when it received it was a question of fact. * * *

The judgment appealed from should be affirmed, with costs.

NOTES AND QUESTIONS

1. A few of the American courts have held that the action for deceit itself will lie for negligent misrepresentations resulting in pecuniary loss. They have either declared outright that the fault of a negligent defendant is equivalent to that of a defendant intending to deceive, or have resorted to the obvious fiction that a duty to learn the facts is the equivalent of knowledge of their existence. See, for example, Mullen v. E. Trust & Banking Co., 81 A. 948 (Me. 1911); Schoefield Gear & Pulley Co. v. Schoefield, 40 A. 1046 (Conn. 1898).

2. As to the dictum in the principal case that "not every casual response, not every idle word * * * gives rise to a cause of action," see Renn v. Provident Trust Co., 196 A. 8 (Pa. 1938) (gratuitous supplying of copy of will, wrong will supplied by mistake); Vartan Garapedian, Inc. v. Anderson, 31 A.2d 371 (N.H. 1943) (casual statement about credit of prospective buyer). Is an attorney or a physician liable to one who is not his client or his patient for "curbstone advice," when it is negligently given? Fish v. Kelly, (1864) 144 Eng. Rep. 78 (Exch.); 17 C.B. (N.S.) 194 (Eng.); Buttersworth v. Swint, 186 S.E. 770 (Ga. App. Ct. 1936); DiMarco v. Lynch Homes, 583 A.2d 422 (Pa. 1990) (liability of physician for negligent advice given to sexual partner of plaintiff) but cf. D'Amico v. Delliquadri, 683 N.E.2d 814 (Ohio Ct. App. 1996) (holding that plaintiff contracting genital warts from boyfriend could not sue boyfriend's physician for negligent advice regarding the communicability of the disease).

3. What if the information, although not volunteered and given without consideration, is supplied in the course of the defendant's business or professional relations? For example, the lessor of a truck gratuitously tells the lessee, in good faith but negligently, that it is covered by insurance? Manock v. Amos D. Bridge's Sons, Inc., 169 A. 881 (N.H. 1934). Cf. Va. Dare Stores v. Schuman, 1 A.2d 897 (Md. 1938) (owner to invitee). The duty may attach to the provider of information who, although not in the business of supplying information, had a pecuniary interest in the transaction contemplated by the parties. See Hawaii v. United States Steel Corporation, 919 P.2d 294 (Haw. 1996). But cf. Fry v. Mount, 554 N.W.2d 263 (Iowa 1996) (duty limited to those in the business of supplying information). Even where a statutory duty of accuracy in business dealings exists, courts may still decline to find a corresponding duty in tort. See Cameron v. Harshbarger, 998 P.2d 221 (Or. 2000). Note that if a duty has been breached, plaintiff must still prove that, given competent advice, on the balance of probabilities, he would have secured effective insurance to cover the loss. Norwest Refrigeration Servs. Pty. Ltd v. Bain Dawes (WA) Pty. Ltd (1984) 157 CLR 149 (Austl.).

4. Representations of fact made in precontractual negotiations may be actionable. Weisman v. Connors, 540 A.2d 783 (Md. 1988) (representations about employment prospects). But cf. Onita Pac. Corp. v. Tr. of Bronson, 843 P.2d 890 (Or. 1992) (duty dependent upon professional relationship and could not be generated in arms-length, pre-contractual negotiations), and Sagent Tech., Inc. v. Micros Sys., Inc., 276 F. Supp. 2d. 464 (D. Md. 2003) (applying Maryland law; requiring contractual privity for a misrepresentation claim).

Winter v. G.P. Putnam's Sons

United States Court of Appeals, Ninth Circuit, 1991.
938 F.2d 1033.

Before SNEED, TANG and THOMPSON, CIRCUIT JUDGES.

SNEED, CIRCUIT JUDGE: * * *

I.

FACTS AND PROCEEDINGS BELOW

The Encyclopedia of Mushrooms is a reference guide containing information on the habitat, collection, and cooking of mushrooms. It was written by two British authors and originally published by a British publishing company. Defendant Putnam, an American book publisher, purchased copies of the book from the British publisher and distributed the finished product in the United States. Putnam neither wrote nor edited the book.

Plaintiffs purchased the book to help them collect and eat wild mushrooms. In 1988, plaintiffs went mushroom hunting and relied on the descriptions in the book in determining which mushrooms were safe to eat. After cooking and eating their harvest, plaintiffs became critically ill. Both have required liver transplants.

Plaintiffs allege that the book contained erroneous and misleading information concerning the identification of the most deadly species of mushrooms. In their suit against the book publisher, plaintiffs allege liability based on products liability, breach of warranty, negligence, negligent misrepresentation, and false representations. Defendant moved for summary judgment asserting that plaintiffs' claims failed as a matter of law because 1) the information contained in a book is not a product for the purposes of strict liability under products liability law; and 2) defendant is not liable under any remaining theories because a publisher does not have a duty to investigate the accuracy of the text it publishes. The district court granted summary judgment for the defendant. Plaintiffs appeal. We affirm.

II.

DISCUSSION

A book containing Shakespeare's sonnets consists of two parts, the material and print therein, and the ideas and expression thereof. The first may be a product, but the second is not. The latter, were Shakespeare alive, would be governed by copyright laws; the laws of libel, to the extent consistent with the First Amendment; and the laws of misrepresentation, negligent misrepresentation, negligence, and mistake. These doctrines applicable to the second part are aimed at the delicate issues that arise with respect to intangibles such as ideas and expression. Products liability law is geared to the tangible world.

A. Products Liability

The language of products liability law reflects its focus on tangible items. In describing the scope of products liability law, the Restatement (Second) of Torts lists examples of items that are covered. All of these are tangible items, such as tires, automobiles, and insecticides. The American Law Institute clearly was concerned with including all physical items but gave no indication that the doctrine should be expanded beyond that area.

The purposes served by products liability law also are focused on the tangible world and do not take into consideration the unique characteristics of ideas and expression. * * *

Although there is always some appeal to the involuntary spreading of costs of injuries in any area, the costs in any comprehensive cost/benefit analysis would be quite different were strict liability concepts applied to words and ideas. We place a high priority on the unfettered exchange of ideas. We accept the risk that words and ideas have wings we cannot clip and which carry them we know not where. The threat of liability without fault (financial responsibility for our words and ideas in the absence of fault or a special undertaking or responsibility) could seriously inhibit those who wish to share thoughts and theories. As a New York court commented, with the specter of strict liability, "[w]ould any author wish to be exposed * * * for writing on a topic which might result in physical injury? e.g. How to cut trees; How to keep bees?" *Walter v. Bauer,* 109 Misc.2d 189, 191, 439 N.Y.S.2d 821, 823 (Sup.Ct.1981) (student injured doing science project described in textbook; court held that the book was not a product for purposes of products liability law), aff'd in part & rev'd in part on other grounds, 88 A.D.2d 787, 451 N.Y.S.2d 533 (1982). One might add: "Would anyone undertake to guide by ideas expressed in words either a discrete group, a nation, or humanity in general?"

Strict liability principles even when applied to products are not without their costs. Innovation may be inhibited. We tolerate these losses. They are much less disturbing than the prospect that we might be deprived of the latest ideas and theories.

* * *

Plaintiffs * * * assert that *The Encyclopedia of Mushrooms* should be analogized to aeronautical charts. Several jurisdictions have held that charts which graphically depict geographic features or instrument approach information for airplanes are "products" for the purpose of products liability law. See Brocklesby v. United States, 767 F.2d 1288, 1294–95 (9th Cir.1985) (applying Restatement for the purpose of California law), cert. denied, 474 U.S. 1101, 106 S.Ct. 882, 88 L.Ed.2d 918 (1986); Saloomey v. Jeppesen & Co., 707 F.2d 671, 676–77 (2d Cir.1983) (applying Restatement for the purpose of Colorado Law). Plaintiffs suggest that *The Encyclopedia of Mushrooms* can be compared to aeronautical charts because both items contain representations of natural features and both are intended to be used while engaging in a hazardous activity. We are not persuaded.

Aeronautical charts are highly technical tools. They are graphic depictions of technical, mechanical data. The best analogy to an aeronautical chart is a compass. Both may be used to guide an individual who is engaged in an activity requiring certain knowledge of natural features. Computer software that fails to yield the result for which it was designed may be another. In contrast, *The Encyclopedia of Mushrooms* is like a book on how to *use* a compass or an aeronautical chart. The chart itself is like a physical "product" while the "How to Use" book is pure thought and expression.

Given these considerations, we decline to expand products liability law to embrace the ideas and expression in a book. We know of no court that has chosen the path to which the plaintiffs point.

B. *The Remaining Theories*

As discussed above, plaintiffs must look to the doctrines of copyright, libel, misrepresentation, negligent misrepresentation, negligence, and mistake to form the basis of a claim against the defendant publisher. Unless it is assumed that the publisher is a guarantor of the accuracy of an author's statements of fact, plaintiffs have made no case under any of these theories other than possibly negligence. Guided by the First Amendment and the values embodied therein, we decline to extend liability under this theory to the ideas and expression contained in a book.

* * * The plaintiffs urge this court that the publisher had a duty to investigate the accuracy of *The Encyclopedia of Mushrooms'* contents. We conclude that the defendants have no duty to investigate the accuracy of the contents of the books it publishes. A publisher may of course assume such a burden, but there is nothing inherent in the role of publisher or the surrounding legal doctrines to suggest that such a duty should be imposed on publishers. Indeed the cases uniformly refuse to impose such a duty. Were we tempted to create this duty, the gentle tug of the First Amendment and the values embodied therein would remind us of the social costs.

Finally, plaintiffs ask us to find that a publisher should be required to give a warning 1) that the information in the book is not complete and that the consumer may not fully rely on it or 2) that this publisher has not investigated the text and cannot guarantee its accuracy. With respect to the first, a publisher would not know what warnings, if any, were required without engaging in a detailed analysis of the factual contents of the book. This would force the publisher to do exactly what we have said he has no duty to do—that is, independently investigate the accuracy of the text. We will not introduce a duty we have just rejected by renaming it a "mere" warning label. With respect to the second, such a warning is unnecessary given that *no* publisher has a duty as a guarantor.

For the reasons outlined above, the decision of the district court is AFFIRMED.

NOTES AND QUESTIONS

1. Section 311 of the Restatement (Second) of Torts (1977) states:

> (1) One who negligently gives false information to another is subject to liability for physical harm caused by action by the other in reasonable reliance upon such information, where such harm results
>
> (a) to the other, or
>
> (b) to such third persons as the actor should expect to be put in peril by the action taken.

(2) Such negligence may consist of failure to exercise reasonable care

(a) in ascertaining the information, or

(b) in the manner in which it is communicated.

Comment *b* to section 311 provides that "[t]he rule . . . extends to any person who, in the course of an activity which is in furtherance of his own interests, undertakes to give information to another, and knows or should realize that the safety of the person of others may depend upon the accuracy of the information."

2. Plaintiff fraudulently misrepresented the safety and lack of danger of white lead pigment. Plaintiff could not prove that it directly relied on the representation, but could prove that the representation led to the injury foreseeably caused to consumers of the white lead pigment. In City of New York v. Lead Indus. Ass., 241 A.D.2d 387 (N. Y. App. Div. 1997), the court found that reliance in cases of bodily injury, in contrast to economic loss, may be indirect.

3. Alm v. Van Nostrand Reinhold Co., 480 N.E.2d 1263 (Ill. App. Ct. 1985), finding no duty to insure the accuracy of instruction manual; plaintiff was injured when tool shattered while following manual's instructions. No duty was found in the following cases: Jones v. J.B. Lippincott, 694 F. Supp. 1216 (D. Md. 1988) (self treatment of constipation following textbook); Smith v. Linn, 563 A.2d 123 (Pa. 1989) (plaintiff's decedent died of malnutrition following diet set forth in defendant's book); and Birmingham v. Fodor's Travel Publ'g, Inc., 833 P.2d 70 (Haw.1992) (plaintiff sued Fodor's for failure to warn of surf conditions in a travel guide). In *Birmingham*, the publisher of the book did not author it, and had no duty to warn of the dangerous conditions at a beach described in the book.

4. The opinion in the principal case distinguished Weirum v. RKO Gen., Inc., 539 P.2d 36, 123 Cal. Rptr. 468 (Cal. 1975) (en banc) wherein defendant ran a promotional contest involving the location of a roving disc jockey. Plaintiff's decedent was killed in an accident caused by teenager speeding to meet the disc jockey. Court found liability. The principal case commented at footnote 8: "A publisher's role in bringing ideas and information to the public bears no resemblance to the *Weirum scenario*."

5. Other cases have distinguished *Weirum* where the communication, albeit not a misrepresentation or misstatement, has caused the plaintiff physical injury. Bill v. Sup. Ct. of San Francisco, 187 Cal. Rptr. 625 (Cal. Ct. App. 1982) (plaintiff shot by gang member after viewing movie "Boulevard Nights"); Yakubowicz v. Paramount Pictures, 536 N.E.2d 1067 (Mass. 1989) (sixteen-year-old boy knifed to death by another youth after viewing a violent movie, "The Warriors"); Herceg v. Hustler Magazine, 814 F.2d 1017 (5th Cir. 1987), *cert. denied*, 485 U.S. 959 (1988) (fourteen-year-old boy died while engaged in "autoerotic asphyxiation" described in defendant magazine); Sanders v. Acclaim Entm't., Inc., 188 F. Supp.2d 1264 (D. Colo. 2002) (Klebold & Harris, both Seventeen, were avid viewers of violent video games and movies; they entered Columbine High School and murdered fellow students and teachers; relatives of victims brought negligence and strict liability claims against producers and manufacturers of the games and videos); on similar

facts, James v. Meow Media, Inc., 300 F.3d 683 (6th Cir. 2002). But cf. cases where Soldier of Fortune Magazine has been sued for deaths and injuries resulting from advertisements for "Gun for Hire": Norwood v. Soldier of Fortune Magazine, 651 F. Supp. 1397 (W.D. Ark. 1987); Eimann v. Soldier of Fortune Magazine, 880 F.2d 830 (5th Cir. 1989), *cert. denied,* 493 U.S. 1024 (1990); Braun v. Soldier of Fortune Magazine, 968 F.2d 1110 (11th Cir. 1992), *cert. denied,* 506 U.S. 1071 (1993); Rice v. Paladin Enter. Inc., 128 F.3d 233 (4th Cir. 1997) (liability for advice on how to commit a murder).

6. Plaintiff, a female high school student, was sexually molested by her teacher. The teacher had been employed by the school after the school board had received a detailed recommendation by the teacher's former employer. The report did not mention the teacher's sexual proclivities known to the former employer. In Randi W. v. Muroc Joint Unified Sch. Dist., 929 P.2d 582 (Cal. 1997), the court held that the "writer of a letter of recommendation owes third persons a duty not to misrepresent the facts in describing the qualifications and character of a former employee, if making the representations would present a substantial and foreseeable risk of physical injury to the third persons." Id. at 591. The half-truths amounted to misrepresentation. But cf. Richland Sch. Dist. v. Mabton Sch. Dist., 45 P.3d 580 (Wash. Ct. App. 2002) (no duty of employee to disclose information not present in recommendation letters).

7. In M.H. & J.L.H. v. Caritas Family Serv., 488 N.W.2d 282 (Minn. 1992), an adoption agency owed a duty of care to disclose information to adoptive parents about the incestuous parentage of a child. However, the courts have drawn back from imposing an affirmative duty to investigate. Meracle v. Children's Serv. Soc. of Wis., 437 N.W.2d 532 (Wis. 1989); Mallette v. Children's Friend & Serv., 661 A.2d 67 (R.I. 1995) (holding agency liable for nondisclosure of genetic or medical information when information of this nature is volunteered; agency must act with reasonable care or refuse to disclose any information); Jackson v. State, 956 P.2d 35 (Mont. 1998) (recognizing a common law duty to disclose concurrent with a statutory obligation). An agency is liable for fraudulent misrepresentation. See Burr v. Bord. of Cnty. Comm'rs, 491 N.E.2d 1101 (Ohio 1986) (knowing misrepresentations as to the background and health risks of child who subsequently became disabled by Huntington's Disease).

Hanberry v. Hearst Corp.

Court of Appeal of California, 1969.
276 Cal.App.2d 680, 81 Cal.Rptr. 519.

[Plaintiff-appellant purchased from defendant Akron a pair of shoes manufactured by defendant Handal. She alleges that the shoes were defective in being "slippery and unsafe" when used on vinyl floor coverings, and that "she stepped on the vinyl floor of her kitchen, slipped, fell and sustained several physical injuries."

She also sues defendant Hearst Corporation on the ground that it had negligently given a Good Housekeeping seal of approval to the shoes as "good ones." Hearst demurred to the causes against it, and the court granted judgment of dismissal to Hearst. Plaintiff appealed from this judgment.]

AULT, ASSOCIATE JUSTICE, PRO TEM. * * * Appellant further alleges respondent Hearst publishes a monthly magazine known as Good Housekeeping in which products, including the shoes she purchased, were advertised as meeting the "Good Housekeeping's Consumers' Guaranty Seal." With respect to this seal the magazine states: "This is Good Housekeeping's Consumers' Guaranty" and "We satisfy ourselves that products advertised in Good Housekeeping are good ones and that the advertising claims made for them in our magazine are truthful." The seal itself contained the promise, "If the product or performance is defective, Good Housekeeping guarantees replacement or refund to the consumer." * * *

In the second and eighth causes of action, appellant seeks to recover on the theory of negligent misrepresentation. * * *

The basic question presented on this appeal is whether one who endorses a product for his own economic gain, and for the purpose of encouraging and inducing the public to buy it, may be liable to a purchaser who, relying on the endorsement, buys the product and is injured because it is defective and not as represented in the endorsement. We conclude such liability may exist and a cause of action has been pleaded in the instant case. * * *

In both the second and eighth causes of action of the complaint under consideration, appellant has alleged respondent extended it certification and permitted the use of its seal in connection with the shoes she purchased without test, inspection or examination of the shoes, or a sample thereof, or if it tested, inspected or examined, it did so in a careless and negligent manner which did not reveal their dangerous and defective condition. If either of the alternative allegations is true, respondent violated its duty of care to the appellant and the issuance of its seal and certification with respect to the shoes under that circumstance would amount to a negligent misrepresentation.

Hearst urges its representation the shoes were "good ones" was a mere statement of opinion, not a statement of a material fact, and therefore not actionable. Since the very purpose of the seal and its certification the shoes were "good ones" was to induce and encourage members of the public to buy the shoes, respondent is in poor position to argue its endorsement cannot legally be considered as the inducing factor in bringing about their sale. [C] Respondent was not the seller or manufacturer of the shoes; it held itself out as a disinterested third party which had examined the shoes, found them satisfactory, and gave its endorsement. By the very procedure and method it used, respondent represented to the public it possessed superior knowledge and special information concerning the product it endorsed. Under such circumstance, respondent may be liable for negligent representations of either fact or opinion. [C]

Respondent argues no basis for liability has been shown because, "It is a matter of common knowledge that brand new soles on brand new shoes have a tendency of being slick and slippery until the shoes have been worn sufficiently long thereafter." The argument may well have merit [c], but it is one addressed properly to the trier of fact. The case is presented to us in the pleading context. We are unwilling to hold as a matter of law that liability will not attach under any circumstance based upon a defectively designed shoe. * * *

The judgment of dismissal is * * * reversed as to the second and eighth causes of action (negligent misrepresentation).

Richard v. A. Waldman & Sons, Inc.

Supreme Court of Connecticut, 1967.
155 Conn. 343, 232 A.2d 307.

COTTER, ASSOCIATE JUSTICE. The plaintiffs, owners of a house and lot in Vernon which they purchased from the defendant corporation, instituted an action * * * for damages for alleged false representations in connection with the sale of land. * * * [Plaintiff obtained] a judgment for damages from which the defendant has appealed. * * *

At the time of the closing, the defendant delivered to the plaintiffs a plot plan prepared by a registered engineer and land surveyor. This plan showed a sideyard of twenty feet on the southerly boundary of the lot which was in compliance with the minimum requirements for this lot according to the zoning regulations on file with the town clerk of Vernon. A permit had previously been granted for the construction of the building, consisting of a house with an attached garage, and the survey submitted at the time the defendant made the application indicated that the structure was to be located twenty feet more or less from the southerly property line. Subsequently, a certificate of occupancy was erroneously issued based on the survey submitted by the defendant. Approximately four months after the delivery of the deed to the plaintiffs, the defendant discovered, when it set pins defining the boundaries of the premises, that the southeast corner of the foundation of the plaintiffs' house was only 1.8 feet from the southerly boundary of the lot. At this time, it was found that trespass upon adjoining property occurred in entering and leaving the plaintiffs' back door and stoop. Prior to this discovery, the parties were unaware that there was a violation of the zoning regulations as to sideyard requirements. The defendant, under a mistaken assumption, had represented by the plot plan that the structure on the lot was twenty feet from the southerly boundary. Unaware of the true fact, the plaintiffs relied on this representation.

The court concluded (1) that the defendant falsely and recklessly represented to the plaintiffs, for the purpose of inducing action, that the premises had a southerly sideyard of twenty feet and that there was no violation of the zoning regulations, and (2) that the plaintiffs were induced to rely on these representations, which were the result of a mistake on the part of the defendant but were not innocent.

The defendant claims that "[a]t most, there was an innocent misrepresentation of fact by the defendant." An innocent misrepresentation may be actionable if the declarant has the means of knowing, ought to know, or has the duty of knowing the truth. [C]

The facts, as properly found, clearly show that the plaintiffs had reasonable grounds upon which to attribute to the defendant accurate knowledge of what it represented as to the location of the structure on the lot. This was a statement of fact about which the defendant as a developer of residential real estate, had special means of knowledge, and it was a matter peculiarly relating to its business and one on which the plaintiffs were entitled to rely. [Cc] The defendant was commercially involved in and responsible for the preliminary and final plans for building and locating the structure which was then constructed on the lot by the defendant in a manner which violated the zoning ordinance. Thereafter, the defendant undertook to provide the plaintiffs with a survey and plot plan which erroneously showed a southerly sideyard of twenty feet. Actual knowledge of the falsity of the representation need not be shown under the circumstances, nor must the plaintiffs allege fraud or bad faith. They have alleged all the facts material to support their claim and demand for damages. It is immaterial whether the wrong which can be legally inferred from the facts arises in contract or in tort. The plaintiffs may seek damages resulting from the defendant's misrepresentation and at the same time retain title to the property. [C] Such a misrepresentation was "in the nature of a warranty" entitling them to a recovery under the contract "as for a breach of warranty." It would be unjust to permit the defendant under these circumstances to "retain the fruits of a bargain induced by" a material misrepresentation upon which the plaintiffs relied. * * *

There was sufficient evidence which supported the court's finding that the plaintiffs were entitled to a recovery based on the rule that the measure of damages was the difference between the actual value of the property and the value of the property had it been as represented. * * *

[In *Rich v. Rankl*, 6 Conn.Cir. 185, 269 A.2d 84 (1969), the court says: "The relief granted in the Richard case was the cost of the construction work and the moving of the house to relocate it on the plaintiffs' lot."]

The facts necessary to establish the defendant's liability were alleged in the complaint, and the conclusions of the trial court are amply supported by the facts found.

There is no error.

NOTES AND QUESTIONS

1. If the plaintiff is seeking to rescind the contract, an innocent misrepresentation that is material is basis for relief. Neither scienter nor negligence is necessary. The action is not in tort, but for restitution. See Seneca Wire & Mfg. Co. v. A.B. Leach & Co., 159 N.E. 700 (N.Y. 1928); Ross v. Harding, 391 P.2d 526 (Wash.1964).

2. The principal case allows recovery for innocent misrepresentation in a tort action. It follows a minority position. The earliest case to carry the strict liability over to a tort action for damages for the misrepresentation was Holcomb v. Noble, 37 N.W. 497 (Mich.1888), where the court appears to have confused equitable relief with an action at law. But Michigan now fully and consciously follows the "doctrine of innocent misrepresentation." U.S. Fidelity & Guar. Co. v. Black, 313 N.W.2d 77 (Mich. 1981).

3. This minority position has been adopted in the RESTATEMENT (SECOND) OF TORTS. SECTION 552C reads as follows:

(1) One who, in a sale, rental or exchange transaction with another, makes a misrepresentation of a material fact for the purpose of inducing the other to act or to refrain from acting in reliance upon it, is subject to liability to the other for pecuniary loss caused to him by his justifiable reliance upon the misrepresentation, even though it is not made fraudulently or negligently.

(2) Damages recoverable under the rule stated in this Section are limited to the difference between the value of what the other has parted with and the value of what he has received in the transaction.

Caveat: The Institute expresses no opinion as to whether there may not be other types of business transactions, in addition to those of sale, rental and exchange, in which strict liability may be imposed for innocent misrepresentation, under the conditions stated in this Section.

4. Is the remedy of rescission adequate to take care of the plaintiff's needs, or should he be able to keep the property and sue for damages? Is a tort action needed if an action for breach of warranty is available? Is the rule in § 552C really a development of the law of torts, or one of the law of restitution, eliminating the requirement of restoring the status quo as a condition for relief? In Growall v. Maietta, 931 A.2d 667, Pa. Super. Ct. 2007, plaintiff sought out-of-pocket losses, but not rescission of the contract in question. In rejecting the claim, the court cited Bortz v. Noon, 729 A.2d 555 (Pa. 1999), refusing monetary relief for innocent misrepresentations. Elucidating the distinction between legal and equitable remedies for misrepresentation, the opinion cites Miller v. Bare, 457 F. Supp. 1359 (W.D. Pa. 1978), in which a federal court (apparently erroneously) determined that Pennsylvania courts would have adopted § 552C in keeping with the trend in that state's case law.

(B) TO THIRD PERSONS

Credit Alliance Corp. v. Arthur Andersen & Co.

Court of Appeals of New York, 1985.
65 N.Y.2d 536, 483 N.E.2d 110, 493 N.Y.S.2d 435.

JASEN, JUDGE. The critical issue common to these two appeals is whether an accountant may be held liable, absent privity of contract, to a party who relies to his detriment upon a negligently prepared financial report and, if so, within what limits does that liability extend.

[In Credit Alliance Corp. v. Andersen & Co., the defendant accountants prepared consolidated financial statements for L.B. Smith, Inc. Credit Alliance had provided financing to Smith for some time, insisting in 1978 upon audited financial statements. Smith supplied statements that had been prepared by defendant. "These statements contained an auditor's report prepared by Andersen stating that it had examined the statements in accordance with generally accepted auditing standards ('GAAS') and found them to reflect fairly the financial position of Smith in conformity with generally accepted accounting principles ('GAAP')." Plaintiff alleged that the statements were inaccurate because of failure to conduct investigations in accordance with proper auditing standards. Special Term denied defendant's motion to dismiss causes of action, based on negligence and fraud. A divided Appellate Division affirmed, 101 A.D.2d 231, 476 N.Y.S.2d 539, and certified to the Court of Appeals the question, "Was the order of the Supreme Court, as affirmed by this court, properly made?"

In European Am. Bank & Trust Co. v. Strahs & Kaye, ("S. & K."), the bank ("EAB") made substantial loans to Majestic Electro Industries. Majestic having become bankrupt, EAB sued S. & K. for seriously exaggerating Majestic's solvency assets. Special Term dismissed the complaint and Appellate Division reversed but certified a similar question to the Court of Appeals. EAB specifically alleges that S. & K. at all relevant times knew that EAB was Majestic Electro's principal lender, was familiar with the terms of the lending relationship and was fully aware that EAB was relying on the statements, and that S. & K. and Majestic were in communication during the entire course of the lending relationship.]

In the seminal case of Ultramares Corp. v. Touche, 255 N.Y. 170, 174 N.E. 441 [1931], this court, speaking through the opinion of Chief Judge Cardozo more than 50 years ago, disallowed a cause of action in negligence against a public accounting firm for inaccurately prepared financial statements which were relied upon by a plaintiff having no contractual privity with the accountants. This court distinguished its holding from Glanzer v. Shepard, 233 N.Y. 236, 135 N.E. 275 [1922], a case decided in an opinion also written by Cardozo nine years earlier. We explained that in *Glanzer,* an action in negligence against public weighers had been permitted, despite the absence of a contract between the parties, because the plaintiff's intended reliance, on the information *directly transmitted* by the weighers, created a bond so closely approaching privity that it was, in practical effect, virtually indistinguishable therefrom. This court has subsequently reaffirmed its holding in *Ultramares* which has been, and continues to be, much discussed and analyzed by the commentators and by the courts of other jurisdictions. These appeals now provide us with the opportunity to reexamine and delineate the principles enunciated in both *Ultramares* and *Glanzer*. Inasmuch as we believe that a relationship "so close as to approach that of privity" [c] remains valid as the predicate for imposing liability upon accountants to noncontractual parties for the negligent preparation of financial reports, we restate and elaborate upon our adherence to that standard today.

The doctrine of privity is said to have had its source in the classic enunciation of its rationale in Winterbottom v. Wright, 10 M. & W. 109, 152 Eng. Rep. 402, [supra page 426]. From *Winterbottom,* the privity doctrine developed into a general rule prevailing well into the Twentieth Century. [Cc]

By the time 90 years had passed, however, this court could note in *Ultramares* that the "assault upon the citadel of privity is proceeding in these days apace." [C] We acknowledged that inroads had been made, for example, where third-party beneficiaries or dangerous instrumentalities were involved. [C] Indeed, we referred to this court's holding in MacPherson v. Buick Motor Co., 217 N.Y. 382, [supra page 428] where it was decided that the manufacturer of a defective chattel—there an automobile—may be liable in negligence for the resulting injuries sustained by a user regardless of the absence of privity—a belated rejection of the doctrine of privity as applied to the facts in *Winterbottom*. Nevertheless, regarding an accountant's liability to unknown parties with whom he had not contracted, the considerations were deemed sufficiently dissimilar to justify different treatment.

Although accountants might be held liable in fraud to nonprivy parties who were intended to rely upon the accountants' misrepresentations, we noted that "[a] different question develops when we ask whether they owed a duty to these to make [their reports] without negligence." Ultramares Corp. v. Touche, supra. Disputing the wisdom of extending the duty of care of accountants to anyone who might foreseeably rely upon their financial reports, Cardozo, speaking for this court, remarked: "If liability for negligence exists, a thoughtless slip or blunder, the failure to detect a theft or forgery beneath the cover of deceptive entries, may expose accountants to a liability in an indeterminate amount for an indeterminate time to an indeterminate class. The hazards of a business conducted on these terms are so extreme as to enkindle doubt whether a flaw may not exist in the implication of a duty that exposes to these consequences." [C]

In *Ultramares,* the accountants had prepared a certified balance sheet for their client to whom they provided 32 copies. The client, in turn, gave one to the plaintiff company. The latter, relying upon the misinformation contained in the balance sheet, made loans to the accountants' client who, only months later, was declared bankrupt. This court, refusing to extend the accountants' liability for negligence to their client's lender, with whom they had no contractual privity, noted that the accountants had prepared a report on behalf of their client to be exhibited generally to "banks, creditors, stockholders, purchasers or sellers, *according to the needs of the occasion*". [C] In reciting the facts, we emphasized that: "*Nothing was said as to the persons to whom these [copies] would be shown or the extent or number of the transactions in which they would be used.* In particular there was no mention of the plaintiff, a corporation doing business chiefly as a factor, which till then had never made advances to the [accountants' client], though it had sold merchandise in small amounts. The range of the transactions in which a certificate of audit might be expected to play a part was as indefinite and wide as the possibilities of the business that was mirrored in the summary." [C]

The accountants' report was primarily intended as a convenient instrumentality for the client's use in developing its business. "[O]nly incidentally or collaterally" was it expected to assist those to whom the client "might exhibit it thereafter". [C] Under such circumstances, permitting recovery by parties such as the plaintiff company would have been to impose a duty upon accountants "enforce[able] by any member of an indeterminate class of creditors, present and prospective, known and unknown." [C]

By sharp contrast, the facts underlying *Glanzer* bespoke an affirmative assumption of a duty of care to a specific party, for a specific purpose, regardless of whether there was a contractual relationship. There, a seller of beans employed the defendants who were engaged in business as public weighers. Pursuant to instructions, the weighers furnished one copy of the weight certificate to their employer, the seller, and another to the prospective buyer. In reliance upon the inaccurately certified weight, the buyer purchased beans from the seller and, thereby, suffered a loss.

Explaining the imposition upon the weighers of a "noncontractual" duty of care to the buyer, this court held: "We think the law imposes a duty toward buyer as well as seller in the situation here disclosed. The [buyer's] use of the certificates was *not an indirect or collateral consequence* of the action of the weighers. It was a consequence which, to the weighers' knowledge, was the *end and aim of the transaction.* [The seller] ordered, but [the buyer was] to use. The defendants held themselves out to the public as skilled and careful in their calling. They knew that the beans had been sold, and that on the faith of their certificate payment would be made. *They sent a copy to the [buyer] for the very purpose of inducing action.* All this they admit. In such circumstances, assumption of the task of weighing was the assumption of a duty to weigh carefully for the benefit of all whose conduct was to be governed. We do not need to state the duty in terms of contract or of privity. Growing out of a contract, it has none the less an origin not exclusively contractual. Given the contract and the relation, the duty is imposed by law." [C]

The critical distinctions between the two cases were highlighted in *Ultramares,* where we explained: "In Glanzer v. Shepard * * * [the certificate of weight], which was made out in duplicate, one copy to the seller and the other to the buyer, *recites that it was made by order of the former for the use of the latter* * * * Here was something more than the rendition of a service in the expectation that the one who ordered the certificate would use it thereafter in the operations of his business as occasion might require. Here was a case where *the transmission of the certificate to another was* not merely one possibility among many, but *the 'end and aim of the transaction,'* as certain and immediate and deliberately willed as if a husband were to order a gown to be delivered to his wife, or a telegraph company, contracting with the sender of a message, were to telegraph it wrongly to the damage of the person expected to receive it * * * The *intimacy of the resulting nexus* is attested by the fact that after stating the case in terms of legal duty, we went on to point out that * * * we could reach the same result by stating it in terms of contract * * * The bond was *so close as to approach that of privity, if not completely one with it.* Not so in the case at hand [i.e., *Ultramares*]. No one would be likely to urge that there was a contractual relation, or *even one approaching it,* at the root of any duty that was owing from the [accountants] now before us to the indeterminate class of persons who, presently or in the future, might deal with the [accountants' client] in reliance on the audit. In a word, the service rendered by the defendant in Glanzer v. Shepard was primarily for the information of a third person, *in effect, if not in name, a party to the contract,* and only incidentally for that of the formal promisee." [C]

Several years subsequent to the decision in *Ultramares,* this court reiterated the requirement for a "contractual relationship or its equivalent" (State St. Trust Co. v. Ernst, 278 N.Y. 104, 111, 15 N.E.2d 416), and more recently, in *White v. Guarente,* 43 N.Y.2d 356, 401 N.Y.S.2d 474, 372 N.E.2d 315, such an equivalent was presented for our consideration. There, the accountants had contracted with a limited partnership to perform an audit and prepare the partnership's tax returns. The nature and purpose of the contract, to satisfy the requirement in the partnership agreement for an audit, made it clear that the accountants' services were obtained to benefit the members of the partnership who, like plaintiff, a limited partner, were necessarily dependent upon the audit to prepare their own tax returns. After outlining the principles articulated in *Ultramares* and *Glanzer,* this court observed that: "[T]his plaintiff seeks redress, not as a mere member of the public, but as one of a settled and particularized class among the members of which the report would be circulated *for the specific purpose of fulfilling the limited partnership agreed upon arrangement.*" [C]

Because the accountants knew that a limited partner would have to rely upon the audit and tax returns of the partnership, and inasmuch as this was within the specific contemplation of the accounting retainer, we held that, "at least on the facts here, an accountant's liability may be so imposed." [C] The resulting relationship between the accountants and the limited partner was clearly one "approach[ing] that of privity, if not completely one with it." (*Ultramares Corp. v. Touche, supra*).

Upon examination of *Ultramares* and *Glanzer* and our recent affirmation of their holdings in *White,* certain criteria may be gleaned. Before accountants may be held liable in negligence to noncontractual parties who rely to their detriment on inaccurate financial reports, certain prerequisites must be satisfied: (1) the accountants must have been aware that the financial reports were to be used for a particular purpose or purposes; (2) in the furtherance of which a known party or parties was intended to rely; and (3) there must have been some conduct on the part of the accountants linking them to that party or parties, which evinces the accountants' understanding of that party or parties' reliance. While these criteria permit some flexibility in the application of the doctrine of privity to accountants' liability, they do not represent a departure from the principles articulated in *Ultramares, Glanzer* and *White,* but, rather, they are intended to preserve the wisdom and policy set forth therein.

We are aware that the courts throughout this country are divided as to the continued validity of the holding in *Ultramares.* Some courts continue to insist that a strict application of the privity requirement governs the law of accountants' liability except, perhaps, where special circumstances compel a different result. * * *

In all of [these] cases, the courts found the facts amenable to the imposition of accountants' liability under the principles of *Ultramares-Glanzer* or extended those principles to permit a more liberalized application. To the extent that the holdings in those cases are predicated upon certain criteria—to wit, a particular purpose for the accountants' report, a known relying party, and some conduct on the part of the accountants linking them to that party—they are consonant with the principles reaffirmed in this decision. To the extent, however, that those cases were decided upon the ground that *Ultramares* should not be followed and, instead, a rule permitting recovery by any foreseeable plaintiff should be adopted, the law in this State, as reiterated today, is clearly distinguishable. * * *

In the appeals we decide today, application of the foregoing principles presents little difficulty. In *Credit Alliance,* the facts as alleged by plaintiffs fail to demonstrate the existence of a relationship between the parties sufficiently approaching privity. Though the complaint and supporting affidavit do allege that Andersen specifically knew, should have known or was on notice that plaintiffs were being shown the reports by Smith, Andersen's client, in order to induce their reliance thereon, nevertheless, there is no adequate allegation of either a particular purpose for the reports' preparation or the prerequisite conduct on the part of the accountants. While the allegations state that Smith sought to induce plaintiffs to extend credit, no claim is made that Andersen was being employed to prepare the reports with that particular purpose in mind. Moreover, there is no allegation that Andersen had any direct dealings with plaintiffs, had specifically agreed with Smith to prepare the report for plaintiffs' use or according to plaintiffs' requirements, or had specifically agreed with Smith to provide plaintiffs with a copy or actually did so. Indeed, there is simply no allegation of any word or action on the part of Andersen directed to plaintiffs, or anything contained in Andersen's retainer agreement with Smith which provided the necessary link between them.

By sharp contrast, in *European American,* the facts as alleged by EAB clearly show that S. & K. was well aware that a primary, if not the exclusive, *end and aim* of auditing its client, Majestic Electro, was to provide EAB with the financial information it required. The prerequisites for the cause of action in negligence, as well as in gross negligence, are fully satisfied. Not only is it alleged, as in *Credit Alliance,* that the accountants knew the identity of the specific nonprivy party who would be relying upon the audit reports, but additionally, the complaint and affidavit here allege both the accountants' awareness of a particular purpose for their services and certain conduct on their part creating an unmistakable relationship with the reliant plaintiff. It is unambiguously claimed that the parties remained in direct communication, both orally and in writing, and, indeed, met together throughout the course of EAB's lending relationship with Majestic Electro, for the very purpose of discussing the latter's financial condition and EAB's need for S. & K.'s evaluation. Moreover, it is alleged that S. & K. made repeated representations personally to representatives of EAB, on these occasions, concerning the value of Majestic Electro's assets. It cannot be gainsaid that the relationship thus created between the parties was the practical equivalent of privity. The parties' direct communications and personal meetings resulted in a nexus between them sufficiently approaching privity under the principles of *Ultramares, Glanzer* and *White* to permit EAB's causes of action.

Finally, disposition of the second cause of action alleged in *Credit Alliance* need not detain us long. The cause of action for fraud repeats the allegations for the negligence cause of action and merely adds a claim that Andersen recklessly disregarded facts which would have apprised it that its reports were misleading or that Andersen had actual knowledge that such was the case. This single allegation of scienter, without additional detail concerning the facts constituting the alleged fraud, is insufficient under the special pleading standards required under CPLR 3016(b), and, consequently, the cause of action should have been dismissed. [Cc].

Accordingly, in *Credit Alliance* both causes of action should be dismissed, the order of the Appellate Division reversed, with costs, and the certified question answered in the negative. In *European American,* the order of the Appellate Division should be affirmed, with costs, and the certified question answered in the affirmative.

Citizens State Bank v. Timm, Schmidt & Co.

Supreme Court of Wisconsin, 1983.
113 Wis.2d 376, 335 N.W.2d 361.

[For the years 1973–76, defendant Timm, Schmidt & Co. (Timm), an accounting firm, prepared financial statements for Clintonville Fire Apparatus, Inc. (CFA), including statements of financial condition, yearly income, retained income and changes in financial condition. These were accompanied by an opinion letter to CFA stating that "the financial statements fairly presented the financial condition of CFA and that the statements were prepared in accordance with generally accepted accounting principles."

In 1975 and 1976 CFA obtained loans from Citizens State Bank amounting to $380,000, relying on Timm's statements. In 1977 Timm discovered mistakes in its statements totaling over $400,000. It notified Security, which called in all of its loans due. CFA went into receivership and was ultimately liquidated and dissolved. Still due to Citizens was $152,214. Citizens sued Timm for that amount.

Timm moved for summary judgment. All persons in the Timm firm who had worked on the CFA statements filed affidavits that they had no knowledge that CFA intended to obtain or had any loans from Citizens. There were some contradictory affidavits, especially from the CFA president, Dando, indicating that he believed that Timm knew of the dealing. The trial court granted the motion for summary judgment, and the court of appeals affirmed. The case is now before the state supreme court.]

DAY, JUSTICE * * * The question on review is whether accountants may be held liable for the negligent preparation of an audit report to a third party not in privity who relies on the report.

This is a question of first impression in this state. However, the issue has received wide consideration in both courts and law journals.

Accountants have long been held not liable for their negligence to relying third parties not in privity under an application of Judge Cardozo's decision in *Ultramares v. Touche,* 255 N.Y. 170, 174 N.E. 441

(1931). In *Ultramares,* Judge Cardozo absolved the defendant accountants from liability for overvaluing the assets of a company in an audit report to a plaintiff who had loaned money in reliance on a certified balance sheet in the report. Judge Cardozo expressed the concern that "if liability exists, a thoughtless slip or blunder * * * may expose accountants to a liability in an indeterminate amount for an indeterminate time to an indeterminate class." [C]

[At one time] *Ultramares* was relied on by every jurisdiction to consider this question to deny accountant liability to third parties. However, in recent years, *Ultramares* has received new attention and courts have started to find accountants liable to third parties.

In Rusch Factors, Inc., v. Levin, 284 F.Supp. 85 (D.C.R.I.1968), the court, citing section 552 of the Restatement, imposed liability on an accountant to a relying third party not in privity. In *Rusch Factors,* the accountant knew the statements he prepared were to be used by his client for the purpose of obtaining credit from a third party even though they did not know of the specific relying third party. Nevertheless, the court allowed liability to be imposed. 284 F.Supp. at 93.

Similarly, in Ryan v. Kanne, 170 N.W.2d 395 (Iowa 1969), the Iowa Supreme Court applying Restatement section 552, determined that an accountant could be held liable to a foreseen third party who had relied upon a negligently prepared audit report. Because the relying third party was "actually known," the court did not address the extent of foreseeability that would be necessary before an accountant could be held liable to a third party not actually known. [C]

In this state, although the liability of accountants to third parties not in privity has not been examined, the liability of an attorney to one not in privity was recently examined in Auric v. Continental Casualty Co., 111 Wis. 2d 507, 331 N.W.2d 325 (1983). This court concluded that an attorney may be held liable to a will beneficiary not in privity for the attorney's negligence in supervising the execution of a will. [C] Part of the rationale for this decision was that the imposition of liability would make attorneys more careful in the execution of their responsibilities to their clients. [C]

That rationale is applicable here. Unless liability is imposed, third parties who rely upon the accuracy of the financial statements will not be protected. Unless an accountant can be held liable to a relying third party, this negligence will go undeterred.

There are additional policy reasons to allow the imposition of liability. If relying third parties, such as creditors, are not allowed to recover, the cost of credit to the general public will increase because creditors will either have to absorb the costs of bad loans made in reliance on faulty information or hire independent accountants to verify the information received. Accountants may spread the risk through the use of liability insurance.

We conclude that the absence of privity alone should not bar negligence actions by relying third parties against accountants.

Although the absence of privity does not bar this action, the question remains as to the extent of an accountant's liability to injured third parties. Courts which have examined this question have generally relied upon section 552 of the Restatement to restrict the class of third persons who could sue accountants for their negligent acts. Under section 552(2)(a) and (b), liability is limited to loss suffered:

"(a) By the person or one of a limited group of persons for whose benefit and guidance he [in this case the accountant] intends to supply the information or knows the recipient intends to supply it; and

"(b) Through reliance upon it in a transaction that he [the accountant] intends the information to influence or knows the recipient so intends or in a substantially similar transaction."

Under section 552, liability is not extended to all parties whom the accountant might reasonably foresee as using the information. Rather, as one commentator noted, "The Restatement's formulation of 'a limited group of persons' extends causes of action to a limited number of third parties who are expected to gain access to the financial statement information in an expected transaction." This limitation is stressed in comment *h* to section 552, where it is noted that:

"It is not required that the person who is to become the plaintiff be identified or known to the defendant as an individual when the information is supplied. It is enough that the maker of the representation intends it to reach and influence either a particular person or persons, known to him, or a group or class of persons, distinct from the much larger class who might reasonably be expected sooner or later to have access to the information and foreseeably to take some action in reliance upon it."

The fundamental principle of Wisconsin negligence law is that a tortfeasor is fully liable for all foreseeable consequences of his act except as those consequences are limited by policy factors. [Cc] The Restatement's statement of limiting liability to certain third parties is too restrictive a statement of policy factors for this Court to adopt.

We conclude that accountants' liability to third parties should be determined under the accepted principles of Wisconsin negligence law. According to these principles, a finding of non-liability will be made only if there is a strong public policy requiring such a finding. [Cc]

Liability will be imposed on these accountants for the foreseeable injuries resulting from their negligent acts unless, under the facts of this particular case, as a matter of policy to be decided by the court, recovery is denied on grounds of public policy. [C] This Court has set out a number of public policy reasons for not imposing liability despite a finding of negligence causing injury:

> "(1) The injury is too remote from the negligence; or (2) the injury is too wholly out of proportion to the culpability of the negligent tort-feasor; or (3) in retrospect it appears too highly extraordinary that the negligence should have brought about the harm; or (4) because allowance of recovery would place too unreasonable a burden on the negligent tort-feasor; or (5) because allowance of recovery would be too likely to open the way for fraudulent claims; or (6) allowance of recovery would enter a field that has no sensible or just stopping point." *Ollerman* [v. O'Rourke Co., 94 Wis. 2d 17, 48, 288 N.W.2d 95 (1980).]

Although in some cases this court has decided at the motion-to-dismiss stage that policy factors preclude the imposition of liability for negligent acts, [c] it has generally been found to be better practice to have a full factual resolution before evaluating the public policy considerations involved. *Ollerman,* [cc].

In this case we conclude that a determination of the public policy questions should be made after the facts of this case have been fully explored at trial. The question of the proper scope of these accountants' liabilities to the third party bank cannot be determined upon the information contained in the record. A full factual resolution is necessary before it can be said that public policy precludes Timm's liability for its allegedly negligent conduct.

The pleadings, affidavits and other information in the record before this court do not establish that Timm was entitled as a matter of law to summary judgment. Under the accepted principles of Wisconsin negligence law, Timm could be liable to Citizens if Timm's actions were the cause of Citizens' injuries and if the injuries were reasonably foreseeable unless public policy precluded recovery.

Timm's affidavits do not dispute that Citizen's reliance upon the financial statements led to the making of the loans and ultimately to the losses which were incurred. Each affidavit recites that Timm employees had no knowledge that the financial statements would actually be used by CFA to apply for a new bank loan or to increase existing loan indebtedness. However, the affidavit of Elmer Timm stated that "as a certified public accountant, I know that audited statements are used for many purposes and that it is common for them to be supplied to lenders and creditors, and other persons."

These affidavits and other information contained in the record do not dispose of the issue of whether it was foreseeable that a negligently prepared financial statement could cause harm to Citizens.

Therefore, Timm having failed to establish a *prima facie* case for summary judgment, we conclude the trial judge erred in granting the motion for summary judgment.

Decision of the court of appeals is reversed and cause remanded to the trial court for further proceedings not inconsistent with this opinion.

NOTES AND QUESTIONS

1. The scope of auditors' liability has been a vexed issue. The two principal cases represent the ends of the spectrum. *Credit Alliance* was thoroughly reexamined and reaffirmed by the Court of Appeals of New York in Sec. Pac. Bus. Credit, Inc. v. Peat Marwick Main & Co., 597 N.E.2d 1080, 586 N.Y.S.2d 87 (N.Y. 1992) (requisite relationship is not established by plaintiff calling auditor and announcing reliance). Elsewhere, the English courts have insisted upon a narrow scope of liability, see Caparo Indus. P.L.C. v. Dickman, (1990) 2 A.C. 605 (H.L.) (Eng.). The duty is limited to where defendant, giving advice or information, was fully aware of the nature of the transaction which the plaintiff had in contemplation, knew that the advice or information would be communicated to him directly or indirectly, and knew that it was very likely that the plaintiff

would rely on that advice or information in deciding whether or not to engage in the transaction in contemplation. Needless to say, the boundaries of the duty have been much debated and remain contentious. Henderson v. Merrett Syndicates Ltd. (No. 1), (1995) 2 A.C. 145 (H.L.) (Eng.).

2. As quoted in the *Citizens State Bank* case [supra at 1107], the Second Restatement takes an intermediate position, confining recovery to a "limited group of persons" and to a transaction or "substantially similar transaction" intended by the defendant. In Bily v. Arthur Young & Co., 834 P.2d 745 (Cal. 1992), the California Supreme Court adopted the Restatement test. The opinion, like that of the House of Lords, supports the criterion of knowledge of the class of persons and transactions that the supplier of the information "intends the information to influence." Unlimited liability is avoided and the scope of liability regulated by the supplier of the information. The court observes that the test is applicable to other professionals supplying information and evaluations for the use and benefit of others, including "attorneys, architects, engineers, title insurers and abstracters." The court formulated the following jury instructions: "The representation must have been made with the intent to induce plaintiff, or a particular class of persons to which plaintiff belongs, to act in reliance upon the representation in a specific transaction, or a specific type of transaction, that defendant intended to influence. Defendant is deemed to have intended to influence [its client's] transaction with plaintiff whenever defendant knows with substantial certainty that plaintiff, or the particular class of persons to which plaintiff belongs, will rely on the representation in the course of the transaction. If others become aware of the representation and act upon it, there is no liability even though defendant should reasonably have foreseen such a possibility."

The California Supreme Court expressly rejected the approaches exemplified in *Credit Alliance* and *Citizens State Bank.* Other cases adopting the Restatement position after close examination of the vying authorities and the policies at play are First National Bank of Commerce v. Monco Agency, 911 F.2d 1053 (5th Cir. 1990) (applying Louisiana law); Nycal v. KPMG Peat Marwick LLP, 688 N.E.2d 1368 (Mass. 1998); ML-Lee Acquisition v. Deloitte & Touche, 463 S.E.2d 618 (S.C. Ct. App. 1995), *aff'd* ML-Lee Acquisition v. Deloitte & Touche, 489 S.E.2d 470 (S.C. 1997).

3. Managers of a corporation engaged in a fraudulent scheme whereby the valuations of inventories were inflated to give a misleading picture of the corporation's wealth. Auditor failed to uncover the fraud. Eventually a corporation officer unmasked the fraud. Should the corporation have a good cause of action against the auditors? Any other person or persons? See Cenco Inc. v. Seidman & Seidman, 686 F.2d 449 (7th Cir. 1982).

4. As suggested, other professionals who proffer advice upon which third parties rely are subject to the same liability as in the auditor cases. Vereins-Und Westbank, AG v. Carter, 691 F. Supp. 704 (S.D.N.Y. 1988) (liability of attorney for opinion letter within the principles in *Ultramares*); Prudential Ins. Co. v. Dewey, Ballantine, 605 N.E.2d 318, 590 N.Y.S.2d 831 (N.Y. 1992) (opinion letter by borrower's lawyers to lender creates a duty of care). But cf. Ackerman v. Schwartz, 733 F. Supp. 1231 (N.D. Ind. 1989) (no liability for opinion letter relied on by non-client). In Robinson v. Omer, 952 S.W.2d 423 (Tenn. 1997), defendant attorney advised his client that to

videotape secretly his sexual encounters would be legally permissible. Plaintiff, after being informed of this advice by the client, agreed to help him videotape the encounters. Plaintiff was sued by a number of the women who had been videotaped and settled the claims at considerable cost. The Tennessee Supreme Court held that no duty was established since the advice was not relied on for a contemplated commercial or business transaction.

During the "great recession" it was claimed that rating agencies had given ratings on securities that were negligently provided or intentionally misleading. Aggrieved parties relied on the ratings of the agencies in making investments. When the market collapsed they claimed that they had reasonably relied on the ratings to their financial detriment. In the first Abu Dhabi Commercial Bank v. Morgan Stanley & Co., 651 F.Supp.2d 155 (S.D.N.Y 2009) case, institutional investors initiated a class action to recover losses stemming from the liquidation of notes issued by the structured investment vehicle ("SIV") between October 2004 and October 2007. The plaintiffs asserted New York common law claims of fraud and negligent misrepresentation. The rating agencies argued that the plaintiffs' misrepresentation claim was not actionable because: "(1) the Rating Agencies are entitled to immunity under the First Amendment and (2) even if the Rating Agencies could be held liable, their ratings are nonactionable opinions." The court pointed out that the rating agencies are protected by the First Amendment "subject to an 'actual malice' exception, from liability arising out of their issuance of credit ratings and reports because their ratings are considered matters of public concern. However, where a rating agency has disseminated their ratings to a select group of investors rather than to the public at large, the rating agency is not afforded the same protection." Here, because the plaintiffs alleged that the SIV's ratings were never widely disseminated, but were provided instead to a select group of investors, the Rating Agencies' First Amendment argument was rejected. The court also rejected the argument that the ratings in this case were nonactionable opinions. The "plaintiffs have sufficiently pled that the Rating Agencies did not genuinely or reasonably believe that the ratings they assigned to the Rated Notes were accurate and had a basis in fact. As a result, the Rating Agencies' ratings were not mere opinions but rather actionable misrepresentations." The court also did not accept, for the same reasons, that the disclaimer stating "that '[a] credit rating represents a Rating Agency's opinion regarding credit quality and is not a guarantee of performance or a recommendation to buy, sell or hold any securities,'" protected them from liability. Id.; see also Abu Dhabi Commercial Bank v. Morgan Stanley & Co., 888 F.Supp.2d 431 (S.D.N.Y. 2012).

5. In M. Miller Co. v. Dames & Moore, 18 Cal.Rptr. 13 (Cal. Ct. App. 1961), an engineering company was hired to prepare a soil report, knowing that it would be used by bidders for work on a sewer system. The report was negligently done and inaccurate, and the successful bidder lost money. He was allowed to recover damages although the report was not made directly to him. Accord, Ossining Union Free Sch. Dist. v. Anderson LaRocca Anderson, 541 N.Y.S.2d 335, 539 N.E.2d 91 (N.Y. 1989) (engineers reporting to architects, reporting to a school district; liability on the basis that the relationship was "the functional equivalent of contractual privity"). But cf. Tex. Tunneling Co. v. Chattanooga, 329 F.2d 402 (6th Cir. 1964), *rev'g*, 204 F. Supp. 821 (E.D. Tenn. 1962); Barrie v. V.P. Exterminators,

Inc., 625 So.2d 1007 (La. 1993) (duty owed by termite inspector to third parties); and Marcellus Constr. Co. v. Broadalbin, 755 N.Y.S.2d 474 (N.Y. App. Div. 2003) (no duty owed by engineer retained by city to contracting company relying on engineer's statements about subsurface conditions; no relationship within test in *Credit Alliance* above).

6. Another line of cases concern the liability of attorneys to disappointed beneficiaries of wills. Does the attorney who negligently causes a testamentary gift to fail owe a duty of care to the disappointed donee? See cases cited in notes 3 and 4, supra page 436 following Clagett v. Dacy, 420 A.2d 1285 (Md. Ct. Spec. App. 1980), supra page 434. The duty was narrowly construed in Noble v. Bruce, 709 A.2d 1264 (1998) (holding that no duty is owed to beneficiaries for negligence leading to large tax liability). Elsewhere, the duty owed to a disappointed beneficiary has been recognized. White v. Jones, (1995) 2 A.C.207 (H.L.) (Eng.).

Ultramares Corp. v. Touche

Court of Appeals of New York, 1931.
255 N.Y. 170, 174 N.E. 441.

[The opinions of Judge Cardozo in Glanzer v. Shepard and Ultramares Corp. v. Touche have been well described in the opinion of Judge Jason in Credit Alliance Co., supra page 1118. The description of *Ultramares* there, however, covered only the holding regarding the accountants' liability to a third person for negligent preparation of financial statements. The *Ultramares* opinion went on to discuss liability in fraud or deceit under the American doctrine in Sovereign Pocohontas Co. v. Bond, 120 F.2d 39 (D.C. Cir. 1941). That part of the *Ultramares* opinion is set forth here.

Touche, Niven's certificate in the case had stated: "We have examined the accounts of Fred Stern & Co. * * * and hereby certify that the annexed balance sheet is in accordance therewith and with the information and explanations given us. We further certify that * * * the said statement in our opinion presents a true and correct view of the financial condition of Fred Stern & Co. * * *."]

CARDOZO, C.J. * * * Our holding [on liability for negligence] does not emancipate accountants from the consequences of fraud. It does not relieve them if their audit has been so negligent as to justify a finding that they had no genuine belief in its adequacy, for this again is fraud. It does no more than say that, if less than this is proved, if there has been neither reckless misstatement nor insincere profession of an opinion, but only honest blunder, the ensuing liability for negligence is one that is bounded by the contract, and is to be enforced between the parties by whom the contract has been made. We doubt whether the average businessman receiving a certificate without paying for it, and receiving it merely as one among a multitude of possible investors, would look for anything more.

The defendants certified as a fact, true to their own knowledge, that the balance sheet was in accordance with the books of account. If their statement was false, they are not to be exonerated because they believed it to be true. [Cc] We think the triers of the facts might hold it to be false.

Correspondence between the balance sheet and the books imports something more, or so the triers of the facts might say, than correspondence between the balance sheet and the general ledger, unsupported or even contradicted by every other record. The correspondence to be of any moment may not unreasonably be held to signify a correspondence between the statement and the books of original entry, the books taken as a whole. If that is what the certificate means, a jury could find that the correspondence did not exist, and that the defendants signed the certificates without knowing it to exist and even without reasonable grounds for belief in its existence. The item of $706,000, representing fictitious accounts receivable, was entered in the ledger after defendant's employee Siess had posted the December sales. He knew of the interpolation, and knew that there was need to verify the entry by reference to books other than the ledger before the books could be found to be in agreement with the balance sheet. The evidence would sustain a finding that this was never done. By concession the interpolated item had no support in the journal, or in any journal voucher, or in the debit memo book, which was a summary of the invoices, or in any thing except the invoices themselves. The defendants do not say that they ever looked at the invoices, seventeen in number, representing these accounts. They profess to be unable to recall whether they did so or not. They admit, however, that, if they had looked, they would have found omissions and irregularities so many and unusual as to have called for further investigation. When we couple the refusal to say that they did look with the admission that, if they had looked, they would or could have seen, the situation is revealed as one in which a jury might reasonably find that in truth they did not look, but certified the correspondence without testing its existence.

In this connection we are to bear in mind the principle * * * that negligence or blindness, even when not equivalent to fraud, is none the less evidence to sustain an inference of fraud. At least this is so if the negligence is gross. Not a little confusion has at times resulted from an undiscriminating quotation of statements in Kountze v. Kennedy, [147 N.Y. 124, 41 N.E. 414 (1895)] statements proper enough in their setting, but capable of misleading when extracted and considered by themselves. "Misjudgment, however gross," it was there observed, "or want of caution, however marked, is not fraud." This was said in a case where the trier of the facts had held the defendants guiltless. The judgment in this court amounted merely to a holding that a finding of fraud did not follow as an inference of law. There was no holding that the evidence would have required a reversal of the judgment if the finding as to guilt had been the other way. Even Derry v. Peek, as we have seen, asserts the probative effect of negligence as an evidentiary fact. We had no thought in Kountze v. Kennedy, of upholding a doctrine more favorable to wrongdoers, though there was a reservation suggesting the approval of a rule more rigorous. * * * No such charity of construction exonerates accountants, who by the very nature of their calling profess to speak with knowledge when certifying to an agreement between the audit and the entries.

The defendants attempt to excuse the omission of an inspection of the invoices proved to be fictitious by invoking a practice known as that of testing and sampling. A random choice of accounts is made from the total number on the books, and these, if found to be regular when inspected and investigated, are taken as a fair indication of the quality of the mass. * * * Verification by test and sample was very likely a sufficient audit as to accounts regularly entered upon the books in the usual course of business. It was plainly insufficient, however, as to accounts not entered upon the books where inspection of the invoices was necessary, not as a check upon accounts fair upon their face, but in order to ascertain whether there were any accounts at all. If the only invoices inspected were invoices unrelated to the interpolated entry, the result was to certify a correspondence between the books and the balance sheet without any effort by the auditors, as to $706,000 of accounts, to ascertain whether the certified agreement was in accordance with the truth. * * * The defendants were put on their guard by the circumstances touching the December accounts receivable to scrutinize with special care. A jury might find that, with suspicions thus awakened, they closed their eyes to the obvious, and blindly gave assent.

We conclude, to sum up the situation, that in certifying to the correspondence between balance sheet and accounts the defendants made a statement as true to their own knowledge, when they had, as a jury might find, no knowledge on the subject. If that is so, they may also be found to have acted without information leading to a sincere or genuine belief when they certified to an opinion that the balance sheet faithfully reflected the condition of the business. * * *

Upon the plaintiff's appeal as to the second cause of action, the judgment [for the defendants in the lower courts] should be reversed, and a new trial granted, with costs to abide the event.

NOTES AND QUESTIONS

1. This part of the *Ultramares* case involves liability for fraudulent, as distinguished from negligent, misrepresentation. The defendant's conduct being more reprehensible, the opinion indicates that a wider circle of liability is required. When the defendant's conduct is not only reckless but also intended to deceive, it would appear that the scope of liability would be even broader.

2. The central requirement of intent in fraudulent misrepresentation or deceit avoids the expansiveness of reasonable foreseeability employed in negligence. The scope of deceit has broadened as the notion of intent has become more liberal but nevertheless, the nexus, as Cardozo recognized, will be close and the duty more narrowly drawn. The Siren call of reasonable foreseeability is thus nicely avoided. For the scope of liability in deceit, see page 1106, note 5.

4. RELIANCE

Williams v. Rank & Son Buick, Inc.

Supreme Court of Wisconsin, 1969.
44 Wis.2d 239, 170 N.W.2d 807.

[Plaintiff went to defendant's used car lot on March 19 and looked at a Chrysler automobile. Plaintiff testified that he was looking for an air-conditioned car; that the salesman told him the car was air-conditioned, and that the particular car had been so described in an advertisement on which he relied. The evidence was, however, that the advertisement was first published two days after plaintiff bought the car, and defendant contended that plaintiff "seized upon an error in the ad to seek a reduction in the price previously paid for the automobile." Plaintiff was invited to take the car out for a test run, and did so, driving it for about an hour and a half. According to plaintiff, however, it was not until several days after the purchase that he discovered that the knobs marked "AIR" were for ventilation, and that the car was not air-conditioned. Plaintiff brought an action for fraud, and received a judgment for $150 damages. Defendant appeals.]

HANLEY, JUSTICE. * * * [T]here is ample evidence to warrant the trial court's finding that the oral misrepresentation of the appellant's salesman was in fact made. * * *

The question of reliance is another matter. Many previous decisions of this court have held that one cannot justifiably rely upon obviously false statements. In Jacobsen v. Whitely (1909), 138 Wis. 434, 436, 437, 120 N.W. 285, 286, the court said:

" * * * It is an unsavory defense for a man who by false statements, induces another to act to assert that if the latter had disbelieved him he would not have been injured. * * * Nevertheless courts will refuse to act for the relief of one claiming to have been misled by another's statements who blindly acts in disregard of knowledge of their falsity or with such opportunity that by the exercise of ordinary observation, not necessarily by search, he would have known. He may not close his eyes to what is obviously discoverable by him. * * * "

It is apparent that the obviousness of a statement's falsity vitiates reliance since no one can rely upon a known falsity. Were the rule otherwise a person would be free to enter into a contract with no intent to perform under the contract unless it ultimately proved profitable. On the other hand, a party who makes an inadvertent slip of the tongue or pencil would continually lose the benefit of the contract.

The question is thus whether the statement's falsity could have been detected by ordinary observation. Whether the falsity of a statement could have been discovered through ordinary care is to be determined in light of the intelligence and experience of the misled individual. Also to be considered is the relationship between the parties. [Cc] In several cases this court has held that the above factors negated the opportunity to inspect and the obviousness of the statement's falsity. [C]

In the instant case, however, no such negating factors exist. The respondent specifically testified that, being a high school graduate, he was capable of both reading and writing. It is also fair to assume that he possessed a degree of business acumen in that he and his brother operated their own business. No fiduciary relationship existed between the parties. They dealt with each other at arms' length. The appellant made no effort to interfere with the respondent's examination of the car, but, on the contrary, allowed him to take the car from the premises for a period of one and one-half hours.

Although the obviousness of a statement's falsity is a question of fact, this court has decided some such questions as a matter of law. [Cc]

In the instant case the respondent had ample opportunity to determine whether the car was air-conditioned. He had examined the car on the lot and had been allowed to remove the car from the lot unaccompanied by a salesman for a period of approximately one and one-half hours. This customers were normally not allowed to do.

No great search was required to disclose the absence of the air conditioning unit since a mere flip of a knob was all that was necessary. If air conditioning was, as stated by the respondent, the main reason he purchased the car, it is doubtful that he would not try the air conditioner. * * *

We conclude that as a matter of law the respondent under the facts and circumstances was not justified in relying upon the oral representation of the salesman. This is an action brought in fraud and not an action for a breach of warranty.

Order reversed [by a vote of 4 to 3].

WILKIE, JUSTICE (dissenting). * * * I would hold that the falsity of the representation was not so obvious that it could be held as a matter of law that the respondent had no right to rely on it. It was for the finder of fact and by finding reliance the trial court, by implication, found respondent had a right to rely thereon. * * *

NOTES AND QUESTIONS

1. In H. Hirschberg Optical Co. v. Michaelson, 95 N.W. 461 (Neb. 1901), plaintiff, buying a pair of glasses, testified that he was told by defendant's salesman that the glass used in them had a special quality which would make them adapt themselves to his eyes. On this evidence, can the plaintiff recover for deceit? See also that foremost classic of legal humor, the sad but fascinating tale of the land of Shalam. Ellis v. Newbrough, 27 P. 490 (N.M. 1891). In Hitachi Credit Am. Corp. v. Signet Bank, 166 F.3d 614 (4th Cir. 1999), Hitachi was persuaded by Signet Bank to participate in the financing of a highly secret, off-shore cigarette venture that had been represented as a venture sponsored by Philip Morris with the cooperation of the United States government. In fact, the venture was a fraud. A former Philip Morris employee falsely represented to Signet and other original parties that he acted for Philip Morris in the venture, but that the venture was so secret it would be denied by Philip Morris. Hitachi was found to have reasonably relied on Signet Bank's representatives about the secret off-shore venture. The touchstone of reasonableness in reliance was "prudent investigation." The case also discusses contractual provisions

relevant to reliance. In this case there was no express disclaimer of responsibility for representations. Cf. Hoover Universal, Inc. v. Brockway Imco, Inc., 809 F.2d 1039 (4th Cir. 1987). A prudent investigation will encompass mounting evidence that a takeover target's financial statements represent a ridiculous overvaluation: Atari Corp. v. Ernst & Whinney, 981 F.2d 1025 (9th Cir. 1992).

2. What if it is made clear by the evidence that plaintiff knew that the representation made to him was false? Cox v. Johnson, 40 S.E.2d 418 (N.C. 1946). Or that he paid no attention to it, and acted for other reasons entirely? McIntyre v. Lyon, 37 N.W.2d 903 (Mich. 1949); Tsang v. Kan, 177 P.2d 630 (Cal. Dist. Ct. App. 1947).

3. Suppose that A and B each make the same false statement to C, and his decision to act is substantially influenced by both. Strong v. Strong, 5 N.E. 799 (N.Y. 1886); Shaw v. Gilbert, 86 N.W. 188 (Wis. 1901). Does it make any difference that either statement alone would have been sufficient to induce the action? What case does this resemble?

4. Does the fact that plaintiff has made an inspection, examination or investigation of his own establish:

A. That he did not believe the representation, and so did not rely on it, but relied instead on his own investigation? See McNabb v. Thomas, 190 F.2d 608 (D.C. Cir. 1951); Savings Banks Ret. Sys. v. Clarke, 258 Md. 501, 265 A.2d 921 (1970).

In Enfield v. Colburn, 63 N.H. 218 (1884), defendant made statements to plaintiffs. Plaintiffs made an expensive investigation, and found that they were false. They sought to recover the expenses of the investigation. Recovery was denied, since "if they relied upon the representations, they did not investigate them; if they investigated them they did not rely upon them. It is a perversion of language to say they did both." Is this right?

B. That he believed the representation, and relied upon it, but sought verification before acting, and in the end relied upon both? John Hancock Mut. Life Ins. Co. v. Cronin, 51 A.2d 2 (N.J. 1947); Fausett & Co. v. Bullard, 229 S.W.2d 490 (Ark. 1950).

5. Purchasers expressed concern about the house's roof, had notice of water spots on its carpet and had personally inspected the roof. Representation was made by sellers that the roof was in good repair. Sellers' assurances that the roof was in good repair were reasonably relied on since the spots were irrelevant to present state of roof and the inspection could not have uncovered the structural defects. Sellers' assurances of repair reasonably precluded the necessity for an independent inspection. Sippy v. Cristich, 609 P.2d 204 (Kan. Ct. App. 1980).

6. *Materiality*. Suppose that defendant, as agent, is selling plaintiff a tract of land on behalf of a principal whom plaintiff never has seen. Defendant falsely states that his principal is left-handed. No other false statements are made. Can plaintiff recover in deceit after he buys the land? Farnsworth v. Duffner, 142 U.S. 43 (1891) (social, religious and political affiliation); Haverland v. Lane, 154 P. 1118 (Wash. 1916) (identity of party).

7. Defendant induces plaintiff to send his daughter to a particular school by false representations that it is attended by her former classmates.

Is this a material representation? Brown v. Search, 111 N.W. 210 (Wis. 1907). What if plaintiff is induced to buy pictures by a false statement that his wife likes them? Washington Post Co. v. Sorrells, 68 S.E. 337 (Ga. Ct. App. 1910). Or he is induced to give money to a college by a statement that it is to be named after one of his friends? Collinson v. Jeffries, 54 S.W. 28 (Tex. Civ. App. 1899). See RESTATEMENT (SECOND) OF TORTS § 538(1)(b).

8. *Contributory Negligence.* Contributory negligence does not bar recovery when the misrepresentation is intentional, Yorke v. Taylor, 124 N.E.2d 912 (Mass. 1955); and Judd v. Walker, 114 S.W. 979 (Mo. 1908) ("the laws of hospitality seem to require that strangers should be taken in in a good sense, but courts should be astute not to permit such a 'taking in' as appears here").

9. What if the defendant's representation is made without scienter or intent to deceive, but is made negligently and the action is one for negligent misrepresentation? Is contributory negligence then a defense? How can plaintiff have reasonably relied if he has failed to take reasonable precautions to protect himself? Does the scope of the defense differ according to whether plaintiff and defendant may interact with one another? Maxwell Ice Co. v. Brackett, Shaw & Lunt Co., 116 A. 34 (N.H. 1921); Gould v. Flato, 10 N.Y.S.2d 361 (N.Y. Spec. Term. 1938); Grand Restaurants of Can. Ltd. v. Toronto, [1982] 39 O.R. 2d 752 (Can.). Greycas, Inc. v. Proud, 826 F.2d 1560 (7th Cir. 1987). Does comparative negligence apply here? Adopting comparative negligence for negligent misrepresentations, see Kramer v. Petisi, 940 A.2d 800 (Con. 2008).

10. The great majority of the cases now hold that the plaintiff has no duty to make inquiry or investigation as to the truth of an apparently reliable statement made to him. This is held even though investigation could be made quickly, with little effort, by means readily at hand. Buckley v. Buckley, 202 N.W. 955 (Mich. 1925). Circumstances, however, may require further investigation. Failure to investigate may persuade the court that the loss was the plaintiff's "own responsibility." Chicago Title & Trust Co. v. First Arlington Nat'l Bank, 73 Ill.Dec. 626, 454 N.E.2d 723 (Ill. App. Ct. 1983).

11. "No rogue should enjoy his ill-gotten plunder for the simple reason that his victim is by chance a fool." Chamberlin v. Fuller, 9 A. 832 (Vt. 1887).

12. Plaintiff, a "gullible young man," whose occupation was that of playing the piano in resorts of ill repute, inherited $40,000 from his mother. On learning this, defendant promptly offered to sell him a disreputable roadhouse, representing that it was worth $35,000. Defendant advised plaintiff not to ask questions of others, because if it got out that the place was for sale other purchasers would probably come and get the bargain away from him. Relying upon these representations, plaintiff made no inquiry, and bought the roadhouse for $35,000. It proved to be practically worthless, and had to be closed down when its license was not renewed. Plaintiff recovered from defendant. Adan v. Steinbrecher, 133 N.W. 477 (Minn. 1911).

5. OPINION

Saxby v. Southern Land Co.

Supreme Court of Appeals of Virginia, 1909.
109 Va. 196, 63 S.E. 423.

Action to recover damages for alleged false and fraudulent representations made in regard to the sale of a certain farm known as "Winslow." A demurrer to the declaration was sustained and the suit dismissed. Plaintiff brings error.

HARRISON, J. * * * The second and third grounds of fraud alleged are that the farm contained at least 150 acres of pine timber of which about 20 acres had been burned over; whereas, there was about 120 acres in timber, of which 60 acres had been burned over.

It is well settled that a misrepresentation, the falsity of which will afford ground for an action for damages, must be of an existing fact, and not the mere expression of an opinion. The mere expression of an opinion, however strong and positive the language may be, is no fraud. Such statements are not fraudulent in law, because * * * they do not ordinarily deceive or mislead. Statements which are vague and indefinite in their nature and terms, or are merely loose, conjectural or exaggerated, go for nothing, though they may not be true, for a man is not justified in placing reliance upon them. An indefinite representation ought to put the person to whom it is made on inquiry. [C]

The declaration states that the farm in question contained 444 acres, 1 rood and 26 poles. It is manifest that the vendor was not asserting a fact in stating the number of acres in timber and the number burned over, but was merely expressing his opinion from appearances. The declaration does not charge him with saying more than that there was about 150 acres in timber and about 20 acres burned over. These expressions indicate that the defendant in error was not making statements of ascertained facts, but was merely expressing his opinion of the acreage in timber and the portion thereof which was burned over. The statements were sufficiently indefinite to have put the plaintiffs in error on their guard to make further inquiry if they regarded the matter as material.

The last two grounds of fraud alleged are that the defendant in error stated that the timber, when cut into cordwood, would readily sell at the local stations on the railroad for $4 per cord, whereas it could be sold only for a much smaller price, and that the land was specially adapted to potato culture, and would by the use of fertilizer yield 100 bushels of potatoes to the acre, whereas, by actual experiment, the land failed to produce anything like that yield by the use of fertilizers.

There is no allegation that the land had produced 100 bushels of potatoes to the acre, or that cordwood had brought $4 per cord at local stations. The production of land in the future and the price of cordwood in the future are dependent upon so many conditions that no assertion of an existing fact could be made with respect thereto.

The statements relied on as grounds of fraud cannot be regarded otherwise than as speculative expressions of opinion—mere trade talk—with respect to matters of an equally uncertain nature. * * *

We are of opinion that the demurrer to the declaration was properly sustained. The judgment complained of must, therefore, be affirmed.

NOTES AND QUESTIONS

1. Suppose that defendant had said that the farm contained "at least 444 acres" when there were only 210? Should it make any difference whether plaintiff saw the land? Is it significant that the plaintiff filed the suit two years after the transaction took place?

2. Which of the following statements, made by a seller to a buyer, are to be regarded as opinion, and which as fact? "This land is worth $5,000." "I paid $5,000 for this land two years ago." Medbury v. Watson, 47 Mass. (6 Met.) 246 (1843). "Property exactly like this is selling for $5,000." Brody v. Foster, 158 N.W. 824 (Minn. 1916). "I have been offered $5,000 for this land by another party." Kabatchnick v. Hanover-Elm Building Corp., 328 Mass. 341, 103 N.E.2d 692 (1952). "The lowest price at which this land can be purchased from my principal is $5,000." Hokanson v. Oatman, 131 N.W. 111 (Mich. 1911).

3. Suppose the statement of opinion as to value is made by the buyer to the seller? The seller has had her car wrecked. She is told by the buyer that in its present condition it is worth only $200, and she sells it for that. Fossier v. Morgan, 474 S.W.2d 801 (Tex. Civ. App. 1971).

4. The statement of any opinion is a statement of at least one fact—the fact that the defendant does have such an opinion. If this is false and dishonest, why should the defendant not be held liable? See W. Page Keeton, Fraud—Misrepresentation of Opinion, 21 MINN. L. REV. 643 (1937).

5. Does a statement of opinion ever imply any other facts? In Simpson v. W. Nat'l Bank of Casper, 497 P.2d 878 (Wyo. 1972), a banker, when asked about the financial condition of a customer for whose benefit the person inquiring was depositing a check, replied that he would come out all right and there was nothing wrong with his financial condition. Held, this "was an implied statement and representation that he knew of no fact incompatible with his opinion." In Wink Enter. v. Dow, 491 S.W.2d 451 (Tex. Civ. App. 1973), an opinion was expressed to a prospective investor that a bank was "a good sound one and will continue to make money." Held, the statement "means that facts exist which lead the maker to believe the statement, or facts actually exist that the bank is in sound condition."

6. Some statements clearly in the form of an opinion are actionable: Hanberry v. Hearst Corp., 81 Cal.Rptr. 519 (Cal. Ct. App. 1969), supra page 1114. Take the following:

A. What about the opinion of an attorney on a point of law, given to a layman with whom he is dealing? Sec. Savings Bank v. Kellems, 9 S.W.2d 967 (Mo. 1928). And what of an attorney's opinion on a point of law when given to an adversary with legal training? Hoyt Prop., Inc. v. Prod. Res. Group, L.L.C., 736 N.W.2d 313 (Minn. 2007).

B. Suppose a violin expert, selling a violin, gives his opinion to a purchaser who knows nothing about such instruments that it is a genuine Stradivarius? Powell v. Flechter, 18 N.Y.S. 451 (N.Y. Gen. Term. 1892). What if the purchaser is another expert? Banner v. Lyon & Healy Inc., 293 N.Y.S. 236 (N.Y. App. Div. 1937). Suppose a so-called "impartial expert" misleads the plaintiff into believing that he is actually impartial? Cf. Oltmer v. Zamora, 94 Ill.App.3d 651, 418 N.E.2d 506 (Ill. App. Ct. 1981).

C. What if the disparity in bargaining power does not arise from any expert knowledge or special information of the defendant, but from the unusual ignorance, inexperience, illiteracy or lack of intelligence of the plaintiff? Ellis v. Gordon, 231 N.W. 585 (Wis.1930).

D. Why is reliance upon statements of opinion, including value, always held to be justified where there is a special relation of trust and confidence between the parties? For example, see Jekshewitz v. Groswald, 164 N.E. 609 (Mass. 1929) (affianced); Allen v. Frawley, 82 N.W. 593 (Wis. 1900) (attorney and client).

Vulcan Metals Co. v. Simmons Mfg. Co.

United States Circuit Court of Appeals, Second Circuit, 1918.
248 Fed. 853.

[Two actions tried together. The Vulcan Metals Company brought action against the Simmons Manufacturing Company for deceit, by reason of misrepresentations in the sale by Simmons to Vulcan of machinery for the manufacture of vacuum cleaners, together with the patents covering their manufacture. The Simmons Company brought action against the Vulcan Company upon notes given for the purchase price, and in this action Vulcan counterclaimed for the same alleged misrepresentations.

The misrepresentations included "commendations of the cleanliness, economy and efficiency of the machine, that it was absolutely perfect in even the smallest detail; that water power, by which it worked, marked the most economical means of operating a vacuum cleaner with the greatest efficiency; that the cleaning was more thoroughly done than by beating or brushing; that, having been perfected, it was a necessity which every one could afford; that it was so simple a child of six could use it; that it worked completely and thoroughly; that it was simple, long-lived, easily operated, and effective; that it was the only sanitary portable cleaner on the market; that perfect satisfaction would result from its use; that it would last a lifetime; that it was the only practical jet machine on the market, and that perfect satisfaction would result from its use, if properly adjusted. The booklet is in general the ordinary compilation, puffing the excellence and powers of the vacuum cleaner, and asserting its superiority over all others of a similar sort." There were further representations that the vacuum cleaner never had been put on the market.

The trial court directed a verdict on each action for the Simmons Company. The Vulcan Company appeals.]

LEARNED HAND, DISTRICT JUDGE. The first question is of the misrepresentations touching the quality and powers of the patented machine. These were general commendations, or, in so far as they included any specific facts, were not disproved; e.g., that the cleaner would produce 18 inches of vacuum with 25 pounds water pressure. They raise, therefore, the question of law how far general "puffing" or "dealers' talk" can be the basis of an action for deceit.

The conceded exception in such cases has generally rested upon the distinction between "opinion" and "fact"; but that distinction has not escaped the criticism it deserves. An opinion is a fact, and it may be a very relevant fact; the expression of an opinion is the assertion of a belief, and any rule which condones the expression of a consciously false opinion condones a consciously false statement of fact. When the parties are so situated that the buyer may reasonably rely upon the expression of the seller's opinion, it is no excuse to give a false one. [C] And so it makes much difference whether the parties stand "on equality." For example, we should treat very differently the expressed opinion of a chemist, to a layman about the properties of a composition from the same opinion between chemist and chemist, when the buyer had full opportunity to examine. The reason of the rule lies, we think, in this: There are some kinds of talk which no sensible man takes seriously, and if he does he suffers from his credulity. If we were all scrupulously honest, it would not be so; but, as it is, neither party usually believes what the seller says about his own opinions, and each knows it. Such statements, like the claims of campaign managers before election, are rather designed to allay the suspicion which would attend their absence than to be understood as having any relation to objective truth. It is quite true that they induce a compliant temper in the buyer, but it is by a much more subtle process than through the acceptance of his claims for his wares.

So far as concerns statements of value, the rule is pretty well fixed against the buyer. * * * It has been applied more generally to statements of quality and serviceability. * * * But this is not always so. * * * As respects the validity of patents it also obtains. * * * Cases of warranty present the same question and have been answered in the same way. * * *

In the case at bar, since the buyer was allowed full opportunity to examine the cleaner and to test it out, we put the parties upon an equality. It seems to us that general statements as to what the cleaner would do, even though consciously false, were not of a kind to be taken literally by the buyer. As between manufacturer and customer, it may not be so; but this was the case of taking over a business, after ample chance to investigate. Such a buyer, who the seller rightly expects will undertake an independent and adequate inquiry into the actual merits of what he gets, has no right to treat as material in his determination statements like these. * * *

As respects the representation that the cleaners had never been put upon the market or offered for sale, the rule does not apply; nor can we agree that such representations could not have been material to Freeman's decision to accept the contract. The actual test of experience in their sale might well be of critical consequence in his decision to buy the business, and the jury would certainly have the right to accept his statement that his reliance upon these representations was determinative of his final decision. We believe that the facts as disclosed by the depositions of the Western witnesses were sufficient to carry to the jury the question whether those statements were false. It is quite true, as the District Judge said, that the number of sales was small, perhaps not 60 in all; but they were scattered in various parts of the Mountain and Pacific states, and the jury might conclude that they were enough to contradict the detailed statements of Simmons that the machines had been kept off the market altogether. * * *

[New trial ordered in the action of deceit.]

NOTES AND QUESTIONS

1. What about a statement that "there is no better land in Vermont"? Nichols v. Lane, 106 A. 592 (Vt. 1919). Or that a machine is "the pride of our line," and "the best on the American market"? Prince v. Brackett, Shaw & Lunt Co., 130 A. 509 (Me.1925). Or that shares of stock are "hot stock," "very good," and "with unlimited possibilities"? Ryan v. Collins, 496 S.W.2d 205 (Tex. Civ. App.1973). Or that a prospect for dancing lessons had "exceptional potential to be a fine and accomplished dancer," that he was a "natural dancer" and a "terrific dancer"? Parker v. Arthur Murray, Inc., 295 N.E.2d 487 (Ill. App. Ct. 1973). See also Letellier v. Small, 400 A.2d 371 (Me. 1979), on "dealer talk"; Schott Motorcycle Supply v. Am. Honda Motor Co., 976 F.2d 58 (1st Cir. 1992) (defendant's assurance of Honda's future commitment to motorcycle business "puffing" and "track talk"); Charpentier v. L.A. Rams Football Co., Inc., 89 Cal. Rptr. 2d 115 (Cal. Ct. App. 1999) (defendant represented no intention "to move the team," plaintiff bought season's tickets in reliance; held jury could conclude representation was "material.").

2. In Bertram v. Reed Automobile Co., 49 S.W.2d 517 (Tex. Civ. App. 1932), the seller of a second-hand automobile described it as a "dandy," a "bearcat," a "good automobile," a "good little car," and a "sweet job." The court said: "Common experience and observation causes one to marvel at the moderation of the selling agent in making his trade talk to appellant. . . . These are relative terms, they may mean anything the orator or the listener wants, and neither may be penalized if the one exaggerates or the other is disappointed. There may be something more definite in the representations that the car had been well taken care of, had good rubber on it, had been driven but 19,000 miles, had not been mistreated, that mechanics had found it in perfect condition."

3. "The rule of law is hardly to be regretted when it is considered how easily and insensibly words of hope or expectation are converted by an interested memory into statements of quality or value when the expectation has been disappointed." in Deming v. Darling, 20 N.E. 107 (Mass. 1889) (Holmes, J.).

6. LAW

Sorenson v. Gardner

Supreme Court of Oregon, 1959.
215 Or. 255, 334 P.2d 471.

LUSK, JUSTICE. This is an action for deceit in which the plaintiffs recovered a judgment for $2,000 and the defendants have appealed.

The action grows out of the sale of a dwelling house. * * * The complaint alleges that the defendants falsely represented to the plaintiffs that the house was well constructed in a workmanlike manner and met all minimum code requirements, particularly with respect to electric wiring, plumbing, septic tank and sewage disposal arrangement. * * * The plaintiff introduced evidence in support of these allegations and evidence tending to show that the representations were false. * * *

* * * [The] general rule [is] that fraud cannot be predicated upon misrepresentations of law or misrepresentations as to matters of law. [C] Thus, misrepresentations concerning the legal effect of an instrument have been held to be not actionable. * * * [Conflicting] reasons [for this] have been repeated, sometimes in the same decision: first, that every man is presumed to know the law, and hence the plaintiff cannot be heard to say that he reasonably believed the statement made to him; and second, that no man, at least without special training, can be expected to know the law, and so the plaintiff must have understood that the defendant was giving him nothing more than an opinion. [C] The basis of the rule has been criticized by courts and textwriters. * * *

The rule of the Restatement of Torts upon this subject is as follows:

"§ 545. Misrepresentation of Law

"(1) If a representation as to a matter of law in a business transaction is a representation of fact the recipient is justified in relying upon it to the same extent as though it were a representation of any other fact.

"(2) If the representation as to a matter of law in a business transaction is a representation of opinion as to the legal consequences of facts known to the maker and the recipient or assumed by both to exist, the recipient is justified in relying upon it to the same extent as though it were a representation of any other opinion as stated in §§ 542, 543."

In the comment on Subsection (1) of the foregoing, it is said, "If a representation concerns the legal effect of facts not disclosed or not otherwise known to the recipient, it may justifiably be interpreted as implying that there are facts which substantiate the statement * * *. So, too, the assertion of title to a particular tract of land asserts the existence of those conveyances or relationships which are necessary to vest the title in the alleged owner. On the other hand, if all the facts believed by the maker to exist are stated to the recipient or otherwise known by him and from these facts the maker of the representation asserts that title vests in the person in question as a legal consequence, the representation is an expression of opinion and the case falls within Subsection (2)." * * *

Here we are dealing with a number of alleged misrepresentations to the effect that the house in question complied with the minimum requirements of state law. * * * There was evidence that in certain particulars the requirements of the code were not met, and evidence from which the jury could find that the defendants knew and the plaintiffs did not what the facts were in this regard. Under the rule as formulated by the Restatement, had the plaintiffs been aware of these facts and had the defendants represented to them that the facts as so known constituted a compliance with the law, then the misrepresentation in question would have been one of law and not of fact. But, the plaintiffs being ignorant of the facts, the representation in the circumstances was one of fact and the case is covered by Subsection (1) of Section 545 of the Restatement of Torts. * * * The plaintiffs are not relying on their ignorance of the law but of the facts, and the alleged representations carried with them the implication that the facts were otherwise than the evidence shows them to have been. They concerned "the legal effect of facts not disclosed or otherwise known to the recipient." * * *

Our own conclusion, which accords with the rule of the Restatement, is that such representations may, and in this case do, relate to matters of fact. Therefore, the contention of the defendants in support of the first ground of the motion for a directed verdict cannot be sustained. * * *

[Reversed, however, and new trial ordered, on the ground of error in instructions to the jury as to the measure of damages.]

NOTES AND QUESTIONS

1. Defendant, a layman, is seeking to settle a claim against plaintiff, and assures him that he is legally liable for his conduct. Plaintiff, relying upon the assurance, settles the claim. He was not in fact liable. Has he a cause of action? Williams v. Dougherty County, 113 S.E.2d 168 (Ga. Ct. App. 1960).

2. Defendant, a layman, sold plaintiff beverages containing 18 to 25 per cent alcohol, assuring him that the local law would permit him to sell them in unbroken packages at retail. In fact, the law did not permit such sales, and plaintiff was arrested and convicted for the unlawful sale of intoxicating liquor. Defendant was held not liable. Ad. Dernehl & Sons Co. v. Detert, 202 N.W. 207 (Wis. 1925). Cf. Gibson v. Mendenhall, 224 P.2d 251 (Okl. 1950) (representation that plaintiff could easily obtain a license).

3. Representations as to the law of another state are treated as statements of fact, upon which the plaintiff may justifiably rely. See, for example, Hembry v. Parreco, 81 A.2d 77 (Mun. App. D.C. 1951); Fireman's Ins. Co. v. Jones, 431 S.W.2d 728 (Ark. 1968) (deception as to foreign statute of limitations).

4. What about a statement that defendant's hospital is legally accredited? Myers v. Lowery, (Cal. Dist. Ct. App. 1920) or that the defendant's title is good? Barnett v. Kunkle, 256 F. 644 (8th Cir. 1919).

5. What about a statement of law made by an attorney to his client? By one member of a family to another? By an insurance company to its policy-holder? Some relationships will demand a disclosure of material facts. Thus fraudulent misrepresentation may be constituted in the absence of an affirmative statement misrepresenting existing fact. Stiley v. Block, 925 P.2d 194, 208 925 P.2d 194 (Wash. 1996) (en banc) (Talmadge, J., concurring); Stark v. Equitable Life Assurance Soc., 285 N.W. 466 (Minn. 1939).

7. PREDICTION AND INTENTION

McElrath v. Electric Investment Co.

Supreme Court of Minnesota, 1911.
114 Minn. 358, 131 N.W. 380.

BROWN, J. Appeal from an order overruling a general demurrer to plaintiffs' complaint. It appears from the complaint that the defendant was the owner of a certain summer hotel property, including the land upon which the building was situated, and certain personal property used in connection with the operation of the hotel, situated at Antlers Park, in Dakota county. On the 15th day of April, 1909, the parties to the action entered into a contract by the terms of which defendant leased the property to plaintiffs for a term of years. * * *

The action is for damages occasioned by the alleged false and fraudulent representations made by defendant for the purpose of inducing plaintiffs to enter into the contract. The complaint alleges: "That for the purpose of inducing said plaintiffs to enter into said contract, Exhibit A, this defendant wrongfully, falsely, and fraudulently stated and represented to these plaintiffs that the Minneapolis, St. Paul, Rochester and Dubuque Electric Traction Company would complete its electric railroad, and would run electric cars over said road from the city of Minneapolis to and beyond said Antlers Park during the summer of 1909, and about July 1st of that year; and said defendant further stated and represented to said plaintiffs that said defendant would, during said summer of 1909 and as soon as said electric railroad should run to said Antlers Park, make of said Antlers Park and surrounding ground an important summer resort for people living at said city of Minneapolis, and further stated and represented to plaintiffs that if they would enter into said contract, Exhibit A, they would make, through the assistance and efforts of said defendant, not less than fifteen hundred dollars ($1,500.00) per annum clear above all expenses of running and management. * * *

It is contended by defendant that the alleged false representations do not constitute a cause of action, for the reason that, when made, they had reference to the future intentions of the traction company, and were not representations of present existing facts, and further, that the complaint contains no allegations that the electric road was not constructed and in operation according to the representations.

We * * * hold that the complaint, in so far as it alleges the making of false representations for the purpose of inducing plaintiffs to enter into the contract, knowing the same to be false, to the effect that the electric road would be completed and in operation by July 1, 1909, states a cause of action. While it is true as a general rule that false representations, upon which fraud may be predicated, must be of existing facts, and cannot consist of mere promises or conjectures as to future acts or events, yet, [c] if in making the representations defendant "intended to create in plaintiffs the belief that it was, as a fact, the then intention of the" traction company to complete the road at the time represented, and "the representations might be understood and were understood by plaintiffs as asserting that fact," then a charge of fraud may be based thereon, though the represented event was to occur in the future. Upon this theory, the complaint, as against a demurrer, states a cause of action. [Cc]

Upon the question of the sufficiency of the other allegations of fraud, the case comes within the general rule that promises or assurances as to future events cannot be made the basis of an action of fraud. In this respect the complaint alleges that defendant represented that it would, as soon as the electric road reached Antlers Park, "make of said Antlers Park and surrounding ground an important summer resort for people living at said City of Minneapolis." This, aside from being a mere promise to do something in the future, namely, "make an important summer resort," rests wholly in conjecture and speculation, depending for its accomplishment upon many facts, of which both parties had, presumptively, equal notice, and depending upon conditions over which neither had control. Whether an important or other summer resort may be established at a particular place depends in the main upon its location and the disposition of the public to make it a place of recreation or pleasure. * * * The naked allegation is of a promise to create a particular condition in the future, a condition surrounded with known uncertainty and beyond defendant's control, and the general rule applies. The other allegations, namely, that plaintiffs would, in the conduct of the leased property, make a specified profit during the season, also rests in conjecture and opinion, and therefore is not open to the charge of actionable fraud.

Affirmed.

NOTES AND QUESTIONS

1. The following have been held not to justify reliance: A prediction that prices will remain unchanged. Coe v. Ware, 171 N.E. 732 (Mass. 1930). That plaintiff will be able to obtain a job. Schwitters v. Des Moines Commercial College, 203 N.W. 265 (Iowa 1925). That building lots next to a highway will prove to be profitable. Campbell County v. Braun, 174 S.W.2d 1 (Ky. 1943). That stock will triple in value within a year. Kennedy v. Flo-Tronics, Inc., 143 N.W.2d 827 (Minn. 1966). That plaintiff will be successful in purchasing property in a foreclosure sale. Spragins v. Sunburst Bank, 605 So.2d 777 (Miss. 1992). That certain adverse consequences would flow from a failure to enter a new agreement and that representor stood to make nothing from the new agreement. Fuller v. Perry, 476 S.E.2d 793 (Ga. Ct. App. 1996). That a construction loan application would be approved. Birt v. Wells Fargo Home Mort., Inc., 75 P.3d 640 (Wyo. 2003) (allegation was "just the sort of 'negligent promise' to which the cause of action should not

be extended,"). That plaintiff's potato chip delivery route would be profitable. Platus Corp. Pension Plan v. Nazareth, 705 N.Y.S.2d 649 (N.Y. App. Div. 2000).

2. In Trustees of Columbia Univ. v. Jacobsen, 574, 148 A.2d 63 (N.J. 1959) cert. denied, 363 U.S. 808, plaintiff, a university student, claimed that the University represented to him that he would acquire "wisdom, truth, character, enlightenment, understanding, justice, liberty, honesty, courage, beauty and similar virtues and qualities; that it would develop the whole man, maturity, well-roundedness, objective thinking and the like. . . ." He failed to graduate because of poor scholastic standing. What result?

3. Contrast Steinberg v. Chicago Medical Sch., 13 Ill.Dec. 699, 371 N.E.2d 634 (Ill. 1977). Plaintiff applied for admission to defendant medical school, paying the application fee, and was rejected. He alleges fraud in the catalog statements regarding selection standards to be applied, and the use of "nonacademic criteria, primarily the ability of the applicant or his family to pledge or make payment of large sums of money to the school." Held, cause of action stated and class action permitted. Recovery allowed "where the false promise or representation of future conduct is alleged to be the scheme employed to accomplish the fraud." See also NECO, Inc. v. Larry Price & Assoc., Inc., 597 N.W.2d 602 (Neb. 1999). Landlord of mixed-use tower induced a fire safety monitoring company to purchase monitoring space in the building with assurances that a newly-installed fire sprinkler system would cover the entire building. In fact, the landlord had previously instructed a renovator to omit installation of sprinklers in significant portions of the building, and did not subsequently revise those instructions. Cause of action found where the party making the representation as to a future event was in control of the event's occurrence or non-occurrence. Not all statements concerning prospective occurrences, without more, are barred from giving rise to misrepresentation claims; some such statements may in fact be representations of present conditions. See Campbell v. Bettius, 421 S.E.2d 433 (Va. 1992) (attorney's false assertion that plaintiffs "would be able" to collect on a guarantee was not a prediction of future events, but a representation of the present effect of contract language).

Burgdorfer v. Thielemann

Supreme Court of Oregon, 1936.
153 Or. 354, 55 P.2d 1122.

Action on the case for deceit by Charles Burgdorfer against Carl Thielemann. From a judgment in favor of plaintiff, defendant appeals.

[Plaintiff charges that defendant fraudulently induced him to exchange a $2,000 note and mortgage (plus two notes totaling $323) for two lots in the Collins View tract, by falsely promising that he would pay a $500 mortgage on the Collins View lot.]

KELLY, JUSTICE. * * * It is further alleged in plaintiff's second amended complaint:

"* * * that the defendant had no intention at the time of making the said promise, or at any time at all, of performing the promise to plaintiff hereinabove set out; * * * that the plaintiff did believe and rely on the said representations and promise of the defendant and did act thereon to his great damage; * * * "

Defendant's first assignment of error imputes error upon the part of the court in allowing plaintiff to testify as to appellant's alleged promise to pay off the mortgage on the Collins View property.

The precise objection which defendant makes is that the alleged promise could not have been performed within one year and, therefore, to be enforceable [under the statute of frauds] it must have been reduced to writing and signed by the party sought to be charged. * * *

We think that, in an action for deceit, [the] provision of the statute [of frauds] does not have the effect of rendering inadmissible testimony of an oral promise made with the fraudulent intent on the part of the promisor at the time the promise was made not to fulfill or perform the same.

One of the reasons leading to this conclusion is that the purpose of such oral testimony is not to establish an agreement, but to prove fraud. The gist of the fraud consists in the false representation of the existence of an intention which in truth and in fact has no existence. * * *

"To profess an intent to do or not to do, when the party intends the contrary, is as clear a case of misrepresentation and of fraud as could be made." Herndon v. Durham & S.R. Co., 161 N.C. 650, 656, 77 S.E. 683, 685. * * *

As stated by Bowen, L.J., in Edgington v. Fitzmaurice, Law Reports, 29 Chancery Division, 459: "There must be a misstatement of an existing fact; but the state of a man's mind is as much a fact as the state of his digestion. It is true that it is very difficult to prove what the state of a man's mind at a particular time is, but if it can be ascertained it is as much a fact as anything else. A misrepresentation as to the state of a man's mind is, therefore, a misstatement of fact." * * *

No error was committed by allowing plaintiff to testify as to defendant's alleged promise to pay off the mortgage on the Collins View property. * * *

The judgment of the circuit court is affirmed.

NOTES AND QUESTIONS

1. Suppose the proof is merely that the defendant made a contract, and after a time broke it. Is this enough for an action of deceit? Williams v. Williams, 18 S.E.2d 364 (N.C. 1942). What if the promise is broken immediately after it is made, with no intervening change in the situation? Guy T. Bisbee Co. v. Granite City Investing Corp., 199 N.W. 14 (Minn. 1924). What about a promise to pay made by one who is completely insolvent at the time? California Conserving Co. v. D'Avanzo, 62 F.2d 528 (2d Cir. 1933).

2. Consider the following possible advantages of the action in deceit over a contract action for breach of the promise itself:

A. The deceit action may avoid the statute of frauds. Channel Master Corp. v. Aluminum Ltd. Sales, 176 N.Y.S.2d 259, 151 N.E.2d 833 (N.Y.

1958). Contra, Cassidy v. Kraft-Phenix Cheese Corp., 280 N.W. 814 (Mich. 1938).

B. It may avoid the difficulties of the parol evidence rule, which prevents any promise not integrated into a written contract from being regarded as a part of the contract. Sabo v. Delman, 143 N.E.2d 906 (N.Y. 1957). Contra: McCreight v. Davey Tree Expert Co., 254 N.W. 623 (Minn. 1934). In Pinnacle Peak Developers v. TRW Invest. Corp., 631 P.2d 540 (Ariz. 1980), Judge Sandra Day O'Connor drew a distinction between contractual parties' "expertise and business sophistication" in the issue of whether the parol evidence rule should be displaced.

C. It may avoid the defense that the promise was without consideration. Daniel v. Daniel, 226 S.W. 1070 (Ky. 1921). But see: Rankin v. Burnham, 274 P. 98 (Wash. 1929).

D. It may avoid the defense that the contract was an illegal one, if the parties are not in pari delicto. See W. Page Keeton, Fraud—Statements of Intention, 15 TEXAS L. REV. 185, 213–216 (1937).

E. It may avoid the defense of the statute of limitations, since a longer period may be applicable in the deceit action, or the statute may run only from the plaintiff's discovery of the fraud. Fidelity-Philadelphia Trust Co. v. Simpson, 293 Pa. 577, 143 A. 202 (1928). But see Brick v. Cohn-Hall-Marx, 11 N.E.2d 902 (N.Y. 1937).

F. It may avoid a limitation of liability contained in the contract itself.

G. It may avoid a defense against the contract action, such as infancy. Wis. Loan & Fin. Corp. v. Goodnough, 228 N.W. 484 (Wis. 1930). Contra, Slayton v. Barry, 56 N.E. 574 (Mass. 1900).

H. It may avoid the necessity of joining parties to a joint contract in one action. Cf. Elliott v. Hayden, 104 Mass. 180 (1870).

8. DAMAGES

Hinkle v. Rockville Motor Co., Inc.

Court of Appeals of Maryland, 1971.
262 Md. 502, 278 A.2d 42.

BARNES, JUDGE. The appellant, Donald Hinkle (Hinkle), purchased a 1969 Ford Galaxie automobile from the appellee, Rockville Motor Company, Inc. (Rockville), in January of 1970. * * * Hinkle alleged that Rockville fraudulently represented to him at the time of sale that the 1969 Galaxie was a new car when, in fact, it had over 2,000 miles on the speedometer and had been involved in an accident in the State of Tennessee. Hinkle discovered the mileage recorded on the speedometer while driving home on the day of the sale. He brought this to the attention of Rockville and an adjustment was made whereby he was compensated in the amount of $109.86, the amount of his first payment, in exchange for a release from any further claims except for those falling within his standard new car warranty. The adjustment for mileage was made on January 27, 1970. Hinkle maintains that it was not until April, 1970, that he learned the automobile had been involved in an accident in Tennessee in July of 1969. It is alleged in the declaration that the front and rear portions of the automobile had been welded together after having been severed in the accident. Hinkle alleged that Rockville had knowledge of the accident but that it "willfully concealed the true circumstances" and "willfully, maliciously and fraudulently misrepresented the quality and condition of the aforesaid Ford vehicle" and that he relied on these misrepresentations to his detriment. Damages were claimed in the amount of $100,000.

At the close of Hinkle's case, Rockville moved for a directed verdict. In granting the directed verdict, the trial court only found it necessary to consider Rockville's argument that Hinkle's failure to produce evidence in regard to the automobile's actual value at the time of sale deprived the jury of the only permissible standard by which the jury could determine the existence or amount of damages. The trial court determined this to be a correct statement of the law and directed a verdict in favor of Rockville notwithstanding the fact that Hinkle had produced expert testimony that the effects of the accident could be remedied and the car returned to new car condition by the expenditure of $800 for repairs. * * *

A majority of States will allow the plaintiffs to recover the "benefit of his bargain" if sufficiently proved. The theory is to compensate the plaintiff as though the transaction had been carried out as represented. [Cc]

Other States restrict the plaintiff to his "out of pocket" losses. The classic formula is the value of the object as represented less its actual value at the time of sale. The theory is to return the plaintiff economically to the position he was in prior to the fraudulent transaction thus allowing him recoupment of actual losses but not expected gain. This rigid limitation on the nature of recovery is often explained as being required because the action is one of tort rather than contract and that it has always been recognized that tort remedies are designed to compensate for actual harm suffered. * * * Maryland is one of those States which has not adopted a rigid stand as far as adopting one of the above theories to the exclusion of the other. Both theories have been used and approved in Maryland. * * *

In summary, the review of the Maryland cases on this question of the proper measure of damages in fraud and deceit cases demonstrates that this Court has applied the so-called "flexibility theory" without heretofore expressly stating the factors to be considered in its application. Selman v. Shirley, 161 Or. 582, 609, 85 P.2d 384, 394, (1938) the first case to define expressly this flexible approach, set forth the following four rules as a guide for the proper measure of damages in these cases.

"(1) If the defrauded party is content with the recovery of only the amount that he actually lost, his damages will be measured under that rule;

"(2) if the fraudulent representation also amounted to a warranty, recovery may be had for the loss of the bargain because a fraud accompanied by a broken promise should cost the wrongdoer as much as the latter alone;

"(3) where the circumstances disclosed by the proof are so vague as to cast virtually no light upon the value of the property had it conformed to the representations, the court will award damages equal only to the loss sustained; and

"(4) where * * * the damages under the benefit-of-the-bargain rule are proved with sufficient certainty, that rule will be employed." * * *

This position was advocated by Professor McCormick who wrote, "In the first place, it seems that in every case the defrauded plaintiff should be allowed to claim under the 'out of pocket' loss theory if he prefers. In the second place, the plaintiff should be allowed to choose the other theory, and recover the value of the bargain as represented, if the trial judge in his discretion considers that, in view of the probable moral culpability of the defendant and of the definiteness of the representations and the ascertainability of the represented value, the case is an appropriate one for such treatment." McCormick, Damages § 122 (1935) at p. 454. Williston on Contracts § 1392 (Rev.Ed.1937) at p. 3886 and Sutherland on Damages § 1172 (4th ed. 1916) at p. 4409 both indicate a preference for allowing the plaintiff to recover the benefit of his bargain in these cases. Sedgewick on Damages § 781 (9th ed.1912) at pp. 1629–31, while recognizing that the majority rule allows "benefit of bargain" recovery, favors a strict adherence to the "out of pocket" remedy in accordance with English common law as set forth in Peek v. Derry, 37 Ch.Div. 541 (1888). The Restatement of Torts, § 549 (1938) also sets forth the "out of pocket" rule of damages.

After the above review of cases and texts on the subject, it is concluded that the trial court erred in directing the verdict against Hinkle for failure to produce evidence upon which damages could be awarded. Hinkle's evidence in regard to the cost of necessary repairs demonstrated the existence of damages and provided an adequate measure upon which they could be predicated.

Judgment reversed and case remanded for new trial, the appellee to pay the costs.

NOTES AND QUESTIONS

1. Does the court in the principal case correctly state the test for the "tort" or "out of pocket" test?

2. "It is the very essence of an action of fraud or deceit that the same shall be accompanied by damage, and neither damnum absque injuria nor injuria absque damnum by themselves constitute a good cause of action." Casey v. Welch, 50 So.2d 124 (Fla.1951). In an action for rescission, it may not be necessary to show pecuniary loss and plaintiff can prevail if he did not receive what he was promised. See Hirschman v. Healy, 202 N.W. 734 (Minn. 1925); Nance v. McClellan, 89 S.W.2d 774 (Tex. Comm'n App. 1936).

3. Auditors' accounts are relied on by plaintiff in taking over a company. The accounts are negligently audited. It is proved that plaintiff would have paid less for the company if the accounts had been accurate. Is this difference recoverable? Or has plaintiff suffered no loss because control of the company has brought an overall benefit? For differing views see opinions in *Scott Group Ltd. v. McFarlane* [1978] 1 N.Z.L.R. 553 (C.A.).

4. Of the two "normal" measures of damages discussed here, the contract or "benefit-of-the-bargain" measure will usually result in greater damages. Thus: Price paid $5,000; Value of property purchased $3,000; Value as represented $7,000. Here the tort, or "out-of-pocket" measure results in damages of $2,000, while the "benefit-of-the-bargain" measure is $4,000.

There may, however, be cases in which the out-of-pocket measure is higher. For example, Estell v. Myers, 56 Miss. 800 (1879), where plaintiff paid $62,500 for land actually worth $27,500, and the value if the representations had been true would have been $50,000. Also Erde v. Fenster, 141 N.Y.S. 943 (1913), where plaintiff was induced to sell a claim for less than it was worth by the buyer's representation that the debtor was totally insolvent.

5. The out-of-pocket measure of damages is adopted in all deceit actions by the English courts, and by a minority of about a dozen American jurisdictions. The "benefit-of-the-bargain" rule has been adopted by about two-thirds of the American courts that have considered the question. Neither group has followed either rule with entire consistency in all cases.

6. The compromise formula, first stated in Selman v. Shirley, 161 Or. 582, 85 P.2d 384 (1938), *reh'g granted as affirmed*, 91 P.2d 312 (Or. 1939), has met general approval by legal writers, and has been followed in some other states. Salter v. Heiser, 239 P.2d 327 (Wash. 1951); Rice v. Price, 164 N.E.2d 891 (Mass. 1960). It has been accepted, in a simplified form, by § 549 of the RESTATEMENT (THIRD) OF TORTS: LIABILITY FOR ECONOMIC HARM (Tentative Draft No. 3, 2014) (concerning § 549).

7. In addition to the "normal" measure of damages, whether it is under the tort or the contract rule, plaintiff can recover for consequential damages resulting from the misrepresentation. Thus one who buys a horse represented to him as gentle may recover for personal injuries if he is kicked by the horse. Vezina v. Souliere, 152 A. 798 (Vt. 1931). And one who buys infected bees, represented to be healthy, may recover for damage to his other bees when the infection spreads to them. Sampson v. Penney, 187 N.W. 135 (Minn. 1922). Plaintiff may recover for expenses to which he has been put, as when he is induced to employ an architect by misrepresentations as to his skill and compelled to incur extra expenses in completing the building as a result. Edward Barron Estate Co. v. Woodruff Co., 126 P. 351 (Cal.1912). In Brooks v. Doherty, Rumble & Butler, 481 N.W.2d 120 (Minn. Ct. App. 1992), the court warned of the possible overlap of contract and tort damages, allowing damages against plaintiff's law firm employer for emotional distress, damage to personal and professional reputation, lost income, and expenses in moving across the country to find a job.

8. Questions of proximate cause can arise in misrepresentation cases, too. Plaintiff is induced to buy stock in a company by defendant's fraudulent statement. The treasurer of the company subsequently absconds with funds that he had been embezzling over a period of time and the company turns out to be insolvent. Defendant knew nothing about the treasurer's misconduct and the misrepresentation did not relate to the value of the stock. Can plaintiff recover in deceit for his loss? Fottler v. Moseley, 70 N.E. 1040 (Mass. 1904), would indicate that the answer is yes. But a majority of the courts would apparently disagree. See Boatmen's

Nat'l Co. v. M.W. Elkins & Co., 63 F.2d 214 (8th Cir. 1933); Morrell v. Wiley, 178 A. 121 (Conn. 1935). Plaintiff would be able to prevail if he sued in rescission. Seneca Wire & Mfg. Co. v. A.B. Leach & Co., 159 N.E. 700 (N.Y. 1928).

9. Damages recoverable as consequential loss under deceit may be broader than those under negligent misrepresentation. See Doyle v. Olby (Ironmongers) Ltd., [1969] 2 Q.B. 158, at 167 (Eng.): "[I]t does not lie in the mouth of the fraudulent person to say [damages] could not reasonably have been foreseen." Can an analogy be drawn with proximate cause in relation to the intentional torts? Cf. RESTATEMENT (THIRD) OF TORTS: LIABILITY FOR ECONOMIC HARM (Tentative Draft No. 3, 2014) (concerning § 548A) (1977), damages recoverable if loss might reasonably be expected to result from reliance on the representation. Punitive damages may be awarded. Warner Comm., Inc. v. Keller, 888 S.W.2d 586 (Tex. App. 1994); Roboserve, Inc. v. Kato Kagaku Co., Limited, 78 F.3d 266, 277 (7th Cir. 1996) (stating the necessity of a showing of "intent to injure constituting gross misconduct or malicious behavior"). Mental anguish is often mentioned as an element in setting damages in actions of deceit and providing a reason for a contractual measure of damages in some cases, see Liberty National v. Sanders, 792 So.2d 1069 (Ala. 2000). The Reporters for the Preliminary draft RESTATEMENT (THIRD) OF TORTS: LIABILITY FOR ECONOMIC HARM, Section 13 would firmly adopt the tort out-of-pocket measure, and provide for mental anguish through resort to actions for intentional and negligent infliction of emotional distress. Do you regard such actions as viable avenues for compensating for such harm?

10. The measure of damages depends on the scope of the duty and rules of causation. The problem is exemplified in Banque Bruxelles Lambert SA v. Eagle Star Ins. Co., [1995] Q.B. 375, *sub nom.* S. Australia Asset Mgmt. Corp. v. York Montague Ltd., [1997] A.C. 191 (H.L.) (Eng.), and Kenny & Good Pty. Ltd. v. MGICA (1992) Ltd. (1999) 199 CLR 413 (Austl.). The English House of Lords and the Australia High Court respectively struggled to establish the correct principle in the following situation. A lends money to B on security of certain real estate. Valuer V is retained by B to value the real estate, knowing that A will rely on the valuation as a basis for advancing the money. V is negligent and the land is worth a fraction of its valuation. A recovers but a fraction of the money loaned to B. It is easy to establish a duty of care owed by V to A, but what is the measure of damages? If A would not have entered the transaction but for the high valuation, could it be said that A should recover from B all the losses necessary to put him back in the position he enjoyed prior to the transaction? That is, the amount of the loan less the money received on foreclosure. (Interest would be calculated.) This measure of damages includes any drop in the market value of the real estate after the loan contract. Should damages, however, incorporate a drop in the market? The House of Lords, describing the scope of the duty, argued that the damages are those caused by the wrongfulness of the valuation: the responsibility extends only to the risk of the negligent advice. To make V liable for the drop in the market would hold him liable for an event that would have occurred even if the valuation had been correct. Thus, the measure should turn on the consequences of the wrong valuation—the difference between the wrong valuation and the correct value. Similar reasoning was employed in the following cases: First Federal Svgs. & Loan Assn. v. Charter

Appraisal Co., Inc., 724 A.2d 497 (Conn. 1999); Movitz v. First Nat'l Bank of Chicago, 148 F.3d 760 (7th Cir. 1998); and in Or. Steel Mills, Inc. v. Coopers & Lybrand, 83 P.3d 322 (Or. 2004).

The Australian High Court found, in *Kenny & Good* above, that the market drop should be included because the scope of the duty (the undertaking) included the assumption of the risk of a drop in the market value of the real estate.

In the cases, the analysis is the same whether the action is in tort or contract. The *Doyle* case, note supra 9, may be justified because fraud requires a strong restitutionary remedy.

In the latest salvo of U.S. Supreme Court cases on punitive damages, Philip Morris USA v. Williams, 549 U.S. 346 (2007), plaintiff pleaded an action in deceit, claiming that defendant tobacco company had systematically misrepresented the risks of smoking. The jury awarded $79.5 million in punitive damages; the ratio of punitive to compensatory damages for the death was about 100:1. The case involved an exquisite dance, over a decade, wherein the case wound through three Oregon courts and was granted certiorari three times and remanded back to the Oregon Supreme Court twice before the United States Supreme Court dismissed the case as improvidently granted. 556 U.S.178 (2009), per curium. Thus is seen in strong relief a struggle for authority between the state and federal law.

The Supreme Court in Dura Pharm., Inc. v. Broudo, 544 U.S. 336 (2005), instructs that lower courts in federal securities fraud cases must seek guidance in "traditional elements of causation and loss," id. at, 346, derived from "common-law deceit and misrepresentation actions," id. at, 343.

CHAPTER 22

INTERFERENCE WITH ADVANTAGEOUS RELATIONSHIPS

1. BUSINESS RELATIONS

(A) INJURIOUS FALSEHOOD

Ratcliffe v. Evans

Court of Appeal, 1892.
[1892] 2 Q.B. 524.

[Plaintiff alleged that he and his father had carried on the business of engineer and boiler maker for many years under the name Ratcliffe & Sons, that the father died but plaintiff carried on the business and that defendant, publisher of the County Herald, "falsely and maliciously" published "certain words" importing "that the plaintiff had ceased to carry on his business * * * and that the firm of Ratcliffe & Sons did not then exist."]

BOWEN, L.J. This was a case in which an action for a false and malicious publication about the trade and manufactures of the plaintiff was tried at the Chester assizes, with the result of a verdict for the plaintiff for 120*l.* Judgment having been entered for the plaintiff for that sum and costs, the defendant appealed to this Court for a new trial, or to enter a verdict for the defendant, on the ground, amongst others, that no special damage, such as was necessary to support the action, was proved at the trial. The injurious statement complained of was a publication in the *County Herald,* a Welsh newspaper. It was treated in the pleadings as a defamatory statement or libel; but this suggestion was negatived, and the verdict of the jury proceeded upon the view that the writing was a false statement purposely made about the manufactures of the plaintiff, which was intended to, and did in fact, cause him damage. The only proof at the trial of such damage consisted, however, of evidence of general loss of business without specific proof of the loss of any particular customers or orders, and the question we have to determine is, whether in such an action such general evidence of damage was admissible and sufficient. That an action will lie for written or oral falsehoods, not actionable per se nor even defamatory, where they are maliciously published, where they are calculated in the ordinary course of things to produce, and where they do produce, actual damage, is established law. Such an action is not one of libel or of slander, but an action on the case for damage wilfully and intentionally done without just occasion or excuse, analogous to an action for slander of title. To support it, actual damage must be shown, for it is an action which only lies in respect of such damage as has actually occurred. It was contended before us that in such an action it is not enough to allege and prove general loss of business arising from the publication, since such general loss is general and not special damage, and special damage, as often has been said, is the gist of such an action on the case.

In an action like the present, brought for a malicious falsehood intentionally published in a newspaper about the plaintiff's business—a falsehood which is not actionable as a personal libel, and which is not defamatory in itself—is evidence to shew that a general loss of business has been the direct and natural result admissible in evidence, and, if uncontradicted, sufficient to maintain the action? In the case of a personal libel, such general loss of custom may unquestionably be alleged and proved. Every libel is of itself a wrong in regard of which the law, as we have seen, implies general damage. By the very fact that he has committed such a wrong, the defendant is prepared for the proof that some general damage may have been done. * * * "It is not special damage, [c] it is general damage resulting from the kind of injury the plaintiff has sustained." [C]

In the case before us to-day, it is a falsehood openly disseminated through the press—probably read, and possibly acted on, by persons of whom the plaintiff never heard. To refuse with reference to such a subject-matter to admit such general evidence would be to * * * involve an absolute denial of justice and of redress for the very mischief which was intended to be committed. * * *

Appeal dismissed.

NOTES AND QUESTIONS

1. This is the leading case giving sufficient scope to the "action on the case for words" to justify the use of the term "injurious falsehood"—a name suggested by Sir John Salmond in his treatise on Torts. Earlier cases had involved "slander of title" or "trade libel," which had developed as isolated torts of a limited scope. Sometimes they were joined together and the term "disparagement" was used. "Injurious falsehood" now denotes a broad general principle of liability for any false and malicious statement resulting in pecuniary loss to another. The principle is generally recognized at the present time, but the courts have been slow to adopt the name.

2. The elements necessary to the cause of action usually have been stated as follows:

A. A false statement of a kind calculated to damage a pecuniary interest of the plaintiff.

B. Publication to a third person.

C. "Malice" in the publication. This element has received much the same treatment, and has caused about as much confusion, as in defamation.

D. Resulting special damage to the plaintiff, in the form of pecuniary loss.

3. The following are illustrations of the broader scope of the principle: Statements that the plaintiff is dead or is not in business or is going out of business. Davis v. New England Railway Pub. Co., 203 Mass.

470, 89 N.E. 565 (1909); McRoberts Protective Agency, Inc. v. Lansdell Protective Agency, Inc., 61 A.D.2d 652, 403 N.Y.S.2d 511 (1978). Or that he does not deal in certain goods. Jarrahdale Timber Co. v. Temperley & Co., 11 T.L.R. 119 (1894). Or that another similar business is "unique," the only one in existence. Dale System v. Time, Inc., 116 F.Supp. 527 (D.Conn.1953). Or that plaintiff is employed by defendant, as a result of which he loses an independent sale and a commission. Balden v. Shorter, [1933] Ch. 427.

See also Gale v. Ryan, 263 A.D. 76, 31 N.Y.S.2d 732 (1941); and Penn-Ohio Steel Corp. v. Allis-Chalmers Mfg. Co., 7 A.D.2d 441, 184 N.Y.S.2d 58 (1959) (defendant made false reports to Internal Revenue of payments made to plaintiff, as a result of which plaintiff had income-tax trouble); Al Raschid v. News Syndicate Co., 265 N.Y. 1, 191 N.E. 713 (1934) (defendant gave false information that plaintiff was not a citizen, subjecting him to deportation proceedings); Bartlett v. Federal Outfitting Co., 133 Cal.App. 747, 24 P.2d 877 (1933) (forged assignment of wages presented to an employer, in consequence of which the employee was discharged); Owens v. Mench, 81 Pa. D. & C. 314 (1953) (false report of a physician on a worker's injury necessitated suit to recover workers' compensation); and Cooper v. Weissblatt, 154 Misc. 522, 277 N.Y.S. 709 (1935) (false statements to church authorities forced the plaintiff to defend a suit).

4. *Special Damage.* Pleading and proof of special damage are held to be essential to any cause of action for injurious falsehood. Personal elements of damage such as mental distress, which are recoverable for defamation, are not sufficient to sustain this action.

5. When the damages claimed consist only of loss of prospective contracts or customers, the older and still prevailing rule is that the plaintiff must identify the particular customers who have refrained from dealing with him, and specify the transactions of which he claims to have been deprived. Wilson v. Dubois, 35 Minn. 471, 29 N.W. 68 (1886). It is not enough merely to show a general decline in plaintiff's business following the false publication. *HipSaver, Inc. v. Kiel*, 464 Mass. 517, 984 N.E.2d 755 (2013) (Manufacturer of hip-protection device brought action alleging claim of commercial disparagement against physician who had written medical journal article concluding that such devices were not effective in preventing hip fractures among nursing home residents. Court found for defendant because plaintiff failed to show it had a reasonable expectation of proving the elements of the claim, one of which was proving it suffered pecuniary loss from the publication). Amerinet, Inc. v. Xerox Corporation, 972 F.2d 1483 (8th Cir.1992), cert. denied, 506 U.S. 1080 (1993); but cf. Imperial Developers, Inc. v. Seaboard Surety Co., 518 N.W.2d 623 (Minn.App.1994) (finding *Amerinet* not persuasive because it did not distinguish between product and business disparagement; the former is not actionable per se while the latter is). Pecuniary Loss is defined in Restatement (Second) of Torts § 633 (1977).

6. The modern tendency, deriving from the principal case, is to require the plaintiff to be specific only when it is reasonable to expect him to do so, and to allow recovery for a general decline in business if all other reasonably possible causes are excluded. Thus in Craig v. Proctor, 229 Mass. 339, 118 N.E. 647 (1918), a general allegation in the complaint was upheld, but it was said that the defendant might compel the plaintiff to furnish before trial such information as he had. If it is impracticable to

prove specific losses, as is often the case, a plaintiff may adduce sufficient evidence by using detailed statistical and expert proof to exclude the influence of other factors causing the loss of general business. Teilhaber Manufacturing Company v. Unarco Materials Storage, 791 P.2d 1164 (Colo. App. 1989), cert. denied, 803 P.2d 517 (1991).

Title

Horning v. Hardy

Court of Special Appeals of Maryland, 1977.
36 Md.App. 419, 373 A.2d 1273.

["The Hardys" filed suit in trespass and ejectment against "the Hornings," claiming that they owned certain real property that the Hornings were developing. The Hornings filed a counterclaim seeking to recover damages on the two bases of slander of title and tortious interference with contract. The trial court held for the Hornings on the initial suit and for the Hardys on the counterclaim, thus allowing neither party to recover. This court agrees with the holding in the suit for trespass and ejectment, on the ground that the Hardys had failed to establish ownership through either deed descriptions or adverse possession.

On the counterclaim, the trial court regarded slander of title and interference with contract as raising the same issues and analyzed the case in terms of slander of title. The Hornings were developing land in the disputed area and had one house ready for sale. On the morning of the settlement, a phone call from the Hardys' attorney advised the parties to the settlement that the Hardys had filed suit claiming ownership on the previous day. The settlement "was immediately aborted and no sales or settlements have been consummated since that day."]

LISS, JUDGE. * * * Prosser * * * suggests that the tort we are here discussing has been incorrectly designated as "slander of title." Such nomenclature derives from the earliest cases—decided before 1600—where it applied primarily to oral aspersions on the plaintiff's ownership of land, which aspersions prevented the owner from leasing or selling the land. Prosser points out that from the beginning the tort was recognized as being only loosely allied to defamation of the person and was considered instead to be an action on the case for the special damage resulting from the defendant's interference. As the years progressed, the tort was expanded to include written aspersions on property, whether land or personalty, and the disparagement of the quality of property. The tort has, therefore, been known as "disparagement of property," "slander of goods," and "trade libel." * * *

A * * * valuable contribution to the clarification of the tort in Maryland was made by Judge Wilson K. Barnes in the case of Beane v. McMullen, 265 Md. 585, 291 A.2d 37 (1972). Quoting extensively from Prosser, Judge Barnes said:

"Injurious falsehood or disparagement, then, may consist of the publication of matter derogatory to the plaintiff's title to his property, or its quality, or to his business in general, or even to some element of his personal affairs, of a kind calculated to prevent others from dealing with him, or otherwise to interfere with his relations with others to his disadvantage. The cause of action founded upon it resembles that for defamation, but differs from it materially in the greater burden of proof resting on the plaintiff, and the necessity for special damage in all cases. The falsehood must be communicated to a third person, since the tort consists of interference with the relation with such persons. But the plaintiff must plead and prove not only the publication and its disparaging innuendo, as in defamation, but something more. There is no presumption, as in the case of personal slander, that the disparaging statement is false, and the plaintiff must establish its falsity as a part of his cause of action. Although it has been contended that there is no essential reason against liability where even the truth is published for the purpose of doing harm, the policy of the courts has been to encourage the publication of the truth, regardless of motive.

"In addition, the plaintiff must prove in all cases that the publication has played a material and substantial part in inducing others not to deal with him, and that as a result he had suffered special damage. * * *

"There is liability when the defendant acts for a spite motive, and out of a desire to do harm for its own sake; and equally so when he acts for the purpose of doing harm to the interests of the plaintiff in a manner in which he is not privileged so to interfere. There is also liability when the defendant knows that what he says is false, regardless of whether he has an ill motive or intends to affect the plaintiff at all. The deliberate liar must take the risk that his statement will prove to be economically damaging to others; and there is something like the 'scienter' found in an action of deceit. Any of these three is sufficient to constitute 'malice' and support the action. But in the absence of any of the three there is no liability, where the defendant has made his utterance in good faith, even though he may have been negligent in failing to ascertain the facts before he made it." Id. at 607–09, 291 A.2d at 49.

* * *

[S]tate law [following *Gertz,* supra page 944 adopts] the standard of negligence as set forth in Restatement (Second) of Torts, § 580B (Tentative Draft #21, 1975), which states that liability may accrue only if the defendant a) knows that the statement is false and that it defames the other, b) the defendant acts in reckless disregard of these matters, or c) acts negligently in failing to ascertain them. The opinion further held that the quantum of proof required of the plaintiff was the usual negligence standard of the preponderance of the evidence.

In the case here being considered, there is one further complicating factor: the assertion of a qualified privilege by the appellees. Prosser * * * states the privilege to be as follows: "If [the defendant] has a present, existing economic interest to protect, such as the ownership or condition of property * * * he is privileged to prevent performance of the contract of another which threatens it; and for obvious reasons of policy he is likewise privileged to assert an honest claim, or bring or threaten a suit in good faith, to exercise the right of petition to public authorities or to settle his own case out of court."

Further justification for the recognition of the conditional privilege is stated in 1 Harper and James, The Law of Torts, § 6.2 (1956): "If, knowing that another is offering or about to offer land or other thing for sale as his own, he fails to take advantage of a readily available opportunity to inform the intending purchaser, or those likely to become purchasers, as where the sale is by auction, of his claim to the thing, he may preclude himself from afterwards asserting it against the purchaser. Therefore, he must be permitted without fear of liability to protect the enforceability of his claim by asserting it before the purchase is made."

Jacron [supra at 962] makes it clear that the adoption of the negligence standard of fault in defamation cases does not make obsolete the defense of conditional privilege. In a case where a common law conditional privilege is asserted and found as a matter of law to exist, "the negligence standard of *Gertz* is logically subsumed in the higher standard for proving malice, reckless disregard as to truth or falsity * * *." Id. at 600, 350 A.2d at 700. If the plaintiff, faced with a conditional privilege, is unable to prove the malice necessary to overcome that defense, the proof of the lesser standard of negligence would not permit a recovery. [C] In conditional privilege cases, the privilege may be lost either by proof of "constitutional malice" in the form of reckless disregard for truth or falsity or knowing falsehood or by proof of common law malice in the form of spite or ill-will.

The question of whether a conditional privilege exists is a matter of law for the court. Whether the privilege has been abused or forfeited by malice is a question of fact for the trier of the facts. [C] The trial court found as a matter of law that the interference by Hardy with the Hornings' title was privileged. It concluded that the "original plaintiffs asserted an honest claim to the land in question which they had reason to believe was part of their property and they therefore had a present economic interest to protect." We hold this conclusion to be correct * * *.

Appellants urge strenuously that the failure of the appellees to act in good faith to verify the boundaries of the land which they claimed and in their failure to secure expert opinion as to the validity of their claim is evidence of a reckless disregard for the truth. This contention ignores, however, our holding in *Kapiloff* [v. Dunn, 27 Md.App. 514, 343 A.2d 251 (1975)], where we said:

"Although the test for reckless disregard does not avail itself of easy application, one point is clear: mere failure to investigate, in and of itself, is not sufficient evidence under the *New York Times* privilege. * * * Since failure to investigate cannot satisfy the constitutional test of reckless disregard, we cannot perceive how mere failure to seek assistance of educational experts, without more, could satisfy that standard." * * *

The trial court found as a fact that there was no abuse of the conditional privilege and we find no plain error in its conclusions. * * *

Judgments affirmed.

NOTES AND QUESTIONS

1. This was the first form of injurious falsehood. See, e.g., Gerard v. Dickenson, Cro. Eliz. 196, 76 Eng. Rep. 903 (1590), a case remarkably similar to principal case, except it was alleged the defendant knew her claim to the castle was based on forgery.

2. Any type of legally protected property interest that can be sold may be the subject of disparagement, including remainders, leases, mineral rights, trademarks, copyrights, patents, corporate shares and literary productions. A common form of "slander of title" is the assertion, as by filing for record, of a false claim to a mortgage or other lien on the property. See, e.g., Wharton v. Tri-State Drilling & Boring, 175 Vt. 494, 824 A.2d 531 (2003), where defendant mistakenly drilled on plaintiff's property and then levied a mechanic's lien on the property in order to force plaintiff to grant a well easement to defendant.

3. *Privileges.* It appears that any absolute or qualified privilege that applies to defamation under the common law applies also to injurious falsehood. Whenever the defendant is privileged to publish a false statement that is personally defamatory, he must be no less privileged to publish one that is not. See Davis v. Union State Bank, 137 Kan. 264, 20 P.2d 508 (1933) (absolute privilege for statements in pleading filed); Bearce v. Bass, 88 Me. 521, 34 A. 411 (1896) (criticism of public building as badly constructed); Mack, Miller Candle Co. v. Macmillan Co., 239 App. Div. 738, 269 N.Y.S. 33 (1934), aff'd, 266 N.Y. 489, 195 N.E. 167 (1934) (report of judicial proceeding). But see Hatch Cos. Contracting v. Arizona Bank, 170 Ariz. 553, 826 P.2d 1179 (Ariz. Ct. App. 1991); Palmer v. Zaklama, 109 Cal. App. 4th 1367, 1 Cal.Rptr.3d 116 (2003) (State legislatures changed this common law rule by statute. Thereby, if a lis pendens is filed with respect to an action that does not affect title to real property, the lis pendens is groundless and is not subject to judicial privilege.).

4. The defendant has a qualified privilege to protect his own interests by the assertion of a bona fide claim to any kind of property. This includes, for example, an assertion that plaintiff is infringing defendant's patent, copyright or trademark rights by the sale of his product. Oil Conservation Engineering Co. v. Brooks Engineering Co., 52 F.2d 783 (6th Cir. 1931); Alliance Securities Co. v. De Vilbiss, 41 F.2d 668 (6th Cir. 1930). The privilege is, however, qualified and is defeated if defendant's motive is shown to be actual malice, as motivated by a desire to do harm. Sinclair Ref. Co. v. Jones Super Service Station, 188 Ark. 1075, 70 S.W.2d 562 (1934); A.B. Farquhar Co. v. National Harrow Co., 102 Fed. 714 (3d Cir. 1900). It is also defeated if the defendant has acted in bad faith, as where it is found that he did not honestly believe his assertions to be true. Hopkins v. Drowne, 21 R.I. 20, 41 A. 567 (1898); Ezmirlian v. Otto, 139 Cal.App. 486, 34 P.2d 774 (1934).

Like other qualified privileges, the defendant will be liable for excessive publication to persons whom it is not reasonably necessary to reach or if he includes statements that he knows to be untrue. Donovan v. Wilson Sporting Goods Co., 285 F.2d 714 (1st Cir. 1961). See generally Restatement (Second) of Torts §§ 635, 646A.

Goods and Trade

More common, and controversial, is the application of the disparagement tort to goods and trade. An early instance of trade disparagement is Dickes v. Fenne, March N.R. 59, 82 Eng. Rep. 411 (1639) ("Defendant having communication with some of the Customers of the Plaintiff, who was a Brewer, said, That he would give a peck of malt to his mare and she should pisse as good beare as Dickes doth Brew"; no recovery because no allegation of special damages).

In Bose Corp. v. Consumers Union of United States, Inc., 466 U.S. 485 (1984), the Supreme Court entertained an action by Bose against the defendant's magazine "Consumer Reports" commenting adversely on Bose's 901 speakers. The court applied the reasoning derived from *New York Times* in deciding that, since Bose was a public figure, it had the burden of showing "actual malice" by "clear and convincing proof" and that an appellate court must exercise independent judgment on this issue. This displaced the usual standard that findings of fact shall not be set aside unless "clearly erroneous." It remains unclear how far constitutional jurisprudence will influence the action for disparagement of a product. The Supreme Court in Central Hudson Gas and Elec. Corp. v. Public Serv. Comm'n of N.Y., 447 U.S. 557 (1980), and in 44 Liquormart, Inc. v. Rhode Island and Rhode Island Liquor Stores Ass'n, 517 U.S. 484 (1996), has clarified the extent to which the state may regulate advertising. Bans on truthful, nonmisleading information require the state to show not merely that they promote a legitimate state interest, but do so "to a material degree." Liability under a disparagement action will tend to promote the reliability and accuracy of information, and unlike the regulation in *Central Hudson* and *44 Liquormart*, it does not, by its intent, suppress truthful and nonmisleading commercial messages. As in defamation, however, that liability may chill the production of information. Political and commercial speech both attract First Amendment scrutiny and the disparagement action is therefore subject to examination under *New York Times.* Reinforcing the constitutional focus is the Supreme Court's opinion in Sorrell v. IMS Health, Inc., 131 S. Ct. 2653 (2011), wherein data miners compiled and sold information about prescription habits of physicians. Vermont attempted to regulate this practice, arguing that it was detrimental to physicians' faithfulness to patients and privacy. The Court struck down the provision as violative of plaintiffs' first amendment rights in commercial speech. The assertion of the state interest could not stand against the merits of a market in this information. To punish the publication of false information, as in falsely claiming to have been awarded military decorations, does not pass muster under the First Amendment that exalts that value against all others. U.S. v. Alvarez,, 132 S. Ct. 2537 (2012).

Intentional Infliction of Harm and Causation

Injurious falsehood requires malice involving a showing of knowledge that the statement was false, or intent to harm the plaintiff or affect his interests in an unprivileged manner. Prosser, Injurious Falsehood: The Basis of Liability, 59 Colum.L.Rev. 425 (1959). See Advance Music Corp. v. American Tobacco Co., 296 N.Y. 79, 70 N.E.2d 401 (1946) (sufficient to allege that defendants "wantonly caused damage to the plaintiff by a system of conduct [that] warrants an inference that they intend harm of that type"); Remick Music Corp. v. American Tobacco Co., 57 F.Supp. 475 (S.D.N.Y.1944) ("defendants deliberately and wilfully indulged in such unfairness"); Dale System v. General Teleradio, 105 F.Supp. 745 (S.D.N.Y.1952) ("intentional publication for the sake of injuring the plaintiff"). The harm identified must have been either intended or the "natural and probable result" of the publication of the false statement. It is not sufficient that the harm is merely reasonably foreseeable. Palmer Bruyn & Parker Pty Limited v. Parsons, 208 C.L.R. 388 (2001) (H.Ct. Australia) (loss of plaintiff's business due to false and malicious letter published to local municipality alderman was harm not caused in the relevant sense); and Clark County Sch. Dist. v. Virtual Educ. Software, Inc., 213 P.3d 496 (Nev. 2009).

Relationship of Injurious Falsehood to Defamation

The wellspring of the tort is deceit, although most attention has been devoted to its overlap with defamation. The same statement may both defame a person and disparage the goods he sells. See Hatchard v. Mege, 18 Q.B.D. 771 (1887). The distinction drawn by the courts is that if the statement made reflects only upon the quality of what the plaintiff has to sell, or the character of his business as such, it is merely injurious falsehood, and proof of special damage is essential to the cause of action. Evans v. Harlow, 5 Q.B. 624 (1844); National Refining Co. v. Benzo Gas Motor Fuel Co., 20 F.2d 763 (8th Cir. 1927); U.S. Healthcare, Inc. v. Blue Cross of Greater Philadelphia, 898 F.2d 914 (3d Cir. 1990). On the other hand, if the statement imputes to the plaintiff reprehensible personal characteristics or misconduct, it is regarded as defamation. Merle v. Sociological Research Film Corp., 166 App. Div. 376, 152 N.Y.S. 829 (1915) (Defendant filmmaker implied that plaintiff factory owner was connected to "white slave traffic"); Kilpatrick v. Edge, 85 N.J.L. 7, 88 A. 839 (1913) (misconduct in a Turkish bath). In appropriate circumstances, if injurious falsehood is established, an injunction may be granted; but cf. defamation. Restatement (Second) of Torts § 626 cmt. b (1977); Restatement (Second) of Torts § 942 cmt. e (1979).

Testing Systems, Inc. v. Magnaflux Corp.

United States District Court, Eastern District of Pennsylvania, 1966.
251 F.Supp. 286.

[Plaintiff and defendant were competing manufacturers of equipment, devices and systems for use in testing industrial and commercial materials. The complaint alleged that defendant circulated to plaintiff's current and prospective customers a false report to the effect that the United States Government had tested plaintiff's product, and found it to be only about 40% as effective as that of the defendant. Plaintiff also claimed that at a manufacturers' convention in Philadelphia defendant's agent, in the presence of plaintiff's current and prospective customers, "did in a loud voice state that * * * [plaintiff's] * * * stuff is no good," and that "the government is throwing them out."]

LORD, DISTRICT JUDGE. This is an action for trade libel or disparagement of property. * * * The matter is now before this Court on defendant's motion to dismiss for failure to state a claim upon which relief can be granted.

For the purposes of this motion, defendant admits the truth of the allegation, but asserts that the action must nevertheless be dismissed because (1) the defendant did no more than make an unfavorable comparison of plaintiff's product with its own; and (2) even assuming that the statements were actionable, plaintiff has failed to allege his damages with the required specificity. * * *

It would serve no useful purpose to dwell at length on the issue of unfavorable comparison. Suffice it to say, as the defendant properly points out, that a statement which takes the form of an unfavorable comparison of products, or which "puffs" or exaggerates the quality of one's own product is not ordinarily actionable. [Cc] This has long been the rule in England, where the action originated, and is now well established in the vast majority of United States jurisdictions. [Cc]

However, this Court is not convinced by the defendant's arguments that his comments amounted to mere unfavorable comparison. The modern history of the doctrine of unfavorable comparison and its permissible use in the conduct of business traces its origin to the leading English case of White v. Mellin [1895] A.C. 154. There the defendant had advertised his product as being far more healthful than plaintiff's. In refusing relief the Court established the precedent that irrespective of their truth or falsity, statements by one competitor which compare his product with that of another are not actionable.

It does not follow from this, however, that every trade disparagement is protectible under the guise of unfavorable comparison merely because the perpetrator was canny enough to mention not only the product of his competitor but also his own. The decision in White v. Mellin, supra, was founded on the near impossibility of ascertaining the truth or falsity of general allegations respecting the superiority of one product over another. To decide otherwise, explained Lord Herschell, would turn the courts "into a machinery for advertising rival productions by obtaining a judicial determination [as to] which of the two was better. [C] One is expected to believe in the superiority of his wares, and he may properly declare his belief to interested parties. It has even been said that he may 'boast untruthfully of his wares.'" Phila. D. Prod. v. Quaker City I. Co., 306 Pa. 164, 172, 159 A. 3 (1932). * * *

The fine line that separates healthy competitive effort from underhanded business tactics is frequently difficult to determine. Apart from the tradesman's right of free speech, which must be vigorously safeguarded, the public has a genuine interest in learning the relative merits of particular products, however that may come about. * * *

Nonetheless, there is an outer perimeter to permissible conduct. The tradesman must be assured that his competitors will not be suffered to engage in conduct which falls below the minimum standard of fair dealing. "[I]t is no answer that they can defend themselves by also resorting to disparagement. A self-respecting business man will not voluntarily adopt, and should not be driven to adopt, a selling method which he regards as undignified, unfair, and repulsive. A competitor should not, by pursuing an unethical practice force his rival to choose between its adoption and the loss of his trade." Wolfe, Unfair Competition, 47 Yale L.J. 1304, 1334–35 (1938).

The defendant's comments in the case presently before this Court do not entitle him to the protection accorded to "unfavorable comparison." There is a readily observable difference between saying that one's product is, in general, better than another's * * * and asserting, as here, that such other's is only 40% as effective as one's own. The former, arguably, merely expresses an opinion, the truth or falsity of which is difficult or impossible of ascertainment. The latter, however, is an assertion of fact, not subject to the same frailties of proof, implying that the party making the statement is fortified with the substantive facts necessary to make it. This distinction has never been seriously questioned. See e.g. Restatement, Torts, §§ 626, 627, 628. The defendant in this case admittedly circulated to plaintiff's present and prospective customers false statements to the effect that the government had tested both products and found the defendant's to be 60% more effective than plaintiff's. This is not the sort of "comparison" that courts will protect.

Apart from this, there is at least one additional factor which withdraws the defendant's comments from the category of unfavorable comparison. Not content with making the admittedly false statements and allowing them to be evaluated independently of any extraneous influence, the defendant here gave added authenticity to its assertions, by invoking the reputation of a third party, the United States Government. It is unnecessary to speculate on the additional force the defendant's remarks must have had when coupled with the purported approval of so highly credible a source. This, of course, is to say nothing of the statements to the effect that plaintiff had been "thrown out," which by no stretch of the imagination could be termed mere comparison.

For all of the above reasons, it is the judgment of this Court that the defendant's remarks are actionable.

NOTES AND QUESTIONS

1. How does this case compare with Vulcan Metals Co. v. Simmons Mfg. Co., supra page 1139?

2. The competitor's "puffing" privilege permits statements of comparison, that the defendant's goods are the best in the market, that they are better than the plaintiff's, or other boasting or exaggeration, even though the defendant is fully aware that what he says is false, and the publication is made for the purpose of injuring the plaintiff by taking business away from him. One of the leading cases is White v. Mellin, [1895] A.C. 154, where the defendant sold packages of plaintiff's baby food with a wrapper affixed to them which stated that defendant's was better. This was held to be privileged. In this respect, there is an obvious difference from personal defamation, which would not be privileged under the same circumstances.

3. Competition for business does not, however, justify intentional false statements of fact concerning the competitor's business or product

when the statements are not confined to comparing the product or conduct of the competitor with that of the plaintiff. Unfair competition is not privileged. U.S. Healthcare, Inc. v. Blue Cross of Greater Philadelphia, 898 F.2d 914 (3d Cir. 1990); Hopkins Chemical Co. v. Read Drug & Chemical Co., 124 Md. 210, 92 A. 478 (1914).

Sometimes the courts have leaned quite far to avoid finding an assertion to be a misstatement of fact. Thus in Nonpareil Cork Mfg. Co. v. Keasbey & Mattison Co., 108 Fed. 721 (E.D. Pa. 1901), a statement that cork covering for steam pipes was a "fraud" was held to be "really but the expression of an unfavorable opinion of the goods" of its competitor. See also Dairy Stores, Inc. v. Sentinel Pub. Co., 104 N.J. 125, 516 A.2d 220 (1986) (applying the distinction between fact and opinion in defamation law). But such expressions are not uncommon among rivals in trade, and their correctness in each instance is for determination by those whose custom is sought, and not by the courts. Is the standard too tolerant of commercial conduct that misleads consumers in the modern marketplace? See Hayden, A Goodly Apple Rotten at the Heart: Commercial Disparagement in Comparative Advertising as Common Law Tortious Unfair Competition, 76 Iowa L. Rev. 67 (1990).

(B) INTERFERENCE WITH EXISTING OR PROSPECTIVE CONTRACTUAL RELATIONS

Lumley v. Gye

Queen's Bench, 1853.
2 El. & Bl. 216, 118 Eng. Rep. 749.

[The declaration alleged: Plaintiff, manager of the Queens Theatre for performing operas, contracted with Johanna Wagner for her to perform in his theatre for a designated time. She agreed not to perform elsewhere during the contract term. Defendant, "knowing the premises and maliciously intruding to injure plaintiff * * *, enticed and procured Wagner to refuse to perform." Defendant demurred.]

ERLE, J. The question raised upon this demurrer is, Whether an action will lie by the proprietor of a theatre against a person who maliciously procures an entire abandonment of a contract to perform exclusively at that theatre for a certain time; whereby damage was sustained? And it seems to me that it will. The authorities are numerous and uniform, that an action will lie by a master against a person who procures that a servant should unlawfully leave his service. The principle involved in these cases comprises the present; for, there, the right of action in the master arises from the wrongful act of the defendant in procuring that the person hired should break his contract, by putting an end to the relation of employer and employed; and the present case is the same. If it is objected that this class of actions for procuring a breach of contract of hiring rests upon no principle, and ought not to be extended beyond the cases heretofore decided, and that, as those have related to contracts respecting trade, manufactures, or household service, and not to performance at a theatre, therefore they are no authority for an action in respect of a contract for such performance; the answer appears to me to be, that the class of cases referred to rests upon the principle that the procurement of the violation of the rights is a cause of action, and that, when this principle is applied to a violation of a right arising upon a contract of hiring, the nature of the service contracted for is immaterial.

It is clear that the procurement of the violation of a right is a cause of action in all instances where the violation is an actionable wrong, as in violations of a right to property, whether real or personal, or to personal security: he who procures the wrong is a joint wrongdoer, and may be sued, either alone or jointly with the agent, in the appropriate action for the wrong complained of. * * * He who maliciously procures a damage to another by violation of his right ought to be made to indemnify; and that, whether he procures an actionable wrong or a breach of contract. He who procures the non-delivery of goods according to contract may inflict an injury, the same as he who procures the abstraction of goods after delivery; and both ought on the same ground to be made responsible. The remedy on the contract may be inadequate * * *.

The result is that there ought to be, in my opinion, judgment for the plaintiff.

[The concurring opinion of CROMPTON, J., and dissenting opinion of COLERIDGE, J., are omitted.]

NOTES AND QUESTIONS

1. The companion case of Lumley v. Wagner, 1 De G.M. & G. 604, 42 Eng. Rep. 687 (1852), a landmark in the law of equitable relief, affirmed injunctions preventing Miss Wagner from breaking the negative covenant in her contract with Lumley by singing for Gye at Covent Garden or elsewhere during the period of her contractual obligation to Lumley. This was a battle in a long war between Lumley and Gye, rival London impresarios. Johanna Wagner, a cantatrice to the King of Prussia and niece of Richard Wagner, finally returned to the London stage five years later, but London audiences were deprived of her voice at its zenith.

2. The principle announced in the principal case was received at first with a great deal of hesitation and disapproval. It was reaffirmed thirty years later in Bowen v. Hall, 6 Q.B.D. 333 (1881), and then by degrees was extended—first to contracts other than those for personal services, and then to a holding that ill-will on the part of the defendant was not essential to the tort. In English law, the principal case was treated as an example of a more "general tort of actionable interference with contractual rights." D.C. Thomson & Co. Ltd. v. Deakin, [1952] Ch. 646. The House of Lords repudiated this line of cases in OBG Ltd. v. Allan, [2008] 1 A.C. 1 [H.L.]; Douglas v. Hello! Ltd. (No. 3); [2003] 1 All E.R. 1087; Mainstream Properties Ltd. v. Young, [2007] 4 All E.R. 545, holding that liability under the principal case turns on defendant "actually" realizing that the action will have the effect of breaching the contract. It is not enough to procure an act that has that effect as a matter of law or construction of the contract. The English law then draws a line between the cases flowing from the principal case and those cases of interference with contract or economic relations that require the use of unlawful means that would be independently actionable or else would have been actionable by a third

party if loss had been suffered. The English law conforms with the law set forth in *Della Penna*, below.

3. Defendant's tortious conduct is not confined to inducing the third person to break the contract. It may apply to other means of preventing the third person from performing. See, e.g., Phez Co. v. Salem Fruit Union, 103 Or. 514, 205 P. 970 (1922) (D refuses to carry out his contract to supply goods to T, to prevent T from supplying them to P).

4. Plaintiff must prove defendant knew of the contract. Imperial Ice Co. v. Rossier, 18 Cal.2d 33, 112 P.2d 631 (1941); Continental Research, Inc. v. Cruttenden, Podesta & Miller, 222 F.Supp. 190 (D.C.Minn. 1963) (circumstantial evidence of knowledge); Mid-Continent Tel. Corp. v. Home Tel. Co., 319 F.Supp. 1176 (D.C. Miss. 1970) (reason to know and reasonable ignorance).

5. A third party beneficiary will be able to recover in tort for interference with the contract if he could have recovered in an action on the contract. Reynolds v. Owen, 34 Conn. Sup. 107, 380 A.2d 543 (1977).

6. If the third party has already broken the contract or decided to do so, and offers to contract with the defendant, defendant has not induced the breach. See Middleton v. Wallichs Music & Entertainment Co., 24 Ariz.App. 180, 536 P.2d 1072 (1975); Northern Wis. Co-op. Tobacco Pool v. Bekkedal, 182 Wis. 571, 197 N.W. 936 (1924).

7. Does the tort interfere with the freedom of a party to a contract to breach and pay contract damages as a result? The theory of *efficient breach* holds that the freedom to breach and recontract more favorably, allows resources to be allocated to a higher valued use. Dean Perlman, Interference with Contract and Other Economic Expectancies: A Clash of Tort and Contract Doctrine, 49 U. Chi. L. Rev. 61 (1982), formulates the tort to avoid this flouting of the efficiency goal of contract law.

But the subject contracts of the tort are relational contracts—employment, leases, professional, and long-term business relationships—where the goal of efficient breach is remote and the goal of maintenance of cooperation more important. Thus the question is whether the tort supports that relational goal. See BeVier, Reconsidering Inducement, 76 Va. L. Rev. 877 (1990) (viewing the tort as promoting parties' value-enhancing behavior) and Partlett, From Victorian Opera to Rock and Rap: Inducement to Breach of Contract in the Music Industry, 66 Tulane L. Rev. 771 (1992) (viewing the tort as filling gaps in contract relationship and obliging the dissemination of information about the existence of the contract). But see Dobbs, Tortious Interference with Contractual Relationships, 34 Ark. L. Rev. 335 (1980) (criticizing the tort for its authoritarian and anti-autonomy tendencies) and Gergen, Tortious Interference: How it is Engulfing Commercial Law, Why This is Not Entirely Bad, and a Prudential Response, 38 Ariz. L. Rev. 1175 (1996) (criticizing economic analysis and supporting application of the tort to avoid unforeseen opportunistic behavior).

Consider how defamation claims could be made as a part of an interference claim. Could freedom of speech be used as a defense? What if the statements were puffery or parody? See King, Defamation Claims Based on Parody and Other Fanciful Communications Not Intended to Be Understood as Fact, 3 Utah L. Rev. 875 (2008).

Bacon v. St. Paul Union Stockyards Co.

Supreme Court of Minnesota, 1924.
161 Minn. 522, 201 N.W. 326.

[Plaintiff's complaint alleges that he was employed by the Drover Livestock Commission Co., engaged in buying, selling and dealing in livestock in the defendant's stockyards, but that the defendant "wrongfully, unlawfully, and willfully excluded plaintiff from its said stockyards, and barred and prevented him from carrying on his occupation therein, and forbade any person, firm, or corporation to employ him in or about" the stockyards. Defendant's demurrer to the complaint was sustained. Plaintiff appealed.]

PER CURIAM. * * * The wrongful interference with the contract relations of others causing a breach is a tort. We are of the opinion that the complaint states a cause of action for wrongful interference with plaintiff's employment. It appears from the complaint that the plaintiff had steady employment, and that defendant wrongfully, willfully, and unlawfully prevented him from continuing in that employment. We think such conduct is in violation of plaintiff's rights. [C] The defendant may have reasons to justify its conduct, but such reasons do not appear in the complaint. * * *

Reversed.

NOTES AND QUESTIONS

1. The principle also applies to conduct making plaintiff's performance of his contract more burdensome or expensive, as by deliberate damage to a highway he is under a duty to repair. McNary v. Chamberlain, 34 Conn. 384, 91 Am. Dec. 732 (1867); See also Cue v. Breland, 78 Miss. 864, 29 So. 850 (1901); Piedmont Cotton Mills v. H.W. Ivey Constr. Co., 109 Ga.App. 876, 137 S.E.2d 528 (1964). Cf. Price v. Sorrell, 784 P.2d 614 (Wyo. 1989) (Court refused to adopt Restatement section 766A finding that causing performance of a contract to be more costly "as an element of proof is too speculative and subject to abuse to provide a meaningful basis for a cause of action).

2. In these "hinderance" cases, under Restatement (Second) of Torts § 766A, the bulk involve a physical interference with person or property and the commission of an independent tort. This duplication of protection, and the uncertain dimensions of liability, grounded the court's reluctance to adopt § 766A liability in Windsor Securities, Inc. v. Hartford Life Ins. Co., 986 F.2d 655 (3d Cir. 1993) (plaintiff investment advisors claim against mutual fund sponsor for restrictions by defendant on investor's ability to transfer investments between accounts finding no liability on the basis that the action was not "wrongful"). The interference must cause plaintiff to lose a right under a contract or make contract rights more costly or less valuable. Thus no action available where defendant induced plaintiff's tenant to vacate premises but lease was not breached. Sampson Investments v. Jondex Corp., 176 Wis.2d 55, 499 N.W.2d 177 (1993).

Della Penna v. Toyota Motor Sales, U.S.A., Inc.

Supreme Court of California, 1995.
11 Cal.4th 376, 45 Cal.Rptr.2d 436, 902 P.2d 740.

ARABIAN, J. We granted review to reexamine, in light of divergent rulings from the Court of Appeal and a doctrinal evolution among other state high courts, the elements of the tort variously known as interference with "prospective economic advantage," "prospective contractual relations," or "prospective economic relations," and the allocation of the burdens of proof between the parties to such an action. We conclude that those Court of Appeal opinions requiring proof of a so-called "wrongful act" as a component of the cause of action, and allocating the burden of proving it to the plaintiff, are the better reasoned decisions; we accordingly adopt that analysis as our own, disapproving language in prior opinions of this court to the contrary. Such a requirement, incorporating the views of several other jurisdictions, much of the Restatement Second of Torts, the better reasoned decisions of the Court of Appeal, and the views of leading academic authorities, sensibly redresses the balance between providing a remedy for predatory economic behavior and keeping legitimate business competition outside litigative bounds. We do not in this case, however, go beyond approving the requirement of a showing of wrongfulness as part of the plaintiff's case; the case, if any, to be made for adopting refinements to that element of the tort—requiring the plaintiff to prove, for example, that the defendant's conduct amounted to an independently tortious act, or was a species of anticompetitive behavior proscribed by positive law, or was motivated by unalloyed malice—can be considered on another day, and in another case.

In this case, after the trial court modified the standard jury instruction to require the plaintiff automobile dealer to show that defendant Toyota's interference with his business relationships was "wrongful," the jury returned a verdict for Toyota. The Court of Appeal reversed the ensuing judgment and ordered a new trial on the ground that plaintiff's burden of proof did not encompass proof of a "wrongful" act and that the modified jury instruction was therefore erroneous. Given our conclusion that the plaintiff's burden does include proof that the defendant's conduct was wrongful by some measure other than an interference with the plaintiff's interest itself, we now reverse the Court of Appeal and direct that the judgment of the trial court be affirmed.

I

John Della Penna, an automobile wholesaler doing business as Pacific Motors, brought this action for damages against defendant Toyota Motor Sales, U.S.A., Inc., and its Lexus division, alleging that certain business conduct of defendants both violated [the] state antitrust statute [c], and constituted an intentional interference with his economic relations. The impetus for Della Penna's suit arose out of the 1989 introduction into the American luxury car market of Toyota's Lexus automobile. Prior to introducing the Lexus, the evidence at trial showed, both the manufacturer, Toyota Motor Corporation, and defendant, the American distributor, had been concerned about the possibility that a resale market might develop for the Lexus in Japan.

* * * Fearing that auto wholesalers in the United States might reexport Lexus models back to Japan for resale, and concerned that, with production and the availability of Lexus models in the American market limited, reexports would jeopardize its fledgling network of American Lexus dealers, Toyota inserted in its dealership agreements a "no export" clause, providing that the dealer was "authorized to sell [Lexus automobiles] only to customers located in the United States. [Dealer] agrees that it will not sell [Lexus automobiles] for resale or use outside the United States. [Dealer] agrees to abide by any export policy established by [distributor]."

Following introduction into the American market, it soon became apparent that some domestic Lexus units were being diverted for foreign sales, principally to Japan. To counter this effect, Toyota managers wrote to their retail dealers, reminding them of the "no-export" policy and explaining that exports for foreign resale could jeopardize the supply of Lexus automobiles available for the United States market. In addition, Toyota compiled a list of "offenders"—dealers and others believed by Toyota to be involved heavily in the developing Lexus foreign resale market—which it distributed to Lexus dealers in the United States. American Lexus dealers were also warned that doing business with those whose names appeared on the "offenders" list might lead to a series of graduated sanctions, from reducing a dealer's allocation to possible reevaluation of the dealer's franchise agreement.

During the years 1989 and 1990, plaintiff Della Penna did a profitable business as an auto wholesaler purchasing Lexus automobiles, chiefly from the Lexus of Stevens Creek retail outlet, at near retail price and exporting them to Japan for resale. By late 1990, however, plaintiff's sources began to dry up, primarily as a result of the "offenders list." Stevens Creek ceased selling models to plaintiff; gradually other sources declined to sell to him as well.

In February 1991, plaintiff filed this lawsuit against Toyota Motor Sales, U.S.A., Inc., alleging both state antitrust claims * * * and interference with his economic relationship with Lexus retail dealers. At the close of plaintiff's case-in-chief, the trial court granted Toyota's motion for nonsuit with respect to the remaining [antitrust] claim (plaintiff had previously abandoned a related claim—unfair competition—prior to trial). The tort cause of action went to the jury, however, under the standard BAJI instructions applicable to such claims with one significant exception. At the request of defendant and over plaintiff's objection, the trial judge modified BAJI No. 7.82—the basic instruction identifying the elements of the tort and indicating the burden of proof—to require plaintiff to prove that defendant's alleged interfering conduct was "wrongful." * * *

II

A

Although legal historians have traced the origins of the so-called "interference torts" as far back as the Roman law, the proximate historical impetus for their modern development lay in mid-19th century English common law. (See, e.g., Sayre, Inducing Breach of

Contract (1923) 36 Harv. L.Rev. 663; Note, Tortious Interference With Contractual Relations in the Nineteenth Century: The Transformation of Property, Contract, and Tort (1980) 93 Harv. L.Rev. 1510.) The opinion of the Queen's Bench in Lumley v. Gye (1853) 2 El. & Bl. 216 [118 Eng. Rep. 749], a case that has become a standard in torts casebooks, is widely cited as the origin of the two torts—interference with contract and its sibling, interference with prospective economic relations[1]—in the form in which they have come down to us. * * *

The opinion in Lumley v. Gye [c] dealt, of course, with conduct intended to induce the breach of an existing contract, not conduct intended to prevent or persuade others not to contract with the plaintiff. That such an interference with prospective economic relations might itself be tortious was confirmed by the Queen's Bench over the next 40 years. In Temperton v. Russell (1893) 1 Q.B. 715 (Temperton), a labor union, embroiled in a dispute with a firm of builders, announced what today would be called a secondary boycott, intended to force a resolution of the union's grievances by pressuring suppliers of the builder to cease furnishing him construction materials. A failure to comply with the union's boycott demands, suppliers were warned, would result in union pressure on those who bought their supplies not to deal with them.

One such supplier of the builder, Temperton, sued the union's leadership, alleging that his business had been injured by breaches of supply contracts and the refusal of others to do business with him, all as a result of the union's threats. A unanimous Queen's Bench upheld the jury's verdict for the plaintiff, reasoning in part on the authority of Lumley v. Gye, supra, 2 El. & Bl. 216, that in the words of Lord Esher, the Master of the Rolls, "the distinction . . . between the claim for inducing persons to break contracts already entered into . . . and . . . inducing persons not to enter into contracts . . . can[not] prevail." (*Temperton*, supra, 1 Q.B. at page 728.)

"There was the same wrongful intent in both cases, wrongful because malicious," Lord Esher wrote. "There was the same kind of injury to the plaintiff. It seems rather a fine distinction to say that, where a defendant maliciously induces a person not to carry out a contract already made with the plaintiff and so injures the plaintiff, it is actionable, but where he injures the plaintiff by maliciously preventing a person from entering into a contract with the plaintiff, which he would otherwise have entered into, it is not actionable." (*Temperton*, supra, 1 Q.B. at page 728.)

As a number of courts and commentators have observed, the keystone of the liability imposed in Lumley v. Gye, supra, 2 El. & Bl. 216, and *Temperton*, supra, 1 Q.B. 715, to judge from the opinions of the justices, appears to have been the "malicious" intent of a defendant in enticing an employee to breach her contract with the plaintiff, and in damaging the business of one who refused to cooperate with the union in achieving its bargaining aims. While some have doubted whether the

[1] Throughout this opinion, in an effort to avoid both cumbersome locutions and clumsy acronyms ("IIPEA"), we use the phrase "interference with economic relations" to refer to the tort generally known as "intentional interference with prospective contractual or economic relations" and to distinguish it from the cognate form, "intentional interference with contract."

use of the word "malicious" amounted to anything more than an intent to commit an act, knowing it would harm the plaintiff (see, e.g., Dobbs, Tortious Interference With Contractual Relationships (1980) 34 Ark. L.Rev. 335, 347, fn. 37), Dean Keeton, assessing the state of the tort as late as 1984, remarked that "[w]ith intent to interfere as the usual basis of the action, the cases have turned almost entirely upon the defendant's motive or purpose and the means by which he has sought to accomplish it. As in the cases of interference with contract, any manner of intentional invasion of the plaintiff's interests may be sufficient if the purpose is not a proper one." (Prosser & Keeton on Torts (5th ed. 1984) Interference with Prospective Advantage, § 130, page 1009.)

It was, legal historians have suggested, this early accent on the defendant's "intentionality" that was responsible for allying the interference torts with their remote relatives, intentional torts of a quite different order—battery, for example, or false imprisonment. More than one account of the rise of the tort has relied on Lord Bowen's statement in an interference with contract case that "intentionally to do that which is calculated in the ordinary course of events to damage, and which does, in fact, damage another in that person's property or trade, is actionable if done without just cause or excuse." (Mogul Steamship Co. v. McGregor, Gow & Co. (1889) 23 Q.B.D. 598, 613.)

One consequence of this superficial kinship was the assimilation to the interference torts of the pleading and burden of proof requirements of the "true" intentional torts: the requirement that the plaintiff need only allege a so-called "prima facie tort" by showing the defendant's awareness of the economic relation, a deliberate interference with it, and the plaintiff's resulting injury. [C] By this account of the matter—the traditional view of the torts and the one adopted by the first Restatement of Torts—the burden then passed to the defendant to demonstrate that its conduct was privileged, that is, "justified" by a recognized defense such as the protection of others or, more likely in this context, the defendant's own competitive business interests. (See, e.g., Restatement, Torts (1939) § 766, coms. *b–m*, pages 50–63 * * *)

These and related features of the economic relations tort and the requirements surrounding its proof and defense led, however, to calls for a reexamination and reform as early as the 1920's. Tracing the origins and the current status of the two interference torts in 1923, Francis Sayre concluded that "a somewhat uncertain law has resulted. . . . Courts still punctiliously repeat the well-known formula which requires 'malice,' or 'without just cause' . . . as one of the requirements of the tort; but there has been such a lack of agreement as to what constitutes 'malice' or 'absence of justification' that such words are becoming little more than empty phrases. . . . Is it not time to formulate the problem of what these worn phrases mean?" (Sayre, Inducing Breach of Contract, supra, 36 Harv. L.Rev. at pages 672, 674–675, fn. Omitted.) The nature of the wrong itself seemed to many unduly vague, inviting suit and hampering the presentation of coherent defenses. More critically in the view of others, the procedural effects of applying the prima facie tort principle to what is essentially a business context led to even more untoward consequences.

Because the plaintiff's initial burden of proof was such a slender one, amounting to no more than showing the defendant's conscious act and plaintiff's economic injury, critics argued that legitimate business competition could lead to time consuming and expensive lawsuits (not to speak of potential liability) by a rival, based on conduct that was regarded by the commercial world as both commonplace and appropriate. The "black letter" rules of the Restatement of Torts surrounding the elements and proof of the tort, some complained, might even suggest to "foreign lawyers reading the Restatement as an original matter [that] the whole competitive order of American industry is prima facie illegal." (Statement of Professor Carl Auerbach at ALI Proceedings, quoted in Perlman, Interference With Contract and Other Economic Expectancies: A Clash of Tort and Contract Doctrine (1982) 49 U. Chi. L.Rev. 61, 79, fn. 89 * * *)

Calls for a reformulation of both the elements and the means of establishing the economic relations tort reached a height around the time the Restatement Second of Torts was being prepared for publication and are reflected in its departures from its predecessor's version. Acknowledging criticism, the American Law Institute discarded the prima facie tort requirement of the first Restatement. A new provision, section 766B, required that the defendant's conduct be "improper," and adopted a multifactor "balancing" approach, identifying seven factors for the trier of fact to weigh in determining a defendant's liability. The Restatement Second of Torts, however, declined to take a position on the issue of which of the parties bore the burden of proof, relying on the "considerable disagreement on who has the burden of pleading and proving certain matters" and the observation that "the law in this area has not fully congealed but is still in a formative stage." (See Rest.2d Torts (1965 ed.) Introductory Note, ch. 37, pages 5–6.) In addition, the Restatement Second provided that a defendant might escape liability by showing that his conduct was justifiable and did not include the use of "wrongful means." (Id., § 768–771.)

B

In the meantime, however, an increasing number of state high courts had traveled well beyond the Restatement Second's reforms by redefining and otherwise recasting the elements of the economic relations tort and the burdens surrounding its proof and defenses. In Top Serv. Body Shop, Inc. v. Allstate Ins. Co. (1978) 283 Ore. 201 [582 P.2d 1365] (Top Service), the Oregon Supreme Court, assessing this " 'most fluid and rapidly growing tort,' " noted that "efforts to consolidate both recognized and unsettled lines of development into a general theory of 'tortious interference' have brought to the surface the difficulties of defining the elements of so general a tort without sweeping within its terms a wide variety of socially very different conduct." [C]

Recognizing the force of these criticisms, the court went on to hold in *Top Service* [c] that a claim of interference with economic relations "is made out when interference resulting in injury to another is wrongful by some measure beyond the fact of the interference itself. Defendant's liability may arise from improper motives or from the use of improper means. They may be wrongful by reason of a statute or other regulation, or a recognized rule of common law, or perhaps an established standard of a trade or profession. No question of privilege arises unless the interference would be wrongful but for the privilege; it becomes an issue only if the acts charged would be tortious on the part of an unprivileged defendant." [C]

Four years later, the views of the Oregon Supreme Court in *Top Service* [c] were adopted by the Utah Supreme Court. In Leigh Furniture and Carpet Co. v. Isom (Utah 1982) 657 P.2d 293, that court underlined the same concerns that had moved the Oregon Supreme Court in *Top Service*: "The problem with the prima facie tort approach is that basing liability on a mere showing that defendant intentionally interfered with plaintiff's prospective economic relations makes actionable all sorts of contemporary examples of otherwise legitimate persuasion, such as efforts to persuade others not to . . . engage in certain activities, or deal with certain entities. The major issue in the controversy—justification for the defendant's conduct—is left to be resolved on the affirmative defense of privilege. In short, the prima facie approach to the tort of interference with prospective economic relations requires too little of the plaintiff." [C]

The Utah Supreme Court went on, however, to reject the alternative, multifactor approach adopted by the Restatement Second: "We concur in the Restatement (Second)'s rejection of the prima facie tort approach because it leaves too much uncertainty about the requirements for a recognized privilege and the defendant's burden of pleading and proving these and other matters. [C] But we also reject the Restatement (Second)'s definition of the tort because of its complexity. We seek a better alternative." [C] That alternative, the court concluded, was the one advanced by the Oregon Supreme Court in *Top Service*, [c], a "middle ground" that requires "the plaintiff to allege and prove more than the prima facie tort, but not to negate all defenses of privilege." [Cc]

Over the past decade or so, close to a majority of the high courts of American jurisdictions have imported into the economic relations tort variations on the *Top Service* line of reasoning, explicitly approving a rule that requires the plaintiff in such a suit to plead and prove the alleged interference was either "wrongful," "improper," "illegal," "independently tortious" or some variant on these formulations. * * *

III

* * *

[O]ur early economic relations cases were principally of two types, either the classic master and servant pattern of the pre-Lumley v. Gye cases (see, e.g., Buxbom v. Smith (1944) 23 Cal. 2d 535, 548 [145 P.2d 305] [hiring away of plaintiff's employees by defendant after plaintiff had built up his business to distribute defendant's publication and defendant had breached distribution contract held actionable as "an unfair method of interference with advantageous relations"]) or those involving circumscribed kinds of business relations in which the plaintiff, typically a real estate broker or attorney working on a contingency, sued to recover fees after defendant had refused to share property sales proceeds or a personal injury recovery (see, e.g.,

Buckaloo v. Johnson (1975) 14 Cal. 3d 815 [122 Cal. Rptr. 745, 537 P.2d 865] [defendant refused to pay plaintiff his broker's commission on the sale of beach property after plaintiff had discussed sale with buyers and directed them to defendant; held, the complaint stated a claim for relief for intentional interference with prospective economic relations].)

* * *

Our opinion in *Buckaloo* [c] reviewed a number of Court of Appeal decisions upholding the applicability of the tort to real estate brokerage situations [C] and concluded by identifying the following elements of the cause of action. "In a real estate brokerage context these are: (1) an economic relationship between broker and vendor or broker and vendee containing the probability of future economic benefit to the broker, (2) knowledge by the defendant of the existence of the relationship, (3) intentional acts on the part of the defendant designed to disrupt the relationship, (4) actual disruption of the relationship, (5) damages to the plaintiff proximately caused by the acts of the defendant." [C]

"In California," we went on to observe, "privilege or justification is an affirmative defense, and the lack thereof need not be shown by the original pleader." [C] A note of caution, however, crept into our formulation of principles at this point. "Perhaps the most significant privilege or justification for interference with a prospective business advantage is free competition," we wrote, "Ours is a competitive economy in which business entities vie for economic advantage. In a sense, all vendees are potential buyers of the products and services of all sellers in a given line, and success goes to him who is able to induce potential customers not to deal with a competitor." [C]

In Seaman's Direct Buying Service, Inc. v. Standard Oil Co. (1984) 36 Cal. 3d 752 [206 Cal. Rptr. 354, 686 P.2d 1158] (Seaman's), overruled in part by Freeman & Mills, Inc. v. Belcher Oil Co. (1995) 11 Cal. 4th 85 [44 Cal. Rptr. 2d 420, 900 P.2d 669], relying on the first Restatement and without reviewing or even mentioning intervening revaluations of the tort by the Restatement Second, other state high courts and our own Court of Appeal, we again endorsed the prima facie tort pleading and burden of proof format, noting that "[o]nly if and when plaintiff establishes an 'intent to interfere' does the issue of 'justification' come into play. [C] '[W]hile defendant's culpable intent is an element of the cause of action to be pleaded and proved by plaintiff, defendant's justification is an affirmative defense. . . .' " [C] We went on to observe that "[defendant] is mistaken when it implies that an improper 'motive' is an element of plaintiff's cause of action rather than a factor in defendant's affirmative defense. It is not." [C]

Although our opinions following *Seaman's*, [c] to the extent they addressed the question at all, continued to enumerate the same prima facie elements of the economic relations tort, the cases consistently denied the plaintiff recovery. * * *

Meanwhile, developments in the Court of Appeal and in the practical administration of such claims in the trial courts had, if anything, outdistanced our own formulations of the elements of the tort and the allocation of the burden of proof in at least two respects. First, several Court of Appeal opinions appeared to engraft onto the elements of the plaintiff's cause of action allegations and proof that the defendant's conduct was "wrongful." * * *

Second, in 1990, BAJI, the Book of Approved Jury Instructions widely used by trial judges in civil cases, relying on the Restatement Second of Torts and Mr. Witkin's account of the tort, included an instruction providing that a defendant in an economic relations tort case could defeat liability by showing that its conduct was not independently "wrongful." [C]

These developments, of course, closely reflect a nearly concurrent change in views both within the American Law Institute and in other jurisdictions. In the face of those twin lines of development, we are thus presented with the opportunity to consider whether to expressly reconstruct the formal elements of the interference with economic relations tort to achieve a closer alignment with the practice of the trial courts, emerging views within the Court of Appeal, the rulings of many other state high courts, and the critiques of leading commentators. We believe that we should.

IV

In searching for a means to recast the elements of the economic relations tort and allocate the associated burdens of proof, we are guided by an overmastering concern articulated by high courts of other jurisdictions and legal commentators: the need to draw and enforce a sharpened distinction between claims for the tortious disruption of an existing contract and claims that a prospective contractual or economic relationship has been interfered with by the defendant. Many of the cases do in fact acknowledge a greater array of justificatory defenses against claims of interference with prospective relations. Still, in our view and that of several other courts and commentators, the notion that the two torts are analytically unitary and derive from a common principle sacrifices practical wisdom to theoretical insight, promoting the idea that the interests invaded are of nearly equal dignity. They are not.

The courts provide a damage remedy against third party conduct intended to disrupt an existing contract precisely because the exchange of promises resulting in such a formally cemented economic relationship is deemed worthy of protection from interference by a stranger to the agreement. Economic relationships short of contractual, however, should stand on a different legal footing as far as the potential for tort liability is reckoned. Because ours is a culture firmly wedded to the social rewards of commercial contests, the law usually takes care to draw lines of legal liability in a way that maximizes areas of competition free of legal penalties.

A doctrine that blurs the analytical line between interference with an existing business contract and interference with commercial relations less than contractual is one that invites both uncertainty in conduct and unpredictability of its legal effect. The notion that inducing the breach of an existing contract is simply a subevent of the "more inclusive" class of acts that interfere with economic relations, while perhaps theoretically unobjectionable, has been mischievous as a practical matter. Our courts should, in short, firmly distinguish the two kinds of business contexts, bringing a greater solicitude to those relationships that have ripened into agreements, while recognizing that relationships short of that subsist in a zone where the rewards and risks of competition are dominant.

* * *

Conclusion

We hold that a plaintiff seeking to recover for an alleged interference with prospective contractual or economic relations must plead and prove as part of its case-in-chief that the defendant not only knowingly interfered with the plaintiff's expectancy, but engaged in conduct that was wrongful by some legal measure other than the fact of interference itself. The judgment of the Court of Appeal is reversed and the cause is remanded with directions to affirm the judgment of the trial court.

MOSK, J. I concur in the judgment.

* * *

[T]he only reasonable choice is reformulation. Indeed, an undertaking of this sort is compelled by the almost unanimous agreement * * * that the interfering party should not be allowed to interfere with impunity at all times and under all circumstances.

To this end, we should clearly define the tort, basing it on stable and circumscribed ground, and eschewing the prima facie tort doctrine, the "protectionist" premise, and the interfering party's motive. Our focus should be on objective conduct and consequences. Further, our concern should be with such conduct and consequences as are unlawful.

General considerations of a formal nature counsel us to take this path. As noted, the tort's rules are "admittedly vague" and their applications "difficult to classify." An objective definition based on unlawfulness, cast in understandable and usable terms, would reduce or remove such weaknesses.

Specific concerns of a substantive kind operate as well. It is plain from the above discussion that the tort is based on the problematic prima facie tort doctrine. In addition, it implicates the "protectionist" premise, which carries internal inconsistency and also threatens the common law's policy of freedom of competition and the First Amendment's guaranty of freedom of speech, freedom of association, and right of petition. Lastly, it has a tendency to yield untoward results, both in individual cases and generally, through its focus on the interfering party's motive. An objective definition based on unlawfulness, developed in light of such facts, would cure or mitigate the deficiency of the doctrine, lessen or eliminate the flaw attributable to the premise, and decrease or neutralize the danger to the policy and the guaranty.

Thus reformulated, the tort requires objective, and unlawful, conduct or consequences.

It follows that the tort may be satisfied by intentional interference with prospective economic advantage by independently tortious means. [Cc]

The interfering party is properly liable to the interfered-with party in such a situation. That is most plainly true when the independently tortious means the interfering party uses are tortious as to the interfered-with party himself. By the tort's very nature, the interfered-with party is an intended (or at least known) victim of the interfering party. [C] But it is true as well when the independently tortious means the interfering party uses are independently tortious only as to a third party. Even under these circumstances, the interfered-with party remains an intended (or at least known) victim of the interfering party—albeit one that is indirect rather than direct. (See Rest.2d Torts, § 767, comment *c*, pages 29–30.) In this situation, the means in question are independently tortious as to the third party "if those elements that pertain to" the interfering party "are present" even if those that pertain to the third party are not. [C]

It also follows that the tort may be satisfied by intentional interference with prospective economic advantage through restraint of trade, including monopolization. [C]

* * *

So reformulated, the tort can be distinctly stated and consistently applied.

The independently tortious means that commonly appear in this context, including assault and battery, defamation, and fraud and deceit. [Cc] Surely, one would not be left to the scant "guidance" of the so-called " 'business ethics' standard" [Cc] which presupposes that "[t]he nature of the conduct which is acceptable today may . . . prove unacceptable tomorrow." [C]

Also, restraints of trade may be "measured by objective economic criteria." [Cc]

Moreover, the tort's internally inconsistent "protectionist" premise is now removed. The interfered-with party is not favored over the interfering party by virtue of their respective status: the former is merely protected against the latter's use of independently tortious means and restraints of trade.

Furthermore, the tort itself does not now impair the common law's policy of freedom of competition. By its very terms, the freedom in question does not extend to the use of independently tortious means or restraints of trade.

Neither does the tort now undermine the First Amendment's guaranty of freedom of speech, freedom of association, or right of petition. That is because, to the extent that speech or association or petitioning is involved, the federal constitutional provision itself limits liability. [C]

Finally, in any action based on the tort, it is the interfered-with party as plaintiff who should bear the burden of pleading and the burden of proof as to whether there has been intentional interference with prospective economic advantage either by independently tortious means or through restraint of trade by the interfering party as defendant.

* * *

It is evident in the analysis presented above that, on many points, I agree with the majority's discussion of the tort of intentional interference with prospective economic advantage and Della Penna's claim against Toyota asserting such a cause of action.

On two major points, however, I am compelled to state my disagreement.

First, I would not adopt the "standard" of "wrongfulness." As I have noted, the term and its cognates are inherently ambiguous. They should probably be avoided. They should surely not be embraced. That is the course we followed in *Buckaloo*. It should be followed here as well.

Second, if I were to adopt such a "standard," I would not allow it to remain undefined. * * * Any definition of the "standard," of course, should avoid suggesting that the interfering party's motive might be material for present purposes. As I have explained, the focus on this issue is inappropriate. [c] A position of this sort, one must acknowledge, would result in the imposition of no liability on a person who is purely, but merely, "malicious"—who acts, to quote Justice Holmes, with "disinterested malevolence" (Amer. Bank & Trust Co. v. Federal Bank (1921) 256 U.S. 350, 358 [65 L. Ed. 983, 990, 41 S. Ct. 499, 25 A.L.R. 971]). Although such a person might be held responsible in conscience, he should not be made answerable in tort.

* * *

NOTES AND QUESTIONS

1. The principal case represents a modern articulation of a tort with ancient roots. Has the court formulated the tort in a way that avoids the vices identified in former formulations? Two later cases, Speakers of Sport, Inc. v. ProServ, Inc., 178 F.3d 862 (7th Cir. 1999) (applying Illinois law) and Wal-Mart Stores, Inc. v. Sturges, 52 S.W.3d 711 (Tex. 2001), confirm the principal case. Citing the principal case, the latter court stresses the importance of "decoupling interference with contract from interference with prospective relations, and of grounding liability for the latter in conduct that is independently tortious by nature or otherwise unlawful," id., at 721. The California Supreme Court has recently explained the principal case and its relationship with *Buckaloo* in Korea Supply Co. v. Lockheed Martin Corp., 29 Cal.4th 1134, 63 P.3d 937, 131 Cal.Rptr.2d 29 (2003).

2. The English courts soon after permitting a cause of action for interference with prospective contractual relations throttled the tort. In Allen v. Flood, [1898] App.Cas. 1, 121, Lord Herschell stated that there was a "chasm" between inducing a breach of contract and inducing a person not to enter a contract.

3. Justice Mosk's challenge in the principal case that wrongful conduct ought to be defined and could not include conduct motivated by malice alone, addresses a long-lingering issue—the "prima facie tort

doctrine." The genesis of this tort is the action on the case. The elements were expressed by Lord Justice Bowen in the English Court of Appeal in Mogul Steamship Co. v. McGregor Gow & Co., 23 Q.B.D. 598, 613 (1889): "[I]ntentionally to do that which is calculated in the ordinary course of events to damage, and which does, in fact, damage another in that person's property or trade, is actionable if done without just cause or excuse." Lord Justice Bowen's formulation resonated with Justice Holmes in launching the "prima facie tort doctrine." See, Taggart, Private Property and Abuse of Rights in Victorian England: The Story of Edward Pickles and the Bradford Water Supply 167–92 (Oxford University Press, 2002). Holmes' ideas influenced legal thought throughout the common-law world. His fault principle as "the fulcrum of liability" led to the formulation of the general principle governing the law of negligence. If there were a general principle for negligence, should there be a general principle for all liability based on intentional wrongdoing? After some shifting in his original position, Holmes accepted the prima facie liability theory as an overarching principle. This theory would account for otherwise separate torts such as interference with business relations and malicious prosecution. But its force as a unifying theory has been weak, even in some jurisdictions where the doctrine was planted by some courts. See Brown v. Missouri Pacific Railroad Co., 720 S.W.2d 357, 361 (Mo. 1986) (en banc) ("No case resulting in a verdict for the plaintiff on a prima facie tort theory has been affirmed by the Missouri appellate courts."); Taylor v. Metzger, 152 N.J. 490, 706 A.2d 685 (1998) (the prima facie tort cause of action cannot be properly pleaded when the essential elements of an established and relevant cause of action are missing).

4. Earlier case law had found liability where the plaintiff had a business or legal right that was intentionally interfered with by the defendant's unlawful activities. In Garret v. Taylor, Cro.Jac. 567, 79 Eng. Rep. 485 (1621), the defendant made threats of mayhem and vexatious suits against customers and workmen. In Tarleton v. McGawley, Peake N.P. 270, 170 Eng. Rep. 153 (1793), where the defendant fired upon Africans with whom the plaintiff was about to trade. The best early statement of the principle is found in Keeble v. Hickeringill, 11 East 574, 103 Eng. Rep. 1127 (1707), where the defendant, inspired by pure malice, fired guns to frighten ducks away from the plaintiff's pond, and so prevented him from taking them.

5. A leading American case is Tuttle v. Buck, 107 Minn. 145, 119 N.W. 946 (1909). Plaintiff's complaint alleged that defendant, a wealthy banker with influence in the community, maliciously established a barber shop, employed a barber to carry on the business, and used his personal influence to attract customers from the plaintiff's barber shop, not for the purpose of serving any legitimate purpose of his own, but for the sole purpose of maliciously injuring the plaintiff; and that as a result of this conduct the plaintiff's business was ruined. The trial court overruled a demurrer to this complaint, and the supreme court affirmed, saying:

"When a man starts an opposition place of business, not for the sake of profit to himself, but regardless of loss to himself, and for the sole purpose of driving his competitor out of business, and with the intention of himself retiring upon the accomplishment of his malevolent purpose, he is guilty of a wanton wrong and an actionable tort. In such a case he would not be exercising his legal right, or doing an act which can be judged separately from the motive which actuated him. To call such conduct competition is a perversion of terms. It is simply the application of force without legal justification, which in its moral quality may be no better than highway robbery."

6. *Restatement of Torts.* Restatement (Second) of Torts § 870 provides: "One who intentionally causes injury to another is subject to liability to the other for that injury, if his conduct is generally culpable and not justifiable under the circumstances. This liability may be imposed although the actor's conduct does not come within a traditional category of tort liability."

The comments spell out in detail the considerations to be balanced by a court in determining whether to declare the existence of a new cause of action or to extend the parameters of an existing cause.

7. *The prima facie tort doctrine* where recognized and applied has protected economic interests. However, in Morrison v. National Broadcasting Co., 24 A.D.2d 284, 266 N.Y.S.2d 406 (1965), Breitel J. extended it to protect the reputational interest of an innocent academic swept up in a notorious scandal involving NBC's rigged quiz show.

8. As noted in the principal case, concern has been voiced about the clash of the tort with the assumptions of the competitive free-market system when the tort is extended to protect "prospective advantage." In the A.L.I. debate on § 766, Restatement (Second) of Torts, Professor Auerbach opined that there was a "fundamental question involved, as to whether we can say in 1969 that all cases decided over more than a 100-year period reach the astounding result that the competitive order which we hold out to the world as a model is prima facie illegal." William L. Prosser, Presentation of Restatement of the Law, Second, Torts, Tentative Draft No. 14, 46 A.L.I. 201 (1969).

9. Dean Wade, after Dean Prosser's proposal was recommitted for further consideration, proposed that the tort was actionable upon proof of the element of "impropriety" measured by a thorough factor balancing test. John W. Wade, Discussion of Restatement of the Law, Second, Torts, Tentative Draft No. 23, 54 A.L.I. 394, 394–435 (1977).

10. Is the tort applicable to a contract terminable at the will of either party? The Restatement § 768 classifies it as prospective advantage. See Roy v. Woonsocket Instit. for Saving, 525 A.2d 915 (R.I. 1987) (bank employee an at will employee, having, at best, an action for interference with prospective advantage); Duggin v. Adams, 234 Va. 221, 360 S.E.2d 832 (1987) (at will employment contract requires proof of (1) knowledge of contract and (2) improper conduct; if for definite term knowledge would suffice).

11. Contracts that are illegal, in restraint of trade, or against public policy, such as those intended to stifle competition, are not protected from interference. Fairbanks, Morse & Co. v. Texas Elec. Serv. Co., 63 F.2d 702 (5th Cir. 1933), cert. denied, 290 U.S. 655.

12. Contracts to marry have received special treatment. Almost without exception, courts have refused to hold that it is a tort to induce the parties to break them. See Nelson v. Melvin, 236 Iowa 604, 19 N.W.2d 685 (1945); Brown v. Glickstein, 347 Ill.App. 486, 107 N.E.2d 267 (1952). The

reason usually given is that contracts to marry are highly personal agreements, and anyone should be free to advise the parties to change their minds.

13. Inducement not to enter into a contract is normally of a third party, not the plaintiff. See Goldstein v. Kern, 82 Mich.App. 723, 267 N.W.2d 165 (1978). But preventing entry into the prospective relation may apply to either the plaintiff or a third person. See Byars v. Baptist Medical Centers, Inc., 361 So.2d 350 (Ala. 1978) (hospital refused to permit nurse to be certified in nurses' registry).

Adler, Barish, Daniels, Levin and Creskoff v. Epstein

Supreme Court of Pennsylvania, 1978.
482 Pa. 416, 393 A.2d 1175, cert. denied, 442 U.S. 907, 99 S.Ct. 2817, 61 L.Ed.2d 272.

ROBERTS, JUSTICE. Appellant, the law firm of Adler, Barish, Daniels, Levin and Creskoff, filed a Complaint in Equity in the Court of Common Pleas of Philadelphia. It sought to enjoin appellees, former associates of Adler Barish, from interfering with existing contractual relationships between Adler Barish and its clients. The court of common pleas entered a final decree granting the requested relief, but a divided Superior Court dissolved the injunction and dismissed Adler Barish's complaint. We granted allowance of appeal. We now reverse and direct reinstatement of the decree of the court of common pleas. * * *

Appellee Alan Epstein's employment relationship with Adler Barish terminated on March 10, 1977. At his request, Epstein continued to use offices of Adler Barish until March 19. During this time, and through April 4, when Adler Barish filed its complaint, Epstein was engaged in an active campaign to procure business for his new law firm. He initiated contacts, by phone and in person, with clients of Adler Barish with open cases on which he had worked while a salaried employee. Epstein advised the Adler Barish clients that he was leaving the firm and that they could choose to be represented by him, Adler Barish, or any other firm or attorney. * * *

He [also] mailed to the clients form letters which could be used to discharge Adler Barish as counsel, name Epstein the client's new counsel and create a contingent fee agreement. Epstein also provided clients with a stamped envelope addressed to Epstein. [Similar actions were taken by other appellees.] * * *

Adler Barish argues that appellees' conduct constitutes an intentional interference with existing contractual relationships between Adler Barish and its clients. According to Adler Barish, appellees' conduct is "deserving of censure, not encouragement." Appellees, on the other hand, contend that their conduct was "privileged," and that therefore no right of action for intentional interference lies. Moreover, they argue that their conduct is protected under the first and fourteenth amendments to the Constitution of the United States.

"[S]peech which does 'no more than propose a commercial transaction'" is no longer outside the protection of the first and fourteenth amendments to the Constitution of the United States.

Virginia Pharmacy Board v. Virginia Consumer Council, 425 U.S. 748, 762 (1976) (striking down state statute deeming licensed pharmacists' advertising of prescription drugs "unprofessional conduct"); see Pennsylvania State Board of Pharmacy v. Pastor, 441 Pa. 186, 272 A.2d 487 (1971) (invalidating Pennsylvania statute prohibiting advertising of "dangerous drugs" dispensible only with a physician's prescription). Accordingly, states are barred from imposing blanket prohibitions against truthful advertising of "routine" legal services. Bates v. State Bar of Arizona, 433 U.S. 350 (1977). Such a blanket prohibition "serves to inhibit the free flow of commercial information and to keep the public in ignorance." Id., 433 U.S. at 365.

Nothing in the challenged decree prohibited appellees from engaging in the truthful advertising protected under *Bates.* Appellees could inform the general public, including clients of Adler Barish, of the availability of their legal services, and thus the "free flow of commercial information" to the public is unimpaired. Moreover, the injunction expressly permitted appellees to announce "formation of their new professional relationship in accordance with the requirements of DR 2–102 of the Code of Professional Responsibility." Appellees therefore were permitted to mail announcements to "lawyers, clients, former clients, personal friends, and relatives." Code of Professional Responsibility, DR 2–102(A)(2). This would include the very clients of Adler Barish whose business appellees sought. See Committee on Professional Ethics of the American Bar Association, Informal Decision No. 681 (August 1, 1963) (permitting departing attorney to send announcements "to those clients of the old firm for whom he had worked").

What the injunction did proscribe was appellees' "contacting and/or communicating with those persons who up to and including April 1, 1977, had active legal matters pending with and were represented by the law firm of Adler, Barish, Daniels, Levin and Creskoff." Our task is to decide whether the conduct of appellees is constitutionally subject to sanction.

The Code of Professional Responsibility, DR 2–103(A) (as adopted, 1974), provides: "A lawyer shall not recommend employment, as a private practitioner, of himself, his partner, or associate to a non-lawyer who has not sought his advice regarding employment of a lawyer." See also Code of Professional Responsibility, DR 2–104(A). Appellees clearly violated this "proscription against self-recommendation." [C] They recommended their own employment, even though clients of Adler Barish did not seek appellees' advice "regarding employment of a lawyer."

Ohralik v. Ohio State Bar Association, 436 U.S. 447 (1978), makes plain that, after *Bates,* states may constitutionally impose sanctions upon attorneys engaging in conduct which violates these disciplinary rules, even though the conduct involves "commercial speech." In *Ohralik,* the state bar association suspended an attorney who "solicited" persons injured in an automobile accident by making visits to the hospital room where the persons were recovering. Mr. Justice Powell, speaking for the Court, emphasized that commercial speech does not enjoy the same constitutional protections traditionally afforded other forms of speech:

"In rejecting the notion that such speech 'is wholly outside the protection of the First Amendment,' Virginia Pharmacy, 425 U.S. at 761, we were careful not to hold 'that it is wholly undifferentiable from other forms' of speech. Id., at 771 n. 24. We have not discarded the 'commonsense' distinction between speech proposing a commercial transaction, which occurs in an area traditionally subject to government regulation, and other varieties of speech. Ibid. To require a parity of constitutional protection for commercial and noncommercial speech alike could invite dilution, simply by a leveling process, of the force of the Amendment's guarantee with respect to the latter kind of speech. Rather than subject the First Amendment to such a devitalization, we instead have afforded commercial speech a limited measure of protection, commensurate with its subordinate position in the scale of First Amendment values, while allowing modes of regulation that might be impermissible in the realm of noncommercial expression. * * *

"[T]he State does not lose its power to regulate commercial activity deemed harmful to the public whenever speech is a component of that activity. Neither *Virginia Pharmacy* nor *Bates* purported to cast doubt on the permissibility of these kinds of commercial regulation." Id., 436 U.S. at 455–456. In rejecting the attorney's constitutional claim, the Court determined that the state's interests were important enough to support regulation of the attorney's conduct. * * * "[The conduct involved solicitation in person.]"

Just as in *Ohralik,* appellees' conduct frustrates, rather than advances, Adler Barish clients' "informed and reliable decisionmaking." After making Adler Barish clients expressly aware that appellees' new firm was interested in procuring their active cases, Epstein provided the clients the forms that would sever one attorney-client relationship and create another. Epstein's aim was to encourage speedy, simple action by the client. All the client needed to do was to "sign on the dotted line" and mail the forms in the self-addressed, stamped envelopes. * * *

Thus, appellees were actively attempting to induce the clients to change law firms in the middle of their active cases. Appellees' concern for their line of credit and the success of their new law firm gave them an immediate, personally created financial interest in the clients' decisions. In this atmosphere, appellees' contacts posed too great a risk that clients would not have the opportunity to make a careful, informed decision. * * * [W]e must reject appellees' argument and conclude that, just as in *Ohralik,* the Constitution permits regulation of their conduct. * * *

Thus, we turn to whether the court of common pleas properly concluded that Adler Barish is entitled to relief. In Birl v. Philadelphia Electric Co., 402 Pa. 297, 167 A.2d 472 (1960), this Court adopted Restatement of Torts § 766 and its definition of the right of action for intentional interference with existing contractual relations. There, we stated:

"At least since Lumley v. Gye [supra at 1148], the common law has recognized an action in tort for an intentional, unprivileged interference with contractual relations. It is generally recognized that one has the right to pursue his business relations or employment free from interference on the part of other persons except where such interference is justified or constitutes an exercise of an absolute right: Restatement, Torts, § 766. * * *

In its continuing effort to provide the judicial system orderly and accurate restatements of the common law, the American Law Institute has reviewed each section of the Restatement of Torts, including Section 766. Restatement (Second) of Torts § 766 (Tent.Draft No. 23, 1977), states the Institute's present view of what constitutes the elements of the cause of action before us:

"*Intentional Interference with Performance of Contract by Third Person.* One who intentionally and improperly interferes with the performance of a contract (except a contract to marry) between another and a third person by inducing or otherwise causing the third person not to perform the contract, is subject to liability to the other for the pecuniary loss resulting to the other from the third person's failure to perform the contract." * * *

An examination of this case in light of Restatement (Second) of Torts § 766, reveals that the sole dispute is whether appellees' conduct is "improper." There is no doubt that appellees intentionally sought to interfere with performance of the contractual relations between Adler Barish and its clients. While still at Adler Barish, appellees' behavior, particularly their use of expected fees from Adler Barish clients' cases, indicates appellees' desire to gain a segment of the firm's business. This pattern of conduct continued until the court of common pleas enjoined it. Indeed, appellees' intentional efforts to obtain a share of Adler Barish's business were successful. The record reveals that several clients signed the forms Epstein prepared on behalf of appellees notifying Adler Barish that the clients no longer wished the services of Adler Barish. Likewise, the record reveals that Adler Barish and its clients were parties to valid, existing contracts.

In assessing whether appellees' conduct is "improper," we bear in mind what this Court stated in Glenn v. Point Park College, 441 Pa. [474,] 482, 272 A.2d [895,] 899, where we analyzed "privileges" in conjunction with the closely related right of action for intentional interference with prospective contract relations:

"The absence of privilege or justification in the tort under discussion is closely related to the element of intent. As stated by Harper & James, The Law of Torts, § 6.11, at 513–14: ' * * * where, as in most cases, the defendant acts at least in part for the purpose of protecting some legitimate interest which conflicts with that of the plaintiff, a line must be drawn and the interests evaluated. This process results in according or denying a privilege which, in turn, determines liability.' What is or is not privileged conduct in a given situation is not susceptible of precise definition. Harper & James refer in general to interferences which 'are sanctioned by the' rules of the game 'which society has adopted', and to 'the area of socially acceptable conduct which the law regards as privileged,' id. at 510, 511, and treat the subject in detail in §§ 6.12 and 6.13."

We are guided, too, by Restatement (Second) of Torts § 767, which focuses on what factors should be considered in determining whether conduct is "improper:"

"In determining whether an actor's conduct in intentionally interfering with an existing contract or a prospective contractual relation of another is improper or not, consideration is given to the following factors:

"(a) The nature of the actor's conduct,

"(b) The actor's motive,

"(c) The interests of the other with which the actor's conduct interferes,

"(d) The interests sought to be advanced by the actor,

"[(e) The social interests in protecting the freedom of action of the actor and the contractual interests of the others,]

"[(f)] The proximity or remoteness of the actor's conduct to the interference and

"[(g)] The relations between the parties."[17]

We find nothing in the " 'rules of the game' which society has adopted" which sanctions appellees' conduct. Indeed, the rules which apply to those who enjoy the privilege of practicing law in this Commonwealth expressly disapprove appellees' method of obtaining clients. * * * We find such a departure from "[r]ecognized ethical codes" "significant in evaluating the nature of [appellees'] conduct." Restatement (Second) of Torts, supra at § 767 comment *c*.[19] All the reasons underlying our Disciplinary Rules' "proscription against [appellees'] self-recommendation," *Berlant Appeal,* 458 Pa. at 443, 328

---

[17] Thus, new Restatement (Second) of Torts focuses upon whether conduct is "proper," rather than "privileged." Compare Restatement of Torts, § 766 (1939) ("[e]xcept as stated in Section 698 [(relating to contracts to marry)], *one who without a privilege to do so,* induces or otherwise purposely causes a third person not to ¶ (a) perform a contract with another, or ¶ (b) enter into or continue a business relation with another ¶ is liable to the other for the harm caused thereby" (emphasis added)). Comment *b* to Restatement (Second) of Torts, supra at § 767, explains the shift in inquiry:

"*Privilege to Interfere, or Interference not Improper.* Unlike other intentional torts such as intentional injury to person or property, or defamation, this branch of tort law has not developed a crystallized set of definite rules as to the existence or non-existence of a privilege to act in the manner stated in §§ 766, 766A or 766B. Because of this fact, this Section is expressed in terms of whether the interference is improper or not rather than in terms of a specific privilege to act in the manner specified. The issue in each case is whether the interference is improper or not under the circumstances; whether, upon a consideration of the relative significance of the factors involved, the conduct should be permitted without liability, despite its effect of harm to another."

[The bracketed material in the list of the factors indicates changes in the section between the Tentative Draft and the published volume. (Ed.)]

[19] Restatement (Second) of Torts, supra at § 767 comment *c*, provides in full:

"*Business Ethics and Customs.* Recognized ethical codes for a particular area of business activity and established customs or practices regarding approved or disapproved actions or methods may also be significant in evaluating the nature of the actor's conduct as a factor in determining whether his interference with the plaintiff's economic relations was improper or not."

A.2d at 474, especially the concern that appellees' contacts too easily could overreach and unduly influence Adler Barish clients with active cases, are relevant here.

Appellees' conduct adversely affected more than the informed and reliable decisionmaking of Adler Barish clients with active cases. Their conduct also had an immediate impact upon Adler Barish. Adler Barish was prepared to continue to perform services for its clients and therefore could anticipate receiving compensation for the value of its efforts. Moreover, * * * Adler Barish's fee agreements with clients were a source of anticipated revenue protected from outside interference.

It is true that, upon termination of their employment relationship with Adler Barish, appellees were free to engage in their own business venture. * * * But appellees' right to pursue their own business interests is not absolute. "[U]nless otherwise agreed, after the termination of the agency, the agent * * * has a duty to the principal not to take advantage of a still subsisting confidential relation created during the prior agency relation". Restatement (Second) of Agency, supra at § 396(d).

Appellees' contacts were possible because Adler Barish partners trusted appellees with the high responsibility of developing its clients' cases. From this position of trust and responsibility, appellees were able to gain knowledge of the details, and status, of each case to which appellees had been assigned. In the atmosphere surrounding appellees' departure, appellees' contacts unduly suggested a course of action for Adler Barish clients and unfairly prejudiced Adler Barish. No public interest is served in condoning use of confidential information which has these effects. Clients too easily may suffer in the end.[21] * * *

In *Ohralik,* MR. JUSTICE POWELL emphasized:

"[T]he state bears a special responsibility for maintaining standards among members of the licensed professions. * * * 'The interest of the States in regulating lawyers is especially great since lawyers are essential to the primary governmental function of administering justice, and have historically been' officers of the courts.' [C] While lawyers act in part as 'self-employed businessmen,' they also act 'as trusted agents of their clients, and as assistants to the court in search of a just solution to disputes.'" Ohralik v. Ohio State Bar Association, 436 U.S. at 460. Our "special responsibility" includes the obligation to assure that persons seeking professional legal assistance

---

[21] Moreover, appellees neither occupied the same status, nor pursued the same goals, as the defendants in Watch Tower Bible & Tract Society v. Dougherty, 337 Pa. 286, 11 A.2d 147 (1940). There, we concluded that defendants, leaders of their church, "cannot be mulcted in damages for protesting against the utterances of one who they believe attacks their church and misrepresents its teachings or for inducing their adherents to make similar protests." 337 Pa. at 288, 11 A.2d at 148. * * *

Appellees suggest that injunctive relief was inappropriate. "It is well settled that equity will act to prevent unjustified interference with contractual relations." Neel v. Allegheny County Memorial Park, 391 Pa. 354, 357, 137 A.2d 785, 787 (1958). Accord, Restatement (Second) of Torts, supra at § 766 comment *t* (approving injunctive relief "in appropriate circumstances"). Given appellees' interest in maintaining the line of credit established on the basis of Adler Barish cases, and appellees' express intent to continue their effort to gain Adler Barish clients, we believe the court of common pleas could properly conclude that equitable relief was necessary to protect all the interests at stake in this case.

receive the quality advocacy and fair treatment they justifiably expect. Our responsibility also includes the duty to provide an atmosphere conducive to proper attorney-client relationships, including those situations where, as here, associates assist other members of a firm in rendering legal services. Consistent with these jurisprudential concerns, our supervisory authority over practitioners in our courts, prior decisions, the Code of Professional Responsibility, and Restatement (Second) of Torts, it must be concluded that the court of common pleas correctly determined that Adler Barish is entitled to relief.

Order of the Superior Court reversed and court of common pleas directed to reinstate its final decree. Each party pay own costs.

MANDERINO, J., filed a dissenting opinion.

NOTES AND QUESTIONS

1. Knowing interference with a valid enforceable contract is usually itself improper. Duggin v. Adams, 234 Va. 221, 360 S.E.2d 832 (1987). The burden then rests on the defendant to justify the interference. The element of impropriety looms when the claim is based on interference with prospective advantage.

In light of the California Supreme Court's opinion in *Della Penna*, supra at 1151, consider the following broad grounds for wrongfulness or impropriety:

A. *Violating Ethical Standards*. See Sustick v. Slatina, 48 N.J.Super. 134, 137 A.2d 54 (1957) (ultimate question is whether the conduct was "both injurious and transgressive of generally accepted standards of common morality or of law," whether it was "sanctioned by the rules of the game," and constituted "right and just dealing"); Leonard Duckworth, Inc. v. Michael L. Field & Co., 516 F.2d 952 (5th Cir. 1975) ("sharp dealing or overreaching or other conduct below the behavior of fair men similarly situated"); Herron v. State Farm Mut. Ins. Co., 56 Cal.2d 202, 363 P.2d 310, 14 Cal.Rptr. 294 (1961) (rules of Nat'l Conf. Comm. on Adjusters); and Gieseke v. IDCA, Inc., 826 N.W.2d 816 (Ct. App. 2013) (confirming the tort of interference of prospective advantage, finding improper conduct in interfering with plaintiff's reasonable expectations); and Nostrame v. Santiago, 61 A.3d 893 (2013) (finding that for an attorney to lure way a client from another may be tortious if the act violates ethics rules.

B. *Other Kinds of Wrongful Conduct*. Physical violence, threats and intimidation: Williams v. Maloof, 223 Ga. 640, 157 S.E.2d 479 (1967). Misrepresentation: Gold v. Los Angeles Democratic League, 49 Cal.App.3d 365, 122 Cal. Rptr. 732 (1975); Johnson v. Gustafson, 201 Minn. 629, 277 N.W. 252 (1938). Defamation: Woody v. Brush, 178 App. Div. 698, 165 N.Y.S. 867 (1917). Threats of suit: Pratt Food Co. v. Bird, 148 Mich. 631, 112 N.W. 701 (1907); Gresh v. Potter-McCune Co., 235 Pa.Super. 537, 344 A.2d 540 (1975). Generally see, Gieseke v. IDCA, Inc., 826 N.W.2d 816 (Ct. App. 2013) (confirming the tort of interference of prospective advantage, finding improper or wrongful conduct in interfering with plaintiff's reasonable expectations; the conduct must be more than unfair).

The United States' 2008 financial crisis provided a modern illustration of this rule. In a deal by Citigroup Inc. to purchase Wachovia Corp.'s failing assets, Wachovia signed an exclusivity agreement requiring it to negotiate only with Citigroup. Before the agreement expired, Wachovia accepted a better buy-out package with Wells Fargo & Co. Citigroup promptly filed suit alleging, amongst other things, tortious interference with contract. At the prompting of federal regulators from the F.D.I.C., the three banks agreed to a legal standstill to negotiate a division of Wachovia's assets. After four days of intense negotiations, Citigroup ceded Wachovia's assets to Wells Fargo but reinstated its lawsuit seeking $60 billion in damages. Wachovia obtained a declaratory judgment that ruled unenforceable its exclusivity agreement with Citigroup. Citigroup has appealed the ruling. See Wachovia Corp. v. Citigroup, Inc., 634 F. Supp. 2d 445 (S.D.N.Y. 2009).

2. Many cases involve conduct designed to prevent or hinder a person entering into a contractual or business relationship. Where a number of persons combine, it is called a boycott, a term that immortalizes a pariah during the Irish "troubles":

> "Captain Boycott, an Englishman, who was agent of Lord Earne and a farmer of Lough Mask, served notices upon the lord's tenants, and they in turn, with the surrounding population, resolved to have nothing to do with him, and, as far as they could prevent it, not to allow anyone else to have. His life appeared to be in danger, and he had to claim police protection. His servants fled from him, and the awful sentence of excommunication could hardly have rendered him more helplessly alone for a time. No one would work for him, and no one would supply him with food. He and his wife were compelled to work their own fields with the shadows of armed constabulary ever at their heels; Justin MacCarthy's England Under Gladstone." Bouvier's Law Dictionary, summarizing statement in State v. Glidden, 55 Conn. 46, 8 A. 890 (1887).

3. Boycotts are "primary," where the defendant himself refuses to deal with the plaintiff, or "secondary," where he seeks to compel third parties to refuse to deal with plaintiff, by refusing to deal with parties dealing with plaintiff. Competition in business was held under the common law to be a sufficient justification for a primary boycott on the part of a single defendant. This has been extensively limited by statute in many jurisdictions. Discrimination in competition has been penalized federally by the Robinson-Patman Act, and by various acts in the states, which are beyond the scope of this book.

Secondary boycotts open up whole areas of law, particularly as to restraints of trade, antitrust acts, and labor disputes, where many complex problems have arisen, also beyond the scope of this book. They are usually dealt with in courses on unfair competition, antitrust or restraint of trade, or labor law. See Smith v. American Guild of Variety Artists, 349 F.2d 975 (8th Cir. 1965).

4. In Bear v. Reformed Mennonite Church, 462 Pa. 330, 341 A.2d 105 (1975), plaintiff alleged that his business collapsed after bishops of the Mennonite Church ordered all members to "shun" him. "Shunning" was a church practice that had been traditionally applied to persons who violated church rules and were excommunicated. Defendant contended that plaintiff fell within that group. Should plaintiff have a claim in tort?

5. When the defendant has no legitimate purpose and acts for a purpose that the law does not accept, he becomes liable if he interferes with a contractual relation of the plaintiff. Thus, there is liability when the defendant procures the discharge of a workman to prevent him from bringing a suit, as in Johnson v. Aetna Life Ins. Co., 158 Wis. 56, 147 N.W. 32 (1914); when defendant forces worker to settle, as in London Guarantee & Accident Co. v. Horn, 206 Ill. 493, 69 N.E. 526 (1903); when defendant attempts to maliciously force debtor to pay a debt. Warschauser v. Brooklyn Furniture Co., 159 App. Div. 81, 144 N.Y.S. 257 (1913); Hill Grocery Co. v. Carroll, 223 Ala. 376, 136 So. 789 (1931). There also is liability when the defendant uses a termination clause in a contract solely for the purpose of injuring subcontractor, without other justification. Alyeska Pipeline Serv. Co. v. Aurora Air Serv., 604 P.2d 1090 (Alaska 1979).

6. The law of civil conspiracy provides that two or more persons will be liable when they act in concert to cause harm to another and such harm results. The significance of the action, and a source of criticism, is that the act, if done alone, would not be actionable.

In Margolin v. Morton F. Plant Hospital Assn., Inc., 342 So.2d 1090 (Fla. App. 1977), the court recognized the action where all the anesthesiologists in a hospital refused to provide services to a particular surgeon, making it impossible for him to practice. It was open to the defendant anesthesiologists to justify by establishing legitimate reasons for their actions. Is the concerted action appropriate considering the potential overlap with antitrust laws? Considering the width of the tortious interference action, the potential overlap with statutory and other common law actions, and the paucity of authorities, some courts have denied the existence of a separate conspiracy tort: e.g., Bloom v. Hennepin County, 783 F.Supp. 418 (D. Minn. 1992).

Brimelow v. Casson

Chancery Division, 1923.
[1924] 1 Ch. 302.

[The case deals with the misfortunes of a burlesque troupe known as the King Wu Tut Revue, which was touring the south counties of England under the managership of one Jack Arnold. Arnold underpaid the chorus girls so badly that they were forced to eke out a living by plying another and an older trade. As the sordid tale was unfolded in court, it appeared that one of the young women had even been compelled by economic necessity to live in "immorality" with a dwarf, who was a member of the company. The secretary of the Actors' Association, named Lugg, took hold of the situation on behalf of the young women, and persuaded the owners of the theaters with which Arnold had contracts to cancel them unless higher wages were paid. This resulted in the troupe being stranded in the town of Maidenhead. A bill in equity was brought on behalf of the owners of the troupe against the representatives of the union to enjoin them from inducing the breaches of contract.]

RUSSELL, J. It is difficult to speak of this condition of things with restraint. A young girl, almost a child, forced by underpayment to continue in sexual association with this abnormal man is, to my mind, a terrible and revolting tragedy, but the question which I have to decide is whether the acts of the defendants make them liable to an action at the suit of the plaintiff, or whether in the circumstances of this case there exists a sufficient justification for the acts which in the absence of such justification would be actionable. * * *

Prima facie interference with a man's contractual rights and with his right to carry on his business as he wills is actionable; but it is clear on the authorities that interference with contractual rights may be justified; a fortiori the inducing of others not to contract with a person may be justified. * * *

[The unions] desire in the interest of the theatrical calling and the members thereof to stop such underpayment with its evil consequences. The only way they can do so is by inducing the proprietors of theatres not to allow persons like the plaintiff the use of their theatres, either by breaking contracts already made or by refusing to enter into contracts. They adopt this course as regards the plaintiff as the only means open to them of bringing to an end his practice of underpayment which, according to their experience, is fruitful of danger to the theatrical calling and its members. In these circumstances, have the defendants justification for their acts? That they would have the sympathy and support of decent men and women I can have no doubt. But have they in law justification for those acts? As has been pointed out, no general rule can be laid down as a general guide in such cases, but I confess that if justification does not exist here I can hardly conceive the case in which it would be present. These defendants, as it seems to me, owed a duty to their calling and to its members, and, I am tempted to add, to the public, to take all necessary peaceful steps to terminate the payment of this insufficient wage, which in the plaintiff's company had apparently been in fact productive of those results which their past experience had led them to anticipate. "The good sense" of this tribunal leads me to decide that in the circumstances of the present case justification did exist. * * *

The result is that the action is dismissed with costs.

NOTES AND QUESTIONS

1. Accord, that a reasonable and disinterested motive for the protection of other individuals, or the public, will justify intentional interference with contract: Caverno v. Fellows, 300 Mass. 331, 15 N.E.2d 483 (1938) (high school supervisor, principal and superintendent reporting on conduct of teacher); RCDI Constr. v. Spaceplan/Architecture, Planning & Interiors P.A., 148 F. Supp. 2d 607 (W.D.N.C. 2001) (unlicensed construction contractor). Porter v. King County Medical Society, 186 Wash. 410, 58 P.2d 367 (1936) (enforcing ethical rules of medical association).

2. Instances of privilege to interfere with prospective advantage, in the interest of others or the public include: NAACP v. Claiborne Hardware Co., 458 U.S. 886 (1982) (picketing and boycott activity to prevent racial discrimination); Harris v. Thomas, 217 S.W. 1068 (Tex. Civ. App. 1920) (acting to protect ethical standards of medical association). The California Supreme Court in *Della Penna*, supra at 1151, canvasses the justification issue, stressing that "free competition" was paramount.

3. On asserting a bona fide claim, see Restatement (Second) of Torts § 773, McReynolds v. Short, 115 Ariz. 166, 564 P.2d 389 (App. 1977); Beane v. McMullen, 265 Md. 585, 291 A.2d 37 (1972); Allen v. Ramsey, 170 Okla. 430, 41 P.2d 658 (1935).

4. Several cases hold that there is a privilege to give disinterested advice to withdraw from a contractual relation. Arnold v. Moffitt, 30 R.I. 310, 75 A. 502 (1910) (electrical inspector's report). But the privilege does not extend to officious intermeddling: Calbom v. Knudtzon, 65 Wash.2d 157, 396 P.2d 148 (1964) (accountant convinced his client to fire her attorney although he was reputable). On whether the advice is disinterested if it also benefits other advisees, see Welch v. Bancorp Management Advisors, Inc., 296 Or. 208, 675 P.2d 172 (1983), and McGanty v. Staudenraus, 321 Or. 532, 901 P.2d 841 (1995).

5. Justification may arise from a contractual or property right or economic interest of sufficient weight to take precedence. See Felsen v. Sol Café Mfg. Corp., 24 N.Y.2d 682, 249 N.E.2d 459, 301 N.Y.S2d 610 (1969) (sole shareholder justified in attempt to protect economic interest). Some courts place the burden on the plaintiff to show that the interference was otherwise improper or malicious: compare M&M Rental Tools, Inc. v. Milchem, Inc., 94 N.M. 449, 612 P.2d 241 (1980) (holding competition sufficient interest to justify interference with prospective but not existing contract), with Johnson & Johnson v. Guidant Corp., 525 F. Supp. 2d 336 (S.D.N.Y. 2007) (competitive business interest sufficient justification for interference with existing contract). Other courts place the burden on the defendant to show that the interference was justified: Lowell v. Mother's Cake & Cookie Co., 79 Cal.App.3d 13, 144 Cal.Rptr. 664 (1978).

Remedies

1. The interference must cause a loss to the plaintiff. In re Alert Holdings, Inc., 148 B.R. 194 (Bkrtcy. N.Y. 1992). Amgro, Inc. v. Lincoln Gen. Ins. Co., 361 F. App'x 338 (3d Cir. 2010) (assessing lost profits). The Court may grant an injunction if the plaintiff shows that damages would be inadequate, such as in the case of a continuing threat of interference. Courts are reluctant to grant an injunction if it would effectively enforce specific performance for a contract for personal services. Beverly Glen Music, Inc. v. Warner Communications, 178 Cal.App.3d 1142, 224 Cal. Rptr. 260 (1986). But see Alan Schwartz, The Case for Specific Performance, 89 Yale L.J. 271, 274–79 (1979) (arguing that specific performance should be a matter of course).

2. Punitive damages are available, in most jurisdictions, on the basis that the defendant's action is intentional and without justification. Envtl. Energy Ptnrs., Inc. v. Siemens Bldg. Techs., Inc., 178 S.W.3d 691 (Mo. Ct. App. 2005) (awarding punitive damages when defendant's actions were "egregious, unwarranted, overbearing, reprehensible, and without justification").

3. Recovery of damages for breach of contract will not preclude the plaintiff's action for tortious interference, although no double recovery will be allowed. Tort damages will include consequential losses to reputation and mental suffering. Duff v. Engelberg, 237 Cal.App.2d 505, 47 Cal. Rptr. 114 (1965). See Farber, Reassessing the Economic Efficiency of Compensatory Damages for Breach of Contract, 66 Va. L. Rev. 1443, 1476–

78 (1980) (arguing that the effects of transaction costs and imperfect information weaken the case for exclusive reliance on compensatory damages).

4. The potency of available remedies was starkly demonstrated in the notorious Texaco, Inc. v. Pennzoil, Co., 729 S.W.2d 768 (Tex. App. 1987). After determining that Texaco knowingly inveigled Getty Oil Co. away from an acquisition agreement with Pennzoil, the jury handed down a verdict in excess of ten billion dollars. Texaco filed for Chapter 11 bankruptcy. The case was finally settled for the sum of three billion dollars. See Baron and Baron, The Pennzoil-Texaco Dispute: An Independent Analysis, 38 Baylor L. Rev. 253 (1986); and S. Coll, The Taking of Getty Oil: The Full Story of the Most Spectacular and Catastrophic Takeover of All Times (1987). The cast of characters reads as if they came from the fertile imagination of a modern Dickens. The issue whether Pennzoil and Getty had entered a binding contract was central. Is there a good reason to be especially wary of concluding that a contract is formed in respect of acquisitions?

Harmon v. Harmon

Supreme Judicial Court of Maine, 1979.
404 A.2d 1020.

NICHOLS, JUSTICE. Somewhere near the frontier of the expanding field of law relating to tortious interference with an advantageous relationship we encounter the legal issue which is paramount in this appeal.

By a complaint entered November 21, 1977, in Superior Court in Cumberland County the Plaintiff, Richard Harmon, asserted that the Defendants, Harold C. Harmon and Virginia S. Harmon (who are the Plaintiff's brother and brother's wife) had by fraud and undue influence induced the Plaintiff's mother, Josephine F. Harmon, while she was 87 years old and in ill health, to transfer to the Defendants valuable property. By her 1976 will and by her more recent statements the mother had indicated her intention that the Plaintiff son should receive at least a one-half interest in this property. Thus, this transfer effectively disinherited the Plaintiff son. The mother, it appears, is still living.

Upon the Defendants' motion the Superior Court dismissed the complaint upon the grounds (a) that the complaint fails to state a claim upon which relief can be granted and (b) that the Plaintiff son lacked standing to proceed against the Defendant son and the latter's wife.

The Plaintiff son has appealed to this Court from that order of dismissal. We sustain his appeal. * * *

In Cyr v. Cote, Me., 396 A.2d 1013 (1979) we recently considered a similar question. There it was after the testator's death that certain legatees under his will commenced their action, alleging that, but for the defendants' fraud and undue influence upon the testator, they would have received the property which by such tortious conduct the Defendants obtained as an intervivos gift. In determining whether the expectancy of receiving a bequest was something which the law would protect, we had occasion to examine Perkins v. Pendleton, 90 Me. 166, 38 A. 96 (1897). There it was held that a plaintiff, employed by a company which had the right to terminate his employment at will, could bring an action against defendants who unlawfully caused the company to discharge the plaintiff. Relying upon *Perkins,* we recognized in Cyr v. Cote an action for the wrongful interference with an expected legacy or gift under a will. * * *

In *Cyr,* the interest we sought to protect was the *expectation,* and not the *certainty,* that the legatees would have received a future benefit under the will. If there had been no undue influence the testator, prior to death, could still have disinherited them or bequeathed the property to another person. Nevertheless, the wrongful conduct deprived the plaintiffs of the possibility that the testator would not have changed his mind, absent the undue influence.

Once the will has been executed an expectancy has been created in the legatee. If the legatee is injured due to some wrongful conduct on the part of a third party against the prospective testator, such act must necessarily occur within the life of the testator. The injury at this point is complete. The problem then becomes the valuation of the chance of benefit that has been lost. On this basis there may be recovery for loss of prospects falling considerably short of certainty. [C]

We find support for the precedent set by *Cyr* in a review of the historical foundations for that precedent.

The law initially proved most ready to protect commercial expectancies, such as that of entering into or continuing a business relation with another. [C] Very early cases protected a merchant whose customers were being driven away and a churchman whose donors were being harassed. [C]

Prospective or potential business relations have been protected from wrongful interference. [C]

Furthermore, it has become a settled rule in the United States that the expectancy of future contractual relations, such as the prospect of obtaining employment or employees, or the opportunity of obtaining customers, will be protected by the law from wrongful interference. [C] Tort liability for damages is the well established remedy in this situation. * * *

The law has, indeed, in the past also proved willing to protect non-commercial interests in a variety of contexts. Dean Prosser has commented:

"On this basis the earlier cases held that recovery would be denied for interference with an expected gift or a legacy under a will, even though the defendant's motives were unworthy and he had resorted to fraudulent means, because the testator might have changed his mind. There is no essential reason for refusing to protect such non-commercial expectancies, at least where there is a strong probability that they would have been realized. * * *

"The problem appears in reality to be one of satisfactory proof that the loss has been suffered, instead of the existence of a ground to tort

liability." W. Prosser, Law of Torts 950–951 (4th ed. 1971) (emphasis added).

Recognition of such a cause of action was made in the Restatement (Second) of Torts § 870 (1939) which declares the imposition of liability for the intended consequences of any tortious act. Comment (b), Illustration 2, is enlightening:

"A, who is zealous in the cause of labor, is about to make a gift to B, a college, when C, for the purpose of preventing the gift, falsely represents that the president of B is opposed to collective bargaining. As a result, A refuses to make the gift, which otherwise he would have made. B is entitled to maintain an action of tort against C."

The parallel between our present factual setting and this illustration is striking indeed. * * *

Likewise, the expectancy of a beneficiary in the proceeds of an insurance policy upon the life of another is an interest which the courts are ready to protect against the wrongful interference of a third person. [Cc]

Such liability in tort is recognized notwithstanding that clearly the beneficiary's interest includes no vested right, but is a "mere" expectancy. [C] The issue is not whether the interest is vested or expectant; rather the issue is whether it is legally protected so that intentional and wrongful interference causing damage to the plaintiff gives rise to liability in tort. [C]

We conclude that where a person can prove that, but for the tortious interference of another, he would in all likelihood have received a gift or a specific profit from a transaction, he is entitled to recover for the damages thereby done to him. * * *

In the case before us, we go one step further than we did in *Cyr*. Here we recognize that one may proceed to enforce this liability, grounded in tort, before the death of the prospective testatrix occurs, even as we have seen that the victim of tortious interference with a contract of employment or with a policy of life insurance has been permitted to proceed.

There are several considerations which strongly favor according the Plaintiff brother an early day in court, notwithstanding the ambulatory nature of the mother's will and the voidable nature of a trust arrangement. These include (a) the availability of witnesses to the allegedly tortious acts while their memories are relatively fresh, (b) the present availability of relevant exhibits, and (c) especially the prospect that the court may gain the testimony of the parties' aged mother, which testimony may determine the outcome here.

While delaying the adjudication until the mother's death could solidify the Plaintiff's position as allegedly a victim of fraud or undue influence, the delay might mean that important evidence would be denied the court. [Cc]

It should be noted that the claim of the Plaintiff son is to a loss of his expectancy, not to a loss of the actual property of his mother.

Having concluded that the Plaintiff son has a justiciable interest upon which he may found this action, it is clear that he has standing to proceed with this action. Therefore, the order of dismissal was in error. * * *

Remanded for further proceedings consistent with the opinion herein.

NOTES AND QUESTIONS

1. Most of the cases dealing with interference with prospective advantage have concerned future contract relations, such as the prospect of obtaining employment or hiring employees, or the opportunity of attracting customers or purchasing property. In these cases there is a background of business experience, on the basis of which it is possible to estimate with some fair amount of success both the value of what has been lost and the likelihood that the plaintiff would have received it if the defendant had not interfered.

2. When the attempt is made to extend liability for interference beyond such commercial dealings to other "expectancies," the courts have found themselves on unfamiliar ground, and frequently have refused to allow the action. The reason usually given is that there is no sufficient degree of certainty that the plaintiff would ever have received the prospective benefits.

3. Some decisions involving interference with an expected gift or legacy under a will have denied recovery on the ground that there was not sufficient certainty that the donor would not have changed his mind. Creek v. Laski, 248 Mich. 425, 227 N.W. 817 (1929) (will destroyed after testator's death); Morton v. Petitt, 124 Ohio St. 241, 177 N.E. 591 (1931) (substitution of a fraudulent will after testator's death).

4. Other cases have granted recovery on the basis of other evidence of a high degree of probability that the testator would have made or changed a bequest. E.g., Brignati v. Medenwald, 315 Mass. 636, 53 N.E.2d 673 (1944); Bohannon v. Wachovia Bank & Trust Co., 210 N.C. 679, 188 S.E. 390 (1936). Morrill v. Morrill, 1998 ME 133, 712 A.2d 1039 (holding that parental relationship established existence of an expectancy, while the extent of expectancy could be evidenced by intestacy of the parents, content of any previous wills, or previous transfers of property during the parents' lifetimes). See also, Latham v. Father Divine, 299 N.Y. 22, 85 N.E.2d 168 (1949) (allowing equitable relief in the form of a constructive trust); ; Allen v. Leybourne, 190 So.2d 825 (Fla. App. 1966); White v. Mulvania, 575 S.W.2d 184 (Mo. 1978). The availability of other sufficient remedies convinced the Supreme Judicial Court of Massachusetts to reject the principal case. Labonte v. Giordano, 426 Mass. 319, 687 N.E.2d 1253 (1997).

5. The reluctance found in will cases has been carried over to cases of other non-commercial expectancies, when there is no high degree of probability. The gambling spirit dies hard as plaintiffs, over a period of a hundred years, have brought, and courts have dismissed, actions for thwarted chances of winning bets on horse racing: Western Union Tel. Co. v. Crall, 39 Kan. 580, 18 P. 719 (1888); Cain v. Vollmer, 19 Idaho 163, 112 P. 686 (1910); and Youst v. Longo, 43 Cal.3d 64, 233 Cal. Rptr. 294, 729 P.2d 728 (1987). See also: Smitha v. Gentry, 20 Ky. L. Rep. 171, 45 S.W. 515 (1898) (chance of obtaining a reward for apprehending a criminal);

Wachtel v. National Alfalfa Journal, 190 Iowa 1293, 176 N.W. 801 (1920) (when based on the number of contestants, plaintiff was "absolutely sure to win a prize").

(C) TORTIOUS BREACH OF CONTRACT

A party to a contract cannot be liable in tort for interfering with his own contract. Applied Equipment Corp. v. Litton Saudi Arabia Ltd., 7 Cal.4th 503, 28 Cal.Rptr.2d 475, 869 P.2d 454 (1994). The interfering conduct must constitute an independent tort, such as fraud. The rule underlines the distinction between tort and contract liability. As tort liability has moved beyond physical interests and focused attention on protecting economic interests, the boundary line between tort and contract has been much debated. Negligence has stretched, as witnessed in Chapter 8, to protect parties in select circumstances from negligent infliction of pure economic loss.

Contract has generally refused to provide protection for non-economic losses arising from breach. This is true despite the fact that in many contracts the parties expose themselves to the risk of the other parties' opportunistic behavior; contracts often expose parties to significant loss not conveniently and adequately measured under the usual rules of breach of contract. Consider that you have contracted with a tour company for a vacation after your first year of law school. Instead of the relaxing, rejuvenating vacation promised, you endure the hardships of Hannibal crossing the Alps. Will a return of the contract price suffice? On occasion, the relationship goes beyond contract to forge a fiduciary relationship, thus, allowing the incidents of equitable remedies. The law may also impose equitable type terms—covenants of good faith—into the contract. The remedy, however, remains in breach of contract.

The law contemplates that parties are free on pain of paying damages in breach of contract to intentionally breach a contract. The last section highlighted that third parties do not have a commensurate freedom. If they should induce a breach of contract, they will be subject to tort liability with its attendant remedies.

One question explored in this section is how far tort law, with its potent remedy of punitive damages, has invaded the domain of contract. Can a breaching party be tortiously liable for interfering with his own contract? Insurance contracts are a well-established exception. Can other contracts be brought within the fold? How is insurance contract to be defined?

Contract assumes the informed, voluntary behavior of the parties. What role does tort play in protecting the integrity of contract formation?

Neibuhr v. Gage

Supreme Court of Minnesota, 1906.
99 Minn. 149, 108 N.W. 884.

ELLIOTT, J. This action was brought to recover damages which the plaintiff claims he suffered by reason of being required while under duress to transfer to the defendant certain shares of stock in a corporation. In the court below he recovered a verdict for $8,478. The trial court denied the defendant's motion for judgment notwithstanding the verdict, but granted a new trial. Both parties appealed. * * *

[Plaintiff possessed 91 shares of stock in Gage, Hayden & Co., having a face value of $9,100. Defendant Gage accused him of the felony of grand larceny and threatened to have him convicted unless he transferred the shares to Gage. Plaintiff alleged that he was innocent and that Gage led him to believe that Gage "would produce false testimony against him, in order to establish and justify [the] false accusation." Under threat of immediate arrest and imprisonment and without opportunity for consultation, plaintiff transferred the shares.]

The defendant contends * * * that if the contract resulted from duress it was voidable, and the sole remedy of the injured party was either to rescind and to restore the benefits, and then bring his action for what he had parted with, or bring his action in equity for a rescission and for such relief as he was entitled to upon rescission. * * *

In form this is an action at law to recover damages for an injury caused by the wrongful act of the defendant Gage. It was so regarded by the trial court, and the plaintiff's evidence was offered and received upon this theory. The pleadings do not raise the question of ratification or laches. The defendant stands squarely upon the proposition that there was no duress and that the plaintiff admitted that he was an embezzler, and for the purpose of paying an acknowledged debt to Gage, Hayden & Co. freely and voluntarily transferred the stock to Gage. * * *

The remedies which are available to one who has been induced to part with his property or execute a contract by ordinary fraud are well understood. He may keep what he has received under the contract and bring an action to recover the damages which he has sustained by reason of the fraud, or he may rescind the contract by his own act, and sue at law for what he parted with by reason of the fraud, or he may sue in equity for a rescission of the contract by the court and recover what he parted with upon such conditions as the court may deem equitable. * * * If he seeks equitable relief, he must proceed promptly and comply with all the conditions which equity imposes. If he elects to rescind by his own act and sue at law for what he parted with by reason of the fraud, he must do all that he reasonably can to place the defendant in status quo. [C]

The plaintiff abandoned his stock to the defendant. He aske [sic] no equitable relief. He ratifies and affirms the contract, but not the fraud by which it was obtained. The equitable doctrine of laches has no application in an action at law to recover damages. * * * In an action for damages where no rescission is sought a return of the consideration received under the contract is unnecessary.

But is a party who has been injured by duress entitled to the same remedies as one who has been injured by deception? We are unable to see why there should be any distinction made between these two classes of cases. Fraud is ordinarily accomplished by deceit, but it is also accomplished by many other practices. As commonly understood, fraud is a wrong accomplished by deception but * * * duress is a species of fraud in which compulsion in some form takes the place of deception in accomplishing the injury. [C]

We find no principle * * * which limits the remedy by reason of some inherent quality found in the definition of the word "deceit." The practice in either case is equally bad, and there is no reason why the remedy should not be as comprehensive and complete in one as in the other. The wrongdoer accomplishes the same wrong in each case, and does it with the same bad intent. The cases are at least analogous and on principle the remedies should be the same. It is not necessary that the law should show any special and extraordinary consideration for the wrongdoer. All he is entitled to is a fair opportunity to make good the damages resulting from his wrong without unnecessary injury to himself. It is not for him to determine the choice of remedies for the injured party. If the remedy of an action at law for damages is available to a person who has been injured by deceit, it should not lie in the mouth of the wrongdoer to say that the remedy is more restricted when the wrong is the result of the more gross and brutal acts which are known as "duress." * * * A party who has been injured by duress is entitled to the same remedies which are available in cases of deceit. * * *

The entire record has been carefully read, and we are satisfied that there is evidence to sustain the verdict. * * *

The order granting a new trial is reversed, with directions to the trial court to enter a judgment in favor of the plaintiff upon the verdict.

NOTES AND QUESTIONS

1. The principal case has not attracted a large following. In accord see Housing Authority of Dallas v. Hubbell, 325 S.W.2d 880 (Tex. Civ. App. 1959) (economic pressure), and State Nat'l Bank of El Paso v. Farah Mfg. Co., 678 S.W.2d 661 (Tex. App. 1984) (lender's liability). The case may suffer from its appellation as "duress" when that term is commonly used in the law of contract and restitution. The English courts have fashioned a more certain, albeit controversial tort, of "intimidation." The tort encompasses those cases in which harm is inflicted by the use of unlawful threats. The threats may interfere with the actions of the plaintiff or of other persons resulting in harm to the plaintiff. Rookes v. Barnard, [1964] A.C. 1129 (appeal taken from Q.B.) (strike threats made by Union, forcing dismissal of plaintiff employee). To threaten to do what one has a legal right to do does not constitute intimidation.

2. The law of fraudulent and negligent misrepresentation plays a similar role in increasing the reliability of information upon which parties act in entering into contracts.

3. Take the following case: Silsbee v. Webber, 171 Mass. 378, 50 N.E. 555 (1898) where defendant threatened to charge plaintiff mother's son with embezzlement before plaintiff's ailing husband. To spare her husband's delicate physical condition, plaintiff transferred property to defendant. Should plaintiff be allowed to recover for her own emotional distress? Should it make any difference whether her son had actually embezzled funds?

The case raises the conundrums surrounding blackmail. Is the criminal law, and therefore tort law building on it, inefficient in foreclosing the blackmailed person's choice to pay for silence? This topic has led to trenchant academic exchanges: Symposium on Blackmail, 141 U. Pa. L. Rev. 1565 (1993). See also Lawrence M. Friedman, Guarding Life's Dark Secrets: Legal and Social Contracts over Reputation, Propriety, and Privacy (2007, Stanford UP), 81–100.

Freeman & Mills, Inc. v. Belcher Oil Company

Supreme Court of California, 1995.
11 Cal.4th 85, 44 Cal.Rptr.2d 420, 900 P.2d 669.

LUCAS, C. J. We granted review in this case to resolve some of the widespread confusion that has arisen regarding the application of our opinion in Seaman's Direct Buying Service, Inc. v. Standard Oil Co. (1984) 36 Cal. 3d 752 [206 Cal. Rptr. 354, 686 P.2d 1158] (Seaman's). We held in that case that a tort cause of action might lie "when, in addition to breaching the contract, [defendant] seeks to shield itself from liability by denying, in bad faith and without probable cause, that the contract exists." [c]

In the present case, the Court of Appeal reversed judgment for plaintiff and remanded the case for a limited retrial, but also suggested that "it is time for the Supreme Court to reexamine the tort of 'bad faith denial of contract.' " We agree, and proceed to do so here. As our order granting review stated, "the issue to be argued before this court is limited to whether, and under what circumstances, a party to a contract may recover in tort for another party's bad faith denial of the contract's existence."

* * *

[W]e have concluded that the *Seaman's* court incorrectly recognized a tort cause of action based on the defendant's bad faith denial of the existence of a contract between the parties. That holding has been widely criticized by legal scholars, has caused considerable confusion among lower courts, and has been rejected by the courts of several other jurisdictions. These critics convincingly argue that the Seaman's decision is confusing and ambiguous, analytically flawed, and promotes questionable policy. After careful review of all the foregoing considerations, we conclude that our *Seaman's* holding should be overruled.

I. Facts

* * * In June 1987, defendant Belcher Oil Company (Belcher Oil) retained the law firm of Morgan, Lewis & Bockius (Morgan) to defend it in a Florida lawsuit. Pursuant to a letter of understanding signed by Belcher Oil's general counsel (William Dunker) and a Morgan partner (Donald Smaltz), Belcher Oil was to pay for costs incurred on its behalf, including fees for accountants. In February 1988, after first obtaining Dunker's express authorization, Smaltz hired plaintiff, the accounting firm of Freeman & Mills, Incorporated (Freeman and Mills), to provide a financial analysis and litigation support for Belcher Oil in the Florida lawsuit.

In March, an engagement letter was signed by both Morgan and Freeman & Mills. At about this time, William Dunker left Belcher Oil and was replaced by Neil Bowman. In April 1988, Bowman became dissatisfied with Morgan's efforts and the lawyers were discharged. Bowman asked Morgan for a summary of the work performed by Freeman & Mills and, at the same time, directed Smaltz to have Freeman & Mills stop their work for Belcher Oil. Smaltz did as he was asked. Freeman & Mills's final statement was for $70,042.50 in fees, plus $7,495.63 for costs, a total of $77,538.13.

Freeman & Mills billed Morgan, but no payment was forthcoming. Freeman & Mills then billed Belcher Oil directly and, for about a year, sent monthly statements and regularly called Bowman about the bill, but no payment was forthcoming. In August 1989, Smaltz finally told Freeman & Mills that Belcher Oil refused to pay their bill. Freeman & Mills then wrote to Bowman asking that the matter be resolved. In September 1989, Bowman responded, complaining that Belcher Oil had not been consulted about the extent of Freeman & Mills's services and suggesting Freeman & Mills should look to Morgan for payment of whatever amounts were claimed due.

Ultimately, Freeman & Mills filed this action against Belcher Oil, alleging (in its second amended complaint) causes of action for breach of contract, "bad faith denial of contract," and quantum meruit. Belcher Oil answered and the case was presented to a jury in a bifurcated trial, with punitive damages reserved for the second phase. According to the evidence presented during the first phase, the amount owed to Freeman & Mills (as indicated on their statements) was $77,538.13.

The jury returned its first phase verdict. On Freeman & Mills's breach of contract claim, the jury found that Belcher Oil had authorized Morgan to retain Freeman & Mills on Belcher Oil's behalf, that Freeman & Mills had performed its obligations under the contract, that Belcher Oil had breached the contract, and that the amount of damages suffered by Freeman & Mills was $25,000. The jury also answered affirmatively the questions about whether Belcher Oil had denied the existence of the contract and had acted with oppression, fraud, or malice. Thereafter, the jury returned its verdict awarding $477,538.13 in punitive damages and judgment was entered consistent with the jury's verdicts.

In three post-trial motions, Freeman & Mills asked for orders (1) "correcting" the jury's verdicts and the court's judgment to reflect compensatory damages of $77,538.13 and punitive damages of $425,000 (on the ground that the jury's questions showed this was its true intent); (2) awarding attorney fees as sanctions for the litigation tactics of Belcher Oil's attorneys; and (3) awarding prejudgment interest on the compensatory damage award. Over Belcher Oil's opposition, all three motions were granted—but with some changes in the course of correcting the judgment—by giving Freeman & Mills $131,614.93 in compensatory damages (the $25,000 actually awarded by the jury, plus the $77,538.13 included in the punitive damage award, plus $29,076.80 for prejudgment interest), and $400,000 (not $425,000 as requested) in punitive damages.

Belcher Oil appealed from the "corrected" judgment. Freeman & Mills cross-appealed from a mid-trial order denying its request to amend its complaint to add a cause of action for fraud, an issue not presently before us. The Court of Appeal majority, finding no "special relationship" between the parties to justify a tort theory of recovery under Seaman's, reversed the judgment and remanded the case to the trial court for a retrial limited to the issue of damages under plaintiff's breach of contract cause of action. (The Court of Appeal dissenting justice would have sustained the tort cause of action and remanded for retrial of the damage issue as to both causes of action.) As will appear, we affirm the judgment of the Court of Appeal, concluding that a tort recovery is unavailable in this case.

II. The Seaman's Decision

The tort of bad faith "denial of contract" was established in a per curiam opinion in *Seaman's* [C]. These were the facts before the court in that case: In 1971, Seaman's Direct Buying Service, a small marine fueling station in Eureka, wanted to expand its operation by developing a marine fuel dealership in conjunction with a new marina under development by the City of Eureka. When Seaman's approached the city about a long-term lease of a large parcel of land in the marina, the city required Seaman's to obtain a binding commitment from an oil supplier. To that end, Seaman's negotiated with several companies and, by 1972, reached a tentative agreement with Standard Oil Company of California.

Both Seaman's and Standard Oil signed a letter of intent setting forth the basic terms of their arrangement, but that letter was subject to government approval of the contract, continued approval of Seaman's credit status, and future agreement on specific arrangements. Seaman's showed the letter to the city and, shortly thereafter, signed a 40-year lease with the city. [C]

Shortly thereafter, an oil shortage dramatically reduced the available supplies of oil and, in November 1973, Standard Oil told Seaman's that new federal regulations requiring allocation of petroleum products to those that had been customers since 1972 precluded its execution of a new dealership agreement. In response, Seaman's obtained an exemption from the appropriate federal agency. Standard Oil appealed and persuaded the agency to reverse the order, but Seaman's eventually had the exemption reinstated contingent on a court determination that a valid contract existed between the parties. [C]

Seaman's then asked Standard Oil to stipulate to the existence of a contract, stating that a refusal would force it to discontinue operations. Standard Oil's representative refused the request, telling Seaman's, "See you in court." Seaman's business collapsed and it sued Standard Oil for damages on four theories—breach of contract, fraud, breach of the implied covenant of good faith and fair dealing, and interference with Seaman's contractual relationship with the city. [C]

The case was tried to a jury, which returned its verdicts in favor of Seaman's on all theories except fraud, awarding compensatory and punitive damages. Standard Oil appealed. [C] We considered "whether, and under what circumstances, a breach of the implied covenant of good faith and fair dealing in a commercial contract may give rise to an action in tort." [C] For purposes of completeness, we quote from *Seaman's* at some length:

"It is well settled that, in California, the law implies in every contract a covenant of good faith and fair dealing. Broadly stated, that covenant requires that neither party do anything which will deprive the other of the benefits of the agreement. California courts have recognized the existence of this covenant, and enforced it, in cases involving a wide variety of contracts. . . . In the seminal cases of Comunale v. Traders & General Ins. Co. [(1958)] 50 Cal. 2d 654 [328 P.2d 198, 68 A.L.R.2d 883], and Crisci v. Security Ins. Co. [(1967)] 66 Cal. 2d 425 [58 Cal. Rptr. 13, 426 P.2d 173], this court held that a breach of the covenant of good faith and fair dealing by an insurance carrier may give rise to a cause of action in tort as well as in contract. [C]

"While the proposition that the law implies a covenant of good faith and fair dealing in all contracts is well established, the proposition advanced by *Seaman's*—that breach of the covenant always gives rise to an action in tort—is not so clear. In holding that a tort action is available for breach of the covenant in an insurance contract, we have emphasized the 'special relationship' between insurer and insured, characterized by elements of public interest, adhesion, and fiduciary responsibility. No doubt there are other relationships with similar characteristics and deserving of similar legal treatment.

"When we move from such special relationships to consideration of the tort remedy in the context of the ordinary commercial contract, we move into largely uncharted and potentially dangerous waters. Here, parties of roughly equal bargaining power are free to shape the contours of their agreement and to include provisions for attorney fees and liquidated damages in the event of breach. They may not be permitted to disclaim the covenant of good faith but they are free, within reasonable limits at least, to agree upon the standards by which application of the covenant is to be measured. In such contracts, it may be difficult to distinguish between breach of the covenant and breach of contract, and there is the risk that interjecting tort remedies will intrude upon the expectations of the parties. This is not to say that tort remedies have no place in such a commercial context, but that it is wise to proceed with caution in determining their scope and application.

"For the purposes of this case it is unnecessary to decide the broad question which Seaman's poses. Indeed, it is not even necessary to predicate liability on a breach of the implied covenant. It is sufficient to recognize that a party to a contract may incur tort remedies when, in addition to breaching the contract, it seeks to shield itself from liability by denying, in bad faith and without probable cause, that the contract exists.

"It has been held that a party to a contract may be subject to tort liability, including punitive damages, if he coerces the other party to pay more than is due under the contract terms through the threat of a lawsuit, made " 'without probable cause and with no belief in the existence of the cause of action.' " There is little difference, in principle, between a contracting party obtaining excess payment in such manner, and a contracting party seeking to avoid all liability on a meritorious contract claim by adopting a 'stonewall' position ('see you in court') without probable cause and with no belief in the existence of a defense. Such conduct goes beyond the mere breach of contract. It offends accepted notions of business ethics. [C] Acceptance of tort remedies in such a situation is not likely to intrude upon the bargaining relationship or upset reasonable expectations of the contracting parties." [C]

Seaman's concluded that, because a good faith denial of the existence of a binding contract is not a tort [c], the trial court's failure to instruct the jury on the requirement of bad faith was error (ibid.) and that error was prejudicial. [C]

* * *

IV. Subsequent Developments

A. California Supreme Court Decisions—Subsequent opinions of this court indicate a continuing reluctance, originally reflected in *Seaman's* itself, to authorize tort recovery for noninsurance contract breaches.

In Foley v. Interactive Data Corp. (1988) 47 Cal. 3d 654 [254 Cal. Rptr. 211, 765 P.2d 373] (Foley), we considered the availability of tort damages for the wrongful termination of a discharged employee. Declining to rely on dictum in *Seaman's* [c] regarding the possible availability of tort remedies for breach of the implied covenant of good faith and fair dealing (hereafter the implied covenant) in the employment context, we refused to afford such remedies for the essentially contractual claim of breach of the implied covenant arising in that context. [C]

In reaching our conclusion in *Foley*, we relied in part on certain basic principles relevant to contract law, including the need for "predictability about the cost of contractual relationships," and the purpose of contract damages to compensate the injured party rather than punish the breaching party. [C] Focusing on the implied covenant, we observed that, with the exception of insurance contracts, "[b]ecause the covenant is a contract term, . . . compensation for its breach has almost always been limited to contract rather than tort remedies." [C]

We acknowledged in *Foley* that "[t]he insurance cases . . . were a major departure from traditional principles of contract law," and we stressed that the courts should take "great care" before extending "the exceptional approach taken in those cases" to "another contract setting." [C] We concluded that "the employment relationship is not sufficiently similar to that of insurer and insured to warrant judicial extension of the proposed additional tort remedies. . . ." [C]

[The Court discusses Hunter v. Up-Right and Applied Equipment v. Litton Saudi Arabia, 6 Cal. 4th 1174, 26 Cal. Rptr. 2d 8, 864 P.2d 88 (1993), 7 Cal. 4th 503, 28 Cal. Rptr. 2d 475, 869 P.2d 454 (1994).]

* * *

Our decisions in *Foley*, *Hunter*, and *Applied Equipment* each contains language that strongly suggests courts should limit tort recovery in contract breach situations to the insurance area, at least in the absence of violation of an independent duty arising from principles of tort law other than denial of the existence of, or liability under, the breached contract. (See also White v. Western Title Ins. Co. (1985) 40 Cal. 3d 870, 901 [221 Cal. Rptr. 509, 710 P.2d 309] (conc. and dis. opn. of Kaus, J.) [observing that "our experience in *Seaman's* surely tells us that there are real problems in applying the substitute remedy of a tort recovery—with or without punitive damages—outside the insurance area," and urging a legislative solution].)

* * *

Without analyzing the particular facts of each case, it is sufficient to observe that our Seaman's holding has presented the lower courts with a number of unanswered questions, and that these courts have reached varying, and often inconsistent, conclusions in response. [Cc]

* * *

[Much] confusion and conflict has arisen regarding the scope and application of our *Seaman's* holding. For example, does the *Seaman's* tort derive from breach of the implied covenant or from some other independent tort duty? [Cc]

Confusion and conflict alone might not justify a decision to abrogate *Seaman's*, for we could attempt to resolve all the uncertainties engendered by that decision. But there are additional considerations that convince us to forgo that predictably Herculean effort. Many of the pertinent Court of Appeal decisions recognize compelling policy reasons supporting the preclusion of tort remedies for contractual breaches outside the insurance context. * * *

Similarly, in Harris [v. Atlantic Richfield Co.], 14 Cal. App. 4th 70 [(1993)], the Court of Appeal denied a tort recovery for bad faith contract breach in violation of public policy. The court elaborated on the applicable policy considerations as follows: "The traditional goal of contract remedies is compensation of the promisee for the loss resulting from the breach, not compulsion of the promisor to perform his promises. Therefore, 'willful' breaches have not been distinguished from other breaches. [C] The restrictions on contract remedies serve purposes not found in tort law. They protect the parties' freedom to bargain over special risks and they promote contract formation by limiting liability to the value of the promise. This encourages efficient breaches, resulting in increased production of goods and services at lower cost to society. [C] Because of these overriding policy considerations, the California Supreme Court has proceeded with caution in carving out exceptions to the traditional contract remedy restrictions." [C]

The *Harris* court set forth as reasons for denying tort recovery in contract breach cases (1) the different objectives underlying the remedies for tort and contract breach, (2) the importance of predictability in assuring commercial stability in contractual dealings, (3) the potential for converting every contract breach into a tort, with accompanying punitive damage recovery, and (4) the preference for legislative action in affording appropriate remedies. [Cc]

[T]he foregoing policy considerations fully support our decision to overrule Seaman's rather than attempt to clarify its uncertain boundaries. (We observe that plaintiff has asked us to take judicial notice of certain records purportedly showing there were only a few jury verdicts involving Seaman's claims during the period from 1981 to 1994. Because jury verdicts are an inconclusive indicia of excessive litigation, and because defendant has raised some doubts regarding the accuracy and completeness of the submitted materials, the application for judicial notice is denied.)

* * *

Ninth Circuit Judge Kozinski expressed his candid criticism of *Seaman's* in a concurring opinion in Oki America, Inc. v. Microtech Intern., Inc. (9th Cir.1989) 872 F.2d 312, 314–317 (Oki America). Among other criticism, Judge Kozinski found the Seaman's holding unduly imprecise and confusing. As he stated, "It is impossible to draw a principled distinction between a tortious denial of a contract's existence and a permissible denial of liability under the terms of the contract. The test . . . seems to be whether the conduct 'offends accepted notions of business ethics.' This gives judges license to rely on their gut feelings in distinguishing between a squabble and a tort. As a result, both the commercial world and the courts are needlessly burdened. . . ." [C]

Judge Kozinski also mentioned the substantial costs associated with Seaman's litigation, and the resulting interference with contractual relationships. "Perhaps most troubling, the willingness of courts to subordinate voluntary contractual arrangements to their own sense of public policy and proper business decorum deprives individuals of an important measure of freedom. The right to enter into contracts—to adjust one's legal relationships by mutual agreement [ ] is too easily smothered by government officers eager to tell us what's best for us." [C] Judge Kozinski concluded by observing that "Seaman's is a prime candidate for reconsideration." [C]

Similarly, in Air-Sea Forwarders, Inc. v. Air Asia Co., Ltd., supra, 880 F.2d at pages 184–185, Judge Hall observed that Seaman's "*ambiguous*" holding had caused widespread confusion among the lower courts. As Judge Hall stated, "Indeed, the *Seaman's* court's failure to explain why it was not necessary to predicate its holding on the implied covenant of good faith and fair dealing, or to justify the dramatically greater liability for the bad faith denial of the existence of a contract as compared to the bad faith dispute of a contract's terms, undoubtedly spawned the confusion in the appellate division cases discussed infra." [C]

[The Court discussed other critical case law and scholarship.]

* * *

As previously indicated, the *Seaman's* decision has generated uniform confusion and uncertainty regarding its scope and application, and widespread doubt about the necessity or desirability of its holding. These doubts and criticisms, express or implied, in decisions from this state and from other state and federal courts, echoed by the generally adverse scholarly comment cited above, convince us that *Seaman's* should be overruled in favor of a general rule precluding tort recovery for noninsurance contract breach, at least in the absence of violation of "an independent duty arising from principles of tort law" (*Applied Equipment*, supra, 7 Cal. 4th at page. 515) other than the bad faith denial of the existence of, or liability under, the breached contract.

As set forth above, the critics stress, among other factors favoring *Seaman's* abrogation, the confusion and uncertainty accompanying the decision, the need for stability and predictability in commercial affairs, the potential for excessive tort damages, and the preference for legislative rather than judicial action in this area.

Even if we were unimpressed by the nearly unanimous criticism leveled at *Seaman's*, on reconsideration the analytical defects in the opinion have become apparent. It seems anomalous to characterize as "tortious" the bad faith denial of the existence of a contract, while treating as "contractual" the bad faith denial of liability or responsibility under an acknowledged contract. In both cases, the breaching party has acted in bad faith and, accordingly, has presumably committed acts offensive to "accepted notions of business ethics." [C] Yet to include bad faith denials of liability within *Seaman's* scope could potentially convert every contract breach into a tort. Nor would limiting *Seaman's* tort to incidents involving "stonewalling" adequately narrow its potential scope. Such conduct by the breaching party, essentially telling the promisee, "See you in court," could incidentally accompany every breach of contract.

For all the foregoing reasons, we conclude that *Seaman's* should be overruled. We emphasize that nothing in this opinion should be read as affecting the existing precedent governing enforcement of the implied covenant in insurance cases. Further, nothing we say here would prevent the Legislature from creating additional civil remedies for noninsurance contract breach, including such measures as providing litigation costs and attorney fees in certain aggravated cases, or assessing increased compensatory damages covering lost profits and other losses attributable to the breach, as well as restoration of the *Seaman's* holding if the Legislature deems that course appropriate. [Cc] Thus far, however, the Legislature has not manifested an intent either to expand contract breach recovery or to provide tort damages for ordinary contract breach.

The judgment of the Court of Appeal, reversing the trial court's judgment in plaintiff's favor and remanding the case for a retrial limited to the issue of damages under plaintiff's breach of contract cause of action, and for judgment in favor of defendant on plaintiff's bad faith denial of contract cause of action, is affirmed.

NOTES AND QUESTIONS

1. As the principal case indicates, the insurance context is the only firm category in which the courts are prepared to find an action in tort for breach of the covenant of good faith. Careau & Co. v. Security Pacific Business Credit, Inc., 222 Cal.App.3d 1371, 272 Cal.Rptr. 387 (1990) (noting the "well-developed history of recognizing" a tort remedy in insurance cases); Roehl Transp., Inc. v. Liberty Mut. Ins. Co., 2010 WI 49,

325 Wis. 2d 56, 784 N.W.2d 542 (tort remedy for failure to settle even when judgment was within policy limits); Willis v. Swain, 129 Haw. 478, 304 P.3d 619 (2013) (extending tort liability even in the absence of an underlying contract under the state's joint underwriting scheme). Courts have refused to extend liability to other contexts: Cates Construction, Inc. v. Talbot Partners, 21 Cal. 4th 28, 86 Cal.Rptr.2d 855, 980 P.2d 407 (1999) (refusing to extend tort liability to breach of surety bond). Intent is not a required element of bad faith: Zoppo v. Homestead Insurance, 71 Ohio St. 3d 552, 644 N.E.2d 397 (1994) (failure to conduct adequate investigation sufficient for finding of bad faith).

2. Should tortious relief be permitted where in-house counsel is dismissed for pursuing a legal agenda that he regards as ethically binding but corporate management finds incompatible with the profit-seeking motive of the corporation? GTE Products Corp. v. Stewart, 421 Mass. 22, 653 N.E.2d 161 (1995).

Other "Business Torts"

There are several fields of the law in the business milieu that involve the imposition of economic injury on a person who is therefore entitled to monetary damages or an injunction against continuing the conduct. These remedies were derived essentially from the philosophy of tort law, but they have now become separate fields of the law developing through statutory provisions, administrative regulations and their own independent concepts. Only a brief reference can be made here.

1. *Copyright and Patent Infringement.* Article I, § 8, cl. 8 of the U.S. Constitution provides that Congress has the power to "promote the Progress of Science and useful Arts by securing for limited Times to Authors and Inventors the exclusive Right to their respective Writings and Discoveries." Congress has exercised this power. See 17 U.S.C.A. §§ 101 et seq. (copyright); 35 U.S.C.A. §§ 1 et seq. (patents).

There are, of course, unsettled problems. Particularly relevant is the issue of federal preemption. See, for example, the twin cases of Sears, Roebuck & Co. v. Stiffel Co., 376 U.S. 225 (1964); and Compco Corp. v. Day-Brite Lighting, Inc., 376 U.S. 234 (1964), holding that there can be no common law protection of the functional design of a product. If it is capable of being patented, compliance with the statutory procedure is necessary; if it is not, it cannot be protected by the common law. "To allow a state by use of its law of unfair competition to prevent the copying of an article which represents too slight an advance to be patented would be to permit the state to block off from the public something which federal law has said belongs to the public." However, provided the torts are not construed to offer patent-like protection, they are not pre-empted. In Rodime PLC v. Seagate Technology, Inc., 174 F.3d 1294, 1306 (Fed. Cir. 1999), the court held that tortious interference and unfair competition protect separate interests: they protect business relationships from wrongful interference or attack "unethical and oppressive business practices."

2. *Trade Marks and Trade Names.* A considerable body of learning has developed regarding trade marks and trade names. Much of it has been common law, but the Lanham Act (Trademark Act of 1946, 15 U.S.C.A. §§ 1051 et seq.) has extensively revised and reorganized it.

3. *Trade Secrets.* Much of this is common law, but there are state statutes and a Uniform Trade Secrets Act. Issues of federal preemption give difficulty here, too.

4. *Unfair Competition.* The three previous topics have often been combined under the generic term "unfair competition," which is also inclusive of such matters as "passing off" of one's goods as another's or misappropriation of another's ideas, news items or unpublished writings. State statutes covering unfair trade practices, false advertising and similar matters are included.

5. *Other Statutes Involving Regulation of Business.* Federal statutes include The Sherman Antitrust Act, 15 U.S.C.A. §§ 1–7 (conspiracy in restraint of trade, attempt to monopolize), Clayton Antitrust Act, 15 U.S.C.A. §§ 12–27 (restraints and monopolies); Robinson-Patman Act, 15 U.S.C.A. §§ 12 et seq. (price discrimination); Federal Trade Commission Act, 15 U.S.C.A. §§ 41–58 et seq., and regulations. There are also various state antitrust statutes.

6. *Labor Law.* Many of the early cases on tortious interference with existing or prospective economic advantage involved contests between employers and employees. Today these have all been incorporated into the law of labor relations, both federal and state, and much of it statutory or based on administrative regulations or rulings.

7. *Civil RICO.* The Racketeer Influenced and Corrupt Organizations Act, 18 U.S.C.A. §§ 1961–1968, is primarily a criminal statute. However, Congress has provided a private cause of action for its breach under § 1964(c). Because of its potent remedies—treble damages and attorney's fees—the statutory cause of action has been increasingly asserted, especially in light of the Section's wide interpretation by the United States Supreme Court in Sedima, S.P.R.L. v. Imrex Co., Inc., 473 U.S. 479 (1985). The action is more thoroughly canvassed infra in Chapter 23.

2. FAMILY RELATIONS

Nash v. Baker

Court of Appeals of Oklahoma, 1974.
522 P.2d 1335.

ROMANG, JUDGE. The appellants, hereinafter referred to as plaintiffs, are five minor children whose mother, Marian Nash, brings this appeal as their natural guardian and next friend. The appellee is hereinafter referred to as the defendant.

Marian Nash filed the petition in her own right and as next friend of the infant plaintiffs, alleging that after Marian Nash and James Nash had been husband and wife for about 18 years and had five children (the minor plaintiffs) of that union, the defendant, a wealthy widow, who knew or should have known of the marriage and children, lured James Nash, the husband and father, away from the plaintiffs by providing said James Nash with a finer home, sexual charms, and other inducements. The plaintiff Marian Nash sought to recover actual and punitive damages in her own right for the alienation of her husband's affections, loss of consortium, and loss of a prospective increased standard of living. In addition, as next friend of her children, she sought recovery of actual and punitive damages under the common law for alienation of their father's affections, interference with their family relationships, and "loss of the society, affection, assistance, moral support and guidance" of their father. The petition also alleged adultery by the defendant with said James Nash.

The trial court sustained the defendant's demurrer as to each of the minor plaintiffs' asserted causes of action and overruled it as to Marian Nash's suit in her own right. The latter suit was tried to a jury, resulting in a verdict for the defendant. The only questions before this court deal with whether any cause of action may be maintained on behalf of the minor children of a marriage, against a woman who entices away their father from the marital home.

The sole question remaining is whether * * * a minor child has in Oklahoma a common law right to sue a third person whose luring away of the father breaks up the parents' marriage and deprives the child of the father's society and guidance. The common law recognized no such right in the child. That the injured spouse has an action for alienation of affections, loss of consortium, or criminal conversation does not require that a cause of action be given to the child. * * * The plaintiffs cite Prosser, Law of Torts 908 (3d ed. 1964) which, although recognizing that the majority of those jurisdictions which passed on the question have denied the child an action, predicts that in the future additional jurisdictions will allow his action. On the other hand, * * * modern statutes abolishing causes of action for alienation of affections, breach of promise to marry, and related actions; the increasing failure of marriages, reportedly more than one in three ending in absolute divorce or permanent separation; and the recent liberalization of divorce in several more states, including a ground or grounds not based on "fault"; and the increase in the number of children whose parents have divorced and remarried; may well prevent the future development predicted by the late Professor Prosser. In addition, there may be a growing feeling that very often the "fault" leading to the breakup of a marriage may not be readily determinable in court, and that the "fault" which caused one spouse to be attracted to a third person was not the magnetism of such third person, but that of an emotional vacuum in the home.

Affirmed.

NOTES AND QUESTIONS

1. The law of torts has been concerned not only with the protection of property and associated interests, but also with what may be called "relational" interests founded upon the relation in which plaintiff stands toward one or more third persons. W. Prosser and Keeton, Torts § 124 (5th ed. 1984); Green, Relational Interests, 29 Ill.L.Rev. 460 (1934). Much development in this area has been based on claims alleging an interference with a family relationship. At early common law, most claims were brought by husbands for loss of economic services of a wife or child. Today there is potential for a claim to be brought by any member of the family unit and the focus is more likely to be on loss of intangible matters such as companionship or affection. The concentration here is on modern remedies.

Claims Based on Intentional Interference

2. *Alienation of Affections.*

A. *Husband and Wife.* In some states today a spouse may bring a claim against a third party for alienation of affections. The plaintiff must show that the spouse's mental attitude and conjugal kindness were converted by the defendant. Pankratz v. Miller, 401 N.W.2d 543, 547 (S.D. 1987) (no liability when alienated wife initiated and pursued the affair).

Most courts have held that it is not necessary to show an act of adultery; in fact, the defendant need not be a romantic rival.

However, parents may be privileged to act when they reasonably believe it to be in the best interest of their child. Compare Koehler v. Koehler, 248 Iowa 144, 79 N.W.2d 791 (1956) (noting parental right to "advise and assist" child in marital decisions), with Glatstein v. Grund, 243 Iowa 541, 51 N.W.2d 162 (1952) (bad faith when husband's mother insisted on sleeping in the same room as the couple, told the wife she was one of "a litter of pigs," and forced the wife to take contraceptives).

While the majority of jurisdictions have abolished the cause of action for alienation of affection, see Helsel v. Noellsch, 107 S.W.3d 231 (Mo. 2003), it lives on in a handful of states, see Fitch v. Valentine, 959 So. 2d 1012 (Miss. 2007) (justifying recognition in the "interest of protecting the marital relationship"). Abolition of the tort of alienation of affections was confirmed in *Helsel*, but cf. the tort of criminal conversation lives in North Carolina, Nunn v. Allen, 154 N.C.App. 523, 574 S.E.2d 35 (2002).

B. *Parent and Child.* If a child is abducted or defendant intentionally deprives a parent of a child's economic services, precedent supports a claim. Most courts have declined, however, to create an alienation-of-affections remedy either on behalf of a parent for loss of a child or a child for loss of a parent. Bartanus v. Lis, 332 Pa.Super. 48, 480 A.2d 1178 (1984) (finding no action for parent absent proof of elements in intentional infliction of emotional distress); Doe v. McKay, 183 Ill.2d 272, 233 Ill.Dec. 310, 700 N.E.2d 1018 (1988) (no cause of action when therapist encouraged daughter to recover memories of sexual molestation by her father). In Wolf v. Wolf, 690 N.W.2d 887 (Iowa 2005): both compensatory and punitive damages were awarded to father, for mother's interference with award of custody.

3. *Criminal Conversation.* This is a tort in which a married person may recover both compensatory and punitive damages by proving that the spouse and the defendant engaged in sexual intercourse. The action became in the 17th Century preliminary to divorce proceedings and, thus, divorce for adultery was introduced into the Law. How should damages be computed? Where both an action for criminal conversation and alienation of affection are pleaded, the jury should be instructed not to allow recovery for the same loss under both. When the crime of adultery has been abolished by the legislature or has been reduced to a misdemeanor with a slight fine, should this affect the tort remedy? Neal v. Neal, 125 Idaho 627, 873 P.2d 881 (App. 1993) (describing the action as an anachronism).

4. *Statutory Abolition of Actions.* Beginning in the late 1930's, legislatures in a substantial number of states have abolished tort actions based on intentional interference with family relations that carry an accusation of sexual behavior. See, e.g., Ala. Code § 6–5–331; Md. Code Ann., Cts. & Jud. Proc. § 5–801; N.Y. Civ. Rights Law § 80–a. The statutes,

known as "Anti-Heart Balm" laws, have generally withstood constitutional challenge. Do you think there should be an action against a spouse or lover for intentional infliction of emotional distress? See Speer v. Dealy, 242 Neb. 542, 495 N.W.2d 911 (1993). For an application of a statute eliminating the action for alienation of affections, see Bailey v. Faulkner, 940 So.2d 247 (Ala. 2006) (action by husband against pastor who had relationship with wife during counseling). What policy reasons support such actions? If a state has an "Anti-Heart Balm" statute, should a child's claim for alienation of affections be automatically barred? See Russick v. Hicks, 85 F.Supp. 281 (W.D. Mich. 1949).

Claims Based on Negligent Interference

5. At common law a husband was legally entitled to his wife's earnings and services. Courts protected the husband's right to these "assets" against negligent interference by third parties. The action is known as one for loss of consortium. The husband also may be able to recover general damages for loss of companionship and sexual relations. Because a wife had no legal interest in her husband's personal property, she was denied a claim.

6. With the growth of legal equality between the spouses, it might be anticipated that the cause of action for loss of consortium would disappear. Instead, beginning with Hitaffer v. Argonne Co., Inc., 183 F.2d 811 (D.C. Cir. 1950), cert. denied, 340 U.S. 852 (1950), courts in many states have permitted both spouses to bring a claim for loss of consortium. See, e.g., Rodriguez v. Bethlehem Steel Corp., 12 Cal. 3d 382, 525 P.2d 669, 115 Cal. Rptr. 765 (1974); Millington v. Southeastern Elevator Co., 22 N.Y.2d 498, 239 N.E.2d 897, 293 N.Y.S.2d 305 (1968). The emphasis on the damage element in the claim has shifted away from economic loss to intangibles such as loss of companionship and affection.

7. Can the claim stand where the marriage has not been formalized? Authority is divided. For a decision insisting on the existence of a formalized marriage, see Elden v. Sheldon, 46 Cal. 3d 267, 758 P.2d 582, 250 Cal. Rptr. 254 (1988) (requiring formalized marriage to prevent burden on courts of determining whether cohabitating couple is "closely related"). New Mexico is the exception to the rule: Loyoza v. Sanchez, 133 N.M. 579, 66 P.3d 948 (2003) (abrogated on other grounds).

8. Although loss of consortium could be viewed as a wholly independent injury, most courts regard it as a derivative claim, subject to all defenses that could be asserted against the spouse who was physically injured. See Buckley v. Nat'l Freight, 90 N.Y.2d 210, 659 N.Y.S.2d 841, 681 N.E.2d 1287 (1997) (discussing various jurisdictions' approaches to joining a loss of consortium claim).

9. Courts have generally declined to allow claims for pure loss of companionship when a child seeks a recovery from a defendant who injured his parent. See, e.g. Mendillo v. Bd. of Educ., 246 Conn. 456, 717 A.2d 1177 (1998) (denying minor child's claim and noting "overwhelming weight of authority" against recognition of the tort). Of the minority of states that have recognized the tort, at least one has done so through statute: La. C.C. Art. 2315 (extending loss of consortium to any party who could have brought an action for wrongful death). See also Taylor v. Beard, 104 S.W.3d 507 (Tenn. 2003) (declining to create a common law cause of action and

leaving the issue to the discretion of the legislature). Claims by parents solely for loss of companionship of their injured children have received similar treatment. Elgin v. Bartlett, 994 P.2d 411, 419 (Colo. 1999). But see Estate of Wells by Jeske v. Mount Sinai Med. Ctr., 183 Wis. 2d 667, 515 N.W.2d 705 (1994) (noting that Wisconsin permits recovery for loss of filial consortium of minor, but not adult, children).

What about siblings? Wachocki v. Bernalillo Cnty. Sheriff's Dep't, 150 N.M. 650, 265 P.3d 701 (2011) (holding that adult siblings may have a cause of action for loss of consortium if they are "mutually dependent").

CHAPTER 23

TORTS IN THE AGE OF STATUTES

The Twentieth Century saw an explosion in the number of statutes enacted by state legislatures and by Congress. The common law of torts is now riddled with statutory inroads. Legislative change has been noted in contributory negligence, contribution between tortfeasors, the abrogation of immunities, limitation periods, and many other topics touched on in the Torts course. This chapter examines those instances where statutes may impliedly or expressly provide or take away a remedy in tort. This chapter is divided into several sections. The first section addresses implied rights of action in from state law, constitutional law, and federal statutes. The next section addresses express rights of action created by federal statute. Finally, the chapter turns to the question of tort reform. It is predictable that our present century will witness no diminution in the pace of legislative enactment, especially as regulation flows from the wreckage of the 2009 financial crisis. Accordingly, the place of tort law within that legislative explosion will continue to present a challenge. As you read the chapter keep in mind that the balance being struck between the legislature and courts in granting, implying, interpreting, and even removing causes of action based upon the Constitution and statutes. What do you think are the important issues to be considered?

1. IMPLIED RIGHTS OF ACTION

(A) IMPLIED RIGHTS OF ACTION FROM STATE LAW

The following cases, both from the Oregon Supreme Court both deal with the question of whether a right of action may be implied from state statutory law, reaching opposite conclusions. How would you distinguish the two cases?

Burnette v. Wahl

Supreme Court of Oregon, 1978.
284 Or. 705, 588 P.2d 1105.

HOLMAN, JUSTICE. Three identical cases have been consolidated for appeal. Plaintiffs are five minor children aged two to eight who, through their guardian, are bringing actions against their mothers for emotional and psychological injury caused by failure of defendant-mothers to perform their parental duties to plaintiffs. Plaintiffs appeal from orders of dismissal entered after demurrers were sustained to the complaints and plaintiffs refused to plead further.

The complaints allege that plaintiffs are in the custody of the Children's Services Division of the Department of Human Resources of the State of Oregon and are wards of Klamath County Juvenile Court.

The complaints are substantially identical, each one being in three counts. Among these counts are strewn various allegations of parental failure upon which the causes of action rest. They are:

"1. Since [date], defendant intentionally, wilfully, maliciously and with cruel disregard of the consequences failed to provide plaintiff with care, custody, parental nurturance, affection, comfort, companionship, support, regular contact and visitation.

"2. She has failed in violation of ORS 109.010[1] to maintain plaintiff, who, due to * * * age and indigency, is poor and unable to work to maintain * * * self.

"3. She has abandoned plaintiff by deserting the child with intent to abandon * * * and with intent to abdicate all responsibility for * * * care and raising, in violation of ORS 163.535.[2]

"4. She has neglected the plaintiff by negligently leaving * * * unattended in or at a place for such period of time as would have been likely to endanger the health or welfare of the plaintiff, in violation of ORS 163.545.[3]

"5. She has refused or neglected without lawful excuse to provide support for plaintiff, in violation of ORS 163.555.[4]

"6. Defendant has maliciously, intentionally, and with cruel disregard of the consequences, deserted and abandoned her child.

"7. Defendant has alienated the affections of the plaintiff in that she has intentionally, wilfully and maliciously abandoned, deserted, neglected and failed to maintain regular contact or visitation, or to provide for the plaintiff and has deprived plaintiff of the love, care, affection and comfort to which plaintiff is entitled."

It is apparent that the first allegation is general in nature and is intended to be all-encompassing. The second, third, fourth and fifth allege violation of statutory duties in which abandonment and desertion comprise the central theme. The sixth allegation is one of abandonment and desertion purportedly based on common law. The seventh allegation is an attempt to allege alienation of affections. Although

---

[1] "ORS 109.010 Duty of Support. Parents are bound to maintain their children who are poor and unable to work to maintain themselves; and children are bound to maintain their parents in like circumstances."

[2] "ORS 163.535 Abandonment of a Child. (1) A person commits the crime of abandonment of a child if, being a parent, lawful guardian or other person lawfully charged with the care or custody of a child under 15 years of age, he deserts the child in any place with intent to abandon it.

"(2) Abandonment of a child is a Class C felony."

[3] "ORS 163.545 Child Neglect. (1) A person having custody or control of a child under 10 years of age commits the crime of child neglect if, with criminal negligence, he leaves the child unattended in or at any place for such period of time as may be likely to endanger the health or welfare of such child.

"(2) Child neglect is a Class A misdemeanor."

[4] ORS 163.555 Criminal Nonsupport. (1) A person commits the crime of criminal nonsupport if, being the parent, lawful guardian or other person lawfully charged with the support of a child under 18 years of age, born in or out of wedlock, he refuses or neglects without lawful excuse to provide support for such child.

"* * *

"(3) Criminal nonsupport is a Class C felony."

these allegations of parental failure allege lack of support and physical care along with affectional neglect, from the allegations of injury in the complaint and the statements made in plaintiffs' brief, it appears that the injuries claimed are solely emotional and psychological.

Preliminary to a more detailed discussion, it should be noted that these claims of parental failure are different from those tort claims usually made upon behalf of children against parents. The adjudicated cases concern physical or emotional injuries resulting from physical acts inflicted upon children such as beatings and rapes and from automobile accidents. Plaintiffs admit they can cite no cases permitting them to recover from their parents for solely emotional or psychological damage resulting from failure to support, nurture and care for them.

The legislature, recognizing the necessity of parental nurture, support and physical care for children, has enacted a vast array of laws for the purpose of protecting or vindicating those rights. These are much more extensive and all-inclusive than are those statutes alleged to have been violated in plaintiffs' allegations of tortious conduct.[5]

ORS ch. 418 establishes extensive provisions for aid to dependent children, and it is under the provisions of this chapter and as wards of the juvenile court that plaintiffs are presently attempting to have their needs met. [The court discusses specific sections of the chapter.]

We recognize that this is not a proceeding to secure parental nurturing, support and physical care for plaintiffs, but rather an action for psychological injury claimed to have been caused by the absence of these services. However, the statutory enactments demonstrate that the legislature has put its mind to the deprivations of which plaintiff children are alleged to be victims and has attempted to remedy such situations by enacting a vast panoply of procedures, both civil and criminal, to insure that children receive proper nurturing, support and physical care. It has never undertaken to establish, however, a cause of action for damages for any emotional injury to the child which may have been caused by a parent's refusal to provide these services. This failure of the legislature to act is significant because this is not a field of recovery which has heretofore been recognized by courts and it would therefore be natural for it to have provided such a remedy if it thought it was wise in view of the social problem it attempts to solve and the statutory provisions it has enacted for that purpose. It has had no difficulty in the past in creating new causes of action for persons aggrieved by conditions which it is attempting to rectify. Examples are the creation of causes of action, including punitive damages, in aid of enforcing ethics in the marketplace, ORS 646.638; actions for compensatory and punitive damages for unlawful discrimination by

[5] Among these laws are ORS 108.040, providing an action against both parents for family necessities; ORS 108.110 *et seq.,* which allow a petition for the support of children to be brought against a parent by the other parent or a state agency for the support of the children; ORS ch. 110, providing both criminal and civil means for reciprocal enforcement between states of the right of support for children; ORS 411.120(4), providing for assistance to dependent children; ORS ch. 416, establishing the relative responsibility law (specifically see ORS 416.090, 416.100, and 416.220 for the means of enforcement); ORS ch. 418, providing for child welfare services (specifically see ORS 418.135(1) and 418.460, concerning enforcement of parental duties); ORS ch. 419, establishing juvenile courts (specifically see ORS 419.513, 419.515, and 419.517 concerning enforcement of support of children by parents).

places of public accommodation, ORS 30.680, and by employers, ORS 659.030 and 659.121; and actions for double and triple damages for timber trespass, ORS 105.810 and 105.815.

The establishment by courts of a civil cause of action based on a criminal or regulatory statute is not premised upon legislative intent to create such an action. It is obvious that had the legislature intended a civil action it would have provided for one, as legislatures many times do. Therefore, the underlying assumption is that it was not intended that the statute create any civil obligation or afford civil protection against the injuries which it was designed to prevent. When neither the statute nor the common law authorizes an action and the statute does not expressly deny it, the court should recognize that it is being asked to bring into existence a new type of tort liability on the basis of its own appraisal of the policy considerations involved. If a court decides to create a cause of action for the act or omission which violates the statute, the interest which is invaded derives its protection solely from the court although the legislative action in branding the act or omission as culpable is taken into consideration by the court in deciding whether a common law action should be established. If a civil cause of action based upon a statute is established by a court, it is because the court, not the legislature, believes it is necessary and desirable to further vindicate the right or to further enforce the duty created by statute.

Because it is plain to the legislature that it could have created the civil liability and it has not, courts must look carefully not only at the particular statute establishing the right or duty but at all statutes which might bear either directly or indirectly on the legislative purpose. If there is any chance that invasion into the field by the court's establishment of a civil cause of action might interfere with the total legislative scheme, courts should err on the side of non-intrusion because it is always possible for the legislature to establish such a civil cause of action if it desires. Courts have no omnipotence in the field of planning, particularly social planning of the kind involved here. Courts should exercise restraint in fields in which the legislature has attempted fairly comprehensive social regulation.

There is no doubt but that the statutory provisions previously cited show a strong state policy of requiring the kind of parental nurturing, support and physical care of children which the defendants here are alleged to have denied their children. As previously indicated, it does not follow as a matter of course that it would be wise or judicious to vindicate that policy by a tort action for damages by children against their mothers. The state also has other policies within its statutory plan of which such a cause of action might well be destructive, particularly the policy of reuniting abandoned children with their parents, if possible. * * *

It is recognized by the statutory scheme that in some instances the reestablishment of a biological family is impossible and it therefore provides for a proceeding to terminate parental rights in order that a new family unit for the child may be formed. * * *

It is significant that plaintiffs' complaints do not allege that proceedings for the termination of the defendants' parental rights have taken place. In such circumstances, it would be exceedingly unwise for this court to step in and to initiate a new and heretofore unrecognized cause of action in a field of social planning to which the legislature has devoted a great deal of time and effort in evolving what appears to be an all-encompassing plan. Those persons designated by statute for aiding the plaintiffs in these cases have not yet taken the step for which the plan provides when there is no longer any hope of reestablishing these children in a family unit with their mothers. Tort actions such as the present ones might well be destructive of any plans the social agencies and the juvenile court might have for these children. It is inappropriate for this court to insert a new cause of action into the picture.

* * * Plaintiffs are unable to point to any literature in the field of child care or family planning which advocates an action for money damages to vindicate a right of the kind asserted here.

In addition, there is a limitation to the extent to which use may be made of tort actions for the purpose of accomplishing social aims. If there is ever a field in which juries and general trial courts are ill equipped to do social engineering, it is in the realm of the emotional relationship between mother and child. It is best we leave such matters to other fields of endeavor. There are certain kinds of relationships which are not proper fodder for tort litigation, and we believe this to be one of them. There are probably as many children who have been damaged in some manner by their parents' failure to meet completely their physical, emotional and psychological needs as there are people. A tort action for damages by emotionally deprived persons against their parents is, in our opinion, not going to solve the social problem in the same manner in which the legislature is attempting to solve it.

In addition to the contention that defendants should be liable for civil damages because of their violation of criminal and regulatory statutes, plaintiffs also contend that defendants are responsible because of the infliction of severe emotional distress by intentional acts. Plaintiffs allege that defendants intentionally deserted and abandoned them; however, they do not contend that defendants deserted them for the purpose of inflicting emotional harm upon them. We recognize that this tort usually also encompasses the infliction of emotional harm under circumstances from which a reasonable person would conclude that harm was almost certain to result. We believe this latter rationale is inapplicable as between parents and children. If it were otherwise, the children of divorced parents would almost always have an action for emotional damage against their parents. Divorce has become a way of life with almost certain emotional trauma of a greater or lesser degree to the children from the legal dissolution of the family and the resultant absence of at least one of the parents and sometimes both.

In addition, plaintiffs contend that the common law tort of alienation of affections is applicable. They argue that because such a cause of action is intended to compensate one spouse for the intentional alienation of the other spouse's affections by a third party, and that because in one case, Daily v. Parker, 152 F.2d 174 (7th Cir.1945), this cause of action has been extended to the children, it should exist against the parent himself. The statement of the argument is its refutation. Also, the tort of alienation of affections has recently been abolished by the legislature, Oregon Laws 1975, ch. 562, § 1.

Plaintiffs generally contend that without respect to previously recognized theories of recovery, we should recognize a new tort of parental desertion. For all the reasons previously given in declining to use recognized theories of recovery, we also decline this invitation.

The judgment of the trial court is affirmed.

TONGUE, JUSTICE, concurring. * * * The doctrine of intrafamily tort immunity has been previously abandoned by this court with respect to intentional torts resulting in physical injuries. In my opinion, however, it does not follow that the doctrine should also be abandoned with respect to intrafamily torts resulting in "mental and emotional injuries" for reasons stated by the majority, although not in the context of intrafamily tort immunity.

LENT, JUSTICE, concurring in part; dissenting in part. I agree with the majority that the asserted cause of action for alienation of affections must fall. I further agree with the majority that from a technical, pleading standpoint plaintiff * * * has failed to state a cause of action for "outrageous conduct" for failure to state that defendant intended to cause the severe emotional distress described in the complaint.

In dissenting, I have joined in the dissent of Linde, J. but desire to add some additional reasons for finding that a civil cause of action for damages should obtain. * * *

At present there are over one-third of a million children in the United States who are dependent upon the community for their parental care. In Oregon during fiscal year 1976–77 the number of dependent children was over 6,000. The future is bleak for the vast majority of these children, at least those in the position of the plaintiffs, whose parents have abandoned them permanently. Only approximately five percent of such children are ever adopted and placed in a permanent parental situation.

* * *

In view of the costs, both tangible and intangible to society of caring for these dependent children who have well been termed the "orphans of the living" and the character of defendant's conduct as admitted by the demurrer, I believe defendant should shoulder so much of the financial burden as her resources permit. Further, I would hold that the emotional harm which the demurrer admits plaintiff has suffered is such as the community should conclude is monetarily compensable. As stated in Justice Linde's dissent plaintiff has alleged a cause of action.

LINDE, JUSTICE, dissenting. * * * The simple issue before us is whether a young child who allegedly has suffered severe mental and emotional injuries as a result of being deserted and abandoned by a parent acting "maliciously, intentionally, and with cruel disregard of the consequences"—conduct which the legislature has declared to be a crime—may upon proper proof hold the parent responsible in damages for these severe mental and emotional injuries. Contrary to the majority opinion, I believe that these allegations, which plead a violation of ORS 163.535, state a claim on which a child so injured may go to trial.[1]

In reaching this conclusion, I differ with the majority's treatment of its two crucial premises: (1) the source of civil liability for violation of criminal laws, and (2) the significance to be accorded to Oregon's child protection laws.

Liability for Damages from Prohibited Conduct. It should be noted at the outset that awarding civil damages for violations of prohibitory laws is not an uncommon or radical theory of recovery. The question when the victim of criminal or otherwise prohibited conduct may recover damages from the wrongdoer is increasingly important in many areas of law. In a number of recent cases the issue has occupied the United States Supreme Court and the federal courts, whose greater attention to statutory premises of liability probably reflects the fact that these courts are not empowered to formulate common law torts unrelated to the Constitution or laws of the United States. [C] Thus the Supreme Court has also referred to potential civil liability under state law as one factor in determining whether such liability arises implicitly from an act of Congress. [C] Apart from these differences, however, federal and state courts face the same question when prohibitory legislation implies a civil liability toward those for whose protection the legislation is enacted and when it does not. The answer depends first on whether a legislative policy to allow or to deny a civil remedy can be discerned in the text or the legislative history of the statute. If neither can be discerned, then it depends on whether the plaintiff belongs to the class for whose special protection the statute was enacted and whether the civil remedy would contribute to or perhaps detract from achieving the object of the legislation. [C]

* * * The American Law Institute's Restatement (Second) of Torts, Tentative Draft No. 23, 1977, lists a number of other illustrations in its discussion of proscriptive or prescriptive statutes as sources of civil liability.[2] Sometimes a common law court will assimilate the statutory

---

1 ORS 163.535:

(1) A person commits the crime of abandonment of a child if, being a parent, lawful guardian or other person lawfully charged with the care or custody of a child under 15 years of age, he deserts the child in any place with intent to abandon it.

(2) Abandonment of a child is a Class C felony.

Since the complaint alleges at least one cause of action, the validity of the other theories of recovery contained in the complaint need not be considered in overruling the demurrer. * * *

2 Restatement (Second) of Torts § 874A (Tentative Draft No. 23, 1977):

"3.A statute makes it a crime to have sexual intercourse with a previously chaste female under the age of 17, even though she factually consents. The court may hold that the tort action of battery will lie, regardless of the consent.

"4.A federal act makes it a crime to intercept and divulge a telephone conversation. The court may 'assimilate' this conduct to the torts of defamation and invasion of the right of privacy and grant damages. * * *

"6.A statute makes it a crime to utter insulting and abusive language to another publicly. The court may hold that a civil action will lie, amounting to the intentional infliction of emotional distress. * * *

"8.A statute makes it a crime to seduce a woman under promises of marriage. The court may hold that this conduct gives rise to a tort action for damages. * * *

duty into an existing principle of liability . . . but that is not always so. See Restatement (Second) of Torts, Tentative Draft No. 23, 1977, § 874A, comment *f*.[3]

Of course, the question of civil recovery for breach of a statutory duty can be an issue only when the legislation itself is silent on the point. If the legislature either provides for a civil remedy or clearly indicates that it means other provisions for enforcement to be complete and exclusive, there is nothing for a court to decide. It would help to clarify not only private rights but also the particular public policy if the legislative assembly as a routine step in the drafting of penal legislation faced the question of its civil consequences, or alternatively, if it were to enact a general formula for determining these consequences when a statute is otherwise silent.

Unfortunately legislatures do neither, but nothing can be inferred from that fact, given the existing practice of recognizing such consequences when the nature of the protective statute appears to imply them. The majority overstates the case when it equates legislative silence with an "underlying assumption * * * that it was not intended that the statute create any civil obligation or afford civil protection against the injuries which it was designed to prevent." Nor does it follow, when a court finds that the duty created or defined by the statute does imply a civil cause of action, that the court is engaged in pronouncing common law. The difference between a new common law theory of recovery in tort or otherwise and a civil claim based on a statute is obvious: The latter claim stands and falls with the statute from which it is implied, and it will disappear as soon as the amendment or repeal of the statute indicates a reconsideration of the previous public policy. Thus, while a court is often left at large to divine the implications of a statutory policy, it is equally an overstatement to say that the court simply makes its own judgment whether to "create a cause of action" deriving "solely" from the court's own appraisal whether additional protection for the claimed interest is "necessary and desirable."[4]

"14. A statute imposes a criminal penalty upon an employer who, upon request of a former employee, fails to supply a 'service letter' providing details of his service. The court may supply a civil action for damages for violation.

[3] As early as 1934, and until 1965, the original Restatement (Second) of Torts, § 286, stated:

"The violation of a legislative enactment by doing a prohibited act, or by failing to do a required act, makes the actor liable for an invasion of an interest of another if:

"(a) the intent of the enactment is exclusively or in part to protect an interest of the other as an individual; and

"(b) the interest invaded is one which the enactment is intended to protect; and,

"(c) where the enactment is intended to protect an interest from a particular hazard, the invasion of the interests results from that hazard; and,

"(d) the violation is a legal cause of the invasion, and the other has not so conducted himself as to disable himself from maintaining an action."

[4] Long ago, Chief Justice Harlan F. Stone deplored the reluctance of "modern courts [to] resort to standards of conduct set up by legislation" as sources of liability or other consequences beyond those provided by the legislation. "The statute was looked upon as in the law but not of it, a formal rule to be obeyed, it is true, since it is the command of the sovereign, but to be obeyed grudgingly, by construing it narrowly and treating it as though it did not

The relevance of criminal or regulatory laws to civil liability is more complex than merely being an element "taken into consideration by the court in deciding whether a common law action should be established," as the majority puts it. Such laws express distinct kinds of policies. First, the most familiar criminal laws are redefinitions of common-law crimes against private persons or property. They have equally familiar civil analogues in common-law torts. Only "victimless crimes" and crimes deemed to endanger the public as a collectivity, such as bribery, counterfeiting, or tax evasion, are likely to lack a corresponding civil liability. Violations of game laws or environmental protection laws may be other examples. Second, regulatory laws specify standards of socially responsible conduct for the protection of persons endangered by the conduct. While the tort standard may go further, we have recognized the force of the criminal or regulatory standard in negligence cases even when it was set by agencies or local governments that presumably could not themselves create civil liability whether or not they had such an intent. [Cc] Third, governmental sanctions, penal or otherwise, may be enacted to add governmental enforcement to the recognized obligations of a relationship existing apart from the legislation. In such a situation the "underlying assumption," to use the majority's phrase, is hardly that the penal sanction makes the civil obligation unnecessary. Rather, the statute shows that the obligation is considered of such importance that it deserves enforcement by public prosecution.

The Child Protection Laws. It can hardly be questioned that a statute like 163.535, which makes it a crime intentionally to desert and abandon a child, is of the third kind. It and the related sections did not enact a novel prohibition against parental neglect for the convenience of the general public or the protection of taxpayers. They enacted a legislative definition and public enforcement of certain minimal obligations of an existing relationship. Jurisprudentially it might be said that parents have a duty not to abandon and desert their young children because ORS 163.535 makes it a crime to do so, but a legislator would surely think ORS 163.535 should make it a crime to abandon and desert a child because the parent's existing duty—the duty to the child, not to the state—deserved governmental reenforcement. It is the parent's duty thus recognized under Oregon law that plaintiffs invoke in these cases.

The majority does not really deny that ORS 163.535 constitutes such a legislative recognition and reenforcement of the parent's private obligation to the child, not of some socially convenient behavior. Rather, the majority would deny a remedy for the intentional breach of this obligation on the ground that other public policies militate against such a remedy. Upon examination, the majority's statutory citations refer to the single policy of maintaining and preserving the position of the child

---

exist for any purpose other than that embraced within the strict construction of its words. It is difficult to appraise the consequences of the perpetuation of incongruities and injustices in the law by this habit of narrow construction of statutes and by the failure to recognize that, as recognitions of social policy, they are as significant and rightly as much a part of the law, as the rules declared by judges." Stone, The Common Law in the United States, 50 Harv.L.Rev. 4 (1936).

within a functioning family as long as this is possible. Without in any way questioning that this is indeed the state's public policy, I do not agree that it supports the conclusion that the legislature meant to deny the child a remedy for injuries from a parent's unlawful acts.

First, it must be kept in mind what conduct violates ORS 163.535. The statute makes it a felony to desert one's child with intent to abandon it. Of course, we have no evidence of the actual facts in these cases, but the allegations are that defendants did desert and abandon their children "maliciously, intentionally, and with cruel disregard of the consequences." If that is true, the parents have in fact ended the family unit, so that solicitude about not impairing it by litigation may sacrifice the children's legal rights to a pious hope. Contrary to the majority, I do not believe it is this court's own judgment of the possible effects of litigation on family relations that matters (a question on which counsel was unable to enlighten us and that, if taken seriously, is hardly within judicial notice) but rather what view of these effects may be attributed to the legislature. More important for interpreting the legislative policy, however, the statute means that a district attorney or grand jury on the alleged facts could prosecute the parents for a felony. It is incongruous to hold that the legislature provided for a felony prosecution of parents who egregiously violate a duty toward their children, but that it meant to exclude civil actions on behalf of the maliciously abandoned children for fear of impairing the family unit. To hold that the plaintiffs cannot invoke this duty, one must assume a legislative policy that a deserted and abandoned child (or a guardian on its behalf) should ask a district attorney to seek the criminal punishment of the parent for this desertion, but that the child should have no claim that would be of any benefit to itself. That seems too unlikely a policy to attribute to the legislature without some showing that it was intended.

Moreover, the majority's premise proves too much. For purposes of the issue of law before us on these demurrers, it can be assumed that the plaintiffs have suffered actual, demonstrable injuries of a kind for which the law provides money damages against defendants other than parents, that defendants have assets from which these real injuries of the plaintiffs could be compensated, and that defendants caused these injuries by intentionally breaching a specific duty toward plaintiffs that is recognized in Oregon law. Perhaps the explanation for the majority's unwillingness to follow these assumptions to their conclusion is that the injuries alleged are psychological and emotional rather than physical. But if a civil remedy is denied on the majority's premise that it is precluded by a state policy of preserving family unity, that premise would apply equally to bar recovery of damages by a child crippled by physical abuse.[5] And despite the majority's reference to statutory

[5] Defendant presented a "parade of horribles" such as actions for psychological or emotional injury from receiving fewer Christmas gifts than a sibling and the like. I note this only to point out that the argument misses the point. The nature of the *breach of duty* in this case is fixed by ORS 163.535 and would not give rise to an expandable common law precedent. As far as the present issue is concerned, the case would be the same if a child had been deliberately abandoned in an unheated mountain cabin and lost a limb to frostbite or suffered other permanent injuries from lack of food or pneumonia.

proceedings for the termination of parental rights, it is at least questionable that a termination proceeding would create rights to a financial recovery to compensate for such very real and costly harm caused before the termination proceeding.

Although the majority does not say so, its premise is the equivalent of the doctrine of intrafamily tort immunity which Oregon has abandoned at least with respect to intentional torts, though attributed here to a supposed legislative policy subordinating legal claims of children against their parents to reliance on "protective social services." I perceive no such prescribed reliance on social services when parents who have deliberately mistreated their children in a manner made criminal by statute have the assets to be responsible for the harm caused thereby. In my view, plaintiffs have alleged at least one triable cause of action arising from an alleged intentional violation of duties recognized in ORS 163.535. Therefore, the demurrers should have been overruled.

LENT, J., joins in this dissent.

Nearing v. Weaver

Supreme Court of Oregon, 1983.
295 Ore. 702, 670 P.2d 137.

LINDE, JUSTICE: In 1977 the Legislative Assembly enacted an "Abuse Prevention Act" to strengthen legal protection for persons threatened with assault by a present or former spouse or a cohabitant. 1977 Or Laws ch 845. The means chosen for this purpose included the use of temporary restraining orders, injunctions, and temporary child custody orders, [C], and mandatory provisions for the warrantless arrest upon probable cause of a person believed to have violated such an order. [C] The present case requires us to decide whether officers who knowingly fail to enforce a judicial order under the 1977 act are potentially liable for resulting harm to the psychic and physical health of the intended beneficiaries of the judicial order, over defenses of official discretion and official immunity. We hold that these defenses do not preclude potential liability.

The case is on appeal from the circuit court's summary judgment for defendants, affirmed by the Court of Appeals. The Court of Appeals did not explain the basis for its decision.

The complaint alleged the following facts. Plaintiffs are Henrietta Nearing and her two children, Robert and Jeanette, respectively 4 and 3 years old. Henrietta Nearing was separated from her husband in November 1979. On April 16, 1980, the husband entered plaintiffs' home without permission and struck Henrietta. She reported this to one of the defendant police officers, Martin Weaver, causing her husband to be arrested and charged with assault. The next day the circuit court

---

Nothing is said here about claims based on other statutes invoked by plaintiffs that deal with general but unintentional neglect or nonsupport of children. The provision of alternative social services relied on by the majority may militate against implying a civil remedy for these less final and culpable violations of parental duty.

issued an order restraining the husband from molesting plaintiffs or entering the family home. The order was served on the husband, and a copy of the order and proof of service were delivered to the police department of defendant City of St. Helens.

On May 12 and 13, 1980, the husband again entered plaintiffs' home without permission, first damaging the premises, and thereafter attempting to remove the children. Henrietta Nearing reported these incidents to defendant Weaver and asked him to arrest her husband because she was frightened of his violent proclivities. The officer confirmed the validity of the restraining order and the damage to plaintiffs' home but declined to arrest the husband on the ground that the officer had not seen the husband on the premises.

On three subsequent occasions in May, 1980, the husband returned to plaintiffs' address, sought entry to the home, and on the last occasion assaulted Henrietta's friend and damaged his van. When Henrietta reported this to defendants Weaver and Sauls on May 27, 1980, Weaver told her that the St. Helen's police would arrest the husband for violating the restraining order "because it was Robert Lee Nearing Sr.'s second offense," but no such action was taken. Two days later, on May 29, Nearing, Henrietta's husband, telephoned her and threatened to kill her friend. On June 1, Nearing intercepted the friend and plaintiffs in front of the home, repeated the threat, and assaulted the friend.

The complaint alleges the defendant officers' knowledge of the relevant facts. It further alleges that as a "proximate result" of their failure and refusal to arrest her husband, Henrietta has suffered "severe emotional distress and physical injuries" further described in the complaint and that the children have suffered "acute emotional distress," have been "upset," have had difficulty sleeping, and have suffered "psychological impairment."

Defendants denied the allegations except for the identity and status of defendants and pleaded affirmative defenses of immunity and discretion. Plaintiffs moved to strike the affirmative defenses and assigned denial of the motion as error on appeal.

* * *

The question, therefore, is whether plaintiffs pleaded an infringement by defendants of a legal right arising independently of the ordinary tort elements of a negligence action. It is clear that plaintiff did so.

The complaint alleges facts that, if proved, obliged the St. Helens police officers to respond to plaintiffs' call for protection against the exact kind of harassment by the elder Robert Nearing that is said to have occurred, and it alleges that the officers refused to enforce the restraining order in the manner prescribed by law. The duty defendants are alleged to have neglected therefore is not an ordinary common law duty of due care to avoid predictable harm to another. It is a specific duty imposed by statute for the benefit of individuals previously identified by a judicial order.

* * *

In this case a duty specifically towards these plaintiffs arises from the statute coupled with the court order. A plaintiff, of course, may plead and argue an action both under a theory of negligence and under another statutory or common law theory if he or she so chooses; actions based on injuries from defective products are a familiar example. When separate legal theories are said to require the same result on the same alleged facts, that contention should be made clear.

In this case, the issue below was the adequacy of defendants' defenses; no objection is raised to plaintiff's complaint. And plaintiff's reference to "negligence" in this case was immaterial to the alleged liability, if "negligence" is used in the sense of "carelessness" or "failure to use due care" rather than merely as a conventional legal totem, because the result would not be different if defendants had acted, or failed to act, willfully or intentionally or with some other state of mind. It must be recalled what role the allegation of "negligence" plays in an ordinary common law case. In general terms that role is to invoke a duty to take reasonable care not to cause a risk of a foreseeable type of harm to a foreseeable class of plaintiffs. Here the risk, the harm, and the potential plaintiff were all foreseen by the lawmaker and, in McEvoy and in this case, by a court. It was not left to the clerk in Brennen, the lawyer in McEvoy, or the officers in this case to foresee a possible risk and to form a "reasonable" opinion as to what "due care" might be required to avoid it. Such ad hoc judgments are exactly what the legislature meant to overcome when it enacted the obligation to enforce judicial orders.

This does not mean that the obligation creates absolute liability for resulting harm. There may be various defenses, for instance that the defendant made a good faith effort to perform, or that he was prevented from doing so by one or another obstacle, either factual or legal. The officer would not be liable, for instance, for failing to make an unconstitutional arrest. Whatever would be a defense under the statute is a defense to civil liability. But such defenses differ from a claim that failing to perform the duty created by the legislature to prevent harm by enforcing court orders is nothing other than a lack of due care toward the world at large and that liability therefore extends only to physical but not psychic or emotional injuries actually caused by that failure.

[The order] clearly gave rise to a duty of defendants toward the plaintiffs under the 1977 act. [The Act] prescribes that a peace officer "shall arrest and take into custody a person without a warrant" when the officer has probable cause to believe that an order under the statute has been served and filed and that the person has violated the order. Subsection (3) appears after two subsections that state when an officer "may" arrest a person without a warrant, and the contrasting use of "shall" in subsection (3) is no accident. The widespread refusal or failure of police officers to remove persons involved in episodes of domestic violence was presented to the legislature as the main reason for tightening the law so as to require enforcement of restraining orders by mandatory arrest and custody. Even though the arrested person is entitled to be released pending an eventual adjudication of a criminal charge or contempt, [c], the temporary removal was deemed essential to emphasize the seriousness of the court's order and to permit the victims of violence to escape further immediate danger.

Defendants argue that an officer's determination of probable cause to believe that a violation has occurred is a "discretionary function or duty" immune from liability [c]. This claim is answered by McBride v. Magnuson, 282 Or 433, 578 P2d 1259 (1978). In that case a police officer claimed immunity for her decision to take a child into custody and to make a report of child abuse. This court held that an officer or employee is not engaged in a "discretionary function or duty" whenever he or she must evaluate and act upon a factual judgment. Discretion, we stated, exists only insofar as an officer has been delegated responsibility for value judgments and policy choices among competing goals and priorities. Patently the purpose of [the section] was to negate any discretion of that kind in enforcing restraining orders issued under the Abuse Prevention Act. This conclusion does not depend on facts in the individual case. The circuit court erred in denying plaintiff's motion to strike this defense.

Defendants also claim immunity by virtue of ORS 133.315, which provides that "[n]o peace officer shall be held criminally or civilly liable for making an arrest pursuant to ORS 133.055(2) or 133.310(3) provided he acts in good faith and without malice." That section provides immunity for making good faith arrests, not for failing to do so, and its obvious purpose is to reinforce the officer's duty to arrest on probable cause. To invert this text so as to grant immunity for failing to make an arrest required by the 1977 act, as defendants propose, would fly in the face of that legislative purpose. This affirmative defense also should have been stricken.

This disposes of the issues actually raised by the parties. We add the following response to assertions introduced by the dissent.

1. The dissent asserts that we "overrule" two cases in which the court declined to find defendants liable for injury resulting from alleged conduct contrary to statutes, Bob Godfrey Pontiac v. Roloff, 291 Or. 318, 630 P.2d 840 (1981), and Burnette v. Wahl, 284 Or. 705, 588 P.2d 1105 (1978). Most of the dissent is devoted to that proposition.

Neither case was cited by defendants. Neither case holds that statutory duties never give rise to civil liability unless the legislature makes that intention explicit in the text or accompanying explanations. We do not overrule either case, as the dissent claims; children still will have no statutory civil claim under the circumstances of *Burnette* nor litigants under the circumstances in *Bob Godfrey Pontiac* unless the legislature makes a change. Those cases relate to this very different statute only because the dissent extends their holdings to a general rejection of all liability whenever the underlying duty is established by the legislature rather than by judges. That conclusion, however, must be reached for different statutes on a case-by-case basis.

The statutes in this case * * * are unique among statutory arrest provisions because the legislature chose mandatory arrest as the best means to reduce recurring domestic violence. They identify with precision when, to whom, and under what circumstances police protection must be afforded. The legislative purpose in requiring the police to enforce individual restraining orders clearly is to protect the named persons for whose protection the order is issued, not to protect the community at large by general law enforcement activity.

2. The dissent states that this decision creates "strict" liability. That is a word of uncertain meaning. It is not liability without fault. We have made it clear that the liability is not absolute; there may be defenses. The governing standard of conduct is set by the statute, not by this decision. If a statute merely calls on its addressee to exercise due care, that is the standard. This statute demands more of officers than the exercise of reasonable judgment whether to respond to requests to enforce known court orders; it mandates that they respond. That is the point of the statute.

3. The dissent asserts that the plaintiffs did not make a claim based on the statute. To the contrary, plaintiffs' argument to the circuit court covered both a common law and a statutory theory.

4. At bottom the dissent simply opposes tort liability for injuries caused by disregard of the statute on policy grounds, because it may cost local governments money. To that there are two answers. First, the same argument can be and no doubt was made against all claims under the Tort Claims Act, but the act was nevertheless enacted. This is a claim under the Tort Claims Act. If a private defendant would be liable for harm caused by failure to carry out a mandatory duty for the benefit of a specific person protected by a court order, * * * the Tort Claims Act makes a public defendant liable in the same manner. That policy decision was made by the legislature; it is not a new policy choice to be made in this case.

The second answer is that there is in fact no liability if the statute is followed. There is here no open-ended invitation to turn courts and juries loose to second-guess local policies. That might be true if all liability can only be negligence liability for lack of "due care," as the dissent seems to argue. But here the statutory duty is too plain to create such unavoidable risks of liability. When compliance with the statute, unless prevented by good cause, will avoid exposure to liability, the argument that there should be no liability because of the potential expense actually is an argument for a privilege not to comply with the statute. But that policy choice, like the policy of the Tort Claims Act, also has been settled by the legislature.

The circuit court's letter order and the arguments made to that court show that the court was persuaded as a matter of law that plaintiff could not recover for psychic and emotional injuries, as distinct from physical injuries that might have resulted from the same inaction by defendants. Because here * * * there was a specific duty toward these plaintiffs, that proposition is incorrect. The decision of the Court of Appeals affirming the summary judgment must be reversed and the case remanded to the circuit court for further proceedings.

Reversed and remanded.

* * *

JUSTICE LINDE concurred with the result but disagreed with the analysis quoted above. * * *

[T]his court still has the power to create a new type of tort liability "on the basis of its own appraisal of the policy considerations involved." *Burnette v. Wahl*, [c]. I do not believe that we should do so today—in this case—for these reasons.

First, the rule of strict liability created in the majority opinion is at variance with the salutary principle that the basis for tort liability normally is unreasonable conduct by the tortfeasor. The common thread in almost all torts is the idea of unreasonable interference with the interests of others. W. Prosser, Torts 6 (4th ed 1971). Although this court has, in the face of manifest need, created strict liability torts, see Wights v. Staff Jennings, Inc., 241 Or 301, 405 P2d 624 (1965), we have rejected new civil torts for violation of statutes under facts similar to those at bar.

Second, this case involves public liability—the liability of the state, its cities and counties, and of peace officers employed by them. We declined to create a right of action against private persons in Burnette v. Wahl, Miller v. City of Portland, and Bob Godfrey Pontiac v. Roloff, all supra. I would tread even more gingerly in creating a new tort against public bodies and their employees. Public monies are scarce, and public responsibilities are multiplying. I do not favor compounding already hefty public problems by creating this new strict liability tort. In addition, the overwhelming weight of authority holds that a breach of duty by a police officer creates no liability on the part of the officer to an individual who is damaged by a lawbreaker's conduct. This is an extremely important question, not heretofore presented in either the trial court or the Court of Appeals, and we should not decide a question not presented.

This court is poorly equipped to make the kind of policy judgments the majority makes. We have no way of knowing how today's decision will affect the ability of municipalities and counties to enforce the law and recruit and hire competent law enforcement officers. We have no way of knowing how much today's decision will exacerbate the fiscal problems of Oregon's cities. Given the prevalence of domestic strife, the effect upon a local government budget could be considerable. Furthermore, we have no way of knowing how today's decision might affect day-to-day law enforcement practices. Although the complaint alleges serious matters for which immediate police action was appropriate, other serious matters of consequence exist. The imposition of personal liability upon officers and upon their employers for failure to arrest could result in an inefficient use of scarce police resources in a period of social crisis or high crime.

Third, this is a new law. We have no information, one way or the other, whether the creation of a strict liability remedy against public bodies and their peace officers is necessary to vindicate the statutory policy. If peace officers are not doing their duty, I favor giving the legislature a further opportunity to look into whether the creation of such a cause of action is necessary. To this day, the public bodies and their employees have not yet been heard from, either by the legislature or any court.

* * *

NOTES AND QUESTIONS

1. An Oregon statute provides: "Any person who is intoxicated or under the influence of controlled substances in a public place may be taken or sent home or to a treatment facility by the police. However, if the person is incapacitated, the health of the person appears to be in immediate danger, or the police have reasonable cause to believe the person is dangerous to self or to any other person, the person shall be taken by the police to an appropriate treatment facility. A person shall be deemed incapacitated when in the opinion of the police officer or director of the treatment facility the person is unable to make a rational decision as to acceptance of assistance." The statute said nothing, however, concerning what consequences could flow if the police failed to act.

The following was enacted simultaneously with the above. It provides in part: "No peace officer * * * shall be held criminally or civilly liable for actions pursuant to ORS 426.450 to 426.470 * * * provided the actions are in good faith, on probable cause and without malice."

Marilyn Scovill was killed when she walked into a city street and was struck by a car. She was badly intoxicated and a short time before had been in the City of Astoria's police station, on the floor unable to talk coherently. Police had discovered three butcher knives on her person and had assured Marilyn Scovill's friend that she would be taken care of. In Scovill v. City of Astoria, 324 Or. 159, 921 P.2d 1312 (1996), the plaintiff's personal representative brought a claim against the city. Three grounds were alleged: negligence, statutory tort, and negligence per se. The court upheld the claim on the statutory tort ground alone.

The court recognized it must decide when a "tort claim for breach of a statutory duty" may be found. Id. at 1319. Since it is rare to find the civil action explicitly spelled out, the court's task was to determine whether the action could be implied. Central in this inquiry was whether a private right of action reinforced the statute's purpose. The court found that the statute intended to protect intoxicated persons who pose a danger to themselves. The court rejected the negligence per se argument because the statute, while it created and imposed a duty to act, did not create a standard of care. Do you agree with this reasoning?

The reasoning of the *Scovill* court appears to give no room for a court to fashion a tort—a private right of action—from a statutory provision where it is not impliedly created by the legislature. See § 874A of the Restatement (Second) of Torts. What factors should determine whether a court should provide a private tort remedy? The court may assimilate the cause of action to the nearest related tort and modify that tort under its common law authority or may create a new tort action. On factors influencing the determination of whether the court should apply a tort remedy, see Restatement (Second) of Torts § 874A cmt. h (1979). And see comment *1c* on the scope of the legislative purpose.

2. The Restatement (Third) of Torts addresses affirmative duty based on statutory provision in § 38. According to Comment C, this section addresses a situation where a statute provides an affirmative duty but neither provides nor bars a private right of action. In this situation, "courts

may consider the legislative purpose and the values reflected in the statute to decide that the purpose and values justify adopting a duty that the common law had not previously recognized." Restatement (Third) of Torts: Phys. & Emot. Harm § 38 cmt. c (2012).

3. Most courts have been laconic in supplying reasons for the implication of tort actions from applicable statutes: Creek v. Laski, 248 Mich. 425, 227 N.W. 817 (1929) (criminal statute on malicious destruction of a will, tort action); Laczko v. Jules Meyers, Inc., 276 Cal.App.2d 293, 80 Cal.Rptr. 798 (1969) (criminal statute against altering mileage on car odometer).

4. Few other courts have clearly examined the statutory cause of action. The Supreme Court of New Hampshire in Marquay v. Eno, 139 N.H. 708, 662 A.2d 272 (1995), considered, among other claims, whether plaintiffs who had been sexually molested at high school by teachers had a cause of action under the New Hampshire child abuse reporting statute. The court held that the statute did not support a private right of action for its violation because it could find no "express or implied legislative intent to create such a civil liability." Id. at 715, 278. The court's reasoning is confined to express or implied rights of action, although some of the reasons for refusing to find a cause of action are more pertinent to judicially created rights of action on the statute. The court had conflated the two types of action.

Courts have been far from clear about the nature of these statutory actions and their relationship to negligence per se. In another reporting statute case, Kansas State Bank & Trust Co. v. Specialized Transportation Services, Inc., 249 Kan. 348, 819 P.2d 587 (1991), plaintiff argued that the statutory violation was negligence per se. The court stated that a "violation of a statute alone does not establish negligence per se. The plaintiff must also establish that an individual right of action for injury arising out of the violation was intended by the legislature." Id. at 370. How should negligence per se be distinguished?

5. In Doe v. Brainerd International Raceway, 533 N.W.2d 617 (Minn.1995), plaintiff, a minor, had become involved in a "wet T-shirt" contest at the defendant's facility. A Minnesota statute prohibited a person from allowing a minor to engage in a sexual performance. The court found that the statute may be relevant in providing a standard of care where a duty of care exists at common law or as creating a civil cause of action. The court found that the latter may arise expressly or impliedly from the construction of the statute. Principles of judicial restraint, the court stated, would preclude the court from creating a new cause of action. In finding no legislative intent to imply a cause of action, the court elicited strong support from the enactment by the legislature four years later of a provision authorizing a civil action based on the use of a minor in sexual performances.

6. Implied rights of action are not divided into accepted categories and thus the application of rules relating to defenses, damages, vicarious liability, and contribution remain problematic.

(B) IMPLIED CONSTITUTIONAL RIGHTS OF ACTION

42 U.S.C. § 1983 creates an express statutory right of action for individuals to sue state and local officials for a depravation of an individual's constitutional rights. The following case implies a functionally equivalent right of action for constitutional violations inflicted by officials of the federal government. In your opinion, does this implied right of action strike the proper balance between the legislature and courts? States and the federal government?

Bivens v. Six Unknown Named Agents of Federal Bureau of Narcotics

Supreme Court of the United States, 1971.
403 U.S. 388, 91 S.Ct. 1999, 29 L.Ed.2d 619.

MR. JUSTICE BRENNAN delivered the opinion of the Court. The Fourth Amendment provides that: "The right of the people to be secure in their persons, houses, papers, and effects, against unreasonable searches and seizures, shall not be violated. * * * "

In Bell v. Hood, 327 U.S. 678 (1946), we reserved the question whether violation of that command by a federal agent acting under color of his authority gives rise to a cause of action for damages consequent upon his unconstitutional conduct. Today we hold that it does. * * *

Petitioner's complaint alleged that * * * respondents, agents of the Federal Bureau of Narcotics acting under claim of federal authority, entered his apartment and arrested him for alleged narcotics violations. The agents manacled petitioner in front of his wife and children, and threatened to arrest the entire family. They searched the apartment from stem to stern. * * *

[H]is complaint [also] asserted that the arrest and search were effected without a warrant, and that unreasonable force was employed in making the arrest, [and, by implication,] that the arrest was made without probable cause. Petitioner claimed to have suffered great humiliation, embarrassment, and mental suffering as a result of the agents' unlawful conduct, and sought $15,000 damages from each of them. The District Court, on respondents' motion, dismissed the complaint on the ground, *inter alia,* that it failed to state a cause of action.[2] 276 F.Supp. 12 (E.D.N.Y.1967). The Court of Appeals * * * affirmed on that basis. 409 F.2d 718 (C.A.2 1969). We granted certiorari. 399 U.S. 905 (1970). We reverse. * * *

Respondents do not argue that petitioner should be entirely without remedy for an unconstitutional invasion of his rights by federal agents. In respondents' view, however, the rights that petitioner asserts—primarily rights of privacy—are creations of state and not of federal law. Accordingly, they argue, petitioner may obtain money

---

[2] The agents were not named in petitioner's complaint, and the District Court ordered that the complaint be served upon "those federal agents who it is indicated by the records of the United States Attorney participated in the November 25, 1965, arrest of the [petitioner]." * * * Five agents were ultimately served.

damages to redress invasion of these rights only by an action in tort, under state law, in the state courts. In this scheme the Fourth Amendment would serve merely to limit the extent to which the agents could defend the state law tort suit by asserting that their actions were a valid exercise of federal power: if the agents were shown to have violated the Fourth Amendment, such a defense would be lost to them and they would stand before the state law merely as private individuals. * * *

We think that respondents' thesis rests upon an unduly restrictive view of the Fourth Amendment's protection against unreasonable searches and seizures by federal agents, a view that has consistently been rejected by this Court. Respondents seek to treat the relationship between a citizen and a federal agent unconstitutionally exercising his authority as no different from the relationship between two private citizens. In so doing, they ignore the fact that power, once granted, does not disappear like a magic gift when it is wrongfully used. An agent acting—albeit unconstitutionally—in the name of the United States possesses a far greater capacity for harm than an individual trespasser exercising no authority other than his own. [Cc] Accordingly, as our cases make clear, the Fourth Amendment operates as a limitation upon the exercise of federal power regardless of whether the State in whose jurisdiction that power is exercised would prohibit or penalize the identical act if engaged in by a private citizen. It guarantees to citizens of the United States the absolute right to be free from unreasonable searches and seizures carried out by virtue of federal authority. And "where federally protected rights have been invaded, it has been the rule from the beginning that courts will be alert to adjust their remedies so as to grant the necessary relief." Bell v. Hood, 327 U.S., at 684. * * *

Our cases have long since rejected the notion that the Fourth Amendment proscribes only such conduct as would, if engaged in by private persons, be condemned by state law. * * *

The interests protected by state laws regulating trespass and the invasion of privacy, and those protected by the Fourth Amendment's guarantee against unreasonable searches and seizures, may be inconsistent or even hostile. Thus, we may bar the door against an unwelcome private intruder, or call the police if he persists in seeking entrance. The availability of such alternative means for the protection of privacy may lead the State to restrict imposition of liability for any consequent trespass. A private citizen, asserting no authority other than his own, will not normally be liable in trespass if he demands, and is granted, admission to another's house. [Cc] But one who demands admission under a claim of federal authority stands in a far different position. [Cc] The mere invocation of federal power by a federal law enforcement official will normally render futile any attempt to resist an unlawful entry or arrest by resort to the local police; and a claim of authority to enter is likely to unlock the door as well. * * *

That damages may be obtained for injuries consequent upon a violation of the Fourth Amendment by federal officials should hardly seem a surprising proposition. Historically, damages have been regarded as the ordinary remedy for an invasion of personal interests in liberty. [Cc] Of course, the Fourth Amendment does not in so many words provide for its enforcement by an award of money damages for the consequences of its violation. But "it is * * * well settled that where legal rights have been invaded, and a federal statute provides for a general right to sue for such invasion, federal courts may use any available remedy to make good the wrong done." Bell v. Hood, 327 U.S., at 684 (footnote omitted). The present case involves no special factors counselling hesitation in the absence of affirmative action by Congress. * * * Finally, we cannot accept respondents' formulation of the question as whether the availability of money damages is necessary to enforce the Fourth Amendment. For we have here no explicit congressional declaration that persons injured by a federal officer's violation of the Fourth Amendment may not recover money damages from the agents, but must instead be remitted to another remedy, equally effective in the view of Congress. The question is merely whether petitioner, if he can demonstrate an injury consequent upon the violation by federal agents of his Fourth Amendment rights, is entitled to redress his injury through a particular remedial mechanism normally available in the federal courts. [Cc] "The very essence of civil liberty certainly consists in the right of every individual to claim the protection of the laws, whenever he receives an injury." Marbury v. Madison, 1 Cranch 137, 163 (1803). Having concluded that petitioner's complaint states a cause of action under the Fourth Amendment * * * we hold that petitioner is entitled to recover money damages for any injuries he has suffered as a result of the agents' violation of the Amendment. * * *

Judgment reversed and case remanded.

MR. JUSTICE HARLAN, concurring in the judgment. * * * I am of the opinion that federal courts do have the power to award damages for violation of "constitutionally protected interests" and I agree with the Court that a traditional judicial remedy such as damages is appropriate to the vindication of the personal interests protected by the Fourth Amendment. * * *

[T]he interest which Bivens claims—to be free from official conduct in contravention of the Fourth Amendment—is a federally protected interest. [C] Therefore, the question of judicial power to grant Bivens damages is not a problem of the "source" of the "right"; instead, the question is whether the power to authorize damages as a judicial remedy for the vindication of a federal constitutional right is placed by the Constitution itself exclusively in Congress' hands. * * *

[I]n suits for damages based on violations of federal statutes lacking any express authorization of a damage remedy, this Court has authorized such relief where, in its view, damages are necessary to effectuate the congressional policy underpinning the substantive provisions of the statute. J.I. Case Co. v. Borak, 377 U.S. 426 (1964). [Cc] * * *

Initially, I note that it would be at least anomalous to conclude that the federal judiciary—while competent to choose among the range of traditional judicial remedies to implement statutory and common-law policies, and even to generate substantive rules governing primary behavior in furtherance of broadly formulated policies articulated by statute or Constitution [cc] is powerless to accord a damages remedy to vindicate social policies which, by virtue of their inclusion in the Constitution, are aimed predominantly at restraining the Government as an instrument of the popular will. * * *

If explicit congressional authorization is an absolute prerequisite to the power of a federal court to accord compensatory relief regardless of the necessity or appropriateness of damages as a remedy simply because of the status of a legal interest as constitutionally protected, then it seems to me that explicit congressional authorization is similarly prerequisite to the exercise of equitable remedial discretion in favor of constitutionally protected interests. Conversely, if a general grant of jurisdiction to the federal courts by Congress is thought adequate to empower a federal court to grant equitable relief for all areas of subject-matter jurisdiction enumerated therein, see 28 U.S.C.A. § 1331(a), then it seems to me that the same statute is sufficient to empower a federal court to grant a traditional remedy at law. * * *

Although conceding that the standard of determining whether a damage remedy should be utilized to effectuate statutory policies is one of "necessity" or "appropriateness," [cc] the Government contends that questions concerning congressional discretion to modify judicial remedies relating to constitutionally protected interests warrant a more stringent constraint on the exercise of judicial power with respect to this class of legally protected interests. [C]

These arguments for a more stringent test to govern the grant of damages in constitutional cases seem to be adequately answered by the point that the judiciary has a particular responsibility to assure the vindication of constitutional interests such as those embraced by the Fourth Amendment. To be sure, "it must be remembered that legislatures are ultimate guardians of the liberties and welfare of the people in quite as great a degree as the courts." [C] But it must also be recognized that the Bill of Rights is particularly intended to vindicate the interests of the individual in the face of the popular will as expressed in legislative majorities * * *.

The question then, is, as I see it, whether compensatory relief is "necessary" or "appropriate" to the vindication of the interest asserted. [Cc] In resolving that question, it seems to me that the range of policy considerations we may take into account is at least as broad as the range a legislature would consider with respect to an express statutory authorization of a traditional remedy. In this regard I agree with the Court that the appropriateness of according Bivens compensatory relief does not turn simply on the deterrent effect liability will have on federal official conduct. Damages as a traditional form of compensation for invasion of a legally protected interest may be entirely appropriate even if no substantial deterrent effects on future official lawlessness might be thought to result. Bivens, after all, has invoked judicial processes claiming entitlement to compensation for injuries resulting from allegedly lawless official behavior, if those injuries are properly compensable in money damages. I do not think a court of law—vested with the power to accord a remedy—should deny him his relief simply because he cannot show that future lawless conduct will thereby be deterred.

And I think it is clear that Bivens advances a claim of the sort that, if proved, would be properly compensable in damages. The personal interests protected by the Fourth Amendment are those we attempt to capture by the notion of "privacy"; while the Court today properly points out that the type of harm which officials can inflict when they invade protected zones of an individual's life are different from the types of harm private citizens inflict on one another, the experience of judges in dealing with private trespass and false imprisonment claims supports the conclusion that courts of law are capable of making the types of judgment concerning causation and magnitude of injury necessary to accord meaningful compensation for invasion of Fourth Amendment rights. * * *

It seems to me entirely proper that these injuries be compensable according to uniform rules of federal law, especially in light of the very large element of federal law which must in any event control the scope of official defenses to liability. [C] Certainly, there is very little to be gained from the standpoint of federalism by preserving different rules of liability for federal officers dependent on the State where the injury occurs. [C]

Putting aside the desirability of leaving the problem of federal official liability to the vagaries of common-law actions, it is apparent that some form of damages is the only possible remedy for someone in Bivens' alleged position. * * *

However desirable a direct remedy against the Government might be as a substitute for individual official liability, the sovereign still remains immune to suit. * * *

The only substantial policy consideration advanced against recognition of a federal cause of action for violation of Fourth Amendment rights by federal officials is the incremental expenditure of judicial resources that will be necessitated by this class of litigation. There is, however, something ultimately self-defeating about this argument. For if, as the Government contends, damages will rarely be realized by plaintiffs in these cases because of jury hostility, the limited resources of the official concerned, etc., then I am not ready to assume that there will be a significant increase in the expenditure of judicial resources on these claims. Few responsible lawyers and plaintiffs are likely to choose the course of litigation if the statistical chances of success are truly de minimis. And I simply cannot agree with my Brother Black that the possibility of "frivolous" claims—if defined simply as claims with no legal merit—warrants closing the courthouse doors to people in Bivens' situation. There are other ways, short of that, of coping with frivolous lawsuits.

On the other hand, if—as I believe is the case with respect, at least, to the most flagrant abuses of official power—damages to some degree will be available when the option of litigation is chosen, then the question appears to be how Fourth Amendment interests rank on a scale of social values compared with, for example, the interests of stockholders defrauded by misleading proxies. See J.I. Case Co. v. Borak, supra. Judicial resources, I am well aware, are increasingly scarce these days. Nonetheless, when we automatically close the courthouse door solely on this basis, we implicitly express a value judgment on the comparative importance of classes of legally protected interests. And current limitations upon the effective functioning of the courts arising from budgetary inadequacies should not be permitted to stand in the way of the recognition of otherwise sound constitutional principles. * * *

For these reasons, I concur in the judgment of the Court.

MR. CHIEF JUSTICE BURGER, dissenting. I dissent from today's holding which judicially creates a damage remedy not provided for by the Constitution and not enacted by Congress. We would more surely preserve the important values of the doctrine of separation of powers—and perhaps get a better result—by recommending a solution to the Congress as the branch of government in which the Constitution has vested the legislative power. Legislation is the business of the Congress, and it has the facilities and competence for that task—as we do not. * * * [The opinion suggests that the problem of a substitute for the "exclusionary rule" might be considered with the problem in this case and legislation recommended to Congress.]

MR. JUSTICE BLACK, dissenting. * * * Congress could create a federal cause of action for damages for an unreasonable search in violation of the Fourth Amendment. Although Congress has created such a federal cause of action against state officials acting under color of state law, it has never created such a cause of action against federal officials. If it wanted to do so, Congress could, of course, create a remedy against federal officials who violate the Fourth Amendment in the performance of their duties. But the point of this case and the fatal weakness in the Court's judgment is that neither Congress nor the State of New York has enacted legislation creating such a right of action. For us to do so is, in my judgment, an exercise of power that the Constitution does not give us.

Even if we had the legislative power to create a remedy, there are many reasons why we should decline to create a cause of action where none has existed since the formation of our Government. The courts of the United States as well as those of the States are choked with lawsuits. The number of cases on the docket of this Court have reached an unprecedented volume in recent years. A majority of these cases are brought by citizens with substantial complaints—persons who are physically or economically injured by torts or frauds or governmental infringement of their rights; persons who have been unjustly deprived of their liberty or their property; and persons who have not yet received the equal opportunity in education, employment, and pursuit of happiness that was the dream of our forefathers. Unfortunately, there have also been a growing number of frivolous lawsuits, particularly actions for damages against law enforcement officers whose conduct has been judicially sanctioned by state trial and appellate courts and in many instances even by this Court. My fellow Justices on this Court and our brethren throughout the federal judiciary know only too well the time-consuming task of conscientiously poring over hundreds of thousands of pages of factual allegations of misconduct by police, judicial, and corrections officials. Of course, there are instances of legitimate grievances, but legislators might well desire to devote judicial resources to other problems of a more serious nature. * * *

But that is not my task. The task of evaluating the pros and cons of creating judicial remedies for particular wrongs is a matter for Congress and the legislatures of the States. * * *

Should the time come when Congress desires such lawsuits, it has before it a model of valid legislation, 42 U.S.C.A. § 1983, to create a damage remedy against federal officers. * * *

NOTES AND QUESTIONS

1. In this, the first Supreme Court case implying a cause of action from a constitutional provision, the Court relied considerably on earlier cases involving actions "implied" from federal statutes, particularly J.I. Case Co. v. Borak, 377 U.S. 426 (1964) (Securities Exchange Act). The Court in Alexander v. Sandoval, 532 U.S. 275 (2001), however, rejected the understanding of private causes of action represented by *Borak*. In Stoneridge Investment Partners v. Scientific-Atlanta, Inc., 552 U.S. 148 (2008), the Supreme Court reaffirmed its rejection of private causes of action as represented by *Borak* by expressly limiting the implied right of action for securities fraud to only one section of the Securites Exchange Act. Observe that *Bivens* established essentially the same cause of action against federal officers as that existing against state officers under 42 U.S.C.A. § 1983. See Chapter 19.

2. Since *Bivens* there have been other Supreme Court cases giving rise to a cause of action deriving from a constitutional provision. See, e.g., Davis v. Passman, 442 U.S. 228 (1979) (5th Amendment—due process and sex discrimination); Carlson v. Green, 446 U.S. 14 (1980) (8th Amendment—cruel and inhuman punishment). Many federal appeals court decisions may be cited. See, e.g., Dunbar Corp. v. Lindsey, 905 F.2d 754 (4th Cir.1990) (5th Amendment); Wilkins v. May, 872 F.2d 190 (7th Cir.1989) (FBI interrogation, 5th Amendment, dicta regarding 4th and 8th Amendments). But cf. Schweiker v. Chilicky, 487 U.S. 412 (1988) (cautioning that *Bivens* action is appropriate only where there are (1) no "special factors counselling hesitation in the absence of affirmative action by Congress"; (2) no explicit statutory prohibition against relief; and (3) no exclusive statutory alternative remedy).

3. An implied cause of action may be maintained to violations of a state constitution: Brown v. New York, 89 N.Y.2d 172, 652 N.Y.S.2d 223, 674 N.E.2d 1129 (1996).

(C) IMPLIED RIGHTS OF ACTION FROM FEDERAL STATUTES

Alexander v. Sandoval

Supreme Court of the United States, 2001.
532 U.S. 275, 121 S.Ct. 1511, 149 L.Ed.2d 517.

SCALIA, J., delivered the opinion of the Court, in which REHNQUIST, C.J., and O'CONNOR, KENNEDY, and THOMAS, JJ., joined. STEVENS, J., filed a dissenting opinion, in which SOUTER, GINSBURG, and BREYER, JJ., joined.

This case presents the question whether private individuals may sue to enforce disparate-impact regulations promulgated under Title VI of the Civil Rights Act of 1964.

I

The Alabama Department of Public Safety (Department), of which petitioner James Alexander is the director, accepted grants of financial assistance from the United States Department of Justice (DOJ) and Department of Transportation (DOT) and so subjected itself to the restrictions of Title VI of the Civil Rights Act of 1964, 78 Stat. 252, as amended, 42 U.S.C. § 2000d *et seq.* Section 601 of that Title provides that no person shall, "on the ground of race, color, or national origin, be excluded from participation in, be denied the benefits of, or be subjected to discrimination under any program or activity" covered by Title VI. 42 U.S.C. § 2000d. Section 602 authorizes federal agencies "to effectuate the provisions of [§ 601] . . . by issuing rules, regulations, or orders of general applicability," 42 U.S.C. § 2000d–1, and the DOJ in an exercise of this authority promulgated a regulation forbidding funding recipients to "utilize criteria or methods of administration which have the effect of subjecting individuals to discrimination because of their race, color, or national origin. . . ." 28 CFR § 42.104(b)(2) (2000).

The State of Alabama amended its Constitution in 1990 to declare English "the official language of the state of Alabama." Pursuant to this provision and, petitioners have argued, to advance public safety, the Department decided to administer state driver's license examinations only in English. Respondent Sandoval, as representative of a class, brought suit in the United States District Court for the Middle District of Alabama to enjoin the English-only policy, arguing that it violated the DOJ regulation because it had the effect of subjecting non-English speakers to discrimination based on their national origin. The District Court agreed. It enjoined the policy and ordered the Department to accommodate non-English speakers. [C] Petitioners appealed to the Court of Appeals for the Eleventh Circuit, which affirmed. [C] Both courts rejected petitioners' argument that Title VI did not provide respondents a cause of action to enforce the regulation. We do not inquire here whether the DOJ regulation was authorized by § 602, or whether the courts below were correct to hold that the English-only policy had the effect of discriminating on the basis of national origin. The petition for writ of certiorari raised, and we agreed to review, only the question posed in the first paragraph of this opinion: whether there is a private cause of action to enforce the regulation. [C]

II

Although Title VI has often come to this Court, it is fair to say (indeed, perhaps an understatement) that our opinions have not eliminated all uncertainty regarding its commands. For purposes of the present case, however, it is clear from our decisions, from Congress's amendments of Title VI, and from the parties' concessions that three aspects of Title VI must be taken as given. First, private individuals may sue to enforce § 601 of Title VI and obtain both injunctive relief and damages. In Cannon v. University of Chicago, 441 U.S. 677 (1979), the Court held that a private right of action existed to enforce Title IX of the Education Amendments of 1972, 86 Stat. 373, as amended, 20

U.S.C. § 1681 *et seq.* The reasoning of that decision embraced the existence of a private right to enforce Title VI as well. "Title IX," the Court noted, "was patterned after Title VI of the Civil Rights Act of 1964." [C] And, "[i]n 1972 when Title IX was enacted, the [parallel] language in Title VI had already been construed as creating a private remedy." [C] That meant, the Court reasoned, that Congress had intended Title IX, like Title VI, to provide a private cause of action. [C] Congress has since ratified *Cannon's* holding. Section 1003 of the Rehabilitation Act Amendments of 1986, 100 Stat. 1845, 42 U.S.C. § 2000d–7, expressly abrogated States' sovereign immunity against suits brought in federal court to enforce Title VI and provided that in a suit against a State "remedies (including remedies both at law and in equity) are available . . . to the same extent as such remedies are available . . . in the suit against any public or private entity other than a State," § 2000d–7(a)(2). We recognized in Franklin v. Gwinnett County Public Schools, 503 U.S. 60 (1992), that § 2000d–7 "cannot be read except as a validation of *Cannon's* holding." [C] It is thus beyond dispute that private individuals may sue to enforce § 601.

Second, it is similarly beyond dispute—and no party disagrees—that § 601 prohibits only intentional discrimination. In Regents of Univ. of Cal. v. Bakke, 438 U.S. 265 (1978), the Court reviewed a decision of the California Supreme Court that had enjoined the University of California Medical School from "according any consideration to race in its admissions process." [C] Essential to the Court's holding reversing that aspect of the California court's decision was the determination that § 601 "proscribe[s] only those racial classifications that would violate the Equal Protection Clause or the Fifth Amendment." [C] In Guardians Assn. v. Civil Serv. Comm'n of New York City, 463 U.S. 582 (1983), the Court made clear that under *Bakke* only intentional discrimination was forbidden by § 601. What we said in Alexander v. Choate, 469 U.S. 287, 293 (1985), is true today: "Title VI itself directly reach[es] only instances of intentional discrimination." [footnote omitted]

Third, we must assume for purposes of deciding this case that regulations promulgated under § 602 of Title VI may validly proscribe groups, even though such activities are permissible under § 601. Though no opinion of this Court has held that, five Justices in *Guardians* voiced that view of the law at least as alternative grounds for their decisions.

Respondents assert that the issue in this case, like the first two described above, has been resolved by our cases. To reject a private cause of action to enforce the disparate-impact regulations, they say, we would "[have] to ignore the actual language of *Guardians* and *Cannon*." The language in *Cannon* to which respondents refer does not in fact support their position. . . . But in any event, this Court is bound by holdings, not language. *Cannon* was decided on the assumption that the University of Chicago had intentionally discriminated against petitioner. In *Guardians*, the Court *held* that private individuals could not recover compensatory damages under Title VI except for intentional discrimination. Five Justices in addition voted to uphold the disparate-impact regulations [C], but of those five, three expressly reserved the question of a direct private right of action to enforce the regulations, saying that "[w]hether a cause of action against private parties exists directly under the regulations . . . [is a] questio[n] that [is] not presented by this case." [C] Thus, only two Justices had cause to reach the issue that respondents say the "actual language" of *Guardians* resolves. Neither that case, nor any other in this Court, has held that the private right of action exists.

* * *

It is clear now that the disparate-impact regulations do not simply apply § 601—since they indeed forbid conduct that § 601 permits—and therefore clear that the private right of action to enforce § 601 does not include a private right to enforce these regulations. See Central Bank of Denver, N.A. v. First Interstate Bank of Denver, N.A., 511 U.S. 164, 173 (1994) (a "private plaintiff may not bring a [suit based on a regulation] against a defendant for acts not prohibited by the text of [the statute]"). That right must come, if at all, from the independent force of § 602. As stated earlier, we assume for purposes of this decision that § 602 confers the authority to promulgate disparate-impact regulations; the question remains whether it confers a private right of action to enforce them. If not, we must conclude that a failure to comply with regulations promulgated under § 602 that is not also a failure to comply with § 601 is not actionable.

Implicit in our discussion thus far has been a particular understanding of the genesis of private causes of action. Like substantive federal law itself, private rights of action to enforce federal law must be created by Congress. Touche Ross & Co. v. Redington, 442 U.S. 560, 578 (1979) (remedies available are those "that Congress enacted into law"). The judicial task is to interpret the statute Congress has passed to determine whether it displays an intent to create not just a private right but also a private remedy. Transamerica Mortgage Advisors, Inc. v. Lewis, 444 U.S. 11, 15 (1979). Statutory intent on this latter point is determinative. [C] Without it, a cause of action does not exist and courts may not create one, no matter how desirable that might be as a policy matter, or how compatible with the statute. [C] "Raising up causes of action where a statute has not created them may be a proper function for common-law courts, but not for federal tribunals." Lampf, Pleva, Lipkind, Prupis & Petigrow v. Gilbertson, 501 U.S. 350, 365 (1991) (SCALIA, J., concurring in part and concurring in judgment).

Respondents would have us revert in this case to the understanding of private causes of action that held sway 40 years ago when Title VI was enacted. That understanding is captured by the Court's statement in J.I. Case Co. v. Borak, 377 U.S. 426, 433 (1964), that "it is the duty of the courts to be alert to provide such remedies as are necessary to make effective the congressional purpose" expressed by a statute. We abandoned that understanding in Cort v. Ash, 422 U.S. 66, 78 (1975)—which itself interpreted a statute enacted under the *ancien regime*—and have not returned to it since. Not even when interpreting the same Securities Exchange Act of 1934 that was at issue in *Borak* have we applied *Borak's* method for discerning and defining causes of action. Having sworn off the habit of venturing beyond

Congress's intent, we will not accept respondents' invitation to have one last drink.

Nor do we agree with the Government that our cases interpreting statutes enacted prior to *Cort v. Ash* have given "dispositive weight" to the "expectations" that the enacting Congress had formed "in light of the 'contemporary legal context.'" [C] Only three of our legion implied-right-of-action cases have found this sort of "contemporary legal context" relevant, and two of those involved Congress's enactment (or reenactment) of the verbatim statutory text that courts had previously interpreted to create a private right of action. [C] In the third case, this sort of "contemporary legal context" simply buttressed a conclusion independently supported by the text of the statute. [C] We have never accorded dispositive weight to context shorn of text. In determining whether statutes create private rights of action, as in interpreting statutes generally, see Blatchford v. Native Village of Noatak, 501 U.S. 775, legal context matters only to the extent it clarifies text.

We therefore begin (and find that we can end) our search for Congress's intent with the text and structure of Title VI. [Footnote omitted] Section 602 authorizes federal agencies "to effectuate the provisions of [§ 601] . . . by issuing rules, regulations, or orders of general applicability." 42 U.S.C. § 2000d–1. It is immediately clear that the "rights-creating" language so critical to the Court's analysis in *Cannon* of § 601, [C], is completely absent from § 602. Whereas § 601 decrees that "[n]o person . . . shall . . . be subjected to discrimination," 42 U.S.C. § 2000d, the text of § 602 provides that "[e]ach Federal department and agency . . . is authorized and directed to effectuate the provisions of [§ 601]," 42 U.S.C. § 2000d–1. Far from displaying congressional intent to create new rights, § 602 limits agencies to "effectuat[ing]" rights already created by § 601. And the focus of § 602 is twice removed from the individuals who will ultimately benefit from Title VI's protection. Statutes that focus on the person regulated rather than the individuals protected create "no implication of an intent to confer rights on a particular class of persons." California v. Sierra Club, 451 U.S. 287, 294 (198), Section 602 is yet a step further removed: It focuses neither on the individuals protected nor even on the funding recipients being regulated, but on the agencies that will do the regulating. Like the statute found not to create a right of action in Universities Research Assn., Inc. v. Coutu, 450 U.S. 754, § 602 is "phrased as a directive to federal agencies engaged in the distribution of public funds," id., at 772. When this is true, "[t]here [is] far less reason to infer a private remedy in favor of individual persons," *Cannon v. University of Chicago, supra,* at 690–691. So far as we can tell, this authorizing portion of § 602 reveals no congressional intent to create a private right of action.

Nor do the methods that § 602 goes on to provide for enforcing its authorized regulations manifest an intent to create a private remedy; if anything, they suggest the opposite. Section 602 empowers agencies to enforce their regulations either by terminating funding to the "particular program, or part thereof," that has violated the regulation or "by any other means authorized by law," 42 U.S.C. § 2000d–1. No enforcement action may be taken, however, "until the department or agency concerned has advised the appropriate person or persons of the failure to comply with the requirement and has determined that compliance cannot be secured by voluntary means." [C] And every agency enforcement action is subject to judicial review. § 2000d–2. If an agency attempts to terminate program funding, still more restrictions apply. The agency head must "file with the committees of the House and Senate having legislative jurisdiction over the program or activity involved a full written report of the circumstances and the grounds for such action." § 2000d–1. And the termination of funding does not "become effective until thirty days have elapsed after the filing of such report." Ibid. Whatever these elaborate restrictions on agency enforcement may imply for the private enforcement of rights created *outside* of § 602 . . . they tend to contradict a congressional intent to create privately enforceable rights through § 602 itself. The express provision of one method of enforcing a substantive rule suggests that Congress intended to preclude others. [C] Sometimes the suggestion is so strong that it precludes a finding of congressional intent to create a private right of action, even though other aspects of the statute (such as language making the would-be plaintiff "a member of the class for whose benefit the statute was enacted") suggest the contrary. 42 U.S.C. § 1983, cases show, some remedial schemes foreclose a private cause of action to enforce even those statutes that admittedly create substantive private rights. [C] In the present case, the claim of exclusivity for the express remedial scheme does not even have to overcome such obstacles. The question whether § 602's remedial scheme can overbear other evidence of congressional intent is simply not presented, since we have found no evidence anywhere in the text to suggest that Congress intended to create a private right to enforce regulations promulgated under § 602.

Both the Government and respondents argue that the *regulations* contain rights-creating language and so must be privately enforceable, but that argument skips an analytical step. Language in a regulation may invoke a private right of action that Congress through statutory text created, but it may not create a right that Congress has not. Touche Ross & Co. v. Redington, 442 U.S., at 577, n. 18 ("[T]he language of the statute and not the rules must control"). Thus, when a statute has provided a general authorization for private enforcement of regulations, it may perhaps be correct that the intent displayed in each regulation can determine whether or not it is privately enforceable. But it is most certainly incorrect to say that language in a regulation can conjure up a private cause of action that has not been authorized by Congress. Agencies may play the sorcerer's apprentice but not the sorcerer himself.

The last string to respondents' and the Government's bow is their argument that two amendments to Title VI "ratified" this Court's decisions finding an implied private right of action to enforce the disparate-impact regulations. See Rehabilitation Act Amendments of 1986, § 1003, 42 U.S.C. § 2000d–7; Civil Rights Restoration Act of 1987, § 6, 102 Stat. 31, 42 U.S.C. § 2000d–4a. One problem with this argument is that, as explained above, none of our decisions establishes (or even assumes) the private right of action at issue here, [C], which is why in *Guardians* three Justices were able expressly to reserve the question. [C] Incorporating our cases in the amendments would thus not help respondents. Another problem is that the incorporation claim itself is flawed. Section 1003 of the Rehabilitation Act Amendments of 1986, on which only respondents rely, by its terms applies only to suits "for a violation of a *statute*," 42 U.S.C. § 2000d–7(a)(2) (emphasis added) . . . Respondents point to Merrill Lynch, Pierce, Fenner & Smith, Inc. v. Curran, 456 U.S., at 381–382, which inferred congressional intent to ratify lower court decisions regarding a particular statutory provision when Congress comprehensively revised the statutory scheme but did not amend that provision. But we recently criticized *Curran's* reliance on congressional inaction, saying that "[a]s a general matter . . . [the] argumen[t] deserve[s] little weight in the interpretive process." Central Bank of Denver, N.A. v. First Interstate Bank of Denver, N. A., 511 U.S., at 187. And when, as here, Congress has not comprehensively revised a statutory scheme but has made only isolated amendments, we have spoken more bluntly: "It is 'impossible to assert with any degree of assurance that congressional failure to act represents' affirmative congressional approval of the Court's statutory interpretation." Patterson v. McLean Credit Union, 491 U.S. 164, 175, n. 1, 132 (1989) (quoting Johnson v. Transportation Agency, Santa Clara Cty., 480 U.S. 616, 671–672 (1987) (SCALIA, J., dissenting)) . . .

The judgment of the Court of Appeals is reversed.

It is so ordered.

NOTES AND QUESTIONS

1. Recall that 42 U.S.C.A. § 1983 provides a cause of action for "the deprivation of any rights, privileges, or immunities secured by the Constitution and laws" of the United States. A § 1983 action is available to a person for both violations of the Constitution and federal statutes. Maine v. Thiboutot, 448 U.S. 1 (1980). However, the statute must create (1) enforceable rights, privileges, or immunities within the meaning of § 1983 and (2) Congress must not have foreclosed such enforcement in the enactment itself. Wright v. City of Roanoke Redevelopment and Housing Authority, 479 U.S. 418 (1987). The first question canvasses a similar inquiry to that engaged by the Supreme Court in the principal case. Did Congress intend to benefit the plaintiff via a private right of action? In Wilder v. Virginia Hospital Association, 496 U.S. 498 (1990), a statutory provision required health care providers to be reimbursed according to rates that were "reasonable and adequate" to meet the costs of "efficiently and economically operated facilities." The Supreme Court found that this was intended to benefit the plaintiffs via a private right of action, especially since, without a private right, the provision would be unenforceable. Consistent with the principal case's gimlet-eyed view of implied private rights of action, the Court in Gonzaga University v. Doe, 536 U.S. 273 (2002) held that § 1983 does not provide the basis of an action to enforce the Family Educational Rights on Privacy Act. Chief Justice Rehnquist, writing for the Court, concluded: "[I]f Congress wishes to create new rights enforceable under § 1983, it must do so in clear and unambiguous terms— no less and no more than what is required for Congress to create new rights enforceable under an implied private right of action." Id. at 290.

2. The Court has not always adopted such a restrictive view of implied rights of action from federal statutes. Specifically, in Cort v. Ash, (422 U.S. 66 (1975)) the Court applied four factors to determine whether a private remedy should be implied from a statute with no express provision for a private right of action. These were: 1) whether the plaintiff was a member of the class intended to be afforded protection by the statute, 2) whether express intent from Congress was present to negate a private cause of action, 3) whether the creation of a private right of action was compatible with the overall legislative scheme and 4) whether the issue in controversy had been "so traditionally relegated to state law as to make it inappropriate to infer a federal cause of action" Transamerica Mortgage Advisors, Inc. v. Lewis, 444 U.S. 11 (1979) (J. White, dissenting). The Court appears to have been more willing to imply a private right of action from statutes adopted when the implication of a private right of action was more commonplace. *See, e.g.* Merrill Lynch, Pierce, Fenner &Smith, Inc. v. Curran, 456 U.S. 353 (1982); Musick, Peeler, & Garrett v. Employers Insurance of Wassau, 508 U.S. 286 (1993).

3. In Franklin v. Gwinnett County Public Schools, 503 U.S. 60 (1992), the plaintiff high school student brought an action for damages. She claimed that, contrary to Title IX of the Education Amendments of 1972, she had been subjected to continued sexual harassment and abuse by a teacher. In Cannon v. University of Chicago, 441 U.S. 677 (1979), cited in the principal case, the Court had held that Title IX was enforceable through a private right of action. The Court then applied the principle that a right is enforceable by the full panoply of judicial remedies. Nothing in Title IX displaced this presumption. Therefore, the plaintiff was entitled to a damages remedy for violation of her private right. Justice Scalia (with whom the Chief Justice and Justice Thomas agreed) concurred but maintained his hostility, criticizing the presumption of expansive remedies. He found a remedy in damages because the legislation in issue was enacted subsequent to *Cannon,* recognizing a private right of action under Title IX.

4. What is the relationship between implied private rights of actions and private rights of action pursuant to § 1983? It is clear that despite the statute upon proper construction providing no implied private right of action, it may support an action under § 1983 by giving rise to an enforceable right by a beneficiary under the statute. Mallett v. Wisconsin Division of Vocational Rehabilitation, 130 F.3d 1245 (7th Cir.1997) (holding that the Rehabilitation Act of 1973, while providing for no implied right of action, supported a § 1983 action.)

2. EXPRESS RIGHTS OF ACTION: CIVIL RICO

Congress expressly created a private right of action for individuals to collect treble damages for injury sustained to their business or property through activities in violation of Section 1962 of the Racketeer Influence and Corrupt Organizations Act ("RICO"). RICO civil actions have evolved expansively since the introduction of the Act. *See* Sedima, S.P.R.L. v. Imrex Co., Inc., 473 U.S. 479 (1985) ("We nonetheless recognize that, in its private civil version, RICO is evolving into something quite different from the original conception of its enactors"). As you read, contrast the role of the courts in construing Civil RICO actions with the inquiry to determine whether there should be an implied right of action. Do you see how the tasks are different?

De Falco v. Bernas

United States Court of Appeals, Second Circuit, 2001.
244 F.3d 286.

[Plaintiffs bought, and proposed to develop, land in the Township of Delaware, Sullivan County, New York. Named defendants were an assortment of public officials and private individuals who were part of, or influenced, local government of the Township. After plaintiffs purchased the property, defendants engaged in a number of threats and intimidation to force plaintiffs to give over property and employ individuals under threat that development approvals would be withheld. Plaintiffs brought an action under 18 U.S.C. § 1962(c) of the Racketeer Influence and Corrupt Organizations Act ("RICO") claiming that plaintiffs' real estate activities were impeded as a result of defendants' operation of the Town of Delaware, New York, as a RICO enterprise.

Plaintiffs claimed that the action arose out of a conspiracy, plan and scheme among the defendants to use the Town of Delaware as a racketeering enterprise to extort money, real property and personal property through misuse of certain public offices, in violation of section 1962(c).]

UNDERHILL, DISTRICT JUDGE* * * * To establish a RICO claim, a plaintiff must show: "(1) a violation of the RICO statute, 18 U.S.C. § 1962; (2) an injury to business or property; and (3) that the injury was caused by the violation of Section 1962." [c] Section 1962(c), the section relevant here, makes it unlawful for any person employed by or associated with any enterprise engaged in, or the activities of which affect, interstate or foreign commerce, to conduct or participate, directly or indirectly, in the conduct of such enterprise's affairs through a pattern of racketeering activity. . . .

To establish a violation of 18 U.S.C. § 1962(c) then, a plaintiff must show "(1) conduct (2) of an enterprise (3) through a pattern (4) of racketeering activity." Sedima, S.P.R.L. v. Imrex Co., 473 U.S. 479, 496, 105 S.Ct. 3275, 87 L.Ed.2d 346 (1985); [Cc] The requirements of section 1962(c) must be established as to each individual defendant. [C]

The terms "enterprise," "racketeering activity," and "pattern of racketeering activity" are defined in 18 U.S.C. § 1961. A RICO enterprise "includes any individual, partnership, corporation, association, or other legal entity, and any union or group of individuals associated in fact although not a legal entity." 18 U.S.C. § 1961(4). "Racketeering activity" is broadly defined to encompass a variety of state and federal offenses including, inter alia, murder, kidnapping, gambling, arson, robbery, bribery and extortion. See 18 U.S.C. § 1961(1). A " 'pattern of racketeering activity' requires at least two acts of racketeering activity, one of which occurred after the effective date of this chapter and the last of which occurred within ten years . . . after the commission of a prior act of racketeering activity." 18 U.S.C. § 1961(5).

Although at least two predicate acts must be present to constitute a pattern, two acts alone will not always suffice to form a pattern. See Sedima, supra.

In short, to establish a violation of 18 U.S.C. § 1962(c), a plaintiff must establish that a defendant, through the commission of two or more acts constituting a pattern of racketeering activity, directly or indirectly participated in an enterprise, the activities of which affected interstate or foreign commerce. See, e.g., Sedima, supra.

We take up each of the RICO elements at issue below.

1. The Town of Delaware as a RICO Enterprise

[Defendant] Dirie [supervisor of the Town of Delaware and a local firewood salesman] claims that the plaintiffs failed to establish that the Town of Delaware was a RICO enterprise and that the plaintiffs failed to establish an enterprise separate from the individual defendants. The plaintiffs argue that an enterprise may be organized for a legitimate and lawful purpose and may include such things as a municipality or town or a subdivision thereof.

As noted above, the RICO statute defines an "enterprise" as "includ[ing] any individual, partnership, corporation, association, or other legal entity, and any union or group of individuals associated in fact although not a legal entity." 18 U.S.C. § 1961(4). The enterprise "is an entity, . . . a group of persons associated together for a common purpose of engaging in a course of conduct." United States v. Turkette, 452 U.S. 576, 583, 101 S.Ct. 2524, 69 L.Ed.2d 246 (1981). A racketeering enterprise is proven through "evidence of an ongoing organization, formal or informal, and by evidence that the various associates function as a continuing unit." Id.; see United States v. Morales, 185 F.3d 74, 80 (2d Cir.1999). Thus, evidence of an ongoing organization, the associates of which function as a continuing unit, suffices to prove an enterprise. See *Turkette, supra.*

Under section 1962(c), a defendant and the enterprise must be distinct. Indeed, "[i]t is well established in this Circuit that, under § 1962(c), the alleged RICO 'person' and RICO 'enterprise' must be distinct." Cedric Kushner Promotions, Ltd. v. King, 219 F.3d 115, 116 (2d Cir.2000) (per curiam) (footnotes omitted). * * *

The requirement of distinctiveness between the defendants and the enterprise, however, was met here. The jury could reasonably have concluded that the RICO persons [the defendants] were a separate and distinct assortment of public officials, private individuals and corporations who used their political power to influence the Town of Delaware's exercise of governmental authority over the plaintiffs' development. From the evidence adduced at trial, there was sufficient evidence from which a reasonable jury could conclude that the named defendants were separate, culpable parties and that the alleged enterprise, the Town of Delaware, was the "passive instrument or victim of [their] racketeering activity." [C]

Moreover, this Court has previously held that a governmental unit can be a RICO enterprise. See United States v. Angelilli, 660 F.2d 23, 30–35 (2d Cir.1981), cert. denied, 455 U.S. 910, 945, 102 S.Ct. 1258, 1442, 71 L.Ed.2d 449, 657 (1982). In *Angelilli,* the defendants were four of approximately eighty New York City marshals appointed by the Mayor of the City of New York as officers of the City's Civil Court. The marshals were charged with mail fraud in a scheme to auction judgment debtors' property at artificially deflated prices. Prior to an auction, the marshals would meet with certain buyers and determine: (1) a deflated price at which property would ostensibly be sold and (2) the amount over the agreed sales price that would be paid to the marshals in return ("top money"). The marshals retained the "top money" and subsequently mailed to judgment creditors amounts reflecting the fraudulently deflated prices. The enterprise in whose activities the marshals were alleged to have participated in a pattern of racketeering activity was the New York City Civil Court.

In concluding that the New York City Civil Court was an enterprise within the meaning of RICO, this Court first noted that, under the language of the statute: "the definition of 'enterprise' is quite broad. We see no sign of an intention by Congress to exclude governmental units from its scope." In reviewing the language of RICO, the Court concluded that, "on its face the definition of an enterprise to 'include any . . . legal entity' is unambiguously broad, and that it does not exclude the Civil Court." [C]

That conclusion was bolstered by certain of RICO's substantive goals, some of which are specifically directed toward governmental entities. [C] Recognizing that "racketeering activity" is defined in section 1961(1) to include bribery and extortion, the Court noted that "bribery is 'a crime which is peculiar to public officials,' " and "[e]xtortion under color of law is a crime which 'can only be committed in the context of governmental activity.' " [C]

By making bribery and extortion RICO offenses, Congress must be said to have understood that these offenses would be committed by governmental officials as a part of their work. Since these offenses can only be committed in the context of the work of a government agency, Congress must be taken to have intended that a governmental agency could be one of the types of "enterprises," the affairs of which are conducted through a pattern of racketeering offenses. [C]

The interpretation of the language of the statute to extend to activities affecting governmental entities is supported by the purpose and legislative history of the Organized Crime Control Act of 1970 ("the Act"), Pub.L. No. 91–452, 84 Stat. 922, of which RICO is Title IX. [C] Both the purpose and legislative history of the Act reflect "concern about the infiltration of local government units." [c] Accordingly, "the language of section 1961(4), defining enterprise, . . . unambiguously encompass[es] governmental units, and . . . the purpose and history of the Act and the substance of RICO's provisions demonstrate a clear congressional intent that RICO be interpreted to apply to activities that corrupt public or governmental entities." [C]

The analysis in *Angelilli* applies with equal force to this case. Throughout this action, the only enterprise alleged by the plaintiffs was the Town of Delaware, and the jury specifically found that the Town of Delaware was a RICO enterprise. [C] Based upon the evidence admitted at trial, the jury could reasonably have concluded that the Town of Delaware's grant or denial of approval for aspects of the plaintiffs' development was conditioned upon complying with the demands of Dirie, the Town Supervisor, and others with influence. As with the New York City Civil Court in *Angelilli,* the jury here could have reasonably found that the Town of Delaware was a "passive instrument" through which the defendants wielded power for their personal benefit and, accordingly, was a RICO enterprise.

2. *Interstate Commerce*

[Defendant] Dirie argues that the plaintiffs offered little, if any, proof of a material impact on interstate commerce of either the enterprise or the RICO predicate crimes. We disagree.

The law in this Circuit does not require RICO plaintiffs to show more than a minimal effect on interstate commerce. [C] Here, one of the extortionate demands caused DeFalco to break an $8800 contract with the Walczak Lumber Company, an out-of-state logger located in Clifford, Pennsylvania. There was also testimony by the Clerk of the Town of Delaware that the regular business of the Town affected interstate commerce. Accordingly, Dirie's contention that the plaintiffs failed to establish that the activities of the enterprise affected interstate commerce is without merit.

3. *Participation in the Conduct of the Town's Affairs*

Section 1962(c) makes it unlawful "for any person employed by or associated with any enterprise . . . *to conduct or participate, directly or indirectly, in the conduct of such enterprise's affairs* through a pattern of racketeering activity. . . ." 18 U.S.C. § 1962(c) (emphasis added). The Supreme Court has interpreted the phrase "to participate . . . in the conduct of [the] enterprise's affairs" to mean participation in the operation or management of the enterprise. See Reves v. Ernst & Young, 507 U.S. 170, 185, 113 S.Ct. 1163, 122 L.Ed.2d 525 (1993). Both Dirie and the Bernas defendants argue that there was insufficient evidence for the jury to find that they conducted the affairs of the Town and that their conduct met the "operation or management" test. We disagree.

In *Reves,* when assessing the RICO liability of an outside accounting firm for racketeering activity carried on by its client, the Supreme Court addressed the question "whether one must participate in the operation or management of the enterprise itself to be subject to liability under this provision." [c] The Supreme Court examined Section 1962(c) and adopted an "operation or management" test to determine whether a defendant had sufficient connection to the enterprise to warrant imposing liability. [C] The Court held that, to conduct or participate, directly or indirectly, in the conduct of an enterprise's affairs, "one must have some part in directing those affairs." [C] The Court stated that "the word 'participate' makes clear that RICO liability is not limited to those with primary responsibility, just as the phrase 'directly or indirectly' makes clear that RICO liability is not limited to those with a formal position in the enterprise. . . ." [C]

The jury specifically found that [individual defendants] each "conducted or participated in the conduct of the affairs of the Town of Delaware through a pattern of racketeering activity," and the record here contains ample evidence from which a reasonable jury could have found that Dirie and the Bernas defendants each had some part in directing the Town of Delaware's affairs.

Dirie was the elected Supervisor of the Town of Delaware from January 1986 to December 1991. In this position, Dirie served as a member of the Town Board and as a member of the Town Legislature. There was evidence at trial that Dirie offered to help guide DeFalco "through the muddy waters" of real estate development in the Town of Delaware, so long as DeFalco followed Dirie's suggestions. There was also evidence that, when DeFalco resisted Dirie's suggestions, Dirie used his authority within the Town of Delaware to affect the plaintiffs' development.

[The Court detailed examples of threats of withholding governmental approvals for failure to enrich defendants.]

* * *

In short, there was ample evidence from which a reasonable jury could conclude that Dirie participated in the operation or management of the Town of Delaware. Indeed, there was more than enough evidence in the record for a reasonable jury to conclude that Dirie had more than just "*some* part in directing those affairs." *Reves,* 507 U.S. at 179, 113 S.Ct. 1163 (emphasis added).

Similarly, a reasonable jury could have found that the Bernas defendants [who were involved in road construction, had extracted gravel from plaintiff's property and demanded a transfer of shares in the business] participated in the operation or management of the Town of Delaware. Although the Bernas, who were involved in road construction, had extracted gravel from the plaintiff's property and demanded a transfer of shares in the business, defendants had no official role in the operation or management of the Town, "RICO liability is not limited to those with primary responsibility for the enterprise's affairs, . . . [or] limited to those with a formal position in the enterprise. . . ." [C] "An enterprise also might be 'operated' or 'managed' by others 'associated with' the enterprise who exert control over it as, for example, by bribery." [C] There was ample evidence from which the jury could have concluded that Bernas played some part in directing the affairs of the Town. . . .

After DeFalco signed over the one-third interest in JOBO, however, Bernas wanted rights to the entire gravel pit and the dedication of the Phase I roads was called into question again. Bernas told DeFalco that, if he did not turn the gravel pit over to him, "[t]hey were going to close the development down." When DeFalco resisted giving Bernas the entire gravel pit, Tax Assessors Ferber and Meckle reassessed certain lots from $20,000 to $45,000 a piece, more than doubling plaintiffs' taxes. When DeFalco asked Dirie how he could get Phase II approved in light of the April 2, 1990 letter from the Town of Delaware Planning Board listing certain uncompleted requirements, Dirie replied, "Give Bernas the gravel pit." * * *

In short, there was ample evidence from which a reasonable jury could conclude that Bernas participated in the operation or management of the Town of Delaware, had at least some part in directing the affairs of the Town and, indeed, exerted some control over it. See *Reves,* 507 U.S. at 179, 184.

4. Predicate Acts

Both Dirie and the Bernas defendants argue that the plaintiffs failed to establish the commission of at least two predicate acts of racketeering by them.

a. William Dirie

Dirie argues that the crimes allegedly constituting racketeering activity by him were all based on extortion. In essence, Dirie argues that extortion requires the wrongful use of force, violence or fear and, in each of these instances, that element is entirely missing. Dirie claims that there was no evidence of a threat from him and that there was no evidence of the requisite fear of adverse consequences with respect to each of the charges of extortion. * * *

Under the Hobbs Act, "[t]he term 'extortion' means the obtaining of property from another, with his consent, induced by wrongful use of actual or threatened force, violence, or fear, or under color of official right." 18 U.S.C. § 1951(b)(2). Extortion through threats of economic loss falls within the Hobbs Act's prohibitions, see United States v. Robilotto, 828 F.2d 940, 944–45 (2d Cir.1987), cert. denied, 484 U.S. 1011 (1988). Extortion may therefore be established on a theory that activities amounted to extortion by wrongful use of fear of economic loss. [C]

In this Circuit, "[t]he cases interpreting the Hobbs Act have repeatedly stressed that the element of 'fear' required by the Act can be satisfied by putting the victim in fear of economic loss." [C] The absence or presence of fear of economic loss "must be considered from the perspective of the victim, not the extortionist; the proof need establish that the victim reasonably believed: first, that the defendant had the power to harm the victim, and second, that the defendant would exploit that power to the victim's detriment." [C]

* * *

[W]e conclude that extortion by Dirie through threats of economic loss was shown in the instant case. Dirie was the elected Supervisor of the Town of Delaware. In this position, Dirie served as a member of the Town Board and as a member of the Town Legislature. As set forth in detail above, there was ample evidence at trial that Dirie offered to help guide DeFalco with his real estate development in the Town of Delaware, provided that DeFalco followed the suggestions that Dirie made to him. There was also considerable evidence that, when DeFalco resisted each of Dirie's suggestions, Dirie used his authority within the Town of Delaware to adversely affect the plaintiffs' development.

* * *

[T]here was sufficient evidence of fear of economic loss with respect to all five predicate acts charged against Dirie for a reasonable jury to conclude that DeFalco believed that Dirie had the power to harm him, and that Dirie would exploit that power to the plaintiffs' detriment.

* * *

The Bernas defendants argue that the plaintiffs failed to establish a pattern of racketeering activity. RICO defines a "pattern of racketeering activity" as requiring "at least two acts of racketeering activity" committed in a 10-year period. [C] To establish a pattern, a plaintiff must also make a showing that the predicate acts of racketeering activity by a defendant are "related, and that they amount to or pose a threat of continued criminal activity." H.J. Inc. v. Northwestern Bell Tel. Co., 492 U.S. 229, 239 (1989). The continuity necessary to prove a pattern can be either "closed-ended continuity," or "open-ended continuity." [Id.]

The Bernas defendants argue that the plaintiffs have failed to establish the requisite minimum period of closed-ended continuity. Here, the Bernas defendants argue, the extortion took place over a period of only a few months: the one-third stock in JOBO was extorted in December 1989, induced by pressure upon DeFalco between may and December 1989; and the extortion of sand and gravel was also complete by December 1989. Thus, the defendants' extortion scheme lasted at most a few months during the last half of 1989, a duration not sufficient to establish a closed-ended pattern of racketeering by these defendants.

The Bernas defendants argue that the plaintiffs have also failed to establish a pattern of open-ended continuity, because the scheme by the Bernas defendants was by its very nature finite—once achieved the scheme would necessarily come to an end and there was no evidence that the predicate acts by the Bernas defendants were a regular way of conducting defendants' ongoing legitimate business.

Since the Supreme Court decided *H.J., Inc.,* this Court has never held a period of less than two years to constitute a "substantial period of time." [C] Other circuits have required similar periods. [C] Although closed-ended continuity is primarily a temporal concept, other factors such as the number and variety of predicate acts, the number of both participants and victims, and the presence of separate schemes are also relevant in determining whether closed-ended continuity exists. [C]

The duration of a pattern of racketeering activity is measured by the RICO predicate acts the defendants commit. [C] Here, the jury found that the Bernas defendants extorted from plaintiffs sand and/or gravel from the JOBO gravel pit and extorted from plaintiffs one-third of the shares of JOBO Associates, Inc.

At best, the evidence in the record indicates that the predicate acts by the Bernas defendants took place between December 1998 and May 1990—a period of approximately a year and a half. This Court has never held that such a short period of activity satisfies the closed-ended continuity requirement. [C] Even viewing the evidence in the light most favorable to the plaintiffs, the period is of insufficient length to demonstrate closed-ended continuity under this Court's precedents.

The plaintiffs argue, however, that they have alternatively established open-ended continuity. To establish open-ended continuity, "the plaintiff need not show that the predicates extended over a substantial period of time but must show that there was a threat of continuing criminal activity beyond the period during which the predicate acts were performed." [C]

In this Circuit, the "cases assessing whether a threat of continuity exists have looked first to the nature of the predicate acts alleged or to the nature of the enterprise at whose behest the predicate acts were performed." GICC Capital Corp., 67 F.3d at 466 (collecting cases). In assessing whether or not the plaintiff has shown open-ended continuity, the nature of the RICO enterprise and of the predicate acts are relevant. [c] Where an inherently unlawful act is performed at the behest of an enterprise whose business is racketeering activity, there is a threat of continued criminal activity, and thus open-ended continuity. See *H.J. Inc.*, 492 U.S. at 242–43 ("[T]he threat of continuity is sufficiently established where the predicates can be attributed to a defendant operating as part of a long-term association that exists for criminal purposes."); However, "where the enterprise primarily conducts a legitimate business, there must be some evidence from which it may be inferred that the predicate acts were the regular way of operating that business, or that the nature of the predicate acts themselves implies a threat of continued criminal activity." [C]

The Bernas defendants argue that the plaintiffs failed to establish a pattern of open-ended continuity against them, because the alleged scheme by the Bernas defendants to obtain stock and gravel was inherently finite and therefore did not pose a threat of repetition.

* * *

[T]here was sufficient evidence from which a reasonable jury could conclude that the escalating nature of the Bernas defendants' demands—such as their demanding an increasing interest in the gravel pit—indicated that they had no intention of stopping once they met some immediate goal. Based on this evidence, the jury could reasonably have concluded that the Bernas defendants would have continued extorting the plaintiffs into the future. Accordingly, the scheme was not "inherently terminable" and the jury could reasonably have found that the nature of the Bernas' predicate acts themselves implied a threat of continued criminal activity.

The private right of action provision of RICO provides that: Any person injured in his business or property by reason of a violation of section 1962 of this chapter may sue therefor in any appropriate United States district court and shall recover threefold the damages he sustains and the cost of the suit, including a reasonable attorney's fee.

18 U.S.C. § 1964(c). " 'The phrase "by reason of" requires that there be a causal connection between the prohibited conduct and [the] plaintiff's injury.' " [C] To show that an injury resulted "by reason of" the defendant's action, a plaintiff must show " 'that the defendant's violations were a proximate cause of the plaintiff's injury, i.e., that there was a direct relationship between the plaintiff's injury and the defendant's injurious conduct.' " First Nationwide Bank v. Gelt Funding Corp., 27 F.3d 763, 769 (2d Cir.1994) (quoting Standardbred Owners Ass'n v. Roosevelt Raceway Assocs., L.P., 985 F.2d 102, 104 (2d Cir.1993)). This requires a showing "not only that the defendant's alleged RICO violation was the 'but-for' or cause-in-fact of his injury,

but also that the violation was the legal or proximate cause." [C] In other words, a plaintiff's injury must be both factually and proximately caused by a defendant's violation of section 1962. [C]

To prove proximate causation, the plaintiffs would have had to offer evidence that they were otherwise entitled to approval of Phase II and that no independent, intervening factors affected their ability to sell the lots. "[T]he less direct an injury is, the more difficult it becomes to ascertain the amount of the plaintiff's damages attributable to the violation, as distinct from other, independent factors." [C]

Thus, even were we to accept the plaintiffs' "enterprise damages" theory, under this Court's RICO precedents, the causal link between the plaintiffs' evidence and the inability to sell the Phase II lots is too weak to satisfy the proximate causation requirement. Thus, the District Court was correct in vacating the $1.6 million award.

CONCLUSION

We have considered the parties' remaining contentions and find them to be without merit. Accordingly, we VACATE the $1,000.00 award against Dirie for the truck wheels and tires extorted for the benefit of Dirie's son, but AFFIRM the judgments of the District Court in all other respects.

NOTES AND QUESTIONS

1. In the principal case, the court finds the defendants were in a relation of control over the township governance. The requisite nexus may be at issue. See University of Maryland at Baltimore v. Peat, Marwick, Main & Co., 996 F.2d 1534 (1993) (finding that the provision of financial services, like auditors and computerization of accounting services relating to purchases and sales, does not form a sufficient "nexus" between "the person and the conduct of the affairs of an enterprise").

2. A person may be liable for conspiracy to violate RICO. Section 1962(d) makes it illegal "to conspire to violate," among other things, § 1962(c). Recall that subsection (c) makes it unlawful for any person employed by an enterprise engaged in interstate commerce "to conduct or participate, directly or indirectly, in the conduct of such enterprise's affairs through a pattern of racketeering activity." In Salinas v. United States, 522 U.S. 52 (1997), the Court addressed conspiracy liability and held, applying general principles of conspiracy law, that a conspirator must intend to further an endeavor which, if completed, would satisfy all the elements of the criminal offense. It suffices, however, that he adopt the goal of furthering or facilitating the crime. It may appear, then, that under subsection (d) one need not participate personally in the operation or management of the enterprise. Could such an argument avoid the nexus requirement under the principal case? In Beck v. Prupis, 529 U.S. 494 (2000), the Court narrowed the scope of RICO conspiracy liability by requiring that the injury be caused by an act of racketeering or independent wrongfulness. This principle was taken from settled common law at the time of congressional enactment of the statute.

3. The provision of treble damages and attorney's fees under civil RICO provided a stimulus to include RICO counts in actions where

traditional claims would lie. Can you suggest actions at common law that may have been available in the principal case?

4. A coalition of anti-abortion groups conspired to shut down abortion clinics. Can pro-choice organizations bring a civil RICO action claiming that the coalition had thus engaged in a pattern of racketeering activity including, as a racketeering predicate act, extortion in violation of the Hobbs Act, 18 U.S.C.A. § 1951? The Supreme Court in National Organization for Women, Inc. v. Scheidler, 510 U.S. 249 (1994) held that the action would lie, finding that the "enterprise" element of the offense did not connote an "economic motive." In a separate opinion Justice Souter, joined by Justice Kennedy, stressed that First Amendment concerns may in the appropriate case delimit the reach of RICO. Ultimately, after remand to the trial court and appeals again to the Court, a judgment for plaintiffs was reversed on the grounds that the elements of the predicate crime of extortion were not met. Scheidler v. National Organization for Women, Inc., 537 U.S. 393 (2003).

3. THE DETERMINATION OF TORT LAW

At the end of the last century and in the first decade of this century, both Congress and the states have become active in tort reform. At the federal level, much activity has been devoted to regulation touching the safety of products. Pharmaceuticals and health care products forming a significant area of tort liability have been closely regulated at the federal level. The debate surrounding health care reform has revivified suggestions that Congress include provisions designed to lessen claim frequency and severity to reduce costs in the provision of medical services. This regulation and reform places at center stage the pre-emption of tort law by congressional lawmaking. You visited the complex issues of pre-emption in the context of products liability. (Chapter 15, Section 4(B).)

State tort reform has gathered pace, fueled by concerns about affordability and availability of liability insurance. Accumulating legislation has often been challenged on the basis that it violates state constitutional provisions. The Kentucky Supreme Court in Williams v. Wilson, 972 S.W.2d 260 (1998) adopted the notion of jural rights derived from the common law to limit reform. Other courts have nullified tort law: e.g., Best v. Taylor Machine Works, 179 Ill.2d 367, 689 N.E.2d 1057, 228 Ill.Dec. 636 (1997) (declaring the Civil Justice Reform Amendments of 1995 unconstitutional under the Illinois constitution); State ex. Rel. Ohio Academy of Trial Lawyers v. Sheward, 86 Ohio St.3d 451, 715 N.E.2d 1062 (1999) (civil justice reform amendments declared unconstitutional under Ohio constitution); Lakin v. Senco Products Inc., 329 Or. 62, 987 P.2d 463 (1999) (cap on noneconomic damages unconstitutional violation of Oregon right to jury trial). But see McDougall v. Schanz, 461 Mich. 15, 597 N.W.2d 148 (1999) (upholding statute setting strict requirements concerning qualifications of experts in medical malpractice cases in face of challenge brought under Michigan constitution).

The following is one court's response to state law reform:

Pulliam v. Coastal Emergency Svcs.

Supreme Court of Virginia, 1999.
257 Va. 1, 509 S.E.2d 307.

CARRICO, CHIEF JUSTICE. In this appeal, we are called upon to consider again the constitutionality of the medical malpractice cap imposed by Code § 8.01–581.15.* We previously upheld the constitutionality of the cap in Etheridge v. Medical Center Hospitals, 237 Va. 87, 376 S.E.2d 525 (1989). * * * Because we conclude that the medical malpractice cap does not violate any constitutional guarantees, we will uphold the cap's constitutionality and reaffirm *Etheridge*.

* * *

[About 3:55 a.m. on December 15, 1995, Mrs. Pulliam arrived at the emergency room of Southside Regional Hospital complaining of "legs aching." She had been diagnosed with influenza two days earlier in the office of her private physician. At Southside Regional, she was examined by Dr. DiGiovanna, who had been retained by defendant Coastal Emergency Services to staff the hospital's emergency room. About 5:00 a.m., Dr. DiGiovanna discharged Mrs. Pulliam after prescribing a muscle relaxant and giving her printed instructions on influenza and additional instructions concerning bedrest. Shortly after 11:00 a.m. the same day, Mrs. Pulliam returned to the emergency room complaining of general weakness, particularly in her lower extremities. Following a physical examination by another doctor, Mrs. Pulliam was started on intravenous fluids and subjected to a CT scan and a lumbar puncture. Thereafter, she was transferred to the intensive care unit, where her condition worsened. She was pronounced dead at 9:08 p.m. An autopsy revealed that the cause of death was bacterial pneumonia and bacteremia. She was survived by her husband, who is the executor of her estate, and a son. After a jury trial based on the medical malpractice of Dr. DiGiovanna, for whom Coastal was vicariously liable, the jury returned a verdict of $2,045,000. Pursuant to the applicable Virginia statute, the trial court judge reduced the verdict to $1,000,000 and this appeal followed.]

A. Constitutionality of Medical Malpractice Cap.

The plaintiff's assignment of error on this point states that "as a matter of law, the trial court erred in failing to conclude that the cap on medical malpractice awards is unconstitutional as applied to Coastal and to Dr. DiGiovanna." (Footnote omitted.) In considering this assignment of error, "we adhere to the well-settled principle that all actions of the General Assembly are presumed to be constitutional. This Court, therefore, will resolve any reasonable doubt regarding a statute's constitutionality in favor of its validity. Any judgment as to the wisdom and propriety of a statute is within the legislative prerogative, and this

* Code § 8.01–581.15 provides that "in any verdict returned against a health care provider in an action for malpractice[,] . . . the total amount recoverable for any injury to, or death of, a patient shall not exceed one million dollars."

Court will declare the legislative judgment null and void only when the statute is plainly repugnant to some provision of the state or federal constitution." [C]

In *Etheridge*, we rejected challenges to the constitutionality of the medical malpractice cap based upon contentions that the cap "violates the Virginia Constitution's due process guarantee, jury trial guarantee, separation of powers doctrine, prohibitions against special legislation, and equal protection guarantee, as well as certain parallel provisions of the Federal Constitution." [C] The plaintiff makes the same challenges here, but amplifies the arguments in several respects. (Footnote omitted.)

It is clear that we cannot grant the plaintiff relief without overruling *Etheridge*. Immediately, therefore, the doctrine of stare decisis is implicated. * * *

The inquiry becomes, therefore, whether flagrant error or mistake exists in the *Etheridge* decision. The plaintiff contends that such error does exist and, therefore, that "the doctrine of stare decisis should not deter this Court from reversing *Etheridge*."

The plaintiff argues that the medical malpractice cap is unconstitutional on each of seven independent grounds. We will consider these grounds seriatim.

1. Right to Trial by Jury.

Article I, § 11 of the Constitution of Virginia provides "that in controversies respecting property, and in suits between man and man, trial by jury is preferable to any other, and ought to be held sacred." In *Etheridge*, we noted that, at the time the Constitution was adopted, the jury's sole function was to resolve disputed facts, that this continues to be a jury's sole function, (footnote omitted) and that the jury's fact-finding function extends to the assessment of damages. [C] We stated, however, that "once the jury has ascertained the facts and assessed the damages, . . . the constitutional mandate is satisfied [and thereafter], it is the duty of the court to apply the law to the facts." [C] The medical malpractice cap, we said, does nothing more than establish the outer limits of a remedy; remedy is a matter of law and not of fact; and a trial court applies the remedy's limitation only after the jury has fulfilled its fact-finding function. Hence, we concluded, the cap does not infringe upon the right to a jury trial. [C]

The plaintiff says, however, that the Court in *Etheridge* "erred by failing to conclude that the mandate of Article I, § 11 includes the right to receive the amount of damages awarded by a jury after a proper jury trial." In this connection, the plaintiff cites two recent Supreme Court decisions.

* * *

The plaintiff says that these two decisions support his conclusion that the medical malpractice cap violates his right to a jury trial. We do not agree. In relying on Hetzel [v. Prince William Cty., 523 U.S. 208 (1998)], the plaintiff attempts to equate remittitur with the medical malpractice cap and argues that, since remittitur without the option of a new trial violates the Seventh Amendment right to a jury trial, application of the cap likewise violates Virginia's right to a jury trial. However, the plaintiff's initial premise is faulty because remittitur and the cap are not equivalent and do not come into play under the same circumstances. Remittitur, as well as additur, is utilized only after a court has determined that a party has not received a fair and proper jury trial. [C] The cap, however, is applied only after a plaintiff has had the benefit of a proper jury trial. In the latter situation, there is no right to a new trial, and the constitutional mandate has been satisfied.

The plaintiff's reliance on Feltner [v. Columbia Pictures Television, Inc., 523 U.S. 340 (1998)] is also misplaced. There, the Court dealt primarily with whether Columbia was entitled to a jury trial even though it elected to seek statutory damages. The Court concluded that Columbia had the right to a jury trial because the common law afforded copyright owners causes of action for infringement, and these actions were tried before juries. The Court recognized that "the Seventh Amendment . . . applies not only to common-law causes of action, but also to 'actions brought to enforce statutory rights that are analogous to common-law causes of action ordinarily decided in English law courts in the late 18th century, as opposed to those customarily heard by courts of equity or admiralty.' " [C] The Court did not address the validity of a cap on the recovery of damages.

Furthermore, while it does not appear that the Supreme Court has addressed the issue of the validity of state statutory caps, it has noted the decisions of two circuit courts of appeals on the subject * * * [and those opinions] have held that district court application of state statutory caps in diversity cases, post verdict, does not violate the Seventh Amendment.

* * *

Concerning the right of trial by jury under the Seventh Amendment, the Fourth Circuit followed our reasoning that it is not the role of the jury but of the legislature to determine the legal consequences of the jury's factual findings. [C] However, the Fourth Circuit assigned this additional reason for upholding the validity of the cap against an assertion that it violated the right of trial by jury: "It is by now axiomatic that the Constitution does not forbid the creation of new rights, or the abolition of old ones recognized by the common law, to attain a permissible legislative object. Indeed, the district court conceded that a legislature's outright abolition of a cause of action would not violate the seventh amendment. If a legislature may completely abolish a cause of action without violating the right of trial by jury, we think it permissibly may limit damages recoverable for a cause of action as well." [Boyd v. Bulala, 877 F.2d 1191 (4th Cir. 1989)] at 1196 (citations and interior quotation marks omitted).

* * *

Nor can it be disputed that, in addition to abolishing a cause of action, a legislature may extinguish a cause of action by the imposition of a statute of limitations, for example, two years from the date of death in the case of an action for wrongful death. Code § 8.01–244. If it is permissible for a legislature to enact a statute of limitations completely barring recovery in a particular cause of action without impinging upon the right of trial by jury, it should be permissible for the legislature to impose a limitation upon the amount of recovery as well.

The courts of other states have upheld medical malpractice caps against assertions that they violate the right to a jury trial. [Cc]

The plaintiff cites several out-of-state cases declaring medical malpractice caps unconstitutional, but we find them inapposite [due to differences between those state's constitutions and Virginia's or unpersuasive]. * * *

2. Special Legislation.

Article IV, § 14 of the Constitution of Virginia provides that "the General Assembly shall not enact any local, special, or private law . . . (18) granting to any private corporation, association, or individual any special or exclusive right, privilege, or immunity." (Footnote omitted.) In *Etheridge*, we noted that we had previously held that laws may be made to apply to a class only, even though the class may be small, provided the classification is reasonable, not arbitrary, and the law is made to apply to all persons in the class without distinction. [C] We also noted that if the classification bears a reasonable and substantial relation to the object sought to be accomplished, it will survive a special-laws constitutional challenge. Id.

We then pointed out that, in enacting the Medical Malpractice Act, the General Assembly, after a careful and deliberate study, had determined health care providers faced increasing difficulty obtaining affordable malpractice coverage in excess of $750,000, thus reducing the number of such providers available to serve Virginia's citizens. We also pointed out that the General Assembly had determined that this significant problem adversely affected the public health, safety, and welfare and necessitated the imposition of a limitation upon the liability of health care providers in medical malpractice actions. [C]

We observed that the General Assembly had decided that damage awards in medical malpractice cases should not exceed $750,000 (now $1,000,000), and we stated that the limitation applied to all health care providers and all medical malpractice patients. [C] We found that the classification was not arbitrary, that it bore a reasonable and substantial relation to the object sought to be accomplished, and that it applied to all persons belonging to the class without distinction. Id. Accordingly, we concluded that the legislation did not violate the prohibition against special legislation. Id.

* * *

[The court then considered plaintiff's argument that the cap was impermissible special legislation.] The remainder of the plaintiff's "as applied" argument is confined to the proposition that the medical malpractice cap concentrates the costs solely upon those whose losses are greatest while identifying "a specific elite class, described as 'health care providers,' to which it accords special privileges and immunities that are given to no other tortfeasors in this Commonwealth." And the plaintiff indicates his agreement with the dissent in *Etheridge* that the General Assembly acted arbitrarily in restricting the cap so that it did not apply to "all plaintiffs and all defendants regardless of their identities." [C] * * *

Here, however, we do not have to assume a set of facts that would sustain the medical malpractice cap. The actual facts were as stated in *Etheridge*: "The General Assembly concluded [after careful and deliberate study] that escalating costs of medical malpractice insurance and the availability of such insurance were substantial problems adversely affecting the health, safety, and welfare of Virginia's citizens." [C] Given these facts, we think the cap bears a reasonable and substantial relation to the General Assembly's objective to protect the public's health, safety, and welfare by insuring the availability of health care providers in the Commonwealth. Accordingly, we conclude that the medical malpractice cap does not constitute special legislation.

3. Taking of Property.

Under the Fifth Amendment to the Constitution of the United States, private property shall not be taken for public use without just compensation. Under art. I, § 11 of the Constitution of Virginia, private property shall not be taken or damaged for public uses without just compensation.

Here, the argument is that the effect of the medical malpractice cap is to take the property of the plaintiff and his son in violation of these constitutional provisions. As the statutory beneficiaries of Mrs. Pulliam, the argument goes, the plaintiff and his son "had a property interest in the full measure of the jury's verdict."

We disagree. * * * [I]t is only when a right has accrued or a claim has arisen that it is subject to the protection of the due process clause * * * "for 'nobody has a vested right in the continuance of the rules of the common law.' " [quoting Hess v. Snyder Hunt Corp., 240 Va. 49, 392 S.E.2d 817 (1990) (citing Munn v. Illinois, 94 U.S. 113, 134, 24 L. Ed. 77 (1877).]. Continuing, we stated that "the fourteenth amendment does not forbid a legislature from abolishing old rights recognized by the common law in order to attain a permissible legislative objective." Id. Finally, we said that "if a legislature can abolish a cause of action for a legitimate legislative purpose, it also may prevent a cause of action from arising by enacting a statute of repose for such a purpose." Id.

This rationale applies with equal force here. The plaintiff's cause of action for wrongful death had not accrued at the time the cap was imposed upon recoveries in medical malpractice cases. One cannot obtain a property interest in a cause of action that has not accrued, and there was nothing to prevent the General Assembly from limiting the remedy, so far as unaccrued causes of action are concerned, to attain a permissible legislative objective without running afoul of the "taking" clauses of the Federal and State Constitutions. Accordingly, we find no violation of the "taking" clauses in this case.

4. Due Process.

* * *

5. Equal Protection.

In oral argument, the plaintiff combined these two subjects and attempted to convince the Court that it should apply an intermediate level of scrutiny, rather than the lower-level rational basis test, in our due process and equal protection analysis of the medical malpractice cap. (Footnote omitted.) However, we ruled in *Etheridge* that, in a due process or equal protection analysis, the rational basis test applies unless a fundamental right or a suspect class is affected. [C] And we noted that those interests that have been recognized as "fundamental" include the right to free speech, the right to vote, the right to interstate travel, the right to fairness in the criminal process, the right to marry, and the right to fairness in procedures concerning governmental deprivation of life, liberty, or property. [C] We noted further that suspect classifications are those based upon race and national origin and that classifications based upon gender, alienage, and illegitimacy are entitled to receive a level of scrutiny between strict scrutiny and the rational basis test. [C] Here, however, no fundamental right or suspect class is affected by application of the medical malpractice cap.

* * *

[The court found that *Etheridge* enunciated the correct level of scrutiny and that the rational basis test continues to provide the proper standard for determining whether there has been a denial of due process or equal protection in a case involving the medical malpractice cap, and that the statute satisfied due process.]

6. Separation of Powers.

* * *

7. Province of the Judiciary.

Because these two subjects are related, we will discuss them together. The plaintiff argues that the medical malpractice cap violates the separation of powers doctrine and also invades the province of the judiciary.

In rejecting a separation of powers challenge in *Etheridge*, we pointed out that under art. VI, § 1 of the Virginia Constitution, the General Assembly, subject to provisions relating to the power and jurisdiction of this Court, has "the power to determine the original and appellate jurisdiction of the courts of the Commonwealth." [C] We also noted that under art. IV, § 14 of the Constitution, the General Assembly's authority extends "to all subjects of legislation not herein forbidden or restricted," and that the common law is one area in which the General Assembly's authority has not been forbidden or restricted. Id.

Accordingly, we said that the legislature has the power to provide, modify, or repeal a remedy. [C] And we concluded that "whether the remedy prescribed in Code § 8.01–581.15 is viewed as a modification of the common law or as establishing the jurisdiction of the courts in specific cases, clearly it was a proper exercise of legislative power." [C]

* * *

Thus, we find no merit in the plaintiff's arguments concerning separation of powers and the province of the judiciary. Accordingly, we reject the arguments. * * *

[The court then ruled that the statutory cap applied to Coastal and that pre-judgment interest was included in the statutory cap.]

Affirmed.

[The concurring opinion of JUSTICE HASSELL is omitted.]

KINSER, JUSTICE (concurring opinion). I agree with the majority's rationale and decision that the medical malpractice recovery cap contained in Code § 8.01–581.15 does not violate any provision of either the Constitution of the United States or the Constitution of Virginia. (Footnote omitted.) I reach this conclusion without considering the role that stare decisis should play in this case. I write separately for the sole purpose of expressing my belief that the medical malpractice cap creates an unwarranted injustice in certain situations.

The General Assembly has the responsibility to protect the health, welfare, and safety of the citizens of this Commonwealth through appropriate legislation. However, the medical malpractice cap works the greatest hardship on those individuals who are the most severely injured by the negligence of health care providers. Nevertheless, I cannot be influenced by such concerns when deciding the constitutionality of a challenged statute. I can only express my views with the hope that the General Assembly will adopt a more equitable method by which to ensure the availability of health care in this Commonwealth.

NOTES AND QUESTIONS

1. The consideration of a catalogue of constitutional challenges by the court in the principal case is typical of the cases challenging state tort reform. Do you agree with the court's ruling on each of the challenges? There are dozens of decisions at various levels by state courts holding state tort reform unconstitutional under state constitutions and even more decisions upholding such laws. For an elegant discussion of the place of tort law in the constitutional law setting, see John C. P. Goldberg, The Constitutional Status of Tort Law: Due Process and the Right to a Law for the Redress of Wrongs, 115 Yale L.J. 524 (2005).

2. As you can see from Justice Kinser's concurring opinion in the principal case, he does not agree with the Virginia legislature's judgment on the propriety of a cap in medical malpractice cases, yet he voted to affirm the trial court's ruling. Why? As Justice Resnick noted in State ex. rel. Ohio Academy of Trial Lawyers v. Sheward, 86 Ohio St.3d 451, 715 N.E.2d 1062, 1072 (1999), "[a]ll arguments going to the soundness of legislative policy choices, however, are directed to their proper place, which is outside the door to this courthouse. This court has nothing to do with the policy or wisdom of a statute. That is the exclusive concern of the legislative branch of the government. The only judicial inquiry into the constitutionality of a statute involves the question of legislative power, not legislative wisdom." (Internal quotations and citations omitted.)

3. A theme in the cases in this chapter is the respective and sometimes conflicting roles of the judiciary and the legislature in declaring tort law. Sometimes the discussion is cast in terms of preference (which body is better suited to resolve the issue) and sometimes in terms of power (which body is authorized to make the decision). See Symposium: Judges as

Tort Lawmakers, 49 DePaul L.Rev. 275 (1999). The substantive issues being considered—whether medical monitoring is a form of damage, the appropriate threshold for punitive damages, the standard for proving punitive damages, whether there should be a cap on damages—are very difficult ones, with compelling arguments on both sides. For example, some investigators have linked tort reform damage caps to a reduction in the intensity of patient care. Rovan Avraham & Max Schanzenbach, *The Impact of Tort Reform on Intensity of Treatment: Evidence from Patients,* 39 J. of Health Econ. 273 (2015). Beyond this the balance may depend on judicial appreciation that the goals and purposes of tort law are separate and independent of the state's regulatory role. Benjamin Zipurski, The New Private Law: Palsgraf, Punitive Damages, and Peemption, 125 Harv. L. Rev. 1757 (2012). Equally challenging is the discernment of the proper role of the two branches of government. How should they work together to make tort law? How do you see their respective roles? This struggle for power between the legislative and judicial branches of the states promises to be an important one, fervently pursued, often on thin data, during the next decade. What will your role in it be? How would you strike the proper balance?

4. When considering product liability, we canvassed the interaction of federal regulation and state tort law. See pages 829 to 831. With increasing Congressional legislation and federal agency regulatory authority, the issue of preemption will remain a dominant arena for considering tort law in the age of the administrative state. Case law has burgeoned. Two recent Supreme Court cases, principal cases in Chapter 15, loom large: Riegal v. Medtronic, Inc., 552 U.S. 312 (2008) and Wyeth v. Levine, 555 U.S. 555 (2009). In the more recent case of *Wyeth*, the Court considered the preemptive effect of agency regulation about warnings given the administration of a prescribed drug, Phenergan. It had been determined at trial that the warning label was inadequate under state tort law. Thus the issue of preemption in FDA regulation again was presented for resolution by the Supreme Court.

In *Wyeth*, a long anticipated decision, the Supreme Court considered Wyeth's two preemption arguments: first, that Wyeth could not have complied with the state-law duty without violating federal law, and second, that recognition of the state tort action created an unacceptable obstacle to the accomplishment and execution of the full purposes and objectives of Congress, in that it substituted a lay jury's decision about drug labeling for the expert judgment of the FDA. The Court relied on two basic tenets in finding no preemption. First, the question depends on the "purpose of Congress," and second, that the assumption that the historic police powers of the States, including tort law, are not superseded unless Congress's intent was clear and manifest. On the evidence, the Court found that Wyeth could have complied with both federal and state requirements. It could have strengthened its warning on the label, even though an earlier warning had been FDA-approved. The responsibility lay with Wyeth. On the second argument—that complying with the tort law would detract from the purpose and objectives of federal drug labeling regulations—the Court found no predicate in the evidence relating to Congressional intent or purpose. However, agency regulations may preempt conflicting state tort law. Two years after Wyeth, the Supreme Court held that state tort law claims against a generic manufacturer in a failure to warn suit were preempted because the FDA regulation prevented the generic drug from having a different warning than the approved pioneer drug. PLIVA v. Mensing, 131 S. Ct. 2567 (2011).

In Wyeth, the Court took the view that the co-existence of state and federal law was complimentary and long standing. Justice Thomas concurred in the Court's opinions but was concerned that the Court's "purposes and objectives" jurisprudence allowed invalidation of state law on broad notions outside the text of the statute. Justice Alito filed a dissenting opinion in which Roberts, C.J. and Scalia, J. joined. The dissent viewed the evidence as establishing that the federal regulation and the state tort law could not co-exist.

After *Wyeth* and *PLIVA*, much will depend on the thoroughness of agency findings. Has the law achieved any stability after *Wyeth*? Is there merit in competing legislative and regulatory findings? Federalism, with its overlapping jurisdictions, some have suggested, has distinct advantages: Robert A. Schapiro, Polyphonic Federalism: Toward the Protection of Fundamental Rights (U of Chicago Press, 2009).

CHAPTER 24

COMPENSATION SYSTEMS AS SUBSTITUTES FOR TORT LAW

Students come to this chapter with a close appreciation of the rambunctious and ramshackle nature of tort law. Although tort law has moved to cover more widely economic interests, its home is its protection of physical integrity. Tort lawyers are usually pictured as inhabiting courtrooms to argue personal injury claims.

This book's cases and materials show that tort law has been subject to both judicial and legislative changes, but these changes have not altered the basic picture of lawyers in the courtroom. About a century ago a more radical change occurred—no-fault workers' compensation. About forty years ago, approaches were suggested and adopted in various states for automobile no-fault compensation systems. These developments are reviewed before turning to other no-fault compensation systems, some targeting particular problems (e.g., vaccine-related injuries) or resulting from catastrophic events (e.g., the 9/11 terrorist attack), others of a broader nature which would replace the entire body of tort liability for personal injury with a governmental no-fault compensation system. As you review these schemes ask about the nature and function of tort liability. What are its purposes and are they adequately reflected in compensation systems? Should those purposes be captured in any tort system or is it appropriate to forfeit some (for example, deterrence) in the interest of maximizing others (for example, compensation to a wide class of injured persons)? Are there ways of formulating the approaches as to preserve the benefits of tort liability while remedying its ills?

1. EMPLOYMENT INJURIES

Negligence was formed in the crucible of the Industrial Revolution. Exponential increase in speed and efficiency of transportation and industrial production resulted in an ever increasing number of personal injuries. Duties of care in negligence were imposed on employers toward their employees. Out of the numerous cases arose an elaborate doctrinal system. Thus, among others, the employer had the general duties of using due care to provide a safe place to work and to supply safe tools and appliances. There were exceptions and counter-exceptions—e.g., the simple-tool doctrine as an exception to the second duty above, and the inexperienced-employee doctrine as an exception to it. See generally J.D. Lee & Barry A. Lindahl, Modern Tort Law: Liability & Litigation (2d ed., 2014), vol. 4.

But the most significant aspect of the doctrinal development was a group of three defenses—assumption of risk, contributory negligence and the fellow-servant rule. This "unholy trinity," added to the requirement of proving the employer's negligence meant that stumbling blocks were placed on recovery of damages by injured workers. Long, drawn-out litigation placed severe financial burdens upon workers.

Even though courts cannot be said to have been uniformly hostile to workers' claims, the realities of wealth and ineffectual representational institutions for workers dictated relatively few instances of compensation.

With the incidence of industrial accidents came social pressure for a system to compensate the many injured. Sometimes the pressure was accommodated through bargains between employers and employees. More widely, Congress took note of the issue and repealed some of the common law doctrines that had frustrated the goal of more adequate compensation for railroad workers. Federal Employees' Liability Act, 1906. The Act did not survive constitutional challenge. The second attempt saw the Federal Employers' Liability Act of 1908 (45 U.S.C.A. § 51 et seq. (1908)). Congress enacted a law easing tort law burdens for longshoremen and harbor workers in 1927 (33 U.S.C.A. § 901 et seq. (as amended 1972)). These acts restructured the tort system making it easier for workers to recover damages. Much later Congress established a compensation system for coal miners commonly called the Black Lung Program (Federal Coal Mine Health and Safety Act of 1969, 30 U.S.C.A. §§ 801–962). Congress, in 1986, enacted the National Childhood Vaccine Injury Act, which provides compensation to certain injuries related to vaccines taken by children. The compensation scheme has been limited to children; the reasons for its enactment, vaccine shortages and litigation costs, were not replicated with respect to adults. U.S. Dep't of Health and Human Services, Public Health Reports No. 3, Vol. 113; p. 236 at 1 (1998).

By far, the boldest scheme is Workers' Compensation legislation that allows workers injured in the course of employment to recover compensation from the employer without having to prove employer fault. The employer is able to insure for these losses. Within each state, a large segment of common law liability was abolished, as the legislation was enacted. Compensation is now ubiquitous in the modern Western Industrial state. It was first introduced in Bismark's Germany in the late 19th Century reflecting the maturity of the industrial revolution, a rise in labor union influence, and the challenge of Marxist ideas. England and other European nations followed the German experiment. New York in 1910 was the first state to adopt workers' compensation legislation. Wisconsin's 1911 legislation was the first to withstand constitutional challenge.

The rallying theme for the movement was that the enterprise should bear the loss rather than permit it to lie on the unfortunate employee who arbitrarily had incurred the injury: "The cost of the product should bear the blood of the workman." The employer was liable to the injured employee regardless of fault, so long as the injury occurred in the course of employment. Early workers' compensation laws only protected employees from work-related injuries, but not occupational diseases. Today these also are included, with some retrenchment in the case of stress-related disease, under the workers' compensation systems. It has been argued that the systems implicitly perform the dual role of tort liability—compensation and optimal deterrence. Deterrence may operate by internalizing the costs of production, thus ensuring an optimal production of goods. The efficacy of internalization depends in part on the sensitivity of the insurance system in discriminating between safe and unsafe producers, the willingness of the political system to face producers with costs of accidents, and the impact of transaction costs, like litigation costs and uncertainty of benefits. In face of these obstacles the internalization process may be weakened as costs are spread to the public at large. Hylton & Laymon, The Internalization Paradox and Workers' Compensation, 21 Hofstra L.Rev. 109 (1992). For historical background, see J. Weinstein, The Corporate Ideal in the Liberal State, 1900–1918, ch. 2 (1968); Epstein, The Historical Origins and Economic Structure of Workers' Compensation Law, 16 Ga.L.Rev. 775 (1982).

Workers' compensation has developed into a complex and highly specialized field of law. Litigation is a feature of the system as each year courts hand down many decisions that mainly concern questions about coverage. Typical questions include whether an injury fell within the scope of employment, see, e.g., Nemchick v. Thatcher Glass Mfg. Co., 203 N.J.Super. 137, 495 A.2d 1372 (App.Div.1985) (employee's injury while driving home from work after completion of an assigned off-premises task occurred in "course of employment"); or whether the injury suffered was caused by conditions of employment. See, e.g., State Accident Ins. Fund v. Noffsinger, 80 Or.App. 640, 723 P.2d 358 (1986) (psychic injury as a result of verbal harassment and horseplay at workplace); Graver Tank & Mfg. Co. v. Industrial Comm'n, 97 Ariz. 256, 399 P.2d 664 (1965) (suicide) Anderson v. Save-A-Lot, 989 S.W.2d 277 (Tenn. 1999) (sexual harassment of employee by supervisor causing injury not in the course of employment). Generally courts consider whether the injury may reasonably be regarded as an incident of employment rather than whether the injury was specifically foreseeable. See, e.g., Burns v. Merritt Eng'g Co., 302 N.Y. 131, 135, 96 N.E.2d 739, 741 (1951).

Advances in medical knowledge have established a causal connection between some diseases and exposure to toxic substances found in the work place. Claims for these diseases have challenged the limits of workers compensation coverage. Indeed, with the recognition of the influence of the workplace on the contraction of disease in general, increasing numbers of claims are brought at the very point where the difficulties of proof are greatest. Dewees, Duff, & Trebilcock, Exploring the Domain of Accident Law: Taking the Facts Seriously 351–352 (1996).

Perhaps the best summary of how these laws function has been provided by the author of the leading treatise in the field:

> "The right to [workers'] compensation benefits depends on one simple test: Was there a work-connected injury? Negligence, and, for the most part, fault, are not in issue and cannot affect the result. Let the employer's conduct be flawless in its perfection, and let the employee's be abysmal in its clumsiness, rashness and ineptitude: if the accident arises out of and in the course of the employment, the employee receives his award. Reverse the positions, with a careless and stupid employer and a wholly innocent employee: the same award issues.
>
> "Thus, the test is not the relation of an individual's personal quality (fault) to an event, but the relationship of an

event to an employment. The essence of applying the test is not a matter of assessing blame, but of marking out boundaries.

"The typical [workers'] compensation act has these features: (a) the basic operating principle is that an employee is automatically entitled to certain benefits whenever he suffers a 'personal injury by accident arising out of and in the course of employment'; (b) negligence and fault are largely immaterial, both in the sense that the employee's contributory negligence does not lessen his rights and in the sense that the employer's complete freedom from fault does not lessen his liability; (c) coverage is limited to persons having the status of employee, as distinguished from independent contractor; (d) benefits to the employee include cash-wage benefits, usually around one-half to two-thirds of his average weekly wage, and hospital and medical expenses; in death cases benefits for dependents are provided; arbitrary maximum and minimum limits are ordinarily imposed; (e) the employee and his dependents, in exchange for these modest but assured benefits, give up their common-law right to sue the employer for damages for any injury covered by the act; (f) the right to sue third persons whose negligence caused the injury remains, however, with the proceeds usually being applied first to reimbursement of the employer for the compensation outlay, the balance (or most of it) going to the employee; (g) administration is typically in the hands of administrative commissions; and, as far as possible, rules of procedure, evidence, and conflict of laws are relaxed to facilitate the achievement of the beneficent purposes of the legislation; and (h) the employer is required to secure his liability through private insurance, state-fund insurance in some states, or 'self-insurance'; thus the burden of compensation liability does not remain upon the employer but passes to the consumer, since compensation premiums, as part of the cost of production, will be reflected in the price of the product." 1 A. Larson, The Law of Workmen's Compensation, 1–2, 5 (1991). (Copyright Matthew Bender and Company, Inc. Reprinted by permission.)

Workers' compensation law has not received the criticism leveled at the common law tort system. Yet burdens of compensation have increased for employers, from $1 billion in 1950 to $2 billion in 1960 to $5 billion in 1970 to $21 billion in 1980, reaching nearly $35 billion in 1986 (reported by the ALI Reporter Study: Enterprise Responsibility for Personal Injury, Vol. 1, p. 106 (1991)). It is estimated that the burden rose to $56 billion in 1990 and to $62 billion in 1992. Schwartz, Waste, Fraud, and Abuse in Workers' Compensation: The Recent California Experience, 52 Md. L. Rev. 983, 984 (1993). The most recent figures from the National Academy of Social Insurance (NASI) show that in 2012 workers compensation costs increased to $83 billion.

Employers have complained about the burden, especially as coverage has extended from injuries to occupational health. Thus, on July 16, 1993, California enacted legislation providing that no compensation shall be paid "for psychiatric injury if the injury was substantially caused by lawful, nondiscriminatory, good faith personnel action." Employees, in contrast, have complained about inadequacy of coverage limits on claims and eroding benefits as levels of compensation are not adjusted for cost of living increases. Eaton, The Bargain is No Longer Equal: State Legislative Efforts to Reduce Workers' Compensation Costs Have Impermissibly Shifted the Balance of the *Quid Pro Quo* in Favor of Employers, 37 Ga. L. Rev. 325 (2002) (arguing that the destruction of the *quid pro quo* of the system makes enhanced employers' tort exposure necessary).

A significant portion of compensation dollars go to pay for hospital and medical expenses. In fact, the health care reforms proposed at the end of 1993 by the Clinton Administration opened the question of whether that component of the workers' compensation system should be shifted to health care plans, leaving the system to deal, in the main, with compensation for lost earnings. However, this question still remains unanswered since the implementation of the Affordable Care Act. What do you see as the advantages or disadvantages of folding the medical expense component of workers compensation into the health care system?

The benefits provided by the workers' compensation system appear to be conspicuously modest in light of the recent developments of expanded liability for tortious conduct. Recall restriction or abolishment of the defenses of contributory negligence, assumption of the risk and the fellow servant rule. In addition, damages for non-economic loss have increased in kind and magnitude. At the same time, constraints on workers' compensation have directly inhibited extension of benefits. Some courts have responded to the disparity by circumventing the workers' compensation immunity shield.

Blankenship v. Cincinnati Milacron Chemicals, Inc.

Supreme Court of Ohio, 1982.
69 Ohio St.2d 608, 433 N.E.2d 572, cert. denied,
459 U.S. 857, 103 S.Ct. 127, 74 L.Ed.2d 110 (1982).

[Eight current or former employees of Cincinnati Milacron Chemicals, Inc. (Milacron) brought an action against Milacron, alleging that exposure to fumes of certain chemicals within the scope of their employment rendered them sick, poisoned, and permanently disabled. The employees alleged that Milacron knew that such conditions existed, failed to correct the conditions, failed to warn the employees of the damages and conditions that existed, and failed to report the conditions to various state and Federal agencies to which they were required to report by law. The employees further alleged that Milacron failed to warn the employees that certain occupational diseases were being contracted and failed to provide medical examinations as required by law, and that Milacron's omissions were intentional, malicious, and in willful and wanton disregard of the duty to protect the health of employees.

The trial court dismissed on the ground that the action was barred by relevant sections of the Ohio Constitution and the Ohio Workers' Compensation Act, which afforded an employer and his employees total immunity from civil suit. Employees appealed the trial court's holding and the Court of Appeals affirmed. The cause is now before this court pursuant to the allowance of a motion to certify the record.]

BROWN, J. * * * The sole issue raised in this appeal is whether the trial court properly granted appellees' motion to dismiss appellants' complaint on the grounds that an employee is barred by Section 35, Article II of the Ohio Constitution, and R.C. 4123.74 and 4123.741 from prosecuting an action at law for an intentional tort. * * *

The primary focus of the dispute between the parties centers upon the question of whether the Workers' Compensation Act (R.C. 4123.35 et seq.) is intended to cover an intentional tort committed by employers against their employees. Section 35, Article II of the Ohio Constitution, serves as a basis for legislative enactments in the area of workers' compensation by providing, in pertinent part:

"For the purpose of providing compensation to workmen and their dependents, for death, injuries or occupational disease, occasioned in the course of such workmen's employment, laws may be passed establishing a state fund to be created by compulsory contribution thereto by employers, and administered by the state, determining the terms and conditions upon which payment shall be made therefrom. Such compensation shall be in lieu of all other rights to compensation, or damages, for such death, injuries, or occupational disease, and any employer who pays the premium or compensation provided by law, passed in accordance herewith, shall not be liable to respond in damages at common law or by statute for such death, injuries or occupational disease. * * * "

The constitutional mandate has been implemented by R.C. 4123.74 which provides: "Employers who comply with section 4123.35 of the Revised Code shall not be liable to respond in damages at common law or by statute for any injury, or occupational disease, or bodily condition, received or contracted by any employee in the course of or arising out of his employment * * * whether or not such injury, occupational disease [or] bodily condition * * * is compensable under sections 4123.01 to 4123.94, inclusive, of the Revised Code." * * *

[W]here an employee asserts in his complaint a claim for damages based on an intentional tort, " * * * the substance of the claim is not an injury * * * received or contracted by any employee in the course of or arising out of his employment within the meaning of R.C. 4123.74 * * *." Id. No reasonable individual would equate intentional and unintentional conduct in terms of the degree of risk which faces an employee nor would such individual contemplate the risk of an intentional tort as a natural risk of employment. Since an employer's intentional conduct does not arise out of employment, R.C. 4123.74 does not bestow upon employers immunity from civil liability for their intentional torts and an employee may resort to a civil suit for damages. [C]

This holding not only comports with constitutional and statutory requirements, but it is also consistent with the legislative goals which underlie the Workers' Compensation Act.

The workers' compensation system is based on the premise that an employer is protected from a suit for negligence in exchange for compliance with the Workers' Compensation Act. The Act operates as a balance of mutual compromise between the interests of the employer and the employee whereby employees relinquish their common law remedy and accept lower benefit levels coupled with the greater assurance of recovery and employers give up their common law defenses and are protected from unlimited liability. But the protection afforded by the Act has always been for negligent acts and not for intentional tortious conduct. Indeed, workers' compensation acts were designed to improve the plight of the injured worker, and to hold that intentional torts are covered under the Act would be tantamount to encouraging such conduct, and this clearly cannot be reconciled with the motivating spirit and purpose of the Act.

It must also be remembered that the compensation scheme was specifically designed to provide less than full compensation for injured employees. Damages such as pain and suffering and loss of services on the part of a spouse are unavailable remedies to the injured employee. Punitive damages cannot be obtained. Yet, these damages are available to individuals who have been injured by intentional tortious conduct of third parties, and there is no legitimate reason why an employer should be able to escape from such damages simply because he committed an intentional tort against his employee.

In addition, one of the avowed purposes of the Act is to promote a safe and injury-free work environment. [C] Affording an employer immunity for his intentional behavior certainly would not promote such an environment, for an employer could commit intentional acts with impunity with the knowledge that, at the very most, his workers' compensation premiums may rise slightly. * * * [The court holds that the question of whether Milacron's conduct and omissions amounted to an intentional tort should have been determined by the trier of fact, and that the trial court improperly dismissed the action. Judgment of the Court of Appeals is reversed and case remanded for further proceedings].

[CELEBREZZE, C.J., and SWEENEY and CLIFFORD F. BROWN, JJ., concur. LOCHER, J., concurs in part and dissents in part. HOLMES and KRUPANSKY, JJ., dissent. The dissenting opinion of Holmes argues that tort actions should be permitted against employers only in cases of actual intent to injure the employees. Krupansky's dissent argues that there should be no judicial creation of an intentional misconduct exception to the employers' tort immunity because there is no express exception in the Ohio Workers' Compensation Act].

NOTES AND QUESTIONS

1. The subsequent evolution of the law in Ohio is tortuous and characterized by legislative initiatives and judicial counterattacks. Immediately after the principal case, the Ohio legislature enacted a statute that attempted to enfold employers' intentional torts within a provision of the Ohio code that precluded common law relief but gave enhanced compensation benefits. The benefits were to be paid from a fund generated by levies against employers. Subsequently, this statute was declared unconstitutional. Brady v. Safety-Kleen Corp., 61 Ohio St.3d 624, 576 N.E.2d 722 (1991). After more case law development, the Ohio legislature again stepped in to define the intentional tort exception more stringently than the judicial definition. Ohio Rev. Code Ann. § 2745.01. The employee

must under this provision prove deliberate and intentional conduct on the employer's part. In yet a further judicial counter attack, the Ohio Supreme Court has found the intentional conduct provision unconstitutional, Johnson v. BP Chemicals, Inc., 85 Ohio St.3d 298, 707 N.E.2d 1107 (1999).

In the absence of a valid statute, Ohio courts have applied the common law claim established in Fyffe v. Jeno's, Inc., 59 Ohio St.3d 115, 570 N.E.2d 1108 (1991). See, e.g., Ulrick v. Kunz, 594 F. Supp. 2d 847 (N.D. Ohio 2009) (applying Ohio law). *Fyffe*, following the rule in Restatement (Second) of Torts § 8A, requires three elements for establishing intentionality: "(1) knowledge by the employer of the existence of a dangerous process, procedure, instrumentality or condition within its business operation; (2) knowledge by the employer that if the employee is subjected by his employment to such dangerous process, procedure, instrumentality or condition, then harm to the employee will be a substantial certainty; and (3) that the employer, under such circumstances, and with such knowledge, did act to require the employee to continue to perform the dangerous task." 59 Ohio St.3d at 115.

2. The Supreme Court of West Virginia created a similar exception for employers' "willful, wanton, or reckless misconduct" in Mandolidis v. Elkins Indus., Inc., 161 W.Va. 695, 246 S.E.2d 907 (1978). Later, the West Virginia legislature modified the *Mandolidis* rule by narrowing the concept of "willful, wanton, and reckless conduct" in an attempt to create greater certainty. Two alternative methods are prescribed for proving deliberate intent. First, the employer is liable if it acts "with a consciously, subjectively and deliberately formed intention to produce the specific result of injury or death to an employee." Second, the employee may establish the requisite intent by proving: (1) unsafe working conditions violative of a statute, or otherwise firmly recognized; and (2) the employer's "subjective realization and appreciation" of that unsafe working condition. The statute established a special "Employer's Excess Liability Fund" under which employers may voluntarily insure against this type of liability. See also Turner v. PCR, Inc., 754 So.2d 683 (Fla. 2000) (intentional tort exception to Florida worker compensation law may be shown by objective standard that employer engaged in conduct substantially certain to result in injury).

3. Other exceptions are:

A. Successor corporations, Billy v. Consolidated Mach. Tool Corp., 51 N.Y.2d 152, 412 N.E.2d 934, 432 N.Y.S.2d 879 (1980). In Billy, the decedent, an employee of Corporation A, was killed by a piece of equipment manufactured by Corporation B. The estate collected workers' compensation benefits, but subsequently sued Corporation A. Prior to the accident, Corporation A had absorbed Corporation B through a merger. But for the merger, Corporation B would have been subject to traditional tort actions. The court held that Corporation A, otherwise immune from suit under the exclusive remedy doctrine, was the successor to the inchoate tort liabilities of Corporation B. The liability survived the merger, "since the obligation upon which [Corporation A] is being sued arose not out of the employment relation, but rather out of [the] independent business transaction" of the merger itself. *Id.* at 940. *Billy*, however, represents the minority view. See Braga v. Genlyte Group, Inc., 420 F.3d 35, 44 (1st Cir. 2005) (criticizing *Billy*; finding that the inchoate tort liability incurred by Corporation B before the merger excluded employees, and that Corporation A should have inherited such immunity).

B. Third party actions for indemnity or contribution against the employer, Lambertson v. Cincinnati Welding Corp., 312 Minn. 114, 257 N.W.2d 679 (1977).

C. Dual capacity of employer, as where a hospital employee is injured in the course of employment, cared for by the employer hospital and the injury is aggravated. Can employee sue at common law for the subsequent injury? Wymer v. JH Properties, Inc., 50 S.W.3d 195 (Ky. 2001) (finding that tort suit is available); but cf. Suburban Hosp., Inc. v. Kirson, 362 Md. 140, 763 A.2d 185 (2000) (tort suit not available).

D. Actions for damages of a kind not covered by the statute, Foley v. Polaroid Corp., 381 Mass. 545, 413 N.E.2d 711 (1980) (injury to reputation resulting from libel).

E. Some state statutes, reflecting recent criticism of the traditional workers' compensation scheme or its costs, allow unions and employers to provide themselves with alternative dispute resolution in some industries. The statutes are described in Moscowitz & Van Bourg, Carve-Outs and the Privatization of Workers' Compensation in Collective Bargaining Agreements, 46 Syracuse L. Rev. 1 (1995).

4. Is the result in the principal case, and the ensuing legislative reform and judicial reaction, likely to occur so long as no-fault compensation systems are islands within the tort litigation system? Ohio is among states with more limited recovery in worker compensation. Would the result have been different if worker compensation awards had been more nearly adequate? Or if, as in England, workers' compensation was not an exclusive remedy but in addition to damages at common law?

2. AUTOMOBILE ACCIDENT INJURIES

Motor vehicle reparation plans, or no-fault automobile insurance as they are commonly called, are schemes under which a policyholder is compensated by his own insurer regardless of his fault in causing his loss. In contrast to the universality of worker's compensation, they have not found fertile ground. Adoption is sporadic and varied, and they have been unable to obtain the widespread adoption of the worker's compensation statutes. Although Judge Marx in 1925 proposed a no-fault reparation scheme, no legislation was enacted until 1971, except in the province of Saskatchewan, Canada. The immediate impetus for automobile no-fault plans was the 1965 book by Professors Robert E. Keeton and Jeffrey O'Connell, titled Basic Protection for the Accident Victim—A Blueprint for Reforming Automobile Insurance. The plan was accompanied by a model no-fault statute. Bolstered by U.S. Department of Transportation, critical of the tort system and ultimately urging no-fault compensation, 24 states and the District of Columbia passed no-fault statutes of various types. Subsequently, a number of states repealed their statutes. As of 2014, twelve states have some form of no-fault insurance. In no state does the insured surrender the right to sue in tort for pain and suffering in exchange for coverage of an economic loss. Modified no-fault is coverage in which benefits are awarded regardless of fault and the right to sue for pain and suffering is permitted only after satisfying a statutory threshold. Some states use a dollar amount; others a verbal threshold (in Florida, for example: "significant and permanent scarring or disfigurement," Fla. Stat.

627.737). These states are Florida, Hawaii, Kansas, Kentucky, Massachusetts, Michigan, Minnesota, New Jersey, New York, North Dakota, Pennsylvania, and Utah. Of the states that are modified no-fault states, three are choice no-fault states. Under this system, a driver may choose to be included in the modified no-fault system or the tort system. States with this form of no-fault coverage are New Jersey, Pennsylvania, and Kentucky. "Add-on" insurance is expanded first-party coverage that has first-party, no-fault benefits for medical expenses and lost wages but does not restrict lawsuits for pain and suffering. The coverage is called "add-on" because it is added on to the existing tort liability system. The ten add-on states are Arkansas, Delaware, Maryland, New Hampshire, Oregon, South Dakota, Texas, Virginia, Washington, and Wisconsin. The District of Columbia also allows for add-on insurance.

Interest in no-fault schemes has been revived with concerns about the cost of compensating victims of auto accidents. At the same time other tort reform initiatives and academic advocacy has further ripened interest in auto no-fault schemes. Congress proposed the Auto Choice Reform Act of 1997 (S. 625, 105th Cong., H.R. 2021, 105th Cong.).

Yet others see little scope for wider adaption of no-fault reforms. See Kenneth S. Abraham, The Liability Century: Insurance and Tort Law from the Progressive Era to 9/11, Harvard Univ Press, 103 (2008) (concluding that auto no-fault "has no prospect of spreading beyond the handful of states where it is now in force"). Read the Rand study described below and ask why, with the identified advantages, the impetus for reform has waned.

In a comprehensive study published by Rand's Institute for Civil Justice entitled, No Fault Approaches to Compensating People Injured in Automobile Accidents, S. J. Carroll et al (R–4019–ICJ) no fault or personal injury protection plans were studied nationally. The authors examined the effects of adopting no fault schemes within the parameters of the following outcomes:

- Total injury coverage costs;
- Transaction costs—lawyer fees and claim processing costs;
- Injured parties' net compensation—after deduction of any lawyer fees;
- How compensation compares with economic loss; and
- Time to payment.

With the goal in mind of providing "policymakers with an empirical framework for thinking about trade-offs implicit in auto insurance compensation schemes," the report conducted on the data and analysis that granting efforts will vary from state to state:

- All no-fault plans reduce transaction costs, regardless of plan provisions. No-fault plans that entirely ban access to the liability system reduce transaction costs by about 80 percent. Those that would allow seriously injured people to pursue liability claims would reduce transaction costs by about 20 to 40 percent; the latter translates into a reduction in total injury coverage costs of approximately 10 percent.

- No-fault plans match compensation more closely with economic loss. No-fault plans do this by increasing the fraction of economic loss that is compensated and by reducing the amount of compensation that exceeds economic loss by reducing payouts for noneconomic loss. Injured people with smaller losses tend to recover amounts approximating their medical costs and lost wages, while those more seriously injured recover a larger share of their losses because they can collect both [personal injury protection plan] PIP and liability compensation.
- No-fault plans eliminate compensation for noneconomic loss, such as pain and suffering, for injured people below the threshold.
- No-fault plans generally speed up compensation. Injured people begin receiving payments on average about two months sooner under no-fault plans than under the traditional system.

The key determinants in design of a scheme are its threshold, its benefits, the offsetting of private insurance, and the deductible.

NOTES AND QUESTIONS

1. *Constitutionality of Automobile No-Fault Schemes.* The personal injury portion of automobile no-fault laws have survived attacks under the due process and equal protection clauses of the Federal Constitution in all state courts of last resort. See Montgomery v. Daniels, 38 N.Y.2d 41, 378 N.Y.S.2d 1, 340 N.E.2d 444 (1975). Most of the decisions have looked to the analogy of workers' compensation laws in order to meet the due process claim. Under those laws in most states a worker can elect to retain his common law rights, and so the analogy is not entirely congruent. (Most workers have declined to make this election).

The equal protection arguments against the no-fault thresholds have given the courts more difficulty, but the thresholds have been sustained. The first major case was Pinnick v. Cleary, 360 Mass. 1, 271 N.E.2d 592 (1971). See also Manzanares v. Bell, 214 Kan. 589, 522 P.2d 1291 (1974) ($500 medical threshold); Lasky v. State Farm Ins. Co., 296 So.2d 9 (Fla.1974) ($500 medical threshold); Fann v. McGuffey, 534 S.W.2d 770 (Ky.1975) ($500 medical threshold); Singer v. Sheppard, 464 Pa. 387, 346 A.2d 897 (1975) ($750 medical threshold). In Gentile v. Altermatt, 169 Conn. 267, 363 A.2d 1 (1975) ($500 medical threshold), the Supreme Court dismissed the appeal, 423 U.S. 1041 (1976). See also Opinion of the Justices, 113 N.H. 205, 304 A.2d 881 (1973) ($1000 medical threshold); In re Requests of the Governor and Senate, Etc., 389 Mich. 441, 208 N.W.2d 469 (1973) ("serious impairment of bodily function" and "permanent serious disfigurement" thresholds); and see Shavers v. Kelley, 402 Mich. 554, 267 N.W.2d 72 (1978).

The Supreme Court of Florida held a no-fault provision regarding damage to the insured vehicle violative of due process when it simply shifted the cost of that risk from the tortfeasor to the injured party. See Kluger v. White, 281 So.2d 1 (Fla.1973). Most no-fault plans do not cover property damage.

The Michigan Supreme Court has upheld the state's statute against numerous equal-protection objections. See O'Donnell v. State Farm Mut. Auto. Ins. Co., 404 Mich. 524, 273 N.W.2d 829 (1979) and Stevenson v. Reese, 239 Mich.App. 513, 609 N.W.2d 195 (2000) (upholding constitutionality of Michigan's no fault legislation that denies recovery of non-economic damages to uninsured motorists).

2. *Deterrence and Costs.* Does the adoption of a no-fault compensation plan for automobile accidents result in increased accident rates? See Landes, Insurance Liability and Accidents: A Theoretical and Empirical Investigation of the Effects of No-Fault Accidents, 25 J.L. & Econ. 49 (1982). Cf. O'Connell & Levmore, A Reply to Landes: A Faulty Study of No-Fault's Effect on Fault? 48 Mo.L.Rev. 649 (1983). The Rand Institute for Civil Justice in 2001 published: The Effect of Non-Fault Automobile Insurance on Driver Behavior and Automobile Accidents in the United States, by David S. Loughran, RAND MR–1384–ICJ, 2001. The study that analyzed accident trends in the United States between 1967 and 1989 found no statistically significant relationship between states' adoption of a no-fault system and the fatal accident rate, overall accident rates, and other measures of driver care. The study found that it was surprising given the lack of any link that the deterrence argument has had such salience. Are some no-fault laws "out-of-balance," in that they cause higher insurance premiums because total no-fault benefits exceed the reduction of tort liability payments? Would it be preferable to introduce a pre-or post-accident choice for the injured parties as to whether they wish to proceed under no-fault or under the common-law liability system? See O'Connell & Joost, Giving Motorists a Choice Between Fault and No-Fault Insurance, 72 Va.L.Rev. 61 (1986). For a similar scheme employing extrapolations from the Rand findings, above, see O'Connell, Carroll, Horowitz, and Abrahamse, Consumer Choice in the Auto Insurance Market 52 Mo.L.Rev. 1016 (1993); O'Connell, Carroll, Horowitz, and Abrahamse, The Costs of Consumer Choice for Auto Insurance in States Without No-Fault Insurance, 54 Md. L. Rev. 281 (1995); and O'Connell, Carroll, Horowitz, and Abrahamse, The Comparative Costs of Allowing Consumer Choice for Auto Insurance in All Fifty States, 55 Md. L. Rev. 160 (1996) and O'Connell et al., A Federal Bill, With Commentary to Allow Choice in Auto Insurance, 7 Conn. Insur. L. J. 511 (2000/2001). The desirability of the elective no-fault scheme promoted by Professor O'Connell and his co-authors turns importantly on the cost to motorists of insurance coverage under the scheme and whether the adoption of the scheme would force an increase in the premiums of those staying with traditional tort coverage. In a study prepared for the Joint Economic Committee of the United States Congress by the Institute for Civil Justice: Rand (April 1997), the authors Allan Abrahamse and Stephen Carroll found that in most states the costs of compensating accident victims for drivers who select elective no-fault would be 60% less than the current system in each state. That would represent a premium savings of about 30% on average for those willing to waive tort rights. In an earlier, 1995 Rand study by the same authors (The Effects of a Choice Auto Insurance Plan on Insurance Costs, Rand, 1995), it was found that the availability of the no-fault option would have no effect on the compensation costs incurred by insurers on their behalf and hence automobile insurance premiums would be uninfluenced. For other aspects, see Cummins et al., The Incentive Effects of No-Fault Automobile

Insurance, 44 J. Law & Econ. 427 (2001); Schwartz, Auto No-Fault and First-Party Insurance: Advantages and Problems, 73 S. Cal. L. Rev. 611 (2000).

3. OTHER NO-FAULT COMPENSATION SYSTEMS

1. The tort system compensates personal injuries and other losses by a system of fault assessment and liability insurance. Even in cases involving strict products liability or abnormally dangerous activities, there is a measure of moral, economic, or legal fault: the product is defective or unreasonably dangerous; the activity involves abnormal risks that outweigh its value to the community. See, e.g., Powers, The Persistence of Fault in Products Liability, 61 Tex.L.Rev. 777 (1983); J. O'Connell, Ending Insult to Injury: No-Fault Insurance for Products and Services 57 (1975); Owen, The Fault Pit, 26 Ga.L.Rev. 703 (1992); Schwartz, The Vitality of Negligence and the Ethics of Strict Liability, 15 Ga.L.Rev. 963 (1981). Litigating fault and using the court system to compensate victims involves substantial transaction costs and expenses of administration. Critics charge that, for reasons of both efficiency and fairness, a no-fault compensation system should replace the traditional tort system's method of compensating accident victims. See, e.g., J. O'Connell, Ending Insult to Injury: No-Fault Insurance for Products and Services (1975); Peter Cane, Atiyah's Accidents, Compensation and the Law, 464–66 (William Twining and Christopher McCrudden eds., 8th ed. 2013).

2. In 1972 New Zealand adopted the first comprehensive administrative system that replaced tort claims with a new no-fault remedy for virtually all accidental injuries. The plan, administered by the government, is a social insurance system that pays limited benefits to all persons who suffer "personal injury by accident." The plan is financed through car-owner, employer, and general tax levies. See G. Palmer, Compensation for Incapacity: A Study of Law and Social Change in New Zealand and Australia (1979); Willy, The Accident Compensation Act and Recovery for Losses Arising From Personal Injury and Death by Accident, 6 N.Z.U.L.Rev. 250 (1975). The New Zealand plan does not replace the tort system in cases involving property damage, non-workplace disease, economic losses or business torts. See Henderson, The New Zealand Accident Compensation Reform, 48 U.Chi.L.Rev. 781 (1981); Franklin, Personal Injury Accidents in New Zealand and the United States, Some Striking Similarities, 27 Stan.L.Rev. 653 (1975); Phillips, In Defense of the Tort System, 27 Ariz.L.Rev. 603, 605 (1986). Under a social insurance compensation plan as in effect in New Zealand, is there a trade-off in lowered accident deterrence and diminished incentives for safety? See T. Ison, Accident Compensation 165 (1980); Love, Punishment and Deterrence: A Comparative Study of Tort Liability for Punitive Damages Under No-Fault Compensation Legislation, 16 U.C.Davis L.Rev. 232 (1983); Klar, New Zealand's Accident Compensation Scheme: A Tort Lawyer's Perspective, 33 U. Toronto L.J. 80 (1983); International Workshop: Beyond Compensation: Dealing with Accidents in the 21st Century, 15 U. Haw. L. Rev. 524 (1993). Is such a plan feasible in the United States? How much would it cost? Constitutionally and culturally, is this large scale reform

feasible? See Goldberg, The Constitutional Status of Tort Law: Due Process and the Right to a Law for the Redress of Wrongs, 115 Yale L. J. 524 (2005).

3. Since 1992, the government, through a series of measures, has shifted the scheme's social welfare objective to one focusing on risk-related insurance. In 1998, for example, employers and the self-employed were given freedom to shop for accident insurance to restrict compensable events and introduce a measure of deterrence into the system. Miller, The 1992 Changes to New Zealand's Accident Compensation Scheme, 5 Canta.L.Rev. 1 (1992) and Miller, An Analysis or Critique of the 1992 changes to New Zealand's Accident Compensation Scheme, 52 Md.L.Rev. 1070 (1993).

The strict risk-related insurance plans relied heavily on stringent, bright-line cut-off limits that left many injuries under-compensated. In New Zealand, public pressure for greater coverage led the 2005 Labour Party-controlled government to liberalize coverage standards that made the question of fault irrelevant. Bright-lines were still required, but medical treatment claims tripled after the first year of enactment while coverage denial rates declined by half. For an in-depth discussion, see Schuck, Tort Reform, Kiwi-Style, 27 Yale L. & Pol'y Rev. 1 (2008).

4. The tide of the comprehensive compensation scheme appears to be ebbing even in its New Zealand home. Todd & Black, Accident Compensation and the Barring of Actions for Damages, 1 Tort L.Rev. 197 (1993). But for an argument from one of the original authors of the compensation scheme, insisting on its endurance despite policy challenges, see Palmer, Accident Compensation in New Zealand: Looking Back and Looking Forward, 2008 NZ Law Review 81.

4. NO-FAULT COMPENSATION IN THE UNITED STATES

In the United States, no-fault approaches to injury compensation have been applied or proposed in a number of contexts other than workers' compensation and automobile accidents:

A. *September 11 Victim Compensation.* Within 10 days of the terrorist attack on September 11, 2001, Congress rushed to action in enacting legislation. The legislation adopted a no-fault compensation scheme for victims suffering personal injuries and the survivors of those who died. (Air Transportation Safety and System Stabilization Act, Pub. L. No. 107–42, 405 (b)(2), 115 Stat. 230, 239–40 (2001)).

The legislation parallels the pattern of other compensation schemes, it trades off a common law claim for a no-fault benefit. Victims were given a choice. The legislation was both designed to free the airline industry of heavy potential claims and to afford swift and fair compensation to victims. In contrast to other no-fault schemes, the extent of compensation was liberal, allowing recovery of economic loss, extending beyond medical expenses and preset earnings, to "loss of business or employment opportunities" to the limits of applicable state law. Non-economic losses were allowed in a broad sweep for "losses for physical and emotional pain, suffering, inconvenience, physical impairment, mental anguish, disfigurement, loss of enjoyment of life, loss of society and companionship, loss of consortium (other than domestic service), hedonic damages, injury to reputation, and all other non-pecuniary loss of any kind or nature." § 402(7).

The terms of the legislation strongly reflect the underlying tort system. Collateral benefits were to be offset; these included "all collateral sources, including life insurance, pension funds, death benefit programs, and payments by federal, state, or local governments related to the attacks." As the Special Master admitted, the deductions from awards "proved to be one of the Funds' most contentious issues." Final Report of the Special Master for the September 11th Victim Compensation Fund of 2001, Volume 1, (2005) p. 44.

The Special Master, Kenneth R. Feinberg, reported that the fund distributed over $7.049 billion to survivors of 2,880 persons killed and to 2,680 injured persons. The average award to families was over $2 million. For injured victims, it was about $400,000.

Most eligible claimants participated in the Fund rather than proceed at common law. The report details the method by which claims were made and compensation determined. Significantly, the Special Master addressed matters of wider public policy for the compensation of victims of catastrophes. Part III of the Report makes the following observations:

> III. OBSERVATIONS AND LESSONS LEARNED
>
> Did the September 11th Victim Compensation Fund of 2001 constitute sound public policy? This question, repeatedly asked by the public, media representatives, public officials and, especially, the September 11th families themselves, is posed in different ways. Did Congress do the right thing in enacting the Victim Compensation Fund? How does one justify the creation of such a Fund limited to September 11th victims and their families, while ignoring the claims of other victims of terrorist attacks at Oklahoma City, the African Embassy bombings, the USS Cole, and the first World Trade Center attack in 1993? Why should Congress provide very generous compensation to a limited number of individuals while excluding other victims of life's misfortunes?
>
> A second question also arises. Even if the Fund can be justified in benefitting only a very small segment of the population, was it a good idea for the Act to require individualized and different amounts of compensation for each eligible claimant? Would it have been wiser to provide a flat payment—the same amount—to each individual claimant? What problems arise when the statutory mandate requires a separate tailored calculation for each individual? What are the strengths and weaknesses, the pros and cons, of the flat payment, one-size-fits-all approach to public compensation?
>
> Finally, the most frequently asked question: In the event of another terrorist attack, should Congress establish a similar victim compensation fund? Is the September 11th Victim Compensation Fund a viable precedent for a similar future program, or should it be viewed as sui generis, a unique response to a unique historical event?

These are the questions considered in a preliminary summary review of the issues posed. The words "preliminary" and "summary" must be emphasized. The September 11th terrorist attacks occurred just nine years ago. They constitute a contemporary event that currently drives public policy. We still lack the benefit of historical perspective. Compounding this difficulty is the fact that the Fund itself is only now beginning to undergo scrutiny by public officials, academics, the September 11th families and the public at large. It will, therefore, be a few years before a comprehensive evaluation of the September 11th Victim Compensation Fund in all of its aspects and complexity can be completed. Nevertheless, it is appropriate and timely to offer the Special Master's personal perspective on these issues as at least a preliminary blueprint to guide policymakers—an initial road map to be modified as we learn more about the impact of this unique Program.

A. The September 11th Victim Compensation Fund of 2001: Sound Public Policy?

* * *

B. The September 11th Victim Compensation Fund of 2001: Different Amounts or the Same for All?

Questions are also posed as to whether Congress acted wisely in providing a statutory compensation scheme that mandated different amounts of compensation for each eligible claimant. Was this a mistake? Why did Congress take this approach and what alternatives might be preferable?

It is easy to understand why Congress did what it did. Since the Act placed limitations on the potential recovery of families and victims in court, the alternative compensation scheme was designed to track the civil justice system in critical respects. Similarly, the definitions of economic and non-economic loss built into the statutory framework tracked traditional tort concepts. The Fund became a familiar conceptual alternative to the tort system and was designed to attract victims and families who otherwise might file thousands of lawsuits against the airlines and others. Individual, tailored awards were designed, at least in large part, to mirror the civil justice system. (Of course, the notion of collateral offsets, also part of the statutory framework, was decidedly not a familiar tort concept, and proved controversial with September 11th families and their lawyers who argued that the offsets severely undercut the very idea of mirroring the tort system.)

But the very idea of individual awards, tailored to the particular circumstances of each eligible claimant, necessitated a more complex analytical approach to the administration of the Fund. That these challenges were overcome, that, ultimately, 97% of eligible families who lost a loved one on September 11 voluntarily participated in the Program, and that the objectives of the Act were accomplished in such a relatively brief period of time and in a cost-effective manner, can be traced in large part to the Regulations which addressed and solved the most serious problems created by the enabling statute. These Regulations, and the day-to-day administration of the Fund, proved to be of critical importance in convincing eligible claimants and the public that this unique Program was a credible and effective alternative to conventional litigation.

* * *

Nevertheless, despite this efficiency and effectiveness, there are serious problems posed by a statutory approach mandating individualized awards for each eligible claimant. The statutory mandate of tailored awards fueled divisiveness among claimants and undercut the very cohesion and united national response reflected in the Act. The fireman's widow would complain: "Why am I receiving less money than the stockbroker's widow? My husband died a hero. Why are you demeaning the value of his life?" The statutory requirement of collateral offsets added to the controversy: "Let me make sure I understand this. Because my wife and I planned our financial future by buying life insurance, you are deducting these life insurance payments from my award. So I am receiving less than my neighbor who never bought life insurance but spent the money on vacations and new automobiles." The statutory requirement that each individual claimant's award reflect unique financial and family circumstances inevitably resulted in finger-pointing and a sense among many claimants that the life of their loved one had been demeaned and undervalued relative to others also receiving compensation from the Fund.

A better approach might be to provide the same amount for all eligible claimants. Such an approach would eliminate the problem of discerning fact from speculation in calculating individual awards. It would also be easier and quicker to process claims since eligibility for compensation would be the sole issue for a Special Master. Most importantly, such an approach might reduce divisiveness among eligible claimants since, by statute, one size would fit all.

But such an approach is not without controversy. Hundreds or thousands of individual claimants could argue that their financial wherewithal and "exceptional circumstances" justify greater compensation than the uniform amount established by Congress. The same amount, whatever it might be, would have a much different impact on the family of the stockbroker or banker than the family of the waiter, policeman or member of the military. Thus, the impact of any flat award would depend upon the financial and family circumstances of the surviving claimant. Providing the same amount for all eligible claimants can easily be criticized as providing no more than "rough justice." But, on balance, I believe that this approach has much to recommend it, especially when one considers the available alternatives.

However, the flat amount approach begs two critically important questions—what exactly is the appropriate amount for an eligible claimant, and should the award come free of any restrictions on the ability of the claimant to access the civil justice system by commencing a lawsuit? These two questions are interrelated. If Congress mandates a flat amount for all, it will likely be relatively modest, tracking, for example, the $250,000 award currently afforded the families of a fireman or police officer killed in the line of duty. This award is mandated by federal law without any restriction on the right of the eligible family to commence a lawsuit against alleged tortfeasors. If the flat amount approach is to be used in the future as the basis for compensating victims of terrorist attacks, it should not be part and parcel of restrictions imposed on the right to litigate in court. Alternatively, the flat amount mandated by statute might arguably be high enough to constitute fair consideration for limiting access to the courtroom. But what is "fair consideration?" Would Congress establish it in the statute or delegate the responsibility to a Special Master? All of these questions and approaches are important food-for-thought in determining the design and contours of any future terrorist compensation program which provides the same amount for all eligible claimants.

C. The September 11th Victim Compensation Fund of 2001: A Precedent for the Future?

* * *

Even considering the generous levels of compensation provided for in the 9/11 victim compensation fund, a small number of claimants, comprising about 60 total lawsuits, still chose to litigate their claims. Most have been bogged down by procedural hurdles and the federal government's refusal to release certain materials. A few cases have settled. See Chanen and Tebo, Accounting for Lives: The 9/11 Victim Compensation Fund Worked. But What About Next Time?, ABA Journal 58, Sept. 2007.

NOTES AND QUESTIONS

1. Do you have an opinion about the strength of the tort claims and the capacity of the courts to handle the litigation? See Effron, Event Jurisdiction and Protective Coordination: Lessons from the September 11th Litigation, 81 S. Cal. L. Rev. 199 (2008). Sebok, What's Law Got To Do With It? Designing Compensation Schemes in the Shadow of the Tort System, 53 DePaul L. Rev. 501 (2003). Kenneth Feinberg was again recruited to administer the Gulf Coast Claims Facility (GCCF) established to compensate persons damaged by the BP Oil Spill imbroglio. The diversity of claimants and the presence of a vigorous class action, militated against an efficient and fair allocation of compensation under the scheme. See Partlett & Weaver, BP Oil Spill: Compensation, Agency Costs, and Restitution, 68 Wash. & Lee L. Rev. 1341 (2011).

Do you agree with Kenneth Feinberg that the September 11 attack and the Fund's establishment is *sui generis*? Dauber, The War of 1812, September 11th, and the Politics of Compensation, 53 DePaul L. Rev. 289 (2003).

Should government sponsor an insurance scheme for victims of terrorism and, by extension, victims of crime? Levmore & Logue, Insuring

Against Terrorism—and Crime, 102 Mich. L. Rev. 268 (2003) (arguing that insurance of terrorist caused injuries may stimulate government-sponsored insurance against crime, thus prompting greater governmental precautions against criminally caused injuries).

A. *Other Federal Compensation Plans.* In 1969, Congress passed the Black Lung Act, 30 U.S.C.A. §§ 901 et seq., to compensate coal miners and their dependents for the disabling respiratory disease known as "black lung." Whether viewed as a compensation system to miners, a subsidy to the mining industry, or as a type of welfare benefit, the federal black lung program represents an innovative solution to compensation in a case in which traditional tort and workers' compensation remedies proved inadequate because of the progressive nature of the disease and the effect of statutes of limitations and workers' compensation statutes that, at that time, failed to cover occupational diseases. See Ramsey & Habermann, The Federal Black Lung Program—The View From the Top, 87 W.Va.L.Rev. 575 (1985); Barth, The Tragedy of Black Lung: Federal Compensation for Occupational Disease (1987) For a history of black lung and the belated public health, regulation, and compensation response, see Derickson, Black Lung: Anatomy of a Public Health Disaster (1998).

Political forces, focused by lawsuits, have prompted Congress to consider schemes consonant with the pattern of the Black Lung legislation. For example, some companies that manufactured products incorporating asbestos have sought legislative compensation schemes disposing with common law litigation, and Vietnam veterans successfully lobbied for wider legislative compensation schemes. Veterans' Dioxin and Radiation Exposure Compensation Standards Act, 38 U.S.C.A. § 354. Congress, however, has been wary of expanding regulatory schemes to provide for private rights of action for personal injuries. See discussion of Superfund legislation noted in Chapter 16. For discussion of these proposals see Gaskins, Environmental Accidents: Personal Injury and Public Responsibility (1989), 253–89.

Chapter 15 noted that liability for the harmful effects of vaccines deterred their beneficial development, production, and use. In order to alleviate this concern a no-fault compensation program was introduced under the National Childhood Vaccine Injury Act of 1986 (42 U.S.C.A. §§ 300aa–10 to 300aa–33). The fund is financed by an excise tax on each dose of vaccine. The statute covers all actual medical expenses as well as costs of rehabilitation, lost wages, if any, based on average earnings in the non-farm sector, and a capped discretionary award for pain and suffering. A claimant may opt for a common law claim but an attempt was made to make this option unappealing by the application of common law principles. (E.g., Restatement (Second) of Torts § 402A, comment *k*.) For a discussion of the shortcomings of the NCVIA and subsequent no-fault vaccine liability schemes, see Apolinsky and Van Detta, Rethinking Liability for Vaccine Injury, 19 Cornell J. L. & Pub. Pol'y 537 (2010).

Who are the winners and losers under these compensation schemes? Could they be the precursors of a general no-fault compensation scheme for all injuries? Harris et al., Compensation and Support for Illness and Injury (1984). Remember that Congress provides a social security "safety net" covering, in varying degrees, unemployment, hospital and medical expenses, disability, retirement and survivor's benefits. Should the tort system be abolished and compensation integrated with a revamped social security system that could deliver benefits more efficiently? Sugarman, Compensation for Accidental Personal Injury: What Nations Might Learn from Each Other, 38 Pepp. L. Rev. 597 (2011); Wagner, Tort, Social Security, and No-Fault Schemes: Lessons from Real-World Experiments, 23 Duke J. Comp. & Int'l L. 1 (2012).

B. *Medical Malpractice.* Periods of high tort claim frequency and severity have, in certain geographical areas, like Dade County, Florida, sharply raised, insurance premium levels or made insurance difficult to obtain. Chapter 4 noted legislative reforms that have ensued. Often the reforms have capped damages, reduced limitation periods, abolished the collateral benefits rule, required arbitration, regulated contingent fees, and provided for periodic payments. For appraisal see Danzon, Medical Malpractice: Theory, Evidence, and Public Policy (1985). Williams, The Cure for What Ails: A Realistic Remedy for the Medical Malpractice "Crisis," 23 Stan. L. & Pol'y Rev 477 (2012).

More thoroughgoing systemic reforms have been suggested. Paul Weiler, Medical Malpractice on Trial (1991), urges the adoption of a no-fault scheme. His work derives from a large empirical study on medical malpractice in New York. Harvard Medical Malpractice Study, Patients, Doctors, and Lawyers: Medical Injury, Malpractice Litigation, and Patient Compensation in New York (1990). Institutional coverage may have advantages over traditional liability insurance, since premiums may be aligned more readily with risk and institutions may effectively monitor physician behavior. Sage, Enterprise Liability and the Emerging Managed Health Care System, 60 Law & Contemp. Prob. 159 (1997); Abraham & Weiler, Enterprise Medical Liability and the Evaluation of the American Health Care System, 108 Harv. L. Rev. 381 (1994); MacCourt and Bernstein, Medical Error Reduction and Tort Reform Through Private, Contractually-Based Quality Medicine Societies, 35 Am. J. L. and Med. 505 (2009).

The American Medical Association has suggested an approach to take adjudication from the hands of the courts. Johnson, Phillips, Orentlicher, and Hatlie, A Fault-Based Administrative Alternative for Resolving Medical Malpractice Claims, 42 Vand. L. Rev. 1365 (1989). One study of Florida closed claims demonstrates that claimants sue for a variety of reasons, including vindication or to uncover information. What does this imply about no-fault reform? Sloan, et al., Suing for Medical Malpractice (1993).

In another study, Viscusi and Born examined the property and casualty insurance files of the National Association of Insurance Commissioners for 1984–1991 to assess the effect of medical malpractice reforms pertaining to damage levels and the degree to which damages are insurable. The authors found the limits on non-economic damages had the most impact on insurance market outcomes. They found also that punitive damage reforms have expected impacts. In consequence, insurer profits were enhanced. Viscusi & Born, Damages Caps, Insurability, and the Performance of Medical Malpractice Insurance, 72 J. of Risk & Ins. 23 (2005). But cf., Baker, Medical Malpractice and the Insurance Underwriting Cycle, 54 DePaul L. Rev. 393 (2005) (examining the insurance underwriting cycle and its influence on medical malpractice insurance premiums and patient safety).

The public prominence of medical malpractice reform highlights the journey of tort law from the fustian courtroom and lawyer's office to the razzmatazz of the political stage. Medical malpractice has been propelled into the political maelstrom of health care reform; reform of medical malpractice is urged as a means of lowering the cost of health care. Unfortunately, rational analysis is often abandoned for the *strum und drang* of slogans and shoddy analysis. For example, in a government study, evaluation of the costs of medical malpractice system turned on reports of physician attitudes and fears. Confronting the New Health Care Crisis: Improving Health Care Quality and Lowering Costs by Fixing our Medical Malpractice Liability System, U.S. Department of Health and Human Services (2002). For a criticism of the methodologies and conclusions of those advocating draconian reform, see Tom Baker, The Medical Malpractice Myth (U. Chi. Press, 2005).

The critical stimulus to good health outcomes is an appropriate array of incentives, including liability rules. It is not enough to say that the liability is costly; the question is whether the costs are justified in preventing bad outcomes and promoting good outcomes.

The claims made about tort reform and no-fault schemes, and modifications thereto, have been episodically examined. Empirical studies concentrate on cost savings, but these are contested, and their savings may be radically less than claimed. Black et al., The Effects of "Early Offers" in Medical Malpractice Cases: Evidence from Texas, 6 J. Emp. Leg. Stud. 723 (2009). Some reforms also produce untoward results in equalities in classes of persons compensated. Moreover, the issue cannot exclusively turn on cost savings, but must be purposed toward the optimal reduction of medical mishaps.

The Patient Protection and Affordable Care Act, Pub. L. No. 111–148, 124 Stat. 119 (2010) is landmark legislation. The reform, during its long gestation period, was roundly attacked for failing to address medical malpractice issues. However, the legislation addresses the reform issue in a deliberate and constructive fashion. Section 10607 provides grant support for "State Demonstration Programs to Evaluate Alternatives to Current Medical Tort Litigation." For an account of early grant projects, see Hafemeister and Porter, The Health Care Reform Act of 2010 and Medical Malpractice Liability: Worlds in Collision or Ships Passing in the Night?, 64 SMU L. Rev. 735 (2011). For a recent proposal, see Raper, Announcing Remedies for Medical Injury: A Proposal for Medical Liability Reform Based on the Patient Protection and Affordable Care Act, 16 J. Health Care L. & Pol'y 309 (2013). Shepherd, Uncovering the Silent Victims of the American Medical Liability System, 67 Vanderbilt Law Rev 151 (2014).

Do you think that the federal government ought to take a role in reforming medical malpractice law? In pondering the desirability of reforms, bear in mind that the capacity to sue at common law not only is justified by compensation and deterrence, but also in according to claimants a sense of vindication and satisfaction in discovering the circumstances surrounding the medical incident causing the injury.

Perhaps, as in non-medical liability, radical changes from the court-based fault liability may be expected only in pockets where liability problems seem intractable. For example, liability for birth-related neurological injuries. In Virginia obstetricians were threatened with denial of coverage for such harms. The Virginia legislature in 1987 passed the

Birth-Related Neurological Injury Compensation Act (Injured Infant Act), Va.Code Ann. §§ 38.2–5000 to 5021. The Act covers

> injury to the brain or spinal cord of an infant caused by the deprivation of oxygen or mechanical injury occurring in the course of labor, delivery or resuscitation in the immediate post-delivery period in a hospital which renders the infant permanently motorically disabled and (i) developmentally disabled or (ii) for infants sufficiently developed to be cognitively evaluated, cognitively disabled. In order to constitute a "birth-related neurological injury" within the meaning of [the act], such disability shall cause the infant to be permanently in need of assistance in all activities of daily living.

Compensation is for all medical expenses not covered by other insurance. Lost wages for ages 18 to 65 are paid on a periodical basis at the rate of one-half of Virginia's average weekly earnings (non-farm). Few claims have been made so far.

Florida enacted similar legislation in 1988. Fl.Code § 766.301–316. Implementation of the Florida scheme has been problematic. The issue in this scheme, as with others, has been to confine the class of injuries and beneficiaries within the no-fault scheme. The pressure to extend common law liability principles to covered injuries is relentless. Sloan, et al., The Road from Medical Injury to Claims Resolution: How No-Fault and Tort Differ, 60 Law & Contemp. Probs. 35 (1997), report on aspects of the no-fault schemes finding them modestly successful.

For commentary, see Duff, Compensation for Neurologically Impaired Infants: Medical No-Fault in Virginia, 27 Harv. J. Legis. 391 (1990); Bovbjerg & Sloan, No-Fault for Medical Injury: Theory and Evidence, 67 U. Cin. L. Rev. 53 (1998) (attempting to assess the success of the Florida and Virginia schemes and concluding that such limited no-fault schemes do not achieve the goals ascribed to no-fault); Martin, NICA-Florida Birth-Related Neurological Injury Compensation Act: Four Reasons Why This Malpractice Reform Must be Eliminated, 26 Nova L. Rev. 609 (2002) (providing a useful history of the legislation and reasons for its repeal).

C. *Products Liability*. As noted in Chapter 15, products liability has received close attention from reformers. Some have suggested a broad departure from strict liability as developed by the courts. Viscusi, Toward a Diminished Role for Tort Liability: Social Insurance, Government Regulation, and Contemporary Risks to Health and Safety, 6 Yale J. on Reg. 65 (1989); Ausness, An Insurance-Based Compensation System for Product-Related Injuries, 58 U. Pitt. L. Rev. 669 (1997) (suggesting and defending a scheme by which product sellers would be obliged to reimburse injured consumers on a no-fault basis for economic losses). Others, however, recommend absolute liability as appropriately fulfilling goals of compensation and deterrence. Hanson & Logue, The First-Party Insurance Externality: An Economic Justification for Enterprise Liability, 76 Cornell L.Rev. 129 (1990); Croley & Hanson, Rescuing the Revolution: The Revived Case for Enterprise Liability, 91 Mich. L. Rev. 683 (1993).

With respect to tobacco-related diseases, Professors Hanson and Logue in The Costs of Cigarettes: The Economic Case for Ex Post Incentive-Based Regulation, 107 Yale L.J. 1163 (1998), note the lack of information available to consumers and in consequence would hold tobacco companies strictly liable in tort for tobacco-related diseases. At the same time, a compensation scheme could be established to process claims under an administrative tribunal. Their proposal is criticized by Professors LeBel and Ausness, Toward Justice in Tobacco Policymaking: A Critique of Hanson and Logue and an Alternative Approach to the Costs of Cigarettes, 33 Ga. L. Rev. 693 (1999). These professors support a tax levy that would support research, education, and health care relating to tobacco use. An immunity would be provided to the companies. They urge that their recommendations are more faithful to the moral or justice dimensions of the law. For a recent discussion of the history and future of tobacco litigation, see Anderson and Twerski, Reaching Equilibrium in Tobacco Litigation, 62 S.C. L. Rev. 67 (2010).

Asbestos litigation has bedeviled the American courts. The claims are high in number and often severe in magnitude, threatening bankruptcy of defendants. Cole, A Calculus Without Consent: Mass Tort Bankruptcies, Future Claimants, and the Problem of Third Party Non-Debtor "Discharge," 84 Iowa L. Rev. 753 (1999). Congress has considered legislation to institute a compensation scheme for asbestos injuries. Asbestos Compensation Act of 2003, 108 H.R. 1586/108 H.R. 1737 and 108 S. 412/1085, 1125. Rabin, Some Thoughts on the Efficacy of a Mass Toxic Torts Administrative Compensation Scheme, 52 Md. L. Rev. 951 (1993). Compensation schemes for product-related injuries are bedevilled by the same requirement as for other schemes: the compensation must be triggered by a defined or compensable event. How is the requirement to be defined for a scheme covering injuries caused by products? A person burns her hand on a stove? Drinks too much liquor? Drives a car off a bridge?

D. *Elective No-Fault Insurance Contracts.* To cover athletic injuries, particularly those sustained in high school football, many school districts purchase insurance contracts that oblige insurance companies to make prompt offers to pay an injured athlete's medical expenses and other economic losses set forth in the policy. But the world of politics did not treat these approaches favorably, and they were opposed by both consumer and business groups.

If the claimant accepts the payment, a release is obtained and no tort suit may be brought. If the payment is not accepted, the victim may proceed with a tort suit. See O'Connell, Elective No-Fault Liability by Contract—With or Without An Enabling Statute, 1975 U.Ill.L.Forum 59–72 (1975).

E. Additional proposals for substituting compensation plans for the tort system have been prepared and forcefully presented. See, for example, Pike, Recovering from Research: A No-Fault Proposal to Compensate Injured Research Participants, 38 Am. J. L. and Med. 7 (2012). For an interesting discussion of contemporary perceptions of no-fault schemes in various contexts, see Sanders et al., Must Torts Be Wrongs? An Empirical Perspective, 49 Wake Forest L. Rev. 1 (2014).

F. Do you agree with Professor John Fleming's assessment of the American compensation picture?

> The overall accident compensation landscape in America is therefore highly fragmented and lacking any systematic plan. The benefits of tort liability are not husbanded for those who are un- or under-compensated from other sources but are distributed

> randomly without regard to the needs or deserts of victims. Its grossly inflated transaction costs add to the remarkable inefficiency of the tort system. Only the affluence of American society has deflected serious misgivings about this wasteful arrangement and about the need to develop a more purposeful compensation policy such as that which other countries, with more limited resources, have been driven to pursue.

J.G. Fleming, The American Tort Process (1988), 30–31.

5. THE FUTURE

The fifth edition of this casebook was published 39 years ago, in 1971. The first automobile no-fault statute had just been passed by the Massachusetts legislature. No cases had been decided on the statute but the concept was being ardently pushed by its proponents and just as strongly opposed by its detractors. The subject could not then be treated in the traditional casebook fashion, but that edition contained a chapter entitled "Automobile Accidents—Tort Law or Reparation System?" The text described the alleged deficiencies in the existing systems, the steps that had been taken in some states to alleviate them, and the various proposals for extensive reform; and it identified the "policy issues" involved in the decisions to be made. It concluded with a reference to the future and presented this challenge:

> "It takes more than a crystal ball to predict what the state of the law will be 20 to 40 years from now. But that is the time when you will be in your prime as a lawyer. Whatever develops, it will be a legal matter and as an attorney you are likely to be deeply involved in it. Speculate now, with the wisdom and background you presently have, both as to what will be the state of the law 30 years from now and as to what [you think] it should be. Why not do it in writing so as to make your thoughts more lucid and concrete? And then you can check yourself as the years roll by to see both how good a legal prognosticator you are and whether your viewpoints on desirable solutions have changed." Prosser and Wade, Cases and Materials on Torts 650 (5th ed. 1971).

The options are greater now than they were then but the limits of reform are more fully appreciated. The pressure for adoption of a reparation system is not as intense at present, but it is steady. We would like to repeat this challenge to you now. You will find the experience a stimulating one. What do you predict as the ultimate outcome, and what do you wish that outcome to be?

INDEX

References are to Pages